Columbia Dictionary of Modern European Literature

Columbia Dictionary of Modern European Literature

HORATIO SMITH, *General Editor*
COLUMBIA UNIVERSITY

Columbia University Press, New York and London

First printing 1947
Fifth printing 1971

ISBN 0-231-01491-0

PRINTED IN THE UNITED STATES OF AMERICA

Preface

THE INTENTION of this Dictionary is to provide a record and signed evaluations of the chief books of the important literary artists of all continental Europe—in the twentieth century and the immediately preceding and closely related decades. It would have made no sense to bow in mechanical respect to chronology, but 1870 or 1880 proved in many instances to be points of departure corresponding to the realities of literary and cultural and political history. Victor Hugo who died in 1885 is not included because he represents earlier generations and moods; Baudelaire who died in 1867 is treated because much of later European poetry stems from him.

The contributors have read the books in the languages in which these were written, ranging from the vernacular of Albania to that of the Ukraine. Thirty-one literatures are represented because that is how many there are, and 239 specialists have done the work because that is how many were qualified and available for what inevitably became a complicated and patience-taxing group enterprise.

The total number of articles is 1167, but here one cannot say blithely because that is how many there are. When is an author important, and why, and to whom, and for how long? In a recent lively and provocative consideration of the problem, *Writers and Their Critics, a Study of Misunderstanding,* Henri Peyre notes that dictionaries are among the least revolutionary of human activities and, in their nature, self-perpetuating. We were indeed less likely in the present instance to turn for authoritative selection of leading writers to earlier compilations of the same scope because these are virtually nonexistent, yet editor, consultants, and contributors might have been tempted to go through the numerous current manuals and perpetuate the choices found there. We encouraged each other not to do so. A Dictionary of Received Ideas is not the object. The constant attitude has been experimental. Collaborators were urged from the very beginning to be bold, free, direct, respectful only of the original documents. In given cases, particularly of course with the extensive literatures of the great and so frequently articulate cultural powers, a number of consultants, all with special experience and knowledge, were invited to draw up independently of each other lists of contemporary writers who were in their minds outstanding. Correspondence within each group was carried on until what could fairly be called a consensus was reached. Five appraisers are not necessarily more right than one, and five conjectures, if you wish to call them that, or five hundred, do not make a certainty. At any rate the lists—let us not say final but those we have ended by using—are honestly representative of common views of thoughtful experts of today.

We did not play the game of quotas. Anyone would agree that there are more writers in Russia important to the whole twentieth-century world than there are in the Faeroe Islands, and neither the principals nor any others are likely to be shocked that the general article on Russian literature runs to 10,000 words and the one on the literature of the Faeroe Islands to 350 words. This is how much Professors Simmons and Einarsson wrote on these subjects. But there were no neatly defined initial pre-assignments, and no scholar, no critic, not even any superhistorian or Supreme Court of Cultural Values could have made them. Names multiplied and distribution of space began to take on a certain pattern as the project grew. Cross references made by contributors in one field to authors in another field reminded us sharply of lacunae. It eventually worked out, to give sample statistics in round numbers, that we have included 200 French authors, 150 Germans, 100 Russians, 100 Italians, 100 Spaniards, 50 Poles, 40 Czechs. Some fields have received attention partly in terms of newness, since no book in English had previously made information about them accessible.

Most of the articles were written directly in English, even though certain contributors more recently established in the United States had done their first living, speaking, and writing in another European language. The English of a man of foreign background and culture often has a freshness of flavor not vouchsafed the native, and if the reader is occasionally startled in this volume by an idiom less than orthodox this may have all the interest and value of shock. Our specialists have been aided and abetted not only to give their own opinions but to do this in their own style. The invaluable assistants of the editor, in the offices of Columbia University Press, were understandably inclined to be more respectful of traditional form; there have been occasions where the editor in the presence of gentle and certainly defensible suggestions from the Press has written firmly in the margin the vigorous four letters of the word "stet"—and of course is responsible for the consequences. The editor favors the principle of a foreign colleague who has learned to write an amazingly effective English: try honestly and hard not to be original and then do not greatly mind if you are. Or as another has put it, true originality is the kind you have in spite of yourself.

The individual manner of the contributor has not been resisted, and within limits neither have his enthusiasms. Any specialist easily develops predilections. Had all superlatives been kept they might have started to cancel each other out, and perspective had to be maintained. But the constant policy has been to choose contributors capable of a thrill about their subjects—even at times a thrill of disagreement—and then not to frustrate them. Some of them as they read this will glance towards the editor a little wryly—in terms of the practice about quotations. How many were eager to share with the reader the savor of a beautifully appropriate and revealing passage! The Dictionary could have expanded rapidly into an Anthology. But the very conditions of high concentration in a single volume forbade this, and everybody finally accepted the discipline of the genre.

To have read all the articles in typescript, revised typescript, proof, revised proof, brings one to the well-known state of encyclopedic ignorance, not to say comprehensive bewilderment. What does the whole thing prove, as the geometrician said after hearing one of Racine's plays. Two complementary observations are offered, for whatever they may be worth.

Issues of nationalism kept emerging, especially with certain less conspicuous and by the same token more assertive countries. This local pride can be accepted sympathetically, and also to our own advantage since the fervor throws light on the real import of the local achievement. We have been told that to consider literature as a document is one of the most fallacious heresies of our times, but one may prefer to remain something of a heretic—like Balzac with his ambition to "faire concurrence à l'état civil." We may still think there is merit in Dorothy Thompson's claim that one gets closer to the truth about American small-town life in Sinclair Lewis's *Main Street* than in the Lynds' *Middletown*. The reader eager to understand the ways of a particular European country in our time will find significant leads in what the contributors have assembled in this Dictionary.

On the other hand there are many cases where one returns to human nature in the large. A critic said not long ago that whether we like it or not "this is a world of particulars and the universal is buried under the specific." After examining details about more than a thousand individual writers and I know not how many thousands of their books, I still doubt the world of particulars. Santayana, who does not like his times, speaks of surrender of essence to miscellany, and a dictionary is surely a miscellany, yet the surrender seems to have been far from total. When we read here, to give only one example, that Unamuno found himself and his Spain in Job and Pascal and Kierkegaard—well, we may remember pleasantly and hopefully that Emerson said that Aristophanes and Hafiz and Rabelais are full of American history. Some of the most authoritative articles reveal such a fusion of the timely and the timeless.

There need be no great objection to being dated, a necessary way of being identified. What is offered here may some day appear a quaint record of contemporary taste; some earnest and painstaking scholar two hundred years from now may make the book the subject of a learned communication to be read before whatever is then the equivalent of a Modern Language Association. We do not know how many of these authors will seem significant then. We have simply done what we could to be faithful to our own values.

Immediately following is a complete list of contributors, with a key to the initials used at the end of each article. Some have written one piece, some twenty, some thirty. I do not know how to select the persons to receive thanks above all others; there is no particular point at which courtesy or justice would permit me to stop. To them all, for industry, punctuality, patience, skill, tolerance of the editorial pencil—and to the staff of Columbia University Press for the same qualities—I offer lasting gratitude.

HORATIO SMITH

Columbia University
June, 1946

Contributors

ARRANGED ALPHABETICALLY ACCORDING TO THE INITIALS WHICH APPEAR AT THE CONCLUSION OF EACH ARTICLE IN THE DICTIONARY

A. B.	Anna Balakian, Syracuse University
A. B. B.	Adolph B. Benson, Yale University
A. Bu.	Adolf Busse, Hunter College
A. C.	Américo Castro, Princeton University
A. C. L.	André C. Lévêque, University of Wisconsin
A. C. R.	Anthony C. Rinaldini, New York City
A. del R.	Angel del Río, Columbia University
A. F.	Albert Feuillerat, Yale University
A. G.	Alrik Gustafson, University of Minnesota
A. I.	Andrés Iduarte, Columbia University
A. J. B.	Adriaan J. Barnouw, Columbia University
A. J. U.	Axel Johan Uppvall, University of Pennsylvania
A. K.	Alexander Kaun,* University of California, Berkeley
A. McV.	Albert McVitty, Falmouth, Mass.
A. M. G.	Anthony M. Gisolfi, New York City
A. P. B.	Angelo Philip Bertocci, Bates College
A. P. C.	Arthur P. Coleman, Columbia University
A. R. F.	Alphonse R. Favreau, University of Michigan
A. S.	Aaron Schaffer, University of Texas
A. Se.	Alfred Senn, University of Pennsylvania
A. Sz.	Albert Schinz,* University of Pennsylvania
A. T. M.	Archibald T. MacAllister, Princeton University
A. V. R.	Alphonse V. Roche, Northwestern University
A. W.	Albin Widén, Minneapolis, Minn.
B. M. W.	Benjamin M. Woodbridge, Reed College
B. P.	Blanche Price, Western College
B. Q. M.	Bayard Q. Morgan, Stanford University
B. R. L.	Bluma Renée Lang, Wells College
C. A. M.	Clarence A. Manning, Columbia University
C. B.	César Barja, University of California, Los Angeles
C. B. C.	Clarissa B. Cooper, New York City
C. E. F.	Charlotte E. Forsyth, College of Notre Dame of Maryland
C. E. W. L. D.	Carl E. W. L. Dahlström, University of Michigan
C. F. W.	Carlo F. Weiss, New York City

* Deceased.

C. K. B.	Carol K. Bang, Baltimore, Md.
C. L. B.	Claude L. Bourcier, Middlebury College
C. M.	Claire Murray, White Plains, N.Y.
C. S. S.	Charles S. Singleton, The Johns Hopkins University
C. W., Jr.	Charles Weir, Jr., Cornell University
C. W. S.	Charles Wharton Stork, Harcum Junior College
D. F.	Daisy Fornacca, New York City
D. K. A.	Doris King Arjona, John B. Stetson University
D. V.	Domenico Vittorini, University of Pennsylvania
E.	René Etiemble, New York City
E. B. M.	Evelyn Beatrice Macht, New York City
E. C.	Ebe Cagli, Cambridge, Mass.
E. C. S.	E. C. Stillman, New York City
E. F.	Ernst Feise, The Johns Hopkins University
E. Fe.	Esther Fenili, Vassar College
E. F. H.	Edith F. Helman, Simmons College
E. Fl.	Eugenio Florit, New York City
E. G. D.	Ernesto G. Da Cal, New York University
E. G. L.	Emilio González-López, Hunter College
E. H.	Einar Haugen, University of Wisconsin
E. H. H.	E. Herman Hespelt, New York University
E. Hof.	Erich Hofacker, Washington University
E. H. W.	Ernest H. Wilkins, Oberlin College
E. J.	Ernst Jockers, University of Pennsylvania
E. J. S.	Ernest J. Simmons, Columbia University
E. Ju.	Elizabeth Judas, New York City
E. M.	Ernst Morwitz, University of North Carolina
E. M. F.	E. M. Fleissner, Wells College
E. M. G.	Elliott M. Grant, Williams College
E. N.	Eduardo Nicol, University of Mexico
E. R.	Ernst Rose, New York University
E. S.	Eugene Sheffer, Columbia University
E. Z.	Edmund Zawacki, University of Wisconsin
F. B.	Fernand Baldensperger, University of California, Los Angeles
F. Br.	Friedrich Bruns, University of Wisconsin
F. de O.	Federico de Onís, Columbia University
F. de P.	Ferran de Pol, Mexico, D.F.
F. D. M.	Ferdinand D. Maurino, Triple Cities College of Syracuse University
F. G. L.	Francisco Garcia Lorca, New York City
F. H. M.	Franz H. Mautner, Ohio Wesleyan University
F. J. W.	Francis J. Whitfield, Harvard University
F. K.	Frances Keene, New York City
F. S.	Frank Spiecker,* University of Illinois

* Deceased.

F. S. y E.	F. Sánchez y Escribano, University of Michigan
F. W. J. H.	Frederick W. J. Heuser, Columbia University
G. B.	Gino Bigongiari, Columbia University
G. Bi.	Gladys Bigongiari, New York City
G. de S.	George de Santillana, Massachusetts Institute of Technology
G. G.	Gaston Gille, New York City
G. I. D.	George I. Dale, Cornell University
G. K.	Günther Keil, Hunter College
G. M.	Gilbert Mignacca, Providence, R.I.
G. M. M.	Gerald M. Moser, University of Wisconsin
G. P.	Giuseppe Prezzolini, Columbia University
G. R. J.	Gertrude R. Jasper, Hunter College
G. R. N.	George R. Noyes, University of California, Berkeley
G. S.	Gioconda Savini, New York City
G. Sh.	Glen Shortliffe, Queen's University, Kingston, Ontario
G. St.	Georg Strandvold, Decorah, Iowa
H. A. L.	Hanna Astrup Larsen,* The American-Scandinavian Foundation
H. B.	Hermann Boeschenstein, University College, Toronto
H. Bf.	Hermann Barnstorff, University of Missouri
H. C.	Halina Chybowska, New York City
H. C. B.	H. Chonon Berkowitz,* University of Wisconsin
H. C. H.	Henry C. Hatfield, Williams College
H. C. R.	Howard C. Rice, Harvard University
H. E. P.	Helen Eitinger Pilla, New York City
H. H.	Hélène Harvitt, Brooklyn College
H. K.	Halvdan Koht, Washington, D.C.
H. M. C.	Haakon M. Chevalier, University of California, Berkeley
H. M. M.	Harold M. March, Swarthmore College
H. P.	Henri Peyre, Yale University
H. R.	Helmut Rehder, University of Wisconsin
H. R. M.	Howard R. Marraro, Columbia University
H. S.	Horatio Smith, Columbia University
H. Sch.	Heinrich Schneider, Cornell University
H. St.	Herbert Steiner, Pennsylvania State College
H. U. F.	H. U. Forest, University of Pennsylvania
H. W. H.-T.	Harvey W. Hewett-Thayer, Princeton University
H. W. L. D.	Henry Wadsworth Longfellow Dana, Cambridge, Mass.
H. W. N.	H. W. Nordmeyer, University of Michigan
H. W. P.	Hugh W. Puckett, Barnard College
I. B.	Irma Brandeis, Bard College
I. C.	Izidor Cankar, Quebec
I. W.	Isabelle de Wyzewa, Barnard College

* Deceased.

J.-A. B.	Jean-Albert Bédé, Columbia University
J.-A. G.	Jan-Albert Goris, New York City
J. B. C. W.	J. B. C. Watkins, The American-Scandinavian Foundation
J. B. O.	John B. Olli, College of the City of New York
J. C.	Joaquín Casalduero, Smith College
J. C. B.	John C. Blankenagel, Wesleyan University
J. C. D. L.	John C. Di Lorenzo, New York City
J. D. Y.	J. David Yarbro, U.S. Naval Academy
J. E. S.	J. E. Shaw, University of Toronto
J. F.	José Famadas, Columbia University
J. F. De S.	Joseph F. De Simone, Brooklyn College
J. F. G.	Jane F. Goodloe, Goucher College
J. F. J.	Joseph F. Jackson, University of Illinois
J. F. M.	James F. Mason, Cornell University
J. G.	Jan Greshoff, Capetown, South Africa
J. M.	Jackson Mathews, Central Washington College of Education
J. M. C.	Joseph M. Carrière, University of Virginia
J. Me.	John Meyer, Chicago, Ill.
J. M. M. i V.	J. M. Miquel i Vergés, University of Mexico
J. N. C.	J. Norton Cru, Williams College
J. O'B.	Justin O'Brien, Columbia University
J. P.	J. Posin, Stanford University
J. R.	Joseph Remenyi, Western Reserve University
J. S.	Joan Sales, University of Barcelona
J. V.	Jeanne Varney, Columbia University
K. H. M.	Karl H. Menges, Columbia University
K. P.	Kurt Pinthus, Washington, D.C.
K. R. W.	Katherine R. Whitmore, Smith College
K. Z.	Krystyna Zbieranska, Toronto
L. A.	Louis Adamic, Milford, N.J.
L. All.	Louis Allard, Harvard University
L. E. S.	Louis E. Sorieri, New York City
L. E. V. N.	Louis E. Van Norman, San Diego, Calif.
L. F.	Leon Feraru, Long Island University
L. G. M.	L. G. Moffatt, University of Virginia
L. K.	Leon Kochnitzky, New York City
L. S.	Leon Stilman, Cornell University
L. T.	Lon Tinkle, Southern Methodist University
L. V.	Léon Verriest, Dartmouth College
M. B.	Marie Buffa, Brooklyn College
M. C. M.	Marie C. Mengers, New York City
M. D.	Mathurin Dondo, University of California, Berkeley
M. de M.	Margarita de Mayo, Vassar College
M. E. C.	Maurice Edgar Coindreau, Princeton University

M. F. Max Fischer, New York City
M. G. Margaret Gilman, Bryn Mawr College
M. H. Milan Herzog, New York City
M. J. B. M. J. Benardete, Brooklyn College
M. M. M. Mespoulet, Barnard College
M. M. C. Marion M. Coleman, New York City
M. P. Mario Pei, Columbia University
M. Pi. Maria Piccirrilli, Vassar College
M. S. Marc Slonim, New York City
M. T. R. Mary T. Ragno, New York City
M. V. H. Marion Vaux Hendrickson, New York City
N. B. A. Nicholson B. Adams, University of North Carolina
N. D. Nelo Drizari, Columbia University
N. J. T. N. J. Tremblay, University of Arizona
N. L. Nancy Lenkeith, New York City
N. L. T. Norman L. Torrey, Columbia University
N. S. Nikander Strelsky,* Vassar College
O. M. Oleg Maslenikov, University of California, Berkeley
O. P. G. Olav Paus Grunt, New York City
O. S. F. O. S. Fleissner, Wells College
P. A. Pauline Albala, New York City
P. A. C. Pierre A. Clamens, Columbia University
P. A. P. Peter A. Pertzoff, Cornell University
P. B. Pierre Brodin, Lycée Français de New York
P. Bo. Paul Bonnet, University of California, Los Angeles
P. M. R. Peter M. Riccio, Columbia University
P. P. M. Peter P. Munisteri, New York City
P. R. Patrick Romanell, Barnard College
P. R. P. Paul R. Pope, Cornell University
P. S. Pedro Salinas, The Johns Hopkins University
R. A. Richard Alewyn, Queens College, New York City
R. Al. Rudolph Altrocchi, University of California, Berkeley
R. B. René Bellé, University of Southern California
R. J. N. R. J. Niess, U.S. Military Academy
R. K. S. Robert K. Spaulding, University of California, Berkeley
R. M. L. Ramón Martínez-López, University of Texas
R. S. Rudolph Schevill,* University of California, Berkeley
R. S. P. M. Ruth Shepard Phelps Morand, New York City
R. T. René Taupin, Hunter College
R. W. René Wellek, Yale University
S. A. R. S. A. Rhodes, College of the City of New York
S. A. V. Sophie A. Vrahnos, New York City
S. B. Stanley Burnshaw, New York City

* Deceased.

S. C. P.	Sheila Cudahy Pellegrini, Barat College
S. E.	Stefán Einarsson, The Johns Hopkins University
S. E. S.	S. Eugene Scalia, Brooklyn College
S. H. C.	Samuel H. Cross, Harvard University
S. L.	Sol Liptzin, College of the City of New York
S. M. S. M.	Sister M. Serafina Mazza, Seton Hill College
S. N.	Samuel Niger, Yiddish Scientific Institute, New York City
S. S.	Sigmund Skard, Washington, D.C.
S. S. W.	Seymour S. Weiner, New York City
S. T.	Signe Toksvig, Bethel, Conn.
T. C.	Teresa Carbonara, Barnard College
T. G. B.	Thomas G. Bergin, Cornell University
T. M.	Thaddeus Mitana, Alliance College
T. M. C.	T. M. Campbell, Northwestern University
V. G.	Vincent Gagliadino, New York City
V. Gu.	Vincent Guilloton, Smith College
V. L.	Victor Lange, Cornell University
W. A. N.	William A. Nitze, University of California, Los Angeles
W. A. R.	Walter A. Reichart, University of Michigan
W. H. B.	W. Hunter Beckwith, Hofstra College
W. H. R.	Winthrop H. Root, Williams College
W. J. E.	William J. Everts, Colgate University
W. J. M.	Walter J. Mueller, New York City
W. J. R.	William J. Rose, University of London
W. K.	Watson Kirkconnell, Hamilton, Ontario
W. K. C.	W. K. Cornell, Yale University
W. K. P.	William K. Pfeiler, University of Nebraska
W. L. F.	William L. Fichter, Brown University
W. L. S.	William L. Schwartz, Stanford University
W. M. F.	Wilbur M. Frohock, Columbia University
W. N.	Werner Neuse, Middlebury College
W. P.	Wolfgang Paulsen, State University of Iowa
W. R. G.	William R. Gaede, New York City

Columbia Dictionary of Modern European Literature

A

Aakjær, Jeppe (1866–1930, Danish novelist and poet), was the son of poor peasants in Jutland. He was hired out as a herd's boy and experienced himself some of the shocking conditions which he afterwards described in *Bondens Søn* (1899; The Peasant's Son) and *Vredens Børn; et Tyendes Saga* (1904; Children of Wrath; the Saga of a Servant). The boy had hardly any schooling, but at 18 went to Copenhagen to study and after 10 years, interrupted by absences in order to earn money to go on, managed to pass the entrance examinations to the university. He then returned to his own people and made his living by writing and lecturing on socialistic lines (which cost him a jail sentence). He was first married, in 1893, to the novelist Marie Bregendahl (*q.v.*), was divorced from her, and later married the artist Nana Krog. About the beginning of the present century he was able to acquire a farm, which he called Jenle (Alone). This he made, a little paradoxically, into a center of folk life and every midsummer held a sort of rustic Chautauqua to which thousands of people came in order to listen to lectures on political and social questions, sing songs, and enjoy a convivial time. Aakjær was not satisfied with the knowledge of the Jutland peasants which he had absorbed from childhood, but applied himself to study of their language, local history, conditions of living, and attitude toward life. He wrote a biography of the leading Jutland writer of an older generation, Steen Steensen Blicher. Aakjær's fiction is strongly agitatorial, though sometimes his short stories are gems of humor and sympathetic understanding. There is no doubt that he contributed to improving the lot of the very poor. At the same time he inspired the common people with a sense of their human worth and with love of the land. He is most nearly classic in his lyrics, which have earned for him the name of the Danish Burns. The best known are *Rugens Sange* (1906; Songs of the Rye). Written sometimes in a Jutland dialect and dealing with the nature and people of Jutland, they have nevertheless become the property of the whole Danish people and, set to music, are sung wherever Danes gather.

See: Waldemar Westergaard, "Jeppe Aakjær," *American-Scandinavian Review,* XII (1924), 665–669.

H. A. L.

Aanrud, Hans (1863–, Norwegian writer of short stories and plays), was born of a peasant family in Gausdal in the central region of the country. Since his début in 1887 he has lived his most active years in Oslo as a critic and literary man. He has written harsh modern comedies on the life of the lower middle class of the capital; but his fame rests on short stories and children's books picturing the peasants of his home valley before the coming of industrialism. Aanrud's horizon is that of his farmers. His conception of society is static, his psychology may have a touch of conventionalism. But within his narrow field he is a master: love makes him seeing. His observation is that of the realist, but he approaches his subject with a respectful devotion which links him to the contemporary "home-soil novelists." In his short stories the valley is reborn with intimate preciseness of detail; landscape, climate and atmosphere, work and play, characters and situations, are portrayed with striking clarity. Aanrud has little interest in the somber and complicated aspects of life. His chef-d'œuvre, "En vinternat" (Eng. tr., "A Winter Night," *American-Scandinavian Review,* Vol. XVI, 1928, pp. 483–491), in *En vinternat og andre fortaellinger* (1896), is a drama of passion and tragedy compressed into a few pages of terrifying reticence; a few of his other stories give surprising glimpses into the subconscious. But what he mostly loves to bring out are the good, solid qualities of his people, their simple wisdom, their patience and stalwart health, described with mild humor and often through a sun haze of memory. With special tenderness he follows the fate of the weak and humble—the old folks, the children, the poor; his charming children's books are pure idyls, almost without a shadow (*e.g., Sidsel Sidsaerk,* 1903, *Sølve Solfeng,* 1910; Eng. tr. of both in *Sidsel Longskirt and Solve Suntrap, Two Children of Norway,* 1935). His style springs from that of the popular tradition, terse, restrained, and suggestive. It is Aanrud who has set the tone for the short story of Norwegian farm life.

S. S.

Aasen, Ivar (1813–1896, Norwegian linguist and poet), born in Ørsta, Sunnmøre, was the son of a tenant farmer. Self-taught, he became the standard-bearer of the Norwegian countryman's movement towards cultural and linguistic self-expression. When 23 years old he staked out his revolutionary life plan: to create for Norway a truly national standard language, based on the speech of the rural districts, which should take the place of the current Dano-Norwegian. He began his dialect studies in 1838, and out of these grew the first systematic grammars and dictionaries of Norwegian dialects, *Det norske folkesprogs grammatik* (1848; Grammar of the Norwegian Popular Language) and *Ordbog over det norske folkesprog* (1850; Dictionary of the Norwegian Popular Language). But Aasen did more than provide the outward structure of the new language which he proposed for his people in 1853 and called Landsmaal (country language). He also proved by eminent example that his language could be a medium of poetry. The cream of his folk lyrics are found in *Symra* (1863; The Anemone) and in his folk play *Ervingen* (1855; The Heir). These works have become household treasures in all Norway, particularly the countryside. Their themes are drawn from the homely, everyday feelings and experiences of the countryman, and they emphasize a love of home and the native culture, a bit on the bleak and sober side, but deeply human.

See: H. Koht, "Ivar Aasen, granskar og maalreisar," in *Minneskrift* (1913); E. Haugen, "The Linguistic Development of Ivar Aasen's New Norse," *Publications of the Modern Language Association*, XLVIII (1933), 558–597, and "Ivar Aasen as a Writer of Dano-Norwegian," *Scandinavian Studies and Notes*, XII (1932), 53–59.

E. H.

Abell, Kjeld (1901–, Danish dramatist), born in Ribe, southwest Jutland, is one of the few really arresting Scandinavian dramatists of our day. His early career seems to have been about equally divided between a serious interest in political science and a remarkable flair for stage designing, the latter interest ultimately leading to his dramatic authorship. His first play, *Melodien, der blev vaek* (1935; Eng. tr., *The Melody That Got Lost*, 1939), with its delicate lyric touch, its gracious, studied charm, and its remarkably skillful use of modern theatrical "revue" techniques, was an instantaneous success in Denmark, where the half-realistic, half-idyllic folk character found the subtle indirections of form and sentiment in the play exactly to its taste. Five other plays have come in rapid succession from Abell's pen, the most important of which is the serious modern problem-play *Anna Sophie Hedvig* (1939; Eng. tr. in *Scandinavian Plays of the Twentieth Century*, Ser. 2, 1944). Here Abell's early penchant for theatrical "modernism" in its most capricious forms gives way to a much more sober, essentially realistic form, and the subtle indirections of dramatic sentiment so characteristic of most of the earlier plays are transformed into certain sharply focused ideas which bear unmistakably upon basic contemporary political problems. The central ethical problem of the play—is it right to commit what society calls "murder" in defense of one's deepest moral sentiments?—is posed specifically with reference to contemporary political developments. Though the main action of the play takes place within the limited confines of a school world in a small Danish provincial town, the obvious "message" of the play (that the individual has the moral right to take a life when his sense of justice has been outraged) is aimed at the political doctrines and practices of European Nazi and Fascist thought. The play contains also a severe arraignment of a modern bourgeois society as such, and the positive position taken is strongly leftist if not actually Communist in its ultimate social and political implications. The Communist thought is not, however, very clearly developed in the play, chiefly perhaps because the play centers its dramatic focus most sharply upon the theme of human protest in its immediate psychological and ethical forms rather than upon the broader concerns of economic, social, and political theory and programs. What the future has in store for Abell as a dramatist is difficult to say. One thing, however, seems clear at present: these six plays bear indubitable witness to the fact that no other living Scandinavian dramatist has such an amazing control of the purely technical resources of the modern stage. And it may be added that such a play as *Anna Sophie Hedvig* suggests that Abell's genius has in it rich reserves of dramatic material which grow immediately and unafraid out of the blood-soaked soil of a contemporary world with all its brutal challenge to serious modern thought.

See: Alrik Gustafson, "Introduction," in *Scandinavian Plays of the Twentieth Century*, Ser. 2 (1944).

A. G.

About, Edmond (1828–1885, French novelist, playwright, and journalist), was born at Dieuze in Lorraine. He attended the Lycée Charlemagne in Paris, where he proved himself a brilliant student, then entered the Ecole Normale Supérieure, and in 1851 won a state scholarship and spent the three next years at the Ecole Française d'Athènes. Although very erudite, he was not destined to remain a mere scholar. On his return to Paris he published a volume of bright, witty, and at times satirical reporting, *La Grèce contemporaine* (1854), which opened to him the doors of the *Revue des deux mondes*. In 1855, however, the novel *Tolla* (Eng. tr., 1855; *Tolla* is apparently an adaptation of Vittoria Savarelli's *Storia del secolo XIX,* 1841) raised a tempest of indignation among critics, who accused him of plagiarism; and the storm had not yet abated when a three-act comedy of his, *Guillery* (earlier title, *L'Effronté*), dismally failed after two performances (1856). In a series of witty and impertinent articles which appeared in the *Figaro* above the signature Valentin de Quévilly, About cheerfully flayed his detractors. In the meanwhile, by his successful *Voyage à travers l'Exposition des Beaux-Arts* (1855) and a succession of amusing sketches in the *Moniteur, Mariages de Paris,* he had fully vindicated himself. His exuberance found another outlet in four novels which to this day are widely read: *Le Roi des Montagnes* (1856; Eng. trs., *The King of the Mountains,* 1861, 1897, 1902), an amusing story of Greek bandits, made into an opera in 1913 by Victor Léon, *Germaine* (1857), *Les Echasses de Maître Pierre* (1857), and *Trente et quarante* (1858).

About had also traveled in Italy, sojourning for a while in Rome, and had written a violent satire against the temporal power of the pope, *La Question romaine* (1859; Eng. tr., *The Roman Question,* 1859), which was first published in Brussels because permission to publish it in France was for a time withheld. He continued his antipapal campaign through weekly articles in the *Opinion nationale,* which were then published under the general title *Lettres d'un bon jeune homme à sa cousine Madeleine* (1861) and of which a new series appeared in 1863. In lighter mood he offered in 1859 a one-act play, *Risette, ou les Millions de la mansarde,* given at the Gymnase, but at the same time he was writing a great five-act drama containing very bold anti-Roman implications. This piece, *Gaetano,* was accepted by the Théâtre Français but not produced there; the Odéon staged it in 1862, and a storm of protests caused it to be withdrawn after only four evenings; it was given repeatedly in provincial cities, never without causing an uproar. About's political activity was kept up in articles, pamphlets, and books (*e.g., Le Progrès,* 1864; *L'ABC du travailleur,* 1868) which have lost interest today. When the Franco-Prussian War broke out, he went as a reporter to the battlefields. After the armistice he joined the ranks of the Republicans, supported Thiers, and together with Sarcey (*q.v.*) and a few others founded the *Siècle* (1871), which was characterized by strong anticlerical and antimonarchistic sentiments. *L'Alsace* (1872) is a severe indictment of the Bismarckian policy and a warning that Alsace will prove to be a vulture tearing the side of the German Empire. About never ceased writing novels: *L'Homme à l'oreille cassée* (1861), an amusing and fanciful episode of the Napoleonic Wars, *Le Nez d'un notaire* (1862), *Le Cas de M. Guérin* (1862), *Madelon* (1863). Some of his earlier plays have been republished in a collection called *Théâtre impossible*. In 1869 appeared *Le Fellah: Souvenirs d'Egypte*.

About presented himself for election to the French Academy in 1870, but his political and religious writings had deeply offended a majority of the members, who denied him their votes. Fourteen years later, in 1884, he was elected to the seat of Jules Sandeau, but died before the official reception.

See: M. Thiébaut, *Edmond About* (1936).

A. Sz.

Abromowitz, Sholem Yakob, *see* Mendele mocher sforim.

Achard, Marcel (1899–, French dramatist), was born at Lyon. His love of the theatre was revealed very early; at the age of seven he told the principal of the school he attended that he would become a dramatist. At the age of 10 a puppet play he wrote was produced. Critics agree that Achard's plays belong to the theatre of fantasy. His first success was *Voulez-vous jouer avec moâ* (Atelier, 1923), in which the characters are clowns and the action takes place in a circus. The dialogue is clever and charming. In *La Vie est belle* (Théâtre de la Madeleine, 1928) the hero is a character, here named Charlemagne, whom Achard introduces in several later plays—a sort of "beloved vagabond." The author throws together, in improbable situations, characters who in ordinary life would have little opportunity to meet. The joy of living is the dominant note of the play. *Jean de la lune* (Comédie des Champs-Elysées, 1929) also enjoyed long popularity as a play and as a film. The principal male character is related to the Charlemagne of *La Vie est belle*. He is an idealist, and although he seems to be a dreamer, he understands human psychology. His faith in the woman he loves, despite her infidelity, triumphs at the end and forces her to accept his philosophy. A more somber note is sounded in *La Belle Marinière* (Comédie Française, 1929). *Domino* (Comédie des Champs-Elysées, 1932; Eng. tr., 1932) was played in New York.

In his criticism of *Pétrus* (Comédie des Champs-Elysées, 1934), Jacques Copeau (*q.v.*), of the Théâtre du Vieux Colombier, uses the words fantasy, imagination, caprice, grace, enchantment, gayety, wit. Achard's plays combine all these traits.

See: L. Delpit, *Paris—Théâtre contemporain,* I (1925), 111, II (1938), 127–130; P. R. Morand, "Marcel Achard and the Modern Stage," *Romanic Review,* XVII (1926), 349–354.

H. H.

Adam, Paul (1862–1920, French novelist), was born in Paris. His great-grandfather and his grandfather were officers in Napoleon's army, and to them he is indebted for his interest in men of action and power. In his first novel, *Chair molle* (1885), Adam shows traces of the naturalistic approach, but he was also closely connected with the symbolists (*see* French symbolism). He founded several magazines, *Carcan* (with Jean Ajalbert), *Symboliste* (with Gustave Kahn and Jean Moréas, *qq.v.*), *Vogue* (with Kahn), and the second series of the *Revue indépendante.* In collaboration with Moréas he wrote *Le Thé chez Miranda* and *Les Demoiselles Joubert* (both 1886). In the year 1889 he actively supported the political party of General Boulanger but, promptly discouraged, he turned back to his literary activities.

A prolific writer, Paul Adam conceived his novels in groups. In a series of 16 volumes entitled *Le Temps et la vie* are found a tale of witchcraft and satanism in the manner of Huysmans (*q.v.*), *Etre, ou les Feux du Sabbat* (1888); an autobiographical story, *Les Images sentimentales* (1893); a powerful tetralogy, *La Force* (1889), *L'Enfant d'Austerlitz* (1902), *La Ruse* (1903), *Au soleil de juillet* (1903); and also *Le Trust* (1910) and *Le Lion d'Arras* (1920). Another group, *L'Epoque,* consists of 20 novels. Besides these cyclic fictions, Paul Adam published 18 volumes of essays (*e.g., Vues d'Amérique,* 1906; *La Morale de la France,* 1908; *La Morale de l'éducation,* 1908), four volumes inspired by the war of 1914, and four dramas. Compact, sometimes overwritten and confused, these works are impressive manifestations of an unusually powerful creative genius. By his cosmic vision, by his ability to analyze the soul of collectivities, to animate crowds and groups of people, Paul Adam appears as a forerunner of what Jules Romains (*q.v.*) named unanimism.

See: Marcel Batilliat, *Paul Adam* (1903); Louis Bertrand, " 'Le Mystère des foules' et l'œuvre de Paul Adam," *Revue hebdomadaire,* Année XXX (1921), Tome I, pp. 133–159; Camille Mauclair, *Paul Adam* (1921); W. Scheifley, "An Epic Genius: Paul Adam," *Sewanee Review,* XXIX (1921), 76–89.

M. E. C.

Adama van Scheltema, Carel Steven (1877–1924, Dutch poet), was born at Amsterdam. He attended the municipal Gymnasium, studied medicine for a short time, went on the stage, became an art dealer, and finally decided to devote himself entirely to literature and to the interests of the Social Democratic Labor Party. His socialism made him an opponent of the editors of *De Nieuwe Gids* (The New Guide), self-centered adherents of "art for art's sake." He was not of the school that believes art to be a cult for the chosen few. To him there could be no art that was not for the many. In one of his songs he likened the hearts of men to rippling brooks which all come together into one glittering stream, a stream of beauty underneath life's turmoil, which carries the voices of all those hearts to the wide, ocean-like, and infinite dream. The poet, in other words, is not the interpreter of his own self, but must, while giving utterance to his emotions, voice in that utterance the feelings that live inarticulate in the community of men. Adama van Scheltema was, indeed, a singer for the people, and the people listened and gave echo to his song. Each new book that was published was seized upon by the composers, who vied with one another in setting his ditties to music. In a vigorously written prose work entitled *Grondslagen eener nieuwe Poezie* (1908; Foundations for a New Poetry) he formulated his ideas of what this poetry for the many should be, but his theory was less effective than his practice. His songs will still be living folk art when his prose is forgotten.

A. J. B.

Ady, Endre (1877–1919, Hungarian poet and writer), was born in Érmindszent and died in Budapest. Among Ady's ancestors there were Calvinist ministers and also members of the minor gentry. He went to secondary school in Nagykároly and Zilah and studied law in Debrecen; he was a journalist in Debrecen and Nagyvárad. In this city he met a highly cultured woman whom he apostrophized as Léda; there was an exultant and pathetic tone in this relationship. In 1915 Ady married Berta Boncza, a woman much younger than he. He traveled a great deal and often visited the Riviera and Paris. His stories and articles sent from Paris to *Budapesti Napló* (Budapest Ledger), a daily paper, and to *Nyugat* (West), a progressive literary bimonthly, aroused considerable discussion; conservative politicians and publicists attacked him as a heretic. Ady opposed the Hungarian ruling classes, their complacency, their indifference to social progress. He also criticized their spiritual immobility, their aesthetic insensitiveness, the wide gulf between the literate and the illiterate. Hailing from a family of puritanic integrity and surrounded by a world in which the profit motive in business and callousness in politics prevailed, he drew his inspiration from these contrasts and expressed himself in a poetic vernacular that irritated those who did not possess his linguistic and creative insight. Although his romantic self-centeredness prevented him from touching the problems of Hungary at every point, yet his basic visions embraced many phases of Hungarian life; rural conditions, urban complexities, class struggles, the issues of the day, all found apocalyptic expression in the rhythms of his poetry. He was also aware of the problems of the Danubian Valley; some of his poems show the vastness of these problems and the poet's ability to approach them with tolerance and understanding. In his strongly personal poems he sang about love, voluptuousness, dissipation, materialism, mysticism, nature, death, and God. His was a tormented soul; Baudelaire's (*q.v.*) battle with the evil spirit of human destiny had its counterpart in Ady's struggle; no wonder that the French poet's art affected him somewhat. Nevertheless his "decadence" was not that of a congenitally sick man but of one whom the world sickened by its wickedness, selfishness, stupidity, and thieving unscrupulousness. By nature he was not a misanthrope; he could love with a childlike warmth, as was shown through his attachment to his mother and to his birthplace. It is reasonable to assume that if the ruling classes of Hungary could have sympathized with his spiritual quest, it would have been easier for him to find a solution for his problems.

Ady's major poems appeared in 11 volumes; his essays, sketches, short stories, articles, in five volumes. After his death, attempts were made to publish his collected works; but the tragic aftermath of the First World War, its desolate accompaniment, a despoiled Hungary, did not favor issuing the collected works of a poet. Adapted editions of Ady's work were published; often political exigencies resulted in an exploitation of Ady's poetry that he would have resented had he been alive. His departure from conventional phrasing was recognized as the prerogative of a poetic genius, and it was also wisely observed that his "modern" idiom echoed the biblical and rural Hungarian language of the 16th, 17th, and 18th centuries. At present Ady's works, once so unreal to many of his compatriots, appear more authentic than those of any other Hungarian poet of the 20th century; he symbolizes an isolated nation's instinct of self-preservation, the need of change, the courage of convictions, the inadequacy of stale traditions. For some time it was fashionable to praise him without discrimination; recently, however, readers have become more critical, more selective. Some of his poetry sounds rhetorical or trite because Ady was prone to succumb too quickly to lyrical impulses; nevertheless what is genuine in his poetry suggests lasting value. No doubt Ady's poetry is better, more original, more exquisite, than his prose. *Vér és arany* (1907; Blood and Gold), *Szeretném ha szeretnének* (1909; I Should Like to Be Loved), *Ki látott engem?* (1914; Who Has Seen Me?), *A halottak élén* (1918; Leading the Dead), and the rest of his poetic volumes show the workings of a mind and of a heart extremely sensitive and imaginative. His images are unexpected and varied. Ady's neurotic disgust with unfairness and platitudes, his prophecy of horror and terror, his pursuit of social and individual values are served in their expression by the strength of a skillful versifier who knew just how to blend the visions and fears of his poetic personality. It has proved difficult to translate Ady into foreign tongues; in English, Watson Kirkconnell, the Canadian poet, has been the most successful. Most translations do not reflect the magic of Ady's poetry. Many books and essays were written about Ady; he has a school of followers; however, he is so original that any imitation immediately betrays the imitator's lack of originality.

See: J. Horváth, *Ady és a legujabb magyar lira* (1909); A. Schöpflin, *Magyar irók* (1917); H. Horváth, *Neue ungarische Lyrik* (1918); J. Horváth, *Aranytol Adyig* (1921); W. Kirkconnell, *The Magyar Muse; an Anthology* (1933); J. Reményi, "Endre Ady, Hungary's Apocalyptic Poet," *Slavonic Review,* Vol. XXII (1944), Part I, pp. 84–105.

J. R.

Afinogenov, Alexander Nikolayevich (1904–1941, Russian dramatist), was brought up at Yaroslavl on the Volga and, with a writer as a father and a school teacher as a mother, turned at an early age to literature. At 15 he started writing, at 16 he edited a paper, while still in his teens he published three small books of verse, and at 19 he began having his plays produced at the Proletkult Theatre in Moscow.

In his first three plays he turned for his subject matter to labor struggles in other countries and earlier periods. *Robert Tim* (1923) dealt with a revolt of the weavers in England in the early 19th century. *Po tu storonu shcheli* (1926; On the Other Side of the Slot) was based on Jack London's story "South of the Slot," about a strike among the workers across the cable line on Market Street in San Francisco during the early years of the 20th century. *Na perelome* (1926; At the Breaking Point) dramatized the unrest in Germany at the end of the First World War.

In his next three plays Afinogenov turned to the life that he found about him in the Soviet Union. *Glyadi v oba!* (1927; Look with Both Eyes!) emphasized the need for the young Communist to keep his eyes open to the snares laid by enemies of the Soviet Union. *Malinovoe varene* (1927; Raspberry Jam) showed the danger of a Red army leader caring too much for the good things of life. *Volchya tropa* (1927; The Trail of the Wolf) depicted an engineer of the old regime trying to cover up his tracks.

In the more mature plays which followed, Afinogenov turned from these external conflicts in order to deal, like Chekhov (*q.v.*), with the inner drama within the characters; but, instead of showing the disintegration of a decaying society, he dealt rather with the birth pangs of a new social order. He had the courage to discuss boldly the problems that were in the minds of his audiences. In *Chudak* (1929; The Crank) he took as his hero a misunderstood but enthusiastic and hard-working non-Communist. In *Strakh* (1931; Eng. tr., *Fear,* 1934) he boldly tackled the theory that the ruling force in the Soviet Union was fear, showing up the fallacy of this belief. Passionately discussed, acted in 390 theatres in the Soviet Union and in those of England and America, this was Afinogenov's greatest success. At this same time he published a book discussing his theories of Soviet drama, called *Tvorcheski metod teatra* (1931; The Creative Method of the Theatre). Another play, *Portret* (1934; Portrait), took up sympathetically the efforts of a woman to break with the evil traditions of her past and to advance with the new socialist society.

During the following years Afinogenov pointed out in his plays the growing menace of fascist aggression. In *Dalyokoe* (1935; Eng. trs., *Remote,* 1936, *Distant Point,* 1941) he showed how important the morale of even a remote Soviet village is to the defense of the motherland. In *Salyut Ispaniya!* (1936; Salute, Spain!) he championed the struggle of the Spanish Loyalists against the fascists and donated his proceeds from the play to the widows and children of the Loyalists killed in the struggle. *Mat svoikh detei* (1940; The Mother of Her Children) symbolized Mother Russia and her devotion to her various children. *Mashenka* (1941; performed by the Harvard Dramatic Club in 1942 and in New York in 1943 under the title *Listen, Professor!*) showed a 15-year-old girl awakening her grandfather to an interest in the new generation and the new Russia.

With the Nazi attack on the Soviet Union in June, 1941, Afinogenov wrote *Nakanune* (performed 1942; Eng. tr., *On the Eve,* in *Seven Soviet Plays,* 1946), depicting a Russian family on the eve of the invasion and their transformation into active resistance immediately afterwards. On November 5, 1941, less than four and a half months after the beginning of the invasion, Afinogenov, while on duty as a member of the Soviet Information Bureau, was killed on the Ilyinka in the heart of Moscow by the explosion of a bomb dropped in a Nazi air raid. He died, as he himself would have said, "full of life."

See: *O "Strakhe"* (1931), the opinions of 24 authors about Afinogenov's *Fear.* H. W. L. Dana, "Afinogenov," *Theatre Arts,* XXVI (1942), 169–176.

H. W. L. D.

Akhmatova, Anna (pseud. of Anna Andreyevna Gorenko, 1888–, Russian poet), was born near Odessa into the family of a merchant marine officer. While still an infant she was taken to Tsarskoye Selo, whither the family moved, and her education began at the Tsarskoye Selo Gymnasium. Before she had finished the Gymnasium curriculum Akhmatova was transferred first to the Smolny Institute and then to Fundukleyev Gymnasium in Kiev, and here she graduated. Subsequently she enrolled in the Kiev College for Women in the faculty of jurisprudence; she also attended the Rayev historical-literary courses in St. Petersburg, where she was a student of the poet Annenski (*q.v.*). In 1910 she married N. S. Gumilyov (*q.v.*), also a poet, and traveled with him in Italy, France, and Germany. In 1918 Akhmatova divorced Gumilyov and married Vladimir Shileyko, an Assyriologist and a poet in his own right. Her home is in Leningrad.

Akhmatova belongs to the "Acmeist" school of Russian poetry and occupies a distinctive place in that group. Akhmatova's genre is lyrical poetry. Its form—with its brittle clarity of description, the direct simplicity of narration, and the musical quality of language—proves an admirable foil for the subject matter, which consists of personal, deeply emotional, pessimistic, and often ironical love lyrics.

Akhmatova began writing poetry before she was 11. Her first published poem appeared in the Russian miscellany *Sirius* (1907), issued in Paris by Gumilyov. Her first book of verse, *Vecher* (Evening), with a warm introduction by the poet Kuzmin, was published in 1912. Subsequent books of verse include the immensely popular *Chyotki* (1914; 9th ed., 1923; Prayer Beads), *Belaya staya* (1917; The White Flock), *Podorozhnik* (1921; The Buckthorn), and *Stikhi* (1922; Verses). After 1922 Akhmatova was silent for the better part of two decades, and only since the outbreak of the Second World War has she returned to poetic activity.

See: B. Eikhenbaum, *Anna Akhmatova* (1923); V. Vinogradov, *Poezia Anny Akhmatovoy* (1925).

O. M.

Alain, *see* Chartier, Emile.

Alain-Fournier, *see* Fournier.

Alarcón, Pedro Antonio de (1833–1891, Spanish novelist), was born in Guadix, Granada, of a noble but impoverished family which claimed a strain of Moorish blood. After receiving his education in the local seminary he chose journalism for his profession. In 1854 with a group of young liberals from Granada, the Cuerda Granadina, he migrated to Madrid, where he became editor of a radical journal, the *Látigo*. Forced to fight a duel with a champion of Queen Isabella II because of his insults to the crown, he found himself on the field of honor deserted by his radical friends, his life spared only by the generosity of his opponent, who fired into the air. The experience led him to reconsider soberly his political creed and to align himself thereafter with the more conservative forces. When the African war broke out in 1859 he went to the front as the first great modern war correspondent. His *Diario de un testigo de la guerra en Africa* (1859–1860), a best seller, made him rich and famous. He traveled through France and Italy, becoming converted in Rome to a militant Catholicism. From 1861 to 1873 he devoted himself to politics as a member of the Unión Liberal, a middle of the road party. Defeated in his campaign for reelection to the Cortes by the ultraconservative candidate, he again took up his pen and during the next 10 years produced all his major works. In 1875 he was elected a member of the Spanish Royal Academy and in his inaugural discourse, *Sobre la moral en el arte,* defended the thesis that the artist cannot be indifferent to the moral implications of his work. This was heresy to the naturalists, and Alarcón found himself outside the main literary current of his day. His serious works found no favor with the critics. Offended by what he thought was their injustice, he resolved in 1882 never to write another novel. In 1887 he suffered an attack of apoplexy, and the last years of his life were spent in complete seclusion.

Alarcón was an eclectic by temperament. He belonged to no school, but wrote sometimes like a belated romantic, sometimes like a *costumbrista,* sometimes like a disciple of Balzac. There is no evidence of a consistent development in his work. He had no gift for inventing a plot or creating characters, but he had great narrative talent. He is at his best in the shorter forms of fiction and with traditional plot material. His first novel, *El final de Norma* (1855), a highly colored tale with an exotic setting, is romantic trash. His later serious novels—*El escándalo* (1875), which tells of the spiritual redemption of a dissolute youth; *El niño de la bola* (1880), which demonstrates the power of religious faith over human passions; and *La pródiga* (1882), which presents an unhappy mixture of love and politics—are unrealistically conceived, often melodramatic and lacking in good taste. Some of his earlier stories, however, especially those set in the background of the Peninsular Wars, such as "El afrancesado" and "El carbonero alcalde" (in *Cuentos, articulos y novelas,* 1859, later reissued in the first of the three volumes of *cuentos, Historietas nacionales,* 1881, *Cuentos amatorios,* 1881, and *Narraciones inverosímiles,* 1882), are models of good storytelling. The unassuming love story of a gruff soldier, *El capitán Veneno* (1882; Eng. tr., *Captain Venom,* 1914), is lighthearted and charming. But Alarcón's claim to immortality is based chiefly upon his incomparable tale of the corregidor's love for the miller's wife, *El sombrero de tres picos* (1874; Eng. trs., *The Three-cornered Hat,* 1891, 1918, 1927) which has become the best-known work of Spanish fiction since *Don Quixote.* In this gay and witty story Alarcón perfectly and seemingly without effort fitted style to theme and produced an almost faultless masterpiece.

In addition to his works of fiction, Alarcón wrote a volume of poems, *Poesías serias y humorísticas* (1870); a drama, *El hijo pródigo* (produced in 1857); several books of travel, *De Madrid a Nápoles* (1861), *La Alpujarra* (1874), *Viajes por España* (1884); a collection of essays, *Juicios literarios y artísticos* (1883); and an autobiographical *Historia de mis libros* (1884).

See: M. Catalina, "Biografía del autor," in Alarcón, *Novelas cortas* (1884), pp. v–xliii; C. Barja, *Literatura española: Libros y autores modernos,* revised ed. (1933), pp. 253–258; E. Pardo Bazán, *Alarcón; estudio biográfico* (n.d.).

E. H. H.

Alas, Leopoldo (pseud. Clarín, 1852–1901, Spanish novelist, essayist, and literary critic), was born at Zamora, but he belongs in every respect to Asturias, where his ancestors came from and where, first as a student, then as a professor of law at the University of Oviedo, he lived most of his life. Asturian also were the basic traits of his literary personality—the cosmopolitan intellectual outlook together with a deep sense of attachment to the regional, the subtle critical analysis, the idealistic aspiration, and the ironic sense of humor.

It was as a literary critic in the field of contemporary literature that Alas, under the pseudonym Clarín, became famous. For this task of literary criticism he was well qualified, adding to his natural gifts of a keen mind and a refined taste the advantages of a broad literary and philosophical background, plus a spirit of wide-awake curiosity that kept him always posted about the most recent cultural developments. His efforts were not always as fruitful as might otherwise have been the case, however, due in part to the exigencies of a daily journalistic task, in part also to what sometimes was an excess of benevolence and other times an excess of passion and of moralistic zeal that caused his criticism to degenerate into a bitter and more or less personal satire. But even with these weaknesses, his criticism is always stimulating, and his influence was among the most powerful in the renovation of the Spanish literary atmosphere at the end of the 19th century. Examples of the author's literary criticism are *Solos de Clarín* (1881), the eight *Folletos literarios* (1886–1891), *Palique* (1893), and *Benito Pérez Galdós* (1889).

While the reputation of Alas as a critic has suffered somewhat, his reputation as a novelist, in spite of the small amount of fiction that he wrote—two novels, two volumes of short stories, and some three volumes of *cuentos*—has constantly increased. This novelistic production falls roughly into two groups, corresponding to the two main phases in the author's literary career, first as a naturalist, then as an idealist and a spiritualist. An admirer of Zola (*q.v.*), Alas was for years not only one of the most enthusiastic exponents in Spain of the naturalistic doctrine but also one of its most faithful practitioners, as evidenced by his long novel *La Regenta* (2 vols., 1884–1885), one of the best novels produced in Spain in the past century. The provincial life of Oviedo (Vetusta in the novel) is woven around a love story of which the *Regenta,* a married woman, is the coveted prize, the contenders being an unsuccessful church dignitary and a finally successful local Don Juan. The canvas here presented is broad, objective, and minutely detailed, reminding one in this case even more of Flaubert (*q.v.*) than of Zola. Traces of the naturalistic influence are also to be found in the author's second full-length novel, *Su único hijo* (1890), as well as in some of the short stories of the volume *Pipá* (1886). Side by side with the naturalistic influence, however, an idealistic tendency begins noticeably to affirm itself in these works, which thus appear as a transition between the naturalism of *La Regenta* and the idealism of the author's last manner. The germs of this idealism were already present in what had always been a romantic and moralistic disposition of the temperament of Alas, and as the years went by, especially under the influence of the idea of death, it tended to assume the form of a religious spiritualism. This idealism became finally the main source of the author's inspiration, and led by it, he wrote some of his most delicate work, short stories such as "Doña Berta" (1892) and, above all, the collections of *cuentos* in the volumes *El Señor y lo demás son cuentos* (1892 or 1893), *Cuentos morales* (1896), and *El gallo de Sócrates* (1901).

See: Azorín, *Clásicos y modernos* (1913), pp. 85–96; P. Sáinz Rodríguez, "'Clarín' y su obra," *Revista de las Españas,* II (1927), 305–311, 441–444, 536–538, 604–613.

C. B.

Albanian literature. Literary works in Albanian, written and published on Albanian soil, became possible only with the rise of a free Albanian state following the Balkan Wars of 1912 and 1913. Up to that time, and throughout the more than four centuries of Ottoman rule which preceded it, writing in the native tongue had been prohibited under stern penalties rigidly enforced by the Turkish gendarmes. Only in Scutari, capital of northern Albania, and there as a result of the special privileges enjoyed by the Roman Catholic clergy, was any exception to this rule permitted.

Yet writing in the Albanian tongue was begun long before 1913, and at first as a consequence of the folk cult which accompanied 19th-century romanticism. The pioneer in this field was Girolamo de Rada (1813–1903), an Italian of Albanian parentage who began his career by collecting the ballads and songs of his countrymen living in Italy and who turned later to writing original verse in which he used the ballad themes as his material. De Rada's principal works are *The Song of Seraphina Thopia, Princess of Zadrima* (1843), an Albanian *Lenore; The Song of Milosaon* (1864), a tale of old Scutari; *Rapsodie albanesi* (1866); and *Skanderbeg* (1873), a song of Albania's greatest national figure. The heir of De Rada on Italian soil was the scholar and poet Giuseppe Schiró (1865–1927), known in literary history for his *Kënga e Mirditës* (1919; The Song of Mirdita) and for his research in Albanian language and literature.

A great spur to literary activity among the Albanians was afforded by the Congress of Berlin (1878), with its high-handed partition of the Albanian lands. Scarcely had the decisions of the Congress been promulgated when, in protest, a league was formed for the defense of Albania's political rights and the promotion of her cultural advance. Soon books in Albanian began to appear wherever Albanians were to be found outside the homeland. Religious differences, which cut deep in Albania, dividing the Moslem from the man of Orthodox faith and both alike from the Roman Catholic, were put aside as representatives of the three faiths met to agree on the principles to be observed in the creation of what seemed desirable to all, a truly national Albanian culture.

One of the leaders in this movement was the historian and patriot Sami Bey Fráshëri (Šems-ed-Dīn Sāmī Frāšerī), author of the first Albanian drama, *Besa* (1901; Pledge of Honor). Another was Pasko Vasa Pasha (pseud. Wassa Effendi, 1827–1892), a Roman Catholic of Scutari who had served under the Porte as governor of Lebanon and the author of Albania's moving hymn of liberation, "Moj Shqypni" (1881; O My Albania). The principal literary figure produced by the movement was Naïm Fráshëri (1846–1900), brother of the above-mentioned Sami. Scion of an aristocratic southern Albanian family and a member of the powerful Bektashi (Bektāšī) sect, Naïm Fráshëri turned from the career of scholar which lay open to him on completion of his studies abroad to dedicate his talents to the Albanian muse. With the pastoral idyl *Bagëti e Bujqësija* (1886; Shepherds and Plowmen), published in Sofia and smuggled into Albania by friendly caravans, Fráshëri won the hearts of his countrymen and made himself their spokesman. Following this with *Fletore e Bektashinjet* (1896; Book of the Bektashis), Naïm Fráshëri turned finally to the theme employed by almost every Albanian writer at one time or another, the story of Skanderbeg, producing a full-length biography in verse—*Istoria e Skënderbeut* (1898; The Story of Skanderbeg). Naïm Fráshëri died abroad in poverty. In 1937, however, when Albania celebrated her first quarter century of independence, his remains were brought to Tirana, the Albanian capital, and a monument was erected to his memory.

The first Albanian verse to be written on Albanian soil was that of Gjergj Fishta (1856–1941), an Albanian of humble Roman Catholic parentage from the Zadrima highland of Scutari. On account of the special conditions, referred to above, which prevailed in the Scutari region, Father Fishta was able to publish his verses, besides his literary review in Albanian *(Hylli i Dritës;* Star of Light), a whole generation before such a thing was possible anywhere else in the realm. Through the publishing house of the Franciscan Order, to which he belonged, Father Fishta was able to serve the Albanian cause well. His principal work, and probably the most authentic lyric note in Albanian literature thus far, was *Lahuta e Malcis* (1899–1909; Highland Strings). Taking its inspiration from popular ballads, the poem links the modern knights of the mountains with their prototypes in the Middle Ages and thus makes all Albanian history one in its heroic struggle for freedom and independence. Fishta died in retirement following the Italian invasion of Albania, stubbornly refusing collaboration with the Fascist "new order." With the name of Fishta is linked that of his fellow Franciscan and coworker, Vinçénc Prenushi, best known for his collection of northern Albanian folk poems, *Kângë Popullore* (1911; Popular Songs).

Two dramatists to be noted are Mihal Grameno (1878–), an Orthodox Albanian of Korça (Koritza), the principal cultural center of southern Albania, whose patriotic tragedy *Vdekja e Piros* (1906; The Death of Pyrrhus) immortalizes not only the great warrior himself but his wife Antigone, daughter of Ptolemy, as well; and Kristo Floqi, also of Korça and also of the Orthodox faith, whose drama *Fé e Kombësi* (1912; Faith and Patriotism) elaborates somewhat melodramatically the popular theme of mixed marriage. A lawyer by profession, Floqi is also a poet. His *Anthollogjia Shqipëtare* (1923; Albanian Anthology), a collection of epic and lyric verse, was used as a textbook in the schools of free Albania.

The two Albanian writers best known abroad are the essayist and critic Faïk Konitza (1875–1942), a member of the Bektashi sect, long editor of the review *Albania* (1896–1909) in Brussels and London, and of the newspaper *Dielli* (Sun), which was published in Boston (1909–); and Fan S. Noli (1881–), bishop of the Albanian Orthodox Church in America. A native of Kyteza, near Adrianople, Bishop Noli received his early education in Turkey and Egypt. Later he came to the United States and was graduated from Harvard University and the New England Conservatory of Music. In 1908 he founded the Albanian Orthodox Church in America. Returning to Albania in the early 20's, Noli served his country as prime minister for six months, only to be forced into exile as a result of the opposition of the feudal lords of the south who objected to his American ideas. Of Bishop Noli's literary works, exclusive of translations, the most important are *Istoria e Skënderbeut* (1921; The Story of Skanderbeg), a biography; the three-act play *Israelite dhe Filistine* (1907; Israelite and Philistine); and *Byzantin Symphony* (1938; The Byzantine Symphony). Probably Noli's greatest contribution to Albanian literature has been his enrichment and expansion of the language itself, through forcing it to express the ideas and sentiments of such world figures as Shakespeare and Ibsen (*q.v.*) and Blasco Ibañez (*q.v.*), to mention but a few of those whose works he has translated.

To the present generation of Albanian writers belong Alexander S. Drenova (pseud. Asdrén), a native of Korça, with his *Psalme Murgu* (1930; Psalms of a Monk), *Rrëzë Dielli* (1904; Facing the Sun), and *Êndëra e Lotë* (1912; Dreams and Tears; and Alí Asllani with his *Hanko Halla* (Aunt Jane), a series of poems full of the homely local wit of Valona. Then there are Skëndér Bardhi, an American of Albanian parentage, a journalist, poet, and teacher, whose poems of the Second World War echo the Albanian's age-old cry of liberty; and Andon Zako (pseud. Çajupi), author of *Babá Tomori,* an anthology of Albanian mountain songs. There is also Midhat Fráshëri (pseud. Lumo Skëndo, 1880–), editor of the literary journal *Diturija* (Education), founded in 1909, and director of the Lumo Skëndo Library in Tirana, whose translation of Schiller's *Wilhelm Tell* has become well known.

Besides these, there are the poet Louis Gurakuqi; Ramíz Harxhi, who wrote poems, *Dëshirat e Zëmërës* (1917; Desires of the Heart), in the idiom of Argyrocastra and Kurveleshi of the south; and Hil Mosi, author of *Zan' i Atdheut* (1913; Voice of the Fatherland). Branko Merxhani, an essayist, was the editor, up to the time of the Italian invasion, of the literary review *Përjkekja Shqiptare* (The Albanian Endeavor), published in Tirana. Foqión Postoli is remembered for the popular novels *Për Mbrojtjen e Atdheut* (1921; In Defense of the Fatherland) and *Lulja e Kujtimit* (1924; The Flower of Reminiscence), as well as for the sentimental play *Dëtyra e Mëmës* (1925; The Mother's Duty). Ilo-Mitkë Qafëzezi has done much to popularize biography. In Milto Sotir-Gurra, a native of Opari, is seen the influence of Maupassant (*q.v.*) and of O. Henry, especially in his *Plagët e Kurbetit* (1938; Wounds of an Exile).

The 30's saw the meteoric rise of a poetic talent in the person of Lasgush Poradeci (1899–), often compared with the Rumanian Mihail Eminescu (*q.v.*). He has been called "a poet of the future"; opinion is divided as to his worth. Like so much of Albanian writing, a good deal of which has been produced abroad, Poradeci's verse has little contact with the real people of Albania. For the true spirit of the land of the Shqipetare, the land of the eagle, as Albanians call their country, one is obliged to turn to the two pioneers of Albanian literature, Naïm Fráshëri and Gjergj Fishta, and, in our own time, to the works of Kristo Floqi.

See: J. Bourcart, "Le Mouvement littéraire en Albanie," *Vie des peuples,* XV (1925), 341–362; S. Shundi, "Lasgush Poradeci," *Balkans,* III (1933), 502–504; X. Lefcoparidis, "L'Albanie intellectuelle," *Balkans,* VI (1934), 79–84; A. Klančar, "Modern Albanian Literature," *Books Abroad,* XVI (1942), 20–23.

N. D.

Alberti, Rafael (1902–, Spanish poet), was born in Puerto de Santa María, Cádiz, and after studying in the Jesuit academy went to

Madrid in 1917. His book *Marinero en tierra* won the National Prize for Literature in 1924. He has never engaged in any other activity except the writing of poetry. During the Spanish civil war he was a fervent supporter of the republic. He has traveled in Europe and visited Soviet Russia. At the end of the civil war and after living some time in Paris, he went to Buenos Aires, where he is continuing his literary work.

Within the total unity of his production, a unity characterized by spiritual grace and technical dexterity, certain stages in his poetry can be distinguished. His first three books, *Marinero en tierra* (1925), *La amante* (1926), and *El alba del alhelí* (1927), are a renovation of the beauties and refinements of the rhythmic poetry of the *cancioneros* of the 16th century, with application to modern and personal themes. A refined treatment of folk themes and a natural exquisiteness are their distinguishing characteristics. In *Cal y canto* (1927) he adds subjects from modern life, represented by the elevator, the telegram, railroad stations, and aviation and presented in a Neo-Gongoristic language of dazzling beauty and novelty of usage. In 1929 his most significant book, *Sobre los ángeles,* was published. Here he deviates from the traditional elements used previously; his angels personify virtues, vices, places, and materials. Each poem has an independent value, but in their totality they convey an impression of distress, of anguish, that is a product of the fatal intimacy between the most beautiful and the most ugly, the most naïve and the most perverse, in that imaginary world of the angels. From that moment the satisfaction he had found in gracefulness was changed to a concern for amplitude and depth. As Alberti declared in 1934, his poetry ceases to serve purely aesthetic reason and now obeys revolutionary reason. *Poesía* (1934) gathers all the aforementioned books under one cover and initiates the period of the social themes; *Trece bandas y cuarenta y ocho estrellas* (*Poema del Mar Caribe*) (1935) and *De un momento a otro* (1937) contain his poetry in defense of the proletarian man in general and of the Spaniard in a struggle for his liberty. His books published since he has been living in Buenos Aires, especially *Entre el clavel y la espada* (1941), seem to temper the immediate aspects of the political theme with a greater insight into its poetical transcription. He has also produced a book in prose, *La arboleda perdida* (1942), which is a series of fanciful recollections of his childhood.

During the first years of his writing Alberti combines with unsurpassed cleverness the two imperatives of literature at the beginning of the century—the folk theme, the essential reality of things Spanish, and the refinements of poetic form which were a part of the program of *modernista* poetry. No one is more skillful in putting into verses of Gongoresque lineage not only the perceptible echo of a historical style, but also the authentic qualities of an entirely contemporary emotion. As he sings of the streetcar ticket, the bullfight, and the football player, all the lyric magic of the baroque period comes to life, vivified in these contemporary themes. From this moment he discards all formal striving for effect based on classic tradition. His poetry is receptive to the torments and incoherences brought to literature by the winds of surrealism. But it is never shapeless or spiritually obscure. On the contrary it is surprising how, even in the depth of his most tortured poetic thought, there still survive the grace and clarity which have characterized his work from the very beginning. Even in his violent and aggressive poems of the modern period, there are continual glimmers of tenderness and delicacy. His crudest moments of expression retain an inevitable verbal charm which constitutes the essence of his poetic personality.

Three of his dramatic works are known: *Fermín Galán* (1931), which exalts the figure of the lieutenant in rebellion against the monarchy; *El hombre deshabitado* (1931), an *auto* of modern thought, descended from the Spanish *auto* theatre; and *La pájara pinta,* a lyrico-farcical fantasy.

See: P. Salinas, *Literatura española siglo XX* (1941), pp. 277–289; E. Proll, "'Popularismo' and 'Barroquismo' in the Poetry of Rafael Alberti," *Bulletin of Spanish Studies,* XIX (1942), 59–86.

P. S.

Albert i Paradis, Catalina, *see* Català, Victor.

Alcover i Maspons, Joan (1854–1926, Catalonian poet), was born in the city of Palma de Mallorca, where he grew up and devoted himself to the practice of law. He did not start to write in Catalan until about 1900; then he found in this particular medium exactly what he needed to produce a truly vigorous literary work. Poems such as "La creu" (The Cross), "Mallorca" (Majorca), "La serra" (The Sierra), "Ramon Llull," "Beethoven," and "Canco de la balanguera" (Song of the Spinning Girl) attracted the attention of critics. The solidarity existing among the

Catalan-speaking countries was shown when the society Rat Penat of Valencia, devoted to the cultivation of literature in the native tongue, made him an honorary member. A deeply felt personal bereavement resulted in elegies of consummate beauty. Manuel de Montoliu has asserted that Joan Alcover is the most profoundly human poet of the Catalonian Renaissance. In 1921 Alcover's poems were collected in a slender volume, *Poesies.*

Alcover has, like other poets of Majorca, a true gift of form. Indeed it is curious that poets so disimilar in regard to themes as Alcover, Costa i Llobera, and Alomar (*qq.v.*) should all show an instinctive Parnassianism. This may be explained in part by the beauties of the land of Majorca and also by the fact that the island is at an intersection of cultural highways running from Italy to Valencia and from France to Barcelona. The language of Joan Alcover has within it a melodic quality difficult to define without examples, and the poet's sensibility is extraordinary. In spite of the leisurely and gentle flow of this verse, Joan Alcover was capable of appreciating the literary revolution which Rubén Darío had begun in Hispanic-American literature and saluted him in notable lines. The Illustracio Catalana has published the complete works of Alcover in three volumes, the first devoted to his poetry, the second to literary-biographical sketches, and the third to his speeches and articles.

See: M. de Montoliu, *Estudis de literatura catalana* (1912); C. Riba, *Escolis* (1921); R. Crossmann, *Katalanische Lyrik der Gegenwart* (1923); A. Schneeberger, *Anthologie des poètes catalans contemporains* (1923); C. Giardini, *Antologia dei poeti catalani contemporanei, 1845–1925* (1926).

F. de P.

Aldanov, Mark Aleksandrovich (pseud. of Mark Aleksandrovich Landau, 1886–, Russian novelist, biographer, and essayist), was born at Kiev, of well-to-do parents, and took degrees in chemistry and law at Kiev University. He left Russia in 1919 and settled in Paris; after the collapse of France he emigrated to the United States (January, 1941). Nearly all of his work has been done abroad.

Aldanov is best known for his historical novels, beginning with the tetralogy, *Myslitel* (The Thinker), which deals with the events of 1793–1821: *Devyatoye termidora* (1923; Eng. tr., *The Ninth Thermidor,* 1926); *Chortov most* (1925; Eng. tr., *The Devil's Bridge,* 1928); *Zagovor* (1927; The Conspiracy); *Svyataya Yelena, malenki ostrov* (1923; Eng. tr., *Saint Helena, Little Island,* 1924). Symbolical devices link the *Myslitel* series to a trilogy centering about the personal problems brought into being by the forces of the Russian Revolution and the attempts of the *émigrés* to cope with life abroad: *Klyuch* (1930; Eng. tr., *The Key,* 1931); *Begstvo* (1932; The Flight); *Peshchera* (2 vols., 1934–1936; The Cave). Some of the themes and one of the characters are carried over into *Nachalo kontsa* (1939; Eng. tr., *The Fifth Seal,* 1943), an interpretation of the general frustration and disillusionment that preceded the Second World War. Aldanov's interest in individual characters and social movements places him squarely in the great tradition of the Russian novel, but he interprets that tradition after his own manner, blending pessimism with irony, realism with symbolical interpretation. A kinship with the 18th century is manifest in the "symbolical tales": the exquisite *Desyataya simfoniya* (1931; The Tenth Symphony, which brings to life Beethoven and the Vienna of his time and presents the eternal problem of human unhappiness and unfulfillment, and *Mogila voina* (1940; Eng. tr., *For Thee the Best,* 1945), a tale of the last years of Byron, of Castlereagh and other statesmen, with the activities of a minor political spy furnishing the necessary links as well as a fresh perspective. The historical novelist's manner reappears in his biographical sketches of significant political personalities—*Sovremenniki* (1928; Contemporaries), *Portrety* (1931; Portraits); there, too, the narrative is leisurely and the canvas large.

See: Charles Ledré, *Trois Romanciers russes* (1935).

P. A. P.

Aleixandre, Vicente (1900–, Spanish poet), born in Seville of a rich family, spent his childhood in Andalusia. Later he moved to Madrid, where he has remained and where for a time he halfheartedly studied law. He has never engaged in any kind of professional activity.

Aleixandre is intensely a poet, who feels the irrepressible urge to write poetry—though he is far from voluminous. *Ambito* (1928) gives evidence of a very personal quality which develops into bitter lyricism with *Espadas como labios* (1932). He belongs to the Spanish generation, rich in good poets, which underwent the literary evolution following the First World War and which learned the lofty poetic discipline and exacting standards of the master, Juan Ramón Jiménez (*q.v.*). Aleixandre's work is less widely known than that of many of his contemporaries, although he yields to none of them in lyrical fervor. His limited appeal is due perhaps to the fact that Aleixandre represents, to a greater degree than the others, a type of poetry which, evolving by means of unusual poetic associations (probably quite conscious with Aleixandre), affords the reader few means of interpreting the poem by any logical criteria. The process of penetrating to the doleful essence of this verse is difficult, not because Aleixandre is related to or sympathetic with any esoteric group of poets, but because of his own attitude of caution and circumspection which makes him delight in clothing the dramatic and ultimate meanings of his human grief in the poetically mysterious. All the verse of Aleixandre forms a sort of mighty elegy within the bounds of desperation; the poet himself is not a victim of this desperation but stoically acceptant. The only thing which balances his ardent romanticism is this willingness to fuse himself, to become one with the mystery and grief of the world—from the light of the star to the palpitation of the insect. The opposition between liberation and servitude, between desire and reality, between poetry and life, are indeed felt romantically; here is a struggle to the death which leaves man and the poet without justification. Love and death are basal themes in his poetry and these naturally have been fused. The constant elegiacal character of his work and the recurrence of certain poetic mannerisms impart a sustained and uniform tone to his poetry which may even obscure for the not completely alert reader the richness of the elements in this poetic world.

Aleixandre's dramatic organization of reality is perfectly expressed in his last book, *La destrucción o el amor* (1935), which won the National Prize for Literature in 1934. If we make allowances for what is merely contemporaneous, certain qualities in this work suggest the great Spanish romantics.

See: P. Salinas, *Literatura española siglo XX* (1941).

F. G. L.

Aleramo, Sibilla (pseud. of Rina Faccio, 1879–, Italian novelist and poet), was born in the city of Alessandria. Her father, a university professor, was forced because of financial difficulties to take a position as director of a chemical factory in a small town in southern Italy. There she spent her adolescent years and at 16 married one of the factory workers. Nine years later she broke the bonds of her loveless marriage, deserting both husband and child for what she thought would be a freer and fuller life.

Sibilla Aleramo's work is for the most part autobiographical. A gifted and very beautiful woman, she writes with fervor of the vicissitudes of her emotional life. Her first novel, *Una Donna* (1906; Eng. tr., *A Woman at Bay*, 1908), was received with much enthusiasm and had great success in Italy and in many other European countries. It has been translated into French, German, Spanish, Swedish, Russian, Polish, and Dutch, as well as English. In this revelation of her youthful life the author touches on various social problems of the time, but is most outstanding in her plea for a forceful assertion of the dignity of womanhood and for woman's right to an existence as a free agent in the social order. This theme is further developed in *Il Passaggio* (1921), but with less success as the author puts too great an emphasis on her own particular frustrations. Her other prose works—*Andando e stando* (1921), *Trasfigurazione* (1922), *Il Mio Primo Amore* (1924), and *Amo, dunque sono* (1927)—are confessions of her innumerable amorous experiences and are saturated throughout with her extreme egocentricity and undiluted sensualism.

Sibilla Aleramo's endeavors in the field of poetry, *Momenti* (1921) and *Poesie* (1929), are all in free verse. They are brief exultations and lamentations too limited and circumscribed by her personal conceit and sensuality to attain any substantial spiritual quality, except in rare instances when, despondent and weary, she pens verses about the delusion and vanity of transient carnal pleasure. *Endimione* (1923) is a poetic drama dealing with one of her many adventures. It was presented at the Théâtre de l'Œuvre, Paris, in 1924, but had only an ephemeral success. More recent works are *Gioie d'occasione* (1930) and the drama *Francesca Diamante* (not published), but her first novel, *Una Donna,* is still considered her best product.

See: L. Russo, *I Narratori* (1923), pp. 140–141; C. Pavolini, "Sibilla Aleramo," *Italia che scrive,* VIII (1925), 133–134; G. Ravegnani, *I Contemporanei* (1930), pp. 60–66.

M. T. R.

Alexis, Paul (1847–1901, French journalist, playwright, and novelist), was born at Aix-en-Provence, where he early formed the attachment for Emile Zola (*q.v.*) which was to dominate his entire life. After attracting attention by passing off some poems of his own as works of Charles Baudelaire (*q.v.*), he entered the world of Parisian journalism and soon found himself in a position to render effective aid to the naturalists, to the impressionistic painters, and to Antoine's (*q.v.*) Théâtre Libre. Alexis laid the foundations of his literary reputation with a short story, "Après la bataille," published in the famous *Soirées de Médan* (1880), an adaptation in the naturalistic manner of the Matron of Ephesus legend. His talent for the short story is, however, better revealed in "La Fin de Lucie Pellegrin" (1880), based on an incident recounted by George Moore, and in such collections as *Le Collage* (1883), *Trente Romans* (1894), and *La Comtesse* (1897). His novels, *Madame Meuriot* (1891) and *Vallobra* (1901), and his plays, most of which conform to the naturalistic pattern, have as their milieu the Parisian *demi-monde* which Alexis, a confirmed noctambulist, knew perhaps better than any man of his time. His devotion to Emile Zola, to whom he later remained faithful in the darkest days of the Dreyfus case, is reflected in his *Emile Zola; notes d'un ami* (1882). Always serious and sincere, Alexis wrote without the irony of the other naturalists; his pictures of life, all based on the *document humain,* are rendered in a dry, incisive style which often recalls Stendhal. His famous telegram to Jules Huret, "Naturalisme pas mort!" typifies his life and career: he sincerely believed that the movement led by Zola was to be deathless, and today it may fairly be said of him that he was the only true and constantly faithful naturalist.

See: J. Huret, *Enquête sur l'évolution littéraire* (1891); R. Dumesnil, *La Publication des Soirées de Médan* (1933); L. Deffoux and E. Zavie, *Le Groupe de Médan,* 2d ed. (n.d.).

R. J. N.

Alibert, François Paul (1873–, French poet), was born at Carcassonne, where he has passed nearly all his life, keeping aloof from literary fads and quarrels and pursuing his own way of perfection. Beginning with *L'Arbre qui saigne* (1907), he has gone on quietly year after year producing distinguished poetry which has never won great popularity but has met with universal respect. His early work was written in melodious free verse, but he soon turned to the classical forms and attitudes that have caused him to be compared to Ronsard, Chénier, and, in more modern times, Moréas (*q.v.*) and Régnier (*q.v.*). His poetry in the main alternates between the ample elegiac and the lapidary epigram and in both styles is marked by nobility, majesty, and great technical mastery. Perhaps it is at its best in his work during the early 20's, *Odes* (1922), *Eglogues* (1923), and *Elégies romaines* (1923). Here, though the classical spirit certainly predominates, it is to a marked degree influenced by symbolism, and the individual line comes very near the density of Mallarmé (*q.v.*) without falling into unintelligibility. The only reproach that can be, and has been, made concerning Alibert's verse is that it is cold, too deliberate and intellectual, without ecstatic vision. Certainly it is austere and marked by a purity of thought and expression that perhaps will not attract a romantic spirit. Nor can it be denied that for the most part it is lacking in "high spots." In his longer poems Alibert's tone is restrained and even, his effect coming rather from the spacious execution of a noble concept than from the brilliance of an individual line or stanza. Historically, however, his place seems certain as one of the major figures between Moréas and Valéry (*q.v.*) in the classical renaissance.

See: Yves-Gérard Le Dantec, "Le Mouvement poétique," *Revue des deux mondes,* November 15, 1937, pp. 450–453; René Lalou, *Histoire de la littérature française contemporaine,* enlarged ed., Vol. II (1940).

C. W., Jr.

Alomar, Gabriel (1873–1941, Spanish poet and essayist), born in Palma de Mallorca in the Balearic Islands, died in Cairo, where he had remained after service as Spanish minister to Egypt. A poet and essayist, he preferred the Catalan language for his poetry and Spanish for his prose. As a poet, although one of the first and most enthusiastic Spanish proponents of futurism, he represents nevertheless a moment of transition between a quasi-French Parnassianism and modernism; his constant concern is the form and style of his compositions. In his essays he manifests an ideology akin to the critical and renovating spirit of the Generation of '98 (*see* Spanish literature). Aware of contemporary European currents, he exerted a great influence in the intellectual circles of the eastern regions of the Spanish Mediterranean (Balearic Islands, Catalonia, Valencia), who saw in Alomar the standard-bearer of a new literary and political faith. Although the majority of his essays are scattered in journals and newspapers, some of them were collected in a volume entitled *Verba* (1917). His book of Catalan poetry is entitled *La columna de foc* (*ca.* 1911).

See: J. Mascaró, "Gabriel Alomar," *Bulletin of Spanish Studies,* XX (1943), 48–54.

E. G. L.

Alonso, Amado (1897–, Spanish philologue and critic), was born in Navarre. He received his training at the Centro de Estudios Históricos in Madrid under Menéndez Pidal and Navarro Tomás (*qq.v.*). With the latter he specialized in phonetics and continued in this science in Germany, where he was lecturer in Spanish at Hamburg. In 1927 he went to Buenos Aires as director of the Instituto de Filología of the University of Buenos Aires, where he now resides permanently. His early work on phonetics and linguistic geography—noteworthy is the emendation of Meyer-Lübke's *La subagrupación románica del catalán* (1926)—acquired new scope and originality in America as he confronted in their totality, and in part answered, the complex problems posed by the Spanish language on this continent. *Problemas de dialectología hispanoamericana* (1930), *El problema de la lengua en América* (1935), *Castellano, español, idioma nacional* (1938; 2d ed., 1943), numerous articles on specific questions, together with the work of Alonso's collaborators and students in the Instituto de Filología de Buenos Aires and in the *Revista de filología hispánica,* of which he is editor, are of fundamental importance, not only for the study of language in America, but for the general history of Spanish. In addition to his study of linguistic history and geography he has devoted himself to problems of style in language, spoken as well as literary. He is the leading exponent in the field of Spanish of the ideas and methods of the new philology and literary criticism which are, in the main, the creation of Karl Vossler. Among his studies in style as a method of literary interpretation, most important by reason of their perfection and depth are his article "Estructura de las sonatas de Valle-Inclán" (in *Verbum,* Buenos Aires, 1928) and his books *Poesía y estilo de Pablo Neruda* (1940) and *Ensayo sobre la novela histórica: El modernismo en "La gloria de don Ramiro" de Enrique Larreta* (1942). He has also published, with Pedro Henríquez Ureña, an excellent *Gramática castellana* (1938–1939; 2d ed., 1940–1941).

See: K. Vossler, review of *El problema de la lengua en América* in *Boletín de la Academia Argentina de Letras,* III (Buenos Aires, 1935), 366–369; L. E. Soto, *Crítica y estimación* (1938), pp. 65–80.

F. de O.

Alonso, Dámaso (1898–, Spanish philologist, critic, and literary historian), born in Madrid, has devoted his life to the study of Spanish philology and literature. He was trained in the Centro de Estudios Históricos, where later he was both a collaborator and a professor. He has taught in various European and North American universities and colleges, such as Berlin, Cambridge, Oxford, Stanford, and Columbia, and is a professor at the University of Madrid.

In the field of literary history and criticism he is to be considered as the most important commentator and critic of all time of Góngora's poetry. In 1935 was published *La lengua poética de Góngora,* a masterly study of that poet's poetic system. Already in 1927 he had produced his edition of the *Soledades* of Góngora, with a modern prose version, a model of illuminating precision. Numerous articles on different aspects of this writer's poetry and style have appeared in periodicals, principally the *Revista de filología.* His short book, *La poesía de San Juan de la Cruz,* was published in 1943. In this work he gives a historical, stylistic, and poetical interpretation of the best poems of the 16th-century mystic. His critical work is outstanding for its preparatory and documental solidity, for the rigor and precision of method, and especially for its fine taste and deep literary sensibility.

Dámaso Alonso brought to criticism and literary history the gifts of the delicate and original writer revealed in his *Poemas puros: Poemillas de la ciudad* (1921) and in verse published in magazines. Certain vivid narratives by Alonso have appeared in literary reviews of a distinctly modernistic tendency. In these the strangeness of theme and a quality of vision combined with a style perfectly organized and of high expressive potentialities provide some of the very best pages of modern Spanish prose.

See: A. Valbuena Prat, *La poesía española contemporánea* (1930), pp. 105–109.

P. S.

Altamira y Crevea, Rafael (1866–, Spanish critic, historian, jurist, and political scientist), was born in Alicante. He has had a long and distinguished academic career, especially at the University of Madrid. He has been president of the Ibero-American Institute of Comparative Law and of other important international organizations and in 1922 was appointed a judge of the Permanent Court of International Justice. He is recognized as one of the most enlightened citizens of modern Spain. He has faced the problems of his country with a realistic approach coupled with a sense of national and international civic responsibility. Altamira's work is characterized by a sane combination of theory and practice in the fields of history and law and in their multitudinous connections and ramifications. At the university of Oviedo he was instrumental in the establishment of the Extensión Universitaria Española, whose main object was to bring the university to the workers of the surrounding region. His earliest work of importance is the *Historia de la propiedad comunal* (1880; revised ed., 1929–). The *Psicología del pueblo español* (1902; 2d ed., 1918) is a notable contribution to the study of the historical events and factors which have made the Spanish people what they are today. Altamira is best known for his solid and trustworthy *Historia de la civilización española* (3 vols., 1901–1906; 4th ed., 4 vols., 1928). His historical method is based on extreme caution in generalizations and on an objectivity properly limited by the use of documentary evidence. He can be considered one of the foremost historians of the first half of the 20th century for his contributions in the history of Spanish law, Spanish colonial history, and the teaching of history. His name is widely known and respected in international circles, and his lectures have taken him to universities in Europe, the United States, and Latin America. Although living in exile today in Mexico, he continues his researches against all odds, and one of his latest publications is the *Técnica de investigación del derecho indiano* (Mexico, 1939).

See: Anonymous, "Notas sobre la vida y obras de Rafael Altamira y Crevea," *Hispania,* XI (1928), 400–406; Havelock Ellis, *The Soul of Spain,* 1931 ed., pp. 399–401.

F. S. y E.

Altenberg, Peter (pseud. of Richard Engländer, 1859–1919, Austrian writer of prose sketches), was born in Vienna and died there. Widely known as a bizarre character frequenting literary cafés, he was also revered as the friend of frank and free souls in the lower walks of life. In his published works and in his famous table talk alike he was a restless apostle of beauty and health and a brilliant philosophical humorist who adored nature and kindness and nonchalantly unmasked the despicable "bourgeois."

Having, in his own words, fervently loved ladies both noble and very ignoble, loitered in the woods, been a law student and a medical student, but never having actually studied either law or medicine, Altenberg published at the age of 37 his first book, *Wie ich es sehe* (1896). "How I see it"—with the stress on *see*—was to be the approach also in his other writings, the *it* always being "life itself" (*Vita ipsa,* 1918), filled with most "real" fairy tales (*Märchen des Lebens,* 1908) and pictures, beautiful and revealing (*Bilderbogen des kleinen Lebens,* 1909). Altenberg wanted to give "extracts of life, dehydrated and canned in two or three pages." Whether these extracts be descriptive or narrative, monologue or dialogue, sublime or abusive, his bohemian existence is their background, explicit or implied. His impressions are submerged in the effort to disclose the values he cared for and to win his readers over to his enthusiastic beliefs—that physiological perfection is the basis of moral, intellectual, aesthetic perfection; that mental genius in men has its counterpart in aesthetic perfection in women; that radical "faithfulness to one's self," accompanied by unselfishness, is the highest good. These convictions pervade the witty and melancholic, shocking and delicate aphorisms, idyls, prose poems and manifestoes of Altenberg's remaining books: *Was der Tag mir zuträgt* (1901), *Pródrŏmŏs* (1906), *Neues Altes* (1911), *Semmering 1912* (1913), *Fechsung* (1915), *Nachfechsung* (1916), *Mein Lebensabend* (1919), *Der Nachlass* (posthumous, 1925). He attacks all that seems hypocritical in a vapid civilization. He praises, with equal enthusiasm, nobleness of mind and of body, finding these in the socially humblest creature as well as in a famous actress. Animals, children, adolescent girls—creatures nearer to nature than the boring world of man—are the preferred objects of his admiration.

Altenberg has a supreme talent for conveying impressions and implications with a minimum of visible effort in concentrated prose or in a revealing dialogue of a few lines. Outstanding is his gift for making silent things resonant and for muffling the loud ones. His last books are full of bitterness and misanthropy. Alone in his sickroom, he turned his power of observation on himself, reflecting upon his passing life, describing the intermittent approach of death—until a few days before the end.

See: E. Friedell, *Ecce Poeta* (1912); A. Polgar, *Der Nachlass von Peter Altenberg* (1925), pp. 149–154.

F. H. M.

Altolaguirre, Manuel (1904?–, Spanish poet), was born in Málaga, Andalusia, where he spent his childhood and part of his youth and where, in 1926, he made a start in literature with his book *Las islas invitadas y otros* *poemas*. With Emilio Prados (*q.v.*) he edited the journal *litoral,* which constitutes an important part of the productive effort of the so-called Southern Group. His *Ejemplo* appeared in 1927 as a supplement to *litoral.* Later he lived in Madrid, Paris, and London without interrupting his poetic production or losing his connections with the new generation headed by García Lorca (*q.v.*). Before founding *litoral* he had founded the journal *Ambos,* and later he established two others, *Poesía* and *Héroe.* These undertakings reveal a great interest in typography, which he made a fine art and which became the favorite occupation of his life. In 1936 the military movement caught him in Madrid. He collaborated with the government, followed it on its odyssey, expressed poetically and with great emotion the feelings of popular heroism, and at the triumph of Franco emigrated to Havana. There he has written many more works and founded the printing establishment "La Verónica."

He has also cultivated lyrical biography (*Garcilaso,* 1932), criticism, the drama, the essay, and has lectured extensively. According to his own declaration his poetry "reveals as a principal influence that of Juan Ramón Jiménez [*q.v.*], has been receptive to but not overwhelmed by that of Góngora, and feels itself to be a younger brother to that of Salinas [*q.v.*]. Moreover, Aleixandre and Cernuda [*qq.v.*] directly influenced his literary and personal formation." As with all of his group, in Altolaguirre the traditionally Spanish elements are combined with all the independence of his own generation. There is to be found in him, also, a gentle and tender sensibility, a childlike uneasiness in the presence of an immense unnamed grief which result in pages deep and exquisite such as those dedicated to his dead mother.

See: Gerardo Diego, *Poesía española (Antología)* (1934), pp. 536–552, 589; *Laurel: Antología de la poesía moderna en lengua española* (1941), pp. 1026–1048, 1133.

A. I.

Alvarez Quintero, Serafín (1871–1938) and **Joaquín** (1873–1944; Spanish dramatists), were born in Utrera, south of Seville, and were Andalusian to the marrow of their bones, not only in the scenes of most of their plays, but also in their sunshiny humor, their zest for life, and their great fecundity. In the development of the short play, the *sainete,* they are definitely in the tradition of the 16th-century Lope de Rueda (*pasos* or curtain raisers), of Cervantes and Quiñones de Benavente (*entremeses* or interludes), and of the 18th-century Ramón de la Cruz (*sainetes*). They continue the romantic tradition of insistence on local color, of the *costumbristas* of the 19th century such as Mesonero Romanos and Estébanez Calderón. The Andalusianism of these attractive brothers can be somewhat more exactly defined by negatives: the alluring region of their birth is not the land of Carmen, not the country of blood, passion, and tragedy described by the poet García Lorca (*q.v.*), not the home of tired descendants of superrefined Arabs with overdelicate sensibilities, and not merely the land of guitars, castanets, gypsy dances, and bullfights. Least of all, to the Quinteros, is it a region beset with dreadful and still unsolved economic, social, and political difficulties, of latifundia and oppressed peasantry. Andalusia is all of those things, but Andalusians are also as the Quinteros present them, a gay—or sad—sentimental folk, with a usually satisfactory adjustment of individual to milieu, a truly splendid sense of humor. Not all Andalusian servants are as amusing as they appear in these plays, and not all Andalusia is quite so picturesquely charming, but spectators are not inclined to protest at artistic heightening of scene or character when the essence is true and valid. Nor do they much mind, either, if the superficial is exalted into the realm of dramatic art.

The Quinteros began in their teens to write plays, which were acted in the patio of their own house. They were still in their teens when their farce called *Esgrima y amor* was acted in the Teatro Cervantes in Seville in 1889. In that year they went to Madrid, where for some time before they became successful they struggled to support themselves with small positions in the Treasury (*Hacienda*) Department. *El ojito derecho* and *La reja* (both 1897), one-act pieces, attracted favorable attention. The musical comedy (*zarzuela*) *La buena sombra* (1898) made them well known. By 1900 they declared they had 51 plays in manuscript, and for a long time they produced five or six a year. *Los galeotes* (1900) is one of their more serious plays. Based on the episode of the galley slaves in *Don Quixote* (Part I, Ch. XXII), it is a study of ingratitude, with the scene laid in a secondhand bookshop in Madrid. The characters are superior to the plot. *El patio* (1900) and *Las flores* (1901) are among the authors' most successful Andalusian genre pictures. The action is slight, the portrayal of types and background masterly. The patio and the flowers acquire real personality of their own. *Pepita*

Reyes (1903) studies a woman who is torn by the lure of the stage and her love for home. The conflict is left unsolved. *El amor que pasa* (1904; Eng. tr., *Love Passes By,* in *Four Comedies,* 1932) shows the sensitive longings of a romantic woman in a provincial town. *Mañana de sol* (1905; Eng. tr., *A Bright Morning,* 1916) is a delightful curtain raiser (*paso de comedia*) based on a *dolora* of Campoamor (*q.v.*). It has been translated into several languages. In *El genio alegre* (1906) an austere household is transformed by the young laughter of the pretty Andalusian heroine. *Las de Caín* (1908) recounts merrily how Professor Caín manages to marry off his five daughters. In its counterpart, *Las de Abel* (1926), which is a better play, marriage is not achieved. *Doña Clarines* (1909; Eng. tr. in *Four Comedies,* 1932) is a serious character study of a blunt and slightly acidulous woman, with a passion for truth and straightforwardness. Based on Bécquer (*q.v.*), *La rima eterna* (1910) is delicate and poetic. *Malvaloca* (1912; Eng. tr., 1916), dedicated to the great scholar Menéndez y Pelayo (*q.v.*) and awarded a prize by the Spanish Academy, is one of the authors' most serious and most famous plays. It portrays the redemption, by a serious Asturian, of the apparently gay and light-hearted Andalusian Malvaloca, whose "life has been a long novel." The sentimental note is highly emphasized. *Puebla de las mujeres* (1912; Eng. tr., *The Women Have Their Way,* in *Four Plays,* 1927), admirably constructed, is all Andalusian gayety and laughter. *Don Juan, buena persona* (1918) presents a new and highly amusing kind of Don Juan, a most kindhearted fellow whose former inamoratas keep coming to him with all their problems, so that he is, as he says, "the slave of his female slaves." He finally marries an excellent woman named Amalia. *La prisa* (1921) contrasts modern haste with sweet Andalusian leisure. If the Quinteros added no new note in subsequent plays, such as *Lo que hablan las mujeres* (1932), *El susto* (1933), and *La inglesa sevillana* (1935), they at least showed that their humor did not diminish with age.

See: Helen and Harley Granville-Barker, introductions to S. and J. Alvarez Quintero, *Four Plays* (1927) and *Four Comedies* (1932); A. F. G. Bell, *Contemporary Spanish Literature,* revised ed. (1933), pp. 180–184.

N. B. A.

Alvaro, Corrado (1889–, Italian novelist), was born in Calabria. He has had what might be called a typical literary career, having been an editor of the *Resto del Carlino* and the *Corriere della sera.* His first book of importance, *L'Uomo nel labirinto* (1922), reveals some influence of Bontempelli (*q.v.*) as well as the author's own predilection for psychological study. Without abandoning his interest in the inner soul of man, he turned to a definite and meticulously portrayed background for two of his later—and still most highly regarded—works, *La Signora dell'isola* and *Gente in Aspromonte.* Both of these volumes appeared in 1930, and the setting was the author's native Calabria. In *Gente in Aspromonte* particularly, the nature of the background, the type of character presented, and the quality of tenseness and concision seemed to indicate that Alvaro could be classified as the Verga (*q.v.*) of his generation, and at this time Italian critics were inclined to place Alvaro in the group—for it is hardly a school—represented by Deledda and Tozzi (*qq.v.*) For this group Pancrazi uses the phrase "lyric regionalism." Actually however it would seem that there remains in Alvaro, in spite of the natural emotion which is apparent when he treats of his native land, more of the purely intellectual interest in the psychology of the individual than is found in either of the other two writers mentioned. *Gente in Aspromonte* was such a competent piece of work and the author was so obviously familiar with his background that it was easy to lose sight of his primary interest. With *L'Uomo è forte* (1938) he returned to the vein that inspired *L'Uomo nel labirinto.* For this is a novel which is entirely of the soul. The locale of the action is not even specified; at the time of publication it was politely assumed to be Russia, but it would not have been hard to imagine another setting. The novel is a study, made with penetration and sympathy, of the mind of man under totalitarian dictatorship. Its defect is an inevitable by-product of the subject: a certain lack of realism in the characters. But within its limits *L'Uomo è forte* is a fine work and one of the few Italian novels of recent years that will bear rereading. One who can write two such books as *Gente in Aspromonte* and *L'Uomo è forte* is a man of rare talent—and promise, for an encouraging thing about Alvaro is his steady growth and development. It is not unlikely that, barring accident, he will be one of the two or three really noteworthy novelists of his generation.

See: Pietro Pancrazi, *Scrittori italiani del novecento* (1934), pp. 186–191.

T. G. B.

Alverdes, Paul (1897–, German poet, story writer, and essayist), was born in Strassburg, where his father, a Prussian officer, was stationed. At 17 he volunteered for service in the First World War, the course and end of which aroused him to an awareness of all the serious problems of individual and national existence. His earliest imperfect efforts in verse and prose, which give expression to his rejection of the literary and political trends of the early 1920's and to his aspirations for the immediate future, found an eager acceptance among the German youth (*Die Nördlichen,* 1922; *Kilian,* 1922; *Die Flucht,* 1923; *Die feindlichen Brüder,* 1923). But with the appearance of the story *Die Pfeiferstube* (1929; Eng. tr., *The Whistlers' Room,* 1930) and the volume of stories *Reinhold oder die Verwandelten* (1931; Eng. tr., *Changed Men,* 1933) Alverdes won his place among the younger members of the group of leading figures in contemporary German literature which gathered annually for a week as the guests of Hans Grimm (*q.v.*) at Lippoldsberg. For *Die Pfeiferstube* he drew upon his own experience to depict three Germans and one Englishman all suffering from severe wounds in the larynx, and he writes a touching memorial to the comradeship of those men whose speech was possible only by means of metal tubes—"whistles"—in their throats. *Reinhold oder die Verwandelten* shows the war itself and the changes it wrought in those who went through it with their whole devotion, as Alverdes himself had done. Between the early works and these two volumes fall the *Deutsches Anekdotenbuch* (1927), which he edited together with Hermann Rinn, and translations from French and English including Cooper's *The Deerslayer.* Subsequently he wrote two enchanting bedtime stories for his children, *Das Männlein Mittentzwei* (1937) and *Das Schlaftürlein* (1938), and a number of dramatizations, imaginary conversations, and radio plays, including *Gespräch über Goethes Harzreise im Winter* (1938).

In 1934 Alverdes together with Karl Benno von Mechow (*q.v.*) founded the monthly magazine *Das Innere Reich.* Since then Alverdes's interests have centered in this journal, for the editing of which his university training and literary gifts and experience admirably fitted him. Within its covers he has introduced to his German readers many contemporary writers of France and Italy, England and other countries, recounting his visits among them and their visits to Munich as his guests; here, too, he has published his own recent works and his numerous and excellent book reviews.

See Herbert Saekel, "Paul Alverdes" (with biography and bibliography), *Die schöne Literatur,* XXVII (1926), 145–150; H. G. Göpfert, "Paul Alverdes" (with bibliography), *Die neue Literatur,* XXXVII (1936), 503–513.

J. F. G.

Ambrus, Zoltán (1861–1933, Hungarian novelist, short-story writer, and critic), was born in Debrecen and died in Budapest. He studied law, then went to Paris. There he learned about French standards of literature, for which he had a natural aptitude, and when he returned to his native country, his critical and creative activities showed a spirit willingly influenced by French taste and clarity. His novels, short stories, critical essays on French writers, and theatrical criticisms displayed aesthetic maturity. Though he was a solitary figure in modern Hungarian literature—he never had a large reading public—his literary significance was never questioned. He received many literary prizes and was a member of the two leading literary societies of Hungary, the Petőfi Társaság (Petőfi Society) and the Kisfaludy Társaság (Kisfaludy Society). His collected works appeared in 20 volumes. From 1916 until 1922 he was the director of the Hungarian National Theatre. As the translator of good French novels and stories he helped to popularize French taste in the Hungarian world. What Georg Brandes (*q.v.*) as a critic and historian of modern European literature set out to do for the propagation of literature in general Ambrus did for French literature in Hungary. His own art was not faultless, but his realism and his irony seem convincing even today, notwithstanding the fact that much of his art has very little in common with European and Hungarian problems that grew out of the First World War. Ambrus was an echo of the French *fin de siècle,* of Flaubert, Maupassant, Anatole France (*qq.v.*).

Ambrus was one of the first Hungarian writers who tried to formulate literary views in which *bon sens* was the professed principle. His reasonableness seemed strange in an environment in which successful authors indulged in sentimentalism. His analytical keenness overlooked nothing that was provocative from an ironic point of view. *Girofle és Girofla* (1901; Girofle and Girofla), *Berzsenyi báró és családja* (1906; Baron Berzsenyi and His Family), *Midas király* (1906; King Midas), *A türelmes Grizeldisz* (1907; The Patient Griselda), *Törpék és óriások* (1908; Midgets and

Giants), and his other short stories and novels were means through which Ambrus discovered the frailties and fallacies of a world in which the reader did not move, or if he did was apt to observe much less than the author observed. The critical works of Ambrus—*Régi és uj szinmüvek* (1914; Old and New Plays), *Szinházi esték* (1914; Theatre Nights), *Vezető elmék* (1914; Leading Spirits), *Költők és irók* (1924; Poets and Writers)—show sharp intelligence and a critical power to translate into lucid sentences the understanding of characters, ideas, and motives expressed and portrayed in Hungarian and foreign creative works. Several of his novels and stories have appeared in French and German translations.

See: F. Szinnyei, *Ambrus Zoltán* (1918).

J. R.

Amiel, Denys (1884–, French dramatist), was born in Villegailhenc, Aude. For many years he was secretary to the playwright Henry Bataille (*q.v.*) and later wrote a critical biography of him. The First World War interrupted Amiel's literary career. Shortly after the war was over, in collaboration with his friend André Obey he wrote his first successful play, *La Souriante Mme Obey* (Nouveau Théâtre, 1921). The subject of this play may not seem very original, but Amiel handles with penetration the psychological study of the husband, a crude, inconsiderate individual, and of the wife, a sensitive, cultured woman. Like Emma Bovary (*see* Flaubert), the wife is bored with her existence in a small provincial town, with a husband who does not understand her. The unexpected turn which the authors give to the relations between the husband and wife is evidence of their dramatic skill. The play was produced in New York with the title *The Wife with the Smile* (Garrick Theatre, 1921).

Amiel belongs to the group of writers which is often called the school of the unexpressed, or the school of silence. Amiel says that the most insignificant moments in life are perhaps the most pregnant with interior drama. One often sees people chatting peacefully, with the gestures of polite and sociable people; yet in their hearts may be stirring the most violent passions of the "ancestral beast." The writer must know how to exploit the dramatic value of the unexpressed. *Le Voyageur,* written in 1912 and produced in 1922, is an application of this theory. It is not in what the characters say, but in what they leave unsaid that lies the drama of their lives. *La Carcasse* (Comédie Française, 1926), also written in collaboration with Obey, *Décalage* (Théâtre Saint-Georges, 1931), *L'Age du fer* (Comédie Française, 1932), *Ma Liberté* (Théâtre Saint-Georges, 1936), and some of his later plays treat such questions as the intellectual and sentimental problems of the young girl of today, the machine age, and the amorous difficulties of man. A strange play, *Trois et une* (1932; Eng. tr., *Three and One,* 1933), had more than 70 performances in New York. Amiel is a keen analyst of the human heart and a keen critic of contemporary society. He is also a clever technician.

See: L. Delpit, *Paris—Théâtre contemporain,* I (1925), 104–106, II (1938), 43–45, 56–59; B. Brisson, *Au hasard des soirées* (1935), pp. 193–199; M. E. Coindreau, *La Farce est jouée* (1942).

H. H.

Amiel, Henri Frédéric (1821–1881, Swiss poet and critic), was born in Geneva of a French family which had been driven there by the revocation of the Edict of Nantes. His mother and his father, a prosperous businessman, died while he was still a boy; he was taken into the family of an uncle, educated in Geneva and Berlin, where he acquired a fondness for German literature and philosophy which he never lost, and provided with the means for extensive European travel. In 1849 he became professor of aesthetics at the Academy of Geneva, in 1854 professor of philosophy; his life was henceforth connected with this institution, which he watched develop into a university. Outwardly his life was a placid and mediocre one, hardly marked even by literary activity. Various critical articles, since collected by Bernard Bouvier in *Essais critiques par Henri-Frédéric Amiel* (1932; included is an essay, *J. J. Rousseau,* which had been translated into English by Van Wyck Brooks, 1922), and a few small volumes of poetry, notably *Grains de mil* (1854) and *Les Etrangères* (1876), translations, chiefly from the English and the German, were his only known productions, until after his death there appeared *Fragments d'un journal intime* (2 vols., 1884; Eng. tr., *The Private Journal of Henri Frédéric Amiel,* enlarged ed., 1935). These are selections from an enormous mass of material (173 notebooks comprising about 16,900 pages) made with the help of Edmond Scherer (*q.v.*) by a friend, Fanny Mercier, to whom Amiel had bequeathed these diaries. The effect of this revelation was immediate. Amiel was everywhere hailed as one of the great observers, analysts, and depicters of the human heart; and the personality which he studied with such absorption for some 35 years has lost little of its attraction with the passing of time.

The secret of Amiel's life is perhaps yet to

be discovered; but at least a tentative analysis is possible. Gifted with both a keen analytic mind and a sympathetic, perceptive nature, undoubtedly poetic in his temperament, he suffered from a lifelong inability to bring any solid, definite work to completion. A strange timidity, an apparent intellectual indolence which delicate health perhaps partly accounts for, an almost neurotic inability to do the *necessary* act, these were drawbacks which he never overcame. Longing for the absolute, he had a distaste for the partial and immediate; fascinated by perfection, he hesitated to take the first step towards it. His reading was remarkable in variety and extent—but only because it was the result of the free and capricious wandering of his desire; as soon as a book *had* to be read for some good reason, the task became almost impossible. The same was true of his poetry: *vers de société* he could produce in profusion, anything else only with enormous effort. The marks of such effort are apparent in his criticism as well; the free and easy outpouring of the *Journal* on books read from day to day disappears, and in its place there is a stiff, labored, almost colorless attempt at complète thoroughness, a criticism, as Scherer remarks, which circles the subject, pursues it into all its relationships and ramifications, and catalogues it completely, without ever really entering into it. Through most of his life, as the *Journal* amply witnesses, Amiel meditated great projects, searched for the field in which his unusual genius could find its fullest expression. Very early he developed a beautifully sensitive intellect; for 30 years his mind remained, like a delicate and perfect piece of apparatus, ready for some rare task; but the will to choose or accomplish was lacking. In part, the keeping of the *Journal* may account for this weakness. Begun at first as a mental and moral discipline, a statement of goals to aim at and a record of success or failure, it became as the years passed perhaps an indulgence, a means of evasion. Here Amiel's tireless mental curiosity could have full play; here his passion for describing, analyzing, and judging himself could compensate for lack of will. Perhaps greater sympathy and encouragement of the right sort from his contemporaries would have made a difference. Amiel had friends in plenty, chiefly feminine, but they were above all admirers, and the incentive to activity which close acquaintance with such a man as Scherer might have provided was always denied him. He himself, with some exaggeration no doubt, traced the roots of his pliancy to a childhood fear of his domineering father. His isolation, too, from the best society of Geneva because of his supposed democratic tendencies undoubtedly helped to turn him in upon himself. But eventually in an attempt to explain, one must return, as he did in the *Journal,* time and again, to an inherent weakness of his own nature.

Nevertheless, it is to that weakness that we owe the *Journal,* his one work of lasting value. Its audience will probably never be wide, but there seems no doubt that it will attract steadily year by year a few thoughtful spirits who will delight in its delicate tints, its psychological nuances. It is certainly not of the highest sort of literature; even among records of spiritual experience it is perhaps not in the first rank. The side of Amiel that for want of a better term one must call feminine is far too predominant; his taste for the pretty and the sentimental exhibits itself in its fullness all too often. He edifies rather than exalts; he is a moralist rather than a mystic, as a comparison of the *Journal* with the *Pensées* of Pascal will make amply clear. Yet there are few who can read Amiel without being moved to reflection, few who after reading him cannot see with a new clearness some part of their own characters. The attacks of Bourget and Brunetière (*qq.v.*) have done little to shake the *Journal's* reputation; one may feel pity, or worse, for the man it reveals; but it still remains the most complete and detailed revelation of a personality to be found in any literature.

See: Paul Bourget, *Nouveaux Essais de psychologie contemporaine* (1885); Edmond Scherer, *Etudes sur la littérature contemporaine,* Vol. VIII (1885); Berthe Vachier, *Vie d'Amiel* (1885); Bernard Bouvier, introductions to *Journal intime d'Henri-Frédéric Amiel* (3 vols., 1923), *Essais critiques par Henri-Frédéric Amiel* (1932), and *La Jeunesse d'Henri-Frédéric Amiel* (1935); Albert Thibaudet, *Intérieurs* (1924).

C. W., Jr.

Amorós, Juan Bautista, *see* Lanza, Silverio.

Andersen, Trygve (1866–1920, Norwegian novelist), was born in the eastern part of the country. His father belonged to the official class, his mother had inherited farmer's traditions, and the son united in himself the two cultural and literary currents whose interplay and sometimes conflict have meant so much to modern Norwegian development. At the University of Christiania he received a good philological and historical education, and he became a fastidious stylist, adapting, with fine taste, words and expressions of the vernacular for the traditional literary language. From about 1890 he was the virtual leader of the neo-romantic group, and his stylistic ideals of conciseness and lucidity influenced many young authors. His own first work, the historical novel *I cancelliraadens dage* (1897; In the Days of the Titled Judge), was a profound study of a milieu and a psychology, picturing the conflicts of Norwegian society at the end of Danish domination. His second novel, *Mot kveld* (1900; Towards Night), is filled with apprehensions of death and forebodings of mental and general collapse. Both novels, each in its particular character, were succeeded by a number of short stories, evidently influenced by Edgar Allan Poe, which proved him the master of this branch of literature in Norway. They are brought together in his *Samlede fortallinger* (3 vols., 1916; Collected Stories).

H. K.

Andersson, Dan (1888–1920, Swedish poet, short-story writer, and novelist), is the greatest poet and one of the most gifted writers of prose fiction among modern Swedish proletarian authors. His life was short and tragic, extreme poverty dogging his every step from childhood to the grave. Born in an isolated district of Dalecarlia, son of a poor folk school teacher, he spent, at the age of 14, some eight months visiting relatives in America. Upon his return to Sweden he became a forest laborer and charcoal burner, at which occupations, except for a short period at Brunnsvik Folk High School, he spent the remainder of his life. His literary work was reasonably prolific, considering the vicissitudes of his life. The best of his poetry was published in two volumes, *Kolvaktarens visor* (1915; The Charcoal Burner's Songs) and *Svarta ballader* (1917; Black Ballads). A collection of short stories, *Kolarhistorier* (1914; Charcoal Burner's Tales), and two novels, *De tre hemlösa* (1918; Three Homeless Ones) and *David Ramms arv* (1919; David Ramm's Heritage), constitute the best of his prose. A selection from his poetry has been translated into English by Caroline Schleef under the title *Charcoal-Burner's Ballad & Other Poems* (1943). Andersson's poetry was strongly influenced on its formal side by Kipling and Service and perhaps to a lesser extent by his countrymen Fröding (*q.v.*) and Karlfeldt (*q.v.*), while his prose in both its spirit and its form owes much to Dostoevski (*q.v.*) and the Hamsun (*q.v.*) of *Hunger* and *Mysteries*. Though his work everywhere reveals a strong sense of solidarity with the lower working classes, he does not directly attack the existing economic and social order and scarcely seems conscious of any sharp class conflicts. His heavy, brooding temperament is concerned primarily with religious and metaphysical problems, though he was never able to resolve the somber disharmonies of the life that was the object of his brooding. He approaches these problems with a fierce primitive intensity, and whatever stray flashes of light he finds in the awesome gloom of human existence become a part of the primitive wilderness mysticism which is essential with him. "His view of life," writes a recent Swedish critic, "is a grim fatalism, and his whole work is a fragmentary theodicy, occasionally lighted by flashes from his innermost soul . . ." His poetry is marked by rich, buoyant rhythms, on occasion softened and subdued, and by a bold, sharp, achingly haunting figurative language eminently appropriate to his somber, restless, ceaselessly searching poetic temperament.

See: Torsten Fogelqvist, introductory essay in Andersson, *Samlade skrifter*, I (1934), viii–lxxvi; E. Kihlman, "Dan Andersson," in *Nordiska profiler* (1935), pp. 69–88; Waldemar Bernhard, *En bok om Dan Andersson* (1941); Anne-Marie Odstedt, *Dan Andersson: en levnadsteckning* (1941).

A. G.

Andrenio, *see* Gómez de Baquero, Eduardo.

Andreyev, Leonid (1871–1919, Russian short-story writer, novelist, and playwright), was born in Orel, studied at the universities of St. Petersburg and Moscow, and graduated from the latter as a lawyer. Having lost the only case he pleaded, he turned to writing, first as a court reporter and subsequently as an author of short stories. His first story, "Bargamot i Garaska" (Eng. tr., "Bargamot and Garaska," in *The Little Angel and Other Stories*, 1916, which also contains translations of many of the stories mentioned later), appeared in a daily Moscow paper in 1898 and drew the attention of young Maxim Gorky (*q.v.*) with its skeptical overtone. Under the influence of Gorky and with his help, Andreyev rapidly acquired fame and success. His reputation as a confirmed doubter was belied during the First World War, when he vehemently championed the Allied cause and bitterly opposed the Bolshevik Revolution. He died in exile, in a small Finnish village, heartbroken and completely disenchanted.

The vogue of Andreyev was due to the fact

that he spoke for the average intellectual at the turn of the century, with his doubts and his bewilderment, characteristic of the twilight of a civilization. Andreyev discussed practically every philosophical, ethical, and social problem of the time, rarely attempting a solution. Even as a court reporter he showed less interest in the verdict than in the presentation of the case itself, from all angles imaginable. A perpetual questioner, Andreyev has prodded the modern man's conscience and consciousness. In story and play he brings to light overt and hidden ailments and follies in their universal aspect, to set us wondering and asking the unanswerable why and wherefore of life and of human existence.

In his early realistic stories Andreyev depicted helpless individuals tormented by fear of life and death ("U okna," 1899, At the Window; "V podvale," 1901, In the Basement), by loneliness and inability to bridge the chasm between fellow men ("Molchaniye," 1900, Silence; "Lozh," 1900, The Lie; "V tumane," 1902, In the Fog), by a sense of inferiority ("Rasskaz o Sergeye Petroviche," 1900, The Story of Sergei Petrovich), and by a craving after illusion and the inevitable disillusionment ("Angelochek," 1899, The Little Angel; "Stena," 1901, The Wall). At this time (1899–1902) he wrote in the traditional style of Russian realism, with a touch of Chekhov's (*q.v.*) impressionism. Gradually Andreyev's tone assumed a higher pitch, as he broadened his scope and deepened his probings. The style of "Zhizn Vasiliya Fiveiskovo" (1903; Eng. tr., "Life of Father Vassily," in *When the King Loses His Head and Other Stories,* 1920) was nervous and gaudy, echoing its Dostoevskian theme of faith versus reason. A similar crescendo could be noticed in "Mysl" (1902, Thought; Eng. tr., *A Dilemma,* 1910), a study of reason turned traitor to its master, who becomes its slave. Andreyev began to attack problems not on any individual and local scale, but in application to humanity and the world—of necessity varying his realism with symbolism and allegory. Thus his "Krasny smekh" (1904; Eng. tr., *The Red Laugh,* 1905) transcended the Russo-Japanese War, its immediate inspiration, and became an arraignment of war in general, with the "red laugh" as a symbol of war's madness and horror. "Tak bylo" (1906, Thus It Was; Eng. tr., "When the King Loses His Head"), though suggested by the revolutionary events in Russia, was a disparaging treatment of the French Revolution and of all revolutions that fail to go beyond the façade and leave man's inner slavery intact. Echoes of the Russian Revolution of 1905 could be felt in such plays as *K zvezdam* (1906; Eng. tr., *To the Stars,* 1907) and *Savva* (1906; Eng. tr., 1914), but the implications again went beyond time and place, touching on such questions as destructive anarchism and the conflict between man's response to the direct demands of the earth, the valley of tears, and the scientist's detached attitude *sub specie aeternitatis.* In *Zhizn cheloveka* (1907; Eng. tr., *The Life of Man,* 1914), a morality play, in which naturalistic passages jostle with vague symbols and obvious allegories, Andreyev attempted an epitome of the folly and futility of man's life, largely in Schopenhauer's vein. The play *Tsar Golod* (1907; Eng. tr., *King Hunger,* 1911) dissected modern society, from the upper classes down to the outcasts, and exposed its moribundity, not sparing even the working class, which was in the eyes of the intelligensia surrounded in those years by a halo. The hopelessness of Andreyev's outlook on individual and collective man was illustrated by most of his later stories and plays, culminating in his last novel, of which he left only a rough draft, *Dnevnik Satany* (1921; Eng. tr., *Satan's Diary,* 1920).

A student of Schopenhauer, Andreyev at times passionately sought to rise above despair by invoking the vision of the *heroischer Lebenslauf* of the hero or the saint. He rose to the peak of his talent in the noble delineation of selfless revolutionists in "Rasskaz o semi poveshennykh" (1908; Eng. tr., *The Seven Who Were Hanged,* 1909) and in the Christlike image of David Leiser in the play *Anatema* (1909; Eng. tr., *Anathema,* 1910). A heartening note may be discerned in the tragedy *Chyornyia maski* (1908; Eng. tr., *The Black Maskers,* in *Plays,* 1915), which ends in the self-immolation of Duke Lorenzo as a triumph of the will to truth. Fugitive though these flashes were, they reappeared persistently on the black horizon of Andreyev's outlook. His last play, *Samson v okovakh* (written in 1914, posthumously published in *Sovremennyia zapiski,* Vol. XXIV, 1925; Eng. tr. from the original manuscript, *Samson in Chains,* 1923), sounds a buoyant note—for Andreyev. The blind Samson rises above carnality and pettiness, and in destroying himself he also brings down the pillars of reigning mediocrity, the temple of Philistia.

See: D. Merezhkovski, "V obezyannykh lapakh," in *Sobraniye sochineni,* XII (1911), 197–242; A. Kaun, *Leonid Andreyev; a Critical Study* (1924).

A. K.

Andrian-Werburg, Leopold, Freiherr zu (1875–, Austrian poet), born in Vienna, came from a family whose lineage goes back to the 12th century. His maternal grandfather was the composer Giacomo Meyerbeer. A diplomatic career led him to Athens, Rio de Janeiro, and St. Petersburg, and during the First World War he represented the Austrian emperor at Warsaw. He had early seen the Hapsburg monarchy threatened by nationalistic and anti-Catholic forces. In July, 1918, he became the *Generalintendant* of the Imperial Theatres of Vienna. After the breakdown of old Austria, he retired. He then lived mainly in Austria and in Nice and, in recent years, in Brazil.

His poems were first published in the *Blätter für die Kunst,* although his ties with its founder, Stefan George (*q.v.*), were anything but close. George never ceased to admire the poems of Andrian's youth for being what they are, an essence of their period (the 90's), and for thus transcending the period. The same can be said of his short prose treatise, *Der Garten der Erkenntnis* (1895), the inner story of a youth, of a haughty and lonely soul—a story impregnated with a very strong feeling for atmosphere, for the promises and threats of life, in a way a *Werther* of its time. It has to be compared and contrasted with Hugo von Hofmannsthal's (*q.v.*) *Märchen der 672. Nacht* or with the youthful treatises of André Gide (*q.v.*). These writings were reedited in 1919 as *Das Fest der Jugend: Des Gartens der Erkenntnis erster Teil und die Jugendgedichte.*

Among Andrian's few essays, the most notable deals with the rebirth of Poland, "Das erniedrigte und das erhöhte Polen" (in *Österreichische Rundschau,* 1921). Here it is the diplomat and the historian who speaks. In two substantial and significant books of Andrian's mature age the point of view is that of the Catholic, the philosopher, the Austrian. The first, *Die Ständeordnung des Alls* (1930), is, as the subtitle has it, "rationales Weltbild eines katholischen Dichters"; the second, *Österreich im Prisma der Idee* (1937), a philosophical dialogue, attempts to establish the existence of an independent Austrian nation. Another work, "De Anima," which may strongly show the author's introspective power as a *moraliste* in the French sense, is as yet unpublished. A booklet on Hofmannsthal, one of his close lifelong friends, was ready for publication when Hitler entered Austria.

See: H. Bahr, *Renaissance* (1897), pp. 41–45; Albert Verwey, *Proza,* III (1921), 173–183; F. Wolters, *Stefan George und die Blätter für die Kunst* (1930), pp. 72–74; C. Du Bos, *Approximations,* Sér. 5 (1932), pp. 143–171.

H. St.

Andrić, Ivo (1892–, Serb short-story writer and poet), was born in Travnik, Bosnia, a Yugoslav region where intermingle influences of different ethnic origins, religions, traditions, and cultures. He went to school in Sarajevo and took part in the movement of nationalistic youth which strove to liberate this province from Austro-Hungarian rule. He studied philosophy in Zagreb, Vienna, and Cracow and for his Yugoslav nationalistic persuasions was put in jail during the First World War, held by the Austrian authorities as a political criminal. In 1918 he became secretary of the National Council in Zagreb, which proclaimed the union of the Croats and Serbs. After the establishment of Yugoslavia, he entered the diplomatic service and served in Rome, Bucharest, Trieste, Geneva, Madrid, Belgrade, Berlin.

During his difficult days in prison, Andrić composed his first series of lyric and philosophic fragments, *Ex Ponto* (1918). This was followed by the volume of short stories *Put Alije Djerzeleza* (1920; partial Eng. tr. in *Slavonic Review,* Vol. XIV, 1935–1936, pp. 13–19, 556–563); by poems entitled *Nemiri* (1921; Disquietudes); by *Pripovetke I* and *II* (1924, 1931; Stories); as well as by numerous other tales in different magazines, especially in *Srpski književni glasnik* (Serbian Literary Herald). *Ex Ponto* and *Nemiri* are really collections of a poetic prose which is mostly autopsychological analysis. They are not lamentations, but rather a man's feverish seeking for a comprehension of life, nature, eternity.

In his later work Andrić turned exclusively to story writing in an effort to depict the conditions, ways, and customs of the people of his very original native country. The gallery of his types is rich: people who are full-blooded, vehement, full of dark instincts and immoderate passions, heroic, quarrelsome; there are monks and dervishes, merchants and craftsmen, Ottoman bigwigs and adventurers, pasha's mistresses and cabaret beauties, Catholics, Orthodox, Moslems, Jews, Gypsies. All these persons have violent longings, but are checked by the petty circumstances of their narrow environment. They are continuously torn between their sensuality and their religious dogma. Andrić is a penetrating observer of these bizarre creatures with their highly oriental coloring, an excellent psychologist, a skillful organizer of his material.

He is definitely a master among modern Yugoslav story writers.

See: M. Bogdanović, "Put Alije Djerzeleza," *Srpski književni glasnik,* September 16, 1920; I. Sekulić, "Istok u pripovetkama Ive Andrića," *Srpski književni glasnik,* December 1, 1925; N. Mirković, "Ivo Andrić," *Srpski književni glasnik,* January–March, 1938.

P. A.

Anghel, Dimitrie (1872–1914, Rumanian poet), studied in Jassy, traveled in Italy, and lived for a long time in Paris. His leisurely youth, due to a rich inheritance, was a rare and precious apprenticeship for his later poetic achievements. Delicate, excessively sensitive, of extraordinary verve and powerful imagination, he wrote his first book of poetry, *In grădină* (In the Garden), in 1903. His prose works *Fantome* (1911; Phantoms) and *Oglinda fermecată* (1911; The Enchanted Mirror), his comedy in verse *Cometa* (The Comet), written in collaboration with St. O. Iosif and produced in 1912, his *Caleidoscopul* (1908; Kaleidoscope), also written with Iosif, as well as numerous poems and poetic sketches, were the product of a distinct individuality.

When Eminescu's (*q.v.*) monument was unveiled at Galatz in 1911, Anghel seized this opportunity to read at the official exercises his "Prinosul unui Iconoclast" (Offerings of an Iconoclast), a short proclamation of independence from the master's sway. With Anghel, a new efflorescence of profuse diversity spread over Rumanian poetry, and many young singers were inspired by him. Maiorescu (*q.v.*), aged and powerful premier, called Anghel's works "fancy bonbons unhealthy for peasants' stomachs," but Iorga (*q.v.*) sensed their suavity and splendor, writing lines of marked appreciation in their favor. An unhappy love life, complicated by poverty and disillusionment, caused Anghel to commit suicide.

See: N. Iorga, *Un poet al florilor* (1914); L. Feraru, *Un manuscris al poetului Anghel* (1922).

L. F.

Annenski, Innokenti Fyodorovich (1856–1909, Russian poet, critic, and translator), was born into the family of an important government official in Omsk, Siberia, but while still a child was taken to St. Petersburg. After studies at the University of St. Petersburg, he intended to continue for a higher degree, but abandoned this plan and accepted a position as instructor in classical languages in a Gymnasium. Eventually he became principal of the Tsarskoye Selo Gymnasium and then director of schools. He also lectured on Greek literature in the Women's College courses in St. Petersburg.

Annenski began his literary career in the 1880's by submitting reviews to various periodicals. In the 1890's he began his work of translating (and popularizing) the works of Euripides. Not until 1904 did Annenski publish a book of his own verses, *Tikhiya pesni* (Quiet Songs)—under the pseudonym Nik. T–O (Nikto = Nobody). His second book of verse, *Kiparisovy larets* (The Cypress Chest), appeared posthumously, in 1910, and soon became a classic among the literary élite. The small amount of his original verse prevented quick recognition of Annenski's poetical talent. Only shortly before his death did he become an influential figure in the St. Petersburg literary circles.

Although Annenski's verse in some respects resembles that of Baudelaire, Verlaine, and Mallarmé (*qq.v.*), it is distinctly Russian in character. His penchant for clarity and his aversion to the diffusiveness of symbolist verse endeared Annenski's poems to the "Acmeist" group of Russian poets. Gumilyov, Akhmatova, Mandelshtam (*qq.v.*), and other lesser poets of this circle were greatly influenced by Annenski.

See: V. Khodasevich, "Ob Annenskom," *Feniks,* I (1922), 122–136.

O. M.

Antoine, André (1858–1943, French actor, theatre director, and dramatic critic), was born in Limoges and went to Paris at the age of eight. He had little or no formal education and at 13 was a clerk in a publishing firm. He used his spare time to educate himself and to satisfy an early passion for the theatre by attending plays every night. He wanted to be an actor, took a course in diction, but failed to enter the Paris Conservatory. After five years of military service (1878–1883) and when employed as clerk in the Paris Gas Company, he joined a group of amateur players. His energy and enthusiasm soon made him their leader, and he was able to realize on a stage, however small, the ideas he had long entertained for a reform of the French theatre whose conventionalism he abhorred. He had meant at first to give plays of all kinds, but found himself welcoming more and more exclusively the dramatists of the naturalist school (*see* French naturalism), the opponents of the "well-made play," who found Antoine the only director in Paris willing to accept their works. His theatre, now called the Théâtre Libre, open only to season-ticket subscribers, was not considered a public place of entertainment, and the often bold dramas of the naturalists thus escaped the censorship. During the seven years of his directorship (1887–1894), Antoine produced 124 new plays by many playwrights later to become famous —Brieux, Curel (*qq.v.*), Henri Lavedan; the contemporary masters of the German, Russian, and Scandinavian drama were likewise introduced by him to French audiences. Many great actors, like Gémier, also began their career under him. Financially, however, the Théâtre Libre never was a success, and in 1894 he abandoned its directorship.

In June, 1896, he was appointed codirector, with Paul Ginisty, of the government-subsidized Odéon, but he resigned at the end of six months after many difficulties with the actors and his associate. In 1897 he opened his own playhouse, the Théâtre Antoine, where for almost 10 years he continued with great success the tradition of the Théâtre Libre. His reputation as a great reformer of the stage was now made; with his troupe he toured Europe and South America. He was appointed an examiner at the Paris Conservatory and received the ribbon of the Legion of Honor. In October, 1906, the minister of education again placed him at the head of the Odéon for a seven-year period, this time as sole director, thus officially crowning his success. Antoine accepted this opportunity of applying his ideas, on a much bigger stage, to the production of the great dramatic masterpieces of the past. The end of his directorship in 1914 marked the end of his active life as a producer. He had the satisfaction of knowing that in spite of much adverse criticism he had achieved his life ambition—to make the French theatre abandon artificiality and conventionalism in favor of truth and naturalness. He served afterwards as dramatic critic on several newspapers and wrote his memoirs. The cinema attracted him for a while, and he directed the screen version of Alphonse Daudet's (*q.v.*) *L'Arlésienne*. Beset all his life by financial difficulties, he died penniless at Camaret in Brittany.

See: A. Thalasso, *Le Théâtre Libre* (1909); Antoine, *Mes Souvenirs sur le Théâtre Libre* (1921) and *Mes Souvenirs sur le Théâtre Antoine et sur l'Odéon* (1928); S. M. Waxman, *Antoine and the Théâtre-Libre* (1926).

V. Gu.

Anzengruber, Ludwig (1839–1889, Austrian playwright, novelist, and short-story writer), was born in Vienna. His father, of Austrian peasant stock, wrote poems and plays in his leisure time and the son inherited his inborn love of the country and the urge to write. He was poor and earned his living first as a clerk in a bookshop, then as an actor. Both attempts were unsuccessful, but they nourished Anzengruber's early interest in literature and the theatre. To amplify his meager income, he wrote plays, librettos, songs, and sketches, though almost despairing of his talent and his future and glad to accept, at the age of 30, a small position with the imperial Austrian police. Thus at last protected against starvation, his spirit liberated from the drudgery of writing for money, he wrote *Der Pfarrer von Kirchfeld* (1870), a *Volksstück* which was immediately successful on the Vienna stage. Its theme, love and tolerant understanding as against narrow religious fanaticism, remained throughout one of Anzengruber's major theses. His reputation established, Anzengruber gave up his tedious office work and in the remaining 19 years of his life wrote nearly 20 plays, two novels, and a great number of short stories, tales, and sketches.

His work is uneven in quality. His best plays, *Der Meineidbauer* (1871; Eng. tr., *The Farmer Forsworn,* 1913–1915) and *Die Kreuzelschreiber* (1874), reveal his strong dramatic gift, his realism touched with humor, his faith in human nature freed from conventions and firmly rooted in the soil. The later plays, however, repeat themselves in plot and characterization; the characters are types rather than individuals. His novel *Der Sternsteinhof* (1884) is perhaps his most original work and is very different from the traditional German *Bauernroman* of his contemporaries Rosegger (*q.v.*) and Auerbach. Helen, the heroine of the novel, represents beauty, health, and ambition which win out in this world over both good and evil. Although a peasant girl, she is a sister in spirit of Becky Sharp in Thackeray's *Vanity Fair,* drawn with a similar detached, almost cruel understanding. Anzengruber's short stories, like most of his plays, deal chiefly with Austrian peasant life, but the themes and problems are also of general significance. His dramatic gift is again revealed in lively dialogue, well-balanced plot, and contrasting sets of characters. At first written only in moments of leisure and relaxation, these stories became Anzengruber's chief means of expression when his success on the stage diminished. Deeply conscious of his ethical responsibility as a *Volksschriftsteller,* Anzengruber considered them, even more than his novels and plays, as expressive of his philosophy of life—a philosophy which matured from traditional idealism into a simple faith in the brotherhood of man, mixed at times with a humorous disdain for the human race as a whole.

See: A. Kleinberg, *Ludwig Anzengruber* (1921).

E. M. F.

Apollinaire, Guillaume (pseud. of Guillaume de Kostrowitski, 1880–1918, French poet), was born either in Rome, where he was baptized, or in Monaco, where he was educated at the Lycée Saint-Charles. His real name was that of his mother, who was of Polish origin. In 1898 he went to Paris, and there his first verses were published in the *Revue blanche* and the *Plume*. At the Soirées de la Plume he met Alfred Jarry (*q.v.*) and "conversed on heraldry, heresies, versification." Symbolism was still alive, and Apollinaire was to inherit some of its tenets, enrich its tradition, and, by embracing its spirit of liberty, develop from it the new movements, modernism, cubism, dada, surrealism.

His laboratory was Paris. His method of studying his times was not unlike Villon's. His poetry, like Villon's, may remain the testament of a man who leaves behind him an agonizing era and who senses ahead of him much that is, at the least, utterly different (for Apollinaire this means the first automobiles, the first moving pictures, the first airplanes, the First World War, all important to poetry). He studied his times like an anthropologist eager to detect in customs and costumes what, for lack of a better word, he called *l'esprit nouveau*. Such was the title he gave to a manifesto published in December, 1918, in the *Mercure de France*. Already, in Italy, his *Antitradition futuriste* (1913) had appeared. He was widely read and developed his erudition throughout his life in different ways, including the editorship of rare books and responsibilities as censor during the First World War. He edited for the Bibliothèque des Curieux erotic books of repute and helped to catalogue the Enfer de la Bibliothèque Nationale.

He became the friend of the great cubists, Picasso, Braque, *et al.*, and saw in cubism the expression of the times, an enrichment of the power of art to seize the present and with it the past and the future, its constituents. He wrote *Les Peintres cubistes* (1913), which founded cubism as a school. Two epithets, ubiquitous and simultaneous, describe the aim of the new art, which abolished the laws of perspective.

Apollinaire has left novels (*Le Poète assassiné*, 1916; *La Femme assise*, 1920, which deals with the Mormons), short stories (*L'Hérésiarque & Cie*, 1910), plays (*Les Mamelles de Tirésias*, staged in 1917; *Couleur du temps*, published in 1920 in the *Nouvelle Revue française*). These are all attempts at humanizing the universe by means of fiction and the limelight.

His most important contributions to literature are the two volumes of poems, *Alcools* (1913) and *Calligrammes* (1918). In *Alcools* there are songs in which Apollinaire's technical skill, his varied versification, now free, now classical, his use of traditional phrases in a new composition, his grouping of images, the absence of punctuation, create an original unity of tone that involves not sentimentality but intimacy, the intimacy resulting from the somewhat casual alternating between the contemporary and the classical. *Calligrammes* goes much further in the direction of the ubiquitous and simultaneous art mentioned; words are used to draw lines, and we are at the confines of the art of writing and the art of drawing. Apollinaire was a soldier in the First World War; he was perhaps the only poet who lived the war poetically. In "A Nîmes" (*Calligrammes*) the seeming haphazard, the seeming disorder under the control of the verses, arranged as heroic couplets, gives the order of military life.

Apollinaire's influence has been great. Some critics have condemned Apollinaire's puns, his playing with words; other poets, including Cocteau (*q.v.*), have borrowed these tricks used by him to allow poetry to take care of itself and to give back to words their own initiative. The surrealists have acknowledged their debt to him; André Breton (*q.v.*) considers him "the last poet," meaning that he has carried the art of poetry to its extreme limits.

See: A. Billy, *Apollinaire vivant* (1923); R. Taupin and L. Zukofsky, *Le Style Apollinaire* (1934).

R. T.

Apukhtin, Aleksei Nikolayevich (1841–1893, Russian poet), born into an old noble family in Bolkhov, Orlov, was educated at an exclusive secondary school and at a select school of jurisprudence. Having in private life close ties with the high society officialdom of St. Petersburg, Apukhtin in his poetry reflected to a great extent the moods of that milieu. His verse (*Stikhotvoreniya*, 1886; Verses) underscores primarily classical motifs and deals with patriotic and historical themes or with rustic idyls. It is frequently light and jocular in tone.

See: S. A. Vengerov, "Etapy neoromanticheskovo dvizheniya," in *Russkaya literatura XX veka*, Vol. I (1914).

O. M.

Aragon, Louis (1897–, French poet, novelist, and essayist), is a brilliant and imaginative writer, gifted with a style that can cut dialectical capers, animated by intellectual curiosity and sentimental quixotism, whose career epitomizes literary and social conflicts of the period between the two World Wars. He started out by participating successively in the cubist and dadaist movements, both of which he repudiated in turn, publishing *Feu de joie,* his first book of poems, in 1920, and following it with fictional pictures of the modern world's anarchy and moral disarray, like the satirical and whimsical *Anicet, ou le Panorama* (1921) and the caustic and erotic *Le Libertinage* (1924). He adhered in 1924 to the surrealist doctrine which, in his view, aimed to accomplish "an unexpected synthesis of the conflicting aspects of the moral world" and "the transmutation of everything into a miracle." He achieved such a "miracle" in *Le Paysan de Paris* (1926), in which his imagination clothes with the enchantments of poetry the commonplace scenes of Parisian reality.

But he criticized subsequently what he termed, in his *Traité du style* (1928), the *néant poétique* he observed in modern, and even surrealist, poetry and its apparent inefficacy in the social sphere. He renounced, finally, the idealistic basis of pure literature, a tainted product, in his eyes, of bourgeois materialism and in 1930 espoused Communism and the concept of "socialist realism." One fruit of this conversion was his inflammatory poem "Front rouge" (1931; Eng. tr., *The Red Front,* 1933), for which he was prosecuted and given a suspended sentence of five years. The surrealists had jumped to his defense, claiming immunity for the poetical as against the political connotations in a poem. This was Communist heresy. Aragon disavowed it, broke definitely with his surrealist friends, and dedicated himself to exalting the social revolution—in his journalistic activities, in publications like *Commune, Humanité,* and *Ce Soir,* of which he was an editor at various times; in his poetry, as in *Persécuteur persécuté* (1931) and *Hourra l'Oural* (1934), in which, conforming to Lautréamont's advice, he aimed to sing "practical truth"; and in novels which describe what he called "the real world." These novels give a complex and somber picture of social and moral decline of bourgeois society and of proletarian struggles, in the years preceding the First World War in France: they consist of *Les Cloches de Bâle* (1934; Eng. tr., *The Bells of Basel,* 1936), *Les Beaux Quartiers* (1936; Eng. tr., *Residential Quarter,* 1938), which won for him the Renaudot literary prize in 1936, and *Les Voyageurs de l'impériale* (1941; Eng. tr., *The Century Was Young,* 1941). In a book of poems published in Paris in 1941, *Le Crève-Cœur,* Aragon sings with the accent of tragic purity his twin passionate loves for his wife, the writer Elsa Triolet, and for fallen France, thus reverting in it to what is the core of his genius—poetry. His other wartime works include, in poetry, *Les Yeux d'Elsa* (1942), *Brocéliande* (1943), *En français dans le texte* (1943), *Le Musée Grévin* (1943), a waxworks gallery of collaborationists, and *La Diane française* (1945), and, in the novel, *Aurélien* (1945). *Le Crève-Cœur* and *Les Yeux d'Elsa* were republished in New York in 1943 and 1944 respectively.

See: Marcel Raymond, *De Baudelaire au surréalisme* (1933), pp. 346–348; M. Cowley, "Louis Aragon," *New Republic,* LXXXVIII (1936), 258; H. Josephson, "Louis Aragon, 'Poet of the War,'" *Saturday Review of Literature,* Vol. XXIV (1941), No. 20, pp. 10–11; H. Josephson and M. Cowley, *Aragon, Poet of the French Resistance* (1945).

S. A. R.

Arany, János (1817–1882, Hungarian poet, writer, and critic), was born in Nagyszalonta and died in Budapest. He was the youngest in a family of ten; his people were poor. Arany is rightly considered as one of the purest Magyar poets—his perceptions, his images, his humor and pensiveness, his very words show indigenous characteristics. He was a strolling actor, a school teacher, a guardsman in the war of freedom in 1848, a notary, a municipal counselor, professor at a Calvinist secondary school, a literary editor, and for a long time secretary of the Hungarian Scientific Academy. His friendship with Sándor Petőfi, the Hungarian Robert Burns, gave the rather shy Arany self-confidence. In 1845 he entered a literary contest of the Kisfaludy Társaság (Kisfaludy Society) with a satirical epic, entitled *Az elveszett alkotmány* (The Lost Constitution), and received the first prize, but it was in 1847 that the attention of the Hungarian literary world was directed to Arany for his *Toldi,* an epic of 12 songs. This was merited recognition of a poetic genius. During his life and after his death his ever-increasing prestige proved the Hungarian nation's need of such a poet; he never struck a false note, and even today he is read not only by students (his poetry is included in textbooks) but by the general public. It is fair to say that Arany exemplifies in his poetic utterances the essence of the Hungarian spirit. In his capacity as the editor of *Szépirodalmi Figyelő* (Belletristic Observer) and *Koszorú* (Wreath), he inaugurated standards of editorial policy which disturbed or silenced the dilettantes of expression. His family life was happy; his son, László, was a poet in his own right. There is nevertheless a note of deep sadness in Arany which was laid bare by his lyric poems, written in old age, but felt in his earlier works too. The tragic lot of the Hungarian nation after the War of Independence in 1848–1849, the enforced passivity of Hungarian leaders, the emphasis on "modernity" which was displeasing and disheartening in its pretense and hollowness, all explain the melancholy of this poet in whom, otherwise, were calm, restraint, and undramatic dignity. His collected works first appeared in 1867; since then there have been several editions, enriched with later writings. Because of its genuineness his poetic voice is still audible despite the fact that the tone of creative realism in which he believed has changed considerably since his time.

Arany was a definitely national poet, but without intolerance. When he presented to the Hungarian world his epics, ballads, satirical and descriptive poems, and brief lyrics, his critical works, and his translation of several comedies of Aristophanes and plays of Shakespeare, he proved that the kind of nationalism which a creatively used language radiates does not ignore man's universal attachments. His epic trilogy, *Toldi* (1847), *Toldi estéje* (1848; Toldi's Night), *Toldi szerelme* (1879; Toldi's Love); his heroic epic, *Buda halála* (1864; Eng. tr., *The Death of King Buda,* 1936); his sardonic *Nagyidai cigányok* (1852; The Gypsies of Nagy Ida); his ballads, *e.g.*, "A Walesi bardok" (The Bards of Wales), "Ágnes Asszony" (Mistress Agnes), "Éjféli párbaj" (Duel at Midnight); his ode, "Széchenyi emlékezete" (In Memory of Szechenyi); his descriptive poem, "A rab gólya" (The Captive Stork); his lyric poems expressing anxiety over the fate of the nation or bashfully revealing the wounds of his soul—these lend support to the view of Hungarian critics that Arany is a confrère of the supreme poets of world literature. It is not presumptuous to say that as a ballad writer he is one of the greatest. The sense of guilt and the tragic shock of his ballads imply an emotive and imaginative force which brings to the surface the deepest conflicts and contradictions of human nature. In its pure Hungarianism his prose is as authentic as his poetry. Arany was an exceptionally intelligent man, widely read, an authority on philological and literary criticism. His translations display a spiritual and verbal sensitiveness which only a real poet and a master of the language can possess. To read Aristophanes or Shakespeare in the translation of Arany is a fascinating experience, especially when one compares the original with the translation and discerns the Hungarian poet's imaginative and literal reliability in the matter of words.

Arany's interest in Attila, the leader of the Huns, or in the era of chivalry in Hungarian history, or in other features of Hungarian life related to the past, was, of course, dictated by poetic curiosity, but also by a desire to stir the people's feeling for the nation's historical greatness. He was apt to conceive romantic issues realistically. The current of nationalism so characteristic of 19th-century Europe had its Hungarian parallel, and in the sphere of poetry Arany's objective was identical with a constructive design of nationalism. Arany perhaps hoped his epics would mean to the Hungarians what the *Kalevala* meant to the Finns. This great and noble poet who never traveled abroad did not narrow the horizon of the world to that of Hungary; in fact through his poetry the horizon of Hungary was widened. He was an excellent craftsman. He conquered despair with the courage of a tragic sense; he conquered formlessness with a flawless sense of form. Some of Arany's work is translated into foreign tongues, including English.

See: P. Gyulai, *Arany életrajza* (1884); F. Riedl, *Arany* (1887); A. Schöpflin, *Irók, könyvek, emlékek* (1925); Arany, *The Death of King Buda,* tr. by W. Kirkconnell (1936).

J. R.

Arbaud, Joseph d' (1874–, Provençal poet and novelist), was born at Meyrargues in Provence. His mother, herself the daughter of a poet, had written a book of Provençal verse long before marrying the comte d'Arbaud. She had joined the Felibrige, an association with the purpose of reviving the language and literature of southern France, and acquired a good reputation under the pen name La Felibresso dóu Cauloun. Thus Joseph d'Arbaud was born and raised in a milieu where poetry and love for the home speech were long-standing traditions. Furthermore, he was encouraged by Mistral (*q.v.*), who always took a keen interest in his literary activities. "You are above them all," once wrote the master comparing him to the other poets of the younger generation. Time has not belied this judgment. Arbaud still holds the foremost place among contemporary Provençal writers.

After finishing his law course at the University of Aix-en-Provence, he remained for some time in the old capital enjoying society life in the company of young writers such as Paul Souchon and Joachim Gasquet, who later made names for themselves in French literature. Having decided to go to the deep sources of Provençal poetry, Arbaud left the "Athènes du Midi" for the remote and solitary Camargue, one of the rare places where the language and traditions were still unimpaired. He owned droves of wild bulls and, for nine years, lived integrally the life of a *gardian* or cowboy. It is to this long and direct contact with primitive nature and rustic people that he owes the best of his work. Back in Aix, he was for many years a very active champion of Provençal regionalism; he contributed articles to both French and Provençal reviews and devoted much of his time to *Le Feu; organe du régionalisme méditerranéen,* of which he was editor or coeditor for various periods between 1917 and 1937.

Arbaud has produced four books in the vernacular, with accompanying French translations. *Lou Lausié d'Arle* (1913; The Laurel of Arles), a volume of verse, was acclaimed by Mistral as a masterpiece comparable to those of Greece and Rome, in which "live again the language and genius of a race." This is fine poetry, remarkable for its power of suggestion, clothed in admirable form, written in a refined and at the same time rich, racy, and colorful language, which the author learned first from the lips of his mother, then from the rough and rustic men of the Camargue. The laurel of Arles, that Provençal tree which must ever root deeper in order to grow higher, is symbolic of the poet's own conception of life. Among his poems published only in reviews or in the form of short pamphlets are a few which must be considered among his best, *Li Cant palustre* (1919; Songs of the Marshes), *Li Rampau d'aram* (1920; The Brazen Boughs), and *La Visioun de l'Uba* (1921; Vision of the North), the last two being partly inspired by the war. Arbaud's philosophy is further developed in *La Bèstio dóu Vacarés* (1924; The Beast of the Vaccares), the story of a *gardian* with his horse and also that of the "beast," a fantastic being, half human, half animal, a voice of the past, the qualified interpreter of Provençal traditions. This work transcends the limits of regional literature. The next two books, *La Caraco* (1926; The Gypsy) and *La Souvagino* (1929; Wild Animals), are collections of short stories, also set in the Camargue and likewise carrying a philosophical and social meaning.

Joseph d'Arbaud has confined himself to the expression of his deepest feelings, and this with the utmost precision, constraint, and sobriety. The classical and somewhat aristocratic quality of his work makes it more appealing to the elite than to the common folk of Provence who speak the language. It is not characterized by the joyous spirit and optimism of the other Felibres, and there is no Rabelaisian laughter—hardly a smile—in his stories. The "most worthy successor of Mistral" is undoubtedly a genuine Provençal and one who has drawn most of his inspiration from the soil of Provence, but he belongs to the serious, reserved, and meditative type that is sketched in his recent study *La Provence; types et coutumes* (1939). It is to this book, the only one he has written in French, that Arbaud owes the crowning of his complete works by the French Academy (Prix Lasserre, 1939). In 1906 he had been elected laureate of the Felibrean *Jeux floraux.* Another and more important literary prize, the award received 33 years later from the Academy, was to establish or rather recognize his great distinction.

See: C. P. Julian and P. Fontan, *Anthologie de Félibrige provençal* (1924); C. Maurras, preface to Arbaud, *La Bête du Vaccarès* (1924); F. Mistral (neveu), "Joseph d'Arbaud, gardian, poète et romancier de Camargue," . . . *Et nous verrons Berre* (1924), pp. 289–296; E. Chauffard, "Un Grand Poète provençal: Joseph d'Arbaud," *Revue de France,* Année X (1930), Tome II, pp. 717–738.

A. V. R.

Arniches y Barrera, Carlos (1866–1943, Spanish playwright), the modern standard-bearer for the *género chico,* was born in the Mediterranean coast city of Alicante. He is next heard of in the employ of the Barcelona newspaper *Vanguardia.* Removing to Madrid at the age of 18 or thereabouts, he endured the usual privations, lightened momentarily by an award for the preparation of a history of the reign of Alfonso XII in the form of a primer. Shortly he scored a success with his (and Gonzalo Cantó's, for he was already writing in the collaboration which was to be so usual later) *Casa editorial* (1888), a literary-musical satire of authors and publishers. Exhibiting the lack of outward cheerfulness which is at least traditional in humorous writers, this *rey del chiste,* "king of jest," continued to write so steadily that by 1927 his creations, including the many done in collaboration (with García Alvarez above all and also with Abati, Asensio Mas, Celso Lucio, Fernández Shaw, Jackson Veyán, López Silva, *q.v.*, and others) numbered approximately 135.

The farce in one act has long held a position of honor in the Spanish theatre, its popularity being such between 1890 and 1900 that new pieces came to the boards at the rate of 150 a year. Arniches was the chief purveyor to the trade during the first two decades of the 20th century. Composed for the *teatros por horas*—in which each number required a ticket and took about an hour to perform—these short dramatic pieces in prose or verse, with or without the accompaniment of music, constitute the *género chico*. Its temple was the Teatro de Apolo in Madrid. The popularity, of some 40 years' duration, of the *género chico* came to an end about 1910.

Arniches's *sainetes* (the term of broadest significance, modernly, for the brief jocose dramatic composition, dealing usually with popular manners or types) were written in the language, somewhat conventionalized, of the lesser citizens of Madrid. They present *cuadros de costumbres* depicting dance halls, restaurants, parks and other places of recreation, fiestas, street scenes, patios, plazas, wherein appear small shopkeepers, itinerant vendors, the policeman on the beat, taxicab or hack drivers, laundresses, seamstresses, hairdressers, lady-killers, district bullies, and indeed all those representatives of society who make up the population of the poorer sections of Madrid. The plots of these sketches are almost never worth recalling, and their literary qualities often nil, but among the earlier successes of Arniches may be mentioned the following: *El santo de la Isidra* (1898), with music by Torregrosa; *El puñao de rosas* (1902), of which the action takes place in Andalusia, the music being by R. Chapí; *Los chicos de la escuela* (1903), *El terrible Pérez* (1904), and *El pobre Valbuena* (1904), all with music by Valverde *hijo; Alma de Dios* (1907), *La alegría del batallón* (1909), and *El trust de los tenorios* (1910), with music by J. Serrano. The titles and characters from some of the productions of Arniches have become almost proverbial, but—though he cannot fairly be dismissed as merely a librettist—some of the specimens of typical music seem more likely to preserve memory of the text. A trifle less hilarious, but with at least equal documentary value and even some philosophy, are *Las estrellas* (1904), *El amigo Melquiades* (1914), and *El chico de las Peñuelas* (1915). When Arniches dilutes his thought to fill the two or three-act farce, the results are less pleasing. The thinness of the plot is harder to conceal, the lack of distinction of idea and expression becomes more obvious, as in *Angela María* (1924) or *El señor Adrián el primo* (1927). The characters, however, are equally recognizable, if no more sharp of outline, the puns are as frequent, and laughs from all causes as plentiful. *La señorita de Trevélez* (1916) leaves the level of the *barrios bajos* and ascends to the middle-class comedy of manners. In the opinion of one—and perhaps only one—critic (Pérez de Ayala, *q.v.*), Arniches has here produced a work of more enduring value.

See J. Cejador, *Historia de la lengua y literatura castellana,* X (1919), 119–120, 126–127; R. Pérez de Ayala, *"La señorita de Trevélez,"* in *Las máscaras,* 1924 ed., II, 171–177.

R. K. S.

Artsybashev, Mikhail Petrovich (1878–1927, Russian novelist, playwright, and essayist), was the son of a district constable from the lesser landed gentry in the Ukraine. Like so many other Russian authors, he began as a painter. His first story to be published was "Pasha Tumanov" (1901; Eng. tr. in *Tales of the Revolution,* 1917). This was followed by other stories of a somewhat Tolstoyan trend. "Smert Lande" (1904; The Death of Lande) was especially noted as a study of moralistic self-perfection, with a disheartening ending. During the revolutionary events of 1904–1905, Artsybashev wrote a number of stories that had an immediate appeal. While they displayed no depth of analysis or understanding of the social and political causes, they depicted the external dramatism of the Revolution. In "Krovavoye pyatno" (Eng. tr., "The Blood-Stain," in *Tales of the Revolution*), "Na belom snegu" (On the White Snow), "Odin den" (One Day), "Chelovecheskaya volna" (The Human Wave), and other stories of that period, the author records the bloodiest episodes of such significant events as the Red Sunday (January 22, 1905), punitive expeditions in the Baltic Provinces, mutiny on the battleship *Potemkin,* December barricades in Moscow. Descriptions of murder, rape, suicide, death, are Artsybashev's strong point.

Fame—and notoriety—came to him after the publication of his novel *Sanin* (1907; Eng. tr., *Sanine,* 1914). In 1903 the manuscript had been rejected by all publishers as false to life. But four years later, after the disenchantment of the abortive Revolution, Sanin, the champion of carnal self-gratification, found an eager hearing among the tired youth of Russia.

Groups of Saninists were formed by schoolboys and schoolgirls for the discussion and emulation of the principle of being unprincipled, so alluringly presented for the first time in Russian literature. As a reaction against the traditional Russian traits of introspection and service to lofty ideals, *Sanin* had novelty and freshness. The author made his hero attractive by the old device of rendering the other characters dull and inferior. The novel breathes a torrid eroticism, which is suggested even in the purely descriptive passages; small wonder that it was proscribed in a number of places, both in and outside of Russia, as pornography.

With the success (*de scandale,* in a certain measure) of *Sanin,* Artsybashev shook himself free from whatever Tolstoyan and revolutionary notions he may have voiced earlier. Later novels such as *Milliony* (1910; Eng. tr., *The Millionaire,* 1915) and plays such as *Revnost* (1913; Eng. tr., *Jealousy,* 1923) and *Zakon dikarya* (1912?; Eng. tr., *The Law of the Savage,* 1923) treat, primarily, sexual problems. Artsybashev has an undeniable gift for bringing out the biological element in human relations. Unfortunately, this gift is one-sided, reducing as it does the complexity of sexual and marital relations to one common denominator. His is also a depressing talent, for outside of a few sun-drenched pages in *Sanin,* his stories and plays are joyless and defeatist. The novel *U posledney cherty* (1912; Eng. tr., *Breaking-Point,* 1915) is a hymn to suicide, as the only dignified way out. Its hero, Naumov, preaches the need of "destroying in men the superstition of life." Artsybashev's gloomy outlook was intensified after his exile from Soviet Russia (1921). During his last years he wrote nothing but venomous articles against the Bolsheviks; these were issued in book form as *Zapiski pisatelya* (Warsaw, 1925; Notes of a Writer).

A. K.

Asch, Sholem (1880–, Yiddish novelist, short-story writer, and playwright), was born in Kutno, a small town in Poland, then part of the Russian Empire. Asch was the 10th child in a family of small-business people. At 19 he went to Warsaw. His schooling had consisted of little more than a limited training in the Hebrew language and its literature, both ancient and modern. Brought up in an orthodox environment, he already considered himself "enlightened." He had inherited from his mother a delicate romanticism, from his father self-confidence and a healthy aggressiveness. He took with him to Warsaw sketches of small-town life, and a year later these sketches appeared in the Yiddish press. In 1904 was published a series of episodes and scenes in lyric prose, under the title *Dos Shtetl* (The Town), issued in book form in 1905. This semi-idyllic, quietly humorous picture of Jewish small-town life represented a kind of romantic realism which was a departure from the pure realism of Mendele mocher sforim (*q.v.*) and other older Yiddish writers—with the exception of Y. L. Peretz (*q.v.*), the father of neo-Yiddish romanticism. Asch introduced a method of idealization to replace the sober and pointed satire practiced by all of them excepting the humorist, Sholem-Aleikhem (*q.v.*) In 1906 he wrote his lyric drama *Moshiakhs Tsaytn* (The Days of the Messiah), in 1907 *Der Got fun Nekome* (Eng. tr., *The God of Vengeance,* 1918), followed by various other dramatic works. These plays were performed not only in the Yiddish theatres of Europe and America, but also on the Russian and Polish stage and in Max Reinhardt's Deutsches Theater in Berlin. Thus Yiddish literature, which until then was known to the world almost exclusively through the translated poems of the American Yiddish poet, Morris Rosenfeld, appeared on the horizon of international literature. Both Asch's novels and his dramas were translated into Russian, German, and Polish, later into English and other languages. Their fascination is due to the freshness of his approach, the intimate humor and the restrained but warm lyricism with which he depicts the mundane experiences of the ordinary person.

The novels which Asch began to write just before the outbreak of the First World War are drawn on an epic scale, covering the social ladder from the lowest to the highest rung, from thieves, brothel inmates, and other underworld characters to revolutionary leaders, martyrs, and saints. The motifs of his works are just as kaleidoscopic. As to the often incompletely rounded central figures, they are mostly people striving to free themselves from inner conflicts, people yearning for a faith. Like the hero of *The God of Vengeance* almost all of them suffer from a sense of guilt, from a deep soul conflict, and they seek security in an ideal, a faith, or a God who will purify them, grant them vigor, wholeness, and inner peace. Like Hans Bodenheimer in *Baim Opgrunt* (1937; Eng. tr., *The Calf of Paper,* American title, *The War Goes On,* both 1936), Asch's other heroes also have "firm faith in a Godhood which is beyond and above the limits of all faiths and confessions, which streams forth from the higher sentiments of faith in eternity which every religious nature possesses."

Asch's most imposing and richest novels are his trilogy *Farn Mabl* (1927–1932; Eng. tr., *Three Cities,* 1933), in which the romanticism of the hero is accentuated by the realistically painted social background; *Der Tilim Yid* (1934; Eng. tr., *Salvation,* 1934), in which Asch sums up the basic themes of almost all his earlier novels and in which he expresses with greater lucidity than anywhere else his faith in faith; *Der Man fun Notseres* (1939; Eng. tr., *The Nazarene,* 1939), which in some important details is a continuation of *Der Tilim Yid* and the main purpose of which is to describe the historical Jewish background of the legend of the founder of Christianity; and *The Apostle* (1943; published in English translation only), based on the life of St. Paul. The last two books attracted great attention by their colorful and meticulous descriptions of the beginning of the Christian era and because in them the author attempts to lift the tragic barrier between Judaism and Christianity.

In 1932 Asch was awarded the Order Polonia Restituta. About the same time he was elected honorary president of the Yiddish P.E.N. Club. In 1937 the Jewish Institute of Religion in New York conferred upon him the degree of Doctor of Hebrew Letters.

Other books by Asch of which there are English translations are *Amerike* (1911; *America,* 1918), *Motke Ganev* (1916; *Mottke the Thief,* 1935), *Mayselekh fun Khumesh* (1923; *In the Beginning,* 1935), *Di Muter* (1925; *The Mother,* 1930), *Dos Gezang fun Tol* (1938; *The Song of the Valley,* 1939). *Three Novels* (1938) contains *Uncle Moses* (*Onkl Moses,* 1920), *Chaim Lederer's Return* (*Chaim Lederer's Tsurikkumen,* 1927), and *Judge Not* (*Toit Urteil,* 1926). *What I Believe* (1941) was first published in German under the title *Woran ich glaube. Children of Abraham* (1942) is a collection of stories about America which had appeared in Yiddish.

See: S. Niger, *Sholem Asch, tsu zayn 6ostn geboyrn-tog* (1940); Charles A. Madison, "Sholem Asch," *Poet Lore,* XLVI (1940), 303–337; A. A. Roback, *The Story of Yiddish Literature* (1940).

S. N.

Aseyev, Nikolai (1889–, Russian poet), is the chief survivor of Russian futurism. In 1939 the 25th anniversary of his first book of poems, *Nochnaya fleita* (Nocturnal Flute), was celebrated throughout the Soviet Union, and the poet, once an extreme individualist and iconoclast, was decorated with the Order of Lenin. Aseyev was one of the closest friends of Mayakovsky (*q.v.*), and one of his more recent efforts is a novel in verse, *Mayakovski nachinayetsa* (1940; Mayakovsky Starts Off), an intimate portrait of the late poet, composed in a style resembling Mayakovsky's. Aseyev, like his friend, began as a poet of a city bohemia—in Vladivostok, instead of Moscow. In 1918 he arrived in Moscow, where as a member of the "Centrofugue" group he attempted to combine "pure" classic lyrics with the innovations of cubo-futurism. He was fond of such bohemian images as "the half-naked moon on a blue couch," the sky a night café, with a star serving oysters and angels smoking cigars. Moscow ripened his talent and imbued him with proletarian, industrial motives. During the New Economic Policy (NEP) and its temporary restoration of private capitalism, Aseyev expressed alarm at the resurgence of everyday-ness—"*la Traviata* languidly sniveling from endless cabarets," and "our time is colored carroty, not red." Typical of Aseyev's concern with industrialism was his volume *Stalnoi solovei* (1922; Steel Nightingale). He reflected the Revolution and the civil war in his epic *Semyon Proskakov* (1928). Primarily Aseyev is a lyricist, however, who records his emotions and observations with a gentle directness that is free both from sentimentality and from the once fashionable Bolshevik Spartanism. His range is wide, his form varies from regular meter to futuristic broken lines and meter, and his vocabulary is fresh and clear, seldom displaying the extreme coinages of the early futurists. As he continues to mature, he may throw off the sobriquet of a lesser Mayakovsky.

A. K.

Asín Palacios, Miguel (1871–1944, Spanish Arabist and philologist), was born in Saragossa. He combined early studies in theology with a profound knowledge of the Arabic language and culture to produce a long series of works on the Christian origins of Islamic mysticism. He made very important contributions to understanding the philosophical and theological views of Hispano-Arabic thinkers of the 12th and 13th centuries and the relation of these men to later European writers. *Abenmasarra y su escuela: Origenes de la filosofía hispanomusulmana* (1914) and *Abenházam de Córdoba y su historia crítica de la ideas religiosas* (3 vols., 1927–1929) are significant studies in the history of philosophy and religion. *La escatología musulmana en la*

Divina Comedia (1919) attracted world-wide attention; this work on the Islamic sources of *The Divine Comedy* became the subject of long and heated discussions (see the answers of Asín Palacios to his critics in "Historia crítica de una polémica," *Boletín de la Academia Española,* Vol. X, 1923, pp. 505–537, Vol. XI, 1924, pp. 5–53, 129–148, and also C. H. Grandgent, "Islam and Dante," *Studi medievali,* Vol. III, 1930, pp. 1–5).

See: Angela González Simón, *Revista de filología,* XXVIII (1944), 349–356, necrology and bibliography.

F. S. y E.

Asnyk, Adam (1838–1897, Polish poet), was born in Kalisz, Russian Poland, of gentry stock recently turned merchant. Unlike the romantic writers of the previous generation, most of whom viewed contemporary struggles from the sidelines, Asnyk took active part, even as a student, in the conflicts of his day. Imprisoned in 1860 in the notorious Warsaw Citadel for conspiracy in connection with the movement for national independence, Asnyk left Poland in 1861 for Paris, London, and eventually Heidelberg, but returned to Warsaw in 1863 to participate in the national uprising and to serve, finally, on the National Council improvised in September of that year by Romuałd Traugutt. Upon the collapse of the uprising, Asnyk fled to Italy and thence to Heidelberg, where in 1866 he received his Ph.D.

After two years in Lwów, where he wrote literary articles for various periodicals, Asnyk finally settled in Cracow (1870). Here he took a leading part in every contemporary movement: in the struggle of Austrian Poland for full political rights—he served for a while as a city councilor and later as a deputy to the Galician Diet; in the "discovery" of the Tatra region as literary material; and in the battle of the Cracow conservatives, known popularly as "Stańczycy" (*see* Polish literature), with the progressive Warsaw positivists, a conflict in which, as editor of *Nowa reforma* (New Reform) from 1882–1894, he took a stand midway between the two.

Asnyk wrote several plays and novels but he is remembered for his lyrics. These appeared in periodicals from 1864 on and were very popular, probably because they suited perfectly the mood of the times. Pleasant, graceful, and never dangerously moving, they met the requirements of a generation suspicious of profoundly stirring poetry, since this, they believed, had led them to the catastrophe of '63, yet desirous of something more nourishing to the spirit than the chill prose of the positivists. Many of Asnyk's lyrics were inspired by the Tatras. His short poem "Do młodych" (To Youth), which begins "Seek out the clear ray of truth . . . Forget the dreams of yesteryear," became the credo of the generation to which belonged, among others, Marie Sklodowska Curie. Two of Asnyk's great admirers were the Polish actress Helena Modjeska, to whom the poet addressed an elegy prematurely in 1871 when she was reported deceased, and Ignace Paderewski. Paderewski, and also his distinguished pupil Sigismund Stojowski, set many of Asnyk's lyrics to music.

See: G. Korbut, *Literatura polska* (1931), IV, 92–95; Z. Nowakowski, *Słownik biograficzny* (1935), I, 171–173.

A. P. C.

Aubanel, Théodore (1829–1886, Provençal poet), was born in Avignon. He belonged to a family of printers, since the 18th century honored by the Holy See with the title Printers to His Holiness. Théodore Aubanel began writing poetry in French, which was the language usually spoken in his home. His shift to Provençal, not an imperative urge, was due principally to the influence of Roumanille (*q.v.*). Having realized that the local speech was a rich, poetical language, closer than French to Provençal reality, he joined that group of young poets who were to be the founders of the Felibrige. As is well known, the purpose of this organization was to bring about the restoration of the Provençal language and literature.

Aubanel's literary production is relatively small in bulk. He is known above all as the author of *La Miougrano entre-duberto* (1860; The Split Pomegranate) and of *Li Fiho d'Avignoun* (1885; The Young Ladies of Avignon), two collections of lyrics, published with an accompanying French translation. The former appeared at a very opportune moment, a year after the epoch-making appearance of *Mirèio,* by Mistral (*q.v.*). It added much to the fast-growing prestige of the Felibrige school. It brought a new element to Provençal lyricism, that of pure passion. Here was found a bold, direct, and realistic expression of intense human suffering caused by frustrated love, the anguish experienced by the author himself after his sweetheart had entered a convent to become a nun. Immediately critics acclaimed Aubanel as having won a place between Mistral and Roumanille. Ever since then, these three names have been regarded as forming a symbolic trinity of Provençal literature, a triumvirate of the Felibrige.

Li Fiho d'Avignoun has been interpreted as a confession of the author's mature age. Here again poetry has its source in the violent conflict between flesh and spirit, Christian principles winning over passion and desire. Although a zealous Catholic and a highly honorable husband and family head, the author had to suffer persecution from the pens of unenlightened censors who accused him of being an impious renegade. It is generally believed that the ordeals he had to undergo in his various attempts to publish the book actually shortened his life. A pure hymn to beauty, *Li Fiho d'Avignoun* contains very fine verses on almost every page. A few of its poems, such as "Lou Bal," "La Venus d'Avignoun," and, above all, "La Venus d'Arle," are little masterpieces by themselves, fine jewels, any one of which would have been sufficient to bring his name to posterity. Aubanel has written three five-act plays in verse. He published one, *Lou Pan dóu pecat* (1882; The Bread of Sin), which was produced in the original text and in a French version by Paul Arène. It is a powerful, violent, grim drama of rustic love. A posthumous collection of poems, *Lou Reire soulèu* (1899; From behind the Sun), does not give anything essentially new about the author or his art. More important from the standpoint of biography is his correspondence with one of his feminine inspirers, *Lettres à Mignon* (1899).

Aubanel is a great lyric poet, second in Provençal literature only to Mistral. His work has not reached a very large public but has been appreciated by those for whom it was written, the select few. His plea, "Luse tout ço qu'es bèu, tout ço qu'es laid s'escounde" (Let beauty shine and ugliness hide), is that of a great artist whose main object has always been to find love and beauty, whether moral or physical, Christian or pagan.

See: L. Legré, *Théodore Aubanel, par un témoin de sa vie* (1894); N. Welter, *Théodore Aubanel, un chantre provençal de la beauté* (1902); J. Vincent, *Théodore Aubanel; la vie et l'homme* (1924); J. L. Vaudoyer, "Avec Zani," in *Beautés de la Provence* (1926).

A. V. R.

Audiberti, Jacques (1900–, French poet and novelist), took his place in his late 30's as one of the most promising of the younger French poets. A reporter on a Parisian newspaper, Audiberti began writing verse about 1933 and made a strong impression with his first book, *Race des hommes* (1937). Since then his work has appeared in several periodicals, notably the *Nouvelle Revue française*, and two novels, *Abraxas* (1938) and *Septième* (1939), have been published. His poetry is distinguished at first glance by an extreme richness of vocabulary; he seems drunk with words, reveling in rare terms and the specialized language of a dozen professions. This extravagance of diction is accompanied by an equally striking use of metaphor and in general a heroic rhetoric that reminds one of Hugo—but a Hugo tempered by Rimbaud (*q.v.*). A closer examination of Audiberti's work reveals a subject matter to match his style. Poetry, he has said, should treat of "la destinée et . . . la grandeur de l'homme." It is modern man, knowing as no man has known before the secrets of time, space, and the elements, probing in his laboratories the very essence of his universe, that Audiberti exalts. He is trying to write the epic of man in a scientific world and to seize and impart the new sort of communion with nature which science has made possible and perhaps even necessary. Audiberti's novels, though probably less important and certainly less original than his poetry, show the same unrestrained imagination, the same preoccupation with rhetoric, and the same verbal profusion.

See: Gabriel Bounoure, *"Race des hommes,* par Audiberti," *Nouvelle Revue française,* XLVIII (1937), 615–617; Marcel Arland, "Quelques Romans français," *Nouvelle Revue française,* LI (1938), 1037–1040.

C. W., Jr.

Aukrust, Olav (1883–1929, Norwegian poet), was born in the mountain valley of Gudbrandsdal, hearth of the ancestral folk culture of Norway. Home, surroundings, and extensive studies early imbued him with the country's national heritage, the literary traditions that go back to ballads and the Edda, the New Norse language, the folk art and material civilization, and the whole popular philosophy; under the influence of the folk high school movement he conceived a religious nationalism in which mystic and realistic elements curiously mingled, as they did in his own mind. His literary work is an attempt to show in poetic images the spiritual growth and destination of the Norwegian people within the eternal framework of Norway's nature.

In two large volumes of loosely connected lyrical poems, *Himmelvarden* (1916; The Mountain Cairn) and *Solrenning* (1930; Sunrise), he attacked the problem from the angle of the individual, symbolizing the development of the nation in his own struggle against the primitive powers of darkness and his own redemption through Christianity. In a remarkable way the psychological interpretation is made to emanate from the landscape, pictured with overwhelming power of visualization. The collections contain striking pictures of folk life and some of the deepest love lyrics in Norwegian literature; they show profundity of thought and feeling, orchestral mastery of the language, and amazing rhythmical inventiveness. Aukrust's other books, *Hamar i hellom* (1926; Spirit from the Mountains) and the unfinished *Norske terningar* (1931; Norwegian Dice), are fragments of a large cycle which was intended in a similar way to consider the nation from the local beginnings of culture through the development of national self-assertion into the universal realm of ideas. The work shows the same poetic power and a baffling knowledge of all manifestations of Norwegian character and life, moving freely from sublime spirituality to broad realism and baroque humor.

In spite of its fragmentary character, Olav Aukrust's poetic work is one of the most original interpretations of the inner history of his nation and one of the strongest expressions of poetic genius in modern Norwegian literature.

See: I. Krokann, *Olav Aukrust* (1933).

S. S.

Averchenko, Arkadi Timofeyevich (1881–1925, Russian short-story writer and dramatist), born at Sevastopol, was a merchant's son and in his youth worked as a clerk. He began his literary career with serious stories, but soon turned to humor, and eventually achieved fame in that genre. He edited the well-known humorous periodical *Satirikon* (1908–13) and contributed frequently to it as well as to other magazines. His short stories and his one-act plays also achieved popularity in such collections as *Vesyolyie ustritsy* (6th ed., 1911; The Gay Oysters), *Rasskazy dlya vyzdoravlivayushchikh* (5th ed., 1913; Stories for Convalescents), and *Chudesa v reshete* (1915; Wonders in a Sieve). Averchenko relied chiefly on broad farce, but his humor has elements of social satire, burlesquing as it does human frailty in fields ranging from friendship to surgery—and not forgetting the plight of an elderly ghost confronted by modern inventions. After the Russian Revolution, Averchenko emigrated and for a time bitterly lampooned the Communists (*Dyuzhinu nozhei v spinu revolyutsii*, 1921; A Dozen Knives into the Back of the Revolution), but in later works reverted to kindlier moods (*Rasskazy tsinika*, 1925; The Stories of a Cynic). English translations of Averchenko are given in B. G. Guerney's *A Treasury of Russian Literature* (1943).

See: "Averchenko," in *Entsiklopediya "Granat,"* Vol. XI (1912), appendix, p. 610; "Averchenko," in *Bolshaya sovetskaya entsiklopediya*, I (1926), 141.

P. A. P.

Aymé, Marcel (1902–, French novelist), was born at Joigny in Burgundy. He was successsively insurance broker, bricklayer, journalist, salesman. After a long illness which put an end to his picaresque existence, he began his literary career. His first novel, *Brûlebois*, was printed at Poitiers in 1926 and later in Paris in 1930. *Aller et retour* (1927) and *Les Jumeaux du diable* (1928) reached a very limited public. The reputation of Aymé began with *La Table-aux-Crevés* (1929), which was unanimously praised by the critics and received the Théophraste Renaudot prize. This robust episode of peasant life was followed every year by a novel or a volume of short stories. The novels are *La Rue sans nom* (1930), *Le Vaurien* (1931), *La Jument verte* (1933), *Maison basse* (1935), *Le Moulin de la Sourdine* (1936), *Gustalin* (1937), *Le Bœuf clandestin* (1939); the short stories are *Le Puits aux images* (1932), *Le Nain* (1934), *Derrière chez Martin* (1938), *Les Contes du chat perché* (1939), which last were rewarded the Chantecler prize. Another volume of short stories, *Le Passe-Muraille*, was added in 1943.

Marcel Aymé's art is thoroughly logical and realistic under a false appearance of eccentricity. His points of departure are often burlesque and sometimes absurd, but the stories develop afterward with a mathematical precision leaving an impression no longer of fantastic pieces of fiction but of scrupulous pictures of a real world. He possesses a broad sense of humor in the best Gallic tradition, particularly in his bawdy tales of country life. *La Jument verte* is the best example of his Rabelaisian verve. But he can also handle grimly tragic subjects or, as in *Les Contes du chat perché*, emulate Charles Perrault and La Fontaine in his presentation of charming fairylands peopled with wise and witty animals. By his multiform talent Marcel Aymé has placed himself among the original authors of his generation.

M. E. C.

Azaña, Manuel (1880–1940, Spanish statesman and critic), born in Alcalá de Henares, was sent when young to the school run by the Augustinian order at the Escorial. There, after finishing his secondary education, he began his studies in law, which he continued at the University of Saragossa. He obtained his doctorate in jurisprudence at the University of Madrid. On his return (1912) to Spain from Paris, where he had been sent on a scholarship, he became a government functionary. Fulfilling his duties soberly and seriously, he remained a government employee, with little interruption, until he entered politics (1930) and established the Partido de Acción Repúblicana.

At a time when the intellectuals of the new literary generation were disinclined to utilize, as they could have, the famous Ateneo de Madrid as a debating society and tribune from which to influence minority opinion, Azaña joined the organization. True to the glorious traditions of the Ateneo, which had shaped so much of the history of Spain from the romantic period down to the end of the past century, he distinguished himself by keeping faith with its political program. From 1913 to 1920 he was its secretary and in 1930 became its president. During the First World War he was a newspaper correspondent in France and Italy. Out of this experience came his book *Estudios de política francesa: La política militar* (1918). Under the mild dictatorship of Primo de Rivera he began his really fecund literary career. A few years before this period he had produced the first Spanish version (1920–1921) of George Borrow's *The Bible in Spain.* With Cipriano Rivas Cherif he founded and directed the literary magazine *Pluma* (1920–1924); in 1922 he took over the political weekly *España,* started originally by Ortega y Gasset (*q.v.*). Azaña came into prominence as a literary critic in 1926 when the coveted National Prize for Literature was bestowed on him for his *Vida de Juan Valera.* His interest in Valera continued. He wrote a copious and valuable introduction to the "Clásicos castellanos" edition (1927) of *Pepita Jiménez;* in 1929 his *Valera en Italia; amores, política, literatura* was published.

With two exceptions, all the writings of Azaña from the advent of the Second Republic until his death deal with politics. The first, *La invención del "Quijote" y otros ensayos* (1934), gives a brilliant interpretation and appreciation of Don Quixote; *Tres generaciones del Ateneo* (1930) is a study on the history and significance of the Ateneo. From 1930 to 1940 Azaña showed energy, great talent, and disciplined leadership in his various posts as minister of war, premier, and president of the republic. In the opinion of many, Azaña was a really great parliamentarian and orator. With the triumph of Franco, he took refuge in France, where, on November 4, 1940, at Montauban, he died a broken man.

Azaña had entered the literary scene late in life. In the two magazines *Pluma* and *España* he engaged in vitriolic criticism of the apolitical attitude assumed by the writers of the Generation of '98, then enjoying prestige and public patronage. His arrogant optimism, his Spanish *soberbia,* made small beer of the claims of those writers. Perhaps he was at his best in studies on Ganivet, Unamuno, and Costa (*qq.v.*). The most ambitious and devastating is "El *Idearium* de Ganivet" (included with the others mentioned in *Plumas y palabras,* 1930), in which he charged this original writer with ignorance of Catholic dogma and with an egregious misconception of Spanish history. The reader, overwhelmed by Azaña's logic and his knowledge of Spanish history, readily acquiesced, if only for the pleasure of anticipating the day when Azaña, a statesman in power, should succeed where the others had failed. But Azaña's optimism, unfortunately, failed too.

In all likelihood his claims to remembrance will rest on his translation of Borrow's *The Bible in Spain,* his sensitive essay on Don Quixote, and, above all, his remarkable recapturing of the essence of his disturbed soul when he studied at the Escorial. Juan Ramón Jiménez (*q.v.*) has well pointed out how the Spaniards of his time cultivated a literary genre which had not enjoyed much prestige in 19th-century Spain, namely, the book of reminiscences of childhood and adolescence. Jiménez himself, Unamuno, Baroja (*q.v.*), Ramón y Cajal, Azorín (*q.v.*), Pérez de Ayala (*q.v.*), and Azaña in his *El jardín de los frailes* (1927) must be included. As a sensitive artist Azaña gave a memorable account of the psychology and moral restlessness of a Spanish adolescent coming from the hallowed Alcalá de Henares (made famous by Cardinal Cisneros and by Cervantes) and going to study at the Escorial where, in spite of the august presence of Philip II, he showed a temperament inimical to the political and religious relics of the past. It is in these recollections that Azaña proved his marvelous grasp of the Spanish language. At a time when all the writers of Spain were swayed by stylistic innovations imported from abroad, he used a style derived from the Spanish theologians and moralists and characterized by a raciness and compactness comparable to Spanish wrought iron. Azaña, whose ideology owed much to the revolutionary and liberal tradition of Europe, is most *castizo* in his style, without being affected or archaic. It was into this resilient Spanish that he translated Borrow's book.

See: E. Giménez Caballero, *Manuel Azaña* (1932); N. González Ruiz, *Azaña; sus ideas religiosas, sus ideas políticas, el hombre* (1932); M. Góngora Echenique, *Ideario de Manuel Azaña* (1936).

M. J. B.

Azorín (pseud. of José Martínez Ruiz, 1873–, Spanish essayist, critic, novelist, and dramatist) cultivated so many genres that he defies precise definition. His early novels are made of intimate remembrances, descriptions of town and country, and criticism of Spanish life; the later *Don Juan* (1922; Eng. tr., 1923) and *Doña Inés* (1925) are evocative vignettes. Evocative in the same manner are attempts at drama such as *Old Spain* (1926) and *Brandy, mucho Brandy* (1927) and short stories such as *Blanco en azul* (1929; Eng. tr., *The Syrens and Other Stories,* 1931). Azorín's many volumes of criticism—the most important aspect of his work—are chiefly short essays, which are a mixture of the newspaper article, the erudite disquisition, and the lyrical impression. What gives unity to all his work is an unmistakable personal tone, certain very definite stylistic traits, quite new and fresh in his time, and a vision of life, literature, and reality in which the aesthetic, the emotional, and the rational are inseparably blended. In the highly personal quality of his writings Azorín appears as the embodiment of the intellectual subjectivism brought forward in Spanish literature by the Generation of '98. Azorín, in fact, was the first writer to adopt this term and the first to define its main characteristics in a series of articles (see "La generación del 98" in *Clásicos y modernos,* 1913). When Azorín spoke of "the men of '98" he was really speaking about himself. He was giving a perfect characterization of his own work and personality when he pointed out the feeling of these men for the Castilian landscape and for the past, their critical attitude toward an academic and pseudoclassical tradition, their love for the primitive poets, their admiration for El Greco and the spirit of such cities as Toledo, their indebtedness to Larra, their varied European influences.

His life has been entirely consecrated to literature except for a few, unsuccessful attempts to enter politics. He was born at Monovar in Alicante province. After attending a religious boarding school (these experiences are the subject of one of his first important books, *Las confesiones de un pequeño filósofo,* 1904), he began the study of law at the University of Valencia. There he wrote his first articles. About 1896 he went to Madrid and very soon became well—and unfavorably—known through the radical character of his writings and campaigns. Between 1893 and 1900 he published, under various pseudonyms, 10 or 12 pamphlets and minor critical works violently attacking accepted social and literary values. With the appearance in 1900 of *Los hidalgos* and *El alma castellana* (*1600–1800*), the real Azorín is revealed. In them were evident that poetic gift for bringing out the "presentness" of the past and that talent for uncovering the lasting significance of the most seemingly insignificant facts which were to form the core of his style. In 1902 and 1903 appeared *La voluntad* and *Antonio Azorín,* two autobiographical novels which contain the full expression of his sensibility and inner life. These two books make up a profound document for the study of the spiritual crisis at the end of the last century in Spain. In describing the perplexities of Antonio Azorín, Martínez Ruiz—who henceforth identified himself with and adopted the name of the character that he had created—analyzed in a moving way the spiritual unrest of the intellectual youth of his time. He showed them torn by an inner conflict between sentiment and reason, between a cult of will and of individual energy and an absolute incapacity for action, looking toward Europe for guidance and trying at the same time to discover the deep roots of the Spanish soul, dissatisfied with the decadent state of Spanish life, rebelling against tradition and yet with a great emotional attachment to that tradition which they wanted to destroy.

The purpose of the greater part of Azorín's works, comprising over 50 volumes, is to give a vision of the eternal values of Spain as perceived by a modern spirit—a poetical and critical vision. He has never abandoned the rational urge for renovation and the "revision of values" which was his point of departure. But on the whole, criticism is more than overbalanced by sentiment. The lyrical impression received when reading his prose is the result of two concentrical emotions, the emotion of the atmosphere of things and the emotion of time. Both find their center in the Castilian landscape and history. Books such as *Los pueblos* (1905), *La ruta de Don Quijote* (1905), and above all *Castilla* (1912) rank with some of Unamuno's essays and certain poems of Antonio Machado (*qq.v.*) as the highest attainments of the typical "Castilianism" in contemporary Spanish literature. In these volumes he detects in the contemplation of silent and often very humble things the shadow of a past which he merges with the present to suggest poetically a feeling of the static emotion of time: everything changes, everything is fleeting; the only permanent thing is this very emotion about the return of things. He brought a similar sensibility to literary criticism in *Lecturas españolas* (1912), *Clásicos y modernos* (1913), *Los valores literarios* (1913), *Al margen de los clásicos* (1915), reawakening an interest in many forgotten authors and books. There is also an exquisite and purely poetic quality in such works as *Don Juan, Doña Inés,* and *Félix Vargas* (1928).

Azorín had an extraordinary influence in the first 20 years of the century. At that time he was acclaimed one of the most original exponents of a new epoch. He owed much to modern European literature, to France especially—Taine, Flaubert (*qq.v.*), the symbolists, and the impressionists. He combined the aesthetic sense and the methods learned from them with a philosophical conception which could be traced indirectly to Germanic sources (*e.g.*, his ideas of time and change, his subjectivism). In addition he had a direct understanding of Spanish spirituality and a profound sense—also Spanish—of the value of the common things of reality.

See: S. de Madariaga, *The Genius of Spain and Other Essays on Spanish Contemporary Literature* (1923), pp. 148–164; Werner Mulertt, *Azorín* (1926, in German; Spanish tr., 1930).

A. del R.

B

Bååth, Albert Ulrik (1853–1912, Swedish poet), appeared first on the literary scene as one of that impressive group of poets from Sweden's rich, southernmost province, Skåne—a group that includes, besides Bååth, Ola Hansson, Anders Österling, and Vilhelm Ekelund (*qq.v.*) Bååth spent his boyhood and youth in a quiet little parish vicarage in southern Skåne, was educated at the University of Lund, and passed a considerable portion of his later life in his native province. Though his career was an essentially academic one (he was an Icelandic scholar, folk high school and university teacher, and director of a museum), the best of his poetry was as little intellectual as poetry can well be. Among the eight published volumes of his verse, covering a span of about 20 years, only the first three are of serious importance—*Dikter* (1879; Poems), *Nya dikter* (1881; New Poems), and *Vid allfarväg* (1884; Along the Great Highway). Some of the poems in these volumes express in rather obvious forms the social sentiments typical of the literature of the day; but the majority of them, and by far the most important, give spontaneous, personal, and direct expression to Bååth's solid animal delight in the folk life and the landscape of his rural Skåne. The strength of these poems lies in their healthy sensualism, their vigorous aliveness to the rich variety of substantial physical forms, colors, odors, and sounds characteristic of the fertile countryside of southern Sweden. Bååth's poems lack, however, any profounder evocative qualities, the philosophical undercurrents and the explosive emotional core of all really great lyric expression; and they are almost entirely devoid of the sensitive musical qualities of Swedish verse at its best. His work is nevertheless of real importance in the development of modern Swedish poetry; for he not only "discovered Skåne" as subject matter for a rich efflorescence of provincial verse, but he pointed the way toward healthy forms of poetic realism for all of Swedish poetry since his day. Such superb lyric poets of the 1890's as Heidenstam, Fröding, and Karlfeldt (*qq.v.*) owe not a little, directly and indirectly, to the example of a new poetic realism in the provincial poetry of Bååth.

See: K. Fredlund, "A. U. Bååths diktning," *Ord och bild,* XXI (1912), 538–547; O. Hansson, "A. U. Bååth," in *Litterära silhuetter, 1885,* in *Samlade skrifter,* II (1920), 9–29.

A. G.

Babel, Isaak Emmanuilovich (1894–, Russian short-story writer), revived the genre of the short story after the Revolution. Uniquely gifted within limits, he is unrivaled for the concentration, impact, and brevity of his stories and for his mastery of dialect. A "fellow traveler," he became a sensation in the first decade of Communism, but since then he has lapsed into relative obscurity. Certain of his tales, however, already belong among the classics and are known by heart by many admirers. Born in Odessa of a typical petty-bourgeois Jewish family, he graduated (1910) from the Odessa School of Commerce. His principal training was received at home, where he studied Hebrew, the Talmud, and the Bible. At 15 he developed a passion for French literature, and he wrote his first stories in that language. In 1916 he went first to Kiev and thence to St. Petersburg, where he suffered hardship because Jews were then denied legal residence. Gorky (*q.v.*) encouraged him by publishing his first two stories in *Letopis* (Chronicle), but rejected his subsequent work as poor and callow. The next seven years Babel wrote nothing, but devoted himself to the Revolution, serving as people's commissar, member of a food expedition, and agent of the Cheka. He fought with Budyonny's cavalry in the Polish campaign of 1921–1922 and with Yudenich's cavalry. Later he operated a printing press in Odessa. He returned to literature (1923) with a number of short stories printed in periodicals. Their instant success led to two volumes of tales, *Odesskie rasskazy* (1923–1924; Odessa Tales) and *Konarmiya* (1926; Eng. tr., *Red Cavalry,* 1929), which brought him international fame. There followed *Bluzhdayushchie zvyozdy* (1926; Wandering Stars), a scenario; *Yevreiskie rasskazy* (1927; Jewish Tales); *Benya Krik* (1927; Eng. tr., 1935), a "film novel"; and two plays, *Zakat* (1928; Sunset) and *Mariya* (1935), produced by the Moscow Art Theatre. Since then he has written other stories and has engaged in a long novel, but he has failed to hold the brilliant popularity won by his earlier work. This is sometimes ascribed to the enforced proletarization of literature under the first Five-Year Plan and to Babel's unwillingness to submit his pen to a dictated tendentiousness.

Babel's subject matter falls into two main cycles, the sufferings of Odessa Jews and the exploits of the Red fighters of Budyonny's cavalry. Benya Krik, a famous Jewish bandit, whose real name was Misha Yaponchik, or Mike the Jap, is the leading character of the first group. Depth and subtlety underlie the concise simplicity of Babel's work, which is a mixture of heroic romance and the utmost naturalism seasoned with irony. All his stories are founded on sharp paradox, violence and serenity, extreme cruelty and lyrical tenderness, humor and tragedy. Apparently crude and fragmentary, in reality they are constructed with the nicest precision, without a superfluous word. His finest things are in dialect, that of the Kuban Cossacks and the Russo-Jewish jargon of Odessa. The speech of such characters is a marvel of phonetic reproduction, impossible to translate. Even so, the foreign reader receives an indelible impression from the story—such is Babel's power. Among the best tales are "Sol" ("Salt"), "Pismo" ("A Letter"), "Smert Dolgushova" ("Death of Dolgushev"), "Zhizn i priklyucheniya Matveya Pavlichenko" ("Life and Adventures of Matvey Pavlitchenko"), all in *Red Cavalry,* and "Korol" (The King, in *Odesskie rasskazy,* 1924, Stories from Odessa) and "Istoriya moei golubyatni" (1926; Eng. tr., "The Story of My Dovecote," *Slavonic Review,* X, 1–11).

See: D. S. Mirsky, "Babel," *Sovremennyia zapiski,* XXXVI (1925), 485–488; A. Kaun, "Babel, Voice of the New Russia," *Menorah Journal,* XV (1928), 400–410.

N. S.

Babits, Mihály (1883–1941, Hungarian poet, critic, novelist, and short-story writer), was born in Szekszárd and died in Budapest. Babits was educated at the Cistercian secondary school in Pécs and at the University of Budapest. In his career as a professor in various provincial towns, in Baja, Szeged, Fogaras, Ujpest, he showed a fine professional conscientiousness; but in his moments of real freedom he was a poet, and gradually his poetic self demanded complete attention. Fortunately the childhood of Babits was spent in a cultural atmosphere; his people belonged to the intellectual middle class. His whole life suggests cultural roots. When his first poems appeared in *Nyugat* (West), they immediately impressed the discriminating readers; they gave the impression of a *poeta doctus.* This first impression was so strong that later it was difficult for readers and critics to recognize the vehemence, the emotional restlessness, the fantastic horizon, the crucified spirit of the poet. Babits never sided with dogmas which narrowed life; he never subordinated the principle of artistic integrity to didacticism or propaganda. By nature he was a contemplative person rather than a man of action; he had the intelligence of a creator and not of a pamphleteer. His neurotic sensitiveness sometimes seemed to be in need of humanization, but in truth he was never so removed from life as to be fairly called an ivory-tower poet. While Freud in psychology, Bergson (*q.v.*) in philosophy, and Julien Benda (*q.v.*) in certain critical norms influenced him, the catholicity of Babits's taste was always such that he could absorb many ideas without paying the tribute of mere resemblance or imitation. He believed in values, not in slogans. His marital life with Sophie Török, a poetess, was ideal; it was a Hungarian version of the Robert Browning–Elizabeth Barrett relationship. Babits was a pacifist, but it is logical to assume that his sense of proportion would have rejected any unreasonable peace.

Babits was not only one of the most gifted poets and writers of modern Hungary, but one of the most erudite and versatile. He made the discursive essay popular in his native country; he translated Sophocles' *Oedipus,* Dante's *The Divine Comedy,* Shakespeare's *The Tempest,* medieval Latin hymns, and the works of many French, German, English, and American poets and writers into Hungarian. His *Az europai irodalom története* (1934; History of European Literature) shows an independent spirit's interpretation of great writers and poets. His plays are book-dramas. After the First World War, Babits became one of the editors of *Nyugat;* he was less radical than his predecessors, but not less strict in his standard of criticism. As a matter of fact, despite increased political nationalism he was unwilling to compromise with his aesthetic doctrines; the hysterical times of course affected him, but he repudiated their standard. The saccharine patriotism of certain Hungarian poets, the conforming rhetorics of certain writers and publicists, the "folkishness" of certain literary or pseudo-literary tendencies, never touched the deepest strings of his heart and his mind. His passion for creative integrity was so honest that his pragmatic compromises were merely matters of inevitable policy and they were not the betrayal of the spirit.

The collected works of Babits were published in 1939. Babits traveled very little, but his work, like that of the non-traveling Immanuel Kant, symbolized his relationship to the cosmos. The sphere of his art and of his thoughts was the universe. He was brought up as Roman Catholic but he did not confine his views to the dogmatic horizon of the Church. His early poems showed ability in poetic symbolism; he was always very fond of Edgar Allan Poe and of certain French and English symbolic poets and emphasized images and workmanship in their fashion. In some respects, like so many other symbolic poets, he was a master of onomatopoeia. When he reached maturity, he felt that even modern terminologies become stereotyped; he dug into his innermost self, and a comparison of his early poems with those of the later period reveal a broader conception of the good life, a deeper understanding of life's experiences. The somewhat "decadent" Babits is best represented by the following volumes of poetry: *Herczeg, hátha megjön a tél is* (1911; But Prince, if Winter Should Come); *Recitativ* (1911; Recitative); *Nyugtalanság völgye* (1917; The Valley of Restlessness); *Sziget és tenger* (1925; Island and Sea). The mellow Babits found his voice in *Versenyt az esztendőkkel* (1928; In Race with the Years) and in *Jónás könyve* (1939; The Book of Jonah). *Halálfiai* (1926; The Sons of Death) is his most ambitious novel; it is a bulky work, written with compassion about the dying gentry and middle class. *Karácsonyi Madonna* (1920; Christmas Madonna), *Timár Virgil fia* (1922; The Son of Vergil Timar), *Kártyavár* (1924; House of Cards), and other stories and novels written by Babits reflect a mind inclined to be fantastic in its psychological orientation and positive in its refusal of the obvious. *Irodalmi problémák* (Literary Problems) shows Babits at his very best as an essayist. His language, rich and sometimes baroque, makes the reading of his works difficult for the uninitiated. Some of his works have been translated into German, Italian, French, and English.

See: H. Horváth, *Neue ungarische Lyrik* (1918); A. Schöpflin, *Irók, könyvek, emlékek* (1925); W. Kirkconnell, *The Magyar Muse; an Anthology* (1933); J. *Reményi,* "The Passing of Mihály Babits," *Books Abroad,* XVI (1942), 36.

J. R.

Bacchelli, Riccardo (1891–, Italian novelist), born in Bologna of a wealthy, well-known family, is one of the few novelists in a literary generation that went in more for lyricism than for narration and that was, until recently, rather wary of construction and plot. Bacchelli's success is due more to his patience and to a persistent will to become a great novelist than to any natural gift. It took him 18 years to acquire any fame at all. His production earned him respect rather than enthusiasm and more authority than popularity. With the exception of *Il Diavolo al Pontelungo* (1927; Eng. tr., *The Devil at the Long Bridge,* 1929), a historical novel, alive and humorous, Bacchelli's work is for the most part ponderous, and his characters are not well enough defined to emerge as living types. *Il Diavolo,* in two distinct parts somewhat separated from each other in tone, is a fictionized account of Bakunin's attempts to introduce socialism in Italy. His early book, *Il Filo meraviglioso* (1910), printed at his own expense, was somewhat mannered, and this same quality persisted throughout all his works. Only once did he try his hand at a light novel, *La Città degli amanti* (1929; Eng. tr., *Love Town,* 1930), in which he tells of a city built for lovers by an American tycoon, but where true lovers cannot really live. This very same invention in the hands of an Anatole France (*q.v.*) or of a Shaw would have resulted in a very amusing satire, but what attracted the critics in *La Città* was a description of the retreat of Caporetto, which entered into the plot only as a side issue. This would indicate that the best qualities of Bacchelli are of a descriptive rather than a narrative nature. Sometimes he gives evidence of a very fine mastery of vocabulary, especially in his tale of fishes, *Lo sa il tonno* (1923), written with satirical intentions in that rather forced style of academic exercise common to the group of the *Ronda*. Occasionally he displays a wealth of detail which goes well with the rather slow and majestic rhythm, earning him the comparison to a river (*scrittore fluviale*).

Bacchelli's most imposing work, a three-volume novel of the time of the Italian *Risorgimento* with his native land of Emilia as background, *Il Mulino del Po* (first published in the *Nuova Antologia*, 1938–1940), is hardly exciting; but it certainly merits consideration for the magnitude of the enterprise, rare among the parsimonious writers of present-day Italy. In *Oggi, domani e mai* (1932), he tried his hand at more serious historical problems (the responsibility of the Reformation for the modern sick political state of Europe) without giving a solution to them, nor creating in the character of Anceschi a true representative of the veteran of the First World War. He merely confirmed the critics' estimation of his qualities as an accomplished academic writer. A few short stories, *Bella Italia* (1928); a tentative retelling in modern words of Hamlet, *Amleto* (1923); some literary memoirs, *Memorie del tempo presente* (1919–1920); one historical essay, *La Congiura di Don Giulio d'Este* (1931); some lyrics in prose, *Poemi lirici* (1914), *Parole d'amore* (1935); and another novel, *Il Rabdomante* (1936), complete the essential achievements of this man of high literary discipline.

See: P. Pancrazi, *Scrittori italiani del novecento*, revised ed. (1939), pp. 221–227; T. G. Bergin, "Riccardo Bacchelli," *Italica*, XVII (1940), 64–68, with bibliography.

G. P.

Bagritsky, Eduard (pseud. of Eduard Dzyubin, 1895–1934, Russian poet), was born in Odessa, of a poor Jewish family. He graduated from a technical school as land surveyor, but never practiced his profession. Bagritsky took part in the civil war as a member of a guerrilla detachment and as a poet attached to the "propaganda train" which was sent to the front by proletarian organizations. Bagritsky started to produce poetry in 1915–1916, but his mature works were written after 1924. He belonged to the group of constructivists whose leaders were his personal friends, but his poetry is by no means an expression of this particular school. Eclectic in scope, it impresses by its romanticism and passionate sense of life. The romantic trend is strongly felt in Bagritsky's imagery and his visions of the far distant past. It was not by mere chance that one of his first collections of poems bore a Dürer drawing on the cover. In the "Ptitselov" (Bird Catcher) Bagritsky proclaimed his utter love for "nature, wind, songs, and freedom." One of his preferred heroes was the exuberant Till Eulenspiegel. He made excellent translations of various poets, especially of Burns and Walter Scott. He also devoted many of his poems to contemporary themes, always choosing colorful scenes and dramatic episodes. Soviet critics praise highly his "Duma pro Opanasa" (Ballad of Opanas), a narrative poem of civil war in which motives of the Ukrainian folklore are skillfully merged into modern rhythms. In spite of its great metric variety and the trace of many conflicting influences, ranging from the classics to Mayakovsky's (*q.v.*) futurism, Bagritsky's poetry has a fundamental unity revealed by the dynamism of its images, the tense rapidity of its rhythms, the sensuous strength of its descriptions, and the general feeling of optimism and vitality. After his death his works were published in *Sobraniye sochineni v dvukh tomakh* (1938; Collected Works in Two Volumes).

M. S.

Bahr, Hermann (1863–1934, Austrian critic, novelist, and dramatist), was born in Linz, Austria, and died in Munich. His closest association was with *Jungwien*, a group of writers which he claimed to have founded or discovered in 1891 and which dominated Austrian literature during the quarter of a century preceding the First World War. This group included Arthur Schnitzler, Hugo von Hofmannsthal, Richard Beer-Hofmann, Peter Altenberg, and Felix Salten (*qq.v.*). Bahr was its most prolific and most versatile member. As a critic (in his *Zur Kritik der Moderne*, 1890) he anticipated the reaction against naturalism, just as this movement was attaining supremacy (*see* German naturalism), and as early as 1891 he espoused in his volume *Die Überwindung des Naturalismus* the cause of the emerging neo-romanticists, symbolists, and decadents. When these finally triumphed, he became the spokesman of the new expressionistic youth, and in his book *Expressionismus* (1916; Eng. tr., *Expressionism,* 1925) he helped to define the characteristics of this literary tendency. As a novelist (*e.g., Theater,* 1897) he was a superb and witty narrator of the charm and the folly of Vienna, when this metropolis was the overrefined capital of a dying empire. As a dramatist he is best remembered for *Das Konzert* (1909; Eng. tr., *The Concert,* 1910), a sophisticated comedy of Vienna, which was successfully produced both on the Continental and on the American stages.

S. L.

Bainville, Jacques (1879–1936, French historian and essayist), was born in Vincennes, Seine. He attended the Lycée Henri IV in Paris, then studied law. He was only 20 when he brought back from a trip to Germany a biography of Ludwig II of Bavaria, the protector of Wagner (*q.v.*).

He wrote short stories and essays of a philosophical nature. *Jaco et Lori* (1927) and *La Tasse de Saxe* (1929) are examples. He was well suited to edit, as he did, the works of Voltaire; the two writers resemble one another in more than one respect—their irony, their scorn for mankind, their pessimism, their admiration of intelligence, their wit, their style.

Bainville's main work, however, was in history and journalism. His historical publications include *Histoire de deux peuples* (1915), *Histoire de trois générations* (1916), *Histoire de France* (1924), and *Napoléon* (1931). As a journalist he contributed political articles to the *Action française* and *Liberté,* economic and political editorials to the *Petit Parisien* and *Nation belge,* and literary essays to the *Revue universelle,* which he founded in 1920 with Henri Massis (*q.v.*). He was able so to expose the most complex problem, the most involved circumstance, as to render them perfectly comprehensible to his many readers. He admittedly looked upon Sainte-Beuve as his model. No matter what the subject matter, his style was one of precision and lucidity. Some of his articles have been collected in *Les Conséquences politiques de la paix* (1920), *La Russie et la barrière de l'est* (1937), and *L'Allemagne* (1939–1940). He was elected a member of the French Academy in 1935, the year before his death.

P. B.

Balart, Federico (1831–1905, Spanish poet and critic), born in Pliego, Murcia, was active in the ranks of the liberal party and held office during the revolutionary period (1868–1874), returning to private life when the monarchy was restored. Before this he had been an outstanding journalist and was considered an extremely able literary and art critic; selections from this phase of his work were collected in 1894 in a volume entitled *Impresiones: Literatura y arte.* That same year, when it seemed as though he had almost passed into oblivion, he achieved one of the greatest literary successes of the day with the publication of a book of poetry entitled *Dolores,* the name of his deceased wife. Her death had occurred in 1879, and the poems dedicated to her had been written between that year and 1891. These verses of marital love were the quiet welling of a wounded heart and were written not for the public but to assuage an inner sorrow. It is to this quality of sincere emotion, expressed in simple, noble, pensive form, in terse nitid language, and tinged with religious resignation that their author owed his late-flowering glory. To this is due the place accorded him as one of the great minor poets of the 19th century. Two later volumes of poetry, *Horizontes* (1897) and *Sombras y destellos* (1905), add nothing to his glory.

See: J. M. Alvarez Sotomayor, "Federico Balart," *Revista católica de Chile,* XLVI (1924) 389–394, 551–554; L. Alas and E. Gómez de Baquero, prologues in Balart, *Poesías completas* (1939).

F. de O.

Baldensperger, Fernand (pseud. Fernand Baldenne, 1871–, French literary historian), born in Saint-Dié, Vosges, is a stalwart Lorrainer who, under a transparent pseudonym, has occasionally extolled in prose and verse the healthy values of local tradition. He is also a scholar of universal knowledge, who has been in recent years engrossed in the preparation of a history of international literature. He has had an extraordinarily full career, producing books by the dozen and articles by the hundreds.

For 36 years (1900–1936) a professor in French universities (Lyon, Strasbourg, Paris), Fernand Baldensperger came to Harvard University in 1936 and has lately been on the staff of the University of California at Los Angeles. Research, lectures, and visiting professorships have taken him to the four corners of Europe, to China and Japan, to both Americas. As early as 1904, when he published his *Goethe en France* and a posthumous, enlarged reedition of Louis Paul Betz's *Littérature comparée; essai bibliographique* (1st ed., 1897), he became a world leader in the field of comparative literature. For his 30th academic anniversary in 1930, 62 scholars from 18 different nations offered him the unprecedented homage of two volumes of *Mélanges* exclusively devoted to comparative studies. Many more contributed to the *Revue de littérature comparée* and its "Bibliothèque" of monographs which he and his foremost disciple, Paul Hazard (*q.v.*), founded together in 1921.

Some of Baldensperger's work is modeled after the pattern set by Gustave Lanson (*q.v.*) and is strictly concerned with national subjects (outstanding in this category are his critical edition of Alfred de Vigny and his two "contributions to the intellectual biography" of the same author, 1912 and 1933). But for the most part his studies have stressed the international viewpoint—*Etudes d'histoire littéraire* (2 vols., 1907–1910), *Le Mouvement des idées dans l'émigration française* (2 vols., 1924), *La Littérature européenne aux XVIIe et XVIIIe siècles* (1930), to quote only a few titles. These works are backed up by a definite philosophy, expressed in a work of 1913 (*La Littérature; création, succès, durée*) and in Baldensperger's important introduction to the very first number of the *Revue de littérature comparée* ("La Littérature comparée; le mot et la chose"). Comparative literature—which crosses at will geographical, linguistic, and cultural boundaries—he characterizes not only as a dynamic conception of literary history but as the possible harbinger of a "new humanism."

See: Emmanuel Beau de Loménie, review of *Le Mouvement des idées dans l'émigration française* in *Revue de littérature comparée,* V (1925), 708–718; Paul Van Tieghem, *La Littérature comparée* (1931), pp. 33–48 and *passim.*

J.-A. B.

Baldini, Antonio (1889–, Italian novelist), was born in Rome. An apathetic son of a prosperous family, he spent his early youth dreaming of poetry. Casting aside any idea of practical employment, he was content to turn over the pages of old and good books, studying, elaborating, and polishing literary forms. He presently achieved a mature literary style saturated with an instinctive, individual humor that distinguishes him from other writers of Italy today. Baldini studied at the University of Bologna and received his doctorate with a thesis on Ariosto, whom he liked to call "Lodovico the tranquil." The First World War interrupted his literary studies and brought him a medal for bravery; in *Nostro Purgatorio* (1918) he records some of his more interesting war experiences. Baldini has been a lecturer, a merchant (in Upper Silesia), and since 1931 the editor of the *Nuova Antologia.*

The three literary works that are most representative of Baldini are *Michelaccio* (1924), *La Dolce Calamita* (1929), and *Amici allo spiedo* (1932). *Michelaccio* is an amusing story of a bad boy. It symbolizes perhaps the natural laziness and mischievousness of the author himself. Michelaccio loves to eat, to drink, and to sleep. So does Baldini. Michelaccio loves women. So does Baldini. Michelaccio is hopelessly indolent. So is Baldini. But here, as the critic Panzini remarks, the analogy must end, for the laziness of Michelaccio is just one characteristic while that of Baldini is a mode of being and of thinking—it is a style, a philosophy. *La Dolce Calamita* contains a series of amusing portraits of women Baldini has known or of women he would like to have known. According to the author, the tools used in constructing this novel were his eyes and his memory, but much of the quality comes from Baldini's fantasy—which he pretends to overlook. In *Amici allo spiedo* he makes fun of many of the leading contemporary luminaries. The quips are those of a good-natured friend; there are indelible portraits of Malaparte (pseud. of Curzio Suckert, *q.v.*), Bacchelli (*q.v.*), Soffici (*q.v.*), Papini (*q.v.*), Giuliotti (*q.v.*), De Chirico, Spadini, Don Benedetto (Croce, *q.v.*), *et al.* To each Baldini devotes a few paragraphs or a chapter, varying the tone and the music, but without ever forgetting the pinch of good humor—the *pizzicata.*

P. M. R.

Baliński, Stanisław (1898–, Polish poet), was born in Warsaw, of Border gentry stock, the son of a one-time mayor of Warsaw. Educated at home and abroad, Baliński came to maturity at the time of the founding of *Skamander* (*see* Polish literature) and was associated with this group until 1939. Baliński's early poems, published mostly in *Wiadomości literackie* (Literary News) and *Skamander,* were slight pieces, but his verses published in exile, after the invasion of Free Poland (*Wielka podróż,* London, 1941; A Great Journey), together with those to be found in the emigration journal *Wiadomości polskie* (London; Polish News), are sincere, moving records of deep spiritual experience.

See: A. P. Coleman, "Polish Literature in Exile," *New York Times Book Review,* June 1, 1941, pp. 8, 18.

A. P. C.

Balmont, Konstantin Dmitriyevich (1867–1943, Russian poet, translator, and essayist), was born into a noble family in the province of Vladimir, Russia. While a student at the Gymnasium, Balmont was temporarily expelled for revolutionary activity. Soon reinstated, he finished the secondary school and enrolled in the faculty of jurisprudence at the University of Moscow (1886); here, however, he studied chiefly German literature and the history of the French Revolution. Within a year he was expelled from the university and exiled to Shuya for leading some of the student outbreaks. In the following year he was permitted to resume studies at the College of Law at Yaroslavl. Given to emotional instability, Balmont at 22 leaped from a window in an attempted suicide and as a result was confined to bed for over a year. He was ever attracted by the lore of strange lands and traveled extensively. In 1904 he visited Mexico; in 1905, because he had written a number of revolutionary poems, Balmont was obliged to emigrate and spent the better part of a decade in Paris, Brussels, and elsewhere. He visited the Orient, Africa, and even Oceania. In 1913 Balmont returned to Moscow. In 1917 he ecstatically greeted the October Revolution; subsequently he was commissioned abroad, where he switched to the *émigré* camp. After that he lived chiefly in France.

When in the middle of the 1890's symbolism as a literary movement had begun in Russia, Balmont supported the new trend and soon was recognized as one of its leaders. Thereafter his name was linked with the symbolists. His first book of melancholy civic verse, *Sbornik stikhotvoreni* (1890; Collection of Verses), reflects the influence—in its content—of the poetry of Nadson (*q.v.*), Nekrasov, Koltsov, Nikitin (*q.v.*), and—in its form—that of Pushkin. Even in his second book, *Pod severnym nebom* (1894; Under Northern Skies), one still finds a similar strain, although here the reader feels that music is used to convey a mood. Balmont's studies of Western verse (eventually he translated into Russian the collected works of Shelley, Whitman, much of Poe, Wilde, Calderón, Hauptmann, *q.v.*) completed a transformation in his poetry. In his *V bezbrezhnosti* (1895; In the Infinite) and *Tishina* (1898; Quietude) Balmont shows a complete break with the traditions of civic poetry and appears as one of the leaders of the new school. His poetry now not only seeks the infinite, but also attempts, through the music of its verse, to convey the ineffable. His next few books, *Goryashchiya zdaniya* (1900; Flaming Buildings), *Budem kak solntse* (1903; Let Us Be like the Sun), *Tolko lyubov* (1903; Love Alone), *Liturgiya krasoty* (1905; The Liturgy of Beauty), reveal Balmont as a spectacular, resplendently colorful, self-centered romanticist. Here he attempts to discard the tenderly melancholy mood of his previous poetry and to become a Nietzschean superman (*see* Nietzsche) whose desires are a law unto themselves. After 1905 Balmont's muse begins to falter, and his poetry becomes repetitious. His verse after 1910 scarcely deserves mention. As a translator Balmont's worth is unequal. His translations suffer from being too free; those he made of Shelley are more paraphrase than translation. Balmont's essays on poetry treat the writing of poetry as a magical process and reflect a typical "symbolist mentality" that prefers to guide itself by inspirational and irrational methods.

Balmont's greatest achievement lies in the mellifluence of his verse; in this he is a master. Although his poetry inspired numerous imitators, most of them were second and third-rate poets, and Igor Severyanin (*q.v.*) alone enjoyed a long period of popularity.

See: Ellis (pseud. of L. L. Kobylinski), *Russkiye simvolisty* (1910); *Zapiski neofilologicheskovo o-va pri Peterburgskom universitete,* 1914, No. 7; E. Anichkov, "Balmont," in S. A. Vengerov, ed., *Russkaya literatura XX veka,* I (1914), 66–100.

O. M.

Bałucki, Michał (pseuds. Elpidon and Załęga, 1837–1901, Polish dramatist), the father of Polish bourgeois comedy, was born in Cracow, and there he spent most of his life. His early writings, poems of love and death in the mood of Słowacki, are all forgotten except for the lyric "Góralu, czy ci nie żal?" (Oh, mountaineer, dost thou not grieve?), which is sung to a popular folk melody. In the 70's Bałucki turned from poetry to the novel, using this form as an instrument of protest against the clergy and aristocracy, whose form of conservatism he hated, against, on the other hand, the growing trend to naturalism in life and literature, and especially against the new freedom accorded women and the mounting popularity of Ibsen (*q.v.*). Bałucki did not find his proper medium until he began to write plays, and even then, although the successful *Radcy pana radcy* (The Counselors of Mr. Councilor) appeared in 1867, it was not until the 80's that he can be said to have mastered that medium. With *Krewniaki* (1879; Kinfolk), the still popular *Grube ryby* (1881; Big Fish),

Dom otwarty (1883; Open House), and *Klub kawalerów* (1890; Bachelors' Club), he provided the Polish theatre of the future with a rich repertory of satirical bourgeois comedy. Bałucki was a man out of tune with his times, his gift of comedy being largely unappreciated by contemporary theatregoers who sought in the drama not amusement, but sublimity and emotional exaltation. Bałucki died a suicide, unable to survive the storm of disapproval that greeted his play *Blagierzy* (1900; The Impostors).

See: G. Korbut, *Literatura polska* (1931), IV, 220–221; Z. Nowakowski, *Słownik biograficzny* (1935), I, 252–254.

A. P. C.

Bandrowski, Juljusz (known also as Kaden, from his mother's name, 1885–1945, Polish novelist and publicist), was born at Rzeszów, in the heart of Austrian Poland, the son of a distinguished and public-spirited physician. Brought up mostly in Lwów, Bandrowski studied in Cracow and later in Brussels, where he specialized in music. He became involved at an early age in the patriotic activities centering around Piłsudski and took a leading part in the exploits of the legionaries during the First World War. After the Piłsudski coup of 1926, Bandrowski became, in effect, the "grand pontiff of official literature" in Poland. His finest work artistically is the tender, autobiographical *Miasto mojej matki* (1925; My Mother's Town). His most ambitious works are *Generał Barcz* (1923), a story of the reconstruction of Polish political and social life in Warsaw immediately following the First World War, and *Czarne skrzydła* (1929; Black Wings), an attempt, only partially successful, to portray fictionally the life of Polish workers in the great Dąbrowa coal basin. In 1938 Bandrowski entered the then officially cultivated field of romantic biography with a fictionized life of Chopin (*Życie Chopina*).

See: Z. Dębicki, *Portrety*, II (1928), 287–302; K. Czachowski, *Obraz współczesnej literatury polskiej*, III (1936), 51–98, 686–690.

A. P. C.

Bang, Herman Joachim (1857–1912, Danish novelist), was born on the island of Als. He came of an old distinguished family which was showing signs of decadence. His father, who was a clergyman, died insane. Herman Bang's mother was his friend and playfellow, but died when he was 14. She figures often in his works, which draw, to an unusual extent, on reminiscences of his childhood. His first important book, the novel *Haabløse Slegter* (1880; Generations without Hope), describes the struggle in himself of the conflicting elements in his heredity. In *Tine* (1889) he uses his own home as the background for his description of the war with Austria and Prussia in 1864 and the retreat from Dannevirke—though actually the family had moved away from the neighborhood the year before. *Det hvide Hus* (1898; The White House) is an idyllic description of his childhood home, with his mother as the central figure.

A sexual abnormality and a morbid sensitiveness placed Bang outside that human fellowship for which he passionately yearned. His own spiritual loneliness is reflected in *De uden Fædreland* (1906; Eng. tr., *Denied a Country*, 1927), though it purports to be the story of a homeless violin virtuoso. It was partly his longing for human contacts and partly his strong love of play-acting that drew Bang in his youth to the stage. When he failed both as actor and playwright, he turned to journalism as a means of livelihood and showed himself a brilliant though subjective critic. No fiction could be less dramatic than Bang's, but no doubt his early failure contributed to his sympathy for those on the periphery of the art world, *e.g.*, the aged danseuse in the tragicomic short story "Irene Holm" (1890). Within this narrow compass Bang's art is almost perfect. *Ved Vejen* (1886; By the Wayside) is generally regarded as his masterpiece. It is a short novel in which, with the slightest means and the subtlest touches, he draws a picture of Danish provincial life and portrays a gentle, shrinking woman who is bound to a coarse, selfish husband. Pity for all who suffered helplessly and loathing of that which he regarded as the most potent cause of human suffering, sexual desire, were the motivating forces in Bang's authorship. Love, he said, always grew into desire; desire brought degradation and misery. His conviction that sexual desire was beyond the control of the will led to rebellion against the idea of a God who placed this devastating impulse at the root of all life and remained coldly aloof and indifferent while his creatures struggled. Bang's art was impressionistic, and he developed a style that exactly fitted his approach. His death was lonely and tragic. He was on a reading tour in the United States when he was found bleeding and unconscious in his berth on the train. He had evidently suffered a stroke and hemorrhage. He was taken to a hospital in Ogden, Utah, but died without regaining consciousness.

See: P. A. Rosenberg, *Herman Bang* (1912); Hans Brix, *Danmarks Digtere* (1925).

H. A. L.

Banville, Théodore de (1823–1891, French poet, dramatist, and prose writer), was born in Moulins, where he had a happy early childhood. From the age of seven on, his life was largely spent in Paris. His family encouraged his literary ambitions from the start, and except for a period of illness and depression his life was serene and uneventful. After a brief liaison with the actress Marie Daubrun, to whom the volume *Améthystes* (1862) is addressed, he found complete happiness in his marriage to Mme Rochegrosse in 1866. On the death of Gautier he became, with Leconte de Lisle (*q.v.*), one of the masters of the younger generation of poets, but lived to see the decline of his popularity.

Banville produced some 20 volumes of verse. In *Les Cariatides* (1842) a romanticism all too reminiscent of Hugo and Musset colors even the Greek themes so dear to Banville and is bridled only by the conscious craftsmanship which marks all his verse. His technique owes much to the poets of the Renaissance, as is evident in *Les Stalactites* (1846), *Odelettes* (1856), and *Le Sang de la coupe* (1857) and particularly in the later volumes in which he rings the changes on a single form such as the ballad or the rondel. From *Les Stalactites* on, Banville's early pessimism gradually disappears, and he becomes the poet of joy, beauty, and love. In the *Odes funambulesques* (1857) and the *Occidentales* (1869) his virtuosity reaches its height as he walks the tightrope of poetic technique. In *Les Exilés* (1867) the poet comes down to earth, to share the misfortunes of his fellow exiles and to speak for them as well as for himself with a depth of feeling and vigor of form rare in Banville's work. *Idylles prussiennes* (1871) is an unfortunate attempt at political satire. Banville's last volumes of poetry reflect a period of disillusionment, followed by renewed optimism.

The dozen or so plays, nearly all in verse, which constitute Banville's dramatic work, are transpositions of his favorite lyric themes. *La Pomme* (1865), *Le Forgeron* (1887), and *Esope* (1893) bring the gods of Greece to the boulevards; *Riquet à la houppe* (1884) and *Le Baiser* (1888) are pure fancy, while *Gringoire* (1866) and *Florise* (1870) glorify the poet in various guises. Banville is almost entirely without dramatic sense, and his plays are armchair drama indeed. During the latter part of his life Banville also wrote a quantity of prose, chiefly journalistic, most of which was collected in *Scènes de la vie* (1859–1888) and *Petites Etudes* (1882–1885). The miniatures of 19th-century Paris, the intimate glimpses of contemporaries, such as are found in *Mes Souvenirs* (1882), have a certain picturesque charm, but all too often the style is diffuse and undistinguished, cluttered with facile formulas and clichés.

Baudelaire (*q.v.*), writing in 1861, noted that Banville's originality lay in the happy and serene quality of his work—a poetry of sunlit hours, of escape from reality to a paradise peopled by his dear Greek gods, where the poet has the place of honor which is his due. But his feeling often lacks intensity, his optimism seems all too facile, and one wearies of the profusion of muses and lyres and of Banville's reiterated reminders to his reader that he is a lyric poet. His pleasure in complicated patterns, his emphasis in the *Petit Traité de poésie française* (1872) on the supreme importance of rhyme, often lead to a Parnassian rigidity. Yet the variations in meter, the rejection of many of the traditional rules of versification, the use of the rhythms and cadences of popular poetry, as in "Nous n'irons plus au bois," make Banville one of the rare artists of his time to anticipate the elusive music of Verlaine (*q.v.*).

See: M. Fuchs, *Théodore de Banville* (1912); J. Charpentier, *Théodore de Banville* (1925); I. Siciliano, *Dal romanticismo al simbolismo* (1927).

M. G.

Barbey d'Aurevilly, Jules Amédée (1808–1889, French novelist and critic), was born at Saint-Sauveur-le-Vicomte near Coutances. He unquestionably belonged to an aristocratic family of the Cotentin peninsula in Normandy. His literary fame now is in the ascendant. The dramatic life, haughty and daring character, famous dandyism (see *Du dandysme et de Georges Brummel,* 1845), unassailable loftiness and unflinching absolutist convictions of this *Connétable des lettres, Sagittaire, Corsaire noir,* etc., who had "a laurel planted in his imagination," can be found in the 50 volumes (besides many uncollected writings) of his work. As a novelist he wrote *Une Vieille Maîtresse* (1851), *L'Ensorcelée* (1854), *Le Chevalier des touches* (1864), *Un Prêtre marié* (1864), *Les Diaboliques* (1874; Eng. tr., *Weird Women,* 1900), *Une Histoire sans nom* (1882; Eng. tr., *The Story without a Name,* 1891, new ed., 1919), *Ce qui ne meurt pas* (1883; Eng. tr. by Sebastian Melmoth, pseud. of Oscar Wilde, *What Never Dies*). As a critic he wrote *Les Œuvres et les hommes,* a series ranging from *Les Prophètes du passé* (1851) to *Le Théâtre contemporain* (1886–1896) and *Portraits politiques et littéraires* (1898). In the 24 volumes of this criticism are collected the most important articles and reviews brought out over a span of 50 years—beginning with his contributions to the *Nouvelliste de Dieppe* (1838) and including those in the *Globe, Revue du monde catholique* (which he founded in 1846), *Journal des débats,* and *Revue indépendante* (1886–1887). His gifts as a letter writer appear particularly in the admirable *Lettres à Trébutien* (*Œuvres complètes,* Vols. XIV–XVII), in the *Lettres à Léon Bloy* (1903), and in the correspondence with Eugénie de Guérin, whose brother Maurice was his admired friend (see *Lettres de M. de Guérin à Barbey d'Aurevilly,* 1928) and whose works he published in 1855 (*Lettres intimes,* 1921).

The novels of Barbey d'Aurevilly bear the imprint of a bold and original genius. They form the most important ensemble of French *romans du terroir.* Barbey made good his wish to become the "Walter Scott of the Cotentin," *i.e.,* the coastal region between Coutances, Valognes, and Saint-Sauveur. "Everything," he declared, "must be Norman with me and be related to Normandy"; such were his novels with their sturdy realism and well-defined historical or legendary events, spacious scenery, and local types—noblemen, peasants, wizards, beggars, priests. All his characters share in the "adhering power" he knew he possessed, as well as in his sometimes Rabelaisian zest for life. Everything in them stands out with a convincing reality due to great creative imagination enhanced by his capacity for remembering, which he prized above all his other gifts. This visionary power, more than his famous descriptions of magic or witchcraft, takes the reader into a weird, mysterious world. On the other hand, those tragic tales "of love, hatred, and deceit" usually are based on some inner drama—the struggle between spiritual forces and the passions at work in his accursed characters, criminals or expiatory victims, out of which rises what Barbey himself termed "the fearful poetry of crime . . . more intellectual than physical."

As a critic he especially revealed his aggressive power, according to Aristide Marie, when dealing with "conflicting social or religious ideas." He is most suggestive when he discusses from a writer's point of view literary schools or forms, the nature of the novel, style, and the like. He is famous for some strongly partial indictments, for his devotion to Balzac (see Balzac, *Œuvres . . . recueillies par Barbey d'Aurevilly,* 1909), and for farsighted divinations, notably of Baudelaire's genius and Hello's spiritual gifts. He "pulverized" nonentities like Feuillet, the third-rate dramatists of his day, the hated bluestockings. He fiercely challenged what appeared to him faked literary or moral literary values. None pointed out more decisively the limitations of naturalism. His always genuine criticism bears witness to the immensity of his reading. At its best it is that of a poet and, like his other writing, has the live quality of a spoken rather than written expression, even though carefully devised and achieved. His lashing irony, buoyancy, tempestuous magnificence, and ever gushing bold images entertain, irritate, and dazzle his readers. His later years were watched over by Mlle Read, "Mademoiselle ma gloire," who undertook the publication of his posthumous works.

See: E. Grelé, *Jules Barbey d'Aurevilly* (1902–1904); *Les Cahiers aurevilliens* (1933), published by the Société Barbey d'Aurevilly; A. Marie, *Le Connétable des lettres, Barbey d'Aurevilly* (1939). There is a "Musée Barbey d'Aurevilly" at Saint-Sauveur-le-Vicomte, where Barbey was buried.

M. M.

Barbusse, Henri (1873–1935, French novelist, journalist, and political writer), was born at Asnières near Paris and died in Moscow during a trip made at the invitation of the Russian government. He made his début in journalism with the *Siècle* in 1889 and became the protégé of Catulle Mendès (*q.v.*), whose youngest daughter he married. The following works were published: *Pleureuses* (1895), poems of a bizarre inspiration; *Les Suppliants* (1903), a novel; *L'Enfer* (1908; Eng. tr., *The Inferno,* 1918), a novel showing an obsession with the sexual instincts and death; *Nous autres* (1914; Eng. tr., *We Others,* 1918), a collection of tales inspired by pity for human stupidity and suffering, together with extreme sentimentality towards animals. None of these books had any success, and Barbusse had to get a living by serving as editor of a popular magazine, *Je sais tout.* The war was needed to bring him public notice, and it found him in a Swiss sanatorium. In August, 1914, fired by patriotism, Barbusse enlisted and, in spite of a new threat of tuberculosis, succeeded in being sent to the trenches. This in itself is meritorious, but biographers of Barbusse have unduly eulogized his record at the front with no more sense of responsibility than the biographers of Dorgelès (*q.v.*) and, in the following decade, those of Erich Maria Remarque (*q.v.*). Barbusse could not stand the hard life under fire and broke down; he also lost the illusions he owed to his utter ignorance of the realities of war. When recuperating in Paris, sometime in 1916, he wrote a war book, *Le Feu,* with the subtitle *Journal d'une escouade,* which was published as a serial in the daily *Œuvre,* beginning in August, 1916. Later, in December, it appeared in book form just in time to be considered for the Goncourt prize. It won the prize for 1916, and if its success was great with some readers, it caused a great scandal with others. It was a brutal piece of realism, the consequence of shattered illusions. Its partial and one-sided presentation of life at the front aroused protests. There are no officers in the book, only privates with their one corporal—no spring, no summer, only a perpetual winter. The applause was, however, louder than the protests, because those ugly pictures were a welcome change from the unreality and optimism of *Gaspard,* the war novel that had received the Goncourt prize the year before. *Le Feu* (Eng. tr., *Under Fire,* 1917) remains the best seller among French war books. Its success oriented the author towards social questions. He founded the *Clarté* group and took the part of a leader in anti-war propaganda colored with socialism and later with communism. His later books benefited from the success of *Le Feu,* but they do not rank above his earlier works. *L'Enfer* was presented anew to the public and had then its first success. *Clarté* (1919; Eng. tr., *Light,* 1919) was a second attempt at depicting the war, with increased prejudice. *Les Enchaînements* (1925; Eng. tr., *Chains,* 1925) is a lengthy string of episodes marking the evolution of civilization and culminating in an episode of the war in 1915. *Force* (1926) and *Jésus* (1927; Eng. tr., 1927) are his last works.

See: H. Hertz, *Henri Barbusse* (1919); J. N. Cru, *Témoins* (1929), pp. 555–565.

J. N. C.

Barlach, Ernst (1870–1938, German dramatist, sculptor, and designer), was born at Wedel in Holstein, the son of a country physician. Because of the early death of his father his education was somewhat irregular, but he eventually succeeded, in 1891, in being admitted to the Academy of Arts at Dresden to study sculpture and design. For 15 years after 1895 he traveled extensively, lived in Hamburg, Berlin, and many other German cities and visited Russia and Italy. Of these trips the stay in Russia in 1906 was decisive, for there he learned "a Christian humility towards all things." In 1910 Barlach established himself permanently at Güstrow, an old Mecklenburg town, famous for its magnificent cathedral. There he lived in solitude and almost complete seclusion until his death.

To speak of Barlach the dramatist is to speak of Barlach the sculptor and designer as well. His characters and figures alike bring back to the mind the great figures of the Romanesque and early Gothic period. With his lithographic illustrations made for some of his plays he achieved an almost perfect unity of the two arts. It was no vain ambition to achieve a double distinction but an eager urge for confession that created the plays of the sculptor Barlach.

Although many literary critics see a representative of expressionism in him, he himself wanted his dramatic characters interpreted as real people, not as visions or reflections of his own condition. It remains true that when he wrote for the theatre he often tried to push forward into metaphysics. His is the old Faustian tradition, emerging here against a Mecklenburg background, and also reminding us of the romanticists Hoffmann and Arnim or even of the strange visions of William Blake. Only his first drama, *Der tote Tag* (1912), is an allegoric story of a son who wants unsuccessfully to break away from his mother, because he perceives the creative paternal spirit in the world outside. The same tension between the world and God, the maternal and paternal powers, is repeated in the plays that followed. His strongest drama, *Der arme Vetter* (1918), reflects this contrast, and the same theme can be found in *Die echten Sedemunds* (1920), *Der Findling* (1922), and *Der blaue Boll* (1926). In *Die Sündflut* (1924) the contrast is expressed in biblical terms: the pious Noah and the refractory Calan contend for God. Some of these plays with their mixture of mysticism, realism, and grotesque humor are surprisingly effective. Barlach himself was a Faustian seeker who was always driven by his longing for God. Tied to the earth he wanted to share in infinity, in order to save himself from resignation or despair.

See: A. Soergel, *Dichtung und Dichter der Zeit,* Neue Folge: *Im Banne des Expressionismus,* 4 Auflage (1927), pp. 742–747; Barlach, *Ein selbsterzähltes Leben* (1930); J. Bithell, *Modern German Literature, 1880–1938* (1939), pp. 450–451.

H. Sch.

Baroja y Nessi, Pío (1872–, Spanish novelist), was born at San Sebastián in the Basque Provinces. He graduated as doctor of medicine from the University of Madrid and for two years was municipal physician of a small Basque town. Because the practice of medicine did not appeal to him he finally gave it up and after some experiences in a small bakery business devoted himself to writing. His first work, *Vidas sombrías,* a collection of charming literary sketches, appeared in 1900. In 1934 he was elected to the Spanish Academy. He lived with his mother until her death (1935) and has never married.

The list of Baroja's publications consists of some 80 titles, of which all are novels except for about a dozen volumes of essays (*e.g., El tablado de Arlequín,* 1904; *Nuevo tablado de Arlequín,* 1917; *La caverna del humorismo,* 1919; *Divagaciones apasionadas,* 1924) and other miscellaneous writings, among them the autobiographical *Juventud, egolatría* (1917; Eng. tr., *Youth and Egolatry,* 1920). Baroja's idea of the novel, however, is elastic enough for him to have included in it all his ideology and all his emotional reactions. In his own words, "it is a sack capable of containing everything," a definition which aptly characterizes the author's type of novel. As to the nature of that ideology, it reflects its double source of inspiration, namely, an exalted spirit of individualism and, in spite of Baroja's rich humoristic vein, a deeply rooted pessimistic sense of life. The two aspects complement each other. It means that, life being the mess of conventions that it is, the highest value goes to the individual, and precisely to the individual strong enough to affirm himself against that mess of conventions. In search of this type of individual, Baroja has descended into the more spontaneous and primitive world of the vagabond, the adventurer, the rebel, and all the picturesque variety of the *golfo* and the picaro and has embodied in such heroes the spirit of rebelliousness and of protest against social abuses, against the church and the state. In their free and dynamic personalities he has also embodied the ideal of a life of action, in which the quiet, sedentary, and intellectual Baroja likes to project his dreams of happiness. It can hardly be said, however, that any of his heroes measures up to the standards of a superman. In the end it is effective will power and a really constructive purpose that they lack. They are thus condemned to final ruin. Though Baroja's novel abounds in such ideological and subjective elements, it is above all as a realistic picture of life, and of Spanish life in particular, that it imposes itself. The picture is an unconventional and a crude one, and to the full rendering of this realistic and vital effect Baroja's novel, with its loose composition, episodic character, and simple and familiar language, is particularly well suited.

The bulk of Baroja's novelistic production can be grouped into two main divisions, the trilogies and the *Memorias de un hombre de acción.* The reason for the grouping into trilogies is obvious in the case of *La lucha por la vida, Agonías de nuestro tiempo,* and *La selva oscura,* the three novels of each being in reality three parts of the same novel. In the other instances the reason is more conventional than real—sometimes only two of the novels are related, as in the trilogies *El pasado, La raza,* and *La vida fantástica,* sometimes the three novels are independent of each other, as in *Tierra vasca* and *Las ciudades. El mar* is a tetralogy, and only two of the novels are related. Though the basic traits of Baroja's personality as a novelist are present in each and all of the novels of these trilogies, the particular kind of novel itself varies somewhat. A good example of the realistic novel is to be seen in the vivid picture of the Madrid underworld in *La lucha por la vida,* comprising *La busca, Mala hierba,* and *Aurora roja* (1904; Eng. tr., *The Quest,* 1922; *Weeds,* 1923; *Red Dawn,* 1924). The philosophic novel is best represented by the somewhat autobiographical *El árbol de la ciencia* (1911; Eng. tr., *The Tree of Knowledge,* 1928). As a psychological novel *Camino de perfección* (1902) deserves mention. Baroja's free play of imagination and good sense of humor are well illustrated in *Aventuras, inventos y mixtificaciones de Silvestre Paradox* (1901) and *Paradox, rey* (1906; Eng. tr., *Paradox, King,* 1931). A good example of the would-be Nietzschean superman who finally ends in ruin is offered in *César o nada* (1910; Eng. tr., *Caesar or Nothing,* 1919). An equally good example of the adventurer type is to be seen in *Zalacaín el aventurero* (1909). As to the *Memorias de un hombre de acción,* it is a series of 22 historical novels covering, though fragmentarily, the first half of the 19th century. The main hero is a second uncle of Baroja's mother, the liberal-minded and adventurous Eugenio de Aviraneta, who played a significant role in many of the political events and intrigues of the time. Two of the novels in the series, all of which can be read separately, are among the author's best—*El aprendiz de conspirador* (1913) and *El escuadrón del Brigante* (1913). Baroja wrote also in a separate volume the biography of his hero, *Aviraneta, o la vida de un conspirador* (1931).

See: J. Ortega y Gasset, *El espectador,* I

(1916), 129–205; Andrenio (E. Gómez de Baquero), *Novelas y novelistas* (1918), pp. 113–216; F. de Onís, "Pío Baroja," *Nosotros,* LIX (1926), 171–182; C. Barja, *Literatura española: Libros y autores contemporáneos* (1935), pp. 299–359; Demuth Helmut, *Pío Baroja: Das Weltbild in seinen Werken* (1937).

C. B.

Barrès, Maurice (1862–1923, French novelist, essayist, journalist, and politician), was born at Charmes-sur-Moselle in Lorraine and died at Neuilly-sur-Seine near Paris. He came to be recognized as one of the two or three most prominent French writers of his time. His first article appeared in a Nancy newspaper in 1881. He left his native province for Paris, where he was to spend the major part of his life, and began to write for several Parisian reviews. He founded one himself, *Les Taches d'encre* (November, 1884–February, 1885), but it was through a humoristic pamphlet, *Huit Jours chez M. Renan* (1885), that he finally attracted the attention of the Paris literary circles. The success of his first novel, *Sous l'œil des barbares* (1888), was partly due to a favorable review by Paul Bourget, who sensed the budding genius of the young author. With *Un Homme libre* (1889) and *Le Jardin de Bérénice* (1891) this volume formed the trilogy entitled *Le Culte du moi.* These three books, of unequal value, contain a number of passages with deep and clear insight into human psychology, cast in a graceful, fluid, and musical language. Their subject is the fascinating investigation of the inner life of a young man who admits but one reality, his own self. However, this egotist begins to meditate on society when he realizes that he cannot cultivate and enrich his personality without communing with his fellow men, whom he professes to despise. The next book of Barrès was *L'Ennemi des lois* (1893).

Having discovered that his "individual soul" was dependent on the "collective soul," Maurice Barrès was led first to accept his own limitations, next to convince himself of the predominance of instinct over reason, finally to believe that French energies would be best revived through the cult of provincial and national traditions and reverence for the soil and the dead. Hence his passage from dream to action, his evolution from pure egotism to regionalism and nationalism. This new aspect of the philosophy of Barrès is illustrated and dramatized in a second trilogy, *Le Roman de l'énergie nationale,* which includes *Les Déracinés* (1897), *L'Appel au soldat* (1900), and *Leurs Figures* (1903). *Les Déracinés* is the story of seven Lorrainers whose lives turn out to be failures because, according to the author, they have been "uprooted" by college education. The book, packed with social and philosophical digressions, has been one of the most influential, and also most discussed, of modern French literature. Like his *Scènes et doctrines du nationalisme* (1902), a collection of articles and essays dealing primarily with the Dreyfus case, *L'Appel au soldat* and *Leurs Figures* were directly inspired by the author's personal experiences in public life. Having been elected deputy of Nancy as early as 1889, he had already played an important role in national politics.

But Barrès also sought inspiration in foreign lands. Two collections of tales and essays, *Du sang, de la volupté, de la mort* (1894), and *Amori et Dolori Sacrum* (1903), the morbid and sensual character of which is accurately suggested by the titles, are the results of travels in Spain and Italy. In these books the author appears again as a peerless artist, dilettante, and romantic seeker of violent sensations. His now well-developed ego, immensely enriched, remains the real subject matter of these as well as of some subsequent works. Inspired by travels abroad are also his *Le Voyage de Sparte* (1905), *Greco, ou le Secret de Tolède* (1912), *Un Jardin sur l'Oronte* (1922), which is a delightful short novel, and *Une Enquête aux pays du Levant* (1923). His third trilogy, *Les Bastions de l'Est* (*Au service de l'Allemagne,* 1905; *Colette Baudoche; histoire d'une jeune fille de Metz,* 1909, Eng. tr., *Colette Baudoche; the Story of a Young Girl of Metz,* 1918; *Le Génie du Rhin,* 1921), is a logical sequence to the novel of national energy. Maurice Barrès, who at the age of eight had seen his home occupied by the enemy and his father and his grandfather taken as hostages, devoted the greater part of his life to the building of those "bastions" or intellectual fortresses meant to protect French civilization from any threatening foreign influences—or armed forces. A book like *Les Amitiés françaises* (1903) as well as numberless speeches and articles had similar aims.

Among other important works of Barrès must also be mentioned *La Colline inspirée* (1913; Eng. tr., *The Sacred Hill,* 1929), a fascinating lyrical and symbolical novel; *La Grande Pitié des églises de France* (1914), a collection of speeches in Parliament; and *Le Mystère en pleine lumière* (1924), a posthumous collection of short stories. Barrès himself, and some critics with him, regarded his *Chronique de la Grande Guerre* (1920–1924) as the most beautiful and deserving of his works. It consists of 14 volumes of collected articles dealing with current events during the war, from 1914 to 1918. Finally, 11 volumes of *Mes Cahiers,* his journal from 1896 to 1918, have also been published posthumously, from 1929 to 1938. These are essential for a full understanding and appreciation of his life and work.

Primarily Maurice Barrès must be considered a great literary artist, an original writer who has created a style of his own and whose influence on young intellectuals has been twofold, in some cases purely literary, in others both literary and ideological. Barrès endowed words and ideas with such an intense life, he marked them with such a personal stamp, that some soon became as inseparable from his name as they were to be from the history of modern thought and literature in France. This applies particularly to *le culte du moi, i.e.,* the best expression of rugged individualism; the theme of *les déracinés* and that of *la terre et les morts,* which are fundamental elements of regionalism; and *le nationalisme,* destined to be the rallying doctrine of all reactionary forces during the last decade of the 19th century. More specifically his main concerns were the return of Alsace-Lorraine to France and, after the First World War, the problem of the Rhineland, considered as a check to the expansion of Pan-Germanism. Toward the end of his life he was widely respected as a sincere and great patriot. Even among his political opponents many admired the man who had tempered his traditionalism and finally given up polemics in an effort to further the realization of national unity during the war.

See: R. Jacquet, *Notre Maître, Maurice Barrès* (1900); H. Bremond, "L'Evolution littéraire de Maurice Barrès," *Revue des deux mondes,* February 15, 1908, pp. 790–824; V. Giraud, *Les Maîtres de l'heure: Maurice Barrès* (1918); E. R. Curtius, *Maurice Barrès und die geistigen Grundlagen des französischen Nationalismus* (1921); A. Thibaudet, *La Vie de Maurice Barrès* (1921).

A. V. R.

Barrili, Anton Giulio (1836–1908, Italian novelist), was born in Savona, but spent most of his life in Genoa. His love of that city and of the Ligurian coast appears in many of his books. In the course of his long life he was a journalist, a professor of literature, a deputy, a soldier in Garibaldi's army, but above all a writer of fiction.

His short stories have an extraordinary grace of style. Their humor, good taste, and great charm brought him at once innumerable readers and made the fortune of his publisher, Treves. Young Italians of Barrili's day were not troubled by what Croce (*q.v.*) calls Barrili's superficiality, nor by his indulgence in digressions. They were immediately delighted by the heroes and heroines of his love stories, who responded to the secret longings of their hearts. The best known of these tales are *Capitan Dodèro* (1865), *Santa Cecilia* (1866), *Val d'Olivi* (1873), *Come un sogno* (1875), *L'Olmo e l'edera* (1877). *Capitan Dodèro* is still read and was translated into English (*The Adventures of Captain Dodèro*) in 1920. *Santa Cecilia,* which deals with a mad organ-grinder, became so popular that every organ-grinder in Genoa was known by the name of its hero.

The faults that Croce finds in Barrili's novels appear also in the story of his campaign days with Garibaldi, *Con Garibaldi alle porte di Roma* (1895), which is a recital of adventures such as war correspondents have made popular today. The portrait of Garibaldi is written with an intensity of emotion and interest that appear nowhere else in Barrili's writings. Other heroes of Italian history also caught his imagination, and he wrote novels about them. *Sorrisi di gioventù* (1898) represents, the author says, the smiles of his youth without the tears. There are few tears in Barrili, but much charm, many happy endings and sentimental dreams, which, if they do not lead to the highest literary pinnacles, enable the reader to share in a pleasant nostalgia.

G. B.

Bartrina, Joaquín María (1850–1880, Spanish poet and journalist), is the voice of doubt, disillusionment, and pessimism in the so-called philosophical school of poetry. He was born at Reus in Catalonia and received his early schooling there. Obliged in his youth to assist in the support of the family, he did not enjoy a university education, but he satisfied his desire for knowledge through wide if desultory reading. Before long he gained prominence in local literary circles as a dynamic journalist and forceful poet. His first collected poems, *Páginas de amor,* already reveal skepticism and independence in his interpretation of emotion and human values in general. Evident, too, is his philosophic approach to poetry. His best-known work, *Algo* (1876), underlines his point of view which led him to seek the meaning of life in terms of reason and the senses. Like other youths of his generation, he was disappointed in the capacity of knowledge to reveal absolute truth, and this made him skeptical and pessimistic. While on occasion he expresses doubt about the material world and scientific progress, in the main his spiritual discomfort derives from his inability to be sustained by faith. Soul, spirit, and conscience mean little to him, but equally meaningless are all forms of human behavior which he sees, as it were, in terms of physiology and biochemistry.

Beneath the banter and irony of his tone, Bartrina is essentially sincere in the expression of his perplexities. His sincerity and his stylistic ingenuity, which is at times more prosaic than poetic, earned for him a rank among the poets of the 19th century in spite of his scant production. After his death, his friend J. Sardá published his collected works —*Obras en prosa y verso* (1881). The volume *Algo* still enjoys wide circulation in Catalonia.

See: J. Roca y Roca, *Memoria biográfica de Joaquín María Bartrina y d'Aixemús* (1916?).

H. C. B.

Basterra, Ramón de (*ca.* 1887–1928, Spanish poet), concerned with both past and future of things Hispanic, wrote with equal fervor about Basque seigniorial and Catholic tradition and about the novelties of the machine age. The scion of a wealthy Bilbao family, he studied in Germany and saw diplomatic service in Rumania, Rome, and Venezuela. His prose studies, *La obra de Trajano* (1921) and *Una empresa del siglo XVIII: Los navíos de la ilustración* (1925), recall his constant pursuit of the centrifugal culture of Spain.

In successive books Basterra's thought—all important in his poetry—becomes more inclusive and moves westward under the dome of Greater Spain which, for him, arches over the Occident from Rome to Manila, "the fringe of the sky." *Las ubres luminosas* (1923) records a pilgrimage to Rome. It is a paean of praise to the Mother City ("most illustrious of wolves") from whom Spain inherits her culture. *La sencillez de los seres* (1923) is a tribute to the people of northern, and especially Basque, Spain. *Los labios del monte* (1924) is a panoramic glorification of their defense of the Catholic faith, from the Reconquest down.

The "Vírulo" of Basterra's last two books represents the peripatetic poet himself. In the morning of *Vírulo, mocedades* (1924) he starts west for the mechanized world of the Hispanic present and future; his finger "turns the pages of the horizons", "tunes the meridians." *Vírulo, mediodía* (1927) finds him at noon in the heart of modernity. His poetry no longer has the classicism of *Las ubres luminosas* or the romanticism of *La sencillez de los seres* and *Los labios del monte*. It is pneumatic, "inflated with the air of the day." It is charged with neo-baroque figures: the sky of the Occident is now "a parasol whose ribs are the meridians." The poet is now "the Aesop of the Machine"; the characters in his fables—a plane, a crane, a truck—"do not speak with jaws, mouths, or beaks, but with escapes, valves, and horns." The book is brilliant, audacious, sometimes puzzling. Its use of image and metaphor displays an inventiveness, worthy of its theme, which allies Basterra to the vanguard poets of his day.

See: A. Valbuena Prat, *La poesía española contemporánea* (1930); F. de Onís, *Antología de la poesía española e hispanoamericana, 1882–1932* (1934).

D. K. A.

Bataille, Henry (1872–1922, French playwright and poet), born in Nîmes, entered the Ecole des Beaux Arts in 1890 to study painting. Four years later, influenced by Robert d'Humières, with whom he had written *La Belle au bois dormant* (1894), he made his début as a dramatist. From 1900 to 1914 Henry Bataille was the most celebrated of the French playwrights. Both the public and the critics praised *L'Enchantement* (1900), *Le Masque* (1902), *Maman Colibri* (1905), *Poliche* (1906), *La Femme nue* (1908), *Le Scandale* (1909), *La Vierge folle* (1910), *L'Enfant de l'amour* (1911), *Les Flambeaux* (1912). In 1913 *Le Phalène,* too obviously inspired by the life of Marie Bashkirtseff, was violently discussed. Three plays, *L'Amazone* (1916), *L'Animateur* (1920), and *La Chair humaine* (1922), mark an evolution towards the theatre of ideas. *L'Homme à la rose* (1920) offered variations on the theme of Don Juan. *La Tendresse* (1921) and *La Possession* (1921) are the last manifestations of a great talent which had gradually degenerated.

The weakness of Bataille's theatre is partly due to the fact that it is the reflection of a period which belongs already to the past. Many of his plays were inspired directly and exclusively by contemporary events and have become dated very rapidly. A romanticist by nature, Bataille felt, moreover, a morbid attraction for exceptional and often repulsive characters. His best dramas are excellent psychological studies of irrepressible passions. They contain powerful scenes, but suffer from an excess of lyricism and from artificialities of style, factors contributing in no small measure to the partial oblivion into which they have already fallen. As a poet Bataille wrote *La*

Chambre blanche (1895), *Le Beau Voyage* (1905), *La Divine Tragédie* (1917), *La Quadrature de l'amour* (1920). Some of his opinions on dramatic art can be found in *Ecrits sur le théâtre* (1917). *L'Enfance éternelle* (1922) contains autobiographical data.

See: D. Amiel, *Henry Bataille* (1912) and *Le Règne intérieur* (1912); P. Lièvre, "Henry Bataille," *Marges*, XV (1918), 203–212; *Herse*, May-June, 1921 (special number); P. Blanchart, *Henry Bataille; son œuvre* (1922); L. Lemonnier, "Le Théâtre d'Henry Bataille," *Grande Revue*, CVIII (1922), 244–262; G. de Catalogne, *Henry Bataille, ou le Romantisme de l'instinct* (1925); E. Seillière, *L'Evolution morale dans le théâtre d'Henry Bataille* (1936).

M. E. C.

Baty, Gaston (1885–, French theatrical director and producer), was born at Pélussin, Loire, and studied at the University of Lyon, where he became interested in the traditional puppet theatres. In 1919, steeped in the theories of Gordon Craig, Adolphe Appia, Georg Fuchs, and Meyerhold, he began to help Firmin Gémier stage vast productions at the Cirque d'Hiver and the Comédie Montaigne. His "Compagnons de la Chimère," formed in 1922, wandered from theatre to theatre until they settled in the small Studio des Champs-Elysées (1924), performing such experimental, and often expressionistic, plays as J. J. Bernard's (*q.v.*) *Martine*, S. Gantillon's *Maya*, and J. V. Pellerin's (*q.v.*) *Têtes de rechange*. Finally the Baty company (probably the best ensemble group in Paris) found the Théâtre Montparnasse, famous for its use by André Antoine (*q.v.*). Constantly protesting against the all-importance of the dramatist's text, he naturally became the godfather of the "theatre of the unexpressed" of Denys Amiel (*q.v.*), J. J. Bernard, *et al.* and strove to enrich his repertory with free adaptations of such novels as *Madame Bovary* (1936), *Manon Lescaut* (1938), *Crime and Punishment* (1932–1933), and *Don Quixote* (1938–1939). Unlike the other contemporary *metteurs en scène* (Dullin, Jouvet, Pitoëff, *qq.v.*), Gaston Baty likes to "adapt" and stamp each detail of a work with his personality, creating thus a series of controversial spectacles which he defends in his essays and prefaces.

See: P. Blanchart, *Gaston Baty* (1939); A. Villeroy, *Dix Ans de théâtre: De la Comédie Montaigne au Théâtre Pigalle* (1930).

J. O'B.

Baudelaire, Charles Pierre (1821–1867, French poet and critic), was born in Paris and spent most of his life there. Soon after his elderly father's death, in 1827, his mother married Colonel Aupick, whom Baudelaire found a difficult and unsympathetic stepfather. After his school years at Lyon and then at the Lycée Louis-le-Grand in Paris, Baudelaire enjoyed a brief period of independence and began his literary career. In 1841 his family sent him off on a long sea voyage, supposedly to India; he returned, however, in less than a year, after short stays on the islands of Mauritius and Bourbon (Réunion). Inheriting his father's fortune on his coming of age, he lived for a time the life of a rich young dandy. But his family, alarmed by the rapidity with which his fortune was disappearing, encumbered him with a financial guardianship. From then on he was burdened with debts, in constant difficulties with publishers and printers, forever moving from one miserable lodging to another. His life was further complicated by his liaison with the mulatto Jeanne Duval, to whom he remained attached for many years. Many of his poems were inspired by her; others belong to a period of idealized devotion to Mme Sabatier, and still others to a brief liaison with the actress Marie Daubrun. After the death of his stepfather in 1857, Baudelaire found some respite from increasing ill-health and financial difficulties in stays with his mother at Honfleur. In 1864 he set out on his unfortunate lecture tour in Belgium. Struck down there by paralysis in 1866, he was brought back to Paris, where he died in 1867.

In *Les Fleurs du mal* (1857) Baudelaire brought together poems on which he had been at work for years, many of which had already appeared in periodicals. The appearance of the volume brought on a trial which resulted in Baudelaire's condemnation for an offense against public morals and the suppression of six of the hundred poems. The second edition (1861) added 35 new poems, and the posthumous edition of 1868 25 more. In the *Petits Poëmes en prose* (1869), most of which had been published during Baudelaire's lifetime, he developed a new form, a spontaneous and natural poetic prose which allowed him more freedom, more detail, than the traditional versification of his earlier poems.

Baudelaire's affiliation with his predecessors, with the Pléiade and Racine as well as with the romantics, is plain, and his passion for perfection of form allies him to the Parnassian poets. But his poetry is intensely personal, marked with a desperate sincerity. The struggle between good and evil, the efforts and failures of the faltering will, the dark and devious attempts to escape from spleen and despair, the passionate devotion to beauty, cry out from the depths of this poetry. Baudelaire's external world is as distinctive as his inner one —the great city with its sordid streets and crowded houses, the vast expanses of sea and sky, the tropical sights and sounds and smells of his early voyage. For him nature is a great storehouse of images; the outer and inner worlds are bound together by mysterious correspondences, not merely between the different senses, but between the visible and invisible worlds. His images are not developed in splendid isolation, like those of the romantic poets, but are symbols in which image and meaning are fused into one. His poetry has a perfection of form and music that gives at times classic simplicity, at times a far-echoing intensity. Undoubtedly the charm is broken sometimes by platitudes, by mediocre lines, by a too heavy and morbid sensualism, but Baudelaire brought to French poetry a dark splendor, a magic density that it had not yet known.

Baudelaire himself said that he considered the poet the best of critics. His own criticism, collected in the two posthumous volumes, *Curiosités esthétiques* (1868) and *L'Art romantique* (1869), is almost entirely of his contemporaries, whom he judged with amazing sureness. The art criticism, centered on Delacroix, includes the *Salons* of 1845, 1846, and 1859, the *Exposition de 1855,* three articles on caricature (1855–1857), *Le Peintre de la vie moderne* (1863), and *L'Œuvre et la vie d'Eugène Delacroix* (1863). In literary criticism there are articles on Poe (1856 and 1857) and Gautier (1859), the series *Poëtes français* (1861–1862), and a number of shorter articles, including one on *Madame Bovary* (1857). In 1861 Baudelaire made his one excursion into musical criticism, with *Richard Wagner et Tannhäuser à Paris.* For him criticism is first of all poetic, the translation of an experience, a reflection of the work of art. Then the intelligence comes into play, and he goes on to "transform delight into knowledge" (*transformer la volupté en connaissance*), to deduce from experience the laws of art, crystallized in his great all-embracing conception of the imagination.

About 1846 Baudelaire discovered Poe, with whom he felt from the first a fraternal affinity. A large part of his literary effort was devoted to his admirable translation of Poe's tales and other works, *Histoires extraordinaires* (1856), *Nouvelles Histoires extraordinaires* (1857), *Aventures d'Arthur Gordon Pym* (1858), *Eureka* (1864), and *Histoires grotesques et extraordinaires* (1864). *Les Paradis artificiels* (1860) comprises an original work, "Poëme du haschisch," and "Confessions d'un mangeur d'opium," an adaptation of De Quincey's work. After Baudelaire's death the *Œuvres posthumes* (1887–1907) gathered together early poems, scattered articles, and unfinished sketches, as well as *Fusées* and *Mon Cœur mis à nu,* the so-called *Journaux intimes.* The publication of the *Lettres 1840–1866* (1907), *Lettres à sa mère* (1918), and *Dernières Lettres à sa mère* (1926) has added much to our knowledge of Baudelaire the man.

Though he died in 1867, one has only to think of Mallarmé and Rimbaud, Claudel and Valéry, Gide and Proust (*qq.v.*), of Swinburne and Yeats, Pound and Eliot, of Stefan George (*q.v.*) and Rilke (*q.v.*), to realize how truly Baudelaire belongs with the moderns.

See: E. and J. Crépet, *Charles Baudelaire* (1907); G. de Reynold, *Charles Baudelaire* (1920); J. Pommier, *La Mystique de Baudelaire* (1932); A. Ferran, *L'Esthétique de Baudelaire* (1933); M. Gilman, *Baudelaire the Critic* (1943).

M. G.

Bazin, René (1853–1932, French novelist), was born and brought up at Angers in Anjou. As a boy he was very fond of country life and read many novels of adventures by Maine Reid and tales of Red Indians. He attended the Catholic University of Angers and in 1875 was appointed professor of law at that institution.

His first novel, *Stéphanette* (1884), was published under the pseudonym Bernard Seigny. Many other novels followed, published under his own name, most of which dealt with country life in Anjou, Poitou, and Vendée. The list includes *Une Tache d'encre* (1888; Eng. trs., *A Blot of Ink,* 1892, *Ink Stain,* 1905), *Les Noellet* (1890; Eng. tr., *This, My Son,* 1909), *La Sarcelle bleue* (1892), *Madame Corentine* (1893; Eng. tr., *Those of His Own Household,* 1914), *Humble Amour* (1894), *De toute son âme* (1897; Eng. tr., *Redemption,* 1897). Particularly successful was a series dealing with the then acute problem of the threatened desertion of the land for the industrial cities: *La Terre qui meurt* (1899; stage version in 1913), *Donatienne* (1903; Eng. tr., *The Penitent,* 1912), *Le Blé qui lève* (1907; Eng. tr., *The Coming Harvest,* 1908), *La Closerie de Champdolent* (1917). Another capital problem which challenged the attention of Bazin was the question of Alsace-Lorraine, in *Les Oberlé* (1901; stage version in 1912; Eng. tr., *The Children of Alsace,* 1912), *Les Nouveaux*

Oberlé (1919), and *Baltus le Lorrain* (1926). This patriotic note was never dissociated from the religious, Roman Catholic note, as well illustrated in the author's last story, *Magnificat* (1931; Eng. tr., *Magnificat*, 1932).

Bazin also wrote books in various other fields: *La Douce France* (1911; Eng. tr., *Gentle France*, 1913), *Charles de Foucauld, explorateur du Maroc, ermite au Sahara* (1921; Eng. tr., *Charles de Foucauld, Hermit and Explorer*, 1923), several collections of short stories, and several accounts of travels in Italy, Spain, and the provinces of France. *Etapes de ma vie* (1936) was published posthumously.

Bazin is an urbane writer, more serious than brilliant, a conscientious and orthodox workman. He was elected to the French Academy in 1903.

See: A. de Bersaucourt, *René Bazin* (1906); Charles Bauman, *René Bazin* (1924); François Mauriac, *René Bazin* (1931).

A. Sz.

Becher, Johannes Robert (1891–, German poet and novelist), was born in Munich, the son of a judge. He studied philosophy and medicine in Munich, Berlin, and Jena and started his literary career with poetry of the most radically expressionistic kind. His first collection of poems and prose, *Verfall und Triumph* (1914), is typical of the explosive and chaotic early expressionism which destroyed the traditional language and syntax as a gesture symbolic of the intellectual destruction of the traditional world. With the critical vehemence of his intellectual attitude Becher soon turned to radical politics; he joined the Communist Party at its inception. In his many books as well as in his personal life he remained a fighter for Communism and Soviet Russia.

Characteristic of his poetry are such works as *An Europa* (1916), *Verbrüderung* (1916), *Gedichte für ein Volk* (1917), *Päan gegen die Zeit* (1918), *Ewig im Aufruhr* (1920), *Am Grabe Lenins* (1925), *Maschinenrhythmen* (1925), and *Der grosse Plan: Epos des sozialistischen Aufbaus* (1931). He published a selection of his early poems in *Ein Mensch unserer Zeit* (1930). His ecstatic eruptions are often of great poetic strength, but he sometimes uses his lyric gifts for the mere presentation of lengthy political effusions. He realized himself that this chaotic and erratic type of expression was not easily understood by the masses for whom his poetry was actually written, and gradually he modified his style. *Gedichte an Lotte* (1920) and *Um Gott* (1921) are written more calmly. He produced a play about and for the masses (*Arbeiter, Bauern, Soldaten*, 1920), as well as a volume of political prose (*Vorwärts, Du rote Front*, 1925) and two novels (*Der einzig gerechte Krieg*, 1925; *Der Bankier reitet über das Schlachtfeld*, 1925), all serving the same radical tendency. Becher is not only the most constant but also the most vigorous of the "political" poets of the left, yet it is a fact that in his poetry written later in Russia there appears a deep longing for Germany and its culture.

Indeed after his emigration to Russia, where he lived in exile from 1932 to 1945, his poetry also began to show classical and traditional forms, at times even the didactic simplicity of a child's reader. During this period he produced some 20 volumes of poetry and prose, *e.g.*, *Neue Gedichte* (1933); *Des Siegs Gewissheit und Sicht auf grosse Tage; Sonette* (1939); *Abschied* (1940), a novel; *Dank an Stalingrad; 53 Balladen* (1943). He returned to Germany with the victorious Russian army in 1945 and became president of the Kulturbund zur Demokratischen Erneuerung Deutschlands.

K. P.

Becque, Henry (1837–1899, French dramatist), was born in Paris and lived there all his life. He was the first playwright successfully to introduce in the French theatre certain aspects of the materialism, immorality, and cupidity current in some parts of Parisian society in his day. His emphasis on a minute and truthful observation of life gave a new and important orientation to a French theatre that had been cluttered with sterilizing artificialities.

Becque's family was impecunious. When he finished his schooling at the Lycée Bonaparte (later the Lycée Condorcet), his father, a government clerk, secured work for him in a railroad office. He did not remain there long, but drifted restlessly from post to post. A maternal uncle, a dramatist and collaborator of Labiche, kept alive Becque's interest in the theatre and saw to it that he became acquainted with the Paris theatres, particularly with the Molière repertory at the Comédie Française. An omnivorous reader and a poet who wrote verse all his life, Becque began to give lessons in literature in preference to filling clerical positions. As secretary to a Polish diplomat who encouraged his literary inclinations, Becque met men in public life, artists, and intellectuals; had it not been for his poverty, he would have seriously considered entering the diplomatic service. He wrote the book for an opera, *Sardanapale* (1868), by a young musician of this milieu. His first serious effort, however, was *L'Enfant prodigue* (1867), a *vaudeville* which was favorably received by the critics and which revealed the dexterity in expression and the vivid dramatic sense that were later to be so highly developed. His second play, *Michel Pauper* (1870), reflected his concern, as he later wrote, "with the innocent and helpless who struggle against force and all tyrannies and injustices." The play is particularly interesting as a commentary on the changing society during the last days of the Second Empire and for the sharply defined characterizations. Becque had to produce this play at his own expense. In 1871 (after service in the Franco-Prussian War) he wrote *L'Enlèvement,* which failed immediately. Impoverished and discouraged, he worked on the stock exchange for the next few years, but was an active member of the Society of Dramatic and Musical Authors. For a while he eked out a living by writing articles on the theatre for *Peuple;* he contributed at various times during his life to other newspapers, among them *Henri IV, Union républicaine, Figaro, Gaulois,* and *Matin* (see the collection entitled *Querelles littéraires,* 1890). The entire year of 1877 he devoted to writing his first masterpiece, *Les Corbeaux,* determined "to defend it against everything." It took him five more years of untiring effort to find a producer for *Les Corbeaux.* During this time he wrote and had presented two successful short plays, *La Navette* (1878) and *Les Honnêtes Femmes* (1880). When *Les Corbeaux* was finally produced in 1882 at the Comédie Française, it was greeted with both hisses and applause. The resulting controversy was not unlike that aroused by Hugo's *Hernani* in 1830. In *Les Corbeaux* the plight of the helpless in the clutch of economic circumstance is again set forth, the helpless being a rich bourgeois family suddenly bereft of the father and at the mercy of former friends who pluck from the mother and daughters all their worldly possessions. The dialogue reflected relentlessly the cupidity and moral weakness of the characters. The play was something new in the French theatre and is still remarkable for its simplicity, for its consistency, for vigorous dramatic effects obtained with the utmost literary economy. Becque's second masterpiece, *La Parisienne,* was produced in 1885. Here, in even sharper, more brilliant dialogue, Becque presented with complete detachment the immorality of one Parisian wife and her particular milieu. A sardonic humor evolves from the characters who not only naturally accept their deviations from accepted morality but rationalize and moralize about them convincingly. After the usual rejections Becque found a producer and rehearsed the play himself. The *première* at the Renaissance Theatre was a sensation. The Comédie Française later performed the play, in 1890, but incompetently; it remained for Antoine (*q.v.*) with the help of a great actress, Réjane, to bring out the full possibilities of the piece. Antoine saw that Becque's dialogue demanded a naturalness and simplicity in acting that were then all but unknown in the French theatre. He systematically cultivated this new acting technique and introduced it in his Théâtre Libre, of which Becque was the literary head. The vitality of the movement Becque inaugurated is evidenced by the dramatists Curel, Brieux, and Courteline (*qq.v.*), all of whom later made their débuts at the Théâtre Libre.

In focusing attention on moral evils of his time Becque was relentless. Therein lie the strength and the limitations of his theatre. Observations are projected with a new vividness, scrupulous honesty, and plausibility. The illusion of reality is achieved with unusual poignancy; the picture is all black, but the particular characters are true to life, their weaknesses and cupidity could not be otherwise, and their actions follow logically and with the inevitability of a Greek tragedy. That Becque had tenderness and tolerance in him, as well as cynicism, appears in his poetry, maxims, and *Notes d'album* (see *Œuvres complètes,* 1924–1926). His qualities of irony and humor and his gift of concision are well represented in *Souvenirs d'un auteur dramatique* (1895), a collection in which he sets down his tribulations as a dramatist and his opinions of producers, critics, and playwrights.

Despite the controversies to which his plays gave rise, Becque won a substantial literary reputation in France. He was admitted to the Legion of Honor in 1886. He enjoyed society and there gave vent to his exuberance and mordant wit. Though he was accepted as a dramatist of the first rank, he achieved no financial success. There was a strange contrast between the brilliant dramatist, the lion of the literary salons, and the poverty and solitude of his private life. Such was his fierce pride that he declined a pension which the government was willing to grant him after his brother and main support died. Becque's plays were especially successful in Italy, to which country he went in 1893 to lecture. Constant poverty and illness prevented Becque from completing his last play, *Les Polischinelles* (1910). A few faithful friends placed him in a private sanatorium, where he died May 15, 1899.

See: A. Antoine, *Mes Souvenirs sur le Théâ-*

tre Libre (1921); E. Dawson, *Henry Becque; sa vie et son théâtre* (1923); A. Arnautovitch, *Henry Becque; sa vie et œuvre* (1927); L. Jouvet, *Réflexions du comédien* (1938).

E. B. M.

Bécquer, Gustavo Adolfo (1836–1870), Spanish lyric poet and author of legends and essays in prose, was born in Seville of noble lineage. His father and his uncle were painters. Bécquer spent his early years in Seville, devoted like his brother Valeriano to the study of painting, but soon he decided in favor of literature. In 1854 he transferred to Madrid, where he lived until his death. He married, had children, and always remained in close touch with Valeriano. His training as a painter, his constant reading in the ancient authors and in the Spanish and foreign writers, together with his trips to Toledo and to the region of the Moncayo, are the most important factors in the formation of his spiritual life. He inspired and directed various cultural works and collaborated in magazines and periodicals. On his death, his friends collected his writings from periodicals and still unedited manuscripts: *Obras de Gustavo A. Bécquer* (2 vols., 1871; 3 vols., 1904). Later, the publication of his works was continued: *Páginas desconocidas de Gustavo Adolfo Bécquer* (3 vols., 1923). In the National Library of Madrid is conserved a notebook entitled "El libro de los gorriones," which is a holograph manuscript of some of his poetry and prose.

In spite of his early death, he created a work as significant as it is brief. His *Rimas* soon made him famous in Spain and in Spanish America. His poetry has an anecdotic background that in sentiment and linear quality expresses the poetic decoration of his period. Brief poems reveal his rare moments of felicity, his constant grief, the suffering and the anguish of a sad love, in an atmosphere typical of the years 1850–1870—a balcony with swallows and honeysuckle vines, a tree-shaded walk, a salon with a harp in an obscure corner. Occasionally he deals with an attitude of strolling lovers, or their angry encounter at a ball, or the poet's own room. His contemporaries felt in this anecdotal manner and matter the complete fulfillment of their sentimental aspirations. They found in this poetry, which departed from tragic romantic desperation, the purest conception of the melancholy, sad, and resigned love of their epoch. The anecdote is the decorative, period element which Bécquer utilizes to present a new sentimental life of the heart. Another theme of the *Rimas* is poetic creation, felt as a conflict between idea and form which can be solved only by means of the word—an inadequate instrument. Bécquer's idealistic realism is preparing and announcing the symbolistic and impressionistic world. His poetry does not capture the fugacity of the present, nor found itself on sensation, nor become a symbol, but seeks to be as fugitive as the present, as light as sensation, and as secret as the symbol. It is the poetry of a will to be, a wish to be one with the beloved, a desire to give form to the ideal which is felt, significantly, as a dream.

Bécquer gives to his poetry a musical rhythm which is at times almost *cantabile.* The sonorous material—accents, pauses, accent and phonetic structure of the word—of the verse is in reality not a form for the voice, yet achieves that form thanks to the voice when the personal sentiment of a man or a woman imbues the material with feeling. Just as the musician indicates the tempo of his melody, so Bécquer points out that his poetry should be softly murmured close to the ear of the fair listener, so that with only the slightest interference of the physical the soul may communicate. It is the poetry of the ineffable, of the intangible, which is still not an allusion to reality, which preserves only the lightest impression of that reality, just as the butterfly leaves on the hands that would detain it only "the golden dust that embellishes its wings." Bécquer demands of his reader an active and a collaborative attention.

The *Rimas* have served as a guide and a stimulus to 20th-century Spanish poetry, and their value is being more and more clarified with the passage of time. Bécquer's prose, on the other hand, has not been looked upon with so much interest; nevertheless it is interesting and has a definite place in the development of 19th-century Spanish prose. Along with his essays—some of which are single and others grouped together by a common theme (*Cartas literarias a una mujer*) or by the place in which they were written (*Cartas desde mi celda*)—appear his *Leyendas.* Although these legends may be narrative or descriptive, they are inspired by the same feeling of mystery which imposes upon all of them a similar pattern of development. Sometimes the mystery expresses the impossibility of capturing the fundamental meaning underlying the creation of life, or the activities of the creative spirit, or the operation of destiny; in other instances, the purgation of sin; and finally, the longing for beauty and love. From the dense shadows which surround him the poet flings himself into the search, representing even in the physical action of his characters the urgency of his spiritual quest. Mystery encircles the earth, hides feelings and things from the profaning glance of the vulgar. At the same time mystery is created by the imagination of the select few with finer sensibilities. Thanks to the imagination, man is transformed into poet, into seer. By means of the imagination, Bécquer succeeds in breaking through the layers of the ordinary daily life of his contemporaries which conceal the virginity of feelings and realities. History is the receptacle of legend. As it recedes from the present, time returns to reality and to life their pristine purity and in this purity lies the essence of their poetry. Imagination is accompanied and is dominated by sentiment. Imagination provides the decoration of his work: brilliant or somber, melancholy or bitter, it forms the labyrinth in which reality is lost; sentiment is the thread of this labyrinth—the constructive element. Bécquer (cf. Pre-Raphaelitism in England, Baudelaire, *q.v.,* in France) enriches the world of the heart and arrives at the moral values through sentiment. He feels death as a form of solitude, of abandon, of oblivion. This solitude is achieved after an extended leave-taking. The feeling that life is a melancholy farewell to time as it passes explains the meaning of his study of types and customs, which do not propose to fix the present, but rather "to preserve the *last word* of an epoch which is vanishing . . . the [provinces] of which tomorrow there will remain only a confused memory." The poet should conserve the traces of an epoch which is disappearing, but his supernatural gift consists in being able to construct with his evocative power that which time and the barbarism of men destroy.

A Bécquer paragraph is extensive and rich in harmony. The enumeration, the symmetrical disposition of equal syntactic groups, the pairing of words and of reiterative or antithetical sentences, the repetition of the last word or words of a sentence at the beginning of the next, are the structures to which he resorts in order to give movement and variation to his paragraph. A certain characteristic of style, the use of a trimember group—subjects, verbs, and complements—was to appear later in Valle-Inclán (see A. Alonso, "Estructura de las 'Sonatas' de Valle-Inclán," *Verbum,* XXI, 6–42). His vocabulary is widely varied and he was proud of his knowledge of technical terms.

See: D. Alonso, "Aquella arpa de Bécquer," *Cruz y raya,* June, 1935, pp. 59–104; J. Guillén, "La poética de Bécquer," *Revista hispánica moderna,* VIII (New York, 1942), 1–42.

J. C.

Bédier, Joseph (1864–1938, French medievalist and literary historian), though born in Paris, prided himself on his Breton origin (the name Bédier is the Arthurian Beduer, Bedivere) and on the fact that his ancestors, involved in the conspiracy of Cellamare, had emigrated to the Ile de Bourbon (Réunion). Expecting to go into secondary teaching, he graduated from the Ecole Normale Supérieure at 22 and then fell under the influence of the famous Gaston Paris (*q.v.*), whose brilliant and original pupil he became. To complete his knowledge of Romance philology he went to Germany, where Hermann Suchier guided him in the acquisition of the latest scientific methods. The University of Fribourg, in Switzerland, next offered him a post (while there he edited the *Lai de l'Ombre* in 1890), which he held until he was recalled to France by the University of Caen. Here at the early age of 27 he presented his theses for the French doctorate and then joined the staff of his alma mater, the Ecole Normale.

The budding medievalist now displayed his scientific temper and perspective by an incursion into the modern field with a volume of studies *(Etudes critiques,* 1903) on Chateaubriand, Diderot, and the *Entretien de Pascal et de M. de Sacy.* Fame came to him, however, with his genial reconstruction in classical modern French of the *Roman de Tristan et Iseult* (1900; first Eng. tr., 1903). Here—at a stroke—the modern troubadour opened up the Middle Ages to the cultivated reading public. Noteworthy is the fact that philology now becomes the handmaid of art and that factual research scores one of its greatest triumphs. This set the pace for all of Bédier's later work.

In 1903, on the death of Gaston Paris, Bédier succeeded him at the Collège de France, an institution which he regarded as the *honneur de l'Europe.* He now devoted himself to the line of research in which Paris had been so much interested, namely, the Old French epic or *chansons de geste.* It is characteristic of Bédier that he planned nothing revolutionary. If he came to uphold a view differing *toto caelo* from his predecessor's, it was due to his unshakable probity (the first asset of a scholar, according to Paris) and his instinctive literary insight. Thus was produced his masterpiece, the four volumes of *Les Légendes épiques* (1908–1913). Bédier's hypothesis is that the French epic was primarily the product of the 11th century, the age of the Crusades, to which the figure of Charlemagne was a heroic "revival" presented as the Christian champion against the threatening Mohammedan world. Hence, according to Bédier, the *Chanson de Roland* is not the survival of an epic song contemporaneous with the defeat of the Franks in 778, but an original composition inspired by the enthusiasm for the First Crusade. The background of the *chansons de geste* he found in the pilgrimage roads to holy places and the monuments (tombs, churches, relics) situated on them, combined with the clerical imagination that was stimulated by them. So arose a new view of medieval literature as expressive of the age from which the extant manuscripts can be dated.

Supplementary to this view is Bédier's stand on textual reconstruction. To him the *Chanson de Roland* is essentially the poem as preserved in the Oxford manuscript (Digby 23). To "reconstruct" medieval literature on the classical theory of Lachmann appeared to Bédier like reconstructing Chateaubriand's *Atala* by mingling the "readings" of the three, separate editions made by Chateaubriand. This fresh approach to the problem has had wide repercussion, for instance in Bédier's own critique of Dom Quentin's reconstruction of the Bible. Bédier did not settle the question, but he established the principle that each text is a problem unto itself which cannot be solved by *a priori* theory.

Like Gaston Paris, Bédier became *administrateur* of his institution, at a time when the Collège de France needed new buildings and a progressive policy. He fulfilled this task surprisingly well. Honors poured in on him; in 1920 he was elected to the French Academy. In 1936 he retired from active teaching. The remaining years of his research he devoted to a critical work—never published—on the history of the editions of the *Roland.*

In appearance Bédier was tall and thin, with clear blue eyes in which were wedded candor and passion, perspicacity and imagination. Shy in manner, with an honesty that refused to compromise, he drove an argument to its basic truth—as in the Dreyfus case, where he became an ardent revisionist. But he was always skeptical of material that he could not himself control. This appears in his *Les Fabliaux* (1893, often revised), in which he takes an anti-folklore attitude in his advocacy of individual literary composition. Yet, despite this limitation, he remains both a traditionalist (in the Cartesian manner) and an outstanding pioneer in the field of pure scholarship. His many pupils and admirers in France and abroad testify to his abiding influence. In this age of propaganda he remains the exemplar of "the disinterested pursuit of truth."

See: Ferdinand Lot, *Joseph Bédier* (1939).

W. A. N.

Bedny, Demyan (pseud. of Yefim Pridvorov, 1883–, Russian poet), born at Gubovka in the former Government of Kherson, is the oldest poet of Soviet Russia; his Bolshevik verse appeared in St. Petersburg periodicals years before the First World War. Previous to 1917 his reputation was based on his political fables, a genre much in vogue under the tsarist regime, when censorship conditions invited the use of an Aesopian language. In these fables Demyan Bedny managed to dodge the censor with his nimble verses about birds, animals, inanimate objects, and rustic simpletons. Their message was perforce subtle, and the very form of fables dictated brevity and precision. Though a university graduate, Bedny likes to pose as a muzhik, and he is, indeed, a master of the colorful folk speech rich in parables, proverbs, unexpected phraseology, and well-aimed epithets.

The Revolution freed Bedny from the fetters of censorship and enabled him to unfold his power fully. It also robbed his verse of subtlety and has rendered it pedestrian and obvious. His services to the Revolution were valuable (he has been decorated several times). Unconcerned about form and hardly sensitive to it, he produced thousands of racy, conversational verses on current issues. He addressed the masses directly on problems of war and of reconstruction, he gave them courage and confidence, entertained them with a bit of coarse humor, whetted their hatred for foreign and inner enemies, and kept them informed, stirred, exhorted, consoled. His *agitki* (bits of agitation, or propaganda) had a tremendous appeal during the civil war; they were recited and sung by soldiers and workers, they penetrated the remote backwoods of Russia and the thick skulls of the peasants. In more recent times, as the Russian public grew more exacting and critical, Demyan Bedny lost his appeal and wrote practically nothing; but with the Second World War his short poems began to appear once more in the periodicals. His verse has been offered to the public in numerous editions.

A. K.

Beer-Hofmann, Richard (1866–1945, Austrian poet, novelist, dramatist), born in Vienna, was most closely associated with *Jungwien,* the literary group that dominated Austrian letters at the turn of the century. He first attracted public notice in 1893 with a slender volume entitled *Novellen,* consisting of two short tales, "Das Kind" and "Camelias." These tales betray the influence of Maupassant (*q.v.*) in subject matter and of Flaubert (*q.v.*) in style. His earliest lyric, *Schlaflied für Miriam* (1898), is the finest philosophic lullaby in German. Eternal chords are touched—the dark origin of life and its unknown end, the blind and lonely path that we tread throughout our days, the impossibility of communicating our deepest experiences even to those nearest to us, and the tragic necessity for each generation to recapitulate the past with all its errors and suffering. Yet behind the apparent chaotic structure of the universe, the poet recognizes a mysterious purpose and a certain continuity of existence. Even as each cell is a necessary part of an organ and each organ has a specialized useful function to perform in the entire organism, so each individual is a necessary link in a historical community of fate; each community of fate has a specific way of life and a definite useful task to perform in man's ascent to an ever higher level of culture. In the poet's only novel, *Der Tod Georgs* (1900), this realization comes to the hero as, in the presence of death, he broods on the meaning of life; he is wrested from his self-centered existence as an aesthetic epicurean and whirled into the midst of his people's struggle for justice.

In *Der Graf von Charolais* (1904), Beer-Hofmann's first and best-known play, the hero, who sees the brittleness of all human relations and the instability of all human emotions, retains to the end his unshakable faith in the bonds linking parents and children to one another. This continuity of existence remains, though all else fails. Our psychic configuration is molded by the past of our ethnic kind and it, in turn, determines the way of life to be lived by our remotest descendants.

Beer-Hofmann was of Jewish origin, and his approach to eternal problems is essentially biblical. His thoughts are ever directed toward God, and his visions are reminiscent of the prophets of the Old Testament. In a biblical trilogy he seeks to restate for modern man the Hebraic position on fundamental questions. The first part, *Jaákobs Traum* (1918), depicts the inner crisis of Jacob, the legendary ancestor of the Jews, during the memorable night at Bethel, when he accepts for himself and his offspring the blessing and the burden of the blessing offered him by God. The second part of the trilogy, *Der junge David* (1933), deals with the testing of David, the descendant of Jacob. Completed shortly before Hitler's rise to power, this play gives the Hebraic answer to Nazi ideology: just as it does not pay for an individual to live solely for himself, so too it does not pay ("Es lohnt nicht!") for a people to think primarily in terms of its own aggrandizement. An individual is valuable only to the extent of his contribution to the well-being of other individuals. A people is important only in so far as it confers its creative gifts upon others, coordinating its own welfare with that of humanity at large. Deprived of this constructive urge, man is but dung of the earth and a people but dust of history.

In 1939 Beer-Hofmann was forced to leave his native land and emigrated to New York. In his 75th year, in 1941, the poet collected in a slender volume, *Verse,* all his lyric production that he cared to see preserved. A new aspect of his creativeness came to the fore on American soil in 1944 in the impressionistic sketches *Aus dem Fragment Paula: Herbstmorgen in Oesterreich.* The poet, who had heretofore spoken only through the masks of his dramatic and fictional heroes, attempted to recapture the autumnal mood of Austria as it interpenetrated his own life and shaped his own personality.

See: R. Reik, *Das Werk Richard Beer-Hofmanns* (1919); S. Liptzin, *Richard Beer-Hofmann* (1936, in English).

S. L.

Belgian literature in Flemish. When the southern Netherlands were separated from the northern provinces, at the end of the 16th century, the intellectual as well as the economic center of the Lowlands moved to the north. For 200 years Flemish literature was reduced to pietist writings of sometimes inane sentimentality and ridiculously detailed symbolism. Literary expression died out. Immediately after the creation of an independent Belgium in 1830, it was revived by the prolific novelist Hendrik Conscience (*q.v.*). His sentimental nationalism, based on what Flanders had achieved in the Middle Ages and on the story of its revolt against tyranny in the 16th century, brought about a renaissance of literary activity. About 1860 his work was well under way, and a number of writers had sprung up who created a literary "climate" in which the fundamental trends of Flemish letters were already plainly visible—

a constant tendency toward cozy provincialism, which finds its expression in the peasant novel, and, on the other hand, a definite longing for universality which uses social and psychological elements. At times these two tendencies intermingle.

About 1880 the majority of the reading public in Flanders belonged to the rural Catholic population. In their struggle against linguistic inequality in the new state, and as a means of self-defense, they took comfort in their local characteristics, their picturesque way of life, their verbal particularities, all of which were employed to prove that Flanders and the Flemish language had a right to exist. Therefore it was quite natural as well as fashionable for the writers of the second half of the 19th century to depict the amenities of life on the farm and in the country in the most lively colors, to exalt the virtues of the rustics, to underline their habits, their wit, and their customs, and to represent them as a touchstone to guarantee the language and personality of the Flemish people. The cult of local expression and idiosyncrasy led to an acute provincialism which manifested itself in the use of dialectic forms and in an opposition to the generally accepted medium of a standard Netherlandish language.

All these handicaps, however, were brilliantly overcome by the one poet of universal stature Flanders produced in the last century, the priest Guido Gezelle (*q.v.*). He embodied the pure gothic spirit; he looked at nature and its botanic details as the miniaturists of the Middle Ages did and with absolute faith in his metaphysical certainties he attained to a mystical familiarity with the Creator which made his art appear as the last flowering of Middle Age devotion. His verse is purely lyrical, although he seldom referred to his personal life, which was at bottom difficult and not devoid of the tragic. Most of his poems deal with the feasts and ceremonies of the Church or with the rural Flemish landscape. They have a charming simplicity and directness and a warmth which was never equaled in Dutch letters except in the 14th century. Nevertheless, he wrote his best poetry on those occasions when he broke the restraint his clerical functions imposed upon him—his verse is then of a very high lyrical quality. It has the unerring musical perfection of the best *Lieder*. He was, indeed, the perfect example of the Franciscan poet, for never was so much joy derived from nature without evident sensuality, never was there in Dutch literature a character as simple in its unity, as forceful in its lyrical power. Reacting against verbose pomposity and pedantic metrical rules, Gezelle adopted an extremely versatile meter for which he found inspiration in the English and Scotch poets. His poems abound in subtle, elegant onomatopoeia, in graceful alliterations, and follow a strictly personal rhythm. Many of them would fit the later formula of "la poésie pure."

A great linguist, he made such an excellent translation (1886) of Longfellow's *Hiawatha* that it became familiar to all Flemish readers. It took his countrymen and the Dutch some time to recognize his significance, to find out his exceptional stature. His localisms had constituted a barrier for both groups, his uncompromising and enthusiastic Catholicism was another. When about 1880 he was introduced to the general public in Holland, his plea for a predominance of the West Flanders tongue was already lost, but he had become the outstanding example of a writer who by the mere contemplation and idealistic description of rural beauties had achieved greatness and even universal recognition. Although some of his poems (*e.g.*, "Dien Avond en die Rooze," That Evening and That Rose; and "O 't ruischen van het Ranke Riet," O Rustling of the Rushes' Throng) have been translated carefully into English, like all great lyrical work, they remain essentially unrenderable.

Parallel to Conscience's enthusiastic prose was the sudden romantic burst of national feeling expressed in the poems of Albrecht Rodenbach (1856–1880). He was the herald of the Flemish political revival. His turbulent, ebullient inspiration was a combination of classicism and Germanic lyricism. Having produced a number of songs and recitation pieces on historical themes and an unfinished drama in verse, *Gudrun* (1882), he died very young, a great promise, a symbol of idealistic youth.

Against the rural idealism of Conscience and Gezelle there reacted a few minor realists like August Snieders (1825–1904) and Domien Sleeckx (1818–1901); a charming essayist, Anton Bergmann (1835–1874); and the interesting novelist, Virginie Loveling (1836–1923). Except for the last-named, their writings had little power in their realism, and their style was conservative and often dull.

It took the revival of Dutch letters, about 1880, to provoke a definite emancipation of Flemish literature. This renewal was prepared by a transitional writer of great dynamism, Pol de Mont (1857–1931), a moderately sensual, highly lyrical, and musical poet who was a true internationalist in his thoughts and a genuine symbolist in his expression. He was the first writer in many decades to feel and speak with the freedom of a well-educated heathen, but this attitude, although closer than that of anybody else in Flanders to the main currents of European thought and sensibility, was never expressed in an aggressive fashion. He discovered and heralded Gezelle's poetry in Holland and in Flanders. He wrote *Rijzende Sterren* (1879; Rising Stars) and *Lentesotternijen* (1881; Spring Follies).

In the 1890's a new generation of writers came to the fore. They rallied around a monthly called *Van Nu en Straks* (Today and Tomorrow) which was definitely internationalist and liberal in its program. The driving spirit, the philosopher of the movement, was August Vermeylen (*q.v.*), a forceful critic with generous views; the literary theorician of the movement was Prosper van Langendonck (1862–1920), a somber, weak, romantic poet; but its real creative geniuses were Cyriel Buysse (*q.v.*), Herman Teirlinck (*q.v.*), Stijn Streuvels (*q.v.*), and, above all, Karel van de Woestijne (*q.v.*).

Buysse was a born narrator of the Maupassant (*q.v.*) school, whom Maeterlinck used to count "among the three or four great rural raconteurs of these last fifty years." He wrote a faithful chronicle of life in the Flemish villages as it evolved rapidly in the last decades.

Undoubtedly, the country baker Stijn Streuvels, a nephew of Guido Gezelle, was the most gifted of the prose writers of that period. There exists an evident synchronism between his early books and the vogue of luminist painting (*e.g.*, *Lenteleven*, 1899; Spring Life). Except when portraying children (*Prutske*, 1922), his psychology appeared rather simple, but his gift for plastic detail and minute yet lyrical description was impressive. In his writings the physical environment, the atmosphere, absorbs man, or rather reduces him to a secondary, even minor role. Man to Streuvels was not the measure of things, he was their plaything. Several of his longer novels, *De Vlaschgaard* (1907; The Flax Field), *Werkmenschen* (1927; Working People), have an epic quality which is very much akin to Scandinavian and Russian literature. In his later work (*e.g.*, *Alma met de vlassen Haren*, 1930; Alma with the Flaxen Hair) the analysis of devotional life was his preoccupation, and he began also to give more attention to the sexual relations and problems of his personages. The exclusive love for the native soil and its inhabitants, which hampered many of his colleagues on their path to greatness and condemned them to provincialism, turned out in his case to be an asset and a starting point for truly universal expression.

All the writers grouped around *Van Nu en Straks* were decided individualists. Like their Dutch colleagues of the 1880's they wanted "to give the most individual expression to their most individual emotions." The outstanding poet of the group, Karel van de Woestijne, succeeded in doing this to such an extent that, had he been writing in one of the major world languages, he could hardly have failed to be universally recognized as one of the greatest lyric poets of his time.

He had no other theme but himself; no other drama to tell but the eternal conflict between mind and matter. His extensive poetical work is little else but a symbolic autobiography. He was as responsive as Gezelle to nature and its thousand details, but his life was dominated by a pendulum movement of attraction and repulsion of the eternal feminine (*Het Vaderhuis*, 1903, The Father House; *De Gulden Schaduw*, 1910, The Golden Shadow). In one of his long poems he sees with Adam "that Eve, in her wickedness, was beautiful." The drama of his life, as expressed in his writings, lies there as well as in a deep conviction of the sinfulness of his spontaneous reactions. He sang his joys and pains with such refined analytic preciseness, such exceptional warmth and tenseness, that there is scarcely anything that approaches his work in European literature. He had the burning heat of the great mystics like St. John of the Cross or St. Theresa, but always, like Paul Verlaine (*q.v.*), he went to the extreme in the humiliating confession of his weakness and frailty. Never in Flemish or Dutch literature had such a great heart witnessed and interpreted the constant conflict between a lucid intelligence and a hypersensitive nature. A good deal of his poetical work exists in a brooding atmosphere in which sensations and thoughts bloom like hothouse flowers of rare and slightly terrifying beauty. Life to him, who harbored a gothic heart in a renaissance body, is but a long conflict between his brilliant intelligence and the toll inevitably exacted by his senses. Woman, who had appeared until then in Flemish poetry and prose either as the devoted mother or the idealized Dulcinea, was to him full of mystery, of charm, of menace, a messenger of destruction and death. The leitmotifs of love and death run through his poems as if they were a verbal transcription of Isolde's *Liebestod.*

Van de Woestijne was a profound humanist. The rare poems which do not refer to his personal life deal with heroes of antiquity (*Interludiën,* 2 vols., 1912; Interludes), especially with Hercules whom he made the symbol of disenchanted grandeur. His goddesses, heroes, and heroines, in their Greek disguise, reveal the split personality, the melancholy, the doubt, and the longing for serene beauty which was characteristic of the atmosphere and literature of the turn of the century. These are decorative poems of moving beauty. In the second period of his life Van de Woestijne became a poet of great metaphysical depth; often his verse had a strange wry sarcasm, *De modderen Man* (1920; The Man of Mud), *God aan Zee* (1926; God at the Sea), *Het Bergmeer* (1928; The Mountain Lake). To such an extent did Van de Woestijne interpret the lyrical sensuality of Rubens, as well as Breughel's irony and keen observation, that his influence dominated Flemish letters for over two decades. Many poets were under his spell and, lacking his subtle balance and genius, devoted themselves to a decadent kind of writing which, by its extremely personal character, provoked a strong reaction in the generation of writers which spoke out during and after the First World War.

The writers of the generation that sprang up between 1917 and 1921 were greatly impressed by social and political problems. Although they recognized the eminence of authors like Van de Woestijne and others, they objected to an ivory-tower attitude, which they condemned as irresponsible and antisocial. They wanted poetry not to be a lyrical confession; they felt that the poet should be the conscience of the world, a seer and prophet like Walt Whitman, always busy drawing the moral of events and—in a broad sense—guiding public opinion. The external elements of the modern world should be incorporated into the poetical vocabulary, no conservative rules of prosody should hamper free expression. They used *vers libre* or they resorted to the psalmodic rhythm so successfully used by Paul Claudel (*q.v.*). For a brief period they indeed succeeded in interpreting the spirit of their time; their expressionist experiments exploded the calm impressionist atmosphere, and literature became unthinkable without humanitarian declamations and modernistic bric-a-brac. Their organ *Ruimte* (Space), which rallied Paul van Ostayen (*q.v.*), Wies Moens (1898–), Achilles Mussche (1896–), Gaston Burssens (1896–), Jan-Albert Goris (*q.v.*), Victor Brunclair (1899–1945) and others, was short-lived, but their influence was decisive for a considerable period.

They were essentially poets. The leader and most versatile of them all, Paul van Ostayen, started out as a young literary dandy, following the footsteps of the *Jungwien* poets. Soon he turned to the political, prophetic genre, in the manner of the German expressionists Werfel, Trakl, and Becher (*qq.v.*), in *Het Sienjaal* (1918; The Signal). Later on he became dadaist for a brief period (*Bezette Stad,* 1921; The City Occupied) and concluded his short life by writing extremely suggestive, highly musical poetry of great refinement and purity. His short stories, burlesque adventures (*Self Defense,* 1933), told with a keenly analytic sarcasm, were a very effective antidote against rhetoric and pomposity. Moens and Mussche, both generous, ardent, lyrical natures, used a biblical and slightly oriental style to express their vivid social reactions, while Goris, after writing a spectacular modernistic baroque piece on St. Francis (*Lof-Litanie vam Sint Franciscus van Assisi,* 1919; Litany in Praise of St. Francis of Assisi), evolved a style which has been considered a reconciliation of expressionism and classic simplicity; in his apparently free verse the discipline is as severe as in the classical meter (*Het Huis,* 1925; The House). Other poets were given to cosmic jugglery, sometimes really impressive. Others still, like Paul Verbruggen (1891–), attained a great purity of expression.

However, this revolt against tradition did not change the aspect of Flemish letters: the cozy rural and small-town novel received a new and powerful endorsement in Felix Timmermans (*q.v.*), a most prolific novelist who expressed a kind of reserved pantheistic joy of life in a very fresh and lyrical book *Pallieter* (1916; Eng. tr., 1924). This dionysian paean was followed by a number of books which were amusing transcriptions of old Flemish paintings and which were sometimes as charming as the products of these *petits maîtres.* He enjoyed a tremendous popularity in Germany, where he was considered a Low-German author. Notwithstanding very humorous, although unorthodox stylistic gifts, he remained a popular author, and one of his recent novels, *Boerenpsalm* (1935; Peasant Psalm), is a remarkably adult and sanguine book. Other authors like Teirlinck, Maurits Sabbe (1873–1938), Ernest Claes (1889–), Lode Baekelmans (1879–), continued the solidly established tradition of charming provincial writing.

Besides the Ruimte group, a number of poets gathered around a tiny review called *Het Fonteintje* (The Little Fountain). They were not humanitarians, but humanists, classicists, and they tried to disengage themselves from Van de Woestijne's grip. They resorted to a humoristic style, inspired by Toulet (*q.v.*) and other French poets. Their master and patron saint was Jan van Nijlen (*q.v.*), a wise, melancholic poet, who wrote fluent, charming verse in which he told people that the world was not exactly "cosmic," but strictly personal. Among them, Raymond Herreman (1896–) was the most outstanding and the most versatile.

The novelist Alfons de Ridder (*q.v.*), whose writings through their merciless humor and grim moral courage are unique in Flemish letters, can also be considered as belonging to this school. He writes in *Villa des Roses* (1913) and *Tsjip* (1934; Cheep) of middle-class people with deep sarcastic anger and a chastely hidden feeling for man's misery. Although he wrote only a few poems, he is also a very remarkable poet.

When the conflict and discussions between the two groups, the humanitarians and the cozy moralists, had subsided, when principles and theories no longer determined literary activity, when the eternal problems of existence had again taken the place of temporary political and social issues, a number of young novelists appeared who brought a new accent into Flemish letters. They had found out that the one and only subject of the novel is man, not the climate or the fauna and flora that surround him. This discovery was responsible for an increase in tempo and a better psychological insight. Among these writers, the most classical-minded is Maurice Roelants (*q.v.*). His novels go back to the great tradition of Benjamin Constant's *Adolphe* and to the works of other keen analysts of the human soul. With less technical perfection, but extreme generosity, Lode Zielens (1901–1944) devotes attention to the Flemish proletariat. He overflows with the milk of human kindness. But the most powerful and productive of them all is Gerard Walschap (*q.v.*). Using all the resources of rhetoric, his story rushes down like a mountain stream. His search is essentially along psychopathological lines. Although his personages often border on the abnormal, the moral of his work is always a belief in the profound goodness and greatness of life and of man. Aside from his torrential tempo, which comes close to the tornado pace James Cain used in *The Postman Always Rings Twice,* the European author he may best be compared with is François Mauriac (*q.v.*).

The great influence of Herman Teirlinck on the Flemish theatre between the two wars should be mentioned. He introduced the modernistic theatrical conceptions with great success.

One of the most remarkable literary facts after the First World War in Flanders was that the influence of Flemish letters on Dutch writing augmented considerably. Most of the young Flemish writers, by increasing the distance between their work and the folklore novelistics of their elders, came close enough to Dutch literature to make their works indistinguishable from Dutch publications.

See: G. Kalff, *Geschiedenis der Nederlandsche Letterkunde* (6 vols., 1906–1910); J. Bithell, *Contemporary Belgian Literature* (1915); J. Persijn, *A Glance at the Soul of the Low Countries* (1916); J. Bithell, *Contemporary Flemish Poetry* (1917); G. L. van Roosbroeck, *Guido Gezelle, the Mystic Poet of Flanders* (1919); P. Hamelius, *Introduction à la littérature française et flamande de Belgique* (1921); A. de Ridder, *La Littérature flamande contemporaine* (1923); A. Vermeylen, *Van Gezelle tot Timmermans* (1923); F. de Backer, *Contemporary Flemish Literature* (1934); M. Gijsen, *De Literatuur in Zuid Nederland sedert 1830* (1940; 3d ed., 1945), *Peripatetisch Onderricht* (1940), and *Vlaamsche Lyriek* (1944).

J.-A. G.

Belgian literature in French. The presence in Belgium of two races of different mentality —the Flemish are of Germanic origin, the Walloons of a Latin tradition—and a glorious common inheritance in the plastic arts have made their mark on the national literature. Many writers of mixed blood use French as their medium of expression, and the Walloons show to some degree traits of their Flemish colleagues. Predominant in the latter is the inspiration drawn from painters. Many scenes, sometimes whole volumes are primarily pictures in words, veritable transpositions of canvases. Color in separate episodes rather than rigidly coherent architecture is sought, and evocation rather than logical thinking. Love of the picturesque contributes to a democratic note, uppermost in fiction. "Go to humble folk," advised De Coster (*q.v.*); "the bourgeois are all tarred with monotony." The Walloons share this interest in the people, but are relatively sober in description; their art reveals more subtle psychology and delicate shades of landscape. Regionalistic fiction, portraying the manners of a city or province, has fascinated the majority of the novelists. This trend comes in part from realistic theories prevalent during the last decades of the 19th century, in part from the historical novel, much in vogue from the moment the desire arose to endow the country with a new glory after independence was won in 1830. Two writers of the following half century have won lasting fame, and between them they represent the two poles of the national temperament—joy in physical vigor and in contemplative sensibility—to become familiar later in Verhaeren and Maeterlinck (*qq.v.*). Charles De Coster's *Ulenspiegel* (1867) is an epic novel culminating the effort to glorify the past in its struggle for freedom. Years of labor had been devoted to the composition; the sources are old chonicles, museums, and folklore; an archaic style lends color to the 16th-century setting. The influence of this novel has been enormous; it was proclaimed the Bible of Belgium by the rising generation. Thus the modern revival of letters starts with a masterpiece of distinctly national inspiration. Octave Pirmez (*q.v.*) was an aristocratic recluse who sought communion with the infinite through nature. Fascinated at once by Pascal, Rousseau, and Chateaubriand, he has left his personal mark on his intuitive philosophy, and his spiritual family includes some of the most distinguished poets. The generation coming of age in 1880, known as Jeune Belgique, hailed De Coster and Pirmez as two of their authentic forerunners.

The great majority of representative Belgian authors are essentially poets, thanks to their aesthetic perception and sheer gusto in living, whatever their mode of expression. A striking example is Camille Lemonnier (*q.v.*), whose voluminous works include no verse; his *La Belgique* (1888), was pronounced too "lyric" for distribution among scholastic prize winners. It was to be an inspiration for his successors in regionalistic fiction. Lemonnier appears as a Proteus with 13 volumes of art criticism, 20 collections of short stories, and 29 novels. He saw in De Coster the supreme painter of the past and advised his younger contemporaries to be the historians of their own time. His counsel has been generally followed except by Eugène Demolder (*q.v.*) who, more than any other Belgian novelist, was fascinated by the old masters of the brush (*La Route d'émeraude*, 1899). Certain critics have sought a sociological trend in Lemonnier. A few novels of his middle period lend color to such an interpretation, but his characterization of himself as an instinctive temperament fascinated by the beauty of life can hardly be bettered. Social revolt marks the vitriolic work of Georges Eekhoud (*q.v.*). He was born of a bourgeois family and spent his mature life in Brussels, but his work is shot through with nostalgia for his native Antwerp countryside and with sympathy for the downtrodden and the outlaws. He would be the interpreter of the peasant soul, expressing sentiments they feel but cannot utter. *La Nouvelle Carthage* (1888, definitive ed., 1893; Eng. tr., *The New Carthage*, 1917) reveals the fascination that Antwerp, in its squalor and its energy, held for him. The novel recalls the attitude of Verhaeren in the poems of the period of *Les Villes tentaculaires* (1895). The question arises as to how much is pure literature in the humanitarianism of certain Belgian writers, but Eekhoud is at least consistent throughout and broke with his friends of *Jeune Belgique* when they championed exclusively the doctrine of "art for art's sake." Still there is ample evidence that he appreciated to the full the picturesqueness of his lusty heroes. Georges Virrès (pseud. of Henri Briers, 1869–) deals with the peasants of Limburg in a different manner. He speaks as a realist, as one who has spent his life among the folk he portrays (*Les Gens de Tiest*, 1903), while Eekhoud is an ideologist whose characters are almost symbols. Nor is the cult of plastic art prominent in Virrès; he resembles the novelists of the Walloon tradition by his finesse of observation of landscape and character. While he is aware of the truculent side of his rustics, he excels in a quiet humor which replaces to advantage the violent hatreds in which Eekhoud indulged. He remarks that Eekhoud often missed the mystic element in peasants and points to apparently supernatural influences which arise from the soil itself and shape character. Yet the work of this Catholic leader is devoid of propaganda; he possesses a sense of structure rare in typical novelists of the Flemish wing. An exaggerated tendency to personify environment may be seen in the once-famous novel of the symbolist poet, Georges Rodenbach (*q.v.*). He states that he intends to make the city an essential and directing personage in *Bruges-la-morte* (1892). Today this work seems singularly artificial beside the vigorous realism of Virrès.

The Walloon novelists are also regionalists but show a conscious effort to distill the universal and to generalize from close observation of familiar scenes and folk. In this sense, and because they are less attracted by color for its own sake, they are truer realists than the Flemings. Hubert Krains (*q.v.*) is an excellent example. By his style and choice of matter he has grasped to the full the classic precept of imitating the majestic simplicity of nature; he is aware that her great plan is always the same across apparent variety. His art is highly selective, eliminating all that is not of structural value. He meditates on every scene until he can evoke it in its most vital features. He wrote relatively little, two short novels and five collections of short stories and a volume of critical essays. His outlook is one of resigned pessimism, yet suffering always arouses his discreet sympathy. Offering no panaceas, defending no theses, he accepts the universe, not as perfect nor as susceptible of becoming so, but as presenting, to those who have eyes to see, the most fascinating of spectacles. A similar ideal characterizes Edmond Glesener (*q.v.*), who extends his observation over a wider range. He barbs his criticism of society with psychological acumen; his objectivity and scourging irony have occasionally brought the charge of cynicism, but *Le Cœur de François Remy* (1904) suffices as refutation. In the stories of *L'Ombre des sapins* (1934) his art lends a tragic grandeur to rustics which makes them symbols of suffering humanity. The popularity of Maurice Des Ombiaux (1868–1943) comes in part from his adaptation of the methods of the Flemish school to the portrayal of Wallonia with its folklore and customs (*Mihien d'Avène,* 1904). Thus he appears as a broadly national novelist. His exuberance recalls Rabelais, yet his naïve paeans to lusty living disarm criticism. If the joy of the spirit gives the measure of its strength, Des Ombiaux is an intellectual titan.

Belgians are at their best in the short story, a genre favored by most of the novelists, whose technique has been profoundly influenced by it; often novels are a series of carefully wrought but loosely connected episodes. Two masters are Hubert Stiernet (1863–1939) and Louis Delattre (1870–1938). Stiernet's originality lies in his use of mysterious forces, not fantastic but springing from the soil, from violation of tradition, or from revival or some past incident. He occasionally recalls Hawthorne. Occult influences skillfully entwined with everyday life appear as prolongations of a word or act which escapes from the subconscious. Once released, they guide the destiny of an individual (*Histoires hantées,* 1906). Delattre, a doctor by profession, is keenly aware of human tragedy yet always fascinated by life observed in its minutest details, which he contrives to forge into drama. He passes for an optimist, but declares that his smile is largely a reaction against the all too prevailing gloom. He succeeds in arousing interest in the apparently commonplace with the maximum simplicity of means (*Le Parfum des buis,* 1911).

Three of the younger novelists deserve special attention. Jean Tousseul (*q.v.*) received his education in the school of hard knocks. Proud of his humble ancestors, he determined, as an artist, to perform his task with the conscientiousness they displayed in theirs. Hence a note at once realistic and idealistic unheard before. The setting of his stories and novels ranges from the prehistoric past to the present of his region; like Michelet, he would resuscitate the common people, and the solidarity with his forebears gives unity to his work. His constant theme is the effort of the downtrodden toward justice for all, but he writes as a poet, not as an agitator. Franz Hellens (*q.v.*) stands apart among Belgian novelists—he has little of the regionalist and nothing of the sociologist. Convinced that the domain of the rational has been thoroughly explored, he turns to the extraintellectual; *Réalités fantastiques* (1923) offers a synthesis of his work. He would use all the techniques of modern psychology in his analyses of the subconscious; the phenomena of involuntary reminiscence fascinate him. He is inspired by music rather than by painting and avows his ambition to create matter by sound. His closest affinity is with his fellow townsman, Maeterlinck, but he appears always as an explorer of purely artistic realms with no didactic purpose. Constant Burniaux (1892–), whom R. T. House has aptly called "the poet of nature's stepchildren," has devoted his life to teaching abnormal waifs. His own sensitive nature is at once repelled and attracted by their degradation, which he is at pains not to gloss over, but, with no illusions about working miracles, he finds a stoic joy in his profession. There is perhaps no truer humanitarian in Belgian literature (see *Crânes tondus,* 1930).

Women have made a significant contribution to letters in Belgium; 70 using French as their medium were represented at an exposition in 1936. In fiction they reveal an acumen in dealing with feminine psychology rare among their masculine colleagues. Marguerite van de Wiele (*Maison flamande,*

1883), who painted Bruges before Rodenbach, and Marie Gevers (*Madame Orpha,* 1934), who gives her version of Eekhoud's Campine, represent the regionalistic wing. Blanche Rousseau (*L'Eventail,* 1906) portrays with exquisite delicacy everyday reality. France Adine (*La Cité sur l'Arno,* 1931) deals with aristocratic, cosmopolitan society; she is interested in the refinement of egoistic males by woman's tact. Julia Frezin (*Le Nid ravagé,* 1937), creates unforgettable characters of both sexes without departing from normal experience. She excels in the portrayal of stoic idealists placed against a realistic background. In poetry Elise Champagne writes with wistful sincerity of the humble citizens of Liége.

A striking phenomenon in Belgium is the number of reviews. The catalogue of the Exposition of 1930 names 166; no less than 25 sprang up in the decade 1874–1884 to defend the cause of literature and art; many others have appeared since. Some were ephemeral, but three require special mention: the *Jeune Belgique, Art moderne,* and *Wallonie.* Most of the writers who were to count in the revival of Belgian letters were affiliated with one or another. In December, 1880, Albert Bauwens and four friends published the first number of *Jeune Revue littéraire,* which became a year later *Jeune Belgique.* At the end of 1881, Bauwens ceded his review to Max Waller, who desired a more agressive attitude. The *Jeune Revue littéraire* had announced itself as a free organ with no other program than that of furthering the cause of literary effort. The policy of its successor varied, but turned more and more to a strict Parnassianism with the exclusive doctrine of "art for art's sake." Hence internal strife and polemics with former friends. Waller, taking for his motto *Fear nought,* quickly won a reputation for spirited impertinence by his attacks on the official and uninspired literature of his time; he did succeed in arousing his countrymen from their lethargy. His collaborators were primarily poets, and while he lived he held his group together. After his death in 1889—he was succeeded in the editorship by the poet Valère Gille (*q.v.*)—inner dissension became violent, culminating in 1895 with the foundation of the short-lived *Coq rouge* by Verhaeren (who was experimenting with free verse), Eekhoud, and other prosateurs. *Jeune Belgique* lasted until 1897; the consummation of the renaissance of Belgian letters is due in large measure to the efforts of its staff. *Art moderne* (1881–1914), whose moving spirit was the lawyer Edmond Picard, aimed at once at the renovation of letters and at a large social reform. Picard was as bellicose as the leaders of *Jeune Belgique* and quite as eager as they to further the cause of a distinctly national art. Accusing his rivals of aping Paris, he sought to foster expression of the "Belgian soul," even if certain niceties of French usage were violated. *Wallonie* (1886–1892), organ of the symbolists, was founded at Liége by Albert Mockel (*q.v.*). Belgian and French poets were among its contributors. The trend of later literary reviews, *e.g., Thyrse,* has been eclectic.

Poets gave to *Jeune Belgique* its distinctive mark. Albert Giraud (*q.v.*) is the unflinching champion of studied Parnassian perfection; he sought in art a refuge from the prevalent vulgarity. *Hors du siècle* (1887), hymning the glories and color of the past, recalls at once Leconte de Lisle and Heredia (*qq.v.*). Giraud's prevailing note is one of pessimism; he was born disillusioned, yet in 1919 he entered the arena with *Les Lauriers* to commune with his countrymen who, he felt, had then met his ideal. His colleague, Iwan Gilkin (*q.v.*) appears as a poet of cosmic interests. He had planned "a sublime journey through Hell, Purgatory and Paradise," but only the first part, *La Nuit* (1897), was written. Here Baudelaire's influence was paramount. But this work seems inspired by a crisis in his career; his subsequent poems, while often accompanied by a subtle note of irony, reveal a joyous acceptance of life. His dramatic poem, *Prométhée* (1899), written in varied meters—he invokes La Fontaine as sponsor—carries out the idea of his unfinished trilogy. The magnificent pantheism of the foreshadowed reconciliation between Zeus and the rebellious Titan seems to symbolize his hope of union between the warring groups of Belgian poets. Only by harmony of endeavor, he felt, could they achieve their goal of giving their country its potential place on Parnassus. He proved his critical acumen when, in the first article published on Maeterlinck's *La Princesse Maleine,* he declared that the piece was certain to mark a date in the history of the theatre (*Jeune Belgique,* December, 1889). Fernand Séverin (*q.v.*) recalls Pirmez by his love of solitude and by the inspiration he found in communion with nature (*Poèmes),* 1930). Some form of pantheism, reached by various means, is a marked trait of Belgian letters. Now it arises from the cult of regionalism, which branches out to embrace ever-widening horizons; Belgians are very conscious of being a tiny nation which has made and is determined to make a noble contribution to the realms of art and civilization. Again it appears as a child of the mystic trend exemplified by Maeterlinck. In Charles Van Lerberghe (*q.v.*) it is inspired by the cult of beauty; his Eve "returns in a smile to the universe she has sung" (*La Chanson d'Eve,* 1904). Van Lerberghe shared the typical Fleming's inspiration from painters, but his ideal was that of Memling and the English Pre-Raphaelites. An idea of the wealth and variety of recent Belgian poetry (*see also* articles on Max Elskamp, Odilon Jean Périer, Eric de Haulleville) may be gained from F. Castillo Nájera's *Un siglo de poesía belga* (1931), in which 78 poets are quoted, discussed, and translated.

The theatre has not received in Belgium the attention devoted to the novel and to poetry. Some critics claim that the Belgian temperament, essentially lyric and descriptive, is unadapted to stage requirements. It is certain that a number of poets, as Van Lerberghe, Rodenbach, Verhaeren, Giraud, and Henri Maubel (pseud. of Maurice Belval, 1862–1919), have written dramatic pieces not primarily intended for the footlights. Other observers find that the wealth of French drama acts as a deterrent to similar efforts in Belgium because producers favor Parisian celebrities. Fernand Crommelynck (*q.v.*) indeed made his reputation with a play first presented in Paris, *La Cocu magnifique* (1921). Yet there is considerable activity in Belgium, and the absence of a national tradition has encouraged originality. The work of Maeterlinck is better known in Anglo-Saxon countries than in his own; Kistemaeckers (*q.v.*) had a certain success in Paris; Picard invented the *monodrame* for the promulgation of his social theses; Marguerite Duterme (1882–), whose first inspiration came from Ibsen, and Gustave Van Zype (1869–), the most gifted of Belgian dramatists, represent the theatre of ideas. Among the younger men, Michel de Ghelderode is experimenting brilliantly with new techniques.

The First World War has been the theme of volumes by most writers who witnessed it: novels, stories, poems, and objective essays abound. Belgium's place among independent nations dates from little more than a century; her men of letters are deeply conscious of their role in giving her artistic autonomy, and Belgian literature is largely inspired by local scenes and by intense regional patriotism. Hence the devastation of the country aroused great indignation. Verhaeren himself discarded for a moment his cosmopolitan doctrines to brand Germany's crime. An anthology of work by those sacrificed in the holocaust appeared in 1922. Among the surviving combatants, Maurice Gauchez (pseud. of Maurice Gilles, 1883–), poet, novelist, and critic, set the example with *Ce que j'ai vu* (1915), and the caustic novelist, Max Deauville (*q.v.*), produced a masterpiece of objective observation, *Jusqu'à l'Yser* (1917).

Poets and novelists vie with scholars in critical essays. The leaders of *Jeune Belgique* did pioneer work here; the first modern Belgian critic, Francis Nautet (1855–1896), whose unfinished *Histoire des lettres belges d'expression française* (1892) is still of value, belonged to the group. Krains's *Portraits d'écrivains belges* (1930) offers penetrating portraits of six; Mockel, Gauchez, and Georges Rency (1875–) divide their efforts between criticism and creative work. Belgian historiography glories in Henri Pirenne's (*q.v.*) magisterial *Histoire de Belgique* (7 vols., 1900–1932); Maurice Wilmotte (1861–1942) was the dean of philological scholarship in his country; Gustave Charlier (1885–), Georges Doutrepont (1868–) and Spoelberch de Lovenjoul (*q.v.*) have made large contributions to both French and Belgian literary history; younger men like J. M. Culot, Léon Sosset, and Gustave Vanwelkenhuyzen are making their mark. There is every evidence that the seed sown by *Jeune Belgique* has not fallen on barren ground.

See: M. Gauchez, *Livre des masques belges* 3 vols., 1908–1911); O. Thiry, *La Miraculeuse Aventure des Jeunes Belgiques* (1911); M. Wilmotte, *La Culture française en Belgique* (1913); J. Bithell, *Contemporary Belgian Literature* (1915); G. Charlier, "Les Lettres belges," in J. Bedier and P. Hazard, *Histoire de la littérature française,* II (1924), 318–326; H. Liebrecht and G. Rency, *Histoire illustrée de la littérature belge de langue française* (1926); B. M. Woodbridge, *Le Roman belge contemporain* (1930).

B. M. W.

Beltramelli, Antonio (1879–1930, Italian novelist), was born at Forli and died in Rome. He first gained recognition as a militant young journalist and later became known as a writer of novels, comedies, poetry, books for children, and travel books. He was made a member of the Italian Academy in 1929. Beltramelli was active in the political strife which followed the First World War in Italy, taking sides finally with the Fascists. In *Il Cavalier Mostardo* (1921), he describes the struggle between republicans and socialists, and in *L'Uomo nuovo* (1923), perhaps his best work, he writes of the atmosphere of his native province Romagna.

Beltramelli's early literary works, such as *Anna Perenna* (1904) and *I Primogeniti* (1905), had seemed to reveal originality. He developed qualities suggestive of the Sicilian writer Verga (*q.v.*). *Solicchio* (1913) is a book of verse in which he attempts to revive legends of Romagna. Later, abandoning the countryside as his subject, he began to write lyric novels in an ultra D'Annunzio (*q.v.*) style, eulogizing past wars and heroic figures. Among his other works are compilations of tales, *L'Alterna Vicenda* (1909), *Le Novelle di Ceppo* (1911), *La Vigna vendemmiata* (1919), and the novels, *L'Ombra del mandorlo* (1921), *Ahi Giacometta la tua ghirlandella* (1921), and *Il Passo dell' ignota* (1927).

See: Arturo Lanocita, *Scrittori del tempo nostro* (1928), pp. 29–38; Giuseppe Ravegnani, *I Contemporanei* (1930), pp. 31–37; Renato Serra, *Scritti* (1938), I, 49–69.

J. C. D. L.

Bely, Andrei (pseud. of Boris Nikolayevich Bugayev, 1880–1934, Russian poet, novelist, critic, essayist, and theoretician of symbolism), was born in Moscow, the only child of one of Russia's leading mathematicians, N. V. Bugayev, dean of the faculty of natural sciences at the University of Moscow. From early childhood he was moved by the music of Schumann, Schubert, Beethoven, and Chopin and by the poetry of Uhland and Goethe. Between 1891 and 1899 he attended the Polivanov Gymnasium, where his inclination toward literature was encouraged. The family of M. S. Solovyov, who was a brother of the poet Vladimir Solovyov (*q.v.*), played a primary role in helping the future poet find himself. Under the guidance of the Solovyovs, Bugayev became interested in philosophy and in literature, particularly in modernistic trends. The poetry of Vladimir Solovyov made a lasting impression on the youth. In 1899 in accordance with his father's wishes he enrolled in the faculty of natural sciences at the University of Moscow. Shortly after his father's death in 1903 he finished his course and transferred to the liberal arts curriculum.

In 1902 Bugayev published his first literary effort, *Dramaticheskaya simfoniya* (The Dramatic Symphony), using the pseudonym Andrei Bely (Andrew the White), under which he became known in literature. Between 1904 and 1909 he acted as member of the editorial board of the symbolist periodical, *Vesy* (The Balance); he was given charge in 1906 of the theoretical and polemical departments of the magazine. In 1909 he became a member of the editorial board of the Mousagethe Press and also organized the Society for the Study of Poetic Rhythm. Bugayev spent several months abroad in 1906, visiting Germany, Switzerland, and France. During 1910–1911, with his wife, Anna Turgeneva, he journeyed to Italy, Sicily, Tunis, Egypt, Palestine. With the collapse of symbolism as a school in 1912 Bugayev became absorbed in the anthroposophical doctrines of Rudolf Steiner and in 1913 went abroad and eventually joined the anthroposophist colony at Dornach, Switzerland. On returning to Russia in 1916, he joined Ivanov-Razumnik and the "Scythian" literary group and, with them, greeted the Revolution. To the Scythians it was a manifestation of the destructive cataclysm that would leave Russia rejuvenated and purified and thus fit for the messianic role which they believed she was destined to play. After the Revolution, Bely took an active part in the various cultural organizations sponsored by the Soviet government—the Moscow Proletkult, Palace of Arts, Theatrical Division of the Department of Education—and organized the Free Philosophical Association. In 1921 he went to Berlin, but returned to Russia two years later.

Bely, throughout his voluminous literary works, appears first of all as an ardent seeker of new truths and, as a result of his searches, a bold experimenter. He created a new literary genre, the "symphony," a novelette written in rhythmic prose and developed in form and content much after the pattern of a musical composition. In his poetry also Bely appears as an innovator, and his early verses served as a first step toward the formal revolution in Russian verse that was achieved by Blok, Akhmatova, and Mayakovsky (*qq.v.*). Bely's talents made him a legendary figure in Russian literature, and he was looked upon as the standard-bearer for those symbolists who regarded the movement as a *Weltanschauung*, rather than mere literary method (*see* French symbolism). In his "symphonies" and verses Bely reveals his belief in the Solovyovan notion that "this world is but a shadow" of another world that is revealed to a poet in moments of creative ecstasy. In his counterpoise of the real with the imaginary Bely constantly denies the empiric reality. He sees objects and people as shadows and caricatures of the prototypes of the ideal world. He is therefore prone to satirize what he sees, and in this he is undeniably a master. In his works, autobiographical to a large extent, Bely appears as an exponent of the realist current in symbolism.

Bely's many works, which reflect in content the influence of Solovyov and also of Nietzsche (*q.v.*), are characterized by their verbal artistry, rhythm, and penchant for "stylization"; his prose therefore approaches poetry. This is illustrated best by his four "symphonies" (1901–1908). His books of verse as well show him as a maker of rhythm; his *Zoloto v lazuri* (1903; Gold in Azure) is Solovyovan in content and distinctly original in form. Subsequently in *Pepel* (1904–1908; Ashes) and *Urna* (1908–1909; Urn) and in the brilliant narrative poem (*Pervoye svidaniye* (1921; The First Meeting), which in part resembles Vladimir Solovyov's *Tri svidaniya* (The Three Meetings), Bely shows in addition a reversion to the poetry of Nekrasov and Pushkin. His critical and theoretical works include *Arabeski* (1911; Arabesques), *Simvolizm* (1910; Symbolism), *Lug zelyony* (1910; Green Pastures), *Ritm, kak dialektika* (1929; Rhythm as Dialectics), *Masterstvo Gogolya* (1932; Gogol's Mastery). Of particular significance are his experiments in rhythm, for they opened the way to the researches of the formalists. Bely's volumes of memoirs, *Vospominaniya ob A. A. Bloke* (Memoirs of Blok; in *Epopeya,* 1922–1923, Nos. 1–4), *Na rubezhe dvykh stoleti* (1929; On the Border of Two Centuries), *Nachalo veka* (1932; The Beginning of a Century), and *Mezhdu dvukh revolyutsi* (1933; Between Two Revolutions), give a brilliant sketch, at times bordering on caricature, of the Russian intellectual circles of the quarter century preceding the October Revolution.

Two of Bely's novels, *Serebryany golub* (1910; The Silver Dove) and *Peterburg* (1912; Petersburg), which resemble some of the best of the fantastic pages of Gogol and Dostoevski (*q.v.*), are regarded by several critics as the masterpieces of 20th-century Russian prose; certainly, although they never achieved widespread popularity, they were assiduously studied by many a young writer. Bely's later novels, *Moskva* (1927; Moscow) and *Maski* (1933; Masks), do not measure up to his earlier works. Bely's influence has been felt by most of the leading Russian novelists of the 1920's and by such poets as Blok, Pasternak (*q.v.*), Aseyev (*q.v.*), and many another younger poet.

See: Ellis (pseud. of L. L. Kobylinski), *Russkiye simvolisty* (1910); R. V. Ivanov-Razumnik, *Vershiny* (1921); Vladimir Orlov, ed., "Aleksandr Blok i Andrei Bely, perepiska," in *Letopisi gosudastvennovo literaturnovo muzeya,* Vol. VII (1940).

O. M.

Benavente, Jacinto (1866–, Spanish dramatist), was born in Madrid. He has always lived there, and his personality and dramatic work are stamped with the unmistakable character of that city. The society of Madrid in which he has lived and moved, particularly the upper middle class and the aristocracy, constitutes the world of most of his comedies and dramas. The title of his second dramatic work, *Gente conocida* (1896), might just as well have been applied to the first, *El nido ajeno* (1894), and to most of those that followed, over a hundred in number. Before devoting himself to the theatre he had begun his literary career with a volume called *Teatro fantástico* (1892), made up of short sketches of a lyrical, imaginative nature not intended for the stage. This was followed the next year by a volume of poetry, *Versos,* and a prose work entitled *Cartas de mujeres* in which already the keen analyst of the feminine soul that Benavente has always been makes his appearance. The lyric and poetic notes also have been present, in a varying degree, in all his dramatic work. These first plays of his, refined and exquisite in their art, initiated certain aspects of the literary revolution of the end of the century, and they definitely place Benavente among the creators of modernism in Spain. His theatre stems, not from that of Echegaray (*q.v.*), against which indeed he reacted, but from the comedy of manners which had evolved in Spain, in varying forms, from Moratín to Pérez Galdós (*q.v.*), with marked influences of contemporary French and English playwrights and, a step removed, of Molière and Shakespeare, whose works he has translated. Though not without difficulty, this new theatre triumphed completely about 1905 and came to replace that of the 19th century in the trend of the writers and the taste of the public.

Outstanding among the works of his early period (1894–1905) are *La comida de las fieras* (1898), *Lo cursi* (1901), and *La gobernadora* (1901; Eng. tr., *The Governor's Wife,* 1918). Almost completely devoid of action, these plays consist of a series of scenes or pictures in which figures and types of Madrid society appear on the stage—while they themselves look on as spectators. The painting was not at all flattering; it was refined satire, faithful and keen in its analysis, always ironical in tone, reserved, and natural, but at heart cruel and implacable, without the slightest attempt at moralizing. In other works of this same period, such as *La noche del sábado* (1903; Eng. tr., *Saturday Night,* 1918) and *La princesa Bebé* (1904; Eng. tr., *Princess Bebé,* in *Plays,* Ser. 2, 1919), Benavente leaves the narrow confines of the society of Madrid and the limitations of reality for a cosmopolitan, international atmosphere, artificial and fantastic, essentially theatrical. In these works his satire takes on a symbolic, transcendental character, allowing him freely to express his ideas, fundamentally skeptical and pessimistic but tolerant and kindly, on love, education, politics, human nature. Other dramas in which symbolism enters the framework of everyday life are a blend of the two foregoing types. *Rosas de otoño* (1905; Eng. tr., *Autumnal Roses,* in *Plays,* 1919) represents the triumph of this superior form of Benavente's drama in which he expresses that conception of life found in varying forms in all his better works. Here the drama of good and evil has as its setting love and marriage; human kindness is incarnated in woman and, as in almost all of Benavente's work, is in keeping with feminine ideas and sentiments. To Benavente kindness is pity, the spirit of self-sacrifice, abnegation, generosity, accepting without protest the unavoidable evils of life, and it is stronger than brute force (*La fuerza bruta,* 1908; Eng. tr., *Brute Force,* 1935), than the evil that is done to us (*El mal que nos hacen,* 1917), stronger even than love (*Más fuerte que el amor,* 1906). This essentially Christian conception of life is in no wise in contradiction to the skeptical, pessimistic, critical, negative character which is found in his first works and which will always be the dominant characteristic of Benavente's writings, for his eye catches with greater precision, fidelity, and acuteness the weaknesses of human nature. But, in spite of this inclination, the fact that there is a touch of sweetness in his bitterness, of sadness and melancholy in his laughter, entitles Benavente to a place among the great modern satirists. Whatever place we or posterity may assign him, his art is related to that of Cervantes, Shakespeare, and Molière. The idealism, kindness, and optimism in his work counterbalance his critical, negative vision of life and humanity and elevate it to the plane of profound, consoling irony.

This moral and aesthetic conception is expressed in a variety of forms in Benavente's later works and achieves its greatest perfection, depth, and intensity in *Los malhechores del bien* (1905; Eng. tr., *The Evil Doers of Good,* in *Plays,* 1917) and *Los intereses creados* (1907; Eng. tr., *The Bonds of Interest,* in *Plays,* 1917), which both the public and the critics have considered his masterpieces. *Los malhechores del bien* presents one of the most deep-rooted and enduring traits of the Spanish character, the idea of moral tolerance. It is expressed through the satirization of outward, pharisaic goodness which smugly sets itself up as an example and rule—that intolerant, inflexible goodness which to Benavente as to the Spanish people is not only not good, but the most unbearable form of evil. In *Los intereses creados,* with classic simplicity, free from the limitations of time and space, is found the quintessence of Benavente's conception of human nature. The use of the device of two characters and two worlds which are really one might lead us to think that Benavente was approaching the aesthetic quality of the *Celestina* or of Cervantes if it were not for the contrast between the vigor and liveliness of his vision of these two worlds, the baser, evil side of humanity being so much better presented than the good.

Two works of Benavente differ markedly in character from those already mentioned—*Señora ama* (1908) and *La malquerida* (1913; Eng. tr. in *Plays,* 1917). These are rustic tragedies, simple yet masterly in their dramatic construction, of classic perfection and power. It was *La malquerida,* together with *Los intereses creados,* that established his national and international prestige and culminated in the award of the Nobel prize in 1922.

See: M. Bueno, *Teatro español contemporáneo* (1909), pp. 129–167; A. González-Blanco, *Los dramaturgos españoles contemporáneos* (1917), I, 27–168; John Dos Passos, *Rosinante to the Road Again* (1922), pp. 182–195; F. de Onís, *Jacinto Benavente; estudio literario* (1923); Walter Starkie, *Jacinto Benavente* (1924, in English); Angel Lázaro, *Jacinto Benavente; de su vida y de su obra* (1925).

F. de O.

Benda, Julien (1867–, French philosopher, essayist, and novelist), has offered in two recent volumes a recapitulation of his life as a "cleric" and a "monk" in the service of what he considers the only true religion, that of Intelligence. *La Jeunesse d'un clerc* (1936) and *Un Régulier dans le siècle* (1938) rank among the most extraordinary books of self-analysis ever written. The cold, clinical lucidity with which the author looks at himself and the world about him, his uninhibited candor, his readiness to flout every social convention that would restrict his freedom of movement, his imperviousness to even the mildest type of sentimentality—all these traits combine to make up an exceptional character whose single but devouring passion is to avoid all passions. "From the life of the heart," Benda declares, "I never expected the full expression of my being nor the satisfaction of my innermost faith. . . . Reason was my choice—reason in its nonhuman aspects."

To the reader of Benda's confessions it will doubtless appear that he had strong dispositions for this type of vocation. "Eleuthère," the Free Man, as he likes to call himself, moved very early indeed in the realm of the "nonhistorical." Born in Paris of unorthodox Jewish parents whose ancestors had been settled in France for no more than two or three generations, he felt from the start no sternly binding attachment to either land or race or religion. As a boy he admired Spinoza who, he was told, lived all alone and had an algebraic mind. As a student he applied himself with unlimited seriousness to both the sciences and the humanities, merely wondering which of the two disciplines would offer the greater guarantee of universality. Having first entered the Ecole Centrale des Arts et Manufactures, he thought better of it and wound up with a literary degree. From then on he clung to the Greco-Roman tradition and the French classical models with such aggressive partiality that cultural nationalism has sometimes been denounced as the weak spot in his "clerical" armor.

Projected against this background, Benda's career shows a remarkable consistency. He began philosophizing at the time and on the subject of the Dreyfus affair (*Dialogues à Byzance,* 1900). Recognition came, rather oddly, with a novel, *L'Ordination* (1912; Eng. tr., *The Yoke of Pity,* 1913), a powerful work the hero of which, having succumbed to the "life of the heart" after a long struggle, becomes that useless phenomenon, "a thing that loves." Then followed in quick succession three massive attacks upon the "man of the hour," Henri Bergson (*q.v.*), and his intuitive metaphysics: *Le Bergsonisme, ou une Philosophie de la mobilité* (1912); *Une Philosophie pathétique* (1913), hospitably received in his *Cahiers de la quinzaine* by the Bergsonian Charles Péguy (*q.v.*); and *Sur le succès du bergsonisme* (1914). Still during the same, fertile period Benda wrote *Belphégor* (1919; Eng. tr., 1929). Placed under the sign of the pagan god of Palestine who once inspired Machiavelli, this "essay on the aesthetics of present-day society" engulfs the vast majority of contemporary writers in a sweeping condemnation of the erratic, emotional, effeminate tendencies of our age. Romain Rolland, Paul Claudel, Maurice Barrès, Paul Bourget, Charles Maurras, Georges Sorel (*qq.v.*), and others, including Benda's former friend, Charles Péguy, and, needless to say, Henri Bergson, are summoned to the bar as utilitarians, obscurantists, and demagogues. The time is not far off when Benda will call them traitors. *La Trahison des clercs,* his most sensational book (1927; Eng. tr., *The Great Betrayal,* American title, *The Treason of the Intellectuals,* both 1928), mourns the defeatist, shameful, fateful surrender of Intelligence. Erasmus is no more. His descendants have sold his sacred trust; they have turned ideas into ideologies; they have become party men, propagandists, organizers of political passions; they adore the particular and the contingent and despise the Eternal.

La Trahison des clercs was widely misinterpreted as meaning that the intellectual must withdraw from temporal affairs. Of course he must not. Far from taking shelter in holy abstention, he enters worldly debates, but he does so as an intellectual, namely, by considering things *sub specie aeternitatis,* from the sole viewpoint of abstract truth and justice, without regard to any practical consequences whatsoever. Having definitely established this point in *La Fin de l'Eternel* (1929) and his *Essai d'un discours cohérent sur les rapports de Dieu et du monde* (1931), Benda added example to precept and offered a "clerical" discussion of such burning topics as that of nationality (*Esquisse d'une histoire des Français dans leur volonté d'être une nation,* 1932), Europeanism (*Discours à la nation européenne,* 1933), and democracy (*La Grande Epreuve des démocraties,* 1942). The manuscript of this last book, a strong, dialectical reaffirmation of the democratic principle, was smuggled out of German-dominated France and published in New York. There is, after all, courage, responsibility—and risk—in Benda's chosen profession.

See: Louis Dumont-Wilden, "Julien Benda, ou l'Idéologue passionné," *Flambeau,* I (1921), 382–413; Constant Bourquin, *Julien Benda, ou le Point de vue de Sirius* (1925); Daniel Halévy, "Deux Livres sur l'apostasie des peuples" [*La Trahison des clercs* and Jacques Maritain's (*q.v.*) *Primauté du spirituel*], *Bibliothèque universelle et revue de Genève,* II (1927), 733–750; H. E. Read, *Julien Benda and the New Humanism* (1930); Jean Malaquais, "Julien Benda et la justice abstraite," *Cahiers du sud,* XVIII (1939), 378–392.

J.-A. B.

Benedictsson, Victoria (pseud. of Ernst Ahlgren, 1850–1888, Swedish novelist and short-story writer), was born in Fru Alstad's parish in southern Skåne. A child of elderly parents whose marriage had been unhappy, she herself married, at the age of 20, a widower much older than herself in order to escape the tyranny of her parents. Later a separation took place. Meantime she had begun to try her hand at literary composition, bombarding editors of newspapers and magazines with immature romantic tales of all kinds. Upon the suggestion of one of these editors she turned soon to an entirely different subject matter, the peasant life of her native Skåne; and in this she immediately succeeded in attracting wide attention. In the course of her very short literary career of some four years were published two volumes of short stories and two novels, in addition to two unimportant plays, one in collaboration with Axel Lundegård (*q.v.*). She took her own life in Copenhagen on the night of July 21–22, 1888, because of her hopeless love for the Danish critic Georg Brandes (*q.v.*).

Despite the weak strain in her nature which precipitated the final catastrophe in her life, Victoria Benedictsson was on the whole one of the most sane and balanced literary figures of her generation. Her short stories and novels reveal a solid, healthy genius which reacted strenuously against the morbid aestheticism of certain of her immediate contemporaries. Though her art is marked by sharp individual traits, she was influenced to some extent by the Danish and Norwegian "problem literature" of her generation as well as by Dickens and George Eliot. Her two volumes of short stories, *Från Skåne* (1884; From Skåne) and *Folklif och småberättelser* (1887; Folk Life and Short Stories), deal primarily with realistic folk motifs from the south of Sweden which she knew so well. She simply describes, with no literary pretensions and no forced obtrusion of "problems" or "themes," a form of life which she had known intimately from childhood. In this description of folk life there is no attempt either to idealize or to brutalize, and hence the tales remain to our day among the most genuine and living literary documents of the 1880's. The two novels published during her lifetime, *Pengar* (1885; Money) and *Fru Marianne* (1887), as well as the posthumous novel *Modern* (1888; The Mother), are more purely in the spirit of the Scandinavian 1880's than are her short stories, particularly in their choice of subject matter, marriage and the relation between man and woman. In *Fru Marianne,* however, Victoria Benedictsson reacts strongly against the tendency of the literature of the day (*e.g., A Doll's House* by Ibsen, *q.v.*) to attack the man and glorify the woman-in-revolt in the marriage relationship. Fru Marianne is, to begin with, a kind of "doll," but she finds salvation ultimately within the marriage relationship in consequence of a growing admiration for her husband's solid though unromantic virtues. The novel becomes a hymn to man at work on the soil. Among the unfinished manuscripts which Victoria Benedictsson upon her death left with her literary executor, Axel Lundegård, were a number of short stories and a play which deal with her tragic relationship with Georg Brandes. They reveal with marvelous intensity and power the nobility of her feelings in that relationship and are among her greatest literary productions. Apart from Strindberg (*q.v.*), it may be said that the 1880's in Sweden produced no more significant literary personality than Victoria Benedictsson.

See: A. Lundegård, *Victoria Benedictsson; en självbiografi ur brev och anteckningar* (1890; 3d ed. revised and enlarged, 2 vols., 1928); F. Böök, *Sveriges moderna litteratur* (1921), also published as Vol. III of O. Sylwan, ed., *Svenska litteraturens historia* (1919–1921), pp. 135–150; Ingrid af Schultén, *Ernst Ahlgren* (1925); S. Linder, *Ernst Ahlgren i sina romaner* (1930); G. Castrén, *Den nya tiden, 1870–1914* (1932), Vol. VII of H. Schück and K. Warburg, *Illustrerad svensk litteraturhistoria,* 3d ed., pp. 176–192.

A. G.

Benediktsson, Einar (1864–1940, Icelandic poet), was born at Elliðavatn near Reykjavík, but he grew up in the North of Iceland. His father was a judge of the superior court, a district magistrate, and a political leader. Emulating the father, the son studied law in Copenhagen (graduating in 1892) and became a political editor (*Dagskrá,* 1896–1898), an attorney, and a district magistrate (1904–1907). After that he lived abroad, often in England, dividing his time between promotion of Icelandic natural resources and writing poetry, until he returned to his homeland shortly before 1930, his health broken. There he stayed in seclusion until his death.

His criticism of the older poets, especially the realists, in *Dagskrá* marks the turning point to a new national romanticism, with renewed stress on the national heritage and an insisting on a new capitalistic development of the country's natural resources. To begin with, he experimented with impressionistic prose sketches, but later he concentrated on poetry, producing the volumes *Sögur og kvæði* (1897; Stories and Poems), *Hafblik* (1906; Smooth Seas), *Hrannir* (1913; Waves), *Vogar* (1921; Inlets), and *Hvammar* (1930; Hollows). He made a translation (1901) of Ibsen's (*q.v.*) *Peer Gynt.*

Einar Benediktsson towers over his contemporaries. He is a great idealist aspiring to material as well as spiritual progress for his nation. His mind is occupied with the science and philosophy of the times, but it is also furnished with an abundance of images and patterns drawn from the native word-stock, and his power over the Icelandic language has become proverbial. His style is aristocratic and ornate, and there is hardly a slipshod note in the whole of his production. His poems are at times hard reading because of the unusually heavy burden of thought that they carry. Like Matthías Jochumsson (*q.v.*), Benediktsson is both broad and profound; but while Jochumsson centers his thought on God and man, Benediktsson starts with nature, whose outer form, land, sea, and sky, he describes with unequaled mastery and whose inner structure, from the electron to the galaxy, he seems to sense in a mystic communion. Indeed this mystic communion with the whole world, this pantheistic feeling, is evident in most of his poetry, whether he writes about the virgin nature of his homeland or the works of man in civilized countries—the forges of Newcastle upon Tyne, an evening in Rome, Stockholm, Fifth Avenue. He has tried to formulate his pantheistic religion in the essay "Alhygð" in *Eimreiðin* (1926).

In the beginning Benediktsson was a progressive national romanticist urging his compatriots not only to conserve the precious part of their heritage, their language and literature, but also to throw off their political yoke and even more so the sloth of centuries in order to join in the rapid progress of industrialization. What he preached he tried to carry out in practice, but without much success. In his later years his philosophical and mystic bent came more to the fore, but he never lost his dream of progress and expansion. In his poetry he roamed vikinglike over many lands in search of subjects, but no amount of foreign influence ever brought him to forget his beloved homeland.

See: K. Andrésson, *Einar Benediktsson sjötugur* (1934); R. Beck, "Iceland's 'Poet Laureate,'" *Books Abroad,* X (1936), 270–271; S. Nordal, "Einar Benediktsson," *Skírnir,* CXIV (1940), 5–23.

S. E.

Benelli, Sem (1875–, Italian dramatist), was born in Prato in Toscana. He has had a long career, writing many plays which commanded attention at the time of their production, but it seems likely that he will be remembered principally as the author of *La Cena delle beffe* (1909; the dates used here are those of presentation, not of publication). In its way this is as good a play as any in the modern Italian theatre; *La Cena* has not the intellectual appeal of a Pirandello (*q.v.*) drama, but it has more feeling, more poetry, and certainly an individuality of its own. The background of the Renaissance with its contrasts of subtlety and violence, refinement and brutality, is brought to a focus in a plot which has something of the flavor of a *novella. La Cena* portrays the traditional astute weakling who gains his terrible vengeance over the bullies who torment him, but the story is told with a psychological awareness which is quite modern and prevents the play from being merely a period piece. Not the least of its qualities is the language; a staccato blank verse, full of imagery and feeling, gives the play its tempo. *La Cena* won international acclaim (Eng. trs., *The Jester's Supper,* 1924–1925, *The Jest,* 1939); in no other play did Benelli show the same technical skill or create the same emotional intensity. The best of his other works, *La Maschera di Bruto* (1908), *L'Amore dei tre re* (1910), *Le Nozze dei centauri* (1915) have, it is true, the same elements, but the fusion of the lyric and the dramatic is not successfully achieved. *Tignola* (1908) is a sort of modern dress version of *La Cena* but lacking its power, and *Il Vezzo di perle* (1926) is a comedy that has charm but is of no particular importance.

Benelli was not merely a dramatist. He served his country as a soldier in the First World War and afterwards entered politics, being elected deputy in 1921. It would seem that the war had an important effect on his inspiration; his post-war plays, though not uninteresting, reveal an unsettled psychology, a restless striving after a new vein. In the late 20's he became manager of a company dedicated to producing plays of real artistic and literary merit on the Italian stage. In this venture Benelli had considerable success; his last noteworthy work, *Orfeo e Proserpina* (1929), was written for and produced by this company. The *Opere* of Benelli, one play to each of the 30 volumes, were published in 1934.

See: C. Lori, *S. Benelli, il suo teatro, la sua compagnia* (1928).

T. G. B.

Bengtsson, Frans Gunnar (1894–, Swedish essayist), born in Tossjö, province of Skåne, is a gentleman scholar with remarkably sensitive and highly developed literary talents. He has tried his hand with very considerable success as a lyric poet (*Tärningskast,* 1923, Throw of the Dice; *Legenden om Babel,* 1925, The Legend of Babel), as a translator (*Paradise Lost, Chanson de Roland*), as a biographer (*Karl XII,* 2 vols., 1935–1936), and, most recently, as a historical novelist (*Röde Orm,* 1942; Eng. tr., *Red Orm,* 1943). But he excels in the informal personal essay, a literary genre which he alone among modern Swedish authors handles with consummate skill and complete mastery. His first volume of essays, *Litteratörer och militärer* (1929; Literary and Military Figures), revealed him as a finished practitioner of informal prose exposition; and three volumes of essays which followed—*Silversköldarna* (1931; The Silver Shields), *De långhåriga merovingerna* (1933; The Long-haired Merovingians), and *Sällskap för en eremit* (1938; Companionship for a Hermit)—have firmly established him as the incomparably most distinguished Swedish exponent of the literary genre developed with so much success in England and France during the 19th century. In form Bengtsson's essays are primarily in the great tradition of the informal essay in England. They are particularly related, it would seem, to the essays of the romantics Lamb and Hazlitt, and perhaps to those of Stevenson, though the Swedish essayist's prose is nowhere slavishly imitative in manner. It is rather a marvelously virile, precise, and flexible medium of expression for a vigorous, many faceted, and astonishingly learned mind. The immense erudition in these essays—which includes a penchant that amounts almost to a passion for unusual, off the beaten track areas of knowledge—is handled lightly, with a grace and ease and a pulsing stylistic flair that one tends to associate with the clever dilettante rather than with the precise thinker or the serious scholar. In subject matter Bengtsson wanders widely over the whole range of human experience and the whole calendar of historical and semihistorical records and events. His earlier essays concerned themselves, apparently by personal preference, with literary figures and military heroes; one essay on Villon and another on General Stonewall Jackson are certainly among the best short prose sketches of these two personalities. His later essays reveal that he can write with fascinating freshness and comprehension on such well-worn themes as the difficulties of maintaining an optimistic view of human existence ("Försök till optimistisk betraktelse") or man's relation to nature ("Vintermänniskan"), or he can indulge in outpourings or apparently inexhaustible whimsicalities on such topics as the curious vagaries of his own literary tastes ("Framför en bokhylla") or the physical and mental habits of semidomesticated cats, rats, and bats ("Det närmaste sällskapet"). Serious or whimsical, penetrating or playful, satiric or constructive in purpose, Bengtsson is always interesting, for his essays give inimitable spontaneous expression to a restless, original mind possessing a natural flair for the unexpected, the unusual, one might almost say the unique. In tone and point of view Bengtsson may be said to combine in his essays something of the whimsicality of a Lamb with the vigor and independence of spirit of a Hazlitt and the heroic-romantic ideal of a Stevenson.

See: O. Bjurling, "Frans Bengtsson poeten och filosofen," *Ord och bild,* XLI (1932), 377–379.

A. G.

Benjamin, René (1885–, French novelist, dramatist, and critic), was born in Paris and educated at the Sorbonne. At the beginning of the First World War he had made a moderate reputation with a novel, *Madame Bonheur* (1909), a comedy, *Le Pacha* (1911), and two volumes of amusing but not very penetrating criticism of French officialdom, *La Farce de la Sorbonne* (1911; enlarged ed., 1921) and *Les Justices de paix* (1913). In 1915, however, his novel *Gaspard,* whose highly conventional hero demonstrated the heroism of the Parisian "little man" against the *boche,* found a ready-made public and won the Prix Goncourt. Since then Benjamin has produced prolifically without greatly adding to his reputation. His most successful work has been not his comedies or novels but the continuation of his satiric attacks on pretentiousness in high places, such as *Aliborons et démagogues* (1927) and *Au soleil de la poésie: Sous l'œil en fleur de Madame de Noailles* (1928). Witty and urbane, catching with a few swift strokes the very accent and visage of his victims, these sketches, whether of professors, judges and lawyers, politicians, or modern poets, cut through the haze of convention and tradition to reveal that it often hides the supremely ridiculous. Benjamin's point of view is essentially that of the rather skeptical bourgeois, and his success consists of applying to more exalted and pretentious circles the standards of common sense by which the average man would judge his neighbor. The results were superficially devastating. But Benjamin is no Voltaire, and the easygoing attitude, the bourgeois good humor, that makes him often more pleasant reading than Voltaire at the same time keeps him from going very deep, from ever grappling with ultimate principles. With *La Prodigieuse Vie d'Honoré de Balzac* (1925; Eng. tr., *Balzac*, 1927) Benjamin entered a new field. He has written since then a large number of popular biographies, notably *Joffre* (1929), *Molière* (1936), and *Marie Antoinette* (1940), marked by an entertaining style and his usual common sense but on the whole not rising greatly above the level of journalism. *Les Sept Etoiles de France* (1942) is a routine glorification of Pétain, and not even very good journalism.

Versatile as he is, in all his work Benjamin seems to be the victim of his own facility and his willingness to capitalize immediately on the undoubted power of his lively, practical, but often superficial mind. He was elected to the Goncourt Academy in 1938.

See: Lucien Dubech, *Les Chefs de file* (1925).

C. W., Jr.

Benn, Gottfried (1886–, German poet and critic), was born in Mansfeld, son of a Protestant minister and a Frenchwoman. Before the First World War intensified his personal problem, Benn, who as physician had specialized in venereal diseases, published his first poems under the significant title *Morgue* (1912). He continued to write while serving in the army, and *Fleisch* (1917) and *Schutt* (1924) evidenced an uncompromising pessimism. Much later, he turned to critical and essayistic prose—*Nach dem Nihilismus* (1932), *Der neue Staat und die Intellektuellen* (1933), *Kunst und Macht* (1934). Meanwhile he had written a number of stories ("Gehirne," "Die Eroberung," "Die Reise," "Der Geburtstag," all in the volume *Gehirne*, 1916) and a few dramatic scenes.

The importance of Benn for German literature transcends by far the value of his individual works, few if any of which may survive. In the unmitigated horror of his images he stands in the forefront of those German expressionists who, scorning the flight from life of the neo-romanticist or the cool impersonality of the impressionist, hurled themselves in passionate rebellion against the demons of a mechanized world, insisting upon the regeneration of man and the rediscovery of God. Benn functions here negatively, so to speak, carrying the work of the literary naturalist one step farther: the horrors he reports must lead to reform and reversal. In his prose he shares in those daring linguistic experiments which triumphantly demonstrated unsuspected possibilities of language.

B. Q. M.

Benoit, Pierre (1886–, French novelist), was born in Albi, Tarn; his childhood was spent in Tunisia and Algeria in the various garrisons to which his father, an army officer, was assigned. This background partly explains his love of travel and his inappeasable curiosity concerning picturesque places and exotic countries. In 1910, having started the study of law in Algiers, completed his military service in a regiment of Zouaves, and obtained his degree in literature in Montpellier, he went to Paris to prepare for a degree in history. His preparation was not, however, of a very serious nature. He much preferred the society of his friends, many of whom were also to make a name for themselves in the world of letters, such as Francis Carco, Pierre Mac-Orlan, and Roland Dorgelès (*qq.v.*). He failed to receive his degree but later, having passed an examination for a position in the Ministry of Public Instruction, became a government employee. During the First World War he served as a lieutenant and was wounded.

At the time of his arrival in Paris, Benoit had already written a play, which has never been published, and several poems, which appeared in 1914 under the title *Diadumène*. His first novel, *Koenigsmark* (1918), enjoyed great success and revealed its author to be a talented novelist. Conceived during the war, it is natural that it should deal with Germany. *L'Atlantide* (1919), one of the first best sellers of the post-war period, was a very well done adventure story. The scene of *Pour Don Carlos* (1920) is Spain, of *Le Lac salé* (1921) Utah, of *La Chaussée des géants* (1922) the Ireland of the Sinn Feiners. *Mlle de la Ferté* (1923) takes place in France, as does *Le Roman des quatre*, published in the same year and written in collaboration with Paul Bourget, Gérard d'Houville (*qq.v.*), and Henri Duvernois.

Because his duties with the Ministry of Public Instruction did not leave him sufficient leisure, Benoit resigned and in 1923 left for a 22-month tour through Turkey and Syria, from which he brought back *La Châtelaine du Liban* (1924) and *Le Puits de Jacob* (1925). A trip to the Far East furnished him with the inspiration for *Le Roi lépreux* (1927). There but remained for him to take a trip around the world, and this he proceeded to do. From Suez he went to Ceylon, Australia, New Caledonia, the New Hebrides, Tahiti, Panama, and the Antilles. Upon his return he wrote *Erromango* (1929), the locale of which is the

New Hebrides. The heroine of *Le Soleil de minuit* (1930) is called Amide, and like all the author's heroines her name begins with the letter A. His *Axelle* (1928) conforms to this rule, and in it he once again treats of Germany and of the camps of war prisoners there. Since 1930 Benoit has every year written a love and adventure story, usually cleverly done and easy to read. He was elected to the French Academy in 1931.

See: René Aigrain, "L'Art et l'érudition de M. Pierre Benoit," *Correspondant*, CCLXXVIII (1920), 701–719; Armand Praviel, "Un Romancier de Gascogne: M. Pierre Benoit," *Correspondant*, CCLXXXVII (1922), 835–847.

P. B.

Berdyayev, Nikolai Aleksandrovich (1874–, Russian theologian, philosopher, and critic), is perhaps the foremost interpreter of modern Russian orthodoxy, whose challenging analyses of the philosophy of religion and history have exerted considerable influence in the Western World, without, however, having founded any school. An eclectic, he has followed no single master, though he has been variously influenced by Marx, Hegel, Schopenhauer, Nietzsche (*q.v.*), and Solovyov (*q.v.*). His thinking is essentially apocalyptic and eschatological. Its emphasis is on the moral and spiritual depths of the contemporary crisis in Western civilization. He attacks the heresies of racialism and collectivism, which in his view mean the end of Renaissance humanism with its basis in individualism and which herald a new Middle Ages. From this will emerge an era of a newly spiritualized man. In this cyclical conception of history Berdyayev is closer to St. Augustine than to Spengler. To Berdyayev history per se is tragic, but its contradictions may be resolved when set against the background of eternity.

Berdyayev was born in Kiev and educated in the Kiev Cadet Corps and in the University of Kiev, first in the faculty of natural sciences, then in the law school. Ever a stormy petrel, he has more than once run afoul of established policy. As a youth he became a student of Marxism. In 1898 he was arrested and expelled from the university. His first article appeared (1899) in *Die neue Zeit,* followed by his first book, *Subektivizm i individualizm v obshchestvennoi filosofii* (1900; Subjectivism and Individualism in Social Philosophy); this brought about a three-year exile in the Vologda region. In 1904 he became editor of *Novy put* (The New Path), and in 1905 editor of *Voprosy zhizni* (Problems of Life). Just before the fall of the monarchy (1917) he was again in jeopardy for having criticized the Erastianism of the governing synod of the Orthodox Church. After the Revolution he founded (1919) in Moscow the Free Academy of Spiritual Culture and was given the chair of philosophy at the University of Moscow. His defense of religion caused first his imprisonment and finally his exile (1922). He went to Berlin and thence to Paris (1934), where he has since resided as director of the Academy of the Philosophy of Religion, first founded by him in Berlin, and as editor of *Put* (Path).

Berdyayev has published a long series of works, widely translated, of which the most important are *Novoye srednevekovie* (1923; A New Middle Ages), *Mirosozertzanie Dostoyevskago* (1923; Eng. tr., *Dostoievsky,* 1934), *O naznachenii cheloveka* (1931; Eng. tr., *The Destiny of Man,* 1935), *Filosofiya svobodnago dukha* (1927; The Philosophy of the Free Spirit), which was awarded a prize by the French Academy, *Smysl istorii* (1923; Eng. tr., *The Meaning of History,* 1936), *Dukh i realnost* (1937; Eng. tr., *Spirit and Reality,* 1939), *Konstantin Leontev* (published in a French tr., 1938; Eng. tr., *Constantine Leontiev,* 1940). Other books, available in English, are *The Russian Revolution; Two Essays on Its Implication in Religion and Psychology* (1931), *The End of Our Time* (1933), *The Bourgeois Mind and Other Essays* (1934), *Freedom and the Spirit* (1935), *The Origin of Russian Communism* (1937), *War and the Christian Conscience* (1938), *Slavery and Freedom* (1943).

See: Eberhard Dennert, *Die Krisis der Gegenwart und die kommende Kultur: Eine Einfuehrung in die Geschichtsphilosophie Berdjajews* (1928); Leo Shestov, "Nikolai Berdyayev: gnosis i ekzistentsialnaya filosofiya," *Sovremennyia zapiski,* LXVII (1938), 196–229; Monroe Beardsley, "Berdyaev: Sybil in Waste Land," *Russian Review,* II (1943), 10–18.

N. S.

Berent, Wacław (1873–1940, Polish novelist), was born in Warsaw, the son of a prominent dealer in optical instruments. A passion for research was Berent's most marked trait, from his boyish excursions into the natural world with the help of his father's microscopes to the final accumulation of primary material for his *Zmierzch wodzów* (1939; Twilight of the Leaders). The same zeal for investigation which won Berent a doctorate in biology from Munich in his early 20's drove him later as a man of letters to undertake the task of revealing through the novel the "genealogy of the Polish soul" from the partitions to the resurrection. His pioneer work in the execution of this task was *Fachowiec* (1898; The Expert), a portrait of Polish society in the epoch of positivism, when youth fled from cultural pursuits into engineering and business. Next came *Próchno* (1901; Rotten Wood), a case study of the Young Poland era and of the *fin-de-siècle* mood in general, based on Berent's own experiences and observations over a wide area, including Munich and Paris, Zurich and Berlin, as well as Cracow and his native Warsaw. After this followed *Ozimina* (1911; Winter Wheat), which Berent intended as an answer to the *Wesele* of Wyspiański (*q.v.*) but which was in reality only a Warsaw counterpart of that Cracovian warning, since in this the author depicted with exact fidelity the *danse macabre* of Polish life in the capital on the eve of the Russo-Japanese War. Finally, in the cycle *Nurt* (The Current), Berent delineated, in order, the buriers of Poland (*Pogrobowcy,* 1934), then certain of her restorers (*Diogenes w kontuszu,* 1937; Diogenes in Polish Dress). Berent's last work, the abovementioned *Zmierzch wodzów*), was a fictionized evocation of certain of Poland's "last leaders," notably General Dąbrowski.

Berent endeavored in all his writings to suit his style to the period in question, and the effort, coupled with the fact that he was an investigator by temperament rather than an artist, made his style often seem labored and artificial. A deep student of Nietzsche (*q.v.*) and an admirer of the Middle Ages—this is seen especially in *Żywe kamienie* (1918; Living Stones)—Berent was also a great Warsaw patriot and to the end of making Warsaw a great intellectual and artistic center founded in 1930 a new literary monthly, *Pamiętnik warszawski* (Warsaw Memoir). Berent lived to see all his dreams for his native city shattered and the city itself in ruins under German occupation.

See: Z. Dębicki, *Portrety,* I (1927), 85–105; reviews in *Wiadomości literackie,* 1934, No. 47, 1937, No. 13, 1939, No. 23; M. Kridl, "Wacław Berent, 1873–1940," *Slavonic Year-Book,* XX (1941), 401–404.

A. P. C.

Bergamín, José (1894–, Spanish essayist), was born in Madrid. He is a prominent figure in the group of writers of the post-war generation who, influenced by current literary taste, tend to adopt shorter forms of prose expression. The most consummate examples of this fragmentation of the literary unit are seen in the "glosses" of Eugenio D'Ors, in the *greguerías* of Ramón Gómez de la Serna (*qq.v.*), and, as its most recent manifestation, in the "aphorisms" of Bergamín.

His first book, *El cohete y la estrella* (1923), and also some of his most felicitous contributions such as *La cabeza a pájaros* (1934) are in this manner. Notwithstanding his very modern sensibility, Bergamín has pronounced Spanish roots; in a sense he directly stems from the Generation of '98 and was influenced by the master Unamuno (*q.v.*), from whom he takes a number of themes; more remotely he is connected with the classic writers of Spanish thought and language. Bergamín at times is closer to the literary processes arising with the Generation of '98 than to the evolution of taste after the First World War. His group posited a whole series of ideological and stylistic problems. Then, as it sought a new linguistic flexibility, as it rejuvenated words by giving them new yet pristine meanings, a rhetoric was evolved in certain sectors of Spanish prose which in successive stages becomes linguistic "wit," the modern "conceptism" of Bergamín. He himself offers us a sagacious interpretation of the related spirit of the 17th century in his work *Mangas y capirotes* (1933).

"Popular" themes are part of Bergamín's inspiration. Popular thought and sentiment are ever present in his work. He frequently starts the development of a theme or the conclusion or analysis of a bit of reasoning with a word used in the sense given it by the people. He often makes use of a saying or a proverb from which he draws all the depth and wisdom that it has lost in the course of being bandied about from mouth to mouth. Sometimes he modifies a proverb by altering its traditional meaning in favor of a new one, or he combines popular expressions to reach an unexpected conclusion. Frequently the best and most attractive part of his prose results from this literary manipulation. Bergamín makes real discoveries, full of philosophic meaning, of a trenchant wit and humor which connects him with certain permanent modalities of the Spanish spirit. This humor, bitter at times, this "intention," his vivaciousness and passionate interest in the current or historical themes that he treats, prevent his work from degenerating into a pure display of cleverness. A militant fervor, an intellectual passion, are constant in his writings. Often, along with the deft selection of expression, there is an echo of the impassioned and lyrical tremor of Unamuno.

From the beginning Bergamín found his norm in a Catholic position, continually vivified by doubt. This is an interior combative position, much in harmony with his temperament. He was the founder in Madrid of *Cruz y raya* (1933–1936), a journal which, besides collecting the most select Spanish literature produced during the years of its publication, reflected the Catholic and liberal, the religious and ideological position of Bergamín, who had close connections with the French and Belgian group of the journal *Esprit*. In the light of his character, he could not help taking a definite position in the Spanish civil struggle, and he was an ardent supporter of the cause of the people. More recently, from his refuge in Mexico City, some of his latest books (*e.g., Detrás de la cruz*, 1941) are devoted to the spiritual drama of the Spanish people. In this city he is continuing his publishing activity as the founder and editor of the publishing establishment "Séneca."

See: P. Salinas, *Literatura española siglo XX* (1941).

F. G. L.

Berger, Johan Henning (1872–1924, Swedish novelist and dramatist), a native of Stockholm, spent the 1890's in the United States, for the most part in Chicago. Later he visited Munich and Paris and after 1902 Copenhagen became his official residence.

Berger's work is founded primarily on his own experiences; *e.g., Ysaïl* (1905) and *Bendel & C:o* (1910), the second novel of the trilogy *Drömlandet* (1909–1911; The Land of Dreams), have settings laid in Chicago. At times Berger seems to be baldly realistic, but his work bears the hallmark of impressionism. There is no deep probing, no profound experiencing; rather, there is a deployment of poignant emotions, with that of pain predominating. Although strong in descriptive powers, Berger revealed weaknesses in plot construction. His outstanding works are *Ysaïl*, the trilogy *Drömlandet, Livets blommor* (1912; Life's Flowers), and the drama *Syndafloden* (1908; produced in the United States in 1917 as *The Deluge*). Berger often depicted Swedish immigrants who could not adapt themselves to the American environment. The figures are sensitive creatures fashioned for intense suffering, even from superficial hurts. They long for the world of dreams and are bitterly disappointed in never attaining it.

See: A. Möller, ed., *Boken om Henning Berger, en minnesgärd av hans vänner* (1924); E. Norling, *Mänskligt* (1930), pp. 149–191, 229–271.

C. E. W. L. D.

Bergman, Bo (1869–, Swedish lyrist, critic, and writer of short stories), was born in Stockholm and educated at Uppsala. At first an official in the Post Office Department, he has mainly worked as a newspaper critic. He made his debut as a poet with *Marionetterna* (1903; Marionettes). This he followed with other volumes of lyrics and of short stories, notably *Skeppet* (1915; The Ship). Bergman is a city recluse, a serene observer of life, who has a deep love for both the past and present of his native city. Although not an outstanding figure, he has a certain mastery in whatever he undertakes: essay, narrative, or verse. Inclined to pessimism, he cultivates the mood of sunset with especial charm. There is something of Wordsworth in Bo Bergman's poetry—an observant eye, a serious trend of thought, and a spirit attuned to the bliss of solitude. In his stories there is a similar fineness of perception and an understanding pity for the victims of complex maladjustments. In this he shows the influence of Hjalmar Söderberg (*q.v.*). Bergman has well deserved the distinction of membership in the Swedish Academy.

See: C. W. Stork, *Anthology of Swedish Lyrics* (1917; revised and enlarged ed., 1930); H. A. Larsen, ed., *Sweden's Best Stories* (1928); G. Bach, *The History of the Scandinavian Literatures*, ed. by Frederika Blankner (1938).

C. W. S.

Bergman, Hjalmar (1883–1930, Swedish novelist and playwright), was born at Örebro, a small residential town in central Sweden. Delicate and sensitive as a child, he suffered all his life from mental depression. He studied at Uppsala and in Italy, specializing in history and philosophy, but the most important part of his education was the knowledge of local life he obtained through the clientele of his father, who was a banker. Marrying into a well-known theatrical family, Bergman became early familiar with the stage and began his literary career as a dramatist. He won a decided success in comedy, having several plays produced at the Royal Dramatic Theatre. His most important piece, *Swedenhielms* (1925; The Swedenhielm Family), is a study of amusing artistic types.

It was, however, in the novel and short story that Hjalmar Bergman attained his fullest expression. From 1910 to 1930 he was the most popular prose writer in Sweden, producing volume after volume of such variety in mood and characterization that he has been called by some a Swedish Dickens. He began in a tragic vein with exotic scenes inspired by his sojourn in Italy and the Near East, notably the volume *Amours* (1910), a group of masterly studies in sex psychology. He then turned to themes in many other times and places, but most significantly to contemporary life in the small Swedish town and in Stockholm. This group of novels may, on a small scale, be compared to *La Comédie humaine* of Balzac. Conspicuous among them are *Markurells i Wadköping* (1919; Eng. tr., *God's Orchid,* 1924); *Farmor och Vår Herre* (1921; The Grandmother and Our Lord); and *Chefen fru Ingeborg* (1924, Madame Directress Ingeborg; Eng. tr., *The Head of the Firm,* 1936). There is in these a sharp cynical tone, much more akin indeed to the French masters than to Dickens, as well as an increasing influence of Freudian abnormality. The result is brilliant and highly sensational, not always agreeable to conventional readers. The plots frequently border on the grotesque and improbable. It is perhaps in his short stories that Hjalmar Bergman is most satisfying. Yet in all his work he shows deep insight and a command of plastic and vivid style that raise him close to the best in modern fiction.

See: R. G. Berg, "Preface," in Bergman, *The Head of the Firm* (1936); G. Bach, *The History of the Scandinavian Literatures,* ed. by Frederika Blankner (1938); E. Linder, *Hjalmar Bergmans ungdom* (1942).

C. W. S.

Bergson, Henri (1859–1941, French philosopher), undoubtedly possessed and illustrated some of the finest qualities of the French genius; yet, to the confusion of race theorists, not a drop of Gallic blood was flowing in his veins. His ancestors had been wealthy, orthodox Jewish merchants of Warsaw, who shipped grain down the Vistula to Danzig. His father, a musician and composer, roamed Western Europe and married an English girl by the name of Katherine Levinson. Their children were British citizens, and the future philosopher, though born and reared in Paris, became a naturalized Frenchman only after receiving his bachelor's degree. As late as 1878–1881 professors and students of the Ecole Normale Supérieure pronounced him *très anglais* in his training and mental bent. Did he not, in a generation newly won over to Kantianism, present the unusual spectacle of remaining faithful to the tenets of John Stuart Mill and Herbert Spencer?

It was not long, however, before the young educator, then in the provinces, underwent a spiritual crisis of his own. It dawned upon him that mechanistic hypotheses, and our ordinary activities as well, rest on a conception of time thoroughly incompatible with the immediate data of consciousness. Time as we perceive it from within is not at all that homogeneous, quantitative substance which the clock parcels out in equal installments. "Lived time," or duration, is irregular, qualitative, indivisible. Valid though they may be, even indispensable, for practical purposes, the mensurations of the dial rob time of its temporal essence; they are indeed but a symbolical substitute borrowed from the categories of space; they transcribe something intensive into something extensive, something alive into something inert, something of the spirit into something of matter.

Such was Bergson's famous "intuition of duration," a truly decisive step in his career since it determined both the method and the content of his doctrine. Starting from the pragmatic assumption that our subservience to the external world tends to standardize and mechanize the processes of the mind, Bergsonian philosophy boldly proceeds to reverse the trend and to remove, as it were, the several layers of materiality accumulated upon us. The *Essai sur les données immédiates de la conscience,* Bergson's doctoral dissertation (1889; Eng. tr., *Time and Free Will,* 1910) proclaims the freedom of the mind as an experimental fact, directly ascertainable by intuition, although most men ignore it and their superficial psychic states are heavily embedded in the law of necessity. *Matière et mémoire* (1896; Eng. tr., *Matter and Memory,* 1911) asserts just as positively that our so-called past recollections preserve an immanent existence and are always present within us or, in other terms, that the mind, being one continuous flow of consciousness, never forgets, never distinguishes between today and yesterday, whereas the brain, supposedly the receptacle of memory, is but an instrument of selection which eliminates and throws into oblivion what is not useful to us. Finally, *L'Evolution créatrice* (1907; Eng. tr., *Creative Evolution,* 1911) defines the mind as undiluted energy, knowing itself intuitively as a genetic impulse, an *élan vital,* ever swelling, ever "becoming," ever participating in the universal creation of forms, despite and against the downward, the deadly pull of instinctive passivity.

Rather foolish doubts have been cast occasionally on Bergson's originality. But these three great, epochal books, however much they may owe to Heraclitus, Plotinus, Maine de Biran (1766–1824), Félix Ravaisson (1823–

1900), Emile Boutroux (*q.v.*), and a score of others, bear in themselves sufficient testimony that he who wrote them knew how to melt a variety of elements in the crucible of his own thought. Other works by him merely strengthen the very personal fiber of his doctrine. *Le Rire*, a little classic (1900; Eng. tr., *Laughter*, 1911), stresses the ridiculous character of whatever in man is grossly reminiscent of the mechanical. *L'Energie spirituelle* (1919; Eng. tr., *Mind-Energy*, 1920) and *La Pensée et le mouvant* (1934) are collections of essays with self-explanatory titles. In *Durée et simultanéité* (1922) Bergson appraises his theories in relation to those of Einstein. As for *Les Deux Sources de la morale et de la religion* (1932; Eng. tr., *The Two Sources of Morality and Religion*, 1935), this book, in many respects the author's testament, effects a near-fusion of Bergsonism and Christianity. The former disciple of Spencer, having demonstrated to his satisfaction the factual immanence of the soul, is now willing to admit of its immortality.

Anti-intellectual in the sense that it grants intelligence the privilege of "thinking matter" but denies it the higher one of "understanding life," the new metaphysics drew heavy fire from the rationalists (*e.g.*, Julien Benda, *q.v.*). When called a mystic, a fetishist, a dreamer, Bergson rebelled, clinging to his tenacious belief in the experimental value of intuition. When called a poet he softened because, after all, he was quite aware of being one—the rediscoverer of some sort of paradise lost, a supreme artisan of words and images, who broke the automatism of language, who, with the help of metaphors, suggested at least, if he could not express, the reality that he had seen. Thus Bergson was a stirrer of souls. His courses at the Collège de France, where he was made a professor in 1900, held spellbound huge crowds of listeners (among them the usual number of snobs and fashionable women) who thronged the lecture room hours before his arrival. In much the same manner *L'Evolution créatrice* fascinated readers all over the world. International from then on, the Bergsonian current ran its unpredictable course far beyond the limits of philosophy proper. Bergsonism outside of Bergson is much less a body of doctrine, faithfully accepted and transmitted as such, than it is an *état d'âme* or, more appropriately still, an *élan vital.* In France alone, it pervaded literature through Charles Péguy and Marcel Proust (*qq.v.*); it entered the field of literary criticism through Albert Thibaudet (*q.v.*) and that of aesthetics through Tancrède de Visan (1878–; see his *Attitude du lyrisme contemporain*, 1911); it made itself felt in psychopathology with Charles Blondel (1876–), in sociology with Maurice Halbwachs (1877–), even in syndicalistic theory with Georges Sorel (*q.v.*). To Edouard Le Roy (1870–), Bergson's successor in the Collège de France (1921), fell the task of achieving the complete merger of Bergsonism and Catholic theology.

Elected to the French Academy in 1914, chosen by the League of Nations as the first chairman of its International Committee on Intellectual Cooperation (1921–1925), awarded the Nobel prize in 1927, Bergson rode on the crest of honors until his health broke down. The last years of his life were a long agony of bedridden invalidism. But as if to crown his evidence with the most triumphant argument of them all, the flame of the spirit shone to the last in the stricken body.

See: Albert Thibaudet, *Trente Ans de vie française*, Vol. III in 2 vols.: *Le Bergsonisme* (1923); Jacques Chevalier, *Bergson* (1926; Eng. tr., 1928); André Metz, *Bergson et le bergsonisme* (1933); Gilbert Maire, *Bergson, mon maître* (1935); Alfredo Coviello, "Bibliografia bergsoniana," *Sustancia* (Tucumán, Argentina), II (1941), 394–440 (also 11 articles by various collaborators, pp. 317 ff.).

J.-A. B.

Bernanos, Georges (1888–, French novelist and political writer), was born in Paris. He suddenly came into the limelight in 1926 with the publication of *Sous le soleil de Satan* (Eng. tr., *The Star of Satan*, 1940), a powerful study of mysticism and satanism, a masterpiece of French fiction. Up to 1926 his literary activity had been limited to occasional articles in the *Action française*, the *Revue universelle*, and less widely known royalist newspapers and magazines. He is both a novelist of rare originality and an effective polemist.

Bernanos can perhaps be best characterized as a firm believer in the essential dignity of man and a militant Christian for whom sanctity constitutes the highest form of adventure and heroism. The comment attributed to him by a critic to the effect that all Dostoevski (*q.v.*) should be done over in a Catholic spirit best illustrates the fundamental aim which he has pursued not only in *Sous le soleil de Satan*, but in the novels *L'Imposture* (1927), *La Joie* (1929), and *Journal d'un curé de campagne* (1936; Eng. tr., *The Diary of a Country Priest*, 1937). Succeeding where Huysmans and Léon Bloy (*qq.v.*) had failed in the final decades of the last century, he has described in these books the mysterious reactions of the human soul to the solicitations of divine grace in a way satisfactory to exacting literary critics and to informed students of mystical theology.

As a polemist Bernanos is strongly opposed to the spirit of parliamentary democracy because, according to him, this form of government is based upon a materialistic philosophy which offers no real check to the greed and selfishness of the financially powerful and leads inevitably to either economic or political tyranny. For France he advocates a return to monarchy as the political regime offering the best guarantees for the harmonious development of a society based upon true honor and justice. The policy of appeasement pursued by the great powers, more particularly by certain elements in his own country, in connection with the conquest of Ethiopia, the destruction of Loyalist Spain by the forces of fascism, and the dismemberment of Czechoslovakia at Munich constitutes in his estimation one of the blackest and most shameful pages in the history of mankind. It is also his earnest conviction that Western civilization can be saved from total disintegration only by a spiritual revival based upon the unequivocal acceptance of the Roman Catholic interpretation of the concepts of justice, honor, and freedom. His plea for a new moral order is not addressed exclusively, or even specifically, to those outside the Catholic Church, but is intended just as much for members of that body. Many Catholic leaders, the author contends, have allowed casuistry and opportunism to lead them into unholy alliances with the forces of reaction. These views, which form the sum and substance of the political creed of Bernanos, have been expressed with great force and earnestness in *La Grande Peur des bien-pensants: Edouard Drumont* (1931), *Les Grands Cimetières sous la lune* (1938; Eng. tr., *A Diary of My Times*, 1938), *Scandale de la vérité* (1939), *Nous autres Français* (1939), and *Lettre aux Anglais* (1942; Eng. tr., *Plea for Liberty*, 1944).

See: Pierre Brodin, "Georges Bernanos," in *Maîtres et témoins de l'entre-deux-guerres* (1943), pp. 183–199.

J. M. C.

Bernard, Jean Jacques (1888–, French dramatist and novelist), born at Enghien-les-Bains, is the son of the well-known playwright Tristan Bernard (*q.v.*) He is the outstanding exponent of the dramatic theory baptized the "school of silence." According to it "the theatre is first and foremost the art of expressing what is unspoken," that is to say, the inaudible but pregnant speech of the heart and soul, what lies inhibited or buried in the subconsciousness, what a pretentious rhetoric befogs or conceals behind a screen of words.

Bernard's talent, first revealed before the First World War, came to flower in his post-war theatre, in *La Maison épargnée* (1919) and especially in *Le Feu qui reprend mal* (1921; Eng. tr., *The Sulky Fire*, 1939), both dramas of soldiers who return from war to face, the one an unsympathetic environment and the other love grown cold through absence and not readily rekindled. His art reached its peak in *Martine* (1922; Eng. tr., 1927), which tells the simple tale of a peasant girl's romance with a city charmer, blighted all too soon. Here is pure drama in its very essence, freed from all rhetoric, ideology, and dramatic trappings. The characters in it are transparent, the passion is both intense and diaphanous.

The same qualities characterize the rest of Bernard's delicately intimate dramas. He has mirrored the illusions and deceptions of life, its pipe dreams, the rainbows of romance and highways of desire, which the imagination builds from the horizons to one's doors and which reality pricks like bubbles; he has painted the tragedies of love, of deep but smothered passion, of soul mates in distress and divided on earth, and the dramas of spiritual and social imperfections and even of industrial strife, in plays like *L'Invitation au voyage* (1924; Eng. trs., *Glamour*, 1927, *Invitation to a Voyage*, 1939), *L'Ame en peine* (1926; Eng. tr., *The Unquiet Spirit*, 1932), *A la recherche des cœurs* (1934), *National 6* (1935). He has rendered as with strings, and in a minor key, the themes and variations the post-war theatre often played as though with wind instruments, sometimes off key. With him poetry catches up with realism and psychology in the theatre. He extracts beauty and pathos out of the most fugitive aspects of life—a look, a sigh, a momentary silence. His insight into the heart is not marred by splashes of jarring passion. The quality of his analysis, the purity of his style, and the sensitiveness of his dramatic climate give to his creations a classic ring. Bernard has also written short stories, as well as novels like *Le Roman de Martine* (1929) and *Madeleine Landier* (1933). After the liberation of France, he published an account of the imprisonment of French Jews in a concentration camp, *Le Camp de la mort lente: Compiègne 1941–1942* (1945).

See: J. L. Palmer, *Studies in the Contemporary Theatre* (1927), pp. 94–111; L. Hommel, "Le Théâtre de Jean-Jacques Bernard," *Revue générale*, XIII (1935), 592–597; J. L. Frith,

"Introduction," in Bernard, *The Sulky Fire* (1939), pp. 7–11.

S. A. R.

Bernard, Tristan (pseud. of Paul Bernard, 1866–, French dramatist, novelist, and wit), was born at Besançon. He changed his given name to Tristan, desiring to suggest, some of his friends have said, the underlying melancholy of his humor. At the beginning of his career he contributed to the *Revue blanche*. In 1889 his novel *Les Mémoires d'un jeune homme rangé* and his well-known short comedy *L'Anglais tel qu'on le parle* both met with great success. His later novels, such as *Le Mari pacifique* (1901), were widely read and exerted through their keen power of observation, sense of the ridiculous, and fundamental pessimism a beneficial influence over the novel of that period which had turned to a rather questionable lyricism.

His fame, however, rests chiefly on his hilarious comedies which have amused several generations of theatregoers both in France and abroad. He has often been compared with Courteline (*q.v.*), while his detached irony and sly humor recall American and English writers of the same school. Essentially a popular dramatist, he has remained apart from any school and has followed the old traditions of the comedy since the time of Plautus, with frequent resort to concealments, disguises, and mistaken identity. One of his best-known plays, *Triplepatte* (1905), shows the difficulty experienced by a man who cannot make any decision as to marriage because of too much advice from his many friends; *Le Prince Charmant* (1921) portrays the familiar type of young man who is sympathetic to everyone but absolutely unreliable in financial matters. *Le Petit Café* (1911) presents the amusing situation of a waiter who is to inherit a fortune on condition that he remain with his employer for 20 years. Some of his other well-known comedies are *Daisy* (1902), *M. Codomat* (1907), *Le Danseur inconnu* (1909), *La Gloire ambulancière* (1913), and *Les Petites Curieuses* (1920).

A familiar figure in both Parisian society and literary circles, Bernard has created many a famous bon mot and has graciously accepted the paternity of many others until he is now not infrequently spoken of as the national humorist.

See: L. Treich, ed., *L'Esprit de Tristan Bernard* (1925).

J. F. M.

Bernstein, Henry (1876–, French playwright), was born in Paris. He is generally thought of as a painter of heartless and brutal characters, hard businessmen, cynical adventurers. This reputation is due to violent dramas such as *La Rafale* (1905), *La Griffe* (1906), and *Samson* (1907). Bernstein, however, had begun his dramatic career with comedies of a milder type, *Le Marché* (1900), *Le Détour* (1902), *Joujou* (1902), *Frère Jacques* (1904; written with Pierre Veber), *Le Bercail* (1904).

After 1913 he wrote a few plays where the emphasis is placed on the characters rather than on a tense and dynamic plot. *Le Secret* (1913), an analysis of a malicious woman who enjoys hurting those whom she pretends to love, and *La Galerie des glaces* (1924), built around a case of inferiority complex and retrospective jealousy, are among his best psychological dramas. Such subtle studies are the exception in Henry Bernstein's theatre. As a rule his characters are dominated by violent passions which they satisfy without any consideration for the usual codes of morality and decency. The public at times reacted unfavorably, as in the case of *Après moi* (1911).

Henry Bernstein is an expert technician who knows how to place his characters in the light which will best intensify the tragic elements of the plot. *Israël* (1908), based on a conflict between Jews and members of the French aristocracy, provides an excellent example of his talent in creating dramatic atmospheres. Aware of the changes in the public's taste Bernstein, while keeping his main characteristics, treats with remarkable ease the most varied subjects. *Judith* (1922), *Mélo* (1929), *Espoir* (1934), are proofs of his versatility.

See: G. Rageot, "Un Nouveau Bernstein," *Revue bleue,* November 15, 1924, and "La Nouvelle Esthétique d'Henry Bernstein," *ibid.*, April 3, 1926; L. Le Sidaner, *Henry Bernstein* (1931).

M. E. C.

Bertrana, Prudenci (1867–1941, Catalonian novelist), was born in the city of Tortosa, received his education in Ampurdan, and spent much of his youth in Gerona, where he contemplated nature and developed gifts as a writer and painter. He originally intended to be a painter, but it was in the literary field that he was to attain real success. His first important work was *Nàufrags* (1907; The Shipwrecked). *Josefat* is characterized by a crude and savage realism he never thereafter abandoned. *Jo* is a passionate and turbulent novel in which one does not know where the fiction ends and libel begins; characters are observed with a stinging sharpness. *Proses* *barbares* are wild stories written in a lively and colorful prose which came to be his habitual manner. *Herois* (Heroes) and *El meu amic Pellini* (My Friend Pellini) followed. In 1931 he won the coveted Crexells prize which the government of Catalonia awarded each year to the best novel, with *L'hereu* (The Heir). Full of biographical references, *L'hereu* reveals Bertrana's predilection for a vigorously portrayed nature, with sharp contrasts brought out with the love of a landscape artist. A later novel is *El vagabund* (The Vagabond). Bertrana also did considerable work as a journalist.

In all of his literary work there is present Bertrana's dual quality of painter and writer. He brought to Catalonian literature a pessimism perhaps less severe that that of Victor Català (*q.v.*) and cultivated a ruralism less full of bitterness, but still acrid. Some of his work has a human quality, blood-warm and vital.

F. de P.

Betteloni, Vittorio (1840–1910, Italian poet and critic), was born in Verona, where, except for university studies in Pisa, he passed almost all his life. He was a teacher and was often in contact with Milanese literary salons and coteries. Carducci (*q.v.*) defined him as the first Italian poet to get away from romanticism. He was a quiet, honest, simple soul and had the courage to remain so when Italian writers began to feel the need of absinthe, the smell of death and the attraction to suicide to stimulate their jaded poetic daemons. (In Italy this phenomenon was known as *scapigliatura.*) His own daemon obtained milder satisfactions from a milliner of Florence and a woman who played cards in the evening with professors and vicars. His poetry is gently sensuous and a little banal, but this very touch of ordinary living and of realistic details, simply and roughly applied from his palette to his idyllic pictures, produced something of a sensation in his time. Romanticists were irritated, and young readers, who had had a taste of the heady, heroic, and magniloquent Carducci, mocked him, but Carducci, the master, recognized him as a poet and wrote one of his rare prefaces for Betteloni's *Nuovi Versi* (1880). Because of these very details—prosaic, realistic—Betteloni in a certain sense is considered the predecessor of the Crepuscular school of poets, without, however, their characteristic heartaches and yearnings.

Cultured and very clever at versification, Betteloni translated with success Byron's *Don Juan,* Goethe's *Hermann und Dorothea,* and Hamerling's *Nero.* Now and then he gives evidence of having been exposed, like almost all Italian poets of that period, to the germ of Heine, but everyone may see how little the resulting malady afflicted him by comparing him with the contemporary Heinian-tainted Stecchetti.

During the last few years of his life Betteloni manifested a degree of irascibility at being neglected when D'Annunzio (*q.v.*), who to him seemed bombastic, Pascoli (*q.v.*), whom he thought a deceiver, and Orsini (pseud. of Domenico Gnoli, *q.v.*), "a mystifier," gathered to themselves all the laurels. Perhaps he was not even mollified by the fervid approbation in 1904 of Benedetto Croce (*q.v.*). In some of his prose essays there are vivid sketches of living people written in a subdued tone of human irony. The best of his poetical production was gathered in a single volume, *Poesie di Vittorio Betteloni* (1914); his prose writings are contained in *Impressioni critiche e ricordi autobiografici* (1914).

See: G. Brognoligo, *Vittorio Betteloni; note biografiche e critiche descritte dal suo carteggio* (1938).

G. P.

Betti, Ugo (1892–, Italian poet, dramatist, and short-story writer), born in Camerino, is a judge by profession. A real poet of the post-war generation (although he began his literary career in 1910 by publishing a translation in the style of Foscolo of the Epithalamium of Catullus), he seems to stand at the confluence of European poetical streams. Critics have found in him traces of the nostalgic weakness of the *crepuscolari,* reminiscences of the glittering display of D'Annunzio (*q.v.*), echoes of the French symbolists (*see* French symbolism) and especially of the weird and uncanny visitations of Maeterlinck (*q.v.*), and imitations of popular ballads. It may be added that certain rapid cadences recall the manner of Jahier (*q.v.*). As for his theatre there come to mind the names of Pirandello (*q.v.*) and his feeling of inescapable human misery; of Georg Kaiser (*q.v.*) and his tendency to universalize; of Chekhov (*q.v.*) and his morbid softness; of Vildrac, Gorki, L. N. Tolstoy (*qq.v.*) and their collectivist thought. In his short stories the staccato style of Verga (*q.v.*) has struck the critics. All this shows that Betti is a cultured man of his epoch. Not one of these tendencies is permanent in his poetical language; and for each of these cultural resonances, there is evidence of a personal thought and feeling.

Betti is, to put it briefly and insufficiently, not so much a decadent, as he has been called, as a neo-romanticist. His poetical creations, which at the beginning had a folkloristic and later gradually assumed a realistic tone, are woven around the assumption that human happiness and pain are without reason or explanation and therefore a stupendous burden to man. His God, like that of Vigny or of Leopardi, is cold and indifferent towards his creation, and life, not guided by reason, is but a marvelous iniquity. This pessimistic view expressed itself in fables, tales, and myths, with a discernible popular rhythm; in ballads of laments of human groups (the little old women, the emigrants, the drinkers, the sleeping lovers); in figures without a name, symbols that bespeak humanity (a sinner without consolation, a worried king, dwellings of men). Later the same desolation reappeared in a realistic form, in short studies of everyday life, in which is felt Betti's vast solicitude, his feeling of being deceived, his presentation of sexual love with such a crude and intense perception of details that the general feeling of pity, commiseration, and ineluctable love for his fellow men is sometimes destroyed. His characters have a tendency to become types, his countries have no frontiers, his epochs no precise time. But even in the most realistic study of the Italian middle class, there is a final poetic inspiration, a current that carries the reader beyond prosaic everyday life. Characteristically enough, not a word of patriotic rhetoric, not a line of flattery for the Duce during the years of Fascism came from the pen of Betti.

Betti produced little between his *Re pensieroso* (1922) and *Uomo e donna* (1937). The *Canzonetta: La Morte* (1932) won him the prize of the Mondadori Academy and, considering the general failure of these prizes in discovering good writers, this exception must be noted. *Caino* (1929) and *Le Case* (1937) are books of short stories. Several plays have been praised by critics and applauded by audiences: *Frana allo scalo nord* (1932), a study of the responsibility or better the irresponsibility of a criminal; *Il Diluvio* (1932); *Il Cacciatore d'anitre* (1937); and *La Padrona* (1927), considered his best play and perhaps symbolical of life, where the "Mistress," Life, is depicted as an attractive, powerful, cynical woman. Several critics have recognized in him a great poet and felt that he has succeeded in overcoming the calligraphic tendency of contemporary Italian lyricism, reverting to a poetry of human content. Some lines of his poems already enjoy a certain popularity and are often quoted.

See: E. De Michelis, *La Poesia di Ugo Betti* (1937); D. Fabbri, "La Drammatica di Ugo Betti," *Rivista italiana del dramma,* Anno IV (1940), Vol. I, No. 2, pp. 129–153.

G. P.

Bezruč, Petr (pseud. of Vladimír Vašek, 1867–, Czech poet), is one of the greatest names in recent Czech literature. Bezruč was born in Opava (Troppau, then in Austrian Silesia), where his father, Antonín Vašek, was a prominent Czech patriot and philologist. For a time he studied classics at the University of Prague, but gave this up and entered the postal service in Brno, Moravia. He retired in 1927. During the First World War, Bezruč was imprisoned for his attacks on the Archduke Frederick. After the war, his voice was heard in favor of an aggressive nationalism and a strong local Moravian patriotism.

Bezruč is the author of only one collection of poems, *Slezské písně* (Silesian Songs), which first appeared in a small edition in 1903 as *Slezské číslo* (A Silesian Number) and then was successively enlarged. It is the most original and powerful group of poems in modern Czech poetry. Bezruč eschewed all expression of the self and created the figure of a popular bard and prophet, Petr Bezruč, who sings the sorrows of his race. He is particularly the poet of the Czechs in Silesia, where national and social oppression was especially strong under the old Austria. Bezruč passionately accuses the German landlords and capitalists, but also pleads for his people, the miners and peasants of Silesia, against the indifference to their fate among the Czechs in Bohemia and Moravia. His rhapsodies have a tragic pathos which succeeds in instilling an apparently local topic with universal content: an outcry for justice, a cry of hatred and anger against the oppressor. Bezruč is a master of an austere rhetoric, of grandiose visions and symbols, of a monumental semi-free verse which is still not completely divorced from popular forms. Only occasionally, in a few poems, there is a note of personal resignation and melancholy reminiscence, but usually the mask of the seer is preserved with dignity and pathos. Bezruč seems almost without ancestors in literature; he knows the folk ballad and uses it sometimes with great effect, as in "Maryčka Magdanova," the story of a girl who commits suicide by drowning. He knows and admires J. S. Machar (*q.v.*), from whom he took some unnecessary classical conventions, and he must have read some of the social poetry of the later Heine. But he stands alone: the fiercest and the finest voice of his nation against national and social oppression.

See: Adolf Veselý, *Peter Bezruč* (1927); J. V. Sedlák, *Petr Bezruč* (1931); Arturo Cronia, *Petr Bezruč* (1932, in Italian); Klementina Rektorisová, *Bezručův verš* (1935). There is a German translation of the Silesian songs by Rudolph Fuchs (*Schlesische Lieder*, 1931).

R. W.

Bezymenski, Alexander Ilyich (1898–, Russian poet and playwright), was born in the city of Zhitomir in the Ukraine and went to the Vladimir Gymnasium and then to the Kiev Commercial Institute in 1916. In 1917, at the age of 19, he fought in the Revolution in Petrograd on the side of the Bolsheviks. As Trotski said of him, "Bezymenski is flesh of the Revolution's flesh." He was a leader of the Vladimir Young Communists League (Comsomol) and retained a perpetual spirit of youth. In one of his youthful poems he told how his mother, who disapproved of his becoming a Bolshevik, threw away his membership card, and he added: "She did not understand that I do not carry my party ticket in my pocket, but in myself." Far from believing in "art for art's sake," he declared: "First of all I am a member of the party, and only afterwards a maker of verses." He was a member of the "October" group of poets who glorified the October Revolution. From its beginning down to its abolition in 1932 he was a director of the Association of Proletarian Writers.

His first book was *Yuny proletari* (1920; The Young Proletarian), a realistic and at the same time epic novel in verse, telling how a young worker became a Communist. His shorter poems are of heroic romantic nature, embodying the spirit of the Young Communists—youthful, cocksure, saucy, but severely self-critical. These poems were collected in a series of volumes whose titles give some indication of their contents: *Oktyabrskie zori* (1920; October Dawns); *K solntsu* (1921; To the Sun); *Kak pakhnet zhizn* (1924; How Life Smells); *Gorodok* (1925; A Little Town); *Gruz* (1926; Cargo); *Put dorogi* (1926; The Way of the Road); *Serdtse cheloveche* (1928; The Human Heart). The style of these poems, somewhat under the influence of Mayakovsky (*q.v.*), is free verse, broken sentences, single words on a line, conversational phrases, staccato effects, hyperboles of metaphor, grotesque, satirical. The subject matter is the joy of work, a reveling in the commonplace, an enthusiasm for the Red army, for collective farms, for factories. "Our soul is a factory. Our heart is a living furnace." For him, flowers are all the more beautiful if they are in factory windows; waterfalls, if they are connected with turbines. The coming of spring is less important than the price of food. A girl's lips do not mean so much as factory chimneys. During a drought, when the fields need rain, the crowd is at the Dynamo Stadium in Moscow watching a football game. Suddenly rain begins to pour, stopping the game, but the crowd rises to applaud the rain.

Once Bezymenski turned to write a verse play for the Meyerhold Theatre. This was called *Vystrel* (1929; The Shot) and represented shock brigades keeping the trolley cars running in spite of the efforts of enemies to destroy them. *Stikhi delayut stal* (1930; Verses Make Steel) shows how Bezymenski uses poems, short verses, slogans on street banners, to help reconstruction and national defense. *Tragedinaya noch* (1931; Tragic Night) was written during the building of the Dneprostroi Dam and introduces an American engineer converted to Communism. More important than the ordering of a new hat is the ordering of a new world. "With the reconstruction of the world goes the reconstruction of emotion." When his master, Mayakovsky, committed suicide in 1930, Bezymenski condemned him as a fabulous tower standing on stilts of mere straw. A bullet ends a man, but not an age. Only he is on the right road who on every front is in the trenches of the great class war, who can in every little thing find a world revolution. In *Kak ponimayu ya lyubov* (1936; How I Understand Love) Bezymenski rejoices in the common everyday task. Since the German invasion of Russia he has thrown the same indomitable spirit into the war effort, but in form he has turned from Mayakovsky back to Pushkin and his war poems are written in regular meters.

See: A. Osenev, *Alexander Bezymenski* (1926); Alexander Kaun, *Soviet Poets and Poetry* (1943), pp. 136–137, 154–163.

H. W. L. D.

Bierbaum, Otto Julius (1865–1910, German poet, novelist, critic, and bibliophile), born at Grünberg, Silesia, was educated chiefly at Dresden and Leipzig and studied philosophy, law, and Chinese at Zurich, Leipzig, Munich, and Berlin. Back in Munich he turned to journalism, entering the circle of M. G. Conrad (*q.v.*), editor of *Die Gesellschaft* and leader of the South German naturalists, but he also championed the art of such romantic painters as Böcklin, Stuck, and others. In 1892 he published an enthusiastic book on Liliencron (*q.v.*), followed by editorial yeoman's service for the "moderns" which in 1894 took him to Berlin. Here his artistic taste and literary talents blended at last perfectly in the creation of the sumptuous art magazine, *Pan* (1895). Four years later, after an interim spent mostly in Southern Tirol, he collaborated with A. W. Heymel in founding the monthly, *Die Insel,* and with it the Inselverlag, known to bibliophiles. The *Goethe-Kalender* is likewise his work (1905 ff.).

Bierbaum's first marriage in 1891 is reflected in several volumes of verse eventually integrated in *Der Irrgarten der Liebe* (1901; revised ed., 1906). This book was a mine for composers (*e.g.,* Richard Strauss, "Traum durch die Dämmerung"). Its unequaled success (86 editions up to 1923) was due only in part to the popularity which the author had attained as editor of *Deutsche Chansons,* the literary expression of the "Überbrettl" movement initiated in 1900. Bierbaum used traditional, even archaic forms and themes, applying, however, all the delicate nuances of a modern impressionistic verse technique and adding the touch of a personal experience. While replacing "Truth" by "Beauty"—lacking only depth—in his lyric work, he remained basically a naturalist in his fiction. Almost all his novels and stories deal with things directly experienced or observed as a child, as a *Korpsstudent,* or as a man of letters (*e.g., Studentenbeichten,* 1892, 1897; *Pankrazius Graunzer,* 1895; *Stilpe,* 1897). Later, after his second marriage to an Italian woman (1901), these were augmented by travel impressions gathered chiefly in Italy (*Empfindsame Reise im Automobil,* 1903, etc.). The intent is humor and satire carried to grotesque extremes, particularly in *Prinz Kuckuck* (3 vols., 1906–1907), a book hardly surpassed for its casual but detailed depiction of moral, social, religious, and political decay. However, there is far too much joy of living and faith in the future in Bierbaum to classify him as a pessimist or a decadent. Combining as he did an ironic sense of facts with a noble cult of aesthetic values, he was a perfect symbol of Germany's well-to-do bourgeoisie before the First World War. After almost another decade in or near Munich, he died at Dresden in 1910.

See: E. Schick, *O. J. Bierbaum* (1903); P. Pollard, *Masks and Minstrels of New Germany* (1911), pp. 121–177; A. Dreyer, "Bierbaum," *Biographisches Jahrbuch und deutscher Nekrolog,* XV (1913), 170–177; E. Darge, *Lebensbejahung in der deutschen Dichtung um 1900* (1934).

H. W. N.

Billinger, Richard (1893–, German poet and dramatist), was born in St. Marienkirchen near Schärding on the Inn, where his peasant ancestors had occupied the same land since the 12th century. He abandoned his university studies preparing him for the priesthood after the discovery, in *Ueber die Aecker* (1921), of his literary talent. He achieved even greater success with his dramas (*Das Perchtenspiel,* 1926; *Rauhnacht,* 1931; *Rosse,* 1933), while continuing with lyric output (*Sichel am Himmel,* 1931; *Der Pfeil im Wappen,* 1932). His best poems have been called baroque or have been likened to woodcuts of the old masters. His main subject fields are traditional or hereditary—the simple piety of his Catholic forebears and environment, the close union with the soil and with nature which the European peasant of every country enjoys. He never wearies of singing the praise of God and of prizing the beauties of his native land. To these motifs may be added, especially in the dramas, the dark and uncanny powers which the country dweller has always been inclined to shape into superstitions or manifestations of the devil. Gifted with a true feeling for stagecraft, he wove these materials together with dance and sorcery into such a compelling piece that Max Reinhardt gave *Das Perchtenspiel* a stirring performance.

Estimates of Billinger are by no means uniform, and he is significantly absent from several recent accounts of German literature; one which gives him brief mention speaks of "der einst vielversprechende Richard Billinger."

See: G. K. Brand, *Werden und Wandlung* (1933), p. 345.

B. Q. M.

Binding, Rudolf Georg (1867–1938, German novelist and poet), was born at Basel, son of the internationally famous jurist Karl Binding. He studied at Leipzig and Berlin, but did not enter upon any professional career. Instead, he devoted his time to horse racing and to travels especially in Italy and Greece. A cavalry captain in the First World War, he was mayor after the war in a small town near Frankfurt am Main and died at Starnberg (Bavaria).

Binding was past 40 when he made his début in German literature. He began with translations from D'Annunzio (*q.v.*) and cultivated the small genre (legends and short stories), in which he soon established himself as a master. Although there are traces of Goethe, Kleist, Keller (*q.v.*), and George (*q.v.*) in his works, he is essentially a literary self-made man, his real "educators" being his father, the Rhine River, horses, the Hermes statue by Praxiteles, and nature itself. For Binding writing is a mission that carries the highest responsibility. It combines romantic longing for the divine with the classical urge to embody the divine in human form. His literary output is relatively small, but excels in deep psychological insight, dramatic condensation, and musical plasticity. His characters, when represented as human, are full-blooded individuals devoted to the pleasures and duties of this world, but humble before their god. When divine, they shine in ethereal beauty, but long for self-realization through earthly love and work. Whether human or divine, however, they all have the same chastity of soul, the same readiness for sacrifice, the same calmness in the presence of fate and death.

In his first publication, *Legenden der Zeit* (1909), inhabitants of heaven and earth meet in helpful understanding (*Coelestina*), occasionally mocking each other about rigoristic dogmas and priests (*St. Georg's Stellvertreter*). Miracles happen in these as in the Christian legends, but instead of detracting from everyday life they lead to a fuller realization of its inherent sanctity. The people in his *Novellen* live their religion through friendship (*Die Waffenbrüder,* 1910), love (*Die Vogelscheuche,* 1910; *Der Opfergang,* 1911; *Angelucia,* 1911; *Unsterblichkeit,* 1921), and service (*Der Wingult,* 1921). *Aus dem Kriege,* a diary written in the war and published in 1925 (Eng. tr., *Fatalist at War,* 1929) without any changes of the original form, is a courageous, realistic, prophetic, and chivalrous book, one of the few war productions with lasting appeal. Three years later appeared his *Erlebtes Leben* (1928), a classical autobiographical gem, symbolic of the best of a generation who in the search for the true meaning of their lives were tragically deceived by the "as if" values of the glittering but shallow Second Reich. In *Rufe und Reden* (1928) Binding discusses the political and cultural problems resulting from the war and warns the German people against increasing materialism, while in his *Antwort eines Deutschen an die Welt* (1933) he defends them against foreign accusations such as those of Romain Rolland (*q.v.*). He strikes a lighter chord in the Apollonian lyric prose hymn *Reitvorschrift an eine Geliebte* (1924), the charming philosophical dialogues *Spiegelgespräche* (1933), the tragicomical anecdote *Wir fordern Reims zur Übergabe auf* (1935), while in *Moselfahrt aus Liebeskummer* (1932) he attempts a new form of the *Novelle* by embodying in a beautiful woman the character of a special landscape, thus making nature the real protagonist of the story. *Vom Leben der Plastik* (1933) is a subtle interpretation of Georg Kolbe's sculptural work and revelatory of Binding's own production.

Although Binding wrote exquisite poetry (*Gedichte,* 1914; *Stolz und Trauer,* 1922; *Ausgewählte und neue Gedichte,* 1932; *Sieg des Herzens,* 1937), he earned his reputation as one of the foremost classical writers in modern German literature through his legends, *Novellen,* and autobiography. His inimitable style has gained, to be sure, through masterful translations of D'Annunzio, Bédier (*q.v.*), St. Francis of Assisi, and Villiers and through the study of the above-mentioned German writers; but essentially it is his own, the true expression of a perfect gentleman, a "virtuoso" whose art is life, because life is his art.

See: F. Lennartz, *Die Dichter unserer Zeit* (1938); T. Stenner, *Rudolf G. Binding; Leben und Werk* (1938); H. Millotat, *Rudolf Georg Bindings erzählerisches Werk* (1939).

E. J.

Björnson, Björnstjerne (1832–1910, Norwegian poet, novelist, dramatist, journalist, and orator), was born in a parsonage high up in the mountains of eastern Norway, but at the age of five moved with his parents to another parsonage at a northwestern fjord. He felt himself a son of this district, Romsdal, mirroring in his character the contrasts of the stormy fjords and the fertile valleys between stern mountains. His father was of farmer stock, his mother of a merchant family, and he combined in himself the different and even conflicting traditions of Norwegian history. It became a chief aim of his career to reconcile the contrasting characters of national life, revealing to his countrymen the live treasures of the farmer society and at the same time freeing the country people from the inhibitions of their isolated existence. The whole task involved the general problems of uniting primitive instincts with conscious self-mastery, of civilizing the human mind by giving spontaneity to its innermost needs, of strengthening both individual liberty and the laws of community. By his broad human sympathies, by the exceptional vigor and vitality of his personality, by his powerful creative imagination, he was able to bring these problems home to his own nation as well as to the other Scandinavian nations, and later to larger parts of the world.

He went to high school at Molde, the small capital of Romsdal, was prepared for the university by courses at Christiania, and started university studies in 1852, but abandoned them very soon for literary work. As early as 1848 he wrote his first newspaper article, inspired by the February Revolution, and for 60 years he was the most assiduous and brilliant journalist of Norway, beginning as a literary critic, by degrees embracing all political, social, moral questions of the day, always in the vanguard for liberal and democratic progress, for mental freedom, for social and national justice. He made his influence felt in the whole political development of Norway from 1859; ultimately, beginning in the 90's, he extended his activities to the foreign press. In 1859 also he began appearing as a public speaker and soon became the greatest orator of the Scandinavian countries; his magnificent voice, his splendid imagery, his dazzling logic, his ever ready wit, made his speeches powerful instruments in all kinds of campaigning.

In 1854 Björnson proclaimed his program for re-creating Norwegian literature. He lifted the banner of Henrik Wergeland, the greatest Norwegian of the first half of the 19th century. Like Wergeland he rebelled against the aestheticism that would keep individuality in severe bondage; he wanted literature to serve ideas, to reveal the intimate unity of life and poetry, to be faithful to truth and to nature. He wished to break absolutely with the literary traditions of the Danish language which, for the last centuries, had dominated Norwegian literature. Björnson won his first victory in this field by a demonstration, the "theatre battle" of 1856, by which he succeeded in stopping the engagement of Danish actors at the theatres of Christiania. The next year he became the director of the theatre at Bergen (for two years, until 1859); later he was the director of the theatre of Christiania (1865–1867), and even managed his own theatre there (1870–1872). The assertion of genuine Norwegian speech was to him only one aspect of his demand for truth in art, and as a stage manager he proved highly effective in teaching young actors to replace fine declamation by psychological realism; in fact, he was the father of a new theatrical school in Norway.

His own first literary work was published in 1857, a modest little novel, *Synnöve Solbakken* (first Eng. trs., 1881; *Sunny Hill, a Norwegian Idyll,* 1932). It was the first of a series of so-called "peasant novels" which, for half a century or more, were the most popular books of the nation. They were written in a style strongly personal, in a Norwegian that was modern and yet akin to the manner of the old sagas. The unbroken connection between ancient Norway and the modern farmer society was indeed a fundamental tenet with Björnson, and he wanted to reveal what still survived of the sagas in the culture of the farmer people—even though they themselves were unaware of it. Therefore, as a natural supplement to his peasant novels, he wrote a series of dramas, epics, and romances built on saga motifs. In all of them the chief theme was the struggle to liberate the suppressed forces of the soul and cultivate them to the advantage of human cooperation. Björnson offered an intimate combination of realism and poetry. He became the great national poet of Norway. It is significant that he published his lyrics under the title *Digte og sange* (1870; Eng. tr., *Poems and Songs,* 1915). Besides intimate personal poems this work contained a number of songs expressing sentiments of the whole nation, among them the song that became the national anthem of Norway. All of them are compactly filled with poetic ideas and images, and they have that peculiar quality of turning household expressions into a most vigorous poetry, as in the first line of the national anthem: "Ja, vi elsker dette laudet" (Yes, we love this country).

Björnson often stayed for long periods abroad (1860–1863 and 1873–1875, mostly in Italy; 1880–1881, in the United States; 1882–1887, in Paris; 1893–1896, in Italy and Germany). During these visits he studied other nations and enriched his own ideas. He sent home the play *En fallit* (1875; Eng. tr., *The Bankrupt,* in *Three Dramas,* 1914), which was really the first social drama in Norway and which had immediate repercussions outside the country, being performed and enthusiastically received in German and other foreign theatres. Its purpose was the revealing of the "lies" of modern society. Of Björnson's later dramas in the same vein none reached higher in art and psychological power than *Over aevne* (1883; Eng. trs., *Pastor Sang,* 1893, *Beyond Our Power* in *Plays,* 1913, *Beyond Human Might* in *Plays,* Ser. 2, 1914), which pictures the overstraining of Christian belief. The drama *Paul Lange og Tora Parsberg* (1898; Eng. tr., *Paul Lange and Tora Parsberg,* 1899) was an indictment of political fanaticism and was filled with mercy for noble weakness. The author's broad humanity emerges also in his gay comedy, *Geografi og kaerlighet* (1885; Eng. tr., *Love and Geography,* in *Plays,* Ser. 2, 1914). Björnson became increasingly known as an international as well as a national fighter for truthful life. He was honored by an annual state stipend from 1863 on and by the Nobel prize in literature in 1903.

From 1875 he made the farm Aulestad in eastern Norway his home, his workshop, and a center of national life. On his last trip abroad he died in Paris, in 1910. His funeral in Christiania was that of a king.

See: Björnson, *Brev,* ed. by H. Koht (6 vols., 1912–1932); C. Collin, *Björnson, barndom og ungdom,* 2d ed. (1923); C. Gierlöff, *Björnstjerne Björnson* (1932); J. Lescoffier, *Björnson, la seconde jeunesse* (1932); Harold Larson, *Björnstjerne Björnson: A Study in Norwegian Nationalism* (1944).

H. K.

Blasco Ibáñez, Vicente (1867–1928), Spanish novelist), was born at Valencia. A republican in politics, a social reformer in economic matters, a freethinker in religion, several times a representative in the Cortes, founder and editor of the radical Valencian newspaper *Pueblo,* above all possessor of a tumultuous temperament—for years Blasco Ibáñez led the life of an agitator and was frequently imprisoned and exiled. His life took a new direction in 1909. Having gone to Argentina for a series of lectures, he finally decided to become a colonizer. The result, after four years of a hazardous, gaucho-like life, was the founding of the two colonies, Cervantes and Nueva Valencia. By 1914 he was back in Paris, and during the First World War he devoted himself to campaigning for the Allies. His outstanding piece of work in this connection was the novel *Los cuatro jinetes del Apocalipsis* (1916). Relatively little known until then as a novelist outside the Spanish-speaking world, with the appearance of the English-American translation of this novel, *The Four Horsemen of the Apocalypse* (1918), he became an international figure and the most translated of all modern Spanish writers (all the novels mentioned in the present article are available in English).

With Blasco Ibáñez the naturalistic novel in Spain reached its highest mark. He is ordinarily referred to as the Spanish Zola (*see* Zola), but the denomination seems only in part correct if one considers the difference in temperament between the French and the Spanish master. At any rate, as stated by Blasco Ibáñez himself, "Zola was a reflective man in literature, and I am an impulsive one. He attained his final result slowly, through perforation, while I proceed through explosion, violently and loudly." By nature a man of action, life was for the Valencian novelist an immediate experience, a direct sensation. By the same token his art was not the product of a patient collection of data systematically classified and elaborated, but a vivid rendition of a series of first impressions of which his senses and his imagination, not his notes—he did not take them—kept the record. This keen sensory perception of things and the capacity to reproduce them in a fresh, vigorous, and colorful picture also characterize his novel, which is, at its best, an essentially descriptive, pictoric novel. Of this the series of Valencian novels (*Arroz y tartana,* 1894; *Flor de mayo,* 1895; *La barraca,* 1898; *Entre naranjos,* 1900; *Cañas y barro,* 1902; also *Los muertos mandan,* 1909, with its setting in the Balearic Islands) is the most perfect example. Though less consistently and in settings less colorful and less well suited to Blasco Ibáñez's sensualistic temperament, other examples are to be found in practically all his novels, including the two war novels, *Los cuatro jinetes del Apocalipsis* and *Mare Nostrum* (1918), especially the first with its pictures of Argentinian land and life and the war scenes. The result is inferior, however, when he deals not with living reality as perceived through his senses but with ideas (as in the social novels *La catedral,* 1903, *El intruso,* 1904, *La bodega* and *La horda,* both 1905, and the more picturesque *Sangre y arena,* 1908) or with psychological problems (*La maja desnuda,* 1906) or with archaeological subjects (*Sónnica la cortesana,* 1901). The same is true of the historical novel cultivated by him during the last years of his life in a series of works conceived as a historical revindication and an epic of Spanish heroes and deeds (*El Papa del mar,* 1925; *A los pies de Venus: Los Borgia,* 1926; and the two posthumous novels *En busca del Gran Kan: Cristóbal Colón* and *El caballero de la Virgen,* both 1929). In these works the epic heroes are more interesting than the superimposed novelistic action.

See: E. Zamacois, *Vicente Blasco Ibáñez* (1910); C. Pitollet, *V. Blasco Ibáñez; ses romans et le roman de sa vie* (1921); Joaquín Ortega, "Vicente Blasco Ibáñez," *University of Wisconsin Studies in Language and Literature,* No. 20 (1924), pp. 214–238; C. Barja, *Literatura española: Libros y autores modernos,* revised ed. (1933), pp. 391–414.

C. B.

Bleibtreu, Karl (1859–1928, German critic, novelist, and dramatist), was born in Berlin of well-to-do parents. His financial circumstances allowed him to devote his life to literary activity and historical researches. After his university years and wide travels through Europe, he settled in Charlottenburg, occupying himself with his writing and studies. In 1908 he made Zurich his home and turned his attention more and more to historical studies. He died in Locarno.

Bleibtreu's important contribution to the development of modern German literature is to be found in his naturalistic period, rather than in the series of narratives of important battles of world history inspired by his father, a well-known painter of battle scenes, or in his historical and literary studies. Outstanding among the theoretic documents of the naturalistic period was his *Revolution der Literatur* (1886), an analysis of German literature from the naturalistic point of view combined with highly subjective criticism of contemporary literary tendencies. Although he takes exception to the more radical tendencies of contemporary German naturalism (*q.v.*), Bleibtreu demands that literature play an active part in contemporary life and treat contemporary social subjects with extreme realism. *Germinal* by Zola (*q.v.*) he cites as the work that converted him to the naturalistic point of view. His later volume of essays, *Der Kampf um das Dasein in der Literatur* (1889), reveals the temperamental and egotistic nature of his criticism, but contributes little to an understanding of the naturalistic movement. Typical of his naturalistic period is the collection of short stories dealing with the bohemian life of Berlin, *Schlechte Gesellschaft* (1885). His Byron tragedies, *Lord Byrons letzte Liebe* and *Seine Tochter* (1886), he looked upon as examples of naturalistic treatment of the problem of heredity. Among his historical works were a history of English literature (1888) and a history of the First World War (1925).

See: H. Merian, *Karl Bleibtreu als Dramatiker* (1892); O. Stauf von der March, *Karl Bleibtreu* (1920).

W. H. R.

Blix, Elias (1836–1902, Norwegian hymnist), was the son of a fisherman in northern Norway. Working his way through a teacher's seminary at Tromsö and the University of Christiania, he became, in 1879, professor of Hebrew in the faculty of theology, was minister for church and education in the first leftist government, 1884–1888, and returned then to his professorship. In 1869 he published anonymously a small collection of hymns, original and translated, in the Norwegian vernacular, the Landsmaal (*see* Norwegian literature), and this, augmented, became the nucleus of the complete hymnbook in this language, published under his name in 1891 and authorized for the Established Church in 1892. His hymns are distinguished by their pure form, simple heartiness, and cheerful temper, their images often adopted from the nature-life of spring. His deep-felt patriotic hymn "Gud signe vaart dyre fedreland" (God Bless Our Dear-loved Fatherland) became a national anthem. In 1882 Blix began a translation of the New Testament in Landsmaal, and, partly translated, partly revised by him, the complete work was published in 1889. As to form it was a little stiff, conforming too strictly to the demand of a literal rendering of the original, but, together with his hymns, it served to make the vernacular fit again for Christian service.

See: L. Eskeland, *Norsk salmesong, Elias Blix* (1904); P. Hognestad, *Evangelisk salmesong og Elias Blix* (1905); E. Berggrav, *Elias Blix* (1936).

H. K.

Blok, Alexander Aleksandrovich (1880–1921, Russian poet, dramatist, critic, and translator), is beyond doubt the greatest poet of the century following Lermontov (1814–1841). He was the supreme exponent of the short-lived symbolist movement, but his creation and his influence far transcend the school that nourished his genius. Endowed with an extraordinary penetration into the inner reality of past and future, he had a genuinely prophetic intuition, but his relationship to his own times remained an insoluble problem for him to the day of his death and colored all his work with deepening pessimism. He was distinguished by a singular personal beauty, by a gentle, unassuming reserve, and by a rare naturalness and simplicity. Those who knew him felt themselves in the presence of a superior being who, for all his talent for friendship, seemed ever apart and alone, as if he were indeed a sojourner from other spheres.

Blok was a product of the most cultivated of the Russian intelligentsia. His father was professor of law at the University of Warsaw; his mother, also a poet, was the daughter of the botanist Beketov, rector of the University of St. Petersburg. Blok's parents were early divorced, and the boy was reared in his grandfather's home, his winters spent in the milieu of the university, his summers at the little estate of Shakhmatovo near Moscow. He was graduated from the Vvedensky Gymnasium (1898) and from the University of St. Petersburg (1906), where he studied with the faculty of history and philology. From 1897 on he traveled extensively throughout Europe. He married (1903) Lyubov, a talented actress and the daughter of the great chemist Mendeleyev. Their one child, Dmitri, died shortly after birth, a loss that had a lasting effect upon the poet.

Blok began writing early and was already well known before his graduation. His first poems appeared (1903) in *Novy put* (The New Path), the journal edited by Merezhkovski and his wife, Zinaida Hippius (*qq.v.*). Like Bryusov, Bely, Vyacheslav Ivanov (*qq.v.*), and the other symbolists, Blok came under the powerful influence of Vladimir Solovyov (*q.v.*), one of the most original thinkers of his time. Blok's first book of lyrics, *Stikhi o prekrasnoi dame* (1904; Verses about the Lady Beautiful), instantly won the younger generation, who found in it the unresolved longings they themselves felt but could not utter. This was the era just before the abortive 1905 uprising, when in literature as well as in life revolt was spreading against the rigid rationalism of the 19th century, so that the renascent mysticism of Blok's poems, with their intensity of vision, their elusive, haunting music, and their expanding concepts, came as a revelation. They invoked the great spirits of the Romantic Age, Pushkin and Lermontov, and at the same time gave form to a profoundly felt, as yet inchoate, presage of the future, one of vast perspectives and of unknown hazards and rewards. They were genuinely a "new word," and they did in fact create a new literature.

Throughout his career Blok's creative passion was inspired by a trinity of the Lady Beautiful, Christ, and Russia. It is impossible to put a clear definition on their significance, for they change in aspect from time to time and in some sense partake of the elements of one another in varying degrees. The tributary sources of these concepts might be indicated, but their main wellspring was in the poet's own nature. The Lady Beautiful was something more than the restatement of the idealized image of medieval chivalry. At first she was an embodiment of Solovyov's vision of Sophia, Divine Wisdom, and for some time Blok experienced a profound and mystical relationship with her as fecund and fulfilling as that of Dante with Beatrice. Suddenly his visions ended, and the blissful communion broke in disillusion.

The political hopes of 1905 broke in disillusion as well. As Blok grew older, the romantic idealization of his immaturity gave place more and more to ironic realism, even to grotesquerie. The Lady Beautiful, no longer divine, became a mocking, carnal figure, while the focus of his passion shifted from a deified feminine abstraction to a messianic, revolutionary vision of Russia. The Communist Revolution set him on the side of the Bolsheviks. In January, 1918, he wrote *Dvenadtsat* (Eng. tr., *The Twelve,* 1920), the most vivid expression of revolution in literature, universally regarded as the supreme utterance of his genius. The edition soon ran into more than 12 million copies. Hoardings and banners bearing extracts from it were scattered all over Russia, though its final image of Christ leading the 12 rioting Red guards through the snowy streets of Petrograd pleased neither the religious nor the Bolsheviks. In the same month Blok wrote "Skify" (1920; Eng. tr., "The Scythians," in *Russian Poetry; an Anthology*, 1927), an implacable, bronze-throated challenge to the Western World, only less powerful than *Dvenadtsat.* This was his last work. His health began to fail, as much from spiritual as from physical exhaustion. Disillusion once more assailed him. Twice in his life he had given his whole passion to an ideal, which in each case had failed him. "Perhaps I am," he said once, *"un enfant perdu."* It had been given him to express both mystically and realistically man's eternal spiritual conflict. The Russian man in his poetry was a metaphysical being, not merely a historical or a geographical figure. At the same time Blok's poems, such as the remarkable *Na pole Kulikovom* (1908; On Kulikovo Battlefield), were historical and clairvoyant, filled with an apocalyptic sense of cataclysm. In a profound sense Blok was a herald of the Revolution. Khodasevich (*q.v.*) said of him that he suffered from an "insomnia of the heart." His terrible awareness of the tragic complexities of life, together with his special sense of its impenetrable mystery, in the end proved a burden too great to bear. After a long cardiac illness, complicated by psychasthenia, he died on August 7, 1921, and was buried in the Smolensk Cemetery in Leningrad, with all the honors accorded a great national poet.

Blok's collected work has been published in five volumes, the first containing the lyrical poems of the early mystical period from 1898 to 1904; the second, those of the transitional and still immature period from 1904 to 1908; the third, his finest lyrics, 1908 to 1916. The fourth volume contains *Dvenadtsat* and an unfinished autobiographical poem, *Vozmezdie* (1922; Retaliation). The fifth is composed of his wonderful lyric dramas. These include a trilogy produced 1906–1907 comprising *Bala-*

ganchik (The Little Booth), a Pierrot comedy bitterly satirizing Blok's own mystical experiences, produced by Meyerhold in the Kommissarzhevskaya Theatre; *Korol na ploshchadi* (Eng. tr., "The King in the Square," *Slavonic Review,* XII, 489–512), a comment on the political and social consequences of the 1905 Revolution; *Neznakomka* (The Unknown Lady), a romantic theme colored by ironic and grotesque realism, wherein a star appears on earth as an alluring woman, tragically unrecognized by the Poet who adores her. There follow *Faïna, Pesnya sudby* (1909; Eng. tr., "The Song of Fate," *Poet Lore,* XLIV, 1–41), a semi-autobiographical drama of the transformation of an isolated dreamer into an active worker in public affairs, with a symbolic connotation of Russia's destiny, and *Roza i krest* (1913; Eng. tr., *The Rose and the Cross,* 1936), the finest poetic drama in Russian, a mystical romance of medieval France and a transcendent utterance of the poet's sense of the inseparable joy and suffering in life. Blok's last play, commissioned by Gorky (*q.v.*), was *Ramzes* (1921; Rameses), scenes of life in ancient Egypt reflecting modern problems of strikes by labor. A translator himself (of Rutebeuf, Byron, Grillparzer, Heine, Jacobson, Hamsun, Finnish and Lettish poets), the works of Blok have been rendered into a dozen languages; many have appeared in English in anthologies and periodicals, by Selver, Noyes, Manning, Deutsch and Yarmolinsky, and others. The best translation of *Dvenadtsat* is the German by Wolfgang Groeger. Blok's letters (*Pisma A. A. Bloka*) were published in Leningrad in 1925.

See: A Bely, "Vospominaniya ob A. A. Bloke," *Epopeya* (Berlin), 1922–1923, Nos. 1–4; N. Volkov, *Aleksandr Blok i teatr* (1926); *Literaturnoye nasledstvo,* 1927–1928, Nos. 27–28; V. Pozner, "Alexandre Blok," in *Panorama de la littérature russe contemporaine* (1929), pp. 159–172; C. M. Bowra, "Alexander Blok," in *The Heritage of Symbolism* (1943), pp. 144–179.

N. S.

Blomberg, Erik (1894–, Swedish poet and art critic), was born and lives in Stockholm. *Ensamhetens sånger* (1928; Songs of Solitude), his first work, was followed by several collections of verse, including *Den fångne guden* (1927; The Captive God) and *Valda dikter* (1928; Selected Poems). His best volumes, however, are *Människan och guden* (1919; The Man and the God) and *Jorden* (1920; The Earth). Blomberg's lyrics comprise not only songs of intimate feeling and pathos, but intellectual, philosophical poems in which the chief motive is the duty of the individual to the whole of which he is a part. A realist and a revolutionary, he has been the most successful of his group in free verse. Among Blomberg's other works are *Tolkningar av engelsk och tysk lyrik* (1926; Translations of English and German Poetry), *Nya tolkningar* (1931; New Translations), and *En antologi av svenska dikter* (1934; An Anthology of Swedish Poetry). He has also written at least three volumes of essays, including *Tidens romantik* (1931; Modern Romanticism).

See: Sten Selander, *Den unga lyriken* (1924); C. W. Stork, *Anthology of Swedish Lyrics,* revised and enlarged ed. (1930).

C. W. S.

Blomberg, Harry (1893–, Swedish poet, novelist, and short-story writer), is among the more productive of that considerable group of Swedish authors of the last generation whose origins are among the poorer working classes and whose work has been concerned largely with conditions among various proletarian groups. Blomberg's published work, beginning in 1917, and including to date about 30 volumes, was in the early years predominantly poetic in form, but later he turned more to prose fiction, with an occasional volume of travels. His most recent work has been of a highly personal, religious-confessional kind. Blomberg's childhood and youth in Stockholm were spent in the deepest poverty and under the influence of pietistic sectarianism of a distinctly tawdry and dubious kind. Upon his escape from this unfortunate early environment, he became something of an irresponsible vagabond. But his feeling of solidarity with the working classes led him during and immediately after the First World War to take an active part in the organized struggle of these classes for better working conditions and for political power. He devoured Kropotkin and Gorki (*qq.v.*) at this time and wrote "Red verse" for extremist labor journals of the day, some of which reappeared in the volume *I revolutionstid: agitatorisk verse* (1919; In Revolutionary Times: Agitation Verse). Later he became a member of the more moderate labor group, the powerful Social Democratic Party.

Finally, in the late 1930's, he became a convert to the Oxford Group movement, partly in consequence of his growing disillusionment with the materialist-Marxist origins of modern socialism and communism. This last phase in Blomberg's development finds expression particularly in the novel *Det brinner i snön* (1935; It Burns in the Snow) and in the highly personal religious-confessional work *Vi måste börja om* (1937; We Must Begin Over Again). *Land, öppna dig!* (1938; Land, Open Your Gates!) reveals that Blomberg's conversion has not, however, resulted in religious quietism, in a passive acceptance of a social and economic and political *status quo* where ultimate comfort lies in the expectation of better things beyond the grave. Blomberg remains social and political minded, but he has finally come to approach the problem of man in his relation to his fellows in terms of a kind of Christian socialism which is in sharp contrast to his previous Marxist point of view. Though he has never been a really leading figure in Swedish working-class circles, his work has undoubtedly left its mark upon the ferment of ideas which has characterized the intellectual life of these circles since the First World War. As literature in the narrower sense, Blomberg's works are definitely not of the very first order, partly because his literary gifts are somewhat limited, partly because his primary concern has always been propagandistic and ideational. His latest books—among the best he has written—are an interesting, if not always profound, reflection of the state of mind of the more sensitive representatives of the proletariat in a world where social, economic, and political ideas are dissolving and rebuilding under the threats of wartime conditions and wartime psychology.

A. G.

Bloy, Léon Marie (1846–1917, French novelist and essayist), was a Catholic pamphleteer in *Le Pal* (1885), *Les Dernières Colonnes de l'église* (1905), and *Belluaires et porchers* (1901), as well as in a large part of his other works, and a novelist in *Le Désespéré* (1886) and *La Femme pauvre* (1897; Eng. tr., *The Woman Who Was Poor,* 1939). He was likewise the author of historical and critical literary essays, among which is an interesting review of Carlyle's *French Revolution* where he found a kindred genius; of the *Journal,* the seven volumes of which extend from the *Mendiant ingrat* (1898) to the *Porte des humbles* (posthumously published, 1918); and of a partly published correspondence, *Lettres de jeunesse* (1920), *Lettres à la fiancée* (1922; Eng. tr., 1937), *Lettres à ses filleuls* (1928), and *Lettres à Véronique* (1933). These volumes of correspondence, together with his two novels and a prophetic vision entitled *Le Salut par les Juifs* (1892), inscribed "to the glory of Israel and of the Christian God," are the high peak of Bloy's achievement.

His work mirrors his life and personality and cannot be considered apart from them. Born of a lower middle-class family of Périgueux in Guyenne, Bloy never could live in harmony with his unbelieving, anticlerical father. His mother, who had Spanish blood, gave him a deeply religious education. He arrived in Paris when 18, having totally lost his faith, and there frequented the art studios while earning his living as a minor employee. He at once became the prey of poverty, which harrowed him to the end. What he experienced as a volunteer at the age of 24 during the Franco-Prussian War is recounted in *Sueur de sang 1870–1871* (1893). Having met Barbey d'Aurevilly (*q.v.*) by chance in 1866, he "contemplated" the master with ecstatic admiration and became his secretary. "Our great and adored Aurevilly, whose language I have endeavored to speak," was to be his leader, model, and introducer to Joseph de Maistre, Balzac, Baudelaire (*q.v.*), and the philosopher Blanc de Saint-Bonnet. He also made Bloy share his hatred for naturalist literature (see *Les Funérailles du naturalisme,* Copenhagen, 1891), rationalism, Victor Hugo, and George Sand. Aurevilly likewise introduced him into literary circles and into journalism and recommended him to publishers. In his preface to his disciple's first published book, *Le Révélateur du globe* (1884), on Christopher Columbus, Aurevilly praised the "new depth, energy, (and) fiery spirit" it revealed and the majesty of its biblical style. Yet he could not endow him with his own capacity to build well-constructed novels or to create characters living independently of their author.

Bloy's novels, filled with essays and disquisitions, are mostly autobiographical. They relate the slightly transformed events of his own life and the amazing and tragic lives of "Véronique" and "Clotilde Maréchal," *i.e.,* Anne Marie Roulé and Berthe Dumont, whose strange fates were dramatically intertwined with his own, and they present a complete gallery of the people he knew. They express the bitterness of an original and powerful writer totally ignored, the agony of the spiritual night which followed the collapse of Véronique's prophecies about impending apocalyptic events when Bloy was to be a new Elijah, and finally the despair caused by the death of his patron-friend, the Reverend Father Tardif de Moidrey, and by the loss of two children due to his poverty. In spite of his tranquilizing marriage to Jeanne Molbeck, the daughter of a Danish poet, and the strength derived from a deepening spiritual life, he never quite recovered from those years of "torture and humiliation." His solitude, spiritual anguish, wounded pride, and violent temperament explain how Bloy came to speak of and to consider himself as an unfailing judge sounding "hosanna and reprobation" on his "twin trumpet"; but he could easily mistake his personal grievances for the sins of others. His chief victims were former friends—Huysmans (see *Sur la tombe de Huysmans,* 1913), Coppée (*qq.v.*), Groux, gentle souls like Louise Read, Aurevilly's guardian angel, those who resented or ignored his demands for financial help (*Mendiant ingrat*), and the majority of contemporary writers. He poured vociferous *réprobations scatologiques* over the rich and powerful, many of his fellow Catholics, including a number of the clergy, and the revelers at Good Friday banquets. On the other hand, he remained deeply attached to Villiers de l'Isle-Adam (*q.v.*), who appears in *La Femme pauvre* as "Bohémon de l'Isle de France," and to Ernest Hello, both companions of his darkest days.

While protesting at his blind fury, one must admit that Bloy was essentially firing at bestiality, cruelty, and injustice and that the true causes for his deserved or undeserved attacks were his devotion to genius, courage, and humility and his burning faith. There is in all his writings a majestic and wild poetry drawn from his very blood. It is due to what Aurevilly termed "a deep, flaming continuous enthusiasm" issuing from his "kingly capacity for love," and especially love of God. It also comes from his self-termed "sepulchral imagination," heightened by his strange hungering for sorrow, and a Baudelairian passion for the absolute (see *Le Pélerin de l'absolu* in the *Journal*). The highest gift of this scorner of poetry was his power to create images, at times decorative allegories, at times emblems as realistic as the paintings of Spanish primitives, again flaming visions. From Father Tardif de Moidrey's exegesis (see *Le Livre de Ruth,* published with a commentary by Paul Claudel, 1938), Bloy derived a conception of universal symbolism linking together "both abysms" with their "correspondences" in which several generating symbols such as Jesus or the Poor, the Cross, or the Paraclete play the chief part. All these images tend to give the reader a sense of the "Inconceivable" and to make him aware of the pervading presence of mystery. Bloy's style, which has the solemnity of Poe's, more and more became "a conflagration in the night," but as he divested himself of anger, pride, and convulsive despair, there stole into it an Edenic tranquillity.

See: J. Maritain, *Quelques Pages sur Léon Bloy* (1927); S. Fumet, *Mission de Léon Bloy* (1935); A. L. Laquerrière and J. Bollery, *Biblio-Iconographie de Léon Bloy* (1935); J. Bollery, *Le Desespéré de Léon Bloy* (1937); Marie Joseph Lory, *Léon Bloy et son époque* (1944) and *Inédits de Léon Bloy* (1945).

M. M.

Blum, Léon (1872–, French statesman and critic), born in Paris, was comfortably reared in a liberal, righteous, Jewish merchant family. The schoolboy was sensitive, brilliant, and insubordinate. Leaving the Ecole Normale Supérieure in 1891 after one year of unsatisfactory work (he had found the discipline burdensome), he earned *licences* in letters and in law and at 23 was appointed to the Conseil d'Etat, where he served with distinction until entering the Chamber of Deputies in 1919. As a youth the future premier was charmingly successful in society and early became a respected and in some cases cherished companion of his literary generation. He was happily married in 1896. In 1892 had begun his tie with the *Revue blanche,* in which appeared the bulk of his writings for a decade—mainly literary reviews and essays, sometimes political articles (his friendship with Lucien Herr and Jaurès was decisive), sometimes autobiographical short stories. The volume *En lisant* (1906) offers a fine selection of his periodical essays. From 1904 to 1911 his dramatic reviews, partly collected with the title *Au théâtre* (4 vols., 1906–1911), regularly appeared in a succession of Paris journals. Here Blum gives free play to his powers of analysis, finds much to arouse enthusiasm, but recognizes no masterpieces. His *Nouvelles Conversations de Goethe avec Eckermann* (1907; in *Revue blanche,* 1897–1901) is written in a style both lucid and fertile with paradoxes; Blum presents, arbitrarily, but with fitting intelligence and gentility, a contemporary Goethe discussing letters, authors, ideas, and politics. Prophetically for Blum, his socialistic Goethe envisions a high role for synthesists—as supercritics and then statesmen, guiding art and science toward the betterment of humanity.

No traditionalist, Blum is still a moralist, like Gide (*q.v.*) whose genius he early noted. He wished his provocative *Du mariage* (1907) to be considered a sincerely moral essay. His literary affinities, aside from the 17th century, are closest with Stendhal, Flaubert (*q.v.*), Marivaux, and, outside France, Tolstoy (*q.v.*), Disraeli, and Hardy. Marivaux he prefers to Molière; he treasures *L'Education sentimentale* and places not only Tolstoy, but also Hardy and D'Annunzio (*q.v.*) above his modern compatriots of the novel. His crowning literary effort, *Stendhal et le beylisme* (1914), resulted from years of devoted scholarship and, though slow to gain recognition, now stands as an excellent example of intuitive, yet objective, literary penetration. Blum claimed Stendhal as a brother, early discovering in himself the qualities of the élite. But his sentimentality does indeed rather recall his other favorite, Marivaux, and his lucidity tends toward intellectuality. His severest critics, literary and political, stress the latter word and go so far as to call him unfeeling. Blum himself, with his race, speaks of "justice" before "charity." Few without prejudice have challenged his passion for that quality.

See: R. L. Stokes, *Léon Blum* (1937); M. Thiébaut, *En lisant M. Léon Blum* (1937); M. Vichniac, *Léon Blum* (1937).

J. D. Y.

Blunck, Hans Friedrich (1880–, German novelist and poet), born in Altona, is in every respect a genuine product of Low German peasantry and is today recognized as the interpreter of the natives along the Baltic and the North Seas and as the exponent of their folklore. For a number of years he was syndic of the University of Hamburg, and from 1933 to 1935 he served as president of the Reichsschrifttumskammer. He has since retired to a farm in Holstein and is devoting his time to writing.

He became known after the First World War through a trilogy of novels published under the collective title *Das werdende Volk,* presenting in the first part the story of the warrior and statesman *Heinz Hoyer* (1920), in the second part the adventures of the roving seaman *Berend Fock* (1921), and in the last part the life history of the farmer and prophet *Stelling Rottkinnsohn* (1923). All three are types of the poet's own people. Another trilogy, *Drei Bücher aus der Frühgeschichte* (1926–1928), is, in its searching qualities, even more subtle and more powerful than its predecessor. With the help of a new technique of combining saga, science, and poetry he re-creates in the first of these three books, *Streit mit den Göttern* (1926), the saga of Weland the smith, who outdistances Wotan in a flying contest. The next book, *Der Kampf der Gestirne* (1926), is written around an old sun myth, and the last, *Gewalt über das Feuer* (1928), deals in a deeply religious mood with the poet's ancestors. Since then he has added to these impressive long novels a volume entitled *Märchen von der Niederelbe* (1931) and two novels based on the journals of his travels through South America, *Die Weibsmühle* (1927) and *Land der Vulkane* (1929). Of his more recent works two important novels portray great historic leaders: *Grosse Fahrt* (1934) deals with the discovery of America by the pirate admiral Pining, and *Der einsame König* (1936) relates the end of Geiserich, the king of the Vandals. Of his dramatic works *Jacob Leisler* (1938), a stage version of the American rebellion headed by Leisler, is the most noteworthy. As a lyricist and writer of epic poetry Blunck has not reached the distinction of his prose works. But his last collection, *Balladen und Gedichte* (1937), which supersedes several previous editions, shows that he masters traditional forms with force and skill. In 1938 Blunck was awarded the German Goethe medal.

See: A. Soergel, *Dichter aus deutschem Volkstum* (1934); F. Lennartz, *Die Dichter unserer Zeit* (1938).

A. Bu.

Boborykin, Peter Dmitriyevich (1836–1921, Russian novelist, short-story writer, and dramatist), born near Nizhni-Novgorod, studied law and chemistry at the University of Kazan and then mathematics and medicine at Dorpat. Although he was the author and translator of some fairly successful textbooks, he soon turned his attention to the theatre and the novel. In 1860 he wrote his first drama, *Odnodvorets* (The Freeholder), and also became known for his *feuilletons* published under the pseudonym Neskazhus. His novel *V put-dorogu* (On the Way) appeared in 1862, and from then on until his death he wrote over 20 novels and some 50 stories on Russian life. He studied in Germany and at the Collège de France and the Sorbonne. In 1872 he brought out *Teatralnoye iskusstvo* (The Art of the Theatre) and for a while in 1891 was director of stock at the Gorevaya Theatre in Moscow. He was a constant traveler. He withdrew from Russia at the triumph of Bolshevism and died in Switzerland in 1921.

For many years a kind of popular dean of Russian letters and constant favorite with most of the reading public, Boborykin did not win the approval of the critics and is not recognized as a really creative artist or thinker. He had a knack for giving a pleasant and somewhat superficial picture of the most recent developments in Russian life, often before the new ideas were fully assimilated by society. His interpretations were often faulty, but they were nonetheless well received. His great subject was the decay of the old aristocratic society and the growing power of the businessman, often drawn from the ranks of the old peasantry or the merchant classes of the Old Believers. Among his most characteristic works are *Zhertva vechernyaya* (1868; Evening Sacrifice), *Solidnyia dobrodeteli* (1870; Solid Virtues), *Deltsy* (1872; Men of Affairs), *Doktor Tsibulka* (1874), *Kitai-gorod* (1882), *Na ushcherbe* (1890; On the Wane), *Vasili Tyorkin* (1892), *Pereval* (1894; The Summit), and *Tyaga* (1898; The Flight).

With some talent for observing the shifting currents of life and one of the first to appreciate the new social trends in Russia, Boborykin hardly tried to penetrate deeply and indeed he remains as a novelist of a type that is rare in Russian literature. He had no message to convey, no doctrine to preach; he was simply able to give a good picture of the world around him and with this to hold the attention of the ordinary citizen of his own day.

See: S. Vengerov, *Kritiko-biografichesky slovar,* IV (1895), 191–241; M. J. Olgin, *A Guide to Russian Literature* (1920).

C. A. M.

Boelsche, Wilhelm (1861–1939, German critic, editor, scientist, and novelist), was born in Cologne. His life was devoted entirely to literary and scientific activities. Boelsche was one of the most active members of the naturalistic group in Berlin, a member of the literary club "Durch" (*q.v.*) and later a leader of the literary group in Friedrichshagen, cofounder of the socialistic *Freie Volksbühne,* and editor of the naturalistic journal *Freie Bühne.* A scientist in his own right and a well-known popularizer of contemporary scientific ideas, Boelsche formulated and defended the naturalistic position on questions of aesthetics and *Weltanschauung* in various articles in the *Freie Bühne* and wrote one of the important documents of the period, *Die naturwissenschaftlichen Grundlagen der Poesie: Prolegomena einer realistischen Aesthetik* (1887). In this he demands that modern literature accept science as its basis, and he analyzes the meaning of science for the special problems of literature. He further discusses in terms of contemporary scientific hypotheses the problems of freedom of will, immortality, and love as they impinge on the literary portrayal of the human being. Primary influences on his thought are Darwin and Zola (*q.v.*). Typically naturalistic are his demand that literature seek vital contact with contemporary life, his emphasis on the evolutionary nature of all human activity, his belief in the influence of heredity and environment, and his desire for extreme objectivity of portrayal. In *Hinter der Weltstadt* (1901) he wrote an important account of the contemporary literary life in Berlin and Friedrichshagen. His best-known novel is *Die Mittagsgöttin* (1891). His later career was devoted largely to popular scientific works, such as *Das Liebesleben in der Natur* (1898–1902). As biographer he wrote *Heinrich Heine* (1887) and edited the works of several well-known literary and scientific writers.

W. H. R.

Böhlau, Helene (1859–, German novelist and writer of short stories), was born in Weimar and there grew to maturity. In love with her literary mentor, a much older man, she followed him to Constantinople, where she married him; her husband became a Moslem under the name of Omar al Raschid Bey. Her early days in Weimar, her flight to Constantinople, and her subsequent idyllic life in the Near East were the significant experiences which shaped her work.

Her writings fall into two main groups, one composed of light, *gemütlich,* and often charming stories of Weimar in the time of Goethe, the other comprising "thesis novels" (and *Novellen*), largely feminist in tendency. Of the first group her *Ratsmädelgeschichten* (1888) is the most successful example. The primary theme of her more serious works is the problem of woman in a world dominated by men (*Das Recht der Mutter,* 1897; *Halbtier,* 1899); but with all her feminism, her male characters are often sympathetically drawn. She proclaims the right of the unhappily married individual to divorce (*Im frischen Wasser,* 1891). *Isebies* (1911) is an autobiographical novel. Helene Böhlau's novels are marked by strong feeling and ethical nobility; they suffer from a too obvious revealing of didactic purpose, from sentimentality, and from the fact that many of the problems which she discusses are no longer of immediate interest. A collection of her works in six volumes appeared in 1915.

H. C. H.

Boito, Arrigo (1842–1918, Italian poet, musician, and librettist), was born in Padua. His father, a good painter of miniatures, abandoned his wife, the Polish countess Giuseppina Radolinska, when Arrigo was about 10 years old and later was killed in a drunken brawl. With the disintegration of his family, young Boito was introduced to a life of want and loneliness. These tragic episodes, however, were mitigated by the companionship of his brother Camillo, who became an eminent architect, and by his mother's intelligent interest in his musical aptitude. Eager to foster this inclination, she went to live in Milan, where she succeeded in having Arrigo admitted to the Conservatory. While still there he composed a cantata, *Il quattro giugno* and a mystery, *Le Sorelle d'Italia.* The lyrics of these two works were entirely Boito's, but the music was in part by Franco Faccio, the poet's inseparable friend. Recognition for the successful presentation of these works at the Conservatory came in the form of a reward from Francesco De Sanctis (*q.v.*), then minister of education, which financed a trip abroad for the two young artists. In Paris they made the acquaintance of Rossini, Verdi, and Berlioz. The atmosphere was charged with the new theories and activities of the Parnassians, realists, and impressionists. It was natural for Boito, who had already shown a penchant for unorthodox phrase and defiant tone in his first works, to identify himself with this world. After Paris, Boito proceeded to Mystki, Poland, where he met his Polish relatives, and from there to Germany, Belgium, and England. He returned to Milan an avowed enemy of all that was smug and materialistic in the literary and musical world of Italy. An admirer of Goethe, Beethoven, and Wagner (*q.v.*), he hoped to infuse new life into Italian poetry by following the pattern of Germanic romantic poetry: the fusion of verse and music. But his real idols were Hugo and Baudelaire (*q.v.*).

Boito never in fact realized his noble intention of lifting Italian literature from its low estate, although he did succeed in introducing new harmonies in Italian music. Like most of the *scapigliati,* a group of eccentric and ultra-romantic writers of the 1860's, he lacked the spiritual insight and creative spark to produce a genuine poetic work. Boito was essentially a virtuoso of rhyme and rhythm, an able craftsman of supple, musical verse. Having led everyone to expect great things of him, Boito worked feverishly in a variety of genres: he translated Polish works, musical dramas of Wagner, and Weber's *Freischutz;* wrote critical articles on music, painting, and sculpture; and, with Emilio Praga, produced a satiric comedy, *Le Madri galanti* (1863). Praga and he also revived the *Figaro,* a critical and polemic review. But the masterpiece never emerged. Instead he only succeeded in presenting his problem, the eternal struggle of good and evil, against a weird and fantastic background, peopling his world with strange and morbid characters and flooding the whole with sonorous verses. Such features appear in *Re Orso* (1865), a dramatic legend and his first major work, and to a lesser degree in the more personal *Libro dei versi* (1877), and in *Ero e Leandro* (1879), music by Bottesini; *La Gioconda* (1876), music by Ponchielli; and in other librettos: *Pier Luigi Farnese* (1891), music by Palumbo; *La Falce* (1875), music by Catalani; and *Amleto* (1865), music by Franco Faccio. In *Otello* (1887) and *Falstaff* (1893), music by Verdi, his vivid imagination appears more disciplined, inspired and also restrained no doubt by Shakespeare's art. It was lack of restraint which caused his original *Mefistofele,* first presented at Milan in 1868, to fail dismally. However, in 1875, abridged and modified, this same opera was generously and warmly applauded at Bologna.

The work upon which Boito lavished many years of thought and effort was the dramatic poem *Nerone* (1901), which he himself set to music. As an opera, it was first presented at La Scala on May 1, 1924, under the direction of Arturo Toscanini. Even this work, which represents both the fruit of a youthful inspiration and mature art, is replete with mystery and ritual, fanfare and pageantry, morbid passions and macabre scenes, depraved and cynical characters. Yet, although this work fails to satisfy and convince, it is somewhat redeemed by the portrayal of the simple, firm faith of the Christian Fanuel and the deep humanity of Rubria.

See: F. Ballo, *Arrigo Boito* (1938).

P. P. M.

Bojer, Johan (1872–, Norwegian novelist and dramatist), a native of Orkdalsøren, near Trondheim, won an international circle of readers by presenting the problems of early 20th-century Norway in entertaining fictional form. He established himself in Norway with *Et folketog* (1896; A Procession), in France and Italy with *Troens magt* (1903, The Power of Faith; Eng. tr., *The Power of a Lie,* 1908), in England and America with *Den store hunger* (1916; Eng. tr., *The Great Hunger,* 1918). These works revolved around rather simple themes, *e.g.,* that many politicians are rascals, that idealists are often self-deceiving egoists, and that material success does not of itself bring happiness. But they were widely acclaimed, even by such prominent and various writers as Brandes, Rolland (*qq.v.*), Tagore, Galsworthy, and Hergesheimer, who found Bojer stimulating and praised him for his realism, his vigorous style, and his original ideas. Norwegian critics, however, refused to recognize him as a major writer, on the grounds that his ideas interfered with his art, his characters were insufficiently motivated, and his style lacked artistic cultivation. They were won over to a somewhat grudging admiration only by his epics of folk life, *Den siste viking* (1921; Eng. tr., *Last of the Vikings,* 1923), which dealt with the Lofoten fishermen, and *Folk ved sjøen* (1929; Eng. tr., *Folk by the Sea,* American title, *The Everlasting Struggle,* both 1931), a story of the poverty-stricken tenants among whom Bojer spent his boyhood. These works, along with some of his fairy tales and the fantasia entitled *Fangen som sang* (1913; Eng. tr., *The Prisoner Who Sang,* 1924), certainly seem to show the best promise of enduring value.

Within his own generation Bojer's grasp on his public was predicated on the immediacy of his writing to the problems that agitated the civilized world. Nowhere else outside the public press could one find so detailed and entertaining a panorama of all the surface aspects of Norwegian life through a generation of pre-war and post-war adjustment. Practically every major event and every topic of discussion between 1890 and 1925 turns up here: the status of women, the relation of labor and capital, the return to the soil, national defense, munitions manufacture, war profiteering, and many others. The characters in his books (in contrast, *e.g.,* to those of Hamsun, *q.v.*) are such as one might conceivably have met in the rapidly advancing Norway of that day, a generation of hard-working and progressive people (the engineer is Bojer's favorite character), national and enthusiastic, liberal and somewhat inclined to overoptimism about the future. This purely sociological value of his writings is fortified by a remarkable skill of observation, which enables him to reproduce creatively the manners and mannerisms of real people, with their quips and anecdotes, their foibles and self-deceptions, as well as their unconscious heroisms. He does not delve deeply into the mechanism of their being, but marches them firmly along toward a dramatic dénouement. The ideas which he advocates through them are never profound, for his views are practically a barometer of liberal bourgeois opinion in his day; he is the mouthpiece of an idealistic individualism which already seems quaintly old-fashioned. It is easy to see the many influences that have played on his thinking—the ethical idealism of Ibsen (*q.v.*), the national and religious liberalism of Björnson (*q.v.*), the poetic exaltation of Victor Hugo, the realistic techniques of Zola and Maupassant (*qq.v.*). He lacks the colossal vigor of these men, and his brew is to some extent a dilution of their doctrines. He lacks those mighty swings of the pendulum that terrify, bewitch, and inspire. His appeal lies in his humanism, his kindliness, and that undogmatic religion which fills his best characters with an abiding faith in the glory of hard work and the mysterious power of love.

See: Carl Gad, *Johan Bojer, the Man and His Works* (1920); A. W. Porterfield, "America Reads Johan Bojer," *American-Scandinavian Review,* IX (1921), 477–481; H. P. Lödrup, "Johan Bojer," *American-Scandinavian Review,* XIV (1926), 207–217; O. E. Rölvaag, "When a Novelist Is in a Hurry," *Scandinavian Studies and Notes,* IX (1926–1927), 61–67; P. G. La Chesnais, *Johan Bojer* (1930, in French; Norwegian tr., 1932).

E. H.

Bölsche, Wilhelm, *see* **Boelsche.**

Bonilla y San Martín, Adolfo (1875–1926, Spanish critic and literary historian), was born at Madrid, where he spent most of his active life as a writer, university professor, academician, lawyer, and counselor of the stock exchange. He lived in an apartment completely choked with books which surrounded him on all sides as he sat at his diminutive table, making his vast frame seem doubly large. His learning was matched by an amazing memory, both being commensurate with the numberless volumes among which he had the habit of writing until early morning hours. His gifts bore a worthy comparison with those of his famous teacher Marcelino Menéndez y Pelayo (*q.v.*), whose favorite disciple he was and in whose inspiring company he frequently spent many hours up to the time of Menéndez y Pelayo's death.

He was professor of philosophy at the University of Madrid, and his most enduring work is to be found in that field. Sound and original are *Luis Vives y la filosofía del renacimiento* (1903), *Historia de la filosofía española* (2 vols., 1908–1911; unfinished), *El Código de Hammurabi y otros estudios de historia y filosofía jurídicas* (1909), and *Fernando de Córdoba (1425–1486?) y los orígenes del renacimiento filosófico en España* (1911). While still a student of the law he published *Concepto y teoría del derecho* (1897); many legal investigations subsequently appeared, such as *Derecho mercantil español* (1904) and *Derecho bursátil* (1924; with D. Emilio Miñana).

In emulation of the vast literary labors of his maestro Menéndez y Pelayo, he edited, with commentaries, a number of Spanish classics. Some of these editions are of service as class texts and all of them reveal, in specific elucidations, his extensive unmatched information in the culture of his country. The most noteworthy are his definitive edition (1910) of Luis Vélez de Guevara's *El diablo cojuelo* and *Clásicos de la literatura española* (12 vols., 1915–1917). He was also coeditor, with R. Schevill, of *Obras completas de Cervantes* (18 vols., 1914–1941); 12 volumes were completed at the time of his death. Two admirable studies may conclude this abbreviated list, *La vida corporativa de los estudiantes españoles en sus relaciones con la historia de las universidades* (1914) and *Las bacantes, o del origen del teatro* (1921).

Bonilla traveled to the United States twice, in 1916 and in 1924, lecturing on Spanish literature at various American universities. Two long sojourns were devoted to courses given at the University of California. He was always greatly respected as a forceful teacher and attracted students by the readiness with which he gave to everyone his time and his unstinted kindly encouragement, he himself being the exemplar of a tireless and devoted worker in the field of Spanish literature and history.

See: J. Puyol y Alonso, *Adolfo Bonilla y San Martín; su vida y sus obras* (1927).

R. S.

Bonsels, Waldemar (1881–, German novelist, poet, and playwright), was born near Hamburg and wandered over Europe, Egypt, India, and much of the Western Hemisphere before finally settling in Ambach on Lake Starnberg. His *Indienfahrt* (written in 1912 but not published until 1916; Eng. tr., *An Indian Journey*, 1928) gave to the German public a new kind of travel literature; in a few simple and lyrically conceived incidents he characterized India, the poverty of its humanity, the lush extravagance of nature. Impressions of the Americas were set forth in two later books, *Brasilianische Tage und Nächte* (with A. von Dungern, 1931) and *Der Reiter in der Wüste; eine Amerikafahrt* (1935).

Bonsel's exceeding popularity rests, however, upon one book in particular, *Die Biene Maja* (1912; Eng. tr., *Maya*, 1922). In this tale, in which the creatures of nature are disarmingly endowed with the most pleasing aspects of human intelligence and emotions, he elaborates an incredibly sentimental gospel of love for nature, for a vaguely conceived God, and for his fellow beings. Three further tales in the same manner (*Das Anjekind*, 1913, Eng. tr., *Angel-Child*, 1926; *Himmelsvolk*, 1915, Eng. tr., *Heavenfolk*, 1924; *Mario und die Tiers*, 1927, Eng. tr., *Adventures of Mario*, 1930) proved to be almost equally popular with a certain public indifferent to the irresponsible and florid qualities of the prose of this minor author. The struggle and search for God and pleasure are enlarged in his "Vagabundentrilogie," *Menschenwege* (1918), *Eros und die Evangelien* (1920), and *Narren und Helden* (1923; Eng. tr., of the trilogy, *Notes of a Vagabond*, 1931). Even in such early "minutiae" as *Ave Vita* (1908, later appearing as *Leben, ich grüsse Dich!*), *Der letzte Frühling* (1905), *Blut* (1905), and the Faust-like *Don Juan* (1919) and in the later *Mario und Gisele* (1930), the theme is an indistinct sort of exuberant love. More attractive and of greater apparent promise are his earliest books, *Der tiefste Traum* (1911) and *Wartalun* (1911), in which the supernatural and German folk themes are happily fused.

See: Fritz Adler, *Waldemar Bonsels: Sein Weltbild und seine Gestalten* (1925); Bonsels, *Tage der Kindheit* (1931); C. R. Goedsche, "Bonsels' Indienfahrt, a Travel Book as a Work of Art," *Monatshefte für deutschen Unterricht*, XXVII (1935), 81–87.

V. L.

Bontempelli, Massimo (1884–, Italian novelist), born in the city of Como, has had an extremely varied literary career. In his early days a teacher in secondary schools, he was a writer in the academic tradition—*Egloghe* (1904), *Settenari e sonetti* (1910), and *Odi* (1910). There is even a tragedy, *Costanza* (1905), included in the production of this early period, which, as critics have noted, had a Carduccian flavor. Indeed like Carducci (*q.v.*) he edited texts for classroom use. At about the same time that he turned from teaching to journalism his artistic outlook underwent a revolutionary change, and he became a convert to futurism. As a journalist Bontempelli had a career of considerable distinction, serving at various times on the staff of the *Piccolo* and the *Mondo* and directing the *Cronaca letteraria* of Florence and the *Fieramosca*. Though he did not long remain faithful to the exaggerations of *futurismo*, this movement has left its mark on his work, and it is reasonable to say that the odd combination of the scholar and the advance guard experimentalist is what gives his books their peculiar charm and vitality. His style is sober and severe, natural, effortless, and eminently readable. His topics or plots, if they may be called that, are the most bizarre imaginable. In this combination of logic and eccentricity he has much in common with Pirandello (*q.v.*) and some of the *grotteschi,* but he is too original and individual to be classed as a member of any school.

Bontempelli is extremely intelligent and ironical, and his work has for the most part a purely intellectual appeal. It is hard to call to mind a really human character in all his novels and stories. On the other hand his comments on life and society in such volumes as *Sette Savi* (1912) or *La Vita intensa* (1919) are penetrating and arresting, and the characters and plots sufficiently well put together to give point to the underlying thesis. There is a certain restlessness in Bontempelli's art, as indeed one might expect from his checkered career, and this restlessness found its clearest expression as well as its most sympathetic audience in the 20's. In that period of post-war uncertainty and readjustment Bontempelli was at the height of his powers. *La Vita operosa* (1920), *Viaggi e scoperti* (1922), and *Eva ultima* (1923), in addition to the titles mentioned above, may be considered as representing the best of his work. Later works of note are *La Vita e la morte di Adria e dei suoi figli* (1930) and *Il Figlio di due madri* (1933). Bontempelli has achieved a recognized eminence among contemporary writers; among other distinctions he is a member of the Italian Academy.

See: R. Serra, *Le Lettere* (1914), pp. 94–95; G. A. Borgese, *Tempo di edificare* (1923), pp. 127–128; G. Antonini, *Il Romanzo contemporaneo in Italia* (1928), pp. 194–204; P. Pancrazi, *Scrittori italiani del novecento* (1934), pp. 102–107.

T. G. B.

Borchardt, Rudolf (1877–1945, German poet, essayist, historian), was born in Königsberg, of a Jewish family which had been Protestant for some generations and had settled in East Prussia. At Berlin, Bonn, and Göttingen he studied the classics; after 1904 he lived in Italy, chiefly near Lucca or Pistoia, with the exception of short periods in Germany and the years of the First World War, in which he took part. His few publications before 1918 and the lectures which he gave during later years aroused passionate interest and opposition.

Borchardt is a poet of high aim, a philologist and historian of genius gifted with the power of evoking the great past, a "revolutionary conservative," a violent fighter generous in love and hate, combining strongly nationalistic tendencies with a rare intuitive sense and an unusual knowledge of the European heritage, a volcanic personality. And such is his work—lava and flame. His style, with its sharp outlines, its Latin periods quivering with passion, its wide historical vistas, has a poetry of its own, heroic and scornful. He is highly individual, even when he seems closest to great models—as if, through their touch and medium, he won access to his deepest self. His anthologies (*Deutsche Denkreden,* 1925; *Ewiger Vorrat deutscher Poesie,* 1926; *Der Deutsche in der Landschaft,* 1927) form an integral part of his work. His translations were born from his vision of the past, of the medieval period as well as of the Greek middle ages. They range from Tacitus' *Germania* (1914) and Hartmann von Aue's *Armer Heinrich* (1925) to the *Homeric Hymns* (*Altionische Götterlieder,* 1924) and to Pindar (*Pindarische Gedichte,* 1930; one of Borchardt's supreme achievements); from Landor's prose (*Imaginäre Unterhaltungen,* 1923) and Swinburne's verse (*Englische Dichter,* 1936—Borchardt in his youth was steeped in English literature) to old Provence (*Die grossen Trobadors,* 1924) and to Dante's *Vita nuova* (1922) and the whole of the *Commedia* (*Dante deutsch,* 1930—the work of decades). For Dante he created a poetical language of his own, a historically unrealized stage between the German of the Middle Ages and the later language—an undertaking in a way analogous to Doughty's in *Arabia Deserta,* isolated, daring, and grand.

Most of these translations as well as the anthologies are followed by essays which shed new light on their subjects. Borchardt has given a new interpretation to Dante and his epoch (*Epilegomena zu Dante I: Einleitung in die Vita nova,* 1923; *Pisa,* 1938). Some of his prose will stand the test of time: *Das Gespräch über Formen und Platons Lysis deutsch* (1905); *Rede über Hofmannsthal* (1907), a fragment; *Der Krieg und die deutsche Selbsteinkehr* (1915); *Der Krieg und die deutsche Verantwortung* (1916); *Prosa I* (1920); *Gartenphantasie* (1925); *Handlungen und Abhandlungen* (1928); *Die Aufgaben der Zeit gegenüber der Literatur* (1929); *Führung* (1931); *Deutsche Reisende, deutsches Schicksal* (1932); *Schriften I, II* (1934, 1935).

Of his poetry and fiction, up to now only a part is known: short plays (*Krippenspiel,* 1922; *Die geliebte Kleinigkeit,* 1923); prologues of tragic import (*Die Päpstin Jutta I: Verkündigung,* 1920; *Staufer I: Alpenübergang,* 1936); a comedy (*Pamela,* 1934); *novelas* and a novel in contemporary setting, of mannered density (*Das hoffnungslose Geschlecht,* 1929; *Vereinigung durch den Feind hindurch,* 1937); tales —some in verse (*Die halbgerettete Seele,* 1920;

Poetische Erzählungen, 1923; *Der ruhende Herakles,* 1924). One of these tales, "Der Durant," published as a fragment, is perhaps the only legitimate continuation of the German medieval epic, remarkable for its somber force. On this tale and on some of his lyrics of love and of despair (*Jugendgedichte,* 1913; *Die Schöpfung aus Liebe,* 1923; *Vermischte Gedichte,* 1924) Borchardt's significance as a poet may be said to rest securely. His poetry as well as the rest of his work—unlike that of any other writer in tone—is at times of highest rank. An anthology of his verse and prose, *Ausgewählte Werke 1900–1918,* was published in 1925.

See: J. Nadler, "Von Bodmer zu Borchardt," *Wissen und Leben,* 1924, pp. 883–892; J. Nadler, *Literaturgeschichte der deutschen Stämme und Landschaften,* Bd. 4 (1928), pp. 730–732; J. Hofmiller, "Borchardts deutscher Dante," *Corona,* 1932, pp. 246–263.

H. St.

Bordeaux, Henry (1870–, French novelist and critic), has been a very prolific writer, following resolutely in the steps of such Roman Catholic authors as Vogüé, Bourget, and Brunetière (*qq.v.*). He was born at Thonon-les-Bains, Haute-Savoie, of an old and distinguished family of magistrates. Although he remained all his life a devoted son of his province, he has spent most of his life in Paris, where he had come early to study law. He published reminiscences of his career as a lawyer in *Carnet d'un stagiaire* (1911).

He has written all through his career an abundance of essays along the most diverse lines—*Ames modernes* (1895), *Les Ecrivains et les mœurs* (three series, 1897–1902), *Vies intimes* (1904). He has composed monographs, books for the young, animal stories. But he is most likely to be remembered as a writer of fiction. A historical novel, *Jeanne Michelin; chronique du XVIIIe siècle* (1896), was soon followed by a series of stories that proved extremely successful with the general public, such as *La Peur de vivre* (1902; Eng. tr., *The Fear of Living,* 1913), *Les Roquevillard* (1906; Eng. tr., *The Will to Live,* 1915), *Les Yeux qui s'ouvrent* (1908; Eng. tr., *The Awakening,* 1914), *La Croisée des chemins* (1909; Eng. tr., *The Parting of the Ways,* 1911), *La Robe de laine* (1910; Eng. tr., *The Woollen Dress,* 1912), *La Neige sur les pas* (1912; Eng. tr., *Footprints beneath the Snow,* 1913). All are what may be called "family novels," with the setting in most cases in Savoy; they have received high praise from some critics and very severe handling from others; there can be no question of their moral earnestness.

In 1914 Henry Bordeaux was mobilized, serving as an infantry captain and then in the Intelligence Department, at General Headquarters. He wrote moving and valuable books on some of the events of these fateful years: *La Chanson de Vaux-Douaumont, I: Les Derniers Jours du Fort de Vaux, II: Les Captifs délivrés* (1916–1917; Eng. tr., *The Last Days of Fort Vaux, March 9–June 7, 1916,* 1917; *The Deliverance of the Captives, Douaumont-Vaux, October 21–November 3, 1916,* 1919); *Le Chevalier de l'air: Guynemer* (1918; Eng. tr., *Guynemer, Knight of the Air,* 1918); *La Bataille devant Souville* (1921); *Le Maréchal Fayolle* (1921).

After the First World War, Bordeaux resumed his career as a novelist, with such works as *La Résurrection de la chair* (1920), *Le Fantôme de la Rue Michel Ange* (1922), *Valombré* (1929). *Murder Party, ou Celle qui n'était pas invitée* (1931; Eng. tr., *Murder Party,* 1931) has a title borrowed from the American society game. In 1938 Bordeaux signed his 50th novel, *Cendres chaudes.* In Montreal in 1942 *La Sonate au clair de lune* was published. From his travels in the East, between the two wars, he had brought back *Yamilé sous les cèdres* (1923; Eng. tr., *The Gardens of Omar,* 1924). Bordeaux contributed to many of the best-known periodicals of the time, and from 1910 to 1921 he was dramatic critic of the *Revue hebdomadaire* (see his 4 vols., *Vie au théâtre*). He was elected to the French Academy to succeed Jules Lemaître (*q.v.*) and officially received in 1920.

See: Fidus, "M. Henry Bordeaux," *Revue des deux mondes,* May 15, 1920, pp. 312–331; Jules Bertaut, *Henry Bordeaux et son œuvre* (1924).

A. Sz.

Borgese, Giuseppe Antonio (1882–, Italian critic, novelist, and publicist), born near Palermo, spent his early years in his native Sicily and went to school until he was 18. He then went to the University of Florence from which he obtained his doctor's degree in 1903, submitting as his thesis a masterly *Storia della critica romantica in Italia* (1905). Borgese was already closely bound in his intellectual development to the method and thinking of Croce (*q.v.*). This alliance, which after an exchange of views was to grow into a progressive, often controversial, relationship, keyed much of his early work.

After a one-year teaching apprenticeship at the University of Turin, Borgese went, in 1910, to the University of Rome, where he taught German literature for the following seven years. During this period his characteristic pace of intense creative activity was set. He wrote with intuition and taste about literature and the arts (much of this criticism was collected in the three-volume work *La Vita e il libro,* 1910–1913). In 1917 he was called to the University of Milan, first as professor of German literature and then, after 1924, as professor of aesthetics and literary criticism. He held this chair until 1931, the year in which he came to the United States. His activity in creative literature had come to the fore with *Rubè* (1921; Eng. tr., 1923), a novel highly praised in Italy and abroad. *Rubè,* summarizing an epoch, centered around its doomed hero the passions of the First World War and the catastrophe of the Armistice, foreboding vaster ruins. He also wrote poems, plays, and short stories (see especially a collection of stories, *Il Pellegrino appassionato,* 1933).

In 1917–1918, under Orlando's premiership, Borgese headed the Press and Propaganda Bureau. His political awareness, which had matured through sharply chastening perception of the pitfalls of demagogy as personified in a former friend, D'Annunzio (*q.v.*), made him recoil from Fascism. During the year when Borgese was teaching and lecturing in the United States, the Fascist oath was imposed on members of the teaching profession. Unwilling to sign and being abroad, he chose exile for the duration of a regime he abominated.

Beginning in 1931 Borgese has taught at the University of California; the New School for Social Research, New York City; Smith College. Since 1936 he has been at the University of Chicago as professor of Italian literature. When, in 1938, he became a citizen of the United States, it meant something more to him than the casual assumption of a title, a new degree; he accepted it as a sign or seal of a new assignment in living. He felt his greatest duty now was to function within the framework of the new society in which he lived as a writer—and in the new language. *Goliath* (1937), *The City of Man* (1940; with Thomas Mann, Lewis Mumford, *et al.*), and *Common Cause* (1943) constitute a valid contribution of material prepared for the well-informed nonspecialist in America.

Integration or Unity—or, as Borgese puts it, "Syntax"—beyond and against a transitional era of fragmentarism and decadence is his leading thought or *idée maîtresse* through all the phases of his career. Since the very start he has rallied directly to De Sanctis's (*q.v.*) example, merging the aesthetic analysis of a single poetic work with its interpretation as a witness to history, and assigning to each its place in the collective unfinished masterpiece which Borgese calls the Bible of Humanity.

See: E. Roditi, "G. A. Borgese," *Sewanee Review,* L (1942), 57–68.

F. K.

Borsi, Giosue-Francesco (1888–1915, Italian journalist and writer), was born in Leghorn, in a Carduccian, anticlerical environment typical of that time. His parents, Averardo Borsi, later editor of the *Telegrafo,* and Verdiana Fabbri, were natives of Castagneto Maremma, later known as Castagneto Carducci. It is not surprising, therefore, that their son became Carducci's (*q.v.*) godchild and that he was named Giosue (Joshua) in honor of his godfather, and not in honor of Moses' successor. Neither is it surprising, since Borsi's father was an ardent anticlerical while his mother was a fervent Catholic, that the name of the recalcitrant pagan-minded poet of the Maremma was coupled with that of the docile Seraphic poet of Assisi. After completing his elementary and secondary education in Leghorn, Giosue, to please his father, matriculated in the faculty of jurisprudence at the University of Pisa. He devoted more time, however, to his literary pursuits than to the study of law and had some difficulty in qualifying for a doctorate in jurisprudence.

As long as his father lived, Giosue led a carefree, dissolute life. He frequented the salons, where he was always welcome because of his literary talent and personal charm. He wrote well and recited even better. As one would expect of a Carduccian disciple, he took delight in classical artistry and in carefully wrought phraseology. This is evident in writings like *Primus Fons* (poems published in 1907), and in the much admired *Il Pappa e i dindi* (1922), a lyric written for his little nephew's birthday, in which there is an apologia of the Italian language. Upon the death of his father in December, 1910, Giosue found himself burdened with manifold cares and responsibilities, the weight of which was augmented by the sorrow caused by the death of his beloved sister, Laura, and of his little nephew, Dino. It was during this period that Borsi underwent the moral and religious crisis recorded in his *Confessioni a Giulia* (1915) which, helped by the beautiful example of his sweet, saintly mother, culminated in his return to the practice of the faith of his baptism. From this time on his writings are decidedly spiritual. They differ from those prior to his conversion not only in content, but also in style. There is no evidence of that fastidiousness of former years. Both in the *Colloqui* (1916; Eng. tr., *A Soldier's Confidences with God,* 1918), and in his *Lettere dal fronte* (1916), one is impressed by the sincerity of his thoughts and the simplicity of his style. Less than a year after his conversion, upon Italy's joining the Allies, Borsi enlisted in the Italian army. Five months later, on November 10, 1915, he was killed at Zagora while leading his men in a daring attack. His heroic death and his startling conversion gave to Borsi's writings a popularity which, under ordinary circumstances, they hardly would have attained.

See: Gustave Cantini, *Giosue Borsi; nuova biografia* (1938).

S. M. S. M.

Botelho, Abel Acácio de Almeida (1854–1917, Portuguese novelist), was born in Taboaço, Beira Alta. He first followed a military career; later he turned to politics and subsequently to diplomacy. Under the republic (1910) he was appointed ambassador to Argentina, where he died. He began his literary career as a journalist; he tried poetry and the drama, without much success, and finally the novel, in which he embraced the Zolaesque realism (*see* Zola) initiated by Eça de Queiroz (*q.v.*). His first novelistic works are found in a compilation of stories, *Mulheres da Beira* (1885–1896; Women of Beira), in which, despite the still romantic character of the themes, already the technical process and the serenity of vision presage the realist. His predominantly visual temperament, his great powers of observation, and his talents as a painter of landscapes are revealed brilliantly in one of the stories, "Corrida de touros no Sabugal" (Bullfight in Sabugal). But the novelistic work to which he owes his fame is the series *Patologia social,* which begins with *O barão de Lavos* (1891; The Baron of Lavos). In the preface he explains the psychological basis of the work: the normal personality is a result of balance between thought, sentiment, and will; when any one of these predominates, a psychological case appears. Each novel proposes to exemplify a special case of disorder, in characters where this derives from a physiological-sexual determinism, from a carnal fatalism. Within this monism all of his work, which reached the extremes of descriptive naturalism, is developed—and limited. *O livro de Alda* (1898; The Book of Alda), *Amanhã* (1902; Tomorrow), and *Os lázaros* (1904; The Lepers) form a part of the *Patologia,* which shocked the public in its time. His style, showing great linguistic richness, is elaborated with medical neologisms. His powers of observation make him a minutely precise painter of attitudes and gestures, and he showed a remarkable feeling for color.

See: F. de Figueiredo, "Abel Botelho," in *História da literatura realista,* 1924 ed., pp. 214–218.

E. G. D.

Bourdet, Edouard (1887–, French dramatist), was born in Saint-Germain-en-Laye, Seine-et-Oise. When still a very young man he wrote a light comedy, *Le Rubicon* (1910), which established him as a master in the genre. Antoine (*q.v.*) expressed his amazement that a beginner should possess such sure touch and also praised Bourdet for his power of observation. For the next 10 years Bourdet was not heard from. He came before the public again in 1920 with *La Cage ouverte,* followed in 1922 by *L'Heure du berger* and in 1924 by *L'Homme enchaîné.* In 1926 he gained general recognition with *La Prisonnière* (Eng. tr., *The Captive,* 1926). *Vient de paraître* (1928) added to his renown. *Le Sexe faible,* produced in 1930 (Eng. tr., *The Sex Fable,* 1931), enjoyed an exceptionally long run, as did *La Fleur des pois* (1932), *Les Temps difficiles* (1934), and *Margot* (1935).

Bourdet is one of the principal contemporary exponents of the comedy of manners. His plays are satirical; the author, without ever losing his tolerant smile, mercilessly exposes the follies and foibles of the society of his day. His work is a gallery of the vices of the time, a clever mixture of fact and satire, which combines the daring of a very personal autobiographer and the prudence of the moralist.

See: F. Porché, "Edouard Bourdet," *Revue de Paris,* Année XLIV (1937), Tome V, pp. 217–228.

P. B.

Bourget, Paul (1852–1935, French novelist and critic), was born at Amiens. He was educated first at the Lycée of Clermont-Ferrand and later, in Paris, at the Lycée Louis-le-Grand and at the Ecole des Hautes Etudes. He began writing poetry, and in 1875 was published *La Vie inquiète,* a book of verse, followed by *Edel* (1877) and *Les Aveux* (1882). Meanwhile he was earning a living by contributing articles to newspapers. A series of essays, written for the *Nouvelle Revue,* published under the titles *Essais de psychologie contemporaine* (1883) and *Nouveaux Essais de psychologie contemporaine* (1885), attracted the attention of the literary world, for those studies marked a new departure in criticism. Adopting

Taine's dictum that literature is a "living psychology," Bourget made a searching analysis of the mental and moral characteristics of certain writers who belonged to the generation preceding his own, and tried to determine to what degree they were responsible for the pessimism which he found everywhere around him. This approach to literature appeared so illuminating that the author was immediately rated as the most original critic since Sainte-Beuve.

But Bourget wanted above all to become a novelist, and he judiciously chose the genre which best permitted the application of his gift of analysis to the study of real life—the psychological novel. His first attempt, *L'Irréparable,* appeared in 1884. *Cruelle Enigme* (1885), *André Cornélis* (1887), *Mensonges* (1887), came next. In these works Bourget not only revived a kind of fiction which is specifically French, but gave it a new form; a minute analysis of human feelings was his chief aim. The author applied the method of precise investigation that had made his *Essais* so convincing, and met the tastes of a generation brought up under the unchallenged domination of realism. Bourget selected as the object of his dissection the wealthy parvenus who were the waifs left behind by the Second Empire. It was not a world in which love can be presented under its innocent aspects. But behind the painter of rather objectionable situations there lurked a stern moralist convinced that "psychology is to ethics what anatomy is to therapeutics." This moralist came out openly in the next novel, *Le Disciple* (1889), an earnest indictment of the deterministic theory. In the preface the author emphasized the lesson he wanted to impart. Asserting that the spiritual values are the important thing in life, he besecched the youth of his time to shun scientific epicurism, a sure road to immorality. Henceforth the ethical note could be heard more distinctly, and Bourget still further enlarged the scope of his novels when he discovered that man, so far the chief object of his interest, cannot be dissociated from the social structure of which he forms a part. This conception found expression in *Cosmopolis* (1893), in which a love story is subservient to a denunciation of cosmopolitism. The political discussions which were the aftermath of the Dreyfus case accelerated Bourget's advance towards the social novel. He became convinced that the only remedy for the moral diseases under which civilization labored was for his country a return to its ancient tradition. He therefore recommended the rehabilitation of an aristocracy, on the model of the English nobility, hereditary but constantly rejuvenated by the admission of men of merit, and a revival of the pristine religion of France. Nearly all the novels he wrote after 1900, *L'Etape* (1902), *Un Divorce* (1904), *L'Emigré* (1907), present different aspects of this belief. In *Le Sens de la mort* (1915), *Cœur pensif ne sait où il va* (1924), *Nos actes nous suivent* (2 vols., 1927), and others he turned his attention to the moral and social problems raised by the First World War.

Bourget wrote also a great number of *nouvelles.* The 22 volumes in which they have been collected exhibit the author's versatility. Bourget has tried all kinds of short stories, from a simple anecdote offhandedly told to a story leisurely unfolded by means of a complicated plot. The variety of subjects in such volumes as *Pastels* (1889), *Complications sentimentales* (1898), *Drames de famille* (1900), *Les Détours du cœur* (1908), *Anomalies* (1920)—to give only a few titles—baffles classification. Bourget's best short stories reach a degree of excellence that has rarely been surpassed.

With *La Barricade* (1910) and *Le Tribun* (1911) Bourget tried his hand at the drama. As their subtitles indicate, these plays are "chronicles" of the years 1910–1911, and they evoke the politico-social atmosphere of that period. A survey of this author's achievements would not be complete without mention of a more graceful side of his talent. Bourget was an indefatigable traveler, and he has related some of his wanderings in *Etudes anglaises* (1889), in *Sensations d'Italie* (1891)—probably the best—and in *Outre-mer* (2 vols., 1895), which is the journal of a tour in the United States.

Few writers have been successful in so many fields of literature, Bourget has a shrine of his own in the pantheon of French criticism. His place in fiction is also assured. In his lifetime he was passionately discussed; caught in the maelstrom of the political dissensions which divided public opinion during the period 1894–1914, to some he became an idol or a prophet, for others he served as a butt for detraction. His intellectual qualities, however—his keenness of mind, his insight into the hidden motives of human actions, the lucidity of his reasoning power, the deftness with which he handled the most complicated plots—have generally been recognized. Bourget had not the vitalizing imagination of Balzac, his chief model; but the minute accuracy of his observation, the sincerity with which he reported his findings, combine to make his works invaluable documents in which future students of manners will find a faithful image of French society between the War of 1870 and the Second World War.

See: Giraud, *Paul Bourget* (1934); A. Feuillerat, *Paul Bourget; histoire d'un esprit sous la IIIe République* (1937).

A. F.

Boutelleau, Jacques, *see* Chardonne, Jacques.

Boutens, Pieter Cornelis (1870–1943, Dutch poet), was born in the city of Middelburg, on the island of Walcheren. He studied classical philology at the University of Utrecht, taught Latin and Greek for some years at Noorthey, a boys' preparatory school at Voorschoten, not far from Leiden, and settled down at The Hague, in the first decade of this century, for a quiet bachelor life of study and poetic creation. He counts among the great poets—some consider him the greatest poet—of his generation. His first book of verse, entitled *Verzen,* appeared in 1898, with an introduction by Lodewijk van Deyssel (*q.v.*), then the leading literary critic of Holland. Van Deyssel's praise brought Boutens immediate recognition. His early poetry revealed a mood steeped in melancholy, a contemplative sadness which is purged of all self-pity and despair by the poet's awareness of visible and invisible beauty and by his gift of turning the seen into meaningful symbols of the unseen. This tendency likewise pervades all his later work, which appeared at regular intervals during the next four decades —*Praeludiën* (1902; Preludes), *Stemmen* (1907; Voices), *Vergeten Liedjes* (1909; Forgotten Melodies), *Carmina* (1912; Songs), *Lentemaan* (1916; Spring Moon), *Liederen van Isoude* (1919; Songs of Isolda), *Sonnetten* (1920; Sonnets), *Zomerwolken* (1922; Summer Clouds), *Bezonnen Verzen* (1931; Thoughtful Poems), *Honderd Hollandsche Kwatrijnen* (1932; One Hundred Dutch Quatrains). He was a deeply religious man, not of the church-going type but keenly sensitive to the divine and eternal beyond the everyday pageantry, and obsessed with a nostalgia for the real life of which the actual is but a token. Hence sorrow and death are his favorite themes, but he sees them transfigured into images of light and beauty.

The secret of his greatness is not merely in this aesthetic revaluation of man's existence. He shares that tendency with other poets. He was in addition past master in the handling of his native language. Being a classical scholar, he possessed an intimate knowledge of ancient Greek literature. But he was equally well read in German, French, and English poetry. Among the poets whom he admired were Goethe and Novalis, Louise Labé and Baudelaire (*q.v.*), Shelley and Dante Gabriel Rossetti. His many publications include a beautifully printed edition of the *Œuvres complètes de Louise Labé Lionoize publiées par P. C. Boutens* (1928). He had a retentive memory for verse and could quote long passages from his favorite poets. There is many a line in his poetry that echoes a remembered note of one of those earlier singers. Hence many and various influences combined in the training and development of this scholarly and deeply artistic poet. Those memories of foreign verse could not fail to leave their mark upon his own poetic diction. He was a daring innovator and often achieved effects that startled the sensitive by their strange beauty and baffled the unresponsive by their enigmatic phrasing. But even when the sense is vaguely guessed, the verse conveys its meaning by its music. Boutens is the most melodious of singers, and the melody is ever in tune with the mood.

Even so, he never was widely popular. Only his *Beatrijs* (1908), a modern version of a medieval Dutch legend, met with nation-wide acclaim and was reprinted 32 times in a period of 25 years. When Queen Wilhelmina celebrated the 40th anniversary of her inauguration, Boutens was asked by the government to voice the nation's feelings in a poem that was to be distributed among the school children of Holland. The choice of the eulogist was unfortunate. The children did not understand the poet's meaning. His tendency towards enigmatic utterance incurred for him the charge of living in an ivory tower. But those who accused him of withdrawing from the common life of his fellow men did not know Boutens. He was neither blind nor indifferent to the injustices of the social order, but being a poet he had no better antidote to offer than the beauty of his verse, which might touch and comfort some of the victims of the social disorder. Its evocation of the glories of the Dutch landscape, of pasture, dune, and sea, and clouded sky, must have given solace in the past few years to thousands of Dutchmen who, with Boutens, shared the pain and agony of the Nazi terror. He did not live to see the hour of liberation. He died, in the 72d year of his life, at his home in The Hague, on March 25, 1943.

See: Oberman, "De hoofdgedachte bij Boutens," *Onze Eeuw,* November, 1919; A. A. M. Stols, *Bibliographie van Boutens' werk* (1926–1930); H. Grierson, *Two Dutch Poets* (1936), Taylorian Lecture; A. J. Barnouw,

"Monthly Letter," published by The Netherland-America Foundation, March, 1943.

A. J. B.

Boutroux, Emile (1845–1921, French philosopher), born in Montrouge near Paris, for 30 years (1877–1907) a professor at the Sorbonne, and from 1912 a member of the French Academy, was in a way the man of a single but highly significant book. At a time (1874) when the fortunes of Taine (*q.v.*), Spencer, and Haeckel were at their apogee, his doctoral dissertation, *De la contingence des lois de la nature* (Eng. tr., *The Contingency of the Laws of Nature,* 1916), conspicuously reversed the current trend and established liberty, instead of necessity, as the fundamental law of creation. This work was profoundly original in that it preserved a critical attitude toward pure metaphysics and adopted the methods of positive science—only to deny that the universe could ever be reduced to mathematical or mechanical unity. There are several worlds, all of which enjoy a certain degree of autonomy. The lower spheres of matter condition but do not produce the higher ones of the spirit. Contingency is what defines this flexible relationship. It spells liberty when the order of things is considered from below, and harmony, or continuity, when the same order is considered from above, *i.e.,* from the point of view of the divine will.

Fairly recognizable here is the inspiration of Pascal, to whom Boutroux devoted an excellent little book (*Pascal,* 1900), and that of Leibnitz, whose *Monadology* he prefaced and translated (1880). A similar vein reappears in his later essays, such as *De l'idée de loi naturelle dans la science et la philosophie contemporaine* (1895; Eng. tr., *Natural Law in Science and Philosophy,* 1914) and *Science et religion dans la philosophie contemporaine* (1908; Eng. tr., *Science & Religion in Contemporary Philosophy,* 1909). Early and persistent as it was, this challenge to determinism had important repercussions. Boutroux shaped in no small measure the ideas of a group of mathematicians which included his own brother-in-law, Henri Poincaré. Moreover, despite a professed hostility to pragmatic principles (*e.g.,* in his *William James,* 1911, Eng. tr., 1912), he definitely foreshadowed the advent of the doctrines of Bergsonism (*see* Bergson, Henri).

See: Léon Brunschvicg, "La Philosophie d'Emile Boutroux," *Revue de métaphysique et de morale,* XXIX (1922), 261–283; Mathieu Schyns, *La Philosophie d'Emile Boutroux* (1923); Lucy Shepard Crawford, *The Philosophy of Emile Boutroux as Representative of French Idealism in the Nineteenth Century* (1924); Raymond Thamin, "La Vie et les travaux d'Emile Boutroux," *Revue internationale de l'enseignement,* LXXXI (1927), 129–145, 213-235.

J.-A. B.

Boy, pseud., *see* Żeleński, Tadeusz.

Boye, Karin (1900–1941, Swedish poet, novelist, and short-story writer), born in Göteborg and who died, apparently a suicide, when she was just past 40, was among the most original and arresting of modern Swedish authors. As a personality she was intent, moody, tautly emotional, rigorously honest; as an artist she was by instinct simple and direct, though her subtle analytical temperament led her not infrequently to employ literary-technical devices which suggest certain strong affinities with modern expressionistic trends in the graphic arts. It was perhaps the rare combination of deep emotionalism and sharp critical intelligence in the same artistic personality that brought about the inner crisis which resulted in her early death. Her last novel, *Kallocain* (1941), reveals clearly enough that she had come to look upon certain developments in modern life (particularly political developments) with such passionate disillusionment that she could not continue to live in a world which at so many essential points inevitably did violence to the deepest and most sensitive of individual values. Her earliest work, two volumes of poems entitled *Moln* (1922; Clouds) and *Glömda land* (1924; Forgotten Land), reveals a young poet of undeniable technical skill, but one who is inspired by what might seem to be a somewhat overstrained youthful idealism. Her later poetry, contained in the volumes *Härdarna* (1927; Hearthstones) and *För trädets skull* (1935; For the Sake of the Tree), maintains with no essential change the austere, rigorous idealism of her earlier verse, though this later poetry has in it much more of the substance of an immediate actual life, and it is moved by a passionately warm feeling for mankind. That which is most characteristic of her best poetry is the note of a fine, dignified personal reserve giving way to a vigorous humanitarianism under the pressure of an overwhelming sense of responsibility to a suffering mankind.

Besides her verse, Karin Boye has written two volumes of short stories as well as five novels. The spirit of high seriousness characteristic of Karin Boye's poetry is just as centrally present in her prose fiction, and in the novels, in fact, her brooding analytical preoccupations come into even sharper relief than in most of her poetry. The novels of the early 1930's—*Astarte* (1931), *Merit vaknar* (1933; Merit Awakens), and *Kris* (1934; Crisis) —are strongly stylized and schematic in form, in part because of the sharp focus on particular moral and psychological problems typical of these stories, in part because of the author's conscious effort to employ contemporary expressionistic literary techniques. The two later novels, *För lite* (1936; Too Little) and *Kallocain,* manage more successfully to avoid the purely schematic and the abstract, telling the central tale more naturally and directly, though they, too, are concerned primarily with psychological and moral problems of a highly complex kind. *För lite* is a strangely gripping tale which illustrates with probing, moody power how a once promising literary figure lives a weary shadow life of evasiveness and frustration because of his inability to rise creatively above the petty domestic fate which is his. *Kallocain* is Karin Boye's contribution to the literature of flaming protest against modern totalitarian politics, written at a time when totalitarianism was everywhere victorious in Europe.

A. G.

Boylesve, René (pseud. of René Tardiveau, 1867–1926, French novelist), took his pen name from his mother's family name. He was born at La Haye-Descartes, in the château country of Touraine, and rarely has a writer's work shown greater debt to the region of his childhood and adolescent experience. Boylesve was by temperament an aristocrat, by birth a bourgeois familiar with peasant life. His work expresses the several aspects of his complex, enigmatic personality, but it is generally agreed that his novels of provincial life in the Touraine region are his major achievement. All of these *romans provinciaux* draw directly upon the author's reservoir of memories from his solitary childhood (his mother died when he was four) and his adolescence, spent in Tours with aged grandparents save for an interlude of study at ecclesiastical schools in Poitiers. After a strict Catholic upbringing, Boylesve went to Paris and enrolled in the school of law at the University of Paris, pursuing his studies in rather dilatory fashion, actively participating in the advance-guard literary life of the capital. Of his early association with the symbolist movement and such experimental periodicals as the *Revue blanche,* slight trace remains in Boylesve's mature writing. Never a man of any school, he relied little on theory or credo and wrote out of his personal experience, though always with an ineradicable discretion and objectivity. The key to his literary point of view lies in his epigraph to his best novel, *La Becquée* (1901), wherein he defines the novelist's role as that of the social historian of manners blended with the insight of the poet. His first published novel, *Le Médecin des dames de Néans* (1896), reveals his great absorption with provincial manners and customs, but also discloses a remarkably subtle lyric gift suggestive of the emotional lucidity of Proust. This study in frustration, of the triumph of mediocrity over poetry, has an expansive lyrical style which Boylesve later abandoned for a tone of severe sobriety and classical restraint, largely because of the merciless pruning of his work by the editor of the *Revue de Paris,* Louis Ganderax.

The provincial novels of Boylesve, as indeed all his work, proceed from studies of character, usually of one dominant person whose life involves others in ever widening circles of experience. Plot counts for little, the development spreading from the central character to tableaux in which the painter's technique seems the basis of Boylesve's composition. Despite his love of music, his work shows little of the modern thematic development and the abandonment of linear treatment. In *La Becquée* he portrays a strong woman determined to preserve the family tradition and the family property, despite the weaknesses or capriciousness of the individual fledglings under her wing. Austere, devoted to duty, inflexible where family interest clashes with individual wish, she dies with no sense of real victory, with only the knowledge that for a time at least she has stemmed the tide of individual disorder and chaos. Her motherbird protectiveness derives not from instinct but from a long traditional consecration to property and to the family. *L'Enfant à la balustrade* (1903), a sequel to *La Becquée,* is again a study of the pettiness and narrowness of provincial life, in which even the strongest characters are forced into compromise if they wish to survive. The earlier *Mademoiselle Cloque* (1899) is another instance of a study in frustration, with an acid portrait of a church quarrel in Tours, wherein the noble, idealistic Mlle Cloque is defeated by the forces of opportunism and hypocrisy. Related to these in content is *La Jeune Fille bien élevée* (1909), a mordant satire despite its suave presentation of the values of small-town life, values in which the tradition of a "good marriage" force unhappiness on a profoundly emotional and gifted young girl. *Madeleine jeune femme* (1912), a work crowned by the French Academy, to which Boylesve was elected in 1918, is a sequel to *La Jeune Fille bien élevée,* continuing the unhappy Madeleine's career in the disturbed and changing Paris of the turn of the century. Here again disillusion is the lot of the heroine still in love with beauty, nobility, and love. Such disenchantment is the almost unvarying mood of Boylesve, a mood reinforced by his work in two other fields: the charming, and licentious, series *Les Leçons d'amour dans un parc* (1902, 1924, 1925) and the novels of straight analysis, such as *Mon Amour* (1908), one of the impressive diary novels in the French language. This courageous, undramatic pessimism is tempered by his poetic sensitivity, but the three factors of a solitary childhood and adolescence largely spent under feminine supervision, an ample family legacy, and a wealthy marriage to a socially inclined family all combine with Boylesve's native reserve and delicacy to make his world one of limited, albeit intense, experience.

See: E. Gérard-Gailly, *Notes sur René Boylesve* (1937); J. Voilquin, *L'Œuvre de René Boylesve* (1938).

L. T.

Bracco, Roberto (1862–1943, Italian dramatist), was born in Naples and lived almost continuously in that city, whose warm exuberance he loved and personified. After attending local secondary schools, he obtained a position in the custom house and then drifted into journalism. As a young reporter he wrote poems in Neapolitan dialect, sketches, and short stories; he then became a musical and dramatic critic—one of the best, indeed, of his time in Italy—and endeavored, among other things, to explain the somewhat exotic beauty, to Italians, of Wagner and Ibsen. He contributed abundantly to local newspapers, such as the *Corriere di Napoli,* and also to the *Capitan Fracassa* of Rome, then the outstanding literary periodical, and later became the editor of *Napoli* and *Piccolo.*

In 1923 he was elected deputy from Campania on the anti-Fascist ticket. Because he upheld with honest tenacity his own convictions and those of his electorate, he was dismissed in 1926 and subjected to repeated persecution and assault; presentation of his plays was forbidden, as well as the sale of his books. He ended his life in poverty. He was married late and had no children.

In 1887 he had been asked by the famous Italian actor Ermete Novelli to write a curtain raiser; this casual request launched him into the drama. At first he wrote merely short, entertaining farces, such as *Non fare ad altri . . .* (1886), *Lui-lei-lui* (1887), *Un'Avventura di viaggio* (1887). He soon saw the opportunity, however, of portraying on a larger and more serious scale the drama of society. His first long play was *Una Donna* (1893), followed by *L'Infedele* (1894). His abundant and varied output totals one volume of verse, three volumes of essays and lectures, four of short stories, and a dozen volumes of plays. He also wrote, in 1887, a libretto, *Le Disilluse.* Many of his plays were translated into several languages.

His drama is based on contemporary life. At times he treated ordinary situations, such as the well-worn triangle, and such social problems as the rights of women and the new claims of the laboring class in Italian democracy. But he also attacked more subtle and even spiritual problems. He followed the tradition which, developed by Ibsen (*q.v.*) and in Italy by Giacosa and Butti (*qq.v.*), became known as *Teatro del pensiero* or "Drama of Ideas." The main characteristic of this genre was that it preferred to treat problems of the spirit rather than of temporary customs or circumstances. Bracco, however, went much farther and, in his later and best work, undertook to delve into problems imbedded in the subconsciousness of his characters. He did this with the conviction that, very often, human actions are based on motives so deep-lying that the person most involved is unaware of them, and that, as he once said, "Drama should be able to express the profoundest and most occult vibrations of the soul." In his "Drama of the Subconscious," he treated, with poetic vision and profound analysis, with an ever-warm compassion for humanity, and with touches of humor, plays of a quality that grip the average theatre audience and that also have a new and subtle technique.

This drama he developed gradually in a series of works: *Il Trionfo* (1895), *Tragedie dell'anima* (1899), *La Piccola Fonte* (1905), *I Fantasmi* (1906), *Il Piccolo Santo* (1909), *L'Amante lontano* (1916), and *I Pazzi* (1922). Of these, the first is somewhat experimental and hardly convincing; the last, which was Bracco's favorite, presents a situation too unusual to be generally appealing. Among the others, *La Piccola Fonte,* the most imaginatively poetic, seems to oppose the selfish, carnal, superman attitude of D'Annunzio's *Gioconda. Il Piccolo Santo* is Bracco's masterpiece and the most remarkable of his studies of the subconscious. In his "Nota" to this play he gives a clear exposition of his intent and method. Among his comedies, *Il Frutto acerbo* (1904) is perhaps the most richly humorous, with the farcical jocosity of so many of his short stories.

The loftiness of his serious plays, his expert familiarity with the stage, his understanding of both the humor and the misery of life, and the fact that he advanced Italian drama, with both popular and literary success, towards new interpretations of mysterious humanity place Bracco at the very top among Italian dramatists of his time.

See: L. MacClintock, *The Contemporary Drama of Italy* (1920); P. Parisi, *Roberto Bracco* (1923); R. Altrocchi, "Bracco and the Drama of the Subconscious," *North American Review,* CCXXIV (1927), 151–162. For a complete list of his works see Bracco, *Il Piccolo Santo,* ed. by R. Altrocchi and M. Bloch (1929).

R. Al.

Braga, Alberto (1851–1911, Portuguese dramatist and short-story writer), was born in Oporto. He settled in Lisbon, where he became secretary of the Instituto Industrial. Such dramas as *Irmã* (Sister) and *A estrada de Damasco* (The Road to Damascus) won him but little fame. He is best known for his *contos,* short stories and sketches which are characterized by a simplicity of style and theme. He chronicles, often in a nostalgic fashion reminiscent of the Spaniard Antonio de Trueba, episodes of the countryside of northern Portugal. His mood is generally melancholy and is hardly relieved by occasional ventures in lighter vein. He possessed definite artistic qualities which can readily be seen in his *Contos da minha lavra* (1879; Short Stories of My Own Making), *Contos de aldeia* (1880; Village Stories), and *Contos escolhidos* (1892; Selected Short Stories).

See: A. F. G. Bell, *Portuguese Literature* (1922), pp. 325–326; F. de Figueiredo, *História da literatura portuguesa,* 2d ed. (1923), pp. 230–231.

G. I. D.

Braga, Teófilo (Joaquim Teófilo Fernandes) (1843–1924, Portuguese literary critic and historian, poet, and polemist), outstanding in politics as the first head of the short-lived Republic of 1910, lives on in literature as one of the earliest humanitarian poets in Portugal and the first man to have attempted a systematic history of Portuguese literature.

Teófilo Braga came from Ponta Delgada, the little capital of the Azores. Although handicapped by poverty and the early death of his mother, he possessed such energy and capacity for work that he made his own way, beginning as a printer's devil. At that time he adopted the name "Teófilo," after the Faust-like clerk who had sold his soul to the devil. In 1861 Braga went to Coimbra to study. There he fell under the spell of Antero de Quental (*q.v.*), also from Ponta Delgada. He became one of the brilliant young men around Antero who, imbued with the philosophy of Hegel and Comte, proclaimed the primacy of science and fought the older generation as "ultraromantic." During this violent war of pens, called the "Coimbra question," hot-blooded Braga, the pale prodigy, who seemed to know everything at the age of 20, attacked the meek but pretentious poet Castilho savagely, making many enemies. He thus failed to obtain the professorship he coveted at Coimbra and had to content himself with a similar position in Lisbon (1872). Further bad luck befell him when his two children died a short time apart and when he himself was struck with blindness in his old age. Yet nothing could break his spirit. On the eve of his death, at the age of 81, he was still planning a "philosophic history of Portugal" in 15 volumes.

Braga had two ambitions as a writer—to fulfill the dream of his elder friend Gomes Monteiro by writing a complete and complex history of Portuguese literature in 32 volumes and to surpass Victor Hugo by composing a gigantic epic on the progress of humankind. Unaided, he battled against the odds of his buoyant temperament and deficient education, of poor or inaccessible source material, and of the apathy reigning in the predominantly illiterate nation for which he labored. Consumed with ambition and heedless of friendly advice, he rushed one volume after the other to the press, with the result that honesty compelled him to revise his hasty hypotheses time and again. Three times he attempted a synthesis of Portuguese literature according to Comte's positivist system (1875, 1885, and 1909–1918). But whereas the pessimism derived from German philosophy had led him in 1870 to conclude that as an "artificial" nation the Portuguese had never had a truly national literature, he later (1909) worked to refute this very idea, seeing in the Portuguese language and literature moral forces that kept the nation alive. Increasingly dominated by an ardent nationalism, he tried at all costs to link the present-day Portuguese to the ancient Lusitanians and considered it the task of the arts, literature, politics, and even of science to make Portugal conscious of her racial heritage, her "lusismo." The latest versions of his theories on "lusismo," on Portuguese lyrics, the Mozarabs, the Amadis novel, the personality of Gil Vicente, may be found in *História da literatura portuguesa* (2 vols., 1909–1914; History of Portuguese Literature) and its continuations, *Os seiscentistas* (1916; 17th-Century Writers) and *Os árcades* (1918; The Arcadians). *As modernas idéias na literatura portuguesa* (2 vols., 1892; Modern Ideas in Portuguese Literature) reveals what he thought about the writings of his contemporaries.

While antagonism against institutions such as the monarchy and personal animosity against fellow writers such as Castilho often biased his judgment, love for the people inspired him to collect and interpret popular literature. In 1867 he began a series of still useful monographs with *História da poesia popular portuguesa* (History of Portuguese Popular Poetry), *Cancioneiro popular* (Popular Songbook), and *Romanceiro geral* (General Ballad Book), adding *Cantos populares do arquipélago açoriano* (1869; Folk Songs of the Azores), *Floresta de vários romances* (1869; Sylva of Several Ballads), and *Contos tradicionais do povo português* (2 vols., 1883; Traditional Tales of the Portuguese People) and summing up his studies on folklore in *O povo português; nos seus costumes, crenças e tradições* (2 vols., 1885; The Portuguese People; Their Customs, Beliefs, and Traditions).

His own poetry was mostly written in the eloquent alexandrine meter. Five years after Hugo's *La Légende des siècles* he began his epic on humankind, *Visão dos tempos* (1864; Vision of the Ages), hailed as a new departure in poetry. But these "sonorous tempests" did not stand the test of time, nor did his short stories and dramas. He has merit, however, as an editor of great writers (Camões, Almeida-Garrett, and Bocage) and of works of his personal friends (João de Deus, *q.v.*, and Antero de Quental).

In spite of their inaccuracy, Braga's teachings bore some good fruit. His enthusiasm was contagious. After him, fellow workers, such as Adolfo Coelho and Michaëlis de Vasconcelos (*q.v.*), and students, such as Hernani Cidade and Fidelino de Figueiredo (*q.v.*), cultivated the field of literary history which he, the uncouth pioneer, had roughly —all too roughly—cleared for them.

See: T. Braga, *Quarenta anos de vida literária* (1903); *Quinquagenário de Teófilo Braga, 1858–1908* (1908); F. de Figueiredo, *História da literatura realista* (1914).

G. M. M.

Brahm, Otto (pseud. of Otto Abrahamson, 1856–1912, German theatrical director, journalist, and literary historian), was a leader of the Berlin group of the German naturalistic movement (*see* German naturalism). He was born in Hamburg. Turning to literature after a brief business career, he studied at the universities of Berlin, Strassburg, and Jena. The greatest influence on his intellectual development was that of Wilhelm Scherer of the University of Berlin. After various journalistic positions, Brahm was dramatic critic (1881–1885) for the *Vossische Zeitung*, where he was closely associated with Theodor Fontane (*q.v.*). From 1855 to 1890 he was an editorial contributor to *Die Nation*. In 1889 he became cofounder and director of the Freie Bühne in Berlin, and, in 1890, editor of the *Freie Bühne für modernes Leben*.

As M. G. Conrad had introduced Zola (*q.v.*), Brahm, in the later naturalistic period, introduced Ibsen to the German public and stage. His reviews, his direction of the Freie Bühne, the Deutsches Theater, and the Lessing Theater, as well as his personal contacts with the literary group in Berlin left an impress on contemporary literary theory; his critical genius and the peculiarly effective nature of his activities in the press and theatre made his influence on contemporary literary development of the greatest importance. His function in the history of naturalism was to produce dramatic criticism of an exceedingly high order, filled with a vivid realization of the needs and meaning of the contemporary scene and a keen awareness of the role of literature, especially the drama, in an age of complex social problems and new scientific theories. He also discovered and presented the works of several of the younger naturalistic dramatists and created a theatre technique along naturalistic lines. His reviews were collected after his death by his friend Paul Schlenther under the title *Kritische Schriften* (2 vols., 1913–1915). Brahm wrote, among other literary historical works, *Heinrich von Kleist* (1884), *Henrik Ibsen* (1887), and *Schiller* (Vol. I, 1888; Vol. II, 1892, incomplete).

See: G. Hirschfeld, *Otto Brahm; Briefe und Erinnerungen* (1925); M. Newmark, *Otto Brahm, the Man and the Critic* (1938).

W. H. R.

Brandes, Georg Morris Cohen (1842–1927, Danish critic and biographer), was born into a cultivated middle-class family and into the cultivated middle-class city of Copenhagen. Its culture did not as yet foster free inquiry, the official mind at least being weather-stripped by an amalgam of orthodox Lutheranism and political conservatism, but an urban 18th-century spirit still throve of which Brandes always remained the inheritor, except for a period in youth when he felt the impact of Søren Kierkegaard. "Yet God preserve me from him, or I shall never be able to live," he wrote in his diary. The opposite of a mystic, but not unlike a castigating prophet in his passionate seriousness, Brandes soon chose what to him was life—the study of creative literature, both psychologically and aesthetically. With his warm, dynamic personality and essentially ethical preoccupation, this widened into what Harald Høffding later was to call Brandes's "fight to liberate and develop the uniqueness of individual personality."

Individual personality expressing its uniqueness in art had his brilliant championship, even in the case of people as unlike Brandes as Selma Lagerlöf, whom he launched, or Hans Christian Andersen, whose portrait is exquisitely done in the book *Danske Digtere* (1877; Danish Writers), one of several books of masterly literary portraits. But the fight for liberation in those days had to be against nearly all accepted ideas. His chief work began in 1871 with the first of the lectures to be published as *Hovedstrømninger i det 19de Aarhundredes Litteratur* (6 vols., 1871–1890; Eng. tr., *Main Currents in Nineteenth Century Literature,* 1901–1905). Previously he had been to Paris, where he had met and known Taine, Renan (*qq.v.*), and John Stuart Mill, acquiring exactly the weapons he longed for, as well as a French clarity of style. He returned to be a "strong, flexible blade" attacking the reaction of the 19th century, and the "Main Currents" lectures, although most vividly about literature, were directed against whatever he saw as holding the human spirit in bondage, the topics being *émigré* literature, romanticism in Germany, reaction in France, naturalism in England, the romantic school in France, and young Germany. These lectures went on, with interruptions, until 1890, helping to deprovincialize all Scandinavia. The joy and hatred stirred up by them were unprecedented. The joy resulted in a new Scandinavian realism in literature. In *Det moderne Gennembruds Mænd* (1883; Men of the Modern Awakening) Brandes describes this and portrays some of the authors he had encouraged and helped to inspire, among them Björnson, Ibsen, Jens Peter Jacobsen, Drachmann (*qq.v.*), Schandorph. But the hatred resulted in a union of clerical and conservative authorities which prevented his getting the professorship in aesthetics at the university, for which he was supremely equipped.

In bitter disappointment he went in 1877 to live in Berlin, where he remained until 1883. From there he wrote the monographs on *Esaias Tegner* (1878), *Benjamin Disraeli* (1878; Eng. tr., *Lord Beaconsfield,* 1880), and *Ferdinand Lassalle* (1881; Eng. tr., 1911). Though he was successful, the Berlin stay was exile for him, and when a number of anonymous Danish admirers offered him a professor's salary, he returned home, this time with leadership demanded of him; the former sodden state had been well leavened, partly by his own ideas. The new Danish radicalism was much aided by his pen. He stood for no compromise. As he wrote to Björnson, "If a deserter or a half-way dishonest writer doesn't lose the sympathy of at least some of his previous associates, you put a premium on slackness and success-hunting." This quality in Brandes, which could make him cry out "Clerical or anticlerical, no other question matters!" roused a similar opposition, which, however great his fame and power at home and in Europe, irked him almost into intolerance of the religious as well as the clerical. Urban he was and remained, and the rise of the Danish farmers with their Grundtvigian ideas (about mass education and folk high schools) was no great pleasure to him. He began to feel isolated. Hence his sympathy for Nietzsche (*q.v.*), whom at the end of the 80's he discovered and lectured on, thus incidentally affecting the work of Strindberg and Hamsun (*qq.v.*). Even the professorship which he received in 1902, with the victory of Danish democracy, did not soothe him. He began to write of misunderstood greatness, producing his *William Shakespeare* (1895–1896; Eng. tr., 1898), considered the finest example of his power of luminous interpretation. His autobiography was published in three parts (1905–1908). In a spurt towards the end he published the popular biographies, *Goethe* (1915; Eng. tr., 1924), *Voltaire* (1916; Eng. tr., 1930), *Caesar* (1918; Eng. tr., 1924), *Michelangelo* (1921). For these he drew largely on his extraordinary memory of a lifetime of reading.

With Voltaire he had much in common, especially the clear fiery anger at injustice, oppression, and hypocrisy, but he was personally frugal, "his furniture was books," and he was capable of devoted friendship. What fitted Brandes for his work as educator-critic was a quality one of his teachers very early discerned in him: he had the freshest, most direct understanding of poetry and art, with a form of presentation which revealed the poetry in his own soul, a requisite for the true aesthetic.

See: H. H. Boyesen, *Essays on Scandinavian Literature* (1895); E. Förster-Nietzsche, *Fr. Nietzsches gesammelte Briefe* (1904), pp. 265–330; E. W. Gosse, *Two Visits to Denmark* (1911); V. Andersen, *Det nittende Aarhundrede anden Halvdel,* Vol. IV (1925) of C. S. Petersen and V. Andersen, *Illustreret dansk Litteraturhistorie,* pp. 158–205; O. Seidlin, "Georg Brandes, 1842–1927," *Journal of the History of Ideas,* III (1942), 415–442.

S. T.

Brecht, Bert (Bertolt) (1898–, German dramatist and ballad writer), was born in Augsburg, Bavaria. His literary ability found early recognition in the award of the Kleist prize (1922). He left Germany in 1933 because he was strongly opposed to Hitlerism. Eventually sojourning in Russia, he edited with Lion Feuchtwanger (*q.v.*) and Willi Bredel a short-lived anti-Nazi magazine, *Das Wort* (Moscow, 1936–1939). He came to the United States in 1941.

With his first dramas, *Trommeln in der Nacht, Baal,* and *Im Dickicht der Städte,* all performed in 1922, Brecht established himself as one of the more important exponents of post-war expressionism, and indeed he was hailed as "the apostle of a new dramatic era." For some time Brecht shared this unique reputation with Arnolt Bronnen (originally Bronner, 1895–, a convert to Nazism), whose dramas *Vatermord* (1925) and *Ostpolzug* (1926) enjoyed great, though transient, success.

Brecht's early dramas differ in two respects from those of his immediate predecessors, which had been either realistic or expressionistic. Stylistically, they are characterized by a queer mixture of realistic and expressionistic elements and by an odd attempt to adapt the technique of the ballad to that of the drama. Philosophically, they are pervaded by a new kind of realism. This new realism is in marked contrast to old-type realism (Ibsen, the young Gerhart Hauptmann, *qq.v.*): its purpose is to combine the rational with the irrational, to depict life in all its incongruities, from determinable, scientifically proved facts to the undeterminable, demoniacal powers of fate. Yet in his propaganda plays, or "Lehrstücke," as he calls them, Brecht attempts to indoctrinate the reader with his own political convictions (*e.g., Die Rundköpfe und die Spitzköpfe,* performed in Copenhagen in 1936, Eng. tr., *Round Heads, Peak Heads,* 1937; published in *Gesammelte Werke,* Vol. II, 1938).

Brecht, so far, has scored his greatest theatrical success with the *Dreigroschenoper* (1928), an adaptation of John Gay's *The Beggar's Opera* (1728). To English literature he is also indebted for his drama *Leben Eduard des Zweiten von England* (1924), for which he draws on Marlowe. The milieu of his comedy, *Mann ist Mann* (1927), is the United States, as it is of his *Die Heilige Johanna der Schlachthöfe* (written in 1922, published in 1938).

After emigrating from Germany, Brecht published his novel, *Dreigroschenroman* (1934; Eng. tr., *A Penny for the Poor,* 1937). *Mother* (1935), a play with music, is based on Gorky's (*q.v.*) novel of the same name. Brecht's *Gesammelte Werke,* in two volumes, printed in Czechoslovakia and published in London, appeared in 1938. They contain copious and detailed commentaries ("Anmerkungen") by Brecht himself. Subsequently, he wrote a number of vigorous one-act plays, radio scripts, and poems against Hitlerism. Most of this material is collected in *Furcht und Elend des Dritten Reiches* (New York, 1945). Several of the playlets, such as *The Informer, The Jewish Wife,* and *In Search of Justice,* had also been included in a book, *The Private Life of the Master Race* (1944; in English only), which Brecht calls a "documentary play." This work, written in a partly expressionistic, partly naturalistic style, portrays with much objectivity the trials and tribulations of the German people under Hitler's yoke. Brecht's ballads are collected in the *Hauspostille* (1927), in *Lieder, Gedichte und Chöre* (1934), and in *Svendborger Gedichte* (1939). Most of his ballads are written in the vein of François Villon and Frank (Benjamin Franklin) Wedekind (*q.v.*), while a few are obviously patterned after the good old "Moritat," naïvely popular examples of the *memento mori* tradition, loose in rhyme and macabre in content.

See: K. Thieme, "Des Teufels Gebetbuch," *Hochland,* XXIX (1932), 397–413; C. Tolksdorf, *John Gays "Beggar's Opera" und Bert Brechts "Dreigroschenoper"* (1934); S. Tretyakov, "Bertolt Brecht," *International Literature,* V (Moscow, May, 1937), 60–70; "Gegenwärtiges Theater," *Mass und Wert,* II (1939), 831–844; E. R. Bentley, "Bertolt Brecht and His Work," in Brecht, *The Private Life of the Master Race* (1944), pp. 117–136.

G. K.

Bregendahl, Marie (1867–, Danish novelist), born in Fly, was 35 years old when she began writing novels dealing with the souls and the lives of the people in the rural part of Jutland, Denmark's mainland. At that time she, herself a daughter of the soil, had seen much, thought much, had married Jeppe Aakjær (*q.v.*), who already had secured an outstanding place in Danish literature of the period, and had been divorced from him. On the bleak background of West Jutland's storm-swept and sand-blown fields, with the thundering music of the North Sea in her ears and with a slowly and painfully acquired experience of life, she had found her special milieu and, in a peculiar sense, made it her own. Her first story, *Ved Lars Skrædders Sygeseng* (1902; At the Sickbed of Lars the Tailor), was soon followed by *Hendrik i Bakken* (1904; Hendrik on the Hill) and *En Dødsnat* (1912; Eng. tr., *A Night of Death*, 1931), powerful, poignant sketches etched in that detached and dispassionate manner which betrays profound sympathy. These shorter novels became, as it were, the introduction to Marie Bregendahl's cycle, *Billeder af Sødalsfolkenes Liv* (6 vols., 1914–1923; Pictures from the Life of the Sea-valley People), and to *Holger Hauge og hans Hustru* (2 double vols., 1934–1935; Holger Hauge and His Wife); these two massive novels are her principal works.

Within a frame of rustic life, of political and social clashes and ferment, Marie Bregendahl emphasizes the irrevocability of fate, the futility of resisting it, the mournful necessity of having to submit to what must be. In nearly all cases emotions and events are closely affiliated with the meager soil and harsh climate of that part of the Danish landscape where she is intimately at home. With Marie Bregendahl, plot is not the essential factor, nor yet style—hers is not always flawless—but the probing of human souls, the sympathetic understanding of deep tragedies and little happinesses.

See: H. G. Topsöe-Jensen, *Scandinavian Literature from Brandes to Our Day* (1929); Helge Kjaergaard, *Die dänische Literatur der neuesten Zeit (1871–1933)* (1934).

G. St.

Bremond, Henri (1865–1933, French historian of religious ideas), offered a unique blending of religious enthusiasm and of literary, nontheological affinities. No one in the long list of modern ecclesiastical authors has produced anything comparable to this erudite writer's *Histoire littéraire du sentiment religieux en France* (11 vols., 1916–1933; unfinished). Born in Aix-en-Provence in a house of pious Roman Catholic traditions, Bremond entered the Society of Jesus, in which other members of his family were prominent; he spent nearly 10 years in England and Wales and came back to France with broader views. His retirement from his order in 1904, his faithfulness to his modernist friend George Tyrrell in 1909, suggested, without casting any doubt upon Bremond's orthodoxy, the evolution from dogma to feeling and, so to say, from Bossuet to Fénelon. He had met Maurice Barrès (*q.v.*) in Athens and had also visited Fogazzaro (*q.v.*). Two collections of essays, both entitled *L'Inquiétude religieuse* (1901, 1909), and numerous contributions to the *Etudes* and the *Correspondant* proved his definite interest in "choice souls," *Newman* (1905) and *Fénelon* (1910) exemplifying the foremost among them. When he was able to give up as a livelihood teaching in Jesuit schools, he devoted most of his time—hampered, however, by poor health—to his lifework, the presentation of religious currents in French literature. In his view an element of mysticism, transcending the matter-of-factness of life, was the indispensable basis for rich, substantial, and vital feeling. It was this conviction which led this man of sunny Provence to take sides in favor of romanticism, in its spiritual sense, and to supplement his learned studies by works of contemporary interest such as *De la poésie pure* (1926), *Prière et poésie* (1926), and *Racine et Valéry* (1930).

As a kind of spiritual adviser of young men of letters, his role during his brief stays in Paris and his contact with circles connected with the French Academy (to which he was elected 1923) made him for a certain time a well-known figure in the world of letters (see interviews and articles in *Nouvelles littéraires*). But he always went back with satisfaction to his winter quarters near Pau and to a life of meditation and research: this "Catholic Sainte-Beuve," as he was called, could not easily dispense with some kind of cell.

See: M. Martin du Gard, *De Sainte-Beuve à Fénelon: Henri Bremond* (1927).

F. B.

Breton, André (1896–, French poet, novelist, and critic), has been since its beginning the great theorist and director of surrealism. The son of modest Norman shopkeepers, Breton was, at the start of the First World War, a medical student, interested especially in mental diseases. As an intern at Nantes in 1916 he met Jacques Vaché, that legendary figure of dada and surrealism, whose complete contempt for society and systematic attempt to turn his life into an extended hallucination had an overwhelming effect on Breton. The work of Rimbaud (*q.v.*) had already deeply attracted Breton, and the result of this dual influence was a theory of life as well as art which combined an extravagant scorn of all accepted values with a corresponding exaltation of the importance of the subconscious. The first of these characteristics was shared by the movement called dada, which after originating in Zurich in 1916, under the direction of Tristan Tzara, invaded Paris in 1919; and it was only natural for Breton and his friends Philippe Soupault and Paul Eluard (*qq.v.*), having already founded the review *Littérature* (1919), to associate themselves with dada.

In the early battles of dada Breton played a leading role, taking full part in such demonstrations as that held in the Salle Gaveau, May 26, 1920, at which the audience pelted the speakers with raw beef; he produced the only important books that can be connected with the movement, *Les Champs magnétiques* (1921), a volume of unconscious writing done in collaboration with Soupault, and *Les Pas perdus* (1924), a collection of critical and autobiographical essays. The essence of dada was negation, a refusal to express or discover any meaning in art or society, and whether it is regarded as a serious affair or as a gigantic parody on all contemporary thought, it is obvious that it was self-destructive. Breton realized this fact more clearly than did Tzara and broke with him in 1921, the rupture being accompanied by the usual demonstrations and counterdemonstrations.

A short period of quiet followed, broken in 1924 by Breton's *Manifeste du surréalisme: Poisson soluble* and the organization in the same year of the review *La Révolution surréaliste*. The leading collaborators with Breton at this time included Soupault, Benjamin Péret, Louis Aragon (*q.v.*), Eluard, Robert Desnos, and René Crevel. In the years that immediately followed, Breton was active as a critic and theorist in *Légitime Défense* (1926) and *Le Surréalisme et la peinture* (1928) and as a creative writer in *Nadja* (1928), one of the most remarkable books in modern literature, the strange, deeply moving story of a love affair between Breton and a woman, Nadja, of marked psychic tendencies. The history of the movement by no means ran smoothly: Breton became more and more inclined to emphasize investigation of psychiatric states and the world of dreams and to look with disfavor on those adherents who were not prepared to embrace surrealism completely, with the result that many former associates, including Desnos and Soupault, were expelled from the group by the *Second Manifeste du surréalisme* (1930). The question of surrealism's relations with the Communist Party was also much debated; in 1930 the title of the official review was changed to *Le Surréalisme au service de la révolution;* but the Communists continued to regard the apparent frivolity of the surrealists with suspicion, with the result that Aragon, the most politically conscious of the group, left surrealism for Communism in 1932, as did Eluard in 1938. Breton continued throughout this period to combine theory and practice, producing *Les Vases communicants* (1932), a study of dreams, and, in collaboration with Eluard, *L'Immaculée Conception* (1930), notable for its attempt to simulate voluntarily various types of mental disease. Breton's short essay, *Qu'est-ce que le surréalisme?* published in Paris in 1934, appeared in English in London in 1936 as *What Is Surrealism?* In spite of internal dissension, the movement received new recruits, notably Salvador Dali and Nicolas Calas, and extended its influence to England and to America, its headquarters at present, with Breton still dominating it, both personally and in his works, *Point du jour* (1934), *L'Amour fou* (1937), and *Fata Morgana* (1942).

Since Breton's own work is so closely connected with surrealism, it is hard to evaluate him without assessing it. Both Eluard and Aragon surpass him in literary ability, and in spite of the merits of *Nadja,* it is as the controlling force of a school that he must take his place in literary history. Surrealism is spun of many yarns and is far from a sudden aberration of French literature. Its way had been prepared by such men as Apollinaire and Jarry, to say nothing of Rimbaud and Lautréamont (*qq.v.*) As a literary practice, it is in large part a logical development of the tendency of French poetry since at least the time of the symbolists (*see* French symbolism) to interest itself in the subconscious, to become more "pure," to use more startling metaphor, to depend less on logical meaning than on the juxtaposition of widely divergent images for the sake of an effect felt *not* by the conscious mind. Nor can the influence of cubism be overlooked, particularly its device of rendering a scene by abstracting its significant elements and recombining them, with possible deformation, into a work of art whose arrangement is purely formal. But surrealism, Breton has always insisted, is not merely an aesthetic theory; it is a philosophy of life. It desires a complete revolution of man's modes of thought—and, it naturally follows, of society as well. The interpretation of the world provided by the intellect does not correspond to anything essential in the true nature of man or the world, and surrealism proposes to replace it by the liberation of the potentialities of the subconscious. The two elements which enter into this position are the spirit of revolt and despair that affected the entire Western World after the First World War (comparable in many ways to the spirit of the romantics in the 1830's) and the desire to escape from a materialistic, scientific world which holds no mystery (also characteristic of much 19th-century poetry). The pure spirit of revolt is more typical of dada than of surrealism; in spite of its political tendency toward the left, surrealism has stressed, as it grew, rather the second element. It is not particularly in nature as the 19th century saw it, however, that surrealism finds an escape, but more often in the trappings of the modern city—factory chimneys, busses, and advertisements, neon signs and wax mannequins, transformed into a fantastic universe by the liberated subconscious. It is likely that surrealism's ultimate value, and Breton's, will reside in this liberation and the stimulus it gave to so much modern literature, whether it called itself surrealism or not.

See: Marcel Raymond, *De Baudelaire au surréalisme* (1933); Guy Mangeot, *Histoire du surréalisme* (1934); David Gascoyne, *A Short Survey of Surrealism* (1935); Herbert Read, ed., *Surrealism* (1936); *New Directions,* 1940 (annual volume); G. E. Lemaitre, *From Cubism to Surrealism in French Literature* (1941).

C. W., Jr.

Březina, Otokar (pseud. of Václav Jebavý, 1868–1929, Czech poet), is the leader of the Czech symbolist movement and possibly the greatest of all recent Czech lyric writers. He was born in Počátky (southern Bohemia), the son of a poor shoemaker, and was a schoolteacher in different towns of Moravia. Březina died in Jaroměřice, where he had resided since 1901.

Recently some of the early poetry and prose of Březina, dating back to his school days, has been unearthed. But his first collection of poetry, *Tajemné dálky* (Mysterious Distances), was published only in 1895 when he was nearing 30, and then within six years he added four more small collections. A volume of essays followed in 1903. After that Březina stopped writing. Late in his life he was interviewed by visitors and friends, and they, especially the Catholic poet Jakub Deml, gave accounts of his later views which excited much disappointment and controversy; he seemed to be characterized chiefly by a disgruntled provincial nationalism. But Březina must be judged on the basis of his poetry, which appeared in five small booklets.

Tajemné dálky is a work of youthful pessimism, only superficially touched by a still largely aesthetic mysticism. The themes are *fin de siècle,* the bitterness of frustration, the sense of guilt, the tragedy of love and friendship, the attraction of death which appears as a distant savior and comforter. In a few poems personal sorrows like the early death of his parents are hinted at, but on the whole solemn tones of prayer prevail. The intricate clusters of images, of which many are drawn from Catholic liturgy, the strangely farfetched, extremely effective rhymes, the use of alexandrines which point to a reading of Baudelaire (*q.v.*), make even this first book unique in Czech poetry. But the truly great Březina begins to emerge only with *Svítání na Západě* (1896; Dawn in the West), though this collection in turn represents only a transition to *Větry od pólu* (1897; Polar Winds), in which Březina appears as a highly original symbolist poet. The early pessimism has almost disappeared and is replaced by a cosmic optimism which has nothing of the shallow belief in progress in it, but is rather the final insight of a mystic who has reached an acceptance of all existence as part of the divine pattern. God's mysterious will works through the striving and the evolution of all created things towards cooperation and unity with Him. Březina, in a highly personal way, manages to combine the insight of all mystics, of whom he was an ardent student, with a monistic optimism which shows traces of reading in Emerson and even Nietzsche (*q.v.*). In these two collections Březina also found his most personal style: free verse, with many dactyls and anapaests, sometimes rhymed, of enormously long lines; clusters of magnificent metaphors which seem to burst one from the other; hymns and dithyrambs which are sometimes put into the mouths of imaginary speakers including "the sun, the earth, the waters, and the mystery of fire." The images from the liturgy have disappeared and are replaced by metaphors drawn from the sciences or ordinary activities such as winegrowing or farming. The next collection, *Stavitelé chrámu* (1899; Builders of the

Temple), represents some backsliding into pessimism. Doubts and uncertainties have arisen in the poet's mind: the suffering of all creation, including inert matter, is voiced in curious poems, and symbolic types such as "prophets," "martyrs," "blind men," "madmen," join their voices in a stupendous oratorio of the whole universe. The last and possibly greatest collection, *Ruce* (1901; Hands), represents a return to certainty and belief. The stress is here stronger than before on the conception of man's cooperation with God and humanity's unity, which is conceived of as including the living, the dead, and the unborn. The innumerable visible and invisible hands, like a magical chain, of the title poem carry out the mysterious laws of His eternal will. One poem sings the "roundelay of hearts," another foresees redeemed man for whose sake "it is joyous to live," and another evokes the time when the "delivered" earth will be extinguished and the mighty current of eternity will roll on. Some of the poems return to traditional stanzas and closed rhyme forms, a change which continues in 13 later scattered poems where Březina even returns to personal problems. The cycle came to an end and the poet imposed silence upon himself, surely because he realized that he had expressed all he had to say. The volume of essays, *Hudba pramenů* (1903; The Music of the Springs), planned as a commentary to his poetry, is rather a paraphrase on a lower stylistic level of his main ideas of art as service to God, of the hidden economy of the universe, of justice and the masses. The highly ornate and metaphorical diction is not illuminated by the same glow of imagination and the same visionary power which uphold even the longest of his poems.

In Březina's work modern Czech poetry has reached its peak, a peak where the air is rarefied and sometimes difficult to breathe. Březina's contacts with ordinary reality are slight, and his social message has little in common with contemporary movements: it breathes the spirit of all mysticism and possibly of general Christianity. His grandiose visions sing the glory of God and the mysteries of the universe in a timeless exaltation.

See: M. Marten, *Otokar Březina* (1903); F. X. Šalda, *Duše a dílo* (1913); J. Staněk, *Otokar Březina* (1918); P. Selver, *Otokar Březina; a Study in Czech Literature* (1921); E. Saudek, *Pod oblohou Otokara Březiny* (1928); A. Veselý, *Otokar Březina* (1928); G. Picková-Saudková, *Hovory s Otokarem Březinou* (1929); J. Deml, *Mé svědectví o Otokaru Březinovi* (1931); A. Pospíšilová, *Otokar Březina* (1936); P. Fraenkel, *O. Březina; genese díla* (1937). There is a German translation of Březina's poetry by O. Pick and E. Saudek (1920), and one in Italian by E. Lo Gatto, *Venti dai poli e I Construttori del tempio* (1930).

R. W.

Brieux, Eugène (1858–1932, French dramatist), was born and reared in one of the working-class districts of Paris, where his father was a carpenter. His limited early education was later complemented with wide reading. He was already interested in the theatre at the time of his stay at Rouen as a journalist; but his first plays worthy of attention were produced by Antoine (*q.v.*)—*Ménages d'artistes* (1890) and especially *Blanchette* (1892), the latter making him known to the public at large. From then on Brieux's literary production was regular and even more than plentiful (40 plays). He was elected to the French Academy in 1910.

If, like most of the playwrights of the Théâtre Libre where he made his début, Brieux has a tendency to unveil with a sometimes cruel realism selfishness and pettiness, particularly of the bourgeoisie, he does it without the bitter irony and pessimism of Becque's (*q.v.*) disciples. Indeed Brieux is something of a missionary. He denounces tirelessly the moral degradation of the individual by other men, by institutions, or by social habits and prejudices, pointing out the ultimate disastrous consequences—and doing this in the mood of a reformer.

Blanchette is about popular education. *La Couvée* (1893) presents a problem dear to Brieux, that of the intervention of parents in the lives of their children. When these parents, influenced by a more or less disguised egoism, try to impose their will on their children, especially where it concerns marriage and the dowry, Brieux's indignation bursts forth. There are similar themes in *Les Trois Filles de M. Dupont* (1897), one of his best plays, and in *La Petite Amie* (1902). In plays like *La Française* (1907), *La Femme seule* (1913), and *Pierrette et Galaor* (1923) Brieux is an ardent defender of women and girls, and in his desire to protect their rights he may seem to go so far as to uphold free union and the illegitimate child. Yet Brieux is at heart a very conservative moralist: if he seems to favor antisocial solutions, it is because for him society as it exists now leaves no alternative. In fact, it is the family he defends in *Le Berceau* (1898), in which he attacks divorce when there are children, and in *Les Remplaçantes* (1901), in which he protests against the practice of wet-nursing. Brieux is somewhat in conflict with himself in *Maternité* (1913), divided between arguments about preventing the birth of unwanted children and the realization that abortion is an antisocial practice. *La Robe rouge* (1900), another outstanding play, develops two themes, the crushing of the individual by the powerful machine of the law and the degradation caused by greed and ambition in a judge; the author demands reform in criminal legislation.

Brieux has been criticized for oversimplifying very complex social problems. He is no deep thinker, nor even always coherent. When he wanders into a world which he does not know very well, the world of science in *L'Evasion* (1896) or the gallant society of *La Régence* (1927), his talent weakens; and when he studies the problem of religion in *La Foi* (1912), his views appear shallow. He has not always avoided rhetoric and melodrama. He does sometimes excel in the portrayal of humble folk, whom he may have had particularly in mind when he said: "I have wished that the amount of suffering upon this earth might be diminished a little because I have lived."

A large number of the plays of Brieux have been translated into English and several were produced in New York.

See: P. V. Thomas, *The Plays of Eugène Brieux* (1915); A. Presas, *Brieux; portrait littéraire* (1930).

A. C. L.

Broch, Hermann (1886–, Austrian novelist, philosopher, and playwright), was born in Vienna. The publication, late in his life, of an amazing prose trilogy (*Die Schlafwandler,* 1930–1932; Eng. tr., *The Sleepwalkers,* 1932) surprised especially those who had known him as mathematician, engineer, and director of a Viennese textile concern. The work is a striking example of a new type of European cultural portraiture in which scientific speculation and poetic imagination are combined to represent the incoherent variety of contemporary experience. In what Broch calls the polyhistoric form of the novel he blends many creative devices, and at least in this resolute attempt to find an adequate medium for the complexity of rational and irrational impulses he belongs in the distinguished company of Joyce and Gide (*q.v.*). In the first volume of the trilogy (*Pasenow, or Romanticism—1888*) the stagnation and disintegration of the spiritual life is revealed beneath the thin ice of a deceptive romantic ideology. The central figure of the second volume (*Esch, or Anarchy—1903*) represents the drift from a pseudobourgeois clerkdom to the despair of a godless and valueless life. *Huguenau, or Realism—1918* finally leaves no doubt of the collapse of all organic coherence and shows, in a more discursive fashion (see the intercalated reflections upon "The Decay of Values"), the escape into substitute forms of belief. This remarkably complex triptych is Broch's central achievement. A drama (*Die Entsühnung,* 1934), another novel (*Die unbekannte Grösse,* 1933; Eng. tr., *The Unknown Quantity,* 1935), and several short stories and essays (*e.g.,* "Eine leichte Enttäuschung" and "Das Böse im Wertsystem der Kunst," both appearing in *Die neue Rundschau,* Jahrgang XLIV, Bd. I, pp. 502–517, Bd. II, pp. 157–191, and the pamphlet, *James Joyce und die Gegenwart,* 1935) reiterate the existential elements in Broch's philosophical position. His latest work, *Der Tod des Vergil* (1945; Eng. tr., *The Death of Virgil,* 1945), is an unusually stirring prose poem which interprets the visions of Vergil and depicts the age from whose bloodshed and convulsions Christianity was soon to be born.

Since coming to America in 1938, Broch has been awarded a Guggenheim Fellowship for 1941–1942, membership in the American Institute of Arts and Letters, 1942, and a Rockefeller Fellowship for Philosophical and Psychological Research at Princeton University, 1942–1944.

See: Fritz Lehner, "Hermann Broch," *Life and Letters To-day,* Vol. XV (1936), No. 6, pp. 64–71.

V. L.

Bródy, Sándor (1863–1924, Hungarian novelist, short-story writer, and playwright), was born in Eger and died in Budapest. His education was superficial. Yet when he raised his voice he attracted many readers and critics, because in relationship to Hungarian literature his voice sounded fresh and his manner of communication seemed new. In fact Bródy was a romantic naturalist who made the mistake of thinking that he was the protagonist of French realism in Hungary. Many readers felt that he went beneath the surface of modern life, and they liked it. It is safe to say that if Bródy had not colored his stories with experiences of poverty, the response of the readers, themselves often poor, would have been less enthusiastic. As the editor of *Fehér Könyv* (White Book) and of *Jövendő* (Future). Bródy recorded the problems of his time with journalistic flexibility. Both magazines expressed the personal whims and convictions of the editor.

Bródy had a prolific pen. He wrote carelessly, but with spontaneity, impressing even readers and critics who might have been in disagreement with his views or literary manners. Generally his work indicates an attempt at the understanding of truth in its social and sensual implications. In a sentimental, seemingly frank fashion he made use of the material that the unfairness of modern conditions offered. The social causes of modern formlessness were unknown to him or only partly understood; his intense subjectivity prevented him from concentration upon specific problems in need of solution. He liked to generalize and preferred rambling wisdoms to truth, which would have required prolonged effort to comprehend. He liked to speak as an eyewitness, but frequently his own bittersweet-gay emotionalism interfered with objectivity in an almost tyrannical fashion. Because of inadequate self-criticism, he did not know or did not care to know the difference between good and mediocre writing; as a consequence much of his work is today on the unused shelves of libraries or in the dusty basements of bookstores. Bródy's promise was not fulfilled. Nevertheless he is entitled to recognition—if only because the vitality of his personality made him for a long time an influential figure in Hungarian literature and because his romantic naturalism paved the way to a freedom of expression on subjects ignored by writers before him. His first important book of short stories, *Nyomor* (1884; Poverty), remained one of his significant works; *Az ezüst kecske* (1898; The Silver Goat) is considered his best novel; *A dada* (1902; The Nurse) and *Tanitónő* (1908; The School Marm) are his best plays. His book on Rembrandt has been translated into English under the title *Rembrandt; a Romance of Divine Love and Art* (1928).

J. R.

Bröger, Karl (1886–, German poet and novelist), was born in Nuremberg, where he has spent much of his life. Of humble origin, Bröger is chiefly known for his contributions to *Arbeiterdichtung* (1929), poetry drawing its subject matter and imagery from the lives of the industrial workers. Bröger's reputation rests mainly upon his lyrics, which are characterized by simplicity, melodiousness, and restraint of style, and express sympathy for the urban proletariat. While vaguely "socialist" in conviction, Bröger is an idealist rather than a materialist, and cannot be classed as a Marxist. (For his development up to the First World War see his autobiographical novel *Der Held im Schatten,* 1920.) In 1914 he supported the war, though in no chauvinistic spirit, and served in the infantry. His poem "Bekenntnis," written in that year, was one of the most popular of German war lyrics. His war experiences are reflected in the volumes of poetry *Kamerad, als wir marschiert . . .* (1916) and *Soldaten der Erde* (1918) and in the realistic and vivid novel *Bunker 17* (1929; Eng. tr., *Pillbox 17,* 1930). Impressed by the horror of the war, Bröger turned increasingly to the ideals of pacifism and universal brotherhood. He was a leader of the Youth Movement. Under the Weimar Republic he gained increased recognition among the writers of the "left." Bröger edited the anthology *Jüngste Arbeiterdichtung* (1925). The scope of his own writing broadened to include the legend in *Die vierzehn Nothelfer* (1923) and the historical novel in *Der Guldenschuh* (1934). His novel *Nürnberg* (1935) shows the impressionable poet as a supporter of Hitler.

H. C. H.

Brunetière, Ferdinand (1849–1906, French professor and critic), born in Toulon, became the outstanding literary judge in France following the death of Taine (*q.v.*). He was a leading professor at the Ecole Normale Supérieure after earlier being refused admission as a student to this exclusive institution, and he was also for many years director of the *Revue des deux mondes.* His work attracts attention by its very mass—some 30 volumes published during his lifetime, not to mention many uncollected and posthumous articles. His career, indeed his life, was almost in its entirety that of a literary critic. The substance of his criticism is found in his *Etudes critiques sur la littérature française* (8 vols., 1880–1907) covering four centuries of French literature. Brunetière was in many ways out of harmony with his age; he yearned for certainty and was dogmatic at a time when, under the influence of science, most of his contemporaries in philosophy, religion, and literature thought and wrote in terms of the relative and the experimental. Yet he himself did not escape the all pervading atmosphere, and he attempted to apply to literary history the new theory of evolution. Assimilating the genres or types in literature to the Darwinian species in the biological world, Brunetière maintains that each genre is born, constitutes itself, is modified, and finally disappears or is transformed into another type, just as with other living organisms. There is, therefore, no spontaneous generation in literature. Hence the importance of adhering closely to the historical method in dealing with literary genres; transition periods should be studied carefully, for it is then that literary types assume new forms. When a professor at the Ecole Normale Supérieure, Brunetière exposed these theories in a course, later published in book form as *L'Evolution de la critique* (1890). The author's plan envisioned a vast work which would treat all literary genres according to the same method; he had time to execute only part of his project, *Les Epoques du théâtre français* (1892) and *L'Evolution de la poésie lyrique* (1894).

Other activities of Brunetière were less purely theoretical. He considered it his duty to wage a relentless war on those whom he called "the enemies of the French soul," especially the literary naturalists (however inconsistent this may seem in a would-be scientific critic) and the romanticists. Art, he thought, should serve a moral or at least a social purpose; the proponents of "art for art's sake" drew biting invective from him; the subjectivism and lack of restraint of the romanticists fared little better. His admiration for 17th-century French classicism, on the other hand, appears excessive. The mind which he brings to criticism is hardly free and open; his preestablished conception of life and of the universe made him singularly narrow. This is true especially of his later articles after his conversion to Catholicism (1900). A moralizing tendency is evident in much of his writing, and in his later works this becomes sheer religious propaganda for the Catholic cause. Studies on Christian apologetics and religious polemics fill almost entirely his last years.

René Doumic (*q.v.*), one of Brunetière's disciples, takes malicious pleasure in drawing up an impressively lengthy and varied list of his master's adversaries. Many of Brunetière's victims were perhaps more than partially right when they accused him of lacking finesse and tact, of being bellicose and vitriolic; his "ego contra" attitude too often bespeaks the pedantic pessimist. In spite of genuine defects, Brunetière's work remains that of a conscientious, erudite scholar; his theory on literary evolution helped to make the study of literature more living and dynamic; his power of generalization enabled him to build countless "palaces of ideas" which he presented in an invariably dialectic and discursive style. He is forever trying to convince. The austerity and tenseness of his criticism are fatiguing, and readers find themselves condemning his didactic manner and even disagreeing with many of his fundamental theories, but few will withhold their admiration for his qualities of order, clarity, intellectual penetration, and, at times, robust common sense.

See: A. Darlu, *M. Brunetière et l'individualisme* (1898); V. Giraud, *Brunetière* (1907); G. Fonsegrive, *Ferdinand Brunetière* (1908); E. Faguet, *Ferdinand Brunetière* (1911); E. Hocking, *Brunetière* (1936).

N. J. T.

Bryusov, Valeri Yakovlevich (1873–1924, Russian poet, critic, novelist, and translator), was born in Moscow into a wealthy merchant family. After graduating from the famous Polivanov Gymnasium, he matriculated with the historico-philological faculty of the University of Moscow. While still in his teens Bryusov resolved to become a littérateur. In 1894–1895 he published at his own expense three booklets entitled *Russkiye simvolisty* (Russian Symbolists), which contained translations from and imitations of some of the more startling examples of Western modernist poetry. By deliberately shocking public taste and critics steeped in the traditional themes and forms of poetry, Bryusov became notorious overnight. Discovering thereupon that no Russian periodical would publish his verse, he undertook a serious study not only of Western modernist poetry but also that of such classical Russian authors as Pushkin, Tyutchev, and Lermontov.

By the end of the 19th century his perseverance won him recognition as a serious critic. In 1899 the publishing house for modernist literature, "Scorpio," was established, and Bryusov was asked to act on its editorial board; later he was virtual director of its policies. By 1904, when he had organized *Vesy* (The Balance), a periodical devoted to symbolist literature, Bryusov became the acknowledged head of the Moscow symbolists. His literary reputation was so well established by 1908 that his verses and prose were welcome even in the traditional "thick" periodicals, and from 1910 to 1912 he even had charge of the literary department of *Russkaya mysl* (Russian Thought). With the outbreak of war in 1914, Bryusov went to the front in the capacity of a war correspondent. He enthusiastically welcomed the October Revolution of 1917 and in 1919 became a member of the Communist Party. Throughout the early years of the Revolution Bryusov tirelessly worked in the various projects of the Department of Education of the Soviet government; he founded the Literary Institute in Moscow in 1921.

Both in his poetry and in his prose Bryusov

appears a classicist of Russian symbolism. His verses, often cold, appear because of their formal perfection "chiseled in marble" or "cast in bronze." Although Bryusov at one time subscribed to the symbolist dictum that poetry was born of magic, yet at heart he was too much of a rationalist to accept fully such a notion. Symbolism to him was a literary style rather than philosophical interpretation of life. Bryusov's influence on symbolist and non-symbolist poets alike has been very great. Much of the "literary hooliganism" of such futurist poets as Mayakovsky (*q.v.*), Burlyuk, and Khlebnikov (*q.v.*) was anticipated in Bryusov's collections, *Russkiye simvolisty;* many a symbolist poet was indebted to Bryusov for his editorial suggestions and for his penetrating critical comments. Such writers as Alexander Blok and Andrei Bely (*qq.v.*) regarded Bryusov as their teacher in poetic form.

Bryusov's literary output has been voluminous. Ideologically it reflects the influence of French and Belgian symbolists (*see* French symbolism)—of Baudelaire, Verlaine, Mallarmé, Rimbaud, Maeterlinck (*qq.v.*), and, after the turn of the century, especially of Verhaeren (*q.v.*). Bryusov's books of verse, *Chefs d'œuvre* (1895), *Me Eum Esse* (1897), *Tertia Vigilia* (1900), *Urbi et Orbi* (1903), *Stephanos* (1906), *Zerkalo tenei* (1912; A Mirror of Shadows), *Posledniye mechty* (1920; Last Wishes), *Mig* (1922; Moment), *Dali* (1922; Distance), *Mea* (1924), reflect the development from a passionate egocentrism toward an impassionate objectivity. His *Opyty* (1918; Experiments) comprises verses of varying worth that illustrate every kind of meter and verse known to prosody. Bryusov's prose includes two semihistorical novels, *Ognenny angel* (1903; The Fiery Angel) and *Altar pobedy* (1913; Altar of Victory), and a number of short stories. His *Dalekiye i blizkiyie* (1912; The Distant Ones and the Near) is a collection of penetrating critical essays on Russian poetry. Bryusov's translations include Verlaine's *Romances sans paroles* (1894); Verhaeren's *Hélène de Sparte* (1909) and his poems (*Stikhi o sovremennosti,* 1907, Poems of Modernity; *Sobranie stikhotvorenii,* 1911, Collected Poems); Maeterlinck's *Pelléas et Mélisande* (1907); D'Annunzio's *Francesca da Rimini* (1908); a number of poems by Oscar Wilde; and a collection, *Frantsuzskiye liriki XIX veka* (1909; French Lyrics of the 19th Century). Bryusov also wrote a number of critical works devoted to Pushkin. His *Dnevniki, 1891–1910* (1927; Diaries, 1891–1910) and a volume of memoirs, *Iz moyei zhizni* (1927), are valuable documentary evidence of an era of intellectual turmoil and seeking.

See: Ellis (pseud. of L. L. Kobylinski), *Russkiye simvolisty* (1910); P. S. Kogan, ed., *Valeriyu Bryusovu* (1924); G. Lelevich, *V. Ya. Bryusov* (1924).

O. M.

Budantsev, Sergei Fyodorovich (1896–, Russian novelist, dramatist, and short-story writer), was born on an estate in the former Government of Ryazan, graduated from a Gymnasium in 1915, and, after a year at the University of Moscow, visited Persia (1916–1918); later he worked for newspapers in Astrakhan and Baku. He had been contributing to the provincial press since 1913, and in 1923 he brought out his *Myatezh* (The Revolt), a typical civil war novel, depicting the triumph of the Red sailors over the Socialist Revolutionaries in a Volga town. A more considerable work is *Sarancha* (1927; The Locusts), with its complex plot, deepened characterization, and convincing description of life and intrigue in the Turkestan steppes. His *Povest o stradaniyakh uma* (1931; A Tale of a Suffering Mind) aroused considerable controversy, for instead of dealing with contemporary Russia, the author had elected to explore the eternal problem of the meaning of human life as it appeared to a young Russian scientist of the 60's.

Budantsev's plays are less known, but his stories have attracted attention and represent a real contribution to Russian literature. Like his novels, they often center about the conflict of sharply differentiated psychological types; they are carefully composed and are written in an expressive language which makes the most of details. These stories have been gathered in several collections (*Yaponskaya duel,* 1927, The Japanese Duel; *Rasskazy,* 1929, Stories; *Lyubov k zhizni,* 1935, Love of Life); the best appear in Budantsev's *Izbrannoye* (1936; Selected Works). The earliest deal with personal tragedy and social injustice among Asiatics ("Zhena"; The Wife); of the later stories, some give a penetrating analysis of ordinary Soviet citizens ("Vesennyaya pesn"; Spring Song), while others, which show the transformation of intellectuals, are psychologically weaker ("Inzhener Vyazemski"; Engineer Vyazemski).

See: G. Gorbachyov, *Sovremennaya russkaya literatura* (1928); "Budantsev," in *Literaturnaya entsiklopediya,* Vol. I (1929); G. Struve, *Soviet Russian Literature* (1935), pp. 142–145.

P. A. P.

Bulgakov, Mikhail Afanasyevich (1891–1940, Russian novelist and dramatist), was born in Kiev, graduated in 1916 from the medical school of the university there, and remained in that city during the following troublous years of the Revolution and civil war, when Kiev changed hands some 10 times. Arriving poor and unknown in Moscow in 1921, he wrote fantastic and satirical stories later collected in *Dyaboliada* (1925; The Deviliad). His two-volume novel, *Belaya Gvardiya* (1925; The White Guard), dealt not unsympathetically with the Turbins, a charming family of the old Russia, undergoing in Kiev the same terrible experiences that Bulgakov had suffered. By condensing this story and in one case combining two characters into one, Bulgakov turned his novel into a play, *Dni Turbinykh* (1926; Eng. tr., *The Days of the Turbins*, 1934). This was beautifully acted by the Moscow Art Theatre and was also produced in England and America; it is often considered the best written of all Soviet plays. It brings in all the different forces then in conflict in Russia—the followers of the tsar, the followers of the Ukrainian hetman, the invading German armies, the outlaws under Petlura. The Bolsheviks themselves never appear, but at the end of the play when they are heard approaching and singing the "Internationale," one of the characters says with evenhanded justice: "To some this is a prologue and to some it is an epilogue." The play has been much discussed and has continued to hold the stage.

Bulgakov also wrote *Zoikina kvartira* (1926; Zoe's Apartment), a comedy making fun of the difficulties of Soviet life, and *Bagrovy ostrov* (1928; The Purple Island), a fantastic allegory on Soviet censorship. For the Moscow Art Theatre he dramatized (1932) Gogol's novel *Mertvie dushi* (*Dead Souls*). For the same theatre he acted as "dramaturge" or selector and arranger of the repertoire. He attempted a sequel to his story about the Turbin family which represented the White Guard officers flying to join the forces of Denikin fighting against the Red armies in the south. This was called *Beg* (1936; Flight). From then on he turned to earlier history and literature. In *Molière* (1936) he dramatized the life of the great French playwright of the 17th century. *Don Quixote* (1940) dramatizes the novel of Cervantes, *Pushkin* (produced in 1943 after Bulgakov's death) the last days in the life of the great Russian poet of the early 19th century.

See: Gleb Struve, *Soviet Russian Literature* (1935), pp. 145–152; *Moskovski Khudozhestvenny Teatr v illyustratsiyakh i dokumentakh* (1938).

H. W. L. D.

Bulgarian literature. Prior to the independence of Bulgaria in 1876, the literature of that country had been didactic or revolutionary in character. Authors such as Father Paisi (1722–?) and Khristo Botev (1848–1876) were more interested in educating their people and rousing them to a knowledge of their past and present than in producing literature as ordinarily defined.

The first real man of letters was Ivan Vazov (*q.v.*). For 50 years he worked in all forms of literature, lyric and epic poetry, short story, novel, and drama, and made himself the leader of a national literature in the best sense of the word. Originally romanticist under the influence of Victor Hugo, he set forth realistically and optimistically the struggles for the liberation and the development of the Bulgarian people. At the same time there developed a group of writers such as Todor Genchov Vlaykov (1865–), Georgi P. Stamatov (1869–), Anton Strashimirov (1872–), Stoyan Mikhaylovski (1856–1927), and Aleko Konstantinov (1863–1897), who pictured in a realistic manner Bulgarian village life with its various manifestations of virtue and of evil, but who believed that with the development of better conditions the good would finally conquer the evil.

As national stability grew and Bulgarian social and political life became better organized, it was only natural that a tendency should arise to bring Bulgarian literature nearer to European models. The leader in this movement, which at first involved an opposition to Vazov and his school, was Pencho Slaveykov (1866–1912). He was the son of the prerevolutionary poet, Petko Rachev Slaveykov, and after some education at home went to Leipzig in 1892 and remained there until 1908. There he came under the influence of German writers, especially Goethe, Heine, and Nietzsche (*q.v.*), and sought to translate into Bulgarian the ideals of modern literature as he understood them. Yet he did it largely through Bulgarian themes in such works as *Epicheski pesni* (1907; Epic Songs), *Son' na shtastie* (1907; Dream of Happiness), and *Korvava pesn'* (1911–1913; Song of Blood). He was the first Bulgarian aesthete and deliberate artist and from his influence developed most of Bulgarian modernism. In the same direction worked two of his younger contemporaries, Peyo Kracholov Yavorov (1878–1914), who leaned heavily upon Russian and French symbolists (*see* French symbolism) in resolving the discords in the human soul, and Petko Yu. Todorov (1879–1916), who introduced Ibsen (*q.v.*) into Bulgaria and reworked many Bulgarian folk themes in a modern psychological manner. Among prose authors in this period, the outstanding name is Elin Pelin (pseud. of Dimitar Ivanov, 1878–), whose short stories reveal Bulgarian life under the impact of modern civilization.

The old optimistic life vanished with the First Balkan War in 1912, when Bulgaria failed to recover Macedonia, and with the heavy losses of the Second Balkan War in 1913. There followed the disastrous entrance of the country into the First World War on the side of the Central Powers, and all these defeats together with the hope of securing territory which all classes of the population believe rightfully theirs led the nation into the Second World War on the side of the Axis, despite the democratic character of the people. All this has had its reflection on modern Bulgarian literature, which since 1912 has shown signs of interest in mysticism, especially the medieval cult of Bogomilism, in symbolism, and in a great development of the historical novel inspired by ancient Bulgarian history. The outstanding poet of this period was Dimcho Debelyanov (1887–1916), who fell in the First World War and who left a small collection of poems which by their quality secured his fame. They number barely 50 but they have made a deep impression upon the Bulgarian literary world. To the same generation belong Ivan Grozev (1872–) with his themes drawn from the supernatural world, and Todor Trayanov (1882–); they are the recognized leaders of the symbolists with a real sense of the problems of Bulgaria, as may be seen *e.g.*, in the latter's *Bulgarski baladi* (1921; Bulgarian Ballads) and *Pesen' na pesnite* (1921; Song of Songs). Other outstanding symbolists are Nikolay Raynov (1888–), a professor of the history of art at the Art Academy, with his *Bogomilski legendi* (1912; Bogomil Legends), and Nikolay Liliev (1885–) with his superb mastery of the music of verse and his yearning for solitude.

In prose Iordan Iovkov (1884–1938) holds the first rank with his stories of peasant life, especially those about his native province of Dobruja. He was an accurate observer and a good student of psychology and had an excellent command of form and style, so that some of his works, such as *Staroplaninski legendi* (1927; Legends of the Staroplanina), can be counted among the best products of Bulgarian literature. His early death was one of the great losses of the modern period. Dobri Nemirov (1882–) is another master painter of village life, as in *Bratya* (1927; The Brothers) which presents conditions at the time of the liberation of the country. He has also worked in the field of the historical novel, *e.g.*, *Angeloglasniyat* (1938; The Angel-voiced Singer). Georgi Raychev (1882–) is the leading psychological novelist and his *Grekh* (1923; Sin) is one of the finest of his works. In general, however, it is fair to say that Bulgarian authors have handled far more satisfactorily the problem of village life and village reaction to modern culture than they have subjects related to the capital or to the leading provincial cities such as Plovdiv. Mention should be made of Angel Karaliychev (1902–) who has gravitated from stories of peasant life to stories of children.

For many years Bulgarian writers were grouped around two literary periodicals, the *Hyperion,* organ of the symbolists, and the *Zlatorog* (Golden Horn), which united those artists who were seeking especially for perfection of form. This second ideal has been supported by critics such as Dr. Kiril Khristich, editor of *Mysl* (Thought), Vladimir Vasilev, Konstantin Galabov, Bozhan Angelov, and Iordan Badev.

Since the beginning of the 20th century women have played a prominent part in Bulgarian literature. Dora Gabe (1886–) won a high reputation before the First World War and has since then devoted herself mainly to poems for children. Elisaveta Bagryana's collection of lyric poems, *Vechnata i svyatata* (Eternity and the Saint), which combine abstract aestheticism and true feeling, were published in 1927. Anna Kamenova (1894–) is the leading woman prose writer.

In a somewhat different vein is Dimitri Shishmanov's (1889–1945), *Blenove kray Akropola* (1938; Shadows on the Acropolis), a series of fictionalized studies on the relations of the ancient and the modern worlds which attracted considerable attention as a type of intelligent sophistication that had not previously appeared in Bulgarian literature. Shishmanov has also written a number of successful novels and dramas.

When we reflect that Bulgarian literature has existed as an independent art only since the liberation of the country, and when we take into account the stormy history of this century, we realize how much Bulgarian writers have achieved. They have acclimated themselves to nearly all the forms and movements of more recent times and have succeeded in leaving their own imprint upon each form that they adopted. Their greatest strength is undoubtedly in the description of peasant life, presented in all periods of its development and in a variety of literary forms.

See: *Bulgarski pisateli,* Vols. I–VI (1929–1930); D. Shishmanov, *A Survey of Bulgarian Literature* (1932); Iordan Badev, *Skitsi na zhivite,* (1934).

C. A. M.

Bull, Olaf (1883–1933; Norwegian lyric poet), born in Christiania, might justly be called the Keats of Norway: he was a dreamer, a pure artist, a passionate lover of truth and beauty, a master of concrete imagery, and a matchless workman who patiently wrought into imperishable form the full wealth of a pensive, restless spirit. He is the one Norwegian poet who was at once (*Digte,* 1909; Poems) recognized as a genius and whose writings bore from birth the stamp of deathlessness. His "Ode to a Grecian Urn" is a poem called "Metope" (1927), wherein melancholy over the fragility of life is woven into a vivid setting which preserves in the "young, eternal alabaster of poetry" a mood like that of Keats's "still unravished . . . quietness." His themes were those of all great lyric writers—nature, love, beauty, death, and the poet's self. He sang the nature of Christiania, particularly the northern spring in its earliest, most auspicious moments, vivifying every nuance of color and light among the shadows. In love he sought the ideal beauty that is glimpsed but never won, dwelling much on memory, concretely and presently imaged, in which he found the true eternity. His goal was to experience poetically the entire universe, and he pursued it by delving deeply into history, biology, geology, and other branches of learning, as well as by direct, acute perception of the outer world. This goal required an intense objectification of his experiences, expressed in life by a completely bohemian, asocial existence, in poetry by a constant veiling of the immediacy of experience in allusion, myth, or poetic imagery. He also hid behind a self-ironic humor which can often be utterly charming. In his last years poems of a less esoteric nature, showing a warmer contact with nation and society, came into being (*De hundrede aar,* 1928, The Hundred Years; *Ignis ardens,* 1932), but in the midst of this new and fruitful development his life was cut short by disease. Bull is generally named in one breath with Norway's masters of lyric verse, Wergeland, Björnson (*q.v.*), Vogt (*q.v.*). He lacks their social stature and their urge to action, but he shares their cosmic feeling and daring imagery and exceeds them in chiseled perfection of form. Some of his most unforgettable poems deal with the laws of fantasy and the poet's difficult art, which he once described as "festively forging parted thoughts together." His published poems are only a fraction compared with what he himself rejected, and not one of them was ever revised after publication. His sense of form extended beyond rhyme and rhythm into the very sound texture of his lines, which he wove together in a rich but subtle assonance. The aristocratic form of his poetry won him admirers among the fastidious rather than the multitude. It is occasionally overloaded with imagery and allusion to the point of unclarity, but is always imaginative, tender, yet virile in its unflinching view of the world. In form and spirit he has much in common with the French symbolists (*see* French symbolism), especially Paul Valéry (*q.v.*), and he has learned from Bergson (*q.v.*), but his own singular genius is apparent in every line.

See: T. Aurell, *et al,* "Olaf Bull," *Samtiden* (1922, 1930, 1933, 1939); K. Elster, "Three Lyric Poets of Norway," *American-Scandinavian Review,* XIII (1925), 653–665; J. Knutzen, "Motiver i Olaf Bulls produksjon," *Nordisk tidskrift,* V (1929), 281–296.

E. H.

Bunin, Ivan Alekseyevich (1870–, Russian novelist, short-story writer, and poet), 1933 winner of the Nobel award, is the most distinguished artist of contemporary Russian letters. In an external sense he belongs to the tradition represented by Aksakov, Leo Tolstoy (*q.v.*), Goncharov, Turgenev (*q.v.*), and Chekhov (*q.v.*); in style and content his work is a culmination of that tradition, broken abruptly by the 1917 Revolution. In a more fundamental sense, however, he is a unique and original figure, closely akin to many of the newest voices in literature, not merely the end of an epoch.

Bunin was born in Voronezh, of landowning nobility, whose ancestors included the poet Zhukovsky. His childhood and youth were spent in rural Central Russia in the atmosphere of a declining gentry. He was educated at the Yelets Gymnasium and the University of Moscow. He made his début in literature with a volume of poems (1891) and a prose volume (1892), besides several brilliant translations, notably of the poems of Byron,

Tennyson, and Longfellow (*The Song of Hiawatha*). In 1903 he was awarded the coveted Pushkin prize, which placed him in the front rank of Chekhov's successors. In 1909 the Russian Academy of Sciences elected him one of 12 honorary members (corresponding to the "Immortals" of the French Academy). During this period Bunin traveled extensively in Italy, Turkey, the Balkans, Greece, North Africa, the Near and Far East. Though associated with the Znanie group of young realists led by Gorky, Bunin avoided affiliation with either political or literary innovators. For this reason and because his first work was largely poetry, he did not acquire fame until his novel *Derevnya* (1910; Eng. tr., *The Village*, 1923) was published. A diptych of peasant life, it inaugurated a long series of works indicting the darkness and barbarity of rural existence, particularly before the 1905 Revolution and the Stolypin agrarian reform. *Sukhodol* (1911–1912; Eng. tr., "Dry Valley," in *The Elaghin Affair and Other Stories*, 1935), in the same genre, a story of the fall of the house of Khrushchov, and *Derevnya* belong among the most powerful examples of Russian prose. *Ioann Rydalets* (1913; Ioann the Weeper) and *Chasha zhizni* (1914; The Cup of Life), collections of poems and stories in the same vein, were followed by *Gospodin iz San Frantsisko* (1916; Eng. tr., *The Gentleman from San Francisco and Other Stories*, 1923), his best-known story noticed especially in the Nobel citation. A miracle of artistic economy, it relates the sudden death of an American millionaire in Capri, its theme that of Ecclesiastes, "Vanity of vanities, saith the preacher, all is vanity."

An intransigent anti-Bolshevik, Bunin emigrated to France (1919), where he has since resided. *Roza Ierikhona* (1923; The Rose of Jericho) and *Solnichnyi udar* (1927; The Sunstroke) are collections of stories and verse. *Mitina lyubov* (1924–1925; Eng. tr., *Mitya's Love*, 1926), a short novel of rare terseness and insight, is a study of early love with its mingled sensuality and idealism. *Zhizn Arseneva; istoki dnei* (1930; Eng. tr., *The Well of Days*, 1933), the first part of a long work, is a novelized autobiography comparable with those of Aksakov and Tolstoy, but more somber and searching. *Bozhie drevo* (1931; God's Tree), short stories, *Osvobozhdenie Tolstovo* (1937; The Liberation of Tolstoy), *Elle* (1938), and *Tyomnye allei* (1943; Dark Alleys) are his most recent works. Bunin has been widely translated and several volumes of his finest stories appear in English —*The Dreams of Chang and Other Stories* (1923), *Grammar of Love* (1934), and *The Elaghin Affair and Other Stories* mentioned above. Besides the title stories, among the most remarkable are "A Night Conversation" (1911) and "A Goodly Life" (1911), both peasant stories of cruelty and violence, the latter told in the vernacular with extraordinary phonetic accuracy; "Brethren" (1914), the tragedy of a Colombo rickshaw man and a bitter comment on imperialism; "Light Breathing" (1916), about the seduction and murder of a well-born young girl; "Gautami" (1919), an Eastern parable on the acceptance of life; and "The Cicadas" (1925; the dates given are those of the original Russian), an exquisite prose poem embodying his artistic credo.

Bunin evades easy category. As a poet he is allied with the Parnassians, rather than with the symbolists. His conception of life is that of a poet, and this attitude informs all his prose. His understanding is primarily a tragic one, but he affirms the eternal beauty and meaning of life. He has a profound sense of its continuity beyond material experience and of the significance of atavistic memory. The supreme mysteries of love and death are the mainsprings of his creative power. For all the searing social criticism implied in much he has written, his chief concern is with the soul of man, which he reveals with marvelous skill and insight. Bunin should not be read hastily. A painter rather than a narrator or an analyst, he is outwardly objective, though actually his personality is never absent. The structure of his work is elemental, bare, and symmetrical, with few characters and little plot. He has a phenomenal faculty of observation, as if endowed with "eagle's eyes for Day and the owl's for Night," and a gift for creating atmosphere, in which all the sensory equipment serves to convey texture, shape, color, taste, and odor. In his descriptions he chooses always the precise word, for its rhythmic and emotional relation to the sentence as well as for its connotation. Since his effects are often those of style, an adequate translation is almost impossible.

The clinical detachment and the merciless veracity of his work, particularly of his early and middle career, relate him to the great realists. In latter years this phase has increasingly given place to one more lyrical and philosophical. His preoccupation with love and death, as well as the sensuous beauty of his language and the exotic element of his many foreign tales, allies him with the romanticists. In his impeccable restraint, in the symmetry and logic of his form and the perfection of his style, he belongs with the classicists. He has been criticized for his uncontemporaneousness, but a less partisan future may revise this opinion. Edmond Jaloux has pointed out the increasing predominance in recent literature of "magic realism," whereby daily experience is made to reveal the signs, the symbols, the poetry of life. Such is Bunin's art, which deals with unchanging verities rather than with the dilemmas, however acute, of a shifting politico-social arena. Controversy aside, he is the acknowledged master of the Russian language and a weaver of tales that for clarity, beauty, and veracity rank with the finest.

See: G. Struve, "The Art of Ivan Bunin," *Slavonic Review,* XI (1932–1933), 423–436; F. Stepun, "Ivan Bunin," *Sovremennyia zapiski,* LIV (1934), 195–211.

N. S.

Burte, Hermann (pseud. of Hermann Strübe, 1879–, German dramatist, novelist, and poet), comes from a South German family of artisans and peasants. His work was determined by race consciousness and interest in aesthetics. He spent years in France and England, studying art. The Renaissance, Shakespeare, Byron and Ruskin, Rabelais and French drama, left deep impressions on him. His one-act plays in *Drei Einakter* (1907) are first attempts, supporting the principle that the world belongs only to the strong and healthy. Love for an English lady inspired the 154 sonnets of *Patricia* (1910), which also present a broad view of the poet's attitude toward God, the world, and man. Despite the occasional use of immaturely exaggerated language, it is a strong poetic creation. A second collection of sonnets, *Die Flügelspielerin* (1913), shows the poet greatly improved in discipline and restraint. Returning from abroad, he decided the Germans were sunk in godless materialism, slavishly subject to all currents of foreign thought. He wrote the novel *Wiltfeber, der ewige Deutsche* (1912), an irate discourse on religion, art, folk, and fatherland, composed in a cyclic arrangement—12 chapters distributed over 24 hours of one day—and written in a language of rhythmic force and beauty. This work, for which Burte received the Kleist prize, tries to show that modern civilization, the ideas of Rousseau and Marx, lead to decay. A change can only come through an anti-Jewish Christianity, through a Nietzschean will to reform, and through a return to life close to the soil. The swastika is hailed, long before Hitler, as the sign of German rebirth. In the dramas *Herzog Utz* (1913) and *Katte* (1914) Burte follows in the path of Kleist and Hebbel. Utz goes on from love of woman to work and duty, the way of a true ruler; Katte is a sacrifice to the ultimate welfare of the state. In his play *Simson* (1917) Burte emphasizes his nationalist-racist attitude by stating that "he who is without folk is without God." In later dramas and poems, though they are mature and well written, he does not strike any particularly new note. He has made an interesting translation of poems of Voltaire, *Gedichte* (1934).

See: A. Soergel, *Dichtung und Dichter der Zeit,* 19. Auflage (1928), pp. 1037–1044.

W. K. P.

Busch, Wilhelm (1832–1908, German humorist and illustrator), was born in Wiedensahl, Hanover, the son of a general-store keeper. His uncommon mathematical ability seeming to indicate engineering as his proper vocation, he attended the polytechnic institute in Hanover. However, his passion for graphic art proved to be dominant, and in 1851 he went to Düsseldorf to study painting. Dissatisfied with the trends he found in vogue there, he transferred in 1852 to Antwerp, where he came permanently under the spell of the great realists of the Netherlands—Rubens, Hals, Brouwer, Teniers, Ostade. The decade 1854–1864 he spent in Munich, then the leading art center, but basically no better suited to his temperament than Düsseldorf. In the art colony he soon attracted attention by his incidental productions, caricatures, costume designs, comic drawings, and also humorous and original writings (an operetta, *Der Vetter auf Besuch,* was performed in the Residenztheater). Thus he came to the notice of Caspar Braun, publisher of the comic weekly *Fliegende Blätter.* Braun's invitation to contribute coincided with an ebb in Busch's funds (1859); it proved to be the hand of fate that beckoned. For it led Busch into a field which was peculiarly his own and in which his undisputed mastery carried him to a unique eminence in German letters. No other German poet before or since has produced work so abounding in familiar quotations of humorous character; keen observation, an uncompromising realism tinged with pessimism, and a gift for terse and pungent utterance combine in these masterpieces of epigrammatic brevity.

Work for the weekly soon led to the creation of pictorial series (the original of the wordless comic strip) and to even more popular—because quotable—versified stories with appropriate illustrations. The first of these, *Max und Moritz* (1865; Eng. tr., *Max and Maurice,* 1871), tapping the inexhaustible theme of the naughty boy, made him a byword in every German household and fixed his literary character, though not quite authentically, for all time. Outstanding among his other picture stories are *Schnurrdiburr oder die Bienen* (1869; Eng. tr., *Buzz a buzz; or, The Bees,* 1872), *Der heilige Antonius* (1870), *Balduin Bählamm, der verhinderte Dichter* (1881), and *Maler Klecksel* (1883). The last two present humorous aspects of his own frustrations. Genuine poetic talent is revealed in *Kritik des Herzens* (1871), philosophic acumen in *Eduards Traum* (1891; Eng. tr., *Edward's Dream,* 1909) exceptional autobiographic ability in "Was mich betrifft" (1886). Busch's preeminence as poet of "superior nonsense" is challenged in the 20th century only by Christian Morgenstern (*q.v.*).

See: Fritz Winther, *Wilhelm Busch als Dichter, Künstler, Psychologe und Philosoph* (1910).

B. Q. M.

Busken Huet, Coenraad (1826–1886, Dutch journalist and critic), born at The Hague, studied theology at Leiden and Geneva and became pastor of the Walloon Church at Haarlem in 1851. He incurred the disapproval of his congregation when he published his *Brieven over den Bijbel* (1858; Letters about the Bible), because the book was too outspoken a confession of his modernism. He resigned from the ministry in 1862 and started on a journalistic career in the editorial office of *De opregte Haarlemsche Courant* (The Outspoken Haarlem Courant). A series of lectures by Huet on Dutch literature of the last decade of the 18th century attracted the attention of Potgieter (*q.v.*), who made him a member of the editorial board of *De Gids* (The Guide). But here again his fiery, uncompromising spirit soon came into conflict with the other editors. They forced him out in 1865, and Potgieter, who sided with Huet, went out with him. Huet became editor of *De Javabode* (The Java Messenger), a daily paper published in Batavia, Java. In 1872 he founded there his own paper, called *Algemeen Dagblad van Nederlandsch Indië* (General Journal of Netherlands India). But in 1876 he retired from newspaper work and settled down with his wife and son in Paris to devote himself entirely to writing and literary criticism. He was a follower of Sainte-Beuve, of whom he wrote in *In Memoriam* (1870): "He has been for many of us an apostle, a mentor, a shepherd." Huet was a relentless critic of Dutch letters, but from his Huguenot ancestry he had inherited a mental agility and grace that enabled him to give the damning verdict the flavor of a compliment. His literary essays and book reviews have been collected in *Literarische Fantasien en Kritieken* (25 vols., 1881–1888; Literary Fantasies and Criticisms). His best-known work is *Het Land van Rembrandt* (1884; The Country of Rembrandt), a history of Dutch culture which is a lasting monument to Rembrandt's country and to the author himself.

See: J. Tielrooy, *Cd. Busken Huet et la littérature française; essai de biographie intellectuelle* (1923).

A. J. B.

Busse, Carl (1872–1918, German lyricist, novelist, and literary critic), was born in Lindenstadt, Posen. After receiving his doctorate from Rostock University (1898; his thesis was *Novalis' Lyrik*), he went to Berlin to devote himself earnestly to a literary career, both as a creative artist and as a literary scholar.

Busse became known to a cultured German public through his *Gedichte* (1892), composed in finished rhythm, distinguished by a sprightly undercurrent of optimism, and characterized by a genuine love of nature. Further collections of poetry followed: *Neue Gedichte* (1895), *Vagabunden* (1901), and *Heilige Not* (1910). The last named, in particular, strikes a note of deep and introspective contemplation. In general, it may be said that Busse's poems are influenced by German romanticism—strongly tempered, however, by the realistic tendencies of Theodor Storm and Detlev von Liliencron (*qq.v.*). His poetry strives toward a combination of romanticism and poetic realism.

In addition to poetry, Busse wrote novels which, for the greater part, deal with life in his native region, the German-Polish boundary areas. His *Schüler von Polajewo* appeared in 1900 and was followed by *Im polnischen Wind* (1906), *Das Gymnasium zu Lengowo* (1907), *Die Hoermanns* (1909), and *Winkelglück* (1918). Busse edited two anthologies, *Neuere deutsche Lyrik* (1895) and *Deutsche Kriegslieder* (1915). He wrote an excellent *Geschichte der deutschen Dichtung im neunzehnten Jahrhundert* (1901) and an impressive *Geschichte der Weltliteratur* (2 vols., 1910–1913).

G. K.

Butti, Enrico Annibale (1868–1912, Italian playwright and novelist), born in Milan of a well-to-do family, was versatile and temperamental. At the University of Pavia his major interests were physics and mathematics. Abandoning these studies, he transferred to the University of Modena where he took a law degree, though his experience in this profession was very short-lived. A musician of more than average ability, he was one of the more ardent admirers of Wagner and helped secure a sympathetic audience for him in Italy. Butti was wracked by chronic illness, and his literary career was blighted by the presentiment that his days would be brief. In spirit and temperament he was a kinsman of the anemic *crepuscolari* who, in plaintive and nostalgic tones, sang of the innocent joys of their sheltered childhood. Essentially an idealist, he cherished an inner sympathy for the positivists and rationalists. Their philosophic theories with their social, economic, scientific, and moral implications appealed to his heart; but the social deterioration of his time dampened his faith. This conflict between his yearning for the ideal and the impact of a stern reality accentuated both his pessimism and his habit of introspection.

Such was Butti the man, and the artist in him faithfully reflects these qualities. It is not surprising therefore to find that the predominant note in Butti's novels (*L'Automa,* 1892; *L'Anima,* 1893; *L'Immorale,* 1894; *L'Incantesimo,* 1897) is a predilection for philosophical musings. The author's incurable preoccupation with ideas still unclarified in his own mind tends to blur his characters and fetter their actions. Turning to the drama, Butti hoped to invest his ideas with dramatic force and elevate the tone of the Italian theatre by neutralizing the influence of the French naturalists and of Antoine's Théâtre Libre (*see* French naturalism; Antoine). However, his early plays *Paolo Ermoli* and *Il Frutto amaro* (both published only in 1912), written in collaboration with Cesare Hanau, as well as *Fiamme nell'ombra* (1907), were in the prevalent naturalistic manner. That his principal aim was not to entertain but to induce his audiences to ponder the problems of the day is shown in *La Corsa al piacere* (1900), *Una Tempesta* (1901), and *Lucifero* (1903), in which he successively treats the themes of pleasure as an end in itself, the theory of socialism, and the soul's need for religion. These plays reverberate with faint echoes from Ibsen's (*q.v.*) world, but the drama never attains the white heat of the Norwegian master. Butti's protagonists, like their creator, are disillusioned rationalists; the vision which animates their thoughts and actions is that of a freer and more humane civilization. Unfortunately, in contrast to Ibsen's determined, virile characters, Butti's creatures give up their lofty designs at the first clash with reality, admitting that they have been deceived and defeated. The same theme of man's struggle to break the shackles of reality and his ultimate capitulation to traditional social forms is found in *L'Utopia* (1894), *La Fine d'un ideale* (1898), and in *Sempre così* (1911). The plays which brought him the greatest success were *Il Cuculo* (1907) and *L'Intermezzo* (1912), which sounded a gay and cheerful note instead of the somber, thoughtful strains so characteristic of most of his work. Other plays are *Il Vortice* (1892), *Il Gigante ed i pigmei* (1903), *Tutto per nulla* (1906), *Nel paese della fortuna* (1911), and *Il Castello del sogno* (1910). This last named, a dramatic poem in four acts, besides epitomizing the author's philosophical creed, contains passages with fresh and arresting images of unsurpassed beauty in which words glow with a new and profound meaning.

See: G. A. Borgese, *La Vita e il libro,* I (1910), 173–183; C. Levi, *Rivista teatrale italiana* (1912), pp. 321–337; A. Tilgher, *La Scena e la vita* (1925), pp. 121–125.

P. P. M.

Buysse, Cyriel (1859–1932, Flemish novelist), was born at Nevele, near Ghent, in the province of East Flanders, the son of a wealthy manufacturer. Originally he worked in his father's weaving mill and for this business spent two years, 1885 and 1886, in the United States. On the ship which took him back to Belgium he wrote his first short novel, *De Biezenstekker* (The Reed Cutter), which was published in 1890 in *De Nieuwe Gids* (The New Guide, Amsterdam), then the leading periodical in the Netherlands. In 1893 appeared Buysse's first great novel, *Het Recht van de Sterkste* (The Right of the Strongest). From that time until his death he wrote numerous novels and short stories. His finest, and also best-known, works are *Het Leven van Roseke van Dalen* (1906; The Life of Rosy van Dalen), *Het Ezelken* (1910; The Little Donkey), and *Tantes* (1924; Aunts).

Buysse was an associate founder of the periodical *Van Nu en Straks* (Today and Tomorrow), and after this was discontinued he established, with Louis Couperus (*q.v.*) and W. G. van Nouhuys, the literary monthly *Groot Nederland* (Great Netherland). This is still in existence. In 1932 he was raised to the peerage by the king of the Belgians with the title of Baron van Deurle. Cyriel Buysse ranks as the greatest narrator of Flanders; in his style he shows some similarity to Guy de Maupassant (*q.v.*). He depicted the life of the farmers and of the middle-class people in the region between the rivers Scheldt and Leie with penetrating accuracy and without compassion.

See: Robert Roemans, *Kritische Bibliografie van Cyriel Buysse* (1931).

J. G.

C

Caillavet, Gaston Arman de (1870–1915, French dramatist), a Parisian by birth and, one might say, by estate, grew up in the charmed circle of his mother's salon where Anatole France (*q.v.*) reigned supreme. There he met Robert de Flers (*q.v.*), with whom he was to form a literary partnership as close and fortunate as that of Meilhac and Halévy a generation before.

Begun under such auspices, the two authors' collaboration could not but retain a distinctively refined quality. Witty, urbane, and tolerant, mildly naughty, mildly romantic, mildly ironical, their librettos (with musical scores by Claude Terrasse, André Messager, Gabriel Pierné) and such light comedies as *Les Sentiers de la vertu* (1903), *Miquette et sa mère* (1906), *L'Ane de Buridan* (1909), and *La Belle Aventure* (1913; in collaboration with Etienne Rey) recall the exquisite daintiness of a Parisian gown or a champagne supper at the Bois. *Primerose* (1911) borders more decidedly on the sentimental, whereas *Monsieur Brotonneau* (1914), their last play, seemed to presage an evolution toward deeper character study. Particularly outstanding, however, is the trilogy *Le Roi* (1908; in collaboration with Emmanuel Arène), hilariously funny as it records the unedifying escapades of visiting royalty; *Le Bois sacré* (1910), a broadside directed at those who worship official titles; and *L'Habit vert* (1912), a humorous caricature of the French Academy. These three plays, more meaningly satirical, yet brimming with a *joie de vivre* that is no more, perhaps evoke best the brilliant and subtle atmosphere of the old Parisian boulevard in its twilight.

See: Cesare Levi, *Autori drammatici francesi* (1923), pp. 275–306; Jeanne Maurice-Pouquet (Mme Gaston de Caillavet by her first marriage), *Le Salon de Mme Arman de Caillavet* (1926); Francis de Croisset, *La Vie parisienne au théâtre* (1929).

J.-A. B.

Câmara, João da (1852–1908, Portuguese dramatist and short-story writer), was a member of the nobility who began his literary career in the 70's of the last century by writing one-act plays for the theatre. Through them he acquired skill for the later dramatic works which placed him among the foremost dramatists of the post-romantic period in Portugal.

Besides pretentious historical dramas in verse, such as *Afonso VI* (1890) and *Alcacer-Kebir* (1891), he enriched the Portuguese stage with some 10 plays in prose, all of which are essentially realistic and present pictures either of Lisbon life or of that of Alemtejo in southern Portugal. In the Lisbon group he is inclined to depict the scandalous, as in *O pântano* (n.d.; The Swamp). Works of the Alemtejo group reveal traits which are characteristic of the rugged rural Portuguese stock. In *A triste viuvinha* (n.d.; The Sad Little Widow) the action takes place in a small town in Baixo Alemtejo, though it might well have occurred in any other small town in Portugal, for it stresses a family trait peculiar to the primitive Catholic society of the country. *Os velhos* (1893; Old People) is genuinely regionalistic and portrays many splendid but simple folks of Alemtejo.

Though Câmara excels in the drama, he also deserves mention as a storyteller with a certain delicacy of style. His single volume of stories is *Contos* (1900; Short Stories), and he is at his best in "As estrêlas do cego" (The Blind Man's Stars), a masterly Christmas sketch, a mood of Christmas as diaphanous and airy as the theme of the story. Though he attempted the novel, his works in that field leave much to be desired.

See: C. de Figueiredo, *Figuras literárias* (1906), pp. 307–308; A. F. G. Bell, *Portuguese Literature* (1922), pp. 311, 326–327.

G. I. D.

Camba, Julio (1884–, Spanish humorist), was born at Villanueva de Arosa in Galicia. He began to write when still in his teens and has since been on the staff of all the most important Madrid papers, but his work was mainly done abroad. He has lived as a special correspondent in several European and American countries and has given, in a particular type of short article created by him, a humoristic and satirical view of the daily life in those countries. He defined himself, adopting the title of one of his books, as a traveling frog. In his works the life of the modern world is seen through the eyes of a typical Spaniard and a man of rare insight. He writes also about Spain, adopting for that the European view acquired in his travels. Camba's literary value rests on a great originality and a sharply cold intelligence which enable him to perceive the contrasts between different countries and the ridiculous side of life in all of them. He is gifted with unfailing logic in examining and showing the absurdity of all national or human prejudice. Apparently a skeptic and often a cynic who laughs at the useless worries of men, Camba nevertheless reveals in his writings a serious and uncompromising respect for real values. He has dealt at times with fundamental Spanish problems in a thoughtful manner. Like other contemporary writers, he has tried to understand Spain in its similarities to and differences from modern Europe. As Federico de Onís (*q.v.*) has pointed out, Camba's comic interpretation of Spain in contrast to Europe is closely related to the profound interpretations made by the great Spanish writers of our epoch such as Costa, Ganivet, Unamuno, Ortega, Azorín (*qq.v.*), and others. His best books, made up of collections of his articles, are *Alemania; impresiones de un español* and *Londres; impresiones de un español* (both 1916); *Un año en el otro mundo* (1917) and *La ciudad automática* (1932), about the United States; *La rana viajera* (1920); *Aventuras de una peseta* (1923); *Sobre casi todo* and *Sobre casi nada* (both 1928); and *Haciendo de república* (1934).

See: F. de Onís, "El humorismo de Julio Camba," *Hispania,* X (1927), 167–175.

A. del R.

Camino, León Felipe, *see* León-Felipe.

Campana, Dino (1885–1932, Italian poet), was born in Marradi, a small town north of Florence. From early youth he gave evidence of peculiarity and even mental disorder. People of his native town spoke of him as that "strange son of the school superintendent." As a young man he became interested in chemistry and for a time studied at the University of Bologna, but because of his unorthodox ideas and his dangerous experiments he was expelled. Then Campana began a series of wanderings to distant lands in Europe, to the Americas, then again across Europe. He volunteered in the First World War, but no sooner was he made a sergeant in the Italian army than he began to show unmistakable signs of derangement and was promptly discharged. His mental instability finally caused his confinement to the insane asylum of Castel Pucci, where he died in 1932. Campana's life was also a constant struggle with material difficulties. He attempted many trades and endured many bitter experiences. He became a kind of modern Ulysses whose journeys took him to the haunts of gauchos, miners, gypsies, beggars, organgrinders, stokers, anarchists, and mountebanks.

In *Canti orfici* (1914; 2d ed., 1928), a collection of poems and his one claim to literary fame, Campana gives expression to the human disappointments that were his and to the spiritual exaltation with which he tried to soothe them. Opposition of pagan and Christian worlds is central in his poetry. Men of letters like Papini and Soffici (*qq.v.*), who were the first to recognize Campana's worth, immediately discerned a deep and vibrant lyrical form in the "fragments" of the *Canti.*

P. M. R.

Campanile, Achille (1900–, Italian humorist), was born and has resided chiefly in Rome, where, beginning in the early 20's, he wrote successively for three newspapers—the *Idea nazionale,* the *Tribuna,* and the *Gazzetta del popolo.* On the *Gazzetta del popolo* he occupied the especially created post of humorous correspondent. He contributed also to the humorous paper *Travaso delle idee,* to the magazine *900,* founded by Bontempelli (*q.v.*) and Malaparte (pseud. of Curzio Suckert, *q.v.*), and to the humorous periodical *Sette bello,* revived and edited under his own direction. In 1925, under the influence of the futurist theatre, he wrote a series of pranks in play form (some were dramatized puns consisting of two speeches apiece), later collected under the title *L'Inventore del cavallo* (1927). In the years 1927–1934 were published a second volume of short pieces, eight novels, and a volume of semiserious prose sketches. Campanile established with these a humorous genre new to Italy, bringing it to perfection and eventually wearing out his initial rich inventiveness within it. In general his writing might remind American readers of Robert Benchley or of James Thurber, for whose sorties into the impossible a special public has gradually been prepared. But it could remind Italian readers of nothing in their literary past; his work was, as far as this may ever be, an absolutely fresh experience, precipitating an utterly new vein of exuberant, inventive, excruciating funniness into Italian literature. Partisanship for and against Campanile was sharp in the early 30's; a considerable army of admirers arose and were angrily challenged by readers who claimed that human intelligence had been insulted by the publication of such nonsense.

Whatever is solemn by tradition or presumption is material for Campanile's special brand of wit-tickling; his books are a long series of hilarious deflations of stock poses and stereotyped manners, notably lacking in that element of cynicism that characterizes most Italian professional humor. The style is serious and elegant, the events and characters preposterous. The reader is given a view of a choice assortment of human foibles which, first reflected by distorting mirrors, are then allowed the full logical development of the new shape. Conversation, mood, and convention are handled with similar pointed disrespect. And plot is always matched to detail. In *Ma che cosa è quest'amore?* (1927), *e.g.*, the plot hinges upon the following situation: five men, traveling in a railroad compartment which harbors also a beautiful lady, are individually seized by speculation as to whether or not it would be advisable to try to kiss her when the train enters a tunnel; the train enters a tunnel, no one dares to kiss the lady, nonetheless a kiss and a resounding slap are heard; all five men now devote as much of their futures as the book recounts to discovering who, indeed, received the distinction of that slap. In the unfolding of this drama we are treated to a horse who is a confirmed equine lady-chaser, a distinguished Latinist who achieved his culture as a result of searching his father's library for money hidden between the leaves of books, a petulant sea captain whose crew teases him, a peroxide-blond young man, a professional thinker, and a character known as the Late-lamented Don Ilario Rossi.

It is difficult to make a comparative evaluation of Campanile's books, since in a genre so special every reader forms his own criteria of excellence. *Ma che cosa è quest'amore?* is one of the best liked and most spontaneous, yet it suffers undeniably from paddings of sheer silliness and from the episodic nature of its construction. *Se la luna mi porta fortuna* (1928) contains passages which are probably slated for a unique immortality, but it is overlong. *Agosto, moglie mia non ti conosco* (1930) seems by all means the most spontaneous, the most pointed, and the most amusingly constructed of all these novels. *Chiarastella* (1934), on the other hand, is certainly the weakest in every respect, giving no hint of the author's real creativity. *Cantilena all'angolo della strada* (1933), which lies outside the humorous classification by intention, is a series of city sketches and impressions of strictly limited and casual interest.

I. B.

Campoamor, Ramón de (1817–1901, Spanish poet, essayist, and politician), was born at Navia in Asturias. An attack of adolescent mysticism made him seek, unsuccessfully, admission into the Society of Jesus. In Madrid he studied in desultory fashion medicine, biological sciences, mathematics, and astronomy. As a politician he was conservative and a staunch monarchist. Enjoying moderate economic comfort, he lived a pleasant and tranquil life. This had a telling effect on his temperament; he was emotionally well poised, spiritually placid, and intellectually serene. He was a solid, contented, middle-class gentleman without deep urges or disturbing preoccupations.

Fundamental to an understanding of Campoamor is his worship of the intelligence. When the study of science failed to reveal to him the ultimate meaning of life, he turned to meditation of a superficially metaphysical character. With a certain amount of philosophic levity he regarded himself as a thinker and metaphysician. He was encouraged by the attention paid to his controversies with Emilio Castelar (*q.v.*) on human progress and with Juan Valera (*q.v.*) on the relation between metaphysics and poetry. A partial record of his intellectual quest is contained in *El personalismo* (1855) and *Lo absoluto* (1865), both in prose, and in *El drama universal* (1869), a pretentious work in verse.

However, Campoamor began his literary career as a poet. In *Ternezas y flores* (1840) and *Ayes del alma* (1842) one can already discern his desire to forge a form appropriate to his temperament, a poetic mold different from the rhetorical style of the traditionalists as well as from the verbalism, eloquence, and artificial enthusiasm of the romanticists. It is not necessary to wait until *Doloras* (1846) and *Pequeños poemas* (1872–1874) to see that Campoamor is concerned less with emotion, spirit, and nature than with subjective and completely personal impressions of human behavior. Not excluding sentiment altogether, he deals with it analytically and even psychologically. Material phenomena and human values have little worth for him as expository or emotional poetic content; he converts everything into philosophic or metaphysical substance. Faithful to his motto of "art for idea's sake," he rarely paints or sings; he comments on life and draws blueprints of it.

Campoamor reveals no unified outlook on life. Disillusioned about the capacity of the intelligence to grasp absolute truths, he aims to demonstrate the relativity of all human values. His observations are frequently contradictory; hence his apparent pessimism and optimism, skepticism and faith, liberalism and conservatism. His equivocal attitudes confused his contemporaries, and his poetry aroused controversies. In retrospect, however, he appears as a genial thinker who found it more pleasant to view life serenely than to be baffled by its mysteries.

Campoamor believed that he created new poetic values in substance and in form. He claimed originality for the *dolora, pequeño poema,* and *humorada,* the molds for his most popular verse. For convenient definition it may be stated that a *humorada* is a brief epigrammatic composition of sculptural contours; a *dolora* is, in Campoamor's own words, a dramatic elaboration of a *humorada;* and a *pequeño poema* is only an extended *dolora.* The poetic quality of all these forms is fairly uniform, predetermined by the author's conviction that rhyme and rhythm alone distinguish poetry from prose and that qualities like cadence, imagery, color, and musicality matter less than brevity, contrast, and dramatic style.

Campoamor's phenomenal popularity during his lifetime is understandable. In the equivocal and oft conflicting tendencies of his so-called philosophical reflections everyone found something to confirm his beliefs or doubts, prejudices or convictions. His pseudoskepticism suited an age that lacked the spiritual energy to sustain long struggles after initial clashes, the more so since this skepticism is cleverly seasoned with sentimentality, mild piety, and surface conformity. Much of Campoamor's verse is inartistic and even unpoetical, and much of his thinking does not rise above the commonplace, but these shortcomings are in part obscured by his broad grace, humor, irony, and homespun wisdom. Few probably were inspired by his poetry of ideas, but none failed to derive momentary satisfaction from it. And an important factor contributing to its popularity is the ease with which it can be memorized because of its epigrammatic form.

Present-day opinion has reacted against Campoamor, perhaps with excessive violence. Even when stripped of poetic values in the light of advanced aesthetic standards, he nevertheless deserves commendation for his independence. He owed nothing to his predecessors and followed no contemporary vogues in poetry. The oft asserted influence of Heine, Hugo, Musset, and Byron can be heavily discounted. Born into a century that valued ideas highly, he sought to express the spirit of his age in philosophic poetry. To condemn the "bourgeois" level of his thinking is to ignore the prominent role of the middle class during the 19th century. Artistically, spiritually, and intellectually Campoamor deserves no worse of posterity than the realistic novelists and dramatists among his contemporaries.

See: E. Pardo Bazán, "Campoamor; estudio biográfico," *Retratos y apuntes literarios,* Ser. 1, in *Obras completas,* XXXII, 5–62; H. Peseux-Richard, *"Humoradas, doloras et petits poèmes," Revue hispanique,* I (1894), 236–257.

H. C. B.

Camus, Albert (1913–, French journalist, essayist, novelist, and dramatist), lived in his native Algiers until 1940. In France during the German occupation, he founded with others the influential underground newspaper *Combat,* distinguished then and after the liberation by Camus's lucid, outspoken editorials.

Before the war his only published book was *Noces* (1939), sympathetic sketches of Algerian life. His first important work, the novel *L'Etranger* (1942; Eng. tr., *The Stranger,* 1946), depicts a hero similar to those of Kafka (*q.v.*) as an alien in a universe whose illogic and illusions he does not share. In his sorry life everything is left to chance and he is supremely indifferent to all that happens because he has no scale of values. This attitude became clear when, later in the same year, appeared *Le Mythe de Sisyphe.* This philosophical essay analyzes a contemporary intellectual malady, the recognition of the absurdity of human life. Starting from the philosophy of Heidegger, Kierkegaard, and Husserl, Camus refuses to accept the existentialist view. He recommends complete lucidity in the face of life's irrationality. His two plays, *Caligula* and *Le Malentendu* (both 1944), illustrate aspects of the same problem: the emperor adds to the absurdity of life consciously and the other hero does so unwittingly. Four brief *Lettres à un ami allemand* (1945) originally appeared clandestinely during the occupation.

Despite the negative attitude of his literary works, Albert Camus has in his editorials taken a positive stand for political purity and social justice.

J. O'B.

Cankar, Ivan (1876–1918, Slovene novelist, dramatist, and poet), was born in the borough of Vrhnika, near Ljubljana, in Slovenia. His father, who had inherited a tiny house, a small field, and his handicraft, was a tailor with a numerous family for which he was not able to provide. When their house burned down the family started moving from one dwelling to another, falling deeper and deeper into misery. The only support of the children was their mother, whom Ivan loved with a tender and almost mystical love all his life. The poverty of his home, combined with many humiliations, and the sublime figure of his mother, whom he called a saint and martyr, left the deepest traces in the mind of the frail and sensitive child. He developed a very early resentment against the "fat," well-off, practical, and successful people and, on the other hand, a permanent admiration, which endured throughout all the crises of his life, for such purity and simplicity as he found in his mother's character; the first trait made him appear, at the very beginning of his literary career, experienced and mature; the second kept him idealistically youthful until his end.

From the primary school at Vrhnika, Cankar was sent to the technical high school at Ljubljana, where he graduated in 1896. In the same year he went with a scholarship to Vienna to study architecture, but soon gave up his studies and his scholarship to devote himself exclusively to literary work. He lived mostly in the workers' quarter of the city where he boarded with the family of a workman while the latter was serving a sentence in jail. Cankar spent 13 years in Vienna writing incessantly; the external monotony of this laborious and hard life was interrupted only once, when in 1907 he entered the electoral contest as Social Democratic candidate in the elections for the Austrian Parliament; he went home for the campaign, although he knew he could not win, and returned after the elections to Vienna. In 1909 he left that city forever, spent a couple of months as guest of the archbishop of Sarajevo with his brother Karlo, who was at that time the archbishop's secretary, then went to Ljubljana, where during the First World War he was for some time interned by the Austrian authorities as politically suspect. He died there after a fall on the stairs. He had been productive as a writer until his last illness. Cankar was physically weak, disorderly in his habits, always in financial embarrassments, high-minded and generous, in conversation brilliant though often hard and sarcastic, inclined to alcoholism; he was slavishly devoted to his work and fully conscious of its value and importance.

Although Cankar read and enthusiastically admired the Russian, French, Scandinavian, and German literature of his time, it is not possible to compare him with any of the famous literary names of the period; he created literary subjects and forms of his own, in the sphere of the international neo-romanticism of the *fin de siècle* and after, consciously opposed to the previous French naturalism (*q.v.*). In his first book, and only volume of poetry, *Erotika* (1899), which the lord bishop of Ljubljana found morally and religiously dangerous and suppressed as well as he could by buying up the first edition, he is still partly dependent on the older Slovene literature, but in his first book of prose, *Vinjete* (1899; Vignettes), a collection of short stories, he opened in Slovenia new literary ways.

In the subsequent and astonishingly fertile period, 1909–1913, Cankar's many books turn on three principal themes, sometimes in tiring repetitions. There are stories about the Slovene artist who is an outcast, a tramp, a nuisance among "decent people," and a foreigner in his own country: *Tujci* (1901; Foreigners), *V mesečini* (1905; In the Moonshine); and the related play, *Pohujšanje v Dolini Šentflorjanski* (1908; Scandal in the Valley of St. Florian). There are stories about "longing souls," yearning for happiness in their misery, for beauty in the dirtiness of their lives: *Na klancu* (1902; On the Slope), *Kriż na gori* (1904; The Cross on the Hill), *Hisa Marije Pomočnice* (1904; The House of Our Lady of Help); and the play *Lepa Vida* (1912; The Beautiful Vida). Finally there are satirical tales criticizing Slovene politics, social organization, and literature: *Za narodov blagor* (1901; For the Nation's Welfare), *Martin Kačur* (1906; a "biography of an idealist"), *Krpanova kobila* (1907; Krpan's Mare), *Hlapec Jernej* (1907; The Farmer's Man Bartholomew), *Hlapci* (1910; Servants).

In his last period Cankar wrote principally what may be called *feuilletons,* in which in fact he reached the peak of his art. There he is, often aware of approaching death, wise, serene, very simple, and expressing himself in a rarely pure and pregnant style. These *feuilletons* are self-analytical studies and personal confessions, memories, scenes of animal life, symbolical stories dealing with personal and national problems rising from the war (the latter were published as *Podobe iz sanj,* 1917;

Parables from My Dreams); in the same form appeared also the charming fragment of his unfinished autobiography, *Moje življenje* (1914; My Life).

Cankar's literary work, published posthumously in 20 volumes, is surprisingly extensive in view of his short life and marks a historical epoch in Slovene literature. In close touch with the vivid idiom of his native village, he created a new, expressive, and sonorous language and a new rhythmic style immediately accepted by the younger generation of writers. Through his work Slovene prose became really an art, and the somewhat provincial literature of his country, which could boast of only one name of really international greatness, Preseren, was lifted to the European level. His ideas and genius also decisively influenced the political attitude of the Slovenes in Yugoslavia and materially strengthened their determination to preserve their cultural and idiomatic individuality in the Yugoslav national unity. A number of his works have been translated into Czech, Russian, German, French and English. There are English translations of *Hlapec Jernej in njegova pravica* (1907; Eng. tr., *Yerney's Justice,* 1926) and of a number of short stories —"Slovene Idylls" (*Slavonic Review,* Vol. XIII, 1934–1935, pp. 494–506), "I Know Now, Mother," "Simple Martin" (both in *Slavonic Review,* Vol. XVII, 1938–1939, pp. 35–41).

See: Ivan Cankar, *Zbrani spisi* (1926–1936), complete edition with introductions and annotations by Izidor Cankar.

I. C.

Cansinos-Asséns, Rafael (1883–, Spanish novelist and critic), was born in Seville. He studied there until 1901, when he left for Madrid to try his luck in the precarious field of creative writing. Unlike many contemporaries, he has not eked out a living by teaching or government employment. In many respects he has been a lonely figure, despite his numerous activities in founding, and contributing to, such literary reviews as *Grecia, Ultra,* and *Perseo,* dedicated to the latest poetical schools that were recruiting disciples in the 20's. As a literary critic he has written for *Correspondencia de España* and *Los lunes del imparcial* and since 1925 for *Libertad.* For his books of literary criticism Cansinos-Asséns was honored by the Spanish Academy with the Chirel prize (1925). The French government honored him in 1926. In the years between 1918 and 1923 he started the so-called *ultraísta* movement in Spanish poetry, a salutary reaction against the *modernista* currents.

Cansinos-Asséns has been a prodigiously prolific writer. His literary criticism is best represented by *La nueva literatura* (4 vols., 1917–1927; *Los hermes, 1898–1900–1916; Las escuelas literarias, 1898–1900–1916; La evolución de la poesía, 1917–1927; La evolución de la novela, 1917–1927*), *Los temas literarios y su interpretación* (1924), and *Literaturas del norte: La obra de Concha Espina* (1924). He has composed poetical and critical works on the Spanish Jews—*España y los judíos españoles* (1919), *Las luminarias de Hanukah* (1924), *Los judíos en la literatura española* (1937). He has made translations from books in a great number of languages, including the writings of the Emperor Julian and the complete works of Dostoevski.

Cansinos-Asséns must be named with Unamuno and Díez-Canedo (*qq.v.*) among the critics who have done most in appreciating the contemporary writers of Iberic America. He has not neglected new names, and yet with all his generosity in recognizing unknown writers, he has discerned and accurately appraised the outstanding figures, such as Rubén Darío, Amado Nervo, Blanco Fombona, Herrera Reissig, Huidobro, Capdevila, and Borges. Cansinos has participated fully in the new movement commenced by Spanish cultural circles on behalf of the Spanish Jews. Following the pioneer work of Senator Angel Pulido, he has sung with nostalgia and love the imperishable genius of Sephardic Jewry.

M. J. B.

Cantoni, Alberto (1841–1904, Italian novelist), was born at Pomponesco in the province of Mantua, where he led a quiet, outdoor life among the countryfolk whom he portrayed in his books. He carefully avoided entering the literary arena of his day and was satisfied to know men without being known by them. His works were not extensively read; they did arouse the interest of a few among the younger generation (particularly Pirandello, *q.v.*) who were to develop a humoristic attitude new in Italian literature. Cantoni died near his birthplace, establishing in his will a fund for the needy.

The novel by which he was to be best remembered, *L'Illustrissimo,* which appeared posthumously in the *Nuova Antologia* (1905), has been termed the northern counterpart of Verga's (*q.v.*) *I Malavoglia.* It pictures the hard life of Lombard peasants, a life which they accept with resignation. A Milanese noblewoman puts her suitor to the test by making him disguise himself as a farm hand and seek employment on his own farm. Thus for the first time he acquires direct knowledge of rural living conditions. Maria, the noblewoman with bucolic illusions, has brought Galeazzo, the landowner, the experimenter, in contact with reality. He has been able to see with his own eyes the evils caused by absenteeism.

Other works of Cantoni, published in his lifetime, are *Il Demonio dello stile* (1887), *Pietro e Paola* (1887), *Un Re umorista* (1891), *L'Altalena delle antipatie* (1893), *Humour classico e moderno* (1899), and *Scaricalasino* (1901). Several short stories appeared in the *Nuova Antologia* under Cantoni's name, but were repudiated by him later.

The seclusiveness of Cantoni's life is somehow communicated to most of his books. Croce (*q.v.*) points out that "Cantoni sounds the river of life here and there, from its banks—without ever plunging into it. He awaits the right moment, which, however, fails to come. . . . You will not obtain from him conclusive and coherent thought, going deep to the root of problems . . . he feels life without taking part in it." On the other hand Cantoni was able to draw from his rustic environment, from real life, vigorous characters, expressing the author's ideas with youthful freshness of sentiment. Blending art and criticism, he strove (this was the aim of his humor) "to make intelligent people smile melancholically." Incapable of improvisation, he worked assiduously. He never quite succeeded in giving unity to his works—unity of thought and of ultimate purpose. Literary and social criticism are intermingled throughout his novels.

See: L. Pirandello, "Alberto Cantoni," *Nuova Antologia*, CC (1905), 233–248; B. Croce, *La Letteratura della nuova Italia*, 3d ed., III (1929), 217–226.

C. F. W.

Čapek, Josef (1887–1945, Czech painter, novelist, and critic), was the elder brother of Karel Čapek (*q.v.*). He was born in Hronov (northeastern Bohemia) and studied painting in Prague and Paris. He was active as an art critic, but following the invasion in 1939 was sent to a German concentration camp. He died at Belsen in April, 1945. Josef Čapek has a considerable reputation as a painter; he first belonged to the cubist school, but later developed his own style of playful primitivism. As a writer he collaborated with his brother in early collections of sketches and stories and in *Adam the Creator*, etc. He himself wrote a utopian play, *Země mnoha jmen* (1923; Eng. tr., *The Land of Many Names*, 1926), and several collections of short stories and sketches. He also produced two short novels: *Stín kapradiny* (1930; The Shadow of the Fern) is a story of poachers in a suggestive nature setting, while *Kulhavý poutník* (1936; The Limping Pilgrim) is more a philosophical meditation than an actual novel. His prose has been hailed as an anticipation of surrealism, largely because of his preoccupation with the subconscious. Josef Čapek was also an art critic whose books such as *Nejskromnější umění* (1920; The Humblest Art) and *Umění přírodních národů* (1938; The Art of Primitive Nations) expound and defend the art of children, savages, and untrained people.

See: V. Nezval, *Josef Čapek* (1937).

R. W.

Čapek, Karel (1890–1938, Czech novelist, playwright, and essayist), was the best-known literary figure of liberated Czechoslovakia after 1918. Čapek was born in Malé Svatoňovice (northeastern Bohemia), the son of a doctor. He studied philosophy at the Czech University of Prague and wrote a graduating thesis on pragmatism (published 1917). He became a journalist and was for a time stage manager of the theatre in Vinohrady. Olga Scheinpflugová, a prominent actress, was his wife. He died on Christmas Day, 1938, of pneumonia.

Čapek is best known as a dramatist. *R.U.R.* (1921; Eng. tr., 1923) and *Ze života hmyzu* (1921; Eng. tr., *The Insect Play*, 1923) took the world by storm and were acted with great success in both London and New York. *R.U.R.* even introduced the word *robot* (from *robotit*, to drudge) into the English language. The main idea was very timely in the 20's: a warning against the dangers of a machine civilization. The automatons moving stiffly like dolls, the tense moments of their great revolt against man, testify to Čapek's vivid sense of the stage. It was easy to overlook the flaw in the structure: the way the robots are changed into men of flesh and blood by a sleight of hand. *The Insect Play* (known in the United States as *The World We Live In*) is possibly better, though the construction is looser. It is almost a ballet or revue. The idea of presenting butterflies as lovers, beetles rolling balls of dirt as capitalists, ants as militaristic imperialists, is carried through with gusto. There is in the vivid scenes with the ants a perfect prophecy of totalitarianism and its canting slogans. Two other less well-known plays are equally ingenious and effective on the stage: *Věc Makropulos* (1922; Eng. tr., *The Makropoulos Secret*, 1925) argues amusingly against the desire for immortality, and *Bílá Nemoc* (1937; Eng. tr., *Power and Glory*, 1938) is an indignant play against dictators. The other plays, *Adam Stvořitel* (1927; Eng. tr., *Adam the Creator,* 1930), written in collaboration with Josef Čapek (*q.v.*), and *Matka* (1938; Eng. tr., *The Mother,* 1939) as well as two early comedies, are less successful.

But Čapek was not merely a dramatist. He was an extremely ambitious and subtle practitioner of the craft of fiction, a philosopher-poet passionately interested in the problems of truth and justice. His early collections of stories (*e.g., Trapné povídky,* 1921; Eng. tr., *Money and Other Stories,* 1929) are still full of youthful pessimism. Life is arbitrary and disconnected, brutal and disconcertingly irrational. The stories are painful and curiously inconclusive. But this was only the first step in his varied career as a writer. Two fanciful romances follow: *Továrna na absolutno* (1922; Eng. tr., *The Absolute at Large,* 1927) and *Krakatit* (1924; Eng. tr., 1925). The weird invention which liberates the Absolute like a gas gives opportunity for much hilarious satire against hypocrisy, while "Krakatit," the deadly explosive which might destroy civilization, becomes the leading theme of an anti-utopian romance. After these two Wellsian pieces, Čapek wrote a number of pleasant, humorous books of sketches and essays and several travel books which give voice to his belief in ordinary man, his sense of the bewildering variety and beauty of the world. His optimism seems sometimes a shade too cheerful, his ridicule of the abnormal and extravagant too complacent. But there is much quiet fun and much insight, especially in *Anglické listy* (1923; Eng. tr., *Letters from England,* 1925) as well as in the similar books on Italy, Holland, Spain, and Scandinavia. Čapek's interests veered more and more to practical politics and to popular art forms. His conversations with President Masaryk (*Hovory s T. G. Masarykem,* 3 vols., 1928–1935; Eng. tr., *President Masaryk Tells His Story,* 1934; *Masaryk on Thought and Life,* 1938) are a little classic in popular biography and political education, and his *Devatero pohádek* (1931; Eng. tr., *Fairy Tales,* 1933) is a veritable treasure house of pure storytelling. *Povídky z jedné kapsy* and *Povídky z druhé kapsy* (1929; Eng. tr., *Tales from Two Pockets,* 1932) try to create a semiphilosophical mystery story rather on the lines of Chesterton. But the poet and writer of tragedy awakens again in the three great novels: *Hordubal* (1933; Eng. tr., 1943), *Povětroň* (1934; Eng. tr., *Meteor,* 1935), and *Obyčejný život* (1935; Eng. tr., *An Ordinary Life,* 1936). Each of these stories tries to tell the same story from a special point of view in order to enhance the variety of its meanings and to suggest the utter mysteriousness of ultimate reality. *Hordubal* on the surface is a story of crime: a peasant who has returned from America to his home in Carpathian Russia dies under mysterious circumstances. *Meteor* is made up of speculative reconstructions of the early history of a pilot whose plane has come down in a crash. The nurse, the doctor, and the poet, all tell their story—with the implication that the poet's exact imagination came nearest to the truth. The last volume, *An Ordinary Life,* is the autobiography of a Czech railway clerk who discovers unexpected hidden selves in his own mind and past. After the great trilogy, Čapek wrote only two books of any length: a new fanciful romance, *Válka s mloky* (1936; Eng. tr., *War with the Newts,* 1937), a satire on modern science and pseudo science as well as international politics, and *První parta* (1937; Eng. tr., *The First Rescue Party,* 1939), a straightforward, almost balladlike story of a pit disaster. The fragment of an unfinished novel, *Život a dílo skladatele Foltýna* (1939; Eng. tr., *The Cheat,* 1941), was published posthumously. It is the story of a young man who marries a rich woman and uses others to build up a fraudulent reputation as a composer.

Čapek is best known for his plays, his visionary romances, and his genial travel books. His finest work is the trilogy of novels which centers around problems of truth and reality and constitutes one of the most successful attempts at a philosophical novel in any language. Čapek has been frequently censured by Czech critics as too international, but a book like *An Ordinary Life* gives a finely drawn picture of the Czech scene, and there is something very representative and national in Čapek's love of the common man, his genuine faith in democracy and humanity.

See: J. Mukařovský, ed., *Výbor z prózy K. Čapka* (1934), selections from Čapek's prose; V. Černý, *Karel Čapek* (1936); René Wellek, "Karel Čapek," *Slavonic Review,* XV (1936–1937), 191–206; Oliver Elton, *Essays and Addresses* (1939).

R. W.

Čapek-Chod, Karel Matěj (1860–1927, Czech novelist), is the most prominent novelist of the Czech naturalist movement. He was born in Domažlice (western Bohemia) and became a reporter and journalist in Prague, where he died. Čapek (who later adopted the name Čapek-Chod) is the Zola (*q.v.*) of Prague—a chronicler of the decay of the Prague bourgeoisie. Čapek's outlook on life is, like that of other naturalists, materialistic and pessimistic. He is a determinist who believes that a malicious fate plays us ugly tricks and thwarts our finest aspirations. Though Čapek has the naturalist's thirst for facts and details, his method is less objective than that of his foreign models: he indulges in the grotesque, uses caricature, and enjoys stylistic juggleries which have an almost Rabelaisian effect. He is not free from vulgarities and trivialities, but has a fantastic vision of the world's tragedy and a rough kind of pity and of humor which make us forget the faults of his loose composition and the lapses of his taste. His vitality and scope put him into the first rank of Czech novelists. His most important books are: *Kašpar Lén, mstitel* (1908; Caspar Lén, the Avenger), a crime story from the Prague periphery; *Turbina* (1916; The Turbine), the tragicomedy of the decay of an upper bourgeois family of Prague; *Antonín Vondrejc* (2 vols., 1917–1918), again a story of decay, this time of a poet forced into the drudgery of journalism; *Jindrové* (1921; The Jindras), a war novel which centers around a conflict between father and son. Čapek-Chod is also the author of several volumes of short stories.

See: H. Jelínek, *Etudes tchécoslovaques* (1927); A. Novák, "K. Matěj Čapek-Chod," in *Almanach České Akademie*, 1928; F. Kovárna, *K. M. Čapek-Chod* (1936). There are French translations of *Antonín Vondrejc* and *Turbina.*

R. W.

Capuana, Luigi (1839–1915, Italian critic and novelist), was born in Mineo, Sicily, the son of a well-to-do farmer. His activity as a writer was long and multifarious, beginning with a dramatic legend in verse, *Garibaldi,* in 1861 and ending with a comedy, *Il Paraninfo,* published posthumously in 1919. He lived a very full life. As novelist, critic, poet, playwright, short-story and fairy-tale writer, parodist (especially of his fellow Sicilian Rapisardi, *q.v.*), student of science (both natural and occult), folklorist, politician (he was twice elected mayor of his native town), teacher (at the Istituto Superiore di Magistero in Rome and later at the University of Catania), amateur photographer, bird fancier, practical joker, and gallant, he never had an idle moment. He was a versatile man, not especially profound. Curiosity and dilettantism are his main intellectual traits. His claim to fame rests mainly on his activity as a critic and fiction writer. In both these capacities he looms large in the history of *verismo,* the Italian counterpart of naturalism.

His criticism is characterized by an innate good taste which enables him to discern and make appraisals correctly and engagingly in an easy-flowing, urbane prose. He came early under the influence of De Sanctis (*q.v.*), but this influence was alloyed with the prevailing scientism of his age and his own mental makeup. Zola's (*q.v.*) naturalism and "experimental" (actually it was "instrumental") novel found in Capuana a warm champion. Later, however, he renounced naturalism and all "isms," going back to the view that in art form is everything. Form and impersonality may be said to be the two main tenets of his critical faith.

When in 1864 Capuana left his native town for Florence in order to drink at the fountainhead of the purest Italian, he did so fully confident that Italy would soon have in him her Shakespeare. By way of apprenticeship, he became dramatic editor of Florence's leading newspaper, the *Nazione.* But right then he "discovered" Balzac and thereupon bade farewell to Shakespeare and all dreams of dramatic glory. Laying aside forever his historical dramas in verse, he proceeded to try his hand at fiction writing. He was then far from thinking that some day all his dramatic talent would be wasted on a dozen or more naturalistic plays, most of them written in his native dialect for the use of some Sicilian actors, who at the time were enjoying a nation-wide vogue, and for the benefit of his creditors, since Capuana had this much in common with Balzac—he always lived beyond his, and his kin's, means. At any rate, in 1865 he wrote his first piece of fiction, *Dottor Cymbalus,* a short story in which is already marked that pseudoscientific background which is to be found in so many of his stories. Then followed a long interlude of critical and political activity, interrupted in 1872 by the appearance of his second short story, *Delfina.* Not until 1877 did Capuana enter the field of fiction as a full-fledged writer. In that year was published his *Profili di donne,* a collection of psychological studies which he, as a bachelor and lady's man, felt competent to give. It was favorably received. In 1879 appeared his first novel, *Giacinta,* composed according to the naturalistic formula. Unfavorably received by the majority of critics, *Giacinta* was recast by Capuana and then again revised. But the judgment remained negative and continued so when it appeared (1890) as a five-act play. *Giacinta* was a failure, even though the author won nation-wide notoriety, a failure because naturalism remained for Capuana a formula, a tool, a prop, because it did not act on him, as it did on his friend Verga (*q.v.*), as a releasing lever, because he used it as a platform rather than as a springboard. Naturalism did not free him from all formalism; he merely substituted another kind, which had little more than novelty to recommend it. The truth of the matter is that Capuana lacked an inner world to which he might give expression. His world was all outside him. His muse was not that imagination which feeds upon an inner world, but the fancy, which loves to sport about with exteriors. His best pages are to be found in those of his works which deal with an outer world into which he has a clear insight—the world of his infancy and youth, the elemental world of his *Paesane* (1894), the best of his several dozen volumes of short stories, and of his *Il Marchese di Roccaverdina* (1901), the best of his five novels.

See: A. Pellizzari, *Il Pensiero e l'arte di L. Capuana* (1919); P. Vetro, *L. Capuana; la vita e le opere* (1922).

S. E. S.

Capus, Alfred (1858–1922, French journalist, novelist, and dramatist), born at Aix-en-Provence, went to Paris to attain renown. As one of the editors of the *Figaro* his short, brilliant articles on political subjects attracted much attention. His more important novels, *Qui perd gagne* (1890), *Faux Départ* (1891), *Robinson* (1910), and *Scènes de la vie difficile* (1921), recall in their classic realism Lesage. Simply though carefully written, they reveal a certain disillusionment and a mild cynicism, but in spite of the melancholy inherent in all his work, they end happily.

Capus views the ordinary man with much indulgence and sympathy. On the stage he portrayed the life of these same people with the same kindly realism, ironic and forgiving. Most of his characters have a Micawber-like trust in a kind Providence or in luck itself which will in the end resolve all difficulties. In *Brignol et sa fille* (1895) a confirmed optimist escapes the ruin planned by one of his creditors when his daughter happens to fall in love with and marry the nephew of the creditor. *La Bourse, ou la vie* (1900) and *La Veine* (1902), one of his most popular and typical comedies, present similar situations. In *La Petite Fonctionnaire* (1901) a young woman, earning her livelihood in a small, provincial post office, is severely criticized by the local townspeople who are quite overcome when she succeeds in marrying a nobleman of the region. Capus's sympathy for those women obliged to earn their living does not, however, preclude his satire of feminism in other plays. In *Les Deux Ecoles* (1903) and *Les Maris de Léontine* (1903) he urges an indulgent attitude in marriage on the part of both parties. His later comedies, while much discussed, met with less success. In general his amusing and optimistic plays preach the doctrine that happiness is the legitimate goal of life, that realities of life, such as food, love, clothes, and money, are perhaps more important to the average man than ideals.

He was elected to the French Academy in 1914 and died at Neuilly-sur-Seine.

See: E. Quet, *Alfred Capus* (1904).

J. F. M.

Caragiale, Ion Luca (1853–1912, Rumanian playwright), was a self-made man. Son and grandson of traveling players, he had no schooling and engaged in a succession of attempts to earn a living at newspaper, office, and other kinds of work. In 1888 he became director general of the Bucharest National Theatre, after a series of successes with his own comedies. Later he tried to be a merchant, opened a beer garden, edited the humoristic weekly *Moftul român* (Rumanian Trifle) with brilliancy and verve, and finally, inheriting a fortune from an aunt, voluntarily exiled himself to Berlin, where he spent the last years of his life in comfort and leisure devoted to music.

Caragiale made his debut in 1874 with a poem in the Bucharest *Revista contemporană* (Contemporary Review). He became famous, however, through his comedies produced in Bucharest and published in *Convorbiri literare* (Literary Conversations). After several years of inactivity, he gave *Năpasta* (1889; False Accusation), a peasant drama which reminds one of Tolstoy's (*q.v.*) *Power of Darkness*. The play, trying to reach deep-down to the foundations of the nation and the pure language "of the soil," does not in fact equal in craftsmanship the author's comedies. It caused, moreover, numerous polemics and made him weary of the stage. He now gave more attention to prose writing and in one of his short stories, "O făclie de Paşte" (1889; An Easter Candle), he rose to the heights of the genre. Another work in prose is his *Momente* (1901; Moments). After the peasant upheaval of 1907 he published a pamphlet, *1907 din primăvară până în toamnă* (1907; 1907 from Spring to Autumn), in which he frankly critized the ruling classes. From Berlin he sent fables, epigrams, and sketches to Bucharest periodicals.

Caragiale caused the first accurate native accents to resound and the first really living figures to move on the stage of the National Theatre. In his comedies of character and manners (*e.g., De ale carnavalului,* 1885, Carnival Adventures), he showed the inherent conflict in an oriental society embracing new occidental customs and laws. In *O scrisoare pierdută* (1884; Lost Letter), one sees liberal politics misinterpreted by a corrupt administration. In *Cuconul Leonida față cu reacțiunea* (1879; Mister Leonida Faces the Reaction), we behold the retired officeholder, imbued with "republicanism," who explains to his wife that "universal suffrage" means that everybody should receive a high salary and no one pay any taxes. The mirth and laughter of these scenes contain a bitter sediment. And the revolted author actually whipped his contemporaries into sobriety and reform.

See: P. Zarifopol, *Introducere la opere de Caragiale* (1930).

L. F.

Carco, Francis (pseud. of François Marie Alexandre Carcopino-Tusoli, 1886–, French novelist, poet, and art critic), was born of Corsican parents at Nouméa, New Caledonia, where his father was superintendent of prisons. The violence of the surroundings—the passionate pent-up emotions of criminals, his father's quick temper and ready hand, the exotic scenery, his nurse's gruesome tales—contributed to enrich an algolagnic penchant. When Carco was nine years old, the family moved to the South of France where the countryside developed his sensuous love of nature and delight in physical sensation. At 14, an indifferent student but an avid reader of the *poètes maudits,* he practiced the technique of versification under the tutelage of Charles de Pomairols. Francis Jammes (*q.v.*) and Henry Bataille (*q.v.*) influenced his first poems. The Lycée of Agen witnessed his cultivation of a bohemian personality. During his military service Carco became organizer and theorist of the group of "fantasist poets" whose kinship was one of temperament and viewpoint rather than one of art and technique. He wrote *La Bohème et mon cœur* (1912; augmented editions, 1922, 1929; complete edition, 1939) under the aegis of Villon, Baudelaire (*q.v.*), and Verlaine (*q.v.*). The tragedy of their destinies, their sordid existence (itself helping them to create beauty), their grandeur rising above social opprobrium, exemplify for Carco the individual unfettering himself from the bourgeois and fulfilling his innermost purity of heart. Both the feeling of spiritual affinity and the problem of environment versus artistic personality produced *Le Roman de Villon* (1926; Eng. tr., *The Romance of Villon,* 1927); *La Légende et la vie d'Utrillo* (1927), in the series "La Vie de Bohème" directed by Carco; and *Verlaine* (1939). Chapters of *Nostalgie de Paris* (1941) are devoted to Baudelaire.

The Montmartre previous to the First World War, with its bohemian life, its milieu of artists and criminals, of pimps and prostitutes and narcotic addicts, is his special province. An apprenticeship as an art critic for the newspaper *Homme libre* preceded the publication of *Jésus-la-Caille* (1914), first of a series in which he defended and explained, sympathetically yet objectively, this marginal society. *Les Innocents* (1916), *Bob et Bobette s'amusent* (1919), *Paname* (1925), are novels of *mœurs* revealing the moral code of a social stratum whose principles are severe though different, the violation of whose tenets induces the chastisement of the offender. The climax, the result of moral disintegration, comes from within rather than from direct punitive efforts of the external world. Inexorable fate cannot be avoided. It is the phosphorescence illuminating the consciences of these elemental beings who, confused by their own murky sense of maladjustment, suddenly find their world made too complex by problems of the spirit. Instinct, clouded by fear (*Perversité,* 1925; Eng. tr., 1928) or premonition of doom (*L'Equipe,* 1919) or an obsession (*Rue Pigalle,* 1927), succumbs to destiny. Carco lacks the sentimentality of a Charles Louis Philippe (*q.v.*); objective and dispassionate in his writing (his economy of structure and precise penetration consistently are termed "classical" by critics), yet fundamentally a moralist, he objects to society's habit of condemning men for its own faults (*L'Amour vénal,* 1924). Nevertheless their degradation aroused in him a feeling of voluptuousness (*La Rue,* 1930), sublimating his personal emotional complexities. Paul Bourget's (*q.v.*) influence, inciting him to write *L'Homme traqué* (1922; Eng. trs., *The Noose of Sin,* 1923, *The Hounded Man,* 1924), which won the Grand Prix of the French Academy, enlarged the scope of his subject matter to include the bourgeois and to emphasize the psychological situation. The essential problem remains one of moral collapse in an individual incapable of escaping his fate. Carco has written about 30 books in this vein, the first few replete with argot.

The passing of his youth has evoked in this member of the Goncourt Academy a nostalgia for his bohemian days. His memoirs, important documents for a consideration of French literary and artistic life since the halcyon days of the cabaret Lapin Agile, reveal intimately the nature and heart of this expressionistic painter in light and shadow of subtle moods. He has said of his work that were the atmosphere removed nothing would remain. *De Montmartre au Quartier latin* (1927; Eng. tr., *The Last Bohemia*, 1928), *A voix basse* (1938), *Bohème d'artiste* (1940), and others show him restrained yet passionate, intelligent though physical, fusing himself with and purging himself by the pain of his protagonists. Francis Carco, the poet vibrantly sensitive to rain and glistening streets, is known as the defender of the *voyou* and the biographer of the prostitute. A definitive edition of the *Mémoires* was published in 1942 in Geneva, near which city Carco resided during a part of the Second World War.

See: H. Martineau, "Francis Carco," *Divan*, XIII (1921), 172–180; A. Thérive, *Opinions littéraires* (1925), pp. 113–129; Marcel Ormoy *et al.*, "Francis Carco, poëte," *Divan*, XXI (1929), 145–212 (whole number); Y. Gandon, *Le Démon du style* (1938), pp. 159–168; A. Rousseaux, *Littérature du XXième siècle* (1939), I, 21–32.

S. S. W.

Cardarelli, Vincenzo (1887–, Italian poet and critic), was born in Corneto (Tarquinia). Self-taught, he has spent most of his life in Rome where he founded and directed the review *Ronda*. His chief collaborators were Bacchelli, Baldini, Barrili, Cecchi, and Ungaretti (*qq.v.*). The *Ronda* represented a reaction against the undisciplined and disintegrating manifestations of futurism and a return to the literary elegance and moral order of the classic writers. Leopardi became Cardarelli's chief idol and master. In *Viaggi nel tempo* (1921) and *Il Sole a picco* (1929), two of Cardarelli's most characteristic works, there is revealed however a certain tormented, moralistic, and somewhat haughty literary style which showed that Leopardi was emulated more as a teacher of letters than of ideas.

See: Pietro Pancrazi, *Ragguagli di Parnaso (1919–1920)* (1920), pp. 119–126.

P. M. R.

Carducci, Giosue (1835–1907, Italian poet, orator, scholar, and critic), was born in the village of Val di Castello in Tuscany and had his schooling in Florence and Pisa. After brief periods of service as a teacher in San Miniato and Pistoia he was appointed, in 1860, to the professorship of Italian literature in the University of Bologna, a position which he held until his retirement in 1904. The years of the first half of his life were the culminating years of the *Risorgimento*, and man of letters though he was, he was passionately concerned for the liberation and unification of Italy and for her establishment in the ways of democracy. The successive phases of the struggle and the unhappy vicissitudes of the newly made Italy are reflected in his writings. Like so many other Latin and Italian poets, he was a master of satire; and his satiric power found plenty of targets in the weaknesses and failures which delayed completion of the national effort and in the inefficiency and corruption of the years that followed that completion. Yet he lived, and lived intensely, not only in the exciting life of his own day, but in the whole vast pageant of classic and Italian history and in the eternal simplicities of human toil and joy and sorrow. These ranges of thought and feeling give breadth and depth and universality to his verse—which is illumined always with beauty seen and rendered, and marked always by flawless artistry.

The successive volumes of his poems are *Rime* (1857), *Levia gravia* (1868), *Poesie* (1871), *Nuove Poesie* (1873), *Odi barbare* (1877), *Nuove Odi barbare* (1882), *Rime nuove* (1887), *Terze Odi barbare* (1889), and *Rime e ritmi* (1899). The second, third, and seventh of these volumes contain old as well as new material. While there are beautiful and striking poems in the three earliest volumes, it was with the fourth, *Nuove Poesie*, that Carducci first established himself on the nobler heights of poetry, in a mastery which he thereafter maintained to the end.

He has been called the poet of history, and he well deserves that title. He must often have stood on Italian summits dominating landscapes that quiver with the life of generations; and it must be from such experience that he derived the recurring phrase by which he expresses his visualization of the past: "I stand upon the mountain of the centuries." From that mountain he directs his vision over the varied land of time and legend that lies below, discerns men and scenes that glow with rich significance, and then, as creator—guided always by a strong sense of epic destiny—evokes those men, those scenes, for the modern world.

Yet he is even more essentially the poet of that basic moral bond *per la quale* (as Dante puts it) *tutti a tutti semo amici*. His favorite word is *pio*, which he uses to express the willing consciousness of interwoven life. Such phrases as *il pio travaglio* and *la giustizia pia del lavoro* are characteristic; and in the most famous of his sonnets he calls even the ox *pio,* as being a willing partner with man. His profound morality is vigorous and aggressive. Often it finds vent in satire; often it exalts wise sacrifice; oftenest it pervades his praise of normal love and toil. Its most perfect and stirring expression is to be found in "Il Canto dell' amore," in which it appears in splendid synthesis with the other major elements of his poetry.

His "long study and great love" of the Greek and Latin classics furnished him with poetic material, held him to fine standards of poetic craftsmanship, and in the latter half of his life led him to extensive and successful experimentation in what he called "barbaric" metrical forms. If the several types of the classic ode are read without regard to the rules of scansion, but with full acceptance of normal verbal stress, the resulting rhythmic patterns differ from the familiar ones, but they are none the less interesting and distinctive. Carducci in his *odi barbare* worked out such patterns in Italian verse, fashioning Italian equivalents for many classic strophes; and the new forms proved to be a perfect vehicle for Carducci's mature poetic genius.

He was often called upon for public addresses; and he never failed to endue his public utterance with a substantial content and a masterly prose form which make his orations worthy companions to his poems. Noblest of all is his oration (1882) on the death of Garibaldi, in which the soaring inspiration reaches a height unsurpassed in ancient or modern oratory. With all his activity in the fields usually regarded as creative, he was no less active—and, in a sense, no less creative—in the fields of scholarship and criticism. The fruits of such labors are to be found in many volumes devoted to literary history and criticism, and in many editions of Italian writers, to which his notes and prefaces give permanent worth. The most notable of his longer studies is that in which he treats "Dello svolgimento della letteratura nazionale"; his editions of Petrarch and of Politian are his most valuable achievements as editor; and his two volumes on Parini constitute the most impressive monument of his indefatigable industry. He proved once and for all that there is no necessary incompatibility between the functions of poetry and of scholarship. His works are collected in a 30-volume National Edition published in Bologna in 1939–1940 by Zanichelli. Much of his poetry has been translated into English.

He was made a senator in 1890 and received the Nobel prize in literature in 1906, the year before his death.

See: G. Chiarini, *Memorie della vita di Giosue Carducci* (1907); A. Jeanroy, *Giosue Carducci, l'homme et le poète* (1911); B. Croce, *Giosue Carducci* (1927).

E. H. W.

Carner, Josep (1884–, Catalonian poet), sums up all of the nonconformity of the generation which, abandoning romantic and archaeological patterns, was identified with countless attempts at poetic renovation. With him Catalonian poetry attains the full flowering of the *Renaixença,* and it is he who effects the fusion between the literary language and the findings of the philological section of the Institut d'Estudis Catalans, until that time without benefit of the voice of an apostle. A language which has suffered the literary prostration of centuries does not recover without pain—as is evident in all the works of the *Renaixença.* But Carner is a very great artist in language as in other respects, and although in his poetry certain archaic forms are still perpetuated, his work represents, from a linguistic point of view, a most important revolution. Indeed the Catalonian linguistic reintegration has been called a literary miracle.

Josep Carner was born in Barcelona, where he received his primary and secondary education in a private academy. He studied law as well as philosophy and letters at the University of Barcelona. His poetic initiation came early; when he was only 12 his first verses were published, and at 15 the journal *Renaixença,* of such great influence in the evolution of Catalonian letters and in reviving the patriotic spirit, was regularly accepting his productions. In *Primer llibre de sonets* (1905; First Book of Sonnets) and *Fruits saborosos* (1906; Delicious Fruit) one sees Carner's great promise as a renovator. He had already produced two books of prose, *L'idil li dels nanyos* (1904; The Idyl of the Dwarfs) and *Deu rondalles de Jesus infant* (1905; Two Serenades to the Child Jesus), of similar importance in the literary evolution of Catalan. There followed, in verse, *Segon llibre de sonets* (1907; Second Book of Sonnets), *La malvestat d'Oriana* (1910), and *Verger de les galanies* (1911; The Garden of Gallantry), while in the pages of the daily paper *Veu de Catalunya* he created a new style of political journalism. *Monjoies* (1912; My Jewels), which shows Carner as the fully matured artist, was followed by *Auques i ventalls* (1914; Easter Prints and Fans) and

La paraula al vent (1916; The Word in the Wind). In 1916 he was elected a member of the Institut d'Estudis Catalans, the highest cultural honor in Catalonia. At that time his literary activity was extraordinary; in addition to composing poems, articles, and essays for numerous publications, he directed the journals *Empori* (Emporium) and *Catalunya* and translated *Prosa catalana* into Spanish, to make known in Spain outstanding manifestations of the *Renaixença;* in this volume he collected short stories of Ixart, Vilanove, Caselles, and others and the *Jacobé* of the master Joaquim Ruyra (*q.v.*).

In 1921 Josep Carner embarked upon a diplomatic career, but continued to maintain his place in the world of Catalonian literature. From this time, many of his works, published in Barcelona, were written in the foreign countries to which his responsibilities as a diplomat took him. Among the works of this period are *L'oreig entre les canyes* (1924; The Breeze among the Canes), *La inutil ofrena* (1924; The Useless Offering), *Les bonhomies* (1928), *El cor quiet* (1931; The Quiet Heart), *El veire encantat* (1933), *La primavera el Poblet* (1935; Spring in Poblet). In prose *La creació d'Eva i altres contes* (1925; The Creation of Eve, and Other Short Stories), and *Les planetes del verdum* (1921) are noteworthy. Among his numerous translations is the *Pickwick Papers* of Dickens (1933). For the stage he prepared Verdaguer's (*q.v.*) poem, "Canigó," translated Molière's *Le Malade imaginaire* and Shakespeare's *Midsummer Night's Dream,* and wrote an original dramatic work, *El giravolt de maig* (1929; The May Pinwheel).

At the time of the invasion of Catalonia, Carner, residing in Brussels as first secretary of the Spanish embassy, had been named minister plenipotentiary to Bucharest, but did not go there. After a short stay in Paris he went to Mexico and now lives in the capital of that country. His literary activities have continued through the medium of the journal *Revista dels Catalans d'Amèrica* (Mexico City, 1939) and of *Full Catala,* a publication which he founded in collaboration with J. M. Miquel i Vergés, Pere Matalonga, and Ferran de Pol. His latest work, the poem *Nabi,* published in Buenos Aires in 1941, was conceived in Hendaye, where he wrote a fragment of the first canto. The originality and force of the poem are outstanding; a poetic objectivity shows how unchanging have been certain characteristics of Josep Carner throughout his evolution. In Mexico City he holds a chair in the university and is a professor in the Centro de Estudios Históricos of the Colegio de Mexico.

See: J. Folguera, *Les noves valors de la poesia catalana* (1919); J. M. Miquel i Vergés, prologue, in Carner, *Nabi.*

J. M. M. i V.

Carossa, Hans (1878–, German prose writer and poet), was born in Tölz, Bavaria. Both his father and his grandfather were physicians. Carossa himself studied medicine and practiced in Passau, Nuremberg, and Munich. In 1916 he joined the German army as *Bataillonsarzt* during the battle of the Somme, but was shifted shortly afterward to the Rumanian front, where he served until the last year of the war. Back on the Western front at the time of Ludendorff's last offensive, he was wounded and sent home. After the war he continued his practice in Munich for a time, then returned to the country.

The combination of physician and poet, not infrequent in German letters, as witness Schiller, Kerner, Döblin (*q.v.*), Schnitzler (*q.v.*), and others, is of particular interest in Carossa. While the family doctor is not exactly in the romantic vanguard of scientific discoverers, he is in most intimate touch with those human values which are the function of literature. Carossa, profiting by the keen observation of the scientist, has made abundant use of such material with the minimum of fiction. His first prose work, *Doktor Bürgers Ende* (1913), represents a modern twist to the Werther theme: a young physician, driven to despair by the suffering of his patients, kills himself when he fails to save his fiancée from death. Carossa drew on his own profession again in *Der Arzt Gion* (1931; Eng. tr., *Doctor Gion,* 1933); indeed, Gion being dialectic for Jean or Hans, the book is confessedly about Carossa himself. In this post-war narrative, which is laid in Munich and has to do with the disruptive effects of the war, the author works, not with political matters or shifting social classes, but with some half-dozen individuals, cases such as any doctor might have had at this period. They are silhouetted against the backdrop of the time with unforgettable effect both for the characters and for the background. *Gion* and the much weaker *Geheimnisse des reiferen Lebens* (1936) are Carossa's nearest approach to the novel. His out and out autobiographical works, *Eine Kindheit* (1922; Eng. tr., *A Childhood,* 1930), *Rumänisches Tagebuch* (1924; Eng. tr., *A Roumanian Diary,* 1929), *Verwandlungen einer Jugend* (1928; Eng. tr., *Boyhood and Youth,* 1930), *Führung und*

Geleit (1933), and *Das Jahr der schönen Täuschungen* (1941), cover the chief events of a life that, with the exception of his participation in the war, was not pitched high with excitement. From Goethe on down to the present, German literature has tended more and more to the idea that confession is the truest form of self-expression. Carossa, in spite of his comparatively uneventful career the autobiographer par excellence, is a classic fruition of that tenet. His confessions are the product of modesty and of that clairvoyance which honesty of intellectual dealing can achieve. They are also noteworthy for the author's reflective strolls along the byways of his narrative.

The doctor appears to be under tribute to the poet. Carossa's amorality despite his mystic bent, his objective judgment of the problems of life, his impartiality toward friend and foe, all derive in some measure from his medical discipline. But there is also a high ethical content in Carossa's writings, a positive *Weltanschauung* that makes them clear and luminous among those of his troubled contemporaries. In contrast to the negation that has characterized so much of European art and letters for the last half century, here is one who bears witness to the art of living without being tormented.

In *Führung und Geleit,* the most formless but most revealing of his works, Carossa mentions many of his fellow writers. His attitude toward them is always one of shy admiration, which, if we may take him at his word, has amounted to an obsession in some cases. The imitation which that would imply is, however, not apparent in his writings, which are characteristic of no one but Carossa and fall into no school. His style, a model of grace and seeming simplicity, is warm and appealing.

Carossa is wont to think of himself primarily as a lyric poet. His output, which has been brought together in a rather slender volume (*Gesammelte Gedichte,* 1938) is of a high order. For one who has written so largely of himself, Carossa's poems are surprisingly objective. They are colored with a straightforward symbolism and are most effective when, as in "Die Fremde auf meiner Bank" and "Der Blinde," the observed is held up against the invisible and imponderable. Sympathy with suffering inspires many of his lyrics, but his choice figures and classic style sometimes seem at variance with the realistic theme. Such poems as "Empfängnis," "Mysterium der Liebe," "An das Ungeborene," among others, fail to strike fire, no doubt because the doctor sees love too much as a complication of physiology.

See: *Buch des Dankes für Hans Carossa* (1928); M. Machate, *Hans Carossa* (1934); A. Haueis, *Hans Carossa* (1935); F. Klatt, *Hans Carossa* (1937).

H. W. P.

Casares, Julio (1877–, Spanish lexicographer and critic), was born in Granada. A student of modern languages, he can translate, it is said, 18 of them, and he is chief of the Language Division in the Spanish Foreign Office. He is also the author of French-Spanish and English-Spanish dictionaries. In the international field he was one of the most active members of the Committee on Intellectual Cooperation in the League of Nations. His work as a linguist consists mainly of newspaper and magazine articles about Spanish words and manners of speech; these contributions are less in the domain of scientific philology than examples of skillful vulgarization as practiced by a man of sound and vast learning. Some of the most important were collected in *Crítica efímera* (2 vols., 1918–1919). Casares entered the Spanish Academy in 1919, reading on the occasion the address *Sobre el nuevo concepto de un diccionario de la lengua* (1921); since then he has been a permanent collaborator in the work of that body, especially as a contributor to the new editions of the dictionary. As a literary commentator he is the author of *Crítica profana* (1915), a volume which attracted special attention for its defense of Castilian purism against the foreignism and stylistic innovations of the modernist writers.

See: M. Bacarisse, "Dos críticos," *Revista de libros,* IV (1920), 11–14.

A. del R

Castelar, Emilio (1832–1899, Spanish statesman, political philosopher, historian, critic, and novelist), was born in Cádiz, cradle of Spanish parliamentarianism, and won fame as Spain's most brilliant parliamentary orator. He made his political début at a rally in Madrid in 1854 with an extemporaneous speech and was at once acclaimed as a magnificent orator and an ardent defender of democracy. His eloquence attracted many listeners to his classes at the University of Madrid, where from 1858 he held the chair in Spanish history, and to his celebrated lectures at the Ateneo, later collected in *La historia de la civilización en los cinco primeros siglos del cristianismo en Europa* (2d ed., 4 vols., 1865). As a historian he showed predilection for broad themes of cultural or ideological synthesis, as in his *Historia del movimiento republicano en Europa* (9 vols., 1875) and *La revolución religiosa* (4 vols., 1880–1883). In the latter work he reveals his own deep religious feeling as a Catholic but, at the same time, his sympathy and tolerance for the great figures of the Reformation, and it was for religious tolerance, for freedom of worship, that he fought in some of his most impassioned addresses before the Cortes. John Hay, who heard him, said: "His speech is like a torrent in its inconceivable fluency, like a raging fire in its brilliancy of color and terrible energy of passion." Castelar also kindled public opinion in the articles he wrote for *Soberanía nacional* and *Discusión* and especially for *Democracia,* an anti-Bourbon newspaper of which he was the editor. His popularity began to wane as his political views became more conservative; as fourth and last president (from September 6, 1873, to January 3, 1874) of the short-lived First Spanish Republic, he was obliged to take strong dictatorial measures, which were not always in harmony with his principles, in order to establish order. In 1888 he withdrew from the political arena and spent his last years in writing and in traveling in France and Italy, the two countries to which he was most devoted throughout his life.

Castelar was a prolific writer. In addition to his political addresses, newspaper articles, and historical works, he wrote a number of novels, from the exceedingly sentimental *Ernesto* (1855) to the somewhat more successful historical novel *Fra Filippo Lippi* (3 vols., 1877–1878). His best writing, however, is to be found in his less ambitious and more personal works (*e.g., Recuerdos de Italia,* 2 vols., 1872–1876) in which travel impressions are intermingled with historical, literary, and artistic reminiscences. In a style that is far less rhapsodic and flowery than that of his public speeches, he conveys his deep emotion on first seeing the Sistine Chapel, or he evokes a historical moment, a landscape, or a great spiritual figure, as in "San Francisco y su convento de Asís." Castelar was the most celebrated Spaniard of the latter part of the 19th century in Europe and in America as well. For years he contributed regularly to the leading newspapers of Spanish America, where he was so widely read that, as Rubén Darío could write on his death, his fame reached virtually every village and hamlet.

See: B. Jarnés, *Castelar, hombre del Sinaí* (1935).

E. F. H.

Castelo Branco, Camilo (1825–1890, Portuguese novelist), first great figure in modern Portuguese fiction, was born in Lisbon, of Trás-os-Montes stock. As the illegitimate child of a romantic love affair, his life was destined to be a current of tumultuous passions, accentuated by a psychopathic constitution. Spontaneous, original, sensual, he showed a curious duality of childish joy and deep melancholy, of tenderness and sarcasm, of kindness and egoism, which was later to produce a brilliant, unequal, and disorganized work. He was an orphan at an early age, a widower almost in his adolescence, an irregular student, a brilliant and scandalous bohemian, imaginative and fantastic, with mystic reactions which nearly led him into the priesthood. All these phases contributed to a melodramatic life which included imprisonment—once for kidnaping, once for adultery—and a bitter and blind old age ending in suicide.

Castelo Branco, author of a hundred volumes, poetic, dramatic, critical, and novelistic, owes his fame to his work in the last-named category. He inaugurated the novel of passion which, with the rural novel, is the bridge between Portuguese historical and realistic fiction; he marks the transition between two epochs and two currents. The Portugal of his earlier years was experiencing the changes which followed civil war; the youth of the period lived in an unrestrained romantic dedication to violence and scandalous love affairs. This atmosphere and his imitation of Sue, Paul de Kock, Soulié, and D'Arlincourt provide the ingredients of his first novelistic works. *Anatéma* (1851; Anathema), *Os mistérios de Lisboa* (1853; The Mysteries of Lisbon), and *O livro negro do Padre Diniz* (1855; The Black Book of Father Diniz) are samples of the gloomy genre with its nocturnal assassinations, gallows, mysterious origins, storming of convents, and the like. But he soon abandoned this sensational manner. At about that time he came in contact with Balzac, for whom he never lost his admiration. *Onde está a felicidade?* (1856; Where Is Happiness?), *Um homem de brios* (1857; A Man of Valor), and *O que fazem as mulheres* (1858; What Women Do) are the first products of his matured genius and place him on the road to fame. His own imprisonment for adultery (1861) produced another definite change in his work, in that it caused him to bring his own passions and misfortunes to the novel. During his incarceration he wrote *Amor de perdição* (1862; Love of Perdition), the most beautiful of his works dealing with passionate love, a veritable autobiographical confession. He retired to village life, harassed by daily necessity, and produced with amazing fecundity, becoming more and more the realist. In *Novelas do Minho* (1875; Novels of Minho), stories of country life in the North, he now gave an objective view of rural primitivism, as opposed to the rose-tinted idealization of the ordinary writers of the rural novel. Even so his romantic formation, his excessive temperament, inclined toward sarcastic, caricatural deformation, his active creativeness, were bound to place him in conflict with the monotonous, platitudinarian writing of formal realism. He was at the height of his fame when Eça de Queiroz (*q.v.*) introduced the realism of Flaubert and Zola (*qq.v.*) in his first novels. Castelo Branco rebelled against the pseudoscientific methods of the experimental novel by publishing *Eusébio Macário* (1879) and *A corja* (1880; The Rabble) as parodies of this technique. Here he attempted to ridicule the new formula and as a result became involved in a violent polemic with the proponents of the new tendency. However, what had begun as literary scoffing ended in a sort of acceptance, indicative of his capacity for assimilation. Thus in *A brazileira de Prazins* (1882; The Brazilian Girl from Prazins) can be detected, beneath his ordinary passionate intensity, a descriptive objectivity and structural balance, unknown in his previous work.

Castelo Branco is the most important representative of the literature of his generation. The over-all significance of his work—58 novels—is comparable in some respects to that of Balzac or Pérez Galdós (*q.v.*); his portrait of the Portuguese society of the period is a permanent record, fixed for all time with emotion and high relief. He limits himself, however, to a single emphasis: love is made the motor center of human personality. He shows a boundless inventive genius and clever analysis of all the shades of amorous passion. Perhaps his most outstanding quality is the rich native texture of his language, "pure marble from the national quarry," a result of multifarious contacts in the course of his eventful life and of a profound knowledge of classic writers. Although he protested that he was not a "lapidary of words," his greatest interest was in style and vocabulary, and this brought about an occasional sacrifice of psychological truth to linguistic brilliance. Inclination to dramatize, emotional intensity, exuberant imagination of action, virulent deforming sarcasm, succulent richness of his prose—these are the most distinguishing characteristics of the novels of Castelo Branco. One limitation, inherent in his temperament, was his inability to disengage himself from his writing; he mixes in the action and takes sides with or against his characters, whom one moment he exalts and the next satirizes cruelly, especially those of the commercial middle class. When he abandons his impetuosity and his sincere emotionalism, he attains a great verisimilitude and naturalness, particularly in the depiction of the humble life of the North, permeated with childhood recollections.

Castelo Branco's work as a dramatist and a poet, although admirable within the frame of its romanticism, is inferior to his novelistic production. A volume of poems, *Nas trevas* (1890; In the Darkness), composed when he was blind, reveals at times a direct and impressive grief. In 1885 he was made a viscount. In 1889 he received a life pension; this he enjoyed only a short time. His spiritual and physical suffering, the insanity of his son, the conviction that his blindness was incurable, and his hereditary, suicidal pessimism can be said to have loaded the pistol with which he took his life a year later.

See: A. Pimentel, *O romance do romancista: Vida de Castelo Branco* (1890); T. Braga, *As modernas idéias na literatura portuguesa* (1892), I, 240–285; F. de Figueiredo, *História da literatura romântica portuguesa, 1825–1870* (1913), pp. 201–227.

E. G. D.

Castro, Américo (1885–, Spanish scholar and critic), born in Brazil of Spanish parents, was taken while a child to Granada, where he had his early education and in 1904 finished his studies for the degree of *licenciado* in literature. For two years (1905–1907) he followed courses in Paris at the Sorbonne, and from that time Castro entered into the living currents of continental European culture. As a result of his studies and travels abroad, he acquired great skill in spoken French and German, in which languages he has lectured with distinction. On his return to Spain he identified himself with the work carried on in the Institución libre de enseñanza, founded by Francisco Giner de los Ríos (*q.v.*). If he owes his spiritual vision to Don Francisco, he is also a faithful disciple and collaborator of Ramón Menéndez Pidal (*q.v.*), who organized at the Centro de Estudios Históricos the program for a disciplined approach in all research connected with the history and culture of Spain. Like

Navarro Tomás (*q.v.*), Solalinde, Alfonso Reyes, and Onís (*q.v.*), Castro was one of the editors of the *Revista de filología española*, and it was in this famous review that some of his memorable work appeared, such as his *Algunas observaciones acerca del honor en los siglos XVI y XVII* in 1916.

Through the Centro de Estudios Históricos and other government agencies, Castro has contributed to the reformation of educational practices and to the diffusion of Spanish culture by training foreigners who came to Spain to study and particularly by placing young Spaniards in the great institutions of learning throughout the world. Besides teaching at the University of Madrid, where he had the chair in the history of the Spanish language, and writing monographs, essays, and books on various subjects, Castro has energetically popularized the findings of Spanish scholars and critics by writing in the *Sol* of Madrid and in the dailies of Buenos Aires. Again like many of his contemporaries, he has lectured at Berlin, Oxford, the Sorbonne, and the universities of the United States and the Argentine. It was in Argentina that he helped Amado Alonso (*q.v.*) found the Instituto de Filología. A liberal in politics, he supported the second Spanish republic, which out of gratitude and admiration sent him to Germany as Spanish ambassador. After 1936 he left for America; he stayed in Buenos Aires for a year and then removed to the United States, where he taught two years at the University of Wisconsin and one at the University of Texas; he has more recently become a professor at Princeton.

Castro's varied and multiple contributions can be classified under four headings: erudite essays on philology (*e.g.*, *Fueros leoneses*, 1916, in collaboration with Onís, and an annotated translation of Meyer-Lübke's book on Romanic linguistics, 1914); interpretative essays, on St. Theresa, Lope de Vega, the Spanish theatre, the Don Juan legend, and other outstanding themes and figures of Spanish literature (*Lengua, enseñanza y literatura*, 1924; *Santa Teresa y otros ensayos*, 1929; the introduction to *El burlador de Sevilla*, 1922, which gives a synthetic vision of the Spanish *comedia*); highly original essays (*El pensamiento de Cervantes*, 1925, the ambitious nature of which created a deep stir among European and American scholars and critics); provocative essays which purport to reach the cultured public at large (*La peculiaridad lingüística rioplatense y su sentido histórico*, 1941).

Castro belongs to the generation of university professors who have combined with their scientific pursuits a sense of the Spanish problem, namely, what meaning is to be given the grandeur that was Spain and her present inchoate state. He is not only a sober investigator in the fields of philology, literature, and culture, but also an acid critic of the dead hand of Spanish traditionalism. At the beginning of his career he showed some of the negativism of the demolishers, but as political fetishes failed, Castro soon discovered the positive elements in the unique culture of Spain.

See: Dámaso Alonso, review of *El pensamiento de Cervantes* in *Revista de la Biblioteca, Archivo y Museo del Ayuntamiento de Madrid*, III (1926), 385–388; C. A. Pastoo, "Américo Castro," *Universitario*, IV (1927), 13–27; Anderson Imbert, "Américo Castro," *Sur*, VII (1937), 86–88.

M. J. B.

Castro, Eugénio de (1869–1944, Portuguese poet), was born in Coimbra, to a family of a very ancient academic and literary tradition. In Lisbon he alternated studies in the liberal arts with newspaper work; later he entered the diplomatic corps and finally became a teacher. After international recognition of his writings and admission to the Portuguese Academy—at the age of 27—Castro was appointed professor of Romance philology in the faculty of philosophy of the University of Lisbon (1914) and then at the University of Coimbra (1916), of which institution he became director.

The earliest literary compositions of Eugénio de Castro, very youthful indeed, showed great verbal talent, along with ingenuousness and a strong poetic temperament. A first trip to France initiated him into the contemporary poetry of that country; this meant for Castro a somewhat involved mixture of Baudelaire (*q.v.*), Gautier, Leconte de Lisle (*q.v.*), Verlaine (*q.v.*), Mallarmé (*q.v.*) and Maeterlinck (*q.v.*) and "art for art's sake." This also meant for him a reaction against the politico-social servitude of Portuguese poetry with its clamorous oratory. Eugénio de Castro and António Nobre (*q.v.*) were to restore Portuguese poetry to aesthetic integrity (*see* Portuguese literature); Nobre, of a deep and morbid sentimentality, changed the poetic substance, Castro, healthy both mentally and physically and with an elegant sense of balance, renovated principally the media of expression.

Upon his return from this first trip to France, he produced *Oaristos* (1890), the first cry of revolt. In the preface-manifesto he declared with provocative aggressiveness that, "with two or three shining exceptions, contemporary Portuguese poetry is based on some few handfuls of feeble and decrepit commonplaces"; he deplored the "Franciscan poverty" of current verse and announced his intention of trying new ways of metrical expression. *Oaristos* and *Horas* (1891; Hours) offered a poetry of aristocratic, formal splendor, Verlainian in tone, polyphonic and rich in imagery. Fashioned only for *os raros*, incomprehensible indeed to the uninitiated, it nevertheless opened a new cycle in Portuguese poetic form. In keeping with his contention—advanced in *Oaristos*—that two thirds of the words in the language lay ignored in the dictionaries, Castro revived a whole archaic, aristocratic, and liturgical vocabulary, replete with brilliant and magnificent images, in a veritable festival of the senses. This refining of the lexicon was accompanied by a new typographical presentation which called for the use of a profusion of capital letters and for special care in the composition of the printed page. Eugénio de Castro is a virtuoso, relying not on the intrinsic meaning of words but on the innumerable possibilities of musical and visual manipulation. At the same time he made no attempt to express the inexpressible with the suggestive verbal penumbra of a Mallarmé; rather, he endeavored to express more richly what is already known.

The later evolution of Castro showed that there remained in his temperament much of the classicist, devoted to clear as well as beautiful forms. Castro and his *nefelibatas* (cloud treaders)—a word which he used and which degenerated into a nickname for the group—took from symbolism its technique and external processes, rather than its essential aesthetic substance. In 1896, to be sure, he returned to France to be consecrated as the leader of Portuguese symbolism at a banquet in his honor, presided over by Catulle Mendès (*q.v.*). And he became identified with the most outstanding elements of the international artistic movement; French and Italian critics introduced him to the world. The *Mercure de France* received and protected him. He exerted an influence on Spanish and Hispano-American modernism and came to be the best-known and most translated Portuguese poet. But beneath the symbolist, the lover of opulent Parnassian graces, the devotee of cosmopolitan and universal art, there throbbed a spirit at once profoundly Portuguese and classical. Little by little he evolved in the direction of a more sober classical art—he knew, admired, and translated Latin and Greek classic authors and Goethe—until he finally moved into the current of the national poetic tradition. Already in *Sagramor* (1895), a dramatic poem, a Faustian incarnation of the *tedium vitae*, are seen a certain rejection of the decadent style and less interest in freakishness and brilliance of rhyme. This work stands in contrast to *Belkiss* (1894), a lyrical prose narration influenced by Maeterlinck which recounts, in a language of Asiatic sumptuousness, the amorous peregrinations of the queen of Sheba through a utopian and legendary Orient. *A nereida de Harlem* (1896; The Nereid of Harlem), *O rei Galaor* (1897; King Galaor), and *Salomé* (1896) continue to show much of the pomp of the earlier manner. *Saüdades do céu* (1899; Longings for Heaven), whose title indicates a national preoccupation, preceded the poem *Constança* (1900), which marked radical withdrawal from his former art. Castro's identification with the amorous and doleful soul of Portugal and its landscape, through the crepuscular figure of the scorned queen, the rival of Inês de Castro, is complete; the channels of his poetical creation and his means of expression are in the most authentic Portuguese. Miguel de Unamuno (*q.v.*) said of *Constança* that it is "a symbol of Portugal itself."

From 1900 to the period following the First World War, Castro alternated his old Parnassian taste, never abandoned completely (*O anel de Polícrates*, 1907, The Ring of Polícrates; *Camafêus romanos*, 1921, Roman Cameos), with a preference for Pre-Raphaelite themes from the national middle ages (*O cavaleiro das mãos irresistíveis*, 1916; The Knight of the Irresistible Hands). His final phase is one of definite devotion to national folk themes, to the Neo-Garrettism that Nobre had initiated in 1892. Without losing its exquisite technique, Castro's poetry gained in depth of sentiment. In a refined and sober language he also sang in his later years of the sadness and joys of family life. The gentle, philosophical pessimism apparent in all his previous work becomes a resigned and indulgent Christian sadness. *Cravos de papel* (1922; Paper Carnations), *Canções desta negra vida* (1922; Songs of This Somber Life), *Descendo a encosta* (1924; Coming Downhill), *Chamas duma candéia velha* (1925; Flames of an Old Lamp), and *Ultimos versos* (1938; Last Verses) are examples of this final phase of tender and intimately Portuguese verse.

The younger poets, who have surpassed him, owe much to Castro. To him is due in great measure the return of Portuguese poetry to dignity, as well as a new cultivation of form and pure aestheticism. He completely renovated the poetic instrument. To this must be added the fact that his recognition in the Latin world gave international voice and prestige to the little-known contemporary Portuguese literature.

See: M. de Unamuno, *Por tierras de Portugal y de España* (1911), pp. 5–13; A. F. G. Bell, *Studies in Portuguese Literature* (1914), pp. 225–232; Rubén Darío, *Los raros* (1918), pp. 245–265.

E. G. D.

Castro, Rosalía (1836?–1885, Spanish poet and novelist), born at Santiago de Compostela in Galicia, was the daughter of Doña Teresa Castro, who was a member of a noble family, and of an unknown father. The air of melancholy which pervades all her writing may well be related to this circumstance. Educated with great care, she early showed remarkable talents for the arts, especially for drawing, music, and singing, and composed her first poems at the age of 12. In poor health, she spent the winters either at the Pazo de Lestrove, ancestral home of the Castros, or at a modest house in the vicinity of Padrón, whose countryside she was to exalt with home-loving devotion in all her poetic work. She moved to Madrid at the age of 20, established relations with the writers of the capital, and became associated with Ventura Ruiz Aguilera, the poet, with Eulogio Florentino Sanz, translator of Heine, and with Gustavo A. Bécquer (*q.v.*). In 1857 was published, in *Museo universal,* her first poem in Galician, a paraphrase of the popular song "Airiños, airiños, aires . . ." (Little airs, little airs, airs . . ."), reflecting her anguish and loneliness. That year also marks the appearance of her first book, *La flor,* a short and unimportant work in Spanish. The following year she married the Galician historian Don Manuel Murguía, one of the best prose writers of his time, accompanied him on his travels through Spain as an archivist, returned several times to Galicia but without happiness, suffered family misfortunes, and finally died in her home at Padrón, July 15, 1885.

Rosalía Castro wrote three books of poetry, *Cantares gallegos* (1863), *Follas novas* (1880), and *En las orillas del Sar* (1884; Eng. tr. of selected poems, *Beside the River Sar,* 1937). The first two are in Galician, the third is in Spanish. The efforts to revive a regional language which had enjoyed such an illustrious past coincide in Galicia with the Provençal and Catalonian literary and cultural revivals; they culminate indeed in this poet, who appropriates all the smooth grace and musicality of the *Cancioneiros* and the *Cantigas* of Alfonso the Wise. She adds her own quality of grief, which is not simply an ephemeral product of the *mal du siècle* but such an absorbing and sincere sentiment that it transcends the world that surrounds her, through a mystic yearning and restlessness of the spirit. This grief becomes the very substance of her life; once when she thought herself free of it, she was tortured by its absence. Her mysticism should be interpreted in the light of this tragic attitude, as is sagaciously pointed out by Unamuno (*q.v.*) in his *Andanzas y visiones españolas.* At times she trembles with a religious fear reminiscent of Baudelaire (*q.v.*); she shows a heroic, tortured religiosity sublimated by remorse. Rosalía typifies the pantheistic interpretation of the *saudade,* the search for perfect communion with the earth which engendered us, with the entire landscape. Some of her poems, with their simple evocative geographic nomenclature, anticipate a poetical idea successful in later Spanish poetry (Unamuno, Machado, Lorca); at other times the poet gives clear shape to the things her eyes behold, re-creating them and vivifying them in a rich system of symbols.

Rosalía Castro is above all the poet of Galicia. In her are all the rebellion, the longings, the complaints, the historical consciousness and aspirations of this Spanish region. It was the Generation of '98—Unamuno, Azorín, Díez-Canedo, Juan Ramón Jiménez (*qq.v.*)—that revealed her to the rest of Spanish-speaking Spain. During her lifetime the Catalonian and Provençal poets had translated and admired her, and the latter even invited her to preside over one of their celebrated Jocs Florals, an honor which the poet's modesty would not permit her to accept. Modern criticism sees in her much more than a forerunner of the metrical innovators of modernism; she is considered a real precursor of poets such as Rubén Darío, Gutiérrez Nájera, Amado Nervo, and Antonio Machado (*q.v.*). Federico García Lorca (*q.v.*) refers to her reverently in one of his *Poemas gallegos.* Her personality is beginning to be disassociated from such figures as Bécquer, Trueba, and Heine, with whom listless critical routine had too long connected her.

Her works in prose—two early novels, *La hija del mar* (1859) and *Flavio* (1861), the novel *Ruinas* (1864), and two exotic tales, *El caballero de las botas azules* (1867) and *El primer loco* (1881)—have suffered an unjust neglect. The shorter stories especially present with originality certain of the disconcerting problems found in the modern psychological novel. Her rhetoric, very typical of her period, is somewhat artificial. But a quality of fantasy and illusion, in the manner of Bécquer, suggests the tradition of the best Spanish romantic prose.

See: C. Barja, *En torno al lirismo gallego del siglo XIX* (1926), pp. 67–91; A. Cortina, "Rosalía Castro de Murguía," *Humanidades* (1930), pp. 161–193; R. Otero Pedrayo, *Discurso de ingreso na Academia Galega* (1931); S. Griswold Morley, "Preface," in Castro, *Beside the River Sar* (1937).

R. M. L.

Català, Victor (pseud. of Catalina Albert i Paradis, 1873–, Catalonian novelist and short-story writer), was born in L'Escala. This little village, a picturesque fishing port, is surrounded by an imposing nature which harmonizes the beauties of the sea and the wildest mountains. The landscape of deep contrasts and the rough people of the district have exerted a marked influence on Victor Català's literary vocation. At first she took part in the poetic competitions which were held each year in Barcelona (Jocs Florals, developed from those celebrated in Toulouse and from those of the late Middle Ages in Barcelona), and although her poetic works did not pass unnoticed, the real field in which she triumphed was in the cultivation of the narrative genre. Her best works are in *Drames rurals* (1902; Rural Dramas), a series of stories or short novels in which she paints, with a marked predilection for the darker hues, different aspects of the simple folk of the country. Her pronounced realism exerted a great influence on a number of important later prose writers. There followed *Caires Vius* (1907), which showed that the literary manner of Victor Català was not a passing caprice or a literary pose, but was grounded in her thought and in her sensibility. The novel *Solitud* (1905; Solitude) was a great triumph; it was awarded the Fastenrath prize in the Jocs Florals and immediately translated into French, Spanish, Portuguese, English, German. The pattern of contrasts and the interplay of the most sublime and the most perverse instincts constitute the essence of this great realistic novel. *La mare balena* (The Mother Whale), a collection of stories, was followed by the three-volume work *Un film* (A Film).

The work of this Catalonian novelist shows great daring not only in the choice of subjects but in the courageous manner of handling them. The new realistic view of life —and the startling fact that the author was a woman—disconcerted the public. But her literary boldness prevailed and a whole group of Catalonian novelists followed in her footsteps, creating a type of rural novel with robust figures and rugged scenes full of grandeur. Prudenci Bertrana (*q.v.*) was one of her outstanding followers. Other writers exaggerated this wild depiction of the country scene, and for some years Catalonian literature was marked by a novel thoroughly rustic in which the characters spoke in the manner of peasants (at times an attempt was made to obtain this effect by the facile recourse of vulgarisms). The devotees of *ruralismo* were legion, if not always distinguished. There has also been in some quarters vigorous resistance to this vogue, but in any event Victor Català gave a great lesson in sincerity. Whatever direction may be taken by the young Catalonian novelist of recent years, her influence will make itself felt as an ardent and deep-felt message of literary integrity.

She has recently been living in retirement in her little village of L'Escala, in that silence which weighs upon all Catalonian writers, unable to write in their language under the regime of General Franco.

See: T. Garcés, "Coversa amb Victor Català," *Revista de Catalunya* (Barcelona), 1926; A. Schmecberger, *Conteurs catalans* (1926).

F. de P.

Catalonian literature, after highly honorable achievements in the Middle Ages and especially in the 15th century, went through a long period of decadence—related to loss of political independence—and at the end of the 18th century Antoni de Capmany had declared the Catalonian idiom "dead for the republic of letters." But precisely at this time was born Antoni Puiz i Blanch (called Puigblanch, 1775–1842), now rightly considered the initiator of a revival (*Renaixença*) of Catalonian writing which has had results reaching down to the present day. Two epic poems which he probably wrote between 1815 and 1820 seem to have circulated in manuscript among the students of the University of Cervera, with copies of a *Gramática y apologia de la lengua cathalana,* published in 1814 by another precursor, De Josep Pau Ballott (1747–1821). These documents deeply influenced contemporary youth.

In 1815 a student, Bonaventura Carles Aribau (1798–1862), was already writing his first poetry in Catalan; somewhat later, in 1833, was published Aribau's famous "Oda a la patria," solemn and noble, the theme of which is homesickness for the native land and melancholy recollections of her lost grandeur. With this poem a romanticism began in Catalonian literature which was a first stage of the *Renaixença.* From 1833 to 1859 certain foreign influences were important (Scotch philosophy, the archaeological manner of Walter Scott, Manzoni, the German romantics), although the poet Joaquim Rubio i Ors (*q.v.*) proclaimed literary independence in the prologue of his book of verse, *Lo gayter del Llobregat* (1841). Catalonian poetry was at that time marked by noble melancholy, profound idealism, and a restrained style which are the sources of its particular charm. These characterstics are especially apparent in the poems of Manuel Milá y Fontanals (*q.v.*) and of Josep Lluis Ponç i Gallarça (1823–1894).

Two important events then occurred, almost simultaneously. In 1858 the Majorcan Marian Aguilo (1825–1897) took up residence in Valencia, as the librarian of the university, and became a true apostle of rejuvenation through his faith in the unity and destiny of the Catalan-speaking countries. His enthusiasm stirred two energetic disciples, Vicente Wenceslao Querol (*q.v.*) and Teodor Llorente (1836–1911). Aguilo was in favor of a literature national to its very depths, removed from all foreign influence (it was to be neither classical nor romantic, as he said). Querol and Llorente laid the foundations of a real Valencian school, distinguished by the autochthonous character of its themes and the noble simplicity of its style. Querol, when he called his poetry "rimas catalanas," marked the literary unity of Catalonia, Valencia, the Balearic Islands. Aguilo exercised a parallel influence in his native country, where soon appeared a Majorcan school. Although there had been precursors in Valencia and in Majorca and the other Balearic Islands, it is indubitable that the great impulse which, in a common desire for revival, cemented all the countries of Catalan speech is to be traced to his crusading spirit.

In 1859 the Jocs Florals of Barcelona, which had been founded by a Catalonian monarch of the 14th century, were reestablished. They represented a tendency to perpetuate, in fixed forms, the subject matter of a somewhat stylized medievalism. The enormous social influence they exerted is undeniable; their anachronistic pomp aroused the interest of "good society" in Catalonian poetry. Most of the poets who began to write in the tradition of the Jocs Florals are forgotten. Victor Balaguer (1824–1901) is one of the exceptions. He was a fiery and declamatory poet, fond of Victor Hugo, enamored of Italy; he had been there at the time of the war for national unity, in which he saw an object lesson for the Catalan-speaking countries since, as he said, just as the Lombards, the Tuscans, etc., form the Italian nation, just so the Catalonians, the Valencians, the natives of the Balearic Islands, etc., form the *patria lemosina.*

The great figure of Catalonian poetry of the 19th century, Jacint Verdaguer (*q.v.*), the son of humble peasants, was still, in many respects, a romantic. Rich Catalonian nature held no secrets for him; he was thoroughly familiar with the names of herbs, birds, and minerals in all the dialects (Ampurdanian, Majorcan, Leridan, Valencian), since he made repeated excursions through this country. Mountains and rivers became living beings to him. His genial intuition gave him a feeling for primitive periods; it was as though he had lived in those times and known their heroes. His genius was predominantly epic in character. His two epics, *La Atlàntida* (1877) and *Canigó* (1885), have been translated into almost all of the literary languages of Europe and some of Asia; one of his charms consists of a highly personal style, characterized by an almost savage energy, which suggests admirably the primitive and barbarous character of the themes (the prehistoric epoch in *L'Atlàntida,* the 9th century in *Canigó*). Verdaguer, specifically with his *Canigó,* really sums up Catalonian romanticism.

Although in this period there was developed the historical novel in the manner of Sir Walter Scott, by and large the only prose of that time which has really survived is in the humorous and *costumbrista* writings of Robert Robert (1840–1905), whose talent, at once tender and ironical, is reminiscent, though in a more subdued tone, of Dickens. The theatre, already somewhat developed by precursors, attained the dignity of true dramatic poetry in this romantic period with the dramas of Frederic Soler (Pitarra) (1839–1895).

Angel Guimerà (*q.v.*) sounds a new note. His *tragedias* add to Catalonian literature—which already boasted, in Verdaguer, an epic genre of great span—another of the great literary genres, the tragic poem. Although by preference he looks for his themes in the Middle Ages, as did the romantics, he handles them in a realistic manner and in a very personal style, distinguished by a concision frequently approaching brutality. He seeks deliberately the unadorned substantive. His sentences are disorderly, hard, hesitating; they give, at times, the sensation of a mere rough draft, of something drawn with force but incomplete, like certain statues of Rodin. His prose drama *Terra Baixa* (1896), widely translated and produced (Eng. tr., *Marta of the Lowlands,* 1914), has been reverently presented by a proletarian wing of the theatre for its social message. In his *Poesies* (1887) he frequently treated macabre themes with a horrifying exactitude of detail.

Joan Maragall (*q.v.*), whose talent was a cultivated one, has become very popular in his country as the author of landscape poetry. He contemplates nature as would a good bourgeois on vacation, and in this is to be found the secret of his extensive success. At times he interwove philosophical ideas (particularly those of Nietzsche, *q.v.*) into his verse, especially in "Comte Arnau" which, according to the author's purpose, was to be the incarnation of the superman. This won him the admiration of Unamuno (*q.v.*), who was responsible for the renown that Maragall obtained in Castile and in the Hispanic-American countries. His "Cant espiritual" is very beautiful, a sort of realistic credo in which the author expresses his candid admiration for the universe as perceived by the senses and deplores the fact that death has to deprive us of them.

The seed sown by Marian Aguilo now bore fruit in the already mentioned Majorcan school, with its classical, Mediterranean style. Costa i Llobera (*q.v.*) is the Majorcan poet par excellence—circumspect, sober, devoid of sentimentalism, impeccable, strong, serene, and an admirer of Horace; even in meter he follows the models of antiquity. Another poet of great talent belonging to this school is Joan Alcover (*q.v.*), whose elegies, nobly moving, are a model in the genre. Along with Verdaguer and Guimerà, they are the Majorcan poets who again carried the Catalan language to literary heights.

The spirit of realism naturally favored the development of the novel. Narcís Oller (*q.v.*) is considered, more or less correctly, as a disciple of Zola (*q.v.*), who made him known in France. Among other initiators of Catalonian realism are Josep Pin i Soler (1842–1927); Joaquim Ruyra (*q.v.*), author of short stories and short novels, whose delightful style won him the admiration of classic writers; Prudenci Bertrana (*q.v.*); and Victor Català (*q.v.*), whose novel *Solitud* (1905) is esteemed by the Catalonians as a masterpiece. New dramatic authors, notably Santiago Rusiñol (*q.v.*) and Ignasi Iglesies (*q.v.*), abandoned the verse drama and cultivated a type of prose comedy which enjoyed a great popular success. Exaggeration of realism even led to the belief that dramatic poetry had died, its place taken by a dialogued prose where the chief ambition was to reproduce, like a phonograph, the conversations of real life.

During this period the philologist Pompeu Fabra (1868–), since exiled in France, carried out his labors directed toward the fixation and purification of the Catalan language. His first grammatical studies appeared in the last quarter of the 19th century, his voluminous *Gramática de la lengua catalana* in 1913. His orthographic system was officially adopted by the Institut d'Estudis Catalans.

In 1914 the Spanish state granted a semblance of autonomy to Catalonia (considered in a strict geographical sense, without Valencia and the Balearic Islands), which was organized with the name *Mancomunitat* under the presidency of Enric Prat de la Riba (1870–1917). He showed himself to be a most devoted patron of Catalonian culture, and with this official stimulus a new literary movement, headed by Eugenio D'Ors (*q.v.*), took over the directing role in the intellectual life of the country. But this movement, while characterized by an unflinching intellectual spirit and by a devastating criticism of realism and all that had preceded it, showed scorn of the national literature of the preceding century and at times an almost slavish admiration for certain foreign schools (in particular French symbolism, *q.v.*); as a result the literature of that moment had scarcely any roots in the national soil. On the other hand it was able to profit by the judicious reforms in the literary language which had been effected by Pompeu Fabra, although it is questionable whether what was gained in the direction of purity of language was a sufficient compensation for what was sacrificed in native genius. There was even a loss in a territorial sense, since the new literature, as distinguished from the former, tended to limit itself to a geographically circumscribed Catalonia.

A multitude of lyric poets then made their appearance, two of whom continue to be admired, Josep Carner (*q.v.*) and Carles Riba. Carner was the poet of the comfortable and elegant life of the bourgeoisie of the beautiful environs of Barcelona; he was likewise the poet of the coquettish modistes and pretty neighborhood girls. More recently an exile in Mexico, Carner is now the dean of Catalonian literature. The Hellenist Riba, recently an exile in France, is above all an intellectual, a university man, often an impediment for his poetry; his *Estances*, however, is profound and subtle and continues to exert a great influence on the younger generation.

The reaction against the realistic prose theatre was carried out by Josep Maria de Sagarra (*q.v.*). He is the most original and at the same time the most popular of the writers of his period; his dramatic poems, of a highly nationalistic tone, enjoyed a noisy triumph on the stage. Unquestionably endowed with genius in his own way, he even undertook an epic poem, *El Comte Arnau* (1928), the first six cantos of which show an astounding vigor and simplicity; unfortunately the last four drag painfully. He has also written various novels, the impudent style of which is charming. The language of Sagarra, extremely rich in native idiom which lend it an inimitable flavor, attains this spontaneous beauty vainly sought in dictionaries and grammars.

Thousands of novels also appeared. The novelist Joan Puig i Ferreter, later an exile in France, introduced to his country the great Russian authors of the 19th century. His *Camins de França*, standing apart from all literary schools, is a collection of highly personal confessions.

In 1931 Catalonia, without Valencia and the Balearic Islands, was organized into an autonomous Generalitat; in 1939 it was invaded by Franco's army. Recent times have seen an implacable persecution of the national culture, which reached the point where aged writers were shot and depositories of Catalonian books were burned. Such a brusque interruption in the literary history of the country has come about that one can rightfully consider the year 1939 as one of those dates which mark the end of a period. The present literary generation is condemned to silence in its own country; one can deduce something of the spirit that animates it from what is produced by that portion of the group which exiled itself voluntarily and is now in free countries. These look forward to another stirring revival of the national spirit, with unity for the Catalan-speaking countries.

See: Manuel de Montoliu, *Manual d'historica critica de la literatura catalana moderna* (1922); Jean Jacques Achille Bertrand, *La Littérature catalane contemporaine, 1833–1933* (1933).

J. S.

Cecchi, Emilio (1884–, Italian art critic, journalist, and essayist), began his literary career with the Florentine group of the *Leonardo* and the *Voce*, but revealed his real personality with the *Ronda* at Rome in the post-war period. He spent 17 years in acquiring that dexterity of expression for which he is now justly esteemed. During those years he wrote *Kipling* (1911) and *Studi critici* (1912). Like many Italians of his generation, he freed himself through the idealism of Croce and Gentile from the sumptuousness of D'Annunzio (*qq.v.*) and from a positivistic conception of life. But he was not a thinker or a man of action, and what remained after this philosophical house cleaning was a sensitive view of the world in delicate colors and a mind capable of examining the universe through a veil of sophisticated culture. Anglo-Saxon readers especially are likely to enjoy his humorous way of expression. He is in the main an essayist and some models of his studied prose can be found in certain modern English writers whom he admired and translated, such as Stevenson, Belloc, and Chesterton.

Since the publication of *Pesci rossi* (1920) revealed him to sophisticated readers, his typical modules have been articles which have served as magazine ornaments and for that characteristic Italian institution, the third page of a newspaper. Be it a criticism of modern or ancient art, a sketch of a street scene, a portrait of a writer, a moral situation, he likes to close himself within the limits of two or three thousand words, starting with a studied simplicity, then prancing around the reader like a Red Indian dancer with that enigmatic smile that makes one wonder if he intends to end with a laugh or with a scalping. This pose earned him the nickname of prankster from critics. His sentences are measured, rhythmical, and he alone knows how many long travels, how many readings, what protracted pipe smokes, went into the finding of a cadenza or a joke, an unexpected resemblance, or the reversal of a commonplace. He is not a spontaneous author but a great worker; and like every personality founded on sensibility, and not on ideas or on a faith, he is at his best when a change offers him new and exciting material which he knows how to absorb without being dominated by it. Editors were shrewd enough to offer him several opportunities to travel. *Qualche Cosa* (1931) is an account of a trip to Holland, *Messico* (1932), of a visit to Mexico, and *Et in Arcadia ego . . .* (1934), his impressions of Greece. He came twice to the United States, once as a professor in the summer school of the University of California at Berkeley, and went even to the Portuguese African colony of Mozambique. He has written only the first volume of a much discussed history of English literature, *Storia della letteratura inglese nel secolo XIX* (1915). His other books are collected pages or essays—*La Giornata delle belle donne* (1924), *L'Osteria del cattivo tempo* (1927), *Corse al trotto* (1936). To the great amazement of the professionals, he wrote many illuminating pages on old and on contemporary painters: *Note d'arte a Valle Giulia* (1911), *La Pittura italiana dell' ottocento* (1927), *Pietro Lorenzetti* (1930), *Giotto* (1937). From his pen has also come *America amara* (1939), which has had six printings; this is a collection of articles on the civilization of the United States, severe but fair.

Above all Cecchi loves his trade and feels for it an ascetic reverence. If he has a morality, it is the morality of form ("you can write in any manner, but not without a manner"); and he is not averse to a political order provided it guarantees the writer the intimate freedom of his room. Like a teacher of good penmanship, he is not interested so much in the meaning of the phrase as in the style. It is quite obvious that he likes to indulge in jokes, and many of his articles or essays were written only for the final jest in them or for some intermingled or recondite quip recounted with jaunty unconcern. Sometimes he pokes fun even at the job of writing, but not too much or his whole world would crumble in ruins about him.

See: A. Gargiulo, "Emilio Cecchi," *Nuova Antologia,* CCCXC (1937), 36–47; P. Pancrazi, *Scrittori italiani del novecento,* revised ed. (1939), pp. 192–197.

G. P.

Čech, Svatopluk (1846–1908, Czech poet and novelist), is usually contrasted with Vrchlický (*q.v.*) as the representative of a definitely nationalistic tradition in poetry. Actually, both in poetic technique and in the ideology of liberalism the two poets were similar, though Čech preached a highly spiritual Pan-Slavism and was far more strongly influenced by Russian romantic literature (Lermontov, Pushkin). Čech was born in Ostředek near Benešov (southeast of Prague), the son of a steward on an estate. He studied law and practiced it for a time, but soon devoted himself only to poetry and the editing of literary journals. Trips to the Caucasus and to Denmark were of importance in his formation. He died in Prague.

Čech's main field was epic poetry, though his talent was rather that of a rhetorical, meditative, and descriptive poet. His best work is in the fresco-like epical poems on themes from Czech history. *Adamité* (1873; The Adamites) depicts the most radical sect of the Hussites who flouted all social and sexual conventions; *Žižka* (1879) centers round the greatest warrior of the Hussites; *Václav z Michalovic* (1880), possibly his best poem, is drawn from the period of oppression after the Battle of the White Mountain (1620); and *Dagmar* (1883) tells the story of a Bohemian princess married to a Danish king in the Middle Ages (here the background is the conflict between Teuton and Slav). All these poems are filled with generous enthusiasm for a future of universal freedom and democracy and are written in magnificent, rather heavily decorative style. Čech's ideas are even better expressed in his artistically less successful allegories, *Evropa* (1878; Europe) and *Slavie* (1882), which present a discussion of communism versus democracy and of Pan-Slavism versus the conflict between the Slavic nations, the poet siding with slow progress and humanity. Čech was most successful in his own time with his political poems. *Jitřní písně* (1887; Morning Songs) and especially *Písně otroka* (1895; The Songs of a Slave) are effective declamation pieces which under thin disguises attack Austrian rule and give voice to the poet's indignation against national and social oppression. A brief epical poem, *Lešetínský kovář* (1883; The Blacksmith of Lešetín), depicts in sharp colors the conflicts between the older homely tradesmen and the encroaching German capitalism.

But it would be a mistake to think of Čech merely as a historical and political poet. He wrote also several humorous and whimsical fairy tales in verse, agreeable and sentimental idyls of Czech country life (*e.g., Ve stínu lípy,* 1879, In the Shade of the Linden Tree), and a whole collection of poems (*Modlitby k Neznámému,* 1896; Prayers to the Unknown) which give expression to a high-minded agnosticism. His prose is less important: it includes many stories, sketches, travel books, two novels, and a very popular series of satirical utopian romances which describe the adventures of a Prague Philistine on the moon and in the 15th century (*Výlet páně Broučkův do měsíce,* 1886, The Excursion of Mr. Brouček to the Moon; *Nový epochální výlet pana*

Broučka tentokrdte do patndctého stoleti, 1888, A New Amazing Excursion of Mr. Brouček, This Time into the Fifteenth Century).

Čech was personally a shy and solitary romantic, who was saved from egoistic pessimism only by his political enthusiasms and his faith in the future victory of humanity and democracy. His ideas and his rhetorical pathos appealed to his contemporaries, who exalted him to the highest rank among Czech poets, but his influence has been on the wane since the advent of critical realism and symbolism.

See: V. Flajšhans, *Svatopluk Čech* (1906); F. Strejček, *O Svatopluku Čechovi* (1908); Arne Novák, *Svatopluk Čech; dilo a osobnost* (2 vols., 1921–1923). There are German translations of *Adamité, Dagmar,* and *Písně otroka.*

R. W.

Cejador, Julio (1864–1927, Spanish scholar and critic), born in Saragossa, entered very young the Society of Jesus, which he left in 1900 to become a secular priest. While still a Jesuit, he studied in France and traveled in the Orient, amassing a considerable amount of erudition in Semitic and Indo-European languages, humanistic studies, and modern literatures. In 1914 he was appointed professor of Latin at the University of Madrid. A tremendous worker, he composed more than 50 large volumes on classical and modern philological matter, constantly engaged in polemics on linguistic and literary points, and never let his pen rest. He expounded certain extravagant theories on the unity of the origin of human languages and on the Basque origin of Castilian. His main contributions to the field of Spanish literature, probably the soundest part of his work, are studies on the language of Cervantes, collections of proverbs and traditional poetry, editions of the Arcipreste de Hita (Juan Ruiz), Quevedo, and others, and the *Historia de la lengua y literatura castellana* (14 vols., 1915–1922). A lack of critical balance and scientific spirit, a questionable literary taste, and the haste in which most of his books were produced invalidate to a great extent his work; it contains, nevertheless, a considerable mass of facts and useful data. He is also the author of novels and autobiographical books.

See: R. F. Giusti, *Critica y polémica,* IV (1930), 157–161.

A. del R.

Céline, Louis Ferdinand (pseud. of Louis Ferdinand Destouches, 1894–, French novelist), has lived a life like that of Bardamu and Ferdinand, the best known of his characters. Born in Paris, of obscure Breton stock, he took a medical degree and became a practicing physician in Paris. Many legends surround him. The known facts are that he has traveled widely in Africa and America and has worked as a ship's doctor, as a hand in a Detroit factory, as a research man for the Rockefeller Foundation. When his first novel was published, he was on the staff of a workingmen's clinic at Clichy, devoting himself, for little or no pay, to the ailing humanity which he reviles in his novels.

Opinions vary as to whether Céline's work has achieved more than a *succès de scandale,* yet even critics who dismiss him as a cheap pornographer admit that as expressions of absolute misanthropy his novels are monumental. The hero of *Voyage au bout de la nuit* (1932; Eng. tr., *Journey to the End of Night,* 1934) stumbles through a life of darkness from one human catastrophe to another. Despite occasional illuminations of decency, love, and human kindness, there is no light at the end. In *Mort à crédit* (1936; Eng. tr., *Death on the Installment Plan,* 1938) the hero (significantly his name is Ferdinand) witnesses the decomposition of everything he touches. Science, love, religion, stand revealed as cruel shams; in this darkness there is not even a glimmer. Céline's conclusion is that the race is divided between the maliciously evil and the insane.

Céline, like Gide (*q.v.*), had hoped that Russia would find a better way of life: a trip there (see *Mea Culpa,* 1937; Eng. tr., 1937) dispelled the hope. Thenceforward his only recourse was to fascism. *Bagatelles pour un massacre* (1938) is a wild diatribe against Jews, and *Ecole des cadavres* (1938) a hymn of hatred of the "degenerate" French. Céline's crude violence, his nihilistic style, the complete filthiness of his vocabulary, are coupled with a fierce sincerity. A plausible analysis would be that his personality, too sensitive to bear the spectacle of daily suffering in the hospital, finds relief in a literary rejection of the flesh which as a physician Céline feels powerless to heal.

See: L. Trotsky, "Novelist and Politician," *Atlantic Monthly,* CLVI (1935), 413–420; G. Truc, "L'Art et la passion de M. Ferdinand Céline," *Revue hebdomadaire,* Année XLVII (1938), Tome VII, pp. 550–565.

W. M. F.

Cena, Giovanni (1870–1917, Italian poet, novelist, and editor), was born at Montanaro Canavese in Piedmont. A kind heart plus sincerity are not sufficient to produce a writer

—especially not a natural and simple one: this is what is learned from reading the works of this honest and well-intentioned soul who in the 90's cut something of a figure in Italian literature. The son of indigent parents, greatly oppressed by misery and maladies, he succeeded, by a rare and lucky stroke, in winning attention through a book of poems, *Madre* (1897), and later a social novel, *Gli Ammonitori* (1904; Eng. tr., *The Forewarners*, 1908). By this time he had become editor of the authoritative Italian magazine *Nuova Antologia*. Wishing to spare others the terrible sufferings of his youth, which had almost made him turn anarchist, he dedicated all his extra time to the education of the poor. He founded private schools for the children of peasants near Rome who had been left by their landowners and by the government in a state of permanent starvation, debasement, and ignorance and under the continuous threat of malaria. They won recognition for him among those who had kind hearts in Italy. These schools have been studied as pedagogical models and were responsible for some of the ideas adopted by Lombardo-Radice in the reform of the elementary school under Gentile.

In the verses of Cena are found, with very few exceptions, only ashes taken from other hearths, residues of other styles. There is nothing simple, nothing genuine, nothing artistically felt, nothing original. Even artificial stones which had fallen from the pasteboard crown of D'Annunzio (*q.v.*) reappear among his prose works. *Gli Ammonitori* was intended as an admonition to the upper classes of the dangerous social situation in the 80's; today it reads like a depressing mixture of dull autobiography and prosaic morality. Nothing better can be salvaged from his letters and critical reviews. In his times the work of Cena had a temporary significance, but it hardly survives an epoch (1880–1900) when social problems predominated.

See: A. Momigliano, *Impressioni di un lettore contemporaneo* (1928), pp. 66–72; G. Lombardo-Radice, *Pedagogia di apostoli e di operai* (1936), pp. 177–204.

G. P.

Čep, Jan (1902–, Czech novelist), is the most gifted among the Czech "ruralists." He was born the son of a poor peasant cottager in Myslechovice near Litovel (northern Moravia) and studied English and French at the University of Prague but without taking a degree. He became reader in a large publishing house and has done much translating, from Joseph Conrad, Bernanos (*q.v.*), Pourrat (*q.v.*), and others. Čep, unlike the other "ruralists," Josef Knap, František Křelina, and F. V. Kříž, is a highly spiritual person who struggles for religious certainty and peace. He depicts usually "the return of the native" who, broken by urban civilization, goes back to his rural home, to the soil, and finally to religion. Čep seems to have been influenced by the early work of Jaroslav Durych (*q.v.*), with whom he shared a sense of the value of the Catholic tradition. There is a strong individual tone, however, in his highly sensitive style—ranking with the best in modern Czech prose—in the magic of his lyrical metaphors, in the refined melancholy which broods over all his little sketches, stories, and fictitious diaries and journals. A certain monotony of themes and lack of invention have prevented Čep from reaching a wider public, but he is one of the most cultivated and genuine of recent Czech writers. His stories are collected as *Zeměžluč* (1931; Bitter Herb), *Letnice* (1932; Whitsuntide), *Děravý plášť* (1934; The Tattered Coat), and *Modrá a zlatá* (1938; Blue and Gold), and there is a fairly long novel, *Hranice stínu* (1935; The Boundary of the Shadow), as well as a shorter piece, *Příbuzenstvo* (1938; Relatives).

See: K. Sezima, "Jan Čep," in *Mládí* (1936).

R. W.

Cernuda, Luis (1904–, Spanish poet), was born in Seville. He studied law in the university of that city and then went to Madrid, where he lived some years. Later he served as an instructor in Spanish at the University of Toulouse. He was identified with the group of poets devoted to the cause of the Spanish republic during the civil war. More recently he has lived in England and has taught Spanish at the University of Glasgow.

His first verse is collected in *Perfil del aire* (1927), a volume that already shows the purity of his poetic vocation despite the occasional faltering note. Here is a poetry of true romantic lineage, of the purified romanticism personified by the poet Bécquer (*q.v.*). The romanticism of Cernuda is deeply felt and also at times reflective, intellectualized. In a second book, *Donde habita el olvido* (1935), his romantic spiritual life is refined to the point of attaining the finest and most delicate shades. Through a pure affinity of temperament, and not owing to any external cause, he leaves the zones of traditional Spanish romanticism and comes into contact with such romantic elements as are represented by Keats and Hölderlin. His world is one of pre-realities and phantoms peopling but not satisfying his solitude. In Cernuda the classic

Spanish sentiment of solitude is repeated with the most modern subtleties and variations. Presentiment, reality, and forgetfulness confuse their limits in a poetic atmosphere which partakes of all three elements. This poetry materializes in verbal form perhaps the strongest immaterializing, spiritualizing force of contemporary Spanish lyric. The purity of his poetic vision is matched exactly by his language, which is light, elegant, and at times deliberately pale. One finds nothing heavy, dull, or abject in this poetry which, above all else, aspires to be essentially poetic.

La realidad y el deseo is the title he has given to the two editions of his complete works, the first of which was published in 1936 and the second in 1940. In the last part of his work the artist leans more toward concrete, exterior realities in time and space. Here his poetry seems to gain in force, in noble serenity and breadth. In London in 1943 was published Cernuda's *Oknos, el affarero,* a collection of prose poems which evoke places and moments of his life in Seville and which are excellent examples of the melancholy charm of nostalgia. During recent years journals have published some of his essays in the field of poetic criticism. Here Cernuda brings to bear the same high purpose and interpretative acumen that characterize his poetry.

See: P. Salinas, *Literatura española siglo XX* (1941), pp. 333–348.

P. S.

Chamson, André (1900–, French regional novelist and essayist), was born in Nîmes, Gard, of a family of peasant origin, and was brought up in the severe Protestant tradition of the Cévennes region, which forms the background and inspiration of his best work. He studied in the *lycées* of Alès and Montpellier, received his degree in history at the Sorbonne, and then took the full course at the Ecole des Chartes, in completion of which he wrote a thesis on the geography of his native region. From this point he has pursued a double career as a novelist and as a student of art, archaeology, geography, and history. *Roux le bandit* (1925; Eng. tr., *Roux the Bandit,* 1929), his first novel; *Les Hommes de la route* (1927; Eng. tr., *The Road,* 1929), his best-known work; *Histoires de Tabusse* (1928); and *Le Crime des justes* (1929; Eng. tr., *The Crime of the Just,* 1930)—all draw a vivid, somber picture of his native region. In *Héritages* (1932) he approaches a more complex world, and *La Galère* (1939) makes a sharp indictment of corrupt French politics. His political essays, *L'Homme contre l'histoire* (1927), *La Révolution de Dix-neuf* (1930) and *Rien qu'un témoignage* (1937), express the point of view of an "advanced democrat." Like so many French writers of the time, Chamson has devoted much attention to contemporary political problems and was associated with the left-wing Association des Ecrivains et Artistes Révolutionnaires. He has also held political posts. He was chief assistant in the Daladier cabinet in 1934 at the time of the February 6 riots and, being an ardent supporter of the Front Populaire, was made assistant curator of the National Museum at the Palace of Versailles under the Blum government, a post which he held until the fall of France. For three years (1935–1938), in association with Jean Guéhenno and Andrée Viollis, he edited the progressive weekly, *Vendredi.*

André Chamson must be numbered among the minor writers of the time, though his quality is authentic. He lacks the originality and color of Jean Giono (*q.v.*), the strength and passion of C. F. Ramuz (*q.v.*). Nevertheless his sober if uninspired style, his intimate knowledge and poetic understanding of the Cevenole peasantry and countryside, his feeling for the common people, joined to his comprehension of history and of contemporary political and social problems, have earned him a place among the novelists and essayists of the period whose work is strongly flavored by the primitivism of regions relatively untouched by modern life. With its note of revolt and heresy reflecting his people's historic struggle for freedom of conscience, his work is simple and austere. As a Protestant he carries on a valuable minority tradition in French literature.

See: Fritz Lehner, "André Chamson," *Deutsch-französische Rundschau,* Vol. III (1930); A. Rousseaux, *Ames et visages du XXe siècle* (1932); John Lehmann, *New Writing in Europe* (1940).

H. M. C.

Chapygin, Aleksei Pavlovich (1870–1937, Russian novelist and short-story writer), was born in a village in the former Government of Olonets and was apprenticed to an icon painter in St. Petersburg. His depressing early stories (1905–1910), dealing with the city poor, were collected in 1912 (*Nelyudimyie;* The Misanthropes), when Chapygin had already turned to his native North, with its enduring traditions and mystic outlook. The primitive peasants of that region were then little known, and his *Bely skit* (1914; The White Hermitage) and *Po zverinoi trope* (1918; Along a Wild

Animals' Trail) attracted attention. In the tales of the Soviet period, Chapygin shows the people he knew so well undergoing the impact of the new social forces. The candid account of his life in *Zhizn moya* (1930; My Life) and *Po tropam i dorogam* (1931; Along the Trails and Roads) contributed to the understanding of his works by disclosing their decidedly autobiographical inspiration.

Meanwhile, in his historical novel *Razin Stepan* (3 vols., 1926–1927), a somewhat theatrical elaboration of his earlier manner, Chapygin had explored the minds of the 17th-century Muscovites, a task for which his life had eminently qualified him; and there is evidence of long study in the rich dialogue, as well as in the reinterpretation of Razin's role in accordance with Soviet ideology. *Gulyashchiye lyudi* (1936; Free Folk), a prologue as well as a sequel to *Razin Stepan,* also deals mainly with peasant uprisings, but is distinguished by a relative simplicity of language. Both novels combine epic sweep with minute detail, and, in spite of the brutalities described, they reveal the author's optimism and testify to his faith in the common people.

See: V. Dynnik, "A. Chapygin," in *Pechat i revolyutsiya* (1928), Book II, pp. 125–134; B. S. Walbe, *Aleksei Pavlovich Chapygin* (1938).

P. A. P.

Chardonne, Jacques (pseud. of Jacques Boutelleau, 1884–, French novelist), was born at Barbezieux, Charente, of a French father and an American mother. He received his early education at home from tutors and later attended school in Barbezieux. He was a sensitive and passionate child and early showed a leaning toward literature. However, he did not start on a literary career until he was 35. He has related the memories of the happy days of his childhood in two books of familiar essays, *Le Bonheur de Barbezieux* (1938) and *Chronique privée* (1940). At the age of 18 he went to Paris, where he attended the university and obtained a law degree. He was married in 1910 and in the same year became a member of the P. V. Stock publishing firm, which he long headed. In 1915 his health failed, and he was sent to Chardonne, a village near Vevey, Switzerland, to recover. It was during this convalescence of five years that he began his first book, a novel, *L'Epithalame* (1921; Eng. tr., *Epithalamium,* 1923). This novel concerns itself with the spiritual problems of married love. Only in marriage, thinks Chardonne, do men and women reveal the secrets of their hearts and show their full and complex personalities. He deals with the same theme in *Eva* (1930; Eng. tr., *Eva; or, The Interrupted Diary,* 1930) and *Claire* (1931) and in all his other works. His outstanding achievement is the cyclical novel, *Les Destinées sentimentales* (1934–1935), in which he presents not only the sentimental problems of husband and wife, but also a faithful picture of French family and business life and of French provincial society.

Chardonne ranks high among the French novelists of today for his fine portrayal of characters, for the restraint and beauty of his style, and for the moral worth of his message.

See: M. Martin du Gard, "Opinions et portraits: Jacques Chardonne," *Nouvelles littéraires,* December 5, 1931; A. Rousseaux, *Ames et visages du XXe siècle* (1936).

R. B.

Charon, *see* Linde, Otto zur.

Chartier, Emile (pseud. Alain, 1868–, French essayist and philosopher), is known as Chartier —just plain Chartier—to numberless generations of students in the *lycées* of Lorient, Rouen, and Henri IV in Paris, as well as to his fellow alumni of the Ecole Normale Supérieure. But to the general public he is the Alain of thousands and thousands of "Propos" which he contributed beginning in 1906, first to the *Dépêche de Rouen* (1906–1914), then to the *Libres Propos* (a weekly edited by himself, 1921–1924), the *Revue des vivants, Revue européenne, Europe, Alsace française, Navire d'argent, Nouvelle Revue française,* etc. The typical *propos* is a short, aphoristic piece of 50 or 60 lines, strewn with concrete or poetical images, pointing, like a fable or parable, to a practical lesson. Though the *propos* as a genre belongs to the art of the "columnist," Alain's essays constitute definitely superior journalism, and through them he enters the long line of French moralists who for centuries meted out to the reader pleasant and digestible pills of worldly wisdom. Roughly one fourth of these sketches were collected in volume form, sometimes under loose titles such as *Les Cent et un Propos d'Alain* (5 vols., 1908–1929), *Les Propos d'Alain* (2 vols., 1920), *Propos sur l'esthétique* (1923), *Propos sur le christianisme* (1924), *Propos sur le bonheur* (1925), *Propos sur l'éducation* (1932), *Propos de littérature* (1934), *Propos de politique* (1934), *Propos d'économique* (1935), sometimes under a more significant heading, indicative of a system. Thus a glance at the remainder of Alain's lengthy bibliography reveals his sustained interest in militant pacifism (*Mars, ou la Guerre jugée,* 1921, Eng. tr., *Mars; or, The Truth about War,* 1930, followed in 1939 by

Convulsion de la force and *Echec à la force*); in democracy and politics (*Eléments d'une doctrine radicale,* 1925; *Le Citoyen contre les pouvoirs,* 1925); in aesthetics (*Système des beaux-arts,* 1920, completed by *Vingt Leçons sur les beaux-arts,* 1931; *La Visite au musicien,* 1927, and *Entretiens chez le sculpteur,* 1937); in psychology and philosophy proper (*Quatre-vingt-un Chapitres sur l'esprit et les passions,* 1915; *Lettres au Docteur Mondor,* 1924; *Sentiments, passions et signes,* 1926; *Esquisses de l'homme,* 1927; *Entretiens au bord de la mer,* 1931; *Les Dieux,* 1934; *Les Saisons de l'esprit,* 1937; *Minerve, ou De la sagesse,* 1939); in philosophical exegesis and literary criticism (*Les Idées et les âges,* 2 vols., 1927; *Introduction aux Passions de l'âme de Descartes,* 1928; *Idées: Platon, Descartes, Hegel,* 1932, reprinted in 1939 with an additional study on Auguste Comte; *Stendhal,* 1935; *Avec Balzac,* 1937; commentary, 1929, on *Charmes* by Paul Valéry, *q.v.,* and another, 1936, on *La Jeune Parque* by the same author). In a class by themselves stand *Histoire de mes pensées* (1936) and *Souvenirs de guerre* (1937).

There is no mystery to the selection of Chartier's pen name. It was chosen in obvious remembrance of his 15th-century homonym, the famous poet, Alain Chartier. From one Norman to another, the greeting appears natural enough. One wonders, however, whether the medieval Alain, polished courtier and much traveled diplomat that he was, would have thought of writing: "I do not just happen to be from Normandy. I am Normandy itself." Such is Emile Chartier's boast—and a fair one indeed. Around Mortagne, his native town, among the hedgerows and the bushes, he found the old "Chouan" spirit still intact and took it as his own. It is an earthy spirit, intent upon real things, sober, unafraid, diffident. With Alain it becomes the "radical" spirit or the faculty, rooted in one's conscience, to resist power—outwardly if power is illegal, inwardly (with due physical obeisance) if power is legal, but to resist in both cases, for all power, according to Alain, is arbitrary in character, and it is of the essence of any power, political or not, to be "regal," to overreach itself, to corrupt and be corrupted. If democracy, for instance, commands his stout respect, it is not that democracy is good government—there are no good governments as such; it is because democracy devised the best means of curbing the excesses of government and setting up the citizen against the powers that be.

A fitting epigraph to Chartier's creed would be found in the sentence, "The minute we think, we should learn how not to die." To live, then, is to be awake. To be awake is to react. Acceptance of ready-made ideas means surrender. Total conformity means death. Is it at all surprising that youth responded to such a stirring call? In fact, Alain's prestige radiated far into academic and literary circles. He was revered and heeded by his disciples as few *lycée* professors have ever been. To be sure, a few older students, such as André Maurois and Henri Massis (*qq.v.*), were stimulated rather than deeply marked; but Jean Prévost (*q.v.*), some 15 years their junior, was fated to represent the Chartier tradition at its sturdiest. This gifted writer joined the French Forces of the Interior during the Second World War and perished in 1944 at the hands of the Germans, thus demonstrating in exemplary fashion that "resistance" in the Alain sense is something other—and something more—than "conscientious objection."

See: Jean Prévost, Albert Thibaudet, Ramon Fernandez, Jean Schlumberger, and Pierre Bost, "L'Œuvre d'Alain," *Europe,* XVI (1928), 129–152; Anonymous, *Alain, professeur* (1932); Denis Saurat, "Alain," *Nouvelle Revue française,* XXXIX (1932), 760–766.

J.-A. B.

Châteaubriant, Alphonse de (1877–, French novelist), was born in Rennes and, except for occasional visits to Paris, has spent most of his life at the Château de la Motte Saint-Sulpice in Vendée. A member of the country nobility, he approached literature with typical detachment and reserve and has preferred the studious and tranquil life of the province rather than the intellectual stimulation of the capital.

Châteaubriant was already 34 when, in 1911, his first novel, *Monsieur des Lourdines* (Eng. tr., *The Keynote,* 1912), was published. Here is related the moving story of an old country gentleman compelled to sell family estates to pay off debts contracted by a prodigal son, whose extravagances ruin his father's life and bring about his mother's death. Poetic language, subdued emotion, and an admirable plot at once revealed the author of this book as a writer of unusual talent. Unspoiled by success, Châteaubriant waited 12 years before offering the public his next novel, *La Brière* (1923; Eng. tr., *The Peat-Cutters,* 1927). This work sets forth a somber but powerful picture of the primitive life of the people of La Brière, a region of peat bogs situated in the most remote section of Brittany, near the mouth of the Loire. The writer has analyzed so convincingly the fears and superstitions of the Briérons and drawn such masterful descriptions of their drab and gloomy countryside that one soon has the impression of reading about people and places long familiar. In *La Brière* Châteaubriant's artistic temperament has found its most perfect expression. *La Réponse du Seigneur* (1933), the author's third novel in 22 years, is the story of a gentleman of the old school, a descendant of the Templars and the last of his family. In his fondness for moralizing, the hero preaches throughout the book a long sermon on the need of a close union of the human soul with the Divinity. This novel falls far below the standards which the author had set himself in *Monsieur des Lourdines* and *La Brière.*

Châteaubriant has produced two other notable books, *La Meute* (1927) and *Au pays de Brière* (1935). *La Meute,* a collection of six short stories, affords an excellent illustration of two divergent aspects of the author's personality. The first three stories contain character sketches of country gentlemen drawn with complete objectivity and detachment. The rest of the book is written in an entirely different spirit. The reader is taken into a world of poetry and dream, at times reminiscent of the atmosphere found in the plays of Maeterlinck (*q.v.*). *Au pays de Brière* is a series of notes describing the few months which the author had spent in La Brière years before. Written in an emotional and subjective style which contrasts strangely with the studiously sober and impersonal style of his previous work about the same region, it displays rare qualities of comprehension and sympathy and presents the country in a mellow and intensely poetic light.

No one would have expected Châteaubriant even temporarily to forsake literature for political propaganda. It is a cruel irony of fate that such a great artist, as the result of a trip to Germany, should have written in 1937 *La Gerbe des forces* (*Nouvelle Allemagne*), an ill-timed and unjudicious praise of National Socialism. In 1938 appeared *Les Pas ont chanté,* a novel based upon memories of Châteaubriant's childhood; this book lacks the originality and the interest that characterized his earlier works.

J. M. C.

Chekhov, Anton Pavlovich (1860–1904, Russian short-story writer and dramatist), the son of a small grocer, a former serf, was born in the little port of Taganrog, on the Sea of Azov. He had to work for the family from his early years, and the tuberculosis he contracted while a medical student at the University of Moscow may have been partly due to overexertion coupled with inadequate nutrition. Shortly after graduation, in 1884, he discovered that the stories he had been writing as a means of subsistence had come to mean more to him than the medical profession. He jestingly remarked that while he regarded medicine as his lawful wife, literature was his irresistible mistress. In 1886 the first collection of his comic tales was published in book form, and that date may be considered as the beginning of his complete dedication to literature. Within the 20 years of his writing activity he composed over a thousand stories, five full-length plays, and about half a dozen one-act plays. One interlude in his career deserves mention. In 1890 he journeyed to the convicts' settlement on Sakhalin Island, and the following year saw the publication of *Sakhalin,* the record of his visit there. Although his first play, *Ivanov,* was produced in 1887, his fame as a playwright came to him only at the end of the century, when the Moscow Art Theatre adopted Chekhov and built its own success on the masterly performances of his plays, beginning with *Chaika* (The Sea Gull) in 1898, following it with *Dyadya Vanya* (Uncle Vanya) in 1899, *Tri sestry* (The Three Sisters) in 1901, and ending with his swan song, *Vishnyovy sad* (The Cherry Orchard), shortly before his death. The Moscow Art Theatre meant much to Chekhov, in more than one way; in 1901 he married one of its most gifted actresses, Olga Knipper.

Chekhov's literary art is apparent in his short stories as much as in his plays; the latter must be seen on the stage to be fully appreciated. There is little action or external dramatism in any of his work, for Chekhov is mainly concerned with bringing out the inner experiences and reactions of his characters. Hence the effectiveness of his plays depends not on traditional acting but on the ability of the actors to live their parts with so deep a sincerity as to infect the audience with their subtly suggested moods and emotions. Chekhov's plays are justly defined as the theatre of mood or atmosphere. This definition might be applied to his stories as well. In most of them plot is reduced to a minimum, often there is no sharply discernible beginning or end, but one is made witness to a momentary yet unforgettable flash of life in its perpetual flow. What makes Chekhov's stories dramatic and what renders his plays enduring literature is the simple dialogue, free from verbosity and blatancy, in which everyday words are so skillfully chosen and placed as to convey the deepest emotion and tragedy. The curtain usually drops on such simple utterances as "If we could only know!" or "It does not matter" (*The Three Sisters*). In "Skuchnaya istoriya" (1889; A Dreary Story) the climax of the professor's tragic loneliness and futility is made to be felt in the words, "Let us have lunch, Kate," which he speaks in reply to her anguished question as to the meaning and purpose of life. In his life and in his work Chekhov detested the garish and loud. He observed the ordinary and commonplace, and he knew how to sift the significant from the vulgar and mean, how to bring it to light without using obvious italics. We come to understand, and therefore to like, most of Chekhov's characters, taken from all walks of life and representing Russia on the eve of the 1905 Revolution. His men are largely failures, weak of will and resolution, incapable of action, most often seeking an outlet in moaning and whimpering, in drinking and gambling, or in suicide. His women, as in the case of Turgenev (*q.v.*), are by comparison stronger and nobler and are kept going by an aptitude for dreams and aspirations. In all events, Chekhov endows his characters with such essential humanness that because of our kinship we feel unable to condemn them. Chekhov's medical training enabled him to diagnose men impartially and objectively, and his mortal malady raised him to a philosophical toleration of human frailties. This impartiality and tolerance he imparts to his readers. But another message is also suggested by this unpartisan artist indirectly—hatred for ugly conditions. By implication we are told not to condemn his miserable and stupid characters, since their faults are not inherent but conditioned by the environment. One sentence in a story by Chekhov became the revolutionary slogan of Russian society in 1904–1905: "One must not live such a life!" The Russian masses translated Chekhov's message dynamically: they destroyed the ugly conditions of life, they changed life itself.

Chekhov's work has been widely translated into English.

See: W. Gerhardi, *Anton Chekhov* (1923, in English); A. Derman, *Tvorcheski portret Chekhova* (1929); P. Kogan, *A. P. Chekhov* (1929); N. A. Toumanova, *Anton Chekhov, the Voice of Twilight Russia* (1937).

A. K.

Chiarelli, Luigi (1884–, Italian playwright), born at Trani, started his literary career as a journalist, but soon turned to the theatre. He became famous with *La Maschera ed il volto,* first presented at the Argentina Theatre in Rome on May 31, 1916. Previous plays, *Vita intima* (1909), *Pasqua delle rose* (1910), *Astuzia* (1910), *La Portantina* (1911), *Extra Dry* (1912), and *Il Record* (1913), had attracted little attention.

In *La Maschera ed il volto,* Chiarelli's chief merit lies in having presented a very ancient subject in a very new and extraordinary dress. A betrayed husband intent upon wreaking vengeance on an adulterous wife—in accordance with the traditional code—suddenly finds he cannot kill her. But he remains conventional enough to affirm that he has done so, and sending his wife out of the country, he stands trial. His acquittal is followed by a series of fantastic complications. A body is found and identified as his wife's, the wife returns to congratulate him on his acquittal, he is likely to go to jail for pleading guilty to a crime not committed, his own pride and his wife's pride become deeply involved. The pair finally take flight together, in the hope of dislodging themselves from an absurdly ritualistic world. Chiarelli is clever in his satire of social fetishes and offers an agreeably shocking amalgam of humorous and tragic incidents. The adjective "grotesque" was applied to the play by clamorous critics, and by many as a paradoxical compliment, and Chiarelli's name was permanently attached to the *grotteschi* movement in the Italian theatre for which the play is the point of departure.

Chiarelli himself continues with the formula in his subsequent plays. In *La Scala di seta* (1917), *Chimere* (1920), *La Morte degli amanti* (1921), *Fuochi d'artificio* (1923), and *Jolly* (1928), he aims again to show the fundamental conflict between appearance and reality, mask and face—but never again with quite the same success. The main action of *La Scala di seta* concerns the inherent antagonism between Roberto, imbued with an unswerving sense of honesty, and Désiré, a vain and silly dancer with extraordinary political ambitions. Désiré actually becomes minister, and then while glibly talking to a huge gathering of people about justice and liberty, instinctively breaks into a dance as the unthinking crowd applauds. *Chimere* shows an even more conscious striving for grotesque effects. The play is redeemed in part by the creation of a "truthful madman" whose cynical quips and caustic humor invest the otherwise trite scenes with a pseudo-philosophical tone. In *La Morte degli amanti,* the grotesqueness is supposed to reside in the fact that Eleonora, having conceived love as a romantic and fatal passion in the grand style, tries in vain to arouse her husband's jealousy.

Other plays of Chiarelli are: *Le Lacrime e le stelle* (1918), *K–41* (1929), *Carne bianca* (1934), *Una Più Due* (1935), and *Pulcinella* (1939).

See: G. Ruberti, *Storia del teatro contemporaneo*, III (1928), 769–772; A. Tilgher, *Studi sul teatro contemporaneo* (1928), pp. 120, 129.

P. P. M.

Chiesa, Francesco (1871–, Italian Swiss poet and novelist), whose works are entirely in Italian, was born at Sagno in the Ticino canton of Switzerland. A graduate of the University of Pavia in jurisprudence and for years director of the canton *liceo* of Lugano, he had his first verse published in 1897. His poetry, chiefly contained in the volumes *La Cattedrale* (1903), *La Reggia* (1904), *Calliope* (1907), and *Consolazioni* (1921), is that of a strict classicist and is much admired for its formal perfection, although it has been censured for a lack of any deep feeling. Chiesa is better known for his prose works. His *novelle* and stories, *Istorie e favole* (1913), *Racconti puerili* (1920), and *Vite e miracoli di santi e profani* (1922), established his reputation as a writer of prose. With his novels *Tempo di marzo* (1925), *Villadorna* (1928), and *Racconti del mio orto* (1929), he has gained a wide recognition for the creation of an original style, which is mobile, built of a constant play of psychological and moral analyses and of moments of lyricism more commonly found in poetry. These last works, in spite of their titles, are hardly novels at all. What they contain as plot has almost no outline, and their substance is rather a weave of successive psychological and moral experiences on the part of the protagonist. In Chiesa's narrative the event is almost always inward and spiritual. He deserves the recognition he has attained—the more so in that his style is strikingly unique in Italian prose. It has qualities more commonly found in French, for example in Anatole France (*q.v.*), though in this respect there is no visible trace of imitation.

See: E. Cecchi, *Studi critici* (1912); A. Momigliano, *Impressioni di un lettore contemporaneo* (1928).

C. S. S.

Chirikov, Yevgeni Nikolayevich (1864–1932, Russian dramatist and journalist), was born in Kazan into the local gentry. In his youth he served several jail sentences for political activity. He studied jurisprudence and medicine at the University of Kazan and in 1887 was expelled for participating in student disturbances and exiled to the provinces. He began his literary career in 1885 and by 1894 had become a regular contributor to the well-known *God's World* and *Russkoye bogatstvo* (Russian Wealth). In 1903 he joined Gorky's (*q.v.*) *Knowledge* group. After the Revolution of 1917 Chirikov emigrated abroad, where he joined the anti-Soviet camp of Russian intelligentsia.

In such stories as *Invalidy* (1897; The Invalids) and *Chuzhestrantsy* (1899; Foreigners) Chirikov portrays life in provincial Russia and the struggle between the supporters of the Populist ideology and the Marxists. Chirikov's better-known dramas include *Yevrei* (1905; The Jews), *Koldunya* (1909; The Witch), *Lesnyie tainy* (1911; Forest Mysteries), and *Tsar Prirody* (1910; Tsar of Nature), which were popular in Russia in the early 20th century.

See: A. Derman, "E. N. Chirikov," in S. A. Vengerov, ed., *Russkaya literatura XX veka*, II (1914), 75–89.

O. M.

Cicognani, Bruno (1879–, Italian novelist), was born in Florence, the son of a magistrate. His mother, Giulia Nencioni, was the sister of Enrico Nencioni, who was a friend of Carducci (*q.v.*) and himself a writer of distinction. It may be said that Cicognani has inherited the gifts of both parents; he has been a magistrate in his native city for years and has managed at the same time to write several books of great merit. His first work, *La Crittogama*, was published in 1909; the date is noteworthy as showing that even at that age he found time for literary composition though he was not a professional writer. The work itself is of no particular importance. The volumes *Sei Storielle* (1917), *Gente di conoscenza* (1918), and *Il Figurinaio* (1920) are of a very different nature. In these the writer's literary skill and gift for psychological analysis are already well developed; his personality has taken shape and, especially in the pages of *Il Figurinaio*, he reveals himself as a true artist and a man of definite individuality. Cicognani at this period was a good deal of a naturalist in his taste for sharp realism, strong phraseology, and rather sordid subjects. Yet even here one is conscious of the two sides of his nature: he is a combination of the keen, scientific, even remorseless student and of the sincerely religious and warm-hearted human being. In *La Valia* (1923), certainly one of the best novels about the modern generation, these qualities are beautifully blended, though the choice of subject is again a little repugnant and the book leaves a somewhat bitter taste in the mouth. In *Villa Beatrice* (1932) is found the same strength and the same humanity, with the humanity being the predominant strain. The novel is no less convincing than *La Velia* for all that; in this study of a frigid woman Cicognani unites all the apparatus of modern realism with an emotional and religious understanding. Both of these books reveal also another characteristic of the author, his robust *campanilismo* (localism): he is a Florentine and every square, every alley, every corner of his native town is real and dear to him—and, it might be added, every conceivable Florentine type. This element is probably the basis of both the realism and the feeling in his art; it may be said to be the essence of the man. As Cicognani has become older he has grown away from fiction and devoted himself to painstaking and charming descriptions of the Florence of his childhood and youth. Such books as *L'Omino che à spento i fochi* (1937) and *L'Età favolosa* are rare in any language; perhaps in some ways they may be compared to Anatole France's (*q.v.*) re-evocations of his boyhood, but they have a Florentine sharpness and color of their own. Cicognani's Tuscan style is impeccable; he has all the virtues of the traditional Tuscan writers without any of the affectations of some of his contemporary fellow townsmen. His language is precise, yet full of warmth, smooth and graceful, yet sturdy and unpretentious. An Italian critic, Moscardelli, has well said of Cicognani that he is not a writer by profession; he is a writer *davvero* (by authentic instinct).

See: N. Moscardelli, *Anime e corpi* (1932), pp. 217–224; P. Pancrazi, *Scrittori italiani del novecento* (1934), pp. 43–53; A. Rommel, *Bruno Cicognani, der Mensch und der Künstler* (1938).

T. G. B.

Clarín, *see* Alas, Leopoldo.

Claudel, Paul (1868–, French poet, dramatist, and essayist), born in the village of Villeneuve-sur-Fère en Tardenois, on the fringe of the old province of Champagne, was the son of a middle-class official and the descendant of a peasant family. He was a brilliant pupil of the Lycée Louis-le-Grand in Paris, where he acquired an excellent knowledge of classical literatures and of philosophy. He soon revolted against his education which he considered pagan and sterile; he rediscovered Catholicism on Christmas night, 1886, in the cathedral of Notre-Dame in Paris and has been ever since an ardent mystic and believer. In 1898 he passed the examination for the French diplomatic service. He was a visitor in the symbolist *cénacles,* but never shared the bookish worship of literature as divorced from life which was then typical of many men of letters. He admired Mallarmé, Verlaine (on whom he wrote a long poem in 1922), and, above all, Rimbaud (*qq.v.*) whom, paradoxically enough, he revered as his religious as well as his literary master. From 1893 to 1934 he lived mostly far from France, first as consul in the United States, China, Germany, and Italy, then as minister in Rio de Janeiro and as ambassador in Tokyo, Washington, and Brussels. His career as a traveler in distant lands increased his conspicuous originality. Since his retirement he has lived in the country, in the province of Dauphiné, and has devoted much of his time to prose writings of a religious character.

Claudel is very widely cultured; he is conversant with Greek and Latin sacred and profane writers, with the Bible, with English poetry, and has displayed a penetrating insight into Dante (*Ode jubilaire,* 1921, on the 600th anniversary of Dante's death), Spain of the 16th century (*Le Soulier de satin,* 1929), the soul of Japan (*L'Oiseau noir dans le soleil levant,* 1927) and that of China (*Connaissance de l'est,* 1900). This last work, a fine series of poems in prose, introduces us to a deeply significant kind of exotic literature. The sources of Claudel's inspiration, however, are not primarily literary, but religious. To his robust and mystical Catholic faith, the world appears as instinct with divine presence and as a harmonious whole singing the glory of God. The task of the poet is to echo that music and to interpret that divine order. Claudel's impersonal and cosmic lyricism sings the beauty of creation, now with impassioned rhetoric and magnificent imagery, now with the tender humility of a naïve prayer. Instead of the traditional alexandrine line, in which his inspiration has always felt cramped, Claudel has substituted a varied rhythm reminiscent of biblical verse. His most ambitious and probably his greatest lyrical poetry is to be found in *Cinq Grandes Odes* (1910) and in *Cette Heure qui est entre le printemps et l'été* (1913; reprinted as *La Cantate à trois voix,* 1931). Two other volumes, *Corona Benignitatis Anni Dei* (1914) and *La Messe là-bas* (1919), also contain moving lyrics of a more humble and familiar character.

Claudel's powerful and synthetizing genius was naturally attracted by the dramatic form, in which his creative imagination, his architectonic gifts, and his profound sense of the inner conflict in man, torn between matter and spirit, were to find full play. Some of his dramas suffer from a formless lack of discipline or from an excessive and monotonous abstraction, such as *La Ville* (1890), *Le Repos du sep-*

tième jour (1901), and *Le Livre de Christophe Colomb* (1930). *L'Otage* (1910) is a well-built tragedy on a purely human plane, but too rigorous in its harsh logic. Two early dramas, *Tête d'or* (1889) and *L'Echange* (1893), the second of which has an imaginary American setting, contain brilliant flashes of strange lyricism and passages of sublime beauty. Claudel's two masterpieces, which rank among the few masterpieces of world drama since Shakespeare and Racine, are *L'Annonce faite à Marie* (1910, originally written as *La Jeune Fille Violaine*) and *Partage de midi* (1906, privately printed), a burning drama of human passion which ends in a hymn of divine love.

Claudel is no less admired as an essayist and as a prose writer. Besides a treatise of abstruse and unorthodox metaphysics, *Art poétique* (1906), and a subtle volume of unconventional sociological discussions, *Conversations dans le Loir-et-Cher* (1937), he has written some illuminating views on poetry and aesthetics in *Positions et propositions* (1928–1934) and beautiful religious, poetical, and humorous meditations in several periodicals (*Nouvelle Revue française, Mesures*) and in *Figures et paraboles* (1936). His French translation (1896–1920) of the Aeschylean trilogy of the *Oresteia* and his numerous commentaries on the Scriptures bear witness to the versatility and originality of a strange genius, one of the greatest in contemporary French literature. Many of Claudel's works have been translated into English.

See: J. de Tonquédec, *L'Œuvre de Claudel* (1917); E. Sainte-Marie Perrin, *Introduction à l'œuvre de Claudel* (1926); J. Madaule, *Le Génie de Paul Claudel* (1933) and *Le Drame de Paul Claudel* (1936).

H. P.

Claussen, Sophus (1865–1931, Danish poet, novelist, and journalist), was born on the island of Langeland, the son of a peasant farmer who rose to be a member of the Danish House of Representatives and served valiantly as such for 30 years. He received classical schooling in Copenhagen. After a sojourn of many years in France and Italy he returned in 1911 to Denmark.

Claussen, probably the most esoteric poet of the Danish school of symbolism and neoromanticism, was deeply influenced by Baudelaire (*q.v.*). He crusaded against conventions, clothed his ideas frequently in paradoxes as well as in symbolism. His most original results were achieved in his poems. *Pilefløter* (1899; Willow Flutes) contains the little masterpiece "Røg" (Smoke), which draws upon the modern industrial world—the symbols (rails, smoke) shifting and re-forming repeatedly. During the next 25 years Claussen put forth some 10 collections of poems. Various thoughts recur again and again: Pan is thus at times the young creative genius, newly sprung from the earth, with whom the poet identifies himself, or Pan is the great generating spirit of nature. Claussen has a neo-romantic conception of the poet's calling; through intuition the poet divines beforehand what science later works out laboriously. The paradoxical "Atomernes Oprør" (The Revolt of the Atoms) constitutes a solemn warning against world dissension. Claussen's Eros is usually a Don Juan in quest of the ideal, but one who definitely extracts honey out of each situation. The writer's style is capricious, perhaps most perfectly so in the lyrical prelude *Frk. Regnveir* (1894; Miss Rainy Weather). The essays, *Løvetandsfnug* (1918; Dandelion Down), *Foraarstaler* (1927; Spring Discourses), give clear, invaluable information on the trends of the times and on Claussen's own aesthetic theories, *e.g.*, his conviction that art, science, and religion represent parallel efforts to express the inconceivable, the true, the eternal. The author's novels, inlaid with lyrical travel descriptions and sprightly adventures generally in France and Spain, are less important than the poems and the essays.

See: H. G. Topsöe-Jensen, *Scandinavian Literature from Brandes to Our Day* (1929); Helge Kjaergaard, *Die dänische Literatur der neuesten Zeit (1871–1933)* (1934).

C. K. B.

Clemenceau, Georges (1841–1929, French statesman), born in Mouilleron-en-Pareds, Vendée, deserves a place in literature not only under the heading of parliamentary eloquence or political journalism (his articles at the time of the Dreyfus affair were collected in no less than seven volumes), but on account of other wide literary interests and almost limitless capacities. He wrote essays and short stories (*La Mêlée sociale*, 1895; *Le Grand Pan*, 1896; *Au fil des jours*, 1900; *Aux embuscades de la vie*, 1903; *Figures de Vendée*, 1903); tried his hand at the novel (*Les Plus Forts*, 1898; Eng. tr., *The Strongest*, 1919) and the drama (*Le Voile du bonheur*, with incidental music by Gabriel Fauré, 1901; Eng. tr., *The Veil of Happiness*, 1920); turned biographer (*Démosthène*, 1926; Eng. tr., 1926) and art critic (*Claude Monet: Les Nymphéas*, 1928; Eng. tr., *Claude Monet: The Water Lilies*, 1930);

assessed in somber and sarcastic tones the disappointing results of a decade of "peace" (*Grandeurs et misères d'une victoire,* 1930; Eng. tr., *Grandeur and Misery of Victory,* 1930); and left a huge philosophical testament entitled *Au soir de la pensée* (2 vols., 1927; Eng. tr., *In the Evening of My Thought,* 2 vols., 1929). Faithfully reminiscent of his intellectual dawn, Clemenceau's twilight is that of a 19th-century positivist who found it possible in theory as well as in practice to reconcile pessimistic materialism with humanitarian ideals.

See: Gustave Geffroy, *Georges Clemenceau; sa vie, son œuvre* (1919); Jean-Albert Bédé, "Paris et Clemenceau," *Renaissance,* I (1943), 391–406; Geoffrey Bruun, *Clemenceau* (1943).

J.-A. B.

Cocteau, Jean (1891–, French poet, dramatist, and novelist), absorbed at a tender age the earlier teachings of André Gide (*q.v.*) and has ever since been "pursuing his own youth." Every conceivable mood or mixture of moods colored in turn this fervent quest. On many occasions there stands revealed a tormented Cocteau almost tragically aware of human weakness, groping for certainty, afraid of love, afraid of life, afraid of death. *Le Potomak,* a fantastic medley of cartoons, prose, and verse composed in 1913 and published in 1919 ("definitive" ed., 1924), was an exploration of the subconscious, attended by gloomy forebodings. The haven of religion tempted him for a while but, after having secured the good offices of that experienced savior of souls, Jacques Maritain (*q.v.*; see *Lettre à Jacques Maritain* and the latter's *Réponse à Jean Cocteau,* 1926), the neophyte flippantly recanted and thumbed his nose at his spiritual director. "Artificial paradises" offered him no better escape (see *Opium: Journal d'une désintoxication,* 1930; Eng tr., *Opium: The Diary of an Addict,* 1932). Thus fortune had it that, despite Cocteau's low critical opinion of his youthful indiscretion, he did ultimately revert to the inspiration of *Le Potomak* (*La Fin du Potomak,* 1940).

More readily remembered, however, will be the sophisticated and exuberant Cocteau, the Prince Charming who, especially in his prime, so captured the fancy of Parisians that they felt powerless to resent his conceit and eccentricities. He became the astute magician and purveyor of his own publicity, whose tricks were legion, whether he permitted an exclusive night club to use the name of one of his works (*Le Bœuf sur le toit*) or decided, one fine morning, to refurbish Jules Verne's old *Tour du monde en 80 jours* and translate it into action (see *Mon Premier Voyage,* 1937; Eng. tr., *Round the World Again in Eighty Days,* 1937). He became, too, the incomparable promoter of new styles and new fashions, whose word in matters of taste was almost law as he sponsored with equal ease the painting of Pablo Picasso and Giorgio de Chirico, Igor Stravinsky and the Ballet Russe, the music of Erik Satie and the "Groupe des Six" (Georges Auric, Louis Durey, Arthur Honegger, Darius Milhaud, Francis Poulenc, Germaine Tailleferre), the first appearances of American jazz, the clown act of the Fratellini brothers, the motion pictures of Charles Chaplin. The story of Cocteau's own modernistic ballets (*e.g., Parade,* score by Erik Satie and scenery by Picasso, 1917; *Le Bœuf sur le toit, ou The Nothing Happens Bar,* score by Darius Milhaud, 1920; *Les Mariés de la Tour Eiffel,* score by the entire "Groupe des Six," 1921) and later of his theatre, is one of gradual progress and ultimate triumph built on a sure knowledge of how and how far the "strong honey" of novelty may be made palatable to the general public. In this Cocteau was helped immeasurably by the fact that he himself is a product of the *bourgeoisie bourgeoisante.* This prodigal son of a wealthy notary, born in Maisons-Laffitte, a prosperous community near Paris, conceals within his nimble mind an ample provision of atavistic shrewdness or even conservatism. It is significant, for instance, that on aesthetic grounds he should call for "order through anarchy" and label himself a "member of the classical left."

The definite pattern of Cocteau's arabesques emerges clearly from his poems (*Poésie 1916–1923,* 1924; *Opéra, œuvres poétiques 1925–1927,* 1927; *Mythologie,* 1934; *Allégories,* 1941) and his critical essays (*e.g., Le Rappel à l'ordre,* 1926, Eng. tr., *A Call to Order,* 1926; *Essai de critique indirecte,* 1932). Often enough he is ranged with the "literary cubists," that is to say, with a group of writers who, mostly through direct acquaintance, underwent the influence of Pablo Picasso. They transfer to literature that painter's contempt of traditional rhetorics, of perspective, of anthropomorphic reality. By treating language as he does his "cubes" they achieve a deformation of speech whereby certain elements ordinarily associated are dissociated, or vice versa. The result is a new, synthetic image suddenly flashed on the screen of the poet's consciousness. Admittedly this image may turn out to be little more than a play on words. At best, however, it is counted upon to shock its creator into a brief mystical trance, thus affording him a glimpse of Beauty asleep in the "meadows of inner silence."

This *art poétique* was substantially that of Max Jacob, André Salmon, and Guillaume Apollinaire (*qq.v.*), all three Cocteau's elders in point of age and performance, all three authentic bohemians and far less hampered than he by artificial constrictions. Cocteau's not inconsiderable role will have been, in the last analysis, to exploit their ideas on a grand scale. Taking a leaf from Baudelaire (*q.v.*), he conceives of all art as poetry and of verse as but one of the wires through which the mysterious "fluid" may pass. Thus he will call his criticism "poésie critique" and his ballets "poésie chorégraphique." Except for *Portraits-Souvenir 1900–1914* (1935), references to his "poésie autobiographique" have been made above. The "poésie de roman" includes *Thomas l'imposteur* and *Le Grand Ecart* (both 1923; Eng. tr., *Thomas the Impostor* and *The Grand Ecart,* both 1925) and *Les Enfants terribles* (1929; Eng. tr., *Enfants terribles,* 1930), a novel of troubled adolescence which many consider Cocteau's masterpiece. The "poésie de théâtre" boasts modernistic adaptations of Sophocles, Shakespeare, and, most recently, Tasso (*Antigone,* with scenery by Picasso and Renaissance costumes by Jean Hugo, 1922; *Roméo et Juliette,* 1924; *Œdipe-Roi,* 1928, unperformed; *Renaud et Armide,* 1943), as well as an original, one-act tragedy, *Orphée* (1926; Eng. tr., 1933). It includes such diversified subjects as *La Voix humaine* (1930), a one-character playlet consisting exclusively of a telephone conversation; *La Machine infernale* (1934; Eng. tr., *The Infernal Machine,* 1936); *Les Chevaliers de la Table Ronde* (1937); *Les Parents terribles* (1938); *Les Monstres sacrés* (1940); *La Machine à écrire* (1941; dates given for Cocteau's plays are those of first performance). Finally, Cocteau's "poésie cinématographique" (*Le Sang d'un Poëte,* 1933; *Tristan et Iseult,* after 1940; *Eternel Retour,* 1944), together with his "poésie graphique" (*Dessins,* 1923; *Vingt-cinq Dessins d'un dormeur,* 1928; *Soixante Dessins pour "Les Enfants terribles,"* 1934), completes the extraordinary picture of an extremely versatile artist.

See: Pierre Dominique, *Quatre Hommes entre vingt: Montherlant, Morand, Cocteau, Drieu La Rochelle* (1924); Marcel Raymond, *De Baudelaire au surréalisme* (1933), pp. 290–308 and *passim;* Edith Sitwell, *A Poet's Notebook* (1943), *passim;* Claude Mauriac, *Jean Cocteau, ou la Vérité du mensonge* (1945).

J.-A. B.

Coelho, José Francisco de Trindade, *see* Trindade Coelho.

Colette, Sidonie Gabrielle (pseud. Colette Willy, 1873–, French novelist), born at Saint-Sauveur-en-Puisaye in Burgundy, was raised in the country and developed a keen understanding of it and a profound love of nature. After her marriage to Henry Gauthier-Villars, a music critic, she lived in Paris among artists and newspapermen. For six years after 1906, the date of her divorce, she acted as a music-hall dancer and mime. A second marriage, to Henri de Jouvenel, brought her back to the literary world, where she rapidly established herself as a distinguished novelist and newspaperwoman.

Her work is essentially subjective. A reflection of her childhood and of her first years of marriage can be found in the Claudine series, *Claudine à l'école* (1900), *Claudine à Paris* (1901), *Claudine en ménage* (1902), *Claudine s'en va* (1903), which she wrote in collaboration with her husband and signed with his penname, Willy. This collaboration stopped in 1904, and from 1904 to 1916 Mme Colette published under the name Colette Willy her remarkable *Dialogues de bêtes* (1904), followed by *Sept Dialogues de bêtes* (1905), and several of her most famous books, *La Retraite sentimentale* (1907), *Les Vrilles de la vigne* (1908), *L'Ingénue libertine* (1909; a reprint of two novels, *Minne* and *Les Egarements de Minne,* published with Willy's signature in 1904 and 1905). Three volumes were inspired by her life in the music hall, *La Vagabonde* (1910), *L'Envers du music-hall* (1913), *L'Entrave* (1913). From 1916 (*La Paix chez les bêtes*) to 1921 Mme Colette signed "Colette (Colette Willy)," and from 1921 on simply "Colette." This latest period marks the climax of her career. *La Fin de Chéri* (1926) provided a pathetic ending to *Chéri* (1920). In *La Maison de Claudine* (1923) and in *Sido* (1929) Colette draws a delightfully candid picture of her childhood. In *Mes Apprentissages* (1936) she recalls her life with Willy and the début of her literary career. *La Naissance du jour* (1928), *La Seconde* (1929), *Duo* (1934), *Bella Vista* (1937), *Chambre d'hôtel* (1940), *Julie de Carneilhan* (1941), and *Le Képi* (1943) are among her latest productions.

The world of Mme Colette is the world of the senses. Her characters follow their instincts with a sort of fatalistic resignation. They are slaves of their impulses, and having no spiritual interests to support them, they drift along in helpless loneliness. These sad specimens of humanity are presented by Colette with a subtle psychological insight and in a style which is unanimously praised for its originality and its power of suggestion. Her descriptions and understanding of animals and nature are unequaled in French contemporary literature, and Mme Colette will always remain one of the greatest stylists of her time.

See: Fernand Keller and André Lautier, *Colette; son œuvre* (1923); Paul Reboux, *Colette, ou le Génie du style* (1925); Jean Larnac, *Colette; sa vie, son œuvre* (1927); Claude Chauvière, *Colette* (1931).

M. E. C.

Collett, Camilla (1813–1895, Norwegian author and feminist), was born in Kristiansand. As the sister of the poet Henrik Wergeland, she belonged to a highly gifted family and was herself possessed of rare beauty, wit, and charm. In 1841 she married Professor Jonas Collett, who died in 1851, but whose influence on her career was very important. He encouraged her to write and sympathized fully with what became the leading purpose of her life—the emancipation of women. At that time no opportunities for education or paying work were open to women, and they were moreover bound by the most rigid conventions of "womanliness." It was the violence done their emotional life that seemed to Camilla Collett to lie at the heart of the problem, and this was the subject of her first book, *Amtmandens døtre* (1855; The Governor's Daughters). It was not only the first cry of feminism but the first modern novel in Norway, and, though imperfect in construction, was so vibrant with noble indignation that it has retained its vitality to this day. It was followed by short stories, sketches, and recollections of her parental home. From 1872 Camilla Collett devoted her authorship entirely to the cause of women. Her most original contribution was *Fra de stummes leir* (1877; From the Camp of the Silent), a series of trenchant reviews in which she essayed to show how a degraded conception of women pervaded all literature, from books intended for bread-and-butter misses to the works of Byron, Goethe, and Dumas *fils*. Even Ibsen (*q.v.*) came in for castigation. In his early heroines, notably Solveig in *Peer Gynt*, she saw the incarnation of a sorry old feminine ideal which she called on Ibsen to destroy rather than exalt. Jonas Lie (*q.v.*), almost alone, won her approval for his self-reliant heroines. Camilla Collett was a personal friend of the Ibsens, and the change in Ibsen's portrayal of women has been traced in part to her influence. Jonas Lie was also indebted to her.

See: A. Collett, *Camilla Colletts livs historie* (1911); I. Grøndahl and O. Raknes, *Chapters in Norwegian Literature* (1923).

H. A. L.

Coloma y Roldán, Luis (1851–1914, Spanish novelist), born in Jerez de la Frontera, in the province of Cádiz in southern Spain, studied law in the University of Seville and then entered the Company of Jesus in 1873.

Padre Coloma occupies a minor position in the group of so-called Spanish naturalists who modified the excesses of French naturalism (*q.v.*) by putting it more in tune with Spanish realistic feeling. His literary production is limited to two novels, a series of stories, and some historical writing. His principal work is the novel *Pequeñeces* (1890), a satire of the aristocracy of Madrid during the period of the restoration of the house of Bourbon. This novel enjoyed an immediate but not enduring success; the author shows skill in a colorful portrayal of society, but the characters are overdrawn and the language too subject to foreign influences. The other novel is *Boy* (1910). Coloma's writings of a historical nature include *Retratos de antaño* (1895) and *Jeromín* (1905–1907).

See: José A. Balseiro, *Novelistas españoles modernos* (1933).

E. G. L.

Comisso, Giovanni (1895–, Italian novelist), was born in Treviso. He fought in the battle for Fiume on the side of Gabriele D'Annunzio (*q.v.*). In *Al vento dell'Adriatico* (1928), he describes his adventures at Fiume and reveals in his literary style strong traces of D'Annunzian sensualism. After the First World War, Comisso went to sea, sailed the Mediterranean, and visited many ports along the Adriatic; in *Gente di mare* (1929) he tells of these experiences. The book is noteworthy for its pungent style and the author's delicate sensitivity to the objects that attract him. In Comisso's writings there is hardly a trace of plot. What strikes the reader is the intense, impressionistic, but somewhat adolescent curiosity of the author concerning the world about him.

See: Pietro Pancrazi, *Scrittori italiani del novecento* (1934), pp. 237–242.

P. M. R.

Conrad, Michael Georg (1846–1927, German critic, novelist, and editor), was born in

Gnodstadt in Franconia. After studying philology, he taught in German schools in Geneva and, for five years, in Naples. His writings during this period were devoted to political and pedagogical subjects and to Freemasonry. In 1876 he gave up his teaching career for one of journalism and literature. Leaving Italy, he went to Paris where he became personally acquainted with Zola (*q.v.*), whose literary activities he discussed in a series of journalistic articles published in German papers, thus becoming with Oskar Welten a pioneer theorist of German naturalism (*q.v.*). His best critical essays were published in this period: "Der Grossmeister des Naturalismus" in *Parisiana* (1880); "Zola und Daudet" in *Französische Charakterköpfe* (1881); "Kritische Zola-Studien" in *Madame Lutetia* (1883). In these articles Conrad, with characteristic enthusiasm, portrays Zola as a courageous and idealistic moralist, a creative novelist of the first rank, and an incisive and fearless critic and defends his scientific and aesthetic theories against the bitter attacks directed against him by contemporary German criticism. Conrad returned to Munich in 1882 and in 1885 founded the first of the naturalistic journals, *Die Gesellschaft,* which gave the growing literary radicalism a rallying point; he gathered around him the various elements of the naturalistic group. With the rise of the Berlin *Freie Bühne* Conrad's influence declined. Two later critical and autobiographical works are important for an understanding of the naturalistic period in Germany, *Von Emile Zola bis Gerhart Hauptmann* (1902) and *Emile Zola* (1905).

Conrad's activity as novelist—extending from his early stories *Lutetias Töchter* (1883) and *Totentanz der Liebe* (1884) through a novel of Munich life, *Was die Isar rauscht* (1887), to a fantastic novel of the future, *In purpurner Finsternis* (1895), and a story of the Bavarian king Ludwig II, *Majestät* (1902)—was of lesser importance in the development of modern German literature. In his later career Conrad sat one term in the Reichstag as deputy for the Demokratische Volkspartei (1893).

See: O. Stauf von der March, *Michael Georg Conrad* (1925).

W. H. R.

Conradi, Hermann (1862–1890, German poet and novelist), of middle-class parentage, grew up a delicate, sensitive child whose ill-health deepened his bookish interests and morbid introspection. By 1880 his poems and critical essays were already appearing in newspapers. His acquaintance with Heinrich and Julius Hart (*q.v.*), whose *Kritische Waffengänge* (1882–1884) gave a critical account of contemporary German literature, was fruitful for his own literary development. In 1884 he settled in Berlin, one of the new literary centers, and soon was writing feverishly. With Wilhelm Arent, who financed the venture and signed as editor, and Karl Henckell (1864–1929), whose extended productivity (poems of nature, love, social injustice) is preserved in five volumes of *Gesammelte Werke* (1923), Conradi published an anthology of contemporary lyric poetry, *Moderne Dichter-Charaktere* (1885). In his introduction he castigated the trivial, shallow, and conventional poetry of the day and expressed the need for a modern literature with new form and new content. He envisaged another era "of great souls and deep feelings." In Conradi's remaining years there were published in quick succession a volume of stories, *Brutalitäten* (1886); a collection of lyrics, perhaps his best work, *Lieder eines Sünders* (1887); two pathological novels of the "Übergangsmensch," *Phrasen* (1887) and *Adam Mensch* (1889); and his psychological evaluation of the age, *Wilhelm II. und die junge Generation* (1889).

An early death cut short a career that gave promise of greater achievement. Conradi was potentially among the most talented of his generation, but left nothing of lasting value. In his work are indications of a deeper understanding of the problems of his age and of a more serious striving for an artistic ideal than he is usually credited with, but his general immaturity and his exaggerated style are fatal limitations. Feeling deeply, but unstable and constantly in conflict with himself and the world, he is perhaps the most articulate representative of his group; intoxicated with his own importance, rebellious and indignant yet inextricably bound to the past, opposed to naturalism (*see* German naturalism) but reflecting many of its characteristics, he saw the conflict and confusion of the times and longed for a vaguely felt but never clearly expressed ideal. He sensed the tragic futility of his unhappy, tempestuous life and characterized himself as "a son of his age, but not its savior" who "like a meteor is lost in the night."

See: P. Ssymank, "Leben Hermann Conradis," in Conradi, *Gesammelte Schriften,* ed. by P. Ssymank and G. W. Peters, I (1911), xix–ccliv; V. B. Kellett, "Hermann Conradi; a Study and Interpretation of the Uebergangsmensch" (unpublished dissertation, Univ. of Michigan, 1943).

W. A. R.

Conscience, Hendrik (1812–1883, Flemish novelist), was born in Antwerp. His significance for his native Flanders is not to be measured by literary standards alone, since his work has also political and moral implications.

The son of a minor Napoleonic official, who had come from France to help in the construction of the French invasion fleet, and of a Flemish mother, Conscience became the herald of a renewed national Flemish feeling in Belgium. While Flemish as a language was officially neglected in a centralized Belgium that had finally attained independence, his romantic masterpiece *De Leeuw van Vlaanderen* (1838; Eng. tr., *The Lion of Flanders,* 1855–1857), dealing with the defeat of the French aristocratic army by the Flemish municipal militias at Kortrijk (Courtrai) in 1302, gave his readers the realization of their former cultural greatness and of their democratic achievements through the ages. All his life he was to be the national hero and the symbol of Flemish intellectual rebirth. It was said of him that "he taught his people to read." He indeed provided them with a great number of historical novels in the tradition of Sir Walter Scott. In these books the dripping sentimentality is nearly always compensated for by a clever and impressive handling of mass movements. His descriptions of battles and of isolated encounters live up to the best models of contemporary fellow romanticists. His psychological analysis is weak, and the pictures of his heroes, and especially his heroines, are schematic and unsatisfactory. They are painted in the traditional black-or-white formula, but this deficiency endeared them all the more to less demanding country readers. With all its defects—faults in the construction as well as consistent weaknesses in the expression—*De Leeuw van Vlaanderen* became a romantic classic, not only in Belgium but in many other countries.

Among the more than a hundred volumes he wrote, many are devoted to pictures of rural felicity. Conscience was an ardent lover of nature, a sentimental botanist. To him the country and its most minute details were the symbols of God's goodness and greatness. It inspired him to a continued gratefulness. The melancholy landscape of the Kempen, north and east of Antwerp, provided the themes for a number of charming and idyllic short novels: *De Loteling* (1850; Eng. tr., *The Conscript,* 1864), *Rikke-Tikke-Tak* (1851; Eng. tr., *Ricketicketack,* 1856), ***Baes Gansendonck*** (Boss Gansendonck). A sincere idealist, he had no fault to find with the peasant folk and their rustic simplicity. He was more critical, although still in a mild fashion, when dealing with provincial town life. He castigated the parvenus in *Siska van Rosemael* (1844; Siska of Rosemael) and objected to the adventurers of his day who left the good old country for San Francisco in 1849. The hero of *Het Goudland* (1854; The Land of Gold) is an exemplary failure.

Conscience wanted to be a moral writer and prided himself upon the fact that by his writings "he never made a maiden blush." It can be added that neither did he ever bore them, which is an even greater achievement. He dealt but little with the social problems of his days. Although he was conscious of their importance, they did not push him to revolt. He was always a conciliatory and charming figure and enjoyed an enormous popularity. His works were translated into many languages, including, in addition to those already mentioned, the following English and American titles: *Sketches from Flemish Life* (1840); *The Progress of a Painter* (1852); *The Good Mother* (1852); *Tales of Flemish Life* (1854); *Tales of Old Flanders* (1855); *Tales and Romances* (6 vols., 1855–1857); *The Poor Gentleman* (1856); *The Miser* (1856); *Tales* (6 vols., 1857); *The Headman's Son* (1861); *The Village Innkeeper* (1867); *The Happiness of Being Rich* (1869); *Tales* (5 vols., 1889); *Popular Tales* (6 vols., 1902–1906).

Victor Hugo and Dumas *père* praised him highly. In the original Flemish his books suffer from a lack of linguistic sensibility and from an overabundance of Gallicisms which he never completely overcame.

See: Emmanuel de Bom, *Hendrik Conscience* (1912); Anton Jacob, *Briefwisseling van, met en over Hendrik Conscience* (2 vols., 1913–1922); Eugeen de Bock, *H. Conscience en de Opkomst van de Vlaamsche Romantiek* (1919).

J.-A. G.

Copeau, Jacques (1879–, French theatrical producer and critic), was born and educated in Paris. He spent a year in Denmark, managed a factory in the Ardennes, and sold modern paintings in a Paris gallery before discovering his vocation. As drama critic for the *Ermitage* (1904–1906) and the *Grande Revue* (1907–1910) he wrote severe, prophetic articles, collected in *Critiques d'un autre temps* (1923). One of the founders and original editors, in 1909, of the *Nouvelle Revue française* he later became the editor in chief of that periodical (1912–1914).

In 1911 the staging of his adaptation of Dostoevski's (*q.v.*) *The Brothers Karamazov* at the Théâtre des Arts of Jacques Rouché brought him into contact with Dullin (*q.v.*), who with Jouvet (*q.v.*) was to second and to continue his revitalization of the French theatre. In the autumn of 1913 he opened the doors of the Théâtre du Vieux Colombier, in the street of the same name in Paris, with a brilliant company of young actors whom he had been training in the countryside. This repertory theatre, animated by a youthful enthusiasm and a disgust for the bombast and conventions of the commercial theatres, inaugurated a new era of simplicity and sincerity. With a more imaginative sense of the theatre than Antoine (*q.v.*) and a more consistent taste than Lugné-Poe (*q.v.*), Copeau effected a revolution, turning the French stage definitively away from the realistic reproduction of life and the confusion of the arts to an authentically poetic interpretation of life. During the first season (1913–1914) a broad repertory, extending from Molière and Shakespeare to Jules Renard (*q.v.*) and Paul Claudel (*q.v.*), from Musset and Henry Becque (*q.v.*) to plays by the young Ghéon, Roger Martin du Gard, and Schlumberger (*qq.v.*), taught Parisian audiences how varied and exciting an "art theatre" could be. In less than a year Copeau had created a community of dramatic workers that can be compared only to Stanislavsky's Moscow Art Theatre. But the war interrupted his effort to create "a refuge for future talent." Fortunately, however, the American financier Otto Kahn and the French government enabled his well-trained company to play in French at the Garrick Theatre in New York (1917–1919), where they set an example for such American groups as the Theatre Guild. Returning to Paris in 1920, the Vieux Colombier enriched its repertory with such important creations as *Cromedeyre-le-Vieil* by Jules Romains, *Le Plaisir du hasard* by René Benjamin, *Saül* by André Gide, and *Le Paquebot Tenacity* by Charles Vildrac (*qq.v.*). In October, 1920, Copeau realized his ideal of establishing a school for the study of all aspects of the dramatic art. The loss of Dullin in 1919 and of Jouvet in 1922, who left to found their own theatres, and Copeau's increasing absorption in his school, while impoverishing the Théâtre du Vieux Colombier itself, only served to spread its influence. Copeau had accomplished his task, for the seed had taken root; and when the theatre closed in 1924 he took a small and young group back to the country "to start all over again from the beginning."

Through his own work and through his disciples Copeau has continued to infuse new life into the French theatre, and most of the groups of the 20's and 30's can be traced directly to him. Named one of the four *metteurs en scène* of the Comédie Française in 1936, he became director of that official theatre in 1940. He occupies a place among such outstanding artists of the modern theatre as Adolphe Appia, Gordon Craig, Max Reinhardt, and Constantin Stanislavsky.

See: W. Frank, *The Art of the Vieux-Colombier* (1918); Copeau, *Souvenirs du Vieux-Colombier* (1931); R. Brasillach, *Animateurs de théâtre* (1936).

J. O'B.

Coppée, François (1842–1908, French poet, playwright, and novelist), was born in Paris, the son of a modest official at the Ministry of War; he could not afford to complete his university studies and himself found employment in the same ministry. He remained there until he was appointed assistant librarian of the Senate (Palais du Luxembourg), two years later becoming archivist of the Théâtre Français. In the meanwhile he had succeeded, thanks to Mendès (*q.v.*), in joining the group of young poets called Parnassians. His election to the French Academy in 1884 allowed him to live, with his mother and sister, on the income from his writings. He had had a great disappointment in love, the aristocratic mother of a young Scandinavian girl having considered the match a *mésalliance*. His philosophy was for a number of years that of an agnostic; a severe illness brought him back to the creed of his younger years. The history of this conversion is related in the preface to *La bonne souffrance* (1898). When Coppée joined the ranks of the anti-Dreyfusards, there resulted a painful estrangement from many of his old friends.

Coppée is known in France chiefly as a poet. He contributed to the successive issues of *Le Parnasse contemporain* (1866, 1869, 1877), but, while he may well be regarded as a Parnassian so far as the metrical form of his poetry is concerned, the epithet does not fit his philosophy. Far from being "impassible" he is, on the contrary, sentimental. Pity for the suffering poor is the fundamental theme of all that came from his pen. This is borne out by the very titles of his works—*Intimités* (1868), *Les Humbles* (1872), *Deux Douleurs* (one-act drama, 1870), *Contes tout simples* (1894). He carried the sentimental note into his *Contes en vers,* which were very popular at the time (*e.g.*, "La Grève des forgerons," "Le Petit Epicier de Montmartre"). He also left several volumes of *Contes en prose,* for which he was, during many years, better known in the United States than for his poetry.

He had achieved sudden fame in 1869 when the Odéon theatre staged a little one-act play in verse, *Le Passant,* the two characters of which (Zanetto and Sylvie) were enacted by the two most applauded French actresses of the day, Mme Sarah Bernhardt and Mme Agard. He wrote other one-act plays, *Le Luthier de Crémone* (1876) and *Le Pater* (1876—a drama of the days of the Commune, which had been suppressed by the censor), as well as two great political dramas, *Severo Torelli* (1883) in five acts and *Pour la couronne* (1895) in three acts. This last was received with great acclaim.

Since his death Coppée's prestige has greatly diminished. His sympathy for the underprivileged has been termed insincere, and his style has sounded bombastic to the cynics of a later generation. Yet, while such a critic as Lalou has not a good word to say of him and speaks of his "detestable sentimental simplicity," Zola (*q.v.*) praises him for having raised the banner of "naturalism in poetry." That Coppée was accepted as a great writer in his day is beyond a doubt, and it seems improbable that the harsh judgments of more recent critics will be regarded as final by posterity.

See: M. de Lescure, *François Coppée; l'homme, la vie et l'œuvre* (1889); L. Le Meur, *La Vie et l'œuvre de François Coppée* (1932).

A. Sz.

Corazzini, Sergio (1887–1907, Italian poet), was born in Rome. He died there of tuberculosis at the age of 20 after a brief period of precocious literary activity from 1904 to 1907. He belongs to that group of "twilight" writers (*i crespuscolari*) which included his friends Aldo Palazzeschi, Marino Moretti, and Fausto Maria Martini (*qq.v.*).

Corazzini's first poetry shows especially the influence of D'Annunzio's (*q.v.*) *Poema paradisiaco,* of Pascoli (*q.v.*), and of the French symbolists (*see* French symbolism). His interest, like Pascoli's, is centered upon the humble things of everyday existence; for Corazzini they are symbols of a monotonous suffering, the visible silence that is the reality of every day and in view of which he rebels against the grandiose passionate world of poets like D'Annunzio. Corazzini's earliest lyrics express this suffering in a tone of bewilderment and childlike simplicity, as in "Dolore" in *Le Dolcezze* (1904), and "A Carlo Simoneschi" in *L'Amaro Calice* (1905). In his later poems, *Libro per la sera della domenica* (1906), this sadness becomes ironic. Sometimes his emotion loses contact with any specific situation, and the poet's suffering dominates what is otherwise a spiritual void. The abstract emotions Melancholy, Hope, and Despair are the actors; the scene is the poet's state of mind. This poetry, unrhetorical in intent and technique, draws its dramatic force from a paradox. Abandoning hope as illusory, the poet finds life meaningless. As suffering is futile, so is the expression of it. Hence the poet should become indifferent, an attitude which would actually render self-expression unnecessary. Thus, aware of his spiritual exhaustion and impotency and not capable of a total indifference, Corazzini turns his irony against himself. Some critics consider Corazzini's poetry as the final expression of the decadence present in the works of D'Annunzio and Pascoli. For others he forms part of that literary twilight after the sun of D'Annunzio has set. It cannot be denied, however, that his state of mind is not merely personal but had meaning and reality for many of his generation; it is echoed by many and finally receives a comprehensive treatment in the poetry of Gozzano (*q.v.*).

See: G. Cuchetti, *Un Antesignano dei crepuscolari* (1929); C. Pellizzi, *La Letteratura del nostro secolo* (1929), pp. 314–316; W. Binni, *La Poetica del decadentismo italiano* (1936), pp. 127, 131, 139.

S. C. P.

Corbière, Tristan (pseud. of Edouard Joachim Corbière, 1845–1875, French poet), was born at Coat-Congar in Brittany. His father, the son of a naval officer, served in the navy, founded several short-lived newspapers, and wrote many books before marrying, at 50, a girl of 18 and becoming the director of the Morlaix branch of a Le Havre steamship company. Young Corbière attended school at Saint-Brieuc and Nantes. At 16, his health seriously impaired, he returned to Morlaix, afterward settling at Roscoff. It was there that, except for a three months' sojourn in Italy, a short trip to Palestine, and less than four years in Paris, he spent the rest of his life. He died before reaching his 30th year.

The fate of Corbière has been a curious one. A central figure in modern French poetry, he has been called the successor to Villon, the brother of Verlaine (*q.v.*), the predecessor of Laforgue (*q.v.*), yet *Les Amours jaunes* (1873) remained virtually unknown until Verlaine devoted to it a chapter of his book *Les Poètes maudits* (1884).

Corbière's poetry takes its place between the romantics and Baudelaire (*q.v.*). The romantics, contemporary with the rise of industrialism, often made of poetry an escape and, Corbière thought, created a fictitious nature. Corbière did not like Hugo at all. His poetry was in direct opposition to the great romantic's gentle, poetic melancholy in *Les Contemplations.* A startlingly sardonic note rings through his work. He caricatures the rhetorics of romanticism and the set romantic feelings. Corbière's sailors are realistic and alive, never shadowy, artificial heroes like Hugo's.

Baudelaire, aware of the unreality of the work of the romantic school, had turned to introspection. His reaction against the anti-intellectualism of the romanticists had led to an abuse of the intellect. Here too, in Corbière's opinion, there was a loss of contact with the outside world. Corbière tried to counteract both tendencies by a genuine return to nature, by going back to the simple primary emotions, by contact with unspoiled sensibility. In reasserting the importance of the life of instinct common to all men, he tried to restore man's confidence in man, to give its proper place to something that was in danger of being denied. His attachment to instinct, the earth, and the sea is an expression of his belief in human nature.

Corbière's poetry may be viewed as a plea for the integrity of man. He believed that the experiences arising out of the changing world were real, as were the old unchanging impulses and needs. If the new feelings are to be seen in their true perspective, he argued, they must be treated as modifications of the great primary emotions and related to them.

See: Paul Verlaine, *Les Poètes maudits* (1884); Rémy de Gourmont, *Le Livre des masques* (1896); René Martineau, *Tristan Corbière* (1925); Alexandre Arnoux, *Une Ame et pas de violon, Tristan Corbière* (1929).

P. B.

Coromines, Pere (1870–1939, Catalonian prose writer), a refugee in America, was the first Catalonian author to die here after the exodus of 1939. In his last impressions, written in France and Argentina, Coromines saw in the Catalonian dispersion something similar to that of the Hebrews; from that fact comes the title of his posthumous notes, unfinished and issued fragmentarily by the publishing branch of the journal *Catalunya* of Buenos Aires, *Diari de la Diàspora* (Diary of the Diaspora). He was born in Barcelona to a family from Ampurias; in that city he obtained his secondary education and pursued studies in law. From his university years date his first contacts with the common people whom he would have liked to inculcate with his theories, a combination of romantic anarchism and an almost mystic goodness. A misunderstanding of his motives brought upon him a death sentence from which he escaped almost miraculously. Upon leaving the fortress of Montjuic, where he had been imprisoned, he produced his first book, *Les presons imaginàries* (1899; The Imaginary Prisons), the title of which was an indication of the author's idealism. The earnest desire for goodness which constituted the guiding star of his whole life was proclaimed in 1911 with the publication of his *Vida austera* (Austere Life), a work which won him the acclaim of critics, a kind of "modern effort in the search for saintliness."

Pere Coromines also played an active role in politics; he was one of the founders of the old *Esquerra catalana* (Catalonian Left), an organ of Catalonianism; his journalistic campaigns, carried on through the medium of *Poble Català* (Catalonian People), are a model of enthusiasm—and not exempt from grave errors in political tact. After many years of a resulting ostracism, during which he dedicated himself to practicing law and to his literary tasks, he returned to active political life with the establishment of the republic in 1931. He was one of those who drew up the statute of autonomy of his country and among the first *consejeros* that the government of Catalonia had. All of his work is stamped with a deep Catalonian spirit, and even in the philosophic themes he attains a popular tone always in good taste. In addition to the works already mentioned, the following, from an extensive list, should be noted: *Les hores d'amor serenes* (1912; The Serene Hours of Love); *Les gràcies de l'Empordá* (1919; The Graces of Empordá); *Cartes d'un visionari* (1921; Letters of a Visionary); *Estudi sobre el pensament filòsofic dels jueus espanyols a l'Edat Mitjana* (1921; Studies concerning the Philosophical Thought of the Spanish Jews in the Middle Ages); *A recés dels Tamarius* (1925; In the Shadow of the Tamarind Tree); a trilogy, *En Tomàs de Bajalta—Silén* (1925), *Pigmalió* (1928), and *Prometeu* (1934); *Interpretació del vuit-cents català* (1937; Interpretation of the Catalonian Penny). Under the title *El perfecte dandi* (The Perfect Dandy), which is the title of the first story in the book, the journal *Catalunya* of Buenos Aires issued in 1940, after his death, some of Coromines's unpublished writings. He belonged to the Institut d'Estudis Catalans, the most important cultural institution of Catalonia, and was head of the scientific section. Some of his works have been translated into French, Italian, and Spanish. In his last essays, left in manuscript in Buenos Aires, one feels the deep homesickness that was oppressing him, offset only by the unshakable faith in the resurrection of his country.

See: "Advertiment," in Coromines, *El perfecte dandi;* J. Pous i Pagès, "Pere Coromines i el seu temps," *Revista de Catalunya* (Barcelonia), No. 97, March, 1940.

J. M. M. i V.

Corradini, Enrico (1865–1931, Italian playwright, novelist, and founder of Italian nationalism), was born at Samminiatello, near Montelupo, in the province of Florence. After graduation from the Royal Institute of Advanced Studies of Florence he began a literary career, attracted by the rising glory of D'Annunzio (*q.v.*). In 1892 Corradini founded a literary review entitled *Germinal,* by means of which he sought to contribute to the efforts that were being made to renovate Italian culture. At first he did not meet with success as a literary journalist and was forced to teach in order to earn a livelihood. Dissatisfied with his teaching, Corradini soon attempted to form a new literary group, larger and more vigorous than the preceding one. The attempt was successful through a combination of fortunate circumstances: the intelligent liberality of his father, the audacity of a young publisher, the unselfishness and courage of the group, and, most of all, the sympathy and support given by D'Annunzio. As he was more inclined toward journalism than the others, Corradini became the director of the review, which, founded in 1896, took the name of the *Marzocco.* Indefatigable and conscientious in his efforts to assure the success of the new enterprise, Corradini never received any compensation for his work as director. Adopting as its motto *multa renascentur,* the *Marzocco* sought to reaffirm the lasting values of the spirit and culture of Tuscany. The unprecedented success of the *Marzocco* gave Corradini the opportunity to train himself in criticism and to develop a robust, sincere, and personal style which later became a permanent characteristic of all his political writings.

Corradini's early critical studies of literature and the theatre evince his desire to lead the Italian theatre back to bourgeois models and more especially to those set up by Ibsen and Maeterlinck (*qq.v.*). His dramatic short story *Dopo la morte* (1894), on which D'Annunzio based his *Gioconda,* shows the author's desire to portray strong emotional conflicts. In his novels *Santamaura* (1896), *La Gioia* (1897), and *La Verginità* (1898) and even in his dramatic composition *La Leonessa* (1899), Corradini shows the influence of D'Annunzio, but more in form than in spirit. His power to portray characters with deep dramatic significance may best be studied in the plays *Giulio Cesare* (1902; Eng. tr., 1929) and *Carlotta Corday* (1908). In *Giulio Cesare,* considered the best of his literary works because of its style and depth of thought, the author presented the hero of Rome as a character of intrinsic value in the history of Italy.

Important as is the place of Corradini in Italian literature and criticism, in the life of his country he occupies a much more significant position as the founder and leader of the Italian nationalist movement which, in November, 1903, resulted in the establishment of the review *Regno.* With its vigorous nationalist program the *Regno* soon attracted several promising young men, including Giovanni Papini, Giuseppe Prezzolini, and Giuseppe Antonio Borgese (*qq.v.*). The articles Corradini published during this period are collected in two volumes, *La Vita nazionale* (1907) and *L'Ombra della vita* (1908). In February, 1905, Corradini abandoned the *Regno,* but several years later resumed expounding his nationalist ideas in the *Idea nazionale,* a review established in 1911 under his directorship.

In addition to two patriotic novels, *La Patria lontana* (1910) and *La Guerra lontana* (1911), in which the author dealt with problems of political importance, Corradini also wrote during this period works in support of Italy's expansionistic program. A synthesis of his political philosophy is contained in *L'Unità e la potenza delle nazioni* (1922) and *Discorsi politici* (1923). Of interest too are his *Diario postbellico* (1924) and *Fascismo vita d'Italia* (1925). In his *Riforma politica d'Europa* (1929) Corradini developed a "biological theory" of the state and individual. A revised edition of *Giulio Cesare* appeared in 1926. He also wrote a new theatrical piece, *L'aurea leggenda di Madonna Chigi* (1931), which enjoyed much success on the stage.

See: P. L. Occhini, *Enrico Corradini; scrittore e nazionalista* (1914) and *Enrico Corradini e la coscienza nazionale* (1915); U. d'Andrea, *I Precursori: Enrico Corradini* (1928); C. Pavoni, *Enrico Corradini nel giornalismo e nella vita nazionale* (1930).

H. R. M.

Correia de Oliveira, António (1879–, Portuguese poet), was born in São Pedro do Sul, Beira, lived there until he was 19 years of age, and then moved to Lisbon, where he tried to follow a career in journalism—without great success. His friendship with the distinguished orator António Cándido brought him, along with a government post in the capital, opportunity to devote himself almost entirely to the writing of poetry. He has been very productive.

In his first works especially (*Ladaínha,* 1897, Lamentation; *Auto do fim do dia,* 1900, Auto of the Day's End; *Alívio dos tristes,* 1901, Relief for the Sad; *Cantigas,* 1902, Couplets; *Raíz,* 1903, Root; *Ara,* 1904, Altar), one can perceive clearly the popular inspiration of his work. *Tentações de S. Frei Gil* (1907; Temptations of S. Frei Gil), *Cravos* (1910; Carnations), and the collections *A minha terra* (1915–1917; My Native Land) and *Nossa pátria* (1920; Our Country) have a certain freshness of language and a quality of simple emotion which have impressed many readers. Although he comes within the realm of Parnassianism and symbolism, nevertheless in some of his later works the rhetorical influence of Eugénio de Castro and Guerra Junqueiro (*qq.v.*) is very apparent. It is in this dualism, which at times assumes an extremely decadent appearance and at others is characterized by a too naïve folklorism, that one finds the reason for the divergent evaluations of his literary work. On the one hand is a middle-class preference for couplets and ballads which he has improved upon and returned to the common treasure of the people, on the other hand the aversion and scorn felt by the more modernistic literati. Traditionalism, popular religiosity, regionalism, and even a certain pedagogical morality and patriotism of primary school type are probably not—except to a great and authentic poetic talent, such as Correia de Oliveira does not possess—the best sources of inspiration for poetry today.

In 1937 he visited Brazil, where he was received with academic honors, the greatest respect and admiration, and the overflowing affection of the Portuguese colony of Rio de Janeiro. A result of this visit was the publication of *Pátria vossa* (1938; Your Country), poems full of fervor for that republic. In 1940 *História pequenina de Portugal gigante* (A Little History of Gigantic Portugal) was added to the author's series of patriotic exhortations for children.

See: M. A. Vaz de Carvalho, *Cerebros e corações* (1903); A. da Veiga Simões, *A nova geração* (1911).

R. M. L.

Cossío, José María de (*ca.* 1895–, Spanish critic), is a reader of taste and a lover of poetry, rather than a professional writer. He has for many years spent much of his time in the province of Santander, alternating between long hours of reading in the Biblioteca de Menéndez y Pelayo (*see* Menéndez y Pelayo) located in the city of Santander and his residence in the "Casona de Tudanca," the house made famous in one of Pereda's (*q.v.*) novels. Cossío is also well known as a competent enthusiast on the subject of bullfighting. All his critical work, which includes several books and a number of erudite articles in learned reviews, is in some way connected with his personal tastes and is marked by a rich erudition and the freedom of interpretation born of a fine sense of poetic value and a nonprofessional critical attitude. It deals mainly with the history of Spanish poetry. Among other books, he is the author of *Los toros en la poesía castellana* (1931; Vol. I, *Estudio,* Vol. II, *Antología*), *Romancero popular de la Montaña* (1933), *La obra literaria de Pereda; su historia y crítica* (1934), *Poesía española: Notas de asedio* (1936), *Siglo XVII: Espinosa, Góngora, Gracián, Calderón, Polo de Medina, Solís* (1940), and *El romanticismo a la vista; tres estudios* (1942). He has been working for a number of years on a history of bullfighting, in several volumes (*Los toros,* Vol. I, 1943, Vol. III, 1944).

A. del R.

Cossío, Manuel Bartolomé (1858–1935, Spanish educator and art historian), born in Haro, Logroño, a fervent disciple of Giner de los Ríos (*q.v.*), devoted most of his life to the reform of public school education in Spain. He taught for almost 50 years—at the Institución Libre de Enseñanza, at the University of Madrid, and at the Museo Pedagógico Nacional, of which he was director from 1883 to 1929. He developed a new kind of teacher, for whom teaching became a creative art and who used the modern intuitive method of awakening the child's sensibility instead of cramming his head with words. Cossío's ideal that opportunities of university education be brought to the rural masses found realization in the Misiones Pedagógicas, traveling schools that along with teachers carried paintings, recordings, and books to the most remote Spanish villages. In his lectures and articles, fragments of which were published under the title *De su jornada* (1929), he constantly pointed out the needs of Spanish education in the light of observations he had made during his extensive travels all over Europe and the United States. In addition to his educational activities Cossío explored and evaluated Spanish art, the popular as well as the fine arts. In his monumental study, *El Greco* (1908)—the product of many years of study and countless excursions with his students—he revealed to the world the extraordinary genius of the Toledan painter and the meaning of his work as an authentic expression of the soul of Spain.

See: *Revista de pedagogía,* September, 1935 (entire issue devoted to Cossío); J. B. Trend, *Origins of Modern Spain* (1934), pp. 192–207.

E. F. H.

Costa, Joaquín (1846–1911, Spanish jurist, historian, and political philosopher), born in Monzón, Huesca, was one of the precursors of the Generation of 1898; with his crusade for the regeneration of Spain he did much to orient Spanish political thought at the beginning of this century. After the disastrous defeat of 1898, he made impassioned speeches all over the country in an effort to arouse his compatriots from their lethargic indifference. At the Ateneo, in his famous lectures later collected in *Oligarquía y caciquismo* (1901), he made a lucid and ruthless analysis of the pseudo-parliamentary regime, showing how it had brought only misery, servitude, and ignorance to the Spanish people, and concluded that the whole oligarchical system must be extirpated by means of a rapid "surgical operation." Costa had a gift of phrase, and many of his pithy mottoes and metaphors at once gained common currency, *e.g.,* his formula "la escuela y la despensa" (school and pantry), which was his terse way of saying that it would take nutrition and education to transform the Spaniard, or his "cirujano de hierro," the surgeon of iron that was to be tutelary dictator until real representative government should be possible. His rallying cry "Desafricanización y europeización de España" became the shibboleth of a whole group of thinkers and writers. Curiously enough Costa, the apostle of Europeanization, was also the untiring investigator of Spain's most ancient traditions. In fact, his political speeches and essays occupied but a small fraction of his life. Most of his effort was spent in digging away at mountains of documents, with characteristic Aragonese diligence and tenacity, and in writing long erudite works on such varied themes as custom as the source of law, in *La vida del derecho* (1876) and *El derecho consuetudinario de España* (1885); the political ideals of the Spanish people as expressed in their popular poetry, in *La poesía popular española y mitología y literatura celtohispanas* (1881); the evolution of Spanish political institutions, in *Estudios jurídicos y políticos* (1884); Spanish cultural origins, in the highly original *Estudios ibéricos* (1891–1894); agrarian problems, in *Colectivismo agrario en España* (1898)—a work that, incidentally, still offers much that remains of universal interest today.

See: C. Aparicio, *Joaquín Costa, el gran fracasado* (1930).

E. F. H.

Costa i Llobera, Miquel (1854–1922, Catalonian poet, prose writer, and sacred orator), was born in the beautiful city of Pollença on the island of Majorca, of a well-to-do family. He moved to Barcelona and then to Madrid to study law, a career which he abandoned for lack of real vocation. In 1874 he competed in the poetic contests, the Jocs Florals, in Barcelona. Later he retired to his native city where he devoted himself leisurely to literature; in 1885 his first volume of poems, *Poesies,* was issued. Then he went to Rome to study in the Gregorian University, was ordained a priest in 1888, and the following year received the degree of Doctor of Sacred Theology. Travels through Italy gave a permament classical stamp to his tastes and manner of thinking. Returning to his native island, he again devoted himself to literature in his native tongue and again took part in the poetic contests of Barcelona. He was named *mestre en gai saber* (master troubadour) in 1902 for having won first prize in each one of the three essential subjects in the celebration of the Jocs Florals—in songs to faith, to love, and to native country. In 1909 he was named canon of the cathedral of Palma de Mallorca. *De l'agre de la terra* (From the Bitterness of the Earth), *Tradicions i fantasies* (Traditions and Fantasies), and *Visions de Palestina* (Visions of Palestine), appeared in 1897, 1903, and 1908 respectively. His crowning work is, without doubt, the volume of poetry entitled *Horacianes* (1906; Poems in the Manner of Horace), in which formal perfection and inspiration were happily joined.

The work of Costa i Llobera, although not voluminous, has exerted a wide influence on Catalonian literature in general and in the development of the so-called Majorcan school, which aimed at formal perfection and felt admiration for the most varied forms of classicism. Costa i Llobera is a poet who is all soul, without indeed a trace of humor or irony, who gives himself up completely to the power of a full-blown emotion. His songs seem to spring tirelessly from a soul full of serenity, as though lost in contemplation of the inexhaustible beauties of the country of Majorca. The reading of the poetic works of Costa i Llobera, and in particular of his *Horacianes,* carries those who can enjoy him in Catalan to magnificent emotional heights. The vital quality of his poetry is comparable to what we enjoy in the great Greek and Latin poets who were his teachers, especially in Horace. Costa i Llobera has enjoyed a European reputation, and his works have been translated into Czech, Hungarian, German, Swedish. An edition of his complete works was published in 1924 by the Illustracio Catalana in four volumes.

See: M. de Montoliu, *Estudis de literatura catalana* (1912); A. Plana, *Antologia de poetes catalans moderns* (1914); C. Giardini, *Antologia dei poeti catalani contemporanei, 1845–1925* (1926).

F. de P.

Coster, Charles de, *see* De Coster.

Couperus, Louis (1863–1923, Dutch novelist), was born at The Hague, but spent his childhood in Java, where his father held an important position in the government service. He was trained to be a high school teacher of Dutch, but although he obtained the certificate that made him eligible for appointment, he never taught. His first novel, *Eline Vere* (1889), scored an immediate success and won for him a prominent place among Dutch writers of fiction. The story is a subtle analysis of the case of a weak, inconstant, aimless woman who feels herself the prisoner of her heredity. In *Noodlot* (1890; Fate), his second novel, the characters are again the helpless victims of an inexorable nemesis. In *Metamorphosis* (1889) Couperus told in fiction form the story of his own growth as an artist and of the genesis of his early novels, *Eline Vere, Noodlot, Extase* (1892), *Majesteit* (1893), and *Wereldvrede* (1895; World Peace). Among his other novels of life at The Hague the most outstanding is *De Boeken der kleine Zielen* (1901–1903; the four volumes comprising this work, published separately in translation, were collected in 1932 in one volume with the title *The Book of the Small Souls*), a story of the type and on the scale of *The Forsyte Saga,* which it antedated by 20 years. From the portrayal of this modern scene he turned to the study of antiquity. In *De Berg van Licht* (1905; The Mountain of Light), *Xerxes* (1919), and *Iskander* (1920) he painted the portraits of three dominant characters of different periods of ancient history: Heliogabalus, the young emperor whose perversities bring about his downfall; Xerxes, the victim of his own ambitions; and Alexander the Great, who is defeated by the vices of the peoples he subdued. But though the scene and the period have changed, the author's philosophy remains the same. He sees in man a will-less creature of his past and his environment. Couperus is not a moralist. He accepts life as an artist enamored of its colors and sounds, he plays with people's destinies as he plays with the language, handling them either with graceful nonchalance or distorting them into something forced and unreal. He possesses a saving sense of humor. In *Van en over Mijzelf en Anderen* (1910; Of and concerning Myself and Others) he smiles with gentle irony at his own idiosyncrasies. These delicate sketches of mocking self-revelation are among his most precious contributions to Dutch literature. Nearly all the works of Couperus have been translated into English and published in the United States.

Couperus, in his early work, was a follower of Flaubert and Zola (*qq.v.*). Yet the artist in him was out of sympathy with naturalism. His creative faculty functioned differently from Zola's. The latter set to work like a scientist, armed with a competent card index and with the blueprint of his story in front of him. Couperus let himself be guided by intuition and the inspiration of the moment. Each life he portrayed was lived by himself. He identified himself with each of his characters.

Couperus lived the greater part of his life abroad. "I do not feel that I am Dutch," he wrote, "although I love my native language, the richest, the loveliest that I know. . . . I feel myself to be an Italian who has been away from his country for a very long time, but who knows immediately on his return who and what he is: a Mediterranean who has pined away in the dim, chilly North." The Javanese blood in his veins had need of sunshine and warmth and blue skies. The outbreak of the First World War forced him to leave Italy. He returned to the dim, cold North and died at Velp near Arnhem in 1923.

See: J. de Graaf, *Le Réveil littéraire en Hollande et le naturalisme français, 1880–1900* (1938), pp. 125–140 and *passim.*

A. J. B.

Courteline, Georges (pseud. of Georges Moinaux, 1860–1929, French novelist and dramatist), was born in the city of Tours. He received his secondary education at Meaux and Paris. Though he was an undisciplined pupil, he gave proof of great creative ability. Finding him incapable of sustained work, his father made him enlist in a cavalry regiment. Georges hated army life and was discharged for poor health at the end of 14 months. He then entered the civil service as a clerk. The job, though tedious, afforded him much time for writing poems and short stories which were published in various periodicals. His first success came with the publication of *Les Gaietés de l'escadron* (1886) and *Le Train de 8h. 47* (1888), both based on his recollections of the humdrum barrack life of peace times. Later, in *Messieurs les ronds-de-cuir* (1893), he ridiculed the civil service and the stultifying routine of bureaucracy. In *Boubouroche,* a short play based on the story of a gullible lover and his clever mistress, first represented at the Théâtre Libre in 1893, Courteline turned his satire against womankind.

A writer of great talent, a pessimist with a Molièresque flair for comedy that appeals both to the few and to the many, Courteline was from the first extremely popular. Many of his novels and stories lent themselves to successful adaptations for the stage that increased his popularity still further. His later years were plagued with illness; in 1925 one of his legs had to be amputated. Official honors were then bestowed on him. In 1926 the French Academy awarded him a literary prize of 15,000 francs, the Goncourt Academy elected him a member, and the French government made him a Commander of the Legion of Honor. He died on June 25, 1929, after a second amputation.

See: J. Vivent, *Les Inspirations et l'art de Courteline* (1921); J. Portail, *Georges Courteline, l'humoriste français* (1928).

V. Gu.

Creangă, Ion (1837–1889, Rumanian popular story teller), was born in the village of Humulești, district of Neamț, about 100 kilometers from Jassy, ancient capital of Moldavia. He was the son of "Stephen, son of Peter the Cobbler" and of "Smaranda, born of David Creangă of the village of Pipirig," and the first of eight children. Creangă preferred the name of his maternal grandfather, adopted it, and made it famous.

He attended the village school, then went to Târgu-Neamț and Folticeni schools, entered and graduated from the Jassy seminary, and became a deacon in 1859. He also took courses at the normal school in Jassy, began teaching, and renounced the priesthood. He joined the Junimea (Youth) society and contributed his popular tales and his *Amintiri din copilărie* (1880; Childhood Reminiscences) to *Convorbiri literare* (Literary Conversations). There he met Eminescu (*q.v.*), with whom he formed a lasting friendship. He spent most of his time in the midst of the people whose language and lore he so successfully assimilated.

The stories he wrote were as ancient as the Moldavian land, and he possessed a genius for enclosing old and quaint sayings and expressions "of the soil" in the structure of his prose. Native and foreign critics agree that Creangă belongs with Andersen, the Grimm brothers, and especially Charles Perrault, whom he resembles in artistry. One finds in the works of these story tellers the same repetition of old tales in a simple popular language, the same life, the same little people, and the same healthy humor. Creangă differs from his predecessors in his realism, and especially in his use of popular proverbs, where he has no equal among European story tellers.

See: J. Boutière, *La Vie et l'œuvre de Ion Creangă* (1930).

L. F.

Croce, Benedetto (1866–, Italian philosopher, critic, scholar, historian, editor, and publicist), born at Pescasseroli, Aquila, is the descendant of a wealthy family of landowners in the Abruzzi and of magistrates under the Bourbons in Naples. He was educated in a private Catholic school restricted to children of families of good social standing. He escaped death in the earthquake of Casamicciola (1883), in which most of his family perished. Together with his brother, who had remained in Naples, he was educated by his uncle, Silvio Spaventa, a well-known conspirator in the *Risorgimento* who after 1860 became an outstanding political figure of united Italy. Croce enrolled in the faculty of law of the University of Rome but never graduated, attending only the courses given by Antonio Labriola, a teacher who awakened many young minds of Italy. Croce made use of his financial independence to dedicate himself to the study, first, of local history (editing the magazine *Napoli nobilissima,* 1892–1907), then of Marxist theories (*Materialismo storico ed economia marxistica,* 1900; Eng. tr., *Historical Materialism and the Economics of Karl Marx,* 1914), then of philosophy and history. He was not very active in the earlier years in the field of politics. His fame was already established when Premier Sonnino made him a senator (1910). After the First World War, Giolitti, the last hope of a confused and embittered Italy, appointed him minister of public instruction, and Croce served from June, 1920 to July, 1921. In this capacity he proposed to Parliament, but without success, a bill which introduced the state examination (*Le Riforme degli esami e la sistemazione delle scuole medie,* 1921), later a part of the famous Gentile Reform. Croce, who is married and has had four children, has always resided in Naples. He is a member of several Italian academies—among which the Pontaniana is particularly to be remembered because in its *Atti* Croce published the first drafts of his most important works. From this academy he withdrew because of Fascism. Oxford (1933) and other universities have bestowed on him the degree of *doctor honoris causa.*

Croce is the great unheeded man of Italy. It remains a puzzle and a paradox why this powerful thinker—the most outstanding Italian since 1900, whose widespread influence is recognizable and found active even in the minds of his opponents—did not exert a greater influence on his own people at critical moments of their history. In 1914 Italy went to war against Germany in spite of admonitions of a neutrally minded Croce, and in 1940, once more against Croce's warnings, sided with Germany. In other matters too his hold on Italians, in spite of his eminence, has been insignificant. The example he has set in matters of methodical work, the lessons he has given as to the necessity of placing humanity above the nation and of being moderate in victory and hopeful in adversity, his modesty in action, his aversion to pomp and rhetoric, his high regard for civic duties, have all had singularly slight effect on his contemporaries. In social matters Italians chose to imitate D'Annunzio (*q.v.*), the charmer, and in politics followed the domineering Mussolini.

Outside of Italy Croce is known particularly in two connections, for his influence as a philosopher of art and for his opposition to Germany and Fascism. Thus limited, an appraisal of him is true to the same extent that a plan representing only two sections of a great and elaborate building would be true. The wings cover a wide expanse: Marxism, philosophy, law, history, criticism, politics, the history of painting and religion, ethics (*e.g., Filosofia della pratica: Economia ed etica,* 1908; Eng. tr., *Philosophy of the Practical: Economic and Ethic,* 1913; *Frammenti di etica,* 1922; Eng. tr., *The Conduct of Life,* 1924). Croce's scores of volumes reveal an accomplished specialist and, at the same time, a universal thinker. Serious matters are often combined with anecdotes and witty remarks. The book reviews and notes published by him in his bimonthly *Critica* (1903–1944) show him at his best in the fields of polemical writing and of brilliant criticism.

Croce has made two clear résumés of his own aesthetics (*Breviario di estetica,* 1913; Eng. tr., *The Essence of Æsthetic,* 1921; and an article, "Aesthetics," first in English in the *Encyclopaedia Britannica,* 14th edition, and then in Italian, *Aesthetics in nuce,* 1929), which give the impression of a perfectly definite, almost axiomatic writer. But if one follows the efforts and development of his thought through his original writings, he is seen to be groping with his problems and making his way only gradually towards the light of truth. He became a philosopher through an active feeling of dissatisfaction with his hard labor of erudition. His system was the fruit of studies of art and history—this must be remembered; and his fundamental conception of "intuition" was twice revised (particularly in *L'Intuizione pura e il carattere lirico dell' arte,* 1908). Although criticisms of opponents provoked these changes, their insertion did not mean the acceptance of the objections, but rather a further free development of his own initial thought.

It is well known that his system is related to the idealistic school of philosophy; *i.e.,* for him the world is Spirit and only Spirit. Spirit is one in its manifestation. Multiplicity is taken account of by Croce's theory of circularity whereby one moment or aspect, which always mirrors the entire unity, passes into the other and yet retains its distinctiveness, to the point that each moment has to be studied separately if a knowledge of its function and of its place is to be acquired. There are four moments or aspects, two theoretic and two practical: aesthetics, or knowledge of the individual; philosophy, or knowledge of the universal; economic, or action for individual aims; and ethics, or action for universal aims. Essential works are *Tesi fondamentali di un'estetica come scienza dell' espressione e linguistica generale* (published first in *Atti dell' Accademia Pontaniana,* 1900, as a separate volume, 1902; Eng. tr., *Æsthetic as Science of Expression and General Linguistic,* 1909), *Lineamenti di una logica come scienza del concetto puro* (1905; Eng. tr., *Logic as the Science of Pure Concept,* 1917), and *Filosofia della pratica* (1908; there are several subsequent editions with important changes).

A dry summary gives but the faintest idea of the richness and the originality of Croce and none at all of the terseness, the clarity, the brilliancy of his writing. His style is very limpid; one may agree or disagree with him, but one always knows what he means. He is direct: he goes straight to his point without rhetorical paddings or ornamental digressions. His prose is an example of intellectual probity and purity, and its beauty is enhanced by a rhythm which seems to be born of the joy of thinking and of discovering. In his minor pieces he is often aggressive, ironic, and hard. His mood is consistently controversial. He has repeatedly asserted that all philosophy must be considered from a controversial viewpoint, and this is, in fact, the impression his writings give.

Croce's philosophy proceeds from Vico (*La Filosofia di Giambattista Vico,* 1911; Eng. tr., *The Philosophy of Giambattista Vico,* 1913) and Hegel (*Ciò che è vivo e ciò che è morto della filosofia di Hegel,* 1907; Eng. tr., *What Is Living and What Is Dead of the Philosophy of Hegel,* 1915), but includes De Sanctis's (*q.v.*) idealism. His Vico, however, is purified of all sociological heaviness, and his Hegel is cleansed of all Prussianism. De Sanctis, too, has been clarified, made smoother and more coherent. Croce is thus a very powerful reviver who has made of Vico, Hegel, and De Sanctis, not to mention other minor luminaries, true living personalities for contemporary Italian thought.

Croce has more importance as a philosopher of art than as a literary critic, but his criticism is remarkable (*Ariosto, Shakespeare e Corneille,* 1920; Eng. tr., *Ariosto, Shakespeare and Corneille,* 1920; *La Poesia di Dante,* 1920; Eng. tr., *The Poetry of Dante,* 1922; *Alessandro Manzoni; saggi e discussioni,* 1930; *Giosue Carducci; studio critico,* 1927; *La Letteratura della nuova Italia,* 4 vols., 1914–1915; 5th vol., 1939; 6th vol., 1940). He has also written essays on English, Spanish, French, German, and even Scandinavian authors, and an anthology of interesting judgments could be collected on others, even in the fields of Latin, early Christian, and Russian literatures. One feels that he is at his best when he comments on poets of the imagination (Ariosto, Shakespeare, Goethe) and at his worst when he deals with extreme lyricism (Leopardi or Baudelaire, *q.v.*). His trend is decidedly antiromantic, and he has shown no mercy for the modern decadent literature in Italy. All told his criticism has exercised a profound renovating influence in Italy (*see* Italian criticism).

He has not always been a friend of democracy nor an adversary of Germany; it would even be correct to say that by his sharp and devastating thoughts on democracy, Freemasonry, pacifism, internationalism (*Pagine sulla guerra,* 1919) Croce, in spite of himself, paved the way for Fascism. His idea of freedom has no connection with what Americans understand by this word. By freedom Croce means that "liberty" of the human mind whereby man strives to actualize those faculties which raise him above the immediate utilitarian interests of the individual person. It is a freedom which is also an obligation: a liberty to do everything that tends to give to the human soul the dignity which an ethical development has bestowed upon humanity. Such liberty easily becomes identical with coercion by parents, teachers, and the state authorities. In politics his liberalism is the doctrine of those who are able to think historically and, therefore, in a certain sense, are above all parties. He has shown in his historical works a tendency to justify all governments and institutions: the Bourbon dynasty in southern Italy (*Storia del regno di Napoli,* Bari 1925), the Spanish Inquisition, and the dictatorship, veneered with democracy, of Giolitti in prewar Italy (*Storia d'Italia dal 1871 al 1915,* 1927; Eng. tr., *A History of Italy, 1871–1915,* 1929). He respects heroes, but he is definitely opposed to revolution and sudden changes. His admiration and respect are reserved for efforts that develop in a ponderously slow rhythm over extended periods of time.

He has an aristocratic liking for unpopularity and has often found himself on the side of minorities; he was the most influential man of culture who in 1914 advocated neutrality for Italy. Likewise he showed till 1925 a certain tolerance towards Fascism (when it could be considered merely in its anti-Communist aspects). But as the movement gained ground he became first silent and then more and more critical. If he did not openly attack Fascism itself (which would not then have been possible), he assailed similar manifestations of the past or of other countries in such a manner that everyone understood to what and to whom he referred. Such was his authority that, whether out of a sense of chivalry, through fear of public opinion abroad, or for some other reason, Mussolini allowed him to continue publishing his *Critica* and many of his major historical works (especially remarkable is the *Storia d'Europa nel secolo decimono,* 1932; Eng. tr., *History of Europe in the Nineteenth Century,* 1933, a defense of the idea of freedom considered as the soul of that century). The survival of an active Croce between 1922 and 1943 in Italy was a thing that would not have been possible in Germany, Russia, or Spain. When Fascism came to an end, the figure of Croce glowed with the light of a solitary preserver of freedom and dignity; but while Italians paid homage to his idealistic figure, they did not follow his political advice, and it seems that his hopes for a strong liberal party in Italy have not aroused enthusiasm. Collections of his articles on politics and ethics and on recent events have been published in the United States but are not especially to be recommended either because their introductions are weak (*Germany and Europe; a Spiritual Dissension,* tr. with introduction by Vincent Sheean, 1944) or because they lack notes which would enable the Anglo-Saxon reader to understand the historical situations that called them forth (*Politics and Morals,* tr. from the Italian by Salvatore J. Castiglione, 1945).

In considering Croce's development it may be said that the direction of his personality has been toward a universal conception of the world; and in more recent years the study of and the translations from Goethe (*Goethe,* 1919; Eng. tr., 1923; *Nuovi saggi sul Goethe,* 1934) are perhaps significant of this trend. In his bitterness concerning recent developments in Europe he has always kept a margin for human considerations and sometimes even for a humorous remark. The reflections he published on Fascism bear this Olympic imprint, as does the moderation in his advice to the political winners in Italy.

Although Croce remains consistent in his philosophical denial of a personal God and of the immortality of the soul, his interest in religious problems and figures has grown, especially as regards the period of the Reformation. He has always believed (like Vico) in a providential power organizing history and entrusting to each man a task which he must actualize for universal ends.

See: G. Castellano, *Benedetto Croce* (1924; 2d ed., 1936); K. Bossler and others, *L'Opera filosofica storica e letteraria di B. Croce; saggi di scrittori italiani e stranieri e bibliografia dal 1920 al 1941* (1941). These two books contain an almost complete bibliography of the works of and on Croce.

G. P.

Croisset, Francis de (pseud. of Franz Wiener, 1877–, French playwright), was born in Brussels. He is known as the author of numerous light comedies, at times objectionable from a moral point of view. These plays, written in a lively style, are typical of the so-called *théâtre du boulevard,* in which sophisticated and witty dialogue makes up for thinness of content. Only in *L'Epervier* (1914) did Croisset attempt to draw a character study, the portrait of a society adventurer reminiscent of Abel Hermant's (*q.v.*) famous vicomte de Courpière. Among his other plays should be mentioned *L'Homme à l'oreille coupée,* also called *Une Mauvaise Plaisanterie,* banned by the censors in 1900; *Chérubin,* three acts in verse, rehearsed at the Comédie Française in 1901 but presented only in 1908 at the Théâtre Femina; *Le Bonheur, mesdames* (1905); and *Le Cœur dispose* (1912).

In collaboration with Emmanuel Arène, Croisset wrote *Paris–New-York* (1907). With Maurice Leblanc he adapted for the stage the well-known detective story *Arsène Lupin* (1908), and, after the death of Gaston de Caillavet (*q.v.*) in 1915, he became the collaborator of Robert de Flers (*q.v.*) in *Le Retour* (1920), *Les Vignes du Seigneur* (1923), *Romance* (1923), *Les Nouveaux Messieurs* (1925), *Ciboulette* (1926), *Le Docteur Miracle* (1930). Croisset has also written a volume of poems (*Nuits de quinze ans,* 1898), novels (*La Féerie cinghalaise,* 1926; *Nous avons fait un beau voyage,* 1930), essays and dramatic criticism (*Pour la langue française,* 1924; *Nos Marionnettes,* 1928; *L'Invasion au théâtre,* 1929; *La Vie parisienne au théâtre,* 1929; *Le Souvenir de Robert de Flers,* 1929). A collection of his aphorisms and wittiest repartees was published in 1930 in a volume entitled *L'Esprit de Francis de Croisset.*

See: L. Maigue, "Une Trilogie de jeunes," *Grande Revue,* March 15, 1906, pp. 453–472.

M. E. C.

Crommelynck, Fernand (1888–, Belgian dramatist), was born in Brussels. His mother was French. His father belonged to a family of modest bourgeoisie connected with theatrical life, and one of his uncles was a famous vernacular actor. Crommelynck received a complete stage training very early, and he probably learned more from the theatre itself than from school or college. Before the outbreak of the First World War, three plays of Crommelynck had already been staged in Brussels, *Nous n'irons plus au bois* (1906), *Le Sculpteur de masques* (1908), and *Le Marchand de regrets* (1913). These early works show his extraordinary skill for creating morbid atmospheres and characters (like the sculptor of masks or the "spleen seller," the dealer of antiques in a small Flemish town) who live, love, hate, and die in the midst of strange surroundings, suggesting the presence of ghosts and witchcraft. *Le Sculpteur de masques* was an inspiration for the French dramatist St. Georges de Bouhélier's *Le Carnaval des enfants.*

Le Cocu magnifique, presented in Paris (1921), brought Crommelynck suddenly into the full light of European glory. The play, entitled by the author a lyrical farce, is an extremely accurate and ruthless study of a lover's jealousy. The protagonist is represented on the stage by two actors, one of whom, Estrugo, is but a shade of the other, a kind of interior Iago, always appearing in time to renew the suspicions and doubts of the husband about his wife's faithfulness. *Le Cocu magnifique* ranks among the most representative plays staged in Europe between the two world wars and has been translated into many languages. Despite the development of the scandalous plot, the play is saved by the stupendous dramatic atmosphere that pervades it and also by the poetical intensity of the dialogue.

Before 1921 Crommelynck earned his livelihood as an actor. The tremendous success of *Le Cocu magnifique* enabled him to devote all his time to the writing of plays. With his wife and children he left Belgium and went to live in Saint-Cloud, near Paris, in the house that had belonged to Emile Verhaeren (*q.v.*), and which the Crommelyncks shared with the poet's widow. *Les Amants puérils* (1923) was not as successful as *Le Cocu magnifique. Tripes d'or* (1930) was a social satire, depicting the vanity of wealth and capitalistic grandeur. This play, translated into Russian, was produced in Moscow with great success. Crommelynck's lyric impetus triumphed again with *Carine, ou la Jeune Fille folle de son âme* (1934), in which the passion of a pure and chaste girl is analyzed. Carine prefers death rather than see her dream of love blemished. The locale of the play is a French provincial chateau, the time is autumn, and the chateau guests are all clad in red hunting coats. *Une Femme qui a le cœur trop petit* (1934) and *Chaud et froid* (1936) were the last works of Crommelynck produced before the Second World War.

Glittering with splendid images, Crommelynck's language is often overweighted with ornamentation. As a whole, it is artificial. The skill with which he surrounds a scene in an atmosphere of mystery and unusual tenseness is on occasion reminiscent of the Elizabethans. He has given to the contemporary theatre a lyrical expression thoroughly novel and sometimes deeply moving.

L. K.

Curel, François de (1854–1928, French dramatist), born at Metz, through his father was descended from a noble family of Lorraine and through his mother from a family of steel magnates, the Wendels. Curel was originally destined for an industrial career, but his plans were altered by the refusal of the German authorities to allow him to participate in the management of the family interests. He decided to devote his enforced leisure to writing. His career as a dramatist began with the sending to Antoine (*q.v.*) of three plays, all of which were accepted by the founder of the Théâtre Libre. From then on, writing only when inspiration prompted him, Curel lived the life of a wealthy nobleman, dividing his time between his Paris residence and his Lorraine forest, the majestic beauty of which he has described in unforgettable terms. He became a member of the French Academy in 1919, succeeding Paul Hervieu (*q.v.*).

The conflicts between ideal and reality, between humanity and animality, between sentiment and instinct, dominate Curel's theatre. One of his first plays, *Sauvé des eaux* (1889), which became in successive versions *L'Amour brode* (1893) and *La Danse devant le miroir* (1913), is a study of the passion of two people in search of an ideal love which, when they are confronted by reality, seems inaccessible. The heroines of *L'Envers d'une sainte* (1892) and *L'Invitée* (1893) also called upon love to satisfy their need for an ideal—and were cruelly disappointed; their proud and tormented souls are analyzed with pitiless lucidity.

After these dramas about love, Curel turned to the "theatre of ideas." But realizing how deficient in dramatic appeal ideas may be in themselves, he always denied that he had intended to use the theatre for the discussion of abstractions; ideas interested him for "the storms which they raise in the soul." It is indeed to an idea, that of the perpetuity of the race in an aristocratic family, that the characters in *Les Fossiles* (1892) sacrifice their happiness, just as Albert Donnat, in *La Nouvelle Idole* (1895), sacrifices a young girl and himself to an idea, that of the progress of science, the "new idol." The industrialist Jean de Miremont, in *Le Repas du lion* (1897), swears to devote his life to a program, the improvement of conditions among the working classes; and the main character in *Le Coup d'aile* (1906) sacrifices his family to his haunting and mad desire for power and glory. The violent internal conflicts in the minds of such heroes of Curel have produced plays of powerful dramatic interest. In *La Fille sauvage*

(1902), on the other hand, the dramatic quality of the story of this girl savage gradually brought into contact with civilization is really subordinated to the author's views on the development of humanity, which constitute the main interest of this work.

During a long period when Curel remained aloof from the theatre, his dramatic genius underwent remarkable changes. A new comic vein, made up of gaiety and irony, appears. The conflicts which had inspired Curel's first dramas now emerge again. Autobiographical details increase. The author has more and more a tendency to put himself on the stage in the guise of various characters which clearly embody at least some aspects of his own personality.

La Comédie du génie (1918) is less a play than an ironic and somewhat disillusioned account of the intellectual and professional adventures of a dramatist in whom it is easy to recognize Curel himself. *L'Ame en folie* (1919) is an entertaining comedy on the conflicting hereditary tendencies in human nature. The ironic *Ivresse du sage* (1922), while exposing opinions on human selection compared with animal selection, makes fun of a philosopher who claims to be free of the tyranny of the flesh. *Terre inhumaine* (1922) shows us how war brings back in the human race the bestial traits which civilization seemed to have crushed; and, when peace comes, the hero of *La Viveuse et le moribond* (1925) succeeds only with difficulty in suppressing the primitive animal resurrected by the war. In his last play, *Orage mystique* (1927), behind an amusing comedy plot Curel attempts to analyze the creation of characters by a dramatist, a subject already studied in his answers to Binet in *L'Année psychologique* (1894).

Curel had no great success with theatre audiences, except in the case of *L'Ame en folie.* Ordinarily, while highly praised by the critics, his plays surprised and interested rather than pleased the public. Never mediocre, Curel is irregular as a dramatist. Capable of attaining greatness, he is at times disconcerting for his awkwardness. He dared to bring ideas upon the stage, and homage must be paid to the nobility of his thoughts and his perfect intellectual honesty.

See: P. Blanchart, *François de Curel* (1924); E. Pronier, *La Vie et l'œuvre de François de Curel* (1934); A. Lévêque, "François de Curel: Observations sur la création dramatique," *Publications of the Modern Language Association of America,* LII (1937), 550–580.

A. C. L.

Curros Enríquez, Manuel (1851–1908, Spanish poet and journalist), was born at Celanova in Galicia and from an early age took part in heated liberal and republican campaigns. He studied law, and as a result of the September Revolution of 1868 he moved to Madrid, where he edited *Imparcial, Porvenir, País,* and other literary and political newspapers and journals. With the publication of his first book the bishop of Orense brought legal action against him, and he was convicted of irreverent attacks against the Catholic religion and the ministers of the Church. A higher court absolved him, and his personal popularity and that of his work became very great. In America especially, in the colonies of Spanish emigrants, there was a succession of editions and expressions of devotion and esteem. He became a Treasury official in Orense and in 1894 moved to Havana, Cuba, where he was editor of the *Diario de la marina.* After his death in Havana, his body was moved to Galicia, where monuments and statues have been erected to him.

Aires d'a miña terra (1879), his first work and the volume which caused his denunciation by the Church, contains the best of his poetry. Three poems in particular were responsible for the official protest. In "Mirando o chau" (Looking at the Ground) God observes his work, the creation, viewing it with the just and liberal spirit of Curros; the poem, admittedly an imitation of Béranger, has attacks on the degenerate church, venal administration of justice, social inequality, hypocrisy. "A igrexa fria" (The Cold Church) depicts licentious ecclesiastical life within sight of the ruins of a monastery. "O divino sainete" (The Divine Farce) is a parody of Dante in the traditional tercets of the medieval Galician lyric, in which the poet accompanied by priests, monks, and fanatics and led by the poet Añon, visits the pope and urges him again to live real Christianity and abandon luxury and pomp. Outstanding in this and similar verse of Curros are extraordinary energy of satire, civic virility, and a flowing naturalness of language, agile and flexible as a whip.

Perhaps the most intense lyrical power of Curros, however, is found in a somewhat different type of verse in the same book. The beautiful Marian legend, "A Virxe d'o Cristal" (The Virgin of the Crystal), could be taken for one of the *Cantigas de Santa María* of Alfonso the Wise. Highly dramatic is the "Nouturnio" (Nocturne), a dialogue between a miserable old man and the haunting croak of a toad, his only companion, which ends in an angry threat against heaven; equally vivid are the poems on emigration and homesickness and those that recall family tragedies. The "complaint" of Rosalía Castro, the vague Celtic argumentation of Pondal (*qq.v.*), have become in Curros a violent revolutionary protest.

See: "Homenaje en honor de Curros Enríquez," *Boletín de la Real Academia Gallega,* May, 1915; César Barja, "En torno al lirismo gallego del siglo XIX," *Smith College Studies in Modern Languages,* Vol. VII (1926), Nos. 2–3, pp. 112–124.

R. M. L.

Czech literature (*see also* Slovak literature). A word about background is particularly necessary for the understanding of recent Czech literature. The Czechs, who are geographically the westernmost of the Slavs, have always had stronger literary and cultural relations with Western and Southern Europe than with the Slavic East (Russian literature became an important influence only during the 19th century). The fine poetic tradition established as early as the 14th century and already Western in quality was interrupted by the Hussite wars and their consequences: Czech literature then became for a long period largely an instrument in the intellectual and social struggle of the nation against Rome. The Czechs, like the Germans, did not have a proper Renaissance. When the old Bohemia came to an end with the defeat of the Bohemian army in the Battle of the White Mountain (1620), an absolutist Hapsburg regime was established and the country was re-Catholicized by force; Bohemia was deprived of its upper classes, cut off from the West, and became, with notable exceptions, a stagnant peasant community. Late in the 18th century, the Czechs began to "awaken," *i.e.,* ideas of the general European Enlightenment began to penetrate into the country and contacts with the West were reestablished. The revival passed through fairly distinct stages: a philological stage in which the Czech language was revived and poetic diction rejuvenated; a poetical one when, early in the 19th century, poetry in the neoclassical and later in the romantic manner was created; and finally, the political stage which led to the abortive revolution of 1848. In 1861, with the reemergence of the Czech nation from a new period of absolutism and oppression, the process of literary revival was accomplished. The romantic movement, which had been particularly strong, inspired as it was by nationalism and enthusiasm for folk poetry, now belonged to the past. One great figure survived until 1876—the historian of Bohemia, František Palacký, born at the end of the 18th century. But new critical and realistic forces were becoming vocal in these last decades. By 1870 the leading literary figures, Jan Neruda, Vítězslav Hálek, and Karolina Světlá (*qq.v.*), exemplified the struggle between the dying romanticism and the emergence of realism. Especially Neruda's terse ironical poetry, inspired by modern scientific ideas, and his humorous prose, lovingly depicting the small people of Prague, anticipated an unromantic future.

Czech literature between 1870 and the First World War was predominantly middle class in social origin and ideology. The old aristocracy, as far as it survived, had turned away from its nation and played no role as a producer or patron of literature. The upper bourgeoisie of wealth and Austrian officialdom were largely German, and the few Czechs who penetrated there had little interest in the literature of their own tongue. The middle class, which produced and consumed Czech literature, was recruited constantly from the peasants and sometimes from the factory workers. But authors who can be described as proletarians or peasants were rare. Practically no literature was written in any dialect, and Prague was almost the only literary center. The majority of authors made their living as teachers, small officials, clerks, and in many cases as journalists and editors, and found their public among the same intelligentsia—the students, doctors, and lawyers scattered over the country. Among those of high literary standing only Jirásek (*q.v.*) can be described as widely popular. Most books were published in small editions, cheaply produced, though there was a limited public for expensively printed books. One notable feature of Czech literature is its close relation with scholarship. When an independent Czech university was reestablished in Prague in 1882, much of the intellectual life of the nation centered round this institution. Masaryk, Vrchlický, Šalda (*qq.v.*), and Beneš were university professors. Even very technical scholars—especially philologists such as Jan Gebauer (1838–1907), who watched over the development of the language, literary historians such as Jaroslav Vlček (1860–1930) and Arne Novák (*q.v.*), and historians such as Josef Pekař (1870–1937) and Josef Šusta (1874–1945) —commanded national attention and took part in contemporary affairs.

Theatrical life was very limited. Actually

only the National Theatre, rebuilt in 1883, was a great stage with fine actors, to which only later was some competition offered by the Municipal Theatre of Vinohrady, a suburb of Prague. The provinces were of little importance to the stage. These social conditions changed somewhat as a result of the First World War and the establishment of the independent republic. Czech literature expanded considerably in mass; the reading public suddenly increased, not only because education awakened in the lower classes a hunger for literature, but also because Czech was again read widely in Slovakia and by the reclaimed minorities. The growth in the number of newspapers and frequently short-lived periodicals was startling. A state-supported expansion of public libraries was added to stimulate a general democratization of literature. Now a whole "proletarian" movement of poets emerged, few of whom, however, were of strictly proletarian origin, and a group of very self-conscious "ruralists" who preached a return to the soil and opposed the centralization of literature in Prague. Thus the earlier, almost absolute monopoly by the middle class and by Prague was, at least partially, broken after 1918. Two new universities, those of Brno and Bratislava, were founded, and academic life spread considerably, without, however, preserving its role of national leadership. The Prague National Theatre also ceased to be the only stage of great artistic pretensions. Small experimental theatres in Prague were centers of excellent stagecraft, and theatres elsewhere, in Brno, Moravská Ostrava, and Bratislava, took serious part in the development of the drama. All told, there was after the war a most impressive expansion—with the concomitant dangers in a break with tradition, in commercialization and nivellization, though these processes scarcely went so far in Czechoslovakia as they did in the West.

Czech literature stands at the crossroads of practically all cultural influences: proximity to Germany, the Slavic language, strong sympathies with the West and Western political ideology have all had their effect. German influence in the early 19th century was considerable, anti-German though the outlook of most writers was. Kindred Slavic literatures played an important and for a time a major role. With the 1870's a flood of French influences arrived, largely through the work of Vrchlický and his school. The "decadents," critics such as Šalda, and, after the First World War, many exponents of the newest movements in poetry were in a large measure dependent on literary fashions in Paris. Only after the war did contacts with the Anglo-Saxon world become more intimate, though Masaryk's orientation had been largely English and American since 1880. Karel Čapek (*q.v.*) especially can be described as sympathetic to the usual Anglo-Saxon mentality. German influences declined at this time; only a group of German writers from Prague —Rilke, Kafka, Werfel (*qq.v.*)—commanded attention. Scandinavia influenced the drama through Ibsen (*q.v.*) and, to a lesser degree, the novel. The relation with the other Slavic literatures was again more intimate. But Polish and Yugoslav literature remained largely the interest of scholars, and Russian literature alone had any popular appeal. Russian romanticism (exemplified in Pushkin) was important for many older (Čech) and even certain much younger poets (Hora); the Russian novel (especially the work of Dostoevski, *q.v.*) commanded a wide reading public and influenced numerous writers. Recently, too, a section of the public has shown strong interest in the new Soviet literature, mostly for political reasons. On the whole, the amazing flood of translations from all literatures and all authors, good and bad, increased after 1918 and showed how avidly the Czech reading public wanted to escape its narrow national limits. Czech literature, like every other small literature, is always confronted with the problem of individuality and nationality. Possibly writers in the post-war years have gone too far in incorporating the general Western cultural pattern into Czech literature. A closer examination shows, however, that a genuine attempt has been made to express something individual and peculiarly Czech. A study of the main figures of Czech literature reveals a great number of original authors who managed to be at once Czech and in some measure universal.

In the late 1870's new figures arose, to dominate Czech literature for some 20 years. In the 90's a new generation matured which revolted very sharply against the preceding group, and similarly, just after the First World War, another new generation enforced a break with the past. So at least three fairly well defined periods of recent Czech literature can be distinguished: from about 1876 to 1894, a period in which rhetorical, decorative poetry fundamentally romantic in outlook prevailed; from 1894 to 1918, when naturalism and symbolism triumphed; since 1918, a time when different movements, vaguely lumped together as "modernism," have dominated the literary scene. One can draw the distinctions on the basis of generations another way. In the first period writers born in the 1840's and 1850's were leaders. In the early part of the second period the generation born in the 60's and 70's made itself felt; just before the First World War a new and less clearly defined group became vocal, writers born in the late 70's and in the 80's who are known as "the lost generation." Post-war literature from 1918 on was dominated by those born in the 90's and in the early 20th century. Of course, there were survivals and anticipations, and within each generation there was conflict. Poetry is the leading genre in Czech literature, and the different periods are most clearly demarcated by its prestige and success. The novel has had a less clear evolution, and the drama, though most successful abroad, was definitely of minor literary importance. Criticism became very influential only after the 1890's.

The early beginnings of realism were interrupted by a new great wave of oratorical poetry which, in technique and outlook, corresponds roughly to that of the great English Victorians. The two leading figures were Jaroslav Vrchlický and Svatopluk Čech (*q.v.*), protagonists of the often contrasted "cosmopolite" and "patriotic" movements. Vrchlický and his numerous followers and imitators were grouped around a quarterly, *Lumír,* edited by J. V. Sládek (*q.v.*), a fine poet and the translator of Shakespeare into Czech; Čech's work had first appeared in an almanac called *Ruch* (1868). The two groups are thus called "Lumírovci" and "Ruchovci," respectively. Actually, however, the contrast between these opposing schools is superficial. Vrchlický stressed the contacts with France and Italy, while Čech was more pro-Russian in his outlook; but in the history of poetry they must both be classed as splendid rhetoricians, in the style sometimes of Hugo and sometimes of the French Parnassians. Ideologically they were also basically similar. Both were good Czech patriots, liberal democrats, believers in progressive evolution, cosmic optimists. Much of their splendid and dazzling work has lost its appeal today, but Vrchlický will survive not only as a virtuoso of all forms and themes, but also as an intimate lyrical poet, who late in life found his way back to a simple, chaste, and even terse style. His historical importance can scarcely be overrated. He definitely broke away from dependence on German romantic models and "opened the windows" to Europe. His enormous activity as a translator of poetry is in itself a major achievement. Somewhat later, in loose association with the "Lumírovci," there appeared another major writer, Julius Zeyer (*q.v.*), who can best be compared to the English Pre-Raphaelites. He is a nostalgic neo-romantic, an aesthete with Catholic and medieval sympathies, a decorative artist with a rather tenuous hold on reality.

While poetry revived romanticism, the novel became more and more realistic and purely descriptive in its techniques. The historical novel, which had been popular among the Czechs, emancipated itself slowly from the model of Sir Walter Scott and achieved real artistic success in the careful work of Alois Jirásek and Zikmund Winter (*q.v.*). Jirásek, who was a genuine student of history, became a great favorite of the masses and a powerful stimulus of national and historical consciousness. The novel of peasant life also assumed new forms in the late 19th century. It became more sociological, more exact, less prone to idealize the peasant. The nostalgic portrait of *Babička* (1855; Grandmother) by Mrs. Božena Němcová (1820–1862) had been the classic of the genre. Now Josef Holeček (*q.v.*) created a great cycle of novels depicting the Czech peasant with realistic technique and preaching a conservative agrarian ideology, rare in a time dominated by 19th-century liberalism. Mrs. Teréza Nováková (*q.v.*) brooded in her novels over the peasants' moral and religious struggles, in the spirit of an earnest investigator of manners and social problems, and numerous other competent writers, such as Karel V. Rais (1859–1926), Alois Mrštík (1861–1925), and Jan Herben (1857–1936), specialized in different regions of the country and in different approaches to the problem of the peasant who was still felt to be the backbone of the nation.

In the 90's a revolution was brought about in Czech literature. The prevailing style and ideology of both the "Lumírovci" and the "Ruchovci" were criticized and condemned by a new generation, which was, however, very sharply divided within itself. One stream of revolt can be described as realist and naturalist; the other, as symbolist and impressionist (there was also a small group of Czech "decadents" who, in practice, were nearest to the symbolists). The realist movement had its intellectual spokesman in Tomáš Masaryk. His importance, especially in his later years, far transcends the field of belles-lettres, but he profoundly influenced literature by his sharp criticisms of the German intellectual tradition, his distrust of rhetoric, of romanticism, and of optimistic liberalism. Masaryk's literary criticism was, on the other hand, too purely moralistic to influence directly the practice of poetry. J. S. Machar (*q.v.*), with his skeptical, satirical, and even dry mind, returned Czech poetic diction to the terse colloquial tradition —interrupted since Neruda—though later in his life Machar surveyed world history poetically in the spirit of an anti-Christian, Nietzschean individualist. Petr Bezruč (*q.v.*), the great poet of Czech nationalism, is stylistically related to Machar. His monumental *Slezské písně* (Silesian Songs) cultivate an austere rhetoric which gives tragic expression to the poet's longing for justice and his hatred and anger for the oppressor. A younger poet, Viktor Dyk (*q.v.*), is also primarily a political poet, a fervent nationalist. He cultivated concise, hard, sharp, even epigrammatic forms and with Machar presents a strongly intellectualistic trend among Czech poets. Karel Toman (pseud. of Antonín Bernášek, 1877–) is another fine poet who, though standing by himself in many ways, must be classed with Dyk, for he too cultivates concise, monumental forms. But he is far more impersonal and matter-of-fact and seems to have no ideology except an instinctive social revolt and a love for his home and nation.

The novel, in accordance with the triumph of naturalism in the West, turned away from history and the countryside to study the town and the bourgeoisie in the light of the positivistic creed. In Czech literature there were, however, few orthodox naturalists; among them Karel Matěj Čapek-Chod (*q.v.*) stands out because he escaped photographic naturalism and rose to write grotesque visions of Prague and the life of its bourgeoisie. Josef K. Šlejhar (1864–1914) is rather a gloomy mystic in the wake of Dostoevski (*q.v.*), and Ignát Herrmann (1854–1935) is a popular genre painter of the small people of Prague.

Czech drama was slow to emancipate itself from romanticism. The closet dramas of the poets were largely failures on the stage, which had to survive on mediocre realistic comedies and florid historical dramas. The change came only when Jaroslav Hilbert (*q.v.*) produced good imitations of Ibsen and later wrote moralistic criticisms of history and Czech society for the stage.

Naturalism and related techniques were rather one tendency of the time than a unified movement. The more purely poetic movements of "decadence" and of symbolism crystallized far more clearly, but here too, surprisingly, it is difficult to distinguish the lines between brands of neo-romanticism, impressionism, and even tendencies called neoclassic. F. X. Šalda was the most influential critic who consistently opposed both the academic art of the "Lumírovci" and the new materialistic naturalism and advocated a highly metaphorical, symbolistic poetry and an art responsible to society, inspired by an idealistic philosophy. Šalda's great influence extended into the 1930's, when he still continued to be the spokesman for the newest art movements. Arne Novák judged and surveyed the whole course of Czech literature from a point of view much more conservative and traditional. A new nonnaturalist poetry began to flourish in the 90's. There was even a small group of Czech "decadents" who cultivated the morbid aestheticism of the *fin-de-siècle* mood with considerable skill and success. Jiří Karásek ze Lvovic (1871–) was the most versatile writer of the group, its critical mouthpiece and organizer, but a proletarian, Karel Hlaváček (*q.v.*), who died early in life, was its most original artist. Nearer to Šalda's ideals were the two great symbolist poets who began to write in the 90's. Antonín Sova (*q.v.*) was a sensitive, moody poet whose roots were in an impressionist, introspective, subjective lyricism; it was only in his later years that he turned to symbolism. He also wrote much high-minded, rhetorical poetry envisaging a utopian socialism. Otokar Březina (*q.v.*), who is usually coupled with Sova, was a far greater and more consistent artist. Březina is possibly the greatest recent Czech poet. He wrote a few volumes of hymns which combine an original Christian mysticism with an ecstatic cosmic optimism, expressed in wonderful cascades of metaphors and majestic free verse. Březina, though he cannot be described as an orthodox Roman Catholic, stimulated the founding of a self-conscious Catholic literary movement; there were several talented poets in this group early in the 20th century, but it is only since the First World War that Jakub Deml (1878–), a poet, and Jaroslav Durych (*q.v.*), the novelist, have here made original contributions of real distinction. Březina, by the very nature of his rare and sublime art, could not have many direct followers. Among the younger poets prominent before 1918, Otakar Theer (*q.v.*) is nearest to him, though Theer attempted to achieve very different classical and even sculpturesque effects in free verse. Otokar Fischer (*q.v.*), an excellent literary historian and translator of verse, is as a poet associated with his friend Theer.

The symbolist movement was, possibly by its very nature, less successful in the field of the novel. Two women stand out, Růžena Svobodová (*q.v.*) and Božena Benešová (1873–1936). Both tried to overcome the forms of realism and naturalism by highly stylized techniques. Mrs. Svobodová is a very ambitious artist who suffers, however, from preciosity and aestheticism, while Mrs. Benešová is preoccupied with ethical problems. Her depth and earnestness are impaired only by an undeniable coldness of imagination. This could not be said of Fráňa Šrámek (*q.v.*), also a lyrical poet of distinction, whose impressionist novels glorify sex and adolescent love with lyrical tenderness. In all these novelists, narrative power and composition are weak; the novel with them somewhat approaches lyrical poetry in its effect and aim. This tendency to lyricism precluded the success of these writers on the stage, though several of them (Šalda, Theer, Fischer, Šrámek) tried to return poetry to the theatre.

Many of these writers lived beyond 1918, producing some of their best work in the years after the First World War, and it would be absurd to deny the continuity of Czech literature through the war years. But the literary atmosphere changed after the establishment of an independent Czechoslovak republic. A stream of self-confidence and buoyant optimism flooded the country. The pre-war writers, exclusively interested in the adventures of their own souls, lost their following. Social questions, sentiments common to the masses of mankind, became the central topic. Subjectivism, individualism, anything that savored of "decadence," were swept away in a great flood of communal experience. The old intellectualism disappeared, and many writers embraced a gospel of life in direct opposition to spirit and mind. Freed as they just were from the prison of the war years, they glorified the pleasures of mere existence, the beauty of the simplest and nearest things. Criticism, still led by Šalda, was prolific in producing manifestoes, programs, and many essays which usually either overrated the peculiar art of the critic's liking or indulged in fierce polemics against the enemy. Only a few critics stand out in this period: F. Götz (1894), an untiring defender of every new movement; B. Václavek (1897–1942), the best among the Marxist critics; and A. Vyskočil (1890–), whose outlook is Catholic. Czech poetry, after 1918, went through three rather clearly marked stages which can be labeled "proletarian" poetry, "poetism," and a return to spiritualism. First, a new social radicalism became the keynote of the young poets, inspired by the successes of the Communist revolution in Russia. The most prominent poet of this movement was Jiří Wolker (*q.v.*), whose early death made him even more than during his life the symbol of the young generation. His poetical technique is traditional. It preserves the lucid simplicity of the folk song and folk ballad. More "modernist" techniques were inspired and practiced by two older poets, S. K. Neumann (*q.v.*), who had his roots in an anarchic individualism and had sung hymns to sensual love before he came to glorify industrial civilization and the Russian Revolution, and Josef Hora (*q.v.*), for whom adherence to the "proletarian" movement was only an episode. Later, Hora developed into a melancholy philosophical poet who returned to the tradition of romanticism, but still preserved his own style. The enthusiasm for "proletarian" poetry began to evaporate about 1924. Social conditions seemed stabilized and a period of peace and prosperity in store. There arose a new movement, headed by Vítězslav Nezval (*q.v.*), which called itself "poetism." This was a new designation for pure poetry devoid of thought and propaganda, for poetry as a play of fancy and association. Nezval was a virtuoso of colorful little pictures, illogical associations, and whole topsy-turvy worlds. Later, his obvious associations with futurism weakened, and he embraced the creed of French surrealism. The reaction against "poetism" came with the general darkening of the international and national horizon. A new group of poets has arisen whose exact achievement and comparative rank it would be difficult to judge at this moment. They have a new spirituality, a new, very abstract style, and a hymnlike rhythm quite different from the little splashes of color and the comic ditties of Nezval. Jan Zahradníček (1905–) and František Halas (1901–) seem to be the most promising of these newcomers. Here are the beginnings of a further development of Czech poetry whose fruits cannot now be predicted. But the Parisian modernism seems dead, and perhaps it is a significant fact that even the poets formerly connected with "proletarian" poetry and "poetism"—Nezval, Hora, and Seifert—have returned to patriotic and philosophic themes.

It is much more difficult to distinguish clear stages in the development of the Czech postwar novel. Certain tendencies of the novel agree with the general trend of literature away from individualism. The old psychological novel disappears almost completely. The old forms of narrative, with a clear chain of events, were largely discarded in favor of forms which tried to grasp a great multitude of events and figures. Experiments in form increased in number, and the themes seemed to cover the universe. The social novel, devoted to a discussion of social problems, has been very much in the forefront of popular attention, but one cannot say that it has achieved great artistic success. Marie Majerová (1882–), a specialist in industrial problems, has a zest and vitality which make us forget her rather crude distribution of light and shade, and there are other competent writers who try to give documentary pictures of social conflicts, largely in the cities. The best recent pictures of the social scene in Czechoslovakia, the novels of Mrs. Marie Tilschová (1873–) and of Mrs. Marie Pujmanová (1893–), are actually revivals or survivals of naturalism. The country has again become the topic of fiction, written in a quite different spirit from the older folklore idyls. The new "ruralists," as they call themselves, have done much for a clearer understanding of the peasant and his struggles. J. Knap (1900–) has been the mouthpiece of the very self-conscious movement, František Křelina (1902–) and J. V. Kříž (1900–) are the best-known names, but Jan Čep (*q.v.*) is the outstanding artist. He is only loosely related to the group as he has no social axe to grind, but rather struggles for inner harmony with a deep melancholy for which the soil and the country are only a symbolic cure. The war novel, also a special field with very different techniques and outlooks, has had its promoters. Jaroslav Hašek (*q.v.*) has drawn a grotesque picture of the Austrian Empire in dissolution and created the type of the "go-slow" Czech in his *Dobrý voják Švejk* (Good Soldier Švejk). But artistically, Hašek is a survival of naturalism, full of low humor and naïve propaganda. The great adventure of the Czechoslovak legions in Russia and Siberia lent itself to different treatment. Rudolf Medek (1890–1940) has written in a heroic spirit novels based on his own experiences, while Josef Kopta (1894–) tried rather, in his *Třetí rota* (1924; Third Platoon), to describe the soul of the masses in a quiet, kindly way which stresses the human side of the war that is missing both in the heroic Medek and the cynical Hašek.

Among the younger fiction writers, Egon Hostovský (1908–) specializes in novels of horror and crime, presented with great skill; indeed in the recent Czech novel the general level of technique, facility, and knowledge of the subject is high. Four authors seem to stand out most conspicuously as personalities with a clearly discernible development and individual style. Ivan Olbracht (*q.v.*) began with subtle psychological novels and has since achieved great success with *Nikolaj Šuhaj, loupežník* (Nikolaj Suhaj, the Robber), a vivid picture of Sub-Carpathian Russia which has rare narrative and epic power. It is difficult to imagine a greater contrast than that between the communist Olbracht and Jaroslav Durych. Durych is a Roman Catholic writer who has, almost singlehanded, revived the Czech historical novel. His great novel on Wallenstein, *Bloudění* (The Erring Quest), is a large-scale fresco of the Thirty Years' War in baroque taste, inspired by a fervid mysticism and otherworldliness which penetrate his poetry and the rest of his prose as well. Another violent contrast in ideology and style is that of Karel Čapek with both Olbracht and Durych. Čapek is best known as a playwright, in collaboration with his painter-brother Josef Čapek (*q.v.*). But his best work is in his fiction, especially in a trilogy of philosophical novels which overshadows his other varied writings—his crime stories, his humorous travel books, fairy tales, essays, etc. Čapek felt in harmony with his age, though he criticized the evils of modern civilization in several anti-utopian utopias. There is something genuinely representative in Čapek's love of the small man, in his belief in democracy and humanity. Of a still different mental type is Vladislav Vančura (*q.v.*), who had nothing of Čapek's optimism. He glories in the merely animal, in the grotesque and repulsive; he became an amazing virtuoso of style and technique who broke with all the traditional forms of the novel. On the whole, the Czech novel after the First World War has presented an astonishingly vivid picture of reality.

Compared to the abundance of good poetry and competent novels, the production of the drama since 1918 seems meager in actual achievement, in spite of the excellent stagecraft of the Prague theatre. The brothers Čapek have made the round of the world's stages with their plays which treat topical problems with great skill. The poetical drama, in spite of ambitious attempts, has failed in this period as everywhere else. Only František Langer (*q.v.*) has scored lasting success with well-constructed—though hardly profound—comedies and dramas from the life of the Prague bourgeoisie on the outskirts of the city.

See: J. Jakubec and A. Novák, *Geschichte der čechischen Literatur* (1907; 2d ed., 1913); A. Novák, *Přehledné dějiny literatury české* (1909; 4th ed., 1939), "Die tschechische Literatur," in O. Walzel, *Handbuch der Literaturwissenschaft* (1931), "Czech Literature during and after the War," *Slavonic Review,* II (1923–1924), 114–132, and "Česká literatura," in *Československá vlastivěda,* Vol. VII (1933); F. X. Šalda, *Moderní literatura česká* (1909; 3d ed., 1929) and *Krásná literatura česká v prvním desitiletí republiky* (1930); H. Jelínek, *La Littérature tchèque contemporaine* (1912), *Etudes tchécoslovaques* (1927), and *Histoire de la littérature tchèque* (3 vols., 1930–1935); F.

Chudoba, *A Short Survey of Czech Literature* (1924); B. Václavek, *Česká literatura XX. století* (1935); K. Polák, *Československá literatura, 1890–1935* (1936); R. Wellek, "Twenty Years of Czech Literature (1918–1938)," *Slavonic Review,* XVII (1938–1939), 329–342, and "The Two Traditions of Czech Literature," in A. Kaun and E. J. Simmons, eds., *Slavic Studies* (1943), 16 essays in honor of G. R. Noyes; P. Selver, *Czechoslovak Literature; an Outline* (1942).

R. W.

D

Dabit, Eugène (1898–1936, French novelist), was born in Paris, the son of a laborer. He attended school only until he was 11 years old. He worked as an apprentice locksmith, as an elevator operator at the Lamarck station of the Paris subway, as a house painter. At 18 he enlisted in the army and was at the front from December, 1916, to November, 1918. Upon his return he completed his education by attending night school, taking courses in drawing and painting. He discovered Balzac, Flaubert (*q.v.*), Zola (*q.v.*), Maupassant (*q.v.*), Huysmans (*q.v.*), Proust (*q.v.*), and Gide (*q.v.*). The works of Vallès (*q.v.*) were a revelation to him. He recognized in them the Paris he knew—its joys, its sorrows, its violence, and its force. Huysmans instilled in him an admiration for a vigorous and precise style. In reading Charles Louis Philippe (*q.v.*), Dabit felt as if he were meeting a friend and a guide who would help him clarify his desires and bring to light his weaknesses. At the time his parents had become the proprietors of a 50-room hotel. Dabit wrote of the lives of those who frequented the place in *Hôtel du Nord* (1929; Eng. tr., 1931), a realistic novel awarded the Populist Prize in 1931. Overnight he became well known. Advised and encouraged by Roger Martin du Gard (*q.v.*) and Gide, he wrote a second book, in part autobiographical, *Petit-Louis* (1930). From then on one or two books appeared every year—*Villa Oasis* (1932), *Faubourgs de Paris* (1933), *Un Mort tout neuf* (1934), *L'Ile* (1934), *La Zone verte* (1935), *Trains de vie* (1936). He died of scarlet fever on August 21, 1936, in a hospital in Sevastopol, after having been ill only four days. He had accompanied Gide and Louis Guilloux (*q.v.*) on a two-month trip to Soviet Russia to attend the funeral of Maxim Gorky (*q.v.*).

Like many writers born of the masses, Eugène Dabit mistrusted—perhaps a little too strongly—those of his associates who wrote for the masses. He doubted the sincerity of the "populist" school of writers and disliked being classed as one of them. The preface to his last book is typical in this respect; in it he declares that literature, without sacrificing any of its value, should be employed as a weapon against a treacherous and cruel world.

P. B.

Dąbrowska, Marja (née Szumska, 1892–, Polish sociologist and novelist), was born in Rusów, Kalisz district, German Poland. She began to write when very young; at 15 her first story was published in the *Gazeta kaliska.* She studied much abroad—natural science in Brussels, social conditions in Switzerland, England, and France, the cooperative movement in Finland—and then returned to Poland to marry a well-known social worker and to dedicate herself to the cause of social and economic reform. After a 10-year apprenticeship as a militant publicist, she turned to fiction, making use for this purpose of memories of her own childhood. The result was the impressive saga of Kalisz, *Noce i dnie* (1932–1934; Nights and Days), which now won for Dąbrowska renown as a literary artist on a par with the fame she had previously enjoyed as a student of social change, thanks especially to an earlier novel, *Ludzie stamtąd* (1925; The Landless). As a result of her challenging *Rozdroże* (1937; The Crossroads), a condensed survey of the peasant problem in Poland from the earliest times to the present, together with its sequel, *Ręce w uścisku* (1939; Hand in Hand), Dąbrowska became the center of a head-on clash between the elements in Poland that desired slow, organic evolution and those demanding immediate change, especially in the relationship of the peasant to the state. In 1939 Dąbrowska turned to the sea as a theme, since the sea was then an important issue in Poland's national life, and produced a drama of the times of King Władysław IV (17th century), *Genjusz sierocy* (Orphan Genius). This was widely praised for its literary qualities as well as for its applicability to an immediate problem.

See: F. Schoell, "Le Roman-Fleuve de Marja Dąbrowska," *Pologne littéraire,* 1933, No. 100; K. Czachowski, *Obraz współczesnej literatury polskiej,* III (1936), 200–228, 690–692; J. Spytkowski, "Sumienie społeczne," *Marchołt,* III (1936–1937), 554–556.

A. P. C.

Danish literature has always accorded an important place to the critic. For a full century Denmark was under the dominion of two critics of widely different principles and outlook. Johan Ludvig Heiberg (1791–1860), who was the literary czar before the advent of Georg Brandes (*q.v.*), was above all else an arbiter of form, and it is noteworthy that he condemned an erratic genius such as Hans Christian Andersen because his style was not according to accepted standards. Brandes, on the other hand, concerned himself with the message of the writer rather than the form. Modern Danish literature may be said to date from 1871 when Brandes began his series of epoch-making lectures on world literature in Copenhagen. He declared that Denmark was 40 years behind the times and needed to be awakened out of her romantic dreaming. To some extent this awakening had already begun. The disastrous war of 1864 had roused the Danes out of their complacency, and in the field of literature the Jutlander Steen Steensen Blicher (1782–1848) and the Jew Meïr Aron Goldschmidt (1819–1887) had been forerunners of realism. The brilliance and aggressiveness of Brandes and his faculty for stirring up discussion made him the leader of a movement for which the times were ripe. Momentous as his influence was, it was due less to any positive contribution than to the general effect of liberation. True, Brandes developed a tyranny of his own, and it is surprising how many writers revolted against the spell he cast over them. But even in revolt they owed to him the incitement that helped them to realize their own individuality. The immediate effect of the movement initiated by him was to make Danish writers see the world afresh and coin new expressions for what they saw. This is especially true of Jens Peter Jacobsen (*q.v.*), the finest spirit in what came to be known as the Modern Awakening (*Det moderne Gennembrud*). His penetration especially into feminine psychology was something new in Danish literature. His novel *Niels Lyhne* (1880; Eng. tr., 1919), though ostensibly placed in the time preceding the war of 1864, actually mirrors the currents of thought in the 70's. Niels Lyhne believes in atheism as the salvation of humanity, but "falls" from atheism in a moment of sore trial. A dreamer but essentially sound, he became the model for many later heroes who had nothing in common with him except inability to fit themselves into organized society. Jacobsen's style also had many imitators. As Brandes pointed out, language "needs to be tuned afresh" a few times in a century, and it was Jacobsen who molded the Danish language into a medium fit for modern ideas. He owed some of its oral quality to the example of Hans Christian Andersen, but the richness of color and texture was all his own and has never been surpassed in Danish literature. His prose is often rhythmic. His poetry, which is thoughtful and psychological rather than lyrical, became the inspiration of Stuckenberg (*q.v.*) and the poets of the 90's.

The finest lyrist of the period and the only poet of rank in the Modern Awakening was Holger Drachmann (*q.v.*). He was drawn to the new movement by his instinct of revolt and his sympathy for the oppressed. Some of his poems about the sweated trades might have been written under the influence of the Russian Revolution. On the other hand, his nationalism, and especially his feeling for the Danes who had so recently come under the German yoke, drew him to the conservative camp. Drachmann has written also popular plays, short stories, and a long autobiographical novel, *Forskrevet* (1890; Signed Away). Sophus Schandorph (1844–1922), under the influence of Zola (*q.v.*), wrote peasant tales in which a somewhat heavy-handed realism is redeemed by a jovial good humor. He may be considered as a forerunner of Henrik Pontoppidan (*q.v.*), the greatest of Danish naturalists. Pontoppidan continued the line from Brandes and Jacobsen in criticizing the Danes for their addiction to dreams, but while Jacobsen concentrated on one character reflected in a few satellite persons, Pontoppidan filled a great canvas with a variety of figures. His fame rests chiefly on three broadly planned novel cycles which, together with his short stories, form an almost complete picture of Danish life in town and country and of Danish religious movements and politics as seen in the span of a long lifetime. The central work in point of time and importance is *Lykke-Per* (2 vols., 1898–1904; Lucky Per). Pontoppidan's style matches his thought, manly and vigorous. In contrast to him, the sensitive, neurasthenic Herman Bang (*q.v.*) had something feminine in his nature. He is most nearly classic in what have been called "tragic idylls," stories depicting the joyless lives of persons—chiefly women—who hang on the fringes of gentility or are victims of social injustice. Under the influence of the French naturalists (*see* French naturalism) and of the Norwegian novelist Jonas Lie (*q.v.*), Bang developed an impressionistic treatment and a scintillating style, sometimes marred by mannerisms, but his subjective approach prevented him from attaining the objectivity of the true naturalist. In the spirit of the age he castigated the complacency and weakness of his countrymen in such works as *Tine* (1889), dealing with the defeat of 1864, and *Stuk* (1887; Stucco), a novel of Copenhagen in which he describes the sons of those who fought at Dybböl as a kind of lost generation, unable to lay hold of life either in honest work or in genuine passion. Most of the men of the Modern Awakening were influenced by English and French thought, but Karl Gjellerup (*q.v.*) pronounced himself a disciple of the Germans. While his contemporaries took their subjects close at hand, he went far afield for exotic themes. His ethical sense revolted against the idea of free love, and he sided with Björnstjerne Björnson (*q.v.*) in the Morality Feud which shook Scandinavia. Study of Old Norse led him to the common Germanic origins and from those to modern Germany; Schiller revealed to him the glory that was Greece, and from Greek thought he went on to that of India, thus completing the "Aryan" cycle. He finally became an exponent of Buddhism.

Peter Nansen (1861–1918), a writer typical of the 80's, imitates Herman Bang in his impressionistic style but without Bang's human sympathy. The literary and bohemian circles, which Holger Drachmann described seriously in his novel *Forskrevet,* the new writers dealt with frivolously. The background of their books is the city, but its life of pleasure, never the workaday world. Erotic themes are treated with blasé cynicism. Akin to Peter Nansen were the Copenhagen dramatists, Edvard Brandes (1847–1931), Otto Benzon (1856–1927), Gustav Esmann (1860–1904), and on a somewhat more serious plane Arne Einar Christiansen (1861–). Gustav Wied (*q.v.*), the author of plays, short stories, and novels, gravitated between naturalism and fantastic caricature. All these writers continued to some extent the traditions of the great 18th-century comedy writer, Ludvig Holberg, but without his didactic purpose. On the whole it must be said that naturalism had become decadent and realism had degenerated into materialism.

The neo-romantic movement of the early 90's, which in Sweden was initiated by Heidenstam and Lagerlöf (*qq.v.*), in Norway by Hamsun (*q.v.*), was represented in Denmark chiefly by the poets. As leaders must be counted the three friends Johannes Jørgensen, Sophus Claussen (*qq.v.*), and Viggo Stuckenberg. Jørgensen was at first an admirer of Brandes and under his influence became a freethinker, but, feeling his spiritual needs unsatisfied, turned to a mystic religion and finally, in 1896, was converted to Catholicism. He has told the story of his conversion in a remarkable autobiography *Mit Livs Legende* (6 vols., 1916–1919; Eng. tr., *Jørgensen, an Autobiography,* 2 vols., 1928–1929.) Jørgensen has written limpid and beautiful poems and voluminous prose. His international fame rests on his biographies of Francis of Assisi and Catherine of Siena. Viggo Stuckenberg collaborated with his friend Jørgensen in establishing, in 1893, the magazine *Taarnet* (The Tower), which was to be the organ of the symbolic school of poetry, but owing to lack of funds was shortlived. In this magazine Stuckenberg began the publication of a dramatic poem, *Den vilde Jæger* (The Wild Huntsman), which in its medieval mysticism marked a very distinct departure from the literary ideals of the preceding decade. Sophus Claussen is first and last a lyric poet. He and Ludvig Holstein (*q.v.*) have written nature lyrics inspired by the gentle, idyllic scenes of the Danish islands. The youngest in the group of poets of the 90's was Helge Rode (*q.v.*), whose lyrics have sometimes been compared to those of Shelley. The best of his poems are contained in a volume which takes its name from a poem entitled *Ariel* (1914). He wrote also plays, notable for intellectual content rather than adaptation for the stage, but he became best known for his subtle essays, one volume of which significantly is entitled *Regenerationen i vort Aandsliv* (1923; The Regeneration in Our Intellectual Life). He made himself the leader in a movement which, in pointed reference to the so-called Modern Awakening (*Det moderne Gennembrud*) he called, in his book of that name, *Det sjælelige Gennembrud* (1928; The Awakening of the Soul). Jørgensen said of him: "Helge Rode had the courage in 1892 to mention a word that was taboo in the highest intellectual circles; he mentioned God." Helge Rode never, like Johannes Jørgensen, accepted an authoritarian religion, but he vindicated the supremacy of the spirit against the materialistic principles of the age. In his book written during the First World War, *Krig og Aand* (1917; War and the Spirit), he attempted to show how the intellectual development of the half century from 1864 to 1914, passing through the phases of naturalism, Darwinism, and Nietzscheism, had led directly to the catastrophe. As the only possible salvation of the world he saw a return to religious faith. To the neo-romanticists belong also two poets of a different trend, Sophus Michaëlis (1865–1932) and Niels Møller (1859–1941), who tended to choose subjects remote in time and place in order to get away from the drabness of modern life. The popular poet Laurits Christian Nielsen (1871–1930), with his subjects from folk life, bridged the gap between the poets of the 90's and the writers of the soil who initiated the new century.

The writers of the soil were natives of Jutland, the mainland of Denmark, which, with its harsher natural conditions of heath and sand dune—perhaps also its proximity to the enemy in the South—has tended to develop a folk of sterner stuff than those who live on the islands. Their movement was a protest against the assumption that all literary values began and ended in Copenhagen. It was a reaction also against the introspection of the neo-romanticists and marked a return to a naturalism somewhat akin to that of Pontoppidan (who was himself a Jutlander), though none of the group had his breadth or his multiplicity of types. They may be classified rather as regional writers, each one cultivating his own small strip with minute care. Somewhat broader than the rest is Jakob Knudsen (*q.v.*), the oldest of the group, though his important literary production does not begin till toward the end of the 19th century. He was originally a teacher and clergyman and was influenced by the great Danish philosopher Søren Kierkegaard. Knudsen's fiction deals primarily with ethical and religious problems, seen from an unconventional point of view. His most significant work, *Den gamle Præst* (1899; The Old Pastor), has for its central figure a patriarchal leader in the parish. Johannes V. Jensen (*q.v.*) in his youth made himself the leader of the Jutland writers in their protest against the sophistication of Copenhagen, and he may be counted as a regional writer in so far as his point of departure has been that region in Jutland where his ancestors had lived for generations. All the harshness and primitiveness of old Jutland is in his masterly *Himmerlands-historier* (3 vols., 1898–1910; Himmerland Stories), but he has an infinitely wider outlook than the other writers of the group. Travels in America and the Orient gave him a marked sympathy for the Anglo-Saxon people and an admiration for American technical achievements. He developed a racial theory by which he traced a connection between his native Jutlanders and the Anglo-Saxon elements in England and America. The assumption that people who went out from Himmerland were the original Cimbri who attacked the Roman Empire is the basis of his greatest work, *Den lange Reise* (1909–1920; The Long Journey), a racial epic of six independent novels in which he tells the history of the Northern race from a time so remote that Scandinavia was in the preglacial tropical age, down to Columbus (whom he counts as a Northerner). It is written with a grandeur of conception and a power of imagination never equaled in Danish literature and rarely in any literature. Though based on historical and scientific studies, it is a creative work which does not pretend to keep within the stockade of known facts. Among the older Jutland writers Johan Skjoldborg and Jeppe Aakjær (*qq.v.*) were definitely enlisted in the service of social reform. Skjoldborg in his novel *Gyldholm* (1902) described with stark realism the life of the pauperized agricultural laborers upon whose toil the luxury and refinement of the Danish manorial estates rested. Jeppe Aakjær in *Vredens Børn; et Tyendes Saga* (1904; Children of Wrath; the Saga of a Servant) painted a dark picture of the life of servants on the peasant farms. He continued to champion reform in books that are sometimes marred by too great zeal, but he is wholly the artist in his lyrics, among which *Rugens Sange* (1906; Songs of the Rye) are best known. Marie Bregendahl (*q.v.*), in her low-toned stories of peasant home life, has created some authentic interiors and fine types of peasant women. All these peasant writers move among elemental realities as they tell the story of people who grapple with the problems of their harsh, simple lives, exhibiting a grim strength that is impressive. The books describing them may at times be monotonous in their sharply narrowed field, but have the integrity that comes from knowledge and sympathy.

The Jutland writers were rooted in tradition. Martin Andersen Nexø (*q.v.*), spokesman of the city proletariat, declared of his hero, Pelle, that it was his purpose to create a hero who should "spring naked out of nothing and conquer the world." He vindicates the sacredness of every human life, however poor and obscure, and fulminates against a world that cares nothing for its poorer children. He sees the world as a constant struggle between the oppressed and the oppressor, the exploited and the exploiter. He is unwilling to concede a spark of humane feeling to the upper classes. It cannot be denied that he is often unjust and in particular that he describes as if they still existed conditions and abuses that have long since been reformed in Denmark, defending himself by saying that he is describing the eternal struggle between those who have and those who have not. Since the Russian Revolution he has looked to Communism as the salvation of humanity. Despite his savage theories, there is in Nexø's writing an element of the idyllic which did much to win international fame for his four-volume novel cycle *Pelle Erobreren* (1906–1910; Eng. tr., *Pelle the Conqueror,* 1913–1917; combined in one volume, 1930), the story of a poor boy who becomes a labor leader. The feminine counterpart, *Ditte Menneskebarn* (5 vols., 1917–1921; Eng. tr., *Ditte: Girl Alive!* 1920; *Ditte, Daughter of Man,* 1921; *Ditte: Toward the Stars,* 1922; combined in one volume, 1931), the story of a poor servant girl, is darker and more poignantly moving. Knud Hjortø (1869–1932), a native of the island of Zealand, has written some regional books, but has done his most distinguished work in philosophical and psychological novels. Otto Rung (1874–) writes novels akin to the English and American with a complexity of characters and plot, drawing sometimes on current conditions, as in his *Paradisfuglen* (1919; The Bird of Paradise), which describes conditions in Copenhagen during the First World War. Harald Kidde's (1878–1918) sensitive and dreamy art was more akin to that of J. P. Jacobsen and was cut short by his early death in 1918. Among women novelists Gyrithe Lemche (1866–) specializes in the solid historical novel, Karin Michaëlis (1872–) excels as an interpreter of feminine psychology, while Thit Jensen (1876–) has turned from vigorous novels of the soil to novels of medieval Denmark. Johannes Anker-Larsen's (1874–) novel *De Vises Sten* (1923; Eng. tr., *The Philosopher's Stone,* 1924) was an expression of the religious unrest following the war. Johannes Buchholtz (1882–) writes stories of provincial life full of humor and with a light touch. Jacob Paludan (1896–) is a striking example of the reaction against modern noisy and strident civilization with its destruction of more quiet values. In his novel *Fugle omkring Fyret* (1925; Eng. tr., *Birds around the Light,* 1928) he describes a fishing hamlet and its simple people being demoralized by the construction of an artificial harbor—which is itself destroyed by the sea. Later he wrote a series of novels about the time of the First World War and after in Denmark, always seeing modern life from a pessimistic point of view. A departure from the preoccupation with the near and immediate was an almost startlingly brilliant historical novel by a young writer, Nis Petersen (1897–1943), entitled *Sandalmagernes Gade* (1931; Eng. tr., *The Street of the Sandalmakers,* 1933) from Rome at the time of Marcus Aurelius.

In the present century a younger group of writers has continued the tradition from the Jutland school, but without the social passion for reform that marked the work of Aakjær and Skjoldborg. The oldest is Thomas Olesen Løkken (*q.v.*), who was born in 1877, but whose first important work did not appear till after the First World War. His three serial novels about the fate of the farmer Nils Hald pictures the disintegrating influence of wartime speculation on rural Denmark. *Klavs Bjerg og Bodil* (1923; Klavs Bjerg and Bodil) deals with more primitive types and is a powerful story of the struggle for survival on the sand dunes along the North Sea. In this book, as often in stories of western Jutland, where life is hard, the influence of the pietistic dissenters is felt. Hans Kirk's (*q.v.*) first novel, *Fiskerne* (1928; The Fishermen), is a subtle study of the form religion takes in each of the simple people that make up the group. Harry Søiberg's (*q.v.*) most important work, the three-volume novel *De Levendes Land* (1916–1920; The Land of the Living) has for its main theme the religious stirrings in a community on the western coast. Marcus Lauesen (1907–), a young writer of South Jutland, found a fresh background for his novels from the Danish-German border. *Og nu venter vi paa Skib* (1931; Eng. tr., *Waiting for a Ship,* 1933) describes the decline of an old family of shipowners whose ships once sailed to China and whose romantic past lent glamour to the little town in South Jutland.

Poetry continues to hold a high place in Danish literature. Valdemar Rørdam (*q.v.*), a very prolific writer, is akin to the romanticists of the early 19th century. Warmly patriotic, he has been especially the spokesman of the South Jutlanders in their sufferings under German rule. He has written plays and long narrative poems, of which the best known is *Gudrun Dyre* (1902), but is finest as a lyrist. Hans Hartvig Seedorf Pedersen (*q.v.*) is a versatile poet who has won popularity by his humorous and sometimes grim ballads, but has written also elegies and poems inspired by his travels around the world. Kai Hoffmann (1874–) is a singer of everyday life and of simple things. Emil Bønnelyche (1893–) is a pioneer of expressionism.

Drama has had fewer votaries. Among the older men, Henri Nathansen (*q.v.*) had one of the finest talents. Best known is his play *Indenfor Murene* (1912; Within the Walls) which gives a picture of the Jewish group in Denmark. Nathansen's contention has been that the Jews have tended too much to give up their special heritage, allowing themselves to be absorbed by the gentiles. In a biography of Brandes he reproaches the great critic with being too Danish and too little Jewish. Svend Borberg (1888–) has written a hyper-modern play in *Circus Juris* (1935), in which he argues that every person has within him several individuals, often at odds, so that one cannot form a just opinion of him merely by his external action. Two playwrights of widely different outlook and choice of subjects, Kaj Munk and Kjeld Abell (*qq.v.*), have dominated the drama of Denmark in recent years. Kaj Munk, a clergyman who has been influenced by the Danish philosopher Søren Kierkegaard, likes to recreate the strong men, one might perhaps say the great criminals, of history with a mixture of fascination and loathing. Among them are Herod in his great play *En Idealist* (1928; An Idealist); Henry VIII in *Cant* (1934), perhaps his most successful play on the stage; Mussolini in *Sejren* (1936; The Victory). He pictures his strong men so convincingly that he sometimes makes us think for a moment that he admires them for their wholeness and singleness of purpose, but he always leads them to their downfall. His real hero is the gentle, unworldly Professor Mensch in *Han sidder ved Smeltediglen* (1938; He Sits by the Melting Pot) who refuses to lend himself to persecution of the Jews. Kaj Munk has himself given the program which he thinks modern drama must follow; if it is to be successful it must learn from the films, where things happen, and must get away from the quiet conversation pieces of the past. Kjeld Abell has also learned from the films. He portrays with a light humorous touch full of grace the common everyday people of his own city, but his humor sometimes hides a bitter satire, as in *Melodien, der blev væk* (1935; Eng. tr., *The Melody That Got Lost*, 1939), a comedy about the poor office proletariat, which has been called a communistic vaudeville. *Eva aftjener sin Barnepligt* (1936; Eva Serves Her Time as a Child) is a delightful comedy about children, ironical on the subject of the joys of childhood. The underlying social theory of Abell's light comedies came out surprisingly in *Anna Sophie Hedvig* (1939; Eng. tr. in *Scandinavian Plays of the Twentieth Century*, Ser. 2, 1944), a drama about a gentle, middle-aged woman teacher in a provincial girls' school, who deliberately murders the principal of the school in order to save a pupil from tyranny. The act is justified by the author and in the last scene is linked with all revolt against injustice through the introduction of the execution of a young revolutionary.

See: Vilhelm Andersen, *Det nittende Aarhundrede anden Halvdel*, Vol. IV (1925) of C. S. Petersen and V. Andersen, *Illustreret dansk Litteraturhistorie;* Hanna Astrup Larsen, ed., *Denmark's Best Stories* (1928); H. G. Topsöe-Jensen, *Scandinavian Literature from Brandes to Our Day* (1929); Helge Kjaergaard, *Die dänische Literatur der neuesten Zeit (1871–1933)* (1934).

H. A. L.

D'Annunzio, Gabriele (1863–1938, Italian poet, novelist, and publicist), is the last of recent Italian literary figures of truly European fame and also occupies a significant place in the political and social history of Italy. He is a kind of last sun and such a burning one that he seems to have left apathy and barrenness behind him, as though instead of providing the country's soil with a gentle heat he had seared it and made it arid. His life might be reconstructed by an admirer as if it were a Dantean journey, which from an Inferno of sensual experience (1883–1910), through the Purgatory of his French exile (1910–1915), finally led him by way of his military exploits and the rescue of Fiume (1915–1920) to assumption in a Paradise of the nation's benefactors where he remained until the end (1938). The eye of the critic can discern something true in this ascent, recognizing especially the signs of a growing need to escape from the distressing and boring sensual dilettantism of the early years, provided it also discerns the indelible print left by that sensuality upon the entire life.

D'Annunzio was born into a patriarchal family of "pure Sabelian race" in the charming town of Pescara, near the mountains and on the Adriatic coast, half-way down the Italian Peninsula. From youth he had a certain kind of handsomeness, and his features were illuminated by a smile of ambiguous quality such as appears on the faces of primitive Etruscan statues. His first period was one of precocious conquest. His eloquence already had the fascination that makes women yield and sweeps men into action; he knew glory at an age when others only dream about it, knew love at an age when it is for most only romantic imaginings, and had money in abundance at a time when it is apt to be only a hope. Later he was to see the Italian aristocratic world at his knees, the masses childishly curious about his every gesture, youth imitating him in his external appearance—even austere representatives of the Soviets finally paid him the tribute of a visit. He unscrupulously used everything and everybody. He was able to choose from among the world's pleasures: his luxuries, his entertainments, his various dwellings, and his innumerable love affairs (especially that with Eleonora Duse, which inspired *Il Fuoco,* 1900; Eng. trs., *The Flame of Life,* 1900, *The Flame,* 1906, 1914) became famous in the current annals of literature and scandal. When nearly 40, driven from his Settignano villa by creditors accumulated through a manner of life more extravagant than truly elegant, D'Annunzio left his country and established himself in France (1910), where he took pleasure in writing works for the theatre (*Le Martyre de St. Sebastien,* 1911) in his own brand of French, conquered with his personal fascination worldly and intellectual elements in Paris, and engaged in his single and highly successful motion-picture enterprise (*Cabiria,* 1914).

He left France in May, 1915, to play his role in the reaction that swept Italy into war against Austria and Germany. At the end of the war he led the expedition which, in opposition to the Treaty of Versailles, restored Fiume to Italy (the March on Ronchi, September 11–12, 1919). He was later obliged by Giolitti's prosaic firmness to leave Fiume. When Fascism came, he accepted it somewhat hesitatingly and lived a life apart in the disdainful, menacing solitude of the Vittoriale, a museum more than an abode. Fortune, which had protected him since birth, granted him the favor of dying before he could witness his country's ruin.

D'Annunzio's life appears restricted after all to a single desire, the search for a new, stimulating, attractive sensation, and a parallel limitation can be found in his art—whatever the abundance of rhymed and free verse, dramas, novels, short stories, apologetic pieces, descriptions, dialogues, diaries, confessions, proclamations, letters, notes. Concerning the one D'Annunzian tone there is fundamental agreement among the critics; they always come back to this theme of the "senses," in evidence from his very earliest compositions.

Primo Vere (1880), which immediately found appreciation, and *Canto novo* (1882), which gave him fame, are poems based on the manner of Carducci (*q.v.*) and Lorenzo Stecchetti (pseud. of Olindo Guerrini, 1845–1916); *Il Libro delle vergini* (1884) and *San Pantaleone* (1886) show him looking towards naturalism and wanting to be an Abruzzian Verga (*q.v.*), although at the same time borrowing freely from Maupassant (*q.v.*). But he really detached himself early from all those masters. A very keen eye was accompanied by a profound indifference to human thought and sorrow, and by an ingenuous barbarism which could be felt in his communion with the sea, the earth, and the sky, without any preoccupations of a historical or reflective character, and with a special delight in sexual imagery (in 1883 the *Intermezzo di rime,* openly aphrodisiac, caused a scandal). Analyses were as precise as they were cruel, descriptions as accurate as they were cold. The subject matter of D'Annunzio's writings was to change, but he never really left this one manner. Some of his masterpieces are already in this earlier work and stand comparison with pages of *Le Laudi* (1903–1912), especially the first book, or the *Notturno* (1921). He always describes. If the scenes are invented, the myth has the precision and the reality of fact; if taken from real life, the description has the enchanted air of the myth. He is forever the painter of bodies and not of souls. The pictures live their own life separate from the ensemble of the book. It is easier to isolate them in the verses and diaries than in the novels, but the result of the reading is consistently this isolation of a page, a detail, a paragraph; the reader is fatally led to neglect the plot, which is pure fiction, to forget the character, who has no life, to skip the thesis, which is artificial. D'Annunzio's art has been compared with that of the Alexandrians and of the Italian Marini; his quality of decadence or excessive romantic individualism is equally the cultural summation of much else, as can be seen from his first novel, *Il Piacere* (1889; Eng. tr., *The Child of Pleasure,* 1898). He continues with this kind of magic, but as one Italian critic says, "In all our literature there is no writer of his rank who is equally lacking in ideas." As to subject matter there are various shifts. From 1890 to 1894 he wavers between Russian influences (*e.g.,* the two novels *L'Innocente,* 1892, Eng. trs., *The Intruder,* 1898, *The Victim,* 1914; and *Giovanni Episcopo,* 1892, Eng. tr., *Episcopo & Company,* 1896; to which corresponds in poetry the *Poema paradisiaco,* 1893) and the influence of Schopenhauer and Nietzsche (*q.v.*) (*Il Trionfo della morte,* 1894; Eng. tr., *The Triumph of Death,* 1896), where we can already perceive the desire to escape sensuality through death. His fundamental manner is the same in his several dramatic efforts, composed especially during his friendship with

Eleonora Duse: *Allegoria della primavera* (1895), *Il Sogno d'un mattino di primavera* (1897; Eng. tr., *The Dream of a Spring Morning,* 1902), *Il Sogno d'un tramonto d'autumno* (1898; Eng. tr., *The Dream of an Autumn Sunset,* 1904). In these as in certain novels he takes up the theme, which was dear to him, of mysterious reincarnations of ancient figures and tragic destinies in modern personages (*La Città morta,* 1898; Eng. tr., *The Dead City,* 1902). In *La Figlia di Jorio* (1904; Eng. tr., *The Daughter of Jorio,* 1907) D'Annunzio wrote his dramatic masterpiece, which won and still keeps public favor, above all on account of the fairy-like character of the folkloristic background. *La Fiaccola sotto il moggio* (1905) is an inferior play about lust, and *La Nave* (1908) is chiefly a drama of collective lust. *Francesca* (1902; Eng. tr., *Francesca da Rimini,* 1902) and *Parisina* (1913) are noteworthy linguistic exercises, and the same may be said of the empty and academic *Vita di Cola di Rienzi* (1913) and of the philological *tour de force* already mentioned, *Le Martyre de St. Sebastien,* a morbid mixture of carnality and exterior Catholicism. The bishop of Paris properly condemned it as blasphemous. Various other attempts to play with Christian thought, especially during the time when D'Annunzio was a neighbor of a M. Bremond in the French Landes (*Contemplazione della morte,* 1912) are not to be taken very seriously.

Italians of recent years have greatly admired in D'Annunzio the public, military, and patriotic poet (*Odi navali,* although these were written in 1892), the eulogist of Garibaldi (1901), Verdi (1901), Victor Hugo (1902), and Carducci (1903), the bard of the *Gesta d'oltremare* (composed for the war in Tripoli, 1912) and later the trumpeting herald of Fiume (1920). In the last period of his life D'Annunzio produced certain fragmentary and diary-like books, where one finds indeed a far lighter, more transparent, and lucid writer (*La Leda senza cigno,* 1916), and even made use of the futuristic technique (*Il Notturno,* 1921), thereby presenting Marinetti (*q.v.*) with a masterpiece in his own style.

The essence of D'Annunzio's art is really in the third book of *Le Laudi, Alcione,* written mostly after 1900 and published in 1907. Here are fables and myths seized in their immediate aspects, without the usual artificial interpositions, direct and impressive. "La Pioggia nel pineto," "Bocca d'Arno," "La Morte del cervo," "La Sera fiesolana," are constantly and rightly cited as samples of a D'Annunzio who now displays, on a vaster scale, the power he had previously shown in the "Falce di lume calante" of the *Canto novo* of 1882. The mature artist and the beginner prove their identity.

The effects D'Annunzio had on Italian life may be traceable to some deep inclination or tradition of the country's ruling classes which has made the so-called "D'Annunzianism" possible, a compound in which it is difficult to say what is the proportion of rhetoric, of affectation, of hardness of heart, of civil indifference, of provincialism, of ignorance, and of arrogance; its analysis would lead back to Petrarch and perhaps even to Cicero. D'Annunzianism was an "Italian disease." Naturally what was first imitated in him was his outward appearance; his necktie, his goatee, his choice of words, his scorn for creditors, his dogs with languorous eyes, his ladies with high-sounding names, his insolent possessiveness, his easy forgetfulness. Then came the more serious deformations, above all the rhetoricism which leads people to think that a thing has been done when it has only been said, albeit in exquisite fashion. In this D'Annunzianism has been lethal to many Italians. Politically, D'Annunzio's influence began in 1915. The famous March on Ronchi of 1919 prevented Fiume from becoming part of the Balkans, but, by provoking the first political revolt in the Italian army, D'Annunzio Balkanized all of Italy and opened the way for the March on Rome of 1922. It has been said that D'Annunzio gave Italy a new aesthetic consciousness, and certainly from his generation dates the conviction, spread throughout Italy, of the beauty of the country and of the importance of this beauty. But perhaps this aesthetic consciousness was gained at the expense of the political consciousness which it had been Carducci's great merit to have aroused.

A complete edition of the works of D'Annunzio has been published by the house of Mondadori at Verona in 49 volumes (1927–1936).

See: G. Borgese, *Gabriele D'Annunzio* (1909); E. Thovez, *Il Pastore, il gregge e la zampogna* (1910); G. Passerini, *Vocabolario dannunziano* (1928); B. Croce, *La Letteratura della nuova Italia,* 3d ed., IV (1930), 7–70; F. V. Nardelli, *L'Arcangelo: Vita e miracoli di G. D'Annunzio* (1931; Eng. tr., *Gabriel, the Archangel,* 1931); A. Sodini, *Ariel armato* (1931); M. Parenti, *Bibliografia dannunziana essenziale* (1939).

G. P.

Dantas, Júlio (1876–, Portuguese dramatist, short-story writer, and poet), is well known in his own country as a brilliant, versatile playwright and an untiring teller of amorous stories. He survives as the youngest member of a generation of dramatists and actors to which Lopes de Mendonça, Mesquita, and the brothers Rosa had belonged. Although born at Lagos, his real home is Lisbon, where he received his schooling. In 1899 he graduated from medical school, and at the same time had his first play produced in the capital. From the outset the psychiatrist and the writer were inseparable in him, as is shown by his doctor's thesis, *Pintores e poetas de Rilhafoles* (1900; Painters and Poets at Rilhafoles), which deals with artists among the insane. As a doctor, Dantas has seen distinguished service in the Portuguese army; as a man of letters, he achieved the distinction of being elected president of the Portuguese Academy of Sciences.

By 1900 four promising works had come from the pen of Dantas, foreshadowing his later career. They were *Nada* (1896; Nothing), a slender volume of materialist poems, whose originality lay in a combination of revived traditional verse forms with modern, nihilistic obsessions and a shocking anatomical vocabulary; *Doentes* (1897; Sick People), a collection of short stories, written in collaboration with Manuel Penteado; and two historical dramas, *O que morreu de amor* (1899; The One Who Died of Love) and *Viriato trágico* (1900; Tragic Viriatus). Soon thereafter, Dantas was to win great success as the author of plays which engaged all his talents—his sense for inner drama, his skill in supplying picturesque detail, his clinical insight, his sensuous lyricism, his gift of telling anecdotes. While remaining faithful to the nationalist and historicizing spirit of the 19th century in taking many of his plots from Portuguese history, he avoided dealing with great events or passions, to which he preferred frivolous but always entertaining subjects. One such vaguely historical drama was *A Severa* (1901; Severa), the melodrama which made him famous. In *A Severa* Dantas succeeded perfectly in creating the enchanted atmosphere of Lisbon's red-light district, the ancient Mouraria, around Count Marialva and the gypsy Severa, two romantic figures beloved by the Lisbonese. The introduction of these two new types on the Portuguese stage showed that the refined archaism of the decadent aristocrat and the slangy vulgarity of the "fado" songstress could be bedfellows. One year later *A ceia dos cardeais* (1902; Eng. tr., *The Cardinals' Collation,* 1927) appeared. It marked a turn to the lyrical one-act drama in verse and proved the author's most popular work in and outside Portugal. A tender emotion, *saüdade,* pervades the play, reaching its highest pitch in the superficial but intense glorification of Portuguese love as the only heartfelt love in the world. Once more Dantas was able to make the lyrical fiber of the Portuguese vibrate when he produced *Rosas de todo o ano* (1907; Eng. tr., *Roses All the Year Round,* 1912), the tender story of two women's love for the same scoundrel. Here, as in his witty short sketches and in his tales, he was at his best, flattering the fair sex. When he aimed higher he failed. In vain he tried to introduce the themes of heredity and social justice, under the influence of the Norwegians and the French. When he tackled great drama—and melodrama—it was through adaptations, from António Ferreira, Tirso de Molina, Shakespeare, Rostand (*q.v.*).

See: F. de Figueiredo, "O sr. Júlio Dantas," in *Revista de história,* VII (1918), 77–96; Wilhelm Giese, *Aspectos da obra literária de Júlio Dantas* (1941?).

G. M. M.

Danvila, Alfonso (1876–, Spanish novelist), has had a career in the diplomatic service, which he entered in 1896, and he has been Spanish ambassador to Argentina and to France. Another example of a not uncommon alliance of diplomacy and letters, he first wrote novels of customs with a refined and worldly atmosphere (*e.g., Lully Arjona,* 1901). He also soon became interested—following probably in the footsteps of his father, Manuel Danvila Collado, a noted historian—in historical studies of the 18th century, and composed monographs such as *Luisa Isabel de Orleans y Luis I* (1902) and *Fernando VI y doña Bárbara de Braganza* (1905). From a combination of both his previous fields came what is considered his most important contribution to literature—a series of historical novels about the peninsular war in the early years of the 18th century, with the meaningful title *Luchas fratricidas de España* (1923–1930), comprising some 14 volumes that begin with *El testamento de Carlos II* and end with *Aún hay Pirineos.* Well documented, written in an entertaining narrative style, rich in incident and anecdote, if they do not reach the level of the *Episodios nacionales* of Pérez Galdós (*q.v.*) they are not unworthy of that model. They have also the interest of focusing attention on the first moment of the tragic civil strife among Spaniards in modern history.

See: E. Suárez Calimano, *21 ensayos* (1926).

A. del R.

Däubler, Theodor (1876–1934, German poet), was born in Trieste, of German parents, and grew up as a bilingual child, equally at home in German and in Italian. One of his grandmothers was Irish. Soon after his final examinations at the Fiume Gymnasium he gave up the striving for a profession and became a vagrant intellectual. In Naples he conceived the plan of his epic poem *Das Nordlicht* (published at Florence in 1910; a much revised edition was published in Geneva in 1922). Later years in Paris were Däubler's really formative period. Although essentially a lonely soul, he there met and became the lifelong friend of Moeller van den Bruck, who in most respects was his spiritual opposite. Däubler spent most of the year 1914 in Italy. In Germany during nearly the entire period of the First World War, he tried repeatedly and unsuccessfully to become a soldier. After the war his homelessness continued; he traveled in Greece and the Near East and visited Egypt and the Scandinavian countries. In 1928 he became a member of the Prussian Academy of Letters. He died in 1934 in a sanatorium in the Black Forest.

Däubler undoubtedly was a creative poet. Under the influence of superstitious servants he early developed a very personal religion. *Das Nordlicht* is conceived as an original cosmic myth. Stylistically, Däubler seems to have been thwarted by the almost insurmountable conflict between the Italian desire for harmony and the German tendency towards the baroque. Only in rare poems did he achieve a perfect expression of his own self (see *Das Sternenkind,* 1917; *Die Treppe zum Nordlicht,* 1920). His travel diaries are of considerable interest. Däubler exercised his greatest influence through his early enthusiasm for expressionism (*Der neue Standpunkt,* 1917; *Im Kampfe um die moderne Kunst,* 1918).

See: S. Heiszel, "Theodor Däubler—ein Schwabe?" *Dichtung und Volkstum,* XXXVIII (1937), 208–224.

E. R.

Daudet, Alphonse (1840–1897, French poet, short-story writer, playwright, and novelist), was born at Nîmes in Languedoc, the son of a royalist father and a deeply religious mother. Because his father, the owner of a silk manufactory, lost his money, the family moved to Lyons, where Alphonse obtained his early schooling. At the age of 16 he was appointed a monitor in the Collège d'Alais, which position promptly became distasteful to his sensitive and gentle nature. The following year he joined his elder brother, Ernest, in Paris, and there his literary career began with the publication of a collection of verse. *Les Amoureuses* (1857), while distinctly adolescent, contained a few graceful poems and gave him entrance into several salons where he met men and women of literary importance. He wrote short articles for several newspapers, notably Villemessant's *Evénement* and *Figaro,* until he received a sinecure in the private offices of the duke of Morny, the emperor's half brother and president of the Corps Législatif (1860–1865). The duke admired the young Southerner greatly and asked him to collaborate on more than one of the plays he was in the habit of writing with other members of his staff. Still other plays composed at this time with the aid of L'Epine met with indifferent success. Morny granted Daudet frequent leaves of absence in search of renewed health. Thus he made several trips to his native Languedoc and one to Algeria, where he gathered the material for numerous later stories and novels. His marriage to Julia Allard (1867) was a great boon, since she calmed his excitable temperament, served him often as a wise collaborator, and eased his later life of pain and ill-health.

Daudet, under the influence of his close friend Mistral (*q.v.*) and other members of the Felibrige movement, soon established himself as a short-story writer of Provence, producing *Les Lettres de mon moulin* in 1866. These portray the author's sensitive nature, his gentle irony, his gift for flashing, brilliantly colored, impetuous prose. There followed a semi-autobiographical work, *Le Petit Chose* (1868), the first part of which contains many details of his early childhood. In 1872 appeared *Les Aventures prodigieuses de Tartarin de Tarascon,* a burlesque of the *méridional* character; as well as the moving tragedy *L'Arlésienne.* With *Fromont jeune et Risler aîné* (1874) Daudet began the writing of full-length novels, which promptly made him one of the most widely read and successful authors of his time. In rapid succession appeared *Jack* (1876), *Le Nabab* (1877), *Les Rois en exil* (1879), *Numa Roumestan* (1881), *L'Evangéliste* (1883), *Sapho* (1884), *Tartarin sur les Alpes* (1885), *L'Immortel* (1888), *Port Tarascon* (1890), and *Soutien de famille* (1898). For the most part the substance of these novels was taken from contemporary life, individuals Daudet knew personally, or events noted in daily newspapers. His habit was to fill numerous notebooks with a vast quantity of heterogeneous material, which he then used at will as he composed. Daudet was more a chronicler of his times than an inventor, reproducing true experiences as he had seen and felt them himself. His chief claim to an established position in French letters lies in his sensibility. His capacity for emotion, so pronounced in his works, set him apart from his master, Flaubert (*q.v.*), and the members of the later naturalistic school. His characters, likened to those of Charles Dickens, are frequently exaggerated under the stimulus of his great sympathy for humanity. His excellent sense of humor, a quality none too common in French authors of his period, restrained a tendency to irony from becoming bitter or didactic. Many of his works have been translated into English.

See: E. Daudet, *Mon Frère et moi* (1882)); R. H. Sherard, *Alphonse Daudet* (1894, in English); Y. Martinet, *Alphonse Daudet; sa vie et son œuvre* (1940).

A. R. F.

Daudet, Léon (1867–1942, French novelist, critic, and journalist), was one of the most colorful figures in modern French letters and politics. Born and raised in Paris, the son of Alphonse Daudet (*q.v.*), he moved in artistic and literary circles from childhood, taking for granted his familiar footing with Zola, the Goncourts, and Mistral (*qq.v.*), looking irreverently at even the old giant, Hugo. He was destined for medicine and studied under Charcot, but the attraction of letters proved too strong, and he entered journalism in 1900, writing at first for the *Gaulois* and *Libre Parole* and then forming a lifelong association with the *Action française* when it became a daily in 1908. A radical, or at least a liberal, in art and politics as a young man, he was led first by his friendship with Edouard Drumont and then by the intellectual spell of Charles Maurras (*q.v.*) into the royalist camp. His activities for the cause, both as an editor of the *Action française* and as a politician (he was deputy for Paris, 1919–1924, and was defeated for senator in 1926), not only provided an ample outlet for his boundless exuberance but also dominated his literary production for the rest of his life.

He was not an original thinker in politics—he himself always acknowledged his complete dependence on Maurras; nor as a critic in such works as *Etudes et milieux littéraires* (1927) and *Flambeaux* (1929) did he formulate or follow a systematic theory of art. Except for *Le Voyage de Shakespeare* (1896), his novels are at best second-rate; the handling of a plausible story and the creation of character are beyond him. But he had himself to give, the perceptions and reflections of an aggressive sensualist gifted with a comic sense who was able to pack a great deal into his life; and he found his true form in the memoir, in which he is justly comparable with Saint-Simon. Daudet wrote great French prose, a blend of the classic and the colloquial (the homely, revealing word), as might be expected of a man whose demigods were Rabelais, Montaigne, and Shakespeare. He was unequaled at portraying in a few phrases yet with the utmost vividness a character, a face, or a scene, and he exploited this gift to the full in his reminiscences, *Souvenirs des milieux littéraires, politiques, artistiques et médicaux* (6 vols., 1914–1921; Eng. tr. of selections, *Memoirs of Léon Daudet,* 1925), and such books of history as *Panorama de la IIIe république* (1936) and *Le stupide XIXe siècle* (1922; Eng. tr., *The Stupid XIXth Century,* 1928).

Yet Léon Daudet's undoubted merits are offset for all but the most blind followers of the *Action française* by grave defects. Even for French political journalism, his daily polemics could be described as nothing but insanely violent, often unfair, generally vulgar, and sometimes obscene. Péguy said of the *Action française,* thinking of Léon Daudet perhaps, that everything about it was 18th century except its manners. Prejudice and hatred run through his work—a literary hatred of Zola and his school, a political hatred of all liberals and radicals, a national hatred of everything German, and an anti-Semitism that has not often been rivaled in France. These prejudices often led him into ridiculous positions as a critic, either of literature, politics, thought, or men: his readers would gather that the work of Flaubert (*q.v.*), Zola, and the whole school of Médan was without value, that all presidents of the republic were corrupt imbeciles, that Bergson (*q.v.*) was of no importance as a philosopher. Yet he was capable of showing unexpected appreciations, as when he was one of the first to hail the work of Proust (*q.v.*). His work remains thus a mixture which will both attract and repel the average reader, by the very fact that it reproduces completely a baffling personality which even his enemies will admit had many of the characteristics of genius. He died at Saint-Rémy de Provence on July 1, 1942.

See: Robert Guillou, *Léon Daudet; son charactère, ses romans, sa politique* (1918); Edouard Mas, *Léon Daudet; son œuvre* (1928).

C. W., Jr.

Dauthendey, Max (1867–1918, German poet and novelist), born in Würzburg, Bavaria, was brought up in a Russian home atmosphere by a father with French ancestry and a Russian mother who are described in *Der Geist meines*

Vaters (1912) and *Gedankengut aus meinen Wanderjahren* (1913). His philosophy of life he later embodied in *Verdensaltet* (published in 1893 with his Swedish friend, Gustaf Uddgren, as collaborator), which contains his theory of artistic creation, and in *Lied der Weltfestlichkeit* (1918), which proclaims the art of finding solace in the beauty and life of animate and inanimate nature. From 1886 until his death he traveled all over Europe, year after year, although often in financial stress, and in 1897 he visited the United States and Mexico. In 1905–1906 he took part in a Cook's Tour around the world. But he always returned gladly to his home town, which inspired many of his poems in *Singsangbuch* (1907), *Der weisse Schlaf* (1907), *Lusamgärtlein* (1909), and *Weltspuck* (1910). Likewise the novel *Josa Gerth* (1893) and several dramas (*e.g., Frau Raufenbarth,* 1911, and the tragedy *Die Heidin Geilane,* 1912) spring from his life in Würzburg. The atmosphere of Sweden is reflected in *Ultra Violett* (1893) and *Reliquien* (1897) and such dramas as *Sun* (1895), *Sehnsucht* (1895), *Der Drache Grauli* (1911), and *Maja* (1911). Memories of his journeys to Paris, Sweden, and Greece found an echo in *Bänkelsang vom Balzer auf der Balz* (1905), and Mexico gave him the idea for his novel *Raubmenschen* (1911). His play *Spielereien einer Kaiserin* (1910; Eng. tr., *Caprices of an Empress,* 1912) had a brief success on the stage. The experiences harvested on his voyage around the world were published as collections of *Novellen* in *Ligam* (1909), *Die acht Gesichter am Biwasee* (1911), and *Geschichten aus den vier Winden* (1915). Likewise his songs in *Die geflügelte Erde* (1910) resulted from this tour. In April, 1914, he set out once more on a world cruise, but the outbreak of the First World War prevented his return. In Java he wrote his last collection of songs, *Des grossen Krieges Not* (1915), and his diaries, on which are based the posthumous works, *Erlebnisse auf Java* (1924) and *Letzte Reise* (1924).

During his lifetime Dauthendey was hardly known in Germany, and even today his recognition as a poet is disputed by literary historians and critics. His orgies of light, color, and sound and his eccentric art forms make this impressionistic and exotic writer at least a *poeta sui generis.*

See: C. Mumm, *Max Dauthendeys Sprache und Stil* (1925); H. G. Wendt, *Max Dauthendey, Poet-Philosopher* (1936).

F. S.

De Amicis, Edmondo (1840–1908), Italian essayist, novelist, and short-story writer), was born at Oneglia in Liguria, but spent the greater part of his life in Turin. As an infantry officer in the Italian army he fought in the campaign against Austria in 1866 and took part in the famous battle of Custozza. He wrote many articles for the army newspaper *Italia militare,* of which he was editor for a time. These articles appeared in book form under the title *La Vita militare* (1868; Eng. tr., *Military Life in Italy,* 1882). In his effort to depict a soldier's life, the author seems to have recourse to every conceivable device for drawing a tear: long marches, thirst, disease, sacrifice, insanity, love, death, are all recurrent themes. Because of this volume the poet Carducci (*q.v.*), always intolerant of the sentimental, termed De Amicis "Edmondo the languorous," long-winded founder of Italian bourgeois prose.

After the publication of a collection of short stories, *Novelle* (1872), De Amicis retired from the army to devote himself entirely to a literary career. Between the years 1872 and 1879 he visited many countries and wrote his well-known books of travel: *Spagna* (1872; Eng. tr., *Spain,* 1881), *Olanda* (1874; Eng. tr., *Holland,* 1880, American title, *Holland and Its People,* 1881), *Ricordi di Londra* (1874; Eng. tr., *Jottings about London,* 1883), *Marocco* (1876; Eng. tr., *Morocco,* 1879, American title, *Morocco, Its People and Places*), *Costantinopili* (1878–1879; Eng. tr., *Constantinople,* 1878), *Ricordi di Parigi* (1879; Eng. tr., *Studies of Paris,* 1879). The most ambitious works of their kind to be written in Italian, often published in beautifully illustrated editions, translated into many languages, they reached a wide audience. Though over-lyrical in style and full of inaccuracies in detail, these books won popularity because of the author's genuine enthusiasm and his sympathetic interpretation of the customs and peoples of other lands.

Cuore (1886; Eng. tr., *Cuore, an Italian Schoolboy's Journal,* 1887) was read in every elementary school in Italy until Fascism came into power. It is widely used today in the United States as a textbook in teaching Italian. *Cuore* is directed to children between the ages of nine and thirteen and is written in finished Tuscan style. True to its name, it goes to the heart. It is sentimental in the extreme, but never undignified. In many touching anecdotes the story brings out the mutual respect that exists between pupil and teacher and cuts through all social prejudices in its portrayal of the deeds and actions of the individual boys. The basic theme of *Cuore* is that there is something fine and lovable in every child, if only it can be reached and developed soon enough. Quite simply, De Amicis has hit upon a fundamental concept in modern education, but in his hands it is shorn of all theory.

His long novel *Sull'oceano* (1889; Eng. tr., *On Blue Water,* 1897) is no more than an extended series of anecdotes depicting the problems and sufferings of illiterate emigrants on their interminable ocean voyage. *Il Romanzo di un maestro* (1890; Eng. tr., *The Romance of a Schoolmaster,* 1892) and *La Maestrina degli operai* (1894; Eng. tr., *Won by a Woman,* 1897) are both concerned with the idealistic but forgotten young schoolteacher, relegated to a country town and at the mercy of inflated politicians and inept superintendents.

Ever in search of the good in the individual and in society, De Amicis in 1890 openly declared himself a Socialist. *Fra scuola e casa* (1892) and *La Carrozza di tutti* (1899), both collections of short stories and anecdotes, reflect the socialistic trend of the author's thinking at this time and are vivid in their defense of the oppressed and in their appeal to human sympathy. But in these and others of his later works the sentiment is laid on too thick, the idealism has become too soft. What in his earlier writings was a genuine gift had now become a too conscious technique.

In 1905 De Amicis's *L'Idioma gentile* was well received. It was written in a new vein and seemed to furnish simple, concrete answers to the ever-debated Italian *questione della lingua.* Following in the footsteps of Manzoni, De Amicis's ideas are in direct opposition to those of the philosopher Benedetto Croce (*q.v.*). De Amicis conceives of language as a tool and urges his readers to love their mother tongue and to perfect their use of it in all its details. Croce, who considers expression intrinsically an individual matter and the idea the main thing, accuses De Amicis of childishness and pedantry. This all too "gentle" volume dissolves under the acute scrutiny of Croce's criticism. The strength of De Amicis lies elsewhere. People who are guided by the heart rather than the mind will no doubt continue to read *Cuore.*

See: J. H. Brovedani, *Edmondo De Amicis; l'homme et l'œuvre* (1914); V. Chialant, *Edmondo De Amicis, educatore e artista* (1911).

M. V. H.

Deauville, Max (pseud. of Maurice Duwez, 1881–, Belgian novelist, war chronicler, playwright, and moralist), was born in Brussels. A doctor by profession, he received early initiation into the world of letters as secretary to the bibliographer Spoelberch de Lovenjoul (*q.v.*). His first novel, *La Fausse Route,* appeared in 1907; his subsequent literary activity, averaging more than a book a year, is unusual among nonprofessional authors. In his pre-war fiction he appears as a detached and slightly ironical observer of the human comedy, but his master novel, *L'Amour dans les ruines* (1910), reveals profound sympathy for its victims. His early plays recall, by their delicate psychology and simplicity of plot, certain of Musset's. The First World War was to bring a profound change. Deauville joined the medical corps at the start and saw active service throughout the conflict. A diary, *Jusqu'à l'Yser* (1917), won international fame when Jean Norton Cru (see below) hailed it as a literary and documentary masterpiece. It is a chronicle, objective as Caesar's *Commentaries.* In a different tone are his two following works, *La Boue de Flandres* (1922) and *Introduction à la vie militaire* (1923), both written, he says, during the war. Here he gives free rein to his irony; his declared aim is to deflate military authority, and it is hard to believe that the manuscript was not revised after the Armistice. A novel, *Jonas* (1923), portraying the immediately succeeding years, is in the same spirit, which also marks his later writings. Irony he holds to be the great source of consolation, capable of alleviating the pain in every human heart. Certainly irony often dominates in contemporary literature, and at times one wonders why so much energy is spent in lashing the despicable and incorrigible gang often presented as humanity. How much is pure pose among these authors? This question rarely comes to mind in reading Max Deauville; he possesses an innate sense of decorum, and his sincerity is manifest. His irony is tinged with pity, and if he laughs it is indeed that he may not weep. He is fundamentally an idealist, embittered by his observation of men's folly and using irony as a stoic armor. "Literature," he says, "is the product of the discord between the life we lead and what should logically be ours." Hence in most of his work discreet pity goes hand in hand with satire. A striking example of this may be seen in his theatrical masterpiece, *Ecce Homo, pièce en sept tableaux* (1931), which is also an original experiment, in both form and matter, in stage craftsmanship. The action is slight; historical color is deliberately sacrificed to accentuate the timelessness of the drama; this, and the mystico-poetic utterances of certain characters, suggest the influence of Maeterlinck (*q.v.*), but the intellectual intention outweighs the emo tional. Christ, whose figure dominates the action, does not appear on the stage; the Galileans are called communists, and Roman officers, in khaki uniforms, use the language of modern barracks. Their unawareness of the significance of what is happening under their eyes recalls *The Procurator of Judea* of Anatole France (*q.v.*). It may be surmised that the latter's *Histoire contemporaine* has had some influence on the disillusioned philosophy of Deauville's post-war work. Keenly alive to the varied trends of contemporary thought, he leaves his personal touch on all his work. His style is marked by classic austerity rather than by the search for color characteristic of the Flemings. He is always more interested in the psychological reactions of his characters than in their actions; hence his plots are never complicated. Many of his "stories" are first cousins of essays intended to propound ideas, and monologues with the same purpose often replace dialogue. Had he lived in the 18th century, he would probably have left memoirs and a collection of maxims. Maurice Gauchez hails him as the La Rochefoucauld of our time.

See: M. Gauchez, *A la recherche d'une personnalité* (1926); J. N. Cru, *Témoins* (1929); *Nervie*, 1931, No. 7 (special number devoted to Max Deauville).

B. M. W.

de Bosis, Adolfo (1863–1924, Italian poet), born in Ancona, settled in Rome in his youth and lived there until his death. His early close friendship with D'Annunzio (*q.v.*) influenced decisively his taste and vocation. Together they were young dandies in Roman society, emulated Wilde and Whistler in manner, and sailed the Adriatic in the spirit of Shelley. Together also, with Giovanni Pascoli (*q.v.*) as a third, they founded in 1895 the periodical *Convito*, in which they published their own and their friends' works (*e.g.*, those of Edoardo Scarfoglio, Francesco Paolo Michetti, Giulio Aristide Sartorio). The foreword by de Bosis outlines their common creed: "Facing the present muddy tide of barbarism, there are still some who keep the faith in the Latin race, in the indestructible power of Beauty, in the sovereign dignity of the spirit, in the necessity of intellectual hierarchies and in the creative power of the Word." Having exhausted his friend's capital, D'Annunzio moved on to new adventures; but de Bosis retired into the orderly life of a successful business lawyer and father of a large family.

Of his own verse he published only two volumes, *Amori ac Silentio* and *Rime sparse* (issued together in 1922). His poetry expresses a despairing love for art and a strong faith in man's progress and is mostly in the vein of stoic consolation. Strangely enough, it also contains one of the first specimens of "social" poetry, "Ode a un macchinista." His verse has been much appreciated for its melody and for the experimenting with new techniques ("Ode ai convalescenti," "La Sera," "Ode al mare," "Eidola"). The name of Adolfo de Bosis remains linked in Italian literature to that of Shelley, whom he worshiped and translated with rare perfection (*Cenci*, 1898; *Prometheus Unbound*, 1922; *Lyrics*, 1928).

See: G. L. Russo, *Adolfo de Bosis* (1922); B. Croce, *La Letteratura della nuova Italia*, 3d ed., IV (1929), 141–156.

G. de S.

de Bosis, Lauro (1901–1931?, Italian poet), was born in Rome, the youngest son of Adolfo de Bosis (*q.v.*) and Lillian Vernon, an American. He grew up in the aesthetic and romantic atmosphere of his father's circle, which left a deep impression upon him. Philosophy and literature remained his lasting interests, although he received a scientific education and took his degree in chemistry at the University of Rome in 1922. Between 1922 and 1926 he translated into Italian verse the *Oedipus Rex* and the *Antigone* of Sophocles, and the *Prometheus Bound* of Aeschylus. He also translated the abridged edition of Frazer's *The Golden Bough* (1924). In 1927 he wrote a lyrical drama, *Icaro*, which received the Olympic prize in Amsterdam in 1928 and was published in Milan in 1930 (Eng. tr., 1933).

Between 1924 and 1930, Lauro de Bosis made several visits to the United States, first as lecturer, then as executive secretary of the Italy-America Society. He also gave a summer course on Italian literature at Harvard. In 1932 was published his *The Golden Book of Italian Poetry*, an anthology preceded by a remarkable historical essay in which the influence of Croce (*q.v.*) is very perceptible.

At the beginning of the Fascist movement, de Bosis, like many young men of his time, was attracted by its reform program; but he soon recognized it as a threat to Italian freedom. In 1930, together with Mario Vinciguerra, Renzo Rendi, and others, he founded the "Alleanza Nazionale," an underground organization which published a bimonthly leaflet. During one of Lauro de Bosis's trips to America, the committee, including his own mother, was arrested. Vinciguerra and Rendi received heavy sentences. "My first instinct," he writes, "was to go to Rome and to share their fate, but I realized that the duty of a soldier is not to surrender, but to fight to the end." He learned to fly and on October 2, 1931, piloted a plane over Rome, scattering leaflets addressed to the population. He managed to escape pursuit planes, but vanished at sea on the return flight in the darkness.

On the night before leaving, he wrote his most important document, *The Story of My Death* (1933), which covers the story of his attempt and carries his message. "No one takes Fascism seriously. Beginning with its leaders, every one counts on its speedy fall, and it seems out of proportion to give one's life to end something that will collapse by itself. That is a mistake. It is necessary to die. I hope that many others will follow me and will at last succeed in rousing public opinion."

G. de S.

De Coster, Charles, (1827–1879, Belgian novelist), was born in Munich; his parents were in the service of a nobleman, who acted as godfather to the child but took small interest in his subsequent career. In all his writings De Coster shows sympathy with the humble people, whom he declares vastly more colorful than the aristocracy. The family soon moved to Brussels, the father died, and Charles was obliged to shift for himself. Artist to the finger tips, he had no interest in bourgeois professions and spent his life in obscure poverty. His ambition was to endow his country with a literary tradition to match its glory in artists of the brush; hence he sought the company of young painters and such men of letters as there were. "I am one of those who know how to wait," he declared, and his long effort toward perfection proves his sincerity. Fame came only after his death, but he had seen his dream fulfilled: his books were illustrated by the most gifted artists of his time. Of his minor compositions, *Légendes flamandes* (1858; Eng. tr., *Flemish Legends,* 1920) attracted some attention from the start and has been translated into several languages. Its style is a discreet imitation of Rabelais's; its matter is based on folklore. The author's preference among the legends was for "Sire Halewyn," perhaps because of its brilliant coloring, but most critics agree with Félicien Rops who gave the palm to "Smets Smee," for which he made all the illustrations. The popular verve of the style, the satire of tyrants, and the sympathy for the rugged sagacity of the humble make this legend the precursor of *Ulenspiegel.*

De Coster's skill in handling Old French brought an appointment in the government archives. He held this post four years (1860–1864), and if his contribution to the editing of ancient laws was not large, the experience was invaluable for the documentation of his masterpiece. *Les Aventures de Tyl Ulenspiegel et de Lamme Goedzak* appeared in a *de luxe* edition at the end of 1867. More than 10 years had been spent in its composition. It is written in the slightly archaic style, handled with greater dexterity than in the *Légendes,* which he regarded as best adapted to reproduce in French the Flemish atmosphere. The author's avowed purpose was to revive yesterday to create tomorrow: "a people is dying," he declared, "when it ignores its past." Peoples whose liberties are threatened by unscrupulous despots, domestic or foreign, have rallied to his book. Ulenspiegel may well claim as his heirs the underground warriors of our day. De Coster was one of the editors of the periodical *Uylenspiegel* (1856–1864)—and made its devise his own: "I walk up and down on the face of the earth, praising all lovely things and hooting at folly." In *Ulenspiegel* he chose a legendary and popular hero, keeping many traditional episodes. These, appearing sporadically throughout the book, figure chiefly in the first part where the urchin, Ulenspiegel, is up to all the pranks ever imagined by the imp of the perverse. But when the Inquisition burns his father and tortures his mother he hears the call, for freedom is the essence of lovely things. Throughout the story scenes of horror are set off by jubilant escapades in which the hero outwits and mocks the oppressor much as his descendants did in the Second World War.

The author's thumbnail review of his book can hardly be bettered: "Above all, this is a joyous, artistic, and literary work, of which history is only the frame and of which love, life, and sentiment, beside the grotesque and the satiric, are the elements." He kept his word and offers the greatest variety. At first sight there seems to be little unity; short chapters, each a picture in itself and often suggesting a painting, present a bewildering number of characters, some historical, some fanciful, but as the story progresses the reader becomes aware that the constantly changing scenes constitute an artfully molded panorama. Ulenspiegel and Lamme belong to folklore: the former had appeared in many chapbooks, the latter was suggested by popular woodcuts. They present a pair often compared to Don Quixote and Sancho Panza. Nele, Ulenspiegel's fiancée, offers the delicate aspect of the love scenes. She is inspired by

De Coster's own betrothed, Elisa Spruyt, whom we know from his posthumously published *Lettres à Elisa* (1894). Satiric bias has doubtless entered into the portraits of certain of the historical characters, *e.g.*, Philip II and the Duke of Alva, whose ghoulish figures enhance the contrast between the Spanish and Flemish temperaments, but they leave an indelible impression on the reader. Among the historical sources for *Ulenspiegel* must be mentioned Van Meteren's *Histoire des révolutions dans les Pays Bas,* which Charles Potvin declares De Coster had read 10 times; Marnix de Sainte-Aldegonde's *Tableau des différens de la religion;* and, of special interest to American readers, John Lathrop Motley's histories of the Low Countries. Less tangible but very real inspiration came from paintings of the old masters; the author haunted museums all his life and appears as the direct forerunner of the next generation of pen-painters such as Lemonnier and Demolder (*qq.v.*). Yet all the study of sources has in no wise challenged De Coster's essential originality; he took his property where he found it, and Ulenspiegel's motto—"I am not body but spirit"—is true in many senses. A new illustrated edition of *Ulenspiegel* was published in New York in 1943.

See: Charles Potvin, ed., *Lettres à Elisa* (1894); Joseph Hanse, *Charles De Coster* (1928); Léon Louis Sosset, *Introduction à l'œuvre de Charles De Coster* (1937).

B. M. W.

Dehmel, Richard (1863–1920, German poet), the most distinguished representative of the transition from extreme naturalism to classic restraint, was born in Wendisch-Hermsdorf, the son of a forester. The landscape of his poetry is that of Brandenburg, a wide, open plain with huge forests of spruce and pine. In it the city of Berlin rises with its factories, forges, and smokestacks. The poet's own landscape has two divergent aspects, on the one hand giant spruce trees battling with the elements, on the other buzzing telegraph wires and blast furnaces belching smoke and flame. The same dualism is evident in the poet: he is both a realistic naturalist and a visionary seer. On the one hand he exemplifies a daring disregard of conventional forms; every poem is a law unto itself. On the other hand his verse displays a painstaking mathematical exactness that recalls Dante. A pure lyric genius, he will sing his social gospel in melodious verse and preach it in impassioned prose.

We see the same dualism in Dehmel's life. While a pupil in a Berlin Gymnasium he comes into conflict with his orthodox teachers. He is ousted and finishes his preparatory training at Danzig. At the university he studies philosophy and literature, as well as the natural sciences. He writes his dissertation in the field of economics, accepts a secretarial position with a fire insurance company. Not until he has published two volumes of poems does he feel he has the right to resign from his position and to devote himself to literature. In 1889 he married Paula Oppenheimer, with whom he collaborated on a volume of verse for children. Frau Paula, he felt, freed his latent powers and showed him the way to serene clarity. But tumultuous passions are seething in the eloquent prophet of a stern ethical code; his first marriage ends in divorce (1899) and Frau Ida (Auerbach) becomes his second wife. Now Dehmel preaches—and practices—rigorous self-discipline and is among the first to see that this is the gospel of Nietzsche (*q.v.*). As a young man Dehmel had been rejected for military service because an excess of nervous energy produced an epileptic condition. Well over 40 he becomes a daring Alpine climber and when almost 51 scales Mont Blanc. The same year the pacifist Dehmel forces the army to accept him for service in the trenches. For him human happiness is the joyful will to sacrifice. When the First World War ends in tragic defeat, he urges the formation of an "iron guard" in which only volunteers would be allowed to serve. This last dream of social service he did not realize; the overexertion of the war years had begun to exact its toll. For some time Dehmel had begun to limp. A bloodclot had developed; he knew his chances for recovery were negligible. What did it matter? To a young friend he remarked: "I have not really been a good man (*ein guter Mensch*), but I believe I have become one." Towards the end he felt he had been privileged to achieve in life what he had long since achieved in his best poetry—the rich harmony of full maturity.

Dehmel's development is clearly visible in his poems from volume to volume; even the titles are significant: *Erlösungen* (1891), *Aber die Liebe* (1893), *Weib und Welt* (1896), *Schöne wilde Welt* (1913). The first three volumes were carefully revised and radically changed in subsequent editions, the last volume was greatly enlarged. A study of these changes reveals the gradual growth of the poet. There can be no doubt that Dehmel has enriched German lyric poetry with a new and significant note. His lyrics show us man in his threefold life as an individual, as a member of society, and as a bit of cosmic life. There is an astounding variety of form and content. Any careful selection will show this and will also show that the variety of form results from the variety of content. His novel in verse *Zwei Menschen* (1903) is the work of a great lyric poet. The meager and conventional plot should not blind the reader to its real significance. Of Dehmel's dramas his last seems the most significant. A "cosmopolitical" comedy, it is the summing up of his war experiences: *Die Götterfamilie* (1921), the fantastic vision of an insane world. A year before his death Dehmel's *Kriegstagebuch* was published with the meaningful subtitle *Zwischen Volk und Menschheit.* For him the poet, as the best of mankind in all nations, stands *zwischen Volk und Menschheit.*

See: J. Bab, *Richard Dehmel* (1926); H. Slochower, *Richard Dehmel, der Mensch und der Denker* (1928).

F. Br.

Deledda, Grazia (1875–1936, Italian novelist), was born in the town of Nuoro, Sardinia, and lived there during the formative years of her life. Most of her stories have the island as a background, and her home remained an inspiration to her perhaps to an even greater degree than in the case of other Italian novelists. She wrote her first short stories at the age of 17, and even these early works show the qualities of a born narrator. She has a simple style and the ability to sketch a situation or a character in a few deft phrases. Her stories have action and movement, and she has an eye for realistic detail that makes the Sardinian tales particularly charming. Because she tells of simple folk, peasants or the rural aristocracy —occasionally contrasted with city life to bring out the full flavor—because she has an interest in the troubles of the lowly and the tormented, and perhaps even more because her work is infused with a tragic sense of destiny, Deledda has been occasionally looked upon as a successor to Verga (*q.v.*). It is a tempting comparison, but it would hardly be a fair one. She is not a "student of life" as Verga is, not a philosopher at all, and if she may be considered an "observer," to use the word of the *veristi,* she is one whose impartiality is continually marred—or relieved—by the lyric impulse. The great scenes and the great characters in her novels are created more through emotional intensity than by the scrupulous cold-blooded concentration of the true naturalist. The characters themselves, though their problems are more complex, are actually less profound than Verga's peasants. The charge has been made that Deledda follows a formula, that from the beginning of her career to the end her novels always contain the same ingredients: a thwarted or obsessed hero or heroine, a dash of Sardinian violence, and a good deal of local color. There is some truth in the charge, though it is fair to point out that in such late works as *L'Incendio nell'oliveto* (1918) and *La Madre* (1920; Eng. tr., *The Woman & the Priest,* 1922, American title, *The Mother,* 1923) there is much more attention paid to psychological atmosphere and character study and less reliance on violence and the picturesque. Deledda was such a serious and conscientious artist that Italian critics have been very well disposed to her and anxious to spare her from being pigeonholed as another regionalist. It would be only reasonable to admit that she is, viewing her work as a whole, precisely that, but she has qualities of perception and human sympathy that raise her far above the level of the writer of provincial vignettes. Her characters do indeed follow a pattern; essentially they are all simple, passionate souls, usually under the influence of some obsession, capable of single-minded egoism relieved by moments of rather romantic self-abnegation. Essentially too they are all feminine, the men—witness Anania in *Cenere* (1904), one of her finest novels—even more perhaps than the women. It follows that such novels as *L'Edera* (1904) or *La Madre,* where the principal character is a woman, seem considerably more realistic psychologically than the others. When all has been said of her limitations, however, the fact remains that Grazia Deledda has to her credit many well-told tales, sincere and moving, and that her whole career was remarkable and admirable in that she realized her faults and wrote novels of increasing merit as she grew older. If her work, taken as a whole, seems repetitious, it also will appear impressive. Some dozen novels of hers will always stand out as competent and inspiring, and it can be said that she never wrote a bad book, taking the adjective in any of its possible senses. Worldwide recognition came to her in 1926 when she was awarded the Nobel prize.

In addition to the titles mentioned above the following should be cited as representing her best work: *Il Vecchio della montagna* (1900), *Elias Portoliu* (1903), *Nostalgie* (1905), *Sino al confine* (1910), *Canne al vento* (1913), *Le Colpe Altrui* (1914), *Il Dio dei viventi* (1922), *La Fuga in Egitto* (1925), *Annalena Bilsini,* (1927).

See: P. Pancrazi, *Venti uomini, un satiro e un burattino* (1923), pp. 89–101; L. Russo, *I Narratori* (1923), pp. 153–156; G. A. Borgese,

La Vita e il libro, 2d ed., II (1928), 78–85, 138, 313; L. Falchi, *L'Opera di Grazia Deledda* (1929); M. Mundula, *Grazia Deledda* (1929).

T. G. B.

De Marchi, Emilio (1851–1901, Italian author of novels and short stories), born at Milan, was a schoolmaster by profession. He had the practical sense of life of the typical Lombard and the didactic inclination of the born teacher. The incurable illness which shortened his life and the loss of a beloved child elicited no complaints from him, but sharpened his sensibility to the hardships of those around him—laborers and farmers and unpretentious citizens of small means like himself—as well as his sympathy with the difficulties and dangers of youth. Many of his earliest publications, such as *L'Età preziosa* (1887), a work devoted to the guidance of young people in the formative period of life, have an unconcealed educative purpose, and in all his literary work the moral preoccupation is fundamental. It finds aesthetic expression because devotion to duty and love of others are the profoundest feelings of the author and the chief subjects of his thought. Literature, he says, should not be an amusement for the idle, but a help to good living. (For De Marchi's reaction to the vogue of D'Annunzio, *q.v.*, see an illuminating interview with Luigi Venturini in the *Rassegna nazionale*, March 16, 1901.)

In the best of his short stories and novels the didactic tendency is transcended by the author's creative imagination. Admirably realistic, sympathetic, and humorous are the *Storie di ogni colore* (1885) and *Nuove Storie di ogni colore* (1895). Of the novels—*Il Cappello del prete* (1888), *Demetrio Pianelli* (1890), *Arabella* (1892), *Giacomo l'idealista* (1897), *Col fuoco non si scherza* (1901)—the masterpiece is *Demetrio Pianelli*. It is the story of an uncouth, middle-aged government clerk who is dragged out of the poor but peaceful life that he has contrived for himself, into the troubled lives of others, by natural affection and an unconscious sense of duty. Demetrio struggles manfully to save from starvation the children of a supercilious half brother who has committed suicide and left his family nothing but debts. He meets with prejudice, obstinate stupidity, duplicity, and, worst of all, with the passion of love. He falls in love with the beautiful and good but stupid widow who, prejudiced against him by her dead husband, was at first the most formidable obstacle to his task. He defends her against the insidiousness of the influential head of his own office who has tried to make use of her poverty for his own guilty pleasure. Demetrio leaves the way open for her to marry a wealthy friend who is also in love with her. His work is now done: he has saved the children and the woman he loves, but he has lost her and has been transferred to an even more wretched position in the government service. Unconscious of his own heroism Demetrio reflects with resignation on his dreary future, comforted only by the trust and affection of the woman, who now understands him. In this novel there is no preaching and no obvious teaching. It ends sadly as do all the others, for life, in the author's experience, is sad. This is a world in which virtue is not often rewarded, and injustice must be borne with resignation: the good that is in human beings, producing affection and devotion to duty, alone makes it worth while.

De Marchi is a romantic realist, like Manzoni. He is often called a *manzoniano* because of the moral sentiment which distinguishes them both and because of the many traces in his own work of the influence of Manzoni's *I Promessi Sposi*. But he lacks the orthodox faith of the latter, as is particularly evident in *Giacomo l'idealista*, which represents the failure of an optimistic philosophy when brought into conflict with the sad reality of life. He is also without that shrinking from the study of sexual love, which is a peculiarity of Manzoni. For De Marchi the passion of love is so common a misfortune that it demands sympathetic study (*Col fuoco non si scherza*). He is inferior to Manzoni as a craftsman in the use of language, but superior in that sympathetic understanding of common people which is a characteristic of Italian romanticism.

Besides stories and novels, De Marchi is the author of some contemplative verse, *Vecchie Cadenze e nuove* (1891), a comedy or two, and critical essays on literature.

See: Benedetto Croce, *La Letteratura della nuova Italia*, III (1915), 155–162; Nino Sammartano, *Emilio De Marchi* (1926); Annibale Pesante, *Due Manzoniani: I. Nievo, E. De Marchi* (1930).

J. E. S.

Demolder, Eugène (1862–1919, Belgian novelist and art critic), was born at Molenbeek-Saint-Jean, a picturesque suburb of Brussels. He dabbled in law, received his doctorate, and spent 10 years as a minor magistrate, but his interests were always artistic and literary. He was associated with Edmond Picard's *Art moderne* and with the brilliant group who created the *Jeune Belgique* (*see* Belgian literature in French) from which, feeling his independence cramped, he revolted to found with others in 1895 the rival review, *Coq rouge.* The same year he married the daughter of the artist Félicien Rops and spent the last third of his life at Essonnes in France (Seine-et-Oise). His thought is not profound, nor is he interested primarily in the creation of character; his personages serve to evoke the atmosphere of a period or of an artistic milieu, but here he gives evidence of wide and accurate scholarship, joined with unequaled sensitivity. His work is first of all an interpretative transposition of plastic art. His friend Albert Giraud (*q.v.*) remarked that one needed blue glasses to read him. Demolder's first volume, *Impressions d'art* (1889), is a collection of essays dealing with both ancient and contemporary masters; it contains in germ all that he was to write. In *Contes d'Yperdamme* (1891) and *Récits de Nazareth* (1893), he would renew subjects treated by old Dutch painters which seemed to him more real on their canvas than in the Scriptures. Like his masters, he places Nazareth in a Flemish landscape. His one experiment in playwriting, *La Mort aux berceaux* (1899), inspired by paintings of the Massacre of the Innocents, recalls Maeterlinck's (*q.v.*) static drama: the forebodings of the mother replace action. In *L'Agonie d'Albion* (1901), he reproduces in words the satiric caricatures aimed at England during the Boer War. His sympathy here is always with the underdog, but it would be an error to attach much political significance to this amusing skit. The one thing he ever took seriously was his love of art. Reminiscences of his experience as a magistrate may be found in *Sous la robe* (1897). Doubtless James Ensor's picture, *Les Bons Juges,* was not foreign to the conception of these memoirs. The humanitarian instincts of the author are strongly marked in *Sous la robe;* he is not composing a plea for reform, but his native good sense should make the book the vade mecum of police magistrates. Two volumes in which the mature colorist appears at his best are *L'Arche de M. Chenus* (1904), a series of sketches in which the author portrays himself and his vague pantheistic dreams, and *L'Espagne en auto* (1906), with its vividly painted landscapes.

Influence of artists is equally strong in Demolder's pure fiction—one volume of short stories, *Quattuor* (1897), and three novels. His masterpiece, *La Route d'émeraude* (1899), is a recreation of the century of Rembrandt, whose figure dominates this panorama of artistic life in old Holland. Many incidents are introduced merely to place before our eyes living models of the master: *e.g., The Rat Killer, The Night Watch;* light effects, so characteristic of Rembrandt, are dramatically used throughout the novel. Minor figures, typical of other aspects of the artistic life of the period, serve for variety and humor. Richepin's (*q.v.*) attempt to dramatize the story offers but an impoverished skeleton. *Les Patins de la reine de Hollande* (1901) reveals Demolder's delight in folklore. He always takes his picturesque where he finds it, with no regard for chronology; in *Les Patins,* among other antitheses is an idyllic love story set off by grotesque antics of the devil. The painter James Ensor, to whom the author devoted a critical essay in 1892, seems to have been the godfather of these *diableries.* One suspects in reading the novel that Demolder preferred art to life; this impression is reinforced by *Le Jardin de la Pompadour* (1904), inspired by the 18th-century painters of sophisticated frivolity. Certain scenes seem suggested also by whimsicalities of Rops. Here is indeed a far cry from the robust disciple of Rembrandt and the old Dutch masters, but Demolder has succeeded admirably in evoking the century of fans and beribboned shepherdesses. He always sought variety, and his first essays revealed a remarkably catholicity of taste. Death seized him while he was at work on a novel set in the period of Louis Philippe.

See: H. Krains, *Portraits d'écrivains belges* (1930), pp. 7–30; B. M. Woodbridge, *Le Roman belge contemporain* (1930), pp. 149–183; L. Bocquet, *La Littérature française de Belgique* (1932), pp. 84–96.

B. M. W.

De Roberto, Federico (1861–1927, Italian novelist and critic), although born in Naples, is considered a Sicilian, both on account of the subject matter of his works and the fact that he spent practically all his life in the region of Catania, whence came Verga (*q.v.*) and Capuana (*q.v.*). With them he forms the triad in whose writings Italian naturalistic fiction achieved its greatest artistic excellence. He started as a critic with a collection of studies called *Arabeschi* (1883). A long period of silence intervened before the publication of his second work, *Documenti umani* (1888), a collection of regionalistic short stories, the title of which already betrays the detached attitude of the historian or sociologist. The youthful critic had turned artist, but his readers immediately perceived that he had taken with him into his art the intellectualism of the critic. Other works of fiction followed one another in rapid succession, in all of which is found the cool self-possession, the cold detachment of the man of science, but none, or not enough, of the warm glow of the artist. Then came his psychological novel *L'Illusione* (1891), the story of an aristocratic Italian Bovary, which, though reminiscent of Flaubert (*q.v.*), is none the less a true work of art, for here the author's imagination does not remain inert, but accompanies and enlivens the probing of his heroine's soul. This was followed by De Roberto's masterpiece, *I Vicerè* (1894), a vast sociological and psychological study depicting, together with a whole eventful epoch, the survival in wealth and power of a princely house amid the degeneration of some of its members and the crumbling of agelong privileges—a survival which follows as the natural consequence of the continuation in other members of the princely house of those predatory instincts which had made it great and the continuation in the people about them of the servile instincts which had kept them subservient. With these two novels De Roberto reached the pinnacle of his art. Thereafter he never again achieved that delicate balance of cold, scientific investigation and imaginative afflatus so frequently met with in the pages of these two voluminous works. The artist succumbed more and more to the psychologist, and his subsequent publications added to the bulk of his production but not to his fame, which, incidentally, owes practically nothing to his activity as a critic.

See: L. Russo, *I Narratori* (1923), pp. 93–97; A. Gatti, "Federico De Roberto nel romanzo italiano," *Nuova Antologia,* CDVI (1939), 123–133.

S. E. S.

De Sanctis, Francesco (1817–1883, Italian critic and literary historian), was born in Morra Irpina, Avellino, not far from Naples. As a boy he went to that city to enter the private school of Basilio Puoti, grammarian and "purist." Later, under the protection of this teacher, young De Sanctis conducted a private school of literature of his own (1838–1848). He soon found his own interests in the study of literature to be quite outside Puoti's narrow precepts and was early in rebellion against all that was Arcadian and academic, convinced that a school should remain always open to the responsibilities of the present. This conviction was shared by his pupils, who worshiped him; they joined him therefore in action in the liberal revolution in Naples in 1848. With the triumphant Bourbon suppression, De Sanctis was watched as a dangerous liberal. Late in 1850 he was seized and taken to the prison of Castel dell'Ovo in Naples, where he was held without trial for two and one half years. He was released in order to be sent in exile to America, but he managed to make his way to Turin to join the many other liberals there preparing for the day of unification. In Turin he resumed his teaching and writing on both literature and politics. Called to the chair of Italian literature in the Polytechnic Institute of Zurich in 1856, he soon won a large audience with his excellent lectures. He continued there his study of German philosophy, but kept in close touch with events in Italy. When the long-awaited moment for action came, he resigned his post and hastened to Naples, where the king had agreed to the institution of a parliament (1860). Garibaldi entered the city in September and promptly appointed De Sanctis governor of his home province of Avellino. The following year he became minister of education in the cabinet of Cavour, a post which he held for only one year on this occasion, but which he again occupied in 1878 and in 1879–1881. During this decade preceding the final unification, De Sanctis wrote much and talked much on the importance of education in the new nation, voicing the persuasion that now new Italians must be created worthy of the new Italy. In 1871 he was appointed to the chair of comparative literature in the University of Naples. In that same year he finished his two-volume *Storia della letteratura italiana* (Eng. tr., *History of Italian Literature,* 1931), to which he planned to add a third volume to bring it up to his own day. This volume as such he never finished, but his courses at the university (since published) were in the direction of preparation for it. He remained at the university until 1877.

De Sanctis's main critical work is contained in his *Saggi critici* (1866), his *Storia della letteratura italiana,* and his *Nuovi Saggi critici* (1872). His complete works contain many essays on politics, essays and polemics on criticism, and the fragment of an autobiography written at the end of his life; but his fame rests upon his criticism of Italian literature (*see* Italian literary criticism). He is now commonly considered to be Italy's foremost literary critic, and his contemporaries knew him as one of her greatest teachers of literature. The best of his published critical work grew out of his classroom lectures, and much of it has kept the style of the spoken lesson.

De Sanctis's criticism is outstanding in its time for its insistence upon poetry as the product of an autonomous faculty of the human spirit, the *fantasia,* which is intuitive, organic, and synthetic. Faithful in his best criticism to this principle of the autonomy of art, he could effectively reject the neoclassic attention to externalities of form, the French concern with the biographical (Sainte-Beuve), and the contemporary German preoccupation with the idea in art (Hegel). In conformity with such a principle, his importance as a teacher and critic of literature resides in his determination to keep his eye on the work of art itself. His greatness lies in his power of analysis and synthesis in the examination of a single work of art. His intuitions of literary qualities in the single work make him one of the great literary critics of modern times. De Sanctis was able to see the literary object almost without distraction and as a whole. He once remarked that good criticism was like the eye which sees objects but does not see itself.

In his *Storia della letteratura italiana,* now generally recognized as a classic and as his greatest work, such a criterion of autonomy and of undistracted attention required grave compromise with other interests. The exclusive attention to the single work of art and the principle of the freedom of that work, as a form, from everything else obviously did not allow at all for the writing of a history with continuity and evolution, either between works of art or between persons and works of art. His new historiographical purpose required that the work of art be used as a document to something else. These conflicts were never reconciled in De Sanctis's work, nor is it clear that they could have been reconciled. In the *Storia,* the essay on the individual form stands grafted into a dialectic which seeks to view it as part of the spiritual journey of a people and the birth of a nation. The *Storia* thus clearly attempts to satisfy a national demand. The romantics had long insisted on viewing society in literature. Now the new nation turns and would see itself in its national literature. The will to re-educate Italians for a new Italy takes over. The result is far from being a work of pure and consistent criticism; but it has proved to be a work of great vitality.

While De Sanctis went far beyond his time in the perception of certain fundamental principles concerning the nature of poetry, he quite naturally brought to the explication of those principles tastes and predilections which were very much of his time. In the *Divine Comedy,* Hell was more poetic than Paradise, Francesca da Rimini more poetic than Beatrice. By the same romantic penchant for the dramatic, Shakespeare's is a greater poetry than Dante's. However, in spite of the discount that the passing of one or two generations must always make in the estimate of a critic, literary history and literary criticism in Italy today constantly return to the *Storia* and to the *Saggi* for certain fundamental perceptions regarding Italian literature.

See: B. Croce, *Estetica come scienza dell'espressione e linguistica generale,* 4th ed., revised (1912), Ch. XV; Croce, *Gli Scritti di F. D. S. e la loro varia fortuna* (1917), and De Sanctis, *Pagine sparse,* ed. by Croce (1934), for complete bibliography; G. A. Borgese, *Storia della critica romantica in Italia,* new ed. (1920), Ch. XVII; L. A. Breglio, *Life and Criticism of Francesco De Sanctis* (1941).

C. S. S.

Descaves, Lucien (1861–, French novelist, dramatist, and critic), was born in Paris in the Montrouge quarter; his father was an engraver of some talent, and Lucien Descaves remained faithful to the atmosphere and to the artisans of the *faubourgs.* He became a bank clerk at the Crédit Lyonnais, which showed him the sordid world of business, and he then spent four years in army service and learned to note with an implacable eye the insipid coarseness and the brutality of the professional noncommissioned officers. When he was able to return to civilian life, he became friends with Edmond de Goncourt, Alphonse Daudet (*qq.v.*), Gustave Geffroy, Séverine, J. K. Huysmans (*q.v.*), and even Zola (*q.v.*). But when Zola's *La Terre* was published, he signed the "Manifeste des Cinq" (*Figaro,* August 18, 1887) and revolted against the extremes of naturalism (*see* French naturalism). In 1889 the publication of *Sous-Offs* was the occasion of a scandal; Descaves was prosecuted and then acquitted after a very eloquent plea made by Alexandre Millerand (1890). But the victory had a Pyrrhic quality since the antimilitaristic author continued to be ostracized by bourgeois opinion. He was able, however, in 1892, when the *Journal* was founded, to use the medium of an important daily newspaper and to give free play to his stormy temperament. He was elected to the Goncourt Academy in 1900, became its *enfant terrible,* and eventually its president (1944).

The writings of Descaves, numerous and varied, show a constant interest in minute observation of everyday reality and warm sympathy for the abundant troubles of humble folk. At first harsh, not to say brutal, in the current naturalistic manner, he gradually freed himself from such heaviness and pessimism and grew to be both ironical and tender, critical and sentimental—in a word, fundamentally Parisian. His novels and stories include *Le Calvaire d'Héloïse Pajadou* (1882), *Une Vieille Rate* (1883), *La Teigne* (1886), all youthful works; *La Caserne* (1887), *Misères du sabre* (1887), and *Sous-Offs*, which are violent satires of military life; *Les Emmurés* (1894), a moving account of the life of the blind; *La Colonne* (1902), an episode of the Commune, and *Philémon, Vieux de la Vieille* (1913), which is the odyssey of a political exile who took refuge in Switzerland after the terrible Bloody Week; *Barabbas* (1914), which is eloquent and heart-rending; and finally the story of Georgin, *L'Imagier d'Epinal* (1919), proof of the author's admiration for the small tradesmen.

His dramatic writing, extensive and uneven, shows that Descaves was again preoccupied with social and moral problems and again full of sympathy for idealistic revolutionaries. Among the plays are *La Pelote* (1889), written with Bonnetain; *Les Chapons* (1890), written with Darien; *La Cage* (1898), production of which was forbidden by the censor; *La Clairière* (1900), written with Donnay (*q.v.*) and very successful; *Oiseaux de passage* (1904), also written with Donnay and containing an analysis, by contrast, of the revolts of occidental idealism and of Slavic mysticism; *L'Attentat* (1906), biting political satire, written with Capus (*q.v.*); *La Préférée* (1906), full of sentiment; *La Saignée* (1913), a tragic picture of the Commune, written with Nozière; *Pierre Dupont* (1922); *L'As de cœur* (1920), a post-war drama; *Le Cœur ébloui* (1926); *Les Fruits de l'amour* (1928).

Descaves also composed, over a period of more than half a century, several thousand articles, often piquant, at times aggressive and formidable and earning him lasting enemies. The best of these pieces are in the *Intransigeant* and the *Journal*, both of which newspapers he long served as literary editor. Although a rebel—and of the line of Jules Vallès (*q.v.*)—he did not always succeed in suppressing delicate sensibilities and authentic enthusiasms, as appears from *La Vie douloureuse de Marceline Desbordes-Valmore* (1911), the devoted pages of *Les Dernières Années de Huysmans* (1941), and especially *Les Mémoires d'un ours* (1946), which is an autobiography.

See: Emile Moselly, *Lucien Descaves; biographie critique* (1910); Léon Deffoux, *Lucien Descaves* (1930).

G. G.

Desjardins, Paul (1859–1940, French philosopher and critic), was born in Paris of a well-to-do family and after a brilliant academic career entered the teaching profession, eventually becoming director of the Ecole Normale de Sèvres. His published work is small, not much more than a half-dozen volumes, of which only *Esquisses et impressions* (1888) and *La Méthode des classiques* (1904) are very large in bulk, but most of it is of the highest quality. His influence on European culture, however, cannot be measured merely in terms of publication. Desjardins, at the end of the 19th century, was one of the many in France who deplored the wave of pessimism which, whether or not the result of the defeat of 1870, had made itself felt more and more in the years that followed it. In *Le Devoir présent* (1891; Eng. tr., *The Present Duty*, 1893) he divided mankind into the positives and the negatives, those with and those without faith in life and civilization, and condemning the latter—the disciples of Renan (*q.v.*), of Darwin, of Zola (*q.v.*)—he called for a *réveil moral* and an association of men of good will who, regardless of race or creed, would unite in affirming the primacy of spiritual values. His first step towards this end was the formation in 1892 of the Union pour l'Action Morale, which in 1898 was split by the Dreyfus affair and, with the schism of Vaugeois and Pujo (founders of the *Action française*), became the Union pour la Vérité.

From 1892 Desjardins's life was one of tireless devotion to the Union and its ideals; in its monthly bulletin and in personal discussions he labored heroically for the cause of humanism and the maintenance of the highest ideals of European culture. In pursuance of this purpose he bought the century-old Cistercian abbey at Pontigny and in 1910 organized the first of the famous "Entretiens d'été de Pontigny," informal discussions of artistic, philosophical, economic, and moral problems by intellectual leaders of all countries. Desjardins preserved throughout these troubled years an intellectual and spiritual integrity and detachment that few could rival; his one vocation was the search for truth, and he believed that it could best be arrived at by free and friendly discussion, by cooperation, faith in mankind, and good will, rather than by suspicion, intolerance, and partisan hatreds. The First World War dealt a serious blow to his ideals, but he persisted; the conferences were resumed in 1922 and during the succeeding years reached a new brilliance. With the Second World War came a new interruption and the death of Desjardins, still hopeful in spite of all. Neither the war nor his death was allowed to put an end to the work, however; during the Second World War the conferences took on a new life at South Hadley, Massachusetts, under the sponsorship of the New York Ecole Libre des Hautes Etudes.

See: Ernst Robert Curtius, *Französischer Geist im neuen Europa* (1925); Jean Dietz, *Paul Desjardins* (1930); M. D. Petre, "Paul Desjardins; a Personal Reminiscence," *Hibbert Journal*, XXXVIII (1940), 505–510.

C. W., Jr.

Deus Ramos, João de (1830–1896, Portuguese poet), was born in São Bartolomeu de Messines, Algarve, of humble parents. In 1849 he went to Coimbra to study law. A contemplative and indolent character, given to self-absorption, he evinced a complete indifference to his academic obligations and gave his time to poetry and bohemian student life. This delayed his law degree 10 years. When he was eventually graduated in 1859, he was so fond of the Coimbra atmosphere that he remained there until 1862. As a result he became attached to the group which, under the name Generation of Coimbra, was to have so much importance in the history of recent Portuguese literature (*q.v.*). A product of romanticism, and also an uncompromising nonconformer and a mystic rebel, he identified himself spiritually with the new revolt, exerted an influence on many of its adherents, and maintained close relations with almost all of them. Later he left for South Portugal and for a period engaged in journalism in Beja. Returning home, he hunted and loitered about the countryside until 1868. João de Deus had never bothered about the publication of his writings; these he composed mentally, and when they took final form he either wrote them down or dictated them to his friends, who collected his scribbled sheets and sent them to the reviews. As early as 1860 some of his friends had thought of collecting his works, and Antero de Quental (*q.v.*) had proclaimed their great artistic worth in an article. In 1868 he published his first collection of poems with the simple title *Flores do campo* (Wild Flowers). Later Teófilo Braga (*q.v.*) was to collect the lyrical works scattered in magazines and newspapers in a volume entitled *Campo de flores* (1893; Field of Flowers), which João de Deus dedicated to "his contemporaries at the University of Coimbra." In 1868 also a group of friends induced the poet to enter politics and sent him to Parliament as a deputy. He accepted indolently but soon became disgusted and gave up the post. He married at this time, and his years of poverty began. He shut himself up in a garret, worked at the sewing machine to help his wife, composed verses on commission for confectionery shops and rural parties, and did the most menial sort of work for bookdealers, lacking the energy to look for a position or even to leave his house.

Flores do campo had been successful but the poverty continued. In 1875 he produced *Fôlhas soltas* (Loose Leaves)—and that same year abandoned poetry to devote himself to the active promotion of a reading method for schools which he had invented (*Cartilha maternal;* Maternal Primer). From that moment his resigned apathy disappeared, and he developed a miraculous self-discipline and great energy and tenacity in his apostleship of popular education. In 1888 his method was officially accepted, and he was appointed to introduce it. In 1896 the youth of the schools paid elaborate homage to him in his home where he lived in semi-poverty. Before the end of that year he died, modest, smiling, and kindly, as he had lived.

Before the publication of the first verses of Quental and before the appearance of a new aesthetic with the polemic of Coimbra, João de Deus—and this is his importance—had already asserted himself as a lyric poet. Chronologically he belongs to realism, but he is separated from this type of poetry by the fact that he does not philosophize. Actually, he is the last great romantic, although also apart from this movement in his scorn for history. He revitalized decadent amorous lyricism, limiting the show of the sentiments and the overfree expansion of the subjective to a pure expression of love. He abolished artificial verbalism and brought to lyricism the only originality possible at that time: a maximum expressiveness within the framework of an eloquent simplicity, which in him reaches the pure folkloric. He renovated the suggestive value of the commonest vocabulary through delicacy of emotion and smooth musicality. A veritable symphonist of words, he created a new metaphysic of love within a new elaboration of Lusitanian rhythms, characterized by extreme fluidity and sweetness. This was an unexpected revelation, and its influence was felt in all subsequent poetry. A succession of images expresses the iridescences of lyric emotion—a method that had been unknown in Portuguese poetry. His poetry contains only contemplative love; there is no anger, hate, or grief. Eça de Queiroz (*q.v.*) referred to "his two interests, woman and divinity: Love and Mysticism." Women never caused him erotic uneasiness, or rather he was able to transform an emotion of voluptu-

active in a number of ways. He served as an accountant for the Royal Swedish Railways for a quarter of a century (during which time he was active in establishing an employees' pension system), was a member of a Swedish Red Cross committee concerned with war prisoners during and after the First World War, and occupied positions of high trust in both the Swedish Authors' Society and the Swedish Dramatists' Society. Just before his death in 1931 he was the recipient of the annual literary prize of Samfundet De Nio, perhaps a rather tardy semiofficial recognition of his long and unselfish if not distinguished service to Swedish literary and cultural life.

See: Ruben Gustafsson Berg, "Ernst Didring," *Ord och bild,* XLI (1932), 209–224.

A. G.

Diego, Gerardo (1896–, Spanish poet), is the most representative of the writers of "pure" poetry who came into prominence about 1919. He is especially associated with the movement dubbed *creacionismo* by the Chilean poet Vicente Huidobro, who believed that the poet should not mirror God's world but create his own. Diego, born in Santander, studied with the Jesuits in Deusto, a district of Bilbao, and at the universities of Salamanca and Madrid. He has taught at the *institutos* of Soria, Gijón, and Santander and lectured widely on literature and music.

Diego's first book, *El romancero de la novia* (1920), was followed by *Imagen* (1922), of capital importance in the "pure" poetry movement, whose creed it states and illustrates. "Does it not seem to you, my brothers, that for a good many years we have lived on Saturday?" asks the poet. "We have been resting because God has given us everything ready-made. Let us shape our own Mondays, Tuesdays, Wednesdays, Thursdays, and Fridays." Poetry has been too long the reflection and plaything of humanity; it must be "dehumanized," freed from narrative, descriptive, and rhetorical preoccupation with the common coin of human experience. Having no emotional substance, it must skip over the surface of life with a kind of cosmic playfulness, catching up images, recombining and refocusing them until they become independent lyric creations.

For Diego, the symbol of poetry is water, which yields its transparence to a multiplicity of images, its eternal rhythm to innumerable melodies, "singing always the same verse, but with different water," "a frieze running forever in the same deliberate posture." The beauty of water informs such musical poems of *Imagen* as "Madrigal" and "Movimiento perpetuo." Tossed into the air it gives title and inspiration to *Manual de espumas* (1924), which is almost pure *creacionismo,* and perhaps reaches its highest point in the fresh and jubilant aspiration of "Paraíso."

Viewed in the order of their publication, Diego's books show an alternation of *creacionismo* with poetry of more or less traditional type. *Imagen* is followed by *Soria* (1923), whose lyrical visions of Castile recall Antonio Machado (*q.v.*). *Manual de espumas* is followed by *Versos humanos* (1925) and *Viacrucis* (1931). *Viacrucis,* a collection of 33 *décimas* in the baroque style, is tender and moving. *Versos humanos,* although largely traditional in character, contains, in the sonnet "El ciprés de Silos," for example, some of Diego's most audacious multiple imagery; it reiterates the assurance that his poetry may be for the moment in captivity to human experience, but will soon leave the cage and resume its lyric flight.

Diego has had great influence among the poets of his group. His *Antología poética en honor de Góngora* (1927) acclaimed one of the most potent sources of their inspiration. His *Poesía española* (1932; new volume, 1934) is an excellent presentation and interpretation of their work.

See: A. Valbuena Prat, *La poesía española contemporánea* (1930); F. de Onís, *Antología de la poesía española e hispanoamericana, 1882–1932* (1934).

D. K. A.

Díez-Canedo, Enrique (1879–1944, Spanish poet and critic), was born in Badajoz. He began his literary work as a poet in the first year of this century, winning a prize in a contest of the newspaper *Liberal.* Three books, *Versos de las horas* (1906), *La visita del sol* (1907), and *Del cercado ajeno* (1907), were soon published. *Del cercado ajeno,* made up of translations of foreign poets, especially French, established his reputation as a translator and a connoisseur of contemporary European poetry. In the same period he began to distinguish himself as a critic—the most constant activity of his life. From 1909 to 1911 Díez-Canedo studied in Paris, becoming acquainted with many Spanish American writers who were living in or visiting the French capital and whom he made known to the Spanish public. He contributed to the most important reviews and papers of the Hispanic world and taught French and history of art. He was also a dramatic critic for *Voz* and *Sol* and for many years was one of the most active and amiable persons in the literary life of Madrid. He lectured in several countries and was in 1931 a visiting professor at Columbia University. As a result of his close friendship with Azaña (*q.v.*), he was ambassador to Uruguay and Argentina during the Republic. In 1935 he entered the Spanish Academy, reading an address on a subject he knew particularly well, the literary relations between Spain and Spanish America (*Unidad y diversidad de las letras hispánicas*). Like many other Spanish writers, he lived in exile in Mexico after the fall of the Republic.

Well equipped by culture, curiosity, and taste for literary criticism, Canedo's work, although fragmentary and circumstantial, is vast and in several respects of very high authority—the evaluation of many contemporary writers, the review of new plays and books, the diffusion of foreign literature in Spain, and the study of current Spanish American literature, a field in which he was a recognized expert. He knew also the literature and plastic arts of the past, and when the pressing duties of the professional critic left him free time, he wrote scholarly studies such as those found in his edition of Boscán and of Garcilaso, those collected in *Conversaciones literarias* (1921) and *Los dioses en el Prado* (1931), and his lecture "España en los umbrales del arte moderno" (*Revista de Indias,* Bogotá, Vol. IV, 1939, pp. 80–94).

Though known primarily as a critic, nevertheless it is probably in poetry that Canedo best expressed his instinctive feeling for perfection in form as well as his fine sensibility of a natural, intimate, and minor-key lyricism, equidistant from the rhetoric of certain modernists and the subtilized expression of more recent pure poetry. Other volumes of his poetry are *La sombra del ensueño* (1916), *Algunos versos* (1924), *Epigramas americanos* (1928), and *El desterrado* (1940).

See: T. Navarro Tomás, *Discurso* (1935), composed for Díez-Canedo's reception into the Spanish Academy.

A. del R.

Di Giacomo, Salvatore (1860–1934, Italian dialectal poet, novelist, and playwright), was born in Naples, where he was educated and spent his life. He began the study of medicine, but was soon lured away by the love of letters and in 1881 wrote his first sonnet in the Neapolitan dialect. All his subsequent poems were written in Neapolitan. He also wrote stories, in the Italian language, most of them having Neapolitan life as a background: *Novelle napoletane* (1919). Di Giacomo became a contributor to the *Corriere del mattino,* the *Pungolo,* and later to the *Corriere di Napoli.* For many years he served as librarian of the Lucchesi-Palli in Naples. As a scholar he was especially erudite in the history of Naples, about which he wrote a total of 34 volumes, in Italian. Like Petrarch he thought his fame would rest on his scholarly work, of which he would often talk, rather than on his poetry, for which in fact his fame spread even beyond national boundaries, notably to Germany and France. One of his famous songs "A Marechiare," set to music by Tosti, is still sung the world over. On March 18, 1929, he was admitted to the Italian Academy.

Di Giacomo matured early as a poet and by 1910 had already written his best poems. His last years were devoted almost entirely to editing his works; the final edition of his complete poems appeared in 1927. In his old age Di Giacomo suffered from both physical and spiritual afflictions. He died alone, away from friends. His publisher, Achille Ricciardi, said he died even away from his poetry and himself.

Di Giacomo began writing when folklore studies and verism had reached their zenith in Italy. His early poems and novels deal directly with the common people. Poems such as "O funneco verde," "Irma," "A Strata," are examples among many of his veristic beginning. Even the great series of sonnets "San Francisco" is to some extent veristic. But he is not the poet of the people. His documentation is not like that of Verga or Capuana (*qq.v.*). His is attenuated, sentimentalized, and even made subjective. Indeed at times he becomes so very personal that one can no longer properly speak of verism. His novels and dramas, however more veristic than his poetry, also show the poet's individuality; they are often mere versions of his poems, keeping not only the subject but also the feeling. Di Giacomo never really wrote prose or verism. The throbbing personality of the author could not remain enchained by either. His poetry is thus lyric, but it unfolds a melancholic lyricism which affects the reader not by a crescendo, but by a sostenuto. It often leaves the reader in tears. His is a sweet and dreamy melancholy, not merely in the subject, but especially in the tone. Poems such as "O Munasterio," "Tutto, tutto se scorda," "Nannina," "Pusilleco," *e.g.*, leave one very sad. He is simple and innocent like a child, and like a child he is easily enchanted by the starry sky or the big moon shining on the sea of Naples. At times he is enthralled by the macabre and the weird; his enchantment gives place to mystification and mystery; he becomes a victim of his own youthful and impetuous fantasy. In his later years Di Giacomo did not write with the same verve; he himself admits it in one of his last poems. The philosophy of his poetry, which shows dissatisfaction with life, is no longer melancholic, but tragic, for the poet ceases to derive appeasement from his own sorrow. Turmoil finally seizes him as well as his characters and readers.

Di Giacomo's poetic language, in Neapolitan dialect, contains earmarks of the poet's culture. His verses are musical, polished, and refined. But the greatness of his poetry lies in the fact that it is warm and refreshing; it does not owe, however, its warmth and freshness to the dialect per se, as it has been claimed; no language is fresh or stale, warm or cold in itself. Di Giacomo's Neapolitan becomes peculiarly his particular channel of expression; it is the reflection of his poetic genius which Croce (*q.v.*) first of all recognized. To Croce, in fact, Di Giacomo owes his rapid rise to fame, but he would have sooner or later surmounted the obstacle of dialect and would have been given recognition just the same because poetry is poetry in any language. Today he is considered not only the outstanding modern Neapolitan poet, but one of Italy's greatest lyric geniuses.

See: F. Gaeta, *Salvatore Di Giacomo* (1911); L. Russo, *Salvatore De Giacomo* (1921); B. Croce, *La Letteratura della nuova Italia,* 2d ed., III (1922), 73–100.

F. D. M.

Döblin, Alfred (1878–, German novelist and essayist), had the greatest narrative talent of any of the members of the German expressionist movement. A writer of tremendous vitality, fertile imagery, and vision, he is thoroughly grounded in modern science and philosophy. He was born in Stettin, but his parents moved to Berlin when he was 10 years of age. He studied in Berlin and Freiburg, obtaining his M.D. in 1905. However, he turned to journalism, and it was not until 1911 that he went back to Berlin to settle down as a psychiatrist in the workers' district around the Alexanderplatz. He married and had four sons. During the first phase of his life his publications were confined to his professional field and to essays on philosophic and aesthetic questions.

Writing was a passion with Döblin; after experiences he needed expression. Most of his early writings remained unpublished. His first public appearance as a writer was made in *Der Sturm,* the expressionist periodical published by Herwarth Walden. The stories there presented were later collected in *Die Ermordung einer Butterblume* (1913). Here vision merges with reality, perspective with distortion, and reflection with symbolism—characteristics revealed also in most of Döblin's later work. His first great success was the "Chinese" novel, *Die drei Sprünge des Wanglun* (1915), which brought him the Fontane prize. It is not a story of adventures or curiosities, although there is a colorful background and exciting incidents abound, but a literary attempt to transplant the soul of the Far East to Europe. Wang-lun, the roaming revolutionary and reformer, must succumb to the crude power of the state, but even in his defeat he demonstrates the victory of the nonviolent spirit over brute force.

In the First World War, Döblin was for three years a physician at the front, but even there he continued his work. *Wadzeks Kampf mit der Dampfmaschine* (1918) poses grotesquely and ironically the problem of man versus machine. The historical novel *Wallenstein* (1920), which varied the philosophical theme of Wang-lun, was also partly written at the front. Stripping history of idealizing embellishments, Döblin shows the collapse of mere power, and is obviously giving his interpretation of the First World War. *Berge, Meere und Giganten* (1924) is a satirical, yet horribly powerful vision of the future of man, a veritable nightmare of expressionist conjuration. Man's modern science without goodness of heart will lead to fantastic apocalyptic doom. Döblin's best-known novel is *Berlin Alexanderplatz* (1929; Eng. tr., *Alexanderplatz, Berlin,* 1931). The best elements of expressionism are fused in this unique work, which though wrongly called an imitation of Joyce nevertheless suggests the Irish writer. The story of the fate of a simple, if rude, proletarian, done with consummate skill and an intimate knowledge of people and locale, has been translated into many languages and has secured the author's fame.

When the anti-Semitic tide rose, Döblin left Germany. His books were burned there, but he continued his work. Some of his writings in exile are: *Babylonische Wanderung* (1934); *Pardon wird nicht gegeben* (1935; Eng. tr., *Men without Mercy,* 1937); two exotic historical novels dealing with the Spanish conquistadores, the Indians, and the Jesuits, *Die Fahrt ins Land ohne Tod* (1937) and *Der blaue Tiger* (1938). *Bürger und Soldaten 1918* (1939) is the first volume of a projected trilogy on the German revolution in 1918. The novelette *Nocturno* (1944) adds little originality to a well-known literary motif. A discriminating essay on German literature written in exile since 1933 is *Die deutsche Literatur* (1938). Döblin and his family lived for a while in Palestine, then moved to the United States. He returned to Germany after the war and in Baden-Baden interested himself in the publishing of a literary magazine.

See: A. Soergel, *Dichtung und Dichter der Zeit,* Neue Folge: *Im Banne des Expressionismus,* 4. Auflage (1927), pp. 871–885; W. Mahrholz, *Deutsche Literatur der Gegenwart* (1930), pp. 425–427; F. Bertaux, *A Panorama of German Literature from 1871 to 1931* (1935), pp. 186–192; H. von Hofe, "German Literature in Exile: Alfred Döblin," *German Quarterly,* XVII (1944), 28–31.

W. K. P.

Dobrogeanu-Gherea, Constantin (1855–1920, Rumanian literary critic), was born and educated in Russia where he took part in revolutionary activities. He suffered imprisonment, escaped to Norway and England, and finally took refuge in Rumania. He contributed to the Jassy *Contemporanul* (The Contemporary) political articles and literary criticisms. His polemics with Titu Maiorescu (*q.v.*) mark an epoch in Rumanian letters. In 1890 he became a Rumanian citizen, the manager of the Ploeşti railroad-station restaurant, and a guiding spirit of political propaganda. When the leaders of the Rumanian Socialist Party renounced their struggle and joined the liberals, Dobrogeanu-Gherea alone continued to uphold socialist theories in his writings. In *Neoiobăgia* (1910; New Serfdom) he gave a searching analysis of the exploitation of the peasantry. His main work, however, is in the three volumes of *Studii critice* (1890–1897; Critical Studies). If politically the seeds of Dobrogeanu-Gherea's ideas fell on stony ground, from a literary point of view they germinated the Poporanist (People's) movement which blossomed in 1906.

See: B. Lăzăreanu, *Ioan Gherea* (1924).

L. F.

Domenchina, Juan José (1898–, Spanish poet and critic), was born in Madrid. Little is known of his early life. With his first volumes of poems—*Del poema eterno* (1917) and *Las interrogaciones del silencio* (1918)—he began to attract attention and to be considered as one of the main poets in the transition between modernism and the "new poetry." From the beginning his poetry had an intellectual bent strangely mixed with a Castilian sense of reality and a baroque form of expression. Díez-Canedo (*q.v.*) defined this as the "corporeity of the abstract," a definition adopted by the poet himself as the title of one of his most characteristic books, *La corporeidad de lo abstracto* (1929), and by most of the critics who have studied Domenchina's poetry. In 1936 he collected his poetic work in the volume *Poesías completas,* which included the books already mentioned as well as the later *Dédalo* (1932) and *Margen* (1933). The early elements of his poetry have not changed, but are rather intensified, acquiring a humane, neo-romantic, and expressionistic character which reaches at times a distorted satiric tone in the best baroque and stoic Spanish tradition of the 17th century. The same can be said of his last book, *Destierro* (1942), written in Mexico, where Domenchina has lived since 1939.

He has also tried narrative prose in two novels, but outside the field of poetry he is best known as a critic for his *Crónicas de Gerardo Rivera* (1935), made up of newspaper articles in which he judged incisively many contemporary writers. In 1941 he published in Mexico an anthology of contemporary Spanish poetry, good as far as the selection of poetry is concerned, but marred by unkind criticism of some fellow poets in the introductory notes.

See: E. Díez-Canedo, "Juan José Domenchina, poeta estoico," in Domenchina, *La corporeidad de lo abstracto* (1929), pp. 9–15.

A. del R.

Donnay, Maurice (1859–1945, French playwright), born in Paris, studied to be an engineer and graduated from the Ecole Centrale in 1885. In 1890 he was a member of the famous Montmartre cabaret, Le Chat Noir, where he presented certain *pièces d'ombres*—*Phryné* (1891), *Ailleurs* (1891). In 1892 he began his real dramatic subjects.

Donnay is one of the most important authors of light comedies. At times he indulged in dramas typical of the *boulevard* theatre (*Education de Prince,* 1900; *La Patronne,* 1908; *La Belle Angevine,* 1922, with André Rivoire; *Le Geste,* 1924, with Henri Duvernois) and even wrote librettos for musical comedies (*Le Mariage de Télémaque,* 1910, with Jules Lemaître, *q.v.,* and *Le Roi Candaule,* 1920). He also contributed plays of deep psychological significance (*Amants,* 1895; *La Douloureuse,* 1897; *L'Autre Danger,* 1902; *Paraître,* 1906) as well as studies of social problems. Among the latter are *La Clairière* (1900; with Lucien Descaves, *q.v.*), an amusing satire of a phalanstery; *Le Retour de Jérusalem* (1903), on the Jewish question; *Oiseaux de passage*

(1904; with Lucien Descaves), on the difficulty people of different races and backgrounds find in understanding each other; *Les Eclaireuses* (1913), on feminism. A skepticism without bitterness and a keen sense of humor prevented Maurice Donnay from giving his social dramas the dull character of problem plays.

Although primarily a playwright, he wrote the *Vie amoureuse d'Alfred de Musset* (1926) and volumes of an autobiographical nature, *Pendant qu'ils sont à Noyon* (1917), *Autour du Chat Noir* (1926), *Mes Débuts à Paris* (1937). Maurice Donnay was elected to the French Academy in 1907.

See: Roger Le Brun, *Maurice Donnay* (1903); Paul Flat, "Maurice Donnay," *Revue bleue,* LII (1914), 359–362; Henry Bidou, "Les Epoques du théâtre contemporain en France: IV, La Période Donnay-Capus," *Revue hebdomadaire,* Année XXX (1921), Tome I, pp. 195–210; P. Bathille, *Maurice Donnay; son œuvre* (1933).

M. E. C.

Dörfler, Peter (1878–, German novelist), was born at Untergermaringen in Württemberg, of an old Catholic peasant family. After completing the Gymnasium at Augsburg, he studied theology and now lives in Munich as a priest and director of an orphanage. A representative of regional literature, Dörfler began with short stories and extensive novels having a Swabian background, almost in the same manner in which Heinrich Hansjacob (1837–1916), also a Catholic priest, had some 20 years earlier told peasant tales of the Black Forest district. His first book—and still one of his best—is *Als Mutter noch lebte* (1912), the story of a young man, a monument to his own mother. It was followed by the novel *Judith Finsterwalderin* (1916), telling in a most simple and clear language the tragic fate of a young peasant girl. Here as well as in the tales which rapidly followed, Dörfler proved to be a genuine writer of and for the people: well he knew how to combine the sense of realism of the Swabians with piety and hearty humor. He originated a genre of fiction which was light but not unrelated to the important problems of life, simple but not superficial.

Dörfler's creative power appears at its best in the two novel-trilogies, *Appolonia* and *Allgäu.* The first stories, *Die Lampe der törichten Jungfrau* (1930), *Appolonias Sommer* (1931), and *Das kommende Geschlecht* (1932), tell of the daughter of a Swabian miller and her sacrifices for three generations of her family. In the second trilogy, *Der Notwender* (1934), *Der Zwingherr* (1935), and *Der Alpkönig* (1936), an outstanding leader risen from the people struggles against the internal and external troubles of his homeland, the Allgäu. Dörfler belongs to the writers of the literature of "race and soil." In spite of his Catholic faith, he was given high honors by Nazi officials.

See: F. Lennartz, *Die Dichter unserer Zeit* (1938), pp. 57–59; J. Bithell, *Modern German Literature, 1880–1938* (1939), p. 490.

H. Sch.

Dorgelès, Roland (pseud. of R. Lécavelé, 1886–, French novelist), was born at Amiens. He attended the Ecole des Arts Décoratifs in Paris, but soon drifted to Montmartre, to live a bohemian life during some 12 years. His name was associated with a famous hoax to fool art critics. When war came, Dorgelès, who like Barbusse (*q.v.*) had not previously been a soldier, volunteered for the front. After a few months in the trenches, disillusion came, and he looked for a change. Flying was an honorable escape: Dorgelès flew, but not at the front. These facts are important to correct the author's imaginary heroics described by his biographers. In 1919 was published his first book and greatest success, *Les Croix de bois* (Eng. tr., *Wooden Crosses,* 1921), a war novel visibly inspired by Barbusse's best seller, *Le Feu.* But he was careful to avoid the brutal realism for which his senior had been blamed. A good critic who had never been a soldier wrote the review that initiated the success. There followed *Le Cabaret de la belle femme* (1919; Eng. tr., *The Cabaret up the Line,* 1930), war tales; *Saint Magloire* (1922; Eng. tr., 1923), the story of a saint in a 20th-century community; *Le Réveil des morts* (1923), the rehabilitation of war-devastated regions; and four travel books, *Sur la route mandarine* (1925; Eng. tr., *On the Mandarin Road,* 1926), *Partir* (1926; Eng. tr., *Departure,* 1928), *La Caravane sans chameaux* (1928), *Entre le ciel et l'eau* (1930). The most sincere and original works of Dorgelès, *Le Château des brouillards* (1932) and *Quand j'étais Montmartrois* (1936), describe the bohemian life he knew so well, a milieu which had not been so vividly presented since Henri Murger gave *Scènes de la vie de Bohême* in 1850. Dorgelès was elected to the Goncourt Academy in 1929, succeeding Georges Courteline (*q.v.*).

See: J. N. Cru, *Témoins* (1929), pp. 587–592; A. Dubeux, *Roland Dorgelès* (1930).

J. N. C.

D'Ors, Eugenio (1882–, Spanish critic and essayist), was born in Barcelona. He is a writer of great artistic and philosophic capacity, always responsive to the conflicts and problems of the modern spirit. The title of one of his most substantial works, *Las ideas y las formas* (1928), suggests his major interests. He is especially attracted to the treatment of aesthetic problems, which he offers the reader in his own disconnected and fragmentary mode of expression—the "glosa." This is a shorter commentary than the essay, rejected as too digressive; the subject is isolated with precision and all the skill of a craftsman. This technique is notable in *El nuevo glosario* (1922), *Diálogos de la pasión meditabunda* (1922), and *Cuando ya esté tranquilo* (1930). The form of the gloss and the enormous field opened to the curiosity of the writer have caused at times a misunderstanding of the great unity of the work of D'Ors. Even those glosses which are the most frivolous from the standpoint of their content or those apparently most removed from the fields of art and thought can be fitted into a system of ideas and into a coherent body of philosophical thought. D'Ors is one of the Spanish thinkers who have tried, with modern sensibility, to overcome the traditional conflicts of philosophy by means of their own solutions. He is really a systematic writer within his "discontinuity." He has an inherent feeling for order—even to giving the word order its architectonic sense; he favors a classifying precision, an established norm. He chooses his themes from among the most lofty and developed forms of human culture much in the manner of a gardener more intent on the perfection of the flower than on its mysterious gestation. He is devoted to intelligence, to reason; he is the enemy of "phantasmagories," as he calls everything that cannot be classified or reduced to method.

In consequence of an antiromantic temperament, D'Ors shuns certain traditional Spanish values which are not in agreement with his attitude. However, he exalts others, since despite his cosmopolitanism D'Ors has a deep concern for Spanish things. Less Hispanized than his immediate predecessors of the Generation of '98 (*see* Spanish literature), he nevertheless turns toward *lo hispánico* from his native Catalonia. He began by being a Catalonian writer employing the Catalan language and signed his work with the pseudonym Xenius, a Catalan diminutive of Eugenio. He then wrote his famous novel *La ben plantada* (1912). Already in 1906 he was collaborating on the important Catalonian newspaper *Veu de Catalunya,* and that same year his *Glosari,* which fascinated the young Catalonian intellectuals, also established the author as a European figure. As a director of public education he took an active part in the movement for the political and intellectual renovation of Catalonia. Then, in 1920, he broke with his Catalonian friends, wrote his following works in Spanish, collaborated only on Madrid newspapers, and finally adhered to the cause of Franco, taking an active part in its political educational program.

D'Ors is a restless and crusading writer who attempts, as he says, to elevate to the rank of a "category" the anecdotal flow of history. His attempt to reconstruct a morphology of culture is interesting, and the classification and connections which he establishes between the apparently different modalities of the spirit are penetrating and fruitful. To him is due in great measure a revaluation of baroque art; he rectifies traditional concepts and establishes the fact that here is a manifestation of culture general during certain periods of history; far from being a deformation of classical taste, here is a forerunner, it is argued, of the romantic attitude. As an art critic the interpretation by D'Ors of the great painters is significant (*Poussin y el Greco,* 1922; *Tres horas en el Museo del Prado,* 1923; *Cézanne,* 1924; *L'Art de Goya,* 1928; *Pablo Picasso,* 1930).

An academic spirit par excellence, attracted by so many currents, D'Ors may be said to have two poles, the aristocratic, ironic, rationalistic, rococo taste of the 18th century on the one hand and the classical Mediterranean values which embody a certain aspect of the Catalan spirit on the other. For although D'Ors still feels *lo hispánico* through the unilateral and exclusive form of the new and already decrepit *falangismo,* he has very deep roots in Catalonian tradition, one of the richest variations of the Hispanic spirit and attitude—witness his cosmopolitan zeal, his "classicism," his plastic capacity, his luminous order. The work of D'Ors is damaged, nevertheless, by a certain affectation of tone, doubtless the result of his purely intellectual adherence to irony, an attitude from which he is temperamentally as removed as he is from humor and jesting.

See: D'Ors, *La filosofía del hombre que trabaja y que juega* (1914), introduction by Manuel G. Morente, commentaries by M. de Unamuno, and other studies; Samuel Putnam, ed., *The European Caravan* (1931).

F. G. L.

Dossi, Carlo (pseud. of Alberto Pisani, 1849–1910, Italian novelist and diplomat), was born at Zenevedro, Pavia. At the age of 19 he won recognition as a literary artist by writing *L'Altrjeri* (1868), the story of his childhood friendship with little Lisa, his pale-faced playmate, and of her death. The simplicity and the grace of this work recall the *Vita nuova;* its poetry is derived from the subtle observation of a world of delicate feelings and kind deeds in which the commonplaces of daily life take on artistic value. In *La Vita d'Alberto Pisani* (1870), a romantic autobiography, his style is often overcast by the clouds of Werther and Orthis. *Elvira* (1872) contains many delightful stories about the little things which make a child's life meaningful and about the joys of innocent love. When Dossi took his place in public life as secretary to Crispi, and later as minister in Bogotá and Athens, the personal poet yielded to the satirist. But he learned little about men; deeply rooted in him were an aristocratic aversion for the vulgarity of the masses—which led him to publish his works in small private editions—and a general distrust and ignorance of the outer world as a whole. *La Colonia felice* (1874) is a poem of ideas which tells of a group of convicts deported to a distant island and there left to themselves, who decide to submit to laws and appoint a ruler in order to build up a natural society and live happily. The three volumes of *I Ritratti umani* (1873–1885) present a series of portraits of a vulgar and sordid world with the habits and faults that Dossi bitterly resented; the first volume, *Il Campionario,* is a loud protest against the dull and the tedious in men and things, and the third, *La Desinenza in A* is a bitter satire of various types of women. The characters are generally as unconcerned with their contemporaries as the author himself; sometimes they are reduced to mere abstractions. *Gocce d'inchiostro* (1880) and *Amori* (1887) are two collections of stories which had already appeared separately in periodicals; the last contains enchanting reflections of his own inner world of youthful memories. At the age of 40 Dossi stopped publishing: "The lamp was soon clogged by too much oil and afterwards it only smoked." He died in 1910 at Cardina, near Como. Posthumously published were his memoirs, the *Note azzure* (1912), and two comedies, *Ona Famiglia de Cilapponi* (1921), *Commediole* (1927).

Dossi belongs to the period of late Lombard romanticism, to the Milanese circle of the painter Tranquillo Cremona from whom he borrowed effects of *delicata sfumatura.* But he also reacted vigorously against the tradition established by the followers of Manzoni, and his own disciple Lucini has regarded him as the master of a new literary style. Dossi tried to enrich the Italian narrative language with obsolete Latin or caustic Milanese or newly coined idioms. He believed that a language became monotonous when nationally adopted and commonly used; he claimed for the writer the right to invent new words as he created new modes and discovered new thoughts. This thirst for a manifold richness of expression tortured him at every page of his work. Croce confirmed him as an artist of merit and has given him a place of importance among the writers of the new Italy. As a poet of simple feelings and quiet scenes, the master of tones and rhythms, Dossi is now widely esteemed.

See: G. P. Lucini, *L'Ora topica di Carlo Dossi; saggio di critica integrale* (1911); B. Croce, *La Letteratura della nuova Italia,* 2d ed., III (1922), 201–217.

N. L.

Dostoevski, Fyodor Mikhailovich (1821–1881, Russian novelist and journalist), born in Moscow, was sent to a military engineering school in St. Petersburg at the age of 17. Dull drill and technical studies bored him and he sought relief in fiction and poetry and in translating Balzac's *Eugénie Grandet.* In 1843 he obtained a commission in the army, but the next year resigned to devote all his time to literature. His first novel, *Bednyie lyudi* (1846; Poor Folk), aroused the enthusiasm of the leading critic, Belinski, who acclaimed the author of this slight tale a coming new force in Russian literature. At the end of the same year (1846) he published his second work, *Dvoinik* (The Double), which disappointed Belinski. Over the next three years Dostoevski wrote some 12 sketches and short stories, concluding with an unfinished novel, *Netochka Nezvanova* (1849). The influence of several authors, particularly that of Gogol, is apparent in these works, but one can also detect some of the characteristic traits of the great novels of the future—the original dramatic method, a deep sympathy with humiliated, oppressed people, and an intense interest in morbid psychology.

During this early period in St. Petersburg, Dostoevski had been a shy, lonely, unsociable individual, always poor and with few friends. Eventually his liberal sympathies brought him into contact with a group of young men, known as the Petrashevski Circle, who met regularly to talk of social and political reforms. No doubt some of these youths, Dostoevski included, were preparing to engage in the illegal printing of controversial writings. At any event, the reactionary government of Nicholas I did not tolerate this kind of activity, however harmless, and in April, 1849, many members of the Petrashevski Circle were arrested and sentenced to death. At the place of execution they were informed that this penalty—really a cruel, theatrical device on the part of the tsar—had been commuted to exile to Siberia. Dostoevski never forgot those terrible moments. He was now to spend four years of hard labor at Omsk. His epilepsy, traces of which had begun to appear earlier, was no doubt aggravated by his severe sufferings at this time. His experiences as a convict played an important part in his development. Any radical leanings were abandoned; he acquired a firmer faith in the teachings of Christ, and his study of the New Testament in prison taught him his notable doctrine of salvation by suffering; he had come in prison to know the common Russian people as never before, and he was convinced that upon them rested the future greatness of Russia.

Dostoevski was released from prison in 1854, but the terms of his sentence obliged him to serve as a private in the ranks. He was quartered in the little Siberian town of Semipalatinsk, where he met and married Marya Isayeva, a widow with one child. An amnesty in 1859 allowed him to return to St. Petersburg. Literature was claiming all his attention once again, for he depended upon his pen for a livelihood. His first new work was *Dyadyushkin son* (1859; Uncle's Dream), an amusing and satirical long short story of a provincial town, quite unlike anything he had done up to this time. In the same year appeared the novelette *Selo Stepanchikovo i evo obitateli* (The Village of Stepanchikovo and Its Inhabitants; Eng. tr. as *The Friend of the Family*), in which he returned to his early method, particularly in the repulsive but brilliantly realized character, Foma Opiskin. His prison experiences began to appear in 1861 in the vivid *Zapiski iz Mertvovo Doma* (Notes from the House of the Dead; Eng. tr. as *Buried Alive, Prison Life in Siberia, The House of the Dead*), a book that Leo Tolstoy (*q.v.*) thought was the author's greatest. In the same year a full-length novel, *Unizhonnyie i oskorblyonnyie* (The Insulted and Injured), was issued in serial form. Once again Dostoevski was regarded by the public as one of the leading novelists.

Meanwhile, in 1861, he had entered the field of journalism with his own periodical *Vremya* (Time). It achieved an immediate success, partly because of his astuteness in steering a middle course between the prevailing extremes of radical and conservative thought. In rather affluent circumstances for the first time, he went abroad, but in 1863, some months after his return, an unfortunate article on the Poles brought about the suppression of his review. The blow left him deeply in debt; yet in the midst of his misfortunes he went abroad to keep a rendezvous in Paris with Polina Suslova, a handsome devotee of the new type of emancipated woman, with whom he had fallen passionately in love, and also to try his fortune at the gaming tables of Wiesbaden. His luck with both was execrable. Upon his return home he revived his review under the name of *Epokha* (The Epoch), but it got off to a bad start and lasted only a short time. He contributed to it his remarkable piece *Zapiski iz podpolya* (1864, Notes from the Underground; Eng. tr. as *Letters from the Underworld*), a kind of prologue to the five great novels that followed.

This same year (1864) his wife and his brother died and, deep in debt, he wrote furiously to pay off creditors. *Prestupleniye i nakazaniye* (Crime and Punishment) appeared in 1866, and the next year *Igrok* (The Gambler). While writing these works he employed a stenographer, Anna Snitkina, whom he married in 1867, one of the most fortunate events of his life. The couple soon went abroad, and this time Dostoevski remained in Europe for four years, living a hand to mouth existence while he indulged his passion for gambling.

He wrote *Idiot* (1868–1869; The Idiot) and began *Besy* (The Demons; Eng. tr. as *The Possessed*) in 1871, the year he returned to Russia. He eventually obtained a position as editor of a conservative weekly (1873–1874), to which he contributed a column, "Dnevnik pisatelya" (The Diary of a Writer), later offered with much success as a separate publication. A novel, *Podrostok* (A Raw Youth), appeared in 1875, and *Bratya Karamazovy* (The Brothers Karamazov) in 1880. The last few years of his life were spent in fairly good financial circumstances. His contemporary fame reached its height upon the occasion of an address delivered at the unveiling of the Pushkin Memorial in 1880, and when he died the following year he was accorded a public funeral.

Dostoevski's fame rests largely upon *Crime and Punishment, The Idiot, The Possessed,* and *The Brothers Karamazov.* He possessed in an extraordinary degree the qualities of the consummate novelist—dramatic construction, psychological insight, convincingness, and the ability to create memorable characters, such as

Raskolnikov, Sonya Marmeladova, Prince Myshkin, Stavrogin, and Dmitri and Ivan Karamazov. He also infused his works with his powerful personality and his ethical and moral thought. Throughout his novels runs his special message of meekness and faith in Christ, whose precepts of suffering and love will enable the Russian people to bring about universal brotherhood. His vision of a purer and finer world was founded on the love and innate goodness that dwell in the hearts of men. This positive doctrine in his novels, however, is always opposed by a negative one, for Dostoevski's own life was a constant struggle between good and evil, and this struggle is reflected in the great characters he created.

There are numerous English translations of Dostoevski's works.

See: N. N. Strakhov, *Biografiya, pisma i zametki iz zapisnoi knizhki Dostoyevskovo* (1883); E. H. Carr, *Dostoevsky* (1931, in English); N. A. Berdyayev, *Dostoievsky: An Interpretation*, tr. by Donald Attwater (1934); Avrahm Yarmolinsky, *Dostoevsky; a Life* (1934); E. J. Simmons, *Dostoevski: The Making of a Novelist* (1940).

E. J. S.

Doumic, René (1860–1937, French critic), born in Paris, made a brilliant record at the Lycée Condorcet and the Ecole Normale Supérieure and taught rhetoric at the Collège Stanislas, engaging in journalism at the same time. In 1897 he abandoned systematic teaching to give all his time to criticism. By then he had written for the *Correspondant,* the *Revue bleue,* and the *Journal des débats,* and, more important, he had established himself solidly at the *Revue des deux mondes,* whose dramatic criticism he continued to write until his death. In 1910 he was elected to the French Academy, and in 1919 he succeeded Frédéric Masson as its *secrétaire perpétuel.* But in 1916 an even more important event had taken place: Doumic became editor of the *Revue des deux mondes,* in which position he remained the rest of his life.

Doumic, like his master Brunetière (*q.v.*), believed that art and morality were inseparable. The task of the critic, as he saw it, was to place writers according to the classic accepted values, to reward those who seemed to work for the spiritual and moral benefit of society and to punish those who, like Baudelaire (*q.v.*), seemed to have aligned themselves with the forces of evil. The critic was a teacher also, improving the public's moral perception as well as its aesthetic, spreading those ideas which were obviously wholesome, handing down the approved verities. To these aims was added, during the later part of Doumic's life, the complementary one of maintaining the prestige of the *Revue* and the Academy. To him the *Revue* in particular seemed the natural guardian of all that was important in the French spirit; it was the living expression of the glories of the French intellect. As its editor he was faced with the problem of keeping it "up to date" without lowering its standards; and his success is amply demonstrated by the fact that he tripled its circulation, though not without suppressing to some degree his own taste in the arts and politics and accepting in literature audacities of form so long as the sense was not contrary to faith and morals. In the Academy, too, his influence was profound.

Though Doumic was most at home in dramatic criticism, collected in such volumes as *De Scribe à Ibsen* (1893) and *Essai sur le théâtre contemporain* (1897), he produced also the useful *Histoire de la littérature française* (1890); a long series of interesting literary essays, *Etudes sur la littérature française* (6 vols., 1896–1908); and three respectable, if not brilliant, studies, *George Sand* (1909; Eng. tr., 1910), *Lamartine* (1911), and *Saint-Simon* (1919). A volume of articles, *Contemporary French Novelists,* was published in English translation in 1899. The most striking characteristics of Doumic's criticism are its bluntness, its deliberate dryness of style, and its constant moral elevation. For all his honesty and high-mindedness, however, Doumic was without any great originality, and it is difficult to see his work as anything more than a weaker continuation of Brunetière.

See: Emile Faguet, *Propos littéraires,* Sér. 4 (1907); John Charpentier, "René Doumic," *Mercure de France,* CCLXXXI (1938), 24–32; Gabriel Hanotaux, "Le Souvenir de René Doumic," *Revue des deux mondes,* November 15, 1938, pp. 266–292.

C. W., Jr.

Drachmann, Holger Henrik Herholdt (1846–1908, Danish poet), was the son of a naval surgeon in Copenhagen. From boyhood he was familiar with the sea and the men who lived by the sea and wanted at first to become a marine painter. His travels as a "journeyman painter" took him to England, and the poverty and misery he saw around the docks of London made him a revolutionary. His first published poem, "Engelske Socialister" (1871; English Socialists), revealed a striking talent. It was followed by two collections, *Digte* (1872; Poems) and *Dæm-*

pede Melodier (1875; Muted Melodies), still under the sign of revolt. Drachmann naturally joined the group of which Georg Brandes (*q.v.*) was the center, but other elements in his rich, complex nature asserted themselves. He made a trip to South Jutland, which had come under German rule in 1864, and wrote a series of travel letters *Derovre fra Grænsen* (1877; Over There from the Border) which had an immense popular success. Incredible as it now seems, the patriotic note—together with the implied strictures on the literary and political squabbles in Copenhagen—offended Drachmann's internationally minded friends. At the same time he expressed his disgust at the "Lenten fare" of the problem literature. He craved romance and heroics. Nevertheless his sea stories, *e.g.*, *I Storm og Stille* (1874; In Storm and Calm) or *Paa Sømands Tro og Love* (1878; On a Sailor's Word and Promise), though somewhat sentimental, show a more sympathetic understanding of the common man than does the work of the professed realists. From this early romantic period are the fairy-tale poem *Prinsessen og det halve Kongerige* (1878; The Princess and Half the Kingdom) and the popular poem *Østenfor Sol og Vesten for Maane* (1880; East of the Sun and West of the Moon). At the same time Drachmann attained his full stature as a lyric poet in *Sange ved Havet* (1877; Songs by the Sea), *Ranker og Roser* (1879; Vines and Roses), and *Ungdom i Digt og Sang* (1879; Youth in Poetry and Song). In these collections he developed to the point of virtuosity that peculiar flexible verse form which is so well suited to express infinitely varied moods. The pretty fairy-tale comedy *Der var en Gang* (1887; Once upon a Time) has retained its place on the Danish stage.

In spite of his charm and his gift for catching the popular imagination, Drachmann remained a lonely man. His South Jutland letters had pleased the conservatives, but his extravagances and the irregularities of his life brought down upon him their censure. His entire life became a swinging back and forth between the mutually hostile intellectual camps of Denmark, just as temperamentally he vibrated between his inherited bourgeois standards and his own bohemian tastes. In his un-bourgeois phase he felt akin to Byron, whose *Don Juan* he translated (1879). In his big two-volume novel of Copenhagen, *Forskrevet* (1890; Signed Away), he personifies the two sides of his nature in two friends, one a vagabond poet, the other a hard-working artist-journalist. The book is formless and chaotic, but rich in profound characterization and written in beautiful lyrical prose. The friends are both inspired by Edith, a singer in a variety theatre modeled after a woman who had great influence over Drachmann for a number of years. She appears under various names in his works, notably as Suleima in a cycle included in *Sangenes Bog* (1889; The Book of Songs), containing some of the finest poems of his maturity. Drachmann was enormously productive. Threescore volumes of prose and poetry reflect the events and the mental and emotional crises of his life. Of uneven merit, they all bear the stamp of his genius and his subjective experience.

See: Georg Brandes, *Det moderne Gennembruds Mænd* (1883); Valdemar Vedel, *Holger Drachmann* (1909).

H. A. L.

Dreyer, Max (1862–, German dramatist and novelist), was born in Rostock, Mecklenburg. After receiving his doctorate in 1884, he became a Gymnasium teacher. Disappointed in his profession because of the rigidity of the educational system, he resigned in the late 80's and became a free-lance writer. School life and pedagogical problems, however, were to play a large part in the best of his literary work.

Dreyer wrote a score of realistic dramas, some of which were very successful on the stage. His drama *Drei* (1894) deals with a triangular marital problem, *Der Winterschlaf* (1896) with a tragic love affair; *In Behandlung* (1897) satirizes the conventional morality of typical small-town society. His greatest stage success was achieved in *Der Probekandidat* (1900; Eng. tr., *On Probation*, 1903), in which a young teacher fights for the maintenance of his intellectual integrity. It is generally considered to be Dreyer's most characteristic and powerful drama.

In the early period of his creative writing, Dreyer is strongly influenced by Ibsen as well as by the earlier works of Gerhart Hauptmann (*qq.v.*). In Dreyer's subsequent plays this influence grows weaker, even though an occasional attempt is made to grapple with "problems," as in *Die Siebzehnjährigen* (1904), which deals with the disturbances of a boy and a girl in adolescence. Most of Dreyer's later plays, however, are written in a lighter vein, *e.g.*, the comedies *Das Tal des Lebens* (1903) and *Des Pfarrers Tochter von Streladorf* (1910).

In addition to his plays, Dreyer wrote a number of novels, the more important of which are *Der deutsche Morgen* (1915), *Nachwuchs* (1917), *Die Siedler von Hohenmoor* (1922), *Das Gymnasium von St. Jürgen* (1925), *Der Weg durchs Feuer* (1930), and *Tapfere kleine Renate* (1932). A volume of poetry, in Low German, *Nah Huus,* appeared in 1904.

G. K.

Drieu La Rochelle, Pierre (1893–, French novelist and critic), was born in Paris of a well-to-do Norman family. Destined for diplomacy, he attended the Ecole des Sciences Politiques; but the First World War soon put an end to that. By the end of the war, he had written two volumes of verse, *Interrogation* (1917), which Barrès thought the best book inspired by the conflict, and *Fond de cantine* (1920). Both were strongly reminiscent of Rimbaud and, even more noticeably, of Claudel (*qq.v.*) in violence and magniloquence of metaphor and sweep of long, free-verse line. In the years following the war, Drieu provided a perfect example of the intellectual confusion and moral bankruptcy of his generation: disoriented, yet passionately desiring order, he jumped from movement to movement with an agility that rivaled Cocteau's (*q.v.*). Communism, surrealism, the Action Française, all at some time counted him as an adherent; he dabbled, like Mauriac (*q.v.*), in Catholic mysticism and, like Montherlant (*q.v.*), sang the praises of the stadium and the bedroom. A volume of short stories, *Plainte contre inconnu* (1924), and two semi-autobiographical novels, *Etat-Civil* (1921) and *Le Jeune Européen* (1927), convey vividly but confusedly the emptiness he and the post-war generation found behind all accepted values, their desire for action and energy, without any distinct idea of the end toward which it was to be directed. In *Mesure de la France* (1923) he surveyed with little hope the political and economic situation of his country, and in *Genève ou Moscou* (1928) he called for a new party of the right, young, authoritarian, and antimaterialist. His novels of this period, *L'Homme couvert de femmes* (1925), *Une Femme à sa fenêtre* (1930), and *Le Feu follet* (1931), continue the theme of disillusion, mixed with a need for the assertion of the individual which finds its outlet in sport, violence, and a monotonous and physical love. In the next decade, however, Drieu discovered his leader in Doriot and his program in the Parti Populaire Français. His position was made clear in such books as *Avec Doriot* (1937), a collection of articles which appeared in Doriot's *Emancipation nationale,* and the novel *Gilles* (1939), the story of a rootless young man who, disgusted with the bourgeois world, finds salvation fighting for Franco in Spain. Immediately after the French defeat of 1940, Drieu became the director of the *Nouvelle Revue française* and stood out, intellectually at least, as the most prominent of the collaborationists.

See: André Rousseaux, *Ames et visages du XXe siècle* (1932); Paul Chauveau, *Caractères* (1933); Beatrice Corrigan, "Drieu La Rochelle: Study of a Collaborator," *University of Toronto Quarterly,* XIV (1945), 199–205; Jean Ehrhard, *Le Roman français depuis Marcel Proust* (n.d.).

C. W., Jr.

Du Bos, Charles (1882–1939, French critic), *anima naturaliter christiana* ever on guard against the spirit of the salon, was born in Paris to the head of the exclusive Jockey Club and his wife, née Eustis, of the family which supplied an American minister to France. The call of the blood, the English poets and Emerson, read at Oxford (1900–1901), successive sojourns (1902–1907) in the Florence of D'Annunzio (*q.v.*) and the Berlin of George (*q.v.*) and Simmel, with a return visit, this time to the England of Henry James, fitted him for the spiritual interpretation of foreign literatures. With the *Nouvelle Revue française* group he labored to develop, through the interpenetration of cultures, the "European," synonymous with the fullest humanity.

The enemy for Du Bos is Cartesian and Voltairian rationalism as well as the (to him) false classical unity trisecting into man, writer, and Christian the oneness of creative personality restored, via Rousseau, by Claudel (*q.v.*). Looking to Bergson (*q.v.*) and the Plato of the transcendent Idea, he combines moralism (without being moralistic), intuition, and ecstasy. Thus, outside of the France of Pascal and Baudelaire (*q.v.*), he feels particularly at home in English, German, and Russian literatures. In a household of faith hospitable to apparent contraries, the Trinity is Shakespeare, Dante, and Keats, with Novalis and Pater as sources of decisive revelation. Nietzsche (*q.v.*) figures as the noblest of adversaries and the dearest of tempters in the years of "individual truths" (1918–1927). But Du Bos "passed beyond" to Catholicism.

Through translations and the editorship of a series of foreign writers, thanks also to unusual powers of conversation and extensive friendships, Du Bos sowed germs of thought and influence freely, like a *grand seigneur* of ideas. The organizing tendency is a view of literature which won him a lodging, not without protest on his part, in Thibaudet's (*q.v.*) *Quartier des philosophes.* Literature is "life becoming conscious of itself when, in the soul of a man of genius, it joins its plenitude of expression." A masterpiece embodies a sense of life, but in its characteristic music a metaphysic speaks. Thus the *Dialogue avec André Gide* (1929) rejects together Gide (*q.v.*), Goethe, and Nietzsche, the whole family of spirits whose art informs the hypothesis, "The end of life is life itself."

Creative criticism results, but with transcendental tendencies. The critic, through analysis-in-ecstasy applied to the tone and tempo of style, re-creates the artist's inspiration and intuits his truth. In rapid formula this criticism is the fusion of Pater, Proust (*q.v.*), and the later James with Du Bos's spiritual fervor and his need to explain. It expects only "approximation" of the artist's essential quality. Judgment is not expressed directly but, at most, overheard in the critic's tone. Du Bos made exhausting efforts to "become the object," and hostile judges will add, "Only to substitute himself too often for it."

The most characteristic work of this self-styled fragmentist is *Extraits d'un journal* (2d ed., augmented, 1931), from which radiate seven volumes of *Approximations* (1922–1937). It marks those "tops of sovereignty" in the presence of literature, music, and painting which led to religion. Other important writings are *Byron et le besoin de la fatalité* (1929; Eng. tr., *Byron and the Need of Fatality,* 1932), three articles, "Du spirituel dans l'ordre littéraire" (in *Vigile,* 1930), and *What Is Literature?* (1940), lectures in English in 1938 before the faculty of Saint Mary's College, Notre Dame, Indiana. Du Bos projected much, completed little—and that in a style uninviting to the general reader. Chronic ill-health, but even more the exquisite sincerities of his form of the religion of art, constricted expression. Friends have suggested that Du Bos is the Sainte-Beuve of the 20th century; in no spirit of derogation one may think more naturally of Mallarmé (*q.v.*).

See: E. R. Curtius, "Du Bos," *Revue nouvelle,* July 15–August 15, 1926; Paul Archambault, *Témoins du spirituel* (1932); André Maurois, "Mon Ami Charles du Bos," *Nouvelles littéraires,* August 12, 1939.

A. P. B.

Ducasse, Isidore Lucien, *see* Lautréamont, comte de.

Dučić, Jovan (1874–1943, Serb poet), was born in the small town of Trebinje, Herzegovina. He attended teachers' colleges in Mostar and Sombor and studied law in Geneva and Paris. Choosing a diplomatic career, he served in Sofia, Rome, Athens, Madrid, Cairo, Geneva, Budapest, Bucharest. After the outbreak of the Second World War, he found refuge in the United States, where he died in Gary, Indiana, in sad and bitter exile.

At the beginning strongly influenced by Russian poets, especially Pushkin, and by the Serbian poet Vojislav Ilić (*q.v.*) as well, Dučić quickly found himself and achieved original expression of his great poetical talent. His stay in France gave him an intimate acquaintance with French literature, and he became enthusiastic about the poetry of the Parnassians and the symbolists (*see* French symbolism), without however any slavish copying of their manners. Dučić was indeed a poet of individualistic tendencies, given to deep introspection. He knew how to turn all his emotions into art. His poetry, often very personal, was extraordinarily subtle, fluid, ethereal, gracious, of a diverse and variable artistic inspiration. He wrote with harmony and elegance, but was never merely conventional or orthodox in his sentiments; on the contrary, his poems abound in rare, delicate feelings, disquietudes, vaguenesses, nuances, mists, and shadows. Very haughty, with a certain scorn for mediocrity and everyday life, he desired his muse "to be too beautiful lest she should please everybody."

Dučić's first book, *Pesme* (1900; Poems), was followed in 1908 by another collection of lyrics and in 1912 by a choice of his best poems; his *Sabrana dela* (1929; Collected Works) comprehend all his poetic as well as his prose writings. The sonnet sequences "Jadranski soneti" (Adriatic Sonnets) and "Carski soneti" (Imperial Sonnets) are masterpieces of poetry. The latter possess moreover a great national value because of their brilliant glorification of the Serbian race, reverence for its past, and belief in its future.

Dučić was also a first-rate prose writer. Besides many critical and aesthetic essays, he published cycles of letters concerning his extensive travels; he describes Geneva, the Alps, the Ionian Sea, Paris, Athens, Madrid. These letters, which reveal an extraordinary pictorial gift and imaginative power, are among the most brilliant pages in Yugoslav literature. *Blago Cara Radovana* (1931; The Treasure of Emperor Radovan), a series of essays on women, love, friendship, poets, prophets, heroes, etc., fascinates one not so much by its thoughts, often commonplace, as by the colorfulness and brightness of its incomparable style. During Dučić's few final years in the United States were published a monograph, *Grof Sava Vladislavić* (1942), and *Federalizam i Centralizam* (1943; Federalism and Centralism), a book of political controversy.

Dučić has appropriately been called "the prince of Serbian poetry and prose" of the 20th century.

See: B. Popović, "Jedna kritička analiza," *Srpski književni glasnik* (1914); P. Albala, "Putopisi Jovana Dučića," *Letopis matice srpske,* August 1, 1928; N. Mirković, "Jovan Dučić," *Slavische Rundschau,* July, 1932; P. Albala, "Jedna knjiga životne mudrosti-Blago Cara Radovana," *Prilozi za književnost, jezik, istoriju i folklor* (1938).

P. A.

Duhamel, Georges (pseud. Denis Thévenin, 1884–, French poet, dramatist, novelist, essayist, and critic), born in Paris, was the son of a physician. He too studied medicine and began to practice shortly before the First World War. He is also an excellent flautist. In 1906 Duhamel, Vildrac (*q.v.*)—later his brother-in-law—and several other young men interested in the arts rented a house at Créteil, which they called the Abbaye. There they planned to live a life in common, working together and devoting themselves to their vocations. They bought a press and printed books, including Duhamel's *Des légendes, des batailles* (1906). In 1907 the group disbanded, due in part to a lack of money. Such an enterprise was destined to fail, since the groundwork had not been carefully prepared. Shortly after leaving the Abbaye, Duhamel became interested in the theatre. In 1911 the Odéon produced his play *La Lumière* (Eng. tr., *The Light,* 1914), in 1912 *Dans l'ombre des statues* (Eng. tr., *In the Shadow of Statues,* 1914). In 1913 the Théâtre des Arts presented *Le Combat* (Eng. tr., 1915). *L'Œuvre des athlètes* was played at the Vieux Colombier in 1920; it is an excellent satire on a literary club of that name and was well received. Duhamel's wife was a member of the Vieux Colombier (founded by Jacques Copeau, *q.v.*). *La Journée des aveux,* played at the Comédie des Champs-Elysées in 1923, illustrates Duhamel's keen powers of observation and a certain sensitivity and delicacy which are characteristic of his entire work.

In 1913 Duhamel accepted the position of literary critic on the *Mercure de France* and wrote a volume on the poetry of Paul Claudel (*q.v.*). Then the First World War broke out, and he left for the front in the capacity of surgeon. The years spent in front-line ambulances revealed another side of Duhamel—the portrayer of suffering and the champion of justice. Two volumes of war stories were written at the front, *Vie des martyrs* (1917; Eng. tr., *The New Book of Martyrs,* 1918) and *Civilisation* (1918; Eng. tr., 1919), for which he was awarded the Prix Goncourt. The descriptions of the suffering of the wounded and dying and the irony with which Duhamel describes the stupidity and heartlessness of those in charge of the hospitals are handled with consummate art and deep-felt sympathy.

Duhamel the novelist has created characters who will surely live in posterity. In his *Cycle de Salavin* (1920–1932; Eng. tr., *Salavin,* 1936) he describes the gropings of a mediocre man, Salavin, who tries hard to adapt himself to life, who is too introspective, too sensitive, too afraid of life to attain happiness. He tries friendship, but it fails him; he tries saintliness, but falls victim to his own generosity; he tries to take an active part in society, but innocently falls into a trap. Finally he leaves France, hoping to change his personality in devoting himself to others, but is wounded by the very boy he tried to protect. Before he dies, he tells his wife that, were he to start life anew, he would know now how to live.

In *Chronique des Pasquier* (Eng. tr., *The Pasquier Chronicles,* 1937–), the first volume of which was published in 1933 and which is still in the course of publication, Duhamel describes a certain bourgeois family of Paris, giving the reader a picture of French life during the early years of the century. The mother is a self-sacrificing, self-effacing woman; the father is an extraordinary and fantastic person, who studied medicine in middle age, after all the children were born, and actually became a practicing if not too effectual physician. Of the five children Laurent, the scientist, represents the ideal towards which Duhamel has always strived.

Duhamel has also written many volumes of essays. Among the first is *La Possession du monde* (1919; Eng. tr., *The Heart's Domain,* 1919), in which he entreats man to appreciate the beauty of nature, to aspire to happiness through the cultivation of his inner life. Duhamel has traveled all over Europe, and his books have been translated into nearly every language. *Scènes de la vie future* (1930) was written after a short and hasty voyage to the United States. Something of a diatribe—although Duhamel did not authorize the title used in the English translation (*America: The Menace,* 1931)—he warns the reader against an overindustrialized civilization, where man allows himself to become a slave of the machine.

In *Querelles de famille* (1931) he shows how France, too, has been too greatly influenced by modern inventions like the radio and telegraph. Man has drifted away from the wholesome, simple life. Before the outbreak of the Second World War, Duhamel produced several volumes of essays in which he warned France against Nazism and made a plea for a strong, united France.

Duhamel's style is sober and free from exaggerations, humorous, in the best tradition of the greatest French writers. His sympathy for his fellow beings has attracted many young writers to him; his influence as a person and as a writer has been great throughout Europe. He is a member of the French Academy.

See: H. Massis, *Jugements*, II (1924), 155–206; André Thérive, *Georges Duhamel, ou l'Intelligence du cœur* (1925) and *Georges Duhamel* (1927); P. Claudel *et al.*, *Duhamel et nous* (1937).

H. H.

Dullin, Charles (1885–, French actor, theatrical director, and *metteur en scène*), fled his native Yenne in Savoie, a clerkship in Lyon, and the cabarets of Montmartre to distinguish himself in the role of Smerdiakov in Copeau's adaptation of *The Brothers Karamazov* (1911). As the associate of Jacques Copeau (*q.v.*) in the Théâtre du Vieux Colombier (1913–1914, 1917–1919) and of Firmin Gémier at the Comédie Montaigne he gathered experience for his own experiments. His Atelier (opened in 1921)—which finally made a financial success with the adaptation by Stefan Zweig and Jules Romains (*qq.v.*) of *Volpone*—began as a rigorous school for actors following the theories of Stanislavsky and Copeau (*q.v.*) and gradually became a school for dramatists as well. Using music by Darius Milhaud and Georges Auric, sets and costumes by Jean Hugo, Touchagues, *et al.*, he has taught the virtues of a stylized simplicity far from the conventional naturalism of the Théâtre Libre and created spectacles containing fairylike qualities. His marked predilection for Aristophanes (*Plutus, Peace*), for the English great (Shakespeare, Jonson, Ford, and Farquhar), and for the Spanish theatre (Cervantes, Calderón, Jacinto Grau) has enriched the Paris stage with beautiful performances.

J. O'B.

Durch, Der Verein. Parallel to M. G. Conrad's activity as naturalistic critic and editor in Munich, there arose in Berlin in 1886 a literary club, "Durch," in which the revolutionary young writers gathered. The name was suggested by Konrad Küster, a leader in university circles and publisher of university journals, who came into contact with the group of young literary rebels through Leo Berg and Eugen Wolff. Other members were Arno Holz (*q.v.*), Johannes Schlaf (*q.v.*), John Henry Mackay, Heinrich and Julius Hart (*q.v.*), Gerhart Hauptmann (*q.v.*), and Adalbert von Hanstein. In the years 1887 and 1888 articles by club members appeared in Küster's *Allgemeine deutsche Universitätszeitung*, the most important of these being Eugen Wolff's "Die 'Moderne,' zur Revolution und Reform der Literatur." The club sought to combat the contemporary mediocrity of German literature and to develop a modern and realistic literature which should treat contemporary social problems frankly and forcefully. Striving to avoid narrow dogmatism, it demanded recognition of contemporary scientific hypotheses and of the complex social conditions of modern life. The club provided a prelude to the later formulation of naturalistic theory.

See: A. von Hanstein, *Das jüngste Deutschland* (1901); W. Liepe, ed., *Verein Durch: Facsimile der Protokolle 1887: Aus der Werdezeit des deutschen Naturalismus* (1932).

W. H. R.

Durkheim, Emile (1858–1917, French sociologist and philosopher), born in Epinal, Vosges, taught at the University of Bordeaux from 1887 to 1902 and at the Sorbonne for the rest of his life. Some 50 years after sociology had received its letters patent from Auguste Comte, he found it—in France at least—still inorganic and undeveloped. At the time of his death he had made it, with the semi-independent help of Lucien Lévy-Bruhl (1857–1939), a thoroughly autonomous science, complete with a charter, a program of studies, a review (*Année sociologique*, 1898–1913, continued by others after 1923 and superseded in 1934 by the *Annales sociologiques*), and, last but not least, an impressive team of workers eager to follow in the master's footsteps (Célestin Bouglé, Henri Hubert, Marcel Mauss, François Simiand, Paul Fauconnet, Maurice Halbwachs, Charles Lalo, Georges Davy, *et al.*).

Durkheim's four main works are: *De la division du travail social*, his doctoral dissertation (1893; Eng. tr., *Emile Durkheim on the Division of Labor in Society*, 1933); *Les Règles de la méthode sociologique* (1895; Eng. tr., *The Rules of Sociological Method*, 1938); *Le Suicide* (1897); and *Les Formes élémentaires de la vie religieuse: Le Système totémique en Australie* (1912; Eng. tr., *The Elementary Forms of the Religious Life*, 1915). Two of these are deserving of special mention. *Les Règles de la méthode sociologique,* somewhat reminiscent in title and purpose of the *Discours de la méthode* of Descartes, effects an abrupt separation between sociology and individual psychology (for an opposite view *see* Tarde, Gabriel) and insists that social facts be considered as "things," that is to say, as entirely original syntheses with no relation to their personal constituents. In *Les Formes élémentaires de la vie religieuse* Durkheim, a deeply religious spirit who counted rabbis among his relatives, asserts that religion is the social fact par excellence, not only because it is social in its essence and origins, but because all collective representations—laws, customs, traditions, fashions, tastes, revolutions—are religious in character, having the same aura of coercion and supra-individual power which surrounds the mystical gatherings of primitive tribes.

See: Maurice Halbwachs, "La Doctrine d'Emile Durkheim," *Revue philosophique,* LXXXV (1918), 353–411; Georges Davy, *Emile Durkheim* (1927); Georges Gurvitch, *Essais de sociologie* (1938), pp. 68–90, 113–169, 189–193, 277–306; Harry Alpert, *Emile Durkheim and His Sociology* (1939).

J.-A. B.

Durych, Jaroslav (1886–, Czech novelist and poet), is the outstanding representative of the Catholic movement in recent Czech literature. He was born in Hradec Králové, studied medicine at the University of Prague and was an army doctor during the First World War. He rose to be a colonel in the medical corps of the Czechoslovak army. Durych's short stories and novels have a great variety of settings, but are variations on one theme: man's desire for divine grace. This grace can be found in mystical union with God, in the love of a pure, simple woman, in the humility of the poorest beggar, and in moments preceding death. Durych, convinced Catholic of the Neo-Thomist persuasion, wants to create a Catholic art which aspires to the Absolute, which would turn the age to God and eternity and revive the Catholic glories of Czech history. But these spiritual aspirations are always crossed by Durych's strong instincts: his sensuality, which struggles with his cult of innocence and purity; his rebellion against social oppression, which seems difficult to reconcile with his glorification of the Counter Reformation; his predilections for the horrible and cruel, grotesque and even brutal, which frequently debase his urge towards mystical ecstasy.

Some of Durych's best work is in small legends and fairy tales, graceful or horrible, whereas his full-length novels suffer from disjointed plots, repetitions, and monotony. The novels include *Na horách* (1919; On the Mountains), a poetic love story set in a dim medieval setting, and *Sedmikráska* (1925; The Daisy), *Paní Anežka Berková* (1931; Mrs. Agnes Berk), and *Píseň o růži* (1934; The Song of the Rose), all three set in small-town surroundings. *Bloudění* (3 vols., 1929; Eng. tr., *The Descent of the Idol,* 1935), the most important, is a large-scale attempt at a historic novel. Its story is set in the time of the Thirty Years' War, and the figures of the great General Wallenstein and of the Emperor Ferdinand II, together with other historical references, are part of the background. In the foreground is the story of a Czech Protestant emigrant and a Catholic girl of Spanish origin whose love finds fulfillment only in the hour of death. Durych enters with sympathy and understanding into the civilization of the Jesuit baroque, but his strained, ornate style, his fantastic landscapes, feverish visions, superhuman passions, and grandiose battle scenes are "expressionism" in a highly modernist manner rather than an imitation of 17th-century art. *Bloudění* is, at least, a welcome reaction against the antiquarian type of historical writing represented by Jirásek (*q.v.*) and Winter (*q.v.*). A set of three stories, *Rekviem* (1930; Requiem), placed just after Wallenstein's assassination, is a particularly successful example of Durych's art on a small scale. His last novel, *Masopust* (1938; The Carnival), is also drawn from history, this time the 16th century; in it his usual motifs of wandering at random and of searching for the one predestined woman are varied with less effect than in the great book on the Wallenstein period.

Durych also wrote distinguished verse, mostly in the simple popular style of ballads and songs (collected as *Básně,* 1930, Poems), and some dramas on themes of martyrdom (*e.g., Svatý Václav,* 1925, St. Wenceslaus) which try to revive the form of the 17th-century Spanish *autos.* His miscellaneous prose includes travel impressions from Germany, Italy, and Spain, reminiscences, and some criticism expounding the Neo-Thomist dogmas or attacking all different contemporary ways of thinking (*e.g., Ejhle, člověk,* 1928, Behold a Man; *Váhy života a umění,* 1933, The Scales of Life and Art). Durych admires Otokar Březina (*q.v.*), to whom he devoted an early pamphlet (1918) in which he declared his allegiance to a symbolist art permeated with the Catholic spirit. He, of all the many Czech

Catholic writers of the last decades, has come nearest to fulfilling this ideal.

See: J. Bartoš, *Kdo jest Jaroslav Durych?* (1930).

R. W.

Dutch literature (*see also* Belgian literature in Flemish). Modern Dutch literature had its beginnings in the 80's of the past century. Each new movement in the history of letters has always been a revolt of the rising generation against the standards and preferences of its immediate predecessor, and the forms in which the modernism of the young rebels found expression have loomed large and alarming to their older contemporaries. In retrospect the contrasts generally fade, and the perspective supplied by the passage of time levels the seemingly jagged line of development into a course of smooth continuity.

But this general truth does not hold for Holland's literary movement of the 80's. This did, indeed, revolutionize Dutch literature and bring about so profound a change in diction and word usage that the cleavage between the periods preceding and following the 80's is still clearly apparent to all readers more than half a century after the breach occurred. It was not only a difference in the handling of the language that set off the new era in such sharp contrast to the past. The general outlook, the attitude towards life and the world, underwent a profound transformation. The first half of the 19th century was an age of emotional stagnation. The Dutch of that period were an orderly, conventional, churchgoing community, whose main concern was the pursuit of commerce. They were keen businessmen, but poor connoisseurs of letters. They lived by sight, rather than by insight. They knew a good picture from a bad one, but they cared little for poetry. Their sense of realism distrusted the genuineness of poetic exaltation. It made them feel embarrassed and uncomfortable. They liked descriptive and didactic verse that portrayed the domestic scene with edifying unction, and, from a patriotic sense of duty, they read and applauded poetry that glorified the national heroes of the past. At the same time they secretly thanked God that heroism was no longer required from their own most unheroic age.

There was, it is true, one poet of great merit, an Amsterdam merchant who had a very uncommercial passion for the cult of letters. E. J. Potgieter (*q.v.*) was the founder and editor of *De Gids* (The Guide), the leading literary monthly, and tried all his life, by criticism and example, to lift the literary output of Holland above the pedestrian level to which it had sunk. He was ably assisted by his fellow editor Coenraad Busken Huet (*q.v.*), a theologian who, unable to reconcile personal belief with traditional doctrine, had left the church to make a living with his pen. It was a trenchant and merciless weapon in his hand. But not even the ablest critic can castigate an artless generation into repentance and creative vigor. When dissension arose between Huet and other members of the editorial board, Potgieter sided with Huet. In 1865 the two men left *De Gids* in charge of respectable mediocrity.

It was 20 years later that a group of young writers at Amsterdam founded a new monthly which, by way of challenge, they called *De Nieuwe Gids* (The New Guide). The name implied that, in their opinion, *De Gids* was superannuated and no longer able to give guidance. *De Nieuwe Gids* would take over that literary mission. In the 20 years preceding their entrance upon the literary scene, rumblings of the revolution they were to bring had reverberated in the writings of Multatuli (*q.v.*), the self-pitying pen name of Eduard Douwes Dekker meaning "I have suffered much." He had won sudden fame in 1860 with his autobiographic novel *Max Havelaar,* a biting satire on the self-satisfied bourgeoisie of Holland which neglected its Christian duty towards the natives of Java for the sake of the profits that the labor of those natives put into Dutch pockets. Multatuli's style struck home by its directness and simple beauty. "I do my best," he wrote, "to write living Dutch, although I have been to school." A rebel by temperament, he hated school for its choking grip on originality. By shaking off the grip of the literary standard upon the language, which squeezed all expression into stereotyped clichés, he prepared the revolutionary movement that was started by the young editors of *De Nieuwe Gids.*

A passion for truth in art was the motive power of their movement. "Whatever one wishes to say, there is only one word to express it, only one verb to animate it, and only one adjective to qualify it." That well-known dictum of Guy de Maupassant (*q.v.*), inspired by Flaubert (*q.v.*), was adopted as the guiding principle of the movement. "Word art" was the favorite name by which these writers called their new style. Each strove for a strikingly individual form of expression. New words were coined and old words were given new syntactic functions. This hunt for the one exact phrase often led to mannerisms and excesses, but even the severest critics of these cannot deny that this word art transformed and permanently enriched the language.

The substance of much of what they wrote has lost the powerful appeal which it possessed for their own generation. The sonnets and the best of the critical prose of Willem Kloos (*q.v.*), the leader of these "Eightiers," as they are called, the bulk of the prose writings of Lodewijk van Deyssel (*q.v.*), critic, essayist, and novelist, the *œuvre* of Frederik van Eeden (*q.v.*), the most versatile among the group, and Albert Verwey's (*q.v.*) first volume of poems have stood the critical test of time.

The revolt of the next generation against the "Eightiers" was voiced by C. S. Adama van Scheltema (*q.v.*). He condemned their movement for its self-centered egotism and its barren adoration of "art for art's sake." Jacques Perk (*q.v.*), the young poet of the sonnet sequence "Mathilde," had turned the Lord's Prayer into an invocation of beauty. He died at the age of 21, four years before *De Nieuwe Gids* was started. But Willem Kloos, who edited his posthumous volume of verse, hailed him as a herald of the movement. Perk's deification of beauty was indeed akin to the "Eightiers's" passionate worship of art. Art is passion, they proclaimed, but Scheltema retorted that art is the memory of passion conventionalized, the styleful re-creation of it, a process in which the intellect must take a part. The "Eightiers," in denying the need for control of the passionate impulse by the unimpassioned reason, did not for long sustain the high excellence to which they rose in their best moments.

In this respect P. C. Boutens (*q.v.*) differs from the "Eightiers," for although he shares their intense individualism, he knows how to purify his emotions in the crucible of the intellect. He is the poet of poets of the introspective mood. His verse technique is unsurpassed by any other living Dutch poet, but owing to his proud aloofness from the passions astir among the people of his own age, his poetry, mysteriously phrased and expressive of intellectualized emotion, appeals to only a small circle of readers.

Another "Eightier" who did not belong to the *Nieuwe Gids* group but was hailed by them as a kindred soul was Herman Gorter (*q.v.*), whose poem *Mei* (May) is considered one of the great poems of modern Dutch literature. It appeared in 1889 and immediately gained for its author a prominent place among the poets of his generation.

In general it is not the theory that makes the poet, but the poet who makes the theory. And this theory should help in the understanding of his poetry. Adama van Scheltema's theory that all art must be for the many is not belied by the fact that Boutens's poetry, which is for the few, is nevertheless great art. Nor does the fact that the poetry of Boutens is greater art than Scheltema's refute Scheltema's conception of the poet's mission. It only proves that, of the two, Boutens is the greater poet. His verse is like a deep, unrippled mountain lake that mirrors the haunting stillness of the dark woods and the infinity of the sky above. Only the lips of those who can climb that height will touch its waters. Scheltema's songs are like running brooks that reflect the varying scenery through which they pass—woods and fields, the villages and the main road, and the city with its splendor and its slums. Like the brook his poetry seeks the valley where the people toil and suffer, to bring them a draught of eternal life.

His protest against the self-cult of the "Eightiers" was echoed by the generation born shortly before or in the 80's. The Social Democratic Labor Party was in the ascendant; the proletariat began to assert itself and found eloquent spokesmen for its cause in the poets of the rising generation. Scheltema joined the party. A. van Collem, a contemporary of the "Eightiers," became a Communist. Henriëtte Roland Holst's (*q.v.*) poetry was the singing voice of the Communist Party.

The same spirit of revolt which animated Roland Holst in political life seems loath to obey the discipline of rhyme and meter. Her artistic conscience evidently constrains her to observe the traditional conventions, but the revolutionist in her finds it difficult to keep within the irksome bounds of prosody. This lends to her verse something rugged and fierce, as if it were on the verge of breaking from its restraint into the lawlessness of free verse.

The "Eightiers" themselves found no lasting satisfaction in their barren worship of beauty, art, and the divine self. They abandoned their egotism for a humanitarian devotion to communal concepts—the nation, the proletariat, mankind. Verwey, who in his youth had written, "Self is the only god," embraced the past of his own and other peoples as it is revealed by their literatures and turned critic and historian; Herman Gorter made the cause of the world's proletariat his own and became an exponent of Marxism; Frederick van Eeden vainly searched for the true life in the footsteps of Thoreau and Tolstoy, until he found it in the bosom of the Church of Rome; Van

Deyssel, child of a devoutly Catholic home, was drawn away from his worship of Zola (*q.v.*) and the naturalistic portrayal of human baseness to the mysticism of Huysmans and Maeterlinck (*qq.v.*) through which he recaptured the lost faith of his infancy. Kloos alone did not change. But the homage that was given him by a younger generation was for the achievement of his youth, which held a promise unfulfilled in riper age.

This diversity of tendencies among the editors found its reflection in the destinies of *De Nieuwe Gids.* Verwey was the first to leave the fold. He was followed by Van Eeden in 1893. Then Van Deyssel resigned and founded with Verwey *Tweemaandelijksch Tijdschrift* (Bimonthly Periodical), which in 1902 was turned into a monthly under the title *De XXste Eeuw* (The 20th Century). Three years later Verwey seceded again and founded *De Beweging* (The Movement). As its editor for 14 years he made it a rallying point of a group of younger poets, who recognized in him their mentor and master. The most prominent among these were Geerten Gossaert (pseud. of Frederik Carel Gerretson), Jakobus Cornelis Bloem, Pieter Nicolaas van Eyck, Adrianus Roland Holst, and Martinus Nijhoff. Verwey alone of the "Eightiers" can be said to have formed a school, although his own verse lacks the emotional quality of that of Kloos, Van Eeden, Gorter, and Boutens. Verwey's poetry seems the happy result of industrious effort, thought turned into verse because the thinker willed it; whereas the poetry of the others, especially Gorter's, impresses one by its inevitability, as thought crystallized into that very form by an impulse stronger than its thinker.

Among the novelists, the epic poets of our time, the late Louis Couperus (*q.v.*) is the only one who has won for himself international recognition. In one of his Roman stories, *De Komedianten* (1917; Eng. tr., *The Comedians; a Story of Ancient Rome,* 1926), he describes a scene in the Theatre of Pompey. A popular mime, the story of a brigand who atones for his crimes on the cross, is being played that day. Instead of the usual life-size doll, a convicted murderer is crucified and lacerated by a bear before the eyes of the horrified audience. Tacitus and Juvenal rise from their seats in disgust and call to Martial, "Come away with us." But Martial answers, "I am staying. This is my own time. I want to look on, that I may know it." "Our time," says Tacitus gloomily, "which one day I shall record that posterity may know." "Indeed," Juvenal joins in, "our time which one day I shall scourge." "And I," replies Martial, "shall no less celebrate it in verse, since I am nothing but a poet."

This threefold attitude towards life, of the chronicler, the moralist, and the poet, defines the chief varieties of the modern novel. That of Couperus is the poet's. He accepts life as an artist enamored of its colors and sounds, even though they are the allurements of corruption. He creates an elegant entertainment out of this Vanity Fair, be it modern or ancient, and plays with people's destinies as he plays with the language, handling them with graceful nonchalance or distorting them into something forced and unreal, as the whim of his playful mood dictates.

Marcellus Emants (*q.v.*), on the other hand, is the Juvenal of modern Dutch literature. Neither he nor Couperus ever identified himself with *De Nieuwe Gids.* They were of The Hague, the worldly resort of diplomacy, of military display, of the idle rich. Emants is the stern critic of that life of leisure, where woman reigns supreme. Woman as the embodiment of insincerity, vanity, and folly is the theme of most of Emants's novels and plays. His novels are masterpieces of psychoanalysis, but they leave the reader chilled by their skeptical denial of all loveliness.

The chronicler's novel is a more common type in Dutch literature. The objective description of everyday life, including the smallest details of the milieu, the thoughts, and the actions with photographic accuracy, is the main subject of what we nevertheless persist in calling fiction. The plot is negligible, the realism and the word art are considered as constituting the essential elements of a good novel. Some of these novels are indeed fine works of art, closely akin to the art of the Dutch genre painters of the 17th century, but whereas those paintings can be taken in at a glance, the picture of the novelist demands sustained attention from the reader which detracts from his aesthetic pleasure. Jacobus van Looy's (*q.v.*) *Jaapje* (1917) is a beautiful instance of this pictorial character of the Dutch novel. Van Looy was a painter by profession, and under his hands the story of little Jaapje's life in the orphanage has become a series of exquisite word pictures rich in action and color. The artist watches the shifting scene of every day, and only by the manner in which his little hero's feelings are affected by that spectacle is Jaapje's inner life disclosed to us.

But this unjudging realism invited reaction. It left the reader unsatisfied because it gave him no other than aesthetic enjoyment. And the Dutch public, whatever the literary connoisseurs may say to the contrary, wants to be edified. It likes a story with an ethical purpose. "Art without a purpose is no art," decreed Nico van Suchtelen. The novelist should not be merely a painter, but also a poet who unveils the eternal behind the shifting pageant of reality. He must reveal to us our fellow men as they might be according to their deepest selves, as they live in their dreams. The descriptive realists, like Couperus's Tacitus, have faithfully and often artistically recorded their own time, that posterity may know. A complete collection of such novels will give some future historian a comprehensive picture of early 20th-century life in Holland. But the school, if so unorganized a movement may be called by that name, of which Van Suchtelen is the chief exponent, wants to interpret this age to itself, depicting its good and its evil not for the sake of the picture, but for the sake of the good in an author's fancy that might be turned into future reality.

A unique figure among Holland's novelists is Arthur van Schendel. He does not take his subject matter from the world in which he lives, but from the world that lives in him. His stories deal with creatures of his fancy, incarnations of an elemental longing for love and wisdom. They tell of dreamed existences in which the abstract outweighs the concrete. His later novels, though, are of the naturalistic school. Still, they create in the reader an impression that the happenings in these stories of actual life are not real but seen in dreams. This is due to Van Schendel's technique, which is that of the impersonal and wholly unemotional recorder. It is only through the words of the recorder that we know what the characters did, said, and thought.

Holland's dramatic output is small in comparison with that of the poets and novelists. The "Eightiers," with the sole exception of Van Eeden, were not interested in the stage. The only playwright whose work has more than ephemeral value is Herman Heijermans (*q.v.*). His mind was quick to perceive dramatic possibilities in the most trifling incidents of everyday life. That facility proved sometimes a pitfall for his artistic conscience. Too often, also, he let his wit outrun the judgment of his taste. But when time will have winnowed the chaff, enough will remain that is of lasting value.

After the First World War a reaction set in against the intellectualized poetry of Verwey's disciples. It was led by Hendrik Marsman (*q.v.*) who, strongly influenced by German expressionism, became the exponent of what he liked to call "vitalism." The "vitalists" longed to merge themselves in the dynamic community of the nameless. To them the poet was one of the millions, but at the same time their spokesman and protagonist. In 1933 Marsman clearly formulated the artistic credo of his youth in an article entitled "De Dood van het Vitalisme" (The Death of Vitalism). The poets of Marsman's generation had their organ first in *Het Getij* (The Tide), afterwards in *De vrije Bladen* (Free Leaflets). Chief among them were Jan Slauerhoff, Hendrik de Vries, Jan Engelman, Anthonie Donker. They opposed to the sensitive refinement and the individualism of *De Beweging* the vehemence and immediacy of actuality. The "vitalists" developed a new rhetoric which, worked to death by their imitators, discredited the movement and called forth a reaction in the periodical *Forum*. This preached clarity, soberness, veracity. The leaders of the *Forum* group were Menno ter Braak, Charles E. du Perron, and Simon Vestdijk, all three of whom had a strong influence upon the youngest generation, Ter Braak through his keen, trenchant style, Du Perron through the charm of his personality even more than through his writings, and Vestdijk through his novels which, together with those of Arthur van Schendel, are among the very best that modern Holland has produced.

Shortly before the German invasion a group of young modernists, under the influence of French surrealism, rebelled against the literalness of *Forum* and pleaded for the irrational as the source of true poetry. Although the various artistic credos of these rival groups create an impression of irreconcilable differences, the practice of the youngest writers does not confirm the existence of a profound cleavage. Bewilderment, despondency, cynicism, hopelessness, are the moods that pervade all their writings, and the manner of voicing these does not strikingly vary from one author to another. What variety there is springs from their individualism rather than from their adherence to some aesthetic dogma.

See: K. H. de Raaf and J. J. Griss, *Zeven Eeuwen; Spiegel der Nederlandsche Letteren*, Vierde Deel: *Stemmingen en Gestalten* (1920); A. J. Barnouw, *Holland under Queen Wilhelmina* (1923); J. de Graaf, *Le Réveil littéraire en Hollande et le naturalisme français, 1880–1900* (1938); J. Greshoff, *Nieuwe Nederlandsche Dichtkunst* (1942).

A. J. B.

Duun, Olav (1876–1939, Norwegian novelist), was born in one of the islands belonging to the district of Namdalen in northern Tröndelag, where fjords, forests, and mountains unite in determining nature and life. He was a farmer's son and participated for some years in the work of farming and fishing, but at 25 left his home to study at a teachers' college. Graduating in 1904, he became a public school teacher, serving most of the time at Botne, near the town of Holmestrand on the Oslo Fjord. He continued to live there in some isolation, even after it was possible for him to give up his teaching position. He began to write books in 1907, first short stories, but soon almost exclusively novels, and after a decade he won fame and recognition as one of the most important authors of Norway. Very few of his books, however, attained a large sale, because he chose to write in the literary form of the vernacular, called Landsmaal (*see* Norwegian literature), from which wide circles of the reading public still kept aloof. To him it was the only natural medium, and also it conformed closely to his home dialect—which was the more necessary to him as his home district was the exclusive scene of all his works. Not that it was the design of his authorship to picture merely local life, but he felt the need of writing only about what he intimately knew; and his novels give proof of profound psychological study which, combined with his masterful, original art, make them human documents of the broadest interest.

The fundamental theme of all his novels is the battle of man with the forces that would dominate his thoughts and acts. The first novels pictured man and the forces of nature. Later we see man struggling against the mental forces within himself created by social surroundings and moral traditions. The monumental work of this order is the series of six relatively short novels, finally collected under the title *Juvikingar* (1918–1923; Eng. tr., *The People of Juvik,* 1930–1935). This is virtually constructed like one of the great Icelandic family sagas, embracing a period of a century and a half and telling of the determined fight of succeeding generations. Culmination is in the story of the last man of the family (presented in the three last volumes), his mental growth from childhood, his ripening, his final victory over the primitive heritage. Wild self-assertion cedes to the nobleness of self-sacrifice; the strength of resignation, however, is really won by virtue of inherited will power. Here, in colorful pictures, is the education of man from barbarism to the highest morality.

The next climax in Duun's authorship was a trilogy of novels—*Medmenneske* (1929; Fellow Beings), *Ragnhild* (1931), *Siste leveåre* (1933; The Last Year of Life)—centered around a single person, a woman, who simply by her innate goodness, in her fight to save the human essence of her soul, is driven to murder, and then finally, through her sufferings, is able to give an example of purity to the world.

Taken together, Duun's novels present a marvelous galaxy of varied and sharply designed characters. In the later ones he made society and surroundings more and more secondary, though they are always distinctly felt, and he never abandoned showing the fight of the individual against the hidden forces of his own soul. He himself defined the idea of his whole authorship by the title of his last book, *Menneske og maktene* (1938; The Man and the Powers). Duun was plainly continuing here the line of Ibsen (*q.v.*). Also, his novels are just as severely and firmly constructed as Ibsen's dramas, and they are like the Icelandic sagas in that the characters reveal the secrets of their nature by their own acts and words, without any interference of the author's pointer. The style of Duun is often surprising for its striking, unaffected paradoxes, of a subtle irony. Without artistry he was an exquisite artist, whose every word served the aim of his work and helped illuminate the eternal psychology of struggling manhood.

See: A. Överland, *Olav Duun* (1926), and "Olav Duun," in *Syn og segn* (1936); R. Thesen, *Menneske og maktene* (1941).

H. K.

Dwinger, Edwin Erich (1898–, German novelist), born in Kiel, the son of a technical officer in the German navy and a Russian woman, is a powerful writer on war experiences. Volunteering to become a cavalry officer, he went to the Eastern front at the age of 17 and in 1915 fell, severely wounded, into the hands of the Russians. After long and painful months he recovered and was gradually moved eastward thousands of miles into Siberia. Later he served against the Bolsheviks in Kolchak's White army and took part in the catastrophic retreat of the Whites through Siberia. In 1920 he succeeded in escaping to Germany, where he settled down to live on a farm in southern Bavaria.

His first attempts to give expression in the

form of fiction to the chaotic wealth of his experiences were the novels *Das grosse Grab* (1920), *Korsakoff* (1926), and *Das letzte Opfer* (1928). He failed. It was not given to him to invent a plot and to create human conflicts, and he was also too much absorbed in the feeling that he had a message for the German people and the world. As he expressed it later: "After Siberia one cannot fight for small objectives; our steel-trained souls must search for something which is worthy of our dead and which breaks up the soil as thoroughly as Bolshevism did in Russia." Dwinger found the form he needed in the "diaries" of the trilogy later called *Die deutsche Passion.* The three parts were *Die Armee hinter Stacheldraht* (1929; Eng. tr., *Prisoner of War,* 1930), *Zwischen Weiss und Rot* (1930; Eng. tr., *Between White and Red,* 1932), and *Wir rufen Deutschland* (1932). Dwinger presents unforgettable scenes of the sufferings of war prisoners in Siberia, of whom 600,000 perished. He reports the derangement and the perversions of the survivors, the insanity and abysmal hopelessness of years of imprisonment, but also the heroic greatness of men in defeat. Thanks to his maternal heritage he is able to give a fair and realistic picture of the Russians, who vacillate between the extremes of cruelty and brokenhearted contrition. In a compact style which abounds in gripping scenes and pictures, Dwinger reports his story as a human being who always sides with the oppressed. The sufferings which he and his comrades endured have meaning in so far as they impede other world catastrophes. Germany must abolish its class distinctions and find a way to socialism of the heart. The third volume of the trilogy reveals a decline of Dwinger's power. He often loses himself in critical and dialectic discussions to show the necessity of a Germany based on an ethnic community.

None of Dwinger's later works, among them the novel *Die letzten Reiter* (1935), can be ranked with the first two books of his trilogy. In his *Spanische Silhouetten* (1937) he gives his impressions of a trip through Spain on Franco's side during the civil war, a piece of journalistic reporting blended with conventional fascist ideology. In The Second World War he served as a war correspondent with a Panzer Division. The book *Panzerführer* (1941) is a glorification of leadership, but also describes ably the work of the staff, the action in the field, and the life of the division when at rest.

See: A. Frisé, "Edwin Erich Dwinger," *Die neue Rundschau,* Jahrgang XLIV (1933), Bd. I, pp. 840–850; W. K. Pfeiler, *War and the German Mind* (1941), pp. 279–285.

W. K. P.

Dygasiński, Adolf (1839–1902, Polish novelist), was born in Niegosławice, Kielce district, Russian Poland. Reaching maturity at the most tragic moment in all Polish history, 1863, he left his studies in the Warsaw Szkoła Główna (*see* Polish literature) to participate in the fatal events of that year. The exigencies of his own temperament, a tendency to aloofness and gloom, coupled with the necessities imposed by the times, made him a perpetual wanderer, earning a poor living however and wherever he could, now as the proprietor of a bookshop in Cracow (1874–1878), now as a journalist and teacher in Warsaw (1879–1888), again as a tutor in various country houses (1889) or a chronicler of emigrant life in South America (1890–1891), finally as a plodding journalist once more in Warsaw. Of the scores of works from his pen—among these translations and manuals for teachers—two will not be forgotten: the letters he wrote from Brazil and later reworked in semi-fictional form as *Na złamanie karku* (1893; Backbreaking Work) and the Kiplingesque *Gody życia* (1902; The Feast of Living). The former is important because of its influence on the better-known portrait of the Brazilian Pole by Konopnicka (*q.v.*), *Pan Balcer w Brazylji* (1892; Mr. Balcer in Brazil), while the latter, an epic of the life cycle of a wren and a prose poem in praise of the life-giving forces of nature, not only possesses great intrinsic beauty, but is, besides, a pioneer work of its kind in Polish.

See: Z. Wasilewski, *Współcześni* (1923), pp. 164–197; K. Czachowski, *Obraz współczesnej literatury polskiej,* I, (1934) 40–49, 303–306.

A. P. C.

Dyk, Viktor (1877–1931, Czech poet, dramatist, and novelist), has written the most important political poetry of the Czechs. A strong nationalism inspires his ironical and satirical spirit. Dyk was born at Psovka near Mělník (north of Prague), the son of a steward on an estate. He became a journalist, taking a prominent part in the editing of several periodicals of the "Radical Progressive" Party which was sharply anti-Austrian. In 1917 he was imprisoned by the Austrian authorities. After the liberation of Czechoslovakia, he became a member of Parliament and later a senator for the National Democratic Party. He died of heart failure while bathing in the Adriatic near Dubrovnik, Yugoslavia.

Skepticism and even nihilism were the main themes of Dyk's early poetry, but his despair was always tempered by irony and satire. He uses stanzaic forms and loves points, paradoxes, and grotesque rhymes. The best collection was called *Marnosti* (1900; Vanities). He then slowly turned away from individual problems of futility and found his themes more and more in political satire and exhortations to his nation. *Satiry a sarkasmy* (1905; Satires and Sarcasms) and *Pohádky z naší vesnice* (1910; Fairy Tales from Our Village) upbraid the nation for abandoning its old traditions and recommend an uncompromising nationalism of a conservative brand. The political verse of Dyk culminates in four collections, *Lehké a těžké kroky* (1915; Light and Heavy Steps), *Anebo* (1918; Or), *Okno* (1920; The Window), and *Poslední rok* (1922; The Last Year), which comment on the war and post-war developments as well as on the author's experiences in an Austrian prison. Among the later books of less importance, *Devátá vlna* (1930; The Ninth Wave) is interesting for its personal tone; the feeling of approaching death unifies a miscellany of intimate lyrics. Besides lyrical poetry, where Dyk is at his best, he attempted also epics on a small scale—a cycle of ballads or romances like that on *Giuseppe Moro* (1911) or a short verse story like *Zápas Jiřího Macků* (1918; The Struggle of George Macků), which deals with a peasant's defiance of death.

As a dramatist Dyk used a technique of effective dialogue, with sharp dialectics, which makes each of his dramas almost a series of epigrams on the stage. *Posel* (1907; The Messenger) is a historical drama which attempts to indict the spirit of Christian pacifism for the loss of the independence of the nation in the Battle of the White Mountain (1620). *Zmoudření Dona Quijota* (1913; Don Quixote Recovers His Reason) is an ironic dramatization of the conflict between romantic dream and sober reality, while *Revoluční trilogie* (1921; The Trilogy of the Revolution) contains three short plays on the French Revolution which bring out the poet's sarcastic attitude towards idealism.

Least successful is the voluminous prose of this author. He wrote some good short stories which vary the theme of romantic illusionism, *e.g., Krysař* (1915; The Pied Piper). But his attempts at satirical and political novels are artistic failures in spite of the interest of the materials, which are based on memories of events and personalities. The composition is loose, and debate and discussion crowd out all imagination. *Konec Hackenschmidův* (1904; Hackenschmid's End) depicts the students' part in the "Progressive" movement; *Soykovy děti* (1929; Soyka's Children) is a chronicle of the war; and *Děs z prázdna* (1932; Horror vacui) attempts to reconstruct Czech political life of the early 19th century. Dyk also wrote polemical prose, a certain amount of criticism, and reminiscences.

Dyk overcame his early nihilism by a fervent nationalism which recommended the most radical measures against Austrian dominion and which after the establishment of the republic turned against socialism and the humanitarian democracy represented by President Masaryk (*q.v.*). Dyk thought of the nation in terms of its historical tradition and conceived of it as a moral absolute. Artistically, he is important as a lyrical poet, because in a time of rhetoric he cultivated concise, hard, and sharp forms. But imagination is too frequently sacrificed to sheer intellect. His dramas seem excogitated, and his novels suffer from too much topical discussion. Though Dyk has been compared to Barrès (*q.v.*), he is far drier, more sober and subdued, and far more narrow.

See: K. H. Hilar, *Viktor Dyk; essay o jeho ironii* (1910); M. Rutte, *Viktor Dyk; portrét básníka* (1931); H. Jelínek, *Viktor Dyk* (1932); A. Novák, *Viktor Dyk* (1936).

R. W.

E

Ebner-Eschenbach, Marie von (née von Dubsky, 1830–1916, Austrian poet and novelist), was born in Moravia (Zdislawitz); her husband, Baron von Ebner-Eschenbach, was like herself a member of the Austrian aristocracy. Much of her life was spent in Vienna, the summers usually on her country estate; and the Austrian metropolis and countryside repeatedly form the background of her narratives.

Influenced largely by Schiller and the performances of the Vienna Burgtheater, she began to write as a young girl. Her lyric verses are of scant importance, and her dramatic attempts, in which she persisted for many years, likewise met with slight success. Even in the field of the *Novelle,* it was not until 1881 that the publication of *Lotti die Uhrmacherin* brought her recognition. In the 80's, however, her reputation grew rapidly; soon Marie von Ebner was considered one of the masters of the 19th-century *Novelle*. Most of her *Novellen* may be described, to quote the title of one of her books, as "village and castle stories," stories of the peasantry and of the landed gentry. Among her best-known shorter narratives are "Die Freiherrn von Gemperlein," "Krambambuli" (Eng. tr., 1913–1915), and "Komtess Muschi" (Eng. tr., *The Two Countesses*, 1893). Perhaps her most important longer work is the novel *Das Gemeindekind* (1887; Eng. tr., *Child of the Parish*, 1893); *Unsühnbar* (1890; Eng. tr., *Beyond Atonement*, 1892) is less convincing and more sentimental. Her works are marked by narrative skill, a generally sympathetic treatment of character, quiet humor, and an emphasis on the development and education of the central figure which places many of them in the tradition of the *Bildungsroman*. The didactic tendency is occasionally all too evident in her fiction; it appears to best advantage in her *Aphorismen* (1880; Eng. tr., *Aphorisms*, 1883). Her female characters follow one of two dominant patterns, the gentle "model girl" or the sport-loving, reckless tomboy. In general, she portrays women and children more successfully than men. The sentimentality of many of the stories is relieved by occasional flashes of psychological insight. An enemy of naturalism, Marie von Ebner strove for that middle ground between realism and idealization which is vaguely described in German literary history as "poetic realism." Socially and politically she was staunchly conservative, a consistent supporter of the family and the church. Though her criticism of the Austrian aristocracy was sometimes incisive, she apparently never questioned the privileges and powers of the nobility. She was by no means devoid of sympathy for the poor and uneducated and felt that the lower classes should be decently treated by their "superiors" in the hierarchy of Austrian society.

Marie von Ebner-Eschenbach has often been compared with Luise von François (1817–1893) who greatly admired her and who also writes largely of the aristocracy and from the aristocratic point of view (see her novel *Die letzte Reckenbürgerin*, 1871).

See: M. Necker, *Marie von Ebner-Eschenbach* (1900); A. Bettelheim, *Marie von Ebner-Eschenbach* (1900) and *Marie von Ebner-Eschenbachs Wirken und Vermächtnis* (1920).

H. C. H.

Eça de Queiroz, José Maria (1845–1900, Portuguese fiction writer and journalist), the indisputable master of the Portuguese novel, was born in Póvoa-de-Varzim, Minho, to a middle-class family. He studied law in Coimbra and was a bosom companion of Antero de Quental (*q.v.*) and an outstanding member of the Generation of 1865. He did not take an active part in the "Coimbra dispute" or in the student struggles, but he did participate in the "Conferências democráticas do Casino de Lisboa" in 1871 (*see* Portuguese literature). After graduation he engaged in political journalism in Evora and practiced law intermittently in Lisbon. In 1869 he attended the opening of the Suez Canal and traveled through the Orient, experiences which he was to use later in his writings. In 1870 he was municipal administrator in Leiria and there familiarized himself with the provincial atmosphere, which he also incorporated subsequently in his work. Finally he entered the Foreign Service, which took him to consular posts in Cuba (1873–1874) and England (1874–1888) and to Paris (1888–1900). The last assignment constituted the realization of a lifelong ambition, nurtured as he was in the Gallophilism of his generation. His long absence from his native land enabled him to judge it dispassionately and at the same time to come in contact with new currents of ideas. This resulted in a richness of intellectual experience which acted as a leaven in his already rich personality.

The articles and stories which were his first work (collected posthumously in *Prosas bárbaras*, 1905, Barbaric Prose) reveal him as under a multitude of youthful influences: he has imagination in the manner of Hoffmann, Parnassian erudition, Poe-like gloominess—transmitted by way of Baudelaire (*q.v.*)—and Germanic lyricism in the manner of Heine. All of this was presented in a provocative new language, Gallicized, twisted, and nebulously lyric. But in Eça's case these influences were only the point of departure for his vigorous originality. In 1871 he undertook with Ramalho Ortigão (*q.v.*), with whom he had already collaborated on a mystery novel, the publication of the monthly review *As farpas* (1871–1883; The Darts), "a monument of criticism and . . . of the social history of its time and country," in which he revealed his biting irony and his bent for reform. After the lectures in 1871 and after having been converted in some measure to French naturalism, he produced *O crime do Padre Amaro* (1875; Father Amaro's Crime), a thesis novel directed against the corruption of the clergy, in which he utilized his observations made in Leiria. The work concerns sacrilegious love in a mean provincial atmosphere, elaborated with all the characteristics of determinism, inheritance, detailed analysis, and psychophysiological description. There is a broader social scene in *O primo Basílio* (1878, Cousin Basil; Eng. tr., *Dragon's Teeth,* 1889), in which, through a case recalling *Madame Bovary* (*see* Flaubert), the moral constitution of a middle-class Lisbon family is analyzed. The panorama of Portuguese society is widened in *Os Maias* (1880; The Maias) to embrace high society, tardily romantic. The great financial, religious, and literary world is depicted with thoroughness and increasing irony. Opposition to these first two novels gave rise to the polemic about the new novelistic art (*see again* Portuguese literature). Eça has been called the Portuguese Zola (*q.v.*), but this is unjust, since naturalism was only a subordinate element from which he soon freed himself to affirm a personal art.

His evolution was slow and harmonious. Observation disciplined his imagination. Eventually he found his distinctive manner, rhythmic, suggestive, and ironic, a mixture of essential romanticism and realistic probity. In *O mandarim* (1880; The Mandarin), a delightful, short, fanciful novel, is a charming view of China gathered through his readings. "On the rugged nakedness of truth—the diaphanous mantle of fancy" are the words which open *A relíquia* (1887; Eng. tr., *The Relic,* 1925); in a sordid novelistic incident of religious hypocrisy he encases an evocation of Palestine, suggestive of Renan (*q.v.*) and having recollections of his own journey, and a poetic reconstruction of the Passion. He had already treated the theme of Christ (see *Prosas bárbaras*), and he returned to it in a delightful story, *Suave milagre* (1891; Eng. tr., *The Sweet Miracle,* 1904), included in the posthumous *Contos* (1902; Short Stories).

Because of his ironic denationalizing criticism a great deal has been said of his foreign sympathies and antipatriotic attitude. But his rebellious satire is only an aspect of his essential Portuguese tenderness, that of a "poor man from Póvoa-de-Varzim," as he defined himself. He treated Portugal ironically because he loved her so much and wished to improve her, and his mockery and dejection are deeply Lusitanian. This tenderness keeps revealing itself; in *A ilustre casa de Ramires* (1900; The Illustrious House of Ramires) it expands lyrically over the essentials of Portuguese life. *A cidade e as serras* (1901; The City and the Mountains) is a hymn to native country and by extension a hymn to primitive simplicity. An aesthete disillusioned and surfeited with civilization, Eça here becomes emotional on contact with nature and simple things. A return to ingenuousness, coupled with the poetically archaeological, is also the explanation of the Pre-Raphaelite hagiology of the "Lendas de Santos" (Saints' Legends), included posthumously in *Ultimas páginas* (1911; Last Pages). He projected the richness of his own human personality as a universal Lusitanian in the type "Fradique Mendes" (*Correspondência de Fradique Mendes,* 1900; Correspondence of Fradique Mendes), the incarnation of the ideal of his generation, a skeptic and sentimental dandy who parades through the world his thirst for artistocratic perfection and his caustic politeness. To Eça, irony was the prism for the analysis of reality, but his smile, devoid of bitterness, reveals a benevolent comprehension of human weaknesses. He is a master in the creation of unexpected relationships between things, an implacable enunciator of the harassing contrast between the aspiration and the reality of the human being; nevertheless his irony is different from that of a Bernard Shaw or an Anatole France (*q.v.*), less corrosive, less cruelly refined.

For his particular art Eça needed a new instrument, ductile and complicated; he had to renew the structure of the language, and indeed he started the greatest revolution that Portuguese prose ever underwent in all its history. He broke up the long oratorical sentence, so dear to the Peninsular ear, joined words in new and subtle combinations, and encompassed in one line a whole series of insinuations, the product of patient observation and synthesis. Uniting abstract elements with concrete images and distilling metaphysical suggestion in lyrical expression, he succeeded in creating a style in which fantasy and reality constantly intermingle. He has been reproached for verbal and syntactical poverty and Gallicisms, but he has a rare intensity of expression. A victim of the "illness of perfection," he changed his thought over and over again, always dissatisfied, ever in search of the ideal, ineffable note. He succeeded in evolving a new aesthetic in a new language; he revealed another world, of vague concepts existing in the subconscious.

Eça's ability to catch an observed totality in a few strokes is comparable to that of Maupassant (*q.v.*). He complained of not having attained either the "sublime note of eternal reality" of Balzac or "the exact note of transitory reality" of Flaubert, but in fact he sometimes achieved both qualities and suggests also the vigor of Zola, the caricatural tenderness of Dickens, the succulent humanity of Thackeray, and the mental aristocracy of Renan. In his very characteristic work as a journalist and a letter writer, collected posthumously in several volumes, is further evidence of his great gifts as an observer of the life and culture of the end of the century. His death marks the end of a period in Portuguese literature. His work has been translated into many European languages, and his influence, discernible not only in the Peninsula but also in all the Hispanic world, is now beginning to be studied as it deserves.

See: F. de Figueiredo, *História da literatura realista* (1914), pp. 117–170; A. Cabral, *Eça de Queiroz; a sua vida e a sua obra* (1920); C. Ramalhete, *Eça de Queiroz* (1942); João Gaspar Simões, *Eça de Queiroz, o homem o artista* (1945).

E. G. D.

Echegaray, José (1832–1916, Spanish dramatist), was born and died in Madrid. He devoted himself with brilliant success to diverse activities, coming to occupy an outstanding position in the scientific, political, and literary life of Spain. Although he was past 40 when he began to cultivate the field of literature, it proved nevertheless the one in which his personality displayed itself in its most original form. He taught at the School of Civil Engineering until the Revolution of 1868 brought him into the political arena. He was elected to the Cortes Constituyentes, was appointed director of public works and minister of the interior, and was considered an authority on economic questions. From 1874, however, when his two first plays, *El libro talonario,* a comedy, and *La esposa del vengador,* a romantic drama, were presented on the stage, he devoted himself almost entirely to the theatre. The success of these works was surpassed the following year by the theatrical, romantic drama *En el puño de la espada,* which definitely established the popularity of its author. From that moment for 30 years Echegaray contributed to the Spanish stage a steady stream of dramas and comedies in prose and verse, and he may well be considered the most genuine and almost exclusive representative of the Spanish theatre during this period. Of all his works there are several besides *En el puño de la espada* which most intensely reflect the quality of his talent—*O locura o santidad* (1876; Eng. trs., *Folly or Saintliness,* 1895, *Madman or Saint,* 1912), *En el seno de la muerte* (1879), *El gran Galeoto* (1881; Eng. trs., *The Great Galeoto,* 1895, *The World and His Wife,* 1908), *Mariana* (1892; Eng. tr., 1895), *Mancha que limpia* (1895), *El loco Dios* (1900; Eng. tr., *The Madman Divine,* 1908). For a complete evaluation of Echegaray's work one of his comedies must be included, as, for example, *Un crítico incipiente* (1891), and also some of his best short stories and articles and speeches.

The dramas referred to can be classified into two different groups, the romantic dramas which are in the nature of historic legends and the dramas which deal with contemporary moral and social problems; the best of his work falls into the latter division. But the difference between the two is more apparent than real. The nature of the dramatic conflict in Echegaray is that of the typical romantic drama. Certain of his later works, such as *El loco Dios* or *El hijo de don Juan* (1892; Eng. tr., *The Son of Don Juan,* 1895), are exceptions; in these he attempted to infuse new life into his theatre by way of a belated Ibsenian inspiration (*see* Ibsen, Henrik). His theatre in general, however, is in the nature of a retrogression. Echegaray stems directly from romanticism, both French and Spanish; but, one step removed, he has as his background and origin the classical Spanish theatre—especially Calderón—and, in a certain sense, Shakespeare. Among all these influences the most important, from the point of view of similarity of results, is that of Calderón. It might be said that just as Calderón was the stylized dramatist of the decadence of the Spanish theatre in the golden age, Echegaray is a belated romantic who appears when romanticism has been completely eclipsed and the powerful reaction of the middle of the century has set in against it. This explains both the good and the bad qualities of Echegaray's theatre. It also explains the popularity and resounding success of his plays, which revived the subject matter and procedure of the romantic and, to a certain extent, the classical theatre, so deeply rooted in the Spanish people. The conflicts assume stark, violent forms, with man and human will the plaything of the more powerful fatalities of chance, and give rise to those calculated, electric, almost physical clashes between individuals. Such is the formula of most of Echegaray's dramas. They revive in modern guise, coldly and with an eye to effect, the old themes and conflicts—a sense of chivalry, honor based on conjugal fidelity which, clouded over by the shadow of a doubt, makes life full of anguish, unbearable. These ideals in their most extreme and unreal forms are the very essence of drama in such of his plays as *O locura o santidad,* the drama of a conscience scrupulous to the point of madness, or *El gran Galeoto,* the drama of public opinion in which there is a spirit of revolt, of horror, and even of redemption with regard to these dominant sentiments. For this reason the two plays have been the most popular and undoubtedly represent the culminating moments of Echegaray's work.

The literary generation that followed him reacted violently against Echegaray at the very moment he was at the height of his national popularity and had been internationally recognized through the award of the Nobel prize (1905). Yet the reputation of Echegaray, within Spain and abroad, is based on positive values which must be judged by the author's own artistic concepts. His talent lies in the way he handles a type of art which is not realistic, which consists in the use of an abstract device whereby themes, oversimplified and at the same time exaggerated, are juxtaposed with intense dramatic effect. There is, as might be expected from one with his mathematical mind, a deliberate withdrawal from reality. The characters are types or simply generic human beings; the passions are abstractions and logical principles; the words are rhetoric. But all this world in which reality is emptied of its content has a perfect harmony of its own, a structural, musical beauty.

See: J. Yxart, *El arte escénico en España* (1894); E. Merimée, *José Echegaray et son œuvre dramatique* (1916); M. Bueno, *Teatro español contemporáneo* (1909–); G. B. Shaw, *Dramatic Opinions and Essays,* 1916 ed., I, 81–89, II, 186–194.

F. de O.

Edschmid, Kasimir (pseud. of Eduard Schmid, 1890–, German novelist), was born in Darmstadt, which has remained his home. He is by and large the real leader of the expressionistic group of German writers. Three short novels, *Die sechs Mündungen* (1915), *Das rasende Leben* (1916), and *Timur* (1917), were the first proclamations of his idea of ecstatic and passionate living in an imaginary world. In a special volume, *Über den Expressionismus in der Literatur* (1918), and in his own periodical, *Tribüne der Kunst und Zeit* (1918–1920), he expounded the artistic, ethical, and technical theories of expressionism. *Die achatnen Kugeln* (1920) "with its hospital routine and erotic minutiae" is his first full-sized novel of considerable length, in which he applies all the newly established principles of form, style, and diction of the expressionistic movement. Nine years later they seem to him still valid, since they are still in evidence in his next novel, *Lord Byron; der Roman einer Leidenschaft* (1929; Eng. tr., *Lord Byron; the Story of a Passion,* Am. tr., *The Passionate Rebel; the Life of Lord Byron,* both 1930); this is not so much a biographical account as a psychological study of the poet's sex life. Repeated journeys to Italy and other Mediterranean countries are later extended to Africa and South America, and after 1929 the observations and experiences of these travels are almost exclusively the background or subject matter of his writings. While language, vocabulary, and style of the earlier works have not essentially changed, his presentation is now more direct and realistic. *Afrika nackt und angezogen* (1929) and *Glanz und Elend Südamerikas; Roman eines Erdteils* (1930; Eng. tr., *South America; Lights and Shadows,* 1932) are the best representatives of this new type of travel writing. Edschmid tries to retain as far as possible the narrative form. Among his products of the last 10 years are four books with very significant titles dealing with Italy and the Mediterranean: *Zauber und Grösse des Mittelmeeres* (1932), *Italien: Lorbeer, Leid und Ruhm* (1935), *Italien: Gärten, Männer und Geschichten* (1937), and *Italien: Inseln, Römer und Cäsaren* (1939).

See: A. Soergel, *Dichtung und Dichter der Zeit,* Neue Folge: *Im Banne des Expressionismus,* 4. Auflage (1927), pp. 346–349, 828–839; J. Bithell, *Modern German Literature, 1880–1938* (1939), pp. 400–489.

A. Bu.

Eeden, Frederik Willem van (1860–1932, Dutch poet, novelist, essayist, and dramatist), was born at Haarlem and studied medicine at the University of Amsterdam, where he took his M.D. in 1886. He started to practice at Bussum, while conducting at the same time a psychotherapeutic clinic at Amsterdam. But gradually his literary work and his interest in social experiments drew him away from the practice of medicine. He was one of the founders and first editors of *De Nieuwe Gids* (The New Guide), in which he published his philosophical fairy tale *De kleine Johannes* (1887; Eng. tr., *Little Johannes,* 1895). This story is a poetical autobiography. Its principal motif is Johannes's longing for the Great Light, *i.e.,* Van Eeden's search for God. The search leads him on to "the great, dark city of humanity and its misery." That is the story of the poet Van Eeden in a nutshell. He turned away from the pride and self-glorification of the *Nieuwe Gids* group to share and alleviate the sufferings of his fellow men. He founded a communal colony, which, ardent admirer of Thoreau as he was, he called Walden. This experiment ended in failure, but Van Eeden, not disillusioned, continued his quest for the true life until he found peace at last in the bosom of the Church of Rome. In his poem *Ellen* (1889) he sang a mystical hymn to divine love, which alone can make man's heart susceptible to beauty. Then followed his great dramatic poem *De Broeders; Tragedie van het Recht* (1894; The Brothers; a Tragedy of Justice), which in the second edition was renamed *De Broederveete* (The Brothers' Feud). In this, perhaps his greatest work, stark realism and mysticism are interwoven into a moving and deeply significant drama. Van Eeden gave the fullest and clearest exposition of his *Weltanschauung* in a long philosophical poem in *terza rima* entitled *Het Lied van Schijn en Wezen* (1895–1910; Song of Semblance and Substance). The novelist Van Eeden is at his best in *Van de Koele Meren des Doods* (1900, Of the Cool Pools of Death; Eng. tr., *The Deeps of Deliverance,* 1902). He was the only one among the "Eightiers" who took an interest in the stage, and his versatility ranged from farce to tragedy, from satirical comedy to the stately historical play. But he was primarily a mystic and philosopher and could portray his inner self much more vividly than he could portray others. Still, some of his plays had a stage success—*IJsbrand* (1908), *In Kenterend Getij* (1910; Change of Tide), *De Heks van Haarlem* (1915; The Witch of Haarlem). His prose essays fill six series of *Studies* (1890–1918). They reveal the wide range of his knowledge and intellectual curiosity.

Van Eeden was indeed the most versatile among the authors of his generation and the one who, more than all others, commands the admiration and the interest of present-day Holland. It is clear from his diaries that Van Eeden felt himself to be a solitary stranger among his fellow men, who failed or refused to understand him. He had, indeed, more enemies than friends among his contemporaries. But two years after his death, a society was founded for the study of his works, the Frederik van Eeden *Genootschap,* with headquarters at Amsterdam. The *Mededeelingen* (Publications) which this organization has issued since February, 1935, contain a mass of valuable information and original documents that throw new light upon this enigmatic figure in modern Dutch literature.

See: A. Lang, "Introductory Essay," in Van Eeden, *Little Johannes* (1895); W. H. Dircks, "Introduction," in Van Eeden, *The Deeps of Deliverance* (1902); G. Kalff, Jr., *Frederik van Eeden; Psychologie van den Tachtiger* (1927); H. W. van Tricht, *Frederik van Eeden, Denker en Strijder* (1934); *Mededeelingen van het Frederik van Eeden Genootschap* (1935–1940).

A. J. B.

Eekhoud, Georges (1854–1927, Belgian novelist), appears as one of the most subjective of Belgian writers. He was born in Antwerp. Little is known of his early years; certain biographers have relied too heavily on references more or less personal in his *La Nouvelle Carthage* (1888) and attributed his anarchistic tendencies to a supposed unhappy childhood. Such inferences are contradicted by his *Souvenirs,* published in 1914. These, however, stop at his 11th year, when his father died; his mother he had scarcely known. His guardian wished him to prepare for a business or professional career, and this may have caused friction. When he came into possession of his heritage, Eekhoud lived for a few months as a gentleman farmer in the rugged Campine around Antwerp. This period was the happiest of his life; it supplied the matter, and especially the inspiration, for many of his future books. Ever afterwards he evoked memories or dreams of that short experience. Hence the nostalgia so marked in his writing. When his financial resources were exhausted, he declined a last offer from his guardian and for the rest of his life eked out a precarious existence as a journalist in Brussels.

He began his literary career in 1877 with a tiny volume of verse, shortly followed by two others. The fanatic lover of independence and of "irregulars" is in bud in certain of these poems. His first prose work was a biography (1881) of the popular Flemish novelist, Hendrik Conscience (*q.v.*), for whom he repeatedly expressed admiration in later years. A note of naïve sentimentality in some of his tales seems to stem from this source. In 1881 Eekhoud joined the vivacious group who, under the leadership of Max Waller, edited the *Jeune Belgique* (*see* Belgian Literature in French). In 1893 he broke with his associates, whose growing Parnassian trend toward aloof objectivity was repugnant to him. Doubtless his own passion for independence was enhanced by this incident. He was accused of abandoning art in the name of an effort toward social reform, but such charges are based on an at least partial misunderstanding. More than his colleagues he had taken to heart De Coster's (*q.v.*) advice: "Go to the humble folk—the bourgeois are all tarred with monotony." He protests repeatedly that he would not change the social status of his beloved vagabonds—that would destroy their picturesqueness—but at last he became aware of dangers inherent in this fascination. In *Le Terroir incarné* (1925) two artists are discussing their principles. One would be the impassive and disinterested interpreter of nature. The other seeks to concentrate and symbolize a whole region in a single individual; he finds his ideal in a simple peasant and loses sight of his pictorial ideal in the obsession unwittingly wrought by his rustic model. Finally he prays for strength to create a work which may immortalize his subject in art and kill it for himself. Thus, at the end of his career, Eekhoud seems to admit the strictures of his former colleagues of the *Jeune Belgique*.

Yet the power of his work comes from his passionate espousal of pariahs and criminals. The stories of *Le Cycle patibulaire* (definitive ed., 1896) are among the most vitriolic he has signed. He would argue that his outcasts are, more or less consciously, unrecognized saints. The last story of the first edition (1892), "Le Suicide par amour," preaches universal charity, but declares that ideal humanity must be created out of dreams. Eekhoud ever defends the most heterodox and brutal ethics provided only that they take their rise in primitive impulse and in revolt from contemptible bourgeois uniformity. His favorite painters are Rubens and Jordaens, whose delight in brawniness he shares; in English literature, it is the Elizabethans who charm him. He translated plays from Webster, Fletcher, and Marlowe and wrote *Au Siècle de Shakespeare* (1893). Unlike Verhaeren (*q.v.*), he can see only evil in "progress" and curses our financial civilization. Striking in this respect is his novel *La Nouvelle Carthage* (Eng. tr., *The New Carthage*, 1917), in which he deplores the modernization of Antwerp and delights in recalling its ancient picturesque squalor. The hero, who has much in common with the author, clashes violently with a social reformer who would "save" what can be saved of the populace and ignore the hopelessly depraved. For Eekhoud the latter are the most precious of the denizens and to change them would be blasphemy against art. Yet he is far from being consistent. He admired the Russian novelists for their revolutionary trends and wrote in 1891: "Literature has been preparing for a long time the social upheaval of tomorrow."

The majority of his short stories (*e.g.*, *Kermesses*, 1884; *Nouvelles Kermesses*, 1887; and *Dernières Kermesses*, 1920), as well as many of his novels (*e.g.*, *Kees Doorik*, 1883; *Les Milices de Saint-François*, 1886; and *Escal Vigor*, 1899), deal with rustic scenes. There is a certain realism in the setting, but the characters, whether peasants or aristocrats, are too often mere symbols destined to personify their creator's visions. The novels, at least when judged by conventional standards, are faulty in structure: they are formed of loosely connected episodes offering dramatic expression of preconceived theories or painting pictures. One cannot forget that Eekhoud, like many of his countrymen, was obsessed by traditions of the brush. He wrote several volumes of art criticism, among which *Les Peintres animaliers belges* (1911) deserves special mention. A similar phenomenon is apparent in his manner of writing. Francis Nautet, the critic of *Jeune Belgique*, remarked that Eekhoud had a language rather than a style. He cares more for colorful words than for harmony of phrase and seeks first to give vent to his robust individuality.

His power lies in his passionate sincerity, in the conflict within himself of the artist and the humanitarian, in his championing of the picturesque helots of civilization, and in his cosmopolitan sympathies. While exalting always his tiny Campine, he would commune in ever widening circles with "tragic and agonized humanity."

See: J. Bithell: *Contemporary Belgian Literature* (1915); H. Krains; *Portraits d'écrivains belges* (1930); G. Vanwelkenhuyzen, *L'Influence du naturalisme français en Belgique* (1930); G. Black, *Bibliographie de Georges Eekhoud* (1931).

B. M. W.

Egge, Peter (1869–, Norwegian novelist), was born in Trondheim. His first success was with a group of stories about his native city and environs. Later he often returns to the same milieu. His books are low-toned, without great events, but with the stress laid on the inner life of the characters. *Inde i fjordene* (1920; By the Deep Fjords) describes the conflict that arises when a professional man's daughter marries into one of the proud, stiff-necked peasant families. *Jægtvig og hans Gud* (1920; Jægtvig and His God) is a study of a poor shoemaker who thinks he is born to create a new religion. *Hansine Solstad* (1925; Eng. tr., *Hansine Solstad, the History of an Honest Woman*, 1929), generally considered the author's masterpiece, describes a peasant girl whose consciousness of an unstained family record sustains her through a lifetime of unmerited disgrace.

Egge is a very productive writer. Besides a great number of novels, some historical, but most of them with modern themes, he has written successful serious dramas as well as comedies in which his sense of humor, restrained in his other works, has free play.

H. A. L.

Ehrenburg, Ilya Grigoriyevich (1891–, Russian journalist, poet, and novelist), is the Soviet Union's most brilliant war correspondent. Extensive travel and long residence abroad have given him a knowledge of Europe which, together with his remarkable powers of observation and his faculty of discerning the inner significance of events, have won him an international reputation in his reporting of both World Wars and of the Ethiopian and Spanish wars. His voluminous literary production, including novels, short stories, poems, translations, articles, plays, and criticism, while artistically uneven and derivative, is regarded in the U.S.S.R. as a valuable source of sociological information on Western countries.

Born in Moscow of poor Jewish parents, Ehrenburg spent his childhood in a suburban brewery and his youth in wandering over Russia, enduring the severest hardships. In 1909 he went to Paris, where he became one of a cosmopolitan group of writers, including his close friend, Francis Jammes (*q.v.*), whose work he translated (1913). At one point his interest in Catholicism nearly led him to join the Benedictine order. In 1917 he returned to Russia, where he remained four years. There he lectured on Russian literature and worked at organizing children's theatres with V. L. Durov, a famous animal trainer and collaborator with the eminent physiologist, Ivan Pavlov. As a writer Ehrenburg belonged to the group once known as "fellow travelers," who accepted the Revolution yet remained its critics. In 1921 he returned to Paris. Expelled at first as a Bolshevik, he was later allowed to return; except for numerous journeys throughout Europe and to the U.S.S.R., he remained in Paris until 1940.

At his best Ehrenburg is a master storyteller of a cinematic, satirical type of adventure tale. His essential rootlessness is both an asset and a liability to his vivid, versatile talent, giving it now perspective, now a cynical superficiality. His chief work includes *Lik voiny* (1920; The Face of War), called the best Russian depiction of the first world conflict; *Neobychainye pokhozhdeniya Khulio Khurenito i yevo uchenikov* (1921; Eng. tr., *The Extraordinary Adventures of Julio Jurenito and His Disciples,* 1930), a picaresque legend after the manner of *Candide,* satirizing several nations in their nihilistic characteristics; *Lubov Zhanny Nei* (1924; Eng. tr., *The Love of Jeanne Ney,* 1929), an ironic story of love and spies with a French-Soviet background; *V Protochnom Pereyulke* (1927; Eng. tr., *A Street in Moscow,* 1932), a richly detailed portrayal of Moscow slums; *Vtoroi den* (1933, The Second Day; Eng. tr., *Out of Chaos,* 1934), a novel dealing with the collective versus the individual will as manifested in the construction of a giant Siberian steel plant; *Ispaniya* (1937) and *Chto cheloveku nado* (1937; What a Man Needs), articles and sketches on the Spanish civil war; *Padenie Parizha* (1942; Eng. tr., *The Fall of Paris,* 1942), a novel of the decay of France from 1935 to 1940, which won the 100,000-ruble Stalin prize and sold 35,000 copies the first week of its publication in London; *Voina* (1942; Eng. tr., *Russia at War,* 1943).

See: Y. Zamyatin, "Ehrenburg," *Rossiya,* 1923; G. Struve, "Ehrenburg," in *Soviet Russian Literature* (1935), pp. 11–13.

N. S.

Ekelund, Vilhelm (1880–, Swedish poet and essayist), began his literary career in the limited lyric manner of the nature poets of Skåne, the province of his birth in the south of Sweden. But since his muse demanded sterner gods to worship, he developed soon into Swedish poetry's most persistent and fanatical seeker after Beauty in the absolute, abstract Platonic sense. Though the early poetry with motifs from Skåne's countryside was a mere preliminary phase in Ekelund's development, it contains some of the most exquisitely beautiful nature poetry in the Swedish language. Indeed, in these early poems—contained in the volumes *Vårbris* (1900; Spring Breeze), *Syner* (1901; Visions), and *Melodier i skymning* (1902; Twilight Melodies)—he outdid his master Ola Hansson (*q.v.*) in the creation of sensitive, mellifluous, nature-intoxicated verse. In his later reaction against the tendency of such verse to become a merely sensuous and passive form of aestheticism, Ekelund turned to other sources of inspiration, first to Nietzsche (*q.v.*) and to Platen and Hölderlin, and then, in his most mature stage of development, to philosophers and mystics such as Swedenborg and Emerson, Pascal and Thomas à Kempis. In Nietzsche he found the heroic ideal, at least partly derivative from the ancient Greeks (Pindar, Heraclitus); and in Platen and Hölderlin he discovered in its purest form a passionate, never satisfied longing for Absolute Beauty, a form of beauty completely dissociated from the world of phenomena and the senses. In the philosophers and mystics he found at first merely certain other spiritual manifestations of a passionate, essentially heroic seeking after Beauty and Truth; but later in his development, when he had come to respond somewhat less to the heroic ideal, he sought in his reading more the quiet and calm of the classical conception of beauty and the Christian conception of truth. Always, however, the object of his quest has been the Absolute; never has he been satisfied with outward beauty alone or with the mere appearance of truth. This has made him the most exclusive of Swedish authors, a restless half-disembodied spirit ranging widely in the most rarefied regions of art and of thought, far distant from the ordinary everyday preoccupations of man.

The best of his mature work is contained in four volumes of poems—*Elegier* (1903; Elegies), *In Candidum* (1905), *Havets stjärna* (1906; The Star of the Sea), and *Dithyramber i aftonglans,* (1906; Dithyrambs in the Splendor of Evening)—and in a long series of volumes of prose aphorisms and essays beginning with *Antikt ideal* (1909; The Antique Ideal). Though for a long time he has not employed verse to any extent to give expression to his thought, his aphoristic prose, with its marvelous compactness of phrase, its flashing metaphors, and its subtle half-rhythmic form, is certainly not wanting in the qualities of pure poetry. He stands today as the one Swedish master of the aphoristic style, and though his influence upon contemporary Swedish literature is difficult to trace with precision, it is unquestionably present, particularly on the younger generation of poets.

See: O. Levertin, *Svensk litteratur* I (1908); A. Werin, "Vilhelm Ekelund som essayist," *Ord och bild,* XXVII (1918), 641–648; A. Österling, *Dagens gärning* (1921); N. Svanberg, "Vilhelm Ekelund's lyrik," *Nysvenska studier,* III (1923), 148–156; F. Böök, *Resa kring svenska Parnassen* (1926) pp. 85–102; G. Castrén, *Den nya tiden 1870–1914* (1932), Vol. VII of H. Schück and K. Warburg, *Illustrerad svensk litteraturhistoria,* 3d ed., pp. 442–447; K. Strömberg, *Modern svensk litteratur* (1932), pp. 108–114; S. Ahlström, *Vilhelm Ekelund* (1940).

A. G.

Elskamp, Max (1862–1931, Belgian poet), was born in Antwerp. This strange and eccentric gentleman of the rich bourgeoisie never left his native town, except during the First World War when he spent four years in Holland. He was born in a part of the city overflowing with Flemish fishmongers and thrift shops. Although he disliked these surroundings, he never went away from this proletarian district. He spent the greatest part of his life in his fine house and collected rare rose trees and sundials for his garden. Between 1892 and 1898 he published several tiny books of poetry. Although very few copies of *Dominicales* (1892) and *Salutations dont d'angéliques* (1893) were printed, they were immediately appreciated in the cenacles of the French symbolists in Paris. Elskamp's French syntax, his modes of expression, and his abundance of rare and unexpected images made him akin to Mallarmé (*q.v.*). But his inspiration was much closer to that of Verlaine's (*q.v.*) *La Bonne Chanson.* He draws the themes of his songs from the life of the simple people of his neighborhood; from their faith, their devotion to the calvaries, the baroque statues of saints placed on artificial rocks around the church. He celebrated the daily toil of the humble, their games and festivities. He uses musical rhythms, repetitions, and alliterations in his short poems, and although, at first sight, they would seem to be songs of folklore, they are in fact extremely intellectual stanzas, chiseled with patience and wit. In 1898 Elskamp collected all his poems in one volume under the title *Louange de la vie* (the same title was adopted a few years later by Gabriele d'Annunzio, *q.v.,* for his great poetical work *Le Laudi*). After that, Elskamp remained silent for 23 years. An exile in Holland during the First World War, he wrote *Sous les tentes de l'exode* (1921), and, after his return to Antwerp, *La Chanson de la rue St. Paul* (1922), glorifying the modest provincial street of his birth. But he never again attained the freshness and purity of his early works.

Elskamp's influence can be retraced in the works of the foremost Catholic poets of France: Charles Péguy and Paul Claudel (*qq.v.*). His influence is to be found also in some of Guillaume Apollinaire's (*q.v.*) songs. In Belgium, Max Elskamp was considered by nearly all the French-writing poets of the 1920–1930 generation as their master.

L. K.

Elsschot, Willem, *see* Ridder, Alfons de.

Elster, Kristian (1841–1881, Norwegian novelist), achieved his first important recognition posthumously with *Farlige folk* (1881;

with God to be made a man, for the sake of a woman; the conflict between emperor and proletarian in revolutionary Paris; small talk of small towns; the fairy tales and ancient lore of the mountains and valleys; the creation of the world. An innovator, a creator of enduring lyric monuments, Eminescu compares favorably with the great European romantic poets.

See: G. Călinescu, *Viața lui Mihail Eminescu* (1932).

L. F.

Engström, Albert (1869–1940, Swedish prose humorist and illustrator), was born in Lönneberga near Kalmar on the southwest coast of Sweden. He studied at Uppsala (1889–1891) and later at the art school of Göteborg under the celebrated master Carl Larsson. In 1897 he founded the humorous weekly *Strix*, after which he published a long succession of volumes consisting mainly of short stories about peasant and seafaring life. Outstanding among these are *En bok* (1905; A Book) and *Bläck och saltvatten* (1914; Ink and Salt Water). It came as a surprise to literary Sweden that Engström was finally elected to the Academy, but few choices have been more popular.

Engström is the nearest that Sweden has come to producing a Mark Twain. He delighted in rough characters, preferring the profane, hard-drinking, loud-laughing sailors of the old school. Old Skipper Isakson, first introduced on his deathbed, was destined to recover and become probably the most appreciated of his heroes. Like the American humorist, Albert Engström was fond of tall stories, the wilder and more extravagant the better. Like him too he enjoyed deflating famous historical personages. Few Swedish authors of importance have been deficient in humor, but Engström raised the national gift to the level of a new art. Many of his books were illustrated by himself, and few authors have been happier in this combination of the arts.

See: F. Böök, *Sveriges moderna litteratur* (1921), also published as Vol. III of O. Sylwan, ed., *Svenska litteraturens historia* (1919–1921), pp. 325–331; H. A. Larsen, ed., *Sweden's Best Stories* (1928).

C. W. S.

Erenburg, Ilya Grigoriyevich, *see* Ehrenburg.

Erlingsson, Þorsteinn (1858–1914, Icelandic poet and short-story writer), was born of well-to-do parents at Stóramörk, Rangárvallasýsla, Iceland. After a happy youth Erlingsson went to school in Reykjavík and then in Copenhagen, where he began by studying law at the university but ended by devoting his time to Icelandic studies and poetry. Here he contracted the tuberculosis of the lungs which finally was to prove fatal. On his return to Iceland, he eked out a meager living by journalism and private teaching.

In Copenhagen, Erlingsson was influenced not only by Brandes's (*q.v.*) realism, but also by the growing socialistic movement. He became an ardent socialist, an antimonarchist, and an intrepid attacker of church and clergy. His satire was as sharp as it was brilliantly executed; it proved very effective in demolishing the fundamentalism of the 19th-century Lutheran Church in Iceland. But Erlingsson was far more than a satirist. Fervent love and nature lyrics also came from his pen. He loved nature in its sunny summer garb, and he expressed his sympathy with birds and beasts not only in poems, but also in exquisite short stories cast in the form of oriental tales. Erlingsson was deeply interested in Icelandic folk poetry; he polished its chief vehicle, the quatrain (*ferskeytla*), to a degree of perfection attained only by the few masters of this form. A high degree of workmanship is characteristic of everything he wrote.

Erlingsson's volume of poems, *Þyrnar* (Thorns), was printed in three editions (1897, 1905, and posthumously, with many additions, in 1918). The poem *Eiðurinn* (1913; The Oath), on the same subject as *The Virgin of Skalholt* by Kamban (*q.v.*), and the animal tales, *Málleysingjar* (1928; The Dumb Ones), complete the list of his productions.

See: Erlingsson, *Þyrnar* (1918), ed. by S. Nordal, with an introduction by several authors.

S. E.

Ernst, Paul (1866–1933, German poet, essayist, and writer of fiction and drama), composed many hundred essays, several hundred short stories, six novels, and 23 works for the theatre (comedies, tragedies, historical dramas, and what he conceived as a new form and called "redemption drama" or "meta-tragedy"). He also produced *Erdachte Gespräche* (1921), two slender volumes of short poems, two epics, the more important of which is *Das Kaiserbuch* (6 vols., 1923–1928), and two volumes of autobiography, *Jugenderinnerungen* (1930) and *Jünglingsjahre* (1932), which are actually a comprehensive account of the economic, social, and political conditions and of the literary trends in the last three decades of the 19th century. He edited with critical prefaces some 50 works from German and other European literatures, in some cases supplying also the translation.

The author of this enormous output of prose and verse, fiction, drama, and criticism was born in Elbingerode and grew up at Clausthal in the stable economic and social conditions of the Harz Mountains, the son of upright parents in modestly comfortable circumstances. His father was a mine foreman possessing all the simple virtues characteristic of the old-fashioned skilled workman and official, to whom Paul Ernst has set up so fine and touching a monument in his *Geschichten von deutscher Art* (1928). The boy was an omnivorous reader. Destined for the ministry, he felt himself repelled by the modern theology professed at Göttingen and Tübingen and by the indifference of its propounders to the social problems and needs that confronted and horrified him in Berlin. He gave up theology for practical social action, writing both literary criticism and essays on economics, politics, and sociology, later editing the Social Democratic, *i.e.*, Marxian, *Berliner Volkstribüne* and making political speeches.

The first of his published works is his essay *Leo Tolstoy und der slawische Roman* (1889). Significant in this essay is the respectful attention he devotes to Tolstoy's criticism and interpretation of the Gospels. Subscribing to Marxian economics, he wrote his doctoral dissertation on *Die gesellschaftliche Reproduktion des Capitals bei gesteigerter Produktivität der Arbeit* (Bern, 1892). Shortly after, he freed himself from his Marxian connections and at the end of the decade turned to creative literature, writing four one-act plays in the naturalistic manner. These satisfied neither the public nor the author. A trip to Italy in 1900 afforded him the necessary clarification of his reflections concerning the principles of art and the laws governing the various genres. There, in the classic forms, both literary and pictorial, he found the intention of poet and artist, and the means they employed, more congenial to his innate conservatism. Thereafter Paul Ernst was to combat naturalism in art as well as Marxism in all its manifestations (*Der Weg zur Form,* 1906; *Ein Credo,* 1912; *Der Zusammenbruch des deutschen Idealismus,* 1919; *Der Zusammenbruch des Marxismus,* 1919; *Grundlagen der neuen Gesellschaft,* 1930).

His political and artistic principles thus clarified, he began his important work as a mature man of 35 with a strong predilection for the drama (which to him was synonymous with tragedy) and a low regard for the novel. Yet some of his novels (*Der schmale Weg zum Glück,* 1904; *Der Schatz im Morgenbrotsthal,* 1926; *Grün aus Trümmern,* 1933; *Das Glück von Lautenthal,* 1933) found their way to the hearts of a public that remained cold to his dramas. *Der schmale Weg zum Glück* has passed through 10 editions. No comparable success greeted his *Brunhild* (1909), the perfect exemplification of his theory of tragedy, or his *Ariadne* (1912), written after he had received the "grace of faith in Jesus Christ" and had decided that tragedy and its essential pessimism must give way to a form "beyond tragedy," to "redemption drama." The same disappointing reception awaited *Das Kaiserbuch,* which he undertook after the First World War hoping by this panorama of the glorious medieval past to give courage to his defeated and despoiled nation. But the very length, 100,000 verses, precluded its becoming the familiar companion of his people. Moreover, Paul Ernst is in no sense what he most ardently aspired to be—a writer for the masses. Though he denied it persistently, he is essentially a thinker with a penchant for abstract thought. This does not detract from his *Novellen,* and here, in the short story of classic construction and brevity with its unexpected point and often two or three turns in as many pages, in this art for an intellectual *élite* which he brought back from Italy and cultivated for 30 years, he became the supreme master. In his *Komödianten- und Spitzbubengeschichten* (1920) the 16th-century Italian setting is so perfect that many Germans speak of the tales as translations. And his *Geschichten von deutscher Art* might more readily and more profitably become a German household book than the great *Kaiserbuch* with its heterodox ideas concerning good and evil.

Paul Ernst is, for all his excellent novels and stories, most stimulating as a critic in matters purely literary and technical. In matters religious and philosophical, subjects which occupied him constantly, his thought remains to the end confused and confusing because, though he was able to free himself from Marxism and naturalism, he was never able to free himself from the intellectual prison of subjectivity and modernism for which Lessing, Kant, the "higher critics," and Tolstoy contributed the foundation stones. However persistently he speaks of God, God is for him not a spirit both transcendent and immanent, not a reality—though also not Vaihinger's "necessary fiction"—but a necessary function of the human mind: "Gott ist kein Ding [an sich], sondern ein Vorgang" (God is no [ultimate] reality, but a process). However deep an experience his own very special "gift of faith in Jesus Christ" was, and it was a deep experience, it did not prevent his denying the historical Jesus of Nazareth. Upon so unstable a foundation and out of theses so uncompelling it was impossible to build great drama or to fulfil as a positive force, except in the practical implications of his best novels and stories, the function of the poet as he conceived it—that of prophet and high priest of his people. But in his very limitations Paul Ernst remains the most significant writer of his day, for his self-contradictions constitute a *reductio ad absurdum* of nominalism and modernism, of post-Kantian philosophy and theosophy. More than any other contemporary German thinker outside the Church, Ernst points the way to the restoration of orthodox Christianity among the intelligentsia.

See: K. A. Kutzbach, "Von Paul Ernsts letzter Lebenszeit" and "Nachwort" (with bibliography), in *Paul Ernst—Gedenkbuch* (1933), pp. 25–28, 212–232; A. Potthoff, *Paul Ernst* (1935); J. F. Goodloe, "Zur Einführung in Paul Ernsts Werke und Weltanschauung," *Monatshefte für deutschen Unterricht,* XXXII (1940), 9–17.

J. F. G.

Ertel, Alexander Ivanovich (1855–1908, Russian novelist), was born near Voronezh, son of the manager of an estate. The boy was prepared for the Gymnasium, but his father refused to allow him to enter, and when he was 13 he was compelled to assist in his father's work. The family moved to the neighborhood of Usman, and there Alexander met a girl of a more cultured milieu and married her in 1875. She educated him and interested him in literature. In 1878 they moved to St. Petersburg to take charge of a library. Troubles accumulated. The library did not succeed; Ertel had a severe illness and was arrested because of some slight contact with revolutionary organizations and forced to settle in Tver (Kalinin). Here he separated from his wife and married a second time. Harassed by material needs, he was forced to take charge of various estates. He gradually gave up writing and died in 1908 after 10 years of silence.

His first important work, *Zapiski stepnyaka* (1890; Memoirs of a Man of the Steppes), was written under the influence of Turgenev (*q.v.*) and Gleb Uspenski. Then came *Volkhonskaya baryshnya* (1883; A Young Lady of Volkhonka) and *Pyatikhiny deti* (1884; The Children of Pyatikhin). Ertel gradually came under the influence of L. N. Tolstoy (*q.v.*) and reached the highest level of his achievement in *Gardininy, ikh dvornya, priverzhentsy i vragi* (1888; The Gardinins, Their House, Adherents, and Enemies). Later came *Smena* (1898; The Change). In spirit and methods of treatment Ertel was very close to the Russian Populists, but he believed instinctively, and also because of his knowledge of estate administration, in a more truthful and realistic approach to the peasant problems. He escaped largely from the direct following of Tolstoy by his increasing appreciation of Western culture. In his later years there was also a growing interest in the essence of religion that separated him from many of the Populists. Ertel was a keen observer of the reality of Russian peasant life, looking at it as one who had been reared in a rural environment; he treated less well the decaying gentry and had no reason for feeling that sense of personal guilt and obligation which marked many of his literary associates. Definitely a minor writer, he nevertheless composed in *The Gardinins* one of the best works of the period and won for his style the compliments of Tolstoy.

See: F. D. Batyushkov, "A. I. Ertel, po neizdannym dokumentam," *Sobraniye sochineni,* I (1909), 1–48; D. S. Mirsky, *Contemporary Russian Literature* (1926).

C. A. M.

Esenin, Sergei Aleksandrovich, *see* Yesenin.

Espina, Antonio (1894–, Spanish poet, novelist, and essayist), was born, studied, and has lived the major part of his life in Madrid, where he has been the editor of various important daily and weekly periodicals and a contributor to the reviews *Pluma, España, Revista de Occidente,* and *Gaceta literaria.* All of his books have been published in that city. These embrace a variety of genres: he started with verses in *Umbrales* (1918) and, after a prose interlude (*Divagaciones,* 1920), continued with the same genre in *Signario* (1923), which is his most characteristic book of poetry. Narrative writing is found in *Pájaro pinto* (1927), in which volume a story, "Xelfa, carne de cera," is outstanding and indispensable for an understanding of his work. The novel *Luna de copas* (1928) was followed by two of a biographical type, *Luis Candelas* (1930) and *Romea, o el comediante* (1935). He is seen as a short-story writer in *Las siete virtudes* (1931), a book prepared in collaboration with other writers. But the newspaper article, literary and political in nature and elevated very often to the category of the essay, has occupied the major part of

Espina's attention. The best examples are to be found in *Lo cómico contemporáneo* (1927) and especially in *El nuevo diantre* (1934). He has made a translation of a work by Benjamin Constant, *Adolfo* (1924), and of a play by Crommelynck (*q.v.*), *El estupendo cornudo* (1926), later presented in Madrid. Some of his writings have been translated into various languages.

Espina says that "poetry is the really unexpressable. The nearer we approach what can actually be expressed, the greater danger there is—without our realizing it—of losing our way." Onís places Espina's poetry "in that stream which represents the total disintegration of modernism, the way for which was prepared by post-modernistic irony," although "his basic art transcends both the former and the latter." His work is characterized by great facility of creation in both verse and prose, the search for the unstable, an apparent puerility, voluntary contradictions, imaginative dissociation, whim, grimace, and caricature; all these qualities are presented in a universal post-war tone which is at the same time deeply Spanish. It has been pointed out that Espina is nearer to the "esperpento" (as created by Valle-Inclán, *q.v.*) than to the newly developed film art; this is another way of affirming that he is a national product rather than an expression of cosmopolitanism. His humor and jesting reveal living depths of sentiment. His literary criticism and political thought are entirely devoid of any meaningless use of word and image and arise from a deep and responsible appreciation of human values.

See: Gerardo Diego, *Poesía española* (*Antología*) (1934), pp. 265–274, 582; Federico de Onís, *Antología de la poesía española e hispanoamericana* (1934), pp. 1046–1052, 1194.

A. I.

Espina de Serna, Concha (1877–, Spanish novelist), was born and bred in Santander. The charming daughter of well-to-do parents, she was given the advantages of a good education and encouragement to develop her taste for writing. The first poems of her girlhood were published in the local newspaper. She married early and went with her husband to Chile. Soon her marriage proved to be a tragic mistake. Unhappy and in need of money, she began to write poems and articles for the *Correo español* of Buenos Aires and for other newspapers. After three years she returned to Spain, where first a volume of lyric poems, *Mis flores* (1904), was published, then a collection of short stories and articles, *Trozos de la vida* (1907), and her first novel, *La niña de Luzmela* (1909). In this story of a Cantabrian Cinderella, Concha Espina's distinctive contributions to the Spanish novel are already apparent—her sensitive interpretation of a woman's mind and heart and her intimate and realistic portrayal of the physical aspects and social customs of her native province. Since 1909 her fertile pen has produced more than 30 volumes, including 14 novels and a dozen collections of short stories as well as poems, essays, one drama (*El jayón,* 1918), and works of other genres. The country around Santander forms the background of the novels *Despertar para morir* (1910), *Agua de nieve* (1912; Eng. tr., *The Woman and the Sea,* 1934), *La rosa de los vientos* (1916), *Dulce nombre* (1921; Eng. tr., *Red Beacon,* 1924), *Altar mayor* (1926), and *La flor de ayer* (1934) and of many short stories. *La esfinge maragata* (1914; Eng. tr., *Mariflor,* 1924) tells of life in an isolated community in the province of León, a district so poor and barren that the men must go south to work through the winter, leaving the women to watch over house and land. This penetrating study of the effect upon women of such poverty and loneliness has become Concha Espina's best-known work.

During the 1920's Concha Espina traveled extensively in Spain, Central Europe, and the United States. The novels *El metal de los muertos* (1920), a sociological study of life in the Río Tinto mines, and *El cáliz rojo* (1923), an exposition of the problem of the Sephardic Jew in Germany, and the short stories in *Tierras del aquilón* (1924) and *Copa de horizontes* (1930) reflect this experience in their backgrounds. Two volumes of American reminiscences are entitled *Singladuras* (1932) and *Alas y leguas.* In 1936–1937, during the Spanish civil war, Concha Espina, whose sympathies were with the *Falangists,* lived in seclusion in her country home in Mascuerras (Luzmela) in territory held by the Loyalists. After the victory of General Franco's forces in the province, she published the diary she had kept during the months of her retirement, *Esclavitud y libertad: Diario de una prisionera* (1938), and some stories of the revolution, *Retaguardia* (*imágenes de vivos y muertos*) (1937), *Luna roja* (1939), and *Princesas del martirio* (1940).

See: R. Cansinos-Asséns, *Literaturas del norte: La obra de Concha Espina* (1924); E. A. Boyd, *Studies from Ten Literatures* (1925), pp. 128–136; *Cuadernos de literatura contemporánea,* No. 1 (1942).

E. H. H.

Estaunié, Edouard (1862–1943, French novelist), was born at Dijon in Burgundy. From early childhood he was brought up by his widowed mother—a woman of exceptional charm and intelligence—and an austere grandfather to whose rigid discipline the child readily submitted. He received his schooling at the hands of Jesuit masters, and it was the memory of his schooldays which suggested to him, in later years, the idea of his best-known novel, *L'Empreinte* (1896). In 1882 he was admitted to the Ecole Polytechnique to study engineering; he was subsequently appointed director of the Ecole d'Application de Télégraphie, a none too flourishing school of engineering in Paris. Here he was fortunate enough to secure the collaboration of such eminent men as Henri Poincaré and Pierre Curie, and very soon the school was infused with new life. Estaunié did other engineering work; during the First World War highly responsible work was entrusted to him, and his services were recognized by the French and the Belgian governments—he was made Commander of the Legion of Honor and received the medal of the Order of Léopold.

He hesitated for some time to let his interest in purely literary pursuits be known. It was the publisher Perrin who brought him before the public. He was from the outset, and remained to the end, what Thibaudet (*q.v.*) called *le romancier de la douleur*. He reminds one of Edouard Rod, who introduced him to the *Revue des deux mondes;* they have the same deep sympathy for all those who suffer their destiny without any morbid self-pity. Estaunié's first novel, *Un Simple* (1891), deals with exactly the same problem as the *Pierre et Jean* of Maupassant (*q.v.*). The two works were published within a few weeks of each other; Estaunié dedicated a later book of his, *Le Ferment* (1899), to Maupassant. In 1892 came a second novel, *La Bonne Dame,* and in 1896 *L'Empreinte,* in which Estaunié used his experience as a pupil of the Jesuits. His apparent thesis is that the education of the Jesuits, widespread in France, leaves so indelible an impression on the young souls of the pupils that they are never able to efface it. The novel was considered by some an attack on religious education; this impression Estaunié promptly corrected by the following novel, *Le Ferment,* in which he stressed the disadvantage of a purely rationalistic upbringing. The later novels and stories of Estaunié never aroused as much discussion, but were esteemed as keen analyses of the varied experiences of interesting and unhappy souls. The best known are *L'Epave* (1902); *La Vie secrète* (1909), which was awarded the Prix Femina; *Les Choses voient* (1913), the *choses* being three pieces of furniture abandoned in an attic which tell the stories of three generations; *L'Ascension de Monsieur Baslevre* (1919), on the ascent of a mediocre soul to a state of ardent spirituality; *L'Appel de la route* (1921), on the inevitableness of suffering. A characteristic story, "L'Infirme aux mains de lumière," gave its title to a collection of shorter narratives (1923); another collection bears the title *Le Silence dans la campagne* (1924). In 1932 appeared Estaunié's last novel, *Madame Clapain.* He also wrote a study of his great Burgundian compatriot, *Buffon* (1924), and was a frequent contributor to such periodicals as the *Revue des deux mondes, Revue de Paris, Grande Revue,* and *Revue bleue.* He was elected to the French Academy in 1923, to succeed Alfred Capus (*q.v.*).

See: André Bellessort, "Un Grand Romancier contemporain," in *Nouvelles Etudes* (1923), pp. 236–264; John Charpentier, *Estaunié, avec . . . un essai de bibliographie par Francis Ambrière* (1932); Camille Cé, *Regards sur l'œuvre d'Edouard Estaunié* (1935); M. H. Ilsey, "Edouard Estaunié's Message," *French Review,* XVI (1942–1943), 461–471.

A. Sz.

Estonian literature. The few Estonians who could afford a university training in the 1820's and 1830's included two men who gave a new direction to Estonian letters for much of the 19th century. F. R. Faehlmann (1798–1850) interested himself in folklore and then, influenced by the success of Lönnrot's *Kalevala* (1835; collected poems about the heroic Kalev), he turned to the Finnish national epic poem based on oral traditions (the Estonian language is related to Finnish). After his death his friend F. R. Kreutzwald (1803–1882) finished the compilation of the *Kalevipoeg* (The Son of Kalev), published 1857–1861. A sense of continuity now stimulated national consciousness to dream of future counterparts of past glories, of a time when, as the poet said, "Kalev comes home to bring happiness to his people." Kreutzwald, although earning the reputation of being the "father of song," did not actually lead literary expression of the expanding national feeling towards great lyrical heights. But Lydia Koidula (1843–1886) achieved altogether admirable literary form in her passionate, triumphant, and poignant patriotic songs. For a short period after the death of Koidula the romantic historical novel was a prevailing genre.

The moods of the next generation were

different and more various. Many wanted hard facts, not exalted feelings. The realistic or naturalistic novel, presenting social data in somber and simple language, met this desire. Eduard Vilde (1865–1933), the master of the new school, was realistic in his early novels and then sharply critical and revolutionary in his later fiction. A similar belligerent tendency prevailed in the short stories of Ernst Peterson (1868–) and in the earlier works of Anton H. Tammsaare (1878–1940) and Mait Metsanurk (1879–). Juhan Liiv (1864–1913) was the only poet among the realists.

Prose writers of a new school called Noor Eesti (Young Estonia) exemplified a great improvement in Estonian literary style, but the very nobility of their language kept them from attaining the popularity of the realistic novelists. Friedebert Tuglas (1886–), the greatest master of this new style, has published several volumes of short stories. Jaan Oksa (1884–1918) was perhaps the most cosmically inspired of this group. Young Estonia also brought about its own renaissance of Estonian lyrics. Gustav Suits (1883–) is a poet of great intensity of thought and an impressive poetical style. Villem Ridala (1885–) is mainly known as an author of nature poems. Ernst Enno (1875–1934) was a pioneer remaining for the most part outside the group.

In its turn also the Young Estonia movement did not go unchallenged. Its modernism was violently attacked by the above-named Eduard Vilde. And, during the First World War, a group of younger lyrical writers, taking up in their own way the modernist and individualist tendencies of Young Estonia, formed themselves into what was known as the Siuru group (Siuru is the name of a mythological bird). Rapturous sensualism gradually gave place to something more idealistic. Marie Under (1883–) has the greatest poetic talent of this group. Henrik Visnapuu (1890–), marked innovator in lyrics, has written nature, love, and patriotic songs and poems of variety and a remarkable ingenuity of form. Johannes Semper (1892–), beginning as a lyrical poet and translator of poetry, turned to literary criticism and in 1935 embarked as a novelist with a definite gift of style. August Gailit (1891–) is an author of fantastical novels. In 1926 A. H. Tammsaare, who has come to be regarded as the master of Estonian fiction, began the publication of his monumental novel *Tõde ja õigus* (Truth and Justice), a vast painting of the social life of Estonia from the last quarter of the 19th century down to the present day. He has been followed by many younger writers.

On the whole the realist revival continues to be dominant, and its representatives are gradually achieving a synthesis of objective description and artistic form. Mait Metsanurk has produced successful war novels; Oskar Luts (1887–) has maintained his position as the foremost Estonian humorist. A. Jakobson and A. Mälk are the most prominent writers among the younger realists. Of the younger poetical generation, J. Sütiste and E. Hiir deserve to be mentioned.

Estonian drama and comedy attained a high level in the works of August Kitzberg (1856–1927), who mostly treated rural subjects. Eduard Vilde wrote at least one drama and one comedy of high quality. A. H. Tammsaare offered in *Judith* (1921) one of the most original treatments of this favored theme, and Hugo Raudsepp (1883–), the wittiest of Estonian essayists, has revealed himself as the writer of comedies in which his humor successfully overshadows his castigating tendency.

See: O. Kallas, *Die Wiederholungslieder der estnischen Volkspoesie* (1901); M. Martna, *L'Estonie* (1920); M. Kampmaa, *Eesti Kirjandusloo Peajooned,* Vol. IV (1936); A. Pullerits, *Eesti Kirjandusest* (1937).

E. Ju.

Eulenberg, Herbert (1876–, German dramatist and short-story writer), was born in Mühlheim am Rhein near Cologne and has remained attached to his Rhenish home country all his life. As a young student he stepped into the arena of naturalism (*see* German naturalism) and whipped up its diminishing enthusiasm by a revival of the ideals of the "storm and stress" of Goethe's youth. Passion is his driving motive, the weird, the uncanny, the sensational, and the grotesque are the aim of his dramatic presentations. *Anna Walewska* (1899), a play with a sex motif involving father and daughter, is the most noteworthy product of his youth and typical of his life's work. Sensuality and sexuality are the themes he discusses in all their variations. In the first decade of the century he is one of the most productive stage writers in Germany and his work possibly the most frequently performed. Among his plays are *Leidenschaft* (1901), a dramatization of his favorite sex theme; *Kassandra* (1903); *Ritter Blaubart* (1905), a fairy play in the Strindberg manner; *Simson* (1910); *Alles um Liebe* (privately printed in 1910), a rather tragic comedy; *Belinde* (1912), awarded the Schiller prize; *Die Insel* (1919), a drama with a truly Shakespearean note. *Sonderbare Geschichten* (1910) is a collection of short stories in the style of the later romanticists, especially in the manner of E. T. A. Hoffmann. Generally speaking, all Eulenberg's prose writings up to the First World War show these same tendencies. Actual post-war conditions are described in *Der Bankerott Europas* (1922) and *Die Hohenzollern* (1928; Eng. tr., *The Hohenzollerns,* 1929). His most recent writings, such as *Pankraz, der Schmoller* (1938), indicate a leaning towards the biographical presentation.

A. Bu.

Euringer, Richard (1891–, German novelist and lyric poet), was born at Augsburg, Bavaria. School and the study of music were followed by military service in 1913. He served as an airplane pilot in the First World War and in 1917 became the head of a Bavarian pilot-training school. After the war he resumed his studies, but soon had to give them up for want of funds, and for some time he tried to make a living as a worker in a sawmill and as an office boy in a bank. During the years of the Weimar Republic, Euringer was a herald and champion of the coming Third Reich; in 1933 he was rewarded for his loyalty to Hitler by being appointed chief librarian of the public library of Essen, without having been professionally trained for library work. He retired in 1936 to a small town in Lippe and since that date has given his time over to writing.

Upon his return from the First World War, Euringer had begun pouring out plays, stories, and visionary verses. Eventually he succeeded in producing one of the better war novels, *Fliegerschule 4* (1929), showing the positive side of the war as well as its tragedy. This novel belongs to those war tales that stress the common adventures of a group of soldiers, here of pilots. Later Euringer took up the problem of unemployment in a novel entitled *Die Arbeitslosen* (1930), but tendentious theories are far too predominant. The same can be said of his historical novel *Die Fürsten fallen* (1935), which pictures the collapse of the old European monarchies between 1793 and 1886, a period of European history which he calls "one hundred years of anarchy." Euringer's lyrics (*Die Gedichte,* 1937) come from a world entirely lacking the classical severity of George's or Rilke's (*qq.v.*) verses; they are original, frequently obscure, at times full of life. His outstanding success was *Deutsche Passion* (1933), a radio play in which he revived some of the traits of the medieval mysteries. For this work he was awarded the first national state prize of the Third Reich.

See: F. Lennartz, *Die Dichter unserer Zeit* (1938), pp. 73–75.

H. Sch.

Evreinov, Nikolai Nikolayevich, *see* Yevreinov.

F

Faeroese literature. In the isolation of the Atlantic the people of the small, rugged Faeroe Islands have preserved not only a dialect, Faeroese, which is closer to Old Norse than any modern language except Icelandic, but also a unique ballad literature, dating from the 13th century. This is the literary expression of their folk dancing (ring dance), from which a renaissance of folk dancing has spread in Scandinavia in recent times. Considering the smallness of the population (approximately 25,000) literary interest and activity have been great.

Up to the late 18th century the ballads were preserved orally only, and nothing was printed until the 19th. Then Venceslaus Ulricus Hammershaimb (1819–1909) virtually created the Faeroese written language with his grammar (1854) and his editions of ballads and folk tales, of which *Færøsk Anthologi* (1884–1891) is the best. His work was carried on by the linguist and folklorist Jakob Jakobsen (1864–1918), whose chief works are *Færøiske Folkesagn og Æventyr* (1898–1901; Faeroese Folk Tales and Märchen) and *An Etymological Dictionary of the Norn Language in Shetland* (2 vols., 1928–1932).

The modern poetry is, as might be expected, predominantly lyric, with a strong strain of the old ballads. Of the modern poets the brothers Jens Hendrik Oliver Djurhuus (1881–) and Hans Andreas Djurhuus (1883–) are perhaps most prominent, the first for his *Yrkingar* (1914; Poems), the second for several volumes of poetry, two plays, and two novels. Even better beloved by his fellow countrymen is the ardent patriot and political leader Jóhannes Paturssson (1866–). He has a volume of poems (*Yrkingar,* 1932) to his credit. Of the prose writers Heðin Brú (pseud. of Hans Jacob Jakobsen, 1901–) has written fine novels (*Lognbrá,* 1930, Mirage; *Fastatökur,* 1936, Firm Grip) in Faeroese itself, while William Heinesen (1900–) and Jörgen Frantz Jakobsen (1901–1937) have written in Danish for a wider public. Heinesen's novel *Nóatún* (1938) was well received, and Jakobsen's *Barbara*

(1939), published after the author's death, became a best seller in Denmark.

See: A. Sigmundsson, "Tunga og bókmenntir Færeyinga," *Skinfaxi,* XXIV (1933), 100–114; E. Krenn, *Die Entwicklung der foeroyischen Literatur* (1940).

S. E.

Faguet, Emile (1847–1916, French critic), was born at La Roche-sur-Yon. After attendance at the Ecole Normale Supérieure, he spent a superficially tranquil life, teaching first at La Rochelle and Bordeaux, then at the Sorbonne, and producing a steady flow of books and articles (he averaged over a book a year for a period of 30 years) which won him both distinction and popularity. He succeeded Jules Lemaître (*q.v.*) as dramatic critic on the *Journal des débats* in 1896 and in 1901 was elected to the French Academy.

As a critic Faguet occupied a middle ground between the classicism of Brunetière (*q.v.*) and the impressionism of Lemaître or Anatole France (*q.v.*). Though not without standards, his criticism did not attempt primarily to distribute rewards and punishments. Books were interesting to him chiefly for what they revealed of an author's character or ideas, and to make the reader join him in apprehending this revelation was the object of his work. Strong in logic, deft in analysis and synthesis, he succeeded best in writing of those men in whom the rational intellect prevailed; weaker in aesthetic sense, he sometimes did badly with poets who were merely poets. He lacked, or rarely showed, the gift of presenting a large picture, the growth or decline through several generations of a literary type or a mode of thought; his chief works of purely literary criticism, *Seizième Siècle* (1894), *Dix-septième Siècle* (1885), *Dix-huitième Siècle* (1890), and *Dix-neuvième Siècle* (1887), are hardly more than a series of individual studies, given a larger unity only by the covers of a book. As he grew older, Faguet's interest turned almost exclusively to the problems of his own day, which he presented in such books as *L'Anticléricalisme* (1906), *Le Socialisme* (1907), and *Le Féminisme* (1910) with his habitual adroitness and precision in grasping and expounding the ideas of others, but without reaching any notable conclusions. His final work, *Jean-Jacques Rousseau* (5 vols., 1911–1913), is an amazing pendant, both in size and in fertility of ideas, to a life so full of literary activity.

There is hardly a great French writer whom Faguet has not analyzed, always with interest, generally with keen intelligence. In particular his championing of the 17th century as against the 18th led to a new interest in the earlier period and, in the minds of many readers, to a wholesome revision of judgment. Perhaps, on the whole, his greatest merit is the fact that, in a period in which criticism seemed likely to be dominated overmuch by the minutiae of historical scholarship on the one hand and the sweeping vistas of the sociologist on the other, he covered erudition with grace and insisted that a proper primary emphasis be put upon the individual writer and his work.

See: Victor Giraud, *Les Maîtres de l'heure* (1911); Alexandre Bélis, *La Critique française à la fin du XIXe siècle* (1926).

C. W., Jr.

Fagus (pseud. of Georges Eugène Faillet, 1872–1933, French poet), was born in Brussels, the son of a Frenchman who had been exiled after the Commune in 1871. The family returned to Paris after the amnesty of 1880. As a youth Fagus was, like his father, a radical, but later became reconciled to the republic and for some time earned his living as an official at the Prefecture of the Seine; he finally turned into a decided reactionary, a fanatic royalist, and an ardent Catholic. Indifferent to recognition by the general public, he remained, until his death in an accident, *un isolé.* He belongs to the generation of the symbolists (*see* French symbolism), who not infrequently could be called bohemians in their writings and gentlemen in their tastes and their way of living. Hostile to all that savored of vulgarity, he insisted on decency in behavior and manners; his language was that of a purist. As an artist he belongs to the family of the Villons, with such writers as Mathurin Régnier, Gérard de Nerval, and Verlaine (*q.v.*), and Gautier would no doubt have added his name to the list of his *Grotesques.*

The titles of his collections of poetry together with the dates of publication are in themselves somewhat revelatory of his evolution towards an ever more orthodox philosophy and creed: *Colloque sentimental entre Emile Zola et Fagus; poèmes* (1898); *Fagus: Testament de sa vie, recueilli et expurgé* (1898); *Ixion; poème* (1903); *Jeunes Fleurs; exercices poétiques* (1906); *Frère Tranquille; dialogue entre la raison et le spectre de la mort* (1918); *La Danse macabre* (1920); *La Prière de 40 heures, ou les 14 Stations sous l'horloge du destin* (1920; republished in *La Guirlande à l'épousée,* 1921); *Les Ephémères* (1925); *Le Sacre des Innocents; poèmes* (1927); *Ballade de Saint Côme offerte à M. Aug.*

Fournier pour tout l'Hôtel-Dieu et les autres hospitaliers (1927). In 1908 was published a small volume, *Aphorismes,* and in 1926 *Clavecin,* comments on the art of writing. As a scholar he translated Vergil's *Eclogues* (1929) and the *Chanson de Roland* (1929). He was a contributor to numerous periodicals and for a time, after 1925, wrote "Chroniques" for the *Evénement.*

See: H. Martineau, "Fagus," *Divan,* XVII (No. 100, May, 1925), 195–312; Adolphe van Bever and Paul Léautaud, *Poètes d'aujourd'hui* (1929).

A. Sz.

Falkberget, Johan (1879–, Norwegian novelist), was born near the small mining town of Röros. Among his forbears on both sides were people who had come from Sweden. They were peasant miners, and the boy began work in the mines when he was only eight years old. It was hard, rough toil in sordid, brutal surroundings, but redeemed by the austere beauty of nature on the treeless mountain plateau. Johan was only 16 when his first stories were published in a local paper. After he had definitely left the mines, he served a short time as editor of a labor paper and then went to Christiania to try his luck as an author. After many rebuffs he placed his first book, *Svarte fjelde* (1907; Black Mountains). It dealt with a remarkable subject matter quite new to Norwegian literature and revealed a narrative gift that has made Falkberget one of the most popular authors in his homeland. Outstanding among his earlier books is *Lisbet paa Jarnfjeld* (1915; Eng. tr., *Lisbeth of Jarnfjeld,* 1930), the story of a woman from the high mountains who marries a man from the lowlands and can never tame her wild nature to pull together with him.

In 1922 Falkberget returned to his home to take over the small farm his father had cleared on the edge of Rugelsjøen. There he lived, writing, studying his background in archives and in present-day life till he had thoroughly mastered it, and identifying himself closely with the people. With *Den fjerde nattevagt* (1923; The Fourth Night Watch) he began writing historical novels, at which he was to excel. The central figure is a clergyman of the early 19th century who comes to the mining community full of a desire to dominate, but who learns charity and humility. The great trilogy *Christianus Sextus* (1927–1935), placed in the 18th century, is the story of the mine of that name and a monument to the simple, hard-working people. In 1940 Falkberget fled before the invading Germans and walked across the plateau to Sweden carrying the manuscript of his latest book, *Nattens brød* (1940; Night Bread.) In this book he takes the story of the mine back to its beginning in the 17th century.

Falkberget's understanding of the life of the poor, their toil and hardships down through the centuries, is deep and genuine, but his work is free from the gospel of hate. In hatred he sees only a negative, corrosive influence. Regeneration must come from work and from love based on Christian faith.

See: T. Freding, "Johan Falkberget," *American-Scandinavian Review,* XXI (1933), 401–406; A. H. Winsnes, *Norges litteratur fra februarrevolutionen til verdenskrigen,* part 2, pp. 561–571, Vol. V (1937) of F. Bull, F. Paasche, and A. H. Winsnes, *Norsk litteraturhistorie.*

H. A. L.

Fallström, Daniel (1858–1937, Swedish poet), was born at Gävle, in central Sweden. He began his career as a journalist, and brought out his first volume of lyrics, *Stockholm och skärgården* (Stockholm and the Coast), in 1881. This book was followed by many others, both of verse and of short stories. There is little originality in the poetry of Fallström. He was neither a thinker nor a pioneer in any way. And yet few poets below the highest rank have had a wider audience in Sweden. A natural singer, he had something of Snoilsky's (*q.v.*) freshness and joy of life. Love songs and pictures of Stockholm, the sea, and the country poured from his pen in melodious abundance, never impressive but seldom insipid. Facile, with neither the firm classic touch of Snoilsky nor the intensity of Fröding (*q.v.*), Fallström is still far from negligible. He was a sort of Swedish Whittier; at all events he was a poet who, like Whittier, found a sure path to the hearts of his people.

See: K. Warburg, *Svensk litteraturhistoria i sammandrag* (1911); C. W. Stork, *Anthology of Swedish Lyrics* (1917; revised and enlarged ed., 1930).

C. W. S.

Fargue, Léon Paul (1878–, French poet), born in Paris, made his début in symbolist circles (*see* French symbolism) and attended Mallarmé's (*q.v.*) receptions. One of his first poems, *Tancrède* (1894), was a characteristic symbolist confession, showing the influence of both La Bruyère and Gide (*q.v.*); it dramatized the plight of the young man as an artist.

Fargue was a frequent contributor to such magazines as *Mesures* and the *Nouvelle Revue française*. It was not until 1912 that a collection of his works, called simply *Poèmes,* was published. Their appearance passed almost unnoticed; they were read only by a select circle of admirers—on whom, indeed, they exerted a strong influence. Though somewhat reminiscent of Rimbaud (*q.v.*) in their imagery, they differ entirely in psychological background. After a second long period during which nothing of Fargue was published there appeared, in 1921, *Espaces* and *Sous la lampe. Espaces* includes "Vulturne," with its fantastic visions, and "Epaisseurs," the name of which suggests the density of the matter through which dreams must penetrate to attain being. *Sous la lampe* comprises "Banalité," a title indicative of the fund of experience from which the poet draws his inspiration, and "Suite familière," a summary of his artistic theories. In 1932 appeared Fargue's *D'après Paris,* in which factual accounts mingle with the dreams, the nightmares, the fantasies, invented in the course of his wanderings through the sleeping city: "J'ai bu le lait divin que versent les nuits blanches."

Basically Fargue is an escapist; he finds a remedy for his sorrow in the dreams that haunt him: "J'ai tant rêvé, j'ai tant rêvé que je ne suis plus ici." His special domain is the visionary penumbra where life is more enjoyable than in hard reality. Through lyrical daydreams pass memories of his childhood, glimpses of ephemeral happiness, short, poignant scenes imbued with a sense of melancholy. He is irrevocably alone. Solitude, death, the tragic inanity of life, darkness and its nightmares, the plight of soul and body, constitute the major themes of these verbal symphonies. Some of Fargue's poems are rhythmic and sensitive in the manner of Chopin's *études.* Others, while finely attuned to every poetic nuance, have a certain firmness which presages Romains (*q.v.*) or a quality which recalls the melancholic yet smiling nonchalance of a lied.

Most of Fargue's work is in prose, but it has little in common with what are generically called prose poems; it is so personal and rich that only the word poetry can properly describe it. A great experimenter with words, images, and sounds, Fargue is one of the links between symbolism and surrealism (*see* Breton, André).

See: Régis Michaud, *Modern Thought and Literature in France* (1934); René Lalou, *Histoire de la littérature française contemporaine,* enlarged ed., Vol. II (1940).

P. B.

Farina, Salvatore (1846–1918, Italian novelist), was born in Sardinia, but spent most of his life in Milan. He studied law at Pavia and Turin, but the publication of his first novel, *Cuore e blasone* (1864), at a very early age started him on a literary career to which subsequently he dedicated all his attention and energy. Farina wrote with great facility and has some 70 titles to his credit. It may be said that they are on much the same plane; almost any novel or, indeed, short story will give the measure of the artist. The best known however are *Il Romanzo di un vedovo* (1871), *Mio Figlio!* (originally appearing in the *Nuova Antologia* as a series of episodes, 1877–1881), *Amore ha cent' occhi* (1883), and *Amore bugiardo* (1893). Farina has a conventional outlook on life; his plots are based on the simple emotional problems of the *Piccola borghesia.* He presents characters that are easily recognizable without necessarily being "types," devoid of psychological complications and treated with sympathy sometimes verging on sentimentalism. It is fair to add that he possesses also a playful irony that keeps the sentimental tendency within bounds and gives to his work a coloring of humor that has made some critics mention Dickens by way of comparison. It is not a comparison that will stand analysis; more revealing of Farina's tone is the fact that his books were very popular in Germany during the later years of the past century. He is not in the least profound, but he is no fool either; his attitude toward life is sane and healthy, and the characters he depicts are always credible. He took no part in the *verismo* controversy; schools and literary camps meant nothing to him. His style is charming; he had a respect for good Tuscan without letting it prevent the frequent use of picturesque regional phraseology. Not a great author, Farina is none the less an honest and accomplished craftsman, and his novels bear rereading today.

See: B. Croce, *Critica,* IV (1906), 186–192, VI (1908), 410–411, IX (1911), 340, XII (1914), 282, and *La Letteratura della nuova Italia,* 2d ed., I (1921), 192–199; Farina, *La Mia Giornata* (3 vols., 1910–1915), his memoirs; L. Russo, *I Narratori* (1923), pp. 47–48; V. Dendi, *Un Romanziere dimenticato, Salvatore Farina* 1921).

T. G. B.

Faure, Elie (1873–1937, French essayist and art critic), was born at Sainte-Foy-la-Grande in the province of Gascony, the country of Montaigne, Montesquieu, and Gobineau; in one of his books, *Les Trois Gouttes de sang*

(1929), he has shrewdly analyzed the ethnic and psychological originality of that region of southwestern France. His father was of peasant stock; his mother came from a well-known Protestant family, the Reclus, and several of his maternal uncles were doctors or geographers. Elie Faure soon revolted against his education and the Protestant environment, to which he owed little except—and the exceptions are notable—an indomitable passion for truth, an austere refusal to compromise, an obstinate independence of character. He studied medicine in Paris, practiced some branches of it all his life, and served as a doctor during the First World War. His main interest, however, was in art and philosophy. The chief formative influences were for him Montaigne, Spinoza, Lamarck, Michelet, Gobineau (*q.v.*), and Nietzsche (*q.v.*); to these should be added the names of the innumerable artists whom he admired, first in the Louvre museum and in the medieval cathedrals, then in Italy, in Spain, and in Asia. Elie Faure's best-known work is his *Histoire de l'art,* in four volumes (1909; revised ed., 1920; Eng. tr., 1921–1924), to which he added in 1926 a fifth volume, on his own theories, *L'Esprit des formes* (Eng. tr., 1930). Scholars and specialists primarily attached to factual objectivity and historical method have often criticized this ambitious work; it is rich in dangerous but pregnant generalizations, dazzling by its piercing intuitions, and always thought provoking. The same original combination of profundity and occasional superficiality, of immense knowledge and of lyrical exaltation, characterizes the other volumes of art criticism written by Elie Faure (*Velasquez,* 1903; *Derain,* 1923; *Cézanne,* 1923; *The Italian Renaissance,* 1929, published in English; *Corot,* 1931; *Ombres solides,* 1934).

It is possible that future readers will rank higher among Faure's works his volumes of philosophical meditations, *La Danse sur le feu et l'eau* (1920; Eng. tr., *The Dance over Fire and Water,* 1926), *Napoléon* (1921; Eng. tr., 1924), *Montaigne et ses trois premiers-nés* (1926), and, above all, *Les Constructeurs* (1914; revised ed., 1921), one of the finest works of critical and personal interpretation of the present century. Toward the end of his life Faure undertook a trip around the world. On his return three volumes appeared, *Mon Périple, Découverte de l'archipel, D'autres terres en vue,* all in 1932, which constitute a genial achievement in that most difficult of all genres, the analysis of the souls of the various peoples and races in the world. The acute and lyrical interpretation of Asia and, to a lesser extent, the pages on North America have been especially admired. Faure's message, through its apocalyptic and at times florid style, through its rejection of bourgeois morality and of spiritual inertia, has antagonized many critics, professors, and snobs. No contemporary French writer has proved more consistently scornful of academic and worldly honors. With Nietzschean fervor, but with more humility than the German thinker, Faure has sung lyrical hymns to adventure and the life of danger, even to wars and revolutions, to a tragic conception of life which honors above all men the hero and the saint. The fame of this courageous and generous prophet is probably destined to rise higher, as posterity recognizes his lucid insight and his fearless faith.

See: "Hommage à Elie Faure" (by several eminent French writers and artists in a special number), *Europe,* December 15, 1937.

H. P.

Federer, Heinrich (1866–1928, Swiss novelist), born in Brienz, was for many years the most popular writer in Switzerland. That a Catholic author—Federer was an ordained priest—could attain such a position is evidence of the conciliatory spirit of his work and of the willingness, on the part of the Protestants, to acknowledge its humane qualities. In Federer, Catholic Swiss literature, which had long been relegated to a secondary role, reached a place equal to that occupied by Protestant writing, falling in line with and strengthening the national tradition of tolerance.

Though all his novels and stories draw extensively on Catholic life and customs, they are nevertheless predominantly Swiss in character, so much so that Federer can be said to typify the high standards of Swiss literary craftmanship, for a number of reasons. He makes his literary occupation to a marked degree a means for pedagogical intentions, for preaching Christian ethics and explaining their application to everyday life. This pedagogical aim Federer attains by the simple expedient of keeping in close touch with such practical problems as the bringing up of children, the political affairs of small communities, the relationship between husband and wife, and by imperceptibly blending his advice into the epic movement of events, without pedantry or dullness. The favorite milieu out of which he fashions his stories is that of the lower middle classes, preferably the inhabitants of mountain districts where he spent many years. *Berge und Menschen* (1911), *Jungfer Therese* (1913), *Das Mätteli-*

seppi (1916), are among the best regional novels Switzerland can show—and there is no dearth in this particular species. An occasional journey into foreign fields, such as *Sisto e Sesto* (1913) and *Patria* (1917), is likewise in the best Swiss tradition, opening as it does a window upon the wider world. Whether it be the Italian scene or his native mountains, Federer always apprehends the outside world with an almost sensuous delight, a *Wirklichkeitsfreude,* characteristic of Swiss literature. Federer's style makes ample use of the Swiss prerogative of spicing German literary diction with ingredients from native dialects. This is of course a process which requires good judgment as to the degree to which the interspersion with local expressions may be carried, without discouraging the non-Swiss German reader. Federer, to judge by his enthusiastic reception in Germany, was able to infuse new blood into a language which, during the second half of the last century, suffered considerably through pollution by stilted official proclamations, sloppy journalism, and a colorless commercial jargon.

See: F. Wagner, *Heinrich Federer; der Mann und das Werk* (1931); O. Floeck, *Heinrich Federer; Leben und Werk* (1938).

H. B.

Fedin, Konstantin Aleksandrovich (1892–, Russian novelist), comes of a lower-middle-class family. He traveled extensively in Western Europe, served in the Red army, and has been publishing since 1913. His early stories, like Gorky's (*q.v.*) first novels, deal extensively with the narrowness and insipidity of middle-class life, but show scant originality. His first major success came with the novel *Goroda i gody* (1924; Cities and Years), in which he developed the theme of culture and the Revolution. Here, though the canvas is broad, including pre-1914 society, the First World War, and the Revolution itself, with scenes in both Germany and Russia, the emphasis is in some degree misleading, since the intellectuals are overweighted and too little attention is given either to the upper middle class or to the masses. The essence of the novel derives from one man's struggle against society: Fedin's hero, an intellectual, unable to reconcile himself with the proletarian revolution, perishes. Soviet critics attribute the weak aspects of the novel to Fedin's personal affinity with this hero, though its rich and figured style, coupled with an appreciably affected language, lends it considerable charm. The hero's psychology is not, however, highly plausible, and the sequence of events is irrationally confused. From the standpoint of socialist realism, the individualistic tendencies exhibited both here and in Fedin's next novel, *Bratya* (1928; Brothers), have also been subjected to some criticism. In the latter novel Fedin discusses the irreconcilability of art and life and endeavors to justify the individualism of his hero, the composer Karev. In *Transvaal* (1928), attacking the official agrarian policy, Fedin even went so far as to idealize the unpopular kulak, or prosperous peasant, against whom the subsequent collectivization program was directed. These fictional works brought Fedin some unpopularity, and it was not until 1930 that he produced another story, entitled *Starik* (The Old Man). A pronounced change in his approach to revolutionary reality was later signalized by his novel *Pokhishchenie Yevropy* (1934; The Rape of Europe). In this, Europe, shaken by crisis, is unfavorably contrasted with the progressive Soviet Union, so that the proletariat, in its new function of leadership is, so to speak, running away with the decadent middle-class continent. The novel is also celebrated for its description of unemployment in the capitalist countries. While Fedin can hardly be regarded as a leading talent, he is distinguished by unusual ability in plot development and by an effective style.

See: G. Reavey and M. Slonim, *Soviet Literature; an Anthology* (1934), pp. 144–163; G. Struve, *25 Years of Soviet Russian Literature* (1944), pp. 33–42, 265–269.

S. H. C.

Feijó, António Joaquim de Castro (1862–1917, Portuguese poet), was Portugal's last Parnassian of rank. He was born in the northern town of Ponte de Lima, home of the "singer of the clear, gentle, haunting river Lima," Diogo Bernardes, whom he counted among his forebears. After studies at Coimbra (1877–1883) Feijó entered the Foreign Service and was sent to Brazil in 1886. In 1891 he went to Stockholm, remaining there, much to his regret, until his death.

Antero de Quental's (*q.v.*) influence predominates in the melancholy attempts at "understanding the modern scientific truths" which Feijó recorded poetically in his first sizable book, *Transfigurações* (1882; Transfigurations). For a time the ironical aesthete and suave diplomat forgot Antero's desperate pessimism in a Parnassian cult of impeccable form and a huge appetite for refined pleasures. In *Líricas e bucólicas* (1884; Lyrics and Bucolics) he thus presents a motley of musical impressions, morbid thoughts, and stanzas as sweet and gentle as folk songs. With other aesthetes of Europe he then turned away from the machine age to the purer art of the Orient and retranslated Judith Gautier's *Livre de jade* into a musical Portuguese of gemlike perfection, giving it the title *Cancioneiro chinês* (1890; 2d ed., improved and enlarged, 1903; Chinese Songbook). *Bailatas* (1907; Little Jumps) shows him as a master in the gentle art of irony, which turns once more to gloom in his last poems, posthumously published as *Sol de inverno* (1922; Winter Sun).

See: J. H. Stabler, tr., *Songs of Li-Tai-Pé from the Cancioneiro chinês of António Castro Feijó* (1922); Francisco Queiroz, *António Feijó e os poetas contemporâneos de Ribeiro Lima* (193?); Luiz de Magalhãis and Alberto d'Oliveira, essays in Feijó, *Poesias completas* (1939?), pp. 297–341.

G. M. M.

Fernández Almagro, Melchor (1895–, Spanish critic), was born in Granada. There he lived the first 20 years of his life, studied law at the university, and began his literary activities in the local newspapers. He finished studies for the doctorate in law in 1913 at Madrid, where he has since lived. In 1921 he became a member of the editorial staff of the conservative paper *Epoca*. More recently he has written, mainly as a dramatic critic, for *Voz, Sol,* and several other papers. His main books are *Vida y obra de Angel Ganivet* (1925); *Origenes del régimen constitucional en España* (1928); *Historia del reinado de don Alfonso XIII* (1933), completed recently with *Historia de la República española (1931–1936)* (1940); and *Jovellanos: Antologia, selección y prólogo* (1940). To several reviews he has contributed literary studies on such figures as Valle Inclán, García Lorca, and Miró (*qq.v.*). All his critical works are distinguished by a sense of objectivity, a wealth of significant details, and a keen perception of cultural and literary values.

A. del R.

Fernández Flórez, Wenceslao (Spanish journalist and novelist), was born, if the literary historian Cejador be correct, in La Coruña in the extreme northwest of Spain. The date of his birth is not forthcoming. One of the several writers of Galician origin looming large on the contemporary Spanish literary horizon, Fernández Flórez cultivated the field of journalistic literature first in his native province, later in Madrid.

In *Volvoreta* (1917), which was awarded a prize by the Circle of Fine Arts of Madrid, the theme is developed by the author with a degree of tenderness and lyricism rarely attained afterward. It shows the trusting male deceived by an altogether unscrupulous daughter of Eve, whose nickname (*volvoreta* = butterfly) the antihero's mother rightly suspects to be indicative of frivolity. Attractive scenes of the damp Galician countryside and of its inhabitants add to the harmony of the effect. *Ha entrado un ladrón* (*ca.* 1920) tells less artistically the same tale of disappointed love in the prosier atmosphere of middle-class Madrid. Jacinto Remesal excites less pity and greater scorn than did the well-studied adolescent, Sergio, of the earlier novel. The material of *Las acotaciones de un oyente* (1916), of *Las gafas del diablo* (1918), which merited a prize from the Royal Spanish Academy, and of *El espejo irónico* (1921) was originally contributed to the conservative Madrid newspaper, *ABC*. The value of these humorous journalistic glimpses of modern Spanish society, however fairly observed, was largely ephemeral. This was justly recognized by their author in the preparation of later editions. The statement of Fernández Flórez that his shorter novels have cost him as much effort as the longer is readily applicable to *Silencio* (1918), an account of the progressive annulment of conscience, of personality, through alcoholism. With its unsmiling humor and excision of irrelevant matter, the unity of this novelette is a positive achievement. *El calor de la hoguera* (*Apuntes para la historia de un pueblo español durante la guerra europea*), which constitutes the final selection in the volume *Silencio,* is utilized to form in part the novel *Los que no fuimos a la guerra* (1930). In these pictures of contemporary customs Fernández Flórez paints with light but revealing strokes the venal publisher, patriots searching for a German spy, the supposed volunteer who is shortly discovered enjoying the sporting life in Madrid, and, above all others, Don Arístides, the zealous boy-scout leader. He who has considered the recent feminine industrial worker will perhaps stifle a yawn at Fernández Flórez's concluding observation that the First World War produced a new race of women. The philosophical novels *El secreto de Barba Azul* (1923) and *Las siete columnas* (1926) probably represent the high point of their author's satirical art. The thesis of the former, an unusually episodical narrative, is that Bluebeard's forbidden chamber was empty, *i.e.*, that human life has no purpose whatsoever. A remedy, thinks Wladimiro Kull, would be to attract the attention of the gods by collective suicide. *Las siete columnas,* another prize winner, is a more cohesive work, done into English by Sir Peter Chalmers Mitchell (*The Seven Pillars,* 1934). It presents and develops the engaging notion that the social edifice, civilization, progress, all are supported by the seven pillars which are the deadly sins. When the columns collapse through a pact entered upon by the Devil and the hermit Acracio Pérez, devastation sweeps the world so thoroughly that Acracio himself joins the procession demanding the restoration of wickedness in its several forms. Among representative works of the not unprolific Fernández Flórez, one of the most recent is *La novela número 13* (1941), so titled, says the author, because it is his 13th novel. (The first one, *La tristeza de la paz,* was published in 1910.) An ostensible account of the adventures of an English detective in Spain, *La novela número 13* serves as a vehicle for altogether unflattering pictures of the Marxist aspects of the republican government. Detective Ring's search for the thoroughbred race horse Wotan ends with the discovery that he himself has consumed part of the animal, meat being scarce in Barcelona. If he is intended to be in any way symbolic, Ring's English tenacity appears more praiseworthy than his perspicacity. It is appropriate at this point to recall that a little earlier Fernández Flórez had printed *Una isla en el Mar Rojo,* a bitter commentary on Spanish civil warfare as seen from the vantage point of an embassy.

The least acute reader of Fernández Flórez will at once be aware that this is an ironically humorous writer. The irony has not, however, as Chalmers Mitchell says, the "suavity of Anatole France [*q.v.*] nor the bitter pathology of Octave Mirbeau [*q.v.*]. It is life seen through the hard and positive eyes of a Spaniard and even the humor is grim." Fernández Flórez has tried his hand particularly at the journalistic essay, the short story, the short novel, the novel of regulation length, psychological, philosophical, and, especially, frivolous. Within the limits of one work several tendencies are in conflict—the "ironic temper;" the partiality for pathetic incidents (in *Volvoreta* the tubercular children of Doña María de Solís die one by one before her eyes); the periodic insertion, in the tradition of the older Spanish novel, of extraneous anecdotes within the bigger framework; the fondness, grown to disturbing proportions in *La novela número 13,* of the author's characters for prolix discourses on problems of human behavior (thus the detective airs his views on nudism and Valdés finds the continuity of human existence in man's desire for trade). In short, the reader may come to feel that a simpler, less diffuse and less varying formula would leave a more lasting flavor, a deeper impression of the obvious inventive talents and satiric powers of Fernández Flórez.

See: J. Casares, *Crítica efímera,* II (1919), 87–101, 181–187; R. Cansinos-Asséns, *La evolución de la novela, 1917–1927,* Vol. IV (1927) of *La nueva literatura,* pp. 139–149.

R. K. S.

Fernández y González, Manuel (1821–1888, Spanish novelist), is known as the Spanish Dumas. He had something of the charm and verve of his native Seville and the curse of uncontrollable fluency. He wrote long and short poems, modeled on those of Zorrilla, but his principal works were novels, of which he produced the astounding number of 300. Since many are long, they fill about 500 volumes. Throughout all of them the reader may normally expect at least one thrill per page. As in the case of the Dumas productions, many of the works of Fernández y González appeared in newspapers, and the voluble Andalusian had no difficulty in dictating the required number of thousands of words per day. Relatively few of the novels are sentimental social works of the Eugène Sue type. Most are based at least distantly on Spanish history and legend, which the author truly loved, especially of the medieval period and the golden age. Examples are *Los siete Infantes de Lara* (1853); *Obispo, casado y rey* (1865), on Ramiro the Monk, king of Aragon; *Men Rodríguez de Sanabria* (1853), on the times of Peter the Cruel; *El pastelero de Madrigal* (1862), on the famous impostor who claimed to be King Sebastian of Portugal; and *El conde-duque de Olivares* (1868). *La historia de los siete murciélagos* (1863) best shows Fernández y González's vivid and brilliant imagination in the realm of the fantastic. His virtues are vigor, rapidity of action, picturesqueness, and color. He was a born storyteller, but not a real literary craftsman. The care and polish of the true artist were unknown to him.

See: A. González-Blanco, *Historia de la novela en España desde el romanticismo a nuestros días* (1909).

N. B. A.

Ferrari, Severino (1856–1905, Italian critic, scholar, and poet), was born in Alberino, Bologna. Beginning his studies in Bologna in 1865, he continued them in Florence, where in 1878 he received the degree of doctor of philosophy. His father had given him a taste for classical literature. He taught in various schools in Italy and finally (1897) was appointed to a chair in the Istituto Magistrale Femminile in Florence; at this time he also assisted Carducci (*q.v.*), who was lecturing at the University of Bologna. In 1877, together with other ambitious young men, he had founded the review *Nuovi Goliardi* to combat pedantic criticism and to satirize the partners of Mario Rapisardi (*q.v.*), who were Carducci's enemies; the conflict between *carducciani* and *rapisardiani* was at the moment tense. Except for financial difficulties the review would undoubtedly have succeeded. Ferrari continued the struggle alone and between 1877 and 1883 he composed a poem in eight cantos, *Il Mago,* published in Rome in 1884. Since his vein was satiric as well as lyric, he was tempted to imitate the poems of Heinrich Heine, whose influence in Italy was then considerable. *Il Mago,* abounding in allusions, allegories, and caricatures, does not often really succeed in being a social and literary satire, but does contain beautiful descriptions of the Romagna countryside. His marriage in 1886 was the inspiration for many of his verses.

It was as a lyrical poet that Ferrari achieved distinction. His lyrics are in three main groups: *I Bordatini* (1885), *Versi* (1892), and *Sonetti* (1901). One finds in them echoes of various schools and a harmonious, happy blending of various elements. Ferrari did not imitate the great classic writers like Dante, Petrarch, Cavalcanti, and Politian from any pedantic motive, but because of a personal, spiritual affinity with them. His discipleship was the natural result of a careful, passionate study. Indeed it is not accurate to speak of imitations when referring to his poems, but rather of original rearrangements. He felt that the old classic poetry was still alive and he wished to continue the glorious tradition by using the most popular Italian forms of poetry since the 14th century—the madrigal and the ballad—which he was convinced had the possibility of expressing the complexity of the modern mind.

A close friend of Carducci, Ferrari was also influenced by him, but his personal horizons are much more limited than Carducci's. Passion for historical or philosophical research was unknown to Ferrari, whose muse was only nourished by the serene springs of domestic affection. In *I Bordatini,* the group of poems dedicated to his wife and to his native countryside, Ferrari reveals his personality: his sane, youthful passion is displayed with potency of inspiration and purity of form. Unlike other lyric poets, he celebrated one love and not love, one woman and not women. Carducci found in Ferrari's poems "much variety and vividness of images and of feelings," and time has more or less vindicated this estimate. Ferrari would be entitled to a higher place in modern literature if his style were always up to the ideas and to the beauty of his inspiration. But his verse often sounds harsh and in the last group, *Sonetti,* he seems unable to exercise control over it. It is not easy to place him in literature. He is neither a romantic nor a sensualist, and his personality is not clearly enough defined to allow him to stand alone. He is a gentle soul, who greatly loved all that was his: his wife, his friends, and his country.

Ferrari's work as a scholar is considerable. He carried on long and patient research on *poesia popolareggiante* from the 14th century on and sponsored its study. Together with Carducci, he commented on Petrarch's *Canzoniere,* some cantos of Dante's *Divine Comedy,* and other classical masterpieces. He compiled many anthologies and made annotated texts for school use. In 1905 he died in a sanitarium at Collegigliato where he had been confined for a nervous ailment.

See: B. Croce, *La Letteratura della nuova Italia,* 2d ed., II (1921), 282–289.

D. F.

Ferrero, Guglielmo (1871–1942, Italian historian and essayist), was born at Portici, near Naples, and died in Geneva. After studying at the universities of Pisa and Turin, he associated himself with Cesare Lombroso, the famous criminologist, whose daughter he later married. Notable among his early works are *L'Europa giovane* (1897) and *Il Militarismo* (1898; Eng. tr., *Militarism,* 1902); Ferrero here begins his passionate advocacy of democracy which he never abandoned. In the first-named book the social situation in northern Europe is studied and a quasi-racialist interpretation of European peoples is given—the northerners are held to be by nature better adapted to industrialism. Ferrero always approached a historical problem with a few simple ideas, adding little or no qualification. This perhaps explains his world-wide journalistic popularity, and on this score too it may be contended that the facts are forced into an arbitrary pattern. Controversial issues reached a polemical stage with the publication of his five volume *Grandezza e decadenza di Roma* (1902–1907; Eng. tr., *The Greatness and Decline of Rome,* 1907–1909). Ferrero states that the Roman histories of Mommsen and Duruy are not read today because they are based on the no longer arresting struggle between republicanism and monarchy. However, his own work is also based on problems of contemporary interest, *i.e.,* the class struggle and extreme concern over economic problems. To this must be added sensational parallels between Roman and modern history: Caesar and Napoleon, Tammany Hall and the organization of the Roman unemployed by demagogues, etc. The work is lively and colorful in style, and it can be said, despite the cold reception Ferrero received from scholars, that thanks to him many read something of ancient history who ordinarily never would have done so.

In *Memorie di un sovrano deposto* (1920) and *La Ruine de la civilisation antique* (1921) Ferrero makes use of the principles of legitimacy, an idea which he develops extensively in his last works. Opposed to Fascism he left Italy in 1930 to become professor of modern history at the University of Geneva. His last writings constitute a trilogy: *Aventure: Bonaparte en Italie 1796–1797* (1935; Eng. tr., *The Gamble: Bonaparte in Italy 1796–1797,* 1939), *Reconstruction: Talleyrand à Vienne* (1940; Eng. tr., *The Reconstruction of Europe—Talleyrand and the Congress of Vienna,* 1941), and, finally published only in America on account of the impossible conditions in Europe, *The Principles of Power: The Great Political Crises of History* (1942). *Aventure* is a most intriguing piece of historical writing. The events of 1796–1797 in Italy are shown to sweep the historical personages beyond their own calculations. The central idea of the three volumes is that force creates fear and instability, the illegitimate government itself feeling insecure. Ferrero does not however state the criteria which determine the legitimacy of a state; at times it seems that a regime or dynasty is legitimate if it has been tolerated for centuries. Ferrero does say that a modern state derives true legitimacy from democratic consent and respect for minority opinion. In general his political outlook suffers grievously because of a lack of consideration for economic matters; an ethico-political structure is formed without regard to what Benedetto Croce (*q.v.*) would call a preceding moment in the hierarchy of life.

See: C. Barbagallo, *L'Opera storica di Guglielmo Ferrero e i suoi critici* (1911).

V. G.

Feuchtwanger, Lion (pseud. J. L. Wetcheek, 1884–, German dramatist and novelist), son of a wealthy manufacturer, was born in Munich. His international reputation can best be explained by his being a scholar, a Jew, and an effective publicist. After having received a Ph. D. in 1907 (his dissertation was on Heine's "Rabbi von Bacharach"), Feuchtwanger started on a literary career with a number of widely performed dramas and adaptations of Greek plays. His fame, however, began with his renewal of the historical novel, in which interesting pictures of the past were given a modern psychological understanding. In 1923 appeared *Die hässliche Herzogin* (Eng. tr., *The Ugly Duchess,* 1928), a story of the 14th century, followed by *Jud Süss* (1925; Eng. tr., *Power,* 1926), a fascinating presentation of the age of absolutism. Feuchtwanger's scholarly interest in the character of the Jewish historian and politician Josephus resulted in the creation of a formidable novel in three massive volumes, *Der jüdische Krieg* (1932; Eng. tr., *Josephus,* 1932), *Die Söhne* (1935; Eng. tr., *The Jew of Rome,* 1935), and *Josephus and the Emperor* (1942, in English only). A by-product of his studies of Roman antiquity, with allusions to present-day conditions, is the novel *Der falsche Nero* (1936; Eng. tr., *The Pretender,* 1937). But Feuchtwanger is also a publicist of contemporary events. *Erfolg* (1930; Eng. tr., *Success,* 1930) gives a clear insight into the life of Munich following the revolution of 1919 and the rise of the Hitler movement. After Feuchtwanger had been driven by the Nazis to France, he published *Die Geschwister Oppenheim* (1933; Eng. tr., *The Oppermanns,* 1933), a story of a Berlin Jewish family before and during the Hitler dictatorship, and *Exil* (1940; Eng. tr., *Paris Gazette,* 1940), a novel about journalism and journalists in Paris. Personal experiences are revealed in the books *Moskau 1937* (1937; Eng. tr., *Moscow, 1937,* 1937) and *Unholdes Frankreich* (1942; Eng. tr., *The Devil in France,* 1941). The latter is an account of his hardships in France after that country collapsed. With great difficulty Feuchtwanger escaped to Spain and finally reached the United States. Here was published the sensational novel *Double, Double, Toil and Trouble* (1943; originally written, but not published, under the title *Die Zauberer*), which is hardly worthy of Feuchtwanger's talent. Far better is the novel *Simone* (1944, in English), which treats the German invasion of France and deals with the timeless topic of the triumph of idealism over selfishness.

See: A. Burkhard, "Thomas Becket and Josef

Süsz Oppenheimer," *Germanic Review,* VI (1931), 144–153; L. Franulic, *Cien autores contemporáneos,* I (Santiago de Chile, 1941), 248–259.

H. Bf.

Fialho de Almeida, José Valentim (1857–1911, Portuguese prose writer), was born in Vilar-de-Frades, Alemtejo. He began to study in Lisbon, but poverty obliged him to work as a pharmacist's clerk. After overcoming great difficulties—giving private lessons and collaborating on obscure publications—he received his medical degree, only to abandon this profession and devote himself wholeheartedly to literary activities. He became well known at once for his political campaigns against the monarchy and attained great popularity. In 1889 he began to publish *Os gatos* (1889–1893; The Cats), a monthly review devoted to Portuguese life and edited exclusively by him. This was a continuation of *As farpas* (1871–1883; The Darts), through which, years before, Eça de Queiroz and Ramalho Ortigão (*qq.v.*) had fustigated the weaknesses of that same society. *Os gatos,* "mewing little, scratching always, and never fearing," launched inexorable attacks against the institutions and the person of the king and his ministers, replacing the delicate humor of *As farpas* by aggressive, defamatory violence. *Os gatos* is the pessimistic reaction of a passionate temperament which sees nothing but a society in ruins, inspiring only hate and scorn. There is lacking the reforming faith and social didacticism of Ramalho, but there are unforgettable pages of journalistic impressions and descriptive prose. In *Pasquinadas* (1890; Pasquinades), *Vida irónica* (1892; Ironical Life), *A esquina* (1903; The Corner), and other books of criticism and journalism, Fialho's biting satire stirred the life of his period with its acid commentary, at once plebeian and aristocratic. His literary initiation coincided with the triumph of realism, to which he adhered, although through personal and literary admiration for Castelo Branco (*q.v.*) there remained in his work much romantic sentimental disorder and subjective expansiveness. If one adds to this the materialism which was a result of his medical training and the bitterness and narrowness of his life, spent at times in the company of an insane brother, one better understands the author's corrosive personality.

His purely literary work is made up of various collections of stories—*Contos* (1881; Short Stories), *A cidade do vício* (1882; The City of Vice), and *O país das uvas* (1893; The Country of Grapes). He was not interested in the soul but in the instincts; a uniform, elemental primitivism permeates all these narratives. In this naturalistic version of rural life Fialho represents the extreme reaction against the falsely idealized vision of romanticism. His literary merit is found in his capacity for apprehending the plastic physiognomy of things. The highly energetic style of his prose and the almost brutal quality of the descriptive coloring reveal a chromatic hypersensitivity. He has recourse even to syntactical distortions, in his vehement desire to give in all its richness the pictorial sensation which his eyes beheld. He would intersperse Gallicisms in his writings when the desired shade was lacking in the vernacular, and he argued the necessity of overcoming by Neo-Latin contributions the rigidity and inadequacy of the old Portuguese language. His influence on modern Portuguese letters in this and other ways has been extensive. In *O país das uvas* he has given, in powerful and palpitating style, a dazzling and luminous vision of the people and the countryside of his native district, Alemtejo.

Expatriation was the bitter end of his life. The clever cajolery of the dictator João Franco had softened him and even made him a fervent supporter; when this regime fell, he found himself surrounded and isolated in a hostile atmosphere. He left for his own province and from there went to Cuba, where he died in 1911.

See: Claudio Basto, *A linguagem de Fialho* (1917); Castelo Branco Chaves, *Fialho de Almeida* (1923); A. Forjaz de Sampaio, "Fialho de Almeida," in *Journal dum rebelde* (1924), pp. 63–93.

E. G. D.

Figueiredo, Fidelino de Sousa (1888–, Portuguese literary critic and historian), a reformer at heart, with an unusually strong philosophic bent, has raised the standards of Portuguese criticism on the basis of individualist principles. Furthermore, he has introduced the study of comparative literature in Portugal.

Born within the bounds of "Pombal's Lisbon," he went to Coimbra to study law and, under Teófilo Braga (*q.v.*), literature. Soon he began to write as a journalist. Dissatisfied over the iconoclast Republic of 1910 and its break with a cherished past, he gathered a group of social-minded traditionalists around his *Revista de história* (1912–1928; Review of History). His hour of action struck when, as a young conservative deputy, he entered the short-lived cabinet (1918–1919) of the dictator-general Sidónio Paes. When Paes was murdered, Figueiredo went into exile. Remaining true to his ideals of enlightened conservatism, he soon found himself outdistanced by Portugal's modern Sebastianists. Like a medieval scholar he wandered from university to university, from country to country, as the intellectual ambassador of his beloved "little backyard." He taught abroad in Rio de Janeiro (1920), visited Madrid (1927–1930) and Berkeley, California (1931, 1937), among other places, returned to Brazil and finally to Portugal.

Guided by ideas received from Benedetto Croce, Paul Bourget (*qq.v.*), and Sainte-Beuve, Figueiredo injected a sound critical spirit into the study of Portuguese literature, till then a favorite ground for national self-glorification. He applied a psychological method, which focused on the individual personality of each author as the primary factor in his works. The practical outgrowth of his theories was *A história literária como ciência* (1912; Literary History as a Science), with its good comparative bibliography, and three standard works, *História da literatura romântica portuguesa, 1825–1870* (1913; History of Portuguese Romantic Literature), *História da literatura realista, 1871–1900* (1914; History of Realist Literature), and *História da literatura clássica, 1502–1825* (3 vols., 1917–1924; History of Classic Literature). Other didactic works included a concise *História da literatura portuguesa* (1919; also published by "Labor," Barcelona, as *Historia de la literatura portuguesa,* 1927). Sincere friendship for Spain speaks through his translations from Unamuno and Menéndez y Pelayo (*qq.v.*) and through two original studies, *As duas Espanhas* (1932; The Two Spains) and *Pirene* (1935; Pyrene). Most of his shorter literary papers are gathered in the four volumes of *Estudos de literatura* (1917–1924; Studies of Literature). Special subjects are taken up in *Características da literatura portuguesa* (1914), in *História dum "vencido da vida"* (1930; History of a "Victim of Life"), a study of Oliveira Martins, in *A épica portuguesa no século XVI* (1931; Portuguese Epics of the 16th Century), and in *Antero* (1942). He has also written works of fiction, including the autobiographic novel *Sob a cinza do tédio* (preface, 1925; Under the Ashes of Disgust).

As a historian Figueiredo laid down his program of militant traditionalism in the handbook *O espírito histórico* (1910; The Historical Spirit). This program was carried out in the 16 volumes of his *Revista de história.* The *Estudos de história americana* (1929) is a contribution to Portuguese-American relations.

Figueiredo himself has provided the best key to his ideas on politics and literature in two volumes of essays that challenge blind, extreme nationalism—*Notas para um idearium português* (1929; Notes for a Portuguese System of Ideas) and *Problemas da ética do pensamento: O dever dos intelectuais* (1936; Problems of Thought Ethics: The Duty of the Intellectuals).

See: Figueiredo, *Notas para um idearium português* (1929), pp. 153–160.

G. M. M.

Finnish literature. The generation of 1880 gave a new impetus and new directions to Finnish literature. Until approximately that date most authors of the country had been educated in Swedish-language schools (Swedish remained the sole official language of instruction in all secondary schools until 1859) and Swedish-language literature had played an important and sometimes a dominant role. In the 1880's a group of new writers began to employ the vernacular, the mother tongue, with new enthusiasm and gave direct and natural expression to the local culture. A distinctly Finnish style developed. These writers also established contacts with the whole world outside, opened up new horizons for their countrymen, suggested new ways of art and life.

The foreign literary influence came mainly from the Scandinavian countries, especially from Norway, and in lesser degree and not as directly from France and from Russia. The general European tendency of the time to stress realities of life in the selection and treatment of literary themes (*see* French naturalism, German naturalism) came to the fore also in Finnish literature. The works of Minna Canth (1844–1897), the pioneer of the new school, are very representative in this respect. In her drama *Työmiehen Vaimo* (1885; The Laborer's Wife) she indicts the upper classes of society for condoning if not actively supporting traditions and laws which kept the poorer classes in hopeless servitude and poverty. In the *Papin Perhe* (1891; The Parson's Family) it is the older generation which is set up in opposition to the younger; the old people appear with all their deep-seated prejudices and narrowness whereas the children demand a healthy, free development of personality.

While Minna Canth wrote with the fervor

the title. This representation of the character and manners of the generation of 1840, based on Flaubert's own experience and observation, a work in grisaille, devoid of positive action and heroics, tinged with irony and disenchantment, is acclaimed by connoisseurs as his masterpiece.

Flaubert's last years were darkened by a succession of misfortunes, private and public—the death of Bouilhet (1869), the Prussian invasion and the occupation of Croisset, the loss of his mother (1872), the bitter struggles between liberals and reactionaries, and family financial difficulties involving tremendous sacrifices (1875–1879). He was also saddened by his failure in the theatre and by general lack of understanding of his work. His *Trois Contes* (1877), the only work published for possible profit, was received with mingled admiration and disapproval. He left unfinished *Bouvard et Pécuchet* (1881, ed. by Maupassant), a savage attack on accepted ideas and a bitter satire of human ignorance, stupidity, prejudice, and ineptitude.

Flaubert's career was a long series of struggles. Seeking in literature an escape from his infirmities and disillusionments, he forced himself to overcome a natural tendency toward excessive lyricism and imagination by a severe application of discipline and restraint. Questions of style and composition tortured him endlessly. He was preoccupied with truthfulness of character and of situation, naturalness of dialogue, and exactness of setting. But he was principally concerned with form. Harmony and rhythm of phrase, logic and solidity of structure, were essential. For Flaubert truth and beauty were inseparable, if not identical. "There are no fine thoughts without beautiful form and vice versa. . . . The Idea exists only by virtue of its form." Flaubert was a perfectionist, spending long years of almost incessant toil in elaborating and revising a single novel. He was completely devoted to his art, which was sacred to him. Because of his disdain for prevailing tastes and conventions, his work was not fully appreciated at first. Uncompromising in his principles, he refused to make concessions for the sake of popular or commercial success. But gradually he came to be recognized as one of the masters of 19th-century prose. He has been classified as a realist, but he himself disclaimed relationship with any literary school. In his ideals he resembles the Parnassians and the partisans of "art for art's sake." Aesthetically he is close to Baudelaire. Flaubert's *Correspondance* (new ed., 9 vols., 1926–1933) gives an intimate picture of the man and an eloquent expression of his ideas and theories. One of the most important literary correspondences of the 19th century, it has been an inspiration for many younger writers. Most of the works of Flaubert have been translated into English.

See: R. Descharmes and R. Dumesnil, *Autour de Flaubert* (2 vols., 1912); R. Dumesnil, *Gustave Flaubert; l'homme et l'œuvre* (1932); A. Thibaudet, *Gustave Flaubert* (1935).

J. F. J.

Flers, Robert Pellevé de La Motte-Ango, marquis de (1872–1927, French dramatist), born in Pont-l'Evêque, of a family prominent in Norman annals since the Middle Ages, spurned the more austere occupations of his forebears and devoted his life to the theatre. In 1901 he married the daughter of the well-known dramatist Sardou (*q.v.*) and began his highly successful collaboration with Gaston de Caillavet (*q.v.*). The latter died during the First World War (1915), and Robert de Flers, having volunteered his services, fulfilled important military and diplomatic missions to Russia and Rumania. Too modestly recorded in his volumes *Sur les chemins de la guerre* (1919) and *La Petite Table* (1920), they were formally eulogized in the Rumanian Parliament. With Francis de Croisset (*q.v.*) as a new associate, he produced another series of plays, at least one of which, the operetta *Ciboulette* (1926; music by Reynaldo Hahn), enjoyed the popularity of his former works. By then he held several influential positions, including that of literary director and dramatic critic of *Figaro*. His election in 1920 to the French Academy, which he had satirized in one of his best-known comedies (*L'Habit vert,* 1912), served notice upon his bewildered ancestors, two of whom had been members of the Institut, that all roads lead to the Coupole.

See: Emmanuel Chaumié, *La Belle Aventure de Robert de Flers: Russie-Roumanie* (1929); Francis de Croisset, *Le Souvenir de Robert de Flers* (1929).

J.-A. B.

Flex, Walter (1887–1917, German poet, novelist, and dramatist), is the poetic representative of the idealist German war volunteer of 1914, the very opposite of Remarque (*q.v.*). Born in Eisenach, Thuringia, he came from a family in which classical culture and idealism had merged with a strong patriotic consciousness. After university studies, the young philologist served for several years as a tutor in the Bismarck family. Early works written between 1909 and 1914—*Demetrius* (1910), *Im Wechsel* (1910), *Zwölf Bismarcks* (1913), *Wallensteins*

Antlitz (1918), and the drama *Lothar* (1920)—showed marked talent, but it is the experience of the war that gave substance to his work. From the standpoint of an idealism which he tried to carry into personal action, Flex wrote his war poems and reflections *Sonne und Schild* (1915), *Vom grossen Abendmahl* (1915), *Im Felde zwischen Nacht und Tag* (1917), and *Leutnantsdienst* (1917). His great success was the story *Der Wanderer zwischen beiden Welten* (1916), in which he depicts a high type of man equal to the war and its problems. The hero, a young lieutenant, wants the German soul and humanity rejuvenated through the spirit of the "Wandervögel," that idealist German youth movement which since the turn of the century tried to fuse the spirit of Rousseau with Nietzsche's (*q.v.*) Dionysian joy of living and with Christian faith and charity; "Stay pure in heart and ripen" is the motto of the story. This was to be followed by a long novel dealing in detail with Flex's own personal development. But in 1917 Flex fell in action, and only two chapters of the novel (*Wolf Eschenlohr,* 1919) were finished; we can see that he meant to offer a non-compromising idealism which was to solve the social question on a national basis. Genuine brotherhood was to remove the cleavage between the classes of the people and create the comradeship of the nation, things for which the war and the experience of the front had paved the way. The work of Flex, more intellectual than passionate, was essentially traditional and conservative. His collected works appeared in 1926.

See: A. Soergel, *Dichtung und Dichter der Zeit,* Neue Folge: *Im Banne des Expressionismus,* 4. Auflage (1927), pp. 503–507; J. Klein, *Walter Flex, ein Deuter des Weltkrieges* (1928); C. Flex, *Walter Flex* (1937); W. K. Pfeiler, *War and the German Mind* (1941), pp. 82–90.

W. K. P.

Fofanov, Konstantin Mikhailovich (1862–1911, Russian poet), was born into the family of a small shopkeeper near St. Petersburg. He received little education. His lyrical verse, somewhat decadent in its mood and devoid of civic ideology, harmonized in content with the antisocial ("art for art's sake") trend that characterized Russian poetry of the 1880's. His work soon became well known throughout Russia. Characteristic collections are *Stikhotvoreniya* (1887; Verses) and *Teni i tainy* (1891; Shadows and Mysteries). A great many of his poems were set to music, and Fofanov became an important literary figure. The greatest weakness of his poetry was its lack of depth, and eventually the symbolists replaced Fofanov in the readers' favor.

See: V. Bryusov, *Dalekiye i blizkiyie* (1912).

O. M.

Fogazzaro, Antonio (1842–1911, Italian novelist), was born in the Venetian city of Vicenza. His family was well-to-do; he never had to earn his living. In his boyhood he had as tutor the gentle and open-minded poet-priest, Giacomo Zanella (*q.v.*), who influenced him deeply in many ways, strengthening the religious interest that was native to him and giving it a somewhat modernistic character. The young Antonio loved music and was not far from seeking a musical career; but lack of really outstanding talent together with a not unsympathetic parental disapproval kept him from entering that field. The failure of the war of 1859 made it unsafe for his family, known for its patriotism, to remain in what was still an Austrian province, and for the seven years that were to intervene before the final liberation of Venetia the family lived in Turin, where Antonio studied law, to little purpose. In 1866 the family returned to Vicenza. Thereafter Fogazzaro's life ran smoothly, divided chiefly, in locale, between two homes, a villa just outside Vicenza, and a villa at the water's edge at Oria, where a mountain valley, the Valsolda, comes down in beauty to the northern shore of the Lake of Lugano.

Fogazzaro came late into literary activity. It was not until 1874, when he was 32 years of age, that he published his first book, *Miranda,* a brief sentimental romance in blank verse; and it was not until 1881 that the series of prose novels, which constitute his only really important work, began with the publication of *Malombra* (Eng. tr., *The Woman,* 1907). His later novels are *Daniele Cortis* (1885; Eng. tr., 1887), *Il Mistero del poeta* (1888), *Piccolo Mondo antico* (1896; Eng. tr., *The Patriot,* 1906), *Piccolo Mondo moderno* (1900), *Il Santo* (1905; Eng. tr., *The Saint,* 1906), and *Leila* (1910; Eng. tr., 1911). *Malombra* and *Il Mistero del poeta* are of slight interest; but the others are all good novels, and *Piccolo Mondo antico* is a masterpiece, generally regarded as the greatest Italian novel of the latter half of the 19th century.

The five successful novels are concerned typically with the love affairs and other problems of high-minded protagonists, of whom one is the more meditative and idealistic, and the other the more energetic and humanly effective. The leading figures are surrounded, always, by an amazing host of secondary characters, depicted with an individualization, a vitality, and an irresistible humor that make them one of the most memorable groups of acquaintances in all modern literature. Fogazzaro's humor, which expresses itself in description, in convincingly real dialogue (sometimes in dialect), and in the ingenious confrontation of fixed habits with chance situations is a type which one associates more readily with English than with Continental fiction. First and foremost, Fogazzaro is a novelist of character: his personages are so real to him that some of them pursue him from book to book, insisting on reappearance—a phenomenon as marked as in the cases of Trollope and Balzac. The five novels all reveal Fogazzaro's preoccupation with religion; and all gain a flavor of melodic reminiscence from the extent and fineness of his musical culture: musical references are as omnipresent in his pages as is the sound of running water in the gardens of an Italian villa.

Piccolo Mondo antico is a study of the mutual influence of a husband, Franco Maironi, who is deeply religious, but rather a dreamer than a man of positive force, and his wife Luisa, who lacks religious faith, but does possess an energetic conviction of moral right and a very strong sense of justice. Their experiences, closely interwoven with those of other members of their families and of the ubiquitous surrounding throng, take them through critical perplexity, through comedy, and through deeply moving tragedy to final integration. The book gains an elevating patriotic tone from the participation of its actors in the preparations for the war of 1859. The three remaining novels proceed from *Piccolo Mondo antico* and form a series with it. Piero Maironi, son of Franco and Luisa, is the hero of *Piccolo Mondo moderno* and *Il Santo.* In the latter book he has left his own social world and reappears as a religious leader, fired with a Franciscan flame of love and abnegation and with a glowing desire for the regeneration of the church from within. One of Piero's disciples is the hero of the less significant final novel, *Leila. Il Santo,* while it has elements of greatness as a novel, is primarily an intense fictional appeal for a turn toward modernism in the policy of the church. As such it found disfavor with the Vatican and was placed upon the Index—as was also the case with the much milder *Leila.*

In addition to his novels Fogazzaro wrote a considerable number of short stories, some of them gems of this form of narrative art. A first collection of such stories, *Fedele,* was published in 1887. A second collection, *Racconti brevi,* was published in 1894 and reissued, with additions, in 1901 under the title *Idilii spezzati.* He also wrote much verse, of placid beauty rather than distinction. An early volume, *Valsolda* (1876), is a collection of lyrics suggested by the sights and sounds of his Alpine valley. A definitive volume, *Le Poesie* (1908), contains all of his verse that he thought worth preserving. He published also four volumes of miscellaneous prose writings and one collection of dramatic sketches, *Scene* (1903). He was made a senator in 1896.

See: S. Rumor, *Antonio Fogazzaro,* 2d ed. (1920); P. Nardi, *Fogazzaro,* 2d ed. (1930); Lucienne Portier, *Antonio Fogazzaro* (1937, in French).

E. H. W.

Fogelqvist, Torsten (1880–1941, Swedish educator, publicist, and critic), born in Lidköping, is one of the most important cultural personalities in 20th-century Sweden. Though he wrote some creditable verse in his earlier years (*På vaxtavla,* 1912, On a Wax Tablet; *Sånger till den förlorade skönheten,* 1915, Songs to Lost Beauty), it is as an educator, publicist, and essayist that he has made his important contribution to modern Swedish life. As a popular lecturer he traveled far and wide in Sweden in the early years of the century, an activity which he continued as time permitted down through his life, even after 1908 when he became first an instructor and then *rektor* at the famous folk high school at Brunnsvik in Dalecarlia. In 1919 he became a member of the editorial staff of the leading liberal newspaper in Stockholm, *Dagens nyheter* (The Daily News) and in 1931 was elected to the Swedish Academy. The view of life which motivated all of his activities as an educator, publicist, and essayist may be called a kind of common-sense humanism, in which the concept of evolution, with its stress upon change and development in man's social, economic, and political life, fuses with a fine sense of the historically organic nature of the intellectual and spiritual sides of human life. His love for the noble spiritual inheritance of man's past in general, and the Swedish past in particular, enabled him to avoid becoming encased in any of the schematic excesses of modern Marxist thought, even though his educational activities brought him into close and sympathetic contact with the younger working classes in modern Sweden.

The rich fruit of his mature thinking is contained in a brilliant series of prose essays and travel sketches, among which may be mentioned *Bok och svärd* (1917; Book and Sword),

Allvarsmän och narrar (1921; Serious Men and Fools), *När stugan blev mig trång* (1922; When the Cottage Became Too Small), *Typer och tänkesätt* (1927; Types and Ways of Thought), and *Svenska och klassiska utsikter* (1940; Swedish and Classical Views). He has also written a group of penetrating biographical and critical monographs on three of his Swedish contemporaries, the artist-caricaturist Albert Engström, and the poets Erik Axel Karlfeldt and Dan Andersson (*qq.v.*). During the difficult days before the outbreak of the Second World War and after, Fogelqvist spoke out strongly with the conviction and eloquence of the great humanistic tradition against the reign of brutality and terror represented in totalitarian thought and action in Europe.

See: B. Bergman, "Torsten Fogelkvist," *Ord och bild,* XXXVI (1927), 177–184; S. Selander, *Européer, amerikaner och annat* (1930), pp. 200–207; V. Spångberg, *Duktigt folk* (1930), pp. 116–119; T. Fogelkvist, *Jag minns den ljuva tiden* (1935).

A. G.

Fontane, Theodor (1819–1898, German novelist), is the master of realism in German fiction. A descendant of French Huguenot refugees, Fontane was born in the little Brandenburg town of Neu-Ruppin, but in his early childhood the family removed to Swinemünde on the Baltic Sea. To prepare for his father's profession he was apprenticed to an apothecary in Berlin; later he worked as an apothecary's assistant in Leipzig, Dresden, and Berlin. While thus employed he wrote numerous articles for newspapers and journals and published a volume of poems (1851). This new apprenticeship introduced him to a new profession. In 1852 he visited England as a special correspondent for a Berlin newspaper and made a longer visit in 1854–1859. After his return to Germany he served on the staff of the *Kreuzzeitung* (1860–1870) and, primarily as a critic of the theatre, on the *Vossische Zeitung* (1870–1889). On the strength of his popular histories of the Prussian wars of the 1860's, a Berlin newspaper commissioned him to write a history of the Franco-Prussian War; he journeyed to the front, where he was captured and held a prisoner for a month. He died in Berlin, September 20, 1898.

Fontane's ballads first brought him recognition in the literary world. His themes were taken from English and Scotch history as well as from legends and historical events of his Prussian fatherland; "Von der schönen Rosamund," "Archibald Douglas," "Der alte Derffling," and "Der Tag von Hemmingstedt" are justly reckoned among the most successful efforts to perpetuate the ballad tradition in modern times. Fontane was in his 60th year when his first novel was published. His experience as a journalist had sharpened his eye in observing the significance of detail in human phenomena; the years had brought also a sanity and balance, a ripening of human understanding, from which his novels derived inestimable profit. His first novels were historical, in the tradition of Scott and of Scott's chief German follower, Willibald Alexis (*Vor dem Sturm,* 1878; *Grete Minde,* 1880; *Ellernklipp,* 1881). His last historical novel, *Schach von Wuthenow* (1883), is a masterly example of the genre; the essential qualities of a historical period, the time immediately preceding the battle of Jena, are embodied in fictitious character and fictitious circumstance. In the meantime with *L'Adultera* (1882) the novelist had entered the field in which he was to become preeminent, the realistic novel of contemporary life in Berlin and the surrounding countryside.

His conception of realism differed sharply from the left-wing realism of the naturalists. "Genuine realism," he said, "will always be full of beauty, for the beautiful belongs to life as well as the ugly," and again, "Art must resort to the ideal to give the impression of completeness." He chose his characters from the everyday world; they enter into normal human relationships and meet with no sensational experiences. He records with extraordinary fidelity the seemingly petty happenings which form the substance of most lives, and in the choice of detail he shows a consummate mastery, revealing the hidden meaning of the apparently insignificant. Fontane's interest centers in character, not in incident; for the most part he avoids scenes of excitement or even ignores the climax of an action, for he is more concerned with the slow process of inconspicuous steps which lead to a crisis. His plots are of extreme simplicity—indeed the last two narratives, *Die Poggenpuhls* (1896) and *Der Stechlin* (1899), hardly present at all the sequence of related events which one calls a plot. Fontane introduces and develops the characters by natural and effortless methods; conversation forms a conspicuous element, and exquisitely subtle and varied are the gradations in speech by which his figures are characterized. The artistic use of foreshadowing devices and his sympathetic relation to the characters of his own creation are not irreconcilable with true realism. The most constant theme in his stories is the problem of a marriage in which some form of inequality or disparity constitutes a latent source of misunderstanding, and the intrusion of a third person raises this to the surface. His masterpiece, *Effi Briest* (1895; Eng. tr., 1913–1915) is a novel of this type. The heroine, daughter of a country gentleman, marries a man of her parents' choosing, a middle-aged government official who had once been a suitor for her mother's hand; from girlish play she is called to the obligations of a new social position. *Effi Briest* is a supreme example of the novelist's ripened art. It is a subdued tragedy of marital error, related with the reticence of a great artist. Other novels present subtle variations of this general problem—*L'Adultera, Graf Petöfy* (1884), *Cécile* (1887), *Unwiederbringlich* (1892). Another distinguished example of Fontane's realism is *Irrungen, Wirrungen* (1888; Eng. tr., *Trials and Tribulations,* 1917). It presents the love of a young aristocrat for a girl of the people, an age-old story, here related in a very modern version. The lovers are separated by barriers of tradition which act as a kind of fate to which one bows in wistful resignation. The heroine, Lene Nimptsch, is one of the most convincing and memorable of Fontane's creations. *Stine* (1890) is a kindred tale, but more distinctly in a minor key, reaching a tragic conclusion in the suicide of the noble lover. In *Frau Jenny Treibel* (1892) the novelist casts an eye upon the plutocratic bourgeoisie. Frau Jenny has risen from humble origins to affluence and social position, and Fontane examines her and her circle with fine irony and amused tolerance. The slight plot is concerned with her plans for an appropriate marriage for her second son. It may be added that two or three of Fontane's novels (*e.g., Unterm Birnbaum,* 1885; *Quitt,* 1891) fall outside the usual pattern and contain some complexity of plot as well as thrilling or even melodramatic incidents.

Among the most engaging of Fontane's works are the autobiographical writings *Meine Kinderjahre* (1894; Eng. tr., of extracts, *My Childhood Days,* 1913–1915), *Von Zwanzig bis Dreissig* (1898), and *Kriegsgefangen* (1871), a delightfully good-humored account of his imprisonment in France; the selections from his journalistic correspondence, *Ein Sommer in London* (1854), *Aus England* (1860), and *Jenseits des Tweed* (1860), show a shrewd and friendly understanding of English life and culture. In his *Wanderungen durch die Mark Brandenburg* (4 vols., 1862–1882) Fontane pays tribute to the neglected beauty of his Prussian fatherland. His letters (various collections, especially 1904, 1910) reveal the distinction and charm of his personality and contain much pertinent comment on life and literature.

See: Franz Servaes, *Fontane* (1900); Joseph Dresch, *Le Roman social en Allemagne (1850–1900)* (1913); Conrad Wandrey, *Theodor Fontane* (1919); Kenneth Hayens, *Theodor Fontane; a Critical Study* (1920); Heinrich Spiero, *Fontane* (1928).

H. W. H.-T.

Forsslund, Karl Erik (1872–1941, Swedish poet and novelist), was born at Örebro and lived most of his life as a schoolteacher at Falun in the mountain region of Dalecarlia. Beginning with narrative prose, he became best known for his lyrics, of which the first collection was *Arbetare* (1902; Workers). He celebrated in particular the old-time Nordic virtues of the mountain folk among whom he taught. His ringing verse is represented in literary anthologies and still more often in socialistic publications. The youthful dreamer, he believed, is the true prophet and molder of the future. The war against oppression and luxury is like the forces of spring returning to rout the cold inertia of winter. A more generous and genial-hearted revolutionary would be hard to find.

See: K. Warburg, *Svensk litteraturhistoria i sammandrag* (1911); C. W. Stork, *Anthology of Swedish Lyrics* (1917; revised and enlarged ed., 1930.)

C. W. S.

Fort, Paul (1872–, French poet), was born in Reims. When he was only 18, *La Petite Bête,* a one-act comedy in prose, was published. In the same year, reacting against the naturalistic theatre and wishing to provide a stage for the "idealistic" drama of the symbolists, he founded the Théâtre d'Art (later the Théâtre de l'Œuvre). A number of his poems appeared in little magazines and *plaquettes;* collected, they formed the first volume of his *Ballades françaises* (1897), for which Pierre Louÿs (*q.v.*) composed a dithyrambic preface. Further books of ballads followed; and Fort found himself master of one of the numerous schools of poetry then flourishing, with headquarters in a café, the Closerie des Lilas. In 1905 he founded the review *Vers et prose,* important in the later history of French symbolism (*q.v.*), and was its editor until 1914. These were years of glory, culminating in his election (1912) as "prince of poets." Mistral (*q.v.*), voting for him, dubbed him *la Cigale du Nord.* The First World War and the years that followed failed to slacken the rhythm of his production: at the end of a 40-year period (1897–1937) no fewer than 38 volumes of the *Ballades françaises et chroniques de France* had been published. Three of the *chroniques,* cast in dramatic form, reached the stage of the Odéon; a fourth, *Les Compères du roi Louis* (1923), that of the Comédie Française. In 1927 Fort was awarded the Prix Lasserre; in the same year he and Louis Mandin published their *Histoire de la poésie française depuis 1850.* It early became evident that, in so voluminous a poetic output, some sort of sifting would be imperative. *Choix de ballades françaises* (1913) was the first of many Paul Fort anthologies, the latest of them having been published since the disaster of 1940 by the poet's friends, in attempted mitigation of his extreme poverty.

Like all poets whose inspiration is abundant, facile, and uneven, Fort tends to repeat himself. Although sometimes reckoned a symbolist, he seems rather a belated romantic strayed into a fog that has some relation to symbolism, and out again. Specialist of the ballad, he makes effective use of the traditional themes of popular poetry. With them he has made many gay and charming songs. He delights in the lively, the colorful, the picturesque; less naïve than it appears, this picturesqueness is not exempt from preciosity and often a rather too complacent (if agreeably ironic) sentimentality. At times he verges on semi-greatness. Although employing rhyme and alexandrines, he takes every kind of liberty with both. His rhymes shade into assonance, his alexandrines into highly rhythmic prose. While he has been acclaimed as a precursor of the vers librists and a creator of new metrical forms, his innovation would appear to consist in the device of printing a ballad stanza in the form of a paragraph of prose. But his poems retain their vitality and freshness, for his exuberance is inexhaustible. He is the Peter Pan of French poetry, with a world of ballads for his Never-Never Land. As poet, chronicler, and animator of literary movements, his measure of fame seems secure.

See: Rémy de Gourmont, *Promenades littéraires,* Vol. IV (1912); Adolphe ven Bever and Paul Léautaud, *Poètes d'aujourd'hui* (1929), Vol. I.

J. Me.

Forzano, Giovacchino (1884–, Italian playwright and librettist), born at Borgo San Lorenzo in Florence province, has had a kaleidoscopic career. He studied medicine, sang as a baritone, and obtained a law degree. In the field of journalism he has been editor and director of small, local newspapers as well as the *Nazione di Firenze.* He has also been stage director of such theatres as La Scala of Milan and Opera Reale of Rome. His talents and experience have been used by the Italian moving picture industry, for which he has directed many films.

Forzano's theatrical production has been prodigious. His buoyant temperament, facile wit, and amazing versatility have made him the idol of the masses and one of Italy's foremost box-office attractions. His immense popularity is due to the wide range and variety of subjects treated, his fertility of invention, and his skill in maintaining the interest of the audience. The scene of *Sly* (1920) is a London tavern of 17th-century England; in *Tien-Hoa* (1924) a Chinese girl commits suicide to keep faith with her dream of love; in *Gutlibi* (1925) a Senegalese boxer becomes involved in the intrigues of Bolshevik politics in Serbia; and in *Jack Broder* (1929) an immigrant Italian girl, masquerading as a young man, becomes a famous American screen star. Forzano is at his best in the creation of light comedies in which the sentimental, comic, and even tragic elements are expertly blended. His *Madonna Oretta* (1918) and *Le Campane di San Lucio* (1916), of a gay, sparkling humor and colorful in their highly flavored Tuscan dialogue, belong to this class. *Sly,* already mentioned, is the offspring of Shakespeare's prologue to *The Taming of the Shrew;* Forzano transforms Christopher Sly, the drunken tinker, into a wine-loving poet who, upon awakening in the lord's palace after his abduction, falls in love with the latter's mistress. In the most powerful scene of the play, Sly professes his love in beautifully sensitive and touching verses which recall Cyrano addressing Roxane (*see* Rostand).

The French Revolution has inspired many of Forzano's historical dramas: *Il Conte di Bréchard* (1923), *I Fiordalisi d'oro* (1924), *Madame Roland* (1926), *Danton* (1930), and *Campo di Maggio* (1930; Eng. adaptation, *Napoleon, the Hundred Days,* 1932). For this last-named play and for *Villafranca* (1931) Mussolini suggested the themes. In *Campo di Maggio,* Napoleon is somewhat extraordinarily portrayed as animated by love of humanity, devoted to family, generous with friend and foe, and inspired by a desire to weld all European nations into a happy, peaceful union.

The more serious critics have deplored Forzano's prolific output and have often classified him as a Scribe or a Sardou (*q.v.*). It is to be regretted that a writer as gifted as Forzano has viewed the theatre solely as a medium for providing entertainment and achieving "success" rather than as a vehicle for the study of real people and their problems. Forzano also wrote many librettos for operas by such famous composers as Mascagni, Franchetti, Puccini, Wolf-Ferrari, Leoncavallo, Randegger, and Lehar.

See: G. Ruberti, *Storia del teatro contemporaneo,* II (1928), 687–689.

P. P. M.

Fournier, Alain- (pseud. of Henri Fournier, 1886–1914, French novelist), was born near Bourges, Cher, at La Chapelle-d'Angillon, where his parents were schoolteachers. His childhood was remarkable chiefly for the intense joy he took in his surroundings, a joy that became nostalgic with the passage of time. After pursuing at Brest studies intended to prepare him for the merchant marine, he abandoned the idea of going to sea and went to the Lycée Lakanal, near Paris, to prepare for the Ecole Normale Supérieure. At Lakanal he met Jacques Rivière, (*q.v.*), later to be his brother-in-law; in 1905, when Fournier spent a summer in England, began the voluminous correspondence, since published, which is such a valuable source of information on the intellectual and spiritual life of the two young men. For two successive years Fournier failed in his entrance examinations for the Ecole Normale. He spent two years in military service, practiced journalism, and in 1913 published *Le Grand Meaulnes,* his only completed novel and the basis of his reputation. Fragments of *Colombe Blanchet,* the novel upon which he was working when war broke out in 1914, were published after the war by the *Nouvelle Revue française* (December, 1922); *Miracles,* a collection of stories and verse, some of them previously published in periodicals, appeared in 1924. Fournier was killed in action in September, 1914.

The first vague plans and sketches for what was to become *Le Grand Meaulnes* date back to about 1902 and seem to have their origin in Fournier's desire to express his emotions about the scenes of his childhood. By 1905 he called the projected book *Les Gens du Domaine.* His literary ideas were under the influence of such writers as Régnier, Mallarmé, Rimbaud, Francis Jammes (*qq.v.;* Claudel and Gide, *qq.v.,* were to come later), and his basic idea was symbolist in character: he planned to write, not about the immediate scene, but about the invisible one behind it. In the final form of the novel, however, this "other landscape" appears only indirectly. *Le Grand Meaulnes* is a story of love and adventure, its protagonists are very human adolescents, its settings basically realistic. But the chief source of its elusive charm is the continual suggestion of deeper significance.

As interesting as the novel is the spiritual adventure which lies behind it and which is revealed by Fournier's letters. In them can be traced the evolution of the "Domain" from a place to a state of mind. They tell of Mlle de Q., or Yvonne de Galais as Fournier was to call her in *Le Grand Meaulnes,* the young woman twice seen in 1905, but at once absorbed into his Domain; they show her becoming a symbol, a Beatrice. Before *Le Grand Meaulnes* was finished, there came a check in this definitely mystical trend; and the refusal, the sense of contamination and of loss which accompanied this check, took their place in the novel beside the suggestion of the Domain.

See: Jacques Rivière, "Introduction," in Alain-Fournier, *Miracles* (1924); Havelock Ellis, *From Rousseau to Proust* (1935), pp. 345–362; Henri Peyre, *Hommes et œuvres du XXe siècle* (1938), pp. 179–212; Harold March, "The 'Other Landscape' of Alain-Fournier," *Publications of the Modern Language Association, LVI* (1941), 266–279.

H. M. M.

France, Anatole (pseud. of Jacques Anatole Thibault, 1844–1924, French novelist, story writer, poet, critic, and historian), was widely regarded in his time as the "prince of letters" and the leading exemplar of French intelligence, wisdom, and wit, on whom had fallen the mantle of Voltaire and of Renan (*q.v.*). While the future will probably not wholly ratify his contemporaries' high estimate, it will certainly rescue him from his present relative disfavor among critics and give him a distinguished place in his country's gallery of literary figures. Though he was not gifted with a powerful creative imagination, he possessed an admirably perceptive, comprehensive, and well-furnished mind and a delicate, responsive sensibility that made him perhaps the most lucid "witness" of his age. His understanding of the traditions and character of his country gave him an impressive authority as its spokesman both at home and abroad.

He was born in Paris, the only son of a bookdealer who had a small shop on the Quai Malaquais. The world of books became his natural habitat, and though he was far from being an exemplary student and failed to graduate from the Marist Collège Stanislas, all his life he was a voracious reader, with a prodigious memory and a sixth sense which made books extraordinarily real and living to him. Rather shy and retiring, yet fond of good conversation and later a brilliant talker in small groups, addicted to "silent orgies of meditation," yet responsive to feminine charm and delighting in the equivocal comedy of sex, he was more at home in the study and the library than in the drawing room or boudoir. His life was almost entirely spent in reading and "scribbling in the margins of old books." Aside from a few trips to Italy, a brief Mediterranean voyage, a lecture tour to Buenos Aires, and a visit to Sweden to receive the Nobel prize in literature, Paris remained his home until he retired, at 70, to his country place, La Béchellerie, in Touraine. His marriage in 1877 to Valérie Guérin, by whom he had a daughter, Suzanne, was at first a happy one; it was at this time that his writing showed a certain sentimental vein and that his first tender reminiscences of childhood and stories for children—*Abeille* (1883) and *Nos Enfants* (1896)—were produced. But incompatibilities led to a divorce in 1892, and during the following 20 years, which form his most productive period, he was inspired and somewhat dominated by Mme Arman de Caillavet, the great love of his life. His last years were melancholy, though he outwardly showed an Olympian serenity. He was given a state funeral that had not been equaled in pomp since that of Victor Hugo 40 years before, while the young generation of writers raised a cry of revolt against one who had held the center of the stage too long and who incarnated a literary ideal on which it had resolutely turned its back.

His first published writings were a study of Alfred de Vigny (1868), a sheaf of critical articles which he contributed to small reviews, and poems in the Parnassian spirit, the best of which he collected in *Les Poèmes dorés* (1872). These show a reverence for the classic tradition, to remain with him throughout his life, and a distinguished if not original poetic talent reaching its peak in a poetic drama, *Les Noces corinthiennes* (1876). His first attempts in prose narrative, *Jocaste* and *Le Chat maigre* (both 1879), show many influences and lack almost wholly the distinctive Anatolian "manner." This is a complex blend of irony, tenderness, sensuality, love of beauty, worldly wisdom, and studied disingenuousness, sprinkled with literary allusions culled from many sources, which first revealed itself in *Le Crime de Sylvestre Bonnard* (1881) and *Le Livre de mon ami* (1885). When in 1888 Adrien Hébrard appointed him to the literary editorship of the *Temps,* he was able for the first time to display his special qualities as a writer—and perhaps also his special limitations—to the full. His excellence, indeed, lies not so much in his ability to meet the demands of sustained work as in the immediate impact of his style, reflecting his many-faceted mind, the infinite play of his fancy and his memory around a great variety of themes. As a critic he was the leading impressionist of the period and affirmed the inescapable subjectivity of all judgments.

In 1897 he was at the height of his fame. He had been elected to the French Academy; *Thaïs* (1890), *L'Etui de nacre* (1892), *La Rôtisserie de la reine Pédauque* (1893), *Le Lys rouge* (1894), and *Le Jardin d'Epicure* (1894), among others, had been published. Master of language, he wrote in a pure classic style, enriched by the cadences and colors of the romantics which he adapted to the taste of the sophisticated, self-indulgent, world-weary intellectual élite of the day. Two things preserved Anatole France from becoming what some have been tempted to see in him, a facile purveyor of literary pleasure: these were a hard core of peasant soundness and a sense of kinship with the common people. Beneath his many moods and apparent contradictions, beneath what frequently could be taken for frivolity and intellectual irresponsibility, he shows attachment to the simple virtues of truth, justice, and goodness. Though he was mild by temperament and his far-roaming intelligence inclined him to detachment, he had a strong social sense which aligned him in the tradition of the French Revolution and led him to take sides in political issues and champion popular causes. With Zola (*q.v.*) he defended Dreyfus in the famous "affair." He flayed superstition, intolerance, injustice, demagogy, and dictatorship, eloquently defended freedom of thought, liberal education, and science, and advocated mass education, the separation of church and state, social reform, labor organization, and the rights of minorities. He became a friend and admirer of the great socialist Jean Jaurès, a supporter of the Russian Revolution, and an advocate of socialism. After 1897 his work increasingly assumed the character of social satire. His strongest and most imaginative writing is contained in the four loosely constructed novels that compose *L'Histoire contemporaine* (1897–1901) and in *L'Affaire Crainquebille* (1901), *L'Ile des Pingouins* (1908), and *La Révolte des anges* (1914), all of which involve broad political and social issues and make sharp, sweeping indictments of contemporary society. His monumental *Vie de Jeanne d'Arc* (1908), in the tradition of Renan's *Vie de Jésus,* is his chief bid for consideration as a historian. Most of the writings of Anatole France have been translated into English.

He was keenly aware of living at the end of an era, in a period of transition when new forces were in germination. Though he brings nothing essentially new to the world of literature, his work as a whole constitutes, with the inevitable limitations of perspective imposed by time and place, a brilliant summation of several centuries of French thought and life. A modern and heretical heir of the Greco-Roman and Christian traditions, in his stories and novels he revives scenes of the Alexandrian period, the Italian Renaissance, the French middle ages, the 18th century, and the period of the French Revolution. He heightens his pictures of the past with adumbrations of the present and those of the present with echoes of the past.

The key to his mind and temper is irony, a disposition to view all things in the double light of appearance and reality, to subject words, acts, institutions, to the test of a displaced perspective which brings out a contrast between the intent and its social projection. His world is one in which such ambivalences have infinite play and in which the relativity of time and place, plus the subjectivity of any human view, give a fleeting and uncertain consistency to phenomena.

See: Gustave Michaut, *Anatole France; étude psychologique* (1913); Léon Carias, *Anatole France* (1931); Haakon M. Chevalier, *The Ironic Temper: Anatole France and His Time* (1932); E. Preston Dargan, *Anatole France, 1844–1896* (1937, in English).

H. M. C.

Frank, Bruno (1886–1945, German novelist, dramatist and poet), born in Stuttgart, studied at several universities in South Germany, taking the Ph.D. degree at Heidelberg. He lived as a writer near Munich until, after 1933, he left Germany; the United States was his home for some years before his death.

Frank began his literary career in 1905 as a poet; *Aus der goldenen Schale* (3d ed., *Gedichte*, 1907) contains graceful but not very original lyrics. Selected poems of the next years were published in *Die Kelter* (1920). Only a few among the many earlier novels, stories, and dramas which Frank wrote were successful, notably the novel *Die Fürstin* (1915) and the drama *Die Schwestern und der Fremde* (1918). It was not until after 1920 that Frank found the artistic formula that made him internationally known. He once wrote, "The masses detest being bored, they need strong stimuli." Adhering to this formula, he builds plots full of action around psychologically modernized historical figures or events, as in *Tage des Königs; drei Erzählungen* (1924; Eng. tr., *The Days of the King*, 1927), *Trenck; Roman eines Günstlings* (1926; Eng. tr., *Trenck; the Love Story of a Favourite*, 1928), the drama *Zwölftausend* (1926; Eng. tr., *Twelve Thousand*, 1928), the novel *Ein Mann namens Cervantes* (1934; Eng. tr., *A Man Called Cervantes*, 1934); or he piques the reader's curiosity by using well-known, if thinly veiled contemporary personalities as subjects for more or less fantastic stories, as in *Der Magier* (1925) and *Politische Novelle* (1928). The novel *Der Reisepass* (1927; Eng. tr., *Lost Heritage*, 1937), a love story among *émigrés*, makes use of popular anti-Nazi feelings to hold the interest of the reader. A novel, *Die Tochter*, was published in Mexico City in 1943 (Eng. tr., *One Fair Daughter*, 1943).

W. R. G.

Frank, Leonhard (1882–, German novelist and dramatist), was born at Würzburg, the son of a cabinetmaker. At the age of 13 he became the apprentice of a bicycle mechanic. For some time he tried to make a living as a factory hand, a chauffeur, a house painter, and a hospital attendant. At 30 he wrote his first novel, *Die Räuberbande* (1914; Eng. tr., *The Robber Band*, 1928), the story of several Würzburg boys who, named after some characters from Karl May's (*q.v.*) books, took part as disguised "brigands" in a series of romantic adventures and pranks. In a sequel to this story, *Das Ochsenfurter Männerquartett* (1927; Eng. tr., *The Singers*, 1932), the revolutionary tunes of *Die Räuberbande* are softened into a bittersweet scherzo on the theme of boys turning bourgeois: we now meet the old "brigands" as middle-aged men who have abandoned their adventurous spirit after the war. Frank's second novel, *Die Ursache* (1920; Eng. tr., *The Cause of the Crime*, 1928), proved his talents as an original narrator. With this book he joined the ranks of those who exploited revolt against the old order as a literary theme; it is full of warlike compassion for the innocently guilty creatures who are the victims of a coercive educational system. There was also a Freudian influence behind this protest inasmuch as it showed that not only moral but also psychological motives of repressed feelings in childhood are the cause of such a rebellious attitude.

When the First World War broke out, Frank left Germany and went to Switzerland as a refugee, where he became a member of a Zurich group of anti-war writers. Here his *Der Mensch ist gut* (1917) was written, a powerful, humanitarian denunciation of the war spirit, the first of its kind in German literature. The book was a great success and even during the war was widely read, in spite of its ghastly picture of suffering. It may have contributed to the weakening of the German home front. In any case it was enough in itself to make Frank again depart from Germany after 1933, when he joined the many recently exiled German writers. In 1924, still impressed by the revolution of 1918, he produced the novel *Der Bürger* (Eng. tr., *A Middle-Class Man,* 1930), less remarkable for its plot than for its style, similar to the technique employed in a movie script with its rapidly changing scenes. After this book Frank was definitely classed with the expressionists. In his short story *Karl und Anna* (1927; Eng. tr., 1929) he succeeded in presenting one of the most original variants of the Enoch Arden motif of the husband's return, but the story is centered primarily around sexual and not patriotic problems. Two years afterward he recast this novel into a very effective and successful play under the same title (1929; Eng. tr., 1929). Of his many short stories *Im letzten Wagen* (1925; Eng. tr., *In the Last Coach and Other Stories,* 1935) seems especially typical of his art, which skillfully combines sensationalism and psychological cruelty. More and more Frank disengaged himself from any allegiance to his native land, and the ground of his narratives became the wide world of international affairs. A large number of his books have been translated into foreign languages.

See: W. Mahrholz, *Deutsche Literatur der Gegenwart* (1930), pp. 399–403; J. Bithell, *Modern German Literature, 1880–1938* (1939), pp. 411–413.

H. Sch.

French literature (*see also* French naturalism, French symbolism). The years between 1870 and 1940 undoubtedly constitute one of the richest periods in the history of French letters. Seldom had French literature proved more boldly original than under the Third Republic. Its prestige and influence abroad rose higher than at any other time except during the age of classicism and the Enlightenment.

Literary evolution does not necessarily coincide with the sharply outlined fluctuations of political, social, and military history. No other date, however, could provide such a logical starting point for an account of modern French literature as the year 1870. The brutal events which then shook France brought to the fore tendencies which might otherwise have remained dormant for many years. Between 1869 and 1876 the last survivors of the great romantic generation died—Lamartine, Sainte-Beuve, Mérimée, Dumas *père,* Gautier, Michelet, Quinet, George Sand. Hugo alone lived on, a universally respected patriarch of French letters, though of little influence on younger poets. Until about 1885 the main intellectual currents were those which had succeeded and opposed romanticism. Positivism was the most widespread philosophical attitude. Science was worshiped by many; mechanistic and determinist explanations of the universe and of man were generally accepted; metaphysical speculation was ridiculed as futile. Emile Littré (1801–1881), Claude Bernard (1813–1878), Marcelin Berthelot (1827–1907), and the psychologist Théodule Ribot (1839–1916) were the chief representatives of scientific positivism, even while another great scientist, Louis Pasteur (1822–1895), asserted his faith in spiritual and Catholic beliefs. The chief influence on literature was that of Taine (*q.v.*), through his critical theories advanced during the Second Empire and his philosophical study, *De l'intelligence* (1870). After the war and the Commune, Taine turned almost exclusively to the writing of history and did not conceal his disapproval of the realistic novelists and the poets of the new school. His ambitious work, in 12 volumes, *Les Origines de la France contemporaine,* suffers in retrospect from his excessive passion for generalization. However, it impressed many French writers (Bourget, Barrès, Maurras, *qq.v.*), through its severe appraisal of the faults of the French Revolution. Until his death in 1893 the prestige of Taine was immense, owing to his encyclopedic knowledge, splendid intellectual integrity, and ardent though somewhat artificial style. Since then it has declined noticeably, while Renan (*q.v.*), often associated with Taine as the chief guiding spirit of the years 1870–1900, remains to this day a powerful influence. His *Souvenirs d'enfance et de jeunesee* (1883) won many readers to his harmonious and lucid prose. As a historian of religion, his work, even when superseded by subsequent research, stands unrivaled for its subtle portrayal of souls and vivid evocation of scenery. As a political thinker he censured the excesses of democracy after 1871, advocating an austere moral and intellectual reform of France; but he soon adopted a more liberal attitude toward the republican regime and branded with prophetic insight the evils which unchecked nationalism and racial ideas would unleash in Europe. His philosophy, which he never tried to organize into a logical system, reacting against positivism and materialism, conceived of the universe as animated by a "mobile becoming" and a mysterious "nisus"—notions which prepared many minds for the *élan vital* of Bergson (*q.v.*). Loti, France, Lemaître (*qq.v.*), and Barrès owed much to Renan's assertion that religious felling should be preserved and purified while religious dogmas were being ruthlessly discarded. "He Christianized us," Barrès wrote of Renan in 1923. Besides Taine and Renan, mention must be made of two important philosophers, Antoine Cournot (1801–1877) and Charles Renouvier (1815–1903), whose influence on literature was relatively slight, and of two original essayists, Henri Frédéric Amiel (*q.v.*) and Louis Ménard (1822–1901), both torn between analysis and reverie, between nostalgia for the past and acceptance of modern science. In literary criticism Montégut (*q.v.*), through his wide curiosity and his refined style, and to a lesser extent Scherer and Weiss (*qq.v.*) seemed the least unworthy successors of Sainte-Beuve. After Taine and Renan the most important prose writer outside the field of fiction, although with a great narrative gift, was Gobineau (*q.v.*). He died in 1882, neglected by his contemporaries, but his fame soon spread, first in Germany, where his influence became considerable on Wagner, Nietzsche (*qq.v.*), and other exponents of racial theories. His philosophy of history hardly stands the test of critical examination; but *Les Pléiades* (1874), *Nouvelles asiatiques* (1876), and some of his posthumously published works are remarkable for their literary charm and the originality of an acute and independent mind, reminiscent of Stendhal at his best.

In the novel the years 1870–1885 saw the triumph of naturalism (*see* French naturalism). Flaubert's (*q.v.*) gospel of artistic and impersonal realism was strikingly reiterated in his posthumous works *Bouvard et Pécuchet* (1881) and *Correspondance* (1884–1892). The Goncourt brothers, Huysmans, and even Alphonse Daudet (*qq.v.*), with his sensitive and humorous realism, have lost much of their earlier appeal. Maupassant (*q.v.*) remains unrivaled in his short stories, but succeeded less conspicuously in the creation of character, although he has been much admired outside of France as a novelist. Zola's (*q.v.*) stature has risen since his death: his pseudoscientific and sociological theories have been exploded, but his epic imagination, his powerful inspiration, his brutal and massive strength, rank him among the great masters of the French novel. Two original temperaments, Jules Vallès and Barbey d'Aurevilly (*qq.v.*), the latter a colorful stylist and a brilliant storyteller rather than a novelist, remained outside of naturalism. A third one, Paul Arène (1843–1896), wrote of his native Provence with a delicate and racy flavor equal to that of Daudet.

The drama of the years 1870–1885 trailed behind the novel. The comedy of manners maintained a conventional technique with Alexandre Dumas *fils* (1824–1895), Edouard Pailleron (1834–1899), Henry Meilhac (1831–1897), and Ludovic Halévy (1834–1908). Eugène Labiche (1815–1888) enjoyed lasting success in light, almost farcical comedy.

Poetry seemed, until 1885, to be chiefly characterized by Parnassian tendencies—worship of art for art's sake, aloofness from the present, colorful and often ponderous evocation of ancient or "barbarian" cultures and religions, emphasis on sculptural beauty and elaborate technique. Leconte de Lisle (*q.v.*), however, occasionally struck a profoundly moving note in his more personal poems, and Heredia (*q.v.*) developed an impeccable technique for the sonnet. The minor Parnassians, including Banville (*q.v.*), whose fanciful and decorative verse Mallarmé (*q.v.*) esteemed, and once overrated talents such as Coppée and Mendès (*qq.v.*) were soon eclipsed by the advent of more original poets. Sully-Prudhomme (*q.v.*) deserves a partial rehabilitation today, as do the philosophical poets Jean Lahor (1840–1909) and, even more, Charles Cros (1842–1888).

A marked change became perceptible in the intellectual atmosphere around 1885–1890. Positivism and determinism no longer satisfied the youth or the scientists themselves. The validity of scientific laws was declared by many thinkers to be merely relative and statistical. Some rash prophets proclaimed "the bankruptcy of science." A formula borrowed from Herbert Spencer, "the Unknowable," was seized upon as making allowance for the mystery in the universe. Hegel and Schopenhauer were repeatedly quoted and occasionally read by French men of letters and were revered as teachers of philosophical idealism. Boutroux (*q.v.*) became the most eminent in a group of philosophers, among whom were Jules Lachelier (1832–1918), Alfred Fouillée (1838–1912), Marie Jean Guyau (1854–1888), and the great mathematician Henri Poincaré (1854–1912), who asserted the relativity of scientific laws and the irreducibility of mental and moral forces to physical phenomena. Bergson, whose first work appeared in 1889, was soon to provide a rallying point for the new tendencies.

The poets, long subdued by the prestige of Hugo (who died in 1885) and of the Parnassian school, suddenly leaped to the vanguard of literary evolution and have remained to this day the boldest and most original element in

French literature. The last 15 years of the 19th century may be called the age of symbolism (*see* French symbolism). Baudelaire (*q.v.*) was hailed as the forerunner of the movement. Rimbaud (*q.v.*), who had abandoned literature in 1873, was discovered. The younger poets grouped themselves around Verlaine (*q.v.*) and Mallarmé. By the close of the century it became clear that a major revolution, affecting both content and technique, had occurred in French poetry.

Prose writers remained comparatively untouched by symbolism, an essentially poetical movement. Villiers de l'Isle-Adam (*q.v.*) is the only important storyteller who invested with a flamboyant and sonorous prose the idealistic visions of the symbolists. Laforgue (*q.v.*) died prematurely, before he could outgrow the humorous boyishness of his bitter talent. The expert artistry of Pierre Louÿs (*q.v.*) was at its best, not in his ingenious tales, but in his rare poems and prose poems. Rémy de Gourmont (*q.v.*), who tried his hand at the novel in a dry, cold manner, proved in criticism a keen expert at "disassociating ideas" and an original interpreter of the new literary tendencies. Marcel Schwob (*q.v.*) had likewise more delicacy of touch and wealth of erudition than imaginative gifts. Teodor de Wyzewa, a Pole, and Edouard Schuré (*qq.v.*), an Alsatian, both passionately fond of music, versed in several foreign literatures, and attracted by esoteric doctrines, were occasionally interesting critics. Vogüé (*q.v.*), whose novels are forgotten, widened the intellectual horizon of his generation through his pioneer work on the Russian novel (1886). The three leading critics of that period opposed symbolism as well as most of the new aspirations of their times: they championed French classicism and extolled the virtues of lucidity and order. Brunetière (*q.v.*), who attempted to judge literary works by dogmatic standards, to carry the notion of evolution into aesthetic history, and to uphold traditional moral values, suffers in retrospect from his conservative prejudices and oratorical style. Lemaître, who stood in sharp contrast to him, displaying nonchalant irony in his impressionistic articles, lacked the vigor and boldness of a great critic. Faguet (*q.v.*) wrote with an overabundant facility, but at his best evinced remarkable gifts as an analyst of ideas and a portrayer of intellectual temperaments, especially in his *Politiques et moralistes* (3 vols., 1891–1900). The most influential dramatic critic of the period, Sarcey (*q.v.*), did little to win the public to innovations of the stage. Fustel de Coulanges (1830–1889), a worthy successor of Taine and Tocqueville in his austere and systematic interpretations of the past, and Albert Sorel (1842–1906) were the most notable historians. Gaston Paris, Lanson, and Bédier (*qq.v.*) renovated literary history through an original combination of solid scientific discipline and artistic taste.

The French novel of the years 1885–1900, sharing in the general reaction against naturalism, shifted its emphasis from the minute description of reality to the analysis of psychological motives and a sympathetic rendering of men's emotions. Irony and pity alternated in the works of the two most popular novelists of the period, France and Loti. Each of them has left three or four masterpieces among a score of less significant works. Neither of them could contrive a dramatic plot, forgetting himself and endowing imaginative characters with life. Bourget was a conscientious builder of novels in the Balzacian manner. His heroes, however, often appear as too logically conceived; they embody intellectual or moral problems, but fail to haunt the reader like the more spontaneous characters of Balzac or Zola. His volumes of criticism, from the early *Essais de psychologie contemporaine* (2 vols., 1883–1885) to *Quelques Témoignages* (1928), show Bourget at his best as an intellectual analyst. Régnier, Hermant, and Marcel Prévost (*qq.v.*) brought to the novel their subtle gifts of irony and style in the best 18th-century tradition, but lacked the imaginative power which the creation of plot and character seems to demand. J. H. Rosny (1856–1940), Renard (*q.v.*), Mirbeau (*q.v.*), and Paul Adam (*q.v.*), who grasped reality with more vigor and tried to depict the contemporary world, failed to fulfill the promise of their early works.

On the French stage the most significant event between 1870 and 1900 was the founding of the Théâtre Libre by Antoine (*q.v.*) in 1887. Becque (*q.v.*) had already given two plays whose brutal truth, skillful characterization, and terse dialogue were not unworthy of Molière. Antoine accustomed Parisian audiences to realistic plays and pioneering innovations in the staging and the acting. His chief claim to fame may well lie in his discovery of several new playwrights—François de Curel, Brieux, Porto-Riche (*qq.v.*)—and to his courageous championing of foreign plays by Ibsen, Tolstoy, Hauptmann (*qq.v.*), *et al.* Soon after, in 1893, Lugné-Poe (*q.v.*) opened his Théâtre de l'Œuvre, which staged many foreign plays and launched several of the boldest French dramatic attempts by Jarry, Crommelynck, Cocteau (*qq.v.*), *et al.* Both the Théâtre de l'Œuvre and Paul Fort's (*q.v.*) Théâtre d'Art, the latter founded in 1891, attempted to revitalize the drama through symbolism. Such a poetical invasion of the stage, though salutary after the realistic excesses of Antoine's Théâtre Libre and the didactic preaching of Curel and Brieux, was bound to be short-lived. Maeterlinck (*q.v.*) was the only dramatist among the symbolists who reached wide popularity: his ethereal dream-like characters, his mechanical suggestion of atmosphere, and the mannerism of his style have been judged severely by later generations. So have the colorful rhetoric and the dazzling verve of Rostand (*q.v.*). Nevertheless *Cyrano de Bergerac* (1897) and *L'Aiglon* (1900) remain the only poetic dramas since Corneille and Hugo which have caught the imagination of the French public at large.

At the turn of the century France was torn by the profound spiritual crisis which resulted from the Dreyfus case. Literature was invaded by political feuds. Historians, political thinkers, moralists, aligned themselves either with the democratic forces which insisted upon extending the liberal gains of the French Revolution farther in the social field or with the conservative elements which preferred traditional order to progress and dreamed nostalgically of the stately hierarchy of prerevolutionary France. In the realm of pure philosophy the years 1900–1913 saw the triumph of Bergsonism. The notions of creative evolution, of the supremacy of intuition over intellectual deduction, of duration as opposed to time, and of the perpetual mobility of a world in which free will was restored and spiritual energy vindicated, corresponded to the aspirations of the generation which had grown up in the days of symbolism. Georges Sorel, Péguy, Thibaudet (*qq.v.*), professional philosophers such as Le Roy (1870–) and Chevalier (1882–), even artistic temperaments like Proust (*q.v.*), came under the spell of the new philosophy, which reshaped and reinforced the deep-seated Pascalian tendencies of French thought. Benda (*q.v.*), a staunch supporter of pure intellectualism, and Maritain (*q.v.*), who discerned a dangerous pantheistic current in a philosophy which seemed to distrust intelligence and Thomist rationalism, were in 1912–1914 the most vigorous opponents of Bergsonism. The other eminent French philosophers of that time were the sociologists Tarde and Durkheim (*qq.v.*). Political thinkers of radical or socialist tendencies were rare in 20th-century France, and the lack was fraught with grave consequences in a country in which ideological doctrines hold much prestige over practical politics. Georges Sorel blended Bergsonism and Marxism in an original system advocating action and violence as more fruitful than theoretical meditation: his socialism has proved influential chiefly on recent totalitarian doctrines. Jaurès (1859–1914), an eloquent orator and a prophetic historian, and Blum (*q.v.*), a subtle literary critic and a refined stylist, failed to develop an original body of thought to support their socialist policies, and this was true also of the champions of "radical" doctrines, Edouard Herriot (1872–, in *Agir*, 1917, and *Créer*, 1919) and the penetrating essayist Alain (pseud. of Emile Chartier, *q.v.*). The first decade of the 20th century was accompanied in France as in other countries (Kipling, Nietzsche and his Pan-Germanist successors, D'Annunzio, *q.v.*) by a revival of nationalist ideas. Barrès, whose group novel *Les Déracinés* had appeared as early as 1897, expounded his romantic religion of the soil, the race, and the dead, in most of his subsequent works. Maurras became the priest of neoclassical paganism in his graceful *Anthinéa* (1901) and of royalist doctrines in his *Enquête sur la monarchie, 1900–1909* (1909; definitive ed., 1924) and in his newspaper, *Action française* (a daily since 1908). His influence on literature has been profound, although his purely literary merits seem to have been much overestimated by partisanship. Bainville (*q.v.*) was the most lucid historian in that group, Léon Daudet (*q.v.*) the most robust and humorous polemist. The cogent but fallacious logic of their reasoning convinced a few critics of dogmatist tendencies, who laid most evils of modern literature to romanticism, itself an offshoot of Rousseauism and revolutionary ideas—Pierre Lasserre (1867–1930), Seillière (*q.v.*), Massis (*q.v.*), and even, more recently, Daniel Halévy (1882–). The greatest essayist of the early 20th century was, however, a thinker more illogical than all these, but nearer to the soul of the people of France and always open to the unpredictable *élan vital* celebrated by Bergson—Charles Péguy. He was at the same time a socialist and a Christian, a fierce patriot, a tireless reasoner, and a mystic. He wrote too much and too hastily and indulged in mannerisms of style which gave a racy flavor to his prose but weakened his poetry. As a literary critic, as a Bergsonian philosopher, as a Catholic interpreter of medieval faith, and as an ardent champion of social justice and Christian charity, Péguy remains to this day the chief representative of France's conflicting aspirations before the First World War.

Those years did not witness any outstanding development in the drama or the novel. The bold innovations of realistic and symbolist drama were followed by a relapse into conventional plays of love, jealousy, and social satire. Tristan Bernard, Capus, Donnay, Flers, and Caillavet (*qq.v.*) were all skillful masters of witty comedy; Henri Lavedan (1859–1940), Bataille (*q.v.*), Sacha Guitry (*q.v.*), and the most expert builder of plots among them, Bernstein (*q.v.*), moved as well as entertained their audiences for several decades. None of their works can lay claim to permanent survival as literature. Courteline (*q.v.*) displayed more racy verve in his ebullient farces with occasionally tragic undertones. The most popular among the French novelists in that decade was Romain Rolland (*q.v.*). His *Jean-Christophe* (1904–1912), however, was more successful in translation with foreign readers than at home: the French have always balked at Rolland's inelegant style, at the loose structure of his serial novel, and at the lack of originality of his psychological revelation. *La Colline inspirée* (1913) by Barrès suffers from just the opposite faults, strained pathos and overwrought prose. The best secondary talents among the novelists who preceded Proust were Renard (*q.v.*), a craftsman in a limited field, Philippe (*q.v.*), who continued and enriched the realistic tradition, Boylesve (*q.v.*), a delicate and modest artist, and Estaunié (*q.v.*), a more moving creator, obsessed with the tragedy of human suffering.

After 1900 poetry was the branch of literature most fertile in bold innovations. Symbolism had been attacked as soon as it seemed to have succeeded in its revolutionary attempts. The different tendencies or "schools" which undertook to replace it all proved abortive or sterile. The Ecole Romane, which advocated a return to classical or medieval models, could boast of only one gifted poet, its standard-bearer, Moréas (*q.v.*). Like most neoclassical tendencies, it mistook prosaic coldness for classical perfection and reiteration of the obvious for lucidity. Régnier and Gérard d'Houville (*q.v.*) reached graceful elegance in their aristocratic evocation of Greek and Alexandrian models, but could not lead the way to a poetical renaissance. Charles Guérin (1873–1907) was a felicitous and often moving successor to the Parnassian tradition; Louis Le Cardonnel (1862–1936) and Alibert (*q.v.*) sang with Vergilian ease and grace of mystic Italy and southern France. Toulet (*q.v.*) blended irony with tenderness in his verse, Fagus (*q.v.*) recaptured a few Villonian accents, and Spire (*q.v.*) proved an original technician and theorist of verse as well as a gifted poet. Two currents opposed symbolism with more success early in the 20th century. The first, naturism, was hardly successful under that name: it advocated the worship of life, reality, nature, and emotion and admired Walt Whitman. It then reappeared as unanimism and celebrated the group and its spiritual roots, the poetry of city life, the sentimental kinship of Europeans, and the fraternity of all men. The inspiration of these poets (Arcos, Chennevière, Martin-Barzun, Duhamel) and their style proved unequal to their great themes. Romains (*q.v.*), who became the theorist of unanimism, never mastered the language of poetry. Vildrac (*q.v.*) wrote more musical verse. The powerful Belgian poet Verhaeren (*q.v.*), Jammes (*q.v.*) in the more truly naïve masterpieces written before he cultivated his simplicity, and Fort in his fresh though monotonous ballads were the true apostles of the return to nature and robust health after the decadent eccentricities—all three were sons and heirs of the symbolist movement. Anna de Noailles (*q.v.*) poured out her tragic and eloquent lamentations on death, old age, and the tortures of love; she celebrated beauty, youth, and nature with pagan fire and romantic exuberance. The form she used lacked originality and subtlety, and her rhetoric lacked the restrained and poignant music which a few readers appreciated in another woman poet, also of foreign origin, Renée Vivien (*q.v.*).

The years 1900–1914 seem today, with the perspective of three decades, to have been dominated by two great poetical figures, Claudel and Apollinaire (*qq.v.*). Claudel is the most powerful Catholic singer ever born in France. As a creator of grandiose images, as a cosmic evocator of a universe all instinct with God's presence, as an eloquent successor to Rimbaud and—little as he would admit it—to Hugo, he stands unrivaled among 20th-century French poets. His best works appeared in 1910 (*Cinq Grandes Odes*) and 1913 (*Cette Heure qui est entre le printemps et l'été*, reprinted in 1931 as *La Cantate à trois voix*). Apollinaire struck a more modest note of melancholy tenderness; he transfigured familiar life with his playful humor and brought the themes and rhythms of the French folk song back into poetry. As an art critic and a champion of all aesthetic innovations he opened most of the new paths of later literary evolution. His friends Salmon, Carco (in *La Bohème et mon cœur*, 1912), and the disconcerting Jacob (*qq.v.*), alternately the humblest mystic and the strangest mystifier, deserve positions beside him.

Suddenly, around 1911–1913, a number of significant works appeared which revealed a true literary renaissance. After a decade of hesitation the new century seemed to have found itself. In painting, Cézanne was belatedly recognized; the "Fauves" and the cubists were struggling for new modes of expression. The Russian ballet had in 1909 revealed a new decorative art, and Stravinsky's *Rites of Spring* (1913) seized the Parisian vanguard with enthusiasm. Dostoevski's (*q.v.*) novels were eagerly read and imitated. The *Nouvelle Revue française* was founded (1909) to voice the emergent literary aspirations, and the theatre of the Vieux Colombier was established (1913). The writers who heralded that literary flowering were in part men in their early 40's who had had to wait 10 or 15 years before gathering their audience and publishing their masterpieces—Proust (*Du côté de chez Swann,* 1913), Gide (*La Porte étroite,* 1909; *Les Caves du Vatican,* 1914), Claudel (*L'Otage,* 1910; *L'Annonce faite à Marie,* 1910), Péguy (*L'Argent, Eve,* 1913). But there were also younger men, born around 1885, who (except for Alain-Fournier, *q.v.,* and Ernest Psichari, killed in the war) were to form in the post-war years one of the most brilliant galaxies of talents France has ever known—Carco, Duhamel, Giraudoux, Jouhandeau, Jouve, Larbaud, Maritain, Roger Martin du Gard, Mauriac, Reverdy, Rivière, Romains, Suarès, Supervielle, Vildrac (*qq.v.*). The First World War matured their talents, inspired the reading public with a freer curiosity, and destroyed their respect for once venerable traditions; it produced a huge crop of war books, only a few of which (those by Duhamel, Maurois, Barbusse, and Dorgelès, *qq.v.*) have any lasting value; but it brought nothing essentially new to French letters, which developed with a fair degree of continuity between 1911 and 1930.

Speed and mobility, the mottoes of the young, were hardly conducive to serene meditation on eternal issues. Philosophical speculation was then in France much less original than purely literary achievement. Bergson remained the great patriarch of French philosophy; his last great work appeared only in 1932. Maritain alone rivals him in personal prestige. His austere advocacy of Thomist Catholicism, his speculations on the problems of free will, knowledge, ethics, education, government, and of a humanism turned toward God, and, even more, his charity and his understanding of art drew many literary and artistic figures to him. The influence of other French thinkers penetrated little outside university circles. Léon Brunschvicg (1869–1944), Lucien Lévy-Bruhl (1857–1939), and Maurice Blondel (1861–) have been the most eminent, and, among their successors, Etienne Gilson (1884–), Gaston Bachelard (1884–), Louis Lavelle, and Jean Wahl (1888–). Two lyrical essayists, Faure (*q.v.*) and Suarès, deserve to rank among the most versatile and occasionally the most penetrating ever produced in the country of Montaigne and Pascal. Henri Focillon (1881–1943) applied his universal and illuminating meditations to art criticism and the philosophy of history. André Siegfried (1875–) and Lucien Romier (1885–1944) have treated of political and economic subjects with literary charm. Literary criticism was practiced by many keen minds, often with brilliance, seldom with the unchallenged authority which critics of earlier eras had possessed. Weekly articles by Souday (*q.v.*), Jaloux (*q.v.*), Henry Bidou (1873–), Lucien Dubech (1882–1941), André Thérive (1891–), while undeniably influential on readers and writers, have proved little more than ephemeral pronouncements. Lalou (*q.v.*), Benjamin Crémieux (1888–1944), and Léon Pierre-Quint (1895–) have done more to mold opinion on living literature. Next to the original "criticism of creators," that of Gide and Valéry (*qq.v.*), the three most important critics of the last 20 years have been Rivière, Du Bos (*q.v.*), and Thibaudet. Bremond (*q.v.*) in his *Histoire littéraire du sentiment religieux en France* (11 vols., 1916–1933) and Charles Andler (1866–1933) in his *Nietzsche* (6 vols., 1921–1930) have come nearest in our time to Sainte-Beuve's encyclopedic *Port-Royal.* André Chevrillon (1864–), Emile Legouis (1861–1937), and Louis Cazamian (1877–) have been Taine's worthiest successors as interpreters of English literature.

The novel received the lion's share in the French literary production from 1911 to 1930. Proust towers above all other novelists of this century because of his power to create life, the depth of his psychological penetration, the originality of his technique, and above all the poetical magic of his prose. The other two novelists of his generation, Gide and Colette (*q.v.*), fell far short of his supreme eminence. Gide is a very great prose writer and perhaps the most characteristic man of letters of France in the last 30 years. His truly Goethian curiosity and sympathy and the purity of his art were, however, ill suited to the novel; his shorter *récits* remain more moving than his ambitious attempts in the manner of Stendhal and Dostoevski. Colette can exquisitely express the world of form and color, of keen sensations, and of feminine emotions, but lacks power to evoke more complex or less purely subjective characters. The most remarkable of the novelists who achieved their main success after the First World War is Mauriac. His intensely Catholic view of life, the provincial atmosphere of his tales of sin and remorse, the absence of social conflicts in his books, and his superbly classical technique have not yet won for him an adequate appreciation outside of France. Jouhandeau, at times hauntingly tragic, and Bernanos (*q.v.*), addicted to imaginative eloquence and too often unequal to his best achievement, are also able novelists of Catholic inspiration. There have been several adepts in the group novel, less traditional in technique and more preoccupied with the Balzacian delineation of an age or society. Romains is the most ambitious of all, and the length of his *Les Hommes de bonne volonté* (1932–) has stretched his creative invention to the breaking point. He knows, analyzes, explains, and organizes life but seldom re-creates it. Duhamel succeeded in conjuring up a compelling character in Salavin, but has since failed to endow his *Chronique des Pasquier* (1933–) with intensity. Roger Martin du Gard related the adventures of *Les Thibault* (1922–1940) with more convincing reality, an unobtrusive technical mastery, and a fluid style, although he cannot be compared, for sheer imaginative force, with the very great masters, Balzac, Flaubert, Zola, Proust. His earlier *Jean Barois* (1913) reached greater heights of intellectual tragedy. René Béhaine (1880–), who was among the first moderns to undertake a saga of the contemporary world, failed to win an audience for his *Histoire d'une société* (12 vols., 1908–1939). Other novelists of the same generation worthy of mention were Jean Richard Bloch (1884–), author of Jewish novels inspired by a robust liberal faith; the Tharaud brothers (*q.v.*), skillful storytellers; André Demaison (1885–), the author of forceful exotic tales on French African colonies; Mac-Orlan (*q.v.*), whose adventure novels retained psychology and style; Pourrat (*q.v.*) and the powerful Swiss writer Ramuz (*q.v.*), who have renovated provincial and peasant fiction. Alain-Fournier had written, one year before the First World War, in which he soon lost his life, an original tale of delicate fantasy, *Le Grand Meaulnes*, which was to be widely but vainly imitated in the post-war years, when the character of the "adolescent" invaded French fiction. Radiguet (*q.v.*), who died at 20, seemed to promise a brilliant career as a skillful and cynical adapter of a Stendhalian tradition. The time-honored French psychological novel was attempted by many in the age of Proust and Gide. Larbaud will probably remain as the most ingenious and touching of those *minores*. Lacretelle (*q.v.*) began with promise but failed to shake off some intellectual coldness, and Maurois, after an adroitly constructed but unconvincing novel, *Climats* (1928), struck a happier vein and a wider success in biography and journalistic essays. Giraudoux and Morand (*q.v.*) will probably provide the future historian of the years 1920–1930 with the most valuable illustrations of the manners and fashions of the age. Giraudoux embodied with fresh charm the perennial French tradition of *préciosité* and sketched a few vivid *jeunes filles* among the gallery of middle-aged women and corrupt young men almost exclusively portrayed in the post-war novel. Morand launched a striking fashion with his abrupt and exotic stories (*Ouvert la nuit*, 1922; *Fermé la nuit*, 1923); he then failed, like many of his brilliant contemporaries, in his attempts at self-renewal, though he drew, in *Air indien* (1932), a striking picture of the South American continent seen "with the eye on the object." Luc Durtain (1881–), after a short-lived success as a superficial novelist of California, wrote a keen and colorful travel book in *Le Globe sous le bras* (1936), which, along with Morand's stories and Faure's lucid analyses, bore evidence of the enlarged cosmopolitan curiosity of post-war France.

The 10 years which followed the First World War are probably the most brilliant the French stage has known for a century. Much credit should go to the impulse given in 1913, and again in 1920, by the Vieux Colombier of Copeau (*q.v.*). The earlier courageous attempts of Antoine, Lugné-Poe, and Gémier were resumed by him with more ardent faith and keener artistic touch; innovations borrowed from great foreign producers (Stanislavsky, Gordon Craig, Reinhardt) were introduced. To technical improvements in the staging, interpreting, and acting of plays, Copeau added an austere insistence upon sincerity, honest workmanship, and art. He avoided the two common pitfalls of vanguard theatres, intellectual snobbery and disconcerting strangeness. Suggestion, rather than realistic illusion, became the motto of his dramatic performances; they aimed at enhancing the poetical virtue of the text. Copeau's lessons proved lastingly fruitful, although he had decided, in 1924, to close the Vieux Colombier. The French dramatic renaissance of the 1920's owed much to his example. The Comédie Française and even the commercial theatres underwent the influence of his reforms. His truest followers were, however, in the best literary theatres of the last 20 years, led by Baty, Dullin, Jouvet, Pitoëff (*qq.v.*), André Obey, *et al.* The most substantial result of that dramatic revival was to achieve a reconciliation between the stage and literature, which would have been unthinkable in the 19th century. The most powerful French dramatist today, though not the most easily staged, is one of the loftiest poets—Claudel. The most original modern tragedies have been written by the most refined of the modern *précieux*, Giraudoux. Romains contrived ingenious comedies as well as elaborate works of fiction. Most of the finest writers of the age (Gide and Rolland before 1914, then Mauriac, Martin du Gard, Duhamel, Giono, *q.v.*), with varied success, brought the homage of their talent to the stage. Cocteau, after Claudel and Giraudoux, displayed some originality in modernizing old tragic themes (in *Antigone, Orphée, La Machine infernale*). Among other attempts at tragedy, those of Lenormand (*q.v.*) utilized the revelations of abnormal psychology and psychoanalysis with ponderous and humorless didacticism. Raynal (*q.v.*), while addicted to declamatory displays of virtuosity, is the author of a powerful psychological drama, *Le Maître de son cœur* (acted in 1920). Simon Gantillon (1890–) in *Maya* (1924) and Passeur (*q.v.*) in several recent plays showed uncommon gifts of stark force and ingenious structure. The attempts of Ghéon and Marcel (*qq.v.*) to revive a Catholic or philosophical drama have been more courageous than successful. The most original note in the drama since the First World War is a delicate blending of humor and poetry, of sentiment tempered with discreet mockery; brutal realism and melodramatic utterances have given way to delicate nuances and an art of suggestion, often through use of "silence." Even more than Achard or Sarment (*qq.v.*), whose early promise is still unfulfilled, J. J. Bernard (*q.v.*) and Vildrac were the most representative of those post-war playwrights who added a strain of Shakespearean fantasy to the tradition of Marivaux and Musset. Pure comedy, which Molière called more difficult than any other kind of writing, has had few adepts in the disillusioned post-war years. Emile Mazáud (1884–) and Crommelynck, on an old and apparently inexhaustible Gallic theme, Denys Amiel (*q.v.*) and André Obey, Pellerin (*q.v.*), in one or two original attempts, and lately Pagnol (*q.v.*) have produced the best recent outbursts of French laughter.

The brightest star in the poetical firmament after the First World War was that of Valéry. While his great contemporary Claudel wrote the best of his lyrical work before 1914, Valéry had been silent for 20 years before he gave the world his masterpiece, *La Jeune Parque*, in 1917. A slender volume, *Charmes*, followed in 1922. In the best of those poems he rivaled Racine and La Fontaine in pure and fluid music, Mallarmé in deliberate and elliptic condensation. They united with miraculous harmony the pangs of the intellect and the thrills of the flesh; only the heart at times remained unmoved. A felicitous fusion of classical, Parnassian, and symbolist elements, Valéry's poetry could not well be imitated. Expressed in a terse epigrammatic prose worthy of the 18th century, the poet's theories, which banished inspiration and the unconscious from artistic creation, fortunately kept pale imitators at a distance. St.-J. Perse (*q.v.*), whose strange, sparkling jewels dazzled T. S. Eliot and Archibald MacLeish, is much nearer to Claudel than to Valéry and even nearer at times to a more musical and more fluid Parnassian tradition. The Lithuanian Milosz (*q.v.*) wrote moving poems. Fargue (*q.v.*) transfigured with humor the familiar mysteries of modern life, and Yvan Goll (1891–) recaptured the charm of old ballads. Cocteau, in his verse as in his plays, novels, and lucid critical essays, is alternately cutting a boyish prank and repressing a bitter sob. There are three true poets, born around 1885, who may rank in future estimates as great poets, second only to Claudel and Valéry in the post-war years—Jouve, Reverdy, and Supervielle. Jouve, after writing clear and direct poems inspired by horror of war and pity for suffering, became engrossed in religious mysticism; his poetical fragments are sometimes rugged and dry, sometimes hauntingly mysterious, as if written by a French brother of Blake or Hölderlin. Reverdy, after sharing the literary nihilism of dada, developed a very original manner, untouched by publicity and coteries, in *Les Epaves du ciel* (1924) and *Ferraille* (1937). In his rendering of restrained emotion and of metaphysical or religious anxiety he is probably one of the most authentic of recent French poets and at times almost Baudelairian. Supervielle is the least revolutionary and difficult of the moderns. His themes are friendship, love, family affections, childhood memories, but also cosmic visions of oceans and planets gravitating through a poet's dreams. A profound philosophical emotion aroused by man's solitude in the universe permeates his finest volume, *La Fable du monde* (1938). None of these poets achieved the reputation won by the surrealists in the era between the two world wars.

The surrealist revolt was fiercely logical in its madness, scornful of traditional moral and aesthetic conventions, skillful in its organized publicity. In spite of its obviously preposterous claims, it constituted the marching wing of French literature after 1920 and recruited the largest number of genuine talents. Its beginnings are often traced back to dada, founded in Zurich in 1916, a radical revision of the essential literary values and a challenge to all rational processes of thought. Yet no first-rate figure emerged from dadaism, although its founder, Tristan Tzara (1896–), made some curious experiments with poetry and one of its members, Ribemont-Dessaignes (1884–), showed promise as a novelist and essayist. In the same year, 1916, in Nantes, independently from the abortive dada movement, the future founder of surrealism, Breton (*q.v.*), met Jacques Vaché (1895–1919) who, though he did not condescend to write anything himself, seems to have possessed fierce originality. The bitter nihilism of Vaché rejected all the traditional elements of Western culture, except for a very few prophets of the new vision, Rimbaud, Lautréamont (*q.v.*), Jarry, Apollinaire. Vaché committed suicide in 1919, as two other members of the surrealist group did later, Jacques Rigaut (1929) and René Crevel (1935). Surrealism (*q.v.*) took shape officially in 1924 under the guidance and strict ferule of Breton, assisted in his early manifestoes and experiments by Soupault, Aragon, and Eluard (*qq.v.*). The original affiliates have since broken with Breton's uncompromising orthodoxy, and new recruits have been added, chiefly from the ranks of painters. The movement became international in character: young English, American, German, and Spanish painters and poets have applied and developed its principles with originality. In its negative aspect surrealism was an all embracing revolt against the whole legacy of the past, aesthetic, moral, even political and social. Hence its provoking audacity, helped somewhat by Freud's discoveries, in doing away with the moral ban on subconscious and erotic visions and also its subsequent and often stormy association with Communist or Trotskyist doctrines, which caused several surrealist schisms. From 1930 on, however, it was clear that surrealism had gone beyond its negative stage and had grown into a constructive attempt to annex new provinces to psychology and literature. The main achievements of the surrealists, often disfigured by childish stunts, may be summarized as: opening the oneiric domain to poetry; breaking the shackles of logic and releasing the forces of imagination, however irrational and humorously absurd the results might be; recovering the purity of a child's vision of the world and the illogical freshness of a spontaneous flow of images; reaching the "super-real" state in which the subjective and the objective, the ego and the universe, are merged in a higher synthesis. In spite of an excess of obstinate reasoning in its very madness and of questionable claims to scientific validity, surrealism appears today a romantic aspiration toward greater sincerity in literature (man's subconscious being less prone to lying or self-deception than his rationalizing ego) and toward liberation of imagination.

The best of recent French poetry derives from the surrealist impulse. Breton, though no mean poet, is chiefly a clear and brilliant master of French prose in his doctrinal manifestoes, his graceful novel, *Nadja* (1928), and the original psychological speculations of *L'Amour fou* (1937). Eluard is the poet of love, conceived as a pathetic struggle against solitude, an aspiration toward purity, and the cosmic center of the universe. His delicate music and his fresh and graceful gift for coining ever renewed images have made him the most widely admired and imitated younger French poet today. Aragon, though apparently a more energetic temperament, is more plastic than Breton or Eluard: his successive works reflect the play of varied fashions or influences. In his early novels a master of satire and a virtuoso of truculent prose, after the Second World War began he suddenly won great popular acclaim through his eloquent restatement of traditional themes—love, the tragedy of war, the bitterness of defeat, patriotic fervor (*Le Crève-Cœur,* 1941; *Les Yeux d'Elsa,* 1943). Raymond Roussel (1877–1933), an original precursor, and Benjamin Péret (1899–) are the other outstanding surrealist poets. In fiction, surrealism has not produced in France works to be ranked with the German novels of Kafka (*q.v.*); Raymond Queneau and Julien Gracq are the only two promising younger novelists who may be attached to the group.

The year 1930 seems to have closed an era of inflation and false security in Europe. The dreams of a permanent Franco-German understanding were shattered; economic and political problems loomed large after the fallacious prosperity of the years 1920–1930. France, the last country to feel the blows of the world-wide depression, was the first to repudiate the literary fashions of the post-war years. Avid newcomers to the world of letters published in literary weeklies manifestoes demanding a new appraisal of the legacy of their elders; about 1930 a few striking works by Céline (*q.v.*), Giono, Malraux (*q.v.*), and Saint Exupéry (*q.v.*) ushered in a new period which, for lack of a better name, may be called "the second pre-war era." The years 1930–1939 discarded some of the more superficial features of the preceding literature: the literary inflation which had led to brief, repetitious volumes devoid of solid content; the excessive intellectuality of many post-war novels; the fashion for adolescent characters deficient in will power and addicted to selfish analysis of their feelings or of their inability to feel; the escapism which had inspired endless travel books, nonchalant reveries, and the subtle games of a new *préciosité*. The new period is marked by the ardent interest taken by men of letters in political and social problems; Gide led the way, with Malraux, Céline, Chamson (*q.v.*), and Drieu La Rochelle (*q.v.*) soon following. On all sides recent writers aspired to a closer communion with the people and repudiated the complacent self-analysis of their predecessors. They sought a new faith and tried to mold a better world or a better man, to build work more solid than the ephemeral volumes of the previous years. The men of this new literary generation, born around 1895–1900, found themselves at 30 or 35. Much may be expected of it, after the tragic experience of the Second World War.

In the novel the outstanding representatives of this generation are six men of striking originality. Céline, the oldest of the group, stands in sharp contrast to Proust and Gide. His power, brutal and truculent like that of a modern Rabelais, marred by mannerism and blatant crudities, is nevertheless haunting. The *Voyage au bout de la nuit* (1932) is a Goyesque nightmare; but his subsequent writing fell far below that startling début. Giono, born in 1895, revealed his full stature in his early masterpieces (*Un de Baumugnes,* 1929; *Jean le bleu,* 1932). With him French fiction has risen to epic heights and recovered a healthy contact with the earth and simple, healthy people. *Le Chant du monde* (1934) and, in parts, *Que ma joie demeure* (1935) are among the most powerful novels of the century, but excessive eagerness to deliver an ideological message has detracted from the later achievement of this spiritual son of Rousseau and Zola. Montherlant (*q.v.*), slightly younger than Giono, began his literary career much earlier and dazzled his contemporaries by his magnificent style and a boyish, cynical insolence alternating with sincere yearning for heroism. His novels are disappointing, but an anthology of his best reflective passages would constitute one of the finest examples of the passionate romanticism concealed behind the bitter dryness of recent French literature. Malraux, born in 1901, has conquered new domains for French fiction: he fled from provincial life and threadbare erotic themes to Asiatic revolutions and European civil wars. His novels, composed with a bold and harsh technique, scornful of traditional rules and even of the average reader's demands, are obsessed by the tragic solitude of the modern hero and his desperate attempts to find a faith for which to live and die. A similar groping search for a faith gives a spiritual meaning to the works of Saint Exupéry. His tales of an airman's life reveal an epic moralist and a creator of dazzling images. Julien Green (*q.v.*), born, like Saint Exupéry, in 1900, has, alone in this group, retained the traditional form of the French novel, swift, condensed, violent, like classical tragedy; his themes are lurid nightmares of terror and hate, at times too close to the mystery story to be fully convincing. Next to these outstanding names, many more testify to the continued vitality of the French novel: Chamson, also born in 1900, is a racy portrayer of peasants in the Cévennes and a refined artist, especially in *Le Crime des justes* (1929). Roger Vercel (1894–), Kessel (*q.v.*), and Edouard Peisson have written skillful tales of sea and air adventures. Paul Nizan (1905–1940), a vigorous novelist and essayist attracted by revolutionary doctrines, was killed in the battle of France. The early tales of Jean Sartre (*q.v.*) blended cynicism and odd metaphysical anxiety (*La Nausée,* 1938; *Le Mur,* 1939). Giono's imaginative or mythical realism has allured many of the younger novelists, while old-fashioned realism counted few adepts in recent French literature. In 1930 a new group headed by André Thérive (1891–) and Léon Lemonnier (1890–) attracted some attention under the name of populism; they advocated a new naturalism, concerned with the common people and the working man instead of the bourgeois or aristocratic heroes of Gide, Mauriac, and Proust. But populism failed to produce any masterpieces. Dabit (*q.v.*) gave the best examples of realistic fiction. Guilloux (*q.v.*) in *Le Sang noir* (1935) displayed, with less power but more sincerity, some of the satiric verve and social bitterness of Céline. Henry Poulaille (1896–) and Malaquais (*q.v.*) have not yet risen to their stature or proved that they can avoid the pitfall of too many realistic novels—lack of art and style and monotonous sordidness of subject.

That same generation born around 1900 has had a number of gifted essayists and critics, but none has yet voiced its aspirations or expressed its original message with undisputed authority. Drieu la Rochelle, whose early works promised much and whose short stories in *La Comédie de Charleroi* (1934) are among the best of their decade, failed to reach a consistent doctrine in politics or literature. Ramon Fernandez (1894–1944) also disappointed those who had expected from him some of the best philosophical criticism of his age. Marcel Arland (1899–) has proved most sensitive to literary values in critical essays on the novel, and Jean Prévost (*q.v.*) is often lucid and sturdy in his intellectual approach. Jean Cassou (1897–) and Rolland de Renéville (1903–) are, with the two Swiss critics Albert Béguin and Marcel Raymond (1897–), the best interpreters of contemporary poetry. Among the younger group Roger Caillois (1913–), René Etiemble (1909–), and Edmonde Magny have shown acumen and courage in their critical judgment. The gifts of Thierry-Maulnier (pseud. of Jacques Talagrand, 1908–) are admirable when political partisanship and youthful paradoxes have not spoiled them.

In the drama Salacrou (*q.v.*) and Jean Anouilh have been the chief representatives of the same generation along with the few dramatists already mentioned who were recognized before 1930—Achard, Pagnol, and Sarment.

In poetry the leaders of surrealism belong to the same age group, and their lasting achievement, following their early revolt, has been effected since 1930. Their influence, often indirect, has left few recent poets untouched: the Belgian Henry Michaux (1899–) is probably the most brilliant of their followers. The tradition of their compatriots, who contributed several leading talents to French symbolism, has been maintained by three other Belgian poets, Eric de Haulleville (1900–1941), Odilon Jean Périer (1901–1928), and Alain Bosquet (1920–), the first an ambitious lyricist, the second moving in his restraint and simplicity, the third an original adapter of the fluid, erotic imagery of surrealism. Audiberti (*q.v.*) is more eloquent and sonorous; his astounding verbal gift is dangerously reminiscent of Hugo's facility and excesses. Georges Pelorson (1908–) attempted in *Connaissance* (1937) to load six-syllable verse with philosophical meaning. La Tour du Pin (*q.v.*), on the eve of the Second World War, was acclaimed the most pleasing and suavely musical of the younger poets: his themes and manner were the most traditional of his generation. In the suffering which followed the German invasion of 1940, French poetry suddenly reached a wide public. Aragon, Eluard, Jouve, rediscovered universal subjects and reintegrated appeal to emotion in their art. Two other poets, Pierre Emmanuel and Lanza Del Vasto, won the audience of the French readers.

At the beginning of the Second World War, French literature, although accused, as it has been regularly for the last hundred years, of being obscure, morbid, decadent, and futile, was characterized by hardy, wholesome qualities. It was at the same time the most traditional in Europe in some aspects and the most revolutionary in many of its experiments. During the tragic years which followed the defeat of 1940, the French people found much comfort in the continued vitality of their literature.

The influence of the war on French letters cannot yet be fully assessed: it was in a sense negative, since it eliminated a number of writers who died between 1940 and 1945 (Giraudoux, Max Jacob, Romain Rolland, Saint Exupéry, Valéry) and others who had thoroughly discredited themselves through collaboration with the enemy and lack of moral courage (Céline, Chardonne, A. de Châteaubriant, Drieu la Rochelle, Maurras, Morand). The war years also created a gulf between the writers admired in the 30's and the youth of France which had grown under the tragic stress of national humiliation and of heroic fight for freedom. Gide, Claudel, even Valéry, have ceased being the masters of the younger generation; Romains counts few admirers, Giraudoux's last play (*Sodome et Gomorrhe,* 1943) was but a weaker repetition of his former manner, Montherlant and Giono had signally failed to apply during times of misery the message that they had preached in happier days. But literature continued active, both underground and in the open, and when France was finally liberated in 1944, the vitality of her letters astonished foreign observers. Some pre-war writers had grown in stature: Mauriac through his courageous role in rallying French Catholics against the clerical hypocrisy of Vichy and through his recent works, notably his play, *Les Mal Aimés* (1945); Chamson, who fought in the *maquis* and in the regular army and penned a vivid picture of life during the enemy occupation in *Le Puits des miracles* (1945); Aragon, who followed his war poetry with a brilliant novel of reminiscences of his youth, *Aurélien* (1945); and above all Malraux. Through his active fight against tyranny and through his *Les Noyers de l'Altenburg* (1943), which contained splendid passages, as well as through his earlier works reread in the light of subsequent events, Malraux appeared as the precursor of the strongest movement of the years 1944–1946.

This movement is often termed existentialism. Its starting point is philosophical, and some of its abstruse doctrines appeal to youth through their very obscurity. The phenomenology of the German Husserl, the metaphysical speculations of two other Germans, Jaspers and Heidegger, and the tragic anguish of the 19th-century Dane, Kierkegaard, have been integrated by these French men of letters into a strange system which proclaims the essential absurdity of life, denounces reason as powerless, rejects the easy refuge of the traditional faith in God and immortality. These negations are accompanied by a fierce determination to endow life with a man-made significance, since it has for them no transcendent meaning, and by the full acceptance of solidarity with other men in misery and in the conquest of freedom. Out of their very pessimism, clearly inspired by the conditions of life in Europe since 1940, these younger French writers emerge with the will to transform the world around them through their pens and through their actions. They reject the ivory-tower conception of the artist's role and maintain that literature is no fancy activity independent of politics, but is bound up with the struggle for liberty and fraternity. Sartre is the acknowledged leader of the new school: two plays, a huge treatise of philosophy, a fictional trilogy, *Les Chemins de la Liberté,* and many articles written since 1940 bear witness to the versatility and the originality of his talent. Beside him, though holding divergent philosophical views, is Albert Camus (*q.v.*), born in a suburb of Algiers, who, after a hard struggle for life and the practice of varied professions, revealed himself as a prose writer of eminence in *Noces* (1939), then in an ideological essay, *Le Mythe de Sisyphe* (1942), in which the Greek myth was reinterpreted as a proud vindication of man's fate against the absurd decrees of the gods, and in a baffling novel, *L'Etranger* (1942). His two plays, *Le Malentendu* and *Caligula* (both 1944), are, in spite of an unconventional and faulty dramatic technique, striking achievements. Camus, even more than Sartre, has proved a bold leader of public opinion through his articles in the newspaper *Combat.* Simone de Beauvoir is another gifted member of the group: her novel, *Le Sang des autres* (1945), which illustrates the thesis of man's responsibility in society, and her play, *Les Bouches inutiles* (1945), have brought existentialist ideas within the reach of a wider public. Michel Leyris and Raymond Queneau in the essay and the novel, Maurice Blanchot as essayist and critic, Anouilh in several plays, Elsa Triolet in the long short story (*Le Premier Accroc coûte 200 francs,* 1944), and Romain Gary, whose first book, *Education européenne* (1945), strikingly evoked the horrors of the Polish underground hunted by the Germans, stand foremost among the new writers of talent in France. Francis Ponge, Loys Masson, and Pierre Seghers are the younger poets who, together with Aragon, Eluard, Emmanuel, and Michaux, promise to assure an era of continued fertility to French poetry. In all its manifestations, recent literature seems today more concerned with philosophical issues and with probing the meaning of life than it had been after the First World War; it is also more socially minded, eager to enrich its substance through communion with other men and through a will to act which repudiates the complacent aestheticism of previous generations. At the same time, it has apparently emerged from the years of distress with no regimentation of the minds: the number and the variety of its individual talents bid fair to make the French writings of tomorrow fully worthy of the literary accomplishments of yesterday.

See: D. Parodi, *La Philosophie contemporaine en France* (1919); B. Crémieux, *XXe siècle* (1924); R. Lalou, *Histoire de la littérature française contemporaine* (1922; enlarged ed., Vol. I, 1941, Vol. II, 1940); I. Benrubi, *Contemporary Thought of France* (1926); John Palmer, *Studies in the Contemporary Theatre* (1927); E. Sée, *Le Théâtre français contemporain* (1928); Edmund Wilson, *Axel's Castle* (1931); R. Michaud, *Vingtième Siècle; an Anthology* (1933) and *Modern Thought and Literature in France* (1934); Marcel Raymond, *De Baudelaire au surréalisme* (1933); G. Truc, *Tableau du XXe siècle,* Vol. III: *La Pensée* (1933); C. Sénéchal, *Les Grands Courants de la littérature française contemporaine* (1934); R. Brasillach, *Animateurs de théâtre* (1936); A. Thibaudet, *Histoire de la littérature française de 1789 à nos jours* (1936); H. Peyre, *Hommes et œuvres du vingtième siècle* (1938); G. E. Lemaitre, *From Cubism to Surrealism in French Literature* (1941); P. Brodin, *Les Ecrivains français de l'entre-deux-guerres* (1942) and *Maîtres et témoins de l'entre-deux-guerres* (1943); M. E. Coindreau, *La Farce est jouée* (1942); S. A. Rhodes, ed., *The Contemporary French Theater* (1942).

H. P.

French naturalism can be defined as a "school" only in most general terms. For its outspokenness and brutality, for its usual (though not exclusive) penchant toward the drab, the vulgar, and the pathological, it strongly resembles naturalism in other countries (*see* German naturalism). Its basic philosophy, reminiscent of Locke, Condillac, and Diderot, holds that there is nothing in the human mind which does not emanate from the senses. By way of consequence, metaphysics are brushed aside, together with psychology as an introspective and analytical instrument of discovery; art, in particular, is but the factual reproduction of the sensation as experienced. The naturalists claim to have fallen heirs to one of the oldest French traditions—that of common sense and matter-of-factness, in short that of realism, as it runs from the fabliau and the farce through Rabelais and Molière to Balzac and Flaubert (*q.v.*). All such views are too sweeping not to require discussion and sometimes contradiction. The healthy hue of French realism is more often than not at variance with naturalist morbidity. Balzac's mysticism and Flaubert's insistence on *le réel écrit* (*i.e.,* on an aesthetic transposition of reality) prove incompatible, if not always with naturalist practice, at least with naturalist theory.

Except for these broad definitions, the naturalist school never boasted a unified doctrine. It would be possible, of course, to build a case for Emile Zola (*q.v.*) as its leader and the *Rougon-Macquart* as its towering achievement. After all, it was Zola who first appropriated the word naturalism (in the preface to the second edition of *Thérèse Raquin,* May, 1868) and came nearest to making it a rallying motto for all those who sought "sincerity in art," namely, a free and total expression of themselves and their beliefs, unhampered by the rules of public taste or the laws of conformism. He befriended Cézanne and Manet and defended them at a time when their paintings were the butt of contempt and derision. He enlisted for himself the moral support of Flaubert, despite their violent differences on artistic grounds. His best novel, and one of his boldest, *L'Assommoir* (1877), appeared in the midst of the political reaction then rampant under the name of "moral order" and touched off a wide "naturalist campaign" against bigotry and intolerance. The same year Zola began gathering in his country house at Médan, near Paris, a group of five—and as yet unknown—disciples, Paul Alexis, Joris Karl Huysmans, Guy de Maupassant (*qq.v.*), Henry Céard (1851–1924), and Léon Hennique (1852–1935). The publication of *Les Soirées de Médan* (1880), a collection of six stories relating to the Franco-Prussian War (one by each member, including Maupassant's "Boule de Suif"), bears striking proof of Zola's ascendancy and stamps the Médan group as the most closely knit of all naturalist associations.

This, however, is only part of the general picture. From the very beginning two trends at least had been apparent within naturalism. Zola's tendency, as is shown at greater length elsewhere in this volume, was to make literature an adjunct of science. In a clumsy sort of way he took to himself Taine's (*q.v.*) determinism and extracted from Claude Bernard's *Introduction à l'étude de la médecine expérimentale* (1865) his own, rather extravagant theory of the experimental novel. Yet the depressingly materialistic atmosphere of this type of novel, or its pseudoscientific method, should not hide the fact that it conveys a broadly humanitarian message. It has a political, democratic tinge—one is reminded of Zola's pronouncement, "The Republic will be naturalist, or it will not *be";* it is optimistic, yes, optimistic as it reveals an almost childish confidence in the possibility of immediate reform and progress. Maupassant said one day that naturalism was a reaction against the verbal and mental incontinence of Victor Hugo. This may be true in terms of Maupassant's works, but there is no denying the link which exists between the *Rougon-Macquart* and, say, *Les Misérables.* On the other hand, in those early days when Zola was still groping in the dark, the literary team of Edmond and Jules de Goncourt (*q.v.*) had given what is generally considered the first true sample of a naturalistic novel, *Germinie Lacerteux* (1864). Rich and independent, connoisseurs and art collectors, attracted to the rare, the exotic, the exquisite, the two brothers stood in strong contrast to the rugged, plebeian Emile Zola. Describing themselves as historians and chroniclers rather than scientists, they probed social evils, but with considerably less gusto, and delved into "popular" subjects, but far more detachedly, than the inventor of the experimental novel. Throughout the course of naturalism the aristocratic reserve and dilettantism of Edmond de Goncourt (Jules died prematurely, in 1870), emulated in many respects by Alphonse Daudet (*q.v.*), was to exert a restraining and somewhat dissolvent influence. In 1885 Edmond opened the doors of his "grenier d'Auteuil" (his studio at Auteuil, a Paris district) to a host of young writers and artists who might otherwise have found their way to the Médan cottage. He and Alphonse Daudet in 1887 inspired, rather underhandedly, the manifesto of five newcomers, all naturalists, Lucien Descaves (*q.v.*), J. H. Rosny *aîné* (1856–1940), Paul Bonnetain (1858–1899), Paul Margueritte (1860–1918), and Gustave Guiches (1860–1935), against Zola's novel, *La Terre* ("Manifeste des Cinq," *Figaro,* August 18, 1887). Finally, Edmond's will provided for the foundation of the Goncourt Academy, which was to become the logical repository of naturalism, but from which Zola was significantly excluded. As things happened, Zola died before the formal inauguration of the Academy in 1903.

Hovering between Zola and Goncourt, devoted to both but seldom in full agreement with either, the younger naturalists soon evolved a philosophy of their own. Age, here, was a decisive factor. Those who had been 20 or thereabouts in the fateful years 1870–1871 felt particularly the terrible impact of the Franco-Prussian War and of the communistic uprising (*la Commune*) which followed. Not without a certain amount of literary pose, they thought of themselves—we have seen this phenomenon repeated and amplified in more recent times—as a "lost generation." Pessimism pervaded their writings. It was tempered no longer by Zola's unshakable faith in science and the future, by Daudet's indulgent smile, or by Edmond de Goncourt's escapist propensities; it was stark pessimism, sheer gloom and despair, a deep sense of utter futility. Schopenhauer had played little or no part in Zola's formation; but these people read him with delight and reveled in such adages of his as "Life is a pendulum which swings from Sorrow to Ennui." To cite a few outstanding examples, Huysmans's novelette *A vau-l'eau* (1882), in which the above maxim is quoted, many of Maupassant's short stories, Henry Céard's *Une Belle Journée* (1881), Georges Darien's antimilitaristic novel *Biribi* (1890), Jules Renard's (*q.v.*) *Poil de carotte* (1894)—such works forced down the reader's throat some of the bitterest "slices of life" that he ever swallowed. From the novel, where naturalism flourished first and foremost, this disillusioned spirit crept upon the stage. Earlier attempts at creating a naturalist theatre had been obscured and doomed to failure by the immense vogue of Alexandre Dumas *fils*, exponent of the "thesis play." Thesis plays represent at best a formula of prenaturalistic vintage. Dumas himself, however, not unlike Flaubert, came to admire at least the courage and independence of his would-be successors. Through his good offices Henry Becque's (*q.v.*) *Les Corbeaux* was admitted to the Comédie Française (1882). This somber work, many offerings of the Théâtre Libre (*see* Antoine, André), Octave Mirbeau's (*q.v.*) dramatic masterpiece, *Les Affaires sont les affaires* (1903), testify to the strange vitality of that pessimist aesthetic which, in the words of the critic Rémy de Gourmont (*q.v.*), "could hardly go farther, or lower, without falling into sheer caricature." This wholesale demoralization Paul Bourget (*q.v.*) saw fit to denounce in *Le Disciple* (1889); away from it finally fled a number of naturalists, some, like Huysmans, into the fold of religion.

Naturalism in general may best be summarized in negative terms. It is a revolt—a bourgeois revolt, by the way, long immune from any trace of Marxism—against the bourgeoisie as it had emerged from half a century of growing prosperity, as it was going to appear at the time of the Dreyfus affair, dull and self-seeking, vain and hypocritical, full of these ready-made ideas which Flaubert had so mercilessly satirized, socially conservative and reactionary in politics, attached to everything "academic" and conventional in art and literature, from the snobbish novels of Octave Feuillet and the spectacular dramas of Victorien Sardou (*q.v.*) to the stilted paintings of Bouguereau. Against this vast bourgeois complacency—to define it in other days the romanticists had used the word *resistance*—naturalism hurls itself, a minority *movement*, noisy to be sure, but a minority movement nevertheless, curiously conscious, because of this fact, of its affinities with other "vanguard" manifestations, such as positivism in philosophy, Darwinian or Spencerian evolutionism in science, symbolism in poetry, realism or impressionism in the fine arts. In this challenge thrown at the society in which they lived, a challenge which they strove to make as blunt and shocking as possible, whether it be constructive (*e.g.*, with Zola) or merely devastating, the naturalists found cause enough, at times, to forget their own quarrels and strength enough to insure their survival.

Despite all assertions to the contrary, naturalism did not die around 1890. It could easily be shown that, at any given moment during the last 50 years, dozens of French novelists of greater or lesser repute (not to mention the dramatists) have been writing in one or another of the naturalist traditions. Wherever the spark of active or passive rebellion is readily discernible—in the industrial novels of Pierre Hamp (*q.v.*), in the peasant novels of Charles Ferdinand Ramuz (*q.v.*), among the literary witnesses of the First World War (*e.g.*, Henri Barbusse, Roland Dorgelès, *qq.v.*), in the vast social frescoes unfolded by Romain Rolland, Roger Martin du Gard, Jules Romains, and Georges Duhamel (*qq.v.*), at the very heart of "populism" (*e.g.*, Léon Lemonnier, Eugène Dabit, *q.v.*), in Louis Ferdinand Céline's (*q.v.*) *Voyage au bout de la nuit* (1932), as late as 1938 in Jean Paul Sartre's (*q.v.*) *La Nausée*—naturalism lives on.

See: Léon Deffoux and Emile Zavie, *Le Groupe de Médan, suivi de deux essais sur le naturalisme* (1920); Pierre Martino, *Le Naturalisme français* (1923); Léon Deffoux, *Le Naturalisme* (1929); Maurice Le Blond *et al.*, "Le Naturalisme et les Soirées de Médan," *Marges,* Spring number, 1930; René Dumesnil, *La Publication des "Soirées de Médan"* (1933) and *Le Réalisme,* Vol. IX (1936) of *Histoire de la littérature française, publiée sous la direction de J. Calvet,* pp. 391–500.

J.-A. B.

French surrealism, *see* surrealism.

French symbolism is a literary movement which exercised a profound influence on the poetry and, to a lesser extent, on the prose, the thought, and the arts of France at the end of the 19th century and which spread from France to several other countries of Europe and America. Precise definition is almost impossible. The achievement of the symbolist poets seldom coincided with what they wanted to do; their theories and manifestoes are often misleading. The use of symbols is only one among many features of their work. Even when the group appeared fairly coherent, the symbolists never constituted a school, heeding or applying the lessons of one master. The most active period of the symbolist movement, though not necessarily the greatest, was between 1885 and 1892 when a dozen literary circles and over 100 poetry magazines flourished in Paris. But more revolutionary and more lasting works had been written by an earlier generation; and long after 1892 the lessons and the influences of symbolism were still felt. Symbolism, second only to romanticism as a force in 19th-century letters, appears above all as an invasion of many fields of art and thought by poetry.

Historically, three main generations of symbolists may be distinguished. The first includes writers born in the early 40's, at the same time as most of the impressionist painters and Rodin—Mallarmé (1842), Verlaine (1844), Corbière (1845), Lautréamont (1846), and the precocious Rimbaud (1854; *qq.v.),* who developed as a poet before the others and gave up literature at 19. To these a lesser but original poet, Charles Cros (1842), and the only great prose writer of symbolism, Villiers de l'Isle-Adam (1840; *q.v.*) should be added. Most of symbolism and "decadentism" is already latent or present in their works. Their common starting point was the *Les Fleurs du mal* (1857) and some of the prose writings of Baudelaire (*q.v.*), the ancestor and founder of symbolism. A second generation coined the words symbolist and decadent, fought the battle for the new poetry as a group, multiplied manifestoes and technical innovations, but produced few poets of the very first rank. Its outstanding representatives were Henri de Régnier and the American-born Vielé-Griffin (*qq.v.*), both of whom produced some of the masterpieces of musical free verse and then developed into more traditional poets. Jules Laforgue (*q.v.*), who died at 27, wrote in a humorous and original familiar vein. Samain (*q.v.*) popularized and often vulgarized symbolist themes. Moréas (*q.v.*), who appeared for a time as the champion and possible leader of the new group, soon deserted it to advocate a return to neo- or pseudo-classicism. Verhaeren (*q.v.*), a more robust talent, outgrew symbolism and sang contemporary life. Two other Belgians, Rodenbach and Van Lerberghe, and the American-born Stuart Merrill (*qq.v.*), wrote graceful and moving lyrics. Maeterlinck (*q.v.*) acquired wide fame in the 90's as the dramatist of the group. A. F. Hérold, Adolphe Retté (*qq.v.*), Ephraim Mikhaël, René Ghil (*q.v.*) and Gustave Kahn (*q.v.*) deserve mention among the minor symbolists, the last two especially as theorists and technical innovators. The critics of the movement were Edouard Dujardin, Teodor de Wyzewa (*q.v.*), and above all Rémy de Gourmont (*q.v.*). These men were all born between 1855 and 1866. Around 1870 a third generation was born, which was to enlarge and revive symbolism, after the movement had been almost stifled in ineffectual literary disputes. It included four writers of great eminence (Claudel, Gide, Proust, and Valéry, *qq.v.*), two important poets (Jammes and Paul Fort, *qq.v.*), and several critics (Schwob, *q.v.*, André Fontainas, Royère, *q.v.*, Camille Mauclair, and the youngest of the group, Thibaudet, *q.v.*), who interpreted symbolism for the 20th century. Bonnard, Vuillard, Matisse, and Rouault were, in painting, their contemporaries.

The symbolists had had predecessors in France and in other countries. In their fight for recognition they hailed as their masters Baudelaire (and sometimes two original poets of the romantic period, Gérard de Nerval and Aloysius Bertrand); E. A. Poe who, as one of the few poets in the English language to express aesthetic and doctrinal ideas on poetry, has had a powerful appeal in France; Shelley and at times Swinburne and Walt Whitman, the last as a master of free or irregular verse; among the Germans, Wagner (*q.v.*) and a few of the romantics, Novalis, Jean Paul Richter. The public and official critics were very reluctant to take the symbolists seriously. It was only in 1884 that the publication of two prose works, Verlaine's *Les Poètes maudits* and Huysmans's (*q.v.*) *A rebours,* attracted attention to them. Several symbolist manifestoes followed (1885–1886), and many reviews, among which *Vogue* (1886–1889), *Revue indépendante* (*nouvelle série,* 1886–1895), *Mercure de France* (since 1890), *Ermitage* (1890–1906), and *Revue blanche* (1891–1903) remain as the most important. In the 20th century, *Vers et prose* (1905–1914) and *Phalange* (1906–1914) continued the justification and the development of symbolism.

The confusion which still obscures today the history of the symbolist movement in France (which has not yet been adequately written) can be easily explained. The poets were all of individualistic temperaments, sometimes in agreement on what they rejected, seldom on what they wanted. No powerful personality, comparable to Victor Hugo among the romantics, won recognition as their accepted leader. Rimbaud had renounced literature, Verlaine was no *chef d'école,* and Mallarmé then seemed too esoteric a writer and too modest a master. No influential critic, comparable to Sainte-Beuve, helped the symbolists to clarify and formulate their ideas. The very word symbol lends itself to many divergent interpretations. While far preferable to decadent, which was for a time popular, and certainly as apt a label for that group of poets as romantic or Parnassian had been for earlier movements, the word symbolist confused the public and misled many poets. The public's general indifference had unfortunate consequences: the symbolists were branded by many contemporaries as a decadent and morbid group of sterile eccentrics. Tolstoy's (*q.v.*) *What Is Art?* (1897–1898; Eng. tr., 1898) and a ponderous and pseudoscientific volume by Max Nordau, *Degeneration* (1892; Eng. tr., 1895), both widely read in the late 90's, Verlaine's wretched life and Oscar Wilde's trial (1895), encouraged this belief in the general public. The unfortunate phrase *fin de siècle* seemed to justify it. Today symbolism appears on the contrary to have been, not an end but a beginning, not an abortive literary movement but one of the most fertile in the last two or three centuries.

Symbolism did not originate in any preconceived doctrine about the part to be played by symbols in literary creation. It was rooted in a profound dissatisfaction felt by the youth of 1870–1890 for the intellectual atmosphere then prevailing and in a desire to vindicate neglected predecessors (Poe, Baudelaire, Wagner) at the expense of official critical opinion. Symbolism involved a reaction of poetry (and of imagination, fancy, intuition, and the free expression of personal sensibility) against prose. It involved very specifically a revolt against the realistic and naturalistic novel which then reigned supreme in France and a parallel revolt against the Parnassian school which had exaggerated the worship of objective and sculptural verse and had reduced poetry to description or to the narrative of ancient mythological legends. On a philosophical plane symbolism was a protest against the bourgeois spirit of the 19th century, against positivism and materialism (followers of Comte and of Taine, *q.v.*), but never became a philosophical movement and produced no great philosopher (the first great work of Bergson, *q.v.,* appeared in 1889). The philosophical culture of the symbolists (even of Mallarmé and Villiers de l'Isle-Adam) was superficial. By borrowing, however, a few sentences from Hegel, Fichte, and Novalis (whom Maeterlinck, *q.v.,* translated) and by taking a convenient formula from Schopenhauer ("The world is my representation"), they rejected the tyranny of the object and proclaimed as their chief credo the ideal character of the world, the superiority of nonrational and intuitive perception over intellectual and scientific knowledge. They quoted the later philosophical writings of Renan (*q.v.*) and those of Herbert Spencer, whose formula of "the Unknowable" seemed to justify their assertion that much, in this mysterious universe, will always resist and deride the efforts of human understanding.

Such a philosophical credo found a ready aesthetic translation in symbolist poems. Since it is vain to describe an elusive reality or to explain an unknowable world, literature should cultivate strangeness, obscurity, dreamlike vagueness. It should express the poet's inner visions through suggestive metaphors and fluid melody. Against the bourgeois worship of activity and success, it should celebrate the rarest and most complex forms of beauty. Above all, in a world where every appearance has a hidden meaning, symbols are the only possible vehicle of eternal mysteries. The symbolists had little difficulty in proving that great geniuses had always expressed themselves symbolically (Pindar, Dante, Shakespeare). They quoted Swedenborg, Balzac's *Louis Lambert,* Emerson's hyperbolic praise of symbols in his essay "Poetry and Imagination," Carlyle, Vigny's attempts at symbolism, Wagner's doctrinal pronouncements, and, especially, Baudelaire's sonnet "Correspondances."

From that sonnet the essence of symbolism was derived. First, nature has a profound hidden meaning, which can only be revealed through "universal analogy." The invisible can be made visible and sensible if re-created by the artist's synthetic magic. These vertical correspondences, as they might be called, will be rendered through a series of symbols (Greek *sumballo,* to throw together) which fuse into one whole the thing which is signified and the sign which signifies it. Second, all arts are parallel translations of one fundamental mystery. Senses correspond to each other; a sound can be translated through a perfume and a perfume through a vision; each vowel suggests a color. Haunted by these horizontal correspondences or *synaesthesiae* and impatient to reach an impossible Wagnerian synthesis of all the arts, the symbolists often fell into sterile technical virtuosity.

The value of the symbolist poets can be measured by their success in giving life, depth, and suggestive power to symbols. Some created only allegories, *i.e.,* inferior symbols, too explicit and too static. Others (especially the poets of the second symbolist generation and even, at times, Mallarmé) made their symbols too voluntary and too intellectual, oversubtle and precious riddles. The greatest among them created symbols spontaneously and intuitively and recaptured the freshness and the mythopoeic power of primitive bards (Nerval, Rimbaud, Claudel; Hopkins, Yeats, Eliot, in England; George, Rilke, *qq.v.,* in Germany). Symbolism, in that sense, lies at the source of all great art: the concluding lines of the second part of Goethe's *Faust* ("Alles Vergängliche—Ist nur ein Gleichnis"), Renan's famous prayer to Athena ("Tout n'est ici-bas que symbole et que songe"), and many other pronouncements were quoted to prove it. Symbolism reintroduced depth of thought and multiplicity of meaning into poetry, the mystical quest for the One hidden in nature behind the Many, and made suggestion, not clear communication, its method. Occasionally the symbolists carried subtlety too far, disguised their meaning artificially, resorted to esoteric allusions and private associations, and opened up the way to much of the obscurity of contemporary poetry.

Much has been made of the technical innovations introduced by the symbolists. Such innovations appeared more revolutionary in France than they would have in other literatures, since the great achievement of French poetry has, in the past, been accomplished by a modest and voluntary submission to traditional rules of versification. Some of these reforms had permanent results, others have been rejected. The vocabulary of the symbolists is intentionally vague and "rare"; many farfetched and over-precious words were coined; archaic words were revived. A new and obscure but suggestive meaning was lent to many adjectives and nouns. The syntax is, especially in Mallarmé, even more revolutionary. The usual sequence of words is purposely altered or upset; orderly rhetorical development is carefully avoided, and Verlaine's advice to "wring the neck of eloquence" is followed. The impression produced is obscurity and strangeness, but often admirable plasticity and new effects of suggestion. The symbolists renounce the elaborate comparisons dear to the Parnassians, omit the first term of the analogy, and emphasize the second, which becomes a symbolic image. Explicit, clear-cut substantives are avoided, adjectives and verbs which suggest subtle motion or delicate vibration are multiplied. In versification, symbolism has been defined by Valéry as an attempt by several poets to "reprendre à la Musique, leur bien." Fluid melody and delicate music were avowedly their aim. Their best poems have a pure singing quality which French poetry had seldom possessed since the 16th century (Verlaine, Régnier). Much theoretical discussion took place in symbolist *cénacles* over free verse. This term designates a varied poetic pattern in which rhymes may disappear, caesuras and accents are capriciously displaced, and the sequence of the lines follows the poet's changing moods. But free verse (sometimes called freed verse, *vers libéré,* and, by Mallarmé, *vers polymorphe*) is not the only or the best innovation of symbolist poetry. The poem in prose enjoyed a wide and, at times, a dangerous vogue; a verse reminiscent of the Bible and of Pascal was revived and given a new splendor by Rimbaud and Claudel, even by Paul Fort and, later on, by St.-J. Perse (*q.v.*). Several poets merely used the traditional alexandrine which they made more supple and more musical. On the whole, metrical innovations introduced by the symbolists were not claims to more facility or to anarchic freedom, but a revolt against dead forms, a search for a new mold, as well as for a new idiom, for poetry.

In painting, the great contemporaries of symbolism were not the symbolist painters, Puvis de Chavannes, Gustave Moreau, Eugène Carrière, Odilon Redon, but the impressionists and the postimpressionists. Rodin, who repeatedly proclaimed that "all is symbol," is not, however, a symbolist, and César Franck, Fauré, and Debussy cannot be characterized truly as symbolist musicians. Even Wagner's relation to French symbolism has been exaggerated, and the powerful vitality of his sonorous orchestration has little in common with the delicate and subtle music of symbolist poets.

French symbolism has proved influential not only in the 19th century, but through the first 30 or 40 years of the 20th century. Numerous reactions tried to attack or to outgrow it around 1900—the neoclassicism of Moréas and Maurras (*qq.v.*); the neo-romanticism of Verhaeren, Rostand (*q.v.*), Mme de Noailles (*q.v.*); the social humanitarianism of Romain Rolland (*q.v.*); unanimism; the gospel of action and heroic life of Nietzsche (*q.v.*), Kipling, Péguy (*q.v.*). But the fame and influence of Baudelaire, Rimbaud, Lautréamont, Mallarmé, have steadily increased.

A latent symbolism or a "diffused mysticism" (Emerson) had long characterized English poetry. The influence of French symbolism in England made it more conscious, provided it with theories and technical innovations, and gave an impetus to English poetry at a time when it seemed to have exhausted its 19th-century vitality. The decadent aspects of symbolism were exaggerated by English imitators or disciples (Oscar Wilde, Ernest Dowson, Lionel Johnson), and an effete aestheticism was encouraged (Walter Pater, George Moore, Charles Morgan). The lessons in art and technique proved more beneficial (Walter de la Mare, Sturge Moore), as did the influence of the most ironical and humorous among the French symbolists (Corbière, Laforgue) on T. S. Eliot and his successors. The Irish literary renaissance, with Yeats, Æ, Synge, had probably the closest affinities with French symbolism.

In America the action of French symbolism (which cannot be clearly distinguished from that of Théophile Gautier and the Parnassians) was felt on the imagist group (1914–1917), on Ezra Pound, Wallace Stevens, *et al.* (Corbière, Laforgue), probably on Hart Crane. In Spain, Portugal, and Spanish America the Parnassian lessons in picturesque form and skillful technique were admired along with the symbolist models of mysterious suggestion: Antonio Machado, Eugénio de Castro, Jorge Guillén (*qq.v.*), who is often compared to Valéry, and most Spanish American poets, above all Rubén Darío, might be mentioned.

An exhaustive study by Enid L. Duthie, *L'Influence du symbolisme français dans le renouveau poétique de l'Allemagne* (1933), has traced the powerful and lasting influence of symbolism on Stefan George and his circle. Baudelaire, Verlaine, Mallarmé, were equally worshiped by Hugo von Hofmannsthal (*q.v.*) and the *Jungwien* group in the early 90's, and the same poets, along with Gide and Valéry, by Rilke. In Russia the stimulating action of French symbolism was keenly felt first in the late 90's by admirers of Baudelaire and decadent literature (Bryusov, Balmont, Annenski, Merezhkovski, *qq.v.*), then by the more mystical and dreamlike Blok and Bely (*qq.v.*) in the first decade of the present century.

The technical experiments and the philosophical aspirations of the symbolists have been among the boldest in the history of literature. They could not but end in partial failures, just as romanticism, a broader movement embracing all literary genres and all the arts and richer in geniuses, had done before. Symbolism, in its flight away from reality, was sometimes lost in the clouds of a rarefied atmosphere; in its flight from its enemy, prose, it often "desperately tried to save its soul from the victor by giving up its body" (Robinson Jeffers) and was too easily content in doing without the earth, the flesh, and its passions; in its contempt for eloquence and communication with a *profanum vulgus,* it became needlessly esoteric and appeared to sing only for the few initiates of a secret cult. But these excesses were the inevitable price of a higher good. Symbolism rediscovered the original tradition of French poetry—a discreet, delicate, and indirect lyricism expressed in a fluid and subtle music. It rediscovered the essence of all great poetry—to feel with intensity and express through pregnant images and suggestive symbols the mystery of existence and the life of the soul.

See: Adolphe van Bever and Paul Léautaud, *Les Poètes d'aujourd'hui* (1900); Ernest Raynaud, *La Mêlée symboliste* (4 vols., 1918–1936); Pierre Martino, *Parnasse et symbolisme, 1850–1900* (1926); John Charpentier, *Le Symbolisme* (1927); Marcel Raymond, *De Baudelaire au surréalisme* (1933). On symbolism in England: Arthur Symons, *The Symbolist Movement in Literature* (1899); W. B. Yeats, *Ideas of Good and Evil* (1903); Louis Cazamian, "Symbolism and Poetry," in *Essais en deux langues* (1938), pp. 187–204. On symbolism in America: Amy Lowell, *Six French Poets* (1915); René Taupin, *L'Influence du symbolisme français sur la poésie américaine, de 1910 à 1920* (1929); Edmund Wilson, *Axel's Castle* (1931).

H. P.

Frenssen, Gustav (1863–1945, German novelist), a chief exponent of regionalism in German fiction, was born at Barlt in Holstein, the son of a local cabinetmaker. After theological studies, he served for 10 years as Lutheran pastor in two villages near his home; a collection of his vigorous but rather unorthodox sermons bears the title *Dorfpredigten* (1899; Eng. tr. of selections, *Village Sermons,* 1924). While working as country pastor Frenssen published three novels, *Die Sandgräfin* (1896), *Die drei Getreuen* (1898; Eng. tr., *The Three Comrades,* 1907), and *Jörn Uhl* (1901; Eng. tr., 1905). The third novel proved a sensational success, and Frenssen resigned his pastorate to devote himself to writing. During these years Frenssen's belief in the orthodox bases for professional service in the church had become radically undermined; this shift of religious opinion appears as a fairly constant factor in his work (*Hilligenlei,* 1905, Eng. tr., *Holyland,* 1906; *Der Pastor von Poggsee,* 1921, Eng. tr., *The Pastor of Poggsee,* 1931).

Frenssen lived for a time at Blankenese on the Elbe near Hamburg, but he returned in his later years to Barlt. With keen understanding and a sympathy which occasionally degenerates into sentimentality, he portrays the peasants, fishermen, and seafaring folk of his homeland who wrest a livelihood from meager acres or seek it in ceaseless struggle with a bleak northern sea. His stories seem to lose validity when he wanders from these narrow confines, as in *Klaus Hinrich Baas* (1909; Eng. tr., 1911), which relates the rise of a Holstein lad to commercial eminence in Hamburg, or in that part of *Lütte Witt* (1924) covering the period before the youthful hero returns from the Ruhr to Holstein. One of the novelist's chief successes, *Peter Moors Fahrt nach Südwest,* (1907; Eng. tr., *Peter Moor's Journey to Southwest Africa,* 1908), hardly forms an exception; its popularity depended in part upon German interest in African colonization. Frenssen was not a voluminous author: a career of nearly 50 years produced 15 works of fiction, three plays, an epic, *Bismarck* (1914), and some miscellaneous writings (*e.g., Briefe aus Amerika,* 1923). Among the novels, *Jörn Uhl* remains the most representative; it is the story of a peasant youth who by sheer strength of character rises to mastery of his fate in conflict with adversity and with sordid and debasing surroundings. In *Hilligenlei* Frenssen sought to explain his new theological position; into the substance of the story the novelist inserts as the work of his hero a rationalized and humanized life of Christ. *Otto Babendiek* (1926; Eng. tr., abridged, *The Anvil,* 1930) is an autobiography in the form of a novel. Frenssen's characters are widely varied within the limits of Holstein types and are vividly conceived. He invests with beauty and charm the rather monotonous landscape of the North Sea shores, and he is capable of highly effective and graphic narrative—the account of the battle of Gravelotte in *Jörn Uhl* is deservedly esteemed. But his novels are weak in construction, are anecdotal and episodic; in this respect the shorter tales (*e.g., Der Untergang der Anna Hollmann,* 1911) show superior craftsmanship. Frenssen's signal talents in portraying the life of a particular region are marred by confused but militant thinking on theology, morals, and politics.

See: H. M. Elster, *Gustav Frenssen* (1912); A. Droege, *Die Technik in Gustav Frenssens Romanen* (1915); W. Alberts, *Gustav Frenssen, ein Dichter unserer Zeit* (1922).

H. W. H.-T.

Freytag, Gustav (1816–1895, German dramatist, novelist, and journalist), was born at Kreuzburg, Silesia, the son of a physician. He studied Germanic philology at the universities of Breslau and Berlin and entered upon a promising career as a scholar at Breslau. But success as a dramatist soon lured him to the literary circles of Dresden and Leipzig. The stirring events of 1848 aroused his political interests, and in that year, together with the historian of literature Julian Schmidt, he became editor of the influential weekly *Die Grenzboten,* a post he occupied for more than 20 years. Though ardently Prussian and nationalistic, Freytag was liberal in his political views and opposed Bismarck's policies with outspoken vigor. He served for a period as a member of the North German Parliament. His liberalism gained for him the friendship of the duke of Coburg, in whose duchy at Siebleben he had a summer home, and of the Prussian crown prince (afterwards Emperor Frederick). The last years of his life Freytag resided in Wiesbaden, where he died in 1895.

Freytag's dramas gained favorable recognition on the stage, but the only play which has stood the test of time is the popular comedy *Die Journalisten* (1854; Eng. tr., 1888), in which the dramatist combines small-town life, local journalism, and local politics with an adroit hand. In spite of technical merits his other plays (*e.g., Die Valentine,* 1847; *Graf Waldemar,* 1850; and *Die Fabier,* 1859, an ambitious historical tragedy) are largely forgotten. As a novelist his reputation rests primarily upon *Soll und Haben* (1855; Eng. tr., *Debit and Credit,* 1856), which is one of the outstanding novels of the mid-century, a work of epic breadth, providing a comprehensive panorama of German life at the time; the solid merits of the middle classes and the dignity of honest labor form the theme of the novel. In *Die verlorene Handschrift* (1864; Eng. tr., *The Lost Manuscript,* 1865) Freytag used the background of university life, to which he had been introduced in his youth. Through the pages of *Die Grenzboten* Freytag sought to communicate to others his own patriotism, and for this purpose he wrote a series of sketches from German history, later published as *Bilder aus der deutschen Vergangenheit* (5 vols., 1859–1867; Eng. tr., *Pictures of German Life,* 4 vols., 1862–1863); in these he presents in brief compass the salient features of a historical epoch, often focused in the career of a commanding personality—Charlemagne, Luther, Frederick the Great. With similar aim he produced *Die Ahnen* (6 vols., 1872–1880; Eng. tr. of selections, *Ingo,* 1873, *Ingraban,* 1873), stories illustrating different periods of German history; the author's narrative gifts and his skill in evoking the spirit of a past epoch do not entirely conceal his pedagogical purpose. Outside of Germany, Freytag is undoubtedly best known through his *Technik des Dramas* (1863; Eng. tr., *Technique of the Drama,* 1895), a study of dramatic structure based mainly upon an examination of the Greeks, Shakespeare, and the German classics; this work was long and widely influential, even authoritative.

Freytag was for decades an outstanding figure in German letters, but his reputation has gradually dimmed. His political opinions have only historical interest. In literature he was not a great spontaneous creator, but a conscious artist of talent, trained in close observation of the masters; in *Soll und Haben,* for example, the patterns of Scott and Dickens are evident. Indeed the very presence among his works of a "technique of the drama" bears testimony to the studied methods which guided his creative imagination.

See: Freytag, *Erinnerungen aus meinem Leben* (1887; Eng. tr., *Reminiscences of My Life,* 1890); F. Seiler, *Gustav Freytag* (1898); H. Lindau, *Gustav Freytag* (1907).

H. W. H.-T.

Friðjónsson, Guðmundur (1869–1944, Icelandic poet, novelist, short-story writer, and essayist), was born at Sílalækur in Þingeyjarsýsla, near the shores of the Arctic. His father was poor, with a large family; but there was talent in the group, and two of the sons became literary figures. Guðmundur Friðjónsson himself had a brief schooling, became a farmer, and, like his father, raised a big family. He lived and died at Sandur, near his birthplace.

In spite of his time- and energy-consuming occupation. Friðjónsson was one of the most prolific recent authors of Iceland. He began as a realist in the 1890's, spurred on by the intellectual atmosphere of his native district. There a spiritual awakening was in progress among the farmers due in large part to the efforts of Benedikt Jónsson, the librarian at Auðnir, and to the early writings of the farmer-novelist Þorgils Gjallandi (pseud. of Jón Stefánsson). Later Friðjónsson became more of a national romantic. Three collections of his essays and lectures have been published, six collections of poems (1902–1942), one novel, and 10 collections of short stories, apart from a host of articles in newspapers and periodicals.

Friðjónsson has the rather narrow point of view of the Icelandic farmer, but within his limited sphere he is a keen observer. His sensitive nature has made him especially able to see and to appreciate the passive heroism so common among the poorer Icelandic farmers. One of his early poems, "Ekkjan við ána" (The Widow at the River), deals with such heroism, and the poet has returned to the theme in many a short story. He appreciates fully the virtues developed through centuries by the farmers in their hard struggle for existence; he has little understanding and less patience with the modern currents of thought and action that tend to sweep away this old culture. The Old Icelandic tradition is very strongly felt in his poems especially; they are as ornate and polyphonous as Bach's music. His prose style, too, is distinguished with the same characteristics; it is rich in images and highly poetical. Like Stephan G. Stephansson (*q.v.*), Friðjónsson exemplifies in his work Icelandic rustic culture at its best.

See: G. Finnbogason, "Guðmundur Friðjónsson," *Vaka,* III (1929), 129–160; S. Einarsson, "Frá Guðmundi Friðjónssyni og sögum hans," *Tímarit Þjóðræknisfélags Íslendinga,* XVIII (1936), 52–66.

S. E.

Fröding, Gustaf (1860–1911, Swedish poet), was born near Karlstad, in the pastoral and mining province of Värmland on the western border of central Sweden. His was the countryside so well known to readers of *Gösta Berlings saga* by Selma Lagerlöf (*q.v.*). Värmland is a district of lakes and forests, far from the turmoil of big cities yet with a gay, high-spirited local aristocracy. The peasants are noted for their hard drinking and rough humor. The loneliness of the region and the rigor of the climate have developed a peculiar sensitiveness in the Värmlander; old legends and superstitions are entwined with his earliest memories.

Mountain trolls, water nixies, and wood spirits are not mere characters of folklore but more than half actual to the popular consciousness.

Fröding came of cultivated and artistic stock on both sides. He was unusually shy and protected himself at school by clowning. His family life was early broken up by an accident to his father and the severe nervous collapse of his mother. There was insanity in his blood. From 1880 to 1883 he was at the University of Uppsala but left without taking a degree. He finally went into newspaper work at Karlstad, where he enlisted on the side of the radicals; this separated him even more from his family. Habits of dissipation formed at the university grew upon him and undermined his already delicate health. It was at this time that he began to contribute poems to his newspaper, his principal models being Burns, Heine, and Byron. His first pieces were mostly pictures of Värmland nature and characters close to the soil. Poetry had been at a low ebb in Sweden, but the success of the oriental sketches of Heidenstam (*q.v.*), *Vallfart och vandringsår* (1888; Pilgrimage and Wanderyears), encouraged Fröding to bring out a volume, the now famous *Gitarr och dragharmonica* (1891; Eng. tr., *Guitar and Concertina; a Century of Poems by Fröding,* by C. D. Locock, 1925). Although it was well received, it did not for some time attain the tremendous popularity it was to command later.

Other collections followed, more personal and fantastic, the influence of Heine predominating over that of Burns, his original inspiration. The visionary and the morbid side of his nature foreboded the mental breakdown which came in 1894 with shattering severity. Although he partly recovered, his creative power was lost, and he wrote little more of importance. He never married. His fame had, in his later years, been growing rapidly, and his funeral was celebrated by a demonstration unequaled in the history of Swedish literature. Today he is the most admired and beloved of all Swedish poets.

It is hard to give a final estimate of Fröding's poetry. Sir Edmund Gosse acclaims him as "one of the few great singing poets whom Europe has produced in the second half of the nineteenth century." He is at least that. His "terrible and enchanting lyrics" attain the highest perfection both in vivid reality of feeling and in spontaneity of rhythm. He is a melodist par excellence, in subtlety as well as in freshness; and yet, as we read him, we never think of him primarily as a virtuoso. Whatever his mood, he carries us with him irresistibly. At times he is almost insupportably intense, and again he will relax into humor, boisterous, grim, or delicate. His emotional range is wide and varied, but through all its gamut he is equally a master of his art. In the whirlwind of his passion, he has the temperance that gives its smoothness.

The keynote of Fröding's appeal is human sympathy, especially for the victims of circumstance, though he enjoys an occasional dig at the "unco guid." His popularity rests chiefly on his scenes from peasant and small-town life, where he is most objective and humorous. A rough hunter, a girl of the streets, an incorrigible small boy, a nasal prayer leader, a gay lieutenant, a drunken recruit, even an old mountain troll may emerge as his central figure. Into all he can project himself. But he has also a more idealistic and universal note. His "Man and Woman," depicting Adam and Eve in the world's first lover's quarrel, sums up the relations of sex from primitive brutality to the final reconciliation in tender forgiveness. The "Poor Monk of Skara" shows us a renegade priest won back to life and love by the beauty of nature. His wonderful fantasy "Dreams in Hades" likewise ends with "a ray of moonlight through Hades' door." To the problem of life's bitterness and cruelty his answer is like that of Shelley, an all pardoning compassion and the hope of a better age to be.

See: F. Böök, *Sveriges moderna litteratur* (1921), also published as Vol. III of O. Sylwan, ed., *Svenska litteraturens historia* (1919–1921), pp. 239–265; E. Gosse and W. A. Craigie, eds., *The Oxford Book of Scandinavian Verse* (1925); M. Hellberg, *Frödingsminnen* (1925). For other translations of his poetry see: Fröding, *Selected Poems,* tr. and with an introduction by C. W. Stork (1916); C. W. Stork, *Anthology of Swedish Lyrics* (1917; revised and enlarged ed., 1930).

C. W. S.

Fucini, Renato (early pseud. Neri Tanfucio, 1843–1921, Italian writer of poems, stories, and sketches), was born at Monterotondo near Pisa. After studying in the various places where his father, a country doctor, happened to be stationed, he attended the university of Pisa, specializing in agriculture. He became inspector of schools near Pistoia, taught in a secondary school, was assistant city engineer, and, for a time, was librarian of the Biblioteca Riccardiana in Florence. He spent most of his life in that city, except for vacations on his farm near Empoli or in his little villa at Castiglioncello, near Leghorn.

It was at Pisa, while a student, that he began to write facetious, witty sonnets in the Pisan dialect. Enthusiastic friends prevailed upon him to publish them; they appeared in 1872 as *Cento Sonetti in vernacolo pisano*. Later he added 50 more sonnets. This book became popular all over Italy and has had some 25 editions. The reason for this immediate and lasting popularity lies in the merry tone, the ease, the benevolent satire, the utter spontaneity of these sonnets, which Miss R. S. Phelps aptly called "little snapshots of 150 aspects of contemporary life." Later he wrote poems in standard Italian and proved that he could treat serious as well as humorous topics in the purest Tuscan with equal spontaneity. In 1878, after a trip to Naples, he published *Napoli a occhio nudo,* a collection of letters to a friend, describing that city with a masterly touch.

A direct result of his country life was *Le Veglie di Neri* (1884), a collection of short stories and sketches of Tuscan scenes and characters, sometimes pathetic, but in a healthy, restrained way, more often humorous, always delightfully genuine and vivacious. A similar volume, *All'aria aperta,* appeared in 1897, and a third, smaller one, *Nella campagna toscana,* in 1908. During his later years he devoted himself to school books (*Mondo nuovo,* 1901; *Mondo vecchio,* 1904). Three of his works appeared posthumously in 1922: *Acqua passata, Foglie al vento,* both containing autobiographical incidents and anecdotes, and *La Maestrina*. For his joyousness, the purity of his Tuscan style, his genuine humanity, his spontaneity, Fucini has a unique place among Italian writers.

See: B. Croce, *La Letteratura della nuova Italia,* III (1915), 139–146; G. Biagi, preface to Fucini, *Acqua passata* (1922); R. S. Phelps, *Italian Silhouettes* (1924), pp. 142–159.

R. Al.

Fulda, Ludwig (1862–1932, German dramatist and translator), was born in Frankfurt am Main, studied in Heidelberg, Munich, and Berlin, visited the United States in 1906 (*Amerikanische Eindrücke,* 1906), and became president of the literary section of the Prussian Academy in 1926. His editing of the works of German poets around 1700 (*Die Gegner der zweiten schlesischen Schule,* 2 vols., 1883, in *Kürschners deutsche Nationallitteratur*) suggested to him the problem of his first drama. The failure of this dramatization of the tragic fate of *Christian Günther* (1882) is almost symbolic of Fulda's own work, since his keen intelligence senses ideals which his amiable, versatile, and facile talent is unable to attain or even to attempt. In spite of his early and courageous espousal of Ibsen's (*q.v.*) cause after the famous performance of *Ghosts* in Augsburg in 1886 and in spite of his membership in the directorate of the Freie Bühne, he deviated little in his own productions from the claptrap of the more ordinary French social drama and *pièce à thèse;* but with an unfailing scent for timely innovations and public demands he infused into them just enough of opportune problems and growing tendencies to insure stage success. Thus, in *Das verlorene Paradies* (1890) he anticipated Hauptmann's (*q.v.*) *Die Weber* (1892) in treatment of a threatening strike, in *Die Sklavin* (1892) he presented a parlor Nora, and in his symbolic drama *Der Talisman* (1893), based upon Hans Christian Andersen's "The Emperor's Clothes," he broke the yoke of naturalism and ushered in the neo-romantic drama. The awarding of the Schiller prize for this last work was vetoed by William II, but Fulda received the Viennese Bauernfeld prize for his comedy *Die Kameraden* (1894). His three score plays show little or no development except in routine. Of lasting value, however, is Fulda's achievement as a translator. In this field his empathic and linguistic talents and his gift of versification (which also comes to light in a collection of epigrams, *Sinngedichte,* 1888) master the most divergent form problems. Notable are his renderings of Ibsen (poems and *Peer Gynt,* 1915), Cavalotti (*Hohes Lied,* 1894), Beaumarchais (*Figaro,* 1894), Rostand, (*Die Romantischen,* 1895, and *Cyrano de Bergerac,* 1898), Molière (*Meisterwerke,* 4 vols., 1897), Shakespeare (*Sonnette,* 1913), and the Spanish dramatists (*Meisterlustspiele der Spanier,* 2 vols., 1926).

See: A. Klaar, *Ludwig Fulda* (1922).

E. F.

Furmanov, Dmitri (1891–1926, Russian novelist), son of a bartender, was born at Sereda, in the former Government of Kostroma, graduated from a technical school, studied literature at the University of Moscow, joined the Communist Party in 1918, and took an active part in the civil war. He was appointed commissar of various fighting units, then political chief on the Turkestan front. He won great popularity in Soviet Russia through his novel *Chapayev* (1923), the first full-scale literary work attempting to depict revolutionary events. Furmanov portrayed Chapayev, an undisciplined guerrilla leader of the southeastern steppes behind the Volga River, as a true representative of the elemental forces of a people in revolt. He used a semi-journalistic method, reporting accurately the facts of the civil war. Furmanov's other books (*Dnevnik,* 1923, Diary; *Myatezh,* 1923, Uprising; *Pozhar,* 1924, Fire) follow the same line of factual naturalism. They lack plot, artistic construction, or elaborate form; they are documentary reports on actuality. In 1923–1925 some enthusiastic critics in Russia acclaimed Furmanov as an initiator of a new "artless literature," asserting that "when the events are as fantastic as they are today, the writer does not need to add anything to them, his goal being merely to state them." Undoubtedly a very gifted man, Furmanov may be considered as a representative of the "factual literature" which flourished in the early period of Soviet art. His novels have hardly any aesthetic value, but they remain as vivid and interesting documents, faithfully reflecting the turbulent years of the Russian Revolution. A very successful film was made out of *Chapayev.*

M. S.

G

Gabriel y Galán, José María (1870–1905, Spanish poet), was born and raised in Frades de la Sierra, a village of Salamanca. He became a schoolteacher, a profession he soon gave up when he married and took up farming in a village of Estremadura, Guijo de Granadilla, isolated and archaic. It was there he lived the traditional life he describes in his poems. He became famous overnight with the poem "El ama," which was awarded first prize in the Juegos Florales held in Salamanca in 1901. In this poem he sang of the life of a ranch in Salamanca, the landscape of Castile, and the austere, traditional character of the Castilian peasant. At the same time he won recognition with another poem, "El Cristu benditu," written in the dialect of Estremadura. These two poems contained all of Galán, and when they were published they sufficed to give him a glory and popularity in which enthusiasm for his work was mingled with protest and with disapprobation of the revolutionary tendencies of the new modernist literature. Nevertheless, this popular traditionalist poetry of Galán's was still another product of the literary revolution that occurred at the end of the century. His glorification of Castile was linked with that of Unamuno, Antonio Machado, and Azorín (*qq.v.*). His classic tendencies were not the conventional ones of the 19th century, but derived from the old rustic and popular poetry, which had been rediscovered by the new school. His traditional sentiments are sincere and deep; he had lived from childhood in the country of Salamanca, where the customs of the peasants still preserved the harmony and grandeur of the great Spain of the past. His traditionalism is therefore healthy, gay, and serene, not sad and pessimistic like that of the modernists. All this holds true of his first poems, both those he called "castellanas" (see *Castellanas,* 1902; *Campesinas,* 1904; *Nuevas castellanas,* 1905) and those he called "extremeñas" (*Extremeñas,* 1902) in which the use of the dialect of Eastern León—very close to Castilian—simplifies and accentuates the rustic, primitive note. As long as Galán keeps to this field he is a great poet, deservedly popular; but in a number of his poems his true originality is smothered by the excess, the vulgarity, and the pedantry of the rhetoric of the 19th century, and for this reason he has had many detractors as well as many admirers.

See: E. Pardo Bazán, *Retratos y apuntes literarios,* Ser. 1 (*ca.* 1908); A. Revilla Marcos, *José María Gabriel y Galán; su vida y sus obras* (1923); F. Iscar Peyra, *Gabriel y Galán, poeta de Castilla* (1936).

F. de O.

Gaeta, Francesco (1879–1927, Italian poet), a solitary man, difficult of approach, lived all his life in Naples, where he was born and where he committed suicide a few moments after his mother's funeral cortege had left the house. He is remote from all trends of Italian contemporary literature, in spite of the fact that his youthful writings (1895–1904) show that at first he tried the forms of Carducci and D'Annunzio (*qq.v.*). Very soon, almost through an effort of will, his style manifested itself in a new direction (*Sonetti voluttuosi,* 1904–1906). With certain strange contortions, twists of verses, interpolations of incidental sentences, and frequent use of Latinisms, he manifested a very modern and personal force of feeling. In his last poems (*Poesie d'amore,* 1906–1920) he had mastered his technique and no longer offered to the reader such a rough and angular surface: smooth, melodious, and at times graceful, he was able to give full expression to his world. It is a world of sensuous, rapturous love which permeates one's very being, full of colors, odors, instances of forsaking all for a great love. But for him pleasure is forever restrained by a certain melancholy and torment.

One of the characteristics of his poetry is the abundance of realistic details: hairpins, underclothes, shawls, the odor of beef stew, cries of children, are all described in an impeccable, classical verse form. He wrote a masterful critical essay on Di Giacomo (*q.v.*), to whom he has been compared because of a common Neapolitan background, but the cultural resonances of Gaeta touch horizons never dreamed of by Di Giacomo, who, on the other hand, is more of a natural poet than Gaeta. The vibrations and agitations of voluptuousness in Gaeta always carry in their wake something that is somber and consuming and, in many instances, the menacing shadow of death. The trend of mind of Gaeta, when he wrote on practical matters, was also rather unusual for an Italian. He was an admirer of old Indian wisdom, convinced of the magnanimity and superior humanity of the Aryans, and in the last years of his life, when his mind was oppressed by cloudy thoughts, he became anti-Semitic (one of his manuscripts was published, posthumously, with the title *Che cosa è la Massoneria,* 1939).

He enjoyed a place in Italian literature but never attained fame and this was partly responsible for his misanthropy. A selection of his works in two volumes, *Poesie* and *Prose,* was published in 1928 by Croce (*q.v.*), who was a true friend and an appreciative critic during his life and after his death.

See: P. Pancrazi, *Scrittori italiani del novecento* (1934), pp. 28–35.

G. P.

Galdós, Benito Pérez, *see* Pérez Galdós.

Ganivet, Angel (1865–1898, Spanish essayist), emerged, at a time when the provincial spirit and the commonplace were dominant in Spain, as an extraordinary nonconformist who contemplated his native country from the north of Europe and aspired to ascertain critically the essence of her peculiar nature and the reasons for her decline. He was born in Granada; there his aesthetic sense of life was formed in the midst of natural beauty and that created by the art of two civilizations. His irregular character was incompatible with the sort of life possible for him at that time—he might have been lawyer or archivist or professor—and he preferred to embark on a diplomatic career in order to live abroad. He resided in Antwerp, Helsinki and Riga. An indefatigable reader, he continued to nourish an intellectual passion which carried him far beyond any cold scientific curiosity—the latter, indeed, being a quality difficult to find in an Andalusian. Ganivet read especially those authors in whom he could find some connection with his Spanish soul: nonconformists or anarchists such as Renan (*q.v.*), Schopenhauer, Nietzsche (*q.v.*), Tolstoy (*q.v.*), Kropotkin (*q.v.*), and certain Scandinavian writers. At the same time he immersed himself in Spanish tradition, beginning with Seneca.

Anguished and pressed for time, he wrote all of his books in some three years: *Granada la bella* (1896); *Idearium español* (1897); *La conquista del reino de Maya* (1897), a rather disconnected satire of modern culture as applied to a people in the center of Africa; *Los trabajos del infatigable creador Pío Cid* (1898), an autobiographical novel which the author left incomplete and in which, in deep intensity of style, he reveals the uncertainty of his character—torn between faith and doubt, impulse and quietist fatalism. The drama *El escultor de su alma* (1904) appeared posthumously, and also *Hombres del norte* (1905), a collection of essays on Jonas Lie, Björnstjerne Björnson, and Henrik Ibsen (*qq.v.*), previously published in a daily paper of Granada, as were Ganivet's *Cartas finlandesas* (1898).

This feverish activity allowed no peace or faith in life to that exuberant and maladjusted temperament, the victim, moreover, of a grave illness, progressive paralysis. In November, 1898, when he was in Riga, Ganivet threw himself into the Dvina from the tug on which he was going to meet his wife, who had borne him a son and was coming to join him. Pulled out of the water he hurled himself in again, confirming what he had written in his books, that he would die when he wished.

Ganivet is considered today the initiator of the reaction against the Spanish 19th century and of the revival of Spanish literature in the 20th century. His works have been republished and made the subject of numerous studies. When his body was moved to Granada in 1925, the intelligentsia organized ceremonies to honor the memory of the unfortunate writer, at a moment in which the country felt itself oppressed by the dictatorship of Primo de Rivera. His most outstanding work remains the *Idearium español,* in which are analyzed the essential characteristics of the Spanish soul. These, according to Ganivet, are Senecan stoicism and religious and poetic exaltation, with the latter traits susceptible of assuming the opposite states of either mysticism or fanaticism. As though he had read Hegel, Ganivet also outlines a geographic theory to explain history: continental nations possess spirit and resistance; insular nations are aggressive (Napoleon was an island that fell on a continent); peninsulas like Spain have a spirit of independence. Spain's error probably consisted in attempting to conduct herself politically as a continental nation, and her capital vice was "collective abulia." As opposed to the programs of Europeanization that Joaquín Costa (*q.v.*) and others were proposing during those years, Ganivet recommends a return to the Spanish way of being. Paraphrasing St. Augustine he writes: "Noli foras ire; in interiore Hispaniae habitat veritas." Without attempting to decide this problem, let us say only that the life of a people cannot be grasped through heterogeneous formulae about Seneca's doubtful influence and geographical conditions; it is juggling history to say that Spain should not have gotten away from herself, since, in explaining that history, it must be taken into account that she did do so, and to a great extent. The interesting thing in Ganivet is not the question whether he was right or wrong "scientifically," but the fact that he brought to a somnolent nation themes that would bestir it, that would oblige people to meditate on the meaning of their own lives and those of others. Ganivet's work gains vehemence and permanence because he himself lived the opposition between Spain and the rest of Europe. On the one hand he recognized the worth of the north of Europe, and on the other he did not abandon hope in the so-called backwardness of his country, in which many people had "the singular good fortune of not being able to read. . . . If the learned have only ideas gleaned from books of diverse origin, it is prudent and safe to be guided by the people, who are more artistic and philosophical than it would seem" (*Granada la bella*). That preference for the spirit, given and expressed in the completeness of life, not merely in books, is an idea which was to take deep root in Unamuno (*q.v.*), who was doubtless greatly influenced by Ganivet. "The people must understand art, since they create it; they are unable to express their thoughts, but they know how to adapt themselves to everything that is grand and beautiful and they are never out of tune" (*Granada la bella*). In this view there is something more than hackneyed romanticism.

Like Spain herself, Ganivet desired both to withdraw from and to enter into the orbit of modern culture; for example, he detested the regimentation and symmetry of such institutions as railway stations and school buildings and even proposed that centers of instruction be developed in the individual farmhouses, the living nuclei of Spain's national existence. In other words, life organically developing from within, not organized from without. The author's inner life was divided between reason, which differentiates, and a tendency toward a total contemplation leading to fatalism, the whole focused on the conviction that human spiritual activity is of value when it is converted into the stuff of life. The living person, not the idea, triumphs. Ganivet diffused the belief, today as generally widespread as it is debatable, that there exists a Senecan basis for Spanish life; he also helped to complicate, usefully, the question of what constitutes the essential nature of progress and civilization. After him came Unamuno, Rodó, and even the theories of Waldo Frank in his *Virgin Spain* (1926).

See: M. Fernández Almagro, *Vida y obra de Angel Ganivet* (1925); H. Jeschke, "Angel Ganivet; seine Persönlichkeit und Hauptwerke," *Revue hispanique*, LXXII (1928), 102–246; A. Espina, *Ganivet; el hombre y la obra* (1942).

A. C.

Garborg, Arne (1851–1924, Norwegian poet, novelist, and essayist), was born in the parish of Time in Jæren, southwestern Norway. He came of a family of poor but independent peasant farmers who had owned their own land for two hundred years. It was a happy household until, when Arne was about eight years old, his father, Eivind Garborg, went through a religious crisis which made him gloomy and tyrannical. He forbade the children going to a "worldly" school or even reading books. But Arne managed to read by stealth. He resolved to leave the farm, to which as eldest son he had *odal* rights, and go to the city. Yet he never ceased to regret the break in that family continuity which he came to value more and more as he grew older.

Garborg afterwards wrote that he was born in the 17th century and had to go through all phases of modern development before he could be himself. In Christiania he studied at the university, supporting himself by writing trenchant, irreverent articles on the questions of the day. He learned to handle the Riksmaal with virtuosity, but in his first important book he returned to the Landsmaal (*see* Norwegian literature). *Bondestudentar* (1883; Peasant Students) describes a phenomenon new in Garborg's day, the peasant boy uprooted from his environs and unable to fit himself into the life of the university. *Mannfolk* (1888; Menfolk) is a naturalistic novel describing young men adrift in the city in the most difficult phase of their lives, that of sex. *Hjaa mor* (1890; At Mother's) is its feminine counterpart, a weaker novel about the dreary life of a young girl who tries to keep respectable. In the natural reaction against the pietism of his home, Garborg had enlisted on the side of the modernists in the two burning questions of the day, free love and atheism. But he soon revolted against the flat negativism of the atheistic theory of life and sickened of the sensuality that masqueraded as free love. *Trætte mænd* (1891; Tired Men), written in diary form, is a record of disintegration in a man whose dissipated life has rendered him incapable of wholehearted love and trust, while he demands unsullied purity in the woman who attracts him. It is written in brilliant Riksmaal well suited to the sophistications of its hero.

Trætte mænd marked Garborg's farewell to the city before he returned to the scenes and subjects of his childhood in Jæren. In *Fred* (1892; Eng. tr., *Peace,* 1929), the story of Enok Hove is based on that of Garborg's own father. It is a tragic and powerful study of a sincere but unlearned peasant nature in the grip of a fire-and-brimstone religion. The chronicles of the Hove family are continued in the drama *Læraren* (1896; The Teacher), *Den burtkomne faderen* (1899; The Lost Father), and *Heimkomin son* (1908; The Son Come Home). Here Garborg evolves an undogmatic religion and a social theory. Paulus, who in *Læraren* had sold his ancestral farm in order to follow literally the commands of Jesus, allows it to come back into the family and consents to work for his nephew as a hired man.

Meanwhile Garborg had written philosophical-religious books, and a translation of the Odyssey into Landsmaal, besides publishing volumes of letters and diaries, and the most popular of all his works, the poetic cycle *Haugtussa* (1895; The Hill Innocent). It tells the story of a young girl who has the mystic power of seeing the souls of the dead, as well as the trolls and sprites that surround human beings, though they are invisible to others. The struggle by which she wins over the powers of darkness is described with a spiritual exaltation which, combined with the lyric beauty of the separate poems, the pictures of Jæren landscapes, and the homely intimate details of peasant life, makes *Haugtussa* the most important poetic work ever published in the Norwegian Landsmaal.

See: I. Grøndahl and O. Raknes, *Chapters in Norwegian Literature* (1923); H. A. Larsen, "Arne Garborg," *American-Scandinavian Review,* XII (1924), 275–283.

H. A. L.

García Lorca, Federico (1899–1936, Spanish poet and dramatist), is the most widely known Spanish writer of recent generations. This is due both to his tragic end and to the expressive power of his inspiration which gained for him in the Spanish-speaking world a popularity unparalleled among first-rank poets. Born near Granada, he found in his native Andalusia the main source of his themes and the charm, passion, and soul which form the permanent basis of his temperament and style. His university studies in Granada in literature and law left no appreciable influence on him, in contrast to the lasting traces of an early artistic self-education as musician and poet. When he arrived at Madrid, at 19, he had already published a book of poetic prose, *Impresiones y paisajes* (1918), and written many poems, selections from which appeared in his *Libro de poemas* (1921). A year before, his first play, *El maleficio de la mariposa,* was presented without success. For some time Lorca wrote much but published little. Nevertheless, through the reading of his poems and his rare personal attractiveness he became known increasingly as one of the most important young writers of the "vanguardia" movement. His standing was confirmed in 1927 by the presentation, with Dalí's scenery, of the historical play *Mariana Pineda* and by the volume *Canciones,* a collection of delicate short poems, some inspired by folkloric and children's songs, others of an exquisite musical impressionism.

Lorca's real success came through the publication of *Romancero gitano* (1928), the only volume of poetry of the period which appealed to the general public and yet at the same time was highly regarded by the selected few for whom the new art was primarily intended. Many of his "romances" were soon recited everywhere; some, sung by the common people, came to enrich the treasure of traditional poetry. It was a repetition of that most characteristic phenomenon of Spanish literature in which a learned poet takes his subjects from the people and the people incorporate the new product into the stream of their living art. Although Lorca's poetry contains many apparently contradictory elements—varying in range from the simple forms of folkloric poetry to the abstract and surrealistic style of his odes ("Oda a Salvador Dalí," "Oda a Walt Whitman")—he probably struck in *Romancero* his most authentic note, that of re-creating the popular spirit of Andalusia, giving it a lyric sense and meaning.

In 1929 Lorca spent a year in New York. The impression made by the modern city upon this poet rooted in the soil and earthly passions is powerfully expressed in *Poeta en Nueva York* (1940; Eng. tr., *The Poet in New York and Other Poems,* 1940). It shows the influence of many contemporary trends, especially of surrealism, but the accent is Lorca's: its rich imagery has the concrete sense of reality, its tone is dramatic. What he misses in the mechanistic civilization is an expression of natural impulses. That is why "El rey de Harlem," one of his great poems, exalts the primitive nature of the Negro, in contrast to the cold soulless sensuality of the city.

The last five years of his life, after his return to Spain, were a succession of triumphs and a proof of his creative power. In 1931 was published *El cante jondo,* a collection of early Andalusian poems, the result of his friendship with De Falla. He directed the "Barraca," a student traveling theatre which carried to rural Spain the best Spanish classical plays, combining modern and classical staging. These were also the years of his great dramatic production—*Amor de don Perlimplín, La zapatera prodigiosa, Doña Rosita la soltera,* and the two rural tragedies *Bodas de sangre* and *Yerma* (Eng. trs. in *From Lorca's Theatre: Five Plays,* 1941; *Blood Wedding,* 1939). Together with certain minor works, they represent the highest attainment of a contemporary poetic theatre along the lines of the tradition of Spanish classic and romantic drama. Like his poetry, his theatre runs a wide gamut, from the "cámara" caprice suggestive of "ballet" technique, to bare tragedy. Like his poetry, it is also lyrical, musical, plastic, and dramatic.

Lorca's final work, *Llanto por Sánchez Mejías* (1935; Eng. tr., *Lament for the Death of a Bullfighter and Other Poems,* 1937), and his last two tragedies represent the plenitude and synthesis of the multiple elements of his art. That art is very complex and gives the impression of absolute spontaneity because, although it is a product of his time and of his country, it is above all the creation of a born poet. At the outbreak of the civil war Lorca was shot in Granada with the tacit consent of the fascist authorities, by one of the irresponsible groups let loose by the military rebellion. Modern and traditional, refined and primitive, Lorca has been appropriately said to be the essence of "living poetry." Though sometimes he skirted a dangerous facility, the strange force of his poetic personality raises his work to a superior plane.

See: R. M. Nadal, "Introduction," in García Lorca, *Poems* (1939); Angel del Río, "García Lorca," *Revista hispánica moderna,* VI (1940), 193–260.

A. del R.

García Morente, Manuel (1888–1941, Spanish philosopher), born in Arjonilla, Jaén, was educated at the University of Madrid. He early came under the influence of Francisco Giner de los Ríos (*q.v.*) and of his Institución Libre de Enseñanza, which was an important contributing factor to the development of new educational doctrines and ideals in Spain. García Morente went to Germany when Neo-Kantian philosophy was still prevalent and studied at the University of Marburg. In 1912 he was appointed professor of philosophy at the University of Madrid; later on he became a member of the Academia de Ciencias Morales y Políticas. Under the influence of José Ortega y Gasset (*q.v.*) his thought evolved towards phenomenology and the philosophy of values. A few years before his death, he became a Roman Catholic and a priest. He visited Argentina twice as a professor; in his second visit (1937) he became the founder and the first dean of the new faculty of philosophy of the University of Tucumán. He applied his excellent qualities as a writer to educational purposes, rather than to the construction of a new personal system. Both his books and his oral teachings were always a model of clearness and careful construction; his vocabulary was rich and classic, his style even and orderly.

García Morente's *La filosofía de Kant* and *La filosofía de Bergson* were both published in 1917; they are the best studies of these philosophers ever written in Spanish. Two of his most important long essays are "Ensayo sobre el progreso" (*Revista de Occidente,* January, February, March, 1932), on the philosophy of values applied to the problem of progress, and "Ensayo sobre la vida privada" (*Revista de Occidente,* January, February,

1935), a phenomenological study on private life. His introduction to philosophy, *Lecciones preliminares de filosofía,* was written and published in Tucumán, in 1937. His last works are *Idea de la hispanidad* (1938) and, with Juan Zaragüeta, *Fundamentos de filosofía* (1943).

E. N.

Gárdonyi, Géza (1863–1925, Hungarian novelist, poet, playwright), was born in Agard and died in Eger. The idealistic habits that Gárdonyi acquired as a young elementary school teacher followed him throughout his life. He was devoted to idealism in its most profound sense; this idealism sustained his spirit when conditions tried his faith in values. He lived in the provinces rather than in Budapest, which he visited only on necessary trips to publishers or theatrical directors. As a rule the setting of his stories and plays is a Hungarian village or a small town, or a historical background is employed. His marriage failed, and this affected his views about women. Either he idealized them, because it was impossible to meet the ideal woman in life, or with the fervor of a misogynist, he assailed them. Though Gárdonyi did not live according to the tenets of an unquestioning faith, he was always inclined to be religious and, like Turgenev (*q.v.*), in the last years of his life he was interested in spiritualism and mysticism. His nation appreciated him; he was a member of several important literary societies, and one of the literary societies of Hungary is named after him. He had a certain international reputation too and in 1899 won first prize in a short-story contest arranged by *Le Journal* in Paris. He was also recognized in Italy. His juvenile stories show the same kind of warmth and understanding heart that is revealed in the juvenile stories of the Italian writer Edmondo de Amicis (*q.v.*).

It is rather ironic that Gárdonyi's popularity started with a series of amusing sketches about a village judge whose name is used as the title: *Göre Gábor* (1895; Gabriel Göre). The comic spirit that permeates these sketches is akin to the farcical gaiety of the fabliau; these sketches, however, would not justify Gárdonyi's literary fame. In his cheerful moods Gárdonyi was apt to turn to stock characters or to plots almost painfully simple. It is said that in his later years he himself felt uncomfortable when some of his early works were mentioned. His lyric poems are rich in sentiment and conventional in phrasing. His best play is *Bor* (1901; Wine). This is delightful, realistic, convincing; it has the charm and freshness of folklore. His other plays are less vital.

Gárdonyi's idealism is successfully expressed in his historical and social novels and stories. In envisaging the Hungarian past he liked to portray the ferocious times of Attila or the heroic times of the Middle Ages or the desolate 16th century. *A láthatatlan ember* (1902; The Invisible Man), *Az egri csillagok* (1905; The Stars of Eger), and *Isten rabjai* (1908; God's Slaves) are his representative historical novels. Gárdonyi understood the soul of historical reality, though sometimes his perspective was not sufficiently reliable and he was apt to stylize history. *Az én falum* (1908; My Village) contains his best short stories: they have humor and idealism. However, a good deal of his work is unsatisfactory; he wrote too much and in consequence many of his writings are more noble in intention than in artistic results.

See: L. Gopcsa, *Gárdonyi Géza élete* (1923); L. Szabolcska, *Gárdonyi élete és költészete* (1926).

J. R.

Garshin, Vsevolod Mikhailovich (1855–1888, short-story writer), was born near Bakhmut in the Ukraine. For some years he lived with his father, an army officer; the parents were estranged. At a Gymnasium in St. Petersburg he was attracted by natural science; but after entering the Institute of Mines he decided to devote himself to literature. Painting of the social scene also became one of his interests, and he formed friendships among the younger painters as well as among the writers. In 1877 the Russo-Turkish War broke out and Garshin, swept up by the desire to share the common man's suffering, volunteered. He was wounded in the leg and a year later left the service. His second story, "Chetyre dnya" (1877; Eng. tr., "Four Days," published, with the other translations mentioned below, in *The Signal and Other Stories,* 1912), brought him immediate fame; but a mental disorder, which had already manifested itself, interrupted his literary activity (1880–1882), and the year of his marriage proved to be only a respite (1883). Thereafter, the periods of his illness recurred with increasing frequency and finally led to his tragic suicide.

The literary output of Garshin is not great, but among his 20-odd stories and sketches are a number of minor masterpieces. Acute sensibility and moral earnestness, qualities which he shares with the giants of Russian literature, compensate for his lack of creative force. Garshin's ideas closely parallel those of the Populists; submerging his ego in the life of the people was with him a consuming desire, particularly in his youth. For a time he found peace in military life, but he never minimized the horror of war; it is his keen awareness of it that gives poignancy to such stories as "Four Days" and "Trus" (1879; Eng. tr., "Coward"). For Garshin war was first of all an unavoidable evil. The wounded man who spends four days on a battlefield does not know the answer to war's fundamental contradictions, and the "coward" simply resolves to undergo that evil without finding the reason for its existence. "Iz vospominani ryadovovo Ivanova" (1883; Eng. tr., "From the Reminiscences of Private Ivanov"), on the same theme, has a larger sweep, but is calmer and pervaded with sadness. The same year saw the appearance of Garshin's acknowledged masterpiece, "Krasny tsvetok" (Eng. tr., "The Scarlet Blossom"); the author's experiences as well as his interest in psychiatry made him particularly qualified to give an accurate portrayal of a madman striving to eradicate all evil, which to him was concentrated in the three poppies growing in the hospital garden. While this story represents Garshin's most direct approach to the problem of evil, the issue pervades much of his work. In "Proisshestviye" (1878; Eng. tr., "An Incident") and "Nadezhda Nikolayevna" (1885; Eng. tr., "Nadezhda Nikolayevna") his idealized prostitutes inspire true love, but nevertheless precipitate tragedies. In "Vstrecha" (1879; Eng. tr., "The Meeting") a predatory individual confronts a well-meaning but ineffective man. In "Khudozhniki" (1879; The Artists) a painter fails because he cannot find moral justification for his art. "Attalea Princeps" (1880; Eng. tr., "Attalea Princeps") is a negation of violence, its symbolism foreshadowing "Skazaniye o gordom Aggeye" (1886; The Tale of the Proud Aggei); the latter, as well as the "Signal" (1887; Eng. tr., "The Signal"), clearly shows the influence of Leo Tolstoy (*q.v.*).

See: V. G. Korolenko, "V. M. Garshin," in D. N. Ovsyaniko-Kulikovski, ed., *Istoriya russkoi literatury XIX veka,* IV (1910), 335–361; G. A. Byaly, *Garshin; literaturnaya borba vosmidesyatykh godov* (1937).

P. A. P.

Geijerstam, Gustaf af (1858–1909, Swedish novelist, short-story writer, and publicist), was born in Västmanland. Brought up in a staid, conservative family tradition with which he broke during his years as a student at Uppsala (in the late 70's and early 80's), Geijerstam became one of the most active proponents of the new realistic and liberal literary movement of the 80's. His first work was a collection of scarcely distinguished short stories *Gråkallt* (1882; Gray Cold), dealing with themes characteristic of the reform-minded literature of the day, such as the conflicts between parents and children and between young men and their beloved resulting from differing views on social and religious questions. Two partly autobiographical novels, *Erik Grane* (1885) and *Pastor Hallin* (1887), develop similar themes at greater length but scarcely with more distinction. Geijerstam's realistic peasant tales—*Fattigt Folk* (2 vols., 1884–1889; Poor People) and *Kronofogdens berättelser* (1890; The District Bailiff's Stories)—are more important, chiefly, perhaps, because they are far more objective, much less concerned with pressing home current ideals of social reform. In some of these tales one finds a strong preoccupation with certain primitive criminal types, studied sympathetically in terms of subconscious and unconscious motivations; in this he was obviously influenced by Dostoevski (*q.v.*). This new emphasis upon a psychological, as distinguished from a social or ethical, approach became characteristic of Geijerstam in the 90's and later. From about the middle of the 90's Geijerstam was very productive, turning out until his death in 1909 a steady stream of novels, short stories, plays (chiefly broad peasant farces in an old Swedish burlesque tradition), and essays. Among the more popular of these later works are the hopelessly sentimental *Boken om lillebror* (1900, 17th ed., 1910; Eng. tr., *The Book about Little Brother,* 1921) and *Kvinnomakt* (1901; Eng. tr., *Woman Power,* 1927). None of this late work, however, weighs at all heavily in the literary scales, though it was exceedingly popular with a broad public (in Germany as well as in Sweden), and though much of it gives apparently sincere, if superficial, expression to the reaction current in the early years of the century against an oversimplified view of human life and human psychology characteristic of the earlier social reform literature of the 80's. Geijerstam may be said to be a first-class journalist and a publicist of some distinction rather than a literary genius of real originality and power.

See: G. Castrén, *Den nya tiden, 1870–1914* (1932), Vol. VII of H. Schuck and K. Warburg, *Illustrerad svensk litteraturhistoria,* 3d ed., pp. 203–208; M. Johnsson, *En åttitalist: Gustaf af Geijerstam, 1858–1895* (1934).

A. G.

Gentile, Giovanni (1875–1944, Italian philosopher, educator, and statesman), was born in

Castelvetrano, Sicily, of poor parents. After studying classics at the Trapani Lyceum, he attended the Normal School of Pisa, where through Donato Jaja he became acquainted with the Hegelian philosophy of Bertrando Spaventa, the most important influence on his intellectual formation. He has held chairs of philosophy at the universities of Naples, Palermo, Pisa, and Rome. In 1903 he began to write for Croce's (*q.v.*) *Critica* and in 1920 started his own *Giornale critico della filosofia italiana.*

Gentile's doctoral thesis, *Rosmini e Gioberti* (1898), the first volume of his series of outstanding contributions on the history of Italian philosophy since the Renaissance, was followed by *Dal Genovesi al Galluppi* (1903), *Studi vichiani* (1915), *Le Origini della filosofia contemporanea in Italia* (1917–1923), *Giordano Bruno e il pensiero del Rinascimento* (1920), *Bertrando Spaventa* (1920), *Studi sul Rinascimento* (1923), *I Profeti del Risorgimento italiano* (1923), and *Il Pensiero italiano del secolo XIX* (1928). His most important works as an educator are *Sommario di pedagogia come scienza filosofica* (2 vols., 1913–1914), *La Riforma dell' educazione* (1920; Eng. tr., *The Reform of Education,* 1922), and *La Riforma della scuola in Italia* (1932). His main books in political philosophy are *La Filosofia di Marx* (1899), *I Fondamenti della filosofia del diritto* (1916), *Che cosa è il fascismo* (1925), and *Origini e dottrina del fascismo* (1929). His contributions in the philosophy of religion include *Il Modernismo e i rapporti fra religione e filosofia* (1909) and *Discorsi di religione* (1920). In the field of æsthetics and literary criticism are *Frammenti di estetica e letteratura* (1921), *Dante e Manzoni* (1923), *Manzoni e Leopardi* (1929), and *La Filosofia dell'arte* (1931).

Gentile's political activities were intensified with the March on Rome in 1922, at which time he was made a senator and became virtually the "official philosopher" of the new Fascist state. This political change was destined to bring about an unfortunate rift between him and his former colleague, Benedetto Croce. Gentile was minister of public instruction under Mussolini from October, 1922 to June, 1924, during which time he devoted himself zealously to the reform of the Italian school system. He was president of the following organizations: Committee to Reform the Italian Constitution; Fascist Institute of Culture, whose organ is *Educazione fascista;* Higher Council of Public Instruction; Leonardo Foundation; and Inter-University Institute. He also directed the monumental work of the new *Enciclopedia italiana.* However, with the Second World War, he lost practically all of his political influence and a considerable amount of his philosophical influence in Italy. He was shot and killed by political enemies outside his house in Florence on April 15, 1944.

Gentile calls his philosophical system by the double name of "actual idealism" or "actualism." This system is developed in *La Riforma della dialettica hegeliana* (1913), *Teoria generale dello spirito come atto puro* (1916; Eng. tr., *The Theory of Mind as Pure Act,* 1922), and *Sistema di logica come teoria del conoscere* (2 vols., 1917). The "actualistic" philosophy represents historically a great and persistent effort to "out-Hegel" Hegel and reach an idealism that is absolutely absolute. Actualism is based on the method of "absolute immanence," in which absolutely nothing is presupposed by the process of thinking because the "thinking ego" posits everything. Reality is "pure experience" or philosophy itself, which is the synthetic "moment" or aspect of the spirit; and art, on the one hand, science and religion, on the other, are respectively the subjective and objective "moments" of spiritual reality, which is at once both the knowing and willing, the thinking and doing of man. The unification of intellectual and practical activities leads Gentile to identify actualism with Fascism. Actual idealism as a philosophy, which is an original form of Hegelian neoidealism, is important for both historical and logical reasons. The Gentilian system remarkably recapitulates the subjectivistic trend of modern thought and thus serves as the crucial test of the entire idealistic tradition, of which it claims to be the "most rigorous form." In this sense, Gentile is the "last" of the moderns.

See: E. Chiocchetti, *La Filosofia di Giovanni Gentile* (1922); V. La Via, *L' Idealismo attuale di Giovanni Gentile* (1925); M. M. Thompson, *The Educational Philosophy of Giovanni Gentile* (1934); R. W. Holmes, *The Idealism of Giovanni Gentile* (1937); P. Romanelli, *Gentile: The Philosophy of Giovanni Gentile* (1938).

P. R.

George, Stefan (1868–1933, German poet), was born in the village of Büdesheim near Bingen on the Rhine. He spent his childhood in Bingen and at the Greek and Latin school in Darmstadt where he completed his schooling in 1888. Subsequently he devoted himself to the study of modern languages, first in French Switzerland and Paris, later at the University of Berlin. During his frequent long stays in Paris, he had personal contacts with Mallarmé, Verlaine, Régnier (*qq.v.*), and Rodin. In London he met Ernest Dowson, and in Belgium and the Netherlands he formed friendships with Van Lerberghe, Verhaeren, Verwey (*qq.v.*), and the painters Ensor and Toorop. His journeys took him north as far as Copenhagen, east to Vienna, west and south to central Spain and to Paestum in Italy. After 1914, he left Germany only for vacations in the Swiss Alps, which he preferred to the windy seashore. He refused honors and funds offered him by the Nazi government and died a voluntary exile in Locarno, Switzerland, on December 4, 1933. He is buried in Locarno.

His work may be divided into five periods. The first period includes poems written up to his 21st year. At this time George intended to become a painter. These poems show that blend of emotion and philosophy dear to youth and are full of tormenting questions about the meaning of life. Some of them were written in a language he himself had invented and later transcribed into German. Only selections are extant, published by George himself in the *Fibel* (1901) and in the last volume of his works.

The second period comprises the *Hymnen* (1890), *Pilgerfahrten* (1891), *Algabal* (1892), and *Die Bücher der Hirten und Preisgedichte, der Sagen und Sänge und der hängenden Gärten* (1895). The poetry of this period may be termed symbolistic and impressionistic. It is in strong opposition to the naturalistic trend of the German poetry of that time. Not only did George incorporate the elements of the French symbolist poets (*see* French symbolism) and impressionist painters, but he also set his stamp on the language of his country. He made it more stern and sparing and utilized the vowel sounds in new and richer combinations. Emotions are not described or analyzed, but conveyed by ear and eye impressions. As is the case with many other works of the poet, the composition of *Hymnen* covers the period of a year, the eternal cycle which nature and the human soul, in tune with the changing seasons, require for their renewal. In *Pilgerfahrten* he is no longer satisfied with the creatures of his imagination, but searches among his contemporaries for a gesture of deeper understanding. It was at this juncture that, together with the young Austrian poet Hugo von Hofmannsthal (*q.v.*) and the Belgian Paul Gérardy, he founded the journal *Blätter für die Kunst* (1892–1919), which was published at irregular intervals and only for subscribers. In *Algabal* he dramatizes the young Roman emperor Heliogabalus, but he deviates from the historical data: his Algabal feels himself close to the passions of the people and is imbued with a sense of remoteness from his environment. "Hirten und Preisgedichte" represents the poet's recovery from this feverish and futile search for companionship. He takes refuge in the world surrounding him, in the unpolluted woods and valleys of his native land and in the simple life of fishermen and shepherds, untouched by the changing centuries. The curves and points and windings of a Gothic town, more French than German, and those aspects of knighthood that are still valid in the modern world form the background for the "Sagen und Sänge." In "Hängende Gärten," an impetuous inner life, in which each moment is savored to the utmost, is set against oriental scenery.

The next sequence, the monochrome and linear period, embraces *Das Jahr der Seele* (1897) and the volume *Der Teppich des Lebens und die Lieder von Traum und Tod, mit einem Vorspiel* (1899). In *Das Jahr der Seele* George is almost reconciled to not finding a companion. An undercurrent of gentle and steadfast melancholy combines even the most contrasting colors into a delicately tinted, homogeneous whole. The poems speak of an "I" and a "you," but more often these terms do not represent two persons but the poet in discussion with himself. From the heights of his solitude he beholds men and objects spread before him like a tapestry of life, and he draws the figures as one sees them on the wall hangings of the Middle Ages, where the most characteristic gesture is arrested at the peak of motion. In the dramatic rise of the "Vorspiel" to "Der Teppich," the poet expresses his philosophy in a dialogue with an angel who is none other than his own soul. "Die Lieder von Traum und Tod" supplies a mystical and transcendent close to this period of despair.

The fourth, his classical period, comprises *Der siebente Ring* (1907) and *Der Stern des Bundes* (1914). The poet found the companion for whom he had been searching in a boy who died at the age of 15, after George had known him for about a year. In the poet's life, this companion, called Maximin, played a role similar to that of Dante's Beatrice. In *Tage und Taten* (1903), George's only volume of prose, he describes his first encounter with Maximin. *Der siebente Ring* reveals the realms thrown open by this friendship. The laws of the new world and the new life are given in *Der Stern des Bundes*. The language of these poems is terse and forceful, and its beauty does not depend on poetic devices or sustaining power of rhyme.

In his last period, George is the judge and seer of his time. *Das neue Reich* (1928) treats of the actual problems of his age. The subject matter is wide in scope, ranging from poems on the basic significance of the First World War to lyrics akin to folk songs in their poignant simplicity of symbols and of meaning.

George translated Shakespeare's *Sonnets* (*Sonette,* 1912), selected cantos from Dante's *The Divine Comedy* (*Göttliche Komödie,* 1909), the major part of Baudelaire's *Les Fleurs du mal* (*Die Blumen des Bösen,* 1901), and poems by Rossetti, Swinburne, Dowson, Jacobsen (*q.v.*), Kloos, Verwey, Verhaeren, Verlaine, Mallarmé, Rimbaud (*q.v.*), Régnier, D'Annunzio (*q.v.*), and Rolicz-Lieder.

See: F. Gundolf, *George* (1930); F. Wolters, *Stefan George und die Blätter für die Kunst* (1930); E. L. Duthie, *L'Influence du symbolisme français dans le renouveau poétique de l'Allemagne; les Blätter für die Kunst de 1892 à 1900* (1933); E. Morwitz, *Die Dichtung Stefan Georges* (1934); Stefan George, *Poems,* tr. by C. N. Valhope and E. Morwitz (1943), German text included; B. von Bothmer, *Stefan George Bibliography* (in preparation).

E. M.

Géraldy, Paul (pseud. of Paul Le Fèvre, 1885–, French poet and dramatist), was born in Paris, where he resides. His poems and plays concern the behavior of men and women of the rich, leisured class. His characters are tense, nervous, fastidious materially if not spiritually; they have no moral code except that they demand integrity from each other in their own relations; they are insecure and desperately seeking momentary happiness with each other.

Petites Ames (1908) reflects the poet's adolescence, *Toi et moi* (1913; Eng. tr., *You and Me,* 1923) his growing concern with the psychological aspects of love between man and woman—a problem which he continues to dissect in *Aimer* (1921), *Robert et Marianne* (1925), and *Christine* (1932), all presented with considerable success at the Comédie Française. In these plays he is more lyrical than profound. *Les Noces d'argent* (Eng. tr., condensed version, *Nest,* 1922) concerns the estrangement of parents and children in a rich middle-class family. It was produced at the Comédie Française in 1917 and failed. In 1928 at the same theatre it was presented again, this time with success, and subsequently appeared in translation all over Europe and in America. The vigorous treatment of the subject is occasionally reminiscent of Henry Becque (*q.v.*), but for the most part *Les Noces d'argent* is just another "well-made play." *Duo* (1938), adopted from the novel of the same name by Colette (*q.v.*), has, on the other hand, not only virile dramatic action but plausible characterization and real pathos. Géraldy has written three pieces with Robert Spitzer, *Do Sol Mi Do* (1925), *L'Homme de joie* (1929), and *Son Mari* (1927), all produced successfully in the boulevard theatres, and one play with Laveline, *La Princesse* (1919), produced at the Odéon. His one-act plays include *Les Spectateurs* (1906), *La Comédie de Famille* (1908), and *Les Grands Garçons* (1922; Eng. tr., *Just Boys: Father and Son,* 1933). "Le Grand-Père," a dramatic poem, was declaimed by Féraudy at the Comédie Française (May 22, 1915). Géraldy has also written the novels *La Guerre, Madame* (1917; Eng. tr., *The War, Madame,* 1917) and *Le Prélude* (1922); *L'Amour* (1929; Eng. tr., *L'Amour; or, The Art of Love,* 1930), maxims; and *Clidindin* (1937), a children's story.

See: John Palmer, *Studies in the Contemporary Theatre* (1937).

E. B. M.

German literature. In the movement of German literature between 1870 and 1940, two themes recur with striking persistence—the gradual emancipation of the writer from the bourgeois tenets of the 19th century and the emerging sense of the artist's increased responsibility within the changing social and political life of the nation. The Franco Prussian War is no casually chosen point of departure; it represents the meaningful date at which, in Germany, the achievement of nationalistic aspirations coincided with the first decisive signs of cultural self-criticism. Soon after the recognition of Germany as a preponderant factor in European politics, German writers themselves began to insist upon the dangers of intellectual isolation and hoped to share in the spiritual life of the continent. None of the German literary movements, in which the endeavors of the three successive generations were to be crystallized, could have taken shape or direction without the influx of ideas, gratefully though never uncritically received, from all parts of Europe. Nationalistic and cosmopolitan tendencies were, at the end of the century, curiously intermingled, and it is well to remember that in the cardinal figure of Friedrich Nietzsche (*q.v.*) elements of Teutonic self-assertion and equally blunt expressions of contempt for the narrow-minded men of the new Reich exist fruitfully side by side.

The 19th century was, in Germany, on the whole, not favorable for the literary artist. In many respects the lingering memory of the idealistic and romantic tradition had paralyzed, rather than enhanced, the creative will, and in spite of many a remarkable individual work the total impression is one of imaginative frustration and indecision; between 1848 and 1870 only one or two novelists contributed to the permanent greatness of the German tradition, and the lyrical achievement of the generation between Heinrich Heine and the realistic poets is platitudinous and uneven. Apart from an academic sort of prose in the considerable body of memoirs, the most vigorous writing of the period and the most distinctly creative intellectual criticism came from the historians and political pamphleteers. The novelists, dramatists, and poets, with a few interesting but hardly striking exceptions, chose, before 1870, to keep aloof from the disquieting preoccupation with the new political issues. Indeed, even where the German writers of the 70's or 80's turned to the pressing subject matter of the changing social scene, they did so with a self-conscious effort of preserving their identity as artists, whose responsibilities were not primarily political.

The German novelist in particular remained ineffectual for so long and his work never reached more than a limited international or even national public because, throughout its history, German fiction has been provincial in setting and parochial in subject matter, whereas the urgent social themes of the advancing century have been predominantly related to the world of the city. In dealing with urban themes and problems the German novelist has, on the whole, been least at ease.

The most distinguished exception to this general observation, and the most urbanely civilized portraitist of Prussian society, both aristocratic and bourgeois, between 1860 and 1890, is Theodor Fontane (*q.v.*). By seizing upon the narrow yet significant Prussian scene, and by the keenness of his observation, he established himself as the one novelist of the age who succeeded in bridging the gulf that usually exists in German fiction between the provincial theme and the craftsmanship of a cosmopolitan storyteller. The motivating elements of his work are a lively sense of historical continuity and a quick perception of the speech and gestures by which the people of his world reveal their special virtues. Moreover, unlike all his other contemporaries, Fontane is wholly unsentimental. In his early journalistic work, he developed a sense of detached and intelligent precision that served him supremely well in his major novels. While it may not be just to compare Fontane to Henry James or Joseph Conrad or, for that matter, to any of his distinguished European contemporaries, he is the only writer of German fiction in the late 19th century who could, now and again, have held his own in their company.

No less significant a narrative artist, though a writer of an entirely different temperament, is Wilhelm Raabe (*q.v.*). In the originality of his idiom, in the breadth of his vision, and in the warmth of his sympathy, he surpasses, at times, Fontane himself, who has much of the cool detachment of Flaubert (*q.v.*) while Raabe continues the fertile tradition of the German baroque imagination. His novels, from *Die Chronik der Sperlingsgasse* (1857) to the somber trilogy *Der Hungerpastor* (1864), *Abu Telfan* (1867), and *Der Schüdderump* (1870), reflect an ever growing concern with the disintegration of the quaint but organic life in the German provinces. As early as 1864 (*Der Hungerpastor*) and 1876 (*Horacker*) and as late as 1891 (*Stopfkuchen*), he interprets apprehensively the implications of the far-reaching achievements of the Prussian armies between 1864 and 1871. Again and again he ponders the disturbing transformation of the nation's emotional life and the conversion of a contemplative people into the efficient but barren organization of the German state. Whatever virtues may illuminate Raabe's world, his is the humor, often bookish and tortuous, of a patient and understanding but never uncritical observer of a society which threatened to substitute sham values for genuine belief.

Few novelists of the time can match the sustained storyteller's craft of Fontane or Raabe. One of them, the Swiss Gottfried Keller (*q.v.*), greatest of all the mid-century realists, issued in 1879 a carefully considered revision of his most impressive novel, *Der grüne Heinrich* (1854–1855); but apart from a late "political" tale, *Martin Salander* (1886), he confined himself at that time to the more congenial medium of the *Novelle,* a form of the short story in which the romantics had excelled and which was now, in the 70's and 80's, once again the favorite German narrative vehicle. Twenty-four volumes of Paul Heyse's (*q.v.*) *Deutscher Novellenschatz* (1871–1876) testify to the popularity of this attractive genre in which genuine fabulists—such as the North German, Theodor Storm (*q.v.*); Gottfried Keller and C. F. Meyer (*q.v.*) in the firm, round manner of the Southwest; and the accomplished Austrians, Ferdinand von Saar (*q.v.*) and Marie von Ebner-Eschenbach (*q.v.*)—spoke authoritatively and appealingly.

It is true that in most of these shorter narratives the provincial themes of German fiction predominate; but the soundness of their form and the steadiness of their human appeal is so striking that, in retrospect, the work of these realistic craftsmen overshadows on the whole the emerging discussion of the new "naturalistic" point of view (*see* German naturalism). Compared to the substantial and lasting achievements of these five or six conservative prose writers, the naturalistic controversy now seems little more than a brief interlude, but —like the subsequent challenge of the "expressionistic" point of view—it served as a climactic shock without which the new "modern" idiom of the 20th century could not have been finally established. This critical skirmish was conducted with vigor and some bitterness, mainly in those cities in which the recent European reorganization had vested economic and social strength—in Berlin, Leipzig, and Munich. Some of the new literary journals sustained the controversy between the rearguard of the idealistic tradition and the cosmopolitan advance of the pseudoscientific and mechanistic-minded forces. In their pages and in the belligerent pamphlets of the outstanding protagonists, the voices of a new generation were first heard, and a distinguished group of European writers (Ibsen, Zola, Tolstoy, Maupassant, Strindberg, Hamsun, Gerhart Hauptmann, *qq.v.*) broke for the first time, with concerted effort, into the established world of bourgeois belief.

The compelling influence of the mid-century's three most persuasive analysts, Taine (*q.v.*), Darwin, and Marx, left the German writers especially preoccupied with the determinist pattern of life. At the beginning of the 80's the fascination of the idealistic tradition seems to be coming to an end: whether optimistic at the prospects of evolutionary progress or resigned to pessimistic immobility, the artist finds himself compelled to abandon the humanistic faith in the creative will of the individual. At a time when German imperialism begins its most aggressive career, the work of Schopenhauer seems, paradoxically, to find its belated fulfillment in the naturalistic philosophy.

At the same time, the earlier predominance of the provincial and idyllic themes now gives way to a deliberate emphasis upon the social issues of the city and of those human types and classes that had not yet actually entered the main stream of self-conscious literature. In the flourishing tradition of the German popular fiction and poetry, the subjects of class conflict and social tension had, of course, not been uncommon. Even the technique of minutely detailed observation and description was not the contribution of the young naturalists alone. But the new matter was now being employed with an aggressive baldness of gesture and design that makes any comparison between the German naturalists and their English, French, or Russian contemporaries difficult. The popularity of the novelist and dramatist Hermann Sudermann (*q.v.*) is not due to the superiority of his achievements; in such works as *Der Katzensteg* (1889) or *Frau Sorge* (1887), he turns the impartial conscientiousness of Zola or Tolstoy into German sentimentality and fails to accomplish more than a transparently crude artifice.

The new and somewhat naïve critical belief in the staccato reproduction of a narrow segment of life, applied, as it was, with the stubbornness of the smaller German naturalistic talents, made any fiction of real distinction impossible. The instrument of the German language which had, since the days of Goethe, become so impressive an organ of thought and eloquence now failed to serve and discipline the narrative artist. Fontane, one of the first to recognize the courage and justice of the naturalistic idiom, bestowed his earliest and generous praise not upon a work of fiction, but upon the paradigmatic play of Arno Holz and Johannes Schlaf (*qq.v.*), *Die Familie Selicke* (1890). It was in the drama—or the theatre— that the nervous manner of meticulous reporting proved to be most effective.

The German drama of the immediate past had not been undistinguished. Still bound to the idealistic conventions of belief and technique, its subject matter had philosophical substance, patriotic fervor, and, here and there, popular appeal. Throughout the age, Richard Wagner's (*q.v.*) influence was compelling, even irresistible. In 1876 his festival house at Bayreuth was finally opened with his *Nibelungen* tetralogy, and six years later *Parsifal* concluded the spectacular career of an artist whose creative work and critical convictions, with all their one-sidedness, were more widely disturbing than those of any other of his European contemporaries.

The naturalistic drama differed in essential respects, however, from Wagner's romantically conceived and emotionally strenuous notion of the *Gesamtkunstwerk*. With something like pedantic consistency, the new playwrights proceeded to dissolve the heroic center of the classical drama into a dull variety of involuntary gestures and episodic situations; even in its subject matter the naturalistic drama was at first tiresome and monotonous, but it soon abandoned the narrow preoccupation with crime, hunger, and disease. In the hands of its most vigorous and gifted artist, Gerhart Hauptmann, it became a remarkably telling and flexible form.

Hauptmann's achievement is not easily summarized. In many respects he has been an awkward and at times even irresponsible artist, whose long career has been filled with surprises and disappointments. But in the company of his more superficial and less courageous—and now generously forgotten—contemporaries, he remains in Germany the only genuine representative of the modern realistic drama. The spectacular aspects of his early success (*Vor Sonnenaufgang,* 1889) are now a matter of record. What gives him lasting distinction is that, within the brief period of 10 or 15 years, he enlarged the indistinct medium of naturalistic speech and action into a variety of impressive dramatic accomplishments. The influence upon him of Ibsen's, Björnson's, (*q.v.*) and Dostoevski's (*q.v.*) religious idealism is strong at first, and compassion remains his most persistent trait. *Die Weber* (1892), a stirring account of exploited and tragically charged human beings, has proved to be Hauptmann's most straightforward work, free of the cliché and claptrap of similar "propaganda" plays. Both in comedy (*Der Biberpelz,* 1893) and in historical tragedy (*Florian Geyer,* 1895), he develops the naturalistic style by the force and detachment of his own temperament into a superbly final type of 19th-century epic-drama. Two later and even more powerful plays, *Fuhrmann Henschel* (1899) and *Rose Bernd* (1903), reaffirmed his skill in human portraiture; but he had then already passed beyond the strict pattern of naturalistic doctrine, for in *Hanneles Himmelfahrt* (1893) and his most widely played lyrical drama in verse, *Die versunkene Glocke* (1897), he had made use of newly developed symbolic poetic devices. Throughout his later career he has shown himself to be resourceful and versatile. Characteristically, he has remained immune to the disturbing influence of Nietzsche—his strength is drawn not from the philosophers, but from a deep sense of the nervous energy and delicate contour of the individual human being.

Hauptmann's work, as well as that of his lesser naturalistic contemporaries, owes much to the flourishing theatrical culture of the time. Three events indicate the memorable advance of the Berlin theatre: the production in 1874, by the duke of Meiningen's troupe, of Shakespeare's *Julius Caesar,* a display of "realistic" staging and mass scenes which was not to be easily surpassed; the establishment, in 1883, of the Deutsches Theater which, under the directorship of A. L'Arronge, was to devote itself both to the classics and to the more drastic new portrayals of Berlin life; and the founding, in 1889, of the Verein Freie Bühne. With its first production (Ibsen's *Ghosts*) and by its sensitiveness to the new contemporary idiom, it gained at once, under its director, Otto Brahm, the respect and enthusiasm of the younger generation. The work of Max Reinhardt (1873–1943), the most agile theatrical talent of the past 50 years, gave to the newly invigorated medium particular distinction. With an extraordinary feeling for the spectacular elements of the old Austrian baroque theatre he combined a metropolitan instinct for the subtleties of poetic effect and a flair for the new function of actor and stage designer. His wide range from Molière to Strindberg, from Gorky's *Night Asylum* to Johann Strauss's *Die Fledermaus,* from Goethe to Georg Kaiser, suggests the measure of his contribution to the vitality and elegance of the stage which long has been, and is especially at the present time, the one artistic area within which the collective devotion of the Germans to the symbols and images of art finds conspicuous public expression.

It was the imaginative strength of the new theatre which directly or indirectly facilitated for the younger writers the transition from the unpromising doctrine of naturalism to more flexible and more specifically poetic forms. Whether the generation of poets, painters, or musicians which now began to reexamine the sources and aims of the work of art declared its allegiance to an "impressionistic," "symbolist," or "neo-romantic" group, its common concern was with the irrational source of the artist's vision. The new poetry did not, of course, at once abandon its preoccupation with the pressing contemporary subject matter of social issues. On the contrary, two of its most forceful representatives, the poets Detlev von Liliencron and Richard Dehmel (*qq.v.*), with all their nervous impressionistic perception were intensely, at times even hectically, concerned with the current issues of sex, social tension, and the city. Those were relevant themes, and the conservative talents assembled in Heyse's *Münchner Dichterbuch* (1882) are the poorer for their want of them. Wilhelm Boelsche in an influential essay, *Die naturwissenschaftlichen Grundlagen der Poesie* (1887), the young Arno Holz (*q.v.*) in his first volume of lyrics, *Das Buch der Zeit* (1885), and the *avant-garde* writers in Arent's *Moderne Dichter-Charaktere* (1885) had stressed the link between the poet and the new "scientific" or the "French" manner of seeing the world. But the stirring example of poetic inspiration and political fervor was Walt Whitman, whose poetry had long been vigorously defended by Freiligrath and was now energetically recognized by Johannes Schlaf (*Walt Whitman,* 1897, 1904). Against the lean and formalized imagery of the German mid-century poets, Whitman represented the voice and rhythm of unself-conscious imagination.

In Dehmel and Liliencron, in the later poetry of Holz (*Phantasus,* 1898–1899), and in one or two minor impressionist poets, the curiously delicate and on the whole unmartial sensibility of the post-Bismarckian era was to find its appropriate idiom. Their perception was not merely precise and accurate, but subtle, and the pulse of their verse was more passionate and restless than might have appeared tolerable, even to the most understanding poets of the older generation. But, for the first time since the flowering of the romantics in the 1820's and 1830's, the poet spoke with the aggressive ardor of the genuinely inspired singer.

The year 1890 indicates the beginning of a far-reaching imaginative movement, of which Hugo von Hofmannsthal, Rainer Maria Rilke, and Stefan George (*qq.v.*) are the most striking representatives. About George's strange and masterly personality gathered the proud apostles of the aristocratic and antimaterialistic faith, who, in the *Blätter für die Kunst* (1892–1919), denounced the pedestrian dullness of naturalism. Hofmannsthal was bound to the new attitude, if not directly at least indirectly, by the patrician delicacy and depth of his intelligence. Rilke, the sensitive Easterner, the *pater seraphicus,* kept cautiously apart from the slowly forming circle of George's followers. But all three, throughout their work, are concerned with the question of the poet's position in an antipoetical world.

In the lyrical poetry at the turn of the century, a feeling of the artist's self-consciousness is especially obvious. To the young Nietzsche, who had met Wagner in 1868, it was axiomatic that civilization and culture should culminate in the artist; with him in 1872 (see *Die Geburt der Tragödie*), as it had also been with Schopenhauer, no creative activity transcended that of the musician. But the poetry of the 90's, whether it came from the East, the West, or the South, reflected the precarious situation of the man of feeling and vision in a fundamentally incoherent society. The Kaiser's refusal to patronize the naturalistic playwrights was merely obtuse, the overwhelming public embarrassment in the face of Baudelaire (*q.v.*), Dehmel, Wedekind, and Strindberg was more serious. The word decadence, which was to become so symptomatic of the intellectual climate of the 90's, meant, of course, more than degeneracy and moral degradation; it conveyed the pathetic increase of spiritual and nervous energies at the expense of biological strength and bourgeois efficacy. Thomas Mann's *Buddenbrooks* (1901), a prodigiously gifted young man's first novel, paraphrases this theme, and his tales, from *Der kleine Herr Friedemann* (1898) to *Der Tod in Venedig* (1913), even the entertainingly moralizing *Königliche Hoheit* (1909), reflect with singular perspicacity some of the spiritual elements which now motivate the young neo-romantics—a lively sense of the irrational heritage of the German past, an insistence upon the traditional responsibility of the man of letters, and the ever more pressing concern with the virtues and destiny of man.

These were, in substance, Nietzsche's problems; and Nietzsche's work is the gigantic gauge by which not only those immediately under his influence but also each generation since his death in 1900 have measured their world. His peremptory challenges, formulated in the most brilliant and disciplined prose of the century, were ultimately directed at the nature of man, at the biological source of his perception, the depth and fiber of his emotional and intellectual constitution, and above all his moral obligation to a society in a state of precarious crisis.

Impressionists, symbolists, and expressionists alike were profoundly affected by Nietzsche's complex work. Among the early impressionists, those who were indebted to the brothers Goncourt (*q.v.*) and the French painters from Monet to Renoir, the preoccupation was, clearly, with a new understanding of the artist's private sensibility. In Germany, Eduard von Hartmann (1842–1906), the philosopher of the "unconscious," had some time before (1869) dissolved the round individuality of the ego into a series of atomic and fleeting perceptions which were, in the subsequent intuitive and metaphysical philosophy of Bergson (*q.v.*) and the psychology of Wundt and Freud, confirmed as the new units of experience. The symbols of Baudelaire and Mallarmé (*q.v.*), the light gestures of Marées and Liebermann, and the "small sensations" of Cézanne and Debussy make up some of the most generally distinctive elements of the intellectual climate of the European *fin de siècle.*

Vienna, always delicate and melancholy in its temper, became the scene of much of the new writing: the emotional refinements of Arthur Schnitzler (*q.v.*) found their most appropriate setting in a society more urbanely, more naïvely preoccupied with the transitoriness of life than was the weary Claudio in Hofmannsthal's *Der Tor und der Tod* (1893). Peter Altenberg (*q.v.*), with his extraordinary feeling for the brittle, revealing detail, is the characteristic Austrian master of a literary chamber music for which Johannes Schlaf's (*q.v.*) Chekhov-like sketches, *In Dingsda* (1892), with their blurring and lyrical overtones, supplied a minor German melody.

Hugo von Hofmannsthal, the most sensitive of the Viennese poets of the 90's, developed the resources of his Austrian heritage into a body of disciplined verse and prose so distinguished that the impressionistic idiom of his early poetry was but the promising beginning of a literary career which surpasses in variety, breadth, and wisdom that of any of his contemporaries. His association with Max Reinhardt and Richard Strauss links him to the baroque theatrical and musical splendor of the post-Wagnerian and neo-romantic generation; his rich, measured, and classical prose is, in modern German literature, unrivaled.

If the gravity of tradition and cultural responsibility dominate Hofmannsthal's work, it is the religious crisis of the age which gives direction and significance to Rilke's poetry. He, too, began as an impressionist. His earliest poems, before *Das Buch der Bilder* (1902), have little specific weight. But the contrasting experiences, first of Russia and later of Rodin's masterly absorption in work, and the instability of his own restless life produced, before the First World War, poetry which for wealth and steadiness of vision is, in retrospect, strikingly consistent and impressive. His cardinal theme, elaborated with an ever more severe measure of self-denial and objectivity, is the loneliness of modern man. The issues of Kierkegaard's Christian radicalism, the religious speculations of subsequent Protestant theologians such as Barth and Brunner, even the prominent psychotherapeutic reflections of men like Jung, are all touched tangentially in Rilke's work. It may be that one source of Rilke's perception was private and romantic; but in an age which was overcharged with a disturbing variety of shifting attitudes and concerns, his total contribution is both unique and convincing. His poetry is never, except by profound implication, "political"; neither in his magnificent late work nor in his voluminous correspondence is there evidence of any concern for the simpler and institutional social ties that hold men together. Even the events of the First World War drove Rilke only into a more intense search for the stable realities in which the supremely conscious man, the poet, could find his place.

In George, the third of the great modern German poets, the paradoxical tensions that sustain the pattern of the past 50 years become most sharply visible. His influence upon the German scene of the last two generations is incalculable. Beginning as the self-willed center of a small group of antipositivist minds, he ended not only as a poet who had achieved an extraordinary manner of his own, but as a prophet of national resurgence. George, the master and seer, and his *Kreis* of devout followers belong in the succession of Nietzsche; aristocratic and pointedly disciplined, but never divorced from the broad current of a common historical heritage—on the contrary, intensely aware of the cultural and traditional responsibilities of the poet—this group represents the extreme measure of the deliberate and stylized, even "heroic" gesture.

The images of past greatness, to which George and his circle were devoted, became the objects of a peculiarly sensitive and exalted form of mythography, and the group's *Blätter für die Kunst,* at first confined to an esoteric circle, provided a guarded platform for men who have since become conspicuous representatives of the new historical sensibility. Few of the disciples attained distinct poetic significance, but George himself, both in his rigorously cultivated idiom and in his gradual focusing upon the political subject matter of the "Reich," achieved an incomparable degree of poetic intensity. His translations from many European poets indicate the range of his spiritual indebtedness.

More palpably than any other major poet George demanded the return to categorical values; indeed, the relativism of the natural sciences and the conciliatory perspectivism of the historical school had gradually given way to a stricter concept of the humanities (*Geisteswissenschaften*), for which the philosopher and historian, Wilhelm Dilthey (1833–1911), had given far-reaching and suggestive definitions and which was now to bear fruit in almost all phases of contemporary thinking. The philosophical writings of the time, whether they are concerned with sociological, aesthetic, or religious problems, are, therefore, of outstanding importance for the appraisal of German literature. Historians not only of the German past, but of the European literatures as well gave new and remarkable impetus to the critical examination of literary patterns and values.

The intellectual currents among the creative writers of the Wilhelmian era are not easily analyzed, but in a comprehensive sense they can be called political, for all impulses of the time spring from a deep-rooted sense of unprecedented change in the outer and inner life of the nation. To divide them into liberal and conservative is perhaps to give unwarranted unity to a large variety of revolutionary attitudes; but the direction of their attack is in almost all cases anti-bourgeois, and much of their aggressive terminology is no less Nietzschean than was the privately poetic temper of the impressionistic and symbolist poets. At the turn of the century, so it seemed, the aftermath of 1870 merged into a premonition of 1914. For their genuine and vigorous comments upon all forms of cultural hypocrisy the South German satirists, with their mocking but prudent strength, were especially effective. *Jugend* and *Simplicissimus,* two of the sharpest and wittiest of the semipolitical papers, both founded in Munich in 1896 provide genuine and biting social criticism; Karl Kraus (*q.v.*) and the belligerent but securely rooted Bavarian, Ludwig Thoma (*q.v.*), were early contributors; the ironical and devastating Biedermeier cartoons of Thomas Theodor Heine became, 25 years after Wilhelm Busch (*q.v.*), the inimitable signature of oblique social pessimism.

In the North, it was Paul Ernst (*q.v.*) who, socialist in politics but conservative in temperament and neoclassicist in form, analyzed in his extensive and varied writings the collapse of German idealism. Nietzsche's influence upon his thinking is unmistakable. With ceaseless energy of thought he challenged, in his austere tragedies as well as in his expert narrative works, the determinism and fatalistic concepts of the naturalistic doctrine. Others (Ferdinand Avenarius, 1856–1923; Arthur Moeller van den Bruck, 1876–1925; Wilhelm von Scholz, Wilhelm Schäfer, Heinrich Mann, *qq.v.*) also stated the case for a more resolutely "political" literature.

Perhaps no part of the literary life profited more from the seriousness with which the place of the arts was now being discussed than German fiction at the turn of the century. Even though the new novel is highly individualistic, it reflects nevertheless the strong interest of the time in matters of a broader cultural kind. Eduard von Keyserling (*q.v.*), in temperament and style related to the widely read Danes, J. P. Jacobsen and Herman Bang (*qq.v.*), observes the oppressively thin atmosphere and the self-conscious paralysis of an enervated and overbred Baltic aristocracy. Even in the work of Thomas Mann, the formal detachment of the Flaubert-Fontane tradition now merges more expressly with the emotional temper of the German romantic heritage. Yet Thomas Mann soon transcends his early proficiency in the impressionistic idiom. The scope and texture of his work have steadily grown; the many memorable figures of his distinguished world, the Tonio Krögers and Buddenbrooks, the Aschenbachs and Castorps, even the recent mythological characters of a recreated past, have appeared before us as ever more urgent reminders of the novelist's concern with the human chance of spiritual self-justification. If, in the earliest tales, it was the socially suspect "artist" who failed to assert himself against an uncomprehending bourgeoisie, the problem of man's adjustment to society and his mastery of the irrational has of late become Thomas Mann's dominant theme. With his work the German novel has undoubtedly attained European rank, but in spite (or because) of the accuracy and refinement of his observation, he has, to some extent, remained the characteristic representative of an atomistic age. When in the late 20's the mood of the time became revolutionary, it seemed to many that his voice and his preceptorial humanism had lost much of their persuasive force. Since his arrival in the United States he has, once again, taken an active part in the discussion of political issues. Many other less brittle novelists may in their work have recorded the changing tide of contemporary feeling more directly and often with more absorbing passion, but in intelligence, moral seriousness, and craftsmanship Thomas Mann has rarely been surpassed.

Of the numerous women writers in whom the delicacy of naturalistic and impressionistic observation is successfully united with a lively sense of plot and character, only one, Ricarda Huch (*q.v.*), has attained lasting significance. Her early patrician novel, *Erinnerungen von Ludolf Ursleu dem Jüngeren* (1893), was followed by a series of broad historical works in which scholarly solidity and expertness of narrative style are happily combined. The sense of obligating tradition, so pronounced in Ricarda Huch, is at the same time one of the dominant traits of the period itself; it is the quality by which many of the impressionist novelists and poets succeeded in giving permanence to their talent.

The initial phases of this return to significant values were inevitably critical of the very foundations of the time. Nietzsche's cultural pessimism, his anticipation of the century of nihilism, his doubts of the validity of current values, his insistence upon biological rather than ideological standards—all merged into an apocalyptic sense of crisis without which neither the generation before nor that after the First World War can be rightly understood. The acid work of the dramatist Frank Wedekind (*q.v.*) is an indication of the cynical despair and skepticism with which, even before the astringent social challenge of Heinrich Mann, Georg Kaiser (*q.v.*), Alfred Döblin (*q.v.*), and Hermann Broch (*q.v.*), all contemporary values were being regarded. In the years between the appearance of Raabe's *Horacker* (1876) and Heinrich Mann's *Der Untertan* (1918), the form of cultural criticism had hardened and its intention had gained in bitterness.

The sense of instability and crisis was, however, not confined to the disillusioned older generation, for the establishment of communal youth organizations and ideologically militant *Bünde*, such as the "Wandervogel" (1896) and the "Pfadfinder" (1911), represents an early and far-reaching mobilization of the younger generation itself; both the hopelessness of youth and its revolutionary mood henceforth remain prominent pathological themes. Even the enormous success of Hans Breuer's songbook, *Der Zupfgeigenhansl* (1908), by which much of the popular poetic feeling and imagery of the subsequent period was being determined, has had considerable political significance.

The lively interest in Strindberg and Kierkegaard, in Rilke and the French symbolist poets (*see* French symbolism), and the ever more fashionable preoccupation with Eastern, especially Russian, literature are sufficiently telling signs. The rebarbative, almost oriental, fiction of Wassermann (*q.v.*) represents in its subject matter the most persuasive statement of the prevailing sense of the individual's merging into humanity or, better, of man's individual responsibility for the whole of mankind. In their form these and other popular novels avoid the radical idiom which was to become characteristic of the expressionistic generation. Impressionistic delicacy and naturalistic determinism had, of course, become equally suspect during the years before 1914. The *Blätter für die Kunst* had prepared the attack upon both attitudes. Now the artist demanded images which were not accidental, but essential and absolutely valid; he insisted not so much upon an adherence to formal principles of external accuracy as upon imaginative re-creation, an "ex-pression" of the commonly concealed core of any given thing or experience. Not the artist's "impression" of a stable world, but the intensity of his intuitive emotional grasp was now to be the source of his work. The reality which he was to represent was not to be a mere copy, a literal transcription of casual living, but a vision different from it in shape and more intensely spiritual in quality.

In music and painting, in the early works of Munch, Gauguin, Van Gogh, Picasso and Kokoschka, the disintegration—or, it would be better to say—the deliberate reorganization of the pattern of things seen and felt, became plainly apparent. In Schönberg's *Pierrot lunaire* (1912) and in the statues of Wilhelm Lehmbruck (1881–1919) and Ernst Barlach (*q.v.*), the characteristic manipulation of purposeful distortion suggested the striking range of the new sensibility. In all of these artists, most movingly, perhaps, in the work of the painter Franz Marc (1880–1916), the ecstatic intensity of feeling breaks conventional forms and a new, inner organ of perception seems to be at work. The "expressionist" idiom was, of course, not confined to German literature—in the poetry of Rimbaud, Claudel, and Jammes (*qq.v.*) it found significant French representatives—but in the revolutionary and hectic decade after the First World War, it had its most enthusiastic supporters in Germany. As early as 1910 some of its tenets were expounded in two periodicals with the indicative titles *Sturm* and *Aktion*. Hermann Bahr (*q.v.*), the mercurial Viennese who had in 1891 proclaimed the end of naturalism, *Die Überwindung des Naturalismus*, now outlined in his brief and popular *Expressionismus* (1916) its main features. A vast literature of enthusiastic and pseudocritical adherence to the new creed paraphrased the anti-bourgeois, pacifist, and revolutionary (activist) nature of the new theses.

But only in the work of the lyrical poets did the expressionistic doctrine release poetic energies that were to become a living part of the literary tradition. Kurt Pinthus's comprehensive and crystallizing anthology, *Menschheitsdämmerung* (1920), reveals the variety of expressionist themes and temperaments. The early poets, the visionary Georg Heym, the evanescent Georg Trakl, the religious Ernst Stadler, and August Stramm (*qq.v.*), prophetically anticipate the apocalyptic shadows of the war years. In the poems of Gerrit Engelke (1892–1918), Max Barthel (1893–), Karl Bröger (*q.v.*), Heinrich Lersch (*q.v.*), and J. R. Becher (*q.v.*), the fervor of inspiration and rebellion against the demons of a mechanized age illuminates proletarian and humanitarian motives. The younger generation, emphatic in their denunciation of war, nevertheless reflect the political currents of the time. Only in the baroque work of a few of these poets does the private experience predominate. The early poetry of Franz Werfel (*q.v.*), with its brilliant musical cadences and its religious groping reminiscent of the young Rilke, has in spite of its anti-war sentiments few of the strident artificialities of the expressionist fraternity. Only now and then does it break into the rebellious cry of the later drama.

For it was in the expressionistic drama that the conventions of feeling and form were most strikingly and most consistently denied. Here, in the lyrical and monodramatic plays of R. J. Sorge, Walter Hasenclever, Fritz von Unruh, and Ernst Toller (*qq.v.*) and in the sharp and bizarre social indictments of Carl Sternheim (*q.v.*), Georg Kaiser, and Arnolt Bronnen (1895–), the shiftless and fearful undercurrents of life were cast into startling images and intellectualized symbols and represented in actions and characters which were stripped of their superficial plausibility. At the same time the typically flamboyant "cry" uttered in an unresponsive "space" demanded new patterns of presentation: the expressionistic theatre (Jessner, Martin, Fehling, Piscator), with its grotesquely dissolved architectural frame and the distorted but intense and rhythmical tones and gestures of its depersonalized actors, provided an adequate if puzzling medium for a revolutionary and uprooted generation. Few of the expressionist plays have survived the psychological climate in which they were conceived. They remain essentially the telling documents of a period of frenzied vertigo and of an idealistic resurgence in which the collective experience of social instability and political defeat found its compensating poetic form in hyperbolic effusion and frantic commotion.

The same measure of formal dissolution was not, perhaps, feasible in the realm of expressionistic prose fiction. But the German novelist of that time shares with his contemporaries in France and England a will to redefine in theory and practice the shape and function of narrative art. In the works of Kasimir Edschmid (*q.v.*), Döblin, E. G. Kolbenheyer (*q.v.*), and Hermann Stehr (*q.v.*), the spirit of social and private rebellion and the quest for a new faith are pressed into an explosive and belligerent narrative idiom. The memory of Nietzsche's intellectual criticism and Freud's insistence upon the symbolic nature of all explicit human acts is now apparent in every form of prose writing, especially in the remarkable neo-romantic and surrealist novels of Franz Kafka (*q.v.*), whose influence upon the present generation, particularly in England and America, has been lasting and profound. Near Kafka and Rilke stands Franz Werfel as the third representative of a specifically Eastern form of religious seriousness and inward idealism.

By 1924, the year in which Thomas Mann's *Der Zauberberg* sums up the conflicting tendencies of a bewildering age, the expressionistic interlude had come to an end. It is true that, for a short time, the radical theses of social revolution continued to be advanced in the shrill and dissonant manner of the political theatre. But the dramatist's voice had lost the dithyrambic note of private agony. If a new social and intellectual order had not yet been found, if a common denominator of accepted beliefs had not been established, there nevertheless began to emerge from among the poets and artists strong and striking signs of a recovery of the emotional equilibrium. The terms "matter-of-factness" (*Neue Sachlichkeit*) and "magic realism" offered themselves conveniently for the critical discussion of the change in perspective. Actually, the firmer and unsentimental frame in which life now seemed to gain coherence and which was to give stability of vision to the poets owed its preliminary strength to more than one element. It was not, certainly, a casual reflection of temporary economic prosperity; rather it was, in the work of the significant writers, a "decision" to survey with utmost soberness the moral resources from which the contemporary life was to derive its validity.

First among these was the attempt to focus more sharply upon the memories of the First World War. The impact of those four cataclysmic years had been immense. To the expressionists, they had conjured up eschatological visions of radical evil; now in a mood of recollection and recovery, the poets of the late 20's seem more disposed to accept the moral challenge of a supremely precarious life. Remarque's justly popular *Im Westen nichts Neues* (1929) may not have been the most substantial of all war books, but in the moving pages of Carossa's unheroic yet resolute and steady *Rumänisches Tagebuch* (1924), in the volume *Kriegsbriefe gefallener Studenten* (1928), in Ludwig Renn's documentary *Krieg* (1928), in R. G. Binding's disciplined *Aus dem Kriege* (1925), and in the sharply realistic and detached work of J. M. Wehner, E. E. Dwinger, and especially Ernst Jünger (*qq.v.*), there emerges a poetic sensibility which in many respects far transcends the mere subject matter of the war and leads away from speculation directly into the stern idiom of what contemporary German critics sometimes broadly term existential issues.

But the war, whether contemplated as an individual experience or a collective effort, is only one of many tentative motives of recollection and reorientation. Among them themes of German history have, especially in the "political" fiction of the past years, become more and more frequent. Spengler's spectacular *Der Untergang des Abendlandes* (1918) produced no more than a cursory wave of pseudohistorical interest; the startling and appalling complexity of its weave left no direct impression upon the poets. Hans Grimm's (*q.v.*) cumbersome but widely discussed *Volk ohne Raum* (1926) and his far superior *Die Olewagen Saga* (1918) represent a popular type of semihistorical fiction in which the pride and tribulation of Germans abroad supply the appealing subject matter. Josef Ponten's (*q.v.*) *Volk auf dem Wege* (5 vols., 1930–1941) and the numerous novels of German life in the diaspora are likely to remain documents of the tenacity of the national character. Most of these works are not easily appreciated and will remain, at best, tempting hieroglyphs to the foreign reader. They lack the transparent ease of such successful writers of historical fiction as Alfred Neumann, Bruno Frank, and Stefan Zweig (*qq.v.*), whose works state not so much the weight of conservatively conceived "perennial" values as, rather, the contemporary problems of liberal living.

In Hermann Hesse's *Der Steppenwolf* (1927), in Broch's broad trilogy, *Die Schlafwandler* (1930–1932), in Robert Musil's (*q.v.*) ironically brittle *Der Mann ohne Eigenschaften* (1930–), even in Erich Kästner's (*q.v.*) *Fabian* (1931), the moral deflation of the age finds its most effective expression: all bourgeois forms of life seem here permanently broken, there remains only (as in the memorable world of Kafka) the oppressive reality of man's preoccupation with the plain business of living. The younger generation, disturbingly dislocated, now surveys the shattered frame of its life; in some of its books, aspects of powerful social criticism are mixed in masterly fashion with elements of demonic force.

At the same time, a curious preoccupation with nature, understood as accepting life not only within the desiccated limits of the city, but in a more loosely defined frame of elemental though deeply civilized obligations, is the subject of much of that literature which has sprung up in the monotonous ideological climate of the past 10 years. Without doubt a few of the younger novelists have produced distinguished, though seldom original, work and have achieved novels with the peculiarly provincial and emotional strength inherent in the tradition of German fiction. But their work, where it promises to remain alive, draws in the main on the literary forms of the past; it owes as much to the serene 19th-century world of Richter, Stifter, and Keller as it does to the ironic formal tradition from Flaubert to Hamsun and Thomas Mann.

The narratives of Binding and the autobiographical tales of Carossa point in another direction; they are, together with the remarkable prose of Jünger, documents of a specifically humanistic concern for the spiritual and moral heritage. Thomas Mann's work, from *Der Zauberberg* to his pointillist portrait of Goethe (*Lotte in Weimar,* 1939) and the most recent Joseph tales (1933–1944), although different in its fundamental premises, indicates this resolution most clearly.

Whatever the sources of the emotional cohesion which the contemporary writer in Germany hopes to establish, whether historical, regional, or religious, whether reasoned or irrational, the idiom of the past 15 years is tranquil and collected. It conveys a calm which is not always free of strain and which is the evidence of something like a deep sense of renunciation. Its dominant character, in remarkable contrast to the experimental temper of the war generation, is a self-conscious obligation to tradition. While the expressionist and revolutionary poets dealt with problems of the social and political crisis in large and metaphysical gestures, many of their less militant contemporaries withdrew deliberately, without even an indication of protest, from a disappointing present. The form of their work, different from the loose, sharp "cry" of the years of the First World War, was severe, their melody restrained. The poetry of the late Rilke, of R. A. Schröder (*q.v.*) and Rudolf Borchardt (*q.v.*) is indicative of a palpable shift from expressionist abandon to the austerity of a disciplined idiom. Another phase of the recent progress of poetry began with Bert Brecht's (*q.v.*) *Hauspostille* (1927), the catching and ironic rhymes of Kästner's "Gebrauchslyrik," and the melancholy and reticent verses of Joachim Ringelnatz (1883–1934). These poets, in form though not in content indebted to Christian Morgenstern (*q. v.*), hoped for the response of a politically alert public; it was their aim to produce "quotable gestures," and whether they represented the ideology of right or left, they advanced, underneath their attitude of deceptive detachment, the strongest claim to political action.

The latest aspect of poetry owes its peculiar character first of all to a striking and not always organic change in subject matter—a change away from collective and "liberal" social themes, towards the more irrational subject of a man's place in the total natural frame of his earthly life. It is a poetry of being and not of speculation and knowledge. After the pungent and caustic short verses of the *Gebrauchslyriker,* the modern poet is once again, in Germany and elsewhere, ready to experiment with more sustained and demanding forms of expression. He cultivates classical meters; hymn, ode, philosophical poem, choral chant, and ballad are popular. But in the more distinguished representatives the quality of this latest poetry is also determined by the confluence of certain impersonal and "objective" elements drawn from Rilke's later elegies and the elevated pathos of Germany's greatest "pure" poet, Hölderlin. In the poems of both of these paradigmatic and widely praised artists, private emotions and the imagery of individualistic experience are subordinated to the acceptance of the inescapable realities of the world. Most of the National Socialist poets lived, of course, only by the artificial inner (and outer) support of a rigid and narrow ideological framework. Their work served the demands of a brief day; and not the limitations of subject matter alone, but their blunt and defective poetic perception has deprived most of them of permanent significance.

Something of the declamatoriness of the poets is also apparent in the more recent drama, for which the early expressionist, Hanns Johst (*q.v.*), has been a vociferous though by no means distinguished spokesman. The combination of modern technical resources (radio, film, mass meeting, open-air stages) and an urgent sense of the dramatist's propagandistic function have produced a peculiar theatrical idiom in which strained solemnity alternates with palpable doctrine and broad popular appeal. Here, as in the novel or ballad, historical themes predominate. In the plays and critical utterances of some of the younger playwrights, there is a lively concern about the relevance to modern tragedy of man's "religious" and political dependence.

Many of the German writers whose work illuminated and reflected the European world between 1914 and 1934 have, during the Nazi decade, lived abroad. Many have passed through years of the deepest despair, some have adjusted themselves in Russia, England, or the Americas to new languages and a new public. German literary magazines abroad have carried the convictions and visions of the exiled across more than 10 years of enforced separation. Among those in Germany who have survived the war and the final collapse of their world, some will again be able to speak freely. The years to come will challenge these poets, young or old, to reassert against the evidence of destruction and incoherence their destined power of evoking and sustaining the permanent signs of human virtue and resolution.

See: Albert Soergel, *Dichtung und Dichter der Zeit,* 1.–3. Folge (1911–1934); Ludwig Lewisohn, *The Spirit of Modern German Literature* (1916); Friedrich von der Leyen, *Deutsche Dichtung in neuer Zeit* (2d ed., 1927; supplement, 1931); Heinz Kindermann, *Das literarische Anlitz der Gegenwart* (1930); Werner Mahrholz, *Deutsche Literatur der Gegenwart* (1930); Arthur Eloesser, *Modern German Literature* (1933); H. Naumann, *Die deutsche Dichtung der Gegenwart (1885–1933)* (1933); T. Roffler, *Bildnisse aus der neueren deutschen Literatur* (1933); Felix Bertaux, *A Panorama of German Literature from 1871 to 1931* (1935); J. W. Nagel and Jakob Zeidler, *Deutsch-österreichische Literaturgeschichte,* Bd. 4 (*1890–1918*), ed. by Eduard Castle (1937); Paul Fechter, *Die deutsche Literatur vom Naturalismus bis zur Literatur des Unwirklichen* (1938); Jethro Bithell, *Modern German Literature, 1880–1938* (1939); Richard Samuel and R. Hinton Thomas, *Expressionism in German Life, Literature, and the Theatre (1910–1924)* (1939); Josef Nadler, *Literaturgeschichte des deutschen Volkes,* Bd. 3 (*1814–1914*), Bd. 4 (*1914–1940*), (1938–1941); Victor Lange, *Modern German Literature, 1870–1940* (1945).

V. L.

German naturalism. In 1880 German literature began to play a role in the European naturalistic movement and in the ensuing two decades contributed some of its outstanding documents. The German movement started in the field of literary theory under the influence of the theory and practice of Emile Zola (*q.v.*). Its first phase was the defense and interpretation of Zola (whom German criticism was vilifying) by four enthusiasts: Michael Georg Conrad (*q.v.*), the only German naturalist to make personal contact with Zola; Oskar

Welten, who gave the most complete German analysis of Zola; and the brothers Heinrich and Julius Hart (*q.v.*). These men offered a favorable interpretation of the French naturalist's activity and explained the theories on which his works were based. In the second phase an attack was launched on the popular German literature of the day for its backward-looking and trivial rumination of the German literary tradition and its lack of contact with the contemporary world. Outstanding in this phase, when with the rise of Germany to the stature of a world power in 1870–1871 there came a desire for a literature commensurate with the nation's new position, were the Harts, Karl Bleibtreu (*q.v.*), Klaus Hermann, and the group of writers gathered in the literary club "Durch" (*q.v.*) and the lyric anthology *Moderne Dichter-Charaktere* (1885). Common to the work of all these writers was the conviction that German literature was not alive to the needs of the day and needed revitalizing. In the third phase there was an attempt to formulate an aesthetic theory along naturalistic lines. Leaders in this endeavor were Wilhelm Boelsche (*q.v.*), a scientist who analyzed literary problems in terms of contemporary scientific hypotheses, and Conrad Alberti, who sought to formulate an even more complete naturalistic theory along social and scientific lines. Around 1890 a final phase developed in which a critical theory arose that was to undermine the naturalistic position. This took the form of an attack on naturalism's demand for extreme objectivity and first appeared as a recognition by Georg Brandes (*q.v.*) of the strongly subjective elements in Zola's works. The tendency was then further developed by Julius Langbehn, Max Nordau, and Hermann Bahr (*q.v.*). Arno Holz (*q.v.*) sought to counter this attack against the naturalistic position by formulation of so-called *konsequenter Naturalismus,* in which he stated a theory of the nature of art that excluded the subjective element; in reality his essay, criticized by his naturalistic colleagues, served to bring about the final downfall of naturalistic theory in Germany.

Naturalistic creative activity was most effective in the fields of the drama and the novel. The lyric played a brief part in the early years of the movement in Germany with Arno Holz's *Das Buch der Zeit* and the anthology *Moderne Dichter-Charaktere,* more important for its introductory essays by Karl Henckell and Hermann Conradi (*q.v.*) than for its poetic offerings. In the later naturalistic period, however, the lyric was considered a genre unsuited to modern needs. The major influence on German naturalistic drama was that of Henrik Ibsen (*q.v.*), whose social dramas were hailed enthusiastically by the German naturalists and produced by the Freie Bühne. The leading dramatic critic of German naturalism was Otto Brahm (*q.v.*), director of the Freie Bühne, outstanding interpreter of Ibsen in Germany, and one of the most incisive of the modern German critics. The founding of the Freie Bühne in 1889 on the model of the Théâtre Libre gave the naturalistic drama a testing ground where the works of Ibsen, Zola, and the German naturalists were brought before the public. Holz and Johannes Schlaf (*q.v.*) collaborated on prose sketches and the drama *Die Familie Selicke,* which, employing an extremely naturalistic treatment of language and detail, played a central role in the rise of the German naturalistic drama. Under their influence, Gerhart Hauptmann (*q.v.*) began his career with *Vor Sonnenaufgang,* which had a stormy presentation by the Freie Bühne, and he produced in the ensuing years the outstanding dramatic works of German naturalism, *Einsame Menschen* and *Die Weber.* Only partly within the naturalistic movement, Hermann Sudermann (*q.v.*) combined the well-made play with naturalistic elements in such dramas as *Die Ehre* and *Heimat.* The naturalistic repertoire was increased by dramas from the pens of Max Halbe (*q.v.*), whose *Jugend* was a contemporary hit, Georg Hirschfeld, Max Dreyer (*q.v.*), Ernst Rosmer, Otto Erich Hartleben (*q.v.*), Paul Ernst (*q.v.*), in his early period, and others. In Austria, Ludwig Anzengruber (*q.v.*) was a forerunner of naturalistic tendencies, and Arthur Schnitzler (*q.v.*), in his early works, a contributor to the naturalistic repertoire. The development of naturalistic drama was broken off by the rise of neo-romanticism around 1896.

Zola's *Rougon-Macquart* novels were the major influence on the German naturalistic novel wherein, after several abortive attempts by Karl Bleibtreu, Conrad Alberti, and Hermann Conradi to portray contemporary life naturalistically, there was a widening of the field of the German prose narrative to include new social subjects and a new interpretation of modern life. Leading novelists were Max Kretzer, author of Berlin novels, Clara Viebig, Wilhelm von Polenz (*qq.v.*), with novels of peasant life, and Georg von Ompteda, novelist of the German artistocracy. Hermann Sudermann once again stood on the periphery of the movement. Again Anzengruber was a forerunner of naturalism with his novels of Austrian village life. Theodor

Fontane (*q.v.*) contributed some of the best novels of the period.

Leading naturalistic journals were *Die Gesellschaft,* edited by M. G. Conrad in Munich from 1885, which gave German naturalism a rallying point and played a major role in its development, and the *Freie Bühne,* published in Berlin under the editorship of Otto Brahm from 1890. The Harts' *Kritische Waffengänge,* a series of essays published 1882–1884, and their short-lived *Berliner Monatshefte* (1885) and *Kritisches Jahrbuch* (1889) were major contributions to German naturalistic journalism.

See: E. Wolff, *Die jüngste deutsche Literaturströmung und das Prinzip der Moderne* (1886); L. Berg, *Der Naturalismus* (1892); A. von Hanstein, *Das jüngste Deutschland* (1901); M. G. Conrad, *Emile Zola* (1906); O. Brahm, *Kritische Schriften* (2 vols., 1913–1915); H. Röhl, *Der Naturalismus* (1927); W. H. Root, *German Criticism of Zola* (1931); Georg Brandes, "Emile Zola," *Deutsche Rundschau,* LIV (1888), 27–44.

W. H. R.

Gershenzon, Mikhail Osipovich (1869–1925, Russian literary historian), born in Kishinev of a Jewish family, graduated from a local Gymnasium in 1887. He studied in Berlin and then at Moscow University, where he followed courses on the history of ancient Greece under P. G. Vinogradov and wrote a thesis, "The Athenian Polity of Aristotle," for which he was awarded a gold medal. In 1893 his articles began to appear in *Russkaya mysl* (Russian Thought). He visited Italy in 1896 as a correspondent of a leading Russian daily. On his return to Russia, Gershenzon became a contributor to a number of the so-called "thick" periodicals. Eventually he became absorbed in the study of Pushkin and his milieu and gained recognition as a leading authority in this field. As a result of these studies Gershenzon published in 1908 a monograph on P. Y. Chaadayev; later came his *Istoricheskiye zapiski (O russkom obshchestve)* (1910; Historical Notes on Russian Society), *Obrazy prochlovo* (1912; Images of the Past), *Griboyedovskaya Moskva* (1914; The Moscow of Griboyedov), *Mudrost Pushkina* (1919; The Wisdom of Pushkin), *Stati o Pushkine* (1926; Essays on Pushkin). Gershenzon also edited *Russkiye Propilei* (6 vols., 1915–1919, The Russian Propylaea).

After the Revolution of 1917 Gershenzon served in the Department of Education, Central Archives; he also organized and was elected first president of the All-Russian Congress of Writers.

See: Andrei Bely, "M. O. Gershenzon," *Rossiya,* 5 (14), 1925.

O. M.

Gezelle, Guido (1830–1899, Flemish poet), was born at Bruges. He studied for the priesthood and after his consecration was appointed an instructor at the Roman Catholic seminary of Roesselare. There he won the lifelong affection of a group of young enthusiasts in whom he stirred that love of poetry which lies dormant in many Flemish souls. But the Francophile higher clergy frowned on his popularity with the boys, in whom he aroused a nationalistic Flemish spirit, and in 1860 he was transferred to Bruges and given the humble office of curate. By that time there had been published *Dichtoefeningen* (1858; Poetic Exercises), which contains his famous poem "O 't ruischen van het Ranke Riet" (O Rustling of the Rushes' Throng), *Gedichten, Gezangen en Gebeden* (1859; Poems, Songs, and Prayers), and *Kerkhofblommen* (1860; Churchyard Flowers). But after his transfer he remained silent for 30 years, perhaps under compulsion of his superiors. He consoled himself with the study of languages —he was an able linguist—and especially of his own beloved Flemish. The love of words was a passion with him. He collected them as an 18th-century virtuoso collected rare cameos. He gathered them out of old books, out of the rough speech of the day laborer by the roadside, no matter where he found them, as long as he thought them beautiful. "Old words are of more value than old jewels," he used to say. He edited for 14 years a linguistic monthly called *Loquela* (1881–1895), in which he published the treasures he discovered. After Gezelle's death this valuable material was rearranged into a dictionary under the same title, *Loquela* (1907). In 1893 the poet broke his long silence with the publication of *Tijdkrans* (Time Garland), which was followed by *Rijmsnoer* (1897; String of Rhymes). In these he gave his very best. He died in 1899, hardly known, outside the circle of his former students, as the great poet he was. It remained for the young leaders of the literary revival, the editors of *Van Nu en Straks* (Today and Tomorrow) in Flanders and of *De Nieuwe Gids* (The New Guide) in Holland, to make him known to lovers of poetry and spread his fame.

The charm of Gezelle's poetry is not in its thought. He was a thinker, though not original enough to create great poetry out of his meditations. But as a visionary and an interpreter of nature's beauty he was original to a great degree. All the innumerable sounds of nature, the rustling of the reed on the water's edge, the calls of birds, the song of the scythe among the wheat, the roar of thunder, are reechoed in his verse; all the variegated hues of his Flemish country, the blues of its summer skies, the grays of its November days, are described with a profusion of words set to melodious rhythms. Among his works is a masterly translation (1886) of Longfellow's *Hiawatha* which shows the best characteristics of his uncommon talent. His native town gave him belated recognition by the erection of a fine statue.

See: A. J. Barnouw, "The Voice of Flanders," *Nation,* C (New York, 1915), 106–107; G. L. van Roosbroeck, *Guido Gezelle, the Mystic Poet of Flanders* (1919); A. de Ridder, *La Littérature flamande contemporaine* (1923).

A. J. B.

Ghéon, Henri (pseud. of Henri Vanglon, 1875–1944, French playwright), was born in Bray-sur-Seine. In spite of a precocious talent for drama (at the age of eight he had written a play entitled *Un Mari trompé*), Henri Ghéon chose medicine as his profession. As early as 1897, however, he contributed articles of literary criticism to various reviews and magazines. In 1899 his play *Le Fils de M. Sage* was published in *Ermitage,* and in 1911 he presented *Le Pain,* a symbolic drama of proletarian and revolutionary character, followed in 1914 by *L'Eau de vie,* a tragic picture of the degrading effect of alcoholism on a family.

André Gide and Jacques Copeau (*qq.v.*), with whom he founded the *Nouvelle Revue française* in 1909, strongly influenced Ghéon. His conversion to Catholicism during the First World War was another powerful element in the development of his art. While still in the army he wrote two religious dramas, *Les Trois Miracles de Sainte Cécile* and *Le Martyre de Saint Valérien* (published in 1922). In 1921 Copeau presented at the Vieux Colombier *Le Pauvre sous l'escalier,* in which Ghéon, mixing comedy and tragedy, uses the familiar and naïve style that remained his favorite means of expression. He believed that the mission of the theatre was a return to the simplicity of the old miracle plays. In order to help the diffusion of his religious dramas Ghéon founded in 1924 a company, the Compagnons de Notre Dame, which became the Compagnons de Jeux in 1931, under the direction of Henri Brochet.

Ghéon not only wrote a considerable number of plays (*Jeux et miracles pour le peuple fidèle,* 2 vols., 1922; *Saint Maurice, ou l'Obéissance,* 1923; *Thomas d'Aquin,* 1924; *Le Comédien et la grâce,* 1925; *La Merveilleuse Histoire du jeune Bernard de Menthon,* 1926; *La Mort de Lazare,* 1931); he also published volumes of poems (*Chansons d'aube,* 1897; *Solitude de l'été,* 1898; *Foi en la France,* 1916), essays (*Nos Directions,* 1911), and novels (*Le Consolateur,* 1903; *Les Jeux de l'Enfer et du Ciel,* 3 vols., 1929; *La Jambe noire,* 1941).

See: Marcel Raymond, *Henri Ghéon; sa vie, son œuvre* (1939); Marcel Raymond, *Le Jeu retrouvé* (1943).

M. E. C.

Ghil, René (1862–1925, French poet), was born in Tourcoing, French Flanders. He studied in Paris at the Lycée Condorcet, where he shared the friendship of Ephraïm Mikhaël, Pierre Quillard, Stuart Merrill (*q.v.*), and André Fontainas, all of whom were soon to play a part in the symbolist movement. His first book of poems, *Légendes d'âmes et de sang* (1885), written under the influence of Mallarmé (*q.v.*), was an attempt at applying his scientific conception of poetry. The following year, in the *Traité du verbe,* he defined and expanded his theories. His main purpose was to submit the art of verse to a scientific method by applying to the sounds of speech the principles of instrumental music, creating thereby what he calls *instrumentation verbale.* Taking Rimbaud's (*q.v.*) "Sonnet des voyelles" as a starting point, Ghil claimed that vowels, and even consonants, not only possess color suggestions, but also a particular timbre corresponding to such and such a musical instrument and capable of evoking by sound alone a variety of emotions. He then began to apply this musical technique to the exposition of his philosophical and scientific concepts, and to that effect several books of poems were published. As if to leave no doubt concerning their unity of design, these works bear a unique title, *Œuvre* (1889–1909), divided into three parts, *Dire du mieux, Dire des sangs, Dire de la loi.* Although verbal orchestration was his main intent, the author dreamed of fusing together all the forms of art, literary, pictorial, plastic, as well as musical. By such means Ghil aimed at giving a complete synthesis of man since his remotest origins. In spite of the elaborate treatises in which he explained his intentions—*De la poésie scien-*

tifique (1909), *La Tradition de la poésie scientifique* (1920), *Les Dates et les œuvres* (1923)—he has had no disciple, but his work remains a curious example of experimentation in the domain of poetic technique.

See: André Barre, *Le Symbolisme* (1912); C. A. Fusil, *La Poésie scientifique* (1918); Adolphe van Bever and Paul Léautaud, *Poètes d'aujourd'hui* (1929).

M. D.

Giacosa, Giuseppe (1847–1906, Italian dramatist), was born and died at Colleretto-Parella, in a mountain valley in Piedmont. The region itself, with its crags and torrents and medieval castles, has been the site through the centuries of plentiful romantic action; it is no wonder that it gave scene and mood to Giacosa for many of his early plays.

After a false start in the law, he turned to the writing which was to be the main business of his life. Within the period 1870–1904 he wrote some 25 plays, most of the earlier ones in verse, the later ones in prose. He was clearly the leading Italian dramatist of the latter part of the 19th century. His first success came with *Una Partita a scacchi* (1872), a brief romantic idyl in a medieval setting. *Il Trionfo d'amore* (1875) is of the same general character. Then came comedies of Goldonian type, of which the best are *Sorprese notturne* (1875) and *Acquazzoni in montagna* (1876). Presently, however, the Middle Ages return—this time not in idyllic form, but in the full panoply of historical romance. The two best plays of this kind are *Il Fratello d'armi* (1877) and *Il Conte rosso* (1880). *Il Fratello d'armi* is perhaps the best product of pure romanticism in Italy. It is somewhat incoherent in structure and uses the romantic stops somewhat too relentlessly, but it is a very good play none the less—stirring, passionate, unexpected, and with more realization of character than one might expect to find in such a work. After 1880 Giacosa reverted occasionally to traditional comedy or historical romance, notably in *La Dame de Challant,* a historical play written in French for Sarah Bernhardt and first produced by her in New York in 1891. But he devoted himself mainly to social dramas, finding his themes among the ordinary problems of modern social and business life (after the naturalist fashion), and treating them, when he is at his best, with a restraint that is almost classic and with a direct simplicity and a common-sense sanity of judgment that are quite his own. The three most notable of these plays are *Tristi Amori* (1888), *Come le foglie* (1900), and *Il Più Forte* (1904). *Tristi Amori* is the best of all, a play so good and so satisfying that it seems to render quite unnecessary and insignificant most of the mass of modern plays that deal with the triangle theme. Giacosa's persons are not of heroic stature: they are everyday people, neither very admirable nor very villainous, mixed in their motives, and not too effectual in their attempts to deal with the forces that play around them and through them. Yet they are well worth knowing and observing, and some of them are permanently likable. Giacosa never preaches, but can at times cut through to remarkably telling statements of essential fact. No triangle play ends with words more memorable than the culminating words of *Tristi Amori:* "Things like this have no ending . . . they just drag on hopelessly."

In collaboration with Luigi Illica, Giacosa wrote the libretti for three familiar operas by Puccini: *La Bohème* (1896), *Tosca* (1899), and *Madama Butterfly* (1903). He wrote also three volumes of good historical and descriptive prose: *Novelle e paesi valdostani* (1886), *Castelli valdostani e canavesani* (1898), and *Impressioni d'America* (1898). The last one was written on the basis of a stay of several months in the United States, to which he came, in 1891, to superintend the rehearsals for *La Dame de Challant.*

See: S. A. Smith, "Introduction," in Giacosa, *Tristi Amori,* ed. by R. Altrocchi and B. M. Woodbridge (1920).

E. H. W.

Gide, André (1869–, French novelist, critic, essayist, and dramatist), is among the most disturbing and controversial of great contemporaries, for hesitations and contradictions mark all his thought. He insists that he writes to be reread; and if he admirably fulfills his function, which is to disturb and provoke the reader, it is also true that each of his books contains the precise antidote for the poison that it apparently distills.

Born in Paris, André Gide descends, on his father's side, from Cévennes Huguenots and, on his mother's, from Norman Catholics recently converted to Protestantism. In these divergent influences he sees the source of his intellectual contradictions and the reason for his writing, since only in art could he harmonize his opposing tendencies. His father's death in 1880 left André in the care of three austere women whose rigid principles did not prevent their pampering the boy—his mother, his Aunt Claire, and the English spinster Anna Shackleton. An indifferent pupil afflicted with nervous disorders, he studied at the Ecole

Alsacienne and under private tutors. The conflict between his intense religious fervor and his awakening to manhood found expression in *Les Cahiers d'André Walter* (1891), begun at 18 and published anonymously as the posthumous diary of an unhappy youth. Though telling in romanticized form the story of his own pure love for his cousin Emmanuèle, this little volume of lyrical prose, soon to be followed by Walter's *Poésies* (1892), also reduced to its essence the philosophico-literary idealism of the epoch and hence opened to its author the doors of the *cénacles.* For two or three seasons Gide circulated among the symbolists, a stiff and artificial figure whose uncomprising intellectualism and devout faith embarrassed his friends. Meanwhile his subtle *Traité du Narcisse* (1892), *Tentative amoureuse* (1893), and *Voyage d'Urien* (1893) further identified him with French symbolism (*q.v.*). But in the fall of 1893 he undertook a trip to North Africa which, as he had foreseen when he left his beloved Bible at home, marked the great turning point in his life. Falling ill at Biskra, he narrowly escaped death, and his convalescence taught him the value of life, of the present moment, and of that ardent fervor which gives life its zest. He also learned the secret of his tormented nature and resolved not to stifle his inclinations. Deliberately he renounced his past, seeking the primitive man under the veneer of education. After a year in the desert he recanted his former life in an ironic epitaph, *Paludes* (1895); in 1897 his break with symbolism was confirmed by *Les Nourritures terrestres,* a breviary of revolt which preaches the joy of living by the senses, restlessly eager for every eventuality. On his return to Paris in 1895 he had witnessed his mother's death and married his cousin. Henceforth, with Paris and his two Norman estates as headquarters, he was to travel frequently, to Africa, Italy, Germany, England, and eventually Russia.

"To free oneself is nothing; it's being free that is hard"—this is the problem which Gide examines from all sides during the next 20 years. The too receptive Saul and the overgenerous Candaulus, heroes of his beautiful verse dramas *Saül* (1903) and *Le Roi Candaule* (1901), together with the Michel of *L'Immoraliste* (1902), end tragically because of breaking with conventional morality in their search for self-fulfillment. The Alissa of *La Porte étroite* (1909), counterpart of *L'Immoraliste,* illustrates the dangers of the other extreme, renunciation. In *Le Retour de l'enfant prodigue* (1907) Gide's prodigal, while admitting his errors, helps his younger brother to escape. Finally, the seductive Lafcadio of *Les Caves du Vatican* (1914) finds himself the prisoner of a free, unmotivated act he has committed to prove his own liberty. Indeed, even during his period of maturity between the two wars, Gide consistently returns to the problem of personal freedom: in his dialogues on the subject of homosexuality, *Corydon* (1924), in his outspoken memoirs, *Si le grain ne meurt* (1926), and in *Les Faux-Monnayeurs* (1926)—the only novel he has written, for he has classified the frankly ironic works as *soties* (*Paludes; Le Prométhée mal enchaîné,* 1899; *Les Caves du Vatican*) and the soberly classical works recounted by one of the protagonists as *récits* (*L'Immoraliste; La Porte étroite; La Symphonie pastorale,* 1919; and a few others). In treating the three themes of his novel—the adolescent revolt, the decaying of bourgeois families, and the creation of a work of art—Gide reveals many of the antinomies upon which his dynamic equilibrium rests: the soul and the flesh, life and art, expression and restraint, the individual and society, classicism and romanticism, Christ and Christianity, God and the Devil. Here, moreover, his predilection for the complex form of a book within a book, which he had originally indulged in his first work, yields its happiest results.

It is natural that his lifelong preoccupation with freedom and his keenly sympathetic nature should have made André Gide a champion of the oppressed. As mayor of a commune in Normandy (1896), later as a juror in Rouen (1912), and finally as a special envoy of the Colonial Ministry (1925–1926), he had ample opportunity to observe social injustice. His *Voyage au Congo* (1927) and *Retour du Tchad* (1928), in fact, led to legal reform and eventually to curbing of the industrial concessions in the colonies. When, in the early 30's, he declared his admiration for Soviet Russia and his sympathy toward Communism, Gide shocked the men of his generation, as he had so often done before, and raised another barrier between himself and official honors. After a trip to Russia his *Retour de l'U.R.S.S.* (1936), which told of his disappointment and criticized the Soviets for abandoning their original principles, momentarily alienated even his young admirers. But Gide has always been an independent.

Gide's critical writings, found chiefly in *Prétextes* (1903), *Nouveaux Prétextes* (1911), *Dostoïevsky* (1923), and *Incidences* (1924), have won him a place as one of the most perspicacious literary critics of his time. His double nature permits him to admire the classical (Goethe, Racine, Bach) while nourishing a predilection for tormented and complicated souls (Nietzsche, *q.v.*, Dostoevski, *q.v.*, Blake, Whitman, Baudelaire, *q.v.*). These and a few others (Montaigne, Browning, Chopin) are the spiritual brothers having most intimate influence on the man who, in a lecture in 1900, made a most eloquent apology for all influences. The same broad sympathies are shown in his clairvoyant criticism of contemporaries, for he has often been the first to discern and encourage authentic talent. In 1909 he was a prime mover in founding the *Nouvelle Revue française,* a focal point in recent French literature. His own influence has been as wide as that of any writer of his generation; suffice it to mention two Academicians and a Nobel prizewinner who have felt that influence, Mauriac, Lacretelle, and Martin du Gard (*qq.v.*), and certain leaders of the group born around 1900, Giono, Green, Malraux, and Saint Exupéry (*qq.v.*).

A skeptic, questioning all values, like Montaigne vaunting his uncertainty and his inconsistencies, Gide early dedicated himself to the study of man. In a style which varies from the colored, ejaculatory prose of his early works to the voluntarily bare understatement of his mature works, he has explored the most complex and most disturbing characters, emotions, and ideas. Though "le gidisme" has frequently exerted an unfortunate influence upon those who failed to read to the end his maxim, "It is good to follow your penchant provided you go upward," nevertheless Gide's position as a moral philosopher only grows with time. He can be best read in the 15-volume edition of the *Œuvres complètes* (1932–1939), to which should be added the 1300 pages of the definitive *Journal* (1939), supplemented by *Pages de journal, 1939–1942* (1944).

See: C. Du Bos, *Le Dialogue avec André Gide* (1929); R. Fernandez, *André Gide* (1931); L. Pierre-Quint, *André Gide; sa vie, son œuvre* (1932); J. Hytier, *André Gide* (1938).

J. O'B.

Gil, Augusto (1873–1929, Portuguese poet), was born near Oporto, in Lordelo de Oiro, but from early childhood lived in A Guarda, Beira. He held important administrative positions in the Department of Public Education.

This poet is perhaps the best Portuguese example in recent times of one who drew his inspiration from folkloric elements. Although literary influences from contemporary modernistic formalism can be seen in his first book, *Musa cérulea* (1894; Cerulean Muse), there are already apparent a simplicity of expression and a spontaneous grace which point to the folkloric orientation of his later work. Indeed, Augusto Gil belonged to a group of poets who passed through the last 10 years of the last century and the first third of the present one without allowing their personalities to become permanently stamped with any of the dominant tendencies, although they continued to appropriate discreetly from each of them. In Gil is another instance of that miracle which at times touches folkloric poets—when their verses are attributed to the people owing to the authenticity of their form and sentiments. The triads of the folk song backed by the tradition of centuries, the quality of the cradle songs, the wittiness of the erotic couplet, the objective emotion which characterizes his treatment of landscape (valley of the Mondego), have made the poet one of the best known and most enjoyed by the Portuguese public. *Luar de janeiro* (1909; January Moonlight), *O craveiro da janela* (1920; The Carnation Pot in the Window), and *Avena rústica* (1927; Rustic Wheat) are his most representative books. In the religious vein, *Alba plena* (1916; Full Dawn) is the story of the Virgin Mary, presented in short poems. At times, owing to the nature of the theme, these deviate somewhat from the poet's characteristic folkloric technique. Gil's *Rosas desta manhã* (This Morning's Roses) was published posthumously in 1931.

See: Agostinho de Campos, *Antologia portuguesa: Augusto Gil* (1923).

R. M. L.

Gil, Ricardo (1855–1908, Spanish poet), was born in Murcia. His poetry is contained in two books, *De los quince a los treinta* (1885) and *La caja de música* (1898), which antedate the appearance of the Spanish poets of the modernist period. He has, therefore, the distinction of being one of the few Spanish forerunners of the great poetic movement at the end of the past century, whose greatest creative figures and precursors were Spanish American, not Spanish. Ricardo Gil distinguished himself in his day as an independent, who drank directly at the fount of French poetry and, under its influence, produced a poetry of his own, characterized by its intimate lyric quality, its delicacy, its elegance. The rest of his work is contained in a posthumous volume, *El último libro* (1909).

See: F. Balart, *Impresiones* (1894), pp. 131–143; E. Díez-Canedo, "Ricardo Gil," *Lectura,* Año VIII (Madrid, 1908), Tomo I, pp. 56–57.

F. de O.

Gilkin, Iwan (1858–1923, Belgian poet and dramatist), was born in Brussels, studied law at the University of Louvain, then lived in Brussels and devoted himself exclusively to literature. He is a purely intellectual poet. His first two volumes of verses, *La Damnation de l'artiste* (1890) and *Ténèbres* (1892; published under the title *La Nuit* in 1897), written with Parnassian correctness, are like an echo of Baudelaire's (*q.v.*) *Les Fleurs du mal,* amplified in the search for perverted sensations. Led on by a pessimism which "darkened his inner life for seventeen years," he describes with diabolical pleasure the perversity of mankind: "If evil were not attractive, evil would not exist." According to him the only outcome of this state of corruption is death, and death itself is fearful because of the mystery of the great beyond. It is hard to believe the assertion of his intimate friend Albert Giraud (*q.v.*) that Gilkin's inspiration was original and not inspired by Baudelaire. *La Nuit* was to be followed by two volumes of a more optimistic and redeeming nature, *L'Aurore* and *La Lumière,* yet these never appeared. *Le Cerisier fleuri* (1899) sounds a more cheerful note. It is a collection of poems written in a lighter vein; the versification is freer, the tone is gay, the general theme is the enjoyment of life. The change in philosophy is complete in *Prométhée,* a dramatic poem, also published in 1899. In this work Gilkin has admittedly been inspired by Goethe's outlook on life as well as by the tragedy of Æschylus. Now the author believes in the final triumph of spirit over matter, and he has gone over to a restricted type of free verse, using occasionally lines of nine or eleven syllables, and rhyming masculine endings with feminine ones or a singular with a plural.

Gilkin has written two dramas in prose: *Savonarole* (1906) and *Les Etudiants russes* (1906). In the first he powerfully evokes the ascetic figure of the great Dominican monk and the irresistible influence of his persuasive personality on the Italian people of his time. *Les Etudiants russes* gives a picture of the various phases of the "Russian soul" at the end of the 19th century, where oriental fatalism is mixed with the social philosophies of the western world.

See: H. Liebrecht, *Histoire de la littérature belge d'expression française* (1910); F. Castillo Nájera, *Un Siècle de poésie belge* (1931; with Spanish translations and notes); G. Doutrepont, *Histoire illustrée de la littérature française en Belgique* (1939).

L. V.

Gille, Valère (1867–, Belgian poet), was born in Brussels. He studied at the University of Louvain and after the death of Max Waller succeeded to the editorship of the *Jeune Belgique* (*see* Belgian Literature in French). Then he became librarian of the Royal Library in Brussels. His weekly critical articles on historical, literary, and artistic subjects in the daily paper *Dernière Heure* were much appreciated. His first volume of verses, *Le Château des merveilles* (1893), is composed of delicate short poems in the manner of Théophile Gautier. *La Cithare* (1897), a collection of beautifully chiseled, plastic and serene pictures of ancient Greece, was crowned by the French Academy; it is reminiscent of the art of Chénier and of Leconte de Lisle (*q.v.*). Gille is a poet of Parnassian correctness and great purity of expression whose constant care seems to have been to keep in check the potential outbursts of his lyricism. The passing touch of Baudelairian pessimism (*see* Baudelaire) found in *Le Coffret d'ébène* (1900) is completely offset by *Le Collier d'opales* (1899), *La Corbeille d'octobre* (1902), and *Joli Mai* (1905), which are like hymns of freshness and youth moderated by an epicurean outlook on life. It is in *La Corbeille d'octobre* that the poet reaches the height of purity in his nobly subdued lyricism. Gille also wrote short plays: *Ce n'était qu'un rêve* (1903) is a fairy tale full of refreshing grace, *Madame reçoit* (1908), a comedy of customs.

See: Henri Liebrecht, *Valère Gille* (1906).

L. V.

Giménez Caballero, Ernesto (1899–, Spanish essayist and journalist), born in Madrid, is one of the most representative prose writers of the generation following the First World War. In 1927 he founded the *Gaceta literaria,* a journal which for several years was an organ of the then so-called *vanguardismo.* As an active littérateur, founder of publishing firms, of clubs, and organizer of banquets, he was one of the most outstanding theorists, propagandists, and directors of this movement—now well forgotten except for its renovating impulse. The books of Giménez Caballero himself which were written according to the ruling patterns of that time—the cult of machinery, the cinema, sports, horror of the romantic and the sentimental, devotion to metaphor and to "the new"—show today a surprising and melancholy oldness (*e.g.*, *Hércules jugando a los dados,* 1929). In Spain, once the brief moment of literary revolution had passed, the young innovators accepted their seniors; in poetry the influence of Juan

Parnassians. One feels his soul vibrate through the cold precision of his style. It is interesting to notice that the first volume of *Hors du siècle* appeared five years before Heredia's *Trophées*. Contemptuous of the commonplaceness of his contemporaries, Giraud likes to evoke in colorful strokes the sumptuous splendor of the past, of ancient Rome, of the bygone glory of his own country of Flanders (*La Frise empourprée,* 1912). At times he reminds the reader of the rhythmical incantation of Baudelaire's (*q.v.*) suggestive phrases. His technical mastery is especially apparent in two collections of his youth, *Pierrot lunaire* (1884) and *Pierrot narcisse* (1891; published together in 1898 under the title *Héros et pierrots*). In these volumes of subtle badinage his mirth is without joy, his gaiety is only external and bears the mark of the misery and hopelessness hidden in his proud soul. Between 1884 and 1921 Giraud wrote all told 10 volumes of verses.

See: J. Chot and R. Dethier, *Histoire des lettres françaises en Belgique* (1910); H. Liebrecht, *Histoire de la littérature belge d'expression française* (1910); G. Doutrepont, *Histoire illustrée de la littérature française en Belgique* (1939).

L. V.

Giraudoux, Jean (1882–1944, French novelist, dramatist, and essayist), was born in Bellac, Haute-Vienne. He was an excellent student, graduated with highest honors from the Ecole Normale Supérieure, and passed the examinations for diplomatic service at the Quai d'Orsay. His earliest publication is *Provinciales* (1909). The First World War, in which Giraudoux saw active service, inspired him to write *Lectures pour une ombre* (1918) and *Adorable Clio* (1920). A mission to the United states resulted in *Amica America* (1918). Following the peace, he resumed his duties as a diplomat, but continued to write. His best-known books of this time, built around charming young girl characters, were *Suzanne et le Pacifique* (1921; Eng. tr., 1923), *Juliette au pays des hommes* (1924), *Bella* (1926; Eng. tr., 1926), and *Eglantine* (1927).

From his very first book it was evident that Giraudoux represented in literature the school of impressionism that had already succeeded in the fields of painting and of music. His masters could only be Claude Monet and Claude Debussy. His earlier works are entirely lacking in plot. They seem to consist merely of trifling incidents, unrelated details, brusque transitions, and lengthy, irrelevant digressions. The merit of these earlier works lies in their style. It is extremely poetic, with striking use of imagery. Figures of speech flow in an unending stream, some poignantly beautiful, some delightfully extravagant, some frankly humorous ("La mort est si ancienne qu'on lui parle latin").

Although such a style would seem eminently unsuited to the drama, the first play of Giraudoux, *Siegfried* (1928; Eng. tr., 1930), adapted from a particularly desultory novel, was highly successful. It was followed by *Amphitryon 38* (1929; Eng. tr., 1938), *La Guerre de Troie n'aura pas lieu* (1935), and *Electre* (1937), all based on ancient Greek myths, but adapted to modern circumstances. The limitations of the stage obliged Giraudoux to discipline the exuberant fantasy which had characterized him as a novelist. On the other hand, he contributed to the freeing of contemporary French drama from the bonds of a pseudo realism. He restored its inherent artistic dignity by the only feasible means, *i.e.*, by the emphasis he placed on dialogue and the magic of his style, at a moment when films clearly pointed to the fact that the rebirth of the theatre depended on its reversion to type. Giraudoux discovered the secret of composition which, in the plays of Racine and of Shakespeare as in those of the ancient Greeks, transforms the puppets on the stage into symbols of humanity.

Giraudoux became commissioner of information just before the Second World War, and his last important work, of a quite different tenor, was a series of political essays, *Pleins Pouvoirs* (1939), concerning the duty of France to remain "a first-rate power."

See: A. Gide, *Nouveaux Prétextes* (1911); R. Brasillach, *Portraits* (1935); A. Rousseaux, *Le Paradis perdu* (1936); G. E. Lemaître, *Four French Novelists* (1938); P. Brodin, *Les Ecrivains français de l'entre-deux-guerres* (1942); C. E. Magny, *Précieux Giraudoux* (1945.)

P. B.

Giuliotti, Domenico (1877–, Italian journalist and religious writer), founder with Federigo Tozzi (*q.v.*) of the *Torre* (Siena) and contributor to Italian and French reviews, was born in San Casciano in Val di Pesa, not far from Greve, in the province of Florence, where he has always resided. He gave up the study of law to devote himself entirely to writing.

His poems, *Ombre d'un ombra* (1910), written prior to his conversion, are romantic in style and pessimistic in tone. After wandering from Catholicism to atheism to theosophy,

Giuliotti was influenced by the reading of French Catholic reactionary authors such as De Maistre, Veuillot, Hello, and Bloy (*q.v.*) and returned to the faith of his childhood. The *Antologia dei Cattolici francesi* (1920), translated from the French, may be considered a tribute to these writers. In his *L'Ora di Barabba* (1920), in a manner not unlike that of Hello and Bloy, he gives vent to his odium for corrupt society, the wealthy bourgeoisie. In forceful and plebeian language he flays those Christians whose lives are not in keeping with the tenets of the faith they profess. The book brought a storm of protests from those offended by his invectives or by his seeming "holier than thou" attitude. Giuliotti was not displeased by this, thinking that he was accomplishing what he had set out to do, shocking the perverted bourgeois back on to the path of righteousness. The *Dizionario dell'omo salvatico* (a first installment published in 1923), written in collaboration with Papini (*q.v.*), brought a still greater storm of protests. This time the authors were really perturbed, for Papini answered with *L'Omo salvatico si difende* (1923), a 45-page explanation, hoping therewith to justify the language and the style of the *Dizionario*. He promised that in the future they would be very careful not to scandalize their faithful coreligionists. Papini closed by asking the readers to pray for the authors. No other part of the *Dizionario* has ever appeared. Indeed one notices a marked change in Giuliotti's subsequent works. In his *Pensieri d'un malpensante* (1936) he is still the fervid and fervent apologist of former years, but not the vehement, bitter polemist of *L'Ora di Barabba*. *Polvere dell'esilio* (1929) has a decided serenity. Papini said this book is "a church on a mountain, built of stones of theology and pillars of prayer, all lighted and embellished by the radiant richness of poetry." Giuliotti's *S. Francesco* (1931) and his *Il Ponte sul mondo* (1932) are so orthodox, both in style and in content, that they were given the imprimatur of the ecclesiastical authorities. The last named book, an explanation and commentary on the Mass, has been translated into English (*The Bridge over the World,* 1935).

See: G. Papini, "Domenico Giuliotti" and "L'Omo salvatico si difende," in *La Scala di Giacobbe* (1932), pp. 299–323, 137–184.

S. M. S. M.

Gjalski, Ksaver Šandor (pseud. of Ljubo Babić, 1854–1935, Croat novelist), was born in the house of the conservative and wealthy vice-governor of Zagorje, Tito Babić. His mother belonged to the aristocratic house of M. S. Gyalya, whence the pen name Gjalski. A lifelong civil servant, he led a sheltered existence, but often changed his residence and thus acquired intimate knowledge of all Croatia. In politics he joined the Serb-Croat coalition against the pro-Hapsburgs and was elected to the Croat Diet. Later he became governor of Zagreb county and after the foundation of Yugoslavia he was sent to the first Yugoslav Parliament.

Gjalski is one of the most fecund Croat writers of the realistic period. His first piece of prose, *Illustrissimus Battorich* (1884), describing the life of the semi-aristocratic Croat bourgeoisie, made him famous. From then on virtually every year a new novel of his appeared and became a best seller. Most of the novels were of patriotic inspiration. In the fight between the younger and older generations Gjalski allied himself with youth and wrote in their reviews, *Mladost* (Youth), *Hrvatski salon* (Croat Salon), and *Život* (Life). His complete works were published by himself in 1913.

See: D. Prohaska, *Pregled savremene hrvatsko-srpske književnosti* (1921).

M. H.

Gjellerup, Karl (1857–1919, Danish novelist), born at Roholte on the island of Zealand, was the son of a clergyman and, true to family tradition, studied theology. But the influence of Brandes (*q.v.*) and reading Darwin and Spencer made him a pronounced atheist, even before he had taken his degree. His first book, *En Idealist* (1878; An Idealist), declared his break with Christianity and foreshadowed the devotion to the German spirit and culture which found full expression in *Germanernes Lærling* (1882; The Disciple of the Teutons). Gjellerup read widely, and many intellectual currents are traceable in his works. He abandoned the naturalism of his Danish contemporaries to worship the humanism of Goethe and Schiller. He essayed tragedies in the grand style with choruses patterned after those of Schiller. Among these the best is his *Brynhild* (1884), in which he endeavors to combine his northern theme with the Greek Spirit. A similar effort is to be traced in his drama on a Greek theme, *Thamyris* (1887). In his novel *Minna* (1889; Eng. tr., 1913), considered his finest work, he pays a tribute to the German spirit in the person of his German-born wife, with the scene laid in Dresden.

Møllen (1896; The Mill) marks a return to

a Danish background. It is a broadly conceived story of crime and atonement and has suggestions of Dostoevski (*q.v.*). At the same time its doctrine of renunciation points to the ideals of Buddhism which engrossed Gjellerup in his last period, when he wrote *Pilgrimen Kamanita* (1896; Eng. tr., *The Pilgrim Kamanita,* 1911) and *Verdensvandrere* (1910; World Wanderers). In the latter he tells the story of a modern Englishman and a German girl, meeting in India, where they learn from an ancient tale of a former incarnation in which they were lovers. The man, whom he calls Sir Edmund Trevelyan, is in part modeled on Byron's piratical friend, Edward John Trelawny, and Shelley figures with Hindu kings and sages among those who were associated in a former incarnation. In spite of much erudition and an exotic imagination hardly equaled in Danish literature, the story leaves the reader rather cold. Gjellerup's last work, *Den gyldne Gren* (1917; The Golden Bough), has the scene laid in ancient Rome at the time of Tiberius. It breathes unrelenting hatred against the Roman world together with an increased sympathy for Christianity. During the last years of his life Gjellerup made his home in Dresden, wrote many of his books simultaneously in German and in Danish, and was an ardent champion of Germany. In 1917 he shared the Nobel prize in literature with Henrik Pontoppidan (*q.v.*).

See: *Karl Gjellerup, der Dichter und Denker; sein Leben in Selbstzeugnissen und Briefen,* I–II (1921–1922); Helge Kjaergaard, *Die dänische Literatur der neuesten Zeit (1871–1933)* (1934).

H. A. L.

Gladkov, Fyodor Vasilyevich (1883–, Russian novelist and dramatist), was born in the former Government of Saratov, of peasant stock. For many years he led a precarious existence, for he did not achieve success until after the Revolution, although he began writing early. Exile to Siberia gave him new material, and in 1912 he wrote *Izgoi* (The Outcasts), a novel of political prisoners, their torments and aspirations, a theme to which he returned in *Staraya sekretnaya* (1927; The Old Dungeon). His drama *Vataga* (1923; The Band), an episode from the 1905 Revolution, portrays the unleashing of violent passions among the primitive Caspian Sea fishermen. *Ognenny kon* (1923; The Fiery Steed), an apocalyptic novel of the civil war, is another characteristic work. The early Gladkov was strongly influenced by Gorky, and more remotely by Dostoevski (*qq.v.*). A proletarian realist, he also showed romantic tendencies; his tone was high-pitched, his language hyperbolic.

In 1926 Gladkov scored his greatest popular success with *Tsement* (Eng. tr., *Cement,* 1929), the first novel devoted to post-revolutionary reconstruction. The hero succeeds in reorganizing a cement factory, but does not solve the problem of his relation to his wife, who represents the "new woman." The over-documented *Energiya* (1933; Energy) deals with similar themes and dwells particularly on the new attitude toward work as expressed in the building of Dneprostroi. *Novaya zemlya* (1931; The New Land) and *Tragediya Lyubashi* (1935; Lyubasha's Tragedy) explore the subject of human relationships against the background of collective society. *Malenkaya trilogiya* (1936; A Little Trilogy) satirizes certain objectionable types among the Communists. *Opalyonnaya dusha* (1943; The Scorched Soul) and *Klyatva* (1944; The Oath), two collections of short stories, represent Gladkov's contribution to war literature, but the emphasis falls on the accomplishments of the home front. His mature work is more subdued in tone, and conforms to the theory of Socialist Realism.

See: *Fyodor Gladkov* (1928); "Gladkov," in *Literaturnaya entsiklopediya,* Vol. I (1929); I. Astakhov, "O tvorchestve F. Gladkova," *Literatura i iskusstvo,* 1931, Nos. 11–12, pp. 56–72.

P. A. P.

Glesener, Edmond (1874–, Belgian novelist), was born at Liége, where he received an excellent education—Greek and Latin, natural sciences, and finally law. In 1900 he entered government service as a clerk at Brussels. When he retired, shortly before the Second World War, he was director of fine arts and letters. His literary work has profited from all his experience: study of the classics enhanced his appreciation of the power of restraint and simplicity in style; scientific method sharpened his observation; his profession gave him insight into political life; while memories of his youth in the provinces have proved an inexhaustible treasure trove. "We wrack our brains for matter," he declares, "and for years the richest of all has been under our eyes." He has written four novels and seven collections of stories, all composed with a meticulous cult of form. He acknowledges study of Flaubert, and the content of his work often recalls Maupassant (*qq.v.*), occasionally Stendhal. He is a realist, as uncompromising as the limits of art allow, but his interest in human nature brings humor, social satire, and vastly more psychological acumen than most realists possess.

His first volume, *Aristide Truffaut* (1898), is almost without plot; it is a whimsical portrait of his father, whose passion for bracket sawing arouses protests from a practical-minded spouse and reflective chuckles from the author. The epigraph is from *Candide,* and at the end Aristide has turned to cultivation of his garden. Voltaire must certainly be included among Glesener's masters. *Le Cœur de François Remy* (1904) is replete with action, chosen for the revelation of character, and with poetry. An ultrasensitive basket weaver, fascinated by a gypsy girl, deserts his home to join a family of nomads. A subordinated side of the author's temperament has found expression here: he avows his youthful passion for the open road. The spell of the Romany alternates with the hero's sense of degradation to form an intensely human drama, and *François Remy* has often been hailed as Glesener's masterpiece. Doubtless life in the capital quickened nostalgia for the Campine around Liége, and this contributes to the poignancy of the work. With the two volumes of *Chronique d'un petit pays* (1913) is found the full-fledged satirist of contemporary manners. The hero, Honoré Colette, is a scion of Maupassant's *Bel Ami,* making his way by impudence and by the fascination he exercises over women. Playing the game according to the rules of organized society, he pushes himself from the slums to a place of dignity and degenerates as he rises. The major interest is in individuals, but politics provide a colorful frame. There is a galaxy of subtly drawn characters, the most amusing being the imperturbable Arthur Boileau, mouthpiece of the author. He indicates *Gil Blas* as his main inspiration and states that he was attempting to revive the picaresque novel. But while Le Sage created a marionette, father of the protagonists of the *contes philosophiques,* Honoré Colette lives by his own right. Complicated psychology would be misplaced in these elemental beings, but each one is adequately presented. *Une Jeunesse,* also in two volumes, appeared in 1927. This is a study of adultery among the bourgeoisie, viewed more from the psychological reactions of the principals than as a triangle. Attention is concentrated on them and on their relations to their families. The action is placed in Liége and in the Ardennes, whose calm beauty contrasts with the unbridled passions of the actors. The author never indulges in moralizing; even his noble priest, l'Abbé Faniel, is content to let life teach its own lesson. Here is adultery in its fairest light, but the lovers soon find the *aliquid amari* which lies in wait for men of honor when they violate their code. The sense of ruin in their career is ever-present to both and is impressed on the reader by the logic of an objective narrative. The hero recalls at times Fréderic Moreau of Flaubert's *L'Education sentimentale.*

Glesener shows the same variety in his short stories as in his novels. The first three collections (1921–1923) center around the First World War, now stigmatizing the atrocities of the invasion or mocking the champions of *Kultur,* now exposing the unedifying activities of Flemish separationists and of profiteers across the Dutch frontier—where, threatened with arrest, the author had taken refuge in 1917. The best of the regionalistic collections, *L'Ombre des sapins,* (1934) represents the complete fruition of his powers. Here his dramatic talent is at its height; objective narrative deepens into terror the pity inspired by *François Remy.* The inevitability of ancient tragedy hovers over peasants caught in the meshes of fate; perennial traits of their class—avarice, sensuality, blind obstinacy—constitute the flaw which draws Nemesis upon them, and they appear as symbols of humanity in agony. The reading of any of Glesener's volumes brings the conviction that, as stylist of the classic tradition and as artisan of the novel, he has not received from foreign critics due meed.

See: B. M. Woodbridge, "Edmond Glesener," *Publications of the Modern Language Association,* LII (1937), 1191–1203 (with bibliography).

B. M. W.

Głowacki, Aleksander, *see* Prus, Bolesław.

Gnoli, Domenico, Conte (pseud. Giulio Orsini, 1838–1915, Italian poet and critic), was born in Rome. He remains known in modern Italian literature for one successful literary deceit—or transformation. He was already a patriarch and a somewhat effete man of letters, whose earlier poems had won him only a respectful silence, when he succeeded in making himself famous under the very well kept and exciting secret of a pseudonym. As a presumably young, fresh, revolutionary poet, he became admired by the generation of the turn of the century, in large part on account of the new lilt of a single quatrain ("Giace anemica la musa. . . .") which was soon on all lips. In a confession published posthumously and similar to that of Poe on the creation of "The Raven," Gnoli has explained that he formed his celebrated quatrain only "for metrical reasons" in one of those "experiments" which are the re-creations of pure artists. From this germ of metric experiment there really sprang a new poet.

The old poet, *i.e.*, the "first" Domenico Gnoli, a charming gentleman in charge of the National Library of Rome and then of the Lancisiana in the same city, wrote, before and also after this literary adventure, several books and an indefinite number of articles (he was editor of the *Nuova Antologia* and created the *Archivio storico dell'arte*) in which erudition is enlivened by a poetical feeling of love for the Eternal City. He had something in common with Ferdinand Gregorovius (1821–1891), German interpreter of Italy, whom he would have been happy to emulate. His poems, well written, in a classical style, and in "pure" Italian, assure him a place of honor among those poets who lived between 1849 and 1870 in the old Rome faithful to Italy and to "purism." They were published in one volume in 1913 by Laterza (*I Poeti della scuola romana, 1850–70*); they are patriotic, dignified—and boring. On the other hand, his three books, published when he was over 60 years old and related to his other and really important poetic personality, *Orpheus* (1901), *Fra terra ed astri* (1903), *Jacovella* (1905), win him a place among the *poeti crepuscolari* who flourished in the new century. These books are full of direct, nostalgic, simple, resigned, and disconsolate poesy.

G. P.

Gobetti, Piero (1901–1926, Italian political writer and critic), born in Turin, was the foremost representative of the intellectual sphere of Turin, where he lived all of his short life. Even in his student days he stood out as an intellectual leader. His first venture was *Energie nuove,* a weekly (1919). He drew for a collaboration on his masters, Francesco Ruffini and Luigi Einaudi, as well as on his fellow students. As a Piedmontese of the educated middle class, he was strongly conscious of the Cavourian classical liberal tradition, which he felt as a "moral religion." Amid the intellectual confusion of the post-war years and many escapes into extremist doctrines, he formed the idea of a thorough revision of Italian political values—a "liberal revolution." He was the first among the writers of the bourgeoisie to study without preconception the Russian Revolution in its background and achievements. Undeterred by the threatening insurrectional atmosphere of Turin in 1920, he established close ties with the group of young Communist intellectuals around Antonio Gramsci and became the literary editor of their paper, the *Ordine nuovo.* In 1922, he founded his own weekly, *Rivoluzione liberale,* which became the chief organ of anti-Fascist intellectuals. In it he subjected to a pitiless critique not only Fascism, but also the many interests, moderate and conservative, which had put themselves at the service of the new regime, and tried to trace the causes of Italian political decadence as a whole. He stood up under the threats and attacks of the local Fascists. But after 1924, the order came from Mussolini "to make life impossible for him." He was repeatedly beaten up, his friends silenced, his presses destroyed, until he realized that the only alternative left was to quit or go abroad. Accordingly, he moved to Paris in 1926. But a few days after his arrival, owing to his frail health and to the maltreatment he had suffered, he died of a heart attack.

The sum of the work that Gobetti put into the 25 years of his life is prodigious and should be multiplied by the work of the whole group which he brought into being and kept going singlehanded (periodicals published later, like the *Caffe* and the *Baretti,* go back to his influence). Apart from incisive polemical articles, which provided memorable analyses of the political scene, he has left *Risorgimento senza eroi* (1926; a series of historical studies), *Giacomo Matteotti* (1924; a biography), and one comprehensive book, *Rivoluzione liberale* (1924), which is an analysis of Italian political life since the time of Cavour and also a statement of Gobetti's doctrine. His revision of values may be defined in his own words: "Marx instead of Mazzini, Cattaneo instead of Gioberti," or, not a society of artificially unified emotional currents and confusions, but instead an active and ordered conflict of "autonomies," *i.e.*, individual and group initiatives, with the statesman as a "diplomat" who steers without suppressing or degrading any of the original forces. Hence his respect and sympathy for the rising young Communists. The sorry experience of Italian Socialism in the first decades of the 20th century, degenerating into demagogy and subsidy-hunting, had not driven him like other liberals into the advocacy of bribery or repression, for he considered fear the cardinal sin of a ruling class; but instead had showed him the need for new energies from the working class to take up the formative struggle of modern society. The role of the liberal is to recognize such forces and give them moral leadership.

G. de S.

Gobineau, Arthur, comte de (1816–1882, French publicist, novelist, and social philosopher), was born in Ville-d'Avray near Paris on Bastille Day, an anniversary he was to deplore all his life. He was brought up in France, then in Switzerland, and then again in France (Lorient and Paris). He became especially interested in oriental languages and, like many a young man, wrote his first verses at the age of 16. Between 1841 and 1849, in which year Tocqueville made Gobineau his *chef de cabinet,* many articles, poems, and novels were published in the most important newspapers and magazines and afterward collected in book form (*e.g., Ternove, Mademoiselle Irnois, Nicolas Belavoir,* all 1847; *L'Abbaye de Typhaines,* 1848).

In 1853 appeared the first part of *L'Essai sur l'inégalité des races humaines,* a work of many weaknesses and considerable charm, which for purely political reasons has up to now made the reputation of Gobineau. After the coup d'état of Napoleon III he entered the diplomatic service and went as first secretary to Persia. While his career took him to Newfoundland, to Teheran again as minister, to Greece, Brazil, and Stockholm, he kept on with literary activities. After retirement from the diplomatic corps he traveled in Italy, England, and Germany; he became an intimate of Wagner (*q.v.*) and was greatly attached to the comtesse de la Tour, for whom he neglected his wife (née Gabrielle Clémence Monnerot). But still he wrote, to the very end of his days, producing a great variety of books, from works as debatable and vulnerable as *Lectures des textes cunéiformes* (1858) and *Histoire d'Ottar Garl et de sa descendance* (1879) to others worthy of esteem and admiration such as *Les Religions et les philosophies dans l'Asie centrale* (1876), *Les Pléiades* (1874; Eng. tr., 1928), and *Nouvelles asiatiques* (1876). Posthumous volumes, which show a letter writer of the highest quality (correspondence with Tocqueville, Prokesch, Keller, Adolphe Franck, Marie Dragoumis; see *Correspondance entre Tocqueville et Gobineau,* 1908, etc.), confirm the true nature of his political and philosophical position, which is very different from common report as built up by the press and misinterpreted by Hitlerian and other fascist propaganda.

Although it is possible to find in the abundance of his writings many contradictory texts (the letters to Prokesch, for example, are inconsistent with *L'Essai,* and the *Deux Etudes sur la Grèce moderne,* 1905, nullify what these same letters affirm about Hellas), the essential Gobineau is not really elusive to impartial scholarship. Gobineau is feudal, accepting nothing which has come since the days of the great barons; autocracy, if reactionary and at the same time "moderate," appears to him the least unsatisfactory solution. The vigorous criticisms in *La Troisième République française et ce qu'elle vaut* (1907) are by no means all unfair. At the same time Gobineau considers it idle to resist democratic degeneration: since the death of the last Aryan, some two thousand years ago, humanity is destined to decrepitude and aestheticism. Germany and Italy are not more estimable than other countries, perhaps less so. It becomes clear that Gobineau is remote from all fascist doctrine; he believes only in a hereditary aristocracy, scorns war and imperialism, speaks of the Jews with sympathy, often with friendliness, at times with admiration. He is not in the least a "discovery" of the Pan-Germans. From his very youth he was celebrated by Frenchmen.

But it is not particularly his political views or his historical fantasies which promise any permanence to Gobineau as a writer—those pages of *L'Essai* which deal with China abound in ignorant mistakes that in themselves destroy the whole thesis of the book. It is for his narrative gift, for his genius as a *conteur,* that this "descendant of kings" is likely to remain known, and also perhaps for the scope of his mind. The originality of his novel *Les Pléiades* (too suggestive of an inferior Stendhal) may be impugned, but Gobineau stands completely on his own in his masterpiece, the *Nouvelles asiatiques.* His style, direct, sober, exact, is never spoiled by the modes of the times; there are none of the defects of romanticism or of realism. With due allowances made for his eccentricity and his nobleman's fanaticism, Gobineau is still definitely one of the geniuses of the French 19th century. When recent conflicts of fascism and liberalism have passed into history, this really great man will have his deserved recognition.

See: R. Dreyfus, *La Vie et les prophéties du comte de Gobineau* (1905); M. Lange, *Le*

Comte de Gobineau (1924); "Gobineau et le gobinisme," *Nouvelle Revue française,* XLII (1934), 161–310 (special number devoted to this author); Etiemble, "Gobineau, juez del fascismo," *Sur,* February, 1942.

E.

Goetel, Ferdynand (1890–, Polish novelist and publicist), was born at Sucha in the Tatras, the son of a poor railroad conductor. Both his parents were of German origin, his father the son of a German colonist in the Bochnia salt mines, his mother the daughter of a retired Austrian soldier, and both parents were intelligent beyond their circumstances. After the death of his father in 1896, Goetel came under the influence of an uncle, the proprietor of the café Pod Pawiem (At the Sign of the Peacock), which was one of the principal meeting places of the Young Poland (*see* Polish literature) group. At school Goetel was lazy and indifferent to routine tasks but, under the influence of socialism, active and enthusiastic in extracurricular projects for spreading enlightenment, especially in the new folk universities. After studying architecture at the Vienna Polytechnic (1908–1912), Goetel abandoned this and went to Warsaw, intending to take up writing as a profession. On the outbreak of the First World War he was interned by the Russians and deported to Turkestan. The experiences he underwent there, first as a common laborer at road construction, later as a highway engineer, together with those he suffered in his subsequent flight by way of Persia and India back to Poland, gave him the material for a series of tales, among these *Przez płonący wschód* (1923; Through the Flaming East), *Kar Chat* (1923), and the widely translated *Z dnia na dzień* (1926; Eng. tr., *From Day to Day,* 1931). Goetel's Eastern stories and also his later description of Iceland, *Wyspa na chmurnej północy* (1928; An Island in the Cloudy North), together with the Icelandic tale *Serce lodów* (1930; Glaciers' Heart), won swift popularity, answering as they did the post-war craving in Poland for something at once exotic and realistic. In the 30's, after an isolated bid for fame as a dramatist with the tendentious *Samuel Zborowski* (1929), Goetel gradually abandoned belles-lettres to become one of Free Poland's leading publicists. Identifying himself with the curious, pseudoarchaic, self-consciously "Old Polish" journal *Merkuryusz* (Mercury), he came to be known as the very high priest of the would-be "Polonizers of Polish literature." With the publication in 1938 of his *Pod znakiem faszyzmu* (Under the Banner of Fascism), in which "an heroic attitude toward life" is held up as an ideal, Goetel's ideological sympathies became suspect and, despite his high position in the P.E.N. Club, he began to be regarded as dangerously reactionary. In 1939, with *Cyklon* (Cyclone), a weak and diffuse tale based on an old journey back from India, Goetel endeavored, without success, to recapture the public that had admired his earlier novels. During the Second World War, Goetel remained in Poland.

See: Z. Dębicki, *Portrety,* II (1928), 351–367; K. Czachowski, *Obraz współczesnej literatury polskiej,* III (1936), 246–258, 692–694; A. P. Coleman, "Ferdinand Goetel Today," *Books Abroad,* XIII (1939), 420–423.

K. Z.

Gojawiczyńska, Pola (pseud. of Apolonia Gojawiczyńska, 1896–, Polish novelist), was born in Warsaw of poor and humble parents. Through her talent for writing, discovered by a teacher, and her great capacity for work, she won the interest and support of Ignacy Matuszewski, then secretary of the treasury. Her semi-autobiographical story "Maryjka" was published in the official *Gazeta polska* (1932) through his help. Thus auspiciously launched, she continued to write, and when a brief residence in Silesia removed her from the center of the literary world, she took advantage of the temporary exile to produce a fine portrait of the mining district and especially of its women in *Ziemia Elżbiety* (1934; The Land of Elizabeth). On her return to Warsaw, Gojawiczyńska proceeded to recreate in the two novels *Dziewczęta z Nowolipek* (1935; The Girls from Nowolipki) and *Rajska jabłoń* (1937; The Apple Tree of Paradise) the hard, drab world from which she herself had sprung, thereby making Warsaw's "lower depths" literary material. Interested primarily in exploring not society as a whole but woman, Gojawiczyńska next pursued, in *Słupy ogniste* (1938; Pillars of Fire), her favorite theme, the tribulations of woman in a man's world. Though this work was distinctly inferior to those which preceded it, Gojawiczyńska was regarded, on the eve of Poland's collapse, as one of the most promising and serious of the younger writers.

See: K. Czachowski, *Najnowska twórczość literacka* (1938), pp. 117–121; A. P. Coleman, "The Literary Scene in Poland," *New York Times Book Review,* April 9, 1939, pp. 8, 24.

A. P. C.

Gómez de Baquero, Eduardo (pseud. Andrenio, 1866–1929, Spanish journalist and critic), was for the first 25 years of this century the leading literary critic in Madrid. He was born in Madrid and studied both law and letters in its university. An attempted political career was ill-starred, for he attained no post of importance either by election or by appointment. His vocation as a writer, however, was soon revealed. When he was but 16 his articles were appearing in the *Revista de España* on such weighty topics as "El panslavismo y la paz europea." Later he wrote for many of the important journals and newspapers of the day: *España moderna; Epoca,* in which he first used the pseudonym Andrenio (1904); *Imparcial,* where he succeeded Clarín (*see* Alas, Leopoldo) as literary critic; *Sol, Voz,* and other publications of Spain and Latin America. In 1924 he was elected to the Spanish Academy.

The variety of subjects on which Andrenio wrote reveals the range of his intellectual interest as well as his competence in diverse fields—legal, social, and historical questions, modes and manners, short fictions, literary topics above all. Andrenio's literary criticisms are uniformly benevolent but not blindly laudatory, for he had the discrimination necessary to select the good qualities of a book, leaving the defects unmentioned. His style is simple, lucid, and gently ironical. His literary studies, such as those in *Novelas y novelistas* (1918), are in no sense exhaustive, but they point out aspects of the subject which are evocative and significant. Andrenio's tranquil objectivity and his real literary insight made it possible for him to write with equally sympathetic appreciation of men of hostile literary schools. *El renacimiento de la novela española en el siglo XIX* (1924) is a brief but excellent résumé of the development of this genre. Taken all together, Andrenio's criticisms form a kind of literary history of the period which is most valuable for its freshness and contemporaneity.

Other published collections of articles include the following: *Letras e ideas* (1905), *Aspectos* (1909), *De Gallardo a Unamuno* (1926), *Pirandello y compañía* (1928), *Nacionalismo e hispanismo* (1928), *Guignol* (1929), *Pen Club* (1929).

See: R. Menéndez Pidal, "Prólogo," in Andrenio, *Guignol* (1929); F. de Onís, introduction to Antonio Alonso, *Antología de ensayos españoles* (1936).

K. R. W.

Gómez de la Serna, Ramón (1891–, Spanish novelist, dramatist, critic, and aphorist), was born in Madrid, a city that was to be the scene of many of his descriptive and interpretative pages. There he studied at the university. Writing is his unmistakable vocation, and few authors have been as prolific. He has lived in Portugal and France and more recently in Buenos Aires. His personality abounds in picturesque characteristics, and in his autobiographical pages he has woven around himself a sort of legend. For many years he had in the old café Pombo in Madrid a literary *tertulia* which without doubt was the most animated and colorful of the period; he wrote the history of this group in his book *Pombo* (1918). His frank and jovial character and eagerness to amuse, so evident in his radio talks and in his lectures, give him the appearance of a modern buffoon, completely anti-academic and lacking in any sort of solemnity.

Gómez de la Serna's inherent need to create has led him to cultivate many different kinds of writing, and in all his peculiar temperament, which he has himself labeled "Ramonismo," is discernible above the characteristics of the genre. "Ramonismo" consists of a grotesquely dramatic vision of the world, ranging from simple caricatural deformation, with an elemental comic intent, to deep insight into the pathetic side of life. His novels, among which *La viuda blanca y negra* (1918), *El doctor inverosímil* (1921), *Cinelandia* (1927; Eng. tr., *Movieland,* 1930), *El torero Caracho* (1927), and *Policéfalo y señora* (1932) are outstanding, are an attempt to express through characters and their actions all the bustling and heterogeneous content of his creative imagination. He finds happiest outlet in books of very personal cast—*El rastro* (1915), *Senos* (1918), *El circo* (1922). Without doubt one of his masterpieces is *El rastro,* in which the author gives us the motley spectacle of the secondhand market in Madrid, a whole world in itself, composed entirely of worn-out things thrown away in their final agonal stage. In these various books the author's span reaches from insignificant details of observation to the weightiest moral considerations. The critico-biographical works, *Oscar Wilde* (1921), *Azorín* (1923), *Goya* (1928), and *El Greco* (1935), are not objective historical treatments, but personal reconstructions of figures whom the author reshapes in order to bring out more fully their natures. His *Retratos contemporáneos* (1942) contains authentic if impressionistic likenesses of some of the best writers of the present day. Among his dramatic works are *El drama del palacio deshabitado* (1909) and *Los medios seres,* which was produced in Madrid in 1929. He has essayed art criticism in his book *Ismos* (1931).

Gómez de la Serna is the inventor of a minor genre, the *greguería,* to which he turns continually and which might be described as the cell of his literary organism. The suggestion of the Spanish word, "confused noise" or "jargon," applies to his fashioning in this small mold of all the phases of his creative restlessness. A *greguería* is necessarily short, aphoristic, and very closely related to the Japanese haikai. Everything can be expressed in the *greguería,* all that is comic, all that is lyric, sudden revelations arising from a new association of ideas, condensed and instantaneous in their effect. The author has composed several books made up entirely of such little pieces; the most important are *Greguerías* (1918) and *Flor de greguerías* (1933), selections from which are translated in *Some Greguerías* (1944). The *greguería* also finds its way, with or without the author's express design, into his novels, his stories, and indeed all his work. Occasionally this form turns into a small poem of lyric intensity.

At first this author was considered merely extravagant and whimsical, yet his total product now shows an urge for literary creation not less serious than fervent. Shunning all appearance of the sacerdotal solemnity inherited from certain 18th-century conceptions, he gives free rein to intellectual capers, but his frivolity, only apparent, hides feelings of torment and desperation about the insolvable problems of human existence. He is a victim of his own profound sense of paradox when he declares that literature is a matter "of working in order not to produce, of working so that everything will be quite destroyed." He typifies the struggle between the propensity for disorder and the need for order in the modern world. By virtue of his desperate individuality, his gift for contrasts, and his plasticity of expression, he is attached today to the Spanish baroque, in the manner of Quevedo; his work is a genial modern version of that tradition.

See: J. Cassou, "La Signification profonde de Ramón Gómez de la Serna," *Revue européenne,* N.S. III (1928), 175–178; M. Pérez Ferrero, *Vida de Ramón* (1935).

P. S.

Goncourt, Edmond de (1822–1896) and **Jules de** (1830–1870; French realistic novelists, diarists, and historians), *les frères Goncourt,* are an amazing example of harmonious unity in literary collaboration. Born one in Nancy, the other in Paris, they were the only children of a cavalry captain who had served Napoleon. Their education at the Collège Bourbon was unusual in that it failed to imbue them with the ordinary national prejudices. In 1848 their dying mother pledged her sons to unite their lives; they never married and, it is said, were separated only once for as much as 24 hours. With a modest inheritance, the Goncourts needed no careers. They first practiced art, later shifted to literature. On December 2, 1851, when their first novel was published, the brothers inaugurated their *Journal,* one of the world's best-known literary diaries. They widened their circle of friends and began to gratify a taste for the unconventionally beautiful by collecting pictures, correspondence, and souvenirs of the 18th century. They were already successful as historians and art critics; their representative works of this period are *Histoire de la société française pendant la Révolution* (1854), *Portraits intimes du XVIIIe siècle* (2 vols., 1857–1858), *L'Art du XVIIIe siècle* (3 vols., 1859–1875). As historians the Goncourts advanced their craft by their new approach to the history of manners, a skillful use of the apparently insignificant document. As writers they laboriously practiced an individual impressionistic style marked by neologisms and labeled by them *le style artiste.* This style, the fruit of their exacerbated nerves and mental *modernité* (a word coined by the Goncourts in 1858), has restricted their circle of readers.

The Goncourts' representative novels appeared in the last decade of Jules's life. They are documentary fiction, with keys duly set down in the *Journal,* and as such they place Edmond and Jules with the 19th-century realists like Murger and Flaubert (*q.v.*), although the brothers' flair for exceptional subjects and pathological cases supports their claim to have anticipated Zola's scientific naturalism (*see* French naturalism). *Charles Demailly* (1860) is a tableau of Parisian journalism and letters, whose themes are extracted from the *Journal. Sœur Philomène* (1861) springs from an incident in a Rouen hospital. *Renée Mauperin* (1864), their most widely read novel, retells their father's biography, and its heroine is drawn after a childhood playmate. *Germinie Lacerteux* (1864) anticipates Zola's proletarian novels; it is based on the posthumous revelation of the "uterine furors" of their own model housekeeper. *Manette Salomon* (1867), perhaps the only adequate novel of artist life in the French language, will always deserve a reading. The tale embodies a Goncourt thesis, that marriage prevents success in art, and contains furthermore the first eulogy of the Japanese color print to be found in European literature. *Madame Gervaisais* (1869) contains the exact story of the life and conversion of an aunt of the Goncourts. Five years after Jules died, prematurely exhausted, Edmond began to publish again—catalogues of Watteau and Prud'hon; the first monographs on the Japanese color-print masters, *Outamaro* (1891) and *Hokousaï* (1896); and his own novels, *La Fille Elisa* (1875) on prostitution, *Les Frères Zemganno* (1879) on the pathetic tragedy of a circus team, *La Faustin* (1882) about a star actress, *Chérie* (1884) about the modern society girl. Dramatizations of nine of these tales were made, a few for the Théâtre Libre of Antoine (*q.v.*).

In 1885 Edmond inaugurated Sunday receptions in the upper story of his Auteuil house, his "grenier," where the opportunity to meet Alphonse Daudet, Zola, and Turgenev (*qq.v.*) served to attract the younger generation of writers and diffuse the cults of *style artiste, le XVIIIe siècle, le japonisme.* This house and its contents are described in *La Maison d'un artiste* (1881). It fostered the fashion of studios hung with Japanese embroideries and overcrowded with *bibelots.* Edmond published three volumes of *Le Journal des Goncourt* in 1887, which were followed by six others. The unexpurgated diary was to have appeared 20 years after the death of the surviving writer. Its entries reflect the humors of their friend Gavarni, preserve the whims and ideals of the brothers, and record the many sayings of Sainte-Beuve, Gautier, Flaubert (*q.v.*), and Renan (*q.v.*), plus gossip about the celebrities of half a century. In 1882 Edmond let it be known that his collections were to be sold to endow an academy of 10 members. The Goncourt Academy, inaugurated in 1900, elects its members without declaration of candidacy. They receive annuities and at an annual luncheon award the coveted Prix Goncourt to the author of "le meilleur ouvrage en prose paru dans l'année."

See: Alidor Delzant, *Les Goncourt* (1889); Marcel Sauvage, *Jules et Edmond de Goncourt; leur œuvre* (1932); Georges de Traz, *Edmond et Jules de Goncourt* (1941).

W. L. S.

Goris, Jan-Albert (pseud. Marnix Gijsen, 1899–, Flemish poet and essayist), was born in Antwerp and studied at Louvain, where he was graduated with the degree of Doctor of History in 1925. He became successively professor at this same university, chief of the cabinet of the mayor of Antwerp, director in the Fine Arts Service of the municipality of Antwerp, chief of the cabinet of the minister of economic affairs, high commissioner for tourism in Belgium, and finally commissioner of information for Belgium in the United States.

After he had spent a year in the United States in his youth (among other things, he studied at Seattle), he paid several visits to this country and in 1927 wrote *Ontdek Amerika* (Discover America; French tr., *Le Cœur de l'Amérique,* 1933). Goris's poetry, collected in one volume entitled *Het Huis* (1925; The House), is not extensive, but of high value and importance. *Het Huis,* regarded exclusively as poetry, contains some of the richest poems written in the Dutch language and has had a profound effect on the development of poetry in the Netherlands. He is without any doubt the greatest of the poets who came to the fore in Flanders after the First World War. His critical and theoretical work is likewise of genuine value and significance.

During the Second World War, his *Belgium in Bondage* (1943) and *Strangers Should Not Whisper* (1945), written in English, and *Du génie flamand* (1943), written in French, were published in New York. At Pretoria, South Africa, there appeared from his pen in 1944 an anthology of Flemish lyric poetry *Vlaamsche Lyriek,* with excellent characterizations of the poets.

J. G.

Gorky, Maxim (pseud. of Aleksei Peshkov, 1868–1936, Russian novelist, playwright, and essayist), had the unique distinction among Russian authors of playing an equally important part in his country before and after the Revolution. He could also claim a practically equal significance as man and as writer. So interwoven were the events of his life with those of Russian history and with his literary expression that both in his life and in his work one loses sight of the borderline between *Dichtung* and *Wahrheit.* Born in Nizhni-Novgorod (now renamed Gorky) on the Mother Volga, the restless wanderer learned to know this great river and all his vast native land by tramping and by plying the widest variety of trades, from errand boy, ragpicker, bird catcher, apple peddler, gardener, kitchen boy on a steamer, to apprentice at a draughtsman's, at an icon shop, in a bakery, to railroad watchman and stevedore. This intimate contact with men and life gave Gorky his sense of reality, which coexisted in him with a perpetual dream of a different world and a better life. Realism coupled with romanticism—such was the outlook of Gorky the man and the author.

In the very first story he published, "Makar Chudra" (1892), he displayed his robust knowledge and understanding of actual conditions among groups as disparate as intellectuals and horse thieves and at the same time his dreamy yearning after a seemingly unattainable fairyland. Similarly in life he lived actively and dreamed dynamically, throwing in his lot with the revolutionary movement, supporting the tsar's opponents with pen and substance, and often risking his freedom and very life in behalf of the people's cause. The contradiction between his realism and romanticism seemed glaring. On the one hand, he knew and portrayed the bulk of humanity as stupid, mean, cruel, stagnant, ignorant, and shortsighted. On the other hand, even from the lowest depths of human degradation he had his Satan proclaim, "Man—that sounds proud!" (*Na dne,* 1902; Eng. tr., *The Lower Depths,* 1912), and in his poem in prose *Chelovek* (1903; Eng. tr., *Man,* 1926) he sang a hopeful hymn to potentially free man, armed with reason and vision, master of nature and machine. In his tramp stories (1895–1902) he exposed truthfully the squalor and brutality of the "Lumpenproletariat," but by implication he expressed his preference for the hobos' freedom from walls and possessions as against the thralldom of things and traditions that weighed down the life of "smug citizens" (*Meshchane,* 1902, Eng. tr., *The Smug Citizen,* 1906; *Foma Gordeyev,* 1899, Eng. tr., 1901; *Troye,* 1901, Eng. tr., *Three of Them,* 1902). Hatred for seamy reality sharpened his yearning for the remote and ideal, for the legendary vistas of such of his early tales as "Old Woman Izerghil" (1895). Free from illusions about the human race as it is and as he so well knew it, Gorky nevertheless kept his faith in man's eventual triumph over his own stupidity and slavery. Only such a faith can explain the fundamental buoyancy of his masterly autobiographical works, notably *Detstvo* (1913; Eng. tr., *My Childhood,* 1915), in which the sunny religiosity of Grandmother lends hope and courage in the face of sordidness, cruelty, and misery. Only such a faith could hearten Gorky in his support of the revolutionary movement at a time when it seemed "impractical" to dream of any positive outcome of the struggle of a handful of idealists against the double enemy of a powerful autocracy above and mass inertia below.

Gorky's faith in man evolved from the naïve individualism of his early tales to the collectivism of his mature productions. *Mat* (1907–1908; Eng. tr., *Mother,* 1907) was the first portrayal in Russian literature of the factory proletariat as a nascent force destined to break down the existing order. One may follow Gorky's gropings in his *Ispoved* (1908; Eng. tr., *The Confession,* 1916), with the seeker Matvei, who discards religion after religion, ideal after ideal, until he finally embraces the one "god"—the people, "creator of all gods . . . creator of miracles." The collective mass of humanity, when organized by an intelligent will, is invincible and knows no barriers on its forward march. Such was the final formula of Gorky's views, at the end of a long and tortuous quest. His faith was put to hard tests again and again, during the mass madness of the First World War and the excesses of the Revolution of 1917 and the resultant civil war. There were times when Gorky vacillated and seemed to reel on the brink of despondency about the human race. He rallied, however, at the lowest ebb of the Bolshevik experiment, when the new state appeared doomed, with war and intervention on 16 fronts and inner breakdown and starvation. Gorky drew strength from the sight of a collective mass united by an intelligent will under the guidance of understanding leaders. The inveterate dreamer once again undertook to champion a "lost cause." Despite his distaste for the Bolshevik methods, he came out in their support, against the opposition of virtually the whole world. His faith in collective man was revived and sustained.

For some 40 years Gorky suffered from tuberculosis of the lungs. He defied medical experts, as he had defied other authorities and institutions, and survived more than one death sentence pronounced by famous specialists. It was necessary for him, however, to reside in a congenial climate, which he found in southern Italy, for many years his second home. In 1928 he threw all considerations of health to the winds and returned to Russia, where he spent his last eight years in variegated activity. He had the rare satisfaction for a dreamer of living to see his dreams come true. The land which had treated him to persecution, prison, and exile received him now with universal enthusiasm. He actually saw the transformation, within a few years, of a backward patriarchal country into a highly industrialized union of numerous nationalities, cemented by a sense of equality and loyalty to an order free from masters and slaves. He saw man rise from darkness, stupidity, and pettiness to the height of his potentialities. It was natural that his spirits were high during these last years and that he eagerly participated in numerous cultural undertakings. Aside from editing various periodicals and editions of classics and foreign authors, Gorky managed to write in this period a prodigious number of essays and much fiction. Most notable is his unfinished dramatic trilogy, the first of which, *Yegor Bulychov* (1932; Eng. tr. in *The Last Plays of Maxim Gorki,* 1937), won considerable success on the stage, and the second, *Dostigayev i drugiye* (1934; Eng. tr., *Dostigaeff and the Others,* in *The Last Plays*), was moderately acclaimed. His four-volume novel, *Klim Samgin—Sorok let* (1927–1936; Eng. tr., *Bystander,* 1930; *The Magnet,* 1931; *Other Fires,* 1933; *The Specter,* 1938), is an ambitious survey of Russian events from 1880 to 1924. Had Gorky lived longer, he would probably have revised and shortened this somewhat lumbering novel. With all its flaws, it is a valuable record and has some of Gorky's memorable portraits.

Both at home and abroad Maxim Gorky remains a living challenge to environment and circumstances, a symbol of dynamic optimism and faith in man.

See: K. Chukovski, *Dve dushi M. Gorkvo* (1925); R. Grigoryev, *M. Gorky* (1925); A. Kaun, *Maxim Gorky and His Russia* (1931); V. Desnitski, *M. Gorky* (1940).

A. K.

Gorter, Herman (1864–1927, Dutch poet), was born at Wormerveer, studied classic philology at the University of Amsterdam, and took his Ph.D. with a dissertation on Aeschylus. He was 25 years old when the publication of *Mei* (1889; May) won him a leading place among the poets of his generation. *Mei* defies all attempts of the literary historians to label it with some descriptive name from their list of genres. It is not an epic, though its length and form make it look like one. The tone is lyrical, and much of its verse is verbal painting of the beauty that is Holland, the Dutch landscape and all that makes it lovely to the artist's eye—meadows, inland lake and seashore, birds, flowers, herds of cattle, and the clouds that graze the pasture of the sky. But *Mei* is also a myth, resembling, not in form but intent, the Icelandic Edda, and it is at the same time a lyrical autobiography. The myth is the story of May, personification of short-lived physical beauty, who seeks to perpetuate herself by marrying the blind God Balder, embodiment of the world soul. But physical beauty cannot immortalize itself through the soul. May is transitory, Balder alone is eternal. He can be realized only through music, and Gorter, the poet, who attempted to marry the beauty of May to the music of his verse only succeeded in expressing his frustration. Language proved inadequate to voice the life of the soul, which can be rendered by music only. Hence Gorter, in *Verzen* (1890), tried the impossible by divorcing his verse from all word meaning, stringing words together that carried no sense, but appealed to the hearer only through the beauty of melodious sound and rhythm. There is much in *Mei* that is equally elusive and must be emotionally savored rather than understood. But it remains, for all that, a magnificent poem that will be read when the bulk of the output of Gorter's generation has ceased to find an echo in the hearts of posterity.

This highly individualized art, however, could not satisfy Gorter for long. In the introduction to *De School der Poëzie* (1897; The School of Poetry) he declared that he strove "to know not only the emotional life of man and the superficial aspect of the world, but the very laws that govern mankind and the world," because he believed that only through that knowledge could he rise to the highest poetry. *Pan* (1912) is the outcome of this ambition. The fundamental idea of this epic, which he expanded in a revised edition to three times its original length, is that the poet, or Pan, the God of the universe and the spirit of mankind, sees the past, present, and future of humanity (represented by the proletariat) pass by him in review and experiences in his mind humanity's oneness with the universe. That concept of unity as the desirable goal became the dominant thought of Gorter's life. He strove for social unity as a theoretical exponent of Marxism. But the intellectual effort was detrimental to the poetry. Gorter published a definitive edition of his verse in 1916. "In these two volumes," he wrote, "I have collected all the poems which were written by me between 1890 and 1906 and which, as attempts, attained a certain degree of perfection." The second volume included *Het kleine Heldendicht* (Brief Epic; originally published in 1906). There are blind admirers of Gorter in

Holland who accept his own estimate of his poetry as final. But it is highly doubtful whether posterity will agree with them. It is more likely that Gorter will live as the poet of *Mei.*

See: W. van Ravesteijn, *Herman Gorter, de Dichter van Pan; een heroisch en tragisch Leven* (1928); J. C. Brandt Corstius, *Herman Gorter* (1934).

A. J. B.

Gött, Emil (1864–1908, German dramatist and philosopher), born in Jechtingen am Kaiserstuhl, strikes the casual observer as being one of those problematic characters whose great gifts never seem to bear full fruit. He completed only a few works: three plays, *Edelwild* (1901), *Der Schwarzkünstler* (1905), and *Mauserung* (1908), and a small number of short stories. The stern demands he made on himself not only left most of his literary projects unfinished—they even induced him to question whether literature in general has more than ephemeral significance. Time and again he tried to escape from reflection and imagination into the sphere of action, as a farmer, as a small manufacturer and inventor. Yet it would be wrong to attribute such restlessness to some subconscious realization of insufficient literary ability, for there is the evidence of his comedies which combine great formal skill with dramatic verve and deep serenity. Worthy of the old Spanish tradition from which they stem, they form a welcome addition to the repertory of the German stage, which is none too abundantly endowed with plays of an entertaining and at the same time thought-provoking character. If Gött could not apply himself exclusively to writing, it was because he felt in all seriousness that more urgent problems were pressing on German civilization, calling for a practical solution rather than for theoretical discussion. However, the seemingly hopeless diffuseness of Gött's interests became, in the form of innumerable entries in his *Tagebücher* (1914), a constructive reckoning with the skepticism of his time and a steady reorientation towards lasting values. These diaries contain stores of ethical wisdom just as Amiel's disseminate psychological insight. With Nietzsche (*q.v.*) and Tolstoy (*q.v.*) as his initial mentors, he visualized a form of culture which would add to the intellectual honesty and fearlessness of the former the Christian candor of the latter, leaving no place for either Nietzsche's brusqueness or Tolstoy's sentimentality. Gött's most cherished vision was of a life which would, in the measure of human possibilities, become a new *imitatio Christi,* with as little dogma and externalized religion as possible, but with the full enactment of the one universal truth that to be good is to know that all men are brothers under the skin. It is not too much to say that in Gött's *Tagebücher* a new spiritual vitality and a fresh confidence in life slowly gain ascendancy over all ancient and modern prophets of gloom.

See: R. Woerner in Gött, *Gesammelte Werke,* I (1910), pp. xii–cx; A. von Grolman, *Werk und Wirklichkeit* (1937), pp. 45–164.

H. B.

Gourmont, Rémy de (1858–1915, French critic, esayist, and writer of fiction), was born in Normandy, of an old aristocratic family. After studying at the Lycée of Coutances and the University of Caen, he went to Paris and became an assistant librarian at the Bibliothèque Nationale, a position which he was forced to resign after the publication of an "unpatriotic" article (1891). He was very active in the literary circles of the capital and soon enjoyed considerable prestige, especially among the poets of the symbolist school. His *Le Livre des masques* (1896) is an interesting portrait gallery of the leading writers of that time. In 1889 he joined the group that was founding the *Mercure de France,* to which he contributed regularly until the time of his death in 1915. When he was in his 30's, a mysterious disease disfigured him almost completely, and thereafter he withdrew more and more among his books to live the semi-recluse life of a lay Benedictine.

Gourmont's numerous writings all bear the mark of a brilliant mind endowed with a wide and eclectic curiosity and often attracted by very esoteric studies. His first book of criticism, *Le Latin mystique* (1892), an essay on medieval hymnology, shows his interest in little-known subjects and gives at the same time a key to his own poetry (*Divertissements,* 1912). "Litanies de la rose," "Les Saintes du Paradis," and "Oraisons mauvaises" are all characterized by a Baudelaire-like (*see* Baudelaire) mixture of mysticism and sensuality and reveal an artist enamored of rare and melodious words rather than a really inspired poet. In his short stories also, in *Le Pèlerin du silence* (1896) and *Couleurs* (1908), he appears more concerned with the artistic arrangement of musical words than with the telling of his sensuous tales. His first novel, *Sixtine* (1890), he himself described as a "novel of the cerebral life," and his later ones, *Les Chevaux de Diomède* (1897), *Une Nuit au Luxembourg* (1906), *Un Cœur virginal* (1907), if they may be called novels at all, are likewise largely cerebral. These strange books evince their author's constant preoccupation with sex: both passionate and cold, ardent and ironical, they leave the reader with a sense of unreality. The heroines especially, fleshly and yet ethereal, have the unsubstantial quality of Pre-Raphaelite virgins. Curiously enough, it is Eve, in *Lilith* (1892), a dramatic treatment of *Paradise Lost,* that one remembers as a real woman.

Gourmont's love for words led him to a study of their derivations. This new interest engendered some of his most original works, *L'Esthétique de la langue française* (1899), *La Culture des idées* (1900), *Le Problème du style* (1902). To him words were not chilly and abstract symbols but living organisms which should be kept alive in all their savor and freshness. From this conception sprang also his theory of the "dissociation of ideas," his desire to break up associations of ideas which have become encysted in stereotyped phrases and threaten to harden a language into deadly woodenness. New fields of study were constantly attracting him—history, philosophy, theology, sociology, biology. His *Physique de l'amour; essai sur l'instinct sexuel* appeared in 1904 when he thought he had discovered a scientific basis for his theory that man's love is only animal instinct. In 1902 was published *Le Chemin de velours,* a reevaluation of the old quarrel between the Jansenists and the Jesuits, favorable in its conclusions to the less inhuman ethics of the latter. He was the most influential of the *Mercure's* collaborators. His articles cover an ever wider range of subjects, further revealing his insatiable curiosity, his truly encyclopedic knowledge, and no matter what their subject, they open new vistas illuminated with flashes of insight. They appeared later in volume form, *Promenades littéraires* (7 vols., 1904–1928), *Promenades philosophiques* (3 vols., 1905–1909). The articles on literature reveal a critic of catholic taste, partial perhaps to the very modern writers or to the lesser known of the distant past—"I feel at home before Boileau and after Baudelaire"—a comprehending judge with no set code or doctrine, whose viewpoint is always novel, whose conclusions are always challenging. In his commentaries on current events, on contemporary life and manners (*Epilogues,* 1903–1907), he often displays an elegant cynicism the detached irony of a modern La Rochefoucauld.

The last years of his life were brightened by the visits of a beloved American woman, "l'Amazone" (*Lettres à l'Amazone,* 1914; *Lettres intimes à l'Amazone,* 1928). But the outbreak of the First World War gave his commentaries a new and sadder tone (*Pendant l'orage,* 1915; *Dans la tourmente,* 1916; *Pendant la guerre,* 1917). This lover of beauty, this hater of the coarse and vulgar, died on September 29, 1915, as he was working on an indignant article protesting the German shelling of Reims Cathedral. Many of Gourmont's works have been translated into English.

See: Legrand-Chabrier, *Rémy de Gourmont; son œuvre* (1925); P. E. Jacob, *Rémy de Gourmont* (1931).

V. Gu.

Gozzano, Guido (1883–1916, Italian poet), was born in Agliè Canavese in the province of Turin. When he entered law school at the University of Turin he was already threatened with tuberculosis, which was to carry him to an early death. Of a restless, dissatisfied nature, he was attracted by distant worlds where he also hoped to recover his health. Gozzano wrote impressions of a journey to India in the form of letters, and these were collected and published posthumously under the title *Verso la cuna del mondo* (1917). Other posthumous works are a series of charming fairy tales for children, *La Principessa si sposa* (1917), and two volumes of not very successful short stories, *L'Altare del passato* (1918), and *L'Ultima Traccia* (1919). But it was through his lyrics —first published in 1907 as *La Via del rifugio* (collected and republished in a revised edition in 1927 as *I Primi e Gli Ultimi Colloqui*)—that Gozzano achieved instant fame and became the most popular of those poets who because of their passive attitude towards life and their predilection for nuances, half tones, and shadows were called *i crepuscolari.* Their poetry, which is sensuous, with no object or ideal, gives evidence of deriving from D'Annunzio (*q.v.*), although in a certain sense it represents a reaction to him.

Besides the decadent D'Annunzio of *Il Piacere* and *Poema paradisiaco,* the French poets Jules Laforgue and Francis Jammes (*qq.v.*) seem to have influenced Gozzano. The poet is melancholic and wants to get away from himself, he yearns for ordinary healthy living, but he cannot achieve this—his inborn love for simplicity has been dissipated by a literary education which has reduced him to indifference and made him a sophist. He is disgusted with being a poet, a refined, modern man, he is tired of affected women and bemoans not having a plain, primitive soul, like his old servant described in "L'Analfabeta." His dreams of purifying himself by marrying a peasant girl and by living in the country never materialize. But if the poet is too weary to make a fresh start toward a realization of his dreams, he is nonetheless able to crystallize them into perfect poetical units, as in "La Signorina Felicità." His beautiful and most popular poem, "L'Amica di nonna Speranza," shows him a real virtuoso in creating verbal effects. With the most commonplace words, by means of redundant repetitions and implacable rhymes, he succeeds in creating an unforgettable poetic picture of the world of 1850. This sentimental bourgeois world of the *Risorgimento,* long since forgotten and considered decadent, appeals to Gozzano's imagination; it affords him pleasure to enumerate the knickknacks, to describe the salons, to report the conversations, to share the dreams of the young girls of that past era. But this poem—like most of the others—ends on a forlorn, desperate note. Gozzano's experiences in the present and his visions of the past—actual everyday life and the life of his dreams—remain vague; he makes a continuous effort to escape from one into the other without finding refuge or peace in either one. He celebrated many erotic adventures, but never real love; he sang of many women, but not one of them appears to have been his spiritual guide or inspiration.

In contrast to Carducci (*q.v.*) who had a passion for heroic deeds and to D'Annunzio who had developed a rhetoric of sensualism, Gozzano had no dominant feeling—only these blurred sensations. He was incapable of setting a goal for himself. His poetry is nothing but the sometimes impressively lyrical outpourings of his ambiguity. He was not averse to displaying his torture, to criticizing himself and his works. He saw clearly what the future held for him; in one of his poems he said that nothing of his would remain save a few verses. These, he said, sprang from his dry heart, like flowers sprouting from a ground which fire has seared. They constitute a mirror in which Gozzano's desperate, poetical soul has come face to face with itself. The critics could add but little.

See: Pietro Pancrazi, *Scrittori italiani del novecento* (1934), pp. 1–13; Giuseppe Petronio, "Poeti del nostro secolo: I Crepuscolari: Guido Gozzano," *Leonardo,* July–August, 1935, pp. 294–303; Benedetto Croce, "Guido Gozzano," *Critica,* XXXIV (1936), 87–95.

D. F.

Graf, Arturo (1848–1913, Italian poet, critic, and scholar), was born at Athens of a German father and an Italian mother. Graf was precocious in his studies, showing particular interest in poetry. At 15 he went to Italy where, in 1870, he received his degree in jurisprudence from the University of Naples. Here he also studied under the critic Francesco de Sanctis (*q.v.*) and formed an enduring friendship with Antonio Labriola, a leading economist and sociologist. The practice of law did not interest him, and he turned to studies in philology and literature, which he was forced to interrupt in order to aid his brother, who had met with financial reverses in Rumania. In November, 1874, Graf returned to Rome, devoting himself entirely to investigations of the literature of the Middle Ages. The following year he began teaching and had such success that in 1876 he was appointed to the professorship of Italian literature at the University of Turin. Graf was a forceful speaker and combined in unusual degree gifts of exposition and scholarship. His *La Crisi letteraria* (1888), *Per la nostra cultura* (1898), and *L'Università futura* (1906) show the development of his ideas on education and culture. He contributed regularly to the important periodical, *Nuova Antologia.* He was the founder and for seven years (1883–1890) the codirector with Francesco Novati and Rodolfo Renier of the *Giornale storico della letteratura italiana.*

The characteristic note in all the poetical production of Graf is the tragic destiny of mankind: evil, sorrow, and death. His lyrics are replete with images of dead monks, dead virgins, dances of skeletons, and abandoned cemeteries. They contain also many mythological and legendary characters who symbolize the mystery of life—Prometheus, Ulysses, Christ, Faust, Charlemagne. The thought of death and sorrow occurs so frequently in his poems that the reader is often reminded of Leopardi, but Graf's pessimism is more intellectual. Like Leopardi he does not believe that man can improve his condition. In *Medusa* (1880, 1881, 1890), his first and most significant book of poems, Graf portrays a world of fearful imagination. Later collections are *Dopo il tramonto* (1893), *Le Danaidi* (1897), *Morgana* (1901), *Poemetti drammatici* (1903), and *Rime della selva* (1906). All his poems were published together under the title *Poesie* in 1922. Graf labored over his verse and not always with success. Some sonnets, such as "Notte di luglio," "La Martire," and certain other pieces do suggest poetical genius.

Graf also wrote fiction. *Il Riscatto* (1901) is a psychological and, in part, autobiographical novel of some quality. His most important works on history, criticism, and literature are *Studi drammatici* (1878), *Roma nella memoria e nelle immaginazioni del medioevo* (1882–1883), *Attraverso il cinquecento* (1888), *Il Diavolo* (1889; Eng. tr., *The Story of the Devil,* 1931), *Miti, leggende e superstizioni del medioevo* (1892–93), *Foscolo, Manzoni, Leopardi* (1898), *L'Anglomania e l'influsso inglese in Italia nel secolo XVIII* (1911).

Graf was intensely interested in researches in the biological sciences and psychology, especially in those topics that concerned the transmutation of the species, heredity, dreams, hypnosis, and the hidden world. He also showed great interest in current ideas on evolution, socialism, mysticism, neoclassicism, and Neo-Catholicism.

See: G. A. Cesareo, *Critica Militante* (1907); R. Renier, "Arturo Graf," in *Annuario della Regia Università di Torino* (1913–1914); V. Cian, "Arturo Graf," in *Atti della Reale Accademia delle Scienze di Torino* (1918) pp. 973–1007; B. Croce, *La Letteratura della nuova Italia,* 2d ed., II (1921), 203–212.

H. R. M.

Grandmontagne, Francisco (1866–1936, Spanish essayist), of French-Basque parentage, was born in the Castilian province of Burgos and combined in personality and style the best features of Basque and Castilian character. When still very young he emigrated to Argentina; he worked in cities and in the Pampa, accepting, at his different tasks, the hard schooling of the emigrant. He became a noted newspaper man in Buenos Aires and one of the editors of *Prensa;* he returned numerous times to Spain (first in 1903), where he stayed only the last years of his life. Highly esteemed by Unamuno (*q.v.*) and other figures of the Generation of '98 for his straightforward, ironic, and critical mind, for his deep feeling of Hispanic values and the force and purity of his style, he interpreted Argentina and the Spanish American world for Spain, and the Spanish world for Argentina. As the poet Antonio Machado (*q.v.*) said of him, he was "the chronicler of two worlds." A great admirer of the Argentine, he studied its modern development, especially in the volume *Origenes del progreso argentino: Una gran potencia en esbozo* (1928). His works, most of them of Argentine background, include two early novels, *Teodoro Foronda* (1896) and *La maldonada* (1898), and books of sketches, stories, and essays about types and customs, such as *Vivos, tilingos y locos lindos* (1901) and *Los inmigrantes prósperos* (1933). He also wrote, perhaps with less sagacity, about Spanish problems.

See: "El escritor y el hombre en Francisco Grandmontagne," *Prensa* (Buenos Aires), February 24, 1935.

A. del R.

Gras, Félix (1844–1901, Provençal poet and novelist), was born in Malemort, a small village of the Comtat Venaissin. Most of his life was spent in Avignon, where he was for many years a justice of the peace. He came of an old family of prosperous farmers and received his education at the Collège of Béziers. While still a student, he became interested in the Felibrige. This literary school, whose object was the revival of the language and literature of Provence, had steadily been growing in influence. Félix Gras was completely won over to its cause after he had seen his sister crowned as "queen of the Felibrige" by Roumanille (*q.v.*), whom she later married. Having joined her in Avignon, he was soon in direct contact with the already famous Felibres, attending their meetings and taking part in their activities. Thus he stands as one of the first Provençal poets to owe their literary vocation to the founders of this movement. Gras is the greatest of the "second generation of Felibres," towering far above the others. In contrast with his masters, however, he was to remain all his life an outspoken "red of the south," *i.e.,* a liberal in politics and religion, a firm believer in the ideals of the French Revolution. He was to enjoy also the distinction of being the Provençal writer most read in the United States—not excepting Mistral (*q.v.*).

His important works in verse consist of two somber epic poems in 12 cantos, *Li Carbounié* (1876; The Charcoal Burners), dramatizing the life of rustic Alpine mountaineers, and *Toloza* (1880), dealing with the Albigensian crusade, as well as *Lou Roumancero prouvençau* (1887), composed of lyrics evoking the history and legend of medieval Provence. Some of these had appeared previously in *L'Armana prouvençau,* the organ of the Felibrige. Having thus established a solid reputation as an epic and lyrical poet, Gras turned to prose. He published *Li Papalino* (1891; Stories of Papal Avignon) and *Li Rouge dóu Miejour* (1 vol., with French tr. on opposite pages, 1896; 3 parts, in French, *Les Rouges du Midi,* 1898–1900; Eng. tr., *The Reds of the Midi,* 1896, *The Terror,* 1898, and *The White Terror,* 1899, the last two being the second and third volumes of the series). He also published a little pamphlet, *Lou Catechisme dou bon felibre* (1892), which defines the ideals of the Felibrige.

Li Papalino comprises picturesque and colorful stories permeated with good humor and gaiety, told in an energetic, yet light and harmonious language. It was *Li Rouge dóu Miejour,* however, that won him a prominent and even original place among the authors of historical fiction. This is the story of the famous battalion of patriots from Marseille to whose enthusiasm we owe the name of the French national anthem. It is extraordinarily alive, rich in color, swift in action, epic-like in its rhythm. It was published simultaneously in Provençal, French, and English. The English translation has had several American editions.

Félix Gras was third *capoulié* (honorary head) of the Felibrige, succeeding Mistral and Roumanille. In that capacity he made many speeches which added not a little to his popularity. He distinguished himself as a French patriot and an intelligent leader of Provençal regionalism.

See: C. P. Julian and P. Fontan, *Anthologie du Félibrige provençal* (1924); M. Jouveau, "Félix Gras," *Feu,* XX (1926), 321–330; F. Bertrand, *Félix Gras et son œuvre* (1935).

A. V. R.

Grau, Jacinto (1877–, Spanish playwright), born in Barcelona, is perhaps Spain's greatest living dramatist. But his plays have been boycotted silently and consistently in Madrid, even while received with glowing acceptance in Paris, Berlin, and Prague. Grau's unflinching sincerity, his deeply rooted purpose to renovate the Spanish stage, and his irascible temperament combined with a self-acclaimed egotism have incurred for him the dislike of many critics and theatre managers among his compatriots. A Spanish commentator said some years ago that there are two literary generations in present-day Spain, the Generation of 1898 (including such men as Unamuno, Ortega y Gasset, Baroja, Benavente, Valle-Inclán, *qq.v.*) and the Unknown Generation. Grau would belong to the latter. In the long run Grau may well emerge, in his measured dignity and even apparent aloofness from social problems, as sounder and more wise and more sincere than many of his contemporaries. With him there have been no fanfares of words, no merely sonorous denunciations; his artistic productions have vigor and a constant eloquence.

Grau has worked diligently during the last 40 years for a new Spanish stage. Younger participants in the conflict over Spanish drama have acclaimed his plays as "vanguardistas." *Trasuntos* (1899) was the first and already very characteristic literary product of this half-Catalonian, half-Andalusian author. In the introduction to this work the great Catalonian poet, Maragall (*q.v.*), pointed out Grau's qualities: a subtle, poetic vision of reality (symbolized in the very title); a strong tendency to philosophize; a really dynamic style. To these must be added a sense of a new way of life, freed from provincialisms and outmoded routines, and the already-mentioned urge to renovate dramatic technique, specifically by combining with contemporary symbolization in stage production the restrained dignity of classical tragedy and the underlying human vitality of the golden-age period of the Spanish theatre. No other modern playwright in Spain has succeeded so well in going back to Calderón. Grau has simplified the baroque complications into a very tense unity and has created situations and characters that transcend prosaic reality; he searches the ultimate meaning of man and all his passions.

Human love in its multitudinous and conflicting aspects is the leitmotif of his plays. His themes are those that constantly recur in dramatic endeavor. The prodigal son is represented in *El hijo pródigo* (1918), a biblical play which attains the human grandeur and desperate dignity of Calderón's tragedies. *El conde Alarcos* (1917), based on an old Spanish ballad, combines poetic medievalism and a "vanguardist" presentation; it suggests Edwin Arlington Robinson's *Tristram.* In *Don Juan de Carillana* (1913) and *El burlador que no se burla* (1930) is found the treatment of the Don Juan theme in two very different aspects, without the baroque complications in style and the eschatological or teleological elements of Tirso's famous play and without the sexually romantic or romantically sexual imitations which followed it. *El burlador que no se burla* exalts natural love. Its ending is disconcerting to squeamish moralists who think of this love as sin: after Don Juan's death, the women he has loved—not deceived—and who have loved him remember him with nostalgic gratitude. Love as triumphant in varying aspects is treated in *El tercer demonio* (1908); in *El caballero Varona* (1929), a play really liked by the Madrid public; in *La Señora guapa* (published 1943 but first produced about 1930). The tragedy of man in relation to the mysteries of illusion, destiny, and death is worked out with a poetic realism and impressive dramatic technique in *Los tres locos del mundo* (1930). *El señor de Pigmalion* (1921), which bears a strong resemblance to Capek's (*q.v.*) *R.U.R.* and was in fact printed before the latter play was performed, had a turbulent stage career; its *première* had to be given at Paris, whence it traveled triumphantly to Berlin and Prague, but Madrid hardly knows it. All these plays and a dozen others show a sensitive, dramatic genius rare in present-day Spain. They are far different from the products of such writers as the Alvarez Quintero brothers, Linares Rivas, and even Benavente (*qq.v.*). They all convey a feeling that they are "new."

Today Grau, an exile in Buenos Aires, is having his plays republished, with commentaries and essays which throw a great deal of light on the Spanish stage of the last 40 years. He has also written more recently a study entitled *Unamuno y la España de su tiempo* (1943), which is an admirable interpretation as well as a tribute to one who like himself suffered much for a nobler Spain.

See: J. Cejador y Franca, *Historia de la lengua y literatura castellana,* XI (1919), 234-244; Federico Navas, "Jacinto Grau," in *Las esfinges de Talia, o encuesta sobre la crisis del teatro* (1928), pp. 55–58; E. Estévez Ortega, "El teatro moderno de Jacinto Grau," in *Nuevo escenario* (1928), pp. 42–49; J. M. de Osma, *"El conde Alarcos,* tragedia de Jacinto Grau," *Hispania,* XII (1929), 179–184.

F. S. y E.

Greek literature. Modern Greece has lacked, almost up to the present, the *sine qua non* of a representative literature, namely, a standardized literary idiom. The spiritual revival of Greece which began about 1800 with the founding of the revolutionary society, Philike Hetairia, produced the War of Independence (1821–1829) and freed most of the Greek realm from political servitude within the Ottoman Empire. It did not, however, free the Greek language. This continued, long after the creation of an independent Greek state (1832), to labor under its old bondage to the classical tongue of Hellas and the language of the New Testament. Through snobbishness and traditionalism the very ones who were most sincere in their desire to see a living native literature in Greece were those most responsible for the trend which actually retarded this. Adamantios Korais (1748–1833), for example, a great patriot, "reformed" the language for literary purposes, but followed the Hellenic pattern, choosing a mold far removed from the living tongue of the klephts whose gallantry had won Greece her freedom. The language of Korais has often been dubbed satirically "korakistika," or "learned jargon."

A pioneer in the countermovement to that represented by Korais was Athanasios Christopoulos (1772–1847), who wrote drinking songs and love verses in the popular idiom, the most popular of which were *Lirika* (1811; Lyrics); but it was Dionysios Solomos (1798–1857) who first made outstandingly successful use of the vernacular (or *demotiki,* as opposed to the *katharevousa,* or pure Greek) as literary material. A native of the Ionian island of Zante, Solomos turned his back on a brilliant career as an Italian poet in order to found a school of Greek poetry deriving its inspiration from the klephtic ballads of his native islands. His own most celebrated work was "E odi tis elephtherias" (1824; Ode to Liberty) which, set to music, has become the national anthem of Greece. To the Ionian school belonged also the gifted poet Andreas Kalvos (1796–1869); the satiric Andreas Lascaratos (1811–1901); and Aristotle Valaoritis (1824–1879), whose poems in praise of the patriot-revolutionaries were widely read and admired.

The outstanding representative of the classical trend in Greek letters was the distinguished scholar, linguist, archaeologist, and diplomat, Alexandros Rizos Rhangavis (1810–1892), generally known as Rangabe. Rangabe's fame as a literary figure is based especially on his dramas, chief among which are the classical tragedy, in verse, *Triakontai tirani* (1866; The Thirty Tyrants) and the Aristophanic comedy *Tou Koutrouli o gamos* (1845; The Marriage of Koutroulis).

At the opposite pole to Rangabe was Iannis (Jean) Psichari (1854–1929), a native of Odessa, who, like so many Greeks of his day, was educated in Paris. Like Iannis Papadiamantopoulos who, under the pseudonym Jean Moréâs (*q.v.*), became one of the poets of the French symbolist school, Psichari aspired to a literary career in French, but turned, under the influence of Emile Legrand, whom he succeeded as professor of philology at the Paris Ecole des Langues Orientales Vivantes, to the propagation of modern Greek. His satirical account of a journey to Greece, *To taxidi mou* (1888; My Journey), written in the demotic tongue, played an immeasureable part in the conversion of Greek writers of his day and later to the vernacular. Besides philological essays, written in French, Psichari wrote plays and short stories in his native tongue. One short story, *Arosti doula* (1907; The Sick Girl), has sociological implications. Outstanding in the field of the short story was Alexandros Papadiamtis (1851–1911). Unlike most of his generation, Papadiamtis kept himself free for the most part from foreign influences, and his short stories, 120 of which are to be found in the collection *Ta rodina akrogalia* (1913; The Happy Shores), possess a native charm and freshness rarely found in modern Greek. To be noted also are the Ionian tales of Argyris Eftaliotis (1849–1923) which appeared under the title *Nisiotikes istories* (1894; Eng. tr., *Tales from the Isles of Greece,* 1897).

The drama, long shackled by the romantic tradition and hampered by the servility of its authors, especially Demetrios Vernadakis (1834–1907) and Spyridon Vasiliadis (1845–1874), to the *katharevousa,* began to emancipate itself with Iannis Kambisis (1872–1902), the Greek Ibsen (*q.v.*), and his realistic, often grimly satirical dramas of Athenian life. Kambisis was followed by Spyros Melas (1880–), a disciple of Gorky (*q.v.*), and Gregorios Xenopoulos (1867–), the outstanding playwright of modern Greece. Best known for his *Stella Violanti* (1909), which has been called the Greek *Doll's House,* Xenopoulos is the dramatist par excellence of the modern woman. All three of the above wrote in the language of the people, as does also Demetrios Tangopoulos (1867–1926), whose *Zontani kai pethameni* (1905; The Live and the Dead) represents the recent trend to symbolism in Greek drama.

Poetry flourished in Greece above all other literary forms in the late 19th century and more recently, especially lyric poetry. The influence of the Ionian school mentioned above is seen in the poems of Stephen Martzokis (1855–1913) and of the French symbolists (*see* French symbolism) in those of Konstantinos Hadzopoulos (1868–), especially in *To phthinoporo* (1917; Autumn). Hadzopoulos is known also for his illuminating critical essays.

The poet to win the highest favor popularly was George Drossinis (1859–), who began by writing in the *katharevousa* with interpolations of verse in the *demotiki.* Later he wrote exclusively in the popular tongue, and his poems from this period—found in the collections *Photera skotadia* (1903–1914; Light Shadows) and *Klista vlephara* (1914–1917; Closed Eyes)—are among the most popular in modern Greek. Less popular with average readers but more widely recognized by the critics both at home and abroad was Kostes Palamas (*q.v.*). A native of Patras and educated in Athens, Palamas began his literary career as a partisan of the *katharevousa,* only to become converted to the *demotiki* at the time of the celebrated linguistic riots, which took place in Athens in 1901 over the publication of Pallis's vulgate translation of the New Testament, and to become, along with Psichari, an advocate of this allegedly sacrilegious translation. One of the most profound and patriotic thinkers of his day, Palamas produced his finest poetry in the series *Assalephti zoi* (1904; Eng. tr. of first part, *Life Immovable,* 1919, of second part, incomplete, *A Hundred Voices and Other Poems,* 1921). In these, as in his *Grammata* (1913; Letters), the lyrical genius of Palamas is often, unfortunately, overshadowed by excessive cerebration and too great use of symbolism. The recent trend to free verse in Greece is represented by the poet Angellos Sikelianos (1884–) whose long poem *Aphierosi* (1922; Consecration) is one of his finest. A leader in the movement to produce Greek classical drama on the modern stage, Sikelianos is master to the young poets of today.

See: H. Pernot, *Etudes de littérature grecque moderne* (1918); D. C. Hesseling, *Histoire de la littérature grecque moderne* (1924); A. Kambanis, *Hystoria tis neas ellinikis logotechnias* (1925).

S. A. V.

Green, Julien (1900–, French novelist), was born in Paris of American parents; his father came from Virginia and his mother from Savannah. Obsessed as he has been by the mysteries of heredity and of remote ancestral influences, he discovered in his sensibility the complex traces of Irish blood (visionary mysticism), of Scottish blood (fear of death and haunting of predestination), and of his American origins (a morbid preoccupation with the violent and supernatural forces of evil, which he shares with Poe, Melville, Hawthorne, and William Faulkner). French was to him not only the language in which he thought and wrote, but also the much needed influence of clarity, sanity, and order which alone could fuse into an artistic whole his conflicting tendencies. He was educated in a Paris *lycée,* enlisted in the French army at the end of the First World War, studied at the University of Virginia from 1919 to 1922, tried painting in Paris, and began his career as a French novelist in 1924. His early volumes, *Le Voyageur sur la terre* (1924; Eng. tr., *The Pilgrim on the Earth,* 1929, and in the volume *Christine and Other Stories,* 1930) and *Mont-Cinère* (1926; Eng. tr., *Avarice House,* 1927), while spoiled by some crude melodramatic elements, give, in the French language, a counterpart to the novels of the Brontë sisters and of Hawthorne. Their theme is hallucination, fear, haunting remorse, and madness. At the same time a series of critical essays (*Suite anglaise,* 1927) was published, on Samuel Johnson, Blake, Charles Lamb, Charlotte Brontë, and in 1928 a study of Hawthorne. His literary and artistic tastes, his inner torments, and his fear of love, of death, and of life after death are discreetly but fully revealed in the two volumes of his *Journal* (1938–1939; Eng. tr., *Personal Record, 1928–1939,* 1939). His best novels are probably *Adrienne Mesurat* (1927; Eng. tr., *The Closed Garden,* 1928), *Léviathan* (1929; Eng. tr., *The Dark Journey,* 1929, and in *Christine and Other Stories,* 1930), *Le Visionnaire* (1934; Eng. tr., *The Dreamer,* 1934), *Minuit* (1936; Eng. tr., *Midnight,* 1936). Between 1940 and 1945 Green lived in the United States, where a novel, *Varouna* (1940; Eng. tr., *Then Shall the Dust Return,* 1941), a volume of reminiscences in English, *Memories of Happy Days* (1942), and translations from Péguy (*q.v.*) were published.

Although he at times recalls Balzac (in his imaginative realism and his haunting evocation of French provincial life) and at times Kafka (*q.v.*), Julien Green stands out as one of the most original novelists of the 20th century. He succeeds in creating a world of his own, weird and unreal, which the reader enters with full suspension of disbelief. Murder, suicide, rape, madness, are the usual incidents in Green's novel of terror and of sadistic violence. No poetic description of nature, no touch of humor, relieves the tense atmosphere. The characters are often morbid and hysterical, and yet convincing, and are conceived with a rare imaginative power. Beneath these tales of horror there runs a strain of metaphysical anxiety: life is a wasteland of perpetual frustration, and man, try as he may, is powerless to escape from a hideous reality and to communicate with other human beings. A skillful technique, which often divides the nightmarish visions into two or three distinct episodes, emphasizing the solitude of the heroes, adds to the credibility of Green's novels. The style lacks originality and power and does not always do justice to the intensity of the author's hallucinations.

H. P.

Grieg, Johan Nordahl Brun (1902–1943, Norwegian poet, novelist, and dramatist), was, while he lived, the foremost exponent of Norwegian fighting spirit in the Second World War and became through his death its most striking symbol. Born in Bergen of a distinguished family, distantly related to Edvard Grieg, and destined for university training, he early showed talents of a stormier kind than would normally lead to a life of scholarship. He interspersed his student days with adventures in journalism, with a voyage as common seaman on a Norwegian freighter, and with tramps across the continent of Europe. The salient traits of his authorship were already present in his first collection of verse, *Rundt Kap det Gode Haab* (1922; Around the Cape of Good Hope)—his eager appetite for adventure, his passionate espousal of the common man, his patriotic, near-bombastic lyricism. A year at Oxford (1923–1924) led to the writing of a long essay on "Rudyard Kipling and the British Empire" (published in *Edda,* Vol. XXVII, 1927, pp. 75–108, 196–249), significant for the kinship which is clearly present between these two poets. Grieg's Anglo-Saxon orientation appears also from an essay collection entitled *De unge døde* (1932; The Young Dead), on Keats, Shelley, Byron, Rupert Brooke, and other English poets who died young. Meanwhile he had tried his hand as columnist, theatre critic, detective-story writer, poet, and novelist. He awakened attention, even scandal, by his frankly naturalistic story of sailor life, *Skibet går videre* (1924; Eng. tr., *The Ship Sails On,* 1927). But the rest of his books from the 20's added little to his stature: two collections of verse, *Stene i strømmen* (1925; Stones in the Stream) and *Norge i våre hjerter* (1929; Norway in Our Hearts); and three plays, *En ung manns kjærlighet* (1927; A Young Man's Love), *Barrabas* (1927), and *Atlanterhavet* (1932; The Atlantic Ocean).

A new phase of his life began when he went to live in Russia (1933–1935). Here he studied the Russian theatre and found his proletarian sympathies strongly reinforced. Social problems became the central theme of his next three plays, which established him as the leading youthful dramatist on the Norwegian stage: *Vår ære og vår makt* (1935; Our Honor and Our Might), attacking the greed of Norwegian ship owners during the

First World War; *Men imorgen* (1936; But Tomorrow—), on the conflict between Nazism and labor; and *Nederlaget* (1937; Eng. tr., *The Defeat,* 1944), a picture of the Paris Commune in 1871. In 1936 and 1937 he carried on the battle against fascism by publishing a periodical, *Veien frem* (The Road Ahead). In 1937 he went to Spain as correspondent and helper behind the front on the republican side. He published a volume of correspondence, *Spansk sommer* (1937; Spanish Summer), but more important was his remarkable novel *Men ung må verden ennu være* (1938; But Young the World Must Be), a panorama of world events from Norway, Russia, and Spain, including an analysis of the Moscow trials.

In 1939 he joined the Norwegian army for neutrality service. He was on furlough in Oslo on April 9, 1940, when the Germans invaded, but stole out to rejoin the army. He was given a special assignment, carried it through at great personal risk, and accompanied the Norwegian government to England in June, 1940. From that time to his death in an American bomber over Berlin on December 2, 1943, he was in constant active service, rising to the rank of captain. His particular task became that of strengthening the spirit of his countrymen in exile and at home. He participated in all the activities of the fighting forces without regard to personal safety and poured into his verse the impression of all that he saw. His lyrics of war, though few in number, were a notable contribution to the Norwegian and Allied cause. That patriotic fervor which sometimes seemed extravagant in peace found its transmutation in times of war. The bombast is gone, leaving only a deep passion for his native land and the shattered values of peace: "We kill, that our children may not become as we are." The appeal of his poetry lies in its immediacy of experience and its breadth of spirit. Grieg was able to keep his idealism intact and his courage young, until he himself joined "the young dead" of whom he once had written.

See: K. Elster, "Johan Nordahl Brun Grieg," in *Norsk biografisk leksikon,* IV (1929), 618–620; Halvdan Koht, "Nordahl Grieg," *American-Scandinavian Review,* XXX (1942), 32–40; Olav Rytter, "Nordahl Grieg," *Norseman,* II (1944), 113–120. There are translations of Grieg's poetry in *American-Scandinavian Review,* XXIX (1941), 109–110, XXXII (1943), 15–16; C. W. Stork, *Anthology of Norwegian Lyrics* (1942); Joy Davidman, *War Poems of the United Nations* (1943); *Norseman,* I (1943), 68, 110, 243–247, II (1944), 112.

E. H.

Griese, Friedrich (1890–, German novelist), was born of an old peasant family at Lehsten, a village in Mecklenburg. After attending the village school there and two teachers' colleges, in 1911 he became a teacher. Immediately after the outbreak of the First World War he volunteered for the front; he went nearly deaf in 1916, was discharged from military service, and resumed teaching. The peaceful life of a village schoolmaster and the solitude of his rural surroundings helped Griese toward literary creation. Since 1921 he has written and published a long series of novels and stories, firmly rooted in the ideas of the rural world and usually located in his homeland Mecklenburg. Griese's place in German literary history is in the long tradition of the regional novel. In an autobiographical sketch he has pointed out that he has always attempted to make transparent the secret background of things, the dark and uncanny powers which, dreaded by the peasant, are still the fountainhead of life. Not unlike another representative of the "Heimatkunst" movement, Timm Kröger (1844–1918), also a native of Lower Germany, Griese became "Heimatdichter" without intention or design, "letting himself be driven where his visions and the flood of his yearning wanted to go."

After a few vigorous tales which he himself regarded later only as a preparation for his spacious sagas and legends, his first well-balanced full novel, *Alte Glocken,* was published in 1925. Soon afterwards he completed a collection of short stories, *Die letzte Garbe* (1927). In the same year appeared his first outstanding novel, *Winter* (Eng. tr., 1929), in which a long winter of almost supernatural cold engulfs a Low German village and elevates men and animals into gigantic mythical dimensions. A number of gloomy and stirring short stories were soon followed by the novels *Der Sohn seiner Mutter* (1929), the mysterious and grave tale of a peasant boy, and *Das Tal der Armen* (1929), in which a remote village is slowly absorbed by the outside world. *Der ewige Acker* (1930) shows how the miserable years during and after the First World War cleansed the earth for a new beginning. Griese's latest novels, *Das letzte Gesicht* (1934), *Bäume im Wind* (1937), and *Die Weissköpfe* (1939), bring him closest to his literary model, Knut Hamsun (*q.v.*). Between 1931 and 1936 his interest in history resulted in impressive and popular historical novels as well as a biography of *Fritz Reuter* (1938). Less successful were three plays *Mensch aus Erde gemacht* (1933), *Wind im Luch* (1937), and *Der heimliche König* (1939).

Griese was elected a member of the Prussian Academy of Letters and awarded the Lessing prize in 1934. The state of Mecklenburg decided to make a present of Rethus, an old water mill near Parchim, "to its greatest living poet." He still resides there, after having resigned from his position at a primary school in Kiel where he had been teaching since 1926. There is no doubt that Griese's literary work makes him preeminent among the many modern German writers whose glorification of peasant life, soil, and countryside is typical of the "Heimatkunst."

See: A. Soergel, *Dichtung und Dichter der Zeit,* Dritte Folge: *Dichter aus deutschem Volkstum* (1934), pp. 207–231; K. Melcher, *Friedrich Griese* (1936).

H. Sch.

Grimm, Hans (1875–, German novelist, short-story writer, and essayist), is widely known, not so much for his strictly creative writing in the field in which he is indisputably the greatest living master—the longer short story—as for the authorship of his stupendous novel *Volk ohne Raum* (1926). The title became instantly a new designation for the German nation and a slogan offering to the German politicians the long-sought "political synthesis." Despite its 1352 pages and the measured tempo of its style which seems to echo the patient, plodding feet of the German peasant and emigrant Cornelius Friebott, despite the epic retardation and the repetition of both narrative and conversational formulae, more than a million copies were sold between its appearance in 1926 and the outbreak of the Second World War in 1939. *Volk ohne Raum* is one of the most harrowingly painful fictionalized records ever penned by an earnest and heart-torn patriot. The suffering recounted is senseless, whether it be that of the Germans in their overcrowded fatherland or of those who emigrated only to become involved in the Boer War and impoverished by it and then dispossessed and shipped like cattle back to a fatherland even less able to contain them at the close of the First World War. It is the suffering of protagonists who are mere struggling victims of a relentless fate, patiently enduring a passion without any scheme of redemption. The same theme is treated, in fact with greater objectivity, conciseness, and artistry, in an earlier and perhaps Grimm's best story, *Die Olewagen Saga* (1918).

Prior to the unexpected success of his novel Hans Grimm had been from 1895 to 1910 a merchant apprentice in England and clerk and independent merchant in Cape Colony. In 1910 he returned to Germany to become a writer. He studied political economy in Munich, fought in the First World War, and then settled at Lippoldsberg on the Weser, to discover subsequently that his new home adjoined the farms and glassworks that had belonged centuries before to his ancestors. Thus his return to Germany, followed closely by the war, with its intensification of his patriotism, and later by his accidental settling near the earliest-known home of his family—that he chanced to be born in Wiesbaden is without significance for him—became in the deepest sense a return of the native and served to shape the "African writer's" determination to become a "German writer," a "political writer."

Regardless of the chronology in which his works appeared, they fall into two distinct, but organically related groups, the creative writing of the artist and the political writing of the patriot. To the latter category belong, besides the political novel *Volk ohne Raum,* the documentary volumes dealing with the sufferings and injustices wantonly inflicted on the South African Germans during and after the First World War, *Der Ölsucher von Duala* (1918), *Die dreizehn Briefe aus Deutsch-Südwest-Afrika* (1928), *Das deutsche Südwester-Buch* (1929). Here also belong the series of 34 short essays which were written between 1911 and 1931 and make up the volume *Der Schriftsteller und die Zeit* (1931); the longer essay *Von der bürgerlichen Ehre und der bürgerlichen Notwendigkeit* (1932); the essays that have appeared in the pages of the magazine *Das Innere Reich,* founded in 1934 by Paul Alverdes and Karl Benno von Mechow (*qq.v.*); and the *Englische Rede: Wie ich den Engländer sehe; Deutsher und englischer Wortlant* (1938).

His purely creative writing consists of the 30-odd stories that make up the volumes *Südafrikanische Novellen* (1913), *Der Gang durch den Sand* (1916), *Der Richter in der Karu* (1930), *Lüderitzland* (1934), and the already mentioned *Olewagen Saga.* All except one of these stories are African in theme, substance, feeling, and style. This preoccupation with the colonial world and its sharp social cleavage is doubtless the direct result of Kipling's influence on Grimm. But Kipling's "white man's burden" is scarcely to be recognized in the realistic race antagonism depicted in "Der Gang durch den Sand." In this story Grimm's conception of race is still that of the white man versus the colored, but subsequently in his political writings it was to develop into the more narrowly exclusive conception of the Nordic man, to all intents and purposes the British and the German man. He did not follow but rather blazed the trail for the still narrower racial theory developed by his younger contemporaries. Grimm is not a party man. He is himself thoroughly sincere and without *arrière-pensée*. What his earlier political writings had lacked—a scheme of redemption to put an end to the German passion—his later essays, and particularly his *Englische Rede,* develop in a plan for understanding between Germany and England. This is but the logical consequence of his inordinate admiration for the British Empire and British justice. The finest paean of praise ever hymned to the British colonial official is "Der Richter in der Karu," and significantly Grimm considers this his finest work. What he expresses here and elsewhere indirectly and subtly he proclaims directly and emphatically in the *Englische Rede.*

See: G. K. Brand, "Hans Grimm" (with biography and bibliography), *Die neue Literatur,* XXVII (1926), 529–537; A. Soergel, *Dichtung und Dichter der Zeit,* Dritte Folge: *Dichter aus deutschem Volkstum* (1934), pp. 43–58; G. H. Danton, "Hans Grimm's Volk ohne Raum," *Monatshefte für deutschen Unterricht, XXVII* (1935), 33–43; W. Steinborn, "Der unbekannte Hans Grimm," *Das Innere Reich,* V (1938), 674–703, 790–816; R. T. House, "The South-African Stories of Hans Grimm," *American-German Review,* VI (1939), 16–17, 34.

J. F. G.

Gripenberg, Bertel (1878–, Finnish poet writing in Swedish), who was born in St. Petersburg, Russia, but comes of the old Swedish-Finnish aristocracy, has brought to Swedish poetry a fire and intensity lacking since the time of Fröding (*q.v.*). Beginning in *Dikter* (1915; Poems) with the perennial themes of love and wine, he turned later to descriptions of nature, to Finland's heroic past, and then to contemporary political and social conflicts, emphasizing in particular the debt of his country to Swedish culture. Gripenberg is temperamentally a modernist, with a clarion ring in his lines. He is a fine sonneteer and has translated effectively Oscar Wilde's "Ballad of Reading Gaol" and Edgar Lee Masters's *Spoon River Anthology.*

See: C. W. Stork, *Anthology of Swedish Lyrics* (1917; revised and enlarged ed., 1930); G. Bach, *The History of the Scandinavian Literatures,* ed. by Frederika Blankner (1938).

C. W. S.

Gröndal, Benedikt Sveinbjarnarson (1826–1907, Icelandic scholar, poet, and dramatist), was born at Bessastaðir near Reykjavík, the son of Sveinbjörn Egilsson, famous Icelandic scholar. He was named after his maternal grandfather, who also was a poet. At home and in the Latin school of his father, Gröndal became imbued with the love of the classics, those of Greek and Roman antiquity as well as the Old Icelandic sagas and Eddas. He grew up into the romantic movement, becoming himself more romantic than most in his poetry. Nature impressed him deeply, and he remained a faithful natural scientist until his death. His artistic nature also found outlet in calligraphy and drawing.

Though brilliantly gifted, Gröndal was an erratic genius. He studied natural history, philosophy, aesthetics, literature, and "northern antiquities" at the University of Copenhagen, becoming an M.A. (the first one) in the last-named subject in 1863. A decade of literary work in Copenhagen followed, after which he went home and taught school for another decade (1874–1883). After that time he was his own master until death overtook him.

Among Gröndal's most important works are the following: *Heljarslóðarorusta* (1861; The Battle of Hel's Field); *Clavis poetica antiquae linguae septentrionalis* (1864), an excellent tool; *Þórðar saga Geirmundssonar* (1891; The Saga of Þórður Geirmundsson), a Rabelaisian satire; *Kvæðabók* (1900; Poems); and *Dægradvöl* (1923; Autobiography). His poetry and prose have many facets, but he is most effective when giving rein to his unbridled imagination. In that mood he wrote some excellent nonsense poems and parodies, as well as Aristophanic plays and Rabelaisian satire. Best of all his works is the inimitable burlesque, *Heljarslóðarorusta,* a mock romance on the battle of Solferino in 1859. It is also his most popular work.

See: *Benedikt Gröndal áttræður* (1906); S. Einarsson, "Benedikt Gröndal and *Heljarslóðarorusta,*" *Journal of English and Germanic Philology,* XXXVI (1937), 307–325, 543–550.

S. E.

Grubiński, Wacław (1883–, Polish dramatist, critic, and short-story writer), was born in Warsaw of a theatrical family. Educated at school in the social sciences, Grubiński steeped himself privately in literature, philosophy, and the arts pertaining to the theatre. In 1909 he began his career by having a somewhat daring play presented on the Warsaw stage (*Pijani,* The Drunks) and was regarded thereafter in bourgeois circles as a bad moral influence. Like his masters Wilde, Anatole France (*q.v.*), Flaubert (*q.v.*), and Przybyszewski (*q.v.*), Grubiński had no desire to be an influence at all, good or bad. "The author," he said in his confession (1925), "exhibits his hero objectively, like a tiger, or bull; you observe how he looks, thinks, and acts, but you make up your own opinion of him, as you would of a bull. . . ." A detached, sybaritic, amused observer of the human animal, Grubiński was a master showman of the animal's foibles and a superb stylist, a fact publicly recognized in 1939 by an Academy award for the "exquisite Polish" of his *Listy pogańskie* (1938; Pagan Letters). Of his short stories, the collection *Człowiek z klarnetem* (1927; Man with Clarionet) is representative, and of his plays, the following are the most popular: *Kochankowie* (1919; The Lovers), *Piękna Helena* (1919; Fair Helen), *Lenin* (1921; a comedy), *Lampa Aladyna* (1923; Aladdin's Lamp), and *Niewinna grzesznica* (1926; The Sinless Sinner). A relic of the last phase of Young Poland (*see* Polish literature), Grubiński was somewhat out of place in the Poland of the 1930's. His plays gradually disappeared from the boards, as the older generation passed from the scene and the neurotic dandyism of the *fin de siècle* went out of fashion.

See: Z. Dębicki, *Portrety,* II (1928), 271–286; K. Czachowski, *Obraz współczesnej literatury polskiej,* II (1934), 171–174, 375–376; J. Lorentowicz, *Teatr Polski w Warszawie* (1938), *passim.*

A. P. C.

Guðmundsson, Kristmann (1902–, Icelandic novelist), was born at Þverfell in Borgarfjörður. His mother's family was deeply rooted in the soil, his father was a temperamental rover. The youth of Guðmundsson was marred by lack of parental care and by sickness, yet he grew up to be a healthy boy whose optimism and enterprising nature nothing could curb. Having been a jack-of-all-trades, he finally (1924) decided to go to Norway and become a writer. Two years later his first book of short stories, *Islandsk kjærlighet* (1926; Icelandic Loves), was an immediate success. Many novels and a host of short stories have appeared in Norwegian. Since 1939 Guðmundsson has lived in Iceland and written in Icelandic.

Kristmann Guðmundsson is a master of the modern romance. Like no other Icelandic novelist he understands the psychology of love, especially young love, and describes it with a realism that nevertheless seems ethereally romantic. With him the spiritual and the physical aspects of love unite in harmony without the bad conscience that troubles some of the pre-war writers, such as Kamban (*q.v.*) who, during the 1920's, fought a struggle of emancipation from the older ideology of love. Next to love, character interests Guðmundsson. This is especially evident in his family sagas: *Brudekjolen* (1927; Icelandic tr., *Brúðarkjóllinn,* 1933; Eng. tr., *The Bridal Gown,* 1931), *Livets morgen* (1929; Icelandic tr., *Morgunn lífsins,* 1932; Eng. tr., *Morning of Life,* 1936), *Det hellige fjell* (1932; The Holy Fell), *Jordens barn* (1934; Children of Earth), and *Gyðjan og uxinn* (1937; Eng. tr., *Winged Citadel,* 1940). The last is a historical romance from the Crete of Minoan times, but it is full of allusions to modern psychoanalysis and modern world politics. Perhaps finest of Guðmundsson's characters is the hero of *Morning of Life;* in him the heroic ideal of the sagas is once more incarnated. Not the least source of Guðmundsson's charm is his facile narrative talent, his obvious joy in telling a story. His books have been translated into many languages.

See: G. G. Hagalín, "Kristmann Guðmundsson, "*Iðunn,* XIV (1930), 55–70.

S. E.

Guerra Junqueiro, Abílio (1850–1923, Portuguese poet), was born in Freixo-de-Espada-à-Cinta, Trás-os-Montes, the son of well-to-do farmers. In 1868 he matriculated in the University of Coimbra. He arrived there in a revolutionary moment and joined the group known as the Generation of Coimbra (*see* Portuguese literature), of which he became an outstanding member. Before he reached the age of 20 some of his writing had already been published, and about the time he entered the university, *Baptismo de amor* (Baptism of Love) appeared. Already he showed verbal opulence, notable metrical flexibility, and a certain oratorical and grandiloquent tendency. Upon obtaining his degree (1873), Junqueiro was employed in government administration. Later he was identified with the republican movement and carried out a violent campaign against the monarchy and the Church.

He matured artistically in a devotion to the Hugo of *La Légende des siècles* and went on to become the most typical and worthy representative of the social and liberal poetry of Portuguese realism. He was one of those who rescued Portuguese poetry from the stagnant waters of an exhausted romantic-Arcadian lyricism. In 1874 was published the work which established his reputation, *A morte de D. João* (Don Juan's Death), a collection of poems without great continuity but held together by the eternal theme of the Seducer, whom he makes the symbol of social corruption, a product of romantic sentimentalism. In these lyrical and satirical poems the main character is grotesquely debased; he is reduced to an extreme state of pauperism and is made to die in an alley, weak and diseased. Junqueiro was immediately charged with degrading poetry and taking the themes of his verses from the privy, the hospital, and the brothel. He retorted that the basis for the new poetry lay in science and not in the transports of romantic lyricism and explained the principles of his aesthetic. Art should express effectively the results of science; it must be progressive and help in giving "a methodical and definite idea" of the universe, its ultimate aim being justice. Everything opposed to justice could be symbolized in Don Juan as corruption and in Jehovah as tyranny. The moral scandal aroused by *A morte de D. João* was followed in 1885 by the religious scandal of *A velhice do Padre Eterno* (The Old Age of the Eternal Father). With the same virulence with which he had attacked the libertinism personified by Don Juan, he now assailed the figure of Jehovah. The Church, religious fanaticism, and intolerance are the targets of these poems, characterized by a rabid sarcasm, in verse of resounding sonorousness and of extraordinarily daring richness of rhythms and images. In both works he definitely incorporated prose into poetry and introduced elements which until then had been considered outside the realm of the poetically beautiful, an extreme reaction against the decorous fastidiousness of the reigning poetry. In the taste for the repulsive and the ugly there is a satanic element reminiscent of Baudelaire (*q.v.*), but by and large the model is Hugo, from whom Junqueiro took the alexandrine, to acclimatize it in Portugal.

On the occasion of the English ultimatum of 1890 Junqueiro's lyre gave expression to national wrath in *Finis Patriae* (1891), a collection of poems, and *Pátria*, a dramatic poem not published until 1896, both full of the fury aroused by the humiliation of his impotent native country. The bitter, lyrically passionate vision of national downfall and the accusation against the supposedly guilty element, the dynasty, furnished a poetic fulfillment of the historical negativism of Oliveira Martins (*q.v.*). *Pátria* was read avidly, and its mysterious and spectral atmosphere, the sinister symbolism of some of its characters—especially O Doido, personification of past Portuguese glory—and its Messianic pessimism made a deep impression. Certain technical characteristics of this lyrical libel, the symbolistic repetitions and the morbid cadences, had a notable influence on much of the poety which followed. Junqueiro's art, essentially pictorial and descriptive, reached its apogee in some of the pages of *Pátria*. In 1892 the publication of *Os simples* (The Simple Ones) marked a new phase in his work. Here, in keeping with the impulses of a new generation, he abandoned social and philosophical themes and with a more intimately contemplative attitude turned his attention to the objects and humble souls of Portuguese rural life. Images lost their oratorical brilliance, were fitted to the candid simplicity of the themes. With a delicately restrained lyricism he gave himself over to an intimate communion with nature, desirous of calm for his disillusioned soul and in search of the tranquil faith of village life. Even so he endeavored to understand by systematic processes the essence and evolution of the surrounding world. His scientific obsession, which he never lost, led him to write a mystico-philosophical poetry of allegorical character, in which he tried to translate poetically the postulates of scientific naturalism and impart a lyric expression to the discoveries of the laboratory. The result is seen in *Oração ao pão* (1902; Prayer to Bread) and *Oração a luz* (1904; Prayer to Light), his last estimable productions.

Shortly after the republic was proclaimed (1910) Junqueiro was sent to Switzerland as minister. There he composed an essay, *Notas sôbre a Suíça* (1911), which is his best work in prose (later included in *Prosas dispersas*, 1921, Collected Prose). The last years of his life, during which he underwent a mystico-Christian evolution, were spent in retirement on his property at Barca d'Avila. In this phase, which has been called Tolstoyan (*see*

Tolstoy, Leo), he devoted himself to the cultivation of his vineyards and to radiological experiments.

See: A. da Veiga Simões, *A nova geração* (1911), pp. 77–83; F. de Figueiredo, *História da literatura realista,* 1924 ed., pp. 112–132; P. Hourcade, *Guerra Junqueiro et le problème des influences françaises dans son œuvre* (1932).

E. G. D.

Guglielminetti, Amalia (1885?–, Italian poetess and novelist), was born in Turin. In her verse she aroused curiosity and interest by her bold treatment of sensuous love and was even hailed by some as a "new Sappho." However, upon a closer scrutiny, it was seen that she was merely recounting personal experiences which she was unable to translate into authentic lyricism or suffuse with the breath of true poetry. The myth of a new, realistic poetess of power was soon dissipated, although she has continued to have readers. What intensity she attained is intellectual rather than emotional. The most passionate and most intimate moments are described with a calculating precision and coldness which make one realize their falseness and lack of sincere human emotion. Her works, sensuous and audacious, lack the human spark which might have made her really great.

Her principal writings are *Voci di giovinezza* (1903), *Le Vergini folli* (1907), *L'Insonne* (1913), *Anime allo specchio* (1917; short stories). *Le Ore inutili* (1919), *Gli Occhi cerchiati d'azzurro* (1920).

E. F.

Guillén, Jorge (1893–, Spanish poet), was born in Valladolid. The external events of the life of this most remarkable lyricist present no special interest. At one time he was a lecturer in Spanish at the University of Paris and later professor of Spanish literature in the universities of Murcia and Seville; more recently he traveled to the United States and has been professor of Spanish at Wellesley College.

If the poetry of a great contemporary, García Lorca (*q.v.*), can be described as the overflow of lights and sounds, as suggestive of juice of fruit bitten when ripe, the art of Guillén can be called a search for the stark, the precise; it always involves care to hit the mark exactly. Guillén has produced only one book, *Cántico* (1928; 3d ed., enl., 1945), yet it is enough to place him among the poets who can confidently await the judgment of posterity. The verses of Guillén are for a limited number of readers and will never attain wide popularity, although this is not because they contain strange words or recondite allusions. On the contrary, his terse lines include scarcely any references to the complicated or the mysterious. His soul retreats candidly within itself, fearful of drawing away from the first bubbling of the poetic spring. There is neither action nor anecdote; there are no catalogued emotions. The difficult thing in his work is the "poetic quality" of the poetry.

In *Cántico* every theme is connected with the anguish or joy caused by impressions received in complete innocence, along with a vehement desire to possess the present moment as part of a vehement longing for eternity. The author is master of his art—of the frame, the portrayal, the coloring. It is almost unbelievable that creative power can reach this degree of intensity with no more ingredients than empty spaces, limiting outlines which encompass the infinite, early lights of dawn, nothings of pre- and of post-existence, fleeting, yet nevertheless eternal, instants.

Guillén's poetry is integrated by a succession of "astonishments" before a world which the poet always contemplates as though in an initial moment, at the beginning of existence. In the 20 lines of "Niño" the child and the world in which he is seen are both children: "An instant without history, obstinately peopled with myths among things: sea alone with its birds." For most poets the world is there, given, present in its primary elements, though indeed these can be combined later in an infinite number of ways. But Guillén shows surprise before something which is not yet completely world, which is not yet experience already created around about him; he stands at the point of intersection between the creative intent and the act of creation, that is to say, at "wild surmise" between nothing and being.

This is difficult poetry, although clear once the reader has grasped its dense meaning. Sequence is obtained through effective chords and cadences, as in a language in which modulations of tone replace stress. We are far removed from the surrealistic seismograph that will register the obscure chaos in the subterranean conscience.

See: Andrenio (E. Gómez de Baquero), *Pen Club: Los poetas* (1929), pp. 109–114; P. Salinas, *Literatura española siglo XX* (1941), pp. 263–277; Frances Avery Pleak, *The Poetry of Jorge Guillén* (1942).

A. C.

Guilloux, Louis (1899–, French novelist), was born in Saint-Brieuc, Brittany, of poor working-class parents. From childhood he was connected with socialism: his father was a leading member of the Socialist Party in Saint-Brieuc, and Guilloux's first position was that of secretary to Augustin Hamon, the socialist, sociologist, and translator of Shaw. The work of Gorky and Romain Rolland (*qq.v.*) had a great influence on him, Guilloux says; and to this must be added the impression made by the philosopher Georges Palante, whose pupil he was at the *lycée* at Saint-Brieuc.

After working on various Parisian newspapers, Guilloux began to write seriously about 1925. His early books, *La Maison du peuple* (1927), *Compagnons* (1931), and *Hyménée* (1932), written in a deliberately simple style and drawing strongly on his early memories of working-class life, can be best described as mystical literature, the expression of the dreams of the pre-war socialist movement, tender, tragic, pervaded by a somewhat inarticulate love for humanity. *Le Sang noir* (1935; Eng. tr., *Bitter Victory*, 1936), his most important work, revealed a new power. This massive, closely packed story of the last day in the life of Merlin, a teacher in an obscure provincial *lycée*, is in one sense an epitome of modern European history. The year is 1917, the soldiers are revolting, the professional patriots of the town are declaiming empty phrases; in the eyes of the intellectual nihilist, Merlin, the town, France, all modern civilization is an obscene, meaningless joke. Yet Merlin himself is made equally impotent by conflicting ideals. Attacking society and the bourgeoisie, he still stores away his money in securities and real estate; believing in nothing, he commits suicide because he feels he has lost his "honor." The one faint ray of hope expressed is Guilloux's rather indefinite suggestion that some of the younger generation, Merlin's pupils, seeing the hollowness in him as well as in the society which surrounds him, will be able to avoid his errors and to carry his confused and tragic negation on into something positive. What this positive position is to be Guilloux does not say, but from his early work and his articles up until the Second World War in *Ce Soir* and André Chamson's leftist weekly *Vendredi*, it is clear that for him the solution is to be found in the political and economic liberation of the working class.

See: Frédéric Lefèvre, "Une Heure avec M. Louis Guilloux, romancier," *Nouvelles littéraires*, December 21, 1935; Eleanor Clark, "Death of a Thinker: A Note on the French Novel, 1925–40," *Kenyon Review*, III (1941), 322–334.

C. W., Jr.

Guimerà, Angel (1849–1924, Catalonian playwright, orator, and poet), was born in Santa Cruz de Tenerife, Canary Islands, of a Catalonian father. At the age of seven he went with his parents to Catalonia and received his first impressions of the landscape of the Bajo Penedés, rich in memories of the passage of the Romans. He studied in Barcelona and returned to his father's village, El Vendrell, to aid his family in the wine business. But he was really interested only in the cultivation of literature and after 1872 lived in Barcelona, since he considered this the most suitable place in which to make himself known in the field of letters. He was an assiduous competitor in the poetic contests called Jocs Florals; in 1877 he was named *mestre en gai saber* (master troubadour) upon winning the three prizes necessary to obtain this title. He was a frequent collaborator on the newspaper *Renaixença*, converted to a magazine by him and other literary men; from 1872 he was the editor of the publication. In 1874 he identified himself with the patriotic organization Jove Catalunya and in 1895, in a memorable presidential speech, in Catalan, he enthroned this language in the Ateneo. Never playing party politics, he dedicated his efforts to preaching the good news of the renaissance of the Catalonian soul, with the breadth of vision shared by all those identified with the *Renaixença* movement. His patriotic speeches are collected in *Cants a la pàtria* (1906; Songs to the Fatherland). Some of his verse had been gathered in *Poesies* (1887); here already he shows himself to be an exalted patriot and employs an energetic language, replete with brusque images and outlines. *Segon llibre de poesies*, which appeared in 1920, is very inferior to the first volume of poems.

For the theatre Guimerà wrote *Gala Placidia* (1879), *Judith de Welp* (1883), and *El fill del mar* (1886; The Son of the Sea), which already reveal a tragic dramatist of full stature. *Mar i cel* (1888; Sea and Sky) has the energy of the great German romantic dramatists, but the psychological verisimilitude of the characters and the humanness and naturalness of the situations elevated it beyond any school. There follow *Rei i monjo* (1890; King and Monk); *L'ànima morta* (1892; The Dead Soul); and *Les monges de Sant*

Aymant (1895; The Monks of Sant Aymant), based on the legend of Count Arnau, a sort of Don Juan, Faust, and Satan rolled into one, whose memory is alive in all Catalonia. *La boja* (1890; The Insane Woman) inaugurates his modern dramas, which include: *En pòlvora* (In Gunpowder); *Maria Rosa* (1894); *La festa del blat* (1896; The Wheat Festival); and *Terra baixa* (1896; Eng. tr., *Marta of the Lowlands,* 1914), a very original play based on the contrast between the purity of the people of the high mountain region and the abject passions which animate those who live in the flatlands. *La farsa* (1899; The Farce), *La filla del mar* (1899; The Daughter of the Sea), *La pecadora* (1902; The Sinner), and others follow. In his final period he cultivated a theatre based on very abstract ideas and of relatively slight value. His *sainetes, La sala d'espera* (1890; The Waiting Room) and *La baldirona,* still appear occasionally on the Catalonian stage. Guimerà's tragedies and dramas were translated into Portuguese, German, Italian, Czech, Dutch, Russian, Spanish, English. Several attempts were made to set his dramas to music, including the German *Tiefland,* based on *Terra Baixa,* with music by D'Albert; *La Catalane,* with music by the French master Leborne; *Euda d'Uriach,* based on *Les monges de Sant Aymant,* in collaboration with the Catalonian composer Vives. Guimerà, genial and irregular, has been criticized frequently as guilty of bad taste. This is occasionally true of both his poetry and plays, but many of his creations are magnificent, and his work is notable for imaginative quality—as well as for a certain predilection for macabre ideas and the presentation of hallucinations. He saw his country submerged, resigned, unaware of its great racial heritage; he devoted all of his life—in literary works, in speeches, in poems—to the task of shaking off its lethargic conformity. He is not only one of the most representative but also one of the noblest men among the instigators of the great movement of revival, the *Renaixença.* As man and artist he never felt that he was a member of a learned caste separate from the people. He died the 18th of July, 1924, the object of the adoration of his compatriots, although opposed until the end of his life by certain literary intellectuals out of touch with the national struggle.

See: J. Prepatx, *La Renaissance des lettres catalanes* (1883); J. Yxart, prologue, in Guimerà, *Poesies* (1887); J. L. Pagano, *Attraverso la Spagna literaria* (1902); M. de Montoliu, *Estudis de literatura catalana* (1912); A. Rovita i Virgili, "Angel Guimerà," *Revista de Catalunya* (Barcelona), August, 1924.

F. de P.

Guitry, Sacha (1885–, French actor and dramatist), son of the famous actor Lucien Guitry, was born at Saint Petersburg (Leningrad). A skillful, versatile artist, he is perhaps the best-known actor on the French stage of recent times. His reputation abroad, where he has played in many countries, is equally great. His more successful roles, most of which he has written and created himself, have been in that light, vivacious comedy so typical of the modern French stage. Following in the tradition of Molière, with whom some of his more ardent admirers have compared him, he has used to good account his extensive knowledge of acting and stagecraft. In the composition of more than a hundred plays, he frankly sets out to amuse and entertain. Fantastic plots and impossible situations are redeemed by sparkling, witty dialogue and excellent dramatic construction. Brilliant rather than profound, he views his fellow men realistically rather than ideally. He has no illusions as to the fundamental egotism of mankind. His frankness and audacity have made him a favorite even with such men as Anatole France, Bergson, Octave Mirbeau, and Tristan Bernard (*qq.v.*), and many other similar and equally important writers have expressed their admiration for him. George Bernard Shaw, in a presentation copy of his *Saint Joan,* wrote: "To Sacha Guitry, who, like myself, does not write in chains and who, indeed, should have written this play."

His earlier plays, such as *Nono* (1905), *L'Illusionniste* (1921), and *L'Amour masqué* (1923), are frequently nothing more than brilliant improvisations. In *Le Veilleur de nuit* (1911) a kindhearted professor refuses to be jealous of his mistress's second lover and in the end finally wins the sympathy of the audience and embarrasses the guilty couple by his generous attitude. *La Prise de Berg-op-Zoom* (1912), in spite of its military title, turns out to be merely a sprightly comedy of gay-hearted philandering. *Jean, ou l'Irrestible Vocation du fils Mondoucet* (1912) shows the stage aspirations of the son of a good bourgeois who is horrified at his son's infatuation with the theatre and finally at the son's appearance in a kingly role. Later Guitry turned to more serious subjects and inaugurated a series of dramatic biographies, such as *Jean de la Fontaine* (1916), *Deburau* (1918), *Pasteur* (1919), and *Mozart* (1925). In each case Guitry has admirably caught the spirit of the titular personage in a number of interesting but detached scenes. *Le Comédien* (1921) and the autobiographical *Un Sujet de roman* (1923) take us to the backstage he knows so well. *Mariette* (1928), with its charming background of the Second Empire, is a good example of his operettas.

He has also collaborated with A. Willemetz in several typical Parisian revues. In more recent years he has become even better known throughout the world by his successes both as director and as actor in the cinema. *Les Perles de la couronne* and *Le Roman d'un tricheur* are typical of his films. In his autobiography, *Souvenirs* (1935), he has given us an amusing account of his life. Both on and off the stage he has earned the reputation of a wit, and his private life as well as his public has entertained France.

J. F. M.

Gullberg, Hjalmar (1898–, Swedish poet and translator of the Greek classics), born in Lund, is among the more sober, intellectual, and disillusioned of contemporary Swedish poets, though his work is not without a strain of deep personal pathos. Aside from his poetic production he has made magnificent translations of Euripides (*Hippolytus,* 1930; *Medea,* 1931; *Alcestis,* 1933) and Sophocles (*Antigone,* 1935) and has collaborated with Ivar Harrie in the translation of Aristophanes (*The Birds,* 1928; *Lysistrata,* 1932) as well as Calderón (*Casa con dos puertas mala es de guardar,* 1934). As a poet Gullberg leaves on a first reading a rather confused impression, partly because of his complex, frequently paradoxical style, partly because his subtle, probing intellectual temperament is little conducive to sharply expressive perspectives or to obvious forms of intellectual or spiritual confessions. That which is most characteristic of both the form and the content of the bulk of his early verse—*I en främmande stad* (1927; In a Strange City), *Sonat* (1929; Sonata), *Andliga övningar* (1932; Spiritual Exercises), *Kärlek i tjugonde seklet* (1933; Love in the 20th Century), and *Ensamstående bildad herre* (1935; Unattached Cultured Gentleman)—is a precarious poetic balance between the ironic-grotesque and the elevated, between the modernity of an age of jazz and sensationalism and the past of a sober classical and humanistic tradition. In form, Gullberg's early verse combines with amazing virtuosity modern slang and banal journalese with echoes of the Bible and of classical drama; in content, his poetry frequently employs the most obvious and trivial of motifs from everyday life as the point of departure for an interpretation of the highest spiritual values. He looks upon the contemporary scene in general with complete disillusionment, with a pessimism which falls short of the most devastating cynicism only because the poet is, in the last analysis, seeking values above and beyond this life. The religious-metaphysical strain has always been more or less apparent in Gullberg's work, in the earliest work in rather baffling and perhaps largely superficial forms, later in somewhat more tangible, clearly defined outlines, and finally (particularly in *Att övervinna världen,* 1937, To Conquer the World) in a wholly elevated and sublime form of lyrical expression which is concerned with purely absolute, nameless, and all but indefinable values beyond both the world of the senses and of thought. In this last phase of Gullberg's development he joins hands with Vilhelm Ekelund (*q.v.*), whose long and restless search for the World of the Absolute beyond the ken of human thought has gained for him the admiration of his countrymen even though it has necessarily left him all but spiritually isolated in the rarified regions of the spirit where the heroic ideal has inevitably led him.

See: S. Ahlgren, "Teknik och poesi: en studie i Hjalmar Gullbergs diktning," *Bonniers litterära magasin,* VII (1938), 26–31.

A. G.

Gumilyov, Nikolai Stepanovich (1886–1921, Russian poet, essayist, short-story writer, and translator), born in Kronstadt into the family of a navy physician, spent his childhood in Tsarskoye Selo. In 1895 he entered the Gurevich Gymnasium in St. Petersburg; several years later the family moved to Tiflis, where Gumilyov became interested in radical political activities. He returned to Tsarskoye Selo in 1903, however, and entered the Gymnasium; here, under the guidance of its principal, I. F. Annenski (*q.v.*), he became interested in Nietzsche (*q.v.*) and symbolism and soon changed his political views. After finishing at the Gymnasium, Gumilyov entered the historico-philological faculty of the University of St. Petersburg and on completing the course in 1906 went to Paris, where he attended lectures at the Sorbonne. While there he published a nonperiodical miscellany, *Sirius.* He traveled extensively, visiting France, Italy, Germany (1906–1912), Egypt (1907), and Abyssinia (1909–1910), where he collected folk songs. In 1908 Gumilyov returned to Tsarskoye Selo once more and soon made fast friends with Annenski and later with Vyacheslav Ivanov (*q.v.*), under whose guidance he organized the Academy of Verse, which eventually became the Society of Enthusiasts of the Artistic Word. With the founding of the periodical *Apollo* (1909–1917), Gumilyov became one of its leading spirits and was soon the acknowledged leader of the "Acmeist" school of poetry centering about the *Apollo*. In 1910 he married A. A. Gorenko (*see* Akhmatova, Anna).

Gumilyov's interest in the ethnography of exotic lands continued to absorb him. In 1913 he headed a scientific expedition to Somaliland for the Museum of Anthropology and Ethnography. With the outbreak of war in 1914 Gumilyov volunteered for army service and went to the front as an officer; here he was twice awarded the cross of St. George for bravery. In the spring of 1917 he was dispatched to Paris by the Provisional Government. He returned to Russia in 1918 and became a member of the editorial board of the "Universal Literature" publications. From 1919 to 1921 he lectured in various studios ("Proletarian Culture," "Baltic Fleet," "Translations") and at the Institute of the Living Word; he also headed the Third Poet Workshop. In June of 1921 he went to Sevastopol. He was accused of complicity in the Tagantsev conspiracy, found guilty, and on August 25, 1921, executed by a firing squad.

Although Gumilyov began his literary career as a disciple of symbolism, he eventually rebelled and led the revolt against its theories. By 1912, together with Gorodetski, he had gained an extensive following among the poets who wished to establish the tangible world, with all its sounds, scents, and colors, as a legitimate province of poetry. To this purpose Gumilyov organized these "Acmeist" poets into a Poet Workshop. The Acmeists countered the mysticism, vagueness, abstractness, and diffusiveness of the symbolists with realism, precision, concreteness, and laconism of expression. Gumilyov and other leading exponents of Acmeism tremendously influenced the verse technique of many of the Leningrad poets.

Gumilyov's first published poem appeared in 1902 in a Tiflis daily. His first book of verse, *Put konkvistadorov* (The Path of the Conquistadors), was published in 1905 and reflected his predilection for what is exotic, romantic, foreign. His subsequent books, *Romanticheskiye tsvety* (1908; Romantic Flowers); *Zhemchuga* (1910; Pearls), *Chuzhoye nebo* (1912; Foreign Skies), *Kolchan* (1916; The Quiver), *Kostyor* (1918; The Campfire), *Ditya Allakha* (1918; Child of Allah), *Shatyor* (1921; The Tent), show this same trait and often contain his own observations made during his many travels. His African scenes and landscapes became famous in Russian poetry. In his last book, *Ognenny stolp* (1921; The Pillar of Flame), Gumilyov returns to the mystical tradition of symbolism, vividly reflected in his poem "Zabludivshisya tramvai" (The Strayed Trolley). His translations include poems of Théophile Gautier, Coleridge's *The Rime of the Ancient Mariner,* a book of Babylonian epics and one of French folk songs. His critical essays are contained in the volume *Pisma o russkoi poezii* (1923; Letters on Russian Poetry).

See: G. Ivanov, "O poezii Gumilyova," *Letopis doma literatorov,* Vol. I (1921); V. Sayanov, "N. Gumilyov," *Na literaturnom postu,* 1927, Nos. 17–18.

O. M.

Gunnarsson, Gunnar (1889–, Icelandic novelist, dramatist, and poet), was born at Valþjófsstaður in Fljótsdalur, East Iceland. His father came of a long line of parsons and sturdy farmers, his mother was the daughter of a picturesque farmer-fisherman on the coast. The boy grew up with his family in Fljótsdalur and Vopnafjörður until 1907, when he went to Denmark to seek his fortune. Though he had little schooling, he worked steadily towards the goal of becoming a writer. He joined the small group of Icelandic writers in Copenhagen who aspired to write in Danish in order to win a wider public, but he was out of tune with their Bohemian life and their Nietzschean aspirations. Yet he shared with them the romantic view of their faraway homeland, and his first work, *Borgslægtens Historie* (4 vols., 1912–1914; Eng. tr. *Guest the One-eyed,* 1920), became an Icelandic family saga. It contained the beautiful legend of Guest the One-eyed and won instant popularity throughout Scandinavia. During the First World War, Gunnarsson struggled bravely, in a series of novels (*Livets Strand,* 1915, The Shore of Life; *Varg i Veum,* 1916, The Outcast; and *Salige er de Enfoldige,* 1920, Eng. tr., *Seven Days' Darkness,* 1930), to find meaning in a war-mad world. In part these novels may have represented his growing pains during the difficult development from the simple faith of his fathers to his own equally simple but newborn faith in the Icelandic race and its immortality; in part he was undoubtedly influenced by the expressionistic tendencies of the time (Strindberg, *q.v.*).

His new faith finds unobtrusive expression

in studies of his nation's history and his own past. *Edbrødre* (1918; Eng. tr., *The Sworn Brothers,* 1920), about the first settlers in Iceland, was the first of a planned series of 12 novels that was to depict on a broad canvas the fate of his people. Six more of these historical novels have appeared, the last being *Graamand* (1936; Gray Man), on a subject from *Sturlunga saga.* The story of *Jón Arason* (1930), last Catholic bishop of Iceland, and the phantasy *Vikivaki* (1932; Vigil Dancing) also belong to this class. But already in the 1920's Gunnarsson had found time to write the story of his own life in *Kirken paa Bjerget* (5 vols., 1924–1928, The Church on the Mountain; Eng. tr. of Vols I–III, *Ships in the Sky,* 1938, and *The Night and the Dream,* 1938). In this great work burns the quiet flame of Gunnarsson's admiration for his heroes in homespun. Here is also eloquent testimony to Gunnarsson's love of the soil, if the rocky coasts and stony plains of his homeland may be given such an epithet. At his best Gunnarsson merges land and people in a single vision of humanity's burning bush in the wilderness. With Hamsun and Duun (*qq.v.*) in Norway and Johannes V. Jensen (*q.v.*) in Denmark, Gunnarsson is one of the great interpreters of the common people of the North. As such he has won a stable reputation in Europe.

In 1938 Gunnarsson went back to his home district to live at Skriðuklaustur in Fljótsdalur. Here he has written his latest work, *Heiðaharmur* (1940; The Heath Laments), in elegant Icelandic despite his long Danish exile. Apart from the novels he has also written several volumes of short stories, plays, and poetry.

See: K. Elfelt, *Gunnar Gunnarsson* (1927); S. Einarsson, "Gunnar Gunnarsson," *Skirnir,* CXII (1938), 138–160, and in *Jón Bjarnason Academy Year Book* (1940), pp. 9–24; H. de Boor, "Gunnar Gunnarsson," *Nordische Stimmen,* IX (1939), 180–183.

S. E.

Günther, Agnes (née Breuning, 1863–1911, German novelist), was born in Stuttgart and died in Marburg; she was the wife of the professor of theology Rudolf Günther. Her one novel, *Die Heilige und ihr Narr* (1913), published posthumously, is a veritable kitchen midden of all the leitmotifs, stage properties, and scenic effects of romanticism unrestrained. The life of the "saint" and her "fool," who appear in the novel only as ghosts, is the subject of the fragment *Von der Hexe, die eine Heilige war.* For a few years the novel topped the list of best sellers and then disappeared.

See: K. J. Friedrich, *Die Heilige: Erinnerungen an Agnes Günther,* 2d ed., (1918).

J. F. G.

Gyulai, Pál (1826–1909, Hungarian critic, story writer, and poet), was born in Kolozsvár and died in Budapest. His father was a government clerk. As a young man Gyulai hesitated between studying law and Calvinistic theology. His solution was to study both. But his real aspirations were literary. He taught in various secondary schools, was a tutor in aristocratic homes, and finally went to Budapest where he became acquainted with the younger writers. In 1858 he married Mária Szendrey, sister of the wife of Sándor Petőfi, Hungary's great lyric poet. His wife died in 1866. Gyulai spent about a year abroad, mostly in Germany and in France, and upon his return to his native land centered his activities exclusively on literature. He assisted in the publication of several literary periodicals, but his critical vigilance was especially felt when he edited *Budapesti Szemle* (Budapest Review), one of the most scholarly literary publications Hungary ever had. Gyulai was a militant critic; his persistent criticism of Móricz Jókai (*q.v.*), the most popular novelist of his time, implied the courage to defy public opinion without fear. Sometimes his righteousness made him seem unpleasant but never to such an extent as to interfere with his prestige. His poems, influenced by Byron and Arany (*q.v.*), reveal him as a minor creator; his stories were more original; it was his critical work that revealed the essence of his nature. His nation respected him: rich and poor knew that he had dedicated his life to Hungarian culture and that his recognition was well merited. He was a member of the Hungarian Scientific Academy, president of the Kisfaludy Társaság (Kisfaludy Society), professor of Hungarian literature at the University of Budapest, a member of the House of Magnates. His collected works appeared in 1902.

There is a resemblance between Gyulai's sense of values and that of the Victorian era in English literature. The complacency of the age in moral matters was less felt in Hungary than in England only because Hungary's social, political, and economic position was less favorable and less secure. Yet the guidance that critics were expected to offer to writers and readers had to be moral, and it was assumed that the social structure was more or less stable. However, it speaks for Gyulai's critical intelligence and desire for impartiality that he never ignored world literature and that he sought an understanding of its organic relationship to Hungarian literature. He allowed, as it were, Western critical ideas to descend upon his spirit and tried to apply them to the creative works of Hungarian writers and poets. But the real source of his work was Hungarian. He was a nationalist, reluctant to identify nationalism with slogans and verbal flag-waving. In such patriotic poems as "Hadnagy uram" (My Lieutenant), in such romantic poems as "Éji látogatás" (Night Visit—in which mother love is glorified), in such stories as "Egy régi udvarház utolsó gazdája" (The Last Owner of the Old Homestead), one senses the romantic, emotional intercourse between national and universal human issues. His elegies, his satirical poems and stories, though greatly prized by his contemporaries, are only slightly above the average of similar works written at that time; most of them probably would have been forgotten without Gyulai's critical reputation. In fact, in their form they are romantic or semi-romantic crumbs of a pre-Victorian age; in their ideas they are a mixture not only of nationalism and humanitarianism, but of puritanism, sentimentalism, and idealism. Gyulai, like many other critics of world literature, served the interests of literature more forcefully in the realm of criticism than in that of creative imagination.

As a critic he had no equal among his contemporaries. His observations were original, his analytical intelligence genuine, his intuitive and acquired knowledge unusual. He wrote political and literary essays; he collected Transylvanian (Székely) folk songs and ballads; he wrote monographs about Arany, Petőfi, Vörösmarty, Katona, Eötvös, and other outstanding Hungarian writers and poets; he participated in critical activities that before him seemed outside the jurisdiction of Hungarian literary critics; indeed through his fruitful criticisms other literary critics were encouraged to remain true to their own aesthetic sensibilities. His best critical essays were published under the title *Birálatok és kritikai dolgozatok* (1854; Criticisms and Critical Essays). Gyulai objected to cleverness, to verbosity, to eccentricity, to seeming modernity. He was conservative in a noble sense, interested in conserving values that deserved to remain precious to a nation's culture. He was the professional critic with insight; this made him intolerant of catchwords and somewhat suspicious about the exhibitionistic propaganda of "progress." He may have been overcautious at times when a more sympathetic understanding of a new writer would have justified a freer approach to his work. Yet even as an old man he did not close his eyes to the compelling and strange poetic personality of Ady (*q.v.*); this shows that as a critic he recognized ability even when it did not meet his taste.

See: S. Galamb, *Gyulai Pál novellái* (1919–1922); T. Dóczy, "Gyulai Pál kritikai elve," *Nyugat* (1922); Gy. Mitrovics, *Gyulai Pál esztetikája* (1926).

J. R.

H

Hagalín, Guðmundur G. (1898–, Icelandic novelist, poet, and playwright), was born at Lokinhamrar in Vestfirðir, of robust farmer-fisherman stock. He soon determined to become a writer and after a brief attendance at school acted as editor of several ephemeral newspapers, thus having an opportunity to indulge in his desire to write. He visited Norway in 1925–1927. In 1930 he became a librarian in Ísafjörður in his home district and has remained there ever since.

Hagalín made his start in the lyric and national romantic period of the early 1920's. Soon he found his field, however, in short stories and novels describing with humor and gusto the life of the fishermen of Vestfirðir. Sometimes he contrasted the old generation with the new, to the latter's detriment. After 1930 Hagalín, like Laxness (*q.v.*), gave up the classical style of his early works for one more redolent of the earth and sea. In rough and robust dialect, assumed in order to depict the primitive characters close to the soil, he has written several short stories and the novels *Kristrún í Hamravík* (1933) and *Sturla í Vogum* (2 vols., 1938). The first pictures an old woman in an isolated cottage facing the Arctic, a widow poor yet perfectly content and self-contained, fearing neither God nor man, a master of her small world. The second describes a rugged, individualistic farmer in his development towards a social consciousness that finds outlet in practical cooperation with his fellow men. Hagalín has also written two adventure biographies of a shark fisherman and a skipper.

See: S. Einarsson, "Guðmundur Gíslason Hagalín," in *Iðunn*, XVIII (1934), 65–88.

S. E.

Halbe, Max (1865–1945, German dramatist and novelist), was born in northeastern Germany near Danzig, in a district where German and Polish racial elements have intermingled for centuries. Growing estrangement between his parents and social ostracism which their Protestant neighbors imposed upon them for being Catholics cast early shadows upon his youth. From 1883 to 1888 he studied first law, then languages and history at the universities of Heidelberg, Berlin, and Munich. In Berlin he became acquainted with Gerhart Hauptmann (*q.v.*) and other naturalistic writers, and their influence, together with that of Ibsen (*q.v.*), is apparent in his first dramatic attempts. In the play *Eisgang* (1892) a social and psychological problem is pictured against the background of a great natural panorama in his homeland. Encouraged by the success of this play, Halbe wrote the drama which was to become his only lasting contribution to German letters, *Jugend* (1893; Eng. tr., *When Love Is Young,* 1904). The new element was the psychology of adolescence: two young people, carried away by their love to a fateful end, express their feelings in highly poetical language. Again the scene was laid in the Polish-German borderland. The performance of the play was given an enthusiastic reception. From then on, however, Halbe's rich dramatic output was a series of bad failures alternating with mild successes. *Mutter Erde* (1897; Eng. tr., *Mother Earth,* 1913–1915), *Haus Rosenhagen* (1901; Eng. tr., *The Rosenhagens,* 1910), and *Der Strom* (New York, 1903; Berlin, 1904) are perhaps the only plays that deserve to be saved from oblivion. In 1895, after a short stay in Switzerland, Halbe went to Munich, which was to become his second home. There he joined the groups of writers who made the Bavarian capital a center of literary activity at about the turn of the century. He was particularly intimate with Frank Wedekind and Graf von Keyserling (*qq.v.*). His theatrical ventures, such as an "Intimate Theatre for Dramatic Experiments" and, in 1899, a "People's Theatre," were rather short-lived. By 1908 Halbe reached the end of his first period. After some sad failures among his plays, he turned to writing fiction which, with the rural novelette *Frau Meseck* (1897), had brought him some success earlier in his career. His two novels, *Die Tat des Dietrich Stobäus* (1910) and *Jo* (1917), are written with a surprising mastery of style and form strangely absent from the historical dramas he wrote during the same period. The publication of his *Gesammelte Werke* (1917–1923) marked the conclusion of Halbe's second period. His later *Jahrhundertwende: Geschichte meines Lebens, 1893–1914* (1935) has significance for its picture of naturalism.

Halbe belongs to those artists who, after initial successes, do not live up to expectation. The reason for his failure is to be seen in a lack of inner balance. Soergel calls him "a naturalist with the soul of a romanticist." In fact, his lyrical and moody tendencies though effectively supporting the dramatic development in *Jugend* tend in many other plays to slow down the action and to divert attention from the main theme. The background of nature is rarely sufficiently integrated with the action and the characters, nor does the racial conflict between Germans and Poles ever attain dramatic significance. His contemplative mood and the plastic descriptions of the landscape stand him in good stead in his prose writings. Yet the great epic of his homeland, West Prussia, which Germans expected of him at the time of its greatest ethnological and territorial tribulations never came from his pen. As a result of his boyhood experiences, Halbe could have been a rebel and a writer of social drama. But his characters only speak about the social conflict, and compared with Wedekind's *Frühlings Erwachen* (1891), his *Jugend* breathes the sad, mellow air of fall. Oddly enough, Halbe tried to give vent to his inner conflicts in the form of comedies, all of which were failures simply because they lack humor. Similarly, his historical plays, *e.g., Das wahre Gesicht* (1907), never succeed in reviving the past and suffer from baroque language and psychological twists. In an introductory poem to his *Gesammelte Werke* Halbe pictures himself as a "wanderer, fighter, and searcher." He never arrived at his goal, and to this day Alfred Kerr's benevolent judgment of him still stands: "What characterizes Halbe is the fact that he never quite succeeded."

See: A. Kerr, *Die Welt im Drama,* I (1917), 163–179; H. von Hülsen, "Max Halbe," *Der Türmer,* XXVIII (1925), 56–61; A. Soergel, *Dichtung und Dichter der Zeit,* 19. Auflage (1928), pp. 394–400.

W. N.

Hálek, Vítězslav (1835–1874, Czech poet, novelist, and dramatist), was born in Dolínek near Mělník (north of Prague), became a journalist, made two trips to Slovakia and to the Balkans and Turkey, and died in Prague. Hálek was at first a romantic poet in the wake of Byron and Heine and in his later work moved towards realism. *Večerni písně* (1858; Evening Songs), a sentimental imitation of Heine, established his local fame as a lyric poet, but his best work is *V přírodě* (1872–

1874; In Nature), which belongs to his last years. These are fine descriptive poems full of a rather naïve nature worship. His epical poetry shows a similar evolution towards realism: from *Alfred* (1856), an imitation of Byron's stories, through different Balkan legends, to a Slovak idyl, *Děvče z Tater* (1871; The Girl from the Tatra Mountains), and *Pohádky z naší vesnice* (1874; Tales from Our Village), which versify little anecdotes and genre pictures of peasant life with skill and charm. His prose also moved away from conventional romanticism to sensitive studies of real social problems of the Czech countryside. *Na statku a v chaloupce* (1871; In the Manor House and in the Cottage) and *Pod pustým kopcem* (1874; Under the Bare Hill) show already traces of his reading of Turgenev (*q.v.*). His dramas, pseudo-Shakespearean history plays, are of little value. Hálek's position in his own time was very considerable, but his prestige declined sharply after his work was attacked by the poet Machar (*q.v.*) in 1894. Recently his historical importance and genuine though narrow talent have again been appreciated.

See: J. S. Machar, *Knihy feuilletonů*, Vol. II (1902); L. Čech, *Literatura česká 19. století*, Vol. III (1907); J. Mukařovský, "Vítězslav Hálek," *Slovo a slovesnost*, I (1935), 73–87.

R. W.

Hallström, Per (1866–, Swedish poet, dramatist, and short-story writer), was born in Stockholm and trained as a scientist. He spent a few years abroad, working as a chemist in London and in Chicago, before settling down in his own country and turning definitely to literature. Hallström made his debut as a lyric poet in 1891, but soon found his perfect medium in the short story. His novel, *En gammal historia* (1895; An Old Tale), a sad and graceful idyl of the late 18th century in Sweden, is in fact an expanded short story. He has also essayed the drama, and his comedy *Erotikon* (1908; Eroticism), an attack on the modern cult of free love, was a decided success. A Shakespearean type of play, *Greven av Antwerpen* (1899; The Count of Antwerp), was better received by the critics than by the public of the theatre. Hallström has more recently been working on a new translation of Shakespeare into Swedish. For some years he has been secretary of the Swedish Academy, to which he was elected in 1908, and chairman of the committee for awarding the Nobel prize in literature.

It is, as suggested, upon his collections of short stories, particularly those in such volumes as *Purpur* (1895; Purple) and *Thanatos* (1900; Death), that Hallström's reputation is most securely based. His type is as far as possible removed from that of his contemporary, Hjalmar Söderberg (*q.v.*); he employs the generous and somehow epic manner of Balzac rather than the crisper idiom of Maupassant (*q.v.*). There is something almost monumental in a Hallström story. "The Falcon," which is set in the Middle Ages, gives a complete picture of the life of certain French nobles, their pride, their cruelty. In "A Florentine Fantasy" is the glow of the Italian Renaissance. "Out of the Dark" presents the mysterious figure of a young girl suddenly brought at midnight into a sophisticated group of modern Swedish artists. Each of these stories is arresting, unforgettable.

There is an underlying philosophy in Hallström's stories. Combined with a strong sense of beauty are a deep pity and a faith in human ideals and character. It is this which gives a peculiar nobility to his art. He is often attracted to the theme of death, which he treats much in the manner of Shakespeare, as not the end but the fulfillment of life. Hallström is not an author likely to appeal to the popular taste of any time, but it is doubtful whether any modern Swedish prose master, not even excepting Verner von Heidenstam (*q.v.*), has a more valid claim on the recognition of posterity.

See: J. Mortensen, *Från Röda rummet till sekelskiftet* (1919); Hallström, *Selected Short Stories*, tr. by F. J. Fielden (1922); C. W. Stork, tr., *Modern Swedish Masterpieces* (1923); H. A. Larsen, ed., *Sweden's Best Stories* (1928); G. Bach, *The History of the Scandinavian Literatures*, ed. by Frederika Blankner (1938).

C. W. S.

Hamp, Pierre (pseud. of Pierre Bourillon, 1876–, French novelist and sociologist), born at Nice, was the son of a *chef-cuisinier* who regarded his art as equal in dignity to any profession—an authentic descendant of the legendary and immortal Vatel. Pierre was brought up in this tradition. He went to Paris for an apprenticeship as pastry cook and chef and was then employed at the Savoy in London and at a hotel in Brighton. Having saved some money, he returned to France, where he began to acquire an education at the then flourishing Université Populaire. His life up to the time when he left the kitchen is told in his capital little book, *Mes Métiers* (1931). It was in England that he had begun to realize the appalling, not to say humiliating, conditions that a youth of his social stratum had to endure, however cheerfully, and to contrast all this with the dignity attached to the condition of the English workingman. Although he was later completely identified with the world of letters and of general ideas, he never disowned his past, saying he would have liked to be known as *Frère Hamp, religieux du travail*, and continuing to advocate honor for servants and workingmen.

Hamp is one of the talented writers of the time who found their way into print through Péguy (*q.v.*) and the *Cahiers de la quinzaine*. He had first been encouraged to take to his pen and become the "narrator for labor" by Paul Desjardins (*q.v.*), author of *Le Devoir présent* and the organizer of the meetings of Pontigny (a literary and social forum, continued during the Second World War at Mount Holyoke College in New England by French scholars in exile). Hamp relates these beginnings in another autobiographical book, *Il faut que vous naissiez de nouveau* (1936), a sequel to *Mes Métiers*. The great social achievement in his view would be happiness for the worker. The series of his books published under the general, and very relevant, title *La Peine des hommes* shows how shockingly distant from this goal we now are. The best known of this dramatic series are *Marée fraîche* (1908), *Vin de Champagne* (1909), *Le Rail* (1912), *Cantique des Cantiques* (1922; on making perfumery), *Le Lin* (1922; on the feminine dress industry), *La Laine* (1931), *Mineurs et métiers de fer* (1932).

For the most part Hamp lets facts speak for themselves; the human lesson is clear enough. Sometimes he cannot refrain from sounding a personal note of indignation or of hope, as in *La Victoire mécanicienne* (1920; partly on conditions in the great markets of Paris) or in *L'Enquête* (1914; an investigation into the starvation wages of the textile workers of Lille).

Hamp's *Trilogie de guerre* (*Le Travail invincible*, 1918; *Les Métiers blessés*, 1919; *La Victoire mécanicienne*), contains a formidable indictment of the German method of systematic destruction of the industries of France during the First World War, a destruction which to Hamp betrays more than anything else the sheer stupidity on the part of the leaders of Germany—since the cooperation of French and German industry could have done wonders for the prosperity of continental Europe. Similar ideas pervade a series called *Gens* (Eng. tr., *People*, 1921), with the following tableaux: *S.A.R. Philippe d'Orléans, L'Epidémie* (on the Goncourt Academy), *Monsieur Curieux, Mlle Moloch, Vieille Histoire.* Hamp has also written a number of plays, *Prologue pour une pièce sans cocu, La Maison avant tout* (a four-act play first published in the *Petite Illustration* in 1923), *La Campagne, Monsieur l'Administrateur, Madame la Guerre.*

The style of Hamp is often pungent because of its very sobriety. His documentation seems faultless and his originality cannot be denied.

See: A. Beaunier, "Les Idées de Pierre Hamp," *Revue des deux mondes*, April 1, 1923, pp. 689–701; T. W. Bussom, "Pierre Hamp, Prophet of the French Proletariat," *South Atlantic Quarterly*, XXVII (1928), 376–390.

A. Sz.

Hamsun, Knut (1859–, Norwegian novelist), is one of the most sharply developed literary personalities in modern Scandinavia. Most of his work, in fact all of his best work, is a direct expression of a highly individualized personality. This accounts for the pulsing intimacy of his work, for its freshness and vigor, its inexhaustible narrative inventiveness, its intensely personal lyric quality, and its impatience with anything that places bonds upon the free development of purely individual values in human life. The figures from Hamsun's generation who have had the greatest significance for him are Strindberg, Nietzsche, and Björnson (*qq.v.*)—Strindberg and Nietzsche because of their passionate, revolutionary individualism, Björnson because of his rich natural vitality and his highly personal literary style. Björnson's almost promiscuous social-mindedness, on the other hand, has always been to Hamsun something to be deprecated. As the mouthpiece for his own highly developed individualism Hamsun has created as the central figure in many of his novels the antisocial vagabond type he calls *en tilvaerelsens udlending* (an outcast from society). Though some of the components of this character type are drawn from the novelist's Strindberg-Nietzsche enthusiasms, Hamsun's early experience of life, with its restless shifts of scene and occupation, suggests the more immediate autobiographical origins of the recurrent vagabond type in his work.

Hamsun was born in the mountain valley of Gudbrandsdal in central Norway, his parents on both sides being of very old peasant stock. When scarcely three years old, he moved with his parents to Hamaröy in the Far North, where he remained until he was 20, except for a year in his early teens in Gudbrandsdalen. At 15 he was again back in the North Country where, for the next five years, he carried on a strenuous wandering existence, being in rapid succession a clerk in a general store, an itinerant merchant, a shoemaker's apprentice, a sheriff's deputy, a schoolteacher, and finally an author in a small local way. At the age of 20 he set out again for more southern parts of Norway, with the intention of establishing himself as a journalist and lecturer. Unsuccessful in these plans, he emigrated in 1882 to America, where he spent some two years at miscellaneous occupations, chiefly in Wisconsin and Minnesota. Finding a semifrontier middle-western United States hardly more appreciative of his talents than the Old World had been, Hamsun returned to Norway in 1884—only to go back to America for another two year period, 1886–1888, during which time he was a streetcar conductor in Chicago, harvest hand in North Dakota, and lecturer on literary and general cultural subjects before small Scandinavian groups in Minneapolis. Though most of his lectures dealt with contemporary European literary figures (Ibsen, Björnson, Strindberg, Lie, Kielland, Garborg, Zola, Dostoevski, Leo Tolstoy, *qq.v.*), he developed in his farewell appearance in Minneapolis his impressions, almost exclusively negative, of the contemporary American scene, a subject on which he shortly afterwards published the book (*Det moderne Amerikas aandsliv,* 1889; The Cultural Life of Modern America) that first attracted to him some general Scandinavian attention.

It was, however, with *Sult* (1890; Eng. tr., *Hunger,* 1899) that he had his first real literary success. *Sult* was an amazingly mature novel for one whose literary apprenticeship had been so miscellaneous and on the whole so unpromising as Hamsun's. Objectively conceived and yet starkly intense in its execution, this novel is a study in the strange vagaries of the human mind under the disintegrating stress of physical starvation. In its preoccupation with purely psychological phenomena, *Sult* represented the young Hamsun's reaction against the current Scandinavian "problem literature" of the 80's. This reaction he further developed in a series of lectures in which he mercilessly satirized the chief Norwegian exponents of this problem literature (Ibsen, Björnson, Lie, and Kielland) and called for a "new literature" whose primary concern would be the individual as such rather than the individual as a mere cog in a piece of social or political machinery. During the two decades following these critical pronouncements, Hamsun wrote almost a score of volumes (including novels and plays as well as one volume of poems), most of which gave direct creative expression to the literary program propounded in his lectures. The plays are prevailingly closet dramas, not easily adapted to the stage. Some of the poems are among the best in Norwegian, particularly the famous tribute to Björnson on his 70th birthday and a number of the nature lyrics.

The novels, 10 in all, contain some of Hamsun's very best work. Of the better novels may be mentioned two early ones, *Mysterier* (1892; Eng. tr., *Mysteries,* 1927) and *Pan* (1894; Eng. tr., 1920), and the later *Under höstsjernen* (1907; Eng. tr., *Under the Autumn Star,* in *Wanderers,* 1922) with its sequel, *En vandrer spiller med sordin* (1909; Eng. tr., *A Wanderer Plays on Muted Strings,* in *Wanderers,* 1922). In Johan Nagel, the central character in *Mysterier,* we are introduced for the first time in Hamsun's work to the typical Hamsun vagabond figure, a young man, sensitive to nature and to love, highly critical of urban society and the pretenses of "civilization," full of irrational impulses and provocative paradoxes. Thomas Glahn is a parallel figure in *Pan,* though Glahn is a far less negative character than is Nagel. He is just as antipathetic to "civilization" as Nagel; but while the latter lives constantly on the periphery of civilization, gaining a kind of perverse pleasure out of his feeling of superiority to it, Glahn expresses his antipathy positively by an escape from society into the great wilderness solitude of arctic Nordland. Both of these novels illustrate Hamsun's prose style at its best, spontaneous, flexible, full of haunting irregular rhythms, an infinitely sensitive instrument which handles with seemingly effortless ease the shifting moods of character and landscape and points of view in these tales. In *Under höstsjernen* and *En vandrer spiller med sordin* we again meet the wanderer-vagabond type—but with a difference. Since he had written *Pan* Hamsun had undergone a profound inner crisis, one associated with the passing of the splendid vigor of youth and the coming of middle age; and this finds central expression in the new novels. Nagel and Glahn, both in the full flower of young manhood, had been sufficient unto themselves, superior to their environment even during moments of partial outward defeat. The hero of *Under höstsjernen* and *En vandrer spiller med sordin* is, in contrast, a man in his 40's, little given to polemics, seeking rather than attacking—seeking his way back to the sources of his youth, sources which he can find now only in part, chiefly in memory and contemplation rather than in fact and action. And unlike Nagel and Glahn, Hamsun's new wanderer-hero is a laborer, a worker with his hands. There is a fine self-irony in the picture, a quiet at least half-resignation to life as it is; and the tale is suffused with a delicate poetic melancholy.

Hamsun's final phase of development as a novelist takes a twofold aspect. In the first group of novels, including *Börn av tiden* (1913; Children of the Time), *Segelfoss by* (1915; Eng. tr., *Segelfoss Town,* 1925), and *Markens gröde* (1917; Eng. tr., *Growth of the Soil,* 1920), he departs from his sharp focus on the individual and takes up problems concerned broadly with society as a whole. In the second group of stories from the last two decades (*Landstrykere,* 1927, Eng. tr., *Vagabonds,* 1930; *August,* 1930, Eng. tr., 1931; *Men livet lever,* 1933, Eng. tr., *The Road Leads On,* 1934; *Ringen slutet,* 1936, Eng. tr., *The Ring Is Closed,* 1937), he again returns to a consideration of the wanderer type; this time it is subjected to a searching, largely negative analysis, though he retains no little sympathy for the type even when he finds its rootlessness essentially sterile in the last analysis if not actually destructive of human values. Hamsun's departure from a preoccupation with the "outcast from society" in *Börn av tiden, Segelfoss by,* and *Markens gröde* reveals him at the height of his powers. The first two of these novels provide a broadly conceived attack on a modern industrial civilization which tends to cheapen human life and destroy society's moral stamina, while *Markens gröde,* a paean of praise to man at work on the soil, is by common consent Hamsun's greatest novel, if not the most impressive peasant novel ever written. In this saga Hamsun has combined a heroic theme with a simplicity of manner and a warm human feeling that make it unique among primitivistic novels. Its action avoids specification in both time and place, and in style it resembles the best of biblical narrative far more than it does the tradition of the modern novel. It is the work which won for its author in 1920 the Nobel prize in literature.

As a very old man Hamsun has had the dubious distinction of being the only Norwegian author of first rank who welcomed the Nazis upon their invasion of Norway in April, 1940. However little one is prepared to condone this step, it should be pointed out that Hamsun was at any rate consistent in thus expressing his sympathy for the German cause in the Second World War. He was an admirer of Prussian militarism in the First World War, and he apparently remained one. It should be noted also that the primitivism which lies at the base of all his social criticism is not without direct points of contact with central tenets in the Nazi philosophy.

See: John Landquist, *Knut Hamsun* (1917, in Swedish); Hanna Astrup Larsen, *Knut Hamsun* (1922, in English); Walter A. Berendsohn, *Knut Hamsun* (1929, in German); Einar Skavlan, *Knut Hamsun* (1929); Alrik Gustafson, *Six Scandinavian Novelists* (1940), pp. 226–285.

A. G.

Handel-Mazzetti, Enrica, Freiin von (1871–, Austrian novelist and poet), was born in Vienna. Her grandfather Heinrich had married an Italian baroness, Carolina Mazzetti of Milan. A posthumous daughter of an Austrian army officer, she was educated by her Hungarian mother and in later years by private tutors. One year (1886–1887) she spent at the institute for the *Englische Fräulein* in St. Pölten. As early as 1892 she was writing her first verse and fiction, but she acquired no literary fame until the appearance of her great historical novels. In these she draws with masterful strokes a picture of the Reformation in her homeland, with all its fury and devotion, its rage and passion. Reminiscences of one of her ancestors who in 1674 was accused as a witch and tortured to death may have influenced her when, in true baroque style, she paints those gruesome scenes of torment with which her work abounds. The first cycle of novels written in this spirit about the Counter Reformation consists of *Meinrad Helmpergers denkwürdiges Jahr* (1900), *Jesse und Maria* (1906; Eng. tr., 1931), *Die arme Margaret* (1910), and the trilogy *Stephana Schwertner* (1913–1914). She returns to her own times in a second group of novels, *Brüderlein und Schwesterlein* (1913), *Ritas Briefe* (5 vols., 1915–1921), and *Ritas Vermächtnis* (1922), in which the social life of Vienna and her favorite idea of the *sponsa Christi* play an important part. Then, perhaps recognizing that her great strength lay in the historical novel, she turned her attention to the Napoleonic era. At short intervals appeared *Der deutsche Held* (1920) and the volumes comprising the trilogy on the murderer of Kotzebue, *Karl Sand* (1924–1926). Her latest works take us back once more to the 18th century. In the *Novelle* entitled *Johann Christian Günther* (1927) she pictures the death of the 18th-century poet, and in another trilogy, *Frau Maria* (1929–1931), the Reichsstift Quedlinburg. As for her lyric poems, mention should be made of the collection *Deutsches Recht und andere Gedichte* (1908).

In her boundless loyalty to the Church she is a fervent defender of the Catholic faith, at the same time treating all problems with greatest charity. As a writer she has found recognition in seeing many of her great novels translated into several languages, in having bestowed upon her (1932) the Goethe medal, and in being elected (1933) a member of the Dichterakademie in Berlin.

See: E. Korrodi, *Enrica von Handel-Mazzetti; die Persönlichkeit und ihr Dichtwerk* (1908); P. Siebertz, *Enrica von Handel-Mazzettis Persönlichkeit, Werk und Bedeutung* (1931).

F. S.

Hansson, Ola (1860–1925, Swedish poet, short-story writer, and critic), was born in Hönsinge in southernmost Skåne. Throughout his literary career he retained no small measure of admiration for the solid, healthy peasant stock from which he came; but an even stronger strain in his art was an extreme tendency toward decadent and pathological themes nurtured by his reading of Jens Peter Jacobsen, Paul Bourget (*qq.v.*), and others. Because of the hostility which much of his early work aroused in Sweden, he came early to live an expatriate's restless, wandering existence, in Germany and France, and late in life in Denmark. His most significant work is doubtless to be found in his two early collections of poems, *Dikter* (1884; Poems) and *Notturno* (1885), in which he gave the most delicate, hypersensitive impressionistic expression to various aspects of life in his native Skåne, particularly to its natural phenomena and its landscape moods. Ola Hansson was the first poet of Skåne to capture its peculiar natural charm in finely modulated, softly melodious verse; and later poets from his province, such as Vilhelm Ekelund and Anders Österling (*qq.v.*) admit freely their indebtedness to Hansson.

The volume which first aroused nearly universal reaction against Ola Hansson in Sweden was *Sensitiva amorosa* (1887), a series of daring "case studies" in pathological eroticism, conceived in terms of the budding pseudo psychiatry of the day and couched in a prose style which was the last word in the overrefined and the *précieux*. In the late 80's and early 90's Hansson was occupied chiefly with prose criticism, writing in rapid succession a considerable number of critical essays published in Germany, Denmark, Norway, and Sweden. These essays were concerned at first with Scandinavian authors of the day, but they soon came to have a wider scope, including lengthy studies of Edgar Allan Poe and a number of French authors (Bourget, Huysmans, Richepin, *qq.v.*) as well as effusive panegyrics on Nietzsche (*q.v.*) and Julius Langbehn, late 19th-century prophet of Pan-Germanism in his *Rembrandt als Erzieher* (1890). Practically everything that Ola Hansson wrote in the 90's was strongly influenced by Nietzsche and Langbehn: they provided him with the metaphysical basis for his rejection of naturalism as an art form in the extended essay *Materialismen i skönlitteraturen* (1892; Materialism in Literature); they inspired the overstrained superman complex as developed in *Ung Ofegs visor* (1892; Eng. tr., *Young Ofeg's Ditties,* 1895); and they were the origin of the racial theories which were at the basis of the social and economic theorizing in *Resan hem* (1895; The Trip Home). None of this work can be said to be of first importance. It is too uncritically enthusiastic, losing itself in apostrophe and paradox and getting nowhere in particular. After 1900 Ola Hansson produced more sparingly and somewhat more solidly; but on the whole his later work rises only occasionally, in his lyric poetry, to something resembling a significant creative art. Despite the falling off in quality of this late work, however, Ola Hansson had the satisfaction during his last years of tardy recognition from his countrymen for the unquestionably important contribution which he had made to Swedish lyric poetry in his early works *Dikter* and *Notturno*.

See: F. Vetterlund, "Ola Hansson," in *Skissblad om poeter* (1914), pp. 205–248; F. Böök, *Sveriges moderna litteratur* (1921), also published as Vol. III of O. Sylwan, ed., *Svenska litteraturens historia* (1919–1921), pp. 347–362; E. Ek, *Ola Hansson* (1925); H. Gullberg, "Ola Hanssons Skåne," in *Skåne: årsbok* (1925), pp. 196–201; E. Ekelund, *Ola Hanssons ungdomsdiktning* (1930).

A. G.

Hardt, Ernst (1876–, German dramatist, story writer, and poet), was born in Graudenz, West Prussia. After graduation from the military academy of Lichterfelde, he traveled for four years in Greece and Spain, then lived as a writer in Dresden and Weimar. From 1919 to 1924 he was director of the Weimar theatre, and after 1924 director of the Cologne radio station. In 1898 appeared his first stories, in the volume *Priester des Todes,* and his first drama, *Tote Zeit.* Never of great originality, he wrote dramas and stories under the influence of Hugo von Hofmannsthal (*q.v.*) and poetry (*Aus den Tagen des Knaben,* 1904) under that of Stefan George (*q.v.*). Hardt became internationally known as a representative of the eclecticism of neo-romanticism and its craving for psychological abnormalities. For his drama *Tantris der Narr* (1907; Eng. trs., *Tantris the Fool,* 1909, *Tristram the Jester,* 1913) he received the national Schiller prize. Of his other dramas, only the tragedy *Gudrun* (1911) and the comedy *Schirin und Gertraude* (1913) were successes. The best among his stories is *An den Toren des Lebens* (1904). *Gesammelte Erzählungen* was published in 1909.

After the First World War, Hardt seems to have felt that his creative days were over. From that time on he has devoted his stylistic gifts to rendering excellent translations from the French (Taine, Flaubert, *qq.v.,* Balzac, Vauvenargues, Rousseau).

See: O. Nieten, *Uber den Neuromantiker Ernst Hardt* (1914). A Soergel, *Dichtung und Dichter der Zeit,* 19. Auflage (1928), pp. 1011-1015.

W. R. G.

Hart, Heinrich (1855-1906) and **Julius** (1859-1930; German critics, dramatists, and poets), were so completely united in their literary careers that it is impossible to treat them separately. Heinrich was born in Wesel and Julius in Münster. After their school and university years, Heinrich left their Wesphalian home and went to Berlin, whither he was soon followed by Julius. The two brothers at once entered actively into the literary life of the Prussian capital, joining forces with the group of young writers who were endeavoring to reform contemporary German literature. They soon became leaders in the early phases of German naturalistic development—as members of the literary club "Durch" (*q.v.*), as contributors to the anthology *Moderne Dichter-Charaktere* (1885), and, later, as members of the Friedrichshagen group gathered around Wilhelm Boelsche (*q.v.*) and Bruno Wille. Throughout the naturalistic revolution they were active as critics and theorists; their critical position was that of a balanced and reasonable aesthetic theory, and they may well be considered with Otto Brahm (*q.v.*) the leading naturalistic critics. Their most important contribution was *Kritische Waffengänge* (1882-1884). This collection of essays gave powerful expression to the demands made by the radical literary youth of the day on contemporary German literature, analyzed Zola (*q.v.*) and his importance for modern German letters, and directed brilliant attacks against the modish literati of the day, Hugo Bürger, Albert Träger, *et al.* Somewhat more conservative than their naturalistic confreres, the Harts none the less worked for a literature that should be contemporary in subject matter and spirit, base its portrayals on a wide understanding of current scientific hypotheses, and, avoiding imitation of outmoded classicism and romanticism, seek to create a balanced realism. Of lesser importance in the history of modern German literature were the short-lived journals edited by the Harts, *Berliner Monatshefte* (1885) and *Kritisches Jahrbuch* (1889), in which they carried on their campaign for a reawakening of contemporary German letters. Their critical activity was continued in the *Freie Bühne* with articles on various aspects of naturalistic aesthetics during the heyday of German naturalism and, after its decline, in *Die deutsche Zeitung, Die tägliche Rundschau,* and other papers. They were also active in various religious and socialistic movements during their later years.

Heinrich Hart's literary works include lyric poetry, *Weltpfingsten* (1878); drama; an unfinished epic of human history, *Das Lied der Menschheit* (1888-1896); and two volumes of short stories, *Kinder des Lichts* (1884) and *Heilige und Tänzerinnen* (1905). His *Gesammelte Werke* appeared in four volumes in 1907.

Julius Hart's literary career led him to the field of the lyric, *Sansara* (1878), *Homo Sum* (1890), *Triumph des Lebens* (1899). In the drama he attempted lyric tragedy, *Juan Tenorio* (1881), and a bourgeois tragedy, *Der Sumpf* (1885). His literary output also includes several volumes of short stories, *e.g., Fünf Novellen* (1888), and an anthology of Spanish poetry.

See: L. H. Wolf, *Die aesthetische Grundlage der Literaturrevolution der achtziger Jahre: Die Kritische Waffengänge der Brüder Hart* (1921); K. Tillmann, *Die Zeitschriften der Gebrüder Hart* (1923).

W. H. R.

Hartleben, Otto Erich (1864-1905, German lyric poet and dramatist), was born at Clausthal, an old mining town in the Harz Mountains where his paternal ancestors had been surveyors of mines for many generations. Early in his life he lost his parents. In 1885 he took up the study of law, which he pursued at the universities of Berlin and Tübingen. He was, however, mainly devoted to the social amenities of university life. Although he had passed the first of two examinations required for admission to the bar, he decided to become a free-lance writer—and combined this with an entirely undisciplined existence. Almost all his literary works owe their production to an occasional sober hour. Later, failing health forced him to give up the merry revels with his boon companions, and he retired to Salo near Lake Garda in northern Italy. There he built his famous villa Halkyone, which was supposed to become the center of a new academy of poetry. But before he was able to carry out this and similar plans Hartleben died, at 41. After his death the literary world witnessed the strange and unhappy spectacle of two women each claiming the legal rights of a wife.

There can be no doubt that Hartleben had great gifts; his humor was genuine, and many of his verses are full of music and almost flawless in form. He began as a disciple of Count A. von Platen (*Meine Verse,* 1895; *Von reifen Früchten; meiner Verse zweiter Teil,* 1904). His first books were two "delightfully nasty" short stories, *Die Geschichte vom abgerissenen Knopf* (1893) and *Der gastfreie Pastor* (1895), in which he looked at small-town ways with the perspective of a skillful but unkind observer. His characters are often caricatures. Of his plays, only one was a real stage success—*Rosenmontag* (1900; Eng. tr., *Love's Carnival,* 1904), more theatrical than truly dramatic. It had merit as an attack upon Prussian militarism.

On the whole Hartleben was only a moderately capable follower of Maupassant (*q.v.*) who never equaled his master. Belonging to the shock troops of his literary generation, he liked to irritate, tease, and alarm the bourgeois, without seriously questioning the latter's form of life and without being really wicked.

See: W. Mahrholz, *Deutsche Literatur der Gegenwart* (1930), pp. 82–83; J. Bithell, *Modern German Literature, 1880–1938* (1939), pp. 68–69.

H. Sch.

Hašek, Jaroslav (1883–1923, Czech novelist and journalist), is the creator of the "Good Soldier Švejk," a humorous type which became the symbol of the Czech "go-slow" attitude towards Austria during the First World War. Hašek was born in Prague and became a journalist. In the First World War he served in the Austrian army and was taken prisoner by the Russians. He joined first the Czech legions in Russia, but later changed over to the Communists. After his return to Prague, he was a free-lance writer leading a merry bohemian life, which gave rise to many legends and anecdotes. Hašek produced a number of ephemeral books of humorous sketches, but *Osudy dobrého vojáka Švejka za světové valky* (4 vols., 1920–1923; Eng. tr., *The Good Soldier Schweik,* 1930) established his reputation at home and abroad. A stage version was a great success in post-war Germany, and some critics hailed Švejk as a second Don Quixote. But *Švejk,* a loosely organized series of coarse farcical scenes interspersed with naïve reflections, is no great work of art. The main figure, Švejk, a fat dogcatcher from the Prague area, is vivid and convincing enough; he gets into trouble with the Austrian authorities for a supposed insult to His Majesty, is drafted, gets to the Russian front, and finally becomes a Russian prisoner. Švejk is a coward and shirker who assumes the innocence and stupidity of an idiot to disarm the railing officers, a happy-go-lucky skeptic as to war and military glory, an endless talker and coarse jester. The many hilarious scenes and the grotesque figures of the Austrian army (insolent officers, drunken chaplains, and the like) pleased a post-war audience which remembered the Austrian Empire and the war as a horrible dream and a bad joke. *Švejk* was unfinished when Hašek died and was concluded, rather lamely, by a fellow humorist, Karel Vaněk.

See: J. Durych, *Ejhle, člověk* (1928); E. A. Longen, *Jaroslav Hašek* (1928); V. Menger, *J. H., zajatec č. 294, 217* (1934) and *J. H. Doma* (1935).

R. W.

Hasenclever, Walter (1890–1940, German dramatist and poet), was born in Aachen. He saw something of the world in his student years, attending not only the University of Leipzig but those of Oxford and Lausanne as well. He was wounded in the First World War and spent a year or more in a hospital.

Hasenclever was nothing if not sensational. His first poems, *Der Jüngling* (1913), were, to be sure, not exciting except for their subject matter: they were the warnings of a confessed libertine. With the play *Der Sohn* (1914), however, the theme of revolt breaks out. A boy of 20 who refuses to be intimidated any longer by his tyrant of a father escapes from home, becomes a revolutionary both socially and politically, and when the bailiffs hale him again before his outraged parent threatens his father with a pistol, with the result that the latter dies of a stroke. This play, produced for the first time in 1916, was one of the early shots fired in the battle of expressionism; it also introduced the motif of father-son hatred which ran like a lurid thread through the literature of the period. As he was drawn into the war in 1915 Hasenclever became more politically conscious. In that year he wrote a dramatic poem, *Der Retter,* in which a poet, prophet of peace and of the brotherhood of man, goes down before the firing squad of the field marshal; his message, we are assured, will live on after him. Spiritual and political leadership is also attributed to the poet in *Der politische Dichter* (1919), which contains poetry of a highly revolutionary sort. The most violent of all Hasenclever's works is his drama *Antigone* (1917). The Greek story is used as a framework for antimilitary arguments: Creon, a mask for William II, becomes the most brutal of tyrants, who is brought to book by the rage of the people; the proud Antigone turns democrat and pacifist.

Eventually Hasenclever found revolution unprofitable. Two experiments with dramatic technique followed, *Die Menschen* (1918), which approaches pantomime since the text consists mostly of interjections, and *Jenseits* (1920), a ghostly tragedy with two characters and an implied spook. Latterly Hasenclever had taken the path of comedy with *Ein besserer Herr* (1927), *Ehen werden im Himmel geschlossen* (1929), and *Napoleon greift ein* (1930). In 1917 he was awarded the Kleist prize.

See: K. Martens, *Die deutsche Literatur unsrer Zeit* (1922), pp. 500 ff.; A. Soergel, *Dichtung und Dichter der Zeit,* Neue Folge: *Im Banne des Expressionismus,* 4. Auflage (1927), pp. 706–716.

H. W. P.

Haulleville, Eric de (1900–1941, Belgian poet, novelist, and essayist), was born in Brussels. He came from a family which for generations had devoted itself to arts and letters. His grandfather, Baron Prosper de Haulleville, a well-known historian and a leader of the Belgian Catholic press, was a personal friend of Montalembert and Louis Veuillot. His father, Baron Alphonse de Haulleville, was one of the founders of the Colonial Museum of Tervueren (near Brussels), devoted to African ethnography. Eric, from his childhood, was familiar with Negro statues and African art. In his first poems, *Dénouement* (1921), he displayed a marvelous imagination together with a Baudelairian "sens de la surprise," a particular taste for the unexpected and for lyrical contrast which constitutes his principal poetic qualities.

Haulleville lived in Paris for nearly 10 years and was intimately connected with the leading personalities of contemporary literature and art. *Le Genre épique* (1928) is an original attempt to render a prismatic view of the visible and the interior world of a poet in short poems, fairy tales, dialogues, and brief dramatic scenes. *Le Voyage aux Iles Galapagos* (1934), a poetic novel in which the influence of the surrealist technique can be retraced, won the Albert I prize in 1935. Haulleville returned to Brussels after his marriage to Rose Nys, Mrs. Aldous Huxley's younger sister. He became the private secretary to Burgomaster Adolphe Max, and after the death of the heroic Brussels mayor remained in the same position with Burgomaster Vandemeulebroeck. In fleeing Belgium during the Second World War, the poet, already worn by a long illness, walked many miles, with his wife and their little girl, through areas devastated by bombs and cities aflame. When at last they arrived in the south of France, there was no longer hope of saving him. He passed the final months of his life in bed correcting the copies of his last manuscript, *L'Anneau des années* (posthumously published, 1941), which contains his best poems. He died in St. Paul de Vence (Var, France) on March 20, 1941.

Haulleville's poetry in his more significant works, despite the ironical fantasy which always gives them a particular color, is inspired by deep and moving thoughts of a metaphysical and cosmic character. More than once his lyrical outcry reaches a Shelleyan grandeur rarely equaled by a poet in this century.

L. K.

Hauptmann, Carl (1858–1921, German dramatist and novelist), was born in Obersalzbrunn, Silesia, the elder brother of Gerhart Hauptmann (*q.v.*). Silesian mysticism, especially the works of Jakob Böhme and Meister Eckhart, early attracted his attention. Interested in the metaphysical approach to natural science, he took his doctorate at Jena under Haeckel in zoology and Avenarius in natural philosophy. Although he gave great promise as a scientist, his brother Gerhart's literary success started Carl on a new career. When the dramas *Marianne* (1894), *Waldleute* (1895), and *Ephraims Breite* (1898; Eng. tr., 1900) appeared, the critics proclaimed him a late naturalist, an imitator of his brother Gerhart, and a talented, forceful writer who, however, might more profitably have confined his endeavors to natural science. But the collection of aphorisms and lyrics, *Aus meinem Tagebuch*

(1900), helped create a better understanding of the man and the poet. In this work he denied all connection with the naturalistic doctrine. He did not share the naturalist's reticence about the "idea"; in fact, the "force of the idea" is a predominant theme in his works.

His dramatic efforts cover an extensive field: tragedy in *Die Austreibung* (1905), realism in the dramatic poem *Moses* (1906), symbolism in *Die Bergschmiede* (1902), Hauptmann's best-known drama. In *Napoleon Bonaparte* (1911), his crowning dramatic achievement, he reconstructed the career of the French emperor within the framework and spirit of Napoleon's own time. Supernatural and realistic elements are interwoven in *Die lange Jule* (1912) and *Die armseligen Besenbinder* (1913). Hauptmann turned to comedy in *Die Rebhühner* (1916), to tragicomedy in *Tobias Buntschuh* (1916), the first play in the trilogy *Die goldenen Strassen,* of which the second and third parts are *Gaukler, Tod und Juwelier* and *Musik* (both 1919). *Der abtrünnige Zar* and *Krieg, ein Tedeum* (Eng. tr., *War, a Tedeum,* in *Drama,* Vol. VI, 1916, pp. 597–653), both published in 1914, predict the coming catastrophe; words are subordinated to plot for a more vivid picture of the nature of things to come.

In the field of prose two works appeared in 1902, the short stories collected under the title *Aus Hütten am Hange* and the novel *Mathilde*—descriptions of milieu and characterizations without the naturalistic undertone of social significance. Hauptmann's striving for perfection in the moral sense reached a climax in the novel *Einhart der Lächler* (1907), in which he portrays the life of a misunderstood artist; here again he combined dream with reality. *Ismael Friedmann* (1913), *Nächte, Schicksale,* and *Das Rübezahlbuch* (all three 1915) have their setting in Silesia. Hauptmann also commanded the lyric form, as in *Der Sonnenwanderer* (1896).

He died in 1921 in his native and beloved Silesian mountains, where he spent the greater part of his life. A sojourn in Italy and a trip to America in 1907 were his only extended travels. Had not his brother Gerhart overshadowed him, Carl would have stood out in clearer relief as the poet he was—a conformer to no literary "ism," a discerning and sensitive master of words, a man whose outlook was tempered by Silesian mysticism and environment, and a soul striving to envisage the future.

See: H. H. Borcherdt, ed., *Carl Hauptmann, er und über ihn* (1911); H. Razinger, *Carl Hauptmann; Gestalt und Werk* (1928); W. Goldstein, *Carl Hauptmann; eine Werkdeutung* (1931).

W. J. M.

Hauptmann, Gerhart (1862–1946, German dramatist and novelist), was born in Obersalzbrunn, Silesia. Reared in Protestant orthodoxy, but early exposed to the more emotional teachings of Moravian pietism, he was as a young man subjected to the impact of an almost religious belief in scientific causality and materialistic determinism, tempered by a vague kind of socialistic meliorism, which at that time attracted the young intellectuals of Germany. A failure as a Gymnasium pupil, he turned to farming, sculpture in Breslau and Rome, desultory academic study in Jena and Berlin, and finally to literature. His marriage to a beautiful young heiress, who supported him throughout the four years of their engagement, freed him from the necessity of literary hack work. Marital incompatibilities and a passionate attachment to a young violinist led to more than 10 years of self-torturing inner conflicts, terminating in divorce and a new marriage in 1904. He received the Nobel prize in literature (1912) and honorary degrees from Oxford (1905), Leipzig (1909), Prague (1921), and Columbia (1932). The Weimar Republic bestowed on him the order Pour le Mérite (1922). The Third Reich ignored him, but he remained one of the most popular dramatists on the German stage.

Hauptmann's work will perhaps go down in history as the most complete artistic expression of the so-called historicism and the relativistic skepticism of the last 50 years. In the fact that he is essentially a product of a time of transition and of uncertain groping lies his distinction as well as his limitations. In a manner unparalleled in German literature he demonstrated a receptivity to the varied intellectual currents of the age and a sensitivity to new literary movements, without persistently following any of them. Few other writers have delved so deeply into the contradictions and irrationalities of human behavior, few have looked at the facts of life and of nature with the same honesty and candor. While he believed in a Supreme Being and felt a cosmic oneness with nature, he could not reconcile with the existence of evil and suffering the Christian concept of God as a loving father. Life was to him a non-rational mystery which must be accepted. It can be portrayed; it cannot be explained.

After dabbling with epigonic dramas, epics, and social ballads, Hauptmann began to experiment with realistic sketches, some unpublished fragments containing painstaking and minute reproductions of various dialects. When he met Arno Holz (*q.v.*) he was already well along the road to the naturalistic style of which Holz claimed to be the originator. What he most owed to Holz was encouragement to apply the new technique to the drama. *Vor Sonnenaufgang* (1889; Eng. tr., *Before Dawn,* 1909) marks the birth of the naturalistic drama. This and the other early plays, except for a greater illusion of realism in speech and in situations, were still reminiscent of Ibsen (*q.v.*) with his emphasis on milieu, heredity, or education. An entirely new dramatic form was evolved in *Die Weber* (1892; Eng. tr., *The Weavers,* 1899). Five seemingly independent tableaux are organically bound together in a climactic action of overpowering force. From the more than 70 characters no individual hero stands out. The hero is in fact the whole proletarian group. A similar structural principle is observed in *Der Biberpelz* (1893; Eng. tr., *The Beaver Coat,* 1912), one of the few great comedies in German literature. The success of *The Weavers* prompted Hauptmann to apply the same technique to a theme from the Peasants' War of the 16th century, *Florian Geyer* (1895; Eng. tr., 1929). The dramatist has succeeded here in combining the speech forms, the psychology, and the cultural and social background of a forgotten age in such a stupendous historic pageant that it took the German public nearly 30 years to appreciate its accuracy and its artistic cogency. Both plays are typical naturalistic tragedies. There is no clash of ideas—only the collision of great natural forces. No divine order of eternal justice and righteousness is vindicated as in the Hegelian type of tragedy. As in *Oedipus Rex* and *King Lear,* the reader is left with the depressing feeling of the senselessness of human events, the brutality of life, and the dominating role played by error and chance. The neo-romantic movement is reflected in the touching dream play *Hanneles Himmelfahrt* (1893; Eng. tr., *Hannele,* 1894), the first drama in world literature making a child the heroine. In this play the romantic supernaturalism could still be explained on purely psychologic grounds as figments of a feverish mind. A complete surrender to romanticism was made in *Die versunkene Glocke* (1897; Eng. tr., *The Sunken Bell,* 1898), the most personal as well as the most popular of Hauptmann's dramas. In most of the plays up to *The Sunken Bell* the tragic outcome is generally the result of man-made causes and could be avoided by man-made reforms. When Hauptmann became more engrossed in his own personal problems, he envisaged tragedy as inherent in human nature itself. Out of man's nature grow not only his most glorious and idealistic impulses, but also the most disgusting and brutal of his instincts. It is largely a matter of chance in which direction nature asserts itself in any given individual. Hence there is no guilt and no poetic justice. And so sex reveals itself in its highest sublimation as self-sacrificing love in Hauptmann's most beautiful verse drama, *Der arme Heinrich* (1902; Eng. tr., *Henry of Auë,* 1914), as well as in one of its most pathological expressions, that of nymphomania, in *Kaiser Karls Geisel* (1908; Eng. tr., *Charlemagne's Hostage,* 1915).

The emphasis on nature and character found its most adequate expression in the two greatest German tragedies of the last 50 years, *Fuhrmann Henschel* (1899; Eng. tr., *Drayman Henschel,* 1913) and *Rose Bernd* (1903; Eng. tr., 1913). As in the other naturalistic plays, dialect predominates, but the structure is more closely knit and the characters are no longer examples of static and plastic analysis. They are human beings undergoing an evolutionary change. As if to escape from the brutality of everyday life, Hauptmann turned more and more to legendary, romantic, and balladesque subjects, even though they were often given a realistic background. The most fascinating and beautiful of these, symbolizing the varied reactions of men to beauty, is found in *Und Pippa tanzt* (1906; Eng. tr., *And Pippa Dances,* 1907), which the poet loved best of all his plays. As a sort of summing up of a lifelong preoccupation with the figure of Christ, he wrote the most profound religious novel of his time, *Der Narr in Christo, Emanuel Quint* (1910; Eng. tr., *The Fool in Christ, Emanuel Quint,* 1911). With sympathetic insight Quint is drawn as a modern mystic who tries to carry out literally the simple social precepts of Jesus and meets with a somewhat similar fate. A journey to Greece produced in the travel diary *Griechischer Frühling* (1908) a unique appreciation of a pastoral, pre-Socratic, essentially Dionysiac Greece with its serenity and joyous acceptance of life even in its most tragic implications. This new outlook was reflected in the forceful drama *Der Bogen des Odysseus* (1914; Eng. tr., *The Bow of Odysseus,* 1917), in which the hero appears at first almost as a dreamy German who has actually lost the sense of his own identity, until he regains his former prowess by contact with his native soil. *Der Ketzer von Soana* (1918; Eng. tr., *The Heretic of Soana,* 1923), a dithyrambic praise of pagan assertion of life and of the senses, is stylistically and structurally the most finished of Hauptmann's narrative works. In a number of books appearing before the outbreak of the First World War he had expressed a presentiment of a catastrophic collapse of Western civilization. The war caused him to withdraw within himself and to continue work on the exotic themes selected earlier. *Der weisse Heiland* (1920; Eng. tr., *The White Saviour,* 1924) is an exquisite tragedy in melodious trochaic tetrameters, holding up to scorn Christian fanatic zeal over against the guilelessness of the Christlike Montezuma. *Indipohdi* (1921; Eng. tr., 1925) is steeped in Buddhistic longing for nonexistence. The epic *Till Eulenspiegel* (1928) is the work which Hauptmann considered his greatest. It contains grandiose and realistic pictures of the depressing and chaotic conditions in post-war Germany and finally takes the hero to Greece, where he lives for a thousand years a characteristically bucolic existence with Baubo, the handmaiden of the gods. After the centaur Chiron has shown him the realm of the Platonic ideas, he returns to the phenomenal world and finally seeks death in the Swiss glacier ice. Later works were two dramas, *Iphigenie in Delphi* (1941) and *Iphigenie in Aulis* (1944).

Hauptmann wrote more than 60 books. It is impossible as yet to trace a definite line of development. Some of his works are known to have gone through long periods of gestation, others were finished years before they were published. Of many others the history is unknown. *Das Abenteuer meiner Jugend* (1937) is a detailed and illuminating autobiography of the first 26 years, but Hauptmann published practically nothing about his later life or about his works. Aphorisms and fragments were brought together in *Ausblicke* (1922), collected speeches in *Um Volk und Geist* (1932). So-called conversations, *Gespräche* (1932), were written down from memory and arranged by Josef Chapiro.

C. F. W. Behl and F. A. Voigt have been at work on a definitive edition of Gerhart Hauptmann's works, of which 17 volumes appeared in 1942.

See: P. Schlenther, *Gerhart Hauptmann* (1897; revised by A. Eloesser, 1922); J. Röhr, *Gerhart Hauptmanns Dramen* (1910); E. Sulger-Gebing, *Gerhart Hauptmann* (1916; revised by W. Linden, 1932); H. von Hülsen, *Gerhart Hauptmann* (1927); V. Ludwig, *Hauptmann-Bibliographie* (1932); Felix A. Voigt, *Antike und antikes Lebensgefühl im Werke Gerhart Hauptmanns* (1935), *Hauptmann-Studien* (1936), and *Hauptmann-Jahrbuch* (1936, 1937).

F. W. J. H.

Hazard, Paul (1878–1944, French scholar and critic), was born in the village of Nordpeene, Nord, the son of a schoolmaster. He became himself one of the most eminent teachers and investigators of his generation, joining high professional competence and scrupulousness with qualities of imagination and grace that endeared him to students in two hemispheres. Trained at the Ecole Normale Supérieure, which he entered in 1900, he was appointed to the chair of comparative literature at the University of Lyon in 1910; he was called to Paris to the Sorbonne in 1919 and became a member of the faculty of the Collège de France in 1925. He lectured extensively abroad and received honorary degrees from the universities of Turin, Santiago (Chile), Mexico, Sofia, Harvard, and Columbia. He was visiting professor at Columbia University in alternate years from 1932 to 1940. Near the end of 1939 he was elected a member of the French Academy.

Hazard's doctoral thesis, *La Révolution française et les lettres italiennes* (1910), has been called a model; here, as constantly in his subsequent writing, he is substantial, documented, but with no suggestion of the ponderous, he is hospitable to general ideas, never irresponsibly affirmative. The multiplicity of his interests is indicated by such titles as *Leopardi* (1913), *Lamartine* (1926), *Stendhal* (1927), *Don Quichotte* (1931). In 1932 appeared *Les Livres, les enfants et les hommes* (Eng. tr., *Books, Children & Men,* 1944), a sensitive appraisal of works written for very young readers, or taken over by them, throughout Europe and through the centuries. The comprehensive *Histoire de la littérature française* (2 vols., 1923–1924), compiled with Joseph Bédier (*q.v.*), ranks with the *Histoire* of Gustave Lanson (*q.v.*). Hazard was long an editor of the highly reputed *Revue de littérature comparée* founded by him and Fernand Baldensperger (*q.v.*).

La Crise de la conscience européenne (3 vols., 1935) is a study of the mind and the heart of Europe in the decades from 1680 to 1715. One reviewer said that the title of the first chapter, "De la stabilité au mouvement," might have served the entire work, but Hazard while he had the boldness of his lucidity—and he has had to endure the not over-devastating reproach of being "un esprit trop clair"—was capable of both seeking and distrusting simplicity. This book is indispensable for any student of the period and of the genesis of a relativistic attitude in modern Europe.

Hazard came to New York for another semester at Columbia University in 1940; he returned to France in January, 1941, to remain with his own people in their tragic ordeal. The enemy refused to accept him for the post to which he was then nominated, the rectorship of the University of Paris. He continued to teach, at Lyon and at Paris, and to study. Before his death in April, 1944, he had completed, in cruel circumstances and with a true humanist's steadiness, a continuation of his report on the European "conscience," a large new work to be entitled *Les Origines intellectuelles de l'Europe contemporaine: Le Dix-huitième Siècle de Montesquieu à Lessing.* A clandestine review, *France de demain,* early in 1944 published Paul Hazard's characteristically moving exhortation to his countrymen, "Pour que vive l'âme de la France" (republished in the *Romanic Review,* December, 1944).

See: Jean Marie Carré, "Paul Hazard," *Revue de littérature comparée,* XX (1940), 5–12; Henri Peyre, "Paul Hazard," *French Review,* XVII (1944), 309–319.

H. S.

Hedberg, Tor Harald (1862–1931, Swedish dramatist, novelist, and poet), born in Stockholm, the son of a writer, served for 10 years as literary and dramatic critic of the newspaper *Svenska dagbladet* (The Swedish Daily Paper), and from 1910 to 1922 was the director of the Dramatic Theatre. He was also a member of the Swedish Academy.

Hedberg's literary career is marked by an early and fruitful beginning. He began writing shortly after leaving Uppsala, and by the time he was 30 had 10 titles to his credit. Although he was a member of the group of writers who called themselves "Det unga Sverige" (Young Sweden), his work was little marked by the views of fellow authors. While his companions were struggling with the problems involved in representing objective reality, Hedberg was concerning himself with psychological studies. His earliest writings were in the field of prose fiction. In works like *Johannes Karr* (1885), *Judas* (1886), and *På Torpa Gård* (1888; At Torpa Estate), he invariably treated the main character from the standpoint of inner stress. In the 90's Hedberg turned his attention to the drama. With *Judas* (1895) he repeated an earlier choice of subject, and the focus once more is on a psychological battle. Judas seemingly can resolve his conflict only by betraying Jesus. In *Gerhard Grim* (1897) there are tendencies that are obviously derived from *Faust.* The most successful of Hedberg's dramas, however, is *Johan Ulfstjerna* (1907). The setting is contemporary and laid in a province of Finland that was formerly Swedish. The figure of Johan Ulfstjerna is very well drawn; indeed, Hedberg has succeeded in investing him with truth and reality. Whereas Judas is the label for a psychological problem presented in dramatic form, Johan Ulfstjerna is a human being who offers himself for the benefit of his fellow men.

See: J. Landquist, *Essayer* (1913); A. Brunius, *Ansikten och masker* (1917); H. Ahlenius, *Tor Hedberg* (1935).

C. E. W. L. D.

Heiberg, Gunnar Edvard Rode (1857–1929; Norwegian dramatist, essayist, and critic), was one of the most defiantly aristocratic individualists of his generation, carrying the spirit of Ibsen (*q.v.*) through the neo-romantic reaction and into the 20th century. Born in Christiania of a highly cultivated family, he was early conversant with European culture, "the first trueborn European in Norwegian literature" (Helge Krog). His first foreign journey took him to Rome, where he met Ibsen; in later years he spent much time in Copenhagen and other European centers, but most of all in Paris, which stood nearest to his own cosmopolitan *esprit.* Even as a university student, he had broken with the family conservatism, making friends with the extreme naturalists, the so-called *bohème,* and choosing, as he said, "two teachers, Johan Sverdrup and Georg Brandes" (*see* Brandes), the bannermen of political and literary radicalism in his day.

His literary début (1878) consisted of two poems in the spirit of Shelley and Wergeland, praising the free human spirit and the pure intellect personified in the rebel Cain. His first drama, *Tante Ulrikke* (1883; Aunt Ulrikke), was Ibsenian in technique, but more violent and explosive. For four years (1884–1888) he was artistic director of the National Theatre in Bergen, doing brilliant work, but being forced out of the position because of his uncompromisingly contemporary choice of repertoire. The play *Kong Midas* (1890; King Midas) was a satire on such dogmatic and self-appointed truthtellers as Björnson (*q.v.*), but with its plea for a more inclusive and artistic humanity in literature it became a turning point in his production. From now on he avoided surface realism and developed a lyric-satiric style of his own, which is often charming, even exalted, but can also be dramatically baffling. A series of plays in the 90's developed his idea that human beings are more important than theories, that mass action is harmful, and that the lone, self-assertive creator is the highest form of human being. The high points of his dramatic production are *Balkonen* (1894; Eng. tr., *The Balcony,* 1922) and *Kjærlighedens tragedie* (1904; Eng. tr., *The Tragedy of Love,* in T. H. Dickinson, *Chief Contemporary Dramatists,* Ser. 2, 1921), both picturing in lyric prose the conflict between erotic passion and intellectual culture; *Jeg vil verge mit land* (1912; I Shall Defend My Land) and *Paradesengen* (1913; Bed of State), satires concerning true and false patriotism. He had a talent for disrespect, mixing the most vicious lampoons with a luxuriant lyricism. His women were creatures of untamable, primitive passions, while his men were delicate, lyrical, overrefined, when they were not brutal and unreflective. His fundamental, almost mystic devotion was to the wholehearted, all-consuming passion, whether in the form of selfless agitation for social justice, uncompromising, defiant patriotism, or the erotic demands of his uncivilizable women. He worshiped the genuine and flayed without mercy every touch of the meretricious.

Heiberg developed his ideas at length in the many brilliant essays and theatrical criticisms which he reprinted in such volumes as *Pariserbreve* (1900; Letters from Paris), *Ibsen og Bjørnson paa scenen* (1918; Ibsen and Björnson on the Stage), *Franske visitter* (1918; French Visits), *Norsk teater* (1920; Norwegian Theatre), *Salt og sukker* (1924; Salt and Sugar). The title of the last-named is suggestive of Heiberg's spirit: an occasionally inorganic blend of scoffer and worshiper, but first and last an artist. His style is nervous, agile, unrhetorical, sometimes jerky and mannered, but always sparkling with malicious wit and dramatic indignation. He is, as one critic remarks, most unlikely ever to be canonized, but he towers high as an uncompromising portrayer of the beauty and the bitterness of life.

See: Schou, *et al,* "Heiberg," *Samtiden* (1917, 1923, 1929, 1937); Julius Bab, *Das Drama der Liebe* (1925); E. Skavlan, "Gunnar Edvard Rode Heiberg," in *Norsk biografisk leksikon,* V (1931), 576–581.

E. H.

Heidenstam, Verner von (1859–1940, Swedish poet and novelist), was born in Västergötland (Olshammar, on Lake Vätter), where, in a magnificently picturesque countryside rich in famous historical traditions from the Swedish middle ages, he spent most of his childhood and youth. After brief attendance at a private school in Stockholm, interrupted by illness when he was 16, he left Sweden to travel for his health in the south of Europe and the Near East. He remained abroad for something over 10 years, not returning permanently to his native land until March, 1887. A year later his first volume of poetry, *Vallfart och vandringsår* (Pilgrimage and Wanderyears) attracted wide and favorable attention in Sweden. During the next few years he composed chiefly in prose a number of relatively unimportant autobiographical volumes and two significant antinaturalistic critical essays, one in collaboration with Oskar Levertin (*q.v.*). His first important volume of poetry, *Dikter* (Poems), appeared in 1895 and firmly established Heidenstam as one of the most significant literary figures of the 90's. In the late 90's and the early years of our century he wrote some distinguished historical fiction, including *Karolinerna* (1897–1898; Eng. tr., *The Charles Men,* 1920), *Heliga Birgittas pilgrimsfärd* (1901; Saint Birgitta's Pilgrimage), and *Folkungaträdet* (2 vols., 1905–1907; Eng. tr., *The Tree of the Folkungs,* 1925). His richest and most mature volume of poems, *Nya dikter* (New Poems), appeared in 1915. Some of his poems have been translated into English (*Sweden's Laureate: Selected Poems,* tr. by C. W. Stork, 1919). In 1916 the Nobel prize in literature was awarded to Heidenstam, with the significant Swedish citation "the leader of a new era in our literature." Only occasional poems and essays came from Heidenstam's pen after 1915. His contribution—one of the most important in modern Swedish literature—had already been made.

Heidenstam's significance in the history of Swedish literature lies chiefly in the fact that he was among the first consciously to break with the spirit of sober reason characteristic of the utilitarian social-reform prose literature of the Swedish 80's, the literature which, following the critical dictum of the Dane Georg Brandes (*q.v.*), had sought primarily "to put problems into debate." Heidenstam's first volume of poems, with its riot of color and its youthful exuberance of feeling and utterance, pointed a new way in terms of creative literature; and his critical essay "Renascence" (1889) contained a direct conscious attack on the realism of the 80's. He maintained that by the early 90's this realism had already exhausted its possibilities and that it was furthermore essentially irreconcilable with the Swedish national temper. In place of the realism of the 80's, deriving largely from foreign sources, Heidenstam championed a new, more purely Swedish literary program, one that would favor the subjective and the personal and would seek to unite the imaginative strain with a sense of the beautiful and also with a bold, racy realism. The challenge of these ideas was met immediately, not only in Heidenstam's own creative work, but also in Selma Lagerlöf's early novels and in the magnificent lyric flowering of such poets of the 90's as Fröding, Karlfeldt, and Levertin (*qq.v.*), Heidenstam's own work illustrates these ideas both in the genre of lyric poetry and in historical fiction—most brilliantly, no doubt, in his lyrics, though his novels and short stories are among the best Swedish historical fiction that there is. His poetry, which early revealed some excesses in the overuse of color and in imaginative exuberance, came with the years to be more disciplined, more concentrated, more firmly classical in form and spirit, though it lost little if any of the essential freshness and vigor of conception that characterized his early poems. In his attitude toward life Heidenstam is essentially pagan, more in the Greek, perhaps, than in the early Scandinavian sense. Though his subjects, particularly in some of the historical novels, are not infrequently drawn from an at least semibarbaric Scandinavian past, he reveals everywhere the sensitive aristocrat's born distrust of barbarism as such, favoring always a kind of harmonious classical humanism, not without a strong admixture of the heroic, as his final cultural ideal. Heidenstam is chiefly indebted for his poetic ideal, it would seem, to the Swedish-Finn Johan Ludvig Runeberg, and, in a lesser degree, to Goethe.

See: John Landquist, *Verner von Heidenstam* (1909); Ruben Gustafsson Berg, *Före 'Vallfart och Vandringsår'* (1919); Fredrik Böök, *Sveriges moderna litteratur* (1921), also published as Vol. III of O. Sylwan, ed., *Svenska litteraturens historia* (1919–1921), pp. 185–211; Alrik Gustafson, *Six Scandinavian Novelists* (1940).

A. G.

Heijermans, Herman (1864–1924, Dutch playwright and short-story writer), was born at Rotterdam. His father intended him for a business career, but he loathed the prospect of spending his life among account books and figures. He went to Amsterdam in 1892 and entered the literary profession as a reporter for the *Telegraaf*. His first dramatic venture, *Dora Kremer* (1893), was a failure. But shortly afterwards another play of his, in one act, scored a sensational success. He had it produced as a translation from the Russian and considered the applause which it earned both from the public and the press as confirmation of his belief that only foreign plays had a chance of success with people who, in their foolish ignorance, judged things by their origin instead of their intrinsic value. But this *Ahasverus* (1893; Eng. tr., 1934), by the fictitious Ivan Jelakowitch, was undeniably a better drama than Heijermans's first play, and the success that he afterwards won in his own name seems to vindicate the public and the critics. The successful presentation of *Ghetto* (1898; Eng. tr., 1899) and its subsequent vogue in London and Paris gave him the certainty of his own power. From then on he wrote for the stage with never lagging productivity. *Het Zevende Gebod* (1899; The Seventh Commandment), a satire on bourgeois morality, *Op Hoop van Zegen* (1900; Eng. tr., *The Good Hope,* 1912), a tragic picture of seafaring life, and a long series of other plays of varying force and quality followed in rapid succession during the next 20 years. Most of these plays have been translated into German. *De rijzende Zon* (Eng. tr., *The Rising Sun,* 1926), in which Meggie Albanesi scored one of her earliest successes in London (1925), completes the list of Heijermans's plays available in English. However, others have been performed before English-speaking audiences: *A Case of Arson* (*De Brand in de Jonge Jan*) and *Links* (*Schakels*) by the London Stage Society (1908); *The Hired Servant* (*De Meid*) by the Pioneer Players in St. Martin's Theatre, London (1917); and *Eva Bonheur* in New York (1925).

The secret of Heijermans's popularity in Holland is in the intensely Dutch character of his work. A fondness for the minute portrayal of reality akin to the art of the Dutch genre painters of the 17th century and coupled with it a strong sense of the humorous and farcical, such as those painters had, made his plays colorful pictures of life in a style that was enjoyed as a truly native art. Their popularity was no doubt due in part to the author's tendency to champion the cause of the underdog and the victims of our social order. Still Heijermans's fame among his countrymen is a distinctly artistic triumph such as no social reformer could have achieved. A social reformer he was and meant to be, but he owed his success in that field to the persuasive power of his art. His most famous play, *The Good Hope,* started an agitation for better government control of seagoing craft, which resulted in the Ships Act of 1909. When Heijermans died, leaving a widow and two little children in straitened circumstances, the crews of Holland's merchant marine contributed to a fund for their relief, in recognition of the great service his art had rendered them and their families.

It would be difficult to say to what extent foreign influences molded Heijermans's art. In his later years he conceived a deep admiration for Gerhart Hauptmann (*q.v.*), which may partly account for his turning from realistic to symbolical drama. *Uitkomst* (1907; *Deliverance*), which deals with the dream visions of a child on its sickbed, shows affinity to *Hanneles Himmelfahrt.* But otherwise he does not seem to have been greatly dependent on literary inspiration. Not literature, but life was his source book.

Heijermans was also a master of the short story. Most of his short stories were written, during his residence in Germany, for the *Telegraaf* and the *Handelsblad,* both Amsterdam dailies. They were published under the pseudonym Samuel Falkland, and the collected edition of these *Falklandjes,* as they are called in Dutch, fills 20 volumes. These alone —and many a precious gem they contain in the midst of less noble matter—would secure for him a place among Holland's writers. The fact that the author's pseudonym in the diminutive has become the recognized name for these stories affords a measure of their popularity.

See: A. J. Barnouw, "Herman Heijermans," New York *Times,* December 21, 1924, Section 7, p. 2, "Herman Heijermans," *Theatre Arts Monthly,* IX (1925), 109–112, and *The Dutch; a Portrait Study of the People of Holland* (1940), pp. 189–214, especially pp. 201–205.

A. J. B.

Heiseler, Henry von (1875–1928, German poet, dramatist, and critic), father of the poet Bernt von Heiseler (1907–), was born and educated in Russia and moved to Germany in 1905. He chanced to be in St. Petersburg at the outbreak of the First World War and had to serve in the Russian army, in a noncombatant capacity. After many harrowing experiences he was able to return to Germany in 1922. Bilingual in the practical, everyday sense of the word and as much at home in German culture as in Russian life, Heiseler nevertheless experienced all the difficulties of a writer who works in a medium which is not fully and utterly his native tongue. His desire to go back to Germany clearly indicated that he was painfully aware of how unsatisfactory it is for a poet to live and to create abroad, severed from direct contact with his cherished tradition. This is not to say that he ever came close to the borderline of dilettantism which is encountered so often in the work of other German writers abroad, notably among those who content themselves with speaking to a linguistic minority whose limited vernacular they acquire or those who drift into a kind of glorified reportage destined for consumption in their faraway home country. Heiseler kept to the high level of neoclassical art, drawing his inspiration from Stefan George (*q.v.*). Nevertheless the trained ear will often discern a lack of native rhythm in his poems (*Der Engel des Krieges,* 1914) or the absence of idiomatic raciness in his stories. Similarly, his preference for Russian scenes and subjects—his best plays (*Peter und Alexéj,* 1906; *Grischa,* 1916; *Die Kinder Godunófs,* 1923) all deal with Russian life and history—accentuates the dualism of his cultural allegiance.

It is in his thought rather than in his emotions that he overcame the handicap of a man with two countries, turning it indeed into the advantage of a well-informed observer of both Russian and German civilization, if not of European life in general. For this reason his critical essays deserve the closest attention; they contain seeds which may yet bear rich fruit in literary criticism and political thought. His fondest hope was for an intimate cultural union of Germany with England and the United States which he felt was bound to issue from their common instinct for order and justice and from the identity of their spiritual aspirations as he discovered them in Shakespeare, Keats, Browning, Walt Whitman, Bach, Goethe, and George. Heiseler's masterly translations of English and also of Russian and French literary works form his practical contribution towards this cultural alliance which would then lead to some sort of political confederation. The spadework was to be done by writers and philosophers; creative writing Heiseler considered to be of immensely greater significance in the evolution of mankind than the doings of so-called men of action, of rulers, conquerors, or industrialists.

See: W. Schneider, *Die auslandsdeutsche Dichtung unserer Zeit* (1936), pp. 120–129; André von Gronicka, *Henry von Heiseler, a Russo-German Writer* (1944).

H. B.

Hellens, Franz (pseud. of Frédéric van Ermengem, 1881–, Belgian novelist, poet, and art critic), was born in Ghent. His father was a university professor; he himself studied law, traveled widely, and has been for years in charge of the Parliamentary Library at Brussels. There is as yet no biography of Hellens, although Belgian critics count him as one of their most original authors, and his books have been much translated. His own writings vividly reflect emotional reactions to his experiences, but, living in the midst of what he calls "réalités fantastiques," he attaches small importance to the concrete facts of his existence. "I have gone through life like a somnambulist," he says. The biographer's task will not be an easy one. Fortunately he gave his own account of the origin of many of his works in *Documents secrets,* published in a limited edition in 1931. From it one learns that he composes with difficulty—a fact hardly to be surmised from a glance at his bibliography. He is among the most productive of Belgian novelists.

His earliest interest was in music, and its influence is clearly traceable in the structure of his stories. But, true to the national tradition, his first literary inspiration came from painters. He mentions specifically two contemporaries, Lemaire and Jules de Bruycker, to whom, and to their common master, the elder Breughel, he was indebted for his initiation into the picturesque quarters of Ghent. His first novel, *En ville morte* (1906), and collections of stories such as *Hors-le-vent* (1909) and *Clartés latentes* (1912) bear titles significantly characteristic of this period. He has written critical studies of artists, *e.g., Gérard Terborch* (1911) and *James Ensor* (1921), but the overtones of music and line rather than color in the plastic arts have held his attention. He avows the fascination that Poe's stories always awoke in him, adding that while Poe proceeds from the unknown to the known, he begins with reality to end in mystery which lies in an inner crisis of consciousness. *Réalités fantastiques* (1923), in which he declares he has put the essence of himself, reveals his kinship with Poe. Of special interest for the conception of his art are his remarks about the composition of *Melusine,* written in 1917, which baffled the publishers and appeared only in 1920. It is distinctly in the surrealist manner. He declares that it was all composed in a feverish trance which lasted for months. The uninitiated would be ill-advised in attempting to make his acquaintance through this novel. *Œil-de-Dieu* (1925) will prove an easier approach. Hellens says that this book was inspired by his admiration for the multiple personality revealed in Charlie Chaplin's art. The hero is at once Harlequin, Pierrot, and Don Quixote. At the start the intention seems to be a parody of the detective novel; little by little the author falls under the spell of his own creation, who is idealized as a champion of frankness, nobility, and courage in a pusillanimous world. Another novel, *Bass-Bassina-Boulou* (1922), is the exteriorization, to use one of his favorite words, of the fascination exercised by an African fetish found in a junk shop. The imagined odyssey of this deity includes tragedy, comedy, and social satire, but there is nothing of the reformer in Hellens; he appears rather as an elfish explorer of the uncanny for its own sake. Another source of inspiration comes from memories of his childhood and youth. *Le Naïf* (1926), *Les Filles du désir* (1930), and *Frédéric* (1935) belong to this group. Autobiography? Doubtless, but in Hellens's peculiar manner. "I have only confused memories of objects, but I cannot forget the atmosphere, which is the sonority of things," he says. This sonority of things, real or imaginary, has always guided him. Two psychological novels in more realistic vein are *La Femme partagée* (1929) and *Grippe-cœur* (1931). The potentially scabrous theme of the first is handled with extraordinary restraint; the second evolves around little ironies that fester in a tormented spirit to breed tragedy, and the slight action exists only to furnish reminiscences which become half-conscious directors of the heroine's life.

There appear in Hellens's work at the same time unity of inspiration—he is always the seeker of untouched realms of mystery within the familiar—and great variety of execution. Alert to every trend in contemporary literature and often himself a forerunner, he is usually less recondite than his fellow craftsmen of the vanguard. The personal mark is easy to distinguish in all his writing; direct literary influences, if they exist, are so subtle as to defy precision.

See: *Nervie,* 1932, No. 6 (special issue on Hellens); M. J. Hachelle, *L'Œuvre de Franz Hellens; essai bibliographique, critique et iconographique* (1937).

B. M. W.

Hellström, Gustaf (1882–, Swedish novelist, short-story writer), educated at the University of Lund, has spent a great deal of his life outside Sweden (in London, Paris, and New York) as foreign correspondent of a leading Swedish newspaper, *Dagens nyheter* (The Daily News). Because of this extensive residence abroad, Hellström has been able to maintain in the later phases of his work a much more objective attitude toward developments in his homeland than most of his Swedish contemporaries. His heavy, rather serious artistic temperament was ill-adapted to the airy skepticism of some of the turn of the century literature in Sweden which he affected in his earliest tales; but soon after his first residence abroad (in London) he had his first real literary success with *Kuskar* (1910; Drivers), a volume of tales which reveals a strong English influence in its direct, unassuming realism and its sensitive responsiveness to the fascinating variety of life in a large modern city. During the First World War he continued his literary work in France, writing in addition to a couple of rather unimportant novels with Parisian backgrounds (*Kring en kvinna,* 1914, About a Woman; *Bengt Blancks sentimentala resa,* 1917, Bengt Blanck's Sentimental Journey) two serious semijournalistic studies on modern France (*Joffre,* 1916; and *Kulturfaktorn: franska stämningar under världskriget,* 1916, The Cultural Factor: French Reactions during the World War). In these he attempted to correct the popular Swedish notion that France was a basically degenerate nation, her higher culture spending itself in a mere play of essentially empty intellectual and artistic subtleties. A clever, broadly ironic book on American upper-class life entitled *Ett rekommendationsbrev* (1920; A Letter of Introduction) brought to an at least temporary close Hellström's books on the foreign scene. He then turned again to Sweden for material in a number of arresting novels, first in a series of fictionalized autobiographical volumes appearing under the collective title *En man utan humor* (1921 ff.; A Man without Humor) and then with two works of more purely literary importance, *Snörmakare Lekholm får en idé* (1927; Eng. tr., *Lacemaker Lekholm Has an Idea,* 1930) and *Carl Heribert Malmros* (1931).

Snörmakare Lekholm får en idé is Hellström's one indubitable masterpiece. It is a detailed, unhurried story of three generations of a typical middle-class Swedish family in all of its fortunate and less fortunate ramifications, with the central action of the tale taking place in a small Swedish garrison town, but with appropriate periphery material from other localities being provided to fill in the broader outlines of the family picture. Its general literary model may well have been Arnold Bennett's *Clayhanger* cycle, though its humor seems to owe more to Dickens and possibly Fielding. Basically, however, Hellström's novel is a fresh, original work, in which comic and half-tragic action are blended in rich human profusion, and in which the elements of narrative structure, characterization, dialogue, and the handling of milieu are everywhere intellectually and aesthetically satisfying. It ranks unquestionably among the few very best Swedish genealogical novels.

See: K. Strömberg, *Modern svensk litteratur* (1932), pp. 69-70, 134–137; H. Ahlenius, *Gustaf Hellström* (1934).

A. G.

Hemmer, Jarl (1893–, Finnish poet and novelist writing in Swedish), born in Vaasa, Finland, is the leading younger poet of his country. He lives at Borgå (now called Porvoo), on the southwestern coast near Helsinki, where Finland's great epic master, J. L. Runeberg, spent his declining years. Traditional in form, there is in Hemmer's lyrics the fresh, unmistakable glow of beauty. Love of nature is his predominant theme. Typical of his many volumes is *Över dunklet* (1919; Above the Dark). Hemmer is also a prose writer of distinction. Best known abroad is his prize novel *En man och hans samvete* (1931; Eng. tr., *A Fool of Faith,* 1935), a strong, highly realistic, psychological tale of suffering and hopelessness, describing the tragic experiences of a priest during the Finnish Revolution, 1917–1918.

See: C. W. Stork, *Anthology of Swedish Lyrics* (revised and enlarged ed., 1930); G. Bach, *The History of the Scandinavian Literatures,* ed. by Frederika Blankner (1938).

C. W. S.

Hémon, Louis (1880–1913, French novelist and short-story writer), was born in Brest. He was educated at the Lycée Montaigne and Lycée Louis-le-Grand of Paris. He then studied law at the University of Paris and at the same time attended courses at the School of Oriental Languages, in preparation for entrance into the colonial service of France, a career which, however, he never pursued. In 1903 he went to England as a commercial clerk, remaining in that country until 1911. He had become a devotee of sports and physical fitness, and during this period he wrote many articles and short stories dealing with these subjects for sporting magazines in France. "Lizzie Blakestone," a *roman-feuilleton* on English life, appeared in 1908 in the *Temps* of Paris.

In 1911 he went to Canada, working as a translator in Montreal. During a sojourn in the back country north of Quebec in 1912, he was profoundly impressed with the life and character of the French Canadian pioneers of that region, and returning to Montreal in

1913, he wrote his great novel of French Canadian life, *Maria Chapdelaine* (Eng. tr., 1921). This was published serially, January–February, 1914, in the *Temps* of Paris, receiving but scant attention from the public and none from the critics. In the meantime Hémon had set out on a walking tour to the Far West. As he was walking along the railroad tracks near the town of Chapleau, Ontario, on the evening of July 8, 1913, he was run over and killed by a train.

His masterpiece, on which his reputation rests, received little attention until it was published in book form in Montreal in 1916 and in Paris by Grasset in 1921. Since then the critics, become enthusiastic, have been practically unanimous in proclaiming it as one of the world's great novels. After his death a number of his short stories were found in manuscript and have been published.

See: René Bazin, "L'Auteur de *Maria Chapdelaine:* Louis Hémon, "*Revue des deux mondes,* October 1, 1921, pp. 528–554; L. J. Dalbis, *Le Bouclier canadien-français* (1928); Allan McAndrew, *Louis Hémon; sa vie et son œuvre* (1936).

L. G. M.

Herczeg, Ferenc (1863–, Hungarian playwright, novelist, and short-story writer), was born in Versecz, but has been a resident of Budapest most of his life. His father was the mayor of Versecz; the family was cultured, and the educational and social opportunities of young Herczeg were very good indeed. He studied law at the University of Budapest, but never practiced. There was a short interlude in his life when he hesitated between German and Hungarian writing; then he chose the Hungarian language as his medium of expression. His life is a success story. While he is not intense, he provides a perfect example of a human destiny governed by a rather exceptional ability and by a sense of decorum that has harmonized with the attitude of the gentry. Herczeg's family belonged to the middle class, but his taste—and perhaps his vanity—induced him to seek the company of the ruling "historical classes"; he was accepted by them, in fact he lived, reflected, and acted exactly as a member of that particular social stratum was expected to live, reflect, and act. He knew how to portray the individuals of this class and their idiosyncrasies; his devotion made him observant and forgiving. As the editor of *Uj Idők* (New Times), a popular weekly, and of *Magyar Figyelő* (Hungarian Observer), a political review under the guidance of Count István Tisza, the Hungarian statesman, Herczeg reached both the "bourgeois" and the "historical" elements of the country. In his capacity of writer he represented that sort of entertaining imagination and observation which stimulates but does not profoundly stir. In his ideology he rarely went a step farther than was permissible for a Hungarian gentleman. He made use of almost every literary genre, but it is difficult to say how much of his work promises permanent value. He was appreciated by his nation, especially by his own class, in various ways—politically, socially, in a literary sense. His collected works appeared in 1926.

Herczeg wrote comedies, farces, tragedies, "light" and "heavy" historical and social novels and stories; some of his work has been translated into foreign tongues. Several of his plays were produced on the English and American stage. Yet despite a certain flavor of *savoir-vivre* that reveals a cosmopolitan temperament, Herczeg wrote as a Hungarian spectator for Hungarian spectators and readers. His literary output is extensive, and few of the foibles of human life and the heroic gestures of its nobility have escaped his observation. With the exception of some short stories, one misses a certain warmth in his work, perhaps the kind of warmth without which one is unable to feel the common lot of mankind. It is this lack of warmth, this detachment, that induced certain critics to call Herczeg a snob, yet it would be wrong to say that he was always emotionally arid. He is the literary gentleman with a monocle, unprepared and unwilling to mingle with those not sufficiently well bred to respect good manners. At first glance it seems that problems interested him merely in relation to his prejudices. A more thorough analysis of his entire work, however, shows that his creative spirit recognized deeper problems, and as a result he has written a few novels, stories, and plays where warmth prevails over his customary aloofness. Trifles and great things alike—in plays as well as in stories—were expressed by Herczeg with a certain mastery of composition, albeit in his earlier works his Hungarian language was sometimes stilted and the manner of phrasing seemed rather Teutonic than Magyar. In his later years he conquered this defect.

Of his gay but superficial stories (several of them dramatized) *Gyurkovics lányok* (1893; The Gyurkovics Girls) and *Gyurkovics fiuk* (1895; The Gyurkovics Boys) are the best known. Ludicrous, hilarious, but essentially meaningless scenes and incidents are appropriately portrayed in a light manner. In dealing with his characters—and this applies to later stories and novels too, *e.g., Szabolcs házassága* (1904; The Marriage of Szabolcs) or *Egy leány története* (1904; The Story of a Girl)—Herczeg does not seem dismayed by the shallow existence of his "heroes" and "heroines." He perceives their emptiness, but is amused by their charm or is detached about them. Gradually the atmosphere of his fiction became more serious. In his historical novels, *e.g., Pogányok* (1902; Pagans) and *Az élet kapuja* (1919; Life's Gate), the writer makes us understand certain problems that the Hungarian nation has had to face during its history; he writes with the conscience of a patriot and with the meticulousness of an artist. In his social novels, *e.g., Idegenek közt* (1900; Among Strangers) and *Az arany hegedü* (1916; The Golden Violin), Herczeg reached a level of creative honesty that did not allow him to be blinded by the prejudices of his class. Of course his sympathies and antipathies were always conditioned by the ironic intelligence of one who belonged to the privileged classes; but greed, selfishness, tactlessness, rudeness, "gogetting," received condemnation from him, even when observed in "gentlemen." His comedies are romantic, pleasant, yet somehow second-rate, though never cheap. Of his psychological plays *Kék róka* (1917; Blue Fox) is the best; his best tragedy is *Bizánc* (1904; Byzantium). Some of his historical plays are paraphrased presentations of modern Hungarian problems, *e.g., A hid* (1925; The Bridge). The play *Ocskay brigadéros* (1901; Brigadier Ocskay) is patriotic pyrotechnics. The most definite criticism one might make of Herczeg is that there is no haunting magic in his art; it is efficient, perplexing, entertaining, biased, but never overwhelming.

See: J. Horváth, *Herczeg Ferenc* (1925); M. Rubinyi, *Herczeg Ferenc* (1926); J. Gassner, *Masters of the Drama* (1940).

J. R.

Heredia, José Maria de (1842–1905, French poet), was, in the words of his biographer Ibrovac, an offspring of the Vikings and the conquistadores: he was born in Cuba to a Spanish father, descendant of Don Pedro de Heredia who in 1532 founded a city on the South American coast, and a French mother, one of whose ancestors, Girard d'Ouville, had been *président à mortier* of the Normandy Parliament under Louis XV. Except for two years at the Royal College of Havana, he received his entire education in France, so that it was easy for him to adopt as his own the country and language of his mother. His financial independence enabled him to devote himself to the career of amateur man of letters. In his early 20's he became associated with a group of young poets who, under the leadership of Leconte de Lisle and Banville (*qq.v.*), launched the Parnassian movement, and it was later to be his proudest boast that he was the *élève bien-aimé* of Leconte de Lisle. The six sonnets which he contributed to the 1866 *Parnasse contemporain* and the 25 printed in that of 1876 furnished the nucleus for his only original literary production, *Les Trophées,* a volume projected as early as 1866 but not published until 1893. This work was composed of 118 sonnets, three poems in *terza rima* on episodes from the Spanish *Romancero,* and a 700-line prologue, in alexandrine couplets, to a projected epic on the conquest of Peru (*Les Conquérants de l'or,* which never advanced beyond this stage). It was enthusiastically received, and in the very next year Heredia was elected to the French Academy, where his *discours de réception* evoked high praise. During his last 20 years his apartment, first in the Rue Balzac and then at the Arsenal, of which he was appointed librarian in 1901, was the rendezvous of the literary *tout Paris.* Of his three daughters, the eldest became the wife of the critic René Doumic (*q.v.*), the second, a poet and novelist in her own right who signed herself Gérard d'Houville (*q.v.*), married Henri de Régnier (*q.v.*), and the third married Pierre Louÿs (*q.v.*).

Heredia's place in the history of literature is unique, resting as it does upon a single volume of poems, all but four of which are written in the same form—the strictly regular Petrarchan sonnet. *Les Trophées* is, in several essential respects, a very remarkable work. Unlike most other lyric poets, Heredia is here, in the main, rigorously impersonal in his treatment of his subject matter which is nothing more or less than the history of civilization. The sonnets, grouped under five rubrics ("La Grèce et la Sicile," "Rome et les barbares," "Le Moyen Age et la Renaissance," "L'Orient et les tropiques," and "La Nature et le rêve"), form a series of thumbnail sketches of episodes, personages, and scenes which make of them a miniature *Légende des siècles.* These sketches are written in a language which, for flamboyance and rarity of vocabulary, for sonority of rhythm and richness of rhyme, and for pictorial and sculptural effect, has rarely been surpassed. The sonnets are marvels of condensation and suggestion; whatever their theme—Perseus' rescue of Andromeda, Anthony and Cleopatra before the battle of

Actium, the visit of the Three Wise Kings, the discovery of a hemisphere, a Breton landscape—they are, at one and the same time, as clear-cut as cameos and as evocative as Chopin preludes. They are poetry transmuted into painting, sculpture, and architecture and as such a supreme achievement in the realm of the *transposition d'art.* What they lack in depth of feeling they compensate for in perfection of form. *Les Trophées* constitutes one of the culminating points in the objective and plastic phases of Parnassian poetry.

Heredia also contributed to periodicals a few poems (not included in *Les Trophées*) and articles and made two translations, *Véridique Histoire de la conquête de la Nouvelle Espagne* (4 vols., 1877–1887) from the Spanish of Bernal Díaz del Castillo and *La Nonne Alferez* (1894) from that of Catalina de Erauso. He was coeditor, with André de Guerne, of Leconte de Lisle's *Derniers Poèmes* (1895), and on his death he left a critical edition of André Chénier's *Les Bucoliques,* which was published in 1905.

See: Miodrag Ibrovac, *José-Maria de Heredia; sa vie, son œuvre* (1923) and *Les Sources des Trophées* (1923).

A. S.

Hermann-Neisse, Max (1886–1941, German poet, novelist, and dramatist), was born in Neisse, Silesia, and as a youth went to Berlin. Here, a little man with a large hunchback and a face like the mask of a very old person, he lived a quiet life, devoted only to his literary work and to his wife Leni, whom he glorified in many poems. He started in the ironic and experimental idiom of certain Berlin groups (*Porträte des Provinztheaters,* 1913; *Sie und die Stadt,* 1914), but soon found his own melody in carefully rhymed verses, far removed from the eccentricities of his expressionistic friends. There is almost no development in his work from the early books (*Empörung, Andacht, Ewigkeit,* 1917; *Verbannung,* 1919; *Die Preisgabe,* 1919; *Im Stern des Schmerzes,* 1924; *Einsame Stimme,* 1928; *Abschied,* 1928; *Musik der Nacht,* 1932) to his last two collections of poems, written in exile (*Um uns die Fremde,* 1936; *Letzte Gedichte,* 1941). He also wrote several novels (*Cajetan Schaltermann,* 1920; *Der Flüchtling,* 1921; *Der Todeskandidat,* 1927) and a number of farcelike comedies. But his true literary achievement lies in his poetry, so full of melancholy, accompanied by a little irony and much admiration for the beauties of this world.

K. P.

Hermant, Abel (1862–, French novelist and playwright), was born in Paris. He entered the Ecole Normale Supérieure in 1880 and left it after a year. In 1883 a volume of his verse, *Les Mépris,* was published. He became an outstanding figure in the field of fiction in 1887 with the publication of his third novel, *Le Cavalier Miserey,* a realistic picture of military life. He was elected to the French Academy in 1927—from which he was ejected in 1945 for his allegiance to the political regime of Marshal Pétain.

One of the most prolific writers of our time, Hermant has made important contributions in every genre. His first novels, *Monsieur Rabosson* (1884), *La Mission de Cruchod* (1885), *Le Cavalier Miserey* (1887), *Nathalie Madoré* (1888), were strongly influenced by his masters, the naturalists. After *Les Confidences d'une aïeule* (1893), he developed a style of his own in the manner of the 18th-century satirical novelists. In 1901 *Souvenirs du vicomte de Courpière, par un témoin* marked the beginning of the *Mémoires pour servir à l'histoire de la société,* which ended in 1937 with *La Dernière Incarnation de Monsieur de Courpière.* The whole series (20 volumes) shows Hermant at his best, always witty, at times bitterly sarcastic (see the five volumes on M. de Courpière; the three volumes on the cadet de Coutras; *Les Grands Bourgeois,* 1906; *Les Renards,* 1912), but also serious and discreetly subjective (the four volumes of confessions; the trilogy *D'une guerre à l'autre guerre,* consisting of *L'Aube ardente,* 1919, *La Journée brève,* 1920, *Le Crépuscule tragique,* 1921). Hermant has also written short stories and novelettes (*Eddy et Paddy,* 1895), 20 comedies of manners, two volumes of memoirs (*Souvenirs de la vie frivole,* 1933; *Souvenirs de la vie mondaine,* 1935), several essays and critical studies, and, in the last 20 years, important contributions to the campaign for the preservation of the French language (*Xavier, ou les Entretiens sur la grammaire française,* 1923; *Lettres à Xavier sur l'art d'écrire,* 1925; *Remarques* and *Nouvelles Remarques de M. Lancelot pour la défense de la langue française,* both 1929; *Les Samedis de M. Lancelot,* 1931; *Ainsi parla M. Lancelot,* 1932).

A strict observer of the classical disciplines, Abel Hermant ranks as an admirable stylist, a keen psychologist, the wittiest and most cruel observer of the society of his time.

See: R. Peltier, *Abel Hermant; son œuvre* (1924); A. Thérive, *Essai sur Abel Hermant* (1926); "Hommage à Abel Hermant," *Divan,* XIX (No. 126, February, 1927), 1–108.

M. E. C.

Hérold, André Ferdinand (1865–, French poet and dramatist), grandson of the composer Louis Joseph Ferdinand Hérold, was born in Paris. There, after completing his classical studies, he received a scholarly training at the Ecole des Hautes Etudes and the Ecole des Chartes, with special emphasis on Sanskrit language and literature. From this erudite culture came the main source of inspiration for his dramatic and poetic writings. With remarkable skill he adapted to the French stage several examples of ancient Hindu drama, among them *L'Anneau de Çakuntala* (1895), from the well-known heroic pastoral of the poet Kalidasa. His translations of the masterpieces of Greek tragedy, presented to the public at the Odéon in Paris, include *Les Perses* (1896), *Electre* (1908), *Les Sept contre Thèbes* (1909), and *Andromaque* (1909).

Steeped in the symbolist movement, Hérold utilized the legends of ancient civilizations to illustrate his philosophical and humanitarian ideas, in such poems as *Les Images tendres et merveilleuses* (1897). However, in other collections, restraining his penchant for erudition and his fondness for the past, he expresses with tenderness his own personal emotions, as in *Au hasard des chemins* (1900). He can also render with delicate feeling his impressions of man and nature seen through his temperament. In this mood were conceived *Les Pæans et les thrènes* (1890), *Chevaleries sentimentales* (1893), and *Intermède pastoral* (1896). In all these poems Hérold combines a wealth of images with a learned and rare vocabulary, which only a trained philologist can fully appreciate and understand. In the matter of technique his verse is more or less emancipated in the manner of Verlaine (*q.v.*), but it never reaches the complete freedom of vers libre, which he considers as an inferior medium, at most an interesting experiment. On the other hand, an ardent champion of the new school of poetry, he is perhaps the best theorician of symbolism, which he defined and illustrated in numerous literary reviews and in a course of lectures at the Ecole des Hautes Etudes.

See: Rémy de Gourmont, *Le Livre des masques* (1896); André Barre, *Le Symbolisme* (1912); Adolphe van Bever and Paul Léautaud, *Poètes d'aujourd'hui* (1929).

M. D.

Hervieu, Paul (1857–1915, French novelist and playwright), born at Neuilly-sur-Seine, had a career as lawyer and diplomat. His first literary contributions were signed Eliacin. He became known first as a short-story writer and a novelist with *Diogène le chien* (1882), *L'Alpe homicide* (1886), *L'Inconnu* (1887), *Flirt* (1890); these early works already showed remarkable qualities of analysis.

In 1890 Hervieu wrote his first play, *Point de lendemain,* and two years later *Les Paroles restent.* Then came his two best novels, *Peints par eux-mêmes* (1893), a bitter satire of French society, and *L'Armature* (1895), a study of the importance of money in the modern world. After 1895 he used the theatre as a constant vehicle to expose social evils and suggest their possible cure—*Les Tenailles* (1893), *La Loi de l'homme* (1897), *L'Enigme* (1901), *La Course du flambeau* (1901), *Le Dédale* (1903), *Le Réveil* (1905), *Modestie* (1909), *Connais-toi* (1909), *Bagatelle* (1912), *Le Destin est maître* (1914). A historical drama, *Théroigne de Méricourt* (1902), was the only interruption to this series of problem plays.

Hervieu treats the eternal themes of divorce, family honor, the relationship between parents and children. He writes with an extreme concision and a strict adherence to rules. He continues the tradition of the classic playwright, but his dramas, impeccably put together, suffer from a sort of mathematical logic, from an oversimplification which results in artificiality. His style has often been criticized for its lack of spontaneity and its unnatural pomposity.

See: Charles Malherbe, *Paul Hervieu* (1912); T. D. Barker, "Reading List on Paul Hervieu," *Bulletin of Bibliography,* VIII (1914), 40; Edmond Estève, *Paul Hervieu, conteur, moraliste et dramaturge* (1917); Claude Ferval, *Paul Hervieu* (1917).

M. E. C.

Herzog, Emile, *see* Maurois, André.

Hesse, Hermann (1877–, German novelist and poet), son and grandson of missionaries in India, was born in the Swabian city of Calw, idyllic background of many of his earlier stories. When 13 years old, he decided to become a poet, lost interest in his schoolwork, and was forced to leave the theological preparatory school at Maulbronn; later, in a similar mood, he left the Gymnasium at Cannstatt. While employed as a mechanic in Calw and as a bookseller in Tübingen and Basel, he relentlessly pursued his education through reading.

Hesse became famous through his novel *Peter Camenzind* (1904), the story of the dreamer from the uplands who, after plunging into the decadent artist's life in Paris, finally discovers in the spirit of St. Francis of Assisi the intimate life with nature for which he longs. Hesse's musical prose and delicate portrayal of natural scenery are the outstanding features of his earlier narratives, *e.g., Unterm Rad* (1905), in which a young boy breaking down under the strain of study drowns himself, and *Nachbarn* (1908), where small-town life is pictured with the sympathetic and humorous touch of a Gottfried Keller (*q.v.*). Hesse's qualities are especially apparent in the touching stories of *Knulp* (1915), the beloved vagabond, who brings to everyone happiness and a little longing for freedom and who dies in the blizzard arguing humbly with the Lord over the "futility" of his life. Here and in other stories young Hesse glorifies childhood as the only period when man can abandon himself to his innocent senses and live a full life. After we have crossed the threshold of puberty, life can never be the same for us. Hence the gentle retrospective melancholy pervading these early stories. In 1911 Hesse left his wife and three sons and the beautiful home on Lake Constance and decided upon an extended trip to India. Hesse's marital difficulties are projected into the figure of the famous painter Veraguth in the novel *Rosshalde* (1914).

The First World War threw Hesse into the severest crisis. When he publicly regretted the terrible bloodshed and hatred, he was treated as a traitor and forsaken by his friends. He began to probe ever deeper into his own soul and assumed his full share of personal responsibility for the savagery rampant in Europe. Before he moved to southern Switzerland in 1919, Hesse lived in Bern, a center of psychoanalysis. His psychoanalytical novel *Demian* (1919; Eng. tr., 1923) made a deep impression on the young people emerging from the war. With subtle and searching insight Hesse traces the mental development of a sensitive individual through childhood and adolescence, through revolt and spiritual loneliness, until occult forces guide him to "Frau Eva," who appears as the symbol of creative and all-embracing life. Hesse's relation to the orthodox world of his father and the poet's absorption in Indian mysticism are reflected in *Siddhartha* (1923), the story of the son who must move ever further away from paternal wisdom into a worldly life before he can find his spiritual self. *Der Steppenwolf* (1927; Eng. tr., *Steppenwolf,* 1929), leading into the pleasure world of large cities, is a severe indictment of our present cultureless age. It lays bare the wolfish, infernal instincts that lurk so closely beside our cultured selves. In its deadly seriousness, in its unremitting introspection and psychoanalytic imagery, it is a bewildering novel that aroused much discussion. *Narziss und Goldmund* (1930; Eng. tr., *Death and the Lover,* 1932) is a masterpiece. Narziss, the abbot and ascetic scholar, who lives in a world of lofty abstract thought, is contrasted with Goldmund, his beloved pupil, who leaves the monastery to experience life's pain in mortal danger and guilt and life's rapture as woman after woman offers her love to him. The thinker and the creative artist, each serving God in his own way, are united by bonds of mutual understanding. A novel by Hesse entitled *Das Glasperlenspiel* was published in 1943. Hesse's poetry (*Gedichte,* 1922; *Trost der Nacht,* 1929), alternately sombre, radiant, and idyllic, very melodious, revealing its depth through subtle symbolism, is popular because, steeped in the tradition of German romanticism, it is yet thoroughly modern and personal.

Hesse, "the last of the German romanticists," is a great individualist. The problem of spiritual loneliness occurs again and again in his works. These constitute a continuous effort on his part to find himself, for "man's soul is his fate."

See: Hugo Ball, *Hermann Hesse* (1927); H. R. Schmid, *Hermann Hesse* (1928).

E. Hof.

Heym, Georg (1887–1912, German lyric poet), was born at Hirschberg in Silesia, of an old family of clergymen and civil servants. Having completed the Gymnasium in Berlin, he studied law at Würzburg and Berlin. In January, 1912, while skating on the Havel river near Berlin, he and a friend were drowned. Not yet 25, flashing with life, he went to a death which he had earlier described many times with gruesome joy.

Influenced by Baudelaire and Rimbaud (*qq.v.*), Heym's verses precede German expressionism like a tragic prologue. He was the first in modern German literature who strove for a new release of his consciousness and innermost experience and whose attitude towards life was entirely distinct from that of the naturalists. In his two books of poetry, *Der ewige Tag* (1911) and *Umbra vitae* (1912), even the somber titles indicate some of the recurrent motifs of his verses, written in an eccentric technique. They were breathtaking visions and unheard-of and gigantic allegories in which he tried to reflect the horror and terrible solitude of the modern large cities. Cruelly and inexorably he spoke in his rhythms of the monster Berlin and its soul-devouring dreadfulness. Envisioning a modern

Inferno, he thrust into eternal pain those condemned to the misery and agony of modern cities. All these motifs were presented even more strikingly in the second volume of his poems, published posthumously. The cities, once a goal of yearning for the poets, are now cursed: they are full of evil and hellish demons, and to live in them means endless torture. Combined with such interpretation of the mercilessness of the cities and the resulting melancholy of their inhabitants is an uncanny foreboding of the horrors of modern warfare. In his volume of short stories, *Der Dieb* (1912), the same outcry of a tormented human heart can be heard. There is more in Heym's verses than mere "glimpses in gloom with the phosphorescence of fine poetry." Many motifs of more recent poetry were anticipated by him.

See: A. Ruest, "Ein toter Sänger des Krieges," (*Literarische Echo,* XVII (1914–1915), pp. 391–396; B. Deutsch and A. Yarmolinsky, *Contemporary German Poetry; an Anthology* (1923), pp. xxii–xxiv, 191.

H. Sch.

Heyse, Paul (1830–1914, German novelist and dramatist), was born in Berlin, where both his father and his grandfather, the compiler of a standard dictionary, had been well-known linguists. Paul's mother came from the family of a well-to-do Jewish court jeweler related to the Mendelssohns. He studied the classics at the University of Berlin for two years, chose Romance languages for his specialty, and took a doctor's degree, with a dissertation on the poetry of the troubadours. In 1852 he made his first journey to Italy, the land of his deepest and most lasting sympathies, in order to do research on Provençal manuscripts and in preparation for his career as university lecturer. He returned to Berlin; at the age of 24 he was called to Munich to the court of the Bavarian king, Maximilian II. Here he became a member of the recently established Round Table of the King, and the guarantee of a generous honorarium freed him for the rest of his life from all financial worries. Although he had at this time published only a few romantic stories and verses, one tragedy, and one short story (his renowned *L'Arrabbiata,* which, from a technical point of view, he never surpassed), Heyse abandoned Romance philology and settled in the Bavarian capital. Soon he shared the honor of being a leading member of the new "Münchener Dichterkreis" with his friend the poet Emanuel Geibel, to whose recommendation he owed the original royal invitation. Shortly after his arrival in Munich, Heyse married, but his wife died in 1862. Though he found happiness in a second marriage in 1867, he went through many personal sorrows; his amazing literary productiveness, however, was not affected. When King Maximilian II died in 1864, his successor, Ludwig II, known for his enthusiastic patronage of Richard Wagner (*q.v.*), generously continued the stipend. In the last years of the century Heyse became one of the most bitter enemies of the naturalistic and impressionistic schools of writers, although he was a good friend of Ibsen's (*q.v.*) during the latter's stay in Munich. He disliked what he considered the naturalistic reveling in the baser aspects of life; he felt that German letters had taken a trend which he was unable to follow. This animosity led to passionate attacks upon him by some of the representatives of other literary schools. After many years of fame Heyse now experienced personal hostility and even oblivion. In 1910, however, the Nobel prize was awarded to him—the first German writer so honored—in recognition of the fact that he was one of the finest craftsmen of the German 19th-century novel. A few months before the outbreak of the First World War, Heyse died in his Munich home.

In the course of his long life Heyse produced about 120 *Novellen,* six large novels, numerous narrative and lyric poems, some 60 plays, and many translations from Italian, Spanish, and English literature. Much of the translation is masterly, above all the versions of modern Italian poets such as Giusti and Leopardi. Among his *Novellen* the best are *L'Arrabbiata* (1855; Eng. tr., 1855), *Das Mädchen von Treppi* (1858; Eng. trs., *The Maiden of Treppi, Love's Victory,* both 1874), *Andrea Delfin* (1859; Eng. tr., 1864), and *Der Weinhüter von Meran* (1864). Many of the tales have an Italian background and served to stimulate the imagination of those who, faithful to the old German yearning, drew their inspiration from Italy. Among his long novels is *Kinder der Welt* (1872; Eng. tr., *Children of the World,* 1882). None of the 60 plays was a stage success. All in all, Heyse was a brilliant if at times unduly conscious representative of German realism.

See: Heyse, *Jugenderinnerungen und Bekenntnisse* (2 vols.; 5th ed., 1912); A. Farinelli, *Paul Heyse* (1913).

H. Sch.

Hilbert, Jaroslav (1871–1936, Czech dramatist), is the most important Czech playwright before the First World War. He was born in

Louny, but spent most of his life in Prague as a journalist and theatre critic and there he died. *Vina* (1896; The Guilt) was one of the greatest successes of the Prague National Theatre. It came at a time when Ibsen (*q.v.*) had begun to penetrate into Bohemia and when the theatre had a group of excellent actors (especially Hana Kvapilová and Edvard Vojan) of this new naturalistic style. *Vina* is an extremely effective imitation of Ibsen and portrays a sensitive, "fallen" girl who perishes by the consciousness of her guilt and the brutality of the man. *O Boha* (1898; Of God), later renamed *Pěst* (The Fist), is a religious drama depicting the revolt of a desperate mother against God and his decrees, while *Psanci* (1900; The Outlaws) analyzes the problems of decadence in a style which attempts symbolism in a realistic setting reminiscent of the later Ibsen. Hilbert outgrew the Ibsen period and turned to history as a source of material for his plays. *Falkenštejn* (1903) has a hero whose desire for liberty is crushed by small-minded neighbors and the treachery of his wife; *Kolumbus* (1915; Columbus) interprets the character of the explorer as that of a great man cheated of his just reward by fate and by his contemporaries. After the war Hilbert turned to plays drawn from the life of the Prague bourgeoisie which he judges with stern, conservative ethical standards and finds corrupt and materialistic. *Druhý břeh* (1924; The Second Shore) is a well-constructed and extremely effective acting play. *Blíženci* (1931; The Twins) is drawn from the heroic story of the Czech legions in Siberia, and *Michael* (1935) turns to the conflict of aristocracy and bourgeoisie. The numerous comedies and some prose are of less importance. Hilbert had a fine sense of the stage; he was a strong moralist with clear conceptions, but the very rationalism of his mind, the hardheaded speculation, make his plays cerebral and, in a curious manner, dated.

See: J. Knap, *Hilbert; případ české dramatiky* (1926).

R. W.

Hille, Peter (1854–1904, German poet, novelist, and playwright), was born in Erwitzen, Westphalia. He was a schoolmate in Münster of Heinrich and Julius Hart (*q.v.*), in whose school paper his first poems appeared and who remained his friends and admirers throughout his strange life. A true poet and mystic, this wayward genius, following an insatiable wanderlust, roamed about Europe as a poor, penniless tramp, happy and content with his lot, having neither wants nor ambitions and enjoying the beauty of the world with childlike faith and wonder. According to his biographer Heinrich Hart, he never lacked ideas. He would jot them down on any available scrap of paper and then stuff the paper into his pocket or into a sack in which he carried his few belongings. It is not surprising that most of Peter Hille's writing was fragmentary and not published until after his death, when it was collected and edited by the Harts. Hille failed whenever he attempted more ambitious works, as in his novels (*Die Sozialisten,* 1887; *Die Hassenburg,* 1905) or in *Des Platonikers Sohn* (1896), the only play he completed. They are deficient in structure and lacking in development. His domain was the prose sketch, marked by striking aphorisms, and the short lyrical poem expressing a variety of moods. To quote Julius Hart: "His art explains too little and does not organize its material, does not subject it to any unifying purpose. It is no art of order and composition, of plans and rules, but full of intangible suggestions and strong sense impressions, born from absorbing observation and sincere emotional response."

See: H. Hart, *Peter Hille* (1904).

O. S. F.

Hippius, Zinaida Nikolayevna (1869–1945, Russian poet, essayist, and critic), born in Belev, Tula Province, came of an old Germanic family of nobles. As a child she traveled much in Russia with her family, to Saratov, Kharkov, St. Petersburg, Moscow. In her youth Hippius was sickly, and the doctors suspected congenital tuberculosis; the family therefore moved to Yalta in 1884. Although she attended no school, Hippius was an avid reader and was particularly fond of Nadson's (*q.v.*) poetry, but her own poetic experiments little resembled his verses. In 1888, while in Tiflis, Hippius met D. S. Merezhkovski (*q.v.*), who had recently launched on his literary career. They were married the following year and moved to St. Petersburg, where they began to cultivate literary friends; their home eventually became a salon for modernist writers and philosophers. Hippius was the life of these gatherings, and it was largely due to her efforts that meetings of the Religious-Philosophical Society were organized in 1901–1902. She also was instrumental in establishing the periodical *Novy put* (1903–1909; The New Path). Her charm, wit, and shrewd analytical ability were greatly esteemed. In 1905–1906 the Merezhkovskis displayed sympathy for the revolutionary movement and were obliged to leave the country for several years. In the course of the next decade, however, their political opinions underwent a definite change, and after the October Revolution they emigrated and joined the anti-Soviet camp of Russians abroad.

Although Hippius wrote some short stories (*Zerkala*, 1897; The Mirrors), novelettes, and dramas (*Chyortova kukla*, 1911, The Devil's Doll; *Roman-Tsarevich*, 1914; *Zelyonoye koltso*, 1914, The Green Ring), her prose fiction is inferior to her poetry and criticism. Her prose works show the influence of Dostoevski (*q.v.*) modified by that of modern decadence. Unlike her prose, which at times shows an awareness of social problems, Hippius's poetry is quite detached from reality. Her verse—she did not create in quantity and wrote only when she "felt she could not do otherwise"—presents a curious blend of devout religious mysticism and decadent aestheticism often touched with perversity. Her first two books of verse, entitled *Sobraniye stikhov* (Vol. I, 1904, Vol. II, 1910; A Collection of Poems), contain her finest poetry. Her critical essays, *Literaturnyi dnevnik* (1911; A Literary Diary), display a penetrating brilliance rare in journalism. After the Revolution, Hippius wrote two books of essays, *Chernaya knizhka* (1924; The Black Book) and *Sinyaya kniga* (1929; The Blue Book), in which she gave vent to her violent antipathy to the Soviet regime. She also produced a series of literary sketches, *Zhivyia litsa* (1924; Living Faces). Her work of the last two decades has little literary merit.

See: V. Bryusov, "Z. N. Hippius," in S. A. Vengerov, ed., *Russkaya literatura XX veka*, I (1914), 178–188.

O. M.

Hlaváček, Karel (1874–1898, Czech poet), was a prominent poet of the Czech "decadence." He was born in a suburb of Prague, the son of a laborer, and made a precarious living as draftsman and illustrator. He died of tuberculosis at the age of 24. His poetry combines the technique of symbolism and the melancholy *fin-de-siècle* mood with a proletarian's hatred for the rich and powerful. *Pozdě k ránu* (1896; Early, towards Morning) contains melodious, dreamy lyrics somewhat in the style of Verlaine (*q.v.*), while *Mstivá kantiléna* (1898; The Revengeful Cantilene) uses the masque of the 17th-century *gueux* to express the poet's desperate struggle against death and his revolt against social oppression. The contrast between the sophisticated and artificial technique and the raw content is frequently remarkable. A collection of prose poems, *Žalmy* (Psalms), was not published until 1934.

See: F. Soldan, *Karel Hlaváček, typ české dekadence* (1930); J. Mukařovský, introduction to Hlaváček, *Žalmy* (1934); F. X. Šalda, *Mladé zápasy* (1934).

R. W.

Hoel, Sigurd (1890–, Norwegian novelist and critic), has two major strings to his bow, the post-war, urban milieu of Oslo and the memories of a rural childhood in Nord-Odal. From a scientific course at the university he turned to teaching, but has mostly worked as a journalist and literary critic. He is noted as a purveyor of European and American literature to his countrymen, having translated such writers as Faulkner, Conrad, and Erskine Caldwell, and having edited a series of translations with introductions, the latter published separately as *50 gule* (1939; 50 Yellow-jacketed Books). These brilliant critiques reveal a subtle, ironic mind, averse to sentimentality, inclined to view the world intellectually rather than emotionally. His novels and short stories show in addition a certain awareness of Freudian doctrine, and in technique they are comparable to the stories of Vicki Baum and Ernest Hemingway. Human problems in a post-war world occupied him from the start, in the short stories of *Veien vi gaar* (1922; The Road We Travel) and the novel *Syvstjernen* (1924; The Pleiades). Hoel's characters are usually rootless figures in earnest search of happiness and are all too often frustrated in their longing. The theme is graciously and amusingly handled in *Syndere i sommersol* (1927; Eng. tr., *Sinners in Summertime*, 1930), wherein a group of intellectual youth attempt in vain to take love lightly and cynically. The young man in *Ingenting* (1929; Nothing) finds exactly what the title states. *En dag i oktober* (1931; Eng. tr., *One Day in October*, 1932) is the tragicomic story of how bourgeois society stamps out happiness because it fears its effects. Both in this book and in *Fjorten dager før frostnettene* (1935; Fourteen Days before the Frost Nights) we meet the intellectual who is unable to assimilate love into his life. *Sesam sesam* (1938; Open Sesame) is a witty and malicious satire on the literary life of a European capital. In the meanwhile Hoel had created a deeper form in his stories of childhood, *Veien til verdens ende* (1933; Road to the World's End), and *Prinsessen på glassberget* (1939; The Princess on the Glass Mountain). Both titles are drawn from well-known Norwegian child's stories, and the books are simply but cleverly told reconstructions of a child's view of the world. Here too there are happinesses and frustrations, the material out of which Hoel's modern world is created.

Hoel wrote critical articles of importance in *Samtiden* (1924, 1925, 1929) and also a defense of his own writing (1932); there followed a caustic analysis by Eugenia Kielland and a reply by Arnulf Överland (*Samtiden*, 1934).

See: K. Elster, "Sigurd Hoel," in *Norsk biografisk leksikon* VI (1934), 171–173.

E. H.

Hofmannsthal, Hugo von (1874–1929, Austrian poet, dramatist, novelist, and essayist), was born in Vienna and died in near-by Rodaun in a charming baroque mansion which he had occupied since his marriage in 1901. Except for summers spent in the Austrian Alps and travels throughout Europe, especially Italy, he did not leave the vicinity of the capital of the old empire whose great literary representative he was. In his own ancestry as in that ancient community of nations were mixed many races and many classes—Austrian peasants, Jewish merchants, and Lombard patricians. In his mind as on the cosmopolitan scene of the Hapsburg Empire lived many regions and many ages—oriental dream, occidental thought, and Mediterranean form. This diversity was to him both a blessing and a burden, but he increasingly realized that it was a part of his Austrian heritage. Such an inheritance, too, was Hofmannsthal's lifelong obsession with the theatre and opera, those great forms of the baroque from which Austrian culture stems. Strengthened by this tradition, Hofmannsthal and his friends of *Jungwien*, Arthur Schnitzler, Richard Beer-Hofmann, and Hermann Bahr (*qq.v.*), were but little affected by the Berlin naturalism. Rather they sailed in that European current which is insufficiently defined as "neo-romanticism" or "symbolism." Hofmannsthal's true contemporaries and his only peers in German letters are Stefan George (*q.v.*), with whom he had a short but significant association (see *Briefwechsel zwischen George und Hofmannsthal*, 1938), and R. M. Rilke (*q.v.*).

Hofmannsthal's beginnings as a writer were marked by astonishing precocity. At the age of 16 his first verses were published, at 17 his first play (*Gestern*) and the first of his illuminating essays on the modern writers of Italy, France, England, and Scandinavia. At 18 he reached maturity as a master of German verse, and a small group of poems and a series of short plays written within the seven following years are of matchless beauty. Among the latter are *Der Tod des Tizian* (1892; Eng. tr., *Death of Titian*, 1913), a hymn on the unity of art and life; *Der Tor und der Tod* (1893; Eng. tr., *Death and the Fool*, 1913), the condemnation and redemption of an aesthete; *Alkestis* (1895), a drama of vicarious death; *Der Kaiser und die Hexe* (1896), an eerie play of enchantment and deliverance; *Das kleine Welttheater* (1897), a mysterious pageant of life; *Der Abenteurer und die Sängerin* (1899; Eng. tr., *The Adventurer and the Singer*, 1917), about the grandeur and the misery of the adventurer; *Die Hochzeit der Sobeide* (1899; Eng. tr., *The Marriage of Sobeide*, 1913), about youthful dream and disenchantment; and *Das Bergwerk von Falun* (1899), an initiation into the mystery of existence. Hardly two of these are alike, but they are all united by their rare blending of grace with wisdom and their intense awareness of the magic of the world.

Hofmannsthal had reached in this early work an apogee; the youthful state of inspiration that had been his could not be prolonged without insincerity. As he emerged from an inner crisis he resumed his work on another plane. Hofmannsthal's middle period is marked by an outward expansion. He strove to master the form of high tragedy reinterpreting old dramatic themes, such as *Elektra* (1903; Eng. tr., *Electra*, 1908), *Ödipus und die Sphinx* (1906), and *Das gerettete Venedig* (1905; Eng. tr., *Venice Preserved*, 1915), after Otway. He entered the field of comedy in *Cristinas Heimreise* (1910; Eng. tr., *Christina's Journey Home*, 1917), *Der Rosenkavalier* (1911; Eng. tr., *The Rose-Bearer*, 1912), and *Ariadne auf Naxos* (1912; Eng. tr., *Ariadne on Naxos*, 1913). The last two, as well as *Elektra*, were set to music by the composer Richard Strauss (see their *Briefwechsel*, 1926, Eng. tr., 1927), for whom Hofmannsthal subsequently wrote *Die Frau ohne Schatten* (1919), *Die ägyptische Helena* (1928), and *Arabella* (1933), all of them literary creations in their own right. The increased interest in the theatre that is manifested in this association resulted also in collaboration with the producer Max Reinhardt, for whom Hofmannsthal translated and adapted plays by Sophocles, Calderón, and Molière as well as the old *Everyman* (*Jedermann*, 1911; Eng. tr., *The Play of Everyman*, 1917). This was the period of Hofmannsthal's greatest public success.

For some years, however, an inner transformation had been preparing in the poet's mind when the outbreak of the war and subsequently the fall of Austria painfully interrupted the outward expansion of his life and work and turned him to introspection into the roots of his existence. He became now more than ever an ardent interpreter and advocate of his native land and its European mission. In *Der Rosenkavalier* and in the novel *Andreas,* begun before the war and published posthumously (1932; Eng. tr., 1936) as a beautiful fragment, he had already returned to the native scene. Now he portrayed the Austrian character in the delightful comedy *Der Schwierige* (1921). In the Salzburg Festivals which he founded with Max Reinhardt he undertook to carry on Austria's theatrical mission as he saw it. To these festivals he dedicated *Das Salzburger Grosse Welttheater* (1922), in which he refashioned Calderón's dramatic allegory into an expression of his enlightened conservatism. He proclaimed a "conservative revolution" in his speech *Das Schrifttum als geistiger Raum der Nation* (1927). His desire to safeguard a European heritage which he saw threatened from below and without now pervades every word of his, written or spoken. Hofmannsthal's production during these years culminates in two works—the symbolic tale *Die Frau ohne Schatten* (1919), a fuller treatment of the subject of his opera and the key to his personal and poetic being, and the gigantic dramatic composition *Der Turm* (1923; new version, 1927), an attempt to interpret the spiritual as well as the political revolution of his time and to ban the evil forces whose rampant growth he watched with clairvoyant anxiety. *Der Turm* is the only one completed of many dramatic plans found in Hofmannsthal's papers (see *Semiramis,* 1933; *Dramatische Entwürfe aus dem Nachlass,* 1936; etc.) in which he seemed to strive for a new dramatic form, a symbolic realism, inspired by Calderón and the drama of the baroque, and full development of which was interrupted by his untimely death.

Rarely has a poet commanded such a wealth of different materials, moods, and manners. There is the magic of the *Arabian Nights* and the severity of the medieval morality, the passionate uproar of Dionysian Greece and the morbid charm of dying Venice, the rustic purity of Carinthian peasants and the mellow abundance of the Renaissance, the naïve grace of Mozartian rococo and the apocalyptic gloom of the baroque. In this pageant of masques, where is the author's own face? This question is relevant, for his was a sensitivity that in great moments endowed him with a feeling of mystical identity with every life however remote from his own. He proclaimed the glory of this state in the characters of emperors and spirits, of artists and lovers, he revealed it in childhood and wealth, in magic and madness. But he is also aware of its ambiguous nature—its inhumanity and its impotence. The aesthete in his ivory tower, the beautiful but barren woman, the actor who is never himself, the adventurer who is not twice the same, are among the symbols which express the doubtful aspects of that privilege. It may become angels or children, but men must accept life, however ugly and sordid it be and even though they may have to pay for it with guilt and pain. The "way into life" now becomes Hofmannsthal's leading theme. It may be achieved by love or by deed, by marriage or parenthood or by assuming one's position in the order of society and in the continuity of history. Thus the mystical strain in Hofmannsthal's work is complemented by another that may truly be called moral. These two knit his work into one, lending it a profundity beneath the beauty of its surface that was overlooked by many of his earlier critics. Since Hofmannsthal's death his greatness as a poet has been increasingly recognized, but the interpretation of his work is only beginning.

Hofmannsthal's *Gesammelte Werke* (3 vols., 1934) are supplemented by a number of posthumous publications in addition to those mentioned above, including *Nachlese der Gedichte* (1934); two volumes of prose, *Loris* (1930) and *Berührung der Sphären* (1931); two volumes of letters, *Briefe 1890–1901* (1935) and *Briefe 1900–1909* (1937); and many miscellaneous papers in the journal *Corona* (1930–1943). A complete edition in 12 volumes, edited by H. Steiner, has begun to appear (1946–).

See: G. Schaeder, *Hugo von Hofmannsthal* (1933); K. J. Krüger, *Hugo von Hofmannsthal und Richard Strauss* (1935); C. J. Naef, *Hugo von Hofmannsthals Wesen und Werk* (1938), with bibliography by Herbert Steiner; Jethro Bithell, *Modern German Literature, 1880–1938* (1939).

R. A.

Högberg, Olof (1855–1932, Swedish novelist and amateur ethnologist), is notable in Swedish literature for one monumental novel, *Den stora vreden* (The Great Wrath), portions of which first appeared as a prize novel in 1906 in the Swedish women's magazine *Idun,* where

Selma Lagerlöf's (*q.v.*) famous *Gösta Berlings saga* had first appeared 15 years earlier. Högberg has written other novels, such as *Baggbölingar* (1911), *Utbölingar* (1912), and *Storfursten av Lappland* (1915; The Grand Duke of Lapland); but these are of no importance as compared with the strange, many-faceted *Den stora vreden,* in part a stirring provincial chronicle from pagan times down to the early 18th century, in part a magnificent fragment of natural history, in part a treasure trove of Arctic mythology and folklore. Högberg was born into an old peasant family from the semi-Arctic province of Ångermanland. After completing his education at the University of Uppsala, he returned to his native province as a teacher and journalist, driven by a never flagging interest in the folk life and folk superstitions of his native province and a consuming desire to give this material adequate literary form. *Den stora vreden* was the result of 20 years of struggle with this strange and diversified material. Though the work lacks literary finish in the usual sense of the term, it is powerfully conceived and written in a bold, harsh, crudely intense prose style that seems the only fitting medium for the fantastic miscellany of material which is poured with such rich and primitive abandon into the book. Important as the book is in itself, it is unquestionably more important as the work which "discovered" the far north of Sweden as a vast, seemingly inexhaustible source of inspiration and of subject matter for imaginative literary treatment. Since Olof Högberg many Swedish writers of prose fiction have employed these materials with success (Ludvig Nordström, Ernst Didring, *qq.v.,* Gustaf Hedenvind-Eriksson, Hildur Dixelius-Brettner, Astrid Väring, and others), and in each case Högberg's *Den stora vreden* has left its imprint upon these authors. Högberg did for this section of the country what Selma Lagerlöf and Gustaf Fröding (*qq.v.*) did for the province of Värmland, what Karlfeldt (*q.v.*) did for Dalecarlia, what A. U. Bååth and Ola Hansson (*qq.v.*) did for Skåne.

Högberg's work is perhaps to be compared most directly with that of Selma Lagerlöf, though *Den stora vreden* differs in certain essential respects from *Gösta Berlings saga.* Högberg's novel, like Selma Lagerlöf's, is primarily a folk epic, in which the author serves simply as the modern literary intermediary in grouping and retelling old tales of the folk. In this retelling both authors are deeply gripped by their materials and treat them with an imaginative intensity and a lyrical fervor seldom found in Swedish prose fiction. But Högberg's work is stylistically far more primitive, more directly the property of "the folk"; and in general structure it is somewhat less unified than is *Gösta Berlings saga,* chiefly because its materials are more diversified and inclusive, going back much farther in time for their origins and including a much more massive and complicated body of folk traditions. As a literary phenomenon it may well be said, indeed, that *Den stora vreden* is all but unique in the annals of Swedish literature. In modern literature in general it finds perhaps its closest counterpart in Alexis Kivi's Finnish folk epic *Seitsemän veljestä* (1870; Eng. tr., *Seven Brothers,* 1929).

See: Ludvig Nordström, "Olof Högberg," *Ord och bild,* XXX (1921), 319–330.

A. G.

Holeček, Josef (1853–1929, Czech novelist and poet), is the author of an enormous 10-volume cycle of novels depicting Czech peasant life. Holeček was born in Stožice near Vodňany (southern Bohemia) and became a journalist. He was a war correspondent and frequent traveler in the Balkans and also visited Russia. He died in Prague. In his early years he wrote much about Yugoslavia, especially Montenegro, an interest which led to his translation of the Yugoslav heroic folk poetry (*Srbská národní epika,* 4 vols., 1909–1926; Serbian National Epics) and to imitation of its style in original poetry about Yugoslav heroes (*e.g., Sokolovič,* 1922). Holeček also translated the Finnish national epic, *Kalevala* (5 vols., 1894–1896). But the cycle of novels, *Naši* (10 vols., 1898–1930; Our People), is his most important work. It attempts to present a complete study of the Czech peasant in southern Bohemia as he was before the advent of industrialization. The action covers the years 1840–1866 and centers around an ideal peasant, a "strong Christian," Kojan. The plot is poorly organized and of little interest compared to Holeček's penetrating analysis of the Czech peasant, of his religious and social problems, and a wonderfully vivid and detailed picture is presented of his customs, superstitions, legends, and beliefs. The book is permeated by a conservative agrarian ideology of strong Christian coloring. Holeček was influenced by the Russian Slavophiles, though his religious thought is primitive general Christianity rather than that of any particular denomination. Holeček preaches love for the soil, for family, community, and nation, with a strong accent on

Pan-Slavism. He depicts the struggle of the peasant with the landlord and the usurer and succeeds in creating sharply individualized types. The books—especially the first three volumes—can be compared with Reymont's (*q.v.*) *The Peasants,* not merely as a documentary novel with folkloristic information, but also as a searching analysis of the peasant's soul which to Holeček was identical with the soul of the nation.

See: J. Voborník, *Josef Holeček* (1913); E. Chalupný, *Dílo Josefa Holečka* (1926).

R. W.

Holstein, Ludvig, Greve (1864–1943, Danish lyrical poet), was born in fertile southern Zealand. He studied in Copenhagen and was for years connected with the publishing firm Gyldendal. His outwardly uneventful life is reflected in his poetry. In his best poems Holstein is one of the finest representatives of Danish neo-romanticism and symbolism, to which Helge Rode (*q.v.*) also belongs. Throughout his whole life Holstein remained close to nature. His themes are preeminently Danish: the beechtree with its "tin-grey" trunk, the apple in bloom in the spring and fragrant with fruit in the fall, the bewitching summer nights, the Northerner's longing for and exultation over "the good sun," "the gentle sun." Holstein's meter is varied, but always musical; alliteration occurs frequently. An aristocratic restraint characterizes his love poems. In one, the poet even warns us that "the heart's happiness" must be cared for like a costly garden, weeded, and protected against scorching rays.

In Holstein's production a lull of almost two decades occurs. During the first period, which brings *Digte* (1895, Poems; included is the haunting "Far, hvor flyver Svanerne hen?" Father, Where Do the Wild Swans Go?) and the lyrical love drama *Tove* (1898), an undercurrent of sadness runs, at times half-hidden below the fresh gayety. In the second period —ushered in by the poet's marriage—from 1915 on, optimism prevails in the poem collections *Løv* (1915; Leaves), *Mos og Muld* (1917; Moss and Mould), *Aebletid* (1920; Appletime), *Hymner og Viser* (1922; Hymns and Songs), and *Jehi* (1929; Become). Sadness, when it does occur, is deepened into sorrow. Decidedly earthy, realistic traits crop up. The poet's conscious feeling of his deeprootedness in Denmark brings abiding happiness. Nature is now clearly pantheistic. One spirit rules behind myriad manifestations (see "Vaaren"; Spring). The feeling of continuity, everlastingness, stands out. The poet meets everywhere the miracles of nature (the only miracles). Holstein's credo is reiterated in the religious-philosophical essay *Den grønne Mark* (1925; The Green Field)—"Root, know your crown; crown, know your root," the poet exhorts. In *Jehi* Holstein's poetry becomes cosmic.

See: C. Ludwigs, "Ludvig Holstein," in Ejnar Skovrup, ed., *Hovedtraek af nordisk Digtning i Nytiden,* I (1920), 129–134; Helge Kjaergaard, *Die dänische Literatur der neuesten Zeit (1871–1933)* (1934).

C. K. B.

Holz, Arno (1863–1929, German poet, literary theorist, and dramatist), was born in the East Prussian city of Rastenburg. In 1875 his family moved to Berlin, and the boy was brought into contact with the modern urban life that he was to make the subject of his first important volume of verse, *Das Buch der Zeit* (1886). His lyric apprenticeship was served in the school of Emmanuel Geibel and Julius Wolff and showed none of his later radicalism (*e.g., Deutsche Weisen,* 1884, with Otto Jerschke).

Holz's real career, typical of the radical and experimental nature of German literature in the last decades of the nineteenth century, started with the naturalistic revolution, of which *Das Buch der Zeit* is an important document with its interest in social problems and the modern city and its enthusiasm for Zola and Ibsen (*qq.v.*). In 1885 Holz was one of the contributors to the naturalistic anthology *Moderne Dichter-Charaktere.* His major contribution to German naturalistic theory was *Die Kunst, ihr Wesen und ihre Gesetze* (1891), an exposition of the theory of so-called *konsequenter Naturalismus.* In this essay Holz attempted to formulate an aesthetic theory which should exclude the subjective element from artistic creation and give naturalism a logical, objective theoretic basis. In reality, its extreme ideas undermined the naturalistic position. More important than his theory was his collaboration with Johannes Schlaf (*q.v.*) in writing, under the joint pseudonym Bjarne P. Holmsen, *Papa Hamlet* (1889), a phonetic and photographic reproduction of reality. This with the drama *Die Familie Selicke* (1890), produced by the Freie Bühne in the same year, and *Neue Gleise* (1892) was of great influence in the development of Gerhart Hauptmann (*q.v.*) and the naturalistic drama in general. With the decline of German naturalism, Holz turned back to the lyric with a volume of modernistic poetry, *Phantasus* (1898–1899). In 1899 was published *Die Revolution der Lyrik,* a theoretic defense of his new poetic technique in which he championed a poetic form that should be a direct expression of the subject matter, avoiding rhyme and strophe, a form that is not "free" but "natural" verse. Typographically the lines are centered on the page and not aligned with the left-hand margin, the so-called *Mittelachse* verse. His later career produced further volumes of lyrics, such as *Dafnis; lyrisches Porträt aus dem 17. Jahrhundert* (1904), and several dramas, among them *Traumulus* (1904), written with Otto Jerschke, and *Sonnenfinsternis* (1908), a tragedy. His works appeared in 10 volumes in 1924 under the title *Das Werk von Arno Holz.*

See: O. E. Lessing, *Die neue Form* (1910); R. Ress, *Arno Holz und seine künstlerische Bedeutung* (1913); K. Turley, *Arno Holz* (1935).

W. H. R.

Hora, Josef (1891–1945, Czech poet), was, next to Wolker (*q.v.*), the most outstanding member of the group who composed "proletarian" verse, and he later developed into a writer of metaphysical reflection and meditation of considerable power. He was born in Dobřín near Roudnice (north of Prague) and became a journalist, first with the Communist and then with the Socialist press. He began as a follower of S. K. Neumann (*q.v.*). Two collections, *Strom v květu* (1920; The Tree in Bloom) and *Pracující den* (1920; The Working Day), established him in the group of proletarian poets. But his enthusiasm for the revolution was even then tempered by a desire for individual integrity and by a frankly contradictory longing for escape from the masses and from towns. *Srdce a vřava světa* (1922; The Heart and the Tumult of the World) constitutes the break with the rhetoric of the proletarians and his return to the forms of folk poetry as well as to themes of nature, home, quiet, and even an unproletarian loneliness. The change is complete in *Italie* (1925; Italy), which is ostensibly a travel diary. In this the poet achieved a style of almost classical serenity and severity. The later collections, among which *Struny ve větru* (1927; Strings in the Wind) is perhaps the best, offer a new metaphysical quality. Meditations on time and the universe, nourished by the reading of William James, Bergson (*q.v.*), and modern physics, acute realizations of the dreamlike character of existence, testify to a degree of spiritualization rare in recent Czech verse. *Máchovské variace* (1936; Variations on a Theme of Mácha) celebrates the great Czech romantic poet on the hundredth anniversary of his death and demonstrates the author's own affinity with romantic themes and forms. This is also obvious in the more recent volume, *Jan houslista* (1940; John the Violinist), a slight, sentimental story with an early-19th-century flavor about the return of a great violinist from America to his downtrodden native country. The convention disguises the author's profound and very personal despair over life and the fate of his nation. Besides these main collections Hora wrote a book of ballads, *Tonoucí stíny* (1933; Drowning Shadows), some verse satires, and some less impressive novelistic prose. In his later years he was extremely successful as a translator of verse; his paraphrase (1937) of Pushkin's *Onegin* is a masterpiece comparable to the finest achievements of Otokar Fischer (*q.v.*). Hora, apparently an out and out modernist and prophet of the coming revolution, found his way back to the sources of poetry in Slavic romanticism, in Mácha and Pushkin and their melancholy. Hora died in July, 1945, and was honored by a state funeral and the newly created title of "national poet."

See: F. X. Šalda, *O nejmladší poesii české* (1928); A. M. Píša, *Proletářská poesie* (1936).

R. W.

Houville, Gérard d' (pseud. of Marie Louise Antoinette de Heredia, 1875–, French poet and prose writer), was born in Paris. Most of the 89 poems that comprise her one volume of poetry were originally published in the *Revue des deux mondes* from 1894 to 1919; others appeared in the *Renaissance latine* and the *Revue hebdomadaire.* The first poems were signed with a triple X, but later she adopted the pseudonym Gérard d'Houville. Her collected verse, entitled *Les Poésies de Gérard d'Houville,* was published in an *édition de luxe* in 1930, in regular edition in 1931. Daughter of the well-known Parnassian poet, José Maria de Heredia, and wife of the symbolist poet, Henri de Régnier (*qq.v.*), Gérard d'Houville shows certain characteristics of both, though she is not directly influenced by either. Like her famous father she was attracted by classical subjects; many of her poems revive the atmosphere and legends of Greek and Roman antiquity with new imagery and interpretations. Like Heredia also she sometimes paints objective, colorful scenes. Strangely enough the daughter of Heredia has written only one sonnet. In the symbolist vein she often demonstrates a love of abstractions and analogies, a preoccupation with musical effects, but, unlike Mallarmé (*q.v.*) and many of his disciples, she is never obscure. Allusions to romantic love are frequent, but her treatment of this passion differs from that of a typically romantic poet such as the comtesse de Noailles (*q.v.*); whereas the latter is inclined to be exalted and tragic, Gérard d'Houville is more often tender and melancholy. Favorite themes are death and the passing of youth, both of which Gérard d'Houville dreads with a very feminine and pagan fervor. Besides elegies in the antique manner and reminiscences of childhood, including nostalgic reveries about her creole ancestors and their land which she never saw, there are impressions of Paris and of travels in foreign lands; three poems inspired by maternal love, and many meditations on the spiritual aspect of human experience. All her poems are modeled on conventional verse forms, and classic clarity of thought and expression is a distinctive quality of her graceful and harmonious style.

As a prose writer Gérard d'Houville has won much admiration and acclaim. In the early part of the century she wrote regular *chroniques* for the *Gaulois;* later she contributed to other Paris periodicals, notably the *Revue des deux mondes* and *Figaro,* where she replaced Robert de Flers (*q.v.*) as dramatic critic after his death in 1927. In 1918 she was the first woman to be awarded the Grand Prix de Littérature by the French Academy. Her prose works include several novels, one of which (*Le Roman des quatre,* 1923) was in collaboration with Paul Bourget, Pierre Benoit (*qq.v.*), and Henri Duvernois, short stories, essays, plays, travel sketches, stories for children, prefaces, and a book of prose poems about flowers (*Le Diadème des flores,* 1925, *édition de luxe* with woodcuts by A. E. Marty).

See: Charles Maurras, "Le Romantisme féminin," in *L'Avenir de l'intelligence* (1905); Jean de Gourmont, *Les Muses d'aujourd'hui* (1910); Y. G. Le Dantec, "Gérard d'Houville, poète," *Muse française,* January 10, 1931.

C. B. C.

Huch, Friedrich (1873–1913, German novelist), born in Braunschweig, was one of the few writers of his time who were able to continue in a classical vein without giving the impression of a weak imitator or of a merely deft virtuoso. To label him a neoclassicist—as is often done—tends to obscure the interesting problem his creative work raises: what is the philosophical attitude which may compel a genuine revival of the older tradition? Can the novel, usually considered to be the most favorable medium for a realistic presentation of life, be made responsive to classical stylization? Huch's first novel, *Peter Michel* (1901), answers these questions once and for all. The hero of this story who starts out as a simple country boy and ends by fitting perfectly into boring bourgeois life is yet, for a number of years between, lifted above his ordinary self by a strong yearning for a more dignified form of existence; to this extent he transcends his particular character and partakes of a more universal if not to say classical impulse which remains the same throughout the ages. To enshrine such transcendence in a novel necessitates a blending of realistic detail and idealistic substance and a resolutely condensed diction, a task which Huch in all his works achieves with supreme skill. The setting of his novels is always contemporary and captivating, while the content touches on general issues of human nature, as when he presents a modern version of "elective affinities" in *Die Geschwister* (1903) or when the essence of human emotions, true love, is gradually evolved out of a welter of lower impulses in *Pitt und Fox* (1909). Even in *Mao* (1907) and in *Enzio* (1911), where a seemingly preponderant psychological interest results in an excellent dissection of decadent characters, closer inspection reveals that Huch again reduces the complexity of modern life to the simplicity of those plots which, to use the terminology of classical criticism, have their roots in the timeless attributes of men.

See: Th. Roffler, *Bildnisse aus der neueren deutschen Literatur* (1933), pp. 208–228; R. Denecke, *Friedrich Huch und die Problematik der bürgerlichen Welt* (1938).

H. B.

Huch, Ricarda (1864–, German novelist and historian), born in Braunschweig, is a sister of the novelist Rudolf Huch (1862–) and a cousin of Friedrich Huch (*q.v.*). Inherited literary talents, the background of a highly cultured home, the opportunity of a university education—a rare privilege then for women—together with an astounding zest for work have enabled Ricarda Huch to become the undisputed leading woman writer in present-day Germany. It is understandable that her work should provide an irresistible challenge to critics of literature, awakening a desire to analyze it from a psychological viewpoint and to throw into high relief its typically feminine qualities. Her creative work, it has been pointed out, shows none of the paralyzing influences which learning and scholarly inclinations quite often have.

Her style, though refined and deliberate in choice of words and structures, remains vigorous and natural; not even the abundance of accurate historical detail displayed in her later novels obstructs the epic flow of tales that are usually gripping. Moreover, while Ricarda Huch is conversant with all current European ideas, nevertheless emotions and strong instincts govern the lives of her characters. The best known among her earlier works, *Erinnerungen von Ludolf Ursleu dem Jüngeren* 1893; Eng. tr., *Recollections of Ludolf Ursleu the Younger,* 1913–1915), at first evokes reminiscences of that long series of European novels portraying the disintegration of a well-to-do family, brought about by an overdose of introspection and intellectual refinement, with an accompanying loss of vitality. With Ricarda Huch, however, disaster results much less from intellectualism than from the onrush of irrational passion.

Much has been made of the fact that after her 50th year she all but ceased to produce creative literature and instead turned to history and philosophy, the inference being that such a shift corresponds to certain biological changes in women. However this may be, it seems that the truly feminine aspects of Ricarda Huch's work still await a more subtle discussion. Ever since she began to write she has made periodic attempts to form a definite philosophy of life and to clarify her social, moral, and political concepts. "Like drops of rain falling from the sky upon the ground we pass through our allotted span of time, tossed about by the winds of fate"—this statement in her first novel was less an abiding conviction than an attitude which Ricarda Huch in all her subsequent works tried to repudiate in favor of a more masculine set of beliefs, possessing ample scope for the exercise of will power. She failed time and again in the attempt. But this failure became her greatest asset and the most intriguing feature of her work—the combining of a truly epic style with the ability to discern, in a welter of conflicts and opposites, the lasting values of beauty and love. No matter to what aspects of life she turns, she always transcends ephemeral phenomena and reconciles the conflicts in a vision of final harmony and beatitude, even when she delves into such a sordid milieu of broken lives as in *Aus der Triumphgasse* (1902). It was only natural that her predestined epic understanding tended to radiate through ever wider spheres of reality and to turn to vast historic panoramas, as in *Die Geschichten von Garibaldi* (1906–1907; Eng. tr., *Defeat,* 1928; *Victory,* 1929), *Das Leben des Grafen Federigo Confalonieri* (1910), and the monumental account of the Thirty Years' War, *Der grosse Krieg in Deutschland* (1912–1914). With the last-mentioned work the end of her creative period is reached. Thereafter she devoted all her energies to historical, critical, and philosophical studies, a field in which she was already well accredited by virtue of her two volumes on the romantic movement, *Die Blütezeit der Romantik* (1899) and *Ausbreitung und Verfall der Romantik* (1902). The crisis affecting this change was fundamentally intellectual. It is as if once more Ricarda Huch had wanted to cast off her womanly, harmonizing role and to fling herself into the man-made world of ideas and polemical issues. But it was in vain; whether she sided with Christianity against neopaganism (*Der Sinn der Heiligen Schrift,* 1919) or with Bakunin's socialism against the bourgeois mentality (*Michael Bakunin und die Anarchie,* 1923), the balance is soon restored as she reveals deep appreciation of personality (*Entpersönlichung,* 1921) or extols the sturdiness of German *Bürgertum* (*Im alten Reich,* 1927). A more recent book, *Das Zeitalter der Glaubensspaltung* (1937), dealing with the age of Reformation and its gigantic inner tensions, shows her power at its best; she experiences life as a bitter struggle and yet she inspires us to release our fondest hopes and warmest sympathies into the world and towards man, notwithstanding his apparent shortcomings. The same maternal instinct with which other woman writers of her time, notably Agnes Sapper (1852–1929) and Helena Christaller (1872–), have sanctified life within the precincts of the family or the small community has in the work of Ricarda Huch extended its beneficial function into far wider spheres of time and place.

See: E. Gottlieb, *Ricarda Huch; ein Beitrag zur Geschichte der deutschen Epik* (1914); O. Walzel, *Ricarda Huch* (1916); E. Hoppe, *Ricarda Huch* (1936).

H. B.

Hungarian literature. In portraying the salient traits of Hungarian literature from 1870 to the present, one must be especially careful not to succumb to comfortable generalizations. The complexities of Hungarian culture cannot be simplified by a few attractive labels. One may at least affirm that in this period Hungarian literature has shown an organic relationship to the main tendencies of Western European literature. It is the tradition of Hungary to be associated culturally with the West. But it should be stressed also that literary schools, like naturalism, realism, impressionism, symbolism, expressionism, futurism, dadaism, surrealism, current for a considerable time in Western Europe, had their exponents in Hungary at considerably later dates. There are two reasons for this delayed action. One is Hungary's geographical and historical position in the Danubian Valley which made her political existence for centuries precarious, so that literature necessarily became above all a weapon of essentially national interests; the other reason is that much of modern literature in Western Europe seemed eccentric, therefore incongruous with the Hungarian spirit. The traumatic effects of Western European writers and poets, the neurotic tendencies of their art, their symbols as a whole, seemed forced and alien; even the anchorites of beauty in Hungarian literature, who withdrew to the seclusion of personal taste, admitting pronounced individualism, found much of exaggerated Western individualism obnoxious or simply undesirable.

While these two reasons appear valid as expressions of a nation's defense mechanism and cultural indigenousness, they contain only half-truth; in fact they also indicate an evasion of responsibility as to an imaginative conception of progress. To be sure, not only the Parnassian adherence to form, as emphasized by Western European creators, but ideological innovations with a sociological perspective implying a need of change in social structure, were considered tenets incompatible with those of Hungarian literature. Consequently writers had too many hurdles to surmount, as too much stress was laid upon conservatism, despite the bargaining technique of a liberal political era. But some change in literary taste was inevitable. The industrial and commercial expansion of Budapest, the conflict that emerged from the contrast of pastoral illusions and urbane sophistication, affected of course the taste and views of writers and readers. On the other hand, the grand style of patriotic pride manifested by the festivities of 1896, when a symbolic expression was given to the fact that the Hungarians had lived in Europe for one thousand years, seems in some respects anachronistic in its enthusiastic tone and color if one considers the social and economic ailments which were causing peasants and proletarians to migrate to America. The dispossessed were symptoms of a chaos that indeed evoked the sympathy of some writers and poets. The analogous social symptoms of Western Europe finally induced some Hungarian writers (*e.g.,* Sándor Bródy, *q.v.*) to devote their attention to the portrayal of the exploited in the manner of Emile Zola (*q.v.*), but it was only in the 20th century that this devotion to the "underdog" achieved real literary significance, though too often it meant subordination of art to didacticism.

Hungary's foremost poet in the 70's, János Arany (*q.v.*), a classicist par excellence (see his *Toldi,* a genuine epic poem) and at the same time close to the people, objected to cosmopolitanism. It would be unfair to accuse Arany of intolerance; he was too powerful a genius for pettiness, and his criticism was directed mainly against journalistic tricks in the name of literature. Nevertheless he stigmatized cosmopolitanism in his own fashion. The leading literary critic of that time, Pál Gyulai (*q.v.*), author of *Petőfi Sándor és lirai költészetünk* (Sándor Petőfi and Our Lyric Poetry), though an ardent nationalist possessed sufficient intellectual flexibility and curiosity to notice the importance of Thackeray, Taine (*q.v.*), and Sainte-Beuve (cf. especially his *Birálatok és kritikai dolgozatok,* 1854, Criticisms and Critical Essays). It is also pertinent to recall the exuberant imagination of Móricz Jókai (*q.v.*), whose narrative genius (see *A fekete gyémántok,* 1870, Eng. tr., *Black Diamonds,* 1896) was recognized by Gyulai, yet whose historical ambiguity and romantic formlessness were severely criticized by the latter. These writers were Hungarians (Magyars) to the very core of their being; they were not insensible to the values of the West but they were inclined to relegate modern aesthetic and sociological theories of literature to a pattern of life which, in their estimation, in its fundamental meaning could not be transferred to Hungary. In truth, they should not be numbered among those who determined the literary character of the last three decades of the 19th century; their literary position was secure when the younger writers were still more or less inarticulate. Arany died in 1882, Gyulai in 1909, Jókai in 1904. They were accepted as literary spokesmen of their country before 1870. Ferenc Toldy, the literary historian, and Ágost Greguss, the critic of aesthetic problems, belong to this generation.

Just as it was immensely difficult for the American South, conditioned by the picturesque and sentimental associations of colonels, juleps, magnolias, plantations, and mammies, to discharge its prejudices in exchange for a democratic concept and a problematical commercial affluence promised by the North, so it was confusing for the Hungarian aristocracy and gentry to associate itself with the idea of progress that meant a refusal of inherited prejudices. The rapid rise of a plutocracy, only too willing to promote its own interests by cooperating with the traditional class distinctions, and rejoicing in nationalism with the eagerness of neophytes, helped to maintain a system which involved pressure upon those now unwilling to accept the new ideology of vested interests and collaboration with the others. Most writers and poets either shared the ethical implication of nationalism without ascertaining its economic unfairness or actually agreed, sometimes in a sheepish way, with the widespread belief that change would be detrimental to the general welfare of the country. The criteria of success resembled those of the American "gilded age"; unfortunately even gifted writers, to whom careerism should have been abhorrent, were compelled to show preference for social and literary norms harmful to the total expression of their creative urge. Only in the 20th century, with the appearance of Endre Ady (*q.v.*) on the horizon of Hungarian literature (see especially his *Vér és arany,* 1907, Blood and Gold), did dissension with petrifying traditions and prejudices reach expression so forceful that the cleavage between the 20th-century Hungarian literary mentality and that of the late 19th century became obvious even to those who as a rule paid little attention to literature.

Hungarian literature also gave frequent evidence, however, of a spiritual mobility akin to that of Western Europe. The romantic pessimism (*Magány,* 1889; Solitude) of Gyula Reviczky (*q.v.*); the philosophical naturalism of János Vajda (*q.v.*); the superman complex of Jenő Komjathy; the oriental sadness (*Költemények,* 1876; Poems) of József Kiss (*q.v.*); the satirical power of László Arany; the mellow sorrow of Gyula Vargha—all implied participation in an utterly modern sensitiveness. These poets grappled as Hungarians and as creators with a fate which expected them to be fugitives from traditions. They were not great poets; they were not carried away by the demoniac power of superhuman restlessness; but they faced life with epical and lyrical courage, and in some of their works they revealed greatness. In the sphere of the novel the style and wit of Zoltán Ambrus (*q.v.*) must be mentioned (*Midas király,* 1906; King Midas), also the naturalistically suggested romantic intensity (*A nap lovagja;* The Knight of the Day) of Sándor Bródy, the erratic and satirical intelligence of Lajos Tolnai, the psychological realism of Zsigmond Justh, and the humor and irony (*Szent Péter esernyője,* 1895; Eng. tr., *St. Peter's Umbrella,* 1900) of Kálmán Mikszáth (*q.v.*). The professional competence of literary historians, philologists, and critics, like Jenő Péterfy (*q.v.*), Lajos Dézsi, Frigyes Riedl, Bernát Alexander, László Négyesy, Zoltán Ferenczi, Pál Hunfalvy, showed an engaging and refreshing mentality, simultaneously studious and human.

But most of the popular writers of these times pictured life with an engaging optimism in order to be enjoyed by conventional readers. It would be wrong to condemn these poets, novelists, short-story writers, and playwrights as mediocre; some were endowed with ability above the average—for instance, Jenő Rákosi, Lajos Dóczy, Károly Eötvös, Géza Gárdonyi (*q.v.*), Ferenc Herczeg (*q.v.*), Victor Cholnoky, Béla Tóth, Gyula Krudy—yet most merely had an aptitude for facile writing. Episodes from Hungarian history, the life of the nobles, the rich, the bourgeoisie, the peasants, and the gypsies, were portrayed sentimentally, anecdotically, or with a restraint of "gentlemanly" humor or superiority. Ferenc Csepreghy, Ede Tóth, Gergely Csiky, Ede Szigligeti, Victor Rákosi, Árpád Berczik, Adolf Ágai, István Tömörkény, István Szomaházy, Antal Váradi, Gyula Pekár, István Bársony, Dezső Malonyai, playwrights and novelists, either ignored or did not understand complex social and aesthetic problems. The archaic usage of a patriotic vocabulary by Sándor Endrődi and Kálmán Thaly was rather an adroit control of a poetic pattern than an organic revelation of the Hungarian spirit in poetry (see Thaly's *Régi magyar vitézi énekek,* Old Hungarian Battle Songs). The religious poems of Gedeon Mindszenty, the rhetorical poems of Emil Ábrányi, the bucolic poems of Mihály Szabolcska, the political poems of Andor Kozma, the patriotic poems of Miklós Bárd and József Lévay, the sentimental poems of Ödön Jakab, Gyula Szávay, and Sándor Sajó, the love poems of Imre Farkas, the cabaret poems of Jenő Heltai, the literary histories of Zsolt Beöthy and Ferenc Badics, all bear witness of an age in which optical illusion was the most successful inspiration and material of creative or pseudo-creative activities.

In the first decade of the 20th century a literary periodical, *Nyugat* (West), edited by the critic and poet Ignotus (*q.v.*) and by Ernő Osvát, brought into its orbit writers and poets dissatisfied with the smugness and conventionalism of the preceding generation. They believed that a work of literature should be a work of art and that love for one's country should not interfere with the freedom of the creative mind. Not all good writers joined *Nyugat,* but the majority did. Some were influenced by French symbolism (*q.v.*), others by the sensualism and the social implications of German, Scandinavian, Italian, and Russian writers, others by the humanitarianism and camaraderie of Walt Whitman. In their social and historical views several of the contributors were inclined to be Marxists. After the experiment of the communist revolution in 1919, many of the communists and their fellow travelers repudiated Marxism; some of the dogmatic communists or socialists indeed remained faithful to their principles and became political refugees. The pragmatism of *Nyugat,* in the service of literary integrity and social progress, became the source of an eclectic literature in which the most contradictory tastes found an opportunity to meet on the common ground of respect for artistic ability. As to workmanship this generation ranks among the foremost in Hungarian literature. The poets Endre Ady, Mihály Babits (*q.v.*), Dezső Kosztolányi (*q.v.*), Gyula Juhász, Árpád Tóth, Zoltán Somlyó, Ernő Szép, Oszkár Gellért, Milán Füst, Anna Lesznai, and among the younger ones, Lörinc Szabó, Tivadar Raith, and Sophie Török; the novelists and short-story writers Zsigmond Móricz (*q.v.*), Géza Csáth, Gyula Szini, Margit Kaffka (*q.v.*), Béla Révész, Dezső Szabó (*q.v.*), Géza Laczkó, Mihály Földi, Ferenc Móra, Irén Gulácsy, Miklós Surányi, Lajos Nagy, Frigyes Karinthy; the playwrights Ferenc Molnár (*q.v.*), Kálmán Harsányi, Dezső Szomory, Lajos Biró, Menyhért Lengyel; the critics and literary scholars Aladár Schöpflin, György Lukács, Lajos Katona, Robert Gragger, János Horváth, Lajos Hatvany, György Király, Zsolt Alszeghy, Jenő Dóczy, József Nagy, Károly Kerényi—all these, irrespective of the conspicuous differences of their talent, must be considered as creators and interpreters who rate high. Naturally the quality of their intentions was sometimes nobler than their execution. Nonetheless their sense of literary orientation was extraordinary, and their spirit loyal to humanity, to art, and to their country.

Among the *avant-garde* poets an iron molder, Lajos Kassák, excelled in manifestoes and sometimes in good free verse (*Máglyák énekelnek;* Singing Pyres). Géza Gyóni, who lost his life in the First World War, and Gábor Oláh were somewhat sidetracked by the conservative pressure of Jenő Rákosi, the powerful jingoistic publicist; but these poets, too, practiced their art with a structural sensitiveness unknown to poets of corresponding ability in the preceding generation. It should be said that most of the poets were also story writers, playwrights, novelists, or critics. In significance and influence Endre Ady towered for some time over the rest of the poets (*Szeretném ha szeretnének,* 1909; I Should Like to Be Loved); after his death in 1919 Mihály Babits symbolized creative maturity in Hungary. It is also important to say that while the *Nyugat* generation was often slandered by the writers of the older generation and was considered "international" in its outlook the really gifted poets and writers never betrayed their Hungarianism. As a matter of fact Ady recaptured the verbal music and spirit of the Reformation in many of his poems, and Kosztolányi (*Erös várunk a nyelv;* Our Language Is Our Fort of Strength) taught his countrymen to distinguish between a "pure" and "impure" Hungarian language. The feverishness of the *Nyugat* generation and of some of the writers independent of *Nyugat* suggested a crisis of the Hungarian spirit and the approach of an upheaval which indeed reached the country in 1918.

The ominous tone that characterized Hungarian literature in the second decade of the 20th century implied need of a revision of the Hungarian spirit; it also implied a Cassandra anxiety about the future. The Trianon peace treaty (June 4, 1920) mutilated Hungary. Hungarians in Czechoslovakia, Yugoslavia, and Rumania (Transylvania), confronted with an alien political and cultural world, learned to attach importance to their regionalistic literature. They soon discovered that their native tongue, used artistically by writers and poets and refreshed by the fecund idioms of the people, might be the main source of their pride and self-confidence as Hungarians in a non-Hungarian world. Meanwhile, in Hungary proper, writers of peasant stock (some exceptionally well educated) rediscovered the richness of folklore and also propagated the need of land reform. What Béla Bartók and Zoltán Kodály did for Hungarian music as an expression of folk characteristics, Gyula Illyés, József Erdélyi, Pál Szabó, János Kodolányi, Péter Veres, and István Sinka did or tried to do in poetry, fiction, plays, and biographies. Attila József, despite his strongly personal voice, expressed the plight of the proletarians and the social outcasts with a sans-culottic temper and authentic poetic ability. Various small literary magazines reflected the need of understanding the "isms" of the West. Urbane sensitiveness and social conscience came out in the poetic works of Miklós Radnóti and István Vas; Sándor Weörös, Zoltán Jékely, Pál Toldalaghy, Pál Gulyás, and Ferenc Jankovich registered the civilized and weary sensibilities of the lost generation. Lajos Zilahy as a playwright and novelist and Sándor Márai as a novelist and writer of sophisticated travel sketches hold to the belief that taste, though expressed in Hungarian, is not incompatible with a cosmopolitan culture. Influenced by Mihály Babits the discoursive essay found intelligent exponents in the works of Gyula Ortutay, György Buday, Albert Gyergyai, László Mátrai, Tibor Joo, László Németh, Dezső Keresztury, László Cs. Szabó, Gábor Halász, and Antal Szerb. Some writers concentrated on "racial" questions in literary reference; Gyula Farkas as a literary historian and Cecile Tormay as a novelist accentuated an ideology that seemed to confirm certain "racial" theories of Germany. There was a Catholic renaissance, influenced chiefly by Sigrid Undset (*q.v.*) and Jacques Maritain (*q.v.*), without works of paramount merit. Sándor Sik was the most notable Catholic poet of these years, and he belonged rather to the preceding generation; Zsolt Aradi represented the Catholic point of view in fiction and journalism. In the realm of literary criticism Elemér Császár, related to the older generation, represented the academic point of view, and in the realm of literary history Jenő Pintér was the voice of traditional nationalism. Many biographies were written; Zsolt Harsányi, in the manner of Emil Ludwig, compiled biographical material (*e.g.*, *És mégis mozog a föld*, The Stargazer) not less interesting because romanticized.

In the Succession States, circumstances and cultural awareness led to the creation of very substantial regionalistic literature; the most admirable work was done by Transylvanian writers centering around a literary periodical, *Erdélyi Helikon* (Transylvania Helicon), first edited by Aladár Kuncz, later by Lajos Áprily, and finally by László Kovács. The folklore collections of János Kriza in the 19th century (*Vadrózhák;* Wild Roses), the "Main Street" stories of István Petelei (*Vidéki emberek;* Men of the Countryside), the fables of Elek Benedek (*Szülöföldem;* My Native Soil), determined the kind of framework within which the writers of the 20th-century Transylvania, though under foreign rule or because of it, remained. The genuine cultural past of Transylvania functioned like a centripetal force, made more powerful by the crucial demands of post-war conditions. In Transylvanian literature as well as in the Hungarian literature of Czechoslovakia and Yugoslavia there were also distinct tendencies of "leftist" character.

The spiritualism of Sándor Remenyik's poetry, the local color of Lajos Áprily, the exquisite imagination of Jenő Dzsida, the disturbing intellectual intensity of Ferenc Szemlér, the pensive energy of László Tompa, afforded poetic experience to those who knew how to differentiate between provincialism and regionalism; the historical novels of Sándor Makkai and Károly Kós, the memoirs of Miklós Kisbán and Aladár Kuncz, the delightful and shrewd folk stories of Áron Tamási and József Nyirö, the enterprising tales of János Kemény and Ernő Ligeti, the critical dissertations of Károly Molter, Miklós Krémer, Géza Tabéry, indicated that the Hungarian language as a medium of creative and critical expression remained authentic in new Transylvania. Hungarian literary regionalism in Czechoslovakia and Yugoslavia seemed less rich. One of the characteristic features of recent Hungarian literature has been a rather abundant translation of foreign works; Árpád Tóth, Lörincz Szabó, Géza Kepes, György Rónay, György Faludy, and others, with varied ability and poetic sensibility, have reproduced in Hungarian the choicest works of Western Europe and America, ancient and modern alike. In the late 19th century János Csengeri, Antal Radó, Károly Szász, and Béla Vikár excelled in this field.

In Hungary proper as well as in the Succession States, especially since 1918, the economic lot of the literati has been anything but enviable. The merciless and frantic logic of poverty offset a great many creative dreams. It was hard to expect writers to have a "healthy" view of life when the disastrous and desolate conditions of their environment ridiculed their private visions. There were scores of "one book" writers and "splendid promises" in modern Hungary and in the Succession States. Nevertheless it is remarkable that they were able to produce as much as they did. Literary work did not necessarily enhance their reputation. The Hungarian spirit, imbued with sorrow, is not decadent in its essence; it is on the contrary vital, chiefly in its indignation and tenderness. But one cannot dismiss from the discussion of Hungarian writers and poets the political and historical intangibles that affect them, and the political, social, and economic tangibles that occupied too much of their energies. The creative instinct that knows how to eliminate unnecessary interferences has its limits; the pressure of political unfairness and poverty almost constant in the past two decades has been apt to destroy the aesthetic zest of very able men and women and compel them to find other objectives in life in order to remain alive.

See: Zs. Beöthy, *Magyar irodalomtörténet* (1900); A. Polignac, *Notes sur la littérature hongroise* (1900); J. Kont, *Geschichte der ungarischen Literatur* (1906); Fr. Riedl, *A History of Hungarian Literature* (1906); H. Horváth, *Neue ungarische Lyrik* (1918); R. Gragger, *Bibliographia Hungariae* (1923); B. Bartók, *Hungarian Folk Music* (1931); K. Viski, *Hungarian Peasant Customs* (1932); J. Pintér, *Magyar irodalomtörténet* (1935); J. Reményi, "Hungarian Writers and the Tragic Sense," *Books Abroad*, XIV (1940), 361–364.

J. R.

Hurban Vajanský, Svetozár (1847–1916, Slovak poet and novelist), was, after Hviezdoslav (*q.v.*), the leading literary figure of Slovakia in the later 19th century. He was the son of the patriot and writer Jozef Miloslav Hurban (1817–1888). He was born at Hlboká, practiced law in different Slovak towns, and later became a journalist and editor. He was frequently fined and even imprisoned by the Magyar authorities. He died in Turčanský Svatý Martin.

Hurban inherited from his father, an associate of L'udevít Štúr, founder of the new Slovak literary language, a strong Slovak nationalism which led him to criticize the Czechs as "Westerners" who had abandoned the true Slavic character. Hurban hoped that the liberation of his nation from the Magyar yoke would be accomplished by Russia. His literary affiliations were largely Russian, especially with Russian Byronism and with Turgenev (*q.v.*) and Goncharov. As a poet Hurban remained in the tradition of Byronic romanticism. A collection entitled *Tatry a more* (1880; The Tatra Mountains and the Sea) expressed his love of Slovakia and her natural beauties as well as his hatred of the Magyar oppressors. In his later poetry (*e.g.*, *Verše*, 1890, Verse) Hurban shows the influence of the Czech poet Vrchlický (*q.v.*): his style has become more rhetorical and decorative. But Hurban Vajanský's prose is far superior to his poetry. His stories and novels give an excellent though somewhat idealized picture of Slovak society, in the style of a moderate realism. Hurban Vajanský depicts the Slovak landed gentry especially in very favorable colors, since he put all hopes of a national regeneration in this class. The titles of his principal novels are: *Letiace tiene* (1883; Flying Shadows), *Suchá ratolest* (1883; The Dry Branch), and *Koreň a výhonky* (1895–1896; The Root and the Shoots). Hurban Vajanský also wrote travel books, reminiscences, and much political and literary journalism, which secured him the position of a leading man of letters in his nation for many decades.

See: A. Pražák, *Studentská léta S. H. Vajanského* (1925); A. Mráz, *Svetozár Hurban Vajanský* (1926).

R. W.

Huysmans, Joris Karl (pseud. of Charles Marie Georges Huysmans, 1848–1907, French novelist and art critic), was born in Paris. He was descended from Dutch painters through his father and from middle-class Burgundians through his mother. In 1866 he became a civil servant at the Ministry of the Interior and remained a "model government officer" until 1898. The only true events in his life are those of his literary achievements, the object of his constant concern, and his reconversion to Catholicism in 1892. With the latter are connected his various sojourns in Benedictine monasteries, particularly at Igny ("Notre-Dame de l'Atre" in *En route*) and Ligugé ("Val des saints" in *L'Oblat*). Apart from a few short journeys taken with his novels in view, he remained a confirmed Parisian (*e.g.*, *Croquis parisiens*, 1880) deeply rooted in the Saint-Sulpice quarter of the capital which is inseparable from his novels. After the *Drageoir aux épices* (1874), in which Banville found him able "to depict by means of harmony and rhythm," he joined the naturalists and contributed "Sac au dos" to the *Les Soirées de Médan* (1880). To this period belong *Marthe; histoire d'une fille* (1876), on the houses of prostitution; *Les Sœurs Vatard* (1879), on the low life of women book stitchers; *En ménage* (1881), relating the pitiful love affairs of drab characters soon stifled by the social structure; *A vau-l'eau* (1882; Eng. tr., *Downstream*, n.d.); and *En rade* (not published before 1887). During this phase Huysmans adhered faithfully to the naturalists' creed as put forth in his apology (1876) of Zola (*q.v.*) which, however, brushed aside the latter's political and scientific preoccupations. On the other hand, he acknowledged Gautier, Flaubert (*q.v.*), the Goncourts (*q.v.*), and later Barbey d'Aurevilly (*q.v.*) as his masters in style. In *L'Art moderne* (1883), his collected "Salons," Huysmans opened up new art vistas, extolled impressionism, and, as later in *Certains* (1889), praised the genius of Degas, Renoir, Whistler, and others through keen analyses and lively descriptions giving proof of an original, inquisitive flair.

In 1884 *A rebours* (Eng. tr., *Against the Grain*, with introduction by Havelock Ellis, 1922) came as a thunderbolt. In this "minute panorama" (preface to the 1903 edition), richly colored and fashioned like a Persian carpet, he remained far from Baudelaire (*q.v.*) though claiming him for his master. His hero, Des Esseintes, whose traits were borrowed from Ludwig II of Bavaria, Robert de Montesquiou, and the author himself, disgusted with his times and his own personality, vainly tries to find a reason to live and a new orientation by searching art and literature. Huysmans's use of "artifice" in this work as a specific for disgust inspired Oscar Wilde in the writing of *The Picture of Dorian Gray*. In *A rebours* Huysmans does for the Latin writers of the decadence and for the new French poets, Corbière, Mallarmé, (*qq.v.*), *et al.*, what in *L'Art moderne* he had done for the impressionists. Zola upbraided Huysmans bitterly for his betrayal of naturalism, but the enthusiastic symbolists opened wide the *Revue indépendante* to him and Barbey's famous review of the book remains an important document for historians of the modern French novel. All the tendencies and "intellectual atmosphere of that period" were embodied in Huysmans's masterpiece, the source of all his future novels (preface to the 1903 edition).

Là-Bas (1891; Eng. tr., *Down There,* 1924), concerning black magic from the Middle Ages to our day, preceded the Catholic tetralogy comprising *En route* (1895; Eng. tr., 1896), which caused many conversions to Catholicism; *La Cathédrale* (1898; Eng. tr., *The Cathedral,* 1898), on the Christian symbology at Chartres; *L'Oblat* (1903; Eng. tr., *Oblate,* 1924), on liturgy; and *Les Foules de Lourdes* (1905; Eng. tr., *Crowds of Lourdes,* 1925). To the end Huysmans prided himself on remaining true to the descriptive, naturalistic method, apparent in *Sainte Lydwine de Schiedam* (1901; Eng. tr., 1923). He has created a single but famous type bearing in turn the names of Folantin, Des Esseintes, and Durtal, whose main prototype was himself, with his hypersensitivity, pessimism, harsh humor, devotion to art, and genuine religious convictions (see his autobiography signed A. Meunier in *Les Hommes d'aujourd'hui* No. 263, 1885). His hero anathematizes what sickens, irks, or scandalizes him with crude, coarse words, in a highly colored, intricate style teeming with picturesque treasure troves, and by his "syntactic irony." He enjoys bringing into relief the oddities, sins, and absurdities of the quaint characters for whom he kept on the lookout. Paul Valéry said of Huysmans in *Variété II:* "He has revealed to many a reader the existence of a hidden, exceptional art, and he derived from mysticism and occultism . . . a somewhat precious literary matter."

See: Havelock Ellis, *Affirmations* (1898); Barbey d'Aurevilly, *Le Roman contemporain* (1902); James Huneker, "The Pessimist's Progress: J.-K. Huysmans," *North American Review,* CLXXXVI (1907), 41–54; L. Descaves, introduction and *postfaces* in Huysmans, *Œuvres complètes* (1928–1934); R. Dumesnil, *La Publication d'En route* (1931); Fr. Lefèvre, *Entretiens sur J.-K. Huysmans* (1931). There is a Société J.-K. Huysmans.

M. M.

Hviezdoslav (pseud. of Pavol Országh, 1849–1921, Slovak poet), was the most prominent Slovak verse writer of the later 19th century. He was born at Vyšní Kubín (in the district of Orava), studied law, was a district judge for some time, and then practiced law in different Slovak towns. He became a member of the first National Assembly after the founding of the Czechoslovak republic. He died in his native village.

Hviezdoslav was fundamentally a romantic in his love for the simple people and the beauties of Slovak nature. In distinction from the usual Slovak verse of the time, however, his did not imitate the style of folk poetry; he developed a highly literary and decorative manner which represents an analogue to the diction of Vrchlický (*q.v.*) and Čech (*q.v.*) in contemporary Czech writing. Hviezdoslav introduced the most difficult stanzaic forms of the West into Slovak and translated much great foreign poetry into excellent Slovak verse. Versions of Shakespeare's *Hamlet* and *A Midsummer Night's Dream,* Madach's *The Tragedy of Man,* Pushkin's *Boris Godunov,* as well as excerpts from Goethe represent a solid achievement which demonstrated that Slovak could be used for the most sublime flights of the imagination. Hviezdoslav also wrote much poetry drawn from Old Testament subjects: two epical poems, *Agar* (1883) and *Ráchel* (1891), and a verse drama, *Herodes a Herodias* (1909). In spite of these systematic moves to escape provincialism in subject matter and form, Hviezdoslav remained an ardent Slovak patriot who strongly believed in the common people and democracy. This democratic outlook made him sympathetic to the Czechs, and he hailed the union of the Czechs and Slovaks after 1918 with genuine enthusiasm. All told, his best work is in the poems with Slovak settings. *Hájnikova žena* (1886; The Gamekeeper's Wife) is a simple story of a gamekeeper's wife who shoots the son of her master when he forces his attentions on her and who then pays with temporary madness. A versified family chronicle, *Ežo Vlkolinský* (1890), and its continuation, *Gábor Vlkolinský* (1899), depict the regeneration by peasant blood of a gentry family and give a vivid picture of Slovak country life. Here Hviezdoslav's power of observation and description, his sonorous verse, his love for his people, have full play and compensate for a lack of deeper powers of characterization or more original handling of ideas and forms.

See: P. Bujnák, *P. Országh-Hviezdoslav* (1919).

R. W.

I

Ibsen, Henrik (1828–1906, Norwegian dramatist and poet), was born in the small town of Skien, in southeastern Norway, of wealthy merchant parents. When he was eight years old, however, his father went bankrupt, and before he was 16 he was apprenticed to a pharmacist in the still smaller town of Grimstad, where he worked for more than six years. He had high ambitions, prepared himself for the university, and went to Christiania in 1850 in order to take his entrance examinations, but did not finish them. When, later in life, he had a doctor's degree, it was an honorary title granted him by the University of Uppsala in 1877.

The characteristic qualities observable in him in his childhood and youth are a vivid sensitiveness and a rebellious mind. Ibsen was early drawn to literary production and tried his hand at many literary forms—poems, novels, dramas—imitating authors of different styles but at the same time strongly self-assertive, endeavoring to protect himself against the pressure of surroundings and satirizing them. He felt his efforts toward mental liberation strengthened by the revolutions of 1848 and in the winter of 1848–1849 wrote the first work that revealed something of his deepest tendencies, the drama *Catiline*. This glorifies the fight of a rebel, and the reason for Catiline's defeat is sought in his failure to keep faith with himself, in the betrayal of his own true personality.

Catiline was published anonymously in 1850, but without the slightest success. An opposition weekly on which Ibsen was collaborating during the next year, still anonymously, had no more success. He was happy to be called as a stage manager to the new Norwegian theatre established at Bergen in 1850 for the purpose of liberating the theatrical art from the Danish traditions, and he worked there for six years (1851–1857). Later he was called as a director for the Norwegian theatre at Christiania, set up with the same program, and there he worked for five years until the theatre went bankrupt (1862).

Meanwhile he had published, now under his own name, three new dramas, all of them complying with the demand of the age for reviving national traditions. But he felt ever more unhappy in all this "servant's work" and at last rebelled. In 1862 was published his first modern drama, *Kaerlighedens komedie* (The Comedy of Love), satirizing the contemporary conventions of betrothal and marriage and thereby scandalizing bourgeois society. The next year he used a theme of history as a call to his nation for truly national action in the drama *Kongs-emnerne* (1863; The Pretenders). But he felt he could not write in full freedom as long as he stayed at home, and in the spring of 1864 he left Norway and went to Rome.

Ibsen remained abroad until 1891, making only short visits to Norway in 1874 and 1885. He was not assimilated in any way by the foreign countries where he lived during all those years, mostly Italy and Germany. His need was to keep free of all influences and pressures that might tend to suppress his mental independence, and the works he sent home from abroad were belligerent dramas intended to raise his nation to moral truth and freedom. He devoted his life to dramaturgical authorship with a singular pertinacity, feeling that the drama form was the natural expression of battles within himself.

The volcanic drama *Brand* (1866), with its transcendental ethical demand for faithfulness to the mission of providence, stirred profoundly the whole Scandinavian world and made Ibsen the moral prophet of these nations. The Norwegian state authorities honored him by an annual stipend like that given to Björnson (*q.v.*). In the next year, 1867, was published the counterpart of *Brand,* the fanciful satire of moral faithlessness and self-betrayal, *Peer Gynt.* This character was pictured as the Norwegian type, and the work was received with both anger and enthusiasm combined. And in a merry comedy, *De unges forbund* (1869; The League of Youth), he pictured a Peer Gynt in politics, representing the traits of several Norwegian politicians.

In an interval after these plays there was published a selection of his poems (*Digte,* 1871; Poems) and a philosophical double drama, *Kejser og Galilaer* (1873; Emperor and Galilean), in which Ibsen tried to clarify his own ideas about the future, in a dialectical way predicting a kind of unity between paganism and Christianity which virtually amounted to a demand for personal moral unity.

Then followed, from 1877 on, the new series of combat dramas which at once won world fame for him. They continued what Björnson had begun in 1875, but with still more dramatic energy and consistency, one work after the other attacking the moral conventions of modern society. In *Samfundets stötter* (1877; The Pillars of Society) Ibsen presented the businessman who betrayed his love and himself for wealth and social power. *Et dukkehjem* (1879; A Doll's House) showed the falseness of a marriage that did not rest upon true comradeship. In *Gengangere* (1881; Ghosts) he pictured the tragic consequences of a marriage enforced by social considerations, not by love. The comedy *En folkefiende* (1882; An Enemy of the People) satirized gaily all the people who did not want to listen to truth that came athwart their personal interests. All these dramas were brilliantly constructed, virtually on the same plan as the Greek tragedies, rushing direct into the catastrophe. They were performed in innumerable theatres and in many languages all over the world, and everywhere they roused heated discussions by virtue of their appeal to the conscience of every individual. At the same time they were profound psychological studies, deeply searching into the secret forces of man's character. In fact, the deepest craving of Ibsen was the moral honesty of man toward himself, and his dramas more and more became purely psychological, seeking the battle and the victory within the souls of man. Such above all were *Vildanden* (1884; The Wild Duck), *Rosmersholm* (1886), *Hedda Gabler* (1890), certainly eminent creations of dramatic authorship, the favorite plays of the greatest actors and actresses.

In 1891 Ibsen returned to Norway and remained at Christiania until his death. Here he wrote a series of dramas of a more introspective nature and finished his life work by what he called a dramatical epilogue, *Nar vi döde vågner* (1899; When We Dead Awaken), a final account of his whole authorship, charging himself with having devoted all his efforts to aesthetical production instead of direct action and thus failing himself to appreciate the far-reaching moral effects of his literary works. His nation and the whole world felt the impact of his insistence upon new moral values and what he himself called the moving of mental boundaries. Ibsen's works have been translated into the principal European languages and into Japanese; an English edition of his collected works by William Archer was published 1906–1912.

See: H. Jaeger, *Ibsen* (1888; Eng. tr., 1890); G. Brandes, *Ibsen* (1898, in Danish); Ibsen, *Breve,* ed. by H. Koht and J. Elias (2 vols., 1904); E. Gosse, *Ibsen* (1907, in English); R. Woerner, *Ibsen,* 2d ed. (2 vols., 1912, in German); Ibsen, *Samlede verker; hundreårs-utgave,* ed. by F. Bull, H. Koht, and D. A. Seip (1928–); H. Koht, *Henrik Ibsen* (2 vols., 1928–1929; Eng. tr., 1931); A. E. Zucker, *Ibsen, the Master Builder* (1929).

H. K.

Icelandic literature. As in no other Germanic country, tradition in Icelandic literature is unbroken, from the time of the Eddic poems (800–1200) and the sagas (13th century) to the present day. From the time of the settlement of the island (874) there is no break in the language; hence people, even children, read the Eddas and sagas with little more difficulty than the daily newspaper. Modern poets still compose their poems according to the alliterative rules valid in Eddic poetry and *Beowulf,* and the saga style is much in evidence in popular literature. Even the heroic spirit of the sagas, though sorely beset through the ages by the church on the one hand and by escapist French romances in prose and in rhyme (*rímur*) on the other, has never quite lost its hold on the people, and in the romantic revival of the 1830's it flared up with renewed vigor.

The romantic movement, of Danish-German origin, had two aspects: admiration for the golden age of the sagas and hopes and demands for increased political independence of the country. Both ideas are still potent in Icelandic literature, though the latter lost its actuality after 1918, when Iceland gained national independence. The pioneers of the romantic movement were Bjarni Thórarensen (1786–1841) and Jónas Hallgrímsson (1807–1845). The tradition was continued by Grímur Thomsen, Benedikt S. Gröndal, Steingrímur Thorsteinsson, and Matthías Jochumsson (*qq.v.*), who was for half a century the leading poet of Iceland. The romanticists created a puristic prose with patterns from the sagas and from popular speech; this style may be called, however paradoxically, classical style of the 19th and 20th centuries. Its greatest early monuments were Sveinbjörn Egilsson's translations of the *Iliad* and the *Odyssey,* Jón Árnason's *Íslenzkar þjóðsögur og æfintýri* (1862–1864; Eng. tr., *Icelandic Legends,* 2 vols., 1864–1866), and Jón Thóroddsen's novels *Piltur og stúlka* (1850; Eng. tr., *Lad and Lass,*

1890) and *Maður og kona* (1876; Man and Wife). Though partly idyllic, these abound, too, in humorous characters. Thóroddsen wrote under the influence of Scott. The playwright Indriði Einarsson (1851–1939) wrote romantic and realistic dramas and worked indefatigably for the stage in Reykjavík.

Under the influence of Georg Brandes (*q.v.*) Icelandic students in Copenhagen inaugurated a movement of realism with the periodical *Verðandi* (1882; The Present). Its individualistic liberalism broke with the narrow fundamentalist outlook of the Lutheran State Church. Social and intellectual criticism marked its beginnings, and Gestur Pálsson (1852–1891), one of *Verðandi's* editors, a brilliant short-story writer, never outgrew this attitude. But Hannes Hafstein (1861–1922), a spirited singer of love, life, and liberty, became a national romantic, and Einar H. Kvaran (*q.v.*) became an apostle of Christian humanitarianism and spiritualism after the turn of the century. Of the realists none were more important than the Icelandic-Canadian Stephan G. Stephansson and Þorsteinn Erlingsson (*qq.v.*). They had similar views, but were of different poetic genius: Erlingsson was a perfectionist in the art of simplicity, while Stephansson was ornate. Stephansson towers over most of his contemporaries, not only in Iceland, but also in Canada.

In the 1870's and 1880's Icelanders flocked to America, especially to Canada, with the greatest settlement in and near Winnipeg. Many others besides Stephansson belong to this group, among them the writer of adventure stories Jóhann Magnús Bjarnason (1867–1945), the humorous poet Kristján Níels Júlíus (1859–1936), the poet and playwright Guttormur J. Guttormsson (1878–), and the poetess Jakobína Johnson (1883–).

In the 1890's reaction set in against the more negative aspects of realism: faith was reborn in a new form (Kvaran), and nationalism was reasserted. The leader of nationalism was Einar Benediktsson (*q.v.*), who ranks with Stephansson as a poet. He was a progressive nationalist as well as a natural philosopher, even a mystic, and a consummate artist. The two geniuses had deep roots in Old Icelandic and were at the same time completely modern. Stephansson was the greater man, Einar Benediktsson the greater artist.

Two farmers emerged as novelists of note: Þorgils Gjallandi (pseud. of Jón Stefánsson, 1851–1915) and Guðmundur Friðjónsson (*q.v.*). While both began as realists, the latter—who wrote mostly short stories and poetry—became a leading interpreter of the farmer's point of view as well as a national romanticist. His style is rich and individualistic. But the greatest novelist of the first two decades of the century, except for Kvaran, was Jón Trausti (*q.v.*). A progressive national romanticist, he was the first to depict social changes on a large canvas (*Halla-Heiðarbýlð*, 4 vols., 1906–1911, Halla and the Heath Cottage; *Leysing*, 1907, Thaw). Later he wrote romantic historical novels. His style is uneven, but his characters are full blooded and sound. Apart from the others stands the Catholic Jón Svenson (*q.v.*), who went to France, became a Jesuit, and later was one of the most important writers of youth literature in Catholic Europe.

At the turn of the century Icelandic writers were shifting their interest from social, national, and political progress to concern with their art, themselves, and man's soul as well as man's dreams. Nationalism remained, to be sure, but it took the form of devotion to folk poetry and folklore and, later, of scrutiny of the national character. In this neo-romantic movement French "decadent" tendencies were mixed with Nietzsche's (*q.v.*) ideas about the genius and the superman. The movement gained momentum in the first two decades of the century. Among the first to reflect the new tendencies were Guðmundur Guðmundsson (1874–1919) and Hulda (pseud. of Unnur Benediktsdóttir, 1881–), lyric poets, the latter more recently a romantic novelist.

A group of writers wrote in Danish to win a wider public. They were led by the gifted playwright Jóhann Sigurjónsson (*q.v.*), whose tragedy *Fjalla-Eyvindur* (1912; Eng. tr., *Eyvind of the Hills*, 1916) instantly won European acclaim. The lyric poet Jónas Guðlaugsson (1887–1916) wrote some short stories as well. Guðmundur Kamban (*q.v.*) turned cosmopolitan social critic in the 1920's, but returned to Icelandic subjects in the 1930's. Gunnar Gunnarsson (*q.v.*) has been strictly loyal to his homeland in choice of subjects. After a romantic start, he wrote somber problem novels during the First World War. But in the post-war period he expressed his faith in the race in a series of autobiographical and historical novels which have won him a European reputation.

Meanwhile there appeared in Iceland the realistic and humorous poets Jakob Thórarensen (1886–) and Örn Arnarson (pseud. of Magnús Stefánsson, 1884–1942) and the pure lyric poets Sigurður Sigurðsson frá Arnarholti (1879–1939), Jakob Jóhannesson Smári (1889–), and Stefán (Sigurðsson) frá Hvítadal (1887–1933). Under Norwegian influence the last named wrote some of the most original lyrics of the second decade of the century (*Söngvar förumannsinns,* 1918; The Songs of the Wanderer); later he turned Catholic. Important as a leader of literary opinion was Sigurður Nordal (*q.v.*), essayist and professor of Icelandic literature since 1918. His exquisite lyric prose fragments have had few imitators, but his interpretation of neo-romantic ideals in contrast to the reigning humanitarianism and liberalism (of Kvaran) as well as his revaluation of the Old Icelandic heritage have both been epoch-making (see the remarkable synthesis in *Íslenzk menning,* 1942–, Icelandic Culture).

A new generation of writers, starting under neo-romantic auspices in the early 1920's, later turned modernistic in various ways which perhaps might be termed neo-realistic. Davíð Stefánsson (*q.v.*) is the most representative and popular poet of this generation—fiery, sensual, with a considerable strain of folk poetry in his lyrics. Of late he has also won acclaim as a novelist and a playwright. Other poets are the ardent nationalist Jón Magnússon (1896–1944) (see his *Bláskógar,* 1925, Blue Forests), the fervid socialist Jóhannes (Jónasson) úr Kötlum (1899–) (*Ég læt sem ég sofi,* 1932, I Pretend to Sleep) as well as the two perfectionists Tómas Guðmundsson (1901–) and Jón Helgason (1899–), who is professor of Old Norse-Icelandic at the University of Copenhagen. Guðmundsson, a humorist, also knows how to endow the commonplace with a romantic tinge (*Fagra veröld,* 1933; Fair World), while Helgason, a satirist, also broods in beautiful verse over his exile and over the rushing away of this our fleeting life (*Úr landsuðri,* 1939; From the South east).

Recent novelists are Guðmundur G. Hagalín, Kristmann Guðmundsson, and Halldór Kiljan Laxness (*qq.v.*). The first two have remained more or less unchanged: Hagalín excels in depicting heroes in homespun, not least the sailors of his home district; Guðmundsson, writing in Norwegian, is a master of the modern romance and a consummate storyteller. Laxness, the most gifted, is the real creator of present-day literary style, reflecting the storm and stress of the turbulent modern age. After a Catholic intermezzo, Laxness turned socialistic, thus joining a movement of the leftists that had been launched by the essayist Þórbergur Þórðarson (*q.v.*) with his *Bréf til Láru* (1924; Letter to Laura). Þórðarson had also rebelled against the lyrical effusions of his romantic contemporaries, and later he was to write a most interesting autobiography in which meet the countercurrents of the sagas and the modern psychological novel (*Íslenzkur aðall,* 1938, Icelandic Nobility; *Ofvitinn,* 2 vols., 1940–1941, The Eccentric). His rich and varicolored writing was a forerunner of a new style in direct contrast to the classic one that had held sway for a century. But it was the privilege of Laxness actually to create the new style in his great novels, beginning with *Vefarinn mikli frá Kasmír* (1927; The Great Weaver from Kashmir). The impact of his work on his contemporaries has been such that not only the beginners imitated him, but older men like Kamban (*Skálholt,* 4 vols., 1930–1935; Eng. tr., of Vols. I and II, *The Virgin of Skalholt,* 1935) and Hagalín (*Kristrún í Hamravík,* 1933) began to experiment with a new, though different, style. In the middle 1930's there was also a flocking to the leftist banner among the younger writers (none of whom is here mentioned). A new literary society, publishing the periodicals *Rauðir pennar* (1935; Red Pens) and *Tímarit Máls og menningar* (1940–; The Journal of Language and Culture), was formed to propagate their ideas. But in spite of their communistic ideals, they were also so nationalistic that they published Nordal's *Íslenzk menning,* the greatest work of the national romantic school. Thus old and new, as always, clasp hands in present-day Iceland.

See: J. C. Poestion, *Isländische Dichter der Neuzeit* (1897); H. Hermannsson, *Icelandic Authors of To-day* (1913), Vol. VI of Islandica; R. Beck, ed., *Icelandic Lyrics* (1930) and *Icelandic Poems and Stories* (1943); G. Finnbogason, "Literature," in Thorsteinn Thorsteinsson, ed., *Iceland* (3d ed., 1936), pp. 151–176; R. Beck, "Icelandic Literature [and] Icelandic-American Literature," in Frederika Blankner, ed., *The History of the Scandinavian Literatures* (1938), pp. 231–287, 368–377; S. Einarsson, "Five Icelandic Novelists," *Books Abroad,* XVI (1942), 254–259.

S. E.

Iglesies, Ignasi (1871–1928, Catalonian dramatist), brought a new manner to the Catalonian theatre—that of individualistic materialism. Born in San Andrés de Palomar (Barcelona) of a laboring family, he knew from childhood the sufferings of this social class, whose representatives he glorified in his work; he came to be known as the "poeta dels humils." Iglesies began his education in Lérida, but soon abandoned his studies in order to dedicate himself to literature. Still very young, he produced *Fructidor* (1897), and *L'escorço* (1902; The Scorpion), works in which one can discern the influence of Ibsen (*q.v.*). The struggles of the workingmen, their economic plight, were presented by Iglesies in numerous works, among which the drama *Els vells* (1903; The Old Ones) is outstanding, and enjoyed an extraordinary success in Barcelona and, translated into French, in Paris. *Lari* and *La mare eterna* (1902; The Eternal Mother) were translated into Italian. Another successful work of Iglesies, also social in nature, is the drama *Les Garces* (The Herons). Still other pieces are: *La Resclosa* (The Canal Lock), in which the routine concept of morality is combated; *El cor el poble* (1897; The Heart of the Humble); *Foc nou* (New Fire); and the comedy of manners *Girasol* (Sunflower). His last productions include *L'encis de la gloria* (The Charm of Glory) and *La llar apagada* (The Cold Hearth). The theatre of Iglesies, while it represented a novelty in the Catalonia of the beginning of the 20th century, seems antiquated today. The plot, which is the crux of his work, is extremely simple, at times even puerile. His desire for social justice, inspired to a certain extent by the thesis-plays of the French theatre, suffers from an exaggerated ingeniousness and is encumbered, moreover, by a special form of depressing sentimentality.

See: R. Darío, "Films fe Paris," *Nación* (Buenos Aires), May 2, 1912; J. Bernat i Duran, *Historia del teatro en Cataluña y Valencia* (1924); R. Tasis i Marca, *La literatura catalana moderna* (1937).

J. M. M. i V.

Ignotus (pseud. of Hugo Veigelsberg, 1869–, Hungarian critic, poet, publicist) was born in Budapest. Son of a noted journalist, he grew up in intellectual surroundings. He contributed to *A Hét* (The Week), a literary weekly published and edited by the poet József Kiss (*q.v.*); he wrote political articles and essays for *Világ* (World), a radical daily, and for its successor, *Magyar Hirlap* (Hungarian Journal). *Nyugat* (West) was established in 1908; Ignotus was one of the editors, and later editor in chief, of this literary periodical. *Nyugat* was considered a rebellious literary publication by the conservatives and by those who lacked ability, and in many respects it did attack static views. In 1919 Ignotus became a political refugee; since then he has sought shelter in Rumania (Transylvania), Czechoslovakia, Austria, and finally America. He arrived in New York in 1941.

The place of Ignotus in modern Hungarian literature is unique. His name is synonymous with critical mobility; he considered eclectic insight indispensable for the proper understanding of creative work and insisted upon the freedom of creative expression. He accepted the right of the poet and the writer to remain true to his own manner or mannerisms; since his own Hungarian was not sufficiently consistent with certain traditions of the Hungarian language, he was unyielding in his view that style is inevitably personal and that verbal idiosyncracies or innovations, if artistically exciting, do not constitute an aesthetic crime. Through the creative spirit he endeavored to find that freedom of man to which the whole of humanity is entitled—and that human dignity. Therefore while he excluded politics from literature, his literary abilities were used to serve politics when progress as he understood it was being furthered.

His critical jottings, aphorisms, and elucidations show wit, knowledge, cultured sensibility, liveliness, universality. *Olvasás közben* (1902; While Reading), *Kisérletek* (1909; Experiments), and other critical or reflective writings of Ignotus have a pioneering significance in Hungarian literature; his *Változatok a G húron* (1907; Variations on a G String) unfold a soul unwilling to compromise with drudgery, dullness, stupidity, pettiness, and conceit. His poems and stories are authentic expressions of a creative spirit; wisdom, feeling, and delight are reflected with urbane sophistication and a somewhat distraught sensitiveness. Ignotus was always a conscientious craftsman, but his own phrasing was often somewhat involved. As a crusader of good literature, he helped many Hungarian writers and poets to become recognized. The aesthetics of Ignotus were really the ethics of a very gifted critic, poet, and literary editor.

J. R.

Ilf, Ilya Arnoldovich (pseud. of Ilya Arnoldovich Fainzilber, 1897–1937, Russian humorist and journalist), was born in Odessa; his father was a Jewish white-collar worker. The son received a technical education and for a time tried various occupations. Reaching Moscow after the Revolution, Ilf became connected with different satiric magazines. A chance suggestion made by Valentin Katayev (*q.v.*) began the well-known collaboration of Ilf with Petrov (*q.v.*), Katayev's brother. Together they wrote *Dvenadtsat stulyev* (1928; Eng. tr., *Diamonds to Sit On,* 1930), a picaresque novel of the adventures of some would-be "capitalists" who seek the diamonds hidden in one of 12 chairs. The plot gives the authors excellent opportunities to poke fun at the various weaknesses of socialist society. The novel ends with the murder of Ostap Bender, "the great combinator," and the revelation that the secret had already been discovered and the diamonds used to build a workers' club. In *Zolotoi telyonok* (1933; Eng. tr., *The Little Golden Calf,* 1932) a resurrected Ostap leads a band of lesser crooks in pursuit of the millions mulcted from Soviet enterprises by another representative of private initiative. The ingenious Bender succeeds, but discovers that money has no power in a socialist state. Here, the vignettes of various types are equally amusing, but the plot is firmer, and the undercurrent of serious satire is more noticeable. After their first novel, Ilf and Petrov wrote and traveled together. A trip to the United States resulted in *Odnoetazhnaya Amerika* (1937; Eng. tr., *Little Golden America,* 1937); it is the work of experienced observers, but its chief interest for us is in its point of view. The two friends also contributed short stories and *feuilletons* to *Pravda* and the humorous magazines, using many pseudonyms including Fyodor Tolstoyevski. The best of these short pieces may be found in *Kak sozdavalsya Robinzon* (1933; How Robinson Was Created), *Chudesnyie gosti* (1935; Wonderful Guests), and *Tonya* (1937; Tonya). As in the novels, the targets for satire are vulgarity, pettiness, greed, hostility to the Soviet state, and bureaucracy; but there is less humor, and the attacks are often direct. With Petrov and Katayev, Ilf collaborated in a scenario and wrote *Bogataya nevesta* (1936; The Rich Bride), a satiric comedy on an old subject in a new setting. After Ilf's death from tuberculosis, Petrov published his friend's notes (*Zapisnyie knizhki,* 1939; Notebooks), adding an illuminating preface.

See: "Ilf," in *Literaturnaya entsiklopediya,* Vol. IV (1930); obituary notices in *Literaturnaya gazeta,* April 15, 1937; L. Levin, "Zametki o satiricheskoi proze," *Molodaya gvardiya,* 1939, No. 9, pp. 151–158.

P. A. P.

Ilić, Vojislav J. (1862–1894, Serb poet), son of the renowned poet Jovan Ilić, had many educational advantages in his father's home in Belgrade, but he was difficult and unadaptable. Later, as a civil servant, he was still undisciplined, and his career was often interrupted by his instability—as well as by his fierce opposition to Serbian administrative authorities.

Ilić wrote a certain amount of prose (notably *Shakespeare-ov Koriolan,* 1882, Shakespeare's *Coriolanus; Shakespeare i Bacon,* 1883, Shakespeare and Bacon), but he is important chiefly as a poet. He started in early youth, and a first volume, *Pesme* (Poems), appeared in 1887, followed by a second volume in 1889; posthumous collections of his verse were published in 1907 and 1909. Ilić broke away, or intended to break away and sometimes did, from romantic conventions both of form and substance; he hated pathos, rhetoric, and subjectivity and tried to make his poems as impersonal, pure, and serene as fine sculpture. He turned to remote countries and above all to classical antiquity whose beauty he deeply felt. He is indeed in some moods a modern classicist and treated such themes as Pythia, the death of Pericles, the Argonauts. He also produced, however, quite subjective, freedom-inspired patriotic ballads and romances. His visual and auditory perceptiveness was exceptional; his poems abound in images and musical effects. Had he lived longer his work might have been of an incomparable variety and richness. The harmony between idea and form in Ilić's best poems is absolute. His art has not been surpassed in Serbia, and he has had a profound influence upon Serb poets.

See: L. Nedić, *In novije srpske lirike* (1893); J. Skerlić, *Vojislav J. Ilić* (1907).

P. A.

Iłłakowicz, Kazimiera (1892–, Polish poet), was born in Wilno of good Polish-Lithuanian gentry stock and reared, after the early death of both parents, by the family of the Counts Plater-Zyberk. Despite her aristocratic upbringing, she was attracted during her student days at the Jagiellonian University (Cracow) to socialism. After finishing her formal education at Oxford, she served as a nurse at the Russian front in the First World War, and from this experience came the passionately humanitarian verses of *Trzy struny* (1917; Three Strings). From 1918 to 1926 she was a clerk in the Foreign Office of the new Polish government, and after the May coup (1926), private secretary to Marshal Piłsudski.

Iłłakowicz strikes in poetry the same note brought by Piłsudski himself to politics: the warm, romantic, expansive, land-loving spirit of the Border gentry. She is a superb lyricist, and whatever shortcomings her poetry may possess are due to carelessness and haste rather than to any lack of the poetic gift. Of her many published volumes, the following should be noted: *Rymy dziecięce* (1923; Childlike Rhymes), charming and whimsical verses written for her nieces; *Płaczący ptak* (1927; Weeping Bird); *Z głębi serca* (1928; From the Heart's Depth); *Popiół i perły* (1930; Ashes and Pearls); *Ballady bohaterskie* (1934; Heroic Ballads); and *Wesołe wierszyki* (1934; Gay Little Verses), a new collection of children's rhymes. In 1939 Iłłakowicz won wide notoriety with her *Ścieżka obok drogi* (A Lane alongside the Highroad), an intimate, personal memoir of Marshal Piłsudski. The Second World War found her in Hungary, employing her time there in the translation of Hungarian classics.

See: K. Czachowski, *Obraz współczesnej literatury polskiej*, III (1936), 118–124, 695–696; A. P. Coleman, "Kazimiera Iłłakowicz," *Books Abroad*, XI (1937), 292–294.

A. P. C.

Ilyin, Mikhail Andreyevich, *see* Osorgin, Mikhail Andreyevich.

Iorga, Nicolae (1871–1940, Rumanian historian, literary critic, and statesman), born in Botoşani, studied in Jassy, Paris, Berlin, and Leipzig, and became a professor of world history at the University of Bucharest in 1885 and a member of the Rumanian Academy in 1900. He was also the director of the Rumanian school in Fontenay-aux-Roses near Paris and a visiting professor at the Sorbonne for several years. In 1903 he took over the editorship of *Sămănătorul* (The Sower) and created a literary movement of national and traditional character. Iorga took part in politics, was a member of the Chamber of Deputies, and for a short time premier of Rumania. In 1940 he was assassinated by Iron Guardists.

Romantic at heart and a historian in his outlook, Iorga glorified the past and emphasized the importance of the peasantry. Opposed to socialism and populism because they preach class antagonism, he believed he had established a brand new school of thought. His "sămănătorism" advocated above everything that the writer should seek inspiration in the villages, where the aboriginal people with their lore and poetry have survived all the vicissitudes of time. Yet the result of this current was a literature impregnated with French and other foreign influences, following a line bordering on Maiorescu's and Dobrogeanu-Gherea's (*qq.v.*) schools.

Iorga was an amazingly prolific writer, and his historical treatises and published documents, literary works and collections of political articles and speeches, pamphlets and translations from world literatures, amount to almost two thousand titles. He mastered several languages, was exceptionally versatile and a spectacular orator. He visited the United States in 1929; *My American Lectures* appeared in English in 1932.

See: S. Meteş, *Ce a scris N. Iorga* (1913).

L. F.

Italian literary criticism (*see also* Italian literature) is often considered the most significant contribution of Italy to letters since 1900. An eminent Austrian scholar, Schlosser, without nationalistic or political bias, wrote in 1924: "Italy, cradle of every theory and history of art, has become as formerly the teacher of the rest of Europe." Schlosser thinks that only future generations will be aware of the importance of the new theories. One may at least record them now as a special feature of recent Italian literature, and apart—as indeed the new doctrines more or less require—from the biographies of recent Italian critics.

The dominance of the ideas of Croce (*q.v.*) becomes immediately apparent. Not a great artist, but certainly a great thinker, he is the hero of this intellectual scene. It is to him that the new criticism is to be attributed—with proper deference to his forerunners Vico and De Sanctis (*q.v.*). Vico and De Sanctis are brilliantly and thoroughly clarified, revised, and brought to life by Croce. The termination of the division between form and content, a heritage of the classical criticism initiated by Plato and Aristotle, is the central idea of the new criticism. In the Vico to Croce sequence, form and content become one and the same unique spiritual act.

The consequences of the principle are many, and here the credit must go entirely to Croce. A mere list of them is bound to seem scholastic and mechanical, especially since what is vital is the spirit. But certain classifiable recommendations do become a part of the new canon, and it is useful to know what they are. Adherence to these recommendations can never by itself make one an expert of the new criticism; the critic must, as in the past, be first of all a man of sensitivity and good taste. The recommendations may then prevent him from attacking artificial problems or entering into futile discussions, in the same way that hygienic measures are an aid to the surgeon against infection even though they will not teach him how to perform an operation.

Here are the new doctrines, which come directly from and are explained by the philosophy of Croce and especially by his concept of intuition. (1) A work of art must be considered in terms of its interior significance, from its auroral birth in the mind of the poet, not in terms of its final and material results. No question of success, of money, of fame, of pleasure, of opportunity, must enter into literary criticism. (2) External to the work of art are all details concerning the times, the personal life, or even the psychology of the artist. The wine of which Carducci (*q.v.*) wrote is not the wine he actually drank. (3) The work of art may be thought of as a historic document, or even as an economic fact, a proper subject for sermons, a good piece of pedagogy, an example of patriotism, but these things do not enter into literary criticism, which must concern itself only with the aesthetic value. In this new criticism art is not indifferent to morality, as in the formula "art for art's sake," but pre-existent and therefore independent of it. (4) The work of art represents an individual moment in the life of the spirit, a form of intuition, and must therefore be studied in itself, not in connection with works similar in external forms. In this criticism, literary genres or forms do not exist. The tragedies of Alfieri, *e.g.*, are to be studied as a moment in the history of Alfieri, not Alfieri as a moment in the history of tragedy. Further, the autobiography of Alfieri must be studied in connection with his other works and not with works similar in subject matter, such as the autobiographies of Cellini or of Goethe. It is perfectly futile to ask if a work of art is a novel or a short story, a lyric or an epic: the only thing that matters is whether it possesses a lyrical feeling, and the nature of this feeling. (5) A work of art is a synthesis, *i.e.*, a new moment of the spirit; and however interesting it may be to consider separately the elements which the synthetic act organized in a new life, this research does not enter into literary criticism, which therefore does not include any study on sources, imitations, and influences. Stones, if they once belonged to an artistic building, or were even already sculptured or made ornate, are again stones when used in a new edifice. (6) Comparison being a general method of research, so-called comparative literature is not to be considered as a science apart, but a method to be used in appropriate cases. Comparisons founded on the "same" subject are false. The Satan of Dante is not the Satan of Milton; there is never the "same" subject under different forms. (7) The ideas of the poet, and especially what has been called his "poetics," are a very interesting subject of study, but cannot be used to determine what the art of the poet is; on the contrary, the artist often arrives where he had no intention of going—like Tasso, who started writing a heroic religious poem and ended by writing instead an amorous, sensuous melodrama. Sometimes poetics are a hindrance to lyricism, as in the case of Dante. (8) Since each author has his own language or technique, literary criticism consists in showing the individual creation, selecting and commenting upon the special characteristic expressions of the artist. One of the critics, Giulio Bertoni (1878–1943), here distinguishes between *lingua*, which is language as expression, and *linguaggio*, which is language as communication. No history of technique (of sonnets, *canzoni*, etc.) is therefore permitted in this literary criticism; and consequently there are no such things as schools of poetry. (9) The principal business of literary criticism is to find the unifying sentiment which underlies the synthesis. The new critics, therefore, have made frequent studies on the unity of important works, but have avoided finding unity in plots, intrigues, characters, events, and have consistently found it in a certain feeling or tone (*e.g.*, the unity of Ariosto's *Orlando Furioso* lies in the feeling of world harmony, and not in the war between Saracens and Christians, or in the love of Ruggero and Bradamante, or in the folly of Orlando, etc.) (10) The work of the critic consists in selecting the pure form from the impure, the living from the dead, in short, what is real art from what is bombastic, or pedagogical, or abstract truth from what is an instant of fatigue or a morality or an arid moment of the poet. (11) New experiences and the development of humanity renovate literary criticism, which can never be final. In many cases the real life of the author begins with his actual death. Every new generation will have its own interpretation of the past, but it will not be disconnected from preceding criticism. Like every scientific work, literary criticism is similar to a chain. Studies on the so-called "fortune of an author," therefore, have been popular with the school of Croce. A successful example is that of Vittore Branca on the fortune of Boccaccio's *Decameron* (*Linee di una storia della critica al "Decamerone,"* 1939). (12) Finally, the consideration of a work of art as individual unique intuition makes it impossible to write a history of literature. A connection between different intuitions does not exist, and any effort to establish it provokes, in the end, a mixture of criticism with the history of culture or of religion or of national feeling which is the too obvious defect in De Sanctis's *Storia della letteratura italiana* (2 vols., 1871; Eng. tr., *History of Italian Literature,* 1931). A history of literature can only be conceived in the form of essays devoted to single authors.

It is easy to see that these tenets run counter to most of the previous criticism and are highly antiprofessional. They reduce all criticism to an aesthetic judgment. It is true that this aesthetic judgment is a historic one, and therefore every fact may be useful in its formation, but the preparation of the judgment is not the judgment itself. Men with little historical preparation, such as De Sanctis by comparison with Carducci, may possess an insight superior to those with a great deal of such erudition—as is evident in the writings on Dante by these two critics. It is quality not the quantity of the documents that is of value.

The new criticism calls for concentration, brevity, search for unity. Generally all appearances of erudition vanish, and several of the best books of this kind have no footnotes. (See Francesco Gaeta, *Salvatore di Giacomo,* 1911; Eugenio Donadoni, *Antonio Fogazzaro,* 1913; Luigi Russo, *Salvatore di Giacomo,* 1921; Piero Nardi, *Antonio Fogazzaro,* 1938.) Some of these critics even write well, which since the generation of the 80's was considered if not actually a sin, at least a luxury. Some do not belong to the professional set, except that they write for newspapers and magazines.

Whatever one may think of this philosophy of art and of this radical rebuilding of the house of criticism, it is a historic fact that after Croce Italian literature has been completely renewed by these ideas. Little by little at the beginning, and more rapidly later, partly through Croce, partly through his disciples, partly even through those who opposed Croce but could not help following in his footsteps, new values enter into the history of literature. There are new names, new characteristics, new problems, new answers to old questions, new shifts of emphasis on authors or periods. These changes were not the result of the discovery of fresh facts and the publication of unknown documents, as was believed by the critics of historic positivism, but came through the critical vigor of Croce.

Many have had a part in this movement, but none perhaps are so outstanding, compared with the master, as to justify extensive treatment here. The best are those nurtured in the new atmosphere created by Croce in those universities where the old system had dominated (see, *e.g.,* the recollections of a Gentile, *q.v.,* in Pisa at the school of D'Ancona, or of a Casella in Florence at that of Rajna). Eugenio Donadoni (1870–1924) in his writings on Foscolo and Fogazzaro (*q.v.*) and Attilio Momigliano (*q.v.*) on Manzoni come first to mind.

A category apart must be made for those writers who were influenced by the criticism of Croce when their minds had already been somewhat definitely formed along traditional lines: such men, Vittorio Rossi (1865–1938), Francesco Flamini (1868–1922), Ernesto Giacomo Parodi (1862–1923), *et al.,* made adjustments.

Another category could be made up for those who tried to go beyond Croce. The most important is certainly Gentile, who insisted on the unity of the spiritual act against the divisions made by Croce between the aesthetic and the philosophic moments. For Gentile the work of art is always also a work of thought. The results of this point of view as seen in his literary essays of more recent years (on Dante, Manzoni, Leopardi) show that to Gentile—and likewise to Mario Casella in his essays on Provençal poets, Dante, and Cervantes—the authors under discussion emerge as if lacking really distinctive personal qualities.

Several trends of course have conflicted with those of Croce. The most original and at times successful among these has been that represented by Renato Serra (*q.v.*). For him and his followers, there are only lyrical fragments in each work of art. Criticism consists in a sensuous reading of these fragments savoring each chosen word to get its flavor. The tendency here is to forget the world of the author for his words; and however much of a display of virtuosity in analyzing single expressions this may provide, the final result today seems aridity and boredom.

See: Luigi Russo, "Richtlinien der literarischen Kritik und der Literaturgeschichte in Italien," *Deutsche Vierteljahrschrift für Literaturwissenschaft und Geistesgeschichte,* X (1932), 534–547.

G. P.

Italian literature. Between 1860 and 1940 Italian culture has in general followed the course of European culture. Like the rest of Europe, Italy adopted the positivistic doctrines and the ingenuous religion of science, with its related agnosticism, which spread over the continent between 1860 and 1890. Then came the swift disappointments and the reactions of the idealists and the historically minded at the outset of the 20th century (1890–1914). In Italy as elsewhere the First World War released an utter confusion of thought rather than new currents of ideas, and it would seem that Italy still lies in the midst of this confusion today. Naturally enough, European transformations had in Italy special aspects, national representatives, and characteristic local problems; though in communion with Europe, Italy lived her own intellectual life, as a brief summary will make abundantly clear.

In 1861 the first kingdom of Italy was formed, still without Venetia (added in 1866) and Rome (taken in 1870); it was formed by virtue of European combinations rather than by the strength, will, and self-sacrifice of the

Italians themselves, although they indeed, since 1848, had given evidence of having at least a ruling class endowed with a certain measure of ability and determination. The rural classes were untouched by the political movements and intellectual life of the country; the directing minds (Cavour, Mazzini, Gioberti, Manzoni) disappeared; and after a kind of unity was achieved Italy went through a period of sadness, mediocrity, turmoil, and lack of faith. The beneficial effects of unity began to be felt only with the rising of a new generation, about 1880.

A French traveler, Hippolyte Taine (*q.v.*), who came to the Peninsula to explore his own country's new political neighbor, thus describes the atmosphere of Naples in his *Voyage en Italie* (1866): "There is the same activity, the same exuberance, in science and religion as in politics. . . . German scholarship and ideas are current, Hegel is widely read, Véra, his most zealous and most highly reputed interpreter, holds an important professorship. Spaventa is trying to discover an Italian philosophy, to reveal Gioberti as a kind of Italian Hegel; national pride enters even the field of pure speculation. . . . The public, especially the younger public, is deeply interested in these investigations. Naples, the home of Vico, has always had an aptitude for philosophy. There has recently been a rush to expositions of the *Phenomenology* of Hegel. They have no trouble in translating the special words, the abstractions, and Heaven knows what these abstractions are! There are various repercussions. Law studies especially, it is said, are well done, and carried on in a thoroughly German manner. The students are still held in by the formulas and classifications of Hegel, but the professors begin to go beyond this, and each in his own way and following his own tendencies. Ideas are still vague, nothing is formed, definitions are only beginning."

Intellectual Italy, at the time of the formation of the kingdom, was indeed Hegelian and romantic, with a somewhat mechanical Hegelianism and a very weary romanticism. As soon as freedom of the press (which only Piedmont had had as early as 1848) opened the gates to foreign publications, the country was quickly overrun by the doctrines which were having their vogue abroad, particularly in France and Germany: positivism in philosophy, realism in literature, the historical method in literary criticism. In a weak Italy, dissatisfied with herself and lacking original thinkers, European vogues met no serious resistance, and just as the chroniclers of the 15th century wrote at the time when Charles VIII made his military promenade from the Alps to Naples, that he "had conquered Italy with chalk," so it may be said that those doctrines conquered Italy with "vulgarization pamphlets."

It is interesting that the first period of political unity seems for the time to have deprived Italy of any capacity for a literature with a universal character. In an Italy divided up into little states and oppressed by foreign nations, Alfieri, Foscolo, Manzoni, and Leopardi had been European voices; in the new united Italy the only real poet, Carducci (*q.v.*), found no echo, then or later, in foreign lands. And whereas Italy coming back to life had aroused enthusiasm in Byron and Hugo, Italy now restored merely aroused interest among journalists, suspicions among politicians, and irony among historians; Mommsen created an epigram about the new Italians who are like flies born from the putrefaction of Rome. The Italians themselves were conscious of inferiority, and their only desire was to look abroad, to set up foreign models, to try to make Italy march with the German goose step, or dress with sober English elegance, or sing with the French spirit of *raillerie;* everything seemed good, save home products. The Italians even forgot that they had altogether superior native talents in such men as the great critic De Sanctis (*q.v.*); if Anglo-Saxon nations gave only belated recognition to De Sanctis (not until 1931 was there an American translation of his chief work), his Italian contemporaries were prompt to forget or deride him.

So for 20 years people spoke of nothing but evolution, realism, naturalistic novels, heredity, and physiology; the god of the period seems to be the "fact." It may be agreed that facts must be the basis of science and history, but surely only on condition that they be not torn from ideas and from life, which confer upon them value and meaning. What seems to dominate in this drab period is the cult of the "little fact" for its own sake. People really thought that it was enough to put "facts" together in order to have science, literary history, and even philosophy. The movement, in literature, had no eminent leadership in Italy. In a university thesis devoted to a minute study of the mediocre polemics of the period, Paul Arrighi is compelled to discuss the theories in terms of De Sanctis, an opponent of the cult, and of Luigi Capuana (*q.v.*), a vague, mediocre advocate who variously imitated French books and articles of uncertain value. The name of Ardigò, the philosopher of Italian positivism, is not even mentioned in the thesis, and rightly so, because in his meditations Ardigò never deigned to take art into consideration.

With the "social-question" emphasis of these years when *verismo* was popular, it was assumed that one could really conceive "experimental" novels and poems that were "social works"; even serious and profound writers like Verga (*q.v.*) believed this. What they actually wrote, to be sure, were pure works of art, neither scientific nor social; only in some little impurity, in the better writers' prefaces or correspondence, can traces of the current mood be perceived. In connection with these delusions, the question of morality in art, or of "art for art's sake," was debated 30 years after it had been considered in France, and without originality; Olindo Guerrini (pseud. Lorenzo Stecchetti, 1845–1916) published the most scandalous of his poems, in which one finds, as in many Italian poets of the period, a taste reminiscent of Heine for irreverence and sentimental irony.

Carducci was Italy's only true poet of the period. He stood indeed for a reaction against the period, he went counter to the official Italy of the moment and, at first in proud solitude, prepared the way for the coming Italian generation. He revealed and restored tradition; he was inspired by a powerful patriotic feeling, he possessed an exact knowledge of every form of literary art and profound understanding of every historical period and of innumerable figures of Italian life. A simple, austere morality of the common people is voiced in every one of his verses. He was not a thinker; indeed he is weaker in his critical writings, where he attempts to found a literary history of Italy based on what he supposes to be its three elements: chivalric, religious, and popular; and in his respect for documents and painstaking documentary research he is positively obsequious. Carducci was more of a historian in his poetry than in his historical writings, a more profound political student in his dreams than in his manifestations, now related to the Masonic mentality, now merely oratorical; he was more of an educator in his example than in his often partisan attempts to influence the school system. All this led to his having as disciples many Italians who did not follow his school or belong to the narrow circle of his so-called students: he was the teacher of the new Italians in general. Very well known in his own day through the abundant polemics, his figure has loomed even larger since his death, and he still appears far superior to any of his contemporaries.

Carducci's fundamental creed was paganism and anticlericalism; from his "Inno a Satana" to his "Fonti del Clitunno" the anti-Christian note is ever-present; in this respect Carducci represented a mood common in his period to scientists, men of learning, men of letters, and politicians. Paradoxically the Italians who were devoting their attention to the Middle Ages showed a profound antipathy for ideas that are either medieval or attributed to the Middle Ages, for asceticism, mysticism, theology, scholasticism, and religious sentiment in general; from Bartoli to D'Ancona, from Comparetti to Novati, the Middle Ages are studied only to find and exalt, as it were, what is antimedieval or least medieval about them, namely, the echoes of classicism and paganism.

Dreams and programs of "reconciliation" between the church and the state, or of "modernization" of the church, had no practical outcome, but in their suppressed hopes, vague idealism, and occasional nostalgia they had literary consequences. The disturbed consciences of believers, who also felt themselves to be patriots and were collaborating with the political organizations of the liberal state, is sensed in the poetry of the priest Giacomo Zanella (*q.v.*) and in the novels of his disciple Antonio Fogazzaro (*q.v.*).

Meanwhile, a particularly important if slow cultural transformation was taking place: the formation of an everyday language, for everyday needs and exchanges; and this language was extending over the entire Peninsula. Powerful factors in its spread were the school system, the newspapers, and compulsory military service with its attendant scattering of youthful recruits over all of Italy and the consequent mingling of their dialects.

The reform of the language, which was part of Manzoni's program, may have been debatable in terms of scientific philology. At all events it brought about (with the support of the schools and of weeklies with an aesthetic leaning, which, from the *Fanfulla della domenica* to the *Rassegna settimanale,* had great importance in Italy) the adoption of a clear, simple, modest prose-form. This lasted until the vogue of D'Annunzio (*q.v.*), about 1900, and even then it was only corrupted rather than destroyed. This reform was a great step forward and meant that Italy's unity, formed in a material way by the political and military class, was now being cemented in the souls of the middle classes and the people.

The school system set up by the Casati Law in 1860 remained generally unchanged until 1923 (when it was fundamentally revised by the Gentile Reform; *see* Gentile). Its efficiency, very high in the secondary schools, very low in the universities, varied in the elementary schools according to the financial means of the local governments to which it was long entrusted, and these means were abundant in the north and distinctly limited in the south. The Daneo-Credaro Law of 1910 brought in state aid everywhere. The effects of liberal-arts schools in Italy were the creation of a ruling class with a common cultural foundation based upon the classics and a satisfactory and progressive decrease in illiteracy, which in some regions of Italy ran above 90 per cent in 1860 and now is somewhere around 15 per cent of the total population.

While the unification of the kingdom led to a certain unification of prose writing, it also saw the resurrection of regional and dialectal forms in poetry, in the novel, and in the artistic consciousness. Even before Italian unity there had existed great dialectal authors, *e.g.*, Meli, Belli, and Porta; but their reading public was limited to their own regions, and few Italian histories of literature looked upon them as artistic writers. With Italian unity the people of Milan learned to love the creations of Angelo Musco's (1872–1937) Sicilian theatre, and the public of Palermo began to listen to Giacinto Gallina's (1852–1897) Venetian comedies. The dialects were modified, and while the school transformed them or dispersed them throughout the younger generation, among the cultured classes they became refined into forms capable of being understood by all Italians. Even novels written in the normal Italian, since realism was in favor, were forced to reproduce the sonorousness, occasionally the syntax, and even the words of dialects. The early short stories of D'Annunzio, the novels and short stories of Capuana, Deledda, Serao, Fucini, and Pirandello (*qq.v.*) are full of local references. Sicilian syntax makes itself felt in Verga's novels, and, used as a realistic and humorous element, lines of dialect make their appearance in the utterances of certain minor characters of Fogazzaro; one great Neapolitan poet, Salvatore Di Giacomo (*q.v.*), made his way to public fame through the medium of a greatly refined and elaborated dialect.

Along with this resumption of regional and dialectal literature went the intellectual and publishing activities of the various Italian centers; in spite of unity, Italy did not become centralized like France, and each great city retained, as in Germany, its own characteristics. One may say that practical matters dominated in Milan, intellectual and artistic things in Florence, official government work in Rome; all centers, indeed even extremely small ones, contributed to maintain that historical Italian variety which goes back to the time of the communes and the oligarchic states (*signorie*).

The first sign of a reaction against realism, positivism, and the historical method came to Italy with a current of aestheticism which had its greatest exponent in Gabriele D'Annunzio. One may or may not admire his art, but one cannot deny his enormous influence in Italy, which could hardly have been so great were it not related to a national quality, a leaning toward rhetoric that ever since Humanism had been very much alive in the Italian upper classes and had been kept in operation by a type of education predominantly classical and Ciceronian in character. D'Annunzio's influence was not merely literary; it extended to social and political life, perhaps in inverse ratio to its artistic originality; the less the originality, the more the oratory grew and affected Italian culture. With an amazing talent for assimilation, a positive genius for imitation, D'Annunzio drank deep at all sources of European culture, from L. N. Tolstoy to Nietzsche (*qq.v.*). Consequently, he was appreciated by foreigners far more than was Carducci, because in his works they found the flavor of their own countries' creations. But fundamentally unchanged by whatever he had acquired from abroad, which never essentially affected his Abruzzian nature, D'Annunzio developed within himself a literary virtuosity almost without precedent, and under the magic of his words, as under a sirocco wind, all forms of corruption grew; the national sentiment degenerated into imperialism, love into sensuality, ornament into the merely baroque, music into exhaustion, literary criticism into love of words, war into a passion for slaughter, politics into dilettantism. His imprint appeared on every phase of the nation's life, and his brand was upon men that one would suppose quite immune to rhetoric, such as bankers and professional soldiers.

There were no such repercussions in the case of another, in his way important, Italian poet of this period, Giovanni Pascoli (*q.v.*); his aestheticism (he wanted to turn the poet into a "little child") started no new movement, his not very definite sense of the mystery of death never assumed a really religious form, his political ideas were limited to borrowing from Enrico Corradini (*q.v.*) the nationalistic concept of an Italy that was a proletarian among the nations.

The time of the reign of King Humbert I (1878–1900) had been thoroughout Europe, and especially in Italy, a period of bad taste: buildings, paintings, statues, eloquence, dress, everything was awkward and bourgeois. Then the wave of aestheticism throughout the cities of Italy resulted in a great eagerness to save from the destruction of the industrial epoch the buildings that bore some sign of artistic nobility; and this preoccupation spread to all fields of human activity. Unfortunately, for a certain length of time nearly all writers, in imitation of D'Annunzio, wrote well, that is to say too well, even when they had nothing to say.

A resumption of studies of the history of art is also due to this aesthetic current; the land of Cennini, Vasari, and Lanzi had allowed the field to be taken over by the Germans (Winckelmann), by the English (Ruskin), by the Americans (Berenson), and even by the French (Muntz). In the general renewal there appear a series of writers, some of whom are artists even with the brush, others simply historians of art, who have given through their research and above all through their interpretation of ancient, modern, and ultramodern art a series of excellent monographs and theories on artistic method. These range from Giovanni Morelli's (1816–1891) studies to the artistic writings of Soffici (*q.v.*), the keen investigations of Roberto Longhi (1890–), the daring explorations of Umberto Boccioni (1882–1916), and even to the uncertain but vast syntheses of Lionello Venturi (1885–).

One of the first signs of awakening from the paralysis which positivism had brought to Italian thought was the interest of the younger elements in socialistic doctrines. It is well known that the Italians favored extreme solutions, including on occasion anarchy (the only section of the First International to support Bakunin was the Italian). After the Socialist Party had made its first conquests, Italy adopted as her favorite writer Georges Sorel (*q.v.*), the theorist of violence as the midwife of a new social order, whom France had already relegated to secondary periodicals and minor publishers. In literature, pink socialism had an echo only in the modest and gentle works of Edmondo De Amicis (*q.v.*).

Young Italians at the beginning of the 20th century eagerly set about the task of renewing culture. This was a period of fervent activity, of innumerable translations, collections, reviews, programs, and polemics; it was the period of the *Leonardo,* futurism, the *Voce,* modernism, of syndicalistic hopes, and of the first appearance of nationalism. Voices of hope, of daring, were sometimes indefinite, often insolent; results did not always come up to the talk about them, realities did not correspond to promises, there was much that was vague and pretentious. But it is certain that Italy in those years underwent radical and rapid changes, at the core of which, one may say, was the importance given to ideas, philosophy, and religion, in contrast with the negation of these values which had been characteristic of positivism.

Of these movements, irregular and confused but significant and full of promise, the most talented representative was Giovanni Papini (*q.v.*), with his autobiography *Un Uomo finito* (1912; Eng. tr., *A Man—Finished,* American title, *The Failure,* both 1924). In this one feels the uncertainty of the period, and the confused aspirations, the spiritual trials sometimes tinctured with dilettantism, of a romantic soul reaching for the absolute and forever dissatisfied with what it achieves from moment to moment. Later, after the First World War, Papini was to write a life of Christ, less pure from a literary standpoint than the autobiography of his youth, but which, with its proclamation of a Catholic faith in the post-war period of uncertainty, struck and even astounded the public and was widely translated all over the world. In other writings, on occasion rich in content, in polemics, or in research, he played a role, sometimes a leading one, in the renewal of Italian culture.

Fundamentally related to Papini, whatever the differences in form, was the sentimental temper of the youthful poetry of the same years, which by reason of its character of uncertainty, nostalgia, reticence, sadness, solitude, fragile style, and opposition to Carducci's magniloquence and D'Annunzio's open sensuality, was called "crepuscular." The important names here are Corazzini, Moretti, Palazzeschi, Gozzano (*qq.v.*); the last two are the more outstanding, Palazzeschi with at times a sharp sense of irony and even malignity, Gozzano with harmonies of sweet resignation and nostalgic memories of women.

Futurism was a noisy phenomenon, important as a sign of the times. Its theories were far from new; they were gathered together with no other desire than to start a clamor. The works to which it gave rise were of varying worth, and the more serious artists who were temporarily affiliated with it, such as Soffici, Palazzeschi, Papini, left it as they had entered it, without contributing anything to it or taking anything from it. As evidence of a desire for an Italy renewed even at the cost of destroying her entire past, futurism struck a responsive chord in the new generations. Its founder, F. T. Marinetti (*q.v.*), having completed his task as herald of the catastrophic times that were to interrupt the peace dating from 1870, survived like the pagans in Roman villages after the triumph of Christianity—as a provincial phenomenon. The war he had prophesied buried his literary movement, which now belongs in a museum showcase.

Both futurism, with its revolutionary and ephemeral vogue of "parole in libertà" ("words at liberty"), and the group of *Voce* writers, with their love for the "fragmentary," contributed to a change observable in contemporary Italian literary prose, a severance from the classical rhythms which had been kept even during romanticism and realism. An important factor in bringing about this change has been the novels, short stories, and plays of Luigi Pirandello, who created the most "spoken" form of prose and dialogue.

In the theatrical field, where two generations of Italian playwrights had done nothing but repeat the formulas of the French bourgeois drama, with a few rare attempts at imitating Ibsen (*q.v.*), the only original Italian figure is in fact Pirandello. Extremely sensitive to the duplicities and secretiveness of the human mind whenever it feels society's eyes fixed upon it, he constructed on that theme an entire series of plays, sometimes tragic, sometimes fantastic, sometimes baldly ironical. They are built up with economy of dialogue and consummate stagecraft; Pirandello is the only recent Italian theatrical creator whom foreign audiences have applauded and foreign playwrights imitated. Sem Benelli (*q.v.*) has also been frequently applauded and imitated, but he brought no original contribution to the theatre.

Partly contemporary, partly subsequent, and essentially opposed to what D'Annunzio represented was the influence of Benedetto Croce (*q.v.*). This influence first emerged in the national life in 1903 with the periodical *Critica,* which began to appear shortly after the publication of Croce's now famous *Estetica* (first in *Atti dell' Accademia Pontaniana,* 1900; first published as a volume in 1902). Here one finds a complement to the political, economic, and intellectual renewal which coincides approximately with Victor Emanuel III's accession to the throne (1900) and with the predominance of the semi-dictator Giolitti. During this period Italy enjoyed an economic prosperity never before experienced, felt the throbbings of a national consciousness at last full-grown, permitting her to look at foreigners with a feeling of independent pride, and now developed an intellectual activity in which she rapidly overtook the contemporary cultures of Europe and America in the fields of philosophy and literary and historical criticism.

No philosopher since the time of Gioberti has had as much influence in Italy as Croce. To explain this phenomenon it must be recalled that this philosopher is also a writer, a man of letters, that his thought, always of a controversial and provocative nature, has reached with originality into the most varied fields. He has treated not only aesthetics (practically the only Croce known abroad), but Marxism and morality, law and economics, history, political life, offending and favoring living passions and interests, with immediate consequences for both individuals and political parties. Furthermore, in the form of his thinking, Croce presses on fearlessly to final conclusions, set forth with great lucidity, accompanied by interesting anecdotes, quickened by quips and paradoxes, and fortified by uncommonly profound learning. In spite of controversies, which have sometimes been extremely personal, he has displayed great honesty and impartiality, and it is understandable that for years he has been in the position of a man superior to parties, whose support was often sought by the most opposed. Although attacked for his resistance to the war against Germany and more recently for his hostility to Fascism, he has maintained his views and his prestige.

A powerful organizer as well as a thinker, Croce is to be credited with the most productive and truly organic cultural work performed during this period. He is mainly responsible for two great collections, the *Scrittori italiani* and the *Classici della filosofia moderna* (which surpasses, in many respects, the older and better-known undertaking of the same nature in Germany).

Among the greatest changes brought about by Croce has been the revival of the writings of Francesco De Sanctis, his own immediate precursor in aesthetic doctrines and literary criticism. De Sanctis now reappears as a great historian of the moral and religious life of the Italian people, the thinker who has drawn from Vico the fundamental germ of a new aestheticism, the literary critic who has been able to make the best use of this aestheticism to interpret authors and place them in a new light, the severe, thoughtful educator whose preoccupation it is to rebuild the character of the Italians. Editions of his works and studies of his life multiplied; from De Sanctis all commentators who were really of any account in the renewal of literary criticism drew their inspiration, even where they did not actually follow Croce's leadership (Serra, Gentile, Momigliano, Borgese, *qq.v.*, equally with Giuseppe De Robertis, Eugenio Donadoni, 1870–

1924, Giulio A. Levi, Luigi Russo, 1892–, *et al.*).

Of secondary importance, but interesting by reason of its political implications, was the vindication of Alfredo Oriani (*q.v.*), a novelist and historian whom the generation of positivism had relegated to comparative obscurity and who after his death (1909) came to be regarded as a pioneer by reason of his concept of the function of aristocracies in national life. There was also a revival of interest in two other writers who had lesser historical and lyrical sense, but greater political precision, Vilfredo Pareto (*q.v.*), the economist, and Gaetano Mosca (1858–1941).

In the educational field, too, there was a new fervor. The secondary school teachers were particularly active. Among a very select minority of these, the criticisms of the agnostic school made by one of their number (Giovanni Gentile) had especial effect. From him and his views on pedagogy there was to spring a complete program of renewal for the schools—which for political reasons could be translated into action only in 1923, and then only in part. The fundamental idea of Gentile, that teacher and pupil are not separate entities and that learning cannot be poured by the one into the other but must be a contemporaneous re-creation in both, was developed in innumerable practical applications in the elementary school, where he wanted religious teaching to be reintroduced, in the university, made for professional training, and in the secondary school, the preparer of men. Gentile later worked out a system of idealism called "actualism," which clashed, partly for personal and political reasons, with the ideas of Croce.

The First World War halted or threw into confusion all movements of higher culture. During that period the so-called "war of ideas" became rather a "war against ideas," and, as was natural, passions perturbed rather than clarified mental processes. Fascism, which came immediately after the war, accentuated the nationalistic note without bringing in any new doctrines; even the corporative state had had its precursors in Catholic thought (Giuseppe Toniolo, 1845–1917).

It is not difficult to relate what Fascism's effect has been upon culture, because it is quite similar to that of other totalitarian regimes. The effects have been of a democratic nature in the sense that they have been for the benefit of the greatest number, and not in terms of quality. Elementary education spread, to the detriment of higher culture. The secondary system does not seem to have suffered unduly. If this period has been without great artistic or philosophical personalities comparable to the ones of earlier periods, possibly one cannot in good faith blame Fascism, but only Providence. The cultural policy of the government, beyond the ever more strict application of Fascist political teachings in the schools, in the press, in books, in official manifestations, was to provide economic means for the outward activities of culture, such as the Fascist-founded Italian Academy, the multiplication of literary and dramatic prizes, the distribution of grants and pensions to writers. The failure of the system is a matter of historical record, even though, as happened in a few rare cases, the awards and pensions were granted to writers of merit independently of their political views.

The "racial" policy inaugurated in 1939 has had no immediate consequences in the literary field, where no writer of the Jewish race had distinguished himself in recent times (the last Jewish writer who aroused considerable interest, but who was deplored by many from an artistic viewpoint, was Guido da Verona). In the field of academic culture, on the contrary, there were serious losses, because here the so-called non-Aryans, especially in the sciences, had many men of value, fully recognized as such by Fascism itself before it adopted the racial policy. In literary criticism racialism has cost Italy the loss of the activities of Attilio Momigliano and Giulio A. Levi, authors of two of the best works on Manzoni and Leopardi.

The poetry and literature of the very youngest writers has not taken on heroic or rhetorical forms (relegated apparently to journalism and official speeches); they have preferred delicate lyricism, have deliberately chosen critical labyrinths, as seen in the so-called "Hermetic" group of poets and critics, gathered in the periodicals *Campo di Marte* and *Letteratura,* whom one might describe as lineal descendants of Mallarmé and Rimbaud (*qq.v.*).

A small number of writers left Italy on account of Fascism, but this emigration had neither the extent nor the importance of the one caused by Bolshevism in Russia or by Nazism in Germany. A single important writer, Borgese, who after the First World War had written a very well-received novel, *Rubè* (1921; Eng. tr., 1923), came to the United States where he has published one, nonliterary, work (*Goliath,* 1937). Ignazio Silone (*q.v.*) is a new writer whose books have had a considerable success due in some measure perhaps to their political tendencies.

See: B. Croce, *La Letteratura della nuova Italia* (4 vols., 1914–1915; 5th vol., 1939; 6th vol., 1940) and *Storia d'Italia* (1928); G. Prezzolini, *La Coltura italiana* (1923); L. Russo, *I Narratori* (1923); G. Papini and P. Pancrazi, *Poeti d'oggi* (1925; an anthology); B. Crémieux, *Panorama de la littérature italienne contemporaine* (1928); G. Volpe, *L'Italia in cammino* (1928); C. Pellizzi, *Le Lettere italiane del nostro secolo* (1929); E. Falqui and E. Vittorini, *Scrittori nuovi* (1930; an anthology); G. Mazzoni, *L'Ottocento* (1934); A. Galletti, *Il Novecento* (1935); P. Arrighi, *Le Vérisme dans la prose narrative italienne* (1937).

G. P.

Ivanov, Vsevolod Vyacheslanovich (1895 or 1896–, Russian short-story writer, novelist, and dramatist), is the most colorful of the "fellow travelers" and a characteristic exponent of the first decade of Soviet literature, when formlessness, local color, extreme outspokenness, and violent paradox supplanted traditional realism. Like Babel, Ivanov owes his start in literature to Gorky (*q.v.*). In its fantastic variety of experience Ivanov's life tallies with the exotic originality of his art. He is a Siberian, born in Lebyazhie on the edge of the Kirghiz steppes. "Ivanov" is a self-chosen name. His father was the illegitimate son of a governor general of Turkestan, and his mother came of mingled Polish and Kirghiz stock. He ran away from the village school to join a circus, and later from an agricultural school, first to wander, then to work as a clerk in a trading outpost. From 1912 to 1918 he alternated a winter job as a typesetter with summer peregrinations; under the name of Ben Ali Bey he posed as dervish and fakir; by turns he was sword swallower, organ-grinder, clown, acrobat, street singer, wrestler. He almost died of typhus, twice he was nearly shot by Red guerrillas and the Cheka, several times he was captured by rival armies. Once in Novonikolayevsk he supervised a labor battalion charged with the burial of 40,000 White soldiers.

His first poems appeared (1916) in a Siberian newspaper. Gorky printed his first story, "Po Irtyshu" (Along the Irtish River), in *Letopis* (Chronicle), but rejected the next 20 with the advice to live and learn more. Ivanov thereupon took an active part in the Revolution, making speeches, setting type, writing articles, even supervising a school, and helping the Red Guard defend Omsk from the advancing Czechs. He managed to reach Petersburg, where he nearly died of hunger until Gorky rescued him and installed him in the House of Scientists. He joined the Serapion Brothers, a group of young Petersburg writers who staunchly affirmed art's independence from political regimentation. His first literary success came with *Partizany* (1922; The Partisans), Siberian civil-war tales, journalistic, uninhibited, and powerful. A novel, *Bronepoyezd 14–69* (1922; Armored Train 14–69), placed him in the front rank of Soviet writers and remains his best-known work. It deals with an episode of Japanese intervention in Siberia in 1919 and proclaims the ideal of social solidarity on a plane equivalent to religious martyrdom. One line became a watchword: "It is for the sake of truth that our Russia is burning!" It was given a brilliant production by the Moscow Art Theatre (1927), thereby marking the Theatre's successful shift from traditional realism to socialized realism. An American version was given in New York (1931) and published in 1933.

Ivanov has since produced more than 25 volumes of tales, novels, and plays, often at the rate of three or four a year. Among the best are *Tsvetnye vertry* (1922; Colorful Winds), *Golubye peski* (1923; Blue Sands), *Puteshestvie v stranu kotoroi yeshcho net* (1930; Journey to a Country That Does Not Yet Exist), and *Povesti Brigadira M. M. Sinitsyna* (1930; Tales of Brigadier Sinitsyn). His last major work is *Pokhozhdeniya fakira* (1935; Eng. tr., abridged, *The Adventures of a Fakir*, 1935), a picaresque semi-autobiographical novel in which the fantastic and the commonplace are exuberantly mingled. His early depiction of man "without a soul" is replaced by a more humanized conception, and his abundant gifts of humor, observation, and narrative skill are revealed at their best. Ivanov has miraculously retained a pristine sense of wonder at life, unmarked by bitterness. Some passages attain a rare quality of aerial ease and freedom, something of a riddle in view of his statement (1934) at a Pan-Soviet literary congress when he avowed the necessity for Bolshevik "tendentiousness," thereby repudiating his Serapion affiliation. Little is known of his work in recent years.

Several early short stories appear in anthologies in English—"The Child" (1925), " 'Merican" (1925), "On the Rails" (1925), "When I Was a Fakir" (1929), "Unfrozen Water" (1932), "The Desert of Toub-Koy" (1933).

See: L. M. Polyak and E. B. Trager, "V. V. Ivanov," in *Literatura XX veka* (1934), pp. 134–140; G. Struve, *Soviet Russian Literature* (1935), pp. 27–31.

N. S.

Ivanov, Vyacheslav Ivanovich (1866–, Russian poet, critic, essayist, and translator), was born in Moscow into the family of a government official. After graduating from the First Moscow Gymnasium, Ivanov spent two years at the University of Moscow, studying classical antiquity under Vinogradov and Guerier. After that he went to Germany, where he studied under Mommsen in Berlin. During his university days he became absorbed in the works of Nietzsche and Vladimir Solovyov (*qq.v.*). In 1895 Ivanov married L. D. Zinovyeva-Hannibal, a distant relative of Pushkin, who made Ivanov conscious of his own poetic ability. He began publishing verse in 1898. During the years 1898–1903 the Ivanovs traveled abroad, visiting London, Athens, Cairo, and Alexandria. In 1903 he delivered a series of lectures in Paris on Dionysus. After they had returned to Russia, the Ivanovs took up residence in St. Petersburg, where their "tower" soon became famous for its "Wednesdays"—informal gatherings of the literary élite. Through the medium of these gatherings Ivanov came to be recognized as leader of the Petersburg symbolists. His eruditeness won him general respect, and in 1909 he was invited to give a course on Roman and Greek literature at the Women's College courses of Rayev. After the October Revolution of 1917 he, like many another poet, took an active part in the Soviet cultural program. In 1921 he was appointed professor at Baku University and in 1924 was sent on a mission to Italy, where he remained.

Ivanov's poetic works, *Kormchiya zvezdy* (1903; Guiding Stars), *Prozrachnost* (1904; Transparency), *Eros* (1907), *Cor Ardens* (1911), are characterized by a ponderous magnificence of language that harks back to the best works of Derzhavin; at the same time they present a curious blend of the literature of ancient Alexandria with that of the most recent modernists. In his collected essays, *Po zvezdam* (1905; Following the Stars) and *Borozdy i mezhi* (1916; Furrows and Borders), Ivanov reveals his belief that art is a mystical religious activity, and he propagandizes for collective art on a monumental scale. His views on culture and civilization are included in the volume written in collaboration with Gershenzon, *Perepiska iz dvnukh uglov* (1921; Correspondence from Two Corners), and in the long philosophical poem, *Chelovek* (1939; Man). His translations include the works of Aeschylus, Dante, Petrarch, Byron, Nietzsche (*q.v.*), and E. T. A. Hoffmann.

See: V. Bryusov, *Dalekiye i blizkiyie* (1912); L. Shestov, "Vyacheslav Velikolepni," *Russkaya mysl*, 1916, No. 10.

O. M.

Iwaszkiewicz, Jarosław (pseud. Eleuter, 1894–, Polish poet, novelist, and playwright), was born near Kalnik, Kievan Ukraine, of Polish gentry stock. Educated at home and in Kiev University, he was early associated, at first through common family interests, later through common tastes, with the composer Karol Szymanowski, for whose opera *King Roger of Sicily* he wrote the libretto. After making his début as a poet in Kiev, Iwaszkiewicz moved at the end of the First World War to Warsaw, where he became one of the founders of *Skamander* (*see* Polish literature). He was often abroad, from 1922, as a state official, in Paris and Copenhagen and at one time in Persia. An artist to the core, called sometimes the Polish Oscar Wilde, Iwaszkiewicz brought to each literary form he essayed the fine poetic sense and feeling for rhythm and color born and bred in him as a son of the Ukraine. *Siedem bogatych miast nieśmiertelnego Kościej* (1924; The Seven Rich Towns of the Immortal Kościej) and *Księżyc wschodzi* (1925; The Moon is Rising) are among his important early works, and among the later ones *Czerwone tarcze* (1934; Red Shields), a fictionized life of the 12th-century Piast prince, Henry of Sandomierz, must be noted. In the 30's Iwaszkiewicz was led, as a result of the many pitfalls facing a writer on contemporary themes, to seek material in the past; from this came two unusual plays, the highly successful *Lato w Nohant* (1936; Summer in Nohant), a series of scenes from the last chapter of the Chopin–George Sand partnership, and the less finely executed *Maskarada* (1939; Masquerade), an improvisation on the life of Pushkin. All Iwaszkiewicz's writings are infected with disillusionment and marked by decadence, especially his last novel, *Pasje Błędomierskie* (1938; The Passions of Błędomierz), but all are redeemed by their style.

See: E. Breiter, review of *Czerwone tarcze* in *Wiadomości literackie*, 1934, No. 48; K. Czachowski, *Obraz współczesnej literatury polskiej*, III (1936), 181–192, 696–698; A. P. Coleman, "The Literary Scene in Poland," *New York Times Book Review*, June 5, 1938, pp. 8, 18.

A. P. C.

J

Jacob, Max (1876–1944, French poet, prose writer, illustrator, and painter), was born at Quimper in Brittany. He attended the Ecole Coloniale, took his law degrees, became a journalist, accompanist, piano teacher, "nursery-maid tutor," "dimestore" salesman, shop sweeper, wanderer in back alleys starved with cold and hunger, honored guest of high aristocracy and wealthy circles, expert in palmistry, horoscopy, and card telling, learned in occultism and astrology. He shared the dire poverty, strenuous work and pursuits, rollicking or rough relaxation of his friends Apollinaire (*q.v.*), Picasso, Salmon (*q.v.*), *et al.*, "that dear gang," during the epoch-making days of the "Rue de Ravignan" at Montmartre, the most celebrated haunt of the post First World War pioneers who were then building "the ascetic provisional shed of the cubist Acropolis." Long before futurism, Freudianism, and surrealism, Max Jacob introduced his "nocturnal nightmares (and) day hallucinations" into poetry which should, in his eyes, express what is deepest and most intimate in man.

The capital event in his subsequent life was his conversion to Catholicism, following two apparitions of Christ, at the Rue de Ravignan in 1909 and at the movies in 1914, which greatly enriched and vivified his poetry. His writings are as surprising as his proteiform life and personality with their variety and many-faceted composition and birdlike mobility. He took a definite stand against Rimbaud (*q.v.*) and also the symbolists, insisting that everything should be given order and place: "Everything that exists is situated, and so is all that transcends matter." To him "gaiety, especially when sad, is divine fire"; and he has the whole range of it from an imperceptible smile to facetiousness, buffoonery, fantastic drolleries, and the joyous, free interplay of mind and imagination. His intellect seems always about to devour the inspired lyricism it lights up. He has experimented with all literary forms. One finds art criticism, biography, translation; a children's book, *Histoire du roi Kaboul et du marmiton Gauvain* (1903); novels, such as *Saint Matorel* (1909), *Le Terrain Bouchaballe* (1923), and *Filibuth, ou la Montre en or* (1924); short stories, *Cinématoma* (1919), *Le Cabinet noir* (1922), and *Le Tableau de la bourgeoisie* (1930), in which the humorist and poet in him classify the bourgeois in families presenting "veiled stupidity, silent cruelty, rivalries, unending backbiting, and illegitimate ambitions." He has done verse portraits in *Le Laboratoire central* (1920); short comedies acted on provincial stages, the work of a born mimic; an operetta, *Isabelle et Pantalon* (1923); a dramatic fantasy, *Le Dos d'Arlequin; petit drame portatif*, "an unactable play, illustrated by the author" (1919); a chronicle of 20th-century painting and literature, "Le Tiers transporté" (*Feux de Paris*, No. 7–8, 1935), including unforgettable portraits of Apollinaire and Marinetti (*q.v.*). There are prose poems like the *Cornet à Dés* (1906), imitated *ad nauseam*, "the subject or picturesqueness of which does not matter," with a preface to its 1916 edition which remains the *vade mecum* of all experimenters in this form, or like the *Visions infernales* (1924), where the devil appears insistently familiar and menacing under the masks of unexpected characters placed in prosaic or fantastic scenes, or again like the *Ballades* (1939), where miracle insensibly spreads over nameless houses and commonplace streets, through the least "distinguished" souls.

His verse poems are even more important, notably those inserted in *Le Siège de Jérusalem; drame céleste* (1912–1914), a hermetic masterpiece which was the author's favorite work; in the prose and verse collection entitled *La Défense de Tartufe* (1919), touching the period of his conversion; and in the "Chansons de Bretagne" (some unpublished), *Fond de l'eau* (1927), *Le Sacrifice impérial* (1928), and *Rivages* (1932), besides an infinite number of uncollected poems, which embody Max Jacob's wish to "recreate earth in the atmosphere of Heaven." His *Art poétique* (1922) expresses the author's loves, hatreds, and intentions as well as the aims and tendencies of modern poetry. While neither strictly built nor metaphysical like Claudel's (*q.v.*), it is the freest, most suggestive treatise on poetical aesthetics published since Baudelaire and Banville (*qq.v.*). The variety of Max Jacob's works is exemplified also in grim dramas shot with sudden flashes of light; in burlesque scenes or cruel, compressed satires contrasted with subtle songs distilling popular ditties of town and country; in heroic actions halted by odd remarks or axioms and proverbs; in celestial or sweet visions blending the crosscurrents of spirit and matter; in harrowing confessions interspersed with shrewd observations; finally in lofty verse sustained as plain song like that of "Le Christ au cinéma" (in *La Défense de Tartufe*), created by the deft juggler of *Les Pénitents en maillot rose* (1926). There is untold variety of interchangeable planes, spaces, and points of view due to the "ubiquity" that this poet demands and possesses. Variety again exists in the synchronism of multiple measures, tones, and accents. Max Jacob hourly works new miracles for "where there is no miracle there is no genius," new soundings of the upper and lower depths, and makes new use of silence and vacuity. He can even renew syntax and the magic of words taken from every manner of speech, with all their pranks, "wanton wiles," and mirages.

In sum, Max Jacob has given a new birth to poetry, which owes him acceleration, translocations, transfigurations, together with new combinations of movements, even explosions. His greater poems vanish into vision. Their darting lightness is accounted for by his saying that "a personality is but a persisting error" and "inspiration is the passing of one world into another, from earth into heaven, from heaven into another heaven." A number of younger poets have named him "the father of modern poetry," and Cocteau (*q.v.*) "that great inspired master of elegance." His influence is felt in Spain, Italy, England. Exhibitions of his paintings in New York in 1930, 1938, and later were greatly admired. There is an anthology of his works (*Morceaux choisis*, 1936). According to R. Lannes, Max Jacob's unpublished works, among which are the important *Méditations*, will provide the matter of at least 10 volumes, and his correspondence, when brought out, will rank among the chief epistolary treasures in French literature.

Since the death of Max Jacob at the Drancy concentration camp a number of his unpublished poems and many articles concerning his work and personality have appeared in the *Arche*, *Cahiers du sud*, *Confluences*, *Orbe*, *Poésie 44*, and other French literary reviews and newspapers.

See: "Max Jacob," *Disque vert* (Brussels) November, 1923 (issue devoted to Jacob); André Salmon, *Max Jacob, poète, peintre mystique et homme de qualité* (1927); Robert Guiette, "Vie de Max Jacob," *Nouvelle Revue française*, XLIII (1934), 5–19, 248–259; A. Billy, *Max Jacob* (1946), with an anthology including previously unpublished letters and poems.

M. M.

Jacobsen, Jens Peter (1847–85), Danish novelist), was born in Thisted, Jutland. His childhood was not unlike that described in his autobiographical novel *Niels Lyhne* (1880; Eng. tr., 1919) in which the hero and a playmate invent endless stories and act them out. Like Niels Lyhne, again, he was divided in allegiance between a practical father and a mother who cherished poetic yearnings. Jens Peter's favorite study was botany—newly introduced into the schools—and he studied it in the open till he knew every plant in the neighborhood. At the same time he read all the Danish classics. In Copenhagen he continued both pursuits; his reading now included Goethe and Schiller, Shakespeare, Kierkegaard, Heine, Byron, Tennyson, and Feuerbach, besides the Bible. He won a gold medal at the university for his thesis on a microscopic marsh plant, and in the same year (1872) his first tale, *Mogens* (Eng. tr., *Mogens and Other Stories*, 1921), was published. Still in the same year he published a translation of Darwin's *The Origin of Species*, following it three years later with a translation of *The Descent of Man*. We know from Jacobsen's words to a friend that the abandonment of all religious faith early in life caused him an agonizing struggle. He embraced evolution as a new faith. For a long time he was in doubt as to whether he would make science or literature his lifework. At 20 he wrote in his diary that if he could "bring into the realm of literature the eternal laws of nature" he felt that his work would be "more than ordinary." These words give the key to his attitude toward life as well as literature.

In *Mogens* Jacobsen first essayed his unique nature descriptions, based on minute, even scientific observation and clothed in a poetic and beautiful language. But it is always nature leading its own life, without the elves and trolls with which the romanticists had peopled the woods and dells and without any sentimental idea of nature as sympathizing with man. *Fru Marie Grubbe; Interiører fra det 17. Aarhundrede* (1876; Eng. tr., *Marie Grubbe; a Lady of the Seventeenth Century*, 1917) was based on a careful study of old documents, and its language is enriched by archaic words and phrases. The heroine was a historical person, a woman who was first married to a king's son and finally found happiness in marriage with a poor ferryman. Jacobsen does not, however, make her last husband a model of rural virtue and does not for a moment take him out of his class, but Søren has that in him which satisfies the woman looking for her master. Marie Grubbe is the first of the women in whom Jacobsen embodies his reaction against the traditional bloodless ideal of femininity. This reaction is more consciously expressed by the modern women in the already-mentioned *Niels Lyhne.* They chafe under the tyranny, disguised as chivalry, which forces into rank growth the qualities once for all established as proper to "the sex," while the qualities they actually possess are crushed out or forced inward by ignoring them. Jacobsen once wrote to a friend that the only subject worthy of literary treatment was "the struggle against that which exists for the right to exist in one's own way." This "right to exist in one's own way" he conceded also to women and endeavored to understand them as individuals instead of projecting his own preconceived ideal of them as the romanticists had done. The hero of *Niels Lyhne,* who "cannot find a handle to life," is in some respects a self-portrait. When Niels tells his mother that nothing but flawless work will satisfy him, it expresses Jacobsen's own ideal, to which he adhered at the cost of labor that is sometimes too apparent in the final result. But unlike his creator Niels never wrote the books he conceived. Not only in the person of his hero but also in the other persons of the book, in Niels's mother and the tutor Bigum—a caricature of himself—Jacobsen scourged himself for "the fair vice of dreams" and reminded himself that "the fairest dreams and the deepest longings do not add an inch to the stature of a human soul." The dogma may be questioned, but it stemmed from his belief in the inexorability of law. This was at the bottom of his revolt against religion; he refused to think that a supernatural power would somehow juggle away the consequences of wrongdoing provided the sinner repented.

In his own life Jacobsen tested his stoical faith, living a life of proud rectitude, patiently bearing poverty and illness, a lovable friend to the few people whom his failing strength allowed him to receive. In his short story *Fru Fønss* (Eng. tr. in *Mogens and Other Stories*), the last in his slender production, there is a letter from a woman who knew she was soon to die. It was his own farewell to "this beautiful earth" and his plea to be remembered. When his illness could no longer be fought off, he went home to his mother in Thisted, where he died, only 38 years old.

See: Georg Brandes, *Det moderne Gennembruds Mænd* (1883); Georg Christensen, *J. P. Jacobsen* (1910); Alrik Gustafson, *Six Scandinavian Novelists* (1940).

H. A. L.

Jahier, Piero (1884–, Italian poet), born in Genoa, has worked most of his life as a railroad employee. He is the author of only three small books, composed between the years 1909–1919, and since then has remained silent. But these slender volumes, while never popular, have won for him the high esteem of critics. What Jahier has written is of a concentrated lyricism, reflects deep experiences of life, reveals strong and original convictions imbued with a high ideal of poetry and humanity. It is not surprising that the name of Jahier is to be found in almost all anthologies and histories of contemporary Italian literature. He is connected with the movement of the *Voce* (*see* Prezzolini); this review discovered him in 1909, and he was one of its most faithful contributors. His three books have that autobiographical flavor that appealed to the *Voce* group (cf. *Uomo finito* of Papini, *q.v., Il Mio Carso* of Slataper, *q.v., Lemmonio Boreo* of Soffici, *q.v.*). They also disclose an inclination towards a fragmentary form of writing, which gives to his art an intensity and a sincerity free of some of the handicaps of more orthodox literary construction. Jahier's lyrical fragments reveal three fundamental life experiences. The first publication, *Ragazzo* (1909), concerns his family, which belonged to that small minority of aboriginal Protestants called Waldensians who have inhabited the western Alpine border of Italy since approximately the 12th century. The second, *Gino Bianchi* (1915), deals with Jahier's work in a railroad office; he gives an excellent, if at times slightly heavy, satire of red tape. The third, *Con me e con gli Alpini* (1919), is dedicated to Jahier's soldiers during the First World War and especially to the most humble and poor of them. Generally these fragments begin with some very simple sentences like notes from a diary, but very soon moral warmth brings them to incandescence. Every word becomes an ethical judgment: Jahier champions the poor, the underdog, the peasant, the mountaineer. At times he goes from prose to a form of poetry, with rhymes and assonances—a very original mixture of church canticle and popular song. Jahier also has made a collection of soldiers' songs, *Canti di soldati* (1919).

His books should not be confused with sketches or memoirs; their high poetic value lies in the power of concentrating in a sentence, and often in a single word, a moral situation, distilled from long repressed feelings of injustice and deprivation. Descriptions, merely incidental details, do not appeal to Jahier, who is more of a sculptor than a painter. Sometimes he may chisel his marble awkwardly, but always with energy. Not often does he find entirely adequate expression for his torment, but when he does his art attains a purity and loftiness that are rare.

See: P. Pancrazi, *Ragguagli di Parnaso (1919–1920)*, (1920), pp. 127–139; G. Prezzolini, *Amici* (1922), pp. 37–59; C. Bo, *Frontespizio* (1938), pp. 297–302.

G. P.

Jaloux, Edmond (1878–, French novelist and critic), was born and educated in Marseille. At the early age of 18 he founded a modest periodical, *Revue méditerranéenne*. Stirred by the ambition to enter upon a literary career, he went to Paris and soon began to contribute articles to such reviews and dailies as the *Mercure de France, Revue hebdomadaire, Candide, Nouvelles littéraires, Revue universelle, Gaulois, Temps, Echo de Paris*. Like many other writers at the beginning of their careers, he wrote verse and in 1906 had accumulated enough material to publish a slender volume of poems, *Une Ame d'automne*. But it was as a novelist that Jaloux was destined to win the esteem of a cultured public. His books, at the same time romantic and realistic, reveal the hidden life of restless souls. This is already true of his very first novel, *L'Agonie de l'amour* (1899), the story of a young man who dreamed of a great love which his own limitations made impossible of attainment. States of mind like this, which are melancholy but can never be characterized as morbid, are analyzed in *Les Sangsues* (1904), *L'Incertaine* (1918), *Au-dessus de la ville* (1920), *L'Alcyone* (1925), and *La Fugitive* (1926). At times a subtle note of symbolism (*see* French symbolism) in the manner of Henri de Régnier (*q.v.*) creeps in, as in *Le Reste est silence* (1909), the tragedy of an ill-matched couple, seen through the eyes of a child. A more pessimistic accent is heard in such novels as *Laetitia* (1929), *La Chute d'Icare* (1936), and *L'Oiseau-lyre* (1938). The last is the story of a young poet who, after being magnificently inspired by the "Lyre Bird" (Violette), meets an adventuress and from that moment is powerless to produce anything but platitudes—life has smothered genius. Among other novels of some importance are *Fumées dans la campagne* (1918) and *La Fin d'un beau jour* (1921), the scenes of which are laid mostly in Aix-en-Provence and in Versailles respectively. The constant avoidance by Jaloux of emphasis, the subdued atmosphere he creates, are in sharp contrast with the vigor and downrightness of writers such as Zola, Bourget, and Barrès (*qq.v.*).

In addition to his novels, Jaloux has written short stories (*La Branche morte*, 1928; *Dessins aux trois crayons*, 1934; *Trois Nouvelles*, 1935) and several volumes of criticism (*L'Esprit des livres*, 1923–1931; *Figures étrangères*, 1926; *Rainer-Maria Rilke*, 1927; *De Pascal à Barrès*, 1928; *Vie de Goethe*, 1933). He composed an important preface in 1935 for the catalogue of the exhibition held at the Bibliothèque Nationale to commemorate the 50th anniversary of the birth of symbolism.

From 1917 to 1923 Jaloux held a responsible position in the Office of Information at the Ministry of Foreign Affairs. In 1909 he was awarded the Prix Femina for *Le Reste est silence*, and in 1920 the Grand Prix de Littérature of the French Academy. He was elected to the Academy to succeed Bourget in 1936 and was received the following year by Lecomte. In 1941 he took refuge in Switzerland; in Fribourg *Le Vent souffle sur le flamme* was published, and in Geneva *Le Pouvoir des choses*.

See: Georges Girard, "Notes bio-bibliographiques: Edmond Jaloux," *Bulletin de la Maison du Livre Français*, June 15, 1922, pp. 223–224.

A. Sz.

Jammes, Francis (1868–1938, French poet), although born in Tournay, Hautes-Pyrénées, came of a colonial family from Guadeloupe. After some years of school at Pau and Bordeaux he served for a time as notary's clerk at Orthez, Basses-Pyrénées, where most of his life was to be spent. These years were marked by inner torment, from which he found relief in poetic composition. Several slender volumes, privately printed at Orthez and entitled simply *Vers* (1891–1894), won him the friendship of a discerning few, among them André Gide (*q.v.*); but it was the publication by the *Mercure de France* of *De l'angelus de l'aube à l'angelus du soir* (1897) which first revealed to the general public an original and, in many respects, a unique poetic talent. It proved to be a prolific talent as well. *Le Deuil des primevères* (1901), *Le Triomphe de la vie* (1902), and *Le Roman du lièvre* (1903) assured him a place in the first rank of the writers of his day. Jammes has been called a *réussite du bon Dieu*. What he brought to French poetry was an entirely fresh "pastoral" note, a new simplicity, a rustic artlessness (and often awkwardness) of which his more self-conscious contemporaries would have been incapable, a sensual, pagan, childlike delight in humble, natural, and minute details which he somehow rendered significant. His literary successes did not alter his way of life. He married (1906), he continued to live in the country; and when finally, after many years, he left Orthez for the

Basque village of Hasparren, it was to lead the same patriarchal existence as before.

With *Clairières dans le ciel* (1906) his writing took on a more militantly Christian and Catholic tinge. Religious themes had, it is true, attracted him from the very beginning; he had written eloquent prayers along with his elegies; but it had always seemed that, to a poet so passionately attached to the visible universe, the Catholic themes must have appealed rather for their picturesque and poetic values than because of their doctrinal implications. Closer contact, however, with the other great Catholic poet of his generation, the unyielding Paul Claudel (*q.v.*), resulted in a stiffening of Jammes's attitude in matters of dogma. His fervor burned more and more brightly. A semi-estrangement from Gide ensued; but Jammes became the darling of the devout. The poet of the elegies now aspired to the role of "Christian Vergil": his "eclogues," *Les Rayons de miel* (1908), were succeded by the three volumes of *Les Géorgiques chrétiennes* (1911–1912). His gifts as storyteller, always remarkable, won him some reputation as a Catholic novelist with *M. le curé d'Ozeron* (1918) and *Le Poète rustique* (1920), the latter created in Jammes's own likeness as he saw it. The First World War appears to have changed him very little: he remained unswervingly naïve, rustic, and Catholic. It failed to diminish his fecundity. He wrote many more books —poetry, novels, and, finally, three delightful volumes of *Mémoires* (1922–1923). In his four *Livres de quatrains* (1923–1925) he essayed, with varying success, stricter form, greater concentration. Almost up to the moment he died, full of years and piety, he was still writing. But these later books, whatever their merits, do not add much that is essential. Very often they merely repeat, less successfully, the usual themes in the usual rural setting. The poet is engaged, one feels, in putting the finishing touches to his lifelong attitudes, in arranging his image for posterity. It is not an unworthy image.

Jammes is one of the most personal of French poets. Whatever lies outside himself, the world beyond his village, leaves him indifferent or even hostile. But his own world is less limited than it might appear because his sense perceptions are so extraordinarily acute and his imagination so vivid. His familiar country landscape always remained for him an enchanted land. A regional poet, he transcends simple regionalism. An occasional exotic note, reminiscent of his colonial heredity, makes itself heard. But he is above all the poet of the humble: people, animals, things. The essentials of the good life consist, for him, in birth, marriage, procreation of children, faithful performance of a few simple tasks and religious duties. Granted all its limitations, Jammes's poetic vision is by no means timid. He dared do the impossible with apparently "unpoetic" subject matter—what other poet has ever prayed to go to heaven in the company of asses? His animals are exquisite creations. So are his *jeunes filles,* Clara d'Ellébeuse, Almaïde d'Etremont, Pomme d'Anis (Jammes remained faithful all his life to his cult of the *jeune fille*). One might trace his literary descent from Rousseau and Bernardin de Saint-Pierre. He is not exempt from the sentimentality in which they habitually overindulge. His vocabulary is extremely rich, especially in terms designating the humbler creatures and objects; his verse is a very flexible instrument. Few vocations have been more authentic. Inspired poet par excellence, he once confided to Gide that he felt he had no right to tamper with a verse after it had been written. Such a method of composition naturally begets blemishes; naïveté becomes coquetry and simplicity turns to artifice. The poet regards his own bearded and patriarchal figure with a too evident complacency. He often becomes monotonous. Devoid of humor, his irony (whenever, in the interest of righteousness, he essays it) is heavy-handed. His *Antigyde* (1932), an attempted satire on the "immoral" influence of Gide, is a case in point. He is too proud of his humility. His later books are often more edifying than satisfying; his poetic wine is diluted with too much holy water. These strictures notwithstanding, he remains one of the chief minor poets of his generation.

See: T. Braun, *Des poètes simples: Francis Jammes* (1900); E. Pilon, *Francis Jammes et le sentiment de la nature* (1908); A. de Bersaucourt, *Francis Jammes, poète chrétien* (1910); L. Moulin, "Etude sur Francis Jammes," in Jammes, *Choix de poèmes* (1922); A. Gide, *Journal* (1939).

J. Me.

Jändel, Ragnar (1895–1939, Swedish poet), born in Jämsjö, Blekinge province, began his literary career as an extremist proletarian poet during the unsettled political years just before and after the close of the First World War. But he very soon outgrew the more excessive phases of his youthful radicalism, and he took no direct polemic part in the social and political program of organized labor in Sweden in the last 20 years, though he maintained throughout these years a warm sense of solidarity with the working classes. His published work is rather extensive, including, besides 13 volumes of poetry, three autobiographical works (*Det stilla året,* 1923, The Quiet Year; *Den trånga porten,* 1924, The Narrow Way; and *Barndomstid,* 1936, Childhood), two volumes of essays on literary and general cultural subjects (*Vägledare,* 1921, Guides; *Jag och vi,* 1928, I and We), and a volume of nature studies (*Blommor,* 1937, Flowers). Neither his prose nor his poetry bear the mark of real greatness; but at their best they give sensitive individual expression to a fine spirit's searching for ultimate values in human life, and even in their less inspired moments they may serve the historian as valuable documents in his investigation of the literary-proletarian contribution to contemporary Swedish cultural trends. Jändel's first two volumes of poems, *Till kärleken och hatet* (1917; To Love and Hatred) and *De tappra* (1918; The Courageous Ones), give a pathos-filled, at times almost hysterical expression to the class consciousness of a small extremist group of the Swedish proletariat fanned into temporary fury by political developments on the Continent, particularly the Bolshevist Revolution in Russia. In these early volumes there is to be found also, however, poems conceived in a quiet, personal, confessional strain, concerned with less urgent social themes—with the home, the Swedish countryside, and with nature in some of its more unassuming idyllic moods. It is this strain that rapidly gains dominance in Jändel's later verse, though on occasion he gives indignant, direct expression to his fundamental social feeling (see "Två dikter till minnet av Sacco och Vanzetti" in *Kämpande tro,* 1928, Fighting Faith). The serene confessional strain which is the mark of most of Jändel's later poetry borders at times dangerously on the sentimental, but for the most part the poet manages to retain a healthy sense of realism, a warm, intimate closeness to the folk and to the earth. With the years he became increasingly concerned with religious problems, a tendency which he had in common with other modern Swedish poets of proletarian origins such as Dan Andersson (*q.v.*). His religious poetry, however, has in it none of the brooding primitive mysticism of Dan Andersson, nor does it find expression in an heroic or ascetic religious idealism. On the negative side it reacts strongly against institutional religion (especially as represented in the Swedish State Church), and it seems equally suspicious of the phenomena of miraculous "conversion" and of modern sectarianism of all kinds. In its positive contents it finds its most characteristic expression in a quiet nondogmatic acceptance of a religious-ethical interpretation of life not without its points of contact with Quakerism on the one hand and Emersonian religious idealism on the other.

A. G.

Janson, Kristofer Nagel (1841–1917, Norwegian author, pastor, and teacher), born in Bergen, is now remembered for but little of his voluminous and once popular production, though he was the first New Norse (Landsmaal) writer to win a poet's stipend (1876). A close friend and imitator of Björnson (*q.v.*), he is said to have been a model of the latter's heroic Pastor Sang in *Beyond Our Power*—and also of Ibsen's (*q.v.*) phrasemaker Hjalmar Ekdal in *The Wild Duck.* His saintly beard, melodious voice, and messianic manner made him a popular reader and lecturer. He taught at Christopher Bruun's folk high school from 1869 to 1878, but his religious development led him into Unitarianism, for which he labored against fearful odds among Lutheran Norwegian immigrants in the United States (1881–1893). His best-known books were the story *Han og ho* (1868; He and She) and the fictionized historical studies *Fraa Dansketidi* (1875; From the Danish Period) and *Vore bedsteforældre* (1882; Our Grandparents); the only important one available in English is *Den bergtekne* (1876; Eng. tr., *The Spell-bound Fiddler,* 1880). He was a sincere, warmhearted, courageous personality, selflessly seeking to urge men "away from strife and wrangling, and forward to brotherhood," but his writings lack artistic power.

See: H. H. Boyesen, "Kristofer Janson and the Reform of the Norwegian Language," *North American Review,* CXV (1872), 379–401; K. Hamsun, *Ny jord,* II (1888), 371–386; Janson, *Hvad jeg har oplevet* (1913), his autobiography; R. B. Anderson, *Life Story of Rasmus B. Anderson* (1915).

E. H.

Jarnés, Benjamín (1888–, Spanish novelist and essayist), was born in Aragon and bears the imprint of this province and of his countryman and guide, Baltasar Gracián. He completed almost all his studies for the priesthood, but then turned to a literary career, to which he brought a genuine predisposition and extraordinary capacity for work. He lived in Madrid until the outbreak of civil war. He went to Valencia and Barcelona in the service of the government; later, with Franco's victory, he went to Mexico, where he now collaborates on newspapers and journals and continues his literary work with undiminished fruitfulness.

The long list of his works, among the most abundant of his period, begins with *Mosén Pedro* (1924), a biographical essay. He became better known with *El río fiel,* which appeared in the *Revista de Occidente* in 1925, and especially with *El profesor inútil* (1926). In the following works, also of novelistic cast, he develops as a stylistic artist and a penetrating psychological analyst, capable of poetic delicacy: *El convidado de papel* (1928); *Paula y Paulita* (1929); *Salón de estío* (1930); *Teoría del zumbel* (1930); *Escenas junto a la muerte* (1931); and *Lo rojo y lo azul* (1932). His introversion also produces essays similar to his novels: *Ejercicios* (1927); *Rúbricas* (1931); *Fauna contemporánea* (1933); and *Cartas al Ebro* (1940), which appeared in Mexico and wherein he announces plans for the publication of numerous other works. He has also cultivated with success the Christian and the pagan legend, as in *Vida de San Alejo* (1928) and *Viviana y Merlín* (1929), both of which were amplified subsequently. His biographical works are important: *Sor Patrocinio, la monja de las llagas* (1929); *Zumalacárregui, el caudillo romántico* (1931); *Castelar, hombre del Sinaí* (1935); and *Doble agonía de Bécquer,* in which the literary critic can be seen in his full stature. He has translated into Spanish *La Chanson de Roland* (*El cantar de Roldán,* 1924), *Bubu de Montparnasse* of C. L. Philippe (*q.v.*), and various other works.

At a time when the literary scene was dominated by lyric poetry with such writers as Salinas, Guillén, García Lorca (*qq.v.*)—and the other genres suffered a passing eclipse, Jarnés proclaimed an earnest desire for a renovation of prose writing. He belongs to a revolutionary generation although, according to his own declaration in *Cartas al Ebro,* "he was the least rebellious of them. . . . Many years of cloistered seclusion drew the sting." In his books, well balanced, poetic, and penetrating, there predominates the student of vast culture, formed by the unhurried reading of Latin authors and Spanish classics and a discriminating appreciation of the foreign literatures of his time.

A. I.

Jarry, Alfred (1873–1907, French dramatist, novelist, and humorist), was born at Laval in central Brittany. To his paternal ancestors—artisans and petty tradesmen—he owed a robust constitution which served for a time to counterbalance a legacy of eccentricity and brilliance from his mother, in whose family there existed a pronounced strain of insanity. He received his early education in the schools of Saint-Brieuc and Rennes before going to Paris in 1891 to pursue his studies at the Lycée Henri IV. After a term of military service he returned to the capital to devote himself to literature. His earliest productions in prose and verse appeared in periodicals of the literary vanguard and were collected in 1894 in a small volume (*Les Minutes de sable mémorial*) remarkable for imaginative intensity and verbal resourcefulness. Lautréamont's (*q.v.*) influence can be discerned; and many passages have the nightmare quality of surrealist texts. In this same year his portrait, complete with parrot and chameleon, was painted by Henri Rousseau and hung in the Salon of the Independents. Jarry undertook to spread the fame of this childlike fellow townsman: brevetted him "Douanier" and commissioned a lithograph—Rousseau's only known print—which appeared in the second issue (January, 1895) of a *de luxe* quarterly, *Ymagier,* founded by Jarry in conjunction with Rémy de Gourmont (*q.v.*).

Sudden and shattering celebrity befell Jarry with the production, on the evening of December 10, 1896, at the experimental Théâtre de l'Œuvre, of his satirical drama *Ubu Roi.* Written at the age of 15 in collaboration with a classmate at the Lycée of Rennes, with the purpose of ridiculing a pompous mathematics teacher, Jarry had recast and expanded the play, while retaining its original Punch and Judy character. This effect he sought to heighten by providing masks for the players, by assigning special voices to each, and by insisting on stylized performances. These innovations, together with the coarseness of the language and the anarchistic implications of the action, outraged the traditionalists in the audience, and the ensuing tumult was later described as "la bataille d'*Hernani* des décadents." In the figure of the ignoble Père Ubu, Jarry created a literary type. Ubu has become the symbol, even in the popular imagination, of bourgeois stupidity grown complacent and irresponsible through abuse of authority. But as if in revenge, this monstrous creation took possession of the personality of its creator; and for the rest of his life Jarry adopted the gestures and intonation of his super-marionette, speaking in clipped, nasal accents, always employing the royal "we."

Until his modest inheritance was exhausted, Jarry continued to write in an involved, strongly personal style characterized by the subtle interplay of humor and lyricism. This manner culminated in *L'Amour absolu* (1899), a novel of almost impenetrable obscurity. Faced finally by the necessity of supporting himself by his writings, he published *Ubu enchaîné* in 1900. Though inferior in verve to the earlier play, the quality of its humor is more cerebral, less gross. It was acted for the first time, with considerable success, at the Paris Exposition of 1937. Like *Ubu Roi* it is in essence a parody of tragedy; together these plays constitute the entire contribution of the symbolist movement (*see* French symbolism) to the field of comedy. More rewarding financially was his novel of ancient Rome, *Messaline*, which appeared in the pages of the *Revue blanche* in the course of the same year (1900). A feat of impeccable and effortless erudition, its sumptuous and richly figured language matched the splendor of its setting and caused it to be regarded by Jarry's contemporaries as his masterpiece. It now seems inferior to its modern counterpart, *Le Surmâle* (1902), the last and best constructed of his novels. Here the style is sober, lucid, and balanced—perfectly adapted to supporting the lurid fantasy of a machine that falls in love with its creator. It has been called the only strictly surrealist novel of our age. With his health undermined by poverty and the systematic overuse of alcohol, Jarry was at length able to contribute only an occasional essay to the reviews. His humor, like that of Swift and Poe, is metaphysical and mathematical, involving the logical demonstration of an absurd proposition. It is displayed to best advantage in *Spéculations* (1911), collected and published after his death, together with an earlier "neo-scientific" novel in the vein of Rabelais, *Les Gestes et opinions du docteur Faustroll.*

The importance of Jarry's literary contribution was for a while obscured by the persistence of the personal legend he had so deliberately cultivated. Interest in his work was revived by the writers of the 20's, who discovered in him a precursor. His books were reissued and reappraised, and his position now seems secure as a writer of remarkable gifts of imagination and verbal facility and as a humorist of the highest order.

See: A. Breton, *Les Pas perdus* (1924), pp. 47–65; Apollinaire, *Il y a* (1925), pp. 223–234; P. Chauveau, *Alfred Jarry* (1932); F. Lot, *Alfred Jarry* (1934).

A. McV.

Jasnorzewska, Marja (known also as Marja Pawlikowska, née Kossak, 1899–1945, Polish poet and playwright), was born in Cracow, the daughter of the well-known painter Wojciech Kossak. Called the queen of Polish lyricists and the Polish Sappho, Jasnorzewska occupies a unique place among Polish poets: she is the one who has brought the short, sensuous lyric close to perfection. Her poems often have the quality of a Japanese flower arrangement, and her ability to communicate the peculiar beauty of her native tongue is remarkable. Of her many volumes, the collections *Śpiąca załoga* (1933; The Sleeping Crew), *Krystalizacje* (1937; Crystallizations), and *Róża i lasy płonące* (1941; The Rose and the Burning Forest) are representative.

As a dramatist Jasnorzewska is more prolific and feminine than deep or universal. She occupies herself generally with artificial situations and bloodless people; yet because of her reputation as a poet and her position in society she was always able to obtain a hearing for her plays, and many of them were staged with a brilliance they did not deserve. Her principal dramas are: *Szofer Archibald* (1924; Chauffeur Archibald); *Egipska pszenica* (1932; Egyptian Wheat); *Niebiescy zalotnicy* (1933; Heavenly Coquettes); *Powrót mamy* (1935; The Mother's Return); *Dowód osobisty* (1936; Personal Evidence); *Nagroda literacka* (1937; Literary Award); the allegorical *Mrówki* (1936; The Ants); and *Baby-Dziwo* (1939), a satire on dictators. Jasnorzewska went to England during the Second World War.

See: K. Czachowski, *Obraz współczesnej literatury polskiej*, III (1936), 393–403, 704–705; K. W. Zawodziński, review of *Krystalizacje* in *Wiadomości literackie*, 1937, No. 42; A. P. Coleman, "Polish Literature in Exile," *New York Times Book Review*, June 1, 1941, pp. 8, 18.

A. P. C.

Jensen, Johannes Vilhelm (1873–, Danish author), was born in the village of Farsø, Himmerland (Northwest Jutland), where his father was the veterinary and his grandfather a farmer and weaver. Jensen studied medicine in Copenhagen, and, although he did not become a doctor, his interest in biological science was one of the two mainsprings of his authorship. The other was his spiritual affiliation with the community, unbookish and close to nature, from which he sprang. In it ancient graves and folkways pointed to the past; his grandfather had a spear hanging over the loom.

After two novels, *Danskere* (1896; Danes) and *Einar Elkjær* (1898), in which he dissected youthful emotions in the manner of the 90's, came the book which he himself regards as his first mature work, *Himmerlandshistorier* (3 vols., 1898–1910; Himmerland Stories). Drawn from his native countryside, their sparkling vigor, freshness, humor, and unsentimental sympathy caused him to be recognized at once as a writer of spontaneous and poetic originality. Stimulated by travels in Europe and voyages to the Far East, he wrote *Exotiske Noveller* (1907–1909; Exotic Stories), *Intermezzo* (1899), and *Skovene* (1904; The Forests) without departing from his own standard; and, beginning his journeys into the past, he wrote *Kongens Fald* (1899–1902; Eng. tr., *The Fall of the King,* 1933), a vivid psychological study of the inner lives of the unfortunate King Christian II and of a simple soldier, a keen experiencer of life. Then, after visiting America, the extravert in Jensen burst forth in the brilliant tales of Chicago and New York, *Madame d'Ora* (1904) and *Hjulet* (1905; The Wheel), rockets of delighted amazement at man's giant efforts in technique and at metropolitan vitality.

After the publication in 1906 of *Digte* (Poems), a book of profound beauty and of great influence in Danish literature (as indeed all his work has been), a new period began for him. Affected in his youth by *The Origin of Species,* his interest in anthropology and biology had concentrated with fervor in the theory of evolution. This resulted in six novels, *Det tabte Land, Bræen, Cimbrernes Tog, Norne-Gæst, Skibet,* and *Christopher Columbus* (1909–1920). In 1938 these were combined in two volumes under the title *Den lange Rejse* (an Eng. tr., *The Long Journey,* had appeared in three volumes, 1922–1924). The main idea, as usual more important to the author than the reader, is the evolution of man from his survival through mere brute force to man as the ship and cathedral builder and man as the yearning, ever-seeking discoverer. The theme centres about the Northmen, but it is not about "Nordics." It is an epic of people who developed hardihood, inventiveness, and even gentleness through pitting themselves against nature, either battling the cold of the ice age or defying the dreaded volcano and bringing down fire from it. Journeys to Norwegian glaciers and Javanese volcanoes gave him his settings; the primitive northern communities were known to him, so to speak, from his childhood countryside. These books are not novels in the usual sense, but they are full of memorable human beings, prehistoric man brought into our comprehension and feeling, individualized convincingly for the first time. The whole work is an ever-playing geyser of beauty, humor, living history, and cosmic fantasy.

Not to be contained in any conventional form, Johannes V. Jensen has published six or seven collections of "myths." A myth is, he says, "every description which brings a bit of nature into relationships with the times"; it is also "the essence and marrow of things." Critics claim that in the myth he has created a form as much his own as the fairy tale was Hans Christian Andersen's. Into it he has poured his observations of landscapes, animals, men, travels, art, and literature, creating many unclassifiable little masterpieces.

Other volumes of poetry and essays have come from his hand, *Dyrenes Forvandling* (1927; The Transformation of Animals) and *Aandens Studier* (1928; Stages in the Development of Mind) being two of the more important collections of essays. In 1933 a bibliography (by Aage Marcus and Frits Johansen) of all he had written included 950 items, most of them having been published in the daily press. He was awarded the Nobel prize in literature in 1944.

Johannes V. Jensen has been criticized for bringing science into the domain of imagination, and inaccuracies in his scientific conclusions have been pointed out, although in some cases he turned out to be right. But it is rather his deep sense of science, or all-including nature, which has aroused his imagination. He has said, "I never felt I was an author," adding that the material meant more to him than the working of it into literature. How is one to classify a writer who is not "literary"? His imitators work in vain; theirs is not his supernormal power of sense perception, nor the gift of conveying what he feels so that we experience it as if we had been just introduced to it in the Garden of Eden. He is at times dogmatic, and no man could attempt to cover what he does without leaving some bare patches, but his philosophy includes both fortitude and tenderness, while as a writer he gives us treasures unsurpassed for their fusing of rare sight and rarer insight.

See: Otto Gelsted, *Johannes V. Jensen* (1913); Alf Henriques, *Johannes V. Jensen* (1938).

S. T.

Jiménez, Juan Ramón (1881–, Spanish poet), outstanding among contemporary poets in the Spanish-speaking world, was born in Moguer, a small Andalusian town whose simple and delicate, dreamlike atmosphere permeates his lyrical work from his very first poems. He studied in a religious college in Santa María, near his home town, and at the University of Seville. His deeply romantic soul was nourished with readings of the Spanish *romancero,* of Góngora and Bécquer, and of the French, English, and German poets of the romantic school, all of whom opened to him the wonders of fantastic imagination and exalted expression of feelings. His early life was burdened with illness, and as a result he developed a love for silence and solitude. At that time he was interested in painting and music; all through his life these two forms of art have been a background to his poetry. In 1901 he went to live in Madrid, where he met the great Latin American poet Rubén Darío, whose role as leader of the *modernista* movement profoundly influenced his work. Several trips and sojourns in France and Switzerland enabled him to become better acquainted with the poetry of the French symbolists (*see* French symbolism). Familiarity with the work of his favorite authors—Verlaine, Samain, Régnier (*qq.v.*), Shakespeare, Keats, Shelley, Browning, Goethe, Hölderlin—added to his poetry that touch of the universal which, together with a deep, true sense of the Spanish lyrical tradition, is the most remarkable feature of his style. After some years spent in Madrid the poet returned to his native Moguer, where he lived until 1912, again in friendly contact with his beloved Andalusian atmosphere. Once more he left Moguer for Madrid, remaining there until 1916, when he journeyed to New York to marry Zenobia Camprubí Aymar, since then his devoted wife and companion in life and letters. In 1917 he wrote *Diario de un poeta recién casado,* of the greatest importance in the development of modern Spanish poetry and still a landmark in Spanish literature because of its freshness of style. The work of this poet has since deepened into a perfect understanding of the inmost sense of the lyrical, being at the same time simple and elaborate, clear and obscure, youthful and mature, as Poetry itself must be. In 1936 Jiménez returned to America after another sojourn in his native land, first living in Puerto Rico and Cuba, where his presence was accepted with great enthusiasm by writers and lovers of poetry and where his direct contact with the young poets deeply influenced their work. He has more recently been living in Washington, D.C., writing and lecturing.

Jiménez's style, both in prose and in verse, differs from that of any other writer in Spanish. A true and independent aesthete, he has never compromised with current fashions in writing. His is a personal pen, always faithful to itself, always sincere to the inspired moment, always translating the profound or even the naïve thoughts of the poet. His treatment of poetical words is appropriate, each of them being a universe of signification. His verse, somewhat ornamental and decorative at its beginning, achieved later an almost naked simplicity; indeed he seemed to reach the very soul of Poetry, whose devoted lover he has always been.

Jiménez has never considered his *Obra,* as he passionately names the entirety of his writings, completed or definite and designates as one of his most interesting tasks the correcting and rewriting of his own work—always in a process of purification. In a sense it is all one diary, for his lyrical, philosophical, or pictorial daily impressions are recorded with a faithfulness, a regularity, that give to the whole an appearance of continuity seldom found in any other poet. This continuity is also shown by the sequence of his publications, which have been almost annual and without interruption since 1900.

The first books of Jiménez, *Almas de violeta* (1900), *Ninfeas* (1900), and *Rimas* (1902), written in his early life, depict what might be called an unrevealed inquietude that, as it develops in maturity, produces the originality of *Arias tristes* (1903), *Jardines lejanos* (1904), and *Pastorales* (1905), together with a dislike for the *modernista* aesthetics. *Pastorales* indeed is written in the Spanish ballad form as a reaction against his own first work. After Jiménez had returned to Moguer, his verse gained in richness and variety. In *Olvidanzas* (1907) and *Baladas de primavera* (1907) the poet is won again by the enchantment of nature; in *La soledad sonora* (1909) and *Poemas mágicos y dolientes* (1909) is found elaborate and often impressive thought; in *Elegías puras* (1908) and *Laberinto* (1913) the variety and richness of expression, still more pronounced, are finally enhanced by depth and intensity. These two qualities are revealed also in *Estío* (1917) and *Sonetos espirituales* (1917), written in Madrid and representing the end of an epoch in his work. The same year, 1917, is marked by the publication of Jiménez's book *Platero y yo,* the best collection of prose poems yet written in Spanish, and by the appearance of the *Diario,* with its new style and final maturity. Since then his work—contained mainly in booklet or broadside form such as *Unidad* (1925), *Sucesión* (1932), and *Presente* (1935) and in such books as *Segunda antología poética* (1922), *Canción* (1936), and *Verso y prosa para niños* (1937)—has reached the pinnacle of literary and human value and has made Jiménez one of the few great figures of contemporary literature.

The Hispanic Society of New York published in 1917 an anthology of Jiménez's lyrical work, *Poesías escogidas,* chosen by the author.

See: A. González-Blanco, "Juan R. Jiménez,"

in *Los contemporáneos,* Ser. 1 (1906); R. Cansinos-Asséns, *La nueva literatura* (2 vols., 1917); F. de Onís, "Juan Ramón Jiménez" in Jiménez, *Platero y yo,* ed. by G. M. Walsh (1922); A. F. G. Bell, *Contemporary Spanish Literature* (1925); Carmen Gómez Tejera and Juan Asencio Alvarez-Torre, preliminary note in Jiménez, *Verso y prosa para niños* (1937).

E. Fl.

Jirásek, Alois (1851–1930, Czech novelist and dramatist), is the most popular novelist of Bohemia. He was born at Hronov near Náchod (northeastern Bohemia), the son of a baker. He studied history at the Czech University of Prague and was a history teacher at a Gymnasium, first in Litomyšl and from 1888 in Prague. During the First World War, Jirásek inspired the manifesto of the Czech writers (1917). After the war he became a member of Parliament and later a senator. He died at Prague.

Jirásek was a historical novelist in the tradition of Sir Walter Scott and roughly comparable to Sienkiewicz (*q.v.*). He was a real scholar who knew a great deal about the past of his nation, especially its customs and folklore. As an artist he excelled in the evocation of scenes and moods, but was, like Scott, weak in psychology and composition. His novels and stories, which fill 47 volumes, cover practically all periods of Czech history. Three groups of novels, *Mezi proudy* (3 vols., 1891; Between the Currents), *Proti všem* (1894; Against the Whole World), and *Bratrstvo* (3 vols., 1899; The Brotherhood), paint a vivid picture of the events leading to the Hussite wars and the wars themselves. The last cycle especially, which tells about the fortunes of the bands of Taborites roaming Hungary and Slovakia, makes a good story. Another group of novels is placed in the time of the Czech defeat after the Battle of the White Mountain (1620). *Psohlavci* (1886; Men with Dog's Heads) was Jirásek's first great success; it is the moving story of a peasants' revolt in western Bohemia and of the heroic death of their leader, Kosina. *Temno* (1915; Darkness) deals in bold fresco-like manner with the later triumph of the Jesuits in Bohemia, the underground Protestant movement, and the Austrian oppression. Another group of novels treats of the Czech national awakening late in the 18th and early in the 19th century. A loosely composed series, *F. L. Věk* (5 vols., 1888–1906), centers round a minor writer of that time whose actual name was Hek, and *U nás* (4 vols., 1896–1903; At Home) is a chronicle of national developments in the district of Jirásek's birth. Among the many short stories, *Filosofická historie* (1878; A Story of Philosophers) is a charming idyl which has achieved great popularity.

Jirásek also wrote *Z mých pamětí* (2 vols., 1911–1913; Memoirs) and several books for young readers. His retelling of old Czech legends, *Staré pověsti české* (1894; Old Czech Myths), is one of the most widely read Czech books. Jirásek was less successful as a dramatist, though some mass scenes in the historical plays (*e.g., Jan Žižka,* 1903), one symbolic play (*Lucerna,* 1905; The Lantern), and several comedies are effective on the stage.

Jirásek must be judged as a great national patriot whose evocation of Czech history has done much to strengthen national feeling and a sense of the national tradition. His novels about the Middle Ages suffer from a lack of imaginative understanding of religion, but the pictures of Bohemia during the ages of serfdom and during the national awakening are both substantially accurate and artistically successful. Jirásek is especially good in genre pictures; his tragic figures and passionate women are still in the conventional romantic manner.

See: Jan Frič, *Alois Jirásek* (1921); M. Hýsek, ed., *Alois Jirásek* (1921); Zdeněk Nejedlý, *Alois Jirásek* (1921); J. Borecký, "Alois Jirásek", in *Almanach České Akademie,* 1933. Several of Jirásek's novels have been translated into German and French.

R. W.

Jochumsson, Matthías (1835–1920, Icelandic poet and playwright), was born at Skógar in Þorskafjörður, of excellent stock. His parents were too poor to send him to school, and he was to become a merchant. But leading men of the cultural center of Flatey, Breiðifjörður, helped him so that he could graduate (1863) from the Latin school in Reykjavík and later (1865) from the school of theology. After that he served as a parson, except for the period from 1874 to 1880 when he edited a newspaper. During the last 20 years of his life he held a government grant as poet laureate of the land. He married three times; the circumstances under which he lost his first two wives caused him great pain. He traveled widely, he visited the United States and the World's Columbian Exposition in Chicago in 1893, and he made friends with prominent men in many lands.

Though Jochumsson composed verse as a boy, it was with the play *Útilegumennirnir* (1864, The Outlaws; later called by the proper name *Skugga-Sveinn*) that he won standing as a poet. It was the first romantic play written in Iceland. Later Jochumsson was to write historical pageants and one historical play, *Jón Arason* (1900), in the manner of Shakespeare, whose *Macbeth, Hamlet, Romeo and Juliet,* and *Othello* he had already turned into excellent Icelandic. He was a great translator; Tegnér's *Friðþjófssaga,* Byron's *Manfred,* and Ibsen's (*q.v.*) *Brand* were among his many poetic translations. His own poems were first published in 1884, his complete poetic works in 1936 (*Ljóðmæli*). He also wrote *Grettisljóð* (1897), a romantic epic on *Grettis saga,* and *Sögukaflar af sjálfum mér* (1922; Stories from My Life), an autobiography.

Jochumsson's lyric poetry ranges from hymns to humorous verse, from eulogies of Iceland to praise of other countries. He witnessed two great national celebrations, the millenary of Iceland in 1874 and the turn of the century in 1900; both occasions he celebrated in odes, hymns, and pageants. He outlived two generations, and every important figure and most of his friends were paid his final respects in a commemorative poem.

The genius of Matthías Jochumsson is at once broad and profound. The essence of his personality is, perhaps, his trust in God or a good Providence and his sympathy with his fellow man. His religion was from an early stage inclined to be nonconfessional; he was influenced in turn by the Unitarian Channing, the philosopher Paul Carus, the "new" German theology, and, at the end of his life, by American-English spiritualism. His hope revolts at atheism and denial of afterlife. His faith has found expression in some of the finest hymns of the Icelandic tongue, including the national hymn of Iceland. As a patriot he loved the nation more than the country—an attitude contrary to that of all his contemporaries. Among his commemorative poems and memorials of historical personages are some of the finest in this common Icelandic genre. His command of the history, literature, and language of the country is phenomenal, and he wields Scaldic and Eddic meters and diction with as much ease as modern mediums. He has written a magnificent eulogy of the language in stately Scaldic measure. The sagas and its figures live again in his work; yet he is no blind admirer of the saga age, and his sympathy with the suffering hero of the Christ type is probably more constant than his love of the brilliant hero of the sagas. Not consistently a good artist, Jochumsson is always an inspired poet. Occasionally his poems sink to mediocrity, but seldom do they lack a flash of genius.

See: S. Nordal, "Matthías við Dettifoss," *Eimreiðin,* XXVII (1921), 1–6; R. Beck, "Matthías Jochumsson—Icelandic Poet and Translator," *Scandinavian Studies and Notes,* XIII (1934–1935), 111–124; S. Einarsson, "Shakespeare in Iceland; an Historical Survey," *ELH; a Journal of English Literary History,* VII (1940), 272–285.

S. E.

Johst, Hanns (1890–, German dramatist, poet, and essayist), was born in Saxony, the son of a grade school teacher. At first he wanted to be a missionary; but then he studied medicine and finally philology and the history of art. His first novel, *Der Anfang* (1917), tells of his youth and early development. By affinity of temperament he was drawn into expressionism; however, contrary to its prevailing ethos of limitless love for all humanity, Johst preached intensity and limitation of personality and came to stress more and more national and ethnic values. The war furnished substance for his first dramatic attempts. His ecstatic *Der junge Mensch* (1916), influenced by Wedekind (*q.v.*), is confessional and full of pathos. Of the same year are the lyrics *Wegwärts,* in which the haste of modern life became the symbol of Johst's dynamics. The play *Der Einsame* (1917) shows in the fate of the poet Grabbe divine redemption after a life of confusion and guilt; it is influenced by Büchner, Wedekind, and Strindberg (*q.v.*). The poems in *Rolandsruf* (1918) and *Mutter* (1921) were expressions of Johst's ethnic consciousness. The drama *Der König* (1920) is the picture of a utopian idealist who perishes because he conceives of action only in the abstract. Maturity gained through stern education by fate is the goal reached in the novel *Der Kreuzweg* (1921), while the drama *Propheten* (1923) shows Luther as the incarnation of the German soul, who with the help of the sword brings about the victory of the spirit. The same year brought also the light comedy of the inflation era, *Wechsler und Händler.* The drama *Die fröhliche Stadt* (1925) scores and satirizes modern materialism disguised as progress. Theoretical writings of a confessional nature were *Wissen und Gewissen* (1924) and *Ich glaube* (1928). *Thomas Paine* (1927) is made the dramatic symbol of the creative leader who, after inspiring the fight for independence, goes to ruin, lonely and forgotten. Johst believed that he had created a German version of this story in *Schlageter* (1933), the symbol of resistance against the enemies of Germany. Fanaticism and unbridled emotions, however, do not replace reasonable motivation. The play is dedicated in "unchanging loyalty" to Hitler. A novel, *Torheit einer Liebe* (1930), is not without some idyllic charm. After 1933 Johst was given practically all the positions of honor that the Third Reich would bestow upon a writer. He even became a brigade leader in Hitler's "SS." For the same period nothing noteworthy can be reported of Johst in the field of literary creation.

See: A. Soergel, *Dichtung und Dichter der Zeit,* Neue Folge: *Im Banne des Expressionismus,* 4. Auflage (1927), pp. 717–728; S. Casper, *Der Dramatiker Hanns Johst* (1935); H. Franke, "Hanns Johst," *Die neue Literatur*, XXXVI (1935), 459–469.

W. K. P.

Jókai, Móricz (1825–1904, Hungarian novelist and short-story writer), was born in Komárom and died in Budapest. He received his elementary and secondary education in his birthplace, then went to school in Pozsony and in Pápa where he befriended Petöfi, the lyric poet. He studied law at the Academy of Kecskemét. His first novel, *Hétköznapok* (Weekdays), appeared in 1846. In 1848 he played an important part in the revolutionary movement of Hungarian youth. That same year he married Róza Laborfalvi, a distinguished actress, who died in 1866. After the collapse of the War of Independence Jókai had to play hide-and-seek in Hungarian villages in order to elude the Austrians; finally, however, he was given amnesty. In 1854 he assisted in the publication of *Vasárnapi Ujság* (Sunday News), a belletristic weekly, and in 1858 he founded a comic paper, *Üstökös* (Comet). He never lost faith in the ability of the nation to regain its independence. In his political activities he scorned the doubters, and as a member of the Hungarian Parliament and later of the House of Magnates he represented the liberal point of view. In recognition of his literary work he was elected to the Hungarian Academy of Sciences and to various literary organizations. He edited several daily newspapers, in 1849 in Budapest *Pesti Hirlap* (Pest Journal) and that same year in Debrecen *Esti Lapok* (Evening News); later, in Budapest, *Magyar Sajtó* (Hungarian Press), *Hon* (Nation), and other newspapers were also under his editorial leadership. His collected works appeared in 100 volumes, and he was the recipient of 100,000 gulden presented to him by the nation. In 1899 Jókai married a second time, again to an actress, Bella Nagy. His career was distinguished and successful; he was idolized by his countrymen. His reputation indeed became world wide. No Hungarian writer before him or since has had such an immense public as Jókai.

In Jókai the universe, dreams, ideals, love, heroic deeds, fantastic possibilities and achievements, historical and contemporary problems, were mingled with pseudoscientific or scientific information, with musings that reached for the infinite, with tones, forms, colors, that were symbolic of an inexhaustible imagination. He found plots where the unimaginative would not have seen even the beginnings of one. His imagination hurdled the obstacles that the Hungarian language, isolated in relationship to the rest of the world, imposes on its writers. His optimism was unbounded, and while the quality of his art is uneven, his most carelessly written stories, his most superficial tales, contain the indubitable sign of narrative genius. Somewhat influenced by French and English romanticists, he very soon was awakened to the demands of his own individuality and followed the voice of his creative temperament. He discovered new provinces for fiction, like Jules Verne and H. G. Wells; natural sciences always interested him, and with an imagination that could be fantastical he also knew how to be scientific. His bent was toward the amazing, the extraordinary; and when necessity and conviction required realism, *e.g.*, in *Az uj földesúr* (1868; The New Squire), it was his romanticism that determined the atmosphere of the story. Generally he was irresistibly attracted to the world of miracles, of magic, of spiritual nobility; consequently the peculiar quality of his art lies not in characterization, not in psychological veracity, not in style, but in the strange universe he was able to create with the freshness and perennial youthfulness of his spirit.

Many of Jókai's themes are Hungarian, but his abundant imagination returned to foreign themes, ancient and modern alike. The gates of the impossible were never closed to him. That was the law of his creative temperament. By nature he was friendly, some sort of survivor of an Atlantis world; he had a voice for the interpretation of sorrow, but he preferred joy. Many of his novels appeared in English; in fact there are translations of Jókai's novels in every civilized tongue. His most popular novels in the English-speaking world are the following: *Erdély aranykora* (1852; Eng. trs., *Midst the Wild Carpathians,* 1894, *The Golden Age in Transylvania,* 1898); *Egy magyar nábob* (1853–1854; Eng. tr., *An Hungarian Nabob,* 1898); *A Janicsárok végnapjai* (1854; Eng. tr., *The Lion of Janina,* 1897); *Szomorú napok* (1856; Eng. tr., *The Day of Wrath,* 1900); *A kőszívű ember fiai* (1869; Eng. tr., *The Baron's*

Sons, 1900); *A fekete gyémantok* (1870; Eng. tr., *Black Diamonds,* 1896); *Az aranyember* (1872; Eng. tr., *A Modern Midas,* 1885); *Nincsen ördög* 1891; Eng. tr., *"There Is No Devil,"* 1891). Indeed in the realm of the imagination Jókai's spirit was never homeless, and even when, as a publicist, he was concerned with realistic problems, he sought union between the exotic world of his imagination and the rational responsibilities of common sense. He was the magnificent storyteller, the creator remembered for his dreams, the illusionist whose ideas and ideals guarded the freedom of his fancy against the encroachments of everyday life. His humor was simple, fostering smiles rather than laughter; his understanding of the people showed an ability to assimilate the images and anecdotes of folklore; his vocabulary was rich, if undisciplined, and always concrete; his sense of composition was uncertain, yet he could shape the unfathomable and could give unimportant experiences the appearance of meaningfulness. As to wealth of imagination, Jokai is unexcelled in Hungarian literature, and here even in world literature he has few competitors.

See: *Jókai Mór önmagáról* (1904); K. Mikszáth, *Jókai Mór élete és kora* (2 vols., 1907); Z. Ferenczi, *Jókai idegen nyelvre forditott műveinek jegyzéke* (1925).

J. R.

Jørgensen, Jens Johannes (1866–, Danish poet, novelist, essayist, and hagiographer), was born in Svendborg, Fyn, the son of a sea captain. After a pious and harmonious home life the youth was rudely jolted in Copenhagen where, in 1886, as a student of zoology, he came under the influence of Brandesian naturalism. Making his debut with *Vers* (1887; Verses), he soon befriended like-minded young poets, of whom Sophus Claussen (*q.v.*) and the couple Ingeborg and Viggo Stuckenberg (*q.v.*) were the most important. This group soon outgrew the social radicalism of Brandes (*q.v.*), following him indeed in his cult of Nietzsche (1888), but parting ways with him in their admiration of the French symbolists (*see* French symbolism). In Nietzsche (*q.v.*) it was not the superman, but his sense of the depth of the world that appealed to them. In the French symbolists it was the keen introspection, the reveling in decadent moods, which struck a responsive chord in their hearts. Jørgensen was even affected by their guilty sense of sin.

Jørgensen's first poetry and prose was in the naturalistic vein, but the note of symbolism was already present in *Stemninger* (1892; Moods) and *Livets Træ* (1893; The Tree of Life). Symbolism was formally launched with the periodical *Taarnet* (1893–1895; The Tower), edited by Jørgensen and supported by his friends. But the new romantic cult of beauty and mysticism as well as the worship of ego failed more and more to satisfy Jørgensen. In the turmoil of financial and spiritual worries he was glad to accept the invitation of a converted Jewish friend, Mogens Ballin, to go with him to Assisi in Italy. This journey, described in *Rejsebogen* (1895; The Book of the Journey), the first of many to the sunny South, was decisive for his spiritual development; he became a Catholic in 1895.

The zeal of the convert, striving for religious truth and the ascetic ideal, is evident in many books of the next five years. But some of his finest poetry also dates from these times—*Digte, 1894–98* (Poems)—and *Lignelser* (1898; Parables) is beautiful prose. A quieter period, after 1900, is marked by the great biography, *Den hellige Frans af Assisi* (1907; Eng. tr., *Saint Francis of Assisi,* 1912), the first in a series of saints' lives (Catherina of Siena, 1915; Don Bosco, 1929; etc.). On the basis of this and his aesthetical writings, including *Essays* (1906) on the symbolistic movement, and *Goethebogen* (1913; The Book on Goethe), he was in 1913 called to the chair of aesthetics at the University of Louvain in Belgium. Forced out by the First World War, he wrote on German atrocities in Belgium (*Klokke Roland,* 1915; Eng. tr., *False Witnesses,* 1916). This estranged him from friends in Germany, but forged his friendship with France and Italy; he once more returned to the latter country, taking up his abode in his beloved Assisi.

In continuation of *Rejsebogen,* Jørgensen has written a great number of books on his journeys and pilgrimages through the length and breadth of Catholic Europe. One of the best is *Pilgrimsbogen* (1903; Eng. tr., *Pilgrim Walks in Franciscan Italy,* 1908). Its popularity in France alone may be judged by the fact that, by 1936, it had appeared in 36 editions.

Jørgensen's chief prose work, however, is *Mit Livs Legende* (6 vols., 1916–1919, 7th vol., 1928; Eng. tr., *Jørgensen, An Autobiography,* 2 vols., 1928–1929). This confessional life is not only valuable for Danish intellectual history in the 1890's, but, like much of Jørgensen's prose, it is rich in lyric beauty, especially in the passages describing the moods of his youth.

Since 1900 Jørgensen has published some five collections of poetry, among which *Blomster og Frugter* (1907; Flowers and Fruits) and *Brig Marie af Svendborg* (1926; The Brig Marie of Svendborg) are notable. His poetry, always simple in form, is a perfect expression of his melancholy moods and continual yearning. It moves from the early nature mysticism, reveling in moonlight and nocturnal romanticism, to the penitential Catholic lyric, stoic in resignation to God's providence. On his long pilgrimage Jørgensen often feels with Odysseus the pangs of nostalgia, for his old home, his old way of life, and his native Denmark. But often, too, he is inspired with his friend Saint Francis to sing the praises of sister nature, the white cell, and the peace that he has finally won in God.

See: Oscar Geismar "Johannes Jørgensen," in Ejnar Skovrup, ed., *Hovedtræk af nordisk Digtning i Nytiden*, I (1920), 140–151; H. G. Topsöe-Jensen, *Scandinavian Literature from Brandes to Our Day* (1929), pp. 126–130; Helge Kjærgaard, *Die dänische Literatur der neuesten Zeit (1871–1933)* (1934), pp. 83–92.

S. E.

Jouhandeau, Marcel (pseud. Marcel Provence, 1888–, French novelist), was born at Guéret in central France. He has been a teacher at the Collège de Passy in Paris. Among contemporary writers he is conspicuous for the bitterness and the cynicism with which he views the world in general and himself in particular. Some of his books are the product of a pitiless introspection—*Monsieur Godeau intime* (1926), *Monsieur Godeau marié* (1933), *Chroniques maritales* (1938); others are cruel portraits of the inhabitants of his native town which appears in his work under the name Chaminadour—*Les Térébinte* (1926), *Tite-le-Long* (1932), *Binche-Ana* (1933), *Chaminadour I* (1934), *Chaminadour II* (1936), *L'Arbre de visages* (Chaminadour III; 1941).

Jouhandeau not only studies the conflicts of man with his own self, but his struggles with God and Satan. At times his stories, detached from the earth, give an impression of unreality due in part to the use of symbolic devices. The ferocious portraits of the citizens of Chaminadour are sketched with the utmost simplicity. He generally ignores nonessential psychological elements and stresses what seems to him the dominant trait of the characters. The same economy of means is noticeable in the plot of his short stories: *Les Pincengrain* (1924), *Prudence Hautechaume* (1927), *Astaroth* (1929), *Le Journal du coiffeur* (1931), *Images de Paris* (1934), *Le Saladier* (1936). These tales are built around insignificant events, and they owe their depth and their intensity to the author's fearless probings into the darkest mysteries of the human soul and to his constant unveiling of the cruelty of life.

Jouhandeau's work includes also *La Jeunesse de Théophile* (1921), *Opales* (1928), *L'Amateur d'imprudence* (1932), *Véronicana* (1933), *Elise* (1933), and a few essays. Under the name Marcel Provence he has written *Les Allemands en Provence* (1919) and *Bauxite et aluminium* (*L'Allemagne et l'après-guerre*) (1920) and has produced an anthology of poems entitled *Amour*.

See: Claude Mauriac, *Introduction à une mystique de l'enfer* (1938).

M. E. C.

Jouve, Pierre Jean (1887–, French poet, novelist, and essayist), was born at Arras in Artois. From the scientific studies of his youth he turned to poetry; he founded with Paul Castiaux, and directed for three years (1907–1910), the magazine *Bandeaux d'or,* which supported the newly formed "Abbaye" group. In the first series of his poems, *Les Muses romaines et florentines* (1910), *Présences* (1912), *Parler* (1913), Jouve already showed a tendency to mingle philosophy and photographic glimpses of reality and dream in a manner somehow foreshadowing surrealism. Although poor health prevented his mobilization in 1914, he volunteered as a hospital orderly, thus gleaning the stories which formed his later book, *Hôtel-Dieu; récits d'hôpital en 1915* (1920). His failing health, however, compelled him to spend the next four years in Switzerland. There his pacifist views, freely aired in the impassioned poetical protests of *Vous êtes des hommes* (1915), *Poème contre le grand crime* (1916), and *Danse des morts* (1917), were fortified by his personal contact with the great figure of Romain Rolland (*q.v.*), to whom he later devoted a book which he himself termed "a poem and act of faith," *Romain Rolland vivant, 1914–1919* (1920). Two collections of a deeper character, *Heures, livre de la nuit* (1919), and *Heures, livre de la grâce* (1920), were later combined with the poetical notations of new trips to Florence, Austria, and Germany, in *Tragiques, suivis du voyage sentimental* (1923). At this point in his poetical evolution he truly was a poet of revolt, whether he evoked the "bitter maze" of his youth, shouted his despair, or cried out his call to love, friendship, art, and beauty. Then his passionate quest for an absolute answer to the mysterious union of contradictory forces in man made him turn to the revelation of the Roman Catholic faith as well as to the study of psychoanalysis, both of which permeate his later work. While still producing poetry, *Prière* (1923), *Les Mystérieuses Noces* (1925), *Nouvelles Noces* (1926), *La Symphonie à Dieu* (1930), *Sueur de sang* (1935), and that moving poem of the birth of anguish in man, *Le Paradis perdu* (1929; new and definitive ed., 1942), Jouve began to write novels and short stories, *Paulina 1880* (1925), whose heroine, a tortured prey to eroticism and mysticism, set the pace for most of his succeeding work, *Le Monde désert* (1926), *Beau Regard* (1927), *Hécate* (1928), *Vagadu* (1931), *Histoires sanglantes* (1932), *La Scène capitale* (1935).

Instead of reviving his pacifist tendencies, the Second World War seems to have intensified Jouve's concern with the ultimate values of life and religion, as is evident in his books recently arrived from Switzerland. His *Porche à la nuit des saints* (1941) reflects the anguish of earlier poems and echoes the tragic destiny of our time, but brings out the true peace that comes only from total submission to God. Two late works of criticism reveal a similar preoccupation, his *Tombeau de Baudelaire* (1941) and, above all, that magnificent piece of music criticism, *Le Don Juan de Mozart* (1942). In it Jouve has succeeded not only in recreating without undue technical language the atmosphere of Mozart's music, but also in giving a new understanding of the musician's genius and a deep insight into the very problem that has haunted the poet himself throughout his life. It is as if, after attempting to further through fiction and poetry his conceptual comprehension of the tragic fate of man dominated by the coupled impulses of love and death, he had found its supreme revelation in the formal product of an art form closely bound to physical necessities and mystical intuition. Mozart's treatment of the myth of love and death as exemplified by Don Juan has become for Jouve the deepest and truly "divine" expression of this excruciating mystery which is the guiding thread of his own inquest and which makes his work an authentic mirror of the tragedy of modern man.

See: S. A. Rhodes, "William Blake and Pierre Jean Jouve," *Romanic Review,* XXIV (1933), 147–149, and "Disciple of William Blake," *Sewanee Review,* XLI (1933), 287–290; *Cahiers du sud,* CLXXXII (April, 1936), 272–304 (number in honor of Jouve).

C. L. B.

Jouvet, Louis (1885–, French actor, theatrical director, and *metteur en scène*), born at Crozon, Finistère, began his career in Paris. Beyond two failures at the Conservatoire, he had had little experience when Jacques Copeau (*q.v.*) established the Théâtre du Vieux Colombier (1913) and found Jouvet indispensable as actor, property man, electrician. When in 1922 Jouvet went to the Comédie des Champs-Elysées (of which he became sole director in 1924), he took many of the best of Copeau's discoveries—Valentine Tessier, Lucienne Bogaert, Michel Simon. He moved his company to the Athénée in 1934, the same year that he became a professor at the Conservatoire. Building his reputation on the total work of such contemporary dramatists as Jean Giraudoux, Jules Romains, Marcel Achard, and Stève Passeur (*qq.v.*), Jouvet has indulged in but few revivals (*e.g.,* Molière and Mérimée) and even fewer foreign plays (*e.g.,* one by the Alvarez Quintero brothers, *q.v.,* and an adaptation of Margaret Kennedy). His taste for original and often complicatedly mechanical sets has necessitated the collaboration of painters like Christian Bérard and the resurrection of 17th-century machinery. In acting as in staging, his striking stylizations have won the enthusiasm of the fashionable world, but if he had done nothing except reveal the dramatic talent of Giraudoux, the literary world would still owe him a great debt. Since he began devoting his vacations to the cinema, Jouvet has been seen in such films as *La Kermesse héroïque, La Fin des jours,* and *Carnet de bal.*

See: C. Cézan, *Louis Jouvet et le théâtre d'aujourd'hui* (1938), with introduction by Jean Giraudoux; Jouvet, *Réflexions du comédien* (1938).

J. O'B.

Jünger, Ernst (1895–, German novelist and essayist), brother of the poet and essayist Friedrich Georg Jünger, was born in Heidelberg. He volunteered at the outbreak of the First World War and, in the course of a distinguished military career, was awarded the highest German order, Pour le Mérite. During the years between the wars he devoted himself to writing and was a widely respected contributor to a number of conservative reviews and newspapers. In 1940 he took part in the French campaign.

The technological and social changes of the last century have not, so it seems to Jünger, decreased the perennial threat with which irrational forces confront the unstable life of man. Only the constant and total exercise of all human virtues, physical as well as moral and intellectual, will establish the vital harmony which can and must sustain a culture. This sense of the perpetual and fearful elemental fascination of the world is one of the most striking qualities of Jünger's work, for which his experience as an officer in the First World War supplied the early substance and material. His first book, *In Stahlgewittern* (1920; Eng. tr., *Storm of Steel,* 1929), struck the characteristic theme of extreme action coupled with insight and soldierly pathos. There followed several volumes essentially observational and reflective rather than narrative in nature. A semi-autobiographical account of earlier experiences in southern France and northern Africa, *Afrikanische Spiele* (1936), suggests the manner of Emil Strauss (*q.v.*); his own proper form, however, is not the novel but the contemplative essay (*Das abenteuerliche Herz, "Figuren und Capriccios,"* 1929, new ed., 1938; *Blätter und Steine,* 1934), in which his "stereoscopic" perception is rendered through imagery of extraordinary "perspective" power.

The political implications of his attitude, in some respects reminiscent of T. E. Lawrence, have had considerable influence upon the present generation. On one occasion he examined in detail the social and emotional structure of the contemporary worker (*Der Arbeiter,* 1932); but it is in the soldier and his reflective counterpart, the poet, that Jünger recognizes the human type in which the supreme qualities of alertness, discipline, intelligence, and sensitiveness appear most strikingly. Jünger is an individualist, and although much of his work is drawn from his experiences of the wars (*e.g., Der Kampf als inneres Erlebnis,* 1922; *Feuer und Blut,* 1925; *Das Wäldchen 125,* 1925, Eng. tr., *Copse 125,* 1930), he should not be accused of the kind of German militaristic thinking that is so justly suspected. Indeed, in two of his recent books, the mythological parable, *Auf den Marmor-Klippen* (1939), and the diary of his months in 1940 as an officer in France, *Gärten und Strassen* (1942), Jünger writes most urgently and with much concern (though not without resorting to an occasional elliptical paraphrase) of the threat to deep-rooted cultural values offered by the forces of undisciplined inhumanity and barbarian dissolution. Yet the vigor of Jünger's philosophical intelligence does not emerge in the bald terms of philosophical propositions. His thought is always conveyed with the precision of one to whom the distinction between the observable fact and the irrational perspective is only one of degree and intensity. Dream imagery is, therefore, one of his most frequent devices, and his vision of nature has, at times, the puzzling coherence of a surrealist landscape. By his devotion to the civilized and civilizing qualities of language (*e.g., Geheimnisse der Sprache,* 1934, revised ed., 1939), he has produced, in a series of successively more significant works, some of the finest prose now being written in Germany; it is lithe, resolute, unsentimental, and radiant. If the term "magic realism" should be applied at all, Jünger's work would most properly deserve it.

See: E. G. Winkler, *Gestalten und Probleme* (1937), pp. 94–133; K. Kamp, *Die Haltung des Frontkämpfers* (1940); W. K. Pfeiler, *War and the German Mind* (1941), pp. 109–116; E. Guerster-Steinhausen, "The Prophet of German Nihilism—Ernst Juenger," *Review of Politics,* VII (1945), 199–209.

V. L.

Junqueiro, Abílio Guerra, *see* Guerra Junqueiro.

K

Kaden, Juljusz, *see* Bandrowski, Juljusz.

Kaffka, Margit (1880–1918, Hungarian poet, novelist, and short-story writer), was born in Nagykároly and died in Budapest during the influenza epidemic at the end of the First World War. Having been reared among the landed gentry, the boldness of her spirit seemed in sharp contrast with traditions that expected women to be interested only in home life. She was educated in the town where she was born and in Budapest. Later she taught in a girls' secondary school in Miskolcz and also in the capital of the country. She was married twice. Her first poems and stories appeared in *A Hét* (The Week) and in *Nyugat* (West). Margit Kaffka ranks among the foremost Hungarian writers, not only compared with Lenke Beniczkyné Bajza, Minka Czobel, and Fruzina Szalay, women writers of the preceding generations, but also compared with her literary contemporaries, regardless of sex. She had an arresting personality; her humanitarian outlook did not permit her to be reconciled to life without protesting, and her artistic disposition made her intense in regard to moral and physical ugliness. Yet she did not write with a didactic temper; she responded passionately to beauty and expressed dissatisfaction in the manner of a creative artist. Even her juvenile stories substantiate her artistic integrity.

Her poems, *Kaffka Margit versei* (1906; The Poems of Margit Kaffka), reveal feminine subtleness and awareness. Many of them are "white" and "pure" in a conventional sense, though Margit Kaffka already showed an ability to free herself from the familiar vocabulary of literary traditions. Gradually the music of her spirit became more modern, and her ideas revealed a successful emancipation from platitudes and prejudices. Her short stories *Levelek a zárdából* (1905; Letters from the Convent), *Csendes válságok* (1909; Quiet Crisis), and *Nyár* (1910; Summer) equal the best short stories ever written by Hungarian women writers; her delicacy recalls Katherine Mansfield, but without the mastery of form so characteristic of the English writer.

Margit Kaffka's talent reached its most mature development in her novels, especially in *Szinek és évek* (1912; Colors and Years). It is comprehensible that a woman with her social outlook should have felt obliged to write about the problem of women in modern times. This particular novel shows Margit Kaffka's ability to see beyond the horizon of a small town; she understands the reasons why people of her class in a Hungarian provincial town should believe in the division of the classes, but she does not approve of their reasons. Her attitude is disruptive of the *status quo;* the problems of her heroines are splendidly portrayed in lyrical and social perspective. *Mária évei* (1913; The Years of Maria), *Állomások* (1917; Signposts), and *Hangyaboly* (1917; Anthill) are incompletely realized novels, but their fragmentary values make them interesting. Margit Kaffka shows the various aspects of human destiny in provincial or metropolitan surroundings with an enlightening understanding of selfish, naïve, or pathetic motives. Her sympathies were always with truth and beauty; it is regrettable that she died so young. Her work breaks off like an unfinished cry.

See: M. Radnóti, *Kaffka Margit művészi fejlődése* (1934).

J. R.

Kafka, Franz (1883–1924, German novelist and essayist), was born in Prague of a well-to-do middle-class Jewish family, in an atmosphere overshadowed by his father's dominant personality (see "Brief an den Vater," 1919) and reminiscent of the earlier years of Proust. After rigid schooling he took, in 1906, his law degree at the German University of Prague and eventually obtained a position in the workmen's compensation division of the Austrian government. Devotion to literature was nevertheless his real concern, and it was only the slowness and conscientiousness of his writing that made it impossible for him to gain a livelihood by it. Severe attacks of tuberculosis compelled him to spend several years in sanatoriums. On two occasions, hopes for a marriage that might have steadied his life failed because of his own sense of inadequacy.

Little of his work was published during his lifetime: none of his three novels, *Der Prozess* (1925; Eng. tr., *The Trial,* 1937), *Das Schloss* (1926; Eng. tr., *The Castle,* 1930), and *Amerika* (1927; Eng. tr., 1938), was completed. Most of his ever increasing reputation rests upon the posthumous publication (happily undertaken by his friend Max Brod against Kafka's own wishes) of an impressive number of short stories, parables, aphorisms, journals, and letters in the *Gesammelte Schriften* (1935–1937).

In his first published work, a collection of prose, *Betrachtung* (1913), and two short stories, *Der Heizer* (1913; later the first chapter of his novel *Amerika*) and *Das Urteil* (1913), he established the main theme of his work, which he soon elaborated in the "ecstatically conceived" story, *Der Verwandlung* (1916; Eng. tr., *Metamorphosis,* 1937). In 1918, during critical months of illness in the country, he began the first chapter of his novel *Das Schloss.* A collection of delicate short stories, *Ein Landarzt* (1919), was followed in 1919 by the significant tale, *In der Strafkolonie* (Eng. tr., "In the Penal Colony," *Partisan Review,* VIII, 98–107, 146–158), and one year before his death he completed a last volume of characteristically lucid and mobile prose, *Ein Hungerkünstler.*

In the words of the editor, Max Brod, Kafka's three incomplete major novels, *Amerika, Der Prozess,* and *Das Schloss,* form "a trilogy of loneliness." Like every other work of Kafka's, they reflect in a profoundly religious sense the experience of human isolation and the pathos of exclusion. Man, forever aware of an inherent sense of "guilt," is compelled to face the "trial" of life in a universe whose pattern and coherence are fundamentally uncertain and incomprehensible (see "In the Penal Colony," *The Trial, The Castle).* The God of Kafka's world is as terrible and fascinating as Jehovah, and however fervently the poet's Job-like characters may wrestle with "the law," there is for them no ultimate consolation. They are but troubled marionettes who can find no escape from the realization of overwhelming frustration. Man's life passes in a series of crises in which the veiled presence of "the law," acting through impersonal agencies (the government, the police, the office, the castle), demonstrates the futility of human effort (*The Trial*). Much of Kafka's imaginative thinking is drawn from Jewish folk literature and the Talmud; but the tenets of his belief should be related to Pascal, the existential philosophy of Kierkegaard, and the contemporary theology of crisis (Karl Barth). In its radically eschatological nature, his symbolic faith is reminiscent of Dostoevski and Strindberg (*qq.v.*), but it lacks the consistency of Dante's or Bunyan's theological frame. The use of minutely detailed irrational dream landscapes, in which strangely related phenomena seem suspended in an unintelligible void, indicates Kafka's nearness to the expressionist and surrealist writers. But even the laconic humor of some of his tales rests upon a powerful faith in what Kafka himself called the "indestructible"; in those grotesque scenes, in which the pathetic human being finds himself caught in the grip of an inescapable mechanism, he reminds us not only of Charlie Chaplin and Walt Disney, but of Poe and Dickens.

In spite of the subtlety and precision of his prose style (Kleist, Hebel, Flaubert, *q.v.*), Kafka is not, compared with his contemporaries (Proust, *q.v.*, Joyce, Thomas Mann, *q.v.*), one of the accomplished novelists; he is rather, with Rilke (*q.v.*), the supremely religious writer of an age in which man, caught in inevitable perplexity and doubt, seems incapable of personal salvation. Ultimately Kafka's theme, like that of all contemporary literature, is the paradoxical human quest for freedom as well as responsibility.

See: M. Brod, *Franz Kafka; eine Biographie* (1937); P. Rahv, "Franz Kafka: The Hero as Lonely Man," *Kenyon Review*, I (1939), 60–74; *A Franz Kafka Miscellany* (1940); A. Warren, "Kosmos Kafka," *Southern Review*, VII (1941–1942), 350–365.

V. L.

Kahn, Gustave (1859–1936, French poet and critic), born at Metz, in the province of Lorraine, went at an early age to Paris and after completing his classical studies indulged his taste for erudition by entering the Ecole des Chartes and the School of Oriental Languages. This was followed by four years of military service in North Africa under conditions favorable to his linguistic and historical studies. Returning to Paris in 1885, he abandoned his scholarly research for the pursuit of a literary career. The review *Vogue*, which he founded with Paul Adam (*q.v.*), was a ready receptacle for his first poems, soon to be published in volume form with the title *Les Palais nomades* (1887). In collaboration with Jean Moréas and Paul Adam (*qq.v.*) he founded also at that period the *Symboliste*, a periodical whose avowed purpose was to encourage the symbolist movement. But Kahn's activities as a critic did not interrupt his poetic production or his experiments with a new form of verse. In the preface to his *Premiers Poèmes* (1897), he lays full claim to the invention of vers libre, yet in fairness that honor should be shared with Rimbaud, Jules Laforgue (*qq.v.*), and others. It must be granted, however, that Kahn was the first theorician of this medium of poetic expression. By methodical and scientific analysis he demonstrated that French verse is not merely constituted by a number of syllables subjected to certain rules, but rather by rhythmic units of equal temporal values governed by the emotional stress of the phrase. Since rhythm is the most adequate expression of individual feelings, the poet's task therefore is to create a form capable of interpreting his own sentiments without being hampered by the arbitrary rules of caesura, hiatus, alternation of rhymes, and other conventions.

In spite of the scholarly precision of its own theories, the verse of Kahn remains too experimental and too hesitating between the syllabic meter and a truly free form to compare favorably with the masterly technique of Vielé-Griffin, Emile Verhaeren, or Henri de Régnier (*qq.v.*). Neither does his poetry reach the high level of these foremost representatives of symbolism. *Les Palais nomades* reveals a delicate sensibility, but too often preciosity and aimless verbiage embarrass the thought and confuse the emotion. However, in *Le Livre d'images* (1897), by means of simple narrative reminiscent of the Germanic *lieder*, he creates a poetic mood which possesses charm and originality.

To the collections of poems can be added several volumes of critical essays, a genre in which Kahn excels. Of particular interest are *Symbolistes et décadents* (1902), an appreciative survey of the literary movement in which he took part, and *Charles Baudelaire* (1925), a penetrating study of the poet with whom he felt some affinities. A distinguished art critic, he is the author of treatises on Boucher, Fragonard, Félicien Rops, Rodin, and other artists.

See: André Barre, *Le Symbolisme* (1912); Tancrède de Visan, *L'Attitude du lyrisme contemporain* (1921); John Charpentier, *Le Symbolisme* (1927); Adolphe van Bever and Paul Léautaud, *Poètes d'aujourd'hui* (1929).

M. D.

Kaiser, Georg (1878–1945, German playwright), was the son of a Magdeburg merchant. He too went into business and eventually established himself in Buenos Aires, but found the climate unhealthy and came back home, where he soon turned to writing. The most sensational event in his career was his trial in 1921 for embezzlement; his plea that as an exceptional man he could not be expected to observe the civil code failed to save him.

His literary career was meteoric. Some of his plays were written as early as 1905, but the first to be published was *Die jüdische Witwe* (1911), a satirical treatment of the Judith theme, and it was not till 1914 that theatregoers made his acquaintance. For the next 10 years Kaiser was the sensation of the German stage; no less than 26 of his dramas were staged. This was the decade of expressionism, and Kaiser was not only the most prolific but also the most representative playwright of that movement. With the passing of expressionism his star waned.

Kaiser spoke of Plato, Schopenhauer, and Nietzsche (*q.v.*) as his spiritual guides. He professed to see in the dialogues of Plato, for instance, the ideal drama. Under this philosophic aegis Kaiser wrote, not *Schauspiele,* but *Denkspiele,* a term reminiscent of Shaw's plays. Despite this designation, however, Kaiser's work does not have the flash of Shaw's wit, nor is it the meditative book drama: it is fast moving theatre, more effective in the acting than in the reading, tense and, at its best, well able to stir human emotions. But each play is the elaboration of an idea developed at the expense of the dramatic form. This formula was a commonplace among the expressionists, who certainly did not need to go back more than two thousand years to find it. In fact, Kaiser's prototypes were Strindberg and Wedekind (*qq.v.*).

The peculiarities of Kaiser's work are essentially those of expressionism. In one of his first successes, *Von Morgens bis Mitternachts* (1916; Eng. tr., *From Morn to Midnight,* 1920), the cashier of a bank, a slave of routine, filches 60,000 marks and runs amuck: a whiff of perfume and the rustle of silk skirts start him off on what he feels to be the first day of his life and what fatefully proves to be the last. His excesses, portrayed in language that has the rhythm of machine-gun fire, make palpitating theatre. But the cashier remains a stranger to us and the other characters are but wraiths. The thought that such abnormal happenings might be expected if suppressed natures acted out their dreams is the chief residue when the fire of the action has burned itself out. The technique of starring the main character and blurring the rest of the cast is perfectly fitted to the *Denkspiel,* which thus becomes practically a monodrama. Even the main character submerges his individuality to become a type without so much as a name: except for some notable historical personages, such as Socrates and Alcibiades (*Der gerettete Alkibiades,* 1920) and Joan of Arc (*Gilles und Jeanne,* 1923), most of the characters in Kaiser's plays are designated merely by rank or function.

The socialistic tendencies of expressionism are found in Kaiser's trilogy on capitalism, *Die Koralle* (1917; Eng. tr., *The Coral,* 1929), *Gas I* 1918; Eng. tr., 1924), and *Gas II* (1920). In the middle member of this trilogy the author has caught very effectively the spirit of the mechanized age and, in posing a great social problem, has created true drama. Less far reaching but equally dramatic is *Die Bürger von Calais* (1917), in which the playwright enhances the tragedy of Froissart's narrative, made famous in Rodin's statuary, by having seven citizens rather than the required six volunteer for death.

Within the atmosphere of expressionism, which is the only environment thinkable for his products, Kaiser evolved a fitting dramatic style of his own which reduces language to a minimum and makes action the real medium for his ideas. In his more ambitious works these ideas became utopian, without, however, carrying true conviction.

Kaiser wrote two novels, *Es ist genug* (1932) and *Villa Aurea* (1940; Eng. tr., *A Villa in Sicily,* 1939).

See: H. F. Königsgarten, *Georg Kaiser* (1928); B. Diebold, *Der Denkspieler Georg Kaiser* (1924); M. Freyhan, *Georg Kaisers Werk* (1926); M. J. Fruchter, *The Social Dialectic in Georg Kaiser's Dramatic Works* (1933).

H. W. P.

Kamban, Guðmundur (1888–1945, Icelandic dramatist and novelist), born on Álftanes near Reykjavík, of poor but enterprising parents, was one of a large family. While working his way through school, Kamban came in contact with the cosmopolitan and humanitarian E. H. Kvaran (*q.v.*); but he went to Copenhagen to study literature and dramatics, and there he joined the group of Jóhann Sigurjónsson (*q.v.*) with enthusiasm and wrote his first play, *Hadda-Padda* (1914; Eng. tr., 1917), under that influence. Hadda-Padda is a woman whose love is her moral guide, a recurrent figure in Kamban's work. The play was a success at the Royal Theatre, but another play in the same national romantic vein was not so successful. After a visit to New York (1915–1917), Kamban turned social critic. In *Marmor* (1918; Marble), a play, and *Ragnar Finnsson* (1922), a novel, he criticized the treatment of convicts in prisons in America. During the 1920's Kamban revolted—as was the fashion of the times—against the conventional morals of love and marriage in a series of plays. *Vi Mordere* (1920; We Murderers) was the most successful of the group. *Sendiherrann frá Júpíter* (1927; The Ambassador from Jupiter) closes this period in Kamban's work with a general challenge to the corruption in Western civilization.

After a decade of cosmopolitan subjects, Kamban returned to native themes and wrote the historical novel *Skálholt* (4 vols., 1930–1935; Eng. tr. of Vols. I and II, *The Virgin of Skalholt,* 1935), about the unhappy love of the proud daughter of Bishop Brynjólfur Sveinson (1605–1675) and about his *mala domestica.* In monumentality of design this work is reminiscent of Undset's (*q.v.*) novels, but the philosophy is totally different: again, as in Kamban's first work, the woman's love is her only conscience. The affinity of this proud type with the women of the sagas is obvious, and in *Jeg ser et stort skønt Land* (1936; Eng. tr., *I See a Wondrous Land,* 1938), Kamban had an opportunity to portray the saga women themselves in his retelling of the stories of the discovery of Greenland and Vínland (America).

Kamban was connected with theatres in Scandinavia and Germany. His stay in Iceland (1927–1930) resulted in the novel *30. Generation* (1933; The Thirtieth Generation), a description of the modern emancipated and cosmopolitan bourgeoisie of Reykjavík, with which Kamban obviously was in sympathy.

During the Second World War, Kamban was in Denmark and Germany, writing several plays. He was killed by mistake by Danish patriots on May 5, 1945.

See: Ø. Ree, "En islandsk dramatiker," in *Nordisk tidskrift för vetenskap, konst och industri utgiven av Letterstedtska Föreningen,* 1921, pp. 39–42; S. Einarsson, "Guðmundur Kamban," *Tímarit Þjóðræknisfélags Íslendinga,* XIV (1932), 7–32.

S. E.

Kamenski, Vasili (1884–, Russian poet, novelist, and dramatist), born aboard a steamboat on the River Kama, was one of the founders of Russian futurism. With Mayakovsky (*q.v.*) and Burlyuk he toured the country on the eve of the First World War, shocking the philistines with unheard-of prose and verse and with outlandish array; Kamenski himself, who was an aviator at the time, appeared with an airplane painted on his brow. Like Khlebnikov (*q.v.*), he took liberties with the Russian language, coined numerous neologisms, and deliberately obscured the meaning of his verse, to produce *zaum* (beyond reason) poetry. His dominant note is carefree exuberance and the joy of living. He refers to himself as "cloudlessly skyey . . . a fierce eagle born in the Urals," whose "narcotic lyricism . . . rings like the carotid aorta" and who knows "no other morals than: Be free and forge ahead!" Aside from his numerous lyrics, Kamenski wrote a long poem, *Stepan Razin* (1916), in which, defying the war censorship, he glorified the spirit of rebellion among 17th-century Cossacks. The poem was dramatized in 1919. A novel of his, *Tango s korovami* (1911; Tango with Cows), gained temporary notoriety. In 1931 was published his autobiographical *Put entuziasta* (The Road of an Enthusiast), valuable for its intimate glimpses at the Russian futurists.

A. K.

Karlfeldt, Erik Axel (1864–1931, Swedish lyric poet), born in Karlbo, Folkärna, was graduated from the Gymnasium at Västerås in 1885 and studied at Uppsala, where he passed his licentiate examination in 1898. He was elected to the Swedish Academy in 1904, became a member of the Nobel committee in 1907 and permanent secretary of the Academy in 1912. In 1917 he received a Ph.D. (*honoris causa*) from the University of Uppsala. The Nobel prize in literature, which he had declined in 1920, was awarded him posthumously in 1931.

Karlfeldt's first work, *Vildmarks- och kärleksvisor* (1895; Ballads of the Woodlands and of Love), with its dedicatory "Fäderna" (My Forefathers) and admirable lyrics like "Sagan om Rosalind" (Rosalind's Saga), suggested the greater things soon to come. In *Fridolins visor* (1898; Fridolin's Ballads) and *Fridolins lustgård och dalmålningar på rim* (1901; Fridolin's Pleasure Garden and Dalecarlian Frescoes in Rhyme) his lyric orchestration is fully developed. The poet now achieves universal popularity; in the person of Fridolin, his alter ego, Karlfeldt becomes a classical figure, and the ballad collection is considered by many to be his masterpiece. *Flora och Pomona* (1906; Flora and Pomona) shows a tendency to loftier diction, to deepening of thought. Notable are poems of personal tone such as "I passionsveckan" (Easter Week), the masterly Dalecarlian rococo "Värdshuset" (The Tavern), and the burlesque "Ode till den höstlige Neptunus" (Ode to the Autumnal Neptune). *Flora och Bellona* (1918; Flora and Bellona) is rich in mirth ("Julia Djuplin"), transcendent beauty ("Zephyrs serenad till Ölands solvända," Zephyr's Serenade to the Öland Rockrose), and satire ("Till Bellona," Ode to Bellona).

The fundamental strains in this collection come from the deeper recesses of the poet's soul: there is a deep, religious undertone in "Systrar i lustgården" (Sisters in the Pleasure Garden), and a logical culmination in "Höstpsalm" (Psalm of Autumn), where the poet reaches the pinnacle of his art. *Skalden Lucidor* (1912; The Poet Lucidor) and *Tal och tankar* (1931, posthumous; public addresses, etc.) reveal a brilliant prose style and genuine oratorical power.

Karlfeldt's major inspiration is nature. Out of the attachment to the soil his song rises and finds unity in the glorification of the seasons and the calendric festivals of the year. The poet at his best is a consummate artist and virtuoso. His astounding mastery of the vernacular, creative imagination, range and intensity of emotion, virility, humor, and pathos have but few parallels in Swedish lyrics. The purely intellectual plays a subordinate part. His magic depends upon immediacy of approach. He appeals to the emotions through the senses by means of color, word witchery, archaisms, varieties of strophic structure, rhyme and rhythm, melody, and delicate and profuse use of the floral pictures. His felicity of metaphor recalls Shakespeare, the lilt of his lines suggests Swinburne.

See: A. M. Carlsson, *Erik Axel Karlfeldt* (1924); T. Fogelqvist, *Erik Axel Karlfeldt* (1931); Carl Mangård, *En bok om Karlfeldt* (1931); Karlfeldt, *Arcadia Borealis*, poems tr. by C. W. Stork (1938).

A. J. U.

Kasprowicz, Jan (1860–1926, Polish poet), was born in Szymborz, a little village in western Poland not far from the celebrated Lake Gopło. His parents were peasants deeply rooted in this historic and almost legendary Polish soil. By birth and ancestry Kasprowicz inherited a cultural tradition which lies at the bottom of almost every Polish peasant's thinking—a firm religious faith and an intuitive, apolitical, almost tribal consciousness of Polish nationality. Upon these two fundamental cultural factors the poet built an imposing intellectual superstructure of erudition in philosophy, classical philology, and comparative literature during his studies in the universities of Leipzig, Breslau, and Lwów. In 1909 he became professor of comparative literature at the University of Lwów. Unlike the great Polish romanticists who first stimulated his poetic spirit, Kasprowicz drew his inspiration from springs deeper than personal or even national fortune and misfortune. True to his peasant tradition he looked at life in the universal and saw man's fleshly existence as a God-ordained mystery of birth and death, as a transient moment between the material eternities of sun and soil and the moral eternities of good and evil, God and Satan. The philosophic depth of Kasprowicz's poetry precluded broad popularity for him in Poland. Yet his position as one of Poland's greatest poets is firmly entrenched, and although he is relatively unknown abroad, he is undoubtedly one of the foremost poets of universal human life and conscience in 20th-century Europe.

It is perhaps because Kasprowicz lived long enough to express himself completely that his poetic output (22 volumes, 1930 ed.) divides itself readily into periods and gives the impression of a drama constructed in logically consecutive acts leading to a climax and a swift inevitable conclusion. Even in his earliest cycles of lyrics in the first published volume of his poetry (1889) and in his sociological tales in verse, *Z chłopskiego zagonu* (1891; From a Peasant's Field), the poet's preoccupation with sociological phenomena assumed a deep moral tone and betrayed the first stirrings of spiritual revolt. This latter is especially noticeable in *Chrystus* (1890; Christ). Kasprowicz's second period marks his departure from sociological themes. Philosophic considerations of good and evil absorb him completely in the cycles collected under the titles *Miłość* (1895; Love) and *Krzak dzikiej róży* (1898; The Wild Rose). Amid doubts, despair, desperate clutchings at faith, and shining moments of decision and strength the poet wrestles with evil, and in *Ginącemu światu* (1902; To a Dying World) he plunges into a tremendous Promethean struggle against God himself. The soaring hymns of this cycle mark the poet's third and climactic period. In Polish literature poetry of comparable lyric intensity, sincerity, and power can be found only in the inspired "Improvisation" of Mickiewicz's *Forefathers' Eve*. The volume *Ballada o słoneczniku* (1908; Ballad of the Sunflower) marks the end of Kasprowicz's revolt and points toward the spiritual calm and consummate artistic simplicity of *Księga ubogich* (1916; The Book of the Poor) and his last book, *Mój świat* (1926; My World). The drama, *Marchołt*, written in 1913 but not published until 1920, is a concentrate of the poet's entire spiritual odyssey from his earliest sociological agitation through his painful philosophic searchings and Promethean revolt to his final, peasantlike, irrational reconciliation with God. Like Marchołt, the poet had fought in earnest without giving or asking quarter and, like Marchołt, was conquered only by God.

Kasprowicz was also a prolific and inspired translator. Among his translations are the complete works of Aeschylus, Euripides, and Shakespeare, Shelley's *Alastor, The Cenci,* and *Prometheus Unbound,* Byron's *Childe Harold's Pilgrimage,* Swinburne's *Atalanta in Calydon* and *Laus Veneris,* Wilde's *Ballad of Reading Gaol,* not to mention copious selections from Marlowe, Blake, Rossetti, Browning, and Yeats. The total of his translations from the German, Italian, and French is scarcely less impressive.

See: Z. Wasilewski, *Jan Kasprowicz; próba wizerunku* (1923); *Wiadomości literackie,* 1926, No. 147 (entire issue); Z. L. Zaleski, *Attitudes et destinées* (1932), pp. 116–138; K. Czachowski, *Obraz współczesnej literatury polskiej,* I (1934), 190–206, 308–313.

E. Z.

Kästner, Erich (1899–, German journalist, poet, and novelist), was born in Dresden. Originally intending to be a teacher, he entered normal school, but left it to be a bank clerk. This was during the post-war inflation, and again he changed his plans and studied literature, taking a Ph.D. degree in 1925. After some years of journalism, he found the income from his collected verse (*Herz auf Taille,* 1928; *Lärm im Spiegel,* 1929; *Ein Mann gibt Auskunft,* 1930) sufficient to set him free, and thereafter he devoted himself to writing. Meanwhile appeared the most popular of all his books, *Emil und die Detektive* (1929; Eng. tr., *Emil and the Detectives,* 1930), which was filmed in the United States; it was followed by *Fabian; die Geschichte eines Moralisten* (1931; Eng. tr., 1932), *Drei Männer im Schnee* (1934; Eng. tr., *Three Men in the Snow,* 1935), also filmed, *Die verschwundene Miniatur* (1936; Eng. tr., *The Missing Miniature,* 1936), and others. The bitterness of the post-war years with their chaos and confusion crops out in his more satiric passages and poems.

Kästner is a versatile and charming writer, whose humor deserves to be given more serious attention, for especially in Germany there has not been too much of it. In his best vein, he writes with a smile which is not frivolous, but merely the obverse of the tragic; he can also produce at will that releasing laughter which is one of the rarest gifts of letters to man.

B. Q. M.

Katayev, Valentin Petrovich (1897–, Russian novelist, short-story writer, and playwright), was born in Odessa, son of a high school teacher. In 1915 Katayev volunteered in the First World War, was wounded and gassed. During the civil war (1918–1920) he was equally ill-treated by the Whites and the Reds. Since 1922 Katayev has lived in Moscow, publishing novels, short stories, and plays. He started his literary career as a poet, but soon gave up poetry and turned definitely to prose. Already in his first books he showed his craftsmanship as a storyteller, both in lighter vein (*Ser Genri i chort,* 1923, Sir Henry and the Devil; *Bezdelnik Eduard,* 1923, The Loafer Eduard) and in serious, realistic portrayal (*Otets,* 1924; Father). His satirical novel *Rastratchiki* (1927; Eng. tr., *The Embezzlers,* 1929), devoted to the period of NEP (New Economic Policy), ranked him as one of the foremost Soviet writers. In *Vremya vperyod!* (1932; Eng. tr., *Time, Forward!* 1933, title in England, *Forward, Oh Time!* 1934) he gave one of the best pictures of the hardships and the pioneer spirit of the first Five-Year Plan. *Beliet parus odinoki* (1936; Eng. tr., *Lonely White Sail,* American title, *Peace Is Where the Tempests Blow,* both 1937) is a delightful story of children's adventures in Odessa during the revolutionary days of 1905–1906, while *Ya syn trudovogo naroda* (1937; I Am the Son of the Working People) is a highly patriotic novel evoking the struggle of Ukrainian partisans during the German occupation of their country in 1918. Katayev's war novel *Zhena* (1944; The Wife) is a strong and pathetic description of a woman who seeks to forget her personal misfortunes in productive work.

Katayev has been influenced by Bunin and Aleksei Tolstoy (*qq.v.*). He carries on successfully the tradition of Russian neo-realism. His novels and short stories have always an interesting plot, a vigorous construction, a sharp sense of humor, a warm humanity, and are written in colorful style. As a playwright Katayev is an amusing and caustic satirist. He drew general attention by his comedies and jests, the best of which are *Kvadratura kruga* (1929; Eng. tr., *Squaring the Circle,* 1934) and *Doroga tsvetov* (1934; The Road of Flowers). Soviet critics reproached Katayev for his comedy *Sini platochek* (1942; Blue Kerchief) because of its dealing with the war situation in a too farcical manner. Several of Katayev's novels and plays have been filmed in the U.S.S.R. Katayev certainly belongs to the most gifted and independent representatives of the Soviet prose of today.

M. S.

Katayev, Yevgeni Petrovich, *see* Petrov, Yevgeni Petrovich.

Kaverin, Venyamin Aleksandrovich (1902–, Russian writer and littérateur), born in St. Petersburg, began to write while still under 20 years of age. He was associated with Vsevolod Ivanov, Mikhail Slonimski, Yevgeni Zamyatin (*qq.v.*), and others in the formation (1921) of the Petersburg literary group known as the Serapion Brothers, which resisted current tendencies toward the regimentation of literature. His first short stories, *e.g.*, "Mastera i podmasterya" (Masters and Apprentices) and "Bubnovaya mast" (The Diamond Suit), were romantic in tendency. In two longer fictional efforts, *Konets Khazy* (The End of Khaza) and *Devyat desyatykh sud'by* (Nine Tenths of Destiny), Kaverin adhered to the so-called formalist school which, in the earlier days of the revolutionary period, made a concerted effort to wall off art from the Revolution itself and, in fact, from all burning political and social problems of the day. In his subsequent novel, *Skandalist* (1928; The Brawler), Kaverin satirized routine middle-class scholars totally cut off from life and, in the author's view, intellectually bankrupt. He approached still closer to Soviet ideology in *Prolog* (The Prologue), written after an extensive visit to the state and collective farms of the steppe country, though he interprets the economic reconstruction of the country as a technical attack by man upon nature. In his story "Khudozhnik neizvesten" (Artist Unknown) Kaverin again remained faithful to his early formalistic convictions and practice, but in his later works, *e.g.*, *Dva kapitana* (1940; Eng. tr., *Two Captains,* 1942), he came nearer to the current Soviet ideal of socialist realism. Kaverin has also experimented with drama in *Ukroshcheniye Robinzona ili Poteryanny Rai* (The Taming of Robinson or Paradise Lost) and wrote the literary monograph *Baron Brambeus: Istoriya Osipa Senkovskogo* (Baron Brambäus: The Story of Osip Senkovski), discussing a fertile but qualitatively insignificant Russian journalist of Pushkin's day.

See: V. Sayanov, "Put V. Kaverina," in Kaverin, *Sochineniya,* I (1930), 5–16; G. Reavey and M. Slonim, *Soviet Literature; an Anthology* (1934), pp. 181–190; G. Struve, *25 Years of Soviet Russian Literature* (1944), pp. 49–55, 271–272.

S. H. C.

Kazin, Vasili (1898–, Russian poet), born in Moscow, comes from a family of peasants and workers and has himself engaged in such crafts as roofing and carpentry. His verse began to appear in print in 1914, but his fame came with the publication of his first slim volume, *Rabochi mai* (1922; The Workers' May). Kazin sees everything through the prism of physical labor, which is evidenced by his similes and images. Such a threadbare theme as a blonde sweetheart is given a new angle in "Rubanok" (Jack Plane), in which the rustling of fragrant shavings reminds the workman of the curls of his beloved, and the grief of parting is like a splinter driven into his heart. Labor is free from drudgery and enslavement when depicted by Kazin. Poetry and the joy of creative effort are in his description of physical exertion, and even fatigue "oozes sweetly down his spine." He regards nature anthropomorphically, and always from the worker's point of view. Thus he sees the sun with the eyes of a bricklayer ("Morning hoisted its brick"), the sounds of awakening spring he perceives in terms of a tin-roofer, while evening is to him an apiarist whose bees are stars. He presents a thunderstorm as a gigantic foundry, with throngs of blacksmiths nimbly setting furnaces aflame and thundering reverberating blows. Kazin is primarily a lyricist, who contemplates the world somewhat sentimentally, even if the sentiment is robust and proletarian. His attempts at longer poems of a broader scope have not been successful.

A. K.

Keller, Gottfried (1819–1890, Swiss novelist), born in Zurich, one of the greatest writers in German of the whole post-Goethian period, is considered by the German Swiss, if not by the whole of Switzerland, to be the most representative national author. Keller's influence among his countrymen in the 20th century is undiminished. His earlier, most productive years coincide with the reconstruction of Switzerland after the Napoleonic Wars, when a vigorous democratic spirit reasserted itself and found expression in numerous progressive measures. Keller took an active part, first, in bringing about some of these measures and, secondly, in fostering, through his writings, the attitude necessary for maintaining and developing democratic standards. Fortunately he combines with such social responsibility a high degree of artistic sensibilities and a sovereign imagination.

Keller for 15 years served his country faithfully as secretary of the cantonal government, a position which entailed many painstaking duties. During these years he had no time to write though ample occasion to gather material and to sift his observations on human life and nature. His best works were either wholly executed after this period or at least then revised and put into final shape. His greatest contribution, *Der grüne Heinrich,* a novel of nearly a thousand pages, was first published 1854–1855, only to be completely recast 25 years later. With the advantage of a seasoned outlook on life Keller was now able to raise this autobiographical account to the level of a representative educational novel; as such it takes its place beside Grimmelshausen's *Simplicissimus* and Goethe's *Wilhelm Meister.*

It is not too much to say that in *Der grüne Heinrich* the Swiss cultural tradition has been developed and refined to a degree which makes this work a model of life among European forms of culture. Man's duty is here conceived by Keller as being first of all towards the reality of this world; his religious, transcendental impulses have to be converted into practical ethics. With that Keller proclaims the sacred duty of making spirit concrete and nature ethical. Hence his joyful abandonment to the physical beauty of our earth, from which we must draw strength and enthusiasm. The fruit of intimate contact with nature and deep confidence in mankind appears in *Der grüne Heinrich* as the hero's decision to devote himself wholly to the social task. He accepts a modest position in the civil service, a step which assumes symbolic significance: in some form or other we must all turn our activities, be they what they may, towards a socially useful purpose. This definition of man's ultimate obligation is repeated in the fate of one of the principal women characters who, likewise after having passed through a period of exuberant naturalism, fulfills her destiny by attending to the poor and sick, sacrificing even her life in the discharge of such duties. Group life, too, has its own characteristic aims and forms; its foremost function is to guarantee freedom, economic well-being, and progress. The emphasis in *Der grüne Heinrich* is, however, less on the acquisition of freedom than on its protection against abuse and deterioration. Progress is something which Keller ardently believes in, though he can by no means be accused of irresponsible optimism. He is enough of a clear-sighted realist to know that constant watchfulness is needed to prevent the exploitation by greed or sly cunning of our human rights. The hero's deceased father, whose memory lives among the neighbors, leaves a shining example of a sturdy, progressive-minded craftsman and citizen; through him the son remains forever pledged to the idea of progress, of a slowly expanding area of good will and reason. Finally, the cornerstone of a sound social structure is education, both in the sense of a solid training in crafts or professions and of keen interest in cultural activities. Less conspicuous for foreign readers but highly interesting for his countrymen is the way in which Keller, in *Der grüne Heinrich,* discusses the relationship between Switzerland and Germany.

Inexhaustible as the vitality and wisdom of *Der grüne Heinrich* proves to be, the reader should turn to other works of Keller, above all to *Das Sinngedicht* (1881) and "Der Landvogt von Greifensee" in *Die Züricher Novellen* (1877), for complementary aspects of his Christian humanism. In these shorter stories Keller takes up some of the more intimate problems of human conduct, reiterating his belief in the absolute value of such qualities as honesty, serenity, mutual sympathy, and castigating as the one unpardonable sin man's inclination to conceit and brutality. A writer of such inner strength cannot fail to produce significant works even in his lighter mood or when giving free rein to humor and imagination, as he does in the two volumes of *Die Leute von Seldwyla* (1856–1874; Eng. tr. of selections, *Seldwyla folks,* 1919).

Recent critics have made much of Keller's last novel, *Martin Salander* (1886), which they declare to be his stern appraisal of democratic institutions. It would, however, seem that Keller's frank criticism takes to task not democracy as such but those of us who through lack of inner effort invite abuse of freedom and of harmonious community life.

See: E. F. Hauch, *Gottfried Keller as a Democratic Idealist* (1916); E. Ermatinger, *Gottfried Kellers Leben, Briefe und Tagebücher* (1924–1925); E. Ackerknecht, *Gottfried Keller* (1939).

H. B.

Kessel, Joseph (1898–, French novelist and journalist), was born in Argentina, in the city of Clara, where his father, a Russian refugee who had completed his medical studies at Montpellier in France, practiced medicine. Kessel himself studied in France, first at the Lycée of Nice, then at the Lycée Louis-le-Grand in Paris. The First World War broke out while he was still studying at the Sorbonne. He enlisted and saw active service as an aviator, receiving the Croix de Guerre. He was then sent to the United States and left France the day the armistice was signed. From New York he went to Los Angeles, crossed the Pacific Ocean, and joined the French general staff in Siberia. It was here he became acquainted with the hetman Semenov and his Cossacks. Upon his return to France *La Steppe rouge*

(1923) was published, a group of short stories dealing with the Terror which accompanied the Russian Revolution. The following year he wrote *L'Equipage,* a war and aviation story, probably his best novel. As a reporter he attempted to reenter Russia and narrowly escaped being shot by the Bolsheviks in Riga. *Les Captifs* (1926), a somber study of the victims of tuberculosis, was awarded the Grand Prix du Roman by the French Academy in 1927. His succeeding works have been, for the most part, inspired by his numerous travels. A vivid book concerning the Second World War, *L'Armée des ombres,* was published in 1944 (Eng. tr., *Army of Shadows,* 1944).

There is in the writing of Kessel a certain savage quality, modified by a classic style of expression. His works echo the world-shaking events to which he has been a witness.

P. B.

Kesten, Hermann (1900–, German novelist and playwright), born in Nuremberg, was educated at Erlangen and Frankfurt am Main. An attack upon Hitlerism in his novel *Der Scharlatan* (1932) made it necessary for him to leave Germany. In Amsterdam, where he fled, he was, from 1933 until 1940, literary editor to the publisher Allert de Lange. In 1940 the German invasion forced him to emigrate to America.

Kesten's talent was early recognized; his first novel, *Joseph sucht die Freiheit* (1927; Eng. tr., *Joseph Breaks Free,* 1930), won for its author the Kleist citation. Its theme—a youth's painful realization that the supposed virtues of his family existed only in his affectionate imagination and his desire to escape from actuality—is, in Kesten's next novel, *Ein ausschweifender Mensch* (1929), enlarged to a man's attempt to break away from his fatherland. His next book, *Glückliche Menschen* (1931; Eng. tr., *Happy Man!* 1935), sentimentally melodramatic at the beginning and fantastic and arbitrary in its sequence of events, is nevertheless characteristic of its author, a moralist disguised as a grim joker. His fictionalized biographies (*Ferdinand und Isabella,* 1936, Eng. tr., *Spanish Fire,* 1937; *König Philipp der Zweite,* 1938, Eng. tr., *I, the King,* 1939) lose none of the reader's interest by Kesten's attention to historical detail and correctness. The confusion and stupidity of the recent Spanish civil war are vividly portrayed in *Die Kinder von Gernika* (1939; Eng. tr., *Children of Guernica,* 1939).

Several of Kesten's plays were produced before he left Germany, *Maud liebt beide* (1928), *Admet* (1929), *Die heilige Familie* (1930), *Babel* (1930), *Einer sagt die Wahrheit* (1931), and, in collaboration with Ernst Toller (*q.v.*), *Wunder in Amerika* (1931; Eng. tr., *Mary Baker Eddy,* in Toller's *Seven Plays,* 1935). In Germany, in the Netherlands during his literary editorship with De Lange, and in America, Kesten published several anthologies of European literature: *24 neue deutsche Erzähler* (1929); *Neue französische Erzähler* (1930), in collaboration with F. Bertaux; *Novellen deutscher Dichter der Gegenwart* (1933), his preference here being, on the whole, for the grim and melancholy, even gruesome aspects of life; and *Heart of Europe* (1943), in collaboration with Klaus Mann (*q.v.*). Kesten has edited, both in German and in English, the poems of Heine (1939, 1943) and has translated Julien Green's (*q.v.*) *Léviathan,* Romains's (*q.v.*) *Le Capitaliste,* Giraudoux's (*q.v.*) *Les Aventures de Jérôme Bardini,* John Gunther's *Inside Asia,* and short prose works of E. Bove, H. Michaux, and Ester Riwkin.

See: F. Bertaux, *A Panorama of German Literature from 1871 to 1931* (1935), pp. 256–257.

V. L.

Key, Ellen (1849–1926, Swedish essayist and moralist), was one of the most provocative cultural personalities in modern Sweden. Her long career as a teacher, popular lecturer, and essayist was punctuated by a number of strenuous cultural controversies because of the frankness with which she spoke her mind on subjects of a highly controversial nature (religion, patriotism, sex, feminine emancipation). All except the most reactionary sections of Swedish society came ultimately to admire her courage and hail her as one of the great feminine cultural forces in Swedish history, a kind of modern St. Birgitta. She has written some 30 volumes of essays, based for the most part directly on lectures which she delivered in Sweden or in various parts of the Continent. These essays develop primarily social, pedagogical, and moral themes of broad, general human interest, but they include also, especially in Ellen Key's early years, a number of extended biographical and critical essays on such Swedish literary figures as C. J. L. Almquist, Victoria Benedictsson (*q.v.*), and Anne Charlotte Leffler-Cajanello.

Much of Ellen Key's central work has been translated into English as well as into German, French, Italian, and other languages. She has had enthusiastic disciples in many countries, particularly in Germany and Italy. In England her work has been highly regarded, though with certain reservations among more critical

English students of modern morals like Havelock Ellis. Herself a product of the movement toward feminine emancipation in the late 19th century, and an enthusiastic champion of some of its ideas, Ellen Key has proved nevertheless to be one of this movement's most severe constructive critics. She reacted particularly strongly against the extreme trend within the movement which sought to deny (by implication at least) any fundamental emotional and physical differences between the sexes. In *Missbrukad kvinnokraft* (1896; Misused Feminine Power) she insists that woman by nature is primarily the mother, and that if she pursues her modern claims of "individualism" and equal rights with man to the point where she denies her fundamental natural function as a mother, she will not only distort her own natural physical and spiritual development but also endanger the whole future of the race. In *Barnets århundrade* (1900; Eng. tr., *The Century of the Child,* 1909) she emphasizes the place of the home as the primary educational and moral institution and in general stresses a natural as opposed to a traditional academic education, in a manner reminiscent of Rousseau. Two other works of central importance in Ellen Key's production are *Tankebilder* (2 vols., 1898, Thought Images) and *Livslinjer* (3 vols., 1903–1906; Life Lines), in which she develops a kind of religious-evolutionary "philosophy" which sharply rejects a traditional Christian asceticism and projects in its place a somewhat vaguely defined, highly optimistic *livstro* (faith in life) as the basis of a new religion. The outbreak of the First World War, with its materialistic motivations and its mass murder, did not destroy Ellen Key's faith in life and humanity, though it made her clothe her ideas henceforth in a somewhat less exuberant prose.

Ellen Key herself is not to be counted among Swedish literary figures in the strictly creative sense, but her ideas have certain undeniable points of contact with the neopaganism of Heidenstam (*q.v.*) and others in the 1890's, and her characteristic prose style, with its lyric effusiveness and its colorful elaboration of imagery, affects one, as a recent Swedish critic has put it, "as an unintentional parody of what the Swedish 1890's meant by a beautiful style." But though her prose style seems to us today stilted and false, and her ideas overoptimistic if not in considerable part actually naïve, Ellen Key as a personality, warm, unselfish, courageous, intensely alive, full of a contagious energy and enthusiasm, has been a very real force in Swedish cultural life in the last half century. The force of her personality has already outlived, and will apparently continue to outlive, details of the specific program of reform for which she fought ceaselessly throughout a long and active life.

See: L. Nystrom-Hamilton, *Ellen Key: en livsbild* (1904, 2d ed., 1917; Eng. tr., *Ellen Key; Her Life and Work,* 1913); J. Landquist, *Ellen Key* (1909); G. Brandes and others, *En bok om Ellen Key* (1919).

A. G.

Keyserling, Eduard, Graf von (1855–1918, German novelist), was born at Paddern, the ancestral estate in the Baltic province of Courland; his distinguished family traced its descent from the Teutonic Knights who had brought Christianity and Western culture to this region in the 13th century. His early education was at the Gymnasium in Hasenpoth, and he attended the university at Dorpat before going to Vienna to live. After some years at Paddern administering the family estate and further travel in Italy, he settled in Munich in 1899, where he lived with two sisters. An invalid since 1897, he was blind the last 10 years of his life.

Keyserling's literary career began late. His first works, the novels *Rosa Herz* (1883) and *Die dritte Stiege* (1890) as well as his dramas, *Frühlingsopfer* (1899), *Der dumme Hans* (1901), *Peter Hawel* (1903), and *Benignens Erlebnis* (1906), influenced by early naturalism, are almost forgotten. His later stories show Keyserling at his best and place him high in the ranks of modern German novelists. His style is reminiscent of Fontane and Turgenev (*qq.v.*). The somber landscape, the melancholy isolation of the baronial estates, reflect the passive mood and aristocratic restraint so fundamental to an understanding of his characters. His delineations are concise and accurate, his narratives realistic and objective. His own social and cultural heritage determined his work. The German nobility in the Baltic provinces had enjoyed a unique position of influence for centuries and controlled internal affairs completely despite the nominal political dependence upon Russia. Even in the late 19th century, after serfdom had been abolished and basic human rights granted to the Lett peasantry, the landed aristocracy dominated. The wide gulf between the masses of people and this small group of cultivated leaders remained unbridged. Keyserling portrayed the life of this select circle. His characters and their outlook are best characterized by Fontane's famous remark that while a weaver may live to be 60 at the most, an aristocratic squire may really be 300 years old. Among Keyserling's best works are the novels *Beate und Mareile* (1903; Eng. tr., *The Curse of the Tarniffs*, 1928), *Dumala* (1907; Eng. tr., *Man of God*, 1930), *Wellen* (1911; Eng. tr., *Tides*, 1929), *Abendliche Häuser* (1913), *Am Südhang* (1916), *Fürstinnen* (1917), and *Feiertagskinder* (1919) and the collections of stories *Schwüle Tage* (1906), *Bunte Herzen* (1908), and *Im stillen Winkel* (1918). His stories are documents of the gradual crumbling of a society that had once been the bulwark of European civilization, but was now an anachronism. He ignored the problems of his time and seemed unaware of the significance of the revolt among the Letts in 1905–1906, which was really a prelude to the final collapse of German supremacy in the Baltic. He portrayed only the daily routine of his own set, "whom life passed by" without actually touching. Its conduct was determined by custom and tradition and had been molded centuries ago. For Keyserling human relationships were significant only within the accepted pattern. His characters feel their position, their privileges, and their duties. Their lives are not easy because custom and tradition dictate procedure in every situation, yet they cannot exist in any world but their own. They have lived too long in an artificial atmosphere and have lost vigor and initiative. They are delicately sensitive and highly cultivated, but their refinement has reached the point of decadence. Love is the motivating factor in Keyserling's narratives, but it is not an elemental passion. Keyserling pictured love as an irrational desire that dislocates the ordinary relationships of life. The scenes are laid on aristocratic estates where gracious living has become a fine art. Against a background of dinners, hunting parties, garden fêtes, and five o'clock teas the disturbing domination of an irrational love affair is pictured. Every story deals with the destructive influence of illicit love in conventional aristocratic circles, yet Keyserling never becomes tiresome in handling such limited materials. He portrays his characters so skillfully with a minimum of detail and artifice that the reader is charmed with the naturalness of his narratives and the economy of his art.

See: A. Soergel, *Dichtung und Dichter der Zeit*, 19. Auflage (1928), pp. 840–845; K. Knoop, *Die Erzählungen Eduard von Keyserlings* (1929).

W. A. R.

Khlebnikov, Velemir (pseud. of Victor Khlebnikov, 1885–1922, Russian poet), born at Kalmytzkaya Step in the former Government of Saratov, was the most prominent member of the cubo-futurist group on the eve of the Russian Revolution. Absent-minded, slovenly, and impractical, he published only a small portion of his voluminous output and died in wretched poverty. A collection of his poems garnered from various publications and from extant manuscripts (he was in the habit of scattering and losing his verses) was issued in 1936 (*Izbrannyie stikhotvoreniya; Selected Poems*). He influenced both his fellow futurists and other poets with his innovations in prosody and especially in language. His intimate knowledge of old and modern Russian, coupled with his inherent penchant for linguistics and his interest in folklore, enabled him to create neologisms free of the absurd trickery that lent unenviable notoriety to such of his associates as Kruchonykh. Khlebnikov's language has its logic and is essentially Russian morphologically, even when the words he uses are nonexistent and have no meaning. A celebrated poem of his, "Zaklyatiye smekhom" (Conjuration by Laughter), is delightful nonsense verse, in which the word *smekh*, laughter, gives birth to nearly a score of fanciful variations—invented nouns, adjectives, verbs, and adverbs—whose total effect on one's risibles is inevitable. His coinage of *zaum* (beyond reason) language is closer to James Joyce's efforts than to the whimseys of Gertrude Stein. Like Joyce, Khlebnikov had a catholic interest in words and linguistics. Hence his preoccupation with Slavic and non-Slavic folklore, epos, and authentic national poets. Among the works that had an influence on him were the *Kalevala, Hiawatha,* oriental epics, the poetry of Pushkin and Walt Whitman.

A mystic megalomania was evidenced in his letters and literary declarations. He took his futurism seriously and referred to himself solemnly as "king of the poets" and "chairman of the globe." His poetry after the Revolution was rather pedestrian.

A. K.

Khodasevich, Vladislav Felitsyanovich (1886–1939, Russian poet and critic), was born and educated in Moscow. In his first book of verse, *Molodost* (1908; Youth), he appears as a minor disciple of symbolism. Although he was an ardent admirer of Andrei Bely (*q.v.*), his poetry came to lean much more toward classicism and reflects rather the influence of Bryusov (*q.v.*)—and through him, of Pushkin. Khodasevich's *Putem zerna* (1920; The Way of Grain) first brought him general recognition as a poet. His finest book of poetry is *Tyazholaya lira* (1922; The Heavy Lyre), in which he appears as a master of classical form. His book of memoirs, *Nekropol* (Paris, 1935; Necropolis), gives brilliant, although not always reliable, sketches of leading personalities of contemporary Russian literature.

See: A. Bely, "V. Khodasevich," *Zapiski mechtatelya,* Vol. V (1922); S. Rodov, "Original-naya poeziya gosizdata," *Na postu,* 1923, Nos. 2–3.

O. M.

Kielland, Alexander Lange (1849–1906, Norwegian novelist, short-story writer, and dramatist), is reckoned as one of the "big four" of Norwegian classic writers, along with Ibsen, Björnson, and Lie (*qq.v.*). He was at one with his contemporaries in attacking the abuses of social life, but he stood apart by virtue of his great personal charm, his brilliant wit, and his unfailing clarity of form. He burst meteorically upon the literary scene in 1879, worked feverishly for a decade, and then stopped writing as suddenly as he had begun. Björnson and Brandes (*q.v.*) hailed him enthusiastically as an ally in the battle for social and intellectual freedom in the North. They were not accustomed to finding men of his caliber on their side, the scion of a wealthy merchant family, "favorite of the gods," large, handsome, elegant. Kielland's attacks on social prejudice did not stem from personal disappointments or disharmonies, but from a deeply founded sincerity of ethical purpose, a logical, rationalistic view of the world, and an absolute conviction of the importance of the cause for which he fought.

His life was outwardly uneventful. After receiving a law degree in 1871, he operated a brick factory (1872–1881) and then spent literary periods in Copenhagen (1881–1883), in his native town of Stavanger (1883–86), and in France (1886–88). He was editor of a Stavanger daily (1889–1890), mayor of Stavanger (1891–1902), and district governor of Romsdal (1902–1906). The really crucial event in Kielland's literary life was his visit to the Paris Exposition in 1878, when he wrote his first short stories and met Björnson. A climax came in 1885, when the Norwegian Storting refused to grant him a poet's stipend, a *cause célèbre* which split the Liberal Party into two irreconcilable wings.

His basic tastes were developed in a pre-capitalistic, patriarchal economy, an atmosphere of small-town merchant princeliness. These are reflected in his courtly manners, the pride and reticence of his character, the deep veneration he nourished for the cultural tradition of his family, and the touch of foppery and *dolce far niente* which he often regretted but never denied. His loving delineation of the ancestral house stands among the high points of his authorship. But Kielland broke decisively with the political and religious tradition of this background. His years as a factory owner opened his eyes to the position of the laboring man; his reading after 1870 gave direction to his life by awakening his anger over the exploitation and inequalities of modern life. The satirical spirit which had been nourished in his student days by Heine and Kierkegaard was now captivated by the ideas of Brandes and John Stuart Mill and inspired by the narrative art of Dickens, Daudet (*q.v.*), Hans Christian Andersen, and Balzac. The theme of his writing, infinitely varied, became the glaring discrepancies between wealth and poverty, the respectable and the outcast. He felt a deep aversion to the anticultural effects of the incoming industrial capitalism and parted company with his own class by sympathizing with its victims instead of its beneficiaries, by seeking to strengthen those who lacked power and encouraging their dissatisfactions. Kielland poured his satiric vitriol above all on the representatives of conservative, institutionalized life, the clergy, the bureaucracy, and the schoolmen. He began with rapier thrusts, but ended with good, hefty blows of the broadsword. He opened with a collection of short stories, *Novelletter* (1879; Eng. tr., *Tales of Two Countries,* 1891; *Norse Tales and Sketches,* 1897); his fame rests chiefly on these and the novels *Garman og Worse* (1880; Eng. tr., *Garman and Worse,* 1885) and *Skipper Worse* (1882; Eng. tr., 1885). The most distinguished of his contemporary satires were the novels *Arbeidsfolk* (1881; Laborers), *Else* (1881; Eng. tr., *Elsie,* 1894), and *Gift* (1883; Poison).

His literary qualities include a cultivation of language that is reminiscent of Flaubert (*q.v.*), a deft, discreet handling of detail which is often loving in its maliciousness, and a lyric vein that grew out of a passionate fondness for the gray, low-lying shores of southwestern Norway and the sea that incessantly pounds them. Kielland's writings offer the most thoroughly and delicately seasoned dish that Norwegian literature has produced, a remarkable blending of the Norwegian milieu with the European outlook. For all the indignation that made him a "partisan of utilitarian poetry" and sometimes misled him to one-sided characterizations, the final impression of his work and his character is that of breadth

—a breadth that included self-irony, tenderness, and an almost sybaritic enjoyment of life's amenities. In Björnson's words, "he was the most perfect representative of Norwegian culture in our day." He has himself joined the characters of his books as a figure in Norwegian literature, living still in the several volumes of his letters published after his death. In them, even more directly than in his works, is reflected a manly soul, gentle, honest, witty, and wise.

See: J. B. Halvorsen, *Norsk forfatter-lexikon,* III (1892), 228–246; G. Brandes, *Samlede Skrifter* (1900); M. Schjødt, *A. L. Kielland* (1904); Kielland, *Breve* (1907), *Breve til hans datter* (1909), and *Samlede digterverker,* ed. by P. L. Stavnem (5 vols., 1919); G. Gran, *Alexander L. Kielland og hans samtid* (1922); O. Storstein, *Kielland på ny* (1936); V. E. Lynner, "Hvem var Alexander Kielland?" *Edda,* XXXVII (1937), 304–337.

E. H.

Kinck, Hans Ernst (1865–1926, Norwegian short-story writer, novelist, dramatist, and essayist), born in Øksfjord in Loppa, was a physician's son who received the determining impulses of his art among the "medieval" country folk of Setesdal (from the age 7 to 11) and the "salty rationalists" of Hardanger (from the age 11 to 17). A classical schooling crowned the development of one of the most original, temperamental, and startling writers in Norwegian letters. Independently, yet in step with other writers and thinkers in the neo-romantic era, he worked his way back to the Middle Ages, seeking there the roots of the nation, "the mystery of a people." Like Bergson (*q.v.*) he praised human vitality, the impulse, the unreflective, the flame of heart and temper. Like Nietzsche (*q.v.*) he saw in history "a series of vast undertakings resulting from the self-willed craving for action of individual personalities." After taking a university degree he won honorable mention for a thesis on the relation between medieval ballad poetry and the mythical-heroic poetry of northern antiquity (1892). This was the first of his many attempts to reach by a magnificent scholarly intuition (too often without adequate support in facts) a conception of Norse "folk psyche" in modern and medieval times. His entire work was founded in mysticism, but he approached it by way of an ironic, almost corrosive wit and a fantastically imaginative intellect. His earliest novels, *Huldren* (1892; The Half-Wit) and *Ungt folk* (1893; Eng. tr., *A Young People,* 1929), were outwardly naturalistic, but their purpose was to reveal the unconscious urges of the soul. A residence in Paris (1893–1894) led to his first genuinely original creation, *Flaggermusvinger* (1895; Bats' Wings), and the two novels about Herman Eek, *Sus* (1896; Soughing) and *Hugormen* (1898; The Adder). He left the public cold, bewildered, or antagonistic; but among authors and connoisseurs he won a faithful, even a frenzied support.

In 1896 Kinck visited Italy for the first time and was so captivated by its charm that he made it his second homeland. From then on his writings in the various genres which he mastered swung back and forth between a Norwegian peasant or medieval background and the Italian Renaissance. His masterpieces in the former include the novel *Emigranter* (1904; Emigrants), the unrhythmical dramatic poem *Driftekaren* (1908; The Drover), numerous volumes of short stories and essays, and the monumental *Sneskavlen brast* (3 vols., 1918–1919; The Avalanche Broke). Class conflicts, the relation of heritage and environment, of race and individual, are their basic themes. His Italian studies led him to set up two polar types in the racial mixture of Italy, the satirist Pietro Aretino, in the drama *Den sidste gjest* (1910; The Last Guest), and the mystic nationalist, Niccolò Machiavelli, in the drama *Mot karneval* (1915; Toward Carnival). Although Kinck was close to Pareto (*q.v.*) in his views on emotion and was affected by the writings of German racialists, he did not follow them into political fascism, remaining sharply opposed to all mechanistic philosophies and mass movements. In his presentation he swung constantly between the lyric and the grotesque, with an overpowering, baroque fantasy which could flare into burlesque or sadism without warning. His style was a Dano-Norwegian such as no one had written before him, shot through with the riches of his childhood dialects, concentrated, impulsive, and difficult of access. Kinck's work flashes with the sovereignty of authentic genius, even when it reveals an incapacity for sustained narrative or dramatic characterization. The best of his extraordinarily prolific work is found in the short stories; less burdened by racial theories, he was here free to be the "pure artist" that Gunnar Heiberg (*q.v.*) once called him.

See: C. Gierløff, *Kinck* (1923); J. Bukdahl, "Hans E. Kinck," *American-Scandinavian Review,* XV (1927), 589–594; A. Harbitz, ed., *Hans E. Kinck; et eftermæle* (1927); H. Jæger, "Hans Ernst Kinck," in *Norsk biografisk leksikon,* VII (1936), 316–329.

E. H.

Kirk, Hans Rudolf (1898–, Danish novelist and journalist), was born the son of a doctor in Hadsund, a fishing town on the Mariager Fjord in Northeast Jutland. Matriculating in 1916 from the old and aristocratic Sorø Academy, he took his degree in law in 1922, entered the civil service for two years, then left abruptly to write. His book reviews for a provincial paper attracted attention. In 1930 he joined the staff of the Copenhagen daily *Social-Demokraten*. From 1938 he was associated with the communistic *Arbejderbladet* (Workers' Journal). He contributed also to radical magazines, including *Clarté* and Nordahl Grieg's (*q.v.*) *Veien frem* (The Road Ahead). With *Fiskerne* (1928; The Fishermen) he won immediate recognition as a novelist of rank. His second novel, *Daglejerne* (1936; Day Laborers), confirmed his position. In both he uses the collective method, substituting for the traditional hero the group—pietistic fishermen forming a new community, farm laborers in the process of becoming factory workers and trade unionists. But groups consist of individuals, and there are few more vivid and memorable in modern literature than Mariane of *Fiskerne* or Cilius of *Daglejerne,* to mention only two of the many characters Kirk has drawn with sympathy and humor in strong, clear prose. His latest novel, *Borgmesteren gaar af* (1942; The Mayor Retires), is a brilliant but not unkindly satire of the officialdom he once so briefly served.

See: O. Friis, "Hans Rudolf Kirk," in *Dansk biografisk Leksikon,* XII (1937), 461–462.

J. B. C. W.

Kirshon, Vladimir Mikhailovich (1902–1937, Russian dramatist), born in St. Petersburg into a family of the Menshevik intelligentsia, became a Bolshevik in 1920, went to Sverdlovsk University in 1921 and to Rostov-on-Don in 1923. He moved to Moscow in 1925 and became one of the leaders of the Association of Proletarian Writers. In 1925 a murder was committed by a Communist student named Korenkov, and a violent discussion arose as to whether the murderer should be pardoned on account of his past services and his possible future usefulness to Communism. Kirshon took this famous case as the subject of his first play, *Rzhavchina* (1927; Eng. tr., *Red Rust,* acted by the Theatre Guild Studio in 1929 and printed in New York in 1930), of which he later changed the title to *Konstantin Terekhin,* the fictitious name of his hero. In the play Kirshon and his collaborator, A. Uspenski, showed the degeneration of a young hero of the Russian Revolution under the corrupting influence of the Nepmen of the New Economic Policy. Kirshon's next play, *Relsy gudyat* (1928; The Rails Are Humming), showed the difficulties of a Communist director in a locomotive repair shop in conflict with reactionary engineers and the final triumph of the workers at the end of the play when the repaired steam engine, giving forth real steam, is set in motion. In *Gorod vetrov* (1929; The City of Winds) Kirshon turned to the Revolution in Baku in 1918 and the story of the 26 Communists who were put to death. The play was made into an opera called *Severny veter* (1930; The North Wind), with music by Leo Knipper. In his next play, *Khleb* (1930; Eng. tr., *Bread* 1934), he turned to the collective farm and the struggle to prevent the kulaks from hoarding wheat and causing starvation. *Sud* (1933; The Trial) took up the struggle in Germany between Social Democrats and Communists. In *Chudesny splav* (1934; The Miraculous Alloy) Kirshon told the story of a brigade of young students who successfully invented a new kind of alloy to be used in making airplanes. In *Bolshoi den* (1937; The Big Day) he depicted the eve of a fascist attack on the Soviet Union and showed a young aviator saving the life of his older rival.

See: A. V. Gurvich, "Kirshon," *Krasnaya nov,* 1934, No. 6; I. Altman, *Dramaturgiya* (1936); A. Gurvich, *Tri dramaturga* (1936), pp. 181–268; Kirshon, "A New Chapter in Dramatic Thought," *Theatre Arts Monthly,* XX (1936), 673–678.

H. W. L. D.

Kiss, József (1843–1921, Hungarian poet), was born in Mezőcsát and died in Budapest. He received rabbinical education and as a young man taught in Hebrew schools in the provinces. In 1868 he went to Budapest and shortly afterwards established his reputation with a volume of poems entitled *Zsidó dalok* (1868; Hebrew Songs). With the exception of Gyula Reviczky (*q.v.*) and János Vajda (*q.v.*), József Kiss was the most genuine poet of his generation. His contemporaries who wrote poetry, *e.g.,* Kálmán Tóth, Árpád Zempléni, Gyula Rudnyánszky, Lajos Palágyi, Lajos Pósa, Elek Londesz, Lajos Bartók, lacked the evoking magic which Kiss sometimes possessed. Yet compared with János Arany (*q.v.*), whom as a poet of ballads he imitated, Kiss was a minor poet; and though he was first acclaimed by Ferenc Toldy who was "the father of Hungarian literary history," he never qualified as a really outstanding creator in terms of comparative literature. In 1890 he founded *A Hét* (The Week), a literary weekly, which influenced the trend of modern Hungarian literature. For some time his assistant editor was Emil Makai, a minor poet and playwright who died in 1901 at the age of 30. Another assistant editor, Tamás Kóbor, was a realistic novelist and writer of short stories of some merit, but chiefly an able journalist. Kiss himself was a member of the Petőfi Társaság (Petőfi Society) and of the Kisfaludy Társaság (Kisfaludy Society).

Influenced by János Arany, Kiss wrote ballads, of which "Simon Judit" (Judith Simon) became the best known. His poems were published in 1876, under the title *Kiss József költeményei* (The Poems of Joseph Kiss). A volume entitled *Ünnepnapok* (1888; Holidays) contained his interpretation of Jewish psalms and other Jewish religious poems. His compassion and imagination was stirred by the plight of girls who had to earn their living in cities. Because of this intense interest in them, he wrote a poetic narrative, *Mese a varrógépről* (1884; A Tale of the Sewing Machine), which found many sympathetic readers. One of his most ambitious attempts was another poetic narrative, *Legendák a nagyapámról* (1888; Legends of My Grandfather). Kiss was fascinated by certain phases of the Jewish past, and it was easy for his imagination to convert these into poetry. His patriotic and pacifistic poems written during the First World War were mediocre ventures of an aging poet who probably thus hoped to regain the fervor of some of his earlier poems.

Kiss was no cosmopolitan. He remained a Hungarian, unable and unwilling to break with his Jewishness; in the world of his spirit and in the world of his emotions both symbols were present. His poetry is a mixture of Hebrew themes, proletarian subjects, Hungarian ideas, and the general topics of love, life, and death. It is rarely inferior poetry, but seldom does it represent highest excellence. Kiss conquered the danger of spiritual uprootal with an understanding of his own place in Hungarian life and literature.

See: M. Rubinyi, *Kiss József stilusa, nyelve, technikája* (1925); W. Kirkconnell, *The Magyar Muse; an Anthology* (1933).

J. R.

Kistemaeckers, Henry (1872–, Belgian dramatist and novelist), was born in Floreffe, in the Walloon section of Belgium, the son of a Brussels publisher. Leaving his own country, he settled in Paris where he devoted himself to writing. Interested mainly in the social drama, he followed the trend of quick wit, irony, and equivocal morality which typified the so-called current "Parisian" literature and lost all traces of the originality which might have linked him with his native country. However, leaving aside the superficial "Parisianism" of plays like *Marthe* (1899), *La Blessure* (1905), *La Rivale* (1907), one finds in them a keen observation of life, a subtle and true psychology, and lyrical outbursts of romantic passion. His masterpiece is *L'Instinct* (1905), a tragically terse and powerful drama. He wrote more than 20 plays, and as many novels, the most successful of which were *L'Illégitime* (1898), *Les Amants romanesques* (1899), and *La Femme inconnue* (1901). At times he used the pseudonyms Janine, Kist, or Kistemaeckers *fils*.

L. V.

Klabund (pseud. of Alfred Henschke, 1890–1928, German novelist, dramatist, and poet) was born in Crossen on the Oder, the son of an apothecary, and enjoyed all the advantages of a good education. At the age of 24 an attack of tuberculosis forced him to abandon his studies. From then on until his death his time was spent, with ever shorter intervals, in the sanitariums of Davos and other health resorts. He married twice. After the early death of his first wife, the "Irene" (peace) of his poems, he wrote the exquisite *Totenklage* (1918–1919).

The critic Alfred Kerr discovered the young Klabund, whose poetry he printed in his periodical *Pan* and whom he staunchly upheld against a scandalized public. Klabund was primarily a lyricist; he was at the same time an expressionist although he never belonged to any of the expressionist groups. He commanded a great variety of types of expression, from the vulgar to the mystic. He was at his best in poems in the popular vein and in songs of a worldly religiosity clothed in the style of Chinese lyrics. Most of his "Chinese" poems are not translations but works of his own imagination. His style, diverse in form, is always restless and impatient. His poetry expresses itself preponderantly in contrasts ("Klabund" means "transformation"), which often led to the grotesque and to satire. Klabund was never a radical. He wrote patriotic war songs as well as pacifist poems. He was attracted by the genuine and the elemental, an inclination evidenced in the subject matter of his novelettes, of which he wrote some 10 and which have, perhaps more than any of his other works, established his popularity. The best known are *Bracke* (1918; Eng. tr., *Brackie the Fool,* 1927), *Pjotr* (1923; Eng. tr., *Peter the Czar,* 1925), and *Borgia* (1928;

Eng. tr., *The Incredible Borgias,* 1929). Klabund was also a successful dramatist, particularly with his version of the Chinese *Kreidekreis* (1924; Eng. tr., *Circle of Chalk,* 1929) and the social comedy *X Y Z* (1926). His work shows indebtedness to Heine, Wedekind, and Rilke.

See: H. Grothe, *Klabund; Leben und Werk eines Poeten* (1933); W. Paulsen, "Klabund", *German Life and Letters,* III (1938–1939), 222–230.

W. P.

Kloos, Willem (1859–1938, Dutch poet and critic), was born at Amsterdam, attended high school there, and studied classical philology at the university of his native city. In 1885 he helped found *De Nieuwe Gids* (The New Guide), of which he was editor in chief and the leading literary critic. Figures of speech, he taught, should never be stereotyped. Each poet has his own way of visualizing thoughts in images. That is why he denied the name of poetry to most of the verse of the preceding generation, which used clichés for their metaphors instead of self-created images. His own poetry was a demonstration of imagery that is seen and not copied. *Verzen,* his first book, was published in 1894. The sonnets it contains are among the finest in the language and assured him at once a high place in Dutch literature. His diction revolutionized the language. Passion and anger and defiance were translated into images that startled by their novelty and unexpectedness. Readers of the present day may still find them beautiful but no longer defiant. What sounded revolutionary in the late 80's set the style for ensuing generations. There is a distinct cleavage between the literary language of present-day Holland and the Dutch that was written before the 90's of the past century. This profound change was brought about by Kloos and his fellow editors of *De Nieuwe Gids.* The success of the "Eightiers," as the rebels were called, was followed by dissension within their own ranks. His colleagues became more and more interested in social rather than literary reform. Kloos alone, staunch individualist and never strongly social-minded, remained all through life the self-expressionist of his poetic début. The definitive edition of his collected verse appeared in 1933 (*Verzen*). His literary critiques and essays were published in *Nieuwere Literatuurgeschiedenis* (5 vols., 1904–1914; Recent Literary History) and *Letterkundige Inzichten en Vergezichten* (22 vols., 1928–1938; Literary Insights and Perspectives).

See: A. Verwey, "Willem Kloos," in *Stille Toernooien* (1901); K. H. de Raaf, *Willem Kloos, de Mensch, de Dichter, de Kriticus* (1934); J. A. Russell, *Dutch Poetry and English* (1939), pp. 156 ff.

A. J. B.

Knudsen, Jakob (1858–1917, Danish novelist, philosopher, and educator), was born at Rødding, Jutland. He was the son of a folk high school teacher who later became parish priest in Aggershus, North Jutland, and here Knudsen spent the formative years of his childhood. Ultimately of a solid stock of Jutland farmers, his father was the son of a sturdy bourgeois family, while his mother was of a nobler but weakened strain. We meet these two families in Knudsen's *To Slægter* (1910; Two Families). His father, who from a timid youth grew up to be a self-righteous man, gave his son a strict puritanical upbringing, managing at the same time to inculcate the essence of Grundtvigianism in the boy, *i.e.,* love for the living word of Christianity and love of his native country. The young man lived up to his father's wishes. Having passed the theological examinations at the University of Copenhagen (in 1881), he became first a teacher at the folk high school at Askov (1881–1890), then a pastor near Randers, Jutland (1890–1897), and finally an itinerant lecturer, mostly for different folk high schools in Denmark.

In his lectures (*Christelige Foredrag,* 1898, Christian Lectures; *Livsfilosofi,* 1908, Philosophy of Life), as well as in his novels, Knudsen evolves his views on life and education. He is a Christian mystic, taking Christ in the orthodox Christian sense; "were he not the Son of God in that sense, but only a human being, he would be, to me, a repulsive type, an anemic wretch, without natural joy in fighting, without eroticism—a megalomaniac." And he has no use for Christian morality as exemplified in the Sermon on the Mount or in Leo Tolstoy's (*q.v.*) teachings; modern humanitarianism is for him an abomination. He favors authority of the few who are able and willing to support not only themselves but also the rest of humanity. The democratic state has too little authority and is far too lenient in its attitude towards lawbreakers and criminals; hence citizens with a feeling of responsibility should not be afraid to take the law into their own hands. But in one point there is too little freedom: children should never be forced to take the subjects which are to mold their character (religion and history of native country), and teachers should be given a free hand in dealing with them. Otherwise children should be brought up in the old-fashioned way, under authority, the stricter the better. In this philosophy of life there may be much inherited farmer's wisdom, but it is also a reaction against the moral laxness of the times, the radical nihilism of the 90's from which Jørgensen escaped into the Catholic Church. Its Nietzschean affinities are obvious (*see* Nietzsche).

Knudsen's first works (1887–) are not significant, but he won instant fame with *Den gamle Præst* (1899; The Old Pastor). Here appear the two types so common in his novels: the criminal moron, dangerous in humanitarian society, and the born nobleman, represented by the too quick-tempered count, and the old pastor, Knudsen's ideal—firm of character, religious, strict, and just, above the law. There followed *Gæring* and *Afklaring* (1902; Ferment and Clarification), dealing with education and the intellectual situation of Knudsen's own generation, and *Sind* (1902; Grit), a fine story of the Jutland lad who, though timid of nature, is so obsessed with asserting his own rights that it carries him directly to a fatal clash with the corrupt authorities. *Inger* (1906) is a novel of married life; *Fremskridt* (1907; Progress) contrasts the old and new peasant culture; and *Lærer Urup* (1909; Schoolmaster Urup) is a bitter indictment of education and lenience towards criminals in modern society. In the family saga *To Slægter* (1910) and *Rodfæstet* (1911; Firmly Rooted), personalities strong by nature and upbringing are set off against weaklings spoilt as children by a Rousseauan education. Morality is the affair of two persons at least, since the moral person must follow an ideal outside himself. Whoever is allowed to follow his own nature becomes an introvert weakling, unable to go through life. It does not matter where a person has his roots, in a faith in God or in the authority exercised by his own family, just so it is outside of himself. It is not always clear whether Knudsen attributes the superiority or the inferiority of persons and families to inheritance or to education, but the two types of people are forever contrasting in his books.

The two-part novel *Angst* (1912; Fear) and *Mod* (1914; Courage) depicts the religious development of Martin Luther and, incidentally, that of Knudsen himself, who not only as an adolescent but also later in life suffered much from depressions and fear. A few more novels and the collection of short stories entitled *Jyllanders* (2 vols., 1912–1917; Jutlanders) complete Knudsen's output.

Artistically Knudsen excels in delineation of characters, often by giving their speech a dialectal tinge. His prose otherwise is straightforward and plain. He is a fine dialectician who drives home his ideas with uncompromising paradoxes. After Grundtvig and Kierkegaard he is by many considered the greatest religious genius that Denmark has fostered. He is still largely unknown outside of Scandinavia and Germany.

See: H. Begtrup, *Jakob Knudsen* (1918); J. Byskov, "Jakob Knudsen" in Ejnar Skovrup, ed., *Hovedtræk af nordisk Digtning i Nytiden,* I (1920), 195–216; Helge Kjærgaard, *Die dänische Literatur der neuesten Zeit (1871–1933)* (1934), pp. 119–130.

S. E.

Koch, Martin (1882–, Swedish novelist and journalist), is the first Swedish author who has depicted Swedish life from below, *i.e.* from the point of view of the proletariat. Born in Stockholm, Koch early had the opportunity of observing the life of the less fortunate lower classes, though he himself came from the lower middle class and his childhood was on the whole a happy one. Upon approaching young manhood, however, he had to become a painter's apprentice instead of taking the coveted "student examination" for entrance to Uppsala; and from this time on his sense of class distinction became acute and his sympathy for the oppressed classes in the city was strongly aroused. Since beginning his literary career in 1911 with an unimportant novel, *Ellen,* he has been reasonably prolific in a number of semi-journalistic literary forms. Though his novels bear undeniable traces of the influence of such Americans as Jack London and Upton Sinclair, and the Russians Gorki and Dostoevski (*qq.v.*), Koch is no mere imitator of earlier foreign literary interpreters of the proletarian scene. He goes to considerable trouble to develop lower-class conditions and themes peculiarly Swedish, and both his local color and the social psychology which forms the interpretative basis of his novels are conceived particularly with immediate Swedish conditions in mind.

His first two important proletarian novels, *Arbetare: en bok om hat* (1912; Workers: a Book about Hatred) and *Timmerdalen: en historia om kultur* (1913; The Timber Valley: a Story about Culture), both draw their materials directly from episodes in the rising class struggle of the day in Sweden, the first apparently from the general strike of 1909, the second from the bloody Sandö Revolt in Norrland. Though the author's sympathies are obviously on the side of the working classes in the new struggle for power in the years just before the First World War, Koch does not overidealize his picture of the proletariat. He is aware of the brutal primitive instincts which too often motivate the actions of workers, and he has a sharp eye for the degenerate sides of lower-class life. This aspect he develops particularly in *Guds vackra värld* (1916; God's Beautiful World), a ghastly picture of the lowest of lower-class life, of social parasites and criminal types from the Swedish "underworld," who batten filthily on petty degeneration of all kinds and who have not the least desire to improve their lot. This completely disillusioned picture has little if anything in it of a type so frequently present in proletarian fiction, the partly idealized lower-class individual who manages somehow to rise at moments above the filth and degradation of his immediate environment. Koch's last important novel, *Fromma människor* (1918; Pious People), is a study in popular religious psychology, an analysis of the conditions which create cheap and sensational sectarianism in various parts of Sweden. He accounts for these curious religious phenomena in terms of various physical and geographical circumstances, much as he had accounted for proletarian excesses in the class struggle depicted in his earlier novels in terms of unhappy economic and social conditions. Because of this broad interpretative basis of his novels, Koch may perhaps be called the first serious social-psychologist in Swedish fiction.

In the last 25 years Koch's literary output has been rather miscellaneous in both form and content, and none of it has been as challenging in its ideas or as vigorous and powerful in its art as are the proletarian novels which he wrote just before and during the First World War. Among the better things in his later work is *Mauritz* (1939), a quiet, objective autobiographical document which outlines with both charm and insight the events of Koch's childhood and youth.

A. G.

Kolbenheyer, Erwin Guido (1878–, German novelist and dramatist), was born in Budapest. His father was for a time a Hungarian government architect. After the father's early death, his widow went with the two-year-old boy back to her home town, Karlsbad. Here Kolbenheyer spent the most impressionable years of his life. Later he moved to Vienna to study philosophy and natural sciences at the university.

Today Kolbenheyer is considered the spiritual exponent of the Sudeten German region. His one-sided overemphasis on Teutonism, which was in tune with the trend of Hitlerism in Germany, was largely the result of his early years in the atmosphere of a German minority group. Not only in his historical novels but also in his theoretical studies (above all *Die Bauhütte,* 1925) he anticipated many ideas of National Socialism.

His work is mainly historical. The heroes of his novels and dramas are what he considers "typical Germans," maintaining themselves against a hostile world. This "typical German" is always a mystic revolting against some form of scholasticism, an exponent of the Reformation rebelling against the fetters of an international church. All Kolbenheyer's historical heroes are in some way or other proclaimers of the spirit of Reformation; such are the central figures in his two most important historical dramas, *Giordano Bruno* (1893; later reissued as *Heroische Leidenschaften,* 1929) and *Gregor und Heinrich* (1934), the Spinoza novel, *Amor Dei* (1902; Eng. tr. *God-intoxicated Man,* 1933), the novel *Meister Joachim Pausewang* (1910; Eng. tr., *A Winter Chronicle,* 1938), evoking the time of Jakob Böhme, and the three-volume *Paracelsus* (1917–1923).

Kolbenheyer does not make any concessions to his reader. His best novels are not only profound historical and philosophical works, permeated with a Germano-mania—even in normal times difficult to appreciate—but in addition some of them are philological experiments. In *Pausewang* and *Paracelsus* Kolbenheyer has tried to reproduce the spirit of the times by creating a semi-archaic language. He has also experimented in his dramas and evolved the theory of a "third stage." In his dramatic conception the stage is to extend over the entire theatre and make the spectator in the audience an integral part of the play. This demand is a continuation of expressionist tendencies, though on a different intellectual and political level. Many other elements have influenced his dramatic development, most of all the work of Ibsen (*q.v.*) and Hebbel.

See: C. Wandrey, *Kolbenheyer, der Dichter und der Philosoph* (1933); L. Schlötermann-Kuffner, *Erwin Guido Kolbenheyers "Dritte Bühne"* (1939).

W. P.

Konopnicka, Marja (née Wasiłowska, 1842–1910, Polish poet and publicist), was born in Suwałki, Russian Poland, the daughter of a government official. She is important chiefly as the archrepresentative of the "free woman" of the positivist era (*see* Polish literature) and as the outstanding poet of militant patriotism in an epoch of appeasement and disillusion. Konopnicka's verses, especially those in which the peasant is fortified in his determination to hold his land and to refuse its sale to the Germans, had much to do with keeping the national faith and the national soil intact in the face of the German *Drang nach Osten*. Like Marja Dąbrowska (*q.v.*) in a later generation, Konopnicka was a passionate partisan of the peasant. She was also a pioneer in the use of peasant themes in literature. Her long pseudo-epic *Pan Balcer w Brazylji* (1892; Mr. Balcer in Brazil) is an idealization of the peasant emigrant based on a work of Dygasiński (*q.v.*). Like countless other items in her vast output, it seemed important when it appeared and when its author, thanks to her "emancipation," was in the public eye, but neither this nor any of her more ambitious works is very highly regarded today.

See: G. Korbut, *Literatura polska* (1931), IV, 101–107.

A. P. C.

Korneichuk, Alexander Yevdokimovich (1910–, Ukrainian dramatist), is the Ukrainian commissar of foreign affairs and the husband of Wanda Wasilewska. He writes in Ukrainian, but his work is best known through Russian translations. He first attracted attention as a playwright with his *Gibel eskadry* (1934; The Sinking of the Squadron), which won second prize at the All-Union Competition for Dramatists (1933). The play is a melodrama concerning the scuttling of the Black Sea fleet in 1918 and was hailed as a blow to Ukrainian nationalism. A more convincing work is *Platon Krechet* (1935), a drama about a doctor who exemplifies the aspirations of the new Soviet intelligentsia and is almost frustrated by a bureaucratic administration. In *Bankir* (1937; The Banker), the story of a self-sacrificing Soviet official, and in *V stepyakh Ukrainy* (On the Ukrainian Steppes) Korneichuk continued to explore contemporary problems, but in *Bogdan Khmelnitski, 1648–1654* (1939; Part I of a trilogy) he turned to a historical theme. This play, however, has its modern implications, for Khmelnitski championed the cause of the Ukrainians against the Poles. Since the outbreak of the Second World War, Korneichuk has written *Partizany y stepyakh Ukrainy* (1942; Eng. tr., *Guerillas of the Ukrainian Steppes*) and *Front* (1942; Eng. tr., *The Front*, both in *Four Soviet War Plays*, 1944), the latter attacking those older generals who had proved incompetent in modern technical warfare. *Platon Krechet, V stepyakh Ukrainy,* and *Front* have been awarded the Stalin prize.

See: "Korneichuk," in *Bolshaya sovetskaya entsiklopediya,* XXXIV (1937), 318; H. W. L. Dana, *Handbook on Soviet Drama* (1938) and *Drama in Wartime Russia* (1943).

P. A. P.

Korolenko, Vladimir Galaktionovich (1853–1921, Russian fiction writer and publicist), was born in Western Russia. His father was a Russian official (a county judge), his mother a Polish woman. This fact tended to plant within the boy the seeds of tolerance and the ability to see both sides of a question. It was made particularly manifest in 1863, during the unsuccessful Polish insurrection, when the sympathies of his parents were divided. Vladimir graduated from the Russian Gymnasium at Rovno and in 1872 entered the University of St. Petersburg. At that time Russia had already entered the period of reaction from the enlightened ideas of the 1860's, and every expression of liberal ideas was persecuted. Korolenko was expelled from the university in 1875 and was later sent into Siberian exile, for what was known as "revolutionary propaganda" but what, in essence, was the expression of the liberal leanings of the man.

Upon his return from Siberia he joined a group of so-called People's Socialists—though he never officially joined that party—in a common undertaking, the editing and publishing of the monthly review *Russkoye bogatstvo* (Russian Wealth). Most of his works as a publicist appeared in the pages of that review. In them a mild liberal and progressive attitude was displayed, as well as a demand for basic justice and tolerance to everybody and condemnation of injustice, violence and brutality.

Korolenko welcomed the February, 1917, Revolution which deposed the tsar and wrote enthusiastic articles about it. However, with the coming of the Bolsheviks to power he turned against the new rulers and their methods and retired to his modest estate in the Ukraine. An attempt by the commissar of education, Lunacharski, to persuade the aged liberal to cooperate with the Soviet government was not successful. In a series of letters Korolenko set forth his objections to the violent and sanguine character of the Bolshevik Revolution, as well as his condemnation of the men engaged therein. Korolenko's health began to decline, and he died an invalid, in 1921.

In his fiction, Korolenko bears marked characteristics of a poet, although he did not write verse. There is delicacy of imagery and expression and a fine rhythmical touch; there is, also, much sentimentality. There can be no doubt that Korolenko's literary types and descriptions wholly originate in his abundantly loving heart and are in no way a product of cool reasoning. The gallery of his types is as vivid as if one had seen them on a canvas. There is the old chimesmaster in the sketch of that title ("Staryi zvonar," 1885), unforgettable in his little steeple, calmly and serenely awaiting the approach of death. The sketch has no social significance, in spite of some hazy symbolic meaning which the most ardent of Korolenko's admirers tried to force into it. There is Pan Tiburtsy from the somewhat autobiographical story "V durnom obshchestve" (1890; Eng. tr., "In Bad Society," with *In Two Moods,* 1891), with his rather confused ideas of right and wrong. There is Makar, from the story "Son Makara" (1885; Eng. tr., title story in *Makár's Dream and Other Stories,* 1892). The setting of this story and Makar himself are presented with rare artistry. The idea of the story—that there is more in everyone's life than appears on the surface—is neither startling nor original, for all its correctness. Just as mediocre is the idea of his novel *Slepoi musykant* (1885; Eng. tr., *The Blind Musician,* 1890) that humility and suffering give content to art. But here again the story, the characters, the descriptions of nature and of events, as well as the psychology of a blind man, are presented with a great deal of artistry.

The extent of Korolenko's social ideas, as revealed both through his fiction and in his work as a publicist, is summarized in his little sketch "Ogni" (1888; Lights). The author tells of a night trip in a rowboat on one of the Siberian rivers. Seeing the lights which appeared to be just ahead of them, the author turned to the oarsman and commented on their proximity. "Far away," came an indifferent reply from the oarsman. Indeed, the lights proved to be far away, the author having been deceived by an optical illusion. This failed to upset him, however. "Still, there are lights ahead!" he concluded his little piece. Among the liberal intelligentsia, this served as an inspiration and a guide.

See: N. Shakhovskaya, *V. G. Korolenko; opyt biograficheskoy kharakteristiki* (1912); Korolenko, *Polnoye sobraniye sochineni* (1914) and *Pisma, 1886–1921* (1922).

J. P.

Kossak, Zofja (1890–, Polish novelist), was born on the estate of Skowródki in Volhynia, of Polish gentry stock already famous through the painter Juljusz Kossak. Reared as a typical daughter of the Borderland, she was early uprooted from her pleasant and sheltered life by the Bolshevik invasion of 1917–1918. This experience she was quick to immortalize in *Pożoga* (1922; Eng. tr., *The Blaze,* 1927). In 1922 she settled in Silesia and soon became deeply interested in the history, folklore, and legendry of that region. The result was a series of Silesian tales, including *Wielcy i mali* (1927; Great Ones and Small), *Legnickie pole* (1930; Legnica Field), *Nieznany kraj* (1932; A Land Unknown), and ultimately, through the fusion of her interest in Silesia with her no less intense interest in the Catholic tradition of her native land, the long novel *Krzyżowcy* (1935; The Crusaders), with its sequels *Król trędowaty* (1937; Eng. tr., *The Leper King,* 1945) and *Bez oręża* (1938; Eng. tr., *Blessed Are the Meek,* 1944). Kossak turned next to the Sandomierian region of Poland, then in the public eye because of the great, new Central Industrialization Project. A series of Sandomierian tales was in preparation when Kossak's literary activities were abruptly stopped by the Second World War. With *Złota wolność* (1928; Golden Freedom), *Trembowla* (1939), and numerous other historical novels to her credit in addition to those mentioned above, Kossak is the outstanding representative of the post-war school of historical fiction in Poland. She was also a leading figure in the Catholic literary renaissance.

See: E. Breiter, review in *Wiadomości literackie,* 1936, No. 26; K. Czachowski, *Obraz współczesnej literatury polskiej,* III (1936), 169–180, 698–700.

A. P. C.

Kosztolányi, Dezső (1885–1936, Hungarian poet, novelist, short-story writer, and critic), was born in Szabadka and died in Budapest. He was educated in a secondary school of his home town, where his father was the principal, and at the University of Budapest. His first literary works appeared in *A Hét* (The Week), *Nyugat* (West), and *Élet* (Life). But even as a writer of daily newspapers, *e.g.*, *Budapesti Napló* (Budapest Ledger), *Pesti Napló* (Pest Ledger), *Pesti Hirlap* (Pest News), he was so much the *homo estheticus* that he introduced into his journalistic utterances ideas and manners of literary significance. Kosztolányi traveled much, loved Latin culture, and while his human convictions were varied and sometimes downright contradictory to his "humaneness," as a literary artist he remained faithful to himself. In the moral and social earthquake that followed the First World War, in the midst of enfeebled ethical concepts, the nonpolitical Kosztolányi was distinctly a stranger; it amazed him to be alive when the secret of living was to escape death and not to enrich life. He drew sustenance for the equilibrium of his spirit from major writers and poets whose works he translated into Hungarian and from a stoic point of view which did not, however, nullify his pity for the terrible lot of mankind. One senses in Kosztolányi's art an almost childish fear of the malevolent forces of fate; one senses the expression of a soul in sore need of learning how to defend itself against the hoodlum slogans and actions of modern times. Unfortunately, in the early 20's Kosztolányi, as a journalist and in the name of patriotism, joined the persecutors; he regretted it later, and he himself became a target of attacks.

Kosztolányi is often considered a decadent poet whose intelligence and subtleness suggest artificiality. This criticism is fair only in part. He was an "art for art's sake" poet, and his relationship to French symbolism (*q.v.*) was undeniable. Nevertheless, since he differentiated between life and art, this does not say that he ignored life. His poems and novels, his critical dissertations and philological essays, his sketches and dialogues, his translations of French, German, English, Italian, and American poetry (published in three volumes), and his translations of Chinese and Japanese lyrics showed not merely a diligent spirit to whom creative expression was vital, but a mentality very much conditioned by the awareness of amorphous reality. *Négy fal között* (1907; Within Four Walls), *Mágia* (1912; Magic), *Mák,* (1916; Poppy), *Kenyér és bor* (1920; Bread and Wine), and his collected poems, which appeared in 1935, tell the story of a man whose poetry and humaneness were intertwined. His two most popular volumes of poetry, *A szegény kisgyermek panaszai* (1910; The Complaints of a Poor Little Child) and *A bús férfi panaszai* (1924; The Complaints of a Sorrowful Man), are, indeed, humane. His volumes of short stories, such as *Boszorkányos esték* (1908; Bewitched Nights), his novels, *A véres költő* (1921; Eng. tr., *The Bloody Poet,* 1927), *Pacsirta* (1924; Lark), *Aranysárkány* (1925; The Golden Dragon), *Édes Anna* (1926; Anna Édes), and all his other works show that Kosztolányi measured life with the yardstick of an artist, but also with a beating heart.

Works of his have appeared in German, Italian, French, and English. *The Bloody Poet,* a story of Nero's sadism, was published in New York. Kosztolányi was one of the best-educated writers in modern Hungary; he was restless, interested in psychology, interested in beauty, and terrified by death. Evidently it was his death complex that determined his uncompromising attachment to pure art. He lost himself in form in order not to be lost in the fear of death.

See: H. Horváth, *Neue ungarische Lyrik* (1918); W. Kirkconnell, *The Magyar Muse; an Anthology* (1933).

J. R.

Krag, Thomas (1868–1913, Norwegian novelist), was one of the leading neo-romanticists of the 1890's, and although his books no longer rouse the enthusiasm they evoked when they first appeared, they still charm by their poetic quality. He grew up in Kristiansand and, together with his brother Vilhelm Krag (*q.v.*), founded the southern school of Norwegian literature, to which Gabriel Scott (*q.v.*) also belonged. Thomas Krag was in part influenced by the Danish authors Jens Peter Jacobsen and Johannes Jørgensen (*qq.v.*). From Jacobsen he learned his colorful style, which now seems somewhat precious. He wrote a number of long novels which are notable for lyric, romantic moods rather than for narrative or characterization. Among them are *Kobberslangen* (1895; The Copper Serpent), *Ada Wilde* (1896), *Ulf Ran* (1897), and *Gunvor Kjeld* (1904).

H. A. L.

Krag, Vilhelm Andreas Wexels (1871–1933, Norwegian poet, novelist, and dramatist), was born into the dying bureaucracy of the gentle, dreamy South of Norway, in the "colonial" town of Kristiansand, which burned soon after his family moved away, leaving in him a trend towards melancholy nostalgia. His début with the frail, elegiac *Digte* (1891; Poems) heralded the neo-romantic movement in Norway and was followed by numerous volumes of romantic poetry and drama and novels from the fictitious past of the Norwegian South. These writings have swiftly paled, however; they often have a bookish taste and lack contact with a living milieu. Krag's most vigorous creation belongs to his later years, when from literary and personal disillusionments he turned to the real life of his home districts. He became their literary spokesman and champion, even in practical matters, and more and more lived there, on a small island given to him by his friends. From this attachment grew a series of sketches and plays from the life of the simple fishing population, filled with life and blood, humor and understanding. In two collections of lyrics, *Sange fra min ø* (1918; Songs from My Island) and *Viser og* *vers* (1919; Ballads and Verses), his sorrows are reconciled in landscape poetry of great and moving beauty. A charming autobiography also belongs to these years (4 vols., 1926–1931). He died on his island, cared for in his last days by his fishermen friends.

See: N. C. Brøgger, "Vilhelm Andreas Wexels Krag," in *Norsk biografisk leksikon,* VII (1936), 624–627; A. H. Winsnes, *Norges litteratur fra februarrevolutionen til verdenskrigen,* part 2, pp. 240–254, Vol. V (1937) of F. Bull, F. Paasche, and A. H. Winsnes, *Norsk litteraturhistorie;* H. Smitt Ingebretsen, *En dikter og en herre: V. Krags liv og diktning* (1942).

S. S.

Krains, Hubert (1862–1934, Belgian novelist), is almost an autodidact. Born of agricultural workers in the village of Les Waleffes (province of Hesbaye), he spent a busy life in the postal service. From 1882 to 1895, the golden age of the *Jeune Belgique* (*see* Belgian literature in French), he lived in Brussels, and the fervid literary activity of the capital awakened his genius. His first collection of stories appeared in 1891, the second in 1895. His fame rests on his subsequent works: *Amours rustiques* (1899), *Le Pain noir* (1904), *Figures du pays* (1908), *Mes Amis* (1920), and *Au cœur des blés* (1934). The second and last are short novels; the others, collections of tales and sketches. The intervals between publication are significant: Krains had caught Flaubert's cult of stylistic perfection and preferred silence to mediocre work. He contributed to many periodicals; a volume of essays, *Portraits d'écrivains belges* (1930), reveals his talent as a literary critic. He lived for 16 years in Switzerland and traveled widely on official business, but memories of his youth continued to inspire his work. Hence in fiction he chose to follow the regionalistic tradition and always dealt with the peasants of his native province. Yet nothing save the landscape is "provincial," and in it too he found a representative setting for human experience. Degrees of latitude do not change the heart, he declared.

In a striking passage of *Mes Amis* he names La Bruyère as his master, but if La Bruyère brought color into the austere prose of his century, Krains is sobriety itself by comparison with his friends Demolder and Eekhoud (*qq.v.*). His first works show occasional traces of their manners: he always shared their sympathy with the downtrodden and their contempt for the self-satisfied bourgeois. From La Bruyère he learned the secret of short, often epigrammatic phrase and of rapid characterization through salient traits rather than by detailed analysis. Then too, Belgians are born painters, and a classicist among them naturally turns to the most picturesque of the 17th-century giants. Krains's technique often recalls Maupassant (*q.v.*); in spite of his apparent objectivity, his choice of incident and grouping of situations reveal a deep sympathy for the wretched. He shuns the satiric trend which occasionally vitiates Maupassant's realism and observes with a poet's insight which is born of complete understanding. He is never sentimental; pathos arises from the studied objectivity of dramatic narrative. Peasants are not given to self-pity; Krains portrays them as he had known them, unconscious of the resignation they learn from nature herself. He has caught every quirk of their angular personalities which he renders with a rare harmony of vividness, sympathy, and objectivity. Acts are often violent; characters come alive by the stark portrayal of their squareheaded and rancorous susceptibility. Although the dominant note is tragic, a discreet note of rugged humor offers relief. This is especially noteworthy in *Mes Amis.* The two pals, Colpin and Benoît, with their wives, Christine and Prudence, live before our eyes. The artist catches them at their most picturesque, and the one necessary artifice is simplicity of style.

In an essay on Eekhoud, Krains remarks that the fiery champion of outlaws lacks the sense of gradation essential to hold alert, without weariness, the reader's emotion. This feeling for architectural composition Krains possessed to an unrivaled degree. The lurid "Ame de la maison" (*Amours rustiques*) is an example. It recalls Flaubert's (*q.v.*) "Un Cœur simple" but has more warmth and intense drama, without sacrifice of objectivity. Barbe is *la mater dolorosa;* the torture of ever sharper pinpricks ends in irreparable disaster, leaving her in a maddened daze. Krains saw everywhere passion leading to tragedy, but of it the stuff of his art is made, and through art the springs of pity and fear are opened and man's vision widened.

See: D. Denuit, *Hubert Krains* (1936).

B. M. W.

Kranjčević, Silvije Strahimir (1865–1908, Croat poet), was born in Senj. His pious parents intended him for the priesthood. He studied in Rome, but turned from the Church, and moved on to Zagreb where he entered a teachers' college. He was a teacher throughout his life, mostly in Bosnia.

His first poems appeared in the reviews *Hrvatska vila* (Croat Fairy) and *Nada* (Hope) in his native Dalmatia. He began as patriotic bard, but soon became negative and pessimistic. Indeed he developed into a despairing individual, deceived by the ideas of the 19th century and inclined to withdraw into himself to brood. He is in fact representative of a certain transition from the 19th to the 20th century in Croat poetry. In the odes in a popular form called *Bugarkinje* (1885) and in *Izabrane pjesme* (1898; Selected Poems), he announced that human and social justice was a lie. Famine, slavery, and tyranny were constant phenomena; "lambs are created to feed the wolf." This conception also drove him to an unfinished satire, *Efeta*. He grew more and more introspective, full of doubt, convinced of the futility of all human efforts, in revolt against all he had written in earlier years. In the long dialogues of the three-part allegory *Prvi grijeh* (1912; First Sin), describing the pains and humiliations a man has to bear, he slowly worked himself up into a mood of cosmic rebellion which is not without dignity and poetic power.

Kranjčević's works first appeared scattered in such periodicals as *Sloboda* (Freedom), *Balkan, Vijenac* (Wreath), *Novi vijek* (New Era), and *Sarajevska nada* (Sarajevo Hope). The last-named review, *Sarajevska nada*, he himself directed from 1895 to 1903; under his auspices it became one of the most important literary periodicals in Croatia and Bosnia. Kranjčević came into conflict with the ruling social order in 1904, when he was promoted to school inspector. The archbishop of Sarajevo, Stadler, protested because Kranjčević was considered a free thinker by the Church. For a short while Kranjčević was excluded from teaching, but under the pressure of powerful intellectual contemporaries, he was renominated professor at the Commercial Academy in Sarajevo.

The Croat literary group Matica Hrvatska published Kranjčević's poetry under the title *Trzaji i Pjesme* (1908; Convulsions and Poems). The Association of Croat Poets printed after his death a selection of his writings, while the complete works were collected in 1912 by Milan Marjanović. Literary critics considered Kranjčević the foremost lyricist of his time and the model for a whole generation of Croat lyrics. His political poetry was Croat rather than Pan-Slav, but still he felt a very close affection for his South Slav brothers in Serbia.

See: A. G. Matoš, *Hrvatsko pravo*, 1908, Nos. 3791–3793; Ela Kranjčević, *Obzor*, 1909, No. 711; Miloš Savković, *La Littérature yougoslave moderne* (1936), pp. 162–165.

M. H.

Kraus, Karl (1874–1936, Austrian essayist, aphorist, and poet), was born in Jičin, Czechoslovakia, but lived mostly in Vienna. After a short career as a brilliant journalist and pamphleteer he was offered an important position with a leading Austrian daily, but inner scruples led him to refuse it. He saw his own intellectual and spiritual integrity as well as the public mind threatened by the corrupt pseudo-liberal press. He therefore founded his own periodical, *Die Fackel* (1899–1936), devoted to social and literary criticism; it was written at first largely, then entirely by himself. This review, in which most of Kraus's works first appeared, became as much admired by the younger generation as it was hated by the established representatives of the bourgeoisie. The fight against intellectual and economic corruption, carried through with devastating wit, soon took on the wider meaning of cultural criticism and grew to a confrontation of the ideal and the reality of man. The perversion of the machine from man's instrument to man's god, the enslavement of nature by commerce, the hypocritical treatment of the sexual instincts, the falsification of literary values, are Kraus's central themes. "Journalism," to Kraus a sort of *Weltanschauung* not confined to the newspapers, remained his chief target. Throughout the years he scathingly attacked "journalese" as the most conspicuous expression of that type of mind.

The emotional impact of the First World War on Kraus was tremendous. Remaining in Vienna, he gave running commentaries, polemic and satirical, directed against those in power who desecrated human dignity, against the unholy mixture of business and "idealism," militarism and religion. His gigantic drama *Die letzten Tage der Menschheit* (1918–1922), a documentary and a visionary panorama at the same time, is the supreme monument of the horror of those years. *Worte in Versen, I–IX* (1916–1930; Eng. tr. of selections, *Poems*, 1930), the embodiment of Kraus's personal experience and philosophy in lyrical, didactic, satirical verses, also began to appear during the war. Before the war Kraus's fame had already been established by two volumes of prose essays, *Sittlichkeit und Kriminalität* (1908) and *Die chinesische Mauer* (1910); to the same literary genre belong *Weltgericht* (1919), *Untergang der Welt durch schwarze Magie* (1922), and *Literatur und Lüge* (1929). Masterpieces of penetrating wit and precision are his books of aphorisms *Sprüche und Widersprüche* (1909), *Pro Domo et Mundo* (1912), and *Nachts* (1919) and his *Epigramme* (1927).

Among minor works in dramatic form are the parody (*Literatur,* 1921) of Werfel's (*q.v.*) *Spiegelmensch,* the satirical version (*Wolkenkuckucksheim,* 1923) of Aristophanes' *Birds,* and the satirical and philosophical reveries *Traumstück* (1923) and *Traumtheater* (1924). In his last book, *Die Sprache* (1937), Kraus discussed with his extraordinary linguistic sensitiveness problems of grammar, style, poetics.

Through all his work runs the conviction of the fundamental moral and aesthetic importance of the way in which words are used; in his own style words and thoughts are inextricably interlocked. While despising the cheap pun, he has made an art of meaningful play on words, sometimes deadly serious. Literary art to Kraus resides in perfect union and mutual enrichment of form and content. This approach to literature he furthered by masterly public readings of Shakespeare, of unorthodox selections from later writers, of his own works; these readings became not only occasions of literary enjoyment, but also satirical tribunals, just as his written work was equally a moral and aesthetic undertaking, a revision of values in every respect. German polemic prose and the essay as a literary genre have won rare power and beauty through Kraus. The superabundance of verbally and factually interdependent allusions, certain mannerisms in his later writings, the revengeful suppression of his name in the press which he so persistently fought—only these have delayed his recognition as the greatest German satirist of the last 150 years.

See: L. Liegler, *Karl Kraus* (1921; reprinted 1933); Kraus, *Poems,* tr. by A. Bloch (1930), pp. 9–21; R. von Schaukal, *Karl Kraus* (1933).

F. H. M.

Kretzer, Max (1854–1941, German novelist and short-story writer), was born in Posen, East Prussia, the son of a prosperous restaurateur. His father's business subsequently failed, however, and the family was forced to move to Berlin, where it merged into the capital's industrial proletariat. Max, then 13, became a factory worker, later a sign painter. An accident he sustained at the age of 25 changed the course of his life, and at that time he took up writing.

Equipped with a keen sense of observation, a facile pen, and an urge to preach on social problems, Kretzer displays an intimate knowledge of Berlin's proletarian life in the 80's and 90's. His first novel, *Die beiden Genossen* (1880), is painted against the background of the activities of the Social Democratic Party; *Die Betrogenen* (1882) dwells on the evils of prostitution; *Die Verkommenen* (1883) describes the fate of the industrial proletariat. In contrast, *Drei Weiber* (1886) pictures the rottenness of high Berlin society. *Meister Timpe* (1888), Kretzer's most characteristic novel, traces the history of a family of artisans from economic security to destruction. A strong religious note is struck in *Die Bergpredigt* (1890) and *Das Gesicht Christi* (1896). The other novels of Kretzer deal mostly, and far less aptly, with the life of the middle class and, while entertaining enough, have but little literary importance. This may also be said of his dramas and poems.

Whether or not Kretzer was influenced by Zola (*q.v.*) is a moot question. Kretzer himself denied it. On the other hand, Kretzer's role as a pioneer of the German naturalistic novel was early recognized by his contemporaries, by Bleibtreu, Conradi, Holz and Schlaf, Gerhart Hauptmann (*qq.v.*), and others. In Kretzer's early naturalistic novels these young writers for the first time found recorded in minute detail the pressing social problems of their day.

It has been conservatively estimated that, by 1928, more than a million copies of Kretzer's works had reached the public. A perusal of catalogues of German publishers from 1928 to 1941 listing numerous reprints of Kretzer's novels would seem to indicate that his reputation as a "Volksschriftsteller" has not waned.

See: G. Keil, *Max Kretzer; a Study in German Naturalism* (1928); H. May, *Max Kretzers Romanschaffen* (1931).

G. K.

Krleža, Miroslav (1893–, Croat novelist, poet, and dramatist), was born in Zagreb. He came of a family of civil servants. His father intended to make him a soldier and placed him in a military school in Hungary where he met a military clique which closely resembled the degenerate Croat bureaucracy of his home town. This experience left a mark on most of his writing. His first inspirations were foreign (especially Nietzsche and Marinetti, *qq.v.*), as is seen in "Zaratustra," published in the review *Savremenik* (Contemporary Review) in 1914, but the truer Krleža was to represent a revolt against the Hapsburgism of the "loyal" Croat bourgeoisie and later against the reactionary ruling classes in general. In 1919 he started a literary review, *Plamen* (Flame), where many of his poems were published; his work was discussed with great interest by the younger reading public. His three volumes of poems, *Pjesme* (1919; Poems), showed Krleža abandoning Nietzschean ideas of a "superman" for a philosophy of collective humanity. He fought for the rights of his collective man in *Plamen* and in that review's successor, *Književna republika* (1924; Literary Republic). After the First World War, Krleža created a new literary school in Croatia with his *Hrvatska rapsodija* (1918; Croat Rhapsody).

His first novel, *Tri kavalira G-djice Melanije* (1920; Three Suitors of Miss Melania), definitely established him as a writer. In the suitors of this novel he interestingly described three members of contemporary Croat society: a mediocre lawyer, an artist dedicated to "art for art's sake" and remote from life, a revolutionary student whose influence becomes fatal to Melania. Krleža's cynicism was the reflection of a new mood among the young Yugoslavs. He wrote partly in the *ekavski* language form, which was currently used for the Serb literature from Belgrade, thus showing his broadmindedness in the quarrel over the dialects of young Yugoslavia. Other novels, *Magyar királyi honvéd* (1921; Royal Hungarian Soldier), *Hrvatski bog Mars* (1922; The Croat God Mars), etc., followed, most of them depicting the world of 1914–1918, which was likewise the world of Jaroslav Hašek's (*q.v.*) famous *Švejk.* But unlike his Czech contemporary, Krleža was bitter and accusing; his officers were guilty fools, and his privates were sheep intended for the slaughterhouse. There is also a whole cycle of novels in which Krleža describes the decadence of the middle class in the post-war period. He created for certain stories a character named Klamfer who is spokesman for the author's views. With novels like *Vražji Otok* (1924; Devil's Island) and *Banket u Blitvi* (Banquet in Blitva) he became the most widely read novelist after the war, and, along with the earlier writer of historical novels, August Šenoa, the most widely read author in Croatia.

Up to 1917 the Zagreb theatre had received six dramas from Krleža and refused them all. In 1920 his drama *Galicija* (Galicia) was accepted, but—evidence of how society feared the revolutionary socialist—it was taken off the bill the very day of its opening. Yet Krleža proved too powerful a dramatist to be kept away permanently from the stage. *Golgota* (1922; Golgotha) was a great success. It was mass drama in a shipyard, indeed a great theatrical experiment with mass movement. In the following years Krleža produced one successful drama after another. Already by 1921 he was an undisputed leader in dramatic artistry. *Agonija* has been constantly played on the Yugoslav stage since its first appearance (1928) and frequently abroad. It is a two-act masterpiece; Act I presents the agony of a former officer who commits suicide because of the loss of ideals he had been taught to believe in; Act II is the agony of the officer's wife, who had stood by her husband but loved another man who proved in the face of disaster to be unworthy and a social coward. Krleža scored another success with the drama *Glembajevi* (1931; The Glembays), another Ibsen-like vivisection of the higher middle-class (*see* Ibsen).

Then for a short time Krleža's talent seemed to be in eclipse, and certain quarrels made him unpopular among many former admirers. But two other major works appeared in the midst of the political crisis that preceded the Second World War. *Petar Križanić* (1934) is a historical novel about the first Croat Pan-Slav. *Petrica Kerempuh* (1936) is about the Croat equivalent of Till Eulenspiegel; Krleža turned to the popular fool in order to compose a satire on society at the verge of Hitler's war. This second book is written in the medieval Croat *kajkavski* language and is a masterpiece in form and style; it was never officially on sale because the dictatorial regime in Yugoslavia tried to suppress it. Even so, at about the same time the collective works of Krleža were being published, and the public subscribed in advance to a record number of sets. The invasion of Yugoslavia caught Krleža off guard. He was repeatedly reported dead. After the liberation of Zagreb he turned up sick, broken, but still alive to mourn the heroic death of many of his pupils.

See: W. Giusti, "Miroslav Krleža," *Rivista di letteratura slave,* III (1928), 163–175; W. Giusti, "Miroslav Krleža," *Europe Centrale,* June, 1928; R. Varnier, "Agonija," *Europe Centrale,* June, 1928.

M. H.

Kropotkin, Peter Alekseyevich, Prince (1842–1921, Russian sociologist, scientist, and revolutionary), was born in Moscow, the son of an officer of the Guards, wealthy and of noble birth. His mother died when he was three. His father's remarriage and futile and despotic character account for the boy's hostility toward him. Kropotkin received an excellent education, first at home, then at the Corps of Pages in St. Petersburg. The radical ideas of the time found their way into this institution, aristocratic and exclusive as it was; their influence made more articulate what in Kropotkin's childhood had been a purely emotional protest against the condition of the serfs. Graduating in 1862, he declined to serve with the Guards, joined instead the Amur

Cossacks, and spent five years in the wilderness of Eastern Siberia as administrator and explorer. In 1867 he returned to St. Petersburg, entered the university to study mathematics, and began his famous work on the surface structure of northern Asia. Soon he was made secretary of the section of physical geography of the Russian Geographical Society which in 1871 sent him to explore glacial deposits in Finland and Sweden. The frenzy of political reaction he found upon his return to the capital dissipated what faith he had in "reforms from above," while his Siberian experience in administration led him to consider all forms of authority based on coercion—and especially centralized government—as an impediment to progress. During a visit to Switzerland in 1872, he established a close and lasting connection with the Jura Federation, of anarchist tendencies. Returning to St. Petersburg, he joined a secret political organization and in 1874 was arrested and incarcerated in St. Peter and Paul's fortress. After more than two years of solitary confinement, he was transferred to a military hospital. This made possible his escape. He went to England; then to Switzerland, whence he was expelled; to France, where he was imprisoned for three years (1883–1886); and finally back to England. He returned to Russia in 1917 and died in his native town.

Kropotkin's creed of anarchist communism derives from his passionate repudiation of oppression in all its forms. In his numerous books—he wrote in French and in English—such as *Paroles d'un révolté* (1885), *La Conquête du pain* (1892; Eng. tr., *The Conquest of Bread,* 1906), *Fields, Factories, and Workshops* 1899), he advocates the abolition not only of capitalism, but also of all governmental authority. He rejected even a transitory dictatorship by the working class, seeing the aim of the revolution not in the seizure, but in the destruction of government. This, he believed, would be immediately followed by the birth of a new society with changing forms of free cooperative associations and federations. This future society would be based on the principle of mutual aid, as universal in social behavior as the struggle for life; it would make full use of science and technology to increase production and thus to satisfy the needs of all.

In *Memoirs of a Revolutionist* (1899) Kropotkin tells the story of his eventful life. In 1901 he visited the United States and delivered a series of lectures later published as *Russian Literature* (1905).

See: G. V. Plechanoff, *Anarchism and Socialism* (1895); E. V. Zenker, *Anarchism* (1897); J. F. Hecker, *Russian Sociology* (1915); Roger Baldwin, ed., *Kropotkin's Revolutionary Pamphlets* (1927).

L. S.

Kruczkowski, Leon (1900–, Polish novelist), a native of Cracow, was the leading "Marxist revisionist of the Polish historical tradition" to express himself through the novel in Free Poland. In 1932 he entered the literary scene with the controversial *Kordjan i cham* (Lord and Churl), a fictional reworking of the celebrated memoir of the peasant Deczyński written at the time of the 1830 uprising. Following this work, which set forth the irreconcilable conflict of interests between landlord and serf, Kruczkowski went on to sketch a portrait of the Galician village on the eve of the First World War in the episodic *Pawie pióra* (1935; Peacock Feathers). Later, in *Sidła* (1937); Snares), Kruczkowski essayed rather unsuccessfully a psychological portraiture of the unemployed in Poland.

See: reviews in *Wiadomości literackie,* 1935, Nos. 13, 15, and 1937, No. 41; K. Czachowski, *Obraz współczesnej literatury polskiej,* III (1936), 623–628.

A. P. C.

Krusenstjerna, Agnes von (1894–1940, Swedish novelist), born in Växjo, is one of the most controversial figures in modern Swedish literature. Born into an old aristocratic Swedish family which on the mother's side had developed serious pathological complications, she spent her childhood and earliest young womanhood in a more or less futile attempt to break the bonds that held her captive in a spiritually sterile and physically and mentally half-degenerate high society. She finally succeeded as a young woman in effecting a complete outward break with this group; but the mark of heredity and early environment was left upon her, and she apparently never succeeded in finding any solid positive values in life outside the class in which she was born, though her marriage with the sensitive critic and translator David Sprengel seems to have been a very happy one. She became in consequence of her break with her own class a tragically isolated figure, particularly after the controversy in the late 1920's and the 1930's of which she was the storm center. This controversy arose out of the bitter attacks upon her work by certain self-appointed "guardians of Swedish morals," who singled out her work as the most patently "immoral" among a group of younger literary figures of the day.

Agnes von Krusenstjerna's novels were especially apt to arouse popular, bigoted "moralists," because these novels focused their attention with such persistent minuteness upon elements of degeneration in a fast disappearing Swedish social class, the lower nobility. Though the attack upon her did not seriously affect the amount of her literary productivity, it did leave its mark upon the tone of her work, which became with the years increasingly dark, hopeless, and brooding, not without a touch of bitterness.

Her total production includes, in addition to her novels, several volumes of short stories and one volume of verse; but she will be remembered in Swedish literature primarily for three long novels, the trilogy under the collective title *Tonyböckerna* (1922–1924; The Tony Books) and two long family-chronicle novels, *Fröknarna von Pahlen* (7 vols., 1930–1934; The Ladies von Pahlen) and *Viveka von Lagercronas historia* (4 vols., 1935–1938; The Story of Viveka von Lagercrona). Of these three novels *Tonyböckerna* is perhaps the best, chiefly because it avoids the confusing multiplicity of characters and the too great preoccupation with matters of mere outward detail that are typical of the two family-chronicle novels. All of Agnes von Krusenstjerna's novels are more or less concerned with manifestations of perversion and semiperversion in the aimless pattern of existence followed by the Swedish aristocracy as she had come to know it in her early years. But she manages usually to avoid a completely morbid effect (except, perhaps, in *Fröknarna von Pahlen*) by her profound understanding of and sympathy for the sensitive, idealistic, dream-loving youth of aristocratic origins who attempt so desperately to realize their ideals in a partly callous, largely degenerate outward environment. Her marvelously sensitive depiction of the childhood and budding puberty of the hapless Tony in *Tonyböckerna* is unique among Swedish novels which deal centrally with crucial phases of the inner life of girlhood and young womanhood. In the matter of style Agnes von Krusenstjerna is nearly always impeccable, one of the great masters of modern Swedish prose. Her sudden death in 1940, the victim of an implacable hereditary disease, suggests something of the terrible reality for herself which the central theme in her novels, degenerate heredity, had.

See: Hagar Olsson, "Agnes von Krusenstjerna," *Bonniers litterära magasin,* VI (1937), 515–526; Stig Ahlgren, *Krusenstjerna studier* (1940).

A. G.

Kuncewiczowa, Marja (née Szczepańska, 1897–, Polish novelist), was born in Samara on the middle Volga, the descendant of a Polish legionary who had fled to Santo Domingo after the 1863 uprising. With the admirable *Cudzoziemka* (1935; Eng. tr., *The Stranger,* 1943), a convincing psychological study of a Polish woman reared in Russia and later transplanted to Poland who feels herself foreign in both countries, Kuncewiczowa represents the trend towards the psychological novel which was quite marked in Free Poland. Dividing her time between Warsaw and the quaint Kazimierz-on-the-Vistula, Kuncewiczowa set forth the peculiar life of the former in *Dyżilans warszawski* (1935; Warsaw Diligence) and represented the latter, with its contrasting populations, artistic and peasant, in the novel *Dwa księżyce* (1933; Two Moons). During the Second World War, Kuncewiczowa served as president of the Polish P.E.N. Club in England.

See: K. Czachowski, *Najnowsza twórczość literacka* (1938), pp. 40–43; review of *Cudzoziemka* in *Wiadomości literackie,* 1936, No. 4, and in *Skamander,* February, 1936.

A. P. C.

Kuprin, Alexander Ivanovich (1870–1938, Russian short-story writer and novelist), born in Narovchat, Penza, was perhaps the last of the traditional realists and one of the few prerevolutionary writers of established reputation to continue in exile their literary productivity in characteristic and undebilitated form. Educated in the Cadet School and the Military School of Moscow, he was commissioned lieutenant (1890), but resigned (1894) to devote himself to writing. For some years he led a vagabond life as dock worker, hunter, fisherman, agronomist, choir singer, actor, and journalist. He entered literature as one of the Znaniye ("knowledge") group led by Gorky, who headed the publishing house of that name. Kuprin's first stories (*Moloch,* 1896), about factory life, and others, chiefly about army officers, made a considerable impression. Fame came with his novel *Poyedinok* (1905; Eng. tr., *The Duel,* 1916), an ironic portrayal of the stupidity and brutality of the military caste and the first uncensored work of that genre. It coincided with the wave of national protest following the Japanese War and was more widely read than Tolstoy's *Resurrection.* Objective and nonpolitical, it excels in characterization and narrative structure.

There followed a long and diverse series of tales and novels, some superlatively wrought, others inferior. Two of the best short stories of their time are *Shtabs-Kapitan Rybnikov* (1906; Eng. tr., "Captain Ribnikov," in *The River of Life and Other Stories,* 1916), a wonderfully told episode of a Japanese spy in St. Petersburg, and *Granatovyi braslet* (1911; Eng. tr., title story in *The Bracelet of Garnets and Other Stories,* 1917), about the love of a poor clerk for a society lady. *Sulamif* (1908; Eng. tr., *Sulamith,* 1923), a reworking of the Song of Songs, and *Yama* (1912; Eng. tr., *Yama: The Pit,* 1922), a journalistic picture of prostitution in Odessa, at first sensationally successful are now dated and neglected. Kuprin's works have been widely translated; many of his short stories appear in anthologies as examples of finished craftsmanship. English collections of his finest tales are *The River of Life* and *The Bracelet of Garnets,* already mentioned, *A Slav Soul and Other Stories* (1916), and *Sasha* (1920). His collected works were published in Berlin (1921) in 12 volumes. After the Revolution, Kuprin emigrated to Paris, where he published *Novye povesti i razskazy* (1927; New Stories and Tales), *Razskazy dlya detei* (1927; Tales for Children), and three short novels, *Koleso vremeni* (1930; The Wheel of Time), *Zhaneta* (1932–1933; Jeannette), both romantic stories of Russian *émigrés* in France, and *Yunkera* (1933; The Junkers), a masterly and charming reminiscence of cadet life in old Russia—all in his best vein. In 1937, ill and homesick, Kuprin returned to Russia, where he was given an elaborate welcome. Fourteen months later, in complete obscurity, he died of cancer.

Kuprin's benevolent, genial personality won him friends among all sorts of people, a trait reflected in the rich diversity of his subject matter. Though his materials and methods are substantially those of his great predecessors, Tolstoy, Chekhov, and Gorky (*qq.v.*), he differs from his contemporaries in his affinity for the story of action, in which he was influenced by Jack London and Kipling. A portrayer, not a theorist, he is never political or metaphysical. Vigorous, prolific, uneven, by his excellences he makes one forget his shortcomings. At his best he is a first-rate narrator with a superlative gift of observation and a strong feeling for the lyrical, colorful elements of everyday existence.

See: Charles Ledré, *Trois Romanciers russes* (1935); Ivan Bunin, "Perechityvaya Kuprina," *Sovremennyia zapiski,* LXVII (1938), 308–324.

N. S.

Kurz, Isolde (1853–, German poet and short-story writer), was born in Stuttgart, daughter of the Swabian novelist Hermann Kurz, who numbered Paul Heyse (*q.v.*) and Eduard Mörike among his friends. Her mother, daringly liberal in her political as well as pedagogical views, instructed her at home and awakened in the child a lifelong love for the masterworks of literature, ancient and modern. After her father's sudden death in 1873, Isolde Kurz began earning her own living. She went to Munich, gave language lessons, and wrote her first short story, which met with considerable success but was sharply criticized on moral grounds by Paul Heyse, a fact which opened her eyes to his artistic limitations. Her conception of art was, in spite of youthful sentimentality and hero worship, fundamentally opposed to Heyse's idealized world. "Life's most beautiful flowers grow by the edge of an abyss," she wrote in *Aus meinem Jugendland* (1922). In 1877 she followed her mother and her brothers to Florence, drawn by a vision of the sea, to her a symbol of freedom. From then on the greater part of her life was spent in Italy until the outbreak of the First World War, when she returned to Munich. Italy became her main source of poetic inspiration. The themes of most of her short stories indicate the Italian subject matter (*Florentiner Novellen,* 1890, Eng. tr., *Tales of Florence,* 1919; *Italienische Novellen,* 1895; *Nächte von Fondi,* 1922). Like C. F. Meyer (*q.v.*) she was attracted by the Italian Renaissance, by the passion and drama of Southern lives, and, like him, she strove to tell about them with conscious, calm detachment. Deeply sensitive to the importance of form, she worked slowly and painstakingly to perfect composition and style, sometimes impairing the warmth and vitality of her writings. Her late novel *Vanadis* (1931) has been linked to the great German tradition of the *Bildungsroman.* Her poems (*Gedichte,* 1899; *Neue Gedichte,* 1905) tend towards excessive reflection, but are outstanding among German *Frauenlyrik* through their straightforward, unsentimental approach to emotions and thoughts. In this respect Isolde Kurz has often been compared to Ricarda Huch (*q.v.*) who is the greater writer but possesses less charm and seems less spontaneous.

See: P. Fechter, *Geschichte der deutschen Literatur,* III (1938), 363–366.

E. M. F.

Kvaran, Einar Hjörleifsson (1859–1938, Icelandic novelist, dramatist and poet), was born at Vallanes in East Iceland, the son of a pastor. He went to study political economy in Copenhagen, but instead he joined the Brandes (*q.v.*) realists among his compatriots and edited (1882) the periodical *Verðandi* (The Present), to which he contributed a rebellious short story. In 1885 Kvaran went to Winnipeg, Canada, where he became an editor of an Icelandic weekly and, in general, a leader of his compatriots. In 1895 he returned to Iceland, there to work as a journalist and political leader until 1906, when he was awarded a governmental grant to devote himself to literature.

The years in Winnipeg mellowed Kvaran's realistic outlook to such an extent that on his return to Iceland he was ready to preach a liberal Christian humanitarianism and to experiment with spiritualism, apostle of which he soon became. Strongly opposed at first, he and his followers gradually won the day; they still have a considerable following, in spite of attacks from the neo-romanticists (Nordal, 1925) and the communists (Laxness, 1936).

Vonir (1888; Hopes) is the first of a long series of short stories, in which Kvaran is at his best. He is especially fine when he writes about individuals least favored in life, a preferred subject with him. These stories are published in the collections *Vestan hafs og austan* (1901; West and East of the Ocean), *Smælingjar* (1908; The Insignificant), and *Frá ýmsum hliðum* (1913; From Various Viewpoints). In the novels *Ofurefli* (1908; The Unconquerable) and *Gull* (1911; Gold), Kvaran describes the impact of new ideas (the "new" theology) on society in Reykjavík. His later novels, *Sálin vaknar* (1916; The Soul Awakens), *Sambýli* (1918; House-mates), *Sögur Rannveigar* (2 vols., 1919–1922; Rannveig's Stories), and *Gæfumaður* (1933; The Fortunate Man), speak eloquently of his humane understanding and breathe the optimism of the convinced spiritualist. Two plays, *Lénharður fógeti* (1913; Eng. tr., "Governor Lenhard," *Poet Lore,* XLIII, 3–55) and *Syndir annara* (1915; The Sins of Others), are partly inspired by the Icelandic struggle for independence, but in *Hallsteinn og Dóra* (1931; Hallsteinn and Dora) the background is spiritualistic. Kvaran has also left a slim volume of poems, thoughtful, melancholy, composed early in life.

As no one else Kvaran represents the optimistic bourgeoisie before the First World War. His style is classical—pure, smooth, often argumentative and tinged with humor or irony. But it is somewhat lacking in vigor, color, and manliness.

See: S. Nordal, "Undir straumhvörf," *Skírnir,* XCIX (1925), 131–149; R. Beck, "Einar H. Kvaran, an Icelandic Novelist and Dramatist," *Poet Lore,* XLIII (1936–1937), 56–63; S. Einarsson, "Þættir af Einari H. Kvaran," *Eimreiðin,* XLIII (1937), 145–160, 287–306, XLIV (1938), 8–16, 178–180, 307–324.

S. E.

L

Lacretelle, Jacques de (1888–, French novelist), was born at Château de Cormatin in Burgundy, of a family already famous in French literature. His great uncle entered the French Academy in 1811; his grandfather, poet and novelist, was also a political figure and a friend of Lamartine. Jacques de Lacretelle studied at the Lycée Janson under André Bellessort, who subjected his romantic tendencies to strong classical disciplines. During a stay at Cambridge he acquainted himself with English literature, and in 1920 *La Vie inquiète de Jean Hermelin* was published. This subjective novel was followed in 1922 by *Silbermann,* the objective story of a Jewish boy in conflict with his classmates. *La Bonifas* (1925) deals with a case of abnormal psychology and definitely placed the author among the best French realists. *Le Retour de Silbermann* (1939) was originally part of *Amour nuptial* (1939), a study of conjugal misunderstanding somewhat similar to André Gide's *L'Immoraliste.* In 1932 was begun the publication of *Les Hauts-Ponts,* a novel in four volumes (*Sabine,* 1932; *Les Fiançailles,* 1933; *Années d'espérance,* 1934; *La Monnaie de plomb,* 1935) based on the passionate attachment of a woman for her family estate.

Lacretelle shows a predilection for lonely characters. He probes into their souls with a fearless interest. His minute analysis and his sense of restraint and proportion make him a true descendant of the 17th-century moralists. Besides his novels he has written short stories (*Quatre Nouvelles italiennes,* 1928; *L'Ame cachée,* 1928), essays (*Lettres espagnoles,* 1926; *Aparté,* 1927; *Le Demi-Dieu,* 1931; *Les Aveux étudiés,* 1934; *L'Ecrivain public,* 1936; *Croisières en eaux troubles,* 1939; *L'Heure qui change,* 1941; *Libérations,* 1945), and translations (*Sarn* by Mary Webb, in collaboration with Mme Guéritte; *La Renarde* by Mary Webb, with Mlle Canavaggia; *Haute Plainte* by Emily Brontë, with Yolande de Lacretelle). Lacretelle became a member of the French Academy in 1938.

See: A. Beaunier, "Un Romancier: M. Jacques de Lacretelle," *Revue des deux mondes,* August 1, 1925, pp. 698–709; R. Bourget-Pailleron, "La Nouvelle Equipe," *Revue des deux mondes,* November 15, 1933, pp. 358–362; A. Hermant, *Réponse au discours de réception de Jacques de Lacretelle à l'Académie Française* (1938); A. Maurois, preface to Lacretelle, *Morceaux choisis* (1938); F. Guirand, "Lacretelle," *Larousse mensuel,* April, 1938, p. 84.

M. E. C.

Laforgue, Jules (1860–1887, French poet and prose writer), was born in Montevideo, Uruguay, of French parentage. His father was a teacher. At the age of six he went to France with his family and lived in Tarbes, a small town at the foot of the Pyrenees, where he attended the *lycée* (1869–1876). There he began to suffer from a disease which never left him—boredom. In 1876 his family moved to Paris, but sometime afterward left him there, first with his sister and then completely alone. He had secured a post as secretary to the director of the *Gazette des beaux-arts,* Ephrussi. That period of solitude in Paris had a great influence on Laforgue's later development. He spent it in a state of sentimental and intellectual exaltation and of physical asceticism. He discovered poetry and philosophy (Schopenhauer was then in vogue). He read furiously: "Two years of solitude in libraries, without love, without friends, the fear of death. Nights spent in meditation in an atmosphere like that of Mount Sinai." He wrote verse and prose; *Le Sanglot de la terre,* a philosophical poem published after his death (in the *Œuvres complètes,* 1903), was composed in this period. Although he was shy and retiring, he made certain friends—Paul Bourget (*q.v.*), Charles Henry, Gustave Kahn (*q.v.*), and a woman poet, Sandah Mahali.

The efforts of Ephrussi gained him the post of reader to the Empress Augusta of Germany, and for five years (1881–1886) Laforgue followed her court wherever she went; Berlin, Potsdam, Baden Baden, and Homburg became the backgrounds of his boredom. Short but frequent trips to Paris alone seemed to sustain his courage. While in Germany he wrote the *Complaintes* (1885) and most of the later published *Moralités légendaires.* His method of writing is revealed by his notebooks (some published among his posthumous works and in the *Nouvelle Revue française,* October, 1920, some still unpublished). His technique in literature is similar to that of the impressionist painters in painting. He was anxious to note the exact and most ephemeral touches of the outside world as well as their immediate repercussions upon his soul. Looking out of an express-train window or watching boats going down the Rhine, he jotted down sentences which he used later in his prose or his poems. The love of a woman, which in Paris had remained in the realm of his dreams, entered his life in Germany. A rather stormy love affair with a person designated in his notebooks by the letter R reached its climax in 1883. It left Laforgue expecting more from life, but he was hardly more mature emotionally. Later when, looking for an English teacher in Berlin, he met Miss Leah Lee, a slender, red-haired English girl, it was love at first sight. In September, 1886, he became engaged to her, resigned his post at the court, and went to Paris to make a living by writing. His *Complaintes* had already won him a certain fame. In January, 1887, he went to London to marry Miss Lee and then settled down with his wife in a small apartment in Paris where he expected to find the happiness he had waited for so long. Instead he found poverty, sickness, and finally, the following summer, death. A cold, caught in London and neglected, had developed into tuberculosis. His wife died a few months later.

Before his death Laforgue had finished the manuscript of *Moralités légendaires* (most of which had earlier appeared in the periodical *Vogue),* but he had been unable to find a publisher. The book appeared posthumously, November, 1887. Two slender books of verses, *L'Imitation de Notre-Dame la Lune* (1886) and *Le Concile féerique* (1886), together with a few articles in symbolist periodicals, are all that were published during his life besides the *Complaintes.* His works appeared in 1901–1903 (3 vols.). Other papers appeared in 1920 (3 vols.). A new edition (5 vols., 1925) added some heretofore unpublished letters.

Laforgue's works should have been the preface to much greater accomplishments, but, as Rémy de Gourmont (*q.v.*) said, it is a preface which can almost make up for the lack of the work itself. He had one of the most original minds of any time. While he lived somewhat apart from the symbolist group, it is clearly seen today that he belongs among them. Following Corbière (*q.v.*), whom he discovered only late and when his manner was well formed, and Verlaine (*q.v.*), he completely renounced the structural principles of classical French verse and created modern free verse. No poet in France or elsewhere can afford to ignore his technical inventions. He also had a tone definitely his own, a sentimental irony which was perhaps the result of the clashing in him of intellectual maturity and emotional immaturity. Irony and verbalism are for Laforgue means of escape. His method consists of a notation of acute personal emotions against a background which evokes his epoch. The ironical treatment of both himself and his background (often his form is that of some *refrain de faubourg*) destroys the romantic strain. It is to be regretted that his poems seldom give the impression of having reached a state of perfection. Not so with his prose, however. *Moralités légendaires,* in which he retells some age-old stories—Perseus and Andromeda, Salome, Lohengrin, Hamlet—lending his characters the psychology of his contemporaries, shows him to be obssessed by Flaubert (*q.v.*). The result is writing which equals the best of the French prose tradition and at the same time deliberately ridicules and attacks that tradition.

The influence of Laforgue on French poets of the next generation, Apollinaire, Salmon (*qq.v.*), *et al.*, and even on recent or contemporary groups like the surrealists, cannot be contested. In America his influence on T. S. Eliot and Ezra Pound, among others, is generally admitted.

See: F. Ruchon, *Jules Laforgue* (1924).

I. W.

Lagerkvist, Pär (1891–, Swedish lyric poet, dramatist, and short-story writer), born in Växjö, was the most arresting figure to appear on the literary scene in Sweden during the First World War, and his early work particularly reflects in both its form and content the half-desperate psychology of a serious, hypersensitive, and brutally frank war generation. Though his later efforts are more mature and satisfying, his work on the whole is characterized by a profound sense of continuity in its development, from his first startling visionary poems down through his late quietly expressionistic dramas. For some years the violently expressionistic form of his poems and early plays (based consciously upon contemporary trends in French painting, naïvism, cubism, and Fauvism, in addition to earlier expressionistic forms, especially those of the religious dramas of Strindberg, *q.v.*) marked him as an exclusive poet, to be read only by the initiated, and served to obscure the high seriousness of his message. But with time his youthful formalistic excesses gave way to a simpler, more concrete, and highly concentrated art, only in part related to expressionism; and at the same time the brutal pessimism of his earlier conception of life gradually yielded to a new, highly individual religious position, in which he comes, obviously after a severe inner struggle, to the conclusion that "good shall at the last triumph, for it is the greatest and the strongest power, however terrifying the world may seem to be."

The development of Lagerkvist's thought, the outlines of which are only partially clear in the volumes of his poetry (from *Motiv,* 1914, Motifs, through *Hjärtats sånger,* 1926, Songs of the Heart) and in his seven plays to date, is given a more precise confessional form in two central autobiographical documents, *Gäst hos verkligheten* (1925; A Guest in the Actual World) and *Det besegrade livet* (1927; Life Conquered). These two volumes express Lagerkvist's final undying faith in the imperishable spirit of man, which against all the fearful odds man faces in his struggle for existence will ultimately triumph. Of recent years Lagerkvist has brought the focus of his art to bear more and more directly upon the modern social and political scene, becoming in the 1930's, particularly in his fiction and his drama, the most eloquent and rigidly uncompromising critic of totalitarianism as a social and political philosophy. He proposes in place of the brutal pretentiousness of totalitarian ideas a kind of heroic humanitarian idealism in which the imperishable human spirit can find its finest and most permanent social and political expression. These ideas are developed most sharply in the sensational short novel *Bödeln* (1934; The Hangman), which has been successfully dramatized, and in the two powerful plays *Mannen utan själ* (1936; The Man without a Soul) and *Seger i mörkret* (1939; Victory in Darkness). Both in technique and themes as a dramatist Lagerkvist is the inspired disciple of the later Strindberg, the Strindberg of the expressionistic plays. In 1940 Lagerkvist was elected to the Swedish Academy, to occupy the chair vacated upon the death of Verner von Heidenstam (*q.v.*), the last of that group of literary figures who created the great literature of the Swedish 1890's.

See: G. M. Bergman, *Pär Lagerkvists dramatik* (1928); K. Strömberg, *Modern svensk litteratur* (1932), pp. 202–211; G. Fredén, *Pär Lagerkvist* (1934); R. Ljungdahl, "Pär Lagerkvist: från 'Ångest' och 'Kaos' till 'Bödeln' och 'Den knutna näven,'" *Finsk tidskrift,* CXVIII (1935), 336–342; H. Ahlenius, "The Dramatic Works of Pär Lagerkvist," *American-Scandinavian Review,* XXVIII (1940), 301–308.

A. G.

Lagerlöf, Selma (1858–1940, Swedish novelist), is incomparably Sweden's greatest storyteller. She was born on the old farmstead

Mårbacka in Värmland, the province with which most of her best fiction is intimately associated and where she lived the greater part of her outwardly uneventful life. She never married. Her first novel, *Gösta Berlings saga* (1891; Eng. tr., 1898), was a fascinatingly original retelling of old Värmland folk legends in an effusive, personal, spontaneously lyric prose, a style in marked contrast to the prevailing fiction of the day in Sweden. The style was suggested by a reading of Carlyle. A number of less important tales appeared from Selma Lagerlöf's pen during the 90's; but it was not until the turn of the century, with the composition of *Jerusalem* (2 vols., 1901–1902; Eng. tr., 1903), that she wrote anything comparable in importance to *Gösta Berlings saga.* In the years that followed she produced steadily (except during the First World War, when her pen was apparently palsied) a large number of novels and short stories (usually in the form of legends and fairy tales) and autobiographical sketches of all kinds. This mass of work was of rather unequal quality on the whole, the most important perhaps being the delightful pedagogical fantasy *Nils Holgerssons underbara resa genom Sverige* (1906–1907; Eng. tr., *The Wonderful Adventures of Nils,* 1907) and the three charmingly modest volumes of Värmland memories from her childhood under the collective title *Mårbacka* (1922–1932; Eng. tr., *Mårbacka,* 1924; *Memories of My Childhood,* 1934; *The Diary of Selma Lagerlöf,* 1936). Her last effort to write extended fiction—the trilogy about Charlotte Löwensköld—reveals a distinct falling off in creative power.

It is impossible to explain Selma Lagerlöf's undeniable eminence as a narrator except by insisting upon the direct, primitive sources of her art. Her best novels and tales spring directly from the Swedish soil, are part and parcel of the Swedish countryside. She had listened breathlessly as a child (and, for that matter, in the years of her maturity) to the whole variegated congeries of tales current on the Värmland countryside; and she has retold these tales with the same breathless naïveté with which she had first listened to them. Her art, in consequence, is scarcely creative in the usual sense. She may be called a creative listener—permitting her fancy, meanwhile, to dance and riot freely in the old folk materials related to her, until out of them come such brilliant tales as *Gösta Berlings saga* and *Jerusalem.* Such novels are probably among the closest approach to genuine folk epics that we have in modern literature. Selma Lagerlöf may thus be looked upon primarily as the infinitely skillful modern medium by which ancient and latter-day Swedish folk tales are brought to the present-day reader. In the naturalness and spontaneity with which she realizes this ideal in fiction she is perhaps unique in contemporary literature. Her conception of life is as naïve as is her art, but less satisfactory to the modern mind. Her characters are frequently oversimplified, as is her view of the forces that govern human life. There is no more insistent optimist among Scandinavian authors than Selma Lagerlöf. The First World War seemed momentarily to shake her faith in the power that goodness ultimately wields over evil on the human scene; but her latest work yields not an iota to the simple childlike optimism of her first novels and tales. There is, in a word, no intellectual development in Selma Lagerlöf's work; but perhaps one should not ask for this (or even wish it) in a narrative genius which could scarcely have come into its own unique and priceless being had it permitted itself to become dominated by what she has, not without irony, referred to in *Gösta Berlings saga* as "the spirit of the age."

See: Johan Mortensen, *Selma Lagerlöf* (1908); W. A. Berendsohn, *Selma Lagerlöf* (1927, in German; Eng. tr., abridged, 1931); Stella Arvidson, *Selma Lagerlöf* (1932); H. A. Larsen, *Selma Lagerlöf* (1936, in English); Alrik Gustafson, *Six Scandinavian Novelists* (1940).

A. G.

Lalou, René (1889–, French critic), was born at Boulogne-sur-Mer and educated in Calais and Paris and at the University of Lille. Before the First World War, in which he served, he taught at the Manchester Grammar School and at the Lycée of Oran; after the war he held a number of *lycée* appointments, the last being in Paris at the Lycée Henri IV. During this period he wrote several novels, of which only one has been published, *Le Chef* (1923), and his *Histoire de la littérature française contemporaine* (1922, enlarged ed., Vol. I, 1941, Vol. II, 1940; Eng. tr., *Contemporary French Literature,* 1924). This handbook, beginning in 1870 with a backward glance at the great romantics and extending in the most recent edition to the Second World War, provides the general public with a useful synthesis, impartial and unprejudiced. Lalou has said that he hopes his criticism can be read with the interest with which one reads a novel, and his infectious enthusiasm for literature, combined with a gift for clear statement and for keeping the main lines of development apparent through a multitude of details, has made that hope more or less a reality. A volume of critical essays, *Défense de l'homme* (1926), a study of Sainte-Beuve, Bertrand, Gérard de Nerval, and Baudelaire (*q.v.*) entitled *Vers une alchimie lyrique* (1927), and a history of modern English literature, *Panorama de la littérature anglaise contemporaine* (1927), have widened his range. His work has been marked in general by a tendency to take a middle ground, not because he hesitates to speak out strongly, but because such a position is natural to his somewhat skeptical intelligence.

See: John Charpentier, "René Lalou," *Mercure de France,* CCXXIV (1930), 343–345.

C. W., Jr.

Landau, Mark Aleksandrovich, *see* Aldanov, Mark Aleksandrovich.

Langer, František (1888–, Czech playwright and novelist), is, next to Karel Čapek (*q.v.*), the most successful Czech dramatist of recent years. He was born in Prague, of Jewish parentage, and became a doctor. In 1916 he was taken prisoner by the Russians, but joined the Czechoslovak legions and took part in their crossing of Siberia as a member of the medical corps. After the First World War he served in the medical corps of the Czechoslovak army, becoming a colonel. In 1939 he succeeded in escaping to England. Before the First World War, Langer wrote a collection of short stories, *Zlatá Venuše* (1910; The Golden Venus), which attracted some attention because of the exquisite sense of form combined with a rather crude sensualism. His plays *Svatý Václav* (1912; St. Wenceslaus) and *Miliony* (performed 1915, printed 1921; Millions) were unsuccessful, though they were both skillfully constructed.

The war changed Langer's outlook completely: he forgot his early aestheticism and neoclassicism and discovered ordinary man and his moral problems. *Velbloud uchem jehly* (1923; Eng. tr., *The Camel through the Needle's Eye,* 1929), his greatest success on the stage, was received with acclaim at home and also in Austria, Germany, and New York. It is clever comedy in praise of victorious robust health and ordinary common sense. *Periferie* (1925; The Outskirts), which followed, is drama on the verge of tragedy; in a technique which imitates that of moving pictures Langer tells the story of a murderer who vainly tries to get convicted by the court. Since these two very effective plays, Langer has descended to farces and sentimental dramas of little value: *Grand Hotel Nevada* (1927—this is the original Czech title) is a satire on the absurdities of rich people, *Obrácení Ferdy Pištory* (1929; The Conversion of Ferda Pištora) presents a rogue from the slums who is converted against his will, and *Andělé mezi námi* (1931; Angels in Our Midst) is a sentimental discussion of euthanasia. Only *Jízdní hlídka* (1935; The Cavalry Watch) represents a new advance. The play is drawn from Langer's experiences as a legionnaire in Siberia and attempts, with some success, a tragedy of collective heroism. *Dvaasedmdesátka* (1937; No. 72) is, like *Periferie,* an interesting reconstruction of a crime, with the technique of a play within a play used to good effect. Langer's later prose is not important; a collection of short stories from Siberia, *Železný vlk* (1920; The Iron Wolf), shows his usual constructive skill, but the attempts at humorous sketches and a novel, *Zázrak v rodině* (1929; The Miracle in the Family), are failures.

Langer has great talent, spoiled by success. He has a flair for stage effects; he handles promising and ambitious themes, but he cannot avoid the pitfalls of sentimentality, easygoing optimism, and sheer triviality. In this respect his fate seems similar to that of the Magyar dramatist Molnar (*q.v.*), who is his nearest analogue in other literatures.

See: Pavla Buzková, "F. Langer," in *České drama* (1932).

R. W.

Lanson, Gustave (1857–1934, French literary historian and critic), was born in Orléans. He entered the Ecole Normale Supérieure in 1876 and, with the exception of some months spent as French tutor to the tsarevitch at the Russian court (1886), had an uninterrupted and most distinguished career as teacher and scholar. In 1887 his doctoral thesis, *Nivelle de la Chaussée,* was highly praised for thoroughness of research and for critical discrimination. When in the 90's it became obvious that university teaching of French literature was not up to the standard of work being done in other fields such as general history and the social sciences, Lanson was the natural choice to remedy the situation. He was appointed professor at the Sorbonne in 1900; he became director of the Ecole Normale Supérieure in 1919.

As an antagonist to easygoing, verbose ways of dealing with the literature of the past, this quiet, bespectacled little man with piercing black eyes was bound to emphasize painstaking exactness, judicious consideration, stubborn resistance to emotional subjectivity. At the same time the discipline and restraint which he constantly showed in his professional work, and even in the modulation of his voice (though he could be sharply sarcastic), probably came quite as much from a serious intensity about his scientific "mission" as from any native poise or calmness of temperament. Adversaries, indeed, accused him of a German dryness, a reproach which, as events proved, became quite fair as applied to certain of Lanson's disciples, all too ready to adopt the merely external aspects of methodical approach. But whoever has listened to Lanson's own impassioned pleas for the pure enjoyment of belles-lettres or to a declamation, in his vibrating voice, of a favorite piece of verse, whoever observed the intensity of his despair when his only son was killed in the First World War, could not imagine how lack of sensibility might ever be charged to him.

At the university he devoted his full effort to modern French "literary history," a study distinct from that form of "criticism" which necessarily includes a large element of personal taste and preference (as shown, indeed, in Lanson's own occasional contributions to the Paris newspaper, *Matin*). *Explication de textes,* study of corrected manuscripts and of changes from edition to edition, discovery of sources which either narrowed or emphasized the originality of a writer, exact knowledge of words in all their connotations at a given moment, thoroughly tested bibliographies where legends about the vogue of a writer yield to the pure truth—all this was simply method. There was a deeper quest. The individual quality in an author, which the theory of Taine (*q.v.*) could not "dissolve," which in the system of Brunetière (*q.v.*) was more of a disturbance than a confirmation, had been emphasized by Sainte-Beuve although often in only secondary figures. Lanson now tried—often with success—to explain the literary titan, as well as lesser personages, by an objective demonstration of his greatness however exceptional and of his style however original.

After numerous individual studies (*e.g., Bossuet,* 1890; *Corneille,* 1895; *Voltaire,* 1906; *L'Art de la prose,* 1908), the *Histoire de la littérature française* (1894; many editions, 17th ed., 1922) and its natural supplement the *Manuel bibliographique de la littérature française, 1500–1900* (1909–1914; new ed., 1921) demonstrated the final importance of this untiring activity. He continued with an admirable hospitality of spirit to make revisions, mainly away from a too philosophical trend and towards more "delight" in the art of fine writing. Benefiting from further study and observation, he tempered his own decided devotion to a rational center of gravity in French literature, "will guided by reason." Leftist tendencies in politics prevented this indefatigable and widely influential scholar and interpreter of French letters from receiving the official recognition of membership in the French Academy.

See: "Bibliographie des œuvres de M. Lanson," in *Mélanges d'histoire littéraire offerts à Gustave Lanson* (1922).

F. B.

Lanza, Silverio (pseud. of Juan Bautista Amorós, 1856–1912, Spanish novelist), a writer today almost forgotten, was once highly esteemed in certain circles as a precursor of contemporary literature in Spain, especially of the Generation of '98 (*see* Spanish literature). Gómez de la Serna (*q.v.*), biographer, admirer, and self-confessed disciple of Lanza, called him "the founder, the revealer, perhaps involuntary . . . of the new literary liberty," adding that "he discovered a greater reality of the Spanish land," that he was "the true successor of Larra . . . the true successor of Goya." Azorín (*q.v.*) admired him greatly also. Lanza was one of the first "raros"—as Rubén Darío called all the strange personalities that carried on in the name of originality and individualism the *fin-de-siècle* artistic rebellion. He studied at the Spanish Naval Academy, abandoning the service shortly after becoming an officer. He was made suddenly famous among a small group of intellectuals by the publication of his first novel, *El año triste* (1883), and although he never attained general public recognition, he kept on writing novels and short stories—now practically unfindable—from Getafe, a small town near Madrid where he led a retired life. Some of his best works are *Cuentos políticos* (1890), *Artuña* (2 vols., 1893–1894), *Ni en la vida ni en la muerte* (1899), and *La rendición de Santiago* (1907).

See: Ramón Gómez de la Serna, ed., *Páginas escogidas e inéditas de Silverio Lanza* (1918).

A. del R.

Larbaud, Valery (1881–, French poet, novelist, and essayist), began his career with an erudite and sensitive verse translation of Coleridge's *The Rime of the Ancient Mariner* (1901). He has been ever since, in whatever he writes, a curious and very personal combination of poet and scholar. Born in Vichy, the international spa, of a wealthy family which sent him first to a private school attended chiefly by the sons of South American millionaires and later (1897) on a grand tour of Germany, Russia, and Turkey, Larbaud first distinguished himself as the poet of luxurious cosmopolitanism. By the time that his *Poèmes par un riche amateur* appeared in 1908, attributed to a fabulous South American, A. O. Barnabooth, he had familiarized himself with Europe and its languages and chosen his intellectual homes—the three principal Latin countries and England. The *Journal d'A. O. Barnabooth* (1913) continues in prose the singing of "Europe, its railways and its theatres and its constellations of cities." Endowed with an ardent idealism, a solid culture, and a shameful fortune, Barnabooth, a kind of Argentine descendant of Henri Brulard, constantly uproots himself physically and morally in a vain effort to dissociate his true personality from fortuitous circumstances.

Larbaud the poet also contains an analyst who, simultaneously with Proust and Pirandello (*qq.v.*), seeks what he calls "self-sapience." Nor is the poet limited by the new dandyism of cosmopolitanism which he bequeaths to Paul Morand, Jean Giraudoux, Jules Romains (*qq.v.*), and so many others; he also delights in the poetry of childhood and adolescence, as in his delicate novel of school life, *Fermina Márquez* (1911), and the sensitive and sympathetic stories of *Enfantines* (1918). The three short novels contained in *Amants, heureux amants* (1924) return to the earlier vein; two of the tales use the form of the interior monologue or stream of consciousness which Larbaud, one of the first (1922) to praise Joyce's *Ulysses,* acclimatized in France.

In his collections of stories and essays—*Jaune, bleu, blanc* (1927), *Technique* (1932), *Aux couleurs de Rome* (1938)—the scholar leads the poet into strange philological byways, when the poet is not interrupting the scholar's labors to record some evanescent aspect of life. The penetrating studies of English writers contained in *Ce Vice impuni, la lecture* (1925), together with his translations of Walt Whitman, Landor, Sir Thomas Browne, and the Samuel Butler of *Erewhon,* have won Larbaud a place among the most perspicacious *anglicistes* of his time. He has also translated from the Spanish and the Italian. On the other hand, his articles for the Buenos Aires *Nación* and for the London *New Weekly* have introduced abroad much of the best in contemporary French literature. He has consistently striven to further intellectual intercourse among nations: the quarterly which he founded with Valéry and Fargue (*qq.v.*) and which abounds in his and others' translations was appropriately called *Commerce* (1924–1932). With characteristic modesty, he is ever ready to efface himself before another writer whom he thinks it his duty to introduce; and humbly he calls upon his patron saint, the compiler of the Vulgate, to establish "the eminent dignity of translators in the Republic of Letters." As a scholar and as a poet Valery Larbaud is a citizen of Europe.

See: J. O'Brien, "Valery Larbaud," *Symposium,* III (1932), 315–334; M. Thiébaut, "Valery Larbaud," *Revue de Paris,* Année XXXIX (1932), Tome VI, pp. 822–858.

J. O'B.

Larsson, Carl Filip (pseud. Carl Larsson i By, 1877–, Swedish poet and novelist), was born in By, Kopparberg (formerly the province of Dalecarlia). Unlike many other self-made literary men of peasant stock, he has remained in his original setting as a tiller of the soil. A number of small collections of poems and short stories reflect the country life he has known from childhood, *e.g., By och bonde* (1907; Village and Villager), *Tionde* (1909; Tithe), *Av jord är du kommen* (1913; Dust Thou Art), *Den sista kärven* (1914; The Last Sheaf), *Bergsmanshistorier* (2 vols., 1915–1918; Stories of Miners), and *Lantliga historier* (1925; Stories of Rural Life). He is fond of the past. His researches concerning his home region constitute a monumental chronicle, *En dalasockens historia* (2 vols., 1920–1939; The History of a Dalecarlian Parish). Popular education has had an enthusiastic trail blazer in Larsson. His contributions to the press on this subject are legion. In *Logen 5455, Morgonvind* (1916; The Lodge No. 5455, Morning Wind) he has presented in novelistic form the history of a temperance society which gives a cross section of one of the idealistic movements that characterized Swedish country life prior to the First World War. As a poet Larsson possesses no brilliant qualities, but his art of storytelling is genuine, and he has a great gift of concision. The environmental descriptions in his stories are always reliable. As both man and author he is, with his idealistic inclinations, representative of a country-wide movement which originated in Sweden as a reaction against the debasement of traditional, rural culture such as had been brought on in part by the inroads of industrialism.

A. W.

Larsson, Hans (1862–1944, Swedish philosopher and aesthetician), is a philosophical thinker by profession with strongly marked literary interests and gifts. Though most of his imposing list of published works (some 30 in all) are technical-philosophical in kind, they are not infrequently concerned with basic aesthetic problems, particularly as applied to phenomena of literary creation; and they are invariably cast in a clear, flexible, exquisitely sensitive Swedish prose. On occasion also the philosophical has given way almost entirely to the literary creative urge in Larsson's production, such volumes as *På vandring* (1909; Afoot), *Hemmabyarna* (1916; The Home Villages), and *Idéerna i Stabberup* (1918; Ideas in Stabberup) being works essentially literary both in form and content. These more purely literary works reveal a creative artist of real originality and of considerable ability, especially in small genre studies of human beings and places in Hans Larsson's native rural Skåne. More important in the history of Swedish literature, however, are Larsson's *Intuition* (1892) and *Poesiens logik* (1899; The Logic of Poetry), penetrating studies in the nature of the creative process, and two collections of essays, *Reflexioner för dagen* (1911; Contemporary Reflections) and *Litteraturintryck* (1926; Literary Impressions). *Intuition* and *Poesiens logik* served in their day to clarify to some extent the whole body of ideas back of the neoromantic strains in the Scandinavian literatures of the 1890's, while *Reflexioner för dagen* contained an essay, entitled "Huvudsak och bisak i litterära brytningar" (The Primary and the Secondary in Literary Transitions), which was perhaps the most sane and balanced contribution to the so-called "Strindbergsfejden" in 1910–1911, one of the most violent literary controversies in the history of Swedish literature. It is the rare combination of literary talents and philosophical acumen in Hans Larsson that has brought him a much larger audience than that of any other professional philosopher in Sweden.

See: Johan Mortensen, "Hans Larsson som diktare," in *Människor och böcker* (1917), pp. 257–269.

A. G.

Lasker-Schüler, Else (1876–1945, German poet, novelist, and essayist), was born in Elberfeld in the Rhineland, of the famous Schüler family. The Rhineland is one of the sources of her inspiration; others are her deep devotion to Judaism and her ecstatic vision of the Orient. After the dissolution of her first marriage with the physician Lasker, she went to Berlin, became the companion of the prophetlike vagabond-poet Peter Hille (*q.v.*), and, after his death, married Herwarth Walden, one of the leaders of the expressionist movement and the editor of the periodical *Der Sturm*. To some she seems always to have remained a bohemian; actually, she lived, in her writings as well as in her personal life, in a world of wonders, colorful images, and fairy-tale adventures suggestive of the *Arabian Nights*. Her only novel is entitled *Mein Herz* (1912); she is the first poet of the contemporary idiom who feels that she and all her fellow beings are crystallizations of the heart. The strength of her imagination, combined with great artistry of language, produced some of the most beautiful and profound modern German poems (*e.g.*, "Ein alter Tibetteppich"). She also possessed the Rhenish humor which often projected her emotional fantasies into the realm of the grotesque.

All these elements caused the young expressionist generation from 1910 to 1920 to recognize in Else Lasker-Schüler a forerunner and a kind of fairy godmother. She, on her part, saw in her many literary admirers strange and fantastic figures of her own wonder world. In some of her books (*Gesichte*, 1911; *Das Konzert*, 1932) one may find a variety of literary genres—poems, essays, grotesques, biographies, fairy tales, and autobiographic novelettes. At times (*Tino von Bagdad*, 1907; *Prinz von Theben*, 1914) she transforms herself into this or that figure of the Orient. Her first book of poems, *Styx*, appeared in 1902; her best poems were collected in *Gedichte* (1914). A later book of poetry is entitled *Die Kuppel* (1925). The Hebraic element became most clearly visible in *Die hebräischen Balladen* (1913) and in the novel *Der Wunderrabiner von Barcelona* (1926). Her Rhenish temperament found its strongest expression in an early social play, *Die Wupper* (1908), produced in the expressionistic style in Berlin in 1919, and in the autobiographical story *Arthur Aronymus: Die Geschichte meines Vaters* (1932). The great hero of her life was Peter Hille, to whom she dedicated the *Peter Hille-Buch* (1906) and whose letters she edited in 1921. There was no room for her in Hitler's world; she found her second home in Palestine, where she wrote *Hebräerland* (1937) and died in 1945.

See: M. Wiener, "Else Lasker-Schüler," in *Juden in der Literatur* (1922).

K. P.

La Tour du Pin, Patrice de (1911–, French poet), was seen by some in the years immediately preceding the Second World War as the chief hope of modern French poetry. Perhaps only those who respond temperamentally to the passionate but rather undisciplined mysticism which has characterized his work can share that opinion. *La Quête de joie* (1933) and *Le Lucernaire* (1936), though marked by an unmistakable talent, must be regarded as promises of genius to come rather than as its mature fruit. The first, a collection of lyric poems, all touching on some aspect of man's search for the answers to two perpetual questions—What is God? and What is man?—is certainly his best work. It is marked by a directness and nobility of statement that has been compared to that of Dante, and if it does not succeed in solving the problems it raises, at least it wins for itself a position among the best religious verse of the present period by its ability to clothe abstract ideas in sensuous garments. *Le Lucernaire,* the first book of what is to be a poem of some length, perhaps suffers from having appeared alone. Nearer to the medieval allegory than to any literary type of the present day, it recounts the soul's search for an ideal purity, more delicious than the joys of the flesh, but to be found only after having passed through these joys and rejected them. The form, the severity of technique, and the nobility of concept again recall Dante; but the poet's meaning is hard to decipher, and unfortunately the concrete sensual quality that marked the early work of La Tour du Pin has been largely replaced by a mass of intellectualized detail.

See: André Fontainas, "Les Poèmes," *Mercure de France,* CCLI (1934), 351–355, CCLXXI (1936), 355–357; Raymond Schwab, "La Poésie," *Nouvelle Revue française,* XLII (1934), 552–554.

C. W., Jr.

Latvian literature, *see* Lettish literature.

Lautréamont, comte de (pseud. of Isidore Lucien Ducasse, 1846–1870, French poet), was born of French parents in Montevideo, where his father was the French consul, and went to Paris at 20 to prepare for the Ecole Polytechnique. His poverty forced him to live in a cheap hotel. His dark room was furnished with a bed, two suitcases full of books, and an upright piano. He wrote at night, consuming innumerable cups of coffee. The manuscript of *Les Chants de Maldoror* was sent to the printers in 1868; only one canto appeared before his death, publishers not daring to put on sale the whole book. He began to write the preface to another volume, to be called *Poésies,* which was never completed. Ducasse, who picked his pen name from one of Eugène Sue's novels, died as mysteriously as he had lived.

Composed under the influence of Byron, Milton, and Poe, the *Maldoror* work is a fantastic epic and reads like a huge nightmare, brightened here and there by beautiful mystic and poetic visions. Ghastly and gruesome, it is a most violent piece of poetic pessimism. From the very first pages of this poem in prose the forces which move the young writer are evident: he is drunk with morbid romanticism, with the funereal grandiloquence of Young and of the pseudo-Ossian, with the satanism of Byron and of the darker novels of Byron's day. A passionate desire for originality results in the exaggeration of this sadistic tendency. Amidst grotesque surroundings the author sees strange visions: in rivers of blood, among lice, vampires, and spiders, the brother of the leech speaks to the toad, apostrophizes Lohengrin, makes love to a female shark, and, transformed into an octopus, defies God. Descending sometimes to the ridiculous, the descriptions are in danger of becoming monotonous and fatiguing; effects are spoiled at times with banal explanations. To Lautréamont, may be applied the words he uses to describe his hero: "Your mind is so ill that you are not aware of the fact and that you believe yourself sane every time you mouth senseless nothings, which are nevertheless filled with an infernal grandeur."

The reader can indeed perceive in this deformed work traces of a masterful imagination. Lyricism shines forth, as in the long, sustained invocation to the ancient sea. The imagery is at times lofty; the irony creates strange, powerful effects. We are transported suddenly to the last days of the world, or we enter, already somewhat baffled, a kingdom of flickering lights and shadows. The poetry is indefinable because it is indefinite; it is in fact "pure poetry."

The influence of Lautréamont on the rising generation of poets was considerable. The surrealists (*see* Breton, André) flocked to his banner and saluted him, with Rimbaud (*q.v.*), as the leader of their revolution. His miraculous force was acknowledged by the great writers of the turn of the century. Many, such as Rémy de Gourmont and Léon Bloy (*qq.v.*), were afraid and declared the author of *Les Chants de Maldoror* a madman. Others, such as Valery Larbaud and **Léon Paul Fargue** (*qq.v.*), openly avowed their admiration. The new generation of poets after the First World War were fully aware of a debt to Lautréamont.

See: Régis Michaud, *Modern Thought and Literature in France* (1934); Albert Thibaudet, *Histoire de la littérature française de 1789 à nos jours* (1936); René Lalou, *Histoire de la littérature française contemporaine*, enlarged ed., Vol. II (1940).

P. B.

Laxness, Halldór Kiljan (1902–, Icelandic novelist, poet, and playwright), was born at Laxnes, near Reykjavík. His parents were farmers. Of the youngest generation of Icelandic writers he is the greatest and at the same time the most consistently modernistic. Like no other writer he represents the youthful urban population of Reykjavík, cut loose from the thousand-year-old farm culture, searching vigorously for a new mode of living among the possibilities of the post-war world. He received his first impulses in the lyric and national romantic atmosphere of the early 1920's, but soon he plunged himself into introspection, philosophy, and religion, following the line of Strindberg and Undset (*qq.v.*). As a youth he steeped himself in expressionism in Germany, in Catholicism in a monastery in Luxembourg, and in surrealism in France (1924–1926), after which he went to Iceland, Canada, and California (1927–1930) to fortify himself in a communism that since has served him as a leading hypothesis. He returned to Iceland in 1930. His books have been written there or wherever his extensive travels have taken him.

From his Catholic period date *Undir Helgahnúk* (1924; Under the Holy Mountain) and *Vefarinn mikli frá Kasmír* (1927; The Great Weaver from Kashmir). The latter book stands as a milestone of a new age in Icelandic novel writing; it is expressionistic and autobiographic, a true picture of the turmoil in the author's mind. In it he shifted his point of view, reducing *ad absurdum* the ideal of the Church, as he understood it. Having returned from California to Iceland in 1930, Laxness aired his communistic views in a book of brilliant essays, *Alþýðubókin* (1930; The Book of the People), and startled the public with a booklet of modernistic lyrics, *Kvæðakver* (1930; Poems). But his greatest work is embodied in three novels, each of many volumes, published during the 1930's. The first unit, *Þú vínviður hreini* (1931) and *Fuglinn í fjörunni* (1932; Eng. tr. of both, *Salka Valka*, 1936), treats of the small fishing village; the next, *Sjálfstætt fólk* (2 vols., 1934–1935; Independent People), is about the poor farmer; and the third, *Ljós heimsins* (4 vols., 1937–1940; The Light of the World), is about the poet of the people. These novels are conceived on a grand scale, the poor but energetic village girl and the independent cottage farmer emerging as heroes of monumental stature, symbols of their class. The poet, though anything but a hero, being the lowly subject and scapegoat of a cruel world, is no less grandly conceived as a symbol of the crucified spirit forever rising in beauty as the light of this world. In these novels Laxness has created a new style, whose storms and stresses contrast vividly with the classic saga-like style of predecessors and contemporaries. A fierce social criticism runs through all his novels; this has alienated readers both at home and abroad. But even his critics have had to admit—and admire—the brilliance of his style, the vigorous symbolism, the high poetic quality of his rich lyric vein, the art with which he fuses characters and scenery into one vast panorama of intensified reality. In his most recent works Laxness has turned to historical subjects.

See: S. Einarsson, "A Contemporary Icelandic Author," *Life and Letters To-day*, Vol. XIV (1936), No. 4, pp. 24–30; H. Spring, review of *Salka Valka* in *Evening Standard* (London), February 6, 1936; S. Nordal, "Tvær miklar skáldsögur," *Lesbók Morgunblaðsins*, November 24, 1940.

S. E.

Lazarević, Laza K. (1851–1890, Serb short-story writer), was graduated from the faculty of law in Belgrade in 1871 and then studied medicine in Berlin, where he received a doctor's degree in 1876. During the Serbo-Turkish War of 1876 he served as a medical assistant in the Serbian army. Later, as a military physician, he lived in Belgrade. He died at the age of 39, before showing the full measure of a very great literary gift.

During his student days in Belgrade, Lazarević had adopted with enthusiasm the current ideas of the Russian socialist reformers, who were very popular in the Serbian milieu, and read and translated several Russian authors, such as Chernischevsky, Gogol, and Pisemsky. He exalted science as the liberator of mankind, translated Darwin and Faraday, and wrote a series of articles in the domain of popular medecine which were definitely useful to his country. But Lazarević was above all by nature a man of letters, sensitive, tender, and delicate. His first collection of tales, *Šest pripovedaka* (Six Stories), was published in 1886; after his death his whole narrative work was published, in 1898–1899, in two volumes (*Pripovetke;* Stories). He wrote about the Serbian region, Mačva, where he himself was born. Although Lazarević had some of the qualities of an excellent realistic writer, a gift for observing characteristic details, and an ability to present vividly and in high relief individuals and environments, he was in essence a poet and a Slavic idealist. In the conflict between the individual who wants liberation from all ties and the family which attempts to preserve tradition, a conflict which he admirably described, he always solved the problem as a conservative, on behalf of the family; the revolter is ever made to yield and to repent, whether or not this seems to square with normal experience. Lazarević conducted his narrative very skillfully, with lively dialogue, unexpected effects, really great art; all his work is infused with discreet emotional warmth. He raised Serbian fiction to the European level, and it was not by chance that his short stories were often translated. He has deservedly been called "the Serbian Turgenev (*q.v.*)."

See: J. Skerlić, *Pisci i knjige,* Vol. II (1907); P. Popović, *Jugo-Slav Stories* (1921).

P. A.

Lechoń, Jan (pseud. of Leszek Serafinowicz, 1899–, Polish poet and essayist), was born in Warsaw and educated at the Russian university in that city. At the age of 19 he burst dramatically upon the literary scene with a moving poem on the romantic poet and liberal of the 19th century, Maurycy Mochnacki, which he delivered at the gala opening of the café Pod Pikadorem (At the Sign of the Picador), the birthplace and home of *Skamander* (*see* Polish literature). Lechoń's performance on this occasion was such as to make it clear not only that Poland had a new poet, but also that the keynote of a whole new literary movement had been sounded, for the poet, while by no means repudiating the past, pleaded for emancipation from the obligation always imposed on the poets of Poland in the past to see in everything only the plight of their country. "In summer," Lechoń entreated, "let the sun be seen shining on the butterflies, and in springtime let it be the spring that I see, not Poland," and his words became the credo of the future Skamandrites.

Lechoń's poetic output was small, consisting principally of the satirical "songs from history" assembled in *Rzeczypospolita Babińska* (1921; The Babin Republic), the important *Karmazynowy poemat* (1920; "Crimson" Poem), and *Srebrne i czarne* (1924; Silver and Black), and for a while it was feared he had developed too quickly, leaving no room for future growth. During the Second World War, however, he returned to poetry with the publishing in 1942 of the volume *Lutnia po Bekwarku* (Lute to Mourning Tuned). A number of excellent critical essays also appeared from his pen in the emigration journal *Wiadomości polskie* (London; Polish News) and in the weekly *Przegląd literacki* (later *Tygodnik Polski*) published by the Polish writers in New York. Lechoń's influence on literary currents in Poland is much greater than the number of his published works would seem to indicate.

See: K. Czachowski, *Obraz współczesnej literatury polskiej,* III (1936), 103–114, 700–701.

A. P. C.

Leconte de Lisle, Charles Marie René (1818–1894, French poet), was born at Saint-Paul, on the island of Réunion. Taken to France at three, he returned to Réunion in 1828, where he spent the next nine years. The beauty of his native isle was deeply impressed on him and later inspired some of his best poetry. This period was also marked by a tragic passion for a young cousin who died prematurely and by the composition of his first verses. In 1837 he went to study law at the University of Rennes, but, more interested in poetry, he joined a group which published the short-lived literary periodical *Variété.* In 1843 he returned to Réunion, but two years later was offered a position with the *Démocratie pacifique* (Parisian Fourierist newspaper). He also contributed poems to the Fourierist monthly, *Phalange,* and thereby made the acquaintance of Thalès Bernard and Louis Ménard, both enthusiastic Hellenists. Through them he met Baudelaire and Banville (*qq.v.*).

Already a convinced republican, Leconte de Lisle was influenced by the Fourierists. He welcomed the Revolution of 1848, joined a political club, and conducted propaganda in Brittany for the *république sociale.* The elections of April 24 returned conservatives in that area. Leconte de Lisle's reaction was bitter; in a famous letter to Ménard he dubbed the people "stupid" and a "race of slaves." Nevertheless he appears to have taken some part in the June Days and to have spent 48 hours in prison. Thereafter he gave up politics, left the *Démocratie pacifique,* and took refuge in his ideal and dream of art. For years his material existence was difficult. Finally in 1864 this ardent republican yielded to "inexorable necessity" and accepted an annuity from the imperial government. When this fact was disclosed in 1870, the poet's embarrassment was acute.

Meanwhile, Leconte de Lisle achieved a commanding position in the domain of poetry. His publications include *Poèmes antiques* (1852; enlarged ed., 1874); *Poèmes et poésies* (1855); *Poésies barbares* (1862), later enlarged and reentitled *Poèmes barbares* (1872); *Les Erinnyes* (1872), a classical tragedy; *Poèmes tragiques* (1884); *L'Apollonide* (1888); *Derniers Poèmes* (1895). The first two volumes brought immediate recognition; the third definitely established him as a leader of the poets known after 1866 as the Parnassians. A group of disciples, including Catulle Mendès (*q.v.*), Léon Dierx, and José Maria de Heredia (*q.v.*), gathered about him. They met every Saturday at his apartment.

From 1852 on Leconte de Lisle turned his back on romantic lyricism and on utilitarianism (see preface to *Poèmes antiques* and to *Poèmes et poésies*). In general, holding that the poet's essential goal should be the creation of beauty and that "art and learning . . . should tend to unite," he sought his inspiration in the great civilizations and legends of the past, especially those of Greece, India, and Scandinavia. But the tropical landscapes of his native isle, the ferocious animals of the jungle, and the rapacious creatures of the ocean depths were sources of inspiration he also frequently exploited. In his evocation of animals he was perhaps influenced by the sculptors Barye and Frémiet who produced some of their best work in the 1840's and 1850's.

Many of Leconte de Lisle's poems are magnificent pictures without much intellectual content (*e.g.*, "Les Elfes," "La Vérandah," "Les Eléphants," "Le Jaguar"); they are triumphs of plastic art or musical effect. Many contain some aspect of the poet's philosophy. His ardent belief in beauty, *la sainte beauté,* is seen in "Hypatie" and "Vénus de Milo." Ancient Greece he preferred to the "industrial Pandemonium" of contemporary France, and he considered the polytheism of the Greeks superior to Christianity, which he viewed as a religion of constraint. But he displayed equal interest in the religious concepts of the ancient Indian sagas (cf. the *Bhagavata,* tr. by Burnouf in 1840; *Rig-Veda,* tr. by Langlois in 1848; *Ramayana,* tr. by Fauché in 1854). Poems such as "Bhagavat," "La Vision de Brahma," "La Maya," and "Midi" reflect in varying degree the notions of detachment, oblivion, absorption into the *néant divin,* which he found in those texts. By nature and experience Leconte de Lisle tended to be disillusioned and pessimistic. The poems "Sacra fames," "Le Vent froid de la nuit," "Solvet seclum," are bitter expressions of his view of human life and his desire to escape from its woes. In such moods he aspired, not for death in the Christian sense, but for complete annihilation. These ideas are set forth in lines so carefully composed, with such precision and restraint of language, as to give the impression of impassibility to the superficial reader. The more attentive realize that genuine passion inspired them.

The Third Republic assured the poet of his material existence by appointing him as one of the librarians of the Senate. In 1886 he was elected to the French Academy to fill the chair left vacant by Hugo. His last years were, therefore, serene and triumphant.

See: J. Dornis, *Leconte de Lisle intime* (1895); F. Calmette, *Un Demi-Siècle littéraire: Leconte de Lisle et ses amis* (1902); M. A. Leblond, *Leconte de Lisle, d'après des documents nouveaux* (1906); E. Estève, *Leconte de Lisle; l'homme et l'œuvre* (1922); I. H. Brown, *Leconte de Lisle; a Study on the Man and His Poetry, with Original Adaptations in English Verse* (1929); P. Flottes, *Le Poète Leconte de Lisle* (1929).

E. M. G.

Le Fort, Gertrud, Freiin von (1876–, German poet and novelist), born in Minden of an aristocratic Huguenot family that had found refuge in Germany, enjoyed a thorough university training in history and philosophy. After editing in 1925 the theological writings of her teacher, the Protestant philosopher Ernst Troeltsch of Heidelberg, she entered the Catholic Church. Her magnificent *Hymnen an die Kirche* (1924; Eng. tr., *Hymns to the Church,* 1937) had already been published. In the novel *Das Schweisstuch der Veronika* (1928; Eng. tr., *The Veil of Veronica,* 1932) she portrays within a single German household living in modern Rome four typical attitudes toward the Church, the "good pagan," the devout daughter of the Church, and two types of conversions. Her two historical novels *Der Papst aus dem Ghetto* (1930; Eng. tr., *The Pope from the Ghetto,* 1934) and *Die magdeburgische Hochzeit* (1939) and one historical story, *Die Letzte am Schaffott* (1931; Eng. tr., *The Song at the Scaffold,* 1933), combine the fruits of extensive research with deep poetic insight and great literary gifts. In contrast to Enrica von Handel-Mazzetti (*q.v.*), Gertrud von Le Fort has chosen historical moments of wide appeal and writes a classically pure and beautiful German that lends itself to unusually fine translation into English. It has been said of her *Hymns to the Church* that the translation is equal to the original. Her moving *Hymnen an Deutschland* (1932) with its Christian appeal to the nation has not been translated, nor has her volume of essays *Die ewige Frau, Die Frau in der Zeit, Die zeitlose Frau* (1934). *Das Reich des Kindes* (1933) is but the introduction to a longer prose epic, *Die drei Kronen,* yet to appear.

See: T. Kampmann, *Gertrud von Le Fort* (1935); G. H. Danton, "Gertrud von Le Fort," *Books Abroad,* XIII (1939), 283–288.

C. E. F.

Léger, Alexis Saint-Léger, *see* Perse, St.-J.

Lemaître, Jules (1853–1914, French critic, dramatist, and short-story writer), was born in Vennecy near Orléans, of very religious parents, teachers in the local school, who sent their son to Catholic institutions, first in Orléans and later in Paris. Lemaître's ambition was to become a professor. A brilliant student, he was admitted to the Ecole Normale Supérieure in 1872 and after graduating held teaching positions in the *lycées* at Havre and Algiers. His doctorate obtained, he taught at the universities of Besançon and Grenoble. He does not seem to have been a good teacher; early in his career belles-lettres attracted him, and he sent contributions, mostly articles of literary criticism, to periodicals such as the *XIXe Siècle* and the *Revue bleue.* In addition two small volumes of verse, Parnassian in form, *Les Médaillons* (1880) and *Petites orientales* (1883), were published. Ironically enough, it was a satirical article on Renan (*q.v.*), the writer who influenced him more than any other ("I admit I was possessed by him"), which brought his name to the attention of a larger public and made him famous almost overnight. In 1885 he succeeded J. J. Weiss (*q.v.*) as dramatic critic on the *Journal des débats.* Later the *Revue des deux mondes* likewise invited his collaboration. The greater part of his essays were collected in a series of volumes under the title *Les Contemporains* (7 vols., 1885–1899; 8th vol., 1918), and his dramatic reviews in *Impressions de théâtre* (10 vols., 1888–1898; 11th vol., 1920). Brilliantly written, they showed strong classical preferences. Lemaître's taste, however, was catholic and his curiosity wide enough to welcome new forms, new *poétiques,* the French symbolists (*see* French symbolism) as well as the Scandinavian dramatists, for instance, although not without the reservations to be expected from a disciple of Sainte-Beuve, always commending order and clarity. In 1884 he resigned his professorship to devote himself entirely to writing.

Besides his critical articles, many original works were published. His only long novel, *Les Rois* (1893), was not a success. Lemaître was at his best in the short story, in which he turned for inspiration to the legends of antiquity or to classical literature. Written in the best Anatole France (*q.v.*) manner, these charming pieces show their author as a consummate stylist, a master of elegant and lucid prose (*En marge des vieux livres,* 2 series, 1905–1907; *La Vieillesse d'Hélène,* 1914). He also tried his hand at drama. Some of his plays, *Le Député Leveau* (1890), *Mariage blanc* (1891), *L'Aînée* (1898), were well received. A definite moralizing tendency in the plays reveals a very serious side to the artist and dilettante. By 1895 Lemaître's fame especially as a critic was considerable, and he was elected that year to the French Academy. When a controversy arose between impressionist and dogmatic critics, that famous debate where "strength was pitted against charm and reason against sensibility," he was the chief impressionist standard-bearer and stood with Anatole France against Brunetière (*q.v.*), whose ponderous blows could not dent the light Heraclitean armor of his adversaries.

The Dreyfus affair marked a turning point in the life of Lemaître. In his youth, after the collapse of the Second Empire, he had hailed the advent of the Third Republic. Now he sided with the reactionaries and put what he conceived as the national interest of France above justice and fairness to a man unjustly accused. Convinced that the nation's fate was at stake, he abandoned literature to give all his time to political action. As founder and president of the Ligue de la Patrie Française he toured the country denouncing the men of the radical bloc then in power as the enemies of France and calling on the voters to elect nationalist deputies to Parliament. It was of no avail. Disappointed and discouraged, Lemaître then went over, heart and soul, to the royalist camp, where he was made most welcome and whence he continued to inveigh against the republic and democracy (*Discours royalistes,* 1908–1911;

Lettres à mon ami, 1909). During that period he was asked to give lectures on literary topics before the Société des Conférences and he chose to discuss the lives and works of great French writers. His lectures appeared later in book form, *J. J. Rousseau* (1907), *Jean Racine* (1908), *Fénelon* (1910), *Chateaubriand* (1912). These are not scholarly books in the strictest sense. Very readable, they bear the mark of having been prepared for Parisian and largely feminine audiences, and the author's political preoccupations weigh heavily on his judgment of Rousseau, the social revolutionary, and of Chateaubriand, the revolutionary in letters. But the book on Racine, who was a perennial favorite with the critic, is unspoiled by such prejudices and is by far the best of the four.

Lemaître died at Tavers in Touraine on August 5, 1914, just as the Third Republic was entering on a war which belied the writer's and his political friends' oft repeated assertion that a democratic France could not wage a victorious war.

See: V. Giraud, *Les Maîtres de l'heure,* Vol. II (1914); H. Morice, *Jules Lemaître* (1924); G. Durrière, *Jules Lemaître et le théâtre* (1934).

V. Gu.

Lemonnier, Camille (1844–1913, Belgian art critic and novelist), born in a suburb of Brussels, led an uneventful life, devoted uniquely to writing. Lovers of biographical anecdote will enjoy the monograph by his friend Maurice Des Ombiaux (*Camille Lemonnier, monographie anecdotique,* 1910). His first work, *Salon de Bruxelles* (1863), inaugurated a series of art criticism which he continued throughout his career. He spoke as a painter rather than as a littérateur and produced studies of Gustave Courbet, Alfred Stevens, Félicien Rops, and others which are still standard. Influence of plastic artists is clearly discernible in all his work. It is often easier to trace the inspiration of his novels to a painter than to any purely literary model. He prided himself on being a Proteus and always gave full vent to his lyric genius: "I have been only a creature of instinct, intoxicated by the beauty of life," he declared. His adoration of nature in all her aspects is the unifying principle of his work; it led him to commune at times with the French naturalistic school (*see* French naturalism), yet his Dionysiac temperament prohibited any suggestion of pessimism. *Le Mâle* (1881), belonging to the early period designated by Léon Bazalgette as unconscious pantheism, remains his masterpiece in fiction and offers a fair synthesis of his large output. It is realistic in the sense that it was conceived and written among the scenes and personages portrayed, but the old Flemish masters, such as Rubens, Jordaens, and Teniers, were ever guiding his eye. The theme is the free, exuberant life of forest and countryside, instinctively enjoyed with no intrusion of debatable social theories. *Le Mort* (dated by author 1878; published 1882), recalls Zola's (*q.v.*) *Thérèse Raquin,* yet an early essay on Courbet (1878) would seem not foreign to its inspiration. In sharp contrast to *Le Mâle,* it stigmatizes the physical and moral depravity of two peasants. In 1883 appeared *L'Hystérique,* beginning a belligerent defense of the claims of nature. It is based on pathological data and perhaps influenced by *La Sorcière* of Michelet, for whom Lemonnier expressed warm admiration. The subject is the misery stemming from ascetic education in a priest and the ruin of his victim in a *béguinage.* This novel marks the transition to what Bazalgette calls the second period, one of uncertain psychological groping.

Sociological tendencies appear in *Happo-Chair* (1886), dedicated to Zola, whose *Germinal* had appeared in 1885, but the Beligan author could claim priority of composition. He studies the wretched life of toilers in a rolling mill whom he had often visited in company with the painter Constantin Meunier. His sympathy is ever with the helots of civilization. At times he felt himself the victim and reacted vigorously. Thus, prosecuted at Paris in 1888 for a short story, he replied with *Le Possédé* (1890), in which he exposes the secret degradation of a magistrate, a lecherous Torquemada persecuting uncompromising art. Certain refinements of corruption here may be traced to the *Diaboliques* of Rops. Another trial, resulting in acquittal, inspired *Les Deux Consciences* (1902)—an analysis of the author's evolution as he saw it. The hero is appropriately named Wildman. There is a series of novels in which he defends the right of woman to full development of individual personality: representative are *L'Arche* (1894), the journal of a mother who rebuilds the family fortunes; *La Faute de Madame Charvet* (1895), the most successful of the psychological group; and *Le Bon Amour* (1900), where an estranged couple reunite in philanthropic activity. *Madame Lupar* (1888), with the subtitle *roman bourgeois,* exposes the mercenary vice of the heroine who dominates the story. *La Fin des bourgeois* (1893) combines naturalistic and sociological trends to conclude that society is in itself an agent of corruption; it must be retempered by a return to a state of nature.

Here then is the germ of the last period in which, led by sympathy with the naïve virtues of peasants, Lemonnier champions a conscious pantheism. Novels like *L'Ile vierge* (1897), *Adam et Eve* (1899), and *Au cœur frais de la forêt* (1900) have something of the freshness of a Theocritean idyl combined with the majesty of biblical poetry; the immediate inspiration may well have been the Edenic scenes of Velvet Breughel and nature painters such as Emile Claus and Corot. Keeping in mind the author's relation to Zola, one may call these novels his *Evangiles.* With *Le Vent dans les moulins* (1901) and *Comme va le ruisseau* (1903), he returns to reality while still remaining lyric. There are reminders that he was a convinced realist and that he dabbled in psychological and sociological fiction, but this remains in the background. He writes from love of the quiet charm of rustic life which he observed closely. His last book, *La Chanson du carillon* (1911), inspired by Rodenbach's (*q.v.*) *Bruges-la-morte* and by the paintings of Memling, crown his work, ever a hymn to the beauty of his country.

A score of collections of short stories reveal again the variety of inspiration and technique noted in the novels. Now Lemonnier presented the national life in a sympathetic, even idyllic light as in the *Contes flamands et wallons* (1875), now in somber and brutal aspects (*Ceux de la glèbe,* 1889). He could write successful children's stories (*Les Joujoux parlants,* 1892), with occasional sallies for their elders, psychological *contes* (*Dames de volupté,* 1902), tales of mystery inspired by Maeterlinck (*q.v.*) and by Poe (*La Vie secrète,* 1898), and sketches of animal life, almost a national genre among the painters. Lemonnier's vocabulary is as extensive as his subject matter, but he rarely borrows from dialect—he seeks primarily picturesque expression and shades. For him a writer is a creator of forms to which all else is subordinated: "The word gives birth to the idea," he declared. His place is among the romantic colorists rather than with thinkers and moralists.

See: G. Rency, *Camille Lemonnier* (1922); G. Vanwelkenhuyzen, *L'Influence du naturalisme français en Belgique* (1930); F. Russell Pope, *Nature in the Work of Camille Lemonnier* (1933); H. Landau, *Camille Lemonnier* (1936).

B. M. W.

Lenéru, Marie (1875–1918, French playwright), was born in Brest, the daughter of a naval officer. She became deaf at an early age and died almost blind. Isolated from the world, she spent her time reading and writing. Her first essays appeared in the *Mercure de France* under the pen name Antoine Morsain.

Marie Lenéru conceived of drama as a means to express ideas and to discuss problems. Six plays established her reputation. She presented the right to love freely in *Les Affranchis* (1910), the crime of treason in *Le Redoutable* (1912), a case of professional jealousy in *La Triomphante* (1918), the question of war and peace in *La Paix* (written in 1915 but not produced until 1921). Two more plays were produced posthumously, *La Maison sur le roc* (1924) and *Le Bonheur des autres* (1925). These pieces belong to the "theatre of ideas" (*see* Curel, François de). Without avoiding entirely the pitfalls of the problem play, they are nevertheless good theatre, the earnest and sincere manifestation of a mature mind, familiar with austere thinkers such as Marcus Aurelius, Pascal, and Barrès (*q.v.*). A picture of Marie Lenéru's physical and spiritual life can be found in the diary she kept from the age of 10, *Journal* (2 vols., 1922).

See: François de Curel, "Marie Lenéru," *Revue de France,* Année I (1921), Tome II, pp. 715–741; *Revue française,* November 13, 1927 (special number); Suzanne Lavaud, *Marie Lenéru; sa vie, son journal* (1932).

M. E. C.

Lenormand, Henri René (1882–, French dramatist), outstanding interpreter of the *théâtre de l'inquiétude,* was born in Paris. He was a son of the composer René Lenormand, whose predilection for oriental music profoundly influenced him and who instilled in him the wanderlust which took the playwright all over the world in search of dramatic material. Following a brief apprenticeship as a writer of melodramatic sketches for the Grand Guignol, Lenormand's first real play, *Les Possédés* (1909), while still immature, gave evidence of the peculiarly searching insight into man's subconscious motivations which forms the mainspring of his theatre (*e.g., Une Vie secrète,* 1929, and *Les Trois Chambres,* 1931, also devoted to analysis of an artist's personality). In 1911 he married the Dutch actress, Marie Kalff, who has since interpreted many roles in his plays. Discharged from the army for reasons of health during the First World War, Lenormand found in the convalescent atmosphere of a Swiss sanatorium a firsthand opportunity to study the psychology of fear and its morbid effect on the human soul (see *Le Lâche,* produced in 1925; Eng. tr., *The Coward,* 1928).

In 1919 Lenormand met the actor-producer Georges Pitoëff (*q.v.*) in Switzerland and formed an association which later expanded to include the leading producers of the *théâtre d'avant-garde,* Firmin Gémier and Gaston Baty (*q.v.*). Pitoëff produced *Le Temps est un songe* (Eng. tr., *Time Is a Dream,* 1923) in Geneva in 1919 and in Paris later the same year. This drama, the first of Lenormand's modern prose tragedies, portrays human destiny chained to the wheel of time in which past, present, and future are telescoped into a tragic dénouement. While this play brought wide critical acclaim, it was Gémier's production of *Les Ratés* (1920; Eng. tr., *Failures,* 1923) which started Lenormand on his world-wide success. *Les Ratés,* later produced in New York by the Theatre Guild in 1924, depicts the tragic career of a playwright and his actress wife, their physical and moral disintegration under the pressure of adversity. *Le Simoun* (1920), a study of the deleterious influence of the tropics on the subconscious incestuous passion of a father for his 18-year-old daughter, develops further the theme of man confronted by the powers of evil. Herein, too, Lenormand analyzes the problem of what the critic Edmond Sée has called "a climatic fatality" which undermines the morale and sanity of its victims. To reflect the elemental in human psychology, the author here and elsewhere has resorted to elemental forces of nature (a soul-sapping desert simoon, a menacing jungle, a mountain peak). Indeed, as some of his very titles suggest (*e.g., A l'ombre du mal,* 1924), Lenormand's plays are bathed in an atmosphere of Baudelairian evil (*see* Baudelaire) where flit the lurking phantoms of the subconscious soul.

The widely acclaimed *Le Mangeur de rêves* (1922; Eng. tr., *The Dream Doctor,* 1928) opens the series of psychoanalytical plays. Although Lenormand has vehemently denied that his theatre is based on Freudian abstractions, it is true that his characters are largely psychopathic. They present remarkably dramatic material to this modern prober of the soul, personified in *Le Mangeur de rêves* by Luc de Bronte, the "devourer of dreams" who delves into the subconscious life of his patients in order to free them from their inhibitions. *L'Homme et ses fantômes* (1924; Eng. tr., *Man and His Phantoms,* 1928) continues the psychoanalytical theme and portrays the subconscious life of a contemporary Don Juan. *Asie* (1931), a reworking of the Medea legend, and *Pacifique* (1937) revert to the climatic theme and analyze the ethnological problem of miscegenation.

Lenormand tries continually to identify himself with an amoral system which, rejecting the ideas of God and Devil, seeks ever, and ever through disillusionment, a natural and self-sufficing truth. In crude phraseology, the conflict is one between faith and science, between conscience (which Sarterre in *Une Vie secrète* calls "the cholera of modern man") and reason, between the dark ages as understood by Lenormand and his interpretation of the 20th century. This is the battlefield of his tragic dramas.

See: Henry Daniel-Rops, *Sur le théâtre de H.-R. Lenormand* (1926); John Palmer, *Studies in the Contemporary Theatre* (1927), pp. 65–93; A. J. Dickman, "Le Mal, force dramatique chez Lenormand," *Romanic Review, XIX* (1928), 218–231.

E. S.

León-Felipe (pseud. of León Felipe Camino, 1884–, Spanish poet), born in the province of Salamanca, has been defined by an American critic, B. D. Wolfe, as "the humblest and simplest of Spain's poets . . . at once mystic and equalitarian." He became known in Madrid with the volume *Versos y oraciones de caminante* (1920). It is a fitting title, for he has spent his life in wandering without apparent purpose, carrying about within him two preponderant emotions which he has unified in his work—poetry and a religious sense of life. Shortly after the publication of his poems he accepted a position as pharmacist (his professional career) in the African possession of Fernando Po. At the time it seems that some of his friends thought of a repetition of Rimbaud's (*q.v.*) flight. Later he established himself in Mexico. He has also lived for some time in the United States (teaching Spanish at Cornell University), in Spain, Panama, and France. His second book, *Versos y oraciones de caminante, Libro II* (1930), was published in New York by the Hispanic Institute. Here, to the intimate lyricism of a man without faith or roots in life which characterized his early poems, was added a strong influence of Whitman, whose work he has recently translated. His poetry now had a deep concern with the destiny of man and a slightly prophetic manner, intensified afterwards in the poem *Drop a Star* (1933) and in the books which followed. In an age of aesthetic and intellectual poetry León-Felipe has been a poet of moral accent. His moral attitude—poetry as a redeeming force of human evils and sorrows—springs from his interior life, but is identified at the same time with an almost mystical feeling for the tormented longings, the faith, and the failures of a quixotic and eternal Spain.

León-Felipe returned to Spain during the civil war thinking that a poet like himself, devoted to the cause of truth, justice, and freedom, had a mission to fulfill in the struggle of his people. At the end he went back to Mexico. In books and poems, written at times with an elegiac, prophetic, and despairing tone, at times with a dark humor (*El payaso de las bofetadas y el pescador de caña,* 1938; *El hacha,* 1939; *El español del éxodo y del llanto,* 1939), he has expressed the anguish of the defeated and exiled Spaniards and mingled it with his own. Poetry has become for him, in a sort of depersonalized lyricism, an arm for the liberation of man whom he sees threatened today by the destructive forces of man's selfishness. He has published recently *Ganarás la luz* (1943), a poetic confession of faith summing up most of his whole work and attitude.

See: B. D. Wolfe, "León Felipe, Poet of Spain's Tragedy," *American Scholar,* XII (1943), 330–338.

A. del R.

Leonov, Leonid (1899–, Russian novelist), born in Moscow, began his literary career by writing short stories in which he gave marked proof of stylistic instinct and versatility, with appreciable reminiscences of Dostoevski (*q.v.*). His first novel, *Barsuki* (The Badgers), appeared in 1924 and deals with the clash between town and village. Still reminiscent of Dostoevski his second novel, *Vor* (1925; Eng. tr., *The Thief,* 1931), describes a man tortured by remorse until he no longer lives sanely and becomes a gangster. In the end he achieves some hopes of recovery by a return to agricultural pursuits. In this novel the trace of Dostoevski is to be found in Leonov's constant search for the individualizing traits in human beings, his humane attachment for his fellow men, and his realistic portrayal of outcasts from bourgeois society. But where Dostoevski's basic philosophy was "salvation through suffering," Leonov pursues a more materialistic and infallible solution.

With *Sot* (1930; Eng. tr., *Sot,* 1931, American title, *Soviet River,* 1932) he offered a characteristic five-year plan construction novel relating to the erection of a paper mill on a North Russian water course, covering the whole project for the electrification and industrialization of the stream. Here the conflict is between the retrograde past and the progressive present. The Communists are opposed by the monks of an adjacent monastery, neighboring peasants instinctively cling to the old and fear the new, and the work of the builders is menaced by saboteurs. In spite of the routine plot, Leonov's character-drawing is as searching as in his earlier fiction.

In *Skutarevski* (1933; Eng. tr., 1936) Leonov discusses the problem of integrating middle-class specialists into socialist life. Skutarevski himself, a world-famous scientist, had always thought of himself as a solitary individual without much community with the surrounding masses. While on a special mission for Lenin he is introduced to a completely new ideology which he learns to understand and love. Through his younger associates Skutarevski comes into contact with factory workers, and his crowning achievement consists in reading to a group of them a treatise he has composed. Only in socialist society has he become fully aware of his existence as a responsible member of the human race instead of an isolated atom.

Leonov's plots appear on the whole schematic, but his psychological adroitness, evidently learned from Dostoevski, lends them additional and sometimes even engrossing interest.

See: G. Reavey and M. Slonim, *Soviet Literature; an Anthology* (1934), pp. 195–203; G. Struve, *25 Years of Soviet Russian Literature* (1944), pp. 42–49, 261–264.

S. H. C.

León y Román, Ricardo (1877–1943, Spanish novelist), was born in Málaga, the son of an officer in the Spanish army. His father's untimely death made it necessary for him to give up early plans for a military career. He found employment, instead, with the Bank of Spain, first in its Málaga branch, later in Santander and in Madrid. His duties at the bank left him some leisure for writing, and he began to contribute poems and articles to the local newspapers. In 1901 his collected poems were published in a volume called *Lira de bronce*. His first novel, the story of a nobly born youth who neglects his ancient heritage for the frivolous gratification of his restless desires, was completed in 1905 and given the title *El alma de las ruinas*. After having been repeatedly rejected by Madrid publishers, it finally appeared in Málaga in 1908 as *Casta de hidalgos* (Eng. tr., *A Son of the Hidalgos,* 1921). It had immediate, overwhelming success. It was followed during the next four years by other novels—*Comedia sentimental* (1909), a tale of a late-flowering passion; *Alcalá de los Zegríes* (1909), the story of a conflict between a man's political ambitions and his domestic responsibilities; *El amor de los amores* (1910), a demonstration of the superiority of sacred to profane love; *Los centauros* (1912), an indictment of the futility and shallowness of modern life—by another book of poems, *Alivio de caminantes* (1911), and by *La escuela de los sofistas* (1910), a series of Socratic dialogues dealing with literature, science, and religion. All these early works are distinguished by a carefully wrought style, a rich background of regional color, and a marked ethical tendency.

Brought up in the conservative tradition of reverence for throne and altar, León was never converted to 20th-century liberalism with its belief in scientific progress and political democracy. Unlike most Spanish writers of his generation who, shocked by the national catastrophe of 1898, thought that their country's hope for the future lay in its gradual Europeanization, León steadfastly maintained that it was Spain's destiny to restore Christian morality to Europe by a rebirth of those virtues which had graced the Spaniards of the golden age. From 1912 to 1922 he wrote no novels, but produced two volumes of essays proclaiming this creed, *La voz de la sangre* (1915) and *Los caballeros de la cruz* (1916), as well as three volumes of his impressions of the First World War, *Europa trágica* (1918–1920). During the war years 1914–1918 he traveled as correspondent through the belligerent and neutral countries of Europe. His political and religious convictions were strengthened by what he saw there. The novels which appeared after 1922 became increasingly works of propaganda, arguments against the evils which he believed to be destroying the world: *Amor de caridad* (1922), against the philosophy of cynicism: *Humos de rey* (1923), against the irreligious frivolity of the younger generation; *El hombre nuevo* (1925), against the fallacies of "progress"; *Los trabajadores de la muerte* (1927), against the international "war makers"; *Jauja* (1928), against the vulgarities of modern life; *Las niñas de mis ojos* (1929), against the exaggerations of feminism; *Bajo el yugo de los bárbaros* (1932), against the revolution of 1931; *Roja y gualda* (1934), against the policies of the Second Republic. The program with which the Falangist Party entered the civil war (1936–1939) embodied the principal tenets of León's creed. After the party's triumph he wrote a novel entitled *Cristo en los infiernos* (1942?).

See: J. Casares, *Crítica profana* (1915), pp. 245–348; Andrenio (E. Gómez de Baquero), *Novelas y novelistas* (1918), pp. 245–270; J. T. Reid, *Modern Spain and Liberalism* (1937), pp. 139–225.

E. H. H.

Lerberghe, Charles van, *see* Van Lerberghe.

Lersch, Heinrich (1889–1936, German poet and novelist), was born at München-Gladbach, learned the trade of his father, a boilermaker, and traveled extensively in Germany, Switzerland, Austria, Italy, Belgium, and Holland. He took part in the First World War and established his literary fame with his song *Soldatenabschied* (1914). After the war he continued his father's business for a while, but gave it up in 1925 in order to devote himself exclusively to his writing. He died at Bodendorf.

Lersch is essentially a lyric writer with a strong tendency towards the philosophical and even the mystical. Although an ardent student of socialistic theories, he never became a member of the powerful Social Democratic Party because he did not believe in class war and revolution. Instead of preaching the destruction of the machine and of the social political system built thereupon (as the expressionistic activists did), he attempted an inner reconciliation of the individual with the machine by depriving both of their absolute power and by making them equally important factors in the creation of a national brotherhood based on love and sacrifice. The spiritual ruler in this ethical community being Jesus Christ, Lersch's original Catholicism assumed the form of a realistic mysticism which sanctifies life and makes of art, science, nature, technics, and industries creative contributors in the divine symphony. The form and style of Lersch's poetry is as undogmatic as his philosophy. Although stanzas and rhymes predominate in his earlier works (*Abglanz des Lebens,* 1914; *Herz, aufglühe dein Blut,* 1916; *Deutschland,* 1917), he never follows conventional patterns, but takes great liberties with rhythm and choice of words, often going to forced extremes. In his later poetic works (*Mensch im Eisen,* 1924; *Stern und Amboss,* 1926; *Mit brüderlicher Stimme,* 1934) he definitely finds his own musical form; the power of Luther, the sublimity of Klopstock, the impetuosity of Beethoven, and the dynamic realism of Walt Whitman are welded together into a forceful symphony. In his prose books (*Hammerschläge,* 1931; *Mut und Übermut,* 1934; *Die Pioniere von Eilenburg,* 1934; *Im Pulsschlag der Ma-*

schinen, 1935) Lersch describes, sometimes with grotesque humor, but always with deep earnestness, experiences of his own wanderings and the sorrows, longings, and pleasures of his fellow workers; in *Manni* (1927) he portrays with striking charm and simplicity the development of his son.

See: A. Soergel, *Dichtung und Dichter der Zeit,* Neue Folge: *Im Banne des Expressionismus,* 4. Auflage (1927), pp. 531–538; W. Mahrholz, *Deutsche Literatur der Gegenwart* (1930), pp. 277–278, 436–437; F. Lennartz, *Die Dichter unserer Zeit* (1938), pp. 175–176.

E. J.

Leśmian, Bolesław (pseud. of Bolesław Lesman, 1878–1937, Polish poet), was born in Warsaw and educated in Kiev. His early poems appeared in *Życie* (Life), the organ of Young Poland (*see* Polish literature), and in its Warsaw counterpart, *Chimera.* A poet of the imagination, divorced from reality and embracing with passion every experience of the senses, Leśmian was one of the few living poets in Free Poland linked with the neo-romantics of the Young Poland movement. A poet not for the masses but for other poets, Leśmian won notice among the latter for his collection *Łąka* (1920; The Meadow). *Napój cienisty* (1936; Shadowy Potion) and the posthumous *Dziejba leśna* (1938; Sylvan Tale) are representative of Leśmian's later style. Several of Edgar Allan Poe's tales have found their way into Polish through Leśmian's translations.

See: K. Czachowski, *Obraz współczesnej literatury polskiej,* II (1934), 64–68, 380–381; A. Szczerbowski, *Bolesław Leśmian* (1938).

A. P. C.

Lettish literature or **Latvian literature.** Under the influence of the German romanticists and the ancient Latin poets studied in school, there arose in the middle of the 19th century a genuine Lettish literature in those parts of the Baltic provinces which in 1918 were to form the republic of Latvia. Launched by the patriots Christian Valdemārs (1825–1891), George Alūnāns (1832–1864), and Christian Barons (1835–1923), Lettish national romanticism (about 1850–1890), often undiscriminating and uncritical in the choice of material, drew its inspiration primarily from folk poetry and legendary antiquities. In spite of serious efforts, none of the poets of that period excelled in their achievement the natural beauty of the folk songs collected by Christian Barons in *Latvju Dainas* (7 vols., 1894–1915; Lettish Folk Songs). After 1890 the Russian socialist movement began to express itself in Lettish, where it was directed against the German ruling class, but German literary movements still continued their influence. The impressionistic movement reached Latvia around the turn of the century and was represented by several persons who later were to play an important role in Lettish letters (especially Aspazija, whose *Sarkanās puķes,* Crimson Flowers, was published in 1897). Rudolf Blaumanis (1863–1908) wrote technically efficient plays in a realistic style, *e.g.,* the comedy *Skroderdienas Silmačos* (1902; Tailoring Days in Silmači) and the tragedies *Pazudušais dēls* (1893; The Prodigal Son), *Indrāni* (1903; The Indrānses), and *Ugunī* (1914; In the Furnace). Neo-romanticism continued the earlier national movement with which it shared a strong interest in folklore. Some of the outstanding Lettish writers are neo-romanticists, *e.g.,* the lyrists Anna Brigadere (1861–1933) and Karl Skalbe (1879–), and, towering over all the others, Rainis (pseud. of John Pliekšāns, 1865–1929).

Rainis, the leading figure in Lettish literature, was both a poet and a political leader; he had to spend part of his life as a refugee abroad. After the establishment of the Latvian republic he was elected to Parliament and in 1927 became minister of education. His literary career began with a translation of Goethe's *Faust* (1898) which was followed by original verse, chiefly lyrical. However, his greatest achievement lies in the dramatic field. His first drama, *Uguns un nakts* (Fire and Night), appeared in 1905, to be followed in later years by *Zelta zirgs* (1910; The Golden Horse), *Induls un Arija* (1911; Induls and Aria), *Pūt, vējiņi* (1913; Blow, Breeze), *Jāzeps un viņa brāļi* (1919; Joseph and His Brethren), *Ilja Muromietis* (1923; Ilja of Murom), and others. Aspazija (pseud. of Elsa Rozenberge, 1868–), the leading woman writer, was Rainis's wife, and the two shared a prestige hardly paralleled in the literature of any other nation. Aspazija, who had started out in 1894 with the drama *Vaidelote* (The Vestal) and soon added socialism and romantic impressionism to her activities, had enriched Lettish literature with an imposing body of poetry and drama. Representative of her later lyric poetry are *Asteru laikā* (1927; In Aster Time) and *Dvēseles ceļojums* (1933; A Soul's Journey). In the field of modern fiction, Andrew Niedra (1871–1942) and Jacob Janševskis (1865–1931) deserve mention. Niedra, a Lutheran pastor, established his reputation with excellent novels and stories dealing with pre-war Lettish life and aspirations.

Since he headed a pro-German government during the German occupation of the First World War, he had to go into exile after the establishment of the independent Latvian republic. Janševskis, who had started in 1890 as a poet in the national vein, obtained prominence as a novelist after the war with *Dzimtene* (1921–25; Native Earth), *Bandava* (1928), and *Mežvidus ļaudis* (1929; Mid-Forest Folk).

The nationalistic trends innate to Lettish literature were even more emphasized after 1934 when Latvia came under an authoritarian regime. A special attempt was made to put dramatic production in the service of the new system. As in Germany, the open-air theatre with gigantic pageants was especially used for this purpose.

See: T. Zeiferts, "Latviešu nacionālā literātūra," in *Latvieši, Rakstu krājums* (1930); U. Katzenelenbogen, *The Daina; an Anthology of Lithuanian and Latvian Folk-Songs with a Critical Study and a Preface* (1935); W. K. Matthews, *The Tricolour Sun; Latvian Lyrics in English Versions, an Essay on Latvian Poetry, and Critical Commentaries* (1936); R. Kroders, *Le Théâtre des fêtes lettonnes* (1937).

A. Se.

Levertin, Oskar (1862–1906, Swedish poet, critic, and writer of prose fiction), was born at Norrköping in the south of Sweden and studied at Uppsala. Later he taught in Stockholm and wrote reviews. He lived under the shadow of ill health and spent much time in Davos, where he became intimate with Verner von Heidenstam. Of Jewish extraction, he early developed the lonely, introspective mood of the Orient. Yet he exerted a wide influence in his time as poet, short-story writer and critic.

There is a rich and haunting grace in his *Legender och visor* (1891; Legends and Songs), although his poetry may often appear somewhat oppressive, like the perfume of hothouse flowers. He is nearly always the self-absorbed visionary, in an ivory tower. The mystic note comes out most strongly in *Kung Saloms och Morolf* (1905; King Solomon and Morolf). In his prose creations, especially in *Rokokonoveller* (1899; Stories of Rococo), he is more objective and even develops a lively wit. An accomplished scholar and teacher, he interested himself deeply in the past of Sweden, writing with charm and penetration of art, literature, and history. The realistic trend of his contemporaries did not please him, and he was slow to recognize even such a genius as Fröding. With Heidenstam he had a greater affinity through the cosmopolitan outlook which they shared.

It is as a lover of beauty, both in prose and verse, that he stands out most conspicuously. His sensitivity is exquisite, his command of phrase and imagery unerring. His most stimulating motif is the joy of his artist solitude on a snow-clad peak lifted far above the common throng, where he "may quaff the blue disdain of the crystal ether." It is a proof of Sweden's catholicity of taste that a writer with Levertin's *morbidezza* is cherished in the country of his spiritual adoption.

See: C. W. Stork, *Anthology of Swedish Lyrics* (1917; revised and enlarged ed., 1930); J. Mortensen, *Från Röda rummet till sekelskiftet* (1919); F. Böök, *Sveriges moderna litteratur* (1921), also published as Vol. III of O. Sylwan, ed., *Svenska litteraturens historia* (1919–1921), pp. 212–238.

C. W. S.

Libedinski, Yuri (1898–, Russian novelist and playwright), was born in the Urals, son of a physician. After graduation from a technical school he joined the Communist Party in 1920 and devoted himself to activity in proletarian literary organizations. In the 20's Libedinski belonged to the October Group and was one of the editors of the literary review *Na postu* (On Guard). In his novels and short stories he attempted to portray various types of Russian Communists (*Nedelya,* 1922, Eng. tr., *A Week,* 1923; *Zavtra,* 1923, Tomorrow; *Komissary,* 1923, The Commissars; *Na povorote,* 1929, The Turning Point). *Nedelya,* which describes revolutionary events in a provincial town, with emphasis on their international implications, was hailed by Soviet critics as a transition from romantic abstraction to concrete realism in Russian modern prose. In *Rozhdeniye geroya* (1930; The Birth of a Hero) Libedinski tried not only to represent his protagonists as men of action absorbed in the gigantic task of reconstruction, but also as human beings, whose life is commanded by love, anxiety, or other emotions. In the controversy on methods of Soviet literature, which divided the writers of the U.S.S.R. in the early 30's, Libedinski declared himself a disciple of the Tolstoyan school (*see* Tolstoy, Leo) of psychological realism. He stated that "spontaneous impressions form the foundations of art." During the war Libedinski published *Gvardeitsy* (1942; The Guards), a broad picture of heroic deeds and hardships of a Red army division on the Russo-German Southern front. Libedinski's main aim is to combine the social novel with the analysis of psychological motivations of human actions. His plays (*e.g.*, *Vysoty*, 1929, The Heights) are less popular in the U.S.S.R. than his novels.

M. S.

Lidin, Vladimir (1894–, Russian novelist and short-story writer), born in Moscow, son of a businessman, was graduated from the Moscow Institute of Oriental Languages and later from the University of Moscow in law. He worked in army auxiliary services during the First World War, served four years in the Red army, traveled extensively throughout the U.S.S.R. and Europe. Lidin started to write before the Revolution. His first two books of short stories, which bore the mark of Chekhov's and Bunin's (*qq.v.*) influence, were published in 1916 and 1917. Since 1923 Lidin has published several novels and hundreds of short stories, closely related in their style and literary devices to the Russian realism of the beginning of the 20th century. His best novels are *Renegat* (1927; The Renegade), a broad picture of Muscovite life during the period of NEP (New Economic Policy); *Iskateli* (1929; The Seekers), devoted to Siberian gold diggers; *Veliki ili Tikhi* (1932; The Pacific), in which the nature and social conditions of the Russian Far East are vividly represented. He is less successful in *Mogila neizvestnogo soldata* (1931; The Unknown Soldier's Grave), an attempt to show the decline and moral disintegration of the ruling classes in France. Lidin is at his best when he depicts the Russian extreme North and the struggle of strong willful men against inhospitable nature. His descriptions of nature also occupy an important part in his short stories. Soviet critics classify Lidin among the representatives of the old intelligentsia who knew how to adapt themselves to the new regime. A skillful and intelligent writer, Lidin however lacks power and originality; his style is heavy and slightly pompous. In 1941–1944 Lidin served as war correspondent on various sectors of the Russo-German front and wrote war stories.

M. S.

Lidman, Sven (1882–, Swedish lyric poet and novelist), born in Karlskrona, is the most striking example of the uncompromising extremist among living Swedish authors. He began his literary career with a number of volumes of poetry and drama (*Pasiphaë*, 1904; *Primavera*, 1905; *Källorna*, 1906, The Springs; *Elden och altaret*, 1907, Fire and the Altar; *Imperia*, 1907; and *Härskare*, 1918, Masters) which express in the most daring forms a philosophy of sensuality combined with a superman complex. But in the middle period of his development Lidman turned to strenuous preaching of concepts of social responsibility, moral duty, and the necessity of sacrifice in a series of genealogical novels on the Silfverstååhl family, beginning with *Stensborg* (1910), and closing with *Tvedräktens barn* (1913; Children of Dissension). This remarkable evolution ended in his becoming a fanatical convert to the present-day Swedish Pentecostal movement. Though there is a fairly obvious psychological consistency in this whirligig of extremist positions, the various rapid metamorphoses that Lidman undergoes are difficult enough otherwise to follow and explain; and the effect on his literary production has not always been happy. Of his work the novels are unquestionably best. Lidman's plays are of no importance. His lyric poetry is vivid and colorful and technically fluid and efficient; but it is frequently overflorid, wordy, and monotonous—at times, indeed, all but hysterical in its strained searching for sensual intensities of an at least half-perverse kind. It is on the whole little more than an immature Swedish rehash of Baudelaire (*q.v.*) and Swinburne.

The Silfverstååhl novels, on the other hand, are much more noteworthy, especially in their handling of episode and milieu, and on occasion in their treatment of character. In general construction they are weaker. It should be mentioned also that the heroic ethical theme of these novels, worked out against an immediate Swedish background, is of some interest as a contribution to a kind of activist nationalism which played a certain interesting if not very important part in internal political discussion in Sweden during the First World War, when Lidman was the publisher of *Svensk lösen* (Swedish Watchword), a periodical devoted to the Swedish activist program of the day. Lidman's growing religious preoccupations during these years, however, are responsible for his best novel, *Huset med de gamla fröknarna* (1918; The House with the Spinsters), a sympathetic and on the whole subtly penetrating account of the withdrawn existences of some elderly ladies of a disappearing gentle class, who find themselves neglected and forgotten by a thoughtless, brutal modern world which worships only material success, but who manage somehow to retain their spiritual identity in the midst of all the hostile forces about them. This quiet, pathos-filled tale is prophetic of Lidman himself, who, in 1921, withdrew from "the things of this world" and became a member of a despised religious sect, Friends of the Pentecost. Since this date his production has restricted itself to strictly religious themes, mostly in the form of devotional works and sermons.

See: O. Levertin, *Svensk litteratur,* I (1908); S. Söderman, *Böcker och författare* (1918); F. Böök, *Resa kring svenska Parnassen* (1926) pp. 116–141; K. Strömberg, *Modern svensk litteratur* (1932) pp. 122–126; G. Castrén, *Den nya tiden, 1870–1914* (1932), Vol. VII of H. Schück and K. Warburg, *Illustrerad svensk litteratur-historia,* 3d ed., pp. 455–461.

A. G.

Lie, Jonas (1833–1909, Norwegian novelist), was born at Eiker, near Drammen, in southern Norway, but when he was only five years old the family removed to Tromsö. This arctic town, with the glamor of its nightless summers and the terror of its winter storms, with the excitement of fishing and seafaring, and with the exotic element furnished by Russian traders, Lapps, and Finns, became the inspiration of the future author. His first book, a short novel entitled *Den fremsynte* (1870; Eng. tr., *The Visionary,* 1894), is a delicate and frangible love story against a Nordland background. After some less successful books came his masterpiece, *Lodsen og hans hustru* (1874; Eng. tr., *The Pilot and His Wife,* 1876), followed by *Rutland* (1880) and *Gaa paa* (1882; Go Ahead). These were novels of the seafaring class, which in Norway is part of the middle class, but were tales of family life rather than sea stories properly speaking, though they contain magnificent descriptions of storms at sea. In *Gaa paa* Jonas Lie created his favorite type of hero, the young enterprising practical man who burns with lust of action and shatters traditions, somewhat on the American late 19th-century order. It was the author's reaction against the academic and bureaucratic traditions that throttled life in Norway.

In *Familien paa Gilje* (1883; Eng. tr., *The Family at Gilje,* 1920) Lie gave a sympathetic picture of life in the milieu to which he himself belonged, the professional and official class. In his early stories he had created a new type of heroine, strong, self-reliant, generous, and warmhearted—removed as far as possible from the romantic Griselda type. In *The Family at Gilje* he shows himself sensitively aware of how women in the educated classes were oppressed. The mother, isolated from all social contacts, is worn out by the endless tasks of a big household with its army of servants and dependents; the daughters are pushed into marriages with elderly suitors, because their young lovers have no prospect of being able to provide homes for them. But in spite of its tragic conflicts *The Family at Gilje* has an idyllic charm which, together with its veracity, places it at the head of Lie's production. *Kommandørens døtre* (1886; Eng. tr., *The Commodore's Daughters,* 1892) is a more bitter arraignment of the social tyranny that ruins the happiness of young girls. *Et samliv* (1887; A Marriage) describes how happiness dribbles out because husband and wife are not companions. *Livsslaven* (1883; Eng. tr., *One of Life's Slaves,* 1895), a story of the slums, and *Maisa Jons* (1888), the tale of a poor seamstress, were Lie's contribution to the social discussion of the day. In general, however, although Lie sympathized with all who suffered, he refused to follow the lead of Copenhagen and turn his stories into a platform of debate on the problems of the day. As a consequence the Brandes brothers ignored him, and his contemporaries at home found fault with him, but to the modern reader he seems to have lost less with the passage of time than those who criticized him.

Jonas Lie won the enduring affection of his countrymen with his clear-eyed stories of everyday family life which always brought a thrill of recognition. As he grew older, however, a submerged mystical quality rose to the surface in his mind and found expression in two volumes of short stories, *Trold* (1891–1892; Trolls), in which Lapp magic and Norwegian superstition are strangely blended. They conceive of human beings as still in part bound by the mysterious forces of nature. Many of these little stories are classics of their kind, written in a simple epic style that contrasts with the scintillating, impressionistic style of his novels. In his later novels, written somewhat in the old manner, there is a new element of pessimism and a persistence of the belief in obscure forces working in the human mind for evil. This is true, for instance, of *Onde magter* (1890; Evil Powers), *Niobe* (1893), and *Dyre Rein* (1896).

Jonas Lie was very happily married to his cousin, Thomasine Lie, who collaborated in his work. They lived for many years abroad, in Rome, Paris, and Berchtesgaden, but returned in 1906 to spend their old age in Norway. It was not for long. She died in 1907, he in 1909.

See: A. Garborg, *Jonas Lie* (1893); H. A. Larsen, "Jonas Lie," *American-Scandinavian*

Review, XXI (1933), 461–471; A. Gustafson, *Six Scandinavian Novelists* (1940), pp. 25–72.
H. A. L.

Liliencron, Detlev von (1844–1909, German poet), was born at Kiel, spent most of his life in North Germany, and died in Hamburg. His father, a baron, lived in straitened circumstances as a customs official; his mother, Adeline von Harten, born in Philadelphia, was the daughter of a general of German origin who had served under George Washington. Liliencron fought and was wounded in the war of 1866 against Austria and in the Franco-Prussian War. To his deep regret, the young officer had to resign from the army because of debts. From 1875 to 1877 he eked out a miserable existence in the United States as a painter, trainer of horses, teacher of piano and language, and pianist in beer halls. After a few years of service as a minor governmental official, he resigned in 1885 and devoted himself to letters. Throughout much of his life he was harassed by creditors.

Liliencron never lost his enthusiasm for military life; his early experiences as a soldier made an indelible impression on him and are portrayed again and again in his writings. He was a lover of music, horses, dogs, hunting, forests, fields, moors, fens, his native North German heath, streams, and the tempestuous North Sea. A man of elemental vigor, he reveled in outdoor life; he viewed nature with senses that were keenly alert, and the impressionistic character of much of his writing is due to this sensibility and a marked gift of vivid reproduction. Although there are elements of naturalism and particularly of impressionism in his writings, he belonged to no school and was not given to theorizing on art.

Liliencron was an ardent admirer of women, of their physical charm, vitality, beauty, and strength of affection. When he wrote of love, it usually was requited love, with its exultation, healthy sensuousness, and vibrant joy. Although he chided human foibles, he had too much energy and joy of living to be a pessimist. His works reveal the repose, freedom, companionship, deepening of life and instinct, that he found in animate nature.

As a writer of longer, sustained works Liliencron had little success. His dramas (*e.g.*, *Knut der Herr*, 1885; *Die Merowinger*, 1888) lack significant character portrayal, compelling motivation, and carefully developed plots. Although they contain occasional elements of poetic beauty, they have not proved effective on the stage. After 1888 he wrote no more plays. In the novel, too, he found it difficult to construct well-rounded, unified plots (*Mäzen*, 1890; *Mit dem linken Ellbogen*, 1899). Their structure is weak and episodical; the characters reflect the author, his experiences, traits, tastes, and desires. As a narrator Liliencron was at his best in short, vivid, impressionistic sketches such as his *Kriegsnovellen* (1895), in which there are momentary pictures with high lights and vivid coloring. Though he loved the life of the soldier, he portrayed its hardships, privations, suffering, and horror as well as its adventuresomeness, comradeship, heroism, and stimulating excitement. His lengthy verse epic, *Poggfred*, written over a long period of years, from 1896 to 1906, lacks unity of form, theme, and structure. It too presents a picture of the author's own inner life, and since he often abandoned himself to the caprice of the moment, form and content are not always in harmony. Much of *Poggfred* represents a compensatory ideal, an escape from the shortcomings of troublesome reality.

In his ballads (*Balladen-Chronik*, 1906) there is much of the eerie gruesomeness of the folk ballad. Many of their themes are drawn from old chronicles and legends, from the history of his ancestors and of Schleswig-Holstein. Liliencron's highest achievement is in the lyric (*Adjutantenritte*, 1883; *Gesammelte Gedichte*, 1897). His best lyrics are spontaneous, their suggestive imagery has a warm, sensuous appeal to eye and ear, their effect is direct and immediate. He had a marked sense of rhythm, used a great variety of stanza forms, disliked impure rimes, and used embellishments of verse with considerable restraint. His wide range of diction was enriched by the vigorous dialect of his region; he derived many daring and sharply pointed verbs from nouns. Fond of music, he had a splendid ear for vowel coloring and varied sound effects. Humor and playful irony are not lacking. He brought renewed life, simplicity, and spontaneity to the German lyric and had considerable influence on minor poets like Otto Julius Bierbaum (*q.v.*), Carl Busse (*q.v.*) and Gustav Falke (1853–1916). Poems by Liliencron were set to music by numerous composers, among them Brahms, Pfitzner, Max Reger, and Richard Strauss. Wide recognition came to him rather late in life.

See: H. Spiero, *Detlev von Liliencron; sein Leben und seine Werke* (1913); H. Maync, *Detlev von Liliencron* (1920).

J. C. B.

Linares Rivas, Manuel (1867–1938, Spanish dramatist), son of a prominent politician, was born in Santiago de Compostela and prepared for a career in law and politics. He soon gave up the law, though he continued his political career as deputy to the Cortes and finally as life senator. All the while he was pouring out a considerable stream of plays. He has written several musical comedies in verse and made a translation of Franz Lehár's *The Merry Widow*. His highly romantic three-act play *Lady Godiva* (1912) is also in verse. Most of the plays of Linares Rivas, however, are brilliant, sometimes militant, and usually witty satires of contemporary Spanish life, of social or political problems. The author is commonly thought of as a follower, even an imitator, of Jacinto Benavente (*q.v.*). It should be pointed out that Benavente, especially in his earlier period, is pessimistic and that he usually satirizes fundamental defects in human character, whereas Linares Rivas is generally cheerful and is likely to attack external or ephemeral mistakes, which a change in a law, for example, might correct. He began with *Aire de fuera* (1903), more tragic in tone than most of his later works. A good woman, bound by law to a bad husband, finds her only solution in suicide, since divorce was impossible in Spain. (It was legalized by the Republic of 1931 and abolished again, of course, by Franco.) *El abolengo* (1904) is a satire against silly family pride. In *María Victoria* (1904) is portrayed a woman who sacrifices love to duty and finds contentment in resignation. *La cizaña* (1905) protests against slander. *El caballero Lobo* (1910), with animal protagonists, was actually prior to the *Chantecler* of Rostand (*q.v.*). *La garra* (1914) is a strong plea for divorce and created considerable excitement in conservative circles. *En cuerpo y alma* (1918) and *La jaula de la leona* (1924) amusingly but firmly teach devotion to duty. Numerous further plays show Linares Rivas as an admirable purveyor of rapidly written, graceful, though not very profound samples of the *alta comedia*.

See: A. González-Blanco, *Los dramaturgos españoles contemporáneos*, Ser. 1 (1917), pp. 171–204; A. F. G. Bell, *Contemporary Spanish Literature*, revised ed. (1933), pp. 178–179.

N. B. A.

Linati, Carlo (1878–, Italian novelist, critic, and translator), born in Como, was seldom far from that region during his lifetime and never separated from it in his thoughts. His first appearance on the literary scene was in magazines of a very advanced and futuristic nature, but his contributions were in marked contrast to the authors generally represented there. Where the tendency of the period was one of boldness, of breaking with tradition, of a deliberate striving for the new, of internationalism, Linati's simple, well-knit prose, his economy of expression, his searching for the right word, his respect for syntax, his nostalgic adherence to the Milanese tradition, might almost be interpreted as a form of reaction and protest. His autobiographical novel *Duccio da bontà* (1913), which has tender passages, shows the anguish and heartaches experienced by a youth in his first encounters with life. Renunciation is reached as a solution to the problem in *Barbogeria* (1917), but it is a renunciation attained more from an adherence to the social code than through any deep-seated moral conviction. In *Sulle orme di Renzo* (1919) Linati's interests—which are for the most part directed at a perfection of style more as a scholarly device rather than as an expression of the mind—are turned towards recapturing the spirit of the region from which Manzoni drew inspiration. His style here acquires real warmth and fervor. The value of the book consists chiefly in the penetrating study of how the characteristics of the Lombardy region affect those sprung from its soil; in the identification of the individual with the countryside, Linati approaches a form of pantheism. The Celtic blood, allegedly flowing in the veins of both the Irish and of the inhabitants of parts of Lombardy, and the Irish countryside, similar in some respects to the Lombardy region, made a strong appeal to a slightly mystic quality in Linati's nature. In the writings of Lady Gregory, Synge, and Yeats he found an answering echo of kindred spirits. He translated W. B. Yeats (*Tragedie irlandesi*, 1914), Lady Gregory (*Commedie irlandesi*, 1916), and Synge (*Il Furfantello dell'Ovest, e altri drammi*, 1917). His interest in Anglo-American culture has expressed itself in a series of very fine critical essays on T. S. Eliot, Ernest Hemingway, Ezra Pound, Herman Melville, Aldous Huxley, Virginia Woolf, and others (*Scrittori anglo americani d'oggi*, 1932). In the *Nuova Antologia* (September 1, 1934), he translated into Italian poems of Emanuel Carnevali, an Italian immigrant in the United States whose verse written in English had elicited the praise of Waldo Frank, Sherwood Anderson, and others. To Linati must go a large share of the credit for first bringing many of these

American authors to the attention of the Italian reading public.

Linati has not in the least changed the flow of Italian letters nor chartered any new courses, yet by faithfully following in the tradition of the Lombardy writers, he most definitely has added new life and vitality to that tradition.

See: G. Papini, *24 Cervelli* (1913), pp. 179–189; P. Pancrazi, *Ragguagli di Parnaso (1919–1920)* (1920), pp. 31–37; L. Russo, *I Narratori* (1923), pp. 158–160.

G. S.

Linde, Otto zur (1873–, German poet), born in Essen, was for many years the leading figure of a literary group which centered around the magazine *Charon,* founded by Linde and Rudolf Pannwitz (1881–) in Berlin in the year 1904. The magazine struggled along under great difficulties and with many personal sacrifices on the part of the editors until the outbreak of the First World War; in 1920 it reappeared as the *Charon-Nothefte.* Although never exerting any lasting influence on the course of modern German literature, *Charon* was in many ways characteristic of the intellectual tendencies at the beginning of the present century. It reacted against naturalism (as did the more important circle of Stefan George, *q.v.*), even though the theories developed by the "Charon" group were largely derived from those of the naturalist lyric Arno Holz (*q.v.*). The relationship of the "Charon" poets to Holz was a mixture of hate and admiration (see Linde's *Arno Holz und der Charon,* 1911). It appears that the influence of Nietzsche (*q.v.*) was particularly strong upon these poets, as on Rudolf Paulsen (1883–), the son of the Berlin philosopher Friedrich Paulsen, on Rudolf Pannwitz and Hanns Meinke (1884–), and on Otto zur Linde himself. Here again a parallel can be drawn to George's circle, with the reservation that "Charon" radically rejected all demands for a new classicism. "Charon" at all times refused to adhere to any dogma, even that of antidogmatism. Hence these poets demanded of the lyricist genuineness and originality and tried to create a verse which would be free of all traces of traditional melodics. They were predominantly lyric poets themselves, yet with a definite interest in philosophic and theoretical problems. The most representative work of the group was Linde's *Die Kugel* (1906–1909; 2d ed., 1923), a "philosophy in verses."

No matter how firmly the philosophy of the "Charon" group was rooted in Nietzsche, in religious and political questions they went their own way. In fact, a deeply religious trend goes through the entire work of the "Charon" poets. This is particularly true of Karl Röttger (1877–), who considered Jesus the exemplary man, and of Rudolf Paulsen in his *Christus und der Wanderer* (1920), in which he tried to harmonize the philosophy of Nietzsche with Christianity. Their religious inclination often led to a modern mysticism, and the "Charon" poets have written an endless number of myths and legends. This mysticism, coupled with a one-sided emphasis on the Teutonic element in intellectual and political matters, has led some of the members of the group to the dim and semimystical ideologies of National Socialism. Karl Röttger is today probably the best known of the "Charon" poets. He has been successful with a number of books of verses and essays, a few novels, and one or two dramas.

W. P.

Lithuanian literature. During the second half of the 19th century the trends of Lithuanian literature were determined by three factors: the Russian government's official ban (1865–1904) on printing in Latin characters, the abolition of serfdom (1861), and the revolutionary movements agitating all parts of the Russian Empire. The first factor, aiming at complete Russification of the country and coupled with deportation of all "dangerous" elements, might have been successful, had it not been for the opposition of the Roman Catholic clergy who recognized in the Russification drive a serious danger to the Church. On account of this active opposition and the passive resistance of the population, the attempts to bring out Lithuanian books printed with Russian characters failed and were given up after 1871. The need for reading material was satisfied by pamphlets and books published in Tilsit, East Prussia, and smuggled into the country. The first to start this practice was Bishop Motiejus Valančius (1801–1875) who, however, had only the interests of the Roman Catholic Church in mind. Twenty years later the first political and literary magazine, *Aušra* (Dawn), liberal in tendency, was founded by Dr. Jonas Basanavičius (1851–1927), a refugee living in Bulgaria who became the patriarch of the Lithuanian national revival. *Aušra,* published in Tilsit, appeared from 1883 to 1886 and had a deep influence upon the life of the nation. Almost equal in importance was *Varpas* (1889–1905; The Bell), a monthly journal of leftist leanings whose guiding spirit was Dr. Vincas Kudirka (1858–1899), the author of the Lithuanian national anthem. The journals *Apžvalga* (1890–1896; The Review) and *Tėvynės sargas* (1896–1904; The Guard of the Fatherland) were organs of the Roman Catholic clergy and had among their collaborators and supporters the inspiring poet and glowing patriot, Maironis (pseud. of Reverend Jonas Mačiulis-Maciulevičius, 1862–1932); the didactic poet, encyclopedist, and literary critic, Adomas Jakštas (pseud. of Reverend Aleksandras Dambrauskas, 1860–1938); and the fiery publicist and successful novelist, Vaižgantas (pseud. of Reverend Juozas Tumas, 1869–1933), founder of *Tėvynės sargas* and its editor, 1897–1902. Quite independently of these magazines, Petras Vileišis (1850–1926) brought out a number of books in St. Petersburg, for which he obtained special permission from the Russian government. He also founded the first Lithuanian daily newspaper in Vilna after the ban on Lithuanian literature had been lifted. For fear of police persecution all publications of the first period had to come out either anonymously or with fictitious names. The use of pseudonyms became so common that it was carried over even into the period when danger was gone.

At the beginning of the Forty Years of Captivity (1865–1905) the Lithuanian spirit was kept alive by the poems of Bishop Antanas Baranauskas (1835–1902), such as *Anykščių šilelis* (1858–1859; The Grove of Anykščiai). About the turn of the century Maironis aroused the nation and became its spiritual leader with his patriotic songs composed in classical meters, the first of which appeared in *Apžvalga* and which were later published in the collection *Pavasario balsai* (1905, 5th ed., 1920, 6th ed., 1927; Voices of Spring). His longer poems include *Lietuva* (1888; Lithuania), *Jaunoji Lietuva* (1895, 1905, 1908, 1921; Young Lithuania), *Raseinių Magdė* (1909; Maggie of Raseiniai), and *Mūsų vargai* (1921; Our Trials).

The older generation is completely dominated by Russian and Polish literature. To be sure, Kudirka translated some of Schiller's dramas (*e.g., Wilhelm Tell*), but that was an outgrowth of the great popularity which this German classic enjoyed in Russia. Influence of Pushkin, Krylov, Tolstoy (*q.v.*), Turgenev (*q.v.*), Gogol, Chekhov (*q.v.*), Mickiewicz, and Kraszewski is notable everywhere. The Russian populist movement with its emphasis upon service to the peasantry was accepted by virtually all, even by those who politically were not in sympathy with it (*Apžvalga* and *Tėvynės sargas*). But to the Lithuanian patroit, "peasant" meant and was identical with "Lithuanian," since the aristocracy of the country, *i.e.*, the landed gentry, was Polish or Russian, and the city population Jewish. Vaižgantas, a most prolific producer of prose of unequal literary value, a man of inconsistency and contradictions, always giving vent to the impressions of the moment, tries to reconcile nihilistic rationalism with his Roman Catholic faith. This liberal tendency and his unbounded vivacity, together with a thoroughly sensual nature which breaks through continually in his writings, more than once earned him rebukes from the Church authorities. In his docile and naïve way he always took the reprimands as deserved and tried to follow the advice received, only to get into some new trouble very soon. In his earlier days he defended the rights of the peasants, but after the establishment of the Lithuanian republic he denounced the agrarian reform and sided with the wealthy landowners. Of permanent significance is his novel *Pragiedruliai* (in 3 parts and 4 vols., 1918–1929; Sunbeams), depicting in a loosely connected series of portraits (the liberal country doctor and his helpers, the Jewish book smuggler, the clergy, the peasants, the decadent aristocrats, the Russian police) the struggle for Lithuanian culture during the latter part of the 19th and the beginning of the 20th century. The introductory chapter portraying symbolically the long and severe "Lithuanian Winter" and the sudden and destructive "Spring Thaws" is a masterpiece both in effectiveness and style. The successful outcome of that battle for cultural emancipation is also presented in the novel *Tėviškė* (2 vols., 1926–1936; Homestead) by Vaidilutė (pseud. of Ona Pleirytė-Puidienė, 1885–1935).

Varpas printed the first literary attempts of Žemaitė (pseud. of Julija Žymantienė, 1845–1921), the first and most successful woman writer of short stories. In a realistic style she portrayed scenes, sometimes serene, but more often gloomy, of Lithuanian peasant life which was just getting free from the chains of serfdom. Three younger women, Lazdynų Pelėda (pseud. of two sisters, Sofija Ivanauskaitė-Pšibilauskienė, 1867–1926, and Marija Ivanauskaitė, 1873–) and Šatrijos Ragana (pseud. of Marija Pečkauskaitė, 1878–1930), followed Žemaitė's example, though in a more optimistic vein.

During the third and fourth decades of the present century, *i.e.*, the period of national independence, Lithuanian literature is dominated by the towering figure of Vincas

Krėvė (Vincas Krėvė-Mickevičius, 1882–). A student of Slavic literature, Sanskrit, European, and Oriental history, and of folklore, he was strongly influenced by the Polish romanticists and the Russian populists. He first wrote poems in the style of the Lithuanian folk songs, then turned to prose, short story and drama becoming his specialty. His prose is rhythmic and melodious, his style based on the language of the folk tales and songs. In his *Dainavos šalies senų žmonių padavimai* (Legends Told by Old People of the Dainava Country), some of which appeared first in 1913 and a complete collection in 1921, and in the historical dramas, *Sarūnas* (1911), *Skirgaila* (1925), and *Mindaugo mirtis* (1935; The Death of Mindaugas), he is a romanticist. His short stories (3 vols., 1921–1922) dealing with modern rural life and his play *Žentas* (1922; The Son-in-Law) display a realistic approach combining fine psychological observation with a tendency to point out existing evils. *Pratjekabuddha,* a Hindu tale, was first published in 1913 and later included in the collection *Rytų pasakos* (1930; Oriental Tales). In *Likimo keliais* (2 vols., 1926 and 1929; On the Paths of Fate), a so-called "dramatic mystery," depicting the struggle for cultural and political liberation from the neighboring powers (Russia, Poland, Germany) and from social suppression by the landowners, Krėvė's art arose to greatness.

In the 20's (1922–1929) Maironis, long famous as the leading lyric poet of the nation, tried his hand at historical dramas centering around Grand Duke Vytautas who is presented as the admired aggrandizer of the Lithuanian Empire. Ever since 1896, when J. Vilkutaitis-Keturakis made a hit with his comedy *Amerika pirtyje* (America in the Bathhouse), the ambition of most authors was directed toward the drama. The most successful of all was Petras Vaičiūnas (1890–) who wrote annually either a satirical comedy or a tragedy for the National Theatre in Kaunas, *e.g., Tuščios pastangos* (1926; Vain Efforts), *Nuodėmingas angelas* (1927; The Sinful Angel), *Patriotai* (1927; The Patriots), *Sudrumstoji ramybė* (1927; The Ruffled Calm), *Sulaužyta priesaika* (1935; The Broken Oath). Other successful playwrights are Sofija Čiurlionienė (1886–), Kazys Binkis (1893–1942), Balys Sruoga (1896–), Vincas Mykolaitis-Putinas (1893–), Vytautas Bičiūnas (1893–). Vydūnas (Vilius Storasta, 1868–), a Prussian Lithuanian dramatist, theosophist, and mystic, stands apart from the others, even in spelling. His most important plays (dramatic mysteries and tragedies) are *Prabočių šešėliai* (1908; Shades of the Ancestors) *Amžina ugnis* (1912–1913; The Eternal Flame), *Pasaulio gaisras* (1928; The World Conflagration).

Vincas Mykolaitis-Putinas, a Roman Catholic priest and a successful lyric poet and dramatist, caused tremendous excitement when he (unlike Vaižgantas but like many other priests) left the Church, married, and wrote the now famous novel *Altorių šešėly* (3 vols., 1933; In the Shadow of the Altars) in which he tried to justify his action. The novel is not only interesting on account of the problem discussed, but also significant for its aesthetic qualities and the expert drawing of the characters. One of the repercussions of this publication was another novel, *Tiesiu keliu* (3 vols., 1934–1935; On the Straight Road), inferior in artistry, which was brought out under the sponsorship of Adomas Jakštas for the purpose of showing how a worthy priest should behave in similar circumstances. The name of its author was given as J. Gintautas which later turned out to be a pseudonym of Bishop Justinas Staugaitis (1886–1943) of Telšiai.

Other prominent writers of fiction of recent times are Vienuolis (pseud. of Antanas Žukauskas, 1882–) with short stories and one novel (see *Rinktiniai raštai,* 1937, Selected Writings); Ignas Jurkūnas-Šeinius (1889–), a novelist; Petras Cvirka (1909–), novelist (*e.g., Žemė maitintoja,* 1935, Mother Earth; Lettish and Russian tr.); Antanas Vaičiulaitis (1906–), a master of the short story.

Lyric poetry has not reached any great height of perfection since Maironis, although there are a number of highly esteemed lyricists, among them Petras Vaičiūnas, Mykolaitis-Putinas, Balys Sruoga, Faustas Kirša (1891–), Juozas Tysliava (1906–), Jurgis Baltrušaitis (1873–1944), and Salomėja Neris (1905–1945). The reason for this lies in the slow development of the Lithuanian standard language which, through the efforts of Professor Jonas Jablonskis (pseud. Rygiškių Jonas, 1861–1930), is now based on the dialect of Northern Suvalkija. The standard form prescribed for the school was not immediately accepted by all authors, some of the older ones (Žemaitė, Krėvė) still holding on to provincial characteristics. Lack of uniformity in word accent, which varies in the main dialects, is especially obstructive in the field of verse poetry. Thus it is impossible to read the inspiring poems of the East Lithuanian Antanas Baranauskas with the accents required by Jablonskis's Grammar without destroying the rhythm. The first collection of poems following strictly the rules of Jablonskis's Grammar is a translation by J. Talmantas of I. A. Krylov's Fables: *Pasakėčios* (1937).

With the First World War the doors were thrown wide open to Western ideas. Many Lithuanian writers spent long years in Western Europe, especially Switzerland (Putinas), France (Tysliava, Vaičiulaitis), Scandinavia (Jurkūnas-Šeinius), Germany (Sruoga, Binkis) where they became acquainted with Western movements and fads. Those who had to stay at home had foreign literatures interpreted to them by competent professors of the University of Lithuania at Kaunas (founded 1922) where literary subjects were taught among others by Maironis, Vaižgantas, Krėvė, Putinas, Sruoga, and Vaičiulaitis. Foreign literatures became also known through a flood of translations. As a result, foreign literary movements, especially that of the futurists (Sruoga, Binkis, Tysliava), cf. *Keturi vėjai* (1924; The Four Winds), temporarily took root in Kaunas during the 20's. A "Collective of Activist Writers" with the journal *Trečias frontas* (1930–31; The Third Front) as its organ was formed in 1930 and included the following young people, all of whom in 1940 became members of the government of Soviet Lithuania: Antanas Venclova, Petras Cvirka, Jonas Šimkus, and Salomėja Neris.

See: M. Biržiška, *Mūsų raštų istorija* (1920), pp. 40–110; J. Tumas (pseud. Vaižgantas), *Lietuvių literatūros paskaitos* (8 vols., 1924–1925) and *Raštai*, Vols. XI–XIV, XIX (1929–1933); A. P. Coleman, "A Survey of Lithuanian Literature," in *Books Abroad*, VIII (1934), 391–393; V. Mykolaitis-Putinas, *Naujoji lietuvių literatūra* (1936); H. Engert, *Aus litauischer Dichtung: Deutsche Nachdichtungen* (1935, 2d. ed., 1938); V. Jungfer, *Litauen: Antlitz eines Volkes* (1938), pp. 228–323; J. Mauclère, *Panorama de la littérature lithuanienne contemporaine* (1938), pp. 91–184; I. Kisinas, *Lietuviškų knygų sistematinis katalogas* (1938), Nos. 4221–6629; A. Vaičiulaitis, *Outline History of Lithuanian Literature* (1942), pp. 22–54.

A. Se.

Løkken, Thomas Olesen (1877–, Danish novelist), was born in Alstrup. He has become one of the important exponents of the regional literature of Denmark, choosing for his special domain that upper part of Jutland known as Vendsyssel, the original home of the fierce and stubborn Cimbrians of ancient days. Modestly, Løkken had to begin life as a cowherd—there are many of them in modern Danish literature—later becoming a cobbler, a bicycle and automobile mechanic, and a book dealer, so that although he is conscious of having wanted to become a writer ever since he was eight years old, he was 43 when his first book, *Bonden Niels Hald* (1920; Farmer Niels Hald), was published. This was followed by *Niels Halds Hustru* (1922; The Wife of Niels Hald) and *Niels Halds Hjem* (1924; The Home of Niels Hald). These three make up his first cycle. Two others have appeared in more recent years: *Povl Dam* (1925), *Kampaar* (1926; Years of Struggle), and *Sejren* (1927; The Victory), all three volumes dealing with the Dam family in Vendsyssel; and *Stormosen* (1929; The Great Swamp), *Mosepigens Søn* (1931; The Son of the Swamp Girl), and *Fra Vildmosens Land* (1934; From the Land of the Wild Swamp). In these trilogies Løkken has described the typical Vendsyssel cotter, the rich and haughty farmer, and the very lowest representatives of peasant life in the huts adjacent to the peat swamps immediately north of the Limfjord. In general, Løkken has confined himself to this part of Jutland (see also one of his earlier books, *Klavs Bjerg og Bodil*, 1923, Klavs Bjerg and Bodil). *Vendsyssel-Noveller* (1925; Vendsyssel Short Stories) and *Sange fra Vendsyssel* (1934; Vendsyssel Songs) by their very titles testify to the deep affection with which he embraces his native province, beyond which he has never had his home.

In Løkken's main works it is possible to detect reminiscences of Nexø (*q.v.*), Thomas Hardy, Reymont (*q.v.*), Zola (*q.v.*), but the virility of style is wholly his own. The particular patch of soil he has tilled was practically nonexistent for writers before him, and his mature perception of human values is a product of many years of rigid self-discipline practiced in the obscurity of manual labor.

See: Jørgen Bukdahl, *Thomas Olesen Løkken* (1927); Helge Kjaergaard, *Die dänische Literatur der neuesten Zeit (1871–1933)* (1934).

G. St.

Løland, Rasmus (1861–1907, Norwegian novelist), was born in the western coastal district of Ryfylke. All through his life he was hampered by neurotic sensitiveness and poor health. His earlier years were spent in shy isolation and in poverty; he suffered from a feeling of uselessness and was definitely eccentric. He found refuge in writing and in a strong intellectual life, influenced by the ideas of science and radical philosophy. His first little book came in 1891 (*Folkeliv;* From the Countryside). Four years later he finally managed to break his bonds and establish himself in Christiania, where he cut his way through as a writer, translator, and editor of a newspaper for children, till disease finally overtook him.

During his short period of literary activity Løland published an astounding number of books, many of them experimental and bearing the marks of his late start as a writer. His creation is limited by his somewhat narrow circle of experience; but one finds character and a deep personal honesty in everything he has done. The real subject of his interest is the fate of the individual within the farm society which he knew from youth, especially the individual isolated within the group—the socially declassed, the weak and crippled, the queer and the gifted, those who "live in the shadow," marked by destiny like himself. His analysis often has a tone of sad resignation toward the inexorable laws of life, but is brightened by unsentimental compassion and a subtle irony. Representative are the autobiographical novel *Aasmund Aarak* (1902) and the posthumous *Hundrad aar* (1910; Hundred Years).

Løland's great achievement, however, which has made him a classic, is his children's books, describing the life of a group of boys in his home district (there is a complete edition in three volumes, *Barnebøker,* 1923–1925; Children's Books). In a masterly way Løland makes the life of these farm children emerge as an autonomous world with other laws and proportions and light and shadows than the clumsy and incomprehensible world of adults, and filled within its own limits with drama and passion, tragedy and deep joy. Løland's intensity in experiencing this world as if he had the senses and soul of the child has been compared to that of the great Russians. But there is no intricacy about his analysis; the narrative is perfectly simple and natural, as is the style. He pictures no idyls. Again and again he points to the insecurity of the child's world, governed by unknown and incontrollable powers, distorted by the transforming forces of imagination. There is the same philosophy in these books as in his novels, a conviction of lawfulness and tragic guilt, of the merciless logic of the "small things." But the keynote is cheerful. His children have health, spontaneous friendliness, sound humor, and a creative, active imagination which promises well for them and shows how little Løland's own fate had shaken his real strength. He is the first of the great portrayers of children in recent Norwegian literature, and in many ways the greatest.

See: S. Eskeland, *R. Løland* (1910); J. Bukdahl, *Det skjulte Norge* (1926), pp. 55–61; O. Bakken, *R. Løland* (1938).

S. S.

Löns, Hermann (1866–1914, German novelist and poet), was born in Kulm on the Vistula, far from the Luneburg Heath which he came to love and on the poetic description of which rests his literary fame. His extensive knowledge of plant and animal life, acquired in his boyhood years, later was the foundation for his scientific investigations. However, in 1891 Löns gave up his medical studies to become a journalist in Hanover and Bückeburg. The journalistic pace is traceable in his works. While his novels are written hastily, his descriptive scenes from nature are inimitable. Never before had the thrills of the born hunter of small game been depicted so vividly and accurately as in *Mein grünes Buch* (1901). The scientist and huntsman are merged with the poet in *Mein braunes Buch* (1906), his first great literary success. Löns was the first to reproduce in literature the infinite variety of colors in the somber moorlands. His stories from animal life are a combination of scientific accuracy and poetic imagination. The former predominates in *Aus Flur und Forst,* originally a commentary for photographs from animal life (1907), the latter prevails in *Mümmelmann* (1909), humorous animal tales, partly influenced by Kipling and Jack London. In his novels on peasant life, *e.g., Der letzte Hansbur* (1909), inspired by Jeremias Gotthelf, Löns wishes to awaken sympathetic understanding for the reticent and proud, hardheaded and loyal peasants of the Luneburg Heath. *Der Wehrwolf* (1910; Eng. tr., *Harm Wulf,* 1931) pictures them in the terse style of an ancient peasant chronicle with many dialect words of old Germanic stock. We see how, in the Thirty Years' War, these heath dwellers are forced to turn into wolves, defending their farms and families against the marauders, killing them from ambush, or pronouncing and executing judgment on them in the old tribal way. It is an exciting though somewhat repetitious novel filled with bloodshed and cruelty. The autobiographical novel *Das zweite Gesicht* (1911) gives an insight into the conflicting forces in Löns's restless mind. *Der kleine Rosengarten* (1911; Eng. tr., *Little Garden of Roses,* 1929) so successfully entered into the spirit and style of the old folk song that its tunes and lyrics captured the popular fancy. More than 400,000 copies have been sold.

Löns was killed before Reims in September, 1914. He had become a favorite of the German Youth Movement. With his emphasis on national literature, race, and soil, he later became an idol of National Socialism.

See: W. Deimann, *Hermann Löns* (1939).

E. Hof.

Looy, Jacobus van (1855–1930, Dutch painter and short-story writer), was born in Haarlem and brought up there in the municipal orphanage. He studied painting at Haarlem, Amsterdam, and Rome and traveled extensively through Italy, Spain, and Morocco before he returned to his native land and to a life of seclusion devoted to study, art, and literature. His first story appeared in *De nieuwe Gids* (The New Guide), which was then in its first year (1885). Van Looy was not so much a narrator as a painter in words of picturesque scenes. Being a painter by profession, he changed his medium but not his manner when he wrote. On his first appearance in print he was recognized as a master of the exact phrase. The painter in words cannot afford to spin too long a yarn. Hence the bulk of his work consists of short stories. Even his tale *Jaapje* (1917), an autobiographic narrative of his boyhood in the Haarlem orphanage, is less a novel than a series of 19 unconnected sketches that have nothing in common except their hero. It is the most popular of his writings. His recollections of life as a charity boy have the air of a highly developed variety of those old-fashioned copperplate penny-prints for children that depicted episodes in the life of some childhood hero. It is not the secret workings of the heart that interest this writer most. The artist in him watches the shifting scene from day to day, and only by the manner in which his little hero's feelings are affected by the beauty and the strangeness of this spectacle is Jaapje's inner life disclosed. The house in Haarlem where Van Looy lived and died is now a museum, where his admirers can study his paintings and get an impression of the home that he guarded so jealously from the curious while he was alive.

A. J. B.

Lopes Vieira, Afonso (1878–, Portuguese poet and critic), was born in Leiria, studied law in Coimbra, and was editor for the Chamber of Deputies. He has traveled extensively in Italy, France, and Switzerland.

In Lopes Vieira's poetry and dramatic attempts as well as in his critical studies and literary reconstructions, Portuguese tradition is his guide and absorbing interest. One of the most prolific contemporary Portuguese writers, he began with books of poetry of modernistic hue, *Para que? Primeiros versos* (1897; Why? First Verses), *O náufrago; versos lusitanos* (1898; The Shipwrecked; Lusitanian Verses), and *O meu adeus* (1900; My Farewell). Later he interrupted his poetic production with three books in prose showing a decided socializing tendency, *Marquês; história dum perseguido* (Marquês; History of a Persecuted Man), *Pedro Kropotkine; a gente nova* (Peter Kropotkin; the Newcomers), and *Conto de natal* (Christmas Story), all published in 1904. He continued then with works which evoked the literature of other periods, not only that of Portugal but—in Portuguese translation—of the whole Peninsula. Outstanding works are those written to focus modern attention on Gil Vicente, the patriarch of the Portuguese theatre, *e.g.*, *A campanha vicentina; conferências e outros escritos* (1910; Vicentian Campaign; Discourses and Other Writings), a book prepared by Lopes Vieira under the guidance of his teacher Carolina Michaëlis de Vasconcelos (*q.v.*); his adaptation of the *Monólogo do vaqueiro* (1910; Cowboy's Monologue) and of the *Auto da barca do inferno* (1911; Mystery Play of the Ship of the Inferno); and his lectures on artistic or historico-literary subjects—Inés de Castro, the Holy Grail, the paintings in the monastery of San Vicente, and studies of Camões and João de Deus (*q.v.*). In a magnificent, though at times too free translation, he has published in Portuguese *O Amadís de Gaula de Lobeira* (1922; The *Amadis of Gaul* of Lobeira), *A Diana de Jorge de Montemôr em português* (1924; The *Diana* of Jorge de Montemayor in Portuguese), and *O poema do Cid* (1925; The Poem of the Cid). The culture of his country is indebted to him for this effort toward the incorporation into Portuguese literature of works written in Spanish by Portuguese authors, of those where the primitive Portuguese version is not known, and of the great medieval epic poetry of the Peninsula. As an anthologist he collected in the *Cancioneiro de Coimbra* (1918; The Songbook of Coimbra) a mass of compositions about the city, its history, and its landscape.

Among his most serious studies on the Portuguese classical writers should be mentioned his critical edition, with introduction, of *Poesias de Francisco Rodrigues Lobo* (1941; Poems of Francisco Rodrigues Lobo) and a new attempt, in *Lettres portugaises; essai de reconstitution du texte français par Charles Culmont, tentativa de texto português* (1941), at reconstructing the text of the famous *Cartas portuguesas* of Soror Mariana de Alcofurado. His poetry is in the manner of the *saüdade* (longing)—he was a member of the *A águia* (The Eagle) group of Teixeira de Pascoais (*q.v.*) and subsequently of the "integralista" group of Sardinha (*q.v.*)—or in the classical tradition, or along lines of folkloric sentimentalism. Of great interest for a study of his aesthetic ideas are his "Aforismos dum estudante de linguagem" (Aphorisms of a Language Student), which are incorporated in *Em demanda do Graal* (1922; In Search of the Grail) and continued in the *Revista de filologia portuguesa* of São Paulo (Nos. 14 and 18, 1925). A dreamy vagueness and verbal musicality—he translated Heine and glossed Schumann—seem to suggest his poetic ideal, but he sometimes shows an excessive formalism of language and theme which is pseudoclassic in nature and directed toward the attainment of archaic effects. His best poetry is found in *Canções de saüdade e de amor* (1917; Songs of Longing and Love), *Ilhas de bruma* (1918; Islands of Mist), and *País lilás; desterro azul* (1922; Lilac Country; Blue Exile).

See: A. da Veiga Simões, *A nova geração* (1911); Agostinho de Campos, *Antologia portuguesa* (1928).

R. M. L.

López de Ayala, Adelardo (1828–1879, Spanish politician, orator, poet, journalist, and dramatist), born at Guadalcanal in the province of Seville, always displayed an Andalusian facility with words and considerable ability along many lines. In politics he was very adaptable, switching from liberalism to conservatism with great ease. He was a cabinet minister after the accession of Alfonso XII and president of the Cortes at the time of his death.

López de Ayala is now best remembered as a dramatist, for his journalistic output was ephemeral and his poems few in number. Like Tamayo y Baus (*q.v.*), he was a dramatist of transition, beginning with historical-romantic plays and ending with more realistic social comedies, somewhat similar to those of Emile Augier. Before he was 21 he wrote a good historical play, *Un hombre de estado,* played at the Teatro Español with great success in 1851. In that play and in several following he showed himself an admirer of Calderón. His versification was supple and his dramatic intrigues well devised. His first period, up to 1856, included four *zarzuelas* or musical comedies.

There are four plays which show Ayala at his best, and they are at least faintly reminiscent of Ruiz de Alarcón, always greatly admired by Don Adelardo. *El tejado de vidrio* (1856) shows a seducer receiving a dose of his own medicine through the infidelity of his own wife. *El tanto por ciento* (1861) has a complicated plot involving financial skulduggery. The grasping tricksters are discomfited, and hero and heroine are happily reconciled and married. *El nuevo don Juan* (1863), not too well constructed, satirizes the modern Don Juan. *Consuelo* (1878) is usually considered Ayala's masterpiece. The protagonist, Consuelo, is presented as a type of selfish and grasping modern woman who sacrifices true love and marries for money alone. She receives condign punishment. Her character is well studied, and the action is plausible, the dénouement logical. Ayala practically always achieves the effect of naturalness, and he avoids the melodramatic exaggerations which mar the theatre of Echegaray. Harmony, balance, fidelity to life, and emphasis on moral themes are his chief qualities.

See: J. O. Picón, "D. Adelardo López de Ayala," in Pedro de Novo y Colson, ed., *Autores dramáticos contemporáneos,* II (1882), 377–399.

N. B. A.

Lòpez-Picó, Josep Maria (1886–, Catalonian poet), extraordinarily fecund writer, has passed through a clearly defined evolution. From an initial exaggerated use of witticisms he moved on to forms of expressive concision, particularly happy in his use of epigrams, keeping, however, an enigmatic tone which in some pieces deliberately without human emotions reaches the point of noncomprehension. When he is, on the other hand, eager to express human qualities, his lyric poetry achieves this through a fine sensibility in which primordial motives remain intact. But his verse often remains cold—although never mediocre. The outstanding virtue of his poetry and that which has exerted a notable influence on the new generations of the Catalan-speaking countries is the constant renovation of images—images of material reality (the house, the landscape) or characterized by a spiritual subjectivism (love, serenity) easily grasped in effective metaphor. The poetry of Lòpez-Picó, in spite of its wide circulation in Catalonia, seems unlikely to outlast his own lifetime; his disciples, decadent symbolists, have emphasized even more the enigmatic tone, which is not in harmony with the general line of development of the race or with the ambition of other modern poets to harmonize the spirit of the authentically national tradition with the poetic gift for the sublime.

Lòpez-Picó was born in Barcelona and pursued his secondary school studies with the Jesuit fathers of that city; he prepared himself in the humanities at the University of Barcelona and received his degree of licentiate in 1902. Among his works, which are very numerous since from 1913 he had published at least a volume a year (a labor interrupted with the invasion of Catalonia in 1939), should be mentioned: *Intermetzzo galant* (1910; Gallant Intermezzo), *Torment froment* (1910; Trembling Torment), *Poemes de port* (1911; Harbor Poems), *Amor, Senyor* (1913; Love, the Lord), *Espectacles i mitologia* (1914; Spectacles and Mythology), *Epigrammata* (1911), *L'ofrena* (The Offering), *Paraules* (1916; Words), *L'instant, les Noces i el càntic serè* (The Instant, the Betrothal and the Serene Song), *El meu pare i jo* (My Father and I), *Primer recull de poesies* (First Collection of Poems), *Moralitats i pretextos* (Moralizings and Pretexts), *Dietari espiritual* (Spiritual Calendar), *L'oci de la paraula* (1927; The Leisure of Words), *Epitalami* (Epithalamium). Upon producing this last book, his 25th, Lòpez-Picó was honored by the *Revista* group, which prepared an anthology of his poetry. He has collaborated on many Catalonian journals, especially on *Vell i nou* (Old and New), *Empori* (Emporium), *Quaderns d'estudi* (Study Cahiers), and *Quaderns de poesia* (Poetry Cahiers). Due to his initiative was the so-called *Almanac de la Poesia* (Poetry Almanac) in which, from 1912, was collected verse published in different books in the course of the year. In 1915, with Joaquim Folguera, he founded the *Revista,* a bimonthly publishing poetry and essays, in which was captured the aesthetic ideals of the generation. Many of the poet's compositions have been translated into English, Italian, Spanish, French, and German. More recently he has been living in Barcelona, obliged to interrupt not only his poetic production but his literary labors on the *Revista* because of the measures tending to blot out even the faintest manifestation of Catalonian spirituality.

See: M. de Montoliu, *Estudi d'història literària de Catalunya* (1912–1914); A. Plana, *Estudi preliminar de l'antologia de poetes catalans* (1915); J. Folguera, *Les noves valors de la poesia catalana* (1919); R. Crossmann, *Katalanische Lyrik der Gegenwart* (1923); C. Giardini, *Antologia dei poeti catalani contemporanei, 1845–1925,* (1926).

J. M. M. i V.

López Pinillos, José (1875–1922, Spanish journalist, novelist, and playwright), was born in Seville and spent his first 20 years in this region, which was to be the principal background of many of his works. Unable to finish his law career for lack of funds, he left his native city for Madrid, where he made his living writing for well-known newspapers. By 1908 his reputation as a keen journalist was well established in the *Heraldo de Madrid,* in which his articles appeared under the pseudonym Parmeno, a character out of the famous *La Celestina* and a symbol of the observer of stark reality who expresses his views without hesitancy or cant. Whether he was writing novels, such as *La sangre de Cristo* (1907), *Doña Mesalina* (1910), *Las águilas* (1911), and *El luchador* (1916), or short stories, as in *Frente al mar* (1914) and *Ojo por ojo* (1915), or dramatic triumphs of the type of *El pantano* (1913), *Nuestro enemigo* (1913), *La otra vida* (1915), and *El embrujamiento* (1923), or newspaper articles as collected in *Hombres, hombrecillos y animales* (1917) and *En la pendiente: Los que suben y los que ruedan* (1920), the technique and the social content are the same. There are Gordian-knot-to-be-cut situations even in the farces or lighter comedies, such as *Hacia la dicha* (1910) or *A tiro limpio* (1918); the author deals always with man's struggle against himself or against man in an Othello-Iago seesaw of passions.

In *Nuestro enemigo* Antolín, the hero, expresses the fundamental suffering of all of Parmeno's characters: "I was deceived by my heart, which is our enemy." His characters forgive, but never forget. Years afterward a word, a gesture, will turn forgiveness into hatred, hatred into death. Most of his works deal with rural or provincial Andalusia or with the lower classes of Madrid, although there are a few exceptions, as in *La otra vida* which deals with the higher classes of the military caste. Between 1910 and 1923 López Pinillos had two or three great dramatic successes, as great as some of Benavente's (*q.v.*), but today he is hardly noticed even in histories of Spanish literature. Perhaps this is an injustice, for he was a first-rate technician comparable to the Galsworthy of *Loyalties* and *The Skin Game.*

See: R. Cansinos-Asséns, "José López Pinillos (Parmeno)," in *Poetas y prosistas del novecientos* (*España y América*) (1919), pp. 191–202, and in *La evolución de la novela (1917–1927)*, Vol. IV (1927) of *La nueva literatura,* pp. 40–52; Mario Méndez Bejarano, *Diccionario de escritores, maestros y oradores naturales de Sevilla y su actual provincia* (1922), I, 410–414, 469–470; Arturo Mori, *Treinta años de teatro hispanoamericano* (1941), pp. 59–61, 224.

F. S. y E.

López Silva, José (1861–1925), Spanish comic poet and playwright), was born in Madrid and died in Buenos Aires. His literary work and his life fit as a casting fits its pattern. Both are romantic, picturesque, full of the local color exemplifying the "roaring 90's" of Spain and the waning of an empire. Both are full of bathos, reminiscent of the Spanish tradition of mingling tragedy and comedy, and true to a national temperament that even in moods of sheer desperation likes to play with reality. Like Arniches (*q.v.*) López Silva started as a clerk in a Madrid dry-goods store—unlike him he always lived among the working classes of Madrid. His early and easy successes in Madrid's comic paper, *Madrid cómico,* enabled him to give up his dry-goods and accounting books in order to compose festive, descriptive poetry about the people he knew so well and loved even more.

His genuinely literary work is found in a series of volumes on passion and death among Madrid's lower classes, written in fluid verse, and in plays on the same subjects. Included in the poetry is *Migajas* (1890), his first book; *Los barrios bajos* (1894), his definite success, in which he showed that he had mastered his own style; *Los madriles* (1896), and finally *La musa del arroyo* (1911). Many of these volumes contain eulogistic introductions by such writers as Benavente, Blasco Ibañez, and Picón, (*qq.v.*) López Silva's plays belong to the *género chico* type. As is characteristic of this genre, he wrote almost all of them in collaboration with some other playwright. Spaniards of this time were in all too frequent disagreement on many matters, especially political and religious, but a group of them collaborated in thousands of *sainetes, pasos,* and *zarzuelas,* written approximately between 1870 and 1915. Among others the Alvarez Quintero brothers (*q.v.*) exemplify this tendency in the Spanish popular drama of this era.

López Silva's three greatest successes, as well as his most representative and best plays, are *Las bravías* (1896); *La revoltosa* (1897), done in collaboration with the prolific Fernández Shaw; and *El barquillero* (1900), written with the no less prolific Jacksón Veyán. Fecundity is in fact a characteristic of these playwrights. Their plays are a joy to the philologist and the sociologist, for they portray linguistically and culturally the whole life of a generation. They are sometimes almost photographic in accuracy; the best of them artistically are bizarre etchings, reminiscent of Goya, in which the most heated arguments then in vogue are portrayed ludicrously and sentimentally. *Las bravías* (The Viragoes) capitalizes on the tempest which feminism was causing in Spain; a subtitle points out that it is a lyrical *sainete* (*i.e.,* with music) "based on Shakespeare's play, *The Taming of the Shrew.*" While writers like Palacio Valdés (*q.v.*) condemned bitterly this theatre in its beginnings, there has since been a general if tempered acceptance of the *género chico* for what it is, for what it strives to do aesthetically. The French critic Mérimée has called López Silva the Homer of the *chulapería* (a *chulapería* is an idiom or expression characteristic of the *chulapo,* the Madrid tough, flashy in talk and dress).

See: Mariano Zurita, *Historia del género chico* (1920); N. Alonso Cortés, "López Silva," in *Quevedo en el teatro y otras cosas* (1930), pp. 45–119 (also published in *Boletín de la Biblioteca de Menéndez y Pelayo,* Vol. XI, 1929, and in *Revista de la Biblioteca, Archivo y Museo del Ayuntamiento de Madrid,* 1929).

F. S. y E.

Loria, Arturo (1902–, Italian picaresque novelist), was born in Carpi, Modena province, but has spent most of his life in Florence, where he became a leading member of the Solaria group of young writers who frequented the Caffè delle Giubbe Rosse. Loria first attracted attention with the publication of a collection of short stories entitled *Il Cieco e la bellona* (1928). Then followed *Fannias Ventosca* (1929) and *La Scuola di ballo* (1932); *La Scuola* won him the coveted literary award of Italia Letteraria for the outstanding novel of the year.

In Loria's stories he obviously turns away from such moderns as Proust (*q.v.*) and Joyce —and Freud—to follow such masters as Cervantes and Balzac. Rogues, beggars, prostitutes, and brigands are his protagonists. He places them, however, in a modern environment and exposes them to the exigencies of the present social order. In spite of the eccentricities of these individuals, Loria depicts their human qualities so vividly and with such delicate irony that almost invariably the reader understands and sympathizes with them. Some critics see in Loria a confirmed pessimist. There is indeed pessimism, yet at the same time few contemporary Italian writers have so vividly portrayed the underlying joys of life. Loria believes that even strange and misshapen humans should have and may have their share of gaiety and amusement. The plots of Loria's stories are thought out with a mathematical accuracy that is calculated to hold the interest of the reader. Yet there is sometimes an overabundance of detail, and the author is too often more preoccupied with minuteness of expression and stylistic effect than with intensity of feeling or action. But whatever the obvious shortcomings in his style, Arturo Loria is one of the most attractive of the younger generation of writers in Italy. His writings—all too few considering the natural talent of the author—reveal a deep and genuinely moving human affection for the unfortunate creatures of this world.

P. M. R.

Loti, Pierre (pseud. of Julien Viaud, 1850–1923, French novelist), has won recognition as a master of colorful, nostalgic descriptions of exotic scenes and as a bard of the grim poetry of the sea, the melancholy of the past, and the majesty of death. Born at Rochefort, of a distinguished Huguenot family, he decided at 15 to become a naval officer and entered the naval school two years later. At the end of a long professional career he was retired in 1910 with the rank of captain, but volunteered (for the army) at the outset of the First World War and was later cited for bravery. He died, at 73, in his solitary villa at Hendaye on the Basque coast. The French navy buried him with national pomp in the grove of his ancestral home at Saint-Pierre d'Oleron. He had been elected to the French Academy in 1891.

From the time he first knew how to write, Loti kept a diary (*Journal intime,* 1926), which later became the fount of his literary production. He wrote more than 40 volumes of touching memories and of impressions gleaned in endless voyages and wanderings. Among the lands he visited, those especially associated with his name are Polynesia (*Rarahu,* later called *Le Mariage de Loti,* 1880), Turkey (*Aziyadé,* 1879; *Les Désenchantées,* 1906; *Suprêmes Visions d'orient,* 1921), Senegambia (*Le Roman d'un spahi,* 1881), Brittany (*Mon Frère Yves,* 1883; *Pêcheur d'Islande,* 1886), Japan (*Madame Chrysanthème,* 1887), China (*Matelot,* 1893), Morocco, the Holy Land (*La Galilée,* 1895), the Basque country (*Ramuntcho,* 1897), India, Persia (*Vers Ispahan,* 1904), Cambodia (*Un Pèlerin d'Angkor,* 1906), and Egypt. *Pêcheur d'Islande* is unquestionably his masterpiece. Many of the works of Loti have been translated into English.

Religious doubts that crept into his mind at a tender age molded Loti's whole life. Bereft of a faith that had promised everlasting communion with his mother—the only woman he ever truly loved—he lived thereafter in mortal dread of losing her. A haunting presentiment of the utter solitude that must one day befall him, the sense of his own fragility and of the futility of life, affected him profoundly. He sought eagerly and enviously, in later life, the secret of the abiding faith of humble folk, through the Orient of the Prophet, in the footsteps of Jesus in Galilee, and at the shrines of the Indian theosophists in holy Benares. On the other hand his life as a sailor hardened his character in some respects—and helped the full blossoming of his talent. By simply confiding in his readers, "unknown friends," he could find a manner of solace for his chagrin and anxiety. Though fleeting as a dream, his emotions run so deep that he easily takes his place among the best of the subjective writers.

Loti is usually considered the initiator of modern exotic fiction, yet the bond between him and the many authors of exotic and regional novels, who more or less consciously derived their inspiration from him, is as slight as his connection with Bernardin de Saint-Pierre and Chateaubriand, with whom he is too readily associated. Whether we consider his works of fiction, in which his characters clearly appear to be projections of his inner self, or his travel books, in which the very universe seems to revolve around his person, we find him in every sense identical with the Loti of those gems of introspective study, *Le Roman d'un enfant* (1890) and *Prime Jeunesse* (1919). A painter of rare genius in the impressionistic style, he captured the symphonies of light with a skill that recalls Debussy's orchestration of incipient and dying harmonies. His depth of human understanding would justify placing his whole production under the title of one of his most stirring books, *Le Livre de la pitié et de la mort* (1890).

See: J. Lemaître, *Les Contemporains* (1898); V. Giraud, *Les Maîtres de l'heure,* Vol. I (1911); N. Serban, *Pierre Loti; sa vie et son œuvre* (1924).

P. A. C.

Louÿs, Pierre (pseud. of Pierre Louis, 1870–1925, French poet and novelist), was born in Ghent, of French parents. He was educated in Paris at the Ecole Alsacienne, a Protestant institution, where he became the friend of André Gide (*q.v.*), at the Lycée Janson-de-Sailly, and at the Sorbonne. He made his entry into the world of letters by founding *La Conque* (1891), a review in which were published his first poems, soon afterwards collected under the title *Astarté* (1891). His chief collaborators were Henri de Régnier (*q.v.*), Gide, and Valéry (*q.v.*). Five years later the same authors founded the sumptuous review *Le Centaure.* Pierre Louÿs was the disciple of Heredia (*q.v.*) and in 1899 married Louise, the youngest daughter of this leading poet of the Parnassian school.

A man of insatiable intellectual curiosity and passionate devotion to art, at once a sensuous pagan and a refined aesthete, he celebrated the free life of ancient Greece and proclaimed sensual fulfillment a condition essential to artistic creation and spiritual development. As a Greek scholar he made the translations *Poésies de Méléagre de Gadara* (1893) and *Scènes de la vie des courtisanes de Lucien* (1894), graceful, piquant works of which the subjects foreshadowed the erotic and Hellenistic tendencies of his later writings. When *Les Chansons de Bilitis, traduites du grec par Pierre Louÿs* (1894) was published, several scholars mistook "ce petit livre d'amour antique" (see the dedication) for an authentic work by a contemporary of Sappho. Indeed these enchanting and licentious poems in prose were harmoniously classic in style and gave evidence of sound archaeological research. When François Coppée (*q.v.*) publicly acclaimed *Aphrodite* (1896) as one of the greatest masterpieces of the French language, Louÿs became famous almost overnight. This novel of Alexandrian manners makes an appeal for the rehabilitation of physical love and the beauty of the nude; though shallow and unreal in psychology, it attests a remarkable historical knowledge and has pages luminously picturesque and exquisitely pure in form. In *La Femme et le pantin* (1898) the interest becomes entirely psychological. Restrained yet vigorous in expression, this Andalusian novel recounts the pathetic experience of a man to whom sensuality brought complete servitude and ruin. Among Louÿs's numerous short stories of classical or fictitious inspiration, *Les Aventures du roi Pausole* (1901) is especially noteworthy as a graceful and spicy bit of drollery.

Though the success of certain of his works was founded as much on their licentious character as on their literary merit, some of the poems of Louÿs (see *Poésies,* 1927) by their grace, by that clear imagery characteristic of the Parnassian school, and by their pure and flexible harmony of style may well become immortal; indeed few poets have ever had a more fervent worship of beauty and a more profound respect for form. The works of Louÿs have inspired several musicians, among whom the most notable is Claude Debussy. With the exception of occasional voyages, Louÿs lived in retirement in his small luxurious home in Paris and remained studious until his death.

See: E. Gaubert, *Pierre Louÿs* (1904) and *Le Tombeau de Pierre Louÿs* (1925); A. Gide, *Si le grain ne meurt* (1926), *passim.*

B. R. L.

Lugné-Poe, Aurélien François (1869–1940, French theatrical producer, director, and actor), championed the cause of young French writers and foreign masters at his Théâtre de l'Œuvre. Born in Paris, he was early attracted to the theatre and while attending the Lycée Condorcet founded the Cercle des Escholiers with Georges Bourdon. He studied at the Conservatory (1888–1892) and acted at the Théâtre Libre (1888–1890) and at Paul Fort's (*q.v.*) Théâtre d'Art (1891–1892). Painters like Bonnard, Denis, Vuillard, and Toulouse-Lautrec offered Lugné stimulating friendship, later contributing their art to his theatre. The production of Maeterlinck's (*q.v.*) *Pelléas et Mélisande* on May 17, 1893, at the Théâtre d'Art, for which Fort had given Lugné-Poe full responsibility, affirmed the scenic value of the Belgian's work and Lugné-Poe's leadership in *avant-garde* theatrical circles. Lugné and his friends determined to prolong their association and, hopeful of discovering a great French masterpiece, called their enterprise the Théâtre de l'Œuvre.

The Théâtre de l'Œuvre opened its first season on October 10, 1893, with Ibsen's (*q.v.*) *Rosmersholm,* inaugurating a vigorous campaign for foreign masterpieces, especially Scandinavian. Until Lugné severed relations with the languishing symbolist movement (1897), the character of the Œuvre remained essentially symbolist, although he always welcomed any play which might stir a sluggish public. Stormy receptions by enemies and by conservative critics merely inspired him to succeed. While still in his 20's Lugné launched playwrights like Henry Bataille (*q.v.*), Maurice Beaubourg, Tristan Bernard (*q.v.*), and Edmond Sée. Wilde's *Salomé* had its world *première* at the Œuvre on February 11, 1896, and Jarry's (*q.v.*) *Ubu Roi* was greeted there noisily on December 10, 1896. The roster of the Œuvre's authors extends brilliantly through the years, including Romain Rolland, Emile Verhaeren, André Gide (*qq.v.*), Jean Jullien, Albert Samain, (*q.v.*), and Paul Claudel (*q.v.*) in the period before 1914, Fernand Crommelynck (*q.v.*), Jean Sarment (*q.v.*), and Stève Passeur (*q.v.*) in the 1920's.

With the loyal cooperation of his actress wife, Mme Suzanne Després, Lugné-Poe supported Parisian productions with the proceeds of tours, at the same time extending the influence of his experimental venture. Eager to meet Ibsen, Lugné, in the first important tour of the Œuvre troupe (1894), dared take French versions of the writer's dramas to Scandinavia. Ibsen's kindness and advice assured in Lugné a lifelong devotion. Other tours carried the troupe to many parts of Europe, South America, and Africa. As impresario Lugné sponsored Parisian appearances of such artists as Eleonora Duse, Ermete Zaccone, Isadora Duncan, and Ruth Draper. After serving in the Intelligence Department (1914–1918), Lugné-Poe won back the important position of the Théâtre de l'Œuvre with no resources except a reputation for imposing foreign masterpieces and the works of promising young Frenchmen. The names of Lugné-Poe and Suzanne Després are interwoven with that of the Œuvre for, undaunted by constant material hardships, they persistently discovered and revealed dramatic talent. The French theatre is richer because of Lugné-Poe's vitality, fearless honesty, liberal interests, and literary discernment.

See: Lugné-Poe, *La Parade* (3 vols., 1931–1933); D. Knowles, *La Réaction idéaliste au théâtre depuis 1890* (1934), pp. 172–208; M. Coindreau, *La Farce est jouée* (1942), pp. 249–262.

G. R. J.

Lundegård, Axel (1861–1930, Swedish novelist), is scarcely a figure of first importance in Swedish literature, but his work (like that indeed of his contemporary Gustaf af Geijerstam, *q.v.*) reflects some of the most characteristic phases of literary development in Sweden in the last 60 years. His first work, a volume of short stories *I gryningen* (1885; At Dawn), reveals him as an extremist exponent of the spirit of the Scandinavian 80's with its strenuous moral feeling (influenced by Kierkegaard and Ibsen's *Brand*) and its rigid realistic techniques. It soon became apparent, however, that this early polemic radicalism was more a half-naïve youthful reflection of the spirit of the day than it was an essential expression of Lundegård's own literary temperament. His first novel, *Röde prinsen* (1889; The Red Prince), provides an early accounting with the orthodoxy of the 80's. Its central character, Max von Rosenberg, is a young author who comes in the course of the novel to lose his early liberal faith in social and political democracy and the current naturalistic literature. He feels that the literature of the 80's had drawn an overidealized picture of the worker and that it had gone too far in its prevailingly dark depiction of human life in general. He calls instead for more light and sunshine in literature and champions an idealistic individualism not without its points of contact with Nietzsche (*q.v.*). In the new program for literature expressed in *Röde prinsen,* Lundegård was in line with the literary ideals of the Swedish 90's (Heidenstam, Lagerlöf, Levertin, *qq.v.*, etc.); but Lundergård himself was not capable of making in the long series of novels that succeeded *Röde prinsen* a really significant creative contribution to the new neoromantic literature that flowered so richly in Sweden around the turn of the century. These novels fall loosely into two classes: first, a group of soft, quietly elegant romantic tales with sentimental erotic themes (*Titania,* 1892; *Prometeus,* 1893; *Tannhäuser,* 1895; *Fru Hedvigs dagbok,* Fru Hedvig's Diary, 1895); and secondly, a number of ambitious but only partially impressive historical novels (*Struensee,* 3 vols., 1898–1900; *Drottning Margareta,* 2 vols., 1905–1906; Queen Margaret; *Drottning Filippa,* 1907; *Drottning Cilla,* 1910; and others).

In his later years Lundegård's creative productivity feel off sharply; but during these years he wrote two pieces of biographical reminiscence (one on Victoria Benediktsson, the other on Strindberg, *qq.v.*) which are among the most valuable documents on literary trends during the 80's in Sweden. In these works Lundegård draws on his experiences as a literary collaborator with both Victoria Benediktsson and Strindberg, particularly with the former, whose literary executor he became.

See: S. Linder, "Axel Lundegård," *Ord och bild,* XL (1931), 482–490.

A. G.

M

Machado, Antonio (1875–1939, Spanish poet), was one of the leading poets of Spain following the renaissance brought about by Rubén Darío's "modernism." Always an admirer of Darío, he rejected the sensual as well as the verbal aestheticism of his school, adopting only the lyrical attitude from which it sprang. From the "modernistic" movement, or rather from its French models, Machado also derived the subjective feeling for the atmosphere of reality which replaced the descriptive representation of reality—or the romantic deviation from it prevailing in the poetry of the preceding period. Except for this debt to the art of his time, Machado's work has a nontemporal accent, the result and expression of an intense concentration in his inner life.

His biography is in perfect accord with the simple austerity of his poetry. Born in Seville, he probably owed to his father, a disciple of Sanz del Río (*q.v.*) and the first scholarly collector of Spanish folklore, an authentic liberalism, a preoccupation with the rebirth of Spain, and a taste for popular lore and wisdom which was—raised to a higher spiritual level—an important part of his work. He studied at the Institución Libre de Enseñanza. Afterward he went to Paris, where at the turn of the century he learned the modes of new poetry and sensibility. In 1907 he became a teacher of French, and years later a teacher of Spanish literature. He taught successively in the *Institutos* of Soria, Baeza, and Segovia. Meanwhile he studied philosophy, first with Bergson (*q.v.*) in Paris, later in Madrid. Respected always as a writer, he shunned recognition and kept aloof from literary groups and passing intellectual fashions. He preferred the friendship of obscure, modest people, appreciating in them, above all, human kindness and honesty. When the republic came, he was transferred to Madrid, elected to the Spanish Academy, and appointed a member of the Consejo de Instrucción Pública. Machado's moral quality—on which so much of the value of his poetry rests —was shown during the civil war. When many intellectuals abandoned the cause of the people, Machado, old and sick, discovered a new energy which he devoted to the struggle. He followed the government to Valencia and Barcelona. Never a prolific writer, he then wrote almost daily for the republican press. He made public appearances and endured the hardships of a chaotic situation. And yet, in a time of unbridled passions, his words were lofty and noble, without a trace of demagogy or hate. In January, 1939, he crossed the Pyrenees afoot, with the mass of exiled refugees, and died a month later in the French village of Collioure. He became a true symbol of the moral strength and aspirations of his people, whom he had never forgotten.

Machado produced little and slowly, first publishing three short books, *Soledades* (1903), *Soledades, Galerías y otros poemas* (1907), and *Campos de Castilla* (1912), reprinted together with some new poems in *Poesías completas* (1917). Then followed *Nuevas canciones* (1924) and three new editions of *Poesías completas* (1928, 1930, 1934). In these were included, besides the later poems, his philosophic and poetic-prose aphorisms, maxims, and fragments, which he attributed to one Juan de Mairena, a creation of his own mind. Other prose fragments of the same type appeared in 1936 with the title *Juan de Mairena: Sentencias, donaires, apuntes y recuerdos de un profesor apócrifo*. His last writings have been collected posthumously in editions published in Mexico and Argentina. In collaboration with his brother Manuel Machado (*q.v.*), also a poet of distinction, he wrote several poetic plays as well as adaptations of Hugo's *Hernani* and of classic plays by Lope, Tirso, and Calderón.

Machado the poet can be characterized by certain objective aspects of his work, such as his themes and ideas. He has a close relationship with the writers of the Generation of '98, especially with Azorín (*q.v.*), for his feeling toward the humble things of life, and with Unamuno (*q.v.*), for his religious and philosophical preoccupations. He is the poet of Castile, with its austere lands and men, its old cities, its history and soul. To Castile he is also bound by the gravity of his character and a deep personal experience in Soria, where he married and lost his young wife, the only love of this solitary poet. This experience had an ever present influence on him. The influence of his native Andalusia is less evident, but not less important. It can be perceived in his melancholy introspectiveness, in the fineness of his sensibility, and in the popular form and substance of his "cantares," proverbs, and maxims. He is also a poet of ideas —a political poet—who reflected in his writings the problems and hopes of modern Spain, and a poet of circumstances, who found his themes in the most immediate and common experiences. He is modern in his thought and aesthetic conception, and at the same time classic and traditional, a direct inheritor of the moral inspiration of poets such as Jorge Manrique. But his real value does not depend on his themes or ideas; it springs from a poetic comprehension of universal human emotions—time, death, and the search for God. These he sees in reality and in life because he is a realist and a stoic who turns towards himself in a continuous soliloquy to seek and find the eternal sources of man's spiritual anxiety and also the moral strength to accept with humble conformity man's destiny. The constant dialogue with himself to which he alludes in "Retrato," one of his most characteristic poems, has a double projection in his poetry, in a remembering and dreaming neither material nor fantastic, but spiritual, to such an extent that were it not for his permanent attachment to reality and vital experience he could almost be characterized as a mystic. In this combination of realism and transcendent illusion, as in everything else, Machado is profoundly Spanish and as such very difficult to classify as belonging to any school or pattern.

See: F. de Onís, *Antología de la poesía española e hispanoamericana, 1882–1932* (1934), pp. 258–292; E. A. Peers, *Antonio Machado* (1940, in English).

A. del R.

Machado, Manuel (1874–, Spanish poet), was born in Seville, as was Antonio Machado (*q.v.*), his brother, from whom he differs profoundly. In Manuel the influence of Seville persists as an essential characteristic of his work, even though he has spent the greater part of his life in Madrid. For this reason, while Antonio is considered the poet of Castile, Manuel is considered a fundamentally Andalusian poet. To this basic Andalusian character there was added the influence of Madrid, and both were later to be fused and refined by the Parisian, acquired through Machado's French readings and the years he spent in Paris between 1898 and 1900. There is no incompatibility in his poetry between these three influences, at first sight so at variance. It was in Paris, under the influence of French symbolism (*q.v.*), that the Spanish personality of Manuel Machado—molded by the two Spanish cities that are at once the most refined and the most popular—revealed itself in its full originality, universal and modern.

The poetry of Manuel Machado, to be found in various works beginning with *Alma* (1902) and collected in *Poesías* (*Opera Omnia Lírica*) (1924), represents at its best one of the supreme forms of contemporary Spanish poetry. Although it seems slight—because his unfailing good taste keeps him from insistence and repetition—it offers great variety and wealth of themes and forms. More than any other Spanish poet he represents the full range of the modernist movement, by reason of his command of the French poetic technique which in him is perfectly fused with the most traditional and popular Spanish forms, by his use of the symbolist themes and sentiments, by his impressionist descriptions, his archaeological primitivism, his transcriptions of paintings, his feeling for the trivial, the commonplace, the decadent, by his abnormal sensitivity and his lack of will power, by his aristocratic interpretation of the popular. All these highly diverse elements are effortlessly combined in every moment of his work through some subtle, indefinable quality which is his originality, something that is grace, lightness, tone, bouquet, air—all contained and precise—elegance, in a word, very Spanish in character and very much of Seville in tone. Because this poetry, which is the essence of poetry, seems so light there are those who do not hold it in sufficient esteem; for this very reason it must be affirmed that it is unique and that its author must be regarded as one of the leading poets of this epoch.

See: A. González-Blanco, "Manuel Machado," in *Los contemporáneos,* Ser. 2 (1908), pp. 83–124; J. Chabás, *Vuelo y estilo* (1924), pp. 97–125.

F. de O.

Machar, Josef Svatopluk (1864–1942, Czech poet and essayist), was the leader of the realist movement in Czech poetry. He was born in Kolín and in 1891 became a bank clerk in Vienna, where he lived till 1918. In 1916 he had been imprisoned by the Austrian authorities for his anti-Austrian underground activities. He became in 1919 inspector general of the Czechoslovak army (largely charged with the educational program), but had to resign in 1924 because of a purely personal affair. This drove him into bitter opposition to his former friend, Masaryk. Machar died in March, 1942, in complete retirement.

The writing career of Machar began with lyrics in the tradition of Heine and Neruda (*q.v.*), later collected in the three volumes of *Confiteor* (1887–1892). In contrast to the decorative diction of poets such as Vrchlický (*q.v.*) and Čech (*q.v.*) Machar wrote in simple, almost prosaic style, and in distinction from their buoyant optimism he sang only of his heart's disillusionments which he bore with ironical skepticism. Many of these early poems, which were followed by a brilliant series of sonnets (1891–1893), are extremely witty as well as genuinely poetic in their sharp outlines, vivid impressionism, and slightly cynical pessimism. A later collection, *Výlet na Krym* (1900; A Trip to the Crimea), is a subjective travel diary in verse which shows a happier mood and an undiminished power of observation and description. But Machar soon widened his themes to include political and social questions. *Tristium Vindobona* (1893) is a series of satirical and skeptical meditations on the politics and ideology of his own nation. Machar suspected romantic nationalism and disliked the ineffectiveness of the Czech parliamentary opposition in Vienna. His early satirical attitude towards women changed. Now he saw them as victims of circumstances and in a volume of sketches and portraits of women called *Zde by měly kvést růže* (1894; Here Should Roses Bloom) pleaded the cause of their emancipation. *Magdalena* (1894; Eng. tr., *Magdalen,* 1916) is a highly amusing verse novel of a prostitute who marries respectably but is forced back to her "establishment" by the relentless persecution of small-town gossips.

With *Golgotha* (1901) Machar embarked on a cycle of volumes which he came to call *Svědomím věků* (The Conscience of the Ages), covering the whole history of the world from Babylon to the First World War. The models of Hugo and Vrchlický were obviously before his eyes. The title poem of *Golgotha* gives the clue to Machar's philosophy of history: Satan upbraids Christ on the Cross for having founded Christianity which will bring only suffering, cruelty, slaughter, and weakness to humanity. Another volume of the series is thus appropriately called *Jed z Judey* (1906; The Poison from Judaea); others glorify the virtues Machar admires—the bright intellect of the Greeks and the power of the Romans. *V záři hellenského slunce* (1906; In the Glow of the Greek Sun), *Barbaři* (1911; Barbarians), *Pohanské plameny* (1911; Pagan Flames), *Apoštolové* (1911; Apostles), *Oni* (1921; They), and *On* (1921; He) are the other titles of the cycle, which is built on the contrast, derived from Nietzsche (*q.v.*), between classical joy and Christian morbidity.

Machar resumed his satirical writing after the war with *Tristium Praga* (1926) and many epigrams and satires against Czechoslovak political conditions. Machar's prose, like his poetry, is always lucid and readable. He is a brilliant polemist and satirist as well as storyteller. Many volumes of reminiscences (*e.g.*, *Konfese literáta,* 2 vols., 1901, The Confessions of a Literary Man; *Kriminál,* 1918, Eng. tr., *The Jail,* 1922; *Pět let v kasárnách,* 1927, Five Years in the Barracks) and portraits (*Vídenšké profily,* 1919; Viennese Profiles) rise above the level of good journalism. In a widely read travel book, *Řím* (1907; Rome), Machar expounded again his philosophy of history, but there his uncritical glorification of antiquity and superficial anticlericalism sounded even more blatant than in the more imaginative verse.

Machar's historical importance is considerable: his return to colloquial diction, his dislike of the 19th-century belief in progress, his hatred of the Hapsburgs and of Catholicism, his plea for the emancipation of woman, left a permanent impress on wide sections of Czech public opinion. But the Nietzscheism and bitter political resentments of his later years again isolated him, and his influence has been steadily on the decline. From an artistic point of view his early work is preferable; the later volumes of "The Conscience of the Ages" are frequently hasty improvisations, and his prose also displays many lapses of taste and power.

See: V. Martínek, *J. S. Machar* (1912); Arne Novák, *Mužové a osudy* (1914); P. Buzková, *Žena v životě a díle J. S. Machara* (1918); J. Šusta, "Macharův Řím," in *Z dob dávných i blízkých* (1924). There are German translations of many of Machar's works.

R. W.

Mac-Orlan, Pierre (pseud. of Pierre Dumarchais, 1883–, French novelist), was born in Péronne, Somme. He attended the *lycée* in Orléans. Prior to 1914 he was one of the bohemians who haunted the slopes of Montmartre, holding innumerable positions, notably one as a cartoonist. It was then he adopted the Scotch pseudonym by which he is now known. At the outbreak of the First World War he had written but a few humorous short stories for various magazines. One of these, *Le Rire jaune* (1914), was a parody on the Martian invasion of the world as described by H. G. Wells; in Mac-Orlan's story the invader is a strange sickness, "yellow laughter," which almost annihilates the human race. In another, *La Bête conquérante* (published in book form with *Le Rire jaune,* 1920), as the result of an operation a pig begins to speak. Thereupon man operates on all the animals, who gradually replace him in performing intellectual tasks. Centuries later man is able to regain his original sovereignty when the animals in turn succumb to their indolence. These two stories reveal the essence of Mac-Orlan's early thought and art: nothing is more unstable than civilization. It is the property of art to visualize ways of life other than the ordinary and to study people living on the margin of civilization—pirates and galley slaves of other days, soldiers of the Foreign Legion and apaches of today. The First World War, in which Mac-Orlan took part, emphasized his original leanings and clarified for him the vague notion on which his antirealism was based: where action is concerned, reality falls far short of the ideal. From this conception stem the two successive phases through which Mac-Orlan has passed in his denying the fitness of reality as subject matter. The first phase is reflected in his adventure stories, the second in his tales of witchcraft. The book he wrote on the war, *Les Poissons morts* (1917), bore witness to his disillusionment, to his conviction that action could never be a satisfactory substitute for dreams. *Le Manuel du parfait aventurier* (1920) crystallized this feeling: the true adventurer is one who without leaving his arm-chair dreams his adventures. *Le Chant de l'équipage* (1918) and *A bord de l'Etoile Matutine* (1920) illustrate this theory. The supernatural elements in *Le Nègre Léonard et Maître Jean Mullin* (1920) are drawn from various works on witchcraft which complete Mac-Orlan's library. *Malice* (1923) is inspired by certain Germanic legends.

Post-war materialism gave new meaning to Mac-Orlan's imaginative powers. He felt more strongly than ever that it was the duty of the poet to create a new set of legends and myths to counteract the barbaric materialism into which humanity was settling. *La Cavalière Elsa* (1921) and *La Vénus internationale* (1923) represent two episodes of this struggle.

See: Georges Girard, "Notes bio-bibliographiques: Pierre Mac Orlan," *Bulletin de la Maison du Livre Français*, January 1, 1922, pp. 140–142; Benjamin Crémieux, "Pierre Mac-Orlan," *Revue européenne*, Vol. IV, October 1, 1924, pp. 16–26.

P. B.

Madariaga, Salvador de (1886–, Spanish essayist and poet), was born at La Coruña in Galicia. Trained as an engineer at the Ecole Polytechnique in Paris, he moved to London in 1916 and devoted himself to journalism. In 1921 he entered the League of Nations Secretariat, becoming in the following year director of the disarmament section (1922–1927). From 1928 to 1931 he occupied the chair of Spanish studies at Oxford University. For the Spanish republic he served as ambassador to the United States (1931) and to France (1932–1934).

A product of three cultures, speaking and writing in Spanish, French, and English with the same perfection (all translations of his books are his own), Madariaga is, of all living Spanish intellectuals, the most cosmopolitan-minded figure. This spirit of cosmopolitanism, or call it rather humanism, is reflected in his political philosophy, based on the double principle of the liberty of the individual and the solidarity of mankind. Hence his interest in the problems of international relations and world organization as means to the realization of this double principle and the attainment of peace, subjects discussed in his political writings (*e.g., Disarmament,* 1929; *Discursos internacionales,* 1934; *Theory and Practice in International Relations,* 1937; *The World's Design,* 1938). Hence also his interest in the problems of national psychology as a political factor in the relations between countries, of which his *Englishmen, Frenchmen, Spaniards* (1928) is the best example. His interest in international affairs, however, has not lessened his preoccupation with Spain and things Spanish in general. Since Madariaga has lived most of the time abroad, especially in England, his task in this respect has consisted mainly in presenting and interpreting Spain—its land and its people, its problems and its values—to the outside world. That he has accomplished his aim in a brilliant manner is well illustrated in his historical essay *Spain* (1930; the second English edition, 1942, covers the period 1930–1942 as well) and in his several writings on different phases of Spanish literature (*Shelley & Calderón,* 1920; *The Genius of Spain and Other Essays on Spanish Contemporary Literature,* 1923; *Guía del lector del "Quijote,"* 1926, Eng. tr., *Don Quixote,* 1934). Also to be mentioned in this connection are the author's two historical biographies, *Christopher Columbus* (1940) and *Hernán Cortés* (1941), which have appeared both in Spanish and in English. Finally, the same Spanish inspiration, in psychological mood as well as in technique, is to be found in Madariaga's creative work as a poet (*Romances de ciego,* 1922; *La fuente serena,* 1928) and, more recently, as a dramatist (*El Toisón de oro,* 1940).

See: H. Petriconi, "Methodische Probleme der Kulturkunde (Zu den Werken Salvador de Madariagas)," *Die neueren Sprachen,* XL (1932), 257–263; A. Aita, "Un espíritu europeo: Salvador de Madariaga," *Nosotros,* LXXX (1933), 62–69.

C. B.

Maeterlinck, Maurice (1862–, Belgian dramatist, poet, and essayist), was born in Ghent, studied law, and even practiced it half-heartedly for a little while. In 1886 he went to Paris, where he joined the phalanx of young symbolist poets who were lining up against the naturalistic sway in literature. In 1889 were published his dream-ridden poems, *Serres chaudes,* and *La Princesse Maleine,* a drama of thwarted love and mystery which, extraordinarily enough, the naturalistic writer Octave Mirbeau (*q.v.*) was the first to herald publicly, and overenthusiastically. Maeterlinck became famous overnight.

His succeeding plays, *L'Intruse* and *Les Aveugles* (1890), *Pelléas et Mélisande* (1892), *Intérieur* (1894), established his reputation. In contrast to the naturalistic theatre, which portrays realistically man's strife with the physical and tangible powers of evil in society, he created a drama which depicts symbolically the conflict the soul wages, "in the presence of eternity and mystery," against the dark and unseen forces of evil in the universe. The brooding pessimism of his early work became tempered, however, in later plays such as *Aglavaine et Selysette* (1896) and *Monna Vanna* (1902). The spell Death cast over his characters yielded gradually to the redeeming power of love, and in *L'Oiseau bleu* (1909), finally, Tyltyl and Mytyl discover that death does not even exist. But they learn also that happiness cannot be found except in the heart of the seeker.

This dramatic evolution had been presaged in his prose work *Le Trésor des humbles* (1896)—especially in the chapters on Ruysbroeck, Novalis, and Emerson, whose mysticism and transcendentalism penetrate him—and parallels the evolution of his thought in his later essays, *La Sagesse et la destinée* (1898) and *Le Temple enseveli* (1902). The spirit, he came to believe, cannot be stained by the mortal sins of the flesh; misfortune, sickness, even death, are external to man's real life, which is spiritual and cannot perish. He found seeming justification for such encouraging optimism in his study of the intelligence and will to live of flowers, bees, termites, ants—*L'Intelligence des fleurs* (1907), *La Vie des termites* (1927)—which bespoke to him the presence in all things as well as in man of a spirit which religions have called divine and which protects life in an otherwise hostile and unknown universe. He holds that even if such a belief were to prove an illusion, it at least lends the heart strength to go to the end of the road. Let evil reign in the universe, justice, goodness, and love in the soul.

As for unterrestrial immortality for the individual soul, Maeterlinck can hold out the hope of survival only in the bosom of the universal conscience, just as the body does in universal matter; he confessed stoically, in *La Mort* (1913), the impossibility of piercing the great secret and found comfort in the thought that a world devoid of mystery would be unbearable. He returned inevitably to the quest, however, and the certainty he could not find in pantheism or established religion he sought through the agency of the occult sciences, in *L'Hôte inconnu* (1917), *Le Grand Secret* (1921). While confirming him in his faith in the spiritual nature of life, they did not dispel his ignorance and doubts regarding the fate of man.

His ultimate attitude is one of melancholy agnosticism in the presence of destiny. His studies represent his poetic explorations in the mystery of life and death rather than a well-coordinated and original philosophical system. In his symbolistic theatre, however, he was the creator of a spiritual and idealistic art, a drama of the soul, which has had universal appeal and influence.

Maeterlinck won the Nobel prize in literature in 1911. In 1920, he came to the United States on a lecture tour. He returned in July, 1940, this time as a refugee from the Second World War. Most of his works are available in English translations.

See: H. Rose, *Maeterlinck's Symbolism: The Blue Bird, and Other Essays* (1911); J. Bithell, *Life and Writings of Maurice Maeterlinck* (1913); U. Taylor, *Maurice Maeterlinck; a Critical Study* (1914); A. Bailly, *Maeterlinck* (1931); G. Harry, *La Vie et l'œuvre de Maurice Maeterlinck* (1932).

S. A. R.

Maeztu, Ramiro de (1876–1936, Spanish journalist and essayist), was born in Vitoria, of a Cuban father and an English mother. A sojourn in Cuba as a lad brought him into contact with the political disturbances there, and his first articles predicted Spain's catastrophe of 1898. Maeztu came into prominence in Spain as a member of the iconoclastic group of young intellectuals later known as the Generation of 1898. His subsequent career was marked by change—change of residence, change of political faith. He traveled much on the Continent. For 15 years he was a news correspondent in London, and his articles published in *Correspondencia* and other Spanish periodicals were influential in arousing the interest of Spaniards in English political and social life. In 1928 the dictator, Primo de Rivera, sent Maeztu, now an arch-conservative, as ambassador of Spain to Argentina. After the fall of the monarchy he became one of the leaders of the reactionary faction, the Acción Española, working always against the liberal forces of the Spanish republic. He was imprisoned after the outbreak of the civil war and, according to report, was killed when he was taken from prison by Loyalist troops on November 7, 1936.

Although Maeztu was an important figure in the literary world of Spain during the first third of this century, much of the value of his writings may be said to be historical and political rather than literary. Their influence was augmented by Maeztu's opportunistic tendency to advocate the popular idea of the moment. From his youthful position of flamboyant anarchism he passed to that of stern defender of hierarchy and discipline. His first book, *Hacia otra España* (1899), urged the reform of Spain by opening its doors to the currents of contemporary European thought, a point of view which he later renounced completely. During his years in London he tended to uphold Anglo-Saxon manners and ideas as models for his fellow countrymen. In *Authority, Liberty, and Function in the Light of the War* (1916), later published in Spanish under the title *La crisis del humanismo* (1919), there is a noticeable shift from the individual to the collective ideal of government. Here he attempts to demonstrate that both authority and liberty have failed as a basis for society, and he maintains that the society of tomorrow must be founded on the principle of function. *Defensa de la hispanidad* (1934) is an eloquent document which the party of General Franco and the Spanish Falange in South America have used as propaganda. It is antiliberal, antidemocratic, anti-Anglo-Saxon, anti-Semitic. In it Maeztu states categorically that the hope of the future is a return to the past. He attributes to the ideals of the French Revolution all the political ills of the past 200 years and for "liberty, equality, fraternity" would substitute "service, hierarchy, brotherhood." He urges all Spanish-speaking countries to unite under the ideal of the ancient Catholic monarchy, the only road to stability and power. *Don Quijote, Don Juan y la Celestina* (1926) is a sociological interpretation rather than a literary criticism of these characters of fiction. Other works of Maeztu are *Inglaterra en armas* (1916), *El arte y la moral* (1932), and *Cinco ensayos sobre don Juan, con un prólogo de A. Castro* (1933).

See: R. Gómez de la Serna, *Azorín,* 1930 ed.; S. de Madariaga, *Spain* (1930); Félix García, *Al través de almas y libros* (1935).

K. R. W.

Magalhães Lima, Jaime de (1857–1936, Portuguese novelist), was born in Aveiro. He devoted himself to politics and social questions and traveled extensively. His literary formation was within the tradition of the realistic school, and he was a friend of the most outstanding figures in this movement. His writing began later, however, when new influences, such as the Russian and the Scandinavian, had come to be felt in the novel. It fell to him to incorporate the first of these tendencies into the Portuguese novel. He was so attracted by the doctrines of Leo Tolstoy (*q.v.*) that he visited this writer in Russia and set about to popularize his ideas in books and articles. *O transviado* (1899; The Mislaid One) is the first attempt in Portugal in the field of the mystico-realistic thesis novel; in its pages a penetrating psychological instinct enhances its quality and interest. Later he wrote other novels and stories of the same evangelical, humanitarian type—*O sonho da perfeição* (1901; The Dream of Perfection), *Na paz do Senhor* (1903; In the Peace of Our Lord), and *Reino da saüdade* (1904; Kingdom of Longing). His work is primarily of interest in that it represents the introduction of this new modality in the modern Portuguese novel.

See: J. Agostinho, *Jaime de Magalhães Lima* (1911).

E. G. D.

Magnússon, Guðmundur, *see* Trausti, Jón.

Maiorescu, Titu (1840–1917, Rumanian literary critic and statesman), studied in Vienna, Berlin, and Paris, and upon returning to his native land, brought with him Western European ideas. Appointed professor of philosophy in the University of Jassy in 1862, he attempted to blend Kantian and Schopenhauerean systems with Hegelianism. He soon realized, however, that in a country hardly emancipated from oriental influences the immediate task was preliminary ground work. He consequently set out to teach fundamentals. The literature of the period had not yet reached its full development, and many were the sins of minor poets. Maiorescu wrote his incisive critical investigation, *Poezia română* (1867; Rumanian Poetry), *Beţia de cuvinte* (1873; Word Intoxication), and his monumental *Critice* (1874; Criticisms).

Maiorescu founded the society Junimea (Youth) of Jassy in 1865, and two years later the *Convorbiri literare* (Literary Conversations). In 1871 he was elected to represent Jassy in the Chamber of Deputies. Establishing himself in Bucharest, Maiorescu practiced law, was named professor of logic and occupied the chair until 1909, became minister of education in 1874 and 1888, minister of justice in 1900, and minister of foreign affairs in 1910. In 1912 he rose to the premiership of Rumania and dictated the Peace of Bucharest (1913), after the Second Balkan War.

An aristocrat and leader of the conservative Junimea (Youth), the former literary society which became a political party, Maiorescu could not accept the Marxian theories of Dobrogeanu-Gherea (*q.v.*). Hence the epochal debate on "art for art's sake" *vs.* "art with a tendency." The two critics exchanged the most skillful thrusts with elegance and fervor. The professor of logic and the former inmate of czarist prisons contributed considerably to the raising of literary polemics to a lofty plane.

See: N. Iorga, *Oameni cari au fost* (1935).

L. F.

Makuszyński, Kornel (1884–, Polish short-story writer, dramatic critic, and novelist), was born of humble parents at Stryj in the oil-bearing foothills of the Carpathians. He was educated in Lwów. His literary career began with the publication of youthful poems and theatrical reviews in *Słowo polskie* (The Polish Word). For 10 years (1904–1914) Makuszyński was dramatic critic for *Słowo;* later he became dramatic director of the Lwów Theatre. He was interned at the outbreak of the First World War and removed to Kiev, where he continued to direct plays. Returning in 1918 to Poland, he lived in Warsaw and in the Tatra mountain resort Zakopane. Within a short time he was the most popular writer in the realm. Poems, novels, short stories, translations, theatrical reviews, *feuilletons,* and children's tales flowed from his pen in an unending flood in response to an apparently insatiable popular craving for "the Makuszyński touch," which was a combination of whimsey and humor plus a large admixture of sincere patriotism. Time will inevitably winnow out much of Makuszyński's enormous output, but his children's stories are likely to live. Typical of his peculiar talent are *Panna z mokrą głową* (1932; The Girl with the Wet Pate), the Jeromesque *Człowiek znaleziony w nocy* (1932; The Man Found in the Night), and *Szatan z siódmej klasy* (1936; The Devil of Class Seven).

See: Z. Dębicki, *Portrety,* II (1928), 183–198; M. Orlicz, *Polski teatr współczesny* (1932), *passim;* K. Czachowski, *Obraz współczesnej literatury polskiej,* II (1934), 278–281, 381–382.

A. P. C.

Malaparte, *see* Suckert, Curzio.

Malaquais, Jean (1908–, French novelist), Polish born, is said to have learned French in three years, mastering it sufficiently to write his novel *Les Javanais* (Eng. tr., *The Men from Java,* 1941, American title, *Men from Nowhere,* 1943) directly in that language. The work was awarded the Théophraste Renaudot prize for 1939. It concerns a community of outcasts who have drifted to a forlorn spot in southern France, where a small mining company offers them work at starvation wages. There are family rebels, international hobos, adventurers, refugees. The author reveals a gift for character analysis and the creation of a tense, somber atmosphere.

In 1939 Malaquais enlisted as a volunteer in the French army. Since his demobilization two works have been published in America, the lurid *Journal de guerre* (1943; Eng. tr., *Jean Malaquais' War Diary,* 1944) and *Tentations* (1943), a group of two short stories.

P. B.

Mallarmé, Stéphane (1842–1898, French poet and aesthetician), was born in Paris and died in Valvins near Fontainebleau. His apparently obscure teacher's life was ruled by the same exclusive "furious vocation" as Villiers de l'Isle-Adam's (*q.v.*). When a child, he endlessly wrote Lamartinian verse. At the *lycée* in Sens, he discovered *Les Fleurs du mal* (*see* Baudelaire) which gave him his true orientation, then Poe and Gautier. About that time he became connected with the new Parnassian group and, at first, joined in their cult of vocables and their endeavor to bring more musical purity and weight to French poetry. He became Banville's admirer and friend, and Villiers appeared to him as "one of the elect." Through the latter he became acquainted with Hegel's philosophy. Having married, he went to London (1862–1864) in order to learn Poe's language—his future means of livelihood—which started him on the road to his linguistic and grammatical investigations (see *Petite Philologie . . . les mots anglais,* 1878). His lifelong interest in English poets and England is shown in his essay on Tennyson (*Vers et Prose*), his *Five Letters to Swinburne* (privately printed, 1922), the Oxford lecture (*La Musique et les lettres*), the essay on *Hamlet* (*Divagations*). Appointed to the Tournon *lycée* as teacher of English in 1863, he lived in the Rhone Valley (except for a year at Besançon) until 1872 and became the friend of Aubanel and Mistral (*qq.v.*). He contributed to *Le Parnasse contemporain* (1866) some poems in which reflections from Nerval and others gleam in a Baudelairian stream. In 1866, having "committed the sin of beholding Dream in its ideal nakedness," he realized the nature and scope of his poetical gifts and with the "fearful vision of the pure poem" before him "laid the foundation" of his "magnificent achievement" (*Lettres à Aubanel,* 1924). Unfortunately sickness and the tedium of his profession endangered the "most divine works" he had envisaged and made him despair. Nevertheless Mallarmé wrote at that time two great works—*Hérodiade,* a drama in verse (in *Le Parnasse contemporain,* 1869), and another in prose, *Igitur, ou la Folie d'Elbehnon* (not published until 1925), both left unfinished. The latter is the active presentation while *Hérodiade,* "the poem of absence," gives the passive aspect of the same theme.

In 1872 Mallarmé went to Paris, where his teaching career ended in 1893. The happier part of his last years was spent at his Valvins cottage. In 1865, at Banville's suggestion, he had written one scene in verse, "L'Après-Midi d'un faune," the first version of which, a "two-voiced poem" (unfinished) meant for the stage, differs largely from the "Eclogue" (1876; final ed., 1887), which inspired Debussy. He gave later a poetic adaptation of G. W. Cox's *Mythology* under the title *Les Dieux antiques* (1880), including an anthology of mythological poems by Banville and Leconte de Lisle.

Mallarmé remained unknown until 1884, when Huysmans (*q.v.*) in *A rebours* and Verlaine (*q.v.*) in his *Les Poètes maudits* paid him homage. Then the future leaders of French art and literature gathered around him, at the famous "Tuesdays" in the "Rue de Rome," and foreigners such as George Moore, Reyes, O'Shaughnessy, Stefan George, and, above all, Whistler, the author of a startling likeness of the poet, and later Gosse, Symons, T. S. Eliot, and others came to share the heroic "sublime madness" of the Prince of Poets.

Poems, from "Le Guignon" (1862) to "Sonnets" (1887), repeatedly revised (collected in *Poésies,* 1887; 2d ed., 1899; 3d ed., 1913; "Poèmes de circonstance" posthumously added, 1920); beautiful translations of Poe's poems (collected 1888); prose poems (partly published in *Pages,* 1891); *Album de vers et de prose* (1887–1888); *Vers et Prose* (1893); articles on the aesthetics of poetry and on style (collected in *Divagations,* 1897, which includes some prose poems and portraits, and in *La Musique et les lettres,* 1894)—these were given to small advance-guard reviews. As Mallarmé progressed, his works became more premeditated and strictly fashioned, hence his growing preference for the sonnet. Villiers said: "Each of his poems should be viewed as one architecture manifesting a concept, otherwise as a general organization." Gourmont found in them the "principle of the ideality of the universe" which had come into French poetry with Baudelaire. A poet's aim is to free the pure idea, "notion pure," from things or appearances, from the unruliness of time or "hazard." His work will be the sum total of the wizard's incantations, which act like a spell gradually transforming the reader into an exalted "diviner." The poems Mallarmé left, though but detached "shreds" of his intended work, are each a perfect symbolic whole wherein everything acts reciprocally, *i.e.,* a complex drama imaging the other drama that is being enacted in the poet's mind. Consequently the nature and possibilities of the theatre were bound to challenge his philosophical and technical powers. His 1876 letters to O'Shaughnessy and various reported discussions prove that he was even then engaged upon a "vast dramatic work" (G. J. Aubry, "Banville, Mallarmé et leurs amis anglais, d'après des documents inédits," *Figaro,* June 2, 1937). His discovery in 1885 of Wagner's opera caused him to define his own position in this respect. Mallarmé claims that the poet alone may create this *drame idéal,* in which converge and unite all other tributary arts and which rejects "outworn" legends or anecdotes and vain scenery. The Wagnerian opera, marred by extraneous elements, remains at mid-height, but Mallarmé aims for the summit, the road to which he traces with remarkable elegance and lucidity in the "Cérémonials" (*Revue indépendante,* 1886–1887, republished in *Vers et Prose*) and in the essays concerning the theatre in *Divagations.* The microcosm or condensation of his ideal drama is the "Book." This throws light upon Mallarmé's famous pronouncements, "Everything in the world exists to be consummated in a book" (*Divagations*) and "There is but one Book" (*Autobiographie*, 1924), to which he had hoped to contribute 20 volumes including four generating tomes of *Un Coup de Dés*. His style harmonized with the Book and the ideal drama he had conceived. This style is, as he intended, new, condensed, suggestive, rich in musical qualities. It has extraordinary variety, while rejecting explanatory and imitative elements. Mallarmé's syntax with its numerous parenthetical clauses is inevitably, at first, difficult for the reader and a source of obscurity through its foreshortenings, unexpected juxtapositions, and displacements; but it has the *équilibre supérieur* he required. His resilient verse, which complies with the rules of traditional prosody, also has a remarkable objective ideal plasticity. The poet said of *Un Coup de Dés*, "Primarily prints." That is why *Un Coup de Dés* as well as every poem he wrote is a figure vivified by music.

In 1897, one year before his death, Mallarmé published *Un Coup de Dés jamais n'Abolira le Hazard* (in *Cosmopolis*, 1897, republished 1914). A cast of the dice symbolizes the creation of the poem that challenges "hazard." The drowning of the ship's master, followed by the like fate of his young successor, portrays the engulfing of the poet by contingencies and the forces of time. We find here no abdication, but instead Baudelaire's exhilaration made up of joy and terror, faith and irony; and *Un Coup de Dés* rises on this twofold basis in the "language of lyricism and satire that lies in the very depths of poetry."

See: J. K. Huysmans, *A rebours* (1884); P. Verlaine, *Les Poètes maudits* (1884); P. Valéry, *Variété II* (1929); E. Noulet, *La Poésie de Stéphane Mallarmé* (1940); P. Beausire, *Essai sur la poésie et la poétique de Mallarmé* (1942); H. Mondor, *Vie de Mallarmé* (1942); Mallarmé, *Œuvres complètes* (1945). Some of Mallarmé's poems have been freely rendered into English by Roger Fry, with commentaries by Charles Mauron (*Poems*, London, 1936, New York, 1937).

M. M.

Malmberg, Bertil (1889–, Swedish poet), was born at Härnösand and studied at Uppsala and in Germany on a traveling scholarship. He has published many volumes of original verse, together with translations of recent German poetry and a study of Schiller. Of his prose the charming interpretation of child life, *Åke och hans värld* (1924; Eng. tr., *Åke and His World*, 1940), is deserving of special mention. In his original poetry he stands alone among present-day Swedish writers. He is a pagan mystic, wholly detached from the life of the moment. The dominant influence in his work is the neoclassical vein of such modern German masters as Stefan George, Hofmannsthal, and Rilke (*qq.v.*). For his devotion to ideal beauty and philosophic introspection the volume *Atlantis* (1916) is typical. His mood is profoundly sad and solitary, changing from misty moonlight to the desolation of autumn, but with occasional gleams of faith in the "supernatural city of beauty" which beckons to him out of the future. In his volume *Sångerne om samvetet och ödet* (1938; Songs of Conscience and Destiny), however, the poet recants his aestheticism and advocates a simple acceptance of duty and human fellowship.

C. W. S.

Malraux, André (1901–, French novelist), was born in Paris, the son of a civil servant. He received his training in the Paris School of Oriental Languages, where he studied Sanskrit, Chinese, and archaeology. Malraux has become a colorful, brilliant, and profound literary exponent of the revolutionary thought and action of his generation. Deeply influenced by Nietzsche, Dostoevski, and André Gide (*qq.v.*), he has explored the human and philosophical meaning of the political struggles of the 20th century that have led, in a series of bloody outbreaks, from the Russian Revolution to the Second World War.

While in Indo-China in 1923 on an archaeological expedition in quest of Khmer statues, he became interested in the problems of colonial peoples and joined the Young Annam League in its fight for dominion status. As associate secretary-general of the Kuomintang, he played a leading role in the National Liberation Movement in 1925 and in the Canton general strike of that same year. In 1926 in Shanghai, Malraux became a member of the Committee of Twelve (of which Chiang Kai-shek was also a member) in a coalition of the Kuomintang and the Communist Party, and during the 1927 revolution he was given the post of propaganda commissioner for the provinces of Kwangsi and Kwantung. It was the experiences of these years and their lessons—at the same time intensely personal and of political and moral import—that Malraux poured into his first three novels, *Les Conquérants* (1928; Eng. tr., *The Conquerors*, 1929), *La Voie royale* (1930; Eng. tr., *The Royal Way*, 1935), and

La Condition humaine (1933; Eng. trs., *Man's Fate, Storm over Shanghai,* both 1934). The last, his masterpiece, won him the Goncourt prize and world-wide fame. In the reaction that followed the successful Shanghai revolution of 1927, Malraux left China for Persia and Afghanistan, where he made important discoveries of Greco-Buddhist art. His next adventure was a flight, in company with his aviation instructor, Captain Corniglion Molinier, over the Arab desert. There, north of Ruba-al-Khali, he discovered what he claimed to be the Queen of Sheba's legendary city. In France during the troubled pre-war years he participated in numerous anti-fascist activities. His disinterestedness, his burning passion, his brilliance, his gift for crystallizing issues in phrases and slogans that were both challenging and charged with far-reaching implications (such as his famous *transformer le destin en conscience*), gave his voice and his writings authority among the politically progressive masses of the world.

Le Temps du mépris (1935; Eng. tr., *Days of Contempt,* American title, *Days of Wrath,* both 1936) is a brief novel dealing with the imprisonment and escape of a leader of the German underground in the days of the Nazi terror. When the Franco revolt broke out on July 18, 1936, Malraux immediately flew down to Madrid and organized an air corps for the Loyalist government. He participated in 65 flights over fascist territory, in the course of which he was twice wounded. In 1937 his novel on Spain, *L'Espoir* (Eng. tr., *Days of Hope,* American title, *Man's Hope,* both 1938), was published. When war came in 1939, he volunteered in the tank corps, was captured, escaped to Unoccupied France, where he completed a book on Colonel Lawrence, "Le Démon de l'absolu," as yet unpublished, and a long novel, *La Lutte avec l'ange* (of which the first volume, *Les Noyers de l'Altenburg,* appeared in Lausanne in 1943 in a limited edition), and was active as a soldier with the French Forces of the Interior.

Malraux writes, as he lives, in a mood of almost superhuman tension. The world of his novels is one of violence and death, of revolutionary upheavals, of oppressed men struggling for their lives and their "dignity." He portrays men at moments when they must face ultimate questions, and it is here that his exceptional gifts seem to come to their sharpest focus. Death and revolution are his main dramatic subjects, and they bring his characters, on both sides of the "barricades," to test their resources of courage and will, their power to endure suffering, to confront the problem of evil. Malraux's revolutionaries, in contradistinction to their bourgeois capitalist enemies, find their strength, not in themselves as individuals, but in their ideal of social purpose and human betterment, in their sense of human brotherhood. Yet, unlike so many proletarian writers, Malraux does not underemphasize individual psychology but treats it, rather, as a function of a social complex. A man of wide culture, he has brought his great resources of knowledge and of imagination to bear upon this problem of man's consciousness in the throes of crisis. Though Malraux is realistic in his respect for and vivid presentation of material reality, his exotic subject matter, the intellectual and emotional range of most of his characters, as well as the dramatic tension and the recurrent mood of exaltation that pervade his work, ally him to the romantics. A serenity, a tenderness, a feeling for the grandeur of human capacity for endurance and sacrifice, underlie the passion and the torment of his novels and lift his work at its best to heights of tragic beauty.

See: Geoffrey Stone, "André Malraux: From Death to Revolution," *American Review,* VII (1936), 287–300; Haakon M. Chevalier, "André Malraux: The Return of the Hero," *Kenyon Review,* II (1940), 35–46; Pierre Brodin, *Les Ecrivains français de l'entre-deux-guerres* (1942).

H. M. C.

Mandelshtam, Osip (1892–, Russian poet), born at Warsaw, a graduate of the University of St. Petersburg, was one of the leaders of the Acmeists, who seceded from the symbolists about 1910. Mandelshtam, in theory and practice, has stood for the expert and reverent use of words, demanding of the writer that he apply the same selective precision as does any craftsman in choosing his working material. Rejecting the verbal fancifulness of the symbolists, he has employed mostly words of common speech, characteristically giving to his first book of verse the title *Kamen* (1913; Stone). "We are introducing Gothic into word relations," he declared, "in the way Bach brought it into music." In a laconic style and classic meter Mandelshtam has sung aloofness, indifference, and a defeatist fatalism. "I have never been anyone's contemporary," he boasted. "All has been, all will recur again. Sweet for us is the moment of recognition only." In a sense he yearned for medievalism, the "noble mixture of rationality and mysticism and the sensation of the world as a living equilibrium." The Revolution left him untouched and sad: "Broken is my spinal cord, my beautiful pitiful century." In 1922 a slim volume of his verse, *Tristia,* was published. He wrote some memoirs in prose, in 1925, and a novel, *Yegipetskaya marka* (1928; Egyptian Stamp).

A. K.

Mann, Heinrich (1871–, German novelist), born in Lübeck, shares with his younger brother Thomas Mann (*q.v.*) acute awareness of the painful contrast between the bourgeois and the artist. In both brothers the paternal conservatism of an old family of North German patricians battled with the inheritance of an artistic mother of Creole blood. While Thomas treated his problems with reserve and detached irony, Heinrich gave himself with intellectual passion to the full expression of his artistic and ethical impulses, whether they welled from the world of beauty-intoxicated Southern sensuality or from the wrathful ethos directed against the sham and rottenness of the society of the German Empire under William II. He studied in Berlin, spent much time in traveling, and lived for long intervals in Italy.

He began his literary career as a disciple of Zola, Maupassant, and D'Annunzio (*qq.v.*), but soon developed an art and style of his own in which naturalism, romanticism, and expressionist-grotesque criticism of the time either fused or were alternately predominant. His first novel, *Im Schlaraffenland* (1901; Eng. tr., *In the Land of Cockaigne,* 1925), is pure naturalism, while the three novels about the duchess of Assy, under the general title *Die Göttinnen* (1902–1903; Eng. trs., *The Goddess,* 1918, *Diana,* 1929), present an orgy of the senses in the successive metamorphoses of the duchess as Diana, Minerva, and Venus. His novel *Professor Unrat* (1904; Eng. trs., *The Blue Angel,* 1932, *Small Town Tyrant,* 1944) shows the decline and debauching of a German schoolmaster. Disgustingly vulgar and blasphemous in parts, it nevertheless shows Mann's art of creating milieu, his ability to unfold psychologic details, and his mastery of pertinent words and phrases. This talent of Mann is turned to an aesthetically more delightful account in the novel *Die kleine Stadt* (1909; Eng. tr., *The Little Town,* 1931), the story of the visit of a company of actors to a small Italian town. One of Mann's masterpieces, it reveals the usually embittered pamphleteer as an able romancer who with benevolence and detachment brings to life the essence of human existence in the happy and tragic fate of little people. It is in glaring contrast to the confessional *Zwischen den Rassen* (1907), a work which attests to the author's difficulty in choosing between ethnic and moral values. This aims, for the benefit of the Germans, at formulating the ideal of a European culture, a goal from which the Germans seemed still remote, as is revealed later by Mann's powerful satire of German society under the empire, the trilogy *Das Kaiserreich;* not released for publication until some time after their writing, the novels *Der Untertan* (1918; Eng. tr., *The Patrioteer,* 1921), *Die Armen* (1917; Eng. tr., *The Poor,* 1917), and a few years later *Der Kopf* (1925; Eng. tr., *The Chief,* 1925) constitute a damning indictment of the ruling class, a skillful if grotesquely distorted pillorizing of the bourgeoisie, and an intellectually sympathetic sketch of the proletariat. The books are documents of political wrath and human indignation, and while their strict confinement to the empire of William II is unjust and untenable —the hypocrisy and selfishness of the *Kaiserreich* was only a specific form of the wave of materialism that had swept Western civilization—they are nevertheless works of a man who, fighting for a civilized humanity, describes with courage and eloquence the faults and weaknesses of his generation.

During the time of the Weimar Republic, Mann was elected president of the writers' section of the Prussian Academy. In this position he continued to work vigorously for the creation of a European culture to which all races would contribute their share. Brilliantly written essays tell of his intellectual leadership. Before Nazi persecution forced him into exile, several novels of widely divergent problems and milieus appeared, *Mutter Marie* (1927; Eng. tr., *Mother Mary,* 1928), *Eugénie oder die Bürgerzeit* (1928; Eng. tr., *The Royal Woman,* 1930), *Die grosse Sache* (1931), and *Ein ernstes Leben* (1932; Eng. tr., *The Hill of Lies,* 1934). Until the Nazis occupied France, Mann lived in Nice. Then he came to the United States.

In exile he continued, with numerous articles and essays, his relentless war against the enslaver of men and culture. In the field of fiction he wrote his "largest and most ambitious" works, the historical novels *Die Jugend des Königs Henri Quatre* (1935; Eng. tr., *Young Henry of Navarre,* 1937) and *Die Vollendung des Königs Henri Quatre* (1938; Eng. tr., *Henry, King of France,* 1939). Dealing with the problem of "human greatness, its questionable value and merit," Mann portrayed on the broad canvas of 16th-century France one of the most interesting figures of

European history. Though magnificent in many parts, the novels are deficient in clearness of plot and sustained excellence of style. The novel *Lidice* (1943) is a curious amalgam of an expressionistic drama and a movie script. As a literary document which is to honor the representative greatness of the martyred Czech town, it is painfully inadequate. His autobiography, *Ein Zeitalter wird besichtigt,* appearing in 1945–1946, was greeted as a critical masterpiece.

Among Mann's attempts at the drama the most worthy of note is his play of the French Revolution, *Madame Legros* (1913); it has effective scenes and is done with a good measure of superb satire. As a champion of a new European humanism and a passionate fighter for intellectual and political freedom, as the master at times of an original, expressive, and cultured style, Heinrich Mann has secured for himself a permanent place in German literature.

See: H. Sinsheimer, *Heinrich Manns Werk* (1921); W. Schroeder, *Heinrich Mann* (1932).

W. K. P.

Mann, Klaus (1908–, German novelist, essayist, and playwright), was born in Munich, son of Thomas and nephew of Heinrich Mann (*qq.v.*). By his 20th year he had written a play (*Anja und Esther,* produced in 1925), short stories (*Vor dem Leben,* 1925), and a novel (*Der fromme Tanz,* 1926), each work promising, if slight, and representative of the diversity of his endeavors. There quickly followed the comedies *Revue zu Vieren* (1926), *Gegenüber von China* (1929), and *Geschwister* (1930; an adaptation for the stage of *Les Enfants terribles* of Cocteau, *q.v.*) and another volume of short stories, *Abenteuer* (1929). But if a certain youthful casualness marred the early works, the vivid recollection of his own childhood now lent understanding and accuracy to his characterizations of Frau Christine's youngsters in *Kindernovelle* (1927; Eng. tr., *The Fifth Child,* 1927) and to the portraits of his family and associates in his "autobiography," *Kind dieser Zeit* (1932). In an *Anthologie jüngster Lyrik* (2 vols., 1927–1929) and an equally provocative *Anthologie jüngster Prosa* (1928) he published characteristic specimens of his contemporaries. With his sister, Erika, he wrote gay accounts of their trips about the world (*Rundherum,* 1929; *Das Buch der Riviera,* 1931), and in 1931 appeared a collection of essays on the predicament of the European literati (*Auf der Suche nach einem Weg*). His next novel, picturesque and startling in its thesis concerning the success of Alexander the Great (*Alexander: Roman der Utopie,* 1929; Eng. tr., *Alexander,* 1930), indicated his interest in semihistorical themes, which he reasserted some years later in his Tchaikovsky novel (*Symphonie pathétique,* 1935; Eng. tr., *Pathetic Symphony,* 1938) and in the tale of Ludwig II of Bavaria (*Vergittertes Fenster,* 1937).

In 1933 Klaus Mann left Germany. Since then he has been actively interested in general cultural issues, has edited the literary anti-Nazi magazine *Die Sammlung* (1933–1935) and *Decision* (1941–1942), and has, time and again, demanded greater political awareness on the part of today's younger writers (see *Escape to Life,* 1939, *The Other Germany,* 1940, both in collaboration with Erika Mann, and his autobiographical commentary on his own generation, *The Turning Point,* 1942). At the same time creative writing has continued to engage him (*Mephisto,* 1936; *Der Vulkan,* 1939); and both as editor (*Heart of Europe,* 1943, an anthology, with Hermann Kesten, *q.v.*) and as critic (*André Gide and the Crisis of Modern Thought,* 1943) he has established himself as one of the most discriminating and intelligent of the younger Germans abroad.

V. L.

Mann, Thomas (1875–, German novelist and essayist), was born in the Hanseatic city of Lübeck, the son of a wealthy grain merchant and his wife, of German-South American extraction. After his father's death, Thomas and his family moved to Munich, where he worked first in an insurance office and later on the staff of the magazine *Simplicissimus,* attended the university, and wrote his early short stories (*e.g.,* "Gefallen," 1894; *Der kleine Herr Friedemann,* 1898). During a stay in Rome with his older brother Heinrich Mann (*q.v.*) he began his first novel, *Buddenbrooks,* which was published in 1900 (imprint, 1901; Eng. tr., 1924). Conceived on a small scale as merely "a protracted finger practice with no ulterior advantages," the book developed into a broad account of the history of a Hanseatic family whose strength and prosperity are gradually being undermined by the disintegrating fascination which the arts, Wagner's (*q.v.*) music, and Schopenhauerian ideas exercise upon its successive generations. J. P. Jacobsen, Turgenev, and Maupassant (*qq.v.*) were some of the formal models of this brilliant naturalistic novel. Its central theme is the emerging relationship between the bourgeois life of the 19th century and the precarious modern sensibility of the artistic temperament—an issue which occupied Thomas Mann throughout his earlier work, especially in his verse drama *Fiorenza* (1906) and in his three superb short stories, "Tonio Kröger" (1903; Eng. tr., 1914), "Bekenntnisse des Hochstaplers Felix Krull" (1911; enlarged, 1937), and *Der Tod in Venedig* (1913; Eng. tr., *Death in Venice,* 1925), the first tale "dearest to my heart," the second, suggested by the memoirs of Manolescu, "the best and happiest thing I have done," and the third one of the most perfect and widely admired *petits romans* written in our time.

The first literary fruit of his marriage in 1905 to the daughter of the mathematician A. Pringsheim was *Königliche Hoheit* (1909; Eng. tr., *Royal Highness,* 1916), "a comedy in the form of a novel," in which the artistically minded aristocratic hero, preoccupied with his private problems, eventually works out his salvation within the social framework of duty and sacrifice instead of becoming a victim of life.

The years during and after the First World War drew Thomas Mann, whose tastes and cultural traditions, as he himself insists, were "moral and metaphysical, not political and social," into an ever greater concern with the issues of the day. A long essay, "Friedrich und die grosse Koalition" (1915; Eng. tr. in *Three Essays,* 1929), and the volume *Betrachtungen eines Unpolitischen* (1918) represent his "war service with the weapon of thought" and the substance of his conservative political speculations during the European conflict. Especially in the essay "Von der Tugend" (in *Betrachtungen*) he deplores the political ineptitude of German writers, and in this and subsequent pleas (*Von deutscher Republik,* 1923) he calls for a genuine mobilization of the German intellectuals in support of the new state.

In 1924 appeared *Der Zauberberg* (Eng. tr., *The Magic Mountain,* 1927), a spectacular novel of ideas, which was begun in 1912 during a three weeks' visit to Davos. The minutely detailed canvas of this characteristically German *Bildungsroman* catches the spiritual pattern of European civilization during the first part of the present century and projects it into the rarefied atmosphere of a Swiss sanatorium. There, drawn into many baffling relationships, a youthfully innocent and impressionable German engineer, Hans Castorp, discovers the problematical nature of life and death. In the midst of sickness and decay and surrounded by exponents of every conceivable human attitude, especially the extremes of devitalized reasoning and overrationalized living, he resolves to respect and maintain the profound distinction between life and death: "For the sake of goodness and love," he concludes in the cardinal chapter "Schnee," "man shall let death have no sovereignty over his thoughts." The breadth of its intelligence, the subtlety of its arguments, the precision of observation, and the consummate craftsmanship of its composition have made *The Magic Mountain* one of the most conspicuous German contributions to the modern European novel.

Work on *Der Zauberberg* was accompanied by the publication of a delightful prose idyl, *Herr und Hund* (1919; Eng. tr., *Bashan and I,* 1923), and the writing of several volumes of critical essays (*Rede und Antwort,* 1922; *Bemühungen,* 1925). Later collections of critical prose (*Die Forderung des Tages,* 1930) reaffirm the subtlety of Thomas Mann's critical perception ("Amphitryon," "Rede über Lessing") and testify to the alertness of his response to the cultural challenges of the time. Apart from frequent tributes to those writers to whom he has felt himself most closely related—Novalis, Heine, Whitman, Fontane (*q.v.*), Ibsen (*q.v.*), Tolstoy (*q.v.*), Joseph Conrad, Gide (*q.v.*)—he has devoted one volume of studies, *Leiden und Grösse der Meister* (1935; Eng. tr., *Freud, Goethe, Wagner,* 1937), to Goethe, Wagner, Platen, and Storm.

During the 20's, Thomas Mann insisted upon the spiritual and political obligations which the humanistic heritage of the European tradition imposed upon the liberal European writers (see *Pariser Rechenschaft,* 1926). His intellectual convictions were based upon Nietzsche (*q.v.*) and the German conservative tradition and sprang from a lively sense of historical continuity and spiritual order. In a delightful story, *Unordnung und frühes Leid* (1925; Eng. tr., *Early Sorrow,* 1929), he portrays, against the background of his own family and with melancholy irony, the moral and social confusion which resulted from the chaotic years of the European inflation of values. In 1930, the year after he was awarded the Nobel prize in literature, there appeared the *Novelle* entitled *Mario und der Zauberer* (Eng. tr., *Mario and the Magician,* 1930), a "tragedy of travel" with "moral and political implications."

In the meantime the plan was being formulated for what will certainly prove to be Mann's most profound and elaborate statement of his vision of man's timeless nature—

though not, perhaps, his most pleasing work. A portfolio of illustrations depicting the story of Joseph, for which he was asked to write an introduction, suggested to him the subject of the novel *Joseph und seine Brüder,* the first volume of which was not published until 1933. Not unlike *Dez Zauberberg,* this impressive tale emphasizes the cultural obligations which a purposeful life imposes upon the human being. The biblical world is seen through the ever sharpening eyes of the young Joseph, another Hans Castorp, whose environment, manners, and language are reproduced with meticulous archaeological accuracy, but who is, at the same time, endowed with the knowing perception of a modern observer. The four bulky volumes, *Die Geschichten Jaakobs* (1933; Eng. tr., *The Tales of Jacob,* American title, *Joseph and His Brothers,* both 1934), *Der junge Joseph* (1934; Eng. tr., *The Young Joseph,* 1935), *Joseph in Aegypten* (1936; Eng. tr., *Joseph in Egypt,* 1938), and *Joseph, der Ernährer* (1944; Eng. tr., *Joseph the Provider,* 1944), represent Mann's most positive treatment of the social frame outside of which civilized living is impossible. The broader problem of cultural unity has thus absorbed in Mann's later work the issue of the artist's personal relationship to society. In *Lotte in Weimar* (1939; Eng. tr., *The Beloved Returns,* 1940), which relates the historic visit in 1816 of Werther's Lotte to the aged Goethe, the stress is not so much upon the problematical figure of the artist as upon the humanistic achievement of a man whose self-denying and stylized life is, to the bourgeois observer, not without strangeness and tragedy. In this book and in the short novel *Die vertauschten Köpfe* (1940, Eng. tr., *The Transposed Heads,* 1941) the delicacy and refinement of Mann's detachment have become disturbing, and his style is often pedantic, pontifical, and mannered, although his talents as storyteller are as apparent as ever.

After 1933 he lived in Switzerland, where he edited the literary journal *Mass und Wert* (1937 ff). Since his arrival in the United States (in 1938), he has taken an active part in the discussion of current political issues (*The Coming Victory of Democracy,* 1938; *This Peace,* 1938) without, however, achieving in the New World the effectiveness of argument or speech for which his earlier German essays had made him so distinguished.

See: Mann, *A Sketch of My Life* (1930); James Cleugh, *Thomas Mann; a Study* (1933); H. J. Weigand, *Thomas Mann's Novel Der Zauberberg* (1933); J. G. Brennan, *Thomas Mann's World* (1942); W. A. Reichart, "Thomas Mann: An American Bibliography," *Monatshefte für deutschen Unterricht,* XXXVII (1945) 389–408.

V. L.

Maragall i Gorina, Joan (1860–1911, Catalonian poet and essayist), was born in the city of Barcelona of a well-to-do, middle-class family and received a very careful education. For some time he was a journalist, imparting to his articles a quality that sometimes gave them the value of literary essays. He revealed himself at once as a poet of lofty inspiration when he participated in the Jocs Florals of Barcelona in the year 1881. His first volume of poetry appeared in 1895 with the title *Poesies,* and this was followed soon by *Visions i cants* (1900; Visions and Songs), *Les disperses* (1904; The Dispersed), *Enlla* (1906), *Seqüències* (1911; Sequences). Elected president of the *Ateneo* of Barcelona in 1903, he read his essay "Elogi de la paraula" (Praise of the World) which, along with his "L'elogi de la poesia," (The Praise of Poetry) stands as a minor masterpiece in this difficult genre. He translated the *Ifigènia a Taurida* from Goethe, who influenced his thought and work so greatly, *Eridon i Amina* (1904) of the same author, *Enric d'Ofterdinger* of Novalis (1907), and *Himnes Homèrics.* His complete works were published by his own sons (*Obres completes,* 21 vols., 1929–1935) with eloquent prologues and essays by distinguished critics.

As a literary theorist Maragall advocates an absolute spontaneity and is opposed to any subsequent retouching of works. His theory of the "living word" influences his disciples considerably, and the danger of approving all that is instinctive and undeveloped was seen when, after his death, his followers found themselves the custodians of his doctrines—without his talent. Living in the Barcelona of the beginning of the century, which was in a state of upheaval and full of class hatreds and struggles between the workers and the powerful middle class, Maragall revealed himself as a very human poet and writer although never going beyond the limits of a broad and Christian sympathy for the humble folk. Barcelona indeed makes itself felt in all his work, is evident in his language, "characterized by a sweet Barcelonian impurity," as has been said, and in his subjects, especially the "Oda a Barcelona" which presents the great Mediterranean city in all its grandeur—and in its defects as he sees them. Verses of his are on all Catalonian lips, either recited or sung to the music by distinguished

Catalonian musicians. The "Cant de la senyera" (Song of the Banner), "La sardana" (Catalan national dance), "La vaca cega" (The Blind Cow), and especially the "Cant espiritual" (Spiritual Song), a vigorous and charming work, are among the best.

Maragall was one of the keenest spiritual guides the Catalonian middle class has ever had and sometimes its severe critic, though never really a radical. His pretended anarchism was purely intellectual in nature and for the most part no more than a certain rebelliousness which ambient reality aroused in his spirit. Some of his observations and intuitive deductions were brilliantly presented, as in his article "L'església cremada" (The Burned Church) when he declared that he sensed God more among the ruins of a church devastated by the fury of the revolutionists than in the churches visited by the mighty. He exerted an immediate influence on various writers. Maragall is a much-read poet in the Catalan-speaking countries. At times he treated expertly themes of extraordinary breadth, as in his "Comte Arnau"; in this traditional figure of Catalonian poetry he saw the incarnation of what for Nietzsche (*q.v.*) was the prototype of the superman. In translation he is much esteemed in Hispanic countries. Miguel de Unamuno (*q.v.*) proclaimed him at his death "the best Peninsular lyric poet."

See: Joaquim Folguera, *Les noves valors de la poesia Catalana* (1919); M. Sants Oliver, prologue, in Maragall, *Obres completes* (1929); Josep Pijoan, *El meu don Joan Maragall* (n.d.).

F. de P.

Marañón, Gregorio (1887–, Spanish essayist), was born in Madrid, where since his youth he has been a well-known figure in the world of science, literature, and high society and later of politics. A physician and scientist by profession, Marañón belongs to that rare type marked by destiny to attain success in several fields. He was, before the civil war, a professor in the faculty of medicine at the University of Madrid; a leading specialist in endocrinology; one of the most esteemed practitioners in Spain; a member of various academies, among them the Academy of Letters; a doctor *honoris causa* in some of the best-known foreign universities. He had also a great political influence in the first years of the republic, heading at the time with Ortega y Gasset (*q.v.*) the Agrupación al Servicio de la República. It is even said that his advice to the persons close to Alfonso XIII was instrumental in bringing about the downfall of the monarchy without bloodshed. Like Ortega, he later grew apart from the republic, left Spain at the outbreak of the civil war, and since then has been bitterly criticized by the republicans for what they term his desertion and even for his pro-Franco sentiment, a charge which he tried to repudiate indirectly in his pamphlet *Liberalismo y comunismo: Reflexiones sobre la Revolución Española* (1938).

As a literary figure Marañón represents, better perhaps than other Spanish scientists who entered the field of literature, a characteristic tendency in contemporary Spanish essay writing, the applying of the knowledge acquired in the study of a scientific discipline to the problems of general culture and, in the case of Spain, to its national and historical problems, the predominant subject in contemporary Spanish thought. A man of wide reading, the owner of a vast and selected library, Marañón's essays and books are numerous. Although cultural in outlook, they are based with few exceptions, on biological facts or doctrines. Some deal with problems of social behavior, such as *Sexo, trabajo y deporte* (1925), *Tres ensayos sobre la vida sexual* (1927), *Amor, conveniencia y eugenesia* (1931), *Vocación y ética* (1935), and *Psicología del gesto* (1937); some are interpretations of literary characters such as Don Juan; some are dedicated to the history of scientific ideas in Spain, especially *Las ideas biológicas del Padre Feijóo* (1934); some are of a general character, such as the essays collected in *Raíz y decoro de España* (1933). There is also another group of biographical and historical studies in which Marañón is probably at his best; among these are the biological essay *Enrique IV de Castilla* (1930), *Amiel: Un estudio sobre la timidez* (1932), *El conde-duque de Olivares* (1936), which Karl Vossler rated as an "extraordinary work of research and exposition," and the more recent *Tiberio: Historia de un resentimiento* (1939) and *Luis Vives, un español fuera de España* (1942).

A. del R.

Marcel, Gabriel (1887–, French dramatist, critic, and philosopher), has succeeded in winning distinction in two widely different fields. As a philosopher he may be accounted one of the leading contemporary idealists, and as a dramatist, though he has never won great popularity, his work has certainly stood in the front rank for the last 30 years. The gap between the two types of endeavor is not so great as it might seem at first glance.

Marcel's plays spring directly from his concept of life, but they can by no means be considered merely as vehicles for the expression of abstract ideas. Indeed, a reader knowing little about Marcel might easily put them down as continuations of Porto-Riche's (*q.v.*) *théâtre d'amour*. He himself acknowledges his technical debt to Porto-Riche and Curel (*q.v.*), to Ibsen (*q.v.*) and Schnitzler (*q.v.*); but he goes on to recognize an intellectual debt as well—to Meredith, Dostoevski (*q.v.*), Nietzsche (*q.v.*), and, above all, Bergson (*q.v.*). Marcel's work as a philosopher has dealt chiefly with epistemological problems and has stressed the importance of intuition, affirmation, and faith. It is not surprising, then, that his plays most often are investigations into the value of faith, the impulse to believe, in the lives of men and women and into the necessity for love, of God and of one's neighbor, as a catalytic agent, if a satisfactory relationship with either God or man is to be achieved. These concepts, in some form, run through all his plays, notably *La Grâce* (1911), *Le Quatuor en fa dièse* (1925), *Un Homme de Dieu* (1925), *La Chapelle ardente* (1925), and *Le Dard* (1938). Marcel has not attempted in these pieces to reach a definite conclusion; he views his material from many angles, making his reader aware of its richness and complexity and leaving him not so much with a moral as with a heightened perception of a spiritual atmosphere. Three books of philosophy, *Journal métaphysique* (1927), *Etre et avoir* (1935), and *Du refus à l'invocation* (1940), give a clear idea of his philosophical development, and numerous uncollected reviews, in particular in the *Nouvelle Revue française,* mark him as a sensitive and intelligent critic.

See: Jean Wahl, *Vers le concret* (1932); Paul Archambault, *Témoins du spirituel* (1933).

C. W., Jr.

Marichalar, Antonio (1893–, Spanish essayist), was born in Logroño, of an aristocratic family. A man of sensitive perception and keen literary curiosity, familiar with various foreign languages, he has devoted his life to the reading and study of literature, with special attention to contemporary authors in English and French. The fruits of his meditation on the aesthetic problems presented by this epoch are his essays on poetry and on such authors as Claudel, Gide (*qq.v.*), James Joyce, Lytton Strachey, and Liam O'Flaherty, among others, which comprise the volume *Mentira desnuda* (1933). He is guided in his analysis of contemporary aesthetics by no literary school or militant position, but by a pure, elevated understanding of the essential values of poetry in all times and all lands. In addition to these essays which have made him a guiding light and an interpreter of foreign literature, he is the author of a book on a Spanish theme with foreign contacts, a biography of the last duke of Osuna (*Riesgo y ventura del duque de Osuna,* 1930; Eng. tr., *The Perils and Fortune of the Duke of Osuna,* 1932).

See: P. Salinas, "Un libro de Marichalar," *Indice literario,* II (Madrid, 1933), 85–89.

F. de O.

Marinetti, Filippo Tommaso (1876–1944, Italian poet, novelist, dramatist, and critic), is best known for his revolutionary theories of criticism, for which he found the name "futurism." These embrace all the arts and invade the domain of politics, calling for war and violence, constituting before the event a program for Fascism. Born in Alexandria, Egypt, he was educated in France at a Jesuit *collège* and at the Sorbonne. He later studied law at Pavia and Genoa, then settled in Milan. Many of his works, written in French, had to be translated into Italian.

Through the *Anthologie-Revue* of Milan he entered into relations with the advance guard of Paris literary circles, and his poem in free verse, "Les Vieux Marins," was awarded first prize at the *samedis populaires* of the Théâtre Sarah Bernhardt. His first important work was an epic poem, *La Conquête des étoiles* (1902), which, like *Destruction: Poésies lyriques* (1904), contained sea poetry of dazzling imagination. His un-French qualities of luxuriance and fury captured the French critics. Paul Claudel (*q.v.*), whose genius was of such an opposite kind, hailed Marinetti as one of the few great poets of his time, and Guillaume Apollinaire (*q.v.*) fell under his influence. In Milan (1905) Marinetti founded *Poesia,* which became the organ of those *grands poètes incendiaires,* the young futurists, raised with their help the flag of lifelong revolt against the tryanny of the past (*passatismo*—"past–ism"), and launched a campaign against French decadence and his own masters, the symbolists, though he was the first to translate Mallarmé (*q.v.*) into Italian. In Paris he was the lion of the literary *salons,* and the *Mercure de France* published (1905) *Le Roi Bombance,* his "hilarious satiric tragedy" dedicated to Paul Adam (*q.v.*), French follower of Nietzsche (*q.v.*), which revealed a powerful but disorganized talent, reminiscent of Rabelais by its coarseness and vitality, but with a disheartening emptiness of meaning. He revisited Africa, which acted upon him like an intoxicant (*La Ville charnelle,* 1908; *Mafarka le futuriste; roman africain,* 1909). On February 20, 1909, he published in *Figaro* his celebrated *Manifeste du futurisme,* which created a furore all over Europe by its artistic iconoclasm and its glorification of *la guerre seule hygiène du monde.* In Paris admiration prevailed over indignation, and on April 3, *Le Roi Bombance,* despite its length and unsuitability to the stage, was performed at the Théâtre de l'Œuvre. D'Annunzio (*q.v.*) became a convert; and when Marinetti was condemned to two months' imprisonment on charges of immorality in the Italian translation of *Mafarka,* Luigi Capuana (*q.v.*), the novelist, defended him in court, expressing regret that he himself was too old to become a futurist. But Marinetti's relentless adversary was always Benedetto Croce (*q.v.*), critic and philosopher, for whom the art of any given period is merely a stage in an endless human tradition that came down to us from the past and will stretch on through us into an immeasurable future. With the *Manifeste* the futurists turned to the methods of politics and war, preaching irreverence, *Irredentismo,* and free verse, despite broken heads, sidewalk affrays and arrests, and carrying their campaign even to Austrian Trieste. Fired by their sense of a mission, they planned to deliver Italy, that museum and mausoleum of the tourists, from her past. They would teach Venice to burn her gondolas and tear down her palaces to make room for factories; they would lead Italian youth to love violence and danger, to despise women and forget the *Divine Comedy;* they would purge Italian literature of tenderness, pity, and age-old moonlit conceptions of beauty, the *sainte pourriture* of romanticism and the traditions of classicism, substituting the new beauty of machinery, airships, and the "demon of speed." They wanted to divest woman of all the trappings of romantic love, religious sentiment, and poetic miasma of Fogazzaro (*q.v.*) and D'Annunzio, stripping her of the importance given her by the old preoccupation with adultery and pursuit, and leaving a mere object of sensuality to be sought by the hero with arrogant assurance in his hours of leisure before returning to man's real life of art and war.

When the First World War, which he had foreseen as well as invoked, came, Marinetti enlisted in the infantry and later became a bombardier, fought at Gorizia and Vittorio Veneto, was wounded and decorated. Although in his literary doctrine he recommends *l'abolizione dell'io,* his poetry is highly personal, and he gives some autobiographical details in *L'Alcòva d'acciaio; romanzo vissuto* (1921) and in the vehement and obscure *8 Anime in una bomba* (1919), which analyzes those eight contradictory spirits in him which shall explode like a bomb in the face of the pedants. His style is always aggressive and extravagant, but clear in his polemic writings. In his fiction and his poetry (a mixture of audacities, defiance, crude sensualism, and splendor of imagery), it is defaced and willfully obscured by *bizarreries* of form, ellipses, and verbal eccentricities (*e.g., L' Imagination sans fils et les mots en liberté,* 1913). His language is often offensive, the wish to outrage always present. The straining after sensationalism betrays itself in various titles: *La Momie sanglante* (1904); *Come si seducono le donne, Elettricità sessuale, Un Ventre di donna; romanzo chirurgico* (all 1919); *Le Monoplane du pape* (1922); *Il Tamburo di fuoco; dramma africano di calore colore rumori odori* (1926); *Novelle colle labbra tinte* (1930).

Futurism repudiates our human heritage, rejects thought and feeling, defies civilization itself. In the arts it led directly to dadism, cubism, and surrealism, in politics to Fascism. Although in 1931 in an English periodical Marinetti denied any relation between his more learned movement and "reactionary" Hitlerism, yet the links and likenesses between them soon became apparent, and futurism clearly helped shape 20th-century counterrevolutionary history.

See: H. B. Samuel, *Modernities* (1914), pp. 212–238; E. Settimelli, *Marinetti; l'uomo e l'artista* (1921); G. d'Arrigo, *Il Poeta futurista Marinetti* (1937); A. Simon, tr., "Poems by Marinetti," *Poet Lore,* XXVI (1915), 707–743.

R. S. P. M.

Maritain, Jacques (1882–, French theologian and philosopher), one of the foremost exponents of Catholic doctrine today, was born in Paris of a Protestant family; his father, who had served as secretary to the statesman Jules Favre, and his mother, Geneviève Favre, brought him up in liberal Protestantism. He was educated at the Lycée Henri IV in Paris, where he met Ernest Psichari, close friend of his youth, and at the Sorbonne, where he met Raïssa Oumançoff, who became his wife and his devoted intellectual partner. After his marriage (1904) and his graduation as *agrégé* in philosophy (1905), he received baptism as a Roman Catholic (1906); he completed his studies in science at Heidelberg and in philosophy under Bergson. But he was deeply dissatisfied with the scientist and phenomenalist attitude then current among philosophers and found comfort and certitude only in the system of St. Thomas Aquinas. He taught for a few years at the Collège Stanislas in Paris, then at the Institut Catholique, lectured widely in Europe and in North and South America, lived and taught in New York during the Second World War, was appointed French ambassador to the Vatican in 1945.

The chief influences on Maritain's youth were those of Léon Bloy (*q.v.*), whose burning faith and charity determined his conversion, of Péguy (*q.v.*), in spite of subsequent estrangement, and of Bergson (*q.v.*), who gave him back the sense of the Absolute. Maritain, however, found Bergson's metaphysics timid and deficient and severely criticized in his first work (*La Philosophie bergsonienne,* 1914; new ed., 1930) Bergson's "irrationalism," his "atheistic pantheism," and his "pragmatism." For several years following his enthusiastic adoption of Thomism, Maritain undertook to attack the chief sources of error of the modern world (chiefly in *Antimoderne,* 1922, and in *Trois Réformateurs,* 1925, Eng. tr., *Three Reformers,* 1928): the Reformation and Luther's religious individualism; Descartes as father of a philosophy divorced from theology and as sponsor of the myth of progress; Rousseau, who disfigured the religious truths which he had rediscovered and bequeathed the mistaken notions of natural goodness and of the omnipotence of the State to modern democracies. Even Pascal, as a poor theologian, a faulty metaphysician, and an empirical pessimist in his political views, has not been immune from Maritain's strictures.

After these combative works, Maritain proceeded to give a more serene exposition of his own philosophy. It is based on St. Thomas, whom Pope Leo XIII had recommended in 1879 to Catholics as the teacher whose inspiration could save intelligence and civilization; but Maritain's Thomism is a living reinterpretation and not a historical or scholarly presentation. It can be defined as Aristotelianism enriched and fulfilled by Christian revelation; it asserts the truth of realism as against Cartesian idealism, branded as "the original sin of modern philosophy." Thomism is also, in Maritain's own words, "a philosophy of intelligence and of being or more precisely of existing considered as the act and perfection of all perfections"; it denies determinism and considers freedom as the very essence of the intellect; it respects mystery as the food, and not the foe, of intelligence and views philosophical progress as a deepening penetration into mystery and not, as in science, as the substitution of some problems for others. Finally, it restores the human mind to order, is the only true and integral humanism not deifying man, but showing him as inhabited by God. Maritain's cardinal principle has been that faith and reason can and must be reconciled, reason being powerless unless it is vivified by faith: he does not contend that Thomism is a ready-made solution to all our problems and does not advocate a return to the Middle Ages, but presents the restoration of the spiritual truths of Thomism as a guiding light in our modern intellectual chaos.

Maritain's most coherent and profound exposition of Thomism is to be found in *Eléments de philosophie* (1923–1930; Eng. tr., *An Introduction to Philosophy,* 1930–1937), *Distinguer pour unir, ou les Degrés du savoir* (1932; Eng. tr., *The Degrees of Knowledge,* 1937), *Humanisme intégral* (1936; Eng. tr., *True Humanism,* 1938), *Ransoming the Time* (New York, 1941), and a convenient summary, *Confession de foi* (New York, 1941), first published in English in a volume by several authors entitled *I Believe* (1939, ed. by Clifton Fadiman). Although Maritain is primarily a metaphysician, his influence has been equally marked in the fields of aesthetics, ethics, and politics. He has tried to evolve an aesthetic out of Scholastic philosophy and has colored it with his personal views on art and his sensitive appreciation of modern writers like Claudel, Cocteau, and Reverdy (*qq.v.*), musicians like Eric Satie, and painters like Severini, Rouault (on whom he wrote brief volumes), and Chagall; his chief work in this domain is *Art et scolastique* (1920; new eds., 1927, 1935; Eng. tr., *Art and Scholasticism,* 1930). His later philosophical criticism of modern poetry (*Situation de la poésie,* 1938) is less luminous.

His ethics and politics derive from his metaphysical position, since man must first of all know who he is and where he is before he can know what he should do. Maritain has vigorously opposed the Rousseauist conception of democracy (in which the general will is the expression of numbers), communism (which frees collective men, but not the human personality), bourgeois and capitalist liberalism (which sets up the selfish interest of the individual as the absolute rule), and all totalitarian, fascist, or reactionary systems (as the most directly opposed to Christian principles). He had condemned the French royalist doctrines as early as 1927, in *Primauté du spirituel* (Eng. tr., *The Things That Are Not Caesar's,* 1930). In several later works, published mostly in English in New York, *Scholasticism and Politics* (1940), *Ransoming the Time, Le Crépuscule de la civilisation* (1941; Eng. tr., *The Twilight of Civilization,* 1943), *The Rights of Man and Natural Law* (1943), Maritain presented democracy as being, in Bergson's phrase, "of evangelical essence and moved by love" and praised it most when, refraining from appealing to appetite and inertia, it proclaimed the dignity of the individual person. He added that such a belief in the worth of the individual can only be rooted in Christian faith and begged Catholics to make democracy more social and, forging new ties between the working classes and the Church, to reintegrate the proletariat in the national community. Equality should be proportional, *i.e.,* afford the possibility for men, in whatever social condition they may be placed, to enjoy the same opportunities of achieving their human fullness. Three other volumes, one on the French defeat of 1940, *A travers le désastre* (1941; Eng. tr., *France, My Country, through the Disaster,* 1941), *Education at the Crossroads* (1943), and *Pour la Justice* (1945), bear witness to Maritain's versatility and keen interest in contemporary problems. He has also written *Christianisme et démocratie* (1943; Eng. tr., *Christianity and Democracy,* 1944).

The value and solidity of Maritain's metaphysics are questioned by many non-Catholic philosophers, and many Catholics refuse to link their faith with one system, however comprehensive it may have been; some even deplore a certain lack of intellectual humility in some of his works. But it is universally acknowledged that the courage of his political attitude, the charity and love of mankind which breathe in his works, the cogent power of his reasoning, and the lucidity of his style when at its best entitle him to be called, in the words of T. S. Eliot, "the most conspicuous figure and probably the most powerful force in contemporary philosophy."

See: Gerald Phelan, *Jacques Maritain* (1937); Raïssa Maritain, *Les Grandes Amitiés* (1941–1944; Eng. tr., *We Have Been Friends Together,* 1942; *Adventures in Grace,* 1945).

H. P.

Marquina, Eduardo (1879–, Spanish dramatist), is generally and properly thought of as the chief exponent of the verse drama in modern Spain. He began his career as a journalist in his native Barcelona, but prose has never been his happiest medium, even though he is the author of various collections of short stories and short novels. He has also translated from Catalan, French (Baudelaire's *Les Fleurs du mal*), Portuguese, and English (Booker T. Washington's *Up from Slavery*). At the age of 20 Marquina published, in collaboration with Luis de Zulueta, a dramatic verse legend called *Jesús y el Diablo,* but his first real achievement was the group of lyric poems, *Odas* (1900), some of which had been previously published in *Publicidad,* of Barcelona. *Eglogas* followed in 1902 and *Elegías* in 1905. These early poems of Marquina placed him among the *modernistas* who, with Rubén Darío at their head, sought to renovate Spanish poetry by extending poetic imagery, by avoiding swollen rhetoric, by perfecting form, by utilizing the innovations of the French Parnassians and symbolists. Marquina did indeed achieve considerable novelty in form, expression, and emotion; but he always maintained his own individuality, and his innovations were received with less shock than that produced by the works of many of his contemporaries. This is probably because he constantly remained serene, optimistic, and sincere. His main theme is love, love for woman first, but also a love toward all created things, as illustrated by *Vendimión* (1909). Marquina was never an ivory-tower poetic recluse, and his growing preoccupation with national problems is shown in successive volumes such as *Canciones del momento* (1910) and *Tierras de España* (1914). His subsequent collections of verse show him still deeply rooted in the Spanish tradition—*Juglarías* (1914), *Breviario de un año* (1918), *La poesía de San Francisco* (1927), *Los pueblos y su alma* (Buenos Aires, 1936), and especially *Por el amor de España* (Buenos Aires, 1937), containing six romances (ballads) and a prose epilogue.

As a dramatist Marquina has written a few plays in prose, such as *Cuando florezcan los rosales* (1914), and several in verse in which the lyric element runs away with the dramatic (*El abanico duende,* 1918; *El pavo real,* 1922); in one case he even dramatized a very poor novel of Blasco Ibáñez (*q.v.*), *Los enemigos de la mujer* (1927). His typical verse dramas, however, place him in the tradition of Lope de Vega and Zorrilla because of his predilection for Spanish history and legend. These historical plays are unquestionably his best. The first was a "dramatic biography in four acts" on a foreign subject, *Benvenuto Cellini* (1906), but in 1908 Marquina showed his real *españolismo* in *Las hijas del Cid,* a not too spirited play based on the third canto of Spain's great epic poem. More dramatic effectiveness is displayed in *Doña María la Brava* (1909). Marquina's most famous play is *En Flandes se ha puesto el sol* (1910), a vivid portrayal of the clash, still continuing, between the spirit of Spain and that of the rest of Europe. Audiences did not care if historical details were false and dramatic structure imperfect, for the play, in ringing verse, is alive. *Las flores de Aragón* (1914) is a vigorous, even somewhat overblown, dramatic treatment of the marriage of Ferdinand and Isabella. *El Gran Capitán* (1916) idealizes the figure of the great Gonzalo de Córdoba and his devotion to Queen Isabella. In 1925 Marquina, in collaboration with A. Hernández Catá, produced a drama in which both theme and subtitle are reminiscent of Spain's golden age, the "legendary cloak and sword play" *Don Luis Mejía,* the best modern Spanish dramatic treatment of the personality of Don Juan. The dramatic technique is admirable, the characterization of the sad and unsatisfied Don Luis excellent. Since 1925 Marquina has continued to write verse dramas (*e.g., Fruto bendito,* 1927; *Salvadora,* 1929; *Fuente escondida,* 1931; *En el nombre del padre,* 1936) and has made an adaptation of Lope de Vega's *La Dorotea* (1935). The success of Marquina's plays, often rhetorical and altisonant in tone, is remarkable in an age dominated in Spain by the quiet, realistic, and apparently undramatic plays of men like Benavente and Martínez Sierra (*qq.v.*).

See: A. González-Blanco, *Los dramaturgos españoles contemporáneos,* Ser. 1 (1917), pp. 297–330.

N. B. A.

Marsman, Hendrik (1899–1940, Dutch poet, critic, and short-story writer), was born at Zeist in the province of Utrecht. He suffered many ailments as a child and never enjoyed robust health. While other boys spent their free time at play, Marsman read and studied. He began to write poetry at the age of 20. His father, who was a well-to-do bookseller, supplied him with the means for travel and for a prolonged sojourn in Germany. That was in 1921, when German youth, demoralized by four years of war and privation, was in turmoil. They were scornful of the intellect and glorified action as the one force that could liberate them from the enervating spell of thought. Marsman's first volume of poetry (*Verzen,* 1923) reflected the rebellious and explosive mood of young Germany, for which he coined the name "vitalism." After his return to Holland he studied law and established himself as a practicing attorney at Utrecht (1929). But he was not strong enough to be both a writer and an attorney. He had to make a choice and chose to devote himself exclusively to a literary career. He was married by that time. The young couple began a wandering life, settling down for longer or shorter periods in France, Spain, Italy, Greece, and Austria, wherever the scene was in harmony with his literary mood. In 1938 was published his *Verzameld Werk* (3 vols., Collected Works), containing selections from his poetry, narrative prose, and critiques that he considered worth reprinting. At the outbreak of the Second World War he was living in the mountains near Bogève, France. In June, 1940, he fled with his wife to Bordeaux, intending to escape via England to South Africa. His ship was torpedoed during the night. Only two of those on board were rescued. One of these was Mrs. Marsman. The poet's life was lost before his great talent had reached maturity.

Marsman ranks among the literary leaders of his generation in Holland. The appearance of his *Verzen* was welcomed as an event of great significance. The spirit of these poems was akin to the revolutionary bewilderment of the German boys who were to form Hitler's hooligan following, But though this mood was alien to Marsman's Dutch contemporaries, they were impressed by the power and the boldness of his imagery. German expressionism was toned down and constrained by the Hollander's pictorial instinct. He was saved from being carried away on the waves of German emotionalism and the animal passions of the age by a native tendency towards self-analysis. He won great distinction as a critic, but he never probed the literary consciences of others as relentlessly as he did his own. This self-probing had a dulling effect on his creative faculty. In the years that followed the publication of *Verzen* he wrote almost exclusively critical and narrative prose. His later poetry is affected by his prose style. It is balder, less ornate; but this simplicity acts as a foil to the force of the imagery. Marsman's egocentric preoccupation with the inner life received a rude shock from the outbreak of the war. His last great poem, *Tempel en Kruis* (1939; Temple and Cross), is a kind of poetic autobiography, the story of his growth as a poet under the impact of the study of world history.

See: J. Greshoff, "Inleiding," *Nieuwe Nederlandsche Dichtkunst* (1942), Vol. II; N. P. van Wyk Louw, "Die Digter Marsman, in Marsman, *Poezie en Proza* (1943).

A. J. B.

Martin du Gard, Roger (1881–, French novelist and dramatist), winner of the Nobel prize in 1937, was born in Neuilly-sur-Seine, of a well-to-do middle-class family. He completed his studies at the Ecole des Chartes in 1906; his thesis, based on excavations at the Norman abbey-church of Jumièges, was published in 1909 under the title *Etude archéologique des ruines de Jumièges.* The same year saw the publication of his first novel, *Devenir!* followed in 1913 by *Jean Barois,* his first work to attract wide attention. After the First World War, during which Martin du Gard served in a motor transport division, he began his major work, *Les Thibault* (complete Eng. tr., *The World of the Thibaults,* 1939–1941), a novel cycle in eight parts, the composition of which filled the period between the two wars (*Le Cahier gris,* 1922; *Le Pénitencier,* 1922; *La Belle Saison,* 1923; *La Consultation,* 1928; *La Sorellina,* 1928; *La Mort du père,* 1929; *L'Eté 1914,* 1936; *Epilogue,* 1940). He has also written *nouvelles* (*Confidence africaine,* 1931; *Vieille France,* 1933). His dramatic works include two peasant farces, *Le Testament du Père Leleu* (performed at the Théâtre du Vieux Colombier 1914) and *La Gonfle* (published 1928), and a drama, *Un Taciturne* (performed 1931 at the Comédie des Champs-Elysées).

Martin du Gard has described himself as "an independent writer who has escaped the fascination of partisan ideologies, an investigator as objective as is humanly possible, as well as a novelist striving to express the tragic quality of individual lives." His novels are in the tradition of the 19th-century realists and naturalists; the seemingly effortless narrative and descriptive technique is the result of patient craftsmanship. He is especially concerned with the conflict of ideas in men's minds: *Jean Barois,* for example, traces the religious and intellectual development of a Frenchman of the 1880–1890 generation who finds himself torn between his heritage of mystic beliefs and the demands of his scientific mind. The two main characters of *Les Thibault,* Jacques and Antoine Thibault, seek in different ways, one through revolt, the other through self-mastery, to define their relationship to their inherited bourgeois environment. Martin du Gard's habit of mingling his fictional characters with historical figures and events—the Dreyfus affair in *Jean Barois,* the First World War in *L'Eté 1914*—makes his novels a valuable commentary on the events and intellectual currents of the early years of the 20th century.

Martin du Gard has never been a conspicuous public figure. Among his friends are Jean Schlumberger and André Gide (*qq.v.*). He was associated with the *Nouvelle Revue française* from its early years, worked and wrote for Jacques Copeau's (*q.v.*) Théâtre du Vieux Colombier immediately before and after the First World War, was a frequent visitor to the symposia held at the Abbaye de Pontigny under the direction of Paul Desjardins (*q.v.*). From 1920 on, his customary residence was his country estate at Bellême in Normandy, where he was known as a friendly host to younger writers. After the events of June, 1940, Martin du Gard lived in Unoccupied France, maintaining a dignified silence in face of the "New Order."

See: A. Houtin, *Un Prêtre symboliste: Marcel Hébert* (1925); R. Lalou, *Roger Martin du Gard* (1937); *Les Prix Nobel en 1937* (Stockholm, 1938); A. Gide, *Journal* (1939); H. C. Rice, *Roger Martin du Gard and the World of the Thibaults* (1941); G. Sadoul, "Rencontres, sous l'occupation, avec Roger Martin du Gard," *Etoiles* (Paris), June 19, 1945.

H. C. R.

Martínez Ruiz, José, *see* Azorín.

Martínez Sierra, Gregorio (1881–, Spanish dramatist), born in Madrid, began his career by writing poems (*e.g., Flores de escarcha,* 1900) and novels (*e.g., Tú eres la paz,* 1907, Eng. tr., *Ana María,* 1921). He took his very first work, *El poema del trabajo* (1899), to the great dramatist Benavente (*q.v.*), who gave the younger man encouragement. Martínez Sierra's first dramatic work consisted of four Maeterlinckian fantasies (*see* Maeterlinck) in dialogue form, published under the title *Teatro de ensueño* (1905). His first attempt actually to reach the stage, *Vida y dulzura* (1908), was in collaboration with the Catalan dramatist Santiago Rusiñol (*q.v.*). *La sombra del padre* (1909) was far more realistic. More successful was *El ama de la casa* (1910), the story of a stepmother who triumphs over difficulties through good sense and sheer goodness. *Canción de cuna* (1911; Eng. tr., *The Cradle Song,* 1917), in two acts with a brief poetic interlude, dedicated to Benavente, is the author's most famous play. It is a poetic idyl rather than a drama, delicately portraying with considerable sentimental charm various feminine types in a convent. It was played in New York in 1921, in London in 1926 (109 performances), again in 1927 in New York (with Eva Le Gallienne; 125 performances). It was on tour in the United States, had several performances in Oxford, Liverpool, and Dublin, and was later made into a movie (1933). *Primavera en otoño* also appeared in 1911. *Mamá* (1912), which would make an audience think contrastingly of Ibsen's (*q.v.*) *The Doll's House,* shows a frivolous mother turned from thoughts of extracurricular pleasures to home and duty, because of the needs of her daughter. *Madrigal* (1913) presents a wayward lover saved from an adventuress and returned to a sane and wholesome life by his pure, sweet fiancée. *El reino de Dios* (1915; Eng. tr., *The Kingdom of God,* in *Plays,* Vol. II, 1923) traces the career of a woman, Sor Gracia, from youth to old age and offers a fine role for a character actress. It was played in London in 1927 and Ethel Barrymore played it in New York in 1928 to open the theatre named for her. *Sueño de una noche de agosto* (1918; Eng. tr., *The Romantic Young Lady,* in *Plays,* Vol. II, 1923) is a typically pleasant Martínez Sierra production, with a romantic heroine, a sophisticated novelist-hero, a sprightly thrice-married grandmother, and amusing situations and dialogue. *Don Juan de España* (1921), in seven acts, presents modern variations on an old theme. In the last act Don Juan, now Brother John, is stabbed in trying to settle a brawl, but he dies in the arms of the sweet and innocent Clara, thus accompanied as always by woman's love. *Triángulo* (1930) presents a man whose supposedly drowned first wife returns after he has married a second. He loves them both equally; so at the end of the play, after the curtain falls, he escapes into the audience, turning "from protagonist into spectator," and there is no solution.

These plays constitute a fair representation of the several score turned out by Martínez Sierra in intervals between managing a theatre (Eslava), running a publishing house (Renacimiento, and later the Biblioteca Estrella), writing poems, novels, short stories, and essays (40-odd volumes of nondramatic works), and translating or adapting plays of Maeterlinck (five volumes), Shakespeare, Goldoni, Dumas *fils,* Brieux (*q.v.*), Björnson (*q.v.*), Ibsen, Dickens, Barrie, and Shaw. In most of his work he has had the collaboration of his distinguished wife, Doña María de la O Lejárraga, and many critics have attributed to her influence the definitely feminine tone of his productions. Like Benavente, he is cosmopolitan in his interests, though typically Madrilene, and it is usually the upper strata of Madrid society which are presented on his stage. He is less bitter and less profound than Benavente. His characters are plausible though not deep, his dialogue always sprightly, his dramatic technique excellent. His very considerable success on the stage was further assured by the talented first lady in his troupe, Doña Catalina Bárcena.

See: Helen and Harley Granville-Barker, "Introduction," in Martínez Sierra, *The Kingdom of God and Other Plays* (1929); J. G. Underhill, "Introduction," in Martínez Sierra, *The Cradle Song and Other Plays* (1929).

N. B. A.

Martini, Fausto Maria (1886–1931, Italian playwright, poet, and novelist), was born in Rome. He seems to have had a pleasant and sheltered childhood; he felt a deep attachment for his mother, and this is a recurring theme in his lyrics and short stories. The novel *Si sbarca a New York* (1930), chiefly autobiographical in character, reveals that Martini was one of a group of young poets who would gather around Sergio Corazzini (*q.v.*) to discuss the latest works of Pascoli and D'Annunzio (*qq.v.*) or to debate the relative merits of Verlaine, Mallarmé, Rodenbach, Maeterlinck, Jammes, and Samain (*qq.v.*), with whom they felt a bond of kinship. When Corazzini died at the age of 20, Martini and two other of Corazzini's admirers, feeling that they had lost their spiritual moorings, set sail for New York. After a series of hardships Fausto returned to Italy, where he entered journalism. He was severely wounded in the First World War.

Although his greatest success was as a playwright, he also wrote several books of verse and prose. Of these, *La Vetrina dell'antichità* (1923), a collection of short stories and reminiscences, is important because it discloses Martini's personality as an artist. It also reveals that spiritual bewilderment which, in the author's lyrical expressions *Le Piccole Morte* (1906), *Panem nostrum* (1906), and *Poesie provinciali* (1910), resolves itself in plaintive and nostalgic tones. In this last-named collection of verse are found the somber colors, the humble and subdued tone, the repressed sentiments, and the languorous and ephemeral musicality of verse that characterize the *poeti crepuscolari.*

In the Italian theatre Martini's position is

unique in that his creations are a product of the blending of three main currents of the artistic expression of his time: the twilight atmosphere of the *crepuscolari,* Pirandello's (*q.v.*) dualistic concept of life, and the wry cynicism of the *grotteschi.* These features are best exemplified in Martini's most successful plays: *L'Altra Nanetta* (1917), *Ridi, pagliaccio* (1919), and *Il Fiore sotto gli occhi* (1922). In *Ridi, pagliaccio,* the protagonist, unable to realize his dream and not possessing the emotional maturity to endure frustration, finds release in suicide. This work, under the title of *Laugh, Clown, Laugh,* was presented in New York by David Belasco and Tom Cushing in 1923–1924. In *Il Fiore sotto gli occhi,* considered by many as Martini's best play, Silvio Aroca, a Latin professor, wants to recapture the romantic, adventurous life of his youth. It is only the heroine's intuitive intelligence and her sense of loyalty to the moral standards of the bourgeois world to which she belongs that avert the catastrophe.

As in his novels and short stories, most of Martini's protagonists in the plays are reflections of the author himself, for they, like him, are products of a well-ordered respectable middle-class society. Yet underneath a placid exterior, there is an emotional unrest and a spiritual groping for something intangible and often indefinable which explains their sense of frustration. It was indeed fortunate that Martini turned to the theatre for the expression of his inner life, because in it his perception of new psychological truths is not blurred by the involved and verbose style of his novels. In his plays, both characters and situations, shorn of any rhetorical cloak, emerge alive in all their frail humanity.

Other plays are *Aprile* (1917), *Il Giglio nero* (1921), *I Drammi dell'insignificante* (1928), *Teatro breve* (1929). *La Porta del paradiso* (1920) and *I Volti del figlio* (1928) are collections of short stories. Martini's best-known novels are *Il fanciullo che cadde* (1920), *Verginità* (1920), and *Il Silenzio* (1932). The author also translated into Italian Rodenbach's (*q.v.*) *Bruges-la-morte* (1907).

See: A. Tilgher, *Voci del tempo,* Ser. 2 (1924), pp. 150–162; A. Galletti, *Il Novecento* (1935), pp. 379–437.

P. P. M.

Martini, Ferdinando (1841–1928, Italian playwright, journalist, and politician), a descendent of an old Tuscan family, was born in Florence. As a boy he attended a private school in Florence which failed to prepare him for the university, although it provided him with ample grounding in rhetoric and prosody. At 15 he left school for the paternal library and the inspiring company of men of letters who frequented his father's house. He prided himself on being a self-educated man.

Interested like his father in the theatre, he wrote a two-act comedy, *L'Uomo propone e la donna dispone* (1862), and a play, *I Nuovi Ricchi* (1863), which won for him a literary prize; other pieces for the stage—*Fede* (1864), *Un Bel Matrimonio* (1864), *L'Elezione di un deputato* (1867)—followed, with varying success. Under the pen name of Fantasio he composed dramatic proverbs (*Chi sa il gioco non l'insegni,* 1871; *La Strada piu' corta,* 1871; *Il Peggio Passo e' quello dell'uscio,* 1873), a story (*Peccato e penitenza,* 1872), and a play (*La Vipera,* 1874) which were extremely well received. Although these are neither masterpieces of characterization nor of invention, nevertheless they represent a genre which, imported from France, was enthusiastically received in Italy.

Martini had a long and colorful political life; a liberal, he was first elected a deputy in 1874 and served until 1919. In 1874 he became undersecretary in the Ministry of Public Education and for a few months was minister (1892–1893). While holding these offices he favored radical reforms. From 1897 to 1900 he was civic commissar of the colony of Eritrea and in 1915–1916 was minister of colonies; he was elected to the Senate in 1923 and became minister of state in 1927. As administrator for Eritrea he displayed wisdom and capacity for organization.

His long political career never caused him to lose interest in literature. The two books *Nell'Affrica italiana* (1891) and *Cose affricane* (1896) are documents of colonial diplomacy and also delightful travel accounts. He collected documentary material on the history of Tuscany and issued *Le Memorie inedite di Giuseppe Giusti* (1890), the *Epistolario di G. Giusti* (1904), and *Il Quarantotto in Toscana* (1918). His main and most important writing activity was however in the field of journalism. He began in 1871 as a correspondent of the daily *Fanfulla* under the pen names of Fantasio and Fox. Later he edited the weekly literary magazine the *Fanfulla della domenica* (1879–1882). He then started the *Domenica letteraria* (February, 1882) and founded the *Giornalino dei bambini* (1880–1882), the first publication of its kind in Italy. He gathered around himself the best writers of his time: Carducci, Pascoli, De Sanctis (*qq.v.*), Collodi, and others. By means of these publications he endeavored to develop cultural interests among his numerous readers and to acquaint the Italian public with European literature. His prose style is worthy of the best literary periodicals of Europe. A wide knowledge of French literature, theatre, and life helped him in developing a manner always clear, precise, modern, appealing to a large public without ever compromising in purity and measure. His prose is a refreshing example of what could actually be done with a language that had been overburdened by a century of classical tradition and too often limited by provincial flavor. Unmistakably a Tuscan, his pages are full of charming anecdotes told with the color, biting irony, and quick wit so characteristic of the people from this region.

His literary criticism is guided by sound instinct and innate good taste if not always by deep aesthetic concepts. His evaluations of D'Annunzio (*q.v.*) and Giovanni Marradi are remarkable instances of the soundness of his taste and of the destructiveness of his apparently stingless appraisals. He discovered and helped artists and writers, admiring cleverness even among those younger authors who somewhat bewildered and shocked him by being so different from him in their scorn for stylistic perfection and their indulgence in vulgarity. Valuing cultured conversation as the highest form of expression, he succeeded in giving to his writings the fluidity, variety, and vivacity of an expert conversationlist.

Martini is at once a modern and a humanist, a Tuscan true to his ancestral blood and a European. His collections of public speeches, articles, and memoirs, such as *Tra un sigaro e l'altro* (1876), *Di palo in frasca* (1891), *Pagine raccolte* (1912), *Confessioni e ricord* (2 vols., 1922–1928), his correspondence, *Lettere, 1860–1928* (1934), offer copious documentation on 80 years of political, literary, and anecdotical life of Italy. Seldom an historian of synthetic vision, he is incomparable as a chronicler and a depicter of bourgeois society.

See: C. Weidlich, *Ritratto di Ferdinando Martini (1841–1928)* (1934).

M. Pi.

Martinson, Harry (1904–, Swedish poet and author of travel sketches and nature studies), is indubitably the most remarkable literary phenomenon among living Swedish authors. While some of his critics have insisted that his work is highly overrated, the general Swedish literary public, judging from the sale of Martinson's books, accept the judgment of those critics who look upon him as the first literary gift to his generation. The strange vagabond story of his childhood, youth, and early manhood is to be found in the two autobiographical novels *Nässlorna blomma* (1935, 9th ed., 1936; The Nettles Bloom) and *Vägen ut* (1936, 5th ed., 1937; The Way Out) and in the two volumes of highly original travel impressions *Resor utan Mål* (1932; Aimless Wanderings) and *Kap Farväl!* (1933; Eng. tr., *Cape Farewell,* 1934) based upon his six years at sea. Born into poverty in the southeast province of Blekinge, a homeless orphan at the age of six, he lived a bleak, wandering early existence, doing what work he could on various farms and estates in his native province, until at the age of 14 he made his way to Göteborg and went to sea as a cabin boy. Despite the unhappy circumstances of his early boyhood and the miscellaneous vagabond experiences of his youth and early manhood, Martinson's work shows on the whole rather few traces of bitterness or of the class consciousness of an author of typical proletarian backgrounds. He is interested in human experience as such rather than in social or political theories; and no Swedish author has given expression to his experience of life in more astonishingly fresh and immediate forms. His work has often been criticized as undisciplined and obscure because of its frequently fantastic, seemingly forced stylistic expressionism. It is undisciplined in the sense that it does not observe the normal rules of Swedish diction and syntax, and it is certainly obscure at points; but not infrequently Martinson's departure from accepted Swedish speech practices is a happy one, and his obscurity (in so far as it exists) seems to result directly from the inability of language to express the overwhelming intensity and complexity of his impressions rather than from any conscious desire on the part of the author merely to experiment with language forms for their own sake.

He has written in both poetic and prose forms, the first two volumes from his pen being poetry (*Spökskepp,* 1929, Ghost Ship; and *Nomad,* 1931), which were followed by the four volumes of autobiographical material. These in turn were succeeded by three volumes of fresh and original if at times somewhat obscure nature studies, *Svärmare och harkrank* (1937; Dreamers and Daddy Longlegs), *Midsommardalen* (1938; Midsummer Valley), and *Det enkla och det svåra* (1939; The Simple and the Difficult).

In 1940 he published a strenuous polemic volume, entitled *Verklighet till döds* (Realism to Death), in which he attacks modern political theories and practices which destroy individual human values. Martinson's two volumes of travel sketches, *Resor utan mål* and *Kap Farväl!* are to date his most artistically well-rounded and satisfactory works. They contain miscellaneous impressions of people, places, and natural phenomena observed during the author's life at sea—impressions projected with an amazing immediacy, so starkly realistic in their employment of sensory material that they break over the bounds of mere sensation into a new-dimensional world clearly related to expressionistic painting. The later nature studies in *Svärmare och harkrank, Midsommardalen,* and *Det enkla och det svåra* retain these new-dimensional patterns, but in somewhat less happy, frequently very obscure forms. This is chiefly because Martinson departs in these volumes from the largely artistic aim merely to regive his impressions and is now searching, not very successfully as yet, for some deeper meaning in the strange world of human experience as he sees it. His "philosophy," a kind of mystical primitivism, is far less impressive than his art. This is apparently however a transitional phase in Martinson's development. The future may reveal him as an original thinker of more consequence than he would seem to be at present.

A. G.

Martinson, Moa (born Helga Svarts, 1890–, Swedish novelist and poet), is the most impressive of women interpreters of rural as well as urban proletarian life in Sweden. Born in extreme poverty in the industrial city of Norrköping, and brought up by a mother who labored for a mere pittance in a textile factory, she married a rather unstable workman at an early age and had five children by him before she was 25. Besides having to face economic uncertainties of all kinds with a constantly growing family, she was early widowed (her husband committed suicide) and two of her young sons lost their lives by drowning. She found work in Stockholm, associated with radical labor groups (syndicalist, communist), began writing occasional articles for the labor press, and in 1929 married the brilliant young proletarian author Harry Martinson (*q.v.*). Her literary career, in the strict sense of the term, did not begin until she was middle-aged—with *Kvinnor och äppelträd* (1933; Women and Apple Trees), followed within a year by its sequel *Sallys söner* (Sally's Sons). These two novels, though not the best of Moa Martinson's work, are in most essential respects typical. They tell the double story of two long-suffering, poverty-stricken women together with the ramifications of their families and their immediate acquaintances. Though the picture of poverty that we get in these novels is at times brutally frank, the author never seeks to play upon the reader's sentiments as such and she never indulges in obtrusive social propaganda aimed at suggesting any specific "program of reform." In form these two novels are almost more chaotic than the miscellany of human fates that they seek to depict, but the story is told with such directness, energy, and fierce realistic intensity that one is scarcely conscious of the absence of normal fictional architectonics. She is not "literary" in the traditional sense simply because she is too close to life itself in all its diverse physical and emotional manifestations.

Since the appearance of *Kvinnor och äppelträd* and *Sallys söner* Moa Martinson has published a half dozen novels and one interesting but not particularly important volume of verse. The novels fall into two classes: three of them *(Mor gifter sig,* 1936, Mother Marries; *Kyrkbröllop,* 1938, Church Wedding; and *Kungens rosor,* 1939, The King's Roses) are directly autobiographical in both inspiration and content; the other three (*Rågvakt,* 1935, Rye Watch; *Drottning Grågyllen,* 1937, Queen Grågyllen; and *Vägen under stjärnorna,* 1940, The Way under the Stars) are broad, warmly realistic chronicle-like novels about peasants and working people from various past periods of Swedish history. Though the autobiographical novels are on the whole more finished and well balanced works of art (*Mor gifter sig* is perhaps Moa Martinson's masterpiece to date), the chronicle novels are in both general conception and in certain details of execution more powerful, and they seem to point the way to a type of novel which is the most natural form of expression for the author's peculiar genius. In these chronicle novels Moa Martinson combines a brutally realistic directness of expression, almost Rabelaisian in its sensuousness, its gusto, and its appetite for life, with an imaginative intensity and sweep and a profound sense for folk traditions and folk superstitions reminiscent of the great epic tradition. Few Swedish novels approach *Rågvakt, Drottning Grågyllen,* and *Vägen under stjärnorna* in color, richness of action, variety of character, and brooding social pathos. If Moa Martinson continues in the way suggested by these novels she is likely to create an epos which will rank in variety of content and intensity of conception with Olof Högberg's (*q.v.*) Norrland folk epic *Den stora vreden,* and her novel will more than likely be cast in a literary form more finally satisfactory than is Högberg's great novel.

See: Marika Stjernstedt, "Om Moa Martinson," *Bonniers litterära magasin,* VIII (1939), 511–521.

A. G.

Masaryk, Tomáš (1850–1937, Czech statesman, philosopher, and critic), widely known national leader and first president of Czechoslovakia (1918–1935), played a significant part in the evolution of Czech ideas on philosophical and sociological subjects and must be included in any consideration of Czech literature. He was an important critic of the history of his country and of its writers. His general intellectual influence can scarcely be overrated; he turned the Czechs away from romantic nationalism and gave them a new ideology with roots in their own past. Masaryk assigned a special role to his own nation in the realization of a high ideal of humanity. He expounded a whole philosophy of Czech history in several books like *Česká otázka* (1895; The Czech Question), *Jan Hus* (1896), and *Karel Havlíček* (1896). The Hussite period appears as the summit of Czech history, and the Bohemian Brethren are presented as the finest embodiment of the ideal of humanity in history. The Czech national revival seems to Masaryk a direct continuation of the Czech Reformation, and the modern Czech democracy preached by him and his followers is to him merely a fulfillment of the early promises of the Czech tradition. These views imply also a conception of Czech literary history which stresses its ideological and theological contents.

Masaryk began to discuss literature in his early writings, attacking the authenticity of the so-called Old Czech Manuscripts, which were actually produced in the early 19th century by Hanka and his associates. He expounded his own literary views in a little pamphlet, *O studiu básnických děl* (1884; On the Study of Poetry), and in a wider context in *Moderní člověk a náboženství* (1898; Eng. tr., *Modern Man and Religion,* 1938), as well as in his many studies of intellectual history, the most important of which is *Rusko a Evropa* (2 vols., 1913; Eng. tr., *The Spirit of Russia,* 1919). Masaryk is first of all a moralist, intensely preoccupied with the ethical and social implications of literature. He sharply criticized romanticism and the related subjectivism and titanism, wherever he found them: in Goethe's *Faust,* in Nietzsche (*q.v.*) and Musset, in Zola (*q.v.*) and Arne Gaborg (*q.v.*). He shocked his contemporaries by a lack of reverence for great names and in particular by his merciless analysis of the intellectual shoddiness of a drama and a poem by his celebrated compatriot, Vrchlický (*q.v.*). He was fascinated though ultimately repelled by Dostoevski (*q.v.*), who seemed to him the *reductio ad absurdum* of romanticism and mysticism. He disliked French romanticism, in which he saw only the symptoms of decadence; he never wearied of praising the sanity, humanity, and Protestant Christianity of the main English tradition. Obviously he had little interest in English poetry, and Byron he criticized severely as a specimen of romantic titanism. He was repelled by writers like Joyce and George Moore, who seemed to him decadent and false. But he loved the main tradition of the English novel from Defoe to Wells, and he was particularly appreciative of women writers like the Brontës and Elizabeth Barrett Browning. It is clear that Masaryk is above all a general critic interested in literature largely as a mirror of society. His rigid moralism and his lack of interest in problems of form frequently led him astray, but the very bluntness with which he expounded his antiromantic point of view profoundly influenced Czech literary criticism, in the 1890's still hidebound in romantic traditions. Whatever may be said about certain deficiencies of his literary insight, he was in literary criticism as elsewhere a leader and a liberator.

See: biographies by J. Herben (3 vols., 1926–1927), K. Čapek (3 vols., 1928–1935; Eng. tr., *President Masaryk Tells His Story,* 1934; *Masaryk on Thought and Life,* 1938), Zdeněk Nejedlý (5 vols., 1930–1937), and P. Selver (1940, in English). For Masaryk as a philosopher see J. L. Hromádka, *Masaryk* (1930); articles in the *Festschrift Th. G. Masaryk zum 80. Geburtstage* (1930); W. P. Warren, *Masaryk's Democracy* (1941); R. Wellek, "The Philosophical Basis of Masaryk's Political Ideals," *Ethics,* LV (1945), 298–304.

R. W.

Massis, Henri (1886–, French critic and essayist), was born and educated in Paris. He attended the Lycée Henri IV, where he came under the spell of Alain (pseud. of Emile Chartier, *q.v.*), the free-lance professor of philosophy who exercised a powerful influence upon many students of his generation. Although not exactly a skeptic, Alain delighted in exploding the doctrines and ideas which his students had accepted during their earlier school days; they generally left his courses without any personal philosophical convictions, but ready to let themselves be carried away by new enthusiasms. So it happened that the very young and very intelligent Massis began by airing his views on Zola (*q.v.*) in *Comment Zola composait ses romans* (1906); he then became interested in Anatole France (*q.v.*) in *Le Puits de Pyrrhon* (1906) and a little later turned his attention to Barrès (*q.v.*) in *La Pensée de Barrès* (1908). These fugitive little books were soon forgotten when he became one of the editors of *Opinion* which was, for a time after the storm raised by the Dreyfus affair, the alert organ of young men in search of new ideas. It was in *Opinion* that Massis and Alfred de Tarde, jointly using the pseudonym Agathon, wrote a series of articles which were reissued in book form in 1911 under the title *L'Esprit de la Nouvelle Sorbonne: La Crise de la culture classique, la crise du français*. Those sensational articles were savage attacks upon Gustave Lanson (*q.v.*) and others who, according to the authors, had replaced the old philosophical appreciation and criticism by an academic, dry-as-dust method imported from Germany. That German method, it may be remarked, went back to Taine and Renan (*qq.v.*). In 1913 there were new attacks (*Les Jeunes Gens d'aujourd'hui, Le Goût de l'action, La Foi patriotique, Une Renaissance catholique, Le Réalisme politique*).

The First World War gave the ardent young protagonist of purely French traditions further occasions to combat German methods and ideas, this time from a political angle. His articles and books at this period breathe an ardent patriotism. *Le Sacrifice: Impressions de guerre* (1914–1916) was officially praised by the French Academy, and Massis wrote a moving book on his personal friend, the author of *Le Centurion* and Renan's grandson, who had died in action, *La Vie d'Ernest Psichari* (1916). He also wrote a pamphlet attacking Rolland, *Romain Rolland contre la France* (1915).

Shortly afterwards, he allied himself momentarily with the Neo-Thomist movement, seeming to find in Jacques Maritain (*q.v.*) the standard by which to judge—more often to condemn—authors who were frequently under discussion at that time: Renan, Gourmont, Gide, Duhamel, Benda (*qq.v.*). His ever impassioned and dogmatic pronouncements of that period were published in two volumes, *Jugements* (1923–1924). In 1920 he founded with Bainville (*q.v.*) the *Revue universelle*, the nationalistic, Catholic, and monarchist fortnightly published by Larousse until 1937.

In *La Défense de l'Occident* (1925; Eng. tr., *Defence of the West*, 1928) Massis tried to give a sort of philosophical unity to all his more recent writings. With utter conviction he declared that the French nation alone is capable of giving the world a civilization worthy of the name, that of "the Occident," while under the designation "the Orient" he classes all that is not what he terms the "Latin inheritance." The Orient includes not only Asia and its peoples who constitute the yellow peril, but the Turks also and the Russians. According to him, it was the Reformation that broke the back of Latin Europe and threw the "white man" into obscurity. What is more, he argued, the Turks and the Eastern powers have found an accomplice in a Germany obsessed by her disaster of 1918. The enemy host is Fichte, Spengler, Keyserling, Steiner, and *tutti quanti*, with whom he associates Gandhi, Tagore, Gobineau (*q.v.*), Kant, and even Seillière and a formidable array of others, with whom the reader is supposed to believe that the author himself is familiar. All this was to arouse France from her inertia. The French Academy awarded him the Grand Prix de Littérature for the total of his publications.

In spite of the enormous output of his own books and articles, Massis found time to publish an important edition of Pascal (1926). In 1937 appeared his *Le Drame de Proust* and *L'Honneur de servir*, wherein he expresses the hope that a revival of 13th-century France will blot out the memory of the France of Renan and of Anatole France. In 1940 he once more expressed his detestation of the Orient, of Germany, and of Gobineau in a series of essays entitled *La Guerre de Trente Ans: Destin d'un age, 1904–1939*. Later in that same year Massis lost no time in turning "collaborationist" (see *Les Idées restent*, 1941).

See: P. Moreau, "Henri Massis," in *Le Victorieux XXe Siècle* (1925).

A. Sz.

Matavulj, Simo (1852–1908, Serb short-story writer and novelist), was born in Dalmatia, in the Adriatic port of Šibenik. After attending school in his native town he was taken by his uncle, an *iguman* or father superior of the Orthodox monastery Krupa, who wanted him to become a monk. But monastic life did not suit him, and he left Krupa after acquiring an unforgettable experience and an insight into this particular milieu. He participated in two Serbian national revolts against the Turkish rule in 1876 and 1881. Then he became a school teacher in Dalmatia and Montenegro and later a language instructor and journalist in Belgrade, where he was elected a member of the Serbian Royal Academy.

Thoroughly familiar with Italian, French, and English, Matavulj was a diligent translator. He translated Molière's *Le Bourgeois Gentilhomme* and *Le Misanthrope,* Zola's *Le Rêve,* tales by Maupassant (*q.v.*), *Bleak House* by Charles Dickens and *De Imitatio Christi* of Thomas à Kempis. There are numerous collections of stories by Matavulj, *e.g., Iz Crne Gore i Primorja* (2 vols., 1888–1889; From Montenegro and the Littoral), *Iz primorskog života* (1890; From Littoral Life), *Sa Jadrana* (1891; From the Adriatic Sea), *Iz beogradskog života* (1891; From Belgrade Life), *Iz raznijeh krajeva* (1893; From Different Regions), *Primorska oblićja* (1894; Figures from the Seashore). These and his two novels *Bakonja fra-Brne* (1892) and *Uskok* (1892; The Guerrilla Fighter), his plays *Zavjet* (1894; The Legacy) and *Na slavi* (1904; House Patron Saint), his autobiography *Bilješke jednog pisca* (1897; Notes of a Writer), and letters about his numerous travels show his manifold talent.

Unlike many other Serb authors, he lived in a number of different provinces and depicted all of them with their characteristics and ways of life, their patricians, monks, intellectuals, and townspeople, as well as their peasants, seamen, and fishermen. An ardent adherent of the French realistic and naturalistic schools, and himself of a rationalistic and positive temperament, with a gift of observation and remarkable understanding of human nature, Matavulj gave a highly adequate reproduction of reality. He is at his best in stories about figures from the Adriatic coast and in the masterful picture of monastic life, *Bakonja fra-Brne.*

See: J. Skerlic, *Pisci i knjige,* Vol. I (1907) and *Brankovo kolo,* Vols. XIII, XIV (1908).

P. A.

Matoš, Antun Gustav (1873–1914, Croat poet, essayist, critic, and journalist), was born in Tovarnik, in the heart of Croatia. He never completed a formal school training. In order to evade the three-year compulsory military service in the Austro-Hungarian army, he fled to Serbia, then to Paris, and then back again to Serbia where he was given friendly shelter until, in 1908, he was pardoned and permitted to return to Zagreb. He lived by his pen, and for a short time by playing the violoncello, in Belgrade.

Matoš was for the turn of the century what Krleža (*q.v.*) became for the post-war Croatian literary world. A bohemian, a lover of elegance and form, he never was a deep thinker. He intensely disliked German heaviness and preferred the lighter touch in literature and art of the French. Unstable and erratic, he was often opposed, but—unquestionably brilliant —he was also extensively admired. Indeed as essayist and journalist he had a great name and a school of followers. The most brilliant pages of all were written in France or about France. Matoš was constantly ill and worked often under pressure of fever and sometimes under threat of hunger.

Politically Matoš was an ardent disciple of the Croat ultranationalist Ante Starčević, and Starčevič's influence is evident in the manner in which Matoš writes of his native province. But Matoš was also always a close friend of the Serbs. An ardent opponent of academic writing, he opposed the Serb professor of literature Jovan Skerlić (*q.v.*). Matoš attracted youth with his revolutionary ideas and founded for them and with them several literary magazines, all of which had short lives.

Matoš's main works are *Iverje* (1899; Waste Wood), *Novo iverje* (1900; New Waste Wood), *Umorne priče* (1909; Tired Tales), and *Vidici i putovi* (1908; Perspectives and Paths). There are other collections of essays and also short stories of nearly perfect form, including the famous *Pereci, friški pereci* (1910; Pretzels, Fresh Pretzels). The poems of Matoš were given wide publicity in the magazines of his time in Belgrade and Zagreb and were collected for the first time in 1923. A selection of his best writing was published by his brother under the title *Dok je srca bit će i Croatie* (1925; While There Is Heart, There Will Be Croatia). Publication of his complete works in 15 volumes, in Zagreb, was interrupted by the invasion of 1941; nine volumes had appeared before that date.

See: A. Venzelides, *Književne studije* (1918); D. Prohaska, *Pregled savremenehrvatsko-srpske književnosti* (1921); A. Barac, *Knjiga Eseja* (1924).

M. H.

Maupassant, Guy de (1850–1893, French short-story writer and novelist), was born in Normandy, where he spent his youth and received his education. His studies were interrupted by service in the Franco-Prussian War, after which he was employed successively in the Ministry of the Navy and the Ministry of Public Instruction. He resigned in 1880 in order to devote himself entirely to writing. Subject to nervous maladies for some time, he eventually experienced hallucinations and obsessions which led to a complete mental breakdown during the final months of his life.

Maupassant's early years were spent in observation and in literary apprenticeship. He accumulated a great store of impressions of the many people he encountered, carefully noting their appearance, manners, gestures, and speech. Norman peasants and fishermen, provincial bourgeois, French and German soldiers, government clerks and other functionaries, members of all classes of Parisian society, are the principal actors of his human comedy. The avowed disciple of Louis Bouilhet and of Flaubert (*q.v.*), he learned a great respect for literary art, the value of precision and consciseness, the necessity of characteristic and accurate detail.

Maupassant's youthful writings were published under various pseudonyms. His first recognized success was "Boule de Suif," a cynical war story appearing in *Les Soirées de Médan* (1880) under the aegis of Zola (*q.v.*). Maupassant was immediately hailed as a master. In the following 10 years he produced nearly 30 large volumes of short stories, novels, plays, and travel books. Among his best-known collections of short stories are *La Maison Tellier* (1881); *Contes de la bécasse* (1883); *Clair de lune* and *Les Sœurs Rondoli* (both 1884); *Toine, Contes du jour et de la nuit,* and *Contes et nouvelles* (all 1885); *Le Horla* (1887); *L'Inutile Beauté* (1890).

The character portrait, the brief but poignant drama, were admirably suited to Maupassant's talent, which excelled in the short story. The painting, achieved in a few bold, rapid strokes, is sober, often somber, occasionally relieved by a touch of ironic humor. There is little real gaiety. The society portrayed is usually the victim of its material interests, of its passions or vanities. Happiness is seldom attained; momentarily glimpsed, it disappears and its loss is a source of perpetual regret. Maupassant seeks truth, "the humble truth," but the mirror which he holds to nature is smoked and uneven. It seldom reflects idealism, spirituality, real generosity. But he often succeeds in elevating the commonplace and the unattractive to the realm of art. His peculiar ability as a *conteur* has generally impaired his technique as a novelist, but in *Pierre et Jean* (1888) he has achieved a rare unity and concentration. The preface contains an important statement of his literary ideas. Other novels are *Une Vie* (1883), a depressing and often revolting story of a Norman woman's life, and *Bel-Ami* (1885), a caricature of an unscrupulously successful Parisian journalist. Identified with the realists and naturalists, Maupassant escapes rigid classification by the scope of his subjects, his preoccupation with form, and his increasing emphasis upon psychology and mental divagations.

Nearly all Maupassant's works have been translated into English.

See: E. Maynial, *La Vie et l'œuvre de Guy de Maupassant* (1907); Ernest A. Boyd, *Guy de Maupassant; a Biographical Study* (1926); R. Dumesnil, *Guy de Maupassant* (1933).

J. F. J.

Maura y Gamazo, Gabriel (1879–, Spanish historian), was born in Madrid. The son of Antonio Maura, the distinguished conservative leader of the reign of Alfonso XIII and founder of the political party bearing his name, he was active as one of the most outstanding members of his father's party. The ideas which he brings to literature do not transcend in scope those of the Maurist party, *i.e.,* the dignification and renovation of national politics within the framework of Spanish tradition. His literary production is limited almost entirely to the field of history. In the beginning his historical studies dealt with past periods, medieval as in *La vida urbana en el siglo XIII* (1909) or modern with *Carlos II y su corte* (1911–1915). Little by little, however, in the face of Spain's political transformation, which was destroying traditional institutions, he became a historian of contemporary events. His narrative is that of a spectator who views with bitterness the disappearance of the most cherished things. This can be seen in his principal works, *Historia crítica de la regencia de doña María Cristina* (1929), *Bosquejo histórico de la Dictadura* (1930), and *Recuerdos de mi vida; confesiones de nuestros tiempos* (1934), which are a valuable source of information for the understanding of contemporary Spain.

E. G. L.

Mauriac, François (1885–, French novelist), was born in Bordeaux, a city in which the scenes of most of his novels are laid. His father died before he was two; his mother gave him a very pious and austere education, which he has described in a small volume, *Commencements d'une vie* (1932). He studied first in a Catholic school, then at the *lycée* and at the University of Bordeaux and, for a brief period, at the Ecole des Chartes in Paris. His books give evidence of a solid classical culture and of constant meditation on the Gospels and on a few great Christian works (*Imitation of Christ,* Pascal's *Pensées*). The chief literary influences on his youth were Maurice Barrès, the Catholic poet Francis Jammes, André Gide (whom he later rejected as a dangerous master of immoralistic temptation), and Paul Claudel (*qq.v.*). He first published a few volumes of verse, a form in which (even in his later and most felicitous poem, *Le Sang d'Atys,* 1940) he never was fully successful. His early novels, while still imperfect, reveal the permanent themes of Mauriac: the turbid age of adolescence; the abysses of sin and of evil; provincial families in which hatred, revenge, and an avid passion for material property are the ruling motives. Human life is presented as a conflict between the treacherous temptations of the flesh and the supreme temptation of God; the latter usually triumphs in the end after the misery of a godless world has aroused remorse and humility in the characters.

Mauriac's first major works were, in 1922 and 1923, *Le Baiser au lépreux* and *Genitrix* (Eng. tr. of both in *The Family,* 1930). Between 1923 and 1941 a dozen more novels, of unequal value, were published. Three undoubtedly stand out as masterpieces of the contemporary novel, *Le Désert de l'amour* (1925; Eng. tr., *The Desert of Love,* 1929), *Thérèse Desqueyroux* (1927; Eng. tr., *Thérèse,* 1928), and *Le Nœud de vipères* (1932; Eng. tr., *Vipers' Tangle,* 1933). Others, especially *La Fin de la nuit* (1935), *Plongées* (1938), and *La Pharisienne* (1941), contain some unforgettable scenes. Mauriac has also proved an able dramatist in *Asmodée* (1938; Eng. tr., *Asmodée; or, The Intruder,* 1939) and *Les Mal Aimés* (1945). He has composed two biographies (*Vie de Racine,* 1928; *Vie de Jésus,* 1936, Eng. tr., *Life of Jesus,* 1937), which do not rank among his best works. Mauriac, unanimously acknowledged in France as a "moralist" of the first order, has written a few remarkable volumes of essays which fully reveal his religious and artistic conception of the novel, *Le Roman* (1928), *Dieu et Mammon* (1929; Eng. tr., *God and Mammon,* 1936), *Le Romancier et ses personnages* (1933). Three volumes of collected articles entitled *Journal* (1934, 1937, and 1940) include some of his finest prose. Although undisputed success came early to Mauriac (he was elected to the French Academy in 1933), he has remained unspoiled by it and independent and has not lost the admiration of the younger literary generation in France. His attitude during the German occupation of France was one of courageous resistance to the invader and the Vichy regime.

The originality of Mauriac as the chief French novelist since Proust lies in his skillful combination of several varied elements: a feeling for poetic and dramatic style, especially conspicuous in the descriptive and evocative parts of his novels; a masterly technique, which owes nothing to English or Russian influences and has reverted to the traditional rigid, condensed, feverish French novel which sprang from Racinian tragedy; a subtle psychology, which never intrudes into the novel but reveals dramatically the bitterest soul conflicts of the characters through their physical appearance, their gestures, and their speech. Reminiscence of the past is a favorite device of Mauriac's novels. A profoundly Christian and Catholic conception of human beings permeates everything; the never-ending conflict—the pagan beauty of the world and the lust for pleasure or possession against remorse, faith, and charity—gives unity and perhaps monotony to these novels. A moving personal book by Mauriac, *Souffrances et bonheur du chrétien* (1929), has revealed the deep sincerity of his austere faith, which does not, like Balzac's or Bourget's (*q.v.*), advocate religion as commendable for political or social reasons.

See: Gérard de Catalogne, *Une Génération* (1930); Charles du Bos, *Mauriac et le problème du romancier catholique* (1933); Amélie Fillon, *Mauriac* (1936).

H. P.

Maurois, André (pseud. of Emile Herzog, 1885–, French biographer, novelist, and essayist), was born at Elbeuf in Normandy, of Alsatian parents. He attended the Lycée Corneille at Rouen; there he studied under the philosopher Alain (pseud. of Emile Chartier, *q.v.*) who was to exercise a profound influence upon his personality and upon his works. Later he studied at the University of Caen and obtained the degree of master of arts in philosophy. Though he would have liked to continue his studies, a sense of duty compelled him to enter the cloth factory his family had founded in Elbeuf. He remained there until 1914, encountering the harsh realities of industrial management. At the beginning of the First World War he was appointed liaison officer and interpreter with the British army. Two books of familiar essays, *Les Silences du colonel Bramble* (1918) and *Les Discours du docteur O'Grady* (1922), portray his British comrades with sympathy, humor, and keen insight. His first biography, *Ariel, ou la Vie de Shelley,* appeared in 1923. In 1926 he again left Elbeuf, where he had resided since the end of the First World War, and went to Paris to devote himself entirely to literature. A series of lectures he gave at Cambridge University in 1928 was later published under the title *Aspects de la biographie* (1928), in which he discusses the technical problems confronting a biographer. According to him, biography should be not only a work of science based on sound erudition, but also a work of art unfolding the development of a human personality and a means of personal expression for the biographer himself. The biographies of Maurois include *La Vie de Disraëli* (1927), *Don Juan, ou la Vie de Byron* (1930), and *Chateaubriand* (1938).

As a novelist Maurois has produced *Bernard Quesnay* (1926), a book which is partly autobiographical, *Climats* (1928), and *Le Cercle de famille* (1932). All relate with penetrating tact and sensitivity the story of a sentimental or moral crisis. He is also the author of fantastic novels, such as *Le Peseur d'âmes* (1931), and of philosophic tales, *La Machine à lire les pensées* (1937).

The alert mind of Maurois has kept in constant touch with the social, political, and ethical problems of the day. He discusses them in essays, *Dialogues sur le commandement* (1924) and *Sentiments et coutumes* (1934). He has been a brilliant and well-qualified interpreter of English civilization in his works of literary criticism, *e.g., Magiciens et logiciens* (1935), and in his historical works, *Edouard VII et son temps* (1933) and *Histoire d'Angleterre* (1937). With the exception of *Sentiments et coutumes,* all the writings of Maurois named in the present article have been translated and published in English.

Maurois was elected to the French Academy on June 23, 1938. At the outbreak of the Second World War he joined the French army. After the military collapse of France he came to the United States, where he lectured and taught. In 1942 he volunteered for the French army in North Africa. Outstanding traits are his keen intelligence, his wide culture, his human sympathy, and his intellectual honesty and courage. Under the influence of his philosophic training and of his personal experience he learned to have a horror of fanaticism, of abstract theorizing, of spectacular simplification. His message is one of friendship and of confident optimism.

See: J. Prévost, "André Maurois," *Nouvelle Revue française,* XLIX (1937), 437–450; G. Lemaitre, *André Maurois* (1939).

R. B.

Maurras, Charles (1868–, French journalist and literary and political critic, leader and theorist of the neo-royalist movement), was born at Martigues in Provence. He moved to Paris after having received his baccalaureate from the Catholic College of Aix-en-Provence, in 1885. Being afflicted with partial deafness since the age of 14, Charles Maurras had become accustomed to an intensely studious and meditative life. He set out to complete his education, and from 1885 to 1890, which he calls his "period of philosophical absorption," he plunged into the study of history, philosophy, and the social sciences. Most of his articles that were published at that time, the first in February, 1886, were critical reviews of books on these subjects. After having made a complete, searching analysis of the doctrine of counterrevolution (in an important essay on "L'Evolution des idées sociales," *Réforme sociale,* January–February, 1891), he turned most of his attention to art and literature, particularly poetry, his *musique intérieure.* During the next period of five or six years, Maurras took an active part in the literary discussions of the day. He wrote numerous articles of criticism, short stories, and poems, some of these in Provençal. He was one of the founders of the short-lived Ecole Romane (1891) and of the Ecole Parisienne du Félibrige (1892). But he never entirely neglected political and social questions.

The Dreyfus affair was in 1898 to throw him entirely into political journalism. Ever since that time the main concern of Maurras has been the elaboration of a system of thought which, in his mind, is destined to solve forever the political and social problems of the French nation. He joined the Action Française soon after its founding, in 1899. This political group, whose initial aim had been limited to the reorganization of republican France, became soon, under his influence, the nucleus of a new royalist movement. It adopted the doctrine of integral nationalism (the placing of the nation's interest above everything else) which, according to Maurras, necessarily entails the restoration of an absolute and hereditary monarchy. The Action Française claims that at least as far as France is concerned only the king and the Catholic Church can secure political and social stability, order in man and in society. In art and literature, Maurras opposes classicism to romanticism and the 16th and 17th centuries to the 18th and 19th. He has naturally contributed his share to the "anti-Rousseauism" crusade. His aim has been to create a deep faith in a new set of values based on tradition and what he calls "reality," *i.e.*, everything that is directly opposed to the principles of the French Revolution. The Action Française supported the government of the French republic during the First World War, but resumed its systematic and relentless attacks on public figures and democratic institutions as soon as the armistice was signed. In spite of some setbacks, such as the temporary condemnation by the pope (the placing of the daily *Action française* and five of Maurras's books on the Index) in 1926, the movement kept growing until 1940. While much of its program was put into force by the Vichy government, it failed in creating the state of mind that might have assured the success of a *coup de force* against the republic. In January, 1945, Maurras was brought to trial as an enemy of the republic and condemned to life imprisonment.

Maurras had previously served sentences in prison, fought duels, and on several occasions narrowly escaped assassination. He was elected to the French Academy in 1938, in his 70th year. Most of his writings have been collected and published in book form. His five-volume *Dictionnaire politique et critique* (1932–1934) is the most convenient work of reference to the ideas he has expressed in practically every field of thought. More strictly limited to the political question are the *Enquête sur la monarchie, 1900–1909* (1909; definitive ed., 1924) and *Mes Idées politiques* (1937), a small compact volume containing the essentials of his teaching. The story of his polemics on the religious question will be found in *La Démocratie religieuse* (1921). His articles on French foreign policy between 1895 and 1905 have formed a volume, *Kiel et Tanger* (1910), which produced a sensation at the time of its publication. There are pages of very fine literary criticism in such books as *Trois Idées politiques* (1898), dealing with Chateaubriand, Michelet, and Sainte-Beuve; *Les Amants de Venise* (1902), on the well-known Sand-Musset love affair, which is Maurras's only book not made up of selected articles and miscellaneous writings; *L'Avenir de l'intelligence* (1905), dealing especially with the concept of order, basic principle of his traditionalism, in all domains of human endeavor; and *L'Etang de Berre* (1915), mostly about Provence and modern Provençal literature. From an artistic and literary point of view must be especially recommended *Le Chemin de Paradis* (1894), a collection of philosophical short stories; *Anthinéa* (1901), letters from Greece, Italy, Corsica, and England; and, above all, *La Musique intérieure* (1925), a selection of poems preceded by a long and interesting biographical essay which contains some of the most beautiful pages Maurras has ever written.

Maurras has pitilessly analyzed the ills of modern society, invariably putting the blame on democracy, romanticism, or "Rousseauism." He is a powerful polemist, one who has aroused much intense hatred among his contemporaries. Yet his sincerity of purpose has rarely been questioned, and the best critics recognize him as one of the ablest thinkers and most forceful prose writers of our time. He has taught many a young man how to think straight—this does not necessarily mean accepting his arguments, either premises or conclusions—and has exerted a deep influence upon modern French thought, whether positively or negatively. Since the appearance of *Anthinéa* Maurras has been considered the foremost representative of the classical spirit in French literature. Through his clear and direct style, vigorous logic, and constant appeal to reason, he has performed the feat of holding the admiration, respect, and even interest of readers who have never been bewitched by the logic of his political philosophy. And this alone would have justified the prominent place that he has been given in the history of French literature.

See: P. Descoqs, S. J., *A travers l'œuvre de Charles Maurras* (1913); A. Ségard, *Charles Maurras et les idées royalistes* (1919); A. Thibaudet, *Les Idées de Charles Maurras* (1920); L. Daudet, *Charles Maurras et son temps* (1930); E. Renauld, *"L'Action Française" contre l'Eglise catholique et contre la monarchie* (1936); E. Roussel, *Les Nuées maurrassiennes* (1937).

A. V. R.

May, Karl (1842–1912, German novelist), was born in Hohenstein-Ernstthal, the son of a weaver. He taught school until discharged for misdemeanors and turned, in 1874, to writing travel and adventure stories. During the rest of his life his literary output was enormous and his popularity has been national, especially among younger readers for whom his work supplied enchanting vistas into romantically conceived distant lands. Although May had no direct experience of America, he conveyed in such books as *Helden des Westens* (1890), *Winnetou* (3 vols., 1893), *Old Surehand* (1894), *Der Schatz im Silbersee* (1894), and many others memorable fictional pictures of a colorful wild West frontier land. With amazing literary agility he published in 1892 alone six long tales with a Near Eastern setting (*Durch Wüste und Harem, Durchs wilde Kurdistan, Von Bagdad nach Stambul, Durch die Schluchten des Balkan, Durch das Land der Skipetaren, Der Schut*). Other parts of the world, charged with mystery and indescribable dangers, are the background of such best sellers as *Das Vermächtnis des Inka* (1895), *Im Lande des Mahdi* (3 vols., 1896), *Im Reich des silberen Löwen* (4 vols., 1898–1902).The Karl-May Stiftung, founded in 1913, has continued to publish (in the *Karl-May-Jahrbuch,* 1918 ff.) the inexhaustible resources of May's literary remains.

In his work memories of the noble savage, aspects of James Fenimore Cooper, and the most striking features of travel and detective literature are effectively intermingled. His tales are fashioned after the black-and-white pattern of a melodramatic chase sustained by treachery and deceit and by the superhuman display of endurance and cunning until Old Surehand or Kara Ben Nemsi fires the redeeming shot. But no matter how transparent his literary devices may be, May represents a significant element in the history of German life at the end of the century. Not only by his insistence upon the indubitable effectiveness of bourgeois values, but also by his attempt to open remote areas of fascinating experience, he contributes to the shift in German imagination from the grand gestures of Wagnerian heroism to the political realities of colonial ambition.

See: May, *Mein Leben und Streben* (1910); Otto Eicke, "Karl May, ein deutscher Volksschriftsteller," *Der Bücherwurm,* XVIII (1933), 206–207; Wolfgang Goetz, "Karl May," *Deutsche Zukunft,* Jahrgang II (1934), No. 19, p. 16.

V. L.

Mayakovsky, Vladimir (1893–1930, Russian poet and playwright), claimed the double distinction of being a leading futurist poet and *the* poet of the Revolution. Before the Revolution his iconoclasm seemed an aim in itself. He hated the existing order, its institutions and standards, its authorities, its aesthetics. His verse had the air of savage anarchism; it spouted indignation, gall, and mockery, and, lacking in a positive goal, it breathed despondency and defeatism. The very form of his verse was a challenge to tradition and convention. After the Revolution of 1917 Mayakovsky changed neither in form nor in substance: but he acquired an ideal, a positive purpose, to which he dedicated himself wholly. He found a meaning in his hatred of the old, and with renewed vigor he now attacked the survivals of the past in the name of the nascent new order. Similarly, his formal innovations came to mean not only a protest against old aesthetics, but also an expression of the new order and its affirmation. Mayakovsky thus personified the odd marriage of futurism and the Bolshevik Revolution.

Mayakovsky was the son of a forester in the village Bagdhady, in the Caucasus. After the death of his father in 1906, the family moved to Moscow. Vladimir, while in high school, joined an underground revolutionary organization and was arrested several times. In 1910 he spent 11 months in a solitary prison cell. He expressed his rebellious spirit as a student in an art school, where he joined a group of extremists, subsequent futurists. His first futurist poem was published in 1912, and in the same year he signed the manifesto of the Moscow cubo-futurists, "A Slap in the Face of Public Taste." Most of his writings before the Revolution were intended to shock the respectable, both in form and in content, but along with boisterous puerilities they displayed the basic robustness of his talent and his healthful resentment to things-as-they-are. Thus in the poem "Oblako v shtanakh" (1915; A Cloud in Pants) he mingled individualistic whims with social motives of daring implications. He addressed the "street thousands," the miserable and destitute, himself as one of the lowly, "vomited by a consumptive night into the palm of Moscow." He exhorted the crowds to straighten out their bent backs, to rise in self-respect, not to beg for alms but to prepare for the pending years. The positive aim of the Revolution was not clear to the poet as yet; he only burned with wrath and vengeance. "On every drop of a flowing tear I have crucified myself," he cried to wretched humanity, to all "who are hungry, sweaty, meek, soured in flea-ridden filth," summoning them to decorate lampposts with "the gory corpses of shopkeepers." This note of rebellion rang out in other long poems of his, as well as in brief lyrics and satires, before and during the First World War. Among the longer compositions of the period there were several outstanding works—"Fleita-pozvonochnik" (1915; Flute-Spinal Cord), "Voina i mir" (1916; War and the World), and the ironical panegyric to himself in "Chelovek" (1917; Man).

From the first, Mayakovsky used a unique style. He despised hackneyed phrases and conventional terms and employed them only in derision. His epithets are fresh and unexpected, his vocabulary is rich and colorfully original, yet his Russian is free from the exaggerated neologisms of his fellow futurists. He achieves novelty by multiplying the potentialities of Russian prefixes and suffixes, by the unexpected juxtaposition of sounds and phrases, by taking such liberties with grammar as changing adverbs into adjectives, verbs into nouns, or vice versa, by omitting prepositions, when the meaning is clear without them, by abbreviating and lengthening words for the sake of euphony, and by other means of avoiding a smooth and obvious language, correct "like the pulse of a corpse." The trim regularity and Tchaikovsky-like melodiousness of the tonic-syllabic Russian verse nauseated Mayakovsky. His verse, not unlike Russian folk poetry, is based on the number of stressed syllables in a line, with no regard for the nonstressed syllables, the result being a flexible tonality and greater freedom of rhythm. His metric irregularity is coupled with typographically broken lines. Since most of his verses are designed for declamation, for street singing and marching, Mayakovsky arranges the lines so as to guide the reader's intonation, making each line an accented unit. Very often his line consists of one word ("Left! Left! Left!"), lending the style a dynamic, elemental rhythm. When his verse is not blank or free, it has the widest variety of rhyming schemes, from subtle inner rhymes to clusters of words combined to echo a preceding line. Equally unexpected and striking are Mayakovsky's metaphors. They are always concrete and sensory, even when he deals with supernatural images, and he deliberately clothes them in a hyperbolic form, humorously exaggerating dimensions and concepts. This feature became more apparent after 1917, when the upheavals and cataclysmal events in Russia lent themselves to hyperbolic treatment, as in the play *Misteriya Buf* (1918; Eng. tr., *Mystery Bouffe*, 1933) or in the long poem *150,000,000* (1920).

During the last 13 years of his life Mayakovsky was extremely active, writing, traveling, reciting, painting, addressing large crowds, throwing himself fully into the fight for the new fatherland. He did not spare himself, nor his everlasting enemies—smugness, pettiness, narrowness, greed, commonplaceness, the vices he found extant even in the new society which he championed. Among his travel verses should be mentioned the cycle *Amerikanskiye stikhi* (1925–1926; American Verses), keen impressions of Mexico and the United States, admiration for technological advancement alternating with revulsion from economic wastage and cruelty. His former preoccupation with his personal self reemerged from time to time, as in "Pro Eto" (1923; Of That) and even in his exuberant hymn to Soviet life, "Khorosho!" (1927; 'Tis Good!). The conflict between his devotion to the new order and his old bohemian leanings may have contributed to his suicide in 1930. His last poem on the death of Lenin, "Vladimir Ilyich Lenin" (1924), showed the progressive ripening of Mayakovsky's gift, his throwing off of his early mannerisms, futuristic trickery, excessive imagery; his personal lyricism became enriched with the broad notes of a national epic. Two prose plays of his, *Klop* (1928; The Bedbug) and *Banya* (1930; The Bathhouse), caustic satires on philistine propensities in Soviet Russia, gave promise of fresh possibilities in the creative mind of Mayakovsky. His premature death was a foolish and cruel loss.

See: V. Pertsov, *Vladimir Mayakovski; kritiko-biograficheski ocherk* (1940); Herbert Marshall, comp., *Mayakovsky and His Poetry* (1942).

A. K.

Mechow, Karl Benno von (1897–, German novelist), born in Bonn in the Rhineland, was the son of a colonel. He himself fought as a cavalry officer in the First World War. Later he acquired an estate near Schwiebus, but the economic situation forced him to give it up. For some time he was employed in a bookstore in Freiburg. Since 1928 he has lived with his wife in southern Bavaria.

Mechow took his time in maturing as a writer, and when he brought out his first novel, *Das ländliche Jahr* (1929), it was a notable success. The work is rooted in a life close to the soil. It shows a rural community in the cycle of one year from winter to winter, but it is singularly free from the falsifying romanticism of the "blood and soil" school. Mechow is an honest writer, and while he describes the phases of nature with loving intimacy and realistic exactness, he shows also the wretchedness of man and his inability to cope with the forces about him. The young manager of an estate, the central figure, has traits of the author's character. Shy, retiring, honest, and not too certain of himself, he grows in dealing with men and problems; Mechow stresses the somewhat resigned attitude of modesty and obedience to the law of life. This is also the basic atmosphere in the noteworthy war novel *Das Abenteuer* (1930), a masterfully graphic description of a "community on horseback." It is the story of the cavalry and its function in the great German thrust into Russia in 1915. Men and horses and landscape gradually slip into the consciousness of the reader until thorough familiarity with the characters and the vast Russian countryside is achieved. The novel *Vorsommer* (1934) had a varied reception. Mechow's ideals of goodness and purity are demonstrated in the chaste love of a young girl, gay and of good will. Through her love an undistinguished man finds meaning and aim in his work and life. The book is more an idyl than a novel. From 1934 to 1938 Mechow was (with Paul Alverdes, *q.v.*) the editor of the periodical *Das Innere Reich*.

See: P. Alverdes, "Karl Benno von Mechow," *Die neue Rundschau*, Jahrgang XLIV (1933), Bd. II, pp. 841–845; G. Haupt, "Karl Benno von Mechow," *Die neue Literatur*, XXXV (1934), 79–83; W. K. Pfeiler, *War and the German Mind* (1941), pp. 240–243.

W. K. P.

Medina, Vicente (1866–1936, Spanish poet), was a native of Murcia, of humble origin. In 1898 he won acclaim with a volume called *Aires murcianos* which initiated a type of regional poetry that was to become widespread and of great influence among local and regional poets of other sections of Spain and Spanish America. Vicente Medina's achievement consisted in creating a new style of rustic poetry. His poetry does not deal with local color, as did the regional literature of the 19th century; nor is he interested in the people because of their unusual or picturesque attributes, as were the romantics, or in the physical and social aspects of their environment, as were the realists. It was the soul of the people he sought to express—their emotions, conflicts, and human qualities as they are manifested in their ingenuous, unstudied, elemental, primitive aspects. For this reason Medina's *Aires murcianos* is regional poetry only in a limited sense. The flavor comes from certain outstanding dialectal characteristics which are perfectly intelligible to anyone who knows Spanish, as Murcia is a region of Castilian origin. The defect of this poetry is its monotony. Medina, throughout his life, merely repeated himself; he was never able to give new dimensions to his poetry, not even by changing the regional theme, as he attempted to do in the popular poems he wrote about the Argentine where he lived for over 20 years. His first creations, however, are masterpieces of an art that is human and unassuming and may well live forever. They have not been surpassed either by their author or his many imitators.

See: A. González-Blanco, *Los contemporáneos* (1906), pp. 240–276; J. Mas y Pi, *Letras españolas* (1911).

F. de O.

Mell, Max (1882, Austrian poet and dramatist), was born in Styria at Marburg (Maribor); his father was made director of the state institute for the blind in Vienna, and the family moved there. Mell took his Ph.D. degree at the University of Vienna, majoring in Germanics, but resolved to devote himself to writing and sought no position or office. While still at the university he published his first book of stories (*Lateinische Erzählungen*, 1904), characterized by polished form and conscious artistry. He continued to improve his style and technical competence by translating and emulating foreign writers, and his prose came to combine Austrian grace and classical purity. His first poems (*Das bekränzte Jahr*, 1911) sing his beloved Styria in all its aspects, seasons, and moods, and a simplicity akin to that of the folk song marks both these and his subsequent lyrics.

More strikingly original and better known is his dramatic production, which won him recognition throughout the German lands for his revival and renewal of the old-time *Laienspiel*. Modeled on the style of the old folk play, inspired by true religious feeling, and rendered more poignant by the destruction and distress of the First World War, Mell's three *Legendenspiele* (*Das Apostelspiel*, 1923, Eng. tr., *Apostle Play*, 1934; *Das Schutzengelspiel*, 1923; *Das Nachfolge Christi-Spiel*, 1927) were played everywhere by professionals and laymen, with reverence in the performance and with profoundly emotional response on the part of the audiences. Reminding one of German expressionism in their affirmation of religious experience, these plays, like many of the lyrics, restored to modern life some of the best aspects of medieval faith and medieval simplicity.

See: A. Soergel, *Dichtung und Dichter der Zeit,* Dritte Folge: *Dichter aus deutschem Volkstum,* (1934), pp. 100–110.

B. Q. M.

Mendele mocher sforim (pseud. of Sholem Yakob Abromowitz, 1836–1917, Yiddish novelist and essayist) was reared in a small town in the province of Minsk, Russia, where he received the traditional orthodox Jewish education with its emphasis upon the Bible, the Talmud, and religious commentaries. At 14, when his father died, he set out as a wandering scholar in search of knowledge. He attended famous rabbinical schools at Slutsk and Vilna. A wandering mendicant who was passing through Mendele's native community fired the young man's imagination with stories of prosperity prevailing in the Ukraine, supposedly a land flowing with milk and honey. Both set out for this promised region, begging their way from town to town, acquiring a fund of experiences, a treasure of folklore, and an insight into Jewish and Russian folkways. Mendele finally managed to break away from the older vagabond and made his way to Kamenets in the Ukrainian province of Podolia. Here the Hebrew poet Abraham Beer Gottlober became interested in him, arranged for his education in Russian, German, and arithmetic, provided him with a position as teacher in a Jewish parochial school, and published his first literary efforts. Encouraged by Gottlober, Mendele decided to devote himself to creative writing.

His first essays in the late 1850's and early 1860's were in Hebrew. But he soon realized that the majority of his fellow Jews did not have sufficient command of Hebrew to read with pleasure works written in the sacred tongue, and so in 1863 he turned to Yiddish as the more suitable vehicle for his popular tales. Unlike his contemporaries, most of whom took great pains with their Hebrew but not with their Yiddish style, Mendele labored no less diligently over his Yiddish, writing and rewriting his essays and stories until they attained their most perfect form. He has been called the creator of classical Yiddish. He is certainly its best prose stylist. His main subject matter is Jewish life in the Russian Pale. He has his intellectual roots in the enlightened humanitarianism of the 18th century and aims not merely to entertain but also to reform his readers. He therefore uses satire as an important vehicle for castigating injustice and for urging reform of intolerable social conditions. In his satirical allegory *Die Klatshe* (1873; The Dobbin) he depicts the hapless lot of Russian Jewry in the figure of a sorry old nag, undernourished, overworked, beset on all sides by the better-fed breed of aristocratic steeds, and becudgeled by ignorant unpitying ragamuffins. In his tale *Fishke der Krume* (1869–1888; Fishke the Lame) he draws upon his youthful experiences as a wandering mendicant and rouses sympathy for the poorest of the poor, for outcasts, vagabonds and thieves. His most ambitious work, *Masoës Benyamin Hashlishi* (1878; The Wanderings of Benjamin the Third), is a prose epic of Eastern European Jewry, modeled after *Don Quixote.* His maturest novel is *Dos Vintshfingerl* (The Wishing Ring), upon which he worked for many years.

Mendele is revered by Yiddish readers as the "grandfather of Yiddish literature." His influence has been enormous upon many younger writers, and his work has been translated into several European tongues.

See: S. Niger, *Mendele mocher sforim* (1936).

S. L.

Mendès, Catulle (pseud., rarely used, C. Valérius, 1841–1909, French poet, novelist, playwright, and critic), was born in Bordeaux. He came of a family of Jewish bankers; his father, having a literary turn of mind, named this son for the Latin poet Catullus. After several changes of residence in France and abroad, Catulle Mendès, still very young, settled in Paris (1860). He very soon threw himself headlong into the literary melee. Romanticism was dead, and poetry was languishing, but the rising generation was eager to bring about its rejuvenation. Mendès was not yet 20 when he launched the very exuberant *Revue fantaisiste* (1861)—whence the name Fantaisistes sometimes given to the group generally called the Parnassians. A heavy fine and imprisonment for an obscene play which appeared in this review (*Le Roman d'une nuit,* published in book form, 1883) sounded the death knell of the periodical. A more successful attempt to give a new impetus to poetry was made by a group of young poets, led by Mendès and Louis Xavier de Ricard, their Maecenas, when they published the first installment of an anthology, *Le Parnasse contemporain* (1866). Mendès has recorded humorously the laborious beginnings of the undertaking in *La Légende du Parnasse contemporain* (1884).

Mendès had a profound admiration for Théophile Gautier, whose daughter Judith he married, but later divorced. He had a great dislike for whatever savored of *littérature utilitaire* or *littérature moralisatrice,* following in that the lead of Gautier, Banville (*q.v.*), and Flaubert (*q.v.*). With a decided leaning towards light poetry, not to say accented *gauloiserie* (*Philomela,* 1863; *Les Vaines Amours; Odelettes et ballades*), Mendès proved himself a virtuoso in almost every form and genre of poetry. The same versatility characterizes his prose stories, with, however, too frequent violation of common decorum. He also tried his hand with moderate success at the theatre (*Briséis,* 1899; *Capitaine Fracasse,* 1878, libretto for an *opéra comique* based on Gautier's story; *La Reine Fiammette,* 1898; *Médée,* 1898; *Scarron,* 1905) and showed an interest in history (*Les 73 Journées de la Commune,* 1871; *Le Roi vierge,* 1881, a novel about Ludwig of Bavaria). He was one of the first enthusiasts of Wagner music in France (*Richard Wagner,* 1886).

Certain critics, *e.g.,* Martino and Souriau, have treated Mendès with great severity. In any case it was sheer injustice that gave Mendès no place in the great four-volume *Anthologie des poètes du XIXme siècle* published by Lemerre in 1888.

See: P. Martino, *Parnassiens et symbolistes* (1925); M. Souriau, *Histoire du Parnasse* (1929); A. Schaffer, *The Genres of Parnassian Poetry* (1944).

A. Sz.

Menéndez Pidal, Ramón (1869–, Spanish philologist and historian of the Middle Ages), born in La Coruña, when still very young attracted the attention of all Romance scholars with his book *La leyenda de los Infantes de Lara* (1896), in which he reconstructs a legend of medieval Spain and traces its development up to the 19th century. His principal works since then are *Gramática histórica* (1904), *El poema del Cid; texto, gramática y vocabulario* (1909), *L'Epopée castillane* (1909), *Poesía juglaresca y juglares* (1924), *Orígenes del español* (1929), *La España del Cid* (1929), *Historia y epopeya* (1934); in addition there are numerous studies on the *Romancero,* the literature of the 17th century, dialectology, etymology. In 1925 appeared three huge volumes, *Homenaje a Menéndez Pidal,* in which philologists and historians from all over the world collaborated as a tribute to the master.

Before Menéndez Pidal, Spanish linguistics was studied by foreigners and not too adequately. Now, as a result of this scholar's great contributions, what the Spanish language is, how it originated and developed historically, can truly be understood. Even more will be revealed upon publication of the monumental *Historia de la lengua española,* on which he has been working all his life. Before Menéndez Pidal, the belief was held that the Spanish epic was meager and not very original; such a situation has changed completely since the sagacious literary archaeologist reconstructed various poems, lost, or scattered in the prose of the medieval chronicles. The particular ability of Menéndez Pidal has consisted in knowing how to combine judiciously a fabulous knowledge of details with a peculiar gift for arriving at great historico-geographic syntheses. Starting, for example, with the diphthongization of the Latin vowels *e* and *o* in the Iberian language, he has been able to reconstruct the successive limits of Basque-Iberian and Latin in the Iberian Peninsula. By comparing 60 local versions of a popular ballad ("Gerineldo"), he has laid the foundations for a folkloric geography, which thus appears to be controlled by social forces analogous to those determining the diffusion of the language.

An unbelievable capacity for work and a rare intuition enable Menéndez Pidal to find his way in the darkness of history. From the shadows are drawn the speech and life of Christian Spain during the 10th and 11th centuries, to produce, in *Orígines del español,* a book without parallel in any modern language. This is the only work, according to Professor Leo Spitzer, that really explains the rise of a Romance national civilization and language; it could have been written, Spitzer says, "only by a polyhistor with a gigantic power of synthesis comparable to that of a Jakob Grimm" (*Modern Language Quarterly,* Vol. IV, 1943, pp. 420–421). Its author is, without any doubt, an essential constituent element of the almost miraculous Spanish revival which centers about the year 1900, and he has been for historical science what S. Ramón y Cajal was for biological science. New interpretations of the art, literature, and thought of Spain were then emerging almost spontaneously; Menéndez Pidal himself really had no teachers. He collected a fund of historical materials which would have overwhelmed anyone but him, endowed as he was with an instinct for logical arrangement and method. At the age of 12, reading the Bible, he tried to understand it in terms of historical maps; later he was to reconstruct the itinerary followed in *El poema del Cid,* the life of the hero, and that of all those who had any importance in the history of the 11th century.

Attracted by the assiduous enthusiasm of this artist of historical precision, a few young Spaniards grouped themselves about him, and with them Menéndez Pidal founded the Centro de Estudios Históricos of Madrid (1910), the important publications of which have blazed new trails for European and American Hispanism. One official organ of the Centro has been the *Revista de filología española,* in which Menéndez Pidal has published some of his best studies on the Spanish *Romancero* and has made known hitherto unpublished poems of the Middle Ages (*Elena y María* and the epic poem *Roncesvalles*). Fascist Spain deprived Menéndez Pidal of the direction of the Centro de Estudios Históricos and of the presidency of the Spanish Academy. But the great scholar continues his task with the same ardor that characterized his youthful years, for the eternal good of Spain.

See: Gaston Paris, *Poèmes et légendes du moyen-âge* (1900), pp. 213–251; H. Morf, *Aus Dichtung und Sprache der Romanen* (1903), pp. 373–396; Homero Serís and Germán Arteta, *Bibliografía hispánica; Ramón Menéndez Pidal,* 2d ed., enlarged (New York, 1938).

A. C.

Menéndez y Pelayo, Marcelino (1856–1912, Spanish historian and critic), was born and died in Santander, in the heart of the primitive nucleus of Castile, a city to which he always came back from Madrid. There he assembled his great library with that bibliophile's passion which characterized him all his life. His entire life was devoted to books. His first works caused a great impression principally because of the amout of reading they represented on the part of an author so young. When he was 22 he won his appointment to the chair of Spanish literature in the University of Madrid, and from 1898 he was the director of the National Library of Madrid. As a young man he was sent with the aid of a grant to study abroad in Portugal, Italy, France, Belgium, and Holland; he visited, in fact, only the libraries, and nothing but books aroused his interest. He was almost altogether self-taught and he had few other teachers than the old and modern books he read, although he was initiated in his studies by Manuel Milá y Fontanals (*q.v.*), whose classes he attended at the University of Barcelona.

His first works were of a polemical nature. Their object was to defend and justify the Spanish tradition against the attacks of which it had been the target since the 18th century in Spain and abroad and which had flared up again in his day on the part of the liberals and progressives of the 19th century. Thus his *Historia de los heterodoxos españoles* (1880–1881) was written to prove that the genuine thought of Spain is Catholic and that only exceptionally has this not been the case in works of real value by Spaniards. *La ciencia española* (1876) is, in turn, a work in which he attempts to reply to the old contention that Spain has contributed nothing to the development of modern science. These apologetic works, which quickly made their author famous, had the defects and merits that might be expected of them: they were full of ardor and emotion, but their arguments were not always entirely valid. The positive and scientific part of these two works was of necessity only the great accumulation of bibliographical material they contained, for it was not possible for a single author to study the history of all the sciences in the one instance, and in the other the history of all religions—except the Catholic. As for literature, the cultural field which Menéndez y Pelayo completely dominated and for the study of which he was extraordinarily gifted and prepared, he produced the most important works that had been written on the subject, so much so that he may be called the creator of the history of Spanish literature in a total conception that aimed to grasp and understand it in its complete development and evaluation. His traditionalism and his Catholicism, once they had ceased to be militant and polemic, became for him the bond with the Spanish past, thus constituting a national sentiment which, united to his deep intuitive sense of beauty and art, gave unity to the whole of his writings.

His first study on Spanish literature, *Historia de las ideas estéticas en España* (1883–1891), he considered an indispensable preliminary work for a projected history of Spanish literature. Though this was never written, many chapters of it are contained in his various other works: the novel prior to Cervantes, in *Orígenes de la novela* (1905–1915); poetry before Garcilaso, in the prologues in the *Antología de poetas líricos españoles* (1890–1908); the theatre, in his prologues to the plays of Lope de Vega in the edition of the latter's *Obras* (1890–1913) published by the Spanish Academy. The vast proportions that his works assumed as they grew have been the reason that nearly all of them remained incomplete on the death of their author. His bibliographical studies extend from the first work he published, entitled *Horacio en España* (1877), to *Bibliografía hispano-latina clásica* (1902), which was left unfinished.

In addition to these larger enterprises, Menéndez y Pelayo wrote works for special occasions, such as addresses or introductions, which of necessity had to be brief and limited. In these, collected under the title *Estudios de crítica literaria* (1884–1908), the reader can appreciate the value of his concisely expressed ideas and opinions on a great variety of topics and writers of Spanish literature.

Throughout his work he displays equal competence, although the field of his preference and most special ability was the golden age, particularly in those of its aspects which derived from the Renaissance and the classics. Menéndez y Pelayo was not a specialist in literary criticism in the sense the word has taken on in modern times, but rather a humanist, like those of the Renaissance. His literary taste was unerring and in his writings he determined the values and rankings of Spanish literature, and his judgments have been generally accepted and have come to constitute the consensus of Spanish literary criticism up to the present moment. This is Menéndez y Pelayo's great talent—his ability to organize and evaluate swiftly a field as broad as is that of the whole civilization of a nation. All this makes him the greatest historian Spain produced in the 19th century. His works may not have achieved perfection; but it would be difficult for anyone to approach any question, large or small, concerning Spanish literature without finding that Menéndez y Pelayo had already taken the initiative in that field and had analyzed it along lines that are almost always definitive.

See: A. Bonilla y San Martín, *Marcelino Menéndez y Pelayo (1856–1912)* (1914); M. Artigas Ferrando, *La vida y la obra de Menéndez y Pelayo* (1939).

F. de O.

Mercier, Louis (1870–, French poet), outstanding representative of the "Ecole Lyonnaise," was born at Coutouvre near Roanne, a town which itself, although in the Forez region, is but a distant suburb of Lyon. The poet's parents lived in comfort on the farm where generations of Merciers had lived and prospered. Mercier was educated at St. Jodard and at the Catholic University of Lyon, where the study of Greek and Latin was inseparable from that of French literature. His academic life was cut short by a period of military service (three years) in North Africa. But he always felt himself an exile there, and in all his works no trace of exoticism is found. Back in his native Forez, his only ambition was to become a writer. He joined the editorial staff of the *Journal de Roanne,* never abandoning his position there and unpholding the most vigorous regionalist and traditionalist views.

Mercier's first book of poems, *L'Enchantée* (1897), a contribution to symbolist literature, has little in common with his later productions. The poet found his real path and struck the right vein for him when love of nature and love of his own homeland inspired him to write his two greatest works, *Voix de la terre et du temps* (1903) and *Le Poème de la maison* (1906). G. M. Witkowski made use of the latter in his symphonic and lyric composition of the same title, first presented in 1921.

The association of the French peasantry with the First World War was recorded by Mercier in two noble, inspired collections, *Poèmes de la tranchée* (1916) and *Les Pierres sacrées* (1920), which more than his *Lazare le Ressuscité* (1909) reveal a "Catholic Vigny." It would perhaps be more appropriate to relate him to Vergil. Though he succeeded, both in verse (*Les Petites Géorgiques,* 1923) and in two novels (*Hélène Sorbiers,* 1912; *Les Demoiselles Valéry,* 1923), in giving probably the best sketches of his native Forez, Mercier is not merely a provincial man of letters. His poetry is a hymn to life, to man's life associated with his ancestors and mother earth. The French peasant lives in close and harmonious contact with the fields and the home of his sires, works hard for his sons, and takes pride in giving life. In his small hedged or walled-in realm he may be forgetful of his hardships, not of his responsibilities.

When Mercier, the first in his family to do so, abandoned the plough for the pen, he took upon himself the task of making his neighbors hear more distinctly the voices of nature and time and become more conscious of the noble beauty of their lives. He never cared to have his poems read and praised by the press and critics of Paris. Mercier's style, in harmony with the subject, is always simple, avoiding all trickery and spotlight effects. Its very flaws—some are obviously deliberate—show the poet's dislike of artifice.

See: F. Gohin, *Le Poète Louis Mercier* (1923.)

P. Bo.

Merezhkovski, Dmitri Sergeyevich (1865–1941, Russian novelist, critic, poet, and essayist), born in St. Petersburg into the family of a nobleman of Ukrainian background, was educated in the Third St. Petersburg Classical Gymnasium. As a boy in his teens Merezhkovski met Dostoevski (*q.v.*), an event that deeply impressed him. He also became acquainted with the poet Nadson (*q.v.*), and a friendship developed between them. In 1884 he finished at the Gymnasium and entered the historico-philological faculty of the University of Moscow. In his student years Merezhkovski was absorbed in the works of Spencer, Comte, Mill, and Darwin; however, the religious urge that was fostered in him since childhood left him dissatisfied with positivist philosophy. Like many another Russian intellectual of the time, Merezhkovski became carried away by a search for "eternal truths." On completing his work at the university, he journeyed to the Caucasus, where he met and soon married Zinaida Hippius (*q.v.*). After his return to St. Petersburg, Merezhkovski began earnestly to pursue a literary career. Aided by his wife, he eventually gathered about himself a number of young authors and philosophers interested in the "God-seeking" trends of that period. Later their informal gatherings took on the aspect of an organization—the Religious-Philosophical Society. Seeking a Neo-Christianity that would supplant the old Russian orthodoxy, Merezhkovski denied equally the church and tsarism and after the Revolution of 1905 was forced to emigrate abroad. With the outbreak of the First World War the Merezhkovskis opposed it on principle; with the ascendancy of the Soviets to power, they took an irreconcilably hostile attitude toward the new regime. In 1919 they succeeded in escaping from Russia and eventually took up residence in Paris, where they became associated with reactionary elements.

Merezhkovski began his literary career as a poet. As early as 1883 he was publishing verses much in the mood of Nadson's melancholy civic poetry. After Nadson's death in 1887 Merezhkovski was regarded for a while as a "civic" poet and possible successor to Nadson. In the early 90's, following a nascent interest in modernism, Merezhkovski published a book of verse, *Simvoly* (1892; Symbols), and a collection of essays, *O prichinakh upadka i o novykh techeniyakh souremennoi russkoi literatury* (1893; On the Causes of the Present Decline and New Currents in Russian Literature), in which he analyzed the spiritual strivings of his contemporaries and also interpreted the works of Russian classics in the light of impressionism, symbolism, and mysticism. In another collection of essays, *Vechnyie sputniki* (1896; Eternal Companions), he pursued this thesis further. Thereafter his reputation as leader of the symbolist movement was established. In 1896 was published *Smert bogov* (Eng. trs., *Julian the Apostate,* 1899, *The Death of the Gods,* 1901, 1929), the first part of his popular trilogy, *Khristos i Antikhrist* (Eng. tr., *Christ and the Antichrist,* 1938). Here Merezhkovski presents his religious-philosophical interpretation of history in a neatly schematized synthesis of thesis and antithesis. Paganism and Christianity, the religion of flesh and the religion of spirit, were the two opposite historical forces that were eventually to resolve themselves into a third, reconciling religion. The second part of the trilogy, *Voskresshive bogi: Leonarao da Vinci* (1901, Resurrected Gods: Leonardo da Vinci; Eng. trs., *The Romance of Leonardo de Vinci,* 1902, 1928), has been the most successful of Marezhkovski's works, although it, too, suffers from subjugation of plot to a philosophical formula. The last part of the trilogy, *Khristos i Antikhrist: Piotr i Aleksei* (1905; Eng. trs., *Peter and Alexis,* 1905, 1931), although historically as authentic as its two predecessors, is less convincing as a literary piece. Merezhkovski's outstanding critical book is his study *Tolstoi i Dostoyevski* (1901–1902; Eng. tr., *Tolstoi as Man and Artist, with an Essay on Dostoïevski,* 1902), in which he analyzes the works of these two authors as antithetical revelations by two "seers"—the one, "of the flesh," being Tolstoy (*q.v.*), and the other, "of the spirit," Dostoevski. During the decade following the Revolution of 1905 were published several collections of essays by Merezhkovski on the social, intellectual, and religious trends in Russia; the essays are full of dialectics, mingled sometimes with prophetic revelations. His other fictional works include such historical novels as *Aleksandr I* (1925) and *14 Dekabrya* (1921; Eng. tr., *December the Fourteenth,* 1923) and the play *Pavel I* (1908; Paul I). After the Revolution of 1917 he attacked Bolshevism in his vitriolic *Tsarstvo Antikhrista* (1922; The Kingdom of Antichrist). Once he had settled in Paris, he undertook a study of ancient Egypt that resulted in a second-rate novel, *Rozhdeniye bogov: Tutankamon na Krite* (1925, The Birth of the Gods: Tutankhamen in Crete; Eng. tr., *The Birth of the Gods,* 1925).

Merezhkovski's most significant contributions to Russian literature were made in the course of a dozen years, ending in 1905. During this time he was an influential figure in an important literary movement; after that his significance declined.

See: A. S. Dolinin, "Dmitri Merezhkovski," in S. A. Vengerov, ed., *Russkaya literatura XX veka,* I (1914), 295–356.

O. M.

Merrill, Stuart (1863–1915, French poet), born in Hempstead, Long Island, New York, went to Paris in his early youth and studied at the Lycée Condorcet. Ephraïm Mikhaël, Pierre Quillard, René Ghil (*q.v.*), and André Fontainas were schoolfellows, who like himself were destined to play an active part in the symbolist movement. In 1884 he returned to America to enter the school of law at Columbia University in New York City. Four years of jurisprudence did not interfere seriously with his poetic vocation, since his first book of poems, *Les Gammes,* appeared in Paris (1887), while in New York were published *Pastels in Prose* (1890) and a volume of translations of contemporary French poetry. Back in France in 1890, Merrill spent the rest of his life in his adopted country, choosing Versailles for his residence and devoting himself to his literary pursuits. An enthusiastic exponent of the new school of poetry, he contributed poems, essays, and critical articles to all the reviews favorable to the symbolist theories. Following the example of René Ghil and deeply influenced by the music of Wagner, Merrill aimed at verbal orchestration, using all the resources of assonance and alliteration as well as the tonal qualities of the vocalic sounds. The result is a complex harmony applied with learned skill to the alexandrine or other syllabic meters. This manner is amply illustrated in *Poèmes* (1887–1897), in which the subtle and refined music of his earlier compositions is followed by the gorgeous sonority of "Les Fastes." The dazzling effect of rare and precious words mingling with the clash of resounding syllables may fail to move our hearts but not to astonish our ears. Soon, however, in *Les Quatre Saisons* (1900) Merrill returned to a more subdued style, one more suited to tender reverie and to the murmured confession of a soul. But the pure artist that he was did not hide from the realities of the world around him, and he took an active interest in socialist organizations as early as his student days in New York. His humanitarian creed finds expression in several of his writings, more particularly in *Une Voix dans la foule* (1909).

See: Rémy de Gourmont, *Le Livre des masques* (1896) ; Vance Thompson, *French Portraits* (1900); André Beaunier, *La Poésie nouvelle* (1902); Marjorie Louise Henry, *La Contribution d'un Américain au symbolisme français: Stuart Merrill* (1927).

M. D.

Mesa y Rosales, Enrique de (1879–1929, Spanish poet and dramatic critic), was born and educated in Madrid. He became known as a writer when he won a prize from a Madrid newspaper in 1903, and from then until his death he devoted himself to the literary profession. He was secretary of the Ateneo and president of its section of literature. As dramatic critic of *Imparcial* he aroused resentment and won respect by his frank appraisals of the work of actors and authors. The best of these criticisms were published under the title *Apostillas a la escena* (1929). Other volumes of his prose are *Flor pagana* (1905), *El retrato de Don Quijote* (1905), and *Andanzas serranas* (1910).

It is as a poet, however, that Enrique de Mesa won fame. His three significant volumes of poetry, *Cancionero castellano* (1911; 2d ed., 1917), *El silencio de la Cartuja* (1916), *El posada y el camino* (1928), form a spiritual whole. *Tierra y alma* (1906) has long been out of print. It is poetry in the traditional manner and meters of the Spanish classical poets. His theme is the Castilian countryside, with its mountains and mountain dwellers, its arid plains, its sense of age and timelessness. His vocabulary consists of precise, realistic words that call country things and places by their popular names. It is a lyric poetry of restrained expression but intense feeling. In a series of plastic word pictures, Enrique de Mesa conveys to the reader a sense of the emotion of the landscape. His exquisite use of color and sound and his evocation of Castile's past reflect the literary mode of his day. He can, however, be classed with no group or school. Rather is he another of the line of truly Spanish poets who perceived the essential quality of his country and gave it beautiful expression.

See: R. Pérez de Ayala, preface to Mesa y Rosales, *Cancionero castellano,* 2d ed. (1917); R. Cansinos-Asséns, *Poetas y prosistas del novecientos* (1919); M. Gardner, "Enrique de Mesa," *Hispania* XIII (1930), 311–314.

K. R. W.

Meyer, Conrad Ferdinand (1825–1898, Swiss poet and story writer), was born in Zurich. A gifted and sensitive child, he grew up in an atmosphere of cultured refinement. After the early death of his father (1840) his education remained in the hands of his melancholy and neurasthenic mother. The poet fell a victim to the same trouble; a neurasthenic fear of reality gripped him, and in 1852 he agreed to enter a sanitarium. He stayed seven months and learned to settle down to a daily task. His first literary work was a translation of Thierry's *Récits des temps mérovingiens,* completed in 1855. The following year his mother committed suicide, a victim of her melancholia. Falling heir to a fair inheritance, Meyer was free. He went to Paris and then to Rome. Much as Meyer admired modern French *esprit* and French art, the stern Calvinist in him rejected what seemed to him French levity. He felt more at home in Rome, and there he found in Michelangelo his ideal, a high seriousness of purpose and an unfailing sense of what is really great. He returned to Zurich, convinced that poetry was his mission.

Meyer presents perhaps the strangest case of delayed development in literary annals. He was 39 when his *Zwanzig Balladen von einem Schweizer* (1864) was published anonymously. At 43 he ventured to give his name to another slim volume, *Romanzen und Bilder* (1871), a collection of ballads and lyrics. At 50 he married. The Franco-German War helped to set free his latent powers, and under the impact of those stirring days he wrote *Huttens letzte Tage* (1871), a sequence of terse ballads forming an epic narrative, his first masterpiece. The laconic couplets seem as if wrought on an anvil. He struggled for a decade with a historical novel, as Michelangelo, his spiritual kinsman, struggled with a block of recalcitrant marble. He was 51 when this novel, *Jürg Jenatsch,* was published (1876). It is his only novel, a panoramic view of the world in the 17th century. The novel centers in Switzerland, but Italy, the France of Richelieu, and the Germany of the Thirty Years' War enter into the picture. The hero is an uncompromising man of action for whom the end must justify the means.

While working on this novel Meyer found the field in which he could most fully satisfy his striving for that final perfection of form his artist's conscience demanded. The shorter *Novelle* with its more closely knit structure, where cause and effect are inexorably linked as in the tragic drama, attracted him. Its very compactness made sterner artistic demands possible, and its relative brevity more readily allowed frequent rewriting and conscientious and conscious artistry. He had entered the field of history in his *Hutten* and his *Jenatsch,* and he stayed there. He sees and depicts human struggles in bygone centuries in their historical aspect. Meyer's production of historical *Novellen* began with *Das Amulett* (1873) and reached its first peak in *Der Heilige* (1880; Eng. tr., *Thomas à Becket the Saint,* 1885). Quite on the same level with this is *Die Hochzeit des Mönchs* (1884; Eng. tr., *The Monk's Wedding,* 1887). Dante tells this story, and from the very beginning we hear the voice that chanted the verse of *The Divine Comedy.* Beside these two supreme achievements stand *Die Leiden eines Knaben* (1883), *Die Richterin* (1885), and *Die Versuchung des Pescara* (1887; Eng. tr., *The Tempting of Pescara,* 1890).

The striving for flawless perfection that marks Meyer's prose is even more evident in his lyrics. An unusually high standard of excellence is maintained throughout, and the very arrangement of the poems is a work of art. Most of these poems stem from the poet's later years. Instead of youthful exuberance are found mellow maturity and conscious restraint, but a sensitive ear will hear the beat of a heart that felt deeply life's joy and grief. Beside the wistful love lyrics of his 30's are the warm and mellow lyrics of his happy marriage. His great ballads are the most direct reflection of his passionate nature, *e.g.,* "In der Sistine" and "Casar Borgias Ohnmacht." Meyer is not only a sensitive interpreter of the various moods of nature, but also of the work of human hands, as in "Der römische Brunnen." In conciseness and perfection of form Meyer is akin to Stefan George (*q.v.*).

See: W. Brecht, *Conrad Ferdinand Meyer und das Kunstwerk seiner Gedichtsammlung* (1918); R. Faesi, *Conrad Ferdinand Meyer* (1925); H. Maync, *Conrad Ferdinand Meyer und sein Werk* (1925); A. Burkhard, *Conrad Ferdinand Meyer; the Style and the Man* (1932).

F. Br.

Michaëlis de Vasconcelos, Carolina Wilhelmina (1851–1925, German philologist, Romanist, and critic), was born in Berlin. At the age of 17 her first work (*Erläuterung zu Herders Cid*) was published, and at 22 she began to write for technical publications such as the *Romanische Forschungen* and the *Zeitschrift für romanische Philologie.* She devoted herself at the start to etymological investigations, chiefly concerning the Spanish language; in her early works the Portuguese language is referred to only when helpful to clarify any particular point under consideration. In Leipzig in 1876 appeared her *Studien zur romanischen Wortschöpfung,* in which she already expounded the theory, later supported by Jespersen and other distinguished linguists, that "each modification of a language is a progressive evolution." She married Joaquim de Vasconcelos, a well-known historian of Portuguese art who had made a long visit to Germany. After 1876 she lived in Portugal.

On the occasion of the third centennial (1880) of the death of Camões she started the publication of her valuable studies about the great Portuguese poet. She was one of the scholars who contributed most to identifying the compositions that had really been written by Camões. She prepared for Gustav Groeber's *Grundiss der romanischen Philologie* (1894) the chapter covering the medieval period of Portuguese literary history. In 1904 was published her famous and scrupulously careful edition of the *Cancioneiro da Ajuda,* a collection of medieval poetry; the glossary did not appear until 1921. She also prepared a critical edition of Sá de Miranda (1885) and valuable studies on Gil Vicente (*Notas vicentinas,* 1912–1917) and on other Portuguese writers and prominent historical personages.

Carolina Michaëlis de Vasconcelos was appointed professor of Germanic philology at the faculty of letters of the University of Lisbon in 1911. One year later, at her request, she was transferred to the chair of Romance philology at the University of Coimbra. She was the editor of the review *Lusitânia* of Lisbon and a contributor to the *Revista de filologia española* of Madrid and to other scholarly publications. She possessed a wealth of scientific information and had a gift for philological research. Her vast knowledge covered the fields of Hispanic linguistics, etymology, literature, ethnology, and folklore. She died at Oporto. In 1933 the University of Coimbra published in her memory a 1156-page volume entitled *Miscelânea de estudos em honra de D. Carolina Michaëlis de Vasconcelos.*

See: J. Mendes dos Remédios, *D. Carolina Michaëlis de Vasconcelos* (1926).

J. F.

Miegel, Agnes (1879–, German poet and short-story writer), was born in Königsberg, East Prussia, the only child of a merchant. She considers herself a genuine *Kolonialdeutsche* since her mother's family had come to East Prussia from Salzburg in Austria in the middle of the 18th century and had been successful farmers there for several generations. In *Kinderland* (1930) she tells of her happy childhood in Königsberg and her first acquaintance with the sea, which made a lasting impression on her. She pays tribute to her parents who introduced her to the best in German and foreign (especially English) literature. She writes of her father's love for their homeland, of his interest in the history of East Prussia, and of her discovery of Prussian folklore and legends, a source of inspiration for her own work. After completing her elementary education in Königsberg, Agnes Miegel attended a girls' finishing school in Weimar and traveled, first to Paris, then to England where she stayed for two years. A number of her ballads deal with themes taken from the history of England and France. She returned from England and spent several years in Berlin doing newspaper work. However, she never felt at home there and longed for East Prussia. Back in Königsberg, where she has lived ever since, she worked on the staff of the *Königsberger Zeitung* until 1927.

Agnes Miegel's talent is essentially lyrical. She expresses her love, suffering, and longing in simple, moving poems, traditional in form. She is best known, however, for her stirring ballads dealing with historical events as well as magic and supernatural forces. They are direct and forceful in style; the fusion of lyrical and narrative elements results in poems quite different in form and appeal from the usual narrative ballad (*Gesammelte Gedichte,* 1927). In her prose tales, the most powerful of which is *Die Fahrt der sieben Ordensbrüder* (1926), she emphasizes detail and description in order to create local color as well as mood and suspense. But although she fully succeeds in thus depicting situations of intense emotional appeal, these are apt to confuse the reader and conflict with the dramatic development of her themes. After the separation of East Prussia from the Reich in 1919, Agnes Miegel became more and more the spokesman of her native land. She voices the hopes and fears of its people (*Herbstgesang,* 1932), "in order that others who will follow may understand their country and their forefathers," and similarly explains her own work in "Gespräch mit den Ahnen" (*Unter hellem Himmel,* 1936).

See: M. Schochow, *Agnes Miegel; eine Studie* (1929); P. Fechter, *Agnes Miegel; eine preussische Frau* (1933).

O. S. F.

Mikszáth, Kálmán (1847–1910, Hungarian novelist and short-story writer), was born in Szklabonya and died in Budapest. Mikszáth went to secondary schools in Rimaszombat and Besztercebánya and studied law at the University of Budapest. For a short time he served as a county official; then he turned to journalism, contributing to newspapers in Szeged and other cities. His social roots were those of the gentry, though his father was an innkeeper and a butcher. Mikszáth's nature was such that he was indulgent with the frailties of human beings, regardless of their social position; this explains his humorous attitude toward the gentry, the Slovak peasants, and the "Palócz" people of County Nográd (descendants of the Bessenyő people, who were absorbed by the Hungarians in the 13th century), toward tradesmen, artisans, windbags, and politicians. His world was a rather simple one, but he saw the complexities of simple or seemingly simple lives. Politically he was attached to the Liberal Party under the leadership of Count Kálmán Tisza; he was also a member of the Hungarian Parliament. His collected works appeared first in 1889, and again in an augmented edition in 1910. Edited by Mózes Rubinyi, 16 volumes were published posthumously. The complete edition of the collected works consists of 46 volumes. The nation appreciated Mikszáth. Every important literary society elected him to its membership; he was a member of the Hungarian Scientific Academy and president of the Society of Hungarian Journalists. At the fortieth anniversary of his literary activities he received the family manor house as a gift from the nation, and his birthplace was named after him. Mikszáth divorced his wife, then remarried her. The death of his young son, János, influenced the character of his children's stories.

Mikszáth was chiefly a humorist, who could laugh and smile and share his fun with the reader, but he had also a mocking intelligence, an ironic vein, and here and there his spirit was darkened by bitterness and uneasiness. One of the reappearing motives in Mikszáth's world of fiction is the illusion of small things being great and great things being small. This does not mean that he was a contortionist in the novel and the short story, but that his observations caught the implications of incongruousness. He wrote much, frequently in the living, vital, direct, and imaginative dialect of the "Palócz" people. From the year 1871, when his first stories appeared, until his death he handled his material with deftness and adroitness. While he did not have the multitude of readers that Jókai (*q.v.*) had, his following was large. Despite dated subject matter, his humor and satire are still lively and refreshing. One of his best novels, *Szent Péter esernyöje* (1895), has appeared in English (*St. Peter's Umbrella,* 1900). His stories were published in French, German, and other languages. Some of his stories were dramatized. He wrote a book about Móricz Jókai, entitled *Jókai Mór élete és kora* (1907; Mór Jókai's Life and His Age). He produced juvenile stories and introductions to a yearbook called *Egyetemes regénytár almanach* (1888; The Almanac of General Fiction), which after his death was named *Mikszáth Kálmán almanachja* (The Almanac of Kálmán Mikszáth).

It is not so much objective critical evaluation as personal taste that decides which of the works of Mikszáth are most admirable. The gusto with which he tells a story is apt to be contagious. Some of his most revealing novels and short stories are the following: *Urak és parasztok* (1904; Gentlemen and Peasants), *A jó Palóczok* (1882; The Good Folks of Palócz), *Vén gazember* (1906; The Old Scoundrel), *Galamb a kalitkában* (1893; A Caged Pigeon), *Katánghy levelei* (1893; The Letters of Katánghy), *Besztercze ostroma* (1895; The Siege of Besztercze), *Kisértet Lublón* (1896; A Ghost in Lublo), *Prakovszky, a siket kovács* (1897; Prakovszky, the Deaf Smithy), *A Noszty fiú esete Tóth Marival* (1907; The Case of the Noszty Boy with Mary Toth), *A fekete város* (1910; The Black City). His political sketches, *e.g., Apróságok a házból* (Trifles from the Parliament), gave him an opportunity to excel in brief, pointed portraits in which the serenity or pompousness of the Parliament was reduced to the level of common humanity. His juvenile story *A ló, a bárányka és a nyúl* (The Horse, the Lamb, and the Rabbit) is enchanting.

From the viewpoint of humor and irony Mikszáth combined many qualities. Jonathan Swift and Mark Twain, Anatole France and Alphonse Daudet, would have enjoyed Mikszáth could they have known him, because each of these authors would have discovered something in the Hungarian writer that would have pleased their sense of humor or their sense of irony. Essentially, however, Mikszáth's charm was the reflection of his originality. Even his anecdotical stories have artistic merit. His characterizations of women are apt to be inferior to those of men, but as a whole this defect does not detract from the general significance of Mikszáth as an important writer of novels and short stories.

See: B. Várdai, *Mikszáth élete és munkái* (1910); P. Gyulai, *Birálatok* (1911); M. Rubinyi, *Mikszáth irói hagyatéka* (1914); A. Schöpflin, *Magyar irók* (1919).

J. R.

Milá y Fontanals, Manuel (1818–1884, Spanish critic and philologist), born in Villafranca del Panadés, was the most brilliant Spanish scholar of the middle 19th century and the founder of modern Spanish scholarship. If his contributions have been unjustly forgotten at times by present-day investigators, this is due partly to the difficulty in obtaining his works, collected in *Obras completas* (8 vols., 1886–1896), which are in fact still far from complete. Very early in life he showed a keen mind, versatile and profound. From 1846 till 1884 he taught with great success at the University of Barcelona. His contributions range from original poetry to significant studies in Romance philology and literature. In keeping with Catalonian tradition Milá was well versed in the classics, a training which tempered his romantic leanings. His *De los trovadores en España: Estudio de lengua y poesía provenzal* (1861) is an outstanding contribution; the *Observaciones sobre la poesía popular con muestras de romances catalanes inéditos* (1853), which later appeared as the *Romancerillo popular catalán* (1882), is one of the first scientific contributions to Spanish folklore; and the *De la poesía heroico-popular castellana* (1874) is the first study to point out the relation between the oldest Spanish ballads and medieval Spanish epic poetry.

See: J. Rubió y Ors, *Noticia de la vida y escritos de D. Manuel Milá y Fontanals* (1887); M. Menéndez y Pelayo, *El doctor D. Manuel Milá y Fontanals; semblanza literaria* (1908); A. Rubió i Lluch, *Manuel Mila i Fontanals; notes biografiques i critiques* (1918); W. J. Entwistle, *European Balladry* (1939).

F. S. y E.

Mille, Pierre (1864–1941, French short-story writer, humorist, and journalist), was born of bourgeois parents in Choisy-le-Roi near Paris. He showed an early interest in journalism, and although he completed a formal law education, his first position, in 1890, was as correspondent in England for the Paris *Temps*. He remained on the staff of the *Temps* until his death, as reporter, colonial editor, and columnist ("En passant"), meanwhile contributing to other newspapers and periodicals. In Madagascar in 1896 he became interested in the problems of the rapidly expanding French colonial empire and subsequently found occasion as a reporter to travel in all France's colonies of the Eastern Hemisphere. He was a recognized authority on colonial problems, advocating a liberal treatment of the natives. He served on the Conseil Supérieur des Colonies from 1912 and became president of the Académie des Sciences Coloniales. Significant reminiscences of all this are found in *Mes Trônes et mes dominations* (1930) and *Mémoires d'un vagabonde en retraite* (1932).

Some 30 volumes of Mille's stories have been published. He was particularly successful with the *nouvelle,* told in a delightfully informal style, tempered with a keen, penetrating humor. He was an independent artist, a humanist who saw permanent values in all life. The settings of his stories are as varied as his travels and are artistically written, but the emphasis is always upon people. His characters are legion. A few are especially significant: Barnavaux, popular French soldier of the Foreign Legion, through whom Mille told many colonial stories, *Sur la vaste terre* (1906; Eng. tr., *Barnavaux,* 1915), *Barnavaux et quelques femmes* (1908; Eng. tr., *Under the Tricolour,* 1915), and *Louise et Barnavaux* (1912; Eng. tr., 1916); Partonneau, a colonial administrator and shrewd observer, *L'Illustre Partonneau* (1924); *Le Monarque* (1914; Eng. tr., *The Monarch,* 1925), a typical French Southerner, sympathetically portrayed without caricature; *Caillou et Tili* (1911; Eng. tr., *Two Little Parisians,* 1913), children whose stories reveal Mille's keen appreciation of childhood; and Nasr-Eddine, a semi-legendary, humorous Turk, whose stories in *Nasr-Eddine et son épouse* (1914) allowed Mille free play for his imagination. Mille ranks among the leaders in French colonial literature.

See: Florian-Parmentier, *Pierre Mille* (1923); André Thérive, *Galerie de ce temps* (1931), pp. 93–116; W. J. Everts, *The Life and Works of Pierre Mille* (1938).

W. J. E.

Milosz, Oscar Wladislas de Lubicz (1877–1939, Lithuanian-French poet, dramatist, and philosopher), was born in Czereia, Lithuania, of an old and noble family. In 1899 he went to Paris, where he attended the Lycée Janson-de-Sailly and then followed courses in the Ecole des Langues Orientales and the Ecole du Louvre, studying Hebrew, Aramaic, and Assyrian. At the same time he was writing and publishing poetry, *Le Poème des décadences* (1899) and *Les Sept Solitudes* (1904), revealing a sensitivity for verbal music and a mystic temperament, but not differing greatly from the work of many other contemporary symbolists (*see* French symbolism). He continued his oriental studies, traveling in the Near East, until the outbreak of the First World War. In 1919 he was named Lithuanian minister to France, a position he held until 1926. In 1930 he became a French citizen.

His work grew in beauty and obscurity as his interest in philosophy and mysticism deepened. Plays, *Mephiboseth* (1914) and *Miguel Mañara* (1912; Eng. tr., 1919), and volumes of verse, *Les Eléments* (1911), *Poèmes* (1915), and *La Confession de Lemuel* (1922), mark a steady increase in preoccupation with spiritual problems and the mystery of the universe. In two books of metaphysics, *Ars magna* (1924) and *Les Arcanes* (1926), Milosz has given some idea of his system, an exotic blend of Catholicism, Swedenborg, Böhme, Eastern tradition, and modern physics. During his later years, he lived in great seclusion at Fontainebleau, engaged in biblical studies and enjoying among his neighbors the reputation of a saint.

Milosz has been accused of pretentiousness and obscurity by some and hailed as one of the greatest modern French poets by others. He himself said that he wrote with *l'âme des mots,* and as he grew older this verbal concentration, combined with the esoteric nature of his subject matter, undoubtedly presented great difficulties to the reader. Whatever Milosz's final position in French literature may be, it cannot be denied that his mastery of the melody and suggestive power of the French language was equaled by few of his contemporaries.

See: Francis de Miomandre, *Le Pavillon du mandarin* (1921); René de Berval, "La Mort d'Oscar W. de L. Milosz-Milasius," *Mercure de France,* CCXCI (1939), 246–247; Francis de Miomandre, "Mort d'un poète: J'ai connu Milosz," *Nouvelles littéraires,* March 11, 1939.

C. W., Jr.

Minski, Nikolai Maksimovich (pseud. of Nikolai Maksimovich Vilenkin, 1855–1937, Russian poet and philosopher), was born of poor Jewish parents at Glubokoye in the former Government of Vilna and took his degree in law at St. Petersburg (1879). Minski began his literary career as a follower of Nekrasov, but soon abandoned "civic" themes for an "art for art's sake" attitude; he became the first of the Russian decadents, among whom he shared leadership with Volynski and Merezhkovski (*q.v.*), particularly as a philosopher. He was one of the organizers of the Religious-Philosophical Society (1902), which attracted the intellectuals among the believers. His ideas are set forth in the Nietzschean *Pri svete sovesti* (1890; By the Light of Conscience) and in *Religiya budushchevo* (1905; The Religion of the Future), which develops his concept of "meonism," the religion of nonbeing, based on a mystic faith in conscience, sacrifice, and love, compounded with elements borrowed from Nietzsche (*q.v.*) and oriental mystics. His poetry is often merely a vehicle for his ideas, though in his later work he occasionally achieved a true synthesis of form and content. Minski was unfortunate in becoming a poet during a period of transition, and his chief importance lies in his preparing the ground for the later symbolists. Curiously enough, 1905 found Minski among the revolutionaries; he became the nominal head of *Novaya zhizn* (The New Life), Russia's first legal Social Democratic newspaper, for which he wrote "A Hymn of the Workers." His arrest terminated that period, and he left Russia for Paris. In exile, he wrote, among other things, a dramatic trilogy and a volume of criticism (*Ot Dante k Bloku,* 1922; From Dante to Blok), and then lapsed into silence.

See: S. A. Vengerov, ed., *Russkaya literatura XX veka,* Vol. I (1914); Aikhenvald, *Siluety russkikh pisatelei,* Vol. III (1923); "Minski," in *Literaturnaya entsiklopediya,* Vol. VII (1934).

P. A. P.

Mirbeau, Octave (1850–1917, French playwright and novelist), was born at Trévières, Calvados, the son of a middle-class doctor. An unhappy childhood, complicated by unfortunate experiences in a school chiefly for young nobles, affected him deeply and may account in part for the bitter tone of much of his mature work. Mirbeau began his literary career as a conservative journalist, but soon became a violent revolutionary. He quickly rose to a position of influence in artistic and literary circles (he was a member of the Goncourt Academy) and gave real support to the efforts of such innovators as Van Gogh, Rodin, Manet, Monet, Cézanne,

Debussy, and Maeterlinck (*q.v.*). After an extremely turbulent journalistic career, during which he provoked numerous duels by his outspoken criticism of conservatives in art and politics, he withdrew to his estate at Cheverchemont, where he died after a long illness.

In his works the note of protest and revolt is dominant. His first great play, *Les Mauvais Bergers* (1897), directed against those dishonest politicians who exploit the laboring man, paved the way for the epoch-making *Les Affaires sont les affaires* (1903), one of the memorable successes of the French stage, a bitter indictment of business ethics and the financial world in general. *Le Foyer* (1908) continues the note of social protest with a sharp attack on deceit and mismanagement in charitable institutions. His early novels, *Le Calvaire* (1886), *L'Abbé Jules* (1888), and *Sébastien Roch* (1889), are largely autobiographical. Of his later novels, *Le Jardin des supplices* (1899), a terrifying study of oriental sadism, and *Le Journal d'une femme de chambre* (1900), the most truly naturalistic of his works, enjoyed the greatest popularity.

Mirbeau's style is peculiarly vivid and intense, his tone nearly always violent and excessive, his execution frequently uneven. Undeniably sincere, he carried on a long crusade for social justice and shocked his age by the reforms he preached. Today, even though many of his ideas are dated, he holds a large audience by the vigor of his prose, by the fearlessness of his attack, and by his love for liberty, justice, and equality.

See: G. Rodenbach, *L'Elite* (1899); E. Pilon, *Octave Mirbeau* (1903); G. Lecomte, "L'Œuvre d'Octave Mirbeau," *Grande Revue*, XCIII (1917), 20–35; M. Revon, *Octave Mirbeau; son œuvre* (1934).

R. J. N.

Miró, Gabriel (1879–1930, Spanish novelist and essayist), born in Alicante, entered the Jesuit College of Orihuela and later the Instituto de Segunda Enseñanza of Alicante. He began the study of law in Valencia and finished these studies in Granada. He lived in Alicante and in 1911 moved to Barcelona, where he worked on a sacred encyclopedia for a publishing firm. Continually in financial straits, he later went to Madrid as secretary of the Concursos Nacionales de Bellas Artes. He died May 27, 1930, in Madrid.

His first work, *Del vivir* (1904), is a book of travels through his own province, in which he seemed to have been mainly impressed by the leprosy existing in certain districts; already he shows vigorous power in the emotional description of persons and places. In the year 1908 his short novel *Nómada* was awarded a prize in a contest sponsored by a Madrid review, and from that moment Miró figures among the group of writers intent upon the renovation of literary style. Novels constitute a good part of his production. The first of these, *La novela de mi amigo* (1902), is marked by profound spiritual anguish and a polished style; *Las cerezas del cementerio* (1914) is characterized by a modernism through which there shines a romantic sensibility. His best novels are *Nuestro padre San Daniel* (1921; Eng. tr., *Our Father San Daniel,* 1930) and *El obispo leproso* (1926). "Ciudad de Oleza" (a name with which he disguises Orihuela in the province of Murcia), episcopal see where the clergy from the convents and the bishop from his palace govern every phase of the people's lives, is, at times, merely the background of his work and of the actions of his characters, but on many occasions this city becomes in its own right a character in these novels. The very typically 19th-century theme of innocent vital instincts stifled by a fanatical conception of morality loses all the appearance of a political thesis in Miró and serves only as a basis for human situations and conflicts.

Although these two major novels of Miró are good examples of modern craftsmanship, the author found the really appropriate expression of his literary temperament in nonfictional forms. This is evident first of all in a series of books—*Libro de Sigüenza* (1917), *El humo dormido* (1919), *El ángel, El molino, El caracol del faro* (1921), *Años y leguas* (1928)—in which he collects impressions and descriptions of landscapes, types, and scenes from the urban and rural life of his region. As the protagonist of almost all these works, Miró invented a double of himself whom he calls "Sigüenza" and who strolls through the recollections of past life or through the present realities of the Mediterranean country. In his figures from the villages and the countryside there is a strict fidelity in the minute descriptions of each object and at the same time a profound poetic sensibility which always extracts a spiritual essence from the material he is describing. His manner suggests Fray Luis de Granada, the mystic of nature of the 16th century; in a deep sense Miró is before all else a poet. His greatest non-novelistic work is *Figuras de la pasión del Señor* (1916; Eng. tr., *Figures of the Passion of Our Lord,* 1924). Against a biblical background this presents scenes from the life of Jesus and portrays the major and minor figures who appeared in it. Doubtless the countryside of Alicante suggested to Miró visions of Palestine, where he had never been. His extensive readings in sacred history, done while he was working in Barcelona, furnished him a documental basis for the work. It is here that Miró's prose reaches its maximum descriptive power; the effects call to mind the magnificent polychrome altarpieces and sculptures of traditional Spain.

Miró really eludes classification. Normal literary genres were never quite appropriate for his intimate quality. He is a *prosista* who, keenly sensitive to the latent beauty of words, would endow prose with all possible potentialities of expression. If in this way his work runs parallel to one of the tendencies of modernism, Miró puts above the merely modernistic a constant use of the "popular" and rural lexicon; this, combined with *cultismos,* produces a prose of a density and richness unmatched in modern Spanish literature.

See: J. Chabás, *Vuelo y estilo* (1930), pp. 17–58; J. Guardiola Ortiz, *Biografía íntima de Gabriel Miró* (1935); M. de Mayo, *Gabriel Miró (1879–1930); vida y obra* (1936).

P. S.

Mistral, Frédéric (1830–1914, Provençal poet), was born, lived, and died at Maillane near Avignon. His father, a well-to-do farmer, felt honor-bound to give him a good classical education. Accordingly Frédéric Mistral was sent to three different boarding schools and given an opportunity to attend courses at the Collège Royal of Avignon. He enjoyed the classics and proved to be an excellent student, but reading Homer and Virgil barely consoled him for the loss of actual contact with country life and people who spoke Provençal, his mother tongue. He had his revenge by composing verses in that speech which was spurned by official education and derided by his schoolmates. One day he was elated to hear one of his teachers, Joseph Roumanille (*q.v.*), recite some poems in the despised tongue. This marked the beginning of a lifelong friendship and fruitful collaboration. Later Mistral went to study law at the University of Aix-en-Provence. After receiving his Licence en Droit (1851), he returned home determined to devote his life to the task of reviving Provençal consciousness among his countrymen. This he hoped to accomplish through the prestige of poetry in the vernacular which, like Roumanille, he was intent upon restoring to literary dignity.

Mistral's first publications had been two French poems written in a period of republican and humanitarian enthusiasm (1848), but he attracted considerable attention only when some of his early compositions in Provençal were included in *Li Prouvençalo* (1852), an anthology of living poets edited by Roumanille. From then on his prestige increased rapidly. He was the most brilliant star of the *pléiade* that founded the Felibrige school (1854), *i.e.,* the association that was to promote the linguistic and literary renaissance of southern France. His first important work, *Mirèio* (1859; Eng. trs., *Mireio,* 1867, *Mirelle,* 1868, *Mirèio,* 1872), established his reputation outside of Provence. This, a long poem in 12 cantos, a rustic idyl cast in the epic form, was a revelation with regard to the richness and poetry of both language and subject matter. It was crowned by the French Academy, later translated into the main European languages, and set to opera by Gounod. Mistral made several trips to Paris but resisted the lure of the capital, his main interest being now to direct the Felibrige toward the realization of a definite social and even political program. Limiting his activities to southern France, he presided over joint meetings of Provençal and Catalan poets, pleading for local and provincial rights. The Franco-Prussian War (1870–1871) modified somewhat the nature of his teaching. Feeling that the real threat to Provençal aspirations and traditions (Mistral is a traditionalist in the best sense of the word) was in the northeast rather than in Paris, he then focused his attention upon the so-called *idée latine,* the idea of uniting the Latin nations, regarded as constituting a "race" or rather group of people with common traditions and ideals, into a kind of peaceful confederation for the defense of Mediterranean civilization. In 1904 Mistral shared the Nobel prize in literature, for both his literary works and his contribution to philology. He used the proceeds of the prize to house the Museon Arlaten, a museum of ethnography which he had just founded and to the enrichment of which he was to devote the last 10 years of his life. When he died, he had been the leading spirit of the Felibrige for nearly 60 years.

Besides *Mirèio* Mistral's works in verse comprise two other poems of the epic type, *Calendau* (1867), symbolizing Provence in its struggle against centralization, and *Lou Pouèmo dóu Rose* (1897; Eng. tr., *Anglore; the Song of the Rhone,* 1937), depicting the life of the Rhone boatmen before the advent of the steamship, as well as two volumes of collected lyrical poems, a versified novelette, and a lyrical tragedy. His prose work includes *Moun espelido; memòri e raconte* (1906; Eng. tr., *Memoirs of Mistral,* 1907); a collection of speeches; and three volumes of *Prose d'almanach* (1926–1930), published posthumously with, opposite the Provençal text, a French translation from the pen of the editor. To these must be added a scholarly work, *Lou Tresor dóu Felibrige; dictionnaire provençal-français embrassant les divers dialectes de la langue d'Oc* (1876–1886), which is indeed a treasure of science and poetry, and a translation of Genesis into Provençal prose. His enormous correspondence has not yet been published, and many scattered poems and articles have still to be collected. Mistral's works are better known to the general public by their French titles, *e.g., Mireille, Calendal, Mes Origines.* The French translations accompanying the original are by the author himself.

While chiefly considered a Provençal patriot and poet of the soil, Mistral has also been studied as a reviver and defender of classical traditions. Served by a powerful genius and a keen artistic sense, he has been able to produce works with a strong and universal appeal, characterized by both perfection of form and the omnipresence of a noble ideal. The greatest qualities of these works are their natural simplicity and freshness and a joyous spirit and reasonable optimism that bear the stamp of their Provençal origin.

See: C. A. Downer, *Frédéric Mistral, Poet and Leader in Provence* (1901); P. Lasserre, *Frédéric Mistral, poète, moraliste, citoyen* (1905); J. Vincent, *Frédéric Mistral; sa vie, son influence, son action et son art* (1918); A. Thibaudet, *Mistral, ou la République de soleil* (1930); C. M. Girdlestone, *Dreamer and Striver: The Poetry of Frédéric Mistral* (1937).

A. V. R.

Moberg, Vilhelm (1898–, Swedish novelist and dramatist), ranks today as one of Sweden's most important novelists. He has been active also as a dramatist, several of his plays (notably *Hustrun,* 1929, The Wife; and *Våld,* 1933, Violence) having had considerable success on the Stockholm stage. Though Moberg left his native rural Småland in early youth to seek a literary career in the city, most of his fiction deals with the folk life of this south-central Swedish province. He attained literary eminence rather slowly, not reaching the heights until the late 1930's, after some 10 years of a persistent and somewhat miscellaneous literary apprenticeship, the most important products of which, aside from one or two of his dramas, were the series of Småland novels *Raskens* (1927), *Långt från landsvägen* (1929; Far from the Highway), and *De knutna händerna* (1930; The Clenched Hands). Though solid in construction and honest in their depiction of folk psychology and folk life, these novels did not rise much above the artistic and intellectual standards of many other Swedish novels of the day. Moberg's first great literary triumph came with his *Knut Toring* trilogy (1935–1939; Eng. tr., *The Earth Is Ours,* 1940). This novel, partly autobiographical, is a sober, penetrating account of how Knut Toring, who had left his native countryside and found success in the city, is driven by spiritual necessity in his maturity to return again to his native village and identify himself again with the way of life there. Though the earlier parts of the trilogy concentrate primarily on the psychological problem posed by Knut Toring's break with the traditions of his peasant ancestors and his subsequent longing to find the way back to these ultimate sources of his spiritual existence, the novel becomes increasingly concerned as it progresses with related general social, economic, and political questions of the day. The last volume of the trilogy has as its immediate background the ominous preliminaries of the Second World War on the Continent, and in it Moberg gives clear and ringing expression to his opposition to modern Continental totalitarian trends. In his next novel *Rid i natt!* (1941; Eng. tr., *Ride This Night!* 1943) Moberg takes his stand even more sharply against totalitarianism and in favor of democracy, though in outward form this novel goes back to the 17th century for its background and its action. In its art this last novel of Moberg's is spare, lean, and muscular, in rather marked contrast with the leisurely, detailed epic manner of most of Moberg's earlier work. The difference is doubtless to be accounted for by the burning actuality, the vital urgency of the theme developed so centrally in *Rid i natt!*

See: A. Gustafson, "'A Dream Worth Dying For—': The Price of Freedom in Vilhelm Moberg's Recent Novels," *American-Scandinavian Review,* XXX (1942), 296–307.

A. G.

Mockel, Albert (1866–1945, Belgian poet, critic, and fableist), was born near Liége and grew up there through school and university. As a "freshman" (1884) he founded a literary society and edited the *Elan littéraire.* Renamed the *Wallonie* (1886–1892), this review introduced symbolism to Belgium and for a time was the principal organ of the symbolist movement. The *Wallonie* inaugurated symbolist drama by first publishing Charles van Lerberghe's (*q.v.*) *Les Flaireurs* (January, 1889), Maeterlinck's (*q.v.*) *L'Intruse* (January, 1890), and Mockel's ideas on the theatre; it published work of nearly all the symbolists, including Mallarmé, Valéry, and Gide (*qq.v.*), and ended by giving its name to the French provinces of Belgium. In the *Wallonie* Mockel developed a critical mind of astonishing clarity, subtlety, and balance, wrote out his rationale of free verse calling on poets to quit the alexandrine and use *rythme intérieur,* and made one of the best efforts of his generation to define the symbol. After 1890 Mockel lived in Paris, where he went regularly to Mallarmé's. He moved to Brussels in 1938 and the next year was president of the Académie Royale.

Propos de littérature (1894) is a mature statement of the ideas developed in *Wallonie,* applied to the poetry of Régnier and Vielé-Griffin (*qq.v.*). This book is perhaps the best source of symbolist aesthetics; its claim is that the symbolists restored music to poetry. In an age of impressionism Mockel used the method of comparison and analysis. Sir Edmund Gosse liked the sophisticated burlesque of *Contes pour les enfants d'hier* (1908) so much that he called Mockel a Belgian Ariosto. The two books on Verhaeren (*q.v.*) (1895, 1917) are a triumph of critical justice done to work not congenial to the critic. His little book on Mallarmé as "a hero" (1899) is definitive in taste and judgment.

Disciple of Wagner (*q.v.*), Mallarmé, and Schopenhauer, Mockel easily moved, both in theory and practice, from music as art to music as idea. In *Chantefable un peu naïve* (1891), of mixed prose, music, and verse (the music to be read, not played), the poet was so absorbed in theory that the technique became the real subject of the work. In his mature poetry, *Clartés* (1901) and *La Flamme immortelle* (1924), music is generalized as means of formal control: rhythm is lyric aspiration toward ideal being.

See: Tancrède de Visan, *L'Attitude du lyrisme contemporain* (1911); A. van Bever and P. Léautaud, *Poètes d'aujourd'hui* (1929).

J. M.

Moe, Ingebret Moltke (1859–1913, Norwegian folklorist and language reformer), born in Krødsherad, was the literary heir of the two great pioneer collectors of Norwegian folk traditions, his own father, Jörgen Moe, and the latter's fellow worker, Asbjörnsen. He started his activities as collector and editor as early as 1877 and became the leading folklorist of all the Scandinavian countries. In 1886 he was appointed professor of folk traditions at the University of Christiania and was the teacher and the industrious advisor of all the younger generations of literary scholars in Norway. With sovereign scholarship and fine poetical taste Moe revised the older editions of fairy tales and legends, espousing and leading the growing demands for a conscious approach to the vernacular, in forms and vocabulary and even more in popular phraseology. From the 1890's he became the real head, often behind the scenes, of the movement for a spelling reform of the traditional literary language, in the same direction, and for the amalgamation of the two literary forms fighting for supremacy. Thus he was the true father of the two spelling reforms of 1907 and 1917; he had worked practically for them, not only by his revisions of the fairy tales, but also by his collaboration in the two most important new primary readers for the schools appearing in the 1890's, that of Nordahl Rolfsen in Bokmaal and that of A. Austlid in Landsmaal. His own authorship, embracing brilliant studies of folk poetry and folk traditions, showed him not only an eminent scholar, a founder of severe methods in his researches, but a stylistic artist of high merit. His writings are available in *Samlede skrifter* (3 vols., 1925–1927; Collected Works).

See: A. Olrik, "Personal Impressions of Moltke Moe," in *Folklore Fellow Communications,* No. 17 (1915), 3–76.

H. K.

Molnár, Ferenc (1878–, Hungarian playwright, novelist, and short-story writer), was born in Budapest. He was reared in well-to-do surroundings; socially and economically he enjoyed advantages that few Hungarian writers have had. He studied law, but preferred journalism, the stage, and literature. He was first acclaimed as a clever and witty journalist and almost simultaneously as a gifted and effective playwright. He also acquired a prominent place in Hungarian literature as a novelist and as a writer of short stories. In 1908 he was elected to the Petőfi Társaság (Petőfi Society), thus receiving official approval of his literary worth. Molnár has been married three times. At present his home is in New York. Much of his time has been spent away from Hungary, yet whatever subject or atmosphere he explored as a writer and as a traveler, he has remained true to his

Budapest background. He has never forgotten the outskirts of Budapest where the poor and the vagabonds live, nor the plutocratic society of his home town.

As a playwright Molnár is internationally famous. His plays are neither enriched nor handicapped by a respect for tradition. His heroes and heroines are apt to encounter difficulties, of course, but these difficulties as a rule are caused by a transgression of conventionalities or by an irrational approach to rational problems, and they rarely reveal those tragic or comic complications which one discerns in the works of the greatest playwrights. Molnár's overtones are apt to be sentimental or cynical. An innate taste has prevented him from being only an effect-seeker, has made him avoid the temptation merely to play tricks, and has enabled him at times in a piece like *Liliom* actually to suppress sentimentalism and to assert a real poetic sensitiveness. It is clear that Molnár has the urge of the genuine creator, but in most of his plays the mingling of realism and romanticism, sometimes assumed mysticism, leads to a heterogeneous sort of artistic experience, betraying an extraordinary aptitude for unexpected scenes, lively dialogues, manufactured excitement. *Az ördög* (1907; Eng. tr., *The Devil,* 1908), *A testőr* (1910; Eng. tr., *The Guardsman,* 1924), *A hattyú* (1920; Eng. tr., *The Swan,* 1922), *Olympia* (1928; Eng. tr., 1928)—to mention a few of his plays produced in the United States—are admirably constructed. However, Molnár's cleverness of composition is inclined to hurt his creative authenticity. The naïveté and poetry of *Liliom* (1909; Lily; Eng. tr., *Liliom,* 1921), though even in this play the sentiments are sometimes dubious, show secrets of Molnár's talent which he neglected or could not recapture in most of his other plays. The symbolism of the play is obvious: the need of goodness and affection is beautifully suggested. Molnár makes us keenly aware of the moods and problems of Liliom, the circus barker. The play is unpretentious, and its legendary atmosphere is within the boundaries of the credible because it is made poetically vivid and convincing. His other plays, despite their skilled technique, their ingeniousness, and in some instances their brilliancy, never rise to the level of supreme literary art. There are, in many other plays of Molnár, unsuspected or sudden echoes of his sincerity, but they cannot make us forget the mannerisms of the playwright, the lack of spontaneousness, the heights he misses.

As a novelist and as a writer of short stories Molnár is, with one or two exceptions, less certain of his composition than in his plays. Yet his unusual ability is demonstrated in a juvenile novel entitled *A Pál-uccai fiuk* (1907; Eng. tr., *The Paul Street Boys,* 1927). In this novel, portraying a phase of Budapest student life, Molnár does not need cleverness in order to conceal bareness. The novel has epic attributes; it is simple and tragic, solid and humane; it has perspective. Most of his novels and stories which were translated into English, such as *Egy gazdátlan csónak története* (1901; Eng. tr., *The Derelict Boat,* 1926), *Éva* (1903; Eng. tr., 1926), *Rabok* (1907; Eng. tr., *Prisoners,* 1925), *Zenélö angyal* (1933; Eng. tr., *Angel Making Music,* 1935), were evidently written with the intention to entertain, but that is all. The fact that Molnár, besides *The Paul Street Boys,* wrote other delightful juvenile stories, *e.g., Gyerekek* (1907; Children) and *Józsi* (1902; Joe), suggests that he could have made better use of his ability had he remained in harmony with those creative instincts here expressed.

One of Molnár's best books has the unpretentious title *Haditudósitó naplója* (1916; The Diary of a War Correspondent). This is the record of a keen observer, of an experienced journalist; but it is also the book of a warmhearted man whose gay and pensive reflections and interpretations of human goodness, decency, and solidarity in the midst of warfare (the First World War) show a passion of the spirit which, regrettably, one often painfully misses in his other works. Compared with some of his successful novels the diary of Molnár as a war correspondent is a modest offering, yet it radiates a humane glow, a forward-looking spirit not found in the hopelessness of these novels.

Molnár's singular ability must be admitted. He was an innovator on the Hungarian stage, and throughout his writings one senses a highly developed sensibility and sophistication.

See: A. Schöpflin, *Magyar irók* (1919); *All the Plays of Molnár,* with a foreword by David Belasco (1937).

J. R.

Molo, Walter von (1880–, German novelist), was born at Sternberg, Moravia. The formative years which he spent in Vienna are charmingly described in *Der kleine Held* (1934). After publishing a few modern novels, Molo gave up his engineering profession to live by his pen. In 1913 he moved to Berlin. The flamboyant titles of his popular Schiller novel in four volumes—*Ums Menschentum,*

—*Titanenkampf, Die Freiheit, Den Sternen zu* (1912–1916)—indicate the author's determination to impress the reader with Schiller's heroic character. Molo depicts the dramatist's milieu in minutest detail, accentuating Schiller's heroic struggle with the petty misery of everyday life. On the other hand, the highly dramatic scenes in which the spiritual development of the hero is revealed in monologues and dialogues are of expressionistic intensity and compactness. However, neither here nor in his Kleist novel *Geschichte einer Seele* (1938) did Molo succeed in creating the spiritual atmosphere in which the genius must live. In his later novels Molo's style becomes even more dramatic, epic progress being expressed by a succession of forceful dialogues linked together by terse narrative passages. The author excels in portraying the Prussian character. In picturing one decisive day of battle, which at first appears hopeless but ends in a great triumph for Frederick the Great, Molo not only holds his reader's constant attention but also presents a complete picture of the king.

Molo's *Holunder in Polen* (1933) describes the plight of the Germans in the territory taken over by the Poles after the Versailles treaty. During those disheartening years following the First World War, many Germans found inspiration in the heroic qualities of great German leaders of the past whom Molo presented so energetically in *Der Roman meines Volkes* with its three parts (*Fridericus,* 1918; *Luise,* 1919; *Das Volk wacht auf,* 1924), in *Mensch Luther* (1928; Eng. tr., *Brother Luther,* 1929), in *Ein Deutscher ohne Deutschland* (1931), presenting the tragic story of the famous German economist Friedrich List, and in *Eugenio von Savoy* (1936).

See: Franz C. Munk, *Walter von Molo; der Dichter und das Leben* (1924).

E. Hof.

Mombert, Alfred (1872–1942, German poet and author of modern "myths"), is an outstanding literary personality not connected with any school or clique. Though little known to a wide public, he has been regarded by poets (Dehmel, *q.v.,* Pannwitz, Benn, *q.v.,* Carossa, *q.v.*) and critics (Moeller van den Bruck, K. H. Strobl, R. Benz, R. von Delius, Ernst Michel) as the outstanding German genius of his generation. Mombert was born in Karlsruhe, Baden, not far from the Rhine, the river which he loved so deeply and which became a kind of homely leitmotif in his most exalted and in his most sublime poetry. He studied law and philosophy at the universities of Heidelberg, Leipzig, Munich, and Berlin. After six years of law practice he retired from all public activities and devoted himself to a life of contemplation. He lived in Heidelberg, absorbed in his books and a collection of minerals which he brought home from trips all over Europe and northern Africa. He was an enthusiastic walker and alpinist, and the greater part of his poetry was written not in his study but while wandering about the country.

Mombert's first volume of verse, *Tag und Nacht* (1894), was influenced by the poets of German romanticism, but at the same time was inspired by a strange psychological insight, making the interior life transparent and mysticism a realistic affair. His next books, *Der Glühende* (1896), *Die Schöpfung* (1897), *Der Denker* (1901) and *Die Blüte des Chaos* (1905), describe the experiences of the human soul in pictures of emotional grandeur and in words of momentous rhythmic power. Many of these poems have been set to music by well-known composers.

In the years that followed, Mombert made the attempt to create a "myth," based on his personal philosophy. His most important work during this period is the trilogy *Aeon* (1907–1911), written in dramatic form. The first part concerns the relations between the world and the human soul, the second the dilemma of our ego placed between chaos and cosmos. The third part deals with the materialization of the human soul in the history of the nations. These dramatic poems with their awe-inspiring impressive dignity are not for the contemporary stage but are meant to be presented to audiences of the future, should the dramatic art ever return to its sacred and solemn beginnings. Of a proposed second trilogy, *Aigla,* the poet finished only two parts (1928–1931). During the same period two of his greatest lyrical works, *Der Held der Erde* (1919) and *Atair* (1925), were published.

In his seventh decade Mombert turned to a new realism. In *Sfaira der Alte* (1936) the wise old poet who is the central figure of this most beautiful book of verse does not have "imagination" and does not talk about things; he is simply the most sensitive and understanding of listeners. The trees, the mountains, the lakes, the parks, the old inns, talk to him. The world is pictured as it looks to them and not from the point of view of a reflective poet. The world of a stalactite cave does not appear through its impressions upon men but is realized, in a superb poem, through the emotions of the cave's gnome when human beings intrude upon his realm. Besides its high artistic value, this book made German history by the deep and tender love it expressed for Germany's landscape, culture, and music at the very time when the Nazis denied the Jew Mombert the right to call himself a German. Friends tried to persuade him to emigrate, but he wanted to die in his beloved homeland.

In the fall of 1940 he was, however, with other so-called "non-Aryans" of western Germany arrested and moved to the concentration camp of Gurs, France, where he fell seriously ill. In 1941 friends succeeded in having him released to reside in Switzerland. He died in Winterthur after celebrating his 70th birthday with his friends. He had finished and revised a second part (1941) to *Sfaira der Alte.*

See: E. Michel, *Der Weg zum Mythos* (1919); R. Benz, *Die Stunde der Musik,* Vol. II (1927); F. D. Benndorf, *Mombert; Geist und Werk* (1932); H. Carossa, *Führung und Geleit* (1933).

M. F.

Momigliano, Attilio (1883–, Italian critic and literary historian), was born in Ceva and was graduated in literature and philosophy from the University of Turin in 1906. From 1919 to 1937 he was one of the editors of the *Giornale storico della letteratura italiana* and was literary critic for the Milanese newspaper *Corriere della sera* from 1926 to 1938. He held the chair of Italian literature in the universities of Catania, Pisa, and Florence from 1920 until 1938, when he was deprived of his post by the race laws against the Jews. In 1946 he was returned to his chair in Florence.

Much of Momigliano's best criticism is contained in the notes and commentaries which he published with his editions of Italian classics: Manzoni's lyrics (1914), Politian's poetry (1921), Alfieri's *Saul* and *Mirra* (1923). Whether in this form or in the separate essay and monograph, as in his *Impressioni di un lettore contemporaneo* (1928), *Studi di poesia* (1938), or the *Saggio sull'Orlando Furioso* (1928) and *Giovanni Verga narratore* (1923), Momigliano's critical effort is devoted exclusively to the work of literature itself. He shows his reader what to look for in the work in hand, how to be alone, one might say, with the work before him. His *Storia della letteratura italiana* (1936) keeps faith with this single intention, with the result that it is outstanding among histories of Italian literature after De Sanctis (*q.v.*). Momigliano makes no attack on the historical and positivist scholars of Italian literature, but he has never forgotten, as they too often did, that the values of a work of literature must be found within itself. His work as teacher and writer by this creed has taught a generation of Italians how to read better their classics.

C. S. S.

Moniz Barreto, Guilherme (1863–1899, Portuguese critic), was born in Goa, Portuguese India, the son of an army officer. He began to study in India and at the age of 17 went to Europe in order to finish his secondary education in Lisbon, where he also followed the Curso Superior de Letras. Very early in his life he began to read intensely, familiarizing himself with the most representative works of European literature, science and philosophy. In spite of his weak physical constitution he made his way through college by teaching philosophy and mathematics.

In 1887 was published in Paris his book *Oliveira Martins,* by which he became well known in Portuguese literary circles. The following year he started his contribution to *O reporter* of Lisbon. In "A crítica," one of the articles he wrote for that periodical (August 9, 1888), he expressed his personal viewpoints concerning the aims and methods of criticism. It was in *O reporter* too that his study on Eça de Queiroz (*q.v.*), among other important articles, was published (July 25, 1888). With "A literatura portuguesa contemporânea," a 40-page article on the Portuguese literature of his time, he opened the first number of the *Revista de Portugal,* which appeared in Oporto in 1889. For three years he wrote for that short-lived review, in which his contributions were issued either under his real name or under the pseudonym G. Côrte Real. In 1893 he went to Paris and began to send articles to the *Jornal do comércio.*

Moniz Barreto was strongly influenced by German philosophical thought, especially by Hegel and Kant. As a critic he was a disciple of Taine (*q.v.*). "He taught me how to write," said he in the tribute he wrote for the *Jornal do comércio* on the occasion of the death of the famous French critic. He was particularly concerned with general ideas and had himself a great power of abstraction. His criticism is dominated by the spirit of system and by the concept of development. A believer in the hierarchy of causes and effects, he always endeavored to see in each literary work a link in the evolution of ideas and feelings of mankind. His views against specialization were expounded in his article "O especialismo," published in *O reporter* (August 16, 1888). His style was convincing, powerful, and precise. He has been regarded as the most outstanding critic of the literary production of the realistic school in Portugal. With the exception of his book on Oliveira Martins, all his studies are scattered in newspapers and periodicals of his time. In 1918, some years after his death, nine such articles were reprinted in the *Revista de história,* under the editorship of Fidelino de Figueiredo (*q.v.*), who wrote a brief introduction to them.

See: Manuel da Silva Gayo, *Os novos; I, Moniz Barreto* (1894); Fidelino de Figueiredo, "Materiais para a história da crítica literária em Portugal: Artigos de Moniz Barreto," in *Revista de história,* VII (1918), 245–276.

J. F.

Montale, Eugenio (1896–, Italian poet and critic), was born in Genoa and spent his youth in that city and on the neighboring Ligurian coast. When Italy entered the First World War, Montale left school to serve with the Italian Alpine troops. On his return to civil life he joined the editorial staff of an Italian publishing house; several years later he accepted the post of chief librarian of the celebrated Gabinetto Vieusseux in Florence. His coolness towards political developments in Italy may have had bearing on the fact that he was quietly relieved of this post, in spite of the luster he shed on it, before the beginning of the Second World War.

As a poet Montale has made an extremely significant and rich contribution to Italian letters, *Ossi di Seppia* (1925), his first published volume, immediately arrested the attention of a poetry-reading public which had retained its taste and interest through many years of predominantly anemic fare. They recognized the true sound and substance of poetry in these unconventional and often cryptic lyrics, and in a period of six years brought about the publication of augmented second and third editions of the little book. In 1931 a lyric entitled "La Casa dei doganieri" won Montale the Antico Fattore prize, yearly award of a group of Florentine artists. The prize poem, together with a small group of new lyrics and half a dozen drawings by artists of the Antico Fattore circle, was subsequently printed in a limited edition pamphlet. At this time a number of critical studies of Montale's work began to make their appearance, his reputation spread abroad, and translations and critical notes were published in both British and American periodicals (*Criterion,* June, 1928; *This Quarter,* April-May, 1930; *London Times Literary Supplement,* June 21, 1934; *Saturday Review of Literature,* July 18, 1936). Foreign readers who watched for his work during this period found his signature under reviews and articles on contemporary French, Italian, and even American literature as well as under his own lyrics in the *Gazzetta del popolo, Italia letteraria, Caratteri,* and other periodicals. His translation of Shakespeare's *The Tempest* was announced before Italy entered the Second World War. In 1940 there appeared a new volume of poems, *Le Occasioni,* reprinted the following year with a few additions and changes.

Montale's poetry communicates a complex experience of external and inner worlds mutually illuminating one another. It is hard, intense, often difficult, with a predominantly tight, dry texture, but musically conceived and musically executed. Like T. S. Eliot, to whom he has often been compared, Montale uses prose rhythms as a basis for poetic structure, like Eliot he has a highly individual and memorable diction, like Eliot he weaves ideas and images with musical rather than prose logic. The comparison, however, should not be given much weight, for in essentials both of sound and sense the two poets are far apart. Montale is concerned above all with the dissidence between man's free hope and his prisoned fate. Life is seen as a chain of events whose links bind and determine one another—and, at the same time, as a spiritual motion away from compulsion, out of the logic of time and place, toward free creation and free vision. This theme is developed or touched upon in almost as many variations as Montale has occasions for poems. It is not stated baldly, but arises from the materials of experience or imagination. And perhaps the outstanding quality of Montale's poetry lies in just this ability to convey the abstract through the concrete and personal without destroying the direct suggestive power of the images. His whole concrete world, its motions and gestures, reflect or interpret an intellectual or emotional content. This is apt to yield strange effects—for the juxtaposition and interplay of things and forces are constrained only by the inner logic of the individual poem—but such strangeness is neither arbitrary nor constructed. Clearly the poet is working toward the crystallization of certain orienting themes in the forms from which he first divined those themes.

Naturally not all the poems in Montale's two volumes and pamphlet reach the same depth or complexity. Some do not pretend to be more than renderings of moments of acute perception. A few are too hermetic even for those readers who prefer the poet in his secret vein.

See: A. Consiglio, *Studi di poesia* (1934); L. Musco, "Montale," *Movimento letterario,* V–VII (1935).

I. B.

Montégut, Emile (1826–1895, French critic), was born at Limoges of a well-to-do bourgeois family. After graduating from the local *lycée,* he went in 1844 to Paris to study law, a purpose from which he was soon turned by the attractions of literature. In 1847, with an article on Emerson, he began a 43-year association with the *Revue des deux mondes.* During that long period he was an indefatigable contributor, ranging through English, American, and European literature, discussing political and social questions, and in his later years writing travel notes and art criticism. Although from 1857 he held the position of chief literary critic of the *Revue,* fame both during his life and after his death seemed to escape him. As a critic he was overshadowed at first by Sainte-Beuve and later by Taine, Renan, and finally Brunetière (*qq.v.*). He received the ribbon of the Legion of Honor in 1865, but he was defeated in three attempts at election to the French Academy, in 1884, 1894, and, most humiliating of all, in 1895 by his former protégé, Brunetière. Nevertheless Montégut deserves a higher place than is generally accorded him. His original work suffers, no doubt, from its miscellaneous character and from the fact that it includes no sustained effort, his books being no more than collections of articles. Yet it has undeniable merit. In a period of literary transition, his criticism had the great virtue of common sense and intellectual flexibility; he was hardly ever wrong in his estimates of what was lasting and what only ephemeral. His tastes were catholic and his reading surprisingly wide. His essays on American literature, particularly on Emerson and Hawthorne, are remarkable considering their date of composition (those on Hawthorne in 1860 and 1864 are still in many ways unsurpassed); and it is unfortunate that they have never been collected. His studies in English literature, collected in *Essais sur la littérature anglaise* (1883), *Ecrivains modernes de l'Angleterre* (3 vols., 1886–1892), and *Heures de lecture d'un critique* (1892), range from Shakespeare, through Aubrey, Pope, and Sterne, to Tennyson and George Eliot; his volumes on European literature, *e.g., Types littéraires* (1882) and *Mélanges critiques* (1888), are no less eclectic, treating as they do such diverse personalities as Dante, Cervantes, Goethe, Hugo, and Michelet. As a translator from the English he was also notable, in particular for his version of Emerson's *Essays, Essais de philosophie américaine* (1851), and of Shakespeare, *Œuvres complètes de Shakespeare* (10 vols., 1867–1873), for long the standard French text.

See: A. Laborde-Milaa, *Emile Montégut* (1922).

C. W., Jr.

Montherlant, Henry de (1896–, French novelist), is a brilliant and perverse writer. He will probably best be remembered as the one prominent French author who during the tragic occupation of his country in the Second World War welcomed and adulated the enemy *pour le plaisir de trahir,* to use his own words—for the sheer pleasure of betraying. Born in Paris of an old French family of Catalan origin, he received an excellent traditional education in a Catholic *collège,* saw service in the First World War and was wounded, and became one of the leading spokesmen of the restless, cynical, and exalted post-war generation. He made a gesture of abandoning literature in favor of life in 1925, traveled in Spain and North Africa for seven years, played an equivocal role as philosopher and prophet during the politically troubled pre-war years, and found in the outbreak of war and the enslavement of his country a complete vindication of the defeatism with which his whole work is saturated.

His first, semi-autobiographical, loosely constructed novels—*La Relève du matin* (1920), *Le Songe* (1925), *Les Bestiaires* (1926; Eng. tr., *The Bullfighters,* 1927), and *Les Olympiques* (1927)—deal with adolescence, war, bullfighting, and sport from the point of view of an aristocratic, highly egotistic, emotionally retarded person, revealing a strong influence of Chateaubriand and an even stronger influence of Barrès (*q.v.*). Preoccupation with tradition, death, and the affinities of blood and lust is at times pushed to the point of caricature. Hating bourgeois democracy with its coddling of the weak and the inept, despising women except as instruments of man's pleasure, exalting the "virile" virtues, professing a philosophy which is an amalgam of stoicism, the patrician code of the Roman Empire, Mithraic sun worship, Nietzscheism (*see* Nietzsche), and physical culture, he constantly skirts the edge of a nihilism which is perhaps best expressed in his *Solstice de juin 1941* (1942).

As writer, as sheer craftsman, he stands above almost all his contemporaries. In *Les Célibataires* (1934; Eng. tr., *Lament for the Death of an Upper Class,* 1935, American title, *Perish in Their Pride,* 1936) and the four volumes of *Les Jeunes Filles* (1935–1940; Eng. tr., *Young Girls,* published with *Pity for Women,* 1937; *The Demon of Good* and *The Lepers,* published in one volume as *The Lepers,* 1940, American title, *Costals & the Hippogriff,* 1940) he shows an evolution from the almost oratorical style of his earlier work toward a hard, brilliant objectivity. Admirably disciplined, with a rare aesthetic integrity, he is a master of character delineation and possesses psychological insight, trenchant wit, and a grasp of the subtlety and complexity of contemporary social relationships. Costals, the hero of *Jeunes Filles,* detestable as he is, is one of the creations of modern fiction, and in this same work there is nothing to compare with his cruel dissection of modern woman.

See: Paul Archambault, *Jeunes Maîtres* (1926); Haakon M. Chevalier, "The Monster, Marriage," review of *Costals & the Hippogriff* in *Kenyon Review,* III (1941), 246–249; Pierre Brodin, *Les Ecrivains français de l'entre-deux-guerres* (1942); Honor Tracy, "The Pleasures of Treason," *Horizon,* VIII (1943), 47.

H. M. C.

Morais, Wenceslau de Sousa (1854–1929, Portuguese prose writer), was born in Lisbon. He embarked upon a career in the Portuguese navy (1871) and eventually became a captain in that service. Then voyages to the Far East so fascinated him that he decided to abandon occidental life. He first obtained the post of Portuguese consul at Kobe, but later (1912) gave up this career too in order to penetrate better the life of the country. He made of Japan—landscape, life, and sentiments—the one theme of his writings and in this was the most characteristic representative of contemporary Portuguese "Japonism." This literary current is totally independent of the influence of Pierre Loti (*q.v.*) or of the Goncourts (*q.v.*); on the contrary it is to be considered as a continuation of a tradition in Lusitanian culture which begins in the 15th century. Morais—who lived in Japan twice as long as Lafcadio Hearn—transformed his life in a passionate effort to identify himself with the Japanese soul. In 1895 he published *Traços do Extremo Oriente* (Sketches from the Far East), in which the most characteristic outlines of life in Siam, China, and Japan are depicted with great serenity of vision. Japan occupies the greatest amount of space, and one senses the author's joy of discovery and his desire for immersion in that exotic world. The work which follows, *Dai-Nippon* (1897; Great Japan), reveals a traveler of an enlarged vision, engaged in an impassioned exegesis of the most individualistic traits of the Japanese spirit, in search of a happy fusion with this spirit. Later he published *Cartas do Japão* (1904–1905; Letters from Japan), in which he outlined for Portugal the Japanese point of view in the conflict with Russia. During this period, after his Buddhist marriage, his compenetration of the Nipponese soul is very profound. There appeared then *O Culto do Chá* (1905; The Cult of Tea) and *Paisagens da China e do Japão* (1906; Landscapes of China and Japan), in which the author continues, with a more controlled style, the interpretation of *Dai-Nippon.* Finally, in his old age, he revealed the melancholy of the occidental disillusioned after the impossible adventure of trying to assimilate himself with the inscrutable Orient. *Bon-Odori em Tokushima* (1918; Bon-Odori in Tokushima) and *O-Yoné e Ko-Haru* (1923; O-Yoné and Ko Haru) are the fruits of this unhappy later mood. As late as 1926 he published *Serões do Japão* (Evenings in Japan) and *Relance da alma Japonesa* (Glances at the Japanese Soul). In 1928 appeared the third series of *Cartas do Japão,* and the following year the author died in Tokushima.

See: F. de Figueiredo, "O homem que trocou a alma," in *Torre de Babel* (1929); A. Pereira and O. César, *Os amores de Wenceslau de Morais* (1937).

E. G. D.

Morales, Tomás (1885–1922, Spanish poet), was born in Moya, a little seacoast town on the Grand Canary. He studied medicine in Cádiz and Madrid and spent several years as a country doctor in Agaete, a town on the island of his birth. There he married and his children were born. He later moved to the capital, Las Palmas, where he became interested in politics. But his principal and unwavering vocation was poetry; this manifested itself in all the phases of his brief existence which, in turn, are reflected in his verses. His infancy is represented by a series of poems entitled "Vacaciones sentimentales," which are subjective in feeling and characterized by a delicate, sentimental prosaicness, typical of the post-modernist period and of the poetry of the Canary Islands. Then comes the poetry of the sea and the waterfront, in its commonplace, everyday aspects, intimate and sentimental in feeling too. And, finally, there is his more ambitious work, represented by the "Oda al Atlántico," the "Canto a la Ciudad Comercial," and other poems with a mythological vision of the sea, at once classic and modern; in these his great rhetorical gifts which stem from the modernists can be appreciated. This poetic production, varied, intense, personal, contained in two books, *Poemas de la gloria, del amor y del mar* (1908) and *Las rosas de Hércules* (1919–1922), has the unmistakable flavor of the region from which he comes and has had a strong influence on the young and gifted poets of the Canary Islands. At the same time its appeal is universal, and its influence is perceived on other poets of Spain and America. All this has combined to make him, it may be claimed, one of the most brilliant examples of the post-modernist poets of Spain.

See: E. Díez-Canedo, review of *Poemas de la gloria, del amor y del mar* in *Lectura,* Año VIII (Madrid, 1908), Tomo II, pp. 315–318, and article in *Pluma,* III (Madrid, 1922), 425–430.

F. de O.

Morand, Paul (1888–, French novelist, diplomat, and writer of travel books), was born in Paris. He attended the Institution Sainte-Marie and in 1899 entered the Lycée Carnot. Having been sent to England every summer to study English, in 1908 he was permitted by his father to spend a full year at Oxford. Upon his return to France he decided to follow a diplomatic career. His military service completed, he entered the Ecole Libre des Sciences Politiques. After a short stay in the Department of the Protocol, Morand was sent first to England (1913–1916), then to Rome (1917) and to Madrid (1918). During the years 1919–1925 Morand was engaged at the Ministry of Foreign Affairs in Paris, and it was then he began to write. His first publications—*Lampes à Arc* (1919) and *Feuilles de température* (1920)—were collections of short poems. *Tendres Stocks* (1921) contained three short stories about three young women, drifting in wartime London. *Ouvert la nuit* (1922) and *Fermé la nuit* (1923) brought Morand instantaneous fame. *Lewis et Irène* (1924), a full-length novel, was not an unqualified success. *L'Europe galante* (1925) presented the same themes as the *Nuits,* but in a more daring key.

In 1925 the Ministry of Foreign Affairs sent him to Siam to assume charge of the legation in Bangkok. To reach his new post, where he remained only a short time, Morand traveled half way round the world. For several years thereafter he spent a large part of his time traveling and devoted the rest to writing. Some of his books were accounts of his travels, *Rien que la terre* (1926), *Le Voyage* (1927), *Paris-Tombouctou* (1928), *Hiver caraïbe* (1929). Others were studies of various human groups, the yellow race in *Bouddha vivant* (1927), the black in *Magie noire* (1928), the American people in *Champions du monde* (1930). In 1932 Morand became the head of the official Tourist Bureau in France. His books since then have been mostly of four kinds: travel books, such as *Flèche d'Orient* (1931), *Air indien* (1932); studies of cities, *New York* (1929), *London* (1931), *Bucharest* (1935); political works, such as *1900* (1931), *France-la-Doulce* (1934), *Rond-Point des Champs-Elysées* (1935); autobiographical works, such as *Papiers d'identité* (1931), *Mes Débuts* (1933). Many of Morand's works have been translated into English.

See: G. E. Lemaître, *Four French Novelists* (1938).

P. B.

Moravia, Alberto (1907–, pseud. of Alberto Pincherle, Italian novelist), born in Rome, has had a rather precocious literary career. His first novel, *Gli Indifferenti* (1929; Eng. tr., *The Indifferent Ones,* 1932), brought him immediate fame and made him one of the most discussed figures among the younger writers in Italy. The chief characteristic of *Gli Indifferenti* is a grim, hopeless realism which seems to be, on the whole, the fundamental note of Moravia's artistic temperament. The personages of this book could be divided into two types: one, unconscious and superficial, lets life overcome him, accepts weakness and compromise, seeming not to know any better; the other looks at his destiny with critical, pessimistic eyes, lacks faith in himself as in others, indulges in psychological self-examinations and confessions, but does not find in himself the energy to escape toward a broader and lighter way of life. The solution to the ethical problems of the characters is thus either negative or pessimistic. This first novel, which struck the critics as a revelation of a powerful and original talent, nonetheless follows the familiar pattern of psychological realism, showing Moravia's derivation from French *réalisme* together with the influence of modern Italian writers such as Pirandello, Tozzi, Svevo (*qq.v.*).

A book of short stories (*La Bella Vita,* 1935), a novel (*Le Ambizioni sbagliate* 1935; Eng. tr., *Wheel of Fortune,* 1937), and a book of *romanzi brevi* (short novels, *L'Imbroglio,* 1937) display the development of Moravia's inspiration; he continues on the road followed in his first book. *Le Ambizioni sbagliate* seems a deeper novel than *Gli Indifferenti.* The author seems to have followed the example of the Russian novelists, mainly Dostoevski (*q.v.*), in the analysis of the slow and inevitable progress of a protagonist toward crime and self-destruction as well as in the technique of painting a constantly somber and haggard atmosphere. Shortcomings of the book are prolixity and a useless repetition of scenes, dialogues, and monologues which are not necessary either to the understanding of the characters or to the development of the plot. The most beautiful pages of Moravia may be found perhaps in some of his short stories where a limited, narrow world is usually painted with a deliberate crudeness. An example of the melancholic cruelty of Moravia's technique may be found in the short story "Inverno di malato," in which the loneliness and utter misery of a sick adolescent are expressed with a sensitive pen. In other stories, *e.g.,* "Delitto al circolo di Tenris," the somber realism degenerates into a morbid love of the sadistic and the grotesque.

See: G. A. Borgese, "Moravia," *Corriere della sera,* July 21, 1929; P. Pancrazi, *Scrittori italiani del novecento* (1934), pp. 313–17.

E. C.

Moréas, Jean (pseud. of Iannis Papadiamantopoulos, 1856–1910, French poet), was born in Athens, where his family was prominent in Greek military and judicial affairs. A French governess inspired young Moréas with a love of French literature which was to dominate his life. When he was allowed to make a European tour as preparation for the study of law, Moréas went to Paris (1872) and was straightway captivated by the metropolis. Returning to Athens, he became increasingly obsessed by love of literature, compiled an anthology of modern Greek verse, and made translations from French and German. In 1878 his first volume of poetry appeared. It contained both Greek and French poems and bore the title *Tourterelles et vipères.* Moréas returned to Paris in 1879, ostensibly to study law, but immediately he began frequenting literary cafés and neglected to study. First identified with the "Hydropathes" and the "Zutistes," he wrote several poems which were published in the *Nouvelle Rive gauche.* His volume of verse *Les Syrtes* (1884), in which the influence of Baudelaire and Verlaine (*qq.v.*) is visible, earned him the esteem of the young poetic generation. The year 1886 saw the appearance of his volume *Les Cantilènes,* of two novels written in collaboration with Paul Adam (*q.v.*), and of a manifesto (in the supplement of *Figaro* on September 18) which defended the symbolists against the accusations of the conservatives. A new manifesto, which appeared as the preface of *Le Pèlerin passionné* (1891), suggests the trend toward classical inspiration which his poetry was to assume. Soon he had founded the Ecole Romane, with Charles Maurras (*q.v.*), Maurice du Plessys, Raymond de la Tailhède, and Ernest Raynaud as disciples. This school called for the return of classic forms, for the inspiration of the Middle Ages, of Ronsard, and of the 17th century. It sought to discredit the romanticists, the Parnassians, and the symbolists, all of whom it accused of breaking the Gallic tradition. In practice this meant the abundant use of mythological references, of archaic words, and of traditional poetic forms. The vices and virtues of this new poetic manner are best demonstrated in Moréas's *Enone au clair visage* (1893) and *Eriphyle* (1894). By virtue of his personality, of his manifestoes, and of these books, Moréas became the recognized leader of a school of poetry. He was encouraged by Léon Deschamps, the director of *Plume,* from whose presses appeared *Les Stances* (Livres I–II, 1899; Livres III–VI, 1901). In 1903 was published *Iphigénie,* a drama in verse which closely followed Euripides in action and content, but which showed originality in images and metrics. Moréas also wrote prose works, of which the best is perhaps *Esquisses et souvenirs* (1908). Ten years after the death of Moréas appeared the *Septième Livre des Stances.*

Moréas's literary reputation is not yet firmly established. Blind adoration from his disciples is offset by accusation that he was only a pedantic and servile imitator. It is certain that his personality had much to do with his position as *chef de file.* A great part of his existence was spent in Parisian cafés where his commanding presence, his incisive voice, his flashing monocle and black mustache, usually dominated a group of admiring young poets. He appears to have been exceedingly vain, but neither to his friends nor in his verse did he yield the secrets of his emotional life. Perusal of his successive volumes of poetry give the impression of a man who suffered much and who became increasingly melancholy and disillusioned, but these are the overtones rather than the matter of his verse. His career was an evolution toward clarity, order, and restraint; had he not been so faithful in imitation of Ronsard and Malherbe, so prone to weight his poems with mythological references, he might have gained a surer reputation. Even detractors will admit his fine sense of rhythm and his ability to lift the commonplace to poetic level.

See: E. Raynaud, *Jean Moréas et les Stances* (1929); R. Georgin, *Jean Moréas* (1930); R. Niklaus, *Jean Moréas, poète lyrique* (1936).

W. K. C.

Moreno Villa, José (1887–, Spanish poet), belongs to the moment of transition from traditional to "pure" poetry, which uses image, metaphor, and allusion, not for the logical expression of ideas, but to dissolve old associations and create new realities stripped of all but purely poetic values. He was born in Málaga and educated there by the Jesuits. In 1904 he went to Germany to prepare himself for a business career, but he soon found that he was more interested in literature and art. In 1910, after his return to Spain, he began the study of archaeology and architecture, which was to have a profound influence on his writing. After five years (1916–1921) of editorial work, he became a librarian, first in the *instituto* of Gijón, then in the University of Madrid. While practicing his profession, he has edited the magazine *Arquitectura*, lectured on architecture and the fine arts, and exhibited his own paintings. He has written plays and edited classics (Juan de Valdés, *Diálogo de la lengua;* Lope de Rueda, *Teatro;* José de Espronceda, *Obras*). In *Pruebas de Nueva York,* which appeared in 1927, are recorded his impressions of a trip to America made in that year.

Garba (1913), Moreno Villa's first book of poetry, is southern in its clarity and grace. It is full of acceptances, of the passing of youth, the limitation of human effort, the triumph of the commonplace. Beginning with his second book, *El pasajero* (1914), the poet enters upon a course of exploration and expostulation, further revealed in the titles of later works—*Luchas de "Pena" y "Alegría"* (1915), *Evoluciones* (1918), *Carambas* (1931), *Puentes que no acaban* (1933), and *Salón sin muros* (1936). *El pasajero* reflects his interest in medieval life and art. Its evocations of old Castilian towns and types recall the work of Antonio Machado (*q.v.*) and others of the Generation of '98. "La selva fervorosa," however, is a spearhead into new realms of poetic sensibility. It is a hymn of human aspiration and despair and divine consolation which might well have been conceived among the stone figures of mingled grotesqueness and beauty crowded under the arches of a Gothic cathedral. It suggests, by a wealth of striking imagery, the mysterious thrust of the unrecognized and uncoordinated thoughts and sensations which struggle constantly within the tangle of man's consciousness. *Evoluciones,* containing both prose and poetry, offers further interpretation of medieval art in "Caprichos románicos" and "Caprichos góticos" and in the "Bestiario," whose animal portraits contain flashes of sharp observation and irony.

Colección (1924), *Jacinta la Pelirroja* (1929), and the three series of *Carambas* have strong vanguard tendencies, including touches of surrealism; "Cuadro cubista" might well be a poetic transcription of Salvador Dalí. The later books, *Puentes que no acaban* and *Salón sin muros,* express unmistakable disillusion with life and art. The poet "devours his life, question by question." He finds the world a mass of absurdities, the line between reality and fantasy impossible to draw. Words seem to him "fragments of broken crystal which cut the truth." Here, as elsewhere, some deep denial in his nature bars him from full allegiance to any spiritual or artistic creed. He remains on the periphery.

See: A. Valbuena Prat, *La poesía española contemporánea* (1930); G. Diego, *Poesía española* (1932; new volume, 1934); F. de Onís, *Antología de la poesía española e hispanoamericana, 1882–1932* (1934).

D. K. A.

Moretti, Marino (1885–, Italian novelist, short-story writer, and poet), was born in Cesenatico, Romagna. After a few years of schooling at Ravenna and Bologna, he went to Florence to study acting. In *Via Laura* (1931) Moretti tells how he turned to poetry when he discovered his inaptitude for the theatre. In spite of his vigorous objections to the title of typical representative of the "crepuscular" school, there can be no doubt that he inaugurated his literary career by adhering to that group of five or six poets (Corazzini, Gozzano, Martini, Palazzeschi, *qq.v.,* Civinini) to whom the critics later attached the label of *crepuscolari.* His first volume of poetry was published in 1905. He followed that with five more, of which *Poesie scritte col lapis* (1910) and *Poesie di tutti i giorni* (1911) are the best. *Poesie* (1919) is the author's own selection of his best poems. By his own admission it was the *Myricae* of Pascoli (*q.v.*) which made him react against the sensual and refined aestheticism of D'Annunzio (*q.v.*). And, indeed, he reminds us of a Pascoli on a small scale, disillusioned and ironically conscious of his own poor world and prosaic destiny. His attention is focused on the petty facts of everyday life and the most elementary sensations, which he envelops in the gray tints of ennui and the minor-key tones of a despairing sadness. A sense of fatigue and desolation pervades everything. Some relief is afforded by a bit of laughter lurking now and then under the general crepuscular melancholy.

Dissatisfied with this prose-poetry, Moretti turned to the short story and wrote four volumes, the most notable being *I Lestofanti* (1909) and *I Pesci fuor d'acqua* (1914). The action is laid almost invariably in the provinces, and the characters are vivid types taken for the most part from the working and lower middle classes and drawn with realistic and psychological directness. Life is painful and meaningless, and the hidden motives underlying human actions are an irrational and incoherent mass of base impulses. There is also a residue of vulgarity and sensuality, which the author fortunately abandoned later.

Barberina, the heroine of his first novel, *Il Sole del sabato* (1916), was destined to be the basic type for several subsequent novels. He offered this poor, ignorant girl almost as a challenge to the glamorous heroines of D'Annunzio and Ibsen (*q.v.*). An exploited and bruised stepchild of life, possessing simple human qualities, she bore patiently the brutality of selfish and vulgar men; and from her long-suffering tale of woe and submission, she learned to love, pray, suffer, and accept life as a duty. With this beautiful example of moral courage Moretti had succeeded in destroying the aimlessness of the crepuscular attitude. From now on his sympathies are almost all for feminine characters. The fundamental sense of sadness, which is the core of his work, comes from an inner striving of these creatures toward a happiness which life invariably denies in one way or another. The heroines of *Guenda* (1918), *La Voce di Dio* (1920), *Nè bella nè brutta* (1921), *I Due Fanciulli* (1922), though drawn from various walks of life, are basically all sisters in search of an illusory happiness. In *I Puri di cuore* (1923) and *Il Trono dei poveri* (1928) the protagonists are men, but the suffering is the same. In *L'Isola dell'amore* (1920) Moretti departs from the realistic descriptions of Romagna and weaves a charming fantasy around a luxurious institute for old maids. Whatever the fantastic atmosphere and the ironic and humoristic tone, the fundamental lesson remains the same: happiness is an illusion and suffering is real. The perfect example of humility, sacrifice, and obedience is found in Clarice, the poor servant girl of *Il Segno della croce* (1926). All these humble and passive people are commendable, to be sure, but their philosophy of nonresistance is a cheerless one. The other characters are rapidly sketched accessory figures. Moretti seems to have sensed the reader's justifiable impatience with this lack of contrast and reaction, and in *L'Andreana* (1935) he creates a character who refuses to succumb completely to life and finally does resist circumstances. This is probably his best novel, a solidly constructed story in which the secondary characters are better delineated and the monotonous gray gives way to the lively colors of desires and instincts let loose. Between novels he wrote innumerable short stories. His prose style expresses itself in a direct, honest, and simple language. The inspiration of his art is preeminently Christian with its message of love for the humble, the defenseless, and the sensitive, adrift in the inevitable evil of the world.

In addition to his creative works, Moretti has written five volumes of reminiscences and autobiographical notes. *Mia Madre* (1924) and *Il Romanzo della mamma* (1924) emphasize the important part that his mother, a humble and kindly elementary school teacher, played in his life and art.

See: F. Cazzamini-Mussi, *Marino Moretti* (1931); P. Pancrazi, *Scrittori italiani del novecento* (1934), pp. 61–67; F. Casnati, "Moretti, laico della misericordia," *Nuova Antologia*, CCCCIV (1939), 190–209.

J. F. De S.

Morgenstern, Christian (1871–1914, German poet-philosopher), admired for his profound spirituality and whimsical humor, was born in Munich, the son and grandson of well-known artists. His philosophical mind was early attracted to Schopenhauer, but in 1893, when Morgenstern's tubercular condition confined him to his room for months, Nietzsche (*q.v.*) first exerted on him the overpowering influence which was to dominate his student years in Berlin. Convinced of the boundless power of the human mind, he expressed his spiritual elation in humorous dithyrambic fantasies *In Phanta's Schloss*

(1895), in which cosmic, mythological, and modern concepts are playfully combined. Morgenstern's lyric talent, revealed also in two subsequent collections, *Auf vielen Wegen* (1897) and *Ich und die Welt* (1898), was recognized by his naturalistic colleagues in Berlin, and Morgenstern was asked to translate Ibsen's (*q.v.*) poems and dramas in verse. This he accomplished in the following years to the great satisfaction of the dramatist. *Ein Sommer* (1899), poems written in Norway, shows a family heritage in the artist's growing appreciation of the physical beauty of this earth. About this time medical examination revealed the certainty of his early death. In his ceaseless search for the meaning of life, with accompanying periods of spiritual helplessness and doubt, he found inspiration in Paul de Lagarde's writings. Beside the impressionistic daintiness of the "silken" verse of Morgenstern, there is in *Melancholie* (1906) the inexorable seriousness of his longing and the awareness of participation in a spiritual realm not yet clearly discerned. The grotesque humor of his *Galgenlieder* (1905) and *Palmström* (1910), which established the poet's widespread popularity among the sophisticated, is just another way of liberating the mind from the world of matter. Morgenstern's "superior nonsense" assigns human attributes and functions to everything, even mere words and sounds. Grotesque scenes are evolved from a literal interpretation of conventional phrases. New objects are created by analogy of mere words, ridiculing the assumption that name and thing are identical.

In the winter of 1905–1906 when Morgenstern studied Buddha, Dostoevski (*q.v.*), and Meister Eckhart, he experienced, through the Gospel of St. John, the crowning realization of many years of meditation: that God, immanent in the world and evolving through it, reaches his highest stage of consciousness in the spiritual man (I and the Father are one). When God becomes conscious of himself in us, all suffering in the world becomes our suffering, time and eternity become one. In the lyrics of his *Einkehr* (1910) we sense the spirit of harmony and gratitude of one who has found his spiritual self, but also the subdued pain of one who is gradually disengaging himself from this physical plane. Morgenstern had reconciled himself to the idea that he must finish his way in solitude when, in 1908, he found through his love for Margarete Gosebruch, who was to become his wife, a companionship and new horizons which transfigured the last years of his life. The sonnets and songs of *Ich und du* (1911) are among the purest and loftiest poems of love in all German literature. Morgenstern became acquainted with Rudolf Steiner through Margarete Gosebruch and seemed admirably prepared to understand Steiner's anthroposophical science. Here he learned that the evolution of the spiritual man was, to be sure, the innermost meaning of this earth, but that man is not the highest stage of God's consciousness. There are, he was told, above him hierarchies guiding man's cosmic evolution as he passes through his earthly reincarnations. The highest cosmic spirit for this earth is Christ. The final phase of Morgenstern's religious development is reflected in his last collection of poems, *Wir fanden einen Pfad* (1914), dedicated to Rudolf Steiner; they rank with the best that George (*q.v.*) and Rilke (*q.v.*) have produced. Two of Morgenstern's posthumous works constitute a priceless record of the poet's inner development and wisdom, a book of aphorisms and notes, called *Stufen* (1918), and *Mensch Wanderer* (1927), a collection of hitherto unpublished poems.

See: Michael Bauer, *Christian Morgensterns Leben und Werk* (1933).

E. Hof.

Móricz, Zsigmond (1879–1942, Hungarian novelist, short-story writer, playwright), was born in Csécse. He received his elementary and secondary education in Debrecen. As a young man he had little chance to learn and practice his craft; for a number of years he did routine work for *Az Ujság* (News), a Budapest daily, and for popular historical and geographical books. *Nyugat* (West) discovered Móricz when he submitted a profoundly moving short story, "Hét krajcár" (Seven Pennies). Debrecen, a predominantly Calvinistic community, the city of Móricz's youth, is in the great Hungarian plains; his own village and the vicinity of this town brought Móricz in contact with wealthy and poor peasants, with farmhands, herdboys, and cattle ranchers. These people and their experiences became the central theme of his brutally realistic art. Later he added other characters to the gallery of his types—small-town tradesmen and artisans, city and county officials, members of the Calvinistic clergy, intellectuals living in villages, ladies and strumpets, and dissipating or unhappy members of the landed aristocracy. This list was completed with historical characters, remote from the contemporary scene but not remote from the fundamental problems of Hungary. Móricz is apt to be sordid in his extreme realism, yet he is also concerned with the lighter side of Hungarian life and can be sincerely humorous.

Móricz is a powerful writer, with an exceptional insight into the rural and provincial realities of his country. He has been accused of exaggerating ugliness and ignoring decency. The truth is that he resented the illusions of the neo-romanticists who preceded him in the description of the village; he was not a propagandist for filth and pauperism but a creative artist and observer opposing such conditions. Móricz is never frivolous, yet sometimes he seems unconvincing because he accentuates spiritual darkness, unfairness, viciousness, vulgarity. His constantly returning theme is frenzied sensuality; sometimes he portrays this psychological and physiological condition in a manner that suggests erotic caricature.

He is widely read as novelist and short-story writer, but a less popular and indeed less capable playwright. At the 25th anniversary of his literary activities his collected works were published. Of his novels *Sárarany* (1910; Golden Mud) is an uncompromisingly frank work; the hero, Dani Turi, is the son of the people, strong, attractive, a peasant Don Juan, outlawed by his own surroundings. *Fáklya* (1925; Eng. tr., *The Torch,* 1931) is the story of a young Calvinist minister, the personification of good will, and of his plight in the village where he preaches the gospel of the Lord. Several other novels and stories of Móricz have been published abroad. *Légy jó mindhalálig* (1922; Be Good Until You Die) is a fine juvenile story. His short stories, *Magyarok* (1926; Hungarians), are penetrating studies and reports of Hungarian types. *Erdély* (1935; Transylvania), a trilogy, represents Móricz as a historical novelist. *Sári Biró* (1910; Judge Sari) and *Buzakalász* (1924; Sheaf of Wheat) are his best plays.

As a social realist and as a master of the Hungarian language Móricz ranks among the foremost Hungarian writers. He was inclined to be a careless craftsman; in his later years he was prolific at the expense of artistic quality. Nevertheless his fiction indicates progress in an honest interpretation of Hungarian life.

See: A. Schöpflin, *Magyar irók* (1919); J. Gassner, *Masters of the Drama* (1940); J. Reményi, "Zsigmond Móricz, Hungarian Realist," *American Slavic and East European Review,* Vol. IV, Nos. 8–9 (1945), 165–181.

J. R.

Morselli, Ercole Luigi (1882–1921, Italian dramatist), born at Pesaro, lived from his seventh to his twenty-first year at Florence, where he studied medicine for two years and also literature, but without receiving any degree. He received mental cultivation and stimulation through contact with such minds as those of Papini and Prezzolini (*qq.v.*). Morselli loved adventure and in 1903 set sail from Genoa with his friend F. Valerio Ratti. After traveling to Cape Town, and spending some time in South America (enlisting to fight against Saravia's army in the civil war in Uruguay) and in England, he turned homewards "the most penitent and happy of prodigal sons."

Morselli's first volume of prose, *Favole per i re d'oggi* (1909), is mild and suffused with a melancholy resignation; there is also a note of derision of contemporary morals. These "little myths" may be considered an anticipation of his two great plays. The myth is the most appropriate means of expression of the inner Morselli, of his delicate and sweetly lyric poetic nature, and provides the unity of his work. His writing is an unmatched phenomenon in Italian literature in that he occupies the unique position of an Italian who had a scant knowledge of Greek and only a smattering of Latin but was a classicist in that spirit which was his by national inheritance. His *Orione* (1910) and *Glauco* (1919) are about mythical heroes. Orione accomplishes gigantic feats: he hunts down wild beasts, insults gods and women, engages in debauchery, derides everything and everybody, even Mother Earth who produced him from a divine seed. Then, the end: a tiny scorpion aroused by the same offended Mother Earth kills the great Orione. *Glauco* is the story of a fine young man who believed in the reality of the only joy granted to mortals, that of a happy home. He leaves the trustworthy love of his Scilla, to travel, to become a king and a god. But landing again at the beach whence he had set sail, he no longer finds his beloved; Scilla, having waited so long and faithfully, has slain herself. Again is heard the lament on the vanity of glory, the futility of a power which cannot revive Glauco's true love who is dead, and the lost reality of human joy. Even the much desired oblivion of death is denied him: "Ah! Cursed be my Glory! Now I see . . . I am immortal!" Glauco then has himself bound to the body of his dearest one, with whom he could no more be united in life and, with her, cast into the sea from where his bewailing may reach mortal ears evermore. Glauco is a defense of the family hearth, an attack upon the much praised "liberty" of the romanticists of the end of the 19th century.

Like his own heroes, Morselli won glory

when it was too late. Having endured the hardships of poverty all his life, in the moment of his triumph with *Glauco* on the Italian stage he was already very ill. The great success of this drama led to an interest in his earlier works, and he seemed to have a wonderful future in prospect. But he died in March, 1921, in Rome, of tuberculosis.

See: R. Rugani, *Ercole Luigi Morselli* (1931); S. D'Amico, *Il Teatro italiano* (1932).

H. E. P.

Multatuli (pseud. of Eduard Douwes Dekker, 1820–1887, Dutch essayist and novelist) was born at Amsterdam, the son of a captain of the Dutch merchant marine. When he was 18 years old, he accompanied his father to Java, where he was given employment in the office of the government comptroller at Batavia. He was quickly promoted and subsequently transferred to the administrative branch of the colonial service. He rose in rank to become secretary of Menado, North Celebes (1848), and three years later was made assistant resident of Amboina, an island of the Moluccas. In 1852 he was given a two-year furlough and returned to Holland. In 1856 he was appointed assistant resident of Lebak, a residency of Java. Here it came to his notice that the native prince impoverished his own people by systematic extortions, and he promptly reported the potentate's misdeeds to his superiors. But the form and the manner of his protest were not approved by his superiors in Batavia. Instead of the praise he expected, he was given a reprimand and temporarily relieved of his office, whereupon Dekker asked for his honorable discharge from the service.

He returned to Europe and settled for a time in Brussels. There in a small inn, Au Prince Belge, he wrote his autobiographical novel *Max Havelaar* (1860; Eng. trs., 1868, 1927), which established his fame as an author and inaugurated a movement for reforms in the methods and practices of colonial administration in the East Indies. The novel bore the curious subtitle *De Koffie-veilingen der Nederlandsche Handelmaatschappij* (The Coffee Auctions of the Netherlands Trading Company). The book was a protest against the commercialism of the Dutch bourgeoisie, which for the sake of financial profits let the Javanese people slave in the coffee plantations and suffer extortion from their princes. He drew an immortal caricature of that bourgeoisie in the person of Batavus Droogstoppel (Drystubble), coffee broker of Amsterdam, who is one of the chief characters in the novel. In 1862 appeared *Minnebrieven* (Love Letters), a correspondence between the author and Fancy, his Muse, containing some of his best parables and satirical tales. In 1862 he brought out a volume entitled *Ideën,* the first of a series of seven, containing a multifarious collection of aphorisms, paradoxes, parables, essays, and fairy tales. The chapters of his uncompleted novel *De Geschiedenis van Woutertje Pieterse* (The Story of Walter Peterson) are scattered through the pages of some of these volumes. They were edited as a consecutive story by his widow in 1890 (Eng. tr., *Walter Pieterse; a Story of Holland, 1904*). He described this whimsical story as a "battle of true poesy against the mendacious prose that offers us the world as truth." Its hero is Multatuli's other self, an honest, romantic, ingenuous boy whose idealism clashes with his petty bourgeois environment. His widow also edited his *Brieven, Bijdragen tot de Kennis van zijn Leven* (1890; Letters, Contributions to the Knowledge of His Life), in which he bared his soul more frankly than any Hollander of his age would have dared or cared to do. Dekker had married, in Java, Everdine Hubertine, Baroness van Wijngaarden, who bore him two children. But his infidelities made life with him unendurable, and she left him in 1872. He remarried after her death and spent his closing years with his second wife in Germany. He chose to live outside his native country, where he felt himself insufficiently appreciated. German romanticism appealed to him, and in Germany he found a final home. He died in Nieder-Ingelheim in 1887.

Multatuli was beyond question the most gifted and most original author of his generation in Holland, and the only one whose writings influenced the movement of the so-called "Eightiers" and *De Nieuwe Gids.* His revolutionary temper was akin to theirs. They shared his contempt for Holland's bourgeoisie, its narrow-mindedness and smugness; they resumed his onslaught on the stereotyped diction of contemporary poetry.

See: A. J. (*i.e.,* Lodewijk van Deyssel), *Multatuli* (1891); P. C. Molhuysen and P. J. Blok, eds., *Nieuw Nederlandsch biografisch Woordenboek,* I (1911), 697–702; D. H. Lawrence, "Introduction," in Multatuli, *Max Havelaar,* tr. by W. Siebenhaar (1927); C. E. du Perron, *De Man van Lebak* (1937); A. J. Barnouw, *The Dutch; a Portrait Study of the People of Holland* (1940), pp. 176–182.

A. J. B.

Münchhausen, Börries, Baron von (1874–1945, German poet and essayist), born in the quaint city of Hildesheim, was doctor of civil and canon law, honorary doctor of philosophy, canon of the Protestant cathedral of Wurzen, captain of the Saxon Guard Cavalry Regiment of the Reserve, senator of the German Akademie der Dichtung, etc., etc. He was not, however, a lineal descendant of the distinguished soldier and world-renowned fabulist Hieronymus von Münchhausen (1720–1797), who left no heirs, though as the head of the widely ramifying Münchhausen clan that traces its descent from one Rembertus von Münchhausen he had in his keeping at Schloss Windischleuba all the family treasures, including the souvenirs of the famous *Lügen-Baron.* As interesting as a work of fiction are his *Geschichten aus der Geschichte einer alten Geschlechtshistorie* (1934), in which he tells of those members of the family who have made it important in the annals of Hanover and two of whom have made it known and loved in two hemispheres.

The poet published his first poems, *Gedichte,* in 1897 and became famous with his sonorous *Juda* (1900) and his first *Balladen* (1901). *Das Balladenbuch* (1924) contains all the ballads, *Das Liederbuch* (1928) all the other poems which had appeared previously in numerous collections. His *Fröhliche Woche mit Freunden* (1922) and *Die Garbe* (1933) contain collections of essays filled with interesting information about the poet, showing the influence that he exerted and that was exerted upon him and setting forth much wholesome appreciation and criticism by an eminently sane practitioner of the art he is judging.

Münchhausen's name is most closely associated with the German ballad. A century and a quarter after Bürger and the Hainbund and while Münchhausen was yet a student at Göttingen, he and a group of his friends infused new life into the form. Acknowledging Strachwitz as his starting point, Münchhausen gave to the ballad a new content, an aristocratic tone which helped to resolve the cacophony of naturalism. This he accomplished as much by his delightful humor (especially in the ballads grouped under the headings "Schwänke und Schnurren" and "Balladen für meine Jungens") as by the "ethical-causal relation between the beginning and the end of the external action" in his *Weltanschauungsballaden* (*e.g.,* "Die Fischer von Svendaland" and "Ballade vom Brennesselbusch"). The astounding range covered by his ballads in time and space is apparent from a glance at the arrangement of them according to subject that precedes the index in *Das Balladenbuch.* What is left over in the world of emotion finds expression in his lyrics, where deep and tender sentiment alternates with captivating humor. The author is a master of the dramatic and onomatopoetic possibilities of the German language. In his *Meister-Balladen: Ein Führer zur Freude* (1923) he analyses 11 great ballads of his precursors and contemporaries. Of more recent date is his preface to *Sammlung deutscher Balladen von Bürger bis Münchhausen* (1934). Sole judge of the Olympic Song Contest in 1935, Münchhausen with his inherited sense of order and documentation subsequently studied patiently all the poems submitted and wrote for private circulation among his friends a lengthy analysis of the total offering and of the psychology of the contestants, many of whom evoked for their temerity the poet's irony, wit, and humor.

See: A. Soergel, *Dichtung und Dichter der Zeit,* 10. Auflage (preface 1919), pp. 707–710; H. Spiero, *Deutsche Köpfe* (1927), pp. 299–308; M. Ritscher, "Börries von Münchhausen" (with biography and bibliography), *Die schöne Literatur,* XXXI (1930), 6–17; W. Kaiser, *Geschichte der deutschen Ballade* (1936), pp. 275–282, 284–289.

J. F. G.

Munk, Kaj (1898–1944, Danish playwright), born in Maribo, is among the more striking figures of contemporary Scandinavian drama. Munk was a clergyman, whose literary production, beginning in the late 1920's, was very prolific and on the whole very uneven in quality. It includes, in addition to eight plays, a travel book on Palestine, two volumes of verse, a sheaf of hunting letters, a large body of articles and essays and sketches for the daily press, and a posthumous volume of sermons. After the Nazi invasion of his homeland in 1939, Munk became one of the most outspoken critics of the invader and all that he stood for, until he was murdered by a band of Nazi assassins early in January, 1944.

In the year before his death Munk wrote his best historical play, *Niels Ebbesen* (Eng. tr. in *Scandinavian Plays of the Twentieth Century,* Ser. 2, 1944), in which he employs as the central figure a Danish national hero who in the late Middle Ages had defied the German oppressors of his homeland. The parallel to contemporary events in Denmark could scarcely be misunderstood. Though there is some necessary bloodletting in the course of the action in *Niels Ebbesen,* this play is less aggressively violent in the main than most of Munk's other historical dramas. These plays reveal a strong predisposition on the dramatist's part to deal with figures of portentous proportions, characters with blood on their hands, and (as Munk conceives them) with deep brooding in their hearts—Herod in *En Idealist* (1928; An Idealist), Henry VIII in *Cant* (1931), King David in *De Udvalgte* (1933; The Elect), Mussolini in *Sejren* (1936; The Victory). In these plays Munk is reacting —not always impressively—against what he considered the "undramatic" modern psychological play in favor of a drama of grandiose scene and violent action reminiscent of the strenuous, full-blooded life of the Renaissance stage. Vividly alive as are some of the individual scenes in these historical plays, Munk is on the whole more successful in two modern dramatic character sketches in a more tempered vein—*I Braendningen* (1929; In the Breakers), a partly symbolical evaluation of Georg Brandes (*q.v.*) as a cultural personality; and *Han sidder ved Smeltediglen* (1938; He Sits by the Melting Pot), a moving study of a fussy old German scholar who has the final moral courage not to prostitute his learning in the service of Nazi doctrine.

Munk is most successful, however, in his one purely religious play, *Ordet* (1932; The Word), which not infrequently employs theatrical devices of a not very subtle kind and yet which moves from scene to scene with a sure dramatic touch and brings its story to a close with an overwhelming cumulation of dramatic power. Its central character is a half-demented youth, who has to show "The Way" to a group of self-righteous religious sectarians who did not have the courage of their convictions in the hour of crisis. Though this youth has a role loosely parallel to that of Eleanora in Strindberg's (*q.v.*) *Easter,* Munk's play seems to be a wholly original dramatic conception, with its alternately satiric and sympathetic treatment of religious sectarianism and its final use of the element of "the miracle" to produce the logical dramatic dénouement. Munk has nowhere else in his dramatic production written anything which can compare with *Ordet* in solid theatrical entertainment, and it is doubtful that he could have done anything as well again had he lived.

See: K. Elfelt, "Kaj Munk og 'Ordet'," *Ord och bild,* XLII (1933), 284–288; H. Kehler, "Kaj Munk," *Bonniers litterära magasin,* IV (May, 1935), 28–37; A. Gustafson, "Introduction," in *Scandinavian Plays of the Twentieth Century,* Ser. 2 (1944).

A. G.

Muñoz Seca, Pedro (1881–1936, Spanish dramatist), was born in Puerto de Santa María, Cádiz, and died in Madrid, a victim of the Spanish civil war. He was professor of the Greek language and of Latin and Greek literature in various academies and private institutes; eventually he entered government service as an employee of a financial board (Tribunal Supremo de Cuentas del Reino). He became one of the cleverest writers of *sainetes* and *comedias de enredo,* in which he constantly created the most improbable and absurd situations. As an Andalusian by birth and a resident of Madrid, he was able to fuse keen Andalusian wit and Madrilenian jocosity. Despite his exaggerated presentation of manners and customs, often approaching caricature, and an excessive use of jokes frequently involving forced humor, his works were a success owing to their cheerful wit, their lively and facile dialogue and clever theatrical devices. Within the dramatic framework of the so-called *género chico,* he was the creator of a special type, the *astrakanada,* in which nonsensical actions, plays on words, and puns, designed to keep the public in a continual state of hilarity, were exploited to their limit. Some of these works were written in collaboration with Pedro Fernández Pérez, and others with García Alvarez. Among his best-known works are *La barba de Carrillo* (1918), *Trampa y cartón* (1920), *Pepe Conde, o el mentir de las estrellas* (1920). In 1919 *La venganza de don Mendo* was staged. This is a parody of the tragic manner, and although it follows the general lines of the *astrakanada* and even accentuates them by the contrast between the tragedy and the comedy, it is written in good verse and parts of it show that its author possessed the potential qualifications for the development of a more serious and lofty dramatic art.

E. G. L.

Musil, Robert (1880–1939, Austrian novelist, dramatist, and essayist), first produced two collections of short stories (*Vereinigungen,* 1911; *Drei Frauen,* 1923), an expressionistic drama (*Die Schwärmer,* 1921), and a comedy (*Vinzenz und die Freundin bedeutender Männer,* 1923). His initial experiment in the novel, *Die Verwirrungen des Zöglings Törless* (1906), dealt with the inner and the outward conflicts of adolescence. Musil's serious claim to greatness rests upon *Der Mann ohne Eigenschaften* (Vol. I, 1930; Vol. II, 1933; Vol. III, 1942), an epic enterprise immense in scope and unique in its execution. Against the background of the disintegrating Austrian Empire it sets the making of a new man and the shaping of a new mind, blending satire with prophesy but without sentimental pathos. Its satire is a subtle dissection of men and manners by the scalpel of an anatomist, its prophesy is the detached determining of a utopian locus by the mind of a mathematician. Because of his probing mind Musil has been compared to Marcel Proust (*q.v.*) and James Joyce. Reminiscent of these two is the sophisticated disintegration of the form of his novel which, with hardly a coherent story, will never have popular appeal but, with its sparkling ironies and striking insights, will always fascinate and delight a few.

R. A.

N

Nabokov, Vladimir Vladimirovich (pseud. Vladimir Sirin, 1899–, Russian novelist, poet, and short-story writer), was born at St. Petersburg of a prominent family, but left Russia after the Revolution. He graduated from Cambridge University (1922), where he wrote Russian verse; he then settled for a time in Berlin and devoted himself primarily to literature, lecturing occasionally, studying butterflies, and playing chess. One of his best novels, *Zashchita Luzhina* (1930; Luzhin's Defense), is the story of a young chess master and his ultimate disintegration, told with sensitiveness and understanding. *Camera Obscura* (1933; Eng. trs., *Camera Obscura,* 1936, *Laughter in the Dark,* 1938) rises above anything merely sensational chiefly because of the author's artistic vision and the virtuosity with which the lethal plot is developed. *Otchainiye* (1934; Eng. tr., *Despair,* 1937), remarkable for its sustained interest, is in the same macabre tradition, which culminated in *Priglasheniye na kazn* (1938; Invitation to an Execution), a phantasmagoria of a topsy-turvy world for all its apparent realism. Unlike most Russian novelists, Nabokov is cold toward his characters and shows little interest in their social backgrounds. His plots are artful and full of surprises, sometimes at the expense of the reader; however, Nabokov's originality lies rather in his imaginative use of language, with which he transfigures reality. All these traits are equally evident in his short stories, some of which have been translated into English.

Since his coming to the United States (1940), Nabokov has divided his time between entomology and literature and has adopted English as his medium. *The Real Life of Sebastian Knight* (1941) may therefore mark the beginning of a new period.

See: G. Struve, "Vladimir Sirin," *Slavonic Review,* XII (1933–1934), 436–444; M. Slonim, "V. Nabokov-Sirin," *Novoye russkoye slovo,* March 21, 1943, p. 8.

P. A. P.

Nadson, Semyon Yakovlevich (1862–1887, Russian lyric poet), born in St. Petersburg, was of Jewish extraction on the side of his father, who was brilliant but mentally unstable. His mother belonged to the noble Mamantov family and was a woman of exceptional charm and energy. After the death of the poet's father, however, a second marriage ended in the suicide of her husband, and she herself died of tuberculosis at the age of 31. The poet's constitutional inheritance was thus not a healthy one, despite his early manifestation of musical and literary talent.

The first poem of Nadson's to be published appeared in print when he was only 15. Regardless of his delicate health, he was schooled for the army, but while still in the military academy he succumbed to a pulmonary infection which necessitated a year's convalescence in the Caucasus and, as subsequent developments proved, was never really cured. His wide popularity began about 1881, when his older friend, the poet A. N. Pleshcheyev, opened to him the pages of *Otechestvennie zapiski* (National Notes), the best-known monthly of the moment. Commissioned in the army the next year, Nadson was at first stationed at Kronstadt, where he seems to have enjoyed military associations and even gathered about him a group of like-minded friends with whom he shared literary experiments, music, and amateur theatricals.

But this contentment was short-lived. In the summer of 1883 Nadson developed a tubercular fistula which necessitated his resignation from the army. He had some thought of becoming a teacher, but his health was so uncertain that physicians advised a milder climate, so that he spent the winter of 1884–1885 in Wiesbaden, Nice, and other resorts. Homesickness drove him back to the dampness of St. Petersburg the next spring, but he was urged to go south again. Residence in Kiev failed to improve his condition, and he refused to endure the loneliness of another stay abroad. In the autumn of

1886 he therefore moved to Yalta, in the Crimea, where he died three months later, in January, 1887.

Nadson was unquestionably the most popular Russian poet of the 80's, and by 1916 the slender volume of his verses (*Stikhotvoreniya*) had sold 28 editions to a total of 197,000 copies. Yet estimates of his work and talent are extremely diverse. Some critics of the day regarded him as the greatest poet since Nekrasov's death; others called him trivial and shallow. As a matter of fact, his talent was moderate, and he died at 25 before it had fully matured. What captivated his contemporaries was his winning personality and the faith he expressed in better things. In an epoch of general depression, Nadson wept with the disconsolate, but tried to arouse within them the hope of a fairer future, so well expressed in his most famous poem "Drug moi, brat moi" (1881; My Friend, My Brother). That is, indeed, Nadson's only theme, but it was what the younger generation of the 80's wanted to hear. They were discouraged in a period of reaction, their intellectual level was not very high. They had ideals which they despaired of realizing, and they needed a poet to tell them the sun would shine sometime. Nadson's own tragic destiny contributed largely to his poetic reputation. But with all due sympathy for his untimely end, one must admit that he owed his popularity to his good fortune in expressing earnestly and sincerely, in acceptable and sometimes brilliant verse, the hopes and aspirations of his generation.

See: A. Luther, *Geschichte der russischen Literatur* (1924), pp. 366–368; D. S. Mirsky, *Contemporary Russian Literature* (1926), pp. 70–71.

S. H. C.

Nałkowska, Zofja (1885–, Polish novelist and dramatist), was born in Warsaw, the daughter of a distinguished geographer, and reared in an unusually scholarly atmosphere. Powerfully stirred by the positivist currents, she began at the age of 15 to take a serious interest in world affairs and especially in social conditions in her own country. After studying the branches which were then so popular—economics, philosophy, and psychology—she made her literary début at 21 with the novel *Kobiety* (1906; Women), a work in which are to be found marked traces of her deep interest in all three of these subjects, especially psychology. A true product of positivism, Nałkowska is devoid of all passion save that of destroying evil and setting the world right. She has given much time to social causes, notably prison reform, and her novels often appear to be mere by-products of these other preoccupations. This is particularly true of *Ściany świata* (1931; Walls of the World), *Granica* (1931; The Boundary Line), and *Niecierpliwi* (1939; The Impatient Ones). With *Choucas* (1927; The Jackdaw), a view of the European mind in general as seen from the vantage point of a Swiss tourist resort, and with *Niedobra miłość* (1928; Unwholesome Love), Nałkowska won considerable fame abroad, as she did also with the two plays *Dom kobiet* (1930; The House of Women) and *Dzień jego powrotu* (1931; The Day of His Return). Nałkowska is greatly respected in Poland, both as a writer and as a person.

See: Z. Dębicki, *Portrety*, II (1928), 251–270; K. Czachowski, *Obraz współczesnej literatury polskiej*, III (1936), 223–224, 370–392, 701–704; Stefanja Podhorska-Okołów, *Kobiety piszą* (1938), Ch. VII.

A. P. C.

Nathansen, Henri (1868–1944, Danish playwright and novelist), was born in the city of Hjörring. His father was a well-to-do merchant, and his family was representative of the highly refined Jewish intellectual aristocracy which has played an important role in Danish life. Nathansen, deeply conscious of his racial affinities, became one of the exemplifications of the claim that in Denmark prosperity and highly developed talent, specific racial characteristics and national traits, have blended remarkably well. The Jewish element in this writer largely determined his life and work—and he ended his life tragically, having been forced by German persecution to flee his native land for Sweden, where in a moment of unbearable anguish he plunged to death from a hotel window.

Nathansen originally studied law at the University of Copenhagen and at the age of 31 published his first book, a novel, *Sommernat* (1899; Summer Night), followed by *Floden* (1901; The River), and *Den forbudne Frugt* (1902; The Forbidden Fruit). In 1905 he began a series of dramas, *Mor har Ret* (1905; Mother is Right), *Den gode Borger* (1907; The Good Citizen), *Daniel Hertz* (1909), *Danas Have* (1910; The Garden of Dana, *i.e.*, Denmark), *Indenfor Murene* (1912; Within the Walls), *Affaeren* (1913; The Affair), and *Dr. Wahl* (1915). Then he turned to novels again, writing *Af Hugo Davids Liv* (1917; From the Life of Hugo David) and *Mendel Philipsen & Søn* (1932). He also composed biographies:

Georg Brandes (1929), *Johannes Poulsen og Poul Reumert* (1918; Johannes Poulsen and Poul Reumert), *Karl Mantzius* (1926), *William Bloch* (1928). For a number of years Nathansen was art director of the national Royal Theatre of Copenhagen, coming into close contact with Poulsen, Reumert, Mantzius, and Bloch.

In everything Nathansen wrote there is an undercurrent of wistfulness, directly due to his racial sensitivity. He had acute perception of the life, and understanding of the thoughts, of the bourgeoisie, a finely developed ear for the music of words, a most accurately registering eye for hidden beauty.

G. St.

naturalism, *see* French naturalism, German naturalism.

Navarro Tomás, Tomás (1884–, Spanish philologist and critic), was born in the province of Albacete. A pupil of Menéndez Pidal (*q.v.*) at the University of Madrid, he later became one of his closest collaborators in the development of modern philological studies in Spain. His first linguistic work was a study of the Aragonese dialect (1908). The following year he entered the National Archives and Library Service, where he reached in 1936 the highest rank as director of the National Library of Madrid. From 1912 to 1914 he had studied phonetics in France, Germany, and Switzerland. After returning to Spain he was a leading figure in the Centro de Estudios Históricos, where he directed the section of phonetics; worked actively in the *Revista de filología española,* and organized the Archivo de la Palabra. An inspiring and respected teacher in the Centro, well known also in foreign universities which he visited at different times, he taught the essentials of Spanish speech to many young Spanish and foreign scholars and guided a group of chosen pupils in the first steps of phonetic and stylistic research. In 1931 he was appointed professor of phonetics at the University of Madrid and in 1934 was elected to the Spanish Academy. During the civil war he was one of the directors of the cultural policy of the republican government, and as a result of his devotion innumerable bibliographical and artistic treasures were saved. He left Spain at the end of the war and has been since then a professor at Columbia University.

Navarro Tomás is the author of many articles and monographs on phonetics and Spanish dialects; a group of them, such as *Doctrina fonética de Juan Pablo Bonet* (1920) and *Manuel Ramírez de Carrión y el arte de enseñar a hablar a los mudos* (1924), deal with the history of linguistic studies in Spain. The *Manual de pronunciación española* (1918), now in its fifth edition, is the standard work in the field. In 1927 he made a complete study of the Spanish language in Puerto Rico, which is now, after a careful revision, in press. He has contributed to literary studies by editing, with critical introduction, the *Moradas* of St. Teresa (1911) and the poetry of Garcilaso de la Vega (1911). His most important work, a "Linguistic Atlas of the Iberian Peninsula," directed and prepared by him with the collaboration of some of his closest pupils, was near completion when interrupted by the civil war.

See: M. Artigas, *Discurso* (1935), composed for Navarro's reception into the Spanish Academy.

A. del R.

Nazor, Vladimir (1876–, Croat poet), was born in Postire, on the island of Brač, studied natural history, and has taught in teachers' colleges in Croatia most of his life. After the First World War he was director of a children's institute, where he found inspiration for his stories and poetry about the very young. In 1926 he was forced to retire because of his political views, but was reinstated as teacher in a women's college the same year.

Nazor's literary activities began when he was still a student. He early translated Yugoslav poetry into Italian and Latin. His first published book was *Slavenske legende* (1900; Slav Legends). Most of his first writings were poetry, lyric and epic, or a kind of simple prose which had lyric connotations—*Knjiga o kraljevima hrvatskijem* (1903; Book about Croat Kings), *Krvava košulja* (1905; Bloody Shirt), *Krvavi dani* (1908; Days of Blood). The next book, *Veli Jože* (1908), a story about Istria, made Nazor's name popular all over Croatia. The volume *Lirika* (1910; Lyrics) lifted him to the rank of a really distinguished poet. The collection *Istarske priče* (1913; Istrian Tales) established his fame as storyteller of the Croat coastland; the poems of *Hrvatski kraljevi* (1912; Croat Kings) made him the national bard of Croatia. Several Croat and Slav nationalistic collections of poetry and prose followed during the years of the First World War. In this period Nazor also published his famous epic for children, *Medvjed Brundo* (1915; Brundo the Bear). Several collections of tales for children followed. As early as 1908 the most competent Croat literary critic, Branko Vodnik, began to publish Nazor's collected works. His lyric poetry was collected in 1922, and in 1925 a representative edition of Nazor's lyrics appeared in Zagreb.

Until about 1920 Nazor was the most discussed author in Croatia. Although he came to fame after his contemporary lyric colleagues Dragutin Domjanić, Mihovil Nikolić, and Vladimir Vidrić, he presently overshadowed all of them. He reached full maturity about 1910. His educational work, particularly for children, grew as his literary work fell off. After the First World War Nazor's fame was in eclipse and emerged again only after Hitler's invasion of Yugoslavia.

When Fascism was imposed on the Croats, the new ruling clique tried to make itself popular by using famous nonpolitical artists for its own purposes. Nazor was slated for such a role. The Quisling of Croatia, Ante Pavelić, nominated Nazor a member of the Croat Academy. But Nazor seemed not to appreciate the honor, and indeed only a few months later there was published a collection of poetry, *Pjesme* (1942; Poetry), which described his disappointment with the new trend of events. Quisling literary critics wrote bitter attacks against the old bard. Then Nazor, not satisfied with writing poems against traitors of his own nation, joined the Partisans in the mountains of his native Dalmatian coastland. Here he created a new kind of prose, wrote stirring appeals to the nation, condemning traitors and extolling the fighters for freedom. He also became president of a local self-governing body of the Partisans in Yugoslavia.

Nazor has had a strong influence on the youth of Croatia and is considered a typical Yugoslav poet, *i.e.*, a poet for all the South Slavs, and not only for his Croat clan. Although not a politician, he always stood for the liberation of the South Slavs from any foreign yoke. While Croatia and Dalmatia were ruled by the Hapsburgs the nationalist poetry of Nazor was in fact a political weapon. During the formative years of Yugoslavia Nazor was less active, but he stirred even the youngest readers to think in terms of Yugoslavia and to reach beyond the narrower national confines.

See: B. Vodnik, "Vladimir Nazor," in preface to *Medvjed Brundo* (1915); A. Barac, *Vladimir Nazor* (1918); A. Venzelidis, *Književne studije* (1918); M. Marjanović, "Vladimir Nazor," in *Carmen Vitae* (1924).

M. H.

Neera (pseud. of Anna Radius Zuccari, 1846–1918, Italian novelist) was born and died in Milan. Her innate introspective tendency became manifest during a childhood devoid of warm maternal affection. When her mother died, her father's cool aloofness further accentuated this trait; the young girl, in her emotional solitude, developed an unusual power of observing life about her and of studying the vicissitudes of real people whom later she was to portray in her novels. Perhaps as a compensation for her loveless childhood, she early decided to make love the exclusive theme of her literary works. But she was not concerned with a somewhat dated romanticism nor with the tawdry and often sordidly tragic passion of certain widely read women novelists; at the outset of her career, Neera chose as her artistic motto: "the ideal through the real," and remained unswervingly faithful to it.

Her many heroines are actual living beings whose passions and actions spring naturally from their inherent character. In *L'Indomani* (1889) she depicts the woman who discovers that motherhood amply compensates her for the passion that matrimony failed to give her. In *Amuleto* (1897) Miriam, already married, renounces love, telling Pietro that while the paths to one's dreams are many, the road to real life lies only in matrimony. Daria, in *La Regaldina* (1884), sacrifices herself to protect her brother's children neglected by an erring sister-in-law. There are many other stories of abnegation in which the chief women characters are at once noble and credible: *Teresa* (1886), *Anima sola* (1894; Eng. tr., *The Soul of an Artist,* 1905), *La Vecchia Casa* (1900), *Una Passione* (1903). The German translator of *Anima sola* claimed to see in the heroine the portrait of Eleonora Duse. In *Senio* (1892) a man falls under the power of a vulgar woman in a manner suggestive of Philip Carey in Maugham's *Of Human Bondage.*

In her score of novels and various short stories as well as in such studies as *Il Libro di mio figlio* (1891), *L'Amor platonico* (1897), *Battaglie per una idea* (1898), and *Un'Idealista* (1898), Neera discusses with warmth and logic her moral philosophy, insisting that our great social evils stem directly from our materialistic concept of happiness. Wrongly accused of antifeminism, she stoutly maintains that neither political nor material equality of the sexes will remedy our social evils, but rather the frank recognition that woman's supreme mission is to create a family and that only through love can man and woman strengthen and improve one another. Neera's style, while often betraying the haste of spontaneity, rises often to poetic beauty and shows sincere creative power. Neera exemplified in her own life the same lofty ideals that she embodied in her literary works.

See: E. Tissot, *Princesses des lettres* (1909); M. Serao, *Ricordando Neera* (1920).

L. E. S.

Negri, Ada (1870–1945), Italian poet and prose writer), is the greatest woman lyricist and one of the great artists both in verse and in prose of modern Italy. She was born in Lodi in Lombardy of extremely poor parents. In her autobiographic story *Stella mattutina* (1921; Eng. tr., *Morning Star,* 1930), by some considered her masterpiece, Negri relates the heroic struggle and self-abnegation by which her widowed mother (slaving 13 hours a day for starving wages in a silk factory) succeeded in putting her promising, gifted daughter through normal school. Her first teaching position took Negri to the village of Motta-Visconti in Pavia where from 1888 to 1892 she taught hundreds of children of poor peasants and factory workers.

In 1892 the publication of *Fatalità* (Eng. tr., *Fate and Other Poems,* 1898), a slender volume of verse which with vehement eloquence exalts the virtues of the hard-working, suffering proletariat and chastises the vices of the idle, effete, parasitic bourgeoisie, skyrocketed her to fame. She was hailed both in Italy and abroad not only as a poetic voice of rich, unique promise, but as the mouthpiece of the oppressed and a champion of the socialist movement then in its heydey in Italy, especially in the highly industrialized North from which Negri came. In 1893 the Italian government, in recognition of her signal poetic achievement, promoted the little schoolmistress of Motta-Visconti to the position of professor of Italian literature in a normal school in Milan.

In 1896 Negri married Giovanni Garlanda, a wealthy Piedmontese industrialist. Marriage gave Negri one supreme, transcending experience—motherhood, whose ecstatic joys and pains she sang eloquently in her volume of verse *Maternità* (1904). But the union between the wealthy bourgeois and the fiery poet of the proletariat was to end in utter failure. In 1910, accompanied by her beloved 12-year-old daughter Bianca, Negri left her husband and Italy. She resided mostly in Switzerland, but traveled extensively to other lands seeking and finding no peace for her wandering ever-yearning spirit. The restless vague longing of this period finds expression in her two volumes of verse *Dal profondo* (1910) and *Esilio* (1914).

At the outbreak of the First World War Negri returned to Italy disillusioned and broken-hearted at the complete failure of the socialist dream of universal brotherhood and lasting peace and justice. This mood of gloomy disenchantment is reflected in her first volume of prose fiction, *Le Solitarie* (1917), which presents a gallery of frustrated modern women "lonely in spite of family, lonely in spite of love." Love is the predominating theme of these short stories. Indeed love is the mainspring of Negri's poetic world. Its unabated longing, occasional fulfillment, and frequent frustration play an all absorbing role in the lives of her characters—women most of them. When in 1919 (after a tempestuous love experience, an experience consumingly intense, total, short-lived, and tragic, which invested her whole passionate being as she was nearing her 50th year) she published *Il Libro di Mara,* Negri gave world literature a breath-taking love poem. This book is aflame with a passion which is frank, devouring, incandescent, essential, elemental like a blind force of nature. It has been placed in the same category as Sappho's lyrics and the Biblical Song of Songs. The same incandescent, ecstatic quality characterizes *I Canti dell'isola* (1925), a series of poems which celebrate the beauty of the island of Capri, beauty so transcending, so overwhelming that the poet becomes "sick with beauty." According to Serao (*q.v.*) these Canti of Negri have said the last word concerning the unearthly beauty of this dream isle.

But neither in the ecstasy of love nor in the ecstasy of beauty did Negri's heart find what it long sought. All the hopes and mirages of her youth and maturity ended in disillusionment. She became convinced that no revolutionary social order could ever establish perfect justice, brotherly love, and lasting peace on earth. No human love and no earthly beauty could give peace to the human heart. The tragedy of human frustration has such deep and distant roots that only God and a supernatural order can heal it. In her last years Negri's works took on an ever deepening mystical and religious tone which reaches its climax in that most beautiful prayer to God entitled "Atto d'Amore," which closes her last volume of poems, *Il Dono* (1936). Resigned acceptance of inescapable suffering which disciplines and purifies the spirit; austere performance of one's daily duties, be they ever so humble; broadening of the heart's charity until it can understand and share all human suffering and in sharing another's pain to forget its own; preparation for and serene expectation of life's supreme ordeal, death—these are the motives that inform Negri's last two volumes of poetry, *Vespertina* (1931) and *Il Dono,* and such prose works as *Le Strade* (1926), *Sorelle* (1929), and *Erba sul sagrato* (1939).

Ada Negri in the course of her career received many literary prizes and distinctions and in 1940 became the first woman member of the Italian Academy.

See: B. Croce, *La Letteratura della nuova Italia,* 3d ed., II (1929), 335–355; A. Mannino, *Ada Negri nella letteratura contemporanea* (1933); V. Schilirò, *L'Itinerario spirituale di Ada Negri* (1938).

T. C.

Nencioni, Enrico (1837–1896, Italian poet and critic), was born in Florence. In his school days he was a fellow pupil of Carducci (*q.v.*) in the Scuole Pie of Florence, and the friendship formed there was destined to be lifelong. Nencioni's early years were not happy; he earned his living as a private tutor in aristocratic families and satisfied the literary urge in him by contributing poems and articles of criticism to ephemeral journals. These writings—and perhaps the friendship of Carducci—secured for him considerable recognition, and in 1879 he was made editor of the *Fanfulla della domenica* in which subsequently appeared most of his best work, including the *Medaglioni* (1883) of famous women. In 1883 he was made professor of Italian literature in the Istituto Superiore di Magistero in Florence. This post he held till his death, meanwhile continuing to contribute to literary periodicals, notably the *Nuova Antologia.* Nencioni was a poet of considerable stature and an outstanding critic, but, perhaps unfortunately for his own reputation, he was endowed as well with such charm of personality that his influence over others, in the last analysis greater than he, tends to overshadow his own substantial merits. He is remembered as the friend of Carducci, to whom he pointed out the beauties of the Northern literatures, thus enriching Carducci's inspiration; he is also remembered as the friend and counselor of the young D'Annunzio (*q.v.*). In their own way both of these writers were at odds with the basic moral and literary attitudes of Nencioni, who was a man of sincere moral conviction and something of a romantic in literature. But though he could hardly make Carducci abandon his classicism and nationalism any more than he could make a Christian of D'Annunzio, his influence is discernible in both. Of his own work it may be said that though the poems (*Poesie,* 1880) are of genuine merit, it is his criticism and essays that are now read, and it is to them that he owes his place in the history of Italian letters. Though less of a historian than Carducci his criticism is nonetheless based on sound research and animated by a sense of poetry and a Tuscan gift of simplicity of style. Perhaps more informational than strictly critical are the various collections of *saggi,* which bear rereading because of their beauty of style and their reflection of a warm personality. The *Saggi critici di letteratura inglese,* collected and published in 1897, contains a preface by Carducci, and the *Saggi critici di letteratura italiana* (1899) has an introduction by D'Annunzio. These volumes contain the best of his work, but the following titles also contain some fine pages: *Nuovi Saggi di letterature straniere* (with a foreword by Ferdinando Martini, 1909), *Nuovi Medaglioni* (1920), and *Impressioni e ricordanze* (1923).

See: F. Pera, *Biografia di Enrico Nencioni* (1896); "A Enrico Nencioni," *Marzocco,* May 13, 1900 (special number devoted to Nencioni); A. Sorbelli, "Gli Amici del Carducci," *Marzocco,* June 24, 1924; M. Praz, *La Carne, la morte e il diavolo nella letteratura romantica* (1930), pp. 248–251; B. Cicognani, *L'Età favolosa* (1940), pp. 73–340.

T. G. B.

Nerman, Ture (1886–, Swedish poet and journalist), is representative of that not inconsiderable group of Swedish literary figures who, despite their middle-class origins and their academic backgrounds, have thrown in their lot with the Swedish proletariat seeking new economic and political power in the last two generations. Born in Norrköping, Nerman received his university education at Uppsala, after which he served his journalistic apprenticeship on the editorial staff of the labor newspaper *Nya samhället* (The New Society) in Sundsvall, center of the sawmill industry in Norrland. Later he was associated with various other liberal and radical newspapers for considerable periods of time as a foreign correspondent. His journalistic assignments took him to the Orient and to America as well as to various parts of the Continent. As a literary figure he was most successful with his poetry, though he tried his hand at the novel (*Olympen,* 1913; *Fem friska,* 1924, Five Healthy Young Men) and at extended interpretative essays on political and cultural subjects (*Kina åt kineserna,* 1914, China for the Chinese; *Borgarkulturens undergång,*

1920, The Decline of Middle-Class Culture). Both as a poet and as a writer of prose he is at his best in a clever, ironic vein strongly reminiscent of Heine, and his verse reveals also an almost Gallic lightness of touch and a remarkable technical virtuosity. Few Swedish poets write with the irrepressible flair and the effortless verbal swing of Nerman at his best. In subject matter his poetry concerns itself almost exclusively with two themes, physical love and labor agitation of one kind and another, though during the First World War he wrote pacifistic verse of considerable originality and power. Nerman has written some half dozen volumes of verse, the most typical being *I brynja och brånad* (1913). Neither his radical labor poetry nor his erotic verse bear the stamp of real greatness: the former is spirited and honest, but it is motivated by the most crass and naïve propagandistic Marxism; the latter, giving expression largely to a callow, youthful sensualism, lacks entirely the note of deep and mature passion. Nerman's loosely composed and on the whole rather superficial novel *Fem friska* (apparently autobiographical in origins) is of some value as a contemporary document in the history of the bohemian-radical side of the Swedish labor movement before and after the First World War.

A. G.

Neruda, Jan (1834–1891, Czech poet and essayist), was the most important poet of his country at the beginning of the 1870's. He was born in Prague, the son of a janitor in the barracks, and grew up in a quaint old quarter, Malá strana (Small Side). For a time he studied at the university and taught school, but subsequently became a journalist. He made his name as a regular essayist for the main Czech daily of the time, *Národní listy* (National Journal). Later in his life he traveled extensively in Europe. He died in Prague.

Neruda was in his own time better known as an essayist and writer of short stories than as a poet. But his poetry contains his most lasting work. His first volume, *Hřbitovní kvítí* (1857; Churchyard Flowers), is still full of conventional romantic pessimism, though the sober and even dry style shows some originality. *Knihy veršů* (1867; Books of Verse), though much superior, is still a romantic volume which contains imitations of folk ballads, echoes of Heine and Musset, and some personal lyrics which hint at silent personal tragedies. *Písně kosmické* (1878; Cosmic Songs), far more original, introduces ideas of modern astronomy and physics into poetry and plays with fanciful analogies between cosmic events and earthly doings in a curious mixture of humor and pathos. In spite of its success it remains a *tour de force*. Two collections published in 1883 contain Neruda's best and most mature work. One, *Balady a romance* (Ballads and Romances), imitating the style of Czech folk ballads, reveals masterpieces of precision and power, and the other, *Prosté Motivy* (Simple Themes), though in the form of simple nature studies, is really the finest expression of a shy and kindly soul who has achieved the peace of smiling resignation. A posthumous volume, *Zpěvy páteční* (1896; Good Friday Songs), shows a surprising change: in hymns full of pathos and with ornate rhetoric are intoned the sufferings and hopes of his nation. Neruda's usually sober nationalism takes on almost mystical fervor.

Neruda's work in prose—voluminous and diffuse—is very different. Many volumes of sketches, essays, and travel impressions (*e.g.*, *Obrazy z ciziny*, 1872, Pictures from Abroad) are only of ephemeral value, though they display his powers of observation, his democratic outlook, and his kindly humor. More important are his short stories, one group collected in *Arabesky* (1864) and another in *Různí lidé* (1871; All Sorts of People), drawn from his travel experiences in the Balkans. By far the best volume, however, is *Malostranské povídky* (1878; Stories from the Small Side). This is his most popular book, based on childhood memories of the quaint old quarter of Prague, its steep and narrow streets and the "originals" which inhabited them. In vividness of description and characterization, in warmth of feeling, these stories approach the art of his master Dickens. A vanished part of Old Prague has found here a lasting monument. Neruda's theatrical and literary criticism, though full of shrewd judgments and sensible reflections on nationalism in literature, is not incisive enough to rise above the level of good journalism. His comedies may be ignored.

Neruda is best as a lyrical poet of intimate sorrows which he expressed, without ostentatious display of feeling, in a sober, subdued, almost classically simple style. His influence, overshadowed in his time by the facile Hálek (*q.v.*) and the brilliant Vrchlický (*q.v.*), has been growing since the turn of the century. Today he is generally acknowledged to be one of the most genuine Czech poets, manly and kindly, disciplined and fervent.

See: F. V. Krejčí, *Jan Neruda* (1902); F. X.

Šalda, *Boje o zítřek* (1905) and *Šaldův zápisník*, VI (1934), 320–345; A. Novák, *Jan Neruda* (1921). There are German translations of *Malostranské povídky, Písně kosmické*, and *Zpěvy páteční*.

R. W.

Neumann, Alfred (1895–, German novelist and poet), was born in Lautenburg, West Prussia. After having attended the Gymnasium in Berlin and in Rostock, he became a reader for the Georg Müller publishing house in Munich (1913–1918) and in 1917 published his *Lieder vom Lacheln und der Not*. From 1918 to 1920 he was *Dramaturg* at the Munich Little Theatre. The most noteworthy of his earlier works is a story entitled *Der Patriot* (1925; Eng. tr., 1928), which deals with the murder of the Emperor Paul of Russia. The dramatic version (1926) was staged in London (1928) under the title *Such Men Are Dangerous*. His first literary recognition, however, came with the Kleist prize for his novel *Der Teufel* (1926; Eng. tr., *The Devil*, 1928), in which lust for power during the reign of Louis XI is the theme. The next year brought *Rebellen* (Eng. tr., *The Rebels*, 1929), with the Carbonari revolution as a background. A kind of continuation is *Guerra* (1928; Eng. tr., 1930), dealing with the leader of the Italian independence movement. The murder of Rathenau in 1922 suggested *Der Held* (1930; Eng. tr., *The Hero*, 1931), and the *Memoiren des Ritters Hans von Schweinichen* led to the composition of *Narrenspiegel* (1932). *Königin Christine von Schweden* (1926; Eng. tr., *The Life of Christina of Sweden*, 1935) represents a historical portrayal of the Swedish queen with some attention to her erotic peculiarities. His dramas, *Königsmaske* (1928), *Frauenschuh* (1929), and *Haus Danieli* (1931), may be mentioned in passing. Under the Nazi regime he left Germany and took refuge in the United States. Among his latest works, written in exile, are *Neuer Caesar* (1934; Eng. tr., 1934), *Kaiserreich* (1936; Eng. tr., *Gaudy Empire*, 1937), and *Goldquelle* (1938).

Neumann has contributed to the revival of the historical novel, using the past, however, to symbolize present political situations and human problems. His lack of hero worship and his tendency to pacifism probably rendered his works, from the Nazi viewpoint, suitable for the notorious holocaust in 1933.

See: A. Neumann, "Autobiographische Skizze," *Blätter der Bücherstube am Museum Wiesbaden*, III (1927), 6–7, "Skizze des Lebens," *Bergische Bühnenblätter*, Vol. VII (1927), No. 28, pp. 4–5, and "Selbstdarstellung," *Die literarische Welt*, Vol. VI (1930), No. 45, p. 1.

F. S.

Neumann, Stanislav Kostka (1875–, Czech poet), is one of the most influential and popular Czech writers of free verse. Neumann was born in Prague, took part in the abortive anti-Austrian conspiracy "Omladina," and for a while cultivated an aristocratic anarchism. He became a journalist and served in the Austrian army during the First World War. After the war he was a member of Parliament for the Czech socialists, but in 1922 he joined the Communist Party and edited their periodicals. In 1945 he was awarded the title "national poet."

Neumann began as the poet of fashionable anarchism and Nietzschean individualism. *Jsem apoštol nového žití* (1896; I Am the Apostle of a New Life) and *Satanova sláva mezi námi* (1897; Satan's Glory among Us) are titles of early verse collections which suggest both the crude ideology and the rhetorical style of the young author. But he soon discovered the social and national question: *Sen o zástupu zoufajících* (1903; A Dream of the Despairing Mass) is a vision of the horrors of social oppression and of the poet's hope for its abolition. Neumann then turned again to individual problems. Possibly his best work is in two collections written before the war. *Kniha lesů, vod a strání* (1914; The Book of Woods, Waters, and Slopes) contains frankly sensual poems in praise of nature, open air, and sex. The rich sonorous free verse, the charmingly vivid and colorful metaphors, convey a sense of zest for life and sheer animal enjoyment rare in Czech poetry. *Horký van a jiné básně* (1918; The Hot Breath and Other Poems) adds a naïve celebration of the pleasures of the marriage bed. But a completely new ideology and technique appear in the collections published just after the war. *Nové zpěvy* (1918; New Songs) suddenly discovers the beauties of machine civilization, and *Třicet zpěvů z rozvratu* (1918; Thirty Songs from the Time of Upheaval) versifies Neumann's experiences in Hungary and the Balkans during the war. The technique of these two collections is futurist—a mosaic of colors and impressions, a flow of free-verse rhetoric which never loses vitality but frequently violates all standards of taste and good sense. *Rudé zpěvy* (1923; Red Songs) and several other later volumes are only versified propaganda, but one collection, *Láska* (1933; Love), returns to the theme of sexual love in sober and mature tones and even uses old-fashioned concise song and stanza forms. Neumann's prose is less important, and much of it is either polemics or propaganda; there are also books of reminiscences from the First World War and two travel books of post-war Czechoslovakia. A love story, *Zlatý oblak* (1932; The Golden Cloud), is trivial, and his histories of love, of woman, and of the French Revolution are mere potboilers.

Neumann's youthful enthusiasm, which outlasted maturity, his frank "pagan" sensualism, his glorification of the wonders of modern civilization, the zest and flow of his rhetorical verse, the color of his metaphors, have endeared him to the generation of readers immediately following the First World War, and he has, more than any other older poet, influenced the young "proletarian" poets. The naïve ideology and the lack of subtler emotions and ideas exclude him from the first rank of Czech poets.

See: B. Polan, *Se St. K. Neumannem* (1919); B. Václavek, *S. K. Neumann, 1875–1935* (1935).

R. W.

Nexø, Martin Andersen (1869–, Danish novelist), the most widely renowned Danish author of his generation and one of the foremost proletarian writers of this century, was born the fourth of 11 children in a rat-infested tenement in a Copenhagen slum. His father, a stonecutter, was of Bornholm peasant stock; his mother was the daughter of an immigrant German blacksmith from Mainz. Relentlessly but without bitterness Nexø has recorded his memories of a proletarian childhood and youth in four volumes which have already become classics of Danish autobiography: *Et lille Kræ* (1932; A Little Mite), *Under aaben Himmel* (1935; Eng. tr., *Under the Open Sky*, 1938, includes this and the preceding volume), *For Lud og koldt Vand* (1937; Roughing It), and *Vejs Ende* (1939; The End of the Road). The first volume presents an appalling picture of the torments of a child of the poor in a big industrial city. The second takes the family to the island of Bornholm, still feudal but kinder to children, where from eight to 14 Martin lived a relatively happy and healthy outdoor life, herding cattle and devouring thrillers by Eugène Sue and others. After confirmation he worked as farm hand, shoemaker's apprentice, and hod carrier for some seven years, during which he became interested in socialism and hungry for education. Two winters in the local folk high school at Rönne were followed by two in the famous Askov school, where he first began to write. From there he went in 1893 to teach in Odense, but developed tuberculosis after a year, and spent most of the next two years in Spain, where he learned "that poverty is international." In *Soldage* (1903; Eng. tr., *Days in the Sun*, 1929) he has recorded his impressions of a second visit to Spain.

To Nexø the cruel poverty in which he grew up seemed as unnecessary as it was unjust, and he threw himself wholeheartedly into the fight against it. As a radical socialist, and since the Russian Revolution as a Communist, he has championed the cause not only of the working people but of all victims of social injustice. He is frankly a propagandist for the ideas in which he believes and has contributed indefatigably to leftist periodicals in many countries. But his most effective contributions to the cause he has served so devotedly are at the same time his finest artistic achievements, the great social epic *Pelle Erobreren* (4 vols., 1906–1910; Eng. tr., *Pelle the Conqueror*, 1913–1917; combined in one volume, 1930) and its feminine counterpart *Ditte Menneskebarn* (5 vols., 1917–1921; Eng. tr., *Ditte: Girl Alive!* 1920; *Ditte, Daughter of Man*, 1921; *Ditte: Toward the Stars*, 1922; combined in one volume, 1931). Pelle spends his boyhood on a Bornholm farm and learns his trade in a small town there. He and his old father, Lasse, are the most vivid and appealing of a whole gallery of superbly drawn Bornholm types. Lasse, gentle and patient, has no heart for the struggle against exploitation, but Pelle, arriving in Copenhagen to find that the machines have taken away his livelihood, becomes the leader of a successful strike and the founder of a cooperative community; his conquest is the modest triumph of Social Democracy in Denmark before the disillusionment of the First World War. In the pathetic story of the little servant girl, Ditte, Nexø shows, as only he can, how unselfishness, tenderness, and even rare delicacy of feeling spring up out of the most unlikely soil. His intimate knowledge of the most wretched of mankind has only strengthened his faith in the fundamental goodness of human nature.

In both these novels as in his short stories (*Samlede Noveller*, 3 vols., 1922–1926), Nexø is at his best in writing of childhood and old age. He is extremely fond of children and was so favorably impressed by Soviet methods of education that he devoted a whole chapter to that subject in his first book on Russia, *Mod Dagningen* (1924; Toward Dawn). A second book on Russia, *To Verdener* (Two Worlds), appeared in 1934. Nexø's third great novel, *Midt i en Jerntid* (1929; Eng. tr., *In God's Land,* 1933), is a satirical study of the more prosperous Danish farmers before and during the First World War—"the dance around the Golden Calf" and its disastrous results when the sudden inflation subsided. Although a powerful novel with many fine characterizations, it lacks the warmth and intimacy of the novels and short stories dealing with the working class and of the autobiography.

In 1923 Nexø went to live in Germany, where he was then very popular, but returned to Copenhagen in 1930. He has made frequent visits to the Soviet Union, where he is still very popular. In 1943 he fled from German-occupied Denmark to Sweden. In his latest novel, *Morten hin Røde* (1945; Morten the Red), he has continued up to 1918 both Pelle's story and his own.

See: O. Friis, "Martin Andersen Nexø," in *Dansk biografisk Leksikon,* I (1933), 405–413; Dorothy Brewster and Angus Burrell, *Modern Fiction* (1934), pp. 283–287; Harry Slochower, *Three Ways of Modern Man* (1937), pp. 105–144; Svend Erichsen, *Martin Andersen Nexø* (1938).

J. B. C. W

Nezval, Vítězslav (1900–, Czech poet, dramatist, and novelist), is the leader of Czech "poetism" and surrealism. Born at Biskupky near Třebíč (western Moravia), the son of a schoolteacher, he went to Prague to study languages and has since earned his living by writing. He has made several visits to Paris and to Russia. In 1945 he became chief of a division in the new Ministry of Information.

Nezval was the founder of a movement which he called "poetism." He had begun as an adherent of "proletarian" poetry, but reacted against its preoccupation with rhetoric and propaganda, though he never gave up his sympathies for Communism. "Poetism" was a new name for pure poetry devoid of thought and of propaganda, for poetry as a play of fancy and association. Nezval carried out his theory in several collections (*e.g., Menší růžová zahrada,* 1927, The Smaller Rose Garden), in which he proved himself an "admirable magician," as one of his poems is called, an astonishing virtuoso in poetical fireworks, an inventor of fantastic rhymes, illogical chains of associations, grotesque fancies, whole topsy-turvy little worlds. The affinities with Italian futurism (*see* Marinetti) and Apollinaire (*q.v.*) are frequently obvious, but Nezval has his own peculiar themes and techniques. About 1928 Nezval's tones began to change and deepen; feverish visions and dreams replace the bright daylight of the early books. His poetry now centers around death, time, inexorable change, and night. His best volume, *Básně noci* (1930; Poems of the Night), is well named, and his masterpiece, "Edison," piquantly combines a celebration of technical civilization with the cult of night and sorrow. Other collections show a decline in inventive power and much repetition, though individual poems are as good as ever. *Snídaně v trávě* (1930; The Breakfast in the Grass), *Jan ve smutku* (1930; John in Mourning), *Skleněný havelok* (1932; The Havelock of Glass), *Zpáteční lístek* (1933; The Return Ticket), *Sbohem a šáteček* (1934; Good-bye and a Handkerchief) are some of the fancifully named volumes which show an increasing lack of self-criticism.

About 1934 Nezval embraced the creed of French surrealism, and he has tried since to write according to the recipes of André Breton (*q.v.*). Poetry is now become a mere overflow of the subconscious, almost automatic writing as practiced by mediums. *Žena v množném čísle* (1936; Woman in the Plural), *Praha s prsty deště* (1936; Prague with the Fingers of Rain), *Absolutní Hrobař* (1937; The Absolute Gravedigger), and *Pět minut za městem* (1939; Five Minutes behind the Town) are the surrealist collections. The last represents a return to public themes; one poem, "Historický obraz" (A Historical Picture), represents an impressive attempt to express the feeling of the Czech people after Munich.

Nezval has done certain verse translations, very free, from Poe, Rimbaud (*q.v.*), and Mallarmé (*q.v.*) and has written verse plays which try to achieve the effect of improvisation in the style of the *commedia dell' arte. Schovávaná na schodech* (1931; Hide-and-Seek on the Stairs) uses a comedy of Calderón, and *Milenci z kiosku* (1932; The Lovers from the Newsstand) is an original entertainment which had considerable success on the stage. Nezval's prose is on a lower artistic level: his novels (*e.g., Posedlost,* 1930, Obsession; *Dolce far niente,* 1931; *Jak vejce vejce,* 1933, As Like as Two Peas) are loosely composed long stories which frequently border on pornography or on Marxist propaganda. A few travel sketches, manifestoes, and essays should be added to this production of bewildering variety.

Nezval is no man of ideas or even intellect, but he has an amazing vitality, a lively play of fancy, an inexhaustible inventiveness in rhyme and metaphor which outweigh his frequent bad taste and schoolboyish coarseness.

See: F. Soldan, *O Nezvalovi a poválečné generaci* (1933); L. Kratochvil, *Wolker a Nezval* (1936).

R. W.

Niccodemi, Dario (1874–1934, Italian dramatist), was born in Leghorn, but the formative years of his adolescence were spent in Buenos Aires. In that city and in the Spanish language his literary career began; while still in his teens he began to write theatre notes and in his early 20's he composed two comedies in Spanish. He might indeed have remained in Argentina but for his connection with the French actress Réjane, who took him to Paris as her secretary. In Paris he remained for some 15 years, from the turn of the century until the outbreak of the First World War. He did a good deal of translation and adaption of Italian comedies and found time also to write several original dramas in French, none of them of really high literary merit but all of them "good theatre." Of these *La Flamme* (1910), *Le Refuge* (1911), and *Les Requins* (1913) are typical. His Italian phase follows; he left France for Italy and during the war years wrote a number of plays in Italian. *L'Ombra,* commonly regarded as his best play, and *Scampolo,* certainly his most popular one, both appeared in 1915. He continued his residence in Italy and his work in the Italian theatre until his death. He was president of the Società Italiana degli Autori for several years and directed for some 10 years (beginning in 1921) a traveling company which gained much success and esteem in Spain and South America. He also continued to write; *La Maestrina* (1918) and the collection of lively one-act plays published under the title of *Teatrino* (1922) should be added to the titles above as representative of his style and technique. Niccodemi had a great deal of facility and, as might be expected, no great profundity, no intellectual content to speak of, though his skill was such as to deceive an occasional contemporary critic. His plays contain good dialogue, vivacity, and just enough realism to make them convincing to the spectator of the moment. Essentially they belong to the Parisian tradition, and they have that combination of wit, melodrama, and sophistication that one finds in Henry Bernstein (*q.v.*). *Scampolo* perhaps stands out above the rest since it contains all these elements nicely combined, plus a real Italian atmosphere lacking in some of the other plays.

See: C. Levi, *Il Teatro* (1921), pp. 33–34.

T. G. B.

Nicolau d'Olwer, Lluis (1888–, Catalonian critic and essayist), is an outstanding figure in Catalonian letters and was also active in liberal-nationalistic politics after the republic was proclaimed in Spain (1931). He was born in Barcelona. His father, a lawyer of that city, was able to provide him with an excellent education. Before finishing his studies, including law, he had already produced several literary essays which gave evidence of a precocious talent: *Sobre les fonts catalanes de "Tirant lo Blanch"* (1907) and *Notes sobre les regles de trobar, de Jofre de Foixà i sobre les poesies que li han atribuit* (1907). He was later elected a member of the Institut d'Estudis Catalans (the most distinguished cultural institution of Catalonia), in which he distinguished himself for his work in the philological section. He became a professor of Greek, and his prestige as a Hellenist led to his appointment as reviser of the Greek and Latin texts of the classics published, with the Catalan version, by the Fundació Bernat Metge of Barcelona. Among his learned and critical works are: *Sobre la influència italiana en la prosa catalana* (Concerning Italian Influence on Catalonian Prose), *Bernat Metge, Francesc Alegre* (1908); *Del classicisme a Catalunya* (1909; On Classicism in Catalonia); *Jaume I i els trobadors provençals* (1909; James I and the Provençal Troubadors); *Gerbert (Silvestre II) i la cuotura catalana del segle X* (1910; Gerbert (Silvestre II) and the Catalonian Culture of the Tenth Century); *Jordi de Sant Jordi* (1915); *Tractat de linguistica* (1917; Treatise on Linguistics) and *Resum de literatura catalana* (1917; Summary of Catalonian Literature).

Nicolau began his political career when he was elected councilman of the municipal government of Barcelona (1918–1921). With his friend Bofill i Mates he founded the party Acció Catalana in 1922. From 1923 to 1930 he worked to harmonize nationalistic and republican ideas; from 1930 to 1939 he filled various representative offices. He continued to be deeply interested in literature and history and produced numerous studies: *Del diàleg de la poesia medieval catalana* (1920; The Dialogue in Medieval Catalonian Poetry); *L'escola poètica de Ripoll en els segles X–XIII* (1920; The Poetic School of Ripoll from the 10th to the 13th Centuries); *L'expansió de Catalunya a la Mediterranea oriental*

(1926; The Expansion of Catalonia in the Eastern Mediterranean); *L'expedició dels catalans a Orient* (1926; The Expedition of the Catalonians to the Near East); *Paisatges de la nostra història* (1929; Landscapes of Our History). Of a political nature are *Comentaris* (1920; Commentaries) and *La llicó de la dictadura* (1931; The Lesson of the Dictatorship). *El pont de la mar blava* (1928), purely literary, consists of impressions of a trip through Tunis, Sicily, and Malta. Nicolau's style is notable for precision, clarity, and simplicity.

A refugee in France in 1939, and his extradition having been demanded, he was obliged to endure incarceration with common offenders. He was finally set at liberty and after living under surveillance in a small village was able to move to the French capital—to await the liberation of his native country.

J. M. M. i V.

Nietzsche, Friedrich Wilhelm (1844–1900, German philosopher), was born at Röcken, Prussian Saxony, the oldest child of a Lutheran minister. His father died in 1849 of a brain affection caused by a fall, and the following year the family moved to Naumburg. There Friedrich attended the Gymnasium (1854–1858) and the Schulpforta (1858–1864). The next year he spent at Bonn in the study of theology and philology and then transferred to Leipzig, where he completed his university course in philology under Ritschl. Among his classmates and intimate friends was Erwin Rohde. While in Leipzig he came under the influence of Schopenhauer and made the personal acquaintance of Richard Wagner (*q.v.*)—two events of great importance in his life. In 1869 he was called to the chair of classical languages at Basel, and in view of his brilliant record as a student, the University of Leipzig conferred the doctor's degree upon him without a formal dissertation. In the Franco-Prussian War he volunteered for ambulance duty and was in the war zone from August till October, 1870. The strenuous work and the sight of suffering proved to be too much for him, and he returned to his teaching after a severe illness. At Basel his favorite colleagues were Franz Overbeck and Jakob Burckhardt. But his most important association was with Wagner at the latter's home in Triebschen, near Lucerne (1869–1872). Both men were interested in the relation of music and tragedy in their bearing on the ethical meaning of life. Wagner regarded Nietzsche as his most brilliant adherent. Coolness developed between the two, however, with Nietzsche's increasing independence. Nietzsche was present at the laying of the cornerstone in Bayreuth (1872), and he attended the opening of the theatre in 1876, but by that time he had definitely if not publicly broken his allegiance to the great composer and was launching out on new ways of his own. For some years Nietzsche's health had been declining, and in 1879 he had to resign his professorship. A small private income, supplemented by a pension from the university, enabled him to live independently on a very modest scale. The next 10 years were spent in growing isolation as Nietzsche traveled about in search of a favorable climate. He suffered a breakdown at Turin in 1889. His mind was beclouded, and he became progressively worse until his death at Weimar in 1900.

Nietzsche's efforts, considered in their totality, were directed to a single goal, the definition of a higher type of human character and its realization in a new frame of existence. He believed that man had come to the end of a long period of civilization and was face to face with a catastrophic dissolution of all his former ideals. It was now a question of complete nihilism or of creating a new goal. The ethical and moral ideas fostered by religions and metaphysics, especially Schopenhauer's pessimism, encouraged an attitude of resignation and held up nirvana or an imaginary future life as our highest hope. Particularly the Christian religion with its doctrine of total depravity broke all that was courageous in man. Psychologically this meant that man was enslaved by a powerful escape complex which unfitted him for the mastery of life and of himself. In opposition, Nietzsche set up the ideal of tragic optimism, or heroic pessimism, which views life as a tragic process but regards tragedy as the source of new life and power. Ethical rank is determined by the capacity to endure suffering and rise superior to it in a new creative effort. The symbol he used for his ideal was the Greek god Dionysus. As a sort of new metaphysical frame, though he ostensibly repudiated metaphysics, he evolved the ideas of the "will to power" and the "eternal return" as his highest expression of the affirmation of earthly existence—in a sense another concept of an "absolute" and another version of immortality. The hypothesis underlying the "will to power" is that in all existence the urge of each vital unit is to secure at every moment the utmost feeling of power, in whatever disguised ways it may be, and according to the "eternal return," life in all its forms will be repeated without change in ever recurring cycles.

Nietzsche first proclaimed his theory of heroic pessimism in *Die Geburt der Tragödie* (1872), which connected the rebirth of the tragic spirit with Wagner's music dramas. At the same time he was advancing new educational ideas in certain public lectures at Basel and in his *Unzeitgemässe Betrachtungen* (4 parts, 1873–1876), all centering around the differences between learning and culture. A new series of analytical studies began with *Menschliches Allzumenschliches* (1878–1880). Rounding out this group were *Morgenröte* (1881) and *Fröhliche Wissenschaft* (1882). At the outset of this period, pure knowledge is represented as man's highest achievement and greatest consolation. Metaphysics, religion, and the aesthetic arts reflecting them are subjected to dispassionate criticism, not without nostalgic relapses. Saint, poet, and philosopher are superseded by the scientist. Biological determinism relieves man of the great burden of responsibility and fear accompanying a "free will." Nietzsche begins his history of moral ideas and shows his hostility to the state as a menace to true culture. As he proceeds he questions the sufficiency of pure knowledge and ends with the idea of "joyful knowledge." This period finds its climax in *Also sprach Zarathustra* (4 parts, 1883–1892), his greatest bid for the popularization of his ideas. The limitations of man in his highest forms are exposed. In the figure of Zarathustra a new type is foreshadowed. He has been through all the "thou shalts" and "thou shalt nots" and, having gained mastery over his baser passions, can now safely entrust himself to a creative morality of "I will."

After *Zarathustra,* Nietzsche again returned to the rational principles of his thinking. In *Jenseits von Gut und Böse* (1886), a fifth part of *Fröhliche Wissenschaft* (1887), and *Zur Genealogie der Moral* (1887), he produced some of his best writing. More and more stress is laid upon the function of the so-called evil forces in the economy of life, and the idea of the "will to power" emerges clearly. What probably would have been Nietzsche's greatest book, in which he intended to develop his ideas in their philosophical and ethical implications, remained unwritten. Materials for it are to be found in Vols. IX–X of his works (*Taschenausgabe*) entitled *Der Wille zur Macht,* compiled by his sister and Peter Gast on the basis of a brief outline left by Nietzsche. The three works written and published in 1888, *Der Fall Wagner, Götzendämmerung,* and *Der Antichrist,* and two others composed in that year but published later, the autobiographical *Ecce Homo* (1900), and *Nietzsche contra Wagner* (1901), represent a final effort to gain general recognition. They are somewhat uneven, frequently rising to Nietzsche's accustomed height but occasionally falling into old ruts of thought, imitation, and ranting. Megalomania appears. Nietzsche regards himself as Dionysus, victor over Christ after two thousand years of dominion.

The complete works of Nietzsche have appeared in English, edited by Dr. Oscar Levy (Edinburg and London, 1909–1913). See: Elisabeth Förster-Nietzsche, *The Young Nietzsche* (1912) and *The Lonely Nietzsche* (1915), tr. from the German; G. B. Foster, *Friedrich Nietzsche* (1931, in English); Ernst Bertram, *Nietzsche* (1933); Karl Jaspers, *Nietzsche: Einführung in das Verständnis seines Philosophierens* (1936); Crane Brinton, *Nietzsche* (1941, in English); G. A. Morgan, Jr., *What Nietzsche Means* (1941).

T. M. C.

Nijlen, Jan van (1884–, Flemish poet), was born in Antwerp. He was originally engaged in his father's banking business, but in 1919 became connected with the Ministry of Justice in Brussels, where he now occupies a high official post.

Van Nijlen's poetry is full of an endless desire to be "elsewhere," full of the eternal homesickness of romanticism, but expressed in a classically governed form. He is the poet of the loneliness of the individual amid the busy turmoil of cities, of the loneliness of older persons amid the bustle of youth, of the loneliness of the poet amid the lively confusion of merchants. In 1938 his poetry was collected in a volume entitled *Gedichten* (Poems). He has also written two extensive studies, one in 1919 on Charles Péguy and one in 1928 on Francis Jammes (*qq.v.*), and has prepared a translation, with explanatory notes and an introduction, of the best essays of Montaigne.

J. G.

Nikitin, Nikolai (1897–, Russian novelist, short-story writer, and playwright), spent his childhood in the extreme North of Russia and his youth in Petrograd. In 1922 he joined the literary group of "Serapion Brothers" led by Gorky and Zamyatin (*qq.v.*). The latter influenced Nikitin's early work (*Kamni,* 1922, Stones; *Rvotny fort,* 1922, Vomiting Fort; *Vosstanye,* 1923, The Revolt; *Russkie nochi,* 1924, Russian Nights), in which the young writer made many stylistic experiments, using all sorts of formal devices—rhythmic prose, folklore elements, symbolistic construction. In general, a combination of romanticism and stylization are characteristic of Nikitin. His novels and short stories are always centered around the events of the Revolution and civil war in Russian villages and small provincial towns. These romantic interpretations of the Revolution, which remind one of Pilnyak (*q.v.*), were gradually superseded by a more direct approach to reality. Nikitin's novel *Prestuplenye Kirika Rudenko* (1927; Kirik Rudenko's Crime) describing ethical problems faced by the Communist youth was written in a more traditional realistic manner. *Shpion* (1930; The Spy), *Linya ognya* (1931; The Line of Fire), and the play *Baku* (1937) deal with life and issues of the reconstruction period. In 1942–1944 Nikitin wrote good short stories on the Russo-German war.

M. S.

Noailles, Anna Elisabeth de Brancovan, comtesse de (1876–1933, French poet), was born in Paris. Her father was Prince Grégoire Bibesco de Brancovan, whose ancestors were rulers of Walachia (now part of Rumania), and her mother was a Greek, born in Constantinople. Anna de Noailles spent most of her life in Paris and at Amphion, the family estate on Lake Geneva in Switzerland. At Amphion, where she lived every summer, even after her marriage to Henri Mathieu, comte de Noailles, in 1897, she took voluminous notes on the tiniest details of nature. As a child she composed verses and extemporized brilliantly in prose before the art-loving society that frequented her parents' home. Educated by private tutors, she read widely and early developed a taste for the philosophies of Taine (*q.v.*), Schopenhauer, and Nietzsche (*q.v.*). She evolved a cult of pleasure and the belief that sensation is the only reality; such convictions caused her to scoff at Christianity and declare herself a pagan. Among the poets who influenced her poetic style were Racine, Hugo, Musset, and Baudelaire (*q.v.*). Her verse is classic in form, but her treatment of the eternal themes of love, nature, and death is a feminized version of that of the early romantic poets, with an added element of Dionysiac fervor. From Baudelaire she learned the evocative power of intuitive imagery to interpret her sensuous appreciation of nature. Pride in her oriental origin and staunch patriotism for France are other favorite themes. Believing inspiration the true guide to poetic creation, Anna de Noailles refused to discipline her thoughts or polish her style. Consequently there is much repetition and exaggeration in the poems comprising her nine large volumes of verse, published 1901–1934. Her early poems express an exuberant *joie de vivre* and evoke a dazzling world of nature, of which she feels herself the center and pivot. Her later books show an ever increasing pessimism and disillusion with life, as she grows older and more aware of death. In general, her prose is greatly inferior to her poetry. Her three novels show a lack of organization and of the objectivity proper to such material. Her other prose works are essays, short stories, a number of prefaces, travel impressions, and an autobiography, *Le Livre de ma vie* (1932).

Anna de Noailles received much literary recognition during her lifetime. When her first book of poems, *Le Cœur innombrable,* appeared in 1901, it was hailed as a chef-d'œuvre, and subsequent collections met with similar success. In 1919 she was invited to join the Nouvelle Pléiade, the other members being Paul Valéry (*q.v.*), Joachim Gasquet, Xavier de Magallon, Pierre Camo, Tristan Derême, and Charles Derennes. In 1921 she was awarded the Grand Prix de Littérature of the French Academy, and in 1922 she was admitted to the Belgian Academy.

See: Jean Larnac, *Comtesse de Noailles; sa vie, son œuvre* (1931).

C. B. C.

Nobre, António (1867–1900, Portuguese poet), born in Oporto, spent his childhood in the company of peasants and fishermen. In 1888 he matriculated in the law school of Coimbra, but failed during his first year. Lack of mental discipline was accompanied by a sickly constitution. He devoted his time to poetry in order to be a "Bachelor Graduated in Illusions from the University of the Chimaera." He then went to Paris to study political science and law, established himself in the Latin Quarter, and, suffering from tuberculosis and also from nostalgia for his Portugal of sea and country, alternated his studies with the writing of poetry. In 1891 he visited Germany and in the following year had published, in Paris, a collection of poems written from 1884 to 1892 with the title *Só* (Alone). This was the lyric autobiography of an ailing spirit tormented by the desire for life. The author himself warned his compatriots against "the saddest book in Portugal." The book in fact aroused sympathy and enthusiasm and began to exert its powerful influence on contemporary Portuguese poetry. A host of imitators appeared, idolaters of "Sósismo." Then Nobre began his wandering and dramatic peregrination in search of better climes, struggling with the consuming illness and with the presentiment of the end. He went to Switzerland (1895), where he sang of that country's beneficent mountains, and to the United States (1897) and finally sought refuge in the Madeira Islands (1898). There his illness became worse. Oppressed by an insatiable thirst for travel—in search of rest—he returned to Switzerland in 1899 and finally, all hope for recovery gone, to Portugal, where he died in Foz, the scene of his childhood, at the age of 33. Nobre's death added to his renown. Two years later his brother published *Despedidas* (Farewells), a collection of the poems written from 1893 to 1899.

Nobre's work—with that of Eugénio de Castro (*q.v.*)—represents in Portuguese poetry the return, following realism, to artistic purity and intimate subjectivity. Essentially a neo-romantic, a sick aesthetician attracted by the latest forms of decadency (through which he had inherited the romantic forms), he combined this neo-romanticism with the candor of a childish soul imbued with devotion to Portuguese folkloric elements. Nostalgia, accentuated by illness, made of Portuguese life and landscape one of the constituent elements of his art. This regionalism, extremely original in its expression, revived the Portuguese lyric and gave birth to the nationalistic poetic movement. Endowed with a remarkable capacity for assimilation, he reduced everything to an extremely personal formula of artistic creation. The synthesis of ingredients as dissimilar as Portuguese folkloric elements and decadence produces alternative attitudes in his work—discernible in a single poem—of satanism and rustic candor; the elemental mysticism of the race appears in fusion with the deliriums of neurosis. The style, which follows these contrasts of angelic sweetness and Luciferian rebellion, connotes a tremendous lack of interior balance, a product of the morbid sensitiveness of the nervous system. There is a deliberate twisting of form, which gives a really astounding variety and flexibility of metric combinations and from which derives the poet's unmistakable manner. Nobre deliberately disregards established rhythmical customs and syntactical laws and utilizes the incoherent to produce that sensation, expressive of the ineffable, sought by the poet. One finds an almost unbelievable richness of images which, owing to extraordinary associative plasticity, open a new metaphoric cycle in contemporary Portuguese poetry.

Nobre's work marked a return to simple folklore and to irrational, mysterious, and Messianic pessimism, perhaps the basal substrata of the Portuguese soul. His dolorous and hopeless song in the sonnet "Ao cair das folhas" (When the Leaves Fall) is the morbid enjoyment of the anticipation of death. In the few published fragments of the epic poem "O Desejado" (The Desired) he associates dramatically the destruction of his physical life with the disaster of Alcácer-Quebir; King Dom Sebastião is simply the symbol of the crumbling of his illusions. The collective cry of renunciation in "Lusitânia no Bairro Latino" (Lusitania in the Latin Quarter) has caused Le Gentil to call him "the great master of discouragement."

See: A. da Veiga Simões, *António Nobre* (1904); Visconde de Vila-Moura, *António Nobre* (1915); Castelo Branco Chaves, *Estudos críticos* (1932), pp. 125–147.

E. G. D.

Noel, Eugenio (1885–1936, Spanish novelist and journalist), was born in Madrid. He became known through his book *Lo que vi en la guerra* (1912), denouncing the Moroccan War of 1909, in which he had served as a private. A picturesque reformer, he acquired a kind of popularity for his bohemian appearance and his campaigns against bullfighting, "flamenco-ism," and other aspects of social life in Spain considered by the intellectuals since the end of the 19th century as national ills. Products of his campaigns were books and pamphlets such as *República y flamenquismo* (1912) and *Escenas y andanzas de la campaña antiflamenca* (1913) as well as the four which were all published in 1915—*Las capeas; Pan y toros; Señoritos, chulos, fenómenos, gitanos y flamencos;* and *Las raíces de la tragedia española.* Of greater literary value are certain books of impressions and travels such as *Semana Santa en Sevilla* (1916), *España nervio a nervio* (1924), and *Aguafuertes ibéricos* (1927) or such novels as *Las siete cucas* (1927). He wrote at times in a forceful although somewhat muddled and baroque style, was gifted with natural talent, and had a varied culture; but a temperamental lack of balance and a deficiency in formal studies prevented his successful development.

See: Azorín, *Los valores literarios* (1913), pp. 231–234.

A. del R.

Nordal, Sigurður (1886–, Icelandic poet, critic, and scholar), was born at Eyjólfsstaðir in Vatnsdalur, North Iceland. He studied Old Norse-Icelandic philology at the University of Copenhagen, taking his M.A. in 1912 and his Ph.D. in 1914 with a study of the Sagas of the Norwegian Kings. He studied psychology and philosophy at Oxford in 1917–1918 and became professor of the Icelandic language and literature at the University of Iceland in 1918, holding the post until 1945. He has frequently lectured in Scandinavia and in England, and in the United States he held the Charles Eliot Norton professorship of poetry at Harvard University in 1931–1932.

Nordal's short stories and prose poems are all contained in one slim volume, *Fornar ástir* (1919; Old Loves). The short stories are of the psychological kind and of no unusual merit. But the prose poem "Hel" is unequaled in Icelandic literature for beauty of style and originality of conception. The influence of French "decadent" masters is obvious. Unfortunately, the work has had no imitators. But as a critic in the tradition of Sainte-Beuve and of Renan (*q.v.*) his favorite, Nordal has been extremely influential in Iceland. In the modern field he has written brilliant essays on the most prominent figures. He has also attacked the pre-war liberalism, especially as mixed with the spiritualism of E. H. Kvaran (*q.v.*), demanding more discipline in thought and action. Finally, he has emphasized the principle of continuity in Icelandic literature and thought and urged deference for national values, whether they date from the golden age of the saga or are more recent, such as the modern rustic culture of Iceland. In the Old Icelandic (Norse) field his studies and essays on Snorri Sturluson (1920), *Völuspá* (1923), and Egill Skallagrímsson (1924) are of fundamental importance. His plan for a new epoch-making literary edition of the sagas is well begun, with many volumes already published (1933–). But his masterpiece will undoubtedly be *Íslenzk menning* (1942–; Icelandic Culture), of which only the first volume has appeared. It is a thoroughly new evaluation of Iceland's contribution to world literature and world civilization, a masterful study of the small nation and a remarkable synthesis of a lifetime of study.

See: S. Einarsson, "Sigurður Nordal," *Tímarit Þjóðræknisfélags Íslendinga*, XIII (1931), 7–18.

S. E.

Nordström, Ludvig (1882–1942, Swedish novelist and short-story writer), began his literary career as a genial teller of full-bodied fisherfolk tales and completed his cycle of development as a literary world-planner in the manner of H. G. Wells. All of his best work finds its setting in and near the harbor town of Härnösand (the Öbacka of his tales and novels), Nordström's birthplace on the Baltic not far from the Polar Circle; but this limitation of scene in no way restricts the rather pretentious, world-embracing imagination which animates the "philosophical" contents of much of Nordström's work, particularly the later novels. Unlike the pure individualist Hamsun (*q.v.*), who also wrote of the life in small harbor communities in the Far North, Nordström is extremely social minded. His late work includes as its central ideational element nothing less than a super-world-plan (named "totalism"), which proposes a Utopian world society based on a world-wide economic solidarity. Into this world society Nordström quite naturally fits his own northern Sweden, whose rapid transformation into a rich modern industrial province he had witnessed in the course of his life. Instead of worshiping the past and that which is peculiar if not unique in the Swede (a form of provincialism not uncommon in Swedish literature: Lagerlöf, Heidenstam, Karlfeldt, *qq.v.*), Nordström worships modern industrial progress as an international phenomenon in which Sweden can play an important part; and his heroes are, in consequence, builders of industry and leaders of finance rather than the military and the ancient ruling classes. He develops these ideas in a very prolific literary production, on a rather abstract and universal plane in such works as *Nya himlar och en ny jord* (1917; New Heavens and a New Earth), *Döda världar i samhällsrymden* (1920; Dead Worlds on Society's Horizon), and *Världsstaden* (1923; The World City), and in a somewhat more immediate and concrete way in a series of novels under the general heading *Petter Svensks historia* (Peter Swede's Story), an attempt to define with some precision Sweden's particular place in the proposed world economic community.

Despite Sweden's remarkable economic and industrial growth in the last two generations, Nordström has found few disciples, literary or otherwise, among his countrymen, chiefly perhaps because his social and economic philosophy is too patently schematic and superficial in its interpretation of national and international developments. As a purely literary figure, however, Nordström is more significant. His Rabelaisian vitality and boundless appetite for life in all its forms, combined with a stylistic gusto of remarkable range and a well-nigh inexhaustible imaginative inventiveness, place him unquestionably high among Swedish authors of the last two generations. His early fisherfolk and harbor town tales (*Fiskare,* 1917, Fisherfolk; *Borgare,* 1909, Citizens; *Herrar,* 1910, Gentlemen; and *De tolv söndagarna,* 1910, The Twelve Sundays), free from the pretentious theorizing of his later work, are on the whole his best work, though his undeniable literary talents not infrequently break through the schematic outlines of the "philosophy" in his late work and provide the reader with some of the best writing in modern Swedish fiction.

See: E. Hedén, *Eros och Himeros* (1917); F. Böök, *Resa kring svenska Parnassen* (1926), pp. 220–236; G. Castrén, *Den nya tiden, 1870–1914* (1932), Vol. VII of H. Schuck and K. Warburg, *Illustrerad svensk litteraturhistoria,* 3d ed., pp. 470–478; K. Stromberg, *Modern svensk litteratur* (1932), pp. 140–148, 159–161; G. Näsström, "Ludvig Nordström," *Ord och bild,* XLVII (1938), 1–11.

A. G.

Norwegian literature. Norwegian literature shows as strong repercussions of the Modern Awakening initiated in 1871 by Georg Brandes (*q.v.*) as does the Danish (*see* Danish literature). The immediate impulse was given by Brandes, but the revolt had long been prepared by the struggle of the Norwegian people to find itself nationally; and the movement in Norway was shaped by national characteristics, by the Norwegian preoccupation with ethical problems, by the tendency to relate literature closely to life, and most of all by the passion for truth and hatred of hypocrisy. The importance of the epoch can hardly be stressed too much. It is possible to trace every new development in modern Norway to the literature which in the 1870's was dominated by four great writers: Henrik Ibsen, Björnstjerne Björnson, Jonas Lie, and Alexander Kielland (*qq.v.*). The liberalizing of the government, the revolt against an authoritarian church, the emancipation of women, the modernizing of education, the new social conscience leading to legislative reforms, and even the development of natural resources which brought expansion of life and somewhat relieved the grim poverty of the 19th century—all have their germs in the literary works of the age.

Björnson's *En fallit* (1875; Eng. tr., *The Bankrupt,* in *Three Dramas,* 1914) and Ibsen's *Samfundets stötter* (1877; Eng. tr., *The Pillars of Society*) introduced the modern realistic drama. Both authors turned from historical subjects to models immediately before them. Both plays deal with dishonesty in business, and both foreshadow that faith in woman as a regenerative influence which was to be so marked in the literature of the future. Jonas Lie created the modern novel picturing family life, sometimes among seafaring people, sometimes in the upper class of business and professional people. Kielland castigated the rich for luxurious living and for exploiting their laborers, but at the same time his novels, such as *Skipper Worse* (1882; Eng. tr., 1885), describe with gusto the activities of seafaring, shipbuilding, trade, and fisheries that were the life of his native town, Stavanger. Both Kielland and Lie satirized the pedantic education of the time as created by bureaucrats to raise more bureaucrats while ignoring preparation for practical life. They even went so far as to suggest that girls of good families could take jobs in offices and had a naïve faith in the efficacy of these measures to solve the woman problem that had been raised by Camilla Collett (*q.v.*) as early as in 1855. Jonas Lie was especially sensitive to the sufferings of women in the upper classes. Ibsen disclaimed the intention of being in any special sense the champion of women, and when the supporters of women's rights appropriated for their cause *Et dukkehjem* (1879; Eng. tr., *A Doll's House*) he stated that he was interested in human beings, not particularly in women. Nevertheless it could not be helped that Nora's refusal to be the plaything of her husband and her insistence on her right to break a marriage in which she could no longer live worthily should start a discussion of the problems relating to women and marriage. The discussion became more stormy on the appearance of *Gengangere* (1881; Eng. tr., *Ghosts*), with its far more somber theme. Here Ibsen posed the question of whether a woman whose husband was diseased and dissolute should still cover up his sins and stay with him. A somewhat undigested Darwinism entered into *Ghosts* and still more into the works of Björnson, leading to a more and more decided repudiation, not only of the church, but of Christianity itself. In its place Björnson would put faith in evolution and in the perfectibility of man.

The decade of the 70's had been that of realism. The decade of the 80's became that of naturalism. It was a period of bitter partisanship, when the nation was divided into two camps, a liberal and a conservative. Families were wrecked and old friendships were broken, while the members of the two camps could hardly speak to each other. But then the liberal camp was split wide open by the issues of religion and morality. Works of literature were no longer judged on the beauty of their style or the profundity of their thought, but on their attitude toward this or that question of the day. Atheism and sex were discussed with a freedom never known before. Zola (*q.v.*) became the model of the naturalistic writers. Absolute unrestraint in matters of sex was urged by Hans Jæger in his novel *Fra Kristiania-Bohêmen* (1885; From the Christiania Bohême). It was a book devoid of literary merit, but the fact that it was confiscated by the police made it an issue to those who demanded freedom of speech, and it precipitated what became known as the Morality Feud. Björnson, although he had renounced the Christian faith, still believed in Christian morality, and made himself the champion of old-fashioned standards. In his drama *En hanske* (1883; Eng. tr., *A Gauntlet,* 1894) he made woman throw down the gauntlet to man, demanding of him the same continence before marriage that he demanded of her. His position led to a break with Brandes and brought down on him the ridicule of younger contemporaries, who mocked the "gauntlet-morality" and were not averse to a little sport at the expense of the sententious elder statesmen of literature. The most gifted of the naturalists, and perhaps the only writer of note who consistently adhered to the naturalistic school throughout her career, was Amalie Skram (*q.v.*). In her novels she essayed to show the demoralizing influence which the conspiracy of silence in matters of sex had on young girls. Arne Garborg (*q.v.*) ranged himself on the side of the naturalists with his novel *Mannfolk* (1888; Menfolk), picturing the miserable existence of the academic and artistic proletariat in Christiania. He blamed poverty and narrow opportunities for the prevailing immorality and urged free relations if marriage was impossible for lack of means. Ibsen, living abroad in distinguished seclusion, had kept aloof from the storm he himself had raised. Beginning with *Vildanden* (1884; Eng. tr., *The Wild Duck*) he had initiated the series of symbolic plays which he continued till his death, delving into the consciousness of the individual rather than castigating the ills of society. However much he might advocate freedom, Ibsen was at heart a puritan, and when he visited Norway in the late 80's his fastidious taste revolted against the shouting from the housetops about matters that had hitherto been considered private. His comment came in *Hedda Gabler* (1890), an analysis of an upper-class woman who likes to toy with erotic subjects and encourages a young man to tell her about his night life, while she herself is a sterile nature, incapable either of loving or of taking a risk.

One of the chief scoffers against Björnson was Gunnar Heiberg (*q.v.*), the most important playwright after Ibsen and a brilliant essayist. Heiberg satirized what he considered the pettiness of Norwegian political life, not sparing the liberal leaders. In other plays, notably *Balkonen* (1894; Eng. tr., *The Balcony,* 1922) and *Kjærlighedens tragedie* (1904; Eng. tr., *The Tragedy of Love,* in T. H. Dickinson, *Chief Contemporary Dramatists,* Ser. 2, 1921), he gave poetic form to the theory of love which had come out in crasser form in the works of the naturalists. He refused to see love as a social factor or a regenerative influence, but looked on it only as a devastating force of nature which must of necessity conflict with work or intellectual interests. The ecstasy of love, and by love he means chiefly the physical, must be weighed against all other life content. The lyrical beauty of Heiberg's style lends a meretricious glamour to a theory of life that is really bald and negative. Most of the books written during the two decades when literature was the vehicle of discussion had been prose. The theory had even been voiced that forms of literature change and perhaps verse was doomed to extinction. Nevertheless the period brought to maturity one of the most distinguished lyric poets of modern Norway, Nils Collett Vogt (*q.v.*). He sought inspiration in nature, and love of the land of Norway always remained a vital element in his verse. During his 50 years of productive work his poetry came to reflect the events and currents of the day, but it never ceases to be lyrical. His plays and novels deal more directly with timely problems. Gunnar Heiberg and Nils Collett Vogt, though each went his own way, are products of the age, with its indignations, its revolt against recognized authorities, its sympathy for those on the shady side of life, and its faith in social reforms to bring happiness to mankind.

Knut Hamsun (*q.v.*) took up the cudgels against this preoccupation with causes and utilitarian purposes. He accused the older authors of reducing life to its simplest factors and leaving vast areas of human experience unexplored. In his first serious book, *Sult* (1890; Eng. tr., *Hunger,* 1899), he described a young writer who went about in Christiania and starved, unable to find work. An author of the preceding decade would have made it an indictment of society which had no use for a young man with "the best brains in the country and shoulders that could stop a truck"—to quote Hamsun's modest description of his alter ego. But Hamsun was not interested in social justice. He cared only for what hunger did to the young man's mind and body and nerves, and he described it in a style which in its lightness and flexibility and capriciousness was as new as his approach. *Hunger* initiated the neo-romantic school in Norway. It was followed by other incarnations of Hamsun's wanderer type, the individual who is always an outsider from life, not from choice, but because his nerves and senses are differently attuned from those of the ordinary citizen. While Hamsun has been the most widely popular contemporary author of Norway, Hans E. Kinck (*q.v.*) has had a small but devoted following. He is at once a romanticist and a scholar. As the son of a country physician, he learned to know the peasants from childhood and later came to see them in the light of his historical studies. He conceived of them as vikings born too late, medieval characters thrown into an age when they could find no outlet for their cravings except drinking and brawling and fighting at weddings. In spite of Kinck's genius, especially evident in his short stories, his countrymen resented the picture of primitive savagery, at times almost bestiality, which he presented as the image of Norwegian peasants.

Toward the end of the 19th and in the beginning of the 20th century, with the movement initiated by Ivar Aasen (*q.v.*), writers became increasingly conscious of the dual nature of the Norwegian people, one element being represented by the peasants who spoke their dialects derived from the Old Norse, the other being the "foreign" official class. Many of the latter were descended from officials who had come in during the union with Denmark, and they spoke a language closely resembling the Danish, called Riksmaal. Garborg was a partisan of the peasantry. Kinck regarded the cleavage between the two folk elements as too deep ever to be bridged. The language problem he endeavored to solve by using the Riksmaal with a more phonetic spelling and incorporating many dialect words. Most Norwegian authors have followed this principle, though with a wide leeway in style and diction. Others have adopted the Landsmaal, a synthesis of peasant dialects. It is probable that the latter have curtailed the circle of their readers by using the Landsmaal. It must be admitted, however, that in the hands of a master like Garborg, as for instance in his lyric cycle *Haugtussa* (1895; The Hill Innocent), the Landsmaal is unsurpassed for poetic beauty and flexibility. Another poet who has used it with success is Per Sivle (*q.v.*). Elias Blix (*q.v.*) and Anders Hovden (1860–) have enriched the Lutheran hymnbook with hymns written in the Landsmaal, which seems well suited to the expression of religious feeling. Among the older authors who used Landsmaal exclusively, Jens Tvedt (*q.v.*) was very productive and popular. With Olav Duun (*q.v.*) the Landsmaal came into its own as the exclusive vehicle of an artist of the first rank. In his books the peasant community is described absolutely from the inside, self-sufficient, resting in itself, without any of the attitude of protest found in Kinck or Garborg. His greatest work is the six-volume novel cycle *Juvikingar* (1918–1923; Eng. tr., *The People of Juvik,* 1930–1935), tracing the history for more than a century of a family of wealthy, landowning peasants. It is a dynasty founded in violence like greater dynasties; and even in the descendants of the "old fellows" there are atavistic impulses, throwbacks to a more savage time, but in the end the Christian and humanitarian impulses win out. The style has a saga terseness well suited to the epic quality of the story. Another author who has written epic works in the Landsmaal is Kristofer Uppdal (*q.v.*). His books signalize the advent of the laboring class into literature. He deals often with the vagrant laborers, in strong contrast with Duun's conservative peasants.

The 20th century shows such volume and variety of literary production in Norway that it is difficult to trace special schools. In general one may say that the first two decades are marked by a strong regionalism, due in part to the increasing number of peasant writers, in part to the geographical conditions in an enormously elongated country pierced by deep fjords and divided by mountain ranges. Garborg, after a long sojourn in the capital, did his best work writing in Landsmaal about the peasants on the small, poor farms of southwestern Norway, where he was born. Hamsun abandoned the story seen through the reflective mind of his wanderer type to describe whole communities of Nordland, as in *Segelfoss by* (1915; Eng. tr., *Segel-*

foss Town, 1925) with its great family, its parvenus, and its lively, reckless fisherfolk. *Markens gröde* (1917; Eng. tr., *Growth of the Soil,* 1920), the book which won its author world fame and the Nobel prize, is an apotheosis of husbandry and is less completely localized, but in his later works, telling the story of his scalawag "hero" August, Hamsun returns to the Nordland background he knew as a child. Thomas Krag (*q.v.*), one of the leading neo-romantic authors, came of an old aristocratic family in southern Norway and drew on his early environs, often picturing in colorful style the decay of such an old family. His younger brother Vilhelm Krag (*q.v.*) wrote novels and poems with the same background. Gabriel Scott (*q.v.*) also draws his themes from southern Norway, but from the life of the poor and humble and simple-minded. His best known novel is *Kilden* (1918; The Fountain), which combines with spiritual beauty an idyllic quality rare in Norwegian literature. Very different are the books picturing the hard, stiff-necked, sturdy people of the interior. Among these a high place is taken by Hans Aanrud (*q.v.*), one of the foremost writers of peasant stories, whose background is the Gudbrandsdal, the heart of Norway from ancient times. Jacob Breda Bull (1853–1930) was at his best in stories of the wooded Österdal, where the people are not only tillers of the soil but know the more adventurous life of lumbering and hunting. Peter Egge (*q.v.*) has described his native Trondheim and environs in vigorous novels, the best known being *Hansine Solstad* (1925; Eng. tr., *Hansine Solstad, the History of an Honest Woman,* 1929). A little to the north lies Olav Duun's Namdalen, the background of his Juvik series. An altogether unique milieu is that of Johan Falkberget (*q.v.*) who writes of the people in the small mining town of Röros on the treeless plateau over toward Sweden. His three-volume novel cycle *Christianus Sextus* (1927–1935), so named from one of the old copper mines, goes back to the first half of the 18th century and pictures a cosmopolitan community of German mining experts, Danish officials, Swedish immigrants from across the border, and Norwegian peasant miners. For multiplicity of types he has been compared to Selma Lagerlöf (*q.v.*). As a regional writer we may also classify Oscar Braaten (1881–), who writes about the proletariat in Oslo's East Side, often using their own dialect.

It is a significant fact that Johan Bojer (*q.v.*) did not completely win the allegiance of his own people before he wrote *Den siste viking* (1921; Eng. tr., *Last of the Vikings,* 1923), a vivid story of the great winter fisheries at Lofoten before the oar and sail had been supplanted by the motor. Much earlier Bojer had won admiration abroad by his psychological problem novels, a characteristic example of which is *Troens magt* (1903, The Power of Faith; Eng. tr., *The Power of a Lie,* 1908), in which a man makes himself believe a lie he has once uttered and finally acts upon it without a twinge of conscience. In *Den store hunger* (1916; Eng. tr., *The Great Hunger,* 1918) he preached an undogmatic religion of forgiveness and love for one's enemies. Coming as it did during the First World War, the book struck a responsive chord, especially in America. A novelist and playwright whose work is akin to Bojer's problem novels is Sigurd Christiansen (1891–), and although he lacks Bojer's gift of vivacious narrative, he far surpasses him in depth and veracity. In *To levende og en død* (1931; Eng. tr., *Two Living and One Dead,* 1932) he satirizes the vicarious heroism of a community which turns a cold shoulder on a man who has refused to throw away his life as a mere heroic gesture in futile defense of money entrusted to him. Modern fiction in Norway shows a wide variety of types. Nini Roll Anker (1873–1942) interprets the problems of women, but is at her best when describing the aristocratic environment in which she grew up. Trygve Andersen (*q.v.*) painted a solid and careful picture of life in official circles in the early 19th century. Hjalmar Christensen (1869–1925) wrote a series of novels dealing with the life of government officials beginning with the end of the 17th century. Kristian Elster (*q.v.*), a competent literary critic and historian, wrote novels of Christiania as well as the countryside. Ronald Fangen (1895–), also a distinguished literary critic, has essayed novels and plays which are thoughtful and written with a pronounced Christian tendency. Sigurd Hoel (*q.v.*) is a flippant and sophisticated satirist possessed of a polished and brilliant style.

By the end of the 19th century it seemed that the wave of revolt which had passed through Norwegian literature had spent itself. Most of the freedoms for which the writers of the period had contended had been won. It followed that the regional writers, described above, settled down to picture objectively the locality or phase of life each knew best, while others, like Bojer, Christiansen, and Fangen, dealt with the moral problems that are common to humanity in any age or under any conditions. Some show a decided turning back to old ideas of religion and morality. In no one is this tendency more pronounced than in Sigrid Undset (*q.v.*), the greatest writer of 20th-century Norway. The scene of her early novels was laid in Christiania (now Oslo). Her heroines are often young girls working in offices, living in dreary lodgings, sometimes seeking satisfaction for their pent-up longing for life and happiness in free love relations, but, because they are at bottom serious and moral, never able to take a light relation lightly, suffering the penalty in disillusionment. Powerful as these low-toned realistic novels were, it was not until she began to choose medieval subjects that the author revealed the full scope of her genius. The magnificent trilogy *Kristin Lavransdatter* (1920–1922; Eng. tr., 1923–1927) differs from the ordinary historical novel in that it does not deal with famous characters or epochal events, but pictures a 14th-century family with a wealth of detail which shows intensive historical study. It is the story of a woman in her relations as daughter, wife, and mother, but above all it is the story of a soul in its relation to God. In the tetralogy *Olav Audunsson* (1925–1927; Eng. tr., *The Master of Hestviken,* 1928–1930) the outer events are quite subordinate to Olav's spiritual development. Though bleaker and harsher than *Kristin Lavransdatter,* it is even more absorbing as a penetrating analysis of sin, retribution, and final redemption. It is Sigrid Undset's great distinction that she has made spiritual experience life's most exalted adventure. In medieval times, with their bolder outlines and sharper contrasts, above all with their conception of wrongdoing not as a mistake but as a sin against God, she found the medium suited to her. After achieving these two great novel cycles, she returned, however, to a modern background. *Gymnadenia* (1929; Eng. tr., *The Wild Orchid,* 1931) and its sequel *Den brændende busk* (1930; Eng. tr., *The Burning Bush,* 1932) describe the conversion of a young Norwegian to the Catholic Church. In her later books the author continues her treatment of family problems, without introducing any distinct religious element, but always along the lines of conservative morality.

Norwegian literature of the 20th century has few dramatists of note, but is rich in lyric poetry. Nils Kjær (1870–1924) was an essayist and dramatist of rather light caliber. Helge Krog (1889–) continues the tradition from Gunnar Heiberg both in his social satires and his conception of love. Nordahl Grieg (*q.v.*), one of the younger authors of Norway, wrote successful plays as well as poetry and novels. He was a champion of the proletariat with decided leftist sympathies, went to sea, and traveled widely. For all his internationalism, he was deeply imbued with patriotism. His lyric cycle *Norge i vore Hjerter* (1929, Norway in Our Hearts) is a homage to the plain people by whose labor the country subsists. Similar tendencies may be found in Arnulf Överland (*q.v.*), considered the most distinguished lyric poet of Norway today. He was one of the first to warn against the dangers of Nazism. Olaf Bull (*q.v.*) launched a passionate attack on German militarism in 1918, predicting that all beauty, culture, and spiritual life would be crushed under a flat-footed soldiery. Olaf Bull is the most intellectual of modern Norwegian poets. Sigbjørn Obstfelder (*q.v.*) and Vilhelm Krag broke with the conventional form of poetry and created a new irregular meter. Herman Wildenvey (*q.v.*) carried this further and developed the long billowing line which C. J. Hambro says is "peculiar to the great wanderers of literature." Wildenvey's light lyrics, often dealing with young love, have won for him a popularity equaled by no Norwegian author except Hamsun. Rolf Hjorth Schøyen (1887–) and Jean Føyen (1878–) are followers of Wildenvey. Among men writing in Landsmaal the visionary Olav Aukrust (*q.v.*) and the epic-lyric poet Tore Ørjasæter (*q.v.*) are most distinguished.

See: F. Bull, F. Paasche, and A. H. Winsnes, *Norsk litteraturhistorie* (5 vols., 1924–1937); K. Elster, d.y., *Illustreret norsk litteraturhistorie* (2 vols., 1923–1924); I. Grøndahl and O. Raknes, *Chapters in Norwegian Literature* (1923); H. G. Topsöe-Jensen, *Scandinavian Literature from Brandes to Our Day* (1929); A. Gustafson, *Six Scandinavian Novelists* (1940); Theodore Jorgenson, *History of Norwegian Literature* (1933).

H. A. L.

Nouveau, Germain (1852–1920, French poet), almost unknown in his own day, will be remembered for having written some of the most beautiful religious poetry of the 19th century. His life was a strange one. Born of poor parents in Pourrières, Var, and never quite free of poverty, during the first half of his life he made a living as best he could, chiefly in Paris, giving drawing lessons, occasionally selling an illustration to a magazine, working sporadically at any odd job that offered itself. Throughout this period he was writing poetry, and though not published, his work was known and praised by Richepin,

Coppée, and Villiers de l'Isle-Adam (*qq.v.*). More important was his friendship with Rimbaud (*q.v.*), whom he had met by 1873 and with whom he traveled in England, and with Verlaine (*q.v.*), whose work strongly influenced him. It was through Verlaine and Verlaine's mother that he returned to Catholicism in 1877. Towards the end of the century, the religious fervor that had steadily increased since his conversion dominated him completely. Repenting of his early bohemian existence, he begged those of his friends who possessed manuscript copies of his poems to destroy them, and cutting himself off completely from the past, he began a period of wandering on foot, begging his bread from church door to church door, journeying to Rome, to St. James of Compostella, and finally up and down the roads of Provence until his death. His whereabouts had been unknown for years, when in 1920 the news came from Pourrières that he had died there, in the public hospital.

Though Nouveau commanded the destruction of his poems, his friends did not heed his order, and in 1904 a collection of his religious verse appeared under the title *Savoir aimer* (reedited and enlarged, 1910, as *Poèmes d'Humilis*). A second volume, *Valentines et autres vers* (1922), early work for the most part, adds little to his stature. Like the work of Verlaine, which it resembles so closely, Nouveau's poetry can be divided into two classes, sacred and profane. The parallel with Verlaine can be made very definitely: it would not be difficult to believe that much of *Poèmes d'Humilis* and *Sagesse,* on the one hand, and of *Valentines* and *Chansons pour elle,* on the other, was the work of a single man. In general, Nouveau's religious poems are not much inferior to those of Verlaine; often they are quite as good; and in a few rare instances they achieve a strength and simplicity, with each word carrying the utmost possible intensity, that recalls no one so much as Villon.

See: Martial Perrier, "A propos de Germain Nouveau," *Mercure de France,* LXXXVIII (1910), 374–377; Marcel Arland, "Poésies d'Humilis," *Nouvelle Revue française,* XXIV (1925), 234–236.

C. W., Jr.

Novák, Arne (1880–1939, Czech critic and literary historian), was the son of the writer Teréza Nováková (*q.v.*). He studied in Prague and Berlin and began teaching at the University of Prague in 1906. In 1920 he became professor of Czech literature at the newly founded Masaryk University at Brno, Moravia. He was its rector when the university was dissolved by the Germans. He died at Polička in November, 1939.

Novák ranks next to Šalda (*q.v.*) as the most important Czech critic. He was a master of psychological portraiture, but he knew that the most important function of the critic is judgment. Novák stressed the national tradition of Czech literature; his political outlook was conservative, and he was cool towards the most modernist literature. But he never forgot that literature is, first of all, an art. His criticisms, written in a somewhat precious style, are collected in many volumes, such as *Mužové a osudy* (1914; Men and Fates), *Myšlenky a spisovatelé* (1914; Thoughts and Writers), *Zvony domova* (1916; Bells of Home), *Krajané a sousedé* (1921; Countrymen and Neighbors), *Duch a národ* (1936; Spirit and Nation), and to these a small handbook, *Literární kritika* (1916; Literary Criticism), should be added. Novák was also a profound student of literary history; he excelled both in monographs, among which studies on Neruda (*q.v.*) and two volumes on Svatopluk Čech (*q.v.*) are most important, and in general histories of Czech literature. His German *Geschichte der čechischen Literatur* (1907; with J. Jakubec) attracted attention by the skill of ordering his materials and the sharp judgments on local celebrities. *Přehledné dějiny české literatury* (1909; A Survey of the History of Czech Literature) was again and again expanded and rewritten until the fourth edition (1936–1939) included all periods of Czech literature. Novák's insight into the movement of ideas as well as into the evolution of the art of literature is as remarkable as the power of characterization and analysis. Novák was also interested in the plastic arts and wrote a book, *Praha barokní* (1916; Baroque Prague), which gives a sympathetic interpretation of the 17th-century architecture and civilization.

See: J. Heidenreich, *Arne Novák* (1940); J. Horák, A. Pražák, *et al., Strážce tradice: Arnu Novákovi na památku* (1940); I. Liškutín, *Arne Novák* (1940); A. Pražák, *Arne Novák* (1940).

R. W.

Nováková, Teréza (née Lanhausová, 1853–1912, Czech novelist), is a prominent woman novelist of peasant life in eastern Bohemia. She was born in Prague and died there, but spent some 20 years in Litomyšl, in eastern Bohemia, where she was married to a teacher at the Gymnasium. She came to take a deep interest in the common people of the region, and this first found expression in good folkloristic and topographical studies. Later she depicted their life in novels, evidencing the same faithfulness with which Karolina Světlá (*q.v.*) and Josef Holeček (*q.v.*) described the peasants of northern and southern Bohemia. In some of her short stories her own voice sounds and the romantic pessimism of her own outlook on life is evident, but her best novels are admirably objective studies of religious and social problems. *Jan Jílek* (1904) tells the story of a Czech at the end of the 18th century who emigrated for religious scruples; *Jiří Šmatlán* (1906) traces the change of a fervent Protestant sectarian into an enthusiastic socialist; *Děti čistého živého* (1909; The Children of the Pure and Living) describes the decay of a remarkable pantheistic sect; and *Drašar* (1914) attempts the portrait of a priest and writer early in the 19th century who was wrecked by his passions. Mrs. Nováková's best work excels, in tightness of composition and penetration of psychological insight, the comparable work of Světlá and Holeček, but she lacks their vitality.

See: F. X. Šalda, "Teréza Nováková," in *Duše a dílo* (1913); J. Novotný, *Kraj a dílo T. Novákové* (1924); A. Novák, *O Teréze Novákové* (1930).

R. W.

Novaro, Angiolo Silvio (1866–, Italian poet and short-story writer), was born in Diano Marina on the Ligurian Riviera. Novaro's first interest was painting, and a work exhibited at the General Exposition of Turin in 1884 was favorably received by the critics, but an eye affliction made him give up the brush for the pen. His promise as a writer had been shown at an early age when several articles and short stories were accepted by the *Gazzetta del popolo della domenica* and the *Gazzetta letteraria* of Turin; the articles, when published in a single volume entitled *Sul mare* (1889), won the praise of Giovanni Verga (*q.v.*), eminent Sicilian novelist. With a brother also inclined to letters he directed an important olive oil company, whose publicity magazine, *Riviera Ligure,* in the years preceding the First World War contained pieces by some of the best young writers of the period, such as Papini, Soffici, and Jahier (*qq.v.*).

Novaro's early poems were gentle, sincere, and light of touch, of a stylistic refinement characteristic of the Carducci (*q.v.*) school. He was acclaimed the poet of the home and garden for his tender treatment of the familiar objects of childhood environment. His only son, Jacopo, fell in battle during the First World War at a very early age, and this bereavement inspired a narrative entitled *Il Fabbro armonioso* (1919) and led to an accentuation of a mystical trend, previously only faintly discernible in Novaro's poetry. Besides *Il Fabbro armonioso,* Novaro wrote *Il Cuore nascosto* (1921; poetry), *La Fisarmonica* (1924; short stories), *Il Piccolo Orfeo* (1929; poetry), but he achieved popularity only with *Il Cestello* (1910), a book of poems for children, some of which are now included in every Italian school anthology. In 1929 he was elected to the Italian Academy.

See: G. A. Borgese, *La Vita e il libro* (1910), pp. 190–195; G. Ravegnani, *I Contemporanei* (1930), pp. 100–109.

C. M.

Novelli, Augusto (1868–1927, Italian dramatist), was born in Florence. His first literary efforts were of a very humble nature, for he began his career as a pamphleteer and his public was the lower-middle-class world. Subsequently he turned his attention to the theatre and wrote a number of comedies, for the most part imitations of the French, characterized by nothing more than a certain superficial facility. He found his true métier toward the turn of the century when he began to compose comedies in the Florentine vernacular dealing with the *piccola borghesia* and the *popolino* of his native town. In this vein he wrote with great charm. It is obvious that such a small world—in all senses of the word—puts its limitations on the artist, and there is certainly no great character that emerges from the theatre of Novelli and no intellectual content to speak of. The plays are amusing, good-natured in tone; here and there one finds a touch of the easy cynicism of the people coupled with the sort of aphoristic morality and conventionality of the world of artisans and shopkeepers. As types the figures in his play are convincing; the dialect is handled with assurance and skill although at times self-consciously; the author is limited not so much by the use of the vernacular as by the characters he portrays and by his own rather conventional attitude towards lfe. The comedies do however give an excellent picture of the Florentine "little man" and are in their way in the sound tradition of Goldoni. Perhaps the best known and the most successful technically is *L'Acqua cheta . . .* (1908). Others of real merit are: *Inferno, Purgatorio e Paradiso* (1894), *Casa mia, casa mia* (1909), *E chi vive si dà pace* (1916), and *La bestia nera* (1909).

See: C. Levi. *Il teatro* (1921), pp. 20–21.

T. G. B.

Novikov-Priboi, Aleksei Silych (1877–, Russian short-story writer and novelist), was born of peasant stock in a village of the Government of Tambov, received an elementary education in the local school, and worked in the fields until his 22d year, when he became a sailor in the Baltic fleet. As a member of the crew of the battleship *Orel,* he participated in the long cruise to the Orient and the fateful battle of Tsushima, during which he was taken prisoner. By then Novikov had become active in the revolutionary movement among the sailors, and consequently he spent the years 1907–1913 in Western Europe, sailing for a time on English commercial ships. He had turned to literature as early as 1906, but because of the censorship found it difficult to publish. After the Revolution he joined the group of proletarian writers known as Kuznitsa (The Smithy) and became a popular author. His first collection of stories, *Morskiye rasskazy* (1917; Sea Stories), was followed by *More zovyot* (1922; The Sea Calls), *Dve dushi* (1923; Two Souls), and others. An adventurous life furnished him with the subject matter of his work: realist and storyteller, he makes the most of the hard life of the sailor, the class struggle, the beauty of nature, and the role that women play in men's lives. His best-known work, *Tsusima* (2 vols., 1933–1934; Eng. tr., *Tsushima,* 1936), is naval history as well as an engrossing account written by an eyewitness of the debacle of the Russian fleet. His latest book, a short novel (*Kapitan 1-vo ranga,* 1943; Captain, Senior Grade), is also retrospective.

See: *A. S. Novikov-Priboi* (1930); "Novikov-Priboi," in *Literaturnaya entsiklopediya,* Vol. VIII (1934).

P. A. P.

Nowaczyński, Adolf (pseuds. Neuwert and Przyjaciel, 1876–1944, Polish dramatist and pamphleteer), was born in Podgórze, a suburb of Cracow, the son of a Polish official in the Austrian service. Educated in Cracow and Munich, Nowaczyński began his career in a manner prophetic of his later iconoclasm, when he publicly proposed a toast to anarchy in a Cracow café on receipt of the news of the Empress Elizabeth's assassination (1898). A tireless, vitriolic pamphleteer, full of eccentricities, spites, and prejudices—many of the latter grossly unworthy of a man of his ability and standing—Nowaczyński was Free Poland's greatest literary curiosity. He would treat any subject under the sun, including many he knew nothing about, such as the American scene, and he wrote in a style that was often turgid, ostentatious, and overloaded with foreignisms. Yet his readers were legion. He liked nothing better than to deflate the reputations of the great and, as in *Warta nad Wartą* (1937; Watch on the Warta), a rehabilitation of several men of western Poland, to extol the neglected. Among his many plays, in all of which history is ruthlessly distorted, are *Car Dymitr* (1908; Tsar Dmitri); *Wielki Fryderyk* (1907; The Great Frederick); *Wiosna narodów* (1929; The Spring of Nations), a satire on 1848; and *Cezar i człowiek* (1937; Caesar and Man), a drama of Copernicus and the Borgias. Nowaczyński's final work before the debacle of 1939 was the fascinating *Młodość Chopina* (1939; Chopin's Youth), a semifictional reconstruction of the early life of the great composer with interesting revelations of the Polish sources of Chopin's genius. Nowaczyński has been called the Polish Daudet.

See: Z. Dębicki, *Portrety,* II (1928), 213–230; K. Czachowski, *Obraz współczesnej literatury polskiej,* I (1934), 262–268, 320–322.

A. P. C.

Núñez de Arce, Gaspar (1834–1903, Spanish poet, dramatist, politician, and journalist), came from middle-class stock of Valladolid. Although a conservative by temperament, he early associated himself with the liberal movement that resulted in the fall of the Bourbons in 1868. He was active in politics throughout his life and rose to the position of colonial minister. As a writer he first attracted attention with his eye-witness impressions of the African war of 1859–1860. Subsequently he wrote for the stage, often in collaboration with Antonio Hurtado. His dramatic writings followed the vogue of the thesis play, but his supreme achievement was *El haz de leña* (1872), a historical drama in verse, dealing with the imprisonment and death of Don Carlos, son of Philip II.

But Núñez de Arce has survived primarily as a poet. Reacting against romanticism, he wrote readily intelligible verse of social and philosophic significance, successfully reflecting the collective ideas and passions, sorrows and joys of his age. His success earned him high popularity, as is attested by the frequent editions of his works. In 1894 Spain paid him official tribute for his patriotic service and for his literary accomplishments, but in recent decades his reputation has been drastically revised downward in the light of modern poetic values.

Núñez de Arce's verse falls into two groups, philosophic and sentimental. Chief examples of the first type are *Gritos del combate* (1875), *Raimundo Lulio* (1875), *La visión de Fray Martín* (1880), *Ultima lamentación de Lord Byron* (1879); the best known of the second category are *Un idilio* (1878), *La pesca* (1884), *Maruja* (1886). In their totality these works reveal a poet of impressive technical versatility but of limited vision and commonplace lyricism. When Núñez de Arce is reflective he is obsessed with doubt; when he is sentimental he lacks personal poignancy. But, whether he expresses the anguish resulting from the conflict between soul and mind, form and spirit, idealism and reality, or whether he interprets familiar reality in terms of readily felt tenderness and delicacy, he is ever conscious of the inherent power of attractive form to furnish an impressive measure of compensation for the inferior quality of substance. Hence his greatest effectiveness derives from rhetoric, eloquence, and conventional poetical adornment in general. His verse lends itself to declamation, and, indeed, public recitals of some of his compositions contributed much to their popularity.

As the poet of doubt Núñez de Arce betrays an intellectual deficiency rather than a philosophic attitude. He is neither a profound nor an inquisitive spirit. The enigmas of life do not intrigue him; his mind is stirred only by what is immediate, clear, and comprehensible. By temperament he liked order, methodicalness, formulas; hence, whatever defied instant penetration stimulated doubt in him. Yet in his day he expressed the dilemma of thinking persons. Brought up to worship liberal political and social ideals, he was grievously disappointed to discover that humanity is manifestly incapable of maintaining the loftiness and purity of an ideal when it is translated into action. He was reluctant to abandon his faith in human perfectibility, but the scant evidence of its realness disheartened him. In austere, patriarchal tones he declaimed against the excesses of rationalism and positivism, voicing the disillusionment of those who found slight comfort in the exchange of faith for reason.

Núñez de Arce's ultimate significance is largely historical. For his contemporaries he had a message of social import, and he delivered it honestly and sincerely, although at times with excessively studied inflection and intonation. For those who, like him, lived in an atmosphere of ideological violence, religious conflicts, and political clashes, his moral zeal and high-pitched earnestness were communicative and contagious; Fernando de Herrera (1534?–1597) and Manuel José Quintana (1772–1857) were revived in his poetic histrionics and patriotic bugling. For posterity he is an illuminating document concerning an age which had a pathetic faith in the power of eloquence to fortify man's spirit in his quest of the good life.

See: J. del Castillo Soriano, *Núñez de Arce* (1904); M. Menéndez y Pelayo, *Estudios de crítica literaria,* Ser. 1 (1927), pp. 291–347.

H. C. B.

Nušić, Branislav (pseud. Ben Akiba, 1864–1938, Serb dramatist, novelist, and humorist), was born in Belgrade, where he studied law. Entering the foreign service he worked for 10 years in the consulates of South Serbia, then under Turkish rule. Later he became a playwright and director of the National Dramatic Theatre, chief of the Serbian Art Division, newspaperman, editor of several newspapers, author, lecturer, initiator of many cultural and national organizations and institutions. "Perpetuum mobile," as he was called, he did not long remain attached to any one task, but in the variety of his activities he was constantly useful and important for his nation. Throughout his whole career he was devoted to literature.

He became one of the most fertile and versatile of Serb writers. From the publication of his first book, *Pripovetke jednog kaplara iz srpsko bugarskog rata 1885* (1886; The Story of a Corporal in the Serbo-Bulgarian War of 1885), to his death, *i.e.,* for more than half a century, he was the most widely read Serb author and a tireless amuser of the Serbian public. The bibliography of his published works contains thousands of items.

A great part of Nušić's production is narrative. Here the best works are *Ramazanske večeri* (1898; The Evenings of Ramazan), *Opštinsko dete* (1902; The Community's Child), *Ben Akiba* (1907), *Devetstopetnaesta* (1921; Nineteen Hundred Fifteen), *Autobiografija* (1924; Autobiography), *Hajduci* (1934; The Haiduks), and several volumes of short stories (1931, 1932, 1936). His *feuilletons* are lively and imaginative, abounding in witticisms, comic situations, interesting anecdotes—to the detriment, it must be confessed, of psychological and genuinely literary elements. During his service in South Serbia, Nušič wrote several good books of travel whose chief value lies in the ethnographic material on this region. Sometimes his work has scientific intention; such is the case with the long study of speech, *Retorika* (1934; Rhetoric).

His greatest contribution is in the drama. He became a master of theatrical technique. A certain number of his plays gained wide popularity because of their patriotic or national tendencies, *e.g., Knez od Semberije* (1900; The Duke of Semberija), *Rastko Nemanjić* (1906), *Danak u krvi* (1907; Tribute in Blood), *Hadži-Loja* (1908), *Nahod* (1923; The Foundling). His serious dramas—*Pučina* (1901; The Main), *Tako je moralo biti* (1910; It Had to Be Thus); *Iza Božjih ledja* (1910; Behind God's Back)—do not represent his highest attainment.

Nušić is important above all as a writer of comedies—*Sumnjivo lice* (1889; A Suspicious Person), *Protekcija* (1889; Pull), *Narodni poslanik* (1896; A National Representative), *Običan čovek* (1900; An Ordinary Man), *Šopenhauer* (1900; Schopenhauer), *Svet* (1906; The World), *Put oko sveta* (1910; A Voyage around the World), *Gospodja ministarka* (1929; The Minister of State's Wife), *Mister Dolar* (1932; Mister Dollar), *Beograd nekad i sad* (1933; Belgrade Then and Now), *Ožalošćena porodica* (1934; The Mourning Family), *Ujež* (1935; The Association of Yugoslav Emancipated Women), *Analfabeta* (1935; The Illiterate), *Doktor* (1936), *Pokojnik* (1937; The Deceased). These are mostly comedies of manners or intrigue, occasionally farces. Nušić knew thoroughly each milieu, the small town as well as the capital, and he saw clearly through his fellow men. He knew society's selfish depths, its ambition, materialism, vanity; he depicted bureaucracy, corruption, the slow tempo of administration, the weaknesses of executives and politicians, and also the relations among the members of a household as well as between the family and society.

His world is the varied one of southeastern Europe, which still shows the traces of a patriarchal tradition, but which already reveals the influences of contemporary materialistic culture. His characters will remain as documents on the Balkan man in an epoch of transition.

Nušić was a constant critic and a mild reformer of customs. Without delivering moral speeches he created comic situations implying conclusions to which the spectator should come by himself. He besprinkled his plays with jolly, carefree humor and laughter; although he touched upon many vices, he did so without emphasis or bitterness. Human sins and foolishness seemed to him altogether pardonable. His characterization was often light, even superficial, as in a film. Only as time went on did his delineation become fuller, deeper, until he achieved the qualitv of a real satirist, an earnest judge of national life. Possessing a marvelously youthful and energetic spirit, tirelessly inventive and active he was in constant contact with his country's life; he participated in its political and social progress and expressed the strivings and thoughts of his environment for many decades.

See: P. Popović, "Srpska drama u XIX veku," *Srpski književni glasnik* (1902); Milan Grol, "Branislav Nušić," *Srpski književni glasnik,* February 16, 1938; B. Kovačević, "Branislav Nušić kao komediograf," *Srpski književni glasnik,* February 16, 1938.

P. A.

O

Obstfelder, Sigbjörn (1866–1900, Norwegian poet), has come to typify the *fin de siècle* in Norwegian poetry as has no one else. Cultivated by only a narrow circle in his lifetime, he has repeatedly been "rediscovered" since his death. He was born in Stavanger, the son of a baker, grandson of a German physician, and his singular talents were apparent already in childhood (original writing in his 11th year). His university studies began in philology, quickly shifted to engineering; he dabbled in painting, played various instruments, and won considerable skill as an improviser on the violin. Split as he was among these various talents, he was unable to strike out on any one of them until his return from an eight-month stay in the United States in 1891 and his recovery from a subsequent nervous breakdown. From 1892 to his untimely death he unfolded one of the most refined and eccentric literary personalities in Norwegian literature, exhibited in such volumes as *Digte* (1893; Poems), *To novelletter* (1895; Two Short Stories), *Korset* (1896; The Cross), *De røde dråber* (1897; The Red Drops), *En præsts dagbog* (1900; A Pastor's Diary), *Efter-*

ladte arbeider (1903; Posthumous Writings). His form was a prose with rhythm and a poetry without rhyme, often seeking to give the effect of music through the sound of words. His themes were the universe, the soul, woman, God, and eternity, all treated in a mystic, brooding spirit, reminiscent of Eduard von Hartmann and Schopenhauer. His overpowering sense of the terror and mystery of life and his own loneliness, as well as his attempts to express the inexpressible, remind one of the paintings of his countryman and contemporary, Edvard Munch. He was a neoromantic of the purest water, but without a trace of the poseur, and even today his slender production is impressive for its limpid depth and the haunting music of its lines.

See: Obstfelder, *Poems from the Norwegian* (1920); C. Claussen, *S. Obstfelder i hans diktning og breve* (1924); C. W. Stork, *An Anthology of Norwegian Lyrics* (1942).

E. H.

Ognyov, Nikolai (pseud. of Mikhail Grigoriyevich Rozanov, 1888–1938, Russian novelist), son of a small-town lawyer, became active in the revolutionary movement as a young man. His first short stories appeared before the First World War. Their somber and morbid fantasy acquired a new significance in the author's later work, in which, as in *Krusheniye antenny* (1923; The Collapse of the Antenna), he contrasted his favorite themes of peasant witchcraft, bestiality, chaos, and death with the organizing and rational principle of the Revolution. His style, like that of many writers of the early 20's, often became overburdened with the unusual and the picturesque. In his wide experience as educator, Ognyov soon found the material for a work purely realistic and remarkably direct, his popular *Dnevnik Kosti Ryabtseva* (2 vols., 1927–1928; Eng. tr., *The Diary of a Communist Schoolboy* and *The Diary of a Communist Undergraduate,* both 1928). It was later completed by his *Tri izmereniya* (1932; The Three Dimensions), which describes an earlier period. The diary is a humorous, vivid, and pathetic story of school life in Soviet Russia in the early 20's, when the new school had to deal with a young generation emerging from the chaos of the civil war. Portrayals of members of the old intelligentsia attempting to find a place in the new society are not always as direct and convincing as those of the younger characters. The series was later abridged by the author and published as *Nachalo zhizni* (1933; The Beginning of Life).

See: E. Rusakova, *N. Ognyov-molodyozhni pisatel* (1933).

L. S.

Ojetti, Ugo (1871–1946, Italian journalist, art critic, novelist, short-story writer, playwright, and essayist), born in Rome, is a perfect example of the gifted and versatile newspaperman. Obviously under the influence of D'Annunzio, he started out on his literary career with the novel *Senza Dio* (1894). He followed that with *Alla scoperta dei letterati* (1895), an inquiry into the most significant currents of Italian literature from Carducci and Verga to Pascoli and D'Annunzio (*qq.v.*). In it were already apparent those qualities of keen observer of the men and events of contemporary life and culture which are the essential characteristic of his work as writer and journalist. His works of fiction (four novels, several volumes of short stories, two comedies) are, with a few exceptions, pleasant but inconsequential, with their typical bourgeois situations and rapidly sketched and poorly motivated characters. The novel *Mio figlio ferroviere* (1922) deserves more consideration. It is a subtly ironic picture of the period of disillusionment, political chaos, and opportunism in Italy immediately following the First World War.

Ojetti finally abandoned light fiction and dedicated himself to his journalist's career, also inaugurated in 1894. Thereafter he wrote for the leading Italian newspapers. It is interesting to note the progressive development of his prose style. He did his most notable writing for the *Corriere della sera,* to which he had contributed from 1898, first with the column *Piccole Verità,* then *Caratteri,* and finally *Cose viste* from 1921 on. These latter articles on contemporary figures and events have been reprinted in six volumes of *Cose viste* (1923, 1924, 1926, 1928, 1931, 1934; partial Eng. tr., *As They Seemed to Me,* 1928). In these Ojetti stands out as one of the most brilliant writers for the literary page or *terza pagina,* which in Italian newspapers has played the important role of bringing literature into contact with daily life and reality. Seldom in his narrative and innumerable critical works is he as keen and literary as in these pictures of men and events. His limpid, fluent, and sharply faceted prose, made up of a happy mixture of the best elements of modernism and classicism, seems a perfect vehicle for his ordered, clear ideas and images. The author's inspiration is sustained; his vigilance, sometimes smiling, sometimes sad, never relaxes. It is fragmentary journalistic art at its best. The subject matter changes continually: distant memories, lively impressions of the moment, portraits and recollections of celebrated men, autobiographical details, pictures of spectacles, crowds, and celebrations, descriptions of historic places, war anecdotes, and graceful fables with a moral. The author is indulgent, ironic, cordial, or skeptical as the occasion demands, and for material he delved into the rich fund of his years of experiences, constant work, meetings with famous people, and travels (Ojetti traveled extensively in Europe, Egypt, Central Asia, and the United States). He was a dilettante in the best sense; no form of human culture was ever a matter of indifference to him. Frank in his likes and dislikes, he maintained a consistent faith in most of his contemporaries and in their striving after ever new expressions.

Ojetti also produced excellent work as an art critic. He conceived and directed two great Italian art exhibitions and founded the reviews *Dedalo* (1920) and *Pegaso* (1929). He waged an untiring campaign against bad taste in the arts and, for all his love and knowledge of the masters, he constantly encouraged and kept his mind open to the new trends.

Ojetti became a member of the Italian Academy in 1930. He was the general editor of two important collections of Italian classics and of the review *Pan*. He also wrote several books of travel and literary essays and two on the United States, *L'America vittoriosa* (1898), on the Spanish-American War, and *L'America e l'avvenire* (1905).

See: L. Russo, *I Narratori* (1923), pp. 173–175; A. Baldini, *Amici allo spiedo* (1932), pp. 97–103; P. Pancrazi, *Scrittori italiani del novecento* (1934), pp. 36–41.

J. F. De S.

Olbracht, Ivan (pseud. of Kamil Zeman, 1882–, Czech novelist), is probably the most gifted of the recent Czech writers of fiction. He was born in Semily (northeastern Bohemia), the son of a writer, Antonín Zeman (1843–1931), who produced early realist novels under the pseudonym Antal Stašek. Olbracht studied law, but became a journalist in the labor movement, writing for Socialist and, later, Communist papers. He spent several short periods in jail because of revolutionary writings and in 1942 was arrested by the Nazis. In 1945 he became chief of the Broadcasting Division of the new Ministry of Information.

Olbracht's first book was a collection of good romantic stories about tramps and circus people, *O zlých samotářích* (1913; Of Evil Solitary Men); but his rise as an artist began only in the First World War, with a strangely powerful novel, *Žalář nejtemnější* (1916; The Darkest Prison), which describes the jealous pangs of a blind man. The next long work, *Podivné přátelství herce Jesenia* (1919; The Strange Friendship of the Actor Jesenius), put him into the front rank of Czech novelists. The story is based on the motif of split personality and is set in extremely vivid scenes of the war and of greenroom life. His moral points toward a victory of collective belief over narrow egotism and barren introspection. Olbracht seems to have taken to heart with a vengeance the lesson of his novel. His next book, *Anna proletářka* (1928; Anne the Proletarian), a story of the Communist revolution, is heavy-handed propaganda, and the prison stories, *Zamřížované zrcadlo* (1930; The Grated Mirror), are also failures. But Olbracht again surprised the admirers of *Jesenius* with his next novel, *Nikolaj Šuhaj, loupežník* (1933; Nikolaj Šuhaj, the Robber), a brisk story of Sub-Carpathian Russia with an epic speed, a tight composition, and a balladlike objectivity. It centers round the deeds and misdeeds of a popular revolutionist who took the law into his own hands against the Czech police authorities. *Golet v údolí* (1937; Golet in the Valley), a series of stories drawn from the lives of the poor Orthodox Jews in Sub-Carpathian Russia, is also excellent. Olbracht's other work is journalistic in nature: it includes an enthusiastic travel book about Soviet Russia (*Obrazy ze soudobého Ruska*, 1920; Pictures of Present-Day Russia) and a good descriptive account of Sub-Carpathian Russia and its social problems (*Hory a staletí*, 1935; Mountains and Centuries). *Bratr Žák* (1938; Brother Žák) is a collection of short stories.

The strong leftist ideology has not marred Olbracht's deep humanity and sure artistry. His evolution from an analytical novelist of the subconscious to a storyteller of epic grandeur is a sign of revolt against the excesses of introspection and heralds the revival of the almost forgotten art of storytelling. For in *Nikolaj Šuhaj* Olbracht succeeded in telling his story interestingly, objectively, in sharp outlines, in fine, clear, model Czech prose, with something of the monumentality of a primitive epic.

See: B. Václavek, *Tvorbou k realitě* (1937).

R. W.

Oliveira Martins, Joaquim Pedro de (1845-1894, Portuguese historian), was born in Lisbon. His father died when he was 10, and he was forced to abandon his studies at an early age and enter business to support his family. In 1870 he went to Spain, and he remained four years as the manager of a mine in the province of Córdoba. From there he went to Oporto, where he was first an employee and later manager of a railroad company until 1888, at which time he moved to Lisbon. In Oporto he became an intimate friend of Antero de Quental (*q.v.*) and established connections with the Coimbra Group (*see* Portuguese literature). This strong-willed autodidact, formed by tireless personal reading, accepted readily the reforms of Coimbra realism. In his youth he had sympathized actively with republicanism—and wrote on socialistic doctrine—but later he abandoned these views, like other members of the Coimbra Group, in the face of the passionate negativism of the republican propaganda. Influenced by German writers, he became an adherent of monarchism in order to attempt national restoration within the framework of the existing regime. This he visualized through economic dictatorship and centralistic Caesarism, in support of the royal authority. These aspirations led him into active politics, and he was a deputy (1887) and secretary of the treasury (1892), but failed in his political purpose. He traveled in Spain and other parts of Europe, represented Portugal at various congresses, and filled different official and honorary positions.

He began his literary career with a historical novel, *Phebus Moniz* (1867)—which he later withdrew from the market—and a historical trilogy in prose and verse, but soon abandoned imaginative literature to devote his efforts to historical writing. He planned an extensive universal and national historical work, projected on a sociological and anthropological basis, which he nearly completed. In this he perpetuated the attitude of Herculano (*see* Portuguese literature) and marked a healthful, though perhaps excessive, reaction against the deceptive optimism as to the historical past and national grandeur, the official attitude of the time. A reexamination of values became imperative. Realism was to confront the romantic eulogy of past glories with the decadence of the moment. Antero de Quental had broken ground in this direction with his lecture in the Casino de Lisboa, and Oliveira Martins was to go the whole way; he represents in Portugal the sifting of historical tradition carried out later in Spain by the Generation of '98—on which he exerted a notable influence. Neither his agitated social life nor his temperament suited him for the slow and laborious task of investigation and accumulation of materials. He utilized the materials of others, from which he extracted and selected data to be passed later through the sieve of his keen sensibility and orderly intelligence. Thus he was able to create a work of artistic reconstruction, of integral revitalization of the past in the manner of Michelet, but with even greater lyric intensity. This is a work characterized by luminous syntheses but also, at times, by hasty or risky generalizations. He was not, strictly speaking, a historian but a man of letters, a poet or dramatist devoted to history—a "great historical artist" in the happy phrase of Menéndez y Pelayo (*q.v.*).

It was Oliveira Martins who initiated the Peninsular point of view in historico-political conceptions. The realism to which he had been somewhat allied had adopted a cosmopolitan attitude as a reaction against romantic nationalism. But this cosmopolitanism, Francophile or Germanophile, was still characterized by ignorance of Spain or prejudice against that nation. Oliveira Martins took a valiant stand in behalf of a deep unity of Peninsular civilization, one which would transcend momentary vicissitudes. Following the English threat of 1890, which led him to a colonial campaign related in *Portugal na Africa* (1891; Portugal in Africa), he succeeded in making Iberism a basis for political action. His stay in Spain and his knowledge of that country doubtless influenced him in his attempt at political *rapprochement,* in which he attempted to replace the traditional English alliance—weakened by the ultimatum—by one with Spain. In 1875 he had founded with Quental the *Revista occidental* to promote a community of interests and collaboration between the two peoples and with the Hispanic American republics.

The influence of Oliveira Martins was very profound. His systematization of national history, which he effected through a subjective interpretation instead of limiting himself to simple recording; the elaboration of a definite and total basis for judgment; his Peninsular theory—all these were new things in Portugal. His success is easily explained if we add a vigorous style, somewhat like that of Taine (*q.v.*), a powerful plastic and psychological imagination, and extraordinary gifts as a literary narrator. But such qualities frequently led him into impressionism, and his work, ardently personal, is less enduring than his historical philosophy. Faithful to his Hegelian tradition, he shows a scrupulous respect for truth, which he depicts from all angles and presents even in contrast with his personal opinions. His evaluation of Portuguese history is painfully negative. His purpose was "to lay it bare of patriotic illusions and fantastic chimeras . . . in an impersonal and objective manner," but, a victim of the national pessimism of all his generation, he viewed the national past in a sad light and painted it à la Goya. In his brilliant and corrosive prose he summed up the eight centuries of Portuguese national development as a mass of abjections and wretchedness and the grandiose epic of the discoveries and the Eastern Empire as a heap of infamies interwoven with plundering and simony.

His first historical work was *O helenismo e a civilização cristã* (1878; Hellenism and Christian Civilization), and there followed in rapid succession *História da civilização ibérica* (1879; Eng. tr., *A History of Iberian Civilization,* 1930), *História de Portugal* (1879; History of Portugal), *Portugal contemporâneo* (1881; Contemporary Portugal) which he himself called "a sad work" and which is a true *de profundis* of the Portuguese nationality—and *Brasil e as colônias portuguesas* (1880; Brazil and the Portuguese Colonies). From 1880 to 1885 he produced a series of works on universal historical anthropology, sociology, and chronology, and in 1889 he returned to national history with *Portugal nos mares* (Portugal in the Seas). From that moment the biographical character of his former work was clear; henceforward he excelled in historical portraits and was an expert in the psychological characterization of personages, groups, and periods. Then there appeared *Os filhos de D. João I* (1891; Eng. tr., *The Golden Age of Prince Henry the Navigator,* 1914), *Vida de Nun'Alvares* (1893; Life of Nun'Alvares), and the single chapter of *O principe perfeito* (The Perfect Prince), published posthumously in 1895. When he left the government (1892) he made a trip to England and wrote *A Inglaterra de hoje* (The England of Today), an appraisal of British society dominated by a confessed Anglophobia. During his last trip to Spain, a little before his death, he wrote a series of impressions entitled *Cartas peninsulares* (1895; Peninsular Letters), also issued posthumously. Aside from his work as a historian he left a large number of very interesting books and tracts on such subjects as literature, economy, politics, and agrarianism.

See: Teófilo Braga, *As modernas idéias na literatura portuguesa* (1892), II, 346–390; Fidelino de Figueiredo, "Oliveira Martins," *Revue hispanique,* LXXV (1929), 54–143.

E. G. D.

Oller i Moragues, Narcís (1846–1930, Catalonian novelist), was born in the city of Valls, near Tarragona, and died in Barcelona. His highly successful participation in Catalonian letters came late and was brought about through the intervention of his cousin, the critic Josep Ixart, who presented him to a group of writers taking part in the Jocs Florals. These poetic competitions, restored some years previously (1859), were contributing to the rebirth of Catalonian literature. He had earlier been a notary. His first works were published in the *Renaixença,* at the beginning in collaboration with Ixart. His reading of Zola's (*q.v.*) works influenced him greatly in his decision to become a novelist. The literary world of the Barcelona of those times was far from able to understand the message of naturalism, and Narcís Oller adapted what he could from the school in the light of his public's taste. In 1875 came his first book, *Croquis del natural* (Sketches from Nature), in which he essayed his powers as a realistic writer. *Sor Sanxa* (Sister Sanxa) was published in 1880, followed by another novel, *Isabel de Galceran.* A little later he wrote *Vilaniu* (1885). Then there appeared one of the author's most popular novels, the one which contributed most to his fame and has been translated into various languages, *La papallona* (1882; The Butterfly), the picture of a masculine character, all movement and madness. *L'escanya pobres* (1884; The Exploiter of the Poor) and the *Febre d'or* (1890; Gold Fever) are the beginning of his thesis works, so dear to naturalism; rather than literary creations they are photographs taken in a sordid milieu of repugnant characters. *La borgeria* (1898; The Bourgeoisie) presents the problem of insanity and its social consequences. Some consider *Pilar Prim* (1906), a novel of middle-class urban life, the crowning point of Narcís Oller's work. Also to be mentioned among his narrative writings are *Notes de color* (Color Notes), *De tots colors* (1888; In All Colors), *Figura i paisatge* (1897; Figure and Landscape), *Rurals i urbanes* (From the Countryside and the City), and *Al llapis i a la ploma* (1929; With Pen and Pencil) which, by their very titles, suggest parallels with the plastic arts, in particular painting and drawing.

In following the French naturalistic school (*see* French naturalism) Narcís Oller developed marked talent as an observer, although, as may happen with the devotees of the naturalistic manner, he frequently presented incarnations of vices and passions rather than men of flesh and bone. Yet his realism never becomes crude, and he shows rather a keen desire to present great social problems in thesis form; this was the genesis of his works on the insane asylum, usury, slander, the desire for wealth. In this sense his work is always moralizing and has an essential didactic purpose. He translated various authors, and his work was in turn translated into Italian, English, Spanish, Russian, and German.

See: A. Savine, *La Littérature catalane* (1888); C. Fortuny, *La novela catalana* (1912); M. de Montoliu, "Estudi critic" (prologue to the complete works of the author published by Gustau Gili, Barcelona, 1928–1930).

F. de P.

Olyosha, Yuri Karlovich (1899–, Russian novelist and dramatist), was born in Odessa. His first novel, *Zavist* (1927; Eng. tr., *Envy*, 1936), based on the conflict between the new society and dying individualism, met with considerable success, but caused much controversy. Olyosha's treatment of the subject seemed equivocal and perplexing. It is true that he represents prerevolutionary individualism by degraded and futile day dreamers, whose impotent hatred finds expression in a fantastic "conspiracy of feelings" against the new social order. On the other hand, his characterization of the director of a food trust, who typifies the new social order, is hardly inspiring; the man's soundness and efficiency exasperate, and a new sort of low-priced sausage that he triumphantly produces symbolizes his main contribution to Soviet society. The author does not make a clear choice between these conflicting types of humanity, and were it not for his introduction of a secondary theme of young love, his attitude could be mistaken for sheer misanthropy. In reality, Olyosha has hardly ever sought to express anything more definite than a belief in the intrinsic value of the psyche and an inability to share in standardized enthusiasms. He is primarily a lyricist and a remarkably brilliant and inventive stylist, whose sensorial acuteness discovers in everyday life fantastic microcosms of unexpected imagery and emotion.

Besides *Envy* and a few short stories, Olyosha has published a longer story, *Tri tolstiaka* (1928; The Three Fat Men), revolutionary in content and somewhat reminiscent of Hans Christian Andersen in form; a play, *Spisok blagodeyani* (1931; List of Blessings), in which he once more turns to the conflict between society and the individual; and two screen plays, one of which, *Walter* (1937), deals with the struggle against facsism. *Zavist* and *Tri tolstiaka* have been adapted for the stage, the latter as a ballet scenario.

See: Gleb Struve, "Current Russian Literature: Yuri Olesha," *Slavonic Review*, XIII (1934–1935), 644–649.

L. S.

Onís, Federico de (1885–, Spanish critic and scholar), was born in Salamanca, where he pursued all his studies up to the time he left for Madrid (1906) to study for the doctorate. At the University of Salamanca, Onís came under the powerful and decisive influence of Miguel de Unamuno (*q.v.*), from whom he acquired an approach to Hispanic culture which differed considerably from the prevailing positivistic perspective, an approach which was responsive to the achievements of all modern European culture without abjuring the indefectible originality of the genius of Spain. In Madrid, Onís came to know the literature of modern Spain and its creators and allied himself with the men determined to renovate cultural Spain. By 1909 he had become professor of Spanish literature at the University of Oviedo, and it was there he read three years later his provocative paper on the historical problem of the Spanish university. Soon Onís was drawn to the new institutions of learning that had been established, especially to the Centro de Estudios Históricos, where under the direction of Menéndez Pidal (*q.v.*) the *Revista de filología española* was started (1914) with his active collaboration and that of Navarro Tomás, Américo Castro (*qq.v.*), Antonio Solalinde, and Alfonso Reyes. At the Residencia de Estudiantes, where students from all over Spain lived and studied, Onís lectured to the future leaders and in 1915 delivered a speech "Disciplina y rebeldía" which breathed the new spirit of renewal controlled by a sturdy discipline of the complete man.

Onís contributed to the new scholarship in his edition (1914–1921, in the "Clásicos castellanos" series) of *De los nombres de Cristo* by Fray Luis de León. In 1916 Columbia University in New York invited him to take charge of graduate work in Spanish. Through new courses, two magazines, *Revista de estudios hispánicos* (1928–1929) and *Revista hispánica moderna* (1934–), the publication of original works and of doctoral theses, the creation of the Hispanic Institute of America (1920) and its Hispanic House, Onís has contributed to the spread of a new vision on matters relating to the culture and civilization of Spain, Portugal, and Iberic America.

Onís has been able to exercise a great deal of influence in Iberic America. His *Antología de la poesía española e hispanoamericana, 1882–1932* (1934) is perhaps the best anthology of its kind in the Spanish language. The enthusiastic response accorded it by outstanding critics in Spain and America indicates its value and importance. In general the pattern of Onís's thought can be traced in the essays "El problema de la universidad española" (1912), "El estudio del español en los Estados Unidos" (1920), and "El concepto del renacimiento aplicado a la literatura española" (1926), all of which were published with other papers in his *Ensayos sobre el sentido de la cultura española* (1932).

See: Azorín, L. Bello, J. Pin y Soler, M. S. Oliver, "Sobre el concepto del patriotismo," in Onís, *Ensayos sobre el sentido de la cultura española* (1932), appendix; M. P. González, *Nuestro camino de Damasco: a propósito de un libro de Federico de Onís* (1935).

M. J. B.

Oriani, Alfredo (1852–1909, Italian historian, critic, and novelist), is a complex and tragic personality, a rich and tormented spirit, who was almost ignored by his contemporaries and then apotheosized by Fascism as one of its major prophets. He was born in Faenza, Romagna, of a noble but impoverished family, the least loved and understood of three children. At the age of 10 he went to Bologna to study with the Barnabites, famous Italian teaching order. In 1868 he went to the University of Rome to study law. Oriani's student years in Rome were the historically stirring years when this ancient mother of civilization was about to become the capital of the youngest national state in Europe. After receiving his law degree from the University of Naples in 1872 he withdrew, to his father's bitter disappointment, to the family villa in Casola-Valsenio to dedicate himself to a literary career. Here Oriani spent the rest of an uneventful but prodigiously prolific literary life. None of the many books into which he poured his passionate soul achieved success during his lifetime. The fame for which he had worked and hungered so came only after he had died a brokenhearted, almost obscure man.

Oriani tried every literary genre. From 1876, when he made his literary debut with an autobiographic novel, *Memorie inutili*, to 1902, when *Olocausto*, his last work of fiction, appeared, he wrote extensively in this field; his novels and short stories gave him the reputation chiefly of a vulgar and disheveled exponent of the naturalist school. Only *Disfatta* (1886), described by Croce as the novel richest in ideas in Italian literature, has escaped oblivion. A volume of verse, *Monotonie* (1878), and the nine plays he produced between 1899 and 1909 caused hardly any stir. Oriani's fame and the considerable influence he exerted on immediate posterity rests mainly on his historical writings. Of these the most important are *Matrimonio* (1886), *Fino a Dogali* (1889), *Lotta politica* (1892), his major work, and *Rivolta ideale* (1908), his last and noblest book.

Matrimonio is an impassioned defense of the integrity of the family against the advancing onslaught of divorce and free love. Dumas *fils* in *La Question du divorce* (1880) had advocated divorce in the name of progress and human happiness. *Matrimonio* refutes Dumas's thesis, maintaining that the essence of life is duty and self-sacrifice, not happiness, and that the family exists for the protection of the child, not for the benefit of the parents. *Fino a Dogali* was inspired by the Dogali disaster, which ended Italy's first colonial venture in Africa. To Oriani expansion into Africa is a historical necessity for Italy, the next inevitable step in her renewed life. His *Africanismo* is an integral part of his vision of history; it informs all his historical works and gives the vantage point from which, in *Lotta politica*, he surveys the entire panorama of Italian and European history. *Lotta politica* is an extraordinary feat of reconstruction embracing three thousand years of Italian history.

Briefly stated, Oriani's vision of history is this: humanity through the blood and toil of the continent of Europe is evolving a world civilization. In the 19th century this civilization attains full maturity as it brings forth the two perfected forms of historic life, the democratic national state and the free citizen of modern society, forms destined to extend to all peoples on earth. The colonial expansion of European states into America, Africa, and Asia is the process whereby Europe is lifting other continents to its own level; the process is completed in America. Italy which by her political renascence has resumed her place in the vanguard of history cannot evade her historic responsibility in Africa. Oriani does not admit imperialism; he has the comfortable theory that even when men think they are furthering their interests they are unconsciously serving an ideal. Oriani's ideal is the triumph of liberty, the establishment of an order wherein free men organize into democratic national states to vie with each other peacefully in the discovery of truth and the creation of beauty—no more master and subject races. Empires will disappear once they have fulfilled their historic function of teaching all peoples democracy. In *Rivolta ideale,* his spiritual testament, Oriani, a careful student of Hegel, warns modern man that liberty does not mean freedom to enrich and indulge himself to the detriment of his brothers; on the contrary liberty means the acceptance of high responsibilities and the willing subordination of interests to ideas and of passions to truth.

See: L. Donati, *La tragedia di Oriani* (1919); G. Pentimalli, *Oriani* (1921); B. Croce, *La Letteratura della nuova Italia,* 2d ed., III (1922), 227–258; P. Zama, *Oriani* (1928); A. Giorgi, *Oriani* (1935).

T. C.

Ørjasaeter, Tore (1886–, Norwegian poet, dramatist, and prose writer), was born in the mountain valley of Gudbrandsdal in central Norway and has lived there most of his life. From early childhood he deeply felt his allegiance to the close-knit farm society with its venerable and overpowering heritage of traditions. But as the son of a schoolteacher he at the same time did not really belong; and his personal development early made him rise in revolt. Long-lasting serious disease emphasized his isolation and intensified his problems.

His literary creations, essentially philosophical, are built on the contrast sharpened by his own experience of the free soul and "the powers." His first collections of verse express spontaneous attachment to his milieu and its secure traditions, with a background of sublime mountain landscapes such as is found in all his poetry. His following books are monuments to crises. In the great verse cycle *Gudbrand Langleite* (3 vols., 1913–1927), within the framework of a loose epic narrative, he runs a gamut of contrasts: the rise of the individual against surroundings and heritage, of man's will against the ensnaring powers of love and home, of the artist's dream against everyday life, of the soul against its fate, the painful doubleness and the struggle of the forces in himself, until the conflict is solved in religious understanding. An independent collection, *Skiringsgangen* (1925; Purgatory), moves within the same circle of ideas. Both works are conceived with intensity and grandeur of thought and emotion, in symbols of original beauty. Similar also are the motifs of Ørjasaeter's two plays, his drama of a legendary mountaineer, symbol of individualistic isolation (*Jo Gjende,* 1917), and his analysis of a girl rising against her inherited tasks (*Anne paa Torp,* 1930; Anne of Torp). The calm and clarity after the storm is charmingly expressed in the allegorical cycle of poems *Elvesong* (1932; Song of the River). In a few highly personal prose works he has analyzed himself and his development with great frankness and a humor which indicates his growing mastery of himself and of his world.

Ørjasaeter is one of the most genuine poets of New Norse literature. His poetry is sometimes monotonous and not always easily accessible. His thought is inquiring and often gropes for expression; his form may be vague and inconclusive. But his best poems have a noble sincerity and a lucid depth of feeling and expression which give them high rank.

See: R. Thesen, *T. Ørjasaeter* (1935).

S. S.

Orkan, Władysław (pseud. of Franciszek Szmaciarz-Smreczyński, 1876–1930, Polish poet and novelist), was born, of peasant stock, in the mountain village of Poręba Wielka in the Podhalan section of the Tatras. He owed everything to his mother, who was determined to give her son an education at whatever cost. By heroic efforts on her part and his. Orkan was able to study at the Jagiellonian University in Cracow. Here he became aware of his potentialities and those of his people through observing the progress of two movements: the "Tatra movement" led by Asnyk (*q.v.*) and Tetmajer (*q.v.*), on the one hand, the neo-romantic "art for art's sake" ferment led by Przybyszewski (*q.v.*), on the other. Orkan stood outside, but derived spiritual nourishment from both movements, and soon he was writing, in his own primitive, somewhat metaphysical style, the first tales of the Tatras to issue from the pen of a real mountaineer. Of his many works, *Drzewiej* (1912; Of Old) was the most significant, standing as a milestone on the long road which, with Reymont (*q.v.*), finally brought the Polish peasant as he is, unidealized, into Poland's limited stock of literary material.

See: Z. Dębicki, *Portrety,* II (1928), 65–82; G. Korbut, *Literatura polska* (1931), IV, 283–284; K. Czachowski, *Obraz współczesnej literatury polskiej,* I (1934), 223–231, 322–324.

A. P. C.

Ors, Eugenio d', *see* D'Ors.

Ortega y Gasset, José (1883–, Spanish essayist and philosopher), was born in Madrid. Like many Spanish liberals, he received an early religious education, and his secondary studies were completed in a Jesuit school. After taking his doctorate in philosophy (Madrid, 1904), he studied in several German universities. In Marburg, Hermann Cohen initiated him into the Neo-Kantian movement. Although his thought later developed along personal lines, Germany left a lasting imprint upon his ideas, affected his approach to all intellectual matters, and awakened his eagerness to create in Spain an adequate atmosphere for philosophical and systematic thinking. The Germanic bent was clearly expressed in his first book, *Meditaciones del Quijote* (1914), in which he compares the Germanic and the Mediterranean culture. The former is for him a culture of "profundity," its instrument the "concept"; the latter is a culture of "surface," its instrument the "impression." He became in 1910 professor of metaphysics at the University of Madrid. Since then, indeed since his return from Germany, Ortega's life has been inseparable from the intellectual life of his country, and he has shared with Unamuno (*q.v.*), outstanding figure of the older generation, the spiritual leadership of Spain.

Ortega's influence grew with the century. His ideas about the "dehumanization" of art, the contemporary spirit, and a new life for Europe and Spain were determining factors in the rise of a new generation which gradually separated itself from the Generation of '98 writers (*see* Spanish literature) and from the modernistic movement. Already in his first essays—collected later in *Personas, obras y cosas* (1916)—Ortega started in earnest the attack against the individualism of his predecessors in literary life. Thus in 1909 in an essay about Renan (*q.v.*), whose intellectualism or idealism had a great influence on the young Ortega, he says: "In general, I cannot conceive that men can be of more interest than ideas, persons than things. . . . The objective is the true, and must interest us above anything else." The disagreement with Unamuno is evident in these lines; later in the same essay the allusions to him become direct, personal, and unflattering.

In other ways too, Ortega was for contemporary Spain an "animator." In fact, his work as writer and thinker is indissolubly bound to his conception of intellectual life as an activity which has to operate on life itself. All his philosophy is built on a concept of human reality already defined in the *Meditaciones del Quijote.* Instead of the thinking ego of Cartesian rationalism, he conceives the first reality to be an ego surrounded by circumstances. "Yo soy yo y mis circunstancias," which could be rendered as "I am my ego plus my circumstances," defining *circunstancias* as the "silent things which are [*i.e.,* which I find] in my immediate surroundings." Accordingly, his first intellectual task was to think about the problems of Spain as a national entity in order to bring it closer to the main currents of European life, which for him represented the highest values of culture. In the *Meditaciones del Quijote* he defines his criticism as a patriotic undertaking, and during the same year, 1914, appeared *Vieja y nueva política,* embodying a real program of intellectual and political action. With the exception of a brief period as a member of the Cortes Constitucionales of the republic, he held no public offices. Throughout the years, however, he considered himself the mouthpiece of an intellectual minority with a superior conception of national life. Its organ was first the review *España,* founded by him in 1915. Later he expounded his ideas on current political events in numerous articles and speeches, some of which he collected in 1931 in such books as *La redención de las provincias y la decadencia nacional* and *Rectificación de la república.* When the civil war began, he left Spain and has been practically silent since then about all Spanish problems. The real field, however, of Ortega's influence has been the intellectual. Through his work as professor, through his books, and through personal contacts with a growing group of devotees, which extended to this side of the Atlantic and especially to Argentina, it can be said that all the intellectual youth of the Spanish-speaking world came at one time or another under his spell. As director of *Revista de Occidente* and of several collections of the publishing house Espasa-Calpe, he made known in Spanish translation an impressive list of books representing the highest attainment of modern European culture, particularly of German thought. For this as well as for his original work, Ernst Curtius could say he was "one of the twelve peers of European intellect."

Ortega has embodied more, perhaps, than any other writer of our time the contemporary spirit. The object of his varied meditations has been the 20th-century scene in all its aspects. He has been a "spectator"—a word he chose as the title of several volumes of essays (*El espectador,* 8 vols., 1916–1934). As such, he defined his mental attitude as that of contemplating things with *amor intellectualis,* trying to find "in a fact, a man, a book, a painting, a landscape, an error, a sorrow . . . the plenitude of its meaning." There is scarcely any important subject of our time that he has not commented upon. He has endeavored to interpret with the same interest and ease the significance of a passing social fashion, the Castilian landscape, the formation and nature of the modern state, the conception of Hegel's philosophy of history, the meaning of time and form in the art of Proust (*q.v.*). Some of his major works contain highly original and controversial ideas which have had great influence and have also provoked sharp reactions against his thought. Such are *España invertebrada* (1922; Eng. tr., *Invertebrate Spain,* 1937), an interpretation of the decadence and anarchy of Spain as owing to the lack of a leading élite (for him, history, as thought and art, is always shaped by selected minorities); *La deshumanización del arte* (1925), an explanation and an implied defense of antirealism in contemporary art; and *La rebelión de las masas* (1930; Eng. tr., *The Revolt of the Masses,* 1932), his most widely read book, in which he explains the modern state of society as an inversion of values due to a crisis in European culture and to the preponderance of a mass mind.

He attempted mainly to systematize his purely philosophical thought in *El tema de nuestro tiempo* (1923; Eng. tr., *The Modern Theme,* 1931), propounding a philosophy based on life itself. The being is conceived as a multiplicity of values which we apprehend through a variety of "perspectives." To the pure reason of idealism he opposes a "vital reason," a logos which is constantly affected by the vital and historical circumstances of life. But he rejects utterly any idea of determinism. The individual, rather than follow circumstances blindly, modifies them in a constant interplay, and life becomes a *quehacer* and a creation, a plurality of tasks that we freely undertake. His thought has a close relation to that of the contemporary German thinkers Dilthey and Scheller and the existentialists. But, on the other hand, it seems to be rooted in a deep Spanish individualism for which man is the supreme reality and the only subject of life and history. To Ortega's thought and influence is added his extraordinary value as a pure writer. In precision, richness, and elegance his style stands out as a model of modern Spanish prose.

See: M. G. Morente, "El tema de nuestro tiempo (Filosofía de la perspectiva)," *Revista de Occidente,* I (1923), 201–217; E. R. Curtius, "Spanische Perspektiven," *Die neue Rundschau,* Jahrgang XXXV (1929), Bd. II, pp. 1229–1248; C. Barja, *Literatura española: Libros y autores contemporáneos* (1935), pp. 98–263; H. L. Nostrand, "Introduction," in Ortega y Gasset, *Mission of the University* (1944), pp. 1–31.

A. del R.

Orzeszkowa, Eliza (née Elżbieta Pawłowska, 1841–1910, Polish feminist and novelist), was born on the family estate at Milkowce near Grodno, Lithuanian Poland, the daughter of a wealthy and cultured country gentleman. Her father died when she was two, and she was brought up by a cold and frivolous mother. She studied for five years (1852–1857) at the famous Convent of the Sisters of the Sacrament in Warsaw—Konopnicka (*q.v.*) was also there at the same time—and then returned to Litwa to marry, at the age of 16, a landowner of Kobryń district in Polesie by the name of Peter Orzeszko. During the conspiratorial period that preceded the uprising of 1863, Orzeszkowa agitated for the national cause among her neighbors in Kobryń district and later, during the uprising, gave invaluable help, it is said, to Romuałd Traugutt, one of its leaders. When her husband was exiled to Siberia after the uprising, Orzeszkowa returned to her native Litwa and proceeded to shock the county population by getting a divorce. She was banished from polite society on this account and in Grodno, to which she moved, became known as a new George Sand.

In 1886 Orzeszkowa began to find the outlet her strong emotional nature needed, with the acceptance of her tales of Lithuanian village life by the Warsaw *Tygodnik ilustrowany* (Illustrated Weekly), a journal more friendly to women than most. Gradually, after this, Orzeszkowa's reputation underwent a change, and soon she was known everywhere as "the Good Lady of Grodno." Of her many works, the most significant were the revolutionary *Meir Ezofowicz* (1878; Eng. tr., 1898), a sympathetic delineation of the struggles of a young Jew to escape from the darkness and superstition of the ghetto, and the prose poem *Nad Niemnem* (1889; Along the Niemen), a picture of Polish-Lithuanian society under Russia notable especially for its descriptions of the Niemen landscape.

A passionate partisan of the peasant, Orzeszkowa strove with all her might to assist him in his struggle for emancipation. To make reading matter available at a cost the peasant could pay, she opened her own publishing house in Wilno, but was blocked in her generous purposes by the ill will of her own class, functioning through the Russian censorship. Orzeszkowa was a true pioneer, both as a champion of woman's right to self-expression outside the home (see her *Kilka słów o kobietach,* 1871, A Few Words about Women) and as a realist in the writing of fiction. She is one of the most interesting and original figures in Polish literature.

See: G. Korbut, *Literatura polska* (1931), IV, 122–126; I. Krzywicka, "Młoda Orzeszkowa," *Wiadomości literackie,* 1936, Nos. 53–54, and "O ciężkiej starości w Polsce," *ibid.,* 1937, Nos. 11, 26; introductions to the collected edition of her works, *Pisma,* 1937–1939.

A. P. C.

Osorgin, Mikhail Andreyevich (pseud. of Mikhail Andreyevich Ilyin, 1878–1942, Russian novelist and journalist), was born at Perm. Long before he took his degree in law at the University of Moscow (1902), he became a frequent contributor to newspapers and magazines. After the abortive Revolution of 1905, he went abroad, but continued to publish in Russia. Among his early works, his studies on Italy attracted attention. A period in Russia (1916–1921) proved unproductive, but during his second and last exile he wrote many remarkable *feuilletons* for the *émigré* newspapers and produced a number of novels, dealing mainly with the Russia he once knew. His best work is *Sivtsev Vrazhek* (1928; Eng. tr., *Quiet Street,* 1930), a novel of gentle people involved in the turmoil of the Revolution of 1917. *Povest o sestre* (1930; Eng. tr., *My Sister's Story,* 1931) is a record of unfulfilled love. In *Svidetel istorii* (1932; The Onlooker of History) and its sequel, *Kniga o kontsakh* (1935; The Book about Ends), Osorgin shows keen sympathy for the early revolutionaries, though he probably identified himself with Father Yakov, the homeless wanderer who loves his land and people. *Volny Kamenshchik* (1937; The Freemason) is about another humble idealist and, like all of Osorgin's work, bears the imprint of a humanitarian and somewhat anarchic spirit.

See: "Osorgin," in *Entsiklopediya "Granat,"* Vol. XI (1912), appendix, p. 681.

P. A. P.

Ossendowski, Ferdynand Antoni (1876–, Polish scientist, traveler, and writer), was born in Vitebsk, of old Polish stock. In 1899, after having studied at the University of St. Petersburg, he made his first trip to Siberia and the Far East, described in *W ludzkiej i leśnej kniei* (1923; Eng. tr., *Man and Mystery in Asia,* 1924). After receiving his doctorate in Paris, he taught chemistry and physics at Tomsk until 1903, when he returned to Eastern Siberia. In *Od szczytu do otchłani* (1924; Eng. tr., *From President to Prison,* 1925) he has recorded his experiences as, successively, chemical expert to the Russian general staff during the Russo-Japanese War, president of a short-lived "Revolutionary Government of the Russian Far East," and political prisoner under the tsarist reaction. On regaining his freedom, he returned to St. Petersburg, where, amidst other work, he served as consulting chemist to the navy until 1917. From 1918 to 1920 he taught chemistry at Omsk, being associated at the same time with the government of Admiral Kolchak. After his escape from the Bolsheviks through Mongolia, described in *Przez kraj zwierząt, ludzi i bogów* (1922; Eng. tr., *Beasts, Men, and Gods,* 1922), he took up residence in Warsaw, where he resumed teaching. He has since traveled extensively, particularly in northern Africa, about which he has written several volumes, among them *Pod smaganiem samumu* (1925; Eng. tr., *The Breath of the Desert,* American title, *Oasis and Simoon,* both 1927), *Płomienna połnoc* (1926; Eng. tr., *The Fire of Desert Folk,* 1926), and *Niewolnicy słońca* (1927; Eng. tr., *Slaves of the Sun,* 1928). Although best known for his books of travel, which have been extensively translated, he has produced many other works, including biographies, plays, novels, and scientific articles.

Ossendowski has described himself as "a writer, wanderer, and weaver of romances," and, against accusations of inaccuracy, he has asserted the traveler's right to be more concerned with his own subjective impressions than with factual detail. His interest in the occult and in local anecdotes and legends gives added color to his memoirs. His political views reflect a deep fear of Bolshevism and Islam and a strong belief that it is the prescribed duty of the "Aryan race" in Europe to lead the less fortunate peoples of the earth to freedom and peace in universal brotherhood.

See: Sven Hedin, *Ossendowski und die Wahrheit* (1925).

F. J. W.

Ossiannilsson, Karl Gustaf (1875–, Swedish poet, novelist, and dramatist), was born at Lund in the south of Sweden, and studied at the University of Lund. He soon became the literary leader of the Socialist Party and was active in the cause of the Allies in the First World War. Though he wrote drama and prose fiction, it is as a lyric poet that he has won his chief recognition, with such volumes as *Örnar* (1902; Eagles) and *Orchester* (1907; The Orchestra). Like Kipling he used repetition effectively, though not the refrain. Sir Edmund Gosse admired his "virile violence in invective." He is fond too, as Sir Edmund's phrase might suggest, of an almost Swinburnian alliteration. He did in fact translate Swinburne and Browning.

Ossiannilsson has been more than a narrow party man; he sees his cause in a perspective of history. One of his most cherished ideas was that the tyrant, in arousing masses to opposition and concentrating their wills, was an involuntary friend of liberty, and Ossiannilsson's best-known poem is "Bismarck." Almost equally memorable is the more smoothly flowing "Pompeii," which begins with a description but develops into a symbol of the idle aristocracy in all ages, careless and secure, while the lava of popular unrest is rising in the crater above them. Ossiannilsson loves the northern winter that is death to the parasites' cowardice and presumption. He has a poem about a woman millworker that is like a modern "Song of the Shirt," and a locomotive lyric that is deafening in its blast and clash, yet he catches equally well the subtle moods of nature's repose, and he has written a delectable drinking song in praise of—water.

See: K. Warburg, *Svensk litteraturhistoria i sammandrag* (1911); C. W. Stork, *Anthology of Swedish Lyrics* (1917; revised and enlarged ed., 1930); E. Gosse and W. A. Craigie, eds., *The Oxford Book of Scandinavian Verse* (1925).

C. W. S.

Ossorgin, Mikhail Andreyevich, *see* Osorgin.

Ostayen, Paul van (1896–1928, Flemish poet and essayist), was born in Antwerp and died in Miavoye-Anhée. He is the most significant experimental poet that Dutch and Flemish literature has had for many years. In three books of poetry, *Music Hall* (1916), *Het Sienjaal* (1918; The Signal), and *Bezette Stad* (1921; The City Occupied), he introduced free verse wherein he combined a great devotion to the political and social problems of his time with an atmosphere of classical and purely aesthetic ivory-tower writing. Abandoning the social themes and his function of political seer and prophet in the manner of Whitman, he then turned to dadaism and finally to "pure poetry." In this last vein he composed poems of great purity and extremely refined musical construction (*Het eerste Boek van Schmoll,* 1929; The First Book of Schmoll). He wrote a number of short stories which are mere intellectual acrobatics, impertinent and witty. They are composed with verbal ingeniousness and constitute powerful antidotes to the bombast and romanticism which are traditional ailments of Flemish literature. As an explorer of literary "realms unknown," his influence was considerable both in Flanders and in Holland. His critical work is extremely personal in tone and phrased in rather abstruse language.

See: G. Burssens, *Paul van Ostayen* (1935).

J.-A. G.

Österling, Anders (1884–, Swedish poet and critic), made his mark as a lyric poet at an early age. When he was scarcely 20, he made a brilliant debut with a volume entitled *Preludier* (Preludes), and during the next three years he added *Offerkransar* (1905; Votive Crowns) and *Hälsningar* (1907; Greetings). Early elected to the Swedish Academy, he became its permanent secretary upon the death of Karlfeldt (*q.v.*) in 1931. His earliest volumes of poetry revealed a sensitive, precociously gifted young poet, filled with infinite longings and an infinite melancholy, and giving expression to his feelings in poems that reflect a marvelous technical virtuosity for one so young. That which he longs for is the ineffable spirit of beauty—beauty with a capital B, the beauty which to the tradition of symbolistic poetry on the Continent was the one source and only aim of the pure poetic mind. Certain things in Ruskin, in the Pre-Raphaelite painting and poetry, and in the verse of Stéphane Mallarmé, Stefan George, and in the early Richard Dehmel (*qq.v.*) were among the chief formative influences in Österling's earliest poetry; while at home, in the example of two contemporaneous poets of Skåne, Ola Hansson and Vilhelm Ekelund (*qq.v.*), he found immediate native models in a sensitive, finely nuanced, and more than a little precious poetic manner. The delicate, subtly varied musical tonalities and the fragile, floating, half-evasive imagery of Continental symbolists was, however, largely an early passing phase in Österling's poetic development. In *Årets visor*

(1907; The Year's Songs) one observes a definite break with the symbolist tradition in poetry. This break is confirmed in *Blommande träd* (1910; Blossoming Trees), is given further and more significant expression in *Idyllernas bok* (1917; Book of the Idylls) and *De sju strängarna* (1922; The Seven Strings), and comes to find a rich, mature, and finally authoritative expression in *Jordens heder* (1927; The Honor of the Earth) and *Tonen från havet* (1933; Tones from the Sea). During all of these years Österling has been occupied also with a rather prolific critical production as literary and theatrical editor of various Stockholm newspapers. Selections from the best of the critical sketches and essays have appeared from time to time in book form under such titles as *Människor och landskap* (1910; Men and Provinces), *Tidsstämningar* (1916; Time Tones), *Dagens gärning* (3 vols., 1921–1931; The Day's Work), and *Tio års teater, 1925–1935* (1936; Ten Years of the Theatre 1925–1935). Österling has also been among the most assiduous and sensitive of Swedish translators of foreign poetry, German, French, and English.

The line of development in Österling's poetry to be noted clearly for the first time in *Årets visor* as early as 1907 is in the direction of a new poetic realism—a realism that involves in its choice of subject matter a return to life and to the soil, and in its form a simple, direct, concrete imagery and word choice. Among Österling's new masters were Francis Jammes (*q.v.*) in France, and, more important, a number of early 20th-century Danish poets; but the chief individual foreign influence on the Swedish poet was unquestionably Wordsworth, whom he came to know early and has translated with a remarkably sensitive feeling for the English poet's essential poetic qualities. It is the quiet, serene, meditative strain in Wordsworth, together with the English poet's interest in common man and his preference for the language of everyday life, that appealed so strongly to Österling's sensitive, restrained poetic temperament. Österling comes to bring this spirit and manner to bear with richly satisfactory results upon the folk life and upon the landscape of his native province of Skåne, effecting, in his best poems, a happy compromise between the half-symbolistic tradition in the contemporaneous poetic tradition in Skåne and the more purely meditative, philosophical manner of Wordsworth. Certain post First World War critics in Sweden have accused Österling of practicing an evasive idyllicism in times which call for poetry of a sterner spirit; but he has gone his own way, as neither reactionary nor revolutionary, quietly meeting the challenge of a changing pattern of life with no fundamental change in point of view or in poetic manner. He, like Wordsworth, feels that true poetic genius draws inspiration from sources beyond those postulated by man's latest fad in thinking or history's most recent phase of development.

See: F. Böök, *Resa kring svenska Parnassen* (1926); A. Gustafson, *Österling's "Arrival" as Landskapsdiktare: from Årets visor (1907) to Blommande träd (1910)* (1938).

A. G.

Ostrovsky, Nikolai Alekseyevich (1904–1937, Russian novelist), has been virtually canonized by Soviet criticism, as much for his extraordinary human accomplishment as for his literary achievement. He lived and died heroically, an example of idealistic youth challenging all obstacles, and his work is ranked among the classics of Soviet literature. Born of a laborer's family in the town of Shepetovka, Volyn (Ukraine), he received only a primary education. At 12 he became a kitchen boy, and then a fireman in an electric station. At 17 he fought in the civil wars in the Western Ukraine. Later a shock-brigade leader, a military commissar, and a regional director of the Young Communists, he lost his health in 1927 when progressive paralysis set in, followed by total blindness. Bedridden, often in agonizing pain, subjected to many operations, he nevertheless resolved (1930) to continue serving the Revolution through writing. The manuscript of his first work was lost in the mails. The second, a novel of the civil wars, *Kak zakalyalas stal* (1936; Eng. tr., *The Making of a Hero,* 1937), won instant recognition as a dramatic and authentic account of the Young Communists of the early Revolution who were, like steel, "forged and hardened" by war, famine, and epidemics. The experiences of Paul Korchagin, the chief character, are largely those of the author. The book sold more than 1,600,000 copies in its first year. *Rozhdyonie burey* (1937; Eng. tr., *Born of the Storm,* 1939), another politico-autobiography, the first half of an uncompleted novel, appeared on the day of his funeral. Dedicated to the struggle of the Ukrainian peasants and proletariat against the Polish lords and the German army of occupation, its main theme is the typical hero of the Revolution. Its last chapters, the personal epic of a man who struggles for his regeneration, attain true moral greatness.

Ostrovsky's narrative power, his skill in creating a vividly realistic background and in handling an intricate plot, are considerable, though his characterizations tend to oversimplification on both national and class lines and his style suffers from clichés. His burning conviction, however, and his heroic will to accomplishment, which for years sustained a ravaged body, offset such faults and lead one to believe his talent would have greatly ripened. He was decorated (1935) with the Order of Lenin. André Gide (*q.v.*) paid him a singular tribute in his *Retour de l'U.R.S.S.*

See: Ostrovsky, *Rechi, stati, i pisma* (1937); M. Serebryanin, "Nikolai Ostrovsky," in Ostrovsky, *Kak zakalyalas stal, Rozhdyonie burey* (1937), pp. 445–460.

N. S.

Överland, Arnulf (1889–, Norwegian poet), has for more than a decade been devoted to the ideal of "forging a sword," *i.e.*, of making his poetry into a social weapon. There was no sign of this ideal in his earliest verse, which appeared in such choice collections as *Den ensomme fest* (1911; The Lonely Feast), *De hundrede violiner* (1912; The Hundred Violins), and *Advent* (1915). These were in the tragic mood of Obstfelder (*q.v.*), but with a tense, compressed power which was unknown to the poets of the 90's. He wrote of his lonely heart, bitterly crying out against the vanity of all things, devoted to the dream which alone satisfies. The poems were acclaimed by critics for their fastidious restraint of form, their elimination of all rhetoric, and their truly monumental use of simple, unadorned words. These qualities have remained characteristic of his verse, which is pale in coloration, with a glint of steel, yet passionately moving because of the angry fire in the poet's heart. That fire was kindled by the First World War and the peace of Versailles, which belied his poetic belief of 1915 that to him "there was nothing more that could happen." He awoke to the existence of social injustice, and it made him cry out in *Brød og vin* (1919; Bread and Wine) that "there are dearer things than life. You shall fight for them!" He turned from the cultivation of his own soul and plunged into contemporary life as a rather obstreperous battler on the extreme left. The collections *Berget det blå* (1927; Blue Mountain), *Hustavler* (1929; Laws of Living), and *Jeg besverger dig* (1934; I Conjure Thee) are not one-sidedly social, for there is love and beauty in them too, but they display a growing faith in the mystic value of sharing life with one's fellow men. This religious devotion to the ideal of socialism became a substitute for the Christianity against which he turned all his acid scorn, using repeatedly its own vocabulary and form, even to the extent of creating a socialistic ritual in the recently published book, *Ord i alvor til det norske folk* (1940; Words in Earnest to the Norwegian People). Many of his poems implied for himself a suffering to come, a crucifixion: "This is my body . . . nailed to the tree of passion; eat, ravens!" Prophetic also was his cry in the poem "Opbrudd" (Breaking Up) of 1934: "Harsh times will come, when each man bears a sword." He quickly found his leading adversary in Hitler, and his poems in *Den røde front* (1937; The Red Front), bearing such flaming titles as "Spain 1936," "Guernica," and "You Must Not Sleep!" were challenges intended to awaken his countrymen to the menace of Nazism. When the German horde actually did invade Norway in 1940, Överland's moment of passion had come. He wrote a series of poems which were anonymously and privately circulated; these became in his countrymen's hands the swords he intended them to be. Such poems as "We Shall Live through All," "They Came as Friends," "Blacked-out Town," "To the Fallen," "Our Men," and "To the King" (since the war's end collected and published in a volume entitled *Vi overlever alt,* 1945, We Shall Live through All) established the pattern of Norwegian resistance, by virtue of the simple but powerful poetic form in which they couched the demand for national integrity. Överland paid for these poems in a German concentration camp, thus giving substance to his own line of 1929: "Words that cost something may long survive." In May, 1945, came his liberation; he has now moved into the Grotto, the old home of Norway's greatest poet, Henrik Wergeland, as the honored guest of the Norwegian state.

See: H. Naeseth, tr., in *American-Scandinavian Review,* XXIX (1941), 331–332; C. W. Stork, *Anthology of Norwegian Lyrics* (1942); E. Haugen, tr., in *American-Scandinavian Review,* XXXI (1943), 5–7; H. Krog, *Nordmannsforbundets Julehefte* (1943).

E. H.

P

Pagnol, Marcel (1895–, French writer and cinema specialist), was born at Aubagne near Marseille. Destined for a career of teaching, he was professor of English in various *lycées* and *collèges* in southern France before being called to the Lycée Condorcet in Paris in 1922. Even in his youth he had shown a marked tendency for creative literary production. During his professorial days in the South of France he edited a literary revue, *Fantasio* (which later became the *Cahiers du sud*), and a theatrical sheet, the *Spectator,* and wrote a pseudoclassical play in verse, *Catulle* (1922), as well as several minor works of small importance. Shortly after his arrival in Paris he deserted the teaching profession in order to throw himself wholly into writing for the stage. In collaboration with Arno Brun he produced the play *Ulysse chez les Phéniciens* (1925). The same year appeared his very successful play, *Les Marchands de gloire,* written in collaboration with Nivoix. In 1926 he produced *Jazz,* and in 1928 the play that brought him especial renown, *Topaze* (presented in New York in English in 1930, English film 1933). His Marseillais trilogy, *Marius* (1929), *Fanny* (1931), and *César* (1936), contributed to the enhancement of his reputation. He also wrote two short novels, *Pirouettes* (1932) and *La Petite Fille aux yeux sombres* (1933). About 1930 he became interested in the possibilities of the cinema and proceeded to the founding of two companies under his direction, one to write and produce moving pictures and the other to market them. He also established a magazine, *Cahiers du film,* which served as a vehicle for the expounding of his cinematographic theories. At the same time he was producing several films, largely adapted from the legitimate stage.

It is in the *Cahiers du film* that are found his theories on the function and art of the cinema. He felt that the sound film represented a new artistic medium and wished to elevate it to the dignity of a separate literary genre which might, in fact, supersede the legitimate stage, and he sought to establish the literary canons for its guidance and development. These canons consist largely of the adaptation of the rules of the French classical theatre to the greater freedom and scenic possibilities of the screen. In 1935 he produced *Merlusse* as an illustration of his cinematographic theories.

See: A. G. Bovée, ed., *Topaze* (1936), pp. ii–iv; Louis Combaluzier, *Le Jardin de Pagnol* (1937); L. G. Moffatt, ed., *Merlusse* (1937), pp. ix–xvi.

L. G. M.

Pailleron, Edouard (1834–1899, French dramatist), the son of wealthy merchants and son-in-law of François Buloz, director of the *Revue des deux mondes,* was a typical Parisian *grand bourgeois* whose fortune allowed him to satisfy a taste for fashionable living and literary endeavor. His dramatic career ran smoothly to the climactic success of *Le Monde où l'on s'ennuie* (1881) and his subsequent election to the French Academy.

Pailleron's works reflect the qualities and limitations of his education and milieu. A conservative at heart, he scorns romanticism as a social disease and extols laughter as a means of self-defense against the disintegration of moral and cultural values (see his "Ode au rire," 1859). As a man of the world, however, he learned how to use his weapons lightly and gingerly. With the exception of some early plays, heavily moralizing and poetized after the manner of Emile Augier (*Les Faux Ménages,* 1869; *Hélène,* 1872), his theatre is remarkable for its witty dialogue and clever characterization (*Le Monde où l'on s'amuse,* 1868; *L'Age ingrat,* 1878; *L'Etincelle,* 1879; *Cabotins,* 1894). *Le Monde où l'on s'ennuie,* his masterpiece, could easily be baptized a social play, a modern replica of Molière's *Les Femmes savantes* as well as a denunciation of the newborn aristocracy of the Third Republic, dull, vulgar, noisy, and self-seeking. Far better justice is done by considering it a superior comedy of intrigue, with just the right mixture of the ironic and the sentimental, a perfect example of Parisian good taste and Gallic sprightliness.

See: Hippolyte Parigot, *Le Théâtre d'hier* (1893), pp. 243–290; Alessandro Lalia-Paternostro, *Edouard Pailleron* (1931).

J.-A. B.

Palacio Valdés, Armando (1853–1938, Spanish novelist, short-story writer, and critic), was born at Entralgo in Asturias, but he passed his youth mostly in neighboring Avilés, where the family took up residence in 1854. After completing his elementary schooling he entered the *instituto* at Oviedo. In 1870 he enrolled in the law school at the University of Madrid. Excelling in philosophy and political science, in which he was more interested than in law, at one time he looked forward to teaching philosophy as a career, but with the encouragement and aid of friends he was attracted to writing and made his début as literary critic and editor. He soon distinguished himself with three series of sketches of Spanish orators, novelists, and poets (*Los oradores del Ateneo,* 1878; *Los novelistas españoles,* 1878; *Nuevo viaje al Parnaso,* 1879). *La literatura en 1881* (1882), a volume he wrote in collaboration with Leopoldo Alas (*q.v.*), was his last critical work. These works contributed more to the crystallization of Palacio's aesthetic concepts than to the development of Spanish literary criticism.

Except for the premature death of his first wife and the loss of his only son, Palacio enjoyed a serene and uneventful life characterized by economic comfort almost unknown among Spanish literary men. His unparalleled popularity abroad—he is the most widely translated modern Spanish novelist—added greatly to the placidity and optimism which permeate most of his works. His relations with other writers were as pleasant as his contacts with life. Few admired him, many esteemed him, and some even appraised him flatteringly. He received many honors at home and abroad. In 1906 he was elected to membership in the Royal Spanish Academy of Language, and in 1917 he was admitted to the Legion of Honor. In the English-speaking world he was regarded as the "dean of Spanish novelists," and he appreciated this admiration as deeply as the enthusiasm of his French devotees who were frequently attracted to his chalet on Cap-Breton.

The essence of Palacio's art may be derived from his own novelistic formula. Free from profound spiritual preoccupations or transcendental aims, he finds his themes and characters in the ordinary ebb and flow of life, which he mirrors with spontaneity and facility. He changes his mood and shifts his view with slight effort, achieving variety at the expense of complexity. His settings are drawn from several regions of Spain, and his choice between city and country is largely capricious. Similarly impulsive would seem to be his unstable attachments to regionalism, naturalism, and idealism. In the matter of following literary fashions Palacio frequently ignored his own injunction against such practice. *Marta y María* (1883; Eng. tr., *The Marquis of Peñalta,* 1886) reflects the concern with religion so prominent in Spanish fiction of the 70's; *La espuma* (1891; Eng. tr., *Froth,* 1891) and *La fe* (1892; Eng. tr., *Faith,* 1892) are naturalistic in a restricted sense of the term; *La Hermana San Sulpicio* (1889; Eng. tr., *Sister Saint Sulpice,* 1890) and *La aldea perdida* (1903) belong to a group of regionalistic novels. However, in preferring to imitate a wisely chosen model rather than striving for originality of doubtful significance, Palacio was more faithful to his own creed. The absence of a strong uniform accent in his art is perhaps due to the fact that he was easily attracted to the sharper tones of his contemporaries. Only once was he able to free himself from artistic opportunism: *La aldea perdida* is a work of genuine inspiration and perhaps the only one in which the author extends his gaze beyond the usual domestic horizon. In the clash between rural life and industrial civilization there is a touch of epic grandeur, and the vigorous conception of the theme overshadows the manipulated characters and the mannered style which is a queer compound of roguishness, banter, euphemism, and transparent humor.

Palacio discovered his stride early and throughout the half century of his career, which was caught between two divergent literary generations, he rarely altered it. He is ever leisurely and diffuse in plot movement, lingering fondly on the episodic and winding pleasantly in the alleys and byways of life. The human beings of his world, which comes close to being the best of possible worlds, are simple, familiar folk whose inner life is as readily comprehensible as their outward behavior is conventional. They cause the author no anxiety, nor do they stir the reader. They are an ingratiating lot capable of transmitting to others their feeling of well-being. They are kindly creatures who offer everyone the hospitality of their restful homes in which pink and pastel shades predominate.

Palacio's impressive success is no surprising phenomenon. Spaniard or foreigner, no reader could fail to derive pleasure or profit from the novels of an author who once (1917) made the following confession: "If I were despoiled of that which belongs to the great masters who have gone before me, I should stand denuded. There is, however, something of which no one in this world can despoil me—the sweet satisfaction of knowing that some of my pages have brought smiles to the lips and others tears of tenderness to the eyes, the comforting certainty that no one has come away from the reading of my novels less pure and less noble than he was." In the light of this confession—which is a bit of sincere autocriticism—the rising literary generations of Spain have been excessively hostile in completely discarding Palacio Valdés.

See: H. Peseux-Richard, "Armando Palacio Valdés," *Revue hispanique,* XLII (1918), 305–480; A. Cruz Rueda, *Armando Palacio Valdés; estudio biográfico* (1925); J. A. Balseiro, *Novelistas españoles modernos* (1933), pp. 382–443.

H. C. B.

Palamas, Kostes (1859–1943, Greek poet), was born in Patras and educated at Missolonghi. He studied at the University of Athens, of which he later became the secretary. He held that post for many years, although efforts were made to oust him at the time of the linguistic riots started by students in 1901 who protested against the translation of the New Testament into the demotic speech. He first began to use the "pure" language (*see* Greek literature), but then turned to the demotic speech, which he brought to the highest stage of its poetical development. With a thorough knowledge of world literature, he welcomed and adapted in modern Greek such various authors as Leconte de Lisle (*q.v.*), Schopenhauer, and Verhaeren (*q.v.*). At the same time he never lost his sense of the continuity of his own Greek literature and life from their earliest days. His first important work in the demotic speech, *Tragoudia tes patridos mou* (1886; Songs of My Fatherland), expresses his aspirations; in the introduction to the *Hymnos sten Athenan* (1889; Hymn to Athena) he asserts categorically the duty of the poet to be a leader of his people. Palamas is far more a philosophical and intellectual poet than he is a pure lyricist, although he can feel deeply, as in *Taphos* (1898; The Tomb), the lament of a father for the death of his favorite child. His most impersonal work is the *Assalephti zoi* (1904, Life Unshakable; Eng. tr. of first part, *Life Immovable,* 1919, of second part, incomplete, *A Hundred Voices and Other Poems,* 1921) in which he glorifies Patras, Missolonghi, Athens, and the eternal qualities of Greece. In such poems as the *Dodekalogos tou Yiphtou* (1907; The Twelve Speeches of the Gypsy) and the *Phlogera tou vasilia* (1910; The Flute of the King) he brings before us the whole pageant of Greek and Byzantine history in the tone of a Byzantine hymn. Elsewhere in the *Dekatetrasticha* (1919; Fourteen Verses) and in his lyric drama *Triseryene* (1903) he again gives the spirit of Greece in its universal aspects. A careful craftsman, protean in his interests, Palamas, more than any other modern Greek writer, embodies the spirit, the aspirations, and the dreams, as well as the enduring sense of the past, of his nation.

See: A. E. Phoutrides, "A New World-Poet," in Palamas, *Life Immovable* (1919); A. Kampanes, *Istoria tes neas ellenikes logotechnias* (1933), pp. 214–239.

C. A. M.

Palazzeschi, Aldo (1885–, Italian poet and novelist), was born in Florence. Manifesting in early youth a pronounced predilection for letters, he soon became an active defender of the futuristic school of poetry which was in vogue in Italy during the years 1908 and 1909 and brought out his first volume of poems, a collection entitled *L'Incendiario,* of which the publisher, Cesare Blanc, was none other than his pet cat. These early poems contained a simplicity and freshness of lyrical inspiration that were bound to attract new readers, even though some found it difficult to distinguish the meaning of such compositions as "Ara mara amara," "Il Segno," "Oro doro odoro dodoro." Yet poems like "Rio Bo," "Chi sono?", "Lo Specchio," "La Fontana malata," "Lasciatemi divertire," revealed a charming delicacy of pathos and a delightful melancholy sweetness, expressed in a style fantastic and almost childlike. The poems also revealed the mischievous, impish, and playful traits of a literary youngster throwing stones at poetic windows.

Palazzeschi's attachment to futurism did not last long. His publications subsequent to *L'Incendiario* show a marked tendency to be independent of any school of literary thought. *Il Codice di Perelà* (1911; English adaptation, *Perelà, The Man of Smoke,* 1936) is the story of a man made of smoke and is considered among the most fantastic and entertaining novels published in Italy in the last 50 years. Here we find Palazzeschi in a gay, mischievous mood, seemingly enjoying the sight of human beings battling the incongruities and impenetrable paradoxes of life. Society for Palazzeschi assumes the character of a three-ringed circus. Like the youngster attending his first performance he laughs heartily at the antics of the clowns before him. His most hearty chuckles are elicited by the somersaults of critics and poets and the tightrope walking of philosophers. Palazzeschi's laughter is interrupted only when he realizes what a ridiculous figure he too has been cutting. Then there is one more hearty laugh, but this time it is at himself. A reviewer of the English version of *Perelà* has called it "an Italian parable of human folly; an Italian version of Gulliver standing on its head."

Since the appearance of *Perelà*, Palazzeschi's most noteworthy publications are *Stampe dell'ottocento* (1932) and *Sorelle Materassi* (1934). The former is autobiographical; the author depicts in colorful nostalgic tones the humorous scenes of his early Florentine childhood. *Sorelle Materassi* contains the same ironic, humorous vein—this time about the world of old maids. The sketches are developed by a more deliberate and mature hand. Critics in Italy have hailed these two novels as among the outstanding achievements of contemporary Italian letters.

See: C. Pellizzi, *Le Lettere italiane del nostro secolo* (1929), pp. 230–234; P. Pancrazi, *Scrittori italiani del novecento,* (1934), pp. 141–147.

P. M. R.

Panferov, Fyodor (1896–, Russian novelist), was born in Central Russia, of a poor peasant family. From early childhood he was compelled to earn his living, as a shepherd, a farm hand, a servant. After the Revolution of 1917 Panferov worked among the peasants as a Communist Party official. He started to write in 1922, but did not gain popularity until 1930 when the first two parts of his long novel *Brusski* (Eng. tr., *Brusski,* 1930; *And Then the Harvest,* 1939) were published. This was the first attempt made in Soviet literature to picture the struggle between the new and the old mode of life in a Russian village. The first and the second parts of *Brusski* have had numerous editions, but the third part (1933), describing the triumph of collectivization in a rhetorical and pompous way, did not appeal to readers. The factual material offered by Panferov was interesting and revealing and it had an undoubtedly large social significance, but the poor organization of the work and the primitiveness of the artistic devices provoked sharp criticism, especially from Gorky (*q.v.*). In 1942 Panferov published a series of short stories on war (*Tyazhelaya ruka,* The Heavy Arm); his book on the industrial effort in the Urals (*Na Urale,* The People of the Urals) appeared in 1943. Panferov's latest work shows that he has followed Gorky's advice and paid more attention to style and literary craftsmanship.

M. S.

Panzacchi, Enrico (1840–1904, Italian poet and critic), was born at Ozzano, near Bologna. He studied at the University of Bologna, and at the University of Pisa where he was taught by two now famous authorities on Italian literature, Pasquale Villari and Alessandro D'Ancona. Panzacchi began his poetical career at the age of 30 with a short volume of verses entitled *Funeralia* (1870). This was followed by *Piccolo Romanziere* (1872), which received the unconditional praises of Carducci (*q.v.*) and which established Panzacchi's fame as a poet. *Lyrica* (1877) had an immediate success. In 1881 appeared *Vecchio Ideale* which became a year later, with additions and minor corrections, *Racconti e liriche;* these poems were written at the height of his inspiration. A later volume is *Nuove Liriche* (1888), and a complete edition of Panzacchi's poetry with a preface by Giovanni Pascoli (*q.v.*) was published in 1908. Panzacchi also tried his hand at writing drama, but here he was a failure.

Panzacchi's poetry consists completely of rapid emotions, not harmonized, not given any lyric unity. He is ready on all occasions, not because of vanity or for mercenary reasons, but because poetry for him is one of the necessities and dignities of life, a noble vocation, an indispensable mode of expression. As lecturer and orator few surpassed him in eloquence.

See: E. Lamma, *Enrico Panzacchi* (1905); B. Croce, *La letteratura della nuova Italia,* 2d ed., II (1921), 119–125; G. Mazzoni, *L'Ottocento* (1934), pp. 1379–1380.

A. C. R.

Panzini, Alfredo (1863–1939), Italian author and teacher), was born in Senigallia, in the Marches, near his beloved Romagna. As a teacher his distaste for scholarly research and publication prevented him from ever getting more than a professorship in a secondary school. A born artist, he loved life far more than archives. In a period in which historical research, positivism, and socialism were in full swing, if it was not exactly a fault to write well, it certainly was no merit, even in university circles. Like Albertazzi and Severino Ferrari (*q.v.*), fellow disciples of Carducci (*q.v.*) with whom he had something in common, Panzini remained a teacher throughout his life, in and outside the classroom. Unlike them, however, he became, in his 50's, a favorite of the Italian ruling class, with its rather obvious hedonistic ideals in art, and also popular with the younger generation of critics, with its rather aristocratic, sophisticated standards. The ruling class and the unruly critics were for once in agreement. His case is a rare example of an outstanding writer ignored by his own generation and made famous by the very generation which delighted in removing the halo surrounding older writers.

His early works (*Libro dei morti,* 1893; *Inganni,* 1895; *Moglie nuova,* 1899; *Piccole Storie del mondo grande,* 1901) were conceived and published in the epoch dominated by Carducci, whose pupil Panzini was proud to acknowledge himself. These books of short stories show all the characteristics of the later Panzini, although at times hazily and clumsily. They were reprinted after Serra (*q.v.*) "discovered" Panzini in 1910 and enjoyed a success almost as great as that of his later works. Panzini's best, however, came at the time of Serra's "discovery," and the enthusiasm of the new generation, which welcomed him in its anthologies (Papini, *q.v.*, and Pancrazi included him in their classic *Poeti d'oggi,* published in 1910), doubtless gave more self-confidence to a man who was by nature rather uncertain, shy, and probably suffering from the public's failure to recognize his merits.

The charm of Panzini's personality is reflected in all his works, even in his dictionary (*Dizionario moderno,* 1906), textbooks, and anthologies. It is a personality impossible to curb or repress. The light plots of his novels (*Santippe,* 1914; *La Madonna di mamà* 1916), the flimsy intrigues of his short stories (*Le Fiabe della vita,* 1911), the kaleidoscopic sequences of his books of history or travel (*La Lanterna di Diogene,* 1907; *Viaggio di un giovane letterato,* 1919, but written in 1913–1914), are no more than springboards and deserve very little attention in an evaluation of his literary art.

Imagine a man of the classic age, fond of simple country life and natural feelings, chaste and moderate of speech, of noble and solemn deeds, revering truth, the family, and his country—imagine such a man risen from the dead in the modern world, hedonistic, money-mad, openly frivolous, sensualist in love, grossly materialistic in its social unrest, rebellious to natural order and tradition. In his simple, childlike heart he cannot but feel that his new contemporaries are wrong, although he cannot bring himself to condemn them. He does not like them, but he is attracted by them; they are impure and absurd—especially the women—but how charming! Like a child, he is slowly overcome with a feeling of wonder. Can it be that he is wrong, that he is a mere provincial, a weakling incapable of making the most of his opportunities? This contrast between the world of classic times, where Panzini has his roots, and the new industrial and materialistic world, wherein it was his lot to live, offers him a good opportunity to carry the reader's imagination with him to the other world and back again into this. Hence follows a style all sparkling with contrasts and ironies, with indecisions, pauses, and resumptions, with personal experiences, with interruptions for a lesson, or with witticisms interrupting a lesson. His easy enthusiasm, which has the cadence of poetry, is often disconnected and fragmentary (this fact endeared him to the *Voce* group, whose gospel was fragmentarism). He is incapable of handling and organizing a complex mass of material and, one may say, incapable of methodically thinking through to a cogent conclusion. Attracted by what glitters, but with a solid attachment for what is fundamental, he has more power of instinct than of reason. When in doubt, he tries to be evasive with a smile or a pleasantry, something for which Croce (*q.v.*) has caustically reproached him. But even this irate philosopher could not but acknowledge the happy moments of pure lyricism in Panzini's fluid and transparent prose. Generally these happy moments are melodious instants in his contemplation of nature, art, and men, idyllic and romantic in their intimate aspirations.

During the First World War, and even more so immediately after it, he was confronted with problems too baffling for him. Peace disappeared from his soul; his mild ironies became sarcasms (*Io cerco moglie,* 1920; Eng. tr., *Wanted—a Wife,* 1922; *Il diavolo nella mia libreria,* 1920; *Signorine,* 1921; *Il Mondo e rotondo,* 1921). His *Il Padrone sono me* (1922) is a frank and bitter expression of the fear of communism dominating the middle classes, which formed the backbone of Fascism in Italy. But the great bulk of his readers was attracted by other qualities of his: his biting ironies, his scathing malice, his veiled criticism of modern life. In his last books Panzini got into the habit of a style made up of contrasts—the so-called "humor" of Panzini which sometimes is rather a formula than a style.

When the crisis brought about by the war and Bolshevism was over in Italy, Panzini turned to recreating the past (*La Pulcella senze pulcellaggio,* 1925; *Tre Re, con Gelsomino buffone del re,* 1927; *Sventurata Irminda,* 1932; *Il Bacio di Lesbia,* 1937) and to the glory of this earth (*Giorni del sole e del grano,* 1929). In these pages there is more academic art and less originality and candor than in previous works. He was made a member of the Italian Academy, and one feels that he deserved this particular honor.

To complete the review of his work, other titles should be mentioned. He wrote two books on Cavour (*Il 1859; da Plombières a Villafranca,* 1909; *Il Conte di Cavour,* 1931) and *La Vera Istoria dei tre colori* (1924). Very gingerly, like a cat approaching water, he touched upon the Jewish question in *Viaggio con la giovane ebrea* (1935). He took up the defense of "noble" Boiardo against "servile" Ariosto (*M. Maria Boiardo,* 1918). Very popular and quite curiously so is the already noticed *Dizionario moderno* (7th ed., 1935), in which he collected for fun all the "garbage" of the current Italian language as it appeared in newspapers, and adding thereto contemporary slogans, slang words and expressions, borrowings from French and English—commenting upon them with caustic spirit, trying at the same time to correct and amend, but sometimes giving up in sheer disgust and helplessness at the violence of what to him were the outpourings of a sewer. He was personally esteemed and loved by many friends.

See: G. Prezzolini, *Amici* (1922) pp. 73–96; G. Mormino, *Alfredo Panzini nelle opere e nella vita* (1937); A. Bocelli, "Alfredo Panzini," *Italia che scrive,* XXII (1939), 95–96 (one of many commemorations of the death of Panzini).

G. P.

Papini, Giovanni (1881–, Italian writer and poet), was born in Florence of a lower-middle-class family; his father was a furniture maker with atheistic views and also an ardent patriot, his mother was a Catholic with simple tastes, devoted to her three children. Papini gives his own picture of his childhood in *Un Uomo finito* (1912; Eng. tr., *A Man—Finished,* American title, *The Failure,* both 1924). These very subjective memoirs show a restless, tormented, and ambitious boy with a devouring passion for information, seeking refuge from a dreary and hostile world in books of every description and in projects for writing an encyclopedia of all knowledge. His formal education completed, Papini became a teacher of Italian at the Anglo-Italian Institute of Santa Reparata (1902–1903) and also served as a library clerk at the Museum of Anthropology (1902–1904). Books lost some of their engrossing charm, and Papini began to crave friendships. With Giuseppe Prezzolini (*q.v.*), to whom Papini was attracted in terms of comradeship, intellectual curiosity, love of ideas, he felt an apostolic urge to lead his countrymen to the acquisition of more culture, more spiritual energy, and more nationalism. Papini believed the time had come for him to emerge from his lowly environment and assert his indomitable personality in the field of thought. With Prezzolini he founded a literary review, the *Leonardo* (1903–1907), which ushered in a nation-wide literary and philosophic renaissance. In politics he played the agitator and the reformer. He joined the ranks of the *Regno* (1903–1905), carrying over from the *Leonardo,* but with added violence, an antagonistic campaign against the Socialists. The articles by Papini and Prezzolini in the *Regno* are among the first documents to express the change that was taking place in the youth of Italy towards nationalism (*e.g., Vecchio e nuovo nazionalismo,* 1914). Papini then carried his restlessness, his gusto for novelty, for social approval, and for self-assertion into the realm of philosophy, proposing to sweep out traditional philosophies and freely pouring forth the bitterness of his own disillusions in *Crepuscolo dei filosofi* (1906). He turned to pragmatism, but this gradually tapered off for him into a strange mixture of vague theosophy, spiritualism, occultism, and mysticism. He wrote short stories where the dramatic torment of his philosophical thought and autobiographical reminiscences served as material for poetic expression: *Il Tragico quotidiano* (1906); *Il Pilota cieco* (1907; Eng. tr. of this and of *Il Tragico quotidiano, Life and Myself,* 1930); *Parole e sangue* (1912); *Buffonate* (1914). In the last two of these books he drifted away from his philosophic abstractions and leaned towards an imitation of Poe and Baudelaire (*q.v.*).

In 1907 Papini married Giacinta Giovagnoli, a peasant girl from Bulciano (Tuscany). He went to Milan where he had some dealings with the religious group known as *Modernista* and then withdrew to Bulciano, to the beauties of nature and the joys of family life, and read and meditated. Towards the end of 1908 Papini returned to Florence where he began to edit a philosophic collection of classics under the title of *Cultura dell'anima.* His most important activity of this period was related to the *Voce* movement (*see* Italian literature). His collaboration was varied: he composed for this periodical articles on political and educational reforms; religious and literary polemics; critical essays on Nietzsche, Count Leo Tolstoy (*qq.v.*), Poe, William James, Vailati, and others (collected in *24 Cervelli,* 1913; Eng. tr., *Four and Twenty Minds,* 1922). With Giovanni Amendola he founded a strictly philosophical monthly, the *Anima* (January–December, 1911). Most of Papini's contributions to the *Anima* were to become chapters of *L'Altra Metà* (1912); some critics have seen in the nihilism and pessimism of this book a first glimmer of Papini's future conversion to Catholicism. He had now reached a crisis in his mental turmoil. He poured out his bitterness against scholars and philosophers in a series of lampoons, satires, and demolitions later collected as *Stroncature* (1916). Then his tempo slowed down in the *Vita di nessuno* (1912). Finally, Papini passed into a lyrical dream, and the result was *Un Uomo finito.* This spiritual autobiography is the author's most complete expression of that belligerent self-assertion which strikes the keynote of his whole literary career.

In January, 1913, Papini, Soffici, Palazzeschi (*qq.v.*), and Tavolato founded a new review, *Lacerba* (1913–1915). This magazine opened its pages to a "futuristic" inundation, and later in 1914 it became an organ of tenacious political propaganda for Italy's intervention in the war on the side of the Allies. Rejected for military service, Papini turned to collect some of his articles previously published in reviews and periodicals. *La Paga del sabato* (1915) contains articles on Papini's disillusion with war; *Testimonianze* (1918), like *Stroncature,* is a collection of literary criticisms; *Maschilità* (1915) contains articles on literary theory. In this fury of publication Papini overlooked nothing. He brought together in *Polemiche religiose* (1918) writings on religious subjects that dated as far back as 1908. In his literary criticism Papini takes over Croce's categories, mixes them with other elements; he is as superficial here as in his treatment of James's pragmatism. His principal offering is "criticism by invective"—with occasional flashes of insight.

Even in an atmosphere of bombastic futurism, war clamors, and fiery polemics, Papini could sometimes achieve such tranquillity as is best represented in his prose poems *Cento Pagine di poesia* (1915) and *Giorni di festa* (1918) and in the poems of *Opera prima* (1917). Here he sought escape from the commonplace sentimentalities of life and from the usual lyrical forms in which they had for centuries been expressed. His concept of pure poetry is probably of French origin, stemming more remotely perhaps from the environment of Rimbaud and Valéry (*qq.v.*), to whom Papini had been introduced by Soffici, an enthusiast. Later, in 1926, when Papini had come forth with his fourth volume of poems, *Pane e vino,* he had become reconciled to the idea that poetry should not consist simply and purely of sound effects for new harmonious pleasure to the ear, but that great poetry could be found solely in eternal truth.

At the end of the First World War, Papini, still feverishly looking for a meaning in life and for a way to be useful to his fellow men, turned to religion and became a convert to Catholicism. His *Storia di Cristo* (1921; Eng. trs., *Life of Christ,* 1923, *The Story of Christ,* 1924) created a sensation. It was translated into many languages, it was financially a tremendous success, it aroused widespread discussion in Italy. The *Storia di Cristo* is Papini's exuberant and highly personal dramatization of Jesus; those hostile critics who have doubted the sincerity of Papini's "conversion" find in the book "no Christian vision of life."

Papini continues to be extraordinarily active. He is a collaborator on the *Frontespizio* and contributes to other periodicals and reviews; he collects essays and articles, produces books such as *Operai della vigna* (1929), *La Scala di Giacobbe* (1932), *La Pietra infernale* (1934), *I Testimoni della passione* (1937). His biographies of *Sant'Agostino* (1929; Eng. tr., *Saint Augustine,* 1930) and *Dante Vivo* (1933; Eng. tr., *Dante Vivo,* 1934) are very interesting in as much as they are strictly "Papinian." *Gog* (1931; Eng. tr., 1931) is a bitter satire on modern society. *Eresie letterarie* (1932) and *Ritratti italiani* (1932) are essays on literary theory and criticism. Papini was made a member of the Italian Academy in 1937.

Papini with his vast ambitions and hasty renunciations remains a typical representative of a period disturbed by great events. His works voice the moods of a whole generation of Italians, a generation that fed too eagerly on abstractions, that hated its masters too cordially, that often sought the short cut to success and the achievement of sound culture, a generation which, nevertheless, struck not a few chords of spiritual revival that echoed throughout the world.

See: G. Prezzolini, *Discorso su Giovanni Papini* (1915); R. Fondi, *Un Costruttore: Giovanni Papini* (1920); E. Palmieri, *Giovanni Papini* (1927); A. Viviani, *Gianfalco* (1934).

M. B.

Pardo Bazán, Emilia, condesa de (1852–1921, Spanish novelist), was born at La Coruña in Galicia. When only 17 years old she married the Galician José Quiroga. Literary success came to her for the first time in 1876 when her essay *Examen crítico de las obras del*

Padre Feijóo won a prize. The fact that she was a woman prevented her election to the Spanish Academy, an honor she was most anxious to have. However, she did have that of being appointed to the chair of modern Romance literatures at the University of Madrid. She was an enthusiastic feminist and an ardent advocate of the education of woman.

Literary criticism and other critical and erudite writings, together with travel books and some dramatic attempts, constitute an important part of the author's 47 volumes of *Obras completas* and stand as a testimony to the variety of talents of this most cultivated lady. By far the largest part, however, consists of novels, and it was as a novelist that she occupied a foremost position among the writers of her time. Her name as a novelist is connected with the rise of the naturalistic movement, of which she was the main Spanish exponent, especially in her essay (originally a series of newspaper articles) *La cuestión palpitante* (1883). Her position in this matter was not an easy one, caught as she was between her literary enthusiasm for the new movement on the one hand and her Catholic faith and rather idealistic philosophy on the other. Curiously, the same year (1882) in which the articles of *La cuestión palpitante* were published saw also the appearance of her two-volume work, *San Francisco de Asís.* What she finally did was to reject the materialistic philosophy of naturalism and accept the realistic principle of its literary orientation, broadening this principle in such a manner, however, as to include the spiritual as well as the natural. Even with these limitations and alterations, her position was ambiguous enough to provoke a reaction on the part of such opponents of naturalism as the Platonist Juan Valera (*q.v.*), who replied to *La cuestión palpitante* with his *Apuntes sobre el nuevo arte de escribir novelas* (1886–1887). Aside from the theoretical aspect of the question, a certain naturalistic tendency is to be seen in such of the author's works as *Un viaje de novios* (1881; Eng. tr., *A Wedding Trip,* 1891), *La tribuna* (1883), *El cisne de Vilamorta* (1885; Eng. tr., *The Swan of Vilamorta,* 1891), *Insolación* (1889), *Morriña* (1889; Eng. tr., *Morriña—Homesickness,* 1891). Of this tendency *Los pazos de Ulloa* (1886) and its sequel, *La madre naturaleza* (1887), in which the primitive instincts and forces of nature play also the role of a deterministic factor, mark the culminating point. Except for *Un viaje de novios* and *Insolación,* all these are regional novels of Galician people, their customs, etc. In them the literary personality of Pardo Bazán as the typical 19th-century painter of Galician life and scenery appears in its true character. The picture is a faithful and colorful one, and of this picture the description of the physical and moral decomposition of the noble house of Ulloa, in *Los pazos de Ulloa,* is the masterpiece. Galician too for the most part are *Una cristiana* (Eng. tr., *A Christian Woman,* 1891) and its sequel, *La prueba* (both 1890). The last novel, however, with its moral of Christian resignation and self-sacrifice, marks a new spiritual, religious orientation in the author's career. Besides her own religious and philosophic background and the antinaturalistic reaction of the closing years of the century, a factor contributing to this new orientation was the reading of Russian literature, in which Pardo Bazán had become interested. Her book *La revolución y la novela en Rusia* (Eng. tr., *Russia: Its People and Its Literature,* 1890), not particularly original yet significant in this connection, had appeared in 1887. Typical of the author's spiritualistic manner are *La quimera* (1905), *La sirena negra* (1908), and *Dulce dueño* (1911), three novels in each of which the disappointments and emptiness of life lead to a religious solution. The lesson is impressively dramatized in the futile life struggle of the hero-artist of *La quimera.* Pardo Bazán's novelistic production includes also several collections of short stories and *cuentos* (*e.g., Cuentos de Navidad y Reyes,* 1902; *Belcebú,* 1912). Outstanding are the Galician short stories and *cuentos* of the two collections *Cuentos de Marineda* (1892) and *Un destripador de antaño* (1900). An English translation of some of her shorter pieces appeared as *Short Stories* in 1933.

See: F. Vézinet, *Les maîtres du roman espagnol contemporain* (1907), pp. 203–231; Andrenio (E. Gómez de Baquero), *Novelas y novelistas* (1918), pp. 293–330; J. A. Balseiro, *Novelistas españoles modernos* (1933), pp. 262–327; C. Barja, *Literatura española: Libros y autores modernos,* revised ed. (1933), pp. 305–322; E. González López, *Emilia Pardo Bazán, novelista de Galicia* (1944).

C. B.

Pareto, Vilfredo (1848–1923, Italian economist, sociologist, and writer), the scion of a noble and patriotic family of Genoa, was born in Paris and died in Céligny, Switzerland. He has a world-wide reputation as an economist and a sociologist, but deserves mention also as a writer. Influenced by Walras, he developed the application of mathematical methods to economic problems in two famous books: *Cours d'économie politique* (1896–1897), *Manuale d'economia politica* (1907). During those years he had criticized the prevailing systems of socialism and had then attempted to treat sociology as a scientific subject in his *Trattato di sociologia generale* (1916), of which there is a notable American version, *The Mind and Society* (4 vols., 1935), edited by Arthur Livingston and translated by him and Andrew Bongiorno.

This is not the place to dwell upon Pareto's theories except to note that all his books are permeated by a spirit of contempt for ordinary, mediocre, and commonly accepted views and opinions. Pareto constructs a veritable barrier between the elite and the common man by creating a world above and beyond any thought of practical or sentimental motives—a world attainable only to superior minds capable of making that rare effort that consists in a pure understanding with no moral implication, hope, or fear. Pareto's thought stemmed directly from two sources of culture, classic Greek and mathematics. His style is precise and crystal clear, like that of Galileo, who had the same fundamental inclination, and like Galileo, Pareto developed from the height of his mental aloofness an unconcealed disdain for careless thinking, for sentimental reasoning, for any appeal to common opinions and authorities. And in so far as Machiavelli was a sort of Galileo, exploring the skies of politics with scientific methods, Pareto has also been called a "Machiavelian," especially because of his study of the role of the ruling class in history. If his works were reduced to the *Cours* and *Manuale,* he would have left only a model of precision, not unlike those of other Italian writers on political economy; but in his *Les Systèmes socialistes* (1903) and in his *Trattato,* both of which deal with historical facts and immediate controversial matters, he had ample opportunity to display his irony and give vent to his onslaughts, disparagements, and invectives, which are by far the most delightful parts of the books.

Perhaps his most vital comments are not to be found in his sociological classifications so much as in his footnotes or in his digressions and comments on quotations of his adversaries or on clippings from newspapers. This is Pareto the writer at his best. His influence has been profound if not extensive, and it is true, although curious, that this writer has contributed to the general devaluation of the domain of the intellect which characterized the beginning of the 20th century. He profoundly disliked the intellectuals. He is to be placed alongside of Bergson, Sorel, and Croce (*qq.v.*) in the category of those thinkers who have used their intelligence to limit the field of the intellect.

He lived for many years in seclusion at Céligny, near Geneva where he taught at the university, and in his aristocratic attitude as well as in his style and in his tastes there is more than one point of contact with Voltaire. He was a great advocate of freedom and among his favorite targets were prudish, hypocritical, and sanctimonious laws and books (*Il Mito virtuista,* 1914).

See: "In memoria di Vilfredo Pareto," *Giornale degli economisti e rivista di statistica,* LXVI (1924), 1–153 (special number devoted to Pareto); G. H. Bousquet, *Vilfredo Pareto, sa vie et son œuvre* (1928); James Burnham, *The Machiavelians* (1943), pp. 169–220.

G. P.

Paris, Gaston (1839–1903, French scholar and critic), born in Avenay, Marne, made a principal part of his life work the conversion of technical philology into living literature in the field of French medievalism. He was the son of Paulin Paris, who was himself an erudite publisher of forgotten treasures as well as commentator. When, before he was 30, Gaston came back from studious semesters in German universities, mainly Bonn and Göttingen, he was well equipped to play a necessary role in high educational circles. He became quickly engaged in a controversy with Désiré Nisard, who had been arguing for complete neglect of the "uncouth attempts at literature before the 16th-century Renaissance." He delivered his first lecture in his father's chair at the Collège de France on December 3, 1866. From that date to his death this energetic scholar, interested in the present and in linking it closely to the past, was faithful to his announced program: "High culture in a nation is at least for a large part that conscience of its continuity which it acquired by the study of its own past." He wrote for the *Revue critique* and the *Revue celtique* and founded the important philological journal *Romania,* a celebrated initial article to the effect that "there are no Latin races" provoking much comment and also disagreement. He taught at the Ecole des Hautes Etudes as well as the Collège de France, carried on a wide correspondence at home and abroad, and was known for his gracious hospitality, combining a highly personal charm and elegance with his linguistic achievements. The loss of one eye did not impede his strenuous existence.

The publication of manuscripts and of etymological studies were the natural by-product of the new presentation of medieval moments. A *Manuel d'ancien français* (1888) was of great help to the growing number of students. Insisting upon the Middle Ages as an essentially poetical epoch, Gaston Paris wrote *La Poésie du moyen âge* (1885), *François Villon* (1901), and *Poèmes et légendes du moyen âge* (1900). In modern literature he dealt with Mistral, Renan, and Sully-Prudhomme (*Penseurs et poètes,* 1896). He was elected to the French Academy in 1896.

Paris accepted the German hypothesis that short songs were in the course of time merged into epics and that very ancient Indo-European tales gradually spread through Western civilizations (*Les Contes orientaux dans la littérature française du moyen âge,* 1875). He was unequaled in pointing out the idiosyncrasies of new renderings of heroic deeds or of everyday stories. His views in *L'Histoire poétique de Charlemagne* (1865) may seem superannuated; a polygenetic or at least a polymorphic origin of folk tales is now often preferred to the notion of a steady diffusion of the primitive stories of the East. His advocacy, in the Congress for Comparative Literature in 1900, of *Stoffgeschichte* now seems too exclusive. But *La Littérature française au moyen âge, XI–XIVe siècles* (1888; never completed) and many essays, studies, and criticisms (in *Journal des savants, Histoire littéraire de la France, Romania,* and *Revue critique*) further testify to the great merit of a scholar who never tired of emphasizing that "science has no other object than truth, and truth for itself."

See: J. Lemaître, *Les Contemporains* (1887); A. G. van Hamel, "Gaston Paris en zijne leerlingen," *De Gids,* June, 1895, pp. 487–528; H. A. Todd, "Gaston Paris, Romance Philologist and Member of the French Academy," *Publications of the Modern Language Association of America,* XII (1897), 341–354; J. Bédier, *Hommage à Gaston Paris* (1904).

F. B.

Pascarella, Cesare (1858–1940, Italian poet and short-story writer), was born in Rome. Having a modest private income, he devoted himself to painting in his earlier years and in the course of these activities he established the contacts which were to lead to his writings in various newspapers and reviews. In his later years, after he was made a member of the Italian Academy, he traveled extensively, going as far as India and America. A growing deafness made him lead in his old age a very retired life.

His literary work, most of which was produced between 1880 and 1890, is of two kinds: poems, in the form of sonnets and sequences of sonnets, composed in the Roman dialect and collected in *Sonetti* (1909); and short stories and sketches of modern Roman life, written in literary Italian, first published for the most part in *Capitan Fracassa, Nuova Antologia,* and *Fanfulla,* and later collected in *Prose* (1920). Although the subject matter is substantially the same in both cases, it is the poems that have given him literary fame.

The Roman dialect in which Pascarella's sonnets appear is a medium which an adroit writer can exploit to great advantage, it being close enough to the normal literary tongue to be readily understood by all Italians (the glossary that accompanies his *Sonetti* consists of less than 40 terms), while at the same time permitting extraordinary freedom of expression. A skilled user can descend deep into the soul of the colorful Roman people. At a slightly earlier period Giuseppe Belli had used the Roman dialect for poetic purposes, but his satiric leanings had prevented him from exploiting its possibilities to the full. Trilussa (pseud. of Carlo Alberto Salustri), almost a contemporary of Pascarella, drew the full flavor from the dialect, but his ultra-cynical and occasionally salacious tendencies limit his achievement, and at best he is only amusing. Pascarella, on the other hand, presents not merely the little comedies, but also the small tragedies of the everyday life of lower-class Romans, and these tragedies are depicted as they really are, that is to say of paramount importance to their participants. Some of these pieces, in the opinion of Italy's foremost literary critics, are of outstanding merit. Carducci (*q.v.*) describes *Villa Gloria* as Italy's highest achievement in dialectal epic while Croce (*q.v.*) extols the author's conscientiousness and seriousness of purpose and his utter and refreshing spontaneity.

Villa Gloria (1885) is a participant's account of one of the ill-fated attempts to seize Rome which preceded the unification of Italy. Scarcely less important is the *Scoperta della America* (1893), in which Columbus, Ferdinand, Isabella, Spanish sailors, and American Indian chieftains speak the colloquial dialect of Rome in its most humorous aspects as they go about the business of negotiations.

voyage, and discovery, in 50 sonnets. *Er Morto de Campagna* (1882) and *La Serenata* (1882) are removed from the sphere of epic action or ludicrous anachronism, but offer tragic episodes of popular Roman life in all their stark, gruesome realism, while *Er Fattaccio* (1904) describes, with graphic yet dispassionate bitterness, the ultra-personal, selfish reactions of five different eyewitnesses to a deed of bloodshed.

See: B. Croce, "Note sulla letteratura italiana nella seconda metà del secolo XIX: Cesare Pascarella," *Critica,* IX (1911), 401–412; E. Cecchi, "Pascarella inedito," *Nuova Antologia,* CDIX (1940), 181–187.

M. P.

Pascoli, Giovanni (1855–1912, Italian poet), was born, the fourth of 10 children, in the village of San Mauro, near Savignano (Romagna), on a princely property of which his father was the respected steward. The poet's affectionate memory clung to that San Mauro hearthside all his life long, its effect upon his writings intensified by the sorrows that early engulfed it. When he was seven a baby sister died, another when he was 10, and when he was 12 fell the tragic blow from which he was never to recover: the father, as he was driving home late at night, was set upon and murdered, a deed for which no one was ever brought to justice. There followed six more deaths, the oldest sister, the mother, two older brothers, two young nephews. At 21 Giovanni found himself head of a family consisting of two younger sisters, still at their convent school at Soriano, and two younger brothers.

Throughout these sad years Pascoli had been receiving an excellent education, especially in Latin, from the brothers of the Scolopi Order, at Urbino, Rimini, and Florence, securing his *licenza* at Cesena in 1873. A scholarship admitted him to the University of Bologna, where he worked well for two years at Greek, Latin, and Italian literature and history, then suddenly dropped out of his classes to join the strong socialist movement of Bologna. When the minister of education visited the university, Pascoli took part in demonstrations which lost him his scholarship, then joined the *Internazionale.* During the turbulent period that followed, his brother Raffaele had to share with him his lodging and a crust. His socialist tendencies—fed by the unjustice of what had befallen his family, his own dire poverty, and the contacts with social problems that city life brought him—led to his arrest and "preventive" imprisonment in the autumn of 1879. This involuntary seclusion gave him time for meditation; he resolved to resume his studies and accept his family responsibilities. His scholarship being restored to him, he was able to begin teaching Greek and Latin at the *liceo* of Matera by 1882. In 1884 he was transferred to Massa and from then on could always make a modest home for his sisters. In 1891 his fame began, with the publication of *Myricae.* That same year he won in the Amsterdam competition the first of his 14 gold medals for Latin poetry, with which he eventually bought a house. In 1895 his sister Ida married, and as a summer home for himself and the other sister he leased (later purchased) a cottage at Castelvecchio di Barga, far up the Tuscan valley of the Serchio, settling there with Maria, who was to be his devoted companion as long as he lived and became his literary executrix (*Poesie varie raccolte da Maria,* 1912–1913, *Traduzioni e riduzioni,* 1913). Throughout the series of academic transferences and promotions (Leghorn, 1887; Bologna, 1895; Messina, 1897; Pisa, 1903), the summers brought them back to Castelvecchio. Out of his childhood memories and the life with Maria came the poems by which he is best known. These intimate subjects he dwells on endlessly: family sorrows, his father's murder, the natural life of growing things that he could watch from his study, the work of the kitchen and the field, the companionship of animals, and a narrow but deep domestic life in which the poet himself took his share of the sacred activities of gardening, drawing water, laying fires, baking bread. He lent a life of their own even to inanimate objects, whose sentiments he imagined and interpreted. *Myricae, Primi Poemetti* (1903), *Canti di Castelvecchio* (1904), *Nuovi Poemetti* (1906), even much of *Odi e inni* (1906), are but sensitive and tender variations upon these plaintive themes; but the antique landscape of the Sicilian years inspired a volume on classical subjects (*Poemi conviviali,* 1903), and after succeeding Carducci in the chair of Italian literature at Bologna (1905), he too turned to historical and patriotic subjects (*Canzoni di Re Enzio,* 1908–1909; *Poemi italici,* 1911; *Poemi del Risorgimento,* ed. by Maria Pascoli, 1913).

The Wordsworthian homeliness of his topics called for a new vocabulary foreign to Italian poetry, and he used dialect, local words, baby talk, pidgin Italian of returning immigrants, onomatopoeia, invented forms, in a great variety of meters (sometimes Latin), whose deceptive simplicity disguises their intricacy and technical skill. By his excessive personalism and his rejection of classical canons, he seems to belong to the romantics, but he owed to a later school his effective use of symbols. Poetry is a staff ("Il Bordone") or a lamp ("La Poesia"), love a sweet mortal poison ("Digitalis purpurea"); "Il Vischio" suggests that the principle of evil may envelop the whole being as the mistletoe stifles the tree; "Il Focolare," a cold forsaken hearth, symbolizes religion; "La Pecora smarrita" is Earth, lost lamb of the universe. He exalts poverty, decries riches. The thought of death is never absent, since the larger number of those dear to him lie in the San Mauro cemetery, "sad and only house of my kinsfolk," seeming still to share the preoccupations of the living family.

In the "Prefazio a Maria" of *Primi Poemetti* he writes: "Recollection is poetry, poesy but recollection," and in the preface to *Nuovi Poemetti* (dedicated to his students): "I sing for you, boys and girls, only for you." Within these two sentences lies his literary doctrine, whose more famous exposition is the essay "Il Fanciullino" (*Pensieri e discorsi,* 1907). Your true poet, he affirms, is a child and should adress himself to the tastes and interests of children—or of the child in all of us—which include nature, family life, military prowess, and adventure. This would exclude love as too dramatic and philosophy as too adult, yet "Il Ciocco" and "La Vertigine" are philosophic poems of cosmic imagination.

Mention should be made of his expositions of the *Divina Commedia,* his anthologies of Italian poetry for youth, and his Latin verse (*Ioannis Pascoli Carmina Recognoscenda Curavit Maria Soror,* 1930). Some of his poetry has been translated into English (*Poems of Giovanni Pascoli,* 1923, 1927, *Selected Poems of Giovanni Pascoli,* 1938).

See: G. L. Passerini, *Vocabolario pascoliano* (1915); A. Simon, "Giovanni Pascoli" (including translations of his poems), *Poet Lore,* XXVII (1916), 191–203; A. Meozzi, *La Vita e la meditazione di Giovanni Pascoli* (1923); A. Gandiglio, *Giovanni Pascoli, poeta latino* (1924); R. S. Phelps, *Italian Silhouettes* (1924), pp. 33–54; A. Zamboni, *Giovanni Pascoli (1885–1912)* (1937).

R. S. P. M.

Passeur, Stève (1899–, French dramatist), born in Sedan, has brought to modern French drama something of the roughness of his native Ardennes. His early work, such as *La Maison ouverte* (1925), was marked by boldness of concept and a strong sense of the theatre, and to these he has added in more recent years greater intelligence and a deeper sense of human values. Passeur is interested in the deepest emotions of his characters; he attempts to shock and surprise his audience by demonstrating that the completely unexpected is very often psychologically quite consistent. His characters, therefore, are almost always thrown into unusual situations, the normal routine of their lives is interrupted and completely upset, the most intense intellectual and moral pressure is piled upon them, and under this strain all that is artificial in their personalities falls away, leaving them psychologically naked before the spectator. In order to facilitate this process, Passeur does not hesitate to resort to the most shopworn tricks of melodrama, but the surprising quality of his work results from the fact that though the situations are often the hackneyed ones of a thousand thrillers and tear-jerkers, the characters' reactions to them are psychologically plausible and hence startling in the extreme. In all his mature work, Passeur excels in thus establishing cynically, brutally, and directly a situation which calls into question conventional values. Too often at first, however, in such plays as *L'Acheteuse* (1930) and *La Chaîne* (1931), he displayed a tendency, once having set his characters in motion, to avoid resolving the problem in an intellectually satisfactory fashion, falling back instead on his mastery of theatrical tricks to provide him with a conclusion. *Les Tricheurs* (1932), however, marked a great advance in this respect. Here one feels that stock devices are used with restraint and are fully justified by the penetration of Passeur's analysis.

See: François Mauriac, *Dramaturges* (1928).

C. W., Jr.

Pasternak, Boris (1890–, Russian poet), born at Moscow, son of a well-known painter, grew up in a highly cultivated environment. His own erudition is broad, and his interests are catholic. He is well versed in literature, painting, music; he studied philosophy at the universities of Moscow and Marburg. In reading his verse one is struck not so much with his versatility and virtuosity as with the freshness and novelty of his approach to life: he reacts to objects and phenomena with the wonderment of one who sees them for the first time and is therefore innocent of hackneyed images and threadbare comparisons. His extremely personal reaction is expressed in a style of his own that makes him difficult to understand at the first reading, but the effort is rewarded by the ultimate pleasure of being able to see with his eyes and hear with his ears. He has been classed for years as a futurist, the only justification for this label being his involved syntax and the resulting "estrangement," a feature advocated by Russian formalists. Actually Pasternak is beyond "school" labels. The form of his verse is regular, the rhythm is varied and rich, the rhymes are extraordinarily original. Though he has influenced a number of young poets, he is essentially inimitable.

It is natural that such a subjective contemplator as Pasternak should remain rather indifferent to political issues. During the most eventful years he suggested that "in times of quick tempo 'tis best to think slowly." The title of his collected verse, 1912–1930, is fittingly enough *Poverkh baryerov* (1931; Above Barriers). In the year of the Revolution, 1917, his volume *Sestra moya zhizn* (Life My Sister) was published in Berlin. "What's the millennium, dear folks, outdoors at the moment?" asks the poet with wide-open eyes. Soviet Russia has inevitably affected his muse, however, as may be seen from his volume *Vtoroye rozhdeniye* (1932; Second Birth). Of late he has made excellent translations from foreign poetry, including his fine version of Shakespeare's *Hamlet,* published in 1941.

A. K.

Pastonchi, Francesco (1877–, Italian poet), born at Riva Ligure, has written poems, one novel, a book of short stories, and in his early years was a literary editor. Fame came to him when he was still a student because of his skill in reciting poems which had a marked tendency to sonority. He started by declaiming the classics but ended by reciting his own, a little like those music conductors who are themselves inspired to compose after a lifetime of hearing the classics. He first became widely known through an intellectual but cold writer of verses, Arturo Graf (*q.v.*). If one is looking only for good style, impeccable form, precise words, measure, polish, adroitness, all sorts of rhymes and rhythms, Pastonchi gives full satisfaction, in any one of his volumes (*Saffiche,* 1892, *Italiche,* 1902, *Belfonte,* 1903, books of poetry; *Il Violinista,* 1908, a novel; *Il Campo di grano,* 1916, short stories). He is an expert technician of Italian verse, and not without reason have his poems been called poetical exercises; he is a kind of general lyricist, ready to exalt water, like Pindar, or wine, like Alceus, to extol patriotism and all kinds of Latin glory, or women, history, heroes, poets. His poems, elegant and precious, are always written to be declaimed; the conscious style and the concern for a surprising rhyme seem to becloud the inspiration—whenever there is any. Pastonchi's charm as a declaimer made him the spoiled child of the wealthy who do not read but enjoy hearing, and he found admirers especially among women of this class. Presently he discovered how empty and shallow this social world is and certain sighs for redemption escaped from him in *Il Randagio* (1920; a poem), but there was no deep feeling. Had he been able to look at the people about him, even the society folk, poetically, he might have produced a real work of art, but when he tried his hand at this (*Versetti,* 1931), only small, fragmentary sketches and bittersweet prints were the outcome. Pastonchi has been classified as a Parnassian of the French school. He definitely has a comparable polish. Fascism turned him into a professor, to the great surprise and consternation of some of the older teachers who did not believe that writing smooth verse guaranteed an ability to teach the history of poetry.

See: P. Pancrazi, *Scrittori italiani del Novecento* (1934), pp. 117–124; U. Ojetti, *Cose viste,* IV (1928), 132–141.

G. P.

Pavlenko, Peter Andreyevich (1899–, Russian novelist), was born in St. Petersburg, into the family of an artisan. He fought in the civil war and in 1919 joined the Communist Party. For several years he served with the Soviet Commercial Agency in Turkey, and his experiences in that country provided him with the subject matter of his volume of short stories, *Aziatskiye rasskazy* (1929; Asiatic Stories). His first novel, *Pustynya* (1931; The Desert), dealing with the irrigation of the Kara Kum Desert in Turkmenistan, is also based on personal experience and observation and is typical of the period of socialist realism. The Paris Commune served as background for his *Barricady* (1932; The Barricades). In *Na vostoke* (1937; Eng. tr., *Red Planes Fly East,* 1938) Pavlenko presents a broad and vigorous picture of life in the Soviet Far Eastern provinces threatened, in their rapid growth, by the ever increasing menace of Japanese imperialism. Though essentially realistic, the novel culminates in a vision of an imaginary conflict; the Japanese army attacks the Soviet border, but meets with disaster, and a vast revolutionary movement spreads from the Asiatic mainland to Japan itself. During the Second World War, Pavlenko published an account of the struggle waged by the partisans against the German invader, *Russkaya povest* (1942; The Russian Story).

See: T. Eventova, "Pavlenko," in *Literaturnaya entsiklopediya,* VIII (1934), 389–392.

L. S.

Pawlikowska, Marja, *see* Jasnorzewska, Marja.

Pea, Enrico (1881–, Italian novelist), has been a sailor, a merchant, the impressario of a provincial theatre, as well as a writer of novels, short stories, poems, and plays. He was born in Versilia, a tiny region of Italy that is in spirit quite apart from the Tuscany to which it belongs geographically; it is impervious to modern civilization, rich in natural talents, poetic geniuses, and interesting persons, with a treasury of popular songs, proverbs, and tales. Two of Pea's books, *Fole* (1910) and *Lo Spaventacchio* (1914), are adult fairy tales. A magic legendary quality colors all his work. Folklore, with a savor of unreality among humble and tragic realities, is in him cultured and artistic, although the origin of this culture and the source of his inspiration are difficult to trace. He was attracted by exotic traditional cultures, especially the oriental, dating from the time when he lived in Egypt selling Italian marble and Egyptian real estate, and by the culture of Versilia to which he finally returned (see *Lo Spaventacchio*). He mixes his personal experiences, always bathed in the light of art, with old literary patterns. In planning a work he takes careful aim beforehand, but his leaning towards that vague world of the imagination frequently causes him to miss fire. One never has the feeling of reality even in characters that he sketches with merciless realism. Religion, not infrequently in the form of superstition, appears often in his dramas and novels, but we cannot say that he seems convinced of his beliefs; angels are not unlike disguised devils.

In late years Pea has frequently tried his hand at the more traditional narrative form of writing, as is seen in his novels *Moscardino* (1922), *Il Volto santo* (1924), *Il Servitore del diavolo* (1931), *Il Forestiero* (1937), and *La Maremmana* (1938). Because of his artistic effort and the strange richness of his vocabulary and the high quality of parts of his writing, his works have always been received with deferential regard, but he has never won the unconditional approval of the critics or a large reading public. In any case he is a personality and has carved his own niche in the literature of contemporary Italy.

G. P.

Péguy, Charles (1873–1914, French man of letters), was born in Orléans of humble working people. His father died while Charles was still less than a year old, and it was the manual labor of his mother, a repairer of chairs, plus numerous scholarships which sent him up the French educational ladder to, in 1894, the Ecole Normale Supérieure. Older than many of his classmates, since he had already voluntarily left school to do his year of military service, and filled with an ardent faith in socialism which he desired to test in action, he was not content with the life of a student; the world outside, and in particular the Dreyfus affair, drew him inescapably. He married, left the Ecole, and in 1897 opened a socialist bookstore and press in the university quarter.

He had already begun to write, and it was only natural that his first two books should come from his own press, *Jeanne d'Arc* (1897), a play, and *Marcel; premier dialogue de la cité harmonieuse* (1898), a noble and ecstatic description of the perfect socialist state. Neither of the books sold, and the shop did not flourish, in spite of subsidies provided by a committee of socialists headed by Lucien Herr. Péguy was intellectually and temperamentally incapable of blindly following a party line, and when the committee, knowing this, refused to back him in his project of founding a review, the inevitable break came. Herr, Blum, and the others withdrew their support; Péguy abandoned the bookstore and went on alone to found the *Cahiers de la quinzaine* (1900), to which he devoted the rest of his life. In its pages most of his work appeared, in its pages he fought, sometimes almost alone, for truth, in its pages he published the work of such young men as Benda (*q.v.*), Daniel Halévy, André Spire (*q.v.*), François Porché, André Suarès (*q.v.*), Romain Rolland (*q.v.*), and the Tharauds (*q.v.*). Constant polemics left him little time for poetry, perhaps his true vocation, till his last years when, as though sensing an impending doom and attempting to pack the work of a lifetime into four years, he produced a series of long poems and poetic plays, in particular *Le Mystère de la charité de Jeanne d'Arc* (1910), *Le Porche du mystère de la deuxième vertu* (1911), *Le Mystère des Saints Innocents* (1912), and *Eve* (1913), which mark him as one of the great French poets. He was killed in action, at Villeroy, September 5, 1914.

Péguy's life, simple as it was, and his thought are full of apparent contradictions. An ardent socialist, he was completely nationalistic; a pugnacious supporter of Dreyfus, he loved the French army and was never happier than when serving his month at maneuvers every summer; a Catholic, devout to the point of saintliness, he was anticlerical, was not married in the Church, did not baptize his children, and, deprived of the sacraments, did not even attend Mass. Actually, however, in great things Péguy was remarkably consistent. His mind was far from universal; it held only a few general ideas, but those it held firmly, comprehended fully, and applied unshrinkingly. Just as Péguy's knowledge of and taste for literature was limited to a few classics instilled in him at school—Sophocles and Homer, Corneille and Hugo—so his basic ideas can be easily traced to his childhood. He was the child of the Church and of the republic, of the state school and of the class in catechism, of Jeanne d'Arc and of the French Revolution. And above all, he was the child of the working class, the people, doing honest labor honestly. His lifelong struggle was an attempt to unite and defend the two idealisms—or, as he would have said, *mystiques* —that of Christianity and that of the French republic. The bond of union he found in the three great virtues, faith, hope, and charity. Péguy loved God and his neighbor, believed in the perfectibility of mankind, fought for truth, attacked falsehood—all falsehood. For him, as for so many, the Dreyfus case was crucial; in it he saw the central event in all modern history, political, religious, intellectual. From it he drew the perfect illustration of his antithesis between *mystique* and *politique:* at first *mystique,* a struggle for truth and truth alone, the case degenerated into *politique* in the retaliatory measures of Combes and Waldeck-Rousseau. It was *politique* that Péguy despised and struck out at, *politique* in the universities, in the Church, in the Socialist Party. To Péguy, Bernard Lazare, who died in poverty, almost forgotten, was a great martyr: he had given his life to the *mystique* of the *affaire.* And Jaurès, mourned by half a nation, was a great Judas: he had sold the *mystique* of the Socialist Party. Péguy's essential task was to see that *mystique* was not devoured by *politique,* that the ideals of France, of democracy, of Christianity, for which generations had given their blood, were not betrayed and defiled. To that task he gave his life.

His prose suffers from being largely occasional, the history of battles whose details escape us with men whose names we no longer recognize. But though at times the quarrel seems petty, behind it the great principles always loom. Péguy's style, too, discourages many. It is simple enough in essence, but it is marked by peculiar repetitions, secular litanies in which the key words and phrases are almost chanted again and again, examined in all their shades of meaning, modified slightly but surely with each repetition, so that the thought seems to progress with the heavy tread of the marching infantryman. The desire to extract the utmost from a single word that led Péguy into repetition led him also into interminable parentheses. He seems unable to choose any one path; he must follow all, include every possible development of an idea. Yet such works as *Notre Patrie* (1905), *Notre Jeunesse* (1910), and *A nos amis, à nos abonnés* (1909) can now be recognized as standing among the greatest in modern French literature.

Péguy's poetic work, whether in the form of the *mystère,* as *La Charité de Jeanne d'Arc,* or the quatrains of *Eve,* is also marked by idiosyncrasies. There is the same repetition, the same slow movement, and hence an almost enormous length. But there is in this poetry a nobility and an acuteness of mystic vision to be found among Péguy's contemporaries only in Claudel (*q.v.*) and a tenderness for suffering humanity, manifest on a verbal level in Péguy's astonishing ability to render the sublime in the words and metaphors of popular speech, which it would be difficult to find anywhere else. Perhaps the highest praise that can be given is to say that in these works Péguy has made God speak and act, and God has not become ridiculous.

Selections from Péguy's prose and poetry have been translated by Ann and Julien Green and appear with French text in *Basic Verities* (1943) and *Men and Saints* (1944).

See: Daniel Halévy, *Charles Péguy et les Cahiers de la quinzaine* (1918); Pierre Lasserre, *Les Chapelles littéraires* (1920); Jérome and Jean Tharaud, *Notre Cher Péguy* (1926); Roger Secrétain, *Péguy, soldat de la liberté* (1941); Ann and Julien Green, introduction to Péguy, *Basic Verities; Prose and Poetry* (1943).

C. W., Jr.

Pellerin, Jean Victor (French dramatist), after writing a novel, *Insulaire* (1920), made his début in the theatre in 1922 with a one-act play called *Intimité.* In it the author used a scenic effect which has served him in good stead since: the characters, husband and wife, are engaged in a conversation that is far from transmitting their true thoughts, which are represented at the rear of the stage by other actors and actresses. The effect is highly satiric. *Le Plus Bel Homme de France* (1925) was slightly less of a success. A deceived husband and his wife's lover are themselves deceived by "the handsomest man in France." The fault of the play lay in the fact that the author strove to transform his characters into symbols; they became lifeless, illogical, meaningless. *Têtes de rechange* (1926) was well received by the critics. Pellerin again made use of the effect which had first won him fame. A young man called Ixe is visited in his office by his uncle, Opéku, who has come to ask his nephew for some financial advice. While the elder man is talking, the young man's mind wanders, and the scenes that follow represent his daydreams. This is typical of the author's predilection for "externalizing" his hero's thoughts. The play cannot really be classified as drama, but rather as a pageant; it calls attention to a certain restlessness characteristic of the era.

It was apparently the author's intention, in *Cris des cœurs* (1928), to present a vast triptych depicting once again this same restless feeling so prevalent among his contemporaries. In the first act a young man is set upon by his ideas come to life. The setting of the second act represents the façade of a home, which fades away to reveal four apartments and four couples. As they are picked out by the spotlight, each character tells of his desires and his sorrows. The theme that runs through their dialogue is the dissatisfaction of modern man who, torn by conflicting instincts and intellectually ill, seeks refuge in love, only to find that it too fails to provide the desired peace. In the third act, a philosophical sculptor proposes a double solution—work and religion. Obviously inspired in part by Francis Jammes and Paul Claudel (*qq.v.*), the play remains rather naïve, arbitrary, and disconcerting.

Pellerin's plays seem to lose with age. Their complement of surprise lost, they already appear dated. Something of their satirical value, however, remains.

See: Edmond Sée, *Le Théâtre français contemporain* (1928), pp. 167–168, and *Le Mouvement dramatique* (1930–1935), I, 85–86, III, 186–190.

P. B.

Pereda y Porrúa, José María de (1833–1906, Spanish novelist and short-story writer), is one of the foremost exponents of regionalism in modern Spanish fiction. He was born in Polanco near Santander, in the heart of the *montaña* (highlands) and close to the Cantabrian Sea, both of which inspired his best works. Of a conservative and moderately wealthy family, he was reared in an atmosphere of chaste Spanish traditionalism. He was educated in Santander and in 1852 went to Madrid to prepare himself for the artillery academy at Segovia. Neither his studies nor life in the national capital attracted him strongly, and in 1854 he returned to Santander, where he soon made himself known as a writer of genre sketches. These appeared first in local papers, but in 1864 a volume of them was published under the title *Escenas montañesas*. Their frankly realistic portrayal of *montaña* life moved Antonio de Trueba, who wrote the prologue for the collection, to accuse the author of imitating the French naturalists. This uncritical opinion had little if any effect on Pereda's literary procedure. In the same vein as his early book was the next volume of sketches, *Tipos y paisajes* (1871), which made its appearance the year before his first novel, *Los hombres de pro* (1872). Pereda had gone to Madrid as deputy in Parliament under the banner of the conservative Carlist Party. Ill fitted for politics by temperament and philosophic conviction, he withdrew into his Polanco retreat in 1872; there he soon fell into the routine of a patriarchal existence and devoted himself exclusively to letters and the management of his financial affairs. Aside from a brief visit to Paris in 1864, a trip to Portugal in the company of Benito Pérez Galdós (*q.v.*) in 1885, and an occasional excursion in Spain, Pereda was almost literally rooted in the *montaña*. In 1897 he was obliged to establish legal residence in Madrid in order to qualify for the Royal Spanish Academy of Language.

Pereda's novels fall into two categories. In those which appeared between 1872 and 1879 (and in an occasional one of later date, notably *La Montálvez*, 1888, and *Nubes de estío*, 1890) he is far more interested in his political, social, and religious prejudices than in the creation of artistic values. Here he attempts to show the evil that comes to man when he removes himself from the wholesome influence of nature and seeks self-realization through experiences provided by modern life—politics, social ambition, religious liberalism. Pereda is controversial, satirical, intolerant, stubborn, and uncompromising. Although his point of view is relentless, he is never convincing, and he inspires in the reader a hostile reaction. More attractive artistically and philosophically are his works between 1881 and 1895, especially *El sabor de la tierruca* (1881), *Sotileza* (1884), and *Peñas arriba* (1894). Written more from the heart than from the head, these novels are the only ones which illustrate fully the author's theory of regionalistic fiction as he formulated it in his speech before the Academy in 1897. Rather than quarrel with a real or imaginary opponent, Pereda has assembled in these works a mass of eloquent evidence to support his philosophy that man's highest goal—moral living—is best realized in close contact with nature, from which he learns many virtues and an occasional vice. There is primitive vigor in the energetically drawn characters, in the throbbing, dramatic canvases of mountain, sea, and valley, and in the incisive, archaically flavored style. In his superior accomplishments Pereda delights with his artless art, free from artifice or strained effect. Philosophically, too, the novels of the second group command respectful attention to their theme of the struggle between man and nature, a struggle in which nature cannot vanquish man because of his infinite power of moral resistance—nor can man subdue nature with the aid of scientific agencies and intellectual strength.

In an appraisal of Pereda's works, his inferior novels are particularly unimportant. Their bias is the expression of a zealous and ardent personality, indifferent to accidental changes, passionate and vehement in matters of the spirit, and profoundly in love with nature and human beings, provided the latter have escaped the effect (or havoc, from Pereda's standpoint) of civilization. Moreover, in several instances (*Pedro Sánchez,* 1883, and *La Montálvez*) Pereda was lured into pitfalls by the leading critics who begrudged him recognition as long as he restricted his vision to the elemental life of the *montaña.* But in his happier and characteristic moments he is a writer of impressive stature. In power of observation and faculty for assimilation of detail he ranks high among modern Spanish realists. His characters may not be psychologically complex, but they are plausible and interesting against their sincerely painted background and in the elemental human situations which shape their lives. Most interesting is their background. Pereda's landscapes are not mere conventional backdrops; they are animated and powerful, often providing the dramatic element of the story. He is an emotional, not a sentimental, painter, and the emotions which he stirs are as deep as the epic grandeur suggested by the vigor and vastness of his pictures.

During his life Pereda's critics emphasized his weaknesses—his tendentiousness, the lack of relief in his plots, the shadowy outlines of his heroines, and his obscurantist ideas. He has fared better with some members of the so-called Generation of '98, largely because of his descriptive skill. Outside of Spain he attracted slight attention because of his self-imposed, chaste regionalism. Yet in the eloquence with which they demonstrate the effect of the *montaña* environment on primal human qualities, Pereda's best works have permanent literary value.

See: R. E. Basset, introduction to Pereda, *Pedro Sánchez,* 1907 ed.; J. M. de Cossío, *La obra literaria de Pereda* (1934); Jean Camp, *José María de Pereda; sa vie, son œuvre et son temps* (1937).

H. C. B.

Peretz, Yitzchok Leibush (1852–1915, Yiddish poet and novelist), was born in Zamość, a town in the province of Lublin, Poland. Besides the traditional education in the Bible, the Talmud, and Hebrew, he received private instruction in Russian, German, and other secular subjects. Brooding over problems of life, death, God, and fate, the youth set out to find an answer in books. Obtaining access to a rich private library, he read the German, Polish, and Russian volumes without much discrimination and then taught himself French so that he could devour the French books as well. Physics and fiction, law and philosophy, were pored over with equal zeal, but his longing for a definitive solution of eternal problems remained unsatisfied.

He began to write at 14. After experimenting with Polish and Hebrew, he finally decided upon Yiddish as a literary vehicle, since only in this tongue could he be adequately understood by the Jewish working masses, whom he was interested in enlightening. His first major Yiddish poem, *Monish,* appeared in 1888, and his first collection of Yiddish tales was published in 1890 under the title *Bekannte Bilder.* During the next quarter of a century he forged ahead as the supreme figure in modern Yiddish literature. The social lyrics of Peretz were recited and his love lyrics were sung throughout Eastern Europe. His short stories stirred to pity and to action. The best known of these, "Bontsie Shvaig" (Bontsie Silent), centered about an inarticulate lowly worker, who found no reward in this world of illusion, but for whom there was reserved in the kingdom of heaven a seat at the side of the saints and patriarchs of Israel.

Peretz pleads the cause of the heart as against the claims of the intellect, the cause of the poor as against the arrogance of the rich, the cause of the Chassidim or mystics as against their deriders, the practical people who lay claim to the goods of this earth. Peretz, Mendele mocher sforim, and Sholem-Aleikhem (*qq.v.*) form the triad of classical Yiddish Literature.

See: A. A. Roback, *I. L. Peretz, Psychologist of Literature* (1935); S. Liptzin, *Peretz* (in preparation; selected stories and essays, English and Yiddish on facing pages).

S. L.

Pérez de Ayala, Ramón (1880–, Spanish novelist, poet, and essayist), was born at Oviedo in Asturias. His early education with the Jesuits was an unpleasant experience which he used later in his satire against that order, *A.M.D.G.* (1910; *Ad majorem Dei gloriam*). Very different was his experience at the University of Oviedo, where he studied law and had the good fortune of meeting a group of sympathetic teachers, among them Leopoldo Alas (*q.v.*), who had a direct influence on his intellectual and spiritual formation. From Oviedo he went to London and there resided for some time. Since then he has spent most of his life in Madrid, though he has traveled frequently in both Europe and America. His wife is a North American. In 1928 he was elected to the Spanish Academy. Like many of his contemporaries, he was finally drawn into politics and in 1931, together with Ortega y Gasset (*q.v.*) and Marañón, founded the political group Agrupación al Servicio de la República. The Spanish republic appointed him ambassador to England (1931–1936).

It was as a poet that Ayala began his literary career in 1903 with *La paz del sendero,* followed in 1916 by *El sendero innumerable.* The two poems, for each volume has the ideal unity of a single poem, are parts of a poetic cycle dealing, respectively, with the two elements, the earth and the sea. Still a third volume, *El sendero andante,* conceived as a link between the two previous poems, appeared in 1921. Showing a sensibility for the most classic as well as the most modern poetic moods and forms, Ayala reveals himself as a poet rich in emotion, imagination, and thought. His is not the simple and uncontrolled sentimental reaction that exhausts itself in the immediacy of the particular experience, but rather the more complex and restrained intellectual emotion that results from the realization of the deeper significance of each single thing as part of a universal and transcendent order. Hence a natural tendency towards both a pantheistic conception of nature—a tendency which in its relation to man resolves itself into a deep sense of humanity—and a symbolic interpretation of things. Yet his art, by virtue of the vividness of the poet's sensations, remains attached to the reality of the surrounding world. Many other poems are interspersed in Ayala's novels, especially in the volume of three "poematic novels," *Prometeo, Luz de domingo, La caída de los Limones* (1916; Eng. tr., *Prometheus: The Fall of the House of Limón: Sunday Sunlight,* 1920), charming short stories, each chapter of which is introduced by a poem which serves as the leitmotif to the episode in question.

A first-rate poet, Ayala is also a first-rate novelist. In truth, the difference between these two aspects of his work is on the whole more formal than real. Characteristic of the author's literary personality is, indeed, this intercrossing in his work of the aspects of the poet, the novelist, and the intellectual (the essayist). Here the poet reflects the intellectual, and the novelist reflects both the poet and the intellectual. The special character of his novel is the result, combining features of a realistic art with the lyric emotions of the poet and the speculations of the intellectual. Somewhat of a difference must be noted in this connection, however, between the two main groups of his novelistic production, namely, the sequence of his first four novels, *Tinieblas en las cumbres* (1907), *A.M.D.G.* (1910), *La pata de la raposa* (1912; Eng. tr., *The Fox's Paw,* 1924), and *Troteras y danzaderas* (1913), on the one hand, and on the other *Belarmino y Apolonio* (1921) and the two novels in two parts each, *Luna de miel, luna de hiel* and *Los trabajos de Urbano y Simona* (both 1923), *Tigre Juan* and *El curandero de su honra* (both 1926; Eng. tr., *Tiger Juan,* 1933). His first four novels are to a large extent still conditioned by both personal and local circumstances, containing as they do elements of a spiritual autobiography and reflecting here and there Ayala's original connection with the spirit of the so-called Generation of 1898. Of such limitations the novels of the second group are for the most part free. The characters, poetically conceived, assume the significance of symbolic representations of the human attitudes they are supposed to embody. The problems, of broad philosophic and educational transcendency, are more universal. The composition is also more organic and more artistic.

Literary criticism, problems of art, and political questions are the subjects commonly discussed by Ayala in his essays. Of special interest, as providing a background for a better understanding of the author's views on the problems presented in some of his novels, is the collection of essays *Las máscaras* (2 vols., 1917–1919).

See: S. de Madariaga, *The Genius of Spain and Other Essays on Spanish Contemporary Literature* (1923), pp. 71–86; F. Agustín, *Ramón Pérez de Ayala; su vida y obras* (1927); J. A. Balseiro, *El vigía*, II (1928), 123–271; C. Barja, *Literatura española: Libros y autores contemporáneos* (1935), pp. 439–466.

C. B.

Pérez Galdós, Benito (1843–1920, Spanish novelist and dramatist), was born in the Canary Islands and went to Madrid in 1863. He devoted his whole life to observing the social reality of which he formed a part and to creating, without rest and without interruption, his vast literary accomplishment of over a hundred volumes. His work, taken as a whole, is a literature in itself which represents the evolution of the novel of his time in Spain and in Europe and which with every day that passes is more unanimously considered the greatest literary achievement of Spain since the golden age.

His first works, *La fontana de oro* and *El audaz*, published in 1871, were historical novels, dealing with the not too remote past, in which Galdós was seeking the beginnings and origin of the present. Then there came to his mind the vast conception of the *Episodios nacionales*, of which the first two series were written between 1873 and 1879 and the last three series 20 years later. In them he gives aesthetic expression to the spiritual unity of a whole nation, not only when this unity existed in fact, as in the War of Independence, but also when, during the whole century that followed, the essential political reality of Spain was its internal discord. At the same time he also wrote four novels, *Doña Perfecta* (1876; Eng. tr., 1880), *Gloria* (1877; Eng. tr., 1883), *Marianela* (1878; Eng. tr., 1883), and *La familia de León Roch* (1878; Eng. tr., *Leon Roch*, 1886), which more than all the rest of his works have influenced the judgment formed of Galdós. These novels, with the exception of *Marianela*, touch upon the heart of what Galdós found to be the basis of the cleavage in the conscience of Spain—the religious problem. The two contending camps in Spain were divided again over these works, and they and their author became a subject of strife. But it was never the intention of Galdós to carry on antireligious propaganda through his novels. Galdós was a profoundly religious spirit. and throughout his work the reader can appreciate his sympathy and affection for all those human beings to whom, in one form or another, religion is a living force.

The second phase of the work of Galdós is represented by a series of novels written between 1881 and 1889 which he calls "contemporary" and which could also be called novels of Madrid. This series, which might properly be considered one single novel with the same characters playing out their lives against the common background of the society of Madrid, represents the zenith of the art of Galdós, most perfectly typified in *Fortunata y Jacinta* (1886–1887). Here is found the perfect harmonization of all the qualities of his genius—his extraordinary capacity for observing and reproducing real life, his humor, and his boundless human understanding and sympathy. The whole range of everyday life in Madrid is portrayed with fidelity and minuteness; but what in the last analysis gives these novels their supreme artistic value is something that transcends time and space and makes of them not only documents of fact and history but also human documents. The characters of these novels live their lives, like everybody, in the inevitable framework of their city and their epoch. But all of them reveal in their commonplace existence a direction, a meaning, which has repeated itself constantly in mankind always and everywhere. As a matter of fact, all these characters are little Quixotes, who are moved by good and generous impulses, by lofty aspiration, by an optimistic, trusting misconception which leads them to believe that everything is better than it really is. There is in all of them so much natural goodness that it redeems them in our eyes from all their mistakes, shortcomings, and badness. But their lives, like that of Don Quixote, are constant failures, "they are," somebody says of one of them, "so good, so good, that they never do anything but blunder." In these novels modern realism and naturalism become fundamentally Spanish, because Galdós's vision of life is not pessimistic but humorous and constitutes the finest example since Cervantes of the Spanish ability to redeem the outcast and the fallen through the gift of understanding, to smile serenely as the last hope fades, and to affirm man's undying worth through his very failure.

In 1889 a change took place in the writings of Galdós, marked by a tendency toward spiritual restlessness and psychological problems. The work manifesting this crisis is *Realidad* (1889), in which the problem raised in *La incógnita* (1889) is solved by eliminating all that we think of as reality and penetrating into the mysterious realm of the soul and the purely subjective world of concept and will. In *Angel Guerra* (1891) Galdós approaches the religious problem anew, from the point of view of an intimate psychological crisis. This spiritual searching, in which there is an influence of the Russian novel, appears in other novels of this period, such as *Nazarín* (1895) and *Misericordia* (1897).

From 1892, when a dramatized version of *Realidad* was put on the stage, until the end of his life, the theatre served Galdós to express those ideological and symbolical concepts which characterized his first novels. Once more the Spanish public was upset and divided by the religious problem of *Doña Perfecta,* dramatized in 1896, also the theme of *Electra* (1900; Eng. tr., 1911) and *Casandra* (1910); but these works, which aroused so much comment for reasons that had nothing to do with literature, were at bottom informed by the same human, conciliatory, deeply artistic and moral significance of *La loca de la casa* (1893), *La de San Quintín* (1894; Eng. tr., *The Duchess of San Quintin,* in B. H. Clark, *Masterpieces of Modern Spanish Drama,* 1917), *Mariucha* (1903), *El abuelo* (1904; Eng. tr., *The Grandfather,* 1910), and the other theatrical works of Galdós which represent the last effort of his creative genius.

See: Clarín (Leopoldo Alas), *Galdós* (1912); Andrenio (E. Gómez de Baquero), *Novelas y novelistas* (1918); S. de Madariaga, *Semblanzas literarias contemporáneas* (1924); Leslie B. Walton, *Pérez Galdós and the Spanish Novel of the Nineteenth Century* (1927); Angel del Río, "Introducción," in Pérez Galdós, *Torquemada en la hoguera* (1932); J. Casalduero, *Vida y obra de Galdós* (1943).

F. de O.

Périer, Odilon Jean (1900–1928, Belgian poet, dramatist, and novelist), was born in Brussels. His family belonged to the upper bourgeoisie, and his grandfather, General Thys, had an important share in the colonization of the Congo. Périer's first poems already gave signs of an unusual personality. His position in Belgian literature is unique, for the young poet's spiritual attitude was a reaction both against the current tendencies of Belgian writers and against the solemn and puritan atmosphere of his family life. However, his best poems are those inspired by his native town, and, curiously enough, his criticism, by its moralizing tone, has forced him into an attitude akin to puritanism.

In contrast to all the Belgian writers of the preceding generation, Périer's language is exceedingly pure, without any superfluous ornament, sober, concise, and always avoiding emphasis and eloquence. In *La Vertu par le chant* (1920), as well as in *Notre Mère la ville* (1922), Périer concentrates in a few lines of blank verse the anxieties of his restless soul. Faith would probably have appeased his anguish, but, although far from being an agnostic, the poet never found the consolation of religion. Therefore the ethical problem that constitutes the background of all his poems remains unsolved. In 1924 he wrote *Le Citadin, ou Eloge de Bruxelles,* a poem in classical French alexandrine verse, in which he draws a vivid description of Brussels and life in Brussels in the 20's, as seen through the eyes of a refined and gentle-hearted young man belonging to the ruling class. *Le Citadin,* Périer's masterpiece, is his best chance of attaining immortality.

The young poet had been very well received in Parisian literary circles. The *Nouvelle Revue française* published his last poems, *Le Promeneur* (1927), and also a curious novel, *Le Passage des anges* (1926). His play, *Les Indifférents* (1925), which reflects his moral attitude and his perpetual scruples, was favorably received in Brussels. Périer, who had always been ailing, died of heart disease in Brussels in January, 1928. He was buried on the very day of the birth of his only child, a son. His poems are to be found in most anthologies of French contemporary poets.

L. K.

Perk, Jacques (1859–1881, Dutch poet), was born at Amsterdam, where his father was a minister of the Walloon Church. While he was yet a student at the University of Amsterdam, a number of his sonnets were published in the weekly *De Nederlandsche Spectator.* They formed part of a sonnet sequence in four books, which he never saw in print. He died before his 22d birthday. The sequence, *Gedichten* (1882; Poems), was edited and posthumously published by his friend Willem Kloos (*q.v.*). The sonnets were inspired by Perk's love for Mathilde, a Belgian girl whom he met, one brief summer vacation, in the Ardennes. She was engaged to be married to another man, and he never saw her again. But in his sorrowing memory she became an embodiment of abstract beauty, the muse who consecrated him poet. A similar idea was expressed by Perk in "Iris," a poem which in its rhythm echoes Shelley's

"Cloud." The rainbow appears when the sun breaks through the weeping clouds; even so beauty is born from sorrow when the latter is illumined by the light of the soul. The sonnets of the Mathilde sequence reflect the changes of the poet's mood as it is affected by his passion and by the mountain scenery that forms the setting of the idyl. Perk's choice of the sonnet form, his diction and imagery, were something new in Dutch literature. The editors of *De Nieuwe Gids* (The New Guide), which began to appear four years after his death, looked upon him as a forerunner, as the herald of the revolt of the "Eightiers."

See: Willem Kloos, "Jacques Perk," in *Veertien Jaar Literatuur-geschiedenis* (1896), pp. 1–24; J. A. Nijland, *Jacques Perk; een Studie* (1906).

A. J. B.

Perse, St.-J. (pseud. of Alexis Saint-Léger Léger, 1887–, French poet), was born on a small coral island near Guadeloupe, Saint-Léger les Feuilles, which belonged to his family. After a childhood spent under the care of a Hindu nurse on West Indian plantations worked by men of all races, Léger went to France for his schooling at the age of 11. Entering the Foreign Service in 1914, he spent the years 1917–1921 in Peking. After the Washington Conference on limitation of armaments (1921–1922), at which Léger served as political expert on Asiatic questions, Briand took him to Paris. For the next decade he served the great peace-loving diplomat, rising rapidly in the Foreign Office until he became General Secretary of the Ministry of Foreign Affairs in 1933. When France capitulated to Germany in June, 1940, Léger came to America.

Rarely has a poet distinguished himself and so deeply influenced contemporary lyricism with so small an output: four thin volumes contain all his work—*Eloges* (1910; Eng. tr., *Eloges and Other Poems,* 1944), *Anabase* (1924), *Amitié du prince* (1924), and *Exil* (1942). The English translation of *Anabasis* by T. S. Eliot (1930) and the German translations by Benjamin and Groethuysen, Rilke (*q.v.*), and Kassner have helped to extend his reputation beyond the borders of France. Vigorous, personal, often obscure, his poetry accumulates rich and unusual images in majestic strophes, like those of Claudel (*q.v.*) or of Rimbaud's (*q.v.*) *Une Saison en Enfer,* with the rhythm strongly marked. His vast and precise vocabulary includes many technical and scientific words. Despite his professed hatred for literary exoticism, Léger's work is saturated with the sun of the Gobi desert, lush with the tropical growth of Polynesian islands, and studded with evocative nautical terms. In the tradition of Rimbaud, St.-J. Perse creates with the subconscious mastered by reason, and his own subconscious—judged by its products—is remarkably rich. To some extent a poet's poet (as is indicated by the list of those who have translated and prefaced his poems, to which list must be added Valery Larbaud, Hugo von Hofmannsthal, and Giuseppe Ungaretti, *qq.v.*), Léger has won for himself a small but fervent audience of the élite.

See: Hugo von Hofmannsthal, *Neue schweitzer Rundschau,* May, 1929; T. S. Eliot, preface to *Anabasis* (1930); Archibald MacLeish, "A Note on Alexis Saint Léger Léger," *Poetry,* LIX (1941–1942), 330–337.

J. O'B.

Perzyński, Włodzimierz (1878–1930, Polish dramatist and novelist), was born at Opoczno, Radom district, Russian Poland, the son of a popular Warsaw editor. After completing his formal education at the Jagiellonian University in Cracow, Perzyński went abroad (1899), first to Italy, later to Paris, where he steeped himself in French literature and mastered, as few of his race have done, the art of dramatic construction. Soon after his return to Poland he published a series of typical poems of young love in *Życie* (Life), the organ of Young Poland (*see* Polish literature), but quickly abandoned poetry for the drama, and through this medium in the next three decades literally "chronicled his epoch." A natural reporter, as his father had been before him, Perzyński was a playwright made to order. His works were popular at once and continued to enjoy favor even after their author's death, his first play, *Lekkomyślna siostra* (1904; The Prodigal Sister), holding the boards to the very end of Free Poland. The scope of Perzyński's interest was not wide nor his concern for humanity deep, but within the limits he set for himself his understanding of human behavior was considerable. His outlook on life, unlike that of most of his contemporaries, was healthy and straightforward. His characters were middle-class intellectuals, mostly Warsawians. Perzyński wrote, besides dramas, many short stories, the best of these being found in the collections *Cudowne dziecko* (1921; The Miraculous Child) and *Znamię* (1928; The Mark). In his last years Perzyński turned to the novel, a form in which he had previously shown skill with *Michalik P.P.S.* (1910) and other tales of the 1905 revolutionaries. *Raz w życiu* (1925; Once in a Lifetime), regarded by many as the finest novel of post-war Warsaw, *Nie było nas, był las* (1927; There Was Only the Forest), and *Klejnoty* (1930; Jewels) show him to have been growing in power rather than declining at the time of his death.

See: Z. Dębicki, *Portrety,* II (1928), 167–182; *Wiadomości literackie,* 1931, No. 371 (entire issue); M. Orlicz, *Polski teatr współczesny* (1932), *passim;* K. Czachowski, *Obraz współczesnej literatury polskiej,* I (1934), 275–285, 324–325.

A. P. C.

Pessanha, Camilo (1871–1926, Portuguese poet), was born in Coimbra. He received a degree in law and practiced this profession; he was also a high school teacher, in Macao (Macáu), Portuguese China. A precursor of the *modernista* group which was to be centered around the review *Presença* (1927), he profoundly influenced these writers. His extremely sensitive poetic nature was even further refined through contacts with Chinese life, art, and literature. Pessanha was the first of the Portuguese writers of his time to begin the cultivation of a pure, inner poetic world by rejecting the emotional inspiration of national lyrical elements. Seeking subtle verbal expression of the utterly subjective, he initiated lyrical formulations of the intimate world of sensations, of what is incoherent and fragmentary in the realm of the psychical, by means of symbols which are both elaborate and partial. The disconnected expression of the disassociated elements of emotional life, a method utilized extensively by those who have followed him, the eagerness to catch in a poem the vague and the fleeting and to achieve revaluation of beauty of form, not as richness but as intensity of expressive power—these are the things which constitute his poetic contribution.

With the exception of one book, *Clepsidra* (1920; Clepsydra), Pessanha's work is scattered in reviews. He wrote in prose on Chinese historical and artistic subjects and translated and annotated Chinese poetry ("Oito elegias chinesas," Eight Chinese Elegies, published in the review *Descobrimento,* Discovery). With Wenceslau de Morais (*q.v.*) he helped maintain the very old orientalist tradition in Portuguese literature.

See: H. Cidade, *Tendências do lirismo contemporâneo* (1939), pp. 67–72.

E. G. D.

Pessoa, Fernando (1888–1935, Portuguese poet), born in Lisbon, spent his childhood in South Africa and received his education in Cape Town University. He is an outstanding member of the first poetic generation of the 20th century in Portugal, a generation which began propitiously with futurism in the review *Orféu* (1915) and developed richly with the *modernista* group represented in the review *Presença* (1927). Pessoa, a link between the two movements, was conspicuous and exceedingly influential—even though his writings were not numerous and are scattered in journals.

His one book, *Mensagem* (1934; Message), distinguished by an official award, is not typical of his poetic bent and represents only a facet of patriotic, Messianic, and irrational mysticism, which links him with the old Lusitanian tradition of the illusion of King Sebastião's return. The rest of his poetic production is truly significant. He unfolded himself by projection into four lyrical personalities, his own and a trio characterized by their individual qualities—Alvaro de Campos, Alberto Caeiro, and Ricardo Reis. These are not pseudonyms, but are four perfectly autonomous entities as regards natures and modes of expression, and the poet has defined them psychologically and biographically. Through them he endeavored to give form to four distinct facets of his being. It is difficult to offer an opinion about the ultimate meaning of this polarization and the boundaries of independence separating those personalities. His poetry, which, like that of his generation, moves in the zones of the inner life, represents an intellectualization of internal emotion. He is the master of intellectual lucidity in the realm of emotion, but beneath the apparent coldness of lyric cerebralism, which at times appears to be only a clever game, one detects a sentimental energy that impels the poet toward direct communication, toward the liberation of verbal expression, and at times toward irrational intuition. His poetic instrument is sensitive to the faintest stimuli coming from the abstract. His form is clear, transparently condensed, and, owing to its precision, almost analytical; his extreme suggestive sensibility recalls Paul Valéry (*q.v.*).

See: A. Casais Monteiro, "Introdução à poesia de Fernando Pessoa," *Bulletin des études portugaises,* Vol. V (Coimbra, 1938), No. 2, pp. 1–14.

E. G. D.

Péterfy, Jenö (1850–1899, Hungarian literary historian, critic, and essayist), was born in Budapest and died, a suicide, on a train near

Fiume. Péterfy studied at the University of Budapest and taught the humanities in one of the secondary schools there. However, his major activities were not didactic in a narrow pedagogical sense: he was a first-rate literary historian, critic, and essayist, sensitive to poetry and to the subleties of philosophy. He was a member of the Kisfaludy Társaság (Kisfaludy Society). He shaped creative and philosophical experiences into meaningful designs at a time when the prevalent tendency was to confine literary and philosophical values within the boundaries of nationalistic phrases. Péterfy loved his country, but he was not content with the critical practice of writers and scholars who identified verbal optimism with courage. Péterfy was a man of letters in the very best sense of the word.

Greek ethos, Hegel's philosophy, and natural sciences were the three factors that determined Péterfy's intellectual outlook. He saw certain ethnical characteristics in creative works and their particular spiritual significance; in his essays on József Eötvös, Zsigmond Kemény, and Móricz Jókai (*q.v.*), he recognized the Hungarianism of these eminent writers. But as culture and beauty were his ideals (he was emphatically an antimaterialist), in his sphere of values the universal elements of man's destiny had to be related to ethnical symbols. Péterfy was a humanist, but not an internationalist as this term is understood today. He was a humanist whose estimations, however, revealed the manifold facets of modernity. His essays written on Hellenic literature (*e.g., Aristophanes,* 1889; *Plato,* 1890) show a spirit that was not enslaved by up-to-date catchwords; with the aid of his analytical intelligence he successfully conveyed to the reader the qualities of the Greek mind; his best efforts were put forth in the service of Greek culture. He translated several works of Plato into Hungarian. The meaning of the tragic spirit, Dante, Ibsen (*q.v.*), Taine (*q.v.*), Gottfried Keller (*q.v.*), Conrad Ferdinand Meyer (*q.v.*), music, the relationship of history to natural sciences, were subjects that he could discuss with insight. His collected works (*Összegyüjtött munkák*) were published in 1903.

Péterfy abhorred a servile acceptance of rules that seemed valid because of tradition and yet were lifeless vestiges of the past. He believed in traditions supported by evidence of merit. He of course recognized adverse material circumstances, but denounced those who ignored culture and who accepted the superficially practical. He addressed his works to the few, failed to reach the many. Péterfy was always honest in his evaluations, sometimes wrong in his conclusions.

See: D. Angyal, *Péterfy Jenö élete* (1903).

J. R.

Petrov, Yevgeni Petrovich (pseud. of Yevgeni Petrovich Katayev, 1903–1942, Russian humorist and journalist), a younger brother of Valentin Katayev (*q.v.*), was born at Odessa into the family of a schoolteacher. In the 20's Petrov went to Moscow, where he worked for satiric journals and published humorous stories. It was here that he met Ilf, with whom he was to engage in a famous collaboration (*see* Ilf, Ilya Arnoldovich). After Ilf's premature death, Petrov continued his journalistic work. During the Second World War he was editor of the popular weekly *Ogonyok* (The Little Light) and a war correspondent of note. He was killed during the siege of Sevastopol. A selection from his informal articles, many of which were addressed to audiences in English-speaking countries, has appeared posthumously as *Frontovoi dnevnik* (1942; Front-Line Diary).

See: "Petrov," in *Literaturnaya entsiklopediya,* Vol. VIII (1934).

P. A. P.

Philippe, Charles Louis (1874–1909, French novelist), was born at Cérilly in Bourbonnais In a letter to Maurice Barrès (*q.v.*), who became one of his influential protectors, he writes: "My grandmother was a beggar; my father, who was a child full of pride, was a beggar when he was too young to earn his daily bread." This father is made the hero of a book, *Charles Blanchard,* Philippe's magnum opus, never completed; it was edited and published after the author's death by Léon Paul Fargue (*q.v.*) with an interesting preface. The father became at first a shoemaker and then started a wood business; he was very thrifty, although never rich, and enjoyed some years of leisure before he died in 1907. The novel offers many autobiographical traits of the author himself. He was brought up in a religious atmosphere and took his first communion at 12; after five years of school at Montluçon, he went to the Lycée of Moulins (1891–1894). He continued his studies and passed his examinations to enter the Ecole Polytechnique, but finally gave up this promising career for no special reason except that he preferred solitude. He wrote this characteristic sentence: "I should have been quite unhappy if I had achieved happiness." He wandered to Paris, and it was not long before he had exhausted the little money he had accumulated. The symbolist poet René Ghil (*q.v.*) had been helpful in getting some of Philippe's articles published (1894–1895). After a few months in Cérilly he returned to Paris (1896), where he found work at a very modest wage as a clerk in an office of the city administration. In 1901 he received a kind of promotion to the Paris department of sanitation, and finally, through the intervention of Barrès, he was appointed to a still better post. After his father's death his mother joined him in Paris, but he never recovered his health, irretrievably damaged by a poor diet, and in 1901 an attack of typhoid fever followed by meningitis took him to the grave.

Philippe's fame rests entirely on the success of his short stories. His favorite theme is the forced resignation of the poor, who are mercilessly trampled under foot by an unhappy fate. The books of Dostoevski (*q.v.*) had been a revelation to him, as were those of Claudel and Nietzsche (*qq.v.*). He had a great admiration also for *La Vie d'un simple* (1904), by Guillaumin, the life of a poor peasant of his own province of Bourbonnais. But nearest to his heart was his friend Jules Renard (*q.v.*), the author of *Poil de carotte* (1894). Like *Poil de carotte,* his *Bubu de Montparnasse* (about the pathetic "cocu") was produced as a play and also as a film. Charles Louis Philippe protested against the not quite undeserved reproach of maudlin sentimentality (*sensiblerie*); it is not altogether easy to explain why he should survive so long in the esteem of later generations while others who sounded the same note of accented pity fell into oblivion or disrepute.

His best stories are found in *Quatre Histoires de pauvre amour* (1897), *Bonne Madeleine et pauvre Marie* (1898), *Mère et enfant* (1900), *Bubu de Montparnasse* (1901), *Père Perdrix, métayer* (1903), *Marie Donadieu* (1904), *Croquignole* (1906). The following books were published after his death: *Dans la petite ville* (1910), *Lettres de jeunesse* (1911), *Charles Blanchard* (1913), *Lettres à sa mère* (1928). Philippe contributed to numerous periodicals, *Art jeune, Revue franco-allemande, Cahiers d'aujourd'hui, Canard sauvage, Mercure de France, Nouvelle Revue française.*

See: A. Gide, "Charles-Louis Philippe," *Grande Revue,* LXIV (1910), 449–467; *Nouvelle Revue française,* III (1910), 139–324 (issue devoted to Philippe); H. Bachelin, *Charles Louis Philippe* (1929); J. Giraudoux, "A propos de Charles-Louis Philippe," *Nouvelle Revue française,* XLIX (1937), 537–549.

A. Sz.

Picard, Edmond (1836–1924, Belgian jurist and author), was a brilliant lawyer, polemist, politician, orator, novelist, poet, playwright, critic, philosopher, traveler, and explorer and played a vital part in the intellectual life of Belgium. He was president of the Belgian bar association and a member of the supreme court of justice. Born in Brussels of a Walloon father and a Dutch-Flemish mother a few years after the birth of his country in 1830 as an independent kingdom, he is considered the creator of the Belgian national spirit in literature, a protagonist of the "Belgian soul."

At the age of 17, interrupting his formal education, he embarked in Antwerp as a cabin boy on a sailing ship bound for New York. For four years he lived the hard life of an ordinary sailor on various sailing vessels cruising the South Atlantic and even rounding Cape Horn. Upon his return to his home country he finished his studies at the law school of the University of Brussels with high honors. While a student he had published a French translation of Goethe's *Faust.* A collection of sonnets (*Rêveries d'un stagiaire*) which he had written about the same time were not published until 1879. An indefatigable worker, he was endowed with a most brilliant and comprehensive intellect. As a lawyer he was known for his vast erudition, the lucidity of his judgment, the ease and fluency of his convincing speeches. Devoting himself entirely for one period to the study of law, he started publication in 1878 of the famous *Pandectes belges* (still continued) which established definitely his reputation as a scholar. Then he turned his attention to the field of art and in *Paradoxe sur l'avocat* (1881), *Mon Oncle le jurisconsulte* (1884), *La Forge Roussel* (1884), *Le Juré* (1887), he tries to draw a parallel between law and art in their ideal achievement of beauty and perfection.

Picard's extraordinary power as a narrative and descriptive writer appears in his novel *L'Amiral* (1884), in which he relates the adventures of his sailor's life. Always in quest of dynamic experiences he undertook a dangerous exploratory journey through the Congo, of which he gave a vivid account in *El Moghreb-al-Aksa* (1889) and *En Congolie* (1896). *Monseigneur le Mont-Blanc* (1900) was written after his climb of that high Alpine peak. Toward the end of his life he turned to the theatre as a means of expression; he wrote seven plays. *La Joyeuse Entrée de Charles le Téméraire* (1905) gives a colorful and well-characterized picture of the great duke of Burgundy and the period of relative autonomy of the Belgian country in the 15th century; *Jéricho* (1901), although tainted with anti-Semitism, is full of wit and dramatic action; *Ambidextre Journaliste* (1904) is a biting satire against the venality of journalism. Some of his plays, *e.g., Psukè* (1903), give the impression of being mainly philosophical dialogues. Picard's theatre is a "théâtre d'idées" forming a logical unity. As in Balzac's *Comédie humaine* the same characters reappear in his various works. Although he himself was of such a very dynamic nature, his general philosophy is one of inner appeasement in the face of the fear-inspiring mysteries of human destiny. Picard has also written some poems of impressive vigor, revealing, besides his temperament as an untiring polemist, a heart sensitive to the deepest emotions (*e.g., Atra Mors,* 1905).

Picard's published works comprise 41 volumes. Yet he was best known to the general Belgian public for the many articles, all of them earmarked with his striking personality, with which he flooded Belgian newspapers and magazines, among others the *Peuple* and the *Art moderne.*

See: J. Chot and R. Dethier, *Histoire des lettres françaises en Belgique* (1910); H. Liebrecht, *Histoire de la littérature belge d'expression française* (1910); G. Doutrepont, *Histoire illustrée de la littérature française en Belgique* (1939).

L. V.

Picón, Jacinto Octavio (1852–1923, Spanish novelist, short-story writer, and critic), was born in Madrid. He was educated first in France and later at the University of Madrid, where he studied law. Essentially a fiction writer, he began his literary career as an art critic. His biography of Velázquez and his book on the evolution of caricature are readable works of sound scholarship.

Picón's early novels are really elongated short stories (*e.g., Lázaro,* 1882), a genre which he cultivated impressively. As a novelist he lacks creative power, although he often achieves effectiveness by sheer intellectual effort. His plots are slight and in their stereotyped artificiality are reminiscent of the classical Spanish *comedia.* Their hesitant progress creates impatience rather than suspense.

More naturalistic than any other Spanish author, Picón had two favorite themes, anticlericalism and unconventional love. Yet his conception of love is romantic in the sense that he presents it as a force justified by its very existence and not to be restrained in its freedom of expression by moral laws or social preoccupations (as in *Dulce y sabrosa,* 1891). Were it not for the veil of delicacy which his cultivated style casts over the details, Picón's fiction might justly be called erotic. Something of Juan Valera's (*q.v.*) interest in the sensuous and his meticulous style can be detected in Picón. His prose is pleasingly dignified and fluent, his diction is sensitively handled, and his sentences fall in soft cadences. Although sparingly humorous, he is always ripplingly ironical. Occasionally his style is self-consciously literary. A pure Madrilenian, Picón builds his scenery out of local vignettes which together with his faithful transcription of the capital's *argot* lend his novels a regionalistic quality.

Picón's strength and weakness derive from his personal formula to which he scrupulously adhered. He aimed to reproduce rather than to create, to appeal to sentiment and not to imagination, to please and not to moralize, and to extract from Castilian as much of its inherent beauty as possible.

See: H. Peseux-Richard, "Un romancier espagnol: Jacinto Octavio Picón," *Revue hispanique,* XXX (1914), 515–585; J. A. Balseiro, *Novelistas españoles modernos* (1933), pp. 338–345.

H. C. B.

Pilnyak, Boris (pseud. of Boris Andreyevich Vogau, 1894–, Russian novelist and short-story writer), was one of the first new literary figures to emerge from the Revolution. Various, complex, and controversial, often an artist of power, he was one of the most brilliant members of the so-called "fellow travelers." As such he accepted the October Revolution as an elemental revolt of the people springing from ancient Russia of the pre-Petrine era—he himself remaining outside orthodox Communism. He was born in Mozhaisk, near Moscow, of well-educated middle-class parents intimately connected with the Populist movement. In his blood mingle four strains—German, Jewish, Slavic, and Tartar. He graduated (1913) from the Nizhni-Novgorod school of positive sciences and (1920) from the Moscow Institute of Commerce, where he specialized in administration and finance. His early years were influenced by a life close to nature and by association with many leaders of the zemstvo and the intelligentsia. His literary beginnings (from 1915) won him no special recognition until he published *Goly god* (1922; Eng. tr., *The Naked Year,* 1928), a panorama of Russia in the chaos of 1921, ravaged by civil war, blockade, and famine. It created a sensation by its tragic realism and its new manner, with its broken rhythms, its flexible language, and its abrupt, strident notes alternating with lyric tenderness. Outwardly formless and non-narrative, its structure is rather that of planes reflecting a complex and violently contradictory scene with the focal emphasis on historical Russia, not on individuals. This was the first major literary depiction of the Revolution.

Many other volumes followed, notably *Ivan-da-Marya* (1923; Ivan and Maria), dealing with the inquisitorial Cheka savagery deriving from sexual perversion; *Tretya stolitsa* (1923; The Third Capital), a contrapuntal *étude* of the spirit of rural Russia, sensitive and redolent of Chekhov and Bunin; *Mashiny i volki* (1925; Machines and Wolves), with its adamant Bolsheviks in leather jackets; and *Mat syra-zemlya* (1926; Mother Damp Earth). Pilnyak's work of these years, while owing much to Bely and Remizov (*qq.v.*), was the most characteristic expression of early Soviet literature, which often took from his style and method. A number of his best-known short stories (see the collection published in English, *Tales of the Wilderness,* 1925) belong to this period. Later his influence waned. *Mahogany* (1929), published in Berlin, was denounced as antirevolutionary and banned in the U.S.S.R. In an altered form it was incorporated into *Volga vpadayet v Kaspiskoye more* (1930; Eng. tr., *The Volga Falls to the Caspian Sea,* 1931), perhaps his most successful and widely known novel, concerned with the building of a dam at Kolomna so as to change the course of the Volga, a project symbolizing the industrial construction of the first Five-Year Plan. The hyperbole of the symbol contains a hidden criticism of the enormous cost in human wreckage entailed in the Revolution. The basic dualism of his attitude to the Revolution appears throughout his work, as in *Rozhdeniye cheloveka* (1935; The Birth of a Man), the heroine of which, a "classical" Communist scorning the "obsolete" family, discovers the joys of motherhood, or as in *Sozrevaniye plodov* (1936; The Ripening of the Fruit), describing the ancient craftsmanship of the villagers of Palekh, for generations devoted to painting icons and, latterly, to secular objects. Pilnyak has traveled extensively throughout Russia and the Far East, as well as in Germany (1922), England (1923), and the United States (1931), where he spent much time in Hollywood. These experiences have unquestionably enriched his thought and his work.

See: V. Lidin, ed., "Boris Pilnyak," in *Pisateli* (1926), pp. 229–233; A. Voronsky, "Boris Pilnyak," in *Literaturnye tipy* (1927), pp. 39–60; B. P. Kozmin, "Boris Pilnyak, in *Pisateli sovremyonnoi epokhi,* Vol. II (1937).

N. S.

Pinto, Júlio Lourenço (1842–1907, Portuguese novelist and critic), was born in Oporto and died there. He studied law at Coimbra and later held various government offices. As a result of opposing the movement to overthrow the liberal government of the duke of Loulé he lost all political preferment. In 1906 he was appointed director of the Banco Comercial of Oporto.

As a writer he cultivated the realistic novel, embraced naturalism wholeheartedly, and became the pupil of Flaubert, Zola, and Eça de Queiroz (*qq.v.*). His first serious attempt in his favored field was *Margarida* (1879), a novel of contemporary customs in which he portrays "a Portuguese Madame Bovary." This work was followed by *Vida atribulada* (1880; Life of Distress), *O senhor deputado* (1882; The District Representative), and *O homem indispensável* (1884; The Indispensable Man). In all these novels he practiced faithfully the tenets of the naturalistic genre, though he is perhaps overzealous in the detailed and methodical treatments of both characters and descriptions. It may be justly said that his work is more imitative of art than of life.

This series of novels was followed in 1885 by his *Estética naturalista* (Aesthetics of Naturalism), subtitled *Estudos sôbre arte* (Studies on Art), wherein he attempts to explain the theory of naturalism, offers a critical analysis of its aesthetic qualities, and defends it vigorously. This work is generally considered a worthy contribution in the field of literary criticism in Portugal.

See: A. F. G. Bell, *Portuguese Literature* (1922), pp. 318–319; F. de Figueiredo, *História da literatura portuguesa* (1923), pp. 230–231.

G. I. D.

Pirandello, Luigi (1867–1936, Italian playwright, short-story writer, and novelist), was born at Girgenti, Sicily, studied at the University of Rome, and took his Ph. D. at the University of Bonn in Germany. Soon after his return to Italy in 1894, Pirandello married Antonietta Portulano, the choice of his father. They settled in Rome, and for 10 years Pirandello was a free-lance author, living on a generous allowance from his father. His unhappy family life with a woman who eventualy lost her mind, his irksome duties when he became a teacher at the Istituto

Superiore Femminile di Magistero in Rome, the indifference of the Italian public to his writings—these details help one understand the pessimism that tinges his art. Fame came to him about 1920. He relinquished his teaching and dedicated himself to the theatre in Italy. He toured Europe and America with his troupe performing his plays, was decorated by the Italian and the French governments, and in 1934 won the Nobel prize in literature. In Italian letters Pirandello was the outstanding personality after the First World War and until his death, of a heart attack in his sleep, in 1936. He owed his first recognition to two foreigners, Benjamin Crémieux, a Frenchman, and James Joyce, an Irishman, both of whom in 1915 called the attention of the literary world to his works. In 1921 his *Sei Personaggi in cerca d'autore* (Eng. tr., *Six Characters in Search of an Author,* 1922) earned him universal acclaim.

The predominating trait of Pirandello's art is humor, but a grim humor with a definite philosophical derivation. He was a thoughtful individual who strolled among his fellow men wondering how he could reconcile life as a cosmic entity with life as enclosed in each being; life as a sublime entity that merged with a sort of religious platonism, and human existence of this planet, a pitiful nothingness that, after a brief interlude of enchantment and beauty, was inevitably destined to wither and perish under the cold hand of death. His art, whether considered in short stories, novels, or plays, is the projection of this dialectical query. If life is a cosmic entity, the very fact that it becomes caught and immobilized in an individual form, be it a tree, an animal, or man, offends it greatly. Ciampa in *Il Berretto a sonagli* (1916) states: "Divine spirit enters into us and becomes dwarfed into a puppet." If life is cosmic in its origin and nature, what is the value of everyday existence and the organization of society with its well-regulated bureaus, its strict laws, and its unbending codes? Why so many temples when there is the universe as a place to worship God? Why so many gods, as many at least as there are religions, if the divine personality of God is one? Why political systems that are bound to become corrupt and perverted? What is the relationship between the cosmic in each man and the mask that he wears when he goes before his fellow men? This is the shout of disgust voiced by Baldovino in *Il Piacere dell'onestà* (1917; Eng. tr., *The Pleasure of Honesty,* 1923). The second act of this dialectical drama presents a sort of rogues' gallery composed of individuals who err by refusing to live according to "sentiment." The author had insisted years before in his study *Umorismo* (1908) that, whatever the illusions, "man does not have an idea, an absolute concept of life, but rather a changing and varied sentiment according to time, cases, and circumstances." He stressed the contrast between concept of life and sentiment of it. Unlike other beings in the universe that live by abandoning themselves to the warm flow of instinct, man is capable of formulating a concept of his existence and of his self, a trait that creates a clash between intellect and instinct. Other beings live, man sees himself live through an infernal machine called logic. Concepts are the chief products of this machine. Man looks at his fellow men, not as individuals but as fixed and unchanging entities in which he crystallizes definite types: this man is moral, that one immoral; another serious, still another funny; and so on through all the categories that have been invented in apprehending and cataloguing a reality that, being made up of individuals, rebels at all these clear-cut and ironclad concepts. The moral and immoral men do not exist in categorically well-defined embodiments. This is the plea of the father in *Sei Personaggi in cerca d'autore.* An individual cannot be categorically said to be serious or lighthearted. The truth is that the same individual can show himself staid and proper with one person and lighthearted with another who awakens the joyous side in his or her nature. This is the main theme in *La Signora Morli, una e due* (1920). Reality does not consist of its material and factual aspects, but of our sentiment of it, *i.e.,* how we mold it to make tolerable an unbearable situation. This is the main motif that runs through *Così è, se vi pare* (1917; Eng. tr., *Right You Are If You Think So,* 1922).

Pirandello began his career as an author by writing short stories and novels. He did so on the advice of Luigi Capuana and Giovanni Verga (*qq.v.*), the leaders of the *verismo* movement in the 90's. These two men had practiced the art of storytelling as the objective study of life in its humble yet dramatic and picturesque aspects. Pirandello, too, presented in his short stories ordinary men and women observed in his native Sicily. Among the best are "L'Eresia catara" and "Il Treno ha fischiato," in which interest is focused on the lamentable plight of the main characters and the power of illusion that allows them to escape it. Yet, in Pirandello's stories (he wrote over 300) there is rarely adequate development of the philosophical intuition that originated them: the clash between the cosmic and the actual. The contrast itself is clearly borne out by many of the titles of the collections: *Amori senza amore* (1894), *Beffe della morte e della vita* (1902), *Bianche e nere* (1904), *Erma bifronte* (1906), *La Trappola* (1915), *Il Carnevale dei morti* (1921). But the humble and elementary characters in whom Pirandello here enclosed his tragic sentiment of life were not big enough nor possessed of an intellectual stature fully to convey it. Though conceived on a wider canvas, and often significant, his novels are weighed down by the clash between the lofty generating motif and the grotesque forms that it assumed in the vicissitudes through which Pirandello led his characters. Such is the case in *L'Esclusa* (1901; Eng. tr., *The Outcast,* 1925), *Il Fu Mattia Pascal* (1904; Eng. tr., *The Late Mattia Pascal,* 1923), *I Vecchi e i giovani* (1913; Eng. tr., *The Old and the Young,* 1928), *Si Gira* (1915; Eng. tr., *Shoot,* 1926), *Uno, nessuno e centomila* (1926). But when Pirandello turned to the stage, he was able to reveal the philosophical motif of his thought untrammeled—and often with the radiance of great art. He then created figures conceived as the reflection of his mature self and capable of carrying the weight of thought and pathos that he entrusted to them. This is true especially in *Il Piacere dell'onestà, Sei Personaggi in cerca d'autore, Enrico IV* (1922; Eng. tr., *Henry IV,* 1922), *Come tu mi vuoi* (1930; Eng. tr., *As You Desire Me,* 1931), and *Quando si è qualcuno* (1933). It was undoubtedly as a playwright that Pirandello found the full measure of himself.

See: W. Starkie, *Luigi Pirandello* (1926; 2d ed., revised and enlarged, 1937); D. Vittorini, *The Modern Italian Novel* (1930), pp. 137–154, and *The Drama of Luigi Pirandello* (1935); F. V. Nardelli, *L'Uomo segreto* (1932); L. Baccolo, *Luigi Pirandello* (1938); B. Croce, *La Letteratura della nuova Italia,* VI (1940), 359–377.

D. V.

Pirenne, Henri (1862–1935, Belgian historian), was born in Verviers. After receiving his doctor's degree at the University of Liége, where he had been the pupil of Godefroid Kurth, he studied in Leipzig, Berlin, and Paris. At the age of 22 he was appointed instructor in paleography at the University of Liége and, two years later, he became professor of history of the Middle Ages at the State University of Ghent, where he remained until 1930, with the exception of the years 1916–1918 which he spent in a German prison camp.

Between the year 1888 and his death he produced more than a dozen works, of which the most important is his monumental *Histoire de Belgique* (7 vols., 1900–1932). The first volume was issued in German in 1899; the French edition began appearing the following year. From the very moment of its publication it put in the shadow all previous studies on the subject. Pirenne's work proclaims the existence of a national Belgian consciousness. His thesis is that Belgium is not a recent creation of European diplomacy, but that its unity and national spirit may be traced back as far as the Treaty of Verdun in the middle of the 9th century. He studies its evolution and its changes through the centuries as being the result of an undeniable ethnological fact. Pirenne is the first historian of that country to give the economic, social, and religious factors a place as prominent as that given to political events in the development of national history, and, differing from his predecessors who used to treat countries as separate entities, he scrutinizes these factors in the light of their connection with the general movement of Western European civilization. In Pirenne's work Belgium has become one of the important elements in Europe's evolution, whether it be in the history of the Crusades, the birth of the communes, the movement of the Renaissance, or in the philosophical, artistic, and scientific fields. Among Pirenne's other publications the following should be noted: *Les Anciennes Démocraties des Pays-Bas* (1909), *Les Villes du Moyen Age; essai historique, économique et social* (1927), *Histoire de l'Europe, des invasions au XVIme siècle* (posthumously published, 1936; Eng. tr., *A History of Europe from the Invasions to the XVI Century,* 1939).

L. V.

Pirmez, Octave (1832–1884, Belgian writer), was born in Châtelet, in the Walloon section of Belgium. His life was uneventful and devoid of material difficulties. Except for travels in France, Germany, and Italy (*Jours de solitude,* 1869; *Lettres à José,* 1884), he led the leisurely life of a solitary country gentleman, reading, studying, and meditating in his Château d'Acoz, near the town of his birth. "My only companions," he said, "are love and death. They converse together at my side without ever fatiguing me." He was a lover of nature and a dreamer, deeply influenced by the melancholy trend of romanticism (*Remo,* 1878), a great reader of Montaigne, Pascal, Rousseau, Chateaubriand; but his "mal du siècle" is sad without despair. It is Christian, exalting, as with Pascal, the power of sentiment above the power of reasoning (see *Heures de philosophie,* 1873). Pirmez is always noble and delicate, his style is clear, flowing in gentle, somewhat sadly harmonious periods; the purity of his mind instills in the reader an aversion for bourgeois commonplaceness and utilitarianism. His first book, *Pensées et maximes* (1862), was republished under the title *Feuillées* in 1870.

See: Paul Champagne, *Octave Pirmez; sa vie et son œuvre* (1925) and *La vie méditative d'Octave Pirmez* (1929).

L. V.

Pitoëff, Georges (1886–1939, French actor, theatrical director, and *metteur en scène*), was born at Tiflis, Georgia, where his father directed a theatre. After acting in St. Petersburg, he formed his own company in Geneva in 1915, whence, already famous, he came to Paris in 1919. At the Comédie des Champs-Elysées, Théâtre des Arts, Vieux Colombier, and finally the Mathurins, he realized a new conception of the theatre dominated by simplicity, subordination of details to the central idea, and emphasis upon psychological overtones. His favorite dramatists were those most characteristic of his age of unrest, Pirandello (*q.v.*), Lenormand (*q.v.*), Shaw, Andreyev (*q.v.*), Gorky (*q.v.*), Claudel (*q.v.*). Before beginning to interpret a work, he lived with the text until he could visualize it upon the stage as if he had written it himself. Brilliant productions, illuminated by his intelligence and the sensitive acting of his wife, Ludmilla Pitoëff, revived Shakespeare, Ibsen (*q.v.*), and Tolstoy (*q.v.*) for the French public. The Pitoëff creations of *Hamlet,* of Bernard Shaw's *Saint Joan,* of Pirandello's *Six Characters in Search of an Author,* are landmarks in the history of the modern stage. With Baty, Dullin, and Jouvet (*qq.v.*) he formed the famous Cartel of four Parisian producers.

See: R. Brasillach, *Animateurs de théâtre* (1936).

J. O'B.

Pogodin, Nikolai Fyodorovich (1900–, Russian dramatist), was born into a peasant family and from childhood worked as a hired hand on a farm and later in blacksmith shops and in bookbinderies. These experiences gave him the raw material first for newspaper sketches and stories and then for plays. From 1930 on, a new play of his was produced nearly every year, and he became the most consistently successful Soviet dramatist. Whereas earlier Soviet playwrights had dealt with the bitter conflicts of the Revolution, Pogodin turned with optimism to the enthusiasm of socialist reconstruction during the first Five-Year Plan. For him dramatic suspense consisted not so much in personal tragedies as in the conquest by the masses of the problems of construction—man's mastery of the machine. His plays were filled with the joy of struggle, rough humor, and friendly teasing among workers busy in a common cause. His themes were drawn from the everyday life of factory or farm. His hero was the common man. This new type of hero, a full-blooded, exuberant, good-natured worker, for whom there is no difference between his private interest and the social good, reveals a very different type from the morbid, introspective heroes so common in Russian plays before the Revolution.

In *Temp* (1930; Eng. tr., *Tempo,* 1936) Pogodin dramatizes the necessity for speed in building the Stalingrad tractor factory, in which feat the Russian workers are helped by a sympathetic young American engineer. In *Poema o topore* (1931; Poem about the Axe) he writes with lyric enthusiasm about the final success of the workers in inventing a stainless steel for axes. *Moi drug* (1932; My Friend) presents a very tolerant picture of the friendly chief of construction of a new factory. In *Sneg* (1932; Snow) is shown the transformation of worthless characters under the ordeal of snow in the Caucasus Mountains. *Posle bala* (1934; After the Ball) transfers the same spirit of good humor to the new life on the collective farm. Pogodin's theories for his new type of drama were given in *O dramaturgii* (1934; About Dramaturgy). With *Aristokraty* (1935; Eng. tr., *Aristocrats,* 1937, acted in London in 1940) Pogodin's optimism goes so far as to represent former criminals and political prisoners, working on the Baltic and White Sea Canal, transformed into real aristocrats of labor. With *Chelovek s ruzhyom* (1937; Eng. tr., *The Man with the Gun,* 1938) Pogodin turned back to the eve of the Russian Revolution and introduced a meeting between a peasant soldier coming from the front and a very human Lenin—the first successful representation of Lenin on the stage. For this play Pogodin was awarded in 1941 the Stalin prize of 100,000 rubles. *Gioconda* (1938) was the story of a patient recuperating at a rest home and caring only for the picture of Mona Lisa and a woman whose smile ressembled hers. *Pad serebryanaya* (1938; The Silver Valley) shifts to the Manchurian frontier and the danger of foreign invasion. For this long series of wholesome portrayals of Soviet life Pogodin was awarded the Order of Lenin in 1939. In *Kremlyovskie kuranty* (1940; The Kremlin Chimes) Pogodin went back again to Lenin and to a half-humorous working man who mended the chimes in the tower of the Kremlin so that they played the "Internationale." After the Nazi attack on Russia, Pogodin's plays took up the question of national defense with the same combination of "tremendous relentless determination and stalwart good humor" which he had shown in his earlier plays dealing with industrialization. *Lodochnitsa* (1943; The Boatwoman) depicted the magnificent courage of the women running the ferry across the Volga River during the siege of Stalingrad. After the invaders had been driven out, Pogodin wrote *Sotvorenie mira* (1945; The Creation of the World), depicting a Russian town wrecked by the Nazis and describing the zeal with which the Russian people turned to the reconstruction of the city as though it were the creation of a new world.

See: Yuri Yuzovski, "Nicholas Pogodin," *Teatr i dramaturgiya,* Vol. I (1933), No. 6, pp. 19–31, No. 7, pp. 56–60, No. 8, pp. 20–24; A. Gurvich, *Tri dramaturga* (1936), pp. 7–111.

H. W. L. D.

Polenz, Wilhelm von (1861–1903, German novelist and dramatist), was born on the country estate of his ancestors at Ober-Cunewalde in the eastern part of Prussia. Though a typical representative of the landed aristocracy by birth, he was attracted by the democratic principles and activities of the naturalistic school. His first novel, *Sühne* (1890), shows the style and form of Zola, Boelsche, Schlaf (*qq.v.*), *et al.* But he soon drifted into a middle of the road course and produced three novels of a type still sociological but in general more cultural. The first, *Der Pfarrer von Breitendorf* (1893), depicts the economic and spiritual afflictions of the country parson; the second, *Der Büttnerbauer* (1895; Eng. tr., *Farmer Büttner,* 1913–1915), presents the milieu of physical misery and constant financial trouble of the small landowner; and the third, *Der Grabenhäger* (1896), outlines the social and political significance of the aristocratic country-estate owners and their economic responsibilities. After *Thekla Lüdekind* (1900), a love story of the triangle type, he discussed in a lengthy autobiographical novel, *Der Wurzellocker* (1902), the struggles and tribulations of his own literary development in the midst of the intellectual confusion of his time. His attempts at self-expression by means of the drama were not very successful; a number of short stories were preparatory steps for his novels. An extensive trip through the United States resulted in his best, and posthumous, work, *Das Land der Zukunft* (1903; Eng. tr., *The Land of the Future,* 1904).

See: E. von Mach, "Wilhelm von Polenz," in *German Classics of the 19th and 20th Century* (1912); W. Tholen, *Wilhelm von Polenz und die deutsche Literatur seiner Zeit* (1924).

A. Bu.

Polish literature in the early 1870's began to be dominated by a new mood, one of romantic humanitarianism, a belated manifestation of the fever which in Western Europe had largely been cured by the events of 1848. The fever had already been known in parts of Poland in the 40's, thanks to emissaries sent from Paris by the Polish exiles to stir up rebellion, but it had not then reached beyond the German and Austrian provinces of that country and its influence on literature had been negligible. When, however, nearly a generation later, romantic humanitarianism actually penetrated the Russian provinces, especially Warsaw and vicinity, it became the principal force animating a literary resurgence whose influence was to be felt for two decades.

The new mood was a natural and logical reaction on the part of youth distrustful of the spirit and ideals which had dominated their elders and which had brought Russian Poland, as a consequence of the uprising of 1863, to an abyss of humiliation. Throughout the three decades following 1831, the year in which the Napoleonic era, so full of buoyancy and hope for Poland, was finally liquidated, the Poles had lived in a dream. They believed, as the romantic poets on whom they were nourished believed, that it is neither "the furrow, nor commerce, nor division of labor" that constitutes a country's wealth, but only "aspiration."

Naturally there were many who, even before the epoch of dreaming was ended by the collapse of the uprising, realized fully that Polish life was an anachronism and that the Polish social organism was in urgent need of revamping; but it was only with the arrival on the scene of a group of young men from the Szkoła Główna, the admirable university in Warsaw founded in 1862 by Alexander Wielopolski, that this feeling was reflected in literature. Having been exposed, in the course of their studies, to Comtian positivism and especially to the writings of the English thinkers of the day—Darwin and Spencer, Buckle and Mill—these young men emerged from the university convinced that it was their duty as patriots to restore "the spiritual equilibrium of the nation, long out of balance through over-emphasis of the artistic," and thus "to reroute the stream of Poland's energy from heart to brain." Even the poets of the Szkoła Główna group sang no longer of nature and love, but of the new ideals of work, reality, and truth.

The Szkoła Główna graduates made their ideals vocal through the various new journals which quickly sprang up in Warsaw. The most influential of these, and the spearhead of the new humanitarianism, was the *Przegląd tygodniowy* (Weekly Review), founded in 1866. The contributors to this journal often crossed swords in the early years of the new literary awakening—which soon came to be known as positivism—with the more conservative *Biblioteka warszawska* (Warsaw Library), a journal dating from the 40's which had grown out of the intensely patriotic *salon* of Deotyma, and also with the Cracow *Przegląd polski* (Polish Review), a monthly founded in 1866 and edited by Stanislaw Tarnowski.

The most important contributor to the *Przegląd tygodniowy* and the very Coeur de Lion of the young writers was Aleksander Świętochowski (*q.v.*) The ideals of the positivists—the nobility of work, the desirability of female emancipation, and the necessity for extending the benefits of education more widely in Poland—were promulgated by Świętochowski in the "Echoes of Warsaw" column of the *Przegląd*. Later he embodied these also in a series of dramas, the best of which was the trilogy of contemporary life *Nieśmiertelne duszy* (1876; Immortal Souls). Because of the excessively cerebral nature of the writing of this most spectacular of the positivist writers, the movement he represented laid itself open to the charge of literary sterility. The credit for giving the lie to this charge, which was in fact an unfair one, goes to that most typical of the positivists, Bolesław Prus (*q.v.*). Prus widened and enriched the stream of Polish literature and turned its course into hitherto unexplored channels of realism.

In Austrian Poland a shock hardly less severe than the one which brought Russian Poland to its senses in 1863 had been felt as early as 1846, with the Metternich-provoked *Jacquerie* throughout the valley of the San; two years later, in 1848, Lwów was bombarded and crushing reprisals followed. In Cracow, early in the 50's, Józef Szujski had issued a challenge to the past when he declared the "epoch of the lyric" was over and the time for the sterner discipline of the drama had arrived. It was not, however, until the late 60's and early 70's that the new day heralded by Szujski actually dawned in literature. Then there took place in Cracow ferment and reorientation like that in Warsaw—similar in purpose, at least, if not in detail.

The literary awakening in Cracow had its origin in an alliance unique in Polish history, an alliance, as the journalist Pruszyński has called it, "of the counts with the professors." Arch-symbol of the alliance, leader of the literary resurgence, and arbiter of taste in Austrian Poland for a long quarter century was Stanisław Tarnowski, a member himself of one of Poland's so-called "nine families" and professor of Polish literature in the Jagiellonian University. Tarnowski and his colleagues, known collectively as "Stańczycy," from the name of a famous 16th-century wit, differed from the Warsaw positivists in their conservatism and religious orthodoxy and in the fact that they were more interested in the past of their country than in its present or future. Their principal contribution was made in the field of historical criticism. Their purely literary works, not excluding Szujski's many and ambitious historical dramas, are today forgotten, but their theory of Polish history, attributing Poland's collapse in the 18th century not alone to the rapacity of Germany and Russia but even more to maladies within the Polish state itself, is a live and burning issue still.

Lwów did not share in the literary awakening of the 70's, yet one Lvovian at least, Władysław Łoziński, adorned his country's literature even in that arid period. With the brilliant and charming historical essays that began in the 70's to flow from his pen, Łoziński established a tradition other Polish writers might well have emulated, and he ultimately won himself the name of being the parent of romantic biography in Poland.

Besides the fascinating, more or less historical figures of the essays of Łoziński, other new material was employed for literary purposes for the first time in the post-1863 epoch. The peasant began to be portrayed as he actually is, first in the moving tales of that pioneer feminist and reformer Eliza Orzeszkowa (*q.v.*), the Polish George Eliot (also called the Polish George Sand), later in the stories of Prus and Sienkiewicz (*qq.v.*). The Jew was represented sympathetically and humanely in the novels of Orzeszkowa, and the whole life of the natural world was for the first time acclimatized to Polish literature by Adolf Dygasiński (*q.v.*). In Cracow at this time also, Michał Bałucki (*q.v.*) pioneered in the use of the city dweller, especially the petty official, as material for the drama.

It is clear that the purpose animating Poland's literary activities in every part of the realm during the post-1863 epoch was a desire to rouse the nation and then to educate it—a purpose manifest in Cracow by a stern evaluation of the past, in Warsaw by a formulation of programs for the future—and no figure is more representative of the era as a whole, none crystallizes its ideals more perfectly, than the one best known and most admired abroad, Henryk Sienkiewicz. For Sienkiewicz was indeed the teacher par excellence of his nation, not alone of his own generation but of the next as well. By bringing tradition brilliantly to life, especially in his trilogy of historical novels, by presenting it in colors that could not fail to thrill and captivate the imagination, Sienkiewicz made tradition seem worthy of perpetuation, not secretly within the hearts of individuals, as in his own day, but openly in the collective heart of a state. Thus, although at first thought Sienkiewicz seems to have little in common with the other writers of his day, with the reformer Świętochowski, the realist Prus, and the conservative, scientifically inclined historians of the Cracow school, he was actually a product of the fusion of the tendencies of all these—and a genius besides. Two widely different monuments bore witness to his greatness: the peasant epic of Reymont (*q.v.*), *Chłopi* (1902–1909; Eng. tr., *The Peasants,* 1924–1925), which owed its inspiration directly to the trilogy, and the free Polish state which arose at the end of the First World War.

One of the most striking phenomena of the epoch immediately following 1863 in Poland was the country's isolation from the West. Travel from Poland to France and Italy fell in this period to an unprecedentedly low state, and the Polish realm "beyond the cordon" erected by the partitioning powers as a result of 1863 took little part in the intellectual life of Western Europe. As Tadeusz Żeleński (Boy) (*q.v.*) put it, "The romantics of the previous generation had been sentenced to vagabondage over the face of Europe and endless yearning for the homeland; their descendants, on the other hand, were obliged to submit to an opposite sentence: to quietly sitting at home and longing endlessly for the almost mythical Europe beyond the border."

In the middle 80's this began to change and Europe found its way once more into the Polish realm, especially, at the beginning, into its Austrian provinces. It arrived first by way of the Cracow theatre, brilliantly cosmopolitan under the administration of Tadeusz Pawlikowski (1894–1899), and later, after the death of Matejko, by way of the Academy of Fine Arts. Even before Poland and Europe had reestablished contact in this manner, however, Cracow had opened up new horizons on its own initiative and found its own way out of isolation. The way, discovered by a band of enthusiastic and lyric young men who soon came to be known collectively as Young Poland (Młoda Polska), led through Poland's hitherto unappreciated and largely unknown southern mountains, the Tatras. The Polish genius has always found its fullest and readiest expression in lyric poetry, yet poetry had been out of fashion in Poland since 1863. Obviously the time had come in the 80's and 90's to set right this unnatural state of affairs, and it fell on the Cracovians to do this. Having found an adequate spring of inspiration in the pure air and the quaint huts of the Tatras, these Young Poles proceeded to restore poetry to the place of honor it had until recently held in the national life. The period was known as "Tatra-ism." There were Asnyk (*q.v.*) with his thoughtful lyrics, Tetmajer (*q.v.*) with his rich verses and authentic if somewhat idealized tales of mountain life, to say nothing of the mountaineer Orkan (*q.v.*) who, though standing apart from Young Poland, nevertheless owed much to it and even contributed his own peculiar genius.

It was not long, however, before the *kawiarnias* (cafés) of Cracow replaced the peaks of Podhale as the center, not only symbolically but actually, of Young Poland's life: "satanism" triumphed over "Tatra-ism" and strange, exotic new colors were introduced. The new colors now came not at all from within Poland itself but entirely from abroad, from the Europe which Cracow had yearned after. They came first by way of Ludwik Szczepanowski, who arrived in 1897 and proceeded to found the journal *Życie* (Life). A little later that "child of Satan," Stanisław Przybyszewski (*q.v.*), returned to his native land from a season in the Berlin circles dominated by Strindberg (*q.v.*) and for the final year and a half of the century reigned in the cafés and monopolized the pages of *Życie.*

Under Przybyszewski's persuasion Young Poland now inscribed on its banners the "art for art's sake" slogan and proclaimed the emancipation of the writer from all moral responsibility. In Warsaw, at the same time, another group of young writers similarly inspired began to proclaim like ideals in a journal appropriately named *Chimera.* Zenon Przesmycki (pseud. Miriam), who founded it in 1901, was the discoverer and rehabilitator of Cyprjan Norwid, little-known romantic. The new agitation, in Warsaw as in Cracow, meant simply that Poland was once more united intellectually and spiritually to the rest of Europe and that she was suffering, along with the West, from the malady called *fin de siècle.* The sober chronicler of this epoch in Poland was the novelist Berent (*q.v.*); its most penetrating satirists were the Cracow dramatist Jan August Kisielewski, disciple of Bahr (*q.v.*) and of Schnitzler (*q.v.*), and Gabrjela Zapolska (*q.v.*), founder of Polish naturalism.

The remarriage of Poland with Europe brought about by Young Poland produced a number of skilled and competent literary figures, among them the dramatists Perzyński (*q.v.*) and Grubiński (*q.v.*) and the great iconoclast-critic Tadeusz Żeleński (Boy), founder of Cracow's most celebrated literary rendezvous, the Zielony Balonik (Little Green Balloon). Besides these, Young Poland produced also the strange and unexpected genius, Stanisław Wyspiański (*q.v.*).

Although Wyspiański far outdistanced Young Poland in his achievements, he nevertheless owed a great deal of his success to this movement: to its Tatra period for having made the native, Slavonic element in Poland's culture not only known, but popular and respected; to its European period for having reopened the sluices that carried the culture of Rome and of the West into Poland; and to the movement as a whole for having restored poetry to Polish life and brought back the imaginative into a position of honor. Wyspiański found the fullest expression for his many-sided genius in poetic drama. Equally at home in a variety of artistic media, he brought into being not only a great body of dramatic literature, but a great theatre in the widest sense of the term. He gave to Polish literature its first original conception in the field of drama, a conception in which he synthesized—as Słowacki and Norwid had unsuccessfully tried to do—all the significant elements of European drama from Aeschylus to his own contemporary Maeterlinck (*q.v.*).

In every nation there are figures outstanding for their enrichment of the symbolism by which the nation thinks and speaks, and Wyspiański was such a figure in Poland. Possessing the insight and understanding necessary to identify the types and symbols peculiar to his nation and recurrent in its experience, Wyspiański had also the skill necessary to evoke these dramatically and in such telling manner as to make them henceforth a part of the national idiom. He belongs, from this point of view, with the creators of Hamlet and Don Quixote, of Werther and Don Juan. Wyspiański's symbols, especially those occurring in his striking folk play *Wesele* (1901; The Wedding)—the peacock feather, the straw man, the golden horn, and the young bridegroom—stand with those of Mickiewicz and Słowacki, immortal and indispensable in the national idiom.

No less powerful in this same respect was the novelist Żeromski (*q.v.*). Like Mickiewicz's Gustav and Słowacki's Kordian, to say nothing of the types found in Wyspiański, Żeromski's Andrzej Radek in *Syzyfowe prace* (1898; Sisyphean Labors), Dr. Judym in *Ludzie bezdomni* (1900; The Homeless), Cezar Baryka in *Przedwiośnie* (1925; Early Spring), Przełęcki in *"Uciekła mi przepióreczka"* (1924; My Little Quail Has Fled), and his evocation of the spirit of the Baltic seacoast in the figure of Smętek in *Wiatr od morza* (1922; The Wind from the Sea)—all have an important and permanent place in the national culture.

The literary awakening noted in Cracow in the 1890's had its counterpart also in Lwów, the political capital of Poland's Austrian provinces, and the movement was due in large measure to the arrival in that city of Jan Kasprowicz (*q.v.*). Poet, professor, journalist, and translator, Kasprowicz possessed not only the enormous virility of the peasant, but the dynamic freshness of a man new to the world of letters. Unlike his contemporary Przybyszewski, with whom Kasprowicz was unhappily linked by the desertion of his wife, Kasprowicz was not the object of a cult, nor did he become a legend, except with the Tatra mountaineers among whom he made his home. Yet after him there flowed out of Lwów an unbroken stream of poetry, first by way of Poland's greatest contemporary lyricist, Leopold Staff (*q.v.*), later through Staff's disciple Kazimierz Wierzyński (*q.v.*). In Kasprowicz's Lwów were bred and nurtured also that prime favorite of both children and grownups in Free Poland, Kornel Makuszyński (*q.v.*) humorist, storyteller and critic, and Stanisław Wasylewski (*q.v.*), leading heir of Łoziński as a historical essayist.

The city of Łódź, Poland's textile capital, experienced no literary revival comparable to that enjoyed by the other cities, yet it had the distinction of contributing to Free Poland her outstanding poet, Juljan Tuwim (*q.v.*). A bard of the present and the future, Tuwim owed more to Russian literature, in which his studies in a Russian Gymnasium thoroughly grounded him, than he did to the literature of the West—though his debt to Whitman and Verlaine (*q.v.*) was by no means small. Tuwim was a brilliant individualist, always to be found in the thick of the literary controversies that kept Warsaw in a stir for the duration of Polish freedom, and he was the leading representative of the post-war cosmopolitan trends in literature which Warsaw warmly supported and which Cracow often resented.

Free Poland inherited from the preceding period of subjection other fully mature writers besides Staff. Some of these, notably the novelist Żeromski and the dramatist Karol Hubert Rostworowski (*q.v.*), a Cracovian bred and born and Wyspiański's principal heir, made a sincere effort to come to terms with the new times and partially succeeded in doing so. Rostworowski was especially successful with his dramas of contemporary life. For the most part, however, the older writers —Tetmajer, Reymont, and Józef Weyssenhoff (*q.v.*), author of the superb prose epic of the Eastern Border, *Soból i panna* (1911; Eng. tr., *The Sable and the Girl,* 1929)—either retired completely from the scene or simply, as one critic has said, "added marginal notes" to their already finished lifework.

So far as new and hitherto untried writers were concerned, these occupied themselves mainly with poetry during the first 10 years of Free Poland; only after about 1928 did they turn to the novel and the drama.

The first group effort to found a literature in the new state took place in Warsaw in 1918, when the First World War was scarcely over and the war with the Bolsheviks was yet to be fought. The movement was known from the name of its journal, *Skamander,* appropriately christened after the youth who was destined to restore the glories of Troy, and its leaders were the young poet and critic Jan Lechoń (*q.v.*), the poet Słonimski (*q.v.*), Tuwin, Kazimiera Iłłakowicz (*q.v.*), and that versatile man of letters, at home in every artistic form and medium, Jarosław Iwaszkiewicz (*q.v.*). The Skamandrites were full of hope and bursting with energy. They desired nothing but the chance to sing of the universal joys and sorrows of mankind, to soar like the poets of other nations, free from the bondage of patriotic themes which seemed ever to shackle the poets of Poland. The youngest talent to ally himself with *Skamander* and to typify its ideals, as these changed and shifted from year to year, was Kazimierz Wierzyński. At the end of Free Poland's existence a still more youthful poet, the Lubliner Józef Łobodowski, became identified with the *Skamander* group.

Life in Poland in the 20's was for most people chaotic and fragmentary, and for years prose writing suffered from the universal lack of time and absence of repose. In the late 20's, however, signs began to appear that the novel was about to come into its own. First came the tales of Juljusz Bandrowski (*q.v.*), some nostalgic, others realistic descriptions of contemporary life in city and industrial center. Besides these there were also numerous "tales from the trek" by Ferdynand Goetel (*q.v.*), including the popular *Z dnia na dzień* (1926; Eng. tr., *From Day to Day,* 1931). Finally, in the 30's, came the imposing *Noce i dnie* (1932–1934; Nights and Days) of Marja Dąbrowska (*q.v.*) and the great medieval canvas of Zofja Kossak (*q.v.*), *Krzyżowcy* (1935; The Crusaders).

In the 30's there also got under way a new generation of playwrights. The Polish stage, after being forced overlong to draw on the balance it had inherited from Young Poland and its descendants—notably from Grubiński, Perzyński, and Nowaczyński (*q.v.*)—was now able to incorporate into its repertory the works of newcomers like Jerzy Szaniawski and Marja Morozowicz-Szczepkowska, Pawlikowska (*see* Jasnorzewska, Marja) and Antoni Cwojdziński.

The psychological novel enjoyed in Free Poland a considerable flowering, in Michał Choromański's *Zazdrość i medycyna* (1932; Jealousy and Medicine), in the many novels of the old writer Zofja Nałkowska (*q.v.*), and in that excellent portrait of the "eternal stranger" by Marja Kuncewiczowa (*q.v.*) *Cudzoziemka* (1935, Forever Foreign; Eng. tr., *The Stranger,* 1943). There are also various studies of womanhood by Pola Gojawiczyńska (*q.v.*) and an autobiographical chart of a boy's growth in Uniłowski's *Dwadzieścia lat życia* (1937; Twenty Years of Life).

Attempts were made by several young writers to force the peasant problem, so crying for solution in Poland, into the limelight by way of the novel, but their success was not conspicuous either artistically or in the consequences for the peasant. A sensational work of this category was Jalu Kurek's *Grypa szaleje w Naprawie* (1934; Influenza Rages in Naprawa). The city slum dweller also became literary material, especially in the novels of Helena Boguszewska and Jerzy Kornacki, and the sea, as a theme for prose and verse, was utilized assiduously by a number of writers in response to official prodding and spontaneous popular urging.

At the end of Free Poland a distinct trend toward the too long neglected art of romantic biography was evident. In line with this were not only the novel *Czerwone tarcze* (1934; Red Shields) by Iwaszkiewicz and the numerous vignettes of Stanisław Wasylewski, but also the controversial *Marysieńka Sobieska* (1938) by Free Poland's eminent writer, Tadeusz Żeleński (Boy). In the field of biography—fictional yet far removed from the romantic—was the portrait of a humble foot soldier in the imperial Austrian army by Józef Wittlin (*q.v.*), *Sól ziemi* (1936; Eng. tr., *Salt of the Earth,* 1939).

A strong trend toward the cultivation of various regional movements in literature manifested itself toward the end of the 30's in Poland, and one can only surmise the consequences had Poland's life as a state not been abruptly cut off by the German invasion of September, 1939.

See: P. Chmielowski, *Zarys literatury polskiej z ostatnich lat szesnastu* (1881) and *Nasza literatura dramatyczna* (1898); K. Wojciechowski, *Przewrót w umysłowości i literaturze polskiej po roku 1863* (1928); W. Borowy, "Fifteen Years of Polish Literature (1918–1933)," *Slavonic Review,* XII (1933–1934), 670–690; K. Czachowski, *Obraz współczesnej literatury polskiej* (3 vols., 1934–1936) and *Najnowsza twórczość literacka* (1938); O. Forst-Battaglia, "The Polish Novel of Today," *Slavonic Review,* XV (1936–1937), 663–674; Z. Grabowski, "Polish Literature between Two Wars," *Free Europe* (London), January 12, 1940, pp. 96–97; W. J. Rose, "The Poets of Young Poland, 1890–1903," *Slavonic Year-Book,* XX (1941), 185–199.

A. P. C.

Pondal, Eduardo (1835–1917, Spanish poet), was born at Ponteceso in Galicia. He studied medicine in Santiago de Compostela and took part in liberal student agitations which culminated in a banquet given for the workers in Conjo, a village near Santiago. He was threatened with punishment by the authorities because of the tone of his fiery anarchical verses. He was graduated as a doctor in 1860 and almost always lived in retirement in his native village. His poetry is contained in two books, *Rumores de los pinos* (1877), written for the most part in Castilian with a few poems in Galician, and *Queixumes dos pinos* (1886; Complaints of the Pines), entirely in Galician. At his death he left unpublished an extensive poem of epic cast, "Os Eoas" (a reference to the seafaring people of the East), written in Galician and relating the deeds of the discoverers of America.

In the renaissance of Galician poetry, Pondal represents the romanticism of the Celtic school and—it might even be said—of Ossianic stripe. He was much given to reading and annotating. His powers of abstraction place him in an almost prehistoric atmosphere, and then the present world adapts itself to his imagination. The murmurs of the pines of Bergantiños resound in his ears like the harps of the ancient singers, and the trees form legions of Celtic warriors; he feels himself to be a bard from other periods before Christianity. Seated by the sea which furiously beats upon the shores of the Galician Finisterre, he carries on a dialogue with the fairy Rouriz or foretells days of glory for the race of Breogán now unchained. Pondal possesses a great humanistic-literary culture (Tasso, Camões, Latin, Greek, mythology), understanding of the Celts and sympathy with the fantastic halo that surrounds them, and exquisite sensibility which allows him to present the remote in terms of the present by symbolic-naturalistic means. He does not, however, adopt the Gaelic literary cycle with its sustained scenes and dramatization, but offers momentary evocations, brief and moving, a miraculous product of an ancestral influence of land and race. No one has written Galician poetry with more austere sonority and grandeur. Discipline in the classical languages has resulted in the most direct of manners put to the service of a primitive solemnity. On rare occasions is seen the nostalgic melancholy common to the Galician poets of his period, in stanzas like those of his most famous composition "A campana d'Anllons" (The Bell of Anllons). Here a captive in Africa grievously evokes his native country under the spell of a hallucination in which he hears the sound of his village bell on a night of full moon. Pondal stands worthily beside Rosalía Castro (*q.v.*) among the poets of his country and time.

See: C. Barja, *En torno al lirismo gallego del siglo XIX* (1926), pp. 92–102; R. Otero Pedrayo, *Discurso de ingreso na Academia Galega* (1931), pp. 109–205.

R. M. L.

Ponten, Josef (1883–1940, German novelist), is one of the foremost representatives of *Sachlichkeit* in modern German literature, chiefly through his portrayal of the life and fate of German emigrant groups in foreign countries, especially Russia. A native of the countryside near Aachen (born at Raeren), he combined the geniality of Rhenish temperament with serious endeavor in the study of geography, philosophy, architecture, and history. Although he spent a large portion of his life "on the road," traveling extensively in Europe, the Americas, Asia, and Africa, and although he chose Munich as his domicile for the last 20 years of his life, he never relinquished the fundamental emotional and spiritual stimuli of his native scene on the Rhine—the simple life of the country folk, the impressive natural environment, the lively river traffic, the celebrated Rhenish art and architecture, the eventful history of one of the oldest provinces of Germany, and last but not least the historical and legendary figure of Charlemagne. These elements furnish, if not the background, at least the poetic and human impulses behind most of his writings.

Ponten's literary significance is primarily based on the extensive series of novels under the collective title *Volk auf dem Wege*, which, composed from 1925 on, began to appear in 1930. But before 1925 Ponten gained considerable repute through several short stories and novels such as *Jungfräulichkeit* (1906; new version, 1920), *Siebenquellen* (1908), *Die Insel* (1918), *Der babylonische Turm* (1918), *Die Bockreiter* (1919), *Der Meister* (1919), *Der Gletscher* (1923), *Die Uhr von Gold* (1923), and *Der Urwald* (1924). In the same group belong *Salz* (1927) and *Die Studenten von Lyon* (1927). Most of these works, participating in the prophetic tone of expressionism without sharing its frenzy, pose in one form or another the problem of the cultural crisis of modern man. They do not voice violent protest or accusation; as long as they can proclaim the continuity of life they are willing to accept the tragic destruction of the individual. Their relative lack of action is balanced by most brilliant description of natural scenery or of cosmic events as well as by calm and concise use of dialogue. Ponten's art of characterization in these books is most successful. Frequently they reveal the author as an attentive disciple of Goethe's physics and Nietzsche's (*q.v.*) metaphysics.

While these earlier works often assumed allegorical dimensions, *Volk auf dem Wege* is grounded more on observation, experience, and source studies. Chancing upon the settlements of Volga Germans in 1920, Ponten planned to present the poetic history of German emigration in various cycles, covering several continents. Only the Russian cycle was completed. In 1930 and 1931 the first volumes appeared (*Wolga, Wolga* and *Rhein und Wolga*); they were soon withdrawn and rewritten. From 1933 on the following volumes were published: *Im Wolgaland* (1933), *Die Väter zogen aus* (1934), *Rheinisches Zwischenspiel* (1937), *Die Heiligen der letzten Tage* (1938), *Der Zug nach dem Kaukasus* (1940, published posthumously). Tracing the various waves of emigration as far back as 1689, Ponten portrays the most diverse causes and motives of "German unrest" and the aspirations and disillusions which accompanied it. With humanistic restraint he pictures historical events as natural processes, as it were, subject to the polarity of being and becoming, of existence and change; but he never succumbs to the lure of narrow-minded nationalism which his subject obviously contained. Similar devotion to objective reality, marked by the absence of sentimental evaluation, pervades Ponten's essays on nature and art, *Studien über Alfred Rethel* (1910; 2d ed., 1922), *Griechische Landschaften; ein Versuch künstlerischer Erdbeschreibung* (1914), *Architektur, die nicht gebaut wurde* (1924), *Europäisches Reisebuch* (1928).

See: Wilhelm Schneider, *Josef Ponten* (1926); L. A. Shears, "The Novellen of Josef Ponten," *Germanic Review*, XI (1936), 50–55; G. Fittbogen, "Pontens volksdeutsches Romanwerk," *Dichtung und Volkstum*, XXXIX (1938), 213–222; H. Rehder, "Josef Ponten, Gestalt und Werk," *Monatshefte für deutschen Unterricht*, XXXIII (1941), 124–137.

H. R.

Pontoppidan, Henrik (1857–1943, Danish novelist), owes his Latinized name to one of his numerous clerical forebears. His father was a clergyman in the Established Church, and although Henrik's childhood in the little Jutland town of Randers seems to have been happy, he reacted against the dominant clerical influence. He wanted a practical profession and chose civil engineering, but when he had almost finished his course, he dropped it in order to become a teacher in his brother's folk high school. Once more he reacted against the religion which here was in the Grundtvigian (*i.e.,* folk high school) pattern and, in Pontoppidan's opinion, was too facile, sentimental, and "joyous." As soon as he had placed his first book, he decided to devote himself entirely to writing. He was on the whole in accord with the principles of Georg Brandes (*q.v.*), but did not feel at home in Copenhagen literary and artistic circles. Many years later he voiced his complete disillusion with the leadership of Brandes in a poem written for the great critic's 70th birthday.

Pontoppidan settled down in the country and married a farmer's daughter. Through his own experiences he learned to know many phases of Danish life. More than any other class he respected the peasants and the small bourgeoisie, but he thought the strongest leaders were likely to come from those who had struggled up from the very bottom. He believed in hate as a potent force for advancement and excoriated his countrymen for their complacency, their easy tolerance of abuses, for their famous "Danish grin," and their addiction to sweetness and light.

In his early books of short stories Pontoppidan painted the life of the very poor in the rural districts with a naturalism that was new at the time. In the three great novel cycles which constitute his chief works he has a wider field and a great variety of types. *Det forjættede Land* (3 vols., 1891–1895; Eng. tr., *The Promised Land,* 1896) tells the story of a clergyman who is imbued with Tolstoyan ideals and tries to put them into practice, but ends in collapse and insanity. The background is that of the Grundtvigian church circles. *Lykke-Per* (2 vols., 1898–1904; Lucky Per) describes life in Copenhagen during the reign of Brandes (who appears in the book as Dr. Nathan). The hero is Per Sidenius, a clergyman's son who revolts against his home and sets out, as a perfectly selfish cad, to conquer the world, but ultimately returns to the ascetic ideal instilled in him from childhood. *De Døødes Rige* (2 vols., 1912–1916; The Kingdom of the Dead) is an utterly pessimistic picture of Denmark at a time when liberalism had conquered outwardly, but, in the opinion of the author, had failed to transform the spirit of the people. Finally, *Mands Himmerig* (1927; Man's Heaven) is an intensely bitter attack on the Danish people at the beginning of the First World War, on the press, the government, the profiteers, and the public which cared about nothing except to keep out of trouble.

No other Danish writer castigated his people as Pontoppidan did. Nevertheless the sense that his anger derived from affection somehow penetrated their minds and won him loyal allegiance in return. The memoirs he published in his old age are mellow and kindly in tone. In 1917 Pontoppidan shared the Nobel prize in literature with his countryman Karl Gjellerup (*q.v.*). The Swedish critic Frederik Böök remarked that instead of half a prize he should have had two.

See: Hanna Astrup Larsen, "Pontoppidan of Denmark," *American-Scandinavian Review,* XXXI (1943), 231–239.

H. A. L.

Popov, Alexander Serafimovich, *see* Serafimovich, Alexander.

Popović, Bogdan (1863–1945, Serb critic and essayist), born in Belgrade, came of a very cultured family and was educated at the University of Belgrade and later in Paris, at the Sorbonne. In 1893 he was made professor of French, comparative literature, and literary theory at the University of Belgrade and soon became a focus of Serbian intellectual life. A university professor during four decades, he contributed to the formation of many writers who later played major roles in the Serbian literary world. As a founder and first editor of the best South Slav review, *Srpski književni glasnik* (1901–1941; Serbian Literary Herald), Popović showed clearly and persuasively which direction his nation should take in writing.

Popović was a man of amazing erudition. Familiar with many European languages and a good classical scholar, he was thoroughly acquainted with much of the world's best literature. Among his numerous translations from English, French, and German are Shakespeare's *The Taming of the Shrew* and Molière's *Le Malade imaginaire.* Besides literature, he understood excellently music, painting, and sculpture, revealing critical gifts in all these domains. His lectures as well as his writings abound in allusions and references taken from a rich artistic treasury out of whose depths he drew countless examples.

Popović was not a fertile or quick writer; he remained a long time considering a problem, analyzing minute details, but the results of his meditations display profoundness of thought, ingenuity of observation, rightness of judgment, and delicacy of taste. His brilliant study *Bomarshe* (1889, 1925; Beaumarchais), his essay *O književnosti* (1894; On Literature), the two volumes of *Ogledi* (1924–1927; Essays), show exceptional writing talent. Outstanding also are articles such as "Walt

Whitman i Swinburne" (Walt Whitman and Swinburne; *Srpski književni glasnik,* January 16, 1925) and "Šta Srbi imaju da nauče of Engleza" (What the Serbs Have to Learn from the English; *Srpski književni glasnik,* September–December, 1929), and the masterly *Antologija novije srpske lirike* (1912; Anthology of New Serbian Lyrics). Popović was more a philosopher of art than an everyday critic, and for him a literary work often served only as an incentive for the development of his aesthetic theories in general. Very significant are his essays on the education of taste, on the principle of harmony, on satire and allegory, on poetical diction. He insists in an essay on criticism upon the scrutiny of "line after line, word after word," until beauty, scientifically tested, becomes real, intense, irresistible. His most important theories have been collected by his disciple Lj. Petrović under the title *Misli i refleksije Bogdana Popovića* (1923; Thoughts and Reflections of Bogdan Popović).

Bogdan Popović's style, vigorous and simple, clear and precise, has served as a model for his numerous disciples. In this way there has come into being the so-called "Belgrade style." Popović is also responsible for the introduction of European criteria and the European spirit into Serbian literature. His judgments often seem sharp and stern, but they are always just and well meant; consequently his influence has been widespread and enduring.

See: I. Sekulić, "'Ogledi' Bogdana Popovića," *Srpski književni glasnik,* Vol. XXI (May–August, 1927); *Zbornik u čast Bogdana Popovića* (1929).

P. A.

Porto-Riche, Georges de (1849–1930, French dramatist), asked to have inscribed on his tomb these words: "The author of *Amoureuse.*" The description is exact, for Porto-Riche is the dramatist of but one play. Presented at the Odéon in 1891 with Réjane in the leading role, *Amoureuse* broke with the fashion of French naturalism (*q.v.*) to return to the French classical tradition of simplicity, penetration, and finesse in the portrayal of passion. Its two principal characters, unlovely but very human, illustrate the fact that it is not enough for two people to love each other if they do not love in the same manner and with something like the same degree of intensity. The fatuous man and the sensual woman whose erotic approaches form the subject of Porto-Riche's comedy of the couple express themselves with cynicism and sometimes with crudity, but they provide insights into the human heart that are reminiscent of Racine. In the violence and predominately sensual quality of the love he depicts, most of Porto-Riche's critics discern a specifically Jewish character.

Georges de Porto-Riche was born in Bordeaux of Italian Jewish parents and was not himself naturalized until 1892, following the triumph of *Amoureuse.* After several volumes of romantic lyrics and some plays, both in bad verse and bad taste, he discovered himself in the one-act *Chance de Françoise* (1888), a foretaste of *Amoureuse.* Later plays—*Le Passé* (1897), *Le Vieil Homme* (1911), *Le Marchand d'estampes* (1917), *Les Vrais Dieux* (1929)—contributed nothing to his initial success. In 1923, after five unsuccessful candidatures, he was elected to the French Academy but never attended a meeting of that august body. He greatly influenced Donnay and Bataille (*qq.v.*).

See: P. Lasserre, *Portraits et discussions* (1914); H. Charasson, *G. de Porto-Riche, ou le Racine juif* (1925); W. Müller, *G. de Porto-Riche* (1934).

J. O'B.

Portuguese literature. By the third quarter of the 19th century, after the long crisis occasioned by the implantation of liberalism and its embodiment into the historical structure of the country, Portuguese romanticism proper had produced everything that could be expected of it. This movement has been divided, with some overlapping, into three periods. An "initial romanticism" (1825–1851) produced three leaders, Almeida-Garrett (1799–1854), Alexandre Herculano (1810–1877), and António Feliciano de Castilho (1800–1875). Upon Garrett's death, the germ of rebellion inherent in the movement was personified in Herculano—he himself called his work "the first attempt at a critical history of Portugal"—but this insurrection disappeared with his retirement to the village of Vale de Lobos in 1867. Then only Castilho remained; around him had collected the greater part of the writers who were to constitute the "second romanticism" (1851–1871). Castilho, a master of the language, a man of verbal opulence but possessing scant creative imagination, personified the adaptation of romanticism to the old culture of Portuguese society. His formation coincided with the dissolution of Arcadian classicism, and he participated in the introduction of romanticism without in fact accepting it entirely. About 1865 he was the pontiff of the pseudoclassic adaptation of romanticism, enthroned as the official, ruling taste. Castilho was the obstacle in the path of the new generation that introduced the "third romanticism" (1871–1890), which soon evolved into a frank realism marking the beginning of contemporary literature. This third movement began with the rebellion of the so-called Generation of Coimbra. The lines were drawn for the battle between the initial romanticism which now enjoyed an official, academic status and the unrestrained, social and critical convictions, highly personal, of the newcomers. The new group revolted not only against the tyranny of officialized taste, represented by Castilho, but also against all its philosophical, aesthetic, and historical concepts—especially against the accompanying national optimism—and stated the necessity of adapting Portugal to European trends.

The young generation broke forth with two noisy manifestations. The first was the famous *"questão coimbrã"* (Coimbra question) presented in the pamphlet *Do bom senso e bom gôsto* (1866; Of Good Sense and Good Taste), and the second the "Conferências democráticas do Casino de Lisboa" (1871; Democratic Lectures in Lisbon's Casino). The young students of Coimbra had shown themselves on several occasions rebellious against the scholastic iron discipline of the University. Two very distinct personalities, Antero de Quental and Teófilo Braga (*qq.v.*), were the visible heads of the university insurgency. Quental had already published *Sonetos* (1861; Sonnets), *Beatrice* (1863), a poem permeated with amorous idealism, and *Fiat Lux* (1863) and *Odes modernas* (1865), in which he attempted to harmonize inspiration and the scientific spirit; Teófilo Braga had also made his appearance in the world of letters with two cyclical poems of Hugoesque inspiration, *Visão dos tempos* (1864; Vision of the Ages) and *Tempestades sonoras* (1864; Sonorous Tempests). The "questão" revealed the abyss separating the two generations. The motive was a trivial one. Castilho, the patriarch of letters, in a letter-preface to the *Poema da mocidade* of Pinheiro Chagas (1842–1895)—spoiled darling of the elect oldsters of Lisbon—had made some references, rather more ironical than malevolent, to the two new poets of Coimbra, attacking the aesthetic tendencies of these representatives of the reforming student youth. Replies were immediately forthcoming, a result of the direct allusion and of the desire for polemical discussion on the part of the young men. Antero de Quental published the acrid brochure mentioned, *Do bom senso e bom gôsto,* in which he attacked Castilho violently. The latter's adherents came forth with a great display of energy; pamphlets flew from the one camp and the other. Quental attacked again with *A dignidade das letras e as literaturas oficiais* (1865; The Dignity of Letters and Official Literature), and Braga published his *Teocracias literárias* (1865; Literary Theocracies).

Camilo Castelo Branco (*q.v.*), the great independent novelist, who was to have subsequent encounters with the same younger generation, took part in the controversy and attacked those of the Coimbra Group with his pungent sarcasm. The polemic lasted until 1866. It was an encounter in which the newcomers saw the opportunity to display themselves in public and try their forces with the enemy. This new romanticism, saturated with French culture and with everything that came through France from the rest of Europe, first took its subject matter from the French thinkers of the group of '48—Michelet, Proudhon, *et al.* Later it broadened its sources and ended in a well-marked realism. Those young men absorbed everything: the satanism of Baudelaire (*q.v.*), the historical erudition of Leconte de Lisle (*q.v.*), the determinism of Taine (*q.v.*), the humanitarian liberalism of Hugo, the apostolic revolutionism of Michelet, the alleged dilettantism of Renan (*q.v.*), and subsequently the realism of Flaubert and Zola (*qq.v.*). All of France overflowed into these rebellious and irreverent youths who, reared in the patriotic optimism of romanticism, had awakened to passionate hypercriticism and denunciation of national historical values. José Maria Eça de Queiroz (*q.v.*), a member of the group and creator of the character "Fadrique Mendes," the ideal type of the generation, said, speaking of "the ardent and fantastic Coimbra" of his day: "Over the railroads which had opened the Peninsula, whole waves of new things descended upon us every day from France, and Germany by way of France: ideas, aesthetic systems, forms, sentiments, humanitarian interests. . . . Each new day brought its revelation like a new sun. Michelet appeared, and Hegel, and Vico, and Proudhon; and Hugo turned prophet and exacting judge of kings; and Balzac with his perverse and languid world, and Goethe, vast as a universe, and Poe and Heine and I believe even Darwin and some others." Everything interested them, folklore, philology, comparative religion, ethnology, archaeology. All the scientific apparatus of the 19th century was brought forward to confront the old flimsy romanticism of Arcadian tendencies. But what really absorbed these young writers was Humanity—in capital letters and still with a romantic coloring. "We began immediately to love Humanity as ultraromanticism had loved Elvira, dressed in muslin in the moonlight," said Eça. Within the resulting ideological confusion two philosophical tendencies were outstanding, the Hegelianism of Quental and the Comtism of Braga. The first of these tendencies was to nourish in Quental the best philosophical poetry of Portugal, and the other was to produce in Braga "the most distinguished victim of the systematic method," whose work as an investigator was impaired by his dogmatism and extravagant syntheses.

The second manifestation of the Generation of Coimbra, now mature, came, as already indicated, in 1871. Some of the members of the original group, with the addition of new elements, had established a *cénacle* in Lisbon, headed by Antero de Quental. Under his leadership they organized the "Conferências democráticas do Casino de Lisboa." Their intention, expressed in the program prepared by Quental, was, in short, to transform Portuguese society by relating the country to the philosophical, aesthetic, and social currents of Europe. Only four lectures were given; three were published the same year. The first, by Quental, dealt with "Causas da decadência dos povos peninsulares" (Causes of the Decay of the Peninsular Peoples)—and was the real point of departure for all the Spanish revisionist literature of the Generation of '98 (*see* Spanish literature). Eça de Queiroz spoke on "Realismo na arte" (Realism in Art). The fifth lecture would have been "Historiadores críticos de vida de Jesús" (Critical Historians of the Life of Jesus), but the government suspended the series as prejudicial to the state religion.

The aged Herculano broke his silence to protest against the official act. Eça soon provided conservative criticism with a motive for attack. Rebellion in the novel was bound to meet violent opposition, owing to the popularity of the genre. Already in 1867 Eça's contributions to the *Gazeta de Portugal,* in a fiercely satanistic tone, had provoked scoffing criticism, and now with the publication of his novel *O crime do Padre Amaro* (1875; Father Amaro's Crime), characterized by a strong psychophysiological social realism in the manner of Zola, the great battle began. A journalist and critic, J. M. da Silva Pinto, a friend of Castelo Branco, published a book praising Eça and the new school, but Branco himself attacked the innovators bitterly and became involved (1881) in an extremely heated controversy with one of the defenders of the new tendencies. Pinheiro Chagas accused Eça of being unpatriotic because of his naturalistic presentation of Portuguese society. Eça's daring realism distressed persons of timorous ethics. Brochures were published addressed to mothers to warn them of the moral pitfalls of the new style. Castelo Branco had carried his belligerency so far as to publish various novels parodying those in the new manner, such as *Eusébio Macário; história natural e social d'uma família no tempo dos Cabraes* (1879; Eusébio Macário; Natural and Social History of a Family in the Time of the Cabrals), and although these purport to be only caricatures of the realistic method, some of them are notable examples of this very technique. Meanwhile the adherents of the new school were explaining and defending it actively. One theorist who expounded its principles was Júlio Lourenço Pinto (*q.v.*)—who as a novelist applied the principles far too rigorously. Another writer, Guilherme Moniz Barreto (*q.v.*), in his literary criticism brought to this type of literature an impartiality of judgment unknown at that time in Portugal. Opposition still continued in 1887 when Pinheiro Chagas, chairman of the prize committee of the Portuguese Academy, caused the rejection of Eça's novel *A relíquia* (1887; Eng. tr., *The Relic,* 1925). The essence of the contention resided in the fact that realism was not a gradual process of evolution from post-romanticism but a weapon imported by a generation for whom "realism meant not only a definite literary school which gave a special interpretation to the novel, but also, and in broader terms, an attitude of protest against a subjective idealism paradoxically without ideals."

This belligerent generation produced three figures of the highest rank—Quental in poetry, Eça in the novel, and Joaquim de Oliveira Martins (*q.v.*) in historical writing. Oliveira Martins was a continuator of the critical thesis of Herculano and a writer who exerted considerable influence on the Spanish thought of the Generation of '98. Also to be mentioned are Abílio Guerra Junqueiro (*q.v.*) and Gomes Leal (1849–1921), eloquent poets with civic-social preoccupations, and João de Deus (*q.v.*), who purifies amorous lyricism through the delicacy of his emotion and the transparency of his methods. In general terms it can be asserted that realism broadened the scope of this poetry by incorporating into it political, social, and philosophical themes.

The poetic vocabulary was expanded, and there was a deliberate seeking after themes and words previously considered unpoetical, as though from a special delight in opposing romantic fastidiousness. In the field of scholarship Téofilo Braga carried out a prodigious work of literary investigation, Francisco de Sousa Viterbo (*q.v.*) untiringly accumulated historical materials, and Gama Barros (1854–1925), Costa Lobo (1840–1913), and Ramos Coelho (1832–1914) elevated historical writing to great heights. The novel reached its apogee at this time with Eça. Other adherents to realism were Francisco Teixeira de Queiroz (*q.v.*), Abel Botelho (*q.v.*), so unflinchingly naturalistic in his *Patologia social* (Social Pathology) series, and Júlio Lourenço Pinto. José Duarte Ramalho Ortigão (*q.v.*) was outstanding in social criticism and travel literature. In collaboration with Eça he published *As farpas* (1871–1883; The Darts), a journal devoted to satire and social education. This type of publication was continued in *Os gatos* (1889–1893; The Cats) by José Valentim Fialho de Almeida (*q.v.*), who replaced fine irony with violent sarcasm. Fialho was also notable as a writer of stories in which he combined a realism characterized stylistically by a plastic striving for great effects and a preoccupation with "écriture artiste." José de Trindade Coelho (*q.v.*) continued his use of country themes and his stylistic scrupulousness. Alberto Braga (*q.v.*) told delightful village tales in a serene and simple manner. Jaime de Magalhães Lima (*q.v.*), who came to literature late, added to realism the humanitarian element of the Russian novel of Leo Tolstoy (*q.v.*), whose doctrines he propounded in a theoretical exposition.

The English threat of war in 1890 and the republican rebellion of Oporto aggravated adverse criticism of the regime and at the same time carried national literary negativism to a systematic denial of historical values. An all but total political impregnation of literature had taken place. Reaction was almost instantaneous, for once again the need was felt to dignify art by removing it from the immediate field of social and political action and from emphasis upon the ugliness of life; it was made to seek the essence of things, not simply to grasp them rationally. This new art, refusing to bow before the alleged scientific veracity of realism, was to seek aesthetic truth. As a reaction against universal and supernational humanitarian liberalism, it was to bring a reversion to the treatment of indigenous themes—a Neo-Garrettism (after Almeida-Garrett, mentioned above). The new movement of aesthetic purification was to affect poetry particularly. No clash comparable to that of 1865–1871 took place, because the newcomers lacked the combative cohesion of the Coimbra Group and in addition their revolution was less profound.

Symbolism began. There was no Parnassian stage, and this is not surprising since the impassive character of that art was in conflict with Portuguese subjectivity and especially since its Hellenic trappings were too reminiscent of the Arcadianism of Castilho. But there were traces of Parnassianism in a certain concern over descriptive accuracy, discernible in the poetry of Cesário Verde and António Feijó (*qq.v.*) and also in the first poems of Gonçalvez Crespo (1846–1883), although he was more closely associated with Brazilian literature. Eugénio de Castro (*q.v.*) was the leader of the *nefelibata* (cloud-treader) movement, the name given to symbolism in the Portugal of that time. His *Oaristos* (1890) was the manifesto. The way had been prepared in many respects by the preceding generation. All the genres had been renovated by foreign influences; poetry alone had made relatively slight progress. Quental, unable to accept satanism, had moved toward a poetry of ideas, extremely personal in nature and expressed through a deep metaphysical lyricism; Junqueiro had imparted eloquent energy to romantic inspiration; and both had supplied new themes, developing a fuller and more sincere poetic language, whose possibilities of expressive simplicity João de Deus had already exploited fully. But none of these things had actually revolutionized poetry, which still followed regular metrical standards and employed an imagery which stopped short of the audacious. A renovation of form was needed and this Castro inaugurated. Entirely new media of expression appeared, the verse line was revolutionized, and an ostentatious vocabulary for fabrics, jewels, perfumes, and rare gems was evolved as a by-product of descriptive Parnassianism. All this was accompanied by a daring system of metaphors, based on bold and unexpected relationships of ideas. Poetry was separated completely from the forum and the market place, and once more the Portuguese bard was concerned with the timeless themes of love and melancholy.

Eugénio de Castro, more receptive to exterior than to local contacts, became one of the Portuguese writers with greatest universal reputation. In Paris he founded an international review, *Arte,* on which Mallarmé and Verlaine (*qq.v.*) collaborated. He established contacts with artists from all over the world who gathered in Paris, and he came to know Rubén Darío. He exerted a profound influence on the Hispanic American *modernista* movement. On the other hand, António Nobre (*q.v.*) was the greatest influence in Portugal and was almost at the opposite pole from the cosmopolitanism of Castro. Exterior contacts caused Nobre to withdraw within himself and to express his subjectivity in a purely Portuguese manner. Combining morbid peasant childishness and literary decadence, he created a regionalism of a certain aesthetic quality which was colored by rustic adolescent recollections in a tormented hypersensitive tone. *Só* (1892; Alone) has been called a "work which marks the return, not only to Garrett, but to all the morbid poetical tendencies and all the picturesque weaknesses of the national spirit."

Two historical events helped restore to literature the impulse for action and the consciousness of national energy—the establishment of the republic (1910) and participation in the First World War. Literature again participated in politics, in a more subtle manner. Manuel da Silva Gaio (*q.v.*) established Neo-Lusitanianism, with the plan, expressed in a symbolic poem, *Chave dourada* (1916; Golden Key), of making the mysticism of the race the basis of national energy. Nationalism branched off in two tendencies, an acceptance of the republic and a desire for counterrevolution. The first was represented in the formation of the group "Renascença Portuguesa" (Portuguese Renaissance), and among its principal leaders were the poets Joaquim Teixeira de Pascoais (*q.v.*) and Jaime Cortesão (1884–), the essayist António Sérgio (*q.v.*), the philosopher Leonardo Coimbra 1883–1936). Pascoais, editor of the group's organ *A águia* (1910; The Eagle), was its spokesman for some time with his doctrine of *saüdosismo*, which endeavored to make of the *saüdade*—national feeling of pleasurable pain in nostalgia—a motive for action. *A arte de sur português* (1915; The Art of Being Portuguese) was the book which expounded this doctrine. Opposition to the republic grouped itself about the historian, poet, and essayist António Sardinha (*q.v.*), who organized the "Integralismo Lusitano" (Lusitanian Integralism) and its organ *A nação portuguesa* (1914; The Portuguese Nation). This movement has been compared with the Action Française and resembles it in many respects; although Sardinha quotes Léon Daudet and Maurras (*qq.v.*), the one to whom he is spiritually akin is Barrès (*q.v.*). The recent authoritarian government (1926–) found its doctrinal basis in this group.

Afonso Lopes Vieira (*q.v.*), founder of the journal *Lusitânia* (1924–1927), on which writers from both groups collaborated, represents purely literary nationalism, and he has sought the national essence not in an artificially picturesque regionalism, but in the roots of his country's literature. In his poetry he has endeavored to effect a fusion between extreme modernity and the archaism of the lyric tradition. A great part of contemporary Portuguese poetry, indeed, has tried to find its formula in an intellectualized vision of folkloric elements, by combining ingenuousness as to theme with skillful elaboration, in what has been called "the democratization of Parnassus and symbolism." Augusto Gil (*q.v.*) describes the pagan-Christian simplicity of the villages in musical Verlainian verses. António Correia de Oliveira (*q.v.*) is carried away by the unadorned and devout graciousness of country life, and, abandoning his devotion to a nebulous pantheism, he becomes the singer of Catholicism and the historic past.

Poetry based on national emotion is disappearing, in favor of themes taken from the intimate zones of personality, from the hermetic seclusion of the inner world, unconcerned by collective destiny. This tendency can already be noted in the next to the last generation, as in the case of Camilo Pessanha (*q.v.*), translator of Chinese poems, whose work is already characterized by a subjective lyricism. Feminine participation in this tendency is notable; among others, Virginia Vitorino (*q.v.*) is an example with her impassioned sonnets. Such poetry presages the *modernista* movement, which had its focal point in Coimbra in the journal *Presença* (1927) and which, after undergoing the momentary influence of futurism (cf. *Orféu*, 1915; Orpheus), has produced poets as delicate as Fernando Pessoa (*q.v.*), Adolfo Casais Monteiro (1908–), Mário de Sá Carneiro (1884–1916), and José Régio (1901–). The influence of Valéry, the ideas of Proust (*qq.v.*), "pure poetry," are discernible in this poetry.

Various attempts at realism in the drama produced little worthy of mention. The nationalistic reaction gave rise to a neoromantic theatre in which the influences of the Scandinavians, of Maeterlinck and Rostand (*qq.v.*), were incorporated. João da Câmara (*q.v.*) is really outstanding in the depiction of regional manners and customs. Amilcar Ramada Curto (*q.v.*) tends toward social criticism. Júlio Dantas (*q.v.*) has brought an elegant, poetic, and heroic Don Juanism to the theatre. A majority of authors have preferred romanticized emotions about the Peninsular past—Fernando Caldeira (1841–1894), Lopes de Mendonça (1856–1931), Marcelino Mesquita (1856–1919), and Eduardo Schwalbach (1856–1919) in addition to the already mentioned Virginia Vitorino, Jaime Cortesão, Correia de Oliveira, *et al.*

The novel is still under the influence of Eça de Queiroz. Themes vary, descriptive naturalism is accentuated, but the structure remains unchanged. Aquilino Ribeiro (*q.v.*) with his copious production is the most consistent follower of Eça. Other novelists are Antero de Figueiredo (1867–), who imparts a certain religious shade to his work, Manuel Ribeiro (1879–1941), in whom can be noted the influence of Huysmans (*q.v.*), and Augusto de Castro (1883–), characterized by psychological tendencies. Oriental exoticism, a part of the old national tradition, reappeared with the Japonism of Wenceslau de Morais (*q.v.*) who, in the desire to "change his soul," may be compared with Lafcadio Hearn. Criticism, since the period of realism, has progressed in all fields, historical, literary, philosophic, etc. The generation of nationalism has produced figures such as Carolina Michaëlis de Vasconcelos (*q.v.*), expert in the study of medieval Romance texts. At the present time a brilliant generation of investigators in numerous special fields is bringing honor to Portugal, alternating works of erudition with the essay and criticism. Above all there is the work of Fidelino de Figueiredo (*q.v.*), indefatigable critic and sagacious essayist, who in the multiplicity of his interests has brought forward the Peninsular point of view in important literary historical writing. There should also be pointed out the work of António Sérgio, whose *Ensaios* (1920–1936) mark a high point in the clarity of Portuguese contemporary thought. Numerous influences can be discerned in the literary production of the moment, though now the French vein seems to be mixed with the English and the Spanish, and to such names as Gide (*q.v.*), Proust, and Valéry should be added those of Thomas Mann, Rilke (*qq.v.*), Joyce, Huxley, Ortega y Gasset (*q.v.*), and Unamuno (*q.v.*). But above the permeations and influences, Portuguese literature can still be heard singing in its unwavering elegiacal range, which after all is the very essence of the ancient national soul.

See: Innocêncio F. da Silva *et al., Dicionário bibliográfico português* (22 vols., 1858–1914); A. de Campos, *Antologia portuguesa* (28 vols., 1919–1926); F. de Figueiredo, *A crítica literária como ciência: Bibliografia portuguesa de crítica literária* (1920), *História da literatura realista,* 1924 ed., and *Depois de Eça de Queiroz* (1938); A. F. G. Bell, *Portuguese Bibliography* (1922) and *Portuguese Literature* (1922); A. J. Anselmo, *Bibliografia das bibliografias* (1923); A. Forjaz de Sampaio, *Coleção patrícia* (51 fascicules, 1923–) and *História da literatura portuguesa ilustrada dos séculos XIX e XX* (1939–); A. F. G. Bell, ed., *Oxford Book of Portuguese Verse* (1925); M. Fonseca, *Aditamentos ao Dicionário bibliográfico português* (1927); J. Mendes dos Remédios, *História da literatura portuguesa desde as origens a atualidade* (1930); G. Le Gentil, *La Littérature portugaise* (1935); H. Cidade, *Tendências do lirismo contemporâneo* (1939).

E. G. D.

Potgieter, Everhardus Johannes (1808–1875, Dutch poet, critic, short-story writer, and essayist), was born at Zwolle, where his father had a draper's business. Everhardus left school when he was 13 years old and was sent to Amsterdam to be employed in the leather trade. In April, 1831, he went on a business trip to Sweden, where he remained till the end of 1832. After his return he established himself as an agent of foreign business concerns. His impressions of that sojourn in Sweden are embodied in *Het Noorden* (2 vols., 1836–1840; The North). In January, 1837, appeared the first issue of *De Gids* (The Guide), a monthly which Potgieter founded and was to edit for the next 28 years. He contributed book reviews, essays, short stories, and poetry. The judgment he passed on contemporary Dutch literature was severe, but deservedly so. He condemned it for its smugness, its pedestrian tone, its lack of moral elevation. *De Gids* came to be known by the nickname *De blauwe Beul* (The Blue Executioner). How feeble and petty, Potgieter thought, were the Dutch of his generation compared to their ancestors of the 17th century. He never tired of reminding his contemporaries of that golden age, in the hope of shaming them into more strenuous activity and emulation of their glorious forebears. *Jan, Jannetje, en hun jongste Kind* (1842; John, Jean, and Their Youngest Child) and *Het Rijksmuseum* (1844; The National Gallery) are his most eloquent pleas for a national revival. In 1863 Coenraad Busken Huet (*q.v.*) joined the editorial board of *De Gids.* He outdid Potgieter in severity when censuring the mediocrity of the monthly literary output. Two articles by Huet in the January issue of 1865 aroused the ire of his fellow editors, who demanded his resignation. Only Potgieter sided with Huet, and when Huet was forced out, Potgieter went out with him. The two friends traveled together to Florence to attend the celebrations in honor of Dante's sexcentenary. This journey suggested to Potgieter the subject of his greatest poem, *Florence* (1868), a poetical life of Dante in *terza rima*. It was included in a volume of his collected poetry, *Poëzy, 1832–1868,* together with another of his major poems, *Gedroomd Paardrijden* (Riding in Dream). Perhaps his most important poetic work is *De Nalatenschap van den Landjonker* (1875, Memories of a Country Esquire), because in this collection of poems he revealed more clearly than elsewhere his inner nature and the hopes, the longings, and disillusions of his life. Potgieter never married. He died in his bachelor home on the Leliegracht at Amsterdam on February 3, 1875.

De Gids, was, thanks to his literary eminence, the leading periodical of its kind in Holland during his lifetime, and it still maintains a place of distinction among Dutch periodicals, although their number has greatly increased since Potgieter's day. He exerted greater influence as a critic than as a writer. Despising the platitudinous and pedestrian writings of most of his contemporaries, he strove, by way of reaction, for a prose style which he meant to be artistic but which impresses a later generation as being ponderous and overornate. His verse was far superior both in form and in content to the poetry of his age, but it is too often marred by the same striving for artistry that vainly parades as art. He was a persistent student of foreign languages, and one of his chief merits was the service he did his countrymen by making them acquainted with the best literature he had found abroad, including the writings of American authors.

See: J. H. Groenewegen, *E. J. Potgieter* (1894); G. Busken Huet, ed., *Brieven van E. J. Potgieter aan C. Busken Huet* (1902); A. Verwey, *Het Leven van Potgieter* (1903); Henry Zylstra, "A Mid-Nineteenth Century Dutch View of American Life and Letters," *Publications of the Modern Language Association of America,* LVII (1942), 1108–1136.

A. J. B.

Pourrat, Henri (1887–, French novelist), was born at Ambert, Puy-de-Dôme, a quiet little town, where prolonged illness has compelled him to spend almost all his life. Under the influence of Jean Angeli, a former schoolmate and an intimate friend endowed with rare artistic sensibility, Pourrat developed at an early date a deep and abiding interest in the picturesque countryside of Auvergne. From the beginning of his literary career his constant preoccupation has been to present a vivid picture of a rural civilization unusually rich in popular lore. His first book, *Sur la colline ronde* (1912), written in collaboration with Angeli, who used the pseudonym Jean l'Olagne, is a series of little sketches depicting life in a village of Auvergne at the beginning of the present century. Since the publication of this work Pourrat has written some 20 volumes dealing with varied aspects of life in his native province and is now recognized by French critics as a master of regionalist literature. His views on this genre are to be found more specifically in *La Ligne verte* (1929) and *Le Bosquet pastoral* (1931), two collections of essays on literature and folklore. In these books he states repeatedly that the regional writer must not use local color as an end in itself, but only as a means. The same idea had already been aptly expressed in *Dans l'herbe des trois vallées* (1927): "True regionalism begins where the picturesque stops." Local color is justified only in so far as it helps the reader better to understand the story. The true artist must avoid sentimentality and introduce a healthy realism and humor in the description of characters and settings.

This is precisely what Pourrat has done with rare success in all his books. Landscapes, people, and customs of his beloved Auvergne have received their most beautiful treatment in his four-volume peasant epic, *Les Vaillances, farces et gentillesses de Gaspard des montagnes* (1922–1931). Perfection of character delineation and depth of poetic feeling combined with the unusual light thrown on popular beliefs and customs, many of which are still current in present-day Auvergne, make this novel one of the masterpieces of contemporary French fiction. Other notable works of Pourrat are *Le Mauvais Garçon* (1926), *Le Meneur de loups* (1930), *La Grande Cabale: Les Sorciers du canton* (1933), *Monts et merveilles* (1934), and *Le Secret des compagnons* (1937).

See: Arno Ringelmann, *Henri Pourrat; ein Beitrag zur Kenntnis der "littérature terrienne"* (1936).

J. M. C.

Prados, Emilio (1899–, Spanish poet), was born in Málaga, Andalusia. Except for a few trips to various Spanish and European cities he lived there until in 1936, when he went to

Madrid to take an active part in the struggle for the republic. In 1939, following the triumph of Franco, he left for Mexico, where he now lives. He was a representative and stimulating member of the Southern Group, which published the journal *litoral* and the works of new poets such as García Lorca, Alberti, Aleixandre (*qq.v.*), and Altolaguirre (*q.v.*)—his inseparable literary associate—as well as the works of Prados himself (*Tiempo,* 1925; *Canciones del farero,* 1925; *Vuelta,* 1927). During the war he reaffirmed his poetic creed and collected the ballads comprising the *Romancero general de la guerra de España* (1937), among which his own ballads are outstanding. His book *Memoria del olvido* (Mexico, 1940) reveals the essential content of his poetry from 1927 and announces the future publication of numerous other works.

In the attitude, inspiration, and form of the Málaga group there has been recognized the stamp of Góngora and the influences of Unamuno, Antonio Machado, Juan Ramón Jiménez—that of the latter in particular—Salinas, and García Lorca (*qq.v.*). With a flavor of the traditional and yet in a most modern and daring manner, Prados brings to literature his own penetrating and serious personality. With as much agility as ardor he interprets his azure and golden countryside of Málaga. The destruction of Spain, in which the lot of Málaga was a particularly painful one, added to his already dramatic sensibility new depths of sorrow and anguish. From that moment his poetry becomes a fever of agony, a tormented dream in which he speaks of death as near and ever present, in which he decries universal injustice in a manner that transcends literary schools and canons, utilizing for these ends a masterful control of classical and popular modes of Spanish poetic expression.

See: *Laurel: Antologia de la poesia moderna en lengua española* (1941), pp. 683–715, 1131.

A. I.

Praga, Marco (1862–1929, Italian playwright), was born in Milan. His father, Emilio Praga, was a prominent member of the *scapigliati,* a group of rebellious and ultraromantic writers of the 1860's. But Marco, who had seen their dream of reviving Italian literature evaporate along with their hazy literary effusions, developed an aversion for romanticism. His father, whose poetic gifts had been vitiated by a life of excesses, died a victim of alcoholism at the age of 36. Marco was then 12 years old. However, he never really forgot the literary glamour which had surrounded the family and tried his hand at play writing while still engaged in the prosaic occupation of accountancy.

His first plays, *L'Incontro* (1883) and *Le Due Case* (1885), both written in collaboration with Virgilio Colombo, gave little indication of the real dramatic gifts latent in this quiet, serious youth. His next play, *L'Amico* (1886), in one act, attracted considerable attention and set the pattern for his subsequent productions. Sensual, illicit love becomes his main theme. *L'Amico* presents the case of a woman who attempts to retrieve letters she had sent her lover, suddenly deceased, and is caught in a trap of her own creation. The dramatic conflict springs from the moral struggle; the dramatic compactness reveals the born playwright. Here in embryonic form are those qualities which become identified with Praga's theatre: a profound analysis of the female character; a dialogue both terse and sober, trenchant in its bitter sarcasm; a faculty for keen and accurate observation; and an aptitude for the faithful and objective representation of life in a few bold strokes.

The people that Praga observed and knew belonged to the aristocratic and well-to-do classes of Milan. It was a society which had enough affluence to permit itself certain luxuries: one of the most costly in human misery was the clandestine and illicit love affair. The prevalence of this immorality may explain Praga's addiction to the theme of adultery. In the projection of his world on the stage he does not preach or inveigh against this moral laxness, nor does he upbraid the transgressors directly. As a playwright his primary interest was to portray life as realistically as possible. Hence his aloofness and his apparent lack of sympathy for his tormented creatures. In this attitude he was an authentic naturalist. In his dramatic creations he is satisfied in letting the spectacle of a humiliated soul consumed by remorse carry its own admonitions. In his more powerful and successful plays, *Le Vergini* (1889), *Il Bell'Apollo* (1894), *La Morale della favola* (1903), *L'Ondina* (1908), and *La Porta chiusa* (1913; Eng. tr., *The Closed Door,* in *The Eleonora Duse Series of Plays,* 1923), the heroine is the victim of man's egotistical nature. Disillusioned and humiliated, she resigns herself to a life of silent expiation of her shame. The male protagonists of most of these plays are self-centered and vain—unworthy of the love and sacrifices they seem to inspire. This contrast between man's selfishness and woman's sacrifice is basic with Praga. But two notable exceptions are found in *La Moglie ideale* (1890) and in *La Crisi* (1901), considered the author's masterpiece. In the first of these an amoral woman contrives to make her husband happy because she possesses the necessary *sang-froid* and cunning to deceive him without compromising herself. In the second it is man who suffers: a husband accepts the humiliation of sharing his wife's embraces with another for fear of losing her. In such plays as these last two the author presents situations that have a definitely grotesque flavor and seems to anticipate by a decade the vogue of the *teatro del grottesco*.

Other plays of Praga are *Giuliana* (1887), *L'Innamorata* (1891), *Alleluja* (1892), *L'Erede* (1893), *La Mamma* (1903), *Il Dubbio* (1903), and *Il Divorzio* (1915). He also wrote the novels *La Biondina* (1893), *Storie di palcoscenico* (1895), and *Anime a nudo* (1920) and a book on the theatre, *Cronache teatrali* (1925).

See: C. Levi, *Autori drammatici italiani* (1921), pp. 69–110; A. Galletti, *Il Novecento* (1935), pp. 417–419.

P. P. M.

Prévost, Jean (1901–1944, French essayist and novelist), attended the Lycée Henri IV. There he studied under Alain (pseud. of Emile Chartier, *q.v.*), whose disciple he remained. In 1919 he entered the Ecole normale supérieure and the Ecole des Langues orientales vivantes. Jacques Rivière (*q.v.*) welcomed him in 1924 to the *Nouvelle Revue française;* in 1925 a short essay, *Tentative de solitude,* was published, in which Prévost attempted to carry isolation and self-analysis to the extreme. The same year he wrote *Plaisirs des sports,* which consisted of a series of analyses of internal sensations and of the movements of the human body. In 1927, in his *Essai sur l'introspection,* he described a series of the intellectual and emotional states commonly believed to be spiritual, in which respect he seemed to adhere to Spinoza's doctrine. Besides a rather inadequate *Vie de Montaigne,* which is in the nature of an educational pamphlet, Prévost had published, in 1926, *Brûlures de la prière,* the fictional diary of a mystic. Editorial secretary on the *Navire d'argent* from 1925 to 1926, then on the staff of the magazine *Europe,* he contributed philosophical essays to those reviews. A novel, *Merlin,* was published in 1928. *Polymnie* (1929) described with almost excessive minuteness the facial and nasal movements of movie actors. The same year also saw the appearance of *Dix-huitième Année,* a volume of Prévost's boyhood souvenirs, which reflects the spirit of his generation. In 1930 was published a "populist" novel, *Les Frères Bouquinquant.* The plot is merely an excuse: the main intention is to show the emotional reactions of members of the working class.

Subsequently Prévost wrote essays (*Les Epicuriens français,* 1931), history (*Histoire de France depuis la guerre,* 1932), short stories (*Nous marchons sur la mer,* 1931; *Lucie-Paulette,* 1935), intelligent but hasty novels (*Rachel,* 1932; *Le Sel sur la plaie,* 1935; *La Chasse du matin,* 1937), and a volume about American civilization (*Usonie,* 1939).

A member of the fighting forces of the Resistance, he fell in the *maquis* of Vercors in 1944.

P. B.

Prévost, Marcel (1862–1941, French novelist, dramatist, and journalist), was born in Paris, the son of a minor government official. Prévost shares with Alexandre Dumas *fils,* who commended his novels, the role of apologist for middle-class moral values. Undoubtedly much of this concern with social law stems from his education in Jesuit schools at Bordeaux and Paris, where high academic honors assured his admission to the Ecole Polytechnique in 1882. Though he had written short stories and articles for *Clairon* as early as 1881, Prévost hesitated to embrace literature as a career, serving as an engineer of the Manufacturiers de Tabacs until 1890, when the success of his first three novels had established his literary reputation. A shrewd psychological insight, flavored by a consciously romantic sensuality reminiscent of George Sand, assured the popularity of *La Confession d'un amant* (1891) and of the *Lettres de femmes* series (1892–1897). Following *Les Demi-Vierges* (1894), which decried moral laxity in the education of young women, Prévost attacked the whole question of feminism in *Les Vierges fortes* (1900), which sought equality for woman within traditional family relationships rather than in independence. His *Lettres à Françoise* (1902), with its sequels, outlined an educational program for the attainment of this feminine ideal. The same mixture of morality and sensuality which led Jules Lemaître to remark that Prévost "loves to dwell on what he condemns" characterizes the long list of novels following his election to the French Academy in 1909. The Vatican denounced *La Retraite ardente* (1927), a somewhat ironic study of spiritual and carnal love which had gained considerable notoriety.

Adaptations of his own novels brought Prévost moderate success as a playwright. An active journalist, he had begun regular contributions to *Figaro* as early as 1902; he directed the publication of the *Revue de*

France until his death at Vianne, Lot-et-Garonne, in April, 1941.

See: Winifred Stephens, *French Novelists of To-day* (1908), pp. 45–81; L. Lemonnier, "Les Romans de Marcel Prévost," *Grande Revue,* CXX (1926), 72–91.

G. Sh.

Prezzolini, Giuseppe (1882–, Italian critic and editor), was born in the city of Perugia. In a land of long-established traditions of formal education he offers the rare example of a self-taught man. Although he came of a family of cultural and literary interests, he left school before obtaining any degree. He found no purpose in life until he went to Florence, where one day he met Giovanni Papini (*q.v.*), in whom he discovered a kindred soul. This meeting marks the turning point in the life of Prezzolini, whose real eagerness to learn in his own way was, through this friendship, given new impetus and an aim. His interest now definitely turned to philosophy and literature. The memory of those days has been indelibly preserved in the tenth chapter of Papini's masterpiece, *Un Uomo finito* (1912), a chapter dedicated to "Giuliano," Prezzolini's pen name in the days of his collaboration with Papini on the famous Florentine review *Leonardo* (1903–1907).

During the days of the *Leonardo,* Prezzolini developed a certain personal inclination towards mysticism under the influence of Bergson (*q.v.*) and James and later of St. Augustine. The experience of the *Leonardo* and the impact of Croce's (*q.v.*) philosophy brought to Prezzolini a feeling of the need of a more earnest way of life for his country. To this end he founded a new review, the *Voce* (1908–1916), dedicated to an intellectual crusade; the aristocracy of culture was to come out of its ivory tower and participate actively in the solution of the problems facing Italy. Prezzolini also attempted to expand Italy's horizons by accounts of the new cultural and philosophical manifestations abroad.

In the *Voce* Prezzolini showed the ability to bring together men who differed not only in character but in political and philosophic thought—Salvemini (*q.v.*) and Mussolini, Gentile (*q.v.*) and Croce (*q.v.*). This ability to discover new men, to interpret the value of new trends in thought and in politics made him an authentic "promoter of culture." It is the same quality which particularly fitted him to direct (1925–1930) the Literary and Information Department of the Bureau for Intellectual Cooperation founded in Paris by the League of Nations, and subsequently to direct (1930–1940) the Casa Italiana of Columbia University in New York. He is now an American citizen.

Prezzolini's great variety of interests has led him into many fields. He tried his hand at allegorical writings in *Il Sarto spirituale* (1906). Having for a while the idea of becoming a systematic philosopher, he began with a study of the inadequacy of language to fully express inward experience (*Il Linguaggio come causa di errore,* 1903) and with a study of the psychological basis of propaganda (*L'Arte di persuadere,* 1905). After the First World War he renounced any attempt to participate actively in the political life of Italy and made up his mind to play the part of impartial judge of men and parties. Invited by the publisher Formiggini to write a biography of Mussolini, he accepted on condition that he also write the biography of Mussolini's chief opponent, Giovanni Amendola; both books appeared in 1923.

Prezzolini is the author of some 20 volumes. He is best known for his interesting study on *Benedetto Croce* (1909), *La Coltura italiana* (1923), his studies on German mystics (*Studi e capricci sui mistici tedeschi,* 1912), his critical essays (*Uomini 22 e città 3,* 1920), and particularly *Amici* (1922), a very readable volume, written in his characteristic unadorned easy-flowing style, devoted to the critical study of certain former collaborators (Jahier, Panzini, Slataper, Soffici, Croce, Salvemini, *qq.v.,* Einaudi, Lombardo-Radice). In 1927 appeared a biography of Machiavelli, widely translated (Eng. tr., 1928). Because of its brilliant, unacademic treatment and entertaining style, it shocked the sedate tastes of some readers, but gave relief to others who were tired of the overdose of ponderous, unimaginative studies on the great Florentine. Since coming to Columbia University (1930) as professor of Italian, Prezzolini has been engaged in the publication of an important bibliography of the history of Italian literary criticism since 1902.

See: C. Pellizzi, *La Letteratura italiana del nostro secolo* (1920); B. Crémieux, preface to the French translation (1925) of Prezzolini, *La Coltura italiana.*

P. M. R.

Prishvin, Mikhail Mikhailovich (1873–, Russian novelist and naturalist), belongs to the older generation, since he was born in Khrushchevo, in the Yelets district of Central Russia, in 1873. He was educated in the local high school and, after some desultory study in Germany, trained himself as an agronomist.

In this capacity his chief contribution to knowledge was *Kartofel* (1905; The Potato), at the time a basic study of tuber culture. Finding agricultural work distasteful, Prishvin made several false starts in letters and then spent some time collecting popular epic poetry in the far northern provinces. The contacts with nature in this area inspired his first successful book, *V krayu nepugannykh ptitz* (1907; In the Land of Unfrightened Birds), followed by *Kolobok* (The Little Round Loaf), inspired by the same experiences. The former book won Prishvin a medal of the Geographic Society and steady journalistic employment. He himself was early to recognize that his chief skill lay in the description of nature, which he instinctively viewed with a painter's eye for color and line. Prishvin's revolutionary experiences were unpleasant, since the local peasants confiscated his small Yelets estate, and he lived for some time in humble circumstances before he acquired a position as schoolteacher in the province of Smolensk.

Prishvin's luck turned in 1923 when Voronski, editor of the magazine *Krasnaya nov* (Red Soil), accepted his episodic novel *Kashcheeva tsep* (The Chain of Kaschei). Having a pronounced autobiographical stamp, this work expressed Prishvin's revolt against superstition and social convention. Its first three parts, after serialization, appeared in book form in 1924 under the group title *Kurymushka* (Prishvin's childhood nickname, roughly "little berry") and gave a fine evaluation of his childhood memories. A fourth part was entitled *Boi* (Battle), and the whole first book appeared in 1927. A second volume in five parts was serialized in 1927–1928 and appeared in book form during the latter year. Prishvin's *Rodniki Berendeya* (1925–1926; Springs of Berendei) is inspired by a love of nature and marked by a talent for the observation of nature rare among Russian authors.

See: D. S. Mirsky, *Contemporary Russian Literature* (1926), pp. 295–296; G. Struve, *25 Years of Soviet Russian Literature* (1944), pp. 17–18.

S. H. C.

Proust, Marcel (1871–1922, French novelist), born in Paris, a scion of the wealthy Parisian bourgeoisie and of Jewish descent on the maternal side, was like Flaubert (*q.v.*)—although much more patently—a genius conditioned by illness. A chronic asthmatic condition, first revealed at the age of nine, cut him off once and for all from the world of action. He literally worshiped his mother, who watched with infinite care over his nervous, sensitive childhood. His father, Adrien Proust, professor at the Paris School of Medicine, promptly decided that the best therapy was to indulge his every whim. Leisurely years on the aristocratic "West Side"; summers at Illiers, a village between Nogent-le-Rotrou and Chartres which he was to immortalize as "Combray," or at Cabourg, the "Balbec" of his novel; brilliant but desultory studies; precocious explorations of the *monde* and *demimonde;* juvenile friendships with a fashionable and literary set—all these circumstances shaped the young man into an aesthete and a snob, charming, eccentric, inordinately curious and observing and yet immensely impractical. In the famous salon of Mme Arman de Caillavet (*see* Caillavet, Gaston Arman de) he brushed elbows with Anatole France (*q.v.*), who condescended to write a preface for Proust's first published work (*Les Plaisirs et les jours,* 1896). Neither this production nor Proust's subsequent journalistic essays (collected as *Pastiches et mélanges,* 1919) proved to be more, however, than the exercises of a fastidious, cultured dilettante.

A trip to Venice (1900) heralded the revelation of Ruskin, whose *Bible of Amiens* (Part I of *Our Fathers Have Told Us*) Proust translated in 1904 (see also his translation of *Sesame and Lilies* in 1906). The deaths in rapid succession of his father and mother (1903, 1905) and a recrudescence of his illness led to the dramatic revulsion from which *A la recherche du Temps Perdu* was born. The former dandy withdrew into quasi seclusion, discharging his social duties through his enormous *Correspondance* (of which six volumes have been printed, 1930–1936). His solitude, unrelieved by any religious faith, turned to art as to "the most austere school of life" and "truly the Last Judgment." Unable to stand the light of day or the noise of the street, Proust wrote by night—mostly in bed—in a cork-walled room filled with the smell of fumigations. Instead of inclining him to concision, the fear of dying too soon caused him to labor feverishly and extend his original three-volume project into a huge cyclic novel of 13 to 16 volumes according to the edition (Eng. tr. by Charles K. Scott Moncrieff and, the last part, by Frederick A. Blossom, *Remembrance of Things Past,* 1922–1932). *Du côté de chez Swann,* the first book and purest gem of the series, came out in 1913 at the author's expense, having been previously refused by several publishers. It went almost unnoticed, in sharp contrast to *A l'ombre des jeunes filles en fleurs* (1918) which won the

Prix Goncourt (1919) and aroused much controversy. Proust's reputation rose to extraordinary heights with *Le Côté de Guermantes* (1920), the four volumes of *Sodome et Gomorrhe* (1921–1923), and the posthumous publication of *La Prisonnière* (2 vols., 1923), *Albertine disparue* (2 vols., 1925), and *Le Temps Retrouvé* (2 vols., 1927) which—as the title indicates—holds the final key to an understanding of the entire work.

That Proust's technique should have been likened by some to that of a *mémorialiste* seems logical enough in view of the fact that *A la recherche du Temps Perdu* records at great length the progressive crumbling of class distinction under the Third Republic and the ultimate abdication of the nobility (or "côté de Guermantes") into the hands of the upper bourgeoisie (or "côté de chez Swann"). Yet Proust himself disclaimed any deliberate ambition on his part to write "the Saint-Simon Memoirs of another epoch." This statement was no mere anticipation of such criticism as would reproach him later for his lack of a political creed, his neglect of the masses, his indifference to economic issues, etc., etc. It sprang from the deep-seated belief that the method commonly termed "realistic" might well be the least realistic of all, since it "decimates" things, satisfies itself with a "puny" inventory of lines and surfaces, and ignores the richer world—the world of inner essences. Unlike the naturalists, Proust did not presume to take "notes" but resorted to "sketches," implying by this that in his eyes the truth of his observations was less a documentary truth inherent in the object than the transient and relative truth of his own successive moods. Thus Proust's analysis never reaches stability or completeness. His cosmos, whether material or moral, and whatever its amazing complexity, consists of an endless chain of approximations.

In such a mobile, atomistic, evanescent universe, the notion of perspective is divested of its spatial content. It comes to represent the angle of incidence of man's emotions; in other words, it takes on a temporal hue. Time, understood in the Bergsonian sense (*see* Bergson, Henri) but not always and not always faithfully; Time, conceived as a "lived" duration but made primarily into an agent of destruction and decay in direct opposition to Bergsonism—Time is the greatest, the most complicated, and, again, the most "approximate" of Proust's characters. In primitive childhood Time is a friend: it stands peaceful and motionless at our side, and the world is ours to have and to enjoy. Presently, however, Time will break this harmony of living: in the wake of our first sorrow, we start on our slow journey toward death and assume the painful task of *comprehending* what we no longer immediately *possess.* Intelligence, therefore, is a fruit of exile grown in a climate of oblivion. The memory of the brain is a faculty most conspicuous by what it forgets, and its very recollections are no recollections at all, rather a system of reference powerless in itself to resuscitate the past. Meanwhile, deep in ourselves, some sort of visceral memory alone challenges the flight of Time, buries all, treasures all, remembers all. Throughout the years the body, this poor, disintegrating machine, renders us the invaluable service of hiding away this one guarantee of our personal identity. Subconscious memory manifests itself in dreams or, during our waking hours, on the occasion of rare "privileged moments" when a chance sensation (it may be the taste of a little cake, the clank of a hammer on a wheel, the peculiar disposition of a group of poplars on the roadside) hauls to the surface its twin sensation of long ago and for a fleeting second abolishes Time by merging our past—the whole living past to which it belongs—into our present.

A la recherche du Temps Perdu is the poem of Oblivion and Memory. It is not, in the manner of Joyce's *Ulysses,* a passive reproduction of the stream of consciousness. It is very much, despite all of Proust's anti-intellectualism, a rational effort at organization and elaboration. The "drops" of transcendental remembrance that fall from the subconscious will be crystallized by means of a mysterious alchemy and linked up in a rigid concatenation of metaphors. In order to give actual relief to the gradual encroachments of death upon life and to the corresponding expansion of reason at the detriment of the heart, the narrator of *A la recherche du Temps Perdu* will use the device of making his prelude poetical like infancy and his finale analytical like old age. These magical transmutations and evocative processes are easily recognizable as those of symbolism and impressionism in all the arts, and the last word to be said about Proust is that he strove—how successfully posterity will tell—to become the Charles Baudelaire (*q.v.*) of French fiction.

See: Léon Pierre-Quint, *Marcel Proust; sa vie, son œuvre* (1925; revised ed., 1928, 1935; Eng. tr., 1927); Arnaud Dandieu, *Marcel Proust; sa révélation psychologique* (1930); Charles Blondel, *La Psychographie de Marcel Proust* (1931); Albert Feuillerat, *Comment Marcel Proust a composé son roman* (1934);

Sybil de Souza, *La Philosophie de Marcel Proust* (1939).

J.-A. B.

Prus, Bolesław (pseud. of Aleksander Głowacki, 1847–1912, Polish journalist and novelist), was born at Hrubieszów, on the Lublin-Volhynian border, of lower gentry stock. His mother died when he was three, and he lived for a time with the grandmother whom he later immortalized in *Kłopoty babuni* (1873; A Grandmother's Woes). Later, on the death of his father, he lived with his aunt, Domicela Olszewska, a remarkable woman whom he used as the model for the good wife and mother in *Omyłka* (1884; The Mistake). Prus was powerfully influenced in his schooldays in Lublin by the example of his brilliant, passionately patriotic older brother Leon, who was in the thick of conspiratorial activities. On the outbreak of the uprising of 1863 Prus enlisted at once, although he was only 16, and saw active service with the Polish forces. Injured by a shell and badly burned, he was later imprisoned by the Russians and released only through the bribes and entreaties of his devoted aunt. Prus's eyesight was permanently impaired by the shell wound, and he was obliged in later years to protect his eyes by the dark glasses which became so characteristic of him.

After the uprising, Prus studied for two years in the excellent Szkoła Główna in Warsaw (*see* Polish literature). When this was made a Russian institution (1869), he left to study in the agricultural institute at Puławy, and also independently. After steeping himself thoroughly in the then popular branches of sociology and economics, he took a job in 1872 in the Warsaw factory of Lilpop and Rau, manufacturers of railroad cars, a common thing for young men of his class to do in those days of industry's novelty. Before this Prus had dreamed of emigrating to America; now he wished only to remain in Poland and serve his country along the lines laid down by the increasingly popular positivist creed.

Soon Prus abandoned the factory lathe for the pen, to expose in a series of articles and stories one sore spot after another in the national life. Many of his articles appeared in Świętochowski's (*q.v.*) famous *Przegląd tygodniowy* (Weekly Review). All segments of Polish life came under his survey, from the industrial workers of Łódź, in *Powracająca fala* (1880; The Returning Wave), to the peasant struggling to hold his land against the German, in *Placówka* (1886; The Outpost). Prus's masterpiece was the great novel of middle-class Warsaw, *Lalka* (1890; The Doll). This work, with its shopkeeper hero, was revolutionary in Polish letters and a herald of the new realism in fiction. It was followed by the widely read and discussed *Emancypantki* (1893; The Emancipated Women), a study of a type new to Polish life and not greatly admired by Prus. In *Faraon* (1895; Pharaoh) Prus resorted to a device popular in Russian Poland, concealing under an Egyptian disguise an exposé of Poland's miseries, and finally, in *Dzieci* (1909; The Children), he brought his life work to a close with a revelation of the intolerable plight of the Pole in the period of reaction following 1905.

A quaint, bespectacled, modest little man, Prus was at heart a reformer, and no finer monument to his memory could possibly be imagined than the embankment along the Vistula bearing his name. Each spring this serves to shield the poor of Warsaw from the swollen river and to remind them of their earliest partisan.

See: L. Włodek, *Bolesław Prus* (1918); G. Korbut, *Literatura polska* (1931), IV, 126–130; *Wiadomości literackie*, 1932, No. 418 (entire issue); T. Żeleński (Boy), "Prus w perspektywie czasu," *Wiadomości literackie*, 1937, No. 25.

A. P. C.

Przybyszewski, Stanisław (1868–1927, Polish novelist, essayist, and dramatist), was born at Łojewo in Kujawy, German Poland, the son of a village schoolteacher and a musical, highly strung, intensely religious mother. His birthplace, near legend-haunted Lake Gopło, the cradle of the Polish state, a melancholy region of peat bogs and willow groves, played a great part in the molding of his nature, heightening a natural tendency to fits of alternate ecstasy and gloom. Przybyszewski himself believed one's birthplace, like one's name, was predestined and prophetic, citing in proof of the latter his own strikingly appropriate name, which means "a destined-for-fame newcomer." A newcomer and an outsider Przybyszewski was from first to last: in Toruń, as a Pole in an almost entirely German Gymnasium (1881–1884); in Berlin (1889–1895), as a member of the suspect Bohemia of the capital; in Cracow, as a denizen of the cafés; in Warsaw, as a man shunned by the more stable elements of society because of his marriage to the estranged wife of the poet Kasprowicz (*q.v.*); and finally in Danzig, as a Polish official in an outpost of militant Germanism.

The most significant period in Przybyszewski's life was that spent in Berlin. Here, at first as a student and later, after a term in Moabite

Prison because of his friendship for a proscribed Polish socialist, as an ex-student earning a precarious living by free-lance writing, Przybyszewski took part in the literary revolution which resulted in the fall of Zola (*q.v.*) and the rise of Strindberg (*q.v.*). He himself was deeply influenced by the Scandinavians. Not only did he now marry a Norwegian, Dagny Juell, and pay a long visit to the Scandinavian states, but it was under Scandinavian influence that he conceived the philosophy of medievalism by which he made himself at once famous and notorious. This philosophy, which repudiates reason and exalts intuition, was embodied first in the famous *Totenmesse* (1893) and *Satanskinder* (1897) and other early works in German. Later Przybyszewski built a temple of Satan in Cracow to promote its proper recognition.

Przybyszewski's influence on Polish literature, which was considerable, was exercised not only through his writings but through his personal association with young Polish talents —Żeleński, Grubiński, Perzyński, etc. (*qq.v.*)— and through his guidance of the editorial policy of the journal *Życie* (Life) during the months of his residence in Cracow from October, 1898, to the end of 1900. It was largely owing to his encouragement that the final blow was dealt to moribund positivism (*see* Polish literature) and the way paved for full acceptance of neo-romanticism. Of Przybyszewski's novels, the most typical is *Homo Sapiens* (1898; Eng. tr., 1915); of his dramas, the most widely influential, among the Czechs and Croatians as well as in Poland, are *Dla szczęścia* (1900; Eng. tr., *For Happiness,* 1912) and *Śnieg* (1903; Eng. tr., *Snow,* 1920).

See: Z. Dębicki, *Portrety,* I (1927), 67–86; A. Guttry, *Unbekannte Literatur* (1932), pp. 29–35; T. Żeleński (Boy), *Znasz-li ten kraj?* (1932).

M. M. C.

psychoanalysis in modern literature. Psychoanalysis has, ever since its consolidation into theoretical and practical psychology, maintained a close contact with art and literature. Sigmund Freud himself gave a definite lead with a number of essays on literature and related topics. Most of these are now contained in his *Psychoanalytische Studien an Werken der Dichtung und Kunst* (1924). In the first place, creative writing supplied him with a source of interesting human material upon which he could test his theories, if indeed he did not extract some of his principles from psychological observations made by novelists and poets. In the second place, literature, as a document and manifestation of life in general, presented excellent material for the psychoanalytic interpretation of cultural evolution as such. Freud's collaborators and early followers have strengthened the bond of interest between psychology and literature. The psychoanalytic viewpoint soon was applied systematically to literature in Wilhelm Stekel's *Dichtung und Neurose* (1909) and in Otto Rank's *Das Inzest-Motiv in Dichtung und Sage* (1912), two books which inaugurated a very active school of psychoanalytic criticism. Foremost among those who demonstrated the general applicability of psychoanalysis to art criticism are C. G. Jung, Oskar Pfister, Charles Baudouin, Albert Mordell, DeWitt Parker, Ernest Jones, F. C. Prescott. It is not difficult to understand why psychoanalysts should veer so conspicuously toward literary problems. The common meeting ground lay, in a broad sense, in the sphere of irrational and subconscious forces. Creative writers throughout the ages have always contended that their works were, in the final analysis, attributable to the prompting of some irrational urge. Psychoanalysts, on the other hand, were quick to claim that their conception of subconscious life was equally applicable to the explanation of art and literature, taking it for granted of course that artists are not noticeably different from the common run of men. Human nature even in our days still remains conditioned, the argument runs, by a set of childhood instincts, mainly of an erotic type, which invariably cause certain psychic problems and disturbances. Artistic production is directly concerned with the transformation of such infantile wishes into socially acceptable or even enjoyable creations.

If we disregard those many modifications which Freud's theory has undergone, certain principles may be set forth as the fundamental tenets on which literary criticism of the more orthodox kind of psychoanalysis is based and which have been widely used for appraisal of both ancient and altogether modern writers.

First. Since all essential manifestations of human conduct must be looked upon as being conditioned by some basic erotic experience and since almost every human action represents the resultant of two opposed forces, of the craving to satisfy our infantile erotic desires and of the more or less keenly felt obligation to suppress, convert, or sublimate such instincts, there can be no hard and fast line of demarcation between art and any other cultural activity; they all constitute so many attempts to cope with the curse of our erotic or, to be quite exact, incestuous nature, leaving in the wake of their efforts a welter of sex symbols, in the form of customs, words, images, institutions, thoughts, handicraft. Similarly, the difference between the most general and anonymous literary products (such as jokes, riddles, myths, fairy tales) and the highly individualistic expressions in towering masterpieces is one of degree rather than of kind. The former are collective confessions of wishful sexual thinking or of clandestine indulgence in incestuous pleasures, while the latter bear witness to the exertion of some conscientious individual to hide or even control his sinful because asocial longings. Gottfried Keller (*q.v.*), in the opinion of psychoanalysts, suffered from a strong mother fixation and was for this reason unable to love another woman; but instead of angrily venting his aversion—to say nothing of yielding to his incestuous impulse—he created a galaxy of beautiful woman-characters too lofty to become the object of erotic attention; these fantasies helped him to purify or at any rate to neutralize his emotional aberrations.

Second. What we commonly call artistic imagination, the ability of some people to weave a motley assembly of thoughts, emotions, and volitions into a pleasing pattern of form and content, is closely related to, though not entirely synonymous with, the faculty of dreaming. The common denominator of both is an ingenious method of evading the censorship invested in social consciousness and of giving more or less free rein to our libidinous drives. But there is this difference between dream and poetic imagination: mere dreaming—daydreaming especially—is bound to result in neurotic mental states with alternating currents of sinning and repenting, whereas the artist somehow manages to stem the tide of incestuous longings and to deflect its soul-destroying power into socially useful channels. Hence the essentially cathartic function of art, ridding individuals and society as a whole of tormenting complexes by substituting an imaginary world for stark reality and by providing relief at least in its imagined world. Few people realize that in witnessing a performance of Wagner's (*q.v.*) *Tannhäuser, Tristan und Isolde,* or *Der fliegende Holländer* their mother complex is being drawn off; yet such is the case, according to psychoanalysts. Wagner's own erotic feelings were focused on his mother, and indeed with such intensity that all his artistic dreams of incest were not sufficient to release him from his complex; on occasion he would actually fall in love with the motherly type of women, with the wives of his best friends.

Third. Since the urge to create is an act of self-defense necessitated by the pressure of incestuous longings, the comprehension of works of literature depends on a thorough analysis of the artist's infantile sex life and not, as traditional literary criticism has assumed, on all the irrelevant details of environment and training. Critics graduating from the Freudian school have produced a new type of biography, in which a few basic psychological data become intimately linked with whatever variety of formal and philosophical characteristics a work of art may possess. For instance, Renan's (*q.v.*) mildly incestuous attachment to his sister is said to reappear in the effeminacy of the author and in the gentleness, the moral tone, of his writings. A murder fantasy discovered among Jane Austen's *Juvenilia* has given rise to the suspicion that many of her works conceal a subconscious desire to do away with her parents and her sister. Père Goriot with his double passion for his daughter and for money enables the analyst to diagnose incestuous impulses and a castration complex in Balzac. *A la recherche du Temps Perdu* gives away, in its very title, Proust's (*q.v.*) dominant longing to go back to the maternal omphalos. But the most revealing authors, for the psychoanalyst, are Baudelaire (*q.v.*), Poe, and Strindberg (*q.v.*). For René Laforgue (*L'Echec de Baudelaire; étude psychanalytique,* 1931) the poems of Baudelaire form a perfect illustration of an acute mother fixation; his hatred for the stepfather—and for his mother in that she preferred a stranger to her own son—assumed such proportions as to make him finally equate all natural things with the abominable. Poe's infantile trauma dates back to two experiences, seeing his mother in the embrace of a strange man and watching her slow death through tuberculosis. According to Marie Bonaparte (*Edgar Poe; étude psychanalytique,* 1933) he became a sadist and necrophile, and his stories must be read as so many dreams through which he relived past horrors or in which he meted out savage punishments. Strindberg, thanks to a long series of autobiographical novels, allows the psychoanalyst to penetrate to a classical bifurcation of the Oedipus complex. Hating his father for having given him a stepmother, he transferred this emotion to all father-surrogates, to teachers, employers, governments. At the same time his aversion from his stepmother made him an inveterate misogynist deriving a morbid satisfaction from being the martyr of numerous marital adventures. From the nature of infantile erotic situations literary critics of the Freudian school finally arrived at a classification of artists into certain types, depending on whether they were bereft of either father or mother or both, on whether they had a stepfather or a stepmother, and on the balance of affection they felt towards their real parents.

Fourth. As it is only natural for psychoanalytic critics to be convinced that in works of art every detail falls into line with the artist's fundamental psychological constitution, there can be no talk of such a thing as an objective style. The old notion, for instance, of objective drama has to be discarded; drama is perhaps the most subjective medium of expression, a perfect external projection of the author's complexes, with more than one member of the dramatis personae appearing as a spokesman of the unconscious drive, or of certain ramifications of this drive, while jointly they reenact the dramatist's struggle between incestuous desires and social conscience. A play thus reveals itself as a series of clever stratagems ending in defeat of, or triumph for, the forces of social responsibility. The ever moving effect of *Hamlet* is attributed by psychoanalysts to a multiple projection of Shakespeare's Oedipus complex. Hamlet embodies this instinct in its broken, intimidated form; his own father, now only a ghost, can no longer be the object of real hatred, and a substitute is therefore created in the person of his stepfather, Claudius. But now the moral censor intervenes, vetoing at least for the time being any drastic expression of Hamlet's pent-up emotions. Another outlet must be found: Laertes appears on the scene to become a perfect disguise for Shakespeare's criminal longings. Laertes' father having been killed—much to Laertes' own satisfaction and to the satisfaction of Shakespeare—the author can now easily deceive the world as to the nature of his feelings by posing as a loving son and as an avenger of his father's death. Moreover, critics point out that in *Hamlet* Shakespeare works off all other concomitant complexes as well, love between brother and sister through the medium of Laertes and Ophelia, love between father and daughter through identification with Polonius and Ophelia.

Fifth. The most startling contribution of psychoanalysis to the criticism of literature was made in the form of a new interpretation of literary historicity. If the word evolution is to carry any meaning with the psychoanalyst, it must imply a steadily growing control over our incestuous desires by means of a strict subjugation of emotions to reason. In this slowly but inexorably maturing sublimation and conversion of harmful instincts literature is playing or, to be more accurate, has played an honorable part. With allowance for repetitions and digressions, the literary guild has in the past centuries discharged its function of universal catharsis in three definite stages which mark the only truly perceptible incisions in the history of creative writing. To recognize the salient features of each successive literary period and of its significance in the growth of Western civilization, psychoanalysts direct us to Sophocles' *Oedipus Rex,* Shakespeare's *Hamlet,* and Schiller's *Don Carlos.* Sophocles, speaking for a primitive age, allowed his incestuous desires to come to the surface almost unsuspected and to be naïvely gratified, if not in reality then at least in the dreamworld of his dramatic vision. Not until after Oedipus has been permitted to kill his father and to marry his mother does the Greek dramatist pause, reflect, and censor the sinful nature of such conduct, to impose on it now the stern punishment of self-inflicted mutilation. Crime and its atonement, sin and repentance, balance one another evenly at this early stage of civilization. It remained for future generations to be more watchful and to intercept the incestuous drive before it has run its course. But ages passed before literature was to record or to suggest a noticeable advance in the control of our infantile impulses. Shakespeare, even if he could not wholly convert or sublimate his sinful promptings, at least knew how to disguise the desire to kill his own father and to marry his mother so well that it takes a trained psychoanalyst to reconstruct the original emotional basis. True, the mother complex is only partly repressed, and to the extent of its being diverted into Hamlet's love for Ophelia. The father complex, on the other hand, has become completely unhooked from its real object and is finding a plausible substitute in Claudius; Hamlet's incestuous hatred, while not exactly transformed into a socially useful purpose, does occasion no great harm, because the stepfather had some punishment due him. Don Carlos brings us considerably closer to successful sublimation; he falls in love with his stepmother, which is a far cry from Oedipus' infatuation with Jocasta, and he would hate the man who happens to be his father even if the latter were a stranger. Yet in the end Schiller, too, feels morally compelled to deliver his seemingly innocent hero into the hands of the executioner, a tacit admission of some lingering feeling of guilt; unless the last vestiges of incestuous motives are eliminated or entirely sublimated there will be no peace for man's conscience, just as there will be no possibility of orderly, rational behavior. An emphatic warning to heed our incestuous urges—this is as far as creative literature can go in helping mankind. Further progress can only be expected from scientific psychology and from the prompt application of its findings. Modern literature has to content itself with making the problems involved apprehensible, rather than evolving the final solution. The same necessity for the most radical rationalization of life, on which our salvation depends, will sooner or later spell the doom of art, just as it spelled the end of religion in earlier times. Art, like religion, had its important duty to fulfill. When this is done, the function which was hitherto entrusted to artists will pass into the hands of the scientists; or rather, the latter must take over where art left off, to lead us into the millennium of scientific control.

Orthodox psychoanalysis has advanced other concepts of literary criticism in addition to those enumerated above. Freud's analysis of the incestuous elements in wit, for instance, was at one time widely discussed. But more important than these are the change which Freud's original views on the nature of our infantile urges has undergone and the influence of this change on literary criticism. Broadly speaking, the tendency among psychoanalysts was to contemplate the presence of other than incestuous or even erotic instincts. Adler's substitution of inferiority and superiority complexes for the Oedipus complex was an invitation to identify the unconscious *Id* with many other nonerotic drives, such as an elemental lust for power or a cannibalistic cruelty. C. G. Jung's preference is for mystic, religious propensities or for collective instincts; still others are ready to accept even innocuous volitions (e.g., a tendency to tell lies) as a fundamental trait, if not of all men at least of all writers. Literary critics who had hesitated to go the whole length of orthodox psychoanalysis availed themselves of the wider scope which these diluted theories of dissenting schools offered to them. Among critical works which employ such eclectic psychoanalytic tenets two deserve mention: Gustav Morf's *The Polish Heritage of Joseph Conrad* (1930) and Walter Muschg's *Gotthelf: Die Geheimnisse des Erzählers* (1931). Morf relies to a considerable extent on Adler's psychology, by attributing to Conrad's work a compensatory function; he had to make good as a writer in order to overcome his inferiority feeling as a foreigner among Englishmen. In other respects the author draws on Freud: Conrad, the motherless boy who was soon also to lose his father, transferred his thwarted love for the parents to Poland; this in turn led to a violent guilt conflict, because he had run away from his native land. *Lord Jim,* apart from having the dreamlike qualities of all great art, is also Conrad's most intimately autobiographical work; here the author atones for his guilt. Jung's influence seems to be suggested by Morf's frequent references to Conrad's instinctive knowledge and use of many universal symbols, for instance of the symbolic meaning of the sea which stands for fate in all its threatening and yet challenging mysteries. If Conrad emerges here as a highly individualistic figure, Gotthelf, as presented by Muschg, appears to be an anonymous spokesman, an outlet not so much of his own personal concerns as of the fundamental urges of his race or of all mankind, an eruption, as it were, of such primal instincts as worship of higher powers, love of the soil, and fear of demons, instincts which were controlled and purified by the fervent desire to sanctify life and to transform reality into an abode of peace and Christian beatitude.

In a preface Muschg acknowledges his indebtedness to Freud; disciples of the Klages school and adherents of the recently propagated "blood and soil" theory, though bitter enemies of psychoanalysis, have yet not hesitated to hail Muschg as a supporter of their own biocentric psychology. This fact goes far to show that there is no strong dividing line between psychoanalysis and other systems of *Tiefenpsychologie.* They are all different phases of a movement which had its origin in German romanticism and which, after having been powerfully amplified by Nietzsche (*q.v.*), was to endure and to gain in influence. Its unifying bond consists in the conviction that the motive for human actions—in life and in literature—must be sought in some unconscious impulse; it is in the exact definition of the unconscious elements that modern psychology begins to split into various factions.

The same civil war raging within the sphere of analytic psychologies has brought to light much valid criticism especially of the orthodox Freudian interpretation of art. Dissenters under the leadership of C. G. Jung protested, first, against the purely genetic approach to art by which nothing is achieved except a slight shift, within the old theory of environment, towards psychological data and, second, against the gloomy conclusion that the days of great art are numbered and that from now on our cultural interests will be in the hands of the scientists. The latter claim is for Jung another instance of causality and science running wild and trespassing into spheres where they are bound to do harm, this time in the sphere of creative imagination and ethical values. As Jung points out, the Oedipus complex and its female counterpart, the Electra complex, may well explain the causes of man's unrest and of the artist's urge to create, but they do not and cannot determine our creative reaction to these inner demons. In the worst cases, the reaction will follow the hedonistic line of a barely concealed resistance, leading to disastrous results; with greater moral fortitude, our response may be directed by some higher vision, creating an entirely new situation. The manly attitude which Oedipus shows when confronted with the consequences of his mistakes is something which could not have been foretold from the nature of his incestuous desires; he rises to an ethical height such as only the imagination and wisdom of Sophocles were able to envisage. To project into the consciousness of mankind such ever nobler ways and means of counteracting the blind force of primitive nature was, is, and forever will be the divine office of art, a task which cannot be taken over, in its entirety, by any other intellectual or spiritual agency. Literary interpretation lacking the intuitive sensitiveness necessary to fathom the possibilities of creative imagination can never do justice either to works of art or to the role which art is playing in civilization. A modern critic relying solely on the analytic approach to art will fall just as short of his goal as would a mineralogist making bold to explain the artistic significance of a marble statue from a purely mineralogical standpoint. Analytic training will enable us to discover in *Faust* the erotic mother fixation of its author; only constructive comprehension can follow Goethe to those new levels of existence on which Faust, impelled by the titanic restlessness of his nature, discovers the essence of human life to lie in social responsibility and in active concern for our fellow men. Great writers have always endeavored to integrate individual life in tasks which by their very difficulty give birth to new inner qualities. Infantile emotions have then no chance to spread. They pass into oblivion.

Recent critics of psychoanalysis go even further than that, by questioning the validity of Freud's main contention that human instincts are basically selfish, pleasure-seeking, and asocial. In 1935 appeared the first edition of I. D. Suttie's book *The Origins of Love and Hate,* a work which may well mark the turning point in modern psychological thought. Much in the same manner in which Pestalozzi, more than a hundred years earlier, emphasized that love in its passive and active form constitutes the first experience of earliest infancy, Suttie holds that the instincts of gentleness and friendliness precede all egoistic sex urges, developing his argument with a medical, psychological, and anthropological knowledge which is more than equal to that of any Freudian. This assumption of the primacy of altruistic emotions over self-interest is one which answers the deepest longings of our time and which may lead to a new social philosophy as well as to a new school of literary critics. By calling attention to the "taboo of tenderness" in European literature Suttie has already indicated the direction which literary research may well follow.

The gauging of the influence that psychoanalysis has had upon recent creative writing will present a task of considerable difficulty to future historians of literature. The problem is not rendered easier by the suspicion—almost amounting to a certainty—that every European and American writer of account in the last four decades has in some form or other become exposed to the psychology of the unconscious. As a preliminary, varying degrees of directness and intensity with which psychoanalysis has affected literature must be distinguished. A tentative stratification may be suggested.

There are, first of all, authors who are more or less expert psychoanalysts and who are fond of introducing a psychoanalytic practitioner among the characters of their literary product. In Italo Svevo's (*q.v.*) *La Coscienza di Zeno* the hero—largely identical with the author—psychoanalyzes his own life in a style suggesting actual clinical case reports. R. E. Sherwood in *Reunion in Vienna* entrusts the psychoanalyst Doctor Krug with the handling and successful solution of an embarrassing family affair. The most direct and almost brazen application of psychoanalytical methods to literature is to be encountered in *Der Seelensucher* by Georg Groddeck who expressly defines his book as a psychoanalytic novel. The technical device he employs is not without hilarious possibilities: a psychoanalytic wolf in the garb of a bourgeois lamb roams through respectable middle-class society and provides, with the bluntness of a fool and the malice of a devil, a running psychoanalytical commentary on our customs and beliefs which shows at every turn that men are not really running their own affairs but are instead being run by that great *Id,* none other, of course, than Eros. Groddeck succeeds in suggesting lascivious intentions even in such trivial acts as the threading of a needle or the striking of a match. Other instances of psychoanalytical practice may be found in the works of the

Swedish novelist Hjalmar Bergman (*q.v.*) and in those of Rebecca West, Eugene O'Neill, and H. R. Lenormand (*q.v.*). It was Lenormand who warned writers against a too literal appropriation of Freudian psychology as the surest way of becoming dated and outmoded.

Other authors, though paying close attention to the findings of psychoanalysis, nevertheless succeed in preserving their intellectual and artistic independence. Thomas Mann (*q.v.*), who wrote a eulogistic essay on Freud's significance for the future of civilization—assigning to him the role of a liberator from all dark, irrational instincts—yet creates his more representative literary figures out of his own psychology. Remarkable is the case of D. H. Lawrence. Overwhelming as the evidence of *Sons and Lovers* and of *Lady Chatterley's Lover* seems to be in favor of direct Freudian influences, in his treatise *Psychoanalysis and the Unconscious* (1921) he not only refutes all such dependence but also ridicules Freud's picture of the unconscious mind.

A large number of modern literary creations in a third group treat boldly of incestuous relationships; the prevalence of this motif may, in the final analysis, be attributable to the stress which Freud has put on the Oedipus complex. May Sinclair, J. D. Beresford, Gabriele D'Annunzio (*q.v.*), Stefan Vacano, J. P. Jacobsen (*q.v.*), Gustav af Geijerstam (*q.v.*), Peter Nansen, Jean Giraudoux (*q.v.*), Catulle Mendès (*q.v.*), Emil Strauss (*q.v.*), Clara Viebig (*q.v.*), Hugo von Hofmannsthal (*q.v.*), Adolf Koelsch, and others may be said to use incest motifs with the responsibility befitting serious writers. The same cannot be claimed of others, for instance of Leonhard Frank (*q.v.*), Arnolt Bronnen, and H. H. Jahn, all of whom hover on the border of pornography.

And finally, just as analysis, the tracing back of manifest behavior to some hidden erotic desire, became a strong trend in modern psychology, so pansexualism, the philosophical complement to psychoanalysis, has infiltrated into innumerable works of literature. But this frank discussion of sex problems for which contemporary literature presents abundant evidence—André Gide, Julien Green, Henry de Montherlant, Gerhart Hauptmann, Frank Wedekind, Arthur Schnitzler, Federigo Tozzi, Corrado Alvaro (*qq.v.*), to mention only a few examples—cannot in every case have been instigated by direct contact with Freudianism; more often it appears to be a result of that general naturalistic current which assumed the proportions of a veritable *Zeitgeist;* of this widely prevailing spirit psychoanalysis itself is only one symptom among many others.

The very diffusion of psychoanalytic influence into every sphere of modern art makes it impossible to discern a psychoanalytic school in the strict sense of a literary movement. A well-defined movement presupposes a common philosophy and the employment of certain stylistic devices and innovations. True enough, the attempt has been made to show that psychoanalysts practice a set of formal characteristics and at the same time have certain views on life in common. The analytic form in drama and fiction, though not of recent origin, seems to meet the exigencies of psychoanalytic problems better than any other, allowing us, as it does, to analyze a conflict breaking out in later life and to run it down to some early, forgotten experience. It has also been pointed out that in life and literature alike psychoanalytic deliverance from a long-hidden complex is most expediently brought about by a confession or by a sudden outburst of self-accusations. Dostoevski's (*q.v.*) technique in *Crime and Punishment*—the slow extraction of a confession—has found many imitators among modern novelists; Jakob Wassermann (*q.v.*) shows a definite preference for this device, E. M. Forster has used it with brilliant effects in *A Passage to India.* Explosive self-revelation was carried to its extreme in expressionistic drama, in which one character often does all the talking while the others are supposed only to be patient and sympathetic listeners. Furthermore, since Freud relied so much on dreams as the royal road into the depth of the unconscious, writers made frequent use of the same expedient, in order to bring to light hidden desires. The sequence of dream scenes alternating with realistic settings in J. M. Barrie's *Dear Brutus* is a striking example of the good use to which dreams may be put for character analysis. Finally, since the past, by virtue of its decisive influence on man, can at any time raise its ugly head and deeply affect the present, psychoanalysts have argued that we must change our conception of time. Literature has taken cognizance of this change by introducing the stream of consciousness technique; James Joyce, Virginia Woolf, and Alfred Döblin (*q.v.*) will always be remembered as chief exponents of this novel method.

All these technical features occur quite frequently, however, aside from psychoanalytic beliefs in the strict sense of this term. In addition, we do not have strong enough evidence of a common approach, among psychoanalysts, to social and political problems. Full agreement prevails on one point only: the obnoxious complex must be converted into a socially useful purpose. Admittedly the definition of such usefulness often coincides with Marxist ideas on progress, and this accounts for the easy amalgamation of psychoanalysis with Marxism—the former explains what human nature is, the latter proclaims what it ought to become. But the two creeds are far from being complementary; one may be a Marxist without taking the slightest notice of Freud, and vice versa.

The prospect of a civilization which will know how to select and control its emotions and how to press them into the service of society remains one of the creative visions by which psychoanalysis deserves to be remembered. These emotions, however, must be located in other than incestuous, egotistic roots. Indications of a growing skeptical view on Freud's basic instincts are as definite among present-day writers as they are among psychologists proper. What is perhaps more revealing is the fact that Gide, a representative novelist of the older generation which was steeped in psychoanalysis, should have recovered his faith in the immanent nature and the everlasting value of altruistic feelings. With gentle insistence he shows in *Les Faux-Monnayeurs* that when all the time-honored emotions of parental love, filial affection, and loyalty among friends have been deflated in true psychoanalytic fashion human beings will at once begin again to crave for the very same emotions. The urge to give love and to receive love is not merely a residue of infantile perversions but must be accepted as a manifestation of cosmic energy. The fact that this universal libido upon occasion deteriorates into incestuous desires or, if we are to believe Adler, into an excessive lust for power does not mean that higher forms of libido such as love, a serene zest for life, social conscience and compassion, are becoming invalidated. It remains for a new generation of writers to rediscover the source of constructive, anagogic inspiration and to reincarnate, both in actuality and in imagination, those lofty, timeless emotions, to borrow an expression from Goethe, which are the very lifeblood of noble thought and action.

See: E. Aulhorn, "Dichtung und Psychoanalyse," *Germanisch-romanische Monatsschrift,* X (1922), 279–292; L. Cazamian, "La Psychanalyse et la critique littéraire," *Revue de littérature comparée,* IV (1924), 449–475; W. Muschg, *Psychoanalyse und Literaturwissenschaft* (1930); F. L. Sack, *Die Psychoanalyse im modernen englischen Roman* (1930); H. Pongs, "Psychoanalyse und Dichtung," *Euphorion,* XXXIV (1933), 38–72; B. De Voto, "Freud in America," *Psychoanalytic Quarterly,* IX (1940), 236–245; C. S. Lewis, "Psycho-Analysis and Literary Criticism," *Essays and Studies by Members of the English Association,* XXVII (1941), 7–21; F. J. Hoffman, *Freudianism and the Literary Mind* (1945).

H. B.

Puccini, Mario (1887–, Italian bookseller, publisher, short-story writer, novelist, critic, and translator), was born in Senigallia. He is a prolific and serious worker who has never attained great fame, although he has always merited attention and praise for his conscientious effort. Characteristic of him are a mild realism and interest in average types. In his first works he followed closely in the footprints of Verga (*q.v.*; see *Foville,* 1914) and noted with sympathy both the literary and political developments of Italy. In a rather studied and fragmentary way he felt the human and national problems of the First World War (*Dal Carso al Piave,* 1918; *Come ho visto il Friuli,* 1919), of the post-war period (*Viva l'anarchia,* 1921; *Dove è il peccato è Dio,* 1922), and of Fascism (*Cola o il ritratto dell'italiano,* 1927). Each of these works has been greeted as a promise, but none has been hailed as a masterpiece. He gives evidence of a religious preoccupation which he has not yet made articulate. He has made good translations from Spanish and South American literature and collected certain critical essays in a volume entitled *Da D'Annunzio a Pirandello* (1928).

See: G. Marcellini, "Mario Puccini," *Nuova Antologia,* CCCXVIII (1925), 84–91; L. Gillet, "M. Mario Puccini et le portrait de l'Italien," *Revue des deux mondes,* September 1, 1928, pp. 207–218; T. G. Bergin, "Mario Puccini," *Italica,* XIII (1936), 129–131.

G. P.

Q

Queiroz, *see* Eça de Queiroz, José Maria; Teixeira de Queiroz, Francisco.

Quental, Antero Tarquinio de (1842–1891, Portuguese poet), was born in Ponta Delgada, Azores, to a noble family of literary and liberal traditions. In 1858 he went to Coimbra to study law. The university was then a center for revolt and for the fermentation of new ideas. Gigantic and kindly, a magnetic personality, with his golden and resplendent shock of hair and beard, he led the school revolts against the medieval Byzantinism of the university and became the guide of a group of restless spirits who, as the Generation of Coimbra, were destined to renovate the spirit of Portuguese literature. In 1861 he made his appearance as a poet with the publication of a volume of poems, *Sonetos de Antero,* which revealed an art of first quality. In the preface he outlined a theory of the sonnet, for him a vehicle of pure lyricism, and urged the rehabilitation of this disciplined metrical form, then out of style, as a link to the tradition of Camões. In the course of 25 years of painful poetic production he was to do the best of his work in the form of sonnets. In 1863 appeared *Beatrice,* a poem full of amorous idealism, showing the influence of the new lyricism of João de Deus (*q.v.*). This poem was included in a later collection of early works, *Primaveras românticas* (1871; Romantic Springs). That same year (1863) he produced *Fiat Lux,* destroyed almost as soon as it was printed—indeed Quental, an essentially sincere and independent spirit, free of all artistic ambition, for whom poetry was an immediate expressive necessity, threw away more of his work than his friends were able to save and publish.

He destroyed the greater part of his verses in romantic vein when, in 1865, he entered the revolutionary phase of *Odes modernas* (Modern Odes); this constitutes a peculiar alliance of Hegelian naturalism and French social humanitarianism. With this extremely original collection he introduced the poetry of struggle into Portugal; later he was also to repudiate this as false, though still recognizing his sincerity in writing it. Now came the famous "Coimbra question" (*see* Portuguese literature). The young Antero was already known outside the university when the noisy polemic, which publicized the incompatibility of the new poets with exhausted post-romanticism, occurred. Then the vigorous polemist, the Antero of the tracts against Castilho, appeared. *Odes modernas* carried a brief note on the mission of poetry, deploring the existing divorce between the prolix, post-romantic lyricism and the complex magnitude of the spiritual life of the century. Influenced by Proudhon, Quental declared that poetry should be the voice of the Revolution. Instead of being an insignificant, personal pastime, it should present the great human problems, the metamorphoses of civilization, and the anxieties of modern conscience. Philistinism viewed all this as an extreme boldness and the odes were called monstrosities and metaphysical pedantry.

Quental had by this time completed his university work, but remained in Coimbra without deciding upon a career. Then began that struggle of will which was to be the great drama of his existence. A constant victim of metaphysical anguish, only in death could he find relief; initiator of all the spiritual movements in the Portugal of his time, he devoted himself with momentary passion to all his ideals, to end finally in the tragedy of neurosis and self-destruction. He started Iberism in 1868 with his brochure *Portugal perante a revolução da Espanha* (Portugal in the Presence of the Spanish Revolution) and later with Oliveira Martins (*q.v.*) founded the *Revista occidental.* He renounced his social position and went to Paris as a typographical worker, but disillusion and poor health obliged him to abandon this proletarian venture. In the sailboat of one of his friends he made a voyage to the United States and to Canada. He took an active part in socialistic propaganda and established the Portuguese branch of the International. In 1871 he again met his fellow students of Coimbra and organized the "Conferências democráticas do Casino de Lisboa" (*see* Portuguese literature), so soon to be suppressed. The polished, satiric pamphleteer appeared again in the "carta" to the marquês de Avila, protesting the suspension. In 1874 neurosis seized him anew, and he gave up all active endeavor and retired to Vila-do-Conde. In this retreat he prepared, with the aid of his faithful friend Oliveira Martins, the edition of the *Sonetos completos* (1886; Eng. tr., *Sonnets and Poems of Antero de Quental,* 1922) as well as a poetic collection for children; in addition, at the request of Eça de Queiroz (*q.v.*), he wrote three articles on the tendencies of contemporary philosophy. He left his seclusion only in 1891, to head the patriotic movement against the English ultimatum. Discouraged by the failure of this final illusion of his active life, he left for his native island; there, one suffocating afternoon, he took his own life in a public park.

Quental's work kept pace with his spiritual evolution. Having lost the Catholic faith of his adolescence, he entered a phase of deistic spiritualism. Later he discovered Hegel and was carried away by the grandiose Hegelian syntheses which he endeavored to combine with the democratic humanitarianism of the French, avoiding the problem of conscience in revolutionary faith. But soon his naturalism and the mystic tendency of his spirit came into conflict. These he tried to reconcile, but slipped into a phase of desolate pessimism—aggravated by disease—which produced the "lugubrious" poems saved by Oliveira Martins. Finally he thought he had discovered interior equilibrium in an optimistic theory of the beatitude of virtue and saintliness, a sort of occidental Buddhism which he called psychodynamism or panpsychism. When he lost hope of the nirvana of moral placidity—reflected in the final sonnets—he sought rest in death. His sonnets are "the autobiography of a thought . . . memoirs of a conscience" which aspires to understand the incomprehensible and express the ineffable. The philosophical sonnet first appeared in *Odes,* and in *Primaveras* there are love sonnets, as there are also in *Raios de extinta luz* (1892; Rays of Vanishing Light), a collection of juvenilia published posthumously.

The aesthetic technique of Antero is extremely personal and consists in the reaching for the most inapprehensible abstraction through the most immediate experience. His imagination was abstract and anti-pictorial. His sonnets, in their dual aesthetic and philosophical quality, give evidence of a sober and luminous art, characterized by deep emotion and sculptured, classic precision. Opposed to art for art's sake, he considered poetry not an end but a "perfectly involuntary means" of satisfying his need for expression. Because of a weakness of will, his production was disproportionately small in comparison with his creative powers, but as for quality "there is not another moment of greater intensity in Portuguese poetry after Camões."

Quental's poetical works have been translated into the principal languages of Europe and take their place beside the best universal philosophical poetry. His philosophical essays, articles, brochures, and similar works collected in *Prosas* (1923–1931; Prose) offer, with his letters, guides to his intimate thought and sentiments and are evidence of his high quality as a prose writer, a role which has been somewhat obscured by the great stature of the poet.

See: Teófilo Braga, *As modernas idéias na literatura portuguesa* (1892), II, 96–223; "Antero de Quental," in *In Memoriam* (1896); Fidelino de Figueiredo, *Antero* (1942).

E. G. D.

Querol, Vicente Wenceslao (1836–1889, Spanish poet), was born in Valencia and while still young wrote a small number of poems which were collected in 1877 in the volume *Rimas* (including also five poems in Catalan with Spanish translations). These were sufficient to give him a place among the best poets of his day. The circumstances of his life which demanded that he devote all his energies to the duties of his post with the Compañía de Ferrocarriles del Mediodía made it impossible for him to dedicate himself to poetry. Though limited in number, the quality and purity of his poems have kept his name alive. Among a select group he commands devotion as a great poet, whose work has not aged like that of some of his more renowned contemporaries. His poetry combines classic regard for form with lyric intimacy. He writes of sentiments that are familiar to all with nobility, tenderness, and delicacy; he writes of staid, chaste love, as in his *Cartas a María.* He feels and expresses with restrained intensity nature, love of country, and moral elevation.

See: J. Valera, *Florilegio de poesías castellanas del siglo XIX* (1902), I, x, IV, 59–68; A. F. G. Bell, *Contemporary Spanish Literature* (1925).

F. de O.

Quintero, Serafín Alvarez and **Joaquín Alvarez,** *see* Alvarez Quintero.

R

Raabe, Wilhelm (1831–1910, German novelist), was born in Eschershausen near Brunswick, the son of a minor official; he left school before finishing and became an apprentice in a Magdeburg bookstore. Even as a child he read avidly (*Robinson Crusoe,* Scott, Hauff, Dumas, Sue, E. T. A. Hoffmann), and before he entered the University of Berlin in 1854, he was acquainted with the English humorists from Sterne to Dickens and Thackeray as well as with the popular German novelists of his day. During the winter of 1854 he wrote his first book, the idyllic novel *Die Chronik der Sperlingsgasse,* which was published in 1857 under the characteristic pesudonym Jacob Corvinus. After three happy years in Wolfenbüttel, he traveled widely, married in 1862, and settled in Stuttgart. There he wrote his most distinguished early novels (*Die Leute aus dem Walde,* 1863; *Der Hungerpastor,* 1864, Eng. tr., *The Hunger-Pastor,* 1885; *Abu Telfan,* 1867, Eng. tr., *Abu Telfan; Return from Mountains of the Moon,* 1882; *Der Schüdderump,* 1870) and two of his most popular collections of short stories (*Ferne Stimmen,* 1865; *Der Regenbogen,* 1869). After 1870 he spent his remaining years in Brunswick, writing in spite of the public's indifference to his later work and living withdrawn from a world that seemed to him in its values ever more confused and unsteady.

Within the intricate history of German fiction, Raabe is one of the few genuine humorists. But his humor, like his characters and their lives, demands from the reader a sympathetic understanding of the depth and breadth of German provincial life. His work indicates the impressive climax and end of the literature of German bourgeois idealism. With Gotthelf, Stifter, and Keller (*q.v.*) he is one of the most representative novelists of the century. A far greater artist than his popular contemporary Freytag, and a less self-conscious craftsman than Fontane (*qq.v.*), he is the most genuine storyteller of his generation. Without being either as romantically subjective or as effusively sentimental as "Jean Paul" Richter, he shares Richter's affection for the minutely revealing detail and the quaint and bizarre characters of a proudly class-conscious society. His language, like that of Richter, is baroque in its warmth, occasionally overcharged with recondite learning, but inexhaustible in its wealth of invention.

His first novel, *Die Chronik der Sperlingsgasse,* is in its subject matter reminiscent of the sensibility of the Biedermeier period, but even in this youthful work Raabe speaks with the seasoned authority of a wise observer of life. Three historical novels, *Nach dem Grossen Kriege* (1861), *Der heilige Born* (1861), and *Unseres Herrgotts Kanzlei* (1862), were followed by the last long work of his early period, *Die Leute aus dem Walde* (1863), in which occurs one often quoted sentence that sums up the idealistic realism of Raabe's belief: "Sieh nach den Sternen! Gib acht auf die Gassen!"

If he found himself in his middle years in agreement with the gist of Schopenhauer's "pessimistic" ideas, he was (long before the remarkable later *Novelle, Pfisters Mühle,* 1884) a critical but positive defender of those threatened cultural values which his gilded age seemed willing to forget (see *Horacker,* 1876). The contemporary socialistic and naturalistic ideologies hardly interested him as such. But in his three best-known novels, *Der Hungerpastor, Abu Telfan,* and *Der Schüdderump,* he foreshadowed the German and European crisis of morals with insight and possibly with greater wisdom than even Nietzsche (*q.v.*) himself. All three works, related in substance but not in plot, portray the eventual triumph of inner strength and integrity of feeling over the forces of dissolution (see the preface to the second edition of *Der Schüdderump,* 1894). Not unlike the world of his North German contemporaries, Storm (*q.v.*), Reuter, and Groth, Raabe's characters demonstrated their bourgeois virtues by their personal solidity and moral substance and not, as in Freytag's *Soll und Haben,* in terms of action and success. With Freytag and the social essayist W. H. Riehl (1823–1897), he shares a pride in the accomplishments of the national past; although he is not primarily a "historical novelist," many of his narratives deal with historical subjects. His short stories, from the early and lyrical "Holunderblüte" (1863) and the dramatic "Die schwarze Galeere" (1860), the humorous "Die Gänse von Bützow" (1865), "Gedelöcke" (1866), and *Wunnigel* (1879), to more complex tales ("Der Marsch nach Hause," 1873, and "Die Innerste," 1874), give him a conspicuous place in the history of the German *Novelle* from Kleist to C. F. Meyer (*q.v.*) and Thomas Mann (*q.v.*).

With his last six novels, *Stopfkuchen* (1891), *Gutmanns Reisen* (1892), *Kloster Lugau* (1894), *Die Akten des Vogelsangs* (1895), *Hastenbeck* (1899), and the fragmentary *Altershausen* (1911), Raabe crowns his work as one of the German masters of the craft of fiction. Without the involved and occasionally precious whimsicality of his earlier prose, these nature works reiterate his tenacious resolve to "remain what we are destined to be": "Wir wollen bleiben was wir sein müssen."

See: W. Fehse, *Wilhelm Raabe* (1937).

V. L.

Radiguet, Raymond (1903–1923, French poet and novelist), because of his personal charm, his precociousness, his considerable promise, and his early death, has become the subject of a legend which his published work hardly warrants. Very few critics today would, on merit alone, give more than passing attention to the two slim volumes of verse, *Joues en feu* (1920) and *Devoirs de vacances* (1921), or to the two short novels, *Le Diable au corps* (1923; Eng. tr., *The Devil in the Flesh,* 1932) and *Le Bal du comte d'Orgel* (1924; Eng. tr., *The Count's Ball,* 1929). Yet they show exceptional merit and maturity for so young a writer and suggest that had he lived he would have produced work of lasting quality and left a mark upon his time.

Nothing is known of Radiguet's earliest years beyond the fact that he was born at

Parc-de-Saint-Maur, a meteorological station some 10 miles from Paris, and that at 14 he was already writing remarkably good poetry. He arrived in Paris in 1918, where he led a hand to mouth existence until presently he was taken up by Max Jacob and Jean Cocteau (*qq.v.*), through whom he was introduced to Aragon, Breton, Soupault (*qq.v.*), and other advance-guard writers. Although he was friendly with these extreme innovators and was invited to contribute to *Sic* and other "new" reviews, he was from the beginning, and remained, addicted to the classic tradition, especially to 18th-century classicism. His verse, both metrically and in subject matter, is conventional, though it has at its best a grace, a felicity, and a restraint that reveal facility and taste, if not original power. *Le Diable au corps* is a highly sophisticated *Daphnis and Chloë* in modern dress and *Le Bal du comte d'Orgel* an almost cynically disillusioned novel of manners, both remarkable for their keen and economical delineation of character, for the extremely skillful handling of complex and elusive human relationships. If they make no striking contribution either to the form or substance of the novel, they reveal in the exceptionally acute and sensitive mind of the author a significant *état d'âme* of that post-war period. It is compounded of traditionalism and an almost nihilistic disillusion, of which the early death of a writer of potential genius is perhaps an appropriately poetic fulfillment.

See: Jean Cocteau, "Préface," in Radiguet, *Le Bal du comte d'Orgel* (1924); M. Martin du Gard, *Feux tournants* (1925), pp. 95–115; Henri Massis, *Raymond Radiguet* (1928); François Mauriac, *Le Roman* (1928); Lawrence Leighton, "An Autopsy and a Prescription," *Hound and Horn,* July–September, 1932, pp. 533–539.

H. M. C.

Rakić, Milan (1876–1938, Serb poet), born in Belgrade, was a son of the writer Mita Rakić, author of an excellent translation of Victor Hugo's *Les Misérables.* He studied law at the University of Paris, where he also added greatly to his knowledge of French literature. In 1904 he entered the foreign service, which led him to South Serbia and Salonika, then under Turkish rule, and later to Bucharest, Stockholm, Copenhagen, Sofia, Rome, and Paris. Rakić began his literary activity by translating the poetry of Victor Hugo and Verlaine (*q.v.*), as well as short pieces from Renan (*q.v.*), but already in 1902 his first original poems had been published. In 1904 appeared his first book, *Pesme* (Poems), and in 1912 *Nove pesme* (New Poems). His entire poetic work was collected in 1922.

Rakić wrote little, a total of some 50 poems, but each one is an artistic achievement. An ardent devotee of Parnassian poetry, he tried to express in harmonious form the sentiment of a heart longing for beauty and alarmed at the inevitability and implacability of fate. His manner of expression is profoundly emotional and personal, but at the same time humanly general. Rakić is a pessimist, to whom life is a burden and an anguish without recognition and without reward, but who believes dignity requires us to bear all, serenely and stoically, with proud resignation.

During his service in South Serbia, in a region the scene of important national historical events, Rakić created a series of poems of patriotic inspiration. His patriotism is unrhetorical, discreet, vibrant, and moving; he inaugurated a significant revival of Serbian patriotic poetry. An extensive musical culture contributed to his success; the rhythm and sonority of his verse are incomparable. Many modern Serbian poets have been attracted both by the spirit and the form of his writing; he has become a model for 20th-century lyric poetry in his own country.

See: J. Skerlić, *Pisci i knjige,* Vols. V (1911), VI (1913); B. Lazarević, "Versifikacija Milana Rakica," in *Impresije iz književnosti,* Vol. II (1924); *Srpski književni glasnik,* July 16–August 1, 1938 (number dedicated to Rakić on the occasion of his death).

P. A.

Ramada Curto, Amílcar da Silva (1886–, Portuguese playwright), lives in Lisbon. Whatever his ambitions may be, he hides them behind a cloak of ironical conceit, resigning himself to the lowly station of an "amateur in belles-lettres."

Since 1916, and especially since 1930, a considerable number of plays have appeared under his name, tragedies and comedies which do not pretend to be anything but honest character studies without frills. Passionate, hopeless love, the traditional Portuguese theme, is a favorite with Ramado Curto. He makes it live in the figures of demonic women who snare helpless puppets of men, but are themselves marionettes in the hands of an unfeeling deity. Such are the sinister Maria in *Demónio* (1930; Demon), the flippant Terezinha in *A boneca e os fantoches* (1930; The Doll and the Puppets), and the fatal Laura in *O sapo e a doninha* (1930; The Toad and the Weasel). The last play, a charming, melancholy idyl, follows the bucolic tradition as it had been revived in the country tales of Almeida-Garrett and Júlio Diniz. Although Ramada Curto does not innovate, he shows courage when, in a country saturated with the glories of the past and in an age of robots, he conceives strong characters and passions without recourse to history.

Besides a dozen or more plays of varying worth, Ramada Curto has published thus far one novel, *Do diário de José Maria* (1942; From Joseph Mary's Diary).

G. M. M.

Ramalho Ortigão, José Duarte (1837–1915, Portuguese prose writer), was born in Oporto. The son of a professor, he followed the same career, combining it with journalism, criticism, and literature. In 1866, while editor of the *Jornal do Pôrto* (Oporto Journal), he took part in the polemic between the post-romantics and the realists which was known as the "Coimbra question" (*see* Portuguese literature). Despite his judicial attitude, the criticism he leveled at Antero de Quental (*q.v.*) in his brochure *A literatura de hoje* (Today's Literature) provoked a duel between the two in which Ramalho was slightly wounded. Later he joined the reform group, and in collaboration with one of its distinguished members, the novelist Eça de Queiroz (*q.v.*), he composed a detective novel in the form of letters to the *Diário de notícias* (Daily News) —*Um mistério na estrada de Cintra* (1870; A Mystery on the Cintra Road)—which caused a sensation since the public believed it dealt with a real happening. The same year his collection of short stories, *Histórias côr de rosa* (Rosy Stories), appeared.

But Ramalho's true literary value found expression in his journalistic work and travel books rather than in fiction. Once more associated with Eça de Queiroz, he began, in 1871, the publication of a monthly journal, *As farpas* (The Darts), which continued at intervals until 1883 and which was to exert an important influence on Portuguese realism. It has been asserted that *As farpas* had its origin in the *Guêpes* of Alphonse Karr, but it must be added that its character is different and richer and its scope much more comprehensive. The journal combined the delicate irony of Eça—whose collaboration continued until 1872—with the balanced, serene, and faithfully didactic spirit of Ramalho. Devoted to elegance and hygiene, both physical and spiritual, Ramalho produced a useful and methodical work of healthful popularization and social education in *As farpas*. With a pleasing encyclopedism the studious Ramalho, eager to teach and reform, treated the most varied subjects, science, politics, literature, in a limpid and flexible style, characterized by ample and delicately ironical sentences. His clear and incisive pen, with a sensible didactic intention, satirizes weaknesses and shortcomings of Portuguese life. The serene balance of his faculties, his artistic good sense, and his spiritual elegance established a tribunal in *As farpas* from which the ideas of the Generation of Coimbra were disseminated. Positivism, determinism, humanitarianism, moral secularism, faith in science, and aesthetic realism were presented in its pages with great coherence. The success of *As farpas* established a "school" which resulted in continuations or imitations, the most significant of which was *Os gatos* (The Cats) of Fialho de Almeida (*q.v.*). *Os gatos,* however, had a very different character, in which defamatory sarcasm was exaggerated.

In the other aspect of his work, travel literature, Ramalho's attitude is not that of the simple observer of beauty who passes on his aesthetic impressions. A product of his period, he imparts scientific importance and practical usefulness to this literature. His aim is to compare societies, draw conclusions, and apply them to the betterment of countries. *A Holanda* (1883; Holland) has this purpose. In an account characterized by great descriptive briskness, indicative of searching powers of observation, he gives us a social and historical study of that country, focused always on comparisons with Portugal. It is Holland and not France that Portugal should observe, since that country represents the solution of a problem more like her own in every respect than that of the great Gallic nation. The book enjoyed a wide acceptance and has remained a model of this type of literature. In 1887 *John Bull* was published. It does not attain the level of excellence of *A Holanda,* either in the system followed or in the attitude; with its Anglophobia, inherited from Herculano and common to the whole realistic generation, it is manifestly hostile to the milieu described. *Ultimas farpas* (1910–1915; Last Darts) is also clearly inferior to the early work. The spiritual and literary personality of Ramalho —progressive and reforming—left a mark of constructive elegance in Portuguese criticism and journalism of the period.

See: Maria A. Vaz de Carvalho, *Alguns homens do meu tempo* (1889), pp. 37–106; J. M. Eça de Queiroz, *Notas contemporâneas*

(1909), pp. 27–54; Ricardo Jorge, *Ramalho Ortigão* (1915).

E. G. D.

Ramuz, Charles Ferdinand (1878–, Swiss novelist), was born at Cully, a small town on Lake Geneva in the canton of Vaud. After completing his studies at the University of Lausanne, he went to Paris where, from 1902 to 1914, he lived in obscurity, known only to a small group of friends and admirers. The books written by him at that time, four volumes of poetry in addition to eight novels and two collections of short stories, failed to attract attention outside his immediate circle. Longing for an atmosphere truly congenial to his artistic temperament, Ramuz decided to go back to his native Cully. This proved to be a momentous step in his life. As he explained in "Raison d'être," published in 1914 in the *Cahiers vaudois,* he now had a clear conception of his purpose as a writer. He at once embarked on what was to be a long and highly successful career.

The 20-odd volumes of fiction written by Ramuz since 1914 contain a searching analysis of the primitive emotions which give the life of the simple folk of his canton its distinctive tonality. Peasants, winegrowers, small craftsmen, and fishermen live again vividly before the eyes of the reader. To mention only the most noteworthy of his books, *La Guérison des maladies* (1917), *Le Règne de l'esprit malin* (1917; Eng. tr., *The Reign of the Evil One,* 1922), *Les Signes parmi nous* (1919), *Salutation paysanne* (1921), *Présence de la mort* (1922; Eng. tr., *The End of All Men,* 1944), *Joie dans le ciel* (1925), *La Grande Peur dans la montagne* (1926), *La Beauté sur la terre* (1927; Eng. tr., *Beauty on Earth,* 1929), and *Derborence* (1935), all very clearly show with what consummate skill he has succeeded in emancipating himself from bookish influences and in merging his personality with that of his characters. His style reveals a remarkable degree of independence from the commonly accepted standards of literary excellence. He readily concedes the presence of regional peculiarities of language in his novels. He also agrees that his word order is often logical rather than grammatical. As critics have pointed out, the rhythm and phrasing of his sentences show not only the influence of the spiritual climate, but even of the geographical features of the canton of Vaud. These varied features make of Ramuz one of the most fascinating figures in contemporary French literature.

See: "Pour ou contre C.-F. Ramuz," *Cahiers de la quinzaine,* XVII (1926), 9–312; Emmanuel Buenzod, *C.-F. Ramuz* (1928); Gertrud Brandner, *C. F. Ramuz, der Dichter des Waadtlandes; ein Beitrag zur Literaturgeschichte der französischen Schweiz* (1938).

J. M. C.

Rapisardi, Mario (1844–1912, Italian poet), is Italy's outstanding contribution to the satanic school of poetry, outstanding for the quantity of his verses if not for the quality. He was born in Catania and taught at its university until his death. If we disregard the poems of his early youth, which he himself rejected, Rapisardi's first production was *Palingenesi* (1868), an epic poem wherein, in keeping with the anticlericalism then current in his country, a religious reform is propounded. Here at the very outset Rapisardi places his art at the service of an ideal. To this practice he adhered all his life. It may have been choice, but one cannot help feeling that for Rapisardi it was a necessity. His vast power of expression could not find adequate scope in his own inward experiences, the paucity of which is further indicated by his labors as a translator (he translated Lucretius, Horace, Catullus, and Shelley's *Prometheus Unbound*) and is borne out by his entire production. Hence the necessity of his looking outside for a peg, as it were, on which to hang a poem —religious reform first, then Darwinism, atheism, socialism, all of which remain mere schematisms which Rapisardi fills in out of the abundance of his vocabulary, reminiscences, and versifying skill.

Today he is remembered chiefly for his polemic (1881) with Carducci (*q.v.*), from which neither his equanimity nor his reputation ever quite recovered. This polemic came on the heels of his *Lucifero* (1877), a miserably conceived epic poem in which fustian, scurrility, blasphemy, and lewdness, compounded with all the commonplaces of Italian poetry and prosody, conspire to move the reader to nausea or, if he is struck by the ludicrous in the author's high pretensions and his performance, to laughter. And to laughter it moved many of his contemporaries, aided and abetted by the parodies it occasioned. Rapisardi, whose vanity, egotism, and self-bestowed role of exalted bard of the new era of universal peace, love, justice, and godlessness could not admit of the slightest sense of humor, became very bitter, but did not relent. Striking the gladiatorial pose best indicated to show to advantage his flowing locks, broad brow, and large, dreamy eyes, he kept open the floodgates of his declamation to give two more epic poems, *Giobbe* (1884) and *Atlantide* (1894). Neither of these did much to dispel the mistaken but widespread belief that the epic was a thing of the past, or to alter the equally widespread conviction that Rapisardi was no epic poet. But is he a poet at all? He is, but only in those rare moments when an inward feeling of wonder, bewilderment, sympathy, or yearning steals into his consciousness and so fills it as to preclude his lapsing into posturing, bombast, or ear-tickling sonorities. These poetic moments are to be found in his shorter lyrics, notably among his *Poesie religiose* (1887), and in several of his *Poemetti* (1885–1907).

See: N. Vaccalluzzo, *Mario Rapisardi; raccolta di poesie scelte con introduzione e commento* (1930); N. Cappellani, *Mario Rapisardi* (1931).

S. E. S.

Raynal, Paul (1890–, French dramatist), born at Narbonne, studied law and passed eventually from jurisprudence to literature. He submitted his first play, *Le Maître de son cœur,* to the Odéon theatre in 1913. But the First World War intervened. The play was laid away and was not produced until 1920, when it was acclaimed a masterpiece of psychological insight, a penetrating analysis of the conflict between love and friendship. In the minds of admiring critics it recalled the art of Racine, Musset, Curel (*q.v.*).

The drama of Paul Raynal has, in fact, become identified with that trend in the postwar theatre in France which drew its inspiration from the classic tradition, from Racine and, especially, Corneille. It is characterized by psychological profundity and moral nobility, by a mood of the tragic and the heroic, two of the essential traits of French tragedy. Raynal had joined his regiment as a simple soldier in 1914. When he came back, four years later, he gave expression to the sufferings and heroisms of all its known and unknown soldiers in his next play, *Le Tombeau sous l'Arc de Triomphe* (1924; Eng. tr., *The Unknown Warrior,* 1928). The drama portrays symbolically the conflict between the desire for peace and its pleasing amenities, on one side, and the tragic call of sacrifice, which is the price of such peace, on the other. It was bitterly assailed and fanatically defended. It has ended by being generally accepted as a masterpiece of the literature inspired by the tragedy of war.

In *Au soleil de l'instinct* (1932) Raynal returned to the vein of his first psychological drama, and in *La Francerie* (1933) to the theme of war, stressing the epic side of it, however, and striking a note of hope for reconciliation among nations. Epic and psychological traits were combined in his portrait of the French emperor, *Napoléon unique* (1936). The lofty nature of Raynal's dramatic talent is strikingly illustrated in his later play, *A souffert sous Ponce Pilate* (1939). Probing the motif for Judas Iscariot's betrayal, he ascribes it not to evil intent but to the disciple's naïveté and limited understanding and less to lack of love than to little faith. The symbol of charity is raised here to the level of the divine.

The art of Raynal stands out for its sumptuous lyric and tragic qualities. He achieves dramatic intensity and the color, the passion, and the movement of life, as in classical tragedy, by virtue of an elevated style which is oratorical but not declamatory, poetic and musical but withal precise, clear, and exact. He drains the complex human passions—love, hate, honor, vengeance, sacrifice—of the dross that collects in them in the maelstrom of daily reality, purifies and lifts them to an exalted mood, and molds through them characters of a heroic stature. He is one of the outstanding dramatists of his generation in France.

See: E. Sée, *Le Théâtre français contemporain* (1928), pp. 72, 157–162; H. M. and A. J. Dickman, "Paul Raynal, Cornelian and Symbolical Theatre—A Critical Essay," *University of Wyoming Publications,* IV (1938), 45–57; K. Wais, "Paul Raynal und die Schöpfung des französischen Kriegsdramas," *Dichtung und Volkstum,* XXXIX (1938), 168–179.

S. A. R.

Régnier, Henri François Joseph de (1864–1936, French poet, novelist, and critic), was born at Honfleur in Normandy, of the lesser French nobility. His paternal ancestors, military men, came from Picardy. Literary inheritance seems to descend from the maternal forebears, Burgundian judges, scholars, men and women writers. Régnier's novel *Les Vacances d'un jeune homme sage* (1903) vividly presents his maternal uncle, a genealogist, who interested him in heraldry (this feature appears in his symbolist poetry). The poet's ancestors are important in his memoirs and novels. His genealogical studies resulted in certain occult and atavistic theories, coloring the novels, making the past and memory outstanding elements of his poetry. In the novel *Le Passé vivant* (1905) the descendants are under fatalistic compulsion, through the survival of mystic forces forming the tissue of their beings, to repeat or be influenced by the destinies of the ancestors living in them. In 1879 Henri wrote his first verses, confiscated by an uncomprehending professor. His friend, the American-born Francis Vielé-Griffin (*q.v.*), another second-generation symbolist, founded the *Entretiens politiques et littéraires,* to which Régnier contributed. A slender volume, *Les Lendemains* (1885), was published by Vanier, the symbolists' editor. Régnier contributed to various little reviews of the period, including *Lutèce* (1885). The pseudonym Hugues Vignix reveals his admiration for Hugo and Vigny, but his early poems indicate especially a Parnassian influence. Sully-Prudhomme and Leconte de Lisle (*qq.v.*) were his first great literary acquaintances.

In *Poèmes anciens et romanesques* (1890) Régnier first manifested the distinctive poetic personality which flowered in *Tel qu'en songe* (1892), *Aréthuse* (1895), and *Les Jeux rustiques et divins* (1897). The last contains the gently crepuscular, sensitive lyrics called "odelettes," an original form, not similar to those of Ronsard or Banville (*q.v.*). He now uses vers libre, rhymed at will or assonanced. The uneven meters, nuances, and wistful musicality of a Verlaine (*q.v.*) are evident, but Régnier's rhythms have a longer flow, his harmonies and art of suggestion are more subtle. There is sumptuous decorativeness and the sadness of a pagan regretting the evanescence of beauty as he clings to memory. His favorite words are *or* and *mort.* He uses all the devices—swans, philtres, enchanted forests, and dream cities—inherited by his great symbolistic predecessors from Wagner, The poem "Le Vase" shows how far he has come from the Parnassians' motionless, chiseled poems of similar title. This remarkable poem, revealing the successive states of an artist while creating, has constant motion. Régnier's sensuousness of sound, perfume, color, and form recalls the "Après-Midi d'un faune" of Stéphane Mallarmé (*q.v.*). Several of Régnier's articles give tribute to that master whose salon he devotedly frequented for years.

Though Régnier's work reveals multiple influences and an eclectic character, he achieves a synthesis that justifies his place as representative symbolist. His importance was officially recognized when he was elected to the French Academy in 1912, but before he had achieved this honor, he had at times veered toward the classic form and given proof of abilities in traditional versification. *Les Médailles d'argile* (1900) was dedicated to André Chénier, as its bucolic tendencies and ancient verses on new themes justified. Here the sonnets also have a touch of the work of José Maria de Heredia (*q.v.*). In 1896 Henri de Régnier married a daughter of Heredia, Marie, who wrote under the pseudonym Gérard d'Houville (*q.v.*).

Versailles, presented as a decorative city of dreamy silence, in its crystallized beauty preserving the past, our only permanence in an ever changing world, is the subject of *La Cité des eaux* (1902). The poet's return to alexandrines and description, said to be an Heredia influence and a bid for Academy election, is more likely a lessening of lyric adolescent revery and originality, a normal growing into maturity's greater realism, a descent from the ivory tower to which his sensitive, haughty soul, wounded by life's imperfection, had retired. His poems, in the works just mentioned and later in *La Sandale ailée* (1906; Eng. tr., *Poems from The Winged Sandal,* 1933), *Vestigia Flammae* (1920), and *Flamma tenax* (1922–28), retain their musical fluidity. There is a tendency to direct expression of sentiments and to less *décor,* but even here the delicately suggestive symbolistic "odelettes" appear.

The prose vein begins with *Contes à soi-même* (1893), symbolic stories with preciosity of style. The first and best-known full-length novel by Régnier, *La Double Maîtresse* (1900), despite its 18th-century setting is said to be the first Freudian novel and thus the precursor of a whole new literature. The main character, among a numerous Dickensian array, suffers from a fixation causing a lifetime of repression. Other novels in 17th and 18th-century style, *Le Bon Plaisir* (1902) and *Les Rencontres de M. de Bréot* (1904; Eng. tr., *The Libertines,* 1929), possess a libertine flavor realistically faithful to the times evoked. However, le comte de Mun, on receiving Henri de Régnier into the Academy, reproached him for their "art for art" realism —and for a lack of moral responsibility towards his readers. *Le Mariage de minuit* (1903) is a beautifully moving, refined modern novel of moral idealism. Its comte de Serpigny portrays the eccentric poet, le comte de Montesquiou-Fezensac, with whom Régnier dueled in 1897. This novel contains reminiscences of Régnier's American tour (1900), as does L'Amphisbène (1912), which also recounts a Mediterranean cruise, described autobiographically in *Escales en Méditerranée* (1931). To a lover of the picturesque past, no city could be more poetic than Venice. Certain of Régnier's modern novels unfold there. *Les Esquisses vénitiennes* (1906) resulted from his visits to Venice; *L'Altana, ou la Vie vénitienne* (2 vols., 1928) relates 25 years of his wanderings about its familiar streets, canals, gardens, and palaces.

As a critic Régnier contributed to the little reviews and to the *Mercure de France, Figaro,* and *Journal des débats.* In his later years he edited the *Roman littéraire,* publishing works by younger writers. Using his memory for things historical, Régnier employs frequent analogies from the past in his criticism. The articles collected in *Figures et caractères* (1901) and *Sujets et paysages* (1906) show the same amused irony present in his novels. *Nos Rencontres* (1931) and *De mon temps* (1933), devoted more to personal memoirs and anecdotes of contemporaries, have less criticism of a man's work, but much deftly delineated portraiture.

See: J. de Gourmont, *Henri de Régnier et son œuvre* (1908); H. Berton, *Henri de Régnier, le poète et le romancier* (1910); A. Lowell, *Six French Poets* (1915); R. Honnert, *Henri de Régnier; son œuvre* (1923).

M. C. M.

Reina y Montilla, Manuel (1856–1905, Spanish poet and politician), was born in Puente Genil, Córdoba. A lawyer by profession, he practiced in Seville, Granada, and Madrid. In politics he was a constitutional monarchist, associated with the liberal party of Sagasta and later with the conservative Maura. Although economically comfortable, he interested himself in the underprivileged, and in Parliament he promoted legislation in behalf of the Spanish wage earners and for the protection of children.

His first verses appeared in *Epoca* and *Ilustración española y americana.* In 1877 *Andantes y alegros* was published, and *Cromos y acuarelas* followed in 1888. His best work is *El jardín de los poetas* (1899), in which he interprets and pays homage to the great poetic figures of the world, from Homer to Spain's Espronceda. *La vida inquieta* (1894) attracted attention because it was published with a prologue by Núñez de Arce (*q.v.*), who presumably influenced Reina.

Reina's poetic qualities may be inferred from the titles of his works—musicality, color, imagery, and emotion. These together with his metrical dexterity, richness of diction, and avoidance of academic molds place him somewhere between his contemporaries and the poets of the following generation. Critics have been fairly unanimous in bestowing praise on this quietly personal and pleasantly independent poet.

See: E. de Ory, *Manuel Reina* (n.d.).

H. C. B.

Rejment, Władysław Stanisław, *see* Reymont.

Remarque, Erich Maria (1898–, German novelist), gained world-wide fame with his war novel *Im Westen nichts Neues* (1929; Eng. tr., *All Quiet on the Western Front,* 1929). He was born the son of a bookbinder in Osnabrück and attended the Gymnasium of his home town. He served and was wounded in the First World War. Later he tried his hand at several professions, finally becoming the editor of a sports journal. When in this position he wrote his famous novel in which he claimed to be the spokesman of "a generation that was destroyed by war, even though it might have escaped its shells." This must be accepted with reserve, for evidence shows (*see* Flex and Dwinger) that the heroes of Remarque are not representative of a whole generation but only of a certain type. Of this type, however, the novel is an authentic record, and it has literary merit. Remarque knows how to draw characters and situations; he engages attention and arouses sympathy. His language is versatile and concise, rich in contrast and interspersed with pertinent reflections. His composition is based upon excellent stage technique. Lyric and idyllic scenes alternate with the coarsest and most lurid realism. The intricate problems of life and of the war are reduced to plain propositions that the poorest in spirit can grasp. Just at the most favorable psychological moment, when Arnold Zweig (*q.v.*) and Georg von der Vring (the latter with his fine war novel *Soldat Suhren;* Eng. tr., *Private Suhren,* 1928) had broken the ice and the universal anti-war sentiment had reached its climax, the story gave eloquent expression to the cry "No more war!" As an ethical document it is not without flaws. It shows adolescent immaturity and, through omissions and through generalizations implied by individual incidents, a partial and narrow outlook.

The fate of the surviving heroes in the chaotic time after the war is told in *Der Weg zurück* (1931; Eng. tr., *The Road Back,* 1931). This novel falls far short of its predecessor, though it has narrative interest. In 1932 Remarque went to live in Switzerland, and in 1939 he came to the United States.

Other successes of his were *Three Comrades* (1937); *Flotsam* (1941), the story of European refugees fleeing from the Gestapo; and *Arch of Triumph* (1946).

See: W. K. Pfeiler, *War and the German Mind* (1941), pp. 140–144.

W. K. P.

Remizov, Aleksei Mikhailovich (1877–, Russian poet and novelist), was born in Moscow into an old merchant family. He received a religious upbringing and in his childhood and youth visited many monasteries. After graduating from the Alexandrovsk Commercial School, he enrolled in the faculty of natural sciences at the University of Moscow. Later he was expelled for political activity and spent several years in exile; he was sent to various provinces, including some very remote corners of Russia. His writings began to be published in 1902, predominately in symbolist periodicals. In 1904 Remizov was freed from police surveillance and permitted to settle in St. Petersburg, where he lived until 1921. At that time he emigrated, first to Germany, then to Paris. His first book appeared in 1907.

Remizov's own philosophical outlook plays an important role in his works. The religious-ethical problem is fundamental for him. He depicts the world as a domain of evil spirits, in which the guiding force is a blind and irrational fate. His tales reflect his own youthful experiences which he represents in images of brutality and fantastic monstrosities. His first novel, *Prud* (1907; The Pond), displays in its bestial nightmares Remizov's revulsion to city life. Many of his works, *Chasy* (1904; Eng. tr., *The Clock,* 1942), *Neugomonny buben* (1909; The Unhushable Tambourine), *Pyataya yazva* (1912; Eng. tr., *The Fifth Pestilence,* 1927), reflect his negative reaction to the life of the provincial towns of Russia. Remizov's aversion to the urbanization of Russia is seen in his *Krestovye Syostry* (1910; Sisters of the Cross) and *Slovo o pogibeli zemli Russkoi* (1917; Lament for the Ruin of Russia), and he blames the Westernizing process begun by Peter for Russia's afflictions.

Although Remizov has not been a popular writer, his works, both in their peculiar peasant style of narration—the *skaz*—and in content, have greatly influenced Russian fiction, particularly that of the postrevolutionary period. The works of such authors as Zamyatin (*q.v.*), Rukavishnikov, Pilnyak (*q.v.*), and Bulgakov (*q.v.*) bear his mark. His own works link him with Gogol and Dostoevski (*q.v.*), and stylistically Remizov is close to Leskov.

See: K. Chukovski, *Psikhologicheskiye motivy v tvorchestve A. Remizova* (1922); D. A. Gorbov, "Mertvaya krasota i zhivucheye bezobraziye," *Krasnaya nov,* 1926, No. 7; D. S. Mirsky, *Contemporary Russian Literature* (1926).

O. M.

Renan, Ernest (1823–1892, French historian and critic), born at Tréguier in Brittany, was intended by a pious mother for the priesthood; he spent long periods of his maturity in the Holy Land, but chiefly in order to examine with a historian's eye the physical setting of a faith which he had determined as he came of age to study scientifically. For most of his life he was a resident of Paris. He had gone there in 1838 to prepare for the great Seminary of Saint-Sulpice, from which he definitely withdrew in 1845; he had been a brilliant and not docile pupil. He turned scholar and teacher and began to write for the *Revue des deux mondes* and the *Journal des débats* with an early developed charm of style which, in a variety of books, was to hold the attention of *tout Paris* for decades. As a Semitist he was appointed to a chair at the Collège de France (1862), gave one lecture, and so offended orthodoxy that the course was stopped and the professor removed; in 1870 the new provisional government restored Renan to his position, and he subsequently (1883) was made director of the famous center of learning. The scandal of 1862 was principally about a reference, in Renan's introductory discourse, to Jesus as an "incomparable man" (not necessarily, for historians, divine); in 1863 was published his most widely known book, the *Vie de Jésus* (Eng. tr., 1863), of which 60,000 copies were bought by an excited public in less than six months and which was attacked by more than 300 different pamphlets in the first three months. Renan was elected to the French Academy in 1878. His outstanding contributions as historian are the *Histoire des origines du christianisme* (1863–1883, including the *Vie de Jésus;* Eng. tr., 1888–1890) and the related *Histoire de peuple d'Israël* (1887–1893; Eng. tr., 1888–1891, 1895). In his later years his reputation was European. He relaxed by composing *Dialogues et fragments philosophiques* (1876; Eng. tr., 1883) and *Drames philosophiques* (1888; Eng. tr., *The Abbess of Jouarre,* 1888; *Priest of Némi,* 1895; *Caliban,* 1896). Many of the ideas developed in Renan's subsequent writings are in his basic *L'Avenir* *de la science; pensées de 1848,* which was not actually published until 1890 (Eng. tr., 1891). The posthumous *Essai psychologique sur Jésus Christ* (1921, written 1845) shows a moralist who was to be as fascinated all his life by essential problems of human nature as were Sainte-Beuve and Taine (*q.v.*)—and this may be the most durable feature of all his works.

Renan said his own ethnic formula would be "a Celt, mixed with a Gascon [his maternal grandfather], with a mongrel dash of Laplander." There is occasional whimsicality allied to much poetry in the enthusiasms and intuitions of this man, most of whose life was given to austere labors of erudition (the total number of his books and articles is 1039), who kept from his early training something of the sacerdotal and who is charged with having become near the end a dilettante, an intellectual voluptuary, an enchanter particularly dangerous to youth. William James, less Celtic, no Gascon, and not flippant, speaks of later days of "sweet decay."

Renan greatly affected literary criticism even though not much of his own writing deals with belles-lettres. Anatole France often composes pieces in a Renan manner, showing, the unfriendly would say, how the manner may be used perversely. Renan is relativistic, devoted to history as newly conceived in the 19th century, enthusiastic about new developments in science and a close friend of the great chemist Berthelot, a disciple of Hegel and an advocate of the doctrine of "becoming" as opposed to "being"—or to go much further back he is definitely Heraclitean rather than Eleatic. One must respect the infinite variety of points of view, expect change, and not believe consistency necessarily a virtue. The essence of criticism, he said, is to enter into modes of life different from our own. He made a study of Galilee as a sort of fifth Gospel, to help understand in their setting the first four. He was tempted, he admits in the widely read and engaging *Souvenirs d'enfance et de jeunesse* (1883; Eng. tr., *Recollections of My Youth,* 1883), always to be of the opinion of his interlocutor. A youthful, fragmentary, somewhat autobiographical novel, *Patrice* (written 1849, published 1908), contains, in a more emphatic style than Renan later approved of, good examples of his critical mind at work. He talked of polychrome printing where varieties of delicate distinctions would be indicated by differences in amount and color of ink. The pages which constitute the famous Prayer at the Acropolis (*Souvenirs*) are an excellent specimen of his consummate art and delight in *nuances* (a key word with Renan); it is here he says that to hate nothing, to love nothing, absolutely, is the part of wisdom. Recent studies of Renan have helped to show underneath the tolerance that may seem to approach flippancy what it is more fair to call an admirable intellectual hospitality and the deep seriousness of a man all his life under the influence of the Church which shaped his early years.

See: L. F. Mott, *Ernest Renan* (1921, in English); J. Pommier, *Renan* (1923); P. Lasserre, *Renan et nous* (1923) and *La Jeunesse de Renan* (1925–1932); H. Psichari, *Renan d'après lui-même* (1937).

H. S.

Renard, Jules (1864–1910, French novelist, playwright, and essayist), was born at Châlons, Mayenne. His father, a contractor, was of peasant stock, and his mother was a somewhat harsh and ill-tempered woman. Two years after his birth the family moved to Chitry-les-Mines in Nièvre. He began his secondary education at Nevers, planned to enter the famous Ecole Normale Supérieure of Paris, and was sent to Paris for further preparation at the Lycée Charlemagne. But he began to visit literary cafés and felt drawn toward writing. After military service he returned to Paris to a modest job, lived simply, and in 1888 married. From this time onward his bourgeois and disciplined existence was dedicated entirely to his family and to writing.

He helped launch the new *Mercure de France* in 1890, contributed critical articles and stories to this review, was noticed by the symbolists (*see* French symbolism). Encouraged by Alphonse Daudet (*q.v.*) and Jean Richepin (*q.v.*), he wrote for the humorous periodicals *Rire* and *Gil Blas* and for important newspapers, *Echo de Paris, Journal,* and *Figaro.* Among his novels, short stories, and essays are *Crime de village* (1888); *Sourires pincés* (1890); *L'Ecornifleur* (1892), which is his masterpiece; *Coquecigrües* (1893); *La Lanterne sourde* (1893); *Le Coureur de filles* (1894); *Le Vigneron dans sa vigne* (1894); *Poil de Carotte* (1894), which depicts a child drudge effectively if with less originality and less color than *Jacques Vingtras* by Jules Vallès (*q.v.*); *Histoires naturelles* (1896); *La Maîtresse* (1896); *Bucoliques* (1898); *Les Philippe* (1907); *Nos Frères farouches* (1908); *Ragotte* (1908). For these numerous productions Renard found his inspiration in the rustic *mœurs* of Nivernais, his home country, and in the intellectual milieu of the Left Bank of Paris. He was at the same time becoming a writer for the stage who frequented the Paris boulevards and developed friendships with Edmond Rostand (*q.v.*), Lucien Guitry, and Marthe Brandès. He composed in succession *La Demande* (1895); *Le Plaisir de rompre* (1898); *Le Pain de ménage* (1899); the play *Poil de Carotte* (1900), which continues to be presented successfully at the Comédie Française; *Monsieur Vernet* (1903); and *La Bigote* (1909), which is a caricature of his own mother. In 1907, through the militant friendship of Lucien Descaves (*q.v.*), he became a member of the Goncourt Academy. But he had kept in touch with the peasant life of Nivernais and had engaged in local politics there. An admirer of Claude Tillier, Victor Hugo, Michelet, and Jaurès, he was if not an ardent socialist at least a very warm believer in the republicanism and the lay movement of the provinces, and he showed the sincerity, the narrow-mindedness, and the stubborness so likely to accompany these ideas. He took very seriously his responsibilities as mayor of Chitry which began in 1904. It is in this village that he was buried, with a civil ceremony, after his death in Paris, May 22, 1910.

The work of Jules Renard is a faithful reflection of his own life and personality. There are episodes of his childhood in *Poil de Carotte, La Bigote, Crime de village;* recollections of his sentimental and laborious youth in Paris in *L'Ecornifleur, La Maîtresse, Le Plaisir de rompre;* pictures of his peaceful bourgeois life in *Le Pain de ménage*. As for his more intimate nature—he was in turn complex and merely commonplace, cynical and naïve—this is revealed in his *Journal* (1925–1927), a posthumous publication of the highest interest for the historian of modern literature in France. Except for a particularly morose and often affected pessimism, which resulted in an abundance of acid comment, his works show no philosophical preoccupation. "I snap my fingers at guiding principles, moral problems, metaphysical fogs. I prefer to a beautiful book a beautiful page and to a beautiful page a beautiful sentence." As a matter of fact his style, which is so deliberate as sometimes to be tense, has been praised for its classical qualities—exactness, sobriety, density, relentlessly minute realism. But he hardly achieves rhythm or movement and certainly not that deep humanity which constitutes the essential contribution of great French writers. One may accept the remark made by André Gide (*q.v.*) concerning the work of Renard: "Not a river, but a distillery."

See: Henri Bachelin, *Jules Renard, 1864–1910; son œuvre* (1930); Léon Guichard, *L'Œuvre et l'âme de Jules Renard* (1935).

G. G.

Renn, Ludwig, (pseud. of Arnold Friedrich Vieth von Golssenau, 1889–, German novelist), born in Dresden, scion of an old and noble family, has Irish and Russian ancestors. Following tradition, he became an officer in 1911 and saw combat and staff service in the First World War. Changed in his whole outlook by the experiences of war, especially after he had "ceased to drink," Renn began to write, in a factual style especially influenced by the travel books of Sven Hedin. After the war he turned to the political left and became a Communist. He studied at the universities of Göttingen, Munich, and Vienna and undertook extensive trips through the Mediterranean lands and Russia.

His fame rests on his first novel, *Krieg* (1928; Eng. tr., *War,* 1929), one of the few great books that came out of the First World War. It presents a simple factual acceptance of the war per se, with a minimum of reflection, sentiment, and didacticism, and as such is a more powerful indictment than any elaborate harangue could be. Wealth of individual experience, rigid discipline in the giving of facts, determined sifting of material, and concentration on the essentials make *Krieg* a true epic of the soldier of the front. The style of Renn is terse, graphic, and clear, revealing a complete mastery of his subject, a mastery which makes the effort of Remarque (*q.v.*) seem puny. Pertinent criticism of the conditions of military life is tempered by an insight into general human weakness, and the distribution of light and shadow is done with fairness and objectivity. The narrative gives in concise delineation the war experience of a straightforward, sympathetic character, and it is to be regretted that political bias and thoughtless criticism have caused wholly incorrect evaluations of Renn's book in Germany and abroad.

In his later works Renn was less successful. *Nachkrieg* (1930; Eng. tr., *After War,* 1931) gives a picture of the hopeless mess of contradictory and aimless political strife in the Weimar Republic. He did not succeed in integrating the huge amount of material. A later volume, *Russland fahrten* (1932), tells of his travels and impressions in Russia. Jailed for several years after Hitler's ascent to power, Renn escaped to Switzerland in

1936, where he wrote *Vor grossen Wandlungen* (1936; Eng. tr., *Death without Battle,* 1937). He took a prominent part in the Spanish civil war, after which he lived in France, writing the treatise *Warfare: The Relation of War to Society* (1939). He now lives in Mexico, where he published his valuable autobiographic novel *Adel im Untergang* (1944).

See: "Ludwig Renn, Germany's Proletarian Novelist," *Living Age,* CCCXLIII (1933), 509–512; W. K. Pfeiler, *War and the German Mind* (1941), pp. 150–164.

W. K. P.

Retté, Adolphe (1863–1930, French poet and religious writer), was born in Paris. His early childhood was spent in Belgium at the home of his maternal grandfather, Professor Borgnet, an eminent historian at the University of Liége. Retté's mother was a talented musician, and from her he seems to have inherited a sensitive and somewhat unstable nature. After a few unhappy years at a Protestant school at Montbéliard, Retté served in the French cavalry for six years. Then, settling in Paris in 1886, he became intensely interested in symbolism; two volumes of poetry, *Cloches en la nuit* (1889) and *Une Belle Dame passa* (1893), were published. Both of these books reflect a strong admiration for Mallarmé and for Gustave Kahn (*qq.v.*). A volume of prose, of strange and hallucinating beauty, entitled *Thulé des brumes* (1891), is an adventure in the world of fantasy and dreams. In 1893 Retté abruptly changed his aesthetic outlook and became interested in anarchism. Violent attacks, bearing Retté's signature, against Mallarmé and against social abuses appeared every month in the magazine *Plume,* and Retté's new outlook is reflected in *Similitudes* (1895) and *La Forêt bruissante* (1896), both of which have a dramatic form. Meanwhile Retté had married and retired with his wife to the little village of Guermantes. Penetrated by the rural atmosphere, Retté gradually became a pantheist, producing two volumes of inspired verse, *Campagne première* (1897) and *Lumières tranquilles* (1901). The death of his wife and that of Léon Deschamps, the director of *Plume,* thrust Retté even more toward nature for consolation, and between 1901 and 1906 he celebrated the beauties of the Forest of Fontainebleau. In 1906 occurred his conversion to Catholicism, an event which he felt to be miraculous and which he described in *Du diable à Dieu* (1907). Thereafter his life was spent in the service of the Church and in the composition of pious volumes, ranging from biographies of saintly figures to personal meditations. Unhappily, in this production, he revealed neither the artistry nor the literary care of his earlier books. When he died, after six years of seclusion at Beaune, he was almost forgotten in the literary world.

See: R. de Smet, *La Vie populaire d'Adolphe Retté* (1933); W. K. Cornell, *Adolphe Retté* (1942, in English).

W. K. C.

Reverdy, Pierre (1889–, French poet), was born at Narbonne, of well-to-do parents who encouraged his desire to become a poet. After leaving the *lycée* in 1910, he went to Paris. There the death of his father in 1911 made him almost wholly dependent on his writing, and he began a bitter struggle to survive. Several small volumes of poetry were published, *Poèmes en prose* (1915), *La Lucarne ovale* (1916), and *Quelques Poèmes* (1916). Little by little his work became known till by 1917 he was director of a review, *Nord-Sud,* presenting the work of such men as Apollinaire, Max Jacob, André Breton, and Louis Aragon (*qq.v.*) and fighting for a poetry which made no pretense of reproducing reality. After the war Reverdy avoided the fascination of dada, cubism, and surrealism and continued on his own way, winning wide recognition with *Les Epaves du ciel* (1924), a collection of his early work, and such books of poetry as *Flaques de verre* (1929), *Pierres blanches* (1931), and *Ferraille* (1937). A volume of criticism, *Le Gant de crin* (1926), has made his purpose clear. Reverdy's eyes are fixed on a spiritual world underlying solid reality; he is the poet of the impalpable, and for him the fleeting impressions of beauty or tragedy felt by the sensitive heart as underlying the most common scenes are the true material of poetry. Gifted with a keen intuition and the ability to make the reader join with him in perceiving the most subtle analogies, Reverdy works with allusion, concentration, half statement, till his poems become almost the overheard murmurs of a mystic rapt in ecstasy. This quality has become more and more pronounced in his verse since 1926, when he returned to the Catholic faith and settled near the Benedictine abbey of Solesmes. His work has had great though indirect effect on the younger French poets, to whom in his unselfish devotion to poetry and in the artistic purity of his work he has seemed the Mallarmé (*q.v.*) of this generation—so much so that Soupault (*q.v.*), Breton, and Aragon have not hesitated to proclaim him *le plus grand poète actuellement vivant.*

See: Régis Michaud, *Modern Thought and Literature in France* (1934); Christian Sénéchal, *Les Grands Courants de la littérature française contemporaine* (1934); G. E. Lemaitre, *From Cubism to Surrealism in French Literature* (1941).

C. W., Jr.

Reviczky, Gyula (1855–1889, Hungarian poet and writer), was born in Vitkóc and died in Budapest. He received his secondary school education in Léva and Pozsony and attended lectures at the University of Budapest. His life is a record of human defeat. He was brought up as a motherless child; poverty, misunderstanding, loneliness, unhappy love, tuberculosis, were his experiences. By nature he was a pessimist, a singer of moods, an introvert, conditioned by a penny-pinching existence that often defied the most elementary principles of a decent livelihood. As a young man he was a tutor, later a journalist. His neo-romanticism seemed a desertion of Hungarian folkish nationalistic literary traditions, and he was therefore accused of being a cosmopolitan when he was merely an unfortunate human being with a broad outlook. He translated some of the works of Kleist and Ibsen (*q.v.*) into Hungarian. His best story is *Apai Örökség* (1884; Parental Heritage). Of his lyrical volumes *Ifjuságom* (1874; My Youth) should be mentioned and also *Magány* (1889; Solitude). His collected poems, in two volumes, appeared in 1895. He somewhat influenced Dezső Kosztolányi (*q.v.*) among the 20th-century Hungarian poets. A literary society in the city of Léva was named after Reviczky.

Reviczky responded to the pessimistic philosophy of Schopenhauer and to the Christian view that this world is but a vale of tears. His nostalgic poems indicated the transitional significance of short-lived illusions. The elegiac tone shows what terrible difficulties Reviczky had when he was facing the grimness of life, and yet with what tender consciousness, sometimes with what pathetic courage he tried to discharge his obligations. Irrespective of whether he wrote about Pan or some other symbol of antiquity, about contemporary themes or about themes purely personal, his feeling of loneliness was the paramount leitmotif. Because of the sentimentality and a certain platitudinous character of his poems, many of them are apt to sound only superficially reflective; and while Reviczky no doubt had an artistic control over the medium of expression, this is not sufficient to make one forget the trite features of his work. As a critic of aesthetic problems (his essays were never published in a volume) he sometimes leaned upon ideas taken from other writers, but even so these essays were essentially expressions of his own taste and views. He could write forcefully when the occasion required; his "cosmopolitanism" formulated some of his theories, but they were also based upon the anti-oratorical, anti-bombastic taste of the poet.

See: P. Koroda, *Reviczky Gyula összegyüjtött müvei* (1895); W. Kirkconnell, *The Magyar Muse; an Anthology* (1933).

J. R.

Reymont or Rejment, Władysław Stanisław (1867–1925, Polish short-story writer and novelist), was born in Kobiele Wielkie, Radom district, Russian Poland, of humble parents. He was one of a family of 10 children, most of them considerably older than he. His childhood, bleak and barren of normal youthful companionship, was spent on an impoverished farm on the outskirts of a depressing village and under the domination of a stern father, who kept his son a virtual prisoner at home, and an excessively pious mother. As a boy his only solace was books, smuggled to him by an older brother who had already left home. The work which fascinated Reymont most in the orgies of reading in which he indulged was Słowacki's fanciful drama of Polish pre-history, *Lilla Weneda,* and especially the scene in which the blind peasant-seer Derwid, prototype of certain characters of his own in *Chłopi,* phrases the national faith in the lines "But even in such nations as our own defeated one, Remains a certain strength . . ." Reymont was looked upon by his parents as the black sheep of the family, and from the record of his successive failures in meeting the tests of life one cannot blame them for holding this view. Not only did he fail in his entrance examinations for the school in Łódź to which he was supposed to be sent, but later he proved unable to remain for long in any school or to keep any position whatever. Finally, a penniless vagabond, he joined a traveling theatrical company and wandered with this for more than a year over the length and breadth of Poland. At the end of this time Reymont's father secured for his son a post in a station on the Warsaw-Vienna railroad. Here Reymont steeped himself in Sienkiewicz (*q.v.*), especially the trilogy of historical novels, and through this, though he did not know it at the time, found not only his proper vocation in life but a master and guide.

Reymont had longed from childhood to break with his family and to fare forth alone into "the great, wide world." Finally, in the autumn of 1893, with a ruble and three kopecks in his pocket, he actually set out. The first two years of freedom were spent in Warsaw in the most bitter poverty. Gradually, however, Reymont began to get a foothold as a writer, through short stories which were published in such journals as the Cracow *Myśl* (Thought) and the Warsaw *Prawda* (Truth) of Świętochowski (*q.v.*). His first significant work, the first also to foreshadow its author's future mastery of the art of mass description, was *Pielgrzymka do Jasnej Góry* (1895; A Pilgrimage to Jasna Góra), a brilliant report of scenes Reymont had witnessed at Częstochowa, the great Polish shrine at which he had thought for a while of becoming a lay brother. In *Komedjantka* (1896; Eng. tr., *The Comédienne,* 1920), a story of a wandering theatrical troupe, Reymont again demonstrated his almost uncanny gift for mass portraiture.

Reymont arrived on the literary scene at a moment of crisis in Polish letters: the positivists (*see* Polish literature) were still in control, but their slogans had already begun to sound somewhat spurious, for industry, in which they had placed their whole faith, was failing, just as poetry and dreams had previously done, to emancipate the Polish people from the dual yoke of poverty and foreign rule. It is not surprising, therefore, that Reymont should have turned, like Sienkiewicz, away from industry or that he should have portrayed the factory, in *Ziemia obiecana* (1899; Eng. tr., *The Promised Land,* 1927), a story of Łódź, as the great debaser and enslaver of mankind. Reymont deplored urbanization, and it was in instinctive revolt against urbanization's rapid advance in Poland that he turned to peasant life for his themes, to produce as his masterpiece the immortal *Chłopi* (1902–1909; Eng. tr., *The Peasants,* 1924–1925). Besides being a vast naturalistic prose drama of village life, *The Peasants* is a veritable encyclopedia of peasant customs and prejudices. Its tone, as might be expected, is generally grim and fatalistic, yet individual scenes are memorable because of their sudden, typically Slavonic bursts of color, movement, and emotional ecstasy.

Following the completion of *The Peasants,* Reymont digressed from the track he had hitherto pursued, to join the ranks of the psychological novelists who were then having a great vogue in Poland. His *Marzyciel* (1910; The Dreamer) and *Wampir* (1911; The Vampire) from this period, both tales growing out of an experience with spiritualism in which Reymont had previously been involved, are decidedly inferior. They prove beyond a doubt that Reymont was great only when he remained faithful to his own genius, which was that of a reporter, not of a psychoanalyst. In *Rok 1794* (1914–1919; The Year 1794), a long novel of the stirring days of the Kościuszko insurrection, he returned to his proper field, the depiction of mass drama.

In 1920 Reymont visited the United States for the purpose of raising money for Poland among the Polish populations of such cities as New York and Chicago. In 1924 he was awarded the Nobel prize in literature. He was living at this time in Poland, devoting his time to writing and to the encouragement of projects leading to the improvement of peasant life. In August, 1925, he took part in the crowning experience of his lifetime, a great folk congress held partly in his honor. Four months later, on the fifth of December, he died at his home in Warsaw.

See: J. Krzyżanowski, *Władysław St. Reymont; twórca i dzieło* (1937); W. Borowy, "Reymont," *Slavonic Review,* XVI (1937–1938), 439–448.

M. M. C.

Ribeiro, Aquilino (1885–, Portuguese novelist), has won fame as the most accomplished fiction writer in modern Portugal, both through the vigor of his style and the diversity of his subjects. He is his most original when true to the life of his native province of Beira. He was born of peasant stock, in a mountain hamlet of the "rough and ascetic" backlands. When a student he was jailed for conspiring against the monarchy, but was able to escape and to continue his studies in Lausanne and at the Sorbonne in Paris. It was perhaps in Paris that he acquired the gentle but irreverent irony recalling Anatole France (*q.v.*) which pervades his stories and cools the ardor of their glorification of life and love. Nevertheless he did not lose the sense of human solidarity that made him join the Seara Nova (New Crop) and devote the best of his talent to recounting the humble lives of Portuguese peasants and fishermen. After 1910 he returned to teach grammar school and administer the ecclesiastic libraries seized by the republic. In 1917 he lectured at the University of Lisbon for a while, later joining the staff of the Lisbon Public Library. Keeping faith with his republican and anticlerical convictions, he has actively opposed the Salazar regime since 1926. Returned from another exile in France (1927–1934), he now lives in Portugal.

His style already attained maturity in his first book, *Jardim das tormentas* (1913; Garden of Storms), 11 tales about human frailty, written from 1910 to 1912 in Paris. Four of the tales introduced the Beira peasants, their worldly priests, haughty fidalgos, and corruptible magistrates. Other regional works followed, written in a rich vernacular and narrating stories of rural passions, relieved now and then by pantheistic landscapes and the pageantry of folklore, such as *Terras do demo* (1917; Lands of the Demon), *Andam faunos pelos bosques* (1926; Fauns Roam the Woods), and the diffuse *Volfrâmio* (1943; Tungsten), his latest, showing how the coveted metal has furnished the Demon with a new means of corruption. Not confined to regionalism, Ribeiro knows also how to analyze modern city life, as in his successful book *O homem que matou o diabo* (1930; The Man Who Killed the Devil). With the same ease he writes animal stories for children, such as *Romance da raposa* (2 vols., 1924; Novel of the Fox), or transplants the theme of *Thaïs* into a Portuguese setting in *S. Banaboião anacoreta e mártir* (1937; Saint Banaboião, Anchoret and Martyr). With a European conscience, he registers French reactions in 1914 and German prostration in 1920. He writes biography and history; he revives glories of past and modern national literature, such as the figures of Francisco Xavier de Oliveira and Brito Camacho.

His lifework is not yet done, but already he has amply fulfilled the hopes of Carlos Malheiro Dias, who in 1913 expected the author of *Jardim das tormentas* to give Portugal "a regional novel swarming with all the rustic figures of Beira."

See: Wilhelm Giese, "Aquilino Ribeiro," *Archiv für das Studium der neueren Sprachen und Literaturen,* CLIV (1928), 259–266; Castelo Branco Chaves, *Aquilino Ribeiro* (1937?).

G. M. M.

Richepin, Jean (1849–1930, French poet, novelist, and dramatist), the son of an army doctor, was born in Médéa, Algeria. His early years were spent in the atmosphere of an army garrison; then followed an education in Parisian *lycées,* a course in medicine at Douai, and, in 1868, the Ecole Normale Supérieure, which he left in 1870 to fight in the Franco-Prussian War. A period of bohemianism ensued, during which Richepin made his headquarters in Montmartre and supported himself by desultory journalism, yielding at intervals to a passion for wandering which took him over much of Europe and during which he worked at a variety of trades, from farm hand to juggler. In these years a group formed around Richepin, including such men as Ponchon, Bouchor, Nouveau (*q.v.*), and even for a while Rimbaud (*q.v.*), calling themselves *les vivants,* scorning conventions, both social and literary, interested in popular poetry and folk song, and believing that the proper material for the artist was the life of the common people and that the artist's achievement could best be estimated by the extent to which he appealed to the uneducated masses.

This revolt against convention and interest in the lower classes are evident in all Richepin's early work, which began typically with *Les Etapes d'un réfractaire* (1872), a study of Jules Vallès (*q.v.*), and are particularly marked in *La Chanson des gueux* (1876), his most famous book. In these poems Richepin continues the portrayal of the vagabond, the *gueux,* which is at least as old as Villon, writing of the lives of these wanderers both in Paris and in the provinces, with an unabashed realism and a use of argot which shocked his contemporaries. He was imprisoned and fined for *outrage aux mœurs,* but the book's reputation, and his, was made. There can be no doubt that Richepin did a great deal to capitalize on this notoriety; his striking physique, handsome face, and grand manner, plus his attitude of romantic defiance, completely satisfied the public's notion of all that a poet should be. Richepin, a born actor, adapted himself to what was expected of him, allowing romantic speculations to spring up as to his ancestry (actually he was descended from perfectly respectable countryfolk of the Ardennes) and encouraging the legend of his vagrant nature, familiarity with the seamy side of life, and excessive virility. *Les Caresses* (1877), poems written in frank praise of physical love, as well as *Les Morts bizarres* (1876), a collection of short stories in the style of Hoffman and Poe, increased his notoriety. In the following years there was no lack of work from his pen —indeed, all his life he was constantly turning out journalistic work of some sort in addition to his more formal productions—notably *La Glu* (1881), a study of a female Don Juan; *Miarka* (1883), the story, rich in local color, of a gypsy girl growing up among townspeople in Richepin's beloved district of Thierache; *Les Blasphèmes* (1884), a group of strident poems proclaiming Richepin's materialism and atheism; and *La Mer* (1886), poetry milder in tone, finding its inspiration in the sea and in the dangerous, humble lives of its followers. At the same time a series of plays were winning him an even wider popularity, especially *Le Flibustier* (1888) and *Le Chemineau* (1897).

Richepin's personal life grew more stable as the years passed (he was received into the French Academy in 1908), and his work, though still in the main concerned with the grotesque and the abnormal, lost much of its truculent style. He continued to be prolific in prose, poetry, and the drama, but none of the work he did after the turn of the century can be considered as having added to his stature, unless it be the charming dramatization—so unexpected from Richepin—of Perrault's *La Belle au bois dormant* (1907). He took with grace and humor the honors with which his later days were decked.

In his own day Richepin's personal charm inevitably influenced his critics; looking back on his work at present and divorcing it from the man, one can judge more soberly. Historically there is no doubt that it is of considerable interest. Richepin's depiction of the lower classes inspired many imitators; *Le Chemineau* can share with Rostand's *Cyrano* the credit for a temporary revival of the romantic drama in verse; and much of Richepin's prose and poetry can be said to have encouraged the development of naturalism (*see* French naturalism). From a purely aesthetic point of view Richepin's work does not fare so well. A few of the novels, *Braves Gens* (1886) and *Le Cadet* (1890) in particular, can hold their own, and there is, no doubt, a considerable body of good poetry scattered through Richepin's plays and volumes of verse. But most of his work seems not only dated but essentially superficial. He exploited his flamboyant personality to the utmost in his work. Fond of simple, direct, sensual pleasures, rough uncomplicated characters, a wandering, rootless life, he was able to present in a forceful way the surface of things but not their depths. His skillful rhetoric is too often hollow; the devices of technique which he perfected as he grew older, his ability to write a sonorous alexandrine or a theatrically effective scene, fail to hide the essential intellectual poverty of his work.

See: Jules Lemaître, *Les Contemporains*, Sér. 3 (1894); Vance Thompson, *French Portraits* (1900); Henri d'Alméras, *Avant la gloire* (1902); F. W. Chandler, *The Contemporary Drama of France* (1920); Alphonse Séché, *Dans la mêlée littéraire* (1935).

C. W., Jr.

Ridder, Alfons de (pseud. Willem Elsschot, 1882–, Flemish novelist), was born in Antwerp. After completing his studies at the Commercial College of his birthplace, he was active for many years at Schiedam (South Holland) and then established an advertising business in his native city.

His first novel, *Villa des Roses* (1913), immediately achieved great success, but more in the Netherlands than in Belgium. Ridder had from the start the pent-up, bitter tone of an excessive emotionality. His second novel, *De Verlossing* (Deliverance), also appeared before the First World War, though it did not receive its first important publication until 1921; and during the occupation of Belgium by the Germans he issued, through an unknown, small publisher at Antwerp, *Lijmen* (republished 1924; Roping-in People)—which passed unnoticed because of the circumstances. Ridder, greatly discouraged thereby, did not set pen on paper for more than 15 years. Only in 1933 appeared *Kaas* (Cheese), and since then he has again been composing regularly: *Tsjip* (1934; Cheep); *Pensioen* (1935; Pension); *Het Been* (1938; The Leg), a sequel to *Lijmen; De Leeuwentemmer* (1940; The Lion Tamer), a sequel to *Tsjip*. A reprint of *Tsjip* and *De Leeuwentemmer* together in one volume was issued in 1943 by Querido in New York.

J. G.

Rilke, Rainer Maria (1875–1926, German poet), was born in Prague, of old Bohemian and Alsatian stock. After a few unhappy early years (1886–1891) at the military academies of St. Pölten and Weisskirchen, a year at school in Linz and four in Prague, he moved to Munich. Untouched by the current naturalistic and impressionistic tendencies, he completed in 1894 a collection of indifferent love poems in the conventional style of the Heine tradition (*Leben und Lieder*). Even in his second and more distinctive volume of poetry, *Larenopfer* (1896), he revealed little beyond a sentimental attachment to his native city, Prague, and a lively though undisciplined sensitiveness to aesthetic impressions. He had not yet brought himself to the intensity of devotion or, above all, to the sharpness of specific observation that became the conspicuous quality of his later poetry. In *Traumgekrönt* (1897), *Advent* (1898), and *Mir zur Feier* (1899) Rilke moved towards a depersonalized idiom in an attempt to convey, in contemplation and suspense, the emotional oneness that henceforth characterizes his poetic landscape of things and creatures. The first part of *Das Stundenbuch* (*Das Buch vom mönchischen Leben,* written in 1899 and published in 1905 together with *Von der Pilgerschaft,* 1901, and *Von der Armuth und vom Tode,* 1903; Eng. tr., *Poems from the Book of Hours,* 1941) intensifies the impression of a fervent though loosely religious imagination.

From 1899 on, he wandered restlessly from one country to another; he traveled in Russia, learned Russian, and, on two occasions, in 1899 and 1900, visited Tolstoy (*q.v.*). Overwhelmed by the immensity of the Eastern landscape, he crystallized his discovery of the immeasurable presence of God in his delightful *Geschichten vom lieben Gott* (1900; Eng. tr., *Stories of God,* 1931). He seemed at home in all parts of Europe; whether in Paris or Munich, Scandinavia, Spain, Italy, or Switzerland, everywhere he developed and realized his characteristic sense of space and physical reality. For two years he lived in the painters' colony at Worpswede (*Worpswede,* 1903), where, determined to rid his poetry of all narrative or merely lyrical elements, he wrote most of the poems that were published under the characteristic title *Das Buch der Bilder* (1902, in two parts; 2d ed., enlarged, 1906). Superbly skillful though most of this work has seemed to some, to Rilke it still lacked that firmness of distinct bodies in space in which he felt most palpably the presence of a moving God.

His association in Paris with the great French sculptor Rodin represents perhaps the most significant turn in his poetic career. He had always found himself in sympathy with much of French culture, and he had translated Maurice de Guérin, Gide (*q.v.*), and Valéry (*q.v.*); but Rodin (like the equally influential Cézanne) became to him a symbol not so much of the French character in general as rather of a hardworking craftsman grappling with the completely significant world of tangible objects. The artist's work, Rodin insisted, is the only satisfactory mode of religious activity. Much of Rilke's happy recognition of this attitude entered into his account of the master (*Auguste Rodin,* 1903; Eng. tr., 1919). But the two volumes of *Neue Gedichte* (1907–1908), the second dedicated to Rodin, "*mon grand ami,*" show the turn in Rilke's conception of the artist even more clearly; they contain his first distinctly mature poetry. In these poems he not only develops a peculiarly objective and sculpturesque form, which has, somewhat misleadingly, become known as *Dinggedicht,* but he advances from his earlier private and impressionistic aestheticism to an integration and transformation of his intense vision into more impersonal symbols. At the same time the poems in *Neue Gedichte* represent, together with the delicate and melancholy prose of his only major narrative work, *Die Aufzeichnungen des Malte Laurids Brigge* (1910; Eng. tr., *Journal of My Other Self,* 1930), the last work in which his impressions, however sublimated and embodied, supplied the material for and the aim of his poetry.

Now his life and his poetry began to change. In spite of his rapidly increasing fame and the astonishing popularity of his earlier, sentimentally melodramatic *Die Weise von Liebe und Tod des Cornets Christoph Rilke* (1906; Eng. tr., *The Tale of the Love and Death of Cornet Christopher Rilke,* 1932) and in spite of a singularly extensive correspondence with a large circle of friends (*Briefe,* 1929 ff.; various parts of Rilke's correspondence have been issued in English translation), there followed years of profound despair, frustration, and helplessness. In August, 1914, for once inspired by a feeling of solidarity with his countrymen, he passed through a brief period of exaltation and wrote, in the ecstatic style of Hölderlin's last poems, *Fünf Gesänge.* But this elation did not last. As early as the winter of 1911–1912 he had begun at the castle of Duino in Istria a series of elegies which he seemed unable to complete until, in an extraordinary burst of inspiration, he finished the last of the 10 poems in 1922, at Castle Muzot in the Swiss Valais. *Duineser Elegien* (1923; Eng. tr., *Duinese Elegies,* 1930) Rilke regarded as his supreme achievement; the elegies are, at the same time, the most impressive sequence of great poetry in modern European literature. Their theme is man's, and particularly the poet's, struggle for clarity and coherence; with two exceptions, they are written in a rhythmically dithyrambic vers libre, and even though they are naturally charged with elements of philosophical reflection, their appeal is, in the main, to the creative and nervous sensibility such as sustained the poet himself. The poems offer the evidence of an overwhelming religious crisis, but, with their recurrent emphasis upon the succession of struggle, death, and regeneration, they represent only one aspect of Rilke's vision. The other, his sense of joy, affirmation, and praise, is the keynote of *Die Sonette an Orpheus* (1923; Eng. tr., *Sonnets to Orpheus,* 1936), a series of 55 brilliant and exuberantly positive "songs," written in a state of astonishing inspiration while he finished the last of the *Elegien*. A few further poems, *Späte Gedichte* (1934; Eng. tr., *Later Poems,* 1938), which reiterate the allegorical manner of the later elegies, were published after his death; but with his two incomparable statements of the cosmic experience, progress, and achievement of the poet, Rilke ended a creative career which is as unique in recent times as it is difficult to appreciate.

To contrast him, as is often done, with his great German contemporary, Stefan George (*q.v.*), is merely to stress the peculiarly personal nature of his imagination. Unlike the rigidly stylized and monumental George, Rilke is ultimately a sensitive and, at his best, supremely realistic poet who succeeded in finding the symbols of a modern religious eloquence. It is perhaps not altogether just to dismiss most of his work prior to the *Neue Gedichte* as unoriginal and dangerously subjective. But it is true that many of even the more popular poems in *Das Stundenbuch* and in *Das Buch der Bilder* lack the authoritative gesture. Rilke was, after all, an artist whose perception and intensity of application were throughout most of his life greater than his powers of resolute mastery. In his earlier poems it is difficult to escape a feeling of glibness and unmerited ease of mystical intuition. The characteristic poetic figure of the "Angel," in which he frequently focuses and through which he realizes the strength of his overpowering inspiration, occurs in his early work as well. It is not until after the years of complete despondency, however, that the symbol of the Angel emerges in the *Elegien,* in severe and peremptory images, as the absolute of vision and completeness. Within the allegorical world of a modern paradise in which, innocently close to the animals, Rilke seeks his way, there is no immediate contact with God, but the Angel appears to the poet as does God to the medieval saint. To approach this source of terrible strength is a task almost too great for man: in children, lovers, and heroes Rilke felt it present, and of them the elegies say much. But the cardinal theme of the *Elegien,* especially of the superb fifth elegy, is the precariousness of human life. And if, as the work draws to a close, the sense of inadequacy gives way to one of trust and affirmation, it is because the poet transmutes what is merely seen or "blindly" lived into the exaltation of a vision (in the seventh elegy) and the acceptance (in the tenth elegy) of death as the final transformer. The experience of grief for the dead was probably for Rilke the most moving human experience (see the series of Requiem poems, 1909; Eng. tr., *Requiem and Other Poems,* 1935). In the *Elegien,* therefore, death resolves the discrepancies of man's life. But in the subsequent *Sonette an Orpheus* Rilke presents the complement to this vision. Here the poet's song serves to transform even the mutability of life into the permanence of absolute creation.

See: F. Olivero, *Rainer Maria Rilke; a Study in Poetry and Mysticism* (1931); F. Dehn, *Rainer Maria Rilke und sein Werk* (1934); F. A. Hünich, *Rilke-Bibliographie* (1935); J. F. Angelloz, *Rainer Maria Rilke; l'évolution spirituelle du poète* (1936); E. C. Mason, *Rilke's Apotheosis* (1938); E. M. Butler, *Rainer Maria Rilke* (1941).

V. L.

Rimbaud, Jean Nicholas Arthur (1854–1891, French poet), was born in Charleville in the northeast of France, the son of self-assertive, mettlesome parents. When 15 he had already written a number of skillful imitations of the romanticists (*Vers de collège,* 1932). The arrival of Izambard (January, 1870), a young anti-imperialist teacher, interested in modern writers, was the most striking event in the school life of Rimbaud. He encouraged the omnivorous reading of living poets and radical writers by his pupil, who became fiercely anticlerical and revolutionary. Thirsting for fame, on May 24, 1870, Rimbaud wrote to Banville (*q.v.*) a letter in which he called himself a "Parnassian," worshiping two goddesses, "the Muse and Liberty." On August 28 he boarded the Paris train without a ticket; for this offense he spent 10 days in jail. To his next flight, through Belgium, are due the series of poems including "Ma Bohême," "La Maline," and "Le Cabaret vert." On February 25, 1871, he again started, this time on foot, for Paris, where he spent about a month in abject poverty; on his return he resolved never to reenter his school. From April 4 to May 5 is the time of a problematic escape to the Paris of the Commune, affirmed by Delahaye, Godschot, *et al.,* denied by Izambard and his followers. He wrote then a plan, now lost, for a communist constitution, his first prose poems "Les Déserts de l'amour," and the two famous *lettres du voyant* (*Lettres de la vie littéraire d'Arthur Rimbaud,* edited by J. M. Carré, 1931) in which he declared his determination "to become a seer." Charles Bretagne, who encouraged his reading of books on occultism and magic, was the promoter of Rimbaud's dramatic "liaison" with Verlaine. The latter called Rimbaud to Paris, where the proud, cynical youth arrived early in September bringing his *Le Bateau ivre.* He found nothing but "emptiness and chaos" among Parisian writers, whom he met with sarcasm or silence, once even with violence, which drew fear and hatred upon him. He was then engaged in writing his first *Illuminations* (not published until 1887).

On July 8, 1871, Rimbaud and Verlaine went to London, where they frequented exiled French communists and led a "stormy, painful life." One can no longer entertain any doubt concerning the abnormal nature of their association. Meanwhile Mme Rimbaud vainly tried to retrieve her son's manuscripts of the "Chasse spirituelle" and "Les Veilleurs," his masterpieces according to Verlaine (*q.v.*), which the latter had left with his wife's parents and which seem to be hopelessly lost. Early in 1873, at Roche, during one of his flights from Verlaine, Rimbaud wrote new *Illuminations* and "atrocious stories [meant for] a pagan or negro book," *i.e., Une Saison en Enfer* (1873). Having again joined Verlaine on July 8, 1873, this time in Brussels, two days later he was shot in the wrist by his friend, who was sentenced to two years' imprisonment. Rimbaud completed *Une Saison en Enfer* at Roche. The whole edition of this work, except a few copies, remained forgotten in the publisher's cellar, where it was found by chance in 1901.

In November, 1873, Rimbaud bade farewell forever to poetry. Between 1873 and 1880 he oscillated between Charleville and many parts of Europe, earning his living in the most various temporary occupations. The remainder of his life Rimbaud passed in Aden and other Red Sea ports, now as the employee of a French exporting house, now as the explorer of the Ogaden and River Web countries, or again as an independent trader leading expeditions to Abyssinia. That he dealt in contraband firearms is certain. The question of his traffic in slaves is disputed (Enid Starkie, *Rimbaud en Abyssinie,* 1938; *Poésie,* November, 1941). In April, 1891, yielding to the increased agony of a fatal disease, Rimbaud began his return journey from Harar to France where, in Marseille, his leg was amputated. He died on November 10, when a number of his poems were about to be published as the *Reliquaire* edited by Darzens. His letters (*Lettres de Jean-Arthur Rimbaud, Egypte, Arabie, Ethiopie,* 1899; there are some factual errors in this edition), relating the progress of his illness, are worthy of the author of *Une Saison en Enfer.* The poems Rimbaud wrote before he was 17 are the offspring of anger and the crying out caused by "the deep and eternal wound" inflicted by life on the delicacy and audacity of youth. At the same time a strong realistic vein appears in condensed, sharply drawn scenes and still lifes. He himself is there with his mistrusts, "profound pities," awakening sensuality, and arrogance. However, these poems are primarily technical studies in which Rimbaud becomes a master of poetic expression. The superiority attained over earlier works by the "Chercheuses de poux" and "Voyelles," with their rich and airy orchestration, and that of *Le Bateau ivre* (1884) are due to the adventure or revolution related in his *lettres du voyant.* Rimbaud is now resolved to be no mere technician, but a seer, and to invent a mode of expression adequate to his visions and science of prosody. *Le Bateau ivre,* with its 100 stanzas of four alternately rhyming alexandrines, sings Rimbaud's soaring into the visionary world. The rush of images expressing flight and release which at the same time impose their physical ponderance hypnotize the reader.

When Rimbaud was writing his first 20 *Illuminations* (May–September, 1871), he was, so he tells us, acquainting himself with "simple hallucination" and noting down "des vertiges, des silences, des nuits," a fact which the *Illuminations* prove conclusively. The verse of these pellucid and poignant poems becomes increasingly freer so that, at last, "Marine" and "Mouvement" realize Banville's wish for free verse. The inventor of the 38 other *Illuminations,* from "Après le déluge" to "Solde," commonly called "prose Illuminations" (dates uncertain), appears both as a "fabulous opera" and a magician contriving festivities and disasters. All flares up in this meteor-like rush compounded of leave-takings, for Rimbaud felt himself "dedicated to a new disorder." Some of these later *Illuminations* are in free verse disposed like prose; in others prose and verse intermingle; others are pure prose poems. The "diamond prose" of this fearful virtuoso seems in turn impalpable, quintessential, or almost brutally material. But this language which Rimbaud called *non-fixé* belongs, first and foremost, to the realm of rhythm.

In *Une Saison en Enfer,* one of the barest and most dramatic human documents, Rimbaud disavows all his former leads. He is now concerned not with vision, but with the stark reality of life and death and primarily with that of his own hell: "I believe myself in hell, hence I am there." Let his race and country with their weakening vices, his "disgusting education" and Christianism, burn up. For when he proclaims "Through the spirit one reaches God," reaffirming a spiritual quest, he does not mean what, to him, has become but an outworn legend. Even under the symbolism of his liaison with Verlaine in "Délires I" or through the analysis of his artist's endeavors in "Délires II," he is solely concerned with the grasping of an immediate and essential reality. Rimbaud, having staked his all on art, has lost, and so let it be. Yet he remains free, scornfully hurling behind him whatever entrapped him. *Une Saison en Enfer* has the "abruptness of thought and style" Chateaubriand saw in Pascal and Bossuet. Its elliptical foreshortenings and compressions contribute extraordinary impact. Here again rhythm commands the diverse elements of style. A comparison of *Ebauches* (ed. by M. Yerta-Méléra, 1937) with the final text makes one realize how aware and deliberate an artist this visionary was and how perfectly articulated and organized his work.

See: P. Berrichon, *La Vie de Jean-Arthur Rimbaud* (1897); P. Claudel, preface to Rimbaud, *Œuvres* (*Mercure de France* ed., 1912); I. Rimbaud, *Reliques* (1922); M. Coulon, *Le Problème de Rimbaud* (1923); E. Delahaye, *Souvenirs familiers* (1925); Rimbaud, *Edition critique,* Vol. I (1939).

M. M.

Rivière, Jacques (1886–1925, French critic and editor), a native of Bordeaux, went to Paris at 17. In spite of an excellent record at the Lycée Lakanal, he was not admitted to the Ecole Normale Supérieure, where he would have prepared for a career of scholarship and teaching. More interested, indeed, in contemporary art, music, and literature than in his studies, he reveals his real preoccupations in letters to his friend and classmate, Alain-Fournier (*q.v.*). When Rivière married Alain-Fournier's sister Isabelle in 1909, he definitely gave up an academic career in philosophy to work with André Gide (*q.v.*) on the newly founded *Nouvelle Revue française.* Rivière first wrote notes on music and the dance, but having already had critical studies published in other magazines, he was soon encouraged to write more lengthy articles. The First World War broke in upon his career. He was taken prisoner in August, 1914, and spent four years in Germany and Switzerland. During his captivity his mind remained active: he observed his captors and his fellow prisoners, kept a journal, *Carnet de guerre* (1929), and made a record of his religious thought in *A la trace de Dieu* (1925). In 1919 he became editor of the *Nouvelle Revue française,* continuing its policy of publishing only the best of contemporary literature, and he preserved from oblivion the works of writers who had been killed in the war. In the midst of literary activity, in February, 1925, Rivière died suddenly of typhoid fever.

Although Rivière wrote two psychological novels, *Aimée* (1922) and *Florence* (unfinished; published posthumously in 1935), most of his work is critical. His first important study, "Paul Claudel, poète chrétien" (1907), which was one of the earliest attempts to explain Claudel's poetry, was first printed in the *Occident.* It was inspired by enthusiasm for the poet and was rewritten after exchanging a number of letters (see Rivière, *Correspondance, 1907–1914,* 1926) with the young diplomat, who, at Rivière's request, was, attempting to show him the Catholic way out of doubt. The revision was included in *Etudes* (1911) with other early studies. Among further critical studies of individual writers are "Alain-Fournier" (1922) and "Rimbaud" (1914) printed first in the *Nouvelle Revue française* and later republished. A series of lectures explaining Marcel Proust was published posthumously as *Quelques Progrès dans l'étude du cœur humain* (1926). Among Rivière's best articles on general literary and philosophical problems are "De la sincérité envers soi-même" (1912) and the "Roman d'aventure" (1913), both published in the *Nouvelle Revue française,* and *Moralisme et littérature,* a lecture published only in 1932. His continued preoccupation with religion is shown in all his correspondence and in "De la foi" (*Nouvelle Revue française,* 1912) and *A la trace de Dieu,* while his interest in political discussions is evident in *L'Allemand* (1918), *Russie* (1927), and *Pour et contre une société des nations* (1930).

Rivière's method of criticism is based upon comprehension of the author's innermost impulsion and upon careful analysis and presentation of the work. He endeavors to reach the center of the philosophical or psychological problem, but never neglects the sensual delight to be found in the resulting work of art. He is usually guided in his choice of subject by deep enthusiasm, ardent curiosity, and keen sympathy. Perhaps the most interesting aspect of his writing is his own subtle and analytical mind. To him his thought had almost a sensual reality. It was also mobile and alive because he wished it to express accurately his nature, varying constantly under accumulated experiences.

See: "Hommage à Jacques Rivière, 1886–1925," *Nouvelle Revue française,* XXIV (1925), 387–829 (issue devoted to this author); Martin Turnell, "The Criticism of Jacques Rivière," *Modern Language Review,* XXXV (1940), 470–482.

B. P.

Rode, Helge (1870–1937, Danish poet, dramatist, and critic), was born in Copenhagen. His mother was the daughter of Orla Lehmann, national liberal leader; his father took active part in the Grundtvigian folk-school movement, but died early. Some of the most impressionable years of the poet's childhood—from the age of 9 to 16—were spent in Norway. Rode's permanent home, however, became Copenhagen, where in the garden suburb of Frederiksberg his tall ascetic figure was a familiar sight.

Rode is perhaps the most versatile writer and the most original thinker of the Danish neo-romantic, symbolistic movement of the 90's, which arose as a reaction against the overrationalization of Georg Brandes (*q.v.*). Rode's first collection of poems, *Hvide Blomster* (1892; White Flowers), reveals the stages of the spiritual awakening, the "breakthrough of the soul," to use the poet's own expression—the feeling of cold desolation over lack of faith, the agonized quest for truth behind the veils of nature, and finally, probably after a sudden mystic vision, the rapturous feeling of the individual "I" as part of the "Great I." In the next important collection of poems, *Ariel* (1914), perhaps the central work in Rode's life, the poet becomes an exulting ethereal being, a messenger, sent to teach man to throw off his bonds and to soar. The enigma of death, however, as seen, for example, in the utter loneliness of the drifting body of the drowned man, exerts gripping fascination. In *Den stille Have* (1922; The Quiet Garden, *i.e.,* the cemetery), which opens with a simple beautiful tribute to the poet's mother, the old Norse belief in the living dead seems merged with Christian resurrection and Hindu mysticism. Death is merely an illusion. Surprising, delightful touches of humor appear in the tribute to the poet's father.

In Rode's dramas ideas are as important as characters. *Kongesønner* (1896; Sons of the King) presents symbolically and in Greek setting the two extremes: boundless exaltation in life versus negation of life; life, but in chastened form, conquers. Pantheism runs through the primitive, prehistoric *Solsagn* (1904; The Legend of the Sun). Ibsen's (*q.v.*) influence is felt in the modern, powerful *Morbus Tellermann* (1907; The Tellermann Plague) and in *Flugten* (1909; The Flight). Envy, hypocrisy, and ambition constitute the driving forces in these two plays, dealing with the scientific medical and the engineering worlds, and in *Det store Forlis* (1917; The Great Shipwreck), where the Titanic disaster and, in a larger sense, the First World War are indicated. Several dramas treat historical figures, one Tolstoy (*q.v.*), one Georg Brandes. The plays of the middle years of Rode's life—even some of his comedies, *e.g., Døden paa Natcafé* (1905; Death in the Night Restaurant)—are bitter, but they are not without hope. Generally there stands out against the mass of climbers a solitary, upright, fearless figure, capable of taking up the gauntlet, a representative of Ibsen's—and Rode's—future "third realm." Rode's women also as a rule are ethical forces. Characteristic again are the kind-hearted ne'er-do-wells, by-passed by Fortune.

Rode's numerous essays, which appeared in the post-war period, constitute mainly dialectical polemic discussions of the burning question of the day, science versus religion. In *Krig og Aand* (1917; War and Intellect) the poet places the blame for the war squarely—not upon man's stupidity, as Brandes does—but upon the tenets of Darwinism, upon naturalism, and the development of the superman morality. Salvation is to be found only in a return to religion, a deep, dogma-free religion, and in the establishment of a union of states.

See: H. C. Topsöe-Jensen, *Scandinavian Literature from Brandes to Our Day* (1929); Helge Kjaergaard, *Die dänische Literatur der neuesten Zeit (1871–1933)* (1934).

C. K. B.

Rodenbach, Georges (1855–1898, Belgian poet), was born in Tournai. Several months after his birth he was taken to Bruges, which he was later to immortalize in what is probably his best-known book, *Bruges-la-morte* (1892). He studied in Ghent, where, at the Collège Sainte-Barbe, he made the acquaintance of Emile Verhaeren (*q.v.*). Having obtained his degree in law, Rodenbach visited Paris (1878–1879). He returned to Belgium and opened a law office, but in 1887 went to live in Paris, where he died.

His first works, published in Belgium, were collections of poems about Flemish life: *Le Foyer et les champs* (1877), *Ode à la Belgique* (1880), *La Mer élégante* (1881), *L'Hiver mon-*

dain (1884). The book which won him general recognition in France was *La Jeunesse blanche* (1886). It was in Paris that he composed his best work, always inspired, however, by his native land. His books include collections of poems: *Le Règne du silence* (1891), *Le Voyage dans les yeux* (1893), *Les Vies encloses* (1896), *Le Miroir du ciel natal* (1898); novels: *La Vocation* (1895), *Le Carillonneur* (1897), *En exil* (1920); plays: *Le Voile* (1894) and *Le Mirage* (1901). All are pervaded by an atmosphere of quiet and introspection. In *Les Vies encloses* he furnishes what is perhaps the key to a state of mind of his generation, shut out from the world, entirely dedicated to "son spectacle intérieur."

See: T. Derème, "La Poésie de Georges Rodenbach," *Revue de Paris*, Année XXXI (1924), Tome I, pp. 674–685; Pierre Maes, *Rodenbach* (1926).

P. B.

Rodríguez Marín, Francisco (1855–1943, Spanish scholar, folklorist, and poet), throughout his long life wrote some 150 volumes, dealing with the three fields he cultivated simultaneously and without interruption. He was also director of the National Library of Madrid and later of the Royal Spanish Academy. His first work, published in Seville, where he was born, was a volume of poetry. This was followed by others from time to time, and a volume of selections was published in 1941 under the title *A la real de España (1871–1941)*. These poems, among which the madrigals and sonnets are especially worthy of mention, are excellent imitations of the poetry of Seville in the golden age. In the field of folklore he published rich and valuable collections of songs, proverbs, metaphors, and popular usages. But the greater part of his work and the most important is that which deals with the history of Spanish literature of the golden age. The merit of these works lies in the author's discovery of biographical data and documents on many classic authors, such as Luis Barahona de Soto, Pedro Espinosa, Mateo Alemán, Fernando de Herrera, and, especially, Cervantes. His editions of works by these authors contain extensive critical, historical, and philological notes. It may be said that no modern critic has known the language and the life of the 16th and 17th centuries as well as he. His wide firsthand knowledge of books and documents of this period enabled him to bring out the most authoritative annotated edition of *Don Quixote* and of several of the *novelas ejemplares*. He also published many articles and pamphlets dealing with a number of concrete points on the life and works of Cervantes. In addition to his erudition, which made him the most competent Cervantes scholar of our time, he was deeply identified with the spirit and character of traditional, popular Spain, as revealed in his witty, expressive, unmistakably Spanish style.

See: G. M. del Río y Rico, *Biografía y bibliografía de don Francisco Rodríguez Marín* (1917); A. Baig y Baños, *Rodríguez Marín, documentador cervantino* (1916) and *Rodríguez Marín, anotador del "Quijote"* (1932).

F. de O.

Rodziewiczówna, Marja (pseud. Zmogas, 1863–1944, Polish novelist), was born at Pieniuha, near Grodno, in Lithuanian Poland, of parents soon to be exiled to Siberia for participation in the uprising against Russian sovereignty in progress at the time of her birth. Reared by the Countess Karolina Skirmunt, Rodziewiczówna was educated in Warsaw at the Kuczyńska pension and later, after her father had inherited an estate at Hruszowa in Polesie, at a convent in Jazłowiec. On the death of her father in 1881, Marja cut her hair, put on men's boots, and, at first solely by the labor of her own hands and those of her peasants, later with aid from her royalties, made the poor, neglected estate of Hruszowa yield a living. She turned to writing not for self-expression, as Orzeszkowa (*q.v.*) did, but in order to preach to her fellow countrymen the gospel of hope and endurance in a hopeless and defeatist age. In a series of more than a dozen novels, the best of which is *Dewajtis* (1889), Rodziewiczówna portrayed with deliberate purpose the full, rich, often violently beautiful life of what she regarded as the citadel of her nation's tradition, her own Eastern Border, believing that an ideal, thus drawn, would win others of her fellow countrymen who were less convinced than she of their tradition's worth and too often were seduced by the foreigner. Heir of Mickiewicz and of Henryk Rzewuski, the author of *The Memoirs of Soplica*, as an immortalizer of the Border spirit, Rodziewiczówna was the most popular novelist with two generations of Poles, despite her dismissal by the cosmopolites and the literati as a mere "character."

See: Z. Dębicki, *Portrety*, I (1927), 231–246; G. Korbut, *Literatura polska* (1931), IV, 152–153; K. Czachowski, *Obraz współczesnej literatury polskiej* (1934), I, 118–124, 339–340.

A. P. C.

Roelants, Maurice (1895–, Flemish poet and novelist), was born in Ghent. After a début as a humanist poet of melancholy refinement and engaging charm (*Het Verzaken,* 1930; Renunciation), Roelants published three novels and a number of short stories which gave him wide renown in Holland and Belgium. He is a classicist, and the drama in his books is essentially internal. His novels reveal a shrewd but sympathetic analyst of human nature and have none of the traditional Flemish rural and folklore elements. Roelants's style is limpid but tense. In *Komen en Gaan* (1927; Come and Go), *Het Leven dat wij droomden* (1931; Life as We Dreamed It), and *Alles komt terecht* (1935; Everything Settles Itself), as well as in *De Jazzspeler* (1928; The Jazz Band Player), painfully acquired wisdom is meted out without condescension and with great subtlety.

J.-A. G.

Roland Holst, Henriëtte (1869–, Dutch poet and writer of prose), was born at Noordwijk near Leiden. She made her poetic début with a book of verse entitled *Sonnetten en Verzen in Terzinen geschreven* (1895; Sonnets and Poems Written in Terza Rima). It was hailed by Willem Kloos (*q.v.*) as a great piece of work that held the promise of greater things to come. In the years that followed her first publication she became an ardent adherent of the socialist cause. Compassion for the underdog and the desire to aid the proletariat in its fight for better living conditions and for organized action were henceforth the dominant motives of her life. She married the artist R. N. Roland Holst—her maiden name was Van der Schalk—and found in him a sympathetic fellow fighter for her social ideals. Her first socialist verses appeared in *De Nieuwe Geboort* (1902; The New Birth). In it she expressed the conflict within her when the loud voice of socialism entered the quiet of her former life, the sense of doubt and perplexity, the pain of nostalgic retrospect when she had followed the voice. In her later poetry, *Opwaartsche Wegen* (1907; Upward Ways) and *De Vrouw in het Woud* (1912; The Woman in the Wood), perplexity and doubt have yielded to an ardent faith in the justice of her cause. In 1910 was published her drama, *De Opstandelingen* (The Rebels), which she described as "an imaginative picture of the essence of the Russian upheaval as a proletarian revolution." This was before the outbreak of the First World War, which led to the seizure of power by the Bolsheviks. She joined the Dutch Communist Party and championed its cause with her ready pen.

She wrote, among other books, *Kapitaal en Arbeid in Nederland* (1902; Capital and Labor in Holland), *Geschiedenis van den proletarischen Klassenstrijd* (1909; History of the Proletarian Class War), a life of Jean Jacques Rousseau (1912), a life of Garibaldi entitled *De Held en de Schare* (1920; The Hero and the Crowd), *Communisme en Moraal* (1925; Communism and Morality). In *Verzonken Grenzen* (1918; Submerged Bounds), written after the triumph of Communism in Russia, she sings the dawn of the new day, in which the bounds that separate man from man and class from class are submerged by the sea of love whose promised tide she saw coming in. The book contains magnificent verse. In the creative impulse of her visions thought blossoms into image as naturally as the bud opens into the rose, and it is to this plastic power that her poetry owes its beauty. We may not believe in the message, we cannot help believing in the poetry. As poetry it will be read when the message will have lost its appeal.

A. J. B.

Rolland, Romain (1866–1944, French novelist, playwright, and musicologist), was born at Clamecy in Burgundy. His poor health as a boy, the early love of music instilled in him by his pious mother, his solitude as a child, and the hero worship fostered by his early reading of Shakespeare—all combined to develop in him a sympathy with artists "the masters of the world, the great Defeated." At the Ecole Normale Supérieure (1886–1889) he specialized in history with Gabriel Monod. In 1886, oppressed by the materialistic life about him, he wrote to the great seer of Europe, Tolstoy (*q.v.*), seeking spiritual guidance. A long letter from Tolstoy (published February, 1902, by Péguy, *q.v.,* in *Cahiers de la quinzaine*) affected his aesthetic profoundly, although he has stated (in an unpublished letter of 1933) that from the beginning he sensed the extreme result of Tolstoy's aesthetic theories and could not acquiesce in Tolstoy's complete "condemnation of art." He lived in Rome from 1889 to 1891 studying at the Ecole Française d'Archéologie et d'Histoire. There he learned from the aged Malwida von Meysenbug, the friend of Kossuth, Mazzini, Louis Blanc, Wagner (*q.v.*), and Nietzsche (*q.v.*), "the intimate relationship between the true France which is hidden and the true Germany which does not raise its voice—the best Germany; it will survive" (preface to

Letters of Romain Rolland and Malwida von Meysenbug, 1933). In Rome he began a cycle of Renaissance drama. From 1891 to 1912 he taught at the Ecole Normale Supérieure and the Sorbonne; in 1895 he published his doctoral thesis, *L'Histoire de l'opéra en Europe avant Lully et Scarlatti* (still a definitive work and the first thesis primarily on music ever accepted by the Sorbonne), and soon began his *Tragédies de la foi: Saint Louis* (1897), expounding the power of faith on a whole people, *Aërt* (1898), illustrating "national exaltation," and *Le Triomphe de la raison* (1899), presenting the typically Romain Rolland heroism, "the conqueror conquered." *Les Loups,* played in March, 1898 (Eng. tr., *The Wolves,* 1937), first published as *Morituri* under the pseudonym Saint Just, was inspired by the Dreyfus affair. The play is noteworthy for its simplicity, rapidity, and directness; it was subsequently incorporated (along with *Le Triomphe de la raison*) in the partially completed cycle of 10 Revolutionary dramas, of which the best known are *Danton* (1900; Eng. tr., 1918), *Le Quatorze juillet* (1902; Eng. tr., *The Fourteenth of July,* 1918), *Le Jeu de l'amour et de la mort* (1924; Eng. tr., *The Game of Love and Death,* 1926), and *Robespierre* (1938). *Le Temps viendra* (1903) is based on an episode in the Boer War. During the writing of these plays Rolland had been clarifying his idea of a People's Theatre and published an essay, *Le Théâtre du Peuple* (1903; Eng. tr., 1918), wherein he found little for the *ouvrier* in the traditional classic or romantic French repertory and proposed the creation of a new form of drama built on the glorious tradition of French history. Rolland's interest in the "great Defeated" inspired his little book, very rare and comparatively unknown, *Millet* (1902), published only in English. This and the very popular, 85-page *Vie de Beethoven* (1903; Eng. tr., 1909), the *Michel-Ange* (1905, rewritten 1906; Eng. tr., 1912), and the *Vie de Tolstoï* (1911; Eng. tr., 1911) are his monuments to his heroes.

The great novel *Jean-Christophe,* conceived in 1886, written in part in Italy in 1889, and published serially in the *Cahiers de la quinzaine* from 1904 to 1912 (in book form, 1905–1913; Eng. tr., 1910–1913), brought Rolland to the fore in the literary world, especially with the youth of all countries. The work has been translated into many languages, including Indian dialects. The novel criticizes contemporary civilization, especially French materialism, through the eyes and thoughts of the German-born musician Jean-Christophe Krafft—Jean, the most common name of man, Christopher, bearing the light of understanding, and Krafft symbolizing the force which the always feeble Rolland admired. It is an uneven work, often called a symphony, with its crashing climaxes of instrumentation and its contrasting andantes and pastorales; Rolland moves through France and Germany with a keenly observant satire, ruthlessly exposing weaknesses. It was complemented, after the war, by a similar novel about a woman, *L'Ame enchantée* (1922–1933; Eng. tr., *The Soul Enchanted,* 1925–1934), of which the first volumes are very fine.

The enemies created by Rolland in *Jean-Christophe* found their revenge in attacking him for his pacifistic papers from 1914 to 1919. The outbreak of the war had found him in retirement in Switzerland, whence he appealed to the intellectual leaders of France, Germany, Spain, Italy, and the United States to campaign for a cessation of hostilities (see *Au-dessus de la mêlée,* 1915, Eng. tr., *Above the Battle,* 1916, and *Les Précurseurs,* 1919, Eng. tr., *The Forerunners,* 1920). His novel *Clérambault; histoire d'une Conscience libre pendant la guerre* (1920; Eng. tr., 1921) presents in readable form the kernel of his ideas on war, even though he denies their autobiographical significance. Rolland was pilloried in many publications and accused of many crimes against the state and civilization; Clemenceau threatened him with imprisonment. After 1919, in addition to the seven-volume novel *L'Ame enchantée,* the play *Robespierre,* and other books already mentioned, Rolland wrote *Mahatma Gandhi* (1924; Eng. tr., 1924), *Vie de Ramakrishna* (1929), and *Vie de Vivekananda* (1930). He was attracted to Communism as a political theory and was an honored guest of Maxim Gorky (*q.v.*) in Russia, but no book resulted. In 1938 he returned to France to live.

Jean-Christophe remains Rolland's most significant work. It is the first great novel in any language about a musician, treating fully the problem of the artist in an alien world. The author's credo centers on the principle that all art manifestations should convey moral truth, which for him seems to be faith in humanity, a pantheistic religion, and continued insistence on the virtues of great artists. He follows Tolstoy in his belief that art should primarily bring men together. He feels that the true greatness of France is the humble man close to the soil and that although France has had questionable leaders its traditions, history, and culture will keep it great.

See: P. Seippel, *Romain Rolland; l'homme et l'œuvre* (1913); P. J. Jouve, *Romain Rolland vivant, 1914–1919* (1920); J. Bonnerot, *Romain Rolland; sa vie, son œuvre* (1921); S. Zweig, *Romain Rolland; The Man and His Work* (1921); C. Sénéchal, *Romain Rolland* (1933).

W. H. B.

Romains, Jules (pseud. of Louis Farigoule, 1885–, French novelist, dramatist, essayist, and poet), was born in a village of Le Velay. He grew up in his native Cévennes Mountains and in Montmartre, where his schoolmaster father had been transferred. After a brilliant record at the Ecole Normale Supérieure (1906–1909), where he received degrees in both science and literature, he held professorships at Laon, Brest, Nice, and Paris (1909–1919). His literary vocation came in 1903 in the form of a poetic revelation of the oneness of even the most fortuitous human groups. The sociological and psychological implications of that experience led Romains to generalize it into a literary theory, unanimism, according to which collective emotions transcend those of the individual and the poet gives groups (the couple, the village, the theatre audience) a keener awareness of their personality. In his early poems—*L'Ame des hommes* (1904), *La Vie unanime* (1908), *Odes et prières* (1913), and the prose poems of *Puissances de Paris* (1911)—he explored the "souls of streets" and raised the group to a status of divinity which he described in *Manuel de déification* (1910). At the same time he illustrated his theory in tales and novels such as *Le Bourg régénéré* (1906), which describes the rebirth of a community inoculated with a revolutionary idea; his masterpiece, *Mort de quelqu'un* (1911; Eng. tr., *The Death of a Nobody,* 1914, reissued, 1944), in which an obscure death creates a new and more interesting life; and *Les Copains* (1913; Eng. tr., *The Boys in the Back Room,* 1937), with its series of youthful pranks upsetting and welding together the inhabitants of two dull towns. In *Donogoo-Tonka* (1920) he again examined, with dry humor, the possibilities of the hoax as a creator of group consciousness. And his first two plays, *L'Armée dans la ville* (1911) and the beautiful *Cromedeyre-le-Vieil* (1920), both in verse, studied the group soul of the city in crisis. During the 20's Romains was to become, with his farces *Knock, ou le Triomphe de la médecine* (1923; Eng. tr., *Doctor Knock,* 1925), *M. Le Trouhadec saisi par la débauche* (1923), and *Le Mariage de M. Le Trouhadec* (1925)—all produced by Louis Jouvet (*q.v.*)—the outstanding comic dramatist of his day. Meanwhile his three-volume *Psyché* (1922–1929; Eng. tr., *The Body's Rapture,* 1933) portrayed the raptures of love on both the physical and the psychic planes.

In 1932 began to appear the monumental cyclic novel, *Les Hommes de bonne volonté* (Eng. tr., *Men of Good Will,* 1933–), which aims to depict modern French life in about 30 volumes. By 1945 no fewer than 24 volumes had appeared. Long developments of thrilling plot illumined by flashes of humor, laborious historical re-creations punctuated with brilliant analyses, and palpitatingly real episodes, contrasting with imaginary interviews of the great, make up a variegated human comedy in which there is no hero unless it be France itself. Romains's unanimistic technique frequently aids him in producing vast frescoes of Paris going to work in 1908, of the armies moving up to Verdun in 1916, of the victory parade in 1919. The high point of the work is reached by the two volumes dealing with the defense of Verdun. While writing this magnum opus, Romains has sought relaxation in well-meaning, elaborately reasoned essays on political subjects; during the 30's, despite Nazism, he ardently sponsored a Franco-German *rapprochement.* But his naïve and vainglorious *Sept Mystères du destin de l'Europe* (1940; Eng. tr., *Seven Mysteries of Europe,* 1940) invalidated his claims as a political thinker. From 1938 to 1941 he served as international president of the P.E.N. Club. As a satirist in fiction and drama, as a powerful creator of a world of characters, as an intellectual force, Jules Romains is one of the most typical and most vigorous writers of the epoch. In 1946 he was elected to the French Academy.

See: B. Crémieux, *XXe Siècle* (1924); A. Cuisenier, *Jules Romains et l'unanimisme* (1935).

J. O'B.

Roman, Ronetti (1853–1908, Rumanian playwright), was educated in foreign lands and upon his return established himself in the town of Roman. From 1868 to 1872 he wrote articles in Hebrew in various periodicals. He taught German in a Bucharest school for some time. In 1877 he gave his first Rumanian satirical sketch, *Domnul Kanitverstan* (Mister Kanitverstan), and in 1878 his poem *Radu* which made him widely known. About that time was published fragments of another poem, "Iwan," in *Convorbiri literare* (Literary Conversations) and in the almanac *Dacia,* edited by Caragiale (*q.v.*). An intimate friend of Caragiale and Eminescu (*q.v.*), he also wrote for the newspaper *Timpul* (Time). In 1893 he took up the Jewish question in Rumania in his pamphlet *Două măsuri* (Two Measures). For a while he acted as translator at the Ministry of Foreign Affairs in Bucharest. The last years of his life he spent on his estate in Moldavia where he managed his farms and wrote his famous *Manasse*. The play was produced in 1900 at the Bucharest National Theatre and created a great stir. Numerous polemics followed, and the question of Jewish assimilation was once more revived.

Manasse is the prototype of the old orthodox Hebrew, who leads a model and respected life among his fellow men. He receives a mortal blow when his only granddaughter marries a Christian. He remains faithful to his tradition and rejects assimilation with Rumanian Christians. The play is enriched by pictures of a world in motion, of the Christian and Jewish communities of a Moldavian town, by portrayals of the many types of business people and officialdom, and particularly of Zelig Shor, the cynic. *Manasse* was produced in many languages and interpreted by celebrated and eminent players; it was played in Saint Louis, Missouri, with the title *New Lamps and Old.* Aside from its racial and religious significance, *Manasse* marks real progress in the development of the Rumanian drama. Its characters are enduring and universal.

See: S. Podoleanu, *60 scriitori români de origină evreiască* (1937).

L. F.

Romanov, Panteleimon (1884–1936, Russian novelist and short-story writer), born in a village near Tula, in Central Russia, of a noble family, studied law at the University of Moscow. Before the Revolution of 1917 Romanov had been dreaming of a vast epic in eight volumes under the general title *Rossiya* (Russia); only the first was actually published (1917). But after years of preparation he abandoned this ambitious project and concentrated on writing short stories, which made him one of the most popular Soviet writers in the 20's. In 1923–1928 his books occupied the first place in lending libraries throughout Russia. His fame was due to the fact that he described the new mode of life resulting from the Revolution. A keen observer, provided with a sense of humor and an extensive knowledge of various strata of Russian society, Romanov gave a broad picture of innumerable changes in social conditions and in the mentality of his fellow countrymen. New bureaucrats, peasants, workmen, party members, young students or old intellectuals, were represented in his sketches with the directness and accuracy of a literary camera. They were often called "the minutes of our times." Romanov, like a literary thermometer, registered all the ups and downs of social temperature in Soviet Russia between 1922 and 1930. A great impression was produced by his collection of short stories on the theory and practice of love during the first period of the Revolution (*Bez cheremukhi,* 1926; Eng. tr., *Without Cherry Blossom,* 1930). His novels dedicated to different aspects of moral conflicts in Soviet Society—*Novaya skrizhal* (1928; Eng. tr., *The New Commandment,* 1933), *Tri pary shelkovykh chulok* (*Tovarishch Kislyakov*) (1931; Eng. tr., *Three Pairs of Silk Stockings,* 1931), *Sobstvennost* (1933; Property)—are badly constructed and lack psychological insight, but they nevertheless can serve as literary illustrations of a certain period. The value of Romanov's work lies in the factual material and the true reflection of everyday life in the U.S.S.R. during the first postrevolutionary decade. Its aesthetic importance is doubtful.

M. S.

Rørdam, Valdemar (1872–, Danish poet), is, like so many of his Danish fellow craftsmen, a product of the idyllic Danish country parsonage—roses, beechwoods, a straw-thatched, rambling house, the singing of nightingales, the "white nights," the gentle melody of golden, waving wheatfields. He was born at Dalby on the island of Zealand. He made his literary début at the age of 23 with a collection of poems, *Sol og Sky* (1895; Sun and Sky); the promise of these came to some fulfillment in his next collection, *Tre Strenge* (1897; Three Chords). There followed his own version of the epic poem, *Bjovulf* (1898; Beowulf); *Dansk Tunge* (1902; Danish Tongue) and a realistic versified novel, *Gudrun Dyre* (1902), which betrayed unusual virtuosity rather than depth of feeling.

Rørdam is one of the most prolific of Danish lyricists. Other important works are *Den gamle Kaptajn* (1908; The Old Captain), imbued with intense patriotism and over-embellished with alliteration; *Jens Hvas til Ulvborg* (1922–1923; Jens Hvas of Ulvborg); *Sangen om Danmark* (1923; The Song of Denmark); *Blomstervers* (1925; Flower Stanzas). These and numerous other collections of flowing verse show a strong influence of Holger Drachmann (*q.v.*) and also a most keenly attuned ear, all his own, for the poetic possibilities of the Danish language. One may say that almost every line in Rørdam's works sings; he has something of the lilt of Swinburne. Rørdam has translated into Danish a number of Kipling's poems; he has also translated Reymont's (*q.v.*) novel-cycle about the peasants of Poland.

In Rørdam one finds a most remarkable blending of an intense, almost chauvinistic Danish nationalism, an astounding gift for anarchistic metrical innovation, and perhaps the most finely strung ear of his time for the sweetness, the gentleness, and the smooth flexibility of his native tongue.

See: Christian Rimestad, *Fra Stuckenberg til Seedorf,* II (1923); Helge Kjaergaard, *Die dänische Literatur der neuesten Zeit (1871–1933)* (1934).

G. St.

Rosegger, Peter (1843–1918, Austrian short-story writer, novelist, and poet), was born in Alpl near Kriegslach in Styria. Rosegger was of peasant stock, but lacked the physical strength for farm work; instead he was apprenticed for four years to an itinerant tailor. In this trade he traveled through the surrounding region, working in the homes of peasants; he came to know the characters, customs, and problems of the country people as intimately as the woods and mountains of his native province (see his autobiographical works *Waldheimat,* 1877, Eng. tr., *Forest Farm,* 1912, and *Als ich jung noch war,* 1895). Almost without formal education, he wrote numerous and varied works in High German and in the Styrian dialect and sent a large bundle of these to Dr. Swoboda, an editor in Graz. Swoboda at once recognized Rosegger's talent and provided the means for his education. Rosegger left school in 1869; in that year two books of dialect poems, *Zither und Hackbrett* and *Tannenherz und Fichtennadel,* were published. Almost immediately he became well known, and throughout his life he was among the most popular writers in German-speaking countries and enjoyed a considerable reputation abroad.

In his depiction of peasant life Rosegger had important predecessors in Berthold Auerbach and Johann Peter Hebel. His work, however, seems to owe more to personal observation and experience than to literary influences. It was primarily the lot of the Austrian peasant which interested Rosegger, and his best work deals with the rural scene. He had great narrative gifts, considerable humor, and a flair for describing eccentric characters. His most successful writing is to be found in such short tales as those in the collections *Neue Waldgeschichten* (1884) and *Allerhand Leute* (1888) and in episodes within his longer works. His full-length novels are often too didactic for modern taste. Even though most of his characters are convincingly and often realistically drawn, they have a tendency to voice the author's own opinions. A favorite theme is the struggle of the peasant against capitalism, especially against the tendency to incorporate the small farms in great estates and to use the land for hunting (*Jakob der Letzte,* 1888). Rosegger's ideal was a patriarchal, pre-industrial society. He was bitterly opposed to factories, socialism, militarism, and above all to modern cities; his attempts to describe urban life are not convincing. The idea of loyalty to traditional morals and customs and to one's family and native farm is a recurrent leitmotif. For all his cult of the peasant, Rosegger's work is clearly distinguished from the "blood and soil" school of the 1930's by its Christian and ethical elements. He was deeply interested in religious problems (*Der Gottsucher,* Eng. tr., *God-Seeker,* 1901; *I.N.R.I.,* 1905, Eng. tr., 1905). Though a Catholic (if far from orthodox), he was a defender of the Protestant cause in Austria. Always didactic in his fiction, Rosegger tended more and more to take an open stand on all problems of the day; he founded the periodical *Der Heimgarten* in 1876 to ensure his influence among the public.

Rosegger was enormously productive; his collected works (1913–1916) fill 40 volumes. His work is of uneven quality: he is weakest in dealing with abstract problems, strongest when telling simple stories of country people. He is generally considered a predecessor of the "Heimatkunst" of the early 1900's.

See: Hermine and Hugo Möbius, *Peter Rosegger* (1903); A. Vulliod, *Peter Rosegger; l'homme et l'œuvre* (1912; German tr. by Moritz Necker, 1913); J. Nadler, "Peter Rosegger," in *Neue österreichische Biographie,* Abt. I (1923).

H. C. H.

Rosso di San Secondo, Piermaria (1887–, Italian playwright and novelist), born in Caltanissetta, Sicily. Despite his travels and a particular fondness for Holland and Germany, Rosso has always cherished a strong attachment for his native island. Even in his early youth he seems to have been especially sensitive to the rugged, tropical beauty of Sicily which nourished and excited his intrinsically sensual nature in no small measure.

From his novels *La Fuga* (1917) and *La Donna che può capire, capisca* (1923) and from his prelude to *Marionette, che passione!* (1918), one is able to get a fairly accurate portrait of Rosso di San Secondo's philosophical and emotional personality. In these writings he sees man bewildered and dazed after his exile from a heavenly world. For man's everyday existence Rosso has a lofty contempt which often finds expression in bitter irony and cynicism; he views man's efforts to attain a measure of happiness on this earth, his temporary abode, as futile and doomed to failure. Only those who rebel against the strictures of society can ever hope to find release from futility. Generally, however, those of his protagonists who do find ultimate release achieve this by self-destruction or by becoming identified with the mentally unbalanced. It was natural for Rosso the dramatist, early in his career, to turn his back on the conventional, bourgeois theatre. He becomes a fellow traveler of the *grotteschi* and a close kinsman of Pirandello (*q.v.*), since the dramatic vision of these writers springs from the same skeptical, negative view of life—although Rosso's outlook is not quite so captious as that of the *grotteschi*. He is determined to infuse a breath of poetry into our apparently vain and useless reality. But temperamentally he is too aloof, too divorced from common humanity to be able to synthesize and transfigure our social, ethical, and psychological concepts into a superior vision of life. His frantic urge to present something vital and significant is dissipated in the projection of lyrical-symbolical situations of an abstract nature. Yet, despite these defects, he has enjoyed a certain popularity, not only in Italy but on the Continent and in South America, and is even considered by serious critics as second in importance only to Pirandello.

The first work to win him widespread acclaim and the one which has remained most characteristic of him is the already mentioned *Marionette, che passione!*, where three anonymous people confess to and conflict with each other in tragical poses in a public place and finally in a restaurant. This is a very clever and original work. Curiosity is piqued from the very beginning and interest is sustained. Yet with the dénouement of the play one remains unconvinced and even baffled. These characters are not the ordinary people they at first seemed to be. Driven by a passion which robbed them of pride, will, and reason, they are on the threshold of insanity. They have been reduced to the status of puppets, and the wire which controls their frenzied movements is their passion. The audience has been duped by the author, who has ingeniously given the illusion of good theatre. *La Bella Addormentata* (1919), considered by many as his second best play, is really a scenic presentation of a folk tale with allegorical implications. Carmelina, a peasant ingenue, jilted by the Tremulous Notary, becomes the village prostitute known widely as the Sleeping Beauty because she appears like one in a trance. As a passive and unwitting instrument in the hands of Bluecheeks, her procuress, she still retains a certain purity which captivates those who gaze upon her. One day she awakens from this state of stupor: a new life is stirring within her. It is to preserve the purity of her unborn child that she rebels against the coercion of Bluecheeks. And it is the Black Man from the Sulphur Pit who comes to her rescue. He is an impetuous romantic figure whose code is the primitive. rustic chivalry of Verga's *Cavalleria rusticana*, except that his interest is purely platonic. This "adventure in colors," as Rosso himself defines this work, comes to an end when the Black Man compels the Tremulous Notary to marry his victim made pregnant by another. Here again Rosso succeeds in casting a spell—but here again there is no drama. In the first two acts of *Il Delirio dell'oste Bassà* (1925), he shows the inner conflict which arises when a widower, having determined to keep intact and unsullied the memory of his idyllic married love, finds that the call of the flesh is stronger than his ascetic determination. As in *Amara* (1919), *Per far l'alba* (1919), and *L'Ospite desiderato* (1921), Rosso displays either an exasperating inability or an almost perverse delight in wasting themes potentially capable of yielding authentic dramas. In these plays which also treat of instinct and frustration he is clever, witty, and even brilliant, but he invariably permits both events and characters to degenerate into a gruesome pattern. *La Danza su un piede* (1923) and *Lazzarina fra i coltelli* (1923) concern themselves with the contrast between Life and Reason. There is no doubt that Rosso's perception of life's values and meaning is unique, startling. Given his remarkable dramatic and poetic gifts, there is little doubt that he would have produced the masterpiece everyone expected of him had he been willing or able to invest his personal world with a more compelling logic and a more genuine humanity.

Other plays are *Primavera* (1927), *La*

Roccia e i monumenti (1923), *L'Avventura terrestre* (1925), *Una Cosa di carne* (1925), *Notturni e preludi* (1926), *Tra vestiti che ballano* (1927), *Febbre* and *Canicola* (1927), *La Fidanzata dell 'albero verde* (1935). Among his novels are *La Morsa* (1918), *La Festa delle rose* (1920), *La Donna senza amore* (1920). His short stories and other prose works include *Ponentino* (1916), *Io commemoro Loletta* (1919), *La Mia Esistenza d'acquario* (1919), *Palamede, Remigia ed io* (1920), *C'era il diavolo o non c'era il diavolo* (1929), and *Luce del nostro cuore* (1932).

See: A. Tilgher, *Studi sul teatro contemporaneo* (1928), 153–185; Arnaldo Bocelli, "Scrittori d'oggi," *Nuova Antologia*, CCCLXVII (1933), 612–614.

P. P. M.

Rostand, Edmond (1868–1918, French poet and dramatist), was born in Marseille, of a well-to-do and cultured family. On marrying the poet Rosemonde Gérard, he presented her with a volume of verse, *Les Musardises* (1890). Soon afterwards, at a time when stark naturalism triumphed on the stage, he undertook to revitalize the old romantic drama in verse, enlisting in the process the friendship and assistance of some of the foremost contemporary actors. Le Bargy interpreted *Les Romanesques* (1894); Sarah Bernhardt at the height of her glory created the title roles of *La Princesse lointaine* (1895), *La Samaritaine* (1897), and *L'Aiglon* (1900); the inimitable Coquelin headed the cast of *Cyrano de Bergerac* (1897), and Lucien Guitry that of *Chantecler* (1910). *Cyrano de Bergerac,* by no means a faithful rendering of the true historical figure but a clever and lively reconstruction of the Louis XIII period in which he lived, enjoyed the most enthusiastic popular reception ever granted a poetic drama and has preserved, despite the rationalizations of hardened critics, its ever fresh and youthful appeal. It spread Rostand's fame far and wide, forced for him—at the age of 33—the doors of the venerable French Academy and, one must add, made him a slave to his tremendous reputation. Laboring under the glare of unwanted publicity, he produced *Chantecler,* his most uneven, yet his most remarkable work, a bold experiment in dramatic technique which carries to the boards the animal world of La Fontaine. *Chantecler* by any standards but those of *Cyrano* would have been called a success; instead, it was pronounced a failure. Shaken in health and spirit, Rostand ended his days in virtual retirement at his luxurious villa "Arnaga" in Cambo (at the foot of the Pyrenees) and lived long enough to see his two sons, Maurice and Jean, enter upon literary careers of their own.

There can be no doubt that Rostand set himself up ostentatiously as the successor of Victor Hugo and shared the latter's exalted conception of the poet as a teacher of lofty ideals. His romanticism, however, retains a distinct Southern flavor. It basks in the dreamy, unreal sun of his native province. Rooted in the ancient tradition of Italo-Provençal chivalric literature, mixing the old themes of love and war, it revels now in pathos and *préciosité,* now in grandiloquence and bombast, only to end with a flourish—*beau geste, panache*—the very arabesque of which carries a suggestion of wistfulness and futility. Thus Rostand's best-known characters, Cyrano, the would-be poet and lover; the eaglet (Napoleon II) deprived of his wings; Chantecler, the cock who discovers that his crowing does not make the sun rise—all illustrate their creator's diffidence and reveal sadness and frustration beneath their superficial bravura. Paradoxically enough, Rostand's theatre, the object of equally extravagant praise and abuse in his lifetime, is being reassessed today in terms of this very sincerity and valued, over and above its emotional thrills, as a lucid and moving dramatization of his own sense of unfulfillment.

Most of the plays of Rostand have been translated into English.

See: Jean Suberville, *Edmond Rostand; son théâtre, son œuvre posthume* (1921); Paul Faure, *Vingt Ans d'intimité avec Edmond Rostand* (1928); M. J. Premsela, *Edmond Rostand* (1933); Rosemonde Gérard, *Edmond Rostand* (1935).

J.-A. B.

Rostworowski, Karol Hubert (1877–1938, Polish tragic dramatist), often called the Polish Mauriac (*q.v.*) and regarded generally as the principal heir of Wyspiański (*q.v.*), was the leading representative in Free Poland of orthodox Catholicism and of the conservative spirit which had its abode principally in Cracow. Born in Rybna near Cracow of a well-to-do gentry family, Rostworowski was early marked for a career as gentleman farmer and sent to study agriculture. He was diverted from this by 10 years (1898–1908) of study abroad, mostly in Germany where he was greatly influenced by Wagner and Kant, and returned to Cracow to make his début as a writer with a drama, *Pod górę* (1910; Uphill), which he himself later withdrew from circulation. Always deeply spiritual, Rostworowski went through formal conversion to the Catholic faith of his fathers at this time, and the experience, together with the horrors of the First World War, left him with an abiding sense of sin and of man's depravity, on the one hand, and of man's unity with the divine, on the other. Man's relationship to God became his sole preoccupation. It was the theme not only of the classic tragedies of his first period—*Judasz z Kariothu* (1912; Judas Iscariot), *Kaligula* (1916), and the mystery *Miłosierdzie* (1920; Charity)—but also of his later trilogy of contemporary life—*Niespodzianka* (1929; The Surprise), *Przeprowadzka* (1930; The Way Up), and *U mety* (1932; At the Goal)—in which the expiation of a crime is traced through three generations of a family "on the way up." A towering figure of a man, "with the profile of a Caesar and the gestures of a Savonarola," Rostworowski became, in his final, somewhat cloistered years just outside Cracow, a kind of legend.

See: E. Breiter, "K. H. Rostworowski," *Wiadomości literackie,* 1938, No. 8; K. Czachowski, "Roztworowski—Polish Tragic Dramatist: 1877–1938," *Slavonic Review,* XVII (1938–1939), 677–688.

A. P. C.

Roth, Joseph (1894–1939, Austrian novelist), was born in Schwabendorf, Volhynia, son of an Austrian and a Russian Jewess. Left to the care of relatives, this unwanted child grew up with a strong desire for social distinction which, he felt, could be attained by a fine education; as he was about to enter the University of Vienna, the First World War broke out, and Roth volunteered. After the war he eked out a scant existence as cinema usher and journalist and for a few years contributed to the distinguished *Frankfurter Zeitung.* In 1933 Roth returned to Vienna and after the move toward *Anschluss* fled in 1936 to Paris. In 1939, overcome by the distress of personal misfortune and exile, Roth committeed suicide.

Roth's unsheltered youth developed in him the understanding and sympathy remarkably apparent in each of his novels. His wisdom, his gentleness, and his strength grew out of the pain and poverty of his childhood and the disappointments of his later life. In his most accomplished novel, *Hiob* (1930; Eng. tr., *Job,* 1931), the story of a "modern wandering Jew," Roth might have been describing himself in the character of the patient and gentle father; and the torment in the soul of the youngest son is the anguish Roth had known as a youth shunned for his poverty and his Jewish blood. His own experiences provide the realistic portraits of human types and the bitter incidents of a life skeptically surveyed: the Jewish clientele of *Hotel Savoy* (1924), the disillusioned Austrian officer returning from the war (*Die Flucht ohne Ende,* 1927; Eng. tr., *Flight without End,* 1930), the gradual moral disintegration during the period of inflation (in a family novel, *Zipper und sein Vater,* 1928; in a political novel, *Rechts und Links,* 1929), the mystical allegory of a Russian army officer seeking his soul's redemption amid the horror of warfare on the Eastern front (*Tarabas, ein Gast auf dieser Erde,* 1934; Eng. tr., *Tarabas, a Guest on Earth,* 1934). His last and strange novel, *Die Legende vom Heiligen Trinker* (1939; Eng. tr., *The Legend of the Holy Drinker,* in K. Mann and H. Kesten, *Heart of Europe,* 1943), is significant for the parallel that could be drawn between Roth and the main character, a destitute foreigner in Paris, depending on chance for a living and spending on drink whatever money came into his hand. In *Juden auf der Wanderschaft* (1927) and *Der Antichrist* (1934; Eng. tr., 1935) Roth pleads for racial and religious tolerance.

In his earliest novels, *Rebellion* (1924), *April; die Geschichte einer Liebe* (1925), and *Der blinde Spiegel* (1925), Roth did not usually achieve the firmness of form and subject matter to be found in his epic-like study of imperial Austria (*Radetzkymarsch,* 1932, Eng. tr., *Radetzky March,* 1933, and its less powerful sequel, *Die Kapuzinergruft,* 1939), in his *Beichte eines Mörders* (1936; Eng. tr., *Confession of a Murderer,* 1937), or in his very original presentation of Napoleon as seen through the eyes of an adoring servant (*Die hundert Tage,* 1936; Eng. tr., *Ballad of the Hundred Days,* 1936).

See: F. Bertaux, *A Panorama of German Literature from 1871 to 1931* (1935), pp. 251–255; A. Werner, "Four Tragic Jews", *Jewish Outlook,* February, 1942.

V. L.

Roumanille, Joseph (1818–1891, Provençal poet and raconteur, promoter of the Felibrige movement), was born at Saint-Rémy-de-Provence, "the town of gardens," near Avignon. Like Frédéric Mistral (*q.v.*), he was an educated man of the soil who had spent his childhood among the country people, speaking their language. He attended the Collège of Tarascon and began his career as an usher and teacher in a private school. He later occupied the position of proofreader in a printing house and finally established himself as a publisher and bookseller in Avignon. His shop became famous as a literary center. Roumanille wrote his first Provençal verses for the mere purpose, he said, of satisfying a literary fancy, of showing what could be done with that home speech which had been "dishonored" by low and coarse rhymesters. He also told how, some time later, he resolved to use it as a sole means of literary expression because his mother had been unable to understand a poem he had written in French. The important fact, however, is that he was living at a time when various trends were leading toward the Provençal renaissance. The rebirth of the provinces was being fostered by scholars, especially historians and philologists, and by the popular poets of the romantic era. Roumanille was still a young man when he conceived the idea of purifying the vernacular of his region. It was with this purpose in mind that, a few years later, he edited an anthology of contemporary poetry, *Li Prouvençalo* (1852). Assuming the role of a Provençal Malherbe, he applied his own simplified system of spelling to all the pieces contained in the book. His next step was to induce those poets who were singing in "the language of their mothers" to attend meetings where the destiny of the home speech, and especially the adoption of a common orthography, would be discussed. Thus he became *lou rampelaire de touti lis ange troubaire* (the recruiting sergeant who drummed up all the angelic troubadours). His activities were to lead to the founding of the Felibrige (1854). The program of this literary school, whose initial aim was the revival of the language and literature of the ancient troubadours, became more ambitious with the rising fame of Mistral, but Roumanille had been its true and active promoter. There lies the principal title to fame of him who was called *le père du félibrige.*

Unlike other Felibres, Roumanille did not publish his works with a face to face translation. He was writing for a limited public, the countryfolk of Provence. His first book, *Li Margarideto* (1847; The Daisies), was a collection of short poems, of a sincere, delicate, and tender realism, written in a light and easy style. He republished them in a larger volume, *Lis Oubreto en vers* (1859; Minor Works in Verse), which contained Christmas carols, didactic stories, and other types of familiar poetry. That same year appeared also *Lis Oubreto in proso,* a book of selected political articles and pamphlets written during the Second Republic. Roumanille displayed much verve and great talent as a defender of traditional order. He was one of the first to use Provençal prose effectively, making everybody laugh, even his opponents. His real fame as a writer, however, rests principally on the short stories that, from 1855 to his death, he contributed to the *Armana prouvençau,* the annual organ of the Felibrige.

Roumanille is not a great poet, but he is an inimitable storyteller, a good observer of human nature, a wholesome "Rabelais de famille," as he has also been called. He was able to raise the popular tale to a certain literary dignity and turn it into a genre that satisfied both the common people and the well-read man, amusing them while teaching a lesson. Some of his best stories were published in book form, *Li Conte prouvençau e li cascareleto* (1883) and *Contes provençaux par Joseph Roumanille avec le texte provençal et la traduction française* (1911). Many of them had previously appeared in Parisian newspapers and reviews, translated and commented on by authors such as Alphonse Daudet (*q.v.*), Paul Arène, and Armand de Pontmartin. Among the best known are "Lou Curat de Cucugnan," "Lou Mege [physician] de Cucugnan," and "L'Ermitan de San Jaque," presented by Daudet as "Le Réveillon de Saint Jacques."

See: Saint-René Taillandier, "La Nouvelle Poésie provençale," *Revue des deux mondes,* October 15, 1859, pp. 807–844; P. Mariéton, F. Mistral, A. de Pontmartin, *et al., Revue félibréenne,* VII (1891), 65–84, 107–118; E. Ripert, *La Renaissance provençale, 1800–1860* (1917), pp. 361–403; J. Aurouze, "Roumanille," *Feu,* XXII (1928), 192–197.

A. V. R.

Roussel, Raymond (1877–1933, French novelist, dramatist, and poet), in his life as well as in his work might almost be mistaken by the casual reader for an invention of the surrealists, who have hailed him as a precursor and a genius. Out of the mass of legend which surrounds him, this much seems clear. He was born in Paris of wealthy parents, and with no necessity of making a living or even of engaging in any useful occupation, he turned to literature as one would to a hobby. Eccentric in the extreme and undoubtedly neurotic (he was for some time under the treatment of Pierre Janet, who has described his case in *De l'angoisse à l'extase,* 1926, Vol. I, pp. 132–138), he wrote with no regard for literary fashion or popular approval, relating in prose or verse fantastic tales of adventure which abounded in the supernatural and were filled with impossible inventions. His great fortune enabled him to have his work published in luxurious format and, since he had a passion for the theatre and eventually adapted most of his work for dramatic presentation, to secure public performances of these plays by first-rate casts. His major works include *La Doublure* (1897), *La Vue* (1904), *Impressions d'Afrique* (1910), *Nouvelles Impressions d'Afrique* (1910), *Locus Solus* (1914), *L'Etoile au front* (1925), and *La Poussière de soleils* (1927). *Comment j'ai écrit certains de mes livres* (1935), left by Roussel to be published posthumously, is of paramount importance in describing his peculiar theory of composition.

It is almost impossible to give in any reasonable compass an adequate idea of the content of Roussel's works; it can only be noted that they suggest more than anything else a weird blend of Roussel's favorite authors, Verne, Loti (*q.v.*), Dumas père, and Camille Flammarion, with overtones of paranoia. Like the *douanier* Rousseau in painting, Roussel depicted the world with a naïve precision, wrote with a directness and lack of sophistication which probably only the most sophisticated can fully enjoy, piled melodramatic cliché upon cliché with the most delightful results. He spent most of his last years in travel and died in Palermo.

See: Roger Vitrac, "Raymond Roussel," *Nouvelle Revue française,* XXX (1928), 162–176; Jean Cocteau, "Note," *Nouvelle Revue française,* XLI (1933), 464–465; Michel Leiris, "Raymond Roussel," *Nouvelle Revue française,* XLIV (1935), 575–582.

C. W., Jr.

Rovetta, Gerolamo (1851–1910, Italian novelist and dramatist), was born in the city of Brescia of a family whose position and affluence permitted him at an early age to mingle with and observe all levels of society in his own and other Italian cities. He spent much of his time in Milan, then, as now, a center of great literary and industrial activity. His easy circumstances may also explain his unwillingness to submit to an artistic discipline which might have raised his best works to the rank of masterpieces. No literary innovator, Rovetta was fortunate in possessing a gift for observation and accurate reproduction which coincided with the requirements of the currently popular *verismo* (*see* Italian literature). Although these qualities are not apparent in his first novel, the excessively sentimental *Mater dolorosa* (1882), they are very evident in his first mature work, *I Barbarò: Le Lacrime del prossimo* (1885). Best and most representative of his novels is *La Baraonda* (1894), which depicts the materialistic society of Milan during the years of economic expansion following political unification. He describes the histrionic expatriot promoter, the quick enthusiasms of the speculating public and their swift and violent disillusionments, the inability of the aristocrat to cope with the unscrupulous parvenu, who, in turn, falls prey to the omnipotent and merciless financier. Virtue means weakness, evil alone is strong; Rovetta's uncompromising adherence to this formula, here as in *Il Tenente dei lancieri* (1896) and *La Signorina* (1900), sometimes brings his characters dangerously close to the level of caricature. This and an overabundance of detail detract from the effectiveness of his considerable gift for simple, unaffectedly powerful narration.

Most of Rovetta's extensive dramatic production exhibits a similarly extreme version of the verist formula (*I Barbarò* and *La Baraonda* were both dramatized by him, in 1890 and 1905 respectively). His *La Trilogia di Dorina* (1889) is not only its best expression but one of the most successful efforts of the *teatro verista.* Here in three rather widely separated moments in his heroine's progress from virtue and helplessness to vice and power, Rovetta presents a brilliant affirmation of his cynical credo. *Alla città di Roma* (1888), *I Disonesti* (1893), *La Realtà* (1895), and *Papà Eccellenza* (1906) are different illustrations of the same theme, with the last-named offering one of his best character studies. In 1896, sensing the renewed interest in the historical drama and, perhaps, seeking relief from the narrowness of naturalism, he turned to the early years of his century for *Principio di secolo.* His second attempt in this genre, *Romanticismo* (1901)—the title was a term contempuously applied by the Austrians to early Italian efforts for freedom—enjoyed immense popularity through its convincing re-creation of the fervor of the struggle for independence so recently completed. With this possible exception, however, his historical manner is definitely inferior to the naturalistic.

Whether Rovetta was primarily a novelist or a dramatist is difficult to decide, largely because he was, himself, almost never able to separate his techniques. His novels make excessive use of dramatic dialogue, a defect which he recognized by describing *L'Idolo* (1898) and *La Signorina* (1900) as *romanzi dialogati;* many of his plays, on the other hand, attempt a breadth of canvas suited only to the novel, which results in a disproportionate number of *macchiette,* characters without intimate life. *La Trilogia di Dorina* is probably his most striking single work, but it is rather in his novels that he makes his greatest contribution, that of a chronicler of his times.

See: B. Croce, *La Letteratura della nuova Italia,* 2d ed., III (1922), 163–167; G. Mazzoni, *L'Ottocento,* (1934), p. 1011; L. Tonelli, *Il Teatro contemporaneo in Italia* (1936), pp. 146–152.

A. T. M.

Royère, Jean (1871–, French poet and critic), was born in Aix-en-Provence and after receiving his Licence ès Lettres at Lyon went to Paris with the intention of studying philosophy. He soon tired of that subject, however, and turned first to politics and then to poetry. In 1905 he became editor of *Ecrits pour l'art* and in 1906 founded the review *Phalange,* which until the First World War was the rallying ground of the successors of symbolism (*see* French symbolism). His first book of verse, *Exil doré,* was published in 1898, and by 1920 he had added to it four small but distinguished volumes. All this work was collected in *Poésies* (1924); since then one more volume of his verse, *Orchestration* (1936), has appeared. In such collections of essays as *Clartés sur la poésie* (1925), *Frontons* (1932), and *Le Point de vue de Sirius* (1935), he has discussed the technique of poetry and criticized most of the chief modern poets with sensitivity and understanding, though with more intellectualism than will please some tastes. Royère can challenge Valéry (*q.v.*) for the distinction of being the most notable disciple of Mallarmé (*q.v.*) and the Abbé Bremond (*q.v.*) for that of the most subtle theorist of "pure poetry." From the point of view of literary history, his chief distinction is undoubtedly that of having more than any other man carried the theory and practice of orthodox symbolism on into the last two decades. As a practicing poet he is interested chiefly in sonorities, verbal music, veiled suggestion, rather than direct statement. Though his work is in the main not excessively "difficult" (certainly much less so than that of Valéry), he has from the very beginning taken as his ideal "une poésie qui contraignît le lisant à autant d'initiative que l'écrivain."

See: Paul Fort and Louis Mandin, *Histoire de la poésie française depuis 1850* (1926); Henry Derieux, *La Poésie française contemporaine, 1885–1935* (1935).

C. W., Jr.

Rozanov, Mikhail Grigoriyevich, *see* Ognyov, Nikolai.

Rozanov, Vasili Vasilyevich (1856–1919, Russian philosopher, publicist, and critic), was an exceptionally original, bold, and controversial figure in Russian letters, scarcely known abroad, but regarded by some critics as the foremost mind of his generation. His chief recognition came from the Right, and he was at first regarded as a Slavophile and a conservative. He transcends these definitions, however, by the extreme independence of his views. He believed in the three principles of individuality, wholeness, and unity, and he attacked the contemporary regime for its failure to uphold these. The Revolution of 1905 evoked in him a passing enthusiasm, but the agnosticism and compulsory sameness of the radicals repelled him. Nevertheless he believed in the apocalyptic significance of the Revolution and the coming regeneration of Russia. At heart Rozanov was nonpolitical, with a profoundly mystical, religious philosophy opposed to systems, and an advocate of the supreme value of the human personality. His attitude toward religion was complex: he was an amoralist who proclaimed the naturalistic religion of procreativeness centered round marriage and the family, and at the same time he was profoundly sympathetic to Christianity. His criticism of the Church attacked its asceticism. Throughout his life there existed in him a painful conflict over the meaning of Christ's teachings, finally resolved on his deathbed in a radiant acceptance. A puzzling dualism characterized many of Rozanov's conceptions, as in his attitude toward Russia, the Revolution, and the Jews. The core of his thinking, however, shows that Rozanov valued most in man his attraction to religion and repulsion from positivism.

Born in Vetluga of a poor, middle-class family, Rozanov graduated (1881) from the faculty of law and philosophy of the University of Moscow. For many years he taught history and geography in provincial secondary schools. Dissatisfied with the academic disciplines, he went to St. Petersburg (1893) to enter the civil service. There he became affiliated with the conservative press, serving on *Novoye vremya* (New Time) until its suppression in 1918. In 1880 he married the extraordinary Apollinaria Suslova, the former mistress of Dostoevski (*q.v.*), then a woman of about 40. It was a singularly unhappy relationship that soon ended, and by 1889 Rozanov had formed a new union with Varvara D. Rudneva, the "Friend" often cited in his pages, who became his perfect companion. He traveled occasionally in Italy, France, and Germany. The 1917 Revolution swept all economic security from under him, and he died in extreme poverty and neglect.

Rozanov's first book was *O ponimanii* (1886; On Understanding), a polemic of 757 pages directed against the University of Moscow and the result of five years' labor. Though unsuccessful, it attracted the attention of Strakhov, the Slavophile publicist, who introduced him to the conservative press. In 1890 he published *Legenda o velikom inkvizitore* (The Legend of the Grand Inquisitor), foremost of his early works, the first attempt to plumb the mind of Dostoevski and a critical analysis of phenomenal intuitive penetration containing some of his most brilliant paradoxes; included is a remarkable chapter on Gogol that placed the latter for the first time in his true relationship to Russian literature. From then on Rozanov issued a series of works on philosophy and religion: *Krasota v prirode i yeya smysl* (1894; Beauty in Nature and Its Meaning), setting forth his historical outlook and containing a valuable chapter on V. S. Solovyov (*q.v.*); *Religiya i kultura* (1899; Religion and Culture); *Literaturnye ocherki* (1899; Literary Sketches); *V mire neyasnago i nereshyonnago* (1901; Among Riddles and Mysteries); *Semeynyi vopros v Rossii* (1903; The Family Problem in Russia); *Okolo tserkovnykh sten* (1906; In the Shadow of Church Walls); *Russkaya tserkov* (1906; The Russian Church); *Kogda nachalstvo ushlo* (1909; When the Authorities Were Away), praising the buoyancy of the 1905 Revolution; *Tyomnyi lik* (1911; The Dark Face) and *Lyudi lunnago sveta* (1913; Moonlight Men), formulating his metaphysics of Christianity; *Solitaria* (1912; Eng. tr., 1927) and *Opavshie listya* (2 vols., 1913–1915; Fallen Leaves), which are the summits of Rozanov's stylistic mastery; *Iz vostochnykh motivov* (1915–1919; Oriental Motives), disclosing the secret of the ancient religions; *Apokalipsis russkoy revolyutsii* (1918–1919; The Apocalypse of the Russian Revolution), on the rebellion against Christianity. One must also note his brilliant preface to Fyodor Shperk's *Ontology; or, The Metaphysics of Pure Being* (London, 1922).

See: E. Gollerbach, *V. V. Rozanov* (1922; this appears in abridged form in Rozanov, *Solitaria,* Eng. tr. by S. S. Koteliansky, 1927); D. S. Mirsky, *Contemporary Russian Literature* (1926), pp. 163–172.

N. S.

Rubió i Ors, Joaquim (1818–1899, Catalonian poet and scholar), is intimately associated with the literary movement known by the name of *Renaixença* (*see* Catalan literature). He abandoned a career in the church for one in letters. In 1847 he was appointed to the chair of general and Spanish literature in the University of Valladolid; in 1858 he moved to the University of Barcelona as occupant of the chair of universal history of literature. His major efforts were directed toward the revival of the Catalonian language and literature. In 1839, under the pseudonym "Lo Gayter del Llobregat," (The Piper of Llobregat) he published his first Catalonian composition in the *Diario de Barcelona* (Barcelona Daily). No one, with the exception of the editor of the newspaper, knew the identity of that new troubadour who, with exemplary faithfulness, kept writing Catalan poems for the most important daily papers of Catalonia. His verse was widely and avidly read. In 1841 he collected in the book now entitled *Lo gayter del Llobregat* the pieces previously published, with other new ones and an important prologue in which he demanded literary independence for Catalonia and urged love and veneration for the native tongue. The prologue had the value of a political-literary manifesto.

Rubió i Ors was one of the restorers of the poetic festival known as the Jocs Florals (*see* Catalan literature) in 1859. He produced works of literary investigation for different Catalonian and foreign journals and with his friend Josep Maria Grau began the publication of a collection of old Catalonian writers. His work has had a wide influence in the Catalan-speaking countries.

See: Francisco Tubino, *Historia del renacimiento literario contemporáneo en Cataluña* (1880); Marcelino Menéndez y Pelayo, prologue, in Rubió i Ors, *Lo gayter del Llobregat* (1889); Manuel de Montoliu, *Manual d'història critica de la literatura catalana moderna* (1922).

J. M. M. i V.

Rueda, Salvador (1857–1933, Spanish poet, novelist, and playwright), was born in Málaga, in the South of Spain, of humble parents. His literary education was scant, and the success he had in the field of Hispanic letters was the result of a powerful and exuberant poetic intuition. Although Rueda cultivated also the novel and drama forms, his literary fame was gained as a poet. From 1885 to 1900 the pen of Salvador Rueda completely dominated the field of Spanish verse.

His poetic production can be described in three words, color, fluidity, and fecundity. A master of easy rhythm, with his tireless pen he exalts all that surrounds him, in a profusion of sonorous, polychromatic effects. The Spanish critic Clarín (*see* Alas, Leopoldo) wrote the prologue for *Cantos de la vendimia* (1891), *En tropel* (1892) appeared with a prologue by Rubén Darío, and the great Spanish writer Unamuno (*q.v.*) is the author of the prologue to *Fuente de salud* (1906). *Mi estética* (1918) is Rueda's last book. It can be said that the work of Salvador Rueda begins and ends with him. He does not follow in the footsteps of the great traditional Spanish poetry, nor does he really create poetic forms which might perpetuate his name. His poetry is neither transcendental in content nor revolutionary in form. It is simply poetry of the senses which, on striking the ear, fills us with melody and rhythm. His poems are never worked out with the technique and discipline which normally go into the making of a literary work; but their richness of sound, their musical quality, may very well account for the almost unprecedented, if not enduring, popularity of Rueda. Very few Spanish poets have attained such fame as he briefly enjoyed, not only in Spain but in all Spanish-speaking countries.

To Salvador Rueda belongs the honor of having introduced to Madrid literary circles the great Nicaraguan poet, Rubén Darío, the real founder of the new literary movement known as *modernismo*. With the growth of *modernismo* Rueda's poetry was relegated to second place, and he lived his last years under the shadow of a really unjust oblivion.

See: A. González-Blanco, *Los grandes maestros, Salvador Rueda y Rubén Darío; estudio cíclico de la lírica española en los últimos tiempos* (1908); F. de Onís, *Antología de la poesía española e hispanoamericana, 1882–1932* (1934).

M. de M.

Rumanian literature. Rumanians have constituted a large and homogeneous population since the year 107, when Trajan conquered Dacia. They have clung to their ancestral traditions; land tillers and shepherds, they have preserved even their ancient costumes of white cloth flowered with gracefully colored patterns. To the Latin foundation and structure of the language, Slavonic and other tongues have contributed amply. Although industrial cities rise here and there, and Bucharest the capital is quite comparable to other European centers, the country has been basically rustic—and possessed of a native folklore the literary possibilities of which have not yet been fully appreciated. Modern Rumanian writers have been particularly interested in occidental fashions, have been eager to avoid the oriental influences normal in this borderland between West and East. Some of them have also known how to exploit, with great success, the resources of the nation itself.

When in 1852 Vasile Alecsandri (1819–1890) wrote *Miorița* (The Lambkin), a popular ballad "corrected" by him, the first native masterpiece saw the light of publicity and the cornerstone of modern Rumanian poetry was laid. The very old song which he adapted is obviously a fragment from a longer poem lost in the vague past. As it appears in Alecsandri's version it preserves its lyric mood. And such lyricism characterizes the subsequent poetry. It was about 30 years after the publication of *Miorița* that Mihail Eminescu (*q.v.*) built the marble palace of his romantic dreams, a monument of verse craftsmanship. Blending his Western education with painstaking study of ancient peasant lore, Eminescu actually molded a poetic language as yet unsurpassed in Rumania. Disappointed in love, fleeing the commonplace and tedious, sinking more and more into his inborn sadness, he was fascinated by Kant and Schopenhauer. Descending deeper into the realm of thought, he included in his poetic world *fin-de-siècle* pessimism and Hindu Nirvana. The mind of this genius darkened in the prime of life, and death, in an insane asylum, cut short the radiance and warmth, richness and depth of Eminescu's verse. In his 60 completed poems occidental technique and village song blend, with unprecedented beauty. Alexandru Macedonski (1854–1920), rival of Eminescu and forerunner of Western inspirations, uses forms which in ultimate development suggest the French manner. Macedonski, in fact, wrote a book of sonnets in that language, *Bronzes* (1897). George Coșbuc (1866–1918) begins the epopee of peasantry, and he is nearer to the soil, singing the daily life of the people and their love for the fields. Dimitrie Anghel (*q.v.*) creates a world of suave sentiments, of gossamer-like flowers scented with charm. Among many others of more or less vitality, Tudor Arghezi (1880–) is markedly original.

Ion Creangă (*q.v.*) establishes a solid native prose. Born of peasants and educated first in his village and later in the capital of Moldavia, Jassy, he excels in retelling the ever refreshing tales of the nation and climaxes his efforts with *Amintiri din copilărie* (1880; Childhood Reminiscences), in which the people's lore and superstitions, work and play, hopes and disappointments, are treated with a somehow primitive and certainly bold skill. Mihail Sadoveanu (1880–) follows Creangă, with an art of his own, enlarging the scope of such fiction, writing of the mountains, forests, valleys, and streams of the land, depicting them with intimate knowledge, and painting vast murals of historic deeds. Sadoveanu's short stories and novels evoke the past, reflect the life of small towns, and above all mingle the temporary feelings of his characters with the eternal palpitation of nature. More impregnated by Western models, Alexandru Vlahuţă (1858–1919) shows other ways for the future novel in *Dan* (1894). Duiliu Zamfirescu (1858–1922) in his serial beginning with *Viața la țară* (1894; Country Life) adds valuable material to the indigenous novel. Of the younger generation, Liviu Rebreanu (1885–) is recognized as an accomplished novelist in his *Ion* (1920), where the passion to own land stands out against a background of Transylvanian farm life, in *Pădurea spânzuraților* (1922; The Forest of the Hanged), an episode of the First World War, and other works.

The aboriginal religious theatre and popular puppet plays are still entertaining the masses in their numerous tiny hamlets and villages. In the larger towns and cities modern theatres produce the world's most recent drama, in translation, and at times the best of the native drama. With Ion Luca Caragiale (*q.v.*) comedy reaches maturity. *O noapte furtunoasă* (1879; Stormy Night) and *Cuconul Leonida față cu reacțiunea* (1879; Mister Leonida Faces the Reaction), followed by *O scrisoare pierdută* (1884; The Lost Letter) and *De ale carnavalului* (1885; Carnival Adventures), comedies of character and manners, show the inherent conflict in an oriental society which is embracing new occidental ways of life; in spite of their age and the change of customs these plays are still successfully produced. In *Năpasta* (1889; False Accusation) Caragiale takes up the peasant drama and, although there are moments in it as profoundly significant as in Tolstoy's (*q.v.*) *Power of Darkness,* the play does not approach in quality the author's comedies. Drama, in the deeply serious sense, comes of age with *Manasse* (1900) by Ronetti Roman (*q.v.*), where the author combines consummate technique and natural dialogue. It is the tragedy of Jewish and Christian misunderstandings, showing Roman's belief in assimilation and humanitarian solutions. Outstanding today, Victor Eftimiu (1889–) refreshes the stage by offering a poem in five acts, *Inşiră-te, mărgărite* (1911; Story without End), in which the people's fairy-tale characters take shape and voice. *Cocoşul negru* (1913; The Black Cock) continues and somehow perfects this theme.

Literary criticism counts two eminent writers, Titu Maiorescu (*q.v.*) and Constantin Dobrogeanu-Gherea (*q.v.*), opponents in the debate on "art for art's sake" *vs.* "art with a tendency." According to Maiorescu, the poet is an individual living in a world of his own, pursuing a dream of perfection conceived only by him and understood by the initiated few. It is thus that he interprets the poetry of Eminescu. In the light of Dobrogeanu-Gherea's conception of art, proceeding from Taine (*q.v.*), Eminescu on the contrary was not the detached genius, indifferent to the struggles of his downtrodden nation whose language he glorified, but the direct result of economic, social and political conditions. Art is the production of environment and time, as well as of race, and should embody a tendency. From the seeds of Dobrogeanu-Gherea's ideas germinated the Poporanist (People's) movement. Constantin Stere (1865–1936), its inspirer and leader, succeeded in bringing together most of the talented authors of the time. Seconded by Garabet Ibrăileanu (1871–1936), he emphasized the importance of the people and also the duty of intellectuals to work for the progress of the villager. Unconsciously leaning towards the Dobrogeanu-Gherea tradition, but more inclined to accept Maiorescu's aesthetics, Nicolae Iorga (*q.v.*), the historian and statesman assassinated by Nazi-inspired Iron Guardists, considering the village as the foundation of Rumaniandom, called his fellow writers to a new crusade for the emancipation of the oppressed. He wanted the man of letters to seek inspiration in the hamlets where the natives with their lore, songs, and tales have survived all the trials of time and shifting conditions. The criticism of the younger set, interesting and versatile, has followed in the main about the same trends.

See: G. Adamescu, *Contribuțiune la bibliografia românească* (1921–1928); L. Feraru, "The Development of the Rumanian Novel," *Romanic Review,* XVII (1926), 291–302, *The Development of Rumanian Poetry* (1929), and "Rumanian Literature," *New International Encyclopaedia Supplement* (1930), Vol. II.

L. F.

Rusiñol, Santiago (1861–1931, Catalonian novelist, dramatist, and essayist), was born in Barcelona. His father was a businessman, and the son followed this example until he was 25. This period of his life and the atmosphere of Barcelona at that time are described in his novel (which was later dramatized) *L'auca del senyor Esteve* (Spanish tr. by G. Martínez Sierra, 1908). From then on until his death he devoted himself to painting and to literature. He died at Aranjuez, a royal country place with which his memory will always be associated, for he was the painter of its gardens. He painted the gardens of all the regions of Spain; it was in this field that he achieved his greatest artistic success, his work showing great originality. His book *Jardins d'Espanya* (1903; Spanish tr., *Jardines de España,* 1914) contains 40 reproductions of these paintings with comments by the author. His literary works, which were almost always written in Catalan and translated into Spanish, were many and varied and achieved great popularity throughout Spain. They include collections of articles on life, travels, and scenery such as *Anant pel mon* (1896), *Oracions* (1897), *Fulls de la vida* (1898), and *L'illa de la calma* (*ca.* 1922; Spanish tr., *La isla de la calma*), the last a description of the island of Majorca. He is the author of novels as well, the most outstanding being *El poble gris* (1902; Spanish tr. by G. Martínez Sierra, 1904), a satirical description of small-town life. But most famous of all are his dramatic works, among them the operetta *L'alegria que passa* (1901; Spanish tr. by Vital Aza, *La alegria que pasa,* 1906), *El pati blau* (1903; Spanish tr., *El patio azul*), and *El mistic* (1904; Spanish tr. by J. Dicenta, *El mistico,* 1904). *El mistic* enjoyed a huge success in all Spain because of its religious and historical significance, dealing as it did with the life of the greatest of Catalonian poets, the priest Jacint Verdaguer (*q.v.*). In all these many and diverse works there exists the unity which comes from the temperament of the author —a blend of humor and sentimentality, of the joy of living and wry skepticism, of brutal realism and romantic idealism.

See: G. Desdevises du Dézert, *Le Théâtre catalan de Santiago Rusiñol* (1906); Rubén Darío, *Cabezas* (1919), pp. 29–35; J. Ochoa, *Santiago Rusiñol; su vida y su obra* (1929); J. Passarell and A. S. Escó, *Vida, obra i anecdotes d'en Santiago Rusiñol* (1931).

F. de O.

Russian literature. The violent death of Tsar Alexander II in 1881 came at the end of Russia's greatest age of fiction. Dostoevski (*q.v.*) died in 1881 and Turgenev (*q.v.*) two years later. Tolstoy (*q.v.*) lived on to 1910, but in 1880, after he had experienced his unique spiritual transformation, he turned his back on the kind of art that had produced *War and Peace* and *Anna Karenina.* In another respect, too, the assassination marked the end of an old and the beginning of a new literary era. There followed a period of black reaction. The revolutionary movement was suppressed, radical publications were banned, and in general progressive intellectual thinking dwindled to a vanishing point.

In such circumstances it was only natural that during the reign of Alexander III (1881–1894) literature should react violently against the utilitarian direction and social significance of the preceding period. Authors eschewed the tendentious and preferred to grapple with a content of more universal implications. The new criticism no longer cried out for literature with a social purpose; it called for more attention to form and beauty.

The towering shadow of the white-bearded prophet Tolstoy dominated the fiction writers between 1880 and 1900. It was the great novels before his spiritual revelation that they sought to imitate and not the occasional but fine tales that seemed to drop from his pen by chance after 1880 amid a sea of religious and didactic works. One of the first and best of the new generation of fiction writers influenced by Tolstoy and partly by Turgenev was V. M. Garshin (*q.v.*). The fame of his tragically brief creative life rests on a series of short stories, the most notable of which, particularly "Krasny tsvetok" (1883; Eng. tr., "The Scarlet Blossom," in *The Signal and Other Stories,* 1912), reveal a moral sensitivity and an infinite compassion for the injured and thwarted victims of man's inhumanity. The matter and not the manner of his narratives pleases, and his fondness for the morbid became the hallmark of so many writers of this feckless age.

If radicalism had a real literary representative during this period of repression, it was V. G. Korolenko (*q.v.*). His first important work, "Son Makara" (1885; Eng. tr., title story in *Makár's Dream and Other Stories,* 1892), written in the year he was allowed to return to Russia from exile in Siberia, is the story of a Yakut. Succeeding tales draw upon his Siberian experiences. With a poet's feeling, and directly in the tradition of Turgenev, he describes the stark beauty of the snowy wastes of the North. His characters are often victims of man's exploitation. At best, Korolenko's radicalism is a form of idealism, a yearning after that state of society when man's innate goodness will finally triumph. Invariably he brings his stories down to earth by a delightful humor, as charming as Gogol's funmaking in his early tales. Korolenko deserves a place as a minor classic among Russian writers.

Indeed, Korolenko's rank as a writer of fiction would have been first among his contemporaries if his principal rival had not been Anton Pavlovich Chekhov (*q.v.*). It was not until "A Dreary Story" in 1889 that Chekhov entered upon his mature period. Here we find that mutual lack of understanding among characters and the psychological development of a mood that combine to form the familiar "Chekhovian state of mind." In this new manner there soon followed those perfect little masterpieces, "The Duel," "Ward 6," "An Anonymous Story," "My Life," and others. They are tight, compact expressions of autumnal moods; subtly contrived emotional and symbolic overtones fit naturally into a marvelously unified construction. His characters lack individuality, for the emphasis is placed on the creation of a poetic atmosphere. This same trait is also very pronounced in his highly popular and unique dramas. The striking undramatic quality of his plays is not an innovation, as is commonly supposed, but simply a further refinement of something already found in certain plays of Ostrovski and especially in those of Turgenev. As in the stories, the dominant note is one of gloom, depression, and futility subtly intensified by an underlying emotional symbolism.

After the golden age of poetry with Pushkin and his immediate disciples (1800–1840), the muse was silenced, or nearly so, by the wonderful flowering of prose fiction. Only the lyric sweetness and exquisite craftsmanship of Tyutchev and Fet and the social realism of the vigorous verse of Nekrasov could compete for public favor with the great novels. In the late 80's and early 90's, however, there was something of a revival in poetry. "Beauty" and "melancholy" became popular themes. The so-called "civic poets" mouthed their melancholy over social injustice in indifferent verse, and the "art for art's sake" poets indulged a melancholy love for pure beauty which they distilled from a variety of lost causes.

The most popular of the civic poets was S. Y. Nadson (*q.v.*). His principal rival for popular favor was A. N. Apukhtin (*q.v.*), whose poetry reflected the same impotent regret, but it was a hedonist's regret for the lost pleasures of youth and was expressed in a more virile, realistic verse.

Rising considerably above the thriving but undistinguished level of poetry during this period was the verse of V. S. Solovyov (*q.v.*). A man of extraordinary contrasts in his intellectual life, Solovyov has won the reputation of being one of Russia's most brilliant philosophical thinkers and cleverest writers of nonsense verse. In poetry he combined the verbal wit and funmaking of a Thomas Hood with the profound mystical experiences of a Blake. His longest poem, *Tri svidaniya* (1891; The Three Meetings), reveals a characteristic thinness of form, but it also combines in a paradoxical manner humorous irreverence with a mystical meaning at once sublime and baffling.

Beneath the oppression and sense of frustration in the 80's and 90's, revolutionary forces were slowly but surely gathering. A new force had also entered the prolonged struggle against autocracy—that of Russian Marxism. The fundamentally scientific doctrine of Marx appealed strongly to disillusioned intellectuals and brought new hope to the whole radical movement. By a miracle of compromise, all liberal and radical forces managed to form a united front against the government; their efforts culminated in the disastrous 1905 Revolution. The high hopes of the revolutionists were blasted, and their disillusion found expression in literature in an antipolitical individualism, in the growth of aestheticism, and often in fiction of a pronounced erotic nature.

The popular school of fiction at this time, and one that drew much of its inspiration from the realism of Chekhov, had as its earliest and most powerful representative Maxim Gorky (*q.v.*). His initial service was to liberate Russian realism from its conservative traditions, for the realism of the great novelists from 1850 to 1900 had been subject to the same restraints and conventions as the realism of English Victorian fiction. Gorky belonged to the provincial proletariat, and he already had had a background of bitter experiences among the lost men and women of Russia's lower depths when he attracted international notice before he was 30 with two volumes of collected stories (1898). The tales strike a characteristic note—profound interest in the misery of Russia's masses. In these forgotten people Gorky sees a poetry, a dignity and beauty, and a strength that will one day enable them to throw off their shackles.

To Gorky's second period belong novels such as *Foma Gordeyev* (1899; Eng. tr., 1901),

Mat (1907–1908; Eng. tr., *Mother,* 1907), and *Matvei Kozhemyakin* (1911), concerned with the vicious life and immorality of provincial Russia. Their somber, bitter realism is only occasionally relieved. Endless talk about the "meaning of life," a penchant for philosophizing of which Gorky never rid himself, is one of the worst features. This same fault serves to make his plays rather bad imitations of Chekhov, although *Na dne* (1902; Eng. tr., *The Lower Depths,* 1912) achieved vast popularity both in and outside of Russia. This period of novels and plays was soon followed by another, in which Gorky devoted himself largely and with great success to autobiographical writing and to a wonderful volume of recollections of the authors he had known.

Gorky's radical activities before 1917 and his declared sympathies for the Communists won him a place as the foremost literary figure of the Soviet Revolution, a place that he retained until his death in 1936. He performed many valuable cultural services for the new regime, and hordes of young Soviet authors regarded him reverentially as their master. Although most of his fiction presents a picture of Russian life that is so dark, cruel, and ugly, it is not essentially pessimistic, for rising above the pervading gloom is always the vision of another brighter and happier Russia. Gorky always leaves one with the feeling that Russia is still the most wonderful country in the world, where "even the fools are original."

Around Gorky and his publishing firm Znaniye there rallied a group of writers who reveled in outspoken realism and went as far in the direction of revolutionary protest as the government authorities would permit. Prominent among them were Y. N. Chirikov, V. V. Veresayev (*qq.v.*), Ivan Shmelyov (1875–), A. Serafimovich (*q.v.*), and Skitalets (S. G. Petrov, 1868–). Of greater stature, however, were three or four authors who belonged to Gorky's generation and in certain respects were influenced by him, but they were all men of original ability, and at least two of them possessed literary talent of a very high order.

Poyedinok (1905; Eng. tr., *The Duel,* 1916) made A. I. Kuprin (*q.v.*) famous over night. This novel of army life was the logical successor of a series of early stories, in which morbid young army officers brood over the meaning of life, and wretched soldiers suffer under the brutality of their superiors. There is more of the influence of Chekhov than Gorky in it, and the character drawing is well done. Kuprin's succeeding novels, such as *Izumrud, Sulamif* (1908; Eng. tr., 1923), and *Yama* (1912; Eng. tr., 1922), also popular, represent a falling off in artistic power. Something of a sensation seeker in subject matter, his considerable ability was often forced to serve themes for which he had no natural aptitude.

I. A. Bunin (*q.v.*) was a nominal follower of Gorky in his youth, but he has closer literary ties with such predecessors as Turgenev, Tolstoy, and Chekhov, and in some respects he is a finer artist than any of the writers of Gorky's generation. Although a poet of some distinction, it is as a novelist that he has achieved his greatest fame. His stories began to appear as early as 1892, but his first novel, *Derevnya,* was not published until 1910 (Eng. tr., *The Village,* 1923). This book was followed by some of his best fiction—*Sukhodol* (1912; Eng. tr., "Dry Valley," in *The Elaghin Affair and Other Stories,* 1935), *Chasha zhizni* (1914; The Cup of Life), and his famous story *Gospodin iz San Frantsisko* (1916; Eng. tr., *The Gentleman from San Francisco,* 1923). In *The Village* Bunin left behind him the sentimental stories of his early period and wrote a bitter realistic social novel of the misery and primitivism of Russian country life. The peasant is faithfully portrayed. Gorky's fault of excessive philosophizing, in *The Village,* is overcome in "Dry Valley," perhaps Bunin's greatest work, the concentrated story of the disintegration of a landowning family told from the point of view of a female servant. Bunin is a strange combination of the realist and the romantic, and at his best he is one of the most original writers of Russian prose today.

The author who for a time became a serious rival of Gorky for popular favor was Leonid Andreyev (*q.v.*). His first short stories show the influence of the new realism of Gorky, and in his favorite themes of death and sex he was inspired by Tolstoy's later fiction. After the failure of the 1905 Revolution, Andreyev catered to the widespread disillusion by treating death and sex in a morbid and sensational manner. He became the leader of a short-lived group of fiction writers whose outlook was entirely nihilistic. His early style, learned from Tolstoy's problem stories, is restrained, logical, and effective; later he is sensational, shrill, rhetorical, and full of bad taste. Yet this second style was tremendously admired in his day as he used it in such famous stories as "Krasny smekh" (1904; Eng. tr., *The Red Laugh,* 1905), "Tak bylo" (1906, Thus It Was; Eng. tr., title story in *When the King Loses His Head and Other Stories,* 1920), "Judas Iscariot" (1907; Eng. tr. in *The Crushed Flower and Other Stories,* 1916), and "Proklyatiye zverya" (1908; The Curse of the Beast). Andreyev became a specialist in madness and horror, and his persistent message was physical death and the annihilation of society, morals, and culture. Occasionally he would revert to his early restraint, as in two of his finest tales, "Gubernator" (1906; The Governor) and "Rasskaz o semi poveshennykh" (1908; Eng. tr., *The Seven Who Were Hanged,* 1909), the latter a story of five terrorists and two common murderers. Although highly representative of one phase of the period in which he lived, Andreyev by no means measured up to the qualities of the best artist. There was more tinsel and fake than sincerity and human sympathy.

In this fiction of pessimism the only popular rival of Andreyev was M. P. Artsybashev (*q.v.*). His enormously successful novel *Sanin* (1907; Eng. tr., *Sanine,* 1914) was a response to the sexual emancipation that reflected one aspect of the nihilism of despair gripping the intelligentsia after the failure of the 1905 Revolution. The theme was one that has been run into the ground in modern fiction—be true to yourself and follow your natural inclinations. With Artsybashev, the natural inclinations were all reduced to carnal desire.

Various forces were at work in the 90's in opposition to the Gorky-Andreyev school and particularly to the dominance of social significance and nihilistic thought in literature. There was a definite turning away from civic morality to aestheticism, from duty to beauty, and cultural and individual values were stressed at the expense of political and social values. Most of the participators in this movement were brilliant intellectuals; their efforts represented a degree of cultural refinement that had never been achieved by any literary group in Russia hitherto. Aesthetic, mystic, and religious philosophers took part in this revolt against the civic-minded intelligentsia, and much of the impetus was provided by those extraordinary painters and writers on art, Diaghilev and Benois, in their lavish monthly magazine, *Mir iskusstva* (The World of Art), founded in 1898.

One of the earliest and most influential of the modernists was D. S. Merezhkovski (*q.v.*). After an initial volume of conventional verse in 1888, he emerged as the champion of the "new ideas" of a group of writers, among whom were prominent his talented wife, Zinaida Hippius (*q.v.*), N. M. Minski (*q.v.*), and Volynski (A. L. Flekser, 1863–1926). A certain vagueness characterized the revolt in its early stages, but over the next few years Merezhkovski devoted a stream of philosophic criticism, historical novels, plays, and pamphlets to elaborating his central idea concerning the opposition of the Greek conception of the sanctity of the flesh and the Christian conception of the sanctity of the spirit and the necessity of synthesis. This antithetical approach in one aspect or another dominated nearly everything he wrote, until it resulted in a kind of ideological madness that seriously vitiated his literary performance. In one of his best-known works, *Tolstoi i Dostoyevski,* Tolstoy becomes the "seer of the flesh" and Dostoevski the "seer of the spirit." Merezhkovski was the founder of the Religious-Philosophical Society which provided, at the turn of the century, a meeting ground for God-seeking intellectuals.

Religious-philosophical speculation became the province of some of the most original minds. As in the case of Merezhkovski, Dostoevski inspired much of this theorizing. V. V. Rozanov (*q.v.*) first attracted general attention by his study *Legenda o velikom inkvizitore* (1890; The Legend of the Grand Inquisitor), a penetrating commentary on the incident in *The Brothers Karamazov.* In a series of later works he went on to attack the ascetic religion of Christ to which he opposed the primitive naturalistic religion that he found in the Old Testament. There was a pronounced amoralism in his thinking that takes the form of a phallic symbolism.

Like him, Leo Shestov (*q.v.*), also an irrationalist and an amoralist, found his starting point in Dostoevski, but he was also much influenced by Nietzsche (*q.v.*), who attracted many Russian writers at this time. Shestov warred against idealism in all its forms (*e.g., Potestas Clavium,* 1916). He was a seeker after God, but it was a God divorced from the good and reason, a God that transcended the traditional standards of morality and logic. Besides being highly independent thinkers, Rozanov and Shestov are remarkable for the excellence of their prose style.

The emphasis upon aesthetics and mysticism in the works of such writers as Merezhkovski, Rozanov, and Shestov provided an easy transition to symbolism, for a mystical interpretation of the world was an aesthetic principle held in common by nearly all the Russian symbolists between 1890 and 1910. Baudelaire and Mallarmé (*qq.v.*) helped to inspire this new movement, but Russian writers, unlike the French, deliberately made a philosophy of symbolism as well as a new form of poetical expression. A new vocabulary or, better, a new way of using old phrases, a subordination of sense to sound, and a symbolic use of words produced that impression of obscurity which became associated with writers of the movement. Everything became significant to them, not in itself, but as a reflection of something else.

Perhaps to V. Y. Bryusov (*q.v.*) belongs the credit for starting the movement with a collection of poems published in *Russkiye simvolisty* (Russian Symbolists) in 1894. For some 10 years he had been regarded as a kind of poetical fraud, and his verses had been the chief butt of the critics, but by 1906 he had won his long battle and was accepted as the head of a school that represented the whole of Russian poetry at the time. His poem *Stephanos,* published in 1906, aroused enthusiasm, and his review, *Vesy* (The Balance), was accepted as the most cultured and authoritative publication in the country. Though a weaver of gorgeous imagery that is often more gaudy than meaningful, Bryusov's poetic and even his prose style frequently bears the traces of chilly, studious premeditation.

K. D. Balmont (*q.v.*) shared with Bryusov the honor of being one of the first of the symbolists in the field by virtue of his early volume of verse, *Pod severnym nebom* (1894; Under Northern Skies). There is more sound than sense in Balmont's poetry, nothing of the intellectual quality of Bryusov's, and very little of the symbolic quality characteristic of the whole school. Succeeding volumes of verse added to his reputation for possessing a sense of form and richness of rhythm almost unique among Russian poets. But in his voluminous later works the richness began to cloy and the patterns of sound became monotonous.

Bryusov and Balmont were more interested in the language of poetry than in its content, and their symbolism was more a matter of theory than practice. With this movement, however, were soon associated a group of writers, some of them of remarkable talent, who brought a subtle intellection and at times a profound philosophical quality to the literature of symbolism. Zinaida Hippius reveals in both her prose and her poetry a fondness for abstract ideas and an unusual skill in psychological observation. A more flawless and delicate symbolist poet was I. F. Annenski (*q.v.*), whose *Kiparisovy lavets* (The Cypress Chest), published in 1910, a year after his death, contains a small collection of lyrics that for compression, subtleness, and precision were scarcely equaled by any of the other symbolist writers.

Annenski was a classical scholar of some note, but he failed to make the Greek spirit as definite a part of his intellectual equipment as did a still greater Greek scholar and contemporary symbolist poet, Vyacheslav Ivanov (*q.v.*). The mystic religions of Greece have left their mark on Ivanov's thought in a curious identification of Christ and Dionysus. Like most of the symbolists, he welcomed the Revolution of 1905 and became the prophet of a new revolutionary philosophy that has been popularly denominated mystical anarchism. Between 1905 and 1911 Ivanov remained the leader of the Petersburg symbolists, opposing his doctrine that art was a mystical religious activity to that of the Moscow symbolists, headed by Bryusov, who believed that the autonomy of art must be preserved against religion and philosophy. His best verse is contained in two volumes entitled *Cor Ardens* (1911), in which the ornate style reaches a high degree of perfection. Ivanov's poetic language has a carefully wrought Byzantine richness about it, and the prevailing subject matter is metaphysical. After the 1917 Revolution he accepted the new order and lent his great talents to the Communist cause.

Of the symbolist writers already mentioned, all had enjoyed the educational and cultural advantages that went with belonging to upper-middle-class families. One of the most remarkable authors in the whole symbolist movement, and one of the most refined poets of the earlier group, came from the lower class and made his way to fame under trying material circumstances. This was Sologub (*q.v.*). He did not receive widespread recognition until the publication of his extraordinary novel, *Melki bes* (1907; Eng. tr., *The Little Demon,* 1916). Sologub's peculiar Manichaean attitude towards life, in which he rejected the visible world as something inexpressibly vulgar for an ideal world of beauty of his own creating, is fully revealed in this novel. In *The Little Demon* the real world is depicted as one of incredible misery and squalor, fearfully symbolized by the hero Peredonov, one of the most striking characters in Russian fiction since Dostoevski. Other novels followed, and also short stories and plays, but the essence of the opposition between Sologub's ideal heaven and the evil diversity of the real world in which he lives is most beautifully and compellingly reflected in his poetry. Unlike the other symbolists, his vocabulary, diction, and meters are traditional, though employed with precision and felicity, but he uses words as symbols, in which the secondary and not the ordinary meaning is consistently emphasized.

Perhaps the most original and at the same time the most difficult of the symbolists was Andrei Bely (*q.v.*). Bely's symbolism is expressed through a curious combination of two planes of existence, the actual and the fantastic or irrational. He dissociates reality, changes its proportions, and then substitutes for it a weird, subjective world of his own that is a blend of naturalism and apocalyptic mysticism, in the realization of which Bely often indulges in delightful flights of humor. Although notable as poet, particularly for his metrical experiments, his most important contributions are in prose fiction. A series of novels, starting with *Serebryany golub* (1910; The Silver Dove) and followed by *Peterburg* (1912) and *Kotik Letayev* (1920), to mention only the more notable productions, reveals Bely as an exceptionally original novelist. The direction of his fiction varies from the most difficult philosophical and symbolic writing to a clear Tolstoyan realism, and his style, in its most extreme form, has some of the characteristics of James Joyce's later prose.

An author often associated with Bely, both as a symbolist and a prose stylist, is A. M. Remizov (*q.v.*). One phase of his creative process is thoroughly dominated by a profound knowledge of folk legends and tales, and his manner is deeply influenced by *skaz, i.e.*, a language based on the living speech of the folk. The other important aspect of his creative process is his realism as exemplified by his novels. Such tales as *Povest o Ivane Semyonoviche Stratilatove—Neuyomny buben* (1909; The Story of Stratilatov), an account of provincial life with some striking character creations, and *Pyataya yazva* (1912; Eng. tr., *The Fifth Pestilence*, 1927), another story of provincial life in all its ugliness, are written in a rich, ornamental, and highly mannerized style. Later novels are deliberately simple. Like Bely, he applies to his prose the infinite care that is customarily applied to poetry, and the results have had a powerful influence on succeeding writers of fiction.

Two clear directions had been manifesting themselves in symbolist literature. The first, aesthetic, emphasized refinement of form; the second laid stress on religious-mystical feelings and the creation of dreamworlds often realistically envisaged. These fuse in the works of the greatest of the symbolist poets, A. A. Blok (*q.v.*). His first volume of poetry, *Stikhi o prekrasnoi dame* (1904; Verses about the Lady Beautiful), contained the history of the poet's mystical "love affair" with a person identified with Sophia, the Divine Wisdom, a feminine hypostasis of the Deity, the subject of Solovyov's *Tri svidaniya*. The meaning evades anyone who is not well versed in the mystical experiences of Blok, but the verbal music of this volume revealed a poet of consummate technique. In a subsequent volume, Blok's mystical mistress deserts him and is replaced by an obsession for a strange woman who haunts his dreams. The poet in his disillusionment turns to more earthy and material themes, many of them effectively handled in a characteristic combination of realistic irony and romantic lyricism.

Blok reached his poetical maturity about 1908. Lyrics and longer pieces of great power followed, in which one occasionally obtains a glimpse of a new love—a love of Russia. With this new love came a dawning political consciousness that manifested itself fitfully between lengthening periods of despair. After the 1917 Revolution he found himself on the side of the Soviets, like Bryusov and Bely, but perhaps for different reasons, since Blok saw in the revolt a great cleansing fire that would purify the soul of Russia. And this conception of the Communist Revolution found expression in his greatest poem, *Dvenadtsat* (1918; Eng. tr., *The Twelve*, 1920), a miracle of revolutionary mysticism and metrical harmony. After this tremendous effort, Blok's revolutionary enthusiasm and poetic fervor gave way again to his chronic despair and passive gloom, and he died three years later (1921), his fame secure as perhaps the greatest Russian poet since Lermontov.

The Twelve was the swan song of symbolism. Blok's own development led him from the abstract in symbolism to the actuality of life. As early as the winter of 1912–1913 new forces began to appear. Two symbolists, Sergei Gorodetski (1884–) and N. S. Gumilyov (*q.v.*), issued a manifesto, in which they declared a revolt against "the mists, shadowy forms, and vague outlines" of symbolism, and announced their intention to "sing the praise of the living world." A new school was formed, called the Acmeists, and its three chief disciples were Gumilyov, a poet of genuine power, Anna Akhmatova (*q.v.*), who wrote brief autobiographical poems notable for their vivid realism and chiseled language, and Osip Mandelshtam (*q.v.*), a poet who laid much stress on form.

Further opposition to symbolism appeared at this time in the declaration and poetry of still another school—the futurists. Igor Severyanin (*q.v.*) was one of the earliest in the field, quickly followed by Velemir Khlebnikov (*q.v.*), with his savage onslaughts on grammar and syntax, and the immensely talented Vladimir Mayakovsky (*q.v.*), who overwhelmed his readers with manifestoes that demanded the destruction of all literary traditions in the name of a new flesh and blood art that would do away with the pale aestheticism of the symbolists and the dry academism of the classics. The poetic program of the original futurist, the Italian Marinetti (*q.v.*), was adopted with Russian variations: verse must now celebrate the modern era of the metropolis, of telephones, cinemas, airplanes, and skyscrapers, and it must do it with a special "wireless imagination" and in a style emancipated from syntax and punctuation.

Meanwhile Russia was plunged into the First World War, which had little immediate effect upon the course of literary development. The February Revolution of 1917 that overthrew the monarchy aroused general enthusiasm, but there was no time for literature. The Bolshevik October Revolution which quickly followed and resulted in the defeat of the Provisional Government was pregnant with all the dark forces of civil war.

The fratricidal struggle lasted from 1917 to 1920, and during these terrible years widespread material privations and the lack of any means of publication almost completely interrupted literary production. Since long prose works were out of the question, poetry was nearly the only literary fare. And much of this was scribbled on scraps of paper and publicly recited by poets to half-fed and half-clothed gatherings in cafés. The man who sprang into sudden fame at this time was Mayakovsky, the futurist, but now he had boisterously accepted the Revolution and roared forth to bewildered listeners a poetry filled with fierce slogans that glorified the proletariat and condemned the bourgeoisie and their effete literature. His principal rival was Sergei Yesenin (*q.v.*), a peasant by birth. Apart from the coarse aggressiveness of his "hooligan poetry," he celebrated in lyrics of ineffable sweetness the joys of the village that would come with the new regime.

The animosities of civil strife and the obvious shape of things to come soon forced nearly all writers to take sides in the bitter struggle. Many of the older writers left the country. Serafimovich, Sergeyev-Tsenski (*q.v.*), and Veresayev stayed behind; Bryusov joined the Communist Party, but was never happy in his allegiance and died in 1924; and Blok embraced the Revolution, but he too lived only a short time after it.

Certain definite tendencies began to manifest themeslves. Marxian critics demanded that a Communist culture should be developed that would reflect the political, social, and economic ideals of the new proletarian regime. In 1920 the Proletkult was organized, to direct the struggle for a proletarian culture on an international scale. The spiritual struggle and tragic sense of futility of the old literature of the intelligentsia were banished and were replaced by a brave acceptance of life and a practical activism.

In their insistence upon the social tasks and duties of the new proletarian literature, the Proletkult authors fell into hopeless wrangling over means and ends. Two schools of thought arose. The moderate school, supported by Trotsky, A. V. Lunacharski, and the critic Voronski, argued that it was impossible to create a proletarian literature by government fiat and that at first much of value could be learned from the old bourgeois art and culture. The extremists, known as the On Guard group, frankly favored the idea of literary dictatorship and demanded a definite class-literature. They were supported by Mayakovsky's LEF (Left Front) group. For a time the moderates won out. One fortunate result was that the pages of the new periodicals were opened to the nonpolitical members of still another group, the Serapion Brothers, founded in 1921. Most of these writers were intellectuals and capable of producing work of high artistic value, but they insisted upon the creative freedom of the individual. At the same time other young authors who, like the Serapion Brothers, accepted the Revolution as an accomplished fact, although they did not personally adhere to Communism, were encouraged to produce by the new dispensation; they were not hostile to the new order, and later most of them definitely accepted it. Trotsky labeled them "fellow travelers" (*poputchiki*), and their efforts helped materially in inaugurating the first positive step forward in Soviet literature.

This first advance manifested itself mostly in fiction and coincided with the period of the NEP (New Economic Policy, 1922–1928). It was almost inevitable that this initial phase should deal with the wealth of material provided by the Revolution and civil war. Stirring events of violence and adventure, many of them lived by the young writers themselves, were eagerly seized upon. One of the earliest works to attract attention for its gruesome depiction of revolutionary violence was *Goly god* (1922; Eng. tr., *The Naked Year,* 1928) by Boris Pilnyak (*q.v.*), who is attracted more by the chaos and the barbaric actions let loose by revolution than by its hopeful ideology.

One of the most brilliant of the early writers on civil war themes is Vsevolod Ivanov (*q.v.*). At first he concentrated his efforts mostly on depicting guerrilla warfare in Siberia in *Partizany* (1922; The Partisans) and

Bronepoyezd 14–69 (1922; Eng. tr., *Armored Train 14–69*, 1933). His civil-war characters are vivid and real, primitive in their emotions and actions, and he has a gift for handling mass scenes.

Another able painter of the romantic side of the civil war is Dmitri Furmanov (*q.v.*), whose best book, *Chapayev* (1923), is an authentic document of a peasant who became the popular commander of a whole division and saved Uralsk from the White forces. Also dealing with authentic material is Isaak Babel's (*q.v.*) *Konarmiya* (1926; Eng. tr., *Red Cavalry*, 1929), a collection of stories based on the author's experiences with Budyonny's Cossacks. These brief sketches are told with extraordinary concentration and a consummate mastery of the racy language of the Cossacks.

On the whole, this early fiction dealing with the Revolution and civil war was concerned with forthright realistic or documentary narrative and eschewed the psychological analysis of the old Russian masters. Although the initial tendency had been to condemn all literature of the past in building a new proletarian culture, the very leaders of the Communist Party stressed the need of learning from the best prerevolutionary writers. And over this early period of the New Economic Policy novelists began to appear who treated themes connected with civil strife, but with a different emphasis and often in the traditional manner of Dostoevski, Tolstoy, and Chekhov.

Konstantin Fedin (*q.v.*) was one of these authors, and his novel *Goroda i gody* (1924; Cities and Years) aroused great interest. It is the story of a Russian prisoner of war in Germany who returns to engage in revolutionary activity. The hero is a self-centered intellectual, and the story concerns his inner struggle, in which he eventually betrays the Revolution. Fedin treats revolution not as a glorious event, but as a profoundly disturbing psychological problem.

There is the flavor of Chekhov's Russia in Fedin's tales and of Dostoevski in the spiritual doubts of his heroes. Dostoevski's influence, however, is much more pronounced in the art of Leonid Leonov (*q.v.*), one of the most distinguished Soviet novelists. In Leonov's first full-length novel, *Barsuki* (1924; The Badgers), a typical Dostoevskian psychological approach is employed in the development of characters cast against a background of revolution. The theme is the fierce antagonism between town and village represented in two brothers, one a city-bred Communist, the other a village kulak.

Leonov's tendency to blend analysis with the description of social events and their implied psychological problems became more pronounced in his later works. Critics praised his fiction as a bridge between Soviet realists and the classics of the past, a compliment that clearly indicated the bankruptcy of the early attempts to create a self-contained proletarian literature by laboratory methods. This link with the past is still more deeply rooted in A. N. Tolstoy (*q.v.*), who had acquired literary fame before the Revolution. Of first-rate importance is his trilogy, *Khozhdeniye po mukam* (1921–1941; partial Eng. trs., *The Road to Calvary*, 1923, *Darkness and Dawn*, 1935; complete tr., *Road to Calvary*, 1946), in which he presents a picture of Russia before, during, and after the Revolution. The picture is authentic, most of the characters are thoroughly alive, and his language, as nearly always with A. N. Tolstoy, is most effective.

Alexander Fadeyev's (1901–) first novel, *Razgrom* (1926, The Rout; Eng. tr., *The Nineteen*, 1929), betrays the obvious influence of Leo Tolstoy in its fresh realism and clear psychological insight. Like Vsevolod Ivanov, Fadeyev exploits his special knowledge of Siberia, for *Razgrom* paints a broad, exciting picture of the civil war in that region. The work won him immediate fame, and he took a place among the leading Soviet writers with his next and longest novel, *Posledni iz Udege* (The Last of the Udegs), which began to appear in 1929. Again the locale is Siberia and the main action concerns the civil war.

These writers of fiction in the early period of Soviet literature vary in their technique, yet it is clear that a well-marked tendency to return to the traditional realistic manner began to increase after 1927. Some authors, however, were confessed followers of the modernistic, almost James Joycean, technique of Bely and Remizov.

The period of the New Economic Policy was succeeded by the first Five-Year Plan which Stalin inaugurated in 1928. The slogan was "Socialism in One Country," and again, as in the days of the Proletkult, an attempt was made to regiment literature. A few interested Communists, with the critic Averbakh in the lead, seized control of the Russian Association of Proletarian Writers (RAPP) and laid down the uncompromising program that the depiction of the Five-Year Plan and of the class war within its framework was the only problem of Soviet literature. An extensive campaign began, and all who refused to hew to the line found themselves outlawed. The results of this "planned literature" were for the most part unsatisfactory. Widespread discontent arose, and finally in 1932, largely through the influence of Gorky, a government edict dissolved the Russian Association of Proletarian Writers, and the literary dictatorship was brought to an end. A general Association of Soviet Writers was formed which was thrown open to all; leading authorities expressed the belief that the majority of Soviet authors sympathized with the efforts of socialist construction and that it was pointless to demand of them outward proofs of political loyalty. The extremists were defeated and once again the lesson was driven home that literature can not flourish in chains.

The Five-Year Plan, in fact, provided plenty of material for fiction, and various writers treated it in various ways. Leonov, after his novel *Vor* (1925; Eng. tr., *The Thief,* 1931), which dealt with the period of the New Economic Policy, turned his attention to socialist reconstruction in two novels *Sot* (1930; Eng. tr., *Sot,* 1931, American title, *Soviet River,* 1932) and *Skutarevski* (1933; Eng. tr., 1936). The first of these deals with the transformation of a northern wilderness into a busy center of the paper industry, and the second concerns a large-scale electrification task. Scientific technicalities abound in these tales of socialist reconstruction, but Leonov's characteristic Dostoevskian concern for the "inner man" and his spiritual doubts over the blessings of the Revolution are everywhere in evidence.

Another fellow traveler, Pilnyak, took up the theme of reconstruction in his novel *Volga vpadayet v Kaspiskoye more* (1930; Eng. tr., *The Volga Falls to the Caspian Sea,* 1931). The plot involves the family tragedies of three engineers who are engaged in the task of diverting the course of a river, and the narrative is freely sprinkled with the technical details of construction, a practice generally adopted by the novelists of this period, and one that may have had an educative value but makes for hard reading. The novel clearly suggests that Pilnyak found it hard to accept the vast industrialization program. In his more recent work, *Sozrevaniye plodov* (1936; The Ripening of the Fruit), he evinces for the first time what seems like a sincere enthusiasm for the aims of the Soviet regime.

One of the most laboriously documented novels of socialist reconstruction was F. V. Gladkov's (*q.v.*) *Energiya* (1933; Energy). He had previously written a tremendously popular novel, *Tsement* (1924; Eng. tr., *Cement,* 1929), that had described the zest with which the workers turned to social and economic reconstruction once civil war had ended. *Energiya* tells the story of Dneprostroi and of the men and women who built the vast construction. What was intended to be a great human epic of socialist labor and triumph runs dangerously close to being simply the excessively detailed reporting of a tremendous feat of engineering.

Much better as a reconstruction novel was Valentin Katayev's (*q.v.*) *Vremya vperyod!* (1932; Eng. tr., *Time, Forward!* 1933), which tells the story of shock brigades competing in the pouring of cement. The action consumes only 24 hours, and the narrative moves with verve and excitement, for Katayev, one of the best Soviet novelists, is a master in depicting external action. While obvious sincerity, real joy, and justifiable pride were manifested in much of this fiction concerning the extraordinary accomplishments in the rapid industrialization of the country, a great many second-rate novels were turned out that pandered to the propaganda motifs of reconstruction at the expense of art. The unvarying pattern of Communist workers frustrating the efforts of bourgeois wreckers grew monotonous and often stupid.

To this period also belongs the flowering of the genius of perhaps the greatest novelist in Soviet literature—Mikhail Sholokhov (*q.v.*). He began his long epic of Cossack life, *Tikhi Don* (The Silent Don) in 1926–1930, but interrupted it to write *Podnyataya tselina* (1932–1933; Eng. tr., *Virgin Soil Upturned,* American title, *Seeds of Tomorrow,* both 1935), a novel dealing with the life of the new collective-farm Cossacks. Sholokhov then returned to his masterpiece, which was not finished until 1940. He is the most Tolstoyan of Soviet novelists. There is much of Tolstoy's epic sweep and his wonderful sense of realism in *The Silent Don* (Eng. tr., 1942; this translation earlier appeared in two volumes, *And Quiet Flows the Don,* 1934, *The Don Flows Home to the Sea,* 1940), and Sholokhov's restraint and sense of proportion, his delicate handling of contrasts and parallels, and the simplicity of his character drawing are qualities that remind one of Tolstoy.

In the whole development of fiction up to this point, there was no lack of criticism of Soviet life, a fact not commonly appreciated abroad. Satire was a favorite weapon, and although it was often directed against capitalist civilization, satire of the vices and foibles of Soviet life and the absurdities of Soviet officialdom was freely tolerated, provided it did not attack the fundamental ideals of the new order.

Y. I. Zamyatin (*q.v.*), an older writer, was a powerful satirist; Ilya Ehrenburg (*q.v.*) combines a clever vein of satire with a bright attractive style; Bulgakov's *Dyaboliada* (1925; The Deviliad) pokes fun, not always good-natured, at Soviet life and bureaucracy; Katayev's fine novel *Rastratchiki* (1927; Eng. tr., *The Embezzlers,* 1929) is a mordant satire on two naïvely irresponsible state officials who steal; and two of the most recently popular satirical and humorous writers and devoted collaborators have been Ilya Ilf and Yevgeni Petrov (*qq.v.*). The most widely read Soviet humorist, however, is Mikhail Zoshchenko (*q.v.*). An early member of the Serapion Brothers, he lately has become a loyal supporter of the Soviet regime. More than 10 volumes of his short stories have been published. Small incidents and comic trifles are most often his themes, but beneath the humor there is always latent a deft criticism of the abuses, foibles, and vices of Soviet life.

During the period of the Five-Year Plan, and even earlier, novelists by no means neglected those vitally real ethical problems that arose from the conflict of the new Communist conscience and ideals with the traditional views on sex, love, marriage, and the family. Such problems concern Sergeyev-Tsenski, a writer of the old school, who has become a prominent Soviet novelist. The transition from bourgeois Russia to the new Soviet society is the principal theme of his series of ambitious novels beginning with *Preobrazheniye* (1923; Eng. tr., *Transfiguration,* 1926). With a somewhat similar theme in mind, Panteleimon Romanov (*q.v.*) designed a series of novels under the general title *Rossiya* (Russia), but he soon abandoned this larger project for separate novels on less complicated aspects of the early period of Soviet life. Yuri Libedinski (*q.v.*) also addresses himself to ethical and social problems, especially in his best work, *Rozhdeniye geroya* (1930; The Birth of a Hero), in which he writes of love, family, and education in Soviet society.

In the early days of the Revolution, Mayakovsky and his followers rang the death knell of symbolism. But the futurism that displaced symbolism soon betrayed its inadequacies. The telegraphic language and wireless imagination of the futurists baffled the proletariat. And Mayakovsky eventually abandoned his poetic excesses, brought his muse down to the proletarian earth, and turned his great talents with a will to the service of the Revolution. He wrote poems about bread prices, the New Economic Policy, the food supply, and international events. He declared war on sensibility, meditation, and tenderness, and no doubt his denying these qualities, which were a genuine part of his nature, contributed to the disillusionment that helped to bring about his unfortunate suicide in 1930.

By insisting upon the communal function of verse, Mayakovsky exercised a tremendous influence on subsequent poetry. His demand that Soviet poets participate in social creation and life was enthusiastically accepted by many younger writers, but none of these followers could equal the effectiveness of his message, and certainly none possessed the unique dynamism of his rhythms.

The poetry of this first period after the Revolution was declarative, spacious in its ideas, and given to abstract heroics. Soon the poets, like the novelists, were split into various factions by the conflicting demands made upon them by authority, Communist conscience, and socialist needs. Poets found their way out of these controversies with much more difficulty than the novelists. Complicated questions of form and poetics in general were stumbling blocks not easily surmounted by the young untrained peasant and proletarian poets who came to the fore. Unlike fiction, Soviet poetry, except for the works of a few first-rate artists, remained for an excessively long time in a transitional stage. In the struggle between rationalism and emotionalism, mere affirmation of faith unsupported by poetic convictions and imaginative vision led to a reiteration of banalities no less flat than those in the bourgeois verse these young Soviet poets so fiercely condemned.

The real early poet laureate of the Revolution was not Mayakovsky, but Demyan Bedny (*q.v.*), a "Bolshevik whose weapon is poetry," as Trotsky described him. Much of his verse (there are more than 15 volumes of it) consists largely of satirical and humorous commentaries on daily events in Soviet life. A good deal of his poetry hardly rises above the level of doggerel, but the best of it has the authentic ring of genuine folk poetry.

The young writers most immediately influenced by Mayakovsky liked to think of themselves as proletarian poets, although their connection with the working class was often tenuous indeed. They began to flourish after 1923, and by far the most popular of them for a time was A. I. Bezymenski (*q.v.*). For all these younger proletarian poets, devotion to the Communist Party took precedence over devotion to the muse. In bombastic verse that had about as much musicality as a loud yawp, Bezymenski arrogantly dismissed the past and geared his numbers to proletarian realities, as in one of his early works, *Kak pakhnet zhizn* (1924; How Life Smells). As he gathered experience, the party and political propaganda were used less ostentatiously as themes, and a growing realization of the sterner tasks confronting the socialist regime began to creep into his verse.

Among this group of proletarian poets, Alexander Zharov (1904–) is a paler and duller disciple of Mayakovsky; Nikolai Ushakov (1899–), in his *Vesna respubliki* (1927; The Spring of the Republic), is authentically Mayakovskian but possesses a more lyric strain; and Mikhail Golodny (pseud. of M. S. Epstein, 1903–), Ivan Doronin (1900–), and Mikhail Svetlov (1903–) are less proletarian in their themes and more romantic in their treatment of them. A proletarian poet with a larger vision and richer talent than any of those already mentioned is Vasili Kazin (*q.v.*).

Bezymenski, in his *Poema o lyubvi* (1932; Poem about Love), had condemned Mayakovsky's unsocial act of suicide, but Nikolai Aseyev (*q.v.*) honored the dead master's memory in his long narrative poem, *Mayakovski nachinayetsa* (1940; Mayakovsky Starts Off). Aseyev, one of the early futurists and followers of Mayakovsky, accepted the Revolution at its outset and is now regarded as one of the foremost Soviet poets.

An offshoot of futurism was constructivism, a vague movement dedicated to subordinating the imagery and vocabulary of poetry to the theme. The principal theoretician is Kornely Zelinski (1896–), and the chief poet of the movement is Ilya Selvinski (*q.v.*). Selvinski is a realist who stresses the social function of poetry, and in several long verse tales he often displays the art of the novelist as much as that of the poet, but he is quite capable of lyric flights. Another constructivist, although many influences worked upon him, was Eduard Bagritsky (*q.v.*), who died young. Highly talented and with a particularly fine lyric gift, he wrote on a large variety of themes, many of them having no relation to the Revolution, though there can be no doubt about his sympathies.

Boris Pasternak (*q.v.*), who began to write under the influence of the futurists, is generally regarded as the leading Soviet poet today. Essentially lyric, his attempts at long verse narratives, such as *Spektorski* (1926) and *God 1905* (1927), are not well sustained. Pasternak finds it difficult to identify his muse with political and socialistic themes, although he has tried on occasion. For he is primarily an individualist—a highly cultured one—and a romantic, who writes with passionate intensity on the traditional subject of nature, which serves so often as a background for personal lyric utterances. His striking originality finds fullest expression in his language and in varied poetic forms. It is a difficult, elliptical, obscure language, with unorthodox syntactical turns, but the musical and rhythmical effects, built up on the intonations and cadences of ordinary speech, are wonderfully successful.

Pasternak's principal rival for top honors in Soviet poetry today is Nikolai Tikhonov (*q.v.*), although this author possesses neither the same sheer poetic power nor equal originality. On the other hand, he is relatively free of the difficult language and complicated handling of themes that have prevented Pasternak from winning wide popularity. It is not easy to place Tikhonov in any particular poetic school, for since the time of his early narrative verse tales—*Orda* (1922; The Horde) and *Braga* (1923; Brew)—to his later ballads on civil-war themes and his recent poems, he has consistently and independently developed his art largely as a medium for treating romantic themes of revolution in a realistic manner.

It is clear that in its performance in Soviet Russia poetry has lagged behind fiction, as indeed in Western Europe and America over the last 20 years. The doubt, despair, and negation of so much of Western European verse, however, have been absent; Soviet poetry has even been characterized by exuberance and an almost excessive determination to mirror life, albeit a socialistic life. In its efforts to condemn a whole world of emotive complexes and values, Soviet poetry inevitably became a literature of fierce conflicts and action. But the constant, driving change of the new life, which was more easily assimilated by fiction, has proved a deterrent to the healthy growth of poetry, which requires periods at least of calm and contemplation. Most recent Soviet verse, however, bears a promise of greatness for the future; form is grasped with more sureness, and a clear vision of the socialist state lends inspiration where doubt and conflict had formerly confused and enervated positive affirmation.

It has become a critical commonplace to observe that the Soviet theatre is perhaps the finest in the world but that a comparable dramatic literature has failed to materialize. Certainly the native repertoire has not kept pace with the outstanding development in the art of the theatre, yet on a comparative basis the whole corpus of Soviet plays written during the last 25 years is not markedly inferior to that of any nation in the West or of America.

As in all Soviet literature, the drama has

also faithfully reflected the rapid political, social, and economic changes. The dramatists earliest upon the scene were mostly of the intelligentsia and in some cases had practiced their art before the Revolution, such as A. N. Tolstoy, K. A. Trenev (1878–), Nikolai Erdman, A. V. Lunacharski (1873–1933), B. S. Romashov (1895–), and Sergei Tretyakov (*q.v.*). Futuristic, romantic, and realistic tendencies are apparent in their plays, none of which, however, won any enduring success.

A second group of dramatists, most of them peasant and proletarian writers, were concerned with propaganda plays, often crudely executed, and also with plays on the civil war and social problems, such as Alexander Neverov's *Povest o babakh* (1923; A Tale of the Womenfolk), Gladkov's *Vataga* (1923; The Band), and Vladimir Bill-Belotserkovski's (1884–) *Ekho* (1924; Echo) and *Shtorm* (1926; The Storm).

A third group of dramatists, to which belong young Soviet writers with a postrevolutionary training, have contributed plays of considerable merit. Among the best of these dramatists are A. N. Afinogenov, Vladimir Kirshon, V. V. Vishnevski, and N. F. Pogodin.

As in fiction, the pronounced tendency of the drama has been in the direction of realism, in which attempts were made to grapple with the conflicts induced by the swiftly changing tempo of Soviet life. People soon wearied of the forthright propaganda plays, such as Mayakovsky's bizarre *Misteriya Buf* (1918; Eng. tr., *Mystery Bouffe,* 1933) and Tretyakov's rather crude drama of imperialism, *Rychi Kitai!* (1926; Eng. tr., *Roar China,* 1931). A few of the civil-war plays, especially Ivanov's *Armored Train 14–69,* Bulgakov's *Dni Turbinykh* (1926; The Days of the Turbins), and Trenev's *Lyubov Yarovaya* (1926), were well constructed and strikingly realistic.

The Five-Year Plan was as prolific in plays as it was in novels, and a monotonous sameness attended both. Plays were formed to a stereotyped pattern and were often hopelessly and boringly didactic. The invariable theme was a bit of villainous wrecking on a construction job or a collectivized farm, in which the counterrevolutionary plotters were foiled and the good Communists triumphant. Afinogenov's (*q.v.*) fine drama *Strakh* (1931; Eng. tr., *Fear,* 1934) was an exception; although the usual counterrevolutionary conspiracy is present, the play also attempts to solve in terms of individual and not mass psychology the significant moral problem of the Revolution's right to terror. Vladimir Kirshon's (*q.v.*) *Khleb* (1930; Eng. tr., *Bread,* 1934) and N. F. Pogodin's (*q.v.*) *Temp* (1930; Eng. tr., *Tempo,* 1936) were also much better than the average Five-Year Plan plays, despite poor construction and careless language. And Olyosha's (*q.v.*) *Spisok blagodeyani* (1931; List of Blessings), very much like Afinogenov's *Fear,* leaves room for the workings of individual psychology in dramatizing the conflict between individualism and socialism.

Most recent tendencies in Soviet drama in no sense lessen the emphasis upon realism, but they are running in the direction of a fuller comprehension of the individual's problems in a collectivist society. There is a deeper searching into the cause and effect of universal human behavior. And coupled with this is an earnest concern with the Russian people as a whole, unconditioned by time, a tendency that is reflected in historical plays and in the dramatic adaptations of great novels of the past, such as Tolstoy's *Anna Karenina* and *War and Peace.*

More sympathetic understanding than critical explanation is required in order to grasp the real significance of the development of Soviet literature. Ever since its existence began Soviet Russia has been in an almost constant state of emergency, and this fact has often dictated the frequent radical changes and sharp reverses in the life and culture of the country. On the surface there was an abiding impermanency. The more enduring values and universal constants of human behavior, however, were never very far beneath the surface, and this was quite true in the swiftly changing literary trends. The highly specialized Communist conscience in the novels, let us say, of Nikolai Ostrovsky (*q.v.*)—*Kak zakalyalas stal* (1936, How the Steel Was Tempered; Eng. tr., *The Making of a Hero,* 1937) and *Rozhdennye burey* (1937; Eng. tr., *Born of the Storm,* 1939)—could give way to ethical and idealistic trends, to the universal emotions and values that transcend all classes, in the works of a score of other novelists.

Thus one may discern in recent trends distinct links with the past, for social idealism and an interest in the human soul had been pronounced aspects in the literary production of the old intelligentsia. Even the historical novel, of which the past furnished some few brilliant examples, has taken on the proportions of a widespread movement in Soviet Russia, as it has recently in America. The tendency of foreign critics to dismiss this eager interest in the historical past as an enforced escape from dangerous contentious themes of the present is hardly justified. It is only natural that Soviet writers should evince a desire to apply their dialectic method in an effort to reinterpret the past in the light of the present. The method is usually the brutal, realistic one, devoid of sentimental romancing, that has been used so successfully in writing on the civil war, and in most cases the documentation is extraordinarily full.

Pyotr Pervy (1929–1934, Peter I; Eng. tr. of Vol. I, *Peter the Great,* 1932) of A. N. Tolstoy is one of the finest of these Soviet historical novels. He treats the period of the great tsar as one of transition, not unlike that of the present-day Russia, and one can see in the sympathetic portrait of Peter a forerunner of Lenin or Stalin. Where A. N. Tolstoy is largely deficient—in the psychology of his characters—another older writer, Sergeyev-Tsenski, admirably succeeds. Since his expansive novel on the Crimean War, he has recently embarked on a theme connected with the First World War, *Brusilovski proryv* (1944; Eng. tr., *Brusilov's Breakthrough,* 1945).

Two other older writers have devoted themselves to historical fiction. Aleksei Chapygin (*q.v.*) has produced *Razin Stepan* (3 vols., 1926–1927), a thrilling tale of the 17th-century Russian Robin Hood, presented as a kind of early "Bolshevik" leader, but with the authentic atmosphere and local color of Stenka Razin's time exactly recreated. The *Tsusima* (1933–1934; Eng. tr., *Tsushima,* 1936) of Aleksei Novikov-Priboi (*q.v.*) is on a quite different theme—a chronicle of the sinking of the Russian fleet in the Russo-Japanese War.

Yuri Tynyanov's (*q.v.*) historical novels are concerned solely with literary figures of the past—*Kyukhlya* (1925), a story of the pathetically comic Decembrist poet and friend of Pushkin, Küchelbecker; *Smert Vazir-Mukhtara* (1929; Eng. tr., *Death and Diplomacy in Persia,* 1938), which tells the story of the famous dramatist, Griboyedov, in the early years of the 19th century; and *Pushkin* (1936), which portrays the great Russian poet. Tynyanov is more of a scholar than a novelist; his documentation is impeccable and the atmosphere of the past is admirably reproduced, but his characters come to life with difficulty. In these historical novels, and in many others of less note, one is impressed by the repeated emphasis upon the patriotic motif. It is not so much an arrant chauvinism or nationalism as a glorification of the unity and heroism of the past with an appeal for similar qualities now in resisting the enemies of the socialist fatherland. For Soviet Russia was well aware of the dangers from without, and this note of patriotic warning against a definite enemy—Japan—was plainly sounded in Peter Pavlenko's (*q.v.*) novel *Na vostoke* (1937, In the East; Eng. tr., *Red Planes Fly East,* 1938).

A new force is apparent in Soviet literature which clearly sets it apart in the last 25 years from the literature of any other country. The total production, which has been enormous, is thoroughly penetrated by social consciousness and a profound responsibility to the people. Despite the constant flux and new demands of the present, Soviet literature has many of its roots in the past, but it ceaselessly endeavors to integrate all the best elements of the past and present in an effort to create the vision of a glorious future.

The new note may perhaps best be described by the much debated critical slogan, "socialist realism," that first appeared in 1932. However new the term, exponents of socialist realism existed in Russia long before the advent of the Soviets. For writers such as Belinski, Herzen, Chernyshevski, and even Tolstoy, who believed that the individual and the community were not opposing but complementary factors in each other's well-being, were in a sense devotees of socialist realism. Of late, bourgeois realism has displayed a degree of defeatism, frustration, and pessimism that suggests a progressive disintegration of the modern society which it describes. With a loss of faith has come a loss of social consciousness, and the bourgeois writer tends to become self-centered and hostile to the community.

The difference between the Soviet realist and the bourgeois realist is essentially a difference between faith in life and lack of faith. Behind the Soviet writer's accurate description of reality is a desire to obtain a clearer understanding of all that must be abolished and all that must be built up. If there is tragedy in his works, there is no pessimism. Socialist realism attempts to integrate literature and life, to direct the creative present towards a more meaningful creative future. Soviet literature has scarcely begun to realize its vast potentialities, but its present vitality, positive affirmation, and soaring faith give promise of a great future.

See: D. S. Mirsky, *Contemporary Russian Literature* (1926); *Literaturnaya entsiklopediya,* Vols. I–IX, XI (1929–1938); M. Maizel, *Kratki ocherk sovremennoi russkoi literatury* (1931); M. Selivanovski, *Ocherki po istorii russkoi sovetskoi poezii* (1936); Janko Lavrin, *An Introduction to the Russian Novel* (1942),

Paul Miliukov, *Outlines of Russian Culture*, ed. by Michael Karpovich (1942), Part II; A. Kaun, *Soviet Poets and Poetry* (1943); E. J. Simmons, *An Outline of Modern Russian Literature, 1880–1940* (1943); Gleb Struve, *25 Years of Soviet Russian Literature, 1918–1943* (1944).

E. J. S.

Ruyra i Oms, Joaquim (1858–1939, Catalonian prose writer), is the author in whom the narrative prose of the *Renaixença* reached its fullest development, an outstanding figure in all Catalonian literature and unquestionably supreme in his genre during the 19th and 20th centuries. His literary initiation came late; it was not until he was 45 that he produced his first book, *Marines i boscatges* (1903; Seascapes and Coppices). These pieces are models of prose, with all the immutable characteristics of his style; they had been awarded prizes in 1895 at the Jocs Florals (the paramount poetic festival of the Catalan-speaking countries, restored, in 1859, through the impulse of the *Renaixença*). The stories "Mar de llamp" (Sea of Lightning) and "Les senyorestes de mar" (The Young Ladies of the Sea) in particular revealed his great narrative talent. The style was hailed as "trail blazing"; and in 1902, when *Jacobé* (Jacob) was awarded a prize at the same poetic festival, Josep Pijoan enthusiastically exclaimed that the Jocs Florals of that year would forever be identified by *Jacobé,* a short novel "evoked from landscapes possessing a soul," with throbbing figures, with tragic shades, profoundly human.

After *Marines i boscatges* Ruyra i Oms became silent; a grave cardiac illness attacked him, and he moved to the Canary Islands in search of rest. It was not until 16 years later that he reaffirmed the first impression with *La Parada* (The Stop), a collection of stories and short novels. During these years there had been notable changes in the literary tendencies of Catalonia; Ruyra, however, true to himself, a real genius and creator, remained faithful to his initial aesthetic creed. He stood apart from the influence of French naturalism (*q.v.*) and still farther away from romantic affectations of a sentimental tendency. He himself confessed that although many times, suspecting a lack of balance in his imagination, he read Zola (*q.v.*), the French author soon began to lose prestige for him, and he finally could not abide a single page of Zola's novels. Ruyra's style, although deeply personal, has a marked classical-Catalonian basis. The unanimously favorable reception which public and critics gave to Ruyra's new work was linked with the success of *Marines i boscatges* and of *Jacobé*—and the fact is that Ruyra's art will be, for all ages, removed from tendencies and schools. "Amidst my suffering," he wrote when he produced his second book, "I have enjoyed a privilege granted to few men: for, having passed a great number of years dead, as one might say, I have had the pleasure of seeing that my work survived."

Joaquim Ruyra i Oms was born in Gerona, where he pursued the studies of his secondary education; in the University of Barcelona he studied law, abandoning it at the moment when he was to get his degree. He retired then to his ancestral house in Blanes, where he was to write, unhurriedly, with the patience of an embroiderer, the marvelous pages in which the figures of his creation—sailors, workmen, farm boys—are observed not only in their external characteristics but also in the most hidden folds of their simple, candid, and frequently contradictory souls. His penchant for mathematics, to which he had recourse as a means of relaxation from his literary labors, explains in part, perhaps, his style, wherein simplicity, harmonized with a perfect clarity and order of thought, is outstanding. All his work, furthermore, reveals a lofty moral purpose, but one, notably, that is never dull. The same combination is found in his poetic production, especially in "El pais del Pler," an allegorical poem. Many short articles of his, which have their own originality, were published in Catalonian journals, such as the *Renaixença, Veu de Catalunya* (The Voice of Catalonia), *Joventut* (Youth), *Ilustració catalana;* all these pieces, along with the works already mentioned, and his latest books, *Pinya de Rosa* (1920; Cone of Roses) and *Entre flames* (In the Flames), were to be collected in a complete edition of his works planned by the Institució de les Lletres Catalanes, but the project was interrupted by the invasion of 1939. In Arenys de Mar, where Ruyra used to spend a part of the summer, he wrote, finally, *En garet a l'enramada,* an adaptation for the stage of one of his short stories, presented in the Poliorama Theatre in Barcelona. He translated into Catalan poems of Mosco, Horace, Dante, Verlaine (*q.v.*), Racine, and tales of Erckmann-Chatrian. Some of his own works have appeared in Spanish, Italian, French, Finnish. He was a member of the Institut d'Estudis Catalans, the most highly esteemed institution of

Catalonia, distinguishing himself in the philological branch of that body, to which he contributed countless idioms gathered from among the people and which were to enrich the great projected language dictionary, patiently prepared by the Institut, a work also interrupted by the events of 1939.

In 1938, at 80 years of age, he was honored by the Catalonian writers and by the *Govern de Catalunya* in a ceremony of intimate simplicity which took place in the Conselleria de Cultura. When the complete invasion of Catalonia took place, Ruyra remained in Barcelona where he died after a short time. During the war, his attitude—much to be admired because Ruyra was ruined by the resulting revolution—was governed by the Christian and patriotic virtues which were a part of his very fiber and soul. He declared that he would feel himself to be less a Christian if, to defend any theologically isolated religious interests, he should resort to the anti-Christian violence of the Falangists and aid in the destruction of the living work of God, his country, his Catalonia. This explains the official silence at the time of his death. A simple family note—in Spanish—announced to the grief-stricken Catalonian people the death of their great prose writer.

See: J. M. Capdevila, "La obra de Joaquim Ruyra," *Hora de España,* XXI (Sept., 1938), 73–82; C. Riba, "Memoria de Joaquim Ruyra," *Revista de Catalunya* (Barcelona), 4th period, No. 95, pp. 9–16.

J. M. M. i V.

Rydberg, Viktor (1828–1895, Swedish philosopher, poet, and novelist), was born in Jönköping, in the south of Sweden, in humble circumstances. After a long and hard struggle he succeeded in obtaining a classical education at the University of Lund and finally became one of the leading scholars of his time in philosophy and the history of religion. It was, however, in fiction that he first achieved prominence. His first novels, *Fribytaren på Östersjön* (1857; Eng. tr., *The Freebooter of the Baltic,* 1891) and *Singoalla* (1858; Eng. tr., 1903) are romantic adventure stories of the Swedish Middle Ages, but in *Den sista Athenaren* (1859; Eng. tr., *The Last Athenian,* 1869), which is reminiscent of Kingsley's *Hypatia,* he describes the conflict between Hellenic Neoplatonism and early Christianity with a decided preference for the former. He then turned to religious and philosophical studies, combatting the narrow "fundamentalist" views of the time. A trip to Italy in 1870 resulted in *Romerska dagar* (1875–1876; Eng. tr., *Roman Days,* 1879), a series of character studies in which he advocates the democratic spirit and attacks the principle of barren aestheticism.

He finally changed from prose to poetry, translating the first part of *Faust* (1876) and publishing an original collection, *Dikter* (1882; Poems). In these we find him at his best, notably in the stirring "Cantata" for a university festival at Uppsala. He describes the march of humanity in terms of the children of Israel's journey through the desert, in which the four academic faculties of theology, law, medicine, and philosophy are brought into play to meet the various crises of the pilgrimage. Most of Rydberg's poems are symbolistic, but they also include pure lyrics and several charming pictures of Swedish domestic life, in particular "The Bathing Children." All the poems, and indeed his prose works as well, are characterized by an extraordinary grace and purity of form. He translated Poe's "The Raven" and developed another motive taken from the same author in "The Two Bells." Lyric beauty in Rydberg is nearly always subservient to an underlying idea.

In his later life Rydberg returned to the Middle Ages in his novel *Vapensmeden* (1891; The Armorer) and to philosophical and mythological studies. There is a firm unity in his product as a whole. He stands out as a seer and prophet in the cause of spiritual progress and freedom of thought. In him we are continually reminded of Arnold's "sweetness and light," but his style exhibits the vigor of the viking as well as the clarity of the classicist.

See: C. W. Stork, *Anthology of Swedish Lyrics* (1917; revised and enlarged ed., 1930); F. Böök, *Sveriges moderna litteratur* (1921), also published as Vol. III of O. Sylwan, ed., *Svenska litteraturens historia* (1919–1921), pp. 3–20; C. W. Stork, "The Poetry of Victor Rydberg," in A. C. Baugh, ed., *Schelling Anniversary Papers* (1923).

C. W. S.

S

Saar, Ferdinand von (1833–1906, Austrian novelist, dramatist, and poet), born in Vienna, has been unjustly neglected in recent literary criticism, both in Germany and abroad. While there is little reason to revive interest in his carefully composed but unoriginal plays or in his poems with their classical echoes, his two collections of short stories *Novellen aus Österreich* (2 vols., 1897) and *Schicksale* (1889) deserve attention both for their intrinsic value and for the place they occupy in the history of German literature.

A plea for their reconsideration may be supported on a number of grounds. Saar's style of writing strikes a happy medium between academic correctness and idiomatic raciness; local dialect elements are admixed in moderate doses only. As a chronicler of Austrian middle- and upper-class life he imparts a deep understanding of the racial, social, and national difficulties under which the old Austro-Hungarian monarchy disintegrated. His characters—artists, officers, businessmen, and civil servants—all foreshadow the decadence and final catastrophe which overtook this overrefined culture, whose final euthanasia Schnitzler (*q.v.*) was to make the dominant theme of his work. And what especially distinguishes Saar is his most serious concern for the impending decline and his attempt to indicate, more by instinct than with clear consciousness, a possible regeneration. Such sources of renewed vitality he taps in at least two of his stories, "Die Steinklopfer" (1874; Eng. tr., *The Stonebreakers,* 1907) and "Die Troglodytin" (1889). The former has been referred to as the first tale of a workingman in German literature—the deeper implication being that the author here senses the inner strength invested in the working classes. The other story contrasts the healthy sensualism of a child of nature with the conventional standards of bourgeois life. While Saar was not enough of a revolutionary to release the full force of naturalism into life and literature, he at least pointed the way for a younger generation.

See: A. Bettelheim, *Ferdinand von Saars Leben und Schaffen* (1909).

H. B.

Sagarra i Castellarnau, Josep Maria de (1894–, Catalonian poet and playwright), born in Barcelona of an aristocratic family, a descendant of one of the branches of the ancient *Comtes-Reis* (Count-Kings), has made on Catalonian letters an imprint of unparalleled sincerity which has imparted an unmistakable tone to the contemporary lyric poetry of his country. After an elementary education from the Jesuits of Barcelona, he studied law at the university of that city. But he never practiced that profession and devoted himself, from an early age and with extraordinary industry, to literature. His first verses were published when he was 12. At the age of 18 he took a trip through Italy which had definite influence upon his taste and his desire to be a writer. An intimacy with outstanding men of the *Renaixença* facilitated his access to the small Catalonian literary world, which saw one of the hopes of its lyric poetry in this pale youth. At the age of 20 he produced his *Primer llibre de poemes* (1914; First Book of Poems), followed by *El mal caçador* (1916; The Bad Hunter), *Cançons d'abril i de novembre* (1918; April and November Songs), *Cançons de taverna i d'oblit* (1922; Songs of the Tavern and of Forgetfulness), *Cançons de rem i de vela* (1924; Songs of the Oar and the Sail), *Cançons de totes les hores* (1925; Songs of All the Hours). In all this verse one feels originality in style and spirit; he touched the sensibility of his compatriots and had numerous imitators. He uses a living language, direct and without pedantry, elevated through its grace to poetic inspiration. His popularity is easily understood; from the time of the *Renaixença* the Catalonian reader had encountered little but archaisms and artifice whereas Sagarra, like Verdaguer and Maragall (*qq.v.*) indeed, drew idioms for his poems from the people. But, in distinction from his predecessors (with whom he has many points of contact, especially with Maragall), he used, daringly, words which would have seemed inadequate for literature to anyone who did not feel the deep desire for sincerity. His particular manner is clearly discernible in his first novel, *Paulina Buxareu* (1919), and in *All i Salobre* (1929; Garlic and Salt), *Cafè copa i puro* (1929; Coffee, Liqueur and Cigar), and *Vida privada* (1932; Private Life). For the last-named work he was awarded the Crexells prize of the Generalitat (1932).

In 1918 he decided to write for the theatre; his first poetic plays, *Rondalla d'esparvers* (1918; Serenade of Blackbirds) and *Dijous*

Sant (1919; Holy Thursday), were an indication of the ease with which he was to progress in dramatic art; the very tone of his poetry seemed the most suitable for the renovation of the Catalonian theatre, which had turned away from verse. The popularity he attained was extraordinary; from *L'estudiant i la pubille* (1921; The Student and the Maid) to *Roserflorit* (1935; Rosebush in Bloom) he was a central figure. Important theatrical works are: *Les veus de la terra* (1923; The Voices of the Soil); *Marçal Prior* (1926); *L'assassinat de la senyora Abril* (1927, in prose; The Slaughter of Lady April); *L'hostal de la glòria* (1931; The Inn of Glory), for which he received the Ignasi Iglesies prize of the Generalitat. These dramatic poems alternated with farces such as *La Llucia i la Ramoneta* (Lucy and Little Raimona) and *Amàlia, Emèlia i Emilia* (1929). He also cultivated the tragic poem in *Judit* (1929; Judith) and *La filla del carmesi* (1930; The Crimson Daughter). As a result of his extraordinary facility and excessive productiveness, his theatre did become somewhat affected, with recurring types and analogous situations, but was constantly redeemed by the grace and originality of his vocabulary. The same eagerness to portray a popular type and present him with qualities of faith and love, intermingled with the most diverse passions—exemplified already in *El mal caçador*—inspires his most famous and long poem, *El Comte Arnau* (1928; Count Arnau), in which Sagarra, in spite of the monotony of some passages, attains real genius. His last book of poems, *La rosa de cristall* (The Crystal Rose), with which he won the Folguera prize of the Generalitat, demonstrates the continuity of his poetic conception.

When the military insurrection broke out in 1936, Josep Maria de Sagarra, who had written in a column entitled "L'Aperitiu" (a model of original prose which deserves to be collected in an anthology) in the weekly journal *Mirador* (Watchtower) certain diatribes against the disturbing elements of the extreme leftist position, became fearful of reprisals and left for France. There he continued his Catalan version of Dante's *Divina Comedia*. General Franco's victory could not ease Sagarra's position, since in addition to belonging to the party Acció Catalana, whose candidate he had been for deputy, he possessed an incorruptible Catalonian nationalistic sense, incompatible with the Castilian idea of assimilation fostered by the new Spanish regime. In 1941 he returned to Catalonia, but his literary life, at least as far as its external expression is concerned, has not found, in his native country, the slightest opportunity to manifest itself.

See: J. Folguera, *Les noves valores de la poesia catalana* (1919); C. Giardini, *Antologia dei poeti catalani contemporanei, 1845–1925* (1926).

J. M. M. i V.

Saint Exupéry, Antoine de (1900–1944, French aviator and writer), was born in Lyon. He came from an old French family, and one of his ancestors fought with the Americans at Yorktown. His books show the clear traces of a good literary and humanistic education and close affinities with the French "moralists" of the 17th century. He was attracted, soon after the First World War, by a life of action and adventure. He flew as a pilot over the most dangerous sections of the air-mail service established by the French over northwest Africa, the South Atlantic, and South America. He narrowly escaped death in several accidents, some of which are related with a modest and moving restraint in his books.

His first volume, *Courrier Sud* (Eng. tr., *Southern Mail,* 1933) revealed him in 1929 as the epic poet in prose of aviation and as an acute analyst of the changes brought about in the modern relationships between man and woman by the self-abnegation of an airman's career. His second novel, *Vol de nuit* (1931; Eng. tr., *Night Flight,* 1932), was not marred, like the first, by a weak plot and unconvincing sentimentality. André Gide (*q.v.*) introduced it in a striking preface, and it was hailed at once as a masterpiece. Underneath an austere and almost Nietzschean picture of the inhuman role of a leader of men, the book reveals a deep reverence for the nobleness of man. The style, terse and laconic, devoid of mannerisms and obscurity, is rich with splendid images. After eight more years of travel, adventure, and silent meditation, Saint Exupéry's best work to date was published, *Terre des hommes* (1939). Lewis Galantière's able translation does not, by its English title (*Wind, Sand, and Stars,* 1939), render the two characteristic features of the book—a new vision of the earth, seen from the air as an insignificant but beloved planet, and a profound affection for the humblest men. The book is not technically a novel, but a series of tales or vignettes, interspersed with moral and psychological reflections. It preaches no message, but an exalted faith in man's courage and heroism, in the beauty of friendship, of wisdom, and of spiritual freedom, is everywhere present. The same qualities are conspicuous in Saint Exupéry's fourth book, published in New York, *Pilote de guerre* (1942; Eng. tr., *Flight to Arras,* 1942). It is the story of a hopeless sortie accomplished by the author as a captain in one of the reconnaissance crews of the French air force in the tragic days of May, 1940. The facts count for little. The book is mostly an introspective analysis of the flyer's mind and a groping but moving attempt at a statement of his philosophy. He asks the harrowing question, "What is the meaning of war and death?" He answers with an earnest reassertion of his faith in his country, in civilization, in the ultimate victory of love and fraternity. Through their unique position among the books of the decade 1930–1940, through their avoidance of facile effect, their incisive simplicity of style, their gospel of sacrifice and heroic hope, Saint Exupéry's works have deserved to be called the "*Chanson de Roland* of our century."

Saint Exupéry was reported missing over southern France in the summer of 1944.

H. P.

Sáinz y Rodríguez, Pedro (1897–, Spanish scholar and critic), was born in Madrid, where he became professor of bibliology in 1926, after teaching at the University of Oviedo. Most of his studies have been in the fields of Spanish mysticism and of the Spanish 19th century, as exemplified by *La mística española* (1926), for which he was awarded the National Prize for Literature; *Introducción a la historia de la literatura mística en España* (1927); *Estudio sobre la historia crítica literaria en España: D. Bartolomé Gallardo y la crítica de su tiempo* (in *Revue hispanique,* Vol. LI, 1921, pp. 211–595); and *Obras escogidas de Bartolomé José Gallardo* (1928). Two other publications, *La evolución política española y el deber social de los intelectuales* (1924) and *La evolución de las ideas sobre la decadencia española; discurso leido en la inauguración del curso académico de 1924 a 1925* (n.d., *ca.* 1925), show a mild political aspiration which was to blossom in 1933 when he became a member of the Agrarian Party. Since Franco's victory he has been made a member of the Spanish Academy, and he was the new regime's minister of education, 1938–1939.

F. S. y E.

Salacrou, Armand (1900–, French playwright), was born in Rouen. He began to work as a journalist, but soon turned his talents to the theatre. The first 10 years of Salacrou's career in the theatre are represented by the program of the student in the later play, *L'Inconnue d'Arras:* "I wish to be compromised with my own generation." Such was Salacrou's own desire. He made his début with a one-act piece, *Le Casseur d'assiettes* (1924). *Tour à terre* (1925) proved disconcerting to the majority of the critics, but was warmly defended by Lugné-Poe (*q.v.*) and Henry Bidou; Pierre Brisson, insisting on its "absolute originality in literature," used a phrase which connotes both high praise and severe criticism. *Le Pont de l'Europe* (1927) was no less heatedly discussed. It consisted chiefly, with slight dramatic action, of a poem in which a king, reminiscent of Hamlet, expressed in eloquent monologues his dream of becoming "the world's passer-by." The principal character of *Patchouli* (1930) was another dreamer for whom love was something else than happiness. In it Salacrou gave unbounded liberty to his imagination, accepting no literary discipline and yet producing a play impressively lyrical and bitter.

Salacrou's sympathy for failures was again evident in *Atlas-Hôtel* (1931). "God himself has failed; all great enterprises fail"—such was the final speech of Auguste, the Don Quixote of the hotel business. *La Vie en rose* (1931), as the author himself admitted, was nothing more than an excuse for songs, costumes, and setting, offered by one born at the beginning of the century who recalled prewar days through the eyes of his childhood. *Les Frénétiques* (1934) was a vigorous satire of the movie world and its conventional characters, although Salacrou himself did not entirely succeed in creating original figures. In *L'Inconnue d'Arras* (1935) he took for his subject the few seconds granted a dying man to see his life pass before him and to evaluate its true worth. This creation, tender and fantastic, gives Salacrou high rank among dramatists of his generation.

P. B.

Salaverría e Ipenza, José María (1873–1943, Spanish essayist), was born in Vinaroz in the region of Valencia. Of a modest family of Basque origin, he supported himself from an early age. He traveled extensively in Spain and throughout America. Although he cultivated the novel, it was in the journalistic article and especially in the essay that he excelled. As distinguished from the other Spanish essayists of his period, principally those of the Generation of '98, who preached a political and social transformation for Spain in accord with the forward movements of

Europe, Salaverría consistently advocated a return to the old national traditions as the only source of Spanish revival. Faithful to this tenet, his principal themes deal with Spain and her heroes, as in *Vieja España* (1907), *Inigo de Loyola* (1909), *Afirmación española* (1917), *España: Pueblos y paisajes* (1936), *Retrato de Santa Teresa de Jesús* (1939), and *A través del Poema de El Cid* (1941). Salaverría had a thorough knowledge of the Hispanic American peoples as a result of his continuous travels, and many articles, some of them published in the *Nación* of Buenos Aires, deal with these countries. All of these works, such as *El poema de la Pampa, Martín Fierro y el criollismo español* (1918), *Los conquistadores: Origen heróico de América* (1919), *Bolívar el Libertador* (1930), and *El castellano en América* (1939), show the same affirmation of faith in traditional Spanish elements. Other essays, *Nuevos retratos* (1930) and *La generación del 98* (1936), consist of appraisals of contemporary Spanish writers from a traditionalistic point of view. Salaverría's family origin led him also to study certain aspects of Basque life, as in *Alma vasca* (1922) and *Iparraguirre, el último bardo* (1932).

See: A. González-Blanco, *Los contemporáneos,* III (1910), 45–86.

E. G. L.

Šalda, František Xaver (1867–1937, Czech critic, poet, and novelist), is the most prominent literary critic in Czech literature. He was born in Liberec (northern Bohemia), the son of a civil servant. He studied law at the University of Prague, but became a free-lance writer and editor of several critical journals. From 1916 he taught the history of French literature at the University of Prague. In 1928 he founded a journal, *Šaldův zápisník* (Šalda's Notebook), which he wrote himself from cover to cover until his death.

Šalda was a practical critic—a master of portraiture, of psychological interpretation, stylistic analysis, and critical judgment—rather than the expounder of a systematic literary theory. He shifted his point of view frequently in his long career and changed his allegiances, but there is continuity behind the baffling variety of his judgments. He always advocated a vital, contemporary art: this made him in the 90's a champion of symbolism against naturalism and after the First World War the godfather of "proletarian" poetry. He wanted a highly poetical, metaphorical poetry and disapproved of all purely naturalist or didactic writing. But in spite of his stress on form and expression, Šalda was never an aesthete pure and simple; he always understood the responsibility of the artist to society and, especially in his later life, saw literature in close connection with religion and philosophy. His work expanded more and more to a general criticism of society and modern civilization, and in his last years his voice was widely listened to as that of a moralist and prophet. Šalda managed to combine a belief in the value of the individual and of individuality with a stress on the necessity for superpersonal values in literature. The scope of his changing interests can be suggested by noting that his studies include all major figures of modern Czech literature and range over many other literatures as well. He has written on Rousseau and Rimbaud (*q.v.*), on Flaubert and Zola (*qq.v.*), on Shakespeare and Dante; he has discussed such subjects as the immortality of a work of poetry and the relation of art and religion. He has surveyed modern Czech literature several times and has made and unmade the reputation of many Czech writers. Šalda has used all forms of criticism, from careful analyses of style to synthetic and wide surveys of development, from fierce polemics to lyrical meditations. His criticism is written in a very personal style which combines in the vortex of a dynamic temperament the most diverse elements; learned terminology is encountered cheek by jowl with trivial colloquialisms, lyrical metaphors with drastic sarcasms. His critical work has been collected under such titles as *Boje o zítřek* (1905; Battles for Tomorrow); *Duše a dílo* (1913; Soul and Work), his best volume; *Juvenilie* (1925; Early Writings); *Mladé zápasy* (1934; Young Struggles); and *Časové a nadčasové* (1936; Matters Ephemeral and Eternal). Much of his best writing, however, is still scattered in pamphlets, buried in files of short-lived periodicals and newspapers, or mixed with ephemeral polemics in the nine volumes of *Šaldův zápisník* (1928–1937).

Šalda was not content with being a literary critic. For a time he was prominent in art criticism largely as an early champion of French impressionism. These articles are collected in *Tajemství zraku* (1940; The Mystery of Sight). Besides, he was himself a creative writer of great ambitions. His poetry is symbolist in style and is preoccupied with problems of death; it sometimes compares with the best work of Sova (*q.v.*) or Březina (*q.v.*), the two Czech poets he admired most. His poetic quality is well represented in a collection of elegies, *Strom bolesti* (1920; The Tree of Pain), written at the death of the novelist Růžena Svobodová (*q.v.*), who was his intimate personal friend. Šalda's long novel, *Loutky i dělníci boží* (1917; Puppets and Laborers of God), seems stilted and cerebral and is overloaded with discussion, but there is good work in his short stories, collected in two volumes, *Život ironický a jiné povídky* (1912; The Ironical Life and Other Stories) and *Dřevoryty staré i nové* (1935; Woodcuts Old and New). A philosophical legend, half essay, half visionary story, *Pokušení Pascalovo* (1928; Pascal's Temptation) is particularly impressive. His three attempts at drama were failures.

See: A. Novák, "F. X. Šalda jako kritik," in *Zvony domova* (1916); R. I. Malý and F. Pujman, eds., *F. X. Šaldovi k padesátinám* (1918); J. Hora, ed., *F. X. Šaldovi k 22. prosinci 1932* (1932); O. Fischer, *Šaldovo češství* (1936); F. Goetz, *F. X. Šalda* (1937); J. Mukařovský, "F. X. Šalda," *Slovo a slovesnost,* III (1937), 65–78; B. Lifka, ed., *Na paměť F. X. Šaldy* (1939).

R. W.

Salinas, Pedro (1892–, Spanish poet and critic), was born in Madrid and graduated from its university. He was lecturer of Spanish in Paris at the Sorbonne from 1914 to 1917 and in 1918 became professor of Spanish literature at the University of Seville. He has taught since then at several Spanish and foreign institutions. In 1936 he established his residence in the United States and holds at present a chair in Johns Hopkins University. One of the most active Spanish intellectuals, he has traveled widely as a lecturer in Europe and America; he organized the section of contemporary literature in the Centro de Estudios Históricos of Madrid and was executive secretary of the Universidad Internacional de Santander (1933–1936). A typical representative of the many-sided contemporary spirit, he is both international and very Spanish in character and taste; a man awakened to the realities of his time and an artist of subtle intellectual—almost abstract—inspiration; a translator of Proust (*q.v.*) and the author of a modern version of the oldest Spanish epic (*Poema de Mio Cid,* 1926).

Salinas belongs to the poetic generation of the post-war period together with García Lorca, Jorge Guillén, and Rafael Alberti (*qq.v.*). They were the four writers who attained early recognition, emerging with a genuine literary value from the confusion of the moment. Lorca and Alberti had a spontaneous inspiration and a direct relation with Spanish traditional poetry; Guillén and Salinas—older and to a great extent fully developed when the new movements began—leaned towards an intellectual type of poetry with an outward simplicity obtained only through complex mental processes. Salinas followed the tendency of spiritual lyricism which in Spain had as the outstanding master Juan Ramón Jiménez (*q.v.*). At his point of departure he could be related also to Unamuno and Antonio Machado (*qq.v.*) and the French current towards "pure poetry." Among the Spanish classics, his sensibility brings him closer to the Neoplatonic poets, Garcilaso, or the mystics. His relation with Góngora—to whom his generation rendered a special cult—is limited to a taste for *conceptismo* and for play with the meaning of words, but he avoids the sensual delight of Gongorism in descriptive imagery. His poetry is made of psychological subtleties, his images are built upon concepts or ideas rather than on sensations. The external world is for him a sort of formless life. The poet's task, his joy, consists in giving it order and sense. Salinas says in *Reality and the Poet in Spanish Poetry* (1940; published only in English), a lucid critical work, that "the poet places himself before reality . . . in order to create something else." Here is the key to the interpretation of Salinas's own poetry. All his books (*Presagios,* 1923; *Seguro azar,* 1929; *Fábula y signo,* 1931; *Amor en vilo,* 1933; *La voz a ti debida,* 1933; *Razón de amor,* 1936) present, when seen in this light, an extraordinary example of unity in the development of a main poetical idea. The themes, often taken from the most modern aspects of city life, may change, but they always express a poetic eagerness to transform the external perception into a superior unchangeable reality from which are derived the emotions—love, happiness, and a kind of metaphysical anguish—that are found in the poetry of Salinas. His poetic method is a sort of "modern, interior *conceptismo,*" as Leo Spitzer defines it, or perhaps a playful exercise of the mind in which humor and wistfulness are delicately blended. Salinas will never be a popular poet, but his work represents an original expression of the spiritual impasse of our time. The poet, lacking a profound faith, re-creates from within a world of ideas and symbols which, however illusive, offers him the joys of certainty.

The two aspects of the personality of Salinas are independent but not unrelated.

His scholarly readings are reflected in his poetry. To teaching and criticism he brought an alert sensibility. His main works in this field, besides those already mentioned, are his edition (1925) of the *Poesías* of Meléndez Valdés and his *Literatura española siglo XX* (1941). An ample selection of his poems has been translated into English by Eleanor L. Turnbull (*Lost Angel and Other Poems,* 1938, *Truth of Two and Other Poems,* 1940, with Spanish and English on opposite pages).

See: Angel del Río, "El poeta Pedro Salinas; vida y obra," Leo Spitzer, "El conceptismo interior de Pedro Salinas," and Margot Arce and Sidonia C. Rosenbaum, "Pedro Salinas; bibliografía," *Revista hispánica moderna,* VII (New York, 1941), 1–32, 33–69, 69–73.

A. del R.

Salmon, André (1881–, French poet, novelist, and critic), son and grandson of artists, was born in Paris and has lived there most of his life, but two trips to Russia profoundly influenced his childhood and adolescence. As one of the artists and poets gathered around Apollinaire (*q.v.*), he qualified as a cubist with his first verse, *Féeries* (1907) and *Le Calumet* (1910), while his articles helped spread cubism. The Russian Revolution and a third trip to Russia brought forth *Prikaz* (1919), a fervent, though dispassionate epic, the feverishness of which Salmon intensified in another epic of his own restless generation, *L'Age de l'humanité* (1922). After a brief incursion into dadaism, Salmon rediscovered his early conviction that "art must be given back to life"; he turned to novels and stories, for which his journalistic training provided the "total realism" of brute facts and his poetic vision the jerky pattern of mythic "illogism." Such was the meaning of the poetic debate of *Le Livre et la bouteille* (1920), in which Salmon had chosen the "bottle," the Dionysiac intuitive grasp of reality, rather than the methodical approach of the "book." Already apparent in *Tendres Canailles* (1913), a novel of an underworld à la Carco (*q.v.*), that tendency burst forth in *La Négresse du Sacré-Cœur* (1920; Eng. tr., *The Black Venus,* 1929), the fantastic kaleidoscope of the new bohemia, painted against a backdrop of pathetic and grotesque gangsterism. Salmon, meantime, had pursued his interest in art, and while producing novels, sketches, and souvenirs, *Le Manuscrit trouvé dans un chapeau* (1919), *L'Entrepreneur d'illuminations* (1921), *Archives du club des onze* (1922), *Voyages au pays des voyantes* (1931), he was becoming, as it were, critic-in-ordinary to the modern painters, with his numerous monographs and essays, especially *L'Art vivant* (1921), *Propos d'atelier* (1923), *Cézanne* (1923), *André Derain* (1923), *Modigliani* (1926), and *Chagall* (1929).

Salmon will remain one of the most authentic poets of his generation. Under a mask of clowning fancy or through the glaring violence of topical events, the broken design of his "poetic reporting" re-creates the turbidity of the modern world, the only justification of which lies in the miraculous blossoming of the ever novel facts, "the true symbol of which is inscribed somewhere else, in some other book."

See: M. Cowley, "André Salmon and His Generation," *Bookman,* LVI (1923), 714–717; G. Bounoure, review in *Nouvelle Revue française,* XXXIII (1929), 839–845; G. E. Lemaitre, *From Cubism to Surrealism in French Literature* (1941), pp. 136–141.

C. L. B.

Salten, Felix (1869–1945, Austrian novelist), was born in Budapest but lived in Vienna from childhood until forced into exile at the age of 70 by the advent of the National Socialist regime in Austria. Salten first became known at the beginning of the 20th century as an able journalist and theatrical critic. His long association with the Viennese *Neue freie Presse,* the most influential organ of the Austro-Hungarian Empire in the years before the First World War, enabled him to wield considerable authority, to make and unmake literary and stage reputations. His own dramatic efforts were unsuccessful. His novels, humorous, satiric, erotic, for a long time found no echo outside his native land. With the appearance of *Bambi* in 1923 (Eng. tr., 1928), however, Salten attained international vogue. This tender tale of a deer's life in the forest had been preceded by *Der Hund von Florenz* (Eng. tr., *Hound of Florence,* 1930) two years earlier and was followed by many other animal tales in which human beings, their passions, and their problems were portrayed through the medium of their four-legged brothers. Salten was the last president of the Austrian P.E.N. Club before its disintegration in 1933 under Nazi attack. During the Second World War he found refuge in Switzerland.

S. L.

Salvemini, Gaetano (1873–, Italian historian and political writer), was born in Molfetta, Apulia, one of 13 children in a family whose support devolved upon him early in his youth. He studied in Florence, with the help of a small scholarship, and started teaching in 1895, first in high schools and then (1900) in the University of Messina. In the Messina earthquake of 1908 he lost his wife and his four children. In 1910 he was called to Pisa and in 1916 to Florence.

His scholarly pursuits, which soon distinguished him as a master in medieval and modern Italian history, did not prevent him from intense political activity. He began by being identified with the Socialists, but his rugged liberal personality and his positivistic training soon made him the agrarian democrat that he has remained ever since. He led the constitutional fight of Apulian peasants against the union of great landholders and government forces and was their candidate in 1911. He was defeated at elections owing to a combination of corruption and strong-arm tactics on the part of the authorities, which he described in a biting pamphlet against Giolitti, *Il Ministro della mala vita* (1910). The subservience of Socialist deputies to Giolittian paternalism was one of his favorite targets. He opposed the Libyan war as imperialistic and economically pointless, but in 1914 he took the side of Bissolati for intervention in the First World War and joined up as a second lieutenant in 1915. Since he consistently maintained that the war was one phase of the fight against imperialism, he put up a staunch opposition to the Right and the nationalists and strongly resisted their annexationist claims on South Tyrol and Dalmatia. Branded as a "renunciator," he was nonetheless elected in 1919 as a deputy of the Rinnovamento party. In 1920 he accused Mussolini of having stolen a large part of the funds gathered in South America for D'Annunzio (*q.v.*); Mussolini thereupon challenged Salvemini to a duel, but refused to clear himself. After the Matteotti crisis and the subsequent emergency laws, Salvemini, together with Carlo Rosselli, who was his friend and pupil, launched the first underground paper, *Non Mollare* (Don't Give Up). He was jailed in 1925, but released before his trial owing to an amnesty and escaped to France. He lived for a few years between Paris and London and in 1932 came to the United States, where he has lectured extensively. In 1934 he was called to the Lauro de Bosis lectureship in Harvard University. The Sereno Medal of London University was awarded to him in 1943.

Salvemini is one of the leading figures, if not the leading figure, of anti-Fascism. Most of the young anti-Fascist leaders of the 1920's were his friends or his pupils. Beginning in 1926 he undertook, almost single-handed, to piece together from abroad the available evidence on Fascist Italy and to provide the first really historical treatment of the material. His political activity since 1938 has become that of an American citizen and of an expert on Italy. Since 1941 he has dedicated himself chiefly to the task of showing, in connection with the Italian problem, in how many ways American and British policies are inconsistent with the idea of a "democratic war." But his influence as an Italian writer in Italy has remained considerable, as has been demonstrated since the liberation of Italy. The initial program of the Action Party, published in 1943, was closely patterned on what Salvemini had taught 20 years before.

Salvemini is a man who has kept telling drastic truths in incisive and often brilliant style. One critic, Nicola Chiaromonte, has said of him: "He is not really a politician, but has been all his life and consistently remains a political pamphleteer of that 18th century stem which had some good shoots in Italy too. Such as he is, Salvemini is for Italians much more of a representative figure than Croce himself."

Salvemini's literary production is enormous, but mostly scattered in articles and pamphlets. Among his major works are: *Magnati e popolani a Firenze* (1899); *Studi storici* (1901); *Mazzini* (1912); *La Politica estera di F. Crispi* (1919); *Tendenze vecchie e necessitá nuove del movimento operaio italiano* (1922); *Mussolini diplomate* (1932); *La Rivoluzione francese* (1905; 2d revised ed., 1924); *Under the Axe of Fascism* (1936); *What to Do with Italy* (1943; in collaboration with G. La Piana).

See: P. Silva, *Chi è Gaetano Salvemini* (1919); E. Rota, *Una Pagina di storia contemporanea: Gaetano Salvemini* (1919); M. D'Andrea (Nicola Chiaromonte), review of Salvemini and La Piana, *What to Do with Italy*, in *Partisan Review*, X (1943), 458–463.

G. de S.

Samain, Albert (1858–1900, French poet and dramatist), was born in Lille, of a lower-middle-class family. Forced by the death of his father to abandon his studies, he went into the sugar brokerage business. Tiring of this occupation which left him too little leisure, he soon obtained a small clerkship in the Department of Instruction in the Prefecture of the Seine. Henceforth he had time to devote himself to literature, as he had long wished. He began to frequent the bohemian group of the period. It was in the journal *Chat noir* that the first of his poems appeared. He took part in the founding of the *Mercure de France* (1890), and a great number of his poems appeared in this review. In 1893, pressed by his friends, he made a selection of his poems which he entitled *Au jardin de l'infante* and which was issued by the Mercure de France in an edition of 350 copies. A few months later (March 15, 1894) a highly favorable article of François Coppée (*q.v.*) in the *Journal* made Samain famous overnight. The first edition, quickly sold out, was followed in 1897 by a new one, which was augmented by a work not yet published, *L'Urne penchée*. The next year the French Academy awarded him the Archon-Despérouses prize. In spite of the fact that he was suffering from tuberculosis, Samain prepared another collection of poems, *Aux flancs du vase*, which was published in 1898. The volume had little success. The death of his mother added to the grief which he felt from this disappointment. His health steadily worsening, he used his last strength to write *Polyphème* (published only in 1906), a poetic drama in two acts. It was his last work. Shortly afterwards, on August 18, he died at Magny-les-Hameaux, at the home of his friend Raymond Bonheur whose hospitality he had accepted. After his death his friends selected his best poems which they published in a posthumous collection, *Le Chariot d'or* (1901). His short stories, collected in one volume and also published by his friends, scarcely add to his fame. *Polyphème* was played successfully for the first time at the Théâtre de l'Œuvre in 1904, then at the Comédie Française, May 19, 1908. A great number of his poems and a manuscript called "Pensées et réflexions" are still unpublished.

The life of Albert Samain was monotonous, discreet, almost colorless; no great passion agitated his soul, and no unusual suffering exposed him to deep unhappiness. Since these sources of inspiration were lacking, he followed a great number of traditional literary themes. Critics have pointed out numerous imitations of literary models. His first poems, many of them unpublished, show the influence of the Parnassian school. The satanism of Baudelaire produced the excessive interest in perversion and the eroto-mystic mania of certain sonnets in *Au jardin de l'infante*. He took up a great number of the themes of romanticism; in fact, he never completely freed himself from this influence. His love for Greece inspired in him the graceful idyls, the rapid little tableaux colored with antiquity, found in *Aux flancs du vase*. He belonged also to his own age: the influence of symbolism, especially that of Verlaine and Mallarmé (*qq.v.*), is perceptible in his works. From the symbolists he accepted the musical conception of poetry. He is not a vers librist, neither does he adhere to the rigid credo of the Parnassians. He helped to facilitate the compromise which was to find its conclusion in what is called the *vers libéré*. In spite of all these influences, he remained an individual and belonged to no school, although he borrowed most judiciously. If one considers symbolism as the conclusion of the different movements succeeding each other in the 19th century, it is evident that Samain is one of its best representatives in that he assimilated not only the best of the romantic and Parnassian doctrines, but also whatever was new and likely to live among the eccentricities and the paradoxes of the new aesthetic.

See: Léon Bocquet, *Albert Samain; sa vie, son œuvre* (1905); Albert de Bersaucourt, *Albert Samain; son œuvre* (1925); Georges Bonneau, *Albert Samain, poète symboliste* (1925).

H. U. F.

Šantić, Aleksa (1868–1924, Serb poet), was born and lived all his life in Mostar, Herzegovina, a province that was occupied by the Austro-Hungarians in 1878 and annexed by them in 1908. After business school training in Ljubljana and Trieste, he settled down in his native town where he became the editor in chief of the review *Zora* (1896–1901; Dawn). In this capacity he came into the focus of the life of this region which, by its cultural and national consciousness, showed a stubborn opposition to the German *Kulturträger*. The product of his patriotic inspiration during the liberating Balkan Wars of 1912–1913 is the book *Na starim ognjištima* (1913; On the Old Hearths). During the First World War he was taken by the Austrians as a hostage, but he survived the war and saw the realization of his dream—the union of the Yugoslav peoples.

During his life Šantić wrote six volumes of poetry (1891, 1895, 1900, 1908, 1911, 1913), as well as some dramatizations in verse, the best of which are *Pod maglom* (1907; In the Fog) and *Hasan-Aginica* (1911). He also translated Heine's *Lyrisches Intermezzo* (1897–1898), prepared an anthology of translated German poets, *Iz nemačke lirike* (1910; From German Lyrics), made a Serbian rendering of Schiller's *Wilhelm Tell* (1922) and translated *Pesme roba* (1919; Poems of a Slave) from the Czech writer Svatopluk Čech (*q.v.*).

Šantić shows two main characteristics:

melancholy concerning the past and an ardent love for his nation, especially for the common man. His lyrics are striking in their emotional sincerity and simplicity; they have vigor, courage, and consolation. Very often the purity of design is classical as well as deeply moving. In his day Šantić gave perhaps the most adequate expression of the collective national soul, of the common sufferings and longings, and in that sense he is his nation's spokesman.

See: S. Petrović, *Aleksa Šantić* (1934); D. Subotić, "Aleksa Šantić," *Slavonic Review*, III (1924–1925), 194.

P. A.

Sanz del Río, Julián (1814–1869), Spanish educator and philosopher), born at Torrearévalo, Soria, is Spain's first modern thinker. His life and thinking were conditioned by four factors. His humble, peasant parentage gave him moral qualities of profound uprightness. His desolate birthplace taught him to revere nature with a religious sense that instilled in him a lasting admiration for science (which for Sanz del Río meant the projection into nature of an anxious soul in quest of the Absolute). He came to feel strongly the impact of romanticism on philosophy, through the Neo-Kantian schools of Schelling, Fichte, and Krause. He was much affected by the antagonism of the Roman Catholic Church and of certain intolerant Catholics, who made a political issue of Sanz del Río's serene, objective method; while he went in quest of the Light that man needs to achieve his full spiritual and intellectual development, his Catholic enemies saw in this quest nothing but rank heresy.

Sanz del Río's determination to uplift his countrymen was so sincere, so little mixed up with petty political or religious issues that his first published work, *Apuntes sobre diezmos* (1837), is written to oppose the idea of suppressing the Church's tithes. Later, in 1854, he indicated to the minister of public instruction, among other university changes, the need of establishing two full chairs of liberal theology, so that the secular priests might have a much better preparation than they were getting in the seminaries. But his *Ideal de la humanidad para la vida* (1860) was put on the Index, and his Roman Catholic adversaries made his life so miserable and precarious that Sanz del Río had to devote much of his time to defending himself.

With the help of an uncle, a liberal priest, Sanz del Río had been able to study the humanities, theology, and law at Granada and Madrid. His moral quality is shown by the early giving up of his law practice, the petty dealings and subterfuges of which he could not stomach, for the study of philosophy. In 1844 he obtained a fellowship to study in Germany and went to Heidelberg, where disciples of Krause were teaching. At Heidelberg he lived with the famous historian Georg Weber, whose *Universal History* he later translated, with a significant introduction and valuable commentaries (4 vols., 1853–1856). One of his friends at Heidelberg was Henri Amiel (*q.v.*). On his return to Madrid, Sanz del Río refused to teach philosophy, for which he did not yet feel adequately equipped, and withdrew to nearby Illescas, where he spent almost 10 years studying and pondering over philosophical problems. In 1854 he did become professor of the history of philosophy at the University of Madrid, and his lectures were attended by the most prominent and best-known scholars and statesmen of his time. In 1867 he resigned because the minister of public instruction had demanded that all professors sign a confession of faith and an oath of allegiance to the Catholic Church.

Sanz del Río became primarily a teacher of teachers who later were to have a tremendous influence in contemporary Spain, such as Francisco Giner de los Ríos, Manuel B. Cossío (*qq.v.*), Adolfo Posada, and many others. In philosophy his most noteworthy contributions are *Sistema de la filosofía metafísica* (1860), *Análisis del pensamiento racional* (1877), and *El idealismo absoluto* (1883). Like Krause, Sanz del Río tries in these works to bring together two categorical imperatives, the psychological and the ontological. He starts with the intuition of the "I" and then tries to determine the general properties or the knowledge of the Absolute Being through this intuition, since perception is the reception of the object and its retention in the "I." In his *Ideal de la humanidad* he discusses a "fundamental human society" in which the same political constitution would bring all men into a permanent peace, a society of families bound by a harmonious alliance with God, reason, and nature. In another work, *Filosofía de la muerte* (1877), he studied the meaning of death, from purely philosophical categories, and here particularly he has shown his fearless thinking, following each step of each syllogism to its ultimate, dauntless conclusions.

See: Gervasio Manrique, *Sanz del Río* (n.d., *ca.* 1934); J. B. Trend, "Sanz del Río, the

Much-abused Philosopher," in *The Origins of Modern Spain* (1934), pp. 30–49; Pierre Jobit, *Les Educateurs de l'Espagne contemporaine: Les Krausistes* (2 vols., 1936).

F. S. y E.

Sarcey, Francisque (1827–1899, French theatrical critic), born in Dourdan, Seine-et-Oise, said that, in 40 years of professional theatregoing, he had attended 15,000 performances without one hour of boredom and without a moment of undue deference to the tyranny of directors and stars. This claim is not without foundation; his real popularity with the French bourgeoisie of his time rests not merely upon his own announced identity with any theatregoer but, perhaps chiefly, upon an individualism and independence to which he was able to give effective expression in his familiar, rather commonplace prose. Most of his comments were published, on innumerable Mondays, in the Paris *Temps*.

His definitely academic training, started at home (his father was the principal of a boarding school at Dourdan) and completed in Paris secondary schools and at the Ecole Normale Supérieure, where he was a classmate of the cerebral Taine (*q.v.*), proved no check at all upon his enjoyment of a neatly spun *vaudeville* or a bombastic heroic play or melodrama. From a great predecessor, Lessing, who was revealed to him by his friend De Suckau, he adopted a motto which helped him in the very midst of realism and naturalism to maintain a kind of middle course: "Nature is one thing; Art, and mainly theatrical Art, is another." Foreshadowing seemed to him the basic essential of a good play; *la scène à faire* was in his view an out and out necessity for any well-developed stage work.

"Uncle Sarcey" became a sure guide for the taste of an immense public and the reliance of playwrights in quest of prompt success—until in the 1890's the trend towards symbolism (*see* French symbolism), to which he was not sympathetic, made him seem out of date. *Quarante Ans de théâtre* (8 vols., 1900–1902) remains as testimony of a continuous and sensible devotion to dramatic criticism. The public lectures which Sarcey gave, mainly in connection with the revival of older plays, were not of the same standard; some of them are remembered as slightly absurd. In the midst of the Second Empire, Sarcey was a liberal and attached to leftist periodicals. Novels (*Etienne Moret*, 1876; *Le Piano de Jeanne*, 1876), memoirs (*Le Siège de Paris*, 1871), and a book entitled *Le Mot et la chose* (1862) complete the record of his publications; they do not add greatly to his importance.

See: J. Claretie *et al.*, introduction to Vol. I (1900) of Sarcey, *Quarante Ans de théâtre*.

F. B.

Sardinha, António (1887?–1925, Portuguese poet and journalist), unexcelled as the singer of rural Portugal, was also the spiritual father of "integralismo," a Portuguese variant of the French "Action Française" (*see* Maurras, Charles). Born in Monforte de Alemtejo, of peasant stock, he always remained attached to his native province, until his premature death at Elvas. Even before leaving the University of Coimbra in 1911 he had embarked on a journalistic career; he became chief editor of the daily *A monarquia* (The Monarchy) and later directed *A nação portuguesa* (The Portuguese Nation). Guided by the critic Moniz Barreto (*q.v.*), he and the poet Lopes Vieira (*q.v.*) founded the movement known as Integralismo Lusitano (1914), advocating a return to the Catholic monarchy and an Atlantic Empire closely allied with Spain. After the murder of Sidónio Paes, the monarchist deputy Sardinha was exiled in 1919 and spent the following three years in Spain. He returned to Portugal, but died before seeing nationalism triumph.

As a poet Sardinha knew how to express pure human emotion. Thus love for a woman moved him to write the sonnets of *Chuva da tarde* (1923; Evening Rain), and grief over the death of a little son the elegies of *Era uma vez um menino* (1926; Once upon a Time There Was a Boy). But most of his verse and prose remained at the service of traditions whose revival, he thought, would save Portugal from disintegration. Not only did he proclaim, like Teixeira de Pascoais (*q.v.*), the revigorating virtues of *saüdade* (sad memories) and the Messianic myth of King Sebastian, but he foreshadowed the "blood and soil" mysticism of the Nazis, when he identified himself with his forebears and the soil of Alemtejo in *Tronco reverdecido* (1910; New Shoots from an Old Trunk) and *A epopéia da planície; poemas da terra e do sangue* (1915; The Epic of the Plain; Poems of Blood and Soil). Exiled in Toledo, the nationalist poet expressed the longings of his "old Lusitanian heart" in the sonnets of *Na côrte da saüdade* (1922; At the Court of Saudade). Also written in exile, *Quando as nascentes despertam . . .* (1921;

When the Springs Awaken . . .) exalts rural Portugal in beautifully tender poems, vibrating with childhood memories and premonitions of early death.

Sardinha devoted most of his energy, however, to political journalism. He developed a fluid, self-possessed style recalling the balanced prose of Eça de Queiroz (*q.v.*) and the subtile, icy rationalizations of Charles Maurras. Having begun his crusade with *O valor da raça* (1915; The Value of Race), he summed up his partisan views on history and politics in *A aliança peninsular* (1926; The Peninsular Alliance).

See: Ramiro de Maeztu, "Prólogo," in *La alianza peninsular* (1930); Mendes dos Remédios, *História da literatura portuguesa,* 6th ed. (1930), p. 574.

G. M. M.

Sardou, Victorien (1831–1908), French dramatist), was born in Paris. After an attempt at medical studies, he undertook various occupations, such as giving private lessons in science; since he wanted to devote himself to his theatrical vocation in spite of his family's opposition and could not expect any assistance from them, he had to earn money to be financially independent. His first play, *La Taverne des étudiants,* given at the Odéon in 1854, was a complete failure. Disgusted, he stayed away from the stage for four years; then, having married an actress, Mlle de Brécourt, he became connected with the famous Déjazet, who agreed to play the main role in *Les Premières Armes de Figaro* (1859). Sardou's productiveness is astonishing, and likewise his versatility which, if we except tragedy, enabled him to write all kinds of plays—vaudeville (*Les Premières Armes de Figaro*), pure comedy (*Les Pattes de mouche,* 1860), high comedy of manners (*Nos Intimes,* 1860; *La Famille Benoiton,* 1865; *Nos Bos villageois,* 1866), comedy of character (*Séraphine,* 1869), historical drama (*Patrie,* 1869; *La Haine,* 1874), historical comedy (*Monsieur Garat,* 1860; *Madame Sans-Gêne,* 1893), a problem play (*Daniel Rochat,* 1880), political satire (*Rabagas,* 1872), farce (*Divorçons,* 1880). There were also farcical plays such as *Les Pommes du voisin,* a dark melodrama perhaps parodical (*Les Diables noirs*), fairy plays such as *Don Quichotte,* plays with showy costumes such as *Les Merveilleuses,* operatic scenarios such as *Les Barbares* for Saint-Saëns, and finally, among the dramas especially written to set off the various gifts of Sarah Bernhardt, *Fédora* (1882), *Théodora* (1884), *La Tosca* (1887), *Gismonda* (1894). His *Thermidor* (1891), against the Terror, evoked a violent uproar, with debates in the Chamber of Deputies, and was suspended after two performances. *Robespierre* (1899) and *Dante* (1903), written for Sir Henry Irving, were never played in French. Sardou was elected a member of the French Academy in 1877.

Perhaps no other 19th-century French dramatist has stirred so many audiences and acquired a comparable reputation in Europe, America, and Asia. At the beginning of the 20th century, Japanese actors were playing *Patrie* in Tokyo in Japanese. On the other hand, there is no dramatic writer who, during his lifetime, has been less spared by critics. University critics were almost ferocious.

In objective appraisal there can be little debate as to Sardou's stagecraft, his talent for endowing a play with life to the least detail. For scenery, costumes, and the setting of the masses in motion, a reconstitution such as *Théodora* at the Porte Saint-Martin remains famous. And if Théodore Barrière, author of *Les Faux Bonshommes,* greeted him in his youth as the incarnation of the theatre, it is because at an early age Sardou showed himself unrivaled, even compared with Scribe, in inventing plays with one dramatic situation after another, in rapid succession, which hold the curiosity of the audience in suspense. His style was lively, sparkling, often biting. In many of his comedies he showed such an understanding of *actualité* that Jules Claretie once called him a "dramatic barometer."

But Sardou tried too exclusively to entertain and carry the onlooker through various emotions by means of the unexpected and thrilling turns of his plots and sacrificed, far too much, character study and real life. This does not mean that he did not thoroughly understand the human heart. Read, for instance, the quarrel between Theodora and Justinien or the great love scene in *Gismonda,* perhaps one of the most beautifully written of the contemporary theatre. A revival of *La Famille Benoiton* at the Odéon made even a severe critic like Doumic (*q.v.*) admit that Sardou had painted from life certain aspects of the manners of the Second Empire. Yet (see his own French Academy speech, published in 1878) he was inclined to study men and events too much from a merely theatrical point of view. His characters are often like silhouettes, and he offers too frequently a rather unreal synthesis of pure comedy in the two first acts and of *drame* and comedy in the last three. A purely comic strain often alternates strangely with an almost caricatural manner. Nor is the too free use of wit in the dialogue true to reality. We observe the author even more than the character, and when he happens to make a show of conventional and sentimental morals, we are surprised at so naïve an outburst from so clever a writer.

Divorçons, undoubtedly one of Sardou's masterpieces, is perhaps also the masterpiece of 19th-century farcical plays. In *Patrie* and in *La Haine* the dramatist rises to heroic heights, lofty emotions. His best comedies, in spite of their defects, will always offer to the student of manners useful documentation; whenever he wanted to be, he was a very good portrayer of his time. Above all, Victorien Sardou—and this is not a minor merit —was able to amuse, charm, and move two generations of Frenchmen and make them forget for a few hours the troubles and worries of everyday life.

See: H. Rebell, *Victorien Sardou* (1903); G. Mouly, *La Vie prodigieuse de Victorien Sardou* (1931).

L. All.

Sarment, Jean (1897–, French actor and dramatist), was born in Nantes. He attended the *lycée* in that city and after finishing his studies went to Paris. His talent attracted the attention of Réjane, the famous actress, and of the popular actor Max Dearly. He studied dramatic art at the Paris Conservatory. In 1917, when Jacques Copeau (*q.v.*), the director of the Vieux Colombier, left for America with a company of actors, Sarment joined the troupe and spent two seasons in New York. On his return to France he joined the company of Lugné-Poe (*q.v.*) at the Théâtre de l'Œuvre and played leading parts in plays by Ibsen and Strindberg (*qq.v.*). Sarment's first two plays, *La Couronne de carton* (1920) and *Le Pêcheur d'ombres* (1921; Eng. tr., *Rude Awakening,* 1939), were produced in that theatre, and the author played the leading roles in both. The plays were very favorably received and are still considered by critics to be among his best. *Le Pêcheur d'ombres,* though its plot bears no resemblance to that of any of Ibsen's plays, has an Ibsenian flavor. The hero of the play is a young poet who is suffering from amnesia and who, when cured, finds life too ugly to endure. There is always a definite romantic tendency, especially in the earlier plays of Sarment. His characters seek to escape from their humdrum existence; it is invariably the idealist for whom Sarment shows his sympathy. Sometimes the characters like to imagine themselves greater than they are, as in *Je suis trop grand pour moâ* (1924). Sarment wrote more than 20 plays in prose and in verse and acted in them as well. They were produced at the Comédie Française, the Odéon, and in many other European theatres.

See: Lucien Dubech, "Le Théâtre de M. Jean Sarment," *Revue universelle,* XVII (1924), 251–255; L. Delpit, *Paris—Théâtre contemporain,* I (1925), 99–101, II (1938), 20–21, 149–151; Edmond Sée, *Le Théâtre français contemporain* (1928), pp. 162–165; M. E. Coindreau, *La Farce est jouée* (1942).

H. H.

Sars, Johan Ernst (1835–1917, Norwegian historian and political essayist), born in Florø, was long a professor at the University of Christiania (from 1874). His father, Michael Sars, was a pioneer in modern zoology, his mother was a sister of one of the leading Norwegian poets in the middle of the 19th century, Johan Sebastian Welhaven, and he received strong impulses both from the methods of science and from the formal demands of poetry. Stimulated to historical thinking by Buckle, to scientific generalizations by Comte and Spencer, to the grasp of laws in historical facts by Guizot, Tocqueville, Fustel de Coulanges, and other French historians, to passionate search for unity in the national history of Norway by Björnson (*q.v.*) and by contemporary politics, Sars created the first great synthesis of Norwegian history in his capital work, *Udsigt over den norske historie* (4 vols., 1873–1891; View of Norwegian History). Here he showed the virtual continuity of national development from the first historical times down to the present, even through the "dark" centuries of foreign domination. Indeed Sars found the germs of decay even in the very elements of greatness and those of a new rise in essentials of the downfall, and arrived at general historical laws of the growth and decline of nations. The immediate effect of his work was the shaping of national thought in Norway. He undertook his historical work with the program of rousing the nation to fight for full political and intellectual independence, and he became a spiritual leader in this fight, popularizing his historical ideas in pamphlets and articles, working as journalist and editor of magazines. In his historical works and essays he proved a brilliant portraitist, often with a touch of irony, and the paradoxical antithesis that was at the foundation of his historical thought, put, as it were, its mark even on his style, which was no doubt influenced by French manners of writing. All this made his essays delightful reading, though they often angered his opponents by their scathing polemics against obsolete conceptions or against undignified servility to authorities. He wanted to throw open the door for all modern science and new ideas, and the magazines of which he was coeditor from 1877 to the end of the century were pioneers in this task.

See: H. Koht, in *Nordmaend i det 19de aarhundrede,* III (1914), 69–98, and in *Forhandlinger i videnskaps-selskapet i Kristiania* (1917), pp. 95–112; J. S. Worm-Müller, in *Norsk historisk videnskap i femti ar* (1920), pp. 25–41.

H. K.

Sartre, Jean Paul (1905–, French philosopher, critic, novelist, and dramatist), a Parisian by birth, wrote between 1936 and 1940 certain studies in the realm of psychology which, though deeply original, remained little known except to initiates (*L'Imagination,* 1936; *Esquisse d'une théorie des émotions,* 1939; *L'Imaginaire,* 1940). A series of critical essays, published in the *Nouvelle Revue française* (on François Mauriac, *q.v.;* John Dos Passos, William Faulkner, *et al.*), introduced him to the general public. There followed a novel, *La Nausée* (1938), which evoked in most somber tones the hopelessness of man's situation in the midst of a universe where "nothing, absolutely nothing, justifies his existence." A volume of short stories (*Le Mur,* 1939) seemed to emphasize further the author's cynicism and despair, his sense of "the absurdity of it all," his blunt and scornful appraisal of human motives and behavior. By and large, Sartre's production of these earlier years, however talented and morbidly fascinating it may have been, received only part of the attention which it deserved.

The situation was sharply modified during the Second World War. Public interest was thoroughly aroused by knowledge of Sartre's valiant role in the French resistance to the German oppressor, and more especially by the manner in which, with his spectacular drama *Les Mouches* (1943), set in Argos under the reign of Aegisthus, he managed to delude Nazi censorship and issue a stirring call on behalf of liberty. Later, audiences listened spellbound to his one-act play, *Huis-Clos* (1944), a remarkably taut and dense symbolization of Hell in the form of a bare, cheap hotel room where three persons—a man, two women—are forever condemned to each other's presence: "l'Enfer, c'est les Autres." In 1943 Sartre also produced his monumental, 700-page philosophical treatise, *L'Etre et le néant.* He now reached a position of singular eminence in the world of French letters. Much was being written, including a novel by his disciple and friend, Simone de Beauvoir (*L'Invitée,* 1943), about the "cénacle" of the Café de Flore of which he had become the principal and most picturesque ornament. His prestige was currently likened to that of Maurice Barrès or André Gide (*qq.v.*) in former days, and some enthusiasts, hastily coining the word "Sartrism," predicted that the new system would displace Bergsonism (*see* Bergson, Henri) as the most modern expression of French philosophical thinking. The fact is that a considerable following, which included a number of fashionable ladies, was converted to existentialism overnight.

Existentialism as propounded in *L'Etre et le néant* is the French naturalization of German phenomenology, itself grafted on the century-old philosophy of Sören Kierkegaard. Sartre fully recognizes his debt to Husserl and Heidegger, but likes to point out that the existential viewpoint is already implicit in the *Cogito* of Descartes. Reality (notwithstanding positivism) has no meaning save *for* the mind—that is the starting point. However, the existentialists add, it does not follow (as idealism would have it) that all reality is *in* the mind. The outer world exists. "Human reality," in fact, is a centrifugal force incessantly directed toward physical objects or other persons treated as physical objects. It yearns to achieve the wholeness and self-identity which is the attribute of things without losing the self-consciousness which is the attribute of man. This, according to Sartre, is a logical contradiction. Human existence, therefore, will be characterized by a lack, a void, a frustration. While it is because of this very incompleteness that we are capable of freedom, our liberty itself is a function of "le néant." It is born in anguish (cf. the "concept of dread" of Kierkegaard) and carries us toward the unpredictable realization of our essence which will not be complete till the day of our death.

It will readily be seen that all of Sartre's works—his treatises, his novels, his dramas—are but different wings of the same "existential" edifice, to be ultimately crowned by a system of ethics. The attitude expressed in *La Nausée* represented a preliminary and indispensable stage. We are now promised a new humanism, the first glimpse of which may be afforded by the triptych of novels entitled *Les Chemins de la Liberté* (*L'Age de raison, Le Sursis, La Dernière Chance,* the first two published in 1945) and the essay entitled *L'Existentialisme est un humanisme* (1946). This new humanism Sartre defines as "without illusions (that is to say, divorced from religious experience), but full of confidence in the grandeur of humanity; hard, but without useless violence; passionate yet restrained; striving to paint the metaphysical condition of man while fully participating in the movements of society."

That a starkly pessimistic writer should emerge as a spiritual leader and a moralist in the old French tradition is not only compatible with existential tenets in general but with Sartre's temperament as well. Of his many complexes some are deeply personal; others he holds in common with his generation—that of the 1920's. The significant fact, however, is that Sartre's intellectual life, though at times "dangerous" in the Nietzschean sense, never sank to the depths of nihilism which engulfed some of his contemporaries. The Ecole Normale Supérieure of his day (1924–1928) was largely under the sway of Alain (*see* Chartier, Emile), whose steady questioning of all accepted values found its own corrective in rugged individualism and dialectical vigor. The "official" teachings of the Sorbonne may have proved repulsive to the student Sartre as they did to his roommate and constant companion, Paul Nizan (see Nizan's *Les Chiens de garde,* 1932). Nevertheless, it is characteristic of him that he should have accepted the yoke and discipline of an academic career, first in the provinces (Lycées of Laon and Le Havre), then in Paris (Lycée Condorcet), until the time when he was satisfied that he had found a plausible answer—universal perhaps, well-integrated at any rate—to the riddle of his own existence. Thus the varied and massive production that followed was not the improvised venture of a dilettante; it was an orderly release of pent-up energy.

See: Simone de Beauvoir, *Pyrrhus et Cinéas* (1944); H. J. Ayer, "Novelists-Philosophers: Jean-Paul Sartre," *Horizon,* XII (London, 1945), 12–26, 101–110; Jean Beaufret, "A propos de l'existentialisme," *Confluences,* N. S. (1945), Nos. 2–6; Claude Edmonde Magny, "Système de Sartre," *Esprit, Année* XIII (1945), pp. 564–580, 709–724; R. Campbell, *Jean-Paul Sartre, ou une Littérature philosophique* (1945).

J.-A. B.

Savinkov, Boris Viktorovich (pseud. V. Ropshin, 1879–1925, Russian terrorist and novelist), born in Kharkov, Ukraine, is one of the most colorful figures in the annals of revolution. As a youth he joined the Social Revolutionists. Deported to Vologda, he escaped via Archangel to Geneva. There he entered the secret terrorist unit of the party, the Fighting Brigade, and returned in disguise to Russia to organize first the assassination (1904) of Von Plehve, minister of the interior, and second that of the Grand Duke Sergei (1905). His prestige in the party exalted by his brilliant daring and inexhaustible resources, he proceeded to engineer a series of conspiracies—including several attempts on the life of Nicholas II—attended by numerous hairbreadth escapes. After the first 1917 Revolution he became Kerensky's minister of war. Violently anti-Bolshevik, he fled in October and thereafter fomented counterrevolutionary activities of wide range and ferocity. In 1924 he reentered the U.S.S.R. and was instantly arrested and tried (August 27–29). Death sentence was commuted to 10 years' imprisonment. Mysterious circumstances yet surround his apparent suicide on May 7, 1925.

Savinkov's literary work is fascinating in a documentary sense rather than as pure literature. His four books, all more or less autobiographical, provide an intimate and indispensable account of the early terrorists' activities and of their macabre psychology. *Kon bledny* (1909; Eng. tr., *The Pale Horse,* 1917) is already a classic example of this genre. This pseudo novel, together with *To chto ne sluchilos* (1913; Eng. tr., *What Never Happened,* 1917), *Kon voronoi* (1923; Eng. tr., *The Black Horse,* 1924), and *Vospominaniya terrorista* (1926; Memoirs of a Terrorist), leaves an indelible impression of the spiritual tragedy of the political destroyer and of his paradoxical mixture of fanaticism, egotism, and self-sacrifice.

See: B. Pares, review of *Delo Borisa Savinkova* (n.d.; The Trial of Boris Savinkov) in *Slavonic Review,* IV (1925–1926), 760–769; Y. Sazonova, review of *Vospominaniya terrorista* in *Sovremennyia zapiski,* XXXI (1927), 463–466; H. Danjou, "Notre Ami l'assassin," *Les Œuvres inédites,* No. 112, October, 1930, pp. 283–324.

N. S.

Savoir, Alfred (1883–1934, French dramatist), born in Łódź, Poland, went to France, where he substituted Savoir for the family name, Posymanski. His *Le Baptême* (1908) and *La Sonate de Kreutzer* (1925) present a bitter and cruel picture of life, quite different from that portrayed in his better-known light and witty comedies such as *La Huitième Femme de Barbe-Bleue* (1921), *La Grande Duchesse* (1924), *Passy 08–45* (1928), and *Lui* (1929; Eng. tr., *He,* 1933). He invented a new type of dramatic entertainment, a kind of symbolic farce or vaudeville of ideas, of which good examples are *Le Dompteur* (1925), *La Couturière de Lunéville* (1923), and *Le Figurant de la gaîté* (1926). *Le Dompteur,* translated into English as *The Tamer; or, English as It Is Eaten,* sets the pattern for this type of play: a brutal lion tamer who believes in strict discipline is set opposite a philosophical Englishman, a firm believer in the freedom of the will. The tyranny of the tamer wins the circus lady whom they both love, while the philosopher is eaten by the animals he pities. Such a grotesque situation offered abundant opportunity for the ingenuity and fantasy of Savoir. Many of his plays were turned into films, and toward the end of his life he was actively engaged in promoting an international association of writers of original plays for the cinema. His plays, well written and cleverly constructed, reflect certain aspects of his epoch, but now seem ephemeral and artificial.

J. F. M.

Scarfoglio, Edoardo (1860–1917, Italian editor and critic), was born at Paganica, Aquila, and died in Naples. He was editor of several newspapers, founder of the *Mattino,* and for a time husband of Matilde Serao (*q.v.*), many of whose works he published. An important figure in politics and letters, he never attained an outstanding position in either. Mixing violent feelings with pessimism and cynicism, he considered himself a buccaneer floundering in nonheroic waters. Frequently his newspaper experiences took the form of piratical adventures in which the sword often proved more effective than the pen. He fought several duels, including a famous one with his old friend D'Annunzio (*q.v.*) and one with Felice Cavallotti, outstanding representative of democracy in politics and romanticism in literature. His first book is the only one of verse he ever wrote (*Papaveri,* 1880), and is no worse than many other Carducci (*q.v.*) imitations of the period; his short stories (*Il Processo di Frine,* 1884) exaggerate the folkloristic, rugged, primitive life of the peasant of the Abruzzi; his several books of travel (*In Levante e a traverso i Balkani,* 1890; *Le Nostre Cose in Africa,* 1895; *Itinerario verso i paesi d'Etiopia,* 1895–1896; *Il Cristiano errante,* 1897) are interesting and vivid reporting, with a nostalgic yearning for the countries described that exhausts itself in the pen rather than in active participation or conquest. Scarfoglio's literary fame is based chiefly on his *Libro di Don Chisciotte* (1885; reprinted 1911, 1925), which is more important as a personal tribute to the Roman literature of the new Italy than for its literary acuteness and insight. He shows his lack of judgment by preferring Capuana to Verga (*qq.v.*)! But in his effective description of the youthful D'Annunzio transformed by Roman Circes into a sort of gigolo he demonstrates his mastery of caricature. In his last few years Scarfoglio's powerful invectives were directed against English imperialism (*Il Popolo dai cinque pasti,* 1915; *La Guerra della sterlina,* 1915).

Much of Scarfoglio's correspondence is in private hands and is of too intimate a character to be published. Many articles may be found in the files of old newspapers, but only an interest in Scarfoglio's bullying, bragging, and boasting prose would warrant examining them. An anthology of his works, prepared by Alberto Consiglio, was published in 1932.

G. P.

Schaeffer, Albrecht (1885–, German poet, novelist, and essayist), was born in Elbing, West Prussia. His childhood was spent in Hanover. He studied in Munich and in Berlin, tried his hand at journalism, but soon gave it up and settled in the Inn valley of southern Bavaria. He was writing poetry at the age of 14, and all his early compositions were in metrical form —poems, romances, verse epics, plays—with the exception of the novel *Helianth* (1920), which established his reputation as a writer. *Helianth* is a three-volume novel of apprenticeship in the tradition of Goethe's *Wilhelm Meister* and Gottfried Keller's (*q.v.*) *Der grüne Heinrich,* deeply concerned with the meaning and value of art. The young author's guiding spirit was Stefan George (*q.v.*). With him he revolted against materialism and cheap opportunism, seeking "the radiant mystery of things" and their adequate poetic expression. A searching study of George forms the major essay in his volume *Dichter und Dichtung* (1923). Schaeffer, like so many of his contemporaries, is also attracted by psychological analysis and naturalistic description of abnormal events and human situations. Some of his short stories, *e.g., Der Hund* (1918), *Der höllische Sebastian* (1928), *Das Opfertier* (1936), as well as episodes in most of his works pay tribute to naturalism (*see* German naturalism, French naturalism) although an undercurrent of mysticism seems to suggest subtler, symbolic meanings.

Religion of a mystical and speculative but emphatically Christian kind, the classics, nature and life close to the soil, are the dominating elements in Schaeffer's work. *Der göttliche Dulder* (1920) retells the adventures of Ulysses; *Parzival* (1922) is a new and brilliantly imaginative adaptation of the medieval epic; *Aphaia: Der Weg der Götter, Völker und Zahlen* (1937) gives a mystical interpretation of certain numbers and their relations to religion, art, and the evolution of national cultures, based on the proportions of an ancient Greek temple. On the other hand, Schaeffer's latest novels, *Cara* (1936) and *Ruhland: Lebensbild eines Mannes* (1937), grew out of the deep contentment which their author had found at last in working the land and sharing the community of country people. They are not "novels of the soil"; their characters' foremost concern is still with problems of the spirit, and their primitive living does not lead to an oversimplified type of human experience. *Ruhland* is Faustian in its restless search for lasting spiritual satisfaction and represents in composition and style as well as in its thought a synthesis of realistic observation, imaginative interpretation, and ethical intent which makes it an outstanding example of the German character novel. Schaeffer left Germany before the Second World War and is at present living in the United States.

See: W. Muschg, *Der dichterische Charakter* (1929); Schaeffer, "Siebengang: Eine Selbstdarstellung," *Die neue Rundschau,* Jahrgang XLV (1934), Bd. II, pp. 312–321.

E. M. F.

Schäfer, Wilhelm (1868–, German novelist and essayist), was born into a peasant family in Ottrau, Hesse-Nassau. He spent his early life near Düsseldorf and for a period of several years was a schoolteacher at Vohwinkel and Eberfeld. Later he had a chance to travel in Switzerland and France; in 1900 he moved to Berlin where, in close friendship with Richard Dehmel (*q.v.*), he worked as a free-lance writer. He soon felt the need for the strength and traditions of his native soil, and in 1900, after having published more than five volumes of narrative prose—some of them influenced by the novels of Björnson (*q.v.*)—he founded the magazine *Die Rheinlande,* in which he gathered together material relating to the history and folklore of western Germany. Schäfer's celebrated versions of the Rhineland sagas (*Rheinsagen*) appeared in 1908, written in his characteristically straightforward and warm prose. At the same time he developed the old literary medium of the short and significant anecdote, of which he and Johann Peter Hebel (1760–1826) have written the most distinguished examples in German literature (*Gesammelte Anekdoten,* 1929; *Wendekreis neuer Anekdoten,* 1937). In all his work a strong sense of the writer's pedagogical responsibility (see his Pestalozzi tale, *Der Lebenstag eines Menschenfreundes,* 1915) is coupled with a lively feeling for historical continuity and pride in the national heritage (*Die dreizehn Bücher der deutschen Seele,* 1922; *Der deutsche Gott,* 1923; *Auf Spuren der alten Reichsherrlichkeit,* 1933; *Deutsche Reden,* 1933; *Theoderich, König des Abendlandes,* 1939). In his many narratives, especially perhaps in his most popular novel, *Der Hauptmann von Köpenick* (1930), he conveys the generosity of his humor, and the seemingly casual skill of a born storyteller, through a language which was originally impressionistic, but has gradually grown more definite in its plasticity and steadiness of rhythm.

Since 1918 Schäfer has lived in Ludwigshafen (Lake Constance). He became an early member of the Prussian Academy of Art and, more recently, of the Akademie der Dichtung.

See: O. Doderer, ed., *Bekenntnis zu Wilhelm Schäfer* (1928); Schäfer, *Mein Leben* (1934) and *Meine Eltern* (1937); H. Langenbucher, "Wilhelm Schäfer zum 70. Geburtstag," *Zeitschrift für deutsche Bildung,* XIV (1938), 32–41; W. Steinborn, "Dichterische Existenz," *Das Innere Reich,* IV (1938), 1208–1237.

V. L.

Schäffer, Albrecht, *see* Schaeffer.

Schaffner, Jakob (1875–1944, Swiss novelist), was born in Basle, raised in an orphanage, and then made to serve an apprenticeship to a cobbler, though his ambition was to become a teacher. As a journeyman cobbler he traveled all over Europe and in the process discovered and developed his ability as a writer and was soon able to live by his pen. The latter fact is a measure of his natural talent; Schaffner possesses indeed an unusually spontaneous power of expression, is a master in bringing to life the greatest variety of European scenes, and enters with astounding psychological understanding into almost any German dialect.

Yet he was far too much interested in social and political life to succumb to the danger of becoming a mere virtuoso. The unfair treatment he received in his youth may have kindled in him that spirit of revolt against bourgeois ideals which permeates the very style of his books, to say nothing of their content. Ever since his early autobiographical novel, *Konrad Pilater* (1910), heralded the dissenter from Swiss middle-class aspirations, Schaffner was different from and often opposed to his countrymen. He is passionate and temperamental to a fault, and his characters show none of the serene tranquillity or exasperating heaviness which is associated with Swiss writing; his women no less openly than his men defy conventional standards and claim the right to follow instinct or intellect. But after the First World War, and no doubt under the influence of pressing social problems, Schaffner's work was marked by a transition from non-cooperative individualism to the serious effort for reconstruction. Unfortunately the remedies he began to advocate only widened the gulf separating him from his compatriots. For Schaffner, who had always been a firm believer in the possibility of combining patriotism with socialism, cast his lot in with German National Socialism whose good points, as he saw it, he tried to interpret for Switzerland. That he was not an uncritical adherent of the German form of totalitarianism is evidenced by his spirited account of a "strength through joy" trip, in *Volk zu Schiff* (1936). Today Schaffner stands fully discredited as a social and political reformer in the eyes of his countrymen, and his reputation as a novelist has suffered proportionately. The time will however come when we can again do justice to his creative work, and it is safe to assume that his voluminous autobiographical novels—*Johannes* (1922), *Die Jünglingszeit des Johannes Schattenhold* (1930), and *Eine deutsche Wanderschaft* (1933)—will then be enjoyed both for their documentary value and for their imaginative and stylistic vividness.

See: R. Faesi, *Gestalten und Wandlungen schweizerischer Dichtung* (1922), pp. 168–203; P. Fässler, *Jakob Schaffner; Leben und Werk* (1937).

H. B.

Schaukal, Richard von (1874–, Austrian poet, novelist, and essayist), was born at Brünn in Austrian Moravia, the son of an apothecary. He studied law at the University of Vienna, entered the service of the Austrian state in 1897, and achieved considerable distinction as a state official; when the Austrian monarchy collapsed in 1918, Schaukal gave up his position and lived thereafter in retirement in a suburb of Vienna. Schaukal's literary production, though not extensive, is of high quality. While his prose fiction (*Eros Thanatos,* 1906; a collection of stories) is respectable, his few essays (*Giorgione,* 1907) noteworthy, and his translations of French poets (Baudelaire, Verlaine, *Nachdichtungen,* 1906) distinguished, he is likely to live longest through his lyric poetry, the first of which was published before he was 20 (*Gedichte,* 1893). It is in this field that a genuine development is discernible in his work. Sloughing off a certain amount of affectation and posing, a blasé weariness and pallor, Schaukal began to come into his own around 1900 and steadily grew thereafter in power and assurance. At the same time he was establishing the principles that were more and more to govern his lyric utterance. These are mainly three, insistence upon the validity and necessity of tradition in life as in art, consistent and conscious advocacy of the "aristocratic" point of view, the conception of artistic form as central and not peripheral. Constantly filing and polishing his poems, he reissued them as if executing a trust (*Ausgewählte Gedichte,* 1909; *Gedichte, 1891–1918,* 1918). There is also a marked trend toward conservatism in style as in subject matter.

See: J. Nadler, *Schaukals lyrisches Werk* (1932).

B. Q. M.

Schaumann, Ruth (1899–, German poet, sculptor, and graphic artist), was born in Hamburg, the daughter of an army officer who was killed in 1917 in the battle of Verdun. At the age of six she became seriously ill and has been in delicate health ever since. While still at school she felt the urge to write. In 1917 she went to Munich to begin her training as an artist, but another serious illness kept her in bed for several years. It was then that she wrote most of her deeply religious poems which appeared in her first book, *Die Kathedrale* (1920). They are expressionistic in style and reveal a fervor of devotion akin to that of the medieval mystics. The same spirit expresses itself in her religious sculpture of that period which is strongly influenced by Gothic art. A trend towards a simpler and more personal style (*volksliedhaft*) is already noticeable in her collection of poems *Der Knospengrund* (1922) and in *Das Passional* (1922), the story of the Passion of Christ. It becomes more and more marked in her later works (short stories, fairy tales, novels, plays) with their faith, childlike humility, and wonder towards God and his creation. In 1924 Ruth Schaumann entered the Catholic Church.

Marriage did not interfere with her literary and artistic endeavors. Her talents are happily combined in books of verse and prose, some of them written for her children and illustrated with her sensitive drawings and woodcuts (*Die Kinder und die Tiere,* 1928; *Die geliebten Dinge,* 1930). The outstanding qualities of her poems and unpresumptuous tales are her convincing sincerity and her quiet and delicate approach. Where she attempts more, the lack of touch with reality and her consciously limited scope of thinking and feeling result in vagueness and absence of color.

See: R. Hetsch, *Ruth Schaumann Buch* (1933).

O. S. F.

Schendel, Arthur van (1874–, Dutch novelist), was born at Batavia, Dutch East Indies. He studied English language and literature, intending to become a high school teacher. He taught for a number of years in England and Holland, but in the 90's began to devote himself exclusively to creative writing. He made his literary début with a short story called "Drogon" (1896), a medieval tale of a shy, passionate eccentric who seduces his brother's wife when her husband has gone to the Holy Land. In 1897 followed "De Schoone Jacht" (The Beautiful Chase), another strange, fantastic tale of medieval life.

Not until 1907 did his peculiar talent show itself in full strength in *Een Zwerver Verliefd* (A Wanderer in Love). It tells of the monk Tamalone's restless longing for distant lands and of his love for the girl who had been entrusted to his protection by her lover. *Een Berg van Droomen* (1913; A Mountain of Dreams) takes the reader into a fairy-tale world of dreamlike imaginings. With the appearance of *Het Fregatschip Johanna Maria* (1930; Eng. tr., *The "Johanna Maria,"* 1935), Van Schendel turned from dream to reality. It is the biography of a sailing vessel, one of the last of Holland's merchant marine that survived the coming of the steamship. The hero of his tale is Jacob Brouwer, the sailmaker of the brave ship. He has known her from the day that she was launched, he has served among her crew with a devotion such as no man gives to a soulless thing, he has at last become her owner and must suffer the pain of parting with the dear one, unable to rescue her from the scrap heap which becomes her burial place. It is a restrained, objective record of a simple life that approaches greatness through its generous surrender to a single devotion. The book was hailed at once as a masterpiece and awarded the annual prize of the Maatschappij der Nederlandsche Letterkunde (Society of Netherlands Literature) as the most distinguished literary work of the year. The best known among his later novels are *De Waterman* (1933; The Waterman), *De Rijke Man* (1936; The Rich Man), and *Grauwe Vogels* (1937; Eng. tr., *Grey Birds,* 1939).

Van Schendel's technique is that of the unemotional recorder. His narrative lacks dramatic quality. It never breaks into dialogue. His characters move speechless through his stories, like figures that one sees in dreams. Van Schendel, nevertheless, is regarded by his Dutch contemporaries as Holland's greatest living novelist. A group of his admirers proposed him, in 1939, as a candidate for the Nobel prize.

A. J. B.

Scherer, Edmond (1815–1889, French critic and publicist), was born in Paris, of Swiss forebears. He was in some respects the Protestant counterpart of Ernest Renan (*q.v.*) An ordained minister in the Reformed Swiss Church, he was one of the many victims of 19th-century science, losing his faith and breaking with the Church in 1861. He left Geneva at that time and made Versailles his home. He was associated until his death with the famous daily, *Temps,* of which he was one of the founders and editors. An unusually prolific writer, Scherer contributed more than 3300 articles of a literary or political nature to the *Temps* and to learned journals and periodicals. Though a politician of some note (he was senator in 1875), his title to fame rests largely on his contributions to the world of letters. Throughout his long career at the *Temps* (26 years), he seldom failed to publish under the heading "Variétés" a substantial weekly article on literature. The most significant of these articles were republished under the title *Etudes sur la littérature contemporaine* (10 vols., 1863–1895). These studies in literature are characterized by their straightforwardness, penetration, literary taste, and cosmopolitan nature. Dealing in the main with French letters, Scherer's studies include outstanding names and works in English, German, Spanish, and Italian literature. His articles on English literature were translated by George Saintsbury under the title *Essays on English Literature* (1891).

When Sainte-Beuve died (1869), the distinction of succeeding the renowned author of the *Lundis* fell upon Scherer. As an admiring disciple of Sainte-Beuve, Scherer was consistently, though not servilely, faithful to his master's method of looking for the man behind the author in a literary work. A book reveals the soul and temperament of its author to the critic who deserves his name; one of the chief tasks of the critic should then be to understand the more or less veiled message about himself which the writer wittingly or unwittingly transmits in his work, and the critic should present it to his readers in a detailed pen picture. Scherer's manner is less circuitous, or less discreet, than that of Sainte-Beuve. With a few bold, well-studied strokes he strives to produce and leave a lifelike, lasting impression on the reader's mind.

Scherer was admittedly influenced by Hegel, on whose work he wrote an article deemed a literary event at the time of its publication in the *Revue des deux mondes* (February 15, 1861). Like many of his contemporaries, Scherer adopted a relativistic philosophy. When he is dealing with literature, however, he for the most part forgets his theories on historical criticism; he is far less interested than many in unearthing the numerous, often doubtful influences that have brought about the genesis and development of a literary work. The finished product itself as a work of art and the author's ideas about life and its gravest concerns—these, above all, attract Scherer's attention. His characteristic qualities are sincerity and literary taste; his neat, sober, rapidly moving and incisive style is that of a thinker whose prime concern is the true and the beautiful.

Though Scherer's contemporaries (among these Sainte-Beuve and Renan) held his work in high esteem, his influence during his lifetime and since has never been very great. Reasons for the relative obscurity of a man who seemed to deserve better of posterity can be conjectured. Scherer's point of view and style were not entirely French, since his background and education were in great part Swiss; his somewhat puritanical approach to literature was not always acceptable to or understood by the Parisians for whom he wrote; a too exclusive independence and "ivory-tower" attitude left Scherer on the margin of social and literary circles where the climate of opinion on belles-lettres often originated; finally, Scherer judged democracy severely at a time when popular hopes ran high in this new experiment, and he expressed undisguised pessimism about the destiny of France under a democratic regime (see *La Démocratie en France,* 1883). In spite of Scherer's unpopularity in his own country, all those who have respect for keen literary taste and refined intellectual honesty may well continue to consult his articles.

See: O. Gréard, *Edmond Scherer* (1890); E. Boutmy, *Taine, Scherer, Laboulaye* (1901); N. Tremblay, *La Critique littéraire d'Edmond Scherer* (1932).

N. J. T.

Schickele, René (1885–1940, German novelist, poet, and dramatist), manifests in his life and works the fate of a citizen in a boundary land between two great cultures. Son of a German father and a French mother, he grew up in Alsace, a country sadly split in its loyalty by the cleavage between Germany and France. He studied in Strassburg, then turned to journalism and the publishing of magazines. His first volumes of poetry were collected in *Der Ritt ins Leben* (1905). Torn between the elemental "natural force" of his paternal ancestry and the greater "historical force" exerted by France, he developed his ideal of the supernational European who is indebted to both "fatherlands." *Der Fremde* (1907), Schickele's first novel, reveals the contradictory elements in the character of its author, who later alternated between expressionist and impressionist modes of style. Several volumes of poetry were followed by the novel *Benkal, der Frauentröster* (1914), an impressive fantastic vision of the coming war and its implicit absurdity. After the outbreak of the war—Schickele was then living in Berlin—he wrote within a few months the successful drama *Hans im Schnakenloch* (1916). The hero, a full-blooded, impetuous farmer, stands between two nations and two women. When the hour strikes, all about him make clear decisions and know where they stand; only Hans is torn within himself. Death in the French army, which he expects to be defeated, is the last hope of the fugitive from home. Soon banned in Germany and condemned in France, the drama gives evidence of the trend of Schickele's development.

In December, 1914, he had become the editor of *Die weissen Blätter.* He transferred the publication from Berlin to Zurich and made it the effective mouthpiece of European anti-war sentiment, counting among its contributors literary leaders from many lands. Schickele himself became an advocate of a revolution which would know no force other than that "of the heart, of persuasion, and of a joyful example." Soon disappointed after the war, he retired to the Black Forest and wrote the trilogy, *Das Erbe am Rhein,* the epic of Alsace and the Alsatians, comprising *Maria Capponi* (1925; Eng. tr., 1928), *Blick auf die Vogesen* (1927; Eng. tr., *Heart of Alsace,* 1929), and *Der Wolf in der Hürde* (1929). The great problems of politics are seen from the point of view of a cultured but kindhearted human being. The brilliancy and clarity of the South are accepted and portrayed as objectively as the mysticism of weaving mists in the Black Forest. To Schickele's way of thinking the solution of the problems between France and Germany may be achieved in terms of concrete humanity.

Driven to France after 1933, Schickele wrote the novel *Die Flaschenpost* (1937), the tragedy of an individualist who in the confusion of modern times finds ultimate peace in an insane asylum. A book on D. H. Lawrence (1934) had shown Schickele as a lucid and passionate interpreter of creative genius.

See: A. Soergel, *Dichtung und Dichter der Zeit,* Neue Folge: *Im Banne des Expressionismus,* 4. Auflage (1927), pp. 324–326, 571–578.

W. K. P.

Schlaf, Johannes (1862–1941, German dramatist and novelist), was born in Querfurt, Saxony, where he received his early education until his parents moved to Magdeburg in 1874. In childhood he showed literary and artistic inclinations which his parents discouraged and suppressed. At the Gymnasium he knew Conradi (*q.v.*), who impressed him greatly. After two semesters at Halle, where he switched quickly from theology to philosophy, he completed his training as a philologist in Berlin (1887). He became a member of the literary group "Durch" (*q.v.*), where young enthusiasts like Heinrich and Julius Hart (*q.v.*), Bruno Wille, Wilhelm Boelsche (*q.v.*), Leo Berg, *et al.* were discussing the requisites of "modern" literature. Already familiar with the new trends and basically in sympathy with them, Schlaf accepted an invitation to collaborate with Arno Holz (*q.v.*) in putting such theories into practice. The winter of 1887–1888 yielded a series of sketches, three of which were published as *Papa Hamlet* (1889), under the joint pseudonym Bjarne P. Holmsen. Their accurate presentation of everyday life in its most prosaic and minute details was carried out with scientific precision and utilized photographic and phonographic techniques. Mannerisms and speech differences of each character were carefully noted and became valuable adjuncts of these milieu studies which aimed not at interpreting but depicting life. They presented, in fact, only the depressing meanness and squalor of bourgeois society. The literary value of these sketches is intrinsically small, but their immediate effect was important: they launched German naturalism (*q.v.*), from which emerged Gerhart Hauptmann (*q.v.*). Earlier and similar sketches, "Die papierne Passion," were finally published in a collection, *Neue Gleise* (1891), together with *Papa Hamlet* and the drama *Die Familie Selicke* (1889). The last, a drab and depressing milieu study of an incompatible bourgeois marriage which gradually killed any hope of happiness for the whole family, set the pattern of consistent naturalism (*konsequenter Naturalismus*).

After 1892 Schlaf and Holz wrote independently and indulged for years in disputes regarding their individual shares in their joint efforts. A reasonable and fair estimate must emphasize that Schlaf had the deeper poetic nature while Holz was the energetic and aggressive theorist who formulated the principal ideas of German naturalism and gave final form to their cooperative writings. Schlaf published *Meister Oelze* (1892; revised 2d ed., 1908), technically perhaps the best naturalistic drama, though never successful in the theatre. Quite in contrast to the crass naturalism of these works are the delicate impressionistic sketches of idyllic contentment far from city turmoil and strife, *In Dingsda* (1892) and *Frühling* (1894). After a serious nervous collapse (1893–1896), Schlaf wrote further dramas and stories, followed by ambitious novels that attempted to combat the decadent spirit of the age and to present the problematic nature of modern man in terms of a new positive faith in spiritual values. He stressed psychological analysis of human character in conflict with the world and itself. These novels, *Das Dritte Reich* (1900), *Die Suchenden* (1901), and *Peter Bojes Freite* (1902), were followed later by another trilogy, *Der Kleine* (1904), *Der Prinz* (1906), and *Am toten Punkt* (1907), in which literary artistry seems secondary to philosophical and religious interests. Schlaf also wrote essays on Whitman, Verhaeren (*q.v.*), and Maeterlinck (*q.v.*) and translated from their works. Religious and metaphysical problems absorbed him more and more until he lost himself in mystical speculations. Less ambitious works like *Miele* (1920) and *Der Weihnachtswunsch und anderes* (1924) are more satisfying because Schlaf is at his best in shorter works where restraint and concentration of effort produced little masterpieces. His place in literary history, however, depends upon his early work with Holz, which profoundly influenced the literature of the 90's.

See: A. Soergel, *Dichtung und Dichter der Zeit,* Neue Folge: *Im Banne des Expression-*

ismus, 4. Auflage (1927), pp. 19–25, and *Dichtung und Dichter der Zeit,* 19. Auflage (1928), pp. 191–201, 384–394.

W. A. R.

Schlumberger, Jean (1877–, French novelist and philosopher), born at Guebwiller in Alsace, belongs to an influential Protestant family of rich industrialists. He counts among his ancestors members of the famous Bernouilli family, and through his mother he is related to a long line of writers from Malezieu to Guizot. Obliged to leave Alsace when he was 15, so as to retain his French nationality, he attended the Lycée Condorcet in Paris. After earning his diploma of Licencié ès Lettres, he became interested in the history of religions, but finally devoted himself entirely to literature. In 1906 appeared, in Péguy's (*q.v.*) *Cahiers de la quinzaine,* Schlumberger's novel *Heureux qui comme Ulysse*—which he was subsequently to work over and lengthen by two parts under the title *L'Inquiète Paternité* (1911). In 1909 he was one of the founders of the *Nouvelle Revue française,* with his friend André Gide (*q.v.*); the two had parted company amicably with Péguy and the *Cahiers.* Both Gide and Schlumberger were of a very well marked Protestant mentality, intellectually rather than emotionally inclined; at the same time both were deeply concerned with the moral aspects of life. They virtually founded what might be called a school of Protestant casuistry (in the sense of a system for dealing with cases of conscience), the most representative novel of which is Gide's *La Porte étroite.* Gide, Schlumberger, and, in his own way, Pierre Loti (*q.v.*) represent the Protestant reaction against the materialistic or pantheistic philosophies which had prevailed for some years in France, just as Bourget (*q.v.*), the author of *Le Disciple,* and his group (Bazin, Bordeaux, *qq.v.,* and others) are the protagonists of a parallel movement among Catholic writers. Both Gide and Schlumberger remained true to their introspective method and consistently opposed individualistic ethics to authority—with this difference, however, that Gide ultimately indulged in very bold theories in his endeavor to escape conventionalism at any cost (*L'Immoraliste, Les Faux-Monnayeurs, Corydon*), while Schlumberger remained more reticent and at least in expression more orthodox.

Most of Schlumberger's novels were published after the First World War: *Un Homme heureux* (1920); *Le Camarade infidèle; roman d'un démobilisé* (1922); *Le Lion devenu vieux* (1924), a *roman historique* in which the author imagines the thoughts that may have been those of the aged Cardinal Retz forced to surrender to the intolerant and despotic Richelieu. The greatest success in the literary career of Schlumberger has been *Saint-Saturnin* (1931). Saint-Saturnin is the name of a family estate in Normandy which its owners consider a sacred trust; the weak-mindedness of the present head of the family jeopardizes the safety of the estate, and the question arises as to how far the irresponsible man should be respected. The discussion of practical problems of life is continued in a novel that may be considered a sort of sequel to *Saint-Saturnin, Histoire de quatre potiers* (1935), in which the successful building up of an industry without involving the enslavement of its employees is discussed.

But the analysis of the problems of the soul remains paramount with Schlumberger, as is testified by his three *traités,* or essays, all of 1927: *L'Enfant qui s'accuse, Césaire, ou la Puissance de l'esprit, Dialogues avec le corps endormi.* The last brings up the eternal problem of body and soul inseparably bound to each other; while the body is asleep, the soul may try to rise to *la contemplation de Dieu.* In 1934 Schlumberger, in *Sur les frontières religieuses,* refers to himself as "un libre croyant"; and in 1936 he rereads Corneille and finds in the old exponent of the *morale du devoir* a real delight (*Plaisir à Corneille; promenade anthologique*). A novel published in 1940, *Stéphane le glorieux,* deals with a very complex *cas de conscience* during the First World War; somewhere in the Balkans the hero Stéphane is almost forced by circumstances to commit a crime, and the memory of this crime remains a burden on his spirit. In 1941 Schlumberger published a volume of essays, *Jalons.*

Schlumberger was interested in the theatre, but did not win much recognition. Two of his plays were given at the Vieux Colombier, *Les Fils Louverné* (1914) and *La Mort de Sparte;* a brief play, *L'Amour, le prince et la vérité,* is presented as a *divertissement.*

In 1942 the French Academy awarded to Schlumberger its Grand Prix de Littérature.

A. Sz.

Schmidtbonn, Wilhelm (pseud. of Wilhelm Schmidt, 1876–, German dramatist, novelist, and poet), was born in Bonn, the son of a merchant. He studied music at Cologne, then literature at the universities of Bonn, Berlin, Göttingen, and Zurich. He was for several years dramaturgist of the municipal theatre at Düsseldorf and editor of the journal *Masken.* For reasons of health he had to leave the Rhineland and now lives in Ascona, Switzerland.

He is a prolific writer. His numerous dramas, novels, and stories show a wide variety, but the line of his development stands out clearly. Beginning under the influence of naturalism (*see* German naturalism), he struggled to find meaning in the realities of life. This struggle is reflected in the stories *Uferleute* (1903) and *Raben* (1902), the novel *Der Heilsbringer* (1906), the dramas *Mutter Landstrasse* (1901), *Der Graf von Gleichen* (1908), and *Der Zorn des Achilles* (1909). Gradually he found himself and experienced the joy of living in a few happy years before 1914. During these years he wrote the dramas *Hilfe! Ein Kind vom Himmel gefallen* (1910), *Der spielende Eros* (1911), and *Der verlorene Sohn* (1912), the poems in *Lobgesang des Lebens* (1911), and 23 legends collected in *Der Wunderbaum* (1913). He was thrown back into doubts and dark moods by the First World War (see the drama *Die Stadt der Besessenen,* 1915, and the translation of a mystery of 1452, *Die Passion,* 1919). After the war his leitmotif became the restoring of human trust and love; he wrote, "Nur der Dichter versteht, der allen Freund ist." Among the dramatic works were *Der Geschlagene* (1920), *Die Schauspieler* (1921), *Die Fahrt nach Orplid* (1922), and *Maruf, der tolle Lügner* (1924). The main narrative works were the story *Die Flucht zu den Hülflosen* (1922), a collection of fairy tales *Der Garten der Erde* (1922), a novel *Der Verzauberte* (1924), a collection of short stories *Geschichten von den unberührten Frauen* (1925), and the novel *Mein Freund Dei; Denkmal eines jungen Lastträgers* (1927). In the two main works of the 30's Schmidtbonn deals with the memories of his home town and his own life. The scene of the novel *Der dreieckige Marktplatz* (1935) is Bonn towards the end of the 19th century; *An einem Strom geboren; ein Lebensbuch* (1935) relates in more than 100 sketches "the fairy tale of my life." The more fantastic side of Schmidtbonn's narrative talents appears again in the novel *Hü Lü* (1936).

See: *Chor um Schmidtbonn* (1926); A. Soergel, *Dichtung und Dichter der Zeit,* Neue Folge: *Im Banne des Expressionismus,* 4. Auflage (1927), pp. 111–118; M. Tau, ed., *Das Wilhelm Schmidtbonn Buch* (1927); H. Pongs, "Rheinische Stammesseele in der Dichtung der Gegenwart," *Dichtung und Volkstum,* XXXIX (1938), 105–106.

W. R. G.

Schnitzler, Arthur (1862–1931, Austrian dramatist and novelist), was born in Vienna and began his career as a physician, a profession in which his father and his brother made records of excellence. He edited the *Internationale klinische Rundschau* from 1887 to 1894 and contributed scientific articles on hypnotism, neurasthenia, telepathy, and psychotherapy. His earliest nonscholarly publications appeared at the close of the 1880's in Viennese periodicals under the pseudonym Anatol, a name that he soon selected for the hero of his first playlets. These playlets appeared in book form in 1892. They were followed by the full-length play *Das Märchen* (1894) and by the more successful drama *Liebelei* (1895; Eng. tr., *The Reckoning,* 1907). Thereafter he devoted himself almost entirely to a literary career, producing plays, novels, and short stories in rapid succession.

At the turn of the century Schnitzler, together with Hermann Bahr, Richard Beer-Hofmann, and Hugo von Hofmannsthal (*qq.v.*), formed the center of a literary movement known as *Jungwien,* a movement that stood in violent opposition to the naturalism of Berlin (*see* German naturalism) as well as to the pseudo-classicism of Grillparzer and his Viennese epigones. *Jungwien* dominated Austrian letters until the First World War.

Schnitzler's medical background is reflected in his literary works. His wisest comments are generally put in the mouths of physicians, his *raisonneurs.* Illness is a favorite theme with him, and the consciousness of death constantly haunts his characters. Indeed, the call of life sounds so alluring to them because they envisage so vividly their inevitable end. They never forge ambitious plans that require decades to mature, but rather seek to experience the fast fleeting moments so intensely that nothing is left for future hours. They never submit to present aches and anxieties for the sake of remote joys that may not materialize. They do not strive for fame, wealth, or power. They eschew grandiloquence. They float on in a continuous intoxication of tenderness and mild passion, adding a little aroma, charm, and friendliness to the bleakest atmosphere.

Schnitzler avoids dogmatic generalizations. Sin, vice, guilt, are for him obsolete expressions. He holds that there are no panaceas for life's ills. Every human being is unique. Hence every relationship between human beings is a unique relationship. It must be studied thoroughly and diagnosed accurately in all its complexities before a specific remedy can be prescribed. The medicine that cures in one case may act as a poison that kills in another. Schnitzler's answers to problems are offered by him merely as possibilities and not as final solutions. Indeed, he often succumbs to the temptation of satirizing good-naturedly in one work the very opinions that his hero or heroine fervently defends in another work. The one theme running through all his plays and novels is that some people are alive while countless others are reposing under the sod. He therefore begs those who live to cease moaning and to avoid darkening with cares their all too few days on earth.

Schnitzler caught in his gentle hand the last golden glow of Vienna's setting glory and converted it to art. In the best of his plays (*Der einsame Weg,* 1903, Eng. tr., *The Lonely Way,* 1915; *Der junge Medardus,* 1910; *Das weite Land,* 1911, Eng. tr., *The Vast Domain,* 1923; *Professor Bernhardi,* 1912, Eng. tr., 1913; *Der Gang zum Weiher,* 1927), in his autobiographic novel *Der Weg ins Freie* (1908; Eng. tr., *The Road to the Open,* 1923), and in numerous short stories, the peculiar culture and atmosphere of this former capital of the Danubian dual monarchy continue to live on, even as in the songs of Franz Schubert and in waltzes of Johann Strauss.

See: J. Körner, *Arthur Schnitzlers Gestalten und Probleme* (1921); R. Specht, *Arthur Schnitzler* (1922); S. Liptzin, *Arthur Schnitzler* (1932, in English).

S. L.

Scholz, Wilhelm von (1874–, German dramatist, novelist, lyric poet, and essayist), is a distinguished writer of versatile talent. As a descendant of the older, conservative bureaucracy (his father was secretary of finance in Bismarck's cabinet), Scholz has striven to maintain for the literary arts a place apart from the turmoil of everyday life, yet accessible enough to exert a formative, cultivating influence upon the sensitive and educated reader. Born and reared in the traditions of the 19th century, he has kept aloof from the changing tendencies of the present, alternating his residence between Berlin and Lake Constance. From 1910 to 1923 he was dramatic director of the stage at Stuttgart. Since then he has remained an independent writer, except for serving as president of the Deutsche Dichterakademie at Berlin for several years.

After symbolistic beginnings in such dramas as *Der Besiegte* (1899) and *Der Gast* (1900), Scholz has consistently interpreted the world of poetry as a net of irrational, magic relations superimposed upon the world of reality. Consequently most of his works deal with dreams, hallucinations, and related demonological topics, achieving at times a singular transparency, especially in the treatment of historical situations of the Middle Ages. Among his dramas, *Der Jude von Konstanz* (1905), *Vertauschte Seelen* (1910), *Gefährliche Liebe* (1913), *Der Wettlauf mit dem Schatten* (1922), and *Die gläserne Frau* (1924) have met with widespread success. His adaptations from Calderón, as well as his revival of the miracle and the marionette play, have been well received. Esoteric impressions are also conveyed in the novels to which the author turned rather late in life. Among these *Perpetua* (1926) and *Der Weg nach Ilok* (1930) express the tragic struggle between the natural and the supernatural in man. His short stories, the genre in which Scholz is a master, appeared in two collections, *Erzählungen* (1924) and *Die Gefährten* (1937).

Aside from a few collections of lyrics (*Der Spiegel,* 1908, and *Neue Gedichte,* 1913) and from several autobiographical works (especially *Wanderungen,* 1934, and *Jahrhundertwende,* 1936), which abound in remarkable nature descriptions, Scholz's significance rests upon his theoretical writings (*Gedanken zum Drama,* 1905, 2d revised ed., 1915; *Der Zufall, eine Vorform des Schicksals,* 1924; *Droste-Hülshoff,* 1904; *Hebbel,* 1905) and upon his many editions of German classics (*Deutsches Balladenbuch,* 1905; *Deutsche Dramaturgie,* 1907–1912; *Deutsche Mystiker,* 1908; *Mörike,* 1922; *Novalis,* 1922; *Hebbel,* 1923; *Eichendorff,* 1924; *Das Bodenseebuch,* 1925; *Das Buch des Lachens,* 1938). He is coeditor of *Die grossen Deutschen* (1935–1937), five volumes of German biographies. As a creative stylist he is a champion of the well-chosen and meticulously presented written word, phrase, or situation.

See: F. Droop, *Wilhelm von Scholz und seine besten Bühnenwerke* (1922); H. M. Elster, "Wilhelm von Scholz; sein Leben und Schaffen," in *Preussische Jahrbücher,* CCXXVIII (1932), 60–78; O. Loerke, "Wilhelm von Scholz," *Die neue Rundschau,* Jahrgang XLVI (1935), Bd. I, pp. 206–214.

H. R.

Schröder, Rudolf Alexander (1878–, German poet and essayist), was born in Bremen, of a patrician family in that republican Hansa town. With his cousin, Alfred Walter Heymel, he founded in 1898 the review *Die Insel* (1898–1902) and the Insel-Verlag, one of the distinguished publishing houses of Germany; in 1912, with Hugo von Hofmannsthal and Rudolf Borchardt (*qq.v.*), he helped to establish the Bremer Presse, which set a high standard for presswork and literary quality. In both undertakings his purpose was to build up a national tradition and at the same time to encourage the revival of arts and crafts, a movement in which he played an important role. He took part in the First World War, in the navy and then in the Brussels administration. As a Protestant and a conservative, Schröder kept aloof from neopagan and totalitarian tendencies. About 1934 he left his home city, and now lives near the Chiemsee, in Bavaria.

Highly gifted in many ways—as an architect and decorator, a painter, a writer of witty and elegant verse (*Hama,* 1908)—he concentrated more and more upon poetry. To him German literature owes translations of *The Rape of the Lock* (1908); the *Odyssey* (1910), the best version since that of Voss, and the *Iliad* (1943); Horace (1935); Vergil's *Georgics* (1924), *Eclogues* (1926), and a canto of the *Aeneid* (in *Corona,* 1931) and Racine (also in *Corona,* 1932), the first adequate versions of both poets; many Flemish and Dutch lyrics (*e.g.,* Guido Gezelle, *q.v.,* 1917, and Geerten Gossaert, 1929); and three plays of Shakespeare. Among his prose translations is *Ciceros Cato der Ältere über das Greisenalter* (1924). He is one of the few German poets who have taken up the great Latin and French tradition (see his essay on Racine).

His prose is stately and leisurely, reflective and meandering (*Der Wanderer und die Heimat,* 1931; *Aus Kindheit und Jugend,* 1934). Some of his most revealing pages deal with the secrets of poetry and of religious faith (*Zur Naturgeschichte des Glaubens, Kunst und Religion,* 1936; *Die Aufsätze und Reden,* 2 vols., 1939). But, first and last, Schröder is a lyric poet, one of the most eminent of his time, more lofty and pure, perhaps, than passionate, faithful to tradition; his style and tone are definitely his own, strangely uninfluenced by his contemporaries, and he—unlike some of them—never overstrains his art. His greatest achievements (the philosophical sonnets "Die Zwillingsbrüder," the elegy "In memoriam," some of his odes and religious poems) he wrung from his profound pessimism. He clings to what may last, country, friendship, poetry, faith. With the years his religious heritage asserted itself strongly; he studied the history of Protestant verse (*Dichtung und Dichter der Kirche,* 1936; *Die Kirche und ihr Lied,* 1937; *Luther und sein Lied,* 1942) and revived the art of hymn writing.

For a time his poems were scarcely noticed and out of print. A new edition of his earlier work has been contemplated (*Unmut,* 1899; *Lieder an eine Geliebte, Empedokles, Sprüche in Reimen,* all 1900; *An Belinde,* 1902; *Sonette zum Andenken an eine Verstorbene,* 1904; *Lieder und Elegien,* 1911). To the collection of his mature poetry, *Die weltlichen Gedichte* (1940), and his religious poems, *Mitte des Lebens* (1930), have been added *Ein Weihnachtslied* (1935), *Ein Lobgesang* (1937), *Osterspiel* (1938), and *Kreuzgespräch* (1939).

See: J. Hofmiller, *Zeitgenossen* (1910), pp. 289–313; J. Nadler, *Literaturgeschichte der deutschen Stämme und Landschaften,* Bd. 4 (1928), pp. 770–772; H. von Hofmannsthal, *Die Berührung der Sphären* (1931), pp. 143–159, 349–351; *Werke und Tage: Festschrift für R. A. Schröder zum 60. Geburtstag* (1938).

H. St.

Schuré, Edouard (1841–1929, French dramatist and critic), was born in Strasbourg, where he received his education, finally taking a degree in law at the university. Instead of settling down to an advocate's practice, however, he traveled in Germany (1864–1865) and Italy (1871–1873), producing meanwhile his first two books, *Histoire du lied* (1868) and *L'Alsace et les prétentions prussiennes* (1871). After his return from Italy he settled in Paris. There he wrote for the *Revue des deux mondes* and the *Nouvelle Revue* and soon became well known for his essays on the history of religions and on the drama.

Like certain other Frenchmen of his generation, Schuré revolted against the materialism of science, the skepticism of Renan (*q.v.*), the determinism of Taine (*q.v.*), the naturalism of contemporary literature. In his opinion the traditional church offered no refuge for such spirits as himself, since, though it had not lost its faith in the divine, it had limited this too much. Schuré at length found his own solution in a poetic nationalism (a *recherche de l'âme celtique*) and in a theosophy which received its final direction from Rudolph Steiner. In art, impressionism and symbolism seemed to him to be respectively a mere rendering of sensation without any shaping concept and a game of analogies with no real metaphysical profundity. He turned, therefore, for inspiration to the Greek tragedies, the poems of Shelley, the operas of Wagner. In *Les Grands Initiés* (1889; Eng. tr., *The Great Initiates,* 2 vols., 1922) and *Précurseurs et révoltés* (1904) he wrote of the great inspired figures of the past, poets and prophets. One of the first French Wagnerites, he fought tirelessly to win a hearing for the German master, in whose work he saw a sense of art as a spiritual force and a recognition of the deep spiritual fountains of the German people. Not content with explaining Wagner's purpose (*Richard Wagner; son œuvre et son idée,* 1875), he attempted himself to perform a similar task. In *Les Grandes Légendes de France* (1891) he presented as an inspiration to his contemporaries those bits of French legend which he felt had the supreme value of representing *un élément essentiel de son âme collective.* At the same time, in a series of mystical plays, *Le Théâtre de l'âme* (3 vols., 1900–1905), he attempted to create a spiritual drama which, like Wagner's at Bayreuth, would approach the status of a religious ceremony. Schuré's criticism may still be read with interest and pleasure, but his plays, though not without occasional happy touches which recall Maeterlinck (*q.v.*), are for the most part so studded with the clichés of the romantic drama as to seem ridiculous to the modern reader.

See: Alphonse Roux and Robert Veyssié, *Edouard Schuré* (1913).

C. W., Jr.

Schwob, Marcel (1867–1905, French scholar, essayist, poet, and novelist), born at Chaville in the Ile-de-France, came of a very cultivated family of rabbis and physicians. His childhood was spent in Nantes. He was given a careful education, was very precocious, and won many prizes; in 1882 he entered the Collège Sainte-Barbe in Paris. He was early familiar with German and English as well as with the classical languages. He became particularly fond of Apuleius, Petronius, and Anacreon; he had a juvenile enthusiasm for Poe and admired Hugo greatly. From Sainte-Barbe he went to the Lycée Louis-le-Grand, where he made friends with Gsell, Léon Daudet (*q.v.*), and Claudel (*q.v.*) and began to dream of great literary achievements—a monumental *Faust* or a *Prometheus.* In 1885, so as to be done with his military duties, he enlisted and served his one year. He became interested in argot and tried to reconstitute the speech of the companions of Villon, a subject which remained near to his heart all his life (*Etude de l'argot français,* 1889; *Le jargon des Coquillards en 1451,* 1890). He began to write poetry (*Mimes; poèmes en prose,* published in 1894), prepared for the Ecole Normale Supérieure, soon became interested in Sanskrit, and pursued his humanistic training in that direction.

Schwob started his journalistic career in the *Evénement,* at the same time sending to the *Echo de Paris* stories which were later included in his collections *Le Beau double* (1892) and *Le Roi au masque d'or* (1893). He was one of the early contributors to the *Mercure de France,* the newly founded organ of the symbolists. Jarry (*q.v.*) dedicated to him his *Ubu Roi.* This multifarious intellectual activity and productivity resulted in a sort of mental anarchy which is reflected in Schwob's most striking but very perplexing *Le Livre de Monelle* (1894; Eng. tr., *The Book of Monelle,* 1929).

Then came the catastrophe. Schwob's health gave way; a serious operation left him an invalid. From that time he was what his biographer calls "the Schwob of legends." His zestful life was only a memory. Like Proust he was a frail human wreck, but with remarkable flashes of genius. He could still put in long hours of study in libraries and in the archives of Paris. He translated *Moll Flanders* (1895), and from old manuscripts and hagiographies he extracted a little masterpiece, *La Croisade des enfants* (1896; Eng. tr., *The Children's Crusade,* 1898), and a series called *Vies imaginaires* (1896), in which he re-creates the lives of interesting men, suggesting that the so-called documented lives of the conventional biographers can only be travesties. In 1896 was published another volume of miscellaneous articles, called *Spicilège,* which is considered, with *Le Livre de Monelle,* particularly representative of his incoherent, mystifying, and suggestive mentality. In spite of his precarious health, Schwob continued to see friends and correspond with them—Meredith, Stevenson, Gourmont (*q.v.*), Valéry (*q.v.*), Mirbeau (*q.v.*), and others. For reasons of health he went to Samoa, where he spent several months (1901–1902). With Paul Morand (*q.v.*) he adapted *Hamlet* for Sarah Bernhardt, for whom he also adapted F. M. Crawford's *Francesca da Rimini.* After a trip to Italy, Spain, and Portugal, he tried once more to complete his work on Villon and opened a course on the *Grand Testament* at the Ecole des Hautes Etudes Sociales, but after a few weeks of illness death overtook him. He also left, unfinished, the *Parnasse satyrique du XVme siècle,* published posthumously in 1905.

Schwob realized that his writings were often cryptic and frequently felt called upon to write prefaces to his books. Even *Le Livre de Monelle* must remain open to almost any interpretation; Pierre Champion calls it a gospel of pity and a manual of nihilism. Schwob had met in 1891 a little prostitute, Louise, who was to die two years later, wasted away by tuberculosis and other diseases; he had taken the greatest care of her and claimed to have remained inconsolable over the loss of that creature whose utter stupidity was an everlasting delight to him and at the same time an incentive to his pity. The echoes of Dickens, Tolstoy, Dostoevski, De Quincey, are obvious. But Schwob's pity led him to utter denial; let man do away with everything: "Destroy, destroy, destroy." There was a constant tug of war between the omniscient Schwob, held by his own accumulated documentation, and the genius who tried to escape the thralldom of mere scholarship. Schwob's case may be compared with that of Baudelaire who, unable to satisfy his ardent idealism, fed his soul on the horror which life inspired in him, on the unfathomable imbecility of mankind, on disgusting sensuality, on the beauty of ugliness.

In 1895, just over a year after Louise's death and eight months before his illness began, Schwob met his second great love in Marguerite Moreno, a distinguished actress of the Comédie Française. They were married in London in 1900; Schwob's letters and travel diaries addressed to her evince his devotion.

Notable among Schwob's last publications was a savage satire on journalism, *Mœurs des diurnales* (1903). Written under the pseudonym Loyson-Bridet, this work is largely inspired by Rabelais; its wit, however, proved too subtle and learned for the general public.

Schwob's complete writings have been edited by Pierre Champion (*Œuvres complètes,* 10 vols., 1927–1930).

See: Pierre Champion, *Marcel Schwob et son temps* (1927).

A. Sz.

Scott, Gabriel (1874–, Norwegian novelist), was born in Leith, Scotland, the son of a Norwegian seamen's pastor. When he was seven years old, the family removed to that part of southern Norway which became the background of his works, a region where nature and people are softer and gentler than in the mountainous interior. Scott wrote a number of rather pale stories, poems, and fairy tales before the First World War seemed to release his latent powers. Two novels under the general title *En saga om fædrelandssind* (A Saga of Patriotism), *Jernbyrden; historien om Jan Vibe* (1915; Ordeal by Fire; the Story of Jan Vibe), and *Enok Rubens levnedsløb* (1917; The Life Story of Enok Ruben), describe the hard times which Norwegians had passed through in the decades following 1770. They were grim tales. The idyllic note which characterizes much of Gabriel Scott's production was struck in *Kilden eller Brevet om fiskeren Markus* (1918; The Fountain, or the Letter about the Fisherman Marcus), the story of a poor fisherman who finds the wellspring of contentment in his own soul. The mystic-religious element is present also in *Stien eller Kristofer med kvisten* (1925; The Path, or Christopher with the Twig), the story of a crippled herdsboy. *Det gyldne Evangelium* (1921; Eng. tr., *The Golden Gospel, a Legend,* 1928) is a fairy tale in book form relating humorously how Our Lord and St. Peter visited the earth and what they saw there. Gabriel Scott has written also novels and short stories about folk life including sympathetic tales of the vagrant gypsies. His memoirs, in the form of a novel *En drøm om en drøm* (The Dream of a Dream), appeared in 1940, and a selection of lyric verse *Årringer* (Annual Rings, as of a tree) in 1945.

H. A. L.

Seedorff Pedersen, Hans Hartvig (1892–, Danish poet, traveler, and journalist), born in Aarhus, Jutland, is a natural lyricist, but one with a fine cultural background. He is par excellence a devotee of joy and beauty, particularly in his early poems, as in the collection *Hyben* (1917; Rose-hips). He appears at times as "Sorgenfri" (Carefree), a bacchant in the "Inn of Gladness," one who hopes for resurrection in the shape of grain, *aqvavit.* Paralleling his conviviality a strong Dionysian strain runs through a few of his other most original poems, showing the mystical, irresistible, well-nigh sleep-walking effect of sex urge (as in "Pigens Møde med Pan"; The Maid's Meeting with Pan). The poet's popular sailor songs, on the other hand (as "Styrmand Anderssons Hjemkomst"; Mate Andersson's Homecoming), roll and rollick. His ballads are rich in baroque humor. In some of the early poems Death appears as the dark foil that accents exulting life. Gradually, however, in later collections Death changes character, becomes Friend, until the poet's belief in immortality shines through. Joy in life—this life—remains.

Seedorff Pedersen's travels (a trip around the world besides various other long expeditions) have borne fruit both in his sometimes langorously sensuous, sometimes socially realistic poems and in his prose travel books (*e.g., To Tredje, Eldorado,* 1929; Two Third-Class, Eldorado). As constant flow and ebb in the poet's life, the outward longing to see and grasp the great rich world is followed by the homeward surge of feeling, the longing and love for Denmark, expressing itself in exquisite poems on Danish nature. Seedorff Pedersen has also written the stirring poem, now a rallying song, "Der rider en Konge" (1943; A King Is Riding), in homage to Christian X on his 73d birthday. And he has worked tirelessly for closer inter-Scandinavian ties.

See: Christian Rimestad, *Fra Stuckenberg til Seedorff,* II (1923); Helge Kjaergaard, *Die dänische Literatur der neuesten Zeit (1871–1933)* (1934).

C. K. B.

Seghers, Anna (pseud. of Netty Radvanyi, 1900–, German novelist), was born in Mainz and educated at Cologne and Heidelberg. In 1925 she married a Hungarian sociologist; with him and their two children she fled to Paris in 1933 and eventually to the anti-fascist colony in Mexico City.

Almost without exception, her novels urge social reforms. She early wrote, in direct and reticent prose, a powerful portrayal of the hopelessness of a village oppressed by monopoly, *Aufstand der Fischer von St. Barbara* (1928; Eng. tr., *The Revolt of the Fishermen,* 1929). There followed less impressive pleas for the German peasantry (*Der Kopflohn,* 1933) and for the German miners (*Die Rettung,* 1934) and then a sympathetic account of the 1934 Socialist uprising in Austria (*Der Weg durch den Februar,* 1935). The insistent anti-fascist message of Anna Seghers is heard again in the novel concerning the refugee problem in Europe, *Die Gefährten* (1932), but above all, and the more emphatically because of her husband's having been in a concentration camp, in a stirring tale written in the flashback manner of the movie scenario and dealing with the German underground, *Das siebte Kreuz* (1942; Eng. tr., *The Seventh Cross,* 1942).

V. L.

Seidel, Ina (1885–, German poet and novelist), was born in Halle an der Saale. She has been steeped in literature throughout all her life. The prolific and successful historical novelist, Georg Ebers (1837–1898), was her mother's stepfather; and her husband, Heinrich Wolfgang Seidel (1876–), who is also something of a writer (*Erinnerungen,* 1912; *Abend und Morgen,* 1934; *Das Seefräulein,* 1937), is the son of Heinrich Seidel (1842–1906), the once popular author of the delightfully sentimental story, *Leberecht Hühnchen* (1881). She married in 1907, hovered for months between death and life after the birth of her first child, and in this period of solitude and spiritual growth her soul turned to self-expression in poetry. Her first beginnings were in the lyric (*Gedichte,* 1914; *Neben der Trommel her,* 1915; *Weltinnigkeit,* 1918). Before the First World War began, however, she had already conceived the nuclear theme of her final masterpiece, and in 1917 she issued her first work of fiction, *Das Haus zum Monde.* Five years later she had already gained enough strength and substance to compose a powerful and significant novel, *Das Labyrinth* (1921; Eng. tr., *The Labyrinth,* 1932), the life story of a strange and enigmatic figure, George Forster, whose career she traced more on the psychic than on the material plane.

But Ina Seidel was not yet fully equipped for the theme which she had first set herself, and definite and ultimate expression came only in 1930, in *Das Wunschkind* (Eng. tr., *The Wish Child,* 1935). This story of a widowed mother, who has literally wrested her child from the reluctant clasp of fate, only to lose him to a more inexorable destiny in the Prussian Wars of Liberation, is one of the great books of its generation, perhaps one of the outstanding documents of our time—a story which only a woman could have written, but one which some woman had to write. It places the author on a level with the greatest women writers of Germany.

See: A. Soergel, *Dichtung und Dichter der Zeit,* Dritte Folge: *Dichter aus deutschem Volkstum* (1934), pp. 149–165.

B. Q. M.

Seifullina, Lidiya Nikolayevna (1889–, Russian novelist), was born at Varlamovo in Orenburg province. She was the daughter of a converted Tartar and a Russian peasant woman and received her education in the high school of Omsk. After teaching school for some years, she went briefly on the stage (1907–1909) and subsequently took up literary work. During the early part of the Revolution (1917–1918) she belonged to the Social Revolutionary Party and long maintained comparative independence. Her literary career began only in 1922 with the novel *Pravonarushiteli* (Criminals) followed by *Peregnoi* (1923; Manure), comprising four stories, and the short novel *Virineya* (1925). Seifullina generally gives a psychologically accurate and objective estimate of her characters, who all belong to the revolutionary period. She makes no effort to embellish her pictures and writes in a direct, lively, and simple style. As in the case of her heroine Virineya, she frequently (and perhaps unconsciously) portrays the emptiness of a soul deprived of faith and moral standards, and not even her loyalty to the prevailing ideology can hide this situation from her. The story *Tanya* (1934) portrays the confused notions of a Communist child.

See: G. Reavey and M. Slonim, *Soviet Literature; an Anthology* (1934), pp. 129–140; G. Struve, *25 Years of Soviet Russian Literature* (1944), pp. 61–63.

S. H. C.

Seillière, Ernest (1866–, French critic and humanist), was born in Paris. He was a brilliant student and in 1886 entered the Ecole Polytechnique. Following his graduation he studied philosophy and history for two years at the University of Heidelberg and perfected his knowledge of German. He made his literary début with a study on Homer, *Une Excursion à Ithaque* (1892). The following year he gave a translation of a famous Swedish poem, *Nadeschda*. Four years later his *Etudes sur Ferdinand Lassalle, fondateur du parti socialiste allemand* (1897) was published, followed by a collection of essays, *Littérature et morale dans le parti socialiste allemand* (1898). He was a very prolific writer, especially well known as an enemy of romanticism. His studies closely parallel the antiromanticist campaign conducted by the much more profound and acute critics, Charles Maurras (*q.v.*) and Pierre Lasserre. Their conclusions are the same as his, but whereas Lasserre and Maurras identify the sources of French romanticism as foreign, Seillière traces it back to the quietist doctrines of Fénelon and Mme Guyon. His antiromanticist works include *Le Mal romantique* (1908), *Les Mystiques du néoromantisme* (1911), *Les Origines romanesques de la morale et de la politique romantiques* (1920), *Du quiétisme au socialisme romantique* (1925), *Sur la psychologie du romantisme français* (1933). Seillière also wrote many volumes to support his theory of "mystic imperialism," such as *La Philosophie de l'impérialisme* (1903–1908) and *Mysticisme et domination: Essais de critique impérialiste* (1913). He was elected to the French Academy in 1946.

See: R. Gillouin, *Une Nouvelle Philosophie de l'histoire moderne et française* (1921); G. M. L. Boudeau, *Ernest Seillière* (1925).

P. B.

Selander, Sten (1891–, Swedish poet and critic), was born and lives in Stockholm. He made his début with *Vers och visor* (1916; Verses and Songs) and *Gryning* (1917; Dawn), followed by several volumes of poems which depict especially the modern city-dweller's restless, critical feeling about life. In general there is a manly seriousness about his work. A sound portrayal of reality and of the duties of the individual, love of home, a feeling of human brotherhood, and a longing for the "twilight of youth" are outstanding elements of his poetry. He is a visionary, rich in color and verbal music, as in his collection *Tystnadens torn* (1918; The Tower of Silence). Selander has translated Fitzgerald's *Rubaiyat* (1919). He is a leader in the new generation of poets and after publishing an anthology of their work under the title *Den unga lyriken* (1924; The Young Lyricists), where a list of his earlier works may be found, he brought out two volumes of *Levande svensk dikt från fem sekel* (1928; Living Swedish Poetry of Five Centuries). As a critic he has shown special interest in the literatures of English-speaking peoples, and has published several collections of essays, including *Europèer, amerikaner och annat* (1930; Europeans, Americans, and Other Subjects).

See: C. W. Stork, *Anthology of Swedish Lyrics* (revised and enlarged ed., 1930); "Selander," in *Nordisk familjebok* (1932).

C. W. S.

Selvinski, Ilya (1899–, Russian poet and playwright), born at Simferopol, became known primarily as the protagonist of constructivism in poetry during the 1920's and early 1930's. Constructivism was an offspring of futurism, with emphasis on the note of modern industry and its technique designed for greater speed, economy, and capacity. The constructivists demanded the "loadification" (*gruzofikatsia*) of the poetic style, "the increased load of functions per unit of material," and the "loadification" of the word—the power unit—with meaning. They also urged "localization," or local semantics: the choice of specific words in their local meanings for characterization or description. The group was disbanded in 1930, but Selvinski persisted for several more years in composing verse in accordance with the principles he had helped to formulate and advocate.

Selvinski's first volume of poetry, *Rekordy* (1926; Records), was followed by a long narrative poem of the civil war, *Ulyalyaievshchina* (1927; The Ulyalyaiev Band), another long poem about the Fur Trade Company (*Pushtor*, 1929), and several plays in verse, such as *Komandarm 2* (1929; Army Commander 2), *Pao-Pao* (1933), and *Rytsar Yoann* (1939; Johann the Knight). Selvinski has kept some of the formalistic features of futurism, the unusual and striking vocabulary and rhymes, the novel and varied rhythm, and the deliberate obscurity ("estrangement," *os-*

traneniye). But he had outgrown the iconoclastic bombast of futurism in the early 1920's and now reflected the postrevolutionary tendencies of constructive organization. Though much concerned about form, he packs or "loads" his form with social content. Selvinski displays an extraordinary avidity for visual and auditory sensations, and he employs his constructivist precision with rare skill, so as to make the reader feel, see, and hear his objects, scenes, and emotions. In the *Rytsar Yoann*, scenes from the Bolotnikov rebellion in the 17th century, Selvinski discards his mannerisms and employs regular iambics in the Pushkin tradition.

A. K.

Sender, Ramón José (1902–, Spanish novelist, critic, and playwright), was born at Alcolea de Cinca in Aragon. The son of country gentry, at 18 he broke with his family, going to Madrid, where he secured employment and attended the university until recalled by his parents. In 1922–1923 he fulfilled his military service, taking part in the ill-fated Moroccan campaign. Returning to civilian life, he resumed the journalistic career begun a few years earlier and in 1924 was appointed to the editorial staff of the *Sol* of Madrid. An advocate of political and social reform, he took an active part in the antimonarchical movement that led to the establishment of the republic (1931). Meanwhile his career as a novelist was initiated with *Imán* (1930; Eng. tr., *Earmarked for Hell,* 1934, American title, *Pro Patria,* 1935), a brilliant first novel. In 1933 he visited Paris, Berlin, and Moscow. When the civil war started in 1936, he enlisted in the Loyalist army, serving as an officer for two years. His wife, who had been captured in rebel territory, was put to death as a republican sympathizer. On the fall of the republic he escaped to France, where he was interned before finding refuge in Mexico. Since 1942 he has lived in the United States.

Sender's work, besides numerous novels, comprises plays (*e.g., El secreto,* 1935, Eng. tr., "The Secret," *One Act Play Magazine,* Vol. I, 1937, pp. 612–626; "La llave," unpublished in Spanish, Eng. tr., "The Key," *Kenyon Review,* Vol. V, 1943, pp. 201–218; *Hernán Cortés,* 1940), short stories (*Mexicayotl,* 1940), and essays and criticism, mostly "leftist" in approach (*e.g.,* "El novelista y las masas," *Leviatán,* Madrid, May, 1936, pp. 31–41; for his present attitude, not necessarily at variance with his earlier outlook, see his important article, "On a Really Austere Aesthetic," *Books Abroad,* Vol. XVI, 1942, pp. 119–123). Sender's outstanding contribution, however, has been as a novelist. *Imán*—based on firsthand knowledge—is an unforgettable picture of the horror and sufferings of war. His preoccupation with social problems, already apparent in *Imán,* comes to the fore in *O.P.* (*Orden público*) (1931), which was inspired by his own experience as a political prisoner in 1927. *El Verbo se hizo sexo* (*Teresa de Jesús*) (1931), a novelized biography of St. Teresa, represents a deviation in his work at this point, yet it is characteristic in its emphasis on human values. His overwhelming interest in the problems of today brought him back to the contemporary scene in his next three novels. *Siete domingos rojos* (1932; Eng. tr., *Seven Red Sundays,* 1936) deals with an abortive workers' revolution in Madrid that supposedly took place after the advent of the republic. *Viaje a la aldea del crimen* (1933) was written in protest against a real event, the brutal repression by state police of a peasant uprising in the Andalusian village of Casas Viejas, a repression so shocking to public opinion that the Azaña cabinet was forced to resign. Moved by the evils and corruption that persisted in the social structure, Sender next wrote one of the most estimable Spanish works of recent years, *La noche de las cien cabezas—novela del tiempo en delirio* (1934), a bitter fantasy which passes in review many of the weak and despicable types met with in modern society; the novel inevitably recalls the magnificent phantasmagoric visions of Quevedo and of Goya. In *Míster Witt en el Cantón* (1935; Eng. tr., *Mr. Witt among the Rebels,* 1937) Sender again turns to the past, depicting this time the gallant but short-lived effort to set up a popular, federalist regime at Cartagena in 1873. From his experiences in the recent civil war came *Contraataque* (1938; Eng. tr. *The War in Spain,* American title, *Counter-Attack in Spain,* both 1937), a straightforward, moving acount of the heroic defense of Madrid. *Proverbio de la muerte* (1939), written under the impact of personal tragedy and of the triumph of fascism in Spain, is Sender's most serious and most ambitious work to date. Overburdened with "scientific" explanations and psychological subtleties, it nevertheless commands respect for its attempt to arrive at a personal, vitalistic philosophy. It marks, too, an important change in the writer's development, in that his concern with the individual, present in his work from the beginning, becomes now the focal point of his writing. This is brought out clearly in the novels that follow. In *El lugar del hombre* (1939; Eng. tr., *A Man's Place,* 1940), though the novelist still sees "man's inhumanity to man" and points it up, moreover, by placing it in a peaceful rural environment, he is preoccupied with the individual's need to find a place of dignity and value in society. *Epitalamio del prieto Trinidad* (1942; Eng. tr., *Dark Wedding,* 1943) shows the individual faced with the cruelty and barbarism of life itself. To the average reader, however, the author's presentation of a Mexican penal colony as a symbol of the world must seem forced, and the book carries, therefore, less conviction than Sender's other works. More recently, Sender has begun to view in retrospect his own life. In *Crónica del alba* (1942; Eng. tr., *Chronicle of Dawn,* 1944) he goes back to his childhood days in Aragon, portraying with tenderness, grace, and humor the unfolding of a boy's character and mind. The novel has been announced as the first of a series that will provide a chronicle of the Spain of our time.

Sender's novelistic work, though still unfinished, assures for him an important place in modern Spanish literature. His writing is at once realistic and imaginative, his characters, in whatever setting, alive and meaningful. His art draws its strength from a deep consciousness of social wrongs and from sympathy with man's long, painful, upward struggle.

See: Sir Peter Chalmers Mitchell, introductory notes to Sender, *Seven Red Sundays* (1936), *Mr. Witt among the Rebels* (1937), and *The War in Spain* (1937); David Lord, "This Man Sender," *Books Abroad,* XIV (1940), 352–354.

W. L. F.

Serafimovich, Alexander (pseud. of Alexander Serafimovich Popov, 1863–, Russian novelist and short-story writer), was born of Cossack parents, in a village of the Don Region. He attended school in a neighboring town that now bears his name. Studying later at the University of St. Petersburg, he came under the influence of Alexander Ulyanov, elder brother of Lenin and revolutionist, who was executed in 1887. The same year Serafimovich was deported to the White Sea where he wrote his first short story, "Na ldine" (1888; On an Ice Floe), followed by many others written after his return to his native Don in 1890. Based on his studies of the lives of fur hunters and fishermen of the North, of peasants, miners, railway and factory workers of Southern Russia, all these stories are devoted to the underprivileged and the exploited. The 1905 Revolution found him in Moscow. His "Sredi nochi" (1906; In the Night), "Zhivaya tyurma" (1907; The Living Prison), and other stories of this period are vibrant with sympathy for the revolutionary movement. Immune to the escapist individualism which prevailed after its defeat, he devoted his first novel, *Gorod v stepi* (1910; The City in the Steppe), to the workers ruthlessly exploited during the early industrial expansion in the Don Region. He was front-line correspondent during the First World War and, writing for *Pravda,* witnessed many of the campaigns of the civil war. One of these campaigns, fought in the Northern Caucasus, is the theme of his *Zhelezny potok* (1924; Eng. tr., *The Iron Flood,* 1935), acclaimed a great achievement of social realism. Member of the Communist Party since 1918, Serafimovich has attained the highest honors in his country.

Serafimovich's style, often colorless and impersonal in his earlier work, later tends to an exaggerated intensity of color and expression and occasionally becomes declamatory. There is, however, a brutal grandeur in some of the scenes of *The Iron Flood;* and though not a master of psychological introspection, Serafimovich can be vigorous and convincing when dealing with mass impulses and passions.

See: V. Veshnev, *A. S. Serafimovich kak khudozhnik slova* (1924); N. Fatov, *A. S. Serafimovich* (1927).

L. S.

Serao, Matilde (1856–1927, Italian novelist), was born in Patras, Greece, of a Greek mother of distinguished family, Paolina Bonely, and a Neapolitan father, Francesco Serao. Brought to Italy at the age of four, she studied in Naples under her mother's direction, attended normal school, obtained a post in the Telegraph Office, and had her first writings accepted by Neapolitan journals. She soon turned her vast energy to journalism and fiction and attained in both a high degree of success and much fame. In 1882 she removed to Rome where, together with Edoardo Scarfoglio, Carducci, and D'Annunzio (*qq.v.*), she helped to make *Capitan Fracassa* the sprightliest Roman paper of its day. In 1884 she married Scarfoglio, and their combined journalistic ventures in Rome and Naples enjoyed varied success for two decades. The Naples *Mattino,* founded and edited by them, was for many years the most substantial newspaper in southern Italy. Upon her separation from her husband in 1904, Serao also left the *Mattino,* and founded her own daily, the

Giorno, which she edited until her death in Naples in 1927.

Matilde Serao's literary production is contained in some 50 volumes which include, besides her widely read novels and short stories of Neapolitan life, many novels in a cinematic style of loves and scandals in high life, books of travel, plays, literary essays, mystery stories, books of religious edification (a volume of prayers, another on San Gennaro, a third on the Madonna and the saints), diaries, letters, a book on etiquette. Her significant work on Neapolitan and also on Roman subjects of the 1880's, which gives her an eminent place in Italian fiction, is to be found in some 10 volumes, all but two of which appeared in the decade 1881–1891.

Fantasia (1883) is a bold psychophysiological study of feminine perversity; its heroine, the neurotic, flighty Lucia, is ever weaving fancies "on God, the Madonna, the affections, on everything." An excellent English translation, *Fantasy,* by the American novelist Henry Harland, with an introduction by the English critic Edmund Gosse, appeared in 1890. *La Virtù di Checchina* (1884) is an engaging narrative about a middle-class wife whose virtue is saved by her fright of a doorman's scrutinizing look. *La Conquista di Roma* (1885; Eng. trs., *The Conquest of Rome,* 1902, 1906), which recounts the failure of a little deputy with Roman ambitions, is notable for its masterly descriptions of the new, tumultuous Rome of the 1880's. *Il Romanzo della fanciulla* (1886) is a collection of stories of middle-class girls and their lives of *decente miseria,* their yearnings for a less restricted existence, their dreams of love. *Vita e avventure di Riccardo Joanna* (1887) tells the story of a turbulent, not too ethical journalism encamped in the new capital. *All'erta, sentinella* (1889; Eng. tr., *On Guard,* 1901), a collection of Neapolitan stories, includes, besides the first one which gives the title and which is a remarkable account of a convict's attachment for the prison warden's child, "Terno secco," a breathtaking tale of three lottery numbers and their effect on the lives of the people of a whole segment of Naples, and "O Giovannino o la morte," a girl's tragic idyl, beautifully told. *Il Paese di cuccagna* (1891; Eng. tr., *The Land of Cockayne,* 1901) again presents Naples and the consuming Neapolitan mania for the lottery. It contains powerful descriptions of the teeming, ragged populace, their endless toil and childbearing, their chronic want, their sunless lives, their fanatic religious fervor, their weekly renewed dream of well-being through the lottery ticket. *La Ballerina* (1899; Eng. tr., *The Ballet Dancer,* 1901) describes the pathetic, sordid life of a chorus girl neither beautiful nor gifted, and *Suor Giovanna della Croce* (1901; Eng. tr., "Sister Giovanna of the Cross," serially in *Living Age,* July–September, 1901) is the tragic tale of a cloistered nun forced back into the world through civil appropriation of her order's properties.

Ventre di Napoli (1884) is Serao's only nonfictional work of unusual merit; it is a social-economic study of the Neapolitan slums of the 80's and was instrumental in bringing about their clearance.

See: Benedetto Croce, "Note sulla letteratura italiana nella seconda meta dal secolo XIX: Matilde Serao," *Critica,* I (1903), 321–351; Henry James, *Notes on Novelists* (1914), pp. 294–313; Ugo Ojetti, *As They Seemed to Me,* tr. by Henry Furst (1928), pp. 208–214.

A. M. G.

Sergeyev-Tsenski, Sergei Nikolayevich (1876–, Russian novelist and short-story writer), born in a little village of the province of Tambovsk, began his career in 1904 in the transitional period between the old realists and the new realist-symbolists. Unlike his contemporaries Andreyev and Artsybashev (*qq.v.*), whose reputations, now faded, were once internationally celebrated, Sergeyev-Tsenski at first won only a moderate acclaim, but his work has quietly and steadily grown in vitality and concentrated excellence until today he is regarded as one of the U.S.S.R.'s most significant literary artists, while yet virtually unknown abroad. Little is known of his personal life. His first work won him serious attention, though it was criticized for an overexuberance of style. Some seven volumes of his tales appeared before 1914. The years of the war and the Revolution he spent in the Crimea pasturing cows and working on a vast trilogy, *Valya* (1923–1926), designed as a history of the mentality of the Russian intelligentsia during the first two decades of this century. The first volume, *Preobrazhenie* (1923; Eng. tr., *Transfiguration,* 1926), concerns a Hamlet-like architect, Aleksei Ivanovich, torn between the desire to avenge his seduced wife and the call of new life, which counsels the futility of vengeance. The Crimean background shows the author's mastery of a richly colorful and evocative landscape. Other tales followed, of increasing artistic distinction. Three of his best short stories have been translated into English: "The Man You Couldn't Kill" (John Cournos, ed., *Short Stories Out of Soviet Russia,* 1929, pp. 101–116, and *A Treasury of Russian Life* *and Humor,* 1943, pp. 309–318); "Womenite Farm" (*Slavonic Review,* XII, 8–12); "The Arákush" (*Slavonic Review,* XVII, 282–296). In 1939–1940 appeared the three volumes of *Sevastopolskaya strada* (The Sevastopol Harvest), a tribute to the heroism of the plain Russian soldier during the defense of that city in the Crimean War. *Brusilovski proryv* (1944; Eng. tr., *Brusilov's Breakthrough,* 1945) is a historical novel of the First World War.

Sergeyev-Tsenski's work as a whole exhibits an interesting evolution in methods, materials, and conception of life. The early phases show his preoccupation with the psychopathology of existence; the principal themes are death, cruelty, the tyranny of fate, the loneliness of man. A growing revitalization alters this fatalistic outlook, and his later work evinces a positive, life-affirming character, realistic, tragic, and humane. Its tensions and conflicts, it is worth noting, are consistently on an individual and nonpolitical plane.

See: D. S. Mirsky, *Contemporary Russian Literature* (1926), pp. 141–144; V. Pozner, *Panorama de la littérature russe contemporaine* (1929), pp. 203–206.

N. S.

Sérgio de Sousa, António (1883–, Portuguese essayist and historian), primarily a rational philosopher and social reformer, has also done writing in many other fields. He was born in Daman (Damão), Portuguese India. When his father, the governor, was recalled, nine-year-old Sérgio went to Portugal with his family. A descendant of aristocrats, colonials, and admirals, he followed the career of a naval officer, abandoning it in 1910 for politics and belles-lettres. Convinced of the urgency of reforms in Portugal, he tried to impress the young élite with his ideas on culture, education, and political economy; he adhered to the group called Renascença Portuguesa (Portuguese Renaissance) and its review *A águia* (The Eagle) in Oporto, founded the review *Pela grei* (For the People's Sake) in 1917 with the economist Ezequiel de Campos, and later, on his return from publishing work in Brazil (1919–1920), participated in the organization of Seara Nova (New Crop), a cooperativist group of educators, economists, and writers, in whom he saw an intellectual élite capable of guiding the republic. Married early to a publisher's daughter, herself an educator, he became editor of her father's *Os serões* (The Soirées) and then of *Lusitânia,* an exemplary review of Portuguese studies. Named librarian at the National Library in Lisbon, he was active founding writers' organizations and promoting the União Cívica (Civic Union), a vast political association. In 1923 he entered the government as secretary of education but soon resigned, unable to carry out any reforms. Because of his leading part in the 1927 revolt against the dictator Carmona, he had to flee to Paris. Later he returned to Lisbon and was temporarily imprisoned on publishing a volume of history in 1941, but he continued to write with the courage of his convictions, a staunch defender of freedom of thought.

He became first known through his *Notas sôbre Antero de Quental* (1909; Notes on Antero de Quental). Besides translations of rationalists such as Spinoza, Leibnitz, Descartes, and Bertrand Russell and countless articles on national problems, he resurrected numerous works of 17th and 18th-century reformers of Portugal, in order to "reform Portuguese mentality." The *Ensaios* (5 vols., 1920–1936; Essays) contain most of his didactic studies, including some on literature (*e.g.,* on Oliveira Martins, *q.v.*). He turned political historian in *O Desejado* (1924; The Longed-for King), attacking with documents the romantically vague and indolent Messianism of the nationalists, abhorrent to him, the disciplined, critical thinker. From then on he eagerly engaged in many personal polemics. He also rewrote Portuguese history from an economic standpoint, starting with the dynamic thesis of a struggle of "the policy of transportation" against "the policy of fixation," *i.e.,* of the maritime city merchants against the landowners in the provinces. He outlined his findings in *Bosquejo da história dc Portugal* (1923; Eng. tr., *A Sketch of the History of Portugal,* 1928) and then expanded them to *História de Portugal* (only in Spanish tr. by J. Moneva y Pujol, 1929, "Colección Labor," VI, No. 206). He has more recently been working on a larger Portuguese edition, the first volume of which was published in 1941.

Sérgio has rightly been called a "universal man," being a poet—his first book was *Rimas* (1908; Rhymes)—a mathematician, philosopher, economist, historian, literary critic, journalist, educator, politician, and, above all, a humanist.

See: Juan Moneva y Pujol, "Prólogo," in Spanish translation (1929) of Sérgio, *História de Portugal,* pp. 7–13; Hernani Cidade, "António Sérgio," *Seara Nova,* August 25, 1932.

G. M. M.

Serra, Renato (1884–1915, Italian critic), was born in Cesena. He graduated from the *liceo* there at the age of 15 and went to study literature with Giosue Carducci (*q.v.*) at the University of Bologna. He graduated in 1904 with a dissertation on Petrarch's *Trionfi*. After some time spent in Florence, he returned to his native city in 1908 and the following year became librarian of the Biblioteca Comunale Malatestiana of Cesena, a post which he held until he was called to arms in April, 1915, as a lieutenant in the infantry. He was killed on the Podgora front in July of that year, leading his company to the attack.

Serra was an assiduous reader from early childhood, and his years of leisure as librarian in the quiet little Malatestiana gave him the time to acquire a very wide range of literary experience. To Serra it was the intimate experience of literature that mattered. For him in fact literature was a way of life. His important work is found in his essays on Pascoli and Panzini (*qq.v.*), an essay on the state of Italian literature in 1913 entitled *Le Lettere* (1914), and his *Esame di coscienza di un letterato,* written as he made ready to enter the war (1915). His published work is contained in two small volumes (*Scritti di Renato Serra,* 1938). In it one enjoys the work of a keen mind, direct and honest, sensitive, and objective. Serra's observations on his contemporaries, on contemporary Italian literature, and above all on the temper and moral fiber of the period do not lose value as time passes. It is clear, however, that his name is known and respected in Italy as much for what he held the promise of becoming as for what he was, and as much for what he seemed capable of writing as for what he wrote. The criticism which he left views its subject with a sure command of its own taste and sensibilities. Serra died at the age of 31. He was already capable of that rare achievement, an ability to enter into a question, literary or otherwise, with his whole soul and yet not to confuse issues. Serra insisted on seeing the whole question, without divisions or abstractions from it. He was persuaded, as he said, that every generation needs sometimes to make its own *esame di coscienza* and to draw up its own moral balance. He came near to fulfilling that need for his own generation, at least for those of it who, like himself, died young in the war.

See: L. Russo, *Problemi di metodo critico* (1930).

C. S. S.

Séverin, Fernand (1867–1931, Belgian poet, essayist, and critic), was born in Grand-Manil, a small village near Gembloux, in the Walloon country. His first poems appeared in the *Wallonie,* and very soon after he joined the Jeune Belgique group (*see* Belgian literature in French). But he never indulged in the Baudelairian and Parnassian imitations that characterized the early works of many of his colleagues and found inspiration in preromantic and early romantic poets such as André Chénier and Lamartine. He was also strongly influenced by Wordsworth and Keats.

A deep love of nature is to be felt in all of Séverin's poems, a pastoral lyricism, pervaded with a sort of pantheistic exhilaration in his early works, and later, clearly under the spell of spiritualism and faith. The poems in *Le Lys* (1888) were already budding into Vergilian blossoms, and these gave their full fragrance in *Le Don d'enfance* (1891). These short poems, written in truly classic verse forms, in simple but harmonious language, struck a chord unknown to the poets of the Jeune Belgique. Séverin, among his companions, represents an idyllic and serene poet, as surprising in their group as La Fontaine among the solemn French classic poets of his time. *Un Chant dans l'ombre* (1895) and *La Solitude heureuse* (1904) developed his innate qualities with a more visible tendency toward a classical style and the traditional meters of French poetry. His inspiration was progressively detaching itself from any link with materiality. He indulged in descriptions of imaginary landscapes which resemble the background of Watteau's pastorals. *Poèmes ingénus* (1909) concludes the pantheistic cycle of his poems.

Long a teacher in several Belgian high schools (*athénées*), Séverin became a professor of French literature at the State University of Ghent in 1907. Among the writers of the Jeune Belgique, his best friend was Charles van Lerberghe (*q.v.*). The two spent their vacations together in the Ardennes and also traveled in Italy. In 1924, 20 years after the death of his friend, Séverin published the letters written to him by the poet of *La Chanson d'Eve*. A year later appeared his own last poems, *La Source au fond des bois* (1925). Séverin has brought into Belgian poetry a sense of Elysian landscape which is distinctly Walloon and in striking contrast to the Promethean tumult pervading the poems of most of the French-writing poets of Flemish descent.

L. K.

Severyanin, Igor (pseud. of Igor Vasilyevich Lotarev, 1887–1942, Russian poet), born in St. Petersburg, was considered at about the time of the First World War to be the leader of the ego-futurist school of poetry. Actually there has always been more of the ego than of the futurist in his verses. From the first volume of his poems, *Gromokipyashchy kubok* (1913; Thunder-seething Cup), through his later collections, such as *Zlatolira* (1914; Golden Lyre), *Ananasy v shampanskom* (1915; Pineapples in Champagne), and *Victoria Regia* (1915), Severyanin espoused "all powerful egoism," free from reticence and convention. "I, genius Igor Severyanin, I am film-screened omni-urbanly, I am ubi-cordially enthroned," is typical of his "I–I–I" poetry. He is on familiar terms with 'Ego-God," and nonchalantly he proclaims: "Venus has given herself to me, and I am universally renowned." His alleged futurism is limited to his facile innovations in word combinations and in the usage of non-Russian terms expressive of Western civilization in its showy externals. His gaudy phrases and words savored of boudoirs and barrooms, and they flattered the taste of middle-class audiences before whom Severyanin recited, or rather chanted, saccharine verses in a titillating rhythm, studded with such foreign exotics as "lilac ice cream," "pineapples in champagne, I am arrayed à la Spain," *"Garçon,* improvise a brilliant five o'clock." After the Revolution, Severyanin lost his ephemeral popularity. He migrated to Estonia, where for a while he produced repetitious verses and then became silent.

Discriminating critics and poets have valued in Severyanin a genuine musical quality and an aptness for fresh images that may be discerned through his loud gaudiness. Were it not for the swift popularity he had gained, Severyanin might have outgrown his vulgar mannerisms. Here and there his poems reveal an authentic talent, as when he takes up Russian rustic themes. Unfortunately such poems, whose high quality roused the admiration of leading symbolists, such as Sologub and Bryusov (*qq.v.*), drown in the mass of garish ostentatiousness.

A. K.

Sforza, Carlo, Conte (1872–, Italian diplomat, statesman, and writer), was born in Montignoso della Lunigiana, north of Lucca. He entered the diplomatic service in 1896. After various other appointments he was attached in 1915 as Italian representative to the Serbian court, took part in the Macedonian campaign, and after the war was Italian high commissioner in Turkey until 1919. He was appointed under-secretary for foreign affairs by Nitti and then became minister of foreign affairs in the Giolitti cabinet of June, 1920, remaining in charge until July 4, 1921. During his tenure of office he negotiated the Treaty of Rapallo with Yugoslavia, thus crowning a policy of friendly understanding with the Eastern neighbors which he had undeviatingly advocated since 1917 and for which he found a valuable friend and ally in Prime Minister Pashich. Sforza's opposition to the expansionist and aggressive designs of Italian nationalism in the Near East earned him the enmity of the group that was to shape the foreign policy of the Fascist Party: he was bitterly denounced as a "renunciator" and public enemy. In 1922 he was appointed ambassador in Paris, but resigned, with a sharply worded telegram, as soon as Mussolini came into power. Thereafter he used the freedom of speech still allowed to him as a senator for documented attacks on Fascist policy, but his life became unsafe, his house was burnt down, and in 1926 he was obliged to leave Italy. He lived mainly in Paris and Brussels and after 1940 settled in the United States, where he wrote and lectured extensively. In 1943, following the Italian armistice, Allied authorities permitted him to return to Italy, where he supported a policy of national union and offered to collaborate with any anti-Fascist government on the single condition that the king be removed as a traitor to the Constitution. His policy met with hostility on the part of the British cabinet, and at last under Allied pressure he entered the Badoglio-Togliatti cabinet in March, 1944, with the full knowledge that he was sacrificing a large part of what he had stood for undeviatingly since 1922, but believing that this was required of him for the good of his country.

Sforza's work as a writer is distinguished by an extensive knowledge of the international political scene and by a wise and civilized perception of the factors which would promote European understanding rather than strife. Never a nationalist, he has tried to reach an unprejudiced appreciation of other countries' problems as well as those of his own, thus living up to a classic tradition of Italian statesmanship. His style is that of a diplomat, sometimes uneven in organization and scholarship, but brilliant and seasoned with firsthand experience.

His principal books have all been written during the period of exile. *Makers of Modern Europe* was published in London in 1930, and *Les Frères Ennemis* appeared in 1933 in Paris. The following have been published in the United States: *Diplomatic Europe since the Treaty of Versailles* (1928); *Europe and Euro-*

peans (1936); *Fifty Years of Diplomacy in the Balkans* (1940); *The Real Italians* (1942); *Contemporary Italy. Its Intellectual and Moral Origins* (1944).

G. de S.

Shaginyan, Marietta Sergeyevna (1888–, Russian poet and novelist), of Armenian descent, was born in Moscow. Her father, a professor of medicine, died early, leaving his family in want. At the age of 15 she began to contribute articles to periodicals, and eventually, supporting herself by journalism, she obtained a degree in philosophy. She continued her studies in Germany, where she undertook a pilgrimage to Weimar; Goethe's thought had a powerful and lasting influence on her. Shaginyan developed in her youth an intensely earnest attitude towards life, an intellectualism which she later struggled to overcome, and a passionate love for learning and for all forms of creative effort.

Shaginyan is the author of several novels, short stories, and dramas and of numerous articles devoted to current events, literary criticism, philosophy, and social problems. Together with her husband, Y. S. Khachatryants, she published studies on Armenian folklore. But it was poetry, which she later abandoned, that first brought her success; her *Orientalia* (1912) was rated among the best productions of the younger symbolists. Her first novel, *Svoya sudba* (1918; One's Own Fate), is largely of philosophical inspiration. Social motives appear in *Peremena* (1922; The Change); they are emphasized in later works, namely in her series *Mess-Mend* (1925–1926), which uses the devices of a mystery novel to present a violently grotesque picture of capitalist society collapsing in a world revolution (for the title the author took at random two words from an English-Russian dictionary). To the literature of socialist realism Shaginyan contributed a novel, *Gidrotsentral* (1931; The Hydroelectric Station), describing with a wealth of technical detail the building of a power plant in Armenia. The more recent *Semya Ulyanovykh* (1938; The Ulyanov Family) is the first part of a novel describing the life of Lenin.

Shaginyan's style is objective and precise. Intricate plots are developed in a manner which is more narrative than directly suggestive of reality. She rightly disclaims any influence of the Russian realistic novel and traces her literary parentage to Voltaire, to Pushkin, and also to Wilkie Collins, whom she greatly admires.

See: V. Kirpotin, "Shaginyan," in *Bolshaya sovetskaya entsiklopediya,* LXI (1934), 788–790; Shaginyan, "Mirovozzreniye i masterstvo (Avtobiografiya)," in *Sobraniye sochineni,* I (1935), 30–71.

L. S.

Shestov, Leo (pseud. of Leo Isaakovich Schwartzmann, 1868–1938, Russian philosopher and critic), was the first Russian philosopher to interest Europe in his thought. Fundamental to him is the idea that God is above good and reason and that the search for this amoral and irrational God is the supreme quest in life. He is a consummate master of polemical style, one who uses logic to refute logic. An internationalist, without roots in any soil, he bears the superficial appearance of a skeptic and a nihilist, but in reality his central idea is a positive one, the shaking free of the human psyche from its ancient bonds.

Shestov was born in Kiev of a wealthy Jewish merchant family and educated in the law faculty of the University of Kiev. He came late to philosophy, by way of literature. His first book was *Shakespeare i yevo kritik Brandes* (1898; Shakespeare and His Critic Brandes), in which he attacked Brandes (*q.v.*) for his positivism and nationalism. Shestov's war against idealism in any form characterized all his later works, beginning with *Dobro v uchenii Tolstovo i Nietzsche* (1900; Good in the Teachings of Tolstoy and Nietzsche) and followed by *Dostoevski i Nietzsche* (1901); these two works contain the whole force of his destructive criticism. Thereafter appeared a long series of books and articles, including many studies of individual figures in literature and philosophy, as Ibsen, Chekhov (*Anton Tchekhov and Other Essays,* 1916), Berdyayev (*qq.v.*), Buber, Plotinus, St. Augustine, Luther, St. Paul, Husserl, and Kierkegaard. Chief among these volumes are *Apofeoz bezpochvennosti* (1905, The Apotheosis of Groundlessness; Eng. tr., *All Things Are Possible,* 1920); *Velikie kanuny* (1910–1912; Great Vigils); *Nachala i kontsy* (Beginnings and Ends); *Potestas Clavium* (1916; The Power of the Keys), in which Shestov passes from modern individualists to the accepted religious leaders of the past, in whom he discovers the same truth as did Dostoevski and Nietzsche (*qq.v.*). In 1917 Shestov left Russia for Paris, where he lived until his death. His last work includes *Les Révélations de la mort: Dostoievski-Tolstoi* (1923); *La Nuit de Gethsémani* (1923), a study of Pascal; *La Philosophie de la tragédie: Dostoievski et Nietzsche* (1926); *Sur les confins de la vie: L'Apothéose du dépaysement* (1927); *Pages choisies* (1931); *Skovannyi Parmenid: Ob istochnikakh metafizicheskikh istin* (1931; The Shackled Parmenides: On the Sources of Metaphysical Truth); *Dans le taureau du Phalaris* (1933); *Kierkegaard i eksistentsialnaya filosofiya: Vox Clamantis in Deserto* (1936; Kierkegaard and Existential Philosophy); *Athènes et Jérusalem* (1938); *Constantine Leontiev,* a study of the Russian philosopher.

See: Boris de Schloezer, preface to Shestov, *Les Révélations de la mort* (1923); D. S. Mirsky. *Contemporary Russian Literature* (1926), pp. 172–175; N. Berdyayev, "Leo Shestov i Kierkegaard," *Sovremennyia zapiski,* LXII (1936), 376–382.

N. S.

Shklovski, Victor Borisovich (1893–, Russian critic and novelist), a prominent exponent of formalism, undertook a series of studies in literature soon after graduation from the University of St. Petersburg. His work was interrupted in 1917 when he was sent to the front as commissar of the Provisional Government. Returning to Petrograd after many wanderings and adventures, he resumed his literary work, but in 1922, implicated in a political conspiracy, he left Russia for two years, which he spent mostly in Berlin. There, among other works, he published his autobiographical *Sentimentalnoye puteshestviye* (1923; Sentimental Journey).

Shklovski presents his critical views in a manner which is often brilliant, if at times rather paradoxical and aggressive; as originally expressed, they are based on the belief that literature is autonomous and that its students should be concerned neither with content in the traditional sense nor with social and economic conditions, but solely and specifically with the form and the structure of a work, with finding out "how it is made." Shklovski, furthermore, interprets literature primarily as a rediscovery of reality. Literature renders new and unusual, and thereby directly visible, a too familiar world, to which we respond with merely automatic recognition. The effect is achieved by breaches of familiar associations, shifts of planes or angles of perception, the use of new words and images, and various other devices which Shklovski calls "rendering strange." His views are presented in a noticeably attenuated form in later works, *Tekhnika pisatelskovo remesla* (1928; The Technique of the Writer's Craft), *Material i stil v romane Lva Tolstovo "Voina i mir"* (1928; Material and Style in Leo Tolstoy's Novel *War and Peace*). These were followed by several historical and biographical narratives, one of which, *Minin i Pozharski* (1940; Minin and Pozharski), is devoted to the traditional liberators of Russia from the Polish invaders in the 17th century. He returned to literary criticism with a vivid and penetrating study of Mayakovsky (*q.v.*), with whom he was closely connected (*O Mayakovskom,* 1940; On Mayakovsky).

See: Gleb Struve, *Soviet Russian Literature* (1935), pp. 201–215.

L. S.

Sholem-Aleikhem (pseud. of Sholem Rabinowitz, 1859–1916, Yiddish novelist and humorist) was born in Pereyaslav, a small town in the province of Poltava, Russia. He received his early education in the neighboring community of Voronkov, the model for Kasrilivke, locale of many of his famous short stories. His talent as humorist was already manifested in his boyhood, when he managed to discover a ridiculous aspect in every situation and a caricature in every person. Until his 13th year his studies were largely limited to the Bible and sacred books, but when in his 14th year he read his first secular novel, Defoe's *Robinson Crusoe,* his imagination was intensely stimulated and he wrote his first immature novel, about a Jewish Crusoe. Encouraged by his father, he continued with the composition of poems, novels, dramas, and aphorisms in Yiddish, Hebrew, and Russian. Before the end of his 20's, his reputation was well established with the Yiddish reading public. As editor of *Die Yiddishe Folksbibliotek* in 1888 and 1889, he attracted the best Yiddish writers, especially since temporary wealth enabled him to play the role of a Maecenas. But soon his wealth came to an end. The ex-banker, ex-broker, and ex-businessman had to devote the last quarter century of his life, his best years, to a desperate struggle for bread. Yet the more difficult his economic plight became and the poorer the state of his health, the more did he seek relief in laughter. In his bitterest years he created the humorous character Tovye der Milchiger (Tovye the Dairyman), the lighthearted pauper who drives his rickety wagon and sorry nag along the dusty road between Kasrilivke and Yehupetz—equivalents of Gotham and Abdera—in search of a bare pittance but whose thoughts traverse the entire globe and reach up to God. Though severest trials assail this simple being, Tovye wipes away the unwelcome tear, strikes up a merry tune, and rejoices that he still lives in God's sunlight on this beautiful earth.

Sholem-Aleikhem taught a people steeped in tragedy to laugh at its troubles. His narratives of small-town life in the ghetto provinces of tsarist Russia are comparable in quality and in kind to Gottfried Keller's (*q.v.*) satiric tales of the petty bourgeoisie of Seldwyla in Switzerland. He loves his men and women for their weaknesses and their follies no less than for their quiet heroism and their inarticulate idealism, but his deepest love is reserved for the children who refuse to grow up and to accept the established order of things. The most attractive of these children is the orphaned boy Motel Peise dem Chazans, who cannot quite adjust himself to adults' concepts and who manages to turn every situation topsy-turvy. Motel Peise is to the Yiddish reader what Tom Sawyer is to the American.

Sholem-Aleikhem died in New York, where he had found a refuge soon after the outbreak of the First World War. His fame has grown constantly since his death and now spans the continents. His tales have been dramatized for the New York stage and for Russian films. Twenty-seven of them have appeared in English translation in *The Old Country* (1946). His anecdotes and aphorisms are retold and reprinted wherever Jews of Eastern European origin congregate. He forms with Mendele mocher sforim and Yitzchok Leibush Peretz (*qq.v.*) the triad of classical Yiddish literature.

See: Maurice Samuel, *The World of Sholom-Aleichem* (1943).

S. L.

Sholokhov, Mikhail (1905–, Russian novelist and short-story writer), is the most substantial artist of Soviet literature, and of its many diverse exponents the one most widely appreciated at home and abroad. He is the first great epic recorder of the Don Cossacks and the poet of their landscape. His work is bulky rather than merely prolific, and unlike many of his colleagues he has never been an experimentalist in form. His fame rests largely on two vast novels, the many excellences of which grow naturally out of the great main stream of objective realism. His distinction derives from the fact that he is a Communist who has taken hitherto untouched material and expressed with abundant virility and historical truth the new Soviet conception of socialist realism. The measure of his power is seen in the complete dominance of the artist over the propagandist.

A Cossack himself, Sholokhov was born in the hamlet of Kruzhlino in the *stanitsa* or township of Veshensk on the banks of the Don. His father was a jack-of-all-trades from Ryazan. His mother, half Cossack, half peasant, learned to read so as to write letters to her son; she was killed by German bombs in 1942. The parents had no property, nor were they formally married until 1912, when the boy was legitimized; thereafter he appeared on official documents as "son of a middle-class citizen." Sholokhov served in various military and civil capacities during the Revolution. He was in turn soldier, handy man, statistician, food inspector, freight handler, mason, bookkeeper, and journalist. In 1923 he began writing for Komsomol newspapers and for periodicals. His first book, *Donskie rasskazy* (1925; Tales of the Don), a group of four short stories, was followed by another, *Lazorevaya Step* (1926; The Azure Steppe), both dealing with the life of the Don Cossacks in the civil war and the first years of NEP. The stories outline the conflicts of class interests among the Cossacks, a theme developed on a heroic scale in the subsequent novels. The endings are uniformly tragic, though not without hope for a happier future. Among the most interesting are "Smertnyi vrag" (Deadly Enemy), "Chervotochina" (Dry Rot), and "Chuzhaya krov" (Alien Blood). Whereas in these early tales the leaders of the village are isolated from the people, in Sholokhov's later work they are wholly integrated with the masses.

In 1926 Sholokhov began working on *Tikhi Don* (The Quiet Don), his major opus, which occupied him 14 years. The first volume (1928) was followed by three others. The whole appears in English as two consecutive novels, *And Quiet Flows the Don* (1934) and *The Don Flows Home to the Sea* (1940), later combined in one volume as *The Silent Don* (1942). Before the appearance of the fourth volume the work had run into 79 editions, totaling four and one-half million copies, printed in 38 separate languages of the U.S.S.R. It was translated in 32 countries abroad, in 14 European and Asiatic languages. With the sensational success of the first volumes Sholokhov became the ranking novelist of the Soviet Union, a position he still occupies and one in which he continues to grow. In its great length (1300 pages), in its panoramic sweep and its numerous characters, as well as in its vitality and veracity, there is much to justify the comparison first made by Maxim Gorky (*q.v.*) with *War and Peace*. On the other hand, it lacks the depth of character analysis and the universality of Tolstoy's masterpiece, and it falls short of attaining the miraculous control of material in the older classic. The reasons for these differences exist apart from Western standards of artistic merit. Sholokhov was following the Marxian line in avoiding subjective emphasis: he is deeply concerned with people, but in the generic sense rather than as individuals. Furthermore, his Cossacks are not complex Europeans, but a primitive race governed by the most elemental instincts in their fighting, mating, cultivating the soil. What is tragic in the book is the inevitable sacrifice that occurs when an ancient, simple way of life is forced by history into a totally new social mold. The main import, however, is not tragic, but life-affirming. The real protagonist is not the Cossacks themselves, with all their exuberant vigor, their savage cruelty, their untapped reserves of social creativeness, nor even the Cossack land, though it is wonderfully portrayed in all its sensuous beauty; rather it is the dynamic unfolding of the dialectical conception of history to which both individuals and groups must adapt or be swept aside. The book depends for its unity on this principle, the most striking demonstration of which is seen in the chief character, Gregor Melekhov. Torn by opposing forces, he fights first on one side, then on the other; he cannot adjust to the new order, however, and he is progressively denuded of his possessions, of his family, and finally of his self-confidence, his integrity, even his animal courage, ending in surrender and probable death. Sholokhov's power is such that there is no trace of schematism or dogma; the clash and struggle are deeply felt, deeply realized. It is of no little significance that owing directly to Sholokhov the Cossacks regained their status as a distinct people, a recognition hitherto withheld by the Soviet government.

In the midst of working on *Tikhi Don,* Sholokhov produced his second novel, *Podnyataya tselina* (1932–1933; Eng. tr., *Virgin Soil Upturned,* American title, *Seeds of Tomorrow,* both 1935), another study of the Cossacks and the tragicomic vicissitudes incident to the organization of collective farming among a pastoral people famous for centuries for their extreme individualism. Strictly sociological, without the thematic grandeur of the first novel, this book nevertheless has its own power, full of racy naturalism, poetic gusto, and naïveté. It quickly sold over a million and a half copies, and by order of the government every supervisor of a collective farm was required to read it. Both novels have been given operatic form with music by Ivan Dzerzhinski and are among the most popular in repertory. *Tikhi Don* has also been filmed, and *Podnyataya tselina* made into a play.

Already assured of a distinguished place in Soviet literature, Sholokhov gives promise of an even finer accomplishment. Until 1941 he lived in Veshensk with his wife and three children, taking an active part in cultural and political affairs. He was awarded the Stalin prize of 100,000 rubles and also the Order of Lenin. He was elected a member of the Academy of Sciences and a deputy to the Supreme Soviet of the U.S.S.R. Like all other Soviet writers he gave himself over wholly to the war effort following the German invasion and served at the front as reporter and in other capacities.

See: V. Goffenshefer, *Mikhail Sholokhov* (1940); Isidor Schneider, "The Quiet Don Flows Home," *Soviet Russia Today,* IX (1941), 10–11, 32.

N. S.

Sienkiewicz, Henryk (1846–1916, Polish journalist, short-story writer, and novelist), was born in the village of Wola Okrzejska, province of Podlasie, Russian Poland, of Polish gentry stock said to have been crossed at some remote date with a strain of Tartar. His mother, Stefanja Cieciszowska, being herself of a poetic temperament, instilled in her son a love of literature and a desire to interpret his country to the world through the written word. In 1866 Sienkiewicz entered the famous Warsaw Szkoła Główna and remained in that institution even after its reorganization as a Russian university in 1869, graduating in 1870 in the same class with Świętochowski (*q.v.*). Sienkiewicz made his literary début in the positivist journal *Przegląd tygodniowy* (Weekly Review; *see* Polish literature) with a critical account of a performance by the popular actor Rapacki in *Nos Intimes* by Sardou (*q.v.*). His first published story, *Na marne* (1872; In Vain), held out little promise of the talent Sienkiewicz was ultimately to display. In 1876 Sienkiewicz journeyed to the United States, partly to carry out his mother's injunction to learn to write by traveling, partly in order to escape the spiritual suffocation of life in Russian Warsaw. For a while he lived in Modjeska's famous Polish "Brook Farm" in California. During his absence from Poland his name was kept alive there by a series of "Listy z podróży" (Travel Letters), written in a manner reminiscent of Dickens and Harriet Martineau and appearing regularly in *Gazeta polska.* From his American experiences came also a number of short stories, the most memorable of which is the immortal "Latarnik" (1882; Eng. tr., "The Light-House Keeper," in *Yanko the Musician and Other*

Stories, 1893), a moving story of a homesick Polish exile.

On his return to Poland, refreshed by his years abroad, Sienkiewicz quickly won a nation-wide reputation. His best works from this period are the realistic *Z pamiętnika korepetytora* (1879; A Teacher's Memoir) and *Janko muzykant* (1879; Eng. tr., *Yanko the Musician, and Other Stories,* 1893), a sympathetic tale of a poor peasant lad who dreamed in vain of possessing a violin.

In 1883 began what may be called Sienkiewicz's heroic period, with the publication in the Warsaw journal *Słowo* of his long novel *Ogniem i mieczem* (Eng. tr., *With Fire and Sword,* 1890). This proved to be but the first of a series of three great historical novels (*Potop,* 1886, Eng. tr., *The Deluge,* 1891, and *Pan Wołodyjowski,* 1888, Eng. tr., *Pan Michael,* 1893) in glorification of Poland's struggle for national existence in the 17th century. The first of the three, a stirring account of the siege of Zbaraż by the Cossack chieftain Chmielnicki and his Turkish ally Tugai Bey, together with the heroic defense of the fortress by Prince Jeremi Wiśniowiecki, calls into bold relief an outstanding Polish trait—military valor. The second dramatizes not only this quality but also the piety of the Pole, as it depicts the defense of the shrine of Jasna Góra by the monk Kordecki. The final volume of the trilogy portrays the defense of still another Polish outpost, the bastion of Kamieniec in Podolia. It was a far cry indeed from the young Sienkiewicz of *Na marne,* with his positivist's aversion to feeling and his repudiation of love as a motive in human affairs, to the mature Sienkiewicz of the trilogy, with his clear implication that blind, unreasoning love is the noblest of all motives. That Sienkiewicz would arrive ultimately at this conviction might, however, have been predicted from 1875, when in his first novel, *Stary sługa* (The Old Servant), he represented blind loyalty and devotion as knightly qualities. While Sienkiewicz always appreciated the praise accorded him by the critics for his psychological novels, *Bez dogmatu* (1891; Eng. tr., *Without Dogma,* 1893) and *Rodzina Połanieckich* (1895; The Polaniecki Family), it was for his historical novels, especially the trilogy, that he preferred to be remembered, since these were the fulfillment of the consuming ambition of his life.

Aside from the trilogy, the novel Sienkiewicz found most difficult to write was *Krzyżacy* (1900; Eng. tr., *Knights of the Cross*), for the story deals with the obscure period of Germany's eastward expansion (13th and 14th centuries), when eyewitness chroniclers were few. Less difficult was the popular *Quo vadis?* (1895; Eng. tr., 1896), a romance of the days of Nero, in the writing of which Sienkiewicz found Tacitus a gold mine of precise detail.

Sienkiewicz is regarded by most Poles as the national interpreter of Poland par excellence. On the 30th anniversary of his literary début (1900), the entire nation arose as one man to do him honor. Five years later (1905) he was awarded the Nobel prize in literature.

During the First World War, Sienkiewicz abandoned work on a novel of Napoleonic times which he had begun, to devote his entire energy to the cause of Polish independence and to the activities of the International Red Cross. He died in Switzerland in the midst of this work.

See: P. Chmielowski, in "Henryk Sienkiewicz," *Nasi powieściopisarze* (1895); L. E. Van Norman, "Henryk Sienkiewicz's Poland," *Bookman,* XLIV (1916–1917), 412–426; *Wiadomości literackie,* 1924, No. 43 (entire issue); M. M. Gardner, *The Patriot Novelist of Poland: Henryk Sienkiewicz* (1926); E. E. Ledbetter, comp., *Polish Literature in English Translation* (1932), pp. 25–27, bibliography of translations; J. Birkenmajer, "Henryk Sienkiewicz," *Thought,* XIV (1939), 579–593.

L. E. V. N.

Sieroszewski, Wacław (1858–, Polish novelist), was born at Wółka Kozłowska in Mazovia, Russian Poland. A brief schooling preceded two years of apprenticeship to a locksmith, after which he was sent to study in the technical school of the Warsaw-Vienna Railroad Company. Attracted, as were so many of his generation, by socialism, Sieroszewski plunged with his whole heart into this movement, only to be arrested in 1878 and sent to Siberia. In Yakutsk, where he was held for 12 years, he turned his enforced leisure to good use by mastering the language and lore of the natives and by collecting material which he was later able to publish through the Petersburg Geographic Association. On his return to Poland in 1891, Sieroszewski occupied himself with writing. In 1902–1903 he made a journey to the Far East. This, like his Siberian experiences, yielded him rich material for a series of novels and tales. Arrested again in 1905, he escaped abroad, returning to Poland in 1914 as a legionary with Piłsudski. A wanderer all his life, Sieroszewski was at home and contented in any part of the world. He was looked upon in Free Poland as the Nestor of the writing guild and was accorded high honors as the figure responsible for making the Orient and the primitive races of the Siberian wilderness literary material in Polish.

See: Z. Dębicki, *Portrety,* I (1927), 51–66; G. Korbut, *Literatura polska* (1931), IV, 155–156; K. Czachowski, *Wacław Sieroszewski; życie i twórczość* (1938).

A. P. C.

Sigurjónsson, Jóhann (1880–1919, Icelandic dramatist and poet), was born at Laxamýri in Þingeyjarsýsla in the North of Iceland. His parents were well to do, and there was poetic talent in his mother's family (*e.g.,* Jónas Hallgrímsson, pioneer of the romantic movement). The boy was able to follow his inclination to study, and, being attracted to natural science, he chose the study of veterinary medicine in Copenhagen (1899). He had almost finished when he determined to devote his whole time and energy to becoming a writer—a great and famous writer it must be. As a short cut to literary fame he decided to write plays in Danish. He was thus the first of his compatriots to cut across the narrow confines of his mother tongue (spoken by a population of about 100,000) to gain a wider audience, and more were to follow his example. He was soon one of the most brilliant members of the bohemian art circle in Copenhagen, a group which tasted the excesses of French *fin-de-siècle* decadence and shared the soaring ambitions of Nietzschean geniuses.

His first two plays, *Dr. Rung* (1905) and *Bóndinn á Hrauni* (1908; Eng. tr., *The Hraun Farm,* 1916), were immature, but the latter treated an Icelandic subject for the first time. With *Bjærg-Ejvind og hans Hustru* (1911; Icelandic, *Fjalla-Eyvindur,* 1912; Eng. tr., *Eyvind of the Hills,* 1916) Sigurjónsson attained meteoric fame. He was acclaimed by the best critics such as Brandes (*q.v.*) and wooed by both the Scandinavian and the German stage (*Fjalla-Eyvindur* was first produced in Reykjavík December 25, 1911, in Copenhagen May 20, 1912). The fame of the play spread even to France, England, and America; a French critic gave the author a seat of honor beside Scandinavia's big three, Björnson, Ibsen, and Strindberg (*qq.v.*). Later Victor Sjöström was to make one of the first artistic films out of the play. *Fjalla-Eyvindur* is based upon an Icelandic folk tale about real 18th-century outlaws (sheep thieves). In the play Fjalla-Eyvindur's wife becomes the true hero, living for her love only and perishing in the end because her love is shattered against the elemental forces of hunger in the wilderness. This great tragedy is projected against the colorful background of Icelandic folkways and magnificent mountains. It is ennobled by the rich lyric expression of the author, who has left other perfect gems of lyric poetry apart from the songs in his plays. His next play, *Ønsket* (1915; Icelandic tr., *Galdra-Loftur,* 1915; Eng. trs., *Loftur,* 1939, "Loft's Wish," *Poet Lore,* XLVI, 99–146), was also based on a folk tale. Loftur is an Icelandic Faust whose towering ambition is to harness the powers of darkness—for higher purposes. He fails utterly because of his selfishness. The same ambition burns in *Løgneren* (1917; The Liar), a play drawn from *Njála,* the most famous of the Icelandic sagas. These two works, though good, did not attain the success of *Fjalla-Eyvindur.*

Sigurjónsson's untimely death cut short a career of unusual brilliance. Those who knew him have all agreed that his life was beautiful poetry even to a greater degree than his written works. He left an unfinished play, *Elsa,* which points to a new, more subdued period in his development.

See: L. Pineau, "Un Poète dramatique islandais, Johann Sigurjonsson," *Revue,* XXV (1914), 52–67, 188–201; A. Møller, "Islandsk Digtning i nyeste Tid og Danmark," in E. Skovrup, ed., *Hovedtræk af Nordisk Digtning i Nytiden* (1921), pp. 356–364; G. Gunnarsson, "Einn sit ég yfir drykkju," in *Rit eftir Jóhann Sigurjónsson,* I (1940), xiii–xlviii; S. Nordal, "Jóhann Sigurjónsson," *Tímarit Máls og menningar,* 1940, pp. 111–124.

S. E.

Silfverstolpe, Gunnar Mascoll (1893–1942, Swedish poet), born in Rytterne, Västmanland, is among the less prolific of modern masters of the Swedish lyric. His total poetic production is contained in five rather slender volumes—*Arvet* (1919; The Heritage), *Dagsljus* (1923; Daylight), *Vardag* (1926; Common Day), *Efteråt* (1932; Afterward), and *Hemland* (Homeland; 1940). This body of poetry was, however, only a part of his quiet and restrained but not unimportant contribution to modern Swedish cultural life. During his life he held many positions of trust directly identified with cultural strivings of the day, among which may be mentioned those of curator of the Royal Art Collections from 1920 to his death, secretary of the Bellman Society, 1919–1934, and officer of the Swedish Pen Club. Besides being active in newspapers and magazines as one of the more sensitive critics of the day, he made more extended critical and scholarly contributions in such works as *Prins Eugens konst* (1935; The Art of Prince Eugene) and *Bokbindare i Stockholm, 1630–1930* (1930; Bookbinders in Stockholm, 1630–1930), and was one of the most active translators of representative English and American verse (*Vers från väster,* 2 vols., 1922–1924; Verse from the West, together with Karl Asplund). In his creative work he is primarily the poet of memories of the past, a poet who has his roots firmly imbedded in the ancient Swedish countryside with all of its finest aristocratic traditions. He never wearies of glorifying the Swedish *herregård* (landed estate), with its gracious culture, its elegance, and its warm basic humanity; he writes of the closed circle of the home, with its solid intimacies and its unspoiled ebb and flow of spontaneous organic life; he sings of simple everyday pleasures in a manner not unlike that of Wordsworth, one of his favorites among the English poets. For Silfverstolpe as for Wordsworth poetry was in essence "emotion recollected in tranquillity," a thing of fine and dignified restraint. In its preoccupation with the simple life and the past Silfverstolpe's work reflects, usually with a most subtle indirection, a sense of homelessness in the brutally complex pattern of modern existence, though his last volume of poems, *Hemland,* reveals that he was not without deep personal feeling for unfortunate victims of the present ghastly world conflagration.

His poetry on the whole is a rather slender but everywhere sensitive and genuine expression of deep spiritual loyalty to an anciently rooted Swedish cultural tradition facing gradual strangulation at the hands of insensitive onrushing modern industrial civilization. As such Silfverstolpe's work takes its modest place alongside of that of Heidenstam and Lagerlöf, Karlfeldt and Österling (*qq.v.*), each of whom worked with similar materials in a similar spirit of fine piety for a past that is rapidly disappearing from the present-day Swedish scene.

A. G.

Silone, Ignazio (pseud. of Secondo Tranquilli, 1900–, Italian novelist and critic), was born in Pescina dei Marsi, Aquila. His family, landed residents of the province, provided him with an education in Catholic schools, but Silone spent most of his boyhood and youth, according to his own preference, in close and working contact with the peasants of the countryside in which he was born. After the death of his mother and five brothers in the 1915 earthquake, he and a surviving brother quit the Abruzzi for Rome, where later Silone edited the youth paper, the *Avanguardia.* In 1921 he visited Russia, returning afterward to Trieste to edit the labor paper, the *Lavoratore.* It was not long before the Fascists seized this paper and issued warrants for the arrest of its editor and his assistants. Silone's brother was captured and subsequently beaten to death in jail. Silone himself escaped pursuit, found shelter with the peasants of his native province, and remained in Italy for a number of years. In 1930 he broke with the Communist Party, in which he had held membership for some time. In 1931 he was smuggled across the border into Germany, traveled from there to other parts of Europe, and settled finally in Switzerland, where he lived until 1944. The fiction, history, and criticism he wrote during those years of exile had the curious distinction of being unknown only in the country to whose literature they made their unique and considerable contribution. In 1944, with the end of Fascism, Silone returned to Italy and resumed political life as a member of the Socialist Party. Soon after, he became editor in chief of the newspaper *Avanti.*

While virtually everything Silone has published up to the present springs from a total rejection of fascism and a corresponding devotion to an ethical conception of socialism, it is as a novelist rather than as a critic of society that his claim upon contemporary attention has been greatest. The cogency of his fiction lies in its humanity, its intelligence, its liveness, and its irony. This last is the over-all tempering element: deeply Italian and appropriate, it is an irony that derives, not from aloofness, but on the contrary from great and offended love. In this, as in his genius for conveying the flavor of peasant life, Silone recalls inevitably another great Italian realist, Giovanni Verga (*q.v.*).

All Silone's writings reveal, with varying stress, the Fascist degradation of Italy and point to the need for an understanding and a solution of her problems arrived at through contact and experience rather than remote reflection and theory. Explicitly he links the idea of socialism with that of liberty, but does not assume liberty to be a necessary or natural outcome of socialism. Like Mazzini, of whom he writes revealingly (in *The Living Thoughts of Mazzini,* 1939; published only in English), he expects his country to be saved not by outside intervention, but from within. Writing in 1939 he declared himself to be a member of no political party, but "an anti-fascist partisan" in the civil war raging throughout the world; and expressed his disappointment with the parties and programs of a Left which had lost all effective contact with reality. As to the Second World War, far from solving the problem of fascism, he saw it as only too likely to result in the "fascistization of the democratic countries," and was unable to condone those socialists who "with the very best possible antifascist intentions . . . put their own theories in mothballs" in order to cooperate with men of opposing ideologies in the struggle against a common enemy. It remained open to the convinced socialist (and Silone's life has born this out) to refuse all compromise and to live in strict accordance with an ethical ideal.

All this is illustrated in the spiritual odyssey of Pietro Spina, protagonist of Silone's *Bread and Wine* (1936; original Italian published later, *Pane e vino,* 1937) and of his *The Seed beneath the Snow* (1942; original Italian version not yet published). Pietro Spina returns from exile to Italy, from realms of revolutionary theory to realms of human reality and, after experiencing some of the blockages and deviations to which man's love of liberty is subject, finds himself home at last in the "poor, barren country" which is "the country of his soul." Spina sheds a falsified social partisanship in favor of a concrete and living Christian morality and shares his life with the humble company of those who can truly break bread with him in poverty, faith, hope, and charity. In *Bread and Wine* the spiritual travels of the principal character are built into the structure of a novel that conveys above all the pulse and color and sound of Italian life. *The Seed beneath the Snow,* its sequel, is less satisfying as a work of art, primarily because it tries to combine satire, symbolism, and realism and fails to fuse them.

Fontamara (1933; Eng. tr., 1934), while simpler in pattern and narrower in scope than those that followed, had a greater popular success. During the first year of publication it appeared in a total of 19 different translations and in 17 languages; it is a brief masterpiece of concrete narration and bitter portraiture recording the lives of a handful of Abbruzese peasants (*cafoni*) under the impact of the "new government."

Notable among Silone's nonfiction writings is his history of Fascism, *Il Fascismo; le sue origini e il suo sviluppo* (published only in Switzerland in its German translation, *Der Fascismus; seine Entstehung und seine Entwicklung,* 1934), a serious and objective account of the beginnings and early years of the Fascist movement in Italy. *The School for Dictators* (1938; published only in English) is a somewhat labored satiric treatise on the proper grooming of modern tyrants. Written in the form of a series of quasi-classic dialogues between an aspirant to American dictatorship, a scholarly American windbag, and a European who styles himself Thomas the Cynic, it treats acidly of the manner, attitudes, dreams, and myths of dictators past and current.

In addition to the books mentioned, Silone has published numerous critical and political articles in American and European periodicals. His most recent work is the drama, *Egli si nascose* (1945; Eng. tr., *And He Hid Himself,* 1946), based in theme and character on the novel *Pane e vino.*

I. B.

Silva Gaio, Manuel da (1860–1934, Portuguese poet, novelist, dramatist, and critic), son of the novelist António de Oliveira da Silva Gaio (1830–1870), was born in Coimbra, where his father was a professor and journalist. He studied law in the university of that city and in 1927 was named secretary of the law school.

The most decisive influence in his first poetical and critical works and in his novels is to be found in the philosophical and scientific doctrines of the unfortunate Guilherme Moniz Barreto (*q.v.*), with whom he was joined by the bonds of a strong friendship and to whom he dedicated a beautiful biographical-critical study, *Os novos: I, Moniz Barreto* (1894; The Newcomers: I, Moniz Barreto). Previously he had composed a carefully written story, *O pecado antigo* (1893; The Ancient Sin), with vivid rural scenes but with too many feuilletonistic surprises and coincidences. In the historical vein, but in a style replete with mannerisms, he made a start in the theatre with *Na volta da India* (1898; The Return from India). The work attracted no attention, though it reveals a certain psychological penetration in its view of India by a Portuguese of the 16th century and in the awakening of the hero's *saüdade* (longing) when confronted with the exotic. The poem "O mundo vive de ilusão" (1896; The World Lives on Illusion) is obscure and confusedly pessimistic. Silva Gaio's first book of poetry, *Mondego* (1900), marks the intelligent revival of the Portuguese pastoral theme in modern times; some of these pieces, such as "Dias correntes" (Ordinary Days; Part III of the eclogue "Lemano"), are the best of their type. He never abandoned his interest in this brilliant Portuguese school, and a little before his death two delicate and elegant studies on the subject were published, *Bucolismo: I, Bernardino Ribeiro; II, Cristoval Falcão* (1932–1933).

Silva Gaio's deep interest in classical literatures and in a revival of humanistic studies in his country is related to another aspect of the Portuguese Renaissance movement. He left evidence of this tendency in works of his own—always very careful, perhaps coldly correct at times, but worthy—in the poetry of *Chave dourada* (1916; Golden Key), *D. João* (1925), and *Sulamite* (1928) and in the essays *Da poesia na educacão dos gregos* (1917; On Poetry in Greek Education) and *De Roma e suas conquistas* (1919; On Rome and Her Conquests). His two novels *Ultimos crentes* (1904; Last Believers) and *Torturados* (1911; The Tormented) merit special mention. In the first of these a strange company of sailors, isolated from the world on a deserted beach, live out the last illusions of the myth of King Sebastian. They await the Encoberto (King Don Sebastião) until they think they see him coming over the horizon, and then all die when they try to save him. In *Torturados* three characters, in a series of renunciations, seek without success a state of intellectual and moral perfection. This affords the author an opportunity to outline extraordinary psychologies that are in conflict with a norm and possessed by a vehement desire to excel, which life itself is sure to overcome. The type seen in the poet Miguel de Gouvêa is of an almost autobiographical richness, and all the characters are described not so much through their acts as by their thoughts and creative plans. Silva Gaio's critical work includes *Eça de Queiroz* (1919), *Eugénio de Castro* (1928), *João de Deus* (1930), and *Os vencidos da vida* (1931; The Failures).

All told, the extensive and varied writings of Silva Gaio are a reflection of the uneasiness and hesitations that the culture of his country felt during the first third of this century. While appreciated only by a select minority of his contemporaries, his art is of the kind which does not disappear. On the one hand it was refined and aristocratic, on the other it had deep roots in Portuguese tradition and a universality due to the author's pervading humanistic ideal.

See: Fidelino de Figueiredo, *Estudos de literatura,* I (1917), 6–22.

R. M. L.

Sirin, Vladimir, *see* Nabokov, Vladimir Vladimirovich.

Sivle, Per (1857–1904, Norwegian poet), was a farmer's son from Voss in western Norway. For years he made his living as a journalist. He published several short stories in the dialect of his home district and a short working-class novel in the traditional literary language, *Streik* (1891; Strike). His chief and lasting work, however, was, from 1884, a number of national poems, some in Riksmaal and some in Landsmaal (*see* Norwegian literature), often taking their subject from national history, all of them battle songs for Norwegian independence. By their epigrammatic form and imaginative power they became classics, standing up like living sculpture and still today stirring Norwegian minds. In particular the one-stanza poem "Vi vil oss et land" (1894; We Will a Country for Us) is a cherished song of the nation. His collected works (*Skrifter*) were published in three volumes, 1909–1910.

See: A. Hovden, *Per Sivle* (1905).

H. K.

Siwertz, Sigfrid (1882–, Swedish prose author and poet), was born in Stockholm and educated at Uppsala. He attracted general attention with his volume of short stories *De gamla* (1909; Old People). With the novel *Selambs* (1920; Eng. tr., *Downstream,* 1923) his promise was fully realized. Since then he has done his best work in collections of short stories, such as *En handfull dun* (1922; A Handful of Feathers). Though dealing usually with artist types, which he handles with great delicacy and humor, Siwertz can also be robust, as in his clever story "The Lady in White," where he contrasts the healthy give-and-take of married life with the sentimental confidences of "spiritual affinity." He is fond of sailing and has done spirited pictures of summer life in the islands of the Stockholm archipelago. In poetry his chief success has been with *Taklagsölet* (1923; Rooftree Ale), a dramatic piece for the dedication of the Stockholm Town Hall. Siwertz has recently been made a member of the Swedish Academy.

It is in *Selambs* (The Selamb Family) that Siwertz has shown greatest authority. This novel is a study of degeneracy through the five members of one family. The description of profiteering as exhibited in the eldest son is a real social document. All the characters of the book are exponents of ruthless selfishness in various forms, from morbid sex inhibition to violent primitivism. It is certainly not cheerful reading, and yet at least a solution is suggested by antithesis with the young men and women who exhibit so clearly what not to be.

In all his work Siwertz is an accomplished stylist. His plastic and colorful prose is a pure delight. What could be better than the scenes in "Leonard and the Fisherman," where the young artist in woodcuts is calmed and reassured by the philosophy of the quaint old fisherman, who turns out to be also, from his former position as a sceneshifter, an addict of grand opera? The two go behind the stage in a performance of *Tristan:* "Like a living, overwhelming stream of actuality the music burst forth through all the dusty rubbish of illusion." It is in such passages that Siwertz proves himself a master equally in perception and expression.

See: C. W. Stork, tr., *Modern Swedish Masterpieces* (1923); H. A. Larsen, ed., *Sweden's Best Stories* (1928); G. Bach, *The History of the Scandinavian Literatures,* ed. by Frederika Blankner (1938).

C. W. S.

Sjöberg, Birger (1885–1929, Swedish poet, novelist, and composer), was for most of his life a resident of Hälsingborg on the south coast of Sweden. No recent volume of Swedish verse has won more immediate popularity than *Fridas bok* (1922; Frida's Book). It pictures with quiet humor and sentiment the life of a small Swedish town. It was followed by *Kriser och kransar* (1927; Crises and Crowns), a collection of poems of great warmth and pathos, of what one may call disharmony of soul, and of lyric imagination, and, posthumously, by *Fridas andra bok* (1929; Frida's Second Book). His popular novel *Kvartetten som sprängdes* (1925; The Dispersed Quartet), though of loose composition, has deep feeling and such a "classical gallery" of characters that it has become one of Sweden's best stories, and was in 1935 successfully dramatized and staged by the author's brother, Gösta Sjöberg.

Sjöberg continued the illustrious tradition of Karl Mikael Bellman, the great 18th-century improviser, who sang his own music to the accompaniment of a guitar. As Bellman pictured the gay life of Stockholm, so does Sjöberg reproduce the homelier scenes of his present-day environment. For some time no musical evening at Stockholm was complete without a performance of "Spanish Moonlight," in which the impetuous hero is carried in imagination to Granada, and then back to the more chaste endearments of his northern sweetheart. Sjöberg's originality has won him a place that is likely to be secure for some time.

See: C. W. Stork, *Anthology of Swedish Lyrics* (revised and enlarged ed., 1930; J. Landquist, "Sjöberg," in *Humanism* (1931).

C. W. S.

Skerlić, Jovan (1877–1914, Serb literary historian, essayist, and national leader), is one of those men who leave their stamp on an era. At the beginning of the 20th century and up to the First World War, all Serbian literature and also the entire public life of the country evolved under the directives and auspices of this great figure.

He was born in Belgrade and became the highest expression and exponent of the strivings and aspirations and ideals of the small Serbian capital. He studied French and comparative literature at the University of Belgrade as a disciple of Bogdan Popović (*q.v.*) and as leader of socialist students took a keen interest in contemporary social and national problems. Serbia and Montenegro were then the only free Yugoslav countries, and the dream was to liberate and unite all the members of the South Slav nations, notably the Serbs, Croats, and Slovenes. Advocating this idea through countless articles and lectures, Skerlić became the most ardent spokesman of a bellicose generation. At the same time, thoroughly acquainted with French political and intellectual life, he wanted the Yugoslav nation to develop on purely democratic lines. Also, as an adherent of the philosophical ideas of the French writers Comte and Guyau, Skerlić emphasized on every occasion the social note in artistic creation and succeeded in discrediting the "art for art's sake" movement.

From 1899 to 1901 Skerlić continued his studies at Paris and Lausanne. He became a follower of Georges Renard, and it was under Renard's influence that his spiritual evolution attained its definite form. His doctor's dissertation, *L'Opinion publique en France d'après la poésie politique et sociale de 1830–1848* (1901), shows the nature of his interests. Beginning in 1901 Skerlić taught French and Yugoslav literature at the University of Belgrade.

As a man of wonderful personal magnetism, and as a gifted orator—he was called "John the Golden-mouthed"—Skerlić acquired very great prestige. Young men from all the provinces of the Yugoslav nation, most of which was under foreign rule at this time, gathered at the University of Belgrade and looked to Skerlić as their prophet. At one word from the master, "Skerlić's youth" was ready for any sacrifice, as indeed was proved in the Balkan Wars of 1912 and 1913 and in the First World War. In his last year Skerlić, made a member of Parliament in 1912, devoted ever more time to politics and was flooded with invitations to visit and lecture in the various unliberated provinces. His sudden and mysterious death, at the age of 36 and when he had seemed in the best of health, was charged by many of his followers to Austro-Hungarian politicians, for whom he obviously was a grave menace.

Skerlić was exceedingly active as an author. First as a collaborator and then as the editor in chief of the best Serbian literary review *Srpski književni glasnik* (Serbian Literary Herald), he was the ever-vigilant chronicler and arbiter of the entire literary production among Yugoslavs. Hundreds of his essays, studies, and reviews were published in *Srpski književni glasnik;* the best were collected in *Pisci i knjige* (10 vols., 1907 ff.; Authors and Books). Other important works, mostly in the domain of literary history, are *Pogled na današnju francusku književnost* (1902; View of Contemporary French Literature); *Uništenje estetike i demokratizacija umetnosti* (1903; Annihilation of Esthetics and Democratization of Art); *Jakov Ignjatović* (1904); *Omladina i njena književnost (1848–1871)* (1906; The Youth Movement and Its Literature); *Vojislav J. Ilić* (1907); *Francuski romantičari i srpska narodna poezija* (1908; The French Romanticists and Serbian Folk Songs); *Srpska književnost u 18om veku* (1909; Serbian Literature in the 18th Century); *Svetozar Marković* (1910); *Istorijski pregled srpske štampe 1791–1911* (1911; Historical Review of the Serbian Press); *Istorija nove srpske književnosti* (1914; History of Modern Serbian Literature, complete ed.); *Današnji srpsko-hrvatski nacionalizam* (1913; Contemporary Serbo-Croatian Nationalism).

As a literary historian Skerlić adopted Taine's (*q.v.*) theory that every work has to be studied as a product of its environment and time. Contemplated from this standpoint, the whole evolution of Serbian literature was illuminated by a new light. Skerlić is famous not only for his scholarship but also for his style. His writings are crystal clear, composed in a vigorous, persuasive, and picturesque manner, full of sparkling wit and vivid imagery. In the white heat of creation he was occasionally incorrect about documents, sometimes hasty. But he left his own mark on whatever he touched.

See: B. Popović, "Jovan Skerlić kao književni kritičar," *Srpski književni glasnik,* September 1, 1920; *Srpski književni glasnik,* May 16, 1924 (whole issue devoted to Skerlić on the 10th anniversary of his death); V. Hilojević, *Jovan Skerlić* (1937).

P. A.

Skjoldborg, Johan (1861–1936, Danish novelist), the son of a poor crofter in Thy, Jutland, became a schoolteacher. His first book, *En Stridsmand* (1896; A Fighter), was a tribute to the men who wrest a living from the stubborn heath land along the North Sea. It was followed by *Kragehuset* (1899; The Crow's Nest). A stronger agitatorial purpose is evident in *Gyldholm* (1902), the novel that brought him recognition in literary circles. It is a dark picture of the misery and degradation of the laborers on Denmark's manorial estates in the 80's and 90's. These estates, he declared, were islands of retrogression in the land. Their laborers were untouched both by the cultural religious forces that centered in the rural folk high schools and by the new socialistic labor movement. But the youngest and strongest of the group, Per Holt, stirred to revolt by a terrible tragedy in his own home, went out from Gyldholm to face a strange world and an unknown fate—symbol of a class emerging from bondage. Skjoldborg is before all else the spokesman of the small crofters. His books have become the property of the very poor and have been a moving force in the Crofter Movement. His early works were all in the service of social reforms. Later he turned not only against the materialism that came with industrialization, but also against what he called the "centrifugal" tendency of modern life. In the midst of an over-organized society, he pleaded for simplicity and singleness of purpose. Love of home, devotion to the land, and absorption in work seemed to him the enduring values. This is the theme of *Nye Mænd* (1917; New Men) and *Jens Jakobs Sønner* (1920; Jens Jakob's Sons). A more definite religious bent is evident in *Præsten i Løgum* (1921–22; The Parson at Løgum). Skjoldborg has a considerable narrative gift and a clear, firm style which in his nature descriptions rises to poetic beauty. But his chief hold over the reader is by virtue of his broad human sympathies.

See: Helge Kjaergaard, *Die dänische Literatur der neuesten Zeit (1871–1933)* (1934).

H. A. L.

Skram, Amalie (1847–1908, Norwegian novelist and dramatist), came from a middle-class family in Bergen. When very young she married a sea captain, whom she divorced after a short and unhappy marriage. Later she married the Danish writer Erik Skram, in whose country she lived the greater part of her life.

Her first important work, *Constance Ring* (1885), reveals her as a disciple of the naturalistic school which at that time, through the influence of Flaubert and Zola (*qq.v.*), had begun to dominate the younger generation of Norwegian writers. It is the story of a tragic marriage, told with all the reveling in minute details which characterizes naturalism. Much more original and intense is *Forraadt* (1892; Betrayed), also a novel dealing with the problems of marriage. Other novels published during this period are *Knut Tandberg* (1886) and *Lucie* (1888), the latter remarkable for its pictures of life in the Christiania of those days. In 1893, after other rather unsuccessful attempts at playwriting, she presented the conflict between an independent, unconventional spirit and a humdrum, Philistine outlook on life in a play, *Agnete* (1893), which has retained all its power of passionate persuasion and remains one of the most remarkable contributions to the 19th-century Norwegian theatre.

The work which has assured for this writer a place among the masters of Norwegian letters is the great epic novel *Hellemyrsfolket* (4 vols., *Sjur Gabriel,* 1887; *To venner,* 1887, Two Friends; *S. G. Myre,* 1890; *Afkom,* 1898, Offspring). This is a family chronicle, the sad tale of generation after generation of miserable people, doomed by their own weakness, seemingly predestined to a life of poverty, squalor, and crime. The background of the novel is the town of Bergen, where the novelist had spent her childhood and youth, and the book is alive with its sights and sounds and smells. An almost uncanny insight into the very depths of human nature makes her reveal to her readers the criss-cross of motives directing the life of her unsavory hero, S. G. Myre, the son of incurable drunkards, himself a vain, weak coward who by devious means succeeds in getting into the middle-class environment he has always wanted to belong to, but who ends his life in prison. A deep, genuine sense of human destiny, of the unescapable logic of fate, permeates this somber epic in which the author's naturalistic conception of a world dominated by biological factors is transformed and illumined by a poet's feeling of tragic necessity.

Among Amalie Skram's other books mention should be made of the polemical novel, *Professor Hieronymus* (1895), the somewhat sentimental *Julehelg* (1900; Christmas), and a collection of short stories, *Sommer* (1899; Summer).

See: Antonie Tiberg, *Amalie Skram* (1910).

O. P. G.

Sládek, Josef Václav (1845–1912, Czech poet and translator of Shakespeare), is the first Czech poet to show intense interest in America. Sládek was born in Zbiroh (west of Prague) and studied science at the University of Prague. In 1868 he came to the United States, where he lived for two years as a teacher and journalist. After his return to Europe he became a teacher of English at the Prague Commercial College. He died, after a long illness, in his native village.

Sládek's personal relations with Vrchlický (*q.v.*) and Zeyer (*q.v.*) as well as his editorship of *Lumír,* the journal of the group, put him into the camp of the "cosmopolites," but his poetic practice was rooted rather in the native tradition of folk poetry. He was most successful as a poet when he wrote short lyrics in the simplest style, some humorous and whimsical, some expressly addressed to children or written as if sung by peasant boys and girls. Sládek was also a good poet of his personal sorrows—the early death of his first wife, his long struggle with disease, his return to traditional religion. He wrote much political verse of distinction, expressing an intense patriotism and a strong belief in the peasants as the core of the nation. Sládek also composed short epics and idyls of country life as well as the more conventional descriptive and meditative poetry. At his best he is a genuine poet who revived the style of folk poetry and filled it with personal content.

His more important volumes are *Básně* (1875; Poems), *Jiskry na moři* (1879; Sparks on the Sea), *Světlou stopou* (1881; On a Bright Trail), *Sluncem a stinem* (1887; In Sun and Shade), *Selské písně a české znělky* (1889; Peasant Songs and Czech Sonnets), and *Starosvětské písničky* (1891; Old-World Ditties). Sládek's stay in America bore fruit in descriptive sketches and informative articles on American life and literature (collected as *Americké obrázky,* 2 vols., 1914, American pictures) as well as in translations of American and English poetry. He translated Longfellow's *Hiawatha* (1872), Bret Harte and Aldrich, Byron and Coleridge, and, with especial success, Burns. Beginning in 1894 he undertook a complete translation of Shakespeare's plays, of which he finished 32. Sládek's Shakespeare is still standard in Czech, faithful, poetic, though somewhat academic, too polished, and not concise enough in the greatest tragedies. Recent translations of individual plays—*Macbeth* by Otokar Fischer (*q.v.*), *Julius Caesar, The Merchant of Venice, A Midsummer Night's Dream,* and *Twelfth Night* by Erik Saudek—are superior, but no one has matched Sládek's general achievement.

See: E. Chalupný, *J. V. Sládek* (1916); F. Strejček, *J. V. Sládek* (1916); R. Wellek, "Vykleštěný Shakespeare," in *Kritika* (1924); F. X. Šalda, *Šaldův zápisník,* IV (1932), 337–352.

R. W.

Slataper, Scipio (1885–1915, Italian poet and free-lance writer), was born of an Italian mother in Trieste, where his father's family, originally Slavic, had become Italianized. He met death on the Podgora front, almost in view of his native city, in the war that gave Trieste to Italy. His name has a prophetic meaning: golden pen. He began writing while very young, but his true spirit did not find expression until, going to Florence to register at the university, he came in contact with the *Voce* group—which served as the spark that lighted his spiritual torch. At times he experienced a feeling of inferiority, coming as he did from a provincial town, finding himself placed on an equal footing with veterans, and suddenly precipitated into the current of the most advanced thought of Italy and the most daring streams of European art criticism. His contribution however was of the highest quality. He brought to the *Voce* a realistic knowledge of the complexities of *Irredentismo;* for the first time Italians were made aware of the complexity of the problem of Trieste, with its Slavic population and its economic rivalry with Venice. He also used his knowledge of German, acquired in an Austrian high school, to translate the *Judith* (1911) and the *Tagebuch* (1912) of Hebbel and to give the first critical appreciation of this tragic playwright in Italian. In addition, he had so completely entered into the spirit of the *Voce* that during an absence of Prezzolini (*q.v.*) he acted as editor of this periodical.

An idealistic love, ending tragically for some unknown reason in the suicide of his beloved, brought him near desperation and made him seek a refuge and solitude in the environs of Trieste, in a region called the Carso. He emerged from this emotional crisis with the book upon which rests his fame, *Il Mio Carso* (1912). It expresses the ideal of the generation of the *Voce,* which tried to find in the sincerity of autobiography an antidote to the rhetoric of D'Annunzio and to the infantilism of Pascoli (*qq.v.*). *Il Mio Carso* is a work in which deep poetic sentiment and crude realism are mingled in a spasmodic and tormented style which seems to take its tone from the harsh, arid, tense character of the region itself. Slataper viewed life and art as a conflict of forces, a token perhaps of the conflict within himself between his Slavic blood, his Italian culture, and his German education. The moral issue dominates all his work; he is an admirer of moral will, which explains his love for Hebbel, and of Ibsen (*q.v.*), about whom he wrote his doctoral dissertation (published by his professor, Arturo Farinelli, posthumously in 1916, though incomplete). The *Lettere* (1931) to three young women—one his first fiancée, the second his future wife, the third a friend—also published posthumously, show him as a young Galahad surrounded by admiration and love. Each woman is treated differently: terrifying love, presented with a certain amount of literary device, for the first, serious love and honest realism for his wife, and a certain friendly compassion for the third.

The lesser contributions, literary (*Scritti letterari e critici,* 1920), and political (*Scritti politici* 1925), made to the *Voce,* the *Resto del Carlino,* and, curiously enough, to a magazine for children, the famous *Giornalino* (of Luigi Bertelli), were dominated by the impulse or necessity of the moment.

For a brief period preceding the First World War he taught Italian in Hamburg at the Colonial Institute. His was a noble life. He successfully overcame numerous financial and political difficulties. His native city, where he had incurred the enmity of many of the inhabitants by speaking the truth, finally became reconciled to him after his heroic death on the field of battle. A street of Rome bears his name.

See: G. Stuparich, *Scipio Slataper* (1922).

G. P.

Słonimski, Antoni (1895–, Polish poet, critic, and playwright), was born in Warsaw, the son of a distinguished Jewish physician. A bitter foe of bigotry, reaction, and especially of racialism, he was also one of the leading pacifists in Free Poland. As a cofounder of *Skamander* (*see* Polish Literature), Słonimski stood at the forefront of the progressive intellectuals of his country. His weekly *feuilletons* in *Wiadomości literackie* (Literary News), appearing under the rubric "Weekly Chronicle," were notable for their common sense, cosmopolitan temper, and fearlessness, as were also his theatrical reviews in the same journal.

Besides several small volumes of verse, Słonimski wrote a number of satirical comedies, among these *Wieża Babel* (1927; The Tower of Babel); *Murzyn warszawski* (1928; The Warsaw Negro), a satire on the literary hack; *Lekarz bezdomny* (1931; The Homeless Physician); and *Rodzina* (1934; The Family), a brilliant take-off on "isms." A collected edition of Słonimski's poems was published in 1929. During the Second World War, Słonimski was active in Polish liberal circles in England; many of his articles appeared in *Robotnik polski* (The Polish Worker), and several volumes of his poetry were published, including *Alarm* (1940) and *Popiół i wiatr* (1941; The Ash and the Wind), a memoir of ruined Warsaw.

See: K. Czachowski, *Obraz współczesnej literatury polskiej,* III (1936), 307–316, 706–707; A. P. Coleman, *New York Times Book Review,* December 22, 1940, pp. 8, 18.

A. P. C.

Slonimski, Mikhail Leonidovich (1897–, Russian novelist and short-story writer), a son of an editor of *Vestnik Yevropy,* was born at Pavlovsk. After graduating from a Gymnasium, he enlisted in the army (1915), and two years later embarked on a literary career, subsequently identifying himself with a group of young writers who called themselves the Serapion Brothers (1921–1922). His impressionistic short stories of that period, which revealed Slonimski as a conscientious and talented artist, reflected the disorganization in human relations brought on by the war and the Revolution (*Shestoi strelkovy,* 1922; The Sixth Fusiliers). In *Mashina Emeri* (1924; Emery's Machine) he first attempted to determine man's significance in an apparently meaningless world, an effort that undoubtedly prepared the ground for the first of his short novels, which deal with Soviet life, *Lavrovy* (1927; The Lavrovs), the story of an intellectual who is unable to find his place in society. This book is also a milestone in Slonimski's transition from impressionism to psychological realism. *Sredni prospekt* (1928; The Middle Avenue), a tight novelette of intrigue, is an excursion into the world of NEP tradesmen demoralized through lack of social consciousness. With *Foma Kleshniov* (1931) Slonimski returned to the characters of *Lavrovy,* but the determined old Bolshevik Kleshniov is less lifelike than the intelligentsia who surround him. After *Povest o Leviné* (1935; The Story of Leviné), a sketch of a leader of the Bavarian Communists, Slonimski reinterpreted some of his early material from a more constructive point of view (*Proshchaniye,* 1937; The Farewell). His *Predsedatel gorsoveta* (1943; The President of the Town Soviet), a collection of stories, deals with people caught in the stresses of the recent war.

See: R. Messer, "O tvorchestve M. L. Slonimskovo," *Zvezda,* 1932, No. 6, pp. 159–172; A. Gorelov, *Put sovremennika; o tvorchestve Mikh. Slonimskovo* (1933).

P. A. P.

Slovak literature (*see also* Czech literature). The Slovaks, a West Slavic nation of about two million, had no distinct literature of their own in earlier centuries but used Czech as their literary language. Their political fate was, however, very different from that of the Czechs: they never had a state of their own and after the destruction of the Great Moravian Empire about 900 formed a part of Hungary. Following the defeat of the Bohemians in the Battle of the White Mountain (1620), Protestantism was suppressed in Bohemia and Moravia. The more tolerant religious conditions of Hungary allowed Czech Protestant literature to continue in Slovakia. A case can even be made out for the statement that the Czech Protestant tradition was preserved in Slovakia. Slovaks writing in Czech certainly played a considerable part early in the 19th century in the Czech national revival. Jan Kollár (1793–1852), an important romantic poet and the founder of Pan-Slavism, and Pavel Josef Šafařík (1795–1861), the founder of Slavonic archaeology, both came from Slovak Protestant homes, wrote in Czech, and felt themselves to be members of the Czechoslovak nation. František Palacký (1798–1876), the great historian of the Czech nation, was born in Moravia, but received his education in Slovakia, which was then attracting Czech Protestants because of its greater religious freedom. A Catholic priest, Antonín Bernolák (1763–1813), had advocated writing in the West Slovak dialect and had found one practicing poet, a Protestant, Jan Hollý (1785–1849), who wrote dreary and extremely artificial imitations of Vergil and Homer in this language. But the movement had failed to take root. Slovak as a literary language was successfully established only in 1844, when L'udevít Štúr (1815–1856) and Jozef Miloslav Hurban (1817–1888), both originally Protestant clergymen, published an almanac, *Nitra,* in the Central Slovak dialect. Štúr developed and defended the language in theoretical writings, and soon gifted poets arose who used it with skill and success. Andrej Sládkovič (1820–1872), Samo Chalupa (1812–1883), Janko Král' (1822–1876), and Ján

Botto (1829–1881 are the outstanding names of a group of highly romantic poets. One good novelist, Ján Kalinčák (1822–1871), can be described as an early realist, a humorous observer of the life of Slovak peasantry and landed gentry.

The reasons for the "separation" from Czech are not far to seek: the Slovaks felt that the Czechs were politically impotent and that no help could be received from them. The use of the local dialect was recommended by good patriots as the best defense against the government-sponsored spread of the Magyar language. Theories about the peculiar value of every local dialect, and especially of Slovak which, according to some scholars, was supposed to be the original language of the Slavs, worked powerfully in the same direction. However deplorable the separation turned out to be from a political point of view, Slovak must be described as a full-fledged literary language; it is used on all stylistic levels for all purposes, even though it is extremely similar to Czech.

After the Austrian-Hungarian Compromise of 1867 the situation for Slovak writers for a time became worse. The Magyars made a determined attempt to eradicate the use of the language, especially for higher purposes. Schools conducted in Slovak were successively closed, and by 1914 there was no education in Slovak beyond the elementary level. Slovak literature was kept alive by a tiny band of enthusiasts who could appeal only to an extremely small reading public. During these worst years two important writers arose, Svetozár Hurban Vajanský (*q.v.*) and Hviezdoslav (*q.v.*). Hurban, with pro-Russian orientation and Pan-Slav romanticism, is most important as a novelist who, under the influence of Turgenev (*q.v.*), wrote fine pictures of the gentry society in Slovakia. Hviezdoslav is largely prominent as an epic poet, best in poems with local rural setting, who also wrote biblical dramas and translated Shakespeare into Slovak. His sympathies were with the Czechs, and his poetry shows the influence of his Czech contemporaries, Čech (*q.v.*) and Vrchlický (*q.v.*).

In 1898 a group of Slovak intellectuals founded a review called *Hlas* (The Voice). With democratic ideals and critical standards largely inspired by Tomáš Masaryk (*q.v.*), they opposed the romantic ideology and the placing of hope in Russia and in the local gentry. Independently of this critical group, the realist novel had found excellent practitioners in Slovakia. Martin Kukučin (pseud. of Matej Bencúr, 1860–1928) depicted Slovak life in extremely vivid sketches and short stories and later, when he had lived for years in Dalmatia and in South America, wrote ambitious novels on the problem of emigration. *Dom v stráni* (published serially in 1904, in book form in 1922; The House on the Slope), with its setting among the Dalmatian peasants, is his acknowledged masterpiece. Jozef Gregor Tajovský (1874–1946) and a woman writer, Timrava (pseud. of Božena Slančíková 1867–), wrote with realistic technique novels and stories which can be called critical and moral studies of Slovak village life. It was not until the early 20th century, and undoubtedly as a belated echo of Western European artistic movements, that a few Slovak poets turned away from didacticism and the depiction of Slovak reality and cultivated a purely personal art. Ivan Krasko (pseud. of Ján Botto, the younger, 1876–) is a refined, melancholy poet touched by the "decadence" of some Western Europeans, while Janko Jesenský (1874–1945) wrote harder, more intellectual and satirical poetry which escaped the conventions of rhetorical romanticism hitherto prevalent in Slovakia. But these were individuals without followers. On the whole, literary life in Slovakia up to 1918 was limited and provincial.

The liberation of the Slovaks and their union with the Czechs in 1918 wrought an almost miraculous change. Slovak suddenly became the official language of the country. A legal and learned terminology was developed. Slovak became the language of the schools from the lowest to the newly founded Comenius University at Bratislava. The reading public expanded so rapidly that Slovak books were published in editions almost 10 times the size of those before 1914. With the exception of strolling companies, no Slovak theatre had existed before the war, but now a national theatre was established at Bratislava and permanent theatres were opened elsewhere. Both poetry and the novel flourished. Poetry, under strong Czech and French influence, became especially diversified and highly cultivated. Among the older poets, two Protestant ministers, Vladimír Roy (1885–1936) and Martin Rázus (1888–1937), stood out. Roy, who had studied in Scotland, translated English poetry and wrote melancholy reflective verse. Rázus was a rhetorical, political writer who became prominent both as politician and as novelist. His novels and autobiography are in fact chronicles full of topical detail and political discussion rather than works of art. The best poetry in Slovak was written by two younger men, who had also studied Protestant theology; these two, Emil Boleslav Lukáč (1900–) and Jan Smrek (pseud. of Jan Čietek, 1898–), present, furthermore, a striking contrast to each other. Lukáč is strongly under the influence of French symbolist poetry (*see* French symbolism), especially that of Claudel (*q.v.*). His inspiration is religious, while his style is highly intellectual and even dialectical. Smrek is melodious, sensuous—even sensual—and glorifies the earth and its pleasures. Smrek in his later work shows the influence of Czech "poetism" which is also dominant in a group of younger poets of leftist political orientation, among whom Laco Novomeský (1904–) is the best known. With this group, which leans toward futurism, certain Catholic poets made another very sharp contrast. Two younger men, Rudolf Dilong (1905–) and Pavel G. Hlbina (pseud. of Pavel Gašparovič, 1908–), both priests, write distinguished verse which shows a knowledge of Březina (*q.v.*), Claudel, and Bremond (*q.v.*). Thus Slovak poetry reflects most of the modern movements and practices with competence and refinement the most diverse techniques.

The novel, which had been largely confined to a realistic analysis of life, also expanded after the First World War with a great variety of themes. An older writer, Ladislav Nadáši-Jégé (1866–1942), created the Slovak historical novel with *Adam Šangala* (1923), a picture of the 17th century; he also wrote less successful, erotic, society novels (*e.g.*, *Cesta životom*, 1930, The Journey through Life). Petr Jilemnický (1901–), a Czech by birth who writes in Slovak, composed social novels of the conflict between the peasant and industry (*e.g.*, *Pole neorané*, 1932, The Unplowed Field) or attempted pictures of Soviet Russia, which he knows from a two-year stay and whose creed he embraced fervently. Milo Urban (1904–) is possibly the most distinguished of the recent Slovak novelists. In three novels (*Živý bič*, 1927, The Living Scourge; *Hmly na úsvite*, 1930, Fogs in the Dawn; *V osidlach*, 1939, Trapped) he is a critical chronicler of the Slovak village during and after the First World War. The picture of the struggle between the primitive mountaineers and the encroaching modern civilization is drawn by Urban without the usual false sentimentality toward the traditional forms of life. All these authors are, in principle, still within the bounds of realistic techniques. Such conventions are broken only by Gejza Vámoš (1901–), a physician, who is preoccupied with the pathology of the middle class and uses burlesque and expressionist techniques reminiscent of Vančura (*q.v.*). Two other genres, Slovak criticism and Slovak drama, lack distinction. Criticism is mostly dependent on Czech models, those of F. X. Šalda (*q.v.*) in particular, and the drama rarely goes beyond realistic comedies or moralizing treatises.

Up to 1918, then, Slovak literature had been constantly handicapped by the political oppression. And there had been no urban centers, no middle class except a rural clergy. The nation was sharply divided into Catholics and Protestants, into gentry and largely illiterate peasants. Literature emancipated itself only very slowly from romanticism and the romantic glorification of the primitive. Since 1918 conditions have changed in favor of a wider outlook and more varied themes, but the sudden expansion and the influx of ideas from abroad have had its dangers. Too many Slovak writers are closely dependent on analogous Czech developments. During the Second World War left-wing sympathizers like Petr Jilemnický and Gejza Vámoš went into exile. Others like Milo Urban adapted themselves. But literary life was almost at a standstill.

See: J. Vlček, *Dejiny literatury slovenskej* (1890, reprinted 1923); S. Krčméry, *Prehľad dejín slovenskej literatúry a vzdelanosti* (1920); D. Chrobák, *Rukoväť dejín slovenskej literatúry* (1932; 2d ed., 1936); A. Pražák, "Literatura slovenská," in *Československá vlastivěda*, Vol. VII (1933); P. Selver, "The Literature of the Slovaks," *Slavonic Review*, XII (1933–1934), 691–703; J. E. Bor, *Poezia povojnového Slovenska* (1934); A. Mráz, *Povojnový slovenský román* (1938).

R. W.

Snoilsky, Carl Grefve (1841–1903, Swedish poet), born in Stockholm, became a diplomatist at the early age of 20. His career took him to Italy at the time of Risorgimento, and he was equally carried away by the splendor of the past and by the exploits of Garibaldi. A strain of Polish blood on the paternal side may help to account for his love of revolution. Aristocratic, vigorous, and healthily sensual, he reminds us of Byron: like his brilliant predecessor he was an intense lover of Italy and Spain, an ardent hater of political and social oppression. He is, however, a gayer, less egocentric spirit.

His *Dikter* (Poems), published in 1869, irradiated Swedish poetry with a joy of life that had been lacking since the time of Tegnér. The grandeur of Roman ruins, the voluptuous charm of Sorrento, the whole glowing pageant of "the land of the myrtle," was caught up and carried to the North in the melody of his verse. Fortunately too he was an admirable craftsman, partly no doubt through the influence of Horace.

But although his early success was so startling, it seems probable (Sir Edmund Gosse to the contrary, notwithstanding) that there is more of enduring worth in his *Sonneter* (1863–1873; Sonnets) and *Svenska bilder* (1886; Pictures of Sweden). The sonnets in particular are masterly, both in design and in execution. He continued to write lyrics and ballads throughout his life, changing to a more compressed and reflective style, with the accent on Sweden's martial achievements and on sympathy with the laboring classes. The mission of poetry, he believed, was to bring beauty to those most in need of it; he provides both the thrill of heroic romance and a high-hearted recognition of present-day humanity. There is a rousing trumpet note in his orchestration as well as the softer strains of flute and violin; he can be at once a Wagner and a Mozart.

See: C. W. Stork, *Anthology of Swedish Lyrics* (1917; revised and enlarged ed., 1930); F. Böök, *Sveriges moderna litteratur* (1921), also published as Vol. III of O. Sylwan, ed., *Svenska litteraturens historia* (1919–1921), pp. 47–65.

C. W. S.

Söderberg, Hjalmar (1869–1941, Swedish dramatist and writer of fiction), was born in Stockholm and studied for a short time at Uppsala. Beginning as a government clerk, he drifted for a time, interesting himself particularly in Anatole France (*q.v.*), whom he translated. He had a decided success with his first novel, *Martin Bircks ungdom* (1901; Eng. tr., *Martin Birck's Youth,* 1930), and later held the stage with his play *Gertrud* (1906), but it was in the very short story that he achieved a unique position. These stories, usually told in the first person, are at times sheer tragedies, after the manner of Maupassant (*q.v.*), but are more often realistic character sketches of penetrating humor. Their disarming simplicity conceals an art that can only be appreciated after many readings, for they sound hidden depths of human consciousness. Söderberg's first collection, *Historietterna* (1898; Little Histories), was followed by several others.

In mood the author is the complete skeptic. "I believe in the lust of the flesh and the eternal loneliness of the soul." But his skepticism is never bitter, as often with Anatole France. There is a cool detachment and impartiality about him. Above all he had a casual rightness of statement, which compels one to believe that everything happens exactly as he says. His favorite subjects are the helpless folk whom circumstances and their own weaknesses entangle in the cobweb filaments of life. But although, as with the modern French masters named, the irony of fate is much in evidence, there are other motifs in the stories of Söderberg. He can be droll, he can indulge in a fairy tale such as "The Accomplished Dragon." And he has a special gift of drawing philosophical conclusions from trivial occurrences, as in "The Cup of Tea," where he is put out of a restaurant for being the only one there not taking stronger drink.

The only regret of Söderberg's many admirers is that he wrote so little. In his later years he turned from fiction to studies of religion, of course in the skeptical vein. He will be remembered chiefly as the portrayer of Stockholm life at the turn of the century. For his particular type of short story, which is in some respects not unlike that of Katherine Mansfield, it would be hard to match him anywhere in modern literature.

See: J. Mortensen, *Från Röda rummet till sekelskiftet* (1919); C. W. Stork, tr., *Modern Swedish Masterpieces* (1923); H. A. Larsen, ed., *Sweden's Best Stories* (1928); Söderberg, *Selected Short Stories,* tr. by C. W. Stork (1935).

C. W. S.

Soffici, Ardengo (1879–, Italian artist, poet, and essayist), was born in Rignano, near Florence. After a long sojourn in Paris as an art student, Soffici returned to Italy and was soon a leading contributor to the *Voce,* the Florentine weekly that was to exert much influence on the subsequent trend of Italian cultural and political life. Through a series of lively articles Soffici made known the works of Degas, Cézanne, Renoir, Gauguin, Van Gogh, Matisse, Picasso, and others. The first exposition in Italy of Europe's most famous impressionists was organized by him.

Soffici really started as a French writer. A decade of Parisian life in artistic milieux and in the company of Guillaume Appollinaire (*q.v.*) had had a marked influence upon him. His first writings were contributions to periodicals like the *Plume, Mercure, Occident,* and above all the *Soirées de Paris.* Later Soffici abandoned his early futuristic sympathies for a gradual but steady return to his native Italian classical traditions. In his Italian writings there is almost no mention of his French literary activity. In *Arlecchino* (1914) and *Giornale di bordo* (1915), Soffici emerged as an attractive and varied Italian literary personality. Nothing he has written since can compare with these two works either in style or human feeling. *Giornale di bordo* is a sort of diary or log of his most intimate thoughts. *Arlecchino* describes Tuscan life in colors as rich and diverse as those on the palette of a painter. The reader accompanies the author on rambles through his beloved Tuscan countryside with nature at all seasons and in all moods. The artist-writer sees green skies, white rain, ashen clouds, orange shadows. He thrills at the fragrance of earth soaked by a heavy rain. He has a Baudelairian sensitivity to odors. No detail of his surroundings escapes him; in fact the small things are for him the great, significant things. The shining flight of an insect, a step in the night, a drop of water reflecting the sky: these are of utmost importance. Soffici writes: "I often feel too much of a poet to like poetry. Nature speaks to me so affectionately that the introduction of any art between me and nature seems to disturb, obscure and falsify our communion."

Reproached by critics for his many contradictory tendencies—he has been liberal and traditionalist, idealist and realist, provincial and cosmopolitan—Soffici retorts that his artistic vision has been sharpened by these contradictions, which, he feels, are characteristic of nature itself. The one permanent quality that permeates every work of Soffici is art. Even *Kobilek* (1918), the story of Soffici's experiences in the First World War, is an artistic experience rather than a military one.

See: G. Papini, *Stroncature* (1916), pp. 261–272; R. Serra, *Le Lettere* (1914); G. Prezzolini, *Amici* (1922), pp. 143–158; A. Baldini, *Amici allo spiedo* (1932), pp. 21–28.

P. M. R.

Søiberg, Harry (1880–, Danish novelist), was born in Ringkøbing on the North Sea coast of Jutland, went to sea as a mess boy, became a bookbinder, and a passionate socialist agitator. His first book, *Syg Slægt* (1904; Sick Generation), published when he was 24, is a not very effective drama. His next volume, *Øde Egne* (1906; Desolate Regions), a collection of short stories, revealed unusual ability to depict nature and to delineate moods and manners as observed in the frugal homes scattered among the sand dunes of the Jutland coast. In *Folket ved Havet* (1906; The People at the Sea), Søiberg is still surer of himself and succeeds in painting a realistic and colorfully vivid canvas of the fisher families and their deep affinity with the rough, stern scenery of the coast. Various minor works followed, and then *De Levendes Land* (1916–1920; The Land of the Living) appeared in the form of a cycle, describing, maturely and deftly, life in the region which Søiberg had chosen for his own. Here is the ancient struggle between broad humanitarianism and religious bigotry, between light and darkness, examined on the dual background of the roaring sea and the First World War. Again fishermen and their families are revealed in their hours of sorrow and joy, of suffering and pleasure, of economic worries, and constant religious friction. *Søkongen* (1926–1930; Eng. tr., *The Sea King,* 1928), a trilogy, follows in the main the same lines, but is more searching, more revealing, and more painstaking in psychological analysis. A number of shorter novels appeared between *De Levendes Land* and *Søkongen,* and also subsequently, but it is in these two works that Søiberg has so far attained the peak of his art. Although there might seem danger of monotony, Søiberg surprises by his ever deeper insight into the thoughts and the souls of the Jutland fishers and constantly finds something which no one else has discovered.

See: K. K. Nicolaisen, "Harry Søiberg," *Illustreret Tidende,* November 11, 1921; Helge Kjaergaard, *Die dänische Literatur der neuesten Zeit (1871–1933)* (1934).

G. St.

Sologub, Fyodor (pseud. of Fyodor Kuzmich Teternikov, 1863–1927, Russian poet and prose writer), was born in St. Petersburg, the son of a tailor. His father died when Sologub was still very young, and his mother was obliged to work as a maid for a well-to-do family. He was educated at the St. Petersburg Teachers' Institute and in 1882 began his career as a teacher. His first literary effort was published in 1884. In 1907 he retired from teaching and dedicated himself entirely to literature. Although Sologub remained aloof from the revolutionary movement of 1917, he stayed in Russia.

Sologub occupies a special niche among the symbolist writers. He was the oldest, in actual age, among them; he also was the first to receive public recognition as a symbolist poet. His poetry, combining realism with fantasy, is ultra-decadent in its themes, favoring motifs of self-deification, demonolatry, and glorification of pain and death. In style Sologub is a master of classical form, and it was this artistry that brought him recognition as a poet. Like his verse, his novels constantly counterpoise the real and the fantastic, thus suggesting the illusory quality of what one normally regards as the real. His prose masterpiece, *Melki bes* (1907; Eng. tr., *The Little Demon,* 1916), first published serially 1892–1902, is a brilliant satire that derives its effect from its symbolism. Peredonov, the name of its hero, became an adjective connoting all that was petty and base. Of Sologub's other novels, *Tvorimaya legenda* (published serially, 1908–1912; The Created Legend) deserves mention, as do *Navii chary* (1912; Phantom Charms) and *Zaklinatelnitsa zmei* (1921; The Charmer of Snakes).

See: A. Gornfeld, "Fyodor Sologub," in S. A. Vengerov, ed., *Russkaya Literatura XX veka,* I (1914) 14–64.

O. M.

Solovyov, Vladimir Sergeyevich (1853–1900, Russian poet and philosopher), most brilliant of the many talented children of Russia's great historian, S. M. Solovyov, was born in Moscow and reared in a patriarchal, severely religious atmosphere. Related, on his mother's side, to the Ukrainian mystic philosopher Skovoroda, Solovyov began early to display a predisposition toward mysticism. Upon finishing the Fifth Moscow Gymnasium, he enrolled in the physico-mathematical faculty of the University of Moscow, but soon transferred to the historico-philological faculty. Although between 14 and 18 he had experienced a period of religious negation, by the time he was 20 he had evolved an anti-positivist, religious philosophy. His master's thesis on "The Crisis of Western Philosophy" reflected the influence of the Slavophiles and the Schelling-Hegelian school of Russian thought; of Schopenhauer and Hartmann, a blending of German philosophy with oriental mysticism; and, finally, of Plato.

In 1875, as docent of the University of Moscow, Solovyov went to England where, in the British Museum, he studied the mystical literature on Sophia, the Divine Wisdom of God. While in London, he saw a vision of Sophia who bade him travel to the Arabian desert, a summons he obeyed. Afterwards he traveled in Italy and France. In 1876–1877 he lectured at the University of Moscow and then went to St. Petersburg, where he delivered a series of public "Lectures on Godmankind." In 1880 he defended his doctoral thesis, "Critique of Abstract Origins," and became professor at the University of Moscow. Following the execution of the assassins of Alexander II in 1881, Solovyov delivered a public address condemning capital punishment and as a result was obliged to give up his professorial career. Thereafter he devoted himself to writing.

Solovyov's philosophical writings are voluminous and reflect his philosophical *Weltanschauung,* yet they have had little influence on Russian literature proper. Not so his single volume of verse, *Stikhotvoreniya* (1891; 7th ed., 1921; Poems). His poetry, marked now by reflective profoundness, now by irreverent wit, conveyed his most intimate thoughts and his mystical interpretation of reality. The "younger generation" of symbolists—Bely, Blok, and Vyacheslav Ivanov (*qq.v.*)—accepted it as the revelation of a poet-prophet, and such a poem as "Mily drug, il ty ne vidish . . ." (Friend Beloved) became a testament for them. Poets who refused to accept the reality of the tangible world as the ultimate reality and sought justification for an irrational belief in another world found support of their beliefs in Solovyov's poetry. Sophia, the Wisdom of God (also the Eternal Feminine Soul), plays a vital part in the philosophy of Solovyov. To her he devoted his seventh lecture on Godmankind and Part III of his dissertation *La Russie et l'Eglise universelle* (1889). Sophia also appears as the Muse that inspires his poetry. Much of the poetry of both Alexander Blok and Andrei Bely is motivated by the symbol of Sophia, appearing as the Beautiful Damsel, or Russia, or under whatever other guise.

See: E. Trubetskoi, *Mirosozertsaniye Vl. Solovyova* (2 vols., 1913); S. M. Solovyov, "Biografiya V. S. Solovyova," in V. S. Solovyov, *Stikhotvoreniya,* 6th ed. (1916).

O. M.

Sorel, Georges (1847–1922, French social philosopher), generally recognized as the outstanding theoretician of revolutionary syndicalism, was born in Cherbourg, of a typical bourgeois family. He entered the Ecole Polytechnique (1865) and became a highway engineer. In 1892, at the age of 45, he abruptly abandoned his profession in order to devote all his time to the study of social problems. His wife, who came from the working class, is said to have done much in bringing about this decision. When she died in 1897, Sorel retired to a modest villa at Boulogne-sur-Seine near Paris, to erect "a philosophical monument worthy of her memory."

By far Sorel's most famous book is his *Réflexions sur la violence* (1908; Eng. tr., *Reflections on Violence,* 1912)—a modified and enlarged version of several articles first published in the Italian *Divenire sociale* (1905) and in the *Mouvement socialiste* (1906–1907). This work offers a curious mixture of Proudhon's economic federalism, Marx's "catastrophic" interpretation of history, Nietzsche's (*q.v.*) hero worship, and Bergson's (*q.v.*) definition of movement as an "indivisible whole." Progress and revolution, according to Sorel, follow a subconscious pattern. Only in action, rebellion, and violence do men discover what they want and why they fight. It is unfair, therefore, to expect from militant syndicalism a precise exposition of its aims and purposes. Militant syndicalism is not rooted in ideas. It constitutes one tremendous intuitive force, a genuine *élan vital* of unpredicted and unpredictable consequences, a spontaneous surge which draws its strength from and finds its symbolical expression in "myths" and "images" such as that of the general strike. Through the incentive of the general strike the workers' collective soul will rise to a "sublime" feeling truly consistent with the exalted mission of the proletariat. At the same time the bourgeoisie, vitally threatened and aroused from its unwholesome lethargy, will resist the growing aggressiveness of labor and undergo in turn a process of rejuvenation.

The startling fact about the *Réflexions sur la violence* is that it does not uphold a class theory. Sorel is much less preoccupied with the proletariat for its own sake than with the proletariat as the catalytic agent of a new social order to be brought about through a war of purification. Should labor weaken in its determination, the same end might still be sought and reached by means of the opposite policy—namely, by bolstering the fighting spirit of the bourgeoisie in order to rekindle the cooling ardor of the working classes. This willingness on Sorel's part to play one side against the other for what he sincerely considers the best interests of both explains to a large extent his many shifts and brazen contradictions. His early association with the parliamentary socialists did not survive the Dreyfus affair, the outcome of which, in his opinion as well as in that of Charles Péguy (*q.v.*), was a "complete moral anarchy" and a drowning in politics of the mystical victory that had been won (see *La Décomposition du marxisme,* 1908; *La Révolution dreyfusienne,* 1909). It was then (about 1898) that Sorel turned to the labor unions as to the standard-bearers of pure, uncompromising socialism (many articles of this period were gathered later in his *Matériaux pour une théorie du prolétariat,* 1919). However, the gospel of "holy violence" did not have the desired effect upon the workers, who seemed more intent on obtaining the immediate satisfaction of higher wages and better living conditions. In 1910 Sorel is found sympathizing with extreme conservatism in the person of Paul Bourget (*q.v.*) whose play, *La Barricade,* "transposed" the Sorelian creed for the benefit of the bourgeoisie. For several years he collaborated on the *Revue critique des idées et des livres* and on the short-lived *Indépendance* (1911–1913), side by side with confirmed nationalists and royalists (Léon Daudet, Charles Maurras, *qq.v.,* Georges Valois, Jean Variot). In the late stages of his career he lavished equal praise on Lenin (see "Pour Lénine," appendix III to the 5th ed. of the *Réflexions sur la violence,* 1921), and on Mussolini whose blueprint of a corporate state was avowedly an extension of Sorelian syndicalism to all classes of society.

Throughout these metamorphoses Sorel maintained the fierce anti-intellectualistic attitude which, early in his crusade, inspired him to condemn Socrates' rationalism for having shaken the heroic traditions of Greece (*Le Procès de Socrate,* 1889). Pluto-democratic ideology, which tends to dissolve the class spirit, appeared to him equally vain and baneful (*Les Illusions du progrès,* 1908). All told, his vision of the world of tomorrow was that of a technician and a moralist. Sorel the engineer, far from being the enemy of industry and production, counted on man-made instruments to free us some day from the deterministic yoke of nature (*Introduction à l'économie moderne,* 1903, and "Les Préoccupations métaphysiques des physiciens modernes," *Revue de métaphysique et de morale,* Vol. XIII, 1905, reprinted in Charles Péguy's *Cahiers de la quinzaine,* 1907). Sorel the moralist—a moralist of almost puritanical mold—dreamed of injecting a high dose of spiritual energy into the material body of present-day civilization. How to moralize technology? That was the question. The multiplicity—or the debatability—of Sorel's answers should not hide from the historian's view the singleness of his purpose.

See: Gaëtan Pirou, *Georges Sorel* (1927); Jacques Rennes, *Georges Sorel et le syndicalisme révolutionnaire* (1936); Victor Sartre, *Georges Sorel: Elites syndicalistes et révolution prolétarienne* (1937); Rainer Heyne, "Georges Sorel und der autoritäre Staat des 20. Jahrhunderts," *Archiv des öffentlichen Rechts,* Neue Folge, Bd. 29 (1938), pp. 129–177, 257–309; Paul Delesalle, "Bibliographie sorélienne," *International Review for Social History,* IV (1939), 463–487; Simone Malvigna, "Il pensiero politico di Sorel e il fascismo," *Rivista internazionale di filosofia del diritto,* XIX (1939), 69–106.

J.-A. B.

Sorge, Reinhard Johannes (1892–1916, German dramatist and poet), born in Flüelen, Switzerland, went to school in Berlin. As a student in Jena he came under the influence of Richard Dehmel and Stefan George (*qq.v.*), but was most deeply stirred by Nietzsche's *Zarathustra* (*e.g., Gericht über Zarathustra; Vision,* posthumously published, 1921). He found his peace in Rome, in his conversion to Catholicism. In 1916 he was killed in action. His first drama, *Der Bettler* (1912), which was honored by the Kleist prize, introduced and influenced the expressionistic movement on the German stage. It was followed, after Sorge's conversion, by religious mysteries, *Guntwar, die Schule eines Propheten* (1914), *Metanoeite* (1915), and *König David* (1915), and by *Mutter der Himmel; Sang in 12 Gesängen* (1915). Posthumously published were *Mystische Zwiesprache* (1922), *Preis der Unbefleckten; Sang über die Begebnisse in Lourdes* (1924), *Der Jüngling: Die frühen Dichtungen* (1925), and *Nachgelassene Gedichte* (1925).

See: W. Spaet, *R. J. Sorge* (1921); M. Rockenbach, *R. J. Sorge* (1923); S. Sorge, *R. J. Sorge: Unser Weg* (1927).

W. R. G.

Souday, Paul (1869–1929, French journalist and critic), born at Le Havre in Normandy, prepared to be a teacher, but chose instead a career of writing. As a reporter for the *Temps* he came into personal contact with many prominent writers. After essaying musical and dramatic criticism, Souday was appointed to the staff of *Opinion,* for which he edited the bimonthly "Chronique littéraire" (1908–1910). In 1912 he became official literary critic of the *Temps,* writing under the caption "Les Livres" (1912–1929). The two collections of essays published 1913–1914 were facetiously entitled *Les Livres du Temps.* A third volume appeared posthumously (1930). Souday also contributed shorter, front-page articles treating a variety of subjects. A fighting tone is apparent throughout all these works.

In 1927 Souday published an edition of Voltaire's *Mémoires* and *Mélanges divers,* containing the startling preface "Voltaire démiurge." The volumes *Marcel Proust, André Gide,* and *Paul Valéry* appeared shortly afterwards. A noteworthy book is *La Société des grands esprits* (1929), in the introduction to which the author significantly remarks: "I have contempt for Disraeli, because he would have preferred to be Alexander rather than Homer." The posthumous *Dialogues critiques* and a *de luxe* Liége edition of *Bossuet* (both 1929) close the series of Souday's publications. The battling critic died suddenly at the peak of his achievement. The sale of his library in March, 1930, brought to light an interesting correspondence with some of the most eminent writers of the day.

Souday fought relentlessly the conception of criticism as an inferior genre. The role of judgment was prominent in his criticism. His militant defense of intellectualism won for him the title "guardian of French culture." Ideologically Souday is a disciple of the 18th-century *philosophes,* with marked faith in the forces of civilization. Like Voltaire he turned against the Church, which he considered an obstacle to progress. In literature and art the critic had well-defined "adorations" and "abominations." His preference was undoubtedly for the *chaîne classique.* He accepted "essential" romanticism, which for him meant the rebirth of both the artistic and critical senses, *i.e.,* Renan as well as Hugo. The "abominations" include all forms of what he called *l'illusion mystico-sentimentale.* Henri Brémond (*q.v.*) and "pure poetry" furnish an example: the mystical *abbé* defined poetry in terms of "ineffable realities." Souday contended that true art is a "construction" and that there is nothing "mysterious" about poetic genius.

See: R. Kemp, "Paul Souday parmi ses livres," *Nouvelles littéraires,* July 13, 1929; F. Ambrière, "Défense de Paul Souday," *Mercure de France,* CCXCIII (1939), 510–511.

G. M.

Soupault, Philippe (1897–, French poet, novelist, critic, and political analyst), born in Chaville near Paris, lived recently in Tunis where, in 1942, he was imprisoned by the Vichy authorities. After his liberation, he spent two years in the United States and is now back in France. The story of his prison days is related in his latest book, *Le Temps des assassins* (1945; Eng. tr., *Age of Assassins,* 1946).

The influence of Lautréamont, Rimbaud, and Apollinaire (*qq.v.*) and his group, as well as Soupault's own disgust with "the bourgeois," led him to play a prominent role in the dadaist revolt and dictated his first poems, collected in *Aquarium* (1917) and *Rose des vents* (1920). But he and Breton (*q.v.*), already dissatisfied with negative dadaism, had just discovered the process of automatic writing, and their joint experiments, bringing forth *Les Champs magnétiques* (1921), engendered surrealism. Soupault, however, did not continue in that direction: his new collections of poems, *Westwego* (1922), *Wang-Wang* (1924), *Georgia* (1926), were not typically surrealist, and he soon devoted himself to the kind of "literature" he despised and wrote novels. Actually these never were anything but lyrical fictions through which Soupault sought to break man's essential bondage and free him from the prison of his personality. Dream, adventure, delusion, vice, even crime—such are the tools to which, in their supreme undertaking, turn the heroes of these fascinating books: *Le Bon Apôtre* (1923), a sort of "Dialogues de Soupault, juge de Philippe"; *A la dérive* (1923), the dream narrative of a restless, adventurous destiny; *En joue* (1925), the ironic satire of the shallow man of letters whose vain efforts at freeing himself lead to insanity; *Le Nègre* (1927), the nightmarish pursuit of a freedom ever denied by ancestral shackles; *Les Dernières Nuits de Paris* (1928; Eng. tr., *Last Nights of Paris,* 1929), the pseudo-detective hallucination whose villain and heroine is Paris herself, with her mysterious ensnaring rites that act like charms over her devotees. Soupault was now extending the scope of his inquest by studying, with powerful insight, those other artists whose creative efforts might also have been directed toward absolute emancipation: *Henri Rousseau, le Douanier* (1927); *William Blake* (1928; Eng. tr., 1928); *Paolo Uccello* (1929); *Charlot* (1931), the lyric image of that true adventurer of the screen, Charlie Chaplin; *Baudelaire* (1931); and *Debussy* (1932). More recently he published *Souvenirs de James Joyce* (1944) in the same vein.

Then, continuing his evolution, Soupault turned to politics. One who already, in his autobiography, *Histoire d'un blanc* (1927), had heralded the coming revolution, now looked at the world and took its pulse; he studied reports and statistics, wrote documented and sagacious articles, lectured, interviewed, reported. It was a weary world, full of anxieties, looking upward to its own liberation, not unlike the psychological world that had been Soupault's: he must have judged it worthy of his solicitude.

See: F. Ribadeau-Dumas, "Carrefour de visages: Philippe Soupault," *Revue des revues,* CLXXIV (1926), 268–273; L. Martin-Chauffier, "Présentation de Philippe Soupault," in Soupault, *Histoire d'un blanc* (1927), pp. 3–11; B. Crémieux, *Inquiétude et reconstruction* (1931), pp. 97–124; H. J. Dupuy, "Philippe Soupault, ou la Poésie spontanée," *Renaissances,* Vol. XVII (1945).

C. L. B.

Sousa Viterbo, Francisco, marquês de (1845–1910, Portuguese historian), was born in Oporto. After preparing himself for a medical career in Lisbon, he abandoned this profession in favor of historical investigation. In 1881 he became a professor in the School of Liberal Arts in Lisbon; illness forced him to relinquish his post in 1901, though he continued to do scholarly work until the time of his death. He was interested in many aspects of history, archaeological, literary, biographical, musical, geographic. In all these fields he collected rich materials with methodical care. Despite the fact that he lacked broad historical vision and, by temperament, shunned dramatizations and interpretative syntheses in the manner of Oliveira Martins (*q.v.*)—Viterbo's work represents a cautious reaction against the dangers of the arbitrary criticism and hasty generalizations of that writer—he was much more than a mere exhumer of data. His prefaces, notes, and commentaries give evidence of a clear conception of historical values, in addition to a delicate sensibility, already evident in his youthful literary works. His work is extensive and varied; enormous masses of documents and data overlooked by archivists were saved by him from destruction. In addition to his biobibliographical works on Camões, Damião de Góis, Friar Luis de Sousa, *et al.,* his most solid contributions include the work on nautical history, *Trabalhos náuticos dos portugueses nos séculos XVI e XVII* (2 vols., 1890–1894; Nautical Works of the Portuguese in the 16th and 17th Centuries), which served to revive interest in the history of the discoveries of the Portuguese navigators, and the *Notícia de alguns pintores portugueses e de outros . . . que exerceram a sua arte em Portugal* (3 vols., 1903–1911; Notes on Some Portuguese Painters and Others . . . Who Practiced Their Art in Portugal), which stimulated the investigation of the history of national art. His studies on the history of industrial trades (*ofícios industriais*) has been called an "epic of national work."

See: V. Ribeiro, *Sousa Viterbo e a sua obra* (1915); F. de Figueiredo, *História da literatura realista,* 1924 ed., pp. 296–301.

E. G. D.

Sova, Antonín (1864–1928, Czech poet and novelist), ranks after Machar (*q.v.*) and Březina (*q.v.*) as the most prominent poet of the generation which began writing in the 1890's and achieved fame and maturity in the early 20th century. Sova was an impressionist who, especially in his later work, used many of the techniques of symbolism. He was born at Pacov (southern Bohemia), the son of a schoolteacher, and entered the service of the Prague Municipal Library, of which he became director late in his life. He died in his native town, after suffering long from a spinal affliction.

Sova started his writing career with realistic sketches in verse and with little landscapes somewhat in the style of Coppée (*q.v.*), but he soon turned to an introspective lyricism in which he gave expression to the struggles, conflicts, and tragedies of a highly sensitive soul. Possibly his best work can be found in the collections of intimate lyrics (*e.g., Zlomená duše,* 1896, A Broken Soul, or *Lyrika lásky a života,* 1907, Lyrics of Love and Life) in which the poet also hints at the tragedy of his unhappy married life. These are mostly song-like verses full of sensitive observations and analyses, with only slight attempts at symbolic implications. This personal poetry, which continued as an undercurrent until the death of Sova, was, at least in the public mind, overshadowed by Sova's increasingly ambitious attempts at symbolist poetry, at grandiose visions and cosmic meditations, written in free verse in a style somewhat resembling the hymns of Verhaeren (*q.v.*). *Ještě jednou se vrátíme* (1900; We Shall Return Again), especially the section "Údolí nového království" (The Valley of the New Kingdom), expresses best his generous hopes of a utopian future of humanity; other collections (*e.g., Krvácející bratrství,* 1920, The Bleeding Brotherhood) voice the poet's faith in democracy and universal socialism. These visions shade off imperceptibly into a considerable mass of political hymns and invectives. The best-known poem ("Theodoru Mommsenovi," 1897) is Sova's sharp answer to the German historian Theodor Mommsen, who had recommended breaking the hard Czech skulls, but much of Sova's work on these themes is rhetorical and even dull. Sova also wrote distinguished ballads in the tradition of Czech folk poetry (*Kniha baladická,* 1915; A Book of Ballads) and a considerable body of prose, which suffers, however, from excessive lyricism and descriptiveness. Among the novels, *Ivův román* 1902; Ivo's Romance) is the study of an unhappy weakling, *Výpravy chudých* (1903; The Campaigns of the Poor) depicts the poet's struggles against poverty and indifference in a slight fictional disguise, and *Toma Bojar* (1910) attempts a social theme from peasant life in his native district. Sova's finest work in prose is found in the bitter short stories *O milkování, lásce a zradě* (2 vols., 1909; Of Flirting, Love, and Betrayal). Sova was primarily a man of feeling, a poet of the most delicate, evanescent shades of emotional conflicts, a sensitive painter of landscapes as states of his mind. He is at his best in traditional song forms, in melancholy meditations, in the "flowers of intimate moods" as he called one of his first collections, *Květy intimních nálad* (1891). His ambition led him into the poetry of ideas, forced him to take the role of a national prophet; but he failed, for his social and religious outlook was vague and too dependent on his shifting emotions. Sova, the original enemy of Parnassian eloquence and bombast, the master of small forms, was seduced into attempting prophetic poetry which turned all too frequently into blurred and even empty rhetorical exercises. But Sova's mastery of nuance, the delicate melody of his early pieces, the sensitive impressionism of his landscapes, have inspired much later verse—like that of S. K. Neumann (*q.v.*)—and constitute an important contribution to the body of Czech poetry.

See: F. X. Šalda, "A. Sova," in *Duše a dílo* (1913), and *A. Sova* (1924); L. N. Zvěřina, *A. Sova* (1919).

R. W.

Spanish literature. Spanish romanticism had a meteoric existence, swift and dazzling. By about 1850 its fire had gone; Larra and Espronceda had died, and the two great survivors of the romantic generation, the duque de Rivas and Zorrilla, simply prolonged for some years themes and attitudes of greater perpetuating than creative force. Already at the apogee of the romantic period certain writers of only ordinary aesthetic stature, the so-called *costumbristas*—Mesonero Romanos and Estébanez Calderón were the most prominent—had sown, in their articles about customs and in their partial descriptions of the society of their day, the seeds of realistic art. Towards 1850 Fernán Caballero utilized these fragmentary visions of the realistic to form something more complex and inclusive, evolving the novel of customs from the scattered *costumbrista* material in the articles and coupling for the first time in Spanish literature of the 19th century the novel and realism—an alliance destined to be mutually inspiring.

There begins then, thanks to Fernán Caballero and to Pedro de Alarcón (*q.v.*), the ascendant curve of the realistic view of life and literature. The complete triumph of this tendency is seen from 1875 to 1885, the great realistic decade. During this period were published *El escándalo* (1875), *El niño de la bola* (1880), and *La pródiga* (1882) of Alarcón; *El sabor de la tierruca* (1881) and *Sotileza* (1884) of José María de Pereda (*q.v.*); *Doña Perfecta* (1876), *Gloria* (1877), *Marianela* (1878), and *Lo prohibido* (1884–1885) of Benito Pérez Galdós (*q.v.*); *Pepita Jiménez* (1874), *Doña Luz* (1879), and *Las ilusiones del Doctor Faustino* (1875) of Juan Valera (*q.v.*); *Un viaje de novios* (1881) and *La tribuna* (1883) of Emilia Pardo Bazán (*q.v.*); *Marta y María* (1883) and *José* (1885) of Armando Palacio Valdés (*q.v.*); a considerable portion of the *Humoradas and Pequeños poemas* of Ramón de Campoamor (*q.v.*); *Gritos del combate* (1875) and *La pesca* (1884) of Gaspar Núñez de Arce (*q.v.*). In these works, taken as a whole, Spanish realism is completely represented; no essential characteristic is lacking. In the realm of literary theory also this decade witnessed the appearance of two works of paramount importance: *La cuestión palpitante* (1883; originally a series of newspaper articles) of Pardo Bazán, in which there is brought forward for public discussion the problem of artistic realism, and the *Poética* (1883) of Campoamor, in which this artist brings dangerously near to one another, within the realm of theory, the concepts of poetry and prose. There is repeated in Spain that phenomenon of the apparently inevitable attraction between the realistic view of life and the novelistic genre. The period produces an abundance of novels and novelists with varying tendencies. Since the 17th century, Spanish literature had not considered the world and man as subject matter worthy of novelistic treatment with the attention and intensity which characterize that era, Fernán Caballero, as successful pioneer, Alarcón, Pereda, and Valera are the top-ranking authors here. The Spanish realistic novel itself seems conditioned by strict laws of place and time. It is always a regional and local novel. Pereda shuts himself in the mountains of Santander, as did his forbears of the first century; there he erects a vigorously regionalistic novel and on these heights raises the banner of a mountaineer conception of life. Galdós, at first glance apparently more national in outlook, cannot conceal his special predilection for the Madrilenian and the Castilian; more than any other writer he is the *costumbrista* of the Madrid of the 19th century, and this characteristic always complements the human quality of his novels. Valera, a man accustomed to living in foreign lands, nevertheless almost always chooses for the scenes of his novels his native Andalusia. So the realistic novel is an enormous storehouse of landscapes, types, and customs of the different regions of Spain; the realistic novelists involuntarily present us with a copious inventory of the elements of Spanish reality, both those which lend themselves to the most casual observation and those which best adapt themselves to detailed description. Pardo Bazán observed of their work in its totality that "they are writing the poem of modern Spain." Indeed by obeying on occasion too servilely the law of the time in which it flourished, the Spanish realistic novel risked the loss of permanent values and in many instances devoted itself too much to the multifarious social and political problems of the moment.

Even more than from disunion, Spain was suffering then from the uprooting of political and social ideals; during the 19th century, civil war never ceased except in appearance and for brief periods. And the realistic novel had its own civil war, centered especially on the clerical problem. The influence of the institutions of the Catholic Church on the life of society and the individual is the theme of this discord. One group—Alarcón, Pereda, and later a novelist of less imposing stature, Padre Luis Coloma (*q.v.*)—defends the position of the Church passionately and unreservedly. Another group, of which Galdós (otherwise a spirit of profound religious sentiment) becomes the leader, attacks the Church position with equal oversimplification, scant reserve, and no less passion. Both of these attitudes should be respected for the element of good faith and earnest desire for the truth that they contained. But it is questionable whether all the polemics and politics have been aesthetically absorbed and advantageously assimilated by novelistic art. In a majority of cases such issues weaken or render entirely impossible the artistic functioning of the novelistic organism and prevent its attaining a result which is general, human, and not restricted to any period. Valera indeed, as a notable exception, was able to escape the tendentious, defending the novel, in his works and in his essay *Apuntes sobre el nuevo arte de escribir novelas* (1886–1887), as a simple work of art and amusement. And Galdós in his later years as a novelist rises far above the limited critical position of his début. Poetry too, like the novel, often descended to the merely timely and circumstantial. Campoamor, in his *Doloras, Pequeños poemas,* and *Humoradas,* throws wide the gates to realism and surrenders unconditionally. The themes and the petty little people of so-called everyday life, sentimentalism in its most conventional form, current skeptical intellectualism, and universally comprehensible and nugatory pragmatic formulas are the worst ingredients of his poetic realism. Núñez de Arce makes naturalistic use of description and sometimes appears to let his poetry be dominated by the current political ideology. Standing apart and on the heights, like an element of less density, without realistic deadweight, is the poetry of Gustavo Adolfo Bécquer (*q.v.*), a solitary and tender romantic voice, remote from the commonplaces of Campoamor and the supplicatory verse of Núñez de Arce. Bécquer's lyric poetry, the expression of a refined romanticism, flowers strangely in this generation. His verse and some verse like it, *e.g.*, that of Rosalía Castro (*q.v.*) and her imitators, should be considered not only as a belated expression of romanticism but as a harbinger of lyric currents of the present day, transmitting romantic sensibility from century to century.

There were comparable tendencies in the theatre. There was a realistic theatre, concerned with the problems of contemporary society, even before the realistic novel had been completely elaborated. From 1856 to 1863 there were presented in Madrid *El tejado de vidrio* (1856), *El tanto por ciento* (1861), and *El nuevo don Juan* (1863) of Adelardo López de Ayala (*q.v.*), works of observation of daily life which, although sometimes written in verse, are the very antithesis of poetry. Another noteworthy dramatist, Manuel Tamayo y Baus (*q.v.*), follows a parallel road in *La bola de nieve* (1856), *Lo positivo* (1862), and *Lances de honor* (1863). But Tamayo is also the author of dramas such as *Locura de amor* (1855) and *Un drama nuevo* (1867) in which logical construction does not exclude pure romantic sentiment. And the great dramatic figure of the period, José Echegaray (*q.v.*), carries human passions as the motivating forces of dramatic action, as well as a deliberate striving for effects, to heights at least as exalted as those of the romantics of 1840. Not even in the midst of realism can the theatre of objective observation and analysis produce notable works free of the great poetic and romantic stage tradition of the Spanish past. The authors of the second half of the 19th century do not succeed in really interrupting the influence of the romantic theatre, and in fact their works—picturesque, replete with theatrical effects and dazzling metrical form—constitute a link between the romantics and the verse dramatists of the 20th century.

The relation of Spanish realism to European realism of the same period, especially in the novel, is a highly controversial matter. For some this relationship is extremely close. Pereda, on the other hand, was almost insulted that one should connect him with anything foreign. Today it is hard to believe that the Spanish novel of the 19th century was an entirely national form of art, surrounded on all sides by the vast expanses of European realism but miraculously saved from any contact with it. But neither can it be considered simply as an offshoot of foreign realism and a faithful imitator of alien accomplishments. With the picaresque novel in the 17th century, Spain had already opened the first laboratory of realistic technique in the novel, and many foreigners had learned much there. But it is certain that Spanish fiction of the more recent period under discussion is neither archaic—save in rare instances, as with Pereda or Estébanez Calderón—nor merely the result of importations. Faithful to a deep-seated and ancient voice of its own, it harmonizes this with the choir of European voices of its period, from which it draws something and to which it in turn makes contribution. A characteristic difference from French naturalism (*q.v.*) and its devotees is found in the reluctance, even the utter unwillingness, of many Spanish novelists to make their novels a literary projection of the prevailing European convictions about determinism, positivism, the promise of experimental science. The Spanish writer does with what he has before him as contemporary French authors are doing: he observes it and describes it. But as soon as he treats of psychological reality and the intimacies of the soul, he draws away from the French school and paints a human being more varied in his reactions. Religious faith, confidence in free will, a vital spontaneity, and anti-nihilism are found in many Spanish novelists along with the most orthodox, realistic conception of novel writing. Thus is to be explained Zola's (*q.v.*) amazement at the fact that Pardo Bazán, militant follower of naturalism, was at one and the same time a sincere Catholic.

From 1885 to the end of the century signs of malaise and omens of change are discernible in the apparent aesthetic unanimity of realism. Even among those who accepted it there is weariness with the positivistic view of humanity; the horizons are scanned in search of beacons. Almost all the great novelists ended their careers in the last years of the century, or early in the following, with their eyes turned in new directions. Thus there is Galdós in *Nazarín* (1895) and in *Halma* (1895) immersing himself in pseudo-mystic subtleties, attenuating his characters until they are mere shadows. Pardo Bazán is no longer the same writer of vigorous realism and in *La quimera* (1905) and *La sirena negra* (1908) allows herself to be seduced by the excesses of spiritual decadence. What realism there is in Valera turns into hyperborean mists in the last and strangest of his novels, *Morsamor* (1899). During these years Palacio Valdés, wisely aware that something in the realistic mechanism had failed to function, enhances his fame and personal influence by abandoning the naturalists' essential pessimism and by turning to what is more moderate and tranquil. The same thing occurs in the theatre. There are echoes of Ibsenism (*see* Ibsen, Henrik) in Echegaray and Galdós. And although in lyric poetry the first dissenting voices come from across the seas, already some Spaniards—Ricardo Gil and Salvador Rueda (*qq.v.*)—emphasize the distance which separates them from the reigning poetry of Campoamor and Núñez de Arce. Clarín (pseud. of Leopoldo Alas, *q.v.*) lives with perhaps more intensity than anyone else the spiritual upheaval of these times; he feels himself between two worlds, neither of them his. After having paid tribute to the naturalistic technique in one of the best Spanish novels in this genre, *La Regenta* (2 vols., 1884–1885), he turns to new interests. In his essays everything becomes a complaint against barrenness, a censure of Spanish isolation, and an appeal for foreign influences. He notes the absence of "lyric rapture" and begs that "the windows be thrown wide to the four winds of the spirit." And in this complaining and longing attitude, this fugitive from realism clasps hands with Angel Ganivet and Miguel de Unamuno (*qq. v.*), those two harbingers, pioneer architects of the future. Of unequaled importance in the betterment of Spanish spiritual life is the silent and austere work of the Institución Libre de Enseñanza, guided by the lofty spirit of Francisco Giner de los Ríos (*q.v.*) and continued until our time by his pupils, among whom Manuel B. Cossío (*q.v.*) is conspicuous. Without being directed to the strictly literary element of Spanish culture, Giner's labors for the refinement of sensibility exerted an influence on some of the most illustrious writers of these years and gave a great impetus to literary renovation.

General chronology and literary chronology coincide in Spain in 1900: a new century begins and a new literature is initiated. The 20th-century writers bring to literature a marked desire for a rebirth. They are customarily considered in terms of "the Generation of 1898" and "modernism." Both terms are exact and representative of quite different but by no means mutually exclusive tendencies. With few exceptions all of these writers are somewhat '98 and somewhat modernist; only the proportion varies. Thus considered, in the interplay of the two impulses the writers of these decades transcend the limitations of any literary school; they represent a new attitude on the part of all Spanish artists and intellectuals, a new view of spiritual problems such as press them with urgency at this time. A new manner of thinking runs parallel with a new manner of feeling; there comes, inevitably, a new manner of writing. The new mission, Azorín (*q.v.*) affirms, is to refine Spanish sensibility. José Ortega y Gasset (*q.v.*) defines it as learning to think more sternly, more austerely. Ramón del Valle-Inclán's (*q.v.*) motto is to write with more artistry and charm. The novelty and richness of the literature of the 20th century come from an infinite variety of elements which in their fusion produce a literary spirit much more complex, profound, and refined than that of the preceding generation.

By "the Generation of 1898" Azorín designated a group of writers who appeared at the turn of the century and who represented the vehement desire for a profound renewal in the national spirit. In his novel *La voluntad* (1902) Azorín is already clearly conscious of the "Generation." In 1913, in his book *Clásicos y modernos,* he offers this designation to literary history in three articles, tracing the genesis and early development of the movement. Some have even questioned its existence. It does seem, however, that the formula or the concept corresponds exactly to a patently clear reality and that it is historically authentic and extremely useful in the comprehension of recent Spanish literature. Ganivet, Unamuno, Jacinto Benavente (*q.v.*), José Martínez Ruiz (Azorín), Pío Baroja (*q.v.*), Antonio Machado (*q.v.*), and, on a plane of inferior literary value, Ramiro de Maeztu (*q.v.*) constitute the first group of the Generation. Some years later Ortega y Gasset and Ramón Pérez de Ayala (*q.v.*), notwithstanding certain new tonalities in their work, maintain faithfully the essential spirit of the Generation of 1898, which is prolonged until the present day by some of the latest writers.

Nothing of importance occurs in Spanish literature during that eponymous year, that famous '98. But in the national history it is the year of the "disaster," of Spain's defeat in the war with the United States and the loss of her last overseas colonies. Through the gaping fissure opened in the self-satisfied and complacent bourgeois society of the Regency there enters the national consciousness a powerful gust of spiritual excitement, of restlessness, discontent, and disillusion, which influences the young men, impelling them toward a common motive for action—the good of Spain. The national tragedy functions as a lens, catching the spiritual energies of the new writers and joining them in concentrated form on a single, shining focal point, *lo español.* For that which distinguishes the "man of '98" is that he thinks Spain, feels Spain, and loves Spain over and above all his other activities, converting it into a completely preferred subject of mental preoccupation, making it the measure of his art, of his life. "Spain is undiscovered," writes Unamuno. The Generation passes through two stages, two moods. One, which is not lasting, immediately follows the disaster: in evidence are seemingly discouraged souls, apparently languid wills, and certainly pitiless criticism of *lo español.* This critical attitude is to be seen in Unamuno, Azorín, and Maeztu in their youthful years. Their devotion to Spain clothes itself in ascetic and disciplinary garb; they castigate the very flesh of the native country—precisely because they aspire to a high spiritual perfection and believe this is the best approach. Already in 1902 Azorín understood the tragic necessity of his generation, the need to consider sternly what they loved most: "perhaps this ferocious analysis of everything is necessary for a synthesis in the more or less near future." But in a few years this manner, only apparently negative, evolves, and notes of affection, esteem, admiration, are heard. Ortega y Gasset says, "Having disowned one Spain we are now in the honorable course of finding another." Azorín interprets tenderly and skillfully the classic authors whom he formerly fustigated. The tonal pessimism of the first stage reveals its motives; there is an almost amorous contemplation of Spain, and one feels the deep devotion to her essential qualities.

A generation of questioners, the favorite queries of these writers were: "Where is Spain?" "What is Spain?" "What is the Spanish soul?" They were a generation of searchers too. The men of '98 set out like quixotic knights-errant in search of the Spain of Dulcinea, the ideal, and were scornful of the material Spain of Aldonza. How and where to find it? One route they rejected, that of the official Spain of the immediate past; its political forms and conventional patriotism constituted an unreal, an untrue Spain, said Ortega. The right way is quite another. Introspection becomes important. Appearances are to be shunned; one must penetrate deeply in search of essentials. Unamuno utters the cry "Within!" and formulates his theory of tradition: this is not to be found in the superficially historical, in the conventionally great deeds of illustrious men, but resides in the historical substrata, conveyed from century to century by the millions of humble beings who live in the fields and villages unmindful of the vain rumblings of historical "events." Those of the Generation of 1898 treat Spain as though they were before a palimpsest; scornful of the visible writing they search in the parchment for the first, original, unadulterated, secret message.

They show a predilection for certain permanent themes. They write of a Castile unadorned, naked, and clean, nearer to the eternal in its almost complete lack of changes through the years. The limitless landscapes without habitation are meant to explain mystic longings and quixotic eagerness, "the land with a soul." The small villages, not contaminated yet by modernity, seem to be standing still, on the fringe of the historic. The humble folk repeat the attitudes of an ancient humanity. The people and the land appear as the unconscious treasurers of the purest Spanish spirit. And the essentially Hispanic leads to the essentially human. The ardor of these men of the Generation of 1898 indeed suggests characteristics of religious life and feeling; they live like the ascetics of a Spanish humanity. This devotion to Spain has nothing of the exaggeratedly patriotic, political, or materialistic in its make-up. They expressly abominate these things. Unamuno, at the conclusion of his essay on Spanish tradition writes: "Man is what we must search for in our souls . . . eternal tradition is universal, cosmopolitan."

Another characteristic of the Generation seems at first glance to be a contradiction—their definite Europeanism. But to be a European is a correlative mandate to being a Spaniard; "Spain is undiscovered, and can be discovered only by Europeanized Spaniards." To be a European is to be receptive to modern currents of thought, to breathe the air of the world with European lungs, to live in a space that is broad and without frontiers. This the men of '98 determined to do. There can be noted a radical difference in their devotion to Spain when it is compared with the romantic attitude, as seen in Rivas and Zorrilla, for example, who were distrustful of foreign things and hostile to them, or with the realistic position of such writers as Alarcón, Pereda, even Galdós. The men of '98 read European literature; they brought to Spain what they considered the best elements of it and lived a life doubly rich and intense. Unamuno was an indefatigable reader of the great literatures; Ortega y Gasset was in the very center of the great currents of the European thought of the day.

This "bilateralism" has other aspects. The Generation couples a sense of aristocracy and spiritual distinction, an abhorrence of the commonplace, with profound devotion to pure folk elements. What is scorned and excluded is a plebeian intellectual mediocrity related to social and official mediocrity. The literature of the men of '98 is never crude or commonplace, no matter how many popular elements it absorbs, and never vaporous or artificial, no matter to what heights it aspires. And there is an analogous bilateralism in the capacity of these writers for utilizing precise observation, minute details, for "strolling and observing" in order to attain spiritual power in the literary product; in the essays of Azorín fineness of line and realistic exactitude account for surprising spiritual effects. There also coexist a highly primitive love for the Middle Ages—*El poema del Cid,* Juan Ruiz (by virtue of considering this period as nearest the fountainhead of the purely Spanish element)—and a passion for modernity, the exaltation of the very latest European writers.

The scrutinizing zeal, the spiritual tenseness of the Generation, are projected predominantly in the essay and in a new kind of lyricism. From the extended essay, such as Unamuno's *Del sentimiento trágico de la vida* (1913) and Ortega y Gasset's *España invertebrada* (1922), to shorter and more various forms, the essay is the genre most favored by the new writers. It serves as a vehicle for the most intellectual element, for the critical attitude embraced in the phrase, of Nietzschean origin, "the reexamination of values." There are essays which are pure confession, an examination of conscience, in an ardent confidential tone, such as the best of Unamuno's; others are more objectively critical, or they are didactic and aspire on a lofty plane to renovate the intellectual repertory of Spain, such as many of those of Ortega y Gasset and of Azorín. A third type of essay brings certain branches of technical knowledge within reach of the lay reader and injects into literature scientific ideas and experimental attitudes (*e.g.*, the essays of the doctors, Gregorio Marañón *et al.*). The essay of this period in all its varieties is directed toward a vast public, offered not only in magazines but in the daily papers—always with a certain dignity of tone and rarely with any excessive simplification. Some of the best pages of literary Spanish of today are to be found here. And the spiritual urge, the interior force which animates the new generation, overflows the essay and ends inevitably in lyricism. Lyricism vibrates in the prose of a man of such intellectual vigor as Ortega y Gasset, and a great essayist such as Unamuno is a true lyric poet. As will be seen, there is a parallel current in modernism.

The spiritual attitude of the time did not leave any comparable imprint on the theatre or the novel. Pío Baroja, the best and most prolific novelist of the 20th century, has quickened greatly the plodding pace of the narrative art of the realistic period. His straightforward and vivid descriptions give evidence of a much more personally selective vision; but there remains apparent in his work a predominance of the realistic conception of the novel and an ideology subservient to the scientific attitude and to the pessimistic conclusions characteristic of realism. Pérez de Ayala, Azorín in some curious attempts, and Valle-Inclán have indeed transcended, sometimes decisively, the novelistic formulas of the 19th century. In the case of the theatre, Benavente figured conspicuously during the first years of the new movement, and his sharp criticism of the bourgeois milieu and his technique of elegant naturalness set him apart as a powerful new force. Then he draws away from the attitude of rebellion maintained by his companions and conforms more and more to average taste. The brothers Serafín and Joaquín Alvarez Quintero and Carlos Arniches (*qq.v.*) maintain a realistic tradition in their best works without seeking innovations, although they may consciously assume attitudes of a popular cast in the manner of the Generation of 1898. Valle-Inclán, of energetic dramatic temperament, charged his admirable "esperpentos" and dialogued works with drama, but did not succeed in creating what could be called, strictly speaking, a theatrical work. There flourishes widely and with numerous variations a verse theatre, almost always an offshoot of the romantic theatre, devoted to national historic themes. Its ablest exponent is Eduardo Marquina (*q.v.*), and it continues more recently with José María Pemán.

With regard to literary style, the Generation has certain definite aims—sobriety, graveness of tone, restrained ardor. Its refinements, and it has them, are not flaunted in the modernistic manner. Fleeing from the pomp and glitter of oratorical prose, these men preserve a natural elegance; they find the distinction and patrician quality of their style, paradoxically, "by immersing themselves in the common people," as Unamuno advised. Instead of the descriptive technique of the realists, who are loosely inclined to set down all they behold, the men of '98 use a descriptive method which deals with essentials, which operates through the delicate selection of detail and through propriety and skill in designations. Just as they search behind the apparent forms of Spanish reality for the soul of Spain, so in their descriptions of persons and places one senses beneath (as in the essays of Gabriel Miró, *q.v.*, and Azorín) a delicate tremor which indicates the presence of something deeper and more abiding.

Before Azorín had coined the name Generation of 1898, it was customary to designate the new literature of the 20th century as "modernism" and its practitioners as "modernists." But it is necessary to distinguish, as already indicated, even though there is cross-fertilization. Modernism is, in its origin, more Hispanic American than Spanish. It was the reigning and resounding literary modality in all Hispanic America from approximately 1890 to 1910. The young Hispanic American writers of that time were dissatisfied with the academic conventionalism of the period which was stifling the poetic spirit; from nonconformity they progress to rebellion, from rebellion to the establishment, as opposed to the discredited *casticista* regime, of something quite new. Their modernism makes its appearance as a mass of explorations, discoveries, and conquests relative to the basic concept of literature and its language, particularly that of poetry. It is the result of a skillful appropriation of various foreign literary currents of the 19th century, principally French, and of the fusion of these diverse elements into a happy synthesis. This work was carried out by a group of poets, scattered over the vastness of all Hispanic America, from the Río Grande to the Plata, who, though separated and not guided by any previously reached agreement, moved in unison. They were impelled by the force of a true spirit of the times, mysteriously shared, which had as its aim the regeneration of Spanish poetry.

The new modernistic sensibility is complex. A parade of opulent aesthetic splendor is harmonized with an affected simplicity in the Pre-Raphaelite manner. Refinement is sought in all its forms. The history of art is retraced in search of beauties already perfected; the hope is to duplicate these in the new literature, which thus takes on many reflected tonalities. Conventional morality becomes outmoded. A show is made of sensuality; it is paraded in affected postures and, in order to be more enticing, is insidiously combined with a refined sentimentalism. There results a brilliant *préciosité,* both in art and in living. A greater contrast to the mediocrity and commonplaceness of the Spain of the Regency could not be imagined.

The modernists dipped into the vast repertory of poetic concepts and language of the French and, to some extent, of the American lyric—Victor Hugo, the Parnassian school, Verlaine (*q.v.*), the decadents, Poe, Whitman. The complexities of the modern foreign lyric act to refine Spanish poetic language, bringing to it graces and subtleties that it had not known for centuries. Certain verse and strophic forms, the alexandrine, the enneasyllabic, the *pareado,* the ballad, are taken from the French; free verse perhaps owes more to North American poetry. Casal and Martí in Cuba, Silva in Colombia, Gutiérrez Nájera and Díaz Mirón in Mexico, are important figures of the modernist movement. But there stands out particularly the Nicaraguan Rubén Darío (1867–1916). In his *Azul* (1888) and *Prosas profanas* (1896) the new poetry is fully formulated. And he transports it to Spain, which was already so aware, in Clarín and Unamuno and especially in Salvador Rueda among the poets, of the sickness afflicting literature.

When Rubén Darío arrived in Spain in 1899, young Spaniards, as eager as the Hispanic Americans to rehabilitate poetry, were fascinated with the magical formulas of salvation which the great poet offered them. Latent Spanish modernism comes out to meet the already existing modernism of the Hispanic Americans. The publication of Darío's *Cantos de vida y esperanza* in the symbolic year 1905, the tercentenary of *Don Quijote de la Mancha,* confirms the sense of a common cause, the liberation of the maiden, Poetry. Spaniards are captivated by a display of qualities hardly present in their national lyric poetry since Góngora—lexigraphic brilliance and novelty, boldness of images, exquisite musicality.

Perhaps the three most important names in Spanish modernism are those of Valle-Inclán, Manuel Machado (*q.v.*), and Juan Ramón Jiménez (*q.v.*).

The modernistic air indeed circulates, with all its perfumed richness and as a vivifying wind, through the whole expanse of Spanish letters and reaches its farthest corners—even though some of the Generation of 1898 resist in terms of simplicity, naturalness, and a strictly national tradition. Certain authors, such as Valle-Inclán, inhale it with the full power of their lungs; Manuel Machado and Juan Ramón Jiménez, while receptive, are already more temperate. If what is artificial in modernism did not altogether penetrate Spanish literature and if so many Spanish authors remained unmoved in their human position as regards eternal values, it is clear that much was integrated, and advantageously. Certain benefits stand out: liberation from *casticismo;* the incorporation into the Spanish thought stream of modern world literature (the great foreign authors of the 19th century who had been thought so revolutionary and extravagant come to be accepted and even highly esteemed); the extensive refinement and enrichment of poetic expression; the sense of collaboration between Spain and the Hispanic American countries in a common endeavor, the labor of innovation. Two distinct and independent forces, modernism and the Generation of 1898, ultimately coalesce in a great final result, the palingenesis of the literary spirit in the Spanish-speaking world.

The results of the zealous renovating efforts can now be clearly seen. Unamuno, Valle-Inclán, Azorín, Antonio Machado, Juan Ramón Jiménez, and Ortega y Gasset have transcended the reputation of eccentricity under which they struggled during their heroic years; the very lights which they lit now play on them fully and reveal them in their greatness as masters and guides. Spanish literature rises considerably in tone. Horizons are enlarged. The new ideas from abroad enter the country as soon as formulated and circulate freely; close attention is paid to outside literary schools and to their efforts; the *Revista de Occidente* and its editorial house, both under the direction of Ortega y Gasset, are instruments of inestimable importance in this work. At the same time the study of Spanish language and literature by new methods, the work principally of the Centro de Estudios Históricos and its school of philologists—Ramón Menéndez Pidal, Américo Castro, Tomás Navarro (*qq.v.*), José F. Montesinos, and Dámaso Alonso (*q.v.*)—reveals to innumerable new writers the import of their relation to their own classics. These authorities, as distinguished from the *casticistas* of a former period, do not invoke from the past rigid models that would subjugate, but rather essential vitalizing elements that serve to amplify the means of more abundant self-expression at the present time.

The decrease in the number of themes not strictly poetic or literary now becomes noteworthy in this 20th-century literature. Fewer sallies are made into social and political fields; there is less of the anxious contemplation of the whole Spanish scene; above all the focus is now on poetic creation. The vastness of the renovating labor of 1900 imposed on that generation the ideal of an extremely wide area of action; the ideal of the new writers involves more concentration. This does not betoken the lack of extensive curiosity on the part of literary youth, but a desire to confine itself to a basic mission and fulfill this conscientiously and with the energy inherent to complete devotion. The aspiration for quality rather than quantity simply means carrying to its ultimate literary conclusion the crusade against the vulgar and the commonplace which Unamuno and Rubén Darío, each from his own pulpit, had for so long been preaching. One result is less cultivation of the genres which lend themselves most readily to extension and digression, the novel and the essay; of more import are the new developments in the genre most capable of quintessences and concentration, lyric poetry. Lyricism, in various forms, is the distinguishing mark of the period.

This lyricism is integrating and straightforward. On the one hand it profits from the great traditions, the *Romancero,* the poetry of the *Cancioneros* of the 15th century, the achievements of Lope de Vega and Góngora; and on the other hand it is aware of the different schools of the new Europe, such as futurism, dadaism, surrealism, and "pure poetry," and revamps all this in its own forms, such as the ultraism of Pedro Garfias and Guillermo de Torre (*q.v.*) and the creationism of Gerardo Diego (*q.v.*) and Juan Larrea. Here is a generation of lyric poets with personalities as varied as they are original. The poetry of Jorge Guillén (*q.v.*) is a lyrical interpretation of the world. Federico García Lorca (*q.v.*), as though heeding the advice of Unamuno, "immerses himself in the Andalusian common people"—and assimilates all of modernism's modes of expression. There merge in Rafael Alberti's (*q.v.*) poetry, always with an original and pleasing result, Hispanic landscape and peasantry, Gongoresque splendors, and strange delvings into the subconscious. A little later, in a new group made up of Luis Cernuda, Vicente Aleixandre, Emilio Prados, and Manuel Altolaguirre (*qq.v.*), appears a poetry of introspective vein, characterized by a refined cultivation of sentimental intimacy, for the expression of which they have recourse at times to surrealistic formulas. This group is now so far removed from the first generation of the 20th century that only at a few certain points of contact—in the poetry of Juan Ramón Jiménez, for example—can one consider it within the limits of this tradition. The lyric attitude which dominates this period overflows poetry and passes into prose. Ramón Gómez de la Serna (*q.v.*) tarries awhile in all the literary genres—is he a novelist, a short-story writer, an essayist, or what?—but the basis of his work is a highly personal lyricism, half hopeless, half jovial. José Bergamín (*q.v.*), an intellectual lyricist, arrives at his thought through fanciful flourishes and poetic conceits in essays. The novel, a fallow genre during these years, is marked with poetic elements in Benjamín Jarnés (*q.v.*). The theatre either is authentically and profoundly poetic in the dramas of García Lorca or pretends to be so, clothing itself in metrical garb in the ancient manner. Literary criticism, not only in its most technical and professional wing with Dámaso Alonso, Amado Alonso (*q.v.*), Valbuena Prat, and Díaz Plaja but also in a freer group with Antonio Marichalar (*q.v.*) and Torre, sets for itself as a favorite task the analysis and elucidation of the poetic phenomenon.

The civil war, begun in 1936, has distorted the natural course of Spanish literature, disarranging all its elements; the consequences and ultimate effects are difficult to discern. Some authors have remained in Spain; others have emigrated. The political question has again erupted into literature. In the writers who favor Franco this is seen in a return to nationalistic *casticismo* and in the frequency of historical themes infused with patriotic or religious sentiment. In the opposing group the authors bend in love and pity over mangled Spain and lean toward a community of feeling with the people in their struggle. It seems predictable that the residence overseas of the large number of writers who have emigrated to the Hispanic American countries and their contact with these lands and peoples will bring to Spanish literature spiritual growth and experiences of significant value.

See: J. Yxart, *El arte escénico en España* (2 vols., 1894–1896); F. Vézinet, *Les Maîtres du roman espagnol contemporain* (1907); R. Cansinos-Asséns, *La nueva literatura* (4 vols., 1917–1927); S. de Madariaga, *The Genius of Spain and Other Essays on Spanish Contemporary Literature* (1923); A. F. G. Bell, *Contemporary Spanish Literature* (1925; revised ed., 1933); H. Petriconi, *Die spanische Literatur der Gegenwart seit 1870* (1926); G. de Torre, *Literaturas europeas de vanguardia* (1927); D. K. Arjona, "'La voluntad' and 'abulia' in Contemporary Spanish Ideology," *Revue hispanique*, LXXIV (1928), 573–672; J. Cassou, *Panorama de la littérature espagnole contemporaine* (1929); Leslie A. Warren, *Modern Spanish Literature* (2 vols., 1929); C. Barja, *Literatura española: Libros y autores modernos*, revised ed. (1933), and *Literatura española: Libros y autores contemporáneos* (1935); H. Jeschke, *Die Generation von 1898 in Spanien* (1934); F. de Onís, *Antología de la poesía española e hispanoamericana, 1882–1932* (1934); P. Salinas, *Literatura española siglo XX* (1941).

P. S.

Spire, André (1868–, French poet), born in Nancy, published his first vers libre after intensive preparation both as a social-minded intellectual and as a literary craftsman. Captivated by Desjardin's (*q.v.*) program for moral regeneration, he founded a society to rehabilitate unfortunates by helping them help themselves. But the Dreyfus affair, in which he fought a duel, converted him from palliative methods, and (with Daniel Halévy) he founded a night school for working-class students. From 1898 to 1902 he specialized in labor problems for the Office du Travail and from 1903 to 1914 organized cooperative banks for the Agricultural Ministry. After serving at the Peace Conference, he continued in social work until he was driven from France by the Nazis. He emigrated to America in 1941.

Dissatisfied with the technical innovations of symbolism, Spire sought a scientific basis for the rhythm of vers libre. Working at the Collège de France he measured the pitch, intensity, and duration of vers libre in order to establish the prosodic system based on accent, which he followed exclusively thereafter.

Et vous riez! (1905) reflects the frustrations of a social ameliorator who takes refuge in creative individualism, realizing he cannot remake society. But his social passion reappears, in limited area, in *Poèmes juifs* (1908), bitter, violent verse of a nonreligious Jew in behalf of his minority. Magnetized by "this eternal tomorrow that draws me on," he turned to ideas in action and exposed the obscurantist dangers fostered by pseudo-Bergsonism (*Vers les routes absurdes*, 1911). Reacting to the 1919 peace with an ironical drama on man's nostalgia for earthly paradise (*Samaël*, 1919), he issued the same year *Le Secret*, his richest collection. Here he has become master of his lyric materials and has achieved the beginnings of serenity. *Poèmes de Loire* (1929) marked the growth of certainty: "The World is desire and yearns to be possessed," and this his subsequent writing translated into lyrical variations.

Despite his preoccupation with social problems, Spire's contribution lies in subjective lyricism—subtle or fierce irony ("Etudiantes," "Acacias," "Ces Grèves"), philosophic reflections ("Immortalité," "Volupté," "Friselis"), passionate cries ("Nudités," "Ecoute Israël!"), and subtle pictures that expand with meaning ("Baisers," "Corps humain"). The unmistakableness of his personal idiom led Richard Aldington to classify him as "not Parnassian, Symbolist, Unanimist, Expressionist; but Spireiste."

See: Richard Aldington, "André Spire," *English Review,* XXXI (1920), 345–348; Frédéric Lefèvre, "Une Heure avec M. André Spire, poëte et essayiste," *Nouvelles littéraires,* January 31, 1931; Stanley Burnshaw, *André Spire and His Poetry* (1933).

S. B.

Spitteler, Carl (1845–1924, Swiss poet and novelist), was born in Liestal near Basel, where he studied before accepting a position as tutor in Russia. Later, he taught and became an editor in Bern and Basel; he died in Lucerne. Spitteler was a most original writer, as bold in his formal innovations as he was in his defiance of traditional ways of thought. Keeping aloof from the fashion of his days which favored the development of realism into consistent naturalism, he for many years directed all his energies toward the creation of one towering epic, *Der olympische Frühling* (first version, 1900–1905; revised, 1910). This work, for which the poet evolved even his own metrical form, has long defied all attempts at aesthetic and historical classification. It appears quite unexpectedly in the evolution of German literature; it is both original and daring in its use of Greek mythology, blending theogony with cosmogony and alternating between a solemn, heroic presentation of the Greek gods and their whimsical reduction to the scale of ordinary mortals. Some critics have hailed this epic as a true successor to the *Iliad* and *The Divine Comedy,* while others can see little more in it than an untimely *tour de force.* The fact that Spitteler was awarded the Nobel prize must be taken as at least a tribute to his courageous independence, if not also to his partial success.

What possible justification could there have been for a poet so utterly to disregard current practice, for a writer to create a work which seemingly has no bearing on modern problems and to choose a form which all historians of literature relegate to the past? For Spitteler the theory of evolution as applied to art holds, if at all, only with second-rate productions; a genius is under no compulsion to fall in step with the so-called tendencies of his time. Epic contemplation is a faculty wholly *sui generis,* characterized mainly by a serene objectivity towards all manifestations of life. The concomitant philosophy indeed is more likely to be a pessimistic realization of the incongruity of man's efforts. If, however, the epic writer finds himself unable to proffer illusory remedies for our ills, he will compensate us with a display of riotous beauty: brilliant imagery and linguistic originality form a sufficient justification for his work and constitute a valuable contribution to civilization.

It can hardly be denied that Spitteler's epic comes close to fulfilling the promise. Yet such is the modern preoccupation with social and political issues that for many readers not even the eruption of sheer imagination and creative will power of *Der olympische Frühling* will satisfy. Spitteler himself must have been aware of some such insufficiency, for prior to and concurrently with his great masterpiece he composed a number of prose works dealing with everyday affairs. True enough, he used to refer to these parerga as mere stylistic exercises or as concessions to the realistic vogue; yet it would seem that through them he established and maintained contact with the tradition of his native country and that he was hoping all the while to effect a final synthesis between austere form and vital content. This he achieved indeed in his late epic *Prometheus der Dulder* (1924), modestly designating it as a recast of his *Prometheus und Epimetheus* (1881). Spitteler now voices his firm belief in the primacy of ethical over aesthetic values, for the second version is as direct in its moral insistence as the first was inconclusive. Prometheus reappears as the embodiment of those basic virtues on which the well-being of society depends; he radiates a perfect integration of classical fortitude with Christian candor, in words and deeds a strong exhortation for us to remain modest while active, magnanimous while firm, and to spare no effort to conquer our impatience with our fellow men.

See: R. Faesi, *Spittelers Weg und Werk* (1933); E. M. Butler, *The Tyranny of Greece over Germany* (1935), pp. 316–322.

H. B.

Spoelberch de Louvenjoul, Charles de (1836–1907, Belgian bibliophile, bibliographer, and critic), was born in Brussels and died in Royat, France. He is the author of remarkable critical and bibliographical studies on George Sand, Alfred de Musset, Charles Sainte-Beuve, Théophile Gautier, Prosper Mérimée, Marceline Desbordes Valmore, and especially on Honoré de Balzac. He possessed to an extraordinary degree the faculty of penetrating the mind and the life of the authors he studied, never deviating from the most positive and strict documentation. His *Histoire des œuvres de Honoré de Balzac* (1879) is a monumental masterpiece of literary and bibliographical scrutiny and criticism. In 1880 he added to it *Un Dernier Chapitre de l'histoire des œuvres de H. de Balzac* and in 1901 *La Genèse d'un roman de Balzac: Les Paysans. Une Page perdue de H. de Balzac* was published in 1903. Endowed with the keenest spirit of research, he discovered and published a number of hitherto unknown manuscripts of the abovementioned romantic authors.

L. V.

Šrámek, Fráňa (1877–, Czech fiction writer, poet, and playwright), was born in Sobotka (eastern Bohemia). Known principally as the leading novelist of Czech impressionism, he is a master in describing and suggesting the most evanescent, momentary emotions and moods. Especially in his later work he successfully evokes the atmosphere of adolescent sexuality, its joys and sorrows, its exaltations and melancholy, when the whole of nature seems to be wrapped in a mist of complete animality. Šrámek's sheer joy in instinctive animal life appealed to a generation which had just gone through the horrors of the First World War and then discovered somewhat naïvely that life goes on and is worth living. The title of his best novel, *Tělo* (1919; The Body), suggests a program, but this story of a girl of strong sexual instincts is little more than a sensitive chronicle of meetings and partings, vacillations and temptations of lovers, against a lightly sketched background of war. An earlier novel, *Stříbrný vítr* (1910; The Silver Wind), largely concerned with students and the problems of puberty, is more of an attack on a society which hampers the free expression of instinct, and some of Šrámek's books of short stories and sketches are filled with an instinctive antimilitarism which condemns war as the enemy of love and life (*e.g., Žasnoucí voják,* 1924, The Perplexed Soldier).

But Šrámek is not a writer concerned with ideas; he is, even in his prose, a lyrical poet. The quintessence of his mood is possibly in the small collections of his poetry, among which *Splav* (1916; The Weir) is the most memorable, and in his lyrical plays, where delicately and compassionately he paints young people in the throes of sexual passion. *Léto* (1915; Summer) and *Měsíc nad řekou* (1922; The Moon above the River) are the two plays which were successful on the stage. Šrámek is a specialist of narrow range, but he is a genuine artist, who has failed only when, as in certain of his recent books and plays, he has attempted contemporary problems and more ambitious complex compositions.

See: J. Knap, ed., *Kniha o Šrámkovi* (1927); J. Durych, *Ejhle, člověk* (1928); F. X. Šalda, *Časové a nadčasové* (1936); J. Knap, *Fráňa Šrámek* (1937).

R. W.

Sremac, Stevan (1855–1906, Serb short-story writer and novelist), was born in Senta, in the province of Bačka, and educated in Belgrade in the house of his uncle, the prominent historian Jovan Djordjević. Through his uncle he became imbued with love for the nation's past and studied history at the University of Belgrade. Later he taught this subject in high school, mostly in the town of Niš, where he lived many years. A fervent patriot, he served in the army as a volunteer during the Serbo-Turkish wars of 1876–1878.

Sremac attempted a series of literary glorifications of the most distinguished personalities of his country's past; he prepared romanticized biographies of Serbian heroes and knights, enveloping them all in a poetic veil and presenting them under the common title *Iz knjiga starostavnih* (6 vols., 1903–1909; From the Ancient Books). He was far more effective in painting contemporary life. His long story *Ivkova slava* (1875; Ivko's House Patron Saint), depicting humorously the picturesque milieu and old stock types of the town of Niš immediately after its liberation from the Turkish yoke, captured the public imagination. He also wrote *Limunacija na selu* (1876; Fireworks in the Village), *Pop Ćira and Pop Spira* (1898; Priest Ćira and Priest Spira), *Božićna pečenica* (1898; The Christmas Roast), *Vukadin* (1903), *Zona Zamfirova* (1907), *Kir Geras* (1908). *Ivkova slava* and *Zona Zamfirova*—the latter, also about life in Niš, is undoubtedly the author's best work—have been dramatized and frequently produced on the Serbian stage.

Thoroughly acquainted with several Serbian provinces, Sremac depicted their local characteristics, their completely different spiritual formation and ways of life. He was interested primarily in the lower classes of this society, in the petty bourgeoisie, sometimes even in failures, believing that in these individuals unrestrained by conventions, human nature is most clearly expressed. He wrote with liveliness and verisimilitude. At the same time he was instinctively a humorist, with the gift of perceiving in every man and every situation the ridiculous aspects. His works are full of witty observations, jokes, unexpected comic developments of character and event. He mocked the human race by drawing its typical foolish figures, but his shafts were not poisoned; the reader doubles up with laughter, but neither despises nor hates these poor fools. Only when the author delineated political circumstances and reformers alien to him, since he was himself an intolerant traditionalist and conservative, did his humor occasionally pass into satire or even caricature. Probably the best Serbian humoristic novelist, Sremac is also an excellent realistic writer whose gallery contains unforgettable portraits.

See: J. Skerlić, "Stevan Sremac," *Pisci i knjige,* Vol. IV (1909); P. Popović, "Stevan Sremac," preface to Sremac, *Pop Ćira i Pop Spira,* revised ed. (1936).

P. A.

Stadler, Ernst (1883–1914, German poet and scholar), was born in Colmar, Alsace, and studied Germanics in Munich and Strassburg. With René Schickele (*q.v.*) he founded the periodical *Der Stürmer* in 1902. In 1903 he studied at Oxford, some years later (1908) began lecturing on Germanics at Strassburg, and in 1910 was appointed professor at Brussels. He was killed in the First World War. Besides well-articulated articles on literature (1910), he wrote two books of poems; the first, *Praeludien* (1904), is not very important, but the other, *Der Aufbruch* (1915), is one of the most beautiful and disciplined examples of the early German expressionistic style. Although this book was influenced by Whitman and Verhaeren (*q.v.*), Stadler adds to their "strömendes Weltgefühl" the deep mysticism of his homeland and an explosive, dynamic quality of his own. In contrast to most of the young expressionists, he never destroys but rather masters language with definite artistry. The visionary poem "Der Aufbruch," which gave the volume its name and in which he foresaw the World War and his own death, was later regarded as symbolic of the emerging generation of expressionist poets.

See: H. Hestermann, *Ernst Stadler* (1929).

K. P.

Staff, Leopold (1878–, Polish poet), was born in Lwów, Austrian Poland, the son of a proprietor of a confectionery shop. Reared in good middle-class surroundings, Staff received his formal education in the Gymnasium and university of his native city. Lwów was the center of great literary and artistic ferment at this time, caused in part by Kasprowicz, and this circumstance, together with the boy's own natural inclination and the city's traditionally buoyant, ecstatic atmosphere, conspired to lead Staff to a literary career. In his youth he was powerfully influenced by the works of Nietzsche (*q.v.*), in his later life no less powerfully by St. Francis of Assisi. Wide travel abroad, in Italy, Germany, and France, and experiences as a prisoner of war in Russia likewise played a part in molding Staff into a poet. He lived a life apart from the angry currents of his times, remote in his scholar's tower, there translating the masterpieces of world literature and fashioning the exquisite lyrics by which he will be forever remembered. A pure poet, and even a poet's poet, Staff was the supreme poet of Free Poland. In the early 30's a uniform collected edition of his works was issued in celebration of his three decades of creative activity.

See: Z. Dębicki, *Portrety,* I (1927), 153–172; *Wiadomości literackie,* 1929, No. 289 (entire issue); W. Borowy, "Leopold Staff," *Slavonic Review,* XI (1932–1933), 145–158; K. Czachowski, *Obraz współczesnej literatury polskiej,* II (1934), 33–44, 391–395; Geoffrey Potocki, tr., *Pologne littéraire,* 1934, No. 91.

A. P. C.

Stanković, Borisav (1876–1927, Serb story writer, novelist, and dramatist), is considered the best Serbian narrative writer in the first decades of the 20th century. Born in South Serbia, in the small town of Vranje, which was till 1876 under Turkish rule, Stanković's mind was pervaded by the patriarchal atmosphere of this region. Even after completing his college studies in Belgrade, becoming a civil servant, and settling down in the capital of Serbia, he felt a deep nostalgia for his native town and dedicated all his efforts to depict it as faithfully as possible.

His first collections of short stories, *Iz starog jevandjelja* (1899; From the Old Gospel), *Božji ljudi* (1902; God's Children), and *Stari dani* (1902; The Old Days), enriched Serbian literature with pictures of an exotic world, fast disappearing, which still presented incarnations of a picturesque oriental sensuality and Slavic sensibility. Although the heroes of these collections have a narrow horizon and limited spheres of action, their interior life is extremely intensive and profound. Their principal motive force is erotic passion, which seldom culminates in happiness and bliss, but almost always in exaltation and pain, storm and suffering, vehemence and fatality. It is rightfully claimed for Stanković that his work was "one great love fever." His play *Koštana* (1902) is about a Gypsy dancer of that name who, after having succeeded in making men fools and disrupting whole families, was forced to marry a ne'er-do-well so that others might escape her dangerous influence. This play is really a most stirring love poem. The novel *Nečista krv* (1911, Impure Blood; Eng. tr., *Sophka,* 1932) perhaps does not succeed in depicting as adequately as was intended the degeneration of a family, but it offers a series of marvelous types of other days, with their mentalities, customs, and ways of life. The play *Tašana* (1915) is much weaker than *Koštana,* although there are high moments and poetically melancholy details as in the earlier drama. The author's last work, *Pod okupacijom* (1929; Under Foreign Occupation), relates the hard years under the Austro-Hungarian occupation during the First World War.

Stanković's work is of limited scope; he portrays local types of a single region. Moreover, his language contains many archaisms and provincial twists. But, although his entire work was written in prose, Stanković is positively the most lyric temperament in Serbian literature, and he does interpret with consummate art one aspect of Serbian life at the very moment of its passing from the patriarchal era to the modern times.

See: J. Skerlić, reviews of Stanković, *Koštana* and *Božji Ljudi,* in *Pisci i knjige,* Vols. I (1907), V (1911); B. Lazarević, "Borisav Stanković," in *Impresije iz književnosti,* Vol. I (1912); M. Grol, "Jubilej Borisava Stankovića," *Srpski književni glasnik,* May 1, 1924.

P. A.

Stefánsson, Davíð (1895–, Icelandic poet, playwright, and novelist), was born at Fagriskógur in Eyjafjörður. His father was a member of Parliament; his mother came of a literary family, her brother being a well-known folklorist and a prolific writer. Soon after graduating from the Gymnasium in Reykjavík, Stefánsson made his literary début with *Svartar fjaðrir* (1919; Black Feathers), a volume of poems, which won him instantaneous acclaim and a stipend to travel to Italy. After that the poet devoted himself for the most part to his art only. Six volumes of poetry have appeared (1919–1936), as well as three plays, *Munkarnir á Möðruvöllum* (1926; The Monks at Möðruvellir), *Gullna hliðið* (1941; The Golden Gate), *Vopn guðanna* (1943; The Weapons of the Gods), and the novel *Sólon Islandus* (2 vols., 1940). For more than a decade he has held the post of librarian at the public library of Akureyri in Eyjafjörður.

Davíð Stefánsson is the best representative of the new national romanticism in Iceland, as he is also the most popular of living Icelandic poets. Especially in his early poetry, he is a hedonist, a proud self-willed poet, who sings of wine and women in passionate, sometimes sadistic tones—though he has, too, the tenderest chords on his lyre. His diction is always easy, his form usually light; the tempo is often borrowed from nursery rhymes, lullabies, and folk dances, and his imagery is saturated with Icelandic folklore. Yet he can use other forms, for instance in his impressions of Italy. He is at his best in his ballad-like poems, sometimes telling a story with sly humor, sometimes abandoning himself to moods of romantic horror or defiance, to nostalgia for mother earth. Rarely is a note of social criticism heard, and then never in the class-conscious way of the leftist poets.

Just as his poetry harks back to folk poetry, ballads, dances, and tales, so his plays are historical, the first a satire of the monks, the second a folk tale embodied in 18th-century beliefs and manners. Most interesting is the novel about Solon Islandus, the Icelandic megalomaniac tramp, whom Stefánsson sees as a symbol of his own small and inferiority-complexed nation. The book is reminiscent in that way of Ibsen's (*q.v.*) *Peer Gynt.* It is done in a quiet, but none the less very effective, realistic manner.

See: S. Nordal, "Tvær miklar skáldsögur," *Lesbók Morgunblaðsins,* November 24, 1940; R. Beck, "Davíð Stefánsson skáld," *Tímarit Þjóðræknisfélags Íslendinga,* XXVII (1945), 51–68.

S. E.

Steffen, Albert (1884–, Swiss novelist, poet, dramatist, and philosopher), born in Murgenthal, is undoubtedly the most interesting figure in contemporary German Swiss literature. Endowed with a deeply compassionate nature and highly sensitive to the problematical aspects of modern civilization, he was in no danger of merely emulating the popular tradition of Alfred Huggenberger (1867–), Jakob Christoph Heer (1859–1925), and Ernst Zahn (1867–), who with their realistic peasant novels or idealizing Alpine stories for a time all but monopolized the sphere of literary entertainment. Steffen's first novel *Ott, Alois und Werelsche* (1907), left no doubt that his literary ancestors were Tolstoy (*q.v.*) and Dostoevski (*q.v.*) rather than Keller (*q.v.*) or Gotthelf, indicating as it did a most fervent desire to make the Sermon on the Mount a practical and strict rule of conduct. Christian humanism, the basis of Swiss intellectual and religious culture, underwent in Steffen's work a profound revival and transformation. His metaphysical novel, *Sucher nach sich selbst* (1931), and even more so his essays, *Frührot der Mysteriendichtung* (1940), give a comprehensive survey of his religious view of existence. For Steffen the mystery of Christ and his redeeming death represent the archetype of all human life; we must all endeavor to atone for the sins of mankind because we are all equally to blame for them. Furthermore he holds that this so-called Christ-impulse in us, once it is awakened and brought to bear on life, will prove the most efficient aid in the solution of contemporary social and political ills. It is not to be wondered at that Steffen, with such mystic leanings and his ardent advocacy of reform, should have identified himself more and more with Rudolf Steiner's anthroposophic movement, of which Steffen became the leader after the death of Steiner in 1925.

Since then Steffen's work has been wholly pressed into the service of anthroposophy, to explore its mystic implications and to propagate its social message; as a result of this he lost his appeal for all but his particular devotees. It is only in recent years, perhaps under the stress of world conditions, that Steffen has been trying again to reach a wider audience by being more explicit and by using symbols and characters which can be generally understood. This is illustrated when he evokes the tragedy of pure idealism exemplified in the life and death of Woodrow Wilson (*Friedenstragödie,* 1936) or when he presents the figure of Pestalozzi to show that in the struggle between Alexander I and Napoleon for world domination the final victory belongs to the tenderhearted humanitarian and friend of all mankind (*Pestalozzi,* 1939). For the moving scenes of this play Steffen's countrymen will forgive him an ocasional excursion into distant mystic lands, since they are evidence enough of his being in tune with the humanitarian tradition of Switzerland.

See: A. von Sybel-Petersen, *Albert Steffen und sein Werk* (1934); R. J. Hofrichter, *Three Poets and Reality* (1942), pp. 73–99.

H. B.

Stehr, Hermann (1864–1940, German poet and novelist), born in Habelschwerdt, started with a number of short stories (*Der Graveur, Meicke der Teufel,* both 1898; *Der Schindelmacher,* 1899) and was quickly labeled a naturalist. But even his earliest works reveal a much more intense reliance on the psychological and psychic qualities of his characters than on their physical environment. Any disturbance in the emotional or intellectual balance seems to have attracted him more than social or political problems, perhaps because he felt his real strength to lie in an almost pedantic but very often truly penetrating power of psychological analysis. His favored theme in these years concerns the explosion of pent-up emotions, usually revenge or hatred dating back to some gross injustice.

This psychological naturalism, though it determined Stehr's style for a long time, was gradually superseded by the religious and mystic tradition of his native Silesian world; it became more and more evident that Stehr was a descendant of Jakob Böhme and Angelus Silesius and the heir of a mysticism further deepened by his study of Lao-tse, Gautama, Ekkehart, Spinoza, and Kant. But the transcendental way of looking at the world in no way thwarted his creative abilities as a novelist. Although one would expect the experience of a mystic union with God to find its chief outlet in brief lyrical utterances, Stehr succeeded in permeating even long novels with his religious fervor. He was not so much interested in stating the final results of his philosophy as in showing the way in which religious longings arise and unfold in human beings. The irresistible growth of the divine spark in us, its flickering and extinction or its triumphant expansion into heavenly light—these are the themes of Stehr's second period, in such novels as *Leonore Griebel* (1900), *Der begrabene Gott* (1905), *Drei Nächte* (1909), and *Geschichten aus dem Mandelhause* (1913). They all purport to show that a genuine desire to establish contact with God enriches even the most earthly and humble existence. How can we live close enough to God so as to partake of his spirit and to understand the world with at least a fraction of his insight and wisdom? To find an answer is the task with which Stehr sends his God-seekers into the world. *Der Heiligenhof* (1918) marks his nearest approach to a solution, to the creation of at least one figure filled to the brim with divine powers. But the result is achieved at the expense of a normal human existence. Little Helen, the daughter of a wealthy farmer, attains an almost saintlike life. She is born blind and is, it first appears, beyond all medical help; shut off from the visible world she turns inward to grasp and absorb God. Other characters around her, spurred on by her vision, catch an occasional glimpse of this higher world. Yet with all these honest efforts the novel ends on a tragic note; saintly Helen is rudely awakened into normal life, through a sudden realization of her own erotic nature. As an immediate result of this she gains her normal sight, only to lose her hold on the supernatural and to become engrossed in the lower desires of mankind. Self-administered death remains her only defense against such degradation. Stehr has retold the same story from the viewpoint of the man who became chiefly responsible for Helen's downfall, in *Peter Brindeisener* (1924). The conclusion remains the same; Peter, who once longed to become initiated through Helen into the mysteries of true existence, also ends by destroying his own life.

Perhaps for a mystic who has trained himself to see all opposites *sub specie aeternitatis* it matters little whether we succeed or fail in this world; crime or virtue, glory or defeat, all are ordained by the will of God. But Stehr's strong instinct balked at such quietism. Discovering as he did that this passive resignation is the result of religious intellectualism, of a tendency to experience religion in terms of philosophy instead of apprehending it by action, he began to experiment with a new set of literary characters who, rather than speculating about religious matters, endeavor to incorporate them in the conduct of their daily lives. His popular violinmaker stories, *Der Geigenmacher* (1926) and *Meister Cajetan* (1931), are attempts in this direction. The religious yearning of these craftsmen is no less intense than it was in Stehr's earlier work; its progress, however, is no longer recorded in the form of philosophical definitions but of manual skill and production; the quality of the instruments created in the workshop is now made to reflect and measure the growth of inner perfection. Perfect as these stories are from an artistic point of view, they do not solve Stehr's most pressing problem of bringing man's religious consciousness to bear on life in a direct and concrete manner.

With his last significant novel, *Nathanael Maechler* (1929), Stehr came much closer to the real absorption of *vita contemplativa* in *vita activa;* in words reminiscent of Goethe's *Faust* he here voices his belief that God looks with favor on man's incessant striving in the realm of human interests, provided it be directed towards the promotion of good will among men and permeated with a feeling of infinite gratitude towards God. A simple and for that reason perhaps all the more convincing enactment of mystic revelations in everyday life is found in *Gudnatz* (1921), a story which treats of the conversion of a war profiteer into a fervent practical Christian.

Stehr's poems illustrate in briefer compass the same development of his mind. They likewise show his original aversion to being satisfied with the impressionistic apprehension of the surface of things, his ability to fathom mystic experience and to create a language capable of expressing religious ecstasy, his final conviction that religion is essentially a practical concern and a powerful incentive to social action.

See: W. A. Reichart, *"Hermann Stehr and His Work," Philological Quarterly,* X (1931), pp. 47–61; E. Freitag, *Hermann Stehr; Gehalt und Gestalt seiner Dichtung,* Vol. I: *Weltanschauung* (1936); G. Blanke, *Hermann Stehrs Menschengestaltung* (1939); K. S. Weimar, *The Concept of Love in the Works of Hermann Stehr* (1945).

H. B.

Stephansson, Stephan Guðmunðsson (1854–1927, Icelandic-Canadian poet), was born at Kirkjuhóll in Skagafjörður, of poor but intellectually alert parents who tried to eke out a living in three different cottages in Iceland before they moved to America in 1873. Here Stephansson took land three times: in Wisconsin, in North Dakota, and finally in Alberta, Canada, near Markerville, where he lived as a hard-working farmer until his death in 1927. He married in 1878 and had eight children, losing two sons before he died. He never had any formal education, but as a boy in Iceland he had read the sagas, which he retained ever after in memory, as his poems show. From the 1890's onward his poems appeared in Icelandic periodicals and weeklies in Winnipeg. His first volume of poems was *Á ferð og flugi* (1900; On the Go), but most of his poems were gradually published in the collection *Andvökur* (6 vols.,

1909–1938; Wakeful Nights), the name referring to the fact that he composed most of his poetry while others slept. Other publications were *Kolbeinslag* (1914; Lay of Kolbeinn), *Heimleiðis* (1917; Homeward Bound), about a trip to Iceland made on the invitation of grateful countrymen, and *Vígslóði* (1920; On the War Path), about the First World War. His letters are being published in Iceland.

Stephansson never assimilated the spirit of English literature, though he read it. He saw the New World from the point of view of the Icelander and of the pioneer. The attitude was, perhaps, one-sided, but certainly not a narrow one, and it was sustained by the unremitting idealism and manliness of the poet. He was an ardent liberal and a thoroughgoing individualist—a king in his farmer's realm. Related to this are his anticlericalism, even atheism, and his hatred of all capitalistic exploitation, whether it was that which he saw rampant in America or that in the imperialistic wars (*e.g.*, the Boer War) of Great Britain. Nor had he any sympathy for either side in the First World War, and he said so in terms that might have cost him dearly had his language been better understood by his ruling fellow Canadians.

But Stephansson was not only a prophet crying in the wilderness. He was also a poet sensitive to the shifting seasons and to the charms of nature even in his adopted land. He has described the prairie, the wide, checkered cornland of the Middle West, and the Canadian Rockies in magnificent poems.

Yet above all he was an Icelandic poet. His homeland is crystallized in beautiful visions in his poems, and figures from the old sagas and romances haunt his mind and take on new symbolic value in his poetry. These and the language had been the sole heritage of the boy when he left his fatherland. They were destined to bear fruit a thousandfold in his new environment. All are agreed that Stephansson is one of the greatest poets that Canada has fostered—perhaps the greatest. Some have even claimed that he is among the most distinguished poets that America has ever had, and one critic, Cawley, rates him as "greater than Poe, greater even than Whitman and Emerson."

See: W. Kirkconnell, "Canada's Leading Poet," *University of Toronto Quarterly,* V (1936), 263–277; F. S. Cawley, "The Greatest Poet of the Western World: Stephan G. Stephansson," *Scandinavian Studies and Notes,* XV (1938–1939), 99–109; S. Nordal, introduction to Stephansson, *Andvökur, úrval* (1939).

S. E.

Sternheim, Carl (1881–1943, German critic, dramatist, and novelist), was born in Leipzig. Although the son of a banker and merchant, he chose the profession of writer. After two unimportant plays, *Ulrich and Brigitte* (1909) and *Don Juan* (1910), he began in his first comedy, *Die Hose* (1911), the exposition of the general theme of all his further productions: the denunciation of the corrupt and intellectually dishonest bourgeois man who constantly perverts art. The various aspects of this theme were depicted in 10 other plays, published with *Die Hose* under the significant title *Aus dem bürgerlichen Heldenleben* (1922). A certain "Bürger Schippel" is here presented as the outstanding bourgeois type that deserves nothing but scorn and ridicule. He and his like, Sternheim suggests, drove Germany into the First World War and lost it, because he is a man without principles and ethical standards. Two books of a critical character, *Berlin oder Juste milieu* (1920) and *Tasso oder Kunst des Juste milieu* (1921), serve as prose commentaries on the ideas of these plays; two novels, *Europa* (1920) and *Fairfax* (1921; Eng. tr., 1923), interpret the same theme on a less national, but more European basis. They are, at the same time, typical specimens of so-called expressionistic prose. In the two novels this medium was worked out with much skill, but in his later writings it became a mannerism. Sternheim continued to ridicule society for its shortcomings in the comedy *Die Schule von Urznach oder die neue Sachlichkeit* (1926), a satire on the modern craze of dancing, in *J. P. Morgan* (1930), a sketch of American life, and in *Aut Caesar, aut Nihil* (1931), a sort of prophecy of the new political ideology. For more than 20 years he virtually exiled himself from Germany, but in the years before his death again made his home in Berlin.

A. Bu.

Stjernstedt, Marika (1875–, Swedish novelist), born in Stockholm, is one of the more eminent of contemporary women novelists in Sweden. Her mature work is everywhere characterized by a sharp intelligence and a warm human feeling, the best traits of a distinguished and romantic ancestry—her father was a Swedish general of fine old military and civil service stock, her mother, a Polish countess, whose lineage can be traced far back into the primitive military aristocracy of the Ukraine and Lithuania. During the First World War Marika Stjernstedt worked untiringly for the cause of France, an evidence of the inclusiveness of her interest in broad human and social values. She is perhaps the most cosmopolitan, in both experience and outlook, of literary women in present-day Sweden. Though her first novels were rather inconsequential efforts in the superficial "psychologizing" manner of Paul Bourget (*q.v.*), she soon found a form more purely her own in the two novels *Landshövdingens dotter* (1911; The Governor's Daughter) and *Daniela Hertz* (1912), twin studies in two sharply contrasting female types, half sisters, the one a person of profound domestic and social instincts, the other a thoroughly antisocial creature, who experiments not unsuccessfully with an extreme form of individualism in conscious head-on revolt against a bourgeois social order. That the First World War deepened Marika Stjernstedt's social conscience as well as her understanding of human nature is evident in the novels which came from her pen in the 20's and 30's, novels that are concerned for the most part with a number of psychologically related but otherwise fairly diverse treatments of the self-supporting unmarried woman who prizes her personal freedom and yet has certain strongly developed moral and social instincts. *Fröken Liwin* (1925) is the tragedy of a young woman textile expert who attempts, in the long run unsuccessfully, to establish a fine mother-daughter relationship with her illegitimate daughter, issue of an unfortunate love affair with a young artist. *Resning i målet* (1925; Higher Aims) is an intelligent though somewhat late-born contribution to the discussion in Scandinavian literature of feminine education, one of the darling themes of the 1880's which had been resurrected, in somewhat different forms, just after the turn of the century by Sigrid Undset (*q.v.*) in Norway and Elin Wägner (*q.v.*) in Sweden.

Three other novels by Marika Stjernstedt should be mentioned: *Von Sneckenströms* (1924), an interesting treatment of a Catholic family's experience in practicing its faith in a modern Protestant environment; *Spegling i en skärva* (1936; Images in a Broken Glass), a finely balanced study of the fate of an upper-class Russian family during and after the Red Revolution; and *Man glömmer ingenting* (1940; One Forgets Nothing), a sober and penetrating analysis of a modern woman's thwarted passion and its consequences upon her later individual development. Of these three novels perhaps *Spegling i en skärva* is most representative of Marika Stjernstedt's art, with its careful building up of milieu, its sensitive treatment of character, and its deep human pathos entirely free of any particular propagandistic leanings.

See: M. Stjernstedt, *Mitt och de mina* (1928); K. Strömberg, *Modern svensk litteratur* (1932), pp. 167–170; S. Ahlgren, *Orfeus i folkhemmet* (1938), pp. 60–73; M. Lindqvist, *Människor* (1938), pp. 115–128.

A. G.

Stoessl, Otto (1875–1936, Austrian novelist and essayist), was born in Vienna, the son of a physician. He studied law and became an official of the Austrian railroads. Soon after the First World War he was pensioned. Though only partly of Austrian origin, he was deeply devoted to Austria. For a long time he was an adherent of Karl Kraus (*q.v.*); however, he eventually rallied to the tendencies of neoclassicism as represented by Paul Ernst (*q.v.*). Politically, his beliefs may have been oppositional, perhaps moderately socialist; but as a slow-working, conscious and conscientious artist, he followed a great tradition, specifically that of Stifter, occasionally giving vent to his pessimism and, less often, to his satirical vein.

He intended to collect and partly to reshape his writings for the edition of his *Gesammelte Werke,* of which only four volumes were published, between 1933 and 1938: *Arkadia, Schelmengeschichten, Geist und Gestalt,* and *Schöpfer.* The first contains some of his verse, the third some of his essays. They are critically and carefully conceived and worth reading, as are his *Gottfried Keller* (1904), *Conrad Ferdinand Meyer* (1906), and *Adalbert Stifter* (1925) and the prose collection entitled *Lebensform und Dichtungsform* (1917). Stoessl scarcely intended to include some early writings (*e.g., Leile* and the plays *Waare* and *Tote Götter,* both in collaboration with Robert Scheu, all 1898), but would not have omitted the delicate dramatic idyl, *Der Hirt als Gott* (1920), and some unpublished plays of his later years (*e.g., Basem der Grobschmied*). His limited but solid fame rests upon the best of his stories and novels. Some of them move slowly, but all are written in a thoughtful and sober language: *Kinderfrühling* (1904), *In den Mauern* (1907), *Sonjas letzter Name* (1908), *Egon und Danitza* (1910), *Allerleirauh* (1911), *Morgenrot* (1912), *Was nützen mir die schönen Schuhe* (1913), *Unterwelt* (1917), *Das Haus Erath* (1920; the story of an Austrian family, one of his best efforts), *Irrwege* (1922), *Sonnenmelodie* (1923), *Menschendämmerung* (1929).

See: J. W. Nagel and Jakob Zeidler, *Deutsch-österreichische Literaturgeschichte,* ed. by Eduard Castle, Bd. 4 (1937), pp. 1739–1740; K. Riedler, *Otto Stoessl* (1939).

H. St.

Storm, Theodor (1817–1888, German lyric poet and story writer), was born in Husum, Schleswig. He completed his law course and settled in his home town as attorney, fully expecting to end his days there. But he took a firm stand against Danish oppression and became an exile in 1853. After three unhappy years in Potsdam he found a new home in a smaller town in rural surroundings, Heiligenstadt, to the southeast of Göttingen. When Schleswig became German in 1864, Storm returned to Husum to practice his profession. In 1880 he retired to near-by Hademarschen to devote himself exclusively to literature. In 1846 Storm had married his cousin Constanze Esmarch. She was his inspiration, his most appreciative and sensitive reader. When she died in 1865 his muse seemed silenced. Then he married Dorothea Jensen, whose ardent love, not entirely unreciprocated, had perturbed the early years of his life with Constanze; only gradually was full happiness with the second wife achieved. One of his finest *Novellen, Viola tricolor* (1873), has its roots in this tragic experience.

Storm's life and art are centered in his home. He is the family man of a small town. And this town is Husum. In an elegiac mood of nostalgic longing it was celebrated by Storm as *die graue Stadt am Meer.* Once an important mercantile center with a busy harbor, Husum had become the home of small tradespeople and a few well-established families for whom the past loomed large. It is for this reason that so many of Storm's stories tell of the past. Storm's fine patriotic pieces spring from a deep love for his home, its immediate landscape and its people. Larger political aspects affect him only as they touch his own life. His first *Novelle, Immensee,* published in 1851 (Eng. tr., 1858), is an idyl in which a deep joy of life is pervaded by a gentle melancholy. A sterner mood is also already apparent: from a dream of lost happiness the old man (Storm himself) turns to his work. A comparison of the first *Novelle* with his last, *Der Schimmelreiter* (1888; Eng. tr., *The Rider of the White Horse,* 1915), reveals the whole change from idyllic renunciation to gripping tragedy. Not only are the hero and the heroine made of sterner stuff, they are also seen in the immediate reality of their busy life. The *Novellen,* more than 30 in number, embrace a wide variety of subject and mood. *Zur Chronik von Grieshus* (1884; Eng. tr., *A Chapter in the History of Grieshus,* 1908), *Ein Fest auf Haderslevhus* (1885; Eng. tr., *A Festival at Haderslevhus,* 1909), and *Aquis Submersus* (1876; Eng. tr., 1910) are based on ancient chronicles. In these as in the old Nibelungenlied love ends in tragedy. *Aquis Submersus,* the story of an artist, is considered Storm's finest by many critics. In sharp contrast to its tragic gloom stand two other tales of artists, *Eine Malerarbeit* (1867) and *Psyche* (1875), the one the victorious struggle of a hunchback against adversity, the other a triumphant song of happy love. Many of Storm's stories deal with family life and its problems. A deep insight into the riddle of human life, a sensuous immediacy of experience and presentation, are coupled with a free play of poetic fancy. There is something subtly lyrical about all of Storm's *Novellen,* even those most intensely realistic, and this is perhaps their greatest charm. In this respect Storm seems akin to his younger Danish contemporary, Jens Peter Jacobsen (*q.v.*).

Indeed, Storm is also a distinguished lyric poet. Many of his poems have a narrative element, but the best of them describe a situation ("Ein Sterbender," "Eine Frühlingsnacht"). Some are tragic, others abound in humor and depict a real joy in life ("Sommermittag," "Juli," "Von Katzen"). Storm depicts his native landscape with impressionistic vividness, the coast line with its shallows at the ebb of tide, the lonely heath wrapped in autumn fogs, or the same heath a purple sea of color under the warm August sun. Of the German lyric poets Storm loved most Eichendorff and Mörike. He was among the very first to discover the latter's rare genius. The perfect lyric poem is for Storm one whose first, immediate appeal is purely sensuous, from which sensuous appeal the inner meaning quite naturally and unobtrusively evolves.

See: Gertrud Storm, *Theodor Storm; ein Bild seines Lebens* (1918).

F. Br.

Stössl, Otto, *see* Stoessl.

Stramm, August (1874–1915, German poet and dramatist), born in Münster, Westphalia, attended the Gymnasium at Eupen and at Aachen. His Catholic mother wanted him to study for the priesthood, but his Protestant father insisted on his entering the federal service. Obeying his father, he nevertheless found time to enroll at the universities of Berlin and Halle; in 1909 he was made a doctor of philosophy. Later in his career he held the position of postal inspector in Bremen and Berlin and still later was called into the Reichspostministerium. In 1914, as a captain in the reserve, he joined the army and the next year died at the Russian front.

For 20 years no publisher accepted his works; in 1913, however, a friend, Herwarth Walden, published the drama *Sancta Susanna* in his periodical *Der Sturm,* and Stramm became a leader in the "Sturmgruppe," a literary circle representing the extreme in expressionism. The next year appeared his love songs, *Du,* and the dramas *Die Haidebraut* (Eng. tr., *The Bride of the Moor,* 1914), *Rudimentär,* and *Die Unfruchtbaren,* which are of a somewhat daring character. Three more plays of a similar type (*Erwachen, Kräfte, Geschehen*) were published in 1915. His war verses were published posthumously with the title *Tropfblut* (1919). His plays are so-called *Schreidramen,* consisting to a great extent of ecstatic ejaculations. His lyric poetry, too, often takes this bizarre form, usually in lines of one syllable. To call these expressionistic explosions genuine poetic atrocities may not be too severe a judgment, but at any rate they should be recorded as phenomena of literary history.

See: H. Jansen, *Der Westfale August Stramm als Hauptvertreter des dichterischen Früexpressionismus* (1928).

F. S.

Strauss, Emil (1866–, German novelist), now generally recognized as outstanding, was born in Pforzheim, Swabia. He studied philosophy, German literature, and economics in Freiburg, Lausanne, and Berlin. After his return from Brazil, where he spent two years (1892–1894) as a farmer and teacher, Strauss devoted his energy to agriculture and writing. As a novelist he remained outside the current literary movements, developing his style and his philosophy of life consistently and independently. Strauss first became widely known through *Freund Hein* (1902), describing the childhood and adolescence of a musical genius who, humiliated and discouraged over his repeated failures in high school mathematics, takes his own life. The book was meant as a psychological novel but was interpreted by the public as an attack upon a heartless school system. Strauss, who is related to the famous Austrian family of musicians, sees in music the purest expression of the divine in human life. This is revealed in *Der Spiegel* (1919), essentially a *Bildungsroman* based on the life of his great-grandfather. A soldier by family tradition, Joseph is seized by a Rousseauistic longing for the simple life, becomes a farmer and then, impelled by an urge to find himself, a monk. A heavenly vision finally reveals to him that he should serve God as a musician. The monastic reform in Austria frees him from his vows. He leads a happy married life until his wife accepts a large legacy in his absence. He dissolves the marriage, since the struggle for existence has become necessary for his happiness. It is part of the heroic conception of life which Strauss presents in his works that man must prove his mettle in the storm and stress of life. We must remain loyal to ourselves and defend our convictions and ideals even against our loved ones. Thus in the historical novel *Der nackte Mann* (1912) Captain Gösslin causes the death of his friend, the margrave, who is about to attack the captain's native city of Pforzheim by night. Thus Colonel Sampiero in the historical drama *Vaterland* (1923) must kill his beloved wife to save his native Corsica from an ignominious peace which her gentle nature hoped to attain.

One of the crucial tests of life, according to Strauss, is to find a life partner who, as if predestined by fate, is the necessary complement of one's own self. This becomes evident especially in the second of the two outstanding collections of *Novellen, Hans und Grete* (1909) and *Der Schleier* (1920), both of which are centered around the theme of love. If we are not wide-awake in the decisive moment, we may forfeit our own and another's happiness, like Baptiste who thus condemned two people to lead a mediocre instead of a full life. By his momentary hesitation Gerard, in "Der Skorpion" of the second collection, so mortally injures the pride of the woman who offers him her love that he brings death upon himself and insanity upon his beloved. The moment when the baroness covers the youthful adventure of her mature husband with her veil, thus winning him back through this token of confidence and unalterable love, is the climax of Strauss's most perfect *Novelle* which gave the second collection its title. The baroness has an earlier though more lowly predecessor in the unforgettable figure of the forgiving wife as she appears in the humorous Swabian tale *Der Engelwirt* (1901). Except for a few scenes in this story and a few early *Novellen,* Strauss's stories have unmistakable South German character and background, and his style grows out of the "hearty" popular idiom of this region, much as Gottfried Keller's (*q.v.*) language is rooted in the Swiss dialect.

Emil Strauss is directly concerned with the welfare of his nation. In the bulky novel *Das Riesenspielzeug* begun in 1924 and finished in 1933 (published 1934), we find the sentiment expressed that the important question is not how to increase our bank account or how to carve out a career for ourselves but what we can do to promote a healthy development of our people. The "Riesenspielzeug" is an experimental farm near the Swiss border conducted by a group of people dissatisfied with the social order in Germany after Bismarck's retirement. Almost all types of Germans are assembled here at one time or another, and many vital social problems are discussed. But the communistic experiment as such proves a failure. In the end we foresee that Dr. Haugh, the practical idealist, will marry Berta, the daughter of an ancient peasant family, and that they will take over the farm.

The fact that some tenets in Strauss's works coincided with those of National Socialism helped to increase the author's popularity, although he personally had never desired this.

See: Fritz Endres, *Emil Strauss* (1936).

E. Hof.

Strauss und Torney, Lulu von (1873–, German poet and prose writer), born in Bückeburg, was married to the publisher Eugen Diederichs in 1916. She is a compatriot of Annette von Droste-Hülshoff to whom, as both her prose and her verse show, she is closely akin. Like Annette she is firmly rooted in the soil of her homeland. Strangely unrevealing as to her emotional experiences and her inner life, even her lyrics are likely to assume an objective quality and approach the ballad. In her narrative prose direct speech plays but a minor role. Her heroes are sparing of words: a thought wells up, a long harbored desire becomes a firm resolve and its sole expression is a firmer setting of the lips while the averted eyes gaze off into the distance. An earthbound realism, which depicts every significant detail, is coupled with a visionary intensity that would pierce this earthly veil. All these things are true both of Annette and of Lulu von Strauss und Torney.

The latter's first published work of importance is a collection of peasant tales, *Bauernstolz; Dorfgeschichten aus dem Weserland* (1901). The theme of the opening story is peasant pride. The daughter of a rich farmer marries a laborer. She is as proud as her father, and her husband is equally proud. This stubborn pride wrecks their lives. A second collection of short stories, *Sieger und Besiegte* (1909), contains her finest and most powerful *Novelle,* "Auge um Auge." It is a story of the days when merry King Jerome ruled over the Kingdom of Westphalia. Blundering oppression and ruthless demands result in sporadic outbursts of revolt. An eye for an eye, a life for a life, is the law of the peasantry. The action moves forward relentlessly to its close, where the old farmer assumes the responsibility for the death of the French officer who has killed the farmer's wife. Though it was the son who had exacted vengeance for the death of his mother, the old man dies so that the son may live and the farm remain in the direct line of descent. A similarly heroic and tragic touch characterizes her longer novels. The first of these is *Luzifer* (1907), in which a 13th-century heretic forsakes the trinitarian doctrine for a belief in four gods. The fourth god is Lucifer, the innocent force of evil that is inherent in all life. The author's next novel is *Judas* (1911). Its setting is the Westphalian countryside in the days when the theories of the French Revolution stirred the peasantry to revolt. The following novel, *Der jüngste Tag* (1921), her masterpiece, has its setting in the same landscape in the days of the Anabaptists.

The verse of Lulu von Strauss und Torney ranks with her prose fiction. In her collected poems and ballads one group bears the significant title "Mutter Erde." Earth is our mother from whose womb we spring and to whose womb we return. Her life is our life. The majestic song of the beeches, "Grüne Zeit," marks the pinnacle of Frau Lulu's lyric art. It is the one forest song in German verse that rivals Gottfried Keller's (*q.v.*) "Waldlied" in concept and in rhythm. Her ballads place her among the very first masters of this form in our time. Many have a historical setting and deal with great heroic figures, others deal with our day and the hero may be an aged peasant who dies content when he has garnered his last sheaf. The collected poems and ballads were published in 1919 in *Reif steht die Saat.* The opening poem struck the keynote. For years the grim reaper had been an all too frequent guest. He had garnered aplenty. Now he listens to the song of the widow Mara who woos him because she loves life's fullness and knows that love and death are inseparable. The final enlarged collection of the author's verse bears the title *Erde der Väter* (1936).

See: A. Soergel, *Dichtung und Dichter der Zeit,* 10. Auflage (preface 1919), pp. 710–712; H. Naumann, *Die deutsche Dichtung der Gegenwart* (1923), pp. 167, 212, 264.

F. Br.

Streuvels, Stijn (pseud. of Frank Lateur, 1871–, Flemish novelist and short-story writer), was born at Heule, near Kortrijk (Courtrai). His mother was a sister of the poet Guido Gezelle (*q.v.*). He was for 15 years the village baker at Avelghem. But in 1906 he moved to Ingoyghem and, from then on, devoted himself entirely to writing. Stijn Streuvels is a product of the Flemish soil, he feels himself part of it, he knows the life of its peasantry because it is his own, and depicts it with the plastic power of a Brueghel. He does not belong to any school, he does not proclaim any program or theory of art, he just writes from the same natural urge that makes his Flemish countryside burst into bloom in the spring. Nature is the dominating power in all his stories. Everything that happens to his characters is predetermined by their subjection to Nature. Hence Streuvels is a fatalist. Nature's dark, incalculable designs shape man's destinies, especially in his earlier tales, *Lenteleven* (1899; Spring Life), *Zomerland* (1900; Summer Land), *Zonnetij* (1900; Sun Tide), *Doodendans* (1901; Dance of Death), and the novel, *Langs de Wegen* (1902, Along the Roads; Eng. tr., *Old Jan,* 1936). The influence of Strindberg and Dostoevski (*qq.v.*) no doubt colored his pessimism. In later stories, however, a serener mood prevails. In *Stille Avonden* (1905; Quiet Evenings) he sounds a note of tenderness and compassion and hope. Here disillusionment gives way to a contented acceptance of life. Nature still dominates the scene but no longer like an inexorable nemesis. In the novel *De Vlaschgaard* (1907; The Flax Field) the story is that of the progress of the seasons through the land, and on that vast scene, against the backdrop of the sky, his characters move charged with passions whose explosion is an intrinsic part of the cosmic drama. There is a biblical grandeur in this story that gives it rank among the great novels of modern times. There is, it is true, a certain similarity among all his tales that results from his exclusive interest in only one phase of life, that of the lowly tiller of the soil. Streuvels, in consequence, is apt to be repetitious. In that respect he is inferior to Balzac, Flaubert (*q.v.*), and Zola (*q.v.*). He has sought strength in limitation. He is a great narrator, but only in his narrowly restricted genre. When he tried for once, in *Dorpslucht* (Village Atmosphere), to paint the village bourgeoisie, or to reanimate the past in his retelling of the legend of Genoveva of Brabant, the result was a failure. He is exclusively the epic poet of the Flemish soil and its humble tiller and, within that limited range, a very great one.

See: A. de Ridder, *Stÿn Streuvels, zÿn leven en zÿn werk* (1908) and *La Littérature flamande contemporaine* (1923).

A. J. B.

Strindberg, Johan August (1849–1912, Swedish dramatist, novelist, short-story writer, poet, and essayist), was born in Stockholm, the fourth in a family of 11 children. Various circumstances of his home life provided the hypersensitive Strindberg with acute and sometimes morbid memories of unpleasantness: a round of births and deaths, stern, unrelenting parents, insufficient funds, a feeling of being unwanted, and a sense of inferiority. At school things were no better until he reached the Stockholm Lyceum, at which institution his intellectual curiosity was awakened by a study of the natural sciences. He made a false start at Uppsala in 1867, returned to Stockholm after a semester, taught grammar school, was a physician's assistant, made an attempt to become an actor, did some writing, and was back at the university for the fall term of 1870. He remained there two academic years, spending much time in reading and writing. By the early spring of 1872, when he gave up his university studies, Strindberg was busy with his ninth literary opus. A play, *I Rom* (1871; In Rome), presented at the Dramatic Theatre, had attracted the attention of King Charles XV, and a grant of money from the royal funds resulted.

Although he expended much time and energy in study and experiments devoted to the sciences, it is as a creative artist that Strindberg has a permanent reputation. All his labor in the sciences was but a getting for literary spending. It took much experience, a great variety of activities, to furnish material for some 70 dramas, a dozen and more novels, many short stories, historical sketches, satires, travel tales, poems, and innumerable essays (the Landquist edition of Strindberg's collected works has 55 volumes). His first outstanding literary composition was the prose version of *Mäster Olof* (Eng. tr.,

Master Olof, 1915), a drama written in 1871–1872 but refused by theaters and publishers alike and hence not printed or produced until 1881. This was a work that revealed Strindberg as a dramatist of the highest rank as well as a master of the Swedish language. His early reputation, however, must be credited to *Röda rummet* (1879; Eng. tr., *The Red Room,* 1913). This book was hailed as the first naturalistic social novel of the Scandinavian North, but it was by no means solely dependent on objective observations. Strindberg, then unacquainted with Zola (*q.v.*), was influenced by Flaubert (*q.v.*) and the Goncourts (*q.v.*). At the same time he also owed much to Rousseau and Dickens. His naturalism was not then or later unqualified.

From 1874 to 1882 Strindberg was an assistant at the Royal Library in Stockholm. During this period he married Siri von Essen, and three children were born of this union. Between 1883 and 1889 he and his family were traveling about Europe, for the most part in France and Switzerland, with Strindberg coming and going even more often than his family. He returned to Stockholm temporarily in October, 1884, to stand trial on charges of blasphemy arising from the publication of *Giftas* (1884; Married), the first collection of stories with this title. Although freed of the charges, Strindberg received a violent nervous shock from which he never fully recovered. The second collection of *Giftas* stories (1885; Eng. tr., one-volume edition of the two collections, *Married,* 1913) reveals a gravitation toward misanthropy. Thenceforward the domestic scene, especially the cruel battle of the sexes, receives prominent attention. Note, for example, *Fadren* (1887; Eng. tr., *The Father,* 1907), *Kamraterna* (1888; Eng. tr., *Comrades,* 1912), *Fröken Julie* (1888; Eng. tr., *Julie,* 1911; later translated as *Miss Julia* and *Countess Julia*), *Bandet* (1893; Eng. tr., *The Link,* 1912), *Dödsdansen* (1901; Eng. tr., *The Dance of Death,* 1912). It must also be remarked that Strindberg was thrice married, thrice divorced, and five times a father.

Among his literary outpourings in the 80's are the four autobiographical novels captioned *Tjänstekvinnans son* (Eng. tr. of the first of these, also entitled *Tjänstekvinnans son, The Son of a Servant,* 1913), all written in 1886, with the first three volumes published during 1886–1887, the fourth in 1909. The novels are an index to the extreme subjectivism of Strindberg's writings, and they are also forerunners of expressionism and "stream of consciousness" books. The later autobiographical sketches *Inferno* (1897; Eng. tr., *The Inferno,* 1913) and *Legenden* (1898; Eng. tr., *Legends,* 1912), derived from a period of intense suffering, are transmuted into the *Till Damaskus* dramatic trilogy (3 parts, 1898–1904; Eng. tr., *To Damascus,* 1933–1935). In the trilogy, experiences are set forth directly from psychic apprehension without correction by reference to a plane of sensuous reality. Artistic manipulation obtains, but subjective distortion is cultivated. In dramas like *Ett drömspel* (1902; Eng. tr., *The Dream Play,* 1912) and *Spöksonaten* (1907; Eng. tr., *The Spook Sonata,* 1916; later translated as *The Ghost Sonata*) the lack of objective analysis is still more pronounced.

Strindberg worked as only a great artist can, exploiting at the same time diametrically opposed moods, settings, and dramatis personae. Thus during the 80's when bitterness dominated so much of his work, he was also writing prose fiction such as the utopian *Lycksalighetens ö* (1884; The Isle of the Blessed); the delightful story with its setting in the Stockholm archipelago, *Hemsöborna* (1887; The Dwellers of Hemsö); the novelette, *Den romantiske klockaren på Rånö* (1888; The Romantic Sexton of Rånö); and the travel sketches, *Bland franska bönder* (1886–89; Among French Peasants).

After his nervous crisis of the 90's Strindberg returned to Sweden to take up permanent residence. Once more he wrote feverishly. There were historical plays such as *Gustav Vasa* (1899; Eng. tr., 1916), *Erik XIV* (1899; Eng. tr., 1931), *Carl XII* (1901), *Kristina* (1901), and *Bjälbo-Jarlen* (1908; The Earl of Bjälbo). And there were chamber plays, written for the Intimate Theatre which he established in 1907—*Oväder* (1907; Eng. tr., *The Thunderstorm,* 1913) and *Brända tomten* (1907; Eng. tr., *After the Fire,* 1913). Likewise during this period he wrote his two most cutting satires, *Götiska rummen* (1904; Gothic Rooms) and *Svarta fanor* (1904; Black Flags).

No simple formula will characterize Strindberg, no brief space can do him justice, and no label of school or literary movement may be unqualifiedly attached to him. He is without doubt the greatest dramatic artist that the Swedes have produced, perhaps the greatest literary genius that has come out of Sweden.

Most of the plays mentioned here may be found in the following collections: *Plays,* tr. by Edith and Wärner Oland (3 vols., 1912–1914); *Plays,* four series, tr. by Edwin Björkman (1912–1916); *Easter and Other*

Plays, tr. by C. D. Locock, E. Classen, E. Palmstierna, and J. B. Fagan (1929); *Lucky Peter's Travels and Other Plays,* tr. by C. D. Locock, E. Classen, Elizabeth Sprigge, and C Napier (1930); *Master Olof and Other Plays,* tr. by C. D. Locock and Joan Bulman (1931).

See: A. Engström, *August Strindberg och jag* (1923); G. Lindblad, *August Strindberg som berättare* (1924); M. Lamm, *Strindbergs dramer* (2 vols., 1924–1926) and *August Strindberg,* Del I: *Före infernokrisen* (1940); C. E. W. L. Dahlström, *Strindberg's Dramatic Expressionism* (1930); A. Jolivet, *Le Théâtre de Strindberg* (1931); J. Bulman, *Strindberg and Shakespeare* (1933).

C. E. W. L. D.

Strug, Andrzej (pseud. of Tadeusz Gałecki, 1873–1937, Polish novelist), was born at Konstantynówka near Lublin, Russian Poland. He was educated in the Lublin Gymnasium, his companions there being the famous pleiad of Lubliners who from 1891 to 1894 kept the University of Warsaw constantly in a patriotic ferment. Strug himself studied not in Warsaw but at the Puławy Agricultural Institute. He was, however, no less ardent a patriot than his friends in Warsaw and was arrested with them in 1894 and deported to Archangel. On being released he engaged even more actively than before in conspiratorial activities, now as a member of the Polish Socialist Party. When the party was forced to go underground after 1905, Strug settled in Paris and devoted himself to the task of recording in fictional form his experiences as a revolutionist. His most important work from this period was *Ludzie podziemni* (1908; Workers Underground). During the First World War, Strug served in the field with Piłsudski and in 1918 settled in Warsaw. Up to 1926 he took an active part in politics but following the May coup found himself in the opposition and withdrew from the political arena. Strug's most ambitious work was the antimilitarist novel of the First World War, *Żółty krzyż* (1933; The Yellow Cross), unfortunately not a success artistically on account of its diffuseness. Strug was a great revolutionist and a man of sterling character, and his chronicles of the revolutionary epoch of 1905 may well assure him literary immortality.

See: Z. Dębicki, *Portrety,* I (1927), 193–212; *Wiadomości literackie,* 1938, No. 10 (entire issue).

A. P. C.

Stuckenberg, Viggo (1863–1905, Danish lyric poet, novelist), was born on Zealand and lived long under straitened circumstances as a teacher in Copenhagen. Stuckenberg's home, however, with the poet's wife Ingeborg as muse, drew a small group of talented youthful writers, Sophus Claussen (*q.v.*), Johannes Jørgensen (*q.v.*), and others.

The problems and the creeds of the 80's and the 90's appear in procession before us in this author's works. Rationalistic realism and the young poet's own high hopes of a new dawn ushered in by enlightenment (*see* Georg Brandes) color *Messias* (1889; The Messiah). Disillusioned naturalism with stress laid upon poverty, sordidness, and the power of inheritance and environment marks *Asmadaeus* (1899). Symbolistic neo-romanticism in the form of haunting medieval mysticism appears, however, in the ballad drama *Den vilde Jaeger* (1894; The Wild Huntsman), showing the effects of the "new awakening of the 90's." Clearly confessional, on the other hand, is the novelette *Fagre Ord* (1895; Fair Words). *Vejbred* (1899; Eng. tr., By the Wayside, 1917) presents in strangely beautiful rhythmic prose youth's eternal quest for high adventure. Stuckenberg is, however, greatest in his poetry, particularly in the collection *Sne* (1901; Snow). The soul of the poet is here laid bare—in the deep straightforward love for Ingeborg, in the despair that shook the roots of his being when she left him, in the confession of his faith. Stuckenberg's philosophy is valiant and well-tried: life is bitter, but woe to him who laments and counts his wounds; go through the flames. Life still deserves all praise. Love in Stuckenberg is a tremendous force, at times a witchery that blasts life, but love is also "the lonely blade of green grass growing on the stony road." As to religion the poet believes that "a God exists somewhere, but One who turns in disgust from those who grovel before Him, a God who watches if man walks unconquered through the gates of life." Certain symbols recur frequently in Stuckenberg, *e.g.,* snow (peace), but the poet's language is infinitely shaded and rich in effects. Life vouchsafed Stuckenberg devoted friends and a second brief spell of happiness when he remarried not long before his death.

See: H. G. Topsöe-Jensen, *Scandinavian Literature from Brandes to Our Day* (1929); Helge Kjaergaard, *Die dänische Literatur der neuesten Zeit (1871–1933)* (1934).

C. K. B.

Suarès, André (1868–, French poet, critic, and essayist), cuts in modern French letters the same quixotic figure which his uncouth appearance and jet black hair worn at shoulder's length presented long ago to his classmates of the Ecole Normale Supérieure (1886–1889). In 1935 the French Academy awarded him its Grand Prix de Littérature as a token of belated recognition for an impressive array of works the unity of which lies in the author's contention that he is first and foremost an errant knight of Beauty. Thus his title *Le Voyage du condottière,* which otherwise covers a three-volume series of Italian impressions (*Vers Venise,* 1910; *Fiorenza,* 1932; *Sienne la bien-aimée,* 1932), takes on a symbolic meaning. It describes the tumultuous journey of a soul naturally inclined toward an earthly, sensuous realism, but dragged down to the depths of negation and despair by the "tragic," bitterly logical realization that the world (and the self) forever escapes our grasp except in the silent possession of death, except, too, in the miracle of poetic vision which alone, in the words of Spinoza, has the power to make things *verae seu reales*—*i.e.,* to transmute transient truth into permanent reality.

Suarès's poems, whether called *Images de la grandeur* (1901) or *Rêves de l'ombre* (1937), presuppose an almost omniscient mind, equally conversant with sciences, especially mathematics and philology, and the arts. Music is an essential ingredient (*Wagner,* 1899; *Debussy,* 1922; *Musique et poésie,* 1928), closely allied to drama which Suarès practices in a semiclassical, semi-Shakespearian vein (*La Tragédie d'Elektre et d'Oreste,* 1905; *Cressida,* 1913; *Polyxène,* 1925). Likewise, he will go to Japan as a model for some of his poetry (*Haï-Kaï d'Occident* and *Soleil de jade,* both 1928), all over Europe in his literary criticism (*Trois Hommes: Pascal, Ibsen, Dostoïevsky,* 1913; *Poëte tragique: Portrait de Prospero,* 1921; *Goethe le grand Européen,* 1932; *Trois Grands Vivants: Cervantes, Tolstoï, Baudelaire,* 1937), through the length and breadth of human experience in his numerous essays (*Voici l'Homme,* 1906; *Sur la vie,* 2 vols., 1912; *Valeurs,* 1936).

With one exception (*Sur la mort de mon frère,* 1904), Suarès the private man withdraws into jealous seclusion. Biographical information about him is extremely scarce and further obscured by his habit of espousing, as it were, the personalities of great figures of the past, of celebrated characters of fiction (Prospero, Don Juan, Manon), even of "doubles" created by his own imagination (André de Séipse, Yves Scantrel, Caerdal). However, despite the fact that Caerdal—the *condottière*—poses as a Celt from Brittany and that, to a German scholar, Suarès exemplifies *der nordisch Mensch,* the truth is that he was born in Vallon-de-l'Oriol, a Marseille suburb, from Portuguese and half-Jewish ancestry. The sonorous magnificence of his style, the healthy quality of his work (for all its somber hues), not to mention a loving "portrait" of his native town (*Marsiho,* 1933), bespeak his Southern origins. His own claim, besides, is that he is, culturally at least, a "Phocaean Greek," an exponent of Hellenistic ideals, forcefully opposed to all forms of "barbaric" hegemony, whether political (Roman) or racial (Germanic). The note which rang through his *Nation contre la race* (2 vols., 1916) reappears, only amplified, in his recent *Vues sur l'Europe.* This, his latest book, was written in 1936 but withheld because of its possibly "dangerous" controversial character. Pathetically enough, it was released in 1939, when it seemed timely and appropriate to throw diplomatic caution to the winds.

See: Frédéric Lefèvre, *Une Heure avec . . .* I (1924), 249–266; Gabriel Bounoure, reviews in *Nouvelle Revue française,* XXXII (1929), 866–875, XLV (1935), 623–627, XLIX (1937), 500–504; M. Martin du Gard, *Harmonies critiques* (1936), pp. 138–148.

J.-A. B.

Suckert, Curzio (pseud. Malaparte, 1898–, Italian publicist and short-story writer), born in Prato in Tuscany, came to prefer his pen name (which is a play on Napoleon's last name) to his own. He was one of the most genuine representatives of the adventurous youth which made Fascism possible in Italy. At 16 he volunteered with an expedition of Garibaldians who went to France. He fought valiantly, was wounded in the Argonne, and later enlisted in the Italian army. After the First World War he was for two years a diplomat, then turned free lance writer and newspaper correspondent. However, he never became an outstanding figure in Fascism and always preserved his own originality and independence of thought—which in 1933 brought him five years of confinement on the island of Lipari and later procured him other annoyances from the Fascist police. As a writer, he enjoys an international reputation as a brilliant political interpreter, as well as a colorful critic, of Fascism. His books, translated into English, French, and Spanish, present Fascism as the reaction of Italy to Europe or as a provincial agricultural traditional country life opposed to a plutocratic bourgeois city life. For some years, with Maccari and Longanesi, he represented the literary school called the *Strapaese,* or ultranational.

In his *Italia barbara* (1925) he championed what foreigners generally objected to in

Italians: poverty, the stiletto, and the lottery. He preferred the inn to the grand hotel, bare legs to silk stockings, street brawls to election fights. One of his books, *Technique du coup d'état* (1931; Eng. tr., *Coup d'état, the Technique of Revolution,* 1932), is replete with paradoxical observations about the means resorted to by Lenin and Mussolini in seizing power. He also wrote stories, half-whimsical, half-realistic, where Tuscany, land of genius and arrogance, plays the title role. Russia, Palestine, and Norway form the background for other tales, *e.g., Sodoma e Gomorra* (1931); in these he enjoys picturing Voltaire attempting to discover what kind of sin was committed by the citizens of Gomorrah; or the Freudian jealousy of a Nordic minister for his daughter who closely resembles his lost wife. Part of the story of his exile in Lipari (*Fughe in prigione,* 1936) was translated: "On the Island of Lipari," *Yale Review,* Summer, 1935. He always writes with a rich vocabulary, a touch of originality, a sort of impudence and directness. There is a decided charm in his adaptations of popular rhythms. Originally he owed much to Soffici (*q.v.*), but more and more he has followed his own bent.

During the Second World War he was sent to Finland, Germany, Rumania, Croatia, and Russia as a correspondent; and from these experiences came forth *Kaputt* (1944), a first-rate book, anti-German, anti-Fascist, full of color, of cruelty, of laughs, of paradoxes, revealing Malaparte as a powerful story-teller, similar to Axel Munthe, author of *San Michele.* From the king of Sweden crocheting beautiful designs to the noble Jews of the ghetto of Warsaw, from the squadron of horses frozen in a lake of Finland to the Spanish ambassador's dog who became frenzied at the sound of airplanes—jailers and jailed, men and animals, parade humorously and humanly before the reader.

See: A. Baldini, *Amici allo spiedo* (1932), pp. 5–11; G. Ravegnani, *I Contemporanei,* Ser. 2 (1936), pp. 341–348.

G. P.

Sudermann, Hermann (1857–1928, German dramatist and novelist), was the son of a brewer whose family, of the Mennonite faith, originally had come from Holland; his mother belonged to a local family. His birthplace, Matziken, lies close to the Russian boundary line of East Prussia where German and Lithuanian racial elements are inextricably mixed. Despite their poverty his parents managed to give him a good education. He attended first the University of Königsberg in East Prussia, then the University of Berlin where he went at the age of 20. Except for short travels he was never to leave the capital of the Reich. Sudermann's development was somewhat influenced by the writer Hans Hopfen, into whose home he came as a teacher for Hopfen's children. After a lean beginning as an editor of a small political weekly, Sudermann began writing short stories. A collection of these appeared in 1886 under the title *Im Zwielicht.* He then wrote two novels, *Frau Sorge* (1887; Eng. tr., *Dame Care,* 1891) and *Der Katzensteg* (1889; Eng. tr., *Regine,* 1894); neither won attention until the overwhelming success of his first play, *Die Ehre* (1889; Eng. tr., *Honor,* 1915).

From then on, one play after another came from his pen in rapid succession. The best known are *Sodoms Ende* (1891; Eng. tr., *The Man and His Picture,* 1903), *Heimat* (1893; Eng. tr., *Magda,* 1896), *Die Schmetterlingsschlacht* (1893; Eng. tr., *The Battle of the Butterflies,* 1914), *Das Glück im Winkel* (1895; Eng. tr., *The Vale of Content,* 1915), *Morituri* (1896; Eng. tr., 1910), *Johannes* (1898; Eng. tr., *John,* 1902), *Die drei Reiherfedern* (New York, 1898, Stuttgart, 1899; Eng. tr., *The Three Heron's Feathers,* 1900), *Johannesfeuer* (1900; Eng. tr., *St. John's Fire,* 1904), *Es lebe das Leben* (1902; Eng. tr., *The Joy of Living,* 1902), and *Blumenboot* (1906). In the last named he returned to a kind of social drama which he had begun with *Sodoms Ende. Sturmgeselle Sokrates* (1903) was meant to be political comedy, *Stein unter Steinen* (1905) is an ex-convict drama. The novel *Das hohe Lied* (1908; Eng. tr., *The Song of Songs,* 1909) and the historical play *Strandkinder* (1909) mark the end of Sudermann's first period. The plays he wrote before the First World War, *Der Bettler von Syrakus* (1911), *Der gute Ruf* (1912; Eng. tr., *A Good Reputation,* 1915), and *Die Lobgesänge des Claudian* (1914), demonstrated somewhat new approaches to the dramatic field, but they were only mildly successful.

When Sudermann turned toward patriotic topics during and after the war (*e.g., Das deutsche Schicksal,* 1921), the public ignored his efforts. But at the same time he found a fertile field for his pen in the stories, legends, and beliefs of his East Prussian home, and his volume of prose *Litauische Geschichten* (1917; Eng. tr., *The Excursion to Tilsit,* 1930) is generally regarded as his best work. In *Frau Sorge* he had attempted to show the inner development of a man, but with insufficient stylistic means; here he is the simple storyteller who forgets most of the tricks of his other trade. The autobiographical *Bilderbuch meiner Jugend* (1922; Eng. tr., *Book of My Youth,* 1923) leads to the third and last phase of his life, during which he produced three important novels, *Der tolle Professor* (1926; Eng. tr., *The Mad Professor,* 1928), *Die Frau des Steffen Tromholt* (1927; Eng. tr., *The Wife of Steffen Tromholt,* 1929), and *Purzelchen* (1928; Eng. tr., *The Dance of Youth,* 1930).

Alfred Kerr, Sudermann's bitterest critic, once said that his successes were the result of his mistakes. There is a great deal of truth in that statement. At the time when his first plays were performed, the public was starving for theatrical fare—ready to overlook the artificiality of his characters and plots, the insincerity of their moralizing, the surprise turns and other theatrical tricks with which the scenes were studded. His plays have made good moving pictures. By the end of his second period the critics had caught up with him. The public began to grow cool toward his plays. Realizing that without worth-while subject matter his plays would keep on being failures, he turned again to prose writing and discovered in the peasants and the folklore of his Lithuanian home a true wellspring of epic material. Although even his later prose is not free from some of the flaws of his early works, his theatrical mannerisms are less disturbing. Thus his prose is likely to live on, but his plays may not survive the sentence pronounced upon them by such critics as Alfred Kerr and Maximilian Harden who likened them to the products of Kotzebue, Augier, Feuillet, or Sardou. More recently, Hans Naumann, in reevaluating Sudermann's *Sodoms Ende,* forecast a more friendly interpretation of his work.

See: A. Kerr, *Das neue Drama,* I (1917), 219–284; K. Busse, *Hermann Sudermann; sein Werk und sein Wesen* (1927); A. Soergel, *Dichtung und Dichter der Zeit,* 19. Auflage (1928), pp. 373–383.

W. N.

Sully-Prudhomme (pseud. of René François Armand Prudhomme, 1839–1907, French poet) was a Parisian by birth. He prepared for the Ecole Polytechnique, thought seriously of entering the Dominican order, worked for a time in the great Schneider factories at Le Creusot, studied law and philosophy, and finally, as a sequel to an unhappy love affair, became a poet. "Le Vase brisé" (in *Stances et poèmes,* 1865) revealed best his "blessure fine et profonde" and proved so popular that it is now a hackneyed piece. *Les Epreuves* (1866), *Les Solitudes* (1869), *Les Vaines Tendresses* (1875), and the posthumous *Epaves* (1907) belong to the same elegiac inspiration, tactfully confidential and equally removed from romantic emotionalism and Parnassian frigidity.

As early as 1869 Sully-Prudhomme's translation of the first book of Lucretius, together with the accompanying preface, heralded a new trend. *Les Destins* (1872), *La Justice* (1886), and *Le Bonheur* (1888) are increasingly ambitious attempts to create the so-called "scientific-philosophic poem" envisioned by André Chénier a century earlier. However disputable the merits of the performance, it must be said for the author that he achieves on occasion a beautiful ethereal quality in his use of symbols and that he is besides the only poet of his times who gives an impression of solid competence in the fields of science and metaphysics. Here again Sully-Prudhomme, although usually classified with the Parnassians, stands athwart the line which divides them from the romanticists. No self-appointed Messiah like Victor Hugo but no nihilist like Leconte de Lisle (*q.v.*), he lifts poetry from some of the gloom into which positivistic pessimism had plunged it for a generation and teaches his belief that the road to happiness lies through pain, self-sacrifice, and brotherly love. "Le Zénith," a poem of circumstance published in the *Revue des deux mondes* in 1876, commemorates the fatal ascent of three balloonists who anticipated present-day excursions into the stratosphere. This lofty composition, dedicated to man's intrepid quest for the truth, gives a cue to Sully-Prudhomme's own lifework and to the reasons why he, a member of the French Academy since 1881, was deemed worthy of the Nobel prize (1901).

See: Camille Hémon, *La Philosophie de M. Sully-Prudhomme* (1907); Ernest Zyromsky, *Sully-Prudhomme* (1907); Edmond Estève, *Sully-Prudhomme, poëte sentimental et poëte philosophe* (1925); Pierre Flottes, *Sully-Prudhomme et sa pensée* (1930).

J.-A. B.

Supervielle, Jules (1884–, French poet, story writer, and dramatist), was born in Montevideo, Uruguay, of a French family which had come originally from the Basque country. He made his first journey to France at the age of eight months; his parents died when he was still an infant. His life has been divided between Spanish America and France. Studies in the law, political science, and modern languages seemed to be leading to a career in diplomacy. Then he married, and dedicated himself to poetry.

"I started from zero," he once wrote to a close friend. His first slender volumes (*Brumes du passé,* 1901; *Comme des voiliers,* 1910) were feeble imitations of the Parnassian manner. His *Poèmes* (1919) and his *Débarcadères* (1922) contain admirable lines and show a definite gift; fuller realization comes with *Gravitations* (1925), not actually surrealist although long considered so. Subsequently, and thanks in part to the friendship and counsel of Jean Paulhan, director of the *Nouvelle Revue française,* Supervielle has made constant progress as a literary artist.

After several experiments in fiction (*L'Homme de la Pampa,* 1923; *Le Voleur d'enfants,* 1926; *Le Survivant,* 1928) he found the right formula for himself in 1931 with his first short stories, *L'Enfant de la haute mer,* which were followed somewhat later by *L'Arche de Noé* (1938) and *Le Petit Bois* (1942). These three collections reveal a narrator whose tone is unique in French letters —a marvelous fusion of the tender and the burlesque, of grandeur and simplicity. Supervielle has also written plays (*Bolivar,* 1936; *La Belle au bois,* 1932; *La Première Famille,* 1936), a volume of souvenirs (*Boire à la source,* 1933), an adaptation of Shakespeare (*Comme il vous plaira,* 1925). But he continues to put into his poetry a considerable part, and perhaps the very best part, of himself: *Le Forçat innocent* (1930), *Les Amis inconnus* (1934), *La Fable du monde* (1938), and finally the wartime *Poèmes de la France malheureuse* (1941) mark finer and finer craftsmanship and increasing depth.

Although Supervielle generally lives in a universe of restless fancy, although he has claimed for poetry a rarely explored domain (that of the most recondite feelings) and produced an abundance of myths, he has never been indifferent to history. The Boer War, the First World War, the Spanish civil war, and the French defeat of 1940 have all had echoes in his poetry. At the same time history never utterly absorbs him; he remains also the poet concerned at once with the humblest objects and with the sweep of the planets through space and the poet of sentiments so elementary as to be too often neglected (the simpler relationships of love, paternity, and the like).

Supervielle is the most unassuming and the least *arriviste* of men, yet his human qualities, coupled with his talent, have won him, especially from about 1930, the admiration and the affection of younger writers. Two testimonial numbers of the periodicals *Avant-Poste* (1935) and *Regains* (1938) prove the impression he has made. At least five or six of the poets who have written about him consider him a foil to Rimbaud (*q.v.*)—which most certainly does not mean an anti-Rimbaud—or at least as complementary to Rimbaud. Supervielle accepts the human situation: he is not one who is "in revolt against death," he is a complete man also (as he writes in a letter), "a literary anarchist" at the outset and in the final stage "classic." Of his total work, which is extensive, part undoubtedly is perishable; the rest is likely to endure as long as our civilization.

See: C. Sénéchal, *Jules Supervielle* (1939).

E.

surrealism. Following close upon political chaos and social upheaval at the end of the First World War, surrealism brought to a head a gradually intensified indictment of some 70 years' standing in French literature and art, directed at the same time against the otherworldly escapism of the romanticists and against naturalism's close adherence to external reality.

The poet had long been represented as a captive trying to tear down his prison walls. Then as science gradually cleared up one after the other the mysteries of the physical world, the ultimate barrier to the unknown assumed an ever greater impermeability. Yet even more resolutely did the poet take up the cry by which, according to the surrealists, Charles Baudelaire (*q.v.*) had launched "the great modern tradition" in the last two lines of his "Voyage": to find something new in the abysses of the unknown whether the adventure lead to heaven or perdition. And as science in the latter part of the 19th century made of the metaphysical or speculative infinite a less satisfactory haven for the seekers of the unknown, the poet was ready to substitute for it what Renan (*q.v.*) called *l'infini réel* and to illustrate in art the concept of an infinite based on the unconditional acceptance of concrete reality. But the word reality gradually ceased to be identified with anything like a stylized "nature" and, on the contrary, was sought in deliberate distortions of accepted views of physical and human nature. The first major examples of this subversive concept of reality were revealed around 1870 in the works of Lautréamont and Rimbaud (*qq.v.*) and in Mallarmé's (*q.v.*) *Igitur.* These were conscious steps towards disregarding natural objects and phenomena by a refusal to imitate them in literature and towards dehumanizing emotions. Here were the beginnings of a mystical atheism that was to form the core of surrealism.

This process of breaking down the accepted concept of nature reached a crisis during the First World War at the hands of a group of notorious demolitionists known as dadaists. But soon a number of young intellectuals, graduating from the excesses of dada, formed their own coterie about 1920, which they called *surréalisme* following Guillaume Apollinaire (*q.v.*) who had used the word *surréaliste* to designate a reality above the accepted and obvious one. André Breton (*q.v.*) was the father of the movement, and he had as his principal co-workers for varying periods of time Philippe Soupault, Louis Aragon (*qq.v.*), Georges Hugnet, René Crevel, E. Mesens, and Paul Eluard (*q.v.*). A host of painters became their associates in this systematic, quasi-scientific experimentation with surreality. Their principal journals were *Littérature,* organized in 1919, about a year before the official advent of surrealism, and *Révolution surréaliste* (1924–1930), transformed in 1930 into *Surréalisme au service de la révolution.* The aims, theories, and quarrels of the surrealists were publicized in two manifestoes in 1924 and 1930 by André Breton. Surrealist experiences with what might be called the fourth dimension in literature involved simulation of mental disorders —which according to Breton was to replace the ballad, the sonnet, and the epic form— spiritualist seances, automatic writing, willful dreaming, and sexual aberrations. In 1928 the surrealists celebrated the 50th anniversary of Jean Martin Charcot's publication of studies in hysteria and accepted him as one of their precursors because he had shown scientifically the possibilities for the human mind to conciliate reality with the dream and to experience this conciliation without exterior stimuli or artificial hypnosis.

Yet it is not in its exhibitionism, psychophysiological theories, and journalistic anarchy that surrealism's contributions to a new mysticism and its effects on literary form are to be found. It is rather in the more authentically literary works, principally Breton's *Nadja* (1928), Aragon's *Le Paysan de Paris* (1926), Crevel's *L'Esprit contre la raison* (1927) and *Le Clavecin de Diderot* (1932), and Eluard's *Les Dessous d'une vie, ou la Pyramide humaine* (1926), that the surrealists crystallized, in a fusion of poetry and prose, a new philosophy of reality. In most of these writings the concept of order is attacked as the primary obstacle in the way of man's exploration here on earth of the infinite. Humanity has been basing its evaluations of natural phenomena, they say, on a preconceived notion of order and then attributing this man-conceived order to the *merveilleux.* It is disorder, then, that has been inconceivable. And now a reliance on Providence, generally considered the manifestation of the mystical order of things, must give way to the worship of hazard or chance, the mystical manifestation of the inconceivable but existent disorder of things. By extracting this "divine" disorder, left so long undisturbed in concrete entities, the surrealists hope to perceive the concrete face of the infinite. "The concrete form of disorder is the outer limit of the mind," said Aragon in *Le Paysan de Paris,* the Bible of this new metaphysics. If the mind can sufficiently free itself from logic to be receptive to this disorder, then it will have overpowered the laws of nature and risen above what Crevel calls *le bric-à-brac réaliste:* gravitation can disappear, fruits and flowers don new colors, night change place with day, the living and the dead hold hands, and the whole movement of existence pause in eternal expectancy. Breton's Nadja, the most authentic of surrealism's brain children, was a product of this mysticism as she loomed on the literary horizon gracefully hiding her face behind the heavy, nonexistent feather of her hat and saw a blue wind passing in the trees.

Glaring peculiarities which exposed the surrealists to criticism and ridicule were the obscurity of language and the antisocial note emanating from many of their manifestoes. Yet neither of these tendencies is a pose or an aim in itself. The oddities of language arise out of an attempt to create a new foundation for literary imagery. For centuries comparison had furnished this basis. Now, dependent as it is on logic, comparison is no longer considered adequate. The poet's eye discerns the *merveilleux* in the contradictions that appear within the generally accepted realities. The new imagery must be based not on comparison but its opposite, contradiction: it is this contradiction in language expressing the disordinate in nature as perceived by the irrational qualities of mind that is the essence of surrealism. As for the antisocial character, it came as a natural consequence of the poet's withdrawal from the ordinate aspects of physical nature: the illogical turn of mind which creates the new reality possesses something of the mystical disorder it sees in inanimate things and in cultivating the inner disorder spurns the qualities of mind and emotions which are the symbols of man's stability—love of home, love of country, love of humanity. But these traits of surrealism were short-lived, and when viewed in relation to the passion and fearless literary experimentation of which they are but the superficial tinsel, they lose the importance that pseudo surrealists and the critics of these have attributed to them.

The historical importance of surrealism lies in the fact that it is not a detached phenomenon in itself but part of a long development in poetic thought. Some of today's most challenging poets passed early in their careers within the wide orbit of this spiritual crisis —Aragon, Breton, Eluard, and others such as Pierre Reverdy and Jules Supervielle (*qq.v.*) who were never officially surrealists. Its bravura days came to a quick end. Many of yesterday's iconoclasts, who were at first touched a little by the insanity they tried to imitate, have become sober literary workmen. But they have not relinquished their dream of representing a materio-mystical experience with its locale somewhere outside both life and death. And on this intermediary plane a new image has been cultivated, freed of the "cheville," released from the bondage of excessive symbolism and pure abstractions, and assuming a stark concreteness without which the surrealists believe that there can be no poetry.

See: M. Raymond, *De Baudelaire au surréalisme* (1933); G. Hugnet, "Préface," in *Petite Anthologie du surréalisme* (1934); A. Béguin, *L'Ame romantique et le rêve* (2 vols., 1937); G. E. Lemaître, *From Cubism to Surrealism in French Literature* (1941). "Interview with André Breton," *View*, October–November, 1941, p. 2; M. Nadeau, *Histoire du surréalisme* (1945).

A. B.

Svensson, Jón (1857–1944, Icelandic novelist), was born at Möðruvellir, Hörgárdalur, North Iceland. As a boy he was offered free education in France by Catholic missionaries in Iceland, with a view to making a convert out of him. He became a Jesuit and a teacher in Denmark. Just before the First World War he began to write down the memories of his youth that he had so often told to his pupils with marked success. The result was the book *Nonni* (1913; "Nonni" was his own pet name as a boy), the first in a long series of *Nonni* books that have become extremely popular reading among boys, especially Catholic boys, all over the world. Written originally in German, they have since been translated into many languages. Of the other books in the series, these may be mentioned: *Nonni und Manni* (1914), *Sonnentage* (1915), and *Die Stadt am Meer* (1922).

Svensson wrote with classic and telling simplicity of the adventures of his childhood, of his first trip to Denmark, of his early days in Copenhagen, of excursions about the smiling Danish islands. His subjects are often seemingly commonplace, but he holds the attention of both young and old as if he were telling an adventure story. He had two aims: to educate young readers in good Christian ways and to impart to them some of his own deep-felt love for his distant homeland. Svensson was an extremely popular lecturer in Catholic Europe and elsewhere. As an octogenarian he went on a lecture trip around the world, visiting America and Japan, where he was hailed by the youngsters as if he were a new Hans Christian Andersen. Returning to Europe just before the Second World War, he died in Cologne on November 1, 1944.

See: P. Bourget, "Introduction," *Récits islandais: Nonni et Manni, Nonni et Elis* (1924); H. Hannesson, "Nonni áttræður," *Eimreiðin*, XLIII (1937), 413–431; J. Hrubý, *Nonni, skald z pulnocni výspy* (1939).

S. E.

Světlá, Karolina (pseud. of Johanna Mužáková, née Rottová, 1830–1899, Czech novelist), is the most important woman novelist of her country in the second half of the 19th century. Světlá came from a well-to-do merchant family in Prague and married a Gymnasium teacher. Her pseudonym is the name of her husband's native village in the Ještěd Mountains of northern Bohemia, where many of her novels are placed. Later in life she became a close friend of Jan Neruda (*q.v.*). She died in Prague.

Světlá's work stands on the brink of modern realism. Her novels are either pictures of the Prague bourgeoisie or canvases of country life in the Ještěd Mountains which on a background of vivid folkloristic details depict moral conflicts, especially of women torn between love and duty. In several books Světlá studies religious problems, for which she offers the solution of religious liberalism. Světlá was a strong and even austere moralist, an ardent patriot, a feminist, a liberal thinker, a lover of the mountains and simple peasants. In some ways she can be compared with George Eliot, but her art is frequently marred by farfetched artificial plots, remnants of conventional romanticism, and undigested moralizing. Her best books are the series devoted to the people in the Ještěd Mountains: *Vesnický román* (1867; A Country Story), *Kříž u potoka* (1868; The Cross at the Brook), *Frantina* (1870), and *Nemodlenec* (1873; The Atheist). Her attempts at historical novels, set in the 18th century, are less successful (*e.g., Zvonečková královna,* 1872, The Queen of Bells). She wrote many short stories as well, among which *Hubička* (1871; The Kiss) has served as the basis of the libretto for an opera by Smetana.

See: T. Nováková, *K. Světlá* (1890); L. Čech, *Karolina Světlá* (1891); A. Novák, *Myšlenky a spisovatelé* (1914).

R. W.

Svevo, Italo (pseud. of Ettore Schmitz, 1861–1928, Italian novelist), was born and, except for five years in a German commercial school (1873–1878), educated in Trieste. After working in a bank until 1897, he became a manufacturer and remained in industry in his native city until his death. James Joyce, who taught him English (1906–1914), discovered his talent and called Svevo to the attention of Larbaud (*q.v.*) and Benjamin Crémieux whose praise brought him great recognition in the 20's. From Paris his fame spread to Italy. He left three novels, a group of short stories, and a play. The novels—*Una Vita* (1893), *Senilità* (1898), and *La Coscienza di Zeno* (1923; Eng. tr., *The Confessions of Zeno,* 1930)—are remarkable chiefly for their scrupulous psychological analysis and their use of the stream-of-consciousness technique. Like Zola (*q.v.*), who influenced him, Svevo aims to reproduce life in the smallest and often most tawdry detail; but his self-questioning heroes are closer to those of Dostoevski (*q.v.*) or to the contemporaneous Salavin of Duhamel (*q.v.*). His chief character is always an ineffectual, mediocre man striving to shape his life despite his own lack of will, showing great ingenuity in overcoming absurdly small obstacles but never coming to grips with the real problems. A peculiar mixture of fundamental pessimism and farcical humor, especially notable in the story *Una Burla riuscita* (1928; Eng. tr., *The Hoax,* 1929), marks all of Svevo's work. His simple, dry style often betrays his Austro-Italian ancestry and his bilingual education.

See: F. Sternberg, *L'Opera di Italo Svevo* (1928); "Omaggio a Svevo," *Convegno,* February 25, 1929.

J. O'B.

Svobodová, Růžena (née Čápová, 1868–1920, Czech novelist), was the leading woman fiction writer of her country in the early 20th century. She was born in Mikulovice near Znojmo (southern Moravia), but spent most of her life in Prague. She married the novelist F. X. Svoboda, who had a good reputation among the early Czech realists. Later she became the intimate friend of the critic F. X. Šalda (*q.v.*). She died in Prague.

Mrs. Svobodová began to write books in the atmosphere of later 19th-century naturalism and feminism: her early books, e.g., *Na písčité půdě* (1895; On Sandy Soil), are studies of sensitive, refined women who are crushed by the brutality of men and the stupidity of conventional society. The tone of accusation is strident, the style rhetorical. Later Mrs. Svobodová changed both her outlook and technique very considerably, and her best work was done early in the 20th century. She became less pessimistic and feminist, less preoccupied with the problem of the "misunderstood" woman. Her themes widen, though she still likes to depict the tragedies of sensitive women's souls and their erotic disillusionments. Mrs. Svobodová now preaches a remedy in collective love and sacrifice. She analyzes the fatal consequences of hedonistic aestheticism—she herself never quite escaped its atmosphere—and even attempts metaphysical themes of death, nature, and immortality. The technique has become that of impressionism: there is much of visual metaphor, delicate observation, knowledge and influence of the plastic arts. The style is most elaborately chiseled, ornate, and frequently precious. The novels suffer from her inability to draw the characters of men and to handle large themes. Especially her most ambitious work, *Zahrada irémská* (1921, The Garden of Irem; in six parts, uncompleted), which attempts a symbolic picture of the whole of our civilization, is lifeless and overburdened by unassimilated discussion. *Zamotaná vlákna* (1898; The Twisted Threads) and *Milenky* (1902; Sweethearts) are much better composed, but have sensational and sentimental plots. Mrs. Svobodová is at her best when she writes short stories, and particularly when she can use forms derived from traditional folk art, such as fairy tales, ballads in prose, and legends. *Plameny a plaménky* (1905; Flames and Little Flames), *Marné lásky* (1907; Frustrate Loves), *Posvátné jaro* (1916; Sacred Spring), and *Po svatební hostině* (1916; After the Wedding Feast) are surpassed only by *Černí myslivci* (1908; Black Foresters), a col lection which is unified by its finely described setting in the Bezkydy Mountains of Moravia. The charming childhood reminiscences, *Ráj* (1920; Paradise), remained a fragment.

Mrs. Svobodová was a sensitive, self-conscious artist of great ambitions who unfortunately, in spite of her ethical and social feelings, never escaped the aestheticism of her youth. Her reputation is today under an eclipse, partly because she has been immoderately overpraised by F. X. Šalda, partly because her problems and outlook (the misunderstood woman, admiration for the aristocracy) as well as her frequently affected style seem remote at this time.

See: F. X. Šalda, two essays in *Duše a dílo* (1913) and *In memoriam R. Svobodové* (1921).

R. W.

Swedish literature from 1830 to about 1870 had been one of middle-class liberalism and had reflected, with more or less intensity, the desire for social betterment. But at the end of this period many of the democratic reforms demanded had been carried out; consequently writers turned from material and political questions to the more religious and philosophical, and polite letters became "nobly realistic" or idealistic. The radical tendencies from abroad did not affect profoundly, if at all, such authors as Snoilsky, Wirsén, and Rydberg (*qq.v.*). Snoilsky, poet, aristocrat, and "Sweden's last classicist," continued during the naturalistic agitation of the 80's to treat historical personalities with sympathy and understanding in his usual elegant form. Wirsén, prolific lyrist, sharp critic, sworn conservative, and long secretary of the Swedish Academy, remained until his death (1912) the determined antagonist of naturalism. Rydberg, Hellenic humanist and sponsor of religious liberalism, wrote reflective lyrics in the style of Goethe and made an excellent translation of the first part of *Faust* (1876). But he was, also, Sweden's greatest novelist before Strindberg, and perhaps of all time. Typical of his humanism in prose form is *Vapensmeden* (1891; The Armorer), which deals with religious intolerance during the Reformation. Prominent dramatists of the Rydberg era were Frans Hedberg (1828–1908) and Harald Molander (1858–1900), who was also a novelist and capable theatre director.

These authors tended to preserve at least a modicum of balance and moderation in Swedish letters during the more turbulent "period of the Eighties," as it was called, when native, classical restraint was battling with new, revolutionary ideas from Denmark, Norway, England, and France. Yet the conservative and radical elements remained coexistent, even at the height of the naturalistic revolt, though this movement predominated for several years and prose fiction even threatened to supplant verse as the prevalent mode of expression. The leader of the movement for naked truth and merciless analyses of all modern problems and conditions was, of course, Strindberg (*q.v.*), Sweden's most stimulating and influential—also most irritating—literary genius and her greatest dramatist. His novel *Röda rummet* (1879; Eng. tr., *The Red Room,* 1913), which is generally considered the convenient starting point of "the Eighties," was followed by several powerful, ultrarealistic products, often pathological, the artistry of which was later to be discarded by the restless author himself for a series of provocative historical dramas, superb stories of the common people, and works of a symbolistic, romantic, or expressionistic character. Strindberg is the personified paradox of changes and contradictions—he was in turn an atheist, a Nietzschean, a Christian, an individualist, and a democrat; the variety and quantity of his output are enormous; yet a vital proportion of his work is one constant, often agonizing, confession. His versatility included poetry, but he is much better in prose, and as for genres he is best of all in the drama. Strindberg's literary policy was pursued, in a more subdued manner, by Anne Charlotte Leffler (1849–1892), who dealt primarily with the woman question; by the more gifted but unhappy Victoria Benedictsson (*q.v.*), who with a deeper understanding of social problems treated the same theme, though glorifying marriage, and in a fresh, humorous tone described the life of her native Skåne; and especially by the productive and widely read Geijerstam (*q.v.*), who at first gloomy and terrifying but interesting, dealing with the abnormally psychological and delving in crime, later turned actually domestic and sentimental, as in *Mina pojkar* (1896; Eng. tr., *My Boys,* 1933), or gay and humorous, as in his popular folk plays. Another eminent writer of the period was Tor Hedberg (*q.v.*), poet, critic, and theatre director, whose fondness for soul analysis is represented in the novel *Judas* (1886) and who subsequently wrote a meritorious political drama, *Johan Ulfstjerna* (1907). The transition from the naturalism of the 80's to the neo-romanticism of "the Nineties," so called, is typified by the lyric poet Ola Hansson (*q.v.*), who after portraying in an original manner and with photographic realism the moods of his native Skåne, later, like Strindberg, proclaimed the superman ideal, and plunged into mystical meditations colored by Catholicism. Another poet from the same province, A. U. Bååth (*q.v.*), shared with Hansson a deep sympathy for the oppressed and neglected people of society.

Swedish literature was not long satisfied with the prospects of lurid realism alone. Even lyric poetry, some of it in a realistic vein, could not be wholly suppressed during the 80's, for Sweden's muse is essentially lyric and the foremost masters of Swedish belles-lettres before Strindberg had generally employed verse as their chief medium. So the demand for a more elevated style, whether in verse or prose, for idealism, beauty, imagination, and the sovereign rights of the individual artist were resuscitated during the last decade of the 19th century. Poetry no longer occupied the exclusive position it had formerly held, and Swedish prose fiction and drama were destined in consonance with modern tendencies everywhere to retain, relatively, a more prominent place than before 1880; with the 1890's came an abundance of both verse and prose, and both of exceptional quality. In fact Swedish literature between 1890 and 1930 attains its highest eminence in history, with four contemporary names of first rank—Lagerlöf, Heidenstam, Karlfeldt, and Fröding (*qq.v.*), the last two pure poets, the first three Nobel prize winners. If we add these names—Hallström (*q.v.*), brilliant master of the short story; Levertin (*q.v.*), Heidenstam's talented Jewish friend and collaborator, the authority on the Swedish rococo period, poet, essayist, and noted critic; and Engström (*q.v.*), unique humorist, caricaturist, and inimitable interpreter of the life of farmers and fishermen—we realize that this was Sweden's richest period. Most of these authors have either wholly or in part been translated into English, as have dozens of others, and the fame of Selma Lagerlöf and Strindberg is universal. Lagerlöf is probably the most beloved of all modern Scandinavian authors and, with the understandable exception of Hans Christian Andersen, the most popular of all time. Most readers of good literature are well acquainted with her saga-and-legend milieu, whether of her native Värmland, as in *Gösta Berlings saga* (1891), or of Italy or Jerusalem. Outstanding qualities are her artistic taste and "naïve geniality," as well as a fairy-tale style, with a delicate balance of the real and the unreal that is truly independent of time or space. Besides, she is an undisputed master in her own story technique, and the effect is that of wholesome, moral idealism. This is true also of Heidenstam's work, in which the colorful romanticism of an oriental background, absorption in foreign travel, and later a serene, optimistic humanism and classicism prevail. Heidenstam is both a first-rank poet and a great novelist, and in the latter capacity especially seeks national themes from the era of Charles XII and the middle ages of Sweden to depict, with universal application, the duty, heroism, suffering, and sacrifice of a struggling people. *Karolinerna* (1897–1898; Eng. tr., *The Charles Men,* 1920) has become a "tragic national epos" of Sweden, with the people as heroes led by their hero king, not to victory but defeat. Karlfeldt, native of Dalecarlia and long secretary of the Swedish Academy, has with great vigor and humor immortalized in poetry the beloved scenes of that province and the solid, proud qualities and traditions of its people. In content he can be either gay or serious, and his plastic form and precise, sonorous language place him, in modern Swedish poetry, next to Fröding in artistic accomplishment. As for the latter, poet and noble philosopher par excellence, he is the greatest verse artist that Sweden has produced. Fröding's faithful, almost naturalistic descriptions of the life of the lower classes, his unsurpassed, and probably unsurpassable, rhymes and rhythms, his lyric beauty, and his extraordinary, profound, yet vagabond humor remind one of the immortal Swedish 18th-century bard, Bellman. Fröding was the first Swedish poet to follow the rhythm of the spoken tongue. Burns is said to have been his teacher; but the simplicity, melodic nuances, and general artistry of his poems are peculiarly his own. Many of those localized in Värmland approach the style of the folk song. He is a true humorist, with gaiety and melancholy blended, and has remained popular in all social circles. Insanity marred his later years, and his early death caused great sorrow in Sweden. In 1897 appeared *Folkskollärare John Chronschoughs memoarer* (The Memoirs of Public School Teacher John Chronschough) by August Bondeson (1854–1906). This was an outstanding, highly original classic of Swedish humor, based on the simple life of a country school teacher. Even the brilliance of so many greater literary luminaries did not wholly eclipse its success.

After 1900 there is no definite single trend in Swedish literature. There is no school: each writer seems to go his own individual way—a Swedish characteristic in most aspects of life—while still remaining sensitive to all winds that blow, whether native or foreign. What impresses the student of the period is, first of all, the number of able creative writers: at least 50 more should be mentioned here, not to speak of a score of gifted authors in related fields. We need only name, *e.g.*, the poets and novelists Dan Andersson, Harry Blomberg, Daniel Fallström, Karl Erik Forsslund, Carl Filip Larsson, Axel Lundegård, Moa Martinson, Ture Nerman, Sten Selander, and the humorist Birger Sjöberg (*qq.v.*). Nor does this include the Finnish group, many of whom have written in Swedish. In general, short stories and novels continue to hold a dominant place, dealing realistically and psychologically with all phases and problems of the present day; several authors, such as Didring, Hjalmar Bergman (*qq.v.*), Hedberg, and Söderberg (*q.v.*), have written successful plays; a new generation of lyricists have described the modern city, since Stockholm has now become a world center; and the southernmost province of Skåne has produced two distinguished poets, Ekelund and Österling (*qq.v.*). There is an abundance of good humor, but the prevailing tone, of the prose literature in particular, is one of dark seriousness, pessimism, and disillusionment, with severe attacks on all forms of hypocrisy and social shortcomings. While it reflects Sweden's economic growth and prosperity, it deals preferably with "earth's stepchildren," such as the church, business, politics, America, the First World War, the labor movement, and various cosmopolitan currents, all furnishing backgrounds for fiction, with critical or ironical analyses of life's problems. Many authors localize their best works in their native province or region, as Selma Lagerlöf, Fröding, and Karlfeldt had done. Thus Olof Högberg (*q.v.*) honors Norrland; Vilhelm Moberg and Elin Wägner (*qq.v.*), Småland; G. Ullman (*q.v.*), Halland; Siwertz (*q.v.*), Stockholm; and the Skåne poets just mentioned extol the beauties of that fertile province. There has developed a special, broad, home-region cult, in Swedish called *hembygdsdikt*, with faithful reproductions, in verse and prose, of the character of the people, local nature scenes, and the traditions of the author's environment.

From 1900 to 1914, says a Danish critic, a certain restlessness prevailed in Swedish letters, but through the softening influence of the 90's their skepticism and realism became more refined and their form more aesthetic. This is illustrated by the works of Söderberg, who first interprets the generation's gloom in the autobiographical novel *Martin Bircks ungdom* (1901; Eng. tr., *Martin Birck's Youth*, 1930). He then turns, with greater success, to short stories, which are brief, elegant masterpieces in plastic, perfected prose, with biting sarcasm hurled at the hypocrisies of sex and religion. Sometimes he can create a really comic scene, as in *Kyrkoherdens kor* (1903; The Parson's Cows). He has received impressions from J. P. Jacobsen and Anatole France (*qq.v.*), whereas his more bitter and intensive contemporary in the same field, Hallström, draws inspiration from Schopenhauer. Equally skeptic and resigned is Bo Bergman (*q.v.*), poet and short-story writer, to whom life is a hopeless existence, but who is more intimate and melancholy. In his fiction he deals, as so many of his confreres do, with less fortunate characters and the tragic incidents of everyday life and in an exquisite manner has reproduced the "fine poetic moods of beautiful Stockholm." Johan Henning Berger (*q.v.*), impressionistic portrayer of big-city life, has located some of his novels among the struggling Swedish immigrants of America, as *Bendel & C:o.* (1910). Ossiannilsson (*q.v.*), poet and prose writer, lover of strong, colorful language and historical supermen, is the militant champion of social democracy, yet he sensationally exposes political conditions and attacks class hatred and party discipline, as in *Barbarskogen* (1908; The Barbarian Forest). He is a revolutionary but patriotic crusader. In 1906 appeared the monumental research novel *Den stora vreden* (The Great Wrath). by Högberg. It is a remarkable historical culture epos, on broad lines, of the Norrland region during the reign of Charles XI and Charles XII. It is a battle between the common people, with their legends and beliefs, on one hand and the ruling clergy and officials on the other. Its *Tendenz* is wholly democratic—the greatest good for the greatest number. Sven Lidman (*q.v.*) began as an author of erotic poems, passed through a stage in which a whole series of novels, in a national, conservative vein, glorified the Silfverstååhl family, and finally entered a religious period, writing novels with penetrating psychology and artistic maturity. Siwertz, an interesting, intellectual artist, was born the same year as Lidman, Elin Wägner, and Nordström (*q.v.*) and is one of the best stylists among the younger Swedish writers. He too made his debut with a collection of poems, but won real distinction in prose fiction, most of it localized about Lake Mälar, as *Mälarpirater*

(1911; Mälar Pirates), a charming, light-hearted, boys' book, like *Tom Sawyer.* Some of his work utilizes the dark background of the First World War, but in America he is best known for his strong, two-volume novel *Selambs* (1920; Eng. tr., *Downstream,* 1923), which exposes the selfishness of wealth. Nordström is a prose-epic portrayer of Norrland, and in particular Ångermanland, the region first made popular, in a more primitive, romantic manner, by Pelle Molin (1864–1896). Nordström is "almost too heavily realistic" in his art, but his descriptions, notably of the fishermen, are based on personal experience. Elin Wägner, now a member of the Swedish Academy, is the good-humored sponsor of the modern woman, for whose moral and social independence she has consistently fought. She has also described the post-bellum Vienna and the Ruhr Occupation. Didring, author of the Norrland drama *Midnattssol* (1897; Midnight Sun), has written a significant novel trilogy, *Malm* (1914–1919; Ore), describing the building of the Lapland railway to the Norwegian border, and as master of dialogue and technique is one of the most successful of modern Swedish dramatists. Hjalmar Bergman, who started his literary career in 1905 with a romantic drama on the Holy Virgin, soon turned to grotesque but human prose pictures of small-town life in Sweden, especially Bergslagen. His greatest success is *Markurells i Wadköping* (1919; Eng. tr., *God's Orchid,* 1924). A play based on this novel is said to be "the generation's best [Swedish] contribution to the drama," and his comedy *Swedenhielms* (1925; The Swedenhielm Family) has been hailed as a real "theatrical triumph." He is the representative of humor and unrestrained fantasy. In lyric poetry Ekelund and Österling were the foremost representatives during the first two decades of the 20th century. Ekelund, author of aphorisms of a pure, severe character, reveals a personality in the style of the antique, while Österling, as an idyllic realist, has a milder, more human attitude of life. Both are influenced by the traditions of their native province, Skåne.

Since the beginning of the First World War, when many old values disappeared, the central idea in Swedish fiction, in so far as there is any, has been to portray the everyday life of the present. This is seen, *e.g.,* in the philosophical "prose poem" *Hemmabyarna* (1916; The Home Villages) by Hans Larsson (*q.v.*), where the author finds comfort for the future in reminiscences of youth and the contemplation of his native Skåne. Inspired by social, political, and moral ideas, many authors have presented and interpreted with talent and artistry not only Swedish but world events and problems. Gustaf Hellström (*q.v.*), the author of profound discussion-novels, living in Paris and London, becomes Sweden's foremost foreign correspondent; Marika Stjernstedt (*q.v.*), who specializes in the modern woman's love and personality problems, writes about France; Anna Lenah Elgström (1884–), fiction writer, treats of America. Martin Koch (*q.v.*) becomes a pioneer of proletarian literature, with powerful descriptions of labor milieus; Fabian Månsson (1872–1938) discusses peoples' movements and writes heavily documented historical narratives; Vilhelm Moberg produces intensive, boldly realistic, and unforgettable novels the scenes of which are laid in Småland; Agnes von Krusenstjerna (*q.v.*) introduces Freudian psychiatry and "sexual romanticism"; and Valdemar Hammenhög (1902–) prefers to describe the workmen bourgeoisie. Other talented prose writers are Harald Beijer (1896–); Frans Bengtsson (*q.v.*), also a poet, who has written an excellent work on Charles XII; Karin Boye (*q.v.*), another poet of ability; Dagmar Edquist (1904–); Olof Hedberg (1899–); Harry Martinson (*q.v.*); Ivan Oljelund (1892–); Ivar Lo-Johansson (1901–); Mathilda Malling (1864–1942); Martin Gunnar Serner (1886–), a prolific novelist who writes under the pseudonym Frank Heller; and Hazze Zetterström (1877–1946), editor and humorist.

During the last generation Swedish poetry, as intimated above, has had to retreat somewhat before the novel, but still it has exhibited remarkable lyric strength. The most original of the younger lyrists, and the leading representative in the 1920's, is Pär Lagerkvist (*q.v.*), who has written metaphysical symbol-poetry in an expressionistic technique. He has also attempted to widen the scope of the drama, believing it should be more imaginative. Erik Blomberg (*q.v.*), journalist and translator of French, German, and English verse, has interpreted the human spirit and defiance à la Lagerkvist; G. M. Silfverstolpe (*q.v.*) has paid special homage to family life; Karl Asplund represents the poetry of love and the sea; Bertil Malmberg (*q.v.*) sounds the contrasts between reality and the world of beauty; Erik Lindorm (1889–1941), a socialist agitator, has described the oppressed poor of Stockholm; the strongly suggestive, musical verse of Hjalmar Gullberg (*q.v.*), characterized by piety, tenderness, and revolt, is said to have had considerable influence since 1930; Ragnar Jändel (*q.v.*) is the representative of religious tension among proletarian poets; Artur Lundkvist (1906–) and Harry Martinson are the leaders of the labor lyricists who are reputed to have made a sensational entree at the end of the 1930's. Both these men delve into sexual romanticism culminating in a form of primitivism. The modern Swedish output in lyric poetry is large and varied, though it may be too early to judge its permanent value.

Remarkable, also, is the quality and quantity of critical studies and literary histories written in Sweden between 1870 and 1940. And still more noteworthy, perhaps, is the high standard of literary reviews maintained by the daily press as well as the wide scope of subjects and countries covered by these reviews. Dramatic criticism—and Sweden has since Strindberg produced a number of highly successful plays not to speak of translations and presentations of foreign works—has ever remained thorough and sympathetic. Here we can mention only a few names of the outstanding Swedish critics and literary historians: Ruben Gustafsson Berg (1876–), Anton Blanck (1881–), Fredrik Böök (1883–), Gunnar Castrén (1878–), Nils Erdmann (1860–), Olof Otto Urban von Feilitzen (1834–1913), Torsten Fogelqvist (*q.v.*), Yrjö Hirn (1870-), Martin Lamm (1880–), John Landquist (1881–, generally regarded as the successor to Levertin), Johan Mortensen (1864–1940), Henrik Schück (1855–, the Nestor of the group), the brothers Torsten and Werner Söderhjelm (1879–1908 and 1859–1931, respectively), Sven Stolpe (1905–), Otto Sylwan (1864–), Fredrik Vetterlund (1865–, Karl J. Warburg (1852–1918), and E. H. G. Wrangel (1863–1940). Of these Castrén, Hirn, and the Söderhjelms are, or were, politically, Finns. To the above list should be added the name of the late Archbishop Nathan Söderblom (1866–1931), liberal author in the field of religious scholarship, and that of Ellen Key (*q.v.*), feminist and renowned writer on social topics.

Brief mention only can be made here of the rich Swedish creative literature of Finland. Zacharias Topelius (1818–1898) continued to publish immortal children's stories after 1870; Karl August Tavaststjerna (1860–1898) wrote fresh, impressionistic lyrics based on his own times; Hjalmar Procopé (1868–1927) was an acknowledged poet of rank; Bertil Gripenberg (*q.v.*) has translated Oscar Wilde; Harald Hornborg (1890–) has written novels with historical background; Runar Schildt (1888–1923) contributed short stories and dramas; Jarl Hemmer (*q.v.*), a poet, has written a powerful novel based on the Finnish civil war, *En man och hans samvete,* (1931), which has been translated as *A Fool of Faith* (1935); the novels of Sally Salminen (1906–), *Katrina* (1937) and *Mariana* (1940), are well known in America; and Mikael Lybeck (1864–1925) distinguished himself as poet, novelist, and dramatist.

See: *Sveriges national-litteratur,* Vols. XV-XXX (1910–1922); Fredrik Böök, *Sveriges moderna litteratur* (1921), also published as Vol. III of Otto Sylwan, ed., *Svenska litteraturens historia* (1919–1921); *Nordisk familjebok* (23 vols., 1923–1937); Henrik Schück and Karl Warburg, *Illustrerad svensk litteraturhistoria* (7 vols., 1926–1932); H. G. Topsöe-Jensen, *Scandinavian Literature from Brandes to Our Day* (1929); *Svensk uppslagsbok* (30 vols., 1930–1937).

A. B. B.

Świętochowski, Aleksander (1849–1938, Polish publicist, historian, and dramatist), was born at Stoczek, a small town in the province of Podlasie, Russian Poland, famous as the scene of an important military victory by Polish peasants in 1831. In 1866 he entered the Szkoła Główna in Warsaw and was graduated from this institution, along with Sienkiewicz (*q.v.*), in 1870, after it had been reorganized as a Russian university. On graduation he became at once a coeditor of the progressive journal *Przegląd tygodniowy* (Weekly Review; *see* Polish literature) and continued to contribute to this even during his absence from Warsaw (1874–1876) as a student of philosophy in Leipzig. Świętochowski was convinced, partly as a result of his studies at home and abroad, partly by the spectacle of collapse at home which followed in the wake of the late insurrection (1863), that revolutionary romanticism, which had sustained the Polish nation since the Partitions, had demonstrated its bankruptcy. Comtian positivism seemed to offer a more effective program, and Świętochowski became the chief apostle in Poland of this philosophy. First by way of the *Przegląd,* later (after 1881) through his own journal *Prawda* (Truth), he waged ruthless warfare on everything that had its roots in the emotions, preaching *urbi et orbi* a gospel of science and "organic work." Away with politics, down with nationalism, was his slogan, let us be realists and citizens of the world. Of his hundreds of polemical exhortations, three may be mentioned as outstanding: "Pasożyty literackie" (1871; Literary Parasites) and "Pleśń społeczna i literacka" (1871; Social and Literary Moldiness), both of which appeared in *Przegląd piśmiennictwa polskiego* (A Review of Polish Writing), and the celebrated call to "Manchesterism" (i.e., dedication of the national energy to economic and social reform rather than to parliamentarianism), "Nasze drogi polityczne" (1876; Our Course Politically), which appeared in the *Przegląd*.

Świętochowski tried his hand at the novel and also the drama, but without success. His failure as a dramatist, notably in the long trilogy *Duchy* (1905; The Spirits), in which he undertook to crystallize man's whole vast struggle from darkness into light, was due to the fact that he was a teacher and not an artist. As a historian, however, Świętochowski achieved conspicuous success with his great *Historja chłopów* (1925–1928; History of the Peasants).

Świętochowski was regarded by his contemporaries, most of whom he outlived, as the very "herald of truth." His keenness and utter ruthlessness in polemic, his passion and skill in advocacy, above all his brilliance as a writer, enabled him to achieve a virtual tyranny over the mind of his generation. At the end of his long life, however, in a swan song bitterly reactionary in its implications, *Genealogja teraźniejszości* (1936; Genealogy of the Present), he repudiated much of his own life's work. Too long withdrawal from the world, coupled with inability to adjust himself to new times, had brought him to the point of claiming for himself the right of sole legislator for mankind and of seeing in the past, as in the work of others, only evil—a blunder which avenged itself on Świętochowski's own work and reputation.

See: Z. Dębicki, *Portrety*, I (1927), 9–32; W. Feldman, *Dzieje polskiej myśli politycznej w okresie porozbiorowym* (1914–1920), pp. 152 ff.; Z. Szwiejkowski, "Alexander Świętochowski," *Slavonic Year-Book*, XIX (1939–1940), 228–236.

W. J. R.

Swiss literature in Alamannic. That part of the population of Switzerland which makes up its Germanic element (approximately three fourths of the total) is bilingual. For the last 200 years their educational system has been based on German, while the colloquial language, the vernacular, is Alamannic or Schwyzertütsch (Swiss-German), which to the average German is just as unintelligible as Luxemburgish, Flemish, and Netherlandish. While many Swiss authors have been prominent in German literature, there has always been a homespun Alamannic literature for home consumption. Primarily supported by the *Heimatschutz* movement, it was favored in its development by several strong factors—the realistic trend in world literature, the deep structural gulf between standard German and the vernacular, the democratic structure of Swiss society where all classes use only the "dialect" in informal conversation. A political factor, opposition to German National Socialism, was added in 1933. A movement to make Alamannic the first of the four administrative languages of Switzerland, replacing German, was launched in 1936 by Emil Baer in his book *Alemannisch, die Rettung der eidgenössischen Seele*. Other important publications supporting this Alamannic movement are Emil Baer and Arthur Baur, *Schribed wien er reded* (1937); Arthur Baur, *Praktische Sprachlehre des Schweizerdeutschen* (2d ed., 1941); Adolf Guggenbühl, *Warum nicht Schweizerdeutsch?* (2d ed., 1937). The movement was and still is opposed by those who fear it might lead to extreme provincialism and deprive the Swiss intellectuals of many opportunities which they now enjoy. A fairly complete account of the lively discussion carried on in the press was given in the *Mitteilungen des deutschschweizerischen Sprachvereins* of 1936 and the following years (see also *Schweizerische Hochschulzeitung*, Vol. XI 1937, pp. 116–154). Professor Eugen Dieth and Catharina Hösli-Streiff have been leading a scientific-linguistic movement called *Schwyzertütsch, Bund zur Pflege der schweizerdeutschen Dialekte*. A monthly magazine for popularization of Alamannic literature, *Schwyzerlüt*, was founded by Dr. G. Schmid at Fribourg in 1939.

Swiss-German literary activities went on independently of the political movement, which itself was possible only because there had been a flourishing Alamannic literature long before. Some Swiss authors who obtained international reputations by their German writings, both in prose and verse form, have in addition occasionally cultivated their "home dialect" for home consumption, *e.g.*, Jakob Burckhardt (1818–1897), Adolf Frey (1855–1920), Otto von Greyerz (1863–1940), all three professional scholars, and Alfred Huggenberger (1867–) and Dominik Müller (pseud. of Paul Schmitz, 1871–). Today no genuine Swiss writer can afford to be out of touch with his own people, and this contact is now more than ever brought about through the use of the "home dialect." In addition to the writers who only occasionally express themselves in their native language, there is an impressive array of intellectual leaders who have deliberately foregone tempting opportunities more international in scope for the less glamorous role of "dialect writers" in the home service. Among these are August Corrodi (1826–1885), who made translations into Swiss from English (the songs of Robert Burns) and from Latin (the *Mostellaria* of Plautus), Rudolf von Tavel (1866–1934), Meinrad Lienert (1865–1933), Zyböri (pseud. of Theodor Bucher, 1868–1937), Simon Gfeller (1868–1943), Josef Reinhart (1875–), Traugott Meyer (1895–), Oskar Eberle (1902–), and T. J. Felix (1900–). In *Die Mundartdichtung der deutschen Schweiz* (1924) Otto von Greyerz discusses the works of 142 recent authors, while G. Schmid's bibliography (*Schwyzerlüt,* Vol. III, 1940–1941, pp. 8–51) lists 219 names. The very existence of these literary patriots and their high significance in the picture of intellectual Switzerland would have completely escaped the eyes of foreign observers had it not been for Josef Nadler (1884–), who in his *Literaturgeschichte der deutschen Schweiz* (1932) gives several strikingly accurate characterizations.

A collection of earlier writings, mostly poetry, was published by Otto Sutermeister (1832–1901) in *Schwyzer-Dütsch: Mundartliche Literatur der Neuzeit in ihren vorzüglichsten Vertretern* (1882–1890), 83 booklets with biographical notes. Selections of lyric poetry were presented by Lesezirkel Hottingen, *Aus allen Gauen* (1896) and *Schwyzerländli* (1915); Otto von Greyerz, *Im Röseligarte* (6 vols., 1908–1912), Swiss folk songs; Robert Faesi, *Die Ernte schweizerischer Lyrik* (1928); Adolf Guggenbühl and Georg Thürer, *Schwyzer Meie* (1938), selections of 50 authors with biographical notes.

Outstanding lyric poets are Meinrad Lienert and Traugott Meyer. The poems of Meinrad Lienert deal with central Switzerland and its history. His collection *'s Schwäbelpfyffli* (3 vols., 1913), by which the dialect was definitely established as a language fit for the best type of poetry, is one large lyric portrait consisting of numerous single songs centering around the same object—his own people. Traugott Meyer (*Mueterguet,* 1929; *Lueg und los,* 1932; *Im Läben inn,* 1935) differs from Meinrad Lienert by a more accented interest in contemporary social problems. But with his sympathy for living and suffering fellow creatures he combines a deep love for nature which he expresses with exceptional skill, making wide use of onomatopoeia. His language is original, free of foreign patterns, genuinely Swiss, and untranslatable. Both Meinrad Lienert and Traugott Meyer have also published well-liked short stories and novels.

Masters in storytelling are Josef Reinhart, with a large number of publications (short stories and novels); Simon Gfeller (1868–1943); Karl Grunder (1880–); Emil Balmer (1890–); and T. J. Felix (*Es mäntschelet,* 1939). All of them have also produced plays, and Josef Reinhart enjoys a high reputation as a lyric poet. The greatest of all the prose writers is Rudolf von Tavel, a Bernese patrician. He is a master of the historical novel in which 500 years of Bernese history are portrayed in an unhurried style with an attitude of both pride and criticism towards the events described. Outstanding among his 15 great novels is *Ring i der Chetti* (1931; Links in the Chain), a colossal picture of 15th-century Bern.

The artistic level of dramatic production, originally limited to comedy, was considerably raised by Otto von Greyerz, who wrote humorous plays still popular today. The younger playwrights and stage managers, Cäsar von Arx (1895–) and Oskar Eberle, who influenced theatrical life decisively, use the dialect even for dramatic composition of serious character.

See: Otto von Greyerz, "Alemannische Mundartliteratur," in P. Merker and W. Stammler, *Reallexikon der deutschen Literaturgeschichte,* I (1925–1926), 9–16; A. Senn, "Verhältnis von Mundart und Schriftsprache in der deutschen Schweiz," *Journal of English and Germanic Philology,* XXXIV (1935), 42–58; A. Senn, "Rudolf von Tavels historische Romane," *Monatshefte für deutschen Unterricht,* XXXVII (1945), 565–570.

A. Se.

Swiss literature in French, *see* Amiel, Henri Frédéric; Ramuz, Charles Ferdinand.

Swiss literature in German, *see* Federer, Heinrich; Keller, Gottfried; Meyer, Conrad Ferdinand; Schaffner, Jakob; Spitteler, Carl; Steffen, Albert.

symbolism, *see* French symbolism.

Szabó Dezső (1879–1945, Hungarian novelist, writer of short stories, essayist, and pamphleteer), was born in Kolozsvár, educated in his home town and in Budapest. For many years he was a professor of literature in various secondary schools in the provinces; but from his youth he was also devoted to creative work and eventually gave up professional teaching. For a time the attention of the reading public of the nation was centered upon him. Szabó was also an excellent orator

His first essays and stories were published by *Nyugat* (West), but his irascible disposition soon put an end to this affiliation. He was always fond of French romantic literature, especially of Victor Hugo; he visited Paris and other parts of France on several occasions. As a raconteur and as a pamphleteer Szabó was spectacular; undisciplined and ridden with malice and distortion, he was capable of brilliance. In recent years his influence has diminished considerably. Some of his work has been translated into Czech and Rumanian.

After the end of the First World War, Hungary's position was desperate. Szabó, a Transylvanian by birth, deeply attached to the folkways of this region of Hungary which was included in enlarged Rumania, decided to write as the conscience of a mutilated Hungary. With the unabashed freedom of a frenzied romanticist he protested against everything that he considered unfair or criminal in relation to the destiny of the Hungarian nation. To outsiders he may have been incomprehensible, but not to many Hungarians. In his verbose yet dynamic novels, *e.g., Az elsodort falú* (1919; The Lost Village), *Csodálatos élet* (1921; Wondrous Life), *Segitség* (1925; Help), *Karácsony Kolozsvárt* (1932; Christmas in Kolozsvár), in his volumes of short stories, *e.g., Napló és elbeszélések* (1918; Diary and Stories), *Mesék a kacagó emberről* (1919; Tales about the Laughing Man), and in his erudite though wordy essays, *e.g., Tanulmányok és jegyzetek* (1920; Essays and Notes), *Egyenes úton* (1920; The Straight Road)—in all these one faces a writer whose purpose evidently was to be a Hungarian literary Savonarola. Szabó was willing to jeopardize his security for his convictions. His impulses and his ideas were thrown with uncompromising vigor into the turmoil of post-war Hungary. Bad taste and fragmentary poetry, melodramatic chaos and clarified truth, bitterness and an epigrammatizing hatred, nihilism and an eudaemonistic realization of the spirit, anxiety and certainty, prejudice and objectivity, mingle in the works of Szabó. All this explains the structural imperfection of his art, and also its controversial character.

See: J. Reményi, "Dezső Szabó, Hungarian Novelist and Pamphleteer," *Slavonic Review*, XXIV (1946), 105–109.

J. R.

T

Taine, Hippolyte (1828–1893, French critic and historian), born in Vouziers, was privately taught at home as a precocious child and then sent to school in Paris at 13, became the number one student of the entering class of 1848 at the Ecole Normale Supérieure, and remained the rest of his life a scholar-critic, perhaps the ranking one of his generation. In philosophy, his first interest (he composed a long essay on human destiny at 20), he was too unorthodox and perhaps too brilliant for the elders in power, but finally satisfied academic requirements by a doctoral thesis on the poetry of La Fontaine—his first philosophizing about literature. He received no early teaching appointment commensurate with his great talents, turned more and more to writing, was famous at 30. Articles on English literature (begun in 1856) became the well-known *Histoire de la littérature anglaise* (1864). An important initial collection of *Essais de critique et d'histoire* appeared in 1858. In 1864 he was made professor of aesthetics and the history of art at the Ecole des Beaux Arts and continued to teach there successfully for 20 years. In *De l'intelligence* (1870, April) he went back to his first love, philosophy—and psychology; then, shocked by French disasters of 1870–1871, he started to apply his analytic methods to the history of his own country and devoted much of the remaining 20 years of his life to *Les Origines de la France contemporaine* (1876–1893). He was given the orthodox blessing of membership in the French Academy at 50 (1878), but his views, in the *Origines,* offended both conservatives and radicals, and one has the impression concerning his final years of "an increasing moral solitude." Always fond of nature, he withdrew more and more to his estate by the mountain lake of Annecy; he was buried, as he had directed, on a secluded hill above this lake.

There was more warmth in the personality of Taine than he and his family have been inclined to reveal. He had attentive, admiring friends. Letters to his family show a tender husband and father. For years before his marriage (at 40) he was devoted to Elise Krinitz, woman novelist, who greatly loved him and undoubtedly influenced his earlier writings; Taine's family insisted upon keeping from the public the 400 letters he had written her (see J. Wright, *Camille Selden,*

1931). An autobiographical novel (*Etienne Mayran*, written about 1861, published 1909), cut short by Taine apparently because he felt he was telling too much, shows an adolescent of amazing will power, vitality, intellectual curiosity; at the point where the story breaks off the young Etienne is beginning "to see an order in all things." This is the same Taine who called a Beethoven sonata as beautiful as a syllogism.

Taine's doctrine is a direct result of his training and temperament—and thus to explain some part of him in terms of his circumstances is to acknowledge validity in his relativism. He follows Hegel, and less directly but quite definitely Spinoza; his essential views are already clearly stated in the preface to the first edition of the *Essais* of 1858 and exemplified in such an article of this early collection as "M. Troplong et M. de Montalembert." The most famous specimen of deterministic generalizations is the introduction to the *Histoire de la littérature anglaise* (Books are products). Already in the *Philosophes français du XIXe siècle* (1857) a vision of an ultimately realized cosmic unity (the Eternal Axiom is pronounced) is offered with something of the fervor of the Hebrew prophets, and the same note is struck even in the later somewhat cynical *Vie et opinions de Graindorge* (1867). At such moments Taine burns with an ardor that makes one forget the relentlessness of the systematizer; he appears as a very authentic *poète de la raison*. A man of this power is likely to dominate contemporaries. Taine did. Twentieth-century France has naturally not remained under the direct spell, but in 1928, the centennial year, the consensus of Paris reviews was that the Taine influence even where no longer identified as his was still all pervading. He has recently been opposed by the American scholar Albert Guérard (*Literature and Society*, 1935) and by the Italian critic Croce (*History as the Story of Liberty*, 1941).

See: V. Giraud, *Essai sur Taine* (1901); A. Chevrillon, *Taine; formation de sa pensée* (1932); M. Leroy, *Taine* (1933); K. de Schaedryver, *Taine; essai sur l'unité de sa pensée* (1938).

H. S.

Tamayo y Baus, Manuel (1829–1898, Spanish playwright), born in Madrid, came of a family of actors and was married to the niece of the great actor Isidoro Máiquez. He wrote a large number of plays prior to 1870. At that time he gave up the stage, becoming librarian first of San Isidro and later of the National Library.

Tamayo was a dramatist of transition, typical of the swing from romanticism to realism. He never recovered from a marked tendency toward sentimentality. His first works, of little note, were translations and adaptations of foreign plays. Later in his career he adapted Schiller's *Kabale und Liebe* and *Die Jungfrau von Orleans*. His early original plays were of the romantic-historical variety then in vogue. *Locura de amor* (prose, 1855) for example, was a successful dramatic treatment of Queen Juana la Loca's sad life.

The effort in France just before the mid-19th century to renew the classic tragedy had its repercussions in Spain. Tamayo's tribute was *Virginia* (1853), which the poet Quintana judged the best of all Spanish tragedies. From 1856 onward Tamayo devoted himself to contemporary problems, to social or thesis plays. *La bola de nieve* (verse, 1856) dramatizes the evils of jealousy. *Lo positivo* (1862), suggested by Léon Laya's *Le Duc Job*, teaches the not very new lesson that love and virtue are more important in marriage than money. *Lances de honor* (1863) attacks the duel. *Los hombres de bien* (1870) suggests that society is over-tolerant toward well-placed evildoers.

Un drama nuevo (1867; Eng. tr., *A New Drama*, 1915) is generally considered Tamayo's masterpiece. A play within a play, it involves Shakespeare in a less than graceful role. Alas! poor Yorick, as an old and jealous husband, tears his passion into more than tatters. There is, however, real intensity beneath the fustian rhetoric, and Tamayo's contemporaries liked melodramatic declamation. Taste has changed, and Tamayo was very much of his time and his milieu. He had real dramatic gifts, and his best scenes are highly effective. He was a man of the theatre who knew his business, a capable and workmanlike dramatist, not a great one. In religion and politics he was a traditionalist, and he always championed good bourgeois virtues.

See: E. Cotarelo y Mori, "Don Manuel Tamayo y Baus," in *Estudios de historia literaria de España* (1901), pp. 363–403; N. Siscars y Salvadó, *Don Manuel Tamayo y Baus; estudio criticobiográfico* (1906).

N. B. A.

Tarde, Gabriel (born Gabriel de Tarde, 1843–1904, French sociologist and philosopher), was long a magistrate in his native town of Sarlat, Dordogne. Several studies in criminology and penology earned him the post of director of criminal statistics at the Ministry of Justice in Paris (1894). Very early, however, Tarde's interest had extended to sociology proper. A series of brilliant works (*Les Lois de l'imitation,* 1890, Eng. tr., *The Laws of Imitation,* 1903; *Les Transformations du droit,* 1892; *La Logique sociale,* 1893; *L'Opposition universelle,* 1897; *Les Lois sociales,* 1898, Eng. tr., *Social Laws,* 1899; *Les Transformations du pouvoir,* 1899) brought about his appointment as a professor in the Collège de France (1899). During his short tenure two more books appeared (*L'Opinion et la foule,* 1901; *Psychologie économique,* 2 vols., 1902).

The almost exact antithesis of Emile Durkheim's (*q.v.*) sociology, that of Tarde remains undogmatic and atomistic. He does not admit of the "social fact" as a supra-individual entity and relies on the laws of "interpsychology" to explain all human relationships. The most fundamental of these laws is that of imitation. Men imitate each other and thereby modify each other. Traditions descend through the ages and fashions sweep throughout space in waves of influence which are subtly "transformed" in proportion as they unfold. When two or more "opposite" waves meet violently, the individual, confronted with a new set of circumstances, adjusts himself by means of an "invention" which is imitated in turn and starts on its course as a social phenomenon. Such, in fact, is Tarde's faith in the ability of the human mind to effect peaceful "adaptations" that a curious utopia of his, written in his youth and posthumously published (*Fragment d'histoire future,* 1904; Eng. tr., *Underground Man,* 1905), envisions an ideal society resting on disinterested love and wholly freed from coercion.

See: Alexandre Lacassagne, Alexis Bertrand, and Nicolas Vaschide, "A la mémoire de Gabriel Tarde," *Archives d'anthropologie criminelle,* XIX (1904), 501–536, 623–660 (contains also the first printing of *Fragment d'histoire future,* pp. 565–621); Célestin Bouglé, "Un Sociologue individualiste: Gabriel Tarde," *Revue de Paris,* Année XII (1905), Tome III, pp. 284–316; Amédée Matagrin, *La Philosophie sociale de Gabriel Tarde* (1910); Maurice Roche-Agussol, "Tarde et l'économie psychologique," *Revue d'histoire économique et sociale,* XIV (1926), 68–114, 273–319.

J.-A. B.

Teirlinck, Herman (1879–, Flemish short-story writer, novelist, and playwright), was born at St. Jans Molenbeek, a part of Brussels. He attended school there, was employed for a time in the municipal department of fine arts, taught Dutch literature in various schools, was manager of a furniture factory, became director of the Institute of Decorative Arts in Brussels, and was appointed by young King Albert his private counselor on matters of art and science. He made his debut as a writer with *De wonderbare Wereld* (1902; The Wondrous World), a collection of three stories of Flemish village life, which was followed by *Het stille Gesternte* (1903; The Still Constellation). Teirlinck did not know village life as does a man who is born and bred on the land. He wove somber and fantastic mysteries around the lives of these primitive souls. These tales have indeed a strange fascination, but lack the convincing power of the village tales by Stijn Streuvels (*q.v.*). From these he turned to his native element in *Het Bedrijf van den Kwade* (1904; The Demon in Action), in which Brussels is the setting of the plot. In *Zon* (1906; Sun) he revealed himself as an impressionist artist of the first order, a word painter of landscape, still life, and interiors closely akin to the old masters of the Dutch school. But his masterpiece, by common consent, is *Mijnheer Serjanszoon* (1908), an evocation of the 18th-century virtuoso: hedonist, aesthete, philanderer, quixotic victim of his love of beauty. Teirlinck's subtle and somewhat mannered style eminently fits the story of this *précieux* character. Then followed *Het ivoren Aapje* (1909; The Ivory Monkey), a novel of Brussels manners portraying the cosmopolitan life of a great city with all its feverish turmoil and its many sorts and conditions of men. It is perhaps this multifarious setting that creates in the reader a sense of bewilderment and incoherence. Teirlinck is an emotional observer devoid of the contemplative calm that can embrace wide vistas. His attention is constantly shifting and eagerly seizes upon each picturesque detail, so that his work lacks massiveness and structure. It is miniature art. That is why he is at his best as a teller of relatively short stories, such as *Johan Doxa* (1917). A gentle irony at play with emotion is the charm of this fine, tragic tale.

In the period following the First World War, Teirlinck turned to the writing of plays. *De vertraagde Film* (1921; Slow-Motion Picture) is enacted under water. The actors are but two: he and she, lovers who have sought death by drowning with the little child whose birth has brought disgrace upon them. During the few minutes that they struggle in the water their past existence, with its joys and sorrows, looms up before them. And reliving their lives, they want to go on living. The child that was the link between them is dead. The two who wanted to die because they could not renounce one another escape death and each other and part as strangers. They return to the city whose turmoil has not been disturbed by the little drama they have enacted. Here is influence of Maeterlinck (*q.v.*), but also, as the title suggests, of the motion pictures. Teirlinck is an innovator and a seeker of new modes of stage art. In *Ik Dien* (1924; I Serve), a dramatization of the Beatrice legend about the runaway nun who, after a life of debauch, returns as a penitent to her convent, medieval miracle play and stage effects from the movies are skillfully combined into a modern drama of great force and suggestive power.

See: A. de Ridder, *La Littérature flamande contemporaine* (1923).

A. J. B.

Teixeira de Pascoais, Joaquim (pseud. of Joaquim Pereira Teixeira de Vasconcelos, 1879–, Portuguese poet), was born in Gatão, Trás-os-Montes, on the river Támega, in the shadow of the Serra do Marão in northern Portugal, and this geography is one of the keys to an understanding of his work. A member of a noble family, he was educated in the University of Coimbra, where he studied law and established intimate contacts with the writers of the period. He has traveled in Spain, France, and England and delivered lectures in Madrid and Barcelona. He divides his time between the ancestral home where he was born and Lisbon, where he holds interesting *tertulias* attended by artists and intellectuals.

When Pascoais produced his first book of poems, *Sempre* (1897; Always), the reigning poetic mood was represented by two very significant books which had appeared five years before—*Só* (Alone) of António Nobre (*q.v.*) and *Os simples* (The Simple Ones) of Guerra Junqueiro (*q.v.*). These, with *Oaristos* (1890) of Eugénio de Castro (*q.v.*), and despite their differing techniques, constitute the high-water mark of the Parnassian and symbolist movements in Portuguese literature. The *Terra proïbida* (1899; Forbidden Land) of Pascoais and his poems "Jesus e Pan" (1903; Jesus and Pan) and "Para a luz" (1904; Towards the Light) continue to reflect the aesthetic preoccupation with form associated with the above tendencies, although from time to time a verse presages his later, more truly characteristic thought. *Vida etérea* (1906; Ethereal Life) is the book in which is clearly seen what Pascoais is going to represent in contemporary poetry. Still showing the expressive elegance of Junqueiro and Eugénio de Castro and a preoccupation with the mystery of his own being and of the exterior world, he makes in fact a clear new start. Two lines reveal the book's dual inspiration, "May our flesh be strengthened by the bright sun of Homer" and "May the sweet and Christian light of the moon move our spirit." The shadows which fill his soul terrify him; anguish sharpens perception of multiple appearances in relation to the unity of being. Human beings and things are only impulses ascending toward his own conscience and approaching God who, thus conceived, is a creature of man and not his creator. What man produces is more important than man himself, and Don Quixote—as Unamuno (*q.v.*) maintained—outlives Cervantes.

It is in the great book *Sombra* (1907; Shadow) that Pascoais develops fully his naturalistic, pantheistic thought, his interpretation of God and the world. Here the poet reveals his dramatic conception of life and creates "a kingdom not of this world," since imperfection cannot constitute the reality of "immaterial but cosmic life." To be captured, this calls for vigorous processes of renunciation and marvelous intuition. Pascoais, for example, does not wish to be the star, but its radiated light; not the lover, but love. The greatness of this poet lies in his sincerity and in the strength of the human emotion with which his philosophical thought springs from his extremely sensitive nature. He is in communion with all existing things, with the living and the dead, with the stones, and with the mountains whose peaceful shadow he envies. Grief also has its shadow, its projection "so that the grief of Humanity be ever present in each human being." This solidarity joins past and future and in the Portuguese man finds its authentic expression in *saüdade,* a word which connotes both recollection and desire, especially of God. Indeed *saüdade* may come to be the authentic spirit of God as realized progressively in the body of the universe (*Deus est in fieri*).

In the year 1912 Pascoais gathered about him the majority of the best youthful elements in his country in the group called Renascença Portuguesa. Their banner was *saüdosismo,* and their vehicle of expression *A águia* (Ser. 1, 1910; The Eagle). Taken as a symbolical and unique characteristic of the Portuguese soul, the *saüdade* concept was connected with the old myth of King Sebastian and led to an exalted affirmation of authentic Portuguese values as a sure solution of the problems which faced the country.

Poets as distinguished as Augusto Casimiro, Jaime Cortesão, Ferreira Monteiro, and especially the poet from Alemtejo, Mario Beirão, were outstanding in the Renascença group. But the division within the group was not long in coming. The new faction, Seara Nova (New Crop), which developed into a group more political than literary, was headed by the notable thinker, António Sérgio. The name was taken from their journal, which first appeared in October, 1921. This review still survives heroically today in the totally adverse political atmosphere created by the dictatorship of Oliveira Salazar. The controversy with Sérgio was long and at times violent. Pascoais published his arguments in the journal *A águia* in 1913 and 1914, as well as in the brochures *O espíritu lusitano* (1912; The Lusitanian Spirit) and *O gênio português na sua expressão filosófica, poética e religiosa* (1913; The Portuguese Genius in Its Philosophical, Poetical, and Religious Expression). While the schism of Sérgio, who was followed by Raul Brandão, Teixeira Gomes, Jaime Cortesão, and Aquilino Ribeiro (*q.v.*), implied a slipping toward liberal rationalism and a reform of political methods very similar to the objectives of *Clarté* of Paris during those years (*see* Barbusse), a further breach completely destroyed the coherence of the Pascoais group when the Integralismo Lusitano, patterned after the ideas of the Action Française of Maurras and Léon Daudet (*qq.v.*) in Paris and guided by a powerful thinker and expert polemist, António Sardinha (*q.v.*), was formed. This organization can be said in the long run to have furnished the political doctrine for the dictatorship inaugurated in 1926.

In the meantime Teixeira de Pascoais continued to produce poetical works, including the great poem *Maranos* (1911), in which converse the shades of Marão, of Don Quixote, the seasons, the *saüdade,* and Maranos himself. Maranos is "the being who wanders through the world, who lives more from his own spirit than from the fruits of the earth," and who hears from supernatural voices the message for the salvation and glory of Portugal. *Regreso ao paraíso* (1912; Return to Paradise) is another great poem in 22 cantos in free verse, perhaps not characterized by as compact and pure emotion as the former, but one that has attracted great attention in Peninsular literature. Among his best and most recent poetic productions are the volumes *O pobre tôlo* (The Poor Fool) and *Painel* (1935; Panel). He has also composed, in prose of an impressively poetic and philosophical quality, three biographies involving great and catastrophic events of the past: he treats the end of Greek and Semitic civilizations in *São Paulo* (1934; Eng. tr., *Saint Paul,* 1937), the fall of the Roman Empire in *São Jeronimo e a trovoada* (1936; St. Jerome and the Thunder Storm), and the tragedy enacted from Waterloo to St. Helena in *Napoleão* (1940). Two dramatic pieces in verse, *D. Carlos* (1924) and *Jesus Cristo em Lisboa* (1917; Jesus Christ in Lisbon), written in collaboration with Raul Brandão, do not attain the level of the poet's really great work. At his best he is without doubt the contemporary writer who has most influenced the Portugal of this century with his thought and art.

See: M. de Unamuno, *Por tierras de Portugal y de España* (1911), pp. 27–35, and introduction to Spanish translation (1935) of Teixeira de Pascoais, *São Paulo;* A. González-Blanco, *Estudio,* Vol. XIX (Barcelona, 1917).

R. M. L.

Teixeira de Queiroz, Francisco (pseud. Bento Moreno, 1848–1919, Portuguese novelist), was born in Arcos de Val-de-Vez, Minho, and received his medical degree at Coimbra in 1878. His positivistic formation led him to embrace the experimental novel introduced into Portugal by Eça de Queiroz (*q.v.*). In 1915 he was a deputy and member of the government. He projected a vast novelistic plan with the intention of duplicating for Portugal *La Comédie humaine* of Balzac. He divided his work into two series of stories and novels: *Comédia do campo* (Comedy of the Countryside), in which he studied life in the villages of his native region, and *Comédia burguesa* (Bourgeois Comedy), in which are interwoven types and sectors from the society of Lisbon. In both series he followed the credo of the experimental school with all faithfulness, making "physiological and social" analyses on the basis of the most minute observation. From *Primeiros contos* (1878; First Short Stories), the first volume of the rural series, to *Ao sol e à chuva* (1916; Under the Sun and the Rain), which closes this cycle, he created beautiful pages reflecting the landscape and customs of the North and interpreting the regionalism of the Minho district by the processes of the realistic school. A facile and capable observer of the country life which he knew very well, he was not equally adept as an observer of urban life. Thus in his novels of the *Comédia burguesa,* which begins with *Os noivos* (1896; The Betrothed), the analysis of types—here of greater psychological complexity—suffers frequently from superficiality, although generally speaking it is redeemed by the minute objectivity of his realism. Perhaps the best of this series are *D. Agostinho* (1894) and *Morte de D. Agostinho* (1895; Death of D. Agostinho), in which are depicted the type of the old, ruined hidalgo in modern society. His style, characterized by great simplicity and impeccable correctness, takes on singular expressive plasticity in the description of rural surroundings.

See: J. Fernandes Costa, *Elógio académico do Dr. Teixeira de Queiroz* (1919).

E. G. D.

Teternikov, Fyodor Kuzmich, *see* Sologub, Fyodor.

Tetmajer, Kazimierz (1865–1940, Polish poet and novelist), was born at Ludzimierz, in the mountainous Podhalan district of the then Austrian province of Galicia. His family on both sides was of the upper gentry. His father, marshal of the gentry of Nowy Targ, had settled in Podhale shortly after the uprising of 1830, in which he had participated. There were several men of letters among Tetmajer's ancestors on his father's side, notably Stanisław, an 18th-century translator of the classics; Karol, grandfather of Kazimierz, a well-known fabulist; and finally the celebrated uhlan, Józef (1814–1880), a poet and a distinguished mathematician. Tetmajer received his early education at home from tutors and from his gifted, high-spirited parents. He had an idyllic childhood, simple, natural, unspoiled by the extremes of either want or luxury. Until he left the mountains for Cracow in order to attend St. Anne's Gymnasium, he was exposed only to the most ideal influences: a countryside unsurpassed for natural beauty, the companionship of highly imaginative and poetic Podhalan mountaineers, and a home atmosphere wholesome and sane. Tetmajer's father died when the boy was still in school, and the family fortune was lost about the same time. Mme Tetmajer stepped into the breach and saw her son safely through his studies, first at the Jagiellonian University, later at Heidelberg.

Tetmajer was temperamentally out of tune with the literary mood of his day. When his first work, *Illa* (1886), was published, poetry was not greatly admired in Poland, and most of those who in an age more friendly to imaginative literature might have been poets were carrying the banners of causes. Tetmajer had no desire to promote causes. He was what would be called today a "pure poet."

Although Tetmajer tried many literary forms—the drama, the novel, the short story—it was in the lyric that he achieved greatness. His lyrics are different from those of the romantic poets who preceded him, having none of the spiritual, transcendental quality dominant in these. Tetmajer was no romanticist. He was a sensualist: women and nature alike he drank in with all his senses, but without romantic imagination. The sensual experience was intense, amounting to intoxication and escape into a kind of nirvana, and the sense of this Tetmajer was able to communicate superbly in the lyric. The works by which, besides his lyrics, Tetmajer will be longest remembered are his tales of the Podhalan mountaineers, among these *Na skalnem Podhalu* (1903–1910; On the Rocky Heights of Podhale); *Bajeczny świat Tatr* (1906; The Fabulous World of the Tatras); and the two-volume cycle *Legendy Tatr* (1910; Tatra Legends), in which the rebel Kostka Napierski and the Tatra Robin Hood, Janosik, play leading parts. A volume of translations, *Tales of the Tatras,* was published in London in 1941 and in New York in 1943. Though not the discoverer of the Tatra Mountains as literary material, Tetmajer was their most affectionate eulogist.

Tetmajer retired from the world about 1920. Almost blind, crushed by a series of personal sorrows and by the onrush of new times, he lived for years in a lonely room in Warsaw, a virtual hermit. He died in January, 1940, in a charity ward of a Warsaw hospital, a casualty of the Second World War.

See: Z. Dębicki, *Portrety,* I (1927), 133–151; K. Czachowski, *Obraz współczesnej literatury polskiej,* I (1934), 177–189, 346–349.

A. P. C.

Tharaud, Jérôme (1874–) and **Jean** (1877–; French journalists and novelists), were born in Saint-Junien, Haute-Vienne, where their father was a notary. Financial difficulties obliged the family to move to Angoulême, and it was in the *lycée* of this city that Jérôme and Jean began their studies. In 1888 Jérôme entered the Lycée Louis-le-Grand in Paris. In 1895 he entered the Ecole Normale Supérieure, but never received his degree. He was sent as a teacher of French grammar and literature to the College of Joseph-Eotvos in Budapest: he was to stay there four years (1899–1903). Jean too had come to Paris and entered the Lycée Saint-Louis, where he remained from 1891 to 1898. He hoped to enter the military academy at Saint-Cyr, but failed in the oral part of the entrance examination. Having completed his year of military service, he returned to Paris to continue his studies. Jérôme, meanwhile, took advantage of his four months' vacation each year to travel in Italy, Russia, Germany, the Balkans, and Turkey, exchanging a voluminous correspondence with Jean, who joined him in his travels whenever possible.

The literary talent of the two brothers was revealed in their first book, *Le Coltineur débile* (1898). As an exercise in literary discipline they next adapted the *Contes de la légende de la Vierge* (published in 1902). Jérôme had formerly transposed into French several Hungarian folk tales. When the Boer War broke out in 1899, Jérôme wanted to serve as a war correspondent. As this was refused him, he followed the newspaper accounts very carefully and drew from them the inspiration for the novel *Dingley,* which he later wrote in collaboration with his brother (1902). As these literary activities were not sufficiently remunerative, the two brothers undertook to write newspaper and magazine articles and continued to do so through the years 1903–1911. They served as secretaries to Maurice Barrès (*q.v.*). In 1906 the Goncourt Academy awarded them its yearly prize. From 1908 to 1911 were published several versions of the life of Ravaillac, and in 1908 they wrote a brief sketch of one of their compatriots, Paul Déroulède. *La Maîtresse servante* was published in 1911, *La Fête arabe* in 1912. When in October, 1912, war broke out between Turkey and Montenegro on the banks of Lake Scutari in Albania, Jérôme left for Cattaro as a reporter. Upon his return he discussed his impressions with his brother, and together they wrote *La Bataille à Scutari d'Albanie* (1913). From April to June, 1914, there appeared in the magazine *Opinion,* under the title *L'An prochain à Jérusalem,* the first of their many novels dealing with conditions in the Jewish communities they had seen. During the First World War, Jean served as a corporal, Jérôme as a simple private. They were sent to Flanders and to Champagne and then took part in an expeditionary mission to Morocco. They were later to write of their experiences in *Rabat* (1918) and *Marrakech* (1920). The Tharauds are excellent reporters and most of their novels are very well written reporter novels.

The French Academy awarded them its Grand Prix de Littérature on June 19, 1919. They were later elected as members of that venerable society, Jérôme in 1940, Jean in 1946.

See: A. Praviel, "Deux Grands Lettrés Limousins: Les Frères Tharaud," *Correspondant,* CCLXXXVIII (1922), 845–860; J. Bonnerot, *Jérôme et Jean Tharaud; leur œuvre* (1927); E. de Lamaze, "Jérôme et Jean Tharaud," *Bulletin des lettres,* 1938, pp. 335–339.

P. B.

Theer, Otakar (1880–1917, Czech poet), attempted, paradoxically, to achieve classical and sculpturesque effects in modern free verse. He was born in Czernowitz (Cernăuţi, Bukovina), the son of an army officer, studied languages at the University of Prague, and joined the staff of the university library.

Theer's first volume of poems, *Háje, kde se tančí* (1897; Groves Where There Is Dancing), expresses a rather crude pagan sensualism. But *Výpravy k Já* (1900; Expeditions to the Ego) begins the development toward a poetry highly speculative and austere yet revealing a fresh sensibility for metaphor. In *Úzkosti a naděje* (1911; Anxieties and Hopes) and especially in his last volume, *Všemu na vzdory* (1916; In Spite of Everything), Theer succeeds in evolving a new type of free verse, according to strict self-imposed rules, and achieves a style of sharp classical outlines. In his thought he leans towards the titanic individualism of Nietzsche (*q.v.*) and cultivates the heroic ideal in life and death. This is also the theme of Theer's only tragedy, *Faëthón* (1917; Phaeton), a remarkably successful attempt to revive the form of the Aeschylean mythical drama and to give it a personal content of heroic frustrate ambition. Theer's early stories, decorative and romantic, were rejected by the mature artist. His criticism is valuable for a quality of sympathy, *e.g.,* with an advocate of heroism like Corneille, rare in Theer's time and place. The pagan sensualism, the strong philosophical content, the striving for a severe classical form in free verse, make an original combination among the modern Czech poets. But Theer's art was too individual to find a wide audience or to exercise profound influence.

See: O. Fischer, A. Novák, O. Šimek, eds., *Na pamět Otakara Theera* (1920); A. M. Píša, *Otakar Theer* (2 vols., 1928–1933).

R. W.

Thibaudet, Albert (1874–1936, French critic), was born at Tournus in Burgundy, prepared himself for teaching, pursued advanced studies at the Sorbonne, and early showed his open-mindedness by taking his *agrégation* in history and geography although his primary concern was with belles-lettres. He taught at first in *lycées,* then lectured successfully in various universities abroad, York, Uppsala, Lausanne, and finally was offered the chair of French literature at the University of Geneva which he held from 1925 to the time of his death.

Always inclined to avoid trodden paths, he became an early contributor to Daniel Halévy's *Cahiers verts* with the study *Paul Valéry* (1924) and was soon a staunch supporter of the *Nouvelle Revue française,* to which he contributed an astounding number of articles. General recognition of his merit as a critic came after publication of *La Poésie de Mallarmé* (1912), which he himself calls an effort to be at once intelligent and equitable and in which he describes Mallarmé as "hanté par l'existence de l'être d'un non-être."

After service in the First World War he recorded his reactions to that conflict in the form of a commentary on the Peloponnesian War (*Campagne de Thucydide,* 1922). The problems of reconstruction of a France which had been upset ever since the Dreyfus affair, "a tumult among intellectuals," were taken up in two books; in *Les Princes lorrains* (1924) he writes of Poincaré and Barrès, and in *La République des professeurs* (1927) of Blum, Painlevé, and Herriot and the contrast between the leftist republic of the professors and the rightist republic of the *littérateurs* of the French Academy. Thibaudet's attitude towards modern poetry, already indicated in *Mallarmé* in 1912, is further developed in 1924 in his *Triptyque de la poésie moderne: Verlaine, Rimbaud, Mallarmé.* He discussed the philosophical trend of his times in *Trente Ans de vie française* (*Les Idées de Maurras,* 1920; *La Vie de Barrès,* 1921; *Le Bergsonisme,* 1923) and in *Intérieurs: Baudelaire, Fromentin, Amiel* (1924).

Thibaudet tried to reach a synthetic view of his own general philosophy in *Histoire de la littérature française de 1789 à nos jours,* never completed, which was edited by two friends (Bopp and Paulhan) soon after the author's death. Here he suggests a new approach to the study of literature, substituting for the usual classification by epochs one by generations: 1789 (with a special chapter on Napoleon), 1820, 1850, 1885, and 1914–1918, "the generation of the mutilated."

In addition to the monographs already mentioned Thibaudet also wrote *Flaubert* (1922), considered particularly good, and *Mistral* (1930), *Stendhal* (1931), and *Montaigne* (1937). Shortly after his death the *Nouvelle Revue française* published, under the title *Chroniques de la Nouvelle Revue française,* four volumes of Thibaudet's contributions (*Réflexions sur la littérature, sur le roman, sur la politique, sur la critique*) as well as several volumes of essays (*Le Liseur de romans, Les Genres, Psychologie et critique, Physiologie de la critique*).

A versatile critic, Thibaudet is representative of his own generation; he is neither dogmatic nor impressionistic, but mainly inquisitive. In his style, as is not infrequently pointed out, he combines dogmatic assertions with a curious hesitancy about making any general philosophic synthesis. An always alert curiosity, with a constant desire to be fair, restrains him here. His reputation may suffer with those who like to list and label their critics, as they can such men as Brunetière, Lemaître, France, Maurras (*qq.v.*). Thibaudet is an ever suggestive and well-informed writer, most definitely a free lance.

See: "Hommage à Albert Thibaudet," *Nouvelle Revue française,* XLVII (1936), 5–176.

A. Sz.

Thoma, Ludwig (1867–1921, German novelist and dramatist), was born in Oberammergau, of old peasant stock. For some years he practiced law in a small Bavarian town, then moved to Munich to become coeditor of Germany's brilliant satirical weekly *Simplicissimus.* Yet he never lost contact with the countryside and all that peasant life stands for. The firsthand knowledge of the Bavarian farmer enabled him to become the foremost regional writer of his native province. A keen observer, sensitive to tragic as well as humorous impressions and boldly using the racy Bavarian dialect, Thoma came to represent the South German modification of the naturalistic movement. But there is nothing doctrinaire about his style, which is controlled by emotion and mood rather than by dogmatic literary technique.

His moods and manners indeed are various. The humorist in him often yields to the temptation of writing for sheer entertainment. *Lausbubengeschichten* (1904), long a favorite in American colleges, is a good example of Thoma's ability to turn almost anything into hilarious comedy. The most opportune medium for the creation and propagation of laughter is, of course, the stage, and Thoma's dialect play *Erster Klasse* (1910) ranks high in German farcical literature, of which there is no great supply on hand. Often a strong desire to extol the beauty of peasant life induces Thoma to content himself with the role of a faithful chronicler of folklore, as in *Hochzeit* (1901), where the epic motif serves as a pretext for the unfolding of old customs prevailing among the Bavarian farmers. As a man of very liberal opinions and with the courage to express his convictions (even if this meant an occasional jail term), Thoma uses the stage as well as the novel to expose the follies of Prussian militarism and of ubiquitous bureaucracy. He preferably employs satire to drive home his lesson, as in *Die Lokalbahn* (1902) or *Moral* (1909; Eng. tr., *Morality,* 1909). Moreover, his deep concern with man directs him to social problems of a more general nature, for instance in *Magdalena* (1912) and especially in *Der Ruepp* (1922), the heartrending account of a once thrifty farmer who becomes a drunkard. Finally, Thoma on occasion succeeds in making all these creative veins subservient to great objectivity and lofty ethical purposes. *Andreas Vöst* (1905), easily his best novel, tells of a farmer who in seeking justice falls afoul of the law and has to serve a prison term. The substance of this work lies in the fearlessness with which Thoma attacks human inertia and hypocrisy; the hero embodies the essential qualities of a tiller of the soil, whose contact with nature sharpens his feelings for the natural rights of man and quickens his impatience with a ruling class which has lost sight of the basic needs of mankind. This peasant novel is far superior to modern specimens of "blood and soil" literature whose heroes are as unreal as the shepherds of the rococo period. Thoma, with all his love for and understanding of the farmer's life was intelligent enough to realize that the salvation of present-day society rests on cooperation among the various classes and between countryside and city.

See: A. Stark, *Die Bauern bei Ludwig Thoma* (1938); E. Cornelius, *Das epische und dramatische Schaffen Ludwig Thoma's* (1939).

H. B.

Thomsen, Grímur (1820–1896, Icelandic poet and essayist), was born at Bessastaðir, a manor near Reykjavík. He studied Hegelian aesthetics and literature at the University of Copenhagen; his Ph.D. dissertation (1845) was on Byron. For a long time he served in the Danish foreign service, but in 1866 he returned to Iceland, bought the place where he was born, and lived there until his death. He wrote several essays on literature and, besides Byron, introduced Runeberg to the Danes and his countrymen. His poems were published late in life: *Ljóðmæli* (1880; Poems), *Ljóðmæli, nýtt safn* (1895; Poems, New Collection), and, posthumously, *Ljóðmæli, nýtt og gamalt* (1906; Poems Old and New) and *Rímur af Búa Andriðarsyni og Fríði Dofradóttur* (1906; Ballads of Búi Andríðarson and Fríður Dofradóttir). The *Ljóðmæli* of 1895 contained translations from the Greek.

In no modern poet is the Old Norse–Icelandic heroic spirit crystallized so purely as in Grímur Thomsen. His ballads on the heroes of the sagas are unequaled in force and in fidelity to the originals. Undoubtedly his deep appreciation of the kindred Greek literature as well as his familiarity with contemporary aristocracy in Europe helped him to paint the proud figures, men and women, chosen from the sagas, the history of his native land, and the history of Europe. His verse is at times stiff and his diction rugged, but his poems are always alive with the heroic spirit.

See: S. Nordal, "Grímur Thomsen," *Eimreiðin,* XXIX (1923), 1–16; R. Beck, "Grímur Thomsen—a Pioneer Byron Student," *Journal of English and Germanic Philology,* XXVII (1928), 170–182.

S. E.

Þórðarson, Þórbergur (1889–, Icelandic essayist and poet), was born at Breiðabólstaður in Suðursveit, an out of the way district of Southeast Iceland. As a boy he earned the epithet *ofviti* (overwise) for his intellectual precocity and consequent eccentricity. He became a sailor and a jack-of-all-trades, to pay for an education that he did not relish until he began the study of Old Icelandic language and literature with the celebrated scholar B. M. Ólsen at the University of Iceland (1913–1918). This study later bore fruit in a collection of folk tales and expressions from colloquial speech.

In 1917 he became interested in theosophy, yoga, and spiritualism, writing under this influence the first of his sparkling essays, "Ljós úr austri" ("Ex oriente lux"), in the periodical *Eimreiðin* (1919). Several years earlier there had appeared a little-noticed sheaf of poems, *Hálfir skósólar* (1915; Half Soles), which was in reality the first harbinger of modernistic (futuristic) poetry in Iceland, written in revolt against the romantic lyric effusions of the time. But it was with *Bréf til Láru* (1924; Letter to Laura) that he struck the first telling blow against the literary conventions, especially the standards of propriety, of the late 19th century. *Bréf til Láru* is a conglomerate of very personal essays, full of humor and satire. It was meant as a manifesto of socialism, and as such it is the first important piece of leftist literature in Iceland. Although it was written in a classical style (even if unusually rich and varicolored), it paved the way towards the new modernistic prose style first really achieved by Laxness. The "letter" created much stir, the author actually being deprived of a teaching job that he held at the time. Two years later he accepted a further consequence of his international socialism by sponsoring the international language Esperanto, to which cause he has devoted much of his time. After visiting Russia he wrote an enthusiastic book about it. His most mature work was yet to come, his own life story in many volumes, of which three have been published: *Íslenzkur aðall* (1938; Icelandic Nobility) and *Ofvitinn* (2 vols., 1940–1941; The Eccentric).

See: S. Einarsson, *Þórbergur Þórðarson fimmtugur* (1939).

S. E.

Thorsteinsson, Steingrímur (1831–1913, Icelandic poet), was born at Arnarstapi, Snæfellsnes, Iceland, the son of a high-ranking civil servant. The intelligent boy was sent as a matter of course to the Latin school in Reykjavík and then to the University of Copenhagen. There he was to study law, but he ended as a student of the Greek and Roman classics, graduating in 1863. After a decade of literary work in Copenhagen he returned to Iceland; he became a teacher and later the headmaster of the Latin school in Reykjavík, a position he held until his death.

In his poetry Thorsteinsson is a romanticist with a strong classical tinge. His lyrics—on love, on Icelandic nature—won a wider public in Iceland because they were used as texts to popular tunes. As a satirist he was even more effective, with epigrams sharp and to the point. His poems (*Ljóðmæli*) were published in 1881, 1893, and 1910.

Thorsteinsson was more significant, however, as a transmitter of culture than as an original poet. He was a gifted translator, and through his pen Icelanders became acquainted with many a poetic masterpiece of Goethe, Schiller, Tegnér, and Byron. He was especially fond of the Hungarian poet Petőfi. Most important of his translations are undoubtedly *The Arabian Nights,* the fairy tales of Hans Christian Andersen, and Shakespeare's *King Lear.*

See: J. C. Poestion, *Steingrímur Thorsteinsson, ein isländischer Dichter und Kulturbringer* (1912).

S. E.

Thovez, Enrico (1869–1925 Italian poet and critic), was born and died in Turin. He was an archeologist, director of the Civic Museum of Modern Art in Turin, and a painter as well as a man of letters. His name appeared for the first time on the literary scene when he discovered and denounced the so-called plagiarisms of D'Annunzio (*q.v.*) in the *Gazzetta letteraria* in 1896; today the sum of these plagiarisms has increased tenfold, but they are likely to be considered not so much thefts as loans that an enterprising individual repays with munificent interest.

Thovez hoped to attain fame as a poet with *Il Poema dell'adolescenza* (1901), but instead he won an important place in modern criticism through the notes, intended first for a preface to his verse, published later as a book on Italian lyricism, *Il Pastore, il gregge e la Zampogna* (1910). This is a highly critical analysis of all Italian poetry but especially of Carducci (*q.v.*) and D'Annunzio, both accused of lacking sincerity, inspiration, actuality, sensitivity. The accusation implied a preponderance of rhetoric, attributed to the influence of the Renaissance which, according to Thovez, had ruined Italian poetry. Dante and Leopardi are cited by him as free from that literary and definitely not lyrical coldness, rigidity, heaviness, characteristic of other Italian poets. Thovez's viewpoint, which has precedents in romantic criticism and even in Baretti and Bettinelli in the 18th century, excited much interest and, of course, much opposition on the part of Croce, Borgese (*qq.v.*), Gargano, and others. The pungent style of his exposition, often in the form of personal memoirs tinged with humor, with well-chosen examples and with skillful and unprejudiced comparisons, had an appeal that survived the transient controversies—and this is confirmed by the number of reprints of the work (1911, 1920, 1926). There is more lyricism in this book of literary analysis than in the poems of Thovez. *Poemi d'amore e di morte* (1922), his second book of poems, was no more successful than the first.

Thovez, in his iconoclastic rebellion, never inclined towards free verse or futurism; indeed he remained always attached to traditional literary forms. A turn of mind rather melancholic and an independence of spirit which permeated also his personal life kept him apart from the literary coteries and made him the target of many personal attacks. Not having succeeded as a poet or as a painter, he was accused of directing his bile against the poets and painters of his time who had been accepted as interpreters of Italy. More over, his attachment to foreign writings and his harsh criticism of the Italian national literature explain the accusations of lukewarm patriotism directed against him. His very name, of Savoyard origin, was an added incentive for this kind of attack.

Certainly Thovez did not enjoy a happy life, and one feels this in his works. Much of the substance of his criticism is now outdated, but the moral consciousness, the strength of his convictions and of his many skillful observations remain. He is the kind of nonconformist who appeals more because of his intransigent attitude than because of the actual message. His other works repeat the same motive of the first one (*e.g., L'Arco di Ulisse,* 1921) or refer principally to modern paintings (*Il Filo di Arianna,* 1924) or criticize certain disagreeable types that sprang up in society during the First World War (*Mimi dei moderni,* 1919; *La Ruota d'Issione,* 1925).

See: F. Durand, *Enrico Thovez* (1933).

G. P.

Tikhonov, Nikolai (1896–, Russian poet and novelist), was born in St. Petersburg. He began to write in 1914, but only after the Revolution did his verse appear in print. His ballads and lyrics, collected in *Orda* (1922; The Horde) and *Braga* (1923; Brew) and in a more complete volume in 1935, are prevailingly narrative in contents. The variegated experiences of Tikhonov are reflected in his poetry—his career as a hussar in the war of 1914–1917, as a carpenter, teacher, actor, and fighter of the Whites. The pathos of war and revolution is felt keenly in his verse, the more intensely because of Tikhonov's reserve. From the Acmeist school (an offspring of symbolism) Tikhonov learned to observe clarity, concreteness of image, severe precision. "Simple—like iron nails" is a characteristic simile of his that might be applied to most of his work, even to his bloodiest and most fantastic ballads.

Though not a member of any party, Tikhonov is sensitive to problems of humanity, and even in his lyrical effusions he shows a deep concern with the world outside of himself. He has shown his wide knowledge of Europe and Russia especially in his prose stories, *Riskovanny chelovek* (1927; Reckless Man), *Kochevniki* (1931; Nomads), and in his novel about the beginning of poison-gas warfare, *Voina* (1931; War). In his cycle of poems about Europe, Tikhonov records his impressions of Europe on the eve of the Second World War. One feels the stifling air of fear and suspense that hovers over the cities and plains of the continent, but one is also aware of the poet's faith in the inevitable victory of free man. The militant optimism of a Soviet citizen dissipates Tikhonov's melancholy musings over the war hysteria of Europe. Since 1941 he has written a number of poems and prose sketches about the war. His *Leningradskiye rasskazy* (1942; Leningrad Tales) raises reportage to the peak of literary art.

A. K.

Timmermans, Felix (1886–, Flemish novelist), born in Lier, is the most important and most typical representative of a constant trend in Flemish literature toward the idyllic and sympathetic presentation of rural and small-town life in Flanders. A born raconteur, his writings are highly flavored with savory expressions. His attitude is moderately but essentially sensuous, and this endears him to his Flemish readers. His love for archaic and folklore elements, which he very cleverly incorporates in his writings (*e.g.,* in *Het Kindeken Jezus in Vlaanderen,* 1917; The Infant Jesus in Flanders; *De Harp van St. Franciscus,* 1936; The Harp of St. Francis), gives his books a Biedermeier atmosphere.

His first literary success came with *Pallieter* (1916; Eng. tr., 1924), a series of sketches about a lyrical, slightly Rabelaisian figure who lives in a strongly idealized Flemish landscape. This aesthetic sensualist spends his time enjoying the physical world and adding to these pleasures the delight of well-chosen readings from poets and mystics. Such frank but still morally conscious sensualism was exactly what the war-weary readers of 1916 desired. In one of his latest books, *Boerenpsalm* (1935; Peasant Psalm), Timmermans almost completely abandoned conventional decorative writing and achieved a novel of peasant life which, although it may be called in a sense synthetic, far surpasses in depth and significance his former works.

His art is devoid of spiritual implications. With Franciscan candor he enjoys life and interprets it with colorful simplicity and sly humor. In many instances his books are literary transcriptions of the illuminations of medieval manuscripts and of the paintings of the masters of the Flemish school. *Pieter Bruegel* (1928; Eng. tr., *Droll Peter,* 1930), a lyrical life of the great painter, is the most striking example of this quality of his writing. The immense popularity of Timmermans is not confined to the Dutch-speaking countries; his work has been translated almost entirely into German, and several of his books exist in English or American versions: *Pallieter* and *Droll Peter* as indicated and also *Drieko-*

ningentryptiek (1923; *The Triptych of the Three Kings,* 1936).

See: M. Rutten, *Felix Timmermans* (1931).

J.-A. G.

Toller, Ernst (1893–1939, German dramatist and poet), was born in Samotschin, in the Prussian province of Posen. After graduating from the Bromberg Realgymnasium (1912), he studied law at Grenoble. At the outbreak of the First World War he joined the German colors, a volunteer. Invalided home in 1916, he continued his studies in Heidelberg and then went to Munich. In 1919 he was elected to the short-lived Bavarian Soviet Republic (*Bayerische Räterepublik*). As a consequence of his revolutionary activities he was sentenced in 1919 to imprisonment for five years. Toller left Germany in 1932. In a mood of despondency he committed suicide in New York City.

Toller has been aptly called "the most dominant and flagrant genius hatched by the German revolution." This is truly reflected in his dramas. Written in an extreme expressionistic style, they are revolutionary and ecstatic in character. Thus in *Die Wandlung* (1919; Eng. tr., *Transfiguration,* in *Seven Plays,* 1935) Toller unfolds in 13 tableaux ("Stationen") the horrors of war as he himself had experienced them. A similar technique is used in *Masse Mensch* (1920; Eng. tr., *Man and the Masses,* 1924), an attack on militarism, capitalism, mechanistic civilization, and other social phenomena, envisaging common brotherhood as the ultimate salvation of mankind. *Die Maschinenstürmer* (1922; Eng. tr., *The Machine-Wreckers,* 1923) deals with the Luddite riots in England in the early 19th century. In *Hinkemann* (1924; Eng. trs., *Brokenbrow,* 1926; *Hinkemann,* in *Seven Plays,* 1935) is pictured the tragic fate, this time not of the masses, but of an individual, a badly wounded war veteran. In *Hoppla, wir leben!* (1927; Eng. tr., *Hoppla!* 1928) Toller satirizes contemporary society. *Feuer unter den Kesseln* (1930; Eng. tr., *Draw the Fires,* 1935) revolves about the mutiny of the German sailors in 1917–1918 which led to the November revolution of 1918. Toller's revealing autobiography, *Eine Jugend in Deutschland,* appeared in 1933 (Eng. tr., *I Was a German,* 1934). His last drama, *Pastor Hall* (1939; in English only), treats of the successful struggle of a pastor to keep his faith, despite Gestapo persecution. This heroic figure represents Pastor Martin Niemöller. Written in realistic style, the drama is "Dedicated to the Day when this drama may be performed in Germany." Toller's outstanding contributions to the expressionistic lyric are *Gedichte der Gefangenen* (1921) and *Das Schwalbenbuch* (1923; Eng. tr., *The Swallow-Book,* 1924), both written in prison.

Toller was fundamentally an idealist, an expressionistic Schiller—exhorting man "to live in the Brotherhood of God, in which all men are equal" (*Pastor Hall*).

See: Paul Singer, *Ernst Toller* (1934); H. Lieberman, *Ernst Toller; la tragedia de un espíritu inquieto* (1939); W. A. Willibrand, *Ernst Toller, Product of Two Revolutions* (1941).

G. K.

Tolstoy, Aleksei Nikolayevich (1882–1945, Russian novelist and man of letters), was born at Nikolayevsk in the province of Samara (now Kuibyshev), on the Volga. As a child he led a solitary life, with abundant opportunity for imaginative dreaming and impressionable observation. Up to the age of 19, when he entered the Technological Institute at St. Petersburg for training as an engineer, he had no great inclination to write; it was contact with the symbolist poetry of Vyacheslav Ivanov, Balmont, and Bryusov (*qq.v.*) that first stimulated him to experiment with verse.

Though a member of the Social Democratic Party during the Revolution of 1905, Tolstoy took no active part in its operations and spent the next two years at the Polytechnic Institute in Dresden. His first collection of verse was published in 1907 under the title *Lirika* (Lyrics), and another collection called *Za sinimi rekami* (Behind Blue Streams) appeared two years later. About 1901 he had begun to write prose, composing stories of provincial life in realistic vein and often drawing for subject matter upon personal experience and acquaintances. With the First World War his style, as revealed in his articles as a war correspondent, gained appreciably in clarity and crispness.

After fighting in the White army, Tolstoy lived in Paris until 1922, when he returned to the Soviet Union. During his residence in Paris he had written dramas and short stories, as well as a novel called *Syostry* (revised 1928; The Sisters), the first part of his trilogy *Khozhdeniye po mukam* (The Road to Suffering; partial Eng. trs., *The Road to Calvary,* 1923, *Darkness and Dawn,* 1935; complete tr., *Road to Calvary,* 1946). In the course of his first years in the U.S.S.R., Tolstoy was clearly not at one either with his material environment or with the prevailing ideology, and his fiction, though often reflecting his education as an engineer, is frequently more fantastic than social in content (*Vosstanie mashin,* The Revolt of the Machines; *Giperboloid inzhenera Garina,* The Hyperboloid of Engineer Garin; *Aelita*). To this period also belong several dramas on events in modern history, including *Zagovor Imperatritzy* (1924; The Plot of the Empress), a wordy picture of Rasputin and his time. In 1928 Tolstoy published the novel *1918* as the second part of his trilogy and by that date was generally accepted as an able, if not entirely regenerate, "fellow traveler."

It was only with the appearance of Tolstoy's masterly historical novel *Pyotr Pervy* (1929–1934, Peter I; Eng. tr. of Vol. I, *Peter the Great,* 1932) that he attained his full stature. In this dramatic re-creation of the past Tolstoy gives the broadest scope to his narrative talents and his gifts of character portrayal and authentic dialogue. Though built around the imposing figure of Peter I, the novel is more than fictionalized biography, since it slights no aspect of Russian existence in the late 17th century during the first 26 years of the tsar's life and even introduces occasional scenes of the Muscovite barbarity which characterized the period. Peter's reign is treated as an age of transition, not unlike pre-war Russia, and there are obvious analogies between the tsar and the more modern innovators Lenin and Stalin. This novel consecrated Tolstoy's status as the foremost contemporary Soviet writer and, since Gorky's (*q.v.*) death, as the recognized spokesman of Russian letters. In 1936 he was thus hailed by Molotov as a loyal Soviet citizen and characterized as "a worthy example of that comradely status which admits of no class distinctions."

In 1938, with *Khleb* (Eng. tr., *Bread,* 1938), Tolstoy proceeded to offer a thrilling record of the defense of Tsaritsyn (Stalingrad), with forceful pictures of the major revolutionary heroes. Since he had experimented with children's stories in his youth, it was not surprising that in 1936 he should have achieved a notable success with a children's play, *Zolotoi klyuchik* (The Golden Key), the dramatized fairy tale of the puppet Buratino, a brilliantly sovietized Pinocchio in search of the golden key that opens the door to a land of happiness for children.

During the years of the Second World War, Tolstoy's writing more and more eloquently expressed his intense awareness of political and social life under the Soviets. The process of conditioning was long, but it eventually turned Tolstoy into a conscious and efficient exponent of Soviet ideology. The war also aroused in him an emotional loyalty toward the country for which his previous attachment had been merely sentimental and intellectual. By 1944 Tolstoy had also become, next to Lenin and Gorky, the author most widely read in Soviet Russia—convincing evidence of rapidly improving Soviet taste. The war demolished the last remnants of Tolstoy's previous ivory tower and inspired him to a strenuous series of official duties and literary tasks in the service of the country to whose rapid intellectual advance and patriotic fervor he so signally contributed. He was an interesting example of a gifted middle-class intellectual who worked his way through to a sympathetic understanding of the socialist environment and carved out for himself a dominant position among proletarian writers who had long viewed him with suspicion because of his background and personal history. Tolstoy's work, will, however, be subject to considerable revaluation when a longer perspective is applied to it.

See: Raisa Misser, *A. N. Tolstoy, istoricheski ocherk* (1939).

S. H. C.

Tolstoy, Count Leo Nikolayevich (1828–1910, Russian novelist and moral philosopher), was born at Yasnaya Polyana, the family country estate in the province of Tula. After the early death of his mother and father, elderly female relatives brought him up. An unusual sensitivity won him the nickname "crybaby Leo," but in most respects he was a normal, healthy child. German and French tutors gave him his first lessons, and at the age of 16 he entered the University of Kazan to study oriental languages but soon transferred to the faculty of jurisprudence. Social life, lack of interest in his work, undermined his studies; he left the university in 1847 without a degree, convinced that the methods of his teachers and the subjects taught were futile. He was already beginning to manifest that anarchical attitude towards established order which characterized so much of his later thought and writing. Vague schemes of scientific farming and of bettering the lot of his serfs came to nothing, and the next few years were passed in visits to Moscow and St. Petersburg, where he frequented high society and sowed his wild oats. He had begun a painful examination of himself in his diaries and also had dreams of a literary career.

In 1851 the young Tolstoy abruptly turned his back on a life of social ease and went to the Caucasus with his brother Nikolai, an army officer at a frontier post. Tolstoy volunteered, saw active service against the mountaineers, distinguished himself for bravery, and eventually won a commission. While in the Caucasus he also completed and published his first novel *Detstvo* (1852; Childhood); its success encouraged him to continue his literary activities. He transferred in 1854 to the army operating against the Turks on the Danube, a few months later was stationed at Sevastopol, and took part in the famous defense of that city. His published Sevastopol tales made a profound impression because of their revelation of the horrors of war and of the suffering and bravery of the common soldiers of Russia. Tolstoy wearied of army life and obtained permission to return to St. Petersburg in 1855 (he eventually resigned his commission in 1857). He was greeted as a literary hero by Turgenev (*q.v.*) and other famous liberal writers, but resisted their friendly attempts to enlist his services in partisan literary efforts. His independence had already become the order of his being. By now his position in literature had been enhanced by the publication of the sequels to *Childhood—Otrochestvo* (1854; Boyhood) and *Yunost* (1856; Youth)—and several tales, *Metel* (1856; The Snowstorm), *Dva Gusara* (1856; Two Hussars), and *Lucerne* (1857).

In 1857 and again in 1860 Tolstoy traveled widely in Western Europe and acquired an abiding dislike for governments, politics, and the materialistic way of life in the West. In 1861 he settled down at Yasnaya Polyana, gave himself up to the affairs of his estate and to teaching peasant children, and developed and published highly original ideas on pedagogy, anticipating in some respects the theories of modern progressive education.

The persistent habit of searching self-analysis intensified and left Tolstoy thoroughly dissatisfied with himself. A spiritual crisis was postponed by his marriage in 1862 to Sofya Andreyevna Bers, a girl of 18. The next 15 years, perhaps the happiest of his life, were spent mostly at Yasnaya Polyana in raising a large family, in managing his estate, and in intense literary efforts. This was Tolstoy's greatest creative period: *Voina i mir* (1865–1869; War and Peace) and *Anna Karenina* (1875–1877) were published, and other works of fiction, *Kazaki* (1863; The Cossacks) and *Polikushka* (1863). He also began two more historical novels on the Decembrists and on Peter the Great, which he never finished, worked on several plays, and published his well-known educational texts, the *Azbuki* (ABC Books).

Tolstoy's world fame rests largely on the masterpieces *War and Peace* and *Anna Karenina*. Modern realism has never equaled the achievement of *War and Peace*. Each of the more than 500 characters on this vast stage has his own distinct personality and speaks his own language. Even the dogs, as one Russian critic remarked, are individualized. Many of the characters he knew in real life, but they are all passed through the alembic of his art. Truth and simplicity, the two canons of his artistic faith, are scrupulously observed. He wrote *War and Peace* in an atmosphere of love and family happiness, and the prevailing spirit of the book is an ecstatic love of life. This exuberance is lacking in *Anna Karenina*, although the novel achieves the same wonderful realism.

After 1876 Tolstoy began to feel more and more dissatisfied with a prosperous, self-centered existence. Indeed, in one mood of despair, he very nearly turned to suicide. He first sought salvation in the religion of the Russian Church, but in vain. The wisdom of the various philosophical systems he studied proved inadequate. Finally, reading of the Gospels convinced him that these sacred books contained the answers to all his questions; with the verse from Matthew (5: 39), "that ye resist not evil," as a cornerstone, he evolved his own conception of Christianity, from which he eliminated all the mystical and nonethical elements. The full account of his conversion, *Ispoved* (1879; A Confession), is a work of extraordinary power and transparent sincerity.

During the last 40 years of his life Tolstoy published much to expound and defend his new faith (see especially *Kratkoye izlozheniye Evangeliya*, 1881, A Short Exposition of the Gospels, and *V chyom moya vera?* 1882, *What I Believe In*). For him God is not personal but the representation of the supreme Good and Reason, and Jesus simply a great man whose ethical teachings happen to accord with the human conscience. The Kingdom of God is within you, Tolstoy maintained, and hence we achieve happiness only by doing right, by loving all men, and by abstaining from all forms of violence, from lust, hate, and anger. Such precepts brought Tolstoy into direct conflict with the state, which he did not hesitate to repudiate, along with war, army service, oath-taking. He applied his ethical and moral principles to social and economic conditions in Russia, and the results are summed up in his unusual book *Tak chto zhe nam delat?* (1886; What Then Must We Do?). He condemned private property, the traditional uses of money, and the exploitation of man by man. His beliefs led him to vegetarianism and an abstinence from intoxicants and tobacco. Followers soon flocked to him, his fame spread throughout the world, and Yasnaya Polyana became a kind of Mecca. The Russian Church excommunicated him; the government feared him and yet wisely left him in peace, although it vigorously persecuted many of his followers.

After his conversion Tolstoy wrote, besides his voluminous controversial works, a great deal of imaginative literature—but now in the light of his new faith. His changed views in this respect he explained in his unique work, *Chto takoye iskusstvo?* (1897–1898; What Is Art?). Art, he argued, is a means of emotional communion, and it is the business of the artist to infect his readers with the feelings he has himself experienced. If the feelings are good, it is good art. New standards obliged Tolstoy to reject or depreciate most of what has generally been considered the greatest art and literature, including his own earlier works. He now labored to achieve a classical simplicity of style and composed a number of short, highly moral tales to teach to the common people his principles. The best of his later works, based on his own inner experiences, are *Smert Ivana Ilyicha* (1886; The Death of Ivan Ilyich), the drama *Vlast tmy* (1886; The Power of Darkness), and the controversial novel on sex, *Kreitserova Sonata* (1889; The Kreutzer Sonata). They are grimly tragic and moving works, in which Tolstoy's artistic powers show no signs of flagging. *Hadji Murad* (1896–1904) and, to a greater extent, *Voskreseniye* (1889–1900; Resurrection) represent a reversion to the richer style of *War and Peace.*

Tolstoy's conversion brought about a marked change in his family life; he strove to live according to his new faith; if his family had permitted, he would have given away all his property. His children, with a few exceptions, and particularly his wife regarded with hostility this abrupt break with their past. Tolstoy's last years were saddened by new domestic tragedies and by a faithful wife now driven to hysteria by the actions of her husband and his disciples. With a vague desire to escape a home life become impossible, Tolstoy stole away secretly one night (October 28, 1910), accompanied by his personal physician, Dr. Makovitski. His health broke down and he died at Astapovo on November 8, 1910.

Tolstoy's works have been widely translated into English.

See: P. I. Biryukov, *Biografiya Lva Nikolayevicha Tolstovo* (1923); N. N. Gusev, *Zhizn Lva Nikolayevicha Tolstovo* (1927–1928); Ernest J. Simmons, *Leo Tolstoy* (1946).

E. J. S.

Torelli, Achille (1841–1922, Italian dramatist), was born at Naples, where his father, Vincenzo Torelli, edited the theatrical magazine *Omnibus.* His mother was Donn'Anna de Tommasi of the princely family of Lampedusa. Until the age of 16 he studied at the French Institute of Isidore Boubée in Naples. He won his first literary award at 17 with his play *Dopo morto.* His very earliest works include *La Verità,* awarded a prize at a contest sponsored by the prince d'Ottaiano, published in 1875, and *Gli Onesti,* published in 1877.

Torelli was but 26 years old when he achieved nation-wide fame with *I Mariti* (1867), which is generally considered not only his masterwork but one of the finest plays of Italian 19th-century drama. It was praised by such critics as Ferrigni, Capuana (*q.v.*), and Manzoni. *I Mariti,* a comedy in five acts, points the moral that it is a good husband that makes a good wife. The play is set in the worldly society of Naples' aristocracy, the author's own environment. In a series of lively tableaus (rather than in a carefully fabricated plot), several married couples appear on the stage. In an atmosphere of idleness, dissoluteness, and extravagance, these couples lead their wretched lives. Confronted with their children's matrimonial failures, the duke and duchess of Herrera, typifying conjugal harmony and loyalty of the good old days, give their youngest daughter, Emma, in marriage to a hard-working, middle-class lawyer, Fabio. A glamorous but worthless naval officer has caught Emma's fancy. Fabio, through his tactful and chivalrous behavior, endeavors to win the love of his capricious young wife. Emma eventually scorns the beau monde, its jealousies and unfaithfulness, and learns to appreciate the man to whom she has been married. This "parable of husbands" was praised by Benedetto Croce (*q.v.*) in particular for its "vividness, gracefulness, and lightness of touch." It has enjoyed uninterrupted popularity in Italy. Encouraged by its sensational success, Torelli wrote *La Moglie* (1869), *Triste Realtà* (1871), *L'Israelita* (1883), *Scrollina* (1885), *Donne antiche e donne moderne* (1886), and many other plays. For the Neapolitan stage he wrote various comedies (*Core d'oro, Nun te ne 'ncaricà,* etc.). Torelli frequently subjected his plays to modifications; *Lo Buono Marito fa la bona mogliera* (1889), *e.g.*, is a dialectal, popularized version of *I Mariti*. Torelli's literary efforts were not confined to the theatre. A collection of his juvenile verses, *Schegge* (1878), was published, as well as a poem, *Alla Vita e alla sua parola* (1898), and a novel, *L'Amore che dura* (1884). As librarian of the Reale Biblioteca di San Giacomo of Naples, he translated and commented the *Song of Songs* (1895). There is also a volume of his lectures on *L'Arte e la morale* (1902).

Torelli is unquestionably seen at his best in *I Mariti*. None of his other works obtained much favor, although his plays are not lacking in skillfully delineated situations and in delicate character sketches here and there. Possibly under the impact of adverse criticism, Torelli aimed at subtleties which brought out his shortcomings. He remains, however, a significant exponent of early naturalism in Italian drama. No longer interested in national political problems, Torelli turned to psychological problems concerning human conduct and relationship. The moral of Torelli's writings is that true love is our main source of strength and consolation in the vicissitudes of life. Shortly after his 80th birthday, on which he was solemnly feted, Torelli died in Naples.

See: L. Tonelli, *L'Evoluzione del teatro contemporaneo in Italia* (1913), pp. 196–212; B. Croce, *La Letteratura della nuova Italia*, I (1914), 333–345; A. Padula, *Commemorazione del socio Achille Torelli* (1924).

C. F. W.

Torre, Guillermo de (1900–, Spanish literary critic and poet), was born in Madrid and studied law in that city. He has recently been living in Argentina. He is one of the outstanding personalities of the vanguard movement in Spanish literature, and his name is associated with the so-called ultraism, of which he was one of the most enthusiastic defenders. His poetry, a reflection of his ultraistic creed, is collected in *Hélices, poemas (1918–1922)* (1923). The major part of his production is in literary criticism and was put to the service of the new conception of literature he had been espousing. In this work he has shown himself to be one of the most penetrating critics of the younger Spanish generation. *Literaturas europeas de vanguardia* (1925) is the most complete and successful of the many Spanish studies upon the varied literary tendencies in the contemporary period. Torre has collaborated actively on most of the Spanish and Argentine literary reviews launched since the end of the First World War and especially on the Spanish journal *Ultra*, an organ of ultraism, and the Argentine journal *Sur*.

See: Nicolas Jiménez, "Guillermo de la Torre y la nueva poesía," *América* (Quito), Vol. IX (1934), Nos. 54–55, pp. 24–33.

E. G. L.

Toulet, Paul Jean (1867–1920, French poet, novelist, essayist, and critic), was born at Pau in Béarn, to which his parents, Creole colonists from the island of Mauritius, had returned so that the child might be born in the ancestral land. An exciting discovery of exotic Mauritius and of mysterious Algiers and, back in his beloved Béarn, the carefree life of a gentleman farmer gave Toulet the vivid memories which enriched his later works. In 1898 he was in Paris, and although his first books remained unnoticed, his nocturnal life, his brilliant conversation, refined, mordacious, soon made him a legendary figure readily identified with his first hero, *Monsieur du Paur, homme public* (1898), the self-analyzing cynic, still capable of grandeur, whose sarcastic maxims are echoed in the bitter aphorisms of the posthumous "Almanach," *Les Trois Impostures* (1922). Under various pseudonyms Toulet then contributed to *Vie parisienne* and other magazines his versatile articles of art criticism and travel notes, his verse, the short stories which were to become *Les Tendres Ménages* (1904), and *Mon Amie Nane* (1905), the novel which probably first introduced the modern courtesan of literature, a precious little trinket, elegant and silly. A translation, *Le Grand Dieu Pan* (1901), of Arthur Machen's strange book and a charming poetical novel, *Le Mariage de Don Quichotte* (1902), complete the summary of his activity for that period. In 1912 Toulet's health compelled him to seek more favorable skies: he settled in the Basque country. He still worked hard, his health permitting, editing and rewriting stories not yet published in book form, incessantly polishing the little poems which had appeared only in magazines, fashioning new ones, reading, translating, and still indulging in brilliant conversation with his ever welcome visitors. *Comme une fantaisie* (1918), *La Jeune Fille verte* (1920), *Les Contes de Béhanzigue* (1921), and the delightful collection of poems, *Les Contrerimes* (1921), were the harvest of the years preceding his death.

His fame grew rapidly: excessive praise was heaped upon a man who certainly deserved more than a reputation for epigrams, but whose only merits apparently had been charm, versatility, and suppleness of style. He often mistakes bitterness for deep thinking. His maxims read like those of a La Rochefoucauld, revised and edited by a Rémy de Gourmont (*q.v.*). His stories bring to mind Stendhal and Laforgue (*q.v.*), and at times their poetic rhythm and richness of imagery announce Giraudoux (*q.v.*). He prided himself on being called a grammaticist because of the many archaic, almost incorrect, syntactic tricks he used and abused. Yet the real title to fame of this "literary dandy" remains the little book of poems, *Les Contrerimes,* in which he was able to mix humor with sadness, despair with tranquillity, simplicity with grandeur, in an exquisite, inimitable way. There is something in them of the haikai and the limerick; exoticism, real or conventional, alternates with the delicate intimacy of childhood memories or the euphuistic urbanism of Parisian gossip; their versatility, their perfection of form, their lack of sensationalism, enhanced by just enough preciosity, give them their charm. They please and irritate; because of them Toulet will remain among the "fantasist poets," although he should fare better. It is through them that he exerted his influence: Jean Pellerin (*q.v.*), Tristan Derême, owed much to them. Yet it is in them, as well as in the best of his prose, that the attentive reader will detect, through the sophisticated irony, the elaborate bitterness and the stylistic virtuosity of the writer, the real feeling, discreet but sincere, of a man who, more than anyone else, perhaps, deserved the title "gentleman of letters."

See: H. Martineau, *La Vie de P.-J. Toulet* (1921); F. Carco, *Amitié avec Toulet* (1934).

C. L. B.

Tousseul, Jean (pseud. of Olivier Degée, 1890–1944, Belgian novelist), was born at Landenne-sur-Meuse, province of Namur. The son of manual toilers, he received only elementary schooling, worked in the quarries, and became interested in agitation for social reform; then, dissatisfied with what he now calls his "years of vagabondage," he turned to literary expression and won fame. His experience gave him an intimate understanding of the problems of the humble. One of the rare Belgian writers who attempted to eke out a living by the pen, he scorned making any compromise with his ideals in order to gain popularity. He sought to copy nature in artless peasants rather than to fathom the subconscious primitive in the supercivilized. Hence the poignant simplicity of his work. A first booklet, never reprinted, appeared in 1916: since then he published 12 collections of stories, nine of sketches and souvenirs, and 12 novels. In his own country he was rewarded by coveted prizes; abroad, there are translations into English, Dutch, German, Czech, and Russian. By the setting of his stories he belongs to the regionalistic tradition. Profoundly conscious of the influence of environment, he evokes primarily the soul of landscape as it may shape the thoughts and emotions of his characters. His village becomes a microcosm in which he discovers humanity. The essential unity of his inspiration proves that he found the center of equilibrium he sought in his days of storm and stress, while the variety of approach and of subject matter bars any suggestion of aloofness.

The title of one of his volumes, *Images et souvenirs* (1931), may stand as epigraph for all his work, for past and present are closely linked in his imagination. Fossils in the stone quarries aroused his interest in the history of the region which he recalls in some of the most successful stories, *e.g.,* "Le Grand Malheur" (in *Le Passé,* 1933). An eclipse of the sun has terrified the villagers, who believe the end of the world at hand. Their reactions are dramatically portrayed in timeless scenes: are we at the beginning of the 15th century or on the eve of a 20th-century invasion of Belgium? Tousseul called *L'Epine blanche* (1936) a fairy story; it is actually set in the 18th century, but no reader can fail to recognize the author in the personage of the apothecary who seeks a "volatile drug" to anesthetize patients on the operating table. Here is a discreet souvenir of his own efforts toward social amelioration—a kind of autobiographical touch frequent in his work. After completing *Jean Clarambaux* (5 vols., 1927–1936), he admitted that the life of his hero and his own had often run parallel ways. His aspirations and ideals are shared by most of his characters. *Jean Clarambaux,* perhaps his masterpiece, and *L'Epine blanche* are his only books which have yet been published in English (1939 and 1944). The first, suggested by Rolland's (*q.v.*) *Jean-Christophe,* perhaps surpasses its predecessor in sustained poetic inspiration. In construction it betrays the technique of the *conteur*—the episodes, artfully wrought to produce a single impression, are loosely bound together. Yet the whole leaves an indelible memory in the reader. Tragedy and heroism alternate with idyllic scenes and homely realism to culminate in a matured philosophy of life. The fourth volume, *La Rafale* (1933), offers glimpses of the First World War seen from a village, the more convincing as friend and foe are impartially scrutinized. Among Jean Tousseul's titles to originality is the enlargement of the scope of fiction by the introduction of quarrymen and the perils of their profession. He never idealizes these helots of civilization but presents them for our admiration and pity as he knew them. Whether he relates incidents of heroism or portrays the brutal fury of intoxication, his realism rings true. It is sprung from sympathy based on dauntless idealism in search of a criterion of life.

See: D. Denuit, *Jean Tousseul* (1937); J. P. Bonnami, ed., *Témoignages sur Jean Tousseul* (1941).

B. M. W.

Tozzi, Federigo (1883–1920, Italian novelist), was born in Siena of lower-middle-class stock. His mother died when he was young, and he does not paint a very pleasant picture of his relations with his father (see *Novale,* 1925). He seems to have been a rather unruly youth, and, although he had opportunities, he lacked the discipline to submit himself to the process of formal education. For a time he worked for the state railways. As early as 1911 Tozzi started contributing to various periodicals and in 1913 at Siena, in collaboration with Giulliotti (*q.v.*), he founded the *Torre,* which was regarded, not without reason, as a reactionary organ. His first book, *La Zampogna verde* (1911), is essentially D'Annunzian in character, which is perhaps hardly remarkable considering the influence of D'Annunzio (*q.v.*) on all the pre-war generation. The same thing may be said of *La Città delle vergini* (1913), the very title of which has a D'Annunzian ring. But with *Tre Croci* (1920; Eng. tr., *Three Crosses,* 1921) and *Il Podere* (1921), Tozzi comes into his own, and it is on these books that his fame rests.

In a way Tozzi is a transition writer, one might almost say a transformer, passing on the current of D'Annunzio and to a more limited extent Verga (*q.v.*) to the post-war generation. Certain elements of D'Annunzio he never shook off; the autobiographical urge, the glorification of some of the more melodramatic aspects of reaction, the taste for the perverse. Yet he shows clearly that he feels the great lack in D'Annunzio, which is moral force, even moral consciousness. It has been remarked that his characters are so many Andrea Sperelli's (protagonist of D'Annunzio's *Il Piacere*) who no longer enjoy the game of pleasure, but are incapable of escaping from themselves. They are in fact somewhere between Sperelli and Rubè (Borgese's, *q.v.,* introspective hero of the early 20's). The subject matter of his novels perhaps more than anything else has led to the comparison with Verga. There is another much more significant resemblance to Verga in that Tozzi too went through a long period of apprenticeship; he had not indeed truly found himself at the time of his death. Like Verga he was of the type that matures slowly and is capable of growth long after other artists have made their work a formula. *Tre Croci* and *Il Podere* are not masterpieces in the sense that Verga's *I Malavoglia* or even D'Annunzio's *Il Piacere* are. But they are fascinating because of their promise and, as a matter of fact, will stand comparison with most novels of the time. It seems likely that, had Tozzi lived another 10 years, his own peasant exuberance and strength might have come more to the fore and forged out of the purely intellectual influences in his career something quite powerful and original.

See: D. Giulliotti, *L'Ora di Barabba* (1920); P. Cesarini, *Vita di Federico Tozzi* (1935); E. De Michallis, *Saggio su Tozzi* (1936).

T. G. B.

Trakl, Georg (1887–1914, Austrian poet), shares with Ernst Stadler (*q.v.*) the rank of leading lyrical talent of German preexpressionism. He was born at Salzburg, Austria, son of a hardware dealer, studied in Vienna and became a druggist at Salzburg, where he met his later friend and protector Ludwig Ficker, in whose magazine *Brenner* he published nearly all his poems. At the outbreak of the First World War he went with an ambulance corps to the Galician front, but soon had to be taken to the military hospital at Cracow for medical treatment. There he died from an overdose of poison, which he apparently had taken to end his suffering.

Trakl is an exclusively lyrical writer, endowed with an almost morbid sensitiveness and an unusually fine feeling for rhythm and color. His first collection of poems, *Gedichte* (1913), shows influences of Dostoevski (*q.v.*), Villon, George (*q.v.*), and Hofmannsthal (*q.v.*). From Nietzsche (*q.v.*) he inherited a deep cultural pessimism which caused him to interpret life in terms of sickness and decay. Unable to find a remedy for this cosmic evil, he indulged in an orgy of somber visions filled with pictures of putrefaction and death. The later poems, published under the title *Sebastian im Traum*

(1915), reveal a more wholesome, although by no means optimistic, concept of life. Under Hölderlin's influence he finds a pantheistic creed and establishes a spiritual community with mankind and nature, life and death. Trakl's language, less rigid than George's and less rhetorical than Hofmannsthal's, is free from expressionistic exaggerations. In the finest examples of this language there is reborn the solemn simplicity and nobleness of Hölderlin, with whom Trakl shows more affinity than with any other poet.

See: A. Soergel, *Dichtung und Dichter der Zeit,* Neue Folge: *Im Banne des Expressionismus,* 4. Auflage (1927) pp. 307–309, 430–433; W. Mahrholz, *Deutsche Literatur der Gegenwart* (1930), pp. 389–393.

E. J.

Trausti, Jón (pseud. of Guðmundur Magnússon, 1873–1918, Icelandic novelist and poet), was born at Rif, the northernmost farm in Iceland, on the shore of the Arctic. His parents were poor, and the famine of 1882 left indelible marks on the mind of the boy. He was, however, steeled by his experiences. In order to get books to read he learned the trade of printing, and he remained a printer to the end of his life. After an apprenticeship in Copenhagen he went to Reykjavík, living there until his death from influenza in the epidemic of 1918.

After two volumes of poetry and one historical play had appeared, Trausti finally found his place as an author in the broad social novel and the short story. In *Halla-Heiðarbýlið* (4 vols., 1906–1911; Halla and the Heath Cottage) he draws on a vast canvas the Icelandic rural scene as he had known it in his youth, teeming with characters, the figure of the poor cotter's wife Halla in the foreground gradually growing into heroic proportions. In *Leysing* (1907; Thaw) he uses economic changes, in *Borgir* (1910; Castles) the advent of new ideas in the church, as a background for his strong, conservative characters. Later he re-creates in *Sögur frá Skaftáreldi* (2 vols., 1912–13; Stories from the Eruption of Skaftá, 1783) the most crucial years in Icelandic history, when the nation almost perished in the terrible famine which was the aftermath of the eruption. After that he wrote a series of romantic novels based on the Icelandic middle ages (14th–16th centuries). As an apostle of progress and rugged individualism he reacted vigorously in *Bessi gamli* (1918; Old Bessi) against the coming socialistic tendencies. Though his style was uneven, Trausti's narrative talent was considerable, and his characters are always vibrantly alive.

See: S. Einarsson, "Jón Trausti," in Trausti, *Ritsafn,* I (1939), 7–39.

S. E.

Tretyakov, Sergei (1892–, Russian poet and playwright), born in Moscow, studied literature at the University of St. Petersburg, joined the group of "formalists" before the Revolution. After 1917 Tretyakov was active as a member of the futuristic movement and one of the leaders of Lef (Left Wing group of proletarian writers). In 1924 he was appointed professor of literature of the Russian department at the National University in Peking. Tretyakov stayed in China for two years and wrote a propaganda play against foreign imperialism in that country, *Rychi Kitai!* (1926; Eng. tr., *Roar China,* 1931), which had a considerable success in Russia. Tretyakov's plays are crude examples of the semi-futuristic, semi-symbolistic style of disciples of Mayakovsky (*q.v.*) in the 20's (*Slushai Moskva,* 1924, Listen Moscow; *Protivogazy,* 1924, Gas Masks). After 1930 Tretyakov was active as a journalist. He produced several books on the collectivization of the Soviet agriculture (*Mesyats v derevne,* 1934, A Month in a Village; *Tysyacha i odin trudoden,* 1934, Thousand and One Workdays), a description of Eastern Siberia (*Strana AE,* 1932; The Land AE), a collection of sketches on Czechoslovakia (*Strana na perekrestke,* 1937; A Country at a Crossroad), and an interesting biography of a Chinese student (*Dinshu-Hua,* 1930). Tretyakov's literary activity was interrupted in 1938 for political reasons.

M. S.

Trigo, Felipe (1864–1916, Spanish novelist), was born in the province of Badajoz (Estremadura), to which he returned after studying medicine in Madrid to practice his profession. It was there he acquired that acquaintance with rural life later depicted in such novels as *El médico rural* (1912) and *Jarrapellejos* (1914). He soon became an army doctor and was stationed in Seville, where he devoted himself to journalism and literature in addition to his military duties and published a book entitled *Etiología moral* (1891). He was ordered to the Philippine Islands and was badly wounded in an uprising of Tagal prisoners. On his return to Spain he continued his journalistic activities, writing a series of articles collected in *La campaña filipina* (*Impresiones de un soldado*) (1897).

Upon being invalided out of the army he resumed the practice of medicine in his native province, and there he wrote his first novel, *Las ingenuas* (1901). This work achieved a great popular success; with it he embarked, fairly late in life, upon the second phase of his literary career, that of a novelist, which he continued in Madrid until he ended his life by his own hand.

The popularity of his first novel and of those which followed in rapid succession—*Le sed de amar* (1902), *La altisima* (1903), *La bruta* (1904)—was due to the boldness with which he handled sex themes. This won him many readers and a dubious fame as a pornographic writer and overshadowed his real literary gifts. There is nothing frivolous or deliberately immoral in his works; on the contrary, there is a fanatical faith in a new morality which is in keeping with the crisis of ideas at the end of the century and which in him was a combination of the materialism engendered by his profession as a doctor and of the idealism of his anarchist belief in free love. He began his career with a book on a moral theme and ended it with others of the same character—*Socialismo individualista* (1906), *El amor en la vida y en los libros* (1908). Neither by reason of his ideas or of his art can he be considered a great writer; but it is equally unjust to look upon him as a writer who has no place in literature. There is strength and originality in his novels which entitle him to a place of his own in the Spanish literature of his day.

See: H. Peseux-Richard, "Un romancier espagnol: M. Felipe Trigo," *Revue hispanique,* XXVIII (1913), 317–389; M. Abril, *Felipe Trigo: Exposición y glosa de su vida, su filosofía, su moral, su arte, su estilo* (1917).

F. de O.

Trindade Coelho, José Francisco de (1861–1908, Portuguese short-story writer), was born in Mogadouro, Trás-os-Montes. From this district, where he passed his childhood in contact with the rural milieu of the North, he was later to draw the materials for his best stories. He went to study law at Coimbra and took his degree in 1885. Subsequently he collected his impressions of student life in a book entitled *In Illo Tempore* (1904). He embarked upon a juridical career and was assigned to Portalegre, Alemtejo. Here he spent four years, and familiarized himself with another of the Portuguese regions characterized by the most typical popular life. In 1890 he was named magistrate in Lisbon. The following year was published the book to which he owes his fame, *Os meus amores* (My Loves), a collection of stories with rural atmosphere. Afterwards he wrote several juridical works and certain brochures on popular culture. He took his own life in 1908, a victim of grief and neurasthenia.

Endowed with marked talents as a storyteller, Trindade Coelho is one of the great regionalists of Portuguese novelistic realism, with a conception of rural life definitely his own. From the rose-tinted version of romantic idealism, writers had passed to the pitiless description of sentiments and brutally elemental passions as the only rural reality. Castelo Branco (*q.v.*) had initiated this phase, members of the realistic school had continued it, and Fialho de Almeida (*q.v.*) had given it its extreme development. Trindade Coelho, temperate in his descriptions, neither idealizes nor degrades. From Fialho, of whom he is considered a follower and whom he indeed admired, he inherits the preoccupation with style which in him makes for a prose of great expressive richness. However, he does not show the violence or disorbed chromatic aberration of Fialho. On the contrary, his style is distinguished by smoothness and delicacy, by an effect of spontaneity and lack of effort. Its sobriety attains a simplicity of which no elements could be suppressed and yet is the result of a conscientious elaboration. *Os meus amores* comprises little sketches of village life which include some of the best pages of Portuguese regionalism. Across a certain tone of kindly irony which permeates his narratives—and which does not prevent his being one of the realists who has known best how to preserve a position of detachment from his work—he translates with great lucidity the relation of the characters to the surroundings. "Tipos da terra" (Local Types), "À lareira" (By the Fireplace), and especially "Idílio rústico" (Idyllic Love) are stories full of simple delicacy, of realism mixed with a subtle lyric sympathy for the milieu, of tragic elements intermingled with patriarchal simplicity. His talents as an objective observer, in combination with the virile calm of his concisely analytical style, his predilection for simple subjects and simple psychology, make of Trindade Coelho, despite his limited output, a writer of strong personality.

See: Luise Ey, *Trindade Coelho* (1918); Fialho de Almeida, "'Os meus amores' de T. C.," *Os gatos,* V (1933), 109–112.

E. G. D.

Tsvetayeva, Marina Ivanovna (1892–, Russian poet), was born in Moscow, the daughter of a professor of art and philology at the University of Moscow. As a child she lived a great deal abroad, attended secondary schools in Lausanne and Freiburg, and in 1898 followed courses in Old French literature at the Sorbonne in Paris. The first years of the Russian Revolution she spent in Moscow, but in 1922 she emigrated abroad and since that time has lived chiefly in Prague, Berlin, and Paris.

Tsvetayeva's poetic talent did not receive due recognition until the 1920's, when several volumes of her mature verse appeared almost simultaneously. Her first three books, *Vecherni albom* (1910; An Evening Album), *Volshebny fonar* (1912; The Magic Lantern), *Iz dvukh knig* (1913; From Two Books), already hint at genuine talent. Her later works, *Versty* (1922; Mileposts), *Tzar-devitsa* (1922; Tsar-Maiden), *Razluka* (1922; Parting), *Stikhi k Bloku* (1922; Poems to Blok), *Molodets* (1924; Bold Fellow), reveal her as a poet of great original creative power and unusual sensitivity to rhythm and sound.

See: I. Ehrenburg, *Portrety russkikh poetov* (1922).

O. M.

Turgenev, Ivan Sergeyevich (1818–1883, Russian dramatist, short-story writer, and novelist), was born in the Central Russian province of Orel. His mother, the wealthy and imperious daughter of serf-owning landed gentry, embittered by an unhappy marriage to an impecunious and dissolute army officer, gave scant thought to the upbringing of Ivan and his two brothers, who were abandoned to the kindly attentions of literate serfs. From Lobanov, his mother's household steward, Turgenev thus learned to read and write Russian and acquired his first taste for Russian literature.

After a year at the University of Moscow (1833–1834), he finished the basic course at the University of St. Petersburg in 1837. Turgenev's earliest literary experiments, dating from his university years, were poetic in form and Byronic in content. His first printed verse was published in 1838 by *Sovremennik* (The Contemporary), a monthly founded by Pushkin. That same spring Turgenev enrolled at the University of Berlin, where for three years he studied philosophy (chiefly Hegel), classics, and history, seasoning his books with considerable travel. In 1842 he passed the St. Petersburg examinations for the master's degree in philosophy but, instead of entering upon a scholarly career, took a minor position in the Ministry of the Interior which he held for two years before turning all his energies to literature.

Since 1843, in fact, Turgenev's interests and associations had been mainly literary. In that year he made the beneficent acquaintance of the great critic Vissarion Belinski and saw in print both his narrative poem *Parasha* and his drama *Neostorozhnost* (Carelessness). He also conceived a lasting attachment for the French opera singer Pauline Viardot-Garcia which was largely responsible for his long residence abroad in later years. Between 1843 and 1856 Turgenev wrote a series of dramas, several of which reflect Gogol's realistic themes of country life, though his dramatic masterpiece, *Mesyats v derevne* (1849; A Month in the Country), exhibits a psychological accuracy and touches of impressionism which foreshadow Chekhov's (*q.v.*) technique. Turgenev's maturity as a realist in prose was signalized in 1847 by the appearance of *Khor i Kalinich* (Khor and Kalinich), a short story of peasant life and actually the first in the series later celebrated as *Zapiski okhotnika* (collected ed., 1852, Notes of a Hunter; Eng. tr. as *Russian Life in the Interior or the Experiences of a Sportsman, A Sportsman's Sketches,* etc.). Upon his mother's death, which made him the self-sufficient master of 15,000 acres and some 2,000 male serfs, Turgenev hastened to mitigate the lot of the latter. He freed the domestic staff, endowing them with fields and woodlands, while the serf farmers previously on forced labor for the owner were given a chance to acquire their own holdings.

The next six years (1850–1856), which Turgenev spent uninterruptedly in Russia, were the period during which he was most closely identified with Russian society and its aspirations. With *A Sportsman's Sketches* he struck a telling blow at the institution of serfdom and all the degeneracy and suffering it entailed. Though not comparable in violence with *Uncle Tom's Cabin,* the *Sketches* give a realistic picture of contemporary country life in an area remote from urban culture, emphasizing the bad effect exercised by serfdom on those who lived by it and with it. In Turgenev's view, it was debasing to the masters, and prevented any recognition of the serfs as human beings. The influence of the *Sketches* was the stronger because of the reserve with which they were written, and Alexander II once said that after he had read them he never lost sight of the necessity for emancipation.

Yet as literature the sketches, however ably composed, were at best genre, and of a type and tendency not uncommon in contemporary and previous Russian letters. Turgenev, though he remained a master of the short story to the end of his days, thus went on to broader portrayals of types which reflect the mood of society as influenced by currents of contemporary thought. *Rudin* (1856), his first major novel, depicts a well-educated intellectual of the 40's whose capacity for analyzing himself and others inhibits all fruitful activity. Even the love of a devoted and energetic girl cannot save him. After several false starts, he proves unable to harmonize word and deed and cannot master his environment. The parallelism between Rudin and Pushkin's Eugene Onegin is immediately apparent, and here Turgenev has been called an "intelligent and creative pupil of Pushkin."

In the summer of 1856 Turgenev left Russia for Western Europe and thereafter never made more than extended visits to his native country—a situation which, though its effect was not immediately sensible, eventually deprived him of intimate contacts with progressive Russian thought. Turgenev's second novel, *Dvoryanskoe gnezdo* (1859; A Nest of Gentlefolk), also treats the 40's and is really the swansong of the old patriarchal provincial life which was fading out with the dawn of a new era. Like Rudin, its hero Lavretzki is still measurably frustrated and wastes eight years in two love affairs, one trivial, the other tragic, before settling down to useful work as a country squire at the age of 45. Liza Kalitina, the heroine, begins the series of Turgenev's great female characters who are important in world literature as descendants of Pushkin's Tatyana and close kinswomen of the heroines of Henry James. She is, first of all, a strong woman contrasted with a generous but essentially weak man.

At bottom, Rudin and Lavretzki are both ineffective in varying degrees. But in his next novel, *Nakanune* (1860; On the Eve), Turgenev endeavored to create a more positive type in the Bulgarian Insarov, who marries a Russian girl but has burnt himself out in the service of his oppressed countrymen. It was perhaps Turgenev's hope that Russian Insarovs would soon appear, but he seems to have chosen a foreigner for his hero because the nature of the rising generation was not yet clear in his mind.

The appearance of this novel coincides with a significant break in Turgenev's friendships. Since 1847 he had published mainly in *Sovremennik,* controlled in the late 50's by the poet Nekrasov but largely dominated by the young and brilliant radical critics Chernyshevski and Dobrolyubov. Turgenev's moderate liberalism was no more to their taste than their bumptious and uncompromising materialism was to his. An unfavorable review of *On the Eve* by Dobrolyubov provoked the final break, and from this point Turgenev published in the moderate *Russki vestnik* (Russian Herald). But his contact with the radical younger generation inspired *Otsy i deti* (1862; Fathers and Sons), the masterpiece among his novels. Bazarov, its hero—no longer an educated nobleman, a reflective country squire, or a resolute foreigner, but a university student of humble origin, a commoner scornful of the past, intolerant of slow-moving contemporary liberalism, eager for a decisive leap into a better future—is the immortal type of the energetic and impatient younger generation, shocking its elders and developing a tremendous head of steam even on the easiest grades. Though with *Fathers and Sons* Turgenev definitively alienated progressive sympathies of his own day, the fact that in such a period Turgenev carried his strong and appealing hero, not to positive triumph, but to accidental and pathetic infection and death, proves only that a novelist is often wiser than his critics. For exile or death would have been, in real life, Bazarov's only conceivable alternatives at the time.

Turgenev's last two major novels, *Dym* (1867; Smoke) and *Nov* (1872; Virgin Soil), though artistically meritorious, failed of popular success because they reflected his basic philosophy of progress step by step and his belief that the revolutionary movement was false and futile. Apart from his major novels, he also composed during his lifetime numerous short stories (some almost of novel length) which reveal his great stylistic gifts and psychological penetration, *e.g., Pervaya lyubov* (1860; First Love), *Stepnoi Korol Lir* (1870; King Lear of the Steppes), *Veshnie vody* (1872; Spring Waters), and *Posle Smerti* (1883; Clara Milich).

From the 50's to his death, Turgenev as an international figure was surpassed by no other Russian author before the appearance of Leo Tolstoy's (*q.v.*) great novels. He it was who first revealed the Russian spirit to the outside world. As the Danish critic Georg Brandes (*q.v.*) wrote, "he gave us the psychology of a whole race." Though seemingly without the neurasthenic depth of Dostoevski (*q.v.*) or the epic sweep of Tolstoy, Turgenev himself suffered from handicaps of character and environment which are reflected in his works. His talent is more lyric than that of either Dostoevski or Tolstoy, and he surpassed them both in his feeling for nature and his capacity to describe it. Beyond that Turgenev still remains the greatest Russian prose stylist of all time. His health began to fail before 1880, and the illness which was to destroy him was finally diagnosed as an inoperable and excruciatingly painful spinal cancer, which caused his death at Paris on September 3, 1883.

There are two full translations of the works of Turgenev in English (by Constance Garnett and by Isabel Hapgood).

See: Edward Garnett, *Turgenev; a Study* (1917); Avrahm Yarmolinsky, *Turgenev; the Man, His Art, and His Age* (1926); André Maurois, *Tourguéniev* (1931, in French); R. A. Gettmann, *Turgenev in England and America* (1941).

S. H. C.

Turkish literature. Classical Turkish literature, extending in its richness from the 16th to the 18th centuries, stood by itself; it exerted no influence upon the literatures of other countries nor was it influenced by them —except that it faithfully followed the patterns of classical Persian literature. The situation became altogether different in the 19th century. Turkey then had to reckon directly with the dynamically expanding European powers and to take into account as never before the complex system of Western cultures. The leaders of the Ottoman Empire, as it retreated from Europe, had to yield to interior and exterior demands for modernization according to patterns from the West. Now came the period of Turkish history called that of the Tanẓīmāt, the reforms; the first step was the liquidation of the Janizaries in 1826. The first newspaper was printed in 1831. Liberal political associations were formed, such as the Jeňi Osmanlylar (New, or Young, Turks) in 1865. Schools of a European model and with European instructors were established, primarily for military purposes but also with a program for higher education; in the 1860's three institutions of major importance were founded—the Galata-Saray Lisesi, the American Robert College, and the Imperial Ottoman University of Constantinople. Definite changes in Turkish literature became apparent, language and style evolved, literary forms very new to the country, in novel and drama, were introduced. The literature was at first that of translation, and French writers exerted the preponderant influence. The "azhar" (flowery) style was abandoned. A multitude of Arabic and Persian words for which there still existed Turkish expressions were replaced by these, although in vocabulary literary Turkish remained, and still does today, overwhelmingly Arabic. An attempt was made to bring the literary language closer to the spoken, even to the colloquial language of the people.

In more recent Turkish literature, to understand which it is necessary to go back to about 1840, three phases are to be distinguished: the literature of the Tanẓīmāt already mentioned; the "New Literature" (Edebijjāt-i Džedīde); and the "National Literature" (Millî Edebiyat). (For earlier Turkish authors and for Turkish works published before the decree of Romanization of modern Turkish in 1928, the Orientalistic transcription is here used, and the new official Turkish orthography for what follows that date.)

Šināsī, the spiritual father of the Young Turkish movement, is the first significant writer of the Tanẓīmāt epoch. He translated French verse, was a poet in his own right, and founded the first two nonofficial newspapers, *Terdžümān-i Aḥvāl* (1860; Interpreter of the Situation) and *Taṣvīr-i Efkār* (1862; Shaping of the Thoughts). Like his literary contemporaries, Ẓijā Paša and Nāmyq Kemāl, he was forced to flee his native country because his progressive ideas were subject to persecution. Nāmyq Kemāl wrote the first national Turkish drama, *Vaṭan jāxud Silistre* (The Fatherland, or Silistria), based on an event of the Russo-Turkish War, and he was soon banished to Cyprus. Writers continued nevertheless to fight the suppression of free thought in Turkey. An important literary critic, dramatist, and poet active a little later was Redžā'ī-Zāde Ekrem (1847–1913), author of a rhetorical essay entitled *Ta'līm-i Edebijjāt* (Instruction in Literature). Abū-ẓ-Ẓijā Tevfīq, littérateur and publisher, compiled a good anthology of Ottoman literature. Aḥmed Midḥat (1844–1913) was a prolific prose writer whose main work consisted of translations and fiction. The Albanian Šems-ed-Dīn Sāmī Frāšerī compiled the famous dictionary *Qāmūs-i Türkī* (Turkish Ocean [of words]) and the Turkish encyclopedia *Qāmūs-el-A'lām* (Ocean of the Sciences). An eminent place among men of letters of this period was occupied by 'Abdu-'l-Ḥaqq Ḥāmid (1852–1937), who introduced into his country European romanticism and European poetical styles. He was both poet and dramatist. Among his works are *Nesteren, Ešber* and *Tezer* (all three narrative); *Ṭāryq,* on the conquest of Spain by the Arabs; collections of poems entitled *Ṣaḥrā* (Desert) and *Maqber* (The Grave); works of fiction, *Ölü* (The Dead [Woman]) and *Belde* (The City, *i.e.,* Paris).

The representatives of the Edebijjāt-i Džedīde formed a literary-political group and published the literary periodical *Servet-i Fünūn* (Riches of Arts). The magazine had been created by Tevfīq Fikret (1867–1915), a poet whose style was modeled after French masters but who sang the praises of the Anatolian peasant. The group was in constant struggle against the reactionary and oppressive measures of the sinister 'Abdu-'l-Ḥamīd. Among its members were the poet Dženāb Šihāb-ed-Dīn (1860–), often called the "Turkish Alfred de Musset," the novelist Meḥmed Ra'ūf (Re'ūf; 1875–1931), Xālid Ẓijā (1866–), and Aḥmed Ḥikmet. Ra'ūf was influenced largely by Feuillet, Daudet (*q.v.*), Flaubert (*q.v.*), and Zola (*q.v.*), as in *Džān-Fezā* (The Lovely One); he wrote many short stories, novels such as *Ejlūl* (September) and *Sijāh Indžiler* (Black Pearls), and a number of plays. Xālid Ẓijā, "the Alphonse Daudet of the Turks," published in the *Servet-i Fünūn* his romances *Māvī ve Sijāh* (Blue and Black) and *Ášq-i Memnū'* (Forbidden Love); numerous letters written during his travels in Germany were published in 1916. Aḥmed Ḥikmet is a novelist; his best-known work is probably *Xāristān ve Gülistān* (Land of Thorns and Garden of Roses), published in Constantinople in 1901. The association Fedžr-i Ātī (The Imminent Dawn) comprised another similarly progressive and antimonarchistic but very individualistic group of writers. These were completely under the influence of French symbolism (*q.v.*). To this group belong Jaḥjā Kemāl (1885–); Aḥmed Hāšim (1885–1933), whose delicate poetry has been published under the titles *Göl Sā'atleri* (Hours of the Lake) and *Pejāle* (The Cup) and whose prose is collected in the volume *Turabā-xāne-ji Laqlaqān* (The Hospice of the Storks); and Šehāb-ed-Dīn Sülejmān (1885–), author of the dramas *Čyqmaz Soqaq* (Dead End), the excited discussion of which led to the foundation of the Fedžr-i Ātī, and *Fyrtyna* (Storm).

The really modern writing is called by the Turks, as already indicated, Millî Edebiyat (National Literature). The term of course has historical as well as aesthetic implications. It became current just prior to the Young Turk revolution of 1908. The Young Turks were a progressive party whose chief aim was less the abolition of the sultanate and the old social structure based on oriental bureaucratic despotism than the creation of a national Turkish state after the pattern of the national states of Europe. The new ideology embraced Pan-Turkism and Pan-Turanism, variations of a totalitarian nationalism; the former was intended to include all Turkic tribes and nations (the majority of the Turkic nations are within the Soviet Union), and the latter was to include tribes and nations which were of "Turanian" origin (*i.e.,* speaking not only Turkic but also Finno-Ugric languages). The Pan-Turanian movement found strong adherents for a time among the young intellectuals of Hungary.

As a result of the retreat of the Ottoman Empire from its former position of conquest in the Balkans, North Africa, Egypt, and Mesopotamia and in view of its obvious disintegration (not only national, as in the Balkans and Egypt, but also economic), the Young Turk movement pledged itself to the creation of a single national Turkish state and to the utmost possible concentration of the national forces, both politically and intellectually.

Unlike the writers of the classical era, the Young Turk authors were mostly not of the upper class. Many of them have been, or still are, teachers of the middle and higher schools. They are consequently much more closely connected with the people. Far better than the classical writers, who enjoyed a life secluded from the *profanum vulgus,* they understand the common man, above all the uncorrupted, valiant Anatolian peasant. They know his positive qualities—his tenacity, his capacity for the endurance of hardships, whether caused by life in a country whose ancient irrigation systems have been destroyed and never rebuilt or by a greedy and corrupt officialdom. They know his fidelity to the *vatan* (Arabic = fatherland); it was the Anatolian peasant who had fought for the glory of the sultans, the rulers of the faithful, and for the expansion of their God-protected empire.

Anatolia, the immediate home of the Turks, and the Turkish people became more and more the subjects of literature. These people were not the refined representatives of the class from which the "pillars of the imperial state" had been recruited; they had different manners and a different education; some of them were even without manners or education and totally illiterate. They did not understand the language of the upper class, almost completely Arabic and Persian; they spoke a more genuinely native language, using a more Turkic vocabulary; their language indeed had been despised by the educated and called *qaba Türkče* (coarse Turkish).

Again there was much translation, and now not only from French but also from German, English, Italian, and Russian. With the elimination of many Arabic and Persian terms, the influence of Islam and of oriental patterns of style decreased. Turkish literature became basically more Europeanized. Fiction and the novel together with political essays formed the bulk of the new writing. Quantitative meter was abandoned in favor of syllabic. The theatre was likewise influenced, both through translations and attempts to copy European patterns.

The Millî Edebiyat has been prolific in writers, but it is still early to appraise them. Many are important now more for political than for aesthetic reasons. Time will be needed to differentiate the really great writers from the journalists or merely political essayists.

The long list begins with the novelist Ömer Sejfeddīn (1882–1920); the poet and chief theorist of Turkish nationalism, Ẓijā Gök Alp (1875–1924); and the publicist Meḥmed Emīn (1869–). It also comprises such writers as Enis 'Avnī (pseud. Aqa Gündüz, 1885–), who wrote novels, *e.g., Qatyrdžy Oγlu,* the story of a robber chieftain of the period of decay under Meḥmed III, 1595–1603; Fāliḥ Ryfqī (now: Falih Rıfkı Atay; 1895–), a gifted essayist who fought for Turkish independence and the Young Turk revolution and whose articles were collected in the *Eski Saat* (Old Hour). Rūšen Ešref (now: Rûşen Eşref), also an essayist, is known for his translation of Vergil. He wrote a study on Tewfīq Fikret and a number of essays, such as *Gečmiš Günler* (Days Passed) and *Damla Damla* (Drop by Drop). Ḥamdullāh Ṣubḥī, an enthusiastic patriot, is a writer of fiction, *e.g., Daγ Jolu* (Mountain Road). Rešād Nūrī (now: Reşad Nuri) became suddenly famous for his great work *Čaly Qušu* ("Le Roîtelet"). He also wrote *Sönmüš Jyldyzlar* (Stars Extinguished), *Dudaqtan Qalbe* (From the Lips to the Heart), *Aqšam Güneši* (Evening Sun). Among his well-known dramas are *Ḥandžer* (The Dagger), *Ümidiṅ Güneši* (The Sun of Hope), and *Bir Gedže Fādžy'asy* (The Tragedy of a Night).

Ja'qūb Qadrī (now: Yakub Kadrî Karaosmanoğlu) is undoubtedly the greatest and most brilliant of living Turkish writers. His significance for Turkish literature will remain outstanding, for his interests, capacities, and subjects reach far beyond the narrow national horizon of the major part of the Millî Edebiyat. He was born in 1889 in Cairo. His father was 'Abdu-'l-Qādyr bej, who belonged to a family of old Turkish nobility. His boyhood and youth were spent in Mağnisa and Cairo and in Smyrna where he met Šehābeddīn Sülejmān, who introduced him into the Fedžr-i Ātī. He went to Constantinople only after the revolution. Maupassant, Daudet, and Bourget (*qq.v.*), whom he admired in his early years, did not continue to exert influence upon him, nor did Turkish men of letters such as Xālid Ẓijā and Meḥmed Re'ūf. His critical ability as well as his truly great artistic capacities was developed very quickly, and this fact was important for his literary independence. Scandinavian literature, especially the work of Ibsen (*q.v.*), influenced his development and personality and is reflected in his work. During the period of the Russian Revolution, he was constantly attracted by the Russian moderns, especially Gorky (*q.v.*), and the younger revolutionary and postrevolutionary writers. The Russian classics were also not without effect upon him. He is perhaps the one Turkish writer who became so seriously and thoroughly acquainted with Russian literature that he was able to interpret it. For clearness and expression his novels may be compared to those of Maupassant and Flaubert (*q.v.*). He accurately describes and interprets the Turkish milieu, especially that of Anatolia; both in his short stories and in his novels he presents a vivid picture of these people, the middle and lower classes, the Anatolian peasant and his language, folklore, and mentality.

Nur Baba (Father Nur [Light]) is his first great story. It contains interesting descriptions of the little-known rites and costumes of the Bektāšī order; for his extreme candor he was attacked by some of the fervent nationalists. Other works are *Bir Serendžām* (An Adventure); *Kiralyq Qonaq* (House for Rent); *Sodom ve Gomore* (Sodom and Gomorrah), which depicts the moral and sentimental crisis of Constantinople during the armistice at the end of the First World War; *Ḥüküm Gedžesi* (Night of Judgment), a history of the opposition under the Young Turk regime (1908–1918); *Jaban* (The World Outside); and *Ankara,* the heroic epopee of the city which became the capital. He also published a volume of prose poems, *Erenler*

Baγyndan (From the Garden of the Initiated), the title being a much used term of the Islamic mystics. He likewise wrote numerous articles and essays on aesthetics and politics, exhibiting profound knowledge of the problems of his time. He was for many years in the diplomatic service of his country and was Turkish envoy plenipotentiary to the government of Czechoslovakia in Prague, until the destruction of that republic in the spring of 1939.

Xālide Edīb (1883–), a strong Pan-Turkist and nationalistic moralist, is important among the women writers. Köprülü-Zāde Meḥmed Fu'ād (1890–) is a fecund critic and the literary historian of modern Turkey, at present professor of Turkish language and literature at both the Ankara and Istanbul state universities. Other authors of some significance are Ṣadrī Ertem, an excellent novelist; Maḥmūd Jesarī (now: Yesarî), a popular literary critic; Pejāmi Ṣafā (now: Peyami Safa), a novelist; and the poets Fārūq Nāfyẓ (1898–), who produced four volumes of verse between 1918 and 1928 (among them *Čoban Češmesi,* The Shepherd's Fountain), and Behdžet Kemāl (now: Behçet Kemāl), who sang of the deeds of Kemal's revolution. There are many young poets—Xālid Faxrī, Naẓīm Ḥikmet, Jašar Nābī, Nedžīb Fāẓyl, and Aḥmed Qudsī. The poet Meḥmed 'Ākif (1873–1936) must be given a separate place. He was the author of the verses of the Turkish national anthem, but he stood alone against the trend of the times, remaining faithful to the Islamic traditions, so that public mention of him was for a while avoided.

Mustafa Kemal, "Atatürk" (1880–1938), first president of the Turkish republic, was a good political writer and stylist. He composed numerous political essays, among them the *Nuṭuq* (Discourse), a magnificent and lengthy speech delivered before the National Assembly.

See: E. J. W. Gibb, *A History of Ottoman Poetry* (6 vols., 1900–1909); O. Hachtmann, *Die türkische Literatur des XX. Jahrhunderts* (1916); Köprülü Zāde Meḥmed Fu'ād, *Bugünkü Edebijjāt* (1923) and *Türk Edebijjāt Ta'rīxi* (1926); Ettore Rossi, "Odierne tendenze literarie e politiche in Turchia," *Oriente moderno,* IX (1929), 580–90; W. Barthold, *Zwölf Vorlesungen über die Geschichte der Türken Mittel-Asiens,* tr. from Osman-Turkish into German by Theodor Menzel (1935); S. Saussey, *Prosateurs turcs contemporains; extraits choisis, présentés et traduits* (1935).

K. H. M.

Tuwim, Juljan (1894–, Polish poet), was born in the factory town of Łódź, of middle-class Jewish stock, and educated in the Russian Gymnasium there. In 1918 he burst upon the literary scene with a poem "Wiosna w mieście" (Spring in the City) that provoked wide discussion and controversy. A leading spirit in the *Skamander* (*see* Polish literature) group, Tuwim has often been called Poland's Walt Whitman. Because of his declared purpose to expand the scope of Polish poetry so that it would sing not only, as in the past, of rural charms and tender sentiments, but "of fortresses, cities, subways, factories, streets, soil, and everything under the sun," Tuwim is regarded as the founder of Polish futurism. A virtuoso of the written word, Tuwim is Poland's outstanding translator from the Russian, his renderings of Pushkin, for example, always equaling and sometimes even excelling the original. A man of the widest interests—bibliophile, anthologist (of "literary trifles"), lexicographer (of Bacchic terms)—Tuwim was Free Poland's most glittering literary phenomenon. A collection of his early poems appeared in 1933, and in 1942 an anthology of all his works was published in New York (*Wybór pism;* A Selection of Writings). One of Tuwim's most successful hobbies was the fashioning of rhymes for children. In this field his *Lokomotywa* (1938; Eng. tr., *Locomotive,* 1940) is to be noted.

See: E. W. Titus, "A Polish Author," *Literary Review of New York Post,* February 16, 1924; K. Czachowski, *Obraz współczesnej literatury polskiej,* III (1936), 280–292, 708–710.

A. P. C.

Tvedt, Jens (1857–1935, Norwegian novelist), was born of a peasant family in Hardanger on the western coast of Norway. After graduating from a teachers' college he lived most of his life as a schoolmaster, journalist, and librarian in Stavanger. Apart from experiments in prose lyrics and plays his writing consists of more than 20 novels published from 1885 to 1928, written exclusively in Landsmaal describing the life of the people of the author's home region. Tvedt is the outstanding representative of the school of the "home-soil novelists." His first books shocked readers by their unvarnished descriptions of life in the small farms along the narrow fjords of the west, so different from previous somewhat roseate pictures of eastern peasant life. But Tvedt's realism is never brutal or morbid. Behind his careful and veracious description there is a strong optimism, a belief in the inherent health and vitality of the people; he shares their own common sense. His "classical realism" is far from naturalism and also far from the pale neo-romanticism of the 90's and is deeply rooted in Norwegian tradition. There is no psychological piquancy in his books, but one finds real life in them, sound feeling, and a natural harmony of subject and form; they are plastic in the classical sense. Outstanding are *Vanheppa* (1891; Bad Luck) and *Madli und' apalen* (1900; Madli under the Apple Tree), stories of everyday endurance of hardship, written with sympathy and genial humor, in a firm New Norse close to the style of the folk narrators. Tvedt's lyrical trend is conspicuous in the love story *Djup jord* (1904; Deep Soil), perhaps his most important work. In his later books the tendency toward didacticism and idyls takes the upper hand. Tvedt has strongly influenced the farm novel in Norway.

See: J. Bukdahl, "Jens Tvedt," in *Norsk aarbok* (1925), pp. 39–59, and in *Det skjulte Norge* (1926), pp. 62–71.

S. S.

Tynyanov, Yuri Nikolayevich (1894–1943, Russian novelist, scholar, critic, and translator), was born at Rezhitsa (Rezekne, Latvia) and graduated from the University of Petrograd (1918). He quickly established himself as a leader of the formalists, who studied literature as form or construction. While lecturing on the history of Russian poetry, he published *Problema stikhotvornovo yazyka* (1924; The Problem of the Poetic Language) and a collection of penetrating studies (*Arkhaisty i novatory,* 1929; Archaists and Innovators), dealing largely with prominent Russian poets. He has also translated Heine (3 vols., 1927–1934).

Tynyanov's creative work is derived from his interest in literary history and theory. His first novel, *Kyukhlya* (1925), which re-creates the quixotic figure of the poet Küchelbecker, friend of Pushkin and one of the Decembrist conspirators, is carefully documented and well constructed, but also manages to convey an air of spontaneity. However, in *Smert Vazir-Mukhtara* (1929; Eng. tr., *Death and Diplomacy in Persia,* 1938) history and theory gain the upper hand. The real hero of the novel is the year immediately preceding the assassination of the dramatist Griboyedov (1795–1829), then on a diplomatic mission to Persia, rather than the dramatist himself. An impressionistic technique is used to show Griboyedov going to his doom through a series of meetings with characters who represent various themes. Of Tynyanov's historical tales, the most original is "Podporuchik Kizhe" (1930; Eng. tr., "Second Lieutenant Also," in *Soviet Short Stories,* 1942); constructed on the premise of the absence of a hero, it is admirable technically but empty of life. The first two parts of the novel *Pushkin* (1936) represent a partial return to the methods of *Kyukhlya;* the development of the youthful poet is shown with realistic simplicity, while the subordinate characters form a rich gallery drawn from what is perhaps the most fascinating period of Russian literary and social history.

See: L. Tsyrlin, *Tynyanov-Belletrist* (1935); Y. Tager, "Tynyanov," in *Literaturnaya entsiklopediya,* Vol. XI (1938).

P. A. P.

U

Ukrainian literature. The last three decades of the 19th century in Russia saw Ukrainian literature laboring under grave political difficulties. The tsarist authorities viewed the development of Ukrainian culture with a jaundiced eye, because of a suspicion that it would lead inevitably to political separatism. As a consequence, a brief lucid interval of toleration in the early 1870's, during which there was a phenomenal upsurge of original work in music, drama, poetry, and scholarship (including monumental collections of folk poetry and folklore), was followed by a drastic ukase of Tsar Alexander II on May 18, 1876, by which Ukrainian books and newspapers were absolutely prohibited and the Ukrainian theatres closed. Only under the milder rule of Austria, in Galicia and in Bukovina, was it possible for Ukrainian literature to develop with any degree of freedom, and even there it had to struggle against strongly Pan-Russian movements that sought to destroy it.

Lemberg (Ukrainian, Lviv; Polish, Lwów) became for more than a generation the chief center of Ukrainian culture, a trend which was assisted especially by the printing projects of the Shevchenko Scientific Society, founded in 1873. The outstanding single figure in creative writing was Ivan Franko

(1856–1916), a poet of remarkable industry and fecundity. Franko was the son of a peasant, originally of German stock, and in his youth suffered three periods of imprisonment for his political activities. He took his Ph.D. degree from the University of Vienna in 1894 and seemed destined for the chair of Ukrainian language and literature in the University of Lemberg, but his past espousal of socialism and Ukrainian nationalism thwarted this hope. He made a lean and precarious living as a hack journalist, yet found time for voluminous translations from German, Russian, and Czech and for a copious output of original work, especially his epic *Moses* (1905), in which the disheartened Hebrew leader symbolizes himself; *Smert Kayina* (1889; The Death of Cain), a misanthropic philosophical poem, influenced by Byron; *Lys Mykyta* (1890; Mickey Fox), a rollicking animal epic; several volumes of lyrics, predominantly melancholy; and a number of historical novels and tales of Galician life. Among Ukrainian poets, Franko is usually ranked second only to Shevchenko. He lacks Shevchenko's Burns-like zest of inspiration, but he has a much broader culture and an unusual capacity for artistic perseverance. So extensive was his output that he may almost be regarded as having created a modern Ukrainian literature single-handed. Among other Ukrainian authors who at this time made Galicia their center of operations were Panteleimon Kulish (1819–1897), poet, novelist, critic, and translator of 10 of Shakespeare's plays, and Alexander Konisky (1836–1900), poet, novelist, and dramatist. Still others whose work, forbidden in Russia, was now published in Galicia were Marko Vovchok (pseud. of Maria Markovich, 1834–1907), a gleaner of folk tales, and Ivan Nechuy-Levitsky (1838–1918), a novelist. In the background of this whole generation, but operating chiefly from exile in Switzerland and Bulgaria, was the notable scholar and political leader, Michael Drahomaniv (1841–1895), formerly professor of history in the University of Kiev. Associated with him as a pioneer was another professor, Volodimir Antonovich (1834–1908).

Bukovina was a secondary center of relatively unfettered activity. Here the chief writer was Osip Yuri Fedkovich (1834–1888), who spent his youth as an officer in the Austrian army. His lyrics and legends are suffused with the tenderness of the folk songs he had learned in his youth and with a sense of the beauty of the Carpathians. Isidore Vorobkevich (1836–1903) was a popular poet of considerable talent.

A striking development in the Greater Ukraine was the creation, after 1880, of a Ukrainian theatre by Marko Kropivnitsky (1841–1910) and a group of gifted associates such as Michael Staritsky (1840–1904) and Ivan Tobilevich (1845–1907). Among the best-known plays of these men are (to give the titles in English): *Olesya, At the Census, Two Sevenths,* and *The Wild One* by Kropivnitsky; *Christmas Night, In the Dark, Bohdan Khmelnitsky, Marusia Bohuslavka,* and *The Last Night* by Staritsky; and *The Vagabond, The Landlord, The Unfortunate One, The Servant Girl, Martin Borula,* and *Conceit* by Tobilevich.

Following close upon the authors already mentioned, and indeed overlapping them, came a younger generation, chiefly in the Greater Ukraine but publishing most of its work in Galicia. Such were the gifted poetess Lesya Ukrayinka (pseud. of Larissa Kvitka, née Kosach, 1872–1913), the author of dramatic poems and of several fine dramas in verse (*Song of the Forest, In the Catacombs, Rufinus and Priscilla, The Drinking Bout, The Babylonian Captivity, In the Ruins*); Mikola Kotsiubinsky (1864–1913), an eminent novelist, author of *The Dream, On the Rock, Fata Morgana, On the Island, By the Minarets, Unknown, Laughter, The Début;* Boris Hrinchenko (1863–1910), a great philologist, author of a four-volume dictionary of the Ukrainian language; Volodimir Samiylenko (1864–1925), poet and satirist; Vasyl Stefanik (1871–1936), a gifted Galician storyteller, graduate in medicine from Cracow University, who wrote such tales as *The Darling, The Blue Book,* and *The Stone Cross;* Agafangel Krimsky (1874–), novelist and translator from Arabic and Persian poets; Pavlo Grabovsky (1864–1902), poet and translator; Olga Kobylianska (1865–1942), a novelist of Bukovina; Bohdan Lepky (1872–1942), lyric poet, critic, and historian; and Alexander Oles (1878–), a lyric poet of great charm. Ultimately to tower above all these, however, was Michael Hrushevsky (1866–1934), the greatest of modern Ukrainian scholars. Trained at the University of Kiev, Hrushevsky was appointed in 1894 to the chair of Ukrainian history in the University of Lemberg. The results of a long life devoted to able research are to be found in his 10-volume *Istoriya Ukrayiny-Rusy* (1898–1937; History of Russian Ukraine) and in his three-volume *Istoriya ukrayins'koyi lyteratury* (1923; History of

Ukrainian Literature). These are indubitably the greatest works in their field. Hrushevsky was in 1917–1918 the first president of the independent Ukrainian nation, with its capital at Kiev. He lived in exile, 1918–1924, but then returned to Russia. He died in 1934, broken by four years of imprisonment at the hands of the Soviet government.

The fate of Hrushevsky is typical of that of most Ukrainian writers under the first 20 years of the Soviet regime. Nationalism, which for nearly a century had been the major motivation of Ukrainian literature, now became a deadly political offense, and the pressure against it grew relentless, especially after 1930. Some of the Ukrainian authors succumbed to this pressure and conformed completely to the new order. Such were the poets Pavlo Tychyna, Maxim Rylsky, and Volodimir Sosiura and the novelists Andrei Holovko, Yuri Yanovsky, and Mikola Bazhan. Others were nominally Communist but struggled by devious means to perpetuate the nationalist point of view; and these, almost without exception, have been liquidated. Examples are the dramatist Mikola Kulish and the novelists Mikola Chvylovy, M. Kosoris, A. Olessich, Volodimir Gsyzky, and O. Dosvitny. Still other authors were deliberately counterrevolutionary and were systematically sought out and shot, *e.g.*, in 1930 Andrei Nikovsky, Sergei Yefremov, L. Starytzka-Cherniachivska, and M. Yevchenko and in 1934 Evhen Pluznyk, Gregory Kosynka, D. Falkivsky, Yuri Shkurupey, and Aleksa Vlysko. Ukrainian literature, in a world where colossal struggles of new orders were impending, had been fatally caught "between the pass and fell incensed points of mighty opposites."

See: B. Lepky, ed., *Struny, antologiya ukrayinskoyi poeziyi* (1922); S. Yefremov, *Korotka istoriya ukrayinskoho pys'menstva* (1924); A. P. Coleman, *Brief Survey of Ukrainian Literature* (1936); D. Doroshenko, *History of the Ukraine* (1939); M. Hrushevsky, *A History of Ukraine* (one-volume abridgment in English, 1941).

W. K.

Ullman, Gustaf (1881–, Swedish poet and short-story writer), born in the province of Halland on Sweden's west coast, restricts his literary motifs almost entirely to the primitive landscape and folk life of his native province. Though in this regional strain in his art he may be compared with Selma Lagerlöf (*q.v.*), greatest of Swedish regionalists in prose fiction, in most other respects Ullman's art is as far removed from Selma Lagerlöf's as it could well be. He lacks completely Selma Lagerlöf's rich, colorful fantasy, her light, playful humor, her love of apostrophe and paradox, her vividly pulsing prose style. Ullman's art is reserved, laconic, severely close to the earth. Even the poetry of his young manhood (*Västkust,* 1903, West Coast; *Caprifol,* 1905; and *Sångarbikt,* 1910, Confessions in Song) indulges in no effusive lyricism, is everywhere sober, severe, restrained. His masters seem to have been the two great painters from Sweden's west coast, Karl Nordström, who has painted the coastal landscape in bare, massive, heroic lines, and Carl Wilhelmson, who has employed an almost equally severe brush in depicting the deep religious character of the people of this region. In Ullman's poetry the landscape dominates, though its folk life also occasionally enters upon the scene. In his prose fiction the people of his province come into a much more sharp focus. Many of these tales are simple straightforward tales of the folk, with no particular problem or theme; but the most successful of them are quietly probing studies of the pietistic religious psychology of the west coast folk, in which Ullman casts up accounts with the severe religious dogmatism ("Schartauism") which for a century has dominated the spiritual life of this region. His most important works on this theme are the collection of short stories *Präster* (1907; Preachers) and the short novel *En flickas ära* (1909; A Girl's Honor). Though Ullman has continued to produce of late years, his work reflects no new developments in either art or subject matter.

See: F. Böök, *Resa kring svenska Parnassen* (1926), pp. 103–115.

A. G.

Unamuno, Miguel de (1864–1936, Spanish philosopher, essayist, poet, and novelist), born in Bilbao of Basque ancestry, became a writer whose art and thought merge, both spontaneously and consciously, into something of the very essence of Spain. At the same time he endowed his country with a new awareness, a new sensitivity, and a new international perspective. For centuries Spain had lived bound by her pitiful attempts to find a position between the divine and the profane, the temporal and the eternal, the particular and the universal. Unamuno hailed the dilemma as a challenge for everyone in Spain and throughout the world who is not content with the dogmatic and nicely turned replies of any science, philosophy, religion, or art. Unamuno made the problem his problem and sought its origins by way of a vital dialectic which is integrated in beauty, in pages of unparalleled prose and verse. From the time of his very first writings the author proposed to stir the conscience of his readers without offering, as a goal, any fixed or systematic doctrine. And in his monumental *Del sentimiento trágico de la vida* (1913; Eng. tr., *The Tragic Sense of Life in Men and in Peoples,* 1921), he says: "My work—I was going to say my mission—is to destroy everyone's faith, faith in affirmation, faith in negation, and faith in abstention, and this because of my faith in faith itself; it is to combat all those who live resigned, be it to Catholicism, to rationalism, or to agnosticism; it is to make everyone live fearfully and hungrily."

Unamuno is close to the despairing souls of history—Job, Pascal, Spinoza, Sénancour, Kierkegaard. In their society he found himself, it may be said, and with their help he found his own Spain; through them, too, his vehement desire to project himself in an eternal perspective was strengthened. The battle represented in his brilliant books was matched by that of his everyday life, in a continual struggle with circumstances. As a young man he held the chair of Greek in the University of Salamanca, although he was never interested in so-called scholarly investigations. His personality overflowed the narrow limits of academic activity to make him a master of souls. He discovered his real milieu less in the university than in the spiritual richness of Salamanca itself, where his Basque character—his tenacious courage, timidity, monodeism, and dryness of expression—became Castilianized in the presence of the clear and open landscapes and in the atmosphere of beauty of one of the most elegant and rhythmical cities which Spain possesses.

From the vantage point of Salamanca, Unamuno, in successive experiences, apprehended and integrated in his soul and style the multifarious variety of enigmatic Iberia. The process gave *Por tierras de Portugal y de España* (1911) and *Andanzas y visiones españolas* (1922). Unamuno was the first to catch in a vital synthesis the essential meaning of Peninsular poetry, in Spanish, in Portuguese, and in Catalan. He did not stop here, because his sensitive and comprehensive understanding extended also to the lands of Hispanic America, whose literary originality he was one of the first to perceive and evaluate. In his work there live cordially side by side all those Hispanic differences which in everyday life have the appearance of mutually repellent dissociations—just as the contradictions and paradoxes in Unamuno, logically irreconcilable, take on meaning in a supreme, vital, and poetic unity.

The author struggled not only against dogmatism and intellectual fetters, but also against any political structure which would not permit the human being the free play of his impulses, even of his errors. Unamuno did not combat the monarchy during the first years of the 20th century, when Spain was living in a sort of "gentle anarchy" and when no one was facing the grave political and social problems which, later appearing as unavoidable questions, were to give rise to the greatest catastrophe in Spanish history. He began to attack Alfonso XIII when the latter showed signs of wishing to govern Spain dictatorially, especially during the dictatorship of General Miguel Primo de Rivera (1923–1930), established with the complicity of the monarch. Unamuno's violent writings cost him a long banishment (1924–1930). Upon his return to Spain he accepted the Republic of 1931 with enthusiasm and was elected a deputy to the Cortes Constituyentes. Soon, however, he showed his disagreement with the new regime because he considered it both too radical and too dogmatic in religious and social matters. Here, it must be admitted, is a real weakness in Unamuno; here he never expressed a single constructive idea and limited himself to the easy role of the iconoclast with both pen and word. Marvelously steady as an artist, in his life as a politician Unamuno was anarchical and the victim of whims. With his negative and harsh criticism he contributed extensively to the confusion of his country. When in 1936 the army rebelled against the republican regime, Unamuno apparently accepted willingly the overthrow of that badly prepared attempt at Spanish democracy. Soon, however, this illusion vanished too, if indeed it can be said that he ever really had it. To him is attributed the prophetic phrase, spoken in a formal university gathering in Salamanca in October, 1936, in the presence of the leaders of the military revolt: "You will conquer but not convince." A short while later he was dying in bitterness and desperation.

Few of the recent writers of Europe have had the full and vitalizing erudition of Unamuno. In him are found effective echoes of world literature, from classic antiquity to

Shakespeare, Cervantes, Leopardi, and Whitman, and to the Dane, Kierkegaard, whose language he learned in order to understand him more fully. He never approached philosophy, science, or literature with a cold intellectual interest; his purpose was to fuse culture with his own anguish over the question of life and death, a basic problem with him and one which renders all else of secondary import. Thus it is that in the characters of his novels *Niebla* (1914; Eng. tr., *Mist*, 1928), *Tres novelas ejemplares y un prólogo* (1920; Eng. tr., *Three Exemplary Novels and a Prologue*, 1930), and *La tía Tula* (1921) he seeks out the essentially "personal" constituent of their make-ups, the ultimate representation of conscience which is sensed to be hovering between today and eternity and which "personalizes" everything about it. But the supreme pages of his work must be sought in his *Ensayos* (8 vols., 1916–1918), replete with profound visions; in them he has touched on a multitude of themes that go to the heart of the essential problems of present-day life. A noble example of his verse is the poem to the star, "Aldebarán" (in *Poesías*, 1907). This magnificent symphony reveals, as in a synthesis, what Luis de León, Pascal, and many others give but fragmentarily. It is characterized by a style the words of which are a ladder leading to the most moving exaltation, an ineffable exaltation in which man feels, at one and the same time, that he is losing and finding himself.

See: S. de Madariaga, *The Genius of Spain and Other Essays on Spanish Contemporary Literature* (1923); J. E. Crawford Flitch, "Introduction," in Unamuno, *Essays and Soliloquies* (1925); M. Romera Navarro, *Miguel de Unamuno, novelista, poeta, ensayista* (1928); H. Daniel-Rops, *Carte d'Europe* (1928), pp. 121–161; J. Marias, *Miguel de Unamuno* (1943).

A. C.

Undset, Sigrid (1882–, Norwegian novelist), is the most distinguished of present-day Scandinavian writers of prose fiction. Born in the charming little Danish town of Kallundborg, Zealand, she moved with her family to Christiania in 1884. Her early childhood in Christiania (treated in the autobiographical work *Elleve år*, 1934, Eng. tr., *The Longest Years*, 1935) was relatively happy; but the death of her father, a well-known archaeologist, when she was only 11 years old, forced the family into the narrowest of economic circumstances. Her education was curtailed, and it was necessary for her to accept employment in an office when she was 16 years of age. The early experience as a self-supporting young woman provided her, however, with much of the material for her early tales. The first of these, *Fru Martha Oulie*, appeared in 1907, to be followed in rapid succession by three more volumes of prose fiction dealing with modern young women, the collection of stories entitled *Den lykkelige alder* (1908; The Happy Age) and two novels, *Jenny* (1911; Eng. tr., 1921) and *Vaaren* (1914; Springtime). During these years was also published her first historical novel, *Vigaljot og Vigdis* (1909; Eng. tr., *Gunnar's Daughter*, 1936). Nearly all of these early tales are concerned with the relation between man and woman, conceived primarily in ultimate ethical terms. She did not fall in line with the neo-romantic Norwegian literary vogue of the day (as represented in Gunnar Heiberg, *q.v.*, and others) where "art" and "love" were looked upon as absolute antisocial concepts that had nothing to do with house and home and all of the practical circumstances of life. Instead Sigrid Undset's early tales conceive of love between man and woman as a matter of quiet everyday growth and development within the immediate limitations and obligations of homemaking. In *Jenny*, the most important of these early stories, the heroine finally meets a tragic fate because she half-consciously "experiments" with love, until it is too late for her to meet love's immediate crucial moral obligations as a mother and homemaker. In the matter of technique, Sigrid Undset's early work is marked by a sober, unpretentious realism, an almost artless directness and simplicity scarcely designed to attract a wide reading public—at least not until the partially sensational contents of *Jenny* made, in 1911, a more sharp and forcible impression. During the First World War Sigrid Undset's production fell off somewhat, and what she did write was of a rather miscellaneous kind: two volumes of tales (*Splinten av troldspeilet*, 1917, one story from which has appeared in an English translation, *Images in a Mirror*, 1938; and *De kloge jomfruer*, 1918, The Wise Virgins); a retelling of the King Arthur romances based on Mallory (*Fortaellinger om Kong Artur og ridderne av det runde bord*, 1915); a literary study dealing with the Brontë sisters (*Tre søstre*, 1917); and a volume of essays on the woman question (*En kvindessynspunkt*, 1919). All of these volumes reveal an increasing preoccupation on the author's part with ethical matters, particularly with a new religious approach to ethical problems; and they serve therefore both as valuable documents in a study of Sigrid Undset's religious development and as an introduction to her later historical novels, in which ethico-religious concerns play such a preeminent part. In 1928 she was awarded the Nobel prize in literature. She took up residence in the United States in 1940.

It is in her two great historical novels, the trilogy *Kristin Lavransdatter* (1920–1922; Eng. tr., 1923–1927) and the tetralogy *Olav Audunsson* (1925–1927; Eng. tr., *The Master of Hestviken,* 1928–1930), that Sigrid Undset's claim to fame primarily lies, though some of her earlier work is to be included in the better prose fiction appearing in Norway in the years before the First World War, and though her later novels (beginning with *Gymnadenia,* 1929, Eng. tr., *The Wild Orchid,* 1931) certainly represent, despite their rather forced strain of religious apologetics, one of the high points in Norwegian fiction in the years before the Second World War. The two great novels reveal an absolute mastery of historical periods, with their dress and food habits, their customs and ways of thought, their broad backgrounds of political and military intrigue; but Sigrid Undset never permits the impedimenta of history in its more antiquarian aspects to interfere with her primary concern with the individual human being in his ceaseless moral struggle with the baffling materials of life. This is what gives her historical novels at one and the same time their warmly human everyday realism and their marvelously sensitive psychological perspective. In their purely narrative movement these novels are slow, leisurely, unhurried, proceeding with a quietly deliberate solemnity, never impatient of detail, ever subtly alert to all those minute forms and phases of outward phenomena which register their impressions upon human character and determine human destiny. This steady stateliness of general movement gathers itself together at times, leaps into a blazing intensity of feeling or of action in certain individual episodes, only to recede again into its unhurried way—as unhurried as the ceaseless processes of nature and eternity and God. Suffusing it all there is a note of unutterable majesty, even of sublimity—the poignant sublimity with which a story of human fate can become invested when a profoundly unhurried artistry touches it and bring it into the delicately penetrating focus of an intensely serious creative imagination. It is to be noted that in these novels the religious emphasis emerges much more sharply than it had in Sigrid Undset's earlier fiction, and not merely because these novels deal directly with a social order dominated by the medieval Church. Sigrid Undset herself became a convert to the Catholic Church shortly after the completion of *Kristin Lavransdatter;* and in most of her authorship since, particularly in *Gymnadenia* and its sequel, *Den brændende busk* (1930; Eng. tr., *The Burning Bush,* 1932), she has not been able to refrain from giving more or less direct expression to a dogmatic Catholic view of the modern human scene. As a recent Norwegian critic has pointed out, we may consider these two late novels dealing with modern life—together with *Ida Elisabeth* (1932; Eng. tr., 1933), *Den trofaste hustru* (1936; Eng. tr., *The Faithful Wife,* 1937), and the very important *Madame Dorothea* (1939; Eng. tr., 1940)—as one of the more important between-the-wars literary "contributions to a fundamental accounting with a materialistic-mechanical philosophy of life." Sigrid Undset has come with the years to find in Catholic dogma the only solution to the problems of a modern world.

See: A. H. Winsnes, *Norges litteratur fra februarrevolutionen til verdenskrigen,* part 2, pp. 528–545, Vol. V (1937) of F. Bull, F. Paasche, and A. H. Winsnes, *Norsk litteraturhistorie;* Alrik Gustafson, *Six Scandinavian Novelists* (1940), pp. 286–361.

A. G.

Ungaretti, Giuseppe (1888–, Italian poet), born of Italian parents in Alexandria, Egypt, spent years in Paris absorbing French culture. From 1915 to 1918 he fought in the First World War, in France and in Italy (beautiful poems tell of this experience in an intense, sharp way, *e.g.,* "Veglia," "Peso," "Soldato," "San Martino del Carso"). He lived for some time in Rome. In late years he has been in South America, teaching Italian literature in the University of São Paulo, Brazil. Ungaretti has collaborated on many literary papers and reviews, among others the *Lacerba* (Florence), *Voce* (Florence), *Popolo d'Italia* (Milan), *Littérature* (Paris), *Ronda* (Rome), *Europe nouvelle* (Paris). In 1916 appeared *Il Porto sepolto* which was followed by *La Guerre* (1919) and *Allegria di naufragi* (1919). *L'Allegria* (1931) contains previous poems reelaborated. More recently Ungaretti has produced a collection of poems, *Sentimento del tempo* (1933), and a book of poems translated from foreign authors, *Traduzioni* (1936).

Ungaretti is the most representative poet of the movement of pure poetry in Italy. Following the path traced by the French symbolists (*see* French symbolism), Rimbaud, Mallarmé, and Apollinaire (*qq.v.*), he searches for a condition of purity and lyrical essence. He aims to restore to words—as the critic Alfredo Gargiulo said—their original virginity and their reconquered lyrical primitivity. To convey in his poetry only the nude essence of his inspiration, Ungaretti tries to concentrate and polish his means of expression by various degrees, employing a complex technique. Therefore he repudiates the traditional metrical and syntactical systems, employing new devices, some of which, such as graphical and typographical innovations, have been identified with the attempts of the *futuristi.* Some extremely short poems ("Sera," "Cielo e mare") are good examples of Ungaretti's effort toward concentration, of his attempt to reach the "state of grace," to express the feeling of "illumination" and the sense of "magic" by which he feels himself possessed. The fundamental note of his lyrical temperament is the striving to reproduce the ineffable. In his elaborate and tortured mode of expression he appears as the central subject of his poetry, as a man in an effort at communication with nature, mystery, and God ("La Pietà," "Cairo," "La Preghiera," "La Morte meditata"). He is the *uomo di pena* (man of sorrow), the poor heart afraid of his ignorance, the creature eternally exiled.

Ungaretti's poetry is still very much discussed: some critics refuse to find in it any serious intellectual meaning and consider it somewhat of a voluptuous playing with words. Others, instead, because of his attempt to transfer into poetry human and essential values, transforming his experiences into a lyrical world at once individual and universal, have connected his name with those of Leopardi and Petrarch.

See: A. Bocelli, "Scrittori d'oggi," *Nuova Antologia,* CCCLXII (1932), 422–428; P. Pancrazi, *Scrittori italiani del novecento* (1934), pp. 162–169.

E. C.

Unruh, Fritz von (1885–, German dramatist and poet), was born at Coblenz. Scion of a noble family, son of a Prussian general, he was educated for a military career at Plön and entered active service in the German army. The young officer pondered over the problem of the soldier, whose profession in times of peace is futile and in times of war seems nothing but subordination. From his musings came the drama *Offiziere* (1912), which Max Reinhardt produced with great success. Feeling that a military career was incompatible with the creative forces of a poet, Unruh resigned his commission and wrote the drama *Prinz Louis Ferdinand von Preussen* (1913), in which duty frustrates the hero's judgment and desire. In 1914 Unruh was called back to the colors and fought through the First World War. His heart, however, battled for peace. The dramatic poem *Vor der Entscheidung* (written 1914, published 1919) was one of the first antiwar creations in Germany. In the narrative *Opfergang* (written in 1916 at Verdun, published 1918; Eng. tr., *Way of Sacrifice,* 1928) a metaphysical reason for war was sought but sadly found wanting. The idea of war was pursued to its mythical depth in the tragedy *Ein Geschlecht* (1916). *Platz* (1920), its sequel, showed that the revolution in Germany was a wrong solution. It did not bring forth the "new being," the dream of the expressionists.

Unruh tried a political career, became a member of the Reichstag, and gave a dithyrambic oration in memory of the murdered Walther Rathenau. When the idea of revenge threatened the understanding between the nations, Unruh worked for greater amity by writing the travel book *Flügel der Nike* (1924), publishing his speeches (*Reden,* 1924), and giving the world the festival play *Heinrich von Andernach* (1925), a great plea for love among men. He foresaw in his drama *Bonaparte* (1927; Eng. tr., 1928) a coming dictatorship and appealed to his countrymen to be alert. The works which followed, *Phaea* (1930), *Berlin in Monte Carlo* (1931), *Zero* (1932), failed to impress. When the Hitler movement gained control, Fritz von Unruh, winner of the Kleist and Schiller prizes, left Germany for Italy and France and finally found refuge in America. Unruh is not a propagandist but a poet; his works offer difficulties because of their expressionistic style and their musical language. He does not want to convince the intellect but grip the feeling of mankind.

See: Fritz Engel, *Fritz von Unruh und seine besten Bühnenwerke* (1922); Wilhelm Geyer, *Fritz von Unruh* (1924); Robert Meister, *Fritz von Unruh* (1925); Richard Samuel and R. Hinton Thomas, *Expressionism in German Life, Literature, and the Theatre* (1939), pp. 47–51, 97–101.

H. Bf.

Uppdal, Kristofer (1878–, Norwegian novelist), was born in an interior valley of northern

Tröndelag, the son of a small farmer who, however, soon moved into a small neighboring town in order to work there. At the age of 18 the son started as a workingman on the construction of railroads and continued at such labor for the better part of the following 15 years. He joined the Workingmen's Trade Union and was for a time a local leader in this movement. In 1905 he made his debut as a poet and during the next 25 years published not a few small volumes of poetry, more and more of a speculative or philosophical character, in a highly personal style, written in the dialect, somewhat normalized, of his home district (*e.g.*, *På galgeberge*, 1930; On the Mountain of the Gallows). His most important work, however, and in fact one of the outstanding products of modern Norwegian literature, was the series of novels he began publishing in 1910, which have for their subject the labor movement of recent years. The series started with five volumes appearing in the years 1911–1914, and was finished with five other volumes published 1919–1924, under a common title, taken from one of them, *Dansen gjenom skuggeheimen* (The Dance through the Shadow World). The plan of these novels is to present the psychological development of the Norwegian labor movement, from the primitive risings of unskilled and uneducated workers in the mines and on the roads up to national organization, the whole of it concentrated in the life, growth, and experiences of a few remarkable characters. The story is told with a flood of gorgeous colors and a red-hot intensity, and the heroes rise up in monumental, sometimes almost Gargantuan shapes. Pictured as the real source of the movement is an indomitable urge for self-assertion and mental expansion. The conflict arises from the double current in the souls of the workers who are making their own progress as a group and breaking away from the class of the farmers, but still always retaining the longing of the farmers for a fixed home. They are radical rebels against private capitalism, but firmly rooted in their peasant heritage, and therefore decidedly nationalistic in outlook. In the last volume of the series, *Domkyrkebyggaren* (The Cathedral Builder), in which the chief hero of the novel rises to national leadership, we can observe distinct traces of a schizophrenia that gradually took hold of the author and for 20 years stopped his production. Yet he had achieved a unique work of truly great dimensions.

H. K.

V

Vajda, János (1827–1897, Hungarian poet), was born in Pest (later Budapest) and died there. He had his secondary school education in Székesfehérvar. At the age of 18 he entered the University of Pest but soon abandoned intellectual pursuits for histrionic ambitions. For about a year he was a strolling actor, with hopes and no recognition. He fought in the Hungarian War of Independence of 1848–1849, and after the war he was sent in retaliation by the Austrians as a soldier to Italy. When in 1853 he returned to Hungary, he naturally sought the company of writers and poets, and was active as a journalist. In 1869 he was elected to the Hungarian Parliament. Vajda had an untamed spirit, a brooding disposition, probably a persecution complex, and his life was very unhappy. His first volume of lyric poems, *Költemények* (Poems), appeared in 1855. *Egy honvéd naplójából* (1869; From the Diary of a Homeguard) is considered one of his most representative works. He failed with his historical drama, *Ildikó* (1857; Ildikó). His poetic narratives, *e.g.*, *Találkozások* (1877; Meetings), *Alfréd regénye* (1883; The Story of Alfred), are of minor importance compared with his lyric poems, but they sustain interest. His love poems, "Gina emléke" (The Memory of Gina), "Szerelem átka" (Curse of Love), "Húsz év múlva" (After Twenty Years), show boundless passion, excitability, misanthropic uneasiness. His philosophical poems, "Öszi tájak" (Autumn Scenes), "Végtelenség" (The Infinite), "A Váli erdőben" (In the Forest of Vál), "Halál" (Death), reveal his absorption in the cosmos and his reflective gratitude towards nature; they also reveal an inevitable loneliness. Vajda's collected poems were published the first time in 1881, and the improved edition in 1895. Endre Ady (*q.v.*) rediscovered him in the 20th century. There is a Vajda János literary society in Budapest.

Though born in a city, Vajda's childhood was spent in Vál, a trans-Danubian village, close to green pastures, fertile fields, woods, and gardens. His father was a forester. It seems that these childhood experiences determined the poet's affection for nature; he felt that nature never deceived him, and it was nature that sometimes consoled his restless, morbid, distrustful spirit. The woman he married disappointed him and some of his friends proved false. There was something of the feverishness of Byron and Lermontov and much of the pessimism of Leopardi in Vajda. True, he was not a master of form; often his yearnings and renunciations were stronger than his ability to give them flawless poetic form. Nevertheless he could reach the heights of a major poet, and when this happened his spirit, nurtured by solitude and melancholy, conquered formlessness with the sure power of a poetic genius.

See: Gy. Kerekes, *Vajda élete és munkái* (1901); P. Gyulai, *Birálatok* (1911); A. Schöpflin, *Magyar irók* (1919); W. Kirkconnell, *The Magyar Muse; an Anthology* (1933).

J. R.

Valera, Juan (1824–1905, Spanish novelist, critic, poet, and diplomat), was born in Cabra, Córdoba, and spent his early years there and at Doña Mencía, where his mother, the marquesa de la Paniega, owned a large estate. His father, José Valera y Viaña, a retired naval officer, recognized his son's ability and spared no expense on his education. After completing his law studies, young Valera was early launched on a diplomatic career when his family secured for him an appointment as *agregado* to the duque de Rivas, ambassador at Naples. During his stay there (1847–1849), Valera studied Italian and Greek and greatly reinforced his native inclination toward the classical in art and literature. All his diplomatic posts—in Lisbon, Rio de Janeiro, and Russia and later as minister to Washington, Brussels, and Vienna—provided him with the opportunity of cultivating his mind and of writing long letters home in which he tells engagingly of his rich experience among the peoples and books of many countries.

Valera's literary work, a matter of 50 volumes, was, he would have us believe, but a parenthesis in his diplomatic career. He began by writing poetry (*Ensayos poéticos,* 1844; *Poesías,* 1858) and was disappointed that the public did not appreciate his verse which, though polished and correct, lacks spontaneity and deep feeling. He found it difficult at first to write prose, and it was not until his diplomatic career was interrupted in 1854 that he decided to try his hand at literary criticism. From then on he wrote for Spanish and later for Spanish American periodicals innumerable articles that fill many volumes of his *Obras completas* (1905; Vols. XIX–XL). These articles are delightful *causeries* that reveal an extraordinary agility and yet constancy of mind, a broad culture, definite artistic criteria, and a detachment rare in Spanish critics. In his reviews of contemporary works, however, Valera is too discreet to be direct; even his famous criticism of *Azul* (1888), which first brought Rubén Darío to the attention of the literary world, is guarded in its enthusiasm and dwells mostly on Valera's oft repeated conviction that the servile imitation of French literature is harmful to Spanish American writers. More significant are his essays on general literary questions, such as *Del romanticismo en España y de Espronceda* (1854), or his studies and academic discourses on masterpieces of the past, such as *Sobre el Quijote y sobre las diferentes maneras de comentarle y juzgarle* (1864) and *Sobre el Fausto de Goethe* (1878). Valera wrote many substantial essays, too, on political, historical, and philosophical themes, *e.g., Sobre el concepto que hoy se forma de España* (1868), *La revolución y la libertad religiosa en España* (1869), *La doctrina del progreso* (1859), and *El superhombre* (1897); in the last two he shows himself to be very skeptical of absolute progress—especially in art—and of evolution toward the superman.

Valera won acclaim as a critic of authority and a master of Spanish prose, but his audience was as yet restricted. It was not until 1874, when he wrote *Pepita Jiménez* (first Eng. tr., 1886)—the novel on which his fame most solidly rests—that he became a popular author. He held consistently, from *De la naturaleza y carácter de la novela* (1860) to *Apuntes sobre el nuevo arte de escribir novelas* (1886–1887), that a novel should be entertaining rather than instructive, that as a form of art it has as its only end to delight with the creation of beautiful form. He berated the sociological and scientific aims of the naturalistic novelists and found intolerable their deterministic philosophy. Valera's most cherished belief was in the capacity of the mind to choose freely between good and evil. In *Pepita Jiménez* the hero, who is about to take holy orders, suddenly discovers his love for the attractive young widow, Pepita; most of the novel is a subtle analysis of his inner conflict which ends in his choosing to renounce divine for human love. This delicate psychological analysis, the natural beauty of the Cordovan setting, the amusing candor of the village folk and the rich popular savor of their language, all contrive to make the novel one of the great classics of modern Spanish literature. Valera's novels—

El comendador Mendoza (1877; Eng. tr., *Commander Mendoza,* 1893) and *Doña Luz* (1879; Eng. tr., 1891) and the later ones he dictated after he had become blind, *Juanita la larga* (1895), *Genio y figura* (1897), and *Morsamor* (1899—are all simple, loosely woven tales, the action of which goes on in the mind or conscience of the main characters. Artistically, tales such as *El pájaro verde* and *Parsondes* (both 1860) and dialogues such as *Asclepigenia* (1878) are his most perfect works. They are written in his most characteristic manner, charming, shrewdly urbane, gently ironical, the manner of the intellectual epicure who ruminates on all the ideas and fancies ever conceived by man, remains in the end serenely and cheerfully skeptical of them all, but has enjoyed himself thoroughly and delighted his reader. In all of his thought Valera strikes a note—somewhat unusual in Spain—of tolerance, moderation, and harmony. Even in politics, as a member of the Cortes and later a senator for life, he always took the position midway between both extremes, and he never joined any party, for he was about equally opposed to the Neo-Catholic reactionaries and to the positivistic progressives. If Valera was not a great or original thinker, he was the greatest writer of Spanish prose since Cervantes, of whom his work is often reminiscent, in its humor, its indulgence toward human weakness, its good cheer, and especially in its style, which is classical without being archaic, naturally elegant, subtle yet luminous, and always delightful.

See: Manuel Azaña, introduction to Valera, *Pepita Jiménez,* "Clásicos castellanos" edition (1927), and *La novela de Pepita Jiménez,* (1929); Edith Fishtine, *Don Juan Valera, the Critic* (1933).

E. F. H.

Valéry, Paul (1871–1945, French poet and critic), was born in the Mediterranean town of Cette, near Montpellier. Son of a French father and an Italian mother, as a boy he spent his vacations in Italy, in particular in Genoa, whose magnificent architecture left a lasting impression on him. His schooling at Montpellier, first at the *lycée* and later at the school of law of the university, he found boring and unprofitable. His two great interests were architecture and poetry, the latter being stimulated by his discovery of Mallarmé and Verlaine (*qq.v.*) in 1889 and encounters with Pierre Louÿs and André Gide (*qq.v.*) in 1890. In 1891, after a month in Paris, during which he was admitted into Mallarmé's circle, and much heart-searching, he decided to give up the study of law. His verses were already being published by such little magazines as the *Ermitage,* the *Conque,* and the *Revue indépendante,* but he showed a strange reluctance to take his place as one of the younger symbolist poets. Instead, he turned from poetry completely. His *Introduction à la méthode de Léonard de Vinci* (Eng. tr., *Introduction to the Method of Leonardo da Vinci,* 1929) was published in the *Nouvelle Revue* (1895), and *La Soirée avec M. Teste* (Eng. tr., *An Evening with Mr. Teste,* 1925) in the *Centaure* (1896); he filled a prosaic post in the War Department from 1897 to 1900 and then, after marrying Mlle Gobillard, niece of Berthe Morisot, took an equally prosaic position with the Havas news agency.

Valéry's long period of silence was not disturbed until the winter of 1912–1913. By that time something of a legend had grown up about him: copies of his early verse and of *La Soirée* were treasured by connoisseurs, and Gide prevailed upon him to make some of this literary material more available by consenting to the publication, in one volume, of his scattered poems. Valéry wished to end the book with a short poem which would be in some sense a valedictory. He turned once again to the art he had abandoned over a decade before; and as he labored, what he had thought of as some 25 lines grew into his major work, *La Jeune Parque,* published by itself in 1917. *La Jeune Parque* is a difficult poem—the most difficult in the French language, Thibaudet (*q.v.*) has said—but even its difficulty and its appearance in a crucial war year did not prevent the critics from recognizing it as a masterpiece. Within the space of a few years Valéry became a major literary figure: *La Soirée* was reedited in 1919, and in 1920 three volumes of poetry, *Odes, Le Cimetière marin* (Eng. tr., *The Graveyard by the Sea,* 1932), and *Album des vers anciens,* appeared. Though even now Valéry could not be termed prolific, his silence, once broken, was not resumed. In the following years were published, besides many fugitive pieces, such important books as the volume of verse *Charmes* (1922) and the prose works *Eupalinos* (1923; Eng. tr., 1932), five collections of essays all called *Variété* (1924, 1929, 1936, 1938, and 1944; Eng. tr., *Variety,* 1927; *Variety: Second Series,* 1938), *Pièces sur l'art* (1934), and *Regards sur le monde actuel* (1931). In 1925 Valéry was elected to the French Academy, taking the chair of Anatole France (*q.v.*).

Had Valéry never written *La Jeune Parque*

and the poems that followed, it would be easy, his prose aside, to label him as a second-rate symbolist (*see* French symbolism) and to dismiss him. Even the most casual acquaintance with this later work, however, will convince the reader, no matter what his final estimate may be, that it cannot be lightly or easily dismissed—or even described. *La Jeune Parque,* taken alone, might be regarded as a continuation of the method and themes of Mallarmé; many of the poems in *Charmes* might suggest a continuation of a classic tradition, with touches of symbolism remaining from Valéry's youth. Perhaps Valéry can be best described as attempting to apply the techniques developed by the symbolists, as well as by modern philosophers and psychologists, to express the movements of man's consciousness and to do it in a strict prosody, since only such a prosody affords the poet adequate scope for a demonstration of his technical powers. Valéry is a great philosophical poet, in the sense that, today, philosophy is more concerned with *how* than with *what* it knows. Philosophy conceived of as didactic is impossible material for poetry—for Valéry at least—but when it becomes analytic he can welcome it with open arms. Here Valéry has the advantage of Mallarmé; the material of symbolism was generally personal and the symbol esoteric; but Valéry's subjects, though studied in him and with the appearance of individuality, are actually universal and in that sense impersonal. *Le Cimetière marin* and *La Jeune Parque* may at times be difficult in sense or expression, but they have the supreme merit of springing from a movement of thought and emotion through which, on some level and in some degree, each intelligent man passes. Even such poems as "Aurore," "Les Pas," and "Palme," specific and limited as their subject, the working of the poetic process, may seem to be, appear on more mature reflection universal as expressing, though necessarily concretely, general psychological truths.

If it can be said that Valéry was esoteric in anything, it was in the unusual, almost morbid importance he placed on the relation of potentiality to action. A series of antitheses characterizes his thought and his verse—appearance and reality, mind and body—but none is more prominent or more important than that of contemplation and action. The concept of an abstract "method" which would represent, in effect, the essence of all human thought, the idea of a being who through such abstraction had attained to the possibility of perfection in all fields, these speculations have constantly fascinated him. In the *Introduction* and *La Soirée* he imagined such a being and drew the necessary conclusion that for one of such pure and absolute potentiality action becomes impossible, except as a revelation of imperfection. To know oneself master of a technique should be enough; to demonstrate one's mastery through the actual writing of a poem or constructing of a building implies a desire to please the crowd or to be admired by them and is in itself admission of less than perfect self-sufficiency. How far such speculations go to explain Valéry's period of silence is hard to say, but it is obvious that besides furnishing him with the theme of much of his poetry they strongly colored his attitude towards his own work and that of others. Through the very fact of being a poet, Valéry chose action, of course, rather than the alternative silence of thought or dream, and in the conclusion of *Le Cimetière marin* he expressed his choice nobly. Yet it must never be overlooked that for Valéry-as-intellect, opposed perhaps to the sensuous Valéry-as-poet, creation is significant only when it is also a demonstration of rigor, of the successful, disciplined working of the intellect, of difficulty met on all levels and overcome. In writing a poem, he in a sense proves his potentiality of doing anything, since the poem is (beyond the individual act which has the value of its own immediate beauty) a demonstration of achievement according to the principles which underlie and make possible achievement in any field into which intelligence may venture.

As was to be expected, Valéry has been greatly admired and greatly attacked. There is a certain unfortunate pontificality about much of his criticism, and the irreverent reader may feel that he makes too great a parade of his interest in philosophy and mathematics, that he carries subtlety of thought to an extreme and unduly complicates simple matters. His emphasis on the poet as a technician as opposed to the romantic concept of him as an inspired mouthpiece has displeased the sentimental and is probably equally far from the mark. Yet there can be little doubt that as a critic his influence in just such matters has been beneficial. Certainly there is no doubt that he is a great poet on any grounds, a master of metrical effects and of language, capable of expressing the most abstract themes with a restrained richness of sensuous imagery almost unrivaled in French poetry.

See: Albert Thibaudet, *Paul Valéry* (1923);

F. Lefèvre, *Entretiens avec Paul Valéry* (1926); L. Estève, "Autour de Valéry," *Revue de métaphysique et de morale,* XXXV (1928), 55–105; V. Larbaud, *Paul Valéry* (1931); Edmund Wilson, *Axel's Castle* (1931); Gustave Cohen, *Essai d'explication du Cimetière marin* (1933); C. M. Bowra, *The Heritage of Symbolism* (1943).

C. W., Jr.

Valle-Inclán, Ramón del (1866?–1936, Spanish novelist, dramatist, and poet), is the supreme example in modern Spanish literature of art for art's sake. Born in Spain's old northwest province of Galicia, he appeared on the Madrid literary scene in the last decade of the 19th century and was soon noted as the most colorful of the younger writers. Legends quickly sprang up about this bizarre, romantic figure with his long beard, unshorn poet's locks, and air of hauteur and mystery, legends which he himself assiduously cultivated. When later he lost his left arm, as the result of an unfortunate altercation in a Madrid café, he stoically accepted the misfortune and characteristically made literature of it. Until his death in 1936 he played, with artistry and gusto, the role of paladin of decadence and aestheticism.

Valle-Inclán's writings—short stories, novels, plays, and poems—are a faithful reflection of his personality. Given his temperament, it is not surprising that he was early attracted to French *fin-de-siècle* literature. The marked influence of the latter is already apparent in his first work, *Femeninas* (1895), six short love stories of a refined and morbid sensualism. In evidence, too, is his stylistic gift, his aptitude for melodious phrasing. It was not, however, until the four short novels dealing with the amorous adventures of the donjuanesque marqués de Bradomín ("ugly, Catholic, and sentimental" and "cynical, unbelieving, and gallant as a cardinal of the Renaissance"), the celebrated *Sonatas* (*Sonata de otoño,* 1902; *Sonata de estio,* 1903; *Sonata de primavera,* 1904; *Sonata de invierno,* 1905), that Valle-Inclán's decadent-symbolist tendencies reached their full expression. The *Sonatas* (Eng. tr., *The Pleasant Memoirs of the Marquis de Bradomín,* 1924) established his position as a master of musical, evocative prose. Meanwhile he had turned for inspiration to the myths and folklore of his native province, creating a poetic vision of a legendary, archaic Galicia in the short novel *Flor de santidad* (1904) and in his first volume of verse, *Aromas de leyenda* (1907). The same background served for the more somber prose plays, termed *comedias bárbaras—Aguila de blasón* (1907), *Romance de lobos* (1908), *Cara de Plata* (1922)—which were centered around the memorable figure of the patriarchal *hidalgo* Don Juan Manuel de Montenegro and his untamed brood of rapacious sons, in a medieval-like setting of barbarity, lust, and superstition. In the trilogy *La guerra carlista,* comprising the novels *Los cruzados de la causa* (1908), *El resplandor de la hoguera* (1908), and *Gerifaltes de antaño* (1909), the author, largely through fictional characters (among them Don Juan Manuel de Montenegro and the marqués de Bradomín) and with characteristic emphasis on the colorful and the dramatic, evokes something of the spirit that animated the lost cause of traditionalism in the last Carlist War (1872–1876).

That Valle-Inclán was still devoted to the symbolist ideal was made clear as late as 1916 in the essay *La lámpara maravillosa,* his longest profession of artistic faith. But even before this time he had begun to change the tone of his work, stressing in certain writings the note of humor, always latent in him. Thus while the prose play *El embrujado* (1913) is still characteristic of his middle period, the new trend is observable in the facetious pirouetting of the verse play *La marquesa Rosalinda* (1913) and in the prose farce *La cabeza del dragón* (1914; Eng. tr., *The Dragon's Head,* 1918). In *La pipa de Kif* (1919), a volume of verse, the humor has become to a considerable extent strident and grotesque, announcing the transition to the next and final stage in his development. In *Luces de Bohemia* (1920), which he designates as an "esperpento" (*i.e.,* a ridiculous, absurd person or thing), Valle-Inclán expounds his new attitude. "The tragic sense of Spanish life," says the author's mouthpiece, "can only be expressed with a systematically deformed aesthetic. . . . My present aesthetic is to transform, with the mathematics of a concave mirror, the classic norms." In consequence, the dominant note of Valle-Inclán's novels and plays from now on is one of burlesque tragedy, and his characters are puppets, ridiculous for the most part, manipulated against a grim, macabre background—the whole reminiscent of the *caprichos* of Goya. It is not only Spanish life that he sees thus; in the novel *Tirano Banderas* (1926; Eng. tr., *The Tyrant,* 1929) he depicts in lurid tones the tragicomedy of revolution in an imaginary Latin American republic (most suggestive of Mexico, which he had several times visited). His most important last works, the novels *La corte de los milagros* (1927) and *Viva mi dueño* (1928), show in similar "esperpento" fashion the corruption of Spanish court and aristocratic life shortly before the Revolution of 1868. They were to have formed part of a large cycle, left unfinished.

Valle-Inclán takes high rank among the writers of his generation (the so-called Generation of '98) as a creator of moods and poetic effects and as a stylist who brought new beauties and rhythms to Spanish prose.

See: S. de Madariaga, *The Genius of Spain and Other Essays on Spanish Contemporary Literature* (1923), pp. 128–147; C. Barja, *Literatura española: Libros y autores contemporáneos* (1935), pp. 360–421.

W. L. F.

Vallès, Jules (1832–1885, French novelist and radical journalist), was born in Le Puy-en-Velay and inherited the fiercely austere virtues of the peasants of that region. His childhood was unhappy, but he proved himself a brilliant student under the severe discipline of his father, a teacher, and was sent to Paris to the Lycée Bonaparte in 1848 to prepare for the Ecole Normale Supérieure. Very soon he was swept away by the revolutionary mood of the capital, took part in the manifestations in favor of Michelet in 1851, resisted the coup d'état of December 2, 1851, was imprisoned as a conspirator at Mazas in 1853. When set free he moved about in bohemian circles, dreamed of poetry and the theatre, cultivated the friendship of Gustave Planche, and finally won attention with a cynical pamphlet, *L'Argent* (1857). As a brilliant chronicler (1858–1868) for the newspaper *Figaro* he did a series of vitriolic portraits, published *Les Réfractaires* in 1865, which were a scathing retort to the sweetish romanticism of Murger; in 1866 was published *La Rue,* a collection of articles which first appeared in the *Evénement* of Villemessant, in the *Epoque* of Feydeau, in the *Liberté* of Girardin. In 1867, with the collaboration of the Goncourts, Zola (*qq.v.*), and Cladel, he started a weekly of high literary quality, also called *La Rue,* in which all traditions were to be smashed. Between 1868 and 1870 he hurled various diatribes against the tottering government of Napoleon III and was again imprisoned and several times fined. In command of a battalion during the siege of Paris, he became a member of the Commune after the defeat, and in his *Cri du peuple* defended the rights of Paris against Thiers and the last remnants of liberty against the most fanatical of the revolutionaries. He was exiled, condemned to death *par contumace* (1872), and resided in England until the amnesty of 1880. While there he wrote *La Rue à Londres* (1883) and the greater part of his admirable trilogy, *Jacques Vingtras.* When he returned to France, he gave the finishing touches to his literary works, wrote excellent chronicles for the *Réveil,* and revived the *Cri du peuple* (1883) with the close cooperation of Séverine and Jules Guesde. He died in Paris on February 14, 1885; the tumultuous funeral ceremonies were both an apotheosis and a public scandal.

Vallès had a hypersensitive nature and was in permanent revolt against all the tyrannies of family, school, and society; he is a symbol of the incorrigible rebel, a pendant to Louis Veuillot and Léon Bloy (*q.v.*). The *Jacques Vingtras* trilogy (*L'Enfant,* 1879; *Le Bachelier,* 1881; *L'Insurgé,* 1886), essentially autobiographical, remains his masterpiece and also one of the most poignant documents of modern French literature. Paul Bourget and Maurice Barrès (*qq.v.*) have hailed Vallès as one of the masters of French prose—a romanticist in his lyrical qualities, realistic in the cruel accuracy of his observing, very modern in tone, always lively. Vallès also has two outstanding classical characteristics, concision and naturalness. It has been said that he is a kind of bridge between the revolutionary romanticism of *Les Misérables* and the truculent realism of Zola and of the first manner of Huysmans (*q.v.*).

See: J. Richepin, *Les Etapes d'un réfractaire* (1872); P. Bourget, "Vallès," in *Etudes et portraits* (1928); G. Gille, *Jules Vallès; ses révoltes, sa maîtrise, son prestige* (1941) and *Jules Vallès; sources, bibliographie, iconographie* (1941).

G. G.

Vančura, Vladislav (1891–1942, Czech novelist, etc.), was the leading prose writer of Czech expressionism. He was born at Háj near Opava (then in Austrian Silesia), served in the First World War in the medical corps of the Austrian army, and became a practicing physician. He was executed by the Nazis on June 1, 1942, one victim of the "reprisal" for the assassination of Heydrich, the German "protector."

Vančura's writings are extremely varied both in subject matter and form. *Pekař Jan Marhoul* (1924; The Baker John Marhoul), his first success, glorifies the "poor in spirit" as well as the poor in earthly goods, in a style which points to the reading of Dostoevski (*q.v.*). *Pole orná a válečná* (1925; Fields and Battlefields) is an anti-war book of unsurpassed bitterness and horror. The following, much weaker book, *Poslední soud* (1929; The Last Judgment), returns to the theme of his very first novel. It depicts a feeble-minded Ruthenian peasant transplanted to the puzzling and cruel urban civilization of Prague. *Markéta Lazarová* (1931) represents a complete change of style and subject matter—the social pathos and the glorification of the "idiot" have disappeared. Vančura now tells a good yarn about robbers and knights, rapes and elopements. Only the display of language and of metaphor suggests that the author has ambitions beyond those of an adventure writer. In addition, the celebration of brute force and lust seems to represent a definite break with the past. *Útěk do Budína* (1932; The Flight to Buda) is, however, a fairly traditional psychological novel of marital difficulties which attempts to bring out the differences between the Czech and the Slovak character in the attitudes of the Czech hero and the Slovak heroine. *Konec starých časů* (1934; The End of Old Times) is again completely different: it is a whimsical revival of the Münchhausen theme, with grotesque setting and veritable fireworks of language and technique. Metaphors, slang, archaic Czech, are used with surprising effect, and the author deliberately breaks any illusion of reality by constant interference and manipulation of his materials. Vančura has become a virtuoso of storytelling and of linguistic inventiveness in these books, but he seems to have given up any attempt at a unified outlook on life or even art. Nevertheless the last book, *Tři řeky* (1936; Three Rivers), though badly composed, is a return to the early themes. It attempts to depict the spiritual growth of its hero through the First World War and the Russian Revolution.

It is difficult to find any unity in Vančura's artistic development: the interest of his work seems largely in the sheer virtuosity with which he managed the language and the technique of storytelling. He is possibly most successful in the short stories of one collection, *Luk královny Dorotky* (1932; The Bow of Queen Dorothy), for there he escapes his evident difficulties with large-scale composition and elaborate characterization. In spite of some deviations and mere *tour de force*, the theme of hatred for war and social oppression runs through his work. Vančura paid with his life for his convictions.

See: F. Götz, "V. Vančura," in *Básnický dnešek* (1931); A. Vyskočil, "V. Vančura," in *Básníkovo slovo* (1933).

R. W.

Van de Woestijne, Karel, *see* Woestijne.

Van Deyssel, Lodewijk, *see* Deyssel.

Van Eeden, Frederik Willem, *see* Eeden.

Vanglon, Henri, *see* Ghéon, Henri.

Van Lerberghe, Charles (1861–1907, Belgian poet and dramatist), was born in Ledeberg, near Ghent, of a father of old Flemish stock, endowed with scholarly and artistic curiosity, and of a very pious mother. He got his secondary schooling at the Collège Sainte-Barbe, a Jesuit institution, in Ghent. There he became a friend of Maurice Maeterlinck (*q.v.*). In 1894 he received his doctor's degree in "philosophie et lettres (philologie classique)" from the University of Brussels, where he had studied intermittently. Van Lerberghe traveled in France (Paris), England (London), Germany (Berlin, Munich), Italy (Rome, Florence), then settled in the historic little town of Bouillon, picturesquely situated among the wood-covered hills of the Belgian Ardennes.

Of a rather timid though gay disposition, he was essentially a dreamer whose exquisite sensitiveness and delicate love of life in all its forms could be summed up in these three lines of his: "Beware, lest thou mightst break anything, Tread upon anything, destroy anything, For life is sweet to all" (*La Chanson d'Eve*). He was a lover of the dreamlike delicacy of primitive painters like Botticelli and the Pre-Raphaelites, particularly of Burne-Jones and Walter Crane. Very well versed in foreign literatures, especially in the English, he was influenced by Shelley and Rossetti. On the French side it was the Parnassians who were his favorites—the delicate Prudhomme, the tenderhearted Coppée, the refined Heredia (*qq.v.*). A Parnassian in his all embracing love for beauty, he is a symbolist through his fluid, dreamlike form, his elusive descriptions of hardly tangible shades ("nuances") of feelings which are more fleeting impressions than actual perceptions of his senses. It is in the mystical beauty of woman that Van Lerberghe finds his greatest inspiration: "Love nothing but beauty, And let this be for you, Woman, the only Truth." This is the essence of his capital work, *La Chanson d'Eve* (1904), a collection of lyrical poems written in fluidly adaptable rhymed free verse, apparently disconnected, but following a straight line of development: the eternal tale of Woman passing through the innocence of childhood, waking up to the urge of love and the secret desire of knowledge followed by the radiant sadness of experience. An earlier volume of lyrics, *Entrevisions,* was published in 1898.

Van Lerberghe wrote one symbolistic drama in prose, *Les Flaireurs* (1889), an impressive, eerie piece of work—Death prowls around its victims—which perhaps inspired Maeterlinck to write *L'Intruse.* He also wrote one comedy, *Pan* (1906), a violent, frolicking satire against conventionalism and hypocrisy, in which this god, having come to live among the peasants of a Flemish village, causes havoc by shocking the traditional authorities.

See: A. Mockel, *Charles Van Lerberghe* (1904); F. Séverin, *Charles Van Lerberghe* (1922); F. Castillo Nájera, *Un Siècle de poésie belge* (1931; with Spanish translations and notes).

L. V.

Van Looy, Jacobus, *see* Looy.

Van Nijlen, Jan, *see* Nijlen.

Van Ostayen, Paul, *see* Ostayen.

Van Schendel, Arthur, *see* Schendel.

Vazov, Ivan (1850–1921, Bulgarian poet, novelist, and dramatist), was born at Sopot of a well-to-do conservative merchant family which had limited intellectual interests. He studied at Sopot and Plovdiv and in the latter place became acquainted with French authors such as Hugo, Lamartine, and Béranger; he also improved his knowledge of Russian. In 1870, while on a business trip to Rumania, he met the revolutionary leaders and writers, Karavelov and Botev, and determined to devote himself to the service of the common people. On the way back he met Petko Rachev Slaveykov, the prerevolutionary poet, in Constantinople. He gave up his plan of studying at the University of Zagreb after he learned of the death of his father during the Bulgarian insurrection and in 1879 became judge of the circuit court in Berkovitsa and later in Vidin. He later played a prominent role in political life in Plovdiv, but in 1886 was compelled to flee to Russia, where he settled in Odessa. In 1889 he returned to Sofia and spent the rest of his life there as a man of letters, the first in free Bulgaria to live by his pen. On October 2, 1920, he was honored by a national jubilee on the completion of 50 years of literary work. A year later he died of a heart attack.

During this half century Vazov worked in almost all fields of literature with marked success. His works were a whole literature in miniature as he set the standards in every form which he employed, lyric, epic, short story, novel, drama. He touched all sides of the national consciousness, whether it was the joy over the liberation, the sorrow over Macedonia, or the despair at the defeat in the First World War. Born to be a romanticist, he felt himself obligated to teach his people through his own kind of literature and he fulfilled his mission.

It is hard to single out individual poems or collections for special mention. In poetry there are such important collections as *Izbavlenie* (1878; Liberation); *Epopeya na zabravenite* (1879; Epos of the Heroes), a glorification of the pre-emancipation leaders of Bulgaria, written in a moment of disillusionment at the new state; *Slivnitsa* (1886), on the Serb-Bulgarian War; *Pod nashete nebe* (1900; Under Our Heaven); *Pesni za Makedoniya* (1914; Songs for Macedonia); *Ne shte zagine* (1920; It Will Not Perish), on the defeat of 1918. His greatest novel is *Pod igoto* (1893; Eng. tr., *Under the Yoke,* 1893), a tale of the beginnings of the Bulgarian revolt against the Turks, which has been translated into nearly all modern languages. There are also the *Nova zemya* (1894; The New Land), a continuation of *Pod igoto; Kazalarskata tsaritsa* (1903; The Empress of Kazalar), a tale of modern Bulgaria; and such studies of the past as *Legendi pri Tsarevets* (1920; Legends at Tsarevets), poems of the Second Bulgarian Empire at Trnovo. In comedy there is the *Mikhalaki chorbadzhi* (1882) and *Sluzhbogontsi* (1903; The Service-Chasers); in historical drama *Borislav* (1909) and *Ivaylo* (1911). Yet these are but a small part of the total output of this prolific writer. As a guide and a teacher he trained many Bulgarian writers and for at least a quarter century he was the accepted authority. More recently younger men have sought to escape from his sway, but Vazov is still generally accepted as the classic Bulgarian author and he bids fair to remain so for years to come.

See: T. Minkov, "Ivan Vazov," *Bulgarski pisateli,* IV (1929), 3–72.

C. A. M.

Vega y Oreiro, Ricardo de la (1839–1910, Spanish dramatist), son of Ventura de la Vega, the well-known writer of comedies of the middle 19th century, was born in Madrid. He became an employee of the Ministry of Public Works. In keeping with the tradition of his family he was devoted to the theatre, but unlike his father, of the Moratín school, he cultivated—with consummate skill—the *sainete* and the *zarzuela*, that is to say the so-called *género chico*. The *sainete* is a short comedy or farce concerning the life of the people or of the middle class; its characters speak the language of everyday life, replete with representative expressions and idioms. The aim is to amuse, not to appraise or moralize. The *zarzuela* is ordinarily a *sainete* with music, dancing, and singing. A traditional Madrid of the people provides the background. Ricardo de la Vega, very familiar with the types and ways of his native city, offers notable portraits, with sharp wit and a gifted realism. The reader or spectator less aware of Madrid will experience some difficulty in understanding the local slang, dialectical forms, intimate plays on words, and continual references to political and social happenings of the author's period. Ricardo de la Vega's most famous *sainete* is *Pepa la frescachona, o un colegial desenvuelto* (1886), and his best-known *zarzuela* is *La verbena de la paloma* (1894).

E. G. L.

Vercors (pseud. of Jean Bruller, 1902–, French novelist and essayist) founded with others in 1941, during the German occupation, the leading clandestine publishing house of France, Les Editions de Minuit. Its first publication was his own work, *Le Silence de la mer* (1942). In this tale and in another, *La Marche à l'étoile* (1943), he revealed by implication the impossibility of collaborating with the enemy and set an example of intellectual resistance that was followed by such writers as Mauriac, Aragon (*qq.v.*), and Cassou. His first work, variously attributed to all the great writers of France, was smuggled to England and America, where it was republished and translated. Since the end of the war a short story, *Le Songe* (1945), and a collection of articles, *Le Sable du temps* (1945), have appeared as well as several prefaces to the works of others.

Known before the war as an original illustrator under his real name, Vercors will keep his new name for his literary activity and continue to use the name Jean Bruller for his satiric drawings.

J. O'B.

Verdaguer i Santaló, Jacint (1845–1902, Catalonian poet, prose writer, and mystic), was born in a small village in the district of Vich called Folguerolas. His father was an obscure stonecutter; his mother could lay claim to no other accomplishment than that of relating to the boy—who listened transported—the stories and tales which village folk tell one another on long evenings before the fire. A stonecutter and a talkative woman gave to the movement of cultural revival of Catalonia, Valencia, and the Balearic Islands known as the *Renaixença* the greatest Catalonian poet of the 19th century.

While studying for the church Verdaguer worked as a farmhand and as a teacher. In 1865 his poetic gifts had their first public acclaim at the recently revived Jocs Florals, where he won two prizes. He became a priest and spent peaceful years among the two hundred parishoners of the village of Vinyoles D'Oris, in his native district. He also made several ocean trips, perhaps owing to delicate health, and was a chaplain on the ships of the Marqués de Comillas from 1873 to 1875. On the high seas he finished his famous epic poem, *La Atlàntida*, awarded a prize in the Jocs Florals in the year 1877—from which time his name spread through Europe and his works began to be translated into various languages. He then abandoned his employment as a ship's chaplain and entered the home of the Comillas as an almoner. His *Idil. lis i cants mistics* (Idyls and Mystic Songs) was published in 1879. He was officially hailed as *mestre en gai saber* (master troubadour) in the year 1880, and indeed the unity of the Catalan-speaking countries has been frequently manifested in their admiration for him. He continued to write important books: *Canigó* (1885); *Excursions i viatges* (1887; Excursions and Trips); *Lo somni de Sant Joan* (1887; The Dream of St. John); *Dietari d'un pelegri a Terra Santa* (Diary of a Pilgrim to the Holy Land); the trilogy dedicated to the child Jesus, *Natzareth* (1890; Nazareth), *Betlem* (1891; Bethlehem), and *La fugida d'Egipte* (1893; The Flight from Egypt).

A period of crisis and suffering then followed. Verdaguer became the victim of intrigues not yet thoroughly studied or understood. Works such as *En defensa propia* (1895; In Self-defense) and *Flors del Calvari: Llibre de consols* (1896; Flowers of Calvary: Book of Consolations) brought the personal drama of Verdaguer to the common people—who rose to support their great poet to the point of idolatry. The strong feelings which had been stirred by his powerful personality persisted and even cast a sinister shadow over his deathbed.

There can be no question of the healthy and virile quality of Verdaguer's writing. His language is selective, if popular in source; he is skillful in the avoidance of archaisms or vulgarisms. Without Verdaguer it would be impossible to explain the work of any of the later Catalonian poets. Even those who at first glance seem to have received all their training in Paris, London, or Berlin are to be numbered among his debtors.

See: M. Milá i Fontanals, prologue, in Verdaguer, *Idil. lis i cants mistics;* A. Vassal, *Mossèn Jacint Verdaguer; sa vie, ses œuvres, sa mort* (1903); V. Serra i Boldu, *Mossèn Jacint Verdaguer* (1915); J. Folguera, *Les noves valors de la poesia catalana* (1919); J. Amade, *Origines et premières manifestations de la renaissance littéraire en Catalogne* (1924).

F. de P.

Verde, Cesário (pseud. of José Joaquim Cesário Verde, 1855–1886, Portuguese poet), was born in Lisbon, where he worked as a businessman and collaborated on various newspapers of the capital and of Brazil. His life was confused and uninteresting. He died in the city of his birth at the age of 31.

Verde's poetic production was scattered in occasional contributions to Lisbon newspapers such as the *Diário da tarde* (Evening Daily) and especially the *Diário de notícias* (Daily News), in journals such as *Renascença* (Rebirth) and *Occidente* (Occident), and in the *Ilustração portuguesa e brasileira* (Portuguese and Brazilian Illustrated Magazine). At the time of his death the critic Manuel José da Silva Pinto collected some of his best poetry in a small volume entitled *O livro de Cesário Verde* (*1873–1886*) (1886; The Book of Cesário Verde), of which there are modern editions (1911, 1926). The importance of Verde in the history of Portuguese literature is based on the fact that he is the first nationalistic poet of his period. He also exerted an influence on the most completely vanguardist poets who, reacting against what had become the artistocratic formalism of modernism, found inspiration and example in his work. His verse is sharply impressionistic, the product of fine analysis and observation of life, and at the same time shows a rich rhythmical facility. He sang of the daily life of Lisbon, of the scenes at its markets and wharves, of the traffic of its streets, of the monotony of its days. From time to time the social revolutionary note in the manner of Proudhon is sounded, as in "Deslumbramentos" (Beguilements), in which the return of justice is foreseen, or the anarchical note, as in "Humilhaçoēs" (Humiliations), an angry protest against armed authority. The best poetry is in such pieces as "Um bairro moderno" (A Modern Quarter) and "Nos" (We), in which the local color is balanced by the perfection of the stanza and the clarity of the metaphors.

See: Manuel José da Silva Pinto, introduction to *O livro de Cesário Verde* (*1873–1886*), 1926 ed.; Hernani Cidade, *Tendências do lirismo português contemporâneo* (1939).

R. M. L.

Veresayev, Vikentii Vikentievich (pseud. of Vikentii Vikentievich Smidovich, 1867–, Russian fiction writer and social critic), was born in Central Russia. The date of his birth is important; by the time he was ready to enter the university the last decade of the 19th century was approaching, and with it came the appearance of the proletariat on the political arena in Russia, the ideas of Karl Marx, and the beginning of Social Democracy. Veresayev's father was of Polish extraction, his mother of pure Russian ancestry. The elder Smidovich was a physician by profession, as well as an amateur scientist. The boy adored him, and this fact may later have been influential in his selecting the career of a physician also. The family lived on a very limited income although Smidovich Sr. had a large practice: it was mostly charity practice. He was also somewhat of a crusader for the rights of the people, to the detriment of his own and his family's welfare. This trait too did not fail to leave its imprint on the mind of the young Vikentii. The elder Vikentii Smidovich died in 1894, after having become infected by one of his typhus patients.

Young Veresayev studied at the University of St. Petersburg in the department of history and philology; after receiving his degree, he entered the university's medical school. His early-acquired scientific traits here received further development. In his *Zapiski vracha* (1900; Memoirs of a Physician) he tells how impressed he was by the scientific scrupulousness and care with which the professors of the medical school approached each problem. Parallel with preoccupation with science, he developed a social philosophy. The time was the early 1890's when the ideas of Social Democracy—the emphasis on the collective effort—had found their way into Russia. In the above-mentioned *Zapiski vracha* Veresayev summed up from his own professional point of view the formidable problem of mutual aid: the medical man cannot hope for a living wage unless his patients receive adequate remuneration, unless there is economic justice for them too—"the only way out is the realization that we are but a small part of one enormous inseparable whole."

Veresayev saw the Russo-Japanese War of 1904–1905 as an army surgeon in Manchuria. The result of that experience was the book *Na voine* (1908; In the War), in which, couched in discreet and dispassionate language, the bitterest indictment is sounded of the incapacity and general debility of the tsar's government. In his purely fictional work Veresayev never forgets the social consciousness he acquired early in his life. Sometimes he is sidetracked. In the story "Bez dorogi" (1895; Without Road) a young physician is mobbed and fatally wounded by the ignorant people whom he had tried to help during an epidemic of cholera. The solution Veresayev offers is to accept the violence in the spirit of Christian submission. He was strongly criticized in his own camp for that. In a long story, "Dva kontsa" (1903; Two Ends), the life of the city proletariat is pictured—poverty, drunkeness, fear of the boss and the foreman, the forcing of the women into shameful relations for the sake of holding their jobs, general cruelty of everyone to everyone else. No definite way out is suggested, possibly because of the rigid censorship.

The social credo of Veresayev is summarized in a little symbolic sketch, "Zvezda" (1897; The Star). It deals with the persistence and discouragements of struggle for the improvement of the human lot. The idea of the sketch is that no matter how apparently hopeless and discouraging the struggle, it must go on until the final victory. In all his work Veresayev's style shuns unnecessary adornment, remaining throughout economical and austere while making use of beautiful and precise Russian language.

The Bolshevik Revolution bewildered and disgusted him at first. He set forth these sentiments in a book entitled *V tupike* (1923, In a Blind Alley; Eng. tr., *Deadlock*). The story concerns itself with the mental and emotional struggles of a young Russian girl, Katia. She finds herself unable to accept either the revolutionary or the counter-revolutionary way out and is left "in a blind alley." Later, Veresayev made his peace with the Soviet government and was restored to favor.

See: Veresayev, *Polnoye sobraniye sochineni* (1913); *V yunye gody,* Vol. XI (1928).

J. P.

Verga, Giovanni (1840–1922, Italian novelist and short-story writer), lived in his native city of Catania throughout childhood and early youth. At the age of 16 he wrote his first novel, *Amore e patria,* which was never published. By the time he was ready to begin the study of law at the university he had finished his second novel, which his father was persuaded to publish with money saved for his schooling. The work appeared in four volumes under the title *I Carbonari della montagna* (1861–1862). It was of the nature of the popular historical novel and of very slight literary merit; but it was well enough received to decide young Verga on his career as a novelist. He went off to Florence in 1865 when that city became temporary capital of the new Italy, to settle down seriously to the business of writing novels. In this same year he published his second, *Una Peccatrice.* During his stay there he finished his third, *Storia di una capinera* (1871), the very sentimental and pathetic story in epistolary form of a young nun in love. This has proved to be one of his most popular novels, though not for reasons of any genuine literary merit. In 1871 Verga removed to Milan, where he remained most of the time during the next 10 years, participating in the artistic, bohemian life of the city and working very hard at his chosen profession of novelist. His works of this period, *Eva* (1873), *Tigre reale* (1873), and *Eros* (1875), are all very much of one style and one taste. Melodramatic, decadently romantic, sentimental, and overemphatic, they reveal little of value as original creation. They catered to the same taste which enjoyed *La Dame aux camélias,* for instance, and which continued to demand more of such fare. These works do, however, form a necessary phase in the development of the young artist. Through them he was freed from an excessive subjectivism and from too much use of the autobiographical. They brought him to desire a new style and another content for his art.

These he found by returning in spirit and in person to his native Sicily. While still in Milan he had written the story *Nedda* (1874), which he called a *bozzetto siciliano* (Sicilian sketch) and which gives clear evidence of his new direction. The story deals with the very hard life of a young peasant girl. Verga is interested in her primitive attitudes, and Nedda is about as far from the erotic aristocrats and bohemians of the Milanese novels as anything could be. After this his visits to Sicily became more frequent, and after his return there for a period of two years (1878–1880) he produced the works which make him one of the most significant prose artists of the century: *Vita dei campi* (1880), a collection of *novelle* of the same world as Nedda's, containing the famous *Cavalleria rusticana* (which gave its own title to later editions of the volume); *I Malavoglia* (1881); *Il Marito di Elena* (1882); *Novelle rusticane* (1883); and *Maestro-don Gesualdo* (1889). (D. H. Lawrence has made the following translations of Verga: *Maestro-don Gesualdo,* 1923; *Little Novels of Sicily* (*Novelle rusticane*), 1925; and *Cavalleria Rusticana and Other Stories,* 1928.) Two volumes of *novelle* followed these works of a decade, *I Ricordi del Capitano d'Arce* (1891) and *Don Candeloro e Ci* (1894), but it was unquestionable that Verga had done his best work in the 80's. The works of that Sicilian period, championed by Luigi Capuana (*q.v.*) as masterpieces of the school of *verismo,* established his name. In 1884 *Cavalleria rusticana* had been rewritten as a play and produced in Turin (the opera by Mascagni, 1890, libretto by Tarzioni-Tozzetti and Menassi, is taken of course from the Verga story). In 1896 *La Lupa,* which probably can be considered Verga's finest story, was also put on the stage. But Verga appeared unable to go on with his announced series of novels, his own *Rougon-Macquart* (*see* Zola), as it were, to which he had given the general title *I Vinti.* In the introduction to *I Malavoglia,* Verga had set forth his grandiose scheme. It was to be a series of novels "studying" realistically, even naturalistically, the "flood of human progress" at its several social levels. This "river" makes use of humanity and makes of it its victim, hence *I Vinti.* In *I Malavoglia* the first impulses toward progress were to be witnessed in a family of humble Sicilian peasants. Next, the greed for riches was to be studied in a bourgeois subject, *Mastro-don Gesualdo.* Beyond these (the only two of the projected series ever published), Verga goes on to speak of three more novels to follow, proceeding very much on schedule up the social ladder: *La Duchessa de Leyra, L'Onorevole Scipione,* and finally *L'Uomo di lusso.* Verga lived through almost the whole of the first quarter of our century. He enjoyed leisure and good health. But he was never able to more than begin *La Duchessa de Leyra,* while the other two novels remained purely in concept. Verga had lived well beyond the triumph of *verismo* and far beyond his own productivity. In his quiet routine life in Catania he was almost forgotten until his death.

The introduction to *I Malavoglia* remarks that style is inherent in the subject. This conception dominated Verga's important work of the Sicilian decade. Verga's greatness lies in his perfection of an art in this sense. *I Malavoglia,* his most significant work in point of style, tends, as do most of the *novelle,* to the complete elimination of the person of the artist. All perceptions and the narration itself are almost completely rerouted through expressions and ways of perception of the characters themselves and of the particular social group of which they are a part. The effort is to give the illusion of emotions and of a lyricism abiding in the very things and events themselves. The result is a style which, in some instances, is almost a dialect in itself, an idiom so intensified in colloquialism as to make adequate translation into another language quite impossible.

Verga was, above all else, an artist. It was surely an encouragement to him that his art should be championed by such a critic as Capuana, that it should receive a name (*verismo*) and that parallels could be drawn with Flaubert's (*q.v.*) and Zola's work. Verga welcomed the doctrines of naturalism and formulated some of his own (see the introductions to *I Malavoglia, Amante di Gramigna, Fantasticheria*). Moreover, regionalism was in ascendance in Italy, helping to support his new Sicilian manner. But the ideas of program, of school, of theory, and of science do not penetrate into his work as an artist as with Zola. It is a mistake to derive Verga's art from either of the great Frenchmen's work. He is more like Flaubert, of course, with his attention on style in prose art. But he is in no sense, in his great works, an imitative artist.

See: A. Momigliano, *Giovanni Verga narratore* (1923); T. G. Bergin, *Giovanni Verga* (1931; in English); L. Russo, *Giovanni Verga* (1934).

C. S. S.

Verhaeren, Emile (1855–1916, Belgian poet and art critic), acclaimed by certain competent foreign critics the supreme poet of the early 20th century, was born at St. Amand on the Scheldt. His father was of Dutch, his mother of French, origin; French was spoken in his home, and he never knew well any other language. Although thoroughly Flemish by temperament—he shares the tenacity and industry as well as the delight in color and in the life of the senses characteristic of the race—he gained a cosmopolitan view by wide travel in France, Spain, England, and Germany. Germans often claim him as a Teutonic poet; his drama *Hélène de Sparte* appeared in Russian and German translations before its publication in French (1912; Eng. tr., *Helen of Sparta,* 1916). He dabbled in law at Louvain, where he associated chiefly with poets and painters. His lifelong passion for plastic art is proved by his verse, by his critical writing in periodicals, and by his monographs on Rembrandt, James Ensor, Rubens, and others. He worked for a time in the law office of Edmond Picard (*q.v.*), to whose *Art moderne* he was a regular contributor. The humanitarian interests of his patron fostered his social philosophy. His first volume, *Les Flamandes* (1883), exalting in colorful description the lusty traditions of Flemish life, was inspired primarily by masters of the brush. In *Les Moines* (1886) the poet seeks initiation into the mystic side of the heroic past. He spent three weeks in a cloister, participating in the daily life of the inmates; they hoped to make a convert, but his interest was only pictorial. At least he learned from the monks devotion to an ideal; he will carry forward the torch with the same courage they show in preserving symbols—such is the role of "poets born too late to be priests." The drama *Le Cloître* (1900; Eng. tr., *The Cloister,* 1915) treats the same subject in more philosophical vein. *Les Soirs* (1888), *Les Débâcles* (1888), and *Les Flambeaux noirs* (1891), a trilogy of gloom at times approaching madness, present the analysis of a poet's neurosis. Verhaeren always feels and expresses himself with the maximum of vigor. Albert Mockel (*q.v.*) once called him a "paroxysist"; these poems justify the epithet. In them he distinctly cultivates suffering as one determined to know by experience all phases of human life. The tone of gloom opens *Les Apparus dans mes chemins* (1891); at the end, the radiant visions of St. George and of four other saints inspire the poet with the noble duty of identifying himself with broad aspirations for the future. "Les Saintes" seems to be his first tribute to Marthe Massin, whom he married in 1891 and to whom he dedicated the trilogy *Les Heures claires* (1896; Eng. tr., *The Sunlit Hours,* 1916), *Les Heures d'après-midi* (1905; Eng. tr., *Afternoon,* 1917), and *Les Heures du soir* (1911; Eng. tr., *The Evening Hours,* 1918)—love poems of poignant sincerity. In an early symbolic poem, "Le Glaive" (in *Les Débâcles*), the spirit of negation utters a challenge: "Thou shalt be nothing, and for thy idle soul the future shall be only regret for the past." The trilogy of sociological trend—the poems *Les Campagnes hallucinées* (1893) and *Les Villes tentaculaires* (1895) and the drama *Les Aubes* (1898; Eng. tr., *The Dawn,* 1898)—hurls back the answer: "The ancient dream is dead, the new is on the forge." The poet is terrified as he witnesses the desertion of the countryside—there are seven "Chansons de fou" in the first collection; then he observes the movement objectively and is finally fascinated by the display of energy in the cities. *Les Aubes* brings the culmination with its vision of reconciliation. Verhaeren is always the poet of energy: the vigor of joy in physical life held him in *Les Flamandes,* the might of an ideal in *Les Moines,* and if, in his crisis he provoked despair, it is because "suffering doubles our strength." Some of his best-known poems, as "Le Passeur d'eau" and "Le Forgeron" (*Les Villages illusoires,* 1895), which exalt into symbols humble folk he had known in his home town, are throbbing with confidence in human effort. Victory is in sight; he celebrates the triumph in the works of his maturity, *Les Visages de la vie* (1899), *Les Forces tumultueuses* (1902), *La Multiple Splendeur* (1906), and *Les Rythmes souverains* (1910). The very names are evocative of the unfolding conquest of the universe by man. The poet forsees the union of humanity through love and admiration joining men in a common purpose and mustering individuals and nations in one cause, the striving for the onward march of life. Thus he reaches a cosmic spirit akin to pantheism. He is often compared to Walt Whitman; they were kindred minds, but there is no evidence of direct influence. The First World War brought the greater indignation to the poet as he saw his cherished ideals turned to mockery by a nation he had believed in the vanguard of progress. Germany's capital crime is to have done to death the idea of human solidarity. The ravage of his beloved Flanders offers a concrete vision of universal horror (*Les Ailes rouges de la guerre,* 1916).

Verhaeren's first volumes are in conventional verse form—the alexandrine—with no more liberties than those common to the French romantic poets. Sonnets are frequent. During his crisis, beginning with *Les Flambeaux noirs,* he uses freer verse with varying rhythms to communicate more vividly overpowering feeling. Although bitterly attacked even by early friends who clung to traditional form and language, he never renounced his independence. He spent much of the last two decades of his life in France, and his work then shows fewer eccentricities, yet he remained a champion of free verse. The first three of his dramas combine prose and verse. The value of his prose writings for the interpretation of his poems as well as for their intrinsic worth has been too often overlooked. Here the monograph of André Fontaine is of special interest.

See: Stefan Zweig, *Emile Verhaeren,* tr. by J. Bithell (1914); A. Mockel, *Emile Verhaeren* (1923); E. Estève, *Emile Verhaeren* (1928); A. Fontaine, *Verhaeren et son œuvre* (1929).

B. M. W.

Verlaine, Paul (1844–1896, French poet), was born in Metz, where his father, an infantry captain, was in garrison. In 1851 the family moved to Paris where, contrary to the legend he tried to create later on in his life, Paul completed substantial studies. At 13 he had discovered Baudelaire (*q.v.*); at 14 the poet was born in him. In 1864 was formed his close association with Louis Xavier de Ricard, Banville (*q.v.*), and Leconte de Lisle (*q.v.*), and he became identified with the Parnassian school; in 1866 and 1869 he collaborated in the first two volumes of *Le Parnasse contemporain.* His first book, *Poèmes saturniens* (1866), marked the miraculous advent of a poet, whose personality was asserted through a wide culture and multiple influences. Already, in this first work of an essentially auditory and visual poet—Verlaine exhibited a passion for music and the plastic arts—the turbulent Verlainian song made itself heard; intrepid rhythms were manifested, an impressionism was linked to a taste for the plastic. Already the varied themes of the *Poèmes saturniens* closely reflected the interior story of Verlaine, the profound distress of his soul. For, in spite of a relatively happy childhood, in a comfortable bourgeois family, Verlaine displayed from early adolescence restless and morbid tendencies. At 14 he was tormented by a sexual crisis which lasted some time. At 18 he began to drink. Later he lost his faith, becoming an atheist, anticlerical, revolutionary. Under a respectable and bourgeois exterior (at that time he was employed in the municipal administration) Verlaine was in a psychological upheaval which influenced his entire future both as man and poet.

In 1869 the Watteau-inspired *Fêtes galantes* appeared, a "troubled mixture of sensation, sentiment, poetry," where scenes eminently melancholy and sensual abound. If, in spite of sadness and "a persistent feeling of irreality," the work is still Parnassian in its impersonality and its perfection of form, it already announces the penetrating musicality of Verlaine. The same year was marked by the poet's meeting and subsequently marrying Mathilde Mauté de Fleurville. The sweetness of the betrothal, the simple joys of marriage, were the themes of his third book, *La Bonne Chanson* (1870), full of intimate verse, essentially personal, in unsophisticated forms without apparent technique, which marked his definite break with the *Parnasse.* Abandoning conventional themes, Verlaine, from this period on, revealed his true self, as the diverse adventures of his life were to make him. Composed during the tormented period of the alliance of the "deux fils du soleil" (in 1872 Verlaine had fled France with Arthur Rimbaud, *q.v.*) and of the rupture with Mathilde, the following book, *Romances sans paroles* (1874), is a masterpiece of impressionistic and subjective poetry where thought, feeling, recollection, and sensation, subtly interwoven, are presented in a vibrant state which puts the reader in intimate contact with the dream, the sentiment, without the intellectual intermediary. An eminently original work, far from the direct lyricism of the preceding book, *Romances sans paroles* illustrates the precepts of Verlaine in his "Art poétique," published subsequently in *Jadis et naguère* (1884)—neither eloquence nor satire, the union of vague and precise, nuance, odd meters, new rhymes, and, more than ever, that glorious, inexpressible Verlainian music.

Then came a long period tragic and unhappy: Verlaine's imprisonment (he had shot Rimbaud in the wrist and was sentenced to two years in prison, 1873–1875), his conversion, deep and sincere, brought about by absolute solitude, his efforts to reform his life, his failures, his wanderings, the sentimental and financial catastrophes, vagrancy, drunkenness, misery, hovels, sickness, hospitals. Alternatives of debauchery and repentance, indices of a strange and mystic soul, of a weak and vacillating spirit, sensual but yet enamored of purity—all this is to be found in the works which follow *Romances sans paroles* and which reveal, simultaneously or in succession, the "desolate and magnificent songs of the poet who, now great sinner, now great repentant, sang with an equal innocence his faults and his remorse." In 1881 appeared *Sagesse,* regarded by some as his masterpiece. This new work embraces sweetly modulated musical pieces where the most intimate secrets of his heart are felt, beautiful hymns where subtle and delicate art puts the poet in immediate contact with those who hear him, where simple and familiar expressions, colloquies, give a note of exquisite intimacy. Then followed, among his most important books, *Jadis et naguère, Amour* (1888), *Parallèlement* (1889), and *Bonheur* (1891).

No work of Verlaine was outstandingly successful. Many, and among the best, passed unnoticed, except in the eyes of a few poets. However, toward 1882, Verlaine once more was in contact with literary circles, and only then did he know success through his studies on *Les Poètes maudits* (1884) and his "Art poétique." The young poets saw in him the leader of the new school. He was active in all the movements of this period. After 1890 he became widely known, was a candidate for the French Academy (and is now one of the great line, beginning with Molière, whom the Academy never received). In 1894, at the death of Leconte de Lisle (*q.v.*), the "younger school" conferred on him the title "prince of poets."

A pure lyrical genius, Verlaine is a poet of absolute originality. His was the art of rendering the unique in sensation, the most fugitive in emotion; he is the poet of the subconscious, the incomplete, the turbulent, the vague; he expressed the inexpressible, perceived the unperceivable. Master of the language, he scorned formalism and rhetoric. He knew all the techniques without ever becoming enslaved by them. If he sought a simple, naïve, familiar form, he was not ignorant of the laws of the purest classicism. To express individuality he dislocated the sentence, which became more and more fluid. Master also of all rhythms, his taste directed him to the "odd"; his bold ear sought for the most tenuous sounds and the most discordant. If the Verlainian music is expressed by minor tonalities, it is enriched also by dissonances, in the modern taste. While he far from scorned the traditional meter, he so disarticulated, disguised, "fluidified," the alexandrine that without him free verse cannot be contemplated.

See: E. Delahaye, *Verlaine* (1919); E. Lepelletier, *Paul Verlaine et son œuvre* (1923); M. Coulon, *Verlaine, poète saturnien* (1929); F. Porché, *Verlaine tel qu'il fut* (1933); A. Adam, *Le Vrai Verlaine* (1936); A. Fontaine, *Verlaine, homme de lettres* (1937); C. Cuénot, *Etat présent des études verlainiennes* (1938).

J. V.

Vermeylen, August (1872–1945, Flemish critic and novelist), was born in Brussels. In the renewal of Flemish literature that took place about 1890, he was the theoretician, the aggressive proponent of a way of writing that would free the artist from complacent provincialism and bigotry. He belonged to the founders of the review *Van Nu en Straks* (Today and Tomorrow) who wanted romanticism replaced by a moderate naturalism and who tried to stress the intellectual element in writing. His philosophical novel *De wandelende Jood* (1906; The Wandering Jew), translated into French, Czech, and German, is written in a language of great plastic beauty and conveys its moral message well. As a critic Vermeylen combated the narrow conservatism of his predecessors and offered also sound criticism of the Flemish movement in his book *Kritiek der Vlaamsche Beweging* (1905; Critique of the Flemish Movement). A professor of the history of art, first at the University of Brussels, then at the State University of Ghent, he composed a remarkable *Geschiedenis der Europeesche Plastiek en Schilderkunst* (1921–25; History of Plastic Art and Painting in Europe). He wrote an excellent history of modern Flemish literature, *Van Gezelle tot Timmermans* (1923; From Gezelle to Timmermans). In 1943 his novel *Twee Vrienden* (Two Friends) was published.

J.-A. G.

Verwey, Albert (1865–1937, Dutch poet, critic, and literary historian), was born at Amsterdam and, after leaving high school in 1883, was employed there in the office of the Maxwell Land Grant Company. He accompanied its vice-president as secretary on an inspection visit to New Mexico. But soon after his return he exchanged this business connection for a literary career. He was among the first editors (1885–1889) of *De Nieuwe Gids* (The New Guide). His *Verzamelde Gedichten* (Collected Poems) appeared in 1889. Five years later he founded with Lodewijk van Deyssel (*q.v.*) *Tweemaandelijksch Tijdschrift* (Bimonthly Periodical), which in 1902 became a monthly under the title *De XXste Eeuw* (The 20th Century). In 1905 he severed his association with Van Deyssel and founded a new monthly which he called *De Beweging* (The Movement). This became the rallying point of a group of younger poets who recognized in Verwey their mentor and master. Without being pontifical he held his followers together by the confidence he inspired in his aesthetic judgment and by their respect for his uncompromising honesty. *De Beweging* was to demonstrate Verwey's conviction that true poetry has a higher vocation than to express individual moods and feelings in musical and picturesque words. That had been his conception of poetry when he was editor of *De Nieuwe Gids*. But in his riper years he saw in poetry a social force by which the successive generations and the members of each generation were welded together and made conscious of their unity. All Verwey's later verse has an intellectual quality that reminds one of the poetry of his German friend Stefan George (*q.v.*). His poems seem to owe their birth to a determined will to compose, rather than to the irresistible urge to sing. *De Beweging* was discontinued in 1919. But five years later Verwey was given an opportunity to influence the nation's youth by his appointment to the vacant chair of Dutch literature at the University of Leiden. When he was forced to retire on reaching his 70th year, he had the satisfaction of seeing himself succeeded by the poet P. N. van Eyck, the most eminent of the *Beweging* group. Among Verwey's contributions to literary history *Het Leven van Potgieter* (1903; Life of Potgieter) deserves mention. His collected *Proza* (1925) fills 10 volumes.

See: M. Uyldert, *Albert Verwey* (1908); A. Verwey, *Mijn Verhouding tot Stefan George* (1934).

A. J. B.

Véry, Pierre (1900–, French novelist), reflects in his first literary manifestations (*Pont-Egaré,* 1929; *Danse à l'ombre,* 1930; *Les Métamorphoses,* 1931) certain tendencies of the period in which he began writing. Rather than novels, they could be called poetic fantasies strongly influenced by the surrealist school. However, under their apparent eccentricity could be detected a brilliant imagination, a gift for dramatic effects and suspense, the consciousness of the mystery of the world and of the ludicrous aspects of human life. Shifting to detective stories was a normal evolution for Véry, who could apply to himself the title of his novel *Le Meneur de jeu* (1934). The games which he invents and directs are the 15 murder stories, filled with his poetical imagination and the whims of his caustic wit. The variety of his inspiration seems inexhaustible. His points of departure are sometimes a popular song (*M. Malbrough est mort,* 1937), an observation or a reminiscence (the resemblance between human and animal faces, already noticed by H. G. Wells, forms the background of *Le Gentleman des Antipodes,* 1936). He even uses personal incidents. He conceived the idea of *Madame et le mort* (1940) after noticing that someone had stolen his wallet. In addition to the novels already mentioned *Monsieur Marcel des pompes funèbres* (1932), *L'Assassinat du Père Noël* (1934), *Goupi-Mains Rouges* (1937), and *Série de sept* (1938) are among his very best. They all show the same qualities, fertility of invention, originality of details, keen sense of observation, vividness of dialogue, and perfect mastery of technique. With Pierre Véry the detective story becomes a true literary genre.

M. E. C.

Vesper, Will (1882–, German poet, novelist, and editor), was born in Wuppertal-Barmen and spent his earliest youth on a farm. His later literary manner and the fields of his intellectual preoccupation (historical and folklore themes, sagas, etc.) reflect the ancient customs and uses, beliefs and sayings, of his western German peasant background. After completing the humanistic Gymnasium, he received no more formal education other than a year's study in history and philology at the University of Munich. Since 1906 he has been literary counselor to the publisher, C. H. Beck, in Munich and from 1918 to 1920 was manager of the literary section of the *Deutsche allgemeine Zeitung.* Recently he has edited with much vigor the literary magazine *Die schöne Literatur,* which became, in 1931, *Die neue Literatur.*

In spite of the remarkable uniformity and even monotony of subject matter, his work is more varied in form, and more voluminous, than can here be enumerated. Between 1906 and 1943 he published with unceasing energy countless popular editions, translations, and modern poetic adaptations of some of the main works of earlier German and European literature (*e.g., Tristan und Isolde,* 1911; *Die Gudrunsage,* 1925). Nearly 15 volumes of his own eclectic, romantic poetry (*Die Liebesmessse,* 1913; *Rufe in die Zeit,* 1936) and more than 20 narrative and historical works (*Martin Luthers Jugendjahre,* 1918; *Gute Geister,* 1921; *Das harte Geschlecht,* 1931) represent the fruits of an ever active and eager literary life. At one time his judicious anthology, *Die Ernte aus acht Jahrhunderten deutscher Lyrik* (1906 ff.), was one of the most widely read collections of German lyrical poetry.

See: K. A. Kutzbach, "Will Vesper" (with bibliography), *Die neue Literatur,* XXXIII (1932), 435–449; A. Soergel, *Dichtung und Dichter der Zeit,* Dritte Folge: *Dichter aus deutschem Volkstum* (1934), pp. 134–148.

V. L.

Viani, Lorenzo (1882–1936, Italian painter and novelist), was born in Viareggio, Lucca, of a very poor peasant family. After a few years of grammar school education he was apprenticed to a Viareggio barber and remained in his shop until, through the interest of a group of clients who had noted Viani's skill in pen and ink drawing (he caricatured everyone who came to the shop), he obtained a scholarship to the Academy of Fine Arts in Lucca. An exuberant youth, acquainted with poverty since childhood, and imbued with revolutionary ideas (his employer had been the Socialist leader in his native town), he soon tired of discipline and quit school, but continued to study. At the age of 23, penniless and friendless, he made his way to Paris and spent several years there in dire poverty, studying and painting. When he returned to Italy, his canvases, some of which had already attracted attention in France, were hung in a number of exhibitions, and his reputation was established. At the outbreak of the First World War, Viani renounced his radical ideas, vigorously urged Italy's intervention on the side of the Allies, volunteered in the army, and served for over three years. As a soldier he continued to use his pen and brush and at the end of the conflict his war drawings were exhibited in Milan. These drawings attracted the attention of Mussolini and resulted in an invitation to Viani to write for the *Popolo d'Italia*. Viani accepted, became a militant Fascist, and remained such until his death.

Viani began to write in 1922, producing first a biography of the poet Ceccardo Ceccardi Roccatagliata and thereafter an average of a book each year. All Viani's works are more or less autobiographical. *Ceccardo* (1922) tells of his friendship with the poet Roccatagliata; *Parigi* (1925) of his experiences in Paris; *Le Chiavi nel pozzo* (1934) recounts his stay in an insane asylum; *Barba e capelli* (1939) is a description of his clients in his barber shop, some of whom, like D'Annunzio (*q.v.*), were famous. These books consist mostly of literary sketches, painted with pen instead of brush—anatomical studies and character dissections—performed with a kind of satanic joy. In these sketches Viani shows a special predilection for lunatics, degenerates, cripples, drunkards, and beggars and a rare mastery in bringing out the grotesque and animal traits of such subjects. He uses a peculiar and expressive language, a jargon of slang and obsolete local terms picked up from the oldest inhabitants of the province of Lucca and at many points incomprehensible to the average reader. He is an adherent of no aesthetic school, he avoids everything that smacks of formal psychology and practices a ruthless and at times cruel realism which does not, however, prevent him from sympathizing with his wretched subjects, feeling for them the solidarity of poverty and suffering. He has had many ardent admirers and some rabid detractors; we are beginning however to have dispassionate appraisal of his work.

See: Krimer (pseud. of C. Mercati) *Sodalizio con V.* (1938); G. Nervini, *L. Viani nella vita e nell'arte* (1939); G. Ravegnani, *I Contemporanei* (1930), pp. 209–223; E. Falqui and E. Vittorini, *Scrittori nuovi* (1930), pp. 651–658.

G. B.

Viebig, Clara (1860–, German novelist), disciple of Zola (*q.v.*), outstanding woman novelist of the naturalistic school, was born at Treves and first became famous by introducing into literature her native region, the bleak and volcanic uplands of the Eifel with its pine forests and its dangerous swamps. How perfectly people and landscape are blended may be seen in her story "Am Totenmaar" from *Kinder der Eifel* (1897), where the austerity of the landscape mirrors the moral rigor of the old shepherd and where its desolation is a symbol of the utter loneliness of his abandoned child. Viebig's early novels could not escape the influence of Gabriele Reuter's courageous and widely discussed novel *Aus guter Familie* (1895), the story of a sensitive girl of the higher middle class whose life is ruined by the conventional narrow-minded prudishness of her religious and social training. But Clara Viebig is more outspoken in her presentation of the erotic side of life which, to cite an early example, is treated with fine humor in the famous novel *Das Weiberdorf* (1900). Except for two short periods of the year when the men return from the steel mills, the women are left alone in this village of the Eifel, where the worthless Pittchen becomes the object of their suppressed desires. When the constable takes him away for petty counterfeiting, the women band together to rescue him, but quickly desert him at the sight of the returning menfolk. The masses which act with collective instinct like one monstrous organism, are pictured here in a masterly fashion, as is the religious ecstasy of the pilgrims to the shrine at Echternach in the Eifel in *Das Kreuz im Venn* (1908) or the suppressed hatred and secret patriotic longing of the servile Polish peasants under German domination, observed during the author's residence in Posen and portrayed in *Das schlafende Heer* (1904; Eng. tr., *The Sleeping Army,* 1929). As a young girl Viebig had lived in Düsseldorf, the scene of her historic novel *Die Wacht am Rhein* (1902). Here the peaceful fusion by marriage of the old Prussian element with the population of the Rhineland is demonstrated in the history of a family through three generations. The novel ends in 1870. Modern Berlin, where Clara Viebig spent her adult years as the wife of the publisher Cohn, is the background of many of her social novels. Among these *Das tägliche Brot* (1900; Eng. tr., *Our Daily Bread,* 1908), depicting the life of a servant girl in the lower middle class, is an example of the author's intense human sympathy which lends abiding value to her novels. Viebig is at her best when portraying characters governed by elemental needs and desires, especially women from the lower classes. Her style is strictly visual, a succession of pictures, vivid and concrete in every detail.

See: C. Scheuffler, *Clara Viebig* (1926).

E. Hof.

Vielé-Griffin, Francis (1864–1937, French poet), whose Huguenot ancestry migrated to the United States at the end of the 17th century, was born in Norfolk, Virginia. His father had been military governor for the Union forces in the Civil War. When eight years old, the boy was taken to France for his education, where he remained the rest of his life, residing now in Paris, now in the provinces, with a preference for Touraine. In his first book of poems, *Cueille d'avril* (1886), one of his most distinguished works, he tells of the charms of country life on the banks of the Loire with the simplicity and musical tenderness of Verlaine (*q.v.*). The soft atmosphere of the region, known as the garden of France, permeates to such an extent the poetic works of Vielé-Griffin that he has been called the poet of Touraine. But he is particularly noted as representative of the symbolist movement and the indisputable master of vers libre. In collaboration with Paul Adam, Henri de Régnier (*qq.v.*), and Bernard Lazare he founded in 1890 the *Entretiens politiques et littéraires,* which became the principal vehicle of expression for the symbolist poets. In this review were formulated on numerous occasions his theories of a new verse, as he strove with Gustave Kahn, Jules Laforgue (*qq.v.*), Edouard Dujardin, and others to liberate French poetry from arbitrary rules. The vers libre which Vielé-Griffin adopted after the publication of *Joies* (1888) is not a mere variation of the alexandrine or any conventional meter, but a rhythmic pattern born out of the emotional movement of the phrase and made perceptible by the appropriate combination of the temporal and quantitative values of syllabic units. His verse thus becomes an original creation expressing by its cadence and musical tonality the whole personality of the poet. It reveals a delicate sensibility which is moved by the multiple aspects of beauty and which a lofty idealism inclines to seek goodness and gladness in man as well as in nature. This optimistic attitude, springing from a belief in life and its spiritual values, is generally maintained in the poetic works collected under the title *Poèmes et poésies* (1886–1893). One may note also the deep religious feeling of *Amour sacré* (1900) and the sincere humanitarian faith of *Clarté de vie* (1897). The frequent use in these poems of the technique of popular song follows a tendency common to the symbolist poets of this period.

Vielé-Griffin's admiration for Keats, Shelley, and particularly Swinburne, whose *Laus Veneris* he translated, not only affected his love for nature but also his interest in Hellenic and medieval legends as symbols of his philosophical thought. In this vein he wrote several narrative poems, the best examples being *Chevauchée d'Yeldis* (1893), *Phocas le jardinier* (1898), and *Légende ailée de Wieland le forgeron* (1900), all imbued with his Neoplatonic conceptions. Too often in these lengthy compositions verbosity and confusion of images render the thought obscure and its expression inadequate. The verse, however, always retains the fluid rhythm and harmonious qualities which characterize the poetry of Vielé-Griffin.

See: Rémy de Gourmont, *Le Livre des masques* (1896); Robert de Souza, *La Poésie populaire et le lyrisme sentimental* (1899); André Beaunier, *La Poésie nouvelle* (1902); Marcel Raymond, *De Baudelaire au surréalisme* (1933).

M. D.

Vildrac, Charles (pseud. of Charles Messager, 1882–, French poet, essayist, and dramatist), was born in Paris. He early began to write poetry. In 1906 he and several of his friends, including Georges Duhamel (*q.v.*), who was later to became his brother-in-law, decided to live cooperatively. They rented an old house at Créteil in the suburbs of Paris and called it the Abbaye. There they hoped to devote themselves to their vocations, writing, painting, music—and to earn their livelihood at the same time. The group disbanded about a year later; each went his own way, enriched, however, by this life in common.

The first volume of poems by Vildrac,

Images et mirages (1908), was printed on the press of the Abbaye. Another volume, *Le Livre d'amour,* appeared in 1910 (Eng. tr., *A Book of Love,* 1923); in 1911 Vildrac published, in collaboration with Duhamel, *Notes sur la technique poétique.* His poetry has been influenced by that of Whitman, both in form and in ideas. Vildrac sees beauty and poetry in the simplest and most humble manifestations of life. Friendship is one of his favorite themes. It is not the social class of his characters which interests him; it is their purely human value. The simplest, plainest people are capable of the highest feelings, of acts of heroism, of nobility of soul, and of poetry. In his play *Le Paquebot Tenacity* (Vieux Colombier, 1920; Eng. tr., *The Steamer Tenacity,* 1921) the plot is almost nonexistent. The character study of the two young men who are about to sail for Canada and the idea of the freedom of the soul form the entire subject of the play. *La Brouille* (Comédie Française, 1930) is also based on a flimsy plot: two friends, one an idealist and the other a realist, have a quarrel over principles. The action is purely psychological.

As an essayist Vildrac again preaches love of fellow man and faith in humanity. *Découvertes* (1912; including a one-act play, *L'Indigent,* of which there is one Eng. tr., *The Art of Making Friends,* 1933) exalts the beauty of human relations, the hunger for human sympathy. Vildrac also has written a charming book for children, *L'Ile rose* (1925).

Vildrac was very active in the resistance movement during the Second World War.

See: L. Savitzky, "Charles Vildrac et le théâtre contemporain," *Mercure de France,* CLXIII (1923), 289–305; C. Sénéchal, *L'Abbaye de Créteil* (1930); M. L. Bidal, *Les Ecrivains de l'Abbaye* (1938).

H. H.

Villaespesa, Francisco (1879–1936, Spanish poet and dramatist), was born in Laujar, Almería. He was a typical Spaniard of the South; in his temperament, his life, and his work he was an improviser, facile and brilliant. When he first attracted attention in Madrid about 1897 it was as the leader of the new modernist poetic movement which, inspired by the example of the poets of Spanish America, was taking shape among the young Spaniards. His home was the gathering point of many of those shy, aloof figures, and the literary reviews that he founded were the organs of expression of the new schools. He always was on the closest terms with the poets of America, first through their books, then through his personal relations with those who came to Spain to live, and later through his own travels and long stays in various countries of the New World. Especially in the latter part of his life, as his reputation declined in Spain, he achieved new triumphs in Spanish America with dramas and poems dealing with American subjects.

His complete works comprise over 50 volumes of poetry and some 30 dramatic works, in addition to a number of novels and short stories. His enduring value lies in the poetic works he wrote before 1912, although it is then that he achieved his great success as a dramatic author with a play in verse on an oriental theme of Granada, *El alcázar de las perlas.* His lyric and poetic gifts are, to be sure, found in this and his other historical dramas of a romantic nature; but they exist in a far purer form in his earlier and essentially lyric compositions. In these appear many of the themes, expressions, and metrical forms of modernism which he took from Rubén Darío and the other Spanish American poets of the period, especially Silva, Lugones, and Herrera y Reissig; it was through them that he received the foreign influences of the epoch already assimilated into Spanish. At times this influence is direct, as in the case of writers akin in language and temperament to the Spanish, such as the Portuguese (especially Eugénia de Castro, *q.v.*) and the Italians (especially D'Annunzio, *q.v.*). In Villaespesa's poetry all these new and foreign elements which characterize modernism are brought into complete accord with traditional Spanish rhetoric. For although modernist in form and content, the poetry and temperament of Villaespesa were romantic, and therefore the writer he most closely resembles is Zorrilla, in his predilection for oriental themes, his conventionally poetic vision of Spain, and his ability to achieve his effects through mere verbal sonority. Aside from this value as a representative of tradition and of his epoch, Villaespesa has a value of his own as a lyric poet. The sadness of life, the intimate experience of love, the moving evocation of places, things, and landscapes, the popular flavor, the eternal dissatisfaction, are the subjective notes of his lyrical creation, poured forth in a multitude of volumes. Careful selection is required if one is to do justice to his originality, which is difficult to perceive because in his poetry the muted, limpid part of his work is the best.

See: P. Gener, "Figuras contemporáneas: Villaespesa," *Cervantes,* Vol. I (Madrid, 1916),

No. 1, pp. 27–40; R. Cansinos-Asséns, *La nueva literatura,* I (1917), 125–137; J. R. Jiménez, "Recuerdo al primer Villaespesa (1899–1901)," *Sol* (Madrid), March 10, 1936; F. de Onís, "Francisco Villaespesa y el modernismo," *Revista hispánica moderna,* III (New York, 1936–1937), 276–278.

F. de O.

Villalón Daoiz y Halcón, Fernando (1881–1930, Spanish poet), was born in Morón de la Frontera, Seville, of an affluent and aristocratic family. From his father he inherited the title of conde de Miraflores de los Angeles and a liking for books. From childhood he lived in close contact with nature in Andalucía la Baja. A vigorous man, an excellent horseman, breeder of fine cattle, friend of bullfighters and of popular singers, he felt and caught all the color and force of his luminous region. His restlessness, born of a penchant for the occult, adds interest to his attractive personality. He was an important figure in the literary journals of his country; a quiet inclination for poetry, familiarity with the classics, contact with the new poets of Spain, as well as articles of his own, were contributing factors. At the age of 46 he published his first book, *Andalucía la Baja* (1927). This was followed by *La Toriada* (1928) and *Romances del 800* (1929). An appreciation of classical poetry, a feeling for the folk elements of Andalusian life which he shared with the young poets of his period and appreciated perhaps even more directly than they—these make of Villalón the authentic poet of his own region, although his verses are noted more for vitality and content than for facility of expression.

See: Gerardo Diego, *Poesía española* (*Antología*) (1934), p. 475; Federico de Onís, *Antología de la poesía española e hispanoamericana* (1934), p. 1066.

A. I.

Villiers de l'Isle-Adam, Jean Marie Mathias Philippe Auguste, comte de (1838–1889, French poet, dramatist, and novelist), was born at St. Brieuc in Brittany. The scion of a noble family illustrious in the annals of French history, he was reared by a chimerical father, who was forever beguiled into quests of impossible treasures he fancied were buried in dungeons, and two saintly women, his mother and his aunt, who idolized him. He grew up into a hypersensitive and dreamy youth inwardly illumined by the splendors of his chivalric heritage and the romantic reflections of an enchanting idyl he had at the age of 17 with a young woman who died soon after, so that henceforth glory, love, and death formed a mystic trinity in his heart.

In 1857, provided with the "sterile riches" of his ancestry, secure in his Catholic faith and legitimist traditions, and his manuscripts in ballast, he followed his literary dreams to Paris. Here the fireworks of his fantasy soon made of him a legendary, but also tragic, figure in the bohemian cafés and cénacles, where his rhapsodic discourses electrified his audiences. He was befriended by the literary élite, especially Baudelaire (*q.v.*), who introduced him to Richard Wagner (*q.v.*) and to the writings of Edgar Allan Poe, two kindred spirits whose works have close affinities with his own. He probed coincidentally the Hegelian philosophy of the Absolute and the arcana of the occult sciences, which seemed to him to be consonant with his own idealism.

His *Premières poésies* (1859) attracted little comment, for he was a great poet only in prose; these verses were but "half a promise," as he himself told Baudelaire, agreeing to send him soon "a prose less immature than his verses." This he did with his novel *Isis* (1862), of which he had already conceived the idea in his adolescent years. Dating from the same period are his two early dramas, *Morgane* and *Elën.* The first to be published, *Elën* (1865), portrays a Circean woman whose lustful love leads to frustration and death. In the second, *Morgane* (1866), love is heightened by ambition; in the end both lovers renounce a throne to be united in the bosom of death. In *Isis* love becomes an unearthly longing which can be fulfilled only in that otherworldliness beyond death which became the omega of all the religious, philosophical, and occult idealisms of the author and which was also the mainspring of his irreconcilable antagonism to modern social and scientific materialisms.

This hostility dictated his sardonic and tragic caricature Tribulat Bonhomet, a kinsman of M. Homais and Bouvard and Pécuchet (*see* Flaubert). Bonhomet is a pseudoscientific, democratic, and antipoetic symbol of crass "common sense," and a terrifying embodiment of moral and spiritual torpidity, whom he opposes to Claire, the creature of faith, in *Claire Lenoir,* novelette published (1867; Eng. tr., 1925) in the *Revue des lettres et des arts.*

Villiers de l'Isle-Adam carried his championship of the spirit to the stage with *La Révolte* (1870), a play with a theme like Ibsen's (*q.v.*) in *A Doll's House* which it antedates, and with his prize-winning play,

Le Nouveau monde (1880). In this play, written in 1876 to celebrate the centenary of the American Revolution but produced only in 1883, two idealisms, the feudal and democratic, battle for country and love with equal heroism. Both plays failed although they deserved a better fate.

Neglected by publishers and public alike, he plumbed at this time frightful depths of misery. But, intrenched in his militant spiritualism, he began to publish, at first in fugitive magazines, his series of tales of terror, mystery, and fantasy which he later brought together in collections such as *Contes cruels* (1883; Eng. tr., *Sardonic Tales,* 1927) and *Histoires insolites* (1888). As with the rest of his work some of them "Vera," "Sentimentalisme," "Akëdysséril"—bespeak his idealistic aspirations, while others—"Les Demoiselles de Bienfilâtre," "La Torture par l'Espérance," "L'Affichage céleste"—echo his irony, humor, and ire against man's spiritual blindness and materialistic presumptions.

Both his high-flown idealism and his humorous realism concurred in the scientific and philosophical novel *L'Eve future* (1886); science creates a living android whose beautiful soul can be, however, only a reflection of her lover's ideal. Thus all creations of science, and reality itself, are but illusions into which the spirit alone can breathe life.

The purest expression of this rarefied idealism is to be found in his poetic drama *Axël* (1890; Eng. tr., 1925), largely written by the year 1872. The heroine, Sara, rejecting the call of religion and heaven, and the hero, Axël, that of the occult world, are tempted by that of life which is symbolized by treasure buried in the crypt under the castle of Auërsperg; they discover upon finding it the greater enchantment of each other's love. Rather than outlive its initial ecstasy and see it tarnished and converted into a deceptive illusion, they resolve to eternize it in the bosom of death. Their ideal, like their creator's, was not of this world.

Villiers de l'Isle-Adam's influence over the symbolistic writers was profound. "Everything I have done I owe to Villiers," Maurice Maeterlinck (*q.v.*) has said, and W. B. Yeats declared that he read *Axël* in his youth, "slowly and laboriously as one reads a sacred book." Verily, he was a "prince de l'esprit."

See: Fernan Clerget, *Villiers de l'Isle Adam* (1913); Arnold Whitridge, *Critical Ventures in Modern French Literature* (1924), pp. 81–101; C. J. C. van der Meulen, *L'Idéalisme de Villiers de l'Isle-Adam* (1925); Peter Quennell, *Baudelaire and the Symbolists* (1929), pp. 99–130; Edmund Wilson, *Axel's Castle; a Study in the Imaginative Literature of 1870–1930* (1931), pp. 258–264; Max Daireaux, *Villiers de l'Isle-Adam; l'homme et l'œuvre* (1936); Vincent O'Sullivan, "The Tales and Stories of Villiers de l'Isle-Adam," *Dublin Magazine* (April–June, 1940), pp. 25–34.

S. A. R.

Vinogradov, Anatoli Korneliyevich (1888–, Russian novelist, biographer, scholar, and librarian), was born at Polotnyany Zavod in the former Government of Kaluga. Although he is best known as a historical novelist, he has published a number of literary studies—*Merime v pismakh k Sobolevskomu* (1928; Mérimée in His Letters to Sobolevski) and biographies of Byron (1936) and Stendhal (1938).

Stendhal is also the subject of a novelette, *Poteryannaya perchatka* (1931; The Lost Glove), based on episodes of the occupation of Moscow by Napoleon's army, and of a long novel, *Tri tsveta vremeni* (1931; The Three Colors of the Times); the colors, of course, are political, and Stendhal is shown as an atheist and a liberal in conflict with clericalism and reactionism. Vinogradov's *Povest o bratyakh Turgenevykh* (1932; The Story of the Brothers Turgenev) concerns itself chiefly with the life abroad of Nicholas and Alexander, champions of progressive ideas during a period of social ferment. Interesting as interpretation is the novel about Toussaint L'Ouverture, *Chyorny konsul* (1933; Eng. tr., *The Black Consul,* 1935), which portrays the sanguinary conflicts in Haiti in the light of the contemporaneous French Revolution. Here, as sometimes elsewhere, the author combines extravagant narration with the meticulous observation of a historian. *Osuzhdeniye Paganini* (1936; The Condemnation of Paganini) has as its protagonist the great violinist, who is shown to be a victim of the unholy machinations of the Jesuits. *Khronika Malevinskikh* (1943; The Chronicle of the Malevinskis), a novel covering the last three generations, offers a view of the development of science and society in Russia. Vinogradov is adept at interpreting sources and presenting his facts in the spirit of socialist realism, now dominant in Russian fiction.

See: *Nauchnyie rabotniki Moskvy* (1930).

P. A. P.

Vitorino, Virginia (1898–, Portuguese poet and dramatist), was born in the historical city of Alcobaça. Her first poetical compositions were published in the daily newspapers of

Lisbon in 1917, and she has collaborated on the most important literary reviews of her native country. The sonnet has been her preferred poetic form, and the collection *Namorados* (1918; Lovers) has had more than 10 editions. In Virginia Vitorino there is a highly elaborated alliance, very appropriate to the sonnet form, of Renaissance rhetorical devices (paradox, metaphorical parallelism) and erotic passion. At times this reminds one very much of the manner of the great South American women poets, Storni and Ibarbourou, because of the ease with which the most elemental sensations are given a universal and absorbing quality. It is not surprising that these sonnets have met with favor in South America. The one entitled "Amor" (Love) is very well known; other pieces of similar inspiration and structure are "Apaixonadamente" (Passionately) and "Renuncia" (Renunciation).

Virginia Vitorino has also made contributions to the Portuguese theatre, in works characterized, at their best, by energy and naturalness, facile dialogue and national popular feeling. *Degredados* (1930; Degraded) is the best known; this was followed by *A volta* (1932; The Return), *Fascinação* (1933; Fascination), *Manuela* (1934), and finally *Camaradas* (1938; Comrades). The last-named work was awarded the Gil Vicente prize by the Secretariado de Propaganda Nacional of her country.

See: A. Forjaz de Sampaio, *História da literatura portuguesa ilustrada dos séculos XIX e XX* (1939).

R. M. L.

Vivanti, Annie (1868–1942, Italian novelist and short-story writer), was born in London, where her father, Anselmo, an Italian patriot, had been forced into exile on account of his active participation in the revolutionary uprisings and political conspiracies in his native Mantua, for which Austria had condemned him to death. With the aid of her mother, Anna Lindau, who was German, the child studied the German poets, especially Goethe and Schiller; from her English governess young Annie learned by heart long passages from the Bible. The home of the Vivantis in London was a meeting place for many German poets and critics, and the child learned to speak both German and English fluently. When she was nine years of age she was taken to Italy to attend school. On the death of her mother in 1880, Annie was sent to Switzerland where she remained two years. After a brief visit to London, she traveled extensively in the United States and studied vocal music in New York.

Upon her return to Italy in 1887 she composed verses in Italian, published in 1890 in a volume entitled *Lirica,* for which Carducci (*q.v.*) wrote the preface. Carducci admired both the poetry and the woman, and a liaison between these two writers lasted for many years. A more impartial criticism of Vivanti's lyrics was made by Benedetto Croce (*q.v.*) who found that her poems suffered from an inadequate artistic elaboration. In 1890 was published a novel, *Marion, artista da caffè concerto,* in which Vivanti depicted a character reminiscent of Carmen, with violent passions and insatiable desires; Marion combines qualities of love and selfishness, modesty and immodesty, compassion and cruelty, pride and baseness; in her perversion and cruelty she is guilty of many crimes.

For two decades Vivanti disappeared from the literary scene. In 1908 she married an Irish lawyer, John Chartres, an active supporter of the Irish Free State movement. Then, in 1910, was published a novel in English entitled *The Devourers,* which she herself translated into Italian under the title of *I Divoratori* (1911). Critics generally agree that this is Vivanti's best novel. It deals with a devoted mother who undergoes many sacrifices for the sake of a young daughter. The success of this novel encouraged Vivanti to write other novels, dramas, short stories, sketches, and articles on a variety of subjects. The most important of these are *Zingaresca* (1918), *Gioia* (1921), *Terra di Cleopatra* (1925), *Perdonate Eglantina!* (1926), and *Mea Culpa* (1927). The quality of her literary production has remained fairly constant. In her stories, always vivid and imaginative, Vivanti enjoys presenting extraordinary events, bewildering and almost fantastic episodes, frightful passions, terrifying wickedness and follies—sometimes combined with extreme kindness, piety, and generosity. Though never great nor profound, she is interesting and most charming. Giuseppe Prezzolini (*q.v.*) has said that of all recent Italian woman writers, "the most vivacious, the most able is Vivanti."

See: B. Croce, *La Letteratura della nuova Italia,* 2d ed., II (1921), 326–333; G. Prezzolini, *La Coltura italiana* (1923), p. 248; L. Russo, *I Narratori* (1923), pp. 201–202.

H. R. M.

Vivien, Renée (née Pauline Tarn, 1877–1909, French poet), was born in London, her father, John Tarn of England, having met and married her mother, Mary Gillet Bennett of

Jackson, Michigan, while on a visit to Honolulu. With the exception of a few unhappy years in England, Renée Vivien spent all her life in Paris, whence she made numerous trips to foreign lands. An ample fortune enabled her to live in luxurious surroundings in a fashionable part of Paris. She loved solitude and study; at 22 she learned Greek in order to read Sappho in the original. While Renée Vivien's prose translations of Sapphic fragments are literal and accurate, her poetic paraphrases are freely fanciful; in fact, her cult of Sappho was purely a pretext for interpreting her own Lesbianism. A fervent disciple of Baudelaire and possessor of a strong inherited strain of Nordic mysticism, she was too obsessed by Christian concepts of chastity and sin to make a convincing pagan. Her Hellenism is anachronistic and artificial, but this does not prevent her evocations of the lives and loves of ancient Greek maidens on the island of Lesbos from having genuine grace and charm. In many of these poems she employs the musical and little-used Sapphic meter. Besides Baudelaire and Sappho, certain poets of her own race contributed to the formation of her poetic manner, especially Swinburne and Rossetti. Furthermore, her symbolism shows the influence of Wagner and Albert Samain (*qq.v.*). From Baudelaire she learned the artistic control of emotions and superb musical technique that make her poetry superior to that of most women poets. From him also she adopted the poetic use of corresponding sensations and the cult of evil. Renée Vivien's best poetry interprets her own deeply felt emotional experiences. It tells of her intense suffering at being treated as a social outcast because of her love of women, of her refusal to see beauty in modern Christian civilization, and of her longing for the pagan life of ancient Greece. She even rented a villa in Mytilene where, for months at a time, she attempted to relive the Golden Age. It is not strange that Renée Vivien, continually haunted by unattainable desires, should have sought the release of death and made it a frequent theme in her poetry; always delicate, she hastened her end by voluntary fasting and died in Paris at 32.

Because of its exaltation of Lesbian love, the poetry of Renée Vivien has been unjustly neglected. Despite this dominating characteristic, her verse merits respect and admiration because of its delicate purity and perfection of form. Originally published in 12 slim volumes (1901–1910), her *Poésies complètes* are now obtainable in two (1934). Her prose, consisting of a novel, two collections of prose poems, a book of tales, and several essays, is mediocre and could be ignored except for its autobiographical interest.

See: Yves-Gérard Le Dantec, *Renée Vivien, femme damnée, femme sauvée* (1930).

C. B. C.

Vogau, Boris Andreyevich, *see* Pilnyak, Boris.

Vogt, Nils Collett (1864–1937, Norwegian poet), was born in Christiania of a bureaucratic engineering father and a sensitive, artistic mother. Even in early adolescence an impulsive individualism led him to revolt against his family so that he might become "a child of the age." Through Georg Brandes (*q.v.*) he found the poetry of Byron, Shelley, and Drachmann, and was thereby prepared for the "dedication to life" which possessed him on hearing Björnson's (*q.v.*) speech at the unveiling of Henrik Wergeland's statue in 1881. His reaction against the "treachery" of the Liberals in 1885 drove him into contact with the radical *bohème* and a nominal adherence to socialistic doctrine. The passionate intellectual rebellion of the 80's and his experiences then remained a recurrent theme in his writings to the very end. His novels and plays deal with little else, and his poetry reverts to them again and again. Already at the age of 30 the sense of memory, of having lived warmly and intensely, of looking back on youth began to fill his poetry. Even when the passage of time had made him less impetuous, he never regretted his stormy youth, and has often sung the glory of youthful idealism, "the fever in our blood," "the dream above the strife of living." His slender first collection, *Digte* (1887; Poems), fell in the midst of a naturalistic, unpoetic era and was severely handled by many of his fellow radicals. But with the 90's came a new spirit more congenial to his lyric muse. In volume after volume he unfolded a genius for lyric-reflective poetry unmatched in Norway for rock-hewn strength, for masculine courage and maturity. *Fra vaar til høst* (1894; From Spring to Autumn) was his first great success, the result of his meeting with the sunlit life of Italy, a warm-blooded confession of pagan faith, the northerner's ego expanding under blue southern skies. But in the long run his meeting with the south led only to a deeper realization of his love for Norway. Although he was frequently critical of his respected contemporaries, he was bound by a mystic sense of identification to the soil of Norway. Already in his earliest collection he wished he might be a "fir tree in the forest"; in *Det* *dyre brød* (1900; The Costly Bread) his friends are likened to sea gulls; in *Septemberbrand* (1907; September Flame) he is the "heather on trackless mountains, flaming most hotly toward rain and autumn"; in *Hjemkomst* (1917; Homecoming) his soul is the "azure wave" which is rolling "gray and somber into the night." Two further collections in 1924 and 1927 completed his poetic production, only to be followed by prose memoirs, the first volume of which, *Fra gutt til mann* (1932; From Boy to Man), tells with superb tolerance and humor the story of his youth, a realistic and tender portrait of a great period. His writings express everywhere a noble and humane spirit, sympathetic, earnest, sadly aware of the passing of spring and youth, for which he nourished so passionate a love. His verse forms are not highly musical, but effective for their forthright, unsentimental vigor. His poems are objective yet personal, thoughtful yet moving, a "unity of perception and reflection" (Winsnes).

See: A. Heiberg *et al.*, "Vogt," *Samtiden* (1915, 1932, 1934); K. Elster, "Three Lyric Poets of Norway," *American-Scandinavian Review,* XIII (1925), 653–665; J. Knutzen, "Tre kantater om Norge," *Edda,* XXVIII (1928), 319–330; bibliography in *Norsk bibliografisk bibliotek* (1937).

E. H.

Vogüé, Eugène Marie Melchior, vicomte de (1848–1910, French critic), was born in Nice and spent his childhood at the ancestral castle of Gourdan in the Ardèche. He received education at the hands of the fathers of Notre Dame at Auteuil. At 20 he left for a trip to Italy, where he was when the Franco-Prussian War broke out in 1870. Rushing back to France, he entered the army in company with an elder brother whom he was to see shot dead at his side during the battle of Sedan. He was later taken prisoner by the Prussians. With his release from Magdeburg his diplomatic career began. He served as secretary to his cousin, ambassador to Turkey. In 1872 Vogüé visited Ephesus, Rhodes, Byblos, and Jerusalem, in 1875 Mt. Athos. His impressions were collected in one volume in 1876. In that same year Vogüé was sent to St. Petersburg, where he remained until his retirement from the diplomatic corps in 1882. His contribution of Russian studies to the *Revue des deux mondes* began in 1879. In 1883 there appeared the earliest of those essays on the Russian novel which, in their collected form, became *Le Roman russe* (1886). In 1889 he was elected to the French Academy; from 1893 to 1898 he sat in the Chamber of Deputies as member for Annonay.

Vogüé, called the Chateaubriand of the Third Republic, was a traditionalist in taste, religion, and politics. The work of Zola (*q.v.*) and his group was distasteful to him. He wrote *Le Roman russe* partly to forward the fall of French naturalism (*q.v.*), partly to exhibit the virtues of Russian fiction from Pushkin to Tolstoy (*q.v.*). The book turned the attention of France to Russian literature and to its religion of human suffering. To Vogüé is due the reappearance of mystery and illusion in French fiction.

See: E. W. Gosse, *Portraits and Sketches* (1912); G. Turquet-Milnes, *Some Modern French Writers* (1921).

P. B.

Voigt-Diederichs, Helene (1875–, German novelist and short-story writer), was born at Marienhoff, a family estate in Schleswig-Holstein, where she received her early education from tutors and lived up to her 14th year, in a rural community, close to nature. Her father died when she was 12. After several years spent traveling, she married, in 1898, the publisher Eugen Diederichs, then of Leipzig, who later moved to Jena. From 1911, she lived, separated from her husband, in Brunswick, but returned to Jena in 1931.

Her literary traits are North German, somber seriousness, relieved occasionally by touches of humor, restraint and aversion to everything strident. In her beginnings she was strongly influenced by the Danish novelist J. P. Jacobsen (*q.v.*), and this is seen in her only volume of lyrics, *Unterstrom* (1901). But her own inclinations and the spirit of her generation led her to keep close to reality in her novels and short stories. Thus her main works are confined to the real experiences of her own life, the rural community, marriage, and children. The most original of her novels and short stories are drawn from the life of peasants and landed gentry in Schleswig-Holstein. Such novels are *Regine Vosgerau* (1901) and *Dreiviertel Stund vor Tag* (1905), prize winner in a contest directed by the poet D. von Liliencron (*q.v.*). Her short stories were later collected in two volumes, *Schleswig-Holsteiner Landleute* and *Schleswig-Holsteiner Blut.* In *Auf Marienhoff; das Leben einer deutschen Mutter* (1925), she described the life of her mother. The stories in *Mann und Frau* (1921) and the novel *Ring um Roderich* (1929) deal with marriage problems. Stories about children are collected in *Kinderland* (1907) and *Der grüne Papagei* (Vol. X of Diederich's *Deutsche Reihe*). The unassuming sobriety of her style gives value and personal charm to her travel books such as *Wandertage in England* (1912) and *Gast in Siebenbürgen* (1936).

See: A. Soergel, *Dichtung und Dichter der Zeit,* 10. Auflage (preface 1919), pp. 758–762.

W. R. G.

Vojnović, Count Ivo (1857–1929, Croat dramatist), was born at Dubrovnik (Ragusa). His father was a noted lawyer and politician; his mother, a woman of fine character, had a deep influence on her son. Though his primary interest was always in literature, Vojnović took the legal course at the University of Zagreb and, after holding various judicial and administrative positions, in 1903 became governor of the island of Brač. His extravagant tastes proved his ruin, for in 1907 an investigating commission found him guilty of misusing public funds. His fault was apparently reckless incompetence rather than calculated dishonesty; the government, perhaps loath to disgrace a distinguished author, merely dismissed him from office without instituting criminal proceedings. Left penniless, Vojnović secured an appointment as literary director of the Zagreb theatre. He had only qualified success and in 1911 ceased to discharge the duties of his office, but his salary was continued up to the First World War on his agreement to write for the theatre one play each year. In July, 1914, the Austrian government arrested Vojnović along with other persons regarded as dangerous to the state. Vojnović was allowed to mingle with the other prisoners, to whom he revealed his best qualities as friend and comrade. In 1915 he was transferred to a hospital in Zagreb, where he underwent an operation on one eye. In 1917 he received an ovation at the Zagreb theatre, where his *Ekvinocijo* (1895; The Equinoctial) was performed in honor of his 60th birthday; the tribute was not only to his literary genius but to the veiled advocacy in his dramas of a union between the Croats and the Serbs in one independent state. From 1919 to 1922 Vojnović was Yugoslav consul at Nice; his last years he spent mainly in Dubrovnik. When friction arose in the new state Vojnović lost some of his popularity among the Croats, but gained in fame among the Serbs, who in 1927 elected him to their Academy and arranged a celebration in Belgrade of his 70th birthday. Vojnović died in a sanitarium in Belgrade. He received a state funeral, after which his body was buried in St. Michael's Cemetery near Dubrovnik.

Vojnović was a man of intense literary temperament, but of rather limited creative power. He did two things with special skill: he portrayed the life of Dubrovnik and its environs, and he paid tribute to motherly devotion and heroism. His far from copious writings consist of seven stories, the longest of which contains less than 150 small pages, of a few sonnets and other lyric poems, and of 15 dramas, seven of which are short one-act plays. In *Geranium* (1880), his first bit of fiction, using a technique imitated from Flaubert, Zola, and Daudet (*qq.v.*), he tells the story of an old maid living near Dubrovnik. The tale foreshadows his whole literary career. He was a product of cosmopolitan culture, showing continually the influence of foreign masters, but he was deeply attached to his own people, to the Serbs as well as to the Croats. His first drama, *Psyche* (1889), is a society comedy of the same type as those by Augier or by Dumas *fils;* the scene is laid in Vienna, and the characters are Polish, English, and Italian. Its success on the Zagreb stage determined his later activity; henceforth he devoted himself almost exclusively to the drama. The already-mentioned *Ekvinocijo,* a melodrama of life on the Dubrovnik coast, is the first of the works on which his fame depends. The plot turns on the love rivalry between a father and his illegitimate son; the father is murdered by the woman whom long ago he betrayed and who, despite her sudden crime, wins our admiration. An equinoctial storm symbolizes the conflict of human passions. Certain details show the influence of Ibsen (*q.v.*).

Dubrovačka trilogija (1902; Eng. tr., *A Trilogy of Dubrovnik,* 1921) is the masterpiece of Vojnović. The tiny commercial republic of Dubrovnik for centuries maintained its independence against both Turks and Venetians; its people were divided into a small, haughty, highly cultured aristocracy and a toiling populace. The *Trilogy*—of which the motto might be, "Men are we, and must grieve when even the Shade of that which once was great, is passed away"—includes three one-act plays; the action takes place in 1806, 1832, and 1900. In the first, *Allons enfants!* (Eng. tr., "The Dying Republic," *Slavonic Review,* Vol. I, 1922–1923), the patrician Orsat vainly exhorts his fellow nobles to resist the French army advancing on the city; when he fails he and his beloved Deša renounce marriage, refusing to raise children who must be slaves of a foreign power. Similar invincible—and futile—pride of race runs through the other two dramas. An epilogue in sonnet form tells of the Dubrovnik patricians moldering in St. Michael's Cemetery. Two propaganda plays, *Smrt majke Jugovića* (1907; The Death of the Mother of the Jugovići) and *Lazarevo vaskrsenje* (1913; Eng. tr., "The Resurrection of Lazarus," *Poet Lore*, Vol. XXXVII, 1926), glorify the heroic resistance of the Serbs to the Turks at the battle of Kosovo in 1389 and in our own times, shortly before the First Balkan War of 1912–1913. The first, written in verse, is based on the Serbian popular ballads, lines of which are woven into the text. Each drama glorifies motherly heroism as well as patriotism. *Gospodja sa suncokretom* (1912; The Lady with the Sunflower), on the other hand, is a decadent cosmopolitan play with an atmosphere reminiscent of D'Annunzio (*q.v.*). *Imperatrix* (1914; printed 1919) is a symbolic play glorifying mother love and protesting against war. Further dramas, *Maškarate ispod kuplja* (1922; Masquerades in an Attic) and *Prolog nenapisane drame* (1929; A Prologue to an Unwritten Drama), show the influence of Maeterlinck and of Pirandello (*qq.v.*). In all his work Vojnović displays brilliant gifts of style; to this in his best plays he adds fine ability in the drawing of character and in dramatic construction. These plays entitle him to a high place, probably the highest place, among dramatists writing in Serbo-Croatian.

See: E. Aničkov, "Les Méditations poétiques d'Ivo Vojnovic," *Monde slave*, 1928, No. 4, 52–76; A. Venzelides, "The Plays of Ivo Vojnović," *Slavonic Review*, VIII (1929–1930), 368–374; J. Goląbek, *Ivo Vojnović* (1932).

G. R. N.

Vollmoeller, Karl Gustav (1878–, German poet and dramatist), was born in Stuttgart, of a wealthy manufacturer's family, studied archaeology and classical philology in Paris, Berlin, Athens, and Bonn, and has lived in Italy. A great part of his life was spent in traveling. He first belonged to Stefan George's (*q.v.*) circle and contributed to *Blätter für die Kunst*. This early poetry, abounding in beautiful images, sounds, and rhythm, is collected in *Parcival, die frühen Gärten* (1903). Later he wrote dramas in the same exaggerated neo-romantic style; a mixture of brutal plot and exuberant lyricism characterizes *Catherina, Gräfin von Armagnac und ihre beiden Liebhaber* (1904) and *Assüs, Fitne und Sumurud* (1906). He tried to be more realistic in the didactic legend *Der deutsche Graf* (1906) and in *Wieland* (1911), the first play in world literature about a flyer. The success he was not able to achieve with his pretentious tragedies came to him with the popular pantomime *Das Mirakel* (1912), a pageant-like dramatization of the old legend of the nun who goes temporarily into the world and whose place is meanwhile taken by the Madonna. Max Reinhardt, with the magic of enchanting settings, costumes, and masses in movement and with a group of distinguished actors, carried *Das Mirakel* through Germany and England as well as to the United States, where the play, set in the gigantic and picturesque decorations by Norman Bel Geddes, was the sensation of New York in 1924. His comedy, *Cocktail* (1930), and the historical drama, *La Paiva* (1931), did not receive as much acclaim as his versions of *Turandot* (1911) and *George Dandin* (1912) and especially his translation of Aeschylus' *Oresteia* (1908).

K. P.

Voloshin, Maximilian Aleksandrovich (full name, Maximilian Aleksandrovich Kirienko-Voloshin, 1877–1932, Russian poet, critic, painter, and translator), was born of a noble family at Kiev, spent his childhood in Crimea, and received his education at Moscow. In 1900 he was expelled from the university for participating in "student disorders" and exiled for six months to Tashkent. Until his final return in 1917 to Koktebel, he traveled and lived a great deal abroad. Contact with the West developed his interest in Catholicism and Latin culture and kept him abreast of the current theories of literature and art, for Voloshin was a painter as well as a man of letters. He translated Verhaeren, Henri de Régnier, Barbey d'Aurevilly (*qq.v.*), and wrote many articles on art and French literature, some of which were collected as *Liki tvorchestva* (1914; The Faces of Creativeness). Voloshin's poetry, which he began to contribute to Russian symbolist periodicals about 1900, is indebted to French models; in particular, the polished form and visual appeal of his verse remind one of Heredia (*q.v.*). Returning to Russia (1909), he became an active collaborator in *Apollon* (Apollo), the organ of the "Acmeists." The publication of his first volume of collected verse established his reputation (1910). The Revolution caused great changes in Voloshin's poetry. Russia and Russian history crowded out esoteric themes; in vigorous verse he indicted the dark forces of destruction and prayed for a spiritual rebirth of his native country (*Demony glukhonemyie*, 1919; The Deaf-mute

Demons). After the civil war he found himself at odds with his Soviet environment, and appears to have published nothing after 1925.

See: B. Deutsch and A. Yarmolinsky, *Russian Poetry; an Anthology* (1927); "Voloshin," in *Literaturnaya entsiklopediya,* Vol. I (1929); M. Tsvetayeva, "Zhivoye o zhivom," *Sovremennyia zapiski,* LII (1933), 238–261, LIII (1933), 215–250.

P. A. P.

Vrchlický, Jaroslav (pseud. of Emil Frida, 1853–1912, Czech poet and dramatist), is the dominant literary figure of the second half of the 19th century in Bohemia. His work is a library in itself: he wrote some 85 volumes of poetry, about 35 plays, and poetic translations filling about 100 volumes. Born in Louny (northwestern Bohemia), the son of a poor tradesman, he studied history at the University of Prague and traveled in Italy as a tutor in 1875–1876. Later he became secretary to the Czech Institute of Technology. In 1893 he was appointed professor of comparative literature in the Czech university at Prague. His health failed in 1908, and four years later he died, paralyzed, at Domažlice. In 1879 he had married Sofie Podlipská, a niece of the writer Karolina Světlá (*q.v.*).

Vrchlický's historical importance cannot be overrated: he definitely broke away from German romantic influences, creating in Czech poetry a new tradition modeled on the achievements of Victor Hugo and also on those of the French Parnassians. He introduced an enormous variety of new themes and forms from all over the world and tried to write a Czech "Legend of the Ages" which gives in innumerable volumes a whole poetic history of the world. The sheer brilliance of his diction, his generous faith in the future of humanity, the panoramic view of world history, the neopagan morality, the vivid coloring of his grandiose visions, the long cadences of his verse, amazed his contemporaries and made Vrchlický easily the foremost Czech poet of the 70's and 80's. In his best pieces contained in such collections as *Epické básně* (1876; Epical poems), *Duch a svět* (1878; Spirit and the World), *Myty* (2 vols., 1879–1880; Myths), and *Zlomky epopeje* (1886; Fragments of an Epopee), Vrchlický created an effective Czech analogue to the best in Hugo and Leconte de Lisle. But he failed in his more ambitious attempts to give new epic versions of Faustian themes, as in *Hilarion* (1882), *Twardowski* (1885), and *Bar Kochba* (1897).

Vrchlický is at his best as an intimate lyrical poet of love and nature. His development from the sensuous verse in praise of his own early married love to a concise, hard, and chaste expression of the ultimate tragedy of life eventually freed him from the shackles of his rhetoric and led him back to a style firmly rooted in the native tradition of intimate lyricism. Especially his last collections (*Strom života,* 1909, The Tree of Life, and *Meč Damoklův,* 1912, The Sword of Damocles), written under the shadow of approaching death, show a new simplicity of expression, a deepening of tone, a greater clarity of form.

Vrchlický's work as a translator of poetry was also of great importance. He always translated in the exact measures of the originals, however complicated, with great skill and verve, though his overproduction sometimes led him into careless routine performances. He translated practically the entire poetical works of Hugo, Leconte de Lisle, and Vigny, the whole of Dante's *The Divine Comedy* in terza rima, Ariosto's *Orlando Furioso,* Tasso's *Jerusalem Delivered,* most of Leopardi and Carducci (*q.v.*), some 15 plays of Calderón, both parts of Goethe's *Faust,* and any number of lyrics from other literatures, including secondhand translations from Persian and Chinese. His translations from English include selections from Browning, Byron, Poe, Swinburne, Whitman, Shelley's *Prometheus Unbound,* and Shakespeare's *Sonnets.*

Vrchlický also wrote much literary criticism, of the "appreciative" type. His enthusiastic studies of Hugo, Carducci, Leopardi, etc., were important introductions to a world remote from Czechs of his time. Vrchlický was least successful as a dramatist. Many of his plays are lifeless closet dramas, but two, a pseudo-Euripidean trilogy, *Hippodamie* (1883–1890), especially effective with the music of Zdeněk Fibich, and a comedy, *Noc na Karlštejně* (1884; A Night on Karlstein), have held the stage.

Vrchlický's brilliant rhetoric, his easy handling of complex verse forms such as sonnets, rondels and sestine, his optimistic pantheism, his strong faith in the future of humanity, his wide range of topics and avid interest in remote countries and ages—all this was at first admired uncritically, but soon evoked sharp reactions. His eclecticism in themes and forms, his faith in progress, came to be rejected by a more fastidious and skeptical generation. Recent critics, however, stress the less flashy side of Vrchlický's work: the expression of his intimate tragedy, the final return to a more chaste and simple diction which continues the tradition of Czech romantic poetry. Vrchlický has suffered from the very vastness of his work and from a lack of self-criticism. But a good anthology like that by Arne Novák (1933), which excludes the derivative and the purely rhetorical, reveals amazing riches and shows him the greatest Czech poet of the 19th century.

See: A. Jensen, *Jaroslav Vrchlický* (1905, in Swedish); J. Borecký, *Jaroslav Vrchlický* (1906); F. V. Krejčí, *Jaroslav Vrchlický* (1913); F. X. Šalda "Jaroslav Vrchlický," in *Duše a dílo* (1913) and introduction to *Dopisy Jaroslava Vrchlického Žofii Podlipské* (1917). Společnost Jaroslava Vrchlického, a Vrchlický society, has published annuals since 1915. There are German anthologies by Eduard Albert (1893) and Friedrich Adler (1895).

R. W.

W

Waggerl, Karl Heinrich (1897–, German novelist), established his reputation with his first book *Brot* (1930; Eng. tr., *Bread,* 1931), and his public has grown with each of his successive novels. Waggerl was born and grew up in Bad Gastein and lives in Wagrain near Salzburg. The poverty of his family forced the boy to operate a hotel elevator, but later means were found to send him to school and prepare him to become a teacher. The hardships of his youth and his captivity in Italy during the First World War undermined his health and prevented him from resuming his teaching. In the picturesque Alpine village he composes his delightful books and pursues his "fourteen hobbies"—he is a master of many skills, photography, drawing, wood carving, hand-hammered metalwork, furniture design, and, above all, bookbinding. With the craftsman's knowledge Waggerl writes of the activities that make up village and farm life in his beloved mountains. Out of the fullness and intimacy of his own observation he portrays the daily and seasonal occupations of his people; with the same understanding and attention to vivid detail he narrates also the manifestations of their inner life, their frailties and virtues, in his genial charity never confusing the misdeed with the doer. It is not without significance that his first novel bore the title *Brot* and that subsequent novels bear the titles *Das Jahr des Herrn* (1934) and *Mütter* (1936), for bread and the farmer's year, motherhood and the "year of the Lord," constitute and frame the life of the peasant villager. In *Das Jahr des Herrn* worship and the Church's ministrations and festivals accompany, hallow, and round out the farmer's year. Bread, children, and freedom of the will in shaping man's destiny—how different from the old naturalistic treatment of such "problems" is Waggerl's understanding of existence and of parenthood. The dark side of life is not wanting. Though Waggerl's people are simple folk, they are in some senses just as complex as their "betters" and just as prone to transgress. The totality of life with the interrelations between individuals, children as sympathetically and as delightfully drawn as those of Booth Tarkington, the problems of chance and of character presented with thoughtful humor and quiet fun—these are Waggerl's subjects. They are treated with a delicate literary art.

See: L. Biermer, "Karl Heinrich Waggerl" (with biography and bibliography), *Die neue Literatur,* XXXVI (1935), 316–324; H. Arens, *Karl Heinrich Waggerl* (1938).

J. F. G.

Wägner, Elin (1882–, Swedish novelist and feminist), was born at Lund in the south of Sweden, but her childhood and much of her later life has been spent in Småland in south central Sweden, where also much of her best fiction finds its natural locale. Her first novels (*Norrtullsligan,* 1908, The North Toll Set; *Pennskaftet,* 1910, The Penholder; *Helga Wisbeck,* 1913) deal primarily, however, with urban conditions, particularly with self-supporting young women of the working classes and professions in Stockholm. Though these are "program novels," with a strenuous feminist point of view, they are lively and clear-headed in their fanatical devotion to the contemporary concept of feminine solidarity, and the style, a sharp, clear literary-journalese, sparkles with irony and pointed witticisms, almost invariably at the expense of men. Unlike Sigrid Undset's (*q.v.*) contemporaneous novels on young working women of Christiania (*Jenny,* etc.), Elin Wägner's early novels are much more concerned with feminism as an economic, social, and political problem than they are with fundamental psychological and moral problems. Elin Wägner's later development, however, leads more and more deeply into certain central moral and religious problems: first, in a series of family novels (*Släkten Jerneploogs framgång,* 1916, The Success of the Jerneploogs; *Silverforsen,* 1924, The Silver Rapids; etc.) in the manner of the contemporary English family novel; and then in that series of Småland novels (*Åsa-Hanna,* 1918; *Den namnlösa,* 1922, The Nameless One; and *Svalorna flyga högt,* 1930, The Swallows Fly High) for which she is chiefly famous. The most significant of the Småland novels is *Åsa-Hanna,* next to Selma Lagerlöf's (*q.v.*) *Jerusalem* and Vilhelm Moberg's (*q.v.*) later *Knut Toring* trilogy perhaps the best peasant novel in Swedish literature. *Åsa-Hanna* is at one and the same time a fascinating study in feminine character and a broad, detailed, sensitive treatment of a whole peasant culture in all of its ancient, deep-rooted ramifications. In 1941 Elin Wägner published *Väckarklocka* (Alarm Clock), an arresting indictment of the failure of women to exercise any salutary determining moral influence upon a morally disintegrating world; and in the years 1942–1943 appeared the two volumes of her warmly human biography of her great countrywoman, Selma Lagerlöf.

See: F. Böök, *Resa kring svenska Parnassen* (1926), pp. 237–248; K. Strömberg, *Modern svensk litteratur* (1932), pp. 170–175; M. Lindqvist, *Människor* (1938), pp. 27–49.

A. G.

Wagner, Richard (1813–1883, German dramatic composer), was born in Leipzig, the ninth child of Friedrich Wagner, not, as some maintain, the natural son of the actor and painter Ludwig Geyer. Friedrich Wagner died when Richard was six months old. Geyer married the widow and gave the family a new home in Dresden. After Geyer's death in 1821 the family returned to Leipzig, where Wagner in his 15th year heard Beethoven's music to Goethe's *Egmont* and was so impressed that he determined to compose music to his own first dramatic attempt, a blood-dripping tragedy, *Leubald und Adelaide* (1828). In school he had shown no musical talent; his tastes were solely literary, his chief interest the classics. Wagner's classical training and his later intensive study of Greek drama determined his subsequent epoch-making conception of the tone drama. His interest in music once aroused through literature, he set out to conquer composition by himself; but fortunately he found a teacher who in six months' instruction, based on analysis of Mozart's and Beethoven's masterpieces, gave him the command of that musical idiom which he perfected in *Tristan* and the *Ring*. In 1833 he began his professional career as chorus master of the Würzburg opera company. Here he composed his first opera, *Die Feen* (1834). He drifted now from one bankrupt opera company to another. At Magdeburg his *Liebesverbot,* an immature work in the spirit of Das Junge Deutschland and patterned after *Measure for Measure,* was composed in 1836. In the hope of conquering the German stage via Paris and the Meyerbeerian grand opera, Wagner spent three years of want and discouragement in the French capital. As there seemed no hope of placing his *Rienzi,* he abandoned the old type opera and completed *Der fliegende Holländer* in seven weeks (1841). He recognized the novelty of his attempt to create a new art form in which music should not be primarily an entertainment but should derive from and interpret a true drama, and he wrote: "Here begins my career as poet; I cease to be a concocter of opera librettos."

Wagner returned to Dresden, where in 1842 *Rienzi* was produced with great success. Fame and fortune seemed assured. To the bitter disappointment of his wife, the actress Minna Planer, Wagner continued the reforms begun with the *Holländer*. At Paris he had read widely in the literature of medieval Germany. This study and his Parisian sojourn had convinced him that his nature was essentially German and that only Germanic sources could inspire him to supreme artistic creation. In *Tannhäuser* (1845) Wagner, on the background of the dull Wartburgkrieg and the Tannhäuser legend, created a powerful psychological love drama in which, as so often in his works, redemption is achieved through a woman's self-sacrificing love. *Lohengrin,* a modernization of the Zeus and Semele theme based on the medieval swan-knight legend, had its *première* under Liszt at Weimar in 1850, after Wagner had fled from Dresden on account of his participation in the May revolution of 1849. In 1848 he had wavered between spoken drama with a historical theme (*Friedrich Barbarossa*) and a musical treatment of the Siegfried myth. He chose mythical rather than historical sources for his following works (with the exception of *Die Meistersinger,* produced in 1868) and documented this decision in a series of expository and propagandistic prose works to which the first years of his banishment at Zurich were devoted and which, especially his

Oper und Drama (1851), elaborate his theories of the new "tone drama." He hoped to create a drama wherein as in Attic tragedy the separate arts should be united in an artistic whole. Unfortunately Wagner's prose style, largely influenced by the philosopher Feuerbach, is often nebulous or ponderous. Meanwhile the original *Siegfried's Tod* (1848) was being expanded into the *Ring* tetralogy. Unlike Hebbel who in writing his drama used only the Middle High German Nibelungenlied, Wagner chose the Scandinavian Eddic poems and the Volsunga Saga and gave a mythical rather than a historical interpretation. The old world of Wotan and Valhalla must perish, a victim of its dishonest greed and lust for power. G. B. Shaw could well call the *Ring* "the work of a social revolutionary." But exaggerated use of alliteration, verbosity, and inconsistencies would have prevented success were it not for the power and wealth of the music. Here the leitmotif, Wagner's new type of musical pattern, is perfected and masterfully employed. By 1857 *Das Rheingold, Die Walküre,* and the first part of *Siegfried* were completed, but Wagner, abandoning hope of any performance of the stupendous cycle and convinced that a single opera might more easily be given a hearing, at the same time inspired by his love for Mathilde Wesendonk and engrossed in Schopenhauer's doctrine of renunciation, turned to the story of *Tristan und Isolde* (completed in 1859). In seeking the ethical kernel he transformed a medieval triangle narrative into a drama of ethical as well as musical sublimity.

The accession to the Bavarian throne of the youthful king, Ludwig, who had been captivated by Wagner's music and ideas, inaugurated a new era for the composer who now became the friend and guest of a monarch. In 1868 Wagner sat in the royal box with Ludwig to witness the *première* of *Die Meistersinger von Nürnberg,* that inspired study of renunciation combined with the symbolical depiction of the eternal conflict of genius and caviling pedantry. Court jealousies, Wagner's indiscretions, his liaison with Cosima, Bülow's wife (daughter of Liszt), necessitated his departure to Triebschen near Lucerne, where he resided until 1872. In that year Bayreuth became his permanent home, and in 1876 it was the scene of the festival performances of the entire *Ring des Nibelungen.* After the performance in 1882 of his last work, *Parsifal,* he went to Venice and there succumbed to a heart attack on February 13, 1883.

Idolized by friends and bitterly attacked by hostile critics, Wagner was all artist, actuated by a demoniac creative urge brooking no opposition, unwilling to compromise with mediocrity, demanding surroundings sybaritic in their luxury, and subordinating everything to his single creative purpose. Not always of complete integrity in his private life, he presented in his tone dramas the highest ethical values, especially the themes of renunciation and of redemption. *Parsifal,* which embodies Wagner's conceptions of Christian and Buddhistic purity, represents Christlike redemption through self-sacrifice and understanding sympathy. This "sinking down at the foot of the Cross" was largely responsible for Nietzsche's (*q.v.*) defection from his formerly beloved and admired master.

Wagner's operatic reforms include the requirement that the text be a consistent drama and form a perfect unity with the interpreting, not merely accompanying, orchestra and the stage picture. Poetic language should harmonize with the nature of the drama. Stylistic unity is attained by the skillful use of the leitmotif. All this was demonstrated in the model festival performances at Bayreuth. Their influence and that of Wagner's music and theories in general have been enormous on all aspects of 19th-century culture. In France in particular, from Baudelaire, Wagner's first staunch advocate, to Claudel (*qq.v.*), writers as well as musicians have been affected. Gide (*q.v.*), in describing one literary circle, says, "Wagner was their God." Rolland and Proust (*qq.v.*) represent the height of this influence, which was potent with the prose writers as well as the lyric poets.

See: H. S. Chamberlain, *Richard Wagner* (1896; Eng. tr., 1897); Max Koch, *Richard Wagner* (3 vols., 1907–1918); W. J. Henderson, *Richard Wagner; His Life and His Dramas* (2d ed., revised, 1923); Ernest Newman, *The Life of Richard Wagner* (4 vols. published 1933–1946); Thomas Mann, *Freud, Goethe, Wagner* (1937, in English).

P. R. P.

Walschap, Gerard (1898–, Flemish novelist), was born at Londerzeel. After work as a journalist he became inspector of public libraries. He made his debut in literature with dramas written in collaboration with Frans Delbeke. In 1928 appeared his first novel, *Waldo,* a disjointed book, which gave no indication that he would come to the fore in the following year, 1929, with a masterpiece, *Adelaide,* the first part of a trilogy which was completed by *Eric* (1930) and *Carla* (1931). In 1939 these novels appeared in one volume under the title *De Familie Roothoofd* (The Roothoofd Family). Walschap has for some time written at least one novel every year. After *Adelaide* his best works are *Sybille* (1934) and *Houtekiet* (1935).

Gerard Walschap is an entirely new phenomenon. From *Adelaide* on, he manifested an individual and strongly personal style which is characterized by two qualities, conciseness and suggestive power. He is a sharp analyst of the human soul and chooses unusual, timid, tormented, eccentric persons and strange situations. He is generally recognized among the younger authors in Flanders as the most important and most original novelist.

J. G.

Wassermann, Jakob (1873–1934, German novelist), was born in Fürth, near Nuremberg. From 1898 until his death he resided in Austria, first in Vienna and later at Alt-Aussee in Styria. His childhood was unhappy, in the army he was treated with scorn, as a young man he lived in Munich on the verge of starvation. Beginning with 1896, short stories and poems of his were published in the magazine *Simplicissimus.* With *Die Juden von Zirndorf* (1897; Eng. tr., *The Dark Pilgrimage,* 1933) began the long series of novels and *Novellen* that made him widely known in Europe and America. His travels took him to various European countries, Africa, and the United States. During his later years he was in demand as a lecturer throughout Europe. As a Jewish liberal, to whom life in a true democracy seemed the only dignified form of human existence, he was dropped from membership in the Prussian Academy of Letters in 1933 with the advent of National Socialism. Among his friends Wassermann counted the pianist Busoni and numerous authors, Richard Dehmel, Alfred Döblin, Hugo von Hofmannsthal, Thomas Mann, and Arthur Schnitzler (*qq.v.*).

Primarily a narrator with the imagination of an oriental fabulist, Wassermann also wrote a few short and undistinguished plays, numerous critical essays, biographies of Christopher Columbus (1929; Eng. tr., 1930) and Henry Morton Stanley (*Bula Matari,* 1932; Eng. tr., *H. M. Stanley, Explorer,* 1932, American title, *Bula Matari,* 1933), and two autobiographical sketches, *Mein Weg als Deutscher und Jude* (1921; Eng. tr., *My Life as German and Jew,* 1933) and *Selbstbetrachtungen* (1933).

In the late 20's and early 30's Wassermann was one of the world's most widely read and translated novelists. Since many of his narratives stress ideas, general problems, and human relationships and are not rooted in German soil, tradition, and customs, they are readily understood by people of different tongues. There are historical narratives, novels of subtle psychological analysis, social novels, imaginative tales, and stories of the First World War and its aftermath. His characters represent various strata of society; frequently they are eccentric, crotchety, impractical, ill-adjusted beings who lead lonely lives of inner torment. Many of them reflect the author's belief that human nature is mysteriously complex and unfathomable. Romantic fancy alternates with crassly realistic portrayal of ugliness and vice. Among numerous recurring motifs are the theme of justice, the general problem of evil, man's slothful indifference to the lot of his fellows, the conflicting views of the older and younger generations, the difficulties confronting post-war youth in Germany, the plight of the Jew, the cruel treatment of criminals in penal institutions, woman's sphere of activity. Such motifs and the author's sense of social mission sometimes stand out too baldly to produce an artistic, harmonious effect. As a result Wassermann's work is of uneven quality. Some of his narratives are of almost exemplary compactness; others are loosely constructed, complex, overcrowded with sensational episodes. Some are couched in simple, refined, restrained diction, while others are marred by extravagance, exaggeration, and violent antitheses. Some are written with objectivity and artistic detachment; others reveal him as an exhorter who would speed social reform by portraying and unmasking human abuses and man's inhumanity to man. As a writer with a strong messianic urge and of great moral earnestness, he aimed to present the deeper significance of life.

Some of Wassermann's more important works are *Caspar Hauser* (1908; Eng. tr., 1928), *Das Gänsemännchen* (1915; Eng. tr., *The Goose Man,* 1922), *Christian Wahnschaffe* (1918; Eng. tr., *The World's Illusion,* 1920), *Ulrike Woytich* (1923; Eng. tr., *Gold,* 1924), *Der Aufruhr um den Junker Ernst* (1926; Eng. tr., *The Triumph of Youth,* 1927), and *Der Fall Maurizius* (1928; Eng. tr., *The Maurizius Case,* 1929).

See: S. Bing, *Jakob Wassermann* (1933); M.

Karlweis, *Jakob Wassermann* (1935); J. C. Blankenagel, *The Writings of Jakob Wassermann* (1942).

J. C. B.

Wasylewski, Stanisław (1885–, Polish essayist), was born in Stanisławów, at the eastern extremity of Austrian Poland, of old and distinguished gentry stock long rooted in the Border. He began his literary career as a theatrical reporter on the Lwów *Gazeta wieczorna* (Evening Gazette) in 1910. After two years with the Polish legions (1915–1917), he founded, and edited from 1918 to 1921, the satirical journal *Szczutek* (Fillip), getting his start in the meantime in the field of the literary-historical essay thanks to the vision and enterprise of the distinguished Poznań publisher Rudolf Wegner, who issued his first efforts in this field under the title *U księżnej pani* (1917; With Her Highness). From that time until the end of Free Poland there flowed from Wasylewski's pen an uninterrupted stream of essays "pleasant yet profound," in which were revealed the private lives, habits, and sentiments of a wide variety of figures, from the ladies of King Stanisław's court (*Na dworze Króla Stasia,* 1919), from the personalities who made Lwów unique in the 19th century (*Bardzo przyjemny miasto,* 1927, A Charming Town, and *Niezapisany stan służby,* 1937, An Unrecorded Condition of Service), to the cloistered Queen Cunegunda (*Ducissa Cunegundis,* 1923) and many others. Often referred to as the Polish Goncourt, Wasylewski owed more in the way of inspiration to Władysław Łoziński (*see* Polish literature), like himself a Lvovian, than to any other.

See: K. Czachowski, *Obraz współczesnej literatury polskiej,* III (1936), 155–160; Wasylewski, *Niezapisany stan służby* (1937).

A. P. C.

Wedekind, Frank (Benjamin Franklin) (1864–1918, German dramatist), was born in Hanover a few months after the return of his parents from America. His emotional intensity and his love of the exotic were a natural heritage: the wanderings of his physician father, a fierce democrat who worshiped Washington and hated Bismarck, extended as widely as Turkey and California; it was in San Francisco that he married a young German actress half his age. Wedekind grew up in Switzerland but spent his maturer years in Germany, where he was variously journalist, playwright, and actor. Political poems published in the satirical magazine *Simplicissimus* resulted in 1899 in his conviction and imprisonment for lèse-majesté.

The keynote of Wedekind's work is eroticism. This is not poetic dalliance with the tender passion, however, for Wedekind sees love as the elemental driving force to which we are all enslaved. To cover up our slavery we practice hypocrisies, and Wedekind, like Friedrich Schlegel in his *Lucinde* days, felt called on to attack this ostrich policy of his fellow men. The Mephistophelean Wedekind cuts a queer figure among the moralists, but however paradoxical he and his works are, no one can doubt his serious intentions. In "Über die Erotik," a preface to his stories in *Feuerwerk* (1905), he sets forth the problem. "Der Brand von Egliswyl" in this volume is an effective example of the power of love. *Frühlings Erwachen* (1891; Eng. tr., *The Awakening of Spring,* 1909), Wedekind's first success and one of his most poetic plays, arraigns the adult world for its misunderstanding and mismanagement of children at puberty. Karl Hetmann, in the drama of that name (1904; first called *Hidalla*), is a fantastic moralist bent on reforming society. Indeed, every work of Wedekind is a thrust at the shams of society, among which moral hypocrisy is the chief.

Wedekind's most notorious creation is his rather appalling version of the eternal feminine whom he presents as the real earth spirit. She is generally known as Lulu, but she answers to any name of Eve's daughters. Through the two dramas *Der Erdgeist* (1895; Eng. tr., *Earth Spirit,* 1914) and *Die Büchse der Pandora* (1903; Eng. tr., *Pandora's Box,* 1918) she runs her course, consuming one man after another until Jack the Ripper puts an end to her. This ageless, amoral incarnation of the sex urge lives in a seething mass of evil and gets down to the dregs of life, but she remains essentially natural and unchanged. Such triumph of primitive nature over civilization is the formula for all Wedekind's work. In *Schloss Wetterstein* (1910) Effie, a lesser Lulu, also makes prostitution on a grand scale her career, and dies at the hands of a pervert. Franziska, in the drama of that name (1912), is a variation of the type. She is a feminine Faust experimenting with love and life at their various levels and—unique ending for Wedekind—finding happiness at last in simple domestic love. Wedekind calls this play a modern mystery.

Woman is not always the protagonist, nor is love the exclusive theme: Wedekind has a predilection for men on the lunatic fringe who lead an existence that, in the eyes of society, is decidedly shady. They, too, are "naturals." The masterpiece in this vein is *Der Marquis von Keith* (1901). Here the hero with his spurious title of nobility is a soldier of fortune, a swindler whose calculations go awry and who at the last curtain, faced with the choice between a revolver and a monetary sop tossed him by his successful rival, grins and takes the money. Into this play the author has smuggled an even weirder collection of people than usual who, in the Wedekind manner, come and go with a happy disregard for probability. Cold, calculating self-interest again inspires Gerardo in *Der Kammersänger* (1899; Eng. tr., *Heart of a Tenor,* 1913), a one-act tragicomedy and Wedekind's most effective and popular work, but, unlike Keith, this quondam paperhanger and now operatic tenor and slave to his art is overwhelmed by success. Wedekind erected a real monument to the tragedy of the artist in *König Nicolo* (1902). The deposed king suffers many humiliations, even to becoming his successor's court fool, but his kingship remains truly inalienable. The play was written in the depression following his imprisonment and is perhaps the most heartfelt of all Wedekind's charges against his fellow man.

Wedekind stood alone in his time. He refused to have truck with the naturalists, and his kind of romanticism had little in common with the prevailing brand. He was a forerunner of expressionism.

See: A. Kutscher, *Frank Wedekind* (3 vols., 1922–1931).

H. W. P.

Wehner, Josef Magnus (1891–, German novelist), was born in Bernbach in the Rhön Mountains (Hesse-Nassau), the son of a village teacher. He studied in Jena and Munich and wanted to become an actor. In the First World War he was severely wounded. He lives in Munich and is editor of the *Münchner neuste Nachrichten.*

Wehner began his literary career in 1921 with *Der Weiler Gottes,* a story in hexameters, praising the Catholic milieu of his Rhön country. Up to 1930 most of his stories were "Heimatkunst," *e.g., Der blaue Berg; Geschichte einer Jugend* (1922) and *Die Hochzeitskuh; Roman einer jungen Liebe* (1928). In another manner are *Die mächtigste Frau; phantastische Novellen* (1923) and *Struensee* (1924). After years of limited success he became famous through his war novel *Sieben vor Verdun* (1930). With its glorification of military heroism, the book made him one of the favorite authors of the Nazi regime. He followed up his success by *Stadt und Festung Belgerad* (1936), which describes the adventures of the heroes of his Verdun book in the Serbian campaign of 1915. He has written patriotic books for children, *A. L. Schlageter* (1934) and *Hindenburg* (1935). A collection of essays and speeches was published under the title *Das unsterbliche Reich* (1933).

See: H. Brandenburg, "Josef Magnus Wehner," in *Die schöne Literatur,* XXXVIII (1929), 49–54; K. Kamp, *Die Haltung des Frontkämpfers* (1940) W. K. Pfeiler, *War and the German Mind* (1941), pp. 216–227.

W. R. G.

Weigand, Wilhelm (1862–, German poet, novelist, and dramatist), was born at Gissigheim in Baden, but early found a congenial home in Munich. There since 1889 he has led a quiet life only occasionally interrupted by trips to the North Sea or the Mediterranean. Although to some extent Weigand can be classified among the neo-romantics, he essentially belongs in the older Munich tradition represented by Paul Heyse and Isolde Kurz (*qq.v.*). From the beginning Weigand has been a consistent enemy of radical naturalism (*see* German naturalism) and instead has always extolled the aristocratic culture of France and Italy of the Renaissance. He started his literary career with several plays; those treating historical subjects (*Florian Geyer,* 1901; *Die Renaissance,* 1899) are superior to those dealing with contemporary matters. But Weigand will chiefly be remembered for his novels (*Die Frankenthaler,* 1889; *Die Löffelstelze,* 1919) and short stories (*Von festlichen Tischen,* 1928). In an exquisite style generously tinged with quiet humor and sometimes reminiscent of Gottfried Keller (*q.v.*), Weigand depicts life in old Franconia and Bavaria. As a lyric poet he has excelled in intimate nature portraits; after the death of his wife a deeper note was added (see *Der verschlossene Garten,* 1909).

See: A. Soergel, *Dichtung und Dichter der Zeit,* 19. Auflage (1928), pp. 734–741.

E. R.

Weinheber, Josef (1892–, Austrian poet), was born in Vienna, the son of a butcher. Losing both parents early in life, he spent six loveless years in an orphanage (see his autobiographic novel, *Das Waisenhaus,* 1925), but was then taken in by an aunt, in whose home his first poems were written (*Der einsame Mensch,* 1920). In 1911 he obtained a position in the postal system, where he continued to earn his living for many years. To his profound disgust, the poems he wrote (*Von beiden Ufern,* 1923; *Boot in der Bucht,* 1926) were virtually ignored. At last the volume *Adel und Untergang* (1932; enlarged, 1934) attracted critical attention; with the award of the Mozart prize in 1935 he suddenly became famous, and critics vied with each other in praising him. With gentle irony he named the following book of poems *Späte Krone* (1936; cf. *Späte Ernte* by Wildgans, *q.v.*).

Weinheber's mastery of form is noted by all who mention him at all, and comparison with Hölderlin has become almost a commonplace. One might well call him a neoclassicist, provided this term is not taken to mean imitative dependence; it expresses rather his conscious espousal of formal perfection as one of the external manifestations of high artistry—as a sculptor might consciously emulate the great Greeks before proceeding to mold his own message in stone or bronze. Aside from this formal element, it seems hardly possible to reduce Weinheber's work to any common denominator. His utterance is impressive, often significant, always competent; his best poems achieve a rare beauty.

See: Adolf Luser, ed., *Josef Weinheber; Persönlichkeit und Schaffen* (1935).

B. Q. M.

Weiss, Jean Jacques (1827–1890, French critic, journalist, and historian), was born at Bayonne, Basses-Pyrénées, where his father, a bandmaster attached to a Swiss regiment, was then stationed. Weiss has related his recollections of his early youth in the preface to *Le Théâtre et les mœurs* (1889); his father moved from garrison to garrison with the various regiments he served, and the boy's education suffered. When the family came to Paris, young Weiss attended the Lycée Louis-le-Grand. He was then to have entered the military school of Saint-Cyr, but successes in his classical studies made him turn to the Ecole Normale Supérieure, where he obtained his *agrégation* in history. For a short time he taught history at the Lycée of La Rochelle. In 1855 he returned to Paris and prepared his Doctorat ès Lettres while writing for the press and from 1856 to 1868 occupied with marked success the chair of French literature at the University of Aix. Weiss joined the editorial staff of the *Journal des débats* as a political writer and contributed articles on literature also. He founded in 1867, with Edouard Hervé, the *Journal de Paris,* a liberal paper which sometimes got into difficulties with the government. In 1877 he opposed the establishment of the republic in articles signed X.Z., but accepted the republican form of government when it was adopted; he once more joined the opposition in 1879 and in his later years was managing editor of the *Gaulois.*

Weiss was a vigorous writer and, in belles-lettres as well as in politics, something of a free lance. His chief contributions to literary history are to be found in his *Essais sur l'histoire de la littérature française* (1865). He professed a great admiration for the society of Louis Philippe's time and regarded the succeeding period as decadent. The year 1857 seemed to him particularly objectionable; it was a year characterized by an unsound pragmatism (*faux moralisme*), the year of Barrière's *Les Faux Bonshommes,* of Baudelaire's (*q.v.*) *Les Fleurs du mal,* of Flaubert's (*q.v.*) *Madame Bovary.* His paradoxical arraignment of Flaubert's style is worth reading. He also contrasts *Madame Bovary* as a novel with Freytag's (*q.v.*) *Soll und Haben.* For a long time he remained true to his favorite age of romanticism. When Nisard began to belittle the romantics, Weiss took up the challenge, asserting that the classical age had been powerless to produce anything comparable to the works of the 18th century, more especially the writings of Voltaire and Rousseau. He even showed a partiality for such writers as Lesage and Gresset, the author of *Ver-Vert.* In discussing foreign literature he avers that since the French Revolution literature has become European rather than national and that Germany because of its *Weltliteratur* should be regarded as the "concertmaster." At the same time, however, he claims that no nation can outdo France in the matter of varied artistic production. Weiss's interest finally turned more especially to the theatre, as demonstrated in his *Feuilletons de critique théâtrale* (1883–1885).

See: B. Stirbey, *J. J. Weiss, conférencier, chroniqueur de théâtre, journaliste, portraitiste, écrivain épistolaire* (1910).

A. Sz.

Wennerberg, Gunnar (1817–1901, Swedish composer-poet), left his only significant mark on Swedish poetry as the creator of *Gluntarne,* most popular and original of all Swedish student songs. Born in Västergötland, where his father was a parish priest, the young Wennerberg came to Uppsala University in 1837, and remained there for the following 11 years. After this he settled down to a career in various departments of the civil service, which led ultimately to his holding some of the most important political positions in the kingdom. Upon coming to Uppsala he was of a rather serious religious temperament; but he was deeply interested in music, secular as well as sacred, and by a lucky accident in his last years at the university he became associated with a happy-go-lucky student group (*juvenalerna*) who spent a good deal of their time at gay musical improvisation, not infrequently under the influence of alcoholic potations. *Gluntarne* was directly inspired by Wennerberg's contact with this group, though most of the songs included in the collection as ultimately published in 1849 and 1850 were composed after *juvenalerna* had broken up. *Gluntarne* consists of 30 pieces, each a duet, sung in part as dialogue, the two singers being Glunten (bass) and Magistern (baritone). The songs, somewhat reminiscent of Bellman's matchless Stockholm ditties, deal with various sides of the student life of the day, its carefree camaraderie, its momentary trials, its relatively harmless bacchanalian excesses, all in keeping with the literary romanticism currently dominant at Uppsala. Both music and text were composed by Wennerberg. Aside from *Gluntarne* Wennerberg wrote a considerable body of verse, most of which, however, is of no particular consequence. Only *Davids psalmer* (1861–1887; Psalms of David), which give expression to Wennerberg's deep religious feelings, are of serious literary importance.

See: S. Taube, *Gunnar Wennerberg* (3 vols., 1913–1916); R. F. von Willebrand, "Gluntarne och deras skald," *Finsk tidskrift,* LXXXIII (1917).

A. G.

Werfel, Franz (1890–1945, Austrian novelist, dramatist, and poet), was born and reared in Prague. While connected with the Kurt Wolff publishing firm in Leipzig (1912–1914), he was cofounder of the important expressionist collection *Der jüngste Tag,* 1913–1921. From 1917 he lived in Vienna until driven out by the Nazi occupation of Austria. After the fall of France in 1940 he escaped to the United States.

Werfel's artistic development shows three phases, the first lyric, the second predominantly dramatic, and the third predominantly epic. Rilke and Whitman may have influenced his lyric, but he soon found his own style. In his poetry he first formulated his basic philosophical conceptions—his faith in a fraternization of humanity and his awareness of the omnipresence of the divine which led him to a transcendental interpretation of reality. Music was another source of his inspiration. Best known of the lyrical works are *Der Weltfreund* (1911), *Wir sind* (1913), *Einander* (1915), and *Gerichtstag* (1919). Forty-nine of Werfel's poetic compositions are translated in a small volume of *Poems* (1946). During his first period Werfel became the exponent of expressionism, and his version of Euripides' *Troerinnen* (1915) was a milestone in the history of the expressionist theatre. Of special importance was his polemic controversy with Kurt Hiller about the role of the poet in the world, in the yearbook *Tätiger Geist* (Munich, 1918). During his second period Werfel wrote a number of dramas which belong to the best of modern German dramatic literature, among them *Spiegelmensch* (1920), *Juarez und Maximilian* (1923; Eng. tr., *Juarez and Maximilian,* 1926), *Paulus unter den Juden* (1926), and *Das Reich Gottes in Böhmen* (1930).

But it was through his prose fiction that Werfel first attained international recognition. In *Verdi; Roman der Oper* (1924; Eng. tr., *Verdi; a Novel of the Opera,* 1925) Werfel paid tribute to the genius of pure music (see also his edition of Verdi's letters, 1926, and his version of *Forza del destino, ca.* 1930). *Barbara oder die Frömmigkeit* (1929; Eng. tr., *The Pure in Heart,* 1931) rather than the better-known *Vierzig Tage des Musa Dagh* (2 vols., 1933; Eng. tr., *The Forty Days of Musa Dagh,* 1934) is Werfel's war novel; in both works the problem of religion and race, which he had approached again and again after his Paulus drama, overshadows the war motif. *Die Geschwister von Neapel* (1931; Eng. tr., *The Pascarella Family,* 1932), epic tale of a family breaking up under the impact of modern times, is perhaps Werfel's purest prose work. An immediate result of Werfel's flight from Europe was his *Lied der Bernadette* (1941; Eng. tr., *The Song of Bernadette,* 1942), a tribute to the saint of Lourdes.

See: R. Specht, *Franz Werfel* (1926).

W. P.

Weyssenhoff, Józef (1860–1932, Polish novelist), was born at Kolano in Podlasie, Russian Poland, of Baltic baron stock long resident in the Eastern Border and thoroughly Polonized. He studied at the University of Dorpat (1884), then settled on an estate he had inherited in Lublin province (Samoklęski) to enjoy for a time the diversions of a country squire. Moving in 1891 to Warsaw, he became associated there with other conservatives and sybarites like himself in the famous Klub Myśliwski (Huntsman's Club). He began his literary career with translations from Heine (1888) and original poems, short stories, and literary reviews in the conservative *Biblioteka warszawska* (*see* Polish literature), of which he was literary editor. Weyssenhoff's reputation as a writer rests on two works: the finely satirical *Żywot i myśli Zygmunta Podfilipskiego* (1898; The Life and Sentiments of Zygmunt Podfilipski) and the magnificent prose poem extolling the beauties of Border life and especially of the chase, *Soból i panna* (1911; Eng. tr., *The Sable and the Girl,* 1929). "A Polish courtier" centuries out of his time, Weyssenhoff was unable to adjust himself to the post-war world. His roots were in pre-war feudal, patriarchal Poland and there his heart was also. He spent his last years in Bydgoszcz, northwestern Poland, a virtual hermit.

See: Z. Dębicki, *Portrety,* I (1927), 33–50; K. Czachowski, *Obraz współczesnej literatury polskiej,* I (1934), 110–117, 349–351; A. Bogusławski, "Kobiety Weyssenhoffa," *Wiadomości polskie* (London), 1941, No. 46.

A. P. C.

Wiechert, Ernst (1887–, German novelist), was born in a lonely forester's home in East Prussia. In *Wälder und Menschen* (1936) he tells about his own childhood spent in close contact with nature, the great woods, the vast moors. These early impressions, together with his memories of his oversensitive, melancholy mother and the powerful hold which the stories of the Bible as well as the weird tales and fantastic legends of the countryside gained on the imaginative child, were to influence all his later writing. At the age of 11 he was sent to school in Königsberg, where he continued his academic studies and took his degree. Teaching in secondary schools left him dissatisfied. Preoccupation with outstanding Russian and Scandinavian writers increased his original leaning toward self-destructive criticism, and in his first novel, *Die Flucht* (1916), the hero significantly takes his own life.

The war did not brighten the young author's views. In his novel *Jedermann* (1931) he gave expression to the enervating experience of endless, despairing waiting, of emptiness and dull patience which scarred every soldier's mind. After the war he did not at first return to teaching but withdrew into the great woods of his homeland. His novels *Der Wald* (1922) and *Der Totenwolf* (1924) reflect the chaotic violence of his reaction against post-war conditions and the spirit of the age. But he soon turned away from hatred and the cult of brutal strength and will power and sought redemption in the universal suffering of man from which love is born. *Der Knecht Gottes Andreas Nyland* (1926) tries to follow Christ's demands to the letter, the hero devoting himself, like Jakob Wassermann's (*q.v.*) *Christian Wahnschaffe,* to all that is miserable and ugly in order to redeem it through love. However, the abundance of human suffering overwhelms his sensitive soul—he realizes the smallness of his attempts and seeks refuge in the woods from the curse of civilization.

From then on, it has been Wiechert's foremost concern to reconcile his deep love of nature, his faith in life close to the soil, with the demands of Christian ethics. Again and again the problem of man's fight against man, be it in war, in politics, or in personal strife, is contrasted with and overcome by the quiet forces of nature which are in league with God. Outstanding among his short stories are *Tobias* (1932), the story of a student who commits a political murder and of his final confession and atonement under the relentless silent accusation of the peaceful life in the old mill and of his grandmother's old-fashioned faith in the Bible, and *Hirtennovelle* (1935), the tale of a boy-shepherd in a poor, remote village who leads the villagers to safety at their enemies' approach but dies trying to save a stray lamb. These two short stories show Wiechert at his best—his gift of imagery, his symbolic interpretation of reality, his intensity of mood and yet simplicity of expression.

Wiechert became best known through his novels *Die Magd des Jürgen Doscozil* (1932) and *Die Majorin* (1934; Eng. tr., *The Baroness,* 1936). The former is obviously influenced by Knut Hamsun's (*q.v.*) *Growth of the Soil.* It is best in its descriptions of primitive living, less convincing in its somewhat sensational plot. *Die Majorin,* psychologically more interesting, deals with the fate of two people, representative of the age, the major's widow, disillusioned and lonely yet bravely administering her estate, and Michael, the soldier, returned from years of war and imprisonment, bitter, burnt out, uprooted. The central problem of the novel, the woman's struggle to win this man back to life, is handled with great tact; characters are fitted into the surrounding landscape as parts of one unified mode of existence.

See: H. Ebeling, *Ernst Wiechert; der Weg eines Dichters* (1937).

E. M. F.

Wied, Gustav Johannes (1858–1914, Danish novelist, dramatist), one of the great humorists in a distinguished comic tradition, was born at Holmegaard, a large farm near Nakskov on the island of Lolland. He died by his own hand a few months after the outbreak of the First World War. His father was a practical, progressive farmer. His mother, who "invented and told the most beautiful fairy tales in the twilight," sturdily championed his infant muse; her idyllic tales of the Denmark of her youth were published by her son as *Bedstemoders Manuscript* (1897; Grandmother's Manuscript). The Lolland farm with its teeming, motley life, both animal and human, supplied material for much of Wied's best work. Of his happy childhood there, to which he looked back nostalgically all his life, of his adolescent years as a book dealer's apprentice, clerk in a lawyer's office, and tutor in a Jutland manor, and of his painful struggle to pass the matriculation examination at the university (he was 28 when he finally succeeded), he has told with charming self-irony in his brief autobiography, *Digt og Virkelighed* (1914; Poetry and Reality). In the novel *Ungdomshistorier* (1895; Stories of Youth), he has described his bohemian days in Copenhagen, teaching for a pittance and writing sketches for the notorious newspaper *København.* One of his stories, judged indecent, landed him in jail for two weeks. There he made up his mind to devote himself henceforth entirely to writing. A few years later he married and settled down in Roskilde, where he built a modest house called "The Castle," brought up a family, and wrote like the diminutive demon he was.

Now Dickensian, now Zolaesque, and often Rabelaisian, Wied was for 20 years the *enfant terrible* of Danish letters and a popular favorite in Scandinavia and Germany. Snobbery, smugness, and sham he loathed and ridiculed wherever he found them. He has been justly called "the quintessential Dane." At bottom he was a Kierkegaardian moralist. The pseudonym "Peter Idealist" with which he signed his first published work, aphorisms on a political scandal almost as grotesque in fact as he made it later in fiction, was significant, as were also two gruesome early tragedies; but few suspected during his lifetime the passionate seriousness and deep pessimism concealed beneath the comic mask. A painstaking craftsman, his industry was prodigious, his creative power phenomenal. Outstanding among his more than 30 published works are the inimitable *Silhuetter* (1891; Silhouettes); two novels of aristocratic decadence, *Slægten* (1898; The Family) and *Fædrene æde Druer* (1908; The Fathers Eat Grapes); two satires of provincial life centering around the now legendary Knagsted, *Livsens Ondskab* (1899; Life's Malice) and *Knagsted* (1902); and the satyr plays, especially *Adel, Gejstlighed, Borger og Bonde, Fire Satyrspil* (1897; Nobility, Clergy, Bourgeoisie, and Peasantry, Four Satyr Plays), called by Georg Brandes (*q.v.*) "one of the great books of our literature, one of the wittiest," and *Dansemus* (1905; Dancing Mice), his most ambitious work, considered by many his masterpiece. In this peculiar fusion of novel and play forms Wied's ironic genius found its most perfect expression. Few of his many stage successes stand the test of time. Toward the end of his life his popularity waned and for some years his reputation was in eclipse. The formation in 1938 of two societies for the publication of works by and about him is substantial if tardy recognition of his permanent place in the literature.

See: Ernest Boyd, *Studies from Ten Literatures* (1925), pp. 267–273; Ebbe Holten-Nielsen, *Gustav Wied; en Bibliografi over Arbejder af og om ham* (1931); Ebbe Neergaard, *Peter Idealist, Studier over Gustav Wieds Ungdom* (1938).

J. B. C. W.

Wierzyński, Kazimierz (1894–, Polish poet), was born at Drohobycz, in the oil-bearing foothills of the Carpathians, Austrian Poland, the son of a railroad-station agent. Identified from his earliest youth with conspiratorial activities whose aim was his country's liberation, Wierzyński served during the First World War in the Eastern Legion until he was captured by the Russians and sent to Ryazan. After the war he settled in Warsaw and became associated with the *Skamander* group (*see* Polish literature). From 1931 to 1932 he edited the *Przegląd sportowy* (Sports Review) and in 1934 became theatrical reviewer for *Gazeta polska.* In 1927 his *Laur olympijski* (Olympic Laurel) won the first international poetry prize at the Amsterdam Olympic games, and from that time on Wierzyński was looked upon as a kind of unofficial poet laureate. His early poems (*Wiosna i wino,* 1919; Springtime and Wine) were buoyant and spirited, while those of later years, in accurate reflection of the times, were more somber and meditative. A collected edition of his works appeared in 1929, and a volume of his best theatrical reviews, *W garderobie duchów* (In the Coatroom of Ghosts), in 1938. Of Wierzyński's later works, *Gorzki urodzaj* (1933; Bitter Harvest) and the three volumes published abroad after the outbreak of the Second World War, *Ziemia wilczyca* (1941; Earth, the She-Wolf), *Barbakan warszawski* (1941; Warsaw Barbakan), and *Róża wiatrów* (1942; Mariners' Rose), are to be noted.

See: K. Czachowski, *Obraz współczesnej literatury polskiej,* III (1936), 293–305, 710–711; A. P. Coleman, "Three Representative Polish Poets," *Books Abroad,* XIII (1939), 161–162, and "Twenty Years of Polish Literature," *ibid.,* XIV (1940), 244–245.

A. P. C.

Wildenbruch, Ernst von (1845–1909, German dramatist, poet, and novelist), was a grandson of the popular and gifted Prince Louis Ferdinand, nephew of Frederick the Great. His father was in the Prussian diplomatic service, and Wildenbruch, born at Beyrouth, Syria, spent much of his childhood in Athens and Istanbul. Entering a military academy, he became a lieutenant in the Guards. But he was not attracted to a military career and resigned his commission in 1865, though he served in the wars of 1866 and 1870. After legal studies at the University of Berlin, he occupied a minor court post at Frankfurt an der Oder, 1871–1876; he was an official in the Foreign Office in Berlin from 1877 until retirement in 1900. He cared little for the brilliant social life to which his birth entitled him and preferred literary and artistic circles; he married a granddaughter of the composer Weber.

Wildenbruch's work is very extensive; plays, novels, *Novellen,* and many poems cover a wide range of subjects, but at the center stands an ardent German and Prussian patriotism. After a modest success with two epic poems celebrating the Franco-Prussian War, *Vionville* (1874) and *Sedan* (1875), he turned to the drama and with indomitable persistence continued to write plays though failing to secure stage performance for them. In 1881, however, the famous Meiningen troupe produced *Die Karolinger,* a drama of the time of Louis the Pious; its success brought other plays before the footlights, *Harold* (Eng. tr., 1891), a tragedy of the Norman Conquest, and two dramas of the Napoleonic period, *Der Menonit* and *Väter und Söhne.* The best of Wildenbruch's plays from German history is probably the double drama *Heinrich und Heinrichs Geschlecht* (1895; Eng. tr. of the first part, *King Henry,* 1913–1914), depicting the medieval struggle between imperial and papal power. In a series of dramas, *Die Quitzows* (1888), *Der Generalfeldoberst* (1889), and *Der neue Herr* (1891), he sought to revivify the Prussian past and glorify the Hohenzollern dynasty. Among the many other dramas are *Christoph Marlow* (1884), *Die Tochter des Erasmus* (1900), and *Die Rabensteinerin* (1907; Eng. tr., *Barseba of Rabenstein,* 1909). The last is perhaps the most popular of his plays, presenting the love of a son of the famous Welser family for the daughter of a robber baron. Wildenbruch had a keen sense of theatrical effect; individual scenes contain tense emotional conflicts, but the plays lack structure and concentration and in the portrayal of character are often weak and inconsistent. Many of the plays are in verse; the language is forceful, at times eloquent, but often rhetorical and artificially archaic. Though the dramas enjoyed for a time both critical and popular acclaim, their general style, that of the poetic historical drama of the Schiller tradition, was little in keeping with the naturalistic tendencies of the day. Wildenbruch's attempts to accommodate his dramatic work to the new trend only proved his limitations (*Die Haubenlerche,* 1891). The novels, like the plays, contain powerful episodes but are diffuse and lack focus (*Das wandernde Licht,* 1893; *Eifernde Liebe,* 1893); the novel *Schwester-Seele* (1894) is in part autobiographical. The best of Wildenbruch's narratives are the pathetic and tragic little stories of childhood and adolescence, *Kindertränen* (1883; Eng. tr. of one story, "Der Letzte," *The Captain's Last Child,* 1909), *Das edle Blut* (1892; Eng. tr., *Noble Blood,* 1896), *Neid* (1900; Eng. tr., *Envy,* 1921). His lifelong love of Mediterranean lands appears in both drama and narrative—in *Der Fürst von Verona* (1887) and *Die Lieder des Euripides* (1905), in the charming story *Der Meister von Tanagra* (1880; Eng. tr., *Master of Tanagra,* 1886).

See: J. Röhr, *Wildenbruch als Dramatiker* (1908); B. Litzmann, *Ernst von Wildenbruch* (2 vols., 1913–1916); H. M. Elster, *Ernst von Wildenbruch* (1919).

H. W. H.-T.

Wildenvey, Herman (1886–, Norwegian poet), is the troubadour of Norwegian verse, the tireless singer of youth, beauty, and summer. Born of farming stock in the community of

Eiker, his real family name being Portaas, he attended secondary school in Norway, then studied for a time at a theological seminary in the United States. His first verse collection after reaching maturity, *Nyinger* (1907; Bonfires), at once established him as a popular idol, and the standard-bearer of a lyric revival in Norwegian letters. He disclaimed all social purpose, and declared that he was a pagan worshiper of life and beauty: "I was washed into the world by a flood of sunshine, that's the word!" Building on the form and spirit of Hamsun's (*q.v.*) poetry, he developed an "ambling" verse line all his own, with an easy billowing cadence produced by the alternation of three and four syllable feet and by the enjambement of sentences over several lines. With this technique he was able to relieve Norwegian verse of its usual sobriety, and give it a new lightness, sometimes merely frothy, but often ingratiatingly charming, as well as witty and daring. He enjoyed irritating the staid and the bourgeois, and he treated love with a flippancy that is reminiscent of Heine (whose *Buch der Lieder* he translated in 1929, *Sangenes bok*), but lacks the latter's tragic undertone. A colloquial, even slangy style, a sudden teasing quip at the end, a glittering, summery love of nature, a ready tenderness for children and the unhappy, these are the qualities his admiring public has come to expect. His prose, chiefly autobiographical, is unimportant, even trivial. But such verse collections as *Kjærtegn* (1916; Caresses), *Ildorkestret* (1923; The Orchestra of Fire), and *Høstens lyre* (1931; The Lyre of Autumn), to mention but a few of his many volumes, reveal a true poet, progressively deepening his formal mastery and the seriousness of his themes. Eternity has begun to play a role in his verse, though still on a poetic, rather than a religious basis: "I believe in the human spirit, that it can reach the stars, and that it yearns for the stars." But along with the new there has persisted the old: "I cannot be profound without a merry smile." One of his frequent visits to the United States led to the appearance of a selection of his verse in English translation by Joseph Auslander, *Owls to Athens* (1934), but it does not convey much of his airy grace.

See: K. Elster, "Three Lyric Poets of Norway," *American-Scandinavian Review,* XIII (1925), 653–665; T. Lunden, *Samtiden,* XL (1929), 578–584; J. Auslander, "Introduction," *Owls to Athens* (1934); P. Houm, *Samtiden,* XLVII (1936), 351–363.

E. H.

Wildgans, Anton (1881–1932, Austrian poet and dramatist), was born in Vienna, the son of a cabinet minister. His childhood was embittered by a stepmother, his adolescence darkened by the tragically protracted death of his father. Love finally induced him to complete his law studies in 1908. When the success of his first book of poems (*Herbstfrühling,* 1909) made him financially independent, he gave up his state position. For a time (1921–1922, 1930–1932) he was director of the famous Burgtheater, one of the leading German theatres. But he devoted himself mainly to writing, in which lyric utterance is prominent; a posthumously published selection of his poems, *Späte Ernte* (1933), attests the fertility and power of his invention. Even greater was the success of his dramatic production, and his tragedy *Armut* (1914) won acclaim such as Vienna had not granted a play for years. Only a little less applause greeted the tragedies *Liebe* (1916) and *Dies irae* (1919).

Because his dramas are coming to be regarded as restatements of ideas set forth in the poems and because they show rather an eclecticism of structure than any one consistent pattern or trend, it seems probable that his strongest claim to lasting esteem will rest on his poetry, some of the best and most authentic of which is to be found in the *Sonette an Ead* (1912). Typically Viennese in the softheartedness, fine sensitivity, and mild humanity of his outlook, he avoided the effeminacy which sometimes characterizes the Austrian Francophiles. More and more he turned to the soil and its toilers and found his motifs in the fundamental experiences of human life—man and nature, man and woman, the spirit and the flesh, the urge to communal living and the longing for solitude. A handful of verses will abide; but these will be worth keeping.

See: J. Soyka, ed., *Das Anton Wildgans-Buch* (1932).

B. Q. M.

Winckler, Josef (1881–, German poet and novelist), was born at Rheine in Westphalia. He studied dentistry at the University of Bonn and started practice in the industrial city of Mörs. At about the same time he founded, with Jakob Kneip and Wilhelm Vershofen, the literary association called Werkleute auf Haus Nyland. Like the workingmen poets of the type of Max Barthel and Gerrit Engelke, the "Werkleute" were devoted to spiritualizing modern industrial civilization. Winckler's *Eiserne Sonette* (1912) was a noteworthy attempt in that direction. Even during the First World War the poet maintained his particular faith in the significance to modern life of the power of the machine (*Ozean, des deutschen Volkes Meergesang,* 1917), but his hopes were completely shattered by the German chaos after 1918. Then Winckler wrote the burlesque-like extravaganza *Irrgarten Gottes* (1922) and the popular drolleries of *Der tolle Bomberg* (1923). The poet now gave up his dental practice and settled in the country. He withdrew to his family traditions (see *Pumpernickel,* 1925) and contemplated the rugged energy of the Westphalian soil (*Doctor Eisenbart,* 1929; *Ein König in Westfalen,* 1934) and the homespun gaiety of the Rhine province (*Die Weinheiligen,* 1935). In his recent epic, *Das Mutterbuch* (1939), the poet celebrates the spirit of motherhood as a remedy for the materialism of our age.

See: A. Soergel, *Dichtung und Dichter der Zeit,* Neue Folge: *Im Banne des Expressionismus,* 4. Auflage (1927), pp. 508–520.

E. R.

Winnig, August (1878–, German statesman and writer of fiction, autobiography, and political essays), is best known for his book *Vom Proletariat zum Arbeitertum* (1930). This book, together with the three volumes of his autobiography (*Frührot,* 1924; *Weiter Weg,* 1932; and *Heimkehr,* 1935) and his essays in *Das Reich als Republik* (1928) and *Wir hüten das Feuer* (1933), offers the most readable and illuminating account of the organization and activities, the personalities and purposes, of the Social Democratic Party in Germany from the promulgation of the laws against the Socialists by Bismarck in 1878 to its dissolution in 1933. But the autobiography contains, besides the politics of half a century, the life story of the most interesting—and, if known to Americans, perhaps the most congenial—figure that attained to distinction in Germany in the period following the First World War. Born in Blankenburg, Harz, youngest of a large family and at an early age fatherless, Winnig experienced in his childhood and youth poverty and disillusionment, which he survived physically and mentally thanks to his mother's wisdom and his own intelligence and character. Organizer of the masons' union and editor of its organ, *Der Grundstein,* Winnig became in 1917 minister plenipotentiary to the Baltic Provinces, later federal commissioner to East and West Prussia, member of the National Assembly at Weimar, and president superior of East Prussia. He retired from active politics in 1923.

His autobiography quite as much as his fiction—10 short stories in the volume *Die ewig grünende Tanne* (1927) and a novel *Wunderbare Welt* (1938)—is written in a style that charms and that would have gained for his *Weiter Weg* the 1933 Carl Schünemann prize had not its classification as autobiography eliminated it from consideration. Winnig's love of nature expresses itself in passages of exquisite lyricism, and his profound religious experiences provide the solid foundation for his deep faith in the German workingman. In 1938 he contributed to *Die Stunde des Christentums,* together with 24 other well-known writers, a significant declaration in support of Christianity implicitly aimed at the current neopagan tendencies. In the same intention he wrote his *Europa* (1937) and published a volume containing a collection of passages from his works to which he gave the transparent title *Die Hand Gottes* (1939).

See: H. Bogner, "August Winnig" (with biography and bibliography), *Die neue Literatur,* XXXIV (1933), 261–266; Fr. Gudehus, *August Winnig* (1938) and *Ein deutsches Gewissen: Dank an August Winnig* (1938).

J. F. G.

Winter, Zikmund (1846–1912, Czech novelist and historian), is, except for Jirásek (*q.v.*), the most important Czech historical novelist. Winter was born in Prague, studied history at the university, and taught that subject at several Gymnasiums in Rakovník and Prague. He was an excellent historian; his books on the history of costume, of the towns, of the University of Prague, of trades and arts and crafts, are mines of information on the social conditions of Bohemia, especially in the 16th and 17th centuries. Winter put his knowledge to good use in his many stories and novels, placed in these two centuries. Winter's method is strictly realistic, devoid of sentimentality. Burghers, clergy, and clerks are his unheroic heroes. They are frequently tragicomic figures, obsessed with lust for money or power. Winter's composition is closely knit, the style frequently archaic, the whole outlook pessimistic. The best collection of stories is called *Bouře a přeháňka* (1907; Storm and Rain). Among the longer books, *Rozina Sebranec* (1905; Rozina, the Foundling) and *Mistr Kampanus* (1909; Master Kampanus), a picture of the persecution of the university after the Battle of the White Mountain (1620), were the most popular.

Though Winter had not the same national importance as Jirásek, he should be preferred to him as an artist.

See: O. Theer, *Časopis Českého Musea* (1904); F. X. Šalda, *Novina* (1912); A. Novák, *Duch a národ* (1936).

R. W.

Wirsén, David af (1842–1912, Swedish poet and critic), was born in the province of Uppland, studied at Uppsala, and became a teacher at Uppsala and Göteborg. His first collections of lyrics, *Dikter* (Poems), appeared in 1876 and 1880. His finished and delicate style won him admission to the Swedish Academy, of which he was long the secretary. In subsequent collections, notably *Toner och Sägner* (1893; Notes and Legends) and *Visor, romanser och ballader* (1899; Songs, Romances, and Ballads), he continued his original style but now showed a greater preference for religious themes. As a critic he did all in his power to combat the rising tendencies of realism and artistic experiment, and to this end used all his authority in the Academy, so that he soon became highly unpopular with the younger generation.

By present-day standards Wirsén would probably be considered a sentimentalist, a Swedish Mid-Victorian. Indeed he called himself a poet of "white roses," as contrasted with the red roses of Snoilsky (*q.v.*). In any case there can be no doubt of his entire sincerity. His idyllic and reflective mood has an appeal independent of contemporary fashion. He may still be read with pleasure for his affirmation of the old human verities of simple human feeling and for the limpid grace of his style. It is curious to note that so polemical a critic should be represented in all anthologies as the poet of tenderness.

See: C. W. Stork, *Anthology of Swedish Lyrics* (1917; revised and enlarged ed., 1930); F. Böök, *Sveriges moderna litteratur* (1921), also published as Vol. III of O. Sylwan, ed., *Svenska litteraturens historia* (1919–1921), pp. 39–46.

C. W. S.

Wittlin, Józef (1896–, Polish poet, translator, and novelist), was born at Dmytrów, Austrian Poland, of Jewish stock, and educated in Lwów. A pacifist by instinct and conviction, Wittlin early embodied his intense aversion to war in a series of poems entitled *Hymny* (1920; Hymns) and endeavored to escape from his horror of war by burying himself in the classical civilization of Greece and by producing eventually a new and admirable translation of the *Odyssey* (1924). Wittlin's principal contribution to Polish literature is the novel *Sól ziemi* (1936; Eng. tr., *Salt of the Earth,* 1939), designed as the initial volume of a long saga devoted to the "patient foot soldier" of the imperial Austrian army. Wittlin's literary work was cut off abruptly by the Second World War, which forced the author to find refuge in the United States.

See: A. P. Coleman, *New York Times Book Review,* July 5, 1936, p. 18, and *Saturday Review of Literature,* August 2, 1941, pp. 10–11; K. Czachowski, *Obraz współczesnej literatury polskiej,* III (1936), 276–279.

A. P. C.

Woestijne, Karel van de (1879–1929, Flemish poet), was born at Ghent, went to school there, studied Germanic philology at the State University of Ghent, and taught Dutch in various schools until he was appointed to the chair of Dutch literature at Ghent. His poetry was a conscious reaction to the vogue of Guido Gezelle (*q.v.*). It gives expression to the questioning bewilderment of the generation that came after Gezelle's placid and self-centered age. Gezelle's provincial self-sufficiency could no longer satisfy these moderns who were alive to currents and movements that stirred the literary world abroad. Van de Woestijne has defined his poetry as "autobiography turned into symbolism." In other words, all his verse is an expression of his conscious and subconscious personality. *Het Vaderhuis* (1903; The Father House) recounts symbolically the story of his boyhood, *De Boomgaard der Vogelen en der Vruchten* (1905; The Orchard of Birds and Fruit) that of his courtship and early marriage, *De Gulden Schaduw* (1910; The Golden Shadow) his family life, after a son is born, in the great city. In *De modderen Man* (1920; The Man of Mud) the aging poet gave expression to the mental pain caused by the struggle between the flesh and the spirit, resurgence of old desires, regret over unrealized dreams. Van de Woestijne's imagery has the quality of sculpture. He carves his figures of speech with bold, powerful strokes from the stone of the language. His poetry is not the kind that one reads for relaxation. His mode of expression is often enigmatic. One has to wrestle with him and wring the meaning from his symbolism. One lives with this poet in a close atmosphere like that of a sultry summer day pregnant with forebodings of an oncoming thunderstorm. His poetry is the expression of a lonely soul tortured by self-analysis and oversensitive nerves. The diction is refined, yet overcharged with decorative imagery. The verse is melodious, but the melody has the somber monotony of organ music. Yet, for all that, he ranks high among Flemish poets, is, in fact, according to present-day estimate, the first among the modern poets of Flanders.

See: A. de Ridder, *La Littérature flamande contemporaine* (1923); M. Rutten. *De Lyriek van Karel van de Woestijne* (1934).

A. J. B.

Wolker, Jiří (1900–1924, Czech poet), the leading poet of the "proletarian" group which became prominent just after the First World War, was born in Prostějov, Moravia, of a good middle-class family. He came to Prague in 1919 to study law, but plunged into the literary life of the new capital city. He died of tuberculosis before he was 24, in his native town.

Wolker is the author of two collections of verse which became very popular and influential. *Host do domu* (1921; The Guest in the House) is a collection of simple poems which dream about the world of the poet's boyhood in the country. Wolker obviously believes in the goodness of man, in the sanctity of poverty, in the complete fundamental identity of all men as it has been preached by French *unanimisme.* The poem "Svatý Kopeček" (The Holy Hill) can be compared with "Zone" of Apollinaire (*q.v.*): the earth melts into the sky, the shadow of death dissolves, silent matter comes alive—everywhere there is unity and continuity. The second collection of Wolker's poetry, *Těžká hodina* (1922; The Grievous Hour), is very different. Wolker has found his allegiance; he has discovered the cause of the proletariat and of communism, which he conceives as an earthly paradise, as the fulfillment of his longing for identification with all humanity. We now have effective social ballads, like "Balada o očích topičových" (Eyes of the Fireman), set in a power station, where gradually the eyes of the fireman change into lights of the city. Wolker has rediscovered the style of the Czech folk ballad and of its greatest master, K. J. Erben. A few poems, published after Wolker's death, give moving expression to his personal tragedy of dying in early youth and knowing all too clearly of his approaching death. His tragic fate, his personal charm, and the popular tone of his lyrics have, however, elevated him to a position in recent Czech poetry which the actual substance of his work does not altogether support. The posthumous, over-complete editions including even his earliest verse, some short plays, and some rather crude prose hardly enhance his reputation with critical readers. There is much adolescent naïveté and sentimentality in Wolker's work. But Wolker had genuine talent, and his historical importance—his rediscovery of the style of the folk ballad, his ardent collectivist faith—can scarcely be overrated. There is a simple charm in his best verse which is beyond sophisticated criticism.

See: V. Nezval, *Wolker* (1925); Z. Kalista, *Kamarád Wolker* (1933); L. Kratochvil, *Wolker a Nezval* (1936).

R. W.

Wyspiański, Stanisław (1869–1907, Polish poet, painter, and dramatist), was born in Cracow, the ancient capital of Poland, where he spent most of his short but fruitful life. The son of a sculptor, the boy was haunted by the many old churches and historical monuments of the "city of living stones." However, it was the royal castle of Wawel, with its gorgeous Renaissance cathedral, that inspired him most of all. After completing the usual training in the Gymnasium, he entered the Cracow Academy of Fine Arts, became a pupil of Poland's greatest painter of historical subjects, Jan Matejko, and, after winning a scholarship from the Academy, continued his studies in France and Italy. Feverishly he studied painting, sculpture, and architecture, as well as literature and the art of the theatre. He found the great tragedies of Corneille, Racine, and Shakespeare as absorbingly interesting as the Italian and French cathedrals. He also threw himself into the study of Greek art and civilization, under the spell of which he was to remain till the very end of his life. Testimony to the many-sidedness of his gifts and interests can be found in some 500 pictorial works, in his mural decorations, in admirable stained-glass windows, in cartoons for the reconstruction of the ancient royal castle in Cracow, in designs of theatrical costumes, in critical reflections on Shakespeare's *Hamlet,* in a version of Corneille's masterpiece, the tragedy of the *Cid,* in illustrations for Homer's *Iliad,* as well as in bold ideas in the field of decorative, applied, and typographical arts. It was this intense overactivity that was undoubtedly responsible for his premature death at the age of 38.

As to his literary achievement, it was bound with his central vision of the theatre. He believed that dramatic poetry is man's greatest accomplishment, and he looked at the theatre as fundamentally a cathedral of the spirit. His 16 plays may be divided into two groups, those definitely Polish and those based on subjects drawn from the literature of ancient Greece. The majority belong to the former group: four powerful dramas, more or less allegorical in character—*Legjon* (1900; The Legion), *Wesele* (1901; The Wedding), *Wyzwolenie* (1903; Deliverance), and *Noc Listopadowa* (1904; November Night) —are considered masterpieces by his countrymen. The tragic problems of freedom, political as well as moral, of national and individual greatness, of heroic attitudes toward life, of the secret of man's wholesome spiritual growth—these are some of the timeless issues that absorbed him. A searcher for heroism and beauty, he turned to the mythology and robust early history of Poland, only to feel all the more bitterly the present political degradation. Determined to get at the roots of the problem, he began to explore the darkest recesses of his nation's character and temperament, its hidden faults and weaknesses, its incapacity for organized action, its deep-rooted habit of substituting misty reflection for clear thinking, and its mood of more or less passive resignation. Although an admirer of the great romantics, Mickiewicz and Słowacki, Wyspiański did not hesitate to voice occasionally his passionate protest against those aspects of their poetry which, in his estimation, induced the Poles to acquiesce in the pathos and beauty of political martyrdom. The intensity of his lyrical fervor is enhanced through his occasional use of the racy speech of the countryside, through irregular lines, rapid movement, colorful idioms, and apt figures of speech.

Wyspiański's lifelong and admiring association with Greek art and its qualities of symmetry and universality did not permit him to remain utterly absorbed in national problems. He frequently used Greek imagery in his Polish plays and wrote four poetic plays round purely Greek subjects. Of these, *Powrót Odyssa* (1907; The Return of Ulysses), Wyspiański's farewell to life, is probably the best.

Austere and rather aloof, completely engrossed in his manifold creative activities, Wyspiański nevertheless exercised a powerful influence upon his generation, having nobly played his role as artist and spiritual leader.

See: S. Srebrny, "Stanisław Wyspiański, *Slavonic Review,* II (1923–1924), 359–380; R. Dyboski, *Modern Polish Literature* (1924); *Wiadomości literackie,* 1928, No. 231 (entire issue); W. Borowy, "Wyspiański," *Slavonic Review,* XI (1932–1933), 617–630.

T. M.

Wyzewa, Teodor de (1862–1917, French critic), was born on his grandmother's estate in the village of Kalusik, Russian Poland. His father was a physician. When the boy was 10 years old, his father decided to move the family to France so that his son could be educated in the French schools which he had learned to prize, having studied there himself while a political exile. The family settled in a village of Normandy, and the young Teodor was sent as a boarding student to the *collège* of Beauvais. Except for vacations, the next years of Wyzewa's life were spent, not happily, in the French schools for which he obtained scholarships. A year of teaching philosophy in the small provincial town of Châtellerault disgusted Wyzewa forever with pedagogy. Having returned to Paris and changed his name from Wyzewski to the more easily pronounced form Wyzewa, he undertook to make a living with his pen. The years of solitude and boredom and the sharp contrast created by recollections of his Polish childhood had already taught Wyzewa to find, in dream, a refuge from drab reality.

In 1885 he and Edouard Dujardin founded the *Revue wagnérienne,* which was to play such an important part in the orientation and the expression of the symbolist movement (*see* French symbolism). Wyzewa was then one of the most brilliant and certainly the most cosmopolitan of a group of young men who gathered every Tuesday at Mallarmé's (*q.v.*) to discuss poetry, music, and philosophy. He knew many languages, had traveled extensively, understood the most difficult poets and philosophers. His knowledge of German and of music was to make him the interpreter of Wagner to his contemporaries and one of the most important critics of his school. Consciously or not Wyzewa attributed to Wagner many of his own ideas, and the series of articles on Wagnerian art published in the *Revue wagnérienne* (1885–1886; later reprinted in *Nos Maîtres,* 1895) is one of the best expressions of symbolist aesthetics as conceived by a disciple of Mallarmé. The influence of this pseudo-Wagnerian philosophy, with its negation of the reality of the outside world ("Alone the 'I' exists and its eternal task is to create"), has been heavy on the generation. *Le Culte du moi* of Barrès (*q.v.*) is an example.

In the *Revue indépendante,* which in 1886 succeeded the *Revue wagnérienne* as a vehicle for symbolist doctrines, Wyzewa found the field in which he was to specialize, the criticism of foreign literature. Leo Tolstoy (*q.v.*) was then superseding Wagner as a model for the idealistically inclined. Wyzewa continued to conduct in the name of Tolstoy and with the label of "anti-intellectualism" the propaganda he had begun in the name of Wagner and with the label of "idealism." His criticism has always been propaganda against naturalism, against materialism, against an undue faith in science. He wrote in *Vogue*, in the *Revue bleu*, and after 1891 in the *Revue des deux mondes*, to which he was called by Brunetière (*q.v.*). Wyzewa's evolution is a reflection of the evolution of the symbolist movement during these years, the end of which was, of course, for many a return to Christianity. That final stage marked by a new generation of poets, Claudel, Péguy, Francis Jammes (*qq.v.*), was reached by Wyzewa about 1900 (*Contes chrétiens*, 1901). At that time, too, he was left a widower, after seven years of dream-like happiness. Abandoning all worldly pursuits, he withdrew into almost complete seclusion, dividing his life between the work which provided for his living (articles in the *Revue des deux mondes*, *Temps*, etc., and translations, many of which were religious in character, such as *The Golden Legend* and St. Francis of Assisi's *Fioretti*) and the music of Mozart, his only solace.

In 1916 he published in collaboration with a friend, G. de St. Foix, an exhaustive study, which had occupied his leisure for 10 years, of Mozart's early works, *La Jeunesse de Mozart*. When in 1917 a sudden illness took him away, his real spirit and all his ambition had long since departed this world.

See: I. de Wyzewa, *La Revue wagnérienne* (1934).

I. W.

Y

Yesenin, Sergei Aleksandrovich (1895–1925, Russian poet), was the most popular poet of the early Revolution and was called by Gorky (*q.v.*) the most gifted since Pushkin. A peasant born in Konstantinov, Ryazan Province, he was educated at an ecclesiastical teachers' school and (1912–1913) at the Shanyavski University, Moscow. In 1915 he went to Petrograd, where he soon became the chief exponent of the imaginists, a group nearer to the vorticists than to the American imagists, who insisted on the image as the "primary pigment of poetry." At first one of the Left Wing Social Revolutionaries, who included Ivanov-Razumnik, editor of *Skify* (The Scythians), Yesenin supported the November Revolution, although he was always more or less hostile to official, orthodox Communism. As an imaginist he declared the independence of poetry and the imagination, a courageous protest against the dictatorship of the early militant period. Later, in Moscow, he became the main attraction of the literary cafés, where his talent together with his rowdyism exercised such a tremendous influence on Soviet youth that "Yeseninism" was declared a dangerous political disease. His marriage to Isadora Duncan (1922) caused world-wide comment, as did their joint tour of Europe and the United States. They separated (1923) and he returned to the U.S.S.R., where some months later he married a granddaughter of Leo Tolstoy (*q.v.*). As a peasant and a revolutionary mystic imbued with the messianism of Blok and Bely, Yesenin suffered progressive disillusion under a proletarian, industrial, and materialistic system. His early dream of the resurrection of the old muzhik "wooden" Russia was unrealizable. His inner maladjustment produced a fatal disintegration of personality, and on December 28, 1925, he slashed his wrists, then hanged himself in a Leningrad hotel room.

Yesenin's was a powerfully lyric genius springing from a religious nature instinct with love for the soil and landscape of Russia. He knew its rich diversity and vastness from his many journeys to Murmansk, Archangel, Turkestan, the Kirghiz steppes, the Caucasus and the Crimea. From *Radunitsa* (1915; Rejoicing) through more than 20 volumes of verse he celebrated this passionate and nostalgic love. Many of his poems are tender, wistful, even pietistic, others brutally blasphemous. His finest songs are among the most lovely and poignant of all Russian poetry, memorable for their simplicity, for their exquisite melodic line, and for the feeling of oneness with nature which they evoke. His best-known works include *Tovarishch Inonia* (1918; Comrade Inonia), which hails the Revolution as the revival of traditional peasant Russia; *Ispoved khuligana* (1921; The Confession of a Hooligan); *Pugachyov* (1922), an epic verse tragedy of the peasant rebel in the reign of Catherine II; *Moskva kabatskaya* (1924; Tavern Moscow); *Rus sovetskaya* (1925; Soviet Russia); *Persidskie motivy* (1925;

Persian Sketches). In 1926 the Soviet Union of Writers established a Yesenin Museum, and the State Publishing House (1926–1927) issued his collected works in four volumes. His poems have been translated into many languages, and a number appear in anthologies in English.

See: Vladislav Khodasevich, "Yesenin," *Sovremennyia zapiski,* XXVIII (1926), 292–322; A. Voronsky, "Sergei Yesenin," in *Literaturnye tipy* (1927), pp. 173–200.

N. S.

Yevreinov, Nikolai Nikolayevich (1879–, Russian dramatist, *régisseur,* and critic and theorist of the drama), was born in Moscow. His father was an engineer and a government official. His mother was descended from a French nobleman who had emigrated to Russia during the French Revolution. Yevreinov himself had a precocious interest in the theatre. At the age of five he was taken to the theatre to see a play; at seven he had written a play of his own; at 13 he had written a novel. At that same age he acted in a theatre and performed as an equilibrist in a circus. He had also studied music under Rimski-Korsakov. He was sent to the Imperial Law School at St. Petersburg and actually graduated from there with a silver medal in 1901. While there, however, he was not so much interested in law as in the Legal Dramatic Circle, for which he acted, wrote plays, and composed an opera. After graduating, he was given a post in the Imperial Ministry of Ways and Communications which he held for 10 years. During that time he continued to write plays; these included a play called *Fundament schastya* (1902; The Foundation of Happiness), which was an episode in the life of gravediggers, and *Krasivy despot* (1906; Eng. tr., *The Beautiful Despot,* 1916), which was acted both in Russia and in England. In 1907 he directed plays from antiquity at the Starinny or Ancient Theatre in St. Petersburg. He took Meyerhold's place in 1908 as *régisseur* for Vera Kommissarzhevskaya at her theatre and, among other plays, directed a remarkable production of Oscar Wilde's *Salomé.* In 1909 he started a theatre of his own called the Merry Theatre for Grown-up Children, where he produced his own play, *Vesyolaya smert* (1909; Eng. tr., *A Merry Death,* 1916), often acted in England and America. This was a short harlequinade in which a woman representing death seems to separate the merry Harlequin from the heartbroken Columbine, until Harlequin finally rises laughing from his deathbed. In *Predstavlenie lyubvi* (1909; The Presentation of Love) Yevreinov produced a monodrama in which all the different characters are interpreted from the point of view of one central character. In connection with this play he published *Vvedenie v monodramu* (1909; Introduction to Monodrama), in which he explained his theory of intense subjectivism and artificiality in drama—a theory which in many ways anticipated expressionism.

In 1910 Yevreinov started another theatre of his own in St. Petersburg called the Krivoe Zerkalo or Crooked Looking Glass, which gave an intentionally distorted and grotesque reflection of life. One of the fantasies which he produced there consisted of five different condensed versions of Gogol's famous play, *The Inspector-General (or "Revizór")*: a classical performance; a lifelike performance in the spirit of Stanislavsky; a grotesque performance in the manner of Max Reinhardt; a mysterious performance in the style of Gordon Craig; a cinematographic performance. He also produced in this theatre some plays of his own. *Shkola etualei* (1911; The School of Stars) represented a director and a number of different types of actresses. In *V kulisakh dusha* (1912; Eng. trs., *The Theatre of the Soul,* 1915, *Behind the Curtain of the Soul,* 1922, *The Back Stage of the Soul,* 1925) a professor reveals three different entities of the soul. The Rational Soul wears spectacles and has a quiet, sober manner. The Emotional Soul wears an artist's blouse and a red tie. The Subliminal Soul wears a black mask. Then are seen the different concepts of the Wife and of the Dancer as they appear to these different entities of the soul. This extravaganza has often been performed in England, America, and other countries and has offered an interesting challenge in its fantastic scenic design and acting. *Schastlivy grobovshchik* (1912; The Happy Coffinmaker), *Kukhnya smekha* (1914; The Kitchen of Laughter), and *Chetvyortaya stena* (1915; The Fourth Wall), in which a parody of *Faust* was given, were all experiments written by Yevreinov for the Crooked Looking Glass.

To go with these plays, Yevreinov wrote a number of theoretical books on the theatre, *Teatr kak takovoi* (1912; The Theatre as Such), *Pro Scena Sua* (1913), and *Teatr dlya sebya* (1915–1917; enlarged and translated into English in 1927 as *The Theatre in Life*). In these treatises Yevreinov explains his theory that all men, whether they know it or not, have a will to dramatize. The child creates his world of make-believe, his theatre. In the childhood of the human race the primitive savage acts out the scene of the hunt in front of the audience gathered around the campfire. All the great men of history have been filled with a desire to act, to play a role before the audience of the world. Religion, revolution, crime—all have something of the theatrical in them. The theatre is greater than life; it heals the wounds that life inflicts.

After the Revolution of 1917 Yevreinov remained in the Soviet Union for several years. In celebration of the third anniversary of the Russian Revolution, he produced his great pageant called *Vzyatie Zimnego Dvortsa* (1920; The Storming of the Winter Palace). This was performed out of doors in Petrograd, in the very square in front of the Winter Palace where the event celebrated had actually taken place three years earlier; of the 8,000 who took part in the pageant many were reenacting realistically what they had actually done on that earlier occasion. Most of the action, however, was symbolic: it took place on a White Stage to the right and a Red Stage to the left with a connecting bridge between them, where the struggle between the two conflicting forces was acted out allegorically as in a sort of political mystery. Yevreinov's later play, *Samoe glavnoe* (1921; Eng. trs., *The Chief Thing,* 1923, *The Most Important Thing,* 1924), was acted as *Quintessence* by the Harvard Dramatic Club in 1925, as *The Chief Thing* by the Theatre Guild in 1926, and as *La Comédie du bonheur* by the Théâtre de l'Atelier in Paris in 1936. It emphasized the idea that in life, as well as in the theatre, illusion is "the main thing" and showed Mr. Paraclete, the Comforter, with his group of actors, providing the occupants of a drab boardinghouse with those illusions which alone will make them happy. In *Korable pravednykh* (1924; Eng. tr., *The Ship of the Saints,* 1926) Yevreinov introduced a series of plays, one inside the other. By this time he had become an *émigré* from Russia, living in Paris and visiting America, writing *Radio-potselui* (1926; Eng. tr., *The Radio Kiss,* 1926) and *Teatr vechnoi voinu* (1928; The Theatre of Eternal War).

See: V. Kamenski, *Kniga o Yevreinove* (1917); B. Arbatov, *Yevreinov i my* (1922); Oliver M. Sayler, *The Russian Theatre,* 2d ed. (1922), pp. 221–244, 258–261; Leo Wiener, *The Contemporary Drama of Russia* (1924), pp. 159–163; B. V. Kazanski, *Metod teatra* (*analiz sistemy N. N. Yevreinova*) (1925).

H. W. L. D.

Yugoslav literature in the narrowest modern sense dates from the political unification of the Serbs, Croats, and Slovenes in 1918, following the First World War. It had its beginnings, however, more than one hundred years ago when Serbia first attained its independence and when the Croats and Slovenes were still under the rule of Austria-Hungary. From the 14th century on, foreign domination under the Turks, Austrians, Hungarians, and Venetians suppressed the brilliant medieval culture of the South Slavs, formerly one of the most advanced in Europe. Except for the remarkable efflorescence of literature and the arts in Dalmatia during the Renaissance, South Slav civilization suffered extreme retardation until recent times. Rigorous repression of native institutions, even of native language, forced the survival of national identity to depend almost wholly upon oral tradition. This tradition, whose vitality has persisted, forms the matrix of all the modern literature. Today Yugoslavia is one of the few remaining regions of the Western world where oral poetry still lives, in spite of the inevitable decline produced by modern civilization. The Serbian ballads, as seen in the famous cycles celebrating the battle of Kosovo (1389), the medieval hero Marko Kraljević, the guerilla warfare of the Haiduks with the Turkish conquerors, and the romances, were recognized more than one hundred years ago by Goethe, the Grimm brothers, Mérimée, Lamartine, Scott, Bulwer-Lytton, Pushkin, Mickiewicz, and other distinguished men of letters as unsurpassed in their genre. They remain today a living folk expression and a prime source of national inspiration.

The first stirrings of national renascence were felt in the 18th century under the leadership of Dositej Obradović (1739–1811), the inaugurator of rationalism and one of the first to arouse the aspiration for liberty and the emancipation of the intellect. Early in the 19th century appeared three great figures on whose work modern South Slav literature is largely based: a Serb, Vuk Stefanović Karadžić (1787–1864); a Croat, Ljudevit Gaj (1809–1872); and, to a less degree, a Slovene, Jernej Kopitar (1780–1844). To these men fell the task of effecting literary reforms. These concerned the basic tools of language, the reform of orthography, the compilation of grammars and dictionaries, the adoption of the vernacular as the literary means of expression, the harmonization of the three dialects—Serbian, Croatian, and Slovenian—and the collection of folk materials, legends, tales, fables, proverbs, epic and lyric songs, that constitute one of the richest treasures of oral literature in Western civilization.

The first half of the 19th century was given to such a forging of means and to the development of a literary audience. The period was characterized by an upsurge of nationalism, specifically expressed in the movement known as "Illyrianism," which had as its goal the cultural and political unification of all South Slavs. This signified in literature as in life the passionate aspiration for liberty and a turning to the heroic past as a source of inspiration and self-affirmation. Until the repressive measures following the 1848 revolt, German influence was dominant in all cultural interchange. Thereafter forcible Germanization from above brought its reaction. French and Russian ideas and literature superseded German; realism and naturalism as a mode took the place of the former romanticism. Whereas cultural progress had been confined to a few isolated places, such as Belgrade, Zagreb, Ljubljana, and Novi Sad, a rapid expansion took place throughout the Slav regions. A multiple development and reform occurred in the theatres, in literary reviews and publishing societies, in academic and other institutions. A great number of translations from French and Russian were made in the fields of the novel, drama, and philosophy.

In mid-century appeared the first South Slav writers to merit the term universal: Prince-Bishop Petar Petrović Njegoš, called the Shakespeare of Montenegro, author of the powerful verse drama *Gorski vijenac* (1847; Eng. tr., *The Mountain Wreath,* 1930), considered the finest work in all Serbian literature and translated into all the principal European languages; the greatly gifted Slovene, France Prešeren (1800–1872), whose genius appeared fully mature yet without native precedent, like that of Pushkin; and the Croat Ivan Mažuranić (1814–1890), author of the epic *Smrt Smaïl-Aga Čengića* (1846; Eng. tr., *The Death of Smail Aga,* 1925). These were the great poets of romanticism, whose fame is secure. Beside them may be mentioned the Slovenes Valentine Vodnik (1758–1819), Fran Levstik (1831–1887), Simon Jenko (1835–1869), Josip Stritar (1836–1923), and Simon Gregorčić (1844–1906); the Croats Stanko Vraz (1810–1851), Dimitrije Demetar (1811–1870), Petar Preradović (1818–1872), and Janko Jurković (1827–1889); and the Serbs Jovan Sterija-Popović (1806–1850), Jovan Ilić (1823–1901), Branko Radičević (1824–1853), Ljubomir Nenadović (1826–1895), Djura Jakšić (1832–1878), Jovan Jovanović-Zmaj (1833–1903), and Laza Kostić (1841–1910) (Kostič's translations introduced Shakespeare to the South Slavs). These men were chiefly poets and romantics who used native materials, such as the epic ballads of oral tradition, as the basis of their inspiration, but they were strongly influenced by such foreign writers as Shakespeare, Heine, Herder, Petőfi, Arany (*q.v.*), Pushkin, Lermontov, Byron, Tennyson, and Goethe. A large number of the works of this period were in verse form, but there was also a considerable body of prose—tales, novels, and essays.

The rise of realism, far from extinguishing the spirit of nationalism and Pan-Slavism, expressed it in new forms. The latter half of the 19th century produced a new social consciousness that reflected the ideas of Western Europe and of the Russians, with whom there had existed a literary affiliation dating from the 18th century. Prose became the favored medium; the Croats became especially accomplished in the novel, while the Serbs excelled in the short story. Writers attacked romantic poetry for what they termed its frivolity and orientalism and insisted on the depiction of the problems of actual, contemporary existence. The old patriarchal, pastoral ways of life were gradually giving way to urban influences. The economic sufferings of the peasantry, the transition from country to town life, the arrogance of the great landowners, the harshness of foreign rule—these were the principal themes of the new realists, whose manner of thought was conditioned by materialist and socialist philosophy, positivism, Darwinism, and the new scientific discoveries.

The precursors of the modern realistic novel among the South Slavs were Jakov Ignatović (1824–1888), August Šenoa (1838–1881), and Josip Jurčić. Ignatović's novels and tales described the society of the Serbian province of Voivodina, especially during the transitional period after 1848, depicting merchants, workers, peasants, students, officers, and churchmen. Šenoa, Croat poet, novelist, and critic, really dominated the literature of his time and effected many reforms. He bitterly criticized German literature and German influence for their suppressive effect on his country and advocated French culture. He was the historian of his epoch and the portrayer of all social classes. His novels give a striking picture of the social and economic decadence of Croat society, showing the conflict of the old patriarchal generation with the new, the struggle of the bourgeoisie with the Church and the nobility, and the relationship of peasant and landlord. Jurčić introduced the realistic novel into Slovene literature. Like others of his generation, he was reared in a romantic, nationalistic atmosphere that instilled in him a belief not only in the ideals of national liberty and unity but also in the usefulness of the struggle and its outcome. His historical novels, his dramatic tragedies, and his novels of contemporary life show a profound insight into the social strata of Slovenia.

Josip Stritar (1836–1923), poet, novelist, and critic, also exerted a powerful influence on the literature of his day. He depicted contemporary Slovene society and predicted the future great role of the Slavs in civilization. In 1870 he founded the review *Zvon* (Bell), which inaugurated Slovene literary criticism. He was the author of many satirical sonnets on the false leaders of the people.

Janko Kersnik (1852–1897) followed Jurčič in the naturalistic observation of modern Slovene society. He satirized false education, the hypocritical aspect of patriotism, intolerant clericalism, and the slackening of political morality. Greed for money and land form the theme of many of his works. Ante Kovačić (1854–1889), a Croat of peasant stock, was also a bitter satirist of social morality who analyzed the transformation of the peasant into townsman, a process that for Kovačić too often spelled individual and social ruin. Josip Tomić (1843–1906), though of secondary literary rank, exerted a considerable influence in poetry, in criticism of the novel, and in the drama. He was a prolific translator, edited reviews, and studied social problems. Using the documentary methods of Šenoa, he wrote many realistic tales of contemporary life and a number of historical novels painting the heroic past.

Among the Serbs, Glišić (1847–1908), Lazarević (*q.v.*), and Veselinović (1862–1905) represent the highest artistic attainment in the short story. Milovan Glišić, often compared with the Russian satirist Saltykov-Shchedrin, wrote a number of excellent village tales setting forth the economic problems of the poor peasantry exploited by usurers and landlords. Laza Lazarević masterfully recorded the beauty of the old patriarchal way of life in many short stories that belong to the classics of South Slav literature. Janko Veselinović, second only to Lazarević, was the author of many short narratives and novels glorifying the moral and material strength of the peasant.

In Croatia the realistic novel was best represented by Kumičić and Gjalski (*q.v.*). Evgenij Kumičić (1850–1904), editor, dramatist, and novelist, dedicated all his work to some 20 novels, plays, and collections of tales, political and literary freedom. Author of he described his native Istria, the life of Zagreb and Vienna, and the fatal role played by foreign cultures in the history of Croatia. Ksaver Šandor Gjalski portrayed the whole social life of Croatia in his many works that constitute a modern épopée and was the founder of the Croatian novel of psychological realism.

Other outstanding writers of the later 19th century include Matavulj (*q.v.*), Kozarac (1858–1906), Novak (1859–1905), Treščec-Borota (1870–1931), Leskovar (1861–), Ranković (1863–1899), Meško (1874–), Sremac (*q.v.*), Draženović (1863–), and Tavčar (1851–1923). Simo Matavulj, a Serb born in Dalmatia, created a gallery of types illustrating the transition from patriarchal to modern life. Josip Kozarac also painted the epoch of transition and proclaimed that the only remedy for current decadence lay in economic relief. Vjenceslav Novak similarly showed the evils of the irrational organization of society. Josip Draženović depicted the people of the Croatian coast, fishermen, sailors, peasants, and artisans. Ivan Tavčar, a Slovene novelist and tale writer of a serene and mature talent, was interested in philosophical problems.

The end of the century produced a reaction against naturalism and the development of psychological realism under the influence of Dostoevski, Leo Tolstoy (*qq.v.*), and contemporary French writers. Man was no longer considered explainable solely by his physiological instincts and his social milieu; more significant were the pattern of his thoughts and the nature of his spirit. The depiction of man in his interior struggle thus enlarged in Yugoslavia, as it did in the rest of Europe, the meaning and scope of literature. The principal writers who represented this new conception of realism were Treščec-Borota and Leskovar in Croatia, Ranković in Serbia, and Meško in Slovenia. Vladimir Treščec-Borota described the crises in the Moslem world brought about through the forcible introduction by Vienna of Western civilization into an oriental milieu fixed in its secular traditions. Janko Leskovar wrote of the *fin-de-siècle* moral and social lassitude, depicting Hamlet-like figures preoccupied with passive subjective analysis and deprived of active will. Svetolik Ranković wrote novels describing the lawless brigands of the mountains and the corruption of monastery life. Franc Ksaver Meško, a Slovene priest, led the reaction against naturalism in his region, calling for a return to God and the supremacy of the spiritual. Stevan Sremac, one of the best South Slav humorists, stands somewhat apart; his finest works are his tales of Niš and its semioriental, semipatriarchal way of life.

The drama of this period was second to poetry and prose literature in attaining marked originality. The growing activity in the theatre derived first from the very considerable and excellent translations of foreign playwrights, such as Molière, Leo Tolstoy, Gogol, Chekhov (*q.v.*), Ibsen (*q.v.*), Björnson (*q.v.*), Hauptmann (*q.v.*), and Schnitzler (*q.v.*). Jovan Sterija-Popović (1806–1856), the first great name in the Belgrade theatre, was the author of many witty and distinguished comedies satirizing society in the manner of Molière. Later Serbian drama developed through the work of Branislav Nušić (*q.v.*), after Sterija-Popović the most admired writer of comedies, Borisav Stanković (*q.v.*), and Aleksa Šantić (*q.v.*). Croatian drama was inaugurated by Julije Rorauer (1859–1912), Marijan Derenčin (1836–1908), Vladimir Mažuranić (1845–1928), Kosta Trifković (1843–1875), Franja Marković (1845–1914), and Stjepan Miletić (1868–1908). Miletić, director of the Zagreb theatre, contributed much through his reforms of repertory, staging, and acting and through his introduction of many European dramas. The name of Count Ivo Vojnović (*q.v.*) leads modern Croat drama; his romantic and nationalistic plays remain favorites of the Yugoslav stage. Other playwrights include Milan Ogrizović (1876–), and Ante Tresić-Pavičić (1867–), both Croats, and the Slovenes Anton Aškerc (1856–1912), Anton Funtek (1862–1932), Anton Medved (1869–1910), and Ivan Cankar (*q.v.*). Cankar, the foremost name in modern Slovene literature, was the author of six powerful plays, four realistic, and two symbolic-realistic.

The poetry of the turn of the century had a number of brilliant exponents whose works have been translated into many European languages. Chief among them are Vojislav Ilić (*q.v.*), Šantić, Silvije Strahimir Kranjčević (*q.v.*), and Aškerc, who formed the South Slav "Parnasse" under the influence of the French school. There was less difference between the older romantic poets, such as Zmaj, Jakšić, and Kostić, who came to maturity at about 1860, and those of the succeeding generation than between the prose writers of the romantic school and their successors in the realistic genre. Šantić, an accomplished stylist, wrote many lyrics of a familiar, provincial character. Ilić, considered by many the finest Serbian poet and the founder of recent Serbian poetry, wrote elegiac verses, a beautiful meditative cycle, and a series of ballads based on classical antiquity. Kranjčević, a Croat, and Aškerc occupy an important place in the transition between the two centuries. Kranjčević's verse is filled with a tragic conception of life in which man's thirst for justice and liberty is forever thwarted by the permanent phenomena of hunger, slavery, and tyranny; while Aškerc, an ex-priest, and the author of some 15 volumes of ballads and epics, gave a modern social accent to national themes.

At the end of the 19th and in the early 20th century the symbolist movement profoundly affected South Slav poetry, as it did other European literatures (*see* French symbolism). Out of this trend came much distinguished work that ranks with the best of modern times, that of the Serbs Jovan Dučić (*q.v.*) and Milan Rakić (*q.v.*), the Croat Vladimir Nazor (*q.v.*), and the Slovene Oton Župančić (*q.v.*). Dučić was accomplished in prose as well as poetry, and his pages belong to the finest of Serbian literature. The originality and harmony of Rakić's verse, though he did not write extensively, place him second only to Dučić. Nazor, both poet and novelist, is prolific and varied; his best work glorifies the heroes of the past, the beauty of the old Adriatic cities, the spirit of man and of nature; the serenity of his philosophy is a contrast to the melancholy of such poets as Kranjčević. Župančić, the director of the National Theatre of Ljubljana until the Second World War, is primarily a lyricist; the force and richness of his language, the complexity and spiritual depth of his thought, make him one of the best of contemporary poets. A place in world literature also belongs to Cankar, whose meditative, lyric poetry clearly falls in the symbolist category, although his wonderful tales and dramas are by turns naturalistic, realistic, and symbolical. To these names must be added those of the Serbian poets Vejlko Petrović (1884–), also known for his short stories, and Sima Pandurović (1883–); the Croats Dragutin Domjanić (1875–1933), Sibe Miličić (1886–), and Vladimir Vidrić (1875–1909); and the Slovene Alojz Gradnik (1882–). The Serb poet and littérateur Svetislav Stefanović (1877–) is renowned also for his translations of Shakespeare, Rossetti, Swinburne, and Browning.

In poetry, the novel, and the drama, South Slav literature now offered materials for comparison and classification, and, moreover, the reading public had reached an adequate degree of intellectual maturity for the development of criticism. Its beginnings had been seen in the work of such men as Šenoa, Stritar and Marković (1846–1875), the first theorists of literature, who were responsible for the introduction of social ideas and the portrayal of actuality. Svetozar Marković was a Serbian publicist profoundly influenced by the ideas of the Russian critics Chernyshevsky, Dobrolyubov, and Pisarev. He was a political and social reformer rather than a true critic, but he did much to found the school of realism. Criticism proper appeared with the work of another Serb, Svetislav Vulović (1847–1898), and after him Ljubomir Nedić (1858–1902), a disciple of German aesthetics and a man of vast culture, who published a series of studies at the end of the century. Surpassing them are Jovan Skerlić (*q.v.*) and Bogdan Popović (*q.v.*), whose judgments formed in the French school reflect all the refinement and subtle penetration of their models. Together with the latter's brother, Pavle Popović (1868–1939), renowned for 40 years as the ablest historian of Yugoslav literature, these men represent the best of South Slav criticism and have had a far-reaching effect on the movement for national unity. In this connection may also be mentioned Božidar Knežević (1862–1905), eminent social philosopher and translator of Carlyle and Macaulay, and the political historian and sociologist Slobodan Jovanović (1869–), whose perfection in literary style has made him a model. Among the foremost Croat literary critics and historians are Milivoj Šrepel (1862–1905), Jakša Čedomil (1868–), Dinko Politeo (1854–1903), Djuro Šurmin (1867–), David Bogdanović (1869–), Antun Matoš (*q.v.*), Dragutin Prohaska (1881–), and Branko Vodnik (1879–); among the Slovenes are Ivan Prijatelj (1875–), Ivan Grafenauer (1880–), Janko Lavrin (1887–), and Josip Vidmar (1895–); other Serb critics include Andra Gavrilović (1864–) and Dragutin Subotić (1887–).

South Slav culture as a whole had by now ripened. Widespread interest existed in philosophy, history, science, ethics, psychology, sociology, and the arts. Cultural interchange with other countries had begun to flourish. Educational institutions had multiplied—Gymnasia, higher schools, and universities—and literary societies, publishing houses, and many reviews all contributed to the enlightenment and refinement of popular taste. The Serbian Academy of Sciences in Belgrade (founded in 1886 as an outgrowth of the older Society of Serbian Letters, founded in 1842 by Sterija-Popović) and the Yugoslav Academy of Science and Arts in Zagreb (founded in 1867 by the great Croat statesman, Bishop Juraj Strossmayer, 1815–1905) printed a mass of historical documents, works of ancient authors, collections of folklore, and at the same time developed closer relations among the provinces. Publishing houses such as the venerable Matica Srpska, the oldest among the South Slavs (founded in Budapest in 1826 and later transferred to Novi Sad), the Zagreb Matica Hrvatska (founded in 1842), and the Ljubljana Matica Slovenska (founded in 1863) issued periodicals and books. From 1900 on, in all South Slavic intellectual centers, the literature began to raise itself to the level of European accomplishment. The years preceding the First World War were a time of aspiration and experiment; nevertheless there was preserved a deep sense of continuity with the tradition of the past.

The Balkan Wars of 1912–1913 produced a fresh impetus, especially in Serbia. Older writers felt a new inspiration, while others hitherto unknown or undistinguished became important. Poetry especially showed the revived spirit of nationalism. Many collections of war poems in the national heroic style were published, as were numerous short stories of the wars. Besides those already mentioned, prose writers who attained recognition before 1918 included among the Serbs Petar Kočić (1877–1916) and Svetozar Ćorović (1875–1919), each the author of many excellent tales and one fine play, Milutin Uskoković (1884–1919), novelist and short-story writer, and Radoje Domanović (1873–1906), a fine satirist; among the Croats were the novelist Viktor Car-Emin (1870–), the poet Milan Begović (1876–), the dramatist, poet, and novelist Josip Kosor (1879–), the dramatist Srgjan Tucić (1873–), and the poet and dramatist Božo Lovrić (1881–); there were besides the Bosnian poet August Harambašić (1861–1911) and the Slovene novelist Ivo Šorli (1877–). Women began to win a place for themselves, *e.g.*, the Croat Ivana Brlić-Mažuranić (1874–1939), whose fairy tales for children have been translated into eight languages, including English; the Slovene feminist and journalist Zofka Kveder (1878–1926); the Serb essayist Isidora Sekulić (1886–); and the Serb poet Desanka Maksimović (1898–).

The immense sufferings and destruction caused by the First World War were reflected in, and to a certain extent counterbalanced by, the upsurge of national enthusiasm created by the political unification of the Serbs, Croats, and Slovenes in the new state of Yugoslavia. The post-war period raised many new problems in literature and produced many new genres, such as futurism, expressionism, and surrealism. Considerable progress was made along the path of dissolving the historical barriers arising from different alphabets (the Serbs employ the Cyrillic, the Croats and Slovenes, the Latin), different religions (the Serbs are predominantly Orthodox while the Croats and Slovenes are predominantly Roman Catholic), and geographical and political alignments. For centuries Serbian life had been turned toward Russia and the oriental world, while the character of Croatian and Slovenian culture was colored by German and Italian ways and ideas, until the middle of the 19th century when, as pointed out, French culture became an important influence upon all South Slav regions. Many obstacles remain, however, beside ancient prejudice, such as the inadequate knowledge in each of the several regions of the literatures of the others. Before the Second World War a closer relationship was clearly developing, as seen in the more intimate association of different authors, the publication of Croatian works in Serbian periodicals, of Serbian in Slovene, and so on in reciprocal fashion, besides the exchange of literary contributions and growing cooperation between the academies of Belgrade and Zagreb.

Perspective is so far lacking for an adequate appraisal of the great number of young writers who have appeared since 1918. Moreover, conditions of war have made the proper materials for study and comparison inaccessible. Certain general observations, however, may be made. In literature as in life a great ferment has been in progress. The reading public has enormously increased, and the book trade compares favorably in proportion with that of any other European country. The best work has continued to be found in poetry and the short story, particularly in Serbia. The novel has had many exponents, especially in Croatia, but so far, with some exceptions, it is of secondary importance. In general the novel may be said to deal with the manners of the several provinces, with social and psychological implications. Russian influence, so strong in the 19th century, has been to some extent replaced by contemporary French, German, and Scandinavian trends, though the Soviet novel has received considerable attention. Autobiography is a rarity, although the biographical novel is growing in popularity. The drama has become completely modernized. Like the novel, it deals principally with the actuality of existence and with the social and psychological problems of contemporary life. Some historical plays and verse dramas have achieved success.

Certain writers appear already to have won an established place. Foremost among them is Miroslav Krleža (*q.v.*), dramatist, novelist, critic, and poet. His is perhaps the strongest and most complete personality of the post-war era, widely popular and with considerable influence. His work has been extensively translated. Others include Misko Kranjec (1908–), a novelist of much power; Fran Bevk (1890–), dramatist and short-story writer; Ivo Andrić (*q.v.*) and Ivan Pregelj (1883–) who have won distinction in the short story; the poets Igo Gruden (1893–), Gustav Krklec (1899–), and Nikola Šop (1904–); and the two novelists Branimir Ćosić (1903–) and Stevan Jakovljević (1890–), whose portrayals of the war years and those following have made them among the most widely read of contemporary Yugoslav writers. This is to name only a few by way of suggestion, rather than as a summary.

A great deal of invaluable work has been done in the collection and study of folk materials, particularly the Serbo-Croatian heroic ballads, while the ballads of Slovenia have received belated attention, and yet more recently studies have been made of the popular poetry of the Moslems of Bosnia and Herzegovina. One of the most important collections of oral poetry in existence was made in 1933–1934 by Professor Milman Parry and Albert Lord on 2,500 double-records of Yugoslav poems, including one of some thirteen thousand lines, about the length of the *Odyssey*, and another of twelve thousand. This remarkable, not to say unique, collection, sponsored at first by Harvard and then by Columbia University, has been edited by the composer Béla Bartók. In this connection it is an interesting fact that the world-renowned Dalmatian sculptor, Ivan Meštrović, himself of peasant stock, knows by heart hundreds of lines of the ancient ballads and that the subjects of some of his most important work are the heroes of the Kosovo cycle.

At the present time a considerable portion of Yugoslav literature exists in translation in a large number of European languages. It has been late in appearing in English translation, though English and American literature has been liberally presented to Yugoslav readers. There exists a very good representation of the heroic ballads done by a number of competent English and American scholars. A fair number of modern short stories many be found in scattered form in periodicals and anthologies; writers thus represented include Karadžić, Jakšić, Lazarević, Ćorović, Matavulj, Stanković, Cankar, Andrić, and Pregelj, to name only a few. Some of the plays of Ivo Vojnović, Nušić, Kosor and Fran Bevk have received able renderings, as have selections from the poems of Prešeren, Levstik, Aškerc, Dučić, Rakić, Ilić, Kostić, Preradović, Nazor, and others. There exists a not inconsiderable body of critical literature in English, largely in periodicals. It is to be hoped that the post-war era will see a rapid expansion of literary interchange between Yugoslavia and the English-speaking world.

See: S. Šurmin, *Povijest književnosti hrvatske i srpske* (1908); P. Popović, *Pregled srpske književnosti* (1909) and *Jugoslovenska književnost* (1918); J. Skerlić, *Istorija nove srpske književnosti* (1914, 1921); D. Bogdanović, *Pregled književnosti hrvatske i srpske* (1915–1916); I. Prijatelj, *Slovenačka književnost* (1920); D. Prohaska, *Pregled savremene hrvatsko-srpske književnosti* (1921); Vasa Stajic, "The Centenary of the 'Matica Srpska'," *Slavonic Review,* VI (1927–1928), 593–602; Josip Vidmar, "Survey of Modern Slovene Literature," *Slavonic Review,* VI (1927–1928), 618–634; J. Grafenauer, *Slovenski biografski leksikon* (1928); P. Popovic and M. Ibrovac, "La Littérature yougoslave," *Monde slave,* 1930, Nos. 7–9, pp. 39–58, 161–185, 335–364; *Monde slave,* 1931, No. 9, pp. 447–469, bibliography of Yugoslav literature by R. Warnier; D. Subotić, *Yugoslav Popular Ballads; Their Origin and Development* (1932); N. Kravtsov, ed., *Serbskii epos* (1933); M. and J. Ibrovac, *Anthologie de la poésie yougoslave* (1935); B. Unbegaun, *Les Débuts de la langue littéraire chez les Serbes* (1935); M. Savković, *La Littérature yougoslave moderne* (1936); A. J. Klančar, "Survey of Yugoslav Literature," *Poet Lore,* L (1944), 37–44; K. and N. Strelsky, *Bibliography of Yugoslav Literature in English Translations and Criticism* (in press).

N. S.

Z

Zaitsev, Boris Konstantinovich (1881–, Russian novelist, short-story writer, and biographer), was born at Orel and spent much of his childhood on the Kaluga estate of his father, a mining engineer. Zaitsev studied at Kaluga and Moscow, but left the university for Italy, returning to Russia in 1904. A brief connection with a Marxist periodical in Moscow did not bear much fruit. Zaitsev was never a true realist: his gift is essentially subjective and lyric. His pre-revolutionary stories are delicately sketched impressions almost lacking in plot and sustained chiefly by a mystic atmosphere. Hostile to the Revolution, he left Russia in 1922 and settled in Paris. The stories included in *Ulitsa sv. Nikolaya* (1923; St. Nicholas Street) and *Strannoye puteshestviye* (1927; A Strange Trip) show an advance in narrative technique, as well as firmer characterization. At the same time Zaitsev embarked on longer works, tempering his subjectivism by the requirements of the novel form. *Zolotoi uzor* (1926; The Golden Pattern) is cast in the form of the autobiography of a singer, but also gives a picture of life in Russia and abroad. *Anna* (1929; Eng. tr., *Anna,* 1937) is a compact narrative of tragic love, set against the background of the Revolution. *Dom v Passy* (1935; The House in Passy), a rambling novel of the Russian *émigrés* in Paris, was a return to an earlier manner, but the unfinished *Puteshestviye Gleba* (Vol. I, 1937; Gleb's Journey) is another step forward. Of autobiographic inspiration and varied approach, this novel is his most promising achievement. Zaitsev's miscellaneous works reflect well his various interests. His accounts of his visits to Mt. Athos and Valaam, some of his stories, and *Prepodobny Sergi Radonezhski* (1925; St. Sergius of Radonezh) testify to his devotion to the Orthodox Church. The retrospective *Italiya* (1923; Italy) and *Moskva* (1939; Moscow) are autobiography as well as description. The book on Turgenev (1932) deals with a kindred spirit in Russian literature.

See: Y. Aikhenvald, *Siluety russkikh pisatelei,* Vol. III (1923); "Zaitsev," in *Literaturnaya entsiklopediya,* Vol. IV (1930); G. Struve, "Boris Zaytsev," *Slavonic Review,* XVII (1938–1939), 445–451.

P. A. P.

Zamyatin, Yevgeni Ivanovich (1884–1937, Russian novelist, dramatist, and naval engineer), was one of the most original and influential figures of the early Revolution. Always a heretic and a satirist, he clashed many times with government authorities. Born in Tambov Province, he graduated (1908) from the Polytechnical Institute of St. Petersburg, where he lectured on naval engineering both before and after the Revolution. He spent 1916–1917 in England constructing icebreakers, notably the famous *Lenin.* His first major work, *Uyezdnoye* (1911; District Tales), markedly influenced by Gogol and Remizov (*q.v.*), was followed by *Na kulichkakh* (1922; At the World's End), which led to the confiscation of the review that printed it. A leader in postrevolutionary cultural activities, he gave to many young writers, particularly the "Serapion Brothers," the pattern of their development. His single long novel, *My* (1922; Eng. tr., *We,* 1924), sometimes compared with Huxley's *Brave New World* in its satirical representation of a collective utopia, was never allowed publication in the U.S.S.R., and in 1929, through an unauthorized Prague edition translated from Czech back into Russian, it made its author the object of anathema at home. In 1931 he was allowed to leave the Soviet Union, and the last years of his life he spent in Paris engaged on a long work on Attila, whose era he saw reflected in the present age. His other works include *Vzroslym detyam skazki* (1922; Fables for Grown-up Children), *Ostrovityane* (1922; The Islanders), *Ogni svetova Dominika* (1923; The Fires of St. Dominic), *Peshchera* (1922; Eng. tr., *The Cave,* 1923), *Mamay* (1922; Eng. tr., 1933), and *Blokha* (1925; The Flea), a dramatization of a story by Leskov. Zamyatin's style is marked for its verbal effects and ornamentalism of speech. Essentially realistic, his work is often characterized by a symbolic grotesquerie and by what has been called a literary "cubism" in its angular, elliptical, and fragmentary structure.

See: G. Struve, *Soviet Russian Literature* (1935), pp. 17–22; A. Remizov, "Stoyat negasimuyyu svechu," *Sovremennyia zapiski,* LXIV (1937), 424–430.

N. S.

Zanella, Giacomo (1820–1888, Italian poet), was born in Chiampo, near Vicenza, in Venetia. Soon after his ordination as a priest in 1842 he was appointed to teach philosophy and belles-lettres at the seminary where he had studied. He displeased the Austrian authorities by his open sympathies with the political uprisings of 1848 and was suspended from his post in 1853 in spite of the protection of his diocesan. He was reappointed in 1857; and when Venetia was liberated he became professor of Italian language and literature at the University of Padua, of which he was rector for the year 1871–1872. Following his mother's death in 1872, the poet suffered a serious nervous breakdown and in 1876 abandoned his professorial duties. He spent the remaining years of his life in the modest villa which he had built on the banks of the Astichello, a few miles from Vicenza, engaging in leisurely literary activities and doing charitable deeds for his fellow villagers of Cavezzale.

While translating as class assignments poems from the ancient classics, Zanella developed a taste and style which came to bear the marks of his own sensitive temperament. Among English and American poets he especially admired Gray, Shelley, and Longfellow, making faithful, though never too literal renderings of such well-known poems as "To a Skylark," "Ode to the West Wind," "The Old Clock on the Stairs," "Excelsior," "The Wreck of the Hesperus." His own first collection, *Versi* (1868), brought him immediate recognition. Besides the usual occasional poems, there were longer compositions revealing the poet's deep concern over the revolutionizing theories of the Darwinian school. Zamella attains perfection of his style and lofty inspiration in the justly famous poem "Sopra una conchiglia fossile nel mio studio," in which, with bold strokes, he paints the successive phases of the evolutionary process, with man appearing on the scene as its culminating point. His unwillingness to accept man as merely an accidental episode in this process is further illustrated in other poems like "La Religione," "La Veglia," and "A mia madre," wherein he reveals a passionate desire to reconcile a deep-seated religious faith with the new scientific theories. Also noteworthy are the dialogue "Milton e Galileo," and the later poems, "L'Evoluzione" and "Le Palme fossili." In the series of charming sonnets, "L'Astichello" (interrupted by his death), the poet reveals a serenity of spirit in the presence of nature, slightly tinged with a kindly irony, which reminds the reader of Horace, Fray Luis de León, and Wordsworth.

Zanella's lyre had a limited number of strings, but his songs on fundamental human themes, social, religious, patriotic, and moral, are characterized by sentiments of profound delicacy, steadied by an abiding faith "in the ways of God to man." His complete *Poesie* were published in Florence in 1928, with a preface by Arturo Graf (*q.v.*). His other writings are *Scritti vari* (1877), *Vita di Palladio* (1880), *Storia della letteratura italiana dalla metà del settecento ai giorni nostri* (1880), and *Paralleli letterari* (1885).

See: F. Lampertico, *Giacomo Zanella* (1895); A. Zardo, *Giacomo Zanella nella vita e nella opere* (1905); G. Vitali, "Giacomo Zanella cinquant'anni dopo la sua morte," *Nuova Antologia,* CCCXCVII (1938), 443–458.

L. E. S.

Zapolska, Gabrjela (pseud. of Gabrjela Korwin-Piotrowska, 1860–1921, Polish novelist and playwright), was born at Kiewierka, a suburb of Łuck in Volhynia, the daughter of Józefa Karska, a famous opera singer and beauty, and Wincenty Korwin-Piotrowski, a well-to-do landowner. In 1878, at the age of 18, she entered into a loveless marriage with Konstanty Śnieżko-Błocki, a cavalry officer, but left him at the end of three years because of the impending birth of a child whose father was Marjan Gawalewicz, the well-known Warsaw writer and editor and founder of the Teatr Mały (Little Theatre). Without means of support, Zapolska turned to the stage, where she made a name for herself in all the cities of Poland. Later, in 1883, she began to write, novels at first and then plays. Her first story, "Jeden dzień z życia róży" (A Day in the Life of a Rose), was published in the *Kurjer krakowski* (Cracow Courier). The rest of her novels, however, appeared not in Cracow but in more liberal Warsaw, where the *Przegląd tygodniowy* (Weekly Review) of Wiślicki and Świętochowski (*q.v.*) was very friendly to her. In 1890 Zapolska left Poland for Paris, where for the ensuing five years she was a member of the famous *Théâtre Libre* of Antoine. The training she received here stood her in good stead in her later years as the founder and creator of the naturalist school of dramatic writing in Poland.

Zapolska disliked Paris intensely, and in 1896 she was back in Poland, there to make a name for herself as a veritable virtuoso of the theatrical art. Play after play flowed from her pen, the characters and situations of all of them being taken, as their creator declared, from scenes she herself witnessed "behind the window curtains" as she passed along the street. In *Kaśka Karjatyda* (1883) Zapolska made the humble, "red-kneed" housemaid dramatic material for the first time in Polish literature and with the two plays *Małka Szwarcenkopf* (1897) and *Jojne Firułkes* (1899) did the same for the Jew. The most popular of Zapolska's many dramas are the celebrated *Moralność Pani Dulskiej* (1907; The Moral Code of Madame Dulska), a "tragi-farce of bourgeois-dom," as Zapolska herself called it; *Skiz* (1909; The Highest Trump); *Ich czworo* (1912; Four of Them); and *Panna Maliczewska* (1912; Miss Maliczewska). All these plays, though at first anathematized by the clergy and shunned by the more conservative elements, were frequently revived in Free Poland and always before a full house. Zapolska has been called "the Polish Sacha Guitry, slightly enlarged."

See: Z. Konarzewski, "Zapolska w życiu i w literaturze," *Wiadomości literackie,* 1936, No. 22; K. Wierzyński, *W garderobie duchów* (1938), pp. 83–86, 101–103; T. Żeleński (Boy), *Romanse cieniów* (1935), pp. 154–159, and *Murzyn zrobił . . .* (1939), pp. 217–223, 264–267.

M. M. C.

Zech, Paul (1881–, German poet, novelist, and dramatist), was born in Briesen Rheinland. His adventurous life has always been the object of much mystery and controversy. The son of a teacher, he studied in Bonn, Heidelberg, and Zurich and later worked as a kind of voluntary proletarian in mines and factories. About 1910 he appeared in Berlin, where he published occasional issues of a luxuriously printed and illustrated periodical, *Das neue Pathos* (1913–1923). His own poetry is as eclectic as this periodical and is influenced by Rilke and Verhaeren, by Rimbaud (*qq.v.*) and the poets of German expressionism. In his many books of poetry he always insists upon attention to form and mastery of language; he never indulges in the explosive words of the expressionists. Most of his early verses are recollections of his proletarian experience: *Schollenbruch* (1910), *Die eiserne Brücke* (1912), *Das schwarze Revier* (1913). This is also true of the short stories published under the title *Der schwarze Baal* (1916). *Das Grab der Welt* (1918) and *Golgatha* (1919) evoke memories of his participation in the First World War. Later his poetry embraces larger issues and even strays into cosmic regions: *Das Terzett der Sterne* (1919), *Die Ballade von mir* (1922), *Die ewige Dreieinigkeit* (1924), and *Gesammelte Gedichte* (1927). Among his novels the following are remarkable: *Die Reise um den Kummerberg* (1924), *Das törichte Herz* (1925), *Die Geschichte einer armen Johanna* (1925), *Ich bin du* (1926), and "Deutschland, dein Tänzer ist der Tod," which was awarded a prize but has not yet been published. His most successful experiment in expressionism has been the "scenic ballad" *Das trunkene Schiff* (1924), a combination of music, drama, and film, dealing with a Negro revolt in Africa and a storm on the ocean and introducing aspects of Rimbaud's life. Other plays are *Steine* (1919), *Das Rad* (1924), *Der Turm* (1924), *Erde* (1925), and *Triumph der Söhne* (1925). When Hitler came to power Zech went voluntarily into exile and has since lived in South America, where he has published some volumes of poetry and an autobiographical novel, *Ich suchte Schmied und fand Malva* (1941).

See: W. Omankowski, "Paul Zech," *Die schöne Literatur,* XXVI (1925), 289–290; "Wer ist Eigentlich dieser Paul Zech?" (autobiography), *Deutsche Blätter,* 1943, Heft 11.

K. P.

Żeleński, Tadeusz (pseud. Boy, 1874–1942, Polish wit, critic, essayist, and translator), was born in Warsaw, the son of Władysław Żeleński, a noted composer, and Wanda Grabowska, an aunt of Kazimierz Tetmajer (*q.v.*). After studying at the Jagiellonian University in Cracow, Boy went to Paris in 1895 to study medicine and while there came under the influence of the brilliant *fin-de-siècle* literary movement. He returned to Poland an unofficial ambassador of French culture. While completing his medical studies in Cracow, he found time to establish the soon famous literary cabaret Zielony Balonik (Little Green Balloon), an imitation of the Parisian Chat Noir. For this he himself provided a stream of witty, satirical, frequently risqué ditties, skits, and lampoons, which were later published in a series of volumes, among them *Piosenki i fraszki Zielonego Balonika* (1908; Ditties and Trifles from the Zielony Balonik) and *Słówka* (1913; Mere Words). Boy's contributions were welcomed by the rebellious Young Poland set of Cracow (*see* Polish literature) as a breath of fresh air in a stifling room.

Boy did not practice medicine for long, but turned rather to translating, producing in this field in the space of three decades some 120 volumes of translations from the French alone (*Biblioteka Boya,* Boy's Library). Besides rendering into flawless Polish all Molière and most of Balzac, this tireless laborer translated also the works of such widely divergent authors as Villon, Rabelais, Montaigne, Descartes, Racine, Marivaux, Voltaire, Beaumarchais, Chateaubriand, Stendhal, Verlaine (*q.v.*), Proust (*q.v.*), and many others, prefacing his translation in each case with an illuminating essay on the author in question. The type of criticism gradually evolved in the course of these essays came to be known as "boyism." Its principal marks were keen psychological penetration, clever and telling use of anecdotes, and great skill in the evocation of personality. Boy's most notable long studies are his *Molière* (1924), *Pani Hańska* (1926), a lively portrait of Balzac's Evelina, and *Marysieńka Sobieska* (1938), a somewhat unorthodox interpretation of the French queen of the Polish national hero, King John III.

Boy was as deeply versed in Polish as in French literature and in this field as in the French often shattered time-hallowed interpretations. He did this by a process he himself christened "de-bronzing," which consisted of scraping ruthlessly away from the figures of the great the accumulated patina of tradition, thus exposing all the passions and foibles that lay underneath, as well as all the virtues and true greatness. A major literary tempest was stirred up in the early 30's when Boy applied this process to Mickiewicz, the great 19th-century romantic poet and patriot (*Bronzownicy,* 1930; Those Who Bronze Over). When the storm had subsided, Boy proceeded to present fresh and revealing sidelights on another great literary figure from the past, namely the dramatist Aleksander Fredro (*Obrachunki Fredrowskie,* 1934; Settling Scores with Fredro).

Boy was Free Poland's outstanding dramatic critic. His articles in this field fill many volumes (*Flirt z Melpomeną,* 20 vols.; *Romanse cieniów,* 1935, Romances of the Shadows; *Murzyn zrobił . . .* 1939, A Hack's Work . . .) and cover the entire theatrical life of post-war Poland. They are invaluable documents for the study of social trends.

A fearless crusader against hypocrisy whether in life or literature, Boy often aroused public sentiment pro and con by his espousal of advanced causes. In *Dziewice konsystorskie* (1929; Virgins before the Bar) he stated the case for divorce and for the marriage of the clergy. In *Piekło kobiet* (1929; Women's Hell) he made a plea for birth control and legalized abortion. The readers of the Warsaw journals *Kurjer poranny* (Morning Courier) and *Wiadomości literackie* (Literary News) looked forward to Boy's *feuilletons,* which were written with French clarity, Polish humor, and a scientist's passion for truth.

Boy refused to leave Poland when the Germans occupied Warsaw in 1939. He fled to Lwów, at first under Soviet occupation, and there continued to write and translate. With the German occupation of Lwów in 1941, he was seized and removed to the concentration camp of Dachau, where he died a martyr's death.

See: F. L. Schoell, "L'Enfant terrible de la Pologne," *La Pologne,* 1931, pp. 580–600; W. Weintraub, "Tadeusz Żeleński (Boy)," *Wiadomości polskie,* 1942, No. 37.

H. C.

Żeromski, Stefan (pseuds. Maurycy Zych and Józef Katerla, 1864–1925, Polish novelist and dramatist), was born at Strawczyna in the Kielce district of Russian Poland, of gentry stock lately impoverished as a consequence of the unsuccessful uprising of 1863. He spent most of his childhood on the estate of Ciekoty in the beautiful Holy Cross Mountains on the River Lubrzanka. Descriptions of this countryside and of his school days in the Russian Gymnasium in Kielce appear repeatedly in Żeromski's writings, the latter especially in the *Nicholas Nickleby* of Polish fiction, *Syzyfowe prace* (1898; Sisyphean Labors). A series of tragic happenings—the death of his adored mother, the collapse of a love affair with his cousin Ludwika Dunin-Borkowska, the scandal of his sister Olesia's severance of home ties (later used by Żeromski as the theme of *Dzieje grzechu,* 1908, The History of a Sin), his father's remarriage and sudden death, climaxed by his own contraction of tuberculosis—all this plunged Żeromski even deeper into the despair to which he had been born as a child of the post-uprising era and caused him abruptly to flee from the scene of so much unhappiness. Without finishing at the Gymnasium, he went to Warsaw and took a course at the veterinary school, hoping that this would fit him quickly to earn a living. In Warsaw, Żeromski became involved at once in conspiratorial activities with the future leader of Polish national thought, Roman Dmowski, and was for a while imprisoned in the Citadel. After this, half-starved and suffering from tuberculosis, Żeromski abandoned Warsaw, to spend the next few years on various estates in the country, where he was able to earn a living by tutoring. After his marriage in 1892, Żeromski left Poland to travel in Western Europe and eventually to spend four years (1892–1896) in Rapperschwil on Lake Zurich as assistant librarian of the Polish National Museum. On his return to Poland in 1897, Żeromski continued to work as a librarian, serving now as assistant to Tadeusz Korzon in the famous Zamoyski Library in Warsaw. It was not until 1904, when he had reached the age of 40, that Żeromski found himself free from the necessity of holding a routine job and able to devote himself entirely to writing.

Though he made his literary début as early as 1889, Żeromski attracted little attention until 1895, with his *Rozdziobią nas kruki, wrony* (Carrion for Crows and Ravens), which was followed in 1896 with the even more striking *Opowiadania* (Tales). The line of thinking marked out in these led naturally to the novel *Ludzie bezdomni* (1900; The Homeless) with which Żeromski climaxed the first epoch of his development. All the works from this period are case studies of the Polish intellectual of the post-positivist era, of the man who, inspired by a Promethean dream of serving his fellows, meets only with inertia and despair in the execution of his dream and becomes in the end, like Prometheus himself, a victim of his own idealism. The classic example of the type, to which Żeromski himself belonged, is Tomasz Judym of *Ludzie bezdomni,* a young physician who, returning to his native village full of ideals of social service, quickly becomes aware of the cleavage between his purposes and the practices of the "pillars of society," including his own father.

After completing his portrait of the Pole of his own generation, Żeromski turned to portray in the epic *Popioły* (1904; Eng. tr., *Ashes,* 1928) the era of "heroic conflict," as he called it, dominated by Napoleon. A vast, chaotic work, crowded with an immense amount of detail and illuminating every aspect of Polish life in that epoch, *Popioły* is at its best in the rapturous descriptions of the Polish landscape with which it abounds. In this, as in *Wierna rzeka* (1912; The Faithful River), a story of the 1863 uprising, in *Wiatr od morza* (1922; The Wind from the Sea), and finally in *Puszcza jodłowa* (1925; The Fir Forest), Żeromski demonstrated beyond doubt that his true talent lay in lyric description.

In his final years Żeromski set himself the task of mastering the dramatic form and again succeeded, in the comedy *"Uciekła mi przepióreczka"* (1924; My Little Quail Has Fled), in depicting his own generation of Poles convincingly. An indefatigable worker till the day of his death, Żeromski was a warrior to the last in the cause of intellectual freedom. Death overtook him in the midst of a bitter controversy over the novel *Przedwiośnie* (1925; Early Spring), which officialdom charged was pro-Communist. With his passing, however, party animosities were forgotten, and Żeromski was given a state funeral. He will go down in literary history as a great stimulator of Polish thought and a great poet of the Polish landscape.

See: *Wiadomości literackie,* 1925, No. 103; Z. L. Zaleski, "Etienne Zeromski," *Le Monde slave,* January, 1926, pp. 25–42; G. Korbut, *Literatura polska* (1931), IV, 289–295; K. Czachowski, *Obraz współczesnej literatury polskiej,* II (1934), 188–233, 234–236, 427–439; W. Borowy, "Żeromski," *Slavonic Review,* XIV (1935–1936), 403–416.

A. P. C.

Zeyer, Julius (1841–1901, Czech poet, novelist, and dramatist), occupies a position roughly analogous to that of the Pre-Raphaelites in England. He was born in Prague, the son of a timber merchant. His father was of Alsatian origin, his mother Jewish. He studied languages at the University of Prague, but soon after left Bohemia to make various journeys —he spent several years in Russia as a private tutor, traveled in Italy and Greece, France and Spain. Later in his life he lived in a southern Bohemian town, Vodňany, in almost complete seclusion. He died in Prague.

As an epic poet Zeyer can best be compared with William Morris. Like Morris he spun out enormously long narrative poems based on themes of medieval literature and legends, in a decorative and even ornate style. One cycle of shorter epics is drawn from legendary Czech antiquity (*Vyšehrad,* 1880), another is an elaborate rewriting of many of the *chansons de geste* (*Karolinská epopeje,* 1896; The Carolingian Epopee), another retells under the title *Z letopisů lásky* (4 vols., 1889–1892; From the Annals of Love) such stories as those of Aucassin and Nicolette, Ghismonda, and Gabriel de Espinosa. Outside of these large cycles, two longer poems deal with Celtic matters; *Ossianův návrat* (1885; Ossian's Return) develops a theme which was suggested by Macpherson's poems, and *Kronika o sv. Brandanu* (1886; The Chronicle of St. Brendan) revives an ancient Irish legend.

Zeyer's prose consists in part of similar retellings of legends and stories drawn from every conceivable country. One volume was appropriately called *Obnovené obrazy* (1894; Restored Pictures), a title which describes excellently the almost antiquarian method. The longest of these restorations is *Román o věrném přátelství Amise a Amila* (1880; The Romance of the True Friendship of Amis and Amile) which revives an Old French theme, while other stories range as far as Japan and China. Possibly the more individual and independent *Tři legendy o krucifixu* (1895; Three Legends of the Cross) represents his greatest success among his short stories. The novels, though loosely constructed and sentimental in tone, express most clearly Zeyer's own personality under the thin disguises of his heroes. *Jan Maria Plojhar* (2 vols., 1888) is placed in Italy and has a hero after Zeyer's own heart: melancholy, homesick, torn by love for two women, dying of tuberculosis, groping his way towards a belief in God. *Dům u tonoucí hvězdy* (1894; The House at the Drowning Star), though ostensibly the story of a Slovak lost in Paris, is a self-portrait which attempts a psychological analysis of a weary and sick soul. The many dramas, though remarkable as uncompromising poetic dramas in verse, are much less successful, as Zeyer's talent was too lyrical and decorative for the stage. Two tragedies, *Doňa Sanča* (1889), a Spanish theme, and *Neklan* (1893), drawn from Old Czech history, are the most impressive on the stage. The other plays, which include fairy tales and legends such as *Radúz a Mahulena* (1896), remain closet dramas, enlivened by lyrical beauties.

Zeyer could be called a precursor of decadence: early in his life he was interested in mysticism and the occult, and he has moved in the direction of a highly aesthetic Catholicism. His mind circled round the conflict between earthly and heavenly love and came to rest on a vague, Christian Platonism. But Zeyer was saved from the ivory tower by his intense nationalism which was, however, a purely elegiac mourning for the sufferings of his nation and the glories of its past. His style was highly cultivated and even decorative and overornate, but at his best Zeyer gave expression to a nostalgic neo-romanticism of rare and even rarefied beauty.

See: J. V. Krejčí, *Julius Zeyer* (1901); J. Voborník, *Julius Zeyer* (1907); Miloš Marten, *Julius Zeyer* (1910); J. Viškovatá, *Ruské motivy v tvorbě Julia Zeyera* (1932). There are German translations of *Jan Maria Plojhar* and *Amis a Amil* and an anthology of short stories, *Florenz im Schnee,* tr. by R. Wellek (1924).

R. W.

Zillich, Heinrich (1898–, Transylvanian-German novelist), was born in Kronstadt, Transylvania. His first literary endeavors deal with childhood recollections, after which he proceeded to treat Transylvanian folklore and peoples, the First World War, cultural relations between Transylvania and Germany, and, most recently, the larger aspects of racial interdependence in Central and Southeastern Europe.

The short story *Der Vater* (1921) was Zillich's earliest publication. Others of this type include *Der Urlaub* (1933), *Die Reinerbachmühle* (1935), and *Der baltische Graf* (1937). Several collections of short stories, *e.g.*, *Der Toddergerch* (1930) and *Sturz aus der Kindheit* (1933), have also been published. Less effective but still indicative of his devotion to Transylvania are the collections of poems, *Strömung und Erde* (1929) and *Komme, was will* (1935). Zillich achieved full literary recognition in Germany with the novel *Zwischen Grenzen und Zeiten* (1936), a semi-autobiographical *Bildungsroman* depicting the part played by Transylvania in the First World War. A later novel, *Der Weizenstrauss* (1938), reveals the complete maturity of the author's style. The aftermath of war provides the subject matter. In 1924 Zillich founded the periodical *Klingsor* (editor, 1924–1936), devoted to German culture in Transylvania. His prose writings incline toward history as it affects and is affected by a small national or racial unit. Zillich represents an active, virulent group of Transylvanian "Heimatdichter."

See: W. J. Mueller, "Heinrich Zillich," *Monatshefte für deutschen Unterricht*, XXXII (1940), 198–204.

W. J. M.

Zola, Emile (1840–1902, French novelist, dramatist, and critic), would according to his own terminology be called the product of two geographical factors. Aix-en-Provence ("Plassans" in his novels), where he spent virtually the first 18 years of his life, and Paris, the city of his birth and his permanent residence after 1858, combined to make him a romanticist at heart notwithstanding his naturalistic label.

"I am only a poet," Zola exclaimed once while on trial at the time of the Dreyfus affair. The poetical streak in him, very deep and very real, was a gift from the South: from his father (1795–1847), an Italian engineer and a naturalized Frenchman, whose head was full of grandiose architectural schemes; from his friends—one of them Paul Cézanne, the future painter—in whose company he roamed the countryside and acquired a love of nature and sunlight which was to permeate his aesthetics, thus creating strong affinities between him and the new school of painting (see *Mon Salon*, 1866; *Edouard Manet*, 1867); from adolescent dreams which find a naïve and sentimental expression in his first published work (*Contes à Ninon*, 1864). Later, the *petite fleur bleue* will never fail to blossom in the corner of even his darkest novels.

Paris, on the other hand, the Paris of the Second Empire, prosperous but politically suppressed, hiding behind a magnificent façade untold depths of vice and misery—Paris stood in his eyes as a symbol of the modern metropolis, where success justifies everything and the Darwinian struggle for life becomes a grim reality. Near-starvation in 1860–1861, then mediocre jobs and journalistic ventures taught him the meaning and value of the word *experience*. Zola was now ready to appreciate the down to earth quality of such authors as Stendhal, Flaubert (*q.v.*), and the Goncourt brothers (*q.v.*), with the all important difference that, unlike them, he felt disinclined to conceal or disguise his personality. He gathered a group of essays and book reviews under the virulent title *Mes Haines* (1866), stating in the text that a work of art was "a corner of Creation seen through a temperament" and in the preface that his duty as an artist was to come forward and "live aloud" (*vivre tout haut*). This, of course, was a romantic motto—the very motto of fighters and would-be reformers like Hugo, Michelet, and even to a certain extent Balzac. It was to remain characteristic of Zola's frame of mind, as opposed to that of the so-called "realists" and to the cynicism and despair of his own naturalistic followers (*see* French naturalism). In the thick of his "campaigns," against a mounting tide of criticism and abuse, he kept on insisting, with seemingly good reason and unquestionable sincerity, that his whole purpose was progressive and educational.

For some 25 years Zola made heroic efforts to double, as it were, his usefulness to mankind by reconciling his reformist zeal with a pretension to scientific accuracy. Having fallen, in more or less orthodox fashion, under the spell of positivism, he fancied himself a practical sociologist or, as he would say, a "physician of the social body." He adapted to his own ends the rigid determinism of Hippolyte Taine (*q.v.*) and considered *Thérèse Raquin* (1867), his first "naturalistic" novel, as the literary counterpart of a surgical autopsy. Dr. Prosper Lucas and his far from reliable *Traité philosophique et physiologique de l'hérédité naturelle* (2 vols., 1847–1850) fired him with the belief that the laws of heredity and the influence of environment could be mathematically ascertained—whereupon he proceeded to draw up the family tree of his Rougon-Macquart, a fictitious collection of 32 individuals, heavily beset with irregularities of blood and nerves, whose "natural and social history under the Second Empire" he would subsequently record in a succession of interlocking volumes. Finally, Claude Bernard's epoch-making *Introduction à l'étude de la médecine expérimentale* (1865) prompted him to apply and later to formulate the famous theory of the "experimental novel" (*Le Roman expérimental,* 1880; Eng. tr., *The Experimental Novel,* 1894). Taken literally, this theory would liken the play and interplay of fictional characters to that of chemical compounds in a test tube. On the strength of these mechanistic premises Zola ingenuously expected to reach definite conclusions which in turn would be of use to the social worker or legislator in wiping out a number of humanity's plague spots.

There is little doubt that the immense cycle of the *Rougon-Macquart,* comprising 20 volumes (1871–1893; Eng. tr. by E. A. Vizetelly, 20 vols., 1885–1907) and several dramatic and operatic adaptations, represents one of the proudest achievements of French literature. To be sure, some installments of the series are now almost completely neglected, including the first and last (*La Fortune des Rougon,* 1871; *Le Docteur Pascal,* 1893), which supply the key to the pseudo-scientific designs of the author. A few survive only because they have an air of scandal about them (*Nana,* 1880; *La Terre,* 1887). Enough others remain, however, to reveal, not indeed an experimental novel, but a gigantic prose poem, a sort of "legend of the century" replete with powerful symbols. Such is the barroom in *L'Assommoir* (1877), Zola's most finished work and that which rightly established his reputation. Such are the central markets of the capital in *Le Ventre de Paris* (1873) and *La Joie de vivre* (1884), the paradisiac garden of Paradou in *La Faute de l'abbé Mouret* (1875), the department store in *Au bonheur des dames* (1883), the dark, twisting coal mines and the mob of maddened strikers in *Germinal* (1885), the unfinished masterpiece of painting in *L'Œuvre* (1886), the locomotive in *La Bête humaine* (1890), the tread of a defeated army in *La Débâcle* (1892). To all practical and poetical purposes *La Débâcle* rather than *Le Docteur Pascal* forms the closing chapter of the *Rougon-Macquart.* In the shadows of Sedan a hated regime crashes to the ground and another arises, bringing with it the promise of a spiritual awakening.

After 1893 Zola, now a prominent, controversial figure, left his "laboratory" and emerged openly as a romantic pilgrim and crusader. The trilogy entitled *Les Trois Villes* (*Lourdes,* 1894; *Rome,* 1896; *Paris,* 1898; Eng. tr. by E. A. Vizetelly, 3 vols., 1894–1898) and the unfinished series called *Les Quatre Evangiles* (*Fécondité,* 1899; *Travail,* 1901; the posthumous *Vérité,* 1903; and the missing panel *Justice;* Eng. tr. by E. A. Vizetelly, 3 vols., 1900–1903) were intended to sing the litanies of a kind of Christian socialism after the manner of Tolstoy (*q.v.*). At the same time the indomitable campaigner entered the Dreyfus fray with his sensational *J'accuse,* an open letter addressed to the president of the republic and charging the whole War Department with having plotted the condemnation of an innocent man. This document was published in Georges Clemenceau's (*q.v.*) newspaper, *Aurore,* on January 13, 1898. Twice brought to trial for "insulting the Army," Zola chose to flee to England in order to escape arrest. He returned in 1899 under cover of a general amnesty, hailed as a hero by the people and by Anatole France (*q.v.*) as "a moment of the human conscience."

On September 28, 1902, Zola was asphyxiated in his sleep by emanations of carbonic acid issuing from a defective chimney. Several years later (1908) the Third Republic rewarded a life of labor and truly "republican" service by transferring his remains to the Panthéon.

See (besides the bibliography under French naturalism and Zola, *Œuvres complètes,* with notes and commentaries by Maurice Le Blond, 50 vols., 1927–1929): Henri Massis, *Comment Zola composait ses romans* (1906); Fernand Doucet, *L'Esthétique d'Emile Zola et son application à la critique* (1923); Matthew Josephson, *Zola and His Time* (1928); Marcel Batilliat, *Emile Zola* (1931); Henri Barbusse, *Zola* (1932; Eng. tr., 1933).

J.-A. B.

Zoshchenko, Mikhail Mikhailovich (1895–, Russian humorist), was born in Poltava, the son of a provincial painter, and studied at the faculty of jurisprudence of the University of St. Petersburg. During the First World War he served as an officer in the imperial forces, but after the October Revolution joined the Red army. In 1922 he joined the Petersburg literary circle, the Serapion Brothers, and since then his work has appeared in various Soviet periodicals. His chief genre is a satirical short story in which he narrates humorous incidents from the daily life of the lower middle class and the petty officialdom of Soviet Russia. The influence of the early Chekhov, of Averchenko, Remizov (*qq.v.*), and Leskov is apparent in Zoshchenko's narratives, told in the slang of the characters whose philistinism he lampoons.

Zoshchenko's short stories have been published in numerous editions and under various titles, the first one of importance being *Uvazhayemyie grazhdane* (Vol. I, 1926, Vol. II, 1940; Respected Citizens). He has also written a few short novels (*e.g.*, *Vozvrashchennaya molodost,* 1933, The Returned Youth) and a few one-act farces (*Svadba,* 1922, The Wedding; *Prestupleniye i nakazaniye,* 1932, Crime and Punishment). Several collections of his short stories have appeared in English (*Russia Laughs,* 1935; *The Woman Who Could Not Read,* 1940).

See: Zoshchenko, *Statyi i materialy* (1928).

O. M.

Zuccoli, Luciano (1870–1930, Italian editor and novelist), was born in Milan, the scion of a noble German family (von Ingenheim) transplanted in Italy. He will remain in Italian contemporary literature as a characteristic figure, although his plots are often melodramatic, his love pages reminiscent of those in pulp magazines, and his prose crude and labored. He will endure because in spite of all these shortcomings he possessed so colorful a personality. In politics he had the courage of his convictions, and against the trends of his epoch he was a militant, outspoken tory, in favor of the military tradition and colonial conquests and opposed to any democratic innovation. He was also one of the few who did not succumb to the lure of decadence in literature and paid no homage to D'Annunzio (*q.v.*), the literary tyrant of his day. Faithful to a half-romantic and half-naturalistic formula, he derived his inspiration from three sources: out of experiences in military life as a cavalry officer he composed one of the few novels sympathetic to soldiers—with certain satirical overtones—*Ufficiali, sottufficiali, caporali e soldati* (1902); from his life in society he created many types of women, always portrayed with penetration and benign indulgence for their weaknesses; and finally he succeeded, sometimes with more depth than might be expected of him, in exploring the feelings of youth in that exciting period of life when love is first discovered, *Le Cose più grandi di lui* (1922; Eng. tr., *Things Greater than He,* 1926). Another of his novels of this genre is *L'Occhio del fanciullo* (1914). Women were his ardent readers, eagerly awaiting his new novels; and Zuccoli, like a good baker, turned one out of his mental oven almost every year, from 1900 to the year of his death. The most famous remain *Il Maleficio occulto* (1901), *L'Amore di Loredana* (1908), *La Freccia nel fianco* (1913). And if he did not strike at the roots of the upper middle class of Lombardy of that period, he was successful in presenting a faithful picture of how the people in that class imagined themselves to be.

See: L. Russo, *I Narratori* (1923), pp. 202–206; P. Pancrazi, "Zuccoli o l'amico delle donne," *Pegaso,* I (1930), 99–101.

G. P.

Zuckmayer, Carl (1896–, German poet, dramatist, and novelist), son of a manufacturer, was born at Nackenheim on the Rhine; he attended the Gymnasium at Mainz until 1914. Four years in the First World War were followed by study at Heidelberg of the natural sciences. Belonging to the young radical literati after the war, Zuckmayer soon devoted his formative years to writing. The inflation forced him to try all kinds of work. After having been a play reader for the Reinhardt theatres he wrote the hilarious comedy *Der fröhliche Weinberg,* (1925), which brought the author the Kleist prize and the dislike of the Nazi party. Zuckmayer settled down, not far from Salzburg in Austria, to an industrious career with his gifted pen. A drama about Germany's famous outlaw, *Schinderhannes* (1927), proved a literary success. German pre-war militarism was satirized in *Der Hauptmann von Köpenick* (1931; Eng. tr., *The Captain of Köpenick,* 1932), and his anti-war feelings were expressed in a number of adaptations, *Rivalen* (1929) from the American play *What Price Glory* by Anderson and Stallings and *Kat* (1931), a dramatization of Ernest Hemingway's novel *A Farewell to Arms.* Since Zuckmayer's plays abound in action, they have found their way into the films, and Zuckmayer has a number of successful movie scenarios to his credit. When the political flood reached Zuckmayer's mountain home and Hitler in 1938 overran Austria, Zuckmayer escaped via Switzerland and France to America. Mention must be made of his prose works (although they never attained the success of his plays): *Der Bauer aus dem Taunus* (1929), *Die Affenhochzeit* (1932), *Salvare oder die Magdalene von Bozen* (1936; Eng. tr., *The Moons Ride Over,* 1937), *Herr über Leben und Tod* (1938). Recollections in autobiographical form under the title *Second Wind* (1940; in English only) tell a vivid story of Zuckmayer's interesting career and his finding a haven in the hills of Vermont.

H. Bf.

Župančič, Oton (1878–, Slovene poet), is the best known of contemporary Slovenian lyricists. Writing in a language used by one of the smallest nations in Europe (Slovenians number less than 1,500,000), a language almost beyond adequate translation into, say, French, German, and English, he has nevertheless won international attention and interest.

He was born on January 23, 1878, in the little town of Vinica, in Bela Krajina, a region which is part of Kranjsko (Krain or Carniola), then and until 1918 a province of Austria. His parents were peasants, somewhat above the average in economic standing. They sent him to the Gymnasium in Novo Mesto, a small provincial city, and later to another Gymnasium in Ljubljana, the capital of Carniola and the cultural center of the Slovenian people. After completing these *srednje šole* (middle schools), he took four years at the University of Vienna, majoring in history and geography, and then continued these studies in Paris. In 1920, after most of Slovenia had been made part of the new state of Yugoslavia, he was appointed art director and manager of the National Dramatic Theatre in Ljubljana, perhaps the most important cultural position in the tiny country. For many years he was also head of the Institute of French Studies in Ljubljana.

While still in the Gymnasium, Župančič began to write little youthful poems about childhood, full of simple charm and unusual insight into the innocently mischievous spirit of very young human beings, communicating their dreamworld to the reader with a beautiful directness. In 1900 some of these early poems were gathered into a volume entitled *Pisanice* (Easter Eggs). Ten years later, as a mature artist, he returned to this sort of poetry, writing for and about his own children, delighting in them and their experiences; and in 1915 there appeared two collections of this juvenile poetry, which may be read as pleasurably by grown-ups as by youngsters, *Ciciban in še kaj* (Ciciban and a Thing or Two Besides) and *Sto ugank* (One Hundred Riddles).

His first book appeared in 1899, *Čaša opojnosti* (Cup of Intoxication), in which, working under the influence of Central and Western European symbolism and decadent concepts, he was not quite himself. In his next two collections, however, in *Cez plan* (1904; Across the Plain) and *Samogovori* (1908; Monologues), he gradually got away from exoticism and artificiality, finally achieving a natural maturity through doubt, unhappiness, and self-examination.

Now, from the late 1900's on, he began to confront his own personal problems and those of his hard-pressed nation with a strange sort of calmness that was much more stirring and stimulating than had been his former symbolic hints of doom. His thought-texture turned confident, almost optimistic; his passions got on an even keel; his poetic form reached a firm lyricism that is a pleasure to read and an intellectual experience. He became a moral force in the life of his people, a very intimate factor in its important spiritual processes, a source of patriotic feeling and thinking, a stabilizing (yet not conservative) influence. This role of the poet became especially clear in *V zarje Vidove* (1920; Toward the Dawn of St. Vitus's Day).

In 1924 he published *Veronika Deseniška* (Veronica of Desenice), a play in verse which failed both as poetry and drama and indicated that his creative talent lay largely in short lyrical outpourings. After this, Župančič tried no new forms. He revised his works, which began to appear in Ljubljana in a four volume edition in 1935. Meantime he translated into superb Slovenian all of the important Shakespeare plays, several John Galsworthy novels, and other books from the English and Russian.

During the first two decades of the 20th century, the average educated person in Slovenia was apt to speak the Slovenian language affectedly. As art director of the National Theatre, Župančič insisted that actors speak naturally, in the manner of the plain people, even when enacting educated characters. This, and the wide reading of his own naturally idiomatic poetry, worked against artificiality and affectation in Slovenian speech—a matter of great moral and national importance to the Slovenian people. There is no doubt that in other respects too Župančič's poetry, written many years before, has played an important part in the development of the amazing Slovenian (and the larger Yugoslav) liberation movement. Much of the success of the Slovenian guerrilla fighting during the Second World War can be traced to Župančič's poems published 15 and 20 years earlier, which were addressed to Slovenian young people, urging them to spend their free days and hours in their native mountains and get acquainted with the cliffs, caves, gorges, and chasms. He himself was throughout his youth and prime a passionate outdoor man and mountain climber.

When, early in May, 1945, Slovenia was liberated by the Slovenian Partisan army, which had come into existence during the four-year Fascist-Nazi occupation, Župančič's poem celebrating the occasion—perhaps his best work—was read by one of the heroes of the War of Liberation to an assembled multitude in Ljubljana as a highlight of the patriotic festivities.

See: A. Cronia, *Ottone Župančič* (1928); L. Sever, *Ottone Župančič* (1928); L. Tesnière, *Oton Joupantchitch, poète slovène; l'homme et son œuvre* (1931); J. Vidmar, *Oton Župančič* (1935).

L. A.

Zweig, Arnold (1887–, German novelist and essayist), was born in Glogau, Silesia, of a Jewish middle-class family. Master of a superior-ironic style and of an apparently innocent approach to the most daring situations, he shows at first an interest in aesthetic mastery of the delicate and refined problems of modern man with his exaggerated sensibility—problems typical not of the great masses, however, but of a thin layer of intellectuals. His initial success was *Novellen um Claudia* (1912; Eng. tr., *Claudia,* 1930), a wreath of short stories that depict the suffering of a young woman from supersensitiveness and inhibitions and the final toilsome conquest of these through instinctive, natural forces. Zweig shows a predilection for the experiences of young people; he detaches himself with an air of benevolent irony, but he is obviously enamored of the world of youth.

The First World War provided the revolutionary experience that turned Zweig away from his preoccupation with the problems of modern intellectualism. It gave substance and ethos to his work and made him the author of one of the greatest war novels, *Der Streit um den Sergeanten Grischa* (1927; Eng. tr., *The Case of Sergeant Grischa,* 1927), published as the central panel of a projected "triptych" intended to give a broad picture and criticism of the war as it resulted from and reacted upon a class-torn, capitalistic society. The series now includes three additional novels (the author has promised still more): *Junge Frau von 1914* (1931; Eng. tr., *Young Woman of 1914,* 1932), *Erziehung vor Verdun* (1935; Eng. tr., *Education before Verdun,* 1936), and *Einsetzung eines Königs* (1937; Eng. tr., *The Crowning of a King,* 1938). In these novels the individual is always the center of interest; from him start all approaches to the problems raised by the war. Community values are recognized in terms of social class and a future socialist society, though references to racial affinities appear not infrequently. A transcendental law is conceived within the teachings of the Torah.

The story of the Russian sergeant, Grischa, who fell victim to a power-intoxicated Prussian war machine, is Zweig's best. While presenting a sequence of events in a well-knit plot, he depicts at the same time the social organism of the German army. Various classes and types appear, from the common man in the labor service to the commander in chief himself. The flight of a Russian prisoner, his adventures, recapture, trial and death sentence as a result of mistaken identity, the establishment of his innocence and his final judicial murder, make up the thread of the plot. It leads with inevitable logic through the various military strata, which thereby become the colorful milieu of a strong narrative.

Here as well as in the other novels, Zweig's mastery of form controls his creative imagination, and freedom of poetic disposition is tempered by his knowledge of persons and situations. Genuine sympathy for suffering humanity is coupled with objective realism. His presentation has that degree of inner probability which reports, describes, and entertains and creates in the reader a true basis for a vicarious experience.

When Zweig was driven out of Germany, the manuscript of *Erziehung vor Verdun* was destroyed, and it had to be rewritten while he struggled heroically against serious eye disease. Zweig now lives and works in Palestine, which is the setting of his novel *De Vriendt kehrt heim* (1933; Eng. tr., *De Vriendt Goes Home,* 1933). Zweig has been successful also as an essayist and editor. He is an active Zionist, and an account of the Jewish contribution to modern German culture is given in *Bilanz der deutschen Judenheit 1933* (1934; Eng. tr., *Insulted and Exiled,* 1937). His latest novel, *The Axe of Wandsbeck* (1946), deals with the Third Reich and was first published in Great Britain in English translation.

See: W. Mahrholz, *Deutsche Literatur der Gegenwart* (1930), pp. 189–191; W. K. Pfeiler, *War and the German Mind* (1941), pp. 129–139.

W. K. P.

Zweig, Stefan (1881–1942, Austrian biographer, novelist, dramatist, and poet), represented a tragically premature cosmopolitan culture. Born into a well-to-do Jewish family, he grew up as a most conscious son of Vienna, the city that harmonized various national, linguistic, and cultural elements into a synthesis of all Western civilization. He found recognition in his teens, when the "Young Vienna" of Schnitzler, Beer-Hofmann, Bahr, Altenberg, and, above all, Hugo von Hofmannsthal (*qq.v.*) ruled the day. At the age of 19 he published the poems *Silberne Seiten* (1901), the first in a series of works written with the *élan* of an intellectual and formative playfulness. Not too self-confident as a writer, he began on Dehmel's (*q.v.*) advice the translation of foreign authors. A turning point toward a deeper conception of his own work came to Zweig in his personal friendship with the Belgian poet Verhaeren (*q.v.*). Mere literary achievement without an immanent ethos ceased to be an attraction to him. He served this master and other European figures for years, by translating and propagating their work. Meanwhile Zweig was able to follow the urgings of his insatiable curiosity by living and traveling all over the world. He was fascinated, as many of his later works show, by the people who were wasteful and almost disdainful of their lives, their time, their money, their health, and their good name.

The poems *Die frühen Kränze* (1907) stand in the shadow of Hofmannsthal and Rilke (*q.v.*). One of his early stories, *Erstes Erlebnis* (1911), Zweig found good enough 10 years later to head a collection of stories of much more profound strength. Three dramas also appeared, *Thersites* (1907), *Das Haus am Meer* (1911), and *Der verwandelte Komödiant* (1912). In *Thersites* Zweig confronts the disfigured, ugly, heart-torn Greek with the handsome and strong Achilles. The drama reveals a certain personal trait in Zweig. He almost never championed the so-called hero but rather the man who succumbed to destiny; in his biographies the interest usually lies with the figure who succeeds not in a worldly way, but in the moral sense. So the suffering Thersites becomes the protagonist instead of Achilles, who makes others suffer through his power and self-assertiveness.

The First World War brought a shock to intellectuals like Zweig who had thought they were doing enough when they fraternized as good Europeans. Zweig served at first in the war archives of Vienna, but only after he had personally seen the horrible face of war was he able to give vehement expression to his humanist, anti-war attitude. Between 1915 and 1917 he wrote the nine scenes of the dramatic poem *Jeremias* (1917; Eng. tr., 1922), the vision of the curse and the bliss of seerhood, his first truly personal creation and a very definite success. Defenseless, misunderstood, and mocked as the fool of God, the prophet stands between the God of his visions and the people who blindly stumble into "sacred" war. In the beginning a warner of the destruction, but in the end the comforter, Jeremiah typifies the fate of all the fighters against the supreme folly of man: war. The drama had its *première* in Zurich, where Zweig spent the latter part of the war period, in spirited intercourse with leading European minds.

From the post-war debacle Zweig came forth as the interpreter of human greatness, confusion, tragedy, and achievement; the poet and scholar merged, and brilliant biographies and essays were the result. In *Drei Meister* (1920; Eng. tr., *Three Masters,* 1930) he treats Balzac, Dickens, and Dostoevski (*q.v.*) as the encyclopedic geniuses of their respective nations; in *Romain Rolland* (1921; Eng. tr., 1921) he shows the greatness and kindness of the French writer (*q.v.*); in *Der Kampf mit dem Dämon* (1923) he pays homage to the demoniac genius of Hölderlin, Kleist, and Nietzsche (*q.v.*) which not only grants the exaltation of divine creation but also drives to insanity and suicide. Casanova, Stendhal, and Tolstoy (*q.v.*) are treated in *Drei Dichter ihres Lebens* (1928; Eng. tr., *Adepts in Self-Portraiture,* 1928). Collected under the title *Baumeister der Welt* (1935; Eng. tr., *Master Builders,* 1939), these biographies are admittedly books of glorification and enthusiasm. Their purpose is to spread "joy and passion" through devotion and worship and to fathom the secret of the power of the creative process.

In the same spirit Zweig wrote excellent stories and essays, among which are *Amok* (1922; Eng. tr., 1931), *Verwirrung der Gefühle* (1926; Eng. tr., *Conflicts,* 1927) and *Sternstunden der Menschheit* (1927; Eng. tr., *The Tide of Fortune,* 1940), a group of historical miniatures depicting fateful moments in the history of man. In his *Gesammelte Erzählungen* (1936) Zweig tried to present a typology of feeling as it is manifested in various forms in passion, age, and time. In addition Zweig wrote the biography *Joseph Fouché* (1929; Eng. tr., 1930), which is an ominous portrait to be published in the years just before the rule of the Gestapo. In *Die Heilung durch den Geist* (1931; Eng. tr., *Mental Healers,*

1932) Zweig presented Mesmer, Mary Baker Eddy, and Freud. The biography *Marie Antoinette* appeared in 1932 (Eng. tr., 1933).

Although without material want since 1933, Zweig went through all the agonies of a man without a country. In 1934 appeared *Triumph und Tragik des Erasmus von Rotterdam* (Eng. tr., *Erasmus of Rotterdam,* 1934). Like *Jeremias* it is a work of innermost personal confession. It is the tragic story of the objective, knowing, all-understanding nonactivist spirit who must give way to the man of passion and action. Zweig, like his hero Erasmus, continued silently on the path of creative writing. Further biographies are *Maria Stuart* (1935; Eng. tr., *Mary, Queen of Scotland and the Isles,* 1935), *Castellio* (1936; Eng. tr., *The Right to Heresy,* 1936), *Magellan* (1938; Eng. tr., *Conqueror of the Seas,* 1938), and *Amerigo* (1942); there are also essays, some stories, and a novel, *Ungeduld des Herzens* (1938; Eng. tr., *Beware of Pity,* 1939), which in a psychological approach treats the indolence of the human heart. In a book on Brazil (1941) he paid tribute to the land that had given him his last refuge. Feeling too old and too tired to start anew, Zweig, the "all-too-impatient one," and his young wife parted voluntarily from life on February 23, 1942. His last work of fiction was the subtle psychological study *Schachnovelle* (1944; Eng. tr., *The Royal Game,* 1944).

Zweig's writings have been translated into some 30 languages. His work was based on studious and sharp observation, tempered with wise and understanding sympathy. His style is animated, subtle, and charming by its innate nobility. His resolve to tell only the essential tightened and clarified the inner structure of his works and thus gave sustenance to their narrative attraction.

See: E. Rieger, *Stefan Zweig* (1928); J. Romains, *Stefan Zweig, Great European* (1941); P. Zech, *Stefan Zweig* (1943); Zweig, *The World of Yesterday* (1943), his autobiography; S. Liptzin, *Germany's Stepchildren* (1944), pp. 211–225.

W. K. P.